American Casebook Series

Hornbook Series and Basic Legal Texts

Nutshell Series

of

WEST PUBLISHING COMPANY

St. Paul, Minnesota 55102

LAW SCHOOL PUBLICATIONS — Continued

COMMON LAW PLEADING

Koffler and Reppy's Text on Common Law Pleading, 663 pages, 1969.
McBaine's Cases, Introduction to Civil Procedure, 399 pages, 1950.
Shipman's Text on Common Law Pleading, 3rd Ed., 644 pages, 1923.

COMMUNITY PROPERTY

Burby's Cases on Community Property, 4th Ed., 342 pages, 1955.
Huie's Texas Cases on Marital Property Rights, 681 pages, 1966.
Verrall and Sammis' Cases on California Community Property, 2nd Ed., 398 pages, 1971.

CONFLICT OF LAWS

Cramton and Currie's Cases—Comments—Questions on Conflicts, 915 pages, 1968.
Ehrenzweig's Text on Conflicts, 824 pages, 1962.
Ehrenzweig's Conflicts in a Nutshell, 2nd Ed., 392 pages, 1970.
Ehrenzweig and Louisell's Jurisdiction in a Nutshell, 3rd Ed., about 255 pages, 1973.
Goodrich's Text on Conflict of Laws, 4th Ed., 483 pages, 1964.
Scoles and Weintraub's Cases on Conflict of Laws, 2nd Ed., 966 pages 1972.

CONSTITUTIONAL LAW

Lockhart, Kamisar and Choper's Cases—Comments—Questions on Constitutional Law, 3rd Ed., 1,487 pages, 1970.
Lockhart, Kamisar and Choper's Cases on The American Constitution, 3rd Ed., 1970.
Lockhart, Kamisar and Choper's Annual Supplement.
See Constitutional Rights and Liberties.

CONSTITUTIONAL RIGHTS & LIBERTIES

Lockhart, Kamisar and Choper's Cases on Constitutional Rights and Liberties, 3rd Ed., 1970.
Lockhart, Kamisar and Choper's Annual Supplement.

CONSUMER CREDIT

Kripke's Cases on Consumer Credit, 454 pages, 1970.
Schrag's Cases on Consumer Credit, 2nd Ed., Pamphlet reprint from Cooper, et al. Law and Poverty, 2nd Ed., about 175 pages, 1973.

CONTRACTS

Calamari & Perillo's Text on Contracts, 621 pages, 1970.
Corbin's Cases on Contracts, 3rd Ed., 1381 pages, 1947. 1953 Supplement, 36 pages.
Corbin's Text on Contracts, Student Edition, 1224 pages, 1952.
Freedman's Cases on Contracts, 658 pages, 1973.
Fuller and Eisenberg's Cases on Contracts, 1043 pages, 1972.
Jackson's Cases on Contract Law in a Modern Society, about 1400 pages, 1973.
Simpson's Cases on Contracts, 592 pages, 1956.
Simpson's Text on Contracts, 2nd Ed., 510 pages, 1965.
White and Summer's Text on the Uniform Commercial Code, 1054 pages, 1972.

COPYRIGHT

Nimmer's Cases on Copyright and Other Aspects of Law Pertaining to Literary, Musical and Artistic Works, 828 pages, 1971.
Nimmer's 1972 Supplement.

CORPORATIONS

Henn's Text on Corporations, 2nd Ed., 956 pages, 1970.
Stevens and Henn's Statutes, Cases on Corporations and Other Business Enterprises, 1448 pages, 1965.
Stevens and Henn's Practice Projects Supplement, 81 pages, 1965.

CORRECTIONS

Krantz' Cases on the Law of Corrections and Prisoners' Rights, about 1085 pages, 1973.

CREDIT TRANSACTIONS

Maxwell & Riesenfeld's California Cases on Security Transactions, 371 pages, 1957.
Maxwell & Riesenfeld's Supplement, 68 pages, 1963.

CREDITORS' RIGHTS

Epstein's Teaching Materials on Debtor-Creditor Relations, 525 pages, 1973.
Epstein's Debtor-Creditor Relations in a Nutshell, 309 pages, 1973.
Riesenfeld's Cases on Creditors' Remedies and Debtors' Protection, 669 pages, 1967.
Riesenfeld's Case and Statutory Supplement, 1972.

R7202—2t II

CRIMINAL LAW

Dix and Sharlot's Cases on Criminal Law, about 1350 pages, 1973.

LaFave and Scott's Text on Criminal Law, 763 pages, 1972.

Miller's Text on Criminal Law, 649 pages, 1934.

Stumberg's Texas Cases on Criminal Law, 505 pages, 1954.

Stumberg and Maloney's Texas Cases Supplement, 117 pages, 1965.

CRIMINAL PROCEDURE

Hall, Kamisar, LaFave and Israel's Cases on Modern Criminal Procedure, 3rd Ed., 1456 pages, 1969.

Hall, Kamisar, LaFave and Israel's Cases on Basic Criminal Procedure, 3rd Ed., 617 pages, 1969.

Hall, Kamisar, LaFave and Israel's Annual Criminal Procedure Supplement.

Israel and LaFave's Constitutional Criminal Procedure in a Nutshell, 423 pages, 1971.

Federal Rules of Civil-Appellate-Criminal Procedure, Law School Edition, 296 pages, 1973.

DAMAGES

Crane's Cases on Damages, 3rd Ed., 337 pages, 1955.

McCormick's Text on Damages, 811 pages, 1935.

See Remedies.

DECEDENTS ESTATES

See Wills, Intestate Succession, Trusts, Gifts and Future Interests.

DICTIONARIES

Black's, one volume.
Bouvier's, two volumes.

DOMESTIC RELATIONS

Clark's Cases on Domestic Relations, 870 pages, 1965.

Clark's Text on Domestic Relations, 754 pages, 1968.

Paulsen's Cases on Family Law and Poverty, 2nd Ed., Pamphlet reprint from Cooper, et al. Law and Poverty, 2nd Ed., about 266 pages, 1973.

See Juvenile Courts.

EQUITY

Cook's Cases on Equity, 4th Ed., 1192 pp., 1948.

McClintock's Text on Equity, 2nd Ed., 643 pages, 1948.

Van Hecke, Leavell and Nelson's Cases on Equitable Remedies and Restitution, 2nd Ed., 717 pages, 1973.

See Remedies.

EVIDENCE

Broun and Meisenholder's Problems in Evidence, about 155 pages, 1973.

Cleary and Strong's Cases on Evidence, 967 pages, 1969.

McCormick, Elliott & Sutton's Cases on Evidence, 4th Ed., 1088 pages, 1971.

McCormick, Cleary, et al., Text on Evidence, 2nd Ed., 938 pages, 1972.

Rothstein's Evidence in a Nutshell, 406 pages, 1970.

FEDERAL ESTATE AND GIFT TAXATION

See Taxation.

FEDERAL INCOME TAXATION

See Taxation.

FEDERAL JURISDICTION AND PROCEDURE

Currie's Cases on Federal Courts, 823 pages, 1968.

Currie's Supplement, 1973.

Ehrenzweig and Louisell's Jurisdiction in a Nutshell, 3rd Ed., about 255 pages, 1973.

Forrester, Currier and Moye's Cases on Federal Jurisdiction and Procedure, 2nd Ed., 933 pages, 1970.

Forrester, Currier and Moye's Supplement, 1973.

Wright's Text on Federal Courts, 2nd Ed., 745 pages, 1970.

Wright's Supplement, 1972.

FUTURE INTERESTS

Gulliver's Cases on Future Interests, 624 pages, 1959.

Powell's Cases on Future Interests, 3rd Ed., 1961.

Simes Text on Future Interests, 2nd Ed., 355 pages, 1966.

See Wills, Intestate Succession, Trusts, Gifts and Future Interests.

GRATUITOUS TRANSFERS

See Wills, Intestate Succession, Trusts, Gifts and Future Interests.

LAW SCHOOL PUBLICATIONS — Continued

HOUSING AND URBAN DEVELOPMENT

Berger's Cases on Housing, 2nd Ed., Pamphlet reprint from Cooper, et al. Law and Poverty, 2nd Ed., about 210 pages, 1973.

Krasnowiecki's Cases on Housing and Urban Development, 697 pages, 1969.

Krasnowiecki's Statutory Supplement 1969.

See Land Use.

INSURANCE

Keeton's Cases on Basic Insurance Law, 655 pages, 1960.

Keeton's Basic Text on Insurance Law, 712 pages, 1971.

Keeton's Case Supplement to Keeton's Basic Text, 398 pages, 1971.

Keeton's Programmed Problems in Insurance Law, 243 pages, 1972.

Keeton & Keeton's Compensation Systems, Pamphlet Reprint from Keeton & Keeton's Cases on Torts, 85 pages, 1971.

Vance's Text on Insurance, 3rd Ed., 1290 pages, 1951.

INTERNATIONAL LAW

Friedmann, Lissitzyn and Pugh's Cases on International Law, 1,205 pages, 1969.

Friedmann, Lissitzyn and Pugh's Supplement, 1972.

INTRODUCTION TO LAW

Fryer and Orentlicher's Cases on Legal Method and Legal System, 1,043 pages, 1967.

Kempin's Historical Introduction to Anglo-American Law in a Nutshell, 2nd Ed., 280 pages, 1973.

Kimball's Historical Introduction to Legal System, 610 pages, 1966.

Kinyon's Introduction to Law Study and Law Examinations in a Nutshell, 389 pages, 1971.

Smith's Cases on Development of Legal Institutions, 757 pages, 1965.

See Legal Method.

JURISPRUDENCE

Christie's Text and Readings on Jurisprudence—The Philosophy of Law, about 1050 pages, 1973.

Wu's Cases on Jurisprudence, 719 pages, 1958.

JUVENILE JUSTICE

Fox's Cases on Modern Juvenile Justice, 1012 pages, 1972.

Fox's The Law of Juvenile Courts in a Nutshell, 286 pages, 1971.

LABOR LAW

Oberer and Hanslowe's Cases on Labor Law, 1091 pages, 1972.

Oberer and Hanslowe's Statutory Supplement, 1972.

Sovern's Cases on Racial Discrimination in Employment, 2nd Ed., Pamphlet reprint from Cooper et al. Law and Poverty, 2nd Ed., about 160 pages, 1973.

LAND USE

Beuscher and Wright's Cases on Land Use, 788 pages, 1969.

Hagman's Cases on Public Planning and Control of Urban and Land Development, about 1025 pages, 1973.

Hagman's Text on Urban Planning and Land Development Control Law, 559 pages, 1971.

LEGAL BIBLIOGRAPHY

Cohen's Legal Research in a Nutshell, 2nd Ed., 259 pages, 1971.

How To Find The Law, with Special Chapters on Legal Writing, 6th Ed., 313 pages, 1965.

How To Find The Law Student Problem Book.

Rombauer's Legal Problem Solving, 2nd Ed., 212 pages, 1973.

Rombauer's Problem Supplement.

LEGAL ETHICS

Mellinkoff's Text on The Conscience of a Lawyer, 304 pages, 1973.

Pirsig's Cases on Professional Responsibility, 2nd Ed., 447 pages, 1970.

LEGAL HISTORY

Kempin's Historical Introduction to Anglo-American Law in a Nutshell, 2nd Ed., 280 pages, 1973.

Kimball's Historical Introduction to Legal System, 610 pages, 1966.

Radin's Text on Anglo-American Legal History, 612 pages, 1936.

Smith's Cases on Development of Legal Institutions, 757 pages, 1965.

LEGAL INTERVIEWING AND COUNSELING

See Clinical Teaching.

LEGAL METHOD—LEGAL SYSTEM

Fryer and Orentlicher's Cases on Legal Method and Legal System, 1043 pages, 1966.

See Introduction to Law.

LEGAL PROCESS

See Legal Method.

LAW SCHOOL PUBLICATIONS — Continued

LEGAL PROFESSION

See Legal Ethics.

LEGAL WRITING STYLE

Weihofen's Text on Legal Writing Style, 323 pages, 1961.
See Legal Bibliography.

LEGISLATION

Nutting, Elliott and Dickerson's Cases on Legislation, 4th Ed., 631 pages, 1969.

LOCAL GOVERNMENT LAW

Michelman and Sandalow's Cases on Government in Urban Areas, 1216 pages, 1970.
Michelman and Sandalow's 1972 Supplement.
Stason and Kauper's Cases on Municipal Corporations, 3rd Ed., 692 pages, 1959.
See Land Use.

MASS COMMUNICATION LAW

Gillmor and Barron's Cases on Mass Communication Law, 853 pages, 1969.
Gillmor and Barron's 1971 Supplement.

MORTGAGES

Osborne's Cases on Secured Transactions, 559 pages, 1967.
Osborne's Text on Mortgages, 2nd Ed., 805 pages, 1970.
See Sales.
See Secured Transactions.

MUNICIPAL CORPORATIONS

See Local Government Law.

NATURAL RESOURCES

Trelease, Bloomenthal and Geraud's Cases on Natural Resources, 1131 pages, 1965.

NEGOTIABLE INSTRUMENTS

Nordstrom and Clovis' Problems on Commercial Paper, 458 pages, 1972.
See Commercial Transactions.

OFFICE PRACTICE

A.B.A. Lawyer's Handbook, 557 pages, 1962.
See Clinical Teaching.

OIL AND GAS

Hemingway's Text on Oil and Gas, 486 pages, 1971.
Huie, Woodward and Smith's Cases on Oil and Gas, 2nd Ed., 955 pages, 1972.
See Natural Resources.

PARTNERSHIP

Crane and Bromberg's Text on Partnership, 695 pages, 1968.
See Agency-Partnership.

PATENTS

Choate's Cases on Patents, 1060 pages, 1973.

PERSONAL PROPERTY

Aigler, Smith and Tefft's Cases on Property, 2 Vols., 1339 pages, 1960.
Bigelow's Cases on Personal Property, 3rd Ed., 507 pages, 1942.
Fryer's Readings on Personal Property, 3rd Ed., 1184 pages, 1938.

PLEADING AND PROCEDURE

Brown, Karlen, Meisenholder, Stevens, and Vestal's Cases on Procedure Before Trial, 784 pages, 1968.
Cleary's Cases on Pleading, 2d Ed., 434 pages, 1958.
Cound, Friedenthal and Miller's Cases on Civil Procedure, 1075 pages, 1968.
Cound, Friedenthal and Miller's Cases on Pleading, Discovery and Joinder, 643 pages, 1968.
Cound, Friedenthal and Miller's Civil Procedure Supplement, 1972.
Ehrenzweig and Louisell's Jurisdiction in a Nutshell, 3rd Ed., about 255 pages, 1973.
Elliott & Karlen's Cases on Pleading, 441 pages, 1961.
Hodges, Jones and Elliott's Cases on Texas Trial and Appellate Procedure, 623 pages, 1965.
Hodges, Jones, Elliott and Thode's Cases on Texas Judicial Process Prior to Trial, 935 pages, 1966.
Karlen and Joiner's Cases on Trials and Appeals, 536 pages, 1971.
Karlen's Procedure Before Trial in a Nutshell, 258 pages, 1972.
McBaine's Cases on Introduction to Civil Procedure, 399 pages, 1950.
Federal Rules of Civil-Appellate-Criminal Procedure, Law School Edition, 296 pages, 1973.

POVERTY LAW

Cooper, Dodyk, Berger, Paulsen, Schrag and Sovern's Cases on Law and Poverty, 2nd Ed., about 1165 pages, 1973.

Cooper and Dodyk's Cases on Income Maintenance, 2nd Ed., Pamphlet reprint from Cooper, et al. Law and Poverty, 2nd Ed., about 400 pages, 1973.

LaFrance, Schroeder, Bennett and Boyd's Text on Law and the Poor, about 520 pages, 1973.

REAL PROPERTY

Aigler, Smith & Tefft's Cases on Property, 2 Vols., 1339 pages, 1960.

Berger's Cases on Housing, Pamphlet reprint from Dodyk, et al. Law and Poverty, 277 pages, 1969.

Browder, Cunningham & Julin's Cases on Basic Property Law, 2d Ed., 1397 pages, 1973.

Burby's Text on Real Property, 3rd Ed., 490 pages, 1965.

Jacobs' Cases on Landlord and Tenant, 2nd Ed., 815 pages, 1941.

Moynihan's Introduction to Real Property, 254 pages, 1962.

Phipps' Titles in a Nutshell—The Calculus of Interests, 277 pages, 1968.

Smith and Boyer's Survey of the Law of Property, 2nd Ed., 510 pages, 1971.

See Housing and Urban Development.

REMEDIES

Cribbet's Cases on Judicial Remedies, 762 pages, 1954.

Dobb's Text, on Remedies, 1067 pages, 1973.

Van Hecke, Leavell and Nelson's Cases on Equitable Remedies and Restitution, 2nd Ed., 717 pages, 1973.

Wright's Cases on Remedies, 498 pages, 1955.

York and Bauman's Cases on Remedies, 2nd Ed., about 1500 pages, 1973.

See Equity.

RESTITUTION

See Equity.
See Remedies.

REVIEW MATERIALS

Ballantine's Problems.
Burby's Law Refreshers.
Smith Reviews.

SALES

Nordstrom's Text on Sales, 600 pages, 1970.

Nordstrom and Lattin's Problems on Sales and Secured Transactions, 809 pages, 1968.

See Commercial Transactions.

SECURED TRANSACTIONS

Henson's Text on Secured Transactions, about 350 pages, 1973.

See Commercial Transactions.
See Sales.

SURETYSHIP AND GUARANTY

Osborne's Cases on Suretyship, 221 pages, 1966.

Simpson's Cases on Suretyship, 538 pages, 1942.

TAXATION

Chommie's Text on Federal Income Taxation, 2nd Ed., about 1000 pages, 1973.

Hellerstein's Cases on State and Local Taxation, 3rd Ed., 741 pages, 1969.

Kragen & McNulty's Cases on Federal Income Taxation, 1,182 pages, 1970.

Lowndes & Kramer's Text on Federal Estate and Gift Taxes, 2nd Ed., 951 pages, 1962.

McNulty's Federal Income Taxation in a Nutshell, 322 pages, 1972.

Rice's Problems in Federal Estate & Gift Taxation, 2nd Ed., 496 pages, 1972.

Rice's Problems in Federal Income Taxation, 2nd Ed., 589 pages, 1971.

TORTS

Green, Pedrick, Rahl, Thode, Hawkins and Smith's Cases on Torts, 1311 pages, 1968.

Green, Pedrick, Rahl, Thode, Hawkins and Smith's Cases on Injuries to Relations, 466 pages, 1968.

Keeton and Keeton's Cases on Torts, 1193 pages, 1971.

Prosser's Text on Torts, 4th Ed., 1208 pages, 1971.

TRADE REGULATION

See Anti-Trust Law.
See Unfair Trade Practices.

TRIAL AND APPELLATE PRACTICE

See Pleading and Procedure.

TRUSTS

Bogert's Text on Trusts, 5th Ed., about 535 pages, 1973.

Powell's Cases on Trusts and Wills, 639 pages, 1960.

See Wills, Intestate Succession, Trusts, Gifts and Future Interests.

UNFAIR TRADE PRACTICES

Oppenheim's Cases on Unfair Trade Practices, 783 pages, 1965.

Oppenheim and Weston's Supplement.

Oppenheim's Robinson-Patman Act Pamphlet, 295 pages, 1967.

WATER LAW

Trelease's Cases on Water Law, 364 pages, 1967.

WILLS

Atkinson's Text on Wills, 2nd Ed., 975 pages, 1953.

Mennell's Cases on California Decedents' Estates, 566 pages, 1973.

Turrentine's Cases on Wills, 2nd Ed., 483 pages, 1962.

See Wills, Intestate Succession, Trusts, Gifts and Future Interests.

WILLS, INTESTATE SUCCESSION, TRUSTS, GIFTS AND FUTURE INTERESTS

Gulliver, Clark, Lusky and Murphy's Cases on Gratuitous Transfers: Wills, Intestate Succession, Trusts, Gifts and Future Interests, 1017 pages, 1967.

WORKMEN'S COMPENSATION

Malone and Plant's Cases on Workmen's Compensation, 622 pages, 1963.

CASES AND MATERIALS

ON

LAW AND POVERTY

SECOND EDITION

By

GEORGE COOPER
Professor of Law, Columbia University

CURTIS J. BERGER
Professor of Law, Columbia University

PAUL M. DODYK
Former Professor of Law, Columbia University
Member of the New York Bar

MONRAD G. PAULSEN
Dean and John B. Minor Professor of Law and Dean,
University of Virginia

PHILIP G. SCHRAG
Professor of Law, Columbia University

MICHAEL I. SOVERN
Dean and Professor of Law, Columbia University

AMERICAN CASEBOOK SERIES

ST. PAUL, MINN.
WEST PUBLISHING CO.
1973

Cooper et al., Cs. Law & Poverty 2d Ed. ACB

PREFACE TO THE SECOND EDITION

The mind boggles at the developments which have swept through this field in the four brief years since publication of the first edition. There is no law without lawyers, and lawyers were sparse indeed in the field of poverty law until the Legal Services Program of the Office of Economic Opportunity and other "public interest" law programs began to have an impact in the late 1960's. Once begun, however, that impact was swift and dramatic. Hundreds of lower court decisions and a myriad of Supreme Court opinions, many of which are set out on the pages which follow, attest to the broad and deep imprint which these programs have had on the law. In 1969, the subject of "Law and Poverty" was more a gleam in the authors' eyes than a developed concept. It is now a fully recognized subject in law school curricula with two published casebooks, and several more casebooks and a treatise forthcoming.

Of course, as noted in the opening pages of this book, there is a very significant gap between this law in the books and its enforcement in practice. Many problems, ranging from the economics of law practice to the politics of legal services, must be overcome before there is a full realization of the legal rights of the poor. But those rights are clearly beginning to take shape and we hope this book can continue to make a modest contribution to that trend by aiding the introduction of new groups of law students to an exciting and personally satisfying area of the law.

This book continues to be, in essence, five individual texts by separate authors. Professor Cooper and Mr. Dodyk are responsible for Chapter 1 (Income Maintenance), Dean Paulsen for Chapter 2 (Family Law), Professor Berger for Chapter 3 (Housing), Dean Sovern for Chapter 4 (Employment Discrimination) and Professor Schrag for Chapter 5 (Consumer Protection). Each chapter deals with a subject which is of special importance to the poor and which offers important rights to which a lawyer for the poor is likely to turn. No effort has been made to integrate the separate chapters or to develop common themes, not because those themes do not exist, but rather because the goal of this book is to provide the raw materials for teaching the various subjects covered rather than to force the emerging law into some particular mold. With this in mind, we have tried to provide a wide variety of secondary materials and supporting data as well as traditional case materials. We have allowed the individual tastes and priorities of the different authors to show through in the selection of materials for the various chapters. We have, however, attempted to minimize any overlap and redundancy. The teacher who covers this entire book will have exposed his students to the basic areas of poverty law and to the major themes which dominate that field, while the teacher who is more selective will find a wide enough variety of materials and topics to develop the theme or approach which he or she prefers.

We are also continuing the practice of making each chapter available as a separate paperback pamphlet for teachers who prefer to focus on only one or two subjects. Each pamphlet contains the full text of one chapter, plus any relevant material from other chapters.

In this rapidly developing field, it is never possible for a bound volume to be fully up to date. For the most part, this book takes account of events occurring through the end of 1972, although some important Supreme Court decisions in 1973 have also been incorporated.

GEORGE COOPER

August, 1973

PREFACE TO THE FIRST EDITION

This volume is an effort on the part of the editors to pool their varying experiences and insights concerning certain areas of the law of relevance to the less affluent members of our society. In compiling these materials, we have attempted to respond promptly to a need which has been expressed with great urgency both by students in American Law Schools and by the increasing numbers of our profession who are engaged in rendering service to the poor. We have attempted to respond to this expressed need by making available a collection of materials which will provide students with the opportunity to ponder problems of law and policy which are, in our judgment, of the greatest importance to the poor.

In assembling these materials there were many difficult choices to be made. Unlike the more traditional areas of legal study, there are few widely accepted criteria to define the body of materials to be included. Doubtless, there are other areas which some will feel equally important in such study. Throughout, our effort has been to raise those problems which we felt of greatest importance to the poor.

More than in many other areas, the legal problems dealt with in this volume are direct reflections of the most pressing social, economic and political issues of our day. Consequently, we have included a greater quantity of secondary material dealing with those issues than might be found in other volumes. We hope that the inclusion of such materials will provide the readers of this volume with a greater opportunity to ponder such underlying issues and to assess the proper role of lawyers, courts and the legal system in responding to these problems.

This volume is designed for classroom use at law schools where a separate course is taught on law and proverty or law and the poor. In order to accommodate classroom requirements at law schools where the subject matter of law and poverty is taught by means of supplementing several presently existing courses, each of the five chapters of this book has been reprinted and made available by the publisher in separate pamphlets.

PAUL M. DODYK
GENERAL EDITOR

July, 1969

*

SUMMARY OF CONTENTS

---

*

TABLE OF CONTENTS

TABLE OF CONTENTS

TABLE OF CONTENTS

TABLE OF CONTENTS

TABLE OF CONTENTS

XXIII

TABLE OF CONTENTS

TABLE OF CONTENTS

TABLE OF CONTENTS

TABLE OF CASES

References are to Pages

TABLE OF CASES

TABLE OF CASES

TABLE OF CASES

TABLE OF CASES

TABLE OF CASES

TABLE OF CASES

†

CASES AND MATERIALS
ON
LAW AND POVERTY

Chapter 1

INCOME MAINTENANCE

THE ROLE OF LAW FOR THE POOR

From Life at the Bottom © 1971
Gregory Armstrong

"This is 1970 isn't it? I think the time has come when people have got to stop making excuses and really get up and do something about things that are going on around here. Every excuse in the book has been given for everything they're doing wrong and as far as I'm concerned there aren't any more excuses or alibis. There's nothing anybody can say that will appease me or pacify me or justify the treatment that goes on towards the black community."

Georgia Jackson,
mother of Jonathan and
George Jackson

"Must we kill to get what we want or what is due to plain human beings."
Victor Martinez
prisoner
Queens House of Detention

One day last year I went to New Haven to visit a photographer who works in the black community. As we walked the streets, kids squirmed all around us, rubbing against our backs and grabbing our hands. "Will you take my picture?" "Will you take my picture?" "Will you take my picture, mister, please?" Just before sunset, we stopped and watched some black kids playing basketball, racing tirelessly back and forth, pounding the ball on the macadam, springing up to pitch the ball into the nets, with an almost machinelike efficiency. No talk, no banter. An almost fanatical determination to control every element of the game.

The next day I went into another section of the black community. It was 10:30 in the morning and already dozens of men were sitting on stoops and leaning against the sides of buildings. Some of them were drinking wine from bottles hidden in paper bags. Their faces were impassive. Their black skin looked as if it had been brushed with ashes. One of the men sitting on a stoop had a gaping wound straight through his cheek. When someone suggested that he should go to the hospital, he lowered his eyes. I drank some wine with a man who had just gotten out of jail after nine years. He explained to me that he had known he was going to prison when he was seven years old. "Every black kid knows he's going to jail when he's just a little child. Look at that kid up there," he said, pointing to a boy playing on a fire escape nearby. "He knows he's going to jail just the same way a white kid born in the suburbs knows he's going to college." The boy was like the kids I had seen the day before. The men leaning against the buildings were only a few years older than the boys who had been playing basketball.

Shortly after I returned from New Haven, I spoke to a man whose older son was about to go on trial for murder. He told me he guessed that one out of every two men in the ghetto were ex-cons. He could identify them by the way they talked and carried themselves. Even though most of them were still young, they were already broken men.

A few weeks later, this man's younger son, Jonathan Jackson, entered a courtroom in San Rafael, California, and attempted to free three black convicts, one of whom was on trial for assaulting a guard. He armed the convicts and took five hostages including the assistant district attorney and the judge, still dressed in his robes. He died a few minutes later in a hail of bullets inside a rented van that was being used for the getaway.

At a press conference, four days later, his mother explained that her son "had done what any other boy his age would do who had gone through what he'd had to go through, growing up in a racist society with his brother in jail, possibly for the rest of his life, for a crime he didn't even commit. Going to trials and hearings since the time he was seven and seeing the kind of justice that is given to black people and poor people of all kinds in this country. Having his brother unjustly accused of murder and seeing him denied even the most elemental human and legal rights."

I think it is very hard for most whites to understand the significance of Jonathan Jackson's action. They see it only as a desperate act by a crazed boy. Blacks regard it in a very different light, almost as if it were the beginning of the end of their subjugation. Jonathan violated one of the most sacred taboos of our society, the sanctity of the court. Where generations of blacks had mutely and fatalistically accepted its total authority over their lives, Jonathan committed the ultimate act of defiance.

"We're taking over," he said. At seventeen, Jonathan Jackson had already come to the conclusion that the only way he could affirm his sense of justice was at the point of a gun. His experience of life in America had convinced him that the only way he could be heard was by an act of suicidal daring. "You can take our pictures. We are the revolutionaries." With these words he announced to the world that he was not a criminal, because he no longer recognized the legitimacy of white law.

When his sister heard the news of his death, she cried out, "But he was only a boy." Her mother corrected her. "Don't say that. He was a man. They killed his father a long time ago. Jonathan wasn't going to let that happen to him. He was going to live like a man." His brother George remarked afterwards that Jonathan had "really been free for a while." Who can say what that moment of pure freedom meant to him?

* * *

Why haven't there been more Jonathan Jacksons in recent history? Why have the poor of all races found it so difficult to organize and move politically in this country? Part of the reason, I would suggest, is that by and large the poor and ostracized minorities have been taught to accept the justice of their debased condition. Black skin, brown skin, powerlessness, poor housing, cheap clothes, bad teeth, chronic debilitating illness, all the other stigmata of poverty, in terms of the actual functioning morality of the American culture—these conditions are the equivalent of criminal acts. Each day of their lives, the poor are guilty of the crime of being themselves. They accept the values of their society and it is these very values which condemn them.

There are two Americas, one governed by law, conferring certain basic human rights on its citizens; the other without law or justice, its citizens completely deprived of even the most rudimentary human rights. Yet both countries judge themselves by the same standards of success and failure. It is because of the disparity between these two Americas that we are entering into a period of revolutionary change.

The poor, black, white, urban, rural, in their deprivation and ostracism, share a common experience of America. Their sense of themselves is formed out of an abyss between what they know firsthand about the reality of their lives and what in effect they are forced to believe about America—the total mythology of America as it is imposed by the media of communication, schools and all the other means of value formation in this country. When the gap between myth and reality grows too great, the social conditioning breaks down. First one Jonathan Jackson breaks out of the mold, then another, and then a thousand.

What are the conditions that have maintained the poor in a state of self-negating passivity for so long? One of the principal reasons is that in America poverty is not just material deprivation, it is moral and spiritual degradation. The absence of money is a state of uncleanliness and contamination, tantamount to a complete loss of identity. This is the legacy of the Protestant work ethic, which forms the basis of capitalist ideology. In terms of analogues, the poor in this country are probably closest to the untouchables of India. In the reality of American daily life they are just as totally excluded from all the rituals and functions that confer the rights and privileges of humanity.

They exist in this country as stateless people with none of the rights possessed by other citizens. Anything they have can be taken away. The entire character of their lives can be altered overnight by changes in government policy. The places where they live can be destroyed and they can be forced to move. Without money to hire lawyers and without access to sources of influence, they have no defense against police brutality and no means of defending themselves adequately against accusations of crime. If they are put in jail they have no money for bail. As declassed and degraded people, they have no way to deal with school and teachers to determine the character of their children's education. To get credit in overpriced neighborhood stores they must beg and wheedle. Nowhere in this country do their voices have any weight or authority. The only time they can be heard, so it would seem, is when they pick up the gun.

The total environment of the poor is an enforced education in self-abasement, powerlessness, worthlessness and rejection. The entire American society is an enormous mirror in which they are forced to see themselves in the image of our fear and loathing of their poverty and helplessness. This image of themselves becomes almost ineradicable. Everything in their world, the total imprinting, conditioning power of society, functions to imbed in them a deep and immutable sense of self-loathing.

The children of the poor learn the lessons of fear and humiliation from their parents. They hear the self-doubt that accompanies everything the parents try to teach them. They see their parents relating with servility to the outside world. They sense the outrageous pain which their parents try to conceal even from themselves. The example of their parents becomes the core to which everything else in their lives relates, particularly when everything else in their environment serves to substantiate and support the sense of life which their parents embody.

Formal education is a long and extended training in worthlessness. Schools define humanity in such a way that the poor can only see themselves as a degraded subspecies of mankind. Establishment schools are chiefly successful in teaching self-hatred and despair.

The teacher told us we should watch how we wear our clothes and try to wash ourselves every day and use brushes on our teeth and eat all those different things on the chart she has. I told my mama, and she said, "Yes, what the teacher says is correct, yes, it is, but you don't always go along because there's no time what with work and life and all that and if you haven't got the shower, you can't take it, and maybe someday it will be different." [1]

School teaches love and respect for the values of democracy. The life of the ghetto teaches the perversion of all democratic ideals and the necessity of a life of suspicion, wariness and pitilessness.

The textbooks tell you how great America is and how they keep people in other countries alive. You know they never said anything about anybody having to starve * * * nothing about people being pushed up from the street looking for jobs * * * nothing about welfare systems. They never told me that the police do hit you. *They Walk You Across the Street* was what I was told. That's crazy! Poor high school kid gets out of school and a cop beats him to death. [2]

* * *

[1] Robert Coles, Uprooted Children (Pittsburgh: University of Pittsburgh Press, 1970).

[2] Todd Gitlin and Nanci Hollander, Uptown (New York: Harper & Row, 1970).

For the poor, the law is further education in their deprivation of rights. We talk about the lawlessness of the poor, yet no group of people has a more juridical, legalistic mentality. Their concern for law is a very serious matter. They have it least and need it most. The poor are without any body of law which relates to their own problems or needs. With no law to sanction their existence, their sense of their own criminality is absolute.

The poor are the chief victims of quasi-legal economic crimes which are committed against them with impunity— the crimes of landlords who don't provide the services they are paid for, the crimes of employers who overwork and underpay, the crimes of storekeepers who overcharge for inferior goods. (The poor pay more in rent per square foot than the middle class. They pay more for the goods they buy. A recent study found that $3,000 in black money would only buy as much as $2,500 to $2,800 worth of goods. The prices in credit stores are as much as fifty-two percent higher. According to a New York study, forty-three percent of those using credit in ghetto stores experienced serious exploitation. Twenty percent were threatened with repossession, garnishment or threat of garnishment.)

The average ghetto resident knows about the law from the small print in installment loan contracts which is turned against him with devastating force. He knows how the law helps to repossess his goods even though they may be almost completely paid for. He knows how the law helps to garnishee his wages to satisfy fraudulent claims.

Most of the poor have firsthand experience of official lawlessness from observing shakedowns, bribes, rigged arrests and payoffs for gambling, prostitution and narcotics. "The police don't want to break it up. They just wants their share."

For the poor, the law is just another way of defining the dimensions of their cages. "They say you get the money and you pay the man, but they don't say how to get it. Now if you use illegal means to obey his ruling to get it, which he's not going to let you do—if you use illegal means to pay your bills according to his ruling—he will put you in jail." [5]

The poor know about the police mostly as an enemy force present in their world to enforce laws which have little or no bearing on the actual problems of their lives as they know them. In the eyes of the law, even their bodies are accorded no dignity or respect. According to a recent study, the police abuse the poor of all minority groups with equal brutality.

They ran into the station and grabbed the Negro man who was inside. Without questioning him, they shoved him into a phone booth and began beating him with their fists and a flashlight. They also hit him in the groin. Then they dragged him out and kept him on his knees. He pleaded that he had just been released from a mental hospital that day and, begging not to be hit again, asked them to let him return to the hospital. One policeman said: "You don't like us, nigger? I like to beat niggers and rip out their eyes." They took him outside to their patrol car. Then they decided to put him on a bus, telling him that he was returning to the hospital; they deliberately put him on a bus going in the opposite direction. [6]

After the policemen got the offenders to the station, although the boys no longer resisted them, the police began to beat them while they were handcuffed in an interrogation room. One of the boys hollered: "You can't beat me like this! I'm only a kid and my hands are tied." Later one of the policemen commented to the observer: "On the street you can't beat them. But when you get to the station, you can instill some respect in them." [7]

It is no wonder that the poor yearn for some kind of binding, obligatory law or moral standard that would guarantee them redress, or at least the prospect of ultimate vindication, a law that would sanction and protect their existence.

Work is another way that the poor find out about themselves and their value to society. The kind of work that is available to the uneducated and unskilled in the cities is so underpaid that often it is only a form of slow economic suicide which serves to intensify feelings of self-hatred and degradation. As the author of *Tally's Corner* observes: "To talk about his job can trigger a deep sense of shame * * * the emptiness of the job experience itself (running an elevator, pushing a mop, digging a hole), only serves to remind him where he stands in society." [8]

The poor learn much of how society would have them regard themselves from dealings with people who are nominally dedicated to helping them. Many doctors, welfare workers and police only recognize the poor as social problems, objects to be manipulated and disposed of. Because of their economic dependency, the poor are vulnerable to emotional abuse and exploitation. When people who are supposed to care about them, the best men in society, treat them with contempt and disdain, it becomes an absolute verdict of their worthlessness.

It's like at city hall, you wait and wait, and they pushes you and shoves you and calls your name only to tell you, you have to wait some more, and

[5] Kenneth Clark, Dark Ghetto (New York: Harper & Row, 1965).

[6] Albert J. Reiss Jr., "Police Brutality—Answers to Key Questions," Trans-action, July/August 1968.

[7] Ibid.

[8] Elliot Liebow, Tally's Corner (Boston: Little, Brown, 1967).

if you tell them you can't stay there all day, they say, "Lady, go home, then." [9]

Sometimes I wonder what goes on in the heads of those doctors. They look you right in the eye, and they're wearing a straight face on, and they tell you you're sick, you've been hurt digging out coal, and you'll never be the same, but you're really not so bad off, because your back isn't so bad you can't be a judge, or a professor, or the president of a coal company or something like that, you know. [10]

It is easy to ignore the fact that the poor really understand what is being said to them, the deep emotional content of our words. Their own sense of their loathsomeness makes them acutely aware of any feelings of distaste and fear on the part of other people.

A woman institutionalized in a mental hospital talks about her doctor:

He tells me I'll be fine, and to take the pills when I get nervous, and if it's especially bad, to take an extra one. If I tell him the pills aren't working, he tells me it takes time for them to work, and I'll be O.K. if I just hold out. I can tell by his face that he doesn't want to hear too much bad news from me. You have to have money to get them to talk with you. [11]

Romantic observers of the poor often assume that the culture of poverty provides strong sensual gratifications and compensations. In fact, sex for the poor is often just another means of experiencing failure. For the woman, it is the prospect of fatherless children. "Your man can bang you, then he just tired of you; he tuk a new girl and leave you. And if you gets a baby it gots to go to the fost' home. That's when the kids ain't got no mother." [12] Young girls learn at an early age "there's too many babies following me now. * * * They follows me up and down the hall, they follow me outside." [13] "When a girl is raised in Harlem and reaches a certain age, she is expected to go along with the crowd. * * * Each boy has a girl friend * * * after going steady with him you go to bed. In most cases the girl becomes pregnant. The girl has her baby and tries to make the most of it." [14] And so the women become matriarchs almost from the time they are born. They pass without any distinction or ceremony from raising their mother's children to having their own.

* * *

Note

The Armstrong essay repeatedly states a theme which must be a matter of great concern to lawyers and law students.

There are two Americas, one governed by law, conferring basic human rights on its citizens; the other without law or justice, its citizens completely deprived of even rudimentary human rights.

* * *

[The poor's] concern for the law is a very serious matter. They have it least and need it most. The poor are without any body of law which relates to their own problems or needs.

* * *

For the poor, the law is just another way of defining the dimensions of their cages.

---

[9] Mary Wright, "The Dusty Outskirts of Hope," Mountain Life and Work, Spring 1964.

[10] Robert Coles, "Life in Appalachia," Trans-action, June 1968.

[11] Robert Coles, "What Poverty Does to the Mind," The Nation, June 20, 1966.

[12] Mary Frances Greene and Orletta Ryan, The Schoolchildren (New York: Pantheon, 1965).

[13] Ibid.

[14] Arthur Simon, Faces of Poverty (St. Louis: Concordia House, 1965).

Can Armstrong be right? Is this really the role of our jealous mistress—at best, to ignore the poor, and, at worst, to oppress them? We can reassure overselves with the thought that these are the words of a polemicist. There *is* obviously a substantial body of law dealing with the rights of tenants and consumers, and there *is* a vast array of government benefit programs aimed at helping the poor. Thus, there is an easy answer to Armstrong, but it is too easy. None of these laws means anything until it is enforced, and this enforcement requires a commitment of legal resources of a magnitude which has never been seriously contemplated. Unless that commitment is made, unless there are lawyers to help convert paper promises into legal rights, the law will offer nothing meaningful to the poor. In that sense, Armstrong is, unfortunately, all too accurate in his perceptions.

This casebook covers five major areas where the law interacts with the poor and offers potential aid and protection. These are the areas of law which a lawyer must know and understand if he is going to apply his professional skills on behalf of the poor.

The law is not a panacea for the poor. But, with skilled lawyers to aid them in using it, the law can be an effective weapon in the fight against poverty.

SECTION 1. INTRODUCTION

AN INTRODUCTION TO AMERICAN INCOME MAINTENANCE INSTITUTIONS

P. M. Dodyk

Central to the legal concerns of the poor are those institutions which have been devised to protect Americans from material deprivation and to maintain income. On one view of American poverty, the social problem which is poverty is quite simply the failure of those institutions to maintain incomes at a civilized level. On this view, the legal problem to be confronted is basically an overhaul of the income maintenance system. Others regard the poor's material insufficiency as but one facet of a problem which goes to the root of the American economic and political system. To them, the material insufficiency of the poor is but a symptom interwoven with other symptoms—materialism, elitism, antiegalitarianism, racism, sexism—which require for their solution a thorough-going restructuring of American society. But even on this view, the simple material insufficiency of the poor remains a problem of immediate concern, the solution of which is a matter of the highest priority. It is, therefore, to the problem of income maintenance that the first section of this book addresses itself.

The cases and materials which constitute Chapter I are devoted in large measure to the Categorical Assistance program. This program, funded in part by the Federal Government under the Social Security Act and administered by state and local governments, constitutes the most comprehensive and well financed of the governmental efforts specifically designed to maintain the income of the poor. It is to reform or replacement of these programs that most people look in their efforts to ameliorate the condition of the poor. The categorical assistance program is, however, but one of many institutions which serve to maintain income and relieve poverty. These institutions are the result of hundreds of years of historical evolution. The purpose of this essay is to provide an historical and institutional perspective for study of the materials which follow by sketching briefly the history and structure of American income maintenance institutions.

I. English Antecedents

Early American methods for dealing with the problems of poverty are customarily traced back to the Elizabethan Act of 1601 For the Relief of the Poor [1] and the Act of 1662 For the Better Relief of the Poor of This Kingdom.[2] Many earlier attempts to deal with persons unable to support themselves can be found in the statute books of England. For example, Edward III prohibited the giving of alms to able-bodied beggars [3] and his successors imposed a succession of laws proscribing vagrancy and begging.[4] Such repressive efforts eventually gave way to a limited recognition of public responsibility for the relief of the poor. One of the earliest forms of such recognition was the sanctioning and regulation of begging by the issuance of licenses to the poor.[5]

During the sixteenth century, it became apparent that more affirmative action was required if the newly perceived public responsibility to the poor was to be effectively discharged. Thus, in 1535, Henry VIII imposed upon borough officers and church wardens the responsibility to collect and distribute alms for the relief of the poor. Throughout the balance of the sixteenth century, various statutes concerning the relief of poverty were from time to time passed and amended, adding the various elements which were finally brought together in the Act of 1601. The central provision of that Act provided:

"That the churchwardens of every parish, and four * * * substan-

[1] 43 Eliz., c. 2 (1601).

[2] 13 & 14 Car. 2, c. 12 (1662).

[3] 23 Edw. 3, c. 7 (1349).

[4] 12 Rich. 2, cc. 3, 7, 8 (1388); 11 Henry 7, c. 2 (1494); 22 Henry 8, c. 12 (1530).

[5] 19 Henry 7, c. 12 (1503).

tial householders there * * * shall be called overseers of the poor of the same parish: and they * * * shall take order from time to time, by and with the consent of two or more * * justices of peace * * * for setting to work all such persons, married or unmarried, having no means to maintain them, and use no ordinary and daily trade of life to get their living by: and also to raise * * * (by taxation of every inhabitant * * * and of every occupier of lands, houses * * * or saleable underwoods in the same parish * * *) a convenient stock of flax, hemp, wool, thread, iron or other necessary ware and stuff, to set the poor on work: and also competent sums of money for and towards the necessary relief of the lame, impotent, old, blind, and such others among them, being poor and not able to work, and also for the putting out of such children to be apprentices. * * * "

The Act of 1601 drew together various pieces of legislation which had been enacted piecemeal during the sixteenth century into an organized program for the relief of the poor. The program contained the central features which have characterized public assistance in England and America to this very day. Most importantly, the Act of 1601 recognized that the relief of poverty was a public responsibility to be discharged from funds raised by taxation. No longer was the State to rely upon private alms giving. Every parish was directed to make provision for the relief of the needy and to levy such taxes as might be required. Beyond its seminal recognition of public responsibility for the relief of poverty, the Act also mandated implementation of that responsibility through means which shaped early American efforts and affected later developments.

Responsibility for the relief of poverty was not assumed by the parliament, but rather imposed upon the Parish and the family. Primary responsibility for the indigent was fastened upon his family. The Act of 1601 provided:

> "That the father and grandfather, and the mother and the grandmother, and the children of every poor, old, blind, lame, and impotent person, or other poor person not able to work, being of a sufficient ability, shall at their own charges relieve and maintain every such person. * * * " [6]

Only in the event that such family support was unavailable did public authorities—the local parish—provide assistance.

The Act also limited direct assistance to "the lame, impotent, old, blind, and such other among them, being poor and not able to work". It did not mandate assistance to all those in need. The similarities in this regard between the limitations imposed in the Act of 1601 and the categorical assistance program established under the Social Security Act of 1935 are striking. Thus, implicit in the Anglo-American system of public assistance from its inception to this very day is the judgment that only certain classes of the needy are to be assisted, a judgment which has long limited the universal and adequate relief of need.

The Act of 1601 reveals the same concern over employment of the poor which informs current debate over income maintenance alternatives. The employable poor are to be provided "necessary ware and stuff, to set the poor on work. * * * " Only those not able to work are to be provided "competent sums of money" for "necessary relief". In the seventeenth century, as in the twentieth, public assistance legislation reflects an insistence that those who are physically able to labor, do so.

Finally, implicit in the Act was the assumption that as a condition for the assistance rendered, governmental authority could and should impose distinctive behavioral requirements upon the recipients. The benefit conferred upon the destitute was not viewed as an unconditional entitlement based on their need alone. Inability to support oneself exposed the public assistance recipient to a variety of constraints thought to redound to the benefit of the recipient or the public. Those constraints impinged upon personal interests of the first importance. The Act of 1601 contemplated the apprenticeship of a recipient's children. Apprenticeship frequently entailed the separation of a child from his or her parents and the indenturing of that child to another for long periods of time. The parents, moreover, could not necessarily recover custody of their children upon regaining self-sufficiency.

The Act of 1662 subjected recipients to another restraint which in various forms survived in this country until very recent times:

> "That it shall and may be lawful, upon complaint made by the churchwardens or overseers of the poor of any parish, to any justice of peace, within forty days after any such person or persons coming so to settle as aforesaid, in any tenement under the yearly value of ten pounds, for any two justices of the peace, whereof one to be * * * of the division where any person or persons that are likely to be chargeable to the parish shall come to inhabit, by their warrant to remove and convey such person or persons to such parish where he or they were last legally settled, either as a native, householder, sojourner, apprentice or servant, for the space of forty days at the least, unless he or they give sufficient security for the discharge of the said parish, to be allowed by the said justices." [7]

---

[6] 43 Eliz., c. 2 § 7 (1601).

[7] 13 & 14 Car. 2, c. 12 § 1(4) (1662).

Enacted to empower parishes to protect their treasuries against the claims of "strangers", the Act of 1662 authorized the bodily removal of a recipient from his current residence to whatever locality was determined to be his domicile or place of settlement. Coupled with widespread criminal punishment of vagrancy,[8] the Laws of Settlement and Removal deprived the poor of their basic freedom to travel and authorized their confinement to a single locality.

II. The Early American Experience

Early American efforts to cope with destitution were based upon approaches with which the colonists were familiar in England. The first comprehensive enactment in the Colonies, the Act of New Plymouth of 1642, contained much the same provisions as its Elizabethan counterpart. Public responsibility for the relief of destitution was recognized. That responsibility was to be discharged by the township. Provision was made for the sick, lame and impotent. Such provision was coupled with punishment of idleness. Powers of removal were granted to local municipalities along with other powers to govern the migration of strangers.[9] Elsewhere in the colonies, English notions of primary family responsibility and apprenticeship of children reappeared.

The Elizabethan inheritance shaped the American response to care of the poor throughout the eighteenth and nineteenth centuries. Recognition of public responsibility for the assistance of the poor, local financing and implementation, limitation of access to public assistance and assumption of the right to dictate behavioral conditions have deeply affected the nature of public assistance in the United States to this very day. The federal character of American Gov-

ernment and the early power of state and local governments reinforced the local tendencies derived from the nation's Elizabethan heritage and agrarian economy.

Although the very assumption of public responsibility for assistance to the poor was subject to periodic challenge, those challenges seem never to have produced any widespread repudiation of such responsibility. The teachings of Thomas Malthus and Herbert Spencer, though doubtless exerting influence over the policies of local authorities, did not result in the dismantling of public assistance. Such influences did, however, reinforce earlier traditions concerning the plenary scope of public authority over public assistance recipients. The most important expression of this tradition prevalent during the nineteenth century was the institutionalization of public assistance recipients. The county almshouse became a familiar American institution. Institutionalization of public assistance recipients was in part a consequence of the necessities of dealing with persons unable to care for themselves physically. It was also due in part to the conviction that the able-bodied poor were personally responsible for their condition—a conviction which drew considerable strength from Social Darwinist doctrines much in vogue. Institutionalization of the able-bodied poor provided a means far more suitable for the enforcement of the disciplinary standards deemed appropriate by many overseers of the poor.

III. Public Assistance in an Industrializing Economy

As the nineteenth century progressed, the social and economic infrastructure upon which the post-Elizabethan public assistance system was based was transformed beyond recognition by the industrial revolution. The largely self-sufficient, multi-generation vertical farm family upon which care of its destitute mem-

---

[8] 27 Henry 8, c. 25 (1535).

[9] 11 Plymouth Colony Records, 26, 30, 32, 38, 40, 41, 44, 108, 110, 111.

bers was originally fastened became an increasing rarity. The increasing mobility of the population and the growth of state government powers made the local government entity less and less an effective focus of public assistance. The growth of an industrial proletariat with its functional specialization, its exposure to the risks of hazardous work and its dependence upon industrial employment furnished by private enterprise gave rise to a variety of new problems beyond the effective reach of traditional measures for the relief of poverty.

A. *Employers' Liability and Workers' Compensation*

One of the earliest causes of destitution to attract governmental effort at the State level was that caused by work injury. The plight of increasing numbers of workers who found themselves disabled and without means of self-support as a result of an industrial accident resulted in widespread demands for legal reform in the late nineteenth and early twentieth centuries. Compensation for work-related injuries under the common law was based on traditional notions of fault. Unless an industrial injury were based upon negligence (or worse) attributable to the employer, no recovery was possible. Moreover, the doctrines of assumption of risk and contributory negligence and the fellow-servant rule, not to mention the formidable problems of securing adequate representation and prosecuting the employee's action, raised serious, frequently insurmountable obstacles to recovery.

Viewed from a broader societal perspective, the fact was that disabling industrial accidents and their impoverishing consequences occurred with an unhappily predictable regularity. The inevitable consequence of relying on traditional common law notions of culpability as a basis for compensating the victims of industrial accidents was a growing number of disabled and destitute workers. Recognition of public responsibility for avoiding the unacceptable results of such impoverishment led to a variety of reforms designed to assure support for those workers whose injuries rendered them incapable of self-support.

First, there came the employer's liability laws which attacked the impoverishment caused by industrial accidents by denying the employer many of the defenses which had been available at common law. Abolition of the doctrines of contributory negligence and assumption of risk and the fellow-servant rule combined with the natural predilections of the jury to endow the injured employee with marked advantages in litigation. There remained, however, the basic necessity of proving that the employee's injury was due to the employer's fault. Combined with the problems of securing adequate representation and the many pitfalls of litigation, that necessity frequently resulted in the uncompensated destitution of disabled workers.

More far reaching was the enactment of workmen's compensation laws which were designed to provide compensation for work-related injuries irrespective of the employer's culpability. Commencing in New York in 1910, workmen's compensation laws were enacted throughout the country during the first third of the century and by 1936 all States other than Arkansas and Mississippi had adopted a compensation law. These laws were designed to make recovery depend solely upon whether an employee's injury was work-related and the character of the injury. The employer's fault or culpability was no longer an issue. The amount of compensation was predetermined. A fixed scale established the compensation to be paid for different types of injuries, taking into account the degree of damage to the worker's physical integrity, the impairment of his earning capacity and the costs and prospects of rehabilitation.

By eliminating the issue of culpability and removing many of the uncertainties involved in the assessment of damages, it was expected that establishment of the employee's entitlement to recovery would be a more orderly, less litigious process. Such expectations have never been fully realized. Contention survived the narrowing of issues and has resulted in extensive litigation under the compensation laws. The adequacy of compensation laws as an income maintenance device has further been undermined by the failure of state legislatures to update, in light of inflation and changing economic conditions, the damages prescribed long ago by statute. Finally, workmen's compensation laws normally exclude from their coverage large groups of workers, most commonly agricultural, domestic and temporary workers. Beyond such commonly excluded categories, coverage varies considerably from State to State. Some statutes are restricted to hazardous employments. Others exclude enterprises employing small numbers of employees. Still others exclude employees of religious and charitable organizations.

Other groups of workers are outside the reach of workmen's compensation laws because they are covered by other bodies of legislation affording some measure of protection against industrial accident. Thus, the estimated 10 million workers employed by State, local and Federal Governments are almost all subject to legislation designed for their particular protection, such as the Federal Employees Compensation Act. Workers engaged in interstate railroad service are covered by the Federal Employees Liability Act whereas maritime workers are governed by Federal admiralty law, with its remedies for unseaworthiness and care and maintenance, and the Jones Act.

Also covered by a distinctive regime relating to disability are veterans of the Armed Forces, who for obvious reasons were early the object of governmental solicitude. Veterans benefits are distributed by the Veterans Administration under three programs: (1) compensation for service-connected disabilities; (2) pensions for nonservice-connected disabilities; and (3) disability benefits payable under Government-issued insurance. In compensation for service-connected disabilities, the Veterans Administration pays statutorily determined amounts for specific disabilities, such as loss of use of limbs or blindness and amounts based on percentage impairment of earning capacity. The latter type of payment is based on the average impairment of earning capacity in civil ocupations as a whole which is deemed to result from a particular disability. No attempt is made to gear the payment to the particular individual's rehabilitation, earnings or need.

The nonservice-connected pension is a monthly payment made by the Veterans Administration by reason of service, age or nonservice-connected disability. To be eligible for such payments by reason of disability, a veteran must have a certain minimum period of wartime service, must be permanently disabled as a result of something other than his own willful misconduct or vicious habits, and must be rendered unemployable to some degree by virtue of the disability. As in the case of compensation for service-connected disabilities, the amount of pension payable by reason of such disability is determined by the average percentage impairment of earning capacity which such disability inflicts on persons employed in civil occupation.

Despite the number of programs thus developed to cope with the economic consequences of disabling injuries, it is estimated by the United States Department of Labor that approximately 20%

of American workers are not protected by compensation legislation. Moreover, such legislation is of course but a partial response to the problem of income failure ensuing from physical disability as, in cases other than the veterans programs, it is limited to work-related disabilities. The limited coverage of the compensation laws, the varying adequacy of benefits payable and the remaining obstacles to successful prosecution of claims has left a significant segment of the disabled needy without assistance.

B. *Mother's Aid Legislation*

Paralleling the enactment of legislation designed to protect individuals against the economic consequence of occupational disability was a resurgence of concern over the condition of needy children. During the history of earlier American efforts to deal with the problems of childhood destitution, provision had been made for needy children within the framework of local general assistance legislation. During most of the nineteenth century, children, like adults, were most often cared for by placement in county almshouses.[10] The other principal methods for the care of needy children were indenturing them to persons who relieved the state of the burden of their support, placing them in public or private institutions designed specifically for the care of children and direct monetary support to the families of needy children.[11] Revelation of the inadequate care received by children in the almshouse environment by Dorothea Dix and many other interested persons eventually led to the enactment of a New York statute in 1864 prohibiting the quartering of children in almshouses.[12] Similar legislation followed in some though not all other states.

The varying and frequently inadequate provision for needy children led President Theodore Roosevelt to call a White House conference to consider the needs of children in 1909. The platform adopted by the conference strongly endorsed the principle that needy children should be cared for in their home environments unless such were not suitable for their proper rearing and education:

"Home life is the highest and finest product of civilization. * * * Children should not be deprived of it except for urgent and compelling reasons. * * * Except in unusual circumstances the home should not be broken up for reasons of poverty but only for considerations of inefficiency or immorality. . . ." [13]

Shortly after the 1909 conference, numerous states began to enact Mother's Aid or Widow's Pension laws providing for "outdoor relief" of women and children who had been deprived of support, that is, direct financial assistance to mothers and children in their homes. In 1911 Illinois and Missouri enacted such legislation. Another 39 states passed such legislation during the second decade of the century and by 1935 all states other than Georgia and South Carolina had enacted such legislation.[14] State Mother's Aid legislation placed administrative and fiscal responsibility for the programs on the county government. Frequently county participation in the programs was optional and less than one-half of the counties in those states which had Mother's Aid legislation elected to maintain such programs. By the mid-nineteen thirties, only 17 state governments were sharing the cost of Mother's Aid programs with the local or county government. The end result of the drive for

---

[10] H. Clarke, Social Legislation 290 (2d Ed. 1957).

[11] Id. at 289–90.

[12] Id. at 291.

[13] Proceedings of the Conference on the Care of Dependent Children, 60th Cong., 2d Sess., S.Doc. 721 (1909).

[14] Abbott, The Child and the State, at Sec. 4 (1938).

widow's pensions at the State level was thus an uneven patchwork of legislation of varying coverage and adequacy.[15]

C. *Old Age Pensions*

The reform movement of the early twentieth century which led to the adoption of Mother's Aid and Workmen's Compensation legislation also focused concern upon the condition of the destitute aged. During the first three decades of the twentieth century, the number of persons over 65 increased far more rapidly (114%) than did the population as a whole (61%).[16] Particularly susceptible to disease and loss of employment, large numbers of the aged, no longer able to rely upon the extended family and local community, found themselves destitute. Seeking alternatives more humane than the county almshouse, many urged adoption of comprehensive income maintenance arrangements for the aged, such as the British Old Age Pension Act of 1908 which provided noncontributorily old-age assistance for needy persons over the age of 70.

The actual results of this drive for old-age income security at the state level were, if anything, even more modest than the results of the efforts for Mother's Aid and Workmen's Compensation. In 1914 the first old age assistance law in the United States was enacted by the State of Arizona, but that statute was promptly declared unconstitutional. It was not until 1923 that Montana enacted the first functioning old age assistance law. Under the pressure of organizations such as the American Association of Old Age Security, established in the mid-nineteen twenties, some 28 states had enacted some form of old age legislation by 1935. In only six of these did the state assume the entire financial burden of the programs, making some contributions to

these burdens in another ten. In only ten of the states was the program statewide and in three the program appears not to have been implemented at all.[17]

Vulnerable to loss of employment and lacking access to means of public support, the aged were particularly exposed to the impact of the Great Depression. It has been estimated that as many as half of the persons over the age of 65 in the United States were dependent on others for support by 1934.[18] Such adversity led to an immense surge of support for the program urged by Dr. Francis E. Townsend which proposed a monthly pension of $200 a month for every person over 60 on the condition that they retire from the work force. The Townsend movement, claiming 2,000,000 members by 1934 and 25,000,000 signatures on petitions urging adoption of the Townsend Plan, profoundly influenced legislators of the period and shaped their efforts at reform.

IV. The Great Depression and the Social Security Act of 1935

At the close of the first third of this century, public provision for the needy thus remained basically dependent upon the locally based and financed post-Elizabethan system of General Assistance. Reform movements of the early twentieth century had supplemented that basic system with a widespread network of workmen's compensation laws and Mother's Aid laws of uneven scope adequacy and the very rudimentary beginnings of laws designed to provide old-age security.

Affording only uncertain relief for destitution arising from predictably recurring causes, American income mainte-

[15] Clarke, supra note 10, at 588–589.

[16] Clarke, supra note 10, at 558.

[17] Leyendecker, Problems and Policies in Public Assistance 55–58 (1955); Clarke, supra note 10, 554–555.

[18] F. Piven & R. Cloward, Regulating the Poor. The Functions of Public Welfare 101 (1971).

nance institutions were wholly unprepared for the massive failure of employment which led to the New Deal administration of President Franklin D. Roosevelt and the adoption of the Social Security Act of 1935.

Unemployment began to rise above normally anticipated levels as early as 1928. By early 1929, the unemployed totaled three million. Another million workers had lost their jobs by January 1930. Unemployment rose further to five million in September 1930, eight million in April 1931 and 15 million in May 1933 by which time one worker of three was unemployed. Between August 1929 and July 1932 seasonally adjusted employment indices had fallen by more than 80%.[19] National income plummeted from 82 billion dollars in 1929 to 40 billion dollars in 1932. Corporate income fell from 11 billion dollars to 2 billion dollars and farm income from 7 billion to 2 billion dollars during that period.[20]

These are a few of the bare statistical parameters of the most severe decline in national production and employment ever experienced in the United States. That decline inevitably resulted in rapid exhaustion of personal financial resources, widespread destitution and unprecedented demands upon existing agencies for relief. There were virtually no state programs providing unemployment compensation at the advent of the Great Depression. It was not until 1932 that the first state unemployment compensation law was passed by the State of Wisconsin. Under these circumstances, the unemployed necessarily turned to private charities and the local general assistance programs.[21] Special campaigns to create job

opportunities and to raise extraordinary private contributions for direct relief sprang up in many communities. The President's Emergency Committee for Employment, organized in October 1930, devoted much of its efforts to publicizing the need for such extraordinary private charitable activities. Local relief expenditures—public and private—multiplied, increasing in the nation's urban areas from $43,745,001 in 1929 to $308,185,543 in 1932.[22]

Demands for public assistance because of unemployment soon outran local fiscal capabilities and gave rise to demands that the Federal Government abandon its traditional noninvolvement in local relief efforts. The Federal Government's first fiscal response to these demands was legislation, contained in the Emergency Relief and Reconstruction Act of 1932, which authorized the Reconstruction Finance Corporation to lend $300,000,000 to State Governments for relief payments. It was not until the Federal Emergency Relief Act of 1933 that the Federal Government authorized direct grants, in the amount of $500,000,000, to support state relief payments. The 1933 Act authorized creation of the Federal Emergency Relief Agency ("FERA") through which more than $3,000,000,000 was distributed to support relief payments during the period from May 1933 through February 1936. During the life of the FERA, approximately two-thirds of public funds expended for relief purposes came from federal sources, with the remainder coming from state and local sources in approximately equal shares.[23]

[19] Nathan, Estimates of Unemployment in the United States 1929–35 (Geneva 1936).

[20] U. S. Bureau of the Census, Statistical Abstract of the United States: 1940 (Wash., D.C., G.P.O.1941).

[21] J. Brown, Public Relief 1929–1939, at 65. (New York 1940).

[22] Expenditures for 120 selected urban areas; E. Winslow, Trends in Different Types of Public and Private Relief in Urban Areas, 1929–35, at 26 (U. S. Children's Bureau No. 237(1937)).

[23] Wells, The Allocation of Relief Funds by the States among Their Political Subdivisions, Monthly Report of FERA, at 57 (June 1936).

The Federal Government's unprecedented involvement in financing direct relief measures under the FERA was generally conceived to be a temporary expedient necessitated by the extraordinary collapse in employment. Necessary as such involvement was, it was viewed with suspicion and the Roosevelt Administration resolved to abandon the direct relief measures of the FERA as soon as possible. In place of the federally supported relief programs of the FERA, the Administration proposed a permanent program of cooperative federal-state action to deal with the problems of economic security and employment. These programs eventually took concrete form in the Works Progress Administration, through which the Federal Government sought to create employment opportunities, and the Social Security Act of 1935, through which the Federal and State Governments implemented the economic security measures which, in amended form, constitute the system of income maintenance upon which the United States relies today.

The President's special message of June 8, 1934, announced that during the fall and winter of 1934, his Administration would attempt to formulate a comprehensive program to further the "security of the citizen and his family through social insurance". The President announced that his greatest concerns were to provide protection against threats to economic security arising from unemployment and old age. By Executive Order 6757, promulgated on June 29, 1934, the President established the Committee on Economic Security whose final report, submitted to the President in January 1935, largely determined the content of what became the Social Security Act of 1935.

The Social Security Act established three major institutions designed to maintain income which provided: (1) unemployment compensation; (2) old age in-

surance; and (3) categorical assistance. The program which came to be known as categorical assistance, to which the materials of the first chapter of this book are largely devoted, provided originally for aid to the aged, the blind and dependent children. Although the system of categorical assistance has attracted great attention in recent years as the last line of defense in providing protection against poverty, it appears to have been of less concern at the time of passage than those measures providing old-age insurance and unemployment compensation.

A. Unemployment Compensation

The provisions designed to establish a system of unemployment compensation were drawn to encourage adoption of unemployment compensation systems by the states and to limit severely the role of the Federal Government, leaving to the States maximum latitude in determining the design and operation of the systems. The basic feature of the program was a federal tax imposed on employers' payrolls against which credits of up to 90% were allowed for employer contributions to state unemployment compensation programs. The tax was imposed at the rate of 1% of payroll for the first year (1936), 2% for the second (1937) and 3% for 1938 and each succeeding year. Exempted from the tax were employers, and excluded from coverage were employees, engaged in governmental service, farm or domestic work, and charitable activity [24] as well as employers having less than 8 employees.[25] The Act required that states deposit funds collected in a federally controlled unemploy-

[24] The Employment Security Amendments of 1970, 84 Stat. 695, added certain categories of eleemosynary employees to the covered population.

[25] As most recently amended, the Act includes employers who during any calendar quarter paid wages of more than $1,560 or employed one or more workers for 20 days during the quarter.

ment trust fund, that the system be administered to assure payment of full compensation when due, that fair hearings be provided for all individuals whose claims for unemployment compensation are denied and that reports be provided the Secretary of Labor containing such information as he may require.

Within the framework of such federal legislation, all states have established unemployment compensation systems. Although the various State programs display considerable variety, virtually all programs contain certain basic elements. Virtually all State programs limit unemployment compensation payments to persons engaged in covered employment.[26] Such limitations mean not only that a person must be engaged in an occupation subject to the Federal payroll tax, but also that he be attached to the work force for a stated period of time. In addition, the States have imposed a variety of other disqualifications which may bar an applicant from compensation—disqualifications most commonly based on determinations that an applicant is not available for work or that he has caused his own unemployment. However, the Social Security Act proscribes disqualifying an applicant for refusal to accept employment which involves substandard conditions or requires joining a company union or refraining from joining a labor union. Prior to receipt of benefits, a waiting period, most commonly of one week, is usually imposed. It is estimated that 80 to 90% of all employed wage and salary workers are presently engaged in covered employment.[27]

Benefits payable during the period of unemployment depend upon the duration of an applicant's period of attachment to the labor force and the level of his

prior earnings. The period over which benefits are payable is restricted to some maximum period, most often 26 weeks. The Employment Security Amendments of 1970, 84 Stat. 695, enacted a Federal-State Extended Unemployment Compensation Program which requires States to make unemployment compensation available for an extended period of 13 weeks beyond the period during which regular unemployment compensation is payable. The State is required to make such payments only during periods of unusually high national or State unemployment: Unusually high national unemployment is defined as insured, seasonally adjusted unemployment in excess of 4.5% for each of the three most recent calendar months. One-half of extended unemployment compensation payments are reimbursed by the Federal Government.

The level of benefits varies from state to state but is most often set at 50% of earnings during the base period subject to prescribed maxima and minima. The benefits so determined are payable irrespective of an individual's needs or resources. The state prescribed minima typically approximate $10 a week and are not designed to provide a minimum subsistence income. A minority of jurisdictions adds a dependents' allowance to a worker's basic compensation. The federal payroll tax which provides financial support for such benefits is currently set at 3.2% of a worker's compensation up to $4,200.

B. *Old Age Income Security Insurance*

The only wholly federal income maintenance program established under the Social Security Act is the Old Age insurance program. Originally devised to provide monthly retirement benefits and lump-sum death benefits, the program has been broadened to provide some measure of income maintenance security when a covered worker's income is interrupted by death, permanent and total

---

[26] Some jurisdictions have expanded coverage in a limited way to cover other employments.

[27] S.Rep.No.91–752, 91st Cong., 2d Sess. 9 (1970).

disability or retirement. Benefits are payable only to workers who have engaged in covered employment for the requisite period of time. Although the old age insurance system, like other programs, originally excluded agricultural, domestic and charitable employees, amendments to the Social Security Act have progressively expanded its reach over the years so that well over 90% of the nation's employees are now subject to the Social Security system.[28] Moreover, the 1965 amendments to the Social Security Act provided for "blanketing-in" all persons over 72; that is, paying minimum benefits to persons over 72 irrespective of their satisfaction of eligibility requirements mandated by the Social Security Act.

The insured status of a worker is dependent on quarters of employment in covered employment. A worker may be fully insured or currently insured. Current insuredness generally qualifies a worker and his family for survivorship and disability benefits and requires that a worker have been employed for six recent calendar quarters. Full insuredness qualifies a worker and his dependents for retirement benefits. Such status requires either 40 quarters of coverage or six quarters and one quarter for every four elapsing after age 21.

The most significant requirement for the receipt of retirement benefits other than requisite attachment to covered employment is that a worker be retired from gainful employment. Deriving from a Depression born concern that older workers retire to increase employment opportunities for younger workers, the retirement criterion has been steadily diluted over the years and is wholly inapplicable to persons over 72.

The retirement benefits payable to an insured worker are determined in rela-

tion to his earnings during a base period. Benefits so determined are payable irrespective of the recipient's need or resources. The percentage of earnings payable is graduated inversely to a worker's base period earnings so that workers with lower earnings receive a higher percentage of those earnings as a pension. For example, pursuant to the statutory provisions effective for 1972, a worker whose average monthly wage was $100 was entitled to receive a monthly pension of $90.60. A worker whose average monthly wage was $700 was entitled to receive a monthly pension of $285.40. The minimum pension payable under the Social Security as of 1972 was $70.40 and the maximum $295.40. The pension payable to an insured worker under age 72 is reduced by the amount of his "excess earnings" which are defined as the worker's earnings for a taxable year in excess of $140 multiplied by the number of months in such year, but excluding one-half of the first $1,200 of such excess.

C. Categorical Assistance

Although the unemployment compensation and old age insurance programs constitute major elements of the American system of income maintenance, neither program is designed for the specific purpose of aiding the needy. Benefits are channeled to persons meeting certain employment-related criteria and are payable irrespective of an individual's need or wealth. The Social Security Act did, however, contain certain provisions designed specifically to relieve need—provisions which established what came to be known as the categorical assistance programs. As described earlier, adoption of the Social Security Act coincided with the growing unpopularity of the Federal Government's involvement in direct relief under the FERA and with the consequent termination of such involvement. In 1934 and 1935, Administration offi-

[28] Gordon, Aging and Income Security, in Handbook of Social Gerontology 229 (1960).

cials were anxious to quit the business of direct relief and return administration of such assistance to State Governments. Accordingly, it was decided by the Committee on Economic Security that federal participation in programs to relieve the needy would be limited to federal grants-in-aid reimbursing State Governments for a portion of the expenses incurred in the relief of the needy.

However, no attempt was made to provide for universal relief of need. Rather, the Federal Government proposed to finance the relief of need only for three categories of the needy whose "entitlement" to public assistance had been recognized in earlier State efforts—the aged (OAA), dependent children (AFDC) and the blind (AB). Indeed, as originally proposed by the Committee on Economic Security, the program envisioned assistance to the aged and dependent children alone, and it was not until Congressional interest had been aroused in the plight of the blind that this group was added as recipients of federally assisted public assistance.

Those eligible for assistance under the Aid to Dependent Children Program are defined in terms of families with at least one "child" who has been "deprived of parental support or care by reason of death, continued absence from home, or physical or mental incapacity of a parent". Adopting the view which informed earlier State Mother's Aid legislation, the Act requires that a dependent child eligible for assistance reside at home with a parent or other specified relative and reimburses assistance for such parent or other person if that person is deemed essential for the care of the dependent child.

Since the initial adoption of the Social Security Act, the Act has been amended to provide financial support for two significant additional groups of persons. In 1950, support was extended to public as-

sistance for the permanently and totally disabled (APTD). In 1961, the aid to dependent children program (AFDC) was expanded to include children deprived of parental support because of the unemployment of a parent (AFDC–U). All States have established and maintain OAA, AB, APTD and AFDC programs. Only 24 States had established AFDC–U programs as of 1969.

In addition, the aid to families with dependent children program was amended to provide federal reimbursement for State expenditures for emergency assistance to "needy families with children" (AFDC–E). Like children in the AFDC program, a child must reside with a statutorily defined "relative"; however, to be eligible a child need not be a "dependent child" as defined in the statute. AFDC–E assistance may be paid only where the child is without available resources and where such assistance is necessary to avoid the destitution of the child or to provide living arrangements in a home for the child. Emergency assistance payments may not be made in respect of a child whose need arose because of a refusal of employment or training by the child or its responsible relative. Emergency payments may not be furnished for a period exceeding 30 days in any 12-month period.

The federal grants-in-aid established under the Social Security Act reimburse State Governments for stated percentages of State public assistance payments up to certain maxima. These reimbursements vary from program to program, and from state to state, but in general the Federal Government bears one-half or more of the cost of grants for categorical assistance.[29]

To qualify for Federal grants-in-aid, the States must comply with certain con-

[29] Prior to the 1972 amendments to the categorical assistance legislation which resulted in federalization of the OAA, AB and APTD programs. See pp. 22–23, infra.

ditions set forth in the Social Security Act. These provisions, particularly those relating to OAA, were the subject of major debate when the Act was originally submitted to Congress. As conceived by Edwin Witte, Executive Director of the Committee on Economic Security, the eligibility requirements to be used in determining who would be eligible for public assistance were to be prescribed in the Act and the States were to be expressly barred from making such requirements more stringent or from legislating additional requirements. Moreover, the bill, as submitted by the Committee, required that old age assistance furnished by the States be sufficient, when added to the income of the aged recipient, to provide a reasonable subsistence compatible with decency and health. Both provisions proved highly objectionable to many Congressmen, particularly those from the South.[30] Accordingly, the provision requiring that assistance be sufficient to provide a reasonable subsistence was deleted and no provision expressly precluding additional or more stringent State eligibility requirements was included.

As enacted by Congress, the Act explicitly required the States only to meet requirements which were largely procedural or administrative in character. Pursuant to these requirements, States are obligated to:

(1) ensure State-wide operation of the plan;

(2) participate in financing assistance payments;

(3) establish a single State agency to administer or supervise the plan;

(4) maintain such methods of administration as are necessary for proper and efficient administration of the plan;

(5) provide that all individuals wishing to make application for assistance

be afforded an opportunity to do so and that all eligible individuals be furnished assistance with reasonable promptness;

(6) provide a fair hearing to any person whose application for assistance is denied or is not acted upon promptly;

(7) maintain the confidentiality of information obtained concerning applicants and recipients;

(8) submit such reports as may be required by the Secretary of Health, Education and Welfare.

In addition, the Act requires that State AFDC programs include procedures which:

(a) provide prompt notice to law enforcement authorities of any dependent child whose dependence arises out of desertion or abandonment or whose home is unsuitable because of neglect, abuse or exploitation;

(b) provide for referral of employable assistance recipients to the appropriate employment or training facility; and

(c) provide for certain prescribed adjustments of the amounts used by the State to determine need and any maxima imposed on the amounts of assistance to reflect cost of living changes since establishment of those amounts and maxima.

The Social Security Act also contains provisions limiting the State's power to disqualify needy applicants by application of age, residence or citizenship standards.

Within the framework of these general requirements, the States exercised considerable discretion in the design and administration of their welfare systems. This discretion was utilized by the States to define with greater stringency the eligibility requirements which must be satisfied before one who is aged, blind, permanently and totally disabled or a de-

30 E. Witte, The Development of the Social Security Act 143–145 (1962).

pendent child may receive public assistance. Drawing upon earlier notions of settlement and removal, States commonly imposed requirements that an applicant have resided in the State for a prescribed period prior to application.[31] Closely related were requirements that the applicant be a citizen of the United States or, in the alternative, satisfy lengthy residence requirements.[32]

Many states impose a variety of requirements designed to regulate a recipient's personal relationships and conduct. Thus, the State of Louisiana terminated assistance to any dependent child who was deemed not to be living in a suitable home, the suitability of which depended largely on the mother's sexual behavior.[33] Similar disqualifications resulted from application of the "substitute father" doctrine whereby a State would deem a child not deprived of parental support and hence not eligible for AFDC assistance if the child's mother were engaged in cohabitation or intimate relations with a man, and such disqualification was imposed irrespective of that man's contributions to the child's support or his obligation to so contribute.[34] Similarly, States such as Connecticut disqualified applicants who did not provide what welfare authorities regarded as satisfactory cooperation in pursuing a deserting spouse and parent.

A pervasive source of State eligibility requirements has been the recurring con-

cern over the employability of the recipient. Over the years since 1935, States have imposed a variety of work requirements upon welfare applicants. The Federal Government itself moved in that direction in 1968 and 1971 by establishing programs relating to the employment of recipients.[35]

While the Department of Health, Education and Welfare, which is responsible for approving state assistance plans, sometimes acted to restrain some of the more outrageous state eligibility restrictions, the Department never challenged the general discretion of the states to impose such restrictions. Recent Supreme Court decisions, as well as lower court rulings, have however cast very substantial doubt on the legality of any state imposed eligibility requirements which deny aid to persons meeting federal categorical requirements. Those recent litigative developments are taken up in the materials which follow.

In addition to the eligibility requirements designed to exclude some category of needy persons or to enforce certain standards of behavior, there are a variety of eligibility requirements incident to the operation of the State welfare procedure itself. States of course require the recipient to furnish certain information and cooperation in order to receive assistance.

To become eligible for public assistance at all, the applicant must submit to the process of inquiry the welfare authorities require. Traditionally, that process has entailed a thoroughgoing inquiry into the applicant's eligibility and condition including the questioning of neighbors and relations in an effort to confirm the statements made by the applicant. Moreover, the scope of inquiry frequently goes far beyond that necessary to determine an applicant's eligibility and need and seeks information thought relevant to the wel-

---

[31] See Shapiro v. Thompson and other materials relating to the constitutionality of durational residence requirements at p. 115 et seq., infra.

[32] See Graham v. Richardson and other materials relating to the constitutionality of citizenship requirements at pp. 127–130, infra.

[33] See p. 139 et seq., infra, for materials relating to the validity of suitable home policies.

[34] See King v. Smith and other materials relating to the legality of the substitute father doctrine at p. 140 et seq., infra.

[35] See materials related to the legality of such procedures at p. 180 et seq., infra.

fare authorities' "rehabilitative" designs. As an alternative some States have adopted a simplified procedure known as the Declaration System whereby inquiry is restricted to those matters directly involved for determination of eligibility and budgetary deficiency and reliance is placed upon the applicant's statement with random verification. Although experimental programs have applied Declaration System procedures to the whole gamut of categorical assistance programs, present federal rules are largely antagonistic to the use of such procedures.[36] Once assistance is granted, public assistance authorities commonly require recipients to admit welfare workers to their homes for purposes of visitation and inspection [37] and to cooperate in a variety of ways. Failure of a recipient to render requisite cooperation may result in termination of assistance.

Once an applicant has shown himself to be a member of that class of the needy to whom federally supported public assistance is payable, there remains the task of determining the amount of assistance to be paid. The threshold determination is one of "need". What does the recipient require to subsist and what does this cost? From a recipient's need, there must be subtracted the "resources" shown or assumed to be available to him. Such resources include income, property and family support obligations. Resource determination is typically pursued with great care and the recipient is required to liquidate all assets of any value not deemed necessary for the recipient's subsistence. In addition, an applicant may be required to enforce the support obligations owed him by children or other relatives under State law. Any assistance paid normally becomes a claim against the recipient recoverable from whatever assets an individual may later acquire. The difference between an individual's need and his resources is his "budgetary deficiency".

Determination of the level of assistance does not stop with determination of need and resources. Various devices are employed by the States to limit the amount of assistance payable to some amount less than an individual's budgetary deficiency. One of these devices is the family maximum whereby the amount payable to any family is limited to a certain stated amount irrespective of the number of persons in the family or their budgetary deficiency. As of 1965, twenty-one States imposed family maxima with levels as low as $81 per month in Florida, $90 in Mississippi and $99 in South Carolina.[38]

Even more frequently used are the practices of percentage reduction and individual maxima. States employing percentage reduction maxima pay recipients only a stated percentage of their budgetary deficiencies. Thus, Mississippi pays AFDC recipients only 30% of their deficiencies, Alabama 50% and Ohio 73%. States applying individual maxima pay no more than a stated amount per person such as the $12 per month paid to the third and subsequent children in Mississippi. Percentage reduction has become an increasingly popular measure in recent years as States have found themselves coming under increasing financial burdens due to rising numbers of AFDC recipients.[39]

This entire structure of federal grant-in-aid assistance will be drastically modified as to OAA, APTD, and AB recipients (the so-called "adult" categories) as

---

[36] See p. 307 et seq., infra, for materials on the Declaration System.

[37] See Wyman v. James and other materials relating to home visits at p. 313 et seq., infra.

[38] See Dandridge v. Williams and other materials relating to the legality of family maxima at p. 77 et seq., infra.

[39] See p. 259 et seq., infra, for materials relating to the legality of percentage and individual maxima.

of January 1, 1974. Effective on that date a new combined program designated Supplemental Security Income (SSI) will replace the existing adult categorical programs. In general, persons who were eligible for assistance under the former adult programs will be eligible under SSI. (Indeed, there is grandfather clause protection for present recipients in adult categories.) However, unlike the former programs this is a federalized program rather than a grant-in-aid arrangement, and thus there is no question that all eligible persons are to be given aid without being subjected to state by state modifications in eligibility standards. This federal aspect also carries over into benefit level. Under SSI, for the first time, there are federally fixed standards of need and benefit levels. SSI guarantees a minimum income of $130 per month to an eligible individual and $195 to a couple both of whom are eligible. The first $20 per month of Social Security or other income is disregarded in computing the benefit payable, as is the first $65 per month of earned income and one-half of all earned income over $65.

Recipients may, without impairing eligibility retain property valued at $1,500 for an individual and $2,250 for a couple exclusive of the value of an individual's house, surrounding property, household effects, personal effects, automobile and property needed for self-support if reasonable.

States are permitted to increase benefit levels above the federal base. Any such state supplementation is to be paid wholly out of state funds, except that a state will be held harmless by the Federal government against any increase in State expenditures above present amounts so long as total benefit levels do not exceed the amount of present levels plus the bonus value of food stamps. The food stamp program, discussed next, is terminated as to SSI recipients.

D. *Food Assistance Programs*

In addition to involving the Federal Government in cash-payment public assistance programs, such as unemployment insurance, old age pensions and categorical assistance, the Great Depression also led to federal involvement in providing food assistance to the poor.[40] The Agricultural Adjustment Act of 1933, as amended in 1935, authorized the Secretary of Agriculture to create a fund for the purpose of increasing consumption of agricultural commodities.[41] Pursuant to the Agricultural Adjustment Act, the Secretary of Agriculture inaugurated a short-lived food stamp program in 1939. That program envisioned two classes of "stamps" issued by the Federal Government to persons in need of food assistance which could be redeemed at retail stores for food. Needy persons were to purchase "orange stamps" which could be used to purchase any type of food. Purchasers of orange stamps would receive "blue stamps" free of charge which could be used to purchase food designated as surplus commodities by the Secretary of Agriculture. This early program was never administered on a nationwide basis. Before its implementation on a comprehensive basis could be achieved, the reorientation of governmental efforts and the improving economic conditions which came with the advent of the Second World War resulted in termination of the program.

During the period since the Second World War, federal food assistance has

[40] This introduction to American income maintenance institutions is focused primarily on sketching the historical development of cash assistance programs. In this subsection and the succeeding subsection, the development of federal programs relating to the provision of food products and medical services is briefly summarized. See also the discussion of the various programs relating to the provision of housing in a later chapter.

[41] 48 Stat. 31 (1933), as amended, 49 Stat. 774 (1935).

taken two principal forms, the distribution of surplus agricultural commodities and the food stamp program. Section 416 of the Agricultural Act of 1949 provides that "in order to prevent the waste of commodities whether in private stocks or acquired through price-support operations by the CCC before they can be disposed of in normal domestic channels * * * the CCC is authorized in the case of food commodities to donate such commodities to * * * the assistance of needy persons * * *." Pursuant to such authorization, the United States Department of Agriculture has made surplus food commodities available to local governments for distribution to needy persons. The decision whether or not to participate in the surplus commodity distribution has been generally made by each county government and need is determined by reference to income levels established by the States in administering the categorical assistance program.

Operation of the post-war food stamp program was first authorized by a 1959 amendment to extend the Agricultural Trade Development and Assistance Act of 1954. On May 29, 1961, the first pilot project food stamp plan was inaugurated in McDowell County, West Virginia, and by May 1964, pilot projects were operating in 40 counties and three large cities and reached a peak of 392,-000 persons during March 1964. Analyses of the pilot projects led President Johnson to recommend implementation of a permanent food stamp program which was authorized on August 31, 1964, by enactment of the Food Stamp Act of 1964.

The Act required that State Governments desiring to participate in the food stamp program submit a plan specifying the method by which the program would operate in the State for approval by the Secretary of Agriculture. The plan was to specify the political subdivisions of the State within which the program was to operate, the standards to be used to determine eligibility for participation and the safeguards to be employed to protect the confidentiality of information supplied by applicants. Eligibility for participation in the program is generally based on the income standards used by the State in administering the categorical assistance program; however, any household determined to be needy with reference to such an income standard is eligible to participate, not just those persons falling within the categories of the categorical assistance program. The Act provided that either a food stamp program or a commodity distribution program, but not both, could be operated in any political subdivision.

Operation of the program envisioned that eligible households would be entitled to buy food stamps having a value in excess of the purchase price. The food stamps could then be used to purchase food (excluding tobacco, alcohol and imported products) at ordinary retail outlets which would redeem the stamps for cash at commercial banks which, in turn, would redeem the stamps at Federal Reserve Banks. The purchase price and value of stamps available to an eligible household varies with the income of the family. Thus, under the price schedule as it existed in the early years of the program, a family of four with a monthly income in the range of 0–$30 was charged $8 per month and received $52 worth of stamps, or "bonus" stamps having a value of $44. A family of four with income in the range of $100–109.99 paid $44 and received stamps worth $78 or a "bonus" of $34. Although the food stamp program was enacted as a solution to the inadequacies of the commodity distribution program, its administration soon came under attack as national awareness of the poor's nutritional deficiencies developed and the program's limitations became more apparent.

In 1967 and 1968 inquiries undertaken by the Citizens' Board of Inquiry into

Hunger and Malnutrition in the United States, the United States Civil Rights Commission and the Senate Subcommittee on Manpower, Employment and Poverty focused national attention on the federal commodity distribution and food stamp programs. Among the inadequacies perceived were the following. Participation in federal food programs was left to local option and many local governments chose not to participate. The Citizens' Board of Inquiry concluded that one-third of the 1,000 counties in the United States with the lowest average per capita income had no federal food program in operation. Eligibility for participation in those counties which had implemented a federal food program was based on the income levels established by the various States for determining eligibility to participate in categorical assistance programs. Those levels varied drastically from State to State and in some States excluded households whose income was clearly insufficient to satisfy minimal nutritional requirements.

Unlike the commodity distribution program, participation in the federal food stamp program required payment of certain amounts for the food stamps, typically at monthly intervals. The charges established for food stamp participation proved beyond the capacity of many households in the relevant income categories. Other potentially eligible households were unaware or incapable of coping with the procedures required for certification to participate in the program. The result was that substitution of the food stamp program for the commodity distribution program in many instances markedly reduced participation in federal food programs. For those families who did participate in the program, the value of the food stamps provided generally fell well below the amount which the Department of Agriculture deemed necessary for minimal nutritional requirements. The Interim Report of the Senate

Select Committee on Nutrition and Human Needs (91st Cong., 1st Sess. 1969) contrasted the Department of Agriculture's low-cost diet of $120 per month for a family of four with the total stamp value currently made available under the food stamp program, which ranged from $60 per month for families having an income of $10 per month to $108 per month for a family having a monthly income of $300.

In response to such criticisms, the food stamp program was significantly reformed by legislation enacted on January 11, 1971. That legislation provided for uniform national eligibility standards and for determination of the eligibility of public assistance recipients upon the applicant's affidavit rather than by the more exacting verification procedures generally employed. It authorized local governments to operate the food stamp and commodity distribution programs concurrently. The purchase price of the stamps was overhauled so that food stamps were distributed without charge to households having an income of $30 per month or less and no household was charged more than 30% of its income. Participants were to be allotted food stamps of sufficient value to procure a nutritionally adequate diet.

The liberalization of the food stamp program and its increasingly widespread implementation has led to rapidly rising enrollments and expenditures. The number of recipients has increased from 392,-000 in March 1964 to 3,600,000 in December 1969 to 6,900,000 in July 1970 to 11,200,000 in July 1971. The value of the bonus stamps distributed during the same period has increased from $30,-479,000 in 1964 to $250,982,000 in 1969 to $1,582,850,000 in 1971. As the food stamp program assumes increasing significance in providing assistance to the poor, its future operation has become more uncertain. The continued existence of the program and its relation to the

Federal Government's cash assistance programs have become increasingly important matters of Congressional concern. As indicated elsewhere, recent discussions concerning substitution of existing categorical assistance programs by new forms of cash assistance have involved the food stamp program and proposals have been made both for its continuation as a supplement to the liberalized cash assistance programs and for its abolition in light of the higher level of cash assistance envisioned. As mentioned above, the newly enacted SSI program ends food stamps for persons under that program, thus setting an important precedent for eventual resolution of the issue as to AFDC recipients.

E. *Medical Services*

The history of the provision of medical services to those unable to bear the costs of such services in many ways resembles the history of public assistance generally. Medical assistance, like cash assistance, has been traditionally provided to the indigent, if at all, through programs of local initiative and private charity. Federal involvement in medical assistance is of even later origin than involvement in cash assistance. Although the original proposals out of which the Social Security Act grew envisioned recommendations by the Committee on Economic Security for health insurance, these provisions were early deleted and no federal health insurance program emerged. Moreover, the categorical assistance provisions of the Act were limited to federal grants-in-aid supporting cash payments. No provision was made for supporting the provision of medical services to categorical assistance recipients. Prior to passage of the Social Security Act, federal involvement in the provision for medical services had been sharply limited, consisting largely of programs dealing with veterans' hospitalization and rehabilitation, maternal and child hygiene and services for crippled children.

Since the early part of the twentieth century there had been repeated efforts to involve the Federal Government in supporting the provision of medical service, but until the closing years of the Second World War, these efforts fell far short of attaining the necessary political support. As the War drew to a close, demands for some form of national health insurance came in increasing numbers. In 1943, Senators Wagner and Murray and Congressman Dingwall introduced proposals for compulsory national health insurance. President Roosevelt's State of the Union message of January 11, 1944, in which he sought to define an Economic Bill of Rights for Americans included the "right to adequate medical care and the opportunity to achieve and enjoy good health". The drive for national health insurance attracted increasing support throughout the late forties, resulting in a major political battle which reached its culmination in 1949 and 1950. However, this movement ultimately proved unable to secure a legislative majority.

What did emerge from the politics of the late forties was the expansion of categorical assistance to include the permanently and totally disabled and the extension of federal grant-in-aid support for medical services rendered on behalf of recipients of categorical assistance. During the ensuing decade of the 1950's there was little significant federal legislative effort affecting the delivery of health services to those unable to purchase them, except for continued support of medical vendor payments made on behalf of categorical assistance recipients which by 1960 had reached the sum of $514 million. Confronted with the continuing impossibility of securing necessary legislative support for compulsory national health insurance, political efforts during the late 1950's and early 1960's narrowed their focus to the health conditions of the aged. Steadily rising medical costs, increased longevity and the concomitant increase in the numbers of the aged unable to purchase needed medical services gave rise to a variety of demands for federal support of the provision of medical services to the aged. The proposals included principally measures to encourage participation in voluntary health insurance programs, compulsory federal health insurance for the aged and subsidization of health services for the aged. During the decade of the 1960's each of these provisions reached legislative fruition in one form or another.

The proposal which earliest secured sufficient support for enactment was federal subsidization of medical services for the aged. The Kerr-Mills Act of 1960 essentially liberalized the provision of federal grants-in-aid in support of medical service payments made on behalf of aged persons in connection with the categorical assistance program. The Kerr-Mills Act liberalized the formula pursuant to which federal grants-in-aid supported medical vendor payments made on behalf of OAA recipients. At the time of enactment of the Kerr-Mills Act, the Federal Government reimbursed State medical expenditures on behalf of categorical assistance recipients to the extent of an amount which was between $41.50 and $46.75 of the first $65 per month of average medical expenses incurred by the State. The Kerr-Mills Act provided federal reimbursement of 50 to 80% of the next $12 of average monthly medical expense incurred on behalf of OAA recipients, the percentage of reimbursement being inversely related to the State's per capita income.

More significantly, the Act also authorized the creation of a medical assistance to the aged program (MAA) pursuant to which the Federal Government offered grant-in-aid support for State vendor payments on behalf of persons over 65 who, although having an income which denied them eligibility for OAA, were sufficiently impecunious that they were unable to meet their medical bills. In 1962, further legislation also made the blind and the permanently and totally disabled eligible for the program. Determination of medical indigence was to be made by the States in accordance with State standards. Federal provisions for administration of the plans by the State were patterned after the existing categorical assistance programs except that the States were barred from establishing durational residency requirements or imposing liens on a recipient's property during his lifetime or that of his or her spouse.

The Kerr-Mills Act also marked the beginning of federal influence over the range of services to be provided by the States. The Act required each State plan to include both institutional and noninstitutional care and provided federal cost-sharing of a wide range of health services, including hospital, physician and nursing home services.

For a variety of reasons, implementation of the Kerr-Mills Act did little more than transfer a greater portion of the cost of providing medical services to the indigent aged to the Federal Government. The standards applied by the States in defining medical indigence were only marginally less restrictive than the standards used to define eligibility for the OAA program. Restrictive eligibility standards and State procedures resulted in keeping the recipient population to a group which was largely composed of persons formerly eligible for needy payment assistance under OAA. The range and quality of services provided was little different from that formerly afforded to OAA recipients.

The failure of Kerr-Mills to improve the delivery of health services to the aged, together with the rapidly rising costs of medical services, created further pressures for legislation which would provide medical services to the aged on a more nearly adequate basis. President Kennedy strongly endorsed the concept of medical insurance for the aged and the King-Anderson bill, although sustaining early defeats, gathered increasing support. The movement of the early 1960's culminated in the Social Security amendments of 1965 pursuant to which the Medicare and Medicaid programs were established.

The Social Security Amendments of 1965 in effect established a three-tiered Federal program to support the provision of medical services to the needy and the aged. Medicare-Part A established a system of compulsory national health insurance, financed through Social Security taxes, pursuant to which all persons eligible for Social Security retirement benefits would be enrolled in a federal health insurance program. The benefits provided for basic hospital in-patient and nursing home services. Pursuant to Medicare-Part B, the Federal Government subsidized the purchase, on a voluntary basis, of health insurance by persons eligible for Social Security retirement benefits to cover the costs of physician and related medical services. Medicare, like the Social Security System of which it became part, was organized as an insurance program. Eligibility is determined without reference to any means test. All persons eligible for Social Security retirement benefits are eligible for Medicare irrespective of their income. Participants receive prescribed benefit coverage in exchange for prescribed contributions.

Title XIX of the 1965 Social Security Amendments established the Medicaid program whereby the Federal Government reconstituted its support for the provision of medical services to the indigent along far more ambitious lines. Like earlier federal involvement, the Medicaid program was built around the categorical assistance program, providing federal grants-in-aid, ranging from 50 to 83%, to

support State provision of medical services for persons covered by the State plan.

The 1965 amendments provided that the State plan must include three categories of persons in the group participating in the program: (1) those persons eligible for categorical assistance; (2) those who would be eligible for categorical assistance but for some State disqualification, such as durational residency, which is proscribed by Medicaid legislation; (3) persons under 21 who would be eligible for categorical assistance if they were under 18. In addition, the State may, if it so chooses, extend medical assistance to: (1) all persons who would be eligible for categorical assistance if the State adopted the broadest possible program; (2) all persons who would be eligible for categorical assistance but for their residence in an institution (other than persons under 65 in mental or tubercular institutions); (3) all persons who would be eligible for categorical assistance if their income were low enough and who have insufficient resources to meet their medical needs; (4) all persons under 21 who are medically indigent irrespective of their eligibility for categorical assistance.

As under the Kerr-Mills Act, States were originally free to determine the level of income which constituted medical indigence. The 1965 amendments proscribed the States from requiring Medicaid beneficiaries who were also receiving cash assistance to share the costs of the services provided, from imposing a lien on the recipient's property until after the death of the recipient and his or her spouse and from asserting liability for the cost of medical services against the recipient's relatives.

The 1965 amendments also went far beyond earlier statutes in establishing requirements designed to ensure the provision of comprehensive health services to Medicaid recipients. States participating in the program were required to provide five basic services: (1) physician's services; (2) in-patient hospital services; (3) out-patient hospital services; (4) skilled nursing home services; (5) laboratory and x-ray services. The State was also permitted to provide any medical or remedial service recognized under State law including fourteen federally recognized services. Moreover, States were required to make a satisfactory showing that they were making substantial progress toward the goal of affording comprehensive health care to all eligible persons by July 1, 1975.

The amendments provided that the level of State payments for hospital services would be equal to the "reasonable cost" of such services. Although the Act did not specify the level at which other services were to be compensated, the prevailing attitude during passage and during the early administration of the program was premised on the notion of bringing Medicaid recipients into the "mainstream" of American medical practice. That policy dictated payment at whatever was the prevailing level of fees to ensure that the services available to Medicaid recipients would be of a quality comparable to that enjoyed by the public at large.

The State response to the Medicaid program was prompt and extensive. All States except Alaska and Arizona implemented Medicaid programs. Moreover, the programs implemented were in some instances of far-reaching scope. In New York, the legislature established an income level of $6,000 to determine Medicaid eligibility and thereby vastly expanded the group of persons eligible for publicly subsidized medical services. The Medi-Cal program implemented in California was restricted to a needier population but contemplated prompt institution of comprehensive health services for those eligible.

The unexpectedly extensive and costly response to the Medicaid program at the State level brought in its wake costs which were far in excess of those which the State and Federal Governments were prepared for. For example, the Federal Government had anticipated that the cost of the Medicaid program for the fiscal year 1968 would be $2.28 billion with 48 States participating. In fact, the program cost with 37 States participating amounted to $3.54 billion. The unexpectedly large costs of the programs established led many in Congress to conclude that certain State plans, such as the New York plan, had gone far beyond the intent of Congress. The history of Medicaid since its passage and the period of immediate post-enactment administration has been a history of retrenchment as State and Federal Governments have sought to back away from the fiscal implications of their original plans.

Fiscal retrenchment of State and Federal commitment to the Medicaid program has affected all dimensions of the program. The number of persons eligible for participation, the scope of services and the original commitment to equal quality of services have all been eroded during the years since adoption of the legislation in 1965. The 1967 amendments to the Social Security Act resulted in imposition of federal restrictions on the States' power to determine the level of income which could constitute medical indigency. Pursuant to these amendments, the income eligibility level established by a state for participation in the Medicaid program cannot exceed 150% of the maximum level of support established under the categorical assistance program. Impelled by more restrictive federal legislation and local fiscal pressures, 11 of the 23 States which had established Medicaid programs to cover persons other than those on categorical assistance reduced their income eligibility levels. The State of New York, whose program had resulted in one of the bell-wether political crises of the program, reduced its eligibility level from $6,000 to $5,000, a reduction which was expected to reduce greatly those not on categorical assistance who would be eligible to participate in Medicaid.

Also the subject of retrenchment was the scope of medical services provided under the program. States were first relieved of the obligation to provide the five basic medical services originally required by Title XIX for Medicaid recipients other than categorical assistance recipients. States were given the option of providing the five basic services (physicians' services, in-patient hospital services, out-patient hospital services, skilled nursing home services and laboratory services) or seven of the fourteen federally prescribed optional medical services. States were later relieved of their obligation to demonstrate progress toward the provision of comprehensive medical services by July 1, 1975. Although this relief took the form of postponing the target date for State provision of comprehensive services until July 1, 1977, the postponement, viewed in the context of related developments in the program, was widely interpreted as a more far-reaching abandonment of the federal effort to require State provision of comprehensive medical services to those unable to afford such services.

Finally, fiscal retrenchment also led to compromising the goal of securing for the indigent medical services of a quality comparable to that afforded the population generally. After consideration of a variety of proposals designed to limit governmental expenditure for medical services, it was determined to limit such support to 75% of the participating physician's normal fee schedule as of January 1969 adjusted for general price increases since that date. Imposition of that limit on the subsidization of medical services coincided with HEW statements

that the goal of securing a single standard of quality medical service for the American population was unrealistic when due consideration was given to the constraints under which the Medicaid program would have to operate.

Recent years of federal involvement in the provision of medical services to those unable to afford them has thus been largely characterized by withdrawal from the objectives of the 1965 Social Security amendments and uncertainty as to the future role of the Federal Government. The shrinking of governmental support has demonstrated the dependence of large numbers of the needy on public subvention while the fiscal demands of such subvention have obstructed adequate provision for medical needs. The shape of future governmental involvement in the provision of medical services for the needy remains obscured in the age-old conflict between perceived need and fiscal constraint.

V. Current Operation of the System

The system of public income maintenance in the United States today consists essentially of the programs described above. Through them an aggregate of some $64.3 billion dollars was disbursed to recipients in 1970. Far and away the most significant component consists of the payments made to retired and disabled workers, their dependents and survivors, through the Social Security system which totaled some $31.6 billion. Another $10.9 billion in retirement benefits was paid to public servants and railroad workers under similar programs. Veterans' pension and compensation payments came to an additional $5.5 billion. In excess of 23 million monthly payments were made to beneficiaries of the Federal Social Security laws during a typical month in 1970 and the average monthly pension disbursed to retired workers was $118.10. Despite the considerable benefits paid to retired workers, the system fell far short of guaranteeing to each aged person an income consistent with minimum standards of health and decency, a fact made plain by the existence of 4.8 million aged persons whom the Federal Government classified "poor". [42]

Unemployment compensation benefits totaled $4.2 billion during 1970 while Workmen's Compensation and temporary disability benefits came to $2.6 billion.[43] An average of 1.5 million beneficiaries drew unemployment benefits during each week of 1970 and 3.4% of those engaged in covered employment found themselves unemployed. Unemployment benefits averaged $50.31 per week and nearly 1.3 million persons exhausted their benefits during the period.

Viewed in general terms, the existing system of unemployment compensation provides limited and temporary income support to those within its reach. The benefits afforded fall short of comprehensive protection against income interruption due to unemployment. The 1.3 million persons who exhausted their benefits in 1970 were confronted with the prospect of continuing uncompensated unemployment. Many of those receiving benefits, which averaged $50.-31, were afforded income maintenance at levels well short of minimum standards of health and decency. And of course many of the unemployed were not attached to covered employment and were therefore beyond the reach of the system altogether.

Federally assisted categorical assistance payments aggregated $8.2 billion in 1970 and were distributed to 13.8 million persons. State-financed general assistance payments aggregated $.6 billion and were paid to slightly over one million persons. Of the recipients of federally assisted

categorical assistance payments, slightly over 2,000,000 were OAA beneficiaries, 81,000 were AB beneficiaries, 935,000 were APTD beneficiaries and 9,659,000 were AFDC beneficiaries. Monthly payments averaged $76.17 for OAA beneficiaries, $104.32 for AB recipients, $97.87 for APTD recipients and $50.52 for AFDC recipients for the nation as a whole. Benefits varied widely from state to state, particularly for the AFDC category where monthly benefits payable averaged $13.75 in Mississippi, $15.64 in Alabama and $19.70 in South Carolina and ranged upwards to $75.83 in New York, $74.04 in Hawaii and $68.64 in Massachusetts.

Over the years, the number of OAA and AB recipients has remained relatively constant:

	1940	1970
OAA	2,070,000	2,082,000
AB	73,400	81,000

The APTD population has increased steadily since inception of the program in 1950 rising from 69,000 in 1950 to 935,000 in 1970. However, it is the AFDC category which has aroused the greatest concern by reason of its rapid growth. The number of AFDC recipients, originally 1,222,000 in 1940, declined substantially during the years of World War II and then increased at a moderate rate to slightly over 3,000,000 in 1960. During the next ten years the AFDC population increased by an unprecedented 320%. What is more, while it took eight years (1960–1968) for the AFDC population to increase by 3,000,-000 persons, the next two years (1968–1970) saw an increase of 3,600,000 persons.

The reasons underlying this rapid and massive increase are many. Continuing migration from southern to northern states brought millions of Americans into states where benefits were higher and

---

[42] See p. 43, infra.

[43] Exclusive of disability benefits payable under the OASDHI provisions of the Social Security Act.

eligibility restrictions less forbidding. Organization and growth of the National Welfare Rights Organization has done much to encourage eligible persons to apply for public assistance and dispel earlier attitudes of reluctance to apply. Access to greatly expanded legal services, made available through appropriations of the Office of Economic Opportunity, made it possible for recipients to challenge the validity of a large number of state-imposed eligibility requirements. As the materials in Chapter I indicate, successive victories invalidated long established restrictions such as those relating to residence, citizenship, substitute fathers and family maxima.

Disquiet over the status of public maintenance institutions arose not only because of the rapidly growing AFDC rolls. President John F. Kennedy's Administration brought renewed attention to the fact that millions of persons were living in poverty and raised questions about the adequacy of the current system of income maintenance. In the 1964 report of the Council of Economic Advisors, the Council adopted a benchmark of $3,000 as the minimum subsistence level for a family of two or more. Shortly thereafter the Department of Health, Education and Welfare developed a more refined "Poverty Index" as a device for measuring the persistence of poverty in the United States. The HEW Index purports to give a measure of the minimum income necessary for subsistence for families of different sizes, ages, sex compositions and places of residence, urban or rural.

The HEW Index is based upon the so-called "economy food plan" devised by the Department of Agriculture to provide a balanced market basket for "temporary or emergency use when funds are low". The Department estimated that $4.60 per person per month could supply the requirements of its economy food plan at the prices prevailing in January 1967.

It is this economy food plan which lies at the basis of HEW's Poverty Index. To derive the Index, HEW merely multiplied the food cost yielded for a family of given composition by three. The HEW multiplier of three is based on empirical studies which demonstrated that lower income families spent approximately one-third of their budgets on food. The Department made no attempt to determine what nonfood items are essential or to estimate the cost of such items.

The HEW Poverty Index figures yielded the following estimates of income necessary for subsistence for nonfarm families for 1969.

Family Size	Poverty Income Level
1	$1,834
2	$2,364
3	$2,905
4	$3,721
5	$4,368
6	$4,921
7	$6,034

Judged by these standards, 24.3 million persons or 12.3% of the population were classified "poor". Of these, 9.8 million were children living in families; 4.4 million of these children lived in female headed families. 1.8 million of the poor were female heads of families. 4.8 million of the poor were at least 65 years of age. Fourteen and nine-tenths percent of all families and unrelated individuals were poor in 1969 including 30.7% of all families and unrelated individuals where the head of the family or individual was over 65. Thirty-one and four-tenths percent of all nonaged female headed white families were poor. Fully 55% of aged black families and 67.8% of black families with an aged female head were poor. Of those black families not headed by an aged person 27.7%

were poor and 50.4% of those headed by a female were poor.

Of 4.9 million heads of poor families, 2.2 million were unemployed throughout the year, 740,000 of whom were disabled or ill and 36,000 of whom were unable to find work. Of those 2.7 million family heads who worked during 1969, 1.6 million worked for 40 weeks or more.

The aggregate poverty gap—that is, the difference between the current income of the poor and the Poverty Index level of income—was $10.1 billion or an average deficit of $1,032 for each poor family and unrelated individual. The average deficit was greatest for female headed black families with children, for whom the poverty gap was $1,718.

The statistics demonstrate that even judged by the spartan standards of the HEW Poverty Index, there remains widespread deprivation which is not remedied by the current system of income maintenance. Such deprivation afflicts one of every seven households in America. Poverty weighs with particular severity upon women, aged persons and blacks. One nonaged female headed family out of three is poor. One aged family of three is poor. One nonaged black family in four is poor. More than half the aged black families are poor and over two out of three families headed by an aged black female are poor.

Concern over American income maintenance institutions comes not only from the failures of those institutions to remedy poverty, but also from other socially disruptive forces which the current system of income maintenance and particularly the AFDC program appears to exert upon the poor. Most important of these forces are those which tend to erode family solidarity and deter employment.

The tendency of the system to erode family solidarity derives from the fact that for a family to qualify for AFDC the dependent child in that family must

be deprived of the support of at least one parent by reason of death, disability or continued absence from home. In 24 States lack of parental support because of involuntary unemployment will also qualify a family for AFDC-U assistance. Consequently, in the 26 States which do not have AFDC-U programs, a father who is unable to find work can obtain categorical assistance for his children only by desertion. The same is true throughout the nation for working fathers whose labor produces an insufficient income.

The categorical assistance program also exerts a powerful disincentive against employment. The budgetary deficiency, pursuant to which the amount of public assistance payable is computed, has traditionally been calculated by subtracting from a person's need his resources, including his earnings. Such computation resulted in reducing an individual's public assistance grant by $1.00 for each $1.00 earned and thus destroyed the economic incentives for employment. The 1968 amendments to the AFDC program sought to ease the disincentive pressures of public assistance by requiring States to "disregard" the first $30 of a recipient's earnings and one-third of the balance in computing the recipient's resources and hence his budgetary deficiency. Although the 1968 amendments did serve to ameliorate disincentive pressures to a degree, the earnings of welfare recipients remained subject to an effective tax rate of $66\frac{2}{3}\%$—a rate which many believe far too high to provide satisfactory employment incentives.

VI. Current Legislative Proposals

Widespread dissatisfaction with the system of public assistance led the Nixon Administration to propose an extensive reform of the categorical assistance program. The most important aspect of the proposed legislation was abolition of the AFDC program and substitution of a new Family Assistance Plan ("FAP") which would have made available for AFDC recipients many of the programatic reforms subsequently provided to adult categories under SSI.

Pursuant to the original version of FAP as introduced in July 1969, the Federal Government proposed to guarantee each family with dependent children a minimum income of $1,600 per year. Such payments were to be made directly by the Federal Government. Unlike AFDC, deprivation of parental support would not have been an eligibility condition under the new program. Families with dependent children were to qualify whether or not both parents reside with the child, and whether or not the parents are employed. The proposal would have extended the reach of public assistance to virtually all persons except married couples without children and unattached individuals who are not aged, disabled or blind. By including working and unemployed fathers, it was hoped to eliminate the disintegrating pressures currently exerted by AFDC on the family structure.

To reduce the employment disincentives of public assistance, it was proposed to expand existing provisions relating to disregard of income to allow the recipient to retain $60 per month plus one-half of the balance of his earnings. Thus, a family earning $2,000 would have been entitled to retain the first $720 of those earnings without any reduction in its public assistance grant. Of the remaining $1,280, $640 would have been applied to reduce the family's $1,600 FAP grant so that the family would have received its earnings of $2,000 plus $960 of the FAP grant or a total of $2,960. This incentive is not as much of a change from the $30 plus one-third exclusion under existing law as might first appear. Although the amount of the exclusion was increased somewhat, no offset was allowed for work related expenses which are deductible under current law. For this reason, the Senate Finance Commit-

tee staff analysis concluded that FAP "provides for an earnings disregard of generally comparable impact" to that under present law. Hearings before Senate Fin.Comm. on H.R. 16311, at 132 (1970). Coupled with the work incentive provisions in FAP were more stringent requirements enforcing participation in the work force.

After some initial vacillation, it was also proposed that FAP recipients be made eligible for the food stamp program pursuant to which they would be able to purchase food coupons worth more than their purchase price.

Although the relationship between State and Federal Governments under FAP was not fully particularized, it was proposed to require that States not reduce current public assistance levels. States were further to be required to spend at least one-half as much as their current expenditures on public assistance, but the Federal Government was to reimburse State expenditures so that no State would be required to spend more than 90% of its current welfare expenditures in complying with the requirement to maintain current benefit levels.

The FAP program would have raised income levels of the poor in rural, largely southern states. The $1,600 benefit level at the time exceeded average public assistance benefits in 20 states. When coupled with the requirement that the State Government spend at least one-half of its current expenditures on welfare, FAP held promise of raising levels in such States substantially. The proposed legislation also envisioned a federally financed payment of $90 per month for the three adult categories, OAA, AB and APTD. The liberalized federal support of assistance in the adult categories combined with the FAP program held forth the prospect of significant improvement in low benefit status.

Such improvements, however, proved insufficient to muster the support needed for passage of FAP. The National Welfare Rights Organization denounced the plan and urged adoption of a minimum income of $6,500. The program lost badly needed support because it promised little fiscal relief to northern industrial States with high benefit levels and nothing at all to the many public assistance recipients in those States. The work requirements of the bill were viewed as overly coercive by some and inadequate by others. The work incentives were perceived as no advance over the income disregard provisions of existing law. Since supplemental State-financed public assistance programs would likely adhere to the contours of the old AFDC program and hence exclude families where both parents reside in the home and neither is unemployed, FAP promised no real escape from the disruptive pressures of categorical assistance on family solidarity. Most importantly the decision to set the FAP benefit level at $1,600 in a year when the Federal Government's spartan poverty index indicated that $3,-721 was required by a family of four for subsistence made plain that FAP promised no solution to the problem of poverty in the United States. In addition, there were a number of procedural and technical objections to FAP which further antagonized potential liberal supporters.

These perceived deficiencies deprived the Administration's original FAP program of the support of those groups whose allegiance was necessary for the bill's passage. Although H.R. 16311, which embodied the Administration proposal, passed the House of Representatives in the spring of 1970, it was rejected by the Senate Finance Committee and did not survive the 91st Congress. A renewed effort at reforming the categorical assistance program, drafted in response to the criticisms made of the original FAP program, took the form of H. R. 1 in the 92nd Congress.

Like the original proposal, the H.R. 1 program was designed to reach all families with dependent children, not only those deprived of parental support. However, such families were divided into two groups, one of which was to be enrolled in the Family Assistance Plan and the other of which was to be enrolled in the Opportunities For Families (OFF) program. The purpose of the division was implementation of the program's emphasis on returning AFDC recipients to employment. Whereas the purpose of the AFDC program is declared to be "encouraging the care of dependent children in their own homes", the purpose of H. R. 1 is stated to be providing for members of "needy families with children the * * * services * * * to * * * prepare them for employment * * * and providing a basic level of financial assistance. * * *" To this end, all families with a member deemed employable must register in the OFF program and receive benefits through the Secretary of Labor. All other needy families with children are enrolled in the FAP program administered by the Secretary of Health, Education and Welfare.

All persons are deemed "employable" except: (1) persons unable to work because of illness, incapacity or age; (2) mothers of children under three; (3) children under 16 or school children under 22; and (4) persons required to care for an ill or incapacitated member of the household. All employable persons must accept any job, job training or rehabilitative program which is assigned to them. No provision is made to permit refusal of the assigned employment on grounds of unsuitability or inadequate child care facilities.

In an effort to attract support from those who had criticized the basic FAP allowance as inadequate, the basic grant for a family of four was raised to $2,400. $800 is allowed for each of the first two family members, $400 for each of the next three, $300 for each of the next two, and $200 for the next three, subject to a maximum of $3,600 per family. An eligible family unit may retain resources of up to $1,500. $800 is deducted from the basic grant for each of the first two members of an OFF family who fail to register for employment or training.

Unlike the earlier FAP proposal families under the H.R. 1 program would not be eligible for food stamps, an entitlement which can be worth as much as $918 per year to an AFDC family.[44] Moreover, the original FAP requirements obligating the States to maintain current benefit levels and to maintain aggregate welfare expenditures at levels at 50% or more of pre-FAP levels were deleted in drafting H.R. 1. The net result of these amendments was to deprive needy families with children of any assurance that they would receive more in assistance than the basic FAP allowance—an amount lower than the amount currently received under the AFDC program in 29 States and lower than the amount of current AFDC payments plus food stamp entitlement in 45 States.

The reaction to H.R. 1 in the 92nd Congress was as mixed as Congressional reaction to the original FAP program. The increased level of payments, when netted against the elimination of food stamp entitlement and the predictably diminished level of State assistance, proved insufficient to rouse the enthusiasm of those seeking a more nearly adequate and universal system of income maintenance. The stiffened work requirements failed to muster the allegiance

of those concerned by the possible disincentive effects of higher benefit levels.

In the end, the 92nd Congress refused to pass H.R. 1. [H.R. 1 is described in more detail and these legislative events are chronicled at pp. 379–395, infra.] It did, however, enact a significant revision of the provisions applicable to the three adult categories—OAA, AB and APTD—in legislating the new SSI program.

The current debate over American income maintenance institutions has, at the time of this writing, resulted in a significant overhaul of support for the blind, the disabled and the aged. The $130 per month payable to an individual under the SSI promises to effect a significant improvement in the level of assistance to those groups, exceeding the national average OAA payment of $78 per month by $52 per month. It remains to be seen how great an inroad the new program will make on the population of 4.8 million aged persons whom the Federal Government recognizes as poor and on the larger group of aged, disabled and blind persons who, by any civilized standard, stand in need of additional assistance.

The vast majority of the categorical assistance population, however, remains beyond the reach of the recent enactment. The 9.7 million AFDC recipients (of a total of 12.7 million categorical assistance recipients) remain governed by an income maintenance system devised in the mid-thirties, which has come under increasing criticisms for the reasons suggested above. The task of overhauling that program has proved to be beyond the capacities of Congress and the President for the past four years. Whether the next Congress proves any more successful in coping with this problem remains to be seen.

44 36 Fed.Reg. 7273 (1971).

THE POVERTY LIVING STANDARD

REPORT OF PRESIDENT'S COMMISSION ON INCOME MAINTENANCE PROGRAMS, POVERTY AMID PLENTY, THE AMERICAN PARADOX 14–16 (1969).

Any discussion of the poor must begin by defining those who are poor and those who are not. But it is obvious that any single standard or definition of poverty is arbitrary, and clearly subject to disagreement. The standard which this Commission has employed is the widely used poverty index, developed by the Social Security Administration. This index is based on the Department of Agriculture's measure of the cost of a temporary low-budget, nutritious diet for households of various sizes. The poverty index is simply this food budget multiplied by three to reflect the fact that food typically represents one-third of the expenses of a low-income family. The resulting figure is the minimum income needed to buy a subsistence level of goods and services; the 25 million people whose incomes fall below the index are poor, while those above it are, officially at least, nonpoor. According to this poverty index, in 1968 a nonfarm family of four required a minimum income of $3,553 per year, or $2.43 per person per day to meet its basic expenses. Table 1–2 shows the poverty index for families of various sizes in 1968.

TABLE 1–2. 1968 Poverty Thresholds

Family size	Poverty index	
	Nonfarm	Farm
1	$1,748	$1,487
2	2,262	1,904
3	2,774	2,352
4	3,553	3,034
5	4,188	3,577
6	4,706	4,021
7 or more	5,789	4,916

How a typical poverty income might be spent can be seen in Table 1–3, which shows the standard of living available to the poor compared with that of a moderate-income family in 1967. In that year the poverty budget was $3,410. A moderate family budget developed by the Bureau of Labor Statistics required an income of $7,836 per year, or $1,300 less than the median family income of $9,120 for nonfarm families of four. Neither budget makes allowance for any costs of employment or taxes paid.

TABLE 1–3. Monthly Budgets, Poor and Moderate-Income Urban Families of Four, 1967

Consumption item	Poor [a]	Moderate [b]
Total	$284	$653
Food	122	175
Housing	91 [c]	199 [d]
Transportation	6	77 [e]
Clothing and personal care	57	82
Medical care	–	40
Gifts and contributions	–	21
Life insurance	–	13
Other consumption (recreation, education, tobacco, etc.)	9	46

[a] Based on budgeted need for an AFDC family of four in Los Angeles, California.
[b] Moderate living standard defined by the Bureau of Labor Statistics for a family of four.
[c] Renter.
[d] Homeowner.
[e] Automobile owner.
Source: State of California, Assembly Committee on Social Welfare, California Welfare: Legislative Program for Reform, February 1969; and U.S. Department of Labor, Bureau of Labor Statistics, Bulletin No. 1570–5, Three Standards of Living for an Urban Family of Four Persons, Spring, 1967.

Clearly, the poor family must do without many of the things that families with an average income consider to be "necessities"—a car, an occasional dessert after meals, rugs, a bed for each family member, school supplies, or an occasional movie. Nothing can be budgeted for medical care or insurance.

This food budget requires more than a third of the poor family's income, but still allows only $1.00 a day for food per person. A family can buy a nutritionally adequate diet for this amount, using the Department of Agriculture's food plan, but it must eat considerably more beans, potatoes, flour and cereal products, and considerably less meat, eggs, fruits, and vegetables than the average family. Each member of the poor family may consume less than one-quarter pound of meat a day.

Unfortunately, the Department's food plan, the basis of the poverty index, is not very realistic. It is estimated that only about one-fourth of the families who spend that much for food actually have a nutritionally adequate diet.[3] The plan calls for skills in meal-planning and buying that are rare at any income level, and it requires extensive efforts by poor families to make the varied and appetizing meals which are ostensibly possible under the plan. Many of the poor lack common kitchen appliances. Moreover, the Department's plan assumes the shopper will buy in economical quantities and take advantage of special bargains, but this is particularly difficult for a poor family with inadequate storage and refrigeration facilities.

The poor family's budget has no provision for eating outside of the home. Any lunches bought by working members or school children will reduce funds available for eating at home, since few outside meals can be bought for the 33 cents per meal allotted to each family member. Many schools charge more than this for a Federally-subsidized lunch.

The poor family's budget provides only $91 a month for all housing costs—including rent, utilities, and household operation—for four persons. No allowance is included for the poor family to purchase household furnishings. In Head Start programs, for example, teachers found that many children never had eaten at a table. Thirty percent of families on welfare live in homes where each family member does not have a bed.[4] A comparative breakdown of the

housing allotments for poor and moderate-income families appears in Table 1–4.

TABLE 1–4. Monthly Housing Budgets, Poor and Moderate-Income Urban Families of Four, 1967

Housing Expenditures	Poor	Moderate
Total	$91	$199
Shelter cost	67 [a]	159 [b]
Household furnishing	–	22
Household operations	12	18
Utilties	12	–

[a] Renter.
[b] Homeowner; includes utilities and allowance for lodging away from home.
Source: See Table 1–3.

The money allotted to transportation for a poor family would not cover even daily transportation for a worker. The moderate-income family not only has more money to spend on recreation, but its automobile permits it to take the children on inexpensive outings, while poor children rarely have access to any form of transportation. Thus, many poor children have never left their own neighborhoods.

Clothing school children is a major problem in poor families. Many poor children wear hand-me-down clothes which they receive from relatives, neighbors, and even teachers. Some clothing may be purchased at second-hand stores. But many poor children have to go to school on rainy days with no boots or raincoats—or stay home.

The poor family has $108 annually— about $9 a month—to spend on "luxuries": reading matter, recreation, education, gifts and contributions, tobacco, alcohol. But it is likely that this money will be spent on necessities, supplementing the meager food, clothing, and housing allowances. There is no room in the budget for luxuries—or emergencies.

Technically, an income at the poverty level should enable families to purchase the bare necessities of life. Yet an itemized budget drawn at that level clearly falls short of adequacy. There are many items for which no money is budgeted,

[3] U. S. Department of Agriculture, Consumer and Food Economics Division.

[4] U. S. Department of Health, Education, and Welfare, National Center for Social Statistics, 1967 AFDC Study: Preliminary Report of Findings from Mail Questionnaire, January 1969.

although those items may be needed. Funds for them can only come out of sums already allotted to the basic necessities of life. As one witness told the Commission, "I either eat good and smell bad, or smell good and don't eat."[5] When another witness was asked how he made ends meet, he simply replied, "They don't meet."[6]

CASEWORKER IN NEW YORK

RATS IN THE CRIB, ROACHES IN THE FOOD

Mary Walton

Village Voice, May 11, 1967.*

By the time you read this it will be over. I don't know where I will be or what I will be doing, but I will no longer be a caseworker for the New York City Welfare Department, and that's all that matters now.

I'm tired. I've had it. I'm not going to do your dirty work any more. Listen.

I'm tired of hearing about rats and roaches, and politely ignoring the latter as they crawl over walls and floors with no thoughts of their own safety. These aren't your upperclass roaches, man, your well-bred insects who dive into the nearest crack at a sudden light or the sound of a voice. These fellows know there's safety in numbers. They've got it made. I'm tired of hearing about babies eating fallen plaster and developing lead poisoning, or, if they're lucky, experiencing only loss of appetite and/or constipation and/or diarrhea, which probably has something to do with the plaster's having

been soaked with insecticide, and the kid's most likely going to develop leukemia or some damn thing sooner or later. I'm tired of broken boilers, toilets, and refrigerators, plumbers who never come, junkies in the halls and junkies who break into apartments and steal clocks, irons, sheets, children's clothes, food—anything they can lay their trembling hands on. I'm tired of hearing about asthma, high blood pressure, anemia, arthritis, toothaches, headaches, and "nervous." And I figure if I stay on the job any longer I'm going to have high blood pressure myself, because those fifth and sixth floors where Welfare clients live (they ought to hang out a "Reserved" sign) are getting harder, not easier, to climb. And I'm not fat.

You know why so many poor people are fat? They fill their aching tummies with rice, beans, and cheap fatty meat. Once a Puerto Rican client asked if there was some way she could get more money for food. I told her only if she obtained a request for a therapeutic diet from a doctor or hospital. Then I asked why she needed more money (!). She ducked her head shyly and didn't answer, but a friend piped up, "She don't like rice and beans." Well, we all had a good laugh over that. I mean, what Puerto Rican doesn't like rice and beans, right? But it seems that this woman was the daughter of a small truck farmer who raised his own vegetables and livestock; then she came to the States and worked for a Jewish family where she had plenty of good, solid . . . food. "She like American food," said the friend. "You know . . . vegetables, meat, potatoes." "She can have all the potatoes she wants," I said. And we all laughed some more. It reminds me, in retrospect, of a panhandler I overheard ask a man for a dime. "I haven't got enough myself," the man said and laughed, and passed by without breaking step. The panhandler looked after him with a per-

---

[5] Witness before Commission, Seattle, Washington.

[6] Witness before Commission, Quincy, Florida.

plexed expression and asked aloud, "What's so funny about that?"

Another thing I don't like about this job is the terrible toughness you acquire. Sit with me while I listen to a woman tell how she sweated for 10 years as a domestic until she'd finally saved enough to make a down payment and two more payments on a two-family house in Brooklyn, planning to live in half and rent the other half, but was never able to make any more payments because her daughters became addicts and stole from her, even as she slept with the money around her waist; how she didn't know they were addicts till the neighbors told her, but still she didn't believe it, and then the junkies started hanging around the hallway—her head bobs up and down in an imitation of the heroin nod and she whispers like the voices which whispered at the door her daughters always made certain to answer—and finally the landlady asked her to move. Then one daughter died from an overdose, and now this woman is caring for her child and the three children of the second daughter, my client, and she's been forced to go on Welfare herself.

And here she's crying and scratching at the same time because she has an outrageous case of hives, and it must be 95 degrees in that apartment, with no fan, as this poor creature goes on crying and scratching, interrupting herself to apologize for the disorder of the apartment and to tell one of her granddaughters to bring me some water, but the fact is I can sit there (are you still with me?) and murmur things like "That's a shame," and "I wish I could do something," but my main desire is to get out of there because I have three more visits to make before 5 p. m., and if I don't get them done I'll be called into the Case Supervisor's office the next morning to explain why not. And as the woman scratches and sobs, I consider saying I've made them, but what if one of the people has

up and died on me or something, when I say I've just seen them? And here this tragic fellow human being, my sister under her black, tormented skin, tells me things that make the Hundred Neediest Cases sound like Horatio Alger success stories, and basically, deep down inside, I don't care any more.

"Any more," because I think I did in the beginning. At least I remember being distinctly moved and upset after visiting my first case, a light-skinned young woman my own age whose husband had deserted her and their two children. She lived in a dirty, poorly lit building on West 118th Street, the whole back of which had been destroyed in a fire some months earlier. She was well-spoken, a high school graduate, and how rare they are I did not realize at the time, but she was completely passive and defeated, and it was this, more than the poverty itself, which kept me awake several nights trying to think of ways to help her. I did not know that at least 75 per cent of my cases would be little different, the main variations being in the number of children involved and the legality of the relationship.

Why do you stop caring? Poverty loses its novelty, I guess. Isn't that awful? It ceases to be interesting or challenging and there's nothing you can do about it anyway. Do you think they don't know that I don't care? Can't you tell when a doctor is more interested in giving you a prescription than in listening to a description of your pain? But hell, he's a doctor, and he's well, and he's being paid to listen. And I'm a social worker, and I'm not poor, and I'm being paid to listen too, though not to the extent that it interferes with my policing duties. ("Rent receipt? Con Ed bill? Clinic card? Relatives? School? Debts? Resources?") I wouldn't really mind if listening did any good.

With 60 cases, a worker who spends half his time in the field as he is expected to do is left with 18 minutes per case per week or slightly over an hour a month of office time per case, which is barely sufficient to do the paper work involved in keeping a case open. I think this pressure from lack of time creates a kind of pettiness in many workers, myself no exception. Like, well . . . listen. I'm going to tell you the worst thing I ever did. It won't absolve me, but it will implicate you, because I am your representative, your paid emissary to the blighted ghettoes you never see.

A man whom I shall call Guillermo Ramos, because that isn't his name, came into the office to see me, his "Investigator." Trained in P.R. as a TV repairman, Mr. Ramos had not found work of that kind here because he cannot drive, which is a requirement. He can't secure a license until he speaks English well enough to pass the written test. The welfare Department enrolled him in a rehabilitation program. On this particular day his wife had just gone into the hospital to have a baby and they needed a layette. I explained to him that he was certainly entitled to the $39 Welfare gives, and he would have the check in a week to ten days; likewise money for the crib he was also requesting. Mr. Ramos complained that he needed the money immediately because there were no clothes and no place for the baby to sleep. I asked why he couldn't make do (magic Welfare words meaning do without for a while) with the clothes which had belonged to his two year old daughter. He replied that they had been worn out and thrown away long ago. Couldn't he borrow some, I asked, becoming increasingly annoyed with this man who had not thought of the problem weeks before, and now that he finally had, was asking of me the extra half hour's work involved in getting an emergency check. No, he knew no one to borrow from. Well, I explained, I was sorry, but he would just have to think of something because that

was the way it was. There was nothing I could do. Mr. Ramos asked to speak to my supervisor, which only intensified my irritation.

I explained the situation to my supervisor, who had two small children of his own, and found him sympathetic to Mr. Ramos. "Give him cash. It only takes a few minutes," he said. I didn't argue. "You don't have to send out the crib now, if you don't want to," he added. And I didn't. Okay, people, several days later I was out to see the family. Looking around their apartment, one of those rats-in-the-crib, roaches-in-the-food, and addicts-in-the-hallways affairs, which was, incidentally, bereft of livingroom furniture because a previous worker for any number of reasons had not issued it, I saw that the new baby was sleeping in a suitcase supported by two straight-backed chairs. There, it's out. That's called the arbitrary use of power, friends, and I ask now to be forgiven. Do you think I asked Mr. Ramos?

But I was not always as you see me, as Peter Sellers says in a very funny movie which none of my clients could afford to see, or any movie for that matter. (Always I'm conscious of doing things THEY cannot do.) A highly unskilled Government major from Radcliffe, I did political research for a time, after which I wrote copy for Comet Cleanser for four months until I found myself actually laughing at the jokes in the commercials and habitually chanting, "Gets out stains far better in one try than other cleansers in two," as I walked along Madison Avenue. I quit suddenly. Stranded for work, I decided I'd rather think about people than things for seven hours a day so I took the Welfare exam and was hired a couple of weeks later. It's very easy to get the job. Any warm body with a college degree will do.

I haven't met any other Ivy Leaguers, male or female, working for the Department, though once I did meet a Yale graduate who told me he had done so some years ago prior to his present banking job. I sometimes wonder what happened to my Cliffie classmates. I only know the whereabouts of two: my former roommate, who is now in medical school, and Maria Livanos, whose name and picture appear occasionally in society pages. Though I never knew her, I remember when Old Maria's slip was the sensation of Cambridge: the year she played the daughter in the pre-off-Broadway production of "Oh Dad, Poor Dad," a part, by the way, my roommate tried out for. She was made assistant stage manager in compensation and was heard as the pirana fish ("Gleep. Gleep.") I was talking, however, about the poor, wasn't I? There's more to tell, even though I suspect you'd rather hear about Maria and "Oh Dad" and All That. Catch you?

I'm also tired of slumlords who complain to me that my clients haven't paid their rent, which forces me to pressure them for an explanation of what they're using their rent money for, thereby associating myself with these wretched men who make their own often wretched livings by keeping others in the same state. (Am I any different?) I'm tired of explaining to martinied taxpayers how it is with the poor, and I'm tired of going cold in the winter because my heavy coat of black dynel shines with the luster of fur, even after four years, and as it is I can't stand the hungry look in their eyes when I remove my fur-lined gloves. Their clothing allowances, parenthetically, do not include gloves. I guess their hands aren't supposed to get cold. I'm tired of demanding support payments from putative fathers making $50 a week if they're working at all, poor bastards. Why should the beauty of making a baby become for poor and ignorant youth a step into poverty, degradation, and deception? And there are those who would call an unwanted and economically ill-

advised marriage the solution. I'm tired of them, too.

I'm tired of hearing people call cheap lineoleum "carpets," and tilt back sofas "Castro Convertibles." Hovering on the fringes of the economy, they know only what they hear: carpets cover floors; couches which become beds are Castro Convertibles. They live and love in your back yard, baby. They listen to your radios, watch your TVs, look in your store windows. But don't worry, New York. They don't have enough of your money to do anything about it.

I don't want to be asked again if Welfare gives anything for Christmas, while round-eyed pickaninnies look hopeful. What do I say? I ask you, I demand to know, what do I say?

As you read, I am no longer there, and I can tell you without risking your wrath that I gave away things. In fact, I gave away as much of your and my tax monies as time permitted. I gave all my clients everything they said they needed, and if I couldn't give them what they asked for I gave them something else. I even ASKED if they needed something: sheets? towels? pots? I gave money for shades, spreads, curtains. . . . lots. (Gave? They're ENTITLED. I am ashamed to remind myself.) By the way, do you know that a broom is budgeted at $1.40? I have a $1.40 broom, made by Lighthouse Industries. I'm on their side, but most of what I sweep up consists of broken broom straws. I issued money for strollers, beds, chairs, lamps. I issued all the clothes I could until they stopped letting us issue clothes; then I issued people things for their apartments which they already had so they could buy clothes * * * or pay utility bills, which in their miserably wired building usually ran half again the $6 or $7 a month allotted in their budgets. And I must have issued hundreds of blankets. Don't be angry. I couldn't have slept at night if I'd thought people didn't have blankets because of me. That's the truth. But I didn't do as much as I could have if I'd had more time, and I regret that. Because I was one of the few chances those people had to get what they needed. And that's the truth, too.

I had too many ambivalent attitudes. Once a woman, spotting my telltale black fieldbook, remarked in a loud voice to her companion on my (warm) boots, "Black boots! Why don't they send us money for those? Hey, black boots!" People turned to stare, and I thought, "I work hard for my money, you black bitch. I didn't lie back and spread my legs instead of learning how to read. I've never asked anybody for anything." But in my favor, what prevails over this very American reaction is the realization that it doesn't matter what kind of person she is or how she got into her present situation. She is a victim. Sure she could get a job: as a salesgirl, scrubwoman, or, if she's lucky, as a waitress, but who would take care of her kids? And how can you EXPECT anyone to take a job like that? Would you? Or might you possibly ask for help, say, from relatives? Is your idea of hard times a lesser office job? Perhaps she should be ashamed of not working, and go to work out of pride? That's funny. These people have been beaten, stepped on, and often treated the worst when they were working the hardest. They have no pride. Knuckling under to the Protestant Ethic doesn't even get them the minimum wage.

Most of all, I think I'm tired of regarding people with suspicion, of having to question everything anyone tells me, of wondering whether Mrs. Burns is lying to me when she says her rent money was stolen and knowing she probably is and I have an obligation to the taxpayer to find out. Well, screw you, taxpayer. It's Christmas and Mrs. Burns doesn't get any money for presents for her five kids and I don't give a damn whether she's lying to me or not. She's telling me what I need to hear; she reported it to the police as required, and she's signed the forms. She should say she used her rent money for toys and clothes? I'd have to let her get evicted. No, thank you. So far as I'm concerned, her rent money was stolen and I'm going to replace it. You want to know something? If Welfare clients were given enough money so that they didn't have to come running to us for special grants for everything besides food, rent, utilities, and basic clothing (sound like a guaranteed mini-income, friends?), you could cut the Welfare staff by three-quarters; whole centers could be closed down. It might even come close to paying for itself. But I'm leaving and I do not have to think about such simple-minded things any more.

No, I'm tiredest of all of having to worry about some 250 people who depend on me for their very existence. I dont' want to see them any more. I don't want to hear the same things: "He just left * * * not enough for * * * I don't know where he * * * like to work but * * * think he's you know, slow * * * not sending up heat * * * some mornings it's so bad. * * * went to the clinic but they * * * do you give money for * * * need * * * teacher sent him home because he * * * only got to the eighth * * * " Poverty jams them into a mold which permits few variations. Lately when the phone rings I pray it isn't the Reception Desk saying a client is waiting to see me.

So, you've come this far with me, which is as much, I guess, as I can ask. I wrote this for two reasons: to unburden myself, and to tell you how it is. Because much of what I read is written from interviews with clients, and that's no good; they don't know how badly off they are. A worker knows both worlds.

So you can forget about those poor people now, though first you really ought to go out to the East Bronx, say, or Williamsburg or Brownsville. Everybody knows about Harlem and Bedford-Stuyvesant, but man, you should see all the other poverty pockets in this city. There are a lot and they're full.

Oh, there's so much more I'd like to tell you. Let me just say this. Our present Welfare system is predicated on the theory that the more unpleasant you make poverty, the fewer poor people there will be. But it doesn't necessarily follow. Deprivation spawns bitterness, frustration, hopelessness, or just sad, unblinking, unrebellious acceptance, but apparently it breeds more, not fewer, poor people, because the relief rolls are going up. Could it be that poverty in some way feeds on itself? Well, something's wrong somewhere, people.

It's not working. Think about that. I can't any more. I want to be like you. I want to turn the page and forget, at least for a little while. I don't know if I can do it, but I'm going to try. Because I'm tired.

THE WHY OF PUBLIC WELFARE

An Outline of the Social Service System in New York State, State Department of Social Service (1970).

The nation faces a massive domestic problem few people understand—widespread poverty side by side with widespread prosperity.

Many of us just can't believe that such deprivation can exist in the United States.

Why can't we believe it? Because most of us—fortunately—are literate, employed, and well housed, and enjoy good health, own cars and all sorts of things, have no long background of want, or any such deprivation.

Besides, few of us know that tens of millions of Americans can't read, don't have the most elementary work skills, are chronically ill or otherwise disabled, live in decayed houses, own practically nothing—and never have—and come from two or three generations damaged by human want.

Consequently in 1970 poverty is still the biggest domestic problem in our country. One measure of that burden, public welfare, involves 10 million public dependents and $10 billion in annual expenditures. And those welfare recipients represent less than half of all Americans living in poverty. How can so many people really be in need? Why don't they go to work like everybody else? Where do "these people" come from? These and other questions are asked of public welfare administrators every day.

All the questions have one answer: the stark facts of life.

What stark facts?

These:
Sickness, accidents, disability, old age, death, unemployment, illiteracy, inadequate work skills, low income, absence of a breadwinner, bad housing, discrimination.

Such adverse conditions affect tens of millions of Americans—Unable Americans—who are the "source of supply" for our welfare rolls.

With a constantly rising population, more and more people are exposed to these social and economic hazards—and the toll, in people and in money, continues to rise. For example, in the last 30 years our population increased by more than 70 million.

To spell it all out—

Sickness and Other Handicaps

Approximately 22 million persons 17 years of age or older are disabled to some extent by a chronic ailment.

Of these, 4 million cannot carry on their major activities—earning a living or keeping house. 12 million others are limited in the kind or amount of work they can do.

Over 29 million persons are admitted to hospitals each year, and at any given time 1,400,000 patients are in these hospitals.

20 million adults and children are afflicted with mental and emotional disorders.

Some 5 million others are mentally retarded.

Another 6½ million suffer from alcoholism to the point where they cannot hold jobs.

115,000 accident victims die each year and 11 million others are disabled—a number of them permanently.

More than 400 million work days are lost annually because of illness.

30 million Americans have no health insurance.

A steady rise in the cost of medical care is prompting many people to risk going without medical attention, and forcing others to turn to Medicaid to pay for medical care.

Sickness and disability are major causes of public dependency, accounting for three-fifths of all public welfare costs.

Inadequate Income

24 million people, or 13 percent of the total population, live in poverty, according to government standards.

10 million are children.

About one-third of the Negro population are poor, and half of them are in families headed by a woman.

Nearly one-fourth of the white poor total of 17½ million are over 65 years of age.

Many who are on the welfare rolls do not get enough assistance to support a minimum subsistence scale of living.

Unemployment and Underemployment

More than 4.5 million persons are totally unemployed.

It is estimated that more than 2 million who want full-time work are able to get only part-time jobs.

It is estimated that only 5 percent of all public assistance recipients are employable in today's labor market.

Illiteracy

Lack of education and lack of work skills needed in today's labor market condemn large numbers of adults and young people to unemployment, under-employment, or low-pay jobs.

More than 3 million adults are illiterate.

Half of all unemployed youth, ages 16–21, are functionally illiterate.

An estimated 10 million children and teenagers have some significant reading difficulty.

About 20 percent of the labor force has only eight years of education or less.

More than 6 million Americans age 25 or over have not completed the fifth grade.

What lack of education means in earning capacity is shown in the following figures:

1969 MEDIAN TOTAL ANNUAL HOUSEHOLD INCOME

Heads of Households with—

Less than 8 years of school	$4,108
8 years of school	5,928
1–3 years of high school	7,687
4 years of high school	9,275

The high school dropout underlines the importance of education. The unemployment rate among workers who failed to finish high school is almost double the rate among those with more education. There are almost 5 million dropouts in the 14–24 age group of the population.

In today's economy fewer and fewer persons can look forward to spending their lives in one occupation or in one location. Workers must be prepared to switch from one type of work to another and, in many cases, move their families to distant points to get jobs. However, lack of education and currently marketable job skills frequently precludes such mobility and opportunity.

Discrimination

Approximately 60 million Americans are age 45 or older; of these, more than 19 million are 65 or older. Workers in both groups find their age is a serious handicap in keeping or finding employment because of discriminatory age deadlines in business and industry.

Discrimination based on color has been another obstacle to employment for many of the nation's 24 million nonwhite citizens, along with lack of education and lack of work skills. The unemployment rate among nonwhites is twice as high as among white workers. And the average income of nonwhite families is 60 percent that of white families.

Poor Living Conditions

Approximately 9 million families live in the slums. It has been demonstrated repeatedly that the incidence of disease, crime, delinquency, and school dropout is greater in the slums than in other neighborhoods. These and other factors combine to limit the employability of young people growing up in the slums and to perpetuate a pattern of life marked by poverty, sickness, and crime.

Over 5 million public assistance recipients, most of them women and children in families receiving aid to dependent children, live in housing that is deteriorating, dilapidated, unsafe, insanitary or overcrowded. In more than 3 million of these households, the average allowance for housing is less than $400 a year. More than 40 percent of all old-age assistance recipients live in deficient housing; in some rural and Southern areas the range is from 45 to 70 percent.

In Summary * * *

These stark facts of life add up to why 10 million Americans are on the nation's welfare rolls at an annual cost of $10 billion, and why some 95 percent of them are too sick, too disabled, too old, too young, too illiterate or too unskilled to hold a job.

SECTION 2. THE CONSTITUTIONAL PARAMETERS

THE CONSTITUTION OF THE UNITED STATES

Amendment I

Congress shall make no law respecting an establishment of religion, or prohibiting the free exercise thereof; or abridging the freedom of speech, or of the press; or the right of the people peaceably to assemble, and to petition the Government for a redress of grievances.

Amendment V

No person shall be held to answer for a capital, or otherwise infamous crime, unless on a presentment or indictment of a Grand Jury, except in cases arising in the land or naval forces, or in the Militia, when in actual service in time of War or public danger; nor shall any person be subject for the same offense to be twice put in jeopardy of life or limb; nor shall be compelled in any criminal case to be a witness against himself, nor be deprived of life, liberty, or property, without due process of law; nor shall private property be taken for public use, without just compensation.

Amendment XIII

Section 1. Neither slavery nor involuntary servitude, except as a punishment for crime whereof the party shall have been duly convicted, shall exist within the United States or within any place subject to their jurisdiction.

Section 2. Congress shall have power to enforce this article by appropriate legislation.

Amendment XIV

Section 1. All persons born or naturalized in the United States, and subject to the jurisdiction thereof, are citizens of the United States and of the State wherein they reside. No State shall make or enforce any law which shall abridge the privileges or immunities of citizens of the United States; nor shall any State deprive any person of life, liberty, or property, without due process of law; nor deny to any person within its jurisdiction the equal protection of the laws.

* * *

Section 5. The Congress shall have power to enforce, by appropriate legislation, the provisions of this article.

A. PROCEDURAL RESTRICTIONS

SMITH v. BOARD OF COMMISSIONERS OF DISTRICT OF COLUMBIA [A]

United States District Court, District of
Columbia, 1966.
259 F.Supp. 423.

HOLTZOFF, District Judge. This is an action brought against the Board of Commissioners of the District of Columbia and the Director and certain other officials of the Department of Public

---

[A] Some footnotes in cases and other borrowed material in this book have been omitted; others have been renumbered.

Welfare of the District of Columbia. The plaintiffs are mothers of children receiving assistance under the provisions of law for aid to families with dependent children, administered by the Government of the District of Columbia through its Department of Public Welfare. The defendants move for summary judgment.

The gravamen of the action is that investigators employed by the Department of Public Welfare at times use harsh, oppressive, illegal, and humiliating methods in making their investigations as to the question whether a particular recipient of assistance is worthy of that aid. The Court is of the opinion, first, that it has no jurisdiction over the internal administration of this agency or any other government department. What the Court is asked to do here is to direct by declaratory or injunctive relief, or both, how the department should be administered. The Court has no such power.

Second, the Court is of the opinion that the administration of relief involves discretion on the part of the agency entrusted with that duty. Payments of relief funds are grants and gratuities. Their disbursement does not constitute payment of legal obligations that the government owes. Being absolutely discretionary, there is no judicial review of the manner in which that discretion is exercised. It must be borne in mind that an individual may not maintain an action to enjoin the day-to-day administration of government functions or the use of government funds. This principle was established in the leading case of Commonwealth of Massachusetts v. Mellon, 262 U.S. 447, 43 S.Ct. 597, 67 L.Ed. 1078.

Third, remedies of the type requested here may not be accorded by a court of equity. This Court may not enjoin a large number of unnamed investigators and instruct them how to conduct their duties, under penalty of being punished for contempt of court. The Court would have no means of supervising and determining the day-to-day compliance or failure to comply with such an injunction. Again, equity does not enjoin unnamed individuals, as equity acts *in personam*.

Counsel for the plaintiffs does not attack the legality or the propriety of the Departmental regulations. He contends, however, that the regulations are being violated by various investigators. In connection with the administration of welfare funds, however, the government has a right, in fact a duty, to make investigations in order to determine whether the money is properly spent, and to make certain that it is not squandered improvidently, and is not obtained on the basis of misrepresentations. If there is any grievance as to the conduct of any particular investigator the matter should be submitted to the administrative agency. There is no showing here that the administrative remedies have been exhausted. If the agency refuses redress appeal can be taken to the Board of Commissioners.

Each of the reasons the Court has just given is in itself separately sufficient to warrant a granting of the defendants' motion for summary judgment.

The defendants' motion is granted. You may submit an order.

THE RULE OF LAW AND THE WELFARE STATE

Harry W. Jones.
58 Col.L.Rev. 143 (1958).

The rise of the welfare state, as it is known today, proceeds from the triumph, in most of our western countries, of a new political philosophy. Changes in conditions and in majority political attitudes have made it the prevailing opinion today that the greater economic and social good of the greater number requires an abandonment of the "hands off" approach and the adoption of public measures directly and explicitly aimed at general economic betterment. The identifying characteristics of the welfare state are chiefly these: (1) a vast increase in the range and detail of government regulation of privately owned economic enterprise; (2) the direct furnishing of services by government to individual members of the national community—unemployment and retirement benefits, family allowances, low-cost housing, medical care, and the like; and (3) increasing government ownership and operation of industries and business which, at an earlier time, were or would have been operated for profit by individuals or private corporations. * * *

For want of a commonly understood American version of the rule of law, I will hazard my own understanding of the term's connotation in the American legal order. The rule of law is a tradition of decision, a tradition embodying at least three indispensable elements: *first,* that every person whose interests will be affected by a judicial or administrative decision has the right to a meaningful "day in court"; *second,* that deciding officers shall be independent in the full sense, free from external direction by political and administrative superiors in the disposition of individual cases and inwardly free from the influence of personal gain and partisan or popular bias; and *third,* that day-to-day decisions shall be reasoned, rationally justified, in terms that take due account both of the demands of general principle and the demands of the particular situation.[5]
* * *

---

[5] "Reasoned" decision is more inclusive than decision "on principle" and has more meaning in administrative context. We forget sometimes that "arbitrary" action can be either an unjustified departure from general policy or an undiscriminating and unjust application of general policy to a concrete situation within its letter but not within its spirit. In the welfare state the greater danger is that administrators, for bureaucratic convenience, may apply general policy in a mechanical and undiscriminating way.

Can this tradition, this adjudicative ideal, be carried over into the welfare state? Manifestly, the welfare state sets a harder and wider task for the rule of law. As government becomes regulator, dispenser of benefits, and mass employer, it draws to itself functions and responsibilities formerly dispersed among such other power centers as private companies, trade and labor associations, and charitable institutions. * * *

Does it follow, then, that the advent of the welfare state is attended, inevitably, by the decline and ultimate disappearance of the rule of law? This is the foreboding thesis of Friedrich A. Hayek's The Road to Serfdom, first published in England in 1944 and since very generally read in the United States and throughout Western Europe. Countless others have written to the same purpose and in the same vein, but it seems safe to say that Dr. Hayek's book is more widely known than any other single statement of the anti-welfare state position. Accordingly, I shall speak elsewhere in this paper of the "Hayek theorem" as a shorthand way of referring to the proposition that the welfare state, by its inherent nature, is incompatible with the rule of law. * * *

Interwoven with Hayek's attack on the egalitarian objectives of central economic planning is a second count of indictment, this one addressed to the crucial role of administrative discretion in the operations of the welfare state. The argument is a familiar one in the literature of administrative law: government regulatory and welfare programs can be carried into effect only by the delegation of discretionary power to "divers boards and authorities"; and the possession and exercise of such discretionary power contravenes the rule of law. Hayek's objections to discretionary power are in part theoretical and in part practical. Broad administrative discretion threatens the Kantian ideal that "man is free if he

needs to obey no person but solely the laws"—an argument strikingly reminiscent of the contention often heard in the United States that discretionary administrative powers undermine a fundamental concept of "government of laws and not of men." In addition, and less philosophically, Hayek develops the charge that the possession of discretionary power destroys the predictability of decision which he sees as a major value of the rule of law. "The important question," says Hayek, "is whether the individual can foresee the action of the state and make use of this knowledge as a datum in forming his own plans * * *." The paradox suggested is that discretion, without which government economic planning is unworkable, prevents reliable planning by the individual. * * *

There is reason and need in the welfare state to devise and perfect safeguards against the always present danger of abuse of administrative authority. Meaningful statutory standards, realistic procedural requirements, and discriminating techniques of judicial review are among the tools of control well along in course of development. Nor is it to be assumed that administrative officers are themselves alien to the tradition of honest judgment and fair decision embodied in the rule of law. It is not to be forgotten, as we admire the achievement of the French Conseil d'Etat, that its superb jurisdictional control of administrative functioning is not wholly external, as in the case of American, English, or German judicial review. A strength of the Conseil d'Etat in the context of French political institutions is that the Conseil itself is *in* the administrative establishment even though it is not entirely *of* it. * * *

In the welfare state, public power becomes an instrumentality for the achievement of purposes beyond the minimum objectives of domestic order and national defense. It is not enough that the national community be secure against internal disorder and external aggression; a society can be thus secure and well ordered and yet lack the attribute of distributive justice. But as social justice becomes a conscious end of state policy there is a vast and inevitable increase in the frequency with which ordinary citizens come into a relationship of direct encounter with state power-holders. The citizen's significant encounter now is not with the policeman or the criminal magistrate but with the official representing a regulatory authority, an administration of social insurances, or a state-operated economic enterprise. It is this dramatically increased incidence of encounter that sets the task of the rule of law in the welfare state.

At the first stage of the welfare state, old rights are subjected to new forms of limitation. Property and contract are the most obvious cases in point. It is not that the right of property or the right to contract were ever absolute; the maxim *sic utere* and the rule that courts will not enforce contracts against public policy are sufficient reminders that every legal system has put outside limits on the autonomy of property owners and contracting parties. But these outer bounds keep moving in as the area of individual decision in proprietary and contractual matters is narrowed in the welfare state. The state's commands must constantly be consulted when the individual is determining the use or disposition of his property, and many matters once left to private bargaining are now foreclosed by public statute or regulation. The doctrines and procedures of what Dicey called the "ordinary law" may give little specific help in working out the ultimate pattern by which old rights are to be adjusted to the social interests given preferred place in the welfare state. If the rule of law is to be fully meaningful in the contemporary setting of detailed regulation, there must be new acts of legal construction as momentous as those un-

dertaken and performed by the great civil law codifiers and common law judges. * * *

Even more important than the regulatory aspect of the welfare state is its office as the source of new rights—for example, the expectations created by a comprehensive system of social insurance. I see no reason why the word "rights," with its unique emotive power, should be deemed inappropriate for these new expectations and preempted for use only in connection with such traditional interests as those in tangible property. For example, studies tell us that the typical middle income American reaches retirement age with a whole bundle of interests and expectations: as homeowner, as small investor, and as social security "beneficiary." Of these, his social security retirement benefits are probably his most important resource. Should this, the most significant of his rights, be entitled to a quality of protection inferior to that afforded his other interests? It becomes the task of the rule of law to surround this new "right" to retirement benefits with protections against arbitrary government action, with substantive and procedural safeguards that are as effective in context as the safeguards enjoyed by traditional rights of property in the best tradition of the older law. * * *

To suggest, as I have, that the reasonable expectations of a social service beneficiary are as meaningful for the rule of law as the interests of an owner of investment securities or real property is in no way to urge a lowering of the standard of protection now extended by law to the more traditional interests. The goal, substantial parity of treatment, can be pursued by levelling up as well as by levelling down. The new expectations progressively brought into existence by the welfare state must be thought of not as privileges to be dispensed unequally or by arbitrary fiat of government officials but as substantial rights in the assertion of which the claimant is entitled to an effective remedy, a fair procedure, and a reasoned decision. Anything short of this leaves one man subject in his essential interests to the arbitrary will of another man who happens to partake of public power; and that kind of unequal and demeaning encounter is repugnant to every sense of the rule of law.

These comments, though impressionistic rather than exhaustive, should have given at least some idea of the magnitude of the task ahead for the rule of law. For centuries our several western legal orders have pursued the ideal that individual rights be kept secure from infringement by other persons and, above all, from the arbitrary exercise of government power. Our concepts and procedures, in their best manifestations, furnish a surer protection than ever before to the essential rights that are first in any heirarchy of individual and social interests: freedom of religion, speech, suffrage, and press, and the related freedom from arbitrary detention. Beyond this, our legal orders have achieved a reasonably effective procedure for the vindication of such other traditional interests as property rights, contract rights, and rights to compensation for injury caused by another's fault. Now the welfare state brings its staggering volume of additional grist to the mills of justice: new rights in vast number and indefinitely more widely dispersed among the citizenship than the old rights ever were. In the scale of legal valuation, these new and more widely asserted rights are outweighed only by the essential civil liberties; they are certainly as dear to their possessors as contract and property rights are to those who possess them.

Mass-produced goods rarely have the quality of goods made in far smaller quantity by traditional hand craftsmanship; an analogous problem challenges the welfare state. In an era when rights are mass produced, can the quality of their protection against arbitrary official action be as high as the quality of the protection afforded in the past to traditional legal rights less numerous and less widely dispersed among the members of society? Dicey accurately perceived it as a great strength of the rule of law in England that most questions of individual right came for decision to a small and homogeneous group of dedicated men, the judges of the "ordinary law." A thousand times as many deciding officers are needed to settle the issues presented by claimants of the new and more widely held rights of the welfare state. Is it beyond hope that this vast new company of officials can, in time, develop a tradition of decision worthy of being called, in Pound's fine phrase, an "ethos of adjudication"?

In the welfare state, the private citizen is forever encountering public officials of many kinds: regulators, dispensers of social services, managers of state-operated enterprises. It is the task of the rule of law to see to it that these multiplied and diverse encounters are as fair, as just, and as free from arbitrariness as are the familiar encounters of the right-asserting private citizen with the judicial officers of the traditional law.

FLEMMING v. NESTOR

Supreme Court of the United States, 1960.
363 U.S. 603, 80 S.Ct. 1367, 4 L.Ed.2d 1435.

Mr. Justice HARLAN delivered the opinion of the Court.

From a decision of the District Court for the District of Columbia holding § 202(n) of the Social Security Act (68 Stat. 1083, as amended, 42 U.S.C.A. § 402(n)) unconstitutional, the Secretary of Health, Education, and Welfare takes this direct appeal pursuant to 28 U.S.C.A. § 1252. The challenged section, set forth in full in the margin,[1] provides for the termination of old-age, survivor, and disability insurance benefits payable to, or in certain cases in respect of, an alien individual who, after September 1, 1954 (the date of enactment of the section), is deported under § 241(a) of the Immigration and Nationality Act (8 U.S. C.A. § 1251(a)) on any one of certain grounds specified in § 202(n).

[1] Section 202(n) provides as follows:

"(n) (1) If any individual is (after the date of enactment of this subsection) deported under paragraph (1), (2), (4), (5), (6), (7), (10), (11), (12), (14), (15), (16), (17), or (18) of section 241(a) of the Immigration and Nationality Act, then, notwithstanding any other provisions of this title—

"(A) no monthly benefit under this section or section 223 [42 U.S.C.A. § 423, relating to "disability insurance benefits"] shall be paid to such individual, on the basis of his wages and self-employment income, for any month occurring (i) after the month in which the Secretary is notified by the Attorney General that such individual has been so deported, and (ii) before the month in which such individual is thereafter lawfully admitted to the United States for permanent residence,

"(B) if no benefit could be paid to such individual (or if no benefit could be paid to him if he were alive) for any month by reason of subparagraph (A), no monthly benefit under this section shall be paid, on the basis of his wages and self-employment income, for such month to any other person who is not a citizen of the United States and is outside the United States for any part of such month, and

"(C) no lump-sum death payment shall be made on the basis of such individual's wages and self-employment income if he dies (i) in or after the month in which such notice is received, and (ii) before the month in which he is thereafter lawfully admitted to the United States for permanent residence.

"Section 203(b) and (c) of this Act shall not apply with respect to any such individual for any month for which no monthly benefit may be paid to him by reason of this paragraph.

"(2) As soon as practicable after the deportation of any individual under any of the paragraphs of section 241(a) of the Immigration and Nationality Act enumerated in paragraph (1) in this subsection, the Attorney General shall notify the Secretary of such deportation."

Appellee, an alien, immigrated to this country from Bulgaria in 1913, and became eligible for old-age benefits in November 1955. In July 1956 he was deported pursuant to § 241(a) (6) (C) (i) of the Immigration and Nationality Act for having been a member of the Communist Party from 1933 to 1939. This being one of the benefit-termination deportation grounds specified in § 202(n), appellee's benefits were terminated soon thereafter, and notice of the termination was given to his wife, who had remained in this country. Upon his failure to obtain administrative reversal of the decision, appellee commenced this action in the District Court, pursuant to § 205(g) of the Social Security Act (53 Stat. 1370, as amended, 42 U.S.C.A. § 405(g)), to secure judicial review. On cross-motions for summary judgment, the District Court ruled for appellee, holding § 202(n) unconstitutional under the Due Process Clause of the Fifth Amendment in that it deprived appellee of an accrued property right. 169 F.Supp. 922. The Secretary prosecuted an appeal to this Court.

* * *

I.

We think that the District Court erred in holding that § 202(n) deprived appellee of an "accrued property right." 169 F.Supp., at 934. Appellee's right to Social Security benefits cannot properly be considered to have been of that order.

The general purposes underlying the Social Security Act were expounded by Mr. Justice Cardozo in Helvering v. Davis, 301 U.S. 619, 640–645, 57 S.Ct. 904, 81 L.Ed. 1307. The issue here, however, requires some inquiry into the statutory scheme by which those purposes are sought to be achieved. Payments under the Act are based upon the wage earner's record of earnings in employment or self-employment covered by the Act, and take the form of old-age insurance and disability insurance benefits inuring to the wage earner (known as the "primary beneficiary"), and of benefits, including survivor benefits, payable to named dependents ("secondary beneficiaries") of a wage earner. Broadly speaking, eligibility for benefits depends on satisfying statutory conditions as to (1) employment in covered employment or self-employment (see § 210(a), 42 U.S. C.A. § 410(a)); (2) the requisite number of "quarters of coverage"—i. e., three-month periods during which not less than a stated sum was earned—the number depending generally on age (see §§ 213–215, 42 U.S.C.A. §§ 413–415); and (3) attainment of the retirement age (see § 216(a), 42 U.S.C.A. § 416(a)). § 202(a), 42 U.S.C.A. § 402(a).[4] Entitlement to benefits once gained, is partially or totally lost if the beneficiary earns more than a stated annual sum, unless he or she is at least 72 years old. § 203(b), (e), 42 U.S.C.A. § 403(b), (e). Of special importance in this case is the fact that eligibility for benefits, and the amount of such benefits, do not in any true sense depend on contribution to the program through the payment of taxes, but rather on the earnings record of the primary beneficiary.

The program is financed through a payroll tax levied on employees in covered employment, and on their employers. The tax rate, which is a fixed percentage of the first $4,800 of employee annual income, is set at a scale which will increase from year to year, presumably to keep pace with rising benefit costs. I.R. C. of 1954, §§ 3101, 3111, 3121(a). The tax proceeds are paid into the Treasury "as internal-revenue collections," I. R.C., § 3501, and each year an amount

equal to the proceeds is appropriated to a Trust Fund, from which benefits and the expenses of the program are paid. § 201, 42 U.S.C.A. § 401. It was evidently contemplated that receipts would greatly exceed disbursements in the early years of operation of the system, and surplus funds are invested in government obligations, and the income returned to the Trust Fund. Thus, provision is made for expected increasing costs of the program.

The Social Security system may be accurately described as a form of social insurance, enacted pursuant to Congress' power to "spend money in aid of the 'general welfare,'" Helvering v. Davis, supra, at 640, whereby persons gainfully employed, and those who employ them, are taxed to permit the payment of benefits to the retired and disabled, and their dependents. Plainly the expectation is that many members of the present productive work force will in turn become beneficiaries rather than supporters of the program. But each worker's benefits, though flowing from the contributions he made to the national economy while actively employed, are not dependent on the degree to which he was called upon to support the system by taxation. It is apparent that the noncontractual interest of an employee covered by the Act cannot be soundly analogized to that of the holder of an annuity, whose right to benefits is bottomed on his contractual premium payments.

It is hardly profitable to engage in conceptualizations regarding "earned rights" and "gratuities." Cf. Lynch v. United States, 292 U.S. 571, 576–577, 54 S.Ct. 840, 78 L.Ed. 1434. The "right" to Social Security benefits is in one sense "earned," for the entire scheme rests on the legislative judgment that those who in their productive years were functioning members of the economy may justly call upon that economy, in their later years, for protection from "the rig-

---

4 In addition, eligibility for disability insurance benefits is of course subject to the further condition of the incurring of a disability as defined in the Act. § 223, 42 U.S. C.A. § 423. Secondary beneficiaries must meet the tests of family relationship to the wage earner set forth in the Act. § 202(b)–(h), 42 U.S.C.A. § 402(b)–(h).

ors of the poor house as well as from the haunting fear that such a lot awaits them when journey's end is near." Helvering v. Davis, supra, at 641. But the practical effectuation of that judgment has of necessity called forth a highly complex and interrelated statutory structure. Integrated treatment of the manifold specific problems presented by the Social Security program demands more than a generalization. That program was designed to function into the indefinite future, and its specific provisions rest on predictions as to expected economic conditions which must inevitably prove less than wholly accurate, and on judgments and preferences as to the proper allocation of the Nation's resources which evolving economic and social conditions will of necessity in some degree modify.

To engraft upon the Social Security system a concept of "accrued property rights" would deprive it of the flexibility and boldness in adjustment to ever-changing conditions which it demands. See Wollenberg, Vested Rights in Social-Security Benefits, 37 Ore.L.Rev. 299, 359. It was doubtless out of an awareness of the need for such flexibility that Congress included in the original Act, and has since retained, a clause expressly reserving to it "[t]he right to alter, amend, or repeal any provision" of the Act. § 1104, 49 Stat. 648, 42 U.S.C.A. § 1304. That provision makes express what is implicit in the institutional needs of the program. See Analysis of the Social Security System, Hearings before a Subcommittee of the Committee on Ways and Means, House of Representatives, 83d Cong., 1st Sess., pp. 920–921. It was pursuant to that provision that § 202(n) was enacted.

We must conclude that a person covered by the Act has not such a right in benefit payments as would make every defeasance of "accrued" interests violative of the Due Process Clause of the Fifth Amendment.

II.

This is not to say, however, that Congress may exercise its power to modify the statutory scheme free of all constitutional restraint. The interest of a covered employee under the Act is of sufficient substance to fall within the protection from arbitrary governmental action afforded by the Due Process Clause. In judging the permissibility of the cut-off provisions of § 202(n) from this standpoint, it is not within our authority to determine whether the Congressional judgment expressed in that section is sound or equitable, or whether it comports well or ill with the purposes of the Act. "Whether wisdom or unwisdom resides in the scheme of benefits set forth in Title II, it is not for us to say. The answer to such inquiries must come from Congress, not the courts. Our concern here, as often, is with power, not with wisdom." Helvering v. Davis, supra, at 644. Particularly when we deal with a withholding of a noncontractual benefit under a social welfare program such as this, we must recognize that the Due Process Clause can be thought to interpose a bar only if the statute manifests a patently arbitrary classification, utterly lacking in rational justification.

Such is not the case here. The fact of a beneficiary's residence abroad—in the case of a deportee, a presumably permanent residence—can be of obvious relevance to the question of eligibility. One benefit which may be thought to accrue to the economy from the Social Security system is the increased over-all national purchasing power resulting from taxation of productive elements of the economy to provide payments to the retired and disabled, who might otherwise be destitute or nearly so, and who would generally spend a comparatively large percentage of their benefit payments. This advantage would be lost as to payments made to one residing abroad. For these purposes, it is, of course, constitutionally irrelevant whether this reasoning in fact underlay the legislative decision, as it is irrelevant that the section does not extend to all to whom the postulated rationale might in logic apply. See United States v. Petrillo, 332 U.S. 1, 8–9, 67 S.Ct. 1538, 91 L.Ed. 1877; Steward Machine Co. v. Davis, 301 U.S. 548, 584–585, 57 S.Ct. 883, 81 L.Ed. 1279; cf. Carmichael v. Southern Coal Co., 301 U.S. 495, 510–513, 57 S.Ct. 868, 81 L. Ed. 1245. Nor, apart from this, can it be deemed irrational for Congress to have concluded that the public purse should not be utilized to contribute to the support of those deported on the grounds specified in the statute.

We need go no further to find support for our conclusion that this provision of the Act cannot be condemned as so lacking in rational justification as to offend due process.

III.

The remaining, and most insistently pressed, constitutional objections rest upon Art. I, § 9, cl. 3, and Art. III, § 2, cl. 3, of the Constitution, and the Sixth Amendment. It is said that the termination of appellee's benefits amounts to punishing him without a judicial trial, on Art. I, §9, cl. 3, and Art. III, § 2, cl. 3, of the Constitution, and the Sixth see Wong Wing v. United States, 163 U.S. 228, 16 S.Ct. 977, 41 L.Ed. 140; that the termination of benefits constitutes the imposition of punishment by legislative act, rendering § 202(n) a bill of attainder, see United States v. Lovett, 328 U.S. 303, 66 S.Ct. 1073, 90 L.Ed. 1252; Cummings v. Missouri, 4 Wall. 277, 18 L.Ed. 356; and that the punishment exacted is imposed for past conduct not unlawful when engaged in, thereby violating the constitutional prohibition on *ex post facto* laws, see Ex parte Garland, 4 Wall. 333, 18 L.Ed. 366. Essential to the success of each of these contentions is the validity of char-

acterizing as "punishment" in the constitutional sense the termination of benefits under § 202(n).

In determining whether legislation which bases a disqualification on the happening of a certain past event imposes a punishment, the Court has sought to discern the objects on which the enactment in question was focused. Where the source of legislative concern can be thought to be the activity or status from which the individual is barred, the disqualification is not punishment even though it may bear harshly upon one affected. The contrary is the case where the statute in question is evidently aimed at the person or class of persons disqualified. * * *

Turning, then, to the particular statutory provision before us, appellee cannot successfully contend that the language and structure of § 202(n), or the nature of the deprivation, requires us to recognize a punitive design. Cf. Wong Wing v. United States, supra (imprisonment, at hard labor up to one year, of person found to be unlawfully in the country). Here the sanction is the mere denial of a noncontractual governmental benefit. No affirmative disability or restraint is imposed, and certainly nothing approaching the "infamous punishment" of imprisonment, as in *Wong Wing*, on which great reliance is mistakenly placed. Moreover, for reasons already given (ante, pp. 611–612), it cannot be said, as was said of the statute in Cummings v. Missouri, supra, at 319; see Dent v. West Virginia, 129 U.S. 114, 126, 9 S.Ct. 231, 32 L.Ed. 623, that the disqualification of certain deportees from receipt of Social Security benefits while they are not lawfully in this country bears no rational connection to the purposes of the legislation of which it is a part, and must without more therefore be taken as evidencing a Congressional desire to punish. * * *

Reversed.

Mr. Justice BLACK, dissenting.

For the reasons stated here and in the dissents of Mr. Justice Douglas and Mr. Justice Brennan I agree with the District Court that the United States is depriving appellee, Ephram Nestor, of his statutory right to old-age benefits in violation of the United States Constitution.

Nestor came to this country from Bulgaria in 1913 and lived here continuously for 43 years, until July 1956. He was then deported from this country for having been a Communist from 1933 to 1939. At that time membership in the Communist Party as such was not illegal and was not even a statutory ground for deportation. From December 1936 to January 1955 Nestor and his employers made regular payments to the Government under the Federal Insurance Contributions Act. 26 U.S.C.A. §§ 3101–3125. These funds went to a special federal old-age and survivors insurance trust fund under 49 Stat. 622, 53 Stat. 1362, as amended, 42 U.S.C.A. § 401, in return for which Nestor, like millions of others, expected to receive payments when he reached the statutory age. In 1954, 15 years after Nestor had last been a Communist, and 18 years after he began to make payments into the old-age security fund, Congress passed a law providing, among other things, that any person who had been deported from this country because of past Communist membership under 66 Stat. 205, 8 U.S.C.A. § 1251(a)(6)(C) should be wholly cut off from any benefits of the fund to which he had contributed under the law. 68 Stat. 1083, 42 U.S.C.A. § 402(n). After the Government deported Nestor in 1956 it notified his wife, who had remained in this country, that he was cut off and no further payments would be made to him. This action, it seems to me, takes Nestor's insurance without just compensation and in violation of the Due Process Clause of the Fifth Amendment. Moreover, it imposes an ex post facto law and bill of attainder by stamping him, without a court trial, as unworthy to receive that for which he has paid and which the Government promised to pay him. The fact that the Court is sustaining this action indicates the extent to which people are willing to go these days to overlook violations of the Constitution perpetrated against anyone who has ever even innocently belonged to the Communist Party.

I.

In Lynch v. United States, 292 U.S. 571, 54 S.Ct. 840, 78 L.Ed. 1434, this Court unanimously held that Congress was without power to repudiate and abrogate in whole or in part its promises to pay amounts claimed by soldiers under the War Risk Insurance Act of 1917, §§ 400–405, 40 Stat. 409. This Court held that such a repudiation was inconsistent with the provision of the Fifth Amendment that "No person shall be * * * deprived of life, liberty, or property, without due process of law; nor shall private property be taken for public use, without just compensation." The Court today puts the Lynch Case aside on the ground that "It is hardly profitable to engage in conceptualizations regarding 'earned rights' and 'gratuities.' " From this sound premise the Court goes on to say that while "The 'right' to Social Security benefits is in one sense 'earned,' " yet the Government's insurance scheme now before us rests not on the idea of the contributors to the fund earning something, but simply provides that they may "justly call" upon the Government "in their later years, for protection from 'the rigors of the poor house as well as from the haunting fear that such a lot awaits them when journey's end is near.' " These are nice words but they cannot conceal the fact that they simply tell the contributors to this insurance fund that despite their own and their employers' payments the Government, in paying the beneficiaries out of the fund, is merely giving them something for nothing and can stop doing so when it pleases. This, in my judgment, reveals a complete misunderstanding of the purpose Congress and the country had in passing that law. It was then generally agreed, as it is today, that it is not desirable that aged people think of the Government as giving them something for nothing. An excellent statement of this view, quoted by Mr. Justice Douglas in another connection, was made by Senator George, the Chairman of the Finance Committee when the Social Security Act was passed, and one very familiar with the philosophy that brought it about:

"It comports better than any substitute we have discovered with the American concept that free men want to earn their security and not ask for doles—that what is due as a matter of earned right is far better than a gratuity. * * *

* * * * *

"Social Security is not a handout; it is not charity; it is not relief. It is an earned right based upon the contributions and earnings of the individual. As an earned right, the individual is eligible to receive his benefit in dignity and self-respect." 102 Cong.Rec. 15110.

The people covered by this Act are now able to rely with complete assurance on the fact that they will be compelled to contribute regularly to this fund whenever each contribution falls due. I believe they are entitled to rely with the same assurance on getting the benefits they have paid for and have been promised, when their disability or age makes their insurance payable under the terms of the law. The Court did not permit the Government to break its plighted faith with the soldiers in the Lynch Case: it said the Constitution forbade such governmental conduct. I would say precisely the same thing here.

The Court consoles those whose insurance is taken away today, and others who may suffer the same fate in the future, by saying that a decision requiring the Social Security system to keep faith "would deprive it of the flexibility and boldness in adjustment to ever-changing conditions which it demands." People who pay premiums for insurance usually think they are paying for insurance, not for "flexibility and boldness." I cannot believe that any private insurance company in America would be permitted to repudiate its matured contracts with its policyholders who have regularly paid all their premiums in reliance upon the good faith of the company. It is true, as the Court says, that the original Act contained a clause, still in force, that expressly reserves to Congress "[t]he right to alter, amend or repeal any provision" of the Act. § 1104, 49 Stat. 648, 42 U.S.C.A. § 1304. Congress, of course, properly retained that power. It could repeal the Act so as to cease to operate its old-age insurance activities for the future. This means that it could stop covering new people, and even stop increasing its obligations to its old contributors. But that is quite different from disappointing the just expectations of the contributors to the fund which the Government has compelled them and their employers to pay its Treasury. There is nothing "conceptualistic" about saying, as this Court did in Lynch, that such a taking as this the Constitution forbids.

II.

In part II of its opinion, the Court throws out a line of hope by its suggestion that if Congress in the future cuts off some other group from the benefits they have bought from the Government, this Court might possibly hold that the future hypothetical act violates the Due Process Clause. In doing so it reads due process as affording only minimal protection, and under this reading it will protect all future groups from destruction of their rights only if Congress "manifests a patently arbitrary classification, utterly lacking in rational justification." The Due Process Clause so defined provides little protection indeed compared with the specific safeguards of the Constitution such as its prohibitions against taking private property for a public use without just compensation, passing ex post facto laws, and imposing bills of attainder. I cannot agree, however, that the Due Process Clause is properly interpreted when it is used to subordinate and dilute the specific safeguards of the Bill of Rights, and when "due process" itself becomes so wholly dependent upon this Court's idea of what is "arbitrary" and "rational." See Levine v. United States, 362 U.S. 610, 620, 80 S. Ct. 1038, 4 L.Ed.2d 989, 997 (dissenting opinion); Adamson v. California, 332 U.S. 46, 89–92, 91 L.Ed. 1903, 1929, 1930, 67 S.Ct. 1672, 171 A.L.R. 1223 (dissenting opinion); Rochin v. California, 342 U.S. 165, 174, 96 L.Ed. 183, 191, 72 S.Ct. 205, 25 A.L.R.2d 1396 (concurring opinion). One reason for my belief in this respect is that I agree with what is said in the Court's quotation from Helvering v. Davis, 301 U.S. 619, 644, 57 S.Ct. 904, 109, 81 L. Ed. 1307, 1317 A.L.R. 1319:

"Whether wisdom or unwisdom resides in the scheme of benefits set forth in Title II, it is not for us to say. The answer to such inquiries must come from Congress, not the courts. Our concern here, as often, is with power, not with wisdom."

And yet the Court's assumption of its power to hold Acts unconstitutional because the Court thinks they are arbitrary and irrational can be neither more nor less than a judicial foray into the field of governmental policy. By the use of this due process formula the Court does not, as its proponents frequently proclaim, abstain from interfering with the congressional policy. It actively enters that field with no standards except its own conclusion as to what is "arbitrary" and what is "rational." And this elastic formula gives the Court a further power, that of holding legislative Acts constitutional on the ground that they are neither arbitrary nor irrational, even though the Acts violate specific Bill of Rights safeguards. See my dissent in Adamson v. California, 332 U.S. 46, 67 S.Ct. 1672, 91 L.Ed. 1903, 171 A.L.R. 1223, supra. Whether this Act had "rational justification" was, in my judgment, for Congress; whether it violates the Federal Constitution is for us to determine, unless we are by circumlocution to abdicate the power that this Court has been held to have ever since Marbury v. Madison (U.S.) 1 Cranch 137, 2 L.Ed. 60.

III.

The Court in part III of its opinion holds that the 1954 Act is not an ex post facto law or bill of attainder even though it creates a class of deportees who cannot collect their insurance benefits because they were once Communists at a time when simply being a Communist was not illegal. The Court also puts great emphasis on its belief that the Act here is not punishment. Although not believing that the particular label "punishment" is of decisive importance, I think the Act does impose punishment even in a classic sense. The basic reason for Nestor's loss of his insurance payments is that he was once a Communist.
* * *

* * *

A basic constitutional infirmity of this Act, in my judgment, is that it is a part of a pattern of laws all of which violate the First Amendment out of fear that this country is in grave danger if it lets a handful of Communist fanatics or some other extremist group make their arguments and discuss their ideas. This fear, I think, is baseless. It reflects a lack of faith in the sturdy patriotism of our people and does not give to the world a true picture of our abiding strength. It is an unworthy fear in a country that has a Bill of Rights containing provisions for fair trials, freedom of speech, press and religion, and other specific safeguards designed to keep men free. I repeat once more that I think this Nation's greatest security lies, not in trusting to a momentary majority of this Court's view at any particular time of what is "patently arbitrary," but in wholehearted devotion to and observance of our constitutional freedoms. See Wieman v. Updegraff, 344 U.S. 183, 192, 73 S.Ct. 215, 97 L.Ed. 216, 222 (concurring opinion).

I would affirm the judgment of the District Court which held that Nestor is constitutionally entitled to collect his insurance.

[Dissenting opinions of Mr. Justice DOUGLAS and Mr. Justice BRENNAN joined by Chief Justice WARREN and Mr. Justice DOUGLAS, omitted].

GOLDBERG v. KELLY

Supreme Court of the United States, 1970.
397 U.S. 254, 90 S.Ct. 1011, 25 L.Ed. 287.

Mr. Justice BRENNAN, delivered the opinion of the Court.

The question for decision is whether a State which terminates public assistance payments to a particular recipient without affording him the opportunity for an evidentiary hearing prior to termination denies the recipient procedural due process in violation of the Due Process Clause of the Fourteenth Amendment.

This action was brought in the District Court for the Southern District of New York by residents of New York City receiving financial aid under the federally assisted program of Aid to Families with Dependent Children (AFDC) or under New York State's general Home Relief program.[1] Their complaint alleged that the New York State and New York City officials administering these programs terminated, or were about to terminate, such aid without prior notice and hearing, thereby denying them due process of law. At the time the suits were filed there was no requirement of prior notice or hearing of any kind before termination of financial aid. However, the State and city adopted procedures for notice and hearing after the suits were brought, and the plaintiffs, appellees here, then challenged the constitutional adequacy of those procedures.

The State Commissioner of Social Services amended the State Department of Social Services' Official Regulations to require that local social services officials proposing to discontinue or suspend a recipient's financial aid do so according to a procedure which conforms to either subdivision (a) or subdivision (b) of § 351.26 of the Regulations as amended.[3] The City of New York elected to

[1] AFDC was established by the Social Security Act of 1935, 49 Stat. 627, as amended, 42 U.S.C.A. §§ 601–610. . . .

Home Relief is a general assistance program financed and administered solely by New York state and local governments. N. Y. Social Welfare Law §§ 157–166 (McKinney 1966). It assists any person unable to support himself or to secure support from other sources. Id., § 158.

[3] The adoption in February 1968 and the amendment in April of Regulation § 351.26 coincided with or followed several revisions by the Department of Health, Education, and Welfare of its regulations implementing 42 U.S.C.A. § 602(a)(4), which is the provision of the Social Security Act that requires a State to afford a "fair hearing" to any recipient of aid under a federally assisted program before termination of his aid becomes final. This requirement is satisfied by a post-termination "fair hearing" under regulations presently in effect. See HEW Handbook of Public Assistance Administration, Pt. IV, §§ 6200–6400. A new HEW regulation, 34 Fed.Reg. 1144 (1969), now scheduled to take effect in July 1970, 34 Fed.Reg. 13595 (1969), would require continuation of AFDC payments until the final decision after a "fair hearing" and would give recip-

promulgate a local procedure according to subdivision (b). That subdivision, so far as here pertinent, provides that the local procedure must include the giving of notice to the recipient of the reasons for a proposed discontinuance or suspension at least seven days prior to its effective date, with notice also that upon request the recipient may have the proposal reviewed by a local welfare official holding a position superior to that of the supervisor who approved the proposed discontinuance or suspension, and, further, that the recipient may submit, for purposes of the review, a written statement to demonstrate why his grant should not be discontinued or suspended. The decision by the reviewing official whether to discontinue or suspend aid must be made expeditiously, with written notice of the decision to the recipient. The section further expressly provides that "[a]ssistance shall not be discontinued or suspended prior to the date such notice of decision is sent to the

ients a right to appointed counsel at "fair hearings." 45 CFR § 205.10, 34 Fed.Reg. 1144 (1969); 45 CFR § 220.25, 34 Fed.Reg. 1356 (1969). For the safeguards specified at such "fair hearings" see HEW Handbook, Pt. IV, §§ 6200–6400. Another recent regulation now in effect requires a local agency administering AFDC to give "advance notice of questions it has about an individual's eligibility so that a recipient has an opportunity to discuss his situation before receiving formal written notice of reduction in payment or termination of assistance." HEW Handbook, Pt. IV, § 2300 (d)(5). This case presents no issue of the validity or construction of the federal regulations. It is only subdivision (b) of § 351.26 of the New York State regulations and implementing procedure 68–18 of New York City which pose the constitutional question before us. Cf. Shapiro v. Thompson, 394 U.S. 618, 641, 89 S.Ct. 1322, 1335, 22 L.Ed.2d 600 (1969). Even assuming that the constitutional question might be avoided in the context of AFDC by construction of the Social Security Act or of the present federal regulations thereunder, or by waiting for the new regulations to become effective, the question must be faced and decided in the context of New York's Home Relief program, to which the procedures also apply.

recipient and his representative, if any, or prior to the proposed effective date of discontinuance or suspension, whichever occurs later."

Pursuant to subdivision (b), the New York City Department of Social Services promulgated Procedure No. 68–18. A caseworker who has doubts about the recipient's continued eligibility must first discuss them with the recipient. If the caseworker concludes that the recipient is no longer eligible, he recommends termination of aid to a unit supervisor. If the latter concurs, he sends the recipient a letter stating the reasons for proposing to terminate aid and notifying him that within seven days he may request that a higher official review the record, and may support the request with a written statement prepared personally or with the aid of an attorney or other person. If the reviewing official affirms the determination of ineligibility, aid is stopped immediately and the recipient is informed by letter of the reasons for the action. Appellees' challenge to this procedure emphasizes the absence of any provisions for the personal appearance of the recipient before the reviewing official, for oral presentation of evidence, and for confrontation and cross-examination of adverse witnesses.[4] However, the letter

4 These omissions contrast with the provisions of subdivision (a) of § 351.26, the validity of which is not at issue in this Court. That subdivision also requires written notification to the recipient at least seven days prior to the proposed effective date of the reasons for the proposed discontinuance or suspension. However, the notification must further advise the recipient that if he makes a request therefor he will be afforded an opportunity to appear at a time and place indicated before the official identified in the notice, who will review his case with him and allow him to present such written and oral evidence as the recipient may have to demonstrate why aid should not be discontinued or suspended. The District Court assumed that subdivision (a) would be construed to afford rights of confrontation and cross-examination and a decision based solely on the record. Kelly v. Wyman, 294 F. Supp. 893, at 906–907.

does inform the recipient that he may request a post-termination "fair hearing." [5] This is a proceeding before an independent state hearing officer at which the recipient may appear personally, offer oral evidence, confront and cross-examine the witnesses against him, and have a record made of the hearing. If the recipient prevails at the "fair hearing" he is paid all funds erroneously withheld.[6] HEW Handbook, Pt. IV, §§ 6200–6500; 18 NYCRR §§ 84.2–84.23. A recipient whose aid is not restored by a "fair hearing" decision may have judicial review. N.Y. Civil Practice Law and Rules, Art. 78 (McKinney 1963). The recipient is so notified, 18 NYCRR § 84.16.

[5] N.Y. Social Welfare Law § 353(2) McKinney (1966) provides for a post-termination "fair hearing" pursuant to 42 U.S.C.A. § 602 (a)(4). See n. 3, supra. Although the District Court noted that HEW had raised some objections to the New York "fair hearing" procedures, 294 F.Supp., at 898, n. 9, these objections are not at issue in this Court. Shortly before this suit was filed, New York State adopted a similar provision for a "fair hearing" in terminations of Home Relief. 18 NYCRR §§ 84.2–84.23. In both AFDC and Home Relief the "fair hearing" must be held within 10 working days of the request, § 84.6, with decision within 12 working days thereafter, § 84.15. It was conceded in oral argument that these time limits are not in fact observed.

[6] Current HEW regulations require the States to make full retroactive payments (with federal matching funds) whenever a "fair hearing" results in a reversal of a termination of assistance. HEW Handbook, Pt. IV, §§ 6200(k), 6300(g), 6500(a); see 18 NYCRR § 358.8. Under New York State regulations retroactive payments can also be made, with certain limitations, to correct an erroneous termination discovered before a "fair hearing" has been held. 18 NYCRR § 351.27. HEW regulations also authorize, but do not require, the State to continue AFDC payments without loss of federal matching funds pending completion of a "fair hearing." HEW Handbook, Pt. IV, § 6500(b). The new HEW regulations presently scheduled to become effective July 1, 1970, will supersede all of these provisions, see n. 3, supra.

I

The constitutional issue to be decided, therefore, is the narrow one whether the Due Process Clause requires that the recipient be afforded an evidentiary hearing *before* the termination of benefits.[7] The District Court held that only a pre-termination evidentiary hearing would satisfy the constitutional command, and rejected the argument of the state and city officials that the combination of the post-termination "fair hearing" with the informal pre-termination review disposed of all due process claims. The Court said: "While post-termination review is relevant, there is one overpowering fact which controls here. By hypothesis, a welfare recipient is destitute, without funds or assets. * * * Suffice it to say that to cut off a welfare recipient in the face of * * * 'brutal need' without a prior hearing of some sort is unconscionable, unless overwhelming considerations justify it." Kelly v. Wyman, 294 F.Supp. 893, 899, 900 (1968). The Court rejected the argument that the need to protect the public's tax revenues supplied the requisite "overwhelming consideration." "Against the justified desire to protect public funds must be weighed the individual's overpowering need in this unique situation not to be wrongfully deprived of assistance. * * * While the problem of additional expense must be kept in mind, it does not justify denying a hearing meeting the ordinary standards of due process. Under all the circumstances, we hold that due process requires an adequate hearing before termination of welfare benefits, and the fact that there is a later constitutionally

[7] Appellant does not question the recipient's due process right to evidentiary review *after* termination. For a general discussion of the provision of an evidentiary hearing prior to termination, see Comment, The Constitutional Minimum for the Termination of Welfare Benefits: The Need for and Requirements of a Prior Hearing, 68 Mich.L. Rev. 112 (1969).

fair proceeding does not alter the result."
Id., at 901. Although state officials
were party defendants in the action, only
the City of New York appealed. We
noted probable jurisdiction, 394 U.S.
971, 89 S.Ct. 1469, 22 L.Ed.2d 751
(1969), to decide important issues which
have been the subject of disagreement
in principle between the three-judge
court in the present case and that convened in Wheeler v. Montgomery, 397
U.S. 280, 90 S.Ct. 1026, 25 L.Ed.2d
307. We affirm.

Appellant does not contend that procedural due process is not applicable to
the termination of welfare benefits. Such
benefits are a matter of statutory entitlement for persons qualified to receive
them.[8] Their termination involves state
action that adjudicates important rights.
The constitutional challenge cannot be
answered by an argument that public assistance benefits are "a 'privilege' and not
a 'right.'" Shapiro v. Thompson, 394

U.S. 618, 627, n. 6, 89 S.Ct. 1322, 1327
(1969). Relevant constitutional restraints apply as much to the withdrawal
of public assistance benefits as to disqualification for unemployment compensation, Sherbert v. Verner, 374 U.S. 398,
83 S.Ct. 1790, 10 L.Ed.2d 965 (1963);
or to denial of a tax exemption, Speiser
v. Randall, 357 U.S. 513, 78 S.Ct. 1332,
2 L.Ed.2d 1460 (1958); or to discharge
from public employment, Slochower v.
Board of Higher Education, 350 U.S.
551, 76 S.Ct. 637, 100 L.Ed. 692
(1956)[9] The extent to which procedural due process must be afforded the
recipient is influenced by the extent to
which he may be "condemned to suffer
grievous loss," Joint Anti-Fascist Refugee
Committee v. McGrath, 341 U.S. 123,
168, 71 S.Ct. 624, 647, 95 L.Ed. 817
(1951) (Frankfurter, J., concurring),
and depends upon whether the recipient's
interest in avoiding that loss outweighs
the governmental interest in summary adjudication. Accordingly, as we said in
Cafeteria & Restaurant Workers Union,
etc. v. McElroy, 367 U.S. 886, 895, 81
S.Ct. 1743, 1748–1749, 6 L.Ed.2d 1230
(1961), "consideration of what procedures due process may require under any
given set of circumstances must begin
with a determination of the precise nature of the government function involved
as well as of the private interest that has
been affected by governmental action."
See also Hannah v. Larche, 363 U.S. 420,
440, 442, 80 S.Ct. 1502, 1513, 1514, 4
L.Ed.2d 1307 (1960).

It is true, of course, that some governmental benefits may be administratively

[8] It may be realistic today to regard welfare entitlements as more like "property"
than a "gratuity." Much of the existing
wealth in this country takes the form of
rights which do not fall within traditional
common-law concepts of property. It has
been aptly noted that

"[s]ociety today is built around entitlement. The automobile dealer has his franchise, the doctor and lawyer their professional licenses, the worker his union membership, contract, and pension rights, the executive his contract and stock options; all
are devices to aid security and independence. Many of the most important of these
entitlements now flow from government:
subsidies to farmers and businessmen, routes
for airlines and channels for television stations; long term contracts for defense, space,
and education; social security pensions for
individuals. Such sources of security, whether private or public, are no longer regarded
as luxuries or gratuities; to the recipients
they are essentials, fully deserved, and in no
sense a form of charity. It is only the poor
whose entitlements, although recognized by
public policy, have not been effectively enforced."

Reich, Individual Rights and Social Wel-
fare: The Emerging Legal Issues, 74 Yale
L.J. 1245, 1255 (1965). See also Reich, The
New Property, 73 Yale L.J. 733 (1964).

[9] See also Goldsmith v. United States
Board of Tax Appeals, 270 U.S. 117, 46 S.Ct.
215, 70 L.Ed. 494 (1926) (right of a certified
public accountant to practice before the
Board of Tax Appeals); Hornsby v. Allen,
326 F.2d 605 (C.A.5th Cir. 1964) (right to obtain a retail liquor store license); Dixon v.
Alabama State Board of Education, 294 F.
2d 150 (C.A.5th Cir.), cert. denied 368 U.S.
930, 82 S.Ct. 368, 7 L.Ed.2d 193 (1961) (right
to attend a public college).

terminated without affording the recipient a pre-termination evidentiary hearing.[10] But we agree with the District Court that when welfare is discontinued, only a pre-termination evidentiary hearing provides the recipient with procedural due process. Cf. Sniadach v. Family Finance Corporation, 395 U.S. 337, 89 S.Ct. 1820, 23 L.Ed.2d 349 (1969). For qualified recipients, welfare provides the means to obtain essential food, clothing, housing, and medical care.[11] Cf. Nash v. Florida Industrial Commission, 389 U.S. 235, 239, 88 S.Ct. 362, 366, 19 L.Ed.2d 438 (1967). Thus the crucial factor in this context—a factor not present in the case of the blacklisted government contractor, the discharged government employee, the taxpayer denied a tax exemption, or virtually anyone else whose governmental largesse is ended— is that termination of aid pending resolution of a controversy over eligibility may deprive an *eligible* recipient of the very means by which to live while he waits. Since he lacks independent resources, his situation becomes immediately desperate. His need to concentrate upon finding the means for daily subsistence, in turn, adversely affects his ability to seek redress from the welfare bureaucracy.[12]

Moreover, important governmental interests are promoted by affording recipients a pre-termination evidentiary hearing. From its founding the Nation's basic commitment has been to foster the dignity and well-being of all persons within its borders. We have come to recognize that forces not within the control of the poor contribute to their poverty.[13] This perception, against the background of our traditions, has significantly influenced the development of the contemporary public assistance system. Welfare, by meeting the basic demands of subsistence, can help bring within the reach of the poor the same opportunities that are available to others to participate meaningfully in the life of the community. At the same time, welfare guards against the societal malaise that may flow from a widespread sense of unjustified frustration and insecurity. Public assistance, then, is not mere charity, but a means to "promote the general Welfare, and secure the Blessings of Liberty to ourselves and our Posterity." The same governmental interests which counsel the provision of welfare, counsel as well its

---

[10] One Court of Appeals has stated: "In a wide variety of situations, it has long been recognized that where harm to the public is threatened, and the private interest infringed is reasonably deemed to be of less importance, an official body can take summary action pending a later hearing." R. A. Holman & Co. v. SEC, 112 U.S.App.D.C. 43, 299 F.2d 127, 131, cert. denied 370 U.S. 911, 82 S.Ct. 1257, 8 L.Ed.2d 404 (1962) (suspension of exemption from stock registration requirement). See also, for example, Ewing v. Mytinger & Casselberry, Inc., 339 U.S. 594, 70 S.Ct. 870, 94 L.Ed. 1088 (1950) (seizure of mislabeled vitamin product); North American Cold Storage Co. v. Chicago, 211 U.S. 306, 29 S.Ct. 101, 53 L.Ed. 195 (1908) (seizure of food not fit for human use); Yakus v. United States, 321 U.S. 414, 64 S.Ct. 660, 88 L.Ed. 834 (1944) (adoption of wartime price regulations); Gonzalez v. Freeman, 118 U.S.App.D.C. 180, 334 F.2d 570 (1964) (disqualification of a contractor to do business with the Government). In Cafeteria & Restaurant Workers Union, etc. v. McElroy, supra, 367 U.S. at 896, 81 S.Ct. at 1749, summary dismissal of a public employee was upheld because "[i]n [its] proprietary military capacity, the Federal Government, * * * has traditionally exercised unfettered control," and because the case involved the Government's "dispatch of its own internal affairs." Cf. Perkins v. Lukens Steel Co., 310 U.S. 113, 60 S.Ct. 869, 84 L.Ed. 1108 (1940).

[11] Administrative determination that a person is ineligible for welfare may also render him ineligible for participation in state-financed medical programs. See N.Y. Social Welfare Law § 366 (McKinney 1966).

[12] His impaired adversary position is particularly telling in light of the welfare bureaucracy's difficulties in reaching correct decisions on eligibility. See Comment, Due Process and the Right to a Prior Hearing in Welfare Cases, 37 Ford.L.Rev. 604, 610– 611 (1969).

[13] See, e. g., Reich, supra, n. 8, 74 Yale L. J., at 1255.

uninterrupted provision to those eligible to receive it; pre-termination evidentiary hearings are indispensable to that end.

Appellant does not challenge the force of these considerations but argues that they are outweighed by countervailing governmental interests in conserving fiscal and administrative resources. These interests, the argument goes, justify the delay of any evidentiary hearing until after discontinuance of the grants. Summary adjudication protects the public fisc by stopping payments promptly upon discovery of reason to believe that a recipient is no longer eligible. Since most terminations are accepted without challenge, summary adjudication also conserves both the fisc and administrative time and energy by reducing the number of evidentiary hearings actually held.

We agree with the District Court, however, that these governmental interests are not overriding in the welfare context. The requirement of a prior hearing doubtless involves some greater expense, and the benefits paid to ineligible recipients pending decision at the hearing probably cannot be recouped, since these recipients are likely to be judgment-proof. But the State is not without weapons to minimize these increased costs. Much of the drain on fiscal and administrative resources can be reduced by developing procedures for prompt pre-termination hearings and by skillful use of personnel and facilities. Indeed, the very provision for a post-termination evidentiary hearing in New York's Home Relief program is itself cogent evidence that the State recognizes the primacy of the public interest in correct eligibility determinations and therefore in the provision of procedural safeguards. Thus, the interest of the eligible recipient in uninterrupted receipt of public assistance, coupled with the State's interest that his payments not be erroneously terminated, clearly outweighs the State's competing concern to prevent any increase in its fiscal and administrative burdens. As the District Court correctly concluded, "[t]he stakes are simply too high for the welfare recipient, and the possibility for honest error or irritable misjudgment too great, to allow termination of aid without giving the recipient a chance, if he so desires, to be fully informed of the case against him so that he may contest its basis and produce evidence in rebuttal." 294 F.Supp., at 904–905.

II

We also agree with the District Court, however, that the pre-termination hearing need not take the form of a judicial or quasi-judicial trial. We bear in mind that the statutory "fair hearing" will provide the recipient with a full administrative review.[14] Accordingly, the pre-termination hearing has one function only: to produce an initial determination of the validity of the welfare department's grounds for discontinuance of payments in order to protect a recipient against an erroneous termination of his benefits. Cf. Sniadach v. Family Finance Corporation, 395 U.S. 337, 343, 89 S.Ct. 1820, 1823, 23 L.Ed.2d 349 (1969) (Harlan, J., concurring). Thus, a complete record and a comprehensive opinion, which would serve primarily to facilitate judicial review and to guide future decisions, need not be provided at the pre-termination stage. We recognize, too, that both welfare authorities and recipients have an interest in relatively speedy resolution of questions of eligibility, that they are used to dealing with one another informally, and that some welfare departments have very burdensome caseloads. These considerations justify the limitation of the pre-termination hearing to minimum procedural safeguards, adapted to the particular characteristics of welfare recipients,

[14] Due process does not, of course, require two hearings. If, for example, a State simply wishes to continue benefits until after a "fair" hearing there will be no need for a preliminary hearing.

and to the limited nature of the controversies to be resolved. We wish to add that we, no less than the dissenters, recognize the importance of not imposing upon the States or the Federal Government in this developing field of law any procedural requirements beyond those demanded by rudimentary due process.

"The fundamental requisite of due process of law is the opportunity to be heard." Grannis v. Ordean, 234 U.S. 385, 394, 34 S.Ct. 779, 783, 58 L.Ed. 1363 (1914). The hearing must be "at a meaningful time and in a meaningful manner." Armstrong v. Manzo, 380 U.S. 545, 552, 85 S.Ct. 1187, 1191, 14 L.Ed.2d 62 (1965). In the present context these principles require that a recipient have timely and adequate notice detailing the reasons for a proposed termination, and an effective opportunity to defend by confronting any adverse witnesses and by presenting his own arguments and evidence orally. These rights are important in cases such as those before us, where recipients have challenged proposed terminations as resting on incorrect or misleading factual premises or on misapplication of rules or policies to the facts of particular cases.[15]

We are not prepared to say that the seven-days notice currently provided by New York City is constitutionally insufficient *per se,* although there may be cases where fairness would require that a longer time be given. Nor do we see any constitutional deficiency in the content or form of the notice. New York employs both a letter and a personal conference with a caseworker to inform a recipient of the precise questions raised

about his continued eligibility. Evidently the recipient is told the legal and factual bases for the Department's doubts. This combination is probably the most effective method of communicating with recipients.

The city's procedures presently do not permit recipients to appear personally with or without counsel before the official who finally determines continued eligibility. Thus a recipient is not permitted to present evidence to that official orally, or to confront or cross-examine adverse witnesses. These omissions are fatal to the constitutional adequacy of the procedures.

The opportunity to be heard must be tailored to the capacities and circumstances of those who are to be heard.[16] It is not enough that a welfare recipient may present his position to the decision maker in writing or secondhand through his caseworker. Written submissions are an unrealistic option for most recipients, who lack the educational attainment necessary to write effectively and who cannot obtain professional assistance. Moreover, written submissions do not afford the flexibility of oral presentations; they do not permit the recipient to mold his argument to the issues the decision maker appears to regard as important. Particularly where credibility and veracity are at issue, as they must be in many termination proceedings, written submissions are a wholly unsatisfactory basis for decision. The second-hand presentation to the decision maker by the caseworker has its own deficiencies; since the caseworker usually gathers the facts upon which the charge of ineligibility rests, the presentation of the recipient's side of the controversy cannot safely be left to him. Therefore a recipient must be allowed to

---

[15] This case presents no question requiring our determination whether due process requires only an opportunity for written submission, or an opportunity both for written submission and oral argument, where there are no factual issues in dispute or where the application of the rule of law is not intertwined with factual issues. See FCC v. WJR, 337 U.S. 265, 275–277, 69 S.Ct. 1097, 1103–1104, 93 L.Ed. 1353 (1949).

[16] "[T]he prosecution of an appeal demands a degree of security, awareness, tenacity, and ability which few dependent people have." Wedemeyer & Moore, The American Welfare System, 54 Calif.L.Rev. 326, 342 (1966).

state his position orally. Informal procedures will suffice; in this context due process does not require a particular order of proof or mode of offering evidence. Cf. HEW Handbook, Pt. IV, § 6400(a).

In almost every setting where important decisions turn on questions of fact, due process requires an opportunity to confront and cross-examine adverse witnesses. E. g., ICC v. Louisville & N. R. R. Co., 227 U.S. 88, 93–94, 33 S.Ct. 185, 187–188, 57 L.Ed. 431 (1913); Willner v. Committee on Character & Fitness, 373 U.S. 96, 103–104, 83 S. Ct. 1175, 1180–1181, 10 L.Ed.2d 224 (1963). What we said in Greene v. McElroy, 360 U.S. 474, 496–497, 79 S. Ct. 1400, 1413, 3 L.Ed.2d 1377 (1959), is particularly pertinent here:

> "Certain principles have remained relatively immutable in our jurisprudence. One of these is that where governmental action seriously injures an individual, and the reasonableness of the action depends on fact findings, the evidence used to prove the Government's case must be disclosed to the individual so that he has an opportunity to show that it is untrue. While this is important in the case of documentary evidence, it is even more important where the evidence consists of the testimony of individuals whose memory might be faulty or who, in fact, might be perjurors or persons motivated by malice, vindictiveness, intolerance, prejudice, or jealousy. We have formalized these protections in the requirements of confrontation and cross-examination. They have ancient roots. They find expression in the Sixth Amendment * * *. This Court has been zealous to protect these rights from erosion. It has spoken out not only in criminal cases, * * bu also in all types of cases where administrative * * * actions were under scrutiny."

Welfare recipients must therefore be given an opportunity to confront and cross-examine the witnesses relied on by the department.

"The right to be heard would be, in many cases, of little avail if it did not comprehend the right to be heard by counsel." Powell v. Alabama, 287 U.S. 45, 68–69, 53 S.Ct. 55, 64, 77 L.Ed. 158 (1932). We do not say that counsel must be provided at the pre-termination hearing, but only that the recipient must be allowed to retain an attorney if he so desires. Counsel can help delineate the issues, present the factual contentions in an orderly manner, conduct cross-examination, and generally safeguard the interests of the recipient. We do not anticipate that this assistance will unduly prolong or otherwise encumber the hearing. Evidently HEW has reached the same conclusion. See 45 CFR § 205.10, 34 Fed.Reg. 1144 (1969); 45 CFR § 220.-25, 34 Fed.Reg. 13595 (1969).

Finally, the decision maker's conclusion as to a recipient's eligibility must rest solely on the legal rules and evidence adduced at the hearing. Ohio Bell Tel. Co. v. PUC, 301 U.S. 292, 57 S.Ct. 724, 81 L.Ed. 1093 (1937); United States & ICC v. Abilene & S. Ry. Co., 265 U.S. 274, 288–289, 44 S.Ct. 565, 569–570, 68 L.Ed. 1016 (1924). To demonstrate compliance with this elementary requirement, the decision maker should state the reasons for his determination and indicate the evidence he relied on, cf. Wichita R. R. & Light Co. v. PUC, 260 U.S. 48, 57–59, 43 S.Ct. 51, 54–55, 67 L.Ed. 124 (1922), though his statement need not amount to a full opinion or even formal findings of fact and conclusions of law. And, of course, an impartial decision maker is essential. Cf. In re Murchison, 349 U.S. 133, 75 S.Ct. 623, 99 L.Ed. 942 (1955); Wong Yang Sung v. McGrath, 339 U.S. 33, 45–46, 70 S.Ct. 445, 451–452, 94 L.Ed. 616

(1950). We agree with the District Court that prior involvement in some aspects of a case will not necessarily bar a welfare official from acting as a decision maker. He should not, however, have participated in making the determination under review.

Affirmed.

Mr. Justice BLACK, dissenting.

In the last half century the United States, along with many, perhaps most, other nations of the world, has moved far towards becoming a welfare state, that is, a nation that for one reason or another taxes its most affluent people to help support, feed, clothe and shelter its less fortunate citizens. The result is that today more than nine million men, women, and children in the United States receive some kind of state or federally financed public assistance in the form of allowances or gratuities, generally paid them periodically, usually by the week, month, or quarter.[1] Since these gratuities are paid on the basis of need, the list of recipients is not static, and some people go off the lists and others are added from time to time. These ever-changing lists put a constant administrative burden on the Government and it certainly could not have reasonably anticipated that this burden would include the additional procedural expense imposed by the Court today.

The dilemma of the ever-increasing poor in the midst of constantly growing affluence presses upon us and must inevitably be met within the framework of our democratic constitutional government, if our system is to survive as such. It was largely to escape just such pressing economic problems and attendant government repression that people from Europe, Asia, and other areas settled this country and formed our Nation. Many of those settlers had personally suffered from persecutions of various kinds and wanted to get away from governments that had unrestrained powers to make life miserable for their citizens. It was for this reason, or so I believe, that on reaching these new lands the early settlers undertook to curb their governments by confining their powers within written boundaries, which eventually became written constitutions.[2] They wrote their basic charters as nearly as men's collective wisdom can do so as to proclaim to their people and their officials an emphatic command that "Thus far and no farther shall you go; and where we neither delegate powers to you, nor prohibit your exercise of them, we the people are left free." [3]

Representatives of the people of the original Thirteen Colonies spent long, hot months in the summer of 1787 in Philadelphia, Pennsylvania, creating a government of limited powers. They divided it into three departments—Legislative, Judicial, and Executive. The Judicial De-

---

[1] This figure includes all recipients of Old-age Assistance, Aid to Families with Dependent Children, Aid to the Blind, Aid to the Permanently and Totally Disabled, and general assistance. In this case appellants are AFDC and general assistance recipients. In New York State alone there are 951,000 AFDC recipients and 108,000 on general assistance. In the Nation as a whole the comparable figures are 6,080,000 and 391,000. U. S. Bureau of the Census, Statistical Abstract of the United States: 1969 (90th ed.), Table 435, at 297.

[2] The goal of a written constitution with fixed limits on governmental power had long been desired. Prior to our colonial constitutions, the closest man had come to realizing this goal was the political movement of the Levellers in England in the 1640's. J. Frank, The Levellers (1955). In 1647 the Levellers proposed the adoption of An Agreement of the People which set forth written limitations on the English Government. This proposal contained many of the ideas which later were incorporated in the constitutions of this Nation. Id. at 135–147.

[3] This command is expressed in the Tenth Amendment:
"The powers not delegated to the United States by the Constitution, nor prohibited by it to the States, are reserved to the States respectively, or to the people."

partment was to have no part whatever in making any laws. In fact proposals looking to vesting some power in the Judiciary to take part in the legislative process and veto laws were offered, considered, and rejected by the Constitutional Convention.[4] In my judgment there is not one word, phrase, or sentence from the beginning to the end of the Constitution from which it can be inferred that judges were granted any such legislative power. True, Marbury v. Madison, 5 U.S. (1 Cranch) 137, 2 L.Ed. 60 (1803), held, and properly, I think, that courts must be the final interpreters of the Constitution, and I recognize that the holding can provide an opportunity to slide imperceptibly into constitutional amendment and law making. But when federal judges use this judicial power for legislative purposes, I think they wander out of their field of vested powers and transgress into the area constitutionally assigned to the Congress and the people. That is precisely what I believe the Court is doing in this case. Hence my dissent.

* * *

The procedure required today as a matter of constitutional law finds no precedent in our legal system. Reduced to its simplest terms, the problem in this case is similar to that frequently encountered when two parties have an ongoing legal relationship which requires one party to make periodic payments to the other. Often the situation arises where the party "owing" the money stops paying it and justifies his conduct by arguing that the

recipient is not legally entitled to payment. The recipient can, of course, disagree and go to court to compel payment. But I know of no situation in our legal system in which the person alleged to owe money to another is required by law to continue making payments to a judgment-proof claimant without the benefit of any security or bond to insure that these payments can be recovered if he wins his legal argument. Yet today's decision in no way obligates the welfare recipient to pay back any benefits wrongfully received during the pretermination evidentiary hearings or post any bond, and in all "fairness" it could not do so. These recipients are by definition too poor to post a bond or to repay the benefits which, as the majority assumes, must be spent as received to insure survival.

The Court apparently feels that this decision will benefit the poor and needy. In my judgment the eventual result will be just the opposite. While today's decision requires only an administrative, evidentiary hearing, the inevitable logic of the approach taken will lead to constitutionally imposed, time-consuming delays of a full adversary process of administrative and judicial review. In the next case the welfare recipients are bound to argue that cutting off benefits before judicial review of the agency's decision is also a denial of due process. Since, by hypothesis, termination of aid at that point may still "deprive an *eligible* recipient of the very means by which to live while he waits," ante, at 1018, I would be surprised if the weighing process did not compel the conclusion that termination without full judicial review would be unconscionable. After all, at each step, as the majority seems to feel, the issue is only one of weighing the Government's pocketbook against the actual survival of the recipient, and surely that balance must always tip in favor of the individual. Similarly today's decision requires only the opportunity to have the

---

[4] It was proposed that members of the judicial branch would sit on a Council of Revision which would consider legislation and have the power to veto it. This proposal was rejected. J. Elliot, Elliot's Debates, vol. I, pp. 160, 164, 214 (Journal of the Federal Convention); 395, 398 (Yates' Minutes); vol. V, 151, 161–166, 344–349 (Madison's Notes) (2d ed. 1836). It was also suggested that The Chief Justice would serve as a member of the President's executive council, but this proposal was similarly rejected. Id., Vol. V, 442, 445, 446, 462.

benefit of counsel at the administrative hearing, but it is difficult to believe that the same reasoning process would not require the appointment of counsel, for otherwise the right to counsel is a meaningless one since these people are too poor to hire their own advocates. Cf. Gideon v. Wainwright, 372 U.S. 335, 344, 83 S.Ct. 792, 796, 9 L.Ed.2d 799 (1963). Thus the end result of today's decision may well be that the Government, once it decides to give welfare benefits, cannot reverse that decision until the recipient has had the benefits of full administrative and judicial review, including, of course, the opportunity to present his case to this Court. Since this process will usually entail a delay of several years, the inevitable result of such a constitutionally imposed burden will be that the Government will not put a claimant on the rolls initially until it has made an exhaustive investigation to determine his eligibility. While this Court will perhaps have insured that no needy person will be taken off the rolls without a full "due process" proceeding, it will also have insured that many will never get on the rolls, or at least that they will remain destitute during the lengthy proceedings followed to determine initial eligibility.

For the foregoing reasons I dissent from the Court's holding. The operation of a welfare state is a new experiment for our Nation. For this reason, among others, I feel that new experiments in carrying out a welfare program should not be frozen into our constitutional structure. It should be left, as are other legislative determinations, to the Congress and the legislatures which the people elect to make our laws.

Mr. Chief Justice BURGER, with whom Mr. Justice BLACK joins, dissenting.

Although I agree in large part with Mr. Justice BLACK's views in No. 62, Goldberg v. Kelly, ante, p. 1022, there are additional factors I wish to mention in dissent from today's unwise and precipitous constitutional holding.

The procedures for review of administrative action in the "welfare" area are in a relatively early stage of development; HEW has already taken the initiative by promulgating regulations requiring that AFDC payments be continued until a final decision after a "fair hearing" is held.[1] The net effect would be to provide a hearing prior to a termination of benefits. Indeed, the HEW administrative regulations go far beyond the result reached today since they require recipients be given the right to appointed counsel,[2] a position expressly rejected by the majority. As the majority notes, see *ante* n. 3, these regulations are scheduled to take effect in July 1970. Against this background I am baffled as to why we should engage in "legislating" via constitutional fiat when an apparently reasonable result has been accomplished administratively.

That HEW has already passed such regulations suggests to me that we ought to hold the heavy hand of constitutional adjudication and allow evolutionary processes at various administrative levels to experiment, given their flexibility to make adjustments in procedure without long delays. This would permit orderly development of procedural solutions, aided as they would be by expert guidance available within federal agencies which have an overview of the entire problem in 50 States. I cannot accept—indeed I reject—any notion that a government which pays out billions of dollars to nearly 12 million welfare recipients is heartless, insensitive or indifferent to the legitimate needs of the poor.

The Court's action today seems another manifestation of the now familiar con-

---

[1] 45 CFR 205.10, 34 Fed.Reg. 1144 (1969).

[2] 45 CFR 220.25, 34 Fed.Reg. 1356 (1969). See also HEW Handbook, Pt. IV, §§ 2300(d) (5), 6200–6400.

stitutionalizing syndrome: once some presumed flaw is observed, the Court then eagerly accepts the invitation to find a constitutionally "rooted" remedy. If no provision is explicit on the point, it is then seen as "implicit" or commanded by the vague and nebulous concept of "fairness."

I can share the impatience of all who seek instant solutions; there is a great temptation in this area to frame remedies which seem fair and can be mandated forthwith as against administrative or congressional action which calls for careful and extended study. That is thought too slow. But however cumbersome or glacial, this is the procedure the Constitution contemplated.

I would not suggest that the procedures of administering the Nation's complex welfare programs are beyond the reach of courts, but I would wait until more is known about the problems before fashioning solutions in the rigidity of a constitutional holding.

By allowing the administrators to deal with these problems we leave room for adjustments if, for example, it is found that a particular hearing process is too costly; the history of the complexity of the administrative process followed by judicial review as we have seen it for the past 30 years should suggest the possibility that new layers of procedural protection may become an intolerable drain on the very funds earmarked for food, clothing, and other living essentials.[3]

Aside from the administrative morass which today's decision could well create, the Court should also be cognizant of the

legal precedent it may be setting. The majority holding raises intriguing possibilities concerning the right to a hearing at other stages in the welfare process which affect the total sum of assistance, even though the action taken might fall short of complete termination. For example, does the Court's holding embrace welfare reductions or denial of increases as opposed to terminations, or decision concerning initial applications or requests for special assistance. The Court supplies no distinguishable considerations and leaves these crucial questions unanswered.

Mr. Justice STEWART, dissenting.

Although the question is for me a close one, I do not believe that the procedures that New York and California now follow in terminating welfare payments are violative of the United States Constitution. See Cafeteria & Restaurant Workers Union v. McElroy, 367 U.S. 886, 894–897, 81 S.Ct. 1743, 1748–1750, 6 L.Ed.2d 1230.

B. EQUAL PROTECTION AND OTHER SUBSTANTIVE RESTRICTIONS

SHERBERT v. VERNER

Supreme Court of the United States, 1963.
374 U.S. 398, 83 S.Ct. 1790, 10 L.Ed.2d 965.

Mr. Justice BRENNAN delivered the opinion of the Court.

Appellant, a member of the Seventh-day Adventist Church, was discharged by her South Carolina employer because she would not work on Saturday, the Sabbath Day of her faith.[1] When she was

---

[3] We are told, for example, that Los Angeles County alone employs 12,500 welfare workers to process grants to 500,000 people under various welfare programs. The record does not reveal how many more employees will be required to give this newly discovered "due process" to every welfare recipient whose payments are terminated for fraud or other factors of ineligibility or those whose initial applications are denied.

[1] Appellant became a member of the Seventh-day Adventist Church in 1957, at a time when her employer, a textile-mill operator, permitted her to work a five-day week. It was not until 1959 that the work week was changed to six days, including Satur-

unable to obtain other employment because from conscientious scruples she would not take Saturday work,[2] she filed a claim for unemployment compensation benefits under the South Carolina Unemployment Compensation Act.[3] That law

day, for all three shifts in the employer's mill. No question has been raised in this case concerning the sincerity of appellant's religious beliefs. Nor is there any doubt that the prohibition against Saturday labor is a basic tenet of the Seventh-day Adventist creed, based upon that religion's interpretation of the Holy Bible.

[2] After her discharge, appellant sought employment with three other mills in the Spartanburg area, but found no suitable five-day work available at any of the mills. In filing her claim with the Commission, she expressed a willingness to accept employment at other mills, or even in another industry, so long as Saturday work was not required. The record indicates that of the 150 or more Seventh-day Adventists in the Spartanburg area, only appellant and one other have been unable to find suitable non-Saturday employment.

[3] The pertinent sections of the South Carolina Unemployment Compensation Act (S.C. Code, Tit. 68, §§ 68–1 to 68–404) are as follows:

"§ 68–113. Conditions of eligibility for benefits.—An unemployed insured worker shall be eligible to receive benefits with respect to any week only if the Commission finds that: * * *

"(3) He is able to work and is available for work, but no claimant shall be considered available for work if engaged in self-employment of such nature as to return or promise remuneration in excess of the weekly benefit amounts he would have received if otherwise unemployed over such period of time. * * *

"§ 68–114. Disqualification for benefits.—Any insured worker shall be ineligible for benefits: * * *

"(2) *Discharge for misconduct.*—If the Commission finds that he has been discharged for misconduct connected with his most recent work prior to filing a request for determination of insured status or a request for initiation of a claim series within an established benefit year, with such ineligibility beginning with the effective date of such request, and continuing not less than five nor more than the next twenty-two consecutive weeks (in addition to the waiting period), as determined by the Commission in each case according to the seriousness of the misconduct * * *.

provides that, to be eligible for benefits, a claimant must be "able to work and * * * available for work"; and, further, that a claimant is ineligible for benefits "[i]f * * * he has failed, without good cause * * * to accept available suitable work when offered him by the employment office or the employer * * *." The appellee Employment Security Commission, in administrative proceedings under the statute, found that appellant's restriction upon her availability for Saturday work brought her within the provision disqualifying for benefits insured workers who fail, without good cause, to accept "suitable work when offered * * * by the employment office or the employer * * *." The Commission's finding was sustained by the Court of Common Pleas for Spartanburg County. That court's judgment was in turn affirmed by the South Carolina Supreme Court, which rejected appellant's contention that, as applied to her, the disqualifying provisions of the South Carolina statute abridged her right to the free exercise of her religion secured under the Free Exercise Clause of the First Amendment through the Four-

"(3) *Failure to accept work.*—(a) If the Commission finds that he has failed, without good cause, (i) either to apply for available suitable work, when so directed by the employment office or the Commission, (ii) to accept available suitable work when offered him by the employment office or the employer or (iii) to return to his customary self-employment (if any) when so directed by the Commission, such ineligibility shall continue for a period of five weeks (the week in which such failure occurred and the next four weeks in addition to the waiting period) as determined by the Commission according to the circumstances in each case * * *.

"(b) In determining whether or not any work is suitable for an individual, the Commission shall consider the degree of risk involved to his health, safety and morals, his physical fitness and prior training, his experience and prior earnings, his length of unemployment and prospects for securing local work in his customary occupation and the distance of the available work from his residence."

teenth Amendment. The State Supreme Court held specifically that appellant's ineligibility infringed no constitutional liberties because such a construction of the statute "places no restriction upon the appellant's freedom of religion nor does it in any way prevent her in the exercise of her right and freedom to observe her religious beliefs in accordance with the dictates of her conscience." 240 S.C. 286, 303–304, 125 S.E.2d 737, 746.[4] We noted probable jurisdiction of appellant's appeal. 371 U.S. 938, 83 S.Ct. 321, 9

[4] It has been suggested that appellant is not within the class entitled to benefits under the South Carolina statute because her unemployment did not result from discharge or layoff due to lack of work. It is true that unavailability for work for some personal reasons not having to do with matters of conscience or religion has been held to be a basis of disqualification for benefits. See, e. g., Judson Mills v. South Carolina Unemployment Compensation Comm'n, 204 S.C. 37, 28 S.E.2d 535; Stone Mfg. Co. v. South Carolina Employment Security Comm'n, 219 S.C. 239, 64 S.E.2d 644. But appellant claims that the Free Exercise Clause prevents the State from basing the denial of benefits upon the "personal reason" she gives for not working on Saturday. Where the consequence of disqualification so directly affects First Amendment rights, surely we should not conclude that every "personal reason" is a basis for disqualification in the absence of explicit language to that effect in the statute or decisions of the South Carolina Supreme Court. Nothing we have found in the statute or in the cited decisions, cf. Lee v. Spartan Mills, 7 CCH Unemployment Ins.Rep.S.C. ¶ 8156 (C.P.1944), and certainly nothing in the South Carolina Court's opinion in this case so construes the statute. Indeed, the contrary seems to have been that court's basic assumption, for if the eligibility provisions were thus limited, it would have been unnecessary for the court to have decided appellant's constitutional challenge to the application of the statute under the Free Exercise Clause.

Likewise, the decision of the State Supreme Court does not rest upon a finding that appellant was disqualified for benefits because she had been "discharged for misconduct"—by reason of her Saturday absences—within the meaning of § 68–114(2). That ground was not adopted by the South Carolina Supreme Court, and the appellees do not urge in this Court that the disqualification rests upon that ground.

L.Ed.2d 273. We reverse the judgment of the South Carolina Supreme Court and remand for further proceedings not inconsistent with this opinion.

I.

The door of the Free Exercise Clause stands tightly closed against any governmental regulation of religious *beliefs* as such, Cantwell v. Connecticut, 310 U.S. 296, 303, 60 S.Ct. 900, 84 L.Ed. 1213. Government may neither compel affirmation of a repugnant belief, Torcaso v. Watkins, 367 U.S. 488, 81 S.Ct. 1680, 6 L.Ed.2d 982; nor penalize or discriminate against individuals or groups because they hold religious views abhorrent to the authorities, Fowler v. Rhode Island, 345 U.S. 67, 73 S.Ct. 526, 97 L.Ed. 828; nor employ the taxing power to inhibit the dissemination of particular religious views, Murdock v. Pennsylvania, 319 U.S. 105, 63 S.Ct. 870, 87 L.Ed. 1292; Follett v. McCormick, 321 U.S. 573, 64 S.Ct. 717, 88 L.Ed. 938; cf. Grosjean v. American Press Co., 297 U.S. 233, 56 S.Ct. 444, 80 L.Ed. 660. On the other hand, the Court has rejected challenges under the Free Exercise Clause to governmental regulation of certain overt acts prompted by religious briefs or principles, for "even when the action is in accord with one's religious convictions, [it] is not totally free from legislative restrictions." Braunfeld v. Brown, 366 U.S. 599, 603, 81 S.Ct. 1144, 6 L.Ed.2d 563. The conduct or actions so regulated have invariably posed some substantial threat to public safety, peace or order. See, e. g., Reynolds v. United States, 98 U.S. 145, 25 L.Ed. 244; Jacobson v. Massachusetts, 197 U.S. 11, 25 S.Ct. 358, 49 L.Ed. 643; Prince v. Massachusetts, 321 U.S. 158, 64 S.Ct. 438, 88 L.Ed. 645; Cleveland v. United States, 329 U.S. 14, 67 S.Ct. 13, 91 L.Ed. 12.

Plainly enough, appellant's conscientious objection to Saturday work constitutes no conduct prompted by religious principles of a kind within the reach of state legislation. If, therefore, the decision of the South Carolina Supreme Court is to withstand appellant's constitutional challenge, it must be either because her disqualification as a beneficiary represents no infringement by the State of her constitutional rights of free exercise, or because any incidental burden on the free exercise of appellant's religion may be justified by a "compelling state interest in the regulation of a subject within the State's constitutional power to regulate * * *." NAACP v. Button, 371 U.S. 415, 438, 83 S.Ct. 328, 9 L.Ed.2d 405.

II.

We turn first to the question whether the disqualification for benefits imposes any burden on the free exercise of appellant's religion. We think it is clear that it does. In a sense the consequences of such a disqualification to religious principles and practices may be only an indirect result of welfare legislation within the State's general competence to enact; it is true that no criminal sanctions directly compel appellant to work a six-day week. But this is only the beginning, not the end, of our inquiry.[5] For "[i]f the purpose or effect of a law is to impede the observance of one or all religions or is to discriminate invidiously between religions, that law is constitutionally invalid even though the burden may be char-

acterized as being only indirect." Braunfeld v. Brown, supra, at 607. Here not only is it apparent that appellant's declared ineligibility for benefits derives solely from the practice of her religion, but the pressure upon her to forego that practice is unmistakable. The ruling forces her to choose between following the precepts of her religion and forfeiting benefits, on the one hand, and abandoning one of the precepts of her religion in order to accept work, on the other hand. Governmental imposition of such a choice puts the same kind of burden upon the free exercise of religion as would a fine imposed against appellant for her Saturday worship.

Nor may the South Carolina court's construction of the statute be saved from constitutional infirmity on the ground that unemployment compensation benefits are not appellant's "right" but merely a "privilege." It is too late in the day to doubt that the liberties of religion and expression may be infringed by the denial of or placing of conditions upon a benefit or privilege. American Communications Assn. v. Douds, 339 U.S. 382, 390, 70 S.Ct. 674, 94 L.Ed. 925; Wieman v. Updegraff, 344 U.S. 183, 191–192, 73 S.Ct. 215, 97 L.Ed. 216; Hannegan v. Esquire, Inc., 327 U.S. 146, 155–156, 66 S.Ct. 456, 90 L.Ed. 586. For example, in Flemming v. Nestor, 363 U.S. 603, 611, 80 S.Ct. 1367, 4 L.Ed.2d 1435, the Court recognized with respect to Federal Social Security benefits that "[t]he interest of a covered employee under the Act is of sufficient substance to fall within the protection from arbitrary governmental action afforded by the Due Process Clause." In Speiser v. Randall, 357 U.S. 513, 78 S.Ct. 1332, 2 L.Ed.2d 1460, we emphasized that conditions upon public benefits cannot be sustained if they so operate, whatever their purpose, as to inhibit or deter the exercise of First Amendment freedoms. We there struck down a condition which limited the avail-

---

[5] In a closely analogous context, this Court said:
"* * * the fact that no direct restraint or punishment is imposed upon speech or assembly does not determine the free speech question. Under some circumstances, indirect 'discouragements' undoubtedly have the same coercive effect upon the exercise of First Amendment rights as imprisonment, fines, injunctions or taxes. A requirement that adherents of particular religious faiths or political parties wear identifying armbands, for example, is obviously of this nature." American Communications Assn. v. Douds, 339 U.S. 382, 402, 70 S.Ct. 674, 94 L. Ed. 925. Cf. Smith v. California, 361 U.S. 147, 153–155, 80 S.Ct. 215, 4 L.Ed.2d 205.

ability of a tax exemption to those members of the exempted class who affirmed their loyalty to the state government granting the exemption. While the State was surely under no obligation to afford such an exemption, we held that the imposition of such a condition upon even a gratuitous benefit inevitably deterred or discouraged the exercise of First Amendment rights of expression and thereby threatened to "produce a result which the State could not command directly." 357 U.S., at 526. "To deny an exemption to claimants who engage in certain forms of speech is in effect to penalize them for such speech." Id., at 518. Likewise, to condition the availability of benefits upon this appellant's willingness to violate a cardinal principle of her religious faith effectively penalizes the free exercise of her constitutional liberties.

Significantly South Carolina expressly saves the Sunday worshipper from having to make the kind of choice which we here hold infringes the Sabbatarian's religious liberty. When in times of "national emergency" the textile plants are authorized by the State Commissioner of Labor to operate on Sunday, "no employee shall be required to work on Sunday * * * who is conscientiously opposed to Sunday work; and if any employee should refuse to work on Sunday on account of conscientious * * * objections he or she shall not jeopardize his or her seniority by such refusal or be discriminated against in any other manner." S.C.Code, § 64–4. No question of the disqualification of a Sunday worshipper for benefits is likely to arise, since we cannot suppose that an employer will discharge him in violation of this statute. The unconstitutionality of the disqualification of the Sabbatarian is thus compounded by the religious discrimination which South Carolina's general statutory scheme necessarily effects.

III.

We must next consider whether some compelling state interest enforced in the eligibility provisions of the South Carolina statute justifies the substantial infringement of appellant's First Amendment right. It is basic that no showing merely of a rational relationship to some colorable state interest would suffice; in this highly sensitive constitutional area, "[o]nly the gravest abuses, endangering paramount interests, give occasion for permissible limitation," Thomas v. Collins, 323 U.S. 516, 530, 65 S.Ct. 315, 89 L.Ed. 430. No such abuse or danger has been advanced in the present case. The appellees suggest no more than a possibility that the filing of fraudulent claims by unscrupulous claimants feigning religious objections to Saturday work might not only dilute the unemployment compensation fund but also hinder the scheduling by employers of necessary Saturday work. But that possibility is not apposite here because no such objection appears to have been made before the South Carolina Supreme Court, and we are unwilling to assess the importance of an asserted state interest without the views of the state court. Nor, if the contention had been made below, would the record appear to sustain it; there is no proof whatever to warrant such fears of malingering or deceit as those which the respondents now advance. Even if consideration of such evidence is not foreclosed by the prohibition against judicial inquiry into the truth or falsity of religious beliefs, United States v. Ballard, 322 U.S. 78, 64 S.Ct. 882, 88 L.Ed. 1148—a question as to which we intimate no view since it is not before us—it is highly doubtful whether such evidence would be sufficient to warrant a substantial infringement of religious liberties. For even if the possibility of spurious claims did threaten to dilute the fund and disrupt the scheduling of work, it would plainly be incumbent upon the appellees to demonstrate that no alternative forms of regulation would combat such abuses without infringing First Amendment rights.[7] Cf. Shelton v. Tucker, 364 U.S. 479, 487–490, 81 S.Ct. 247, 5 L.Ed.2d 231; Talley v. California, 362 U.S. 60, 64, 80 S.Ct. 536, 4 L.Ed.2d 559; Schneider v. State, 308 U.S. 147, 161, 60 S.Ct. 146, 84 L.Ed. 155; Martin v. Struthers, 319 U.S. 141, 144–149, 63 S.Ct. 862, 87 L.Ed. 1313.

In these respects, then, the state interest asserted in the present case is wholly dissimilar to the interests which were found to justify the less direct burden upon religious practices in Braunfeld v. Brown, supra. The Court recognized that the Sunday closing law which that decision sustained undoubtedly served "to make the practice of [the Orthodox Jewish merchants'] * * * religious beliefs more expensive," 366 U.S., at 605. But the statute was nevertheless saved by a countervailing factor which finds no equivalent in the instant case—a strong state interest in providing one uniform day of rest for all workers. That secular objective could be achieved, the Court found, only by declaring Sunday to be that day of rest. Requiring exemptions for Sabbatarians, while theoretically possible, appeared to present an administrative problem of such magnitude, or to afford the exempted class so great a competitive advantage, that such a requirement would have rendered the entire statutory scheme unworkable. In the present case no such justifications underlie the determination of the state court that appellant's religion makes her ineligible to receive benefits.

[7] We note that before the instant decision, state supreme courts had, without exception, granted benefits to persons who were physically available for work but unable to find suitable employment solely because of a religious prohibition against Saturday work. E. g., In re Miller, 243 N.C. 509, 91 S.E.2d 241.

IV.

In holding as we do, plainly we are not fostering the "establishment" of the Seventh-day Adventist religion in South Carolina, for the extension of unemployment benefits to Sabbatarians in common with Sunday worshippers reflects nothing more than the governmental obligation of neutrality in the face of religious differences, and does not represent that involvement of religious with secular institutions which it is the object of the Establishment Clause to forestall. See School District of Abington Township v. Schempp, ante, p. 203. Nor does the recognition of the appellant's right to unemployment benefits under the state statute serve to abridge any other person's religious liberties. Nor do we, by our decision today, declare the existence of a constitutional right to unemployment benefits on the part of all persons whose religious convictions are the cause of their unemployment. This is not a case in which an employee's religious convictions serve to make him a nonproductive member of society. See note 2, supra. Finally, nothing we say today constrains the States to adopt any particular form or scheme of unemployment compensation. Our holding today is only that South Carolina may not constitutionally apply the eligibility provisions so as to constrain a worker to abandon his religious convictions respecting the day of rest. This holding but reaffirms a principle that we announced a decade and a half ago, namely that no State may "exclude individual Catholics, Lutherans, Mohammedans, Baptists, Jews, Methodists, Non-believers, Presbyterians, or the members of any other faith, *because of their faith, or lack of it,* from receiving the benefits of public welfare legislation." Everson v. Board of Education, 330 U.S. 1, 16, 67 S.Ct. 504, 91 L.Ed. 711.

In view of the result we have reached under the First and Fourteenth Amendments' guarantee of free exercise of religion, we have no occasion to consider appellant's claim that the denial of benefits also deprived her of the equal protection of the laws in violation of the Fourteenth Amendment.

The judgment of the South Carolina Supreme Court is reversed and the case is remanded for further proceedings not inconsistent with this opinion.

It is so ordered.

Mr. Justice HARLAN, whom Mr. Justice WHITE joins, dissenting.

* * *

The South Carolina Supreme Court has uniformly applied this law in conformity with its clearly expressed purpose. It has consistently held that one is not "available for work" if his unemployment has resulted not from the inability of industry to provide a job but rather from personal circumstances, no matter how compelling. The reference to "involuntary unemployment" in the legislative statement of policy, whatever a sociologist, philosopher, or theologian might say, has been interpreted not to embrace such personal circumstances. See, e. g., Judson Mills v. South Carolina Unemployment Compensation Comm'n, 204 S.C. 37, 28 S.E.2d 535 (claimant was "unavailable for work" when she became unable to work the third shift, and limited her availability to the other two, because of the need to care for her four children); Stone Mfg. Co. v. South Carolina Employment Security Comm'n, 219 S.C. 239, 64 S.E.2d 644; Hartsville Cotton Mill v. South Carolina Employment Security Comm'n, 224 S.C. 407, 79 S.E. 2d 381.

In the present case all that the state court has done is to apply these accepted principles. Since virtually all of the mills in the Spartanburg area were operating on a six-day week, the appellant was "unavailable for work," and thus ineligible for benefits, when personal considerations prevented her from accepting employment on a full-time basis in the industry and locality in which she had worked. The fact that these personal considerations sprang from her religious convictions was wholly without relevance to the state court's application of the law. Thus in no proper sense can it be said that the State discriminated against the appellant on the basis of her religious beliefs or that she was denied benefits *because* she was a Seventh-day Adventist. She was denied benefits just as any other claimant would be denied benefits who was not "available for work" for personal reasons.

With this background, this Court's decision comes into clearer focus. What the Court is holding is that if the State chooses to condition unemployment compensation on the applicant's availability for work, it is constitutionally compelled to *carve out an exception*—and to provide benefits—for those whose unavailability is due to their religious convictions.

* * *

* * * [T]he implications of the present decision are far more troublesome than its apparently narrow dimensions would indicate at first glance. The meaning of today's holding, as already noted, is that the State must furnish unemployment benefits to one who is unavailable for work if the unavailability stems from the exercise of religious convictions. The State, in other words, must *single out* for financial assistance those whose behavior is religiously motivated, even though it denies such assistance to others whose identical behavior (in this case, inability to work on Saturdays) is not religiously motivated.

It has been suggested that such singling out of religious conduct for special treatment may violate the constitutional limitations on state action. See Kurland, Of Church and State and The Supreme Court, 29 U. of Chi.L.Rev. 1; cf. Cammarano v. United States, 358 U. S. 498, 515, 79 S.Ct. 524, 3 L.Ed.2d 462 (concurring opinion). My own view, however, is that at least under the circumstances of this case it would be a permissible accommodation of religion for the State, if it *chose* to do so, to create an exception to its eligibility requirements for persons like the appellant. The constitutional obligation of "neutrality," see School District of Abington Township v. Schempp, ante, p. 222, is not so narrow a channel that the slightest deviation from an absolutely straight course leads to condemnation. There are too many instances in which no such course can be charted, too many areas in which the pervasive activities of the State justify some special provision for religion to prevent it from being submerged by an all-embracing secularism. The State violates its obligation of neutrality when, for example, it mandates a daily religious exercise in its public schools, with all the attendant pressures on the school children that such an exercise entails. See Engel v. Vitale, 370 U.S. 421, 82 S.Ct. 1261, 8 L.Ed.2d 601; School District of Abington Township v. Schempp, supra. But there is, I believe, enough flexibility in the Constitution to permit a legislative judgment accommodating an unemployment compensation law to the exercise of religious beliefs such as appellant's.

For very much of the same reasons, however, I cannot subscribe to the conclusion that the State is constitutionally *compelled* to carve out an exception to its general rule of eligibility in the present case. Those situations in which the Constitution may require special treatment on account of religion are, in my view, few and far between, and this view is amply supported by the course of constitutional litigation in this area. See, e. g., Braunfeld v. Brown, supra; Cleveland v. United States, 329 U.S. 14, 67 S. Ct. 13, 91 L.Ed. 12; Prince v. Massachusetts, 321 U.S. 158, 64 S.Ct. 438, 88 L.Ed. 645; Jacobson v. Massachusetts, 197 U.S. 11, 25 S.Ct. 358, 49 L.Ed. 643;

Reynolds v. United States, 98 U.S. 145, 25 L.Ed. 244. Such compulsion in the present case is particularly inappropriate in light of the indirect, remote, and insubstantial effect of the decision below on the exercise of appellant's religion and in light of the direct financial assistance to religion that today's decision requires.

For these reasons I respectfully dissent from the opinion and judgment of the court.

[The concurring opinions of Mr. Justice DOUGLAS and Mr. Justice STEWART are omitted.]

DANDRIDGE v. WILLIAMS

Supreme Court of the United States, 1970.
397 U.S. 471, 90 S.Ct. 1153, 25 L.Ed.2d 491.

Mr. Justice STEWART delivered the opinion of the Court.

This case involves the validity of a method used by Maryland, in the administration of an aspect of its public welfare program, to reconcile the demands of its needy citizens with the finite resources available to meet those demands. Like every other State in the Union, Maryland participates in the federal Aid to Families with Dependent Children (AFDC program, 42 U.S.C.A. § 601 et seq., which originated with the Social Security Act of 1935.[1] Under this jointly financed program, a State computes the so-called "standard of need" of each eligible family unit within its borders. See generally, Rosado v. Wyman, 397 U. S. 397, 90 S.Ct. 1207, 25 L.Ed.2d 442. Some States provide that every family shall receive grants sufficient to meet fully the determined standard of need. Other States provide that each family unit shall receive a percentage of the determined need. Still others provide

[1] 49 Stat. 620, as amended, 42 U.S.C.A. §§ 301–1394.

grants to most families in full accord with the ascertained standard of need, but impose an upper limit on the total amount of money any one family unit may receive. Maryland, through administrative adoption of a "maximum grant regulation," has followed this last course. This suit was brought by several AFDC recipients to enjoin the application of the Maryland maximum grant regulation on the ground that it is in conflict with the Social Security Act of 1935 and with the Equal Protection Clause of the Fourteenth Amendment. A three-judge District Court, convened pursuant to 28 U.S.C.A. § 2281, held that the Maryland regulation violates the Equal Protection Clause. 297 F.Supp. 450. This direct appeal followed, 28 U.S.C.A. § 1253, and we noted probable jurisdiction, 396 U.S. 811, 90 S.Ct. 62, 24 L.Ed.2d 64.

The operation of the Maryland welfare system is not complex. By statute [2] the State participates in the AFDC program. It computes the standard of need for each eligible family based on the number of children in the family and the circumstances under which the family lives. In general, the standard of need increases with each additional person in the household, but the increments become proportionately smaller.[3] The regulation here in issue imposes upon the grant that any single family may receive an upper limit of $250 per month in certain counties including Baltimore City, and of $240 per month elsewhere in the State.[4] The ap-

pellees all have large families, so that their standards of need as computed by the State substantially exceed the maximum grants that they actually receive under the regulation. The appellees urged in the District Court that the maximum grant limitation operates to discriminate against them merely because of the size of their families, in violation of the Equal Protection Clause of the Fourteenth Amendment. They claimed further that the regulation is incompatible with the purpose of the Social Security Act of 1935, as well as in conflict with its explicit provisions.

"2. $240—for local departments under any 'Plan B' of Shelter Schedule
"*Except that*:
"a. If the requirements of a child over 18 are included to enable him to complete high school or training for employment (III–C–3), the grant may exceed the maximum by the amount of such child's needs.
"b. If the resource of support is paid as a refund (VI–B–6), the grant may exceed the maximum by an amount of such refund. This makes consistent the principle that the amount from public assistance funds does not exceed the maximum.
"c. The maximum may be exceeded by the amount of an emergency grant for items not included in a regular monthly grant. (VIII)
"d. The maximum may be exceeded up to the amount of a grant to a person in one of the nursing homes specified in Schedule D, Section a.
"3. A grant is subject to any limitation established because of insufficient funds." Maryland Manual of Dept. of Social Services, Rule 200, § X, B, at 23, formerly Md. Manual of Dept. of Pub.Wel., Part II, Rule 200, § VII, 1, at 20.

In addition, AFDC recipients in Maryland may be eligible for certain assistance in kind, including food stamps, public housing, and medical aid. See, e. g., 42 U.S.C.A. § 1396 et seq. (1964 ed., Supp. IV); 7 U.S.C.A. §§ 1695–1697. The applicable provisions of state and federal law also permit recipients to keep part of their earnings from outside jobs. 42 U.S.C.A. §§ 630–644 (1964 ed., Supp. IV); Md.Manual of Dept. of Social Services, Part II, Rule 200, § VI, B(8)(c)(2). Both federal and state law require that recipients seek work and take it if it is available. 42 U.S.C.A. § 602(a)(19)(F) (1964 ed., Supp. IV); Md.Manual of Dept. of Social Services, Rule 200, § III(D)(1)(d).

---

[2] Maryland Ann.Code, Art. 88A, § 44A et seq. (1969).

[3] The schedule for determining subsistence needs is set forth in an Appendix to this opinion.

[4] The regulation now provides:
"B. *Amount*—The amount of the grant is the resulting amount of need when resources are deducted from requirements as set forth in this Rule, subject to a maximum on each grant from each category:
"1. $250—for local departments under any 'Plan A' of Shelter Schedule

In its original opinion the District Court held that the Maryland regulation does conflict with the federal statute, and also concluded that it violates the Fourteenth Amendment's equal protection guarantee. After reconsideration on motion, the court issued a new opinion resting its determination of the regulation's invalidity entirely on the constitutional ground.[5] Both the statutory and constitutional issues have been fully briefed and argued here, and the judgment of the District Court must, of course, be affirmed if the Maryland regulation is in conflict with either the federal statute or the Constitution.[6] We consider the statu-

---

[5] Both opinions appear at 297 F.Supp. 450.

[6] The prevailing party may, of course, assert in a reviewing court any ground in support of his judgment, whether or not that ground was relied upon or even considered by the trial court. Compare Langnes v. Green, 282 U.S. 531, 538, 51 S.Ct. 243, 246, 75 L.Ed. 520, with Story Parchment Co. v. Paterson Parchment Paper Co., 282 U.S. 555, 567–568, 51 S.Ct. 248, 252, 75 L.Ed. 544. As the Court said in United States v. American Ry. Express Co., 265 U.S. 425, 435–436, 44 S.Ct. 560, 564, 68 L.Ed. 1087: "[I]t is likewise settled that the appellee may, without taking a cross-appeal, urge in support of a decree any matter appearing in the record, although his argument may involve an attack upon the reasoning of the lower court or an insistence upon matter overlooked or ignored by it. By the claims now in question, the American does not attack, in any respect, the decree entered below. It merely asserts additional grounds why the decree should be affirmed." When attention has been focused on other issues, or when the court from which a case comes has expressed no views on a controlling question, it may be appropriate to remand the case rather than deal with the merits of that question in this Court. See Aetna Cas. & Sur. Co. v. Flowers, 330 U.S. 464, 468, 67 S.Ct. 798, 800, 91 L.Ed. 1024; United States v. Ballard, 322 U.S. 78, 88, 64 S.Ct. 882, 887, 88 L.Ed. 1148. That is not the situation here, however. The issue having been fully argued both here and in the District Court, consideration of the statutory claim is appropriate. Bondholders Committee, Marlborough Inv. Co., etc. v. Commissioner of Internal Revenue, 315 U.S. 189, 192, n. 2, 62 S.Ct. 537, 539, 86 L.Ed. 784; H. Hart & H. Wechsler, The Federal Courts and the Federal System 1394 (1953). See also

---

tory question first, because if the appellees' position on this question is correct, there is no occasion to reach the constitutional issues. Ashwander v. TVA, 297 U.S. 288, 346–347, 56 S.Ct. 466, 482–483, 80 L.Ed. 688 (Brandeis, J., concurring); Rosenberg v. Fleuti, 374 U.S. 449, 83 S.Ct. 1804, 10 L.Ed.2d 1000.

I

The appellees contend that the maximum grant system is contrary to § 402 (a)(10) of the Social Security Act, as amended,[7] which requires that a state plan shall

"provide * * * that all individuals wishing to make application for aid to families with dependent children shall have the opportunity to do so, and that aid to families with dependent children shall be furnished with reasonable promptness to all eligible individuals."

The argument is that the state regulation denies benefits to the younger children in a large family. Thus, the appellees say, the regulation is in patent violation of the Act, since those younger children are just as "dependent" as their older siblings under the definition of "dependent child" fixed by federal law. See King v. Smith, 392 U.S. 309, 88 S.Ct. 2128, 20 L.Ed.2d 1118. Moreover, it is argued that the regulation, in limiting the amount of money any single household may receive, contravenes a basic purpose of the federal law by encouraging the parents of large families to "farm out" their children to relatives whose grants are not yet subject to the maximum limitation.

It cannot be gainsaid that the effect of the Maryland maximum grant provision

---

Jaffke v. Dunham, 352 U.S. 280, 77 S.Ct. 307, 1 L.Ed.2d 314.

[7] 64 Stat. 550 (1950), as amended 76 Stat. 185 (1962), 81 Stat. 881 (1968), 42 U.S.C.A. § 602(a)(10).

is to reduce the per capita benefits to the children in the largest families. Although the appellees argue that the younger and more recently arrived children in such families are totally deprived of aid, a more realistic view is that the lot of the entire family is diminished because of the presence of additional children without any increase in payments. Cf. King v. Smith, supra, at 335 n. 4, 88 S.Ct. at 2142. It is no more accurate to say that the last child's grant is wholly taken away than to say that the grant of the first child is totally rescinded. In fact, it is the *family* grant that is affected. Whether this per capita diminution is compatible with the statute is the question here. For the reasons that follow, we have concluded that the Maryland regulation is permissible under the federal law.

In King v. Smith, supra, we stressed the States' "undisputed power," under these provisions of the Social Security Act, "to set the level of benefits and the standard of need." Id., at 334, 88 S.Ct. at 2142. We described the AFDC enterprise as "a scheme of cooperative federalism," id., at 316, 88 S.Ct. at 2133, and noted carefully that "[t]here is no question that States have considerable latitude in allocating their AFDC resources, since each State is free to set its own standard of need and to determine the level of benefits by the amount of funds it devotes to the program." Id., at 318–319, 88 S.Ct. at 2134.

Congress was itself cognizant of the limitations on state resources from the very outset of the federal welfare program. The first section of the Act, 42 U.S.C.A. § 601, provides that the Act is

"For the purpose of encouraging the care of dependent children in their own homes or in the homes of relatives by enabling each State to furnish financial assistance and rehabilitation and other services, *as far as practicable under the conditions in such State,* to needy dependent children and the parents or relatives with whom they are living to help maintain and strengthen family life and to help such parents or relatives to attain or retain capability for the maximum self-support and personal independence consistent with the maintenance of continuing parental care and protection, * * *" (Emphasis added.)

Thus the starting point of the statutory analysis must be a recognition that the federal law gives each State great latitude in dispensing its available funds.

The very title of the Act, the repeated references to families added in 1962, Pub. L. No. 87–543, § 104(a) (3), 76 Stat. 185, and the words of the preamble quoted above, show that Congress wished to help children through the family structure. The operation of the statute itself has this effect. From its inception the Act has defined "dependent child" in part by reference to the relatives with whom the child lives.[9] When a "dependent child" is living with relatives, then "aid" also includes payments and medical care to those relatives, including the spouse of the child's parent. 42 U.S.C.A. § 606(b). Thus, as the District Court noted, the amount of aid "is * * * computed by treating the relative, parent or spouse of parent as the case may be, of the 'dependent child' as a part of the family unit." 297 F.Supp., at 455. Congress has been so desirous of keeping dependent children within a family that it amended the law in 1967 to provide that aid could go to children whose need arose merely from their parents' unemployment, under federally determined standards, although the parent was not incapacitated. 42 U.S.C.A. § 607 (1964 ed., Supp. IV).

9 42 U.S.C.A. § 606(a), supra, n. 8, formerly c. 531, § 406, 49 Stat. 629 (1935), as amended, c. 836, § 321, 70 Stat. 850 (1956). See also S.Rep.No.628, 74th Cong., 1st Sess., 16–17 (1935).

The States must respond to this federal statutory concern for preserving children in a family environment. Given Maryland's finite resources, its choice is either to support some families adequately and others less adequately, or not to give sufficient support to any family. We see nothing in the federal statute that forbids a State to balance the stresses which uniform insufficiency of payments would impose on all families against the greater ability of large families—because of the inherent economies of scale—to accommodate their needs to diminished per capita payments. The strong policy of the statute in favor of preserving family units does not prevent a State from sustaining as many families as it can, and providing the largest families somewhat less than their ascertained per capita standard of need.[10] Nor does the maximum grant system necessitate the dissolution of family bonds. For even if a parent should be inclined to increase his per capita family income by sending a child away, the federal law requires that the child, to be eligible for AFDC payments, must live with one of several enumerated relatives.[11] The kinship tie may be attenuated but it cannot be destroyed.

The appellees rely most heavily upon the statutory requirement that aid "shall be furnished with reasonable promptness to all eligible individuals." 42 U.S.C.A. § 602(a)(10) (1964 ed., Supp. IV).

But since the statute leaves the level of benefits within the judgment of the State, this language cannot mean that the "aid" furnished must equal the total of each individual's standard of need in every family group. Indeed the appellees do not deny that a scheme of proportional reductions for all families could be used which would result in no individual's receiving aid equal to his standard of need. As we have noted, the practical effect of the Maryland regulation is that all children, even in very large families, do receive some aid. We find nothing in 42 U.S.C.A. § 602(a)(10) that requires more than this.[12] So long as some aid is provided to all eligible families and all eligible children, the statute itself is not violated.

This is the view that has been taken by the Secretary of Health, Education, and Welfare, who is charged with the administration of the Social Security Act and the approval of state welfare plans. The parties have stipulated that the Secretary has, on numerous occasions, approved the Maryland welfare scheme, including its provision of maximum payments to any one family, a provision which has been in force in various forms since 1947. Moreover, a majority of the States pay less than their determined standard of need, and 20 of these States impose maximums on family grants of the kind here

[10] The Maryland Dept. of Social Services, Monthly Financial and Statistical Report, Table 7 (Nov. 1969), indicates that 32,504 families receive AFDC assistance. In the Maryland Dept. of Social Services, 1970 Fiscal Year Budget, the department estimated that 2,537 families would be affected by the removal of the maximum grant limitation. It thus appears that only one thirteenth of the AFDC families in Maryland receive less than their determined need because of the operation of the maximum grant regulation. Of course, if the same funds were allocated subject to a percentage limitation, no AFDC family would receive funds sufficient to meet its determined need.

[11] 42 U.S.C.A. § 606(a), n. 8, supra.

[12] The State argues that in the total context of the federal statute, reference to "eligible individuals" means eligible applicants for AFDC grants, rather than all the family members whom the applicants may represent, and that the statutory provision was designed only to prevent the use of waiting lists. There is considerable support in the legislative history for this view. See H.R. Rep.No.1300, 81st Cong., 1st Sess., 48, 148 (1949); 95 Cong.Rec. 13934 (1949) (remarks of Rep.Forand). And it is certainly true that the statute contemplates that actual payments will be made to responsible adults. See, e. g., 42 U.S.C.A. § 605. For the reasons given above, however, we do not find it necessary to consider this argument.

in issue.[13] The Secretary has not disapproved any state plan because of its maximum grant provision. On the contrary, the Secretary has explicitly recognized state maximum grant systems.[14]

Finally, Congress itself has acknowledged a full awareness of state maximum grant limitations. In 1967 Congress amended 42 U.S.C.A. § 602(a) to add a subsection, (23):

> "[The State shall] provide that by July 1, 1969, the amounts used by the State to determine the needs of individuals will have been adjusted to reflect fully changes in living costs since such amounts were established, and *any maximums that the State imposes on the amount of aid paid to families will have been proportionately adjusted.*" (Emphasis added.)

This specific congressional recognition of the state maximum grant provisions is not, of course, an approval of any specific maximum. The structure of specific maximums Congress left to the States, and the validity of any such structure must meet constitutional tests. However, the 1967 amendment does make clear that Congress fully recognized that the Act permits maximum grant regulations.[15]

For all of these reasons, we conclude that the Maryland regulation is not prohibited by the Social Security Act.

II

Although a State may adopt a maximum grant system in allocating its funds available for AFDC payments without violating the Act, it may not, of course, impose a regime of invidious discrimination in violation of the Equal Protection Clause of the Fourteenth Amendment. Maryland says that its maximum grant regulation is wholly free of any invidiously discriminatory purpose or effect, and that the regulation is rationally supportable on at least four entirely valid grounds. The regulation can be clearly justified, Maryland argues, in terms of legitimate state interests in encouraging gainful employment, in maintaining an

---

[13] See Department of Health, Education, and Welfare, Report on Money Payments to Recipients of Special Types of Public Assistance, Table 4 (NCSS Report D–4 1967). See also Hearings on H.R. 5710 before the House Committee on Ways and Means, 90th Cong., 1st Sess., pt. 1, at 118 (1967).

[14] Department of Health, Education, and Welfare, State Maximums and Other Methods of Limiting Money Payments to Recipients of Special Types of Public Assistance 3 (1962):

"When States are unable to meet need as determined under their standards they reduce payments on a percentage or flat reduction basis * * *. These types of limitations may be used in the absence of, or in conjunction with, legal or administrative maximums. A maximum limits the amount of assistance that may be paid to persons whose determined need exceeds that maximum, whereas percentage or flat reductions usually have the effect of lowering payments to most or all recipients to a level below that of determined need."

See also Department of Health, Education, and Welfare, Interim Policy Statement of May 31, 1968, 33 Fed.Reg. 10230 (1968); 45 CFR § 233.20(a)(2)(ii), 34 Fed.Reg. 1394 (1969).

[15] The provisions of 42 U.S.C.A. § 1396b(f), also added in 1967, 81 Stat. 898, are consistent with this view. That section provides that no medical assistance shall be given to any family which has a certain level of income. The section, however, makes an exception, 42 U.S.C.A. § 1396b(f)(1)(B)(ii): "If the Secretary finds that the operation of a uniform maximum limits payments to families of more than one size, he may adjust the amount otherwise determined under clause (i) to take account of families of different sizes."

These provisions have particular significance in light of the Administration's initial effort to secure a law forcing each State to pay its full standard of need. See Rosado v. Wyman, supra.

This recognition of the existence of state maximums is not new with the 1967 amendments. In reporting on amendments to the Social Security Act in 1962, 76 Stat. 185 (1962), the Senate committee referred to "States in which there is a maximum limiting the amount of assistance an individual may receive." S.Rep.No.1589, 87th Cong., 2d Sess., 14 (1962 U.S.Code Cong. and Admin. News, p. 1956.

equitable balance in economic status as between welfare families and those supported by a wage-earner, in providing incentives for family planning, and in allocating available public funds in such a way as fully to meet the needs of the largest possible number of families. The District Court, while apparently recognizing the validity of at least some of these state concerns, nonetheless held that the regulation "is invalid on its face for overreaching," 297 F.Supp., at 468—that it violates the Equal Protection Clause "[b]ecause it cuts too broad a swath on an indiscriminate basis as applied to the entire group of AFDC eligibles to which it purports to apply, * * * " 297 F.Supp., at 469.

If this were a case involving government action claimed to violate the First Amendment guarantee of free speech, a finding of "overreaching" would be significant and might be crucial. For when otherwise valid governmental regulation sweeps so broadly as to impinge upon activity protected by the First Amendment, its very overbreadth may make it unconstitutional. See, e. g., Shelton v. Tucker, 364 U.S. 479, 81 S.Ct. 247, 5 L.Ed.2d 231. But the concept of "overreaching" has no place in this case. For here we deal with state regulation in the social and economic field, not affecting freedoms guaranteed by the Bill of Rights, and claimed to violate the Fourteenth Amendment only because the regulation results in some disparity in grants of welfare payments to the largest AFDC families.[16] For this Court to approve the invalidation of state economic or social regulation as "overreaching" would be far too reminiscent of an era when the Court thought the Fourteenth Amendment gave it power to strike down state laws "be-cause they may be unwise, improvident, or out of harmony with a particular school of thought." Williamson v. Lee Optical of Oklahoma, Inc., 348 U.S. 483, 488, 75 S.Ct. 461, 464, 99 L.Ed. 563. That era long ago passed into history. Ferguson v. Skrupa, 372 U.S. 726, 83 S.Ct. 1028, 10 L.Ed.2d 93.

In the area of economics and social welfare, a State does not violate the Equal Protection Clause merely because the classifications made by its laws are imperfect. If the classification has some "reasonable basis," it does not offend the Constitution simply because the classification "is not made with mathematical nicety or because in practice it results in some inequality." Lindsley v. Natural Carbonic Gas Co., 220 U.S. 61, 78, 31 S.Ct. 337, 340, 55 L.Ed. 369. "The problems of government are practical ones and may justify, if they do not require, rough accommodations—illogical, it may be, and unscientific." Metropolis Theatre Co. v. City of Chicago, 228 U.S. 61, 69–70, 33 S.Ct. 441, 443, 57 L.Ed. 730. "A statutory discrimination will not be set aside if any state of facts reasonably may be conceived to justify it." McGowan v. Maryland, 366 U.S. 420, 426, 81 S.Ct. 1101, 1105, 6 L.Ed.2d 393.

To be sure, the cases cited, and many others enunciating this fundamental standard under the Equal Protection Clause, have in the main involved state regulation of business or industry. The administration of public welfare assistance, by contrast, involves the most basic economic needs of impoverished human beings. We recognize the dramatically real factual difference between the cited cases and this one, but we can find no basis for applying a different constitutional standard.[17] See Snell v. Wyman,

16 Cf. Shapiro v. Thompson, 394 U.S. 618, 89 S.Ct. 1322, 22 L.Ed.2d 600, where, by contrast, the Court found state interference with the constitutionally protected freedom of interstate travel.

17 It is important to note that there is no contention that the Maryland regulation is infected with a racially discriminatory purpose or effect such as to make it inherently

D.C., 281 F.Supp. 853, aff'd, 393 U.S. 323, 89 S.Ct. 553, 21 L.Ed.2d 511. It is a standard that has consistently been applied to state legislation restricting the availability of employment opportunities. Goesaert v. Cleary, 335 U.S. 464, 69 S.Ct. 198, 93 L.Ed. 163; Kotch v. Board of River Port Pilot Com'rs, 330 U.S. 552, 67 S.Ct. 910, 91 L.Ed. 1093. See also Flemming v. Nestor, 363 U.S. 603, 80 S.Ct. 1367, 4 L.Ed.2d 1435. And it is a standard that is true to the principle that the Fourteenth Amendment gives the federal courts no power to impose upon the States their views of wise economic or social policy.[18]

Under this long-established meaning of the Equal Protection Clause, it is clear that the Maryland maximum grant regulation is constitutionally valid. We need not explore all the reasons that the State advances in justification of the regulation. It is enough that a solid foundation for the regulation can be found in the State's legitimate interest in encouraging employment and in avoiding discrimination between welfare families and the families of the working poor. By combining a limit on the recipient's grant with permission to retain money earned, without reduction in the amount of the grant, Maryland provides an incentive to seek gainful employment. And by keying the maximum family AFDC grants to the minimum wage a steadily employed head of a household receives, the State maintains some semblance of an equitable balance between families on welfare and those supported by an employed breadwinner.[19]

suspect. Cf. McLaughlin v. Florida, 379 U.S. 184, 85 S.Ct. 283, 13 L.Ed.2d 222.

[18] See Developments in the Law—Equal Protection, 82 Harv.L.Rev. 1065, 1082–1087.

[19] The present federal minimum wage is $52–$64 per 40-hour week, 29 U.S.C.A. § 206 (1964 ed., Supp. IV). The Maryland minimum wage is $46–52 per week, Md.Code Ann., Art. 100, § 83.

It is true that in some AFDC families there may be no person who is employable.[20] It is also true that with respect to AFDC families whose determined standard of need is below the regulatory maximum, and who therefore receive grants equal to the determined standard, the employment incentive is absent. But the Equal Protection Clause does not require that a State must choose between attacking every aspect of a problem or not attacking the problem at all. Lindsley v. Natural Carbonic Gas Co., 220 U.S. 61, 31 S.Ct. 337, 55 L.Ed. 369. It is enough that the State's action be rationally based and free from invidious discrimination. The regulation before us meets that test.

We do not decide today that the Maryland regulation is wise, that it best fulfills the relevant social and economic objectives that Maryland might ideally espouse, or that a more just and humane system could not be devised. Conflicting claims of morality and intelligence are raised by opponents and proponents of almost every measure, certainly including the one before us. But the intractable economic, social, and even philosophical problems presented by public welfare assistance programs are not the business of this Court. The Constitution may impose certain procedural safeguards upon systems of welfare administration, Goldberg v. Kelly, 397 U.S. 254, 90 S.Ct. 1011, 25 L.Ed.2d 287. But the Constitution does not empower this Court to second-guess state officials charged with the difficult responsibility of allocating limited public welfare funds among the myriad of potential recipients. Cf. Charles C. Steward Mach. Co. v. Davis, 301 U.S. 548, 584–585, 57 S.Ct. 883, 889–890, 81 L.Ed. 1279; Helvering v. Davis, 301 U.S. 619, 644, 57 S.Ct. 904, 909, 81 L.Ed. 1307.

The judgment is reversed.

[20] It appears that no family members of any of the named plaintiffs in the present case are employable.

APPENDIX

The following was the schedule for determining subsistence needs, exclusive of rent, at the time this action was brought. Maryland Manual of Dept. of Pub. Welfare, Part II, Rule 200, Sched. A, 27:

STANDARD FOR DETERMINING COST OF SUBSISTENCE NEEDS

Number of persons in assistance unit (include unborn child as an additional person)	I	II	III	IV	V
	Monthly costs when				
	No heat or utilities included with shelter	Light and/ or cooking fuel included with shelter	Heat with or without light included with shelter	Heat, cooking fuel and water heating included with shelter	Heat and all utilities included with shelter
1 person living:					
Alone	$51.00	$49.00	$43.00	$40.00	$38.00
With 1 person	42.00	41.00	38.00	36.00	35.00
With 2 persons	38.00	37.00	35.00	34.00	33.00
With 3 or more persons ...	36.00	35.00	34.00	33.00	32.00
2 persons living:					
Alone	84.00	82.00	76.00	72.00	70.00
With 1 other person	76.00	74.00	70.00	68.00	66.00
With 2 or more other persons	72.00	70.00	68.00	66.00	64.00
3 persons living:					
Alone	113.00	110.00	105.00	101.00	99.00
With 1 or more other persons	108.00	106.00	101.00	99.00	97.00
4 persons	143.00	140.00	135.00	131.00	128.00
5 persons	164.00	162.00	156.00	152.00	150.00
6 persons	184.00	181.00	176.00	172.00	169.00
7 persons	209.00	205.00	201.00	197.00	193.00
8 persons	235.00	231.00	227.00	222.00	219.00
9 persons	259.00	256.00	251.00	247.00	244.00
10 persons	284.00	281.00	276.00	271.00	268.00
Each additional person over 10 persons	24.50	24.50	24.50	24.50	24.50

Modification of standard for cost of eating in restaurant: Add $15 per individual.

Other schedules set the estimated cost of shelter in the various counties in Maryland. See id., Sched. B—Plan A, 29; Sched. B—Plan B, 30. The present schedules, which are substantially the same, appear in the Maryland Manual of Dept. of Social Services, Part II, Rule 200, at 33, 35.

———◆———

Mr. Justice BLACK, with whom THE CHIEF JUSTICE joins, concurring.

Assuming, as the Court apparently does, that individual welfare recipients can bring an action against state welfare authorities challenging an aspect of the State's welfare plan as inconsistent with the provisions of the Social Security Act, 42 U.S.C.A. §§ 601–610, even though the Secretary of Health, Education, and Welfare has determined as he has here that the federal and state provisions are consistent, cf. Rosado v. Wyman, 397 U.S. 397, 90 S.Ct. 1207, 25 L.Ed.2d 442 (1970) (Black, J., dissenting), I join in the opinion of the Court in this case.

Mr. Justice HARLAN, concurring.

I join the Court's opinion, with one reservation which I deem called for by certain implications that might be drawn from the opinion.

As I stated in dissent in Shapiro v. Thompson, 394 U.S. 618, 658–663, 89 S.Ct. 1322, 1344–1347, 22 L.Ed.2d 600 (1969), I find no solid basis for the doctrine there expounded that certain statutory classifications will be held to deny equal protection unless justified by a "compelling" governmental interest, while others will pass muster if they meet traditional equal protection standards. See also my dissenting opinion in Katzenbach v. Morgan, 384 U.S. 641, 660–661, 86 S.Ct. 1731, 1732–1733, 16 L.Ed. 2d 828 (1966). Except with respect to racial classifications, to which unique historical considerations apply, see *Shapiro,* 394 U.S. at 659, 89 S.Ct. at 1344, I believe the constitutional provisions assuring equal protection of the laws impose a standard of rationality of classification, long applied in the decisions of this Court, that does not depend upon the nature of the classification or interest involved.

It is on this basis, and not because this case involves only interests in "the area of economics and social welfare," at 1161, that I join the Court's constitutional holding.

Mr. Justice DOUGLAS, dissenting.

Appellees, recipients of benefits under the Aid to Families with Dependent Children program (AFDC), brought this suit under 42 U.S.C. § 1983 to declare invalid and permanently enjoin the enforcement of the Maryland maximum grant regulation, which places a ceiling on the amount of benefits payable to a family under AFDC. They alleged that the regulation was inconsistent with the Social Security Act and that it denied equal protection of the laws in violation of the Fourteenth Amendment. I do not find it necessary to reach the constitutional argument in this case, for in my view the Maryland regulation is inconsistent with the terms and purposes of the Social Security Act.

The Maryland regulation under attack, Rule 200, § X, B, of the Maryland Department of Social Services, places an absolute limit of $250 per month on the amount of a grant under AFDC, regardless of the size of the family and its actual need.[1] The effect of this regulation is to deny benefits to additional children born into a family of six, thus making it impossible for families of seven persons or more to receive an amount commensurate with their actual need in accordance with standards formulated by the Maryland Department of Social Services whereas families of six or less can receive the full amount of their need as so determined. Appellee Williams, according to the computed need for herself and her eight children, should receive $296.15 per month. Appellees Gary should receive $331.50 for themselves and their eight children. Instead, these appellees received the $250 maximum grant.

[Justice DOUGLAS went on to argue at length that the legislative history of the Act demonstrated an intent to aid "individuals", not families, and the Maryland maximum grant rule offended that intent by denying aid to some of the children in large families.]

Mr. Justice MARSHALL, whom Mr. Justice BRENNAN joins, dissenting.

For the reasons stated by Mr. Justice DOUGLAS, to which I add some comments of my own, I believe that the Court has erroneously concluded that Maryland's maximum grant regulation is consistent with the federal statute. In my view, that regulation is fundamentally in conflict with the basic structure and purposes of the Social Security Act.

More important in the long run than this misreading of a federal statute, however, is the Court's emasculation of the Equal Protection Clause as a constitutional principle applicable to the area of social welfare administration. The Court holds

---

[1] In certain counties the applicable maximum grant is $240 per month. All of the appellees in this case are residents of Baltimore City, where the $250 month maximum grant applies.

today that regardless of the arbitrariness of a classification it must be sustained if any state goal can be imagined which is arguably furthered by its effects. This is so even though the classification's under- or over-inclusiveness clearly demonstrates that its actual basis is something other than that asserted by the State, and even though the relationship between the classification and the state interests which it purports to serve is so tenuous that it could not seriously be maintained that the classification tends to accomplish the ascribed goals.

The Court recognizes, as it must, that this case involves "the most basic economic needs of improverished human beings," and that there is therefore a "dramatically real factual difference" between the instant case and those decisions upon which the Court relies. The acknowledgment that these dramatic differences exist is a candid recognition that the Court's decision today is wholly without precedent. I cannot subscribe to the Court's sweeping refusal to accord the Equal Protection Clause any role in this entire area of the law, and I therefore dissent from both parts of the Court's decision.

I

At the outset, it should be emphasized exactly what is involved in determining whether this maximum grant regulation is consistent with and valid under the federal law. In administering its AFDC program, Maryland has established its own standards of need, and they are not under challenge in this litigation. Indeed, the District Court specifically refused to require additional appropriations on the part of the State or to permit appellees to recover a monetary judgment against the State. At the same time, however, there is no contention, nor could there be any, that the maximum grant regulation is in any manner related

to calculation of need.[1] Rather, it arbitrarily cuts across state-defined standards of need to deny any additional assistance with respect to the fifth or any succeeding child in a family.[2] In short, the regulation represents no less than the refusal of the State to give any aid whatsoever for the support of certain dependent children who meet the standards of need which the State itself has established.

Since its inception in the Social Security Act of 1935, the focus of the federal AFDC program has been to provide benefits for the support of dependent children of needy families with a view toward maintaining and strengthening family life within the family unit. As succinctly stated by the Senate Committee on Finance, "[t]he objective of the aid to dependent children program is to provide cash assistance for needy children *in their own homes.*"[3] In meeting these objectives, moreover, Congress has pro-

[1] The Court is thus wrong in speaking of "the greater ability of large families—because of the inherent economies of scale—to accommodate their needs to diminished per capita payments." Those economies have already been taken into account once in calculating the standard of need. Indeed, it borders on the ludicrous to suggest that a large family is more capable of living on perhaps 50% of its standard of need than a small family is on 95%.

[2] Because of minor variations in the calculation of the subsistence needs of particular families, and because the maximum grant varies between $240 and $250 per month, depending upon the county in which a particular family resides, the cutoff point between families which receive the full subsistence allowance and those which do not is not precisely families of more than six members. In practice, it appears that the subsistence needs of a family of six members are fully met. The needs of the seventh member (i. e., the fifth or sixth child, depending upon whether one or both parents are within the assistance unit), as defined by the State are met, if at all, only to a very small extent. In the usual situation, no payments whatever would be made with respect to any additional eligible dependent children.

[3] S.Rep.No.165, 87th Cong., 1st Sess., 6 (1961). (Emphasis added.)

vided the outlines that the AFDC plan is to follow if a State should choose to participate in the federal program. The maximum grant regulation, however, does not fall within these outlines or accord with the purposes of the Act. And the Court by approving it allows for a complete departure from the congressional intent.

The phrase "aid to families with dependent children," from which the AFDC program derives its name, appears in § 402(a)(10) of the Act, 42 U.S.C.A. § 602(a)(10), and is defined in 42 U.S.C.A. § 606(b) as, *inter alia,* "money payments *with respect to* * * * dependent children." (Emphasis added.) Moreover, the term "dependent child" is also extensively defined in the Act. See 42 U.S.C.A. § 606(a). Nowhere in the Act is there any sanction or authority for the State to alter those definitions—that is, to select arbitrarily from among the class of needy dependent children those whom it will aid. Yet the clear effect of the maximum grant regulation is to do just that, for the regulation creates in effect a class of otherwise eligible dependent children with respect to whom no assistance is granted.

It was to disapprove just such an arbitrary device to limit AFDC payments that Congress amended § 402(a)(10) in 1951 to provide that aid "shall be furnished with reasonable promptness *to all eligible individuals.*" (Emphasis added.) Surely, as my Brother DOUGLAS demonstrates, this statutory language means at least that the State must take into account the needs of, and provide aid with respect to, *all* needy dependent children. Indeed, that was our assessment of the congressional design embodied in the AFDC program in King v. Smith, 392 U.S. 309, 329–330, 333, 88 S.Ct. 2128, 2139–2140, 2141, 20 L.Ed.2d 1118 (1968).

* * *

II

Having decided that the injunction issued by the District Court was proper as a matter of statutory construction, I could affirm on that ground alone. However, the majority has of necessity passed on the constitutional issues. I believe that in overruling the decision of this and every other district court that has passed on the validity of the maximum grant device,[10] the Court both reaches the wrong result and lays down an insupportable test for determining whether a State has denied its citizens the equal protection of the laws.

The Maryland AFDC program in its basic structure operates uniformly with regard to all needy children by taking into account the basic subsistence needs of all eligible individuals in the formulation of the standards of need for families of various sizes. However, superimposed upon this uniform system is the maximum grant regulation, the operative effect of which is to create two classes of needy children and two classes of eligible families: those small families and their members who receive payments to cover their subsistence needs and those large families who do not.[11]

[10] The lower courts have been unanimous in the view that maximum grant regulations such as Maryland's are invalid. See Dews v. Henry, supra; Westberry v. Fisher, 297 F.Supp. 1109 (D.C.D.Me.1969); Lindsey v. Smith, 303 F.Supp. 1203 (D.C.W.D.Wash. 1969); Kaiser v. Montgomery, 319 F.Supp. 329 (D.C.N.D.Cal.1969). See also Collins v. State Board of Social Welfare, 248 Iowa 369, 81 N.W.2d 4 (1957) (family maximum invalid under equal protection clause of state constitution); Metcalf v. Swank, 293 F.Supp. 268 (D.C.N.D.Ill.1968) (dictum).

[11] In theory, no payments are made with respect to needy dependent children in excess of four or five as the case may be. In practice, of course, the excess children share in the benefits which are paid with respect to the other members of the family. The result is that support for the entire family is reduced below minimum subsistence levels. However, for purposes of equal protection analysis, it makes no difference

This classification process effected by the maximum grant regulation produces a basic denial of equal treatment. Persons who are concededly similarly situated (dependent children and their families), are not afforded equal, or even approximately equal, treatment under the maximum grant regulation. Subsistence benefits are paid with respect to some needy dependent children; nothing is paid with respect to others. Some needy families receive full subsistence assistance as calculated by the State; the assistance paid to other families is grossly below their similarly calculated needs.

Yet, as a general principle, individuals should not be afforded different treatment by the State unless there is a relevant distinction between them and "a statutory discrimination must be based on differences that are reasonably related to the purposes of the Act in which it is found." Morey v. Doud, 354 U.S. 457, 465, 77 S.Ct. 1344, 1350, 1 L.Ed.2d 1485 (1957). See Gulf, Colorado & Santa Fe Ry. v. Ellis, 165 U.S. 150, 155, 17 S.Ct. 255, 256, 41 L.Ed. 666 (1897). Consequently, the State may not, in the provision of important services or the distribution of governmental payments, supply benefits to some individuals while denying them to others who are similarly situated. See, e. g., Griffin v. County School Board of Prince Edward County, 377 U.S. 218, 84 S.Ct. 1226, 12 L.Ed.2d 256 (1964).

In the instant case, the only distinction between those children with respect to whom assistance is granted and those children who are denied such assistance is the size of the family into which the child permits himself to be born. The class of individuals with respect to whom

payments are actually made (the first four or five eligible dependent children in a family), is grossly underinclusive in terms of the class which the AFDC program was designed to assist, namely *all* needy dependent children. Such underinclusiveness manifests "a *prima facie* violation of the equal protection requirement of reasonable classification,"[12] compelling the State to come forward with a persuasive justification for the classification.

The Court never undertakes to inquire for such a justification; rather it avoids the task by focusing upon the abstract dichotomy between two different approaches to equal protection problems which have been utilized by this Court.

Under the so-called "traditional test," a classification is said to be permissible under the Equal Protection Clause unless it is "without any reasonable basis." Lindsley v. Natural Carbonic Gas Co., 220 U.S. 61, 78, 31 S.Ct. 337, 340, 55 L.Ed. 369 (1911).[13] On the other hand, if the classification affects a "fundamental right," then the state interest in perpetuating the classification must be "compelling" in order to be sustained. See, e. g., Shapiro v. Thompson, supra; Harper v. Virginia State Board of Elections, 383 U.S. 663, 86 S.Ct. 1079, 16 L.Ed.2d 169 (1966); McLaughlin v. Florida, 379 U.S. 184, 85 S.Ct. 283, 13 L.Ed.2d 222 (1964).

This case simply defies easy characterization in terms of one or the other of these "tests." The cases relied on by the Court, in which a "mere rationality" test was actually used, e. g., Williamson v. Lee Optical of Oklahoma, Inc., 348 U.S. 483, 75 S.Ct. 461, 99 L.Ed. 563 (1955), are most accurately described as involv-

whether the class against which the maximum grant regulation discriminates is defined as eligible dependent children in excess of the fourth or fifth, or, alternatively, as individuals in large families generally, that is, those with more than six members.

[12] Tussman & tenBroek, The Equal Protection of the Laws, 37 Calif.L.Rev. 341, 348 (1949).

[13] See generally Developments in the Law —Equal Protection, 82 Harv.L.Rev. 1065, 1076–1087 (1969).

ing the application of equal protection reasoning to the regulation of business interests. The extremes to which the Court has gone in dreaming up rational bases for state regulation in that area may in many instances be ascribed to a healthy revulsion from the Court's earlier excesses in using the Constitution to protect interests which have more than enough power to protect themselves in the legislative halls. This case, involving the literally vital interests of a powerless minority—poor families without breadwinners—is far removed from the area of business regulation, as the Court concedes. Why then is the standard used in those cases imposed here? We are told no more than that this case falls in "the area of economics and social welfare," with the implication that from there the answer is obvious.

In my view, equal protection analysis of this case is not appreciably advanced by the *a priori* definition of a "right," fundamental or otherwise.[14] Rather, con-

centration must be placed upon the character of the classification in question, the relative importance to individuals in the class discriminated against of the governmental benefits which they do not receive, and the asserted state interests in support of the classification. As we said only recently, "In determining whether or not a state law violates the Equal Protection Clause, we must consider the facts and circumstances behind the law, the interests which the State claims to be protecting, and the interests of those who are disadvantaged by the classification." Kramer v. Union Free School District No. 15, 395 U.S. 621, 626, 89 S.Ct. 1886, 1889, 23 L.Ed.2d 583 (1969), quoting Williams v. Rhodes, 393 U.S. 23, 30, 89 S.Ct. 5, 10, 21 L.Ed.2d 24 (1968).[15]

It is the individual interests here at stake which, as the Court concedes, most clearly distinguish this case from the "business regulation" equal protection cases. AFDC support to needy dependent children provides the stuff which sustains those children's lives: food, clothing, shelter.[16] And this Court has already recognized several times that when

---

[14] See generally Van Alstyne, The Demise of the Right-Privilege Distinction in Constitutional Law, 81 Harv.L.Rev. 1439 (1968). Appellees do argue that their "fundamental rights" are infringed by the maximum grant regulation. They cite, for example, Skinner v. Oklahoma ex rel. Williamson, 316 U.S. 535, 62 S.Ct. 1110, 86 L.Ed. 1655 (1942), for the proposition that the "right of procreation" is fundamental. The statement is no doubt accurate as far as it goes, but the effect of the maximum grant regulation upon the right of procreation is marginal and indirect at best, totally unlike the compulsory sterilization law which was at issue in *Skinner*.

At the same time the Court's insistence that equal protection analysis turns on the basis of a closed category of "fundamental rights" involves a curious value judgment. It is certainly difficult to believe that a person whose very survival is at stake would be comforted by the knowledge that his "fundamental" rights are preserved intact.

On the issue of whether there is a "right" to welfare assistance, see generally Graham, Public Assistance: The Right to Receive; the Obligation To Repay, 43 N.Y.U.L.Rev. 451 (1968); Harvith, Federal Equal Protection and Welfare Assistance, 31 Albany L.

Rev. 210 (1967): Note, Welfare Due Process: The Maximum Grant Limitation on the Right to Survive, 3 Ga.L.Rev. 459 (1969). See also Universal Declaration of Human Rights, Art. 25.

[15] This is essentially what this Court has done in applying equal protection concepts in numerous cases, though the various aspects of the approach appear with a greater or lesser degree of clarity in particular cases. See, e. g., McLaughlin v. Florida, supra; Rinaldi v. Yeager, 384 U.S. 305, 86 S.Ct. 1497, 16 L.Ed.2d 577 (1966); Carrington v. Rash, 380 U.S. 89, 85 S.Ct. 775, 13 L. Ed.2d 675 (1965); Douglas v. California, 372 U.S. 353, 83 S.Ct. 814, 9 L.Ed.2d 811 (1963); Skinner v. Oklahoma ex rel. Williamson, supra.

For an application of this approach to several welfare questions, see Note Equal Protection as a Measure of Competing Interests in Welfare Litigation, 21 Me.L.Rev. 175 (1969).

[16] See also Rothstein v. Wyman, 303 F. Supp. 339, 346–347 (D.C.S.D.N.Y.1969): Harvith, supra, n. 28, at 222–226.

a benefit, even a "gratuitous" benefit, is necessary to sustain life, stricter constitutional standards, both procedural [17] and substantive,[18] are applied to the deprivation of that benefit.

Nor is the distinction upon which the deprivation is here based—the distinction between large and small families—one which readily commends itself as a basis for determining which children are to have support approximating subsistence and which are not. Indeed, governmental discrimination between children on the basis of a factor over which they have no

[17] See Sniadach v. Family Finance Corp., 395 U.S. 337, 340–342, 89 S.Ct. 1820, 1822–1823, 23 L.Ed.2d 349 (1969) (relying on devastating impact of wage garnishment to require prior hearing as a matter of due process); Goldberg v. Kelly, 397 U.S. 254, 264, 90 S.Ct. 1011, 1018, 25 L.Ed.2d 287 (1970): "Thus the crucial factor in this context—a factor not present in the case of the blacklisted government contractor, the discharged government employee, the taxpayer denied a tax exemption, or virtually anyone else whose governmental largesse is ended—is that termination of aid pending resolution of a controversy over eligibility may deprive an *eligible* recipient of the very means by which to live while he waits."

[18] Compare Shapiro v. Thompson, supra, 394 U.S. at 627, 89 S.Ct. at 1327, striking down one-year residency requirement for welfare eligibility as violation of equal protection, and noting that the benefits in question are "the very means to subsist—food, shelter, and other necessities of life," with Kirk v. Board of Regents, etc., Cal. App., 78 Cal.Rptr. 260, 266–267 (1969), appeal dismissed, 396 U.S. 554, 90 S.Ct. 754, 24 L. Ed.2d 747 (1970), upholding one-year residency requirement for tuition-free graduate education at state university, and distinguishing *Shapiro* on the ground that it "involved the immediate and pressing need for preservation of life and health of persons unable to live without public assistance, and their dependent children."

These cases and those cited n. 17, supra, suggest that whether or not there is a constitutional "right" to subsistence (as to which see n. 14, supra), deprivations of benefits necessary for subsistence will receive closer constitutional scrutiny, under both the Due Process and Equal Protection clauses, than will deprivations of less essential forms of governmental largesse.

control—the number of their brothers and sisters—bears some resemblance to the classification between legitimate and illegitimate children which we condemned as a violation of the Equal Protection Clause in Levy v. Louisiana, 391 U.S. 68, 88 S.Ct. 1509, 20 L.Ed.2d 436 (1968).

The asserted state interests in the maintenance of the maximum grant regulation, on the other hand, are hardly clear. In the early stages of this litigation, the State attempted to rationalize the maximum grant regulation on the theory that it was merely a device to conserve state funds, in the language of the answer, "a legitimate way of allocating the State's limited resources available for AFDC assistance." Indeed, the initial opinion of the District Court concluded that the sole reason for the regulation, as revealed by the record, was "to fit the total needs of the State's dependent children, as measured by the State's standards of their subsistence requirements, into an inadequate State appropriation." 297 F.Supp., at 458. The District Court quite properly rejected this asserted justification, for "[t]he saving of welfare costs cannot justify an otherwise invidious classification." Shapiro v. Thompson, *supra,* 394 U.S. at 633, 89 S.Ct. at 1330. See Goldberg v. Kelly, *supra,* 397 U.S. at 266, 90 S.Ct. at 1019.

In post-trial proceedings in the District Court, and in briefs to this court, the State apparently abandoned reliance on the fiscal justification. In its place, there have now appeared several different rationales for the maximum grant regulation, prominent among them being those relied upon by the majority—the notions that imposition of the maximum serves as an incentive to welfare recipients to find and maintain employment and provides a semblance of equality with persons earning a minimum wage.

With regard to the latter, Maryland has urged that the maximum grant regulation serves to maintain a rough equality between wage earning families and AFDC families, thereby increasing the political support for—or perhaps reducing the opposition to—the AFDC program. It is questionable whether the Court really relies on this ground, especially when in many States the prescribed family maximum bears no such relation to the minimum wage.[19] But the Court does not indicate that a different result might obtain in other cases. Indeed, whether elimination of the maximum would produce welfare incomes out of line with other incomes in Maryland is itself open to question on this record.[20] It is true that government in the United States, unlike certain other countries, has not chosen to make public aid available to assist families generally in raising their children. Rather, in this case Maryland, with the encouragement and assistance of the Federal Government, has elected to provide assistance at a subsistence level for those in particular need—the aged, the blind, the infirm, and the unemployed and unemployable, and their children. The only question presented here is whether, having once undertaken such a program, the State may arbitrarily select from among the concededly eligible those to whom it will provide benefits. And it is too late to argue that political expediency will sustain discrimination not otherwise supportable. Cf. Cooper v.

[19] See Department of Health, Education, and Welfare, Report on Money Payments to Recipients of Special Types of Public Assistance, Table 4 (NCSS Report D–4, 1967).

[20] The State of Maryland has long spoken with at least two voices on the issue of the maximum grant regulation. The Department of Public Welfare has taken the position, over a number of years, that the regulation should be abolished and has made several proposals to that effect. In so doing, the Department has taken the position that its proposals would not set welfare benefits out of line with household incomes throughout the State. See, e. g., Minutes of State Board of Public Welfare Meeting, September 26, 1958, printed in the Appendix in this case, at 130–132.

Aaron, 358 U.S. 1, 78 S.Ct. 1401, 3 L. Ed.2d 5 (1958).

Vital to the employment-incentive basis found by the Court to sustain the regulation is, of course, the supposition that an appreciable number of AFDC recipients are in fact employable. For it is perfectly obvious that limitations upon assistance cannot reasonably operate as a work incentive with regard to those who cannot work or who cannot be expected to work. In this connection, Maryland candidly notes that "only a very small percentage of the total universe of welfare recipients are employable." The State, however, urges us to ignore the "total universe" and to concentrate attention instead upon the heads of AFDC families. Yet the very purpose of the AFDC program since its inception has been to provide assistance for dependent *children*. The State's position is thus that the State may deprive certain needy children of assistance to which they would otherwise be entitled in order to provide an arguable work-incentive for their parents. But the State may not wield its economic whip in this fashion when the effect is to cause a deprivation to needy dependent children in order to correct an arguable fault of their parents. Cf. Levy v. Louisiana, supra; King v. Smith, supra, 392 U.S. at 334–336, 88 S.Ct. at 2141–2143 (Douglas, J., concurring); Doe v. Shapiro, 302 F.Supp. 761 (D.C.D.Conn.1969), appeal dismissed, 396 U.S. 488, 90 S.Ct. 641, 24 L.Ed.2d 677 (1970).

Even if the invitation of the State to focus upon the heads of AFDC families is accepted, the minimum rationality of the maximum grant regulation is hard to discern. The District Court found that of Maryland's more than 32,000 AFDC families, only about 116 could be classified as having employable members, and, of these, the number to which the maximum grant regulation was applicable is not disclosed by the record. The State objects that this figure includes only families in which the father is unemployed and fails to take account of families in which an employable mother is the head of the household. At the same time, however, the State itself has recognized that the vast proportion of these mothers are in fact unemployable because they are mentally or physically incapacitated, because they have no marketable skills, or most prominently, because the best interests of the children dictate that the mother remain in the home.[21] Thus, it is clear, although the record does not disclose precise figures, that the total number of "employable" mothers is but a fraction of the total number of AFDC mothers. Furthermore, the record is silent as to what proportion of large families subject to the maximum have "employable" mothers. Indeed, one must assume that the presence of the mother in the home can be less easily dispensed with in the case of large families, particularly where small children are involved and alternative provisions for their care are accordingly more difficult to arrange. In short, not only has the State failed to establish that there is a substantial or even a significant proportion of AFDC heads of households as to whom the maximum grant regulation arguably serves as a viable and logical work incentive, but it is also indisputable that the regulation at best is drastically *overinclusive* since it applies with equal vigor to a very substantial number of persons who like appellees are completely disabled from working.

Finally, it should be noted that, to the extent there is a legitimate state interest in encouraging heads of AFDC households to find employment, application of the maximum grant regulation is also grossly *underinclusive* because it singles out and affects only large families. No reason is suggested why this particular group should be carved out for the purpose of having unusually harsh "work incentives" imposed upon them. Not only has the State selected for special treatment a small group from among similarly-situated families, but it has done so on a basis—family size—which bears no relation to the evil that the State claims the regulation was designed to correct. There is simply no indication whatever that heads of large families, as opposed to heads of small families, are particularly prone to refuse to seek or to maintain employment.

The State has presented other arguments to support the regulation. However, they are not dealt with specifically by the Court, and the reason is not difficult to discern. The Court has picked the strongest available; the others suffer from similar and greater defects.[22] Moreover, it is relevant to note that both Congress and the State have adopted other measures which deal specifically with exactly those interests the State contends are advanced by the maximum grant regulation. Thus, for example, employable AFDC recipients are required to seek employment through the congressionally established Work Incentive Program which provides an elaborate system of counseling, training, and incentive pay-

---

[21] Indeed, Rule 200 IX A(2)(b)(5) of the Manual of the Maryland State Department of Social Services prohibits the referral for employment of AFDC mothers who are needed in the home. And the unsuitability of many AFDC mothers has been well chronicalized in Maryland Department of Social Services. Profile of Caseloads, Research Report No. 5, at 6 (1969). See also Carter, The Employment Potential of AFDC Mothers, 6 Welfare in Review, No. 4, at 4 (1968).

[22] Thus, the State cannot single out a miniscule proportion of the total number of families in the State as in need of birth control incentives. Not only is the classification effected by the regulation totally underinclusive if this is its rationale, but it also arbitrarily punishes children for factors beyond their control, and overinclusively applies to families like appellees' that were already large before it became necessary to seek assistance. For similar reasons, the argument that the regulation serves as a disincentive to desertion does not stand scrutiny.

ments for heads of AFDC families. See generally 42 U.S.C.A. §§ 630–644.[23] The existence of these alternatives does not, of course, conclusively establish the invalidity of the maximum grant regulation. It is certainly relevant, however, in appraising the over-all interest of the State in the maintenance of the regulation.

In the final analysis, Maryland has set up an AFDC program structured to calculate and pay the minimum standard of need to dependent children. Having set up that program, however, the State denies some of those needy children the minimum subsistence standard of living, and it does so on the wholly arbitrary basis that they happen to be members of large families. One need not speculate too far on the actual reason for the regulation, for in the early stages of this litigation the State virtually conceded that it set out to limit the total cost of the program along the path of least resistance. Now, however, we are told that other rationales can be manufactured to support the regulation and to sustain it against a fundamental constitutional challenge.

However, these asserted state interests, which are not insignificant in themselves, are advanced either not at all or by complete accident by the maximum grant regulation. Clearly they could be served by measures far less destructive of the individual interests at stake. Moreover, the device assertedly chosen to further them is at one and the same time both grossly underinclusive—because it does not apply

at all to a much larger class in an equal position—and grossly overinclusive—because it applies so strongly against a substantial class as to which it can rationally serve no end. Were this a case of pure business regulation, these defects would place it beyond what has heretofore seemed a borderline case, see e. g., Railway Express Agency, Inc. v. New York, 336 U.S. 106, 69 S.Ct. 463, 93 L.Ed. 533 (1949), and I do not believe that the regulation can be sustained even under the Court's "reasonableness" test.

In any event, it cannot suffice merely to invoke the spectre of the past and to recite from Lindsley v. Natural Carbonic Gas Co. and Williamson v. Lee Optical of Oklahoma, Inc. to decide the case. Appellees are not a gas company or an optical dispenser; they are needy dependent children and families who are discriminated against by the State. The basis of that discrimination—the classification of individuals into large and small families—is too arbitrary and too unconnected to the asserted rationale, the impact on those discriminated against—the denial of even a subsistence existence—too great, and the supposed interests served too contrived and attenuated to meet the requirements of the Constitution. In my view Maryland's maximum grant regulation is invalid under the Equal Protection Clause of the Fourteenth Amendment.

I would affirm the judgment of the District Court.

Note on Dandridge v. Williams and the Present State of the Art in Equal Protection Challenges

Dandridge v. Williams has been widely regarded as the turning point in litigation designed to use the equal protection clause as a device to broaden the reach of existing welfare programs. The earliest cases, Thompson v. Shapiro, 270 F.Supp. 331 (D.C.Conn.1967) and Smith v. King, 277 F.Supp. 31 (D.C.M.D.Ala.

---

[23] Likewise, the State, with the encouragement of Congress see 42 U.S.C.A. §§ 602(a)(21), 610, has developed extensive statutory provisions to deal specifically with the problem of parental desertion. See generally 3 Md.Code Ann., Art. 27, §§ 88–96. And Congress has mandated, with respect to family planning, that the States provide services to AFDC recipients with the objective of "preventing or reducing the incidence of births out of wedlock and otherwise strengthening family life." 42 U.S.C.A. § 602(a)(15).

1967), were rather narrowly defined applications of the equal protection clause. *Thompson* challenged the constitutionality of the widespread rule which denied AFDC assistance to any family which had not resided in a state for a given period of time, most commonly a year. The court ruled that there was no rational basis for distinguishing the needy long-term resident of a state from the needy short-term resident and that such a distinction imposed unconstitutional burdens on the freedom to travel. *Smith* challenged one of the more egregious forms of what is called the "substitute father rule", a rule which denied AFDC assistance to a family wherein a mother had established some form of relation with a man to whom she was not bound in legal matrimony. Stressing the fact that many such liaisons could not rationally be thought productive of support for the children of such a family, the district court found it violative of equal protection to presume that the children of such a "substitute father" were as likely to receive support as children of a natural or adoptive father.

The United States Supreme Court affirmed both decisions and the odyssey of welfare-oriented equal protection litigation was launched. There were limitations to be sure. In Shapiro v. Thompson, 394 U.S. 618, 89 S.Ct. 1322, 22 L. Ed.2d 600 (1968) the Court placed a rather great degree of stress upon the fact that durational residence restrictions inhibited the constitutionally protected freedom of travel. The Supreme Court affirmed King v. Smith, 392 U.S. 309, 88 S.Ct. 2128, 20 L.Ed.2d 1118 (1968), upon grounds of statutory construction. (Both these decisions are set out in full, infra.) But still, the Court's decisions seemed to presage a hostile attitude toward distinctions which afforded support to some needy persons and denied support to other equally needy persons because of some reason unrelated to their need.

The promise of that judicial hostility seemed unbounded. It opened the possibility of eventual obliteration of any distinction which served to exclude discrete groups of needy persons from public assistance or to limit them to a level of support below that accorded to similarly needy groups. To take but a few examples: How could a state provide public assistance equal to a person's need if this need arose from old age, but deny it to children whose need arose from loss of parental support? See Ward v. Winstead, 314 F.Supp. 1225 (D.C.N.D. Miss.1970), appeal dismissed 400 U.S. 1019, 91 S.Ct. 587 (1971). How could the state provide public assistance equal to need to a child deprived of parental support by reason of a parent's death, disability or absence, but deny it altogether to a child whose failure of support was due to the fact that his parents were involuntarily unemployed or that his fully employed parent earned less than the amount paid to a family deprived of family support? See Macias v. Finch, 324 F.Supp. 1252 (N.D.Calif.1970), aff'd per curiam sub nom., Macias v. Richardson, 400 U.S. 913, 91 S.Ct. 180 (1970). Finally and, as it then appeared, most clearly, how could a state provide support equal to need in a three-child family, but limit support to some amount less than need in a five-child family, as did Maryland?

That series of rhetorical questions and their confidently anticipated answers were profoundly exciting; for each question challenged the impoverishing validity of a distinction which preferred one group of needy persons to another equally needy group for reasons which had nothing to do with their need. If successful, such litigation could spell the end of distinctions which had the effect of limiting public assistance to preferred groups of the needy. If successful, such litigation could spread the reach of public assistance to all needy persons irrespective of what other distinctions could be drawn to disqualify them.

In the spectrum of cases which could be brought to challenge such distinctions, Dandridge v. Williams was widely thought to be one of the easier. A challenge to the constitutionality of family maxima carried fairly limited social and economic repercussions. The effect would be merely to bring children in large families to the level of support which the state had decided to accord to children of smaller families. That result was nowhere near as revolutionary as deciding that needy children were entitled to the same level of support as the needy aged; nor as expensive. The result anticipated in *Dandridge* was insignificant compared to the possibility that a court would rule that an impoverished child was entitled to support even though not deprived of parental support within the meaning of the AFDC statutes. Moreover, when *Dandridge* arrived at the Supreme Court, four federal district courts and one state supreme court had already ruled family maxima unlawful. See note 10 to Mr. Justice Marshall's dissent, supra. And so, the reversal of *Dandridge* came as somewhat of a shock. The cases which followed, some of which are set out in these materials, seemed to confirm the significance of *Dandridge* in bringing the expansive potentialities of the equal protection clause to an end so far as welfare litigation was concerned.

But perhaps that was a short-sighted reaction. Developments in equal protection doctrine have been so rapid in the past few years that nothing can be set down with certainty. One constitutional concept with vast potential for welfare recipients is that classifications burdening the poor might be considered constitutionally suspect in much the same manner as racial classifications. See note 17 to the majority opinion in *Dandridge*. While this concept has never squarely commanded a majority of the court, there is enough peripheral support for it in cases such as Harper v. Virginia Bd. of Elections, 383 U.S. 663 (1966) (poll tax unconstitutional burden on right to vote) and Boddie v. Connecticut, p. 456, infra (mandatory fees and cost for obtaining divorce unconstitutional burden on poor) that it could easily emerge at any time as a full blown constitutional principle. See dissenting opinion of Mr. Justice Brennan in *Boddie*. But cf. United States v. Kras, 409 U.S. 434, 93 S.Ct. 631, 34 L.Ed.2d 626 (1973) (fees for filing of bankruptcy petition upheld despite claimed inability to pay); Ortwein v. Schwab, —— U.S. ——, 93 S.Ct. 1172, 35 L.Ed.2d 572 (1973) (fees charged to welfare recipients appealing agency decisions on benefits upheld).

Another development is a growing indication that rigid compartments of protected rights provoking strict judicial review and unprotected rights justifying only lax review, may no longer be the order of the day. See Weber v. Aetna Cas. and Sur. Co., p. 461, infra; Gunther, Foreword: In Search of Evolving Doctrine on a Changing Court: A Model For a Newer Equal Protection, 86 Harv. L.Rev. 1 (1972).

All of these lines of constitutional development are implicated in the two cases which follow. Unfortunately, this is not a book devoted to constitutional law and it is therefore not possible here to do more than touch on many of these evolving equal protection and related decisions which may bear on poverty law. It is clear, however, that the Constitution as it is mined by creative lawyers and read by American courts offers a wealth of possibilities for protecting the interests of the poor. Many of these constitutional principles will be raised, as appropriate, elsewhere in this book.

SAN ANTONIO INDEPENDENT SCHOOL DIST. v. RODRIQUEZ

United States Supreme Court, 1973.
— U.S. —, 93 S.Ct. 1278, 36 L.Ed.2d 16.

[Public elementary and secondary education in Texas is financed by a joint state and local program. The state contribution comes from the Minimum Foundation School Program, which accounts for half of the total educational expenditure in the state. This program is funded 80% from state general revenues and 20% from special contributions by school districts. These contributions, designated the Local Fund Assignment, are based on a complex formula aimed at placing heavier burdens on school districts with greater paying ability. The amounts distributed to each school district from the Foundation Program are in turn determined by another formula designed to provide a minimum number of teachers and supporting personnel paid at a state supported minimum salary level. Each school district raises funds for its Local Fund Assignment through an ad valorem property tax levied within its jurisdiction. Surplus revenues from this tax are used to provide direct local school financing to supplement monies received from the Foundation Program.

An example of the operation of this program can be seen by comparing two districts in San Antonio—the least and most affluent. (These are the districts which the parties and the court used for comparison.) The poorer district, Edgewood, is a core-city district with a student population 90% Mexican-American and 6% Negro. Its per pupil assessed property value is $5,960 and its median family income is $4,686. Alamo Heights, the wealthier district, has only 18% Mexican-Americans and less than 1% Negroes in its student population. Its per pupil assessed property value exceeds $49,000 and its median family income is $8,000. For 1967–68 Edgewood expended $356 per pupil, $222 from the Foundation Program, $26 from surplus local property tax revenues, and $108 from supplementary Federal funds. The local property tax rate was $1.05 per $100 of assessed value. The contrast, Alamo Heights expended $558 per student, $225 from the Foundation Program, $333 from surplus local revenue, and $36 from Federal sources. The local property tax rate was $.85 per $100. For 1970–71, the disparity in Foundation Program grants was more marked—$356 per pupil to Edgewood and $491 to Alamo Heights. This disparity was due primarily to the fact that Alamo Heights had a larger proportion of experienced teachers with advanced degrees whose state supported salary level was consequently higher. The equalizing effect of the Local Fund Assignment for 1970–71 was also noted by the Court. Edgewood contributed $8.46 per pupil and Alamo Heights contributed approximately $100 per pupil to the Foundation Program, making Edgewood's net benefit approximately $348 per pupil and Alamo Heights' $391 per pupil.

This system of school financing was attacked on behalf of school children in districts having a low property tax base, claiming that it deprived them of equal protection because of the manner in which it led to a less well financed education for them. The Supreme Court, per Mr. Justice Powell, rejected these claims. Justices Brennan, White, Douglas and Marshall dissented. The following is an excerpt from the opinion of the Court.]

Texas virtually concedes that its historically rooted dual system of financing education could not withstand the strict judicial scrutiny that this Court has found appropriate in reviewing legislative judgments that interfere with fundamental constitutional rights or that involve suspect classifications. * * *

This, then, establishes the framework for our analysis. We must decide, first, whether the Texas system of financing public education operates to the disadvantage of some suspect class or impinges upon a fundamental right explicitly or implicitly protected by the Constitution, thereby requiring strict judicial scrutiny. If so, the judgment of the District Court should be affirmed. If not, the Texas scheme must still be examined to determine whether it rationally furthers some legitimate, articulated state purpose and therefore does not constitute an invidious discrimination in violation of the Equal Protection Clause of the Fourteenth Amendment.

II

The District Court's opinion does not reflect the novelty and complexity of the constitutional questions posed by appellees' challenge to Texas' system of school finance. In concluding that strict judicial scrutiny was required, that court relied on decisions dealing with the rights of indigents to equal treatment in the criminal trial and appellate processes, and on cases disapproving wealth restrictions on the right to vote. Those cases, the District Court concluded, established wealth as a suspect classification. Finding that the local property tax system discriminated on the basis of wealth, it regarded those precedents as controlling. It then reasoned, based on decisions of this Court affirming the undeniable importance of education, that there is a fundamental right to education and that, absent some compelling state justification, the Texas system could not stand.

We are unable to agree that this case, which in significant aspects is *sui generis*, may be so neatly fitted into the conventional mosaic of constitutional analysis under the Equal Protection Clause. Indeed, for the several reasons that follow, we find neither the suspect classification nor the fundamental interest analysis persuasive.

A

The wealth discrimination discovered by the District Court in this case, and by several other courts that have recently struck down school financing laws in other States, is quite unlike any of the forms of wealth discrimination heretofore reviewed by this Court. Rather than focusing on the unique features of the alleged discrimination, the courts in these cases have virtually assumed their findings of a suspect classification through a simplistic process of analysis: since, under the traditional systems of financing public schools, some poorer people receive less expensive educations than other more affluent people, these systems discriminate on the basis of wealth. This approach largely ignores the hard threshold questions, including whether it makes a difference for purposes of consideration under the Constitution that the class of disadvantaged "poor" cannot be identified or defined in customary equal protection terms, and whether the relative—rather than absolute—nature of the asserted deprivation is of significant consequence. Before a State's laws and the justifications for the classifications they create are subjected to strict judicial scrutiny, we think these threshold considerations must be analyzed more closely than they were in the court below.

The case comes to us with no definitive description of the classifying facts or delineation of the disfavored class. Examination of the District Court's opinion and of appellees' complaint, briefs, and contentions at oral argument suggests, however, at least three ways in which the discrimination claimed here might be described. The Texas system of school finance might be regarded as discriminating (1) against "poor" persons whose incomes fall below some identifiable level of poverty or who might be characterized as functionally "indigent," or (2) against those who are relatively poorer than others, or (3) against all those who, irrespective of their personal incomes, happen to reside in relatively poorer school districts. Our task must be to ascertain whether, in fact, the Texas system has been shown to discriminate on any of these possible bases and, if so, whether the resulting classification may be regarded as suspect.

The precedents of this Court provide the proper starting point. The individuals or groups of individuals who constituted the class discriminated against in our prior cases shared two distinguishing characteristics: because of their impecunity they were completely unable to pay for some desired benefit, and as a consequence, they sustained an absolute deprivation of a meaningful opportunity to enjoy that benefit. In Griffin v. Illinois, 351 U.S. 12, 76 S.Ct. 585, 100 L. Ed. 891 (1956), and its progeny, the Court invalidated state laws that prevented an indigent criminal defendant from acquiring a transcript, or an adequate substitute for a transcript, for use at several stages of the trial and appeal process. The payment requirements in each case were found to occasion *de facto* discrimination against those who, because of their indigency, were totally unable to pay for transcripts. And, the Court in each case emphasized that no constitutional violation would have been shown if the State had provided some "adequate substitute" for a full stenographic transcript. [citations omitted]

Likewise, in Douglas v. California, 372 U.S. 353, 83 S.Ct. 814, 9 L.Ed.2d 811 (1963), a decision establishing an indigent defendant's right to court-appointed counsel on direct appeal, the Court dealt only with defendants who could not pay for counsel from their own resources and who had no other way of gaining representation. *Douglas* provides no relief for those on whom the burdens of paying for a criminal defense are relatively speaking, great but not insurmountable. Nor does it deal with relative differences in the quality of counsel acquired by the less wealthy.

Williams v. Illinois, 399 U.S. 235, 90 S.Ct. 2018, 26 L.Ed.2d 586 (1970), and Tate v. Short, 401 U.S. 395, 91 S.Ct. 668, 28 L.Ed.2d 130 (1971), struck down criminal penalties that subjected indigents to incarceration simply because of their inability to pay a fine. Again, the disadvantaged class was composed only of persons who were totally unable to pay the demanded sum. Those cases do not touch on the question whether equal protection is denied to persons with relatively less money on whom designated fines impose heavier burdens. The Court has not held that fines must be structured to reflect each person's ability to pay in order to avoid disproportionate burdens. Sentencing judges may, and often do, consider the defendant's ability to pay, but in such circumstances they are guided by sound judicial discretion rather than by constitutional mandate.

Finally, in Bullock v. Carter, 405 U.S. 134, 92 S.Ct. 849, 31 L.Ed.2d 92 (1972), the Court invalidated the Texas filing fee requirement for primary elections. Both of the relevant classifying facts found in the previous cases were present there. The size of the fee, often running into the thousands of dollars and, in at least one case, as high as $8,900, effectively barred all potential candidates who were unable to pay the required fee. As the system provided "no reasonable alternative means of access to the ballot" (id., at 149, 92 S.Ct. at 859), inability to pay occasioned an absolute denial of a position on the primary ballot.

Only appellees' first possible basis for describing the class disadvantaged by the Texas school finance system—discrimination against a class of definably "poor" persons—might arguably meet the criteria established in these prior cases. Even a cursory examination, however, demonstrates that neither of the two distinguishing characteristics of wealth classifications can be found here. First, in support of their charge that the system discriminates against the "poor," appellees have made no effort to demonstrate that it operates to the peculiar disadvantage of any class fairly definable as indigent, or as composed of persons whose incomes are beneath any designated poverty level. Indeed, there is reason to believe that the poorest families are not necessarily clustered in the poorest property districts. * * *

Second, neither appellees nor the District Court addressed the fact that, unlike each of the foregoing cases, lack of personal resources has not occasioned an absolute deprivation of the desired benefit. The argument here is not that the children in districts having relatively low assessable property values are receiving no public education; rather, it is that they are receiving a poorer quality education than that available to children in districts having more assessable wealth. Apart from the unsettled and disputed question whether the quality of education may be determined by the amount of money expended for it, a sufficient answer to appellees' argument is that at least where wealth is involved the Equal Protection clause does not require absolute equality or precisely equal advantages. Nor indeed, in view of the infinite variables affecting the educational process, can any system assure equal quality of education except in the most relative sense. Texas asserts that the Minimum Foundation Program provides an "adequate" education for all children in the State. * * * No proof was offered at trial persuasively discrediting or refuting the State's assertion.

For these two reasons—the absence of any evidence that the financing system discriminates against any definable category of "poor" people or that it results in the absolute deprivation of education —the disadvantaged class is not suscep-

tible to identification in traditional terms.

As suggested above, appellees and the District Court may have embraced a second or third approach, the second of which might be characterized as a theory of relative or comparative discrimination based on family income. Appellees sought to prove that a direct correlation exists between the wealth of families within each district and the expenditures therein for education. That is, along a continuum, the poorer the family the lower the dollar amount of education received by the family's children.

The principal evidence adduced in support of this comparative discrimination claim is an affidavit submitted by Professor Joele S. Berke of Syracuse University's Educational Finance Policy Institute. The District Court, relying in major part upon this affidavit and apparently accepting the substance of appellees' theory, noted, first, a positive correlation between the wealth of school districts, measured in terms of assessable property per pupil, and their levels of per-pupil expenditures. Second, the court found a similar correlation between district wealth and the personal wealth of its residents, measured in terms of median family income. 337 F.Supp., at 282, n. 3.

If, in fact, these correlations could be sustained, then it might be argued that expenditures on education—equated by appellees to the quality of education— are dependent on personal wealth. Appellees' comparative discrimination theory would still face serious unanswered questions, including whether a bare positive correlation or some higher degree of correlation is necessary to provide a basis for concluding that the financing system is designed to operate to the peculiar disadvantage of the comparatively poor, and whether a class of this size and diversity could ever claim the special protection accorded "suspect" classes. These questions need not be addressed in this case, however, since appellees' proof fails to support their allegations or the District Court's conclusions.

Professor Berke's affidavit is based on a survey of approximately 10% of the school districts in Texas. His findings, set out in the margin,[63] show only that the wealthiest few districts in the sample have the highest median family incomes and spend the most on education, and that the several poorest districts have the lowest family incomes and devote the least amount of money to education. For the remainder of the districts—96 districts comprising almost 90% of the sample—the correlation is inverted, i. e., the districts that spend next to the most money on education are populated by families having next to the lowest median family incomes while the districts spending the least have the highest median family incomes. It is evident that, even if the conceptual questions were answered favorably to appellees, no factual basis exists upon which to found a claim of comparative wealth discrimination.

This brings us, then, to the third way in which the classification scheme might be defined—*district* wealth discrimination. Since the only correlation indicated by the evidence is between district property wealth and expenditures, it may be argued that discrimination might be found without regard to the individual income characteristics of district residents. Assuming a perfect correlation between district property wealth and expenditures from top to bottom, the disadvantaged class might be viewed as encompassing every child in every district except the district that has the most assessable wealth and spends the most on education. Alternatively, as suggested in Mr. Justice MARSHALL's dissenting opinion, *post*, [omitted], the class might be defined more restrictively to include children in districts with assessable property which falls below the statewide average, or median, or below some other artificially defined level.

However described, it is clear that appellees' suit asks this Court to extend its most exacting scrutiny to review a system that allegedly discriminates against a large, diverse, and amorphous class, unified only by the common factor of residence in districts that happen to have less taxable wealth than other districts. The system of alleged discrimination and the class it defines have none of the traditional indicia of suspectness: the class is not saddled with such disabilities, or subjected to such a history of purposeful unequal treatment, or relegated to such a position of political powerlessness as to command extraordinary protection from the majoritarian political process.

We thus conclude that the Texas system does not operate to the peculiar disadvantage of any suspect class. But in recognition of the fact that this Court has never heretofore held that wealth dis-

63.	Market Value of Taxable Property Per Pupil	Median Family Income in 1960	State & Local Expenditures Per Pupil
	Above $100,000 (10 districts)	$5,900	$815
	$100,000–$50,000 (26 districts)	$4,425	$544
	$50,000–$30,000 (30 districts)	$4,900	$483
	$30,000–$10,000 (40 districts)	$5,050	$462
	Below $10,000 (4 districts)	$3,325	$305

crimination alone provides an adequate basis for invoking strict scrutiny, appellees have not relied solely on this contention. They also assert that the State's system impermissibly interferes with the exercise of a "fundamental" right and that accordingly the prior decisions of this Court require the application of the strict standard of judicial review. [citations omitted] It is this question—whether education is a fundamental right, in the sense that it is among the rights and liberties protected by the Constitution—which has so consumed the attention of courts and commentators in recent years.

B

In Brown v. Board of Education, 347 U.S. 483, 74 S.Ct. 686, 98 L.Ed. 873 (1954), a unanimous Court recognized that "education is perhaps the most important function of state and local governments." Id., at 493, 74 S.Ct., at 691. What was said there in the context of racial discrimination has lost none of its vitality with the passage of time:

> "Compulsory school attendance laws and the great expenditures for education both demonstrate our recognition of the importance of education to our democratic society. It is required in the performance of our most basic responsibilities, even service in the armed forces. It is the very foundation of good citizenship. Today it is a principal instrument in awakening the child to cultural values, in preparing him for later professional training, and in helping him to adjust normally to his environment. In these days, it is doubtful that any child may reasonably be expected to succeed in life if he is denied the opportunity of an education. Such an opportunity, where the state has undertaken to provide it, is a right which must be made available to all on equal terms." Ibid.

This theme, expressing an abiding respect for the vital role of education in a free society, may be found in numerous opinions of Justices of this Court writing both before and after Brown was decided. [citations omitted]

Nothing this Court holds today in any way detracts from our historic dedication to public education. We are in complete agreement with the conclusion of the three-judge panel below that "the grave significance of education both to the individual and to our society" cannot be doubted. But the importance of a service performed by the State does not determine whether it must be regarded as fundamental for purposes of examination under the Equal Protection Clause. Mr. Justice Harlan, dissenting from the Court's application of strict scrutiny to a law impinging upon the right of interstate travel, admonished that "[v]irtually every state statute affects important rights." Shapiro v. Thompson, 394 U.S. 618, 655, 661, 89 S.Ct. 1322, 1342, 1345, 22 L.Ed.2d 600 (1969). In his view, if the degree of judicial scrutiny of state legislation fluctuated depending on a majority's view of the importance of the interest affected, we would have gone "far toward making this Court a 'super-legislature.'" Ibid. We would indeed then be assuming a legislative role and one for which the Court lacks both authority and competence. But Mr. Justice Stewart's response in Shapiro to Mr. Justice Harlan's concern correctly articulates the limits of the fundamental rights rationale employed in the Court's equal protection decisions:

> "The Court today does *not* 'pick out particular human activities, characterize them as "fundamental," and give them added protection. * * *' To the contrary, the Court simply recognizes, as it must, an established constitutional right, and gives to that right no less protection than the Constitution itself demands." 394 U.S., at

642, 89 S.Ct., at 1335. (Emphasis from original.)

* * *

Lindsey v. Normet, 405 U.S. 56, 92 S.Ct. 862, 31 L.Ed.2d 36 (1972), decided only last Term, firmly reiterates that social importance is not the critical determinant for subjecting the state legislation to strict scrutiny. The complainants in that case, involving a challenge to the procedural limitations imposed on tenants in suits brought by landlords under Oregon's Forcible Entry and Wrongful Detainer Law, urged the Court to examine the operation of the statute under "a more stringent standard then mere rationality." Id., at 73, 92 S.Ct., at 874. The tenants argued that the statutory limitations implicated "fundamental interests which are particularly important to the poor," such as the " 'need for decent shelter' " and the " 'right to retain peaceful possession of one's home.' " Ibid. Mr. Justice White's analysis, in his opinion for the Court is instructive:

"We do not denigrate the importance of decent, safe and sanitary housing. But the Constitution does not provide judicial remedies for every social and economic ill. We are unable to perceive in that document any constitutional guarantee of access to dwellings of a particular quality or any recognition of the right of a tenant to occupy the real property of his landlord beyond the term of his lease, without the payment of rent. * * * *Absent constitutional mandate,* the assurance of adequate housing and the definition of landlord-tenant relationships are legislative, not judicial, functions." *Id.,* at 74, 92 S.Ct. at 874. (Emphasis supplied.)

* * *

The lesson of these cases in addressing the question now before the Court is plain. It is not the province of this Court to create substantive constitutional rights in the name of guaranteeing equal protection of the laws. Thus the key to discovering whether education is "fundamental" is not to be found in comparisons of the relative societal significance of education as opposed to subsistence or housing. Nor is it to be found by weighing whether education is as important as the right to travel. Rather, the answer lies in assessing whether there is a right to education explicitly or implicitly guaranteed by the Constitution. [citations omitted].

Education, of course, is not among the rights afforded explicit protection under our Federal Constitution. Nor do we find any basis for saying it is implicitly so protected. As we have said, the undisputed importance of education will not alone cause this Court to depart from the usual standard for reviewing a State's social and economic legislation. It is appellees' contention, however, that education is distinguishable from other services and benefits provided by the State because it bears a peculiarly close relationship to other rights and liberties accorded protection under the Constitution. Specifically, they insist that education is itself a fundamental personal right because it is essential to the effective exercise of First Amendment freedoms and to intelligent utilization of the right to vote. In asserting a nexus between speech and education, appellees urge that the right to speak is meaningless unless the speaker is capable of articulating his thoughts intelligently and persuasively. The "marketplace of ideas" is an empty forum for those lacking basic communicative tools. Likewise, they argue that the corollary right to receive information becomes little more than a hollow privilege when the recipient has not been taught to read, assimilate, and utilize available knowledge.

A similar line of reasoning is pursued with respect to the right to vote. * * *

We need not dispute any of these propositions. The Court has long afforded zealous protection against unjustifiable governmental interference with the individual's rights to speak and to vote. Yet we have never presumed to possess either the ability or the authority to guarantee to the citizenry the most *effective* speech or the most *informed* electoral choice. That these may be desirable goals of a system of freedom of expression and of a representative form of government is not to be doubted. These are indeed goals to be pursued by a people whose thoughts and beliefs are freed from governmental interference. But they are not values to be implemented by judicial intrusion into otherwise legitimate state activities.

Even if it were conceded that some identifiable quantum of education is a constitutionally protected prerequisite to the meaningful exercise of either right, we have no indication that the present levels of educational expenditure in Texas provide an education that falls short. Whatever merit appellees' argument might have if a State's financing system occasioned an absolute denial of educational opportunities to any of its children, that argument provides no basis for finding an interference with fundamental rights where only relative differences in spending levels are involved and where —as is true in the present case—no charge fairly could be made that the system fails to provide each child with an opportunity to acquire the basic minimal skills necessary for the enjoyment of the rights of speech and of full participation in the political process.

Furthermore, the logical limitations on appellees' nexus theory are difficult to perceive. How, for instance, is education to be distinguished from the significant personal interests in the basics of decent food and shelter? Empirical examination might well buttress an assumption that the ill-fed, ill-clothed, and ill-

housed are among the most ineffective participants in the political process and that they derive the least enjoyment from the benefits of the First Amendment. If so appellees' thesis would cast serious doubt on the authority of Dandridge v. Williams, supra and Lindsey v. Normet, supra.

We have carefully considered each of the arguments supportive of the District Court's finding that education is a fundamental right or liberty and have found those arguments unpersuasive. In one further respect we find this a particularly inappropriate case in which to subject state action to strict judicial scrutiny. The present case, in another basic sense, is significantly different from any of the cases in which the Court has applied strict scrutiny to state or federal legislation touching upon constitutionally protected rights. Each of our prior cases involved legislation which "deprived," "infringed," or "interfered" with the free exercise of some such fundamental personal right or liberty. * * * Every step leading to the establishment of the system Texas utilizes today—including the decisions permitting localities to tax and expend locally, and creating and continuously expanding the state aid—was implemented in an effort to *extend* public education and to improve its quality. Of course, every reform that benefits some more than others may be criticized for what it fails to accomplish. But we think it plain that, in substance, the thrust of the Texas system is affirmative and reformatory and, therefore, should be scrutinized under judicial principles sensitive to the nature of the State's efforts and to the rights reserved to the States under the Constitution.

C

It should be clear, for the reasons stated above and in accord with the prior decisions of this Court, that this is not a case in which the challenged state action must be subjected to the searching judicial scrutiny reserved for laws that create suspect classifications or impinge upon constitutionally protected rights.

We need not rest our decision, however, solely on the inappropriateness of the strict scrutiny test. A century of Supreme Court adjudication under the Equal Protection Clause affirmatively supports the application of the traditional standard of review, which requires only that the State's system be shown to bear some rational relationship to legitimate state purposes. This case represents far more than a challenge to the manner in which Texas provides for the education of its children. We have here nothing less than a direct attack on the way in which Texas has chosen to raise and disburse state and local tax revenues. We are asked to condemn the State's judgment in conferring on political subdivisions the power to tax local property to supply revenues for local interests. In so doing, appellees would have the Court intrude in an area in which it has traditionally deferred to state legislatures. * * *

In its reliance on state as well as local resources, the Texas system is comparable to the systems employed in virtually every other State. The power to tax local property for educational purposes has been recognized in Texas at least since 1883. When the growth of commercial and industrial centers and accompanying shifts in population began to create disparities in local resources, Texas undertook a program calling for a considerable investment of state funds.

The "foundation grant" theory upon which Texas educators based the Gilmer-Aiken bills, was a product of the pioneering work of two New York educational reformers in the 1920's, George D. Strayer and Robert M. Haig. Their efforts were devoted to establishing a means of guaranteeing a minimum statewide educational program without sacrificing the vital element of local participation. The

Strayer-Haig thesis represented an accommodation between these two competing forces. As articulated by Professor Coleman:

> "The history of education since the industrial revolution shows a continual struggle between two forces: the desire by members of society to have educational opportunity for all children, and the desire of each family to provide the best education it can afford for its own children."

The Texas system of school finance is responsive to these two forces. While assuring a basic education for every child in the State, it permits and encourages a large measure of participation in and control of each district's schools at the local level. * * *

Appellees further urge that the Texas system is unconstitutionally arbitrary because it allows the availability of local taxable resources to turn on "happenstance." They see no justification for a system that allows, as they contend, the quality of education to fluctuate on the basis of the fortuitous positioning of the boundary lines of political subdivisions and the location of valuable commercial and industrial property. But any scheme of local taxation—indeed the very existence of identifiable local governmental units—requires the establishment of jurisdictional boundaries that are inevitably arbitrary. It is equally inevitable that some localities are going to be blessed with more taxable assets than others. Nor is local wealth a static quantity. Changes in the level of taxable wealth within any district may result from any number of events, some of which local residents can and do influence. For instance, commercial and industrial enterprises may be encouraged to locate within a district by various actions—public and private.

Moreover, if local taxation for local expenditure is an unconstitutional method of providing for education then it may be an equally impermissible means of providing other necessary services customarily financed largely from local property taxes, including local police and fire protection, public health and hospitals, and public utility facilities of various kinds. We perceive no justification for such a severe denegration of local property taxation and control as would follow from appellees' contentions. It has simply never been within the constitutional prerogative of this Court to nullify statewide measures for financing public services merely because the burdens or benefits thereof fall unevenly depending upon the relative wealth of the political subdivisions in which citizens live.

In sum, to the extent that the Texas system of school finance results in unequal expenditures between children who happen to reside in different districts, we cannot say that such disparities are the product of a system that is so irrational as to be invidiously discriminatory. * *

NEW YORK v. RICHARDSON

United States Court of Appeals,
Second Circuit, 1973.
473 F.2d 923.

KAUFMAN, Circuit Judge. This sprawling, multi-party, multi-claim appeal, presents a broadside constitutional attack upon certain provisions of the Social Security Act of 1935, 42 U.S.C.A. § 301, et seq., and New York State's Social Services Law, See New York Social Welfare Law (McKinney 1966 and Supp. 1972) particularly those provisions concerned with the financing and reimbursement policies established by the Acts. Plaintiffs are the City of New York, and three individuals—John V. Lindsay, The Mayor of the City of New York, Jule Sugarman, the Commissioner of Social Services of the City of New York, and Ola Bryant, a taxpaying citizen and resident of New York City. The federal defendants are the Secretary of Health, Education and Welfare of the United States, the Secretary of the Treasury of the United States, and two regional officers of HEW. The state defendant is the Commissioner of Social Services of the State of New York. The district court granted motions to intervene as parties plaintiff in behalf of Westchester, Nassau and Suffolk counties, their County Executives, and other county officials,[1] in their individual and official capacities.

Invoking the protection of the Fifth, Ninth, Tenth and Fourteenth Amendments, as well as the General Welfare Clause of Article I, Section 8, Clause 1 of the Constitution, and various unenumerated safeguards—such as the right to travel—thought to inhere in that document, plaintiffs sought declaratory, injunctive and other appropriate relief, and the convocation of a three-judge court. Judge McLean, after motion by the federal and state defendants to dismiss for failure to state a claim for relief, and for lack of subject matter jurisdiction, dismissed the complaint. This appeal followed.

I.

Public assistance laws, as incorporated in the Social Security Act, in rules and regulations of the Department of Health, Education and Welfare, and in various state social service programs, present as complex a legislative mosaic as could possibly be conceived by man. The provisions complained of here, which appear to contain, as far as we have been able to

---

[1] Although granted leave to intervene, and given permission to argue orally before the court below, the county plaintiffs did not file their complaints until after Judge McLean rendered his decision in this case. The intervenors filed a timely notice of appeal from the judgment below. They have fully participated in this appeal by briefing the issues and arguing orally before the court. Accordingly, they are bound by our decision today.

determine, no traps for the unwary, present the following pattern.

The Social Security Act provides, inter alia, for public assistance to the aged, Title I, 42 U.S.C.A. § 301, et seq., to families with dependent children, Title IV, 42 U.S.C. § 601, et seq., to the blind, Title X, 42 U.S.C.A. § 1201 et seq., and to the permanently and totally disabled, Title XIV, 42 U.S.C.A. § 1351 et seq. Funds provided in accordance with the Social Security Act are not distributed directly to individuals eligible for assistance; instead, as part of what has been called a "scheme of cooperative federalism," King v. Smith, 392 U.S. 309, 316 (1968), federal funds are made available on a matching-fund basis, for administration by the states. No state is required to participate in any program offered under the Social Security Act, but those states that wish to receive federal financial aid for local public assistance must submit to the Secretary of HEW, and have approved by him, a state plan for such assistance. Each plan, to obtain approval, must comply with certain provisions of the Social Security Act and with rules and regulations issued by HEW. Thus, subject to certain limited exceptions, a state plan will not be approved unless it provides "for the establishment or designation of a single state agency with authority to administer or supervise the administration of the plan." 45 C.F.R. § 205.100(a) (1). The plan must be in effect "on a statewide basis in accordance with equitable standards for assistance and administration that are mandatory throughout the State." 45 C.F.R. § 205.120(a). State funds must be used for both assistance and administration and on no account may State participation total less than 40% of the non-federal share of the total expenditure, 45 C.F.R. 205.130(a) (1), (c). There is no requirement that local governments contribute to the cost of a state's welfare expenditure, but "if there is local financial

participation there [must] be a method of apportioning State and Federal funds among the political subdivisions of the State on an equalization or other basis that will assure that lack of funds from local sources does not result in lowering the amount, duration, scope, or quality of care and services or level of administration under the plan in any part of the State." 45 C.F.R. § 205.130(c) (2).

States submitting an approved plan to the Secretary of HEW may choose between two reimbursement formulae. The first of these, see 42 U.S.C.A. §§ 303, 603, 1203, 1353, 1383, is based upon a sliding percentage calculation of certain fixed dollar allotments for each of the four public assistance programs covered by the Social Security Act. The second, the "Medicaid" formula, see 42 U.S.C.A. § 1318, takes into account not fixed but actual payments made by a state for public assistance and is based upon a sliding percentage scale, with a minimum reimbursement level to the states of 50%. The Medicaid formula contains a factor based upon the ratio of the square of the state's per capita income to the square of the per capita income of the nation as a whole. Under this formula relatively "poorer" states are reimbursed at a higher percentage than relatively "richer" states. New York State, whose plan was approved by the Secretary of HEW, opted for the Medicaid formula under which the federal government reimburses New York for 50% of its total welfare costs.[2]

New York State's approved plan, divide's the state into geographic social services districts. New York City is one

[2] The federal appellees' brief states:

The average monthly payment to a New York AFDC [aid to Families with Dependent Children] recipient in May 1972 was $71.21. Under the original formula, which is still in use by many states, New York would receive $22 per recipient from the federal government. Under the Medicaid method, New York receives $36.50 per recipient. * * *

such social service district, *see* Social Services Law § 61(1), and is consequently "responsible for the assistance and care of any person who resides or is found in its territory and who is in need of public assistance and care which he is unable to provide for himself." Social Services Law § 62(1). The state plan sets standards for eligibility, payments schedules and the conditions of administration, and requires each local social service district to finance its own public assistance needs,[3] subject to the following reimbursement provision in New York Social Services Law, § 153:

> Reimbursement and advances
> by the state.
>
> 1.   *   *   *
>
> There shall be paid to each such [public welfare] district, city or town
>
> a. the amount of federal funds, if any, properly received or to be received on account of such expenditures;
>
> b.   *   *   *
>
> c. fifty percentum of the amount expended for public assistance and care for local charges, after first deducting therefrom any federal funds properly received or to be received on account thereof.

[3] New York Social Services Law, § 91, provides:

> *   *   * The legislative body of the city social services district shall appropriate the amount necessary for such purpose [public assistance and care] and shall cause taxes to be levied for the amount of such appropriation.

We stress here that local financing of statewide public assistance programs is not required by the federal statute and New York State, were it so inclined, could decide to bear the full cost of public assistance and still be eligible for a 50% reimbursement from the federal government. Statistics for fiscal year 1970 indicate that sixteen states have assumed the full burden of financing public assistance expenditures. United States Dep't of Health, Education and Welfare National Center for Social Statistics: NCSS Report F-1 (1971).

The net effect of the combined federal-state programs is that payments for assistance in federally-aided categories are provided as follows:

Federal revenue:	50%
State revenue:	25%
Local revenue:	25%

Appellants challenge this financing formula on a number of constitutional grounds and we turn now to a discussion of that challenge.

*   *   *

III.

We come, finally, to claims raised by the individual plaintiffs against the state defendant, the Commissioner of Social Services of the State of New York. Although the district court denied the application for a three-judge court and dismissed this portion of the complaint for lack of subject matter jurisdiction, we deal first with the substantive merits of the claim, and then with problems of standing and jurisdiction.

The challenge presented here is novel and appears to be one of first impression. To best illustrate the nature of the Equal Protection argument advanced in this litigation we may, for the moment, put aside the claims of the county intervenors and focus on the New York City plaintiffs. It is undisputed that the state Social Services Law compels residents of New York City to pay 25% of the cost of public assistance payments made to welfare recipients residing in the city, see New York Social Services Law §§ 62, 91 and 153. These costs are mandated by authority of the state Legislature, as is the level of payments required to be made to each welfare recipient. The inequity complained of is that the manner in which the state has drawn the boundaries of social service districts tends to discriminate, arbitrarily and without rational justification, against New York City by imposing a disproportionately heavy tax burden upon city residents. Statistics for the year 1969 appear to bear out this claim. Although only 45% of New York State's residents live in New York City, the City is financially responsible for 74% of the state's welfare recipients.[7] 12.52% of New York City's residents receive public assistance, as against an average of 3.49% for the balance of the state. New York City clearly bears a greater burden of the costs of welfare in the State because it has, vis-a-vis other State social service districts, a proportionately greater percentage of welfare recipients living within its social service jurisdiction.

The Equal Protection clause of the constitution requires that any discrimination between individuals, if there be such, must be rationally based and not invidious. The question we must ask is whether the state's decision to distribute the financial burden of public assistance on a geographic basis, which does not take into account gross disparities in the number of welfare recipients residing in each local district and which imposes proportionately greater financial obligations on the taxpaying citizens of certain districts, is reasonably related to a legitimate state objective and thus able to withstand constitutional attack.

Although this is indeed the question we ask, we need not fully resolve it at the present time. This issue arises in the context of an appeal from a denial of an application to convene a three-judge court. Our function, upon review of that decision, assuming for the moment no insurmountable jurisdictional obstruction, is simply to inquire whether the question raised is "wholly" or "clearly insubstantial", see Goosby v. Osser, 452 F. 2d 39, —— U.S. ——, 93 S.Ct. 531, 41 U.S.L.W. 4167 (January 16, 1973); Powell v. Workmen's Compensation Board of the State of New York, 327 F. 2d 131, 138 (2 Cir. 1964); Astro Cinema Corp., Inc. v. Mackell, 422 F.2d 293, 298 (2 Cir. 1970); see also, Ex parte Poresky, 290 U.S. 30 (1933); California Water Service Co. v. City of Redding, 304 U.S. 252, 255 (1938) ["The lack of substantiality in a federal question may appear either because it is obviously without merit or because its unsoundness clearly results from the previous decisions of this Court as to foreclose the subject."]; and Wright, Law of Federal Courts 191 (2 ed. 1970). If the constitutional question is substantial, further proceedings before a three-judge district court are required. 28 U.S.C.A. § 2281.

Since we deal here neither with alleged violations of fundamental interests, compare Shapiro v. Thompson, 394 U.S. 618 (1969) (interstate travel) and Harper v. Board of Elections, 383 U.S. 663 (1966) (voting), with Lindsey v. Normet, 405 U.S. 56 (1972;) (housing not a fundamental interest); nor with suspect classifications, see Korematsu v. United States, 323 U.S. 214 (1944) (race) and Graham v. Richardson, 403 U.S. 365 (1971) (alienage), we do not subject the statutory provisions of New York's Social Services law to a "strict scrutiny" or "compelling state interest" test. Nevertheless, even a cursory reading of recent Equal Protection cases emanating from the Supreme Court indicates that the traditional "rational relationship" standard, under which "a statutory discrimination will not be set aside if any state of facts reasonably may be conceived to justify it,"

---

[7] New York City's estimated population in 1969 was 8,110,000; New York State's estimated population was 18,262,000, see New York State Statistical Yearbook (1970), but see The World Almanac (1972): census figures for 1970 indicate that New York City's population is approximately 7,868,000. 1,016,405 persons received public assistance benefits in New York City as against 354,742 persons in the remaining social service districts of the State. By the end of November, 1972, New York City welfare rolls accounted for 1,260,135 out of 1,786,814 persons receiving public assistance in the State, i. e., slightly more than 70%. The New York Times, January 21, 1973, at 21, col. 1.

McGowan v. Maryland, 366 U.S. 420, 426 (1961), has been modified. The two-tiered equal protection doctrine seems to have begun to give way to a more graduated, sliding-scale test, see generally, Gunther, The Supreme Court, 1971 Term, Foreword: In Search of Evolving Doctrine on a Changing Court: A Model for A Newer Equal Protection, 86 Harvard L.Rev. 1 (1972); Note, Legislative Purpose, Rationality and Equal Protection, 82 Yale L.J. 123 (1972); see also, Aguayo v. Richardson, supra. In Reed v. Reed, 404 U.S. 71 (1972), a unanimous Court, in an opinion written by the Chief Justice, applied a more demanding version of the traditional "rational relationship" test and held that a state purpose that clearly had "some legitimacy" still ran afoul of the Equal Protection Clause, Id. at 76. The Court in Eisenstadt v. Baird, 405 U.S. 438, 448 (1972), announced that a statutory discrimination that concededly had a "marginal relation" to a legitimate state objective was, nevertheless, constitutionally impermissible under the Equal Protection Clause. And in Weber v. Aetna Casualty and Surety Company, 406 U.S. 164, 170, the Court held that legislative discrimination could be justified only upon a showing that the state interest furthered by the statute was "substantial."

Clearly, these decisions seem to foreshadow an expanded judicial inquiry under the Equal Protection Clause, although the outer boundary of that inquiry remains ambiguous. The State appellee, however, has not seen fit to offer this Court even a minimally rational explanation for the statutory discrimination which inheres in New York's Social Service Law. This, in itself, suggests that the question presented is sufficiently substantial to merit the convening of a three-judge court.

Of course, were the residents of New York City in some way "responsible" for the city's disproportionately large number of public assistance recipients the State might justifiably decide to levy costs where the fault lies or where it could be shown that the locality gained some special benefit or service. But when the issue involves assistance for the aged, the blind, the disabled and the dependent, we believe the concept of "fault" would appear to be irrelevant. Moreover, unrebutted statistics presented by the appellants clearly establish that a large percentage of public assistance recipients residing in New York City have migrated from other states,[8] drawn to New York, perhaps by a dream of a better life but in part, one suspects, by the high level of assistance payments, relative to other states, that obtains throughout New York State.[9] New York City neither controls this payment schedule, nor may it, consistent with the Constitution, interfere with the right of welfare recipients to travel interstate and settle in New York City. Shapiro v. Thompson, supra.

We believe, moreover, that the State Social Services program cannot be justi-

---

[8] In 1968, 78.2% of the mothers receiving AFDC payments in New York City were born out of state. U. S. House of Representatives, 91st Congress, 1st Session, Comm. on Ways and Means. Report of Findings of Special Review of Aid to Families with Dependent Children in New York City, Table 20 (1969).

[9] Consider the following statistics:

Average Monthly Payments (December 1970)

	Old Age Assistance	Aid to Dependent Children	Aid to the Blind	Aid to the Permanently and Totally Disabled
National	$ 78	$187	$104	$ 97
New York State	$105	$292	$136	$127

Statistics for New Jersey and Connecticut, states adjacent to New York, and for California, a comparably large state, appear below:

New Jersey	$ 78	$253	$100	$107
Connecticut	$101	$242	$101	$130
California	$117	$193	$160	$139

See United States Department of Commerce, Statistical Abstract of the United States, at 294 (1971).

fied on the ground that it is designed to promote efficiency of administration. Governmental efficiency has never been thought to legitimize unconstitutional discrimination, see Reed v. Reed, supra, at 76; cf. Goldberg v. Kelly, 397 U.S. 254, 264–266 (1970) (governmental interest in conserving fiscal and administrative resources does not override welfare recipient's due process right to pre-termination hearing), nor would we expect it to do so in this case.

Inasmuch as the state-appellee has not offered any rational justification for a discrimination which results from the joint requirement that the state be divided into geographic districts, and that each district finance 25% of its welfare expenditures, and since the Court does not readily perceive what justifying considerations may have motivated the State legislature to devise a system that appears on the surface discriminatory, we are of the view that the Equal Protection claim advanced here is sufficiently substantial to require the convening of a three-judge district court. Of course, at that time it will be open to the state to present whatever explanation it concludes may preserve the statute in question against constitutional attack.[10]

* * *

[10] One case of marginal relevance to the issue before us is Hargrave v. McKinney, 413 F.2d 320 (5 Cir. 1969), where the Court of Appeals reversed a denial by a district court judge of an application for a three-judge district court to consider the constitutionality of a Florida statute providing that any county imposing upon itself more than 10 mills ad valorem property taxes for educational financing would be ineligible to receive state funds for the support of its public schools. The plaintiffs argued that the tax limitation statute unconstitutionally discriminated against property-poor districts by preventing them from spending as much

What result should be anticipated on remand, in light of the intervening Supreme Court decision in San Antonio Independent School Dist. v. Rodriquez, *supra*?

as rich districts for education. Noting that the argument was novel, the Court of Appeals concluded that the claim was "substantial" within the meaning of Ex Parte Poresky, supra.

On remand, the three-judge district court held the Florida statute unconstitutional, 313 F.Supp. 944 (M.D.Fla.1970). Although the court was invited to apply a strict "compelling state interest" Equal Protection test, on the theory that the statutory classification denied equality of educational opportunity, an interest the plaintiffs termed "fundamental," the court declined to do so. In its view, Florida's Millage Rollback Act— the statute in question—failed even to satisfy the "rational relationship" test. The decision was vacated and remanded on other grounds in Askew v. Hargrave, 401 U.S. 476 (1971).

The compulsion *to tax* in the instant case is clearer than the compulsion *not* to tax involved in *Hargrave*. The appellants here have argued that the relatively heavier public assistance tax burden which they sustain deprives them of revenues needed for local services such as education, sanitation and police or, at least, makes raising additional funds for these purposes difficult. In light of certain recent cases and trends, see, e. g., Serrano v. Priest, 5 Cal.3d 584, 487 P.2d 1241 (1971); Rodriguez v. San Antonio Independent School District, 337 F.Supp. 280 (W.D.Texas 1972), probable jurisdiction noted, 406 U.S. 966 (1972); but cf. McInnis v. Shapiro, 293 F.Supp. 237 (N.D.Ill.1968), aff'd sub nom. McInnis v. Ogilvie, 394 U.S. 322 (1969) (without opinion); Burrus v. Wilkinson, 301 F.Supp. 1237 (W.D.Va.1968), aff'd 397 U.S. 44 (1970) (without opinion), it would be unwise to foreclose the plaintiffs from presenting their claim in its strongest posture at this time. We fully recognize that the cases cited in this footnote are not controlling, and are only generally relevant to the issue presented whether the constitutional question is "insubstantial." In directing the convening of a three-judge court we intimate no views on the ultimate merits of the constitutional claim to be adjudicated by that court.

SECTION 3. ELIGIBILITY CONDITIONS

A. IN GENERAL

One approach to the question of welfare eligibility is that of the following excerpt—that need alone should be the criterion. While that approach is not generally followed in the United States today, the country is, as will appear in the pages that follow, somewhat closer to it now than it was in 1966 when this excerpt was published. This excerpt is included to give some historical perspective on the changes which have occurred in recent years. These changes are largely the result of law reform litigation and an examination of this history teaches much about what can be accomplished through the courts.

A SINGLE ELIGIBILITY REQUIREMENT: NEED

Report of Advisory Council on Public Welfare Administration, Dept. of Health, Educ. and Welfare, "Having the Power, We Have the Duty" 23–27, 30–31 (1966).

" * * * * *the major purpose of public assistance programs, that of helping people, is made unnecessarily difficult to achieve. This is because we have segregated human need into fragments based on causal or associated factors and have not attempted to deal with the fact of need itself."*

> Maurice P. Beck, *Exec. Dir.*, Michigan Welfare League Advisory Council Hearing—Chicago March 26, 1965

ELIGIBILITY REQUIREMENTS for public assistance under the Social Security Act were designed to deal with needs and circumstances of some 30 years ago. Since that time they have undergone the elaboration of repeated efforts to adapt once-useful concepts to changed economic facts, new social pressures, developing knowledge, broadened national goals, and limited State financial resources.

Today, lack of Federal provision for large groups of needy people, plus further limiting requirements for groups that are included, prevent many of the most destitute from receiving needed assistance. The innumerable fine distinctions, sometimes rigid and arbitrary definitions and interpretations, and an avalanche of technicalities consume much time and energy of staff that could be far better spent in aiding people in trouble. Moreover, applicants should be able to establish initial eligibility by statements or simple inquiry relating to their financial situation and family composition, subject only to appropriate sample reviews.

Federal action extending coverage to all needy people with available income falling below established levels and eliminating artificial barriers such as categories, imposition by States of provisions narrower than in Federal law, and restrictions not specifically mentioned or proscribed in Federal law, would represent a giant step forward in securing for all needy Americans the assistance necessary to sustain life and hope.

THEREFORE: *The Advisory Council on Public Welfare Recommends*

A Nationwide Comprehensive Program of Public Assistance Based Upon a Single Criterion: Need

Only a relatively small segment of the needy are now helped by public assistance programs—about one-fifth of those in families having an annual income of less than $3,000.

This is largely because (1) there are gaps in the categories of needy people included within the public assistance titles of the Social Security Act; (2) some States are not financially able or do not wish to participate in all programs provided under Federal law; (3) some States, for similar reasons, impose limitations that result in provisions narrower than those in Federal law or add additional restrictions not expressly prohibited by Federal law; and (4) standards of assistance in some States are so low as to exclude many persons with incomes beyond the State standard but far less than the currently accepted poverty level.

Among the poor not being helped by any federally-aided public assistance program are:

most needy adults under 65 years of age who are unemployed or unable to earn an adequate income;

most needy children living with both parents or someone other than a close relative;

needy disabled adults who are not both permanently and totally disabled;

many children in need because of the unemployment of a parent;

needy otherwise eligible persons who have not resided in a particular State for a specified period of years;

needy mothers who are employable but for whom no jobs are available; and

persons rapidly losing their vision but not yet blind enough to qualify for assistance for the blind.

Note on General Assistance [1]

Needy persons who do not qualify for assistance under one of the federal categorical programs may be eligible for state general assistance (sometimes called home relief or general relief). These state programs vary greatly in eligibility requirements, procedural protections and benefits. Despite the application of due process standards to New York Home Relief in Goldberg v. Kelly, programs in many states, including California, Colorado, Florida and Missouri, still fail to mandate such basic protections as notice and hearing.[2] Louisiana and Oklahoma impose state durational residency requirements [3] and other states impose or permit local durational residency requirements contrary to constitutional prohibitions which apply with equal force to state and federal programs.

General assistance programs which tend to be most similar to the federal categorical programs are administered directly by the state through the same offices used to administer categorical programs. Most of these programs are funded by the states without local assistance. Seventeen states scattered over the country have this type of program, including Hawaii, Louisiana, Missouri, Pennsylvania and Washington. The District of Columbia, Puerto Rico, Guam and the Virgin Islands also have this type of program.[4] State and federal programs are often covered by the same budget manuals, and changes in federal regulations may be applied to state programs for simplicity and efficiency in administration. However, most state-run programs vary in substantial respects from the federal model. For example, Missouri General Relief is limited to unemployables, and has no provisions for hearing or appeal.[5] Washington General Assistance to Unemployables (GAU) has benefits and protections similar to the federal programs, but Washington General Assistance to Employables (GAE) is

[1] It is difficult to maintain accurate and up-to-date information on the multitude of state and local general assistance programs. The information in the text, based on Federal Government publications and sources in the excellent specialized collection of the Center on Social Welfare Policy and Law, is believed to reflect practices as of the spring of 1972.

[2] United States Dep't of Health, Education and Welfare, Characteristics of General Assistance in the United States 15, 17, 25, 59 (Public Assistance Report No. 39, 1970 ed.).

[3] Id. at 44, 80.

[4] See generally, id.

[5] Missouri Public Assistance Manual, pt. V, at 46, Revised 1/71.

a non-continuing form of emergency relief intended mainly to meet food requirements.[6] Louisiana General Assistance is primarily for persons who are temporarily disabled, and pays a maximum of $60 per month to individuals, or up to $79 per month to assistance groups of two or more persons, as compared with an Old Age Assistance maximum of $100 per month per person and $94 per month per person for assistance groups of two or more persons, and an Aid to Needy Blind maximum of $101 per month per person.[7] As a result of these and other limitations, few of these state-run programs completely fill the gaps in categorical programs. Other types of programs are even less likely to approach this ideal.

A second type of program, found in seventeen states, is administered by local political jurisdictions without state agency responsibility.[8] Only two of these programs receive any state funds; the rest are supported entirely by local funds. Local autonomy is so highly valued in some states that state law provides that the state welfare agency cannot even investigate or report on local welfare programs [9]; in most other states the guidance provided by state law or regulation is minimal. Many local programs, especially in New Hampshire, Indiana and Iowa, still resemble Elizabethan poor relief, with settlement and removal laws, overseers of the poor and suits between towns to determine responsibility for individual cases. See New Hampshire Children's Aid Society v. Morgan, 107

N.H. 246, 249–50, 221 A.2d 238 (1966). Delayed assistance is not unusual, although some states require localities to provide immediate relief for the applicant, and permit later determination of municipal responsibility. Local programs, especially in rural areas, usually confer broad discretion upon the director or board to determine who is eligible, how much assistance is needed, and how long assistance will continue. For example, in Texas, limitations on assistance are at the discretion of local officials, and payments are usually limited to minimum grocery orders, and vendor payments for shelter, fuel and utilities. Local programs in many states are reluctant to provide recipients with cash, and make all payments directly to stores and businessmen. Benefit levels are generally lower than federal programs and cover fewer items, but levels may vary greatly even within a single state. For example, in Georgia's urban counties, the standards are generally the same as for the federal programs, while in other counties no assistance is provided at all, because of lack of appropriations.[10]

A third type of general assistance, found in sixteen states, is a joint state-local program, with the amount of state financial assistance and supervisory responsibility varying greatly from state to state.[11] Compliance with state regulations is usually a precondition for reimbursement by the state. Some of these programs, like New York Home Relief, are administered through the same offices as the categorical programs; others, like New Jersey General Assistance, are administered separately by local officials, in accordance with state budget manuals.[12]

[6] Washington Manual for County Offices of the Department of Public Assistance, II, § 12.151, Effective 12/69.

[7] Louisiana Department of Public Welfare Manual of Policies and Procedures, § 2–1026, Reissued 4/71 (GA); § 2–1022, Reissued 4/71 (OAA); § 2–1024, Reissued 4/71 (AMB); § 2–1023, Reissued 4/71 (ADC-percentage reduction, no monthly maximum).

[8] Characteristics of General Assistance in the United States, supra note 2, at 114.

[9] See Burns' Indiana Stat.Ann. 52–176a (1964).

[10] Georgia Dept. of Family and Children Services, Annual Report, July 1968–June 1969, at 54.

[11] Characteristics of General Assistance in the United States, supra note 2, at 114.

[12] New Jersey Division of Welfare Manual of Assistance for General Assistance, § 2.-300A at 1, Revised 1/52.

When general assistance has a separate budget manual, as in New Jersey, it tends to be revised less often than the federally supervised categorical assistance budget manuals; for example, allotments for some items are based on price estimates which have not been changed for ten or fifteen years.[13] As with the first two types of programs, it is difficult to generalize about benefit levels. The standard of need and level of payments in New York Home Relief are identical to New York AFDC;[14] the standard of need in Kansas General Assistance is identical to the standard in the categorical programs, but the actual level of payments in General Assistance is reduced by a percentage of the difference between income and budgeted need, and receipt of aid is limited to one month in twelve;[15] New Jersey General Assistance has a lower standard of need than categorical assistance, and short-term budgets often fail to include standard categorical assistance needs such as clothing.[16]

Many of the state, local and joint programs are not really "general" assistance, but instead are a narrow form of categorical assistance. For example, Alabama Temporary Aid is for persons "in need of temporary care because of an emergency such as illness."[17] Oklahoma General Assistance is limited to unemployables. Other programs, more "general" in their eligibility requirements, fail to fill the gaps in categorical assistance mainly because of low payment levels and

limitations on the number of months a person may receive aid. For example, Arkansas General Relief provides up to $20 per month per person, while maximum grants in Arkansas AFDC vary from $86 to $151 per month, depending on family size and $105 per month is the maximum in AABD.[18] While categorical assistance is continuous, receipt of Arkansas General Assistance is generally limited to three consecutive months.[19] Some programs are both categorical and parsimonious. Alabama Temporary Aid provides residents with up to $12.50 per month, with a twelve-month maximum of $37.50. Non-residents may receive a maximum of one $12.50 grant.[20] Oklahoma General Assistance provides a flat $10 grant per month to eligible individuals, or a flat grant of $20 per month to eligible families, regardless of size, with no specific limitation on the number of months a person may receive assistance.[21] General Assistance to Employables in Washington and Virginia and many local programs, especially in rural areas, also fit into the categorical and limited model.

B. RESIDENCE AND RELATED REQUIREMENTS

SHAPIRO v. THOMPSON

Supreme Court of the United States, 1969.
394 U.S. 618, 89 S.Ct. 1322, 22 L.Ed.2d 600.

Mr. Justice BRENNAN delivered the opinion of the Court. These three appeals were restored to the calendar for reargument. 392 U.S. 920, 88 S.Ct. 2272, 20 L.Ed.2d 1381 (1968). Each

---

[13] Id., § 2.300A at 23, Revised 10/58.

[14] New York Dep't of Social Services Bulletin No. 134 at C-5a, Issued 5/13/71.

[15] Kansas Public Assistance Manual, § 2260, Revised 7/71; § 1512.2, Revised 5/70.

[16] N.J.G.A. Manual, § 2.300A at 5, Revised 11/56; Compare Monthly Allowance for Restaurant Meals, N.J.G.A. Manual, § 2.300A at 20, Revised 5/67 with N.J. Categorical Assistance Budget Manual, Appendix § I at 4, Revised 3/67.

[17] Alabama Manual for Administration of Public Assistance, pt. I, § II–7, Revised 1/71.

[18] Arkansas Department of Public Welfare Manual, § 2360.3, Revised 4/71.

[19] Id., § 5410, Revised 7/68.

[20] Ala. Manual, pt. I, § 111–49a, Revised 5/70.

[21] Oklahoma Department of Public Welfare Manual, § 360, Revised 11/66.

is an appeal from a decision of a three-judge District Court holding unconstitutional a State or District of Columbia statutory provision which denies welfare assistance to residents of the State or District who have not resided within their jurisdictions for at least one year immediately preceding their applications for such assistance.[1] We affirm the judgments of the District Courts in the three cases.

I.

In No. 9, the Connecticut Welfare Department invoked § 17–2d of the Connecticut General Statutes [2] to deny the ap-

---

[1] Accord: Robertson v. Ott, 284 F.Supp. 735 (D.C.D.Mass.1968); Johnson v. Robinson (D.C.N.D.Ill.1968); Ramos v. Health and Social Services Bd., 276 F.Supp. 474 (D. C.E.D.Wis.1967); Green v. Dept. of Pub. Welfare, 270 F.Supp. 173 (D.C.D.Del.1967). Contra: Waggoner v. Rosenn, 286 F.Supp. 275 (D.C.M.D.Pa.1968); see also People ex rel. Heydenreich v. Lyons, 374 Ill. 557, 30 N.E.2d 46, 132 A.L.R. 511 (1940).

All but one of the appellees herein applied for assistance under the Aid to Families with Dependent Children Program (AFDC) which was established by the Social Security Act of 1935. 49 Stat. 620, as amended, 42 U.S.C.A. §§ 301–1394. The program provides partial federal funding of state assistance plans which meet certain specifications. One appellee applied for Aid to the Permanently and Totally Disabled which is also jointly funded by the States and the Federal Government, 42 U.S.C.A. §§ 1351–1355.

[2] Conn.Gen.Stat.Rev. § 17–2d (1966), now § 17–2c provides:

"When any person comes into this state without visible means of support for the immediate future and applies for aid to dependent children under chapter 301 or general assistance under part I of chapter 308 within one year from his arrival, such person shall be eligible only for temporary aid or care until arrangements are made for his return, provided ineligibility for aid to dependent children shall not continue beyond the maximum federal residence requirement."

An exception is made for those persons who come to Connecticut with a bona fide job offer or are self-supporting upon arrival in the State and for three months thereafter.

---

plication of appellee Vivian Marie Thompson for assistance under the program for Aid to Families with Dependent Children (AFDC). She was a 19-year-old unwed mother of one child and pregnant with her second child when she changed her residence in June 1966 from Dorchester, Massachusetts, to Hartford, Connecticut, to live with her mother, a Hartford resident. She moved to her own apartment in Hartford in August 1966, when her mother was no longer able to support her and her infant son. Because of her pregnancy, she was unable to work or enter a work training program. Her application for AFDC assistance, filed in August, was denied in November solely on the ground that, as required by § 17–2d, she had not lived in the State for a year before her application was filed. * * *

In No. 33, there are four appellees. Three of them—appellees Harrell, Brown, and Legrant—applied for and were denied AFDC aid. The fourth, appellee Barley, applied for and was denied benefits under the program for Aid to the Permanently and Totally Disabled. The denial in each case was on the ground that the applicant had not resided in the District of Columbia for one year immediately preceding the filing of her application, as required by § 3–203 of the District of Columbia Code.[3]

---

1 Conn.Welfare Manual, c. II, §§ 219.1–219.2 (1966).

[3] D.C.Code Ann. § 3–203 (1967) provides:

"Public assistance shall be awarded to or on behalf of any needy individual who either (a) has resided in the District for one year immediately preceding the date of filing his application for such assistance; or (b) who was born within one year immediately preceding the application for such aid, if the parent or other relative with whom the child is living has resided in the District for one year immediately preceding the birth; or (c) is otherwise within one of the categories of public assistance established by this chapter." See D. C. Handbook of Pub. Assistance Policies and Procedures, HPA–2, EL 9.1, I, III (1965) (hereinafter cited as D. C. Handbook).

Appellee Minnie Harrell, now deceased, had moved with her three children from New York to Washington in September 1966. She suffered from cancer and moved to be near members of her family who lived in Washington.

Appellee Barley, a former resident of the District of Columbia, returned to the District in March 1941 and was committed a month later to St. Elizabeths Hospital as mentally ill. She has remained in that Hospital ever since. She was deemed eligible for release in 1965, and a plan was made to transfer her from the Hospital to a foster home. The plan depended, however, upon Mrs. Barley obtaining welfare assistance for her support. Her application for assistance under the program for Aid to the Permanently and Totally Disabled was denied because her time spent in the Hospital did not count in determining compliance with the one-year requirement.

Appellee Brown lived with her mother and two of her three children in Fort Smith, Arkansas. Her third child was living with appellee Brown's father in the District of Columbia. When her mother moved from Fort Smith to Oklahoma, appellee Brown, in February 1966, returned to the District of Columbia where she lived as a child. Her application for AFDC assistance was approved insofar as it sought assistance for the child who had lived in the District with her father but was denied to the extent it sought assistance for the two other children.

Appellee Legrant moved with her two children from South Carolina to the District of Columbia in March 1967 after the death of her mother. She planned to live with a sister and brother in Washington. She was pregnant and in ill health when she applied for and was denied AFDC assistance in July 1967.

* * *

In No. 34, there are two appellees, Smith and Foster, who were denied AFDC and on the sole ground that they had not been residents of Pennsylvania for a year prior to their applications as required by § 432(6) of the Pennsylvania Welfare Code.[5] Appellee Smith and her five minor children moved in December 1966 from Delaware to Philadelphia, Pennsylvania, where her father lived. Her father supported her and her children for several months until he lost his job. Appellee then applied for AFDC assistance and had received two checks when the aid was terminated. Appellee Foster, after living in Pennsylvania from 1953 to 1965, had moved with her four children to South Carolina to care for her grandfather and invalid grandmother and had returned to Pennsylvania in 1967. * * *

II.

There is no dispute that the effect of the waiting-period requirement in each case is to create two classes of needy resident families indistinguishable from each other except that one is composed

[5] Pa.Stat., Tit. 62, § 432(6) (1968). See also, Pa.Public Assistance Manual, §§ 3150–3151 (1962). Section 432(6) provides:

"Assistance may be granted only to or in behalf of a person residing in Pennsylvania who (i) has resided therein for at least one year immediately preceding the date of application; (ii) last resided in a state which, by law, regulation or reciprocal agreement with Pennsylvania, grants public assistance to or in behalf of a person who has resided in such state for less than one year; (iii) is a married woman residing with a husband who meets the requirement prescribed in subclause (i) or (ii) of this clause; or (iv) is a child less than one year of age whose parent, or relative with whom he is residing, meets the requirement prescribed in subclause (i), (ii) or (iii) of this clause or resided in Pennsylvania for at least one year immediately preceding the child's birth. Needy persons who do not meet any of the requirements stated in this clause and who are transients or without residence in any state, may be granted assistance in accordance with rules, regulations, and standards established by the department."

of residents who have resided a year or more, and the second of residents who have resided less than a year, in the jurisdiction. On the basis of this sole difference the first class is granted and the second class is denied welfare aid upon which may depend the ability of the families to obtain the very means to subsist—food, shelter, and other necessities of life. In each case, the District Court found that appellees met the test for residence in their jurisdictions, as well as all other eligibility requirements except the requirement of residence for a full year prior to their applications. On reargument, appellees' central contention is that the statutory prohibition of benefits to residents of less than a year creates a classification which constitutes an invidious discrimination denying them equal protection of the laws.[6] We agree. The interests which appellants assert are promoted by the classification either may not constitutionally be promoted by government or are not compelling governmental interests.

III.

Primarily, appellants justify the waiting-period requirement as a protective device to preserve the fiscal integrity of state public assistance programs. It is asserted that people who require welfare assistance during their first year of residence in a State are likely to become continuing burdens on state welfare programs. Therefore, the argument runs, if such people can be deterred from entering the jurisdiction by denying them welfare benefits during the first year, state programs to assist long-time residents will not be impaired by a substantial influx of indigent newcomers.

There is weighty evidence that exclusion from the jurisdiction of the poor who need or may need relief was the specific objective of these provisions. In the Congress, sponsors of federal legislation to eliminate all residence requirements have been consistently opposed by representatives of state and local welfare agencies who have stressed the fears of the States that elimination of the requirements would result in a heavy influx of individuals into States providing the most generous benefits. See, e. g., Hearings on H.R. 10032 Before the House Committee on Ways and Means, 87th Cong., 2d Sess., 309–310, 644 (1962); Hearings on H.R. 6000 Before the Senate Committee on Finance, 81st Cong., 2d Sess., 324–327 (1950). * * *

We do not doubt that the one-year waiting period device is well suited to discourage the influx of poor families in need of assistance, An indigent who desires to migrate, resettle, find a new job, start a new life will doubtless hesitate if he knows that he must risk making the move without the possibility of falling back on state welfare assistance during his first year of residence, when his need may be most acute. But the purpose of inhibiting migration by needy persons into the State is constitutionally impermissible.

This Court long ago recognized that the nature of our Federal Union and our constitutional concepts of personal liberty unite to require that all citizens be free to travel throughout the length and breadth of our land uninhibited by statutes, rules, or regulations which unreasonably burden or restrict this movement. * * *

We have no occasion to ascribe the source of this right to travel interstate to a particular constitutional provision.[8] It

---

[6] This constitutional challenge cannot be answered by the argument that public assistance benefits are a "privilege" and not a "right." See Sherbert v. Verner, 374 U.S. 398, 404, 83 S.Ct. 1790, 1794, 10 L.Ed.2d 965 (1963).

[8] In Corfield v. Coryell, 6 Fed.Cas. pp. 546, 552 (No. 3230) (C.C.E.D.Pa.1823), Paul v. Virginia, 8 Wall. (75 U.S.) 168, 180, 19 L.Ed. 357 (1808), and Ward v. Maryland, 12 Wall.

suffices that, as Mr. Justice Stewart said for the Court in United States v. Guest, 383 U.S. 745, 757–758, 86 S.Ct. 1170, 1178, 16 L.Ed.2d 239 (1966):

> "The constitutional right to travel from one State to another * * * occupies a position fundamental to the concept of our Federal Union. It is a right that has been firmly established and repeatedly recognized.
>
> "[The] right finds no explicit mention in the Constitution. The reason, it has been suggested, is that a right so elementary was conceived from the beginning to be a necessary concomitant of the stronger Union the Constitution created. In any event, freedom to travel throughout the United States has long been recognized as a basic right under the Constitution."

Thus, the purpose of deterring the inmigration of indigents cannot serve as justification for the classification created by the one-year waiting period, since that purpose is constitutionally impermissible. If a law has "no other purpose * * * than to chill the assertion of constitutional rights by penalizing those who choose

(79 U.S.) 418, 430, 20 L.Ed. 449 (1870), the right to travel interstate was grounded upon the Privileges and Immunities Clause of Art. IV, § 2. See also Slaughter-House Cases, 16 Wall. 36, 79, 21 L.Ed. 394 (1872); Twining v. New Jersey, 211 U.S. 78, 97, 29 S.Ct. 14, 18, 53 L.Ed. 97 (1908). In Edwards v. California, 314 U.S. 160, 181, 183–185, 62 S.Ct. 164, 170, 171–172, 86 L.Ed. 119 (Douglas and Jackson, JJ. concurring), and Twining v. New Jersey, supra, reliance was placed on the Privileges and Immunities Clause of the Fourteenth Amendment. See also Crandall v. Nevada, 6 Wall. (73 U.S.) 35, 18 L.Ed. 744 (1868). In Edwards v. California, supra, and Passenger Cases, 7 How. 283 (1849), a Commerce Clause approach was employed.

See also Kent v. Dulles, 357 U.S. 116, 125, 78 S.Ct. 1113, 1118, 2 L.Ed.2d 1204 (1958); Aptheker v. Rusk, 378 U.S. 500, 505–506, 84 S.Ct. 1659, 1663, 12 L.Ed.2d 992 (1964); Zemel v. Rusk, 381 U.S. 1, 14, 85 S.Ct. 1271, 1279, 14 L.Ed.2d 179 (1966), where the freedom of Americans to travel outside the country was grounded upon the Due Process Clause of the Fifth Amendment.

to exercise them, then it [is] patently unconstitutional." United States v. Jackson, 390 U.S. 570, 581, 88 S.Ct. 1209, 1216, 20 L.Ed.2d 138 (1968).

Alternatively, appellants argue that even if it is impermissible for a State to attempt to deter the entry of all indigents, the challenged classification may be justified as a permissible state attempt to discourage those indigents who would enter the State solely to obtain larger benefits. We observe first that none of the statutes before us is tailored to serve that objective. Rather, the class of barred newcomers is all-inclusive, lumping the great majority who come to the State for other purposes with those who come for the sole purpose of collecting higher benefits. In actual operation, therefore, the three statutes enact what in effect are non-rebuttable presumptions that every applicant for assistance in his first year of residence came to the jurisdiction solely to obtain higher benefits. Nothing whatever in any of these records supplies any basis in fact for such a presumption.

More fundamentally, a State may no more try to fence out those indigents who seek higher welfare benefits than it may try to fence out indigents generally. Implicit in any such distinction is the notion that indigents who enter a State with the hope of securing higher welfare benefits are somehow less deserving than indigents who do not take this consideration into account. But we do not perceive why a mother who is seeking to make a new life for herself and her children should be regarded as less deserving because she considers, among others factors, the level of a State's public assistance. Surely such a mother is no less deserving than a mother who moves into a particular State in order to take advantage of its better educational facilities.

Appellants argue further that the challenged classification may be sustained as an attempt to distinguish between new and old residents on the basis of the contribution they have made to the community through the payment of taxes. We have difficulty seeing how long-term residents who qualify for welfare are making a greater present contribution to the State in taxes than indigent residents who have recently arrived. If the argument is based on contributions made in the past by the long-term residents, there is some question, as a factual matter, whether this argument is applicable in Pennsylvania where the record suggests that some 40% of those denied public assistance because of the waiting period had lengthy prior residence in the State.[9] But we need not rest on the particular facts of these cases. Appellants' reasoning would logically permit the State to bar new residents from schools, parks, and libraries or deprive them of police and fire protection. Indeed it would permit the State to apportion all benefits and services according to the past tax contributions of its citizens. The Equal Protection Clause prohibits such an apportionment of state services.[10]

We recognize that a State has a valid interest in preserving the fiscal integrity of its programs. It may legitimately attempt to limit its expenditures, whether for public assistance, public education, or any other program. But a State may not accomplish such a purpose by invidious distinctions between classes of its citizens. It could not, for example, reduce expenditures for education by barring indigent children from its schools. Similarly, in the cases before us, appellants must do more than show that denying welfare benefits to new residents saves money. The saving of welfare costs cannot be an independent ground for an invidious classification.[11]

In sum, neither deterrence of indigents from migrating to the State nor limitation of welfare benefits to those regarded as contributing to the State is a constitutionally permissible state objective.

IV.

Appellants next advance as justification certain administrative and related governmental objectives allegedly served by the waiting-period requirement.[12] They argue that the requirement (1) facilitates the planning of the welfare budget; (2) provides an objective test of residency; (3) minimizes the opportunity for recipients fraudulently to receive payments from more than one jurisdiction; and (4) encourages early entry of new residents into the labor force.

At the outset, we reject appellants' argument that a mere showing of a rational relationship between the waiting period and these four admittedly permissible state objectives will suffice to justify the classification. See Lindsley v. Natl. Carbonic Gas Co., 220 U.S. 61, 78,

[9] Furthermore, the contribution rationale can hardly explain why the District of Columbia and Pennsylvania bar payments to children who have not lived in the jurisdiction for a year regardless of whether the parents have lived in the jurisdiction for that period. See D.C.Code § 3–203; D. C. Handbook, EL 9.1, I(C) (1965); Pa.Stat., Tit. 62, § 432(6) (1968). Clearly, the children who were barred would not have made a contribution during that year.

[10] We are not dealing here with state insurance programs which may legitimately tie the amount of benefits to the individual's contributions.

[11] In Rinaldi v. Yeager, 384 U.S. 305, 86 S.Ct. 1497, 16 L.Ed.2d 577 (1966), New Jersey attempted to reduce expenditures by requiring prisoners who took an unsuccessful appeal to reimburse the State out of their institutional earnings for the cost of furnishing a trial transcript. This Court held the New Jersey statute unconstitutional because it did not require similar repayments from unsuccessful appellants given a suspended sentence, placed on probation, or sentenced only to a fine. There was no rational basis for the distinction between unsuccessful appellants who were in prison and those who were not.

[12] Appellant in No. 9, the Connecticut Welfare Commissioner, disclaims any reliance on this contention. In No. 34, the District Court found as a fact that the Pennsylvania requirement served none of the claimed functions. 277 F.Supp. 65, 68 (1967).

31 S.Ct. 337, 340, 55 L.Ed. 369 (1911); Flemming v. Nestor, 363 U.S. 603, 611, 80 S.Ct. 1367, 1372, 4 L.Ed.2d 1435 (1960); McGowan v. Maryland, 366 U.S. 420, 426, 81 S.Ct. 1101, 1105, 6 L.Ed.2d 393 (1961). The waiting-period provision denies welfare benefits to otherwise eligible applicants solely because they have recently moved into the jurisdiction. But in moving from State to State or to the District of Columbia appellees were exercising a constitutional right, and any classification which serves to penalize the exercise of that right, unless shown to be necessary to promote a *compelling* governmental interest, is unconstitutional. Cf. Skinner v. Oklahoma, 316 U.S. 535, 541, 62 S.Ct. 1110, 1113, 86 L.Ed. 1655 (1942); Korematsu v. United States, 323 U.S. 214, 216, 65 S. Ct. 193, 194, 89 L.Ed. 194 (1944); Bates v. Little Rock, 361 U.S. 516, 524, 80 S.Ct. 412, 417, 4 L.Ed.2d 480 (1960); Sherbert v. Verner, 374 U.S. 398, 406, 83 S.Ct. 1790, 1795, 10 L.Ed. 2d 965 (1963).

The argument that the waiting-period requirement facilitates budget predictability is wholly unfounded. The records in all three cases are utterly devoid of evidence that either State or the District of Columbia in fact uses the one-year requirement as a means to predict the number of people who will require assistance in the budget year.

The argument that the waiting period serves as an administratively efficient rule of thumb for determining residency similarly will not withstand scrutiny. The residence requirement and the one-year waiting-period requirement are distinct and independent prerequisites for assistance under these three statutes, and the facts relevant to the determination of each are directly examined by the welfare authorities. Before granting an application, the welfare authorities investigate the applicant's employment, housing, and family situation and in the course of the

inquiry necessarily learn the facts upon which to determine whether the applicant is a resident.

Similarly, there is no need for a State to use the one-year waiting period as a safeguard against fraudulent receipt of benefits; [18] for less drastic means are available, and are employed, to minimize that hazard. Of course, a State has a valid interest in preventing fraud by any applicant, whether a newcomer or a long-time resident. It is not denied however that the investigations now conducted entail inquiries into facts relevant to that subject. In addition, cooperation among state welfare departments is common. * * * Since double payments can be prevented by a letter or a telephone call, it is unreasonable to accomplish this objective by the blunderbuss method of denying assistance to all indigent newcomers for an entire year.

Pennsylvania suggests that the one-year waiting period is justified as a means of encouraging new residents to join the labor force promptly. But this logic would also require a similar waiting period for long-term residents of the State. A state purpose to encourage employment provides no rational basis for imposing a one-year waiting-period restriction on new residents only.

We conclude therefore that appellants in these cases do not use and have no need to use the one-year requirement for the governmental purposes suggested. Thus, even under traditional equal protection tests a classification of welfare applicants according to whether they have lived in the State for one year would seem irrational and unconstitutional.[20] But,

[18] The unconcern of Connecticut and Pennsylvania with the one-year requirement as a means of preventing fraud is made apparent by the waiver of the requirement in reciprocal agreements with other States. See n. 15, supra.

[20] Under the traditional standard, equal protection is denied only if the classification is "without any reasonable basis,"

of course, the traditional criteria do not apply in these cases. Since the classification here touches on the fundamental right of interstate movement, its constitutionality must be judged by the stricter standard of whether it promotes a *compelling* state interest. Under this standard, the waiting period requirement clearly violates the Equal Protection Clause.[21]

V.

Connecticut and Pennsylvania argue, however, that the constitutional challenge to the waiting period requirements must fail because Congress expressly approved the imposition of the requirement by the States as part of the jointly funded AFDC program.

Section 402(b) of the Social Security Act of 1935, as amended, 42 U.S.C.A. § 602(b), provides that:

"The Secretary shall approve any [state assistance] plan which fulfills the conditions specified in subsection (a) of this section, except that he shall not approve any plan which imposes as a condition of eligibility for aid to families with dependent children, a residence requirement which denies aid with respect to any child residing in the State (1) who has resided in the State for one year immediately preceding the application for such aid, or (2) who was born within one year immediately preceding the application, if the parent or other relative with whom the child is living has resided in the

State for one year immediately preceding the birth."

On its face, the statute does not approve, much less prescribe, a one-year requirement. It merely directs the Secretary of Health, Education, and Welfare not to disapprove plans submitted by the States because they include such a requirement.[22] The suggestion that Congress enacted that directive to encourage state participation in the AFDC program is completely refuted by the legislative history of the section. That history discloses that Congress enacted the directive to curb hardships resulting from lengthy residence requirements. Rather than an approval or a prescription of the requirement in state plans, the directive was the means chosen by Congress to deny federal funding to any State which persisted in stipulating excessive residence requirements as a condition of the payment of benefits.

One year before the Social Security Act was passed, 20 of the 45 States which had aid to dependent children programs required residence in the State for two or more years. Ten other States required two or more years of residence in a particular town or county. And 33 States required at least one year of residence in a particular town or county. Congress determined to combat this restrictionist policy. Both the House and Senate Committee Reports expressly stated that the objective of § 402(b) was to force "[l]iberality of residence requirement." Not a single instance can be found in the debates or committee reports supporting the contention that § 402(b) was enacted to encourage participation by the States

---

Lindsley v. National Carbonic Gas Co., 220 U.S. 61, 78, 31 S.Ct. 337, 340, 55 L.Ed. 369 (1911); see also Flemming v. Nestor, 363 U. S. 603, 80 S.Ct. 1367 (1960).

[21] We imply no view of the validity of waiting period *or* residence requirements determining eligibility to vote, eligibility for tuition-free education, to obtain a license to practice a profession, to hunt or fish, and so forth. Such requirements may promote compelling state interests on the one hand, or, on the other, may not be penalties upon the exercise of the constitutional right of interstate travel.

[22] As of 1964, 11 jurisdictions imposed no residence requirement whatever for AFDC assistance. They were Alaska, Georgia, Hawaii, Kentucky, New Jersey, New York, Rhode Island, Vermont, Guam, Puerto Rico, and the Virgin Islands. See Dept. of HEW, Characteristics of State Public Assistance Plans under the Social Security Act (Pub. Assistance Rep.No.50, 1964 ed.).

in the AFDC program. To the contrary, those few who addressed themselves to waiting-period requirements emphasized that participation would depend on a State's repeal or drastic revision of existing requirements. A congressional demand on 41 States to repeal or drastically revise offending statutes is hardly a way to enlist their cooperation.[25]

But even if we were to assume, *arguendo,* that Congress did approve the imposition of a one-year waiting period, it is the responsive *state* legislation which infringes constitutional rights. By itself § 402(b) has absolutely no restrictive effect. It is therefore not that statute but only the state requirements which pose the constitutional question.

Finally, even if it could be argued that the constitutionality of § 402(b) is somehow at issue here, it follows from what we have said that the provision, insofar as it permits the one-year waiting-period requirement, would be unconstitutional. Congress may not authorize the States to violate the Equal Protection Clause. Perhaps Congress could induce wider state participation in school construction if it authorized the use of joint funds for the building of segregated schools. But could it seriously be contended that Congress would be constitutionally justified

[25] Section 402(b) required the repeal of 30 state statutes which imposed too long a waiting period and 11 state statutes (as well as the Hawaii statute) which required residence in a particular town or county. See Social Security Board, Social Security in America 235–236 (1937).

It is apparent that Congress was not intimating any view of the constitutionality of a one-year limitation. The constitutionality of any scheme of federal social security legislation was a matter of doubt at that time in light of the decision in Schecter Poultry Corp. v. United States, 295 U.S. 495, 55 S.Ct. 837, 79 L.Ed. 1570 (1935). Throughout the House debates congressmen discussed the constitutionality of the fundamental taxing provisions of the Social Security Act, see e. g., 79 Cong.Rec. 5783 (1935) (remarks of Rep. Cooper), but not once discussed the constitutionality of § 402(b).

in such authorization by the need to secure state cooperation? Congress is without power to enlist state cooperation in a joint federal-state program by legislation which authorizes the States to violate the Equal Protection Clause. Katzenbach v. Morgan, 384 U.S. 641, 651, 86 S.Ct. 1717, 1723, 16 L.Ed.2d 828, n. 10 (1966).

VI.

The waiting-period requirement in the District of Columbia Code involved in No. 33 is also unconstitutional even though it was adopted by Congress as an exercise of federal power. In terms of federal power, the discrimination created by the one-year requirement violates the Due Process Clause of the Fifth Amendment. "[W]hile the Fifth Amendment contains no equal protection clause, it does forbid discrimination that is 'so unjustifiable as to be violative of due process.'" Schneider v. Rusk, 377 U.S. 163, 168, 84 S.Ct. 1187, 1190, 12 L.Ed.2d 218 (1964); Bolling v. Sharpe, 347 U.S. 497, 74 S.Ct. 693, 98 L.Ed. 884 (1954). For the reasons we have stated in invalidating the Pennsylvania and Connecticut provisions, the District of Columbia provision is also invalid— the Due Process Clause of the Fifth Amendment forbids Congress from denying public assistance to poor persons otherwise eligible solely on the ground that they have not been residents of the District of Columbia for one year at the time their applications are filed.

Accordingly, the judgments in Nos. 9, 33, and 34 are

Affirmed.

Mr. Justice STEWART, concurring.

In joining the opinion of the Court, I add a word in response to the dissent of my Brother HARLAN, who, I think, has quite misapprehended what the Court's opinion says.

The Court today does *not* "pick out particular human activities, characterize them as 'fundamental,' and give them added protection * * *." To the contrary, the Court simply recognizes, as it must, an established constitutional right, and gives to that right no less protection than the Constitution itself demands.

"The constitutional right to travel from one State to another * * * has been firmly established and repeatedly recognized." United States v. Guest, 383 U.S. 745, 757, 86 S.Ct. 1170, 1178, 16 L.Ed. 2d 239. This constitutional right, which, of course, includes the right of "entering and abiding in any state in the Union," Truax v. Raich, 239 U.S. 33, 39, 36 S. Ct. 7, 9, 60 L.Ed. 131, is *not* a mere conditional liberty subject to regulation and control under conventional due process or equal protection standards.[1] "[T]he right to travel freely from State to State finds constitutional protection that is quite independent of the Fourteenth Amendment." United States v. Guest, supra, at 760, 86 S.Ct. at 1179, n. 17.[2] As we made clear in *Guest,* it is a right broadly assertable against private interference as well as governmental action.[3] Like the right of association, NAACP v. Alabama, 357 U.S. 449, 78 S.Ct. 1163, 2 L.Ed.2d 1488, it is a virtually unconditional personal right,[4] guaranteed by the Constitution to us all.

It follows, as the Court says, that "the purpose of deterring the in-migration of indigents cannot serve as justification for the classification created by the one-year waiting period, since that purpose is constitutionally impermissible." And it further follows, as the Court says, that any *other* purposes offered in support of a law that so clearly impinges upon the constitutional right of interstate travel must be shown to reflect a *compelling* governmental interest. This is necessarily true whether the impinging law be a classification statute to be tested against the Equal Protection Clause, or a state or federal regulatory law, to be tested against the Due Process Clause of the Fourteenth or Fifth Amendment. As Mr. Justice Harlan wrote for the Court more than a decade ago, "[T]o justify the deterrent effect * * * on the free exercise * * * of their constitutionally protected right, * * * a 'subordinating interest of the State must be compelling.'" NAACP v. Alabama, supra, at 463, 78 S.Ct. at 1172.

The Court today, therefore, is not "contriving new constitutional principles." It is deciding these cases under the aegis of established constitutional law.[5]

---

[1] By contrast, the "right" of international travel has been considered to be no more than an aspect of the "liberty" protected by the Due Process Clause of the Fifth Amendment. Kent v. Dulles, 357 U.S. 116, 125, 78 S.Ct. 1113, 1118, 2 L.Ed.2d 1204; Aptheker v. Secretary of State, 378 U.S. 500, 505—506, 84 S.Ct. 1659, 1663, 12 L.Ed.2d 992. As such, this "right," the Court has held, can be regulated within the bounds of due process. Zemel v. Rusk, 381 U.S. 1, 85 S.Ct. 1271, 14 L.Ed.2d 179.

[2] The constitutional right of interstate travel was fully recognized long before adoption of the Fourteenth Amendment. See the statement of Chief Justice Taney in the Passenger Cases, 7 How. 283, 492, 12 L.Ed. 702:

"For all the great purposes for which the Federal government was formed, we are one people, with one common country. We are all citizens of the United States; and, as members of the same community, must have the right to pass and repass through every part of it without interruption, as freely as in our own States."

[3] Mr. Justice Harlan was alone in dissenting from this square holding in Guest. 383 U.S., at 762, 86 S.Ct. 1170.

[4] The extent of emergency governmental power temporarily to prevent or control interstate travel, e. g., to a disaster area, need not be considered in these cases.

[5] It is to be remembered that the Court today affirms the judgment of three different federal district courts, and that at least four other federal courts have reached the same result. See ante, p. 1324, n. 1.

Mr. Chief Justice WARREN, with whom Mr. Justice BLACK joins, dissenting.

In my opinion the issue before us can be simply stated: may Congress, acting under one of its enumerated powers, impose minimal nationwide residence requirements or authorize the States to do so? Since I believe that Congress does have this power and has constitutionally exercised it in these cases, I must dissent.

I.

The Court insists that § 402(b) of the Social Security Act "does not approve, much less prescribe, a one-year requirement." Ante, at 1334. From this reading of the legislative history it concludes that Congress did not intend to authorize the States to impose residence requirements. An examination of the relevant legislative materials compels, in my view, the opposite conclusion, i. e., Congress intended to authorize state residence requirements of up to one year.

* * *

II.

Congress has imposed a residence requirement in the District of Columbia and authorized the States to impose similar requirements. The issue before us must therefore be framed in terms of whether Congress may create minimal residence requirements, not whether the States, acting alone, may do so. See Prudential Insurance Co. v. Benjamin, 328 U.S. 408, 66 S.Ct. 1142, 90 L.Ed. 1342 (1946); In re Rahrer, 140 U.S. 545, 11 S.Ct. 865, 32 S.Ct. 572 (1891). Appellees insist that a congressionally mandated residence requirement would violate their right to travel. The import of their contention is that Congress, even under its "plenary" [4] power to control interstate commerce, is constitutionally prohibited from imposing residence requirements. I reach a contrary conclusion for I am convinced that the extent

of the burden on interstate travel when compared with the justification for its imposition requires the Court to uphold this exertion of federal power.

Congress, pursuant to its commerce power, has enacted a variety of restrictions upon interstate travel. It has taxed air and rail fares and the gasoline needed to power cars and trucks which move interstate. 26 U.S.C.A. § 4261 (air fares); 26 U.S.C.A., 1952 ed., § 3469, repealed in part by P.L. 87–508, § 5(b) (rail fares); 26 U.S.C.A. § 4081 (gasoline). Many of the federal safety regulations of common carriers which cross state lines burden the right to travel. 45 U.S.C.A. §§ 1–46 (railroad safety appliances); 49 U.S.C.A. § 1421 (air safety regulations). And Congress has prohibited by criminal statute interstate travel for certain purposes. E. g., 18 U.S.C.A. § 1952. Although each of these restrictions operates as a limitation upon free interstate movement of persons, their constitutionality appears well settled. See Texas & Pacific Railway Co. v. Rigsby, 241 U.S. 33, 41, 36 S.Ct. 482, 485, 60 L.Ed. 874 (1916); Southern Railway Co. v. United States, 222 U.S. 20, 32 S.Ct. 2, 56 L.Ed. 72 (1911); United States v. Zizzo, 338 F.2d 577 (C.A.7th Cir., 1964), cert. denied, 381 U.S. 915, 85 S.Ct. 1530, 14 L.Ed.2d 435 (1965). As the Court observed in Zemel v. Rusk, 381 U.S. 1, 14, 85 S.Ct. 1271, 1279, 14 L.Ed.2d 179 (1965), "the fact that liberty cannot be inhibited without due process of law does not mean that it can under no circumstances be inhibited."

The Court's right-to-travel cases lend little support to the view that congressional action is invalid merely because it burdens the right to travel. Most of our cases fall into two categories: those in which *state* imposed restrictions were involved, see, e. g., Edwards v. California, 314 U.S. 160, 62 S.Ct. 164, 86 L.Ed. 119 (1941); Crandall v. Nevada, 6 Wall. 35, 18 L.Ed. 744 (1867), and those concerning congressional decisions to remove impediments to interstate movement, see, e. g., United States v. Guest, 383 U.S. 745, 86 S.Ct. 1170, 16 L.Ed.2d 239 (1966). Since the focus of our inquiry must be whether Congress would exceed permissible bounds by imposing residence requirements, neither group of cases offers controlling principles.

* * *

The core inquiry is "the extent of the governmental restriction imposed" and the "extent of the necessity for the restriction." Id., at 14, 85 S.Ct. at 1279. As already noted, travel itself is not prohibited. Any burden inheres solely in the fact that a potential welfare recipient might take into consideration the loss of welfare benefits for a limited period of time if he changes his residence. Not only is this burden of uncertain degree,[5] but appellees themselves assert there is evidence that few welfare recipients have in fact been deterred by residence requirements. See Harvith, The Constitutionality of Residence Tests for General and Categorical Assistance Programs, 54 Calif.L.Rev. 567, 615–618 (1966); Note, Residence Requirements in State Public Welfare Statutes, 51 Iowa L.Rev. 1080, 1083–1085 (1966).

The insubstantiality of the restriction imposed by residence requirements must then be evaluated in light of the possible congressional reasons for such requirements. See, e. g., McGowan v. Maryland, 366 U.S. 420, 425–427, 81 S.Ct. 1101, 1104–1105, 6 L.Ed.2d 393 (1961). One fact which does emerge with clarity from the legislative history is Congress' belief that a program of cooperative federalism combining federal

aid with enhanced state participation would result in an increase in the scope of welfare programs and level of benefits. Given the apprehensions of many States that an increase in benefits without minimal residence requirements would result in an inability to provide an adequate welfare system, Congress deliberately adopted the intermediate course of a cooperative program. Such a program, Congress believed, would encourage the States to assume greater welfare responsibilities and would give the States the necessary financial support for such an undertaking. Our cases require only that Congress have a rational basis for finding that a chosen regulatory scheme is necessary to the furtherance of interstate commerce. See, e. g., Katzenbach v. McClung, 379 U.S. 294, 85 S.Ct. 377, 13 L.Ed.2d 290 (1964); Wickard v. Filburn, 317 U.S. 111, 63 S.Ct. 82, 87 L.Ed. 122 (1942). Certainly, a congressional finding that residence requirements allowed each State to concentrate its resources upon new and increased programs of rehabilitation ultimately resulting in an enhanced flow of commerce as the economic condition of welfare recipients progressively improved is rational and would justify imposition of residence requirements under the Commerce Clause. And Congress could have also determined that residence requirements fostered personal mobility. An individual no longer dependent upon welfare would be presented with an unfettered range of choices so that a decision to migrate could be made without regard to considerations of possible economic dislocation.

* * *

III.

The era is long past when this Court under the rubric of due process has reviewed the wisdom of a congressional decision that interstate commerce will be fostered by the enactment of certain regulations. Compare Adkins v. Children's

---

[5] The burden is uncertain because indigents who are disqualified from categorical assistance by residence requirements are not left wholly without assistance. Each of the appellees in these cases found alternative sources of assistance after their disqualification.

Hospital, 261 U.S. 525, 43 S.Ct. 394, 67 L.Ed. 785 (1923), with United States v. Darby, 312 U.S. 100, 61 S.Ct. 451, 85 L.Ed. 609 (1941). Speaking for the Court in Helvering v. Davis, 301 U.S. 619, 644, 57 S.Ct. 904, 910, 81 L.Ed. 1307 (1937), Mr. Justice Cardozo said of another section of the Social Security Act:

"Whether wisdom or unwisdom resides in the scheme of benefits set forth * * * is not for us to say. The answer to such inquiries must come from Congress, not the courts. Our concern here, as often, is with power, not with wisdom."

I am convinced that Congress does have power to enact residence requirements of reasonable duration or to authorize the States to do so and that it has exercised this power.

The Court's decision reveals only the top of the iceberg. Lurking beneath are the multitude of situations in which States have imposed residence requirements including eligibility to vote, to engage in certain professions or occupations or to attend a state-supported university. Although the Court takes pains to avoid acknowledging the ramifications of its decision, its implications cannot be ignored. I dissent.

[Dissenting opinion of Mr. Justice HARLAN omitted].

Notes on Shapiro v. Thompson

1. * Statutory attempts to restrict the movement of the working man and indigents have been present in our Anglo-Saxon legal system since the Fourteenth Century. In order to cope with the increased mobility and concomitant economic insecurity resulting from the decline of the rural feudal system and the growth of the

*This note paragraph is excerpted from a brief filed by the Center on Social Welfare Policy and Law of Columbia University in the case of Shapiro v. Thompson, supra.

towns, Parliament provided that no worker was to go "out of the town where he dwelleth in the winter, to serve in the summer, * * *". This and other restrictions on mobility imposed over the years culminated in the Settlement Act of 1662.

The 1662 Act was largely passed in response to the metropolitan members of Parliament, who wanted to prevent the poor from coming to the city. The act provided that any newcomer to a parish could be returned within 40 days to the parish where he was last legally settled, whether or not he applied for relief or was likely to do so. To avoid such expulsion, the individual could provide security or pay an exorbitant rent (£10), far beyond the ability of most (90%) of the population. The result was the legal restriction of all people without substantial wealth or property to the narrow area in which they were born. This Act was the prototype for subsequent English and American Poor Laws.

The English principle of public responsibility for the local indigent was brought to North America by the British settlers and took root. Towns were closely knit, independent, insular and isolated. Hardly off the boat, the people of Charlestown settlement in Massachusetts determined in 1634 "that none be permitted to * * * dwell in this town without the consent of the town first obtained."

The Seventeenth Century also saw the development of "warning out" laws in New England and, later elsewhere, by which all newcomers who might become chargeable were to leave the local town. In practice many people did not leave but never acquired a legal settlement and therefore were ineligible for aid.

Toward the end of the seventeenth century and throughout the eighteenth century, the population increased in size and mobility. It became more and more difficult to prevent movement, and more rigorous devices were believed necessary to determine who would be eligible for relief.

The first general poor laws in the colonies, enacted at the close of the eighteenth century, dealt with the problems of settlement and residence, in much the same manner as their predeccessors. But from the beginning these statutes lacked the uniformity that was the key to the English system of relief. In the more complex American laws, each jurisdiction could define the period necessary to gain settlement. As now, legal settlement could be lost in one jurisdiction prior to being gained in another.

The Ohio Territorial Law of 1795 formed the basis for Poor Law administration throughout the sparsely populated but enormous Northwest Territory. The statute was copied from the Pennsylvania Poor Law, which itself was adapted from Elizabethan Poor Law. There was extraordinary similarity in wording and intent between the 1662 Law of Settlement, set forth above, and the Ohio Territorial Law of 1795:

> "Upon complaint being made by the overseers of the poor * * * any two justices * * * [may] by their warrant or order * * * remove and convey such person, or persons, to the country, township, place or state, where he, she or they was or were last legally settled, unless such person or persons shall give sufficient security to discharge and indemnify the said township."

Elizabethan philosophical and administrative concepts were indelibly impressed upon nearly all of the country, except Louisiana.

Although there was some variation from state to state, means of gaining legal settlement were patterned after English law. A man who had paid taxes for one or two years, paid a yearly rental of not less and $25.00, had lived for a year on his own property, or held public office acquired a legal settlement and became eligible for relief.

The laws of settlement remained largely unchanged into the Twentieth Century, despite the continuing opposition of persons working in the field of social welfare. The Social Security Act of 1935, as amended, effected a substantial reduction of the period of residence required in many states and changed the emphasis from settlement to residence for the categorical programs.

In addition to the residence requirements a number of other statutes typical of the early English and American poor law have persisted on our statute books well into the twentieth century and in more than one instance up to the present time. Officials in Iowa may now obtain a court order requiring a person not receiving assistance but likely to become a charge to leave the county or state. Enforcement is by contempt proceedings or physical removal by the sheriff. Intrastate removal may be compelled without any judicial proceedings whatever in Minnesota; the chairman of the county welfare board need merely serve an order on the sheriff. Similar statutes may well be on the books of other states. Officials "have often engaged in the practice of dumping or passing on nonresidents who apply for aid, in the hope that the next community will accept responsibility for their care." Other familiar statutes from Elizabethan times, such as penalties for aiding travel of indigents and "warning out" still exist or have recently been repealed.

2. In Graham v. Richardson, 403 U. S. 365, 91 S.Ct. 1848, 29 L.Ed. 534 (1971), two years after *Shapiro,* a Supreme Court with much altered membership was called upon to reinterpret the principles underlying the decision. The issue in Graham was whether a state could condition welfare benefits on either (a) a person's possession of United States

citizenship or (b) if a person is an alien, upon his having resided in this country for a specified number of years. The Court, in a unanimous opinion written by Mr. Justice Blackmun, held both of these conditions to be in violation of the Fourteenth Amendment, as indicated in the following excerpt:

The appellants argue initially that the States, consistent with the Equal Protection Clause, may favor United States citizens over aliens in the distribution of welfare benefits. It is said that this distinction involves no "invidious discrimination" such as was condemned in King v. Smith, 392 U.S. 309, 88 S.Ct. 2128, 20 L.Ed.2d 1118 (1968), for the State is not discriminating with respect to race or nationality.

The Fourteenth Amendment provides, "[N]or shall any State deprive any person of life, liberty, or property, without due process of law; nor deny to any person within its jurisdiction the equal protection of the laws." It has long been settled, and it is not disputed here, that the term "person" in this context encompasses lawfully admitted resident aliens as well as citizens of the United States and entitles both citizens and aliens to the equal protection of the laws of the State in which they reside. [citations]. * * * [T]he Court's decisions have established that classifications based on alienage, like those based on nationality or race, are inherently suspect and subject to close judicial scrutiny. Aliens as a class are a prime example of a "discrete and insular" minority (see United States v. Carolene Products Co., 304 U.S. 144, 152–153, n. 4 (1938)) for whom such heightened judicial solicitude is appropriate. Accordingly, it was said in Takahashi, 334 U.S., at 420, that "the power of a state to apply its laws exclusively to its alien inhabitants as a class is confined within narrow limits."

Arizona and Pennsylvania seek to justify their restrictions on the eligibility of aliens for public assistance solely on the basis of a State's "special public interest" in favoring its own citizens over aliens in the distribution of limited resources such as welfare benefits. It is true that this Court on occasion has upheld state statutes that treat citizens and noncitizens differently, the ground for distinction having been that such laws were necessary to protect special interests of the State or its citizens. * * *

Takahashi v. Fish & Game Comm'n, 334 U.S. 410 (1948), however, cast doubt on the continuing validity of the special public-interest doctrine in all contexts. There the Court held that California's purported ownership of fish in the ocean off its shores was not such a special public interest as would justify prohibiting aliens from making a living by fishing in those waters while permitting all others to do so. It was said:

"The Fourteenth Amendment and the laws adopted under its authority thus embody a general policy that all persons lawfully in this country shall abide 'in any state' on an equality of legal privileges with all citizens under nondiscriminatory laws." 334 U.S., at 420.

Whatever may be the contemporary vitality of the special public-interest doctrine in other contexts after *Takahashi,* we conclude that a State's desire to preserve limited welfare benefits for its own citizens is inadequate to justify Pennsylvania's making noncitizens ineligible for public assistance, and Arizona's restricting benefits to citizens and longtime resident aliens. First, the special public interest doctrine was heavily grounded on the notion that "[w]hether is a privilege, rather than a right, may be made dependent upon citizenship." People v. Crane, 214 N.

Y., at 164, 108 N.E., at 430. But this Court now has rejected the concept that constitutional rights turn upon whether a governmental benefit is characterized as a "right" or as a "privilege." Sherbert v. Verner, 374 U.S. 398, 404 (1963); Shapiro v. Thompson, 394 U. S., at 627 n. 6; Goldberg v. Kelly, 397 U.S. 254, 262 (1970); Bell v. Burson, 402 U.S. 535, 539 (1971). Second, as the Court recognized in *Shapiro:*

"[A] State has a valid interest in preserving the fiscal integrity of its programs. It may legitimately attempt to limit its expenditures, whether for public assistance, public education, or any other program. But a State may not accomplish such a purpose by invidious distinctions between classes of its citizens. * * * The saving of welfare costs cannot justify an otherwise invidious classification." 394 U.S., at 633.

Since an alien as well as a citizen is a 'person' for equal protection purposes, a concern for fiscal integrity is no more compelling a justification for the questioned classification in these cases than it was in *Shapiro.*"

The Court also held that these state imposed burdens on aliens improperly encroached upon Federal powers to regulate immigration and nationality, with a footnote that the question of Congressional power to impose a "uniform nationwide residency requirement" as a condition of federally funded welfare benefits for aliens was left open.

3. In *Shapiro* and *Graham's* wake, no type of durational residency requirement for the receipt of public assistance has been able to withstand an assault on its constitutionality.

During its 1970 term, the Supreme Court, in a curt per curiam opinion simply citing *Shapiro,* affirmed a judgment based on *Shapiro's* dictum that a state may not seek to "fence out" those indigents who migrate solely in pursuit of large welfare benefits. Wyman v. Bowens, 397 U.S. 49 (1970), aff'g per curiam sub nom. Gaddis v. Wyman, 304 F.Supp. 717 (S. D.N.Y.1969). The district court had invalidated a New York statute providing that no one could receive either aid to dependent children or general assistance within one year of his arrival in New York unless he could establish by "clear and convincing proof" that he had not entered the state in order to secure its welfare benefits. The next year, the Supreme Court held that durational residency requirements were as impermissible under locally funded general assistance programs as they were under federally supported categorical aid programs like those involved in *Shapiro.* Pease v. Hansen, 92 S.Ct. 318, rev'g per curiam 157 Mont. 99, 483 P.2d 720 (1971). More recently, the Supreme Court upheld without opinion the invalidation of two state statutes establishing five year "emergency periods" during which durational residency requirements would be imposed for the receipt of public assistance. Wyman v. Lopez, 404 U.S. 1055 (1972), aff'g mem., Civil No. 1971–308 (W.D.N.Y., Aug. 9, 1971); Dunn v. Rivera, 404 U.S. 1054 (1972), aff'g mem., 329 F.Supp. 554 (D.Conn.1971). Both the New York and Connecticut legislatures had claimed that in a time of rapidly growing governmental burdens, cutting into spiraling welfare costs through durational residency requirements was "an essential step in protecting * * * the economic and social viability" of their states.

Relying on *Shapiro,* several federal lower courts have proceeded to strike down durational residency requirements for the receipt of public services ordinarily provided for the poor on other than a cash basis.

The First Circuit has found that a two year residency requirement for admission to public housing is constitutionally impermissible. Cole v. Housing Authority of City of Newport, 435 F.2d 807 (1st Cir. 1970). A similar five year requirement has also been invalidated by the Second Circuit. King v. New Rochelle Municipal Housing Authority, 442 F.2d 646 (2d Cir. 1971), cert. denied 404 U.S. 863 (1971).

In Crapps v. Duval County Hospital Authority, 314 F.Supp. 181 (M.D.Fla. 1970), and Valenciano v. Bateman, 323 F.Supp. 600 (D.Ariz.1971), district courts struck down state laws requiring indigents to be county residents for a year before becoming eligible for medical care at county hospitals. A somewhat different statute limiting the provisions of free medical assistance was struck down in Vaughan v. Bower, 313 F.Supp. 37 (D. Ariz.1970), aff'd mem., 400 U.S. 884 (1970). The statute had permitted the superintendent of the Arizona state mental hospital to return patients with less than one year of Arizona residency to the homes of friends or relatives or to proper authorities in their former states of residence.

In none of the cases mentioned above were the courts able to discern a significant distinction between the impact of the governmental policies under consideration and those that had been invalidated in *Shapiro*. They also failed to find that either economic or administrative considerations provided any better justification for restricting the availability of medical care or housing than for restricting public assistance payments.

In the *Valenciano* case, supra, and in both of the housing cases, supra, some, but not all, of the plaintiffs had moved into the jurisdictions of the housing or medical authorities from communities within the states in which those authorities were located. In none of the cases, however, did the courts choose to differentiate among the plaintiffs' rights on the basis of whether they were intra- or inter-state migrants. All of the courts either expressly or implicitly assumed that *Shapiro's* enunciation of a right of "interstate travel" indicated the existence of a correlative right to travel within a state.

Durational residency requirements in areas completely apart from welfare benefits have also been invalidated in reliance on *Shapiro*. See Dunn v. Blumstein, 405 U.S. 330 (1972) (residence requirement for voting limited to minimum administrative period), Carter v. Gallagher, 3 CCH Emp.Prac.Dec. ¶ 8339 (D.Minn. Aug. 6, 1971) (five year residency for civil service veteran's preference); Corkey v. Edwards, 322 F.Supp. 1248 (W. D.N.C.1971), judgment vacated on other grounds, 41 U.S.L.W. 3462 (Feb. 27, 1973) (four months residency for therapeutic abortion); Keenan v. Board of Law Examiners, 317 F.Supp. 1350 (E.D. N.C.1970), (one year residency for bar admission). See also, Stevens v. Campbell, 332 F.Supp. 102 (D.Mass.1971) (residency requirements for civil service veteran's preference held violative of traditional equal protection standards).

What, then, are the ultimate implications for welfare recipients of the right to travel as enunciated in *Shapiro*?

In Galvan v. Catherwood, 324 F.Supp. 1016 (S.D.N.Y.1971), one district court suggested that *Shapiro* has not swept away all restraints on travel. At issue in *Galvan* were the policies adopted by New York State for the administration of its unemployment insurance program. By various interstate agreements, New York State unemployment benefits may be collected by a claimant after he has moved away from New York provided that he is "ready, willing and able to work." In 1967, the Industrial Commissioner of New York determined that a claimant's removal to an area of "high persistent unemployment" constituted convincing evidence that he was unavailable for work and, therefore, ineligible for unemployment benefits. Areas with "high persistent unemployment" were subsequently defined as those Department of Labor "major labor areas" with unemployment rates of over twelve percent. As a practical matter, only two labor areas fell into this category, both of them in Puerto Rico.

The *Galvan* plaintiffs had both had their unemployment benefits terminated when they traveled to Puerto Rico after having lost their jobs in New York. They contended among other things, that New York's actions violated their fundamental right to travel as established by *Shapiro.*

The district court refused to accept the plaintiffs' position. Instead, it ruled that *Shapiro* left a state free to impose "reasonable" penalties on individuals leaving its borders.

> We do not deem it clear in the context of this case * * * that the unlimited right to travel out of the state as asserted by plaintiffs falls within the ambit of constitutional protection. The Court in *Shapiro* relied heavily on the fact that the restriction involved created an 'invidious distinction' between residents of the state. In this case, plaintiffs concededly have left the state from time to time to take up residence in Puerto Rico; conceivably, the benefits or obligations owed by the State of New York to its former residents are not co-equal with those owed to its present residents. Indeed it may be that New York is not constitutionally required to provide unemployment benefits for anyone who leaves the state.

> In any event, the right to travel freely throughout the several states is not an absolute right. American citizens are 'free to travel * * * uninhibited by statutes, rules or regulations which unreasonably burden or restrict this movement.' [citing *Shapiro*] * * * In the case before us, the restriction involved is a minor one * *

Furthermore, at least on the record before us, this limitation is reasonably and directly related to the long-standing and valid policy of the unemployment insurance provisions of New York law * * * 324 F.Supp. at 1019.

Galvan of course draws strength from the out-migrant status of the plaintiffs.

Another, more significant limitation of the impact of *Shapiro* has been suggested by the California Court of Appeal. In Kirk v. Board of Regents, 273 Cal.App. 2d 430, 78 Cal.Rptr. 260 (1969), appeal dismissed, 396 U.S. 554 (1970), the plaintiff had moved from Ohio to California after marrying a man who lived and worked there. When she enrolled at the University of California two and a half months later, she was classified as a "non-resident" student because she had not been living in California for a year, and was charged higher tuition than "resident" students. Subsequently, the plaintiff brought suit claiming that the durational residency requirement for reduced tuition had an unconstitutional "chilling effect" on her right to travel.

The Court of Appeal refused to accept her position. Instead, it ruled that the scope of *Shapiro* is limited to proscribing only that discrimination against in-migrants which deprives them of the basic necessities of life:

> While we fully recognize the value of higher education, we cannot equate its attainment with food, clothing and shelter. Shapiro involved the immediate and pressing need for preservation of life and health of persons unable to live without public assistance, and their dependent children. Thus, the residence requirements in Shapiro could cause great suffering and even loss of life. The durational residence requirement for attendance at publicly financed institutions of higher learning

do not involve similar risks. Nor was petitioner (unlike the families in Shapiro) precluded from the benefit of obtaining higher education. 78 Cal.Rptr. at 266–7

Accord, Starns v. Malkerson, 326 F.Supp. 234 (D.Minn.1970), aff'd per curiam, 401 U.S. 985 (1971).

Problems

1. Under New York's medical assistance (Medicaid) program, benefits are paid only to a person who

"is a resident of the State, or while temporarily in the State, requires immediate medical care which is not otherwise available, provided that such person did not enter the State for the purpose of obtaining such medical care * * * " N.Y.Soc.Serv.L. § 366–1 (b).

Can the final cause in this statute stand after *Shapiro*, Gaddis v. Wyman and Wyman v. Lopez (discussed in the preceding note)?

2. To what extent does *Shapiro* limit the imposition of even a simple, nondurational, residency requirement? For example, does the *Shapiro* principle require that aid be given to migrant workers while they are in a state even though it is clear that they are not "residents" and do not intend to remain?

3. The newly enacted SSI program raises a number of troublesome residency problems. Section 1611(f), 42 U.S.C.A. § 1382, terminates payments to a recipient who is outside the United States for a full month. Section 1616(c)(1), 42 U.S.C.A. § 1382, permits states to impose certain residence requirements as conditions to receipt of state funded supplements to the basic SSI grant. Examine these provisions (set out in full in the appendix). How might either or both be defended against a Shapiro v. Thompson attack?

4. The following is the statement of facts from the Wisconsin Supreme Court opinion in Vanden Broek v. Reitz, 53 Wis.2d 87, 191 N.W.2d 913 (1971), app. dismissed sub nom. Reitz v. Vanden Broek, 406 U.S. 902 (1972):

The petition alleged that Harold and Isabell Reitz, husband and wife, (defendants-appellants) have legal settlement in the petitioning town and therefore if public relief is granted to them it must be paid by the town; that defendants reside in Milwaukee county and first obtained relief from Milwaukee county in October, 1967, and have been dependent persons and on relief since that time pursuant to the provisions of sec. 49.01(4), Stats.; that from October of 1967 to date of petition (July 14, 1970), defendants have received relief from Milwaukee county; that the petitioning town offers and is able to provide employment for defendants in the township so that it will not be necessary for them to be on public relief in Milwaukee county; that petitioner has invited them to return to the town, but they have refused and neglected to come back; that the petitioner is informed that unemployment in Milwaukee county is very high and that there is no immediate or prospective opportunity for defendants to secure employment in Milwaukee county and that petitioner believes that in view of the fact that defendants remain unemployed in Milwaukee county after residing there since February of 1967, and being on relief most of the time, that they should be required to return to their place of legal settlement, i. e., petitioning town; that their return to the township will not substantially reduce the employment and earning opportunities of the defendants, will not materially disrupt family ties, and will not work any material injustice upon them.

Sections 49.01 to 49.17, Stats., constitute a plan for general relief to provide eligible dependent persons with necessary commodities, services and money. As applied to the facts of this case, the plan is financed by the taxpayers of the municipality of the recipient's legal settlement, and is totally distinct from state and federal categorical aid plans such as old-age assistance, aid to the blind, aid to families with dependent children, and aid to totally or partially disabled. Legal settlement is established in a municipality by residing therein for one year without receiving assistance of public or private aid, sec. 49.10. Once legal settlement for relief purposes is established in the particular municipality, it continues until it is lost by residing outside the municipality without support as a dependent person for one year.

Thus, since defendants' legal settlement for general relief purposes has been established in the Town of Vanden Broek, so it continues until they have been absent therefrom for one year without receiving general relief. The Town of Vanden Broek bears the ultimate cost of assistance, notwithstanding that the defendants reside in another municipality or county. Absent a removal proceeding, the municipality of legal settlement may be chargeable for general relief furnished to a recipient residing in another municipality for an indefinite number of years.

This appeal concerns sec. 49.09(1) and (2), Stats., which provide:

"49.09 Removal of dependents. (1) When a dependent person, other than a recipient of old-age assistance, aid to blind, aid to families with dependent children, or aid to totally and permanently disabled persons is receiving relief elsewhere than at his place of settlement and refuses to re- turn thereto, the officer or agency of the place administering relief or of the place of settlement may petition the judge of the county court or the judge of any other court of record of the county in which the relief is furnished for an order directing such person to return to his place of settlement. The petition shall state specifically the reasons upon which the order is sought and copies shall be served upon the dependent person, the officer or agency of the place of residence or the place of legal settlement. Notice of hearing shall be served upon the same parties at least 10 days in advance of the hearing. Service may be made personally or by registered mail with return receipt requested.

"(2) If the judge finds that return to the place of legal settlement does not substantially reduce the employment and earning opportunities of the dependent person, does not materially disrupt family ties, and does not work any material injustice to him, he may order the dependent person to return to his place of settlement. The order of the judge for removal shall specify a time beyond which no further relief shall be granted the dependent person unless he returns to the place of his legal settlement and shall further specify the conditions to be complied with by the petitioning municipality to provide suitable transportation to the place of settlement. The cost of transportation shall be chargeable to the place of legal settlement and may be recovered as any other relief costs, pursuant to section 49.11. * * * ''

Appellants advance three arguments in support of the proposition that the procedure embodied in sec. 49.09(1) and (2), Stats., is unconstitutional: (1) Denial of equal protection, (2) interferes with the right of privacy, and (3) infringes on the right to travel.

What decision is appropriate in the *Reitz* case? Does the decision in Fenster v. Leary which follows these problems suggest any other line of argument which the appellants in *Reitz* might pursue?

FENSTER v. LEARY

New York Court of Appeals, 1967.
20 N.Y.2d 309, 282 N.Y.S.2d 739, 229 N.E.2d 426.

BURKE, J.: On three occasions in late 1964, each about a month apart, the plaintiff, Charles Fenster, was arrested by the New York City police and charged with violation of subdivision 1 of § 887 of the Code of Criminal Procedure (New York's vagrancy statute). Fenster was charged under the language of this section with being "a person who not having visible means to maintain himself, lives without employment." Following each arrest he was acquitted of the violation charged, but conviction on such charges would have subjected him to possible imprisonment for up to six months. (Code of Cr.Proc. § 892.)

The record does not indicate why this plaintiff was singled out for such treatment by the police, especially in the face of previous acquittals, but Fenster, apparently concerned at the likelihood of further arrests on this same charge, sought, following his third arrest, an order in the nature of prohibition against the Criminal Court of the City of New York barring that court from hearing and determining the charge of vagrancy levelled against him following his third arrest. In this action he attacked the constitutionality of the statute, but prohibition was denied in our lower courts, and in this Court the decisions below were affirmed on the sole ground that the remedy of prohibition was discretionary (Matter of Fenster v. Criminal Court of the City of New York, 17 N.Y.2d 641, 269 N.Y.S.2d 139, 216 N.E.2d 342).

After our decision in this earlier action and following his third acquittal on this vagrancy charge, plaintiff applied to a three-judge federal court in the Southern District of New York for a declaration of the statute's unconstitutionality. This was denied on the ground that plaintiff had a state remedy by way of an application to the New York courts for a declaratory judgment (264 F.Supp. 153), and the United States Supreme Court affirmed (see 386 U.S. 10, 87 S.Ct. 862, 17 L.Ed. 2d 701).

Plaintiff next initiated the present action seeking declaratory relief in the Supreme Court, New York County (Lupiano, J.). He is again before this Court on a direct appeal from the judgment of the Supreme Court, at Special Term, denying his motion for summary judgment declaring subdivision 1 of § 887 unconstitutional and dismissing his complaint. He urges that we at last strike down this law.

Plaintiff's appeal is appealable directly to this Court as the sole question raised and decided below and the sole issue on this appeal is the constitutionality of subdivision 1 of our vagrancy statute (see CPLR § 5601(b)(2)) and declaratory relief of the kind here sought is available in our courts under the circumstances here presented (see The Bookcase, Inc. v. Broderick, 18 N.Y.2d 71, 271 N.Y.S.2d 947, 218 N.E.2d 668).

Plaintiff's arguments against the constitutionality of this statute are as follows: 1) It interferes with and impairs the liberty of a citizen to exercise his faculties so long as he does not interfere with others; 2) It requires involuntary servitude in violation of the Thirteenth Amendment; 3) It denies plaintiff the equal protection of the laws; 4) It imposes cruel and unusual punishment on a person because of his status; and 5) It deprives plaintiff of his privileges and immunities guaranteed by the Federal Constitution.

We are in agreement with plaintiff that subdivision 1 of § 887, Code of Criminal Procedure, is unconstitutional, on the ground that it violates due process and constitutes an overreaching of the proper limitations of the police power in that it unreasonably makes criminal and provides punishment for conduct (if we can call *idleness* conduct) of an individual which in no way impinges on the rights or interests of others and which has in no way been demonstrated to have anything more than the most tenuous connection with prevention of crime and preservation of the public order (on which ground the Attorney General would have us sustain the statute), other than, perhaps, as a means of harassing, punishing or apprehending suspected criminals in an unconstitutional fashion. We do not reach any of the other arguments for invalidity urged by plaintiff.

The crime of common law vagrancy, which is what subdivision 1 of our statute involves, contains three elements: 1) being without visible means of support, 2) being without employment, and 3) being able to work but refusing to do so. (See Note, The Vagrancy Concept Reconsidered, 37 N.Y.U.L.Rev. 102, 109.) In a more homely fashion our statute has been described as directed against the "loafer or lazy man, the one who hangs about streets and public places without employment or visible means of support when he could with effort obtain something to do." (People v. Sohn, 269 N.Y. 330, 334–335, 199 N.E. 501, 502.) Such statutes have their origins in feudal laws aimed against runaway serfs and the English poor laws" (see Douglas, Vagrancy and Arrest on Suspicion, 70 Yale L.J. 1; Lacey, Vagrancy and Other Crimes of Personal Condition, 66 Harv.L.Rev. 1203; Note, The Vagrancy Concept Reconsidered, 37 N.Y. U.L.Rev. 102) and were originally designed as a means of regulating the economic life of the populace. The modern emphasis or stated justification for re-

taining such laws has shifted, however, to the prevention or control of crime and common law vagrancy remains a crime in virtually all American jurisdictions. (See, e. g., Lacey, op. cit. supra. Note, The Vagrancy Concept Reconsidered, supra.)
* * *

As a number of commentators have observed, common law vagrancy, in contrast to most other crimes recognized in our law, is not defined in terms of an *act* or *acts* but in terms of a *status* or *condition of being* (see, e. g., Lacey, op. cit. supra, at 1203). The essential element of this crime, as well as of other *status* crimes, is "the accused's having a certain personal condition or being a person of a specified character." (Ibid.) Other crimes of *status* would include "gangster statutes" (such as was involved in Lanzetta v. New Jersey, 306 U.S. 451, 59 S. Ct. 618, 83 L.Ed. 888) or statutes making it criminal to be a narcotics addict (such as was involved in Robinson v. California, 270 U.S. 660, 82 S.Ct. 1417, 8 L.Ed. 758). Under our own § 887, a number of other "personal conditions" are declared to make one a vagrant and thus subject to imprisonment, e. g., that of being a prostitute or panderer (§ 887, subd. 4) or of being a beggar on the public ways (§ 887, subd. 5). Such statutes can not stand if they would make criminal a condition, such as one resulting from illness, over which the accused has no control (Robinson v. California, supra; see, also, People v. Sohn, supra) or if the class of persons coming within their ambit is so vaguely defined as to make it unclear to potential violators just what conduct will subject them to criminal liability and what will not (Lanzetta v. New Jersey, supra). Such constitutional problems would not appear to be directly involved in the instant case, however, as under our *Sohn* decision (supra) it seems clear that physical or even *psychological* inability to work would bar conviction as a vagrant and plaintiff does not appear to attack the statute as void for vagueness (for which reason we need not reach this point). Another constitutional problem, of major proportions does, however, appear in this case, namely, whether our statute constitutes a valid exercise of the police power.

Initially, it must be observed that a strong presumption of validity attaches to statutes and that the burden of proving invalidity is upon those who challenge their constitutionality to establish this beyond a reasonable doubt (see Matter of Van Berkel v. Power, 16 N.Y.2d 37, 40, 261 N.Y.S.2d 876, 209 N.E.2d 539 and the cases cited therein), but it must likewise be noted that a statute whose effect is to curtail the liberty of individuals to live their lives as they would and whose justification is claimed to lie in the exercise of the police power of the state must bear a reasonable relationship to, some proportion to, the alleged public good on account of which this restriction on individual liberty would be justified. As Judge Fuld (as he was then) observed in People v. Bunis (9 N.Y.2d 1, at 4, 210 N.Y.S.2d 505, 172 N.E.2d 273), "The police power is 'very broad and comprehensive' and in its exercise 'the conduct of an individual and the use of property may be regulated so as to interfere, to some extent, with the freedom of the one and the enjoyment of the other', * * *. But, in order for an exercise of the police power to be valid, there must be 'some fair, just and reasonable connection' between it and the promotion of the health, comfort, safety and welfare of society."

The Attorney General of New York, appearing herein pursuant to § 71 of the Executive Law in defense of the statute's constitutionality, cites to us various statements from our own decisions and from the decisions of our lower courts in support of vagrancy statutes as a valid exercise of the police power. The general thrust of these decisions is that in order to prevent their coming into existence a "class of able bodied vagrants * * *

[supporting] themselves by preying on society and thus [threatening] the public peace and security" (People ex rel. Stolofsky v. Superintendent, 259 N.Y. 115, 118, 181 N.E. 68), to "compel individuals to engage in some legitimate and gainful occupation from which they might maintain themselves, and thus remove the temptation to lead a life of crime or become public charges," People v. Banwer, 22 N.Y.S.2d 566 (Mag.Ct.Brooklyn, 1940), the able bodied poor may be made, subject to the sanctions of the criminal law, to accept available employment. This view of the matter does, of course, raise the possibility of interesting Thirteenth Amendment problems, and plaintiff strenuously urges these as grounds for reversal, and it also raises an interesting "equal protection" question as to whether persons of means are entitled any more than the poor to enjoy the allegedly debilitating effects of idleness, but, on a more fundamental level, we feel the statute is defective on the ground that, whatever purpose and role it may or may not have served in an earlier day, and however valid or invalid may be the proposition that the able bodied unemployed poor are a likely source of crime, in this era of widespread efforts to motivate and educate the poor toward economic betterment of themselves, of the "War on Poverty" and all its varied programs, it is obvious to all that the vagrancy laws have been abandoned by our governmental authorities as a means of "persuading" unemployed poor persons to seek work (the Attorney General does not even suggest that the vagrancy laws would be invoked against such people today). It is also obvious that today the only persons arrested and prosecuted as common-law vagrants are alcoholic derelicts and other unfortunates, whose only crime, if any, is against themselves, and whose main offense usually consists in their leaving the environs of skid row and disturbing *by their presence* the sensibilities of residents of nicer parts of the community, or suspected criminals, with respect to whom the authorities do not have enough evidence to make a proper arrest or secure a conviction on the crime suspected. (See Foote, Vagrancy-type Law and its Administration, 104 U. of Pa.L.Rev. 603; Lacey, op. cit. supra, at 1217–1219. See, also, People v. Robinson, 13 N.Y.2d 296, 246 N.Y.S.2d 623.) As to the former, it seems clear that they are more properly objects of the welfare laws and public health programs than of the criminal law and, as to the latter, it should by now be clear to our governmental authorities that the vagrancy laws were never intended to be and may not be used as an administrative short cut to avoid the requirements of constitutional due process in the administration of criminal justice. If it is only to allow arrests and criminal prosecutions for vagrancy to continue against individuals such as these that the Attorney General would have us uphold the statute, then it must fall. And despite certain fairly recent cases upholding similar statutes (see Hicks v. District of Columbia, 197 A.2d 154 [D.C.Ct.App.1963], certiorari dismissed as "improvidently granted", 383 U.S. 252, 86 S.Ct. 798, 15 L.Ed.2d 744 [1966]; Dominguez v. City and County of Denver, 147 Colo. 233, 363 P.2d 661 [Col.Sup.Ct., 1961], we can, in fact, see no other purpose in our statute today and therefore find it invalid.

The judgment below should be reversed and judgment directed for plaintiff as demanded in the complaint.

SCILEPPI, J. (dissenting):

I disagree and would affirm. A strong presumption of validity attaches to a statute and the heavy burden of proving its invalidity rests upon the appellant who is attacking its constitutionality (e. g. New York State Thruway Authority v. Ashley Motor Court, 10 N.Y.2d 151, 218 N.Y. S.2d 640, 176 N.E.2d 566; Matter of Roosevelt Raceway v. Monoghan, 9 N.Y. 2d 293, 213 N.Y.S.2d 729, 174 N.E.2d 71).

In my opinion, the appellant has not discharged his burden.

As Chief Judge Fuld said in People v. Bunis (9 N.Y.2d 1, 210 N.Y.S.2d 505, 172 N.E.2d 273): "the police power is 'very broad and comprehensive' and in its exercise 'the conduct of an individual and the use of property may be regulated so as to interfere, to some extent, with the freedom of the one and the enjoyment of the other' * * *. But, in order for an exercise of the police power to be valid, there must be 'some fair, just and reasonable connection' between it and the promotion of the health, comfort, safety and welfare of society. * * *" (People v. Bunis, supra, at p. 4). There can be no doubt that the State has a legitimate interest in discouraging able bodied men who are capable of working from becoming loafers and public charges (People v. Sohn, 269 N.Y. 330, 199 N.E. 501); Hicks v. District of Columbia, 197 A.2d 154 [D.C.Ct.App.1964]; certiorari dismissed 383 U.S. 252, 86 S.Ct. 798, 15 L.Ed.2d 744). The state has chosen to achieve that end by imposing criminal penalties on those who are vagrants. It is argued that this end might be better achieved through social welfare legislation rather than through criminal sanctions. This may be so, but the relative merit of one approach over another is for the Legislature to decide and not the courts. As long as the exercise of the state's police power bears a reasonable relationship to the ends sought to be accomplished, the constitutionality of the statute must be upheld. We cannot strike down the statute because we feel another approach would be better. In my opinion, the appellant has failed to prove that there is no reasonable relationship between the statute in question and the ends it seeks to accomplish. Accordingly, the statute must stand and the judgment below should be affirmed.

* * *

Judgment reversed, with costs, and judgment directed to be entered for plaintiff as demanded in the complaint. Opinion by Burke, J. All concur except Scileppi, J., who dissents and votes to affirm in a memorandum in which Van Voorhis, J., concurs.

C. RELATIONSHIP BETWEEN FEDERAL ELIGIBILITY AND STATE DISCRETION

Note on Suitable Homes and Kindred Constraints

The "suitable home" and "substitute father" conflicts, reproduced below, are the most widely publicized of state attempts to control the personal behavior of public assistance recipients, and to enforce such control by termination of the grant. Sexual activity and procreation are common targets.

Closely related is the so-called "minor unmarried mother rule" which is in force in a number of states. Pursuant to this rule, a minor unmarried mother is required to live with her parents (the AFDC "child's" grandparents) to be eligible for public assistance. She may be required to do so even though she is judicially emancipated, even though typically, a minor married mother is not required to live with her parents, though deserted by her husband. State regulations may go on to make one of the grandparents the payee of the grant. They may also make eligibility determinations with reference to the extended household which they have created, either by treating the grandparents as the AFDC child's "parent" (and so disqualifying the unmarried mother and her child from AFDC if both "grandparents" are present) or by indulging in questionable assumptions regarding the availability of the grandparents' income.

Some of these related practices may raise litigable issues to the extent they deviate from the construction of "parent" adopted by the Supreme Court in King v. Smith, infra. Also raised is the threshold issue whether the state may legitimately condition the disbursement of assistance benefits upon the mother's residence with her parents. What legitimate state interest is served by the requirement? Is it sufficient to say that minor unmarried mother can be presumed to be in greater need of parental supervision? Can the state offer this justification even though its policy of enforcing parental supervision is limited to public assistance recipients? Even if the end in question is a legitimate one, are the means utilized, termination of public assistance, consistent with the central purpose of the Social Security Act: to relieve need?

Moreover, what of the minor unmarried mother's children? Do they have a basis for complaint wholly apart from their mother's? The notion of "punishing" children for the acts of their parents is hardly one with much moral or juridical appeal. Is this practice properly so characterized, and, if so, can one's objections be translated into some respectable form of constitutional or statutory argument?

These questions as well as a number of related issues stemming from state decisions to curtail relief to accomplish some ulterior purpose are raised by the materials which follow. The subsequent section on Welfare and Employment is closely related.

KING v. SMITH

Supreme Court of the United States, 1968.
392 U.S. 309, 88 S.Ct. 2128, 20 L.Ed.2d 1118.

Mr. Chief Justice WARREN delivered the opinion of the Court.

Alabama, together with every other State, Puerto Rico, the Virgin Islands, the District of Columbia, and Guam, participates in the Federal Government's Aid to Families With Dependent Children Program (AFDC), which was established by the Social Security Act of 1935. 49 Stat. 620 (1935), as amended, 42 U.S.C.A. §§ 301–1394. This appeal presents the question whether a regulation of the Alabama Department of Pensions and Security, employed in that Department's administration of the State's federally funded AFDC program, is consistent with Subchapter IV of the Social Security Act, 42 U.S.C.A. §§ 601–609, and with the Equal Protection Clause of the Fourteenth Amendment. At issue is the validity of Alabama's so-called "substitute father" regulation which denies AFDC payments to the children of a mother who "cohabits" in or outside her home with any single or married able-bodied man. Appellees brought this class action against appellants, officers, and members of the Alabama Board of Pensions and Security, in the United States District Court for the Middle District of Alabama, under 42 U.S.C.A. § 1983, seeking declaratory and injunctive relief. A properly convened three-judge District Court correctly adjudicated the merits of the controversy without requiring appellees to exhaust state administrative remedies,[4] and found

the regulation to be inconsistent with the Social Security Act and the Equal Protection Clause. We noted probable jurisdiction, 390 U.S. 903, 88 S.Ct. 821, 19 L.Ed.2d 869 (1968), and for reasons which will appear, we affirm without reaching the constitutional issue.

I.

The AFDC program is one of three major categorical public assistance programs established by the Social Security Act of 1935. See U. S. Advisory Commission Report an Intergovernmental Relations, Statutory and Administrative Control Associated with Federal Grants for Public Assistance 5–7 (1964) (hereafter cited as Advisory Commission Report). The category singled out for welfare assistance by AFDC is the "dependent child," who is defined in § 406 of the Act, 49 Stat. 629 (1935), as amended, 42 U.S.C.A. § 606(a), as an age-qualified "needy child * * * who has been deprived of parental support or care by reason of the death, continued absence from the home or physical or mental incapacity of a parent, and who is living with" any one of several listed relatives. Under this provision, and insofar as relevant here, aid can be granted only if "a parent" of the needy child is continually absent from the home. Alabama considers a man who qualifies as a "substitute father" under its regulation to be a nonabsent parent within the fed-

[4] We reject appellants' argument that appellees were required to exhaust their administrative remedies prior to bringing this action. Pursuant to the requirement of the Social Security Act that States must grant AFDC applicants who are denied aid "an opportunity for a fair hearing before the State agency," 42 U.S.C.A. § 602(a)(4), Alabama provides for administrative review of such denials. Alabama Manual for Administration of Public Assistance, Part I, § II,

Parts V–5 to V–12. Decisions of this Court, however, establish that a plaintiff in an action brought under the Civil Rights Act, 42 U.S.C. § 1983, 28 U.S.C.A. § 1343, is not required to exhaust administrative remedies, where the constitutional challenge is sufficiently substantial, as here, to require the convening of a three-judge court. Damico v. California, 389 U.S. 416, 88 S.Ct. 526, 19 L.Ed.2d 647 (1967). See also McNeese v. Board of Education, 373 U.S. 668, 83 S.Ct. 1433, 10 L.Ed.2d 622 (1963); Monroe v. Pape, 365 U.S. 167, 180–183, 81 S.Ct. 473, 480–482, 5 L.Ed.2d 492 (1961). For a general discussion of review in the federal courts of state welfare practices, see Note, Federal Judicial Review of State Welfare Practices, 67 Col. L.Rev. 84 (1967).

eral statute. The State therefore denies aid to an otherwise eligible needy child on the basis that his substitute parent is not absent from the home.

Under the Alabama regulation, an "able-bodied man, married or single, is considered a substitute father of *all the children of the applicant* * * * mother" in three different situations: (1) if "he lives in the home with the child's natural or adoptive mother for the purpose of cohabitation"; or (2) if "he visits [the home] frequently for the purpose of cohabiting with the child's natural or adoptive mother"; or (3) if "he does not frequent the home but cohabits with the child's natural or adoptive mother elsewhere." Whether the substitute father is actually the father of the children is irrelevant. It is also irrelevant whether he is legally obligated to support the children, and whether he does in fact contribute to their support. What is determinative is simply whether he "cohabits" with the mother.

The testimony below by officials responsible for the administration of Alabama's AFDC program establishes that "cohabitation," as used in the regulation, means essentially that the man and woman have "frequent" or "continuing" sexual relations. With regard to how frequent or continual these relations must be, the testimony is conflicting. One state official testified that the regulation applied only if the parties had sex at least once a week; another thought once every three months would suffice; and still another believed once every six months sufficient. The regulation itself provides that pregnancy or a baby under six months of age is prima facie evidence of a substitute father.*

* [Editor's Note] The full text of the Alabama regulation was set out in the District Court opinion:

"V. Child Ineligible If There is a Father or Mother Substitute

"A. *Father Substitute*: An able-bodied man, married or single, is considered a sub-

Between June 1964, when Alabama's substitute father regulation became effective, and January 1967, the total number of AFDC recipients in the State declined by about 20,000 persons, and the

stitute father of *all* the children of the applicant/recipient mother living in her home, whether they are his or not, if: (1) he lives in the home with the child's natural or adoptive mother for the purpose of cohabitation; or (2) though not living in the home regularly, he visits frequently for the purpose of cohabiting with the child's natural or adoptive mother; or (3) he does not frequent the home but cohabits with the child's natural or adoptive mother elsewhere. Pregnancy or a baby six months or under is prima facie evidence of a substitute father as indicated above.

"When there appears to be a substitute father, disapprove an application or terminate aid unless the mother establishes that one of the following situations exists: (1) she and/or the substitute father meets the criteria of disability as described under 'Physical or Mental Incapacity'; (2) the substitute father is no longer living in the home or visiting the home for the purpose of cohabiting with her; or (3) the relationship is broken between the mother and a man who has not been living in the home or frequenting the home.

"Evidence showing that the relationship has been discontinued includes proof such as: the father has married another woman; or he is in a public institution; or, if he has been living in the home, he is now living at another address; or a notarized statement by the mother and substitute father that they have discontinued their relationship. This evidence must be corroborated by at least two acceptable references in a position to know. Examples of acceptable references are: law-enforcement officials; ministers; neighbors; grocers. If needed, the mother will be given 30 days to present her evidence before her application is disapproved or her case closed unless additional time is needed. If additional time is needed, another 30 days may be allowed. In no instance shall more than 60 days be allowed. Although the burden of proof rests with the mother, the worker will assist in any way possible to help the mother establish that she has broken a relationship. Also, before rejecting an application or closing a case, the worker will talk with the mother about reasons for the agency's action and about her right to reapply at any time that she does break the relationship. If the family is otherwise eligible, the case should be recertified for aid immediately."

number of children recipients by about 16,000 or 22%. As applied in this case, the regulation has caused the termination of all AFDC payments to the appellees, Mrs. Sylvester Smith and her four minor children.

Mrs. Smith and her four children, ages 14, 12, 11, and 9, reside in Dallas County, Alabama. For several years prior to October 1, 1966, they had received aid under the AFDC program. By notice dated October 11, 1966, they were removed from the list of persons eligible to receive such aid. This action was taken by the Dallas County welfare authorities pursuant to the substitute father regulation, on the ground that a Mr. Williams came to her home on weekends and had sexual relations with her.

Three of Mrs. Smith's children have not received parental support or care from a father since their natural father's death in 1955. The fourth child's father left home in 1963, and the child has not received the support or care of his father since then. All the children live in the home of their mother, and except for the substitute father regulation are eligible for aid. The family is not receiving any other type of public assistance, and has been living, since the termination of AFDC payments, on Mrs. Smith's salary of between $16 and $20 per week which she earns working from 3:30 a. m. to 12 noon as a cook and waitress.

Mr. Williams, the alleged "substitute father" of Mrs. Smith's children, has nine children of his own and lives with his wife and family, all of whom are dependent upon him for support. Mr. Williams is not the father of any of Mrs. Smith's children. He is not legally obligated, under Alabama law, to support any of Mrs. Smith's children.[10] Further, he is

not willing or able to support the Smith children, and does not in fact support them. His wife is required to work to help support the Williams household.

II.

The AFDC program is based on a scheme of cooperative federalism. See generally Advisory Commission Report, supra, at 1–59. It is financed largely by the Federal Government, on a matching fund basis, and is administered by the States. States are not required to participate in the program, but those which desire to take advantage of the substantial federal funds available for distribution to needy children are required to submit an AFDC plan for the approval of the Secretary of Health, Education, and Welfare (HEW). 49 Stat. 627 (1935), 42 U.S.C.A. §§ 601, 602, 603, and 604. See Advisory Commission Report, supra, at 21–23. The plan must conform with several requirements of the Social Security Act and with rules and regulations promulgated by HEW. 49 Stat. 627 (1935) as amended, 42 U.S.

---

10 Under Alabama statutes, a legal duty of support is imposed only upon a "parent," who is defined as (1) a "natural legal parent," (2) one who has "legally acquired the custody of" the child, and (3) "the father of

such child, * * * though born out of lawful wedlock." 34 Ala.Code §§ 89, 90; 27 Ala.Code §§ 12(1), 12(4). Law v. State, 238 Ala. 428, 191 So. 803 (1939). The Alabama Courts have interpreted the statute to impose a legal duty of support upon one who has "publicly acknowledged or treated the child as his own, in a manner to indicate his voluntary assumption of parenthood" irrespective of whether the alleged parent is in fact the child's real father. Law v. State, 238 Ala. 428, 191 So. 803 (1939). It seems clear, however, that even a stepfather who is not the child's natural parent and has not acquired legal custody of him is under an obligation of support only if he has made this "voluntary assumption of parenthood." See Chandler v. Whatley, 238 Ala. 206, 189 So. 751 (1939); Englehardt v. Yung's Heirs, 76 Ala. 534, 540 (1884); Nicholas v. State, 32 Ala.App. 574, 28 So.2d 422 (1946). Further, the Alabama Supreme Court has emphasized that the alleged father's intention to support the child, requisite to a finding of voluntary assumption of parenthood, "should not be slightly nor hastily inferred * * *." Englehardt v. Yung's Heirs, 76 Ala. 534, 540 (1884).

C.A. § 602. See also, HEW, Handbook of Public Assistance Administration, Pt. IV, §§ 2200, 2300 (1967) (hereafter cited, as Handbook).

One of the statutory requirements is that "aid to families with dependent children shall be furnished with reasonable promptness to all eligible individuals * * *." 64 Stat. 550 (1950), 42 U.S. C.A. § 602(a)(9) [now § 602(a)(10)]. As noted above, § 406(a) of the Act defines a "dependent child" as one who has been deprived of "parental" support or care by reason of the death, continued absence or incapacity of a "parent." 42 U.S.C.A. § 606(a). In combination, these two provisions of the Act clearly require participating States to furnish aid to families with children who have a parent absent from the home, if such families are in other respects eligible. See also Handbook, Pt. IV, § 2200(b)(4).

The State argues that its substitute father regulation simply defines who is a nonabsent "parent" under § 406(a) of the Social Security Act. 42 U.S.C.A. § 606(a). The State submits that the regulation is a legitimate way of allocating its limited resources available for AFDC assistance, in that it reduces the caseload of its social workers and provides increased benefits to those still eligible for assistance. Two State interest are asserted in support of the allocation of AFDC assistance achieved by the regulation: first, it discourages illicit sexual relationships and illegitimate births; second, it put families in which there is an informal "marital" relationship on a par with those in which there is an ordinary marital relationship, because families of the latter sort are not eligible for AFDC assistance.[13]

13 Commencing in 1961, federal matching funds have been made available under the AFDC subchapter of the Social Security Act for a State which grants assistance to needy children who have two able-bodied parents living in the home, but who have been "deprived of parental support or care by reason

We think it well to note at the outset what is *not* involved in this case. There is no question that States have considerable latitude in allocating their AFDC resources, since each State is free to set its own standard of need [14] and to determine the level of benefits by the amount of funds it devotes to the program. See Advisory Commission Report, supra, at 30–59. Further, there is no question that regular and actual contributions to a needy child, including contributions from the kind of person Alabama calls a substitute father, can be taken into account in determining whether the child is needy.[16] In other words, if by reason of

of the unemployment * * * of a parent." 42 U.S.C.A. § 607. Participation in this program for aid to dependent children of unemployed parents is not obligatory on the States, and the Court has been advised that only 21 States participate. Alabama does not participate.

14 HEW's Handbook, in Pt. IV, § 3120, provides that: "A needy individual * * * [under AFDC] is one who does not have income and resources sufficient to assure economic security, *the standard of which must be defined by each State.* The act recognizes that *the standard so defined depends upon the conditions existing in each State.*" (Emphasis added.) The legislative history of the Act also makes clear that the States have power to determine who is "needy" for purposes of AFDC. Thus the Reports of the House Ways and Means Committee and Senate Finance Committee make clear that the States are free to impose eligibility requirements as to "means." H.R.Rep.No.615, 74th Cong., 1st Sess. 24 (1935); S.Rep.No.628, 74th Cong., 1st Sess., 36 (1935). The floor debates corroborate that this was Congress' intent. For example, Representative Vinson explained that "need is to be determined under the State law." 79 Cong.Rec. 5471 (1935).

16 Indeed, the Act requires that in determining need the state agency "shall * * * take into consideration any other income and resources of any other child or relative claiming aid to families with dependent children * * *." 42 U.S.C.A. § 602(a)(7). Regulations of HEW, which clearly comport with the statute, restrict the resources which are to be taken into account under § 602 to those "that are, in fact, available to an applicant or recipient for current use on a regular basis. * * *" This regulation properly excludes from consideration resources which

such a man's contribution, the child is not in financial need, the child would be ineligible for AFDC assistance without regard to the substitute father rule. The appellees here, however, meet Alabama's need requirements; their alleged substitute father makes no contribution to their support; and they have been denied assistance solely on the basis of the substitute father regulation. Further, the regulation itself is unrelated to need, because the actual financial situation of the family is irrelevant in determining the existence of a substitute father.

Also not involved in this case is the question of Alabama's general power to deal with conduct it regards as immoral and with the problem of illegitimacy. This appeal raises only the question whether the State may deal with these problems in the manner that it has here by flatly denying AFDC assistance to otherwise eligible dependent children.

Alabama's argument based on its interests in discouraging immorality and illegitimacy would have been quite relevant at one time in the history of the AFDC program. However, subsequent developments clearly establish that these state interests are not presently legitimate justifications for AFDC disqualification. Insofar as this or any similar regulation is based on the State's asserted interests in discouraging illicit sexual behavior and illegitimacy, it plainly conflicts with federal law and policy.

A significant characteristic of public welfare programs during the last half of the 19th century in this country was their preference for the "worthy" poor. Some poor persons were thought worthy of public assistance, and others were thought unworthy because of their supposed incapacity for "moral regeneration." Leyendecker, Problems and Policy in Public

Assistance, at 45–57 (1955); Wedemeyer and Moore, The American Welfare System, 54 Calif.L.Rev. 326, 327–328 (1966). This worthy person concept characterized the mothers' pension welfare programs, which were the precursors of AFDC. See Bell, Aid to Dependent Children, at 3–19 (1965). Benefits under the mothers' pension programs, accordingly, were customarily restricted to widows who were considered morally fit. See Bell, supra, at 7; Leyendecker, supra, at 53.

In this social context it is not surprising that both the House and Senate Committee Reports on the Social Security Act of 1935 indicate that States participating in AFDC were free to impose eligibility requirements relating to the "moral character" of applicants. H.R.Rep.No.615, 74th Cong., 1st Sess., 24 (1935); S.Rep. No.628, 74th Cong., 1st Sess., 36 (1935). See also 79 Cong.Rec. 5679 (statement by Representative Jenkins) (1935). During the following years, many state AFDC plans included provisions making ineligible for assistance dependent children not living in "suitable homes." See Bell, supra, at 29–136 (1965). As applied, these suitable home provisions frequently disqualified children on the basis of the alleged immoral behavior of their mothers. Ibid.

In the 1940's, suitable home provisions came under increasing attack. Critics argued, for example, that such disqualification provisions undermined the mother's confidence and authority, thereby promoting continued dependency; that they forced destitute mothers into increased immorality as a means of earning money; that they were habitually used to disguise systematic racial discrimination; and that they senselessly punished impoverished children on the basis of their mothers' behavior, while inconsistently permitting them to remain in the alleged unsuitable homes. In 1945, the

are merely assumed to be available to the needy individual. Handbook, Pt. IV, § 3131 (7). See also §§ 3120, 3123, 3124, 3131(10), and 3131(11).

predecessor of HEW produced a state letter arguing against suitable home provisions and recommending their abolition. See Bell, supra, at 51. Although 15 States abolished their provisions during the following decade, numerous other States retained them. Ibid.

In the 1950's matters became further complicated by pressures in numerous States to disqualify illegitimate children from AFDC assistance. Attempts were made in at least 18 States to enact laws excluding children on the basis of their own or their siblings' birth status. See Bell, supra, at 72–73. All but three attempts failed to pass the State legislatures, and two of the three successful bills were vetoed by the governors of the States involved. Ibid. In 1960, the federal agency strongly disapproved of illegitimacy disqualifications. See Bell, supra, at 73–74.

Nonetheless, in 1960, Louisiana enacted legislation requiring, as a condition precedent for AFDC eligibility, that the home of a dependent child be "suitable," and specifying that any home in which an illegitimate child had been born subsequent to the receipt of public assistance would be considered unsuitable. Louisiana Acts, No. 251 (1960). In the summer of 1960, approximately 23,000 children were dropped from Louisiana's AFDC rolls. Bell, supra, at 137. In disapproving this legislation, then Secretary of Health, Education, and Welfare Flemming issued what is now known as the Flemming Ruling, stating that as of July 1, 1961.

*"a state plan * * * may not impose an eligibility condition that would deny assistance with respect to a needy child on the basis that the home conditions in which the child lives are unsuitable, while the child continues to reside in the home. Assistance will therefore be continued during the time efforts are being made either to im-*

prove the home conditions or to make arrangements for the child elsewhere."

Congress quickly approved the Flemming Ruling, while extending until September 1, 1962, the time for state compliance. 75 Stat. 77 (1961), as amended, 42 U. S.C.A. § 604(b). At the same time, Congress acted to implement the ruling by providing, on a temporary basis, that dependent children could receive AFDC assistance if they were placed in foster homes after a court determination that their former homes were, as the Senate Report stated, "unsuitable because of the immoral or negligent behavior of the parent." S.Rep.No.165, 87th Cong., 1st Sess., 6 (1961), U.S.Code Cong. & Admin.News 1961, p. 1721. See 75 Stat. 76 (1961), as amended, 42 U.S.C.A. § 608.

In 1962, Congress made permanent the provision for AFDC assistance to children placed in foster homes and intended such coverage to include children placed in child-care institutions. 76 Stat. 180, 185, 193, 196, 207 (1962), 42 U.S.C.A. § 608. See S.Rep.No.1589, 87th Cong., 2d Sess., 13 (1962), U.S.Code Cong. & Admin.News, p. 1943. At the same time, Congress modified the Flemming Ruling by amending § 404(b) of the Act. As amended, the statute permits States to disqualify from AFDC aid children who live in unsuitable homes, provided they are granted other "adequate care and assistance." 76 Stat. 189, 42 U.S. C.A. § 604(b) (1962). See S.Rep.No. 1589, 87th Cong., 2d Sess., 14 (1962), U.S.Code Cong. & Admin.News, p. 1943.

Thus, under the 1961 and 1962 amendments to the Social Security Act, the States are permitted to remove a child from a home that is judicially determined to be so unsuitable as to "be contrary to the welfare of such child." 42 U.S.C.A. § 608(a)(1). The States are also permitted to terminate AFDC assistance to a child living in an unsuitable home, if they provide other adequate care and assistance for the child under a general welfare program. 42 U.S.C.A. § 604(b). See S.Rep.No.1589, 87th Cong., 2d Sess., 14 (1962). The statutory approval of the Flemming Ruling, however, precludes the States from otherwise denying AFDC assistance to dependent children on the basis of their mother's alleged immorality or to discourage illegitimate births.

The most recent congressional amendments to the Social Security Act further corroborate that federal public welfare policy now rests on a basis considerably more sophisticated and enlightened than the "worthy person" concept of earlier times. State plans are now required to provide for a rehabilitative program of improving and correcting unsuitable homes, 42 U.S.C.A. § 602(a), as amended, § 201(a)(1)(B)(14), 81 Stat. 877 (1968); 42 U.S.C.A. § 606, as amended, § 201(f), 81 Stat. 880 (1968); to provide voluntary family planning services for the purpose of reducing illegitimate births, 42 U.S.C.A. § 602(a), as amended, § 201(a)(1)(C)(15), 81 Stat. 878 (1968); and to provide a program for establishing the paternity of illegitimate children and securing support for them, 42 U.S.C.A. § 602(a), as amended, § 201 (a)(1)(C)(17), 81 Stat. 878 (1968).

In sum, Congress has determined that immorality and illegitimacy should be dealt with through rehabilitative measures rather than measures that punish dependent children, and that protection of such children is the paramount goal of AFDC. In light of the Flemming Ruling and the 1961, 1962, and 1968 amendments to the Social Security Act, it is simply inconceivable, as HEW has recognized,[23] that Ala-

bama is free to discourage immorality and illegitimacy by the device of absolute disqualification of needy children. Alabama may deal with these problems by several different methods under the Social Security Act. But the method it has chosen plainly conflicts with the Act.

III.

Alabama's second justification for its substitute father regulation is that "there is a public interest in a State not undertaking the payment of these funds to families who because of their living arrangements would be in the same situation as if the parents were married, except for the marriage." In other words, the State argues that since in Alabama the needy children of married couples are not eligible for AFDC aid so long as their father is in the home, it is only fair that children of a mother who cohabits with a

---

[23] Both before and after the Flemming Ruling, the Alabama and federal authorities corresponded with considerable frequency concerning the State's suitable home and substitute father policies. In April 1959, HEW by letter stated that "suitable home" legislation then being proposed by Alabama raised substantial questions of conformity with the Social Security Act, because it seemed to deprive children of AFDC assistance on the basis of illegitimate births in the family. In May 1959 and again in August 1959 new suitable home policies were submitted and were rejected by HEW. Negotiations continued, and in June 1961, HEW responded that the newest legislative proposal was inconsistent with Congress' statutory approval of the Flemming Ruling because (1) assistance would be denied to children on the basis that their homes were unsuitable but they would be permitted to remain in the homes; and (2) a home could be found unsuitable simply on the basis of the child's birth status. Still later, on June 12, 1963, HEW rejected another Alabama suitable home provision on the ground that it provided for denial of AFDC assistance while the child remained in the home without providing for other "adequate care and assistance," as required by the 1962 amendment to the Federal Act. The evidence below establishes that soon after appellant King's appointment as Commissioner, he undertook a study that led to the adoption of the substitute father regulation. When this regulation was submitted to HEW, it responded that the regulation did not conform with 42 U.S.C.A. § 604(b) for the same reasons as its predecessor legislative proposals. Additional correspondence ensued, but HEW never approved the regulation.

man not her husband and not their father be treated similarly. The difficulty with this argument is that it fails to take account of the circumstance that children of fathers living in the home are in a very different position from children of mothers who cohabit with men not their fathers: the child's father has a legal duty to support him, while the unrelated substitute father, at least in Alabama, does not. We believe Congress intended the term "parent" in § 406(a) of the Act, 42 U.S.C.A. § 606(a), to include only those persons with a legal duty of support.

The Social Security Act of 1935 was part of a broad legislative program to counteract the depression. Congress was deeply concerned with the dire straits in which all needy children in the Nation then found themselves. In agreement with the President's Commission on Economic Security, the House Committee Report declared, "the core of any social plan must be the child." H.R.Rep.No.615, 74th Cong., 1st Sess., 10 (1935). The AFDC program, however, was not designed to aid all needy children. The plight of most children was caused simply by the unemployment of their fathers. With respect to these children, Congress planned that "the work relief program and * * * the revival of private industry" would provide employment for their fathers. S.Rep.No.628, 74th Cong., 1st Sess., 17 (1935). As the Senate Committee Report stated: "Many of the children included in relief families present no other problem than that of providing work for the breadwinner of the family." Ibid. Implicit in this statement is the assumption that children would in fact be supported by the family "breadwinner."

The AFDC program was designed to meet a need unmet by programs providing employment for breadwinners. It was designed to protect what the House Report characterized as "one clearly distinguishable group of children." H.R.

Rep.No.615, 74th Cong., 1st Sess., 10 (1935). This group was comprised of children in families without a "breadwinner," "wage earner," or "father," as the repeated use of these terms throughout the Report of the President's Commission, Committee Hearings and Reports and the floor debates makes perfectly clear. To describe the sort of breadwinner that it had in mind, Congress employed the word "parent." 49 Stat. 629 (1939), as amended, 42 U.S.C.A. § 606 (a). A child would be eligible for assistance if his parent was deceased, incapacitated or continually absent.

The question for decision here is whether Congress could have intended that a man was to be regarded as a child's parent so as to deprive the child of AFDC eligibility despite the circumstances: (1) that the man did not in fact support the child; and (2) that he was not legally obligated to support the child. The State correctly observes that the fact that the man in question does not actually support the child cannot be determinative, because a natural father at home may fail actually to support his child but his presence will still render the child ineligible for assistance. On the question whether the man must be legally obligated to provide support before he can be regarded as the child's parent, the State has no such cogent answer. We think the answer is quite clear: Congress must have meant by the term "parent" an individual who owed to the child a state-imposed legal duty of support.

It is clear, as we have noted, that Congress expected "breadwinners" who secured employment would support their children. This congressional expectation is most reasonably explained on the basis that the kind of breadwinner Congress had in mind was one who was legally obligated to support his children. We think it beyond reason to believe that Congress would have considered that providing employment for the paramour of a deserted mother would benefit the mother's children whom he was not obligated to support.

By a parity of reasoning, we think that Congress must have intended that the children in such a situation remain eligible for AFDC assistance notwithstanding their mother's impropriety. AFDC was intended to provide economic security for children whom Congress could not reasonably expect would be provided for by simply securing employment for family breadwinners. We think it apparent that neither Congress nor any reasonable person would believe that providing employment for some man who is under no legal duty to support a child would in any way provide meaningful economic security for that child.

A contrary view would require us to assume that Congress, at the same time that it intended to provide programs for the economic security and protection of *all* children, also intended arbitrarily to leave one class of destitute children entirely without meaningful protection. Children who are told, as Alabama has told these appellees, to look for their food to a man who is not in the least obliged to support them are without meaningful protection. Such an interpretation of congressional intent would be most unreasonable, and we decline to adopt it.

Our interpretation of the term "parent" in § 406(a) is strongly supported by the way the term is used in other sections of the Act. Section 402(a)(10) requires that, effective July 1, 1952, a state plan must:

"provide for prompt notice to appropriate law-enforcement officials of the furnishing of aid to families with dependent children in respect of a child who has been deserted or abandoned by a *parent.*" 64 Stat. 550 (1950), 42 U.S.C.A. § 602(a)(10). (Emphasis added.)

The "parent" whom this provision requires to be reported to law enforcement officials is surely the same "parent" whose desertion makes a child eligible for AFDC assistance in the first place. And Congress obviously did not intend that a so-called "parent" who has no legal duties of support be referred to law enforcement officials (as Alabama's own welfare regulations recognize for the very purpose of such referrals is to institute non-support proceedings. See Handbook, Pt. IV, §§ 8100, 8149. Whatever doubt there might have been over this proposition has been completely dispelled by the 1968 amendments to the Social Security Act, which provide that the States must develop a program:

"(i) in the case of a child born out of wedlock who is receiving aid to families with dependent children, to establish the *paternity of such child and secure support for him,* and

"(ii) in the case of any child receiving such aid who has been deserted or abandoned *by his parent, to secure support for such child from such parent (or from any other person legally liable for such support)* * * *.*" 42 U.S.C.A. § 602(a), as amended, § 201(a)(1)(C)(17), 81 Stat. 878 (1968). (Emphasis added.)

Another provision in the 1968 amendments requires the States, effective January 1, 1969, to report to HEW any *"parent * * * against whom an order for the support and maintenance* of such [dependent] child or children has been issued by" a court, if such parent is not making the required support payments. 42 U.S.C.A. § 602(a), as amended, § 211(a)(21), 81 Stat. 896 (1968). (Emphasis added.) Still another amendment requires the States to cooperate with HEW in locating any *parent* against whom a support petition has been filed in another State, and in securing compliance with any support order issued by another State, 42 U.S.C.A. § 602(a), as amended, § 211(a)(22), 81 Stat. 897 (1968).

The pattern of this legislation could not be clearer. Every effort is to be made to locate and secure support payments from persons legally obligated to support a deserted child. The underlying policy and consistency in statutory interpretation dictate that the "parent" referred to in these statutory provisions is the same parent as that in § 406(a). The provisions seek to secure parental support in lieu of AFDC support for dependent children. Such parental support can be secured only where the parent is under a state-imposed legal duty to support the child. Children with alleged substitute parents who owe them no duty of support are entirely unprotected by these provisions. We think that these provisions corroborate the intent of Congress that the only kind of "parent," under § 406(a), whose presence in the home would provide adequate economic protection for a dependent child is one who is legally obligated to support him. Consequently, if Alabama believes it necessary that it be able to disqualify a child on the basis of a man who is not under such a duty of support, its arguments should be addressed to Congress and not this Court.

IV.

Alabama's substitute father regulation, as written and as applied in this case, requires the disqualification of otherwise eligible dependent children if their mother "cohabits" with a man who is not obligated by Alabama law to support the children. The regulation is therefore invalid because it defines "parent" in a manner that is inconsistent with § 406(a) of the Social Security Act. 42 U.S.C.A. § 606(a).[34] In denying AFDC assist-

ance to appellees on the basis of this invalid regulation, Alabama has breached its federally imposed obligation to furnish "aid to families with dependent children * * * with reasonable promptness to all eligible individuals * * *." 42 U.S.C.A. § 602(a)(9). Our conclusion makes unnecessary consideration of appellees' equal-protection claim, upon which we intimate no views.

We think it well, in concluding, to emphasize that no legitimate interest of the State of Alabama is defeated by the decision we announce today. The State's interest in discouraging illicit sexual behavior and illegitimacy may be protected by other means, subject to constitutional limitations, including state participation in AFDC rehabilitative programs. Its interest in economically allocating its limited AFDC resources may be protected by its undisputed power to set the level of benefits and the standard of need, and by its taking into account in determining whether a child is needy all actual and regular contributions to his support.

All responsible governmental agencies in the Nation today recognize the enormity and pervasiveness of social ills caused by poverty. The causes of and cures for poverty are currently the subject of much debate. We hold today only that Congress has made at least this one determination: that destitute children who are legally fatherless cannot be flatly denied federally funded assistance on the trans-

---

[34] There is of course no question that the Federal Government, unless barred by some controlling constitutional prohibition, may

impose the terms and conditions upon which its money allotments to the States shall be disbursed, and that any state law or regulation inconsistent with such federal terms and conditions is to that extent invalid. See Ivanhoe Irrigation District v. McCracken, 357 U.S. 275, 295, 78 S.Ct. 1174, 1185, 2 L.Ed. 2d 1313 (1958); State of Oklahoma v. United States Civil Service Commission, 330 U.S. 127, 143, 67 S.Ct. 544, 553, 91 L.Ed. 794 (1947). It is equally clear that to the extent HEW has approved any so-called "man-in-the-house" provision which conflicts with § 406 (a) of the Social Security Act, 42 U.S.C.A. § 606(a), such approval is inconsistent with the controlling federal statute.

parent fiction that they have a substitute father.

Affirmed.

Mr. Justice DOUGLAS (concurring).

The Court follows the statutory route in reaching the result that I reach on constitutional grounds. It is, of course, traditional that our disposition of cases should, if possible, be on statutory rather than constitutional grounds, unless problems of statutory construction are insurmountable. E. g., Harmon v. Brucker, 355 U.S. 579, 581, 78 S.Ct. 433, 434, 2 L.Ed.2d 503.

We do have, however, in this case a long-standing administrative construction that approves state AFDC plans containing a man-in-the-house provision. Certainly that early administrative construction, which so far as I can ascertain has been a consistent one, is entitled to great weight. E. g., Power Reactor Development Co. v. International Union of Electrical, Radio and Machine Workers, 367 U.S. 396, 408, 81 S.Ct. 1529, 1535, 6 L.Ed.2d 924.

The Department of Health, Education, and Welfare balked at the Alabama provision only because it reached all nonmarital sexual relations of the mother, not just nonmarital relations on a regular basis in the mother's house. Since I cannot distinguish between the two categories, I reach the constitutional question.

The Alabama regulation describes three situations in which needy children, otherwise eligible for relief, are to be denied financial assistance. In none of these is the child to blame. The disqualification of the family, and hence the needy child, turns upon the "sin" of the mother.[4]

First, if a man not married to the mother and not the father of the children lives in her home for purposes of cohabitating with her, the children are cast into the outer darkness.

Second, if a man who is not married to the mother and is not the father of the children visits her home for the purpose of cohabitating with her, the needy children meet the same fate.

Third, if a man not married to the mother and not the father of the children cohabits with her outside the home, then the needy children are likewise denied relief. In each of these three situations the needy family is wholly cut off from AFDC assistance without considering whether the mother's paramour is in fact aiding the family, is financially able to do so, or is legally required to do so. Since there is "sin," the paramour's wealth or indigency is irrelevant.

In other words, Alabama regulations are aimed at punishing mothers who have nonmarital sexual relations. The economic need of the children, their age, their other means of support, are all irrelevant. The standard is the so-called immorality of the mother.[5]

The other day in a comparable situation we held that the Equal Protection Clause of the Fourteenth Amendment barred discrimination against illegitimate children. We held that they cannot be denied a cause of action because they were conceived in "sin," that the making of such a disqualification was an invidious discrimination. Levy v. Louisiana, 391 U.S. 68, 88 S.Ct. 1509, 20 L.Ed.2d 436. I would think precisely the same result

---

[4] Whether the mother alone could constitutionally be cut off from assistance because of her "sin" (compare Glona v. American Guarantee & Liability Insurance Co., 391 U.S. 73, 88 S.Ct. 1512, 1515, 20 L.Ed.2d 441) is a question not presented. The aid is to the needy family, and without removing the children from their mother because of her unfitness—action not contemplated here,

as far as the record indicates—there is no existing means by which Alabama can assist the children while ensuring that the mother does not benefit.

[5] This penalizing the children for the sins of their mother is reminiscent of the archaic corruption of the blood, a form of bill of attainder, which I have discussed recently in a different context. George Campbell Painting Corp. v. Reid, 392 U.S. 286, 88 S.Ct. 1978, 20 L.Ed.2d 1094 (dissenting opinion).

should be reached here. I would say that the immorality of the mother has no rational connection with the need of her children under any welfare program.

I would affirm this judgment for the reasons more fully elaborated in the opinion of the three-judge District Court. Smith v. King, 277 F.Supp. 31, 38–40.

APPENDIX

States which, according to HEW, currently have "man-in-the-home" policies in their plans for the Federal-State program of Aid to Families with Dependent Children.

State and effective date of approved State policy.	Status of subsequent revisions submitted for approval and incorporation in the State's plan.
Alabama ....Dec. 1962	Revision dated July 1964 and all subsequent revisions including an Administrative Letter of Nov. 13, 1967, are being held pending approval.
Arizona ....Nov. 1963	Latest revision incorporated May 24, 1967.
Arkansas ....Aug. 1959	
District of Columbia.　　　Jan. 1955	A revision dated 12/27/60 was incorporated into the approved plan on Jan. 13, 1961; however, when the District's plan manual system was revised and resubmitted as the State's plan, in June 1964, the "man-in-the-home" provisions were not accepted and together with subsequent revisions are still pending approval.
Florida ....July 1959	
Georgia ....April 1952	
Indiana	A "man-in-the-home" provision, not previously in the State's plan, was submitted in September 1964, to be effective August 1964, and is still being held pending approval.
Kentucky ....June 1962	Revised State plan pages including these provisions were approved for incorporation in 1964 and 1965.
Louisiana ....Jan. 1, 1961	Revisions submitted in 1962 and 1964 are still being held pending approval.
Michigan ....July 1955	Revisions dated 4/2/63 were approved 6/4/63.

State and effective date of approved State policy.	*Status of subsequent revisions submitted for approval and incorporation in the State's plan.*
Mississippi ....Feb. 1954	Revisions submitted in 1966 and subsequently are being held pending approval.
Missouri ....Oct. 1951	
New Hampshire 1948	
New Mexico ....April 1964	A revised State plan page including this provision was approved for incorporation 6/16/67.
North Carolina ....Sept. 1955	
Oklahoma ....May 1963	A revised State plan page including this provision was approved for incorporation March 1964 and a correction of a clerical error which would have changed the sense of the provision was made and accepted February 1967.
South Carolina ....Oct. 1956	
Tennessee ....June 1955	Three revisions, beginning in 1964, are being held pending approval.
Texas ....Nov. 1959	
Virginia ....July 1956	A revision dated July 1962 is still held pending approval.

Note: Eligibility Regulations of the Department of Health, Education and Welfare

45 C.F.R. § 233.90. (1971)

[The following regulation was promulgated by H.E.W. after King v. Smith.]

PART 233 COVERAGE AND CONDITIONS OF ELIGIBILITY IN FINANCIAL ASSISTANCE PROGRAMS

§ 233.90 Factors specific to AFDC.

(a) *State plan requirement.* A State plan under title IV–A of the Social Security Act must provide that the determination whether a child has been deprived of parental support or care by reason of the death, continued absence from the home, or physical or mental incapacity of a parent, or (if the State plan includes such cases) the unemployment of his father, will be made only in relation to the child's natural or adoptive parent, or in relation to the child's stepparent who is ceremonially married to the child's natural or adoptive parent and is legally obligated to support the child under State law of general applicability which requires stepparents to support stepchildren to the same extent that natural or adoptive parents are required to support their children. Under this requirement, the inclusion in the family, or the presence in the home, of a "substitute parent" or "man-in-the-house" or any individual other than one described in this paragraph is not an acceptable basis for a finding of ineligibility or for assuming the availability of income by the State. In establishing financial eligibility and the amount of the assistance payment, only such net income as is actually available for current use on a regular basis will be considered, and the income only of the parent described in the first sentence of this paragraph will be considered available for children in the household in the absence of proof of actual contributions.

(b) *Condition for plan approval.* A child may not be denied AFDC either initially or subsequently "because of the conditions of the home in which the child resides", or because the home is considered "unsuitable", unless "provision is otherwise made pursuant to a State statute for adequate care and assistance with respect to such child". (Section 404(b) of the Social Security Act.)

(c) *Federal financial participation.* (1) Federal financial participation under title IV–A of the Social Security Act in payments with respect to a "dependent child", as defined in section 406(a) of the Act, is available within the following interpretations:

(i) *Needy child deprived by reason of.* The phrase "needy child * * * deprived * * * by reason of" requires that both need and deprivation of parental support or care exist in the individual case but does not require an affirmative showing that a causal relationship exists in the individual case. The phrase encompasses the situation of any child who is in need and otherwise eligible, and whose parent— father or mother—either has died, has a physical or mental incapacity, or is continually absent from the home. This interpretation is equally applicable whether the parent was the chief breadwinner or devoted himself or herself primarily to the care of the child, and whether or not the parents

were married to each other. The determination whether a child has been deprived of parental support or care is made in relation to the child's natural parent or, as appropriate, the adoptive parent or steppparent described in paragraph (a) of this section.

(ii) *Death of a parent.* If either parent of a child is deceased, the child is deprived of parental support or care, and may, if he is in need and otherwise eligible, be included within the scope of the program.

(iii) *Continued absence of the parent from the home.* Continued absence of the parent from the home constitutes the reason for deprivation of parental support or care when the parent is out of the home, the nature of the absence is such as either to interrupt or to terminate the parent's functioning as a provider of maintenance, physical care, or guidance for the child, and the known or indefinite duration of the absence precludes counting on the parent's performance of his function in planning for the present support or care of the child. If these conditions exist, the parent may be absent for any reason, and he may have left only recently or some time previously.

(iv) *"Physical or mental incapacity".* "Physical or mental incapacity" of a parent may be deemed to exist when one parent has a physical or mental defect, illness, or disability, whatever its cause, degree, or duration, or accompanying factors.

(v) *"Living with [a specified relative] in a place of residence maintained * * * as his * * * own home".* (*a*) A child may be considered to meet the requirement of living with one of the relatives specified in the Act if his home is with a parent or a person in one of the following groups:

(1) Any blood relative, including those of half-blood, and including first cousins, nephews, or nieces, and persons of preceding generations as denoted by prefixes of grand, great, or great-great:

(2) Stepfather, stepmother, stepbrother, and stepsister.

(3) Persons who legally adopt a child or his parent as well as the natural and other legally adopted children of such persons, and other relatives of the adoptive parents in accordance with State law.

(4) Spouses of any persons named in the above groups even after the marriage is terminated by death or divorce.

(b) A home is the family setting maintained or in process of being established, as evidenced by assumption and continuation of responsibility for day to day care of the child by the relative with whom the child is living. A home exists so long as the relative exercises responsibility for the care and control of the child, even though either the child or the relative is temporarily absent from the customary family setting. Within this interpretation, the child is considered to be "living with" his relative even though

(1) He is under the jurisdiction of the court (e. g., receiving probation services or protective supervision); or

(2) Legal custody is held by an agency that does not have physical possession of the child.

(vi) *"Regularly attending a school, college, or university, or regularly attending a course of vocational or technical training designed to fit him for gainful employment."* A child may be considered in regular attendance at school or a training course in months in which he is not attending because of official school or training program vacation, illness, convalescence, or family emergency, and for the month in which he completes or discontinues his school or training program.

(2) Federal financial participation is available in:

(i) Initial payments made on behalf of a child who goes to live with a relative specified in section 406(a) (1) of the Social Security Act within 30 days of the receipt of the first payment, provided payments are not made for a concurrent period for the same child in the home of another relative or as AFDC–FC;

(ii) Payments with respect to an unborn child when the fact of pregnancy has been determined by medical diagnosis;

(iii) Payments made for the entire month in the course of which a child leaves the home of a specified relative, provided payments are not made for a concurrent period for the same child in the home of another relative or as AFDC–FC; and

(iv) Payments made to persons acting for relatives specified in section 406(a) (1) of the Act in emergency situations that deprive the child of the care of the relative through whom he has been receiving aid, for a temporary period necessary to make and carry out plans for the child's continuing care and support.

(3) Federal financial participation (at the 50 percent rate) is available in any expenses incurred in establishing eligibility for AFDC, including expenses incident to obtaining necessary information to determine the existence of incapacity of a parent or pregnancy of a mother.

Note on Constitutional Status of Substitute Parent and Related Rules

The three-judge district court in King v. Smith, sub nom. Smith v. King, 277 F.Supp. 31 (M.D.Ala.1967) had struck down the Alabama substitute father rule on equal protection grounds rather than the statutory grounds relied upon by the Supreme Court:

"This Court concludes that the Alabama 'substitute father' regulation is an arbitrary and discriminatory classification which results in the denial of financial benefits to needy children who are clearly eligible and entitled to receive such benefits under both the federal and State statutes and constitutional regulations and that said children are denied for reasons unrelated to and in conflict with the purposes of these statutes. For this reason, on its face and as the evidence reflects it has been applied in this case, the Alabama 'substitute father' regulation deprives those children of the equal protection of the laws in violation of the Fourteenth Amendment to the Constitution of the United States."

What is the status of this equal protection approach after Dandridge v. Williams, Section 2B, supra?

King v. Smith does not present the only context in which the Fourteenth Amendment has been raised as a possible barrier against state laws bearing on private familial activity. For example, in Griswold v. Connecticut, 381 U.S. 479, 85 S.Ct. 1678, 14 L.Ed.2d 510 (1965), a state law barring use of contraceptives was struck down on the ground that it violated a concept of family privacy protected by various constitutional provisions incorporated in the Fourteenth Amendment. Most recently, this right of privacy has been extended in Roe v. Wade, —— U.S. ——, 93 S.Ct. 705, 35 L. Ed.2d 147 (1973), to limit state anti-abortion statutes. Mr. Justice Blackmun, writing for the Court in Roe, explained the right in the following terms.

The Constitution does not explicitly mention any right of privacy. In a line of decisions, however, going back perhaps as far as Union Pacific R. Co. v. Botsford, 141 U.S. 250, 251 (1891), the Court has recognized that a right of personal privacy, or a guarantee of certain areas or zones of privacy, does exist under the Constitution. In varying contexts the Court or individual Justices have indeed found at least the roots of that right in the First Amendment, Stanley v. Georgia 394 U.S. 557, 564 (1969); in the Fourth and Fifth Amendments, Terry v. Ohio, 392 U.S. 1, 8–9 (1968), Katz v. United States, 389 U.S. 347, 350 (1967), Boyd v. United States, 116 U.S. 616 (1886), see Olmstead v. United States, 277 U. S. 438, 478 (1928) (Brandeis, J. dissenting); in the penumbras of the Bill of Rights, Griswold v. Connecticut, 381 U.S. 479, 484–485 (1965); in the Ninth Amendment, id., at 486 (Goldberg, J., concurring); or in the concept of liberty guaranteed by the first section of the Fourteenth Amendment, see Meyer v. Nebraska, 262 U.S. 390, 399 (1923). These decisions make it clear that only personal rights that can be deemed "fundamental" or "implicit in the concept of ordered liberty," Palko v. Connecticut, 302 U.S. 319, 325 (1937), are included in this guarantee of personal privacy. They also make it clear that the right has some extension to activities relating to marriage, Loving v. Virginia, 388 U.S. 1, 12 (1967), procreation, Skinner v. Oklahoma, 316 U.S. 535, 541–542 (1942), contraception, Eisenstadt v. Baird, 405 U.S. 438, 453–454 (1972); id., at 460, 463–465 (WHITE, J., concurring), family relationships, Prince v. Massachusetts, 321 U.S. 158, 166 (1944), and child rearing and education, Pierce v. Society of Sisters, 268 U.S. 510, 535 (1925), Meyer v. Nebraska, supra.

This right of privacy, whether it be founded in the Fourteenth Amendment's concept of personal liberty and restrictions upon state action, as we feel it is, or, as the District Court determined, in the Ninth Amendment's reservation of rights to the people, is broad enough to encompass a woman's decision whether or not to terminate her pregnancy. The detriment that the State would impose upon the pregnant woman by denying this choice altogether is apparent. Specific and direct harm medically diagnosable even in early pregnancy may be involved. Maternity, or additional offspring, may force upon the woman a distressful life and future. Psychological harm may be imminent. Mental and physical health may be taxed by child care. There is also the distress, for all concerned, associated with the unwanted child, and there is the problem of bringing a child into a family already unable, psychologically and otherwise, to care for it. In other cases, as in this one, the additional difficulties and continuing stigma of unwed motherhood may be involved. All these are factors the woman and her responsible physician necessarily will consider in consultation.

On the basis of elements such as these, appellants and some *amici* argue that the woman's right is absolute and that she is entitled to terminate her pregnancy at whatever time, in whatever way, and for whatever reason she alone chooses. With this we do not agree. Appellants' arguments that Texas either has no valid interest at all in regulating the abortion decision, or no interest strong enough to support any limitation upon the woman's sole determination is unpersuasive. The

Court's decisions recognizing a right of privacy also acknowledge that some state regulation in areas protected by that right is appropriate. As noted above, a state may properly assert important interests in safeguarding health, in maintaining medical standards, and in protecting potential life. At some point in pregnancy, these respective interests become sufficiently compelling to sustain regulation of the factors that govern the abortion decision. The privacy right involved, therefore, cannot be said to be absolute. In fact, it is not clear to us that the claim asserted by some *amici* that one has an unlimited right to do with one's body as one pleases bears a close relationship to the right of privacy previously articulated in the Court's decisions. The Court has refused to recognize an unlimited right of this kind in the past. Jacobson v. Massachusetts, 197 U.S. 11 (1905) (vaccination); Buck v. Bell, 274 U.S. 200 (1927) (sterilization).

We therefore conclude that the right of personal privacy includes the abortion decision, but that this right is not unqualified and must be considered against important state interests in regulation.

* * *

Where certain "fundamental rights" are involved, the Court has held that regulation limiting these rights may be justified only by a "compelling state interest," Kramer v. Union Free School District, 395 U.S. 621, 627 (1969); Shapiro v. Thompson, 394 U.S. 618, 634 (1969), Sherbert v. Verner, 374 U.S. 398, 406 (1963), and that legislative enactments must be narrowly drawn to express only the legitimate state interests at stake. Griswold v. Connecticut, 381 U.S. 479, 485 (1965); Aptheker v. Secretary of State, 378 U.S. 500, 508 (1964);

Cantwell v. Connecticut, 310 U.S. 296, 307–308 (1940); see Eisenstadt v. Baird, 405 U.S. 438, 460, 463–464 (1972) (WHITE, J., concurring).

In the recent abortion cases, cited above, courts have recognized these principles. Those striking down state laws have generally scrutinized the State's interest in protecting health and potential life and have concluded that neither interest justified broad limitations on the reasons for which a physician and his pregnant patient might decide that she should have an abortion in the early stages of pregnancy. Courts sustaining state laws have held that the State's determinations to protect health or prenatal life are dominant and constitutionally justifiable.

* * *

In view of all this, we do not agree that, by adopting one theory of life, Texas may override the rights of the pregnant woman that are at stake. We repeat, however, that the State does have an important and legitimate interest in preserving and protecting the health of the pregnant woman, whether she be a resident of the State or a nonresident who seeks medical consultation and treatment there, and that it has still *another* important and legitimate interest in protecting the potentiality of human life. These interests are separate and distinct. Each grows in substantiality as the woman approaches term and, at a point during pregnancy, each becomes "compelling."

With respect to the State's important and legitimate interest in the health of the mother, the "compelling" point, in the light of present medical knowledge, is at approximately the end of the first trimester. This is so because of the now established medical fact, referred to above at p. 34, that until the end of the first trimester mortality in abortion is less than mortality in normal childbirth. It follows that, from and after this point, a State may regulate the abortion procedure to the extent that the regulation reasonably relates to the preservation and protection of maternal health. Examples of permissible state regulation in this area are requirements as to the qualifications of the person who is to perform the abortion; as to the licensure of that person; as to the facility in which the procedure is to be performed, that is, whether it must be a hospital or may be a clinic or some other place of less-than-hospital status; as to the licensing of the facility; and the like.

This means, on the other hand, that, for the period of pregnancy prior to this "compelling" point, the attending physician, in consultation with his patient, is free to determine, without regulation by the State, that in his medical judgment the patient's pregnancy should be terminated. If that decision is reached, the judgment may be effectuated by an abortion free of interference by the State.

With respect to the State's important and legitimate interest in potential life, the "compelling" point is at viability. This is so because the fetus then presumably has the capability of meaningful life outside the mother's womb. State regulation protective of fetal life after viability thus has both logical and biological justifications. If the State is interested in protecting fetal life after viability, it may go so far as to proscribe abortion during that period except when it is necessary to preserve the life or health of the mother.

Measured against these standards, Art. 1196 of the Texas Penal Code, in restricting legal abortions to those "procured or attempted by medical advice for the purpose of saving the life of the mother," sweeps too broadly.

The statute makes no distinction between abortions performed early in pregnancy and those performed later, and it limits to a single reason, "saving" the mother's life, the legal justification for the procedure. The statute, therefore, cannot survive the constitutional attack made upon it here.

This holding, we feel, is consistent with the relative weights of the respective interests involved, with the lessons and example of medical and legal history, with the lenity of the common law, and with the demands of the profound problems of the present day. The decision leaves the State free to place increasing restrictions on abortion as the period of pregnancy lengthens, so long as those restrictions are tailored to the recognized state interests. The decision vindicates the right of the physician to administer medical treatment according to his profesional judgment up to the points where important state interests provide compelling justifications for intervention. Up to those points the abortion decision in all its aspects is inherently, and primarily, a medical decision, and basic responsibility for it must rest with the physician. If an individual practitioner abuses the privilege of exercising proper medical judgment, the usual remedies, judicial and intra-professional, are available.

Decisions such as these have major, although as yet undefined, implications for welfare law. However, the decisions in Dandridge v. Williams, supra, and in Wyman v. James, 400 U.S. 309, 91 S.Ct. 381, 27 L.Ed.2d 408 (1971), reprinted at p. 319, infra, suggest that sympathy for the concept of privacy does not fully extend to welfare families. It remains to be seen how the Court will reconcile these conflicting lines of authority.

Another related recent case is Weber v. Aetna Casualty & Surety Co., 406 U.S. 164, 92 S.Ct. 1400, 31 L.Ed.2d 15 (1972). There the Court struck down a Louisiana statute discriminating against unacknowledged, illegitimate children in paying workmen's compensation benefits on the death of their father. The Court was confronted with two conflicting lines of authority. In Levy v. Louisiana, 391 U.S. 68, 88 S.Ct. 1509, 20 L.Ed.2d 436 (1968), discrimination by Louisiana against illegitimates in granting rights to sue for wrongful death had been held to violate the Fourteenth Amendment. But in Labine v. Vincent, 401 U.S. 532, 91 S.Ct. 1017, 28 L.Ed.2d 288 (1971), the Court had sustained the Louisiana statute barring illegitimate children from intestate succession. Mr. Justice Powell, writing for an 8 to 1 majority in *Weber*, came out squarely behind the older *Levy* rule and rejected the notion that an acknowledged state interest in protecting "legitimate family relationships" was rationally served by curbing rights to workmen's compensation. The full opinion in *Weber* is reprinted at p. 461, infra.

Problem

Consider whether any constitutional objections could be successfully raised against the legislative action proposed in this excerpt from a recent staff report of the Senate Finance Committee:

On June 17, 1968, the Supreme Court ruled in King v. Smith (392 U.S. 309) that a State could not consider a child ineligible for aid to families with dependent children when there was a substitute parent with no legal obligation to support the child. The Court decision was based on its interpretation of congressional intent as expressed in the Social Security Act and its legislative history. The decision states: "We believe Congress intended the term 'parent' in section 406 (a) of the act * * * to include only those persons with a legal duty of support." In a similar vein, the Supreme Court in Lewis v. Martin (397 U.S. 552, decided April 20, 1970), denied the right of a State, in determining need for assistance, to assume that the income of a man assuming the role of spouse is available to the family.

In Shapiro v. Solman, the Supreme Court affirmed a lower court decision (300 F.Supp. 409) prohibiting a State from denying AFDC to a family when there is a stepfather in the house.

Possible legislative action.—The Court decision was based on an interpretation that Congress did not intend for the income and resources of a man in the house to be taken into account in determining a family's eligibility for welfare. H.R. 16311, in effect, writes the Court decision on the man-in-the-house rule into law. The committee may wish instead to permit States to take into account the presence of a man in the house in determining eligibility for welfare by specifying the kinds of circumstances under which an individual may be considered a man in the house.

The existence of any of the following circumstances between any child and any individual not related to him could be considered as positive indications that there exists between them a continuing parent-child relationship:

(1) They are frequently seen together in public;

(2) The individual is the parent of a half-brother or half-sister of the child;

(3) The individual exercises parental control over the child;

(4) The individual makes substantial gifts to the child or to members of his family;

(5) The individual claims the child as a dependent for income tax purposes;

(6) The individual arranges for the care of the child when his mother is ill or absent from the home;

(7) The individual assumes responsibility for the child when there occurs in the child's life a crisis such as illness or detention by public authorities;

(8) The individual is listed as the parent or guardian of the child in school records which are designed to indicate the identity of the parents or guardians of children;

(9) The individual makes frequent visits to the place of residence of the child; and

(10) The individual gives or uses as his address the address of such place of residence in dealing with his employer, his creditors, postal authorities, other public authorities, or others with whom he may have dealings, relationships, or obligations.

TOWNSEND v. SWANK

Supreme Court of the United States, 1971.
404 U.S. 282, 92 Sup.Ct. 502, 30 L.Ed.2d 448.

Mr. Justice BRENNAN delivered the opinion of the Court.

Appellants, two college students and their mothers, brought this class action in the District Court for the Northern District of Illinois alleging that § 4–1.1 of the Illinois Public Aid Code, Ill.Rev.Stat., c. 23, § 4–1.1 (1967) and implementing Illinois Public Aid Regulation 150 violate the Equal Protection Clause of the Fourteenth Amendment, and, because inconsistent with § 406(a)(2)(B) of the Social Security Act, 42 U.S.C.A. § 606 (a)(2)(B), also violate the Supremacy

Clause of the Constitution.[1] Under the Illinois statute and regulation needy dependent children 18 through 20 years of age who attend high school or vocational training school are eligible for benefits under the federally assisted Aid to Families with Dependent Children program (AFDC), 42 U.S.C.A. § 601 et seq. but such children who attend a college or university are not eligible.[2] Section 406(a)

[1] Section 4–1.1 of the Illinois Public Aid Code, Ill.Rev.Stat., c. 23, § 4–1.1 (1967), provides:

"Child Age Eligibility. The Child or Children must be under 18, or age 18 or over but under age 21 if in regular attendance in high school or in a vocational or technical training school. 'Regular Attendance,' as used in this Section, means attendance full time during the regular terms of such schools, or attendance part time during such regular terms as may be authorized by rule of the Illinois Department for the purpose of permitting the child to engage in employment which supplements his classroom instruction or which otherwise enhances his development toward a self-supporting status."

Illinois Department of Public Aid Regulation 150 provides:

"§ 150. Age Requirements:

"A. D. C. Dependent children under 18 years of age, unless 18 through 20 years of age and in regular attendance in high school or vocational or technical training school. (This does not include 18 through 20 year old children in college.)"

[2] Appellant Loverta Alexander lives with her son Jerome in Chicago. Jerome reached his 18th birthday in August 1968 and enrolled in junior college about a month later. In early October a Cook County welfare officer notified Mrs. Alexander that the AFDC benefits received by her since 1963 would be terminated as of November 1, 1968. Though Mrs. Alexander was able to obtain general assistance benefits from the State, the termination of AFDC payments resulted in a loss of $23.52 per month in the family's income. The only reason given by the State for the termination was that Jerome had reached his 18th birthday and was not attending high school or vocational school.

Appellant Georgia Townsend is the sole support of Omega Minor, her only child. Mrs. Townsend, who is disabled, received AFDC benefits for herself and her daughter from 1953 through 1960. Thereafter she received AFDC grants for Omega, and bene-

(2) of the Social Security Act, on the other hand, defines "dependent child" to include a child " * * * (B) under the age of twenty-one and (as determined by the State in accordance with standards prescribed by the Secretary) a student regularly attending a school, college, or university, or regularly attending a course of vocational or technical training designed to fit him for gainful employment." A three-judge district court held that neither constitutional contention had merit and sustained the validity of the Illinois statute and regulations. 314 F.Supp. 1082 (1970). We noted probable jurisdiction, 401 U.S. 906 (1971). We hold that the Illinois statute and regulation conflict with § 406(a)(2)(B) and for that reason are invalid under the Supremacy Clause. We therefore reverse on that ground without reaching the Equal Protection issue.

I

Section 402(a)(10) of the Social Security Act provides that state participatory

fits for herself under the Aid to the Disabled provisions of the Social Security Act, 42 U.S.C.A. § 1351 et seq. In September 1966, Omega enrolled in junior college. Two months later a Cook County welfare officer notified Mrs. Townsend that Omega's monthly AFDC payment would be canceled as of January 1967. While Mrs. Townsend's disability payments were increased to meet her own needs, the loss of AFDC benefits resulted in a reduction of $47.94 per month in family income. Again the only reason given was the failure to comply with the Illinois statute and regulation.

This action was brought by Mrs. Alexander under the Federal Civil Rights Act, 42 U.S.C.A. § 1983, seeking declaratory and injunctive relief against the termination of her AFDC benefits. Mrs. Townsend intervened as a plaintiff on behalf of herself and her daughter Omega, and as a member of the class described in Mrs. Alexander's complaint. The three-judge court, convened pursuant to 28 U.S.C.A. §§ 2281, 2284, held that appellants' complaint stated a cause of action under the Civil Rights Act, and was a proper class action under Rule 23, Federal Rules of Civil Procedure. Those holdings are not challenged in this Court.

plans submitted under the AFDC program for the approval of the Secretary of HEW must provide "that aid to families with dependent children shall be furnished with reasonable promptness to *all eligible* individuals." (Emphasis supplied.) In King v. Smith, 392 U.S. 309 (1968), we considered whether a State participating in an AFDC program may, consistently with the Supremacy Clause, adopt eligibility standards that exclude from benefits needy dependent children eligible for benefits under applicable federal statutory standards. There was before us in that case a regulation of the Alabama Department of Pensions and Security that treated a man who cohabited with the mother of needy dependent children in or outside the home as a nonabsent "parent" within the federal statute. Since aid can be granted under § 406(a) of the Federal Act only if a "parent" of the needy child is continually absent from the home, Alabama's regulation resulted in the ineligibility of the children for benefits. We held that the Alabama regulation defined "parent" in a manner inconsistent with § 406(a) of the Social Security Act and therefore that in "denying AFDC assistance to [children] on the basis of this invalid regulation, Alabama has breached its federally imposed obligation to furnish 'aid to families with dependent children * * * with reasonable promptness to all eligible individuals. * * * *'" 392 U.S., at 333.

Thus King v. Smith establishes that, at least in the absence of congressional authorization for the exclusion clearly evidenced from the Social Security Act or its legislative history, a state eligibility standard that excludes persons eligible for assistance under federal AFDC standards violates the Social Security Act and is therefore invalid under the Supremacy Clause. We recognize that regulations of the Department of Health, Education, and Welfare seem to imply that States

may to some extent vary eligibility requirements from federal standards.[3] However, the principle which accords substantial weight to interpretation of a statute by the department entrusted with its administration is inapplicable insofar as those regulations are inconsistent with the requirement of § 402(a)(10) that aid be furnished "to *all eligible* individuals." (Emphasis supplied.) King v. Smith, 392 U.S., at 333 n. 34.

II

It is next argued that in the case of 18–20-year-old needy dependent children, Congress authorized the States to vary eligibility requirements from federal standards. In other words, it is contended that Congress authorized the States to discriminate between these needy dependent children solely upon the basis of the type of school attended. Our examination of the legislative history has uncovered no evidence that Congress granted the asserted authority. On the contrary, we are persuaded that the history supports the conclusion that Congress meant to continue financial assistance for AFDC programs for the age group only in States that conformed their eligibility requirements to the federal eligibility standards.

Section 406(a)(2)(B) makes dependent 18–20-year-olds eligible for benefits whether attending a college or university, or attending a course of voca-

[3] See, e. g., HEW's so-called "Condition X" embodied in a regulation found in 45 CFR § 233.10(a)(1)(ii):

"The groups selected for inclusion in the plan and the eligibility conditions imposed must not exclude individuals or groups on an arbitrary or unreasonable basis, and must not result in inequitable treatment of individuals or groups in light of the provisions and purposes of the public assistance titles of the Social Security Act." See also HEW, Handbook of Public Assistance Administration, "Green Sheets," Part IV, G–4210 (1965); Note, Welfare's "Condition X," 76 Yale L.J. 1222 (1967).

tional or technical training. The only discretion written into the statute permits a State to determine, "in accordance with standards prescribed by the Secretary," whether a particular student, without regard to whether his attendance is at a college or vocational school, is a student "regularly attending" a bona fide school.[4] This particularization of the area of state authority is itself cogent evidence that Congress did not also authorize the States to limit eligibility to students attending vocational school.

Nor is there anything in the legislative history of the evolution of § 406(a)(2)(B) to support appellee's argument.[5] That history does show that whenever Congress extended AFDC eligibility to older children—from those under 16 to those 16–17, and finally to those 18–20 —Congress left to the individual States the decision whether to participate in the program for the new age group. There is no legislative history, however, to support the proposition that Congress also gave to the individual States an option to tailor eligibility standards within the age group, and thus exclude children eligible under the federal standards.

The original Social Security Act provided aid only to dependent children under the age of 16. 49 Stat. 629 (1935). A 1939 amendment extended aid to children age 16–17 "regularly attending school," 53 Stat. 1380. The States were not however required to extend their AFDC programs to the 16–17-year age group. See H.R.Rep. No. 728, 76th Cong., 1st Sess., 28–29. But if a State chose to do so, not a word in the legislative history suggests that it might limit its choice to students attending schools selected by the State, and exclude children of the age group attending other schools.

In 1956 Congress deleted the school attendance requirement and provided for benefits for all dependent children of the 16–17 age group. 70 Stat. 850. The Senate Report on this bill stated that the bill would "*permit* Federal sharing in assistance to such children" and also that the bill would "*make* some additional needy children eligible for aid." S.Rep. No. 2133, 84th Cong., 2d Sess., 30 (1956). (Emphasis supplied.) The Conference Report stated that the bill would "*eliminate* the requirement that a needy child between 16 and 18 years of age must be regularly attending school in order to be eligible for aid to dependent children." H.R.Rep. No. 2936, 84th Cong., 2d Sess. 42 (1956). Significantly nothing in the legislative history of that change indicates that the States were at liberty to continue to limit eligibility to 16–17-year-olds attending school.[6]

The first provision for the age group 18–20 came in 1964 when benefits were authorized but limited to children attending high school or vocational school. 78 Stat. 1042. As in the case of the 1939

---

4 See HEW Handbook "Green Sheets," supra, n. 3, Part IV, G–3220; cf. Conf.Rep.No. 682, 89th Cong., 1st Sess., 69–70 (1965).

5 The United States, as *amicus curiae*, cites sections of the Social Security Act as supporting Illinois' contention that its college-vocational school distinction is authorized. For example, the United States refers to § 406(a) which originally defined "dependent child" to include a child living with his "father, mother, grandfather, grandmother, brother, sister, stepfather, stepmother, stepbrother, stepsister, uncle or aunt." 49 Stat. 629. A statement by Senator Harrison during debate on this provision, 79 Cong.Rec. 9269 (1935), is said to establish that the States were not required to extend assistance for every relative listed in the section. Section 407(b) is also cited as explicitly reserving to the States a choice whether to participate in certain parts of the AFDC program. But these are express authorizations to depart from federal eligibility standards; there is no express authorization in this case.

6 It appears that some States and the District of Columbia continued to limit payments to 16–17-year-olds attending school and to handicapped children prevented from doing so. HEW Public Assistance Report No. 50, Characteristics of State Public Assistance Plans under the Social Security Act (1964 ed.).

amendments extending aid to children 16–17 regularly attending school, the States had the choice whether to participate in this new program; S.Rep. No. 1517, 88th Cong., 2d Sess., 2 (1964), expressly stated that "extension of the program in that manner would be optional with the States." When in 1965 Congress amended § 406(a)(2)(B) in the form now before us nothing was said to indicate that States which had adopted the 1964 program limited to children attending vocational schools were free to continue that limited program and not extend it to children 18–20 attending a college or university. The relevant Senate Report, S.Rep. No. 404 Part I, 89th Cong., 1st Sess., 147, implies the contrary, stating:

> "Under existing law States, at their option, may continue payments to needy children up to age 21 in the aid to families with dependent children program, providing they are 'regularly attending a high school in pursuance of a course of study leading to a high school diploma or its equivalent, or regularly attending a course of vocational or technical training designed to fit him for gainful employment.' The committee added an amendment extending this provision so as to include needy children under 21 who are regularly 'attending a school, college, or university.' "

Moreover, the Report notes that one of the purposes of the extension was to bring AFDC in line with the Old Age Survivors and Disability Insurance provisions of the Social Security Act, 42 U.S.C.A. § 401 et seq. Under that program an insured's child is eligible for insurance benefits if he is a full-time student under 22 years of age, and under § 402(d)(7) this includes a student attending a college or university. S.Rep. No. 404 attributed to the provision under both programs a purpose to "assure as far as possible, that

children will not be prevented from going to school or college because they are deprived of parental support." S.Rep. No. 404, supra, at 147. This theme carried through the Conference Committee Report: "This Amendment would broaden the type of schools that children over the age of 18 and under the age of 21 may attend and receive aid to families with dependent children payments in which the Federal Government will participate." Conf.Rep. No. 682, 89th Cong., 1st Sess., 69 (1965).[7]

In sum, when application of AFDC was extended to a new age group—in 1939 to 16–17-year-olds and in 1964 to 18–20-year-olds—Congress took care to make explicit that the decision whether to participate was left to the individual States. However, when application of AFDC within the age group was enlarged—in 1956 to all 16–17-year-olds and in 1965 to 18–20-year-olds attending college or a university—the evidence, if not as clear, is that financial support of AFDC programs for the age group was to continue only in States that conformed their eligibility requirements to the new federal standards. Any doubt must be resolved in favor of this construction to avoid the necessity of passing upon the equal protection issue. "Congress is without power to enlist state cooperation in a joint federal-state program by legislation which authorizes the States to violate the Equal Protection Clause." Shapiro v. Thompson, 394 U.S. 618, 641 (1969). Notwithstanding the view of the majority of the District Court, 314 F.Supp., at 1088–1089, we think there is a serious question whether the Illinois classifica-

---

7 HEW itself states: "Within the age limit set by the State, there should be a choice of attending a school, college or university or taking a course of vocational or technical training for gainful employment." HEW, Handbook of Public Assistance Administration, "Green Sheets," supra, n. 3. Part IV, G–3220.

tion can withstand the strictures of the Equal Protection Clause. The majority justified the classification as designed to attain the twin goals of aiding needy children to become employable and self-sufficient, and of insuring fiscal integrity of the State's welfare program. We doubt the rationality of the classification as a means of furthering the goal of aiding needy children to become employable and self-sufficient; we are not told what basis in practical experience supports the proposition that children with a vocational training are more readily employable than children with a college education. And a State's interest in preserving the fiscal integrity of its welfare program by economically allocating limited AFDC resources may not be protected by the device of adopting eligibility requirements restricting the class of children made eligible by federal standards. That interest may be protected by the State's "undisputed power to set the level of benefits * * *." King v. Smith, 392 U.S., at 334. See Dandridge v. Williams, 397 U.S. 471 (1970).[8]

Reversed.

---

[8] The concurring opinion below acknowledged that the reasonable basis for the classification would not be apparent if incentives to learn white and blue collar trades and the supply and demand for professional and labor positions were the same. The opinion concluded, however, that the classification could be reasonable in the context of a labor market in which "the skills of manual laborers are in short supply," because in such a market, "as a means of utilizing limited state funds in an effort to channel persons into those employment positions for which the society has great need, the statutory discrimination between college students and post-high school vocational trainees is not purely arbitrary or invidious, but rather, a rational approach designed to correct a perceived problem." 314 F.Supp., at 1091. Apart from the fact that nothing appears about the nature of the market, a classification which channels one class of people, poor people, into a particular class of low paying, low status jobs would plainly raise substantial questions under the Equal Protection Clause.

Mr. Chief Justice BURGER, concurring.

I concur in the result reached by the Court, but add this brief comment. In dealing with this case—and the other AFDC cases on the Court's docket—it seems appropriate to keep clearly in mind that Title IV of the Social Security Act governs the dispensation of federal funds and that it does no more than that. True, Congress has used the "power of the purse" to force the States to adhere to its wishes to a certain extent; but adherence to the provisions of Title IV is in no way mandatory upon the States under the Supremacy Clause. The appropriate inquiry in any case should be, simply, whether the State has indeed adhered to the provisions and is accordingly entitled to utilize federal funds in support of its program. Cf. Rosado v. Wyman, 397 U.S. 397, 420 (1970). I agree that the answer to that inquiry in this case must be in the negative; I therefore concur in the judgment of the Court.

Note on the Judicial Federalizing of Categorical Assistance Programs

The argument contra to the conclusion reached in *Townsend* is set out in the following excerpt from the brief for the United States as amicus curiae.

Excerpt from Brief of the United States as Amicus Curiae in Townsend v. Swank

I. **The Social Security Act Does Not Require The States To Provide AFDC Benefits For All Persons With Respect To Whom Federal Matching Payments Can Be Made.**

   A. *Section 402 is the sole provision specifying the requirements of state plans for Aid to Families with Dependent Children.*

   Section 402 of the Social Security Act provides that in order to obtain the Secretary's approval, a state AFDC plan "must" meet twenty-three elaborate criteria, most of which are designed to insure efficient and equitable administration of the state plans. Although a number of the provisions require that eligibility requirements be uniformly imposed throughout the state, Section 402 does not suggest that a plan, in order to qualify for approval, need include any specific class of persons in its definition of eligibility. Indeed, when Title IV was first enacted, Section 402 contained no reference to the question of eligibility for assistance, except that it prohibited excessive residency requirements.[8]

[8] The original provision provided:

Section 402. (a) A State plan for aid to dependent children must (1) provide that it shall be in effect in all political subdivisions of the State, and, if administered by them, be mandatory upon them; (2) provide for financial participation by the State; (3) either provide for the establishment or designation of a single State agency to administer the plan, or provide for the establishment or designation of a single State agency to supervise the administration of the plan; (4) provide for granting to any individual, whose claim with respect to aid to a dependent child is denied, an opportunity for a fair hearing before such State agency; (5) provide such methods of administration (other than those relating to selection, tenure of office, and compensation of personnel) as are found by the Board to be necessary for the efficient operation of the plan; and (6) provide that the State agency will make such reports, in such form and containing such information, as the Board may from time to time require, and comply with such provisions as the Board may from time to time find necessary to assure the correctness and verification of such reports.

(b) The Board shall approve any plan which fulfills the conditions specified in subsection (a), except that it shall not approve any plan which imposes as a condition of eligibility for aid to dependent children, a residence requirement which denies aid with respect to any child residing in the State (1) who has resided in the State for one year immediately preceding the application for such aid, or (2) who was born within the State within one year immediately preceding the application, if its mother has resided in the State for one year immediately preceding the birth.

The Senate Report which accompanied the original bill made it clear that Congress intended at that time to impose only minimal requirements on state plans:

> It may be pointed out that these provisions impose only a few, reasonable, minimum requirements upon the States, and give recognition to the principle of State rights. The supervision given to the Federal agencies in charge has been carefully circumscribed so that there may be no unreasonable encroachment upon the States from Washington. Less Federal control is provided than in any recent Federal aid law. The conditions provided in the bill deal with such matters as the requirement of State matching, financial participation by the State government, the submission of reports, and residence requirements. These conditions are entirely appropriate and are, in fact, essential if the Federal Government is to bear a part of the burden. [S.Rep. No. 628, 74th Cong., 1st Sess. 4 (1935)]

The broad flexibility which Congress intended to leave to the states in defining eligibility was emphasized in the reports on Section 402(b), which dealt with the prohibition of residence requirements greater than one year:

> The State may be more lenient than this, if it wishes. It may, furthermore, impose such other eligibility requirements—as to means, moral character, etc.—as it sees fit. * * * [H.Rep. No. 615, 74th Cong., 1st Sess. 24 (1935); S.Rep. No. 628, 74th Cong., 1st Sess. 35–36 (1935)]

In the Department's view, none of the subsequent additions to Section 402, many of which deal more specifically with aspects of state plan administration than the original provision, indicates any modification of Congress' original intention to leave the basic determination of eligibility to the states.

In contrast to the mandatory language of Section 402, Sections 406, 407 and 408 of the Act merely define certain classes of persons with respect to whom state payments will be federally matched. The Department has from the beginning read these Sections as giving the states broad discretion to determine the classes of persons included in their assistance programs with federal matching. The Department's general view that states have broad latitude in determining AFDC program coverage is now made explicit by regulation:

> States have substantial latitude and corresponding responsibility for determining the coverage, nature and scope of their public assistance programs. Although the public assistance titles define the coverage in which the Federal Government will participate financially, a State may provide coverage on a broader or more limited basis. However, it may not impose any eligibility condition that is prohibited under the Social Security Act. [45 C.F.R. 233.10(a)(1)(i)]

Since the onset of the AFDC program, the Department has approved state plans which set eligibility requirements which are narrower in various ways than the definitions set forth in Section 406. The Department's interpretation and practice in this area, which are, of course, entitled to considerable weight in construction of the statute, are strongly supported by the legislative history of the definitional provisions of the Act, and, as we show in the following section, especially by the history of the definition of "dependent child" in Section 406(a).

B. *The legislative history of Section 406(a) indicates that state plans are not required to include all persons whom the definitions in that provision cover.*

The legislative history of the criteria for federal matching in Section 406(a), including those relating to age and school attendance, reveals that Congress has never viewed these definitional provisions as mandatory. With respect to age and school attendance criteria, for example, the original Social Security Act set sixteen as the maximum age for a dependent child. 49 Stat. 629. The age provision has since been liberalized several times, and each time Congress made it clear that extension of benefits to the new group of eligible persons was optional with the states. In 1939, Section 406(a) was broadened to include needy children "under the age of eighteen if found by the State agency to be regularly attending school * * *." 53 Stat. 1380. Committee reports on the measure explicitly stated that the amendment imposed no new requirement on the states:

> The age limit for Federal grants is raised from 16 to 18 if the State agency finds that the child is regularly attending school. This will enable most children to finish high school. Six States already provide aid to children up to the age of 18 and six additional States have the necessary legislation to take advantage of this amendment immediately. It is estimated that about 100,000 additional children may obtain aid by virtue of this change, provided all States amend their laws accordingly.

> *   *   *   *   *

> The additional cost to the Federal Government of these three amendments is difficult to estimate due to

the fact that the amendments are effective only at such time and to the extent that the States match the Federal funds * * *. [H.Rep. No. 728, 76th Cong., 1st Sess. 28–29; S.Rep. No. 734, 76th Cong., 1st Sess. 30.]

In 1956, federal matching became available for state assistance to all needy children under 18, regardless of school attendance. But the removal of the school attendance requirement did not signal mandatory inclusion in state AFDC plans of all needy children 16–17. The change "would permit Federal sharing" only if the state chose to extend the program. S.Rep. No. 2133, 84th Cong., 2d Sess. 30 (1956).

In 1964, Congress again enlarged the definition of "dependent child" to include needy children between 18 and 21 who were regularly attending high school or a vocational or technical school. 78 Stat. 1042. Again, the congressional reports made it clear that "The extension of the program in this manner would be optional with the states." S.Rep. No. 1517, 88th Cong., 2d Sess. 2 (1964).[9]

In 1965, Congress amended Section 406(a) to read as it now does. A needy child between 18 and 21 is eligible to receive AFDC payments if he is attending any sort of school, college, or university. The applicable Senate Report stated:

Under existing law States, *at their option, may* continue payments to needy children up to age 21 in the aid to families with dependent children program, providing they are 'regularly attending a high school in pursuance of a course of study leading to a high school diploma or its equivalent, or regularly attend-

ing a course of vocational or technical training designed to fit him for gainful employment.' The committee added an amendment extending this provision so as to include needy children under 21 who are regularly 'attending a school, college, or university.' Federal sharing for this purpose would thus be *available to States who implement such a program for payments to children regularly attending a college,* or university, as well as those attending high school or a vocational school, thus bringing this provision more nearly in line with the provision of the bill relating to the continuation of a child's benefit under the OASDI system. * * * [S.Rep. No. 404, Part I, 89th Cong., 1st Sess. 147 (1965 (emphasis added)].[10]

The legislative history of other definitional elements of Section 406(a), and of other definitional provisions of the Act, also supports the Department's view that the definitions are not mandatory. The original Social Security Act, for example, defined "dependent child" to include a child living with his "father, mother, grandfather, grandmother, brother, sister, stepfather, stepmother, stepbrother, stepsister, uncle, or aunt * * *." Explaining the effect of this provision on the floor of the Senate, Senator Harrison, chairman of the Senate Finance Committee, stated:

A State will not have to aid every child which it finds to be in need. Obviously, for many States, that would be too large a burden. It

---

[9] See also remarks made on the floor of the House by Congressman Mills, 110 Cong., Rec. 23701 (1964).

[10] See also Committee on Ways and Means, House of Representatives, Eighty-Ninth Congress, First Session, Summary of Major Provisions of H.R. 6675, The Social Security Amendments of 1965 as Reflected by the Agreement Reached between the House and Senate Conference together with Actuarial Data, July 24, 1965, p. 19.

may limit aid to children living with their widowed mother, or it can include children without parents living with near relatives. The provisions are not for general relief of poor children but are designed to hold broken families together. [79 Cong.Rec. 9269 (1935).]

In 1956, when Congress expanded this list of relatives to include first cousins, nephews, or nieces of the dependent child, it again indicated that it considered additional coverage optional.[11] Congressional pronouncements on other definitional sections of the Act, such as Sections 406(b) ("aid to families with dependent children"),[12] 407 ("dependent children of unemployed fathers"),[13] and 408 ("foster home care of dependent children") [14] reiterate the non-mandatory nature of the definitions contained therein.[15] Indeed, Section 407(b) of the Act itself,

dealing with children of unemployed fathers, explicitly recognizes that states need not provide assistance to the class of individuals defined in that section.[16]

* * *

II. The Illinois * * * Limitations On AFDC Eligibility In Question Here Are Not Prohibited By The Social Security Act.

A. *The standard for testing state limitations on eligibility is whether the limitation is rational and consistent with the purposes of the Act.*

Although we believe that the Social Security Act's definitions delimiting the scope of federal fund matching under AFDC do not require states that receive federal funds to extend such aid to all persons included in those definitions, state discretion to limit eligibility is not unlimited. The Department has always taken the position that in considering State AFDC plans, the Secretary has "the inherent authority to reject a state plan which bears no rational relation to any purpose of the federal act." Note, Welfare's Condition X, 76 Yale L.J. 1222, 1224 (1967). This concept is now embodied in a Department regulation:

> The groups selected for inclusion in the plan and the eligibility conditions imposed must not exclude individuals or groups on an arbitrary or unreasonable basis, and must not result in inequitable treatment of individuals or groups in the light of

[11] See S.Rep.No.2133, 84th Cong., 2d Sess. 30 (1956). The Handbook of Public Assistance Administration, Part IV; § 3433, states:

Requirements for State Plans

State plans shall indicate which of the relatives specified in the act are recognized by the State as relatives of the child for purposes of aid to families with dependent children. If the State desires to recognize relatives of adoptive parents, the plan shall indicate which of the relatives specified in the act are determined in accordance with State practice to be relatives of the adopted child.

[12] See S.Rep.No.1589, 87th Cong., 2d Sess. 12 (1962).

[13] When the AFDC program for unemployed parents was extended in 1962 a House Report observed that by January of that year "15 states had programs in effect under the [unemployed father] * * * provision * * *." H.Rep.No.1414, 87th Cong., 2d Sess. 14 (1962). The report did not question the right of the remaining states not to initiate these programs.

[14] As of 1969, assistance to children in foster care became mandatory, but, significantly, the provision requiring assistance to that category of children was placed in Section 402(a), not in Section 408.

[15] See H.Rep.No.1414, 87th Cong., 2d Sess. 16 (1962).

[16] It provides: "The provisions of subsection (a) [of section 407] shall be applicable to a State if the State's plan approved under section * * * [402] * * * requires the payment of aid to families with dependent children with respect to a dependent child as defined in subsection (a) * * *." If a state elects to participate in the unemployed fathers program, however, Section 408 requires it to use the federal definition of unemployment.

the provisions and purposes of the public assistance titles of the Social Security Act. [45 C.F.R. 233.10(a)(1)(iii).]

The Secretary has rejected plans which included eligibility limitations that were unreasonable because based on such factors as race, illegitimacy, and the unsuitability of the dependent child's home [17]—factors that were not reasonably related to the purposes of the Social Security Act.[18] The basis for these actions has been the Department's view that the several provisions of the public assistance titles of the Social Security Act, in combination, require that a state plan provide for equitable treatment of individuals assisted under it. By the same token, the Secretary would not approve classifications if he believed that the Act intended the class denied benefits to have a higher priority than the class made eligible under state law.

In King v. Smith, 392 U.S. 309, this Court struck down as violative of the purposes of the Act Alabama's "substitute father regulation," under which AFDC benefits were denied to the children of a mother who "cohabits" with a man. The Alabama regulation considered any man who has sexual relations with a mother of children who receive AFDC a substitute father regardless of whether he is legally obligated to support the children and whether he actually contributes to their support. The Court pointed out (392

U.S. at 320–327) that although the Social Security Act may at one time have permitted the states to deprive children of eligibility for AFDC on the basis of their parents' immorality, Congress, through a series of amendments to the Act,[19] "has determined that immorality and illegitimacy should be dealt with through rehabilitative measures rather than measures that punish dependent children, and that protection of such children is the paramount goal of AFDC." 392 U.S. at 325. With respect to Alabama's argument that its regulation simply recognized that families in which the mother cohabited with a man were in the same position as families in which the children's parents were married, the Court concluded that Alabama had failed.

to take account of the circumstance that children of fathers living in the home are in a very different position from children of mothers who cohabit with men not their fathers: the child's father has a legal duty to support him, while the unrelated substitute father * * * does not. We believe Congress intended the term "parent" in § 406(a) * * * to include only those persons with a legal duty of support. [392 U.S. at 327.]

We submit that the Department's long-held view of the scope of state discretion to set AFDC eligibility standards is consistent with King v. Smith.[20] The opinion in *King* focused

---

[17] See Note, Welfare's Condition X, 76 Yale L.J. 1222, 1222–1223, n. 7.

[18] Section 401, 42 U.S.C.A. 601, describes the purposes of the Act as

encouraging the care of dependent children in their * * * homes or in the homes of relatives * * * [first] to help maintain and strengthen family life and [second] to help such parents or relatives to attain * * * independence consistent with the maintenance of continuing parental care and protection * * *.

[19] See 392 U.S. at 322–325. These measures include Section 404(b) of the Act, which permits states to disqualify children who live in unsuitable homes *only* if they are granted other "adequate care and assistance."

[20] The Department did not approve the Alabama substitute father regulation, and at the time of King v. Smith, the Department was engaged in a lengthy correspondence with the state of Alabama concerning its suitable home and substitute father policies. See 392 U.S. at 326, note 23.

specifically on the arbitrary nature of the distinction for AFDC purposes between children whose mothers cohabited with a man not legally obligated to support them and those whose mothers did not. The Court emphasized that "We hold today only that Congress has made at least this one determination: that destitute children who are legally fatherless cannot be flatly denied federally funded assistance on the transparent fiction that they have a substitute father." 392 U.S. at 334. Furthermore, as the Court stated, "There is no question that States have considerable latitude in allocating their AFDC resources, since each State is free to set its own standard of need * * *." 392 U.S. at 318. See also Dandridge v. Williams, 397 U.S. 471, 478–483.

The opinion does not suggest that all state eligibility standards which fall short of the federal definitions are invalid. Indeed, in view of the longstanding administrative interpretation and the legislative history of the definitional provisions of the Act, it is difficult to believe that the Court would have implicitly so concluded without explicit discussion of the issue. We believe that King v. Smith implies, at most, that state eligibility restrictions in areas where Congress has not specifically indicated that states have broad discretion must be scrutinized with special care.

Appellants base their argument that King v. Smith imposes federal eligibility standards on the states (see, e. g., Appellants' Br. in No. 70–5021, pp. 37–51) primarily on two sentences of the Court's opinion which we think have been taken out of context and misinterpreted. After its lengthy discussion of the inconsistency between the Alabama regulation and the purposes of the Act, the Court concluded:

> The regulation is therefore invalid because it defines "parent" in a manner that is inconsistent with § 406 (a) of the Social Security Act. * * * In denying AFDC assistance to appellees on the basis of this invalid regulation, Alabama has breached its federally imposed obligation to furnish "aid to families with dependent children * * * with reasonable promptness to all eligible individuals * * *" [citing the provision which is now Section 402 (a)(10) of the Act]. [392 U.S. at 333]

For the reasons stated above, we do not think that the Court's reference to the Alabama definition as "inconsistent with § 406(a)" may fairly be read as implying that the states must provide AFDC to all categories of children included in that Section of the Act. Rather, we interpret this sentence to mean simply that § 406(a) (as well as other provisions of the Act) expresses a congressional policy which the Alabama substitute father rule, for the specific reasons discussed in the opinion, violated.

Nor do we believe that the Court's reference to Section 402(a)(10), which requires the states to furnish "aid to families with dependent children * * * with reasonable promptness to all eligible individuals," implies that the states must furnish aid to all persons meeting the federal standard of eligibility. To the contrary, the legislative history of that Section indicates that Congress intended merely to eliminate the frequent state practice of putting families deemed eligible for AFDC *under state eligibility standards* on "waiting lists" until other eligible persons had been removed from the rolls.[21]   Thus, although we agree that there are instanc-

[21] In 1950, Section 402 of the Act was amended by the addition of the following plan requirement:

> [A State AFDC plan must] provide, effective July 1, 1951, that all individuals wishing to make application for aid to dependent children shall have opportunity to do so, and that aid to dependent children shall be furnished with reasonable promptness to all eligible individuals.

The House Report described the particular practice at which this new requirement was designed to strike as follows:

> Shortage of funds in aid to dependent children has sometimes, as in old-age assistance, resulted in a decision not to take more applications or to keep eligible families on waiting lists until enough recipients could be removed from the assistance rolls to make a place for them. As noted in the discussion of this problem in the section on old-age assistance, this difference in treatment accorded to eligible people results in undue hardship on needy persons and is inappropriate in a program financed from Federal funds. The requirement that State plans must provide opportunity to apply to all persons wishing to do so and that assistance shall be furnished promptly to all eligible families is included in the proposed amendments to title IV of the Social Security Act. [H.R.Rep.No.1300, 81st Cong., 1st Sess. 48 (1949).]

In describing the situation existing at the time this bill was under consideration, the House Report refers to "eligible" people not receiving assistance. Congress was concerned with persons, *determined to be eligible under standards set by the State*, who nonetheless were not receiving assistance.

The House debates further support the position that the eligibility referred to in this amendment is that defined by the States:

Improvements in Administrative Requirements

> The public assistance programs in which the Federal Government shares in the costs are administered or supervised by the States. The Social Security Act provides minimum requirements for the operation of programs by the States. The State-Federal partnership for aiding needy persons established in 1935 has functioned well. H.R. 6000 contains no provision to alter the basic relationship between the States and the Federal Government. The changes that would be made in the Federal requirements by the bill are designed to improve administrative practices in the State with the view of affording more

es, such as King v. Smith, in which the state may be required to alter its eligibility standard because of an inconsistency with the purposes of the Social Security Act, such a requirement is not rooted in Section 402(a) (10), which is neutral with respect to the content of the state eligibility definition.

B. *The eligibility limitations in question here are valid.*

1. *The Illinois provision.* In view of the foregoing discussion, we believe that the Illinois AFDC plan, which provides aid to persons between 18 and 21 who attend high school or vocational school but not to those who attend college, is a valid exercise of state discretion to define AFDC eligibility. As we have shown, supra pp. 16–18, Congress has repeatedly indicated that state adoption of the broadened age and school attendance aspects of the dependent child definition is optional. In view of these explicit statements, including those made when the definition was expanded to include 18 to 20 year-olds attending college, the Illinois limitation is not contrary to the purposes of the Act. Indeed, two district courts have upheld stricter age and school attendance limitations than the one in question here.[22]

Although the Department considers it highly desirable for states to provide

equitable treatment to the needy on the State-Federal assistance rolls. [95 Cong. Rec. 13934 (1949) (Remarks by Congressman Forand)].

Since 1950 the Department has consistently implemented Section 402(a)(10) in accordance with this interpretation; it has never viewed that plan requirement as prescribing mandatory eligibility criteria on the states.

[22] McClellan v. Shapiro, No. 13,627, decided April 20, 1970 (D.Conn.) (limitation of AFDC assistance to 19-year-olds attending secondary schools); Barksdale v. Shea, No. C. 1967, decided March 1, 1971 (D.Colo.) (limitation to children under 18 who attend school).

funds for needy children to attend whatever school they choose . . . it cannot be said that in allocating its welfare resources Illinois has distinguished irrationally between the importance of providing at least high school or vocational school training for dependent children and the importance of providing education at a more advanced level. When viewed in this light, Illinois' determination that eligibility should be limited to vocational and high school students is closely related to its undisputed right to determine standards of need; in other words, Illinois may have made the judgment that children age 18 or older who have attained a sufficient level of education to allow them to enroll in a college or university are not "needy" enought to justify their inclusion in that state's AFDC program.

In rejecting the government's approach, the Supreme Court may to some extent have read the specific legislative history of the 1965 amendment (enlarging the eligible 18–20 year-old group to include college students) differently from the government, but the Supreme Court also seems to have adopted a much different view from that of the government regarding the scope of state discretion in fixing eligibility requirements. In so doing, the Court was following the lead of several three-judge district courts which had held that "need" and "dependency" are the only permissible eligibility criteria in state AFDC programs. Noteworthy among these lower court decisions are several which struck down state attempts to coerce AFDC mothers into providing information regarding the fathers of their children or otherwise cooperating in collecting monies from those fathers. This requirement of cooperation, the courts indicated, was the imposi-

tion of an authorized eligibility condition. See, e. g. Doe v. Shapiro, 302 F.Supp. 761 (D.C.Conn.1969), appeal dismissed 396 U.S. 488, 90 S.Ct. 641, 24 L.Ed.2d 677 (1970), rehearing denied 397 U.S. 970, 90 S.Ct. 991, 25 L.Ed.2d 264 (1970).

Make no mistake about it. *Townsend,* at least on its face, is a sharp rebuke to H.E.W. policies evolved over four decades. The basic premise of *Townsend*— that AFDC is presumptively a program based on Federal standards—seems fundamentally inconsistent with the basic premise of the government's brief—that AFDC is a grant-in-aid program based primarily on state standards.

In analyzing *Townsend* you should consider whether the Court's result is logically compelled by a reading of the statute, or whether the government's view might not also be justified. If the government's alternative is possible, why did a Court which showed itself to be relatively unsympathetic to welfare recipients in Dandridge v. Williams, supra, and other contexts join unanimously here? What theoretical, practical, and constitutional problems would be raised by implementation of the "rational relation" approach proposed by the government? Does the result in *Townsend* suggest any strategy for future constitutional litigation in this field?

These are but a few of the questions which the *Townsend* decision raises. But even more urgent is the very practical question of how far the *Townsend* principle will be extended to other issues. *Townsend* may require major revision of virtually every state AFDC program and even of state OAA, AB and APTD programs. Can this be so? Or does the *Townsend* decision somehow turn upon its particular facts?

There was not long to wait for the beginnings of an answer to this question. Later in the same term the Court turned its attention to Carleson v. Remillard. The issue there was the lawfullness of a California rule that the absence of a father to serve on military duty was not a "continued absence from the home" so as to make the family eligible for AFDC. See 42 U.S.C.A. § 606(a). The government struggled mightily in its *Remillard* brief to limit the implications of *Townsend*, as indicated in the following excerpt.

Excerpt from Brief of the United States as Amicus Curiae in Carleson v. Remillard

In spite of the language in *Townsend* indicating that state AFDC plans are required to include persons eligible to receive federal matching funds, we believe that the California AFDC limitation under consideration in this case is distinguishable from the limitation held invalid in *Townsend*, and that the Court's holding in *Townsend* does not require the Court to hold the California provision invalid. The basic distinction between the two cases is that the restriction on aid to 18–20 year-old college students held invalid in *Townsend* conflicts with a provision of the Social Security Act which specifically declares persons in that category eligible for federal matching funds. In the Court's view, this specific provision reflects Congress' conclusion that the states should have no discretion to provide assistance to a class of children more narrowly defined in terms of age and school attendance.

In contrast to the specific provisions defining the age and school attendance aspects of AFDC eligibility, the Social Security Act does not elaborate on the scope of the term "continued absence." In our view, Congress' failure to define the federal standard applicable to this aspect of AFDC eligibility indicates that the states were intended to have considerable discretion in de-

termining what sort of parental absence justifies AFDC assistance. Furthermore, the Court in *Townsend* found the Illinois restriction on AFDC in conflict with the Social Security Act not only because of the specific language in the Act covering the omitted category of children, but also because the legislative history of the amendment to the Act adding 18–20 year-old college students, in the Court's view, indicates a clear Congressional intent to require the states to provide assistance to the newly qualified class. By contrast, there is virtually no legislative history indicating either the scope of the federal standard of "continued absence" or whether the states are required to incorporate into their AFDC plans the broadest permissible reading of the term as used in the Social Security Act.

*   *   *   If the Court construes *Townsend* to require states to extend AFDC coverage to all classes of persons for whom federal matching funds are available, even where the Social Security Act provides only a broad general standard of eligibility, the impact on the administration of the Act would be substantial. There are numerous general terms like the term "continued absence" involved here in the provisions of the Act setting forth eligibility criteria for federal matching funds, and if all state plans are required to implement these terms by providing coverage to the largest class of persons with respect to whom HEW approves the payment of federal matching funds, HEW believes that nearly every state plan will be invalid. This may well include not only AFDC plans, but state plans for administering the other public assistance programs established by the Social Security Act.

*   *   *

In our view, a sweeping change of this magnitude in the administration of the Social Security Act and the relationship of federal eligibility provisions to state plans is more appropriately left to the Congress. Indeed, the welfare reform bill currently under consideration in Congress, H.R. 1, contains uniform provisions establishing federal eligibility criteria for assistance to needy families and to the needy aged, blind, and disabled.

. . . Accordingly, we believe that the California regulation precluding AFDC assistance to families in which parental absence is due to military service ought to be judged according to the standard which HEW has traditionally applied in approving state plans; thus, if the classification reflected in the regulation is reasonable and not inconsistent with the purposes of the Act, the regulation ought to be held valid. We believe that the regulation reflects California's view that AFDC is designed primarily to assist families in which parental absence represents not simply a temporary physical separation of parent and child, but "a substantial severance of marital and family ties that deprives the child of at least one of its natural parents." Cal.Dept. of Soc. Wel.Reg. EAS § 42–350.1. In California's view, such a severance exists where there is a "definite interruption of or marked reduction in marital * * * responsibilities and relationships compared to previously existing conditions." *Id.* Thus California excludes from its AFDC program children whose parents are away from home in connection with current or prospective employment, and military service is considered for these purposes a type of employment. Cal.Dept. of Soc.Wel.Reg. EAS § 42–350.11.

Although HEW encourages states to include dependent children whose parents are absent due to military service in their AFDC plans, and recognizes the serious financial difficulties faced by many servicemen's families, we believe that California has made a reasonable judgment that absence due to employment, including military service, is not ordinarily as disruptive of the family structure and not as likely to result in the child's being deprived of parental support as absence due, for example, to parental desertion. Moreover, we believe that the regulation may also reflect California's view that the financial problems generated by absence of a parent due to military service are more properly the responsibility of the military pay and allotment system. We believe that both of these considerations are reasonable, and that the regulation is not an abuse of California's discretion to define AFDC eligibility.

A unanimous Supreme Court, however, hewed to its *Townsend* line in *Remillard*. That decision and some problems on the issues which it raises now follow.

———

CARLESON v. REMILLARD

Supreme Court of the United States, 1972.
406 U.S. 598, 92 S.Ct. 1932, 32 L.Ed.2d 352.

Mr. Justice DOUGLAS delivered the opinion of the Court.

Appellees are mother and child. The husband enlisted in the United States Army and served in Vietnam. The mother applied for AFDC benefits at a time when the amount of the monthly allotment she received by virtue of her husband's military service was less than her "need" as computed by the California agency and less than the monthly AFDC grant an adult with one child receives in California. She was denied relief. Although the Social Security Act, 42 U.S.C.A. § 301–1394, grants aid to families with "dependent children," and includes in the term "dependent child" one "who has been deprived of parental support or care by reason of * * * continued absence from the home." 42 U.S.C.A. § 606(a), California construed "continued absence" as not including military absence. It is unquestioned that her child is in fact "needy."

When the husband's allotment check was stopped, appellee again applied for AFDC benefits. She again was denied the benefits, this time because California had adopted a regulation [1] which specifically prohibited the payment of AFDC benefits to needy families where the absence of a parent was due to military service.

This action is a class action seeking a declaration of the invalidity of the regulation and an injunction restraining its enforcement on the ground that it conflicts with the Social Security Act and denies appellees the Fourteenth Amendment rights of due process and equal protection.

A three-judge District Court was convened and by a divided vote granted the relief sought. 325 F.Supp. 1272. The case is here by appeal. 28 U.S.C.A. §§ 1253, 2101(b). We noted probable jurisdiction, 404 U.S. 1013, 92 S.Ct. 670, 30 L.Ed.2d 660.

Section 402(a)(10) of the Social Security Act, 42 U.S.C.A. § 602(a)(10), places on each State participating in the AFDC program the requirement that "aid to families with dependent children shall be furnished with reasonable promptness to all eligible individuals." "Eligibility," so defined, must be measured by federal standards. King v. Smith, 392 U.S. 309, 88 S.Ct. 2128, 20 L.Ed.2d 1118. There, we were faced with an Alabama regulation which defined a mother's paramour

as a "parent" for § 606(a)(1) purposes, thus permitting the State to deny AFDC benefits to needy dependent children on the theory that there was no parent who was continually absent from the home. We held that Congress had defined "parent" as a breadwinner who was legally obligated to support his children, and that Alabama was precluded from altering that federal standard. The importance of our holding was stressed in Townsend v. Swank, 404 U.S. 282, 286, 92 S.Ct. 502, 505, 30 L.Ed.2d 448:

"* * * King v. Smith establishes that, at least in the absence of congressional authorization for the exclusion clearly evidenced from the Social Security Act or its legislative history, a state eligibility standard that excludes persons eligible for assistance under *federal* AFDC standards violates the Social Security Act and is therefore invalid under the Supremacy Clause." (Emphasis supplied.)

In *Townsend,* we also expressly disapproved the HEW policy which permitted States to vary eligibility requirements from the federal standards without express or clearly implied congressional authorization. 404 U.S., at 286, 92 S.Ct. 502.

Townsend involved § 406(a)(2)(B) of the Act, 42 U.S.C.A. § 606(a)(2) (B), which includes in the definition of "dependent children" those "under the age of twenty-one and (as determined by the State in accordance with standards prescribed by the Secretary) a student regularly attending a school, college, or university, or regularly attending a course of vocational or technical training designed to fit him for gainful employment." Illinois had defined AFDC eligible dependent children to include 18–20-year-old high school or vocational school children but not children of the same age group attending college. We held that § 606(a)(2)(B) precluded that clas-

---

[1] Calif.Dept.Soc.Welfare Reg. EAS 42–350.-11 provides:

"When one parent is physically absent from the home on a temporary basis. Examples are visits, trips made in connection with current or prospective employment, active duty in the Armed Services."

sification because it varied from the federal standard for needy dependent children. Involved in the present controversy is another eligibility criterion for federal matching funds set forth in the Act, namely the "continued absence" of a parent from the home. If California's definition conflicts with the federal criterion then it, too, is invalid under the Supremacy Clause.

HEW's regulations for federal matching funds provide [2] that:

"Continued absence of a parent from the home constitutes the reason for deprivation of parental support or care when the parent is out of the home, the nature of the absence is such as either to interrupt or to terminate the parent's functioning as a provider of maintenance, physical care, or guidance for the child, and the known or indefinite duration of the absence precludes counting on the parent's performance of his function in planning for the present support or care of the child. If these conditions exist, the parent may be absent for any reason, and he may have left only recently or some time previously."

The Solicitor General advises us that although HEW reads the term "continued absence" to permit the payment of federal matching funds to families where the parental absence is due to military service, it has approved state plans under which families in this category are not eligible for AFDC benefits.[3] HEW has included "service in the armed forces or other military service" as an example of a situation falling under the above definition of "continued absence." HEW Handbook of Public Assistance Administration, Part IV, § 3422.2.

[2] 45 CFR § 233.90(c)(1)(iii).

[3] The present record reveals that 22 States and the District of Columbia do furnish AFDC benefits to needy families of servicemen, while 19 States and Puerto Rico do not.

Our difficulty with that position is that "continued absence from the home" accurately describes a parent on active military duty. The House Report speaks of children "in families lacking a father's support," H.R.Rep.No.615, 74th Cong., 1st Sess., 10, and the Senate Report refers to "children in families which have been deprived of a father's support." S.Rep.No.628, 74th Cong., 1st Sess., 12. While the Senate Report noted that "these are principally families with female heads who are widowed, divorced, or deserted," id., at 12, it was not stated nor implied that eligibility by virtue of a parent's "continued absence" was limited to cases of divorce or desertion.

We agree that "continued absence" connotes, as HEW says, that "the parent may be absent for any reason." We search the Act in vain, moreover, for any authority to make "continued absence" into an accordion-like concept, applicable to some parents because of "continued absence" but not to others.

The presence of the parent in the home who has the legal obligation to support is the key to the AFDC program, King v. Smith, supra, 392 U.S. at 327, 88 S.Ct. at 2138; Lewis v. Martin, 397 U.S. 552, 559, 90 S.Ct. 1282, 1285, 25 L.Ed.2d 561. Congress looked to "work relief" programs and "the revival of private industry" to help the parent find the work needed to support the family. S.Rep.No. 628, supra, at 17, and the AFDC program was designed to meet a need unmet by depression-era programs aimed at providing work for breadwinners. King v. Smith, supra, 392 U.S. at 328, 88 S.Ct. at 2139. That need was the protection of children in homes without such a breadwinner. Ibid. It is clear that "military orphans" are in this category, for, as stated by the Supreme Court of Washington, a man in the miliatry service

"[H]as little control over his family's economic destiny. He has no labor union or other agency to look to as a means of persuading his employer to pay him a living wage. He is without access to collective bargaining or any negotiating forum or other means of economic persuasion, or even the informal but concerted support of his fellow employees. He cannot quit his job and seek a better paying one. * * [T]here is no action he could lawfully take to make his earnings adequate while putting in full time on his job. His was a kind of involuntary employment where legally he could do virtually nothing to improve the economic welfare of his family." Kennedy v. Dept. of Public Assistance, 79 Wash. 2d 728, 732, 733, 489 P.2d 154, 157.

Stoddard v. Fisher, D.C., 330 F.Supp. 566, held a Maine regulation invalid under the Supremacy Clause which denied AFDC aid where the father was continually absent because of his military service. Judge Coffin said:

"We cannot help but note the irony of a result which would deny assistance to the family of a man who finds that family disqualified from receiving AFDC on the ground that he has removed himself from the possibility of receiving public work relief by voluntarily undertaking, for inadequate compensation, the defense of his country." Id., 571, n. 8.

We cannot assume here, anymore than we could in King v. Smith, supra, that while Congress "intended to provide programs for the economic security and protection of *all children*," it also "intended arbitrarily to leave one class of destitute children entirely without meaningful protection." 392 U.S., at 330, 88 S.Ct. at 2140. We are especially confident Congress could not have designed an Act leaving uncared for an entire class who became "needy children" because their father was in the Armed Services defending their country.

We hold that there is no congressional authorization for States to exclude these so-called military orphans from AFDC benefits. Accordingly we affirm the judgment of the three-judge court.

Affirmed.

Mr. Chief Justice BURGER, concurring.

I join in the opinion and judgment of the Court but on the assumption, not expressly articulated in the opinion, that a State may administratively deduct from its total "need payment" such amount as is being paid to the dependents under the military allotment system. It would be curious, indeed, if two "pockets" of the same government would be required to make duplicating payments for welfare.

The administrative procedures to give effect to this process may be cumbersome, but the right of the State to avoid overlapping benefits for support should be clearly understood.

Problems

1. The Department of Health, Education and Welfare defines the "incapacity" of a parent necessary to bring a family under AFDC as being any physical or mental incapacity, "whatever its cause, degree, or duration, or accompanying factors." 45 C.F.R. 233.90(c)(iv). Pursuant to this definition, New York treats an intact, two-parent family with a working father as being eligible for AFDC when the mother is pregnant, i. e., the pregnancy is deemed an incapacity. Do *Townsend* and *Remillard* compel all states to do the same?

2. Several states treat a fetus as being a "dependent child" within the meaning of AFDC beginning with the sixth month of pregnancy or even as early as the pregnancy is verified. The Department of Health, Education and Welfare has traditionally approved such state plans. Is this interpretation now mandated on all

states? See Parks v. Harden, 354 F.Supp. 620 (N.D.Ga.1973); Wilson v. Weaver, —— F.Supp. ——, No. 72C 1960 (N.D.Ill.1972).

3. Assuming that a state has adopted an AFDC–UP program pursuant to 42 U.S.C. § 607, can it refuse aid to families where the father is unemployed because of a strike? The Department of Health, Education and Welfare permits such a family to be included. 45 C.F.R. § 233.-100. See Francis v. Davidson, 340 F. Supp. 351 (D.C.Md.1971) (three judge ct.), aff'd per curiam, 409 U.S. 904, 93 S.Ct. 223, 34 L.Ed.2d 168 (1972).

4. Is a state permitted to adopt the AFDC emergency assistance program, provided in 42 U.S. § 606(e), for only limited purposes or must that program be adopted in its fullest scope if adopted at all? In this regard, examine *Townsend* and *Remillard* carefully; do the decisions have any applicability at all to the emergency assistance program?

————

D. WELFARE AND PERSONAL FREEDOM

————

Many eligibility conditions are phrased not in terms of the applicant's status but in terms of his personal behavior. As in Wilkie v. O'Connor, infra, they require the applicant to conform to certain behavioral norms not required of the society as a whole. In so doing, they raise issues as to the wisdom and legality of imposing such constraints. Practices such as these have led Professor Ten Broek and others to speak of two systems of law, one governing the poor and another the balance of society. Constraints on individual capacity may also be imposed by imposing charges which are beyond the financial ability of the poor. Both forms of constraint give rise to grievances for which redress is often sought.

However much one may bemoan the existence of such a pattern of constraints, it is a different matter to translate that concern into an effective legal argument. Where the individual is required to surrender one's freedom of religion or his protection against unreasonable searches and seizures, or his privilege against self-incrimination, the argument to be made is fairly well defined. However, the behavioral constraints spread far beyond such clearly protected areas and so raise more difficult problems. The materials thus far have developed various bases for challenge of overzealous administrative behavior. Can the *Wilkie* case be fitted into the mold of those authorities? What other constitutional or statutory alternatives might there be on which to base a legal attack?

————

WILKIE v. O'CONNOR

Supreme Court, Appellate Division, Fourth Department, 1941.
261 App.Div. 373, 25 N.Y.S.2d 617.

CROSBY, Presiding Justice. The appellant, by petition dated March 29, 1940, commenced this proceeding to obtain an alternative mandamus order to show cause why the Commissioner of Public Welfare of Seneca County should not deliver to petitioner a check for $24.-50, being the amount of "old age assistance," under the Public Welfare Law, which petitioner had been receiving for some time.

The Commissioner's answer alleges that petitioner, despite all efforts to dissuade him, insists upon his right to sleep under an old barn, in a nest of rags to which he has to crawl upon his hands and knees. The answer further alleges that petitioner has been offered suitable living quarters and an increase in pension sufficient to enable him to maintain a so-called civilized standard of living.

The record discloses that the justice in Special Term made a personal inspection of petitioner's sleeping quarters before denying the prayer of his petition.

The remedy of mandamus, by that name at least, was abolished September 1, 1937, by Article 78, § 1283 et seq., of the Civil Practice Act. However, no objection is made to the form of the petition or to the practice followed. We shall treat the matter, therefore, as a proceeding under Article 78. Section 1285 (sub. 4) of that Article provides that the procedure under Article 78 is not available to a party where the determination complained of "can be adequately reviewed by an appeal to a court or to some other body or officer."

An appeal from the determination of the Commissioner of Public Welfare to the State Department of Public Welfare is specifically provided for in the Public Welfare Law (Section 124–d). Section 124–e provides that: "All grants of assistance under this article shall be reconsidered from time to time", and "it shall be within the power of the public welfare official at any time to cancel and revoke assistance for cause, and he may for cause suspend payments thereof for such periods as he may deem proper, subject to review by the state department, as provided in section one hundred twenty-four-d."

Section 124–f provides that not only the public welfare officer, and the pensioner, but "any person" may apply to the State department for the correction of any errors committed by the local welfare officer.

Indeed appellant, in his brief, cites section 124–f and complains that the welfare officer did not appeal to the State department. The same appeal, at much less expense than the appeal to this Court, was available to the appellant. It follows that he is improperly in Court. Sec. 1285 subd. (4), Civil Practice Act.

However, we are tempted to go further, in view of the public interest, as well as the human interest involved in this proceeding. One of appellant's arguments, gathered from his brief, is that after the local welfare officer has once granted the petitioner a pension he has no control over the matter, and that his only duty is to pay the pension regularly, and that his power is limited to the performance of that duty. The Public Welfare Law clearly negatives that argument. Appellant also argues that he has a right to live as he pleases while being supported by public charity. One would admire his independence if he were not so dependent, but he has no right to defy the standards and conventions of civilized society while being supported at public expense. This is true even though some of those conventions may be somewhat artificial. One is impressed with appellant's argument that he enjoys the life he lives in his humble "home" as he calls it. It may possibly be true, as he says, that his health is not threatened by the way he lives. After all he should not demand that the public, at its expense, allow him to experiment with a manner of living which is likely to endanger his health so that he will become a still greater expense to the public.

It is true, as appellant argues, that the hardy pioneers of our country slept in beds not better than the one he has chosen. But, unlike the appellant, they did it from necessity, and unlike the appellant, they did not call upon the public to support them, while doing it.

Another of appellant's arguments is entirely fallacious. In his brief he says that to a man who has "lived a good life for sixty-five years * * * this old age assistance statute should be viewed in the light of a reward." There is nothing in the record to show that appellant has lived a "good life." In any case his old age pension is not given as a reward, it is given to satisfy a human need regardless of the kind of a life the man has lived, and, in accepting charity, the appellant has consented to the provisions of the law under which charity is bestowed. There is nothing in the record to show that the welfare law has, in this case, been improperly administered.

The order appealed from should be affirmed without costs.

Order affirmed without costs. All concur.

Problem

Issues of the kind raised by *Wilkie* are not of purely historical interest. Consider, for example, section 1611(e)(3) (A) of the SSI program newly enacted by Congress in 1972, 42 U.S.C.A. § 1382 (e)(3)(A), this provision (set out in full in the statutory appendix) requires any recipient who is "medically determined to be a drug addict or an alcoholic" to be "undergoing any treatment that may be appropriate for his condition." Similarly, section 1615(b) of this new law, 42 U.S.C.A. § 1382d(b), (also in appendix) requires a blind and disabled recipient to "accept such rehabilitation services as are made available to him under the State plan for vocational rehabilitation services." Are either of these provisions vulnerable to constitutional attack?

E. WELFARE AND EMPLOYMENT

Work requirements have long been an integral feature of public assistance programs. In a sense, these requirements represent a further example of eligibility conditions and an analysis of them can be seen as a review of all the material above. But more than this the imposition of work requirements goes to the heart of welfare policy. Should an able bodied person have a *right* to assistance or is assistance to be only a last resort after all self-help sources of income have been exhausted? There are probably no more fundamental questions of social policy in work ethic America than those raised in this section.

1. Work Programs—In General

LESSONS FROM THE PAST *

Joel F. Handler.
New Generation, Winter 1970, at 10–12.

It should come as no surprise that what has been billed as the most significant proposed reform in welfare since the Social Security Act should emphasize work more than anything else. In this respect (and there are others), Nixon's Family Assistance Plan is being sold on the same basis as all previous proposals to deal with the problem of poverty.

The problem, it appears, is to reduce or eliminate poverty by getting people to work. In a society that reveres initiative, work and individual capacities, there has always been the fear that the indiscriminate giving of outright relief would encourage people to forsake jobs for the dole. Conditions of relief for those presumed to be in the labor market have always been onerous and stigmatic compared with welfare programs for those not considered to be in the work force. In the words of the late Professor ten Broek, welfare systems are "an indispensable part of the overall system of labor legislation."

The immediate political problem facing the Nixon Administration was the Aid to Families with Dependent Children program. This is the program that has produced the "crisis in welfare" and the one that has led the more urbanized northern states to demand federal relief. This is our largest single relief program, a program that continues to grow in numbers and in costs at alarming rates, and the program that raises issues of race, sex, religion and family responsibility. However, since the clients of this program are husbandless mothers and their children, the question of who should work and who should receive aid has proved to be extremely difficult to resolve. So far, it has always been decided at the local level in a more or less ad hoc fashion.

It has often been assumed that when AFDC programs were first started at the beginning of this century we were fairly clear on the issue of work and welfare—i. e., mothers should stay home and take care of their children. This was not the case, however, for the *class* of husbandless mothers in poverty. The original statutes (then called Mothers' Pensions) were broadly cast; aid could be granted to dependent children of mothers who were divorced, separated, deserted or unwed, as well as widowed, provided these mothers were "fit and proper" to raise children. But relief was, in fact, given primarily to widows, which meant that local administrators (usually county court judges) decided that within the *class* only widows were "fit and proper" and that the other husbandless mothers should use relief programs that had work requirements, find other means of taking care of their families or give up their children.

Even within the group that qualified for AFDC, there was a work test. In 1917, four years after Wisconsin enacted its program, county court judges were given permission to require recipients to work as a condition of receiving assistance. In other words, mothers of dependent children have always been considered part of the work force. They never fully qualified as "deserving poor" (that is, impoverished through no fault of their own and therefore not required to work), but there was no general agreement or standard by which one could decide which mothers should stay at home and which mothers should work. Consequently the issue was left to local administrators to apply their own or the community's sense of morality.

Requiring husbandless mothers to work as an alternative to aid or as a condition of receiving aid did not really become a national issue until the 1950's. During the Depression the primary concern was to find jobs for able-bodied males. AFDC (or ADC, as it was then called) was considered a residual welfare program that would "wither away" as prosperity returned to the country.

The attitude toward the program changed during the last two decades as relief rolls continued to rise despite periods of relatively low unemployment, costs of the programs rose dramatically in the urbanized northern states, and widows were replaced by families where the principal cause of dependency was that fathers *abandoned* their children. In the popular mind, AFDC was a program supporting black mothers, for the most part unwed, who were spawning more and more illegitimate children and traveling north to take advantage of high-benefit states. By 1960 we had a "crisis in welfare."

The first national response to the crisis in welfare was the 1962 social service amendments of the Kennedy Administration. Hailed as a landmark and a new philosophy in welfare by HEW Secretary Ribicoff, the amendments were designed to encourage state welfare agencies to institute social service rehabilitative programs for AFDC families; the bait was that the federal government would pick up an additional 25 per cent of the administrative costs, including the caseworker's salary. The amendments were sold to Congress on the basis that rehabilitation was the way to move people off the welfare rolls permanently and thereby cut costs.

The basic technique of the 1962 amendments followed the standard pattern of federal welfare legislation. The states were given permission to institute programs; they were perfectly free to forgo the additional federal money. And for those states that accepted, federal standards were so vague that the participating states (and local agencies) had almost unlimited discretion as to how to spend the additional money.

The results of the "landmark" approach were predictable: there was never really enough money to do anywhere near the job of rehabilitation; it was impossible to find enough trained people to do the job; many states increased their staff and made formal compliance with federal requirements, but very little happened. It is commonly conceded that there are no social services in public assistance. The situation was not helped by the War on Poverty's general and largely unfair discrediting of social services and social workers.

NOTE

The continued growth of welfare rolls in the late 60's and early 70's, accompanied by the disillusionment with the rehabilitative approach of 1962, has led to an ever increasing emphasis on work as the panacea for "the welfare problem." In examining the following materials, consider two questions:

(1) to what extent are work rules lawful? and (2) to what extent can work rules be effective?

ANDERSON v. BURSON

United States District Court, N.D.
Georgia, 1968.
300 F.Supp. 401.

Before BELL, Circuit Judge and MORGAN and SMITH, District Judges.

PER CURIAM: These cases involve the employable mother regulation promulgated under the Georgia plan for Aid to Families with Dependent Children. Plaintiffs sought a judgment declaring certain portions of the regulation facially unconstitutional and as applied to them and other members of their class. They also sought injunctive relief with respect thereto. In Civil Action No. 10,991, ancillary relief was sought against Secretary Gardner and Regional Representative Perry of the United States Department of Health, Education and Welfare based on their approval of the Georgia regulation in question. The Secretary and Regional Representative were also made parties in Civil Actions Nos. 10,443 and 10,882. Honorable William H. Burson succeeded Mrs. Bruce Schaefer as Director of the Georgia Department of Family and Children Services and was substituted in her place and stead as a party defendant in Nos. 10,443 and 10,-882.

The matters have been heard and are now ripe for final disposition. Upon consideration of the stipulated issues, facts, and exhibits together with the motions and memoranda of the parties and the arguments of counsel for the parties, the court makes the following findings of fact and conclusions of law:

FINDINGS OF FACT

1. Defendant William H. Burson is the director of the State Department of Family and Children Services in Georgia. All of the remaining defendants in Action Nos. 10,443 and 10,882, except defendants Gardner and Perry, are officials of county boards of welfare and departments of welfare in Georgia, and as such are responsible for the implementation and operation of the state program of Aid to Families with Dependent Children (AFDC) in their respective counties. Defendants Mary Louise Maxwell and Dorothy Foreman are directors of county departments of Family and Chil-

dren Services, and as such are employees of the state department.

2. Defendant Burson, in his position as director, is responsible for the direct supervision and control of county departments and officials and has among his duties the promulgation, implementation, and interpretation of rules and regulations under which county officials administer the state program.

3. Defendant Burson, in his position as director, is responsible for developing a state plan for Aid to Families with Dependent Children.

4. In order to receive federal matching funds for assistance payments made as part of the state's AFDC program, the state plan must be submitted for approval to and approved by the Secretary of Health, Education and Welfare, as provided by Title IV of the Social Security Act, 42 U.S.C.A. §§ 601 et seq.

5. The State of Georgia has a currently approved plan for AFDC and is operating a program pursuant thereto which provides assistance payments to families with dependent children.

6. The state plan for AFDC includes a regulation, known as "the employable mother" regulation (Part III, Section V–C(3)(b)(2) of the Georgia Manual of Public Welfare Administration), which at the time of the initiation of these actions provided, in effect:

a. that a mother who is receiving assistance payments must accept available "suitable" employment subject to certain exceptions designed primarily to safeguard the well-being of her children;

b. that in those counties where seasonal employment exists, the county boards will designate such periods as periods of full-time employment; during such periods all applications for assistance are denied and all current cases are closed where the mother is subject to the condition that she must accept employ-

ment. Such applications are denied and closed regardless of whether a mother was in fact employed or had received a bona fide offer of employment;

c. that the burden of proof is upon the mother to show that suitable employment is not available;

d. that wages from "full-time" employment will not be supplemented by assistance payments regardless of the amount of those wages whereas wages from "part-time" or "irregular" employment may be supplemented;

and contains other related provisions which need not be dealt with to dispose of these actions.

7. The state plan for AFDC provides that where unearned income, or income derived from part-time or irregular employment does not meet the full financial needs of the recipient, such income is supplemented with assistance payments.

8. Defendant John Gardner is the Secretary of Health, Education and Welfare; defendant Wave Perry is the administrative official in the Atlanta regional office of the Department of Health, Education and Welfare to whom state plan material is initially submitted. In their official capacities, they, or their agents and employees, have approved the Georgia state plan which includes the employable mother regulation. As a result of that approval, federal funds have been given to Georgia for the administration of their AFDC program to the extent that approximately 75% of the funds expended by the State of Georgia have been from the Federal government.

9. Plaintiffs are mothers who, with their children, are eligible for assistance payments under the Georgia program except for the employable mother regulation.

10. Plaintiffs in Nos. 10,443 and 10,882 sought a declaratory judgment and

injunctive relief against the state and local defendants for violation of their constitutional and statutory rights based upon the text and implementation of the employable mother regulation. Defendant Gardner was ordered joined as a party-defendant by the court. Plaintiffs then commenced No. 10,991 against defendants Gardner and Perry individually. No. 10,991 was consolidated with the other two actions.

11. Subsequent to the commencement of these actions, the employable mother regulation was amended by deleting those portions which provided that employment is presumed to be available to everyone during certain seasons designated by the county welfare agencies and that the burden of proof is at all times on the recipient to establish that employment is not available (those policies described in paragraphs 6(b) and (c) above).

12. Prior to the hearing before this Court on October 6, 1967, the State of Georgia proposed a new employable mother regulation. This regulation deleted the provision that income from full-time employment would not be supplemented. Rather, it put into effect a formula under which income from employment could be supplemented, but on a different basis from income from other sources such as Veterans' benefits, social security benefits, contributions from family members, etc. The effect of the proposed new regulation is that a person whose income comes from employment would in most cases receive less in AFDC benefits than a person whose income came from other sources.

13. The new regulation proposed by the State was not agreed to by the United States Department of Health, Education and Welfare (HEW) on the grounds that it improperly discriminated between AFDC recipients in the calculation of the amount of their grants on the basis of the sources of their income.

14. By suggestion of the court, the state and federal departments attempted to reach an agreement on a substitute employable mother regulation. They have been unable, however, to do so.

CONCLUSIONS OF LAW

1. That portion of the "employable mother" regulation which provides that a mother must accept suitable employment, assuming adequate safeguards to the mother and her children, such as the availability of adequate child care plans and other such limitations, does not violate any of plaintiffs' constitutional or statutory rights, there being no federally protected right of a mother to refuse employment while receiving assistance and remaining at home with her children.

2. That portion of the employable mother regulation which prohibits the supplementation of wages derived from full-time employment violates plaintiffs' constitutional rights established by the equal protection clause of the Fourteenth Amendment to the Constitution in that, although plaintiffs are as needy as other recipients of assistance who also have income, the regulation operates to the financial disadvantage of plaintiffs on the basis of the source of their income and the character of their employment; namely, earned income derived from full-time employment, a basis which bears no reasonable relationship to plaintiffs' financial needs and therefore to the purposes of the Social Security Act. See Gulf, Colorado and Santa Fe Railway Company v. Ellis, 165 U.S. 150, 17 S.Ct. 255, 41 L.Ed. 666 (1896); Morey v. Doud, 354 U.S. 457, 77 S.Ct. 1344, 1 L.Ed.2d 1485 (1957).

3. Similarly, the state's proposed substitution for the employable mother regulation violates plaintiffs' rights under the equal protection clause since it also discriminates between persons on the basis of their source of income without any

relation to their actual financial needs in that persons with income from employment receive less in AFDC benefits than persons with the same amount of income from other sources. On and after April 15, 1968 welfare payments in connection with the AFDC program shall be made without such discrimination and this may be accomplished through the application of any and all income, from whatever source derived, in determining the assistance to be granted.

4. With respect to the burden of proof question, see Findings of Fact ¶¶ 6(c) and 11, in addition to having deleted the requirement, the state director has agreed to employ the following safeguards in the administration of the employable mother regulation: No aid to a mother will be terminated without a showing of a bona fide offer of suitable employment, or referral thereto having been made; and provision will be made for the mother to show good cause grounds for rejecting specific employment and for a hearing, where requested, on those grounds.

5. Since the substance of plaintiffs' complaint pertaining to the employable mother regulation arises from the regulation itself rather than from its improper implementation or application and presents substantial issues arising under the Federal Constitution, plaintiffs are not required to exhaust any administrative remedies, even assuming that any such remedies in fact exist. Damico v. California, 389 U.S. 416, 88 S.Ct. 526, 19 L.Ed.2d 647 (1967).

6. No relief is warranted against the directors and members of the county welfare boards named as defendants in Nos. 10,443 and 10,882.

7. The motion of the defendant Secretary and Regional Representative to dismiss for lack of jurisdiction over the particular subject matter now existent in

Civil Action Nos. 10,443, 10,882, and 10,991 will be granted.

FINAL JUDGMENT

1. The motion of defendant William H. Burson to dismiss Nos. 10,443 and 10,882 for failure of plaintiffs to exhaust their administrative remedies is denied.

2. The defendants in Nos. 10,443 and 10,882 who are directors and members of the board of the Grady County Department of Family and Children Services and the Dougherty County Department of Family and Children Services are hereby dismissed.

3. The motion of defendants John Gardner and Wave Perry to dismiss for lack of jurisdiction over the particular subject matter now existent in Nos. 10,-443, 10,882 and 10,991 is granted and they are hereby dismissed.

4. The defendant William H. Burson, his agents and successors, shall not, on and after April 15, 1968, give any force or effect to that portion of the "employable mother" regulation (Georgia Manual of Public Welfare Administration Part III. Section V–C(3)(b)(2)) which prohibits the supplementation of income derived from full-time employment. Thereafter such income shall be supplemented on the same basis and in accordance with the same standards as other income is supplemented.

PEOPLE v. PICKETT

Court of Appeals of New York, 1967.
19 N.Y.2d 170, 278 N.Y.S.2d 802, 225 N.E.2d 509.

FULD, Ch. J. This case is the first to reach our court in which a strong argument is made that some aspect of social welfare legislation conflicts with traditional concepts of civil liberties. (See, generally, Jones, The Rule of Law and the Welfare State, 58 Col.L.Rev. 143; Reich, Individual Rights and Social Welfare: The Emerging Legal Issues, 74 Yale L.J. 1245.) More particularly, we are called upon to consider whether a welfare recipient may be imprisoned for his refusal to accept available employment.

It is a basic tenet of the Social Welfare Law that "No assistance or care shall be given to an employable person who has * * * refused to accept a position for which he is fitted and which he is able to accept" (Soc.Wel.L., § 131, subd. 4; see 18 NYCRR, §§ 352.6, 385.4, 385.7). However, the termination of public assistance in such a situation may not always be desirable, particularly if the welfare payments were being provided primarily for the benefit of the recipient's dependents. In an effort to avoid visiting the sins of the parent on the heads of his children, the State has taken the position here that it is authorized to prosecute a father for his unjustified refusal to work in lieu of depriving his dependents of welfare assistance.

In the Spring of 1966, the defendant Pickett was unemployed and was a recipient of Temporary Aid to Dependent Children, a form of welfare assistance provided for the benefit of minors whose "parents are unemployed" (Soc.Wel.L., § 349, subd. B [1–a]; see U.S.Code, tit. 42, § 607). Although he had looked for work, he had not actually had a job since the summer of 1964, just before he got married, and, in the interim, he was trained at public expense, as provided for by the Social Welfare Law (§ 350–b), in a landscape gardening school. On April 18, 1966, the New York State Employment Service referred him to a job as a "landscape laborer" at $1.50 an hour, 25¢ an hour above the minimum wage then required by law (Labor Law, § 652, subd. 1[a]). On prior occasions when he had been referred to a job by the State Employment Service, the defendant had sought employment at the places where work was said to be available. On

this occasion, however, he said that "it wasn't enough money" and that he "wanted to look on his own". It was his testimony at the trial that he told the employment official he desired to investigate the possibility of working for one Carter in a construction job and he asked that his referral to a landscaping firm "be put * * * off a week". He was told to return a week later and a notation to that effect was made on his employment referral form.

When the Welfare Department learned of the incident, the defendant's welfare assistance was cut off, although payment of benefits to his wife and children was thereafter resumed. At any rate, on the same day the payments were stopped, an official of the Welfare Department went to the City Court of Niagara Falls and, with the help of the clerk of the court, instituted criminal proceedings against the defendant for violating section 145 of the Social Welfare Law—a provision which makes it a misdemeanor to commit "any wilful act designed to interfere with the proper administration of public assistance and care". In somewhat greater detail, the pertinent part of the section, captioned "Penalties", reads as follows:

"Any person who by means of a false statement or representation or by deliberate concealment of any material fact, or by impersonation or other fraudulent device, obtains or attempts to obtain, or aids or abets any person to obtain public assistance or care to which he is not entitled, or does any wilful act designed to interfere with the proper administration of public assistance and care, shall be guilty of a misdemeanor."

The defendant was arrested but, shortly thereafter, was released pending trial. He immediately went back to the State Employment Office and accepted the same kind of job, landscaping, that he had previously turned down.

He was found guilty, after trial, of violating section 145 and sentenced to 30 days in jail—of which he actually served 20—for his "refusal * * * to go to work" and, on appeal, the Niagara County Court affirmed the judgment of conviction.

It is not clear from the legislative history of section 145 exactly what was meant by the proscription against "any wilful act designed to interfere with the proper administration of public assistance." This language first appeared in our statutes in 1929 as part of the former Public Welfare Law in a section which was entitled "Penalty for fraud; false representation and false swearing" (L.1929, ch. 565, § 148). In 1940, the provision was substantially re-enacted in the Social Welfare Law as section 145 which, as noted above, bears the simple title, "Penalties". Nothing in the documents associated with the passage of the Social Welfare Law suggests that a substantive change was effected by the abridgment of the title to the section dealing with penal sanctions. Indeed, the Legislature subsequently described section 145 as "relating to penalties and prosecution for obtaining public assistance * * * by fraud" (L.1954, ch. 63; see L.1950, ch. 344) or by "deliberate concealment of material facts" (L.1950, ch. 293). All of this would seem to indicate that the Legislature intended a penal sanction to attach to a "wilful act designed to interfere with the proper administration of public assistance" *only if* the act were committed in furtherance of some fraudulent scheme to obtain undeserved welfare payments.

It is of high significance that the provision has been consistently so interpreted by the public officials who are charged with the duty of administering the welfare law. The regulations of the Department of Social Welfare discuss criminal prosecutions under section 145 only in connection with fraud (see 18 NYCRR

pt. 346) and, in a 1962 Report on "Controls and Safeguards in the Administration of Public Assistance and Care", the Social Welfare Board made no mention of any penal "controls and safeguards" provided by section 145 except for fraud. Nor did the 1963 Moreland Commission in its "Report on Public Welfare in the State of New York" give the slightest indication that a prosecution such as the one before us was viewed by it or by welfare officials as being authorized by the statute. Finally, research discloses that in the nearly 40 years that section 145 or its predecessor has been in force, there have been no succesful prosecutions except for fraud and all but one of the reported prosecutions have involved some element of fraud. (See, e. g., People v. Pellerito, 262 N.Y. 465, 188 N.E. 22; People v. George, 279 App.Div. 878; People v. Hurkin, 266 App.Div. 966; People v. Miller, 255 App.Div. 1026, 9 N.Y.S.2d 578; People v. Scalise, 246 App.Div. 799, 285 N.Y.S. 1056).[1]

Although the statutory language of section 145 is exceedingly broad, we believe that the Legislature meant to provide penal sanctions only for acts motivated by fraudulent intent. Since the defendant was neither charged with fraud nor was proof of fraud on his part introduced upon the trial, his conviction must be reversed and the information dismissed.

This view is strengthened by the settled canon of construction that a statute

[1] The sole exception is People v. La Fountain (21 A.D.2d 719, 249 N.Y.S.2d 744) where, during very cold weather, welfare recipients in a work-relief program (Soc.Wel.L., § 164) refused to cut brush alongside a county road in exceedingly deep snow. Although they were indicted and convicted for doing a "wilful act designed to interfere with the proper administration of public assistance", the Appellate Division reversed the conviction and dismissed the indictment on the ground that no 'wilful' act within the meaning of section 145 and none, certainly, 'designed' to interfere with welfare administration" had been proved (p. 720).

"should be construed when possible in manner which would remove doubt of its constitutionality". (New York Post Corp. v. Leibowitz, 2 N.Y.2d 677, 687, 163 N.Y.S.2d 409, 143 N.E.2d 256; see People v. Lo Cicero, 14 N.Y.2d 374, 378, 251 N.Y.S.2d 953, 200 N.E.2d 622.) Absent a requirement that there be proof of fraudulent intent, the portion of section 145 under consideration here might well be regarded as unconstitutional on the ground of vagueness (see, e. g., Keyishian v. Board of Regents of U. of N. Y., 385 U.S. 589, 87 S.Ct. 675, 17 L.Ed.2d 629, 35 USLW 4152 [decided Jan. 23, 1967]; People v. Caswell-Massey Co., 6 N.Y.2d 497, 501, 100 N.Y.S. 2d 649, 160 N.E.2d 895; People v. Diaz, 4 N.Y.2d 469, 176 N.Y.S.2d 313, 151 N.E.2d 871; People v. Firth, 3 N.Y.2d 472, 169 N.Y.S.2d 949, 146 N.E.2d 682; People v. Grogan, 260 N.Y. 138, 183 N.E. 273) or because it sanctions "involuntary servitude" and "peonage". (U.S.Const., 13th Amdt.; U.S.Code, tit. 18, § 1581(a); see, e. g., Pollock v. Williams, 322 U.S. 4, 17–18, 64 S.Ct. 792, 88 L.Ed. 1095; United States v. Gaskin, 320 U.S. 527, 64 S.Ct. 318, 88 L.Ed. 287; Taylor v. Georgia, 315 U.S. 25, 62 S.Ct. 415, 86 L.Ed. 615; United States Plaintiff in Error v. Reynolds, 235 U.S. 133, 35 S.Ct. 86, 59 L.Ed. 162; Bailey v. Alabama, 219 U.S. 219, 31 S. Ct. 145, 55 L.Ed. 191; Thompson v. Bunton, 117 Mo. 83, 22 S.W. 863.)

The judgment of conviction should be reversed and the information dismissed.

* * *

Judgment reversed and the information dismissed. Opinion by Fuld, Ch. J. All concur; Van Voorhis, J., in the result upon the ground that section 145 of the Social Welfare Law is ambiguous for the reasons stated in the opinion of Chief Judge Fuld and, therefore, supplies an insufficient foundation to support a criminal charge.

PEOPLE v. PICKETT

Excerpt from the Brief.

POINT I

SECTION 145, AS INTERPRETED AND APPLIED IN THIS CASE, VIOLATES RIGHTS GUARANTEED TO APPELLANT BY THE THIRTEENTH AMENDMENT TO THE UNITED STATES CONSTITUTION AND THE FEDERAL ANTI-PEONAGE ACT.

The question here is the state's power, through the Welfare Department, to prosecute, convict and imprison a public assistance recipient for his refusal to accept a particular offer of private employment. We shall demonstrate in this Point that such power violates—at the very least—two fundamental provisions of law: The Thirteenth Amendment to United States Constitution, and Title 18 U.S.C.A. § 1581, the federal Anti-Peonage Act, adopted by Congress as a means of implementing the Thirteenth Amendment.

The Thirteenth Amendment provides:

"Section 1. Neither slavery nor involuntary servitude, except as a punishment for crime whereof the party shall have been duly convicted, shall exist within the United States or within any place subject to their jurisdiction."

"Section 2. Congress shall have power to enforce this article by appropriate legislation".

Title 18 U.S.C.A. § 1581(a) provides:

"(a) Whoever holds or returns any person to a condition of peonage, or arrests any person with the intent of placing him in or returning him to a condition of peonage, shall be fined not more than $5,000 or imprisoned not more than five years, or both."

The decisions of the United States Supreme Court dealing with the Thirteenth Amendment and the Anti-Peonage Act evince two overriding objectives: (1) The prohibition of labor compelled by threats of criminal punishment, even though such labor is performed or promised for the purpose of paying debts; (2) the preservation of a free and voluntary labor system in the United States, with all its attendant benefits to society. Initially we examine the decided cases and, thereafter, consider the inescapable consequences of those cases for the question presently before this Court.

The Supreme Court early considered the nature of compulsion under the Thirteenth Amendment. United States v. Reynolds, 235 U.S. 133, 35 S.Ct. 86, 59 L.Ed. 162 (1914), a prosecution under the federal Anti-Peonage Act, involved Alabama statutes which authorized agreement between a person against whom a court had assessed a fine and a "surety" who would pay the fine. * * * The Court described the vicious cycle of debt, work agreement and intimidation which the statutes made possible and held that fear of criminal punishment brought the employment within the prohibition of the Thirteenth Amendment (235 U.S. at 146).

> This labor [under the surety agreement] is performed under the constant coercion and threat of another possible arrest and prosecution in case he violates the labor contract which he has made with the surety; and this form of coercion is as potent as it would have been had the law provided for the seizure and compulsory service of the convict. Compulsion of such service by a constant fear of imprisonment under the criminal laws renders the work compulsory, as much so as authority to arrest and hold his person would be if the law authorized that to be done.

In Bailey v. Alabama, 219 U.S. 219, 31 S.Ct. 145, 55 L.Ed. 191 (1911), the Court, upon striking down a statute which compelled performance of work contracts by creating a presumption of criminal fraud in the event the employee refused or failed to perform the work, made the critical distinction between the right of the employer to sue for breach of contract and a statute which compelled performance of the contract through threat of criminal punishment for breach. Said the Court of the federal Anti-Peonage statute (219 U.S. at 243–244):

> "It is the compulsion of the service that the statute inhibits, for when that occurs, the condition of servitude is created, which would be not less involuntary because of the original agreement to work out the indebtedness. The contract exposes the debtor to liability for the loss due to the breach, but not to enforce labor." 219 U.S. at 242.

> "The Act of Congress, nullifying all state laws by which it should be attempted to enforce the 'service of labor of any persons as peons, in liquidation of any debt or obligation, or othwise,' necessarily embraces all legislation which seeks to compel the service of labor by making it a crime to refuse or fail to perform it. Such laws would furnish the readiest means of compulsion * * *

> "It does not permit slavery or involuntary servitude to be established or maintained through the operation of the criminal law by making it a crime to refuse to submit to the one or render the service which would constitute the other. The state may impose involuntary servitude as a punishment for crime, but it may not compel one man to labor for another in payment of a debt, by punishing him as a criminal if he does not perform the service or pay the debt." * * *

Pollock v. Williams, 322 U.S. 4, 64 S.Ct. 792, 88 L.Ed. 1095 (1944) is the latest case in which the Supreme Court has examined the question of peonage.

There, the Court spoke most directly of the central concern of the Thirteenth Amendment: The preservation of a completely free and voluntary system of labor throughout the United States. There again, the federal Anti-Peonage Act was invoked as a shield to protect an individual from conviction under a state statute. The Court held that the statute in question was void as a whole because the existence and potential operation of the law were intimidatory and coercive. Said the Court (322 U.S. at 17–18):

"The undoubted aim of the Thirteenth Amendment as implemented by the Anti-Peonage Act was *not merely* to end slavery *but to maintain a system of completely free and voluntary labor throughout the United States.* Forced labor in some special circumstances may be consistent with the general basic system of free labor. For example, forced labor has been sustained as a means of punishing crime, and there are duties such as work on highways which society may compel. But in general the defense against oppressive hours, pay, working conditions, or treatment is the right to change employers. When the master can compel and the laborer cannot escape the obligation to go on, there is no power below to redress and no incentive to work. * * * Whatever of social value there may be, and of course it is great, in enforcing contracts and collection of debts, Congress has put it beyond debate that no indebtedness warrants a suspension of the right to be free from compulsory service. *This congressional policy means that no state can make the quitting of work any component of a crime, or make criminal sanctions available for holding unwilling persons to labor. The federal statutory test is a practical inquiry into the utilization of an act as well as its mere form and terms."* 323 U.S. at 17–18. (Emphasis supplied)

In the case at bar, Section 145—as interpreted and applied below—serves as a classic illustration of the peonage condemned by the Thirteenth Amendment. An individual, in financial need, seeks and receives a grant from the welfare department. By statute, as we show below, a debtor-creditor relationship with the welfare department is thereby created. The creditor (welfare department) demands the individual perform particular work for a particular private employer. The individual (allegedly) refuses. He is prosecuted. The individual then accepts the work. Indeed, so bald is the work compulsion here involved that the District Attorney's representative argued below—for the purpose of demonstrating the alleged crime—that Appellant accepted the landscaping job only because of his arrest! Thus: (T. 29):

"Mr. DiFlorio: If the Court please, I think the evidence presented * * * show there was an actual refusal on the part of the defendant of employment which had been offered to him * * * *Evidence shows also that it was only after this defendant was picked up by the police that he cooperated with the Welfare authorities and then accepted this same particular job which had been offered to him before at the same salary."* (Our emphasis)

Involuntary servitude is no less unlawful when compelled on behalf of particular private employers by a welfare department than when compelled by the private employers themselves. Indeed, it is even more dangerous to our democratic society when compelled under such circumstances. * * *

Nor is it relevant whether or not the state has an affirmative duty to provide welfare benefits to its destitute citizens as an original proposition. Whatever the conflicting views may be about welfare programs—and they are sometimes rancorous—the federal and state governments have all recognized their responsibility toward the poor. It is an ancient, not novel, practice.* But as this case demonstrates, there are conflicting points of view concerning the correlative duties of the recipients of the state's welfare. Thus, the prosecution here has demonstrated its belief that the recipient's duty to relieve welfare costs—and to repay what statute has deemed an implied loan in a debtor-creditor relationship—can be enforced with the harsh sanction of imprisonment. Likewise, the legislatures of Alabama and Georgia believed that agreements to discharge private debts could be enforced through forced labor, but the Supreme Court held otherwise. This court can do no less.

No matter how the facts in this case are turned, they come down to this: First, the state has undertaken to provide money payments to persons who are unemployed and whose families would otherwise be destitute. If the head of the household is not employable, the payments are not conditioned upon his taking work. If, however, the head of the household is employable, the state requires by statute that he accept employment and that the cost of welfare be thereby lowered; in the event the employable person refuses, assistance is to be terminated (See § 131(4) of the Social Welfare Law). Second, when assistance is accepted, the statute declares that "an implied contract" between the recipient and the welfare department is created. The recipient stands as a debtor and is expected to repay the amount of assistance should he gain other funds at a later date. For a period of ten years after granting assistance, the welfare department is authorized to bring an action to recover the amount paid from either the recipient or his estate whenever such other funds are gained. Indeed, the statute declares that when such a claim against a former re-

* In the Anglo-Saxon world, they have been recognized by law since the first Poor Laws were adopted in England in 1601.

cipient is asserted, the welfare department "shall be deemed a preferred creditor". See § 104, Social Welfare Law. So far, so good.

By its next step, however, through the mechanism of § 145 as interpreted below, the state has crossed the line that separates forced labor from free labor. The state has chosen to prosecute one of its debtor-public assistance recipients for not immediately accepting an offer of a particular job with a particular employer. Simultaneously, the state has asserted its power to act in the same manner against any welfare recipient it deems employable. The state was satisfied not simply with a termination of assistance because of the alleged job refusal. It did not seek to institute a civil suit to compel Appellant to support his family as it was authorized to do (See § 102, Social Welfare Law). The remedy sought was a criminal prosecution; the consequence was forced labor.

It should be emphasized that while the status of the public assistance recipient as a *debtor* makes the criminal prosecution in this case squarely analogous to previous peonage cases, recognition of that status is by no means necessary to the inescapable conclusion that § 145 as interterpreted violates the Thirteenth Amendment. Assuming that Appellant Pickett did not stand in the relation of debtor to the welfare department, his criminal prosecution for refusing a job offer is even more obviously and blatantly a violation of the Thirteenth Amendment. The debtor relationship has been merely part of the rationale used by states in previous peonage cases to justify their statutes. It is the threat of criminal punishment that "renders the work compulsory" and thereby causes a violation of the Thirteenth Amendment and the Anti-Peonage Act. See *Reynolds,* supra, 235 U.S. at 146. * * *

"One of the most valuable rights of man is to work where he pleases, and to quit one employment and go to another, subject, of course, to civil liability for breach of contract obligations." Peonage Cases, 123 F.2d 671, 686 (M.D.Ala. 1903). The state may offer an elaborate explanation to distinguish this case from peonage or involuntary servitude. But it remains that the Anti-Peonage Act "means that no state can make the quitting of work any component of a crime, or make criminal sanctions available for holding unwilling persons to labor". Pollock v. Williams, supra, 323 U.S. at 18. We urge this Court to condemn the forced labor which the welfare department sought in this case as a violation of the Thirteenth Amendment. * * *

2. The Federal Work Incentive Program (WIN)

THE MECHANICS OF WIN

From Comment, 119 U.Pa.L.Rev. 485, 489–92 (1971).

WIN is administered by HEW and the Department of Labor. Each department is responsible for different aspects of the program. The process begins when the state welfare' agency evaluates adult AFDC recipients to determine which are "appropriate" [22] for referral to the program. Federal regulations require that the states evaluate individuals in a specified order,[23] beginning with AFDC unemployed fathers. Mothers and other caretaker relatives who volunteer for WIN and are currently in a program under title V of the Economic Opportunity Act [24] or in a CWT program are evaluated next. Presumably these in-

dividuals are already motivated to work or to be trained and have access to child care programs. The third group comprises "[d]ependent children and essential persons age 16 or over who are not in school, at work, or in training, and for whom there are no educational plans under consideration." [25] Mothers who volunteer but are not already in existing training programs constitute the next group if they have no pre-school-age children, and the fifth group if they do. Thereafter, the state welfare agency may evaluate for referral any other recipients.

Of the five groups, the regulations require assessment of only the first (unemployed fathers) and third (youth and essential persons 16 or over).[26] States need not assess any other individuals, but if they do, they must follow the prescribed order.

Welfare caseworkers interview recipients and ostensibly select for enrollment in WIN only those most likely to succeed in the program.[27] The caseworker is familiar with the history, work experience, family needs, emotional stability, and other factors relevant to the recipient's appropriateness. But caseworkers are not manpower employment specialists and the standards of employability or trainability are not objective; thus the complex decision of appropriateness is left largely to the caseworker's intuition. The number of recipients referred by the state welfare agencies as appropriate consequently varies greatly from state to state,[28] and only 43.9 percent of those

---

[22] Social Security Act §§ 402(a)(19)(A)(i), (ii), 42 U.S.C.A. §§ 602(a)(19)(A)(i), (ii) (Supp. V, 1970).

[23] U. S. Dep't of Health, Educ., & Welfare, Guidelines for the Work Incentive Program § 61.1 (1969).

[24] 42 U.S.C.A. §§ 2921–33 (Supp. V, 1970).

[25] 45 CFR § 220.35(a)(3)(iii) (1970).

[26] Id. §§ 220.35(a)(iv)–(v).

[27] The selection process is described in Manpower Admin., U. S. Dep't of Labor, Bureau of Work and Training Programs Manual ch. 9 (WIN Handbook), § 19 (1968) [hereinafter cited as BWTP Manual].

[28] The variations among the states in finding AFDC recipients appropriate are staggering. Nevada and New Hampshire are the lowest states, finding only 5.8% and 6.1% of their recipients appropriate; West Vir-

referred by the state agencies are ultimately enrolled in WIN.[29]

Recipients found appropriate by the state agencies are next referred[30] to the Local Bureau of Employment Services (under the supervision of the Department of Labor), which conducts its own assessment of appropriateness. This reevaluation determines whether the individuals are immediately employable or suitable for other manpower programs or need specialized services[31] (or are inappropriate for WIN, in which case they are referred back to the welfare agencies). This assessment is conducted by an employability team comprising a counselor, manpower training specialist, job developer, and coach. The team draws up an

employability development plan for each individual which "will best meet the needs for employment in a job the trainee desires and is capable of performing. The team concept provides for a controlled caseload allowing sufficient time for work with the trainees."[32]

As the employability development plan progresses, individuals are separated into three "priorities."[33] Those who are immediately employable and have work skills needed in the local labor market, or who can enter on-the-job training positions in existing federal programs,[34] are either found employment or placed in federal manpower programs. These enrollees receive supportive services (such as counseling) for a minimum of ninety days[35] and, in computing their welfare needs, may disregard the first thirty dollars of their earned income and one third of the remainder.[36]

The second priority includes enrollees needing special training to be employable.[37] Enrollees in this priority fall into either occupational or pre-occupational training. The former includes union apprenticeships, advanced institutional training in a particular skill,[38] or institutional training in a new basic skill such

ginia and Oregon are highest, finding 93.0% and 91.0% appropriate. U. S. Dep't of Health, Educ., & Welfare, Social and Rehabilitation Services Monthly Status Reports for WIN (May 31, 1970) [hereinafter cited as Monthly Status Reports for WIN (May 31, 1970)].

[29] Id.

[30] Many recipients considered appropriate for referral by the state agencies are not actually referred. See text accompanying note 67 infra (table I). The disparity may be explained in part by

the fact that some individuals found appropriate become inappropriate before they can be referred; and a reluctance on the part of the local welfare agencies to refer additional individuals as enrollments approach the maximum number of training spaces available.

J. Lynch, Statistical Data on Welfare Aspects of Work Incentive Program for AFDC Recipients, Selected Periods Within Fiscal Year 1969, at 2, 1969 (Nat'l Center for Social Statistics, Social & Rehabilitation Service U. S. Dep't of Health, Educ., & Welfare, Rep. H–2(69)). As of March 1970, however, these factors only accounted for approximately 25% of the appropriate AFDC recipients never ultimately referred to WIN by the local Bureau after reassessment. Staff of the Senate Comm., on Finance, 91st Cong., 2d Sess., Material, Related to Work and Training Provisions of Administration Revision of H.R. 16311, at 5 (Comm.Print 1970) [hereinafter cited as Finance Comm. Staff Material].

[31] BWTP Manual §§ 511–12.

Cooper et al., Cs. Law & Poverty 2d Ed. ACB—13

[32] U. S. Dep't of Labor, Work Incentive Briefing Paper 2, Dec. 15, 1969.

[33] S.Rep.No.744, supra note 18, at 147–55. The statutory provision incorporating these priorities is Social Security Act § 432(b), 42 U.S.C.A. § 632(b) (Supp. V, 1970).

[34] S.Rep.No.744, supra note 18, at 149.

[35] U. S. Dep't of Labor, Work Incentive Briefing Paper 2, Dec. 15, 1969.

[36] Social Security Act § 402(a)(8)(A)(ii), 42 U.S.C.A. § 602(a)(8)(A)(ii) (Supp. V, 1970).

[37] S.Rep.No.744, supra note 18, at 149.

[38] U. S. Dep't of Labor, The Work Incentive Program: First Annual Report of the Dep't of Labor to the Congress on Training and Employment Under Title IV of the Social Security Act 9, June 1970 [hereinafter cited as WIN First Annual Report]; BWTP Manual § 514.3.

as simple typing or filing,[39] or training for a job requiring no formal skill,[40] such as nurse's or teacher's aide. Pre-occupational programs provide extensive preparatory training, including basic orientation to work experience [41] (how to act during a job interview, how to relate to fellow employees, employers' expectations), exploration of ability by job try-outs and work samples,[42] and acquisition of basic educational tools.[43] All enrollees in this second priority receive a monthly incentive payment of thirty dollars in addition to their welfare grants.[44]

Recipients who cannot benefit from training and for whom jobs in the economy cannot be located—but who have nonetheless been found appropriate for WIN—are placed in "special works projects," the third priority. Public agencies or private nonprofit agencies organized for a public purpose can employ these enrollees, who "in most instances * * * would no longer receive a welfare check." [45] Instead, they receive a payment from an employer for services performed. A supplemental grant will be made, if necessary, to bring their wages to a level twenty percent above their welfare grant level. They are also reimbursed for any expenses incurred due to participation in the program. If an enrollee's employability development plan bogs down, he may be sidetracked, perhaps for months, in a "holding" status; no incentive payments are made to these enrollees.

In some respects WIN is an innovative manpower program. The financial incentive is a noteworthy departure from previous antipoverty programs, and WIN provides an organized approach to provision of manpower services which other antipoverty manpower programs provide separately. The concept of an employment team has been found particularly effective in providing assistance to multiproblem welfare recipients.

NEW YORK STATE DEPARTMENT OF SOCIAL SERVICES v. DUBLINO

Supreme Court of the United States, 1973.
—— U.S. ——, 93 S.Ct. ——, —— L.Ed.2d ——.

Mr. Justice POWELL delivered the opinion of the Court.

The question before us is whether the Social Security Act of 1935 bars a State from independently requiring individuals to accept employment as a condition for receipt of federally funded aid to families with dependent children. More precisely, the issue is whether that part of the Social Security Act known as the federal Work Incentive Program, pre-empts the provisions of the New York Social Welfare Law commonly referred to as the New York Work Rules. A brief description of both the state and federal programs will be necessary.

The Work Rules were enacted by New York in 1971 [1] as part of Governor Rock-

---

[39] See WIN First Annual Report 9; BWTP Manual § 514.3.

[40] See WIN First Annual Report 11: BWTP Manual § 514.4.

[41] WIN First Annual Report 8; BWTP Manual § 514.5.

[42] WIN First Annual Report 10–11; BWTP Manual § 514.2.

[43] WIN First Annual Report 9; BWTP Manual § 515. "Educational services are provided to those recipients lacking the minimum education necessary to obtain a job or participate in further training." WIN First Annual Report 9. One part of the educational training provides a high school equivalency diploma ("General Educational Development," or GED); this type of education may continue even after the educational level of the enrollee enables him to begin training. See id. 5.

[44] Social Security Act § 402(a)(19)(D)(i), 42 U.S.C.A. § 602(a)(19)(D)(i) (Supp. V, 1970).

[45] S.Rep.No.744, supra note 18, at 150.

[1] The basic provisions of the Work Rules at the time this action was brought are set

efeller's efforts to reorganize the New York Welfare Program. Their aim, as

forth in § 131 of the New York Social Services Law (52A McKinney's Cons.Laws § 131 (4)):

"4. No assistance or care shall be given to an employable person who has not registered with the nearest local employment agency of the department of labor or has refused to accept employment in which he is able to engage.

"A person shall be deemed to have refused to accept such employment if he:

"a. Fails to obtain and file with the social services district at least once in every two-week period a new certificate from the appropriate local employment office of the state department of labor stating that such employment office has no order for an opening in part-time, full-time, temporary or permanent employment in which the applicant is able to engage, or

"b. wilfully fails to report for an interview at an employment office with respect to employment when requested to do so by such office, or

"c. wilfully fails to report to such office the result of a referral to employment, or

"d. wilfully fails to report for employment. Such wilful failures or refusal as above listed shall be reported immediately to the social services district by such employment office.

"For the purposes of this subdivision and subdivision five, a person shall be deemed employable if such person is not rendered unable to work by: illness or significant and substantial incapacitation, either mental or physical, to the extent and of such duration that such illness or incapacitation prevents such person from performing services; advanced age; full-time attendance at school in the case of minor, in accordance with provisions of this chapter; full-time, satisfactory participation in an approved program of vocational training or rehabilitation; the need of such person to provide full-time care for other members of such person's household who are wholly incapacitated, or who are children, and for whom required care is not otherwise reasonably available, notwithstanding diligent efforts by such person to obtain others to provide such care. A person assigned to and participating in a public works project under the provisions of section one hundred sixty-four or three hundred fifty-k of this chapter shall be deemed to be employable but not employed.

"Every employable recipient of public assistance or person who is deemed not to be employable by reason of full-time satisfactory participation in an approved program of vocational training or rehabilitation shall receive his public assistance grants and al-

explained by the Governor, is to encourage "the young and able-bodied, temporarily in need of assistance through no fault of their own, to achieve the education and the skills, the motivation and the determination that will make it possible for them to become increasingly self-sufficient, independent citizens who can contribute to and share in the responsibility for their families and our society." [2]

To achieve this, the Work Rules establish a presumption that certain recipients of public assistance are employable [3] and require those recipients to report every two weeks to pick up their assistance checks in person; to file every two weeks a certificate from the appropriate public employment office stating that no suitable employment opportunities are available; to report for requested employment interviews; to report to the public employment office the result of a referral for employment; and not to fail willfully to report for suitable employment, when available. In addition to establishing a system of referral for employment in the private sector of the economy, the Work Rules permit the establishment of public works projects in New York's social service districts.[4] Failure of "employable" persons to participate in the operation of

lowances in person from the division of employment of the state department of labor, in accordance with regulations of the department."

Section 350(k) of New York Social Services Law (52A McKinney's Cons.Laws 350(k) provides for public works project employment for employable recipients of AFDC who cannot be placed in regular employment.

[2] Special Message to the New York State Legislature, March 29, 1971 (Brief for Appellants, p. 9).

[3] For the statutory definition of persons deemed "employable" see n. 1, supra.

[4] See n. 1, supra. These provisions for employment of recipients in public works projects have not been implemented, as the HEW Regional Commissioner indicated that such projects would not be approved for federal aid. Appellant's Brief, p. 13.

the Work Rules results in a loss of assistance.[5]

Like the Work Rules, the federal Work Incentive Program (WIN) is designed to help individuals on welfare "acquire a sense of dignity, self-worth, and confidence which will flow from being recognized as a wage-earning member of society * * *," 42 U.S.C.A. § 630. The program was enacted as part of the 1967 amendments to the Social Security Act,[6] whereby States were required to incorporate the Work Incentive Program into their AFDC plans. 42 U.S.C.A. § 602 (a)(19), § 630 et seq. Every state AFDC plan must provide that certain "employable" individuals, as a condition for receiving aid, shall register for manpower services, training, and employment under regulations promulgated by the Secretary of Labor. 42 U.S.C.A. § 602(a)(19) (A).[7] Available services, to be provided by the State, must include "such health, vocational rehabilitation, counseling, child care, and other such supportive services as are necessary to enable such individuals to accept employment or receive manpower training * * *." 42 U.S.C.A. § 602(a)(19)(G). After the required services have been provided, the State must certify to the Secretary of Labor those individuals who are ready for employment or training programs, 42 U.S.C.A. §§ 602(a)(19)(G), 632, 633.[8] Employment consists both of work in the regular economy and participation in public service programs. 42 U.S.C.A. §§ 630, 632, 633. As with the Work Rules, cooperation in WIN is necessary for employable individuals to continue to receive assistance.

In the court below, appellees, New York public assistance recipients subject to the Work Rules, challenged those

---

[5] See n. 1, supra, and Social Services Administrative Letter, 71 PWD—43 which reads in relevant part:
"* * * the Laws of 1971 place a renewed and expanded emphasis on restoring all employable recipients of public assistance to employment in the regular economy. Accordingly, all unemployed employable persons applying for or receiving public assistance are not only required to register at the New York State Employment Service district office in their community, and report there regularly for appropriate employment counseling services and job referral; but, effective July 1, they will also pick up their assistance checks there. The penalty for not cooperating in this procedure is ineligibility for public assistance whether the individual is the grantee head of family, single person living alone, or non-grantee non-head of family."

[6] In 1971, further amendments dealing with the WIN program were enacted. Act of Dec. 14, 1971, Pub.L. 92–223, 85 Stat. 803.

[7] 42 U.S.C.A. § 602(a):
"§ 602. State plans for aid and services to needy families with children; contents; approval by Secretary
"(a) A State plan for aid and services to needy families with children must.

. . . . .

"(19) provide—
"(A) that every individual, as a condition of eligibility for aid under this part, shall

register for manpower services, training and employment as provided by regulations of the Secretary of Labor, unless such individual is—
"(i) a child who is under age 16 or attending school full time;
"(ii) a person who is ill, incapacitated, or of advanced age;
"(iii) a person so remote from a work incentive project that his effective participation is precluded;
"(iv) a person whose presence in the home is required because of illness or incapacity of another member of the household;
"(v) a mother or other relative of a child under the age of six who is caring for the child; or
"(vi) the mother or other female caretaker of a child, if the father or another adult male relative is in the home and not excluded by clause (i), (ii), (iii), or (iv), of this subparagraph (unless he has failed to register as required by this subparagraph, or has been found by the Secretary of Labor under section 633(g) of this title to have refused without good cause to participate under a work incentive program or accept employment as described in subparagraph (F) of this paragraph)."

[8] States are penalized by a reduction in assistance if they fail to certify to the Secretary of Labor at least 15% of the average number of those registered each year. 42 U.S.C.A. § 603(c).

Rules as violative of several provisions of the Constitution and as having been pre-empted by the WIN provisions of the Federal Social Security Act. The three-judge District Court rejected all but the last contention. 348 F.Supp. 290 (1972). On this point, it held that "for those in the AFDC program, WIN preempts" [9] the New York Work Rules. Id., at 297.[10] As this holding not only affected the continued operation of the New York rules but raised serious doubts as to the viability of the supplementary work programs in 22 States, we set the cause for argument, 409 U.S. 1123 (1973).[11] We now reverse this holding.

[9] The District Court and the parties in this case have used the word "pre-emption" in a rather special sense. This is not a case involving arguable federal pre-emption of a wholly independent state program dealing with the same or a similar problem. Cf., e. g., Huron Portland Cement Co. v. Detroit, 362 U.S. 440, 446 (1959). AFDC is a federal statutory program, of which the WIN program is a part. The State Work Rules also were promulgated as part of the implementation of AFDC, and are therefore not wholly independent of the federal program. With this caveat, however, we will preserve the District Court's usage, which has the advantage of focusing attention on the critical question: whether Congress intended the WIN program to provide the exclusive mechanism for establishing work rules under AFDC.

[10] The court found additional points of conflict between the state and federal programs with regard to procedures for termination of benefits and the presence of certain hearings and counseling services under WIN which were absent from the Work Rules. 348 F.Supp., at 295–297.

[11] We postponed consideration of the question of jurisdiction to the hearing on the merits. We now conclude that the constitutional questions raised by appellees were not so insubstantial as to deprive the three-judge District Court of jurisdiction.

As to appellees' due process claim, the court below directed the State to implement suitable means of informing Home Relief recipients of their hearing rights. 348 F.Supp., at 299. The State stipulates that this has been done. Tr. of Oral Arg., pp. 19–20. The only issue which we address on this appeal is whether the state program is superseded in whole or in part by federal law.

I

The holding of the court below affects the Work Rules only insofar as they apply to AFDC recipients. 348 F.Supp., at 297, 300, and n. 5. New York's Home Relief program, for example—a general state assistance plan for which there is no federal reimbursement or support [12]—remains untouched by the Court's pre-emption ruling. As to AFDC participants, however, the decision below would render the Work Rules inoperative and hold WIN "the exclusive manner of applying the carrot and stick" in efforts to place such recipients in gainful employment. 348 F.Supp., at 300.[13]

This is a sweeping step that strikes at the core of state prerogative under the AFDC program—a program which this Court has been careful to describe as a "scheme of cooperative federalism." King v. Smith, 392 U.S. 309, 316 (1968); Dandridge v. Williams, 397 U.S. 471, 478 (1970); Jefferson v. Hackney, 406 U.S. 535, 542 (1972). It could impair the capacity of the state government to deal effectively with the critical problem of mounting welfare costs and the increasing financial dependency of many of its citizens. New York has a legitimate interest in encouraging those of its citizens who can work to do so, and thus contribute to the societal well-being in addition to their personal and family support. To the extent that the Work Rules embody New York's attempt to promote self-reliance and civic responsibility, to assure that limited state welfare funds be spent on behalf of those genuinely incapacitated and most in need, and to cope with the fiscal hardships envelop-

[12] The AFDC program is jointly financed by the States and Federal Government. Dandridge v. Williams, supra, at 473.

[13] Appellees' position is also one of "complete exclusion" of the Work Rules, at least with regard to AFDC recipients. Tr. of Oral Arg., p. 34; Brief for Appellees in Response to Brief for the United States as amicus curiae, pp. 2–3.

ing many state and local governments, this Court should not lightly interfere. The problems confronting our society in these areas are severe, and state governments, in cooperation with the Federal Government, must be allowed considerable latitude in attempting their resolution.

This Court has repeatedly refused to void state statutory programs, absent congressional intent to pre-empt them.

"If Congress is authorized to act in a field, it should manifest its intention clearly. It will not be presumed that a federal statute was intended to supersede the exercise of the power of the state unless there is a clear manifestation of intention to do so. The exercise of federal supremacy is not lightly to be presumed." Schwartz v. Texas, 344 U.S. 199, 202–203 (1952).

[Citations omitted.]

This same principle relates directly to state AFDC programs, where the Court already has acknowledged that States "have considerable latitude in allocating their AFDC resources, since each State is free to set its own standard of need and to determine the level of benefits by the amount of funds it devotes to the program." King v. Smith, supra, at 318–319; Dandridge v. Williams, supra, at 478; Jefferson v. Hackney, supra, at 541. Moreover, at the time of the passage of the federal work incentive program in 1967, 21 States already had initiated welfare work requirements as a condition of AFDC eligibility.[14] If Congress had intended to pre-empt state plans and efforts in such an important dimension of the AFDC program as employment referrals for those on assistance, such intentions would in all likelihood have been expressed in direct and unambiguous language. No such expression exists, however, either in the federal statute or in the committee reports.[15]

Appellees argue, nonetheless, that Congress intended to pre-empt state work programs because of the comprehensive nature of the WIN legislation, its legislative history,[16] and the alleged conflicts between certain sections of the state and federal laws.[17] We do not agree. We reject, to begin with, the contention that pre-emption is to be inferred merely from the comprehensive character of the federal work incentive provisions, 42 U.S.C. § 602(a)(19), § 630 et seq. The subjects of modern social and regulatory legislation often by their very nature require intricate and complex responses from the Congress, but without Congress necessarily intending its enactment as the exclusive means of meeting the problem, cf. Askew v. American Waterways, —— U.S. —— (1973). Given the complexity of the matter addressed by Congress in the federal work incentive program, a detailed statutory scheme was both likely and appropriate, completely apart from any questions of pre-emptive intent. This would be especially the case when the federal work incentive provisions had to be sufficiently comprehensive to authorize and govern programs in States which had no welfare work requirements of their own as well as cooperatively in States with such requirements.

[14] See Brief for the United States as *amicus curiae*, p. 12. The information was derived from a survey of state plans conducted by the Department of Health, Education, and Welfare.

[15] No express intention to eliminate co-existing state work programs appears either at the time of the original 1967 enactment of the WIN program, see S.Rep.No.744, 90th Cong., 1st Sess., at 26, 145–157; H.R.Rep.No. 1030, 90th Cong., 1st Sess., at 58–59, or at the time of the 1971 amendments, n. 6, supra.

[16] The court below also asserted that the legislative history was supportive of a pre-emptive intent, 348 F.Supp., at 297, but no legislative history is cited for that proposition.

[17] In view of our remand, Part III, infra, we do not reach the issue of specific alleged conflicts. In sum, however, they are not sufficient to indicate pre-emptive intent, especially in light of the impressive evidence to the contrary.

Appellees also rely, as did the District Court, on the legislative history as supporting the view that "the WIN legislation is addressed to all AFDC recipients, leaving no employable recipients to be subject to state work rules." Brief, p. 29. The court below pointed to no specific legislative history as supportive of its conclusion. Appellees do cite fragmentary statements which we find unpersuasive. Reliance is placed, for example, on a statement in the report of the House Ways and Means Committee on the WIN legislation as follows:

"Under your committee's bill, States would be required to develop a program *for each appropriate* relative and dependent child which would assure, to the maximum extent possible, that each individual would enter the labor force, *in order to become self-sufficient.* To accomplish this, the states would have to assure that *each* adult in the family, and each child over age 16 who is not attending school is given, when appropriate, employment counselling, testing and job training." (Emphasis supplied by appellees.) H.R.Rep.No. 544, 90th Cong., 1st Sess., at 16 (1967).[18]

At best, this statement is ambiguous as to a possible congressional intention to supersede all state work programs.[19] "Ap-

propriateness," as used in the Committee Report, may well mean "appropriateness" solely within the scope and confines of the WIN program. Furthermore, the language employed by Congress in enacting the WIN program must be considered in conjunction with its operational scope and level of funding, which, as will be shown, is quite limited with respect to the total number of employable AFDC recipients, Part II, infra.

In sum, our attention has been directed to no relevant argument which supports, except in the most peripheral way, the view that Congress intended, either expressly or impliedly, to pre-empt state work programs. Far more would be required to show the "clear manifestation

---

[18] Other citations to similar effect appear in Appellee's Brief, pp. 29–30.

[19] Perhaps the most revealing legislative expressions confirm, subsequent to enactment, a congressional desire to preserve supplementary state work programs, not to supersede them. In the wake of the invalidation of the New York Work Rules by the three-judge District Court, members of the New York congressional delegation became concerned that the court had misconstrued the intent of Congress. The following colloquy occurred between Senator Buckley of New York and Senator Long of Louisiana, Chairman of the Finance Committee which considered the WIN program prior to approval by the Senate:

"Mr. Buckley: Was it ever the intention of Congress at that time to have the provisions of the WIN statutes preempt the field of employment and training for ADC recipients?

"Mr. Long: I did not have that in mind.

* * *

"Mr. Buckley: * * * So far as the distinguished chairman is concerned was it ever the intention of at least this body to have a preemption in the field?

"Mr. Long: It was never our intention to prevent a State from requiring recipients to do something for their money if they were employable. * * *" 118 Cong.Rec.S. 18492, Oct. 17, 1972.

In the House of Representatives, a similar dialogue took place between Congressman Carey of New York and Congressman Mills, Chairman of the House Ways and Means Committee, which considered the WIN program:

"Mr. Carey: My specific question for the chairman has to do with the intent of the Congress in authorizing the WIN program in 1967 and in amendments to that program in subsequent years. It is my understanding that Congress intended, through the WIN program merely to assist the States in the critical area of guiding able bodied welfare recipients toward self-sufficency—and not to supersede individual State programs designed to achieve the same end. Under this interpretation, New York and other States could operate their own programs as supplementary to the Federal WIN program. Is my understanding of the congressional intent in this area correct?

"Mr. Mills: I agree with the interpretation of my friend, the gentleman from New York, on the matter, so long as the State program does not contravene the provisions of Federal law." 118 Cong.Rec., H. 10212, Oct. 17, 1972.

of [congressional] intention" which must exist before a federal statute is held "to supersede the exercise" of state action. Schwartz v. Texas, supra, 202–203.

II

Persuasive affirmative reasons exist in this case which also strongly negate the view that Congress intended, by the enactment of the WIN legislation, to terminate all existing state work programs and foreclose additional state cooperate programs in the future. We note, first, that the WIN program itself was not designed on its face to be all embracing. Federal work incentive programs were to be established only in States and political subdivisions

"in which he [the Secretary of Labor] determines there is a significant number of individuals who have attained age 16 and are receiving aid to families with dependent children. In other political subdivisions, he shall use his best efforts to provide such programs either within such subdivisions or through the provision of transportation for such persons to political subdivisions of the State in which such programs are established." 42 U.S.C.A. § 632(a).

This section constitutes an express recognition that the federal statute probably would be limited in scope and application.[20] In New York, this has meant operation of WIN in only 14 of New York's 64 social service districts, though these 14 districts do service approximately 90% of the welfare recipients in the State. Yet the Secretary of Labor has not authorized additional WIN programs for the other districts, resulting in a lack of federal job placement opportunities in the more lightly populated areas of States

and in those without adequate transportation of potential enrollees to districts with WIN programs.[21]

Even in the districts where WIN does operate, its reach is limited. In New York, according to federal estimates, there are 150,000 WIN registrants for the current fiscal year, but the Secretary of Labor has contracted with the State to provide services to only 90,000 registrants, of whom the majority will not receive full job training and placement assistance.[22] In fiscal 1971, New York asserts that "17,511 individuals were referred for participation in the WIN program, but the Federal Government allowed only 9,600 opportunities for enrollment."[23] California claims "over 122,000 employable AFDC recipients" last year, but only 18,000 available WIN slots.[24]

It is evident that WIN is a partial program which stops short of providing adequate job and training opportunities for large numbers of state AFDC recipients. It would be incongruous for Congress on the one hand to promote work opportunities for AFDC recipients and on the other to prevent States from undertaking supplementary efforts toward this very same end. We cannot interpret federal statutes to negate their own stated purposes. The significance of state supple-

---

[20] The WIN guidelines, issued by the United States Department of Labor, provide, according to appellants, for establishment of WIN programs only in those areas where there are at least 1,100 potential WIN referees, Brief, p. 37.

[21] See Appellant's Brief, pp. 37–38. 42 U.S.C.A. § 602(a) (19) (A) (iii) may also have contemplated limited application of the federal work incentive program, since it exempts from WIN registration "a person so remote from a work incentive project that his effective participation is precluded."

[22] See Brief for the United States as *amicus curiae*, p. 15, citing U.S.Dept. of Labor, Manpower Administration, Contract No. 36–2–0001–188, modification No. 3, June 20, 1972. The Government contends further that "the current level of WIN funding is such that no more than one-fifth of the WIN registrants will receive the full job training and placement assistance contemplated by the Act." Brief, p. 15.

[23] Appellant's Brief, p. 38, 17.

[24] Brief for California as *amicus curiae*, p. 3.

mentation is illustrated by the experience in New York, where the Work Rules have aided the objectives of federal work incentives: from July 1 through September 30, 1971, the first months of the Work Rules' operation, the State Employment Service claimed job placements for approximately 9,376 recipients.[25]

Moreover, the Department of Health, Education, and Welfare, the agency of Government responsible for administering the Federal Social Security Act—including reviewing of state AFDC programs—has never considered the WIN legislation to be pre-emptive. HEW has followed consistently the policy of approving state plans containing welfare work requirements so long as those requirements are not arbitrary or unreasonable.[26] Congress presumably knew of this settled administrative policy at the time of enactment of WIN, when 21 States had welfare work programs. Subsequent to WIN's passage, HEW has continued to approve state work requirements. Pursuant to such approval, New York has received federal grants in aid for the operation of its AFDC plan, in-

cluding its work provisions.[27] In interpreting this statute, we must be mindful that "the construction of a statute by those charged with its execution should be followed unless there are compelling indications that it is wrong. * * *" Red Lion Broadcasting Co. v. FCC, 395 U.S. 367, 381 (1969); Dandridge v. Williams, supra, at 481–482. In this case, such indications are wholly absent.

New York, furthermore, has attempted to operate the Work Rules in such a manner as to avoid friction and overlap with the WIN program. Officials from both the State Department of Labor and a local Social Service Department testified below that every AFDC recipient appropriate for a WIN program was first referred there, that no person was to be referred to the state program who was participating in a WIN program, and that only if there was no position available for him under WIN, was a recipient to be referred for employment pursuant to state statute.[28] Where coordinate state and federal efforts exist within a complementary administrative framework, and in the pursuit of common purposes, the case for federal pre-emption becomes a less persuasive one.

In this context, the dissenting opinion's reliance on Townsend v. Swank, 404 U.S. 282 (1971), Carleson v. Remillard, 406 U.S. 598 (1972), and King v. Smith, supra, is misplaced. In those cases it was clear that state law excluded people from AFDC benefits whom the Social Security Act expressly provided would be eligible. The Court found no room either in the Act's language or legislative history to warrant the States' additional eligibility

---

[25] Appellant's Brief, p. 15; appendix, p. 192. Appellants claim further that from January to June 1972, "there were 2,657 job placements under the WIN program," and 5,323 placements under the Work Rules. Brief, p. 18. These figures must be qualified, however, with the observation that many of the job placements are temporary; many of those placed under the Work Rules may have been recipients of forms of assistance other than AFDC (while the number of WIN placements counts only AFDC recipients); and that single recipients may have been referred or placed—and thus statistically tabulated—on more than one occasion. See Appellee's Brief, pp. 33–36. None of these observations, however, obscures the basic fact that the Work Rules materially contribute toward attainment of the objective of the WIN program in restoring employable AFDC recipients as wage-earning members of society. See 42 U.S.C.A. § 630.

[26] See Brief for the United States as *amicus curiae*, p. 3, filed by the Solicitor General and joined in by the General Counsel of HEW.

[27] Ibid.

[28] Excerpts from Depositions of Nelson Hopper, Director of the Employment Service Bureau of the New York State Dept. of Labor, and George Demmon, Senior Employment Counsellor, Erie County Dept. of Social Services, appendix, pp. 226, 234. See also Appellant's Brief, p. 17, and Tr. of Oral Arg., p. 7.

requirements. Here, by contrast, the Act allows for complementary state work incentive programs and procedures incident thereto—even if they become conditions for continued assistance. Such programs and procedures are not necessarily invalid, any more than other supplementary regulations promulgated within the legitimate sphere of state administration. See Wyman v. James, 400 U.S. 309 (1971); Snell v. Wyman, 281 F.Supp. 853, aff'd, 393 U.S. 323 (1969). See also Dandridge v. Williams, supra; Jefferson v. Hackney, supra.

III

We thus reverse the holding below that the federal work incentive program preempts the New York Work Rules. Our ruling establishes the validity of a state work program as one means of helping AFDC recipients return to gainful employment. We do not resolve, however, the question of whether some particular sections of the Work Rules might contravene the specific provisions of the Federal Social Security Act.

This last question we remand to the court below. That court did not have the opportunity to consider the issue of specific conflict between the state and federal programs, free from its misapprehension that the Work Rules had been entirely pre-empted. Further, the New York Legislature amended the Work Rules in 1972 to provide, among other things, for exemption of persons engaged in full-time training and vocational rehabilitation programs from the reporting and check pickup requirements (Chapter 683, N.Y.Laws of 1972), for monthly rather than semi-monthly payments of shelter allowances (id., c. 685) and, most significantly, for a definition of an "employable" AFDC recipient which is claimed by New York to be identical to that now used under WIN (id., c. 941). Inasmuch as the court below did not have the opportunity to consider the 1972 amendments as they related to the issue of po-

tential state-federal conflict, the remand should afford it.

We deem it unnecessary at the present time to intimate any view on whether or to what extent particular provisions of the Work Rules may contravene the purposes or provisions of the WIN program. Such a determination should be made initially by the court below, consistent with the principles set forth in this opinion.[29]

The judgment of the three-judge District Court is reversed and the case remanded for further proceedings in accord with this opinion.

Mr. Justice MARSHALL, with whom Mr. Justice BRENNAN joins, dissenting.

Because the Court today ignores a fundamental rule for interpreting the Social Security Act, I must respectfully dissent. As we said in Townsend v. Swank, 404 U.S. 282, 286 (1971), "in the absence of congressional authorization for the exclusion clearly evidenced from the Social Security Act or its legislative history, a state eligibility standard that excludes persons eligible for assistance under federal AFDC standards violates the Social Security Act and is therefore invalid under the Supremacy Clause." See also King v. Smith, 392 U.S. 309 (1968); Carleson v. Remillard, 406 U.S. 598, 600 (1972). The New York Work Rules fall squarely

[29] In considering the question of possible conflict between the state and federal work programs, the court below will take into account our prior decisions. Congress "has given the States broad discretion," as to the AFDC program, Jefferson v. Hackney, supra, at 545; see also Dandridge v. Williams, supra, at 478; King v. Smith, supra, at 318–319, and "so long as the State's actions are not in violation of any specific provision of the Constitution or the Social Security Act," the courts may not void them. Jefferson, supra, at 541. Conflicts, to merit judicial rather than cooperative federal-state resolution, should be of substance and not merely trivial or insubstantial. But if there is a conflict of substance as to eligibility provisions, the federal law of course must control. King v. Smith, supra; Townsend v. Swank, supra; Carleson v. Remillard, supra.

within this statement; they clearly exclude persons eligible for assistance under federal standards, and it could hardly be maintained that they did not impose additional conditions of eligibility.[1] For example, under federal standards, it is irrelevant to a determination of eligibility that a recipient has or has not filed every two weeks a certificate from the local employment office that no suitable employment opportunities are available, yet under the Work Rules, a recipient who fails to file such a certificate is "deemed" to have refused to accept suitable employment, and so is not eligible for assistance. N.Y.Social Services Law § 131(4)(a) (McKinney 1971).[2] Thus, according to the rules of interpretation we have heretofore followed, the proper inquiry is whether the Social Security Act or its legislative history clearly show congressional authorization for state employment requirements other than those involved in the federal Work Incentive Program.

* * *

COMMENT, THE FAILURE OF THE WORK INCENTIVE (WIN) PROGRAM

119 U.Pa.L.Rev. 485, 492–501 (1971).

Like the CWT Program, which was intended "to enrich and expand [manpower] programs and provide various services which would help rehabilitate the * * * recipients"[51] but which actually

resulted in "little training and meaningless work experience,"[52] WIN has encountered numerous difficulties.[53] A recent evaluation indicates that the chronically unemployed rarely successfully complete the WIN training programs and find stable employment.[54] What were innovations on paper have often not materialized. For example, the highly touted concept of an employability team providing individualized attention has frequently not been realized. "Some [local WIN offices] use 'assembly line' tactics, keeping enrollees together in 'classes' and sending them through the same sequence of [pre-occupational training] components at the same pace."[55] In some areas the team concept has been altogether abandoned, sometimes because of friction among team members over seniority rights in decisionmaking.[56] When teams are used, enrollee contact with all of the members (particularly with the manpower specialist) is often negligible.[57]

Ideally the employability development plan would bring to an enrollee's aid the combined talent of the members of the team. But such plans may never be drawn for some enrollees. In the "great majority" of cases examined by one group

---

a portion of this Comment excerpted at pp. 192–194, supra.]

[52] Hausman, The AFDC Amendments of 1967: Their Impact on the Capacity for Self-Support and the Employability of AFDC Family Heads, 19 Lab.L.J. 496, 506 (1968). WIN is "an old program under a new label." Id. Other older work relief programs have manifested similar failures. See S. Levitan, supra note 49, at 74.

[53] Auerbach Corporation, Report on WIN Program: Supplement to Oral Presentation, pt. 2, at 4, Apr. 24, 1969 [hereinafter cited as Auerbach Report].

[54] Id.

[55] Auerbach Briefing 6. But see Division of Program Review & Analysis, Office of Evaluation, U. S. Dep't of Labor, WIN Program Review After One Year 2, Oct. 22, 1969 [hereinafter cited as WIN Review].

[56] Auerbach Report, pt. 2, at 5.

[57] Cf. id.; WIN Review 25.

[1] Appellants state that the Work Rules do not "constitute an additional condition of eligibility for public assistance." Reply Brief for Appellants New York State Departments, at 9. The arguments they present, however, relate entirely to the purported congressional authorization for additional conditions of this sort.

[2] The federal conditions of eligibility relating to registration for employment are found at 42 U.S.C.A. § 602(a)(19) (Supp. I, 1971).

[51] S. Levitan, supra note 49, at 68. [Ed.: This and some other footnotes refer back to

of researchers, the files contained no employability plans at all.[58]

The orientation component of pre-occupational training in most cases apparently serves the highly useful function of introducing previously unemployed recipients to the world of work. But "[o]rientation is sometimes used thoughtlessly as a convenient catch-all for enrollees which enables the WIN staff to 'buy time' to develop employability plans." [59] When this component is incorrectly used, its value is quickly lost. In some cases orientation training appears to the enrollees as merely a personal attack or stigma where the employability team is "trying to tell me I don't dress right, or talk right" for little reason at all.[60]

The educational training component is likewise used as a holding ground for enrollees. Its relation to employability is sometimes doubtful.[61] Some WIN offices use traditional classroom techniques which may make some recipients feel that they are "going back to school" rather than training for a job. On the other hand, some WIN education programs begin at too advanced a level for the recipients.[62]

The occupational training programs have also run into trouble. Studies suggest that job training has not taken into account enrollees' existing skills, and that enrollees are forced to enter training classes below their level.

[V]irtually no accommodations are made for either unconventional past experience or past training. * * * Little attempt was made to build on past enrollee experience, even though some enrollees listed "substantial work experience in the field of his (their) vocational choice." After duly noting same, [employability teams] went right ahead and enrolled people in training for that very field: a machinist in a machinist's course * * *. Previously trained people fared worse. Despite protestations, one young lady who had taken typing in high school and graduated less than a year ago was enrolled in a clerk-general course and promptly typed fifty-seven words per minute in the first of twenty-six weeks. Other clients fully or partially trained by OIC [Opportunities Industrialization Centers], EOA [Economic Opportunity Act], and other agencies were often assigned to the same fields they had allegedly trained for. On the basis of test results, all started at the beginning of these courses. Three months in clerk-general at OIC * * * counted nothing.

* * *

Behind the WIN program lay Congress' belief that many adult AFDC recipients were immediately employable without training or at least immediately trainable for work.[64] By the end of fiscal 1970, 150,000 AFDC recipients were to have been trained by WIN; by the end of fiscal 1971, an additional 190,000. By the end of fiscal 1972, a cumulative total of 757,000.[65] These estimates appear slightly ridiculous today: in fact the WIN selection process has not uncovered a size-

---

[58] Auerbach Report, pt. 2, at 6; see WIN Review 2.

[59] Auerbach Report, pt. 2, at 7.

[60] Id.

[61] Id., pt. 1, at 9.

[62] Id., pt. 2, at 7. "Programs for both Basic Education and High School Equivalency have been largely 'standard' packages, which may fail to meet the needs of welfare recipients." WIN First Annual Report 30–31.

[64] See notes 18–20 supra & accompanying text.

[65] Conf.Rep.No.1030, supra note 18. To date, "the program has had a history of missed estimates and revised estimates, only to be missed again." F. Arner, supra note 18, at 74. For other estimates of the number of WIN enrollees, see note 18 supra.

able body of recipients appropriate for the program.[66] Table I shows the number of recipients eliminated from consideration at each step of the selection process. The figures include the first two years of WIN's operation, when presumably most of the appropriate recipients would be discovered and enrolled in WIN.

TABLE I [67]
AFDC RECIPIENTS AND WIN ENROLLEES

Total Adult AFDC Recipients	AFDC Recipients Assessed	Appropriate for Referral by State Welfare Agency	Actually Referred by State Welfare Agency	WIN Enrollees After Labor Dep't Reevaluation
2,150,000	1,810,578 (84.2% of total)	374,177 (17.4% of total) (20.7% of assessed)	282,380 (13.1% of total) (15.6% of assessed)	164,348 (7.6% of total) (9.1% of assessed)

Figures as of May 31, 1970

As the figures illustrated, the high elimination rate at each stage of the selection process means that only a small percentage of the adult AFDC population is ultimately enrolled in WIN for either work or training. Of the 1,810,578 assessed as of May 31, 1970, only 164,348 adults—7.6 percent of the adult AFDC population, 9.1 percent of those assessed —have been found enrollable in WIN. To meet the prediction of 757,000, the number of appropriate recipients must increase dramatically; but, barring an unforeseen growth in AFDC rolls, the potential for expansion of the program appears slight.

The error of the congressional assumption about the nature of the AFDC population is also demonstrated by comparing the number of enrollees placed in jobs with the number placed in occupational and pre-occupational training.

TABLE II [68]
PLACEMENT OF ENROLLEES

WIN Enrollees After Labor Dep't Reevaluation	Employed	Occupational Training	Pre-occupational Training	Holding	Dropout
209,761	34,181 (16.3%)	31,318 (14.9%)	32,237 (15.4%)	27,118 (12.9%)	84,907 (40.5%)

Figures as of October 31, 1970

As shown by Table II, as of October 31, 1970, only 34,181 were employed.

This represents 16.3 percent of the total enrollment, 1.9 percent of the total as-

[66] The Labor Department's estimate of 150,000 trainees by the end of fiscal 1970 was revised in 1969 to 77,000. The actual number of trainees by the end of fiscal 1970 was 42,000. Finance Comm. State Material, 2-3.

[67] Monthly Status Reports for WIN (May 31, 1970).

[68] The data appears in Division of Reports Analysis, Office of Manpower Mgmt. Data Systems, Manpower Admin., U. S. Dep't of Labor, WIN Program Data, Transmittal No. 97, at 1 of 15, Dec. 16, 1970 [hereinafter cited as WIN Program Data], except for the "employed" figure. This figure was calculated by adding 12,881 participants who have not completed their follow-up counseling to the 20,397 who have completed the job entry period and the 903 in special works projects.

sessed (that is, of the total assessed as of May 31, 1970, as indicated in Table I; the percentage would be less as of October 31, 1970, because more recipients will have been assessed),[69] and 1.6 percent of the total adult AFDC population (also as of May 31, 1970). Moreover, 24 percent of the AFDC recipients referred to WIN (as of August 1969) had been out of work fourteen weeks or less,[70] indicating that they likely could have returned to the labor market without WIN's efforts or training.

Of those referred but not employed, 31,318 (14.9 percent) were receiving occupational training and 32,237 (15.4 percent) were receiving pre-occupational training. Thus, of those in training, 50.7 percent were involved in pre-occupational training, not yet ready for occupational training. Of those 32,237 in pre-occupational training, 21,552[71] (33.9 percent of all those in training) were in the basic education and general educational development programs. Thus, of the total WIN program, presumably filled with the most employable or trainable of the adult AFDC population, 10.3 percent of those enrolled have been placed in programs indicating that they need basic educational skills before job training or employment can even begin.

The dropout rate of WIN enrollees is another indication of the erroneous assumptions made about the employability or trainability of the adult AFDC recipients. There have been 84,907 dropouts as of October 31, 1970. Of these, 21,-400 (25.2 percent) left without good cause and 63,507 (74.8 percent) left for

good cause.[72] The high rate of failure for good cause may indicate that too many referrals are in fact inappropriate for WIN. Those dropouts without good cause may also have been inappropriate for referral and, once forced into WIN training, so frustrated and demeaned that they risked the loss of welfare grants rather than continue.

Supporting the assertion that many dropouts were inappropriately referred is the correlation of the dropout rate with the length of time spent in holding.[73] Enrollees in holding often present difficult training problems which rather than solved are avoided by delay. "The difficult cases continue to be in holding * * without any immediate goal."[74] The WIN dropouts generally had spent more time in holding than had the successful enrollees. The median holding time for WIN graduates was about six weeks; for dropouts, thirteen weeks.[75]

Thus the congressional assumption of a large body of employable and trainable AFDC recipients has not proved correct. Not only have very few AFDC recipients been found appropriate for referral to WIN, but those who have been referred are likely to require fundamental pre-vocational training prior to vocational training or employment. Further, the number of referrals with even the same low level of skills as the current enrollees may be expected to drop rather than rise because most of the employable recipients have already been taken from the welfare rolls.

The congressional assumption that WIN would train its enrollees in skills or jobs for which there is a demand in the economy has also proved wrong: WIN training often fails to provide the enrollees with new skills, and the skills that

---

Telephone interview with Richard Shirey, Manpower Specialist, Manpower Admin., U. S. Dep't of Labor, Jan. 4, 1971.

[69] The figures on assessments are available only as of May 31, 1970. Shirey interview, supra note 68. Thus the comparisons made are not exact.

[70] WIN Review 3.

[71] WIN Program Data 1 of 12.

[72] Id. 1 of 15.

[73] See text accompanying note 48 supra.

[74] Auerbach Report, pt. 1, at 9.

[75] WIN First Annual Report 18.

it does provide are those least in demand in the economy,[76] especially during this period of economic retrenchment.

As already noted,[77] WIN enrollees are not being trained for the right jobs for their skills, and are often enrolled in training classes below their skill level. And even after they have purportedly been trained, they do not easily enter the labor market.

A notably increasing proportion of the growing numbers in component holding are those reported to have been last engaged in institutional training. The August 1969 report shows 18.4% in this situation. One wonders if these enrollees generally are job ready. Having been trained through institutional vocational education, the next step normally is placement.   *   *   * [S]pecial attention is needed in local offices in order that institutional training will be relevant to live employment opportunities and that WIN enrollees will be exposed to such job opportunities.[78]

The Department of Labor has adopted the policy that WIN training must be oriented toward jobs in the "demand occupations" either in the long or short run, and toward "career ladder" jobs rather than dead-end, low-paying jobs.[79] But WIN training programs have been modelled after earlier programs also intended to train the chronically unemployed. Studies made during the first eighteen months of WIN's operation indicate that WIN does not vary substantially from these past programs, which have been criticized for providing "little training experience and meaningless work experience." [80] And the preponderance of women enrollees has created a serious problem in training enrollees for "demand occupations":

> The local job market   *   *   * particularly the rural areas, hold[s] few jobs for women without advanced cleri-

---

[76] The three leading occupational categories for employed WIN enrollees are: clerical and sales (21.5% of total employed), service (20.6%), and structural work (14.2%). Office of Manpower Mgmt. Data Systems, Manpower Admin., U. S. Dep't of Labor, Results of Special Occupational and Wage Survey of Employed WIN Program Participants in Follow-up Status Conducted in Six States as of August 31, 1969, at 3 [hereinafter cited as Six-State Study], discussed at note 89 infra. In October 1970, the unemployment rate for clerical workers was 4.7%, up 1.3% from October 1969; for sales workers, 4.3%—up 0.8%. These two categories had the highest unemployment rate and showed the largest increase of all white-collar occupations. The unemployment rate for service workers was 5.8%, up 1.6%. Among construction workers, the rate was 11.9% in October 1970, up 4.6% from the preceding October, the highest rate and highest rise of any industry. Monthly Lab.Rev., Dec. 1970, at 69 (table 8) (published by Bureau of Labor Statistics, U. S. Dep't of Labor).

[77] Text accompanying notes 58–63 supra.

[78] WIN Review 13.

[79] For example, the Manpower Administration does not approve training programs for domestics. When Delaware attempted to establish such a training program Louis Day, WIN Regional Director, Manpower Administration, stated that the intent of WIN was to assist enrollees in securing and retaining employment with possibilities for advancement. The purpose of WIN is not just training or employment; it is employment with a future. Interview with Louis Day, Middle-Atlantic Regional Director of WIN, Manpower Admin., U. S. Dep't of Labor, in Phila., Dec. 15, 1969. An examination of the Connecticut WIN program in 1969 found that 473 recipients were in some kind of training; only 233 in vocational training and the rest in prevocational training. Of the 233, 75 were being trained as hairdressers (raising the question whether the Connecticut job market could absorb 75 more hairdressers). Other major categories included 17 being trained as licensed practical nurses, 20 as keypunch operators, and 15 as clerk-typists. Arthur D. Little Co., Connecticut Welfare Study 190, 193 (1969). Louis Houff, WIN Manpower Development Specialist, Manpower Administration, indicated that the jobs for which many enrollees were being trained in Connecticut did not comply with the career ladder criteria. Telephone interview with Louis Houff, Mar. 2, 1970.

[80] Hausman, supra note 52, at 506.

cal skills. WIN staff in these areas anticipated that it would be a matter of years bringing most WIN enrollees up to the required skill levels. The few jobs available to most of the women enrollees were primarily limited to low paying, highly unstable service jobs such as domestics or charwomen.[81]

Furthermore, those most liable to be laid off or unemployed, especially in a slumping economy, are those who populate the WIN program. The President's Commission on Income Maintenance found that "young people without work experience, people with low educational attainments, and members of minority groups subject to discrimination will be particularly handicapped in their search for employment." [82] In April 1970, the WIN population was 71 percent female,[83] 40 percent black,[84] and 22 percent Spanish surnamed; [85] 68 percent had not completed high school, 25 percent had not even entered high school,[86] and 22 percent were under the age of 22.[87]

The economic slowdown has also caused a reduction in on-the-job training programs which are no longer supported by employers forced to lay off longtime employees.[88]

The second assumption has thus proven incorrect. The failure can be ascribed partly to inadequate training programs which fail to prepare enrollees properly,

and must be ascribed partly to the contradictory policies of training people for jobs while attempting to eliminate those jobs from the economy.

The third assumption—that the participants in the WIN program who found employment would earn enough to make assistance unnecessary—has likewise proved unwarranted. A special six-state Department of Labor survey of 4,623 employed WIN participants [89] in follow-up status [90] found that only 42.2 percent of the men and 9.9 percent of the women had sufficient earnings to be ineligible for assistance. Median hourly wages for men were $2.47 but only $2.02 for women.[91] The low figures for women enrollees reflect the generally lower earnings of women in our society,[92] but they are es-

---

[81] Auerbach Report, pt. 2 at 9.

[82] President's Comm'n on Income Maintenance Programs, Poverty Amid Plenty: The American Paradox 25–26 (1969) [hereinafter cited as President's Comm'n on Income Maintenance].

[83] WIN First Annual Report, table 2. On employment difficulties for women heading families, see President's Comm'n on Income Maintenance 30.

[84] WIN First Annual Report, table 2.

[85] Id.

[86] Id.

[87] Id.

[88] See id. 31.

[89] Six-State Study 1. The six states were California, Colorado, Illinois, New York, Pennsylvania, and Washington. Of the 4,623 individuals surveyed, 2,100 were from California.

[90] For a description of "follow-up" status, see text accompanying note 35 supra.

[91] Six-State Study 7. Average hourly earnings were as follows:

Average Hourly Earnings	Number of Participants	Percent
under $1.60	180	3.9
$1.60–1.99	1,312	28.4
$2.00–2.49	1,493	32.3
$2.50–2.99	887	19.2
$3.00 or more	751	16.2

[92] More than one third of the 26.9 million women employed in the United States in 1967 had a "low-paying" position, such as saleswoman, service worker, laborer, and farm worker. In 1965, the median annual income of women who worked full-time at such jobs was $2,784. Carter, The Employment Potential of AFDC Mothers: Some Questions and Some Answers, 6 Welfare in Rev., July-Aug. 1968, at 1, 3 (citing Women's Bureau, U. S. Dep't of Labor, Women in the Labor Force, 1966 and 1967, Jan. 31, 1968). Women from poor families are even more limited: "In 1966 almost 50 percent of all employed white women heading poor families and 75 percent of nonwhite women heading poor families worked in service occupations, one of the lowest paid groups. For many such women, Public Assistance offers a more secure existence." President's Comm'n on Income Maintenance 30.

pecially significant for the WIN program: 71 percent [93] of WIN enrollees and 95 percent of all adult AFDC recipients are women.[94]

Finally, Congress also assumed, as indicated by the statement of goals in the Act itself, that "the example of a working adult in these [AFDC] families will have beneficial effects on the children in such families." [95] Apparently these beneficial effects were presumed to flow from the "sense of dignity, self-worth, and confidence" an AFDC parent would derive "from being recognized as a wage-earning member of society," [96] or simply from the mere fact that the parent worked. But one study suggests that "the mother's working is only one of many factors impinging on children and * * * on the whole it is a secondary rather than a primary factor, so far as child development and adjustment are concerned." [97] Another researcher states:

> Probably much depends upon the nature of the mother's work and the status it confers. Perhaps the example of serious interest in outside work on the mother's part makes both her sons and her daughters value such work more highly.[98]

The WIN program is not altogether conducive to inspiring in recipients either a "serious interest" in or respect for work. A mother in effect forced by the WIN program to leave her children for a substantial part of the day and work at a possibly demeaning job is unlikely to bring home at the end of the day an appreciation of the inherent value of work. If the mother is bitter and resentful about her job, her children will probably not grow up enamored of the world of work. The "dignity, self-worth, and confidence" assumed by Congress to flow from "being recognized" as a worker will in fact never attach to a mother unhappy with her mandatory job and her loss of supervision over her children. Her perception of herself may change only to the extent that her estimate of her helplessness increases. As a WIN consultant to the Department of Labor concluded:

> There is a tendency to feel that any job is better than no job at all. This is not necessarily the view held by the recipients, nor is it a valid axiom around which a vocational program can be built. In the first place, certain classes of jobs are viewed as dead-end and meaningless by applicants * * *. Forcing people to accept unappealing, low-pay, dead-end jobs will not result in program success.[99]

CONCLUSION

Were the WIN program simply a well-intentioned failure to provide jobs for the country's indigent, that would be cause enough for lament. But WIN may indeed produce positive harm. For example, the WIN incentive payments, on the whole probably an advantage of the program, result in unfairness to the nonwelfare working poor (and may exacerbate any present hostility between the welfare and nonwelfare poor) because a WIN participant working at a job paying the same wage as a nonparticipant has a higher income than the latter (because the

---

[93] WIN First Annual Report, supra note 38, at table 2 (as of Apr. 30, 1970). "The data suggest that many welfare mothers, after training and employment, will not be able to make enough wages to bring their families entirely out of poverty." Id. 22–23.

[94] WIN Review 2.

[95] Social Security Act § 430, 42 U.S.C.A. § 630 (Supp. V, 1970).

[96] Id.

[97] E. Herzog, Children of Working Mothers 30 (Children's Bureau, Social Security Admin., U. S. Dep't of Health, Educ., & Welfare Pub. No. 382–1960, 1960).

[98] Maccoby, Effects Upon Children of Their Mothers' Outside Employment, in Work in the Lives of Married Women 157 (1958) (Nat'l Manpower Council Conference proceedings).

[99] Auerbach Briefing, supra note 18, at 4.

WIN participant receives an incentive payment in addition to his wage).[100]

The mandatory character of WIN is another harmful aspect of the program, resulting in yet another encroachment on recipient autonomy by those purporting to know recipients' best interests best. This point was made in various forms during the congressional hearings. Secretary of Labor Willard Wirtz stated:

> [I]n my judgment * * * an absolute statutory conditioning of welfare payments on the acceptance of work or work training would be unwise and impracticable.
>
> * * *
>
> I note * * * the lesson of experience from the administration of most of the existing work and work training programs. One of the hardest problems is getting through with these programs to those who need them most. This problem could well be aggravated rather than made easier by a general rule of compulsory training.[101]

Mitchell Ginsberg, presently Dean of Columbia University School of Social Work, stated:

> There is no doubt that employment and training programs * * * are desirable, and that aggressive efforts to educate low-income families to their value are crucial. But to require, rather

than to make available, these resources as a condition for continued financial assistance opens such a wide area of discretion that it constitutes an open invitation to abuse.[102]

That these voices were not heeded is perhaps indicative of the most harmful aspect of WIN: its reiteration and propagation of erroneous assumptions about welfare recipients and about the causes of poverty. WIN intervenes in the poverty cycle at the locus of the individual rather than the labor market. So long as poverty is viewed as simply a manifestation of personal failure, congressional antipoverty programs will be a waste of bureaucratic energy.

Stephen F. Gold

Note on 1971 WIN Amendments

While major Federal welfare reform, in the form of the Nixon Administration Family Assistance Program (see pp. 380–395 infra), was stalled, disenchantment with the existing work requirements in WIN grew. The consequence was the Talmadge Amendments which swept quickly through Congress in late 1971 and were enacted with virtually no discussion or review. The full text of relevant portions of these amendments to sections 602(a) (15), 602(a) (19), 603, 607, 630–644 is set out in the statutory appendix hereto which gives both the pre-1971 version and the amendments. The following is a brief description of the amendments which is virtually all that is available by way of legislative history:

IMPROVEMENT OF THE WORK INCENTIVE PROGRAM

117 Cong.Rec. 21641 (daily ed. Dec. 14, 1971)

(comments of Senator Russell Long)

The first of these Senate amendments, introduced by Senator Talmadge, makes a number of changes designed to improve

---

[100] Congress clearly recognized this problem, but decided that the remedy was too expensive:

The committee appreciates the objections to this type of situation which can be made; but the alternative would have increased the costs of the proposal about $160 million a year by placing people on the AFDC rolls who now have earnings in excess of their need for public assistance as determined under their State plan. In short, the various provisions included in the committee's bill are designed to get people off AFDC rolls, not put them on.

S.Rep.No.744, supra note 18, at 158.

[101] Senate WIN Hearings, supra note 19, pt. 2, at 796.

[102] Id. 945.

the work incentive program for welfare recipients under the Social Security Act. I am pleased to say that these provisions were accepted by the conferees with very few changes. As agreed to by the conferees, the amendments would:

Insure that welfare recipients are provided the services they need, including child care, to participate effectively in the work incentive program.

Emphasize employment-based rather than institutional training under the program.

Relate institutional training much more closely to actual jobs available.

Set priorities for participation in the work incentive program, giving high priority to mothers who volunteer to participate in the program.

Ease the fiscal burden on the States by increasing Federal matching from 80 to 90 percent for expenses under the work incentive program and from 75 to 90 percent for child care, family planning, and other services needed to permit an individual to participate in the WIN program. Often States will be able to put up their entire 10-percent matching in kind, so this increase in the matching percent should enable them to make significant progress in developing these needed services.

Increase Federal matching for the public service employment component of the work incentive program to 100 percent for the first year of employment, 75 percent for the second year, and 50 percent for the third year.

Institute an orderly registration procedure for participation in the WIN program and make a number of other changes to improve the operation of the program.

I would like to single out one aspect of the conference agreement for comment because it concerns a matter that is critical to the success of the work incentive program. The major failings of the WIN program at the local level have been due to a lack of coordination between the employment service and the welfare agency. The Senate amendment would have mandated coordination between these two agencies by requiring that they prepare a joint employability plan for each WIN participant.

The Labor Department argued strongly that a joint plan was not feasible. The conferees agreed to drop the statutory requirement, but this was done with the understanding that the lack of coordination which has plagued the program would come to an end. We cannot understand why bureaucratic rivalry should be allowed to undermine a worthwhile program aimed at helping people to help themselves, and I want to assure the Labor Department that we will be following very closely their activities to insure that they make good their promise to make coordination work without a statutory mandate.

One final word on this amendment. As the Senate knows, we will be legislating next year on extensive changes in the welfare system. I have views of my own, as I am sure other Senators do, about what we might do to improve the welfare programs; but in the meantime, I am pleased to see the Congress take this forward step in improving the work incentive program under existing law so that it can be more effective in enabling welfare recipients to become employed. As we know from a number of studies that have been conducted by the Department of Health, Education, and Welfare, most adults in families receiving welfare would prefer to work rather than remain on welfare. It is my hope that the amendments contained in the conference report will help these recipients in their efforts to become independent—efforts that are all too often frustrated today by the welfare system that is supposed to be helping them.

How effective will these amendments be in correcting the defects in the WIN program? Consider the following regulations promulgated by the Dept. of Labor in carrying out its responsibilities under the program.

WIN REGULATIONS OF THE DEPARTMENT OF LABOR

29 C.F.R. Part 56 (1972).

PART 56—WORK INCENTIVE PROGRAMS FOR AFDC RECIPIENTS UNDER TITLE IV OF THE SOCIAL SECURITY ACT

AUTHORITY: The provisions of this Part 56 are issued under 85 Stat. 803, 808, 42 U.S.C.A. sections 602 and 639, unless otherwise noted.

§ 56.1   Definitions.

As used in this part and in contracts entered into pursuant to this part:

(a) "Act" means title IV of the Social Security Act as amended by Public Law 92–223, December 28, 1971.

(b) "AFDC" (Aid to Families with Dependent Children) means a program authorized by title IV of the Social Security Act to provide financial assistance and social services to needy families with children.

(c) "Applicant" means a person who applies to the State or local Income Maintenance Unit for AFDC benefits.

(d) "Appraisal" means the interview of a registrant by WIN staff and Sepa-[. . . ?] mine employability potential and suitability for participation in the appropriate WIN service level.

(e) "Certification" means a written statement by the Separate Administrative Unit that requested self-support services are provided or arranged for a specific participant and that the individual is ready for employment or training or that no self-support services are needed and that the individual is at that time ready for employment or training.

(f) "Child" means dependent members of the family under age 21.

(g) "Commuting time" means the time spent traveling to and from a place of residence and an employment or training site.

(h) "DOL" means the U.S. Department of Labor.

(i) "Exempt" means an AFDC recipient who is not legally required to register for employment or training under the WIN program.

(j) "Grievance" means participant complaints concerning matters within the power of the WIN sponsor to change.

(k) "HEW" means the U.S. Department of Health, Education, and Welfare.

(l) "Incentive payments" means cash payment up to $30 per month, paid semimonthly to a WIN participant who is participating in an activity for which such payments are authorized.

(m) "Income Maintenance Unit" means the office where the applicant applies for AFDC benefits.

(n) "Institutional training" means skill training for a specific occupational area conducted by an instructor in a non-work site setting.

(o) "Manpower services" means those services provided by WIN project staff designed to result in the training or employment of participants.

(p) "Participant" means a registrant who has been appraised and for whom an employability plan has been initiated by local WIN project and Separate Administrative Unit staff.

(q) "Placement" means the process of successfully moving participants who are job-ready into appropriate work.

(r) "Public Service Employment" (PSE) means a WIN component which provides subsidized, transitional employ-ment for WIN participants with public or private nonprofit agencies.

(s) "Recipient" means an individual who is receiving AFDC benefits.

(t) "Registrant" means an AFDC recipient who has registered for manpower services, training, and employment as provided by the Act.

(u) "Registrant pool" means the entire group of registrants.

(v) "Registration" means the process whereby an AFDC applicant or recipient signs a completed registration card.

(w) "Social and Rehabilitation Service Regional Commissioner" means the Regional Commissioner of the Social and Rehabilitation Service of the U.S. Department of Health, Education, and Welfare.

(x) "RMA" means Regional Manpower Administrator for the U.S. Department of Labor.

(y) "SAU" means Separate Administrative Unit of the social service agency established pursuant to section 402(a)(19)(G) of the Social Security Act, as amended, to administer the WIN program for that agency.

(z) "Secretary" means the Secretary of Labor.

(aa) "Self-support services" means those services provided or arranged by the SAU, such as child care and medical services, necessary to enable the participant to enter employment or training.

(bb) "State" means the 50 States, the District of Columbia, the Commonwealth of Puerto Rico, the Virgin Islands, and Guam.

(cc) [Reserved]

(dd) "Training-related expenses" means those reimbursable expenses incurred by participants in order to participate in work experience and training.

(ee) "Unemployed fathers" means those fathers who apply for or receive

AFDC benefits under section 407 of the Act.

(ff) "Volunteer" means any AFDC recipient who is legally exempt from registration who chooses to register for manpower training and employment services.

(gg) "WIN" means Work Incentive program.

(hh) "WIN sponsors" means the State Employment Service or other public or nonprofit private agency with which the RMA contracts to administer the WIN program at the State or local level.

§ 56.2   Purpose and scope.

This part contains the policies, rules, and regulations of the Department of Labor for implementing and administering the registration requirements of section 402(a)(19)(A) of the Act, as amended, and the requirements of part C, title IV of that Act, as amended. The applicable regulations of the Secretary of Health, Education, and Welfare relating to title IV of the Act may be found in 45 CFR Parts 220, 233, and 234.

(a) Under the Act the Secretary of Labor prescribes the regulations for registering individuals for manpower services, training and employment as a condition of eligibility for aid to families with dependent children and provides grants to and enters into agreements with public sponsors for the purpose of establishing Work Incentive programs for placing as many of such individuals in employment or on-the-job training, in institutional and work experience training, in public service employment, or in other activities which would enable them to become self-supporting employees in the regular economy.

(b) This part sets forth the requirements for registration of individuals for manpower services; the standards for selection, appraisal, and certification of,

and development of employability plans for such individuals; the responsibilities and functions of the WIN project staff in administering and carrying out the purposes of the Work Incentive program; the responsibilities and functions of the Labor Market Advisory Councils, the Regional Coordination Committees, and the National Coordination Committee; requirements of and policies for the development of and approval of Local and Statewide Operational Plans; the requirements for use of Federal funds and for non-Federal share under part C of the Act; the requirement for allocation of funds; requirements as to compensation and working and training conditions of participants; recordkeeping and reporting requirements; and other pertinent conditions and standards.

§ 56.3   Administration.

(a) Within DOL, the Regional Manpower Administrator shall, in accordance with his delegated authority, act on behalf of the Secretary. When authority is delegated to the Regional Manpower Administrator in the regulations in this subchapter, such authority may be exercised by him or by his designee.

(b) The State WIN agency or other sponsors with whom the Secretary has entered into an agreement shall be responsible for the administration of the programs established under part C of the Act and the responsibilities and functions set forth in this subchapter.

§ 56.4   Registration and exemptions of AFDC applicants.

(a) The Income Maintenance Unit of the local welfare agency, as agents of the RMA, shall register AFDC applicants and recipients for manpower services, training and employment as required under section 402(a)(19)(A) of the Act. It shall determine whether the applicant or recipient and members of his family are required to register as a condition for receiving AFDC benefits. Each individual must register unless he is—

(1) Under age 16 with proof of age;

(2) Attending school full time and age 16 but not yet age 21, unless a State AFDC requirement specifies a lower cut-off age, with proof of age and verification from an appropriate school official that the person is enrolled or has been accepted for enrollment for the next school term as a full-time student;

(3) Ill with medical evidence that the illness or an injury temporarily prevents entry into employment or training; (This exemption shall not exceed 90 days. A request for continuing exemption for illness or disability due to injury after 90 days shall be reviewed for medical determination of "incapacity").

(4) Incapacitated, when verified by the Income Maintenance Unit that a medically determinable physical or mental impairment, which by itself or in conjunction with age prevents the individual from engaging in employment or training under WIN, and the impairment is expected to exist for a continuous period of at least 3 months; (Except where determined to be permanently incapacitated, the individual shall notify the Income Maintenance Unit when he has been discharged by the attending physician).

(5) 65 years of age or older with verification of age;

(6) Residing at a location which is so remote from a WIN project so that more than a total of 10 hours would be required for a normal work or training day including round trip by reasonable available public transportation from his home to the WIN project;

(7) A caretaker in the home and the Income Maintenance Unit has verified that a medically determinable condition of another member of the household, without regard to expected duration, requires the individual's presence in the home on a substantially continuous basis; (A person exempt as "needed in the home" shall be subject to registration when no longer needed in his caretaker role.)

(8) A mother or other caretaker relative of a child under age 6, with proof of age and relationship;

(9) A mother or other female caretaker of a child, when the nonexempt father or other nonexempt adult male relative in the home is registered and has not refused to participate in the program or employment without good cause.

(b) Exemptions granted under paragraph (a)(9) of this section shall be withdrawn when the Income Maintenance Unit is informed that the nonexempt father or other nonexempt adult male relative in the home is not registered or has been found to have refused without good cause to participate in the program or accept employment.

(c) The Income Maintenance Unit shall establish standards of proof required for determining an individual's exemption under paragraph (a) of this section. Such standards shall be submitted in writing to the RMA for his review and approval at the earliest practicable date. The approved standards shall be applied in determining whether the individual is or is not exempt. Modifications of approved standards shall be processed in a similar manner.

(d) Exempt persons are required to notify the Income Maintenance Unit of any changes affecting their exempt status within 5 days of the change. The Income Maintenance Unit shall conduct periodic reviews of exempt status as a part of the redetermination process, except where the individual has been determined to be permanently incapacitated.

(e) An individual claiming to be exempt from the registration requirement may request the Income Maintenance

Unit to reconsider its determination or request a hearing by the State welfare agency.

(f) All persons exempt in accordance with criteria set forth in paragraph (a) of this section may volunteer for registration for manpower services, training, or employment. An exempt individual who volunteers for registration may cease to participate at any time, without loss of AFDC benefits, provided his status in the interim has not changed in a way which would require him to register in accordance with the Act.

§ 56.5 Selection, appraisal, and certification of participants.

(a) Registrants will be selected for appraisal of their employability potential and their needs, if any, for manpower, self-support and job placement services by WIN project and SAU staff on the basis of information obtained during the registration process. The following call-in order shall be followed, taking into account the individual's employability potential as determined from the registration form—

(1) All unemployed fathers without the application of selection factors;

(2) Mothers who volunteer for participation;

(3) Other mothers and pregnant women under 19 years of age who are required to register;

(4) Dependent children and relatives who have attained age 16 and who are not in school or engaged in work or manpower training;

(5) All others.

(b) The appraisal interview shall be conducted by WIN project and SAU staff at a time and place designated by them. Testing may be utilized to the extent it is required to determine whether or not the individual is employable. An employability plan for each registrant shall be initiated at the appraisal interviews by the WIN project staff and SAU in consultation with the participant. The employability plan shall be designed to lead to appropriate employment and shall contain a definite employment goal attainable in the shortest time period consistent with the participant's needs and qualifications, project resources, and job market opportunities. All information which has a bearing upon his vocational objective shall be included. The plan shall specify the steps for the participant to reach the goals established in the plan and shall identify the major barriers to employment or training and propose remedial action. The employability plan shall be reviewed periodically and modified as circumstances warrant. After appraisal, participants will be placed into the appropriate service level. As appropriate employment opportunities or openings in WIN manpower service programs become available, WIN project staff will request the SAU to certify those individuals, for whom such self-support services are identified in their employability plan, in the same order as prescribed above.

(c) The WIN project staff shall initiate all requests for certification. The requests shall be made only for participants who are to be entered into WIN training or placement and for participants who are enrolled in other manpower training programs: *Provided, however,* That certification will be requested for all unemployed fathers within two weeks of registration irrespective of whether an employability plan has been developed. In the event that certification has not been requested within this period, the SAU will proceed to certify the unemployed father on its own initiative. The determination of the participant's need for self-support services shall be made jointly by WIN and SAU staff. In the event of disagreement, the WIN staff shall make the final determination of the need for services. When needed self-support services have been made available or when the participant is not in need of such services to enable him to participate in training or employment, the SAU shall certify him to the WIN project. When so certified, he shall be referred by the WIN project staff to employment in the private sector, to on-the-job training or to institutional and work experience training or public service employment which is likely to lead to regular employment. Every effort shall be made to place participants in employment. All participants who are not employed or in training will be periodically exposed to available employment opportunities.

§ 56.6   [Reserved]

§ 56.7   Changes in status affecting welfare benefits.

The WIN project staff shall promptly notify the Income Maintenance Unit of any work placement or change of status which may affect the payment of welfare benefits to the participant.

§ 56.8   Allowances to certain WIN registrants/participants.

(a) A participant assigned to an institutional or work experience training component may be eligible to receive the following allowances—

(1) Incentive payments at a rate not to exceed $30 a month; (Unless waived by the WIN project staff, deductions may be made from the incentive payment for failure to meet attendance requirements established and posted by the sponsor.)

(2) Incidental daily training-related expenses to cover such items as lunches and transportation at the rate of $2 for each day that he attends such training during a training payment period; (Such amount shall be increased by the amount of excess daily travel cost where the cost of daily transportation exceeds $1 a day. This amount may be increased in in-

stances of extreme hardship upon prior approval of the RMA.)

(3) A subsistence allowance, in addition to a training-related expense allowance, to qualified participants for their separate maintenance when they are assigned to a training facility beyond daily commuting distance from their homes at the rate of $8 a day ($10 in Alaska) for each calendar day within the training payment period during which they were participating in training; (If the training facility makes available food and lodging, the subsistence allowance will be computed by multiplying the number of days in training in the period, plus intervening days of no training, by the daily rate charged for food and lodging plus $1 per day for incidentals, rounded to the next higher dollar.)

(4) A transportation allowance to a training facility located beyond commuting distance for the cost of his initial trip to the training facility and for his final trip home at the completion or other termination of his training program. (The amount of the transportation allowance will be the cost of the most economical public transportation available or at the rate of 6 cents per mile, if private transportation is used.)

(b) Allowances for nonrecurring expenses may be authorized by the Secretary, such as payments to cover necessary expenses incurred by a registrant in order to report for the appraisal interview.

§ 56.9   Relocation assistance.

The Secretary may assist participants to relocate their place of residence when he determines such relocation is necessary in order to enable them to become permanently employable and self-supporting. Such assistance shall be given only to participants who concur in their relocation and who will be employed at their place of relocation at wage rates which will meet at least their full need as determined by the State to which they will be relocated. Assistance under this section shall not exceed the reasonable costs of transportation for participants, their dependents, and their household belongings plus such relocation allowance as the Secretary determines to be reasonable.

§ 56.10 Overpayments.

The participant shall be required to repay the amount of any overpayment to him under part C of the Act. Overpayments not repaid shall be set off against any future allowance or other training payment under the Act to which the participant shall become entitled. Where the overpayment was made in the absence of fault on the part of the participant, recovery may be waived where such recovery would be against equity and good conscience.

§ 56.11 [Reserved]

§ 56.12 Agreements for WIN program services.

The State or local WIN sponsor shall by agreements with public or private agencies or organizations, including Indian tribes with respect to Indians on a reservation, carry out on-the-job training and work experience programs, and such other activities or programs as approved or developed by the Secretary. No agreement, however, shall be entered into with a private employer for profit, or with a nonprofit employer not organized for a public purpose, for purposes of a work experience project.

§ 56.13 Local Operational Plans.

(a) Local WIN Project staff shall develop an annual Local Operational Plan in cooperation with the local SAU. The plan shall describe how the local project will operate and will be administered and shall include—

(1) A list of all manpower activities which will be undertaken such as the anticipated number of direct placements, institutional training related to jobs of the type which are likely to become available in the area, on-the-job training and public service employment, and the estimated level of activity for each such component;

(2) The extent to which manpower training and employment services and opportunities under other Acts are to be utilized and an estimate of costs of such services and opportunities not otherwise available on a nonreimbursable basis;

(3) The number and kinds of self-support services which will be available and the extent to which such resources must be supplemented to meet projected needs;

(4) Identification of the agency, unit or subcontractor who will be responsible for providing manpower and self-support services and activities to be performed under the program; and

(5) A description of the manner in which information provided by the Labor Market Advisory Council (LMAC) will be utilized in the planning and operation of the local project.

(b) Local Operational Plans shall be forwarded to the State WIN agency for incorporation into the Statewide Operational Plan. Simultaneously, copies of the plan shall be sent to the appropriate mayors or chief executives of the areas involved for their review and submission of their comments directly to the local and State WIN agency and SAU. The State WIN agency shall maintain a copy of the local plan for use of regional and national monitors.

§ 56.14 Statewide Operational Plans.

(a) Statewide Operational Plans shall be jointly developed and approved by the State WIN agency and the State SAU. The RMA shall issue instructions to the State WIN agency for the development of that portion of the Statewide Operational Plan pertaining to manpower services and activities. The State WIN agency, in cooperation with the State SAU, will consolidate the WIN agency's State Level Plan which describes the operation to be carried out by the State WIN agency, the SAU's counterpart plan, and the Local Operational Plans.

(b) The plan shall describe how the WIN program will be administered and operated at the State and local levels, the total amount of the manpower and self-support services and activities which are to be provided during the fiscal year, the agencies or organizations which will be responsible for providing the services or conducting the activities enumerated, and the manner in which information provided by the Labor Market Advisory Council was utilized in planning and will be utilized in the operation of the program.

(c) The State WIN agency and the State SAU shall forward four copies of the approved Statewide Operational Plan to the appropriate RMA for distribution to each member of the Regional Coordination Committee. The agency shall also forward a copy of the plan to the Governor's Manpower Planning Council, or its equivalent, for review and comment. Any comments made by the Governor's Council should be forwarded directly to the Regional Coordination Committee by the date and to the address indicated by the Committee. Copies of such comments should also be sent to the State WIN agency, the State SAU, and other interested agencies.

§ 56.15 Labor Market Advisory Councils.

(a) For the purpose of advising the Secretary of employment opportunities, a Labor Market Advisory Council shall be established or designated in each State, municipality, or other appropriate geographic area in which a WIN project is located. The council shall consist of not more than a total of 18 persons, including representatives of industry, labor, and public service employers from the area to be served by the council, and of such other groups as the Secretary may designate.

(b) In those areas where Manpower Area Planning Councils or Ancillary Manpower Planning Boards have been established, the Secretary may designate such groups as Labor Market Advisory Councils for specific areas.

(c) The Councils shall be responsible for preparing quarterly reports on the types and numbers of jobs available or likely to become available in the area and such other data as required by the Secretary. Copies of the quarterly reports shall be forwarded to the Regional Manpower Administrator, the State WIN agency and the local WIN project(s) in the area.

§ 56.16 Regional Coordination Committees.

(a) The Regional Coordination Committee in each region shall consist of the Regional Manpower Administrator, or his designee, and the Social and Rehabilitation Service Regional Commissioner, or his designee. The Committee shall review and approve all Statewide Operational Plans and major modifications of such plans covering the States in its region. Copies of the approved Statewide Operational Plan will be distributed to each member of the RCC, the State WIN agency, the State SAU, and the Governor's Council.

(b) Any disagreement concerning the approval or disapproval of a Statewide Operational Plan between the Departmental representatives serving as members of the Regional Coordination Committee shall be referred promptly to the National Coordination Committee for resolution.

§ 56.17 National Coordination Committee.

(a) The National Coordination Committee shall be composed of members designated by the Secretaries of Labor, and Health, Education, and Welfare.

(b) It shall establish uniform reporting and other requirements for the effective administration of the WIN program and shall prepare and publish a monthly report on WIN operations.

§ 56.18 [Reserved]

§ 56.19 [Reserved]

§ 56.20 Allocations of Federal funds.

(a) The Secretary shall allocate not less than 50 percent of the sums appropriated to carry out the provisions of the Work Incentive Program among the States in accordance with a formula under which each State receives (from the total available for such allotment) an amount which bears the same ratio to such total as—

(1) In the case of the fiscal years ending June 30, 1973, and June 30, 1974, the average number of recipients of aid to families with dependent children in such State during the month of January last preceding the commencement of such fiscal year bears to the average number of such recipients during such month in all the States; and

(2) In the case of any fiscal year thereafter, the average number of individuals in such State who, during the month of January last preceding the commencement of such fiscal year, are registered pursuant to section 402(a)(19)(A) of the Social Security Act, as amended, bears to the average number of individuals in all States who, during such month, are so registered.

(b) The Secretary shall allocate the balance of the sums not allocated under paragraph (a) of this section in such manner which he determines would best serve the objectives to be attained by the program.

(c) Of the sums allocated to the States under paragraphs (a) and (b) of this section, not less than 33⅓ percent thereof shall be expended for carrying out the programs of on-the-job training and public service employment established under the Act.

§ 56.21 Use of Federal funds.

(a) Except where otherwise specified, Federal funds allocated by the Secretary to the State WIN agencies may be used to meet not more than 90 percent of the cost of the work incentive programs established by the Act. No funds, except in cases of public service employment under the Act, may be used for any reimbursement for time spent by participants in work, training, or other participation in the program.

(b) Such funds shall be expended only for purposes (1) permitted under the provisions of Subpart 1–15.7 of Title 41 of the Code of Federal Regulations, entitled "Principles for Determining Costs Applicable to Grants and Contracts" and (2) not barred under the remaining provisions of this part.

§ 56.22 Non-Federal share.

(a) The non-Federal share arranged for by the State public assistance agency may be provided in cash or in kind, fairly evaluated, including, but not limited to plant, equipment or services.

(b) The non-Federal share must be expended for a purpose which is allowable under the provisions of Subpart 1–15.7 of Title 41 of the Code of Federal Regulations.

(c) The fair market value of services provided, when such services are determined to be allowable costs in support of the WIN program and when such services are provided at no cost or at a cost below the fair market value, may be included as in-kind non-Federal share.

(d) Other Federal funds or resources, whether in cash or in-kind, may not be used for the non-Federal share, except when specifically permitted by the law under which other Federal funds were made available. State funds or resources that have been used to match other Federal funds also may not be used for this purpose.

(e) The Secretary shall report the failure of any State to meet its obligation of arranging for 10 percent of the costs of the work incentive program to the Secretary of Health, Education, and Welfare for action as prescribed by section 443 of the Act.

§ 56.23 Period of participation.

(a) The average duration of institutional and work experience training established pursuant to the Act shall not exceed 6 months, with a maximum duration of 1 year. The RMA may allow an exception to this limitation for training in high paying occupations with a high placement record.

(b) Manpower services provided under the WIN program may be provided to an individual until he has completed his employability plan or for such other period the WIN project staff determines is necessary to qualify him fully for employment even though his earnings disqualify him from aid under a State plan approved under section 402 of the Act: *Provided,* That such period does not exceed 30 days in duration.

§ 56.24 [Reserved]

§ 56.25 Public service employment.

The State WIN sponsor shall, in developing public service employment opportunities in jobs which would not oth-

erwise be performed by regular employees, enter into agreements with—

(a) Units of Federal, State, or general local governments;

(b) Public agencies and institutions which are subdivisions of State or general local government, and institutions of the Federal Government;

(c) Indian tribes or combination of tribes on a Federal or State reservation; or

(d) Private nonprofit organizations established to serve a public purpose.

§ 56.26 Standards for appropriate work or training.

(a) A mandatory certified participant must accept assignment to employment, training, or manpower services as determined appropriate by the WIN project staff. The standards in paragraph (b) of this section must be met before a WIN participant can be required to accept an assignment to any WIN activity. An assignment is construed to include not only the referral and the first physical reporting of the participant to the work or training site, but also, to regular participation until the assignment is completed.

(b) The following standards are common to assignments to both work and training—

(1) The job or training assignment must be within the capability of the participant performing the task on a regular basis, without adverse effects on his physical or mental health; (A finding of adverse effect shall be based, as a minimum, on a physician's statement indicating that participation would impair the individual's health.)

(2) The total commuting time to and from the work or training site to which the participant is assigned shall not normally exceed 2 hours, including deposit and pick-up of a child at an approved child care location, unless a longer com-

muting distance and time is generally accepted in the community; (The total participant day shall not exceed 10 hours including work or training time.)

(3) When child care is required, it must be made available during the hours the participant is working or in training plus any additional time which is required to deposit and pick-up the child;

(4) The work or training site to which the individual is assigned must not be in violation of established Federal, State, or local health and safety standards.

(c) The determination of "appropriate work" shall be made at the local project level. The following shall be applied in determining "appropriate work"—

(1) When income disregard or other income supplementation is available, the wage shall meet or exceed the Federal or State minimum wage law, whichever is applicable, or if such laws are not applicable, a wage which is not substantially less favorable than the wage normally paid for similar work in that labor market but in no event less than three-fourths of the Federal minimum wage;

(2) When, as a result of becoming employed, no income disregard or other income supplementation is available to the participant, the wage shall provide an income equal to or exceeding the individual's AFDC benefits, plus employment-related expenses such as transportation, lunches, special work clothes or tools;

(3) The daily hours of work and the weekly number of hours of work shall not exceed those customary to the occupation;

(4) No participant shall be required to accept employment if—(i) The position offered is vacant due to a strike, lockout, or other labor dispute; (ii) as a condition of being employed, the individual would be required to join a company union or to resign from or refrain from joining any bona fide labor organization; (iii) the job offered would interrupt a program in progress for permanent rehabilitation or self-support, or would conflict with an imminent likelihood of re-employment at the person's regular work if such work would provide adequate income to make the person self-supporting.

(d) The standards set forth in paragraph (b) of this section shall apply to training assignments. In addition, any institutional training shall be in conformance with the recommendations of the local Labor Market Advisory Council. The quality of the training provided must meet local employer's requirements so that the participant will be in a competitive position within the local labor market.

§ 56.27 Participants enrolled in other manpower programs.

Participants attending a WIN component shall be compensated according to these regulations and procedures. A WIN participant referred to a slot in other federally or State funded training programs and meeting all the eligibility requirements under those programs shall be temporarily suspended from the WIN program. Those participants assigned to an institutional training program under the Manpower Development and Training Act shall be compensated in accordance with the provisions of title II of that act. Those participants assigned to programs developed under the Economic Opportunity Act will be compensated in accordance with the provisions of that act in lieu of WIN incentive payments and other WIN allowances.

§ 56.28 [Reserved]

§ 56.29 [Reserved]

§ 56.30 Project work rules and grievances.

(a) The WIN sponsor shall establish rules, subject to the approval of the RMA, governing attendance, conduct, and grievances. Each participant shall be given a copy of the rules and grievance procedure which shall include the names, addresses, and phone numbers of the persons he may contact if he believes he has a grievance.

(b) Written complaints of grievances may be filed with either the local WIN project office or the State WIN agency and shall be processed at the level at which they are submitted. All grievances must be resolved within 14 days of the receipt of the complaint by the local project or State WIN office. A registrant/participant may appeal to the RMA if he is not satisfied with the disposition of the complaint or if the complaint is not resolved within the prescribed time limit. The RMA's decision shall be the final decision in the matter.

§ 56.31   Nondiscrimination.

(a) No person in the United States shall, on the grounds of race, creed, color or national origin, be excluded from participation in, be denied the benefits of, or be subjected to discrimination under any program or activity receiving Federal financial assistance under this Act.

(b) Grievances involving discrimination under paragraph (a) of this section shall be processed according to the equal opportunity provisions established by the Secretary and in compliance with title VI of the Civil Rights Act of 1964 (78 Stat. 252) and the regulations issued thereunder (Part 31 of this subtitle).

§ 56.32   Political activity.

No funds allocated under the Act shall be used for any partisan political activity or to further the election or defeat of any candidate for public office; nor shall they be used to provide services, or for the employment or assignment of personnel in a manner supporting or result-

ing in the identification of programs conducted pursuant to the Act with—

(1) Any partisan or nonpartisan political activity or any other political activity associated with a candidate, or contending faction or group, in an election for public or party office;

(2) Any activity to provide voters or prospective voters with transportation to the polls or similar assistance in connection with any such election; or

(3) Any voter registration activity.

§ 56.33   Participant status.

A participant in a WIN project shall not be deemed an employee of the Federal Government, and shall not be subject to the provisions of laws relating to Federal employees, including those relating to hours of work, rates of compensation, leave, unemployment compensation, and Federal employee benefits.

§ 56.34   Reports.

State and local WIN sponsors shall submit periodic reports as required by the Secretary.

§ 56.35   [Reserved]

§ 56.36   Records, financial statements, and audits.

The WIN sponsor and subcontractors shall maintain such records and accounts, including records of property purchased with non-Federal share, and personnel and financial records, and submit such financial statements as are required by the Secretary to assure proper accounting for all program funds, including the non-Federal share. Such records and accounts shall be made available for audit purposes to the Department of Labor or the Comptroller General of the United States or any authorized representative of either, and shall be retained for 3 years after the completion of or final payment under the agreement, whichever is later. The records shall be retained beyond the 3-year period if audit findings have not been resolved.

§ 56.37 Adjustments in payments to sponsors.

(a) If any funds are expended by a State WIN sponsor or by a public service employer in violation of the Act, the regulations, or contract conditions, the Secretary may make necessary adjustments in payments to the sponsor or the employing agency on account of such unauthorized or illegal expenditures. He may draw back unexpended funds which have been made available in order to assure that they will be used in accordance with the purposes of the Act, or to prevent further unauthorized or illegal expenditures, and he may withhold funds otherwise payable under the Act in order to recover any amounts expended illegally or for unauthorized purposes in the current or immediately prior fiscal year. If no further payments would otherwise be made under the Act during the current or subsequent fiscal year, the Secretary may request a repayment of funds used for unauthorized or illegal expenditures, and within 30 days after receipt of such request such repayment shall be made.

(b) No action taken by the Secretary under paragraph (a) of this section shall entitle the sponsor to reduce program activities or allowances for any participant or to expend less during the effective period of the contract than those sums called for in his operational plan. Any such reduction in expenditures may be deemed sufficient cause for termination under § 56.38.

§ 56.38 Termination of contract.

(a) If a WIN sponsor or Income Maintenance Unit violates any provision of the Act or the regulations or contract terms or conditions which the Secretary has issued or shall subsequently issue during the period of the contract, the Secretary may terminate the contract in whole or in part unless the agency which caused the violation corrects it within a period of 30 days after receipt of notice specifying the violation or—

(b) In his discretion, the Secretary may terminate the contract in whole or in part;

(c) Termination shall be effected by a notice of termination which shall specify the extent of termination and the date upon which such termination becomes effective. Upon receipt of a notice of termination the agency shall—

(1) Discontinue further commitments of contract funds to the extent that they relate to the terminated portion of the contracts;

(2) Promptly cancel all subcontracts utilizing funds under the contract to the extent that they relate to the terminated portion of the contract;

(3) Settle, with the approval of the Secretary, all outstanding claims arising from such termination;

(4) Submit, within 6 months after the receipt of the notice of termination, a termination settlement proposal which shall include a final statement of all unreimbursed costs related to the terminated portion of the contract, but in case of terminations under paragraph (a) of this section will not include the cost of preparing a settlement proposal. Allowable costs shall be determined in accordance with the provisions of Part 1–15.7 of Title 41 of the Code of Federal Regulations.

Effective date. This part shall become effective July 1, 1972.

3. Proposals for Reform of Work Rules

Introductory Note

President Nixon has asserted that the nation "can work its way out of poverty," and labelled his welfare reform proposals, embodied in H.R. 1, 92d Cong., as a "workfare" plan to achieve this goal. The work aspects of the proposed replacement for AFDC have been discussed as follows:

The new plan would substitute exact rules to determine who must register for work or training for the haphazard system today under which each state decides who is required to register. Under the bill, any member of an eligible family who did not meet specific criteria would be considered available for employment and would have to register with the Secretary of Labor for work and training.

Any person who did not register or take work or training as required would subject the family to an $800 per year reduction in benefits. [Ed: This is equal to the total grant per person under the plan.] Every person taking training would receive about $30 per month as an additional incentive to stay in the training. (Thus, the monetary difference between refusing or taking training could be $1,160 per

year.) The same penalties and allowances would apply to people who are offered vocational rehabilitation services.

As an incentive for work the first $720 plus one-third of the remainder of annual earnings would not be used to reduce family benefits. H.Rep.No. 92–590, 92d Cong., 1st Sess. 160 (1971).

The incentive side of this is largely unchanged from existing law; although the basic incentive is increased from $360 per year to $720 per year there is an accompanying cutback on the allowance of offsets for work related expenses. Thus, the reform emphasis is on the requirement side (a pattern since adopted in the Talmadge Amendments, see pp. 210–212 supra. In a recent article, Professor Joel Handler and Ellen Jane Hollingsworth suggested that incentives are more likely to reduce welfare rolls than are requirements, and closed with this comment on the Nixon proposals:

One would think that a conservative administration would have more faith in the market and less faith in government regulation.

Does this puzzle you as well?

The following materials are included to aid in your evaluation of the Nixon proposals and other reform suggestions. However, such evaluations are not easy because the empirical data are so limited.

WELFARE MYTHS vs. FACTS

Social and Rehabilitational Service, Dep't of
Health, Education and Welfare, Welfare
Myths vs. Facts (SRS) 71–127 (1971).

MYTH:

The welfare rolls are full
of able-bodied loafers!

FACT:

Less than one percent of welfare recipients are able-bodied unemployed males:
some 126,000 of the more than 13 million Americans on Federal/State-sup-
ported welfare (April 1971 statistics).
Most of them—80 percent—want work,
according to a Government-sponsored
study; about half the men are enrolled
in work training programs.

The largest group of working-age adults
on welfare are 2.5 million mothers of
welfare families, most of whom head
families with no able-bodied male present. About 14 percent of these mothers
work, and 7 percent are in work training.
Many of the other mothers confront
serious barriers to employment under
the existing welfare system. But if day
care were available for their children,
and if job training and jobs were to be
had, it is estimated that another 35
percent would be potential employees.
An additional 4 to 5 percent of mothers
have some employment potential, but
require more extensive social rehabilitative service to prepare them. (The proposed welfare reform program includes
provisions for day care, job training,
public service jobs, and more extensive
service for welfare recipients.)

The remaining 40 percent of welfare
mothers have little or no employment

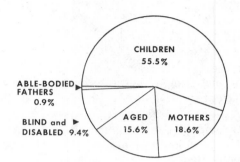

FEDERALLY ASSISTED WELFARE POPULATION
(as of April 1971)

CHILDREN 55.5%

ABLE-BODIED FATHERS 0.9%

BLIND and DISABLED 9.4%

AGED 15.6%

MOTHERS 18.6%

potential because they care for small
children at home, have major physical
or mental incapacities, or other insurmountable work barriers. In spite of this,
70 to 80 percent of welfare mothers
consistently report they would work if
present barriers to employment are
overcome.

Factors in the Employability of Welfare Mothers
(From a 1969 study)

● Needed at home to care for small children,
  have a long-term disability, etc........ **40%**

● Employable if job training, jobs, and
  day care were made available **35%**

● Already employed full- or part-time...... **14%**

● In work-training programs or waiting
  to be accepted **7%**

● Need extensive medical or rehabilitative
  services before becoming
  employable **4%**

[A7342]

NOTE: The term "welfare" in this leaflet refers to Aid to Families with Dependent Children (AFDC), the largest public assistance program.

CHARACTERISTICS AND WORK EXPERIENCE OF AFDC RECIPIENTS

S. Levitan, M. Rein, D. Marwick.
(From Work and Welfare Go Together, 1972).

The distinction made by the Social Security Act between those who can support themselves and those who cannot is not based upon actual labor market operations, for work and welfare are closely intertwined.* AFDC family heads need not make an "all or nothing" choice, but may select the best combination of the two. The decision to accept welfare neither precludes participation in the labor force nor necessitates a long duration on public assistance.

The Revolving Door

Welfare recipients are not unable or unwilling to work, nor do they languish on the rolls forever. Steady growth of the rolls masks a tremendous turnover. Some of the families who leave the rolls later return, but there is nevertheless great dynamism in the caseload. During 1970 some 750,000 cases were closed— including nearly 40 percent of the 1.9 million AFDC households on the rolls at the beginning of the year. Thus, the 1.3 million families who received AFDC payments during all of 1970 accounted for less than one-half of the caseload at the beginning of 1971.

* The National Center for Social Statistics of the U. S. Department of Health, Education, and Welfare's Social and Rehabilitation Service makes periodic surveys of AFDC recipients, gathering data on demographic, health, and financial characteristics of recipients and on program characteristics. During the last decade these surveys have been conducted in 1961, 1967, 1969, and 1971. Most of the data in this [excerpt] are derived from these surveys.

Most families join and leave the AFDC rolls quickly. In recent years approximately one-quarter of the cases left within six months; 30 percent left within a year; half closed within two years; and three-fifths closed within three years.

The instability of the AFDC population reflects the fact that poverty is also frequently transitory. While there was a net decline of 2 percent in the poverty population between 1965 and 1966, one-third of the poor in 1965 rose above the poverty threshold in 1966. An equal proportion of the poor in 1966 were non-poor the previous year.[1]

The high proportion of AFDC clients who have previously received public assistance is another indication of the interdependence between work and welfare. In both 1961 and 1971 one AFDC family in three had previously received assistance. Of those in 1967 who had previously received aid, two-thirds had been on the rolls only once before and one-third had been on at least twice. Moreover, one-fifth had been denied assistance at some time.

The number of AFDC recipients mirrored national unemployment trends until the 1960s, with drops during the tight labor markets of both World War II and the Korean War. Moreover, until recently, the effect of seasonality in employment was also evident in AFDC caseloads. The greater availability of jobs during spring and summer months was reflected in slower growth or even declines in the recipient population (Chart 7).

[1] Terence F. Kelly, "Factors Affecting Poverty: A Gross Flow Analysis," in The President's Commission on Income Maintenance Programs, Technical Studies (Washington: Government Printing Office, 1970), p. 24.

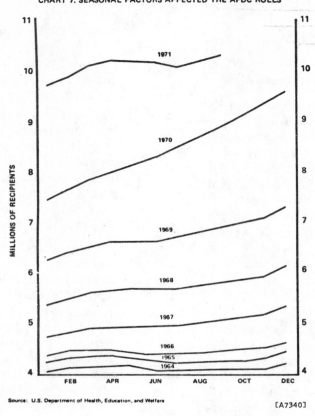

CHART 7. SEASONAL FACTORS AFFECTED THE AFDC ROLLS

Source: U.S. Department of Health, Education, and Welfare

[A7340]

EMPLOYABILITY OF AFDC FATHERS

Nearly one-fifth of AFDC families include a father, but two-thirds of these men are incapacitated. The others qualified for AFDC under the Unemployed Fathers (UF) component added in 1961. Only half of the states even enacted an UF component and several of these have since eliminated it.

These men, who worked in noncovered employment or must have exhausted their unemployment insurance and have been out of work for a substantial period of time to qualify for AFDC–UF, have been forced to rely upon welfare because of their inability to compete in the labor market. Just over one in five was a high school graduate in 1969, as contrasted with nearly three of every five adult males in the civilian labor force in 1970. About one-half of the unemployed fathers, but less than one-fifth of the civilian labor force, had failed to complete more than eight years of education (Table 5). Moreover, the unemployed fathers have few skills. Only 2 percent have never worked full time. But even among those who have been employed, only 5 percent usually held white-collar

TABLE 5. AFDC UNEMPLOYED FATHERS ARE POORLY EDUCATED

Educational attainment (in years)	AFDC unemployed fathers, 1969	All males in the labor force 18 and over in 1970
Median	8.4	12.4
Less than 8	31%	10%
8	15	10
9 to 11	33	17
12	17	35
More than 12	4	28

SOURCE: U.S. Department of Health, Education, and Welfare, and Labor.

jobs, as opposed to 47 percent nationally. Fully 64 percent were service workers or laborers, while only 13 percent of the national labor force were in these low-skilled groups (Table 6). Thus, these men are at a disadvantage in both education and skills and are usually confined to the "secondary" labor market jobs requiring few skills but offering little job stability and wages at or below the poverty level.

TABLE 6. AFDC UNEMPLOYED FATHERS ARE CONCENTRATED IN UNFAVORABLE OCCUPATIONS

	AFDC unemployed fathers, by current or usual occupation, 1967	Male family heads, by longest occupation during 1970
Total	100%	100%
Professional, technical, managerial	2	35
Clerical and sales	3	12
Craftsmen and operatives	30	40
Service workers	6	7
Laborers	58	7

SOURCE: U. S. Department of Health, Education, and Welfare and U. S. Bureau of the Census.

EMPLOYABILITY OF AFDC MOTHERS

As the burden of the rolls became financially onerous, public assistance for dependent children and their parents came under increasing attack. Not only was the AFDC-UF component providing support for employable male heads of families, but the role of women, especially married women, in the labor force was undergoing substantial change.

The public debate dealing with AFDC has been frequently concerned more with rhetoric than reality. The issue of whether welfare mothers *can* work has been confused with the issue of whether they *should* work and at what rate of pay. And because of the insistence that work and welfare be treated as mutually exclusive, the ability of welfare mothers to enter the labor market and earn some money has been confused with their ability to achieve economic self-support.

The original social security legislation provided assistance to mothers so that they would not be forced to work, not because they were unemployable, but because jobs were scarce. Barriers to employment, such as the physical impediments of the aged, blind, and disabled, were rare. The problem of child care, however, was and continues to be significant. Although there were few jobs available in the 1930s, even for those who sought employment, the attitude that mothers should not be forced out of the home to work prevailed into the mid-1960s.

Few married women, and especially mothers, worked prior to World War II. In 1940 only 15 percent of married women with husbands present and only 9 percent of mothers were in the work force. The succeeding three decades witnessed a continuing rise in labor force participation by women. In 1970 half of all mothers with their husbands present had work experience, including 44 percent of mothers with children under six and 58 percent of mothers with children aged six to seventeen. Exempting welfare mothers from employment when half of all mothers were working no longer seemed justified.

Though public debate continues as to whether welfare mothers should be required to work, the conclusion has generally been reached that AFDC mothers can work and should be encouraged to do so. Over the last decade, about one welfare mother in five was consistently in the labor force; moreover, the proportion in part-time work declined and that in full-time employment increased (Chart 8). A closer examination of these data reveals wide variation among states. In 1971, when 28 percent of all AFDC mothers were in the labor force or training, state rates ranged from 12 percent in Pennsylvania to 42 percent in Florida.

An examination of the characteristics of recipients suggests that for many on relief, achieving full economic independence is an unrealistic goal. However, given opportunities, suitable work incentives, and supportive services, many more

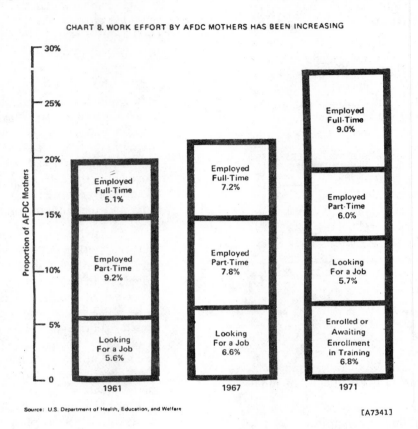

CHART 8. WORK EFFORT BY AFDC MOTHERS HAS BEEN INCREASING

Source: U.S. Department of Health, Education, and Welfare

[A7341]

welfare mothers could work and earn, though these earnings could only supplement and perhaps partially substitute for public assistance, not completely replace it.

Employability is a complex balance of economic, social, and psychological factors, and attempts at precise measurement must be inconclusive. On the supply side, employability is usually associated with work experience, education, and skills, and the absence of certain barriers, including health problems, child care responsibilities, and work disincentives.

For employability and desire to work to result in a job, a demand for labor is also necessary.

Child Care

The presence of young children is the most obvious barrier to the employment of all mothers and certainly no less a problem for those on AFDC. Of all married women, husband present, with children under three, some 27 percent are in the labor force. Of AFDC women with children under three, some 14 percent are in training or at work; when the unemployed are included, the participation rate approaches 18 percent. It is increasingly acceptable for mothers to leave their children in another's care while they work. For some mothers the limited supply of day care facilities is a severe constraint, but many others have managed, nevertheless, to make arrangements.

Of every eight welfare mothers in 1971, about five had a child under six; another two had no child under six but one under thirteen; the balance had only children over thirteen. This means that more than 60 percent of the mothers might need full-time, year-round day care if they were to work; and another quarter might need care in the afternoon during the school year and all day during the summer. But according to HEW estimates, the total capacity of licensed day care centers and family day care homes in 1971 was only 750,000. In the same year there were 2.3 million AFDC children under six who presumably would need full-time care and another 2.8 million between six and twelve requiring part-time care, if their mothers were not available to care for them. Licensed facilities fell far short of being able to accommodate the children of welfare mothers. And, of course, another thirteen million working mothers might be competing for such facilities.

Nevertheless, the mothers of nearly twenty-six million minor children, including six million under six years of age, were working in March 1970.[2] These working mothers have accommodated themselves in a variety of ways to the paucity and cost of licensed facilities. The amount and types of child care arrangements used depend primarily on the number and age of the children and on the availability of relatives to provide inexpensive services. Of all employed mothers, ages thirty to forty-four, with minor children in a nationwide survey, only two in five reported the need to make regular child care arrangements; but of mothers with children under six, the proportion rose to seven in ten. Few

[2] U. S. Bureau of Labor Statistics, Children of Women in the Labor Force, March 1970, Special Labor Force Report 134, 1971.

of the mothers surveyed used facilities that might be licensed. Only one mother in eleven used a child care center. The others used, equally, relatives and non-relatives, in either the child's or the caretaker's home. Thus, informal arrangements—which are not subject to licensing—constitute the bulk of child care.

Because preschool children must be supervised for a larger part of the day and also more carefully, daily costs rise substantially when a child under six is present (Table 7). Costs of child care also depend more heavily on the availability of relatives and others who can provide free services than on the type of services. For those who paid for child care, daily costs ranged from $2.50 to $3.50 for care by a relative, from $3.00

TABLE 7. CHILD CARE COSTS ARE HIGHER FOR YOUNG CHILDREN

Number of children under 6	Median daily cost	
	White	Black
None	$2.06	$0.70
One	3.01	1.35
Two or more	3.31	0.19 a

a Apparently child care is so expensive that few black mothers with more than one preschool child work unless they can arrange for free child care.
SOURCE: Herbert Parnes et al., Dual Careers, Volume 1, U. S. Department of Labor, Manpower Research Monograph No. 21, 1970, p. 125.

to more than $4.00 for care by a nonrelative, and to about $2.75 for school or group care centers. Because half of the relatives, but few of the others providing care did so without charge, the median daily costs overall were reduced to under 50 cents for care by a relative but not lowered much for other types of service. Expenditures for child care also rise with earnings. Not only can parents with higher incomes afford to spend more money, but better-paying jobs may require more reliable, more consistent, and longer care. Black mothers spend significantly less on child care than do white mothers. Not only are their incomes lower but they are also more likely to have access to relatives who will provide services without charge. Furthermore, reflecting their lower earnings, blacks are forced to choose less expensive forms of care and have lower costs for each type or child care arrangement. However, the extent to which lower costs reflect only inferior services is not known.[3]

Largely because the potential demand is so much greater than the available supply, child care has been hailed as the panacea for the employment problems of welfare mothers. Emphasizing the scarcity of child care facilities, however, may divert attention from the ability of these mothers to locate such services on their own. A woman's willingness to bear the costs of leaving her child(ren) depends largely on the expected benefits of doing so, especially on the potential earnings. A survey for the Department of Health, Education, and Welfare of AFDC in ten cities found that of all the welfare mothers sampled, two of every three "said they could make 'arrangements' (for child care) to work if a good job were available."[4]

Health

Poor health is another handicap to employment. The health problems of poor people—reinforced by inadequate diet, poor housing, and deficient medical care are well documented. A nutrition study conducted by HEW in ten states found that persons below the poverty line were twice as likely to be low or deficient in several important nutrition criteria, including hemoglobin, that may lead to anemia.[5] A study of labor force participation in New York City poverty areas found that the incidence of disability or ill health was substantially higher than nationally. Of the population twenty-five and over, 10 percent of all men and 15 percent of all women in the poverty areas were not participating in the labor force because of health problems, as compared with 4 percent of the men and 9 percent of the women for the rest of the population.[6]

However, the impact of ill health on labor force participation by AFDC mothers is difficult to assess. About one of every nine mothers cited, in response to HEW surveys, physical or mental incapacity as the primary reason for not being in the labor force. Studies in 1968 by the Social and Rehabilitation Service indicate a higher incidence of health problems. About two mothers in five answered "yes" to the question, "Are there some kinds of jobs you can't get because of your health?" One in five answered "yes" to the question, "Does your health keep you from working altogether?"[7]

Education

The median educational attainment of welfare mothers increased between 1961 and 1971 from less than nine years to

[3] Herbert Parnes et al., Dual Careers: A Longitudinal Study of Labor Market Experience of Women, Volume 1, U. S. Department of Labor, Manpower Research Monograph No. 21, 1970, pp. 121–27, and John R. Shea et al., Years for Decision: A longitudinal Study of the Educational and Labor Market Experience of Young Women, Volume 1, Center for Human Resource Research, The Ohio State University (Columbus, Ohio, 1971), pp. 132–40.

[4] Andrew K. Solarz, "Effects of Earnings Exemption Provision on AFDC Recipients," Welfare in Review (January-February 1971): 19.

[5] Department of Health, Education, and Welfare, Public Health Service, Ten-State Nutrition Survey in the United States, 1968-1970, April 1971.

[6] U. S. Department of Labor, Bureau of Labor Statistics, Poverty Area Profiles: Working Age Nonparticipants: Persons Not in the Labor Force and Their Employment Problems. Middle Atlantic Regional Report Number 22, June 1971.

[7] Perry Levinson, "How Employable Are AFDC Women," Welfare in Review (July-August 1970): 15–16.

more than ten years, but still trailed by two years other adult females. The proportion who had completed eight or fewer years of schooling declined from 56 percent to 31 percent (Table 8). While education is viewed by economists as "investment in human capital" that is supposed to lead to improvement in earnings ability, the added educational attainment

TABLE 8. THE EDUCATIONAL ATTAINMENT OF AFDC MOTHERS HAS RISEN BUT STILL LAGS BEHIND THAT FOR ALL WOMEN

Educational attainment (in years)	AFDC mothers		All women, 16 to 64, in the labor force, 1970
	1961	1971	
Median	8.7	10.4	12.4
Less than 8	38%	19%	6%
8	18	12	8
9 to 11	29	41	17
12	13	24	46
More than 12	2	4	24

SOURCE: Departments of Health, Education, and Welfare, and Labor.

of welfare recipients does not necessarily result in rising returns. Studies have found that blacks benefit substantially less than whites from education and that in urban ghettos the returns to nonwhites are extremely small, neither increasing earnings nor decreasing unemployment.[8]

Work Experience

Reflecting the rising female participation in the labor force and the increasing interdependence of work and welfare, the work experience of AFDC mothers improved between 1961 and 1971. Although the proportion of mothers employed remained stable at about 15 percent, the proportion who had never worked dropped sharply from about one in three in 1961 to less than one in four in 1971. In addition to the mothers then working, another one-fifth had worked within the previous year and one-tenth more in the past two years. Only one

[8] Bennett Harrison, Education, Training and the Urban Ghetto (Baltimore: The Johns Hopkins Press, 1972).

mother in five had not worked at all in the last five years.

Race

The proportion of nonwhites among AFDC mothers increased substantially until the 1960s, but during the decade of greatest expansion of the rolls changed little:

	1948	1961	1971
White	69	52	52
Nonwhite	31	48	48

There is little question that blacks, chicanos, Indians, and other minority groups encounter disproportionate labor market difficulties. This discrimination is important for present purposes because these problems not only make nonwhites more likely to rely on AFDC but also decrease their ability to earn enough to escape relief.

The manifestations are many. White female family heads experience less unemployment, work in better-paying occupations, and, accordingly, are less likely to be in poverty if they are in the work force. In March 1970 almost twice as many black female family heads with minor children were unemployed as among whites. The average weekly earnings of sixteen- to forty-four-year-old female family heads in May 1969 were nearly one-fifth better for whites ($88) than for nonwhites ($74); this differential held true for all educational levels. Not only were nonwhite female family heads more likely to work in lower paying occupations, but within every occupation they were more likely to be poor. Faced with more and lengthier periods of unemployment, fewer black female family heads worked full time, year round; but more worked full time for at least half the year or part time year round. Similarly, among AFDC mothers, nonwhites are about 50 percent more likely to work than whites. For each level of labor force effort, Negroes were far more likely to be in poverty (Table 9). Thus, because of more unemployment and lower earnings for each occupation and educational level, nonwhite female family heads are about twice as likely to be poor and also about twice as likely to receive AFDC as whites.

Obviously, a group of female family heads who encounter such pervasive unfavorable conditions will be less able to earn enough to avoid depending upon

TABLE 9. FEMALE-HEADED FAMILIES: WORK EXPERIENCE OF HEAD, RACE, AND POVERTY, 1970

		(Percent)		
	All families		Families in poverty	
	White	Negro	White	**Negro**
Total	100%	100%	25%	**54%**
With work experience	60	62	17	42
Worked at full-time job:				
50 to 52 weeks	34	27	5	18
27 to 49 weeks	8	10	17	39
26 weeks or less	6	8	50	68
Worked at part-time job:				
50 to 52 weeks	4	6	22	54
27 to 49 weeks	3	5	18	57
26 weeks or less	6	6	46	85
With no work experience	40	38	38	76

welfare and once they qualify for assistance to become economically self-supporting. Consequently, as the proportion of nonwhites increases, the earnings potential and capacity for self-support declines among AFDC mothers.

Demand

Even if welfare mothers were not constrained in their labor force activity by child care, health, and similar problems, their earning ability would be quite limited. Although there was some improvement between 1961 and 1971, welfare mothers are concentrated in the most unfavorable occupations and, even in comparison with all female family heads, are at a significant disadvantage. Of all AFDC mothers, 27 percent have never worked. Even those who have held jobs are concentrated in the least attractive occupations, many of them in the low-skilled, poorly-paying, transitory secondary labor market. These limited skills impede the escape of welfare mothers from poverty (Table 10).

TABLE 10. AFDC MOTHERS ARE CONCENTRATED IN LOW-PAYING JOBS

	Ever-employed AFDC mothers 1967	Female family heads with work experience in 1970	
		Distribution by occupation	Proportion in poverty
Total	100%	100%	100%
Professional, technical, managerial, official	2	17	9
Clerical and sales	14	33	12
Craftsmen and operatives	12	12	46
Private household workers	20	8	56
Other service workers	28	22	34

SOURCE: U. S. Department of Health, Education, and Welfare and U. S. Bureau of the Census.

The occupational distribution of AFDC mothers will prove even more unfavorable in the future, according to projections by the Department of Labor. Their estimates suggest that welfare mothers' usual occupations are those which will increase least during the current decade. For the 27 percent of mothers who have never been employed, the shift to more highly skilled occupations is especially ominous.

Location

Fears that the suburbanization of employment would decrease employment opportunities for AFDC recipients who increasingly live in central cities may be exaggerated. It is true that employment is growing more in suburbs than in central cities and that the proportion of jobs located in suburbia is increasing. At the same time, however, central city employment has continued to grow, while population has generally stagnated, if not declined. Hence, the number of jobs per central city resident has been increasing. Moreover, there is evidence that the mix of central city employment has changed, with an increasing proportion of low-skill jobs. Thus, more of the central city jobs are within the capabilities of residents there generally, and AFDC recipients specifically. Unfortunately, low-skill jobs usually pay low wages and are not likely to be much more rewarding or remunerative than welfare.[9]

The increasing concentration of AFDC recipients in certain areas may have significant labor market implications. Such large dependence on AFDC may precipitate withdrawals from the work force, thus decreasing the supply of labor and increasing its price. Accordingly, the incomes of the working poor may increase, but this also implies a rise in production costs.

Although AFDC mothers in rural areas are slightly less likely to work than those in urban areas, participation decreases as city size grows. This is consistent with the generally more adequate benefit levels in larger industrialized areas. However, assertions that people move from the south to large northern cities in order to qualify for welfare are not well supported. A study for the House Ways and Means Committee of New York City's welfare population concluded the size of welfare payments may be a significant factor in a migrant's choice of destination, but indicated that the evidence was not adequate to assert that many recipients migrated "intentionally seeking public assistance."[10]

Work Incentives

A final consideration is the structure of work incentives. The treatment of income earned by AFDC recipients is a crucial variable in the choice between, or combination of, work and welfare. Factors reviewed above provide an indication of the extent to which welfare recipients *can* compete for employment and earnings in the labor market. But in the absence of a work requirement their decision to enter the labor force—whether they *will* compete—hinges on the incentives offered for working, which include both financial and psychological factors and can be studied from three perspectives: the relationship between work effort and existing incentives, interviews with welfare recipients and others, and the results of social experimentation.

The importance of financial incentives and alternatives to employment is underscored by the difference in labor force participation of three groups of mothers with children under three. For married

9 Wilfred Lewis, Jr., Urban Growth and Suburbanization of Employment—Some New Data, mimeographed, 1969.

10 U. S. Congress, House Committee on Ways and Means, Report of Findings of Special Review of Aid to Families with Dependent Children in New York City, 91st Cong., 1st Sess. (Washington: Government Printing Office, 1969), p. 35.

women, husbands present, in this category the participation rate in 1969 was 27 percent. For other married mothers, the rate was 44 percent; after adjustments to exclude AFDC women from this group, the rate rose to about 50 percent. For AFDC mothers, the proportion either in training or at work was 18 percent. Thus, mothers of young children who have no alternative to employment are far more likely to work or seek employment than are those who can rely on a husband's income or on AFDC. Within the latter two groups, the tax bite of the AFDC women who may earn, say, $2,000 annually, including the "$30 plus one-third" disregard, is equal to the tax of other working women on an annual taxable income of over $40,000.

Despite the bias toward self-support, government policy long stifled initiative by welfare mothers. During its first three decades earnings of most AFDC recipients were treated as income available toward fulfilling predetermined needs, and assistance payments were reduced by the full amount of the earnings in the states that provided for each family the amount designated by the state as the full standard of need. This "100 percent tax" on earnings inevitably forestalled attempts to achieve financial independence. Work expenses were typically not subject to this tax. But allowing a recipient one dollar of earnings for each dollar he spent on transportation or clothes adds nothing to his disposable income and the tax robs the relief recipient of any pecuniary incentive to work. Some other states, however, paid only a proportion of the full standard. Before the 1967 amendments became effective, Indiana, for example, specified the full standard for a family of four as $287, but paid no more than $150 or 52 percent. Accordingly, the family could earn the difference of $137 without penalty, but for each additional dollar earned the

welfare benefit was decreased by a dollar, constituting effectively a 100 percent tax on earnings.

States which paid less than full needs and permitted recipients to keep earnings up to the full standard provided a financial incentive to work. Public assistance recipients in these states had higher labor force participation rates than those in states that paid full needs (Table 11). But states that did not pay full needs also forced recipients to work to supplement incomes which were insufficient for subsistance living, regardless of the incentive offered.[11] About half of the welfare mothers in Alabama, Florida, and Mississippi were employed at least part of the year, because their payments were no more than 50 percent of the "basic needs" for a family of four. Southern states have also been accused of "en-

TABLE 11. AFDC MOTHERS' LABOR FORCE PARTICIPATION WAS HIGHER IN STATES PAYING LESS THAN FULL NEEDS, 1967

Percent of standard of needs paid	Number of states	Proportion of AFDC population	Average labor force participation rate of AFDC mothers
100	25	56%	17%
90 to 99	5	18	20
75 to 89	3	4	20
60 to 74	6	7	26
45 to 59	9	12	40
Less than 45	3	4	37

SOURCE: U. S. Department of Health, Education, and Welfare.

couraging" welfare recipients to do farm labor at harvest time in order not to jeopardize their eligibility for public assistance during the rest of the year and of keeping payments low to increase this leverage. This may also explain the higher employment rates in these states.[12]

[11] Irene Cox, "The Employment of Mothers As a Means of Family Support," Welfare in Review (November-December 1970): 14–15.

[12] Lester M. Salamon, "Family Assistance: The Stakes in the South," New Republic, February 20, 1971, and Richard Armstrong, "The Looming Money Revolution Down South," Fortune, June 1970.

There were other less significant work incentives. About half of the states allowed earnings to be retained for "future identifiable needs" of a child, such as school or health. Between 1965 and 1967 one-third of the states disregarded up to $5 a month of any income, enacted so that the increase in social security payments in 1965 would not be balanced by a decrease in public assistance. A 1965 provision allowed states to disregard earnings of teenage youth up to $50 per child or $150 per family.

The 1967 Social Security Amendments provided the first general work incentives for AFDC recipients. Whether these incentives are adequate to induce relief welfare recipients to seek employment is crucial to any contemplated design for the overhauling of AFDC.

Efforts to study work incentives have also included interviews with welfare and nonwelfare recipients. Surveys conducted by Leonard Goodwin of the Brookings Institution reveal that AFDC recipients have essentially the same attachment to the work ethic as members of families with regular workers.[13]

Social experimentation has been heralded as a basis for policymaking, and federal agencies have initiated a series of such projects in the field of income maintenance. The designs called for exploring the impact of income maintenance upon welfare recipients and working poor, whites and blacks, female-headed families and male-headed families under urban and rural settings and under a variety of benefit levels, tax rates, child care, training and other services, HEW's projects in Gary, Indiana; Seattle, Washington; Denver, Colorado; and in rural counties in Iowa and North Carolina were started too recently to yield results yet. However, the earliest and most prominent

of the projects is the Office of Economic Opportunity's much heralded New Jersey Experiment, which focuses on urban male-headed families. OEO rushed to announce that preliminary findings in early 1970 supported President Nixon's Family Assistance Plan. Their conclusions, however, may have been based more on the investigator's biases than on hard facts, and they were challenged as premature by the General Accounting Office. More recent information suggests that the experimental families' earnings have kept pace with those of the control group. Hourly earnings of experimental family heads have increased enough to compensate for a slight decline in their own hours and a larger drop in the hours worked by their wives and children. The income support apparently enabled these family heads to seek out better-paying jobs than they might have obtained in the absence of aid. Firm conclusions will not be possible until the five-year project is completed. Whether this experiment, and others begun more recently, can provide a sound basis for policy formulation remains a matter of debate.

———

WELFARE IN NEW YORK CITY: THE AVAILABILITY OF JOBS

Blanche Bernstein.
City Almanac,* February 1970, at 5–8.

THE AVAILABILITY OF JOBS

Before we conclude that the current size of the welfare caseload is reasonable in the light of the number of families and individuals in the city with incomes below the poverty level, we must examine the question of availability of jobs, the level of earnings they provide, and the ability of the welfare recipient to fill them. Clearly, if there are not jobs in

[13] Leonard Goodwin, Do the Poor Want to Work: Studies in the Work Orientation of the Poor and the Non-Poor (Washington: Brookings Institution, 1972).

* Published by Center for New York City Affairs, New School for Social Research.

the city for the men, women and older adolescents on welfare, society should continue to carry the burden of welfare at whatever level necessary and do so without whimpering about it.

It has been frequently stated by public officials, representatives of minority groups, and some leaders of civic and voluntary agencies that the loss of unskilled jobs in the city, the racial discrimination which excludes Blacks and Puerto Ricans from decent paying jobs, and the low educational and skill levels prevent the employables on welfare from obtaining the jobs which are available. This is all true to some extent but it does not fully explain the situation.

No one who rides the subways can fail to see the numerous ads for electricians helpers (about $7,000 per year) subway patrolmen (around $8,000 per year) Office Temporaries and Kelly Girls. The New York Telephone Company urges people to join them and be trained by them. No one who walks down Madison, Lexington or Third Avenue will miss the signs for Help. No one who has had the misfortune of staying in a hospital recently, or even visiting one, is untroubled by the shortage of auxiliary and service personnel, a situation which persists despite the long overdue salary increase obtained by the union in recent years. And any one who rides taxis with any frequency is aware of the number of taxis in the garage despite the industry's efforts to recruit additional drivers. According to industry spokesman, taxi drivers earn about $7,000 a year including tips. One of the fascinating statistics about New York City is that fewer persons were employed in domestic service in 1968 than in 1960. This is surely not the result of diminished demand but of a refusal to accept such employment. Yet the rate of pay for domestic workers is $2.00 or more per hour and carfare is extra. The jobs which have been men-

tioned do not require a college education, some do not even require high school graduation, entering skills are often not necessary and racial discrimination is absent or minimal.

These impressions of the labor market in recent years are confirmed by official data. According to the Director of the State Employment Service in the city, jobs were available which welfare recipients could fill if they would be willing to accept the job offer. About 11,400 job openings registered with the Employment Service remained unfilled for 30 days or more as of the end of November, 1968, of which approximately 2,700 were for unskilled workers such as janitors, porters and cleaners, jobs which could be filled by either men or women. The demand for women domestics was great.

Even more startling is the figure which comes out of a recent survey conducted by the Bureau of Labor Statistics of the total number of job vacancies in the city. Herbert Bienstock, Director of the New York Regional Office estimates that there are 50,000 to 75,000 job vacancies in the city; about half have been vacant for 30 days or more. Some of the heaviest demands are for nurses, secretaries, clerks, typists and messengers.

With this number of jobs available one must ask why the welfare recipients are not taking them. The question seems to have a three fold answer: 1/ expectations, 2/ the impact of welfare on the incentive to work and, 3/ the "employability" of the welfare recipients.

In his book *Maximum Feasible Misunderstanding,* Daniel P. Moynihan quotes Lloyd Ohlin as saying "—the adult migrant, lacking secure conceptions of the new cultural norms, induce in their children unrealistic expectations which are unrelated in any case to observable relevant structures of opportunities by which these expectations may be achieved". Moynihan goes on to say that "as the 1960's wore on the problems of unrealistic expectations began to be compounded by a seeming depreciation of heretofore decent-enough jobs which the poor were now said to find unacceptable". Another factor has been that the wholly worthwhile idea of new careers or career ladders has, to some extent, been turned into an ideology which justifies the refusal of jobs involving necessary and dignified work if they do not lead ever upward. Somehow an air of immorality has been created about the idea of working as a porter or janitor or taxi driver and certainly about urging any one to do so. Yet we know that while efforts to improve educational and skill levels must be intensified, many tens of thousands of people are going to remain taxi drivers, grocery clerks or sales clerks all their working lives. Further, these and many other unskilled and semi-skilled jobs are essential to the reasonable working of the economy and indeed to the lives of the people who inhabit the city. One can just think for a moment of what work is required to get some food on to the table in a New York City home, restaurant or sandwich shop. Further, not all welfare recipients are uneducated and lacking in skills. Fully 25 percent of the AFDC mothers have a high school education or better and thus a variety of decent paying jobs are available to them. Many job vacancies have an advancement potential.

It may be worthwhile pointing out that whatever may be the impact in New York during the coming year of the Nixon Administration anti-inflation program, it had not, by the end of 1969 had any significant adverse effect on the employment situation in the city. According to reports of the New York State Department of Labor, total employment of 4,160,000 in the city in November, 1969 was the highest for any November on record, reflecting an increase of 41,000 jobs over the previous year. Unemployment, however, rose slightly, from 130,800 to 139,000 or from 3.0 to 3.2 per cent. The total number of payroll jobs in the city rose by about 250,000 between 1961 and 1969 with the largest gain of 71,000 taking place in 1968. As one looks a bit into the future,—to 1975—the prospects are far from grim. Total employment is expected to increase and while it is anticipated that the number of blue collar jobs will diminish, the number of service workers needed will increase and the net drop in the two categories combined will be less than two percent compared to 1965. In the meantime, it is not unreasonable to assume a significant upgrading in the skills of the population as more people complete high school, college and work training programs.

The high rate of unemployment or sub-employment of youth in ghetto areas despite the widespread affluence of the society has been the subject of particular concern. A recent Bureau of Labor Statistics study in the Poverty Area Profiles series, covering the four major poverty areas of New York City, show an unemployment rate of 25.3 percent among the teenagers 16–19 years old living in the areas. A report of a study of youth in the ghetto areas of Houston and Chicago, published in the Fall 1969 issue of Public Interest, by Edwin Harwood, raises some serious question, however, as to whether this unemployment is justified by the situation in the labor market. He points out that Appalachian adult migrants had no trouble finding jobs at $90 to $130 per week but that the "adolescent Appalachian worked just enough to get by." The southern white teenager knew they could get jobs anytime they wanted to but since they did not have to support families they worked only enough "to support their street-corner activities, pay for room and board, and buy occasional luxury items." With similar experiences coming out of the study in Houston, the author suggests some new assumption about unemployed youth, to wit:

"Many boys are underemployed and subemployed because they value leisure as much as money, which leads them to seek only as much work as is needed to get by with enough of each."

"Because many youth support only themselves, their preference for under-employment may be based on a reasoned calculation of self interest. Why expect ghetto youth to settle down at 17 or 18 to the discipline of a year-round-full-time job, that, in effect, denies them the leisure for 'identity building' we extend to college youths."

If, as the evidence indicates, jobs are available for which welfare recipients are qualified why are they not taking them? To some extent, of course, they are, as indicated by data on turnover in the case-load. Turnover is indeed substantial in all the programs; data based on analysis of 1967 cases indicate that on TADC and General Assistance cases the median duration of relief is less than a year but on ADC it is 2–3 years. More recent data are unfortunately not available but it can only be assumed that the average duration of cases has substantially risen; since the largest increases in caseload occurred in 1967 and 1968, and a further increase was noted in 1969, the passage of time must be reflected in a lengthening of the average duration of a case.

It has indeed been generally assumed that welfare recipients prefer work to welfare. This notion has been subjected to recent scrutiny in a number of studies of the impact of current welfare stand-ards on the incentive to work.

The problem arises with particular acuteness in New York State which has a welfare standard among the highest in the country. Thus a wage earner who can obtain only an unskilled job at the minimum wage of $1.60 can earn only $64 for a 40-hour week but if he is the father in a family of four, he can obtain about $75 a week on welfare. Even at $2.00 per hour, the difference between his wages and welfare will be more than absorbed by work expenses and such taxes as he may pay. The problem for the AFDC mothers is compounded by the need to arrange and pay for the care of the children while she is at work.

Elizabeth Durbin in her study, *The Effect of Welfare Programs on the Decision to Work*, points out that the increase in the welfare allowance in recent years and particularly in 1966, has been substantially greater than the increase in wages. She adds that there is evidence indicating it is more difficult now to find people willing to work at low wages than to find low wage job openings. She assumes people will behave rationally in economic terms and that they will not be drawn to work, if they can get as much income without working.

The recent study on the Administration of Aid to Families with Dependent Children in New York City came to a similar conclusion. Its data indicate that as the AFDC grant approaches what the women can actually receive as a wage, more and more of them tend to choose AFDC. "When the AFDC grant level is so far below their already low best wages, the poor women choose (when they have a choice) the barely adequate wage, rather than the less than adequate AFDC grant. After deducting all work re-lated expenses from wages, the size of the AFDC grant in cities like New York must actually be higher than the wages they could earn. This being true, it is not surprising to find that women who can get at best low paying and *at worst*, irregular, part time exhausting jobs choose public assistance over employ-ment when it pays more."

Eveline Burns, in a paper on the Future Course of Public Welfare, has summed up the situation succinctly in stating "For those whose work is unpleasant or uninteresting, or for whom the rewards of working are meager, it is likely that the availability of an income equal or almost equal to their potential earnings will indeed have some effect on willingness to work".

Attention must be focused, therefore, on whether as a matter of public policy the individual should have the right to refuse a job at $70, $80 or $90 a week because he can get as much on welfare. In answering this question one must take account of the fact that quite a lot of people are working at jobs that pay such wages. In fact, about 30 percent of the jobs in the city pay less than $90 a week. Not all these jobs, however, are held by heads of four person households who could get as much as welfare. Many are held by young people living alone or in families where they are supplementary earners, many by wives who are supplementary earners, and some by men whose wives are working and adding to the family income. The question of supplementary earners is crucial to understanding the income situation of families and the standard of living they can achieve, and will be discussed at a later stage.

At this point, it becomes necessary to consider the employability of the people on welfare. Much has been made of the fact, that 80 percent of the persons on welfare are children under the age of 21 years or the adults who are taking care of them, and that of the remaining 20 percent, many are old, disabled, or sick, or in fact working and receiving supplementation. It has been frequently stated that only 4 percent of those on welfare are employable. The argument has an air of reality about it, but it is to a substantial degree a spurious one. No one is arguing that children under the age of 16 or 17 should be working. The question is to what extent is it reasonable to expect the 186,000 mothers on AFDC to work to help support their families and

to what extent one can look to the youngsters 17–19 years of age to work part time to contribute to the family's support.

As we have noted earlier, 50 percent of the AFDC mothers have only one or two children so that arrangements for their care might not be too difficult; a large proportion are in the most employable age group and about 25 percent have a high school education or better. It is in considering this question that we become acutely aware of the impact of current welfare grants on incentives to work. Recognizing the problem of incentives, the Congress in amendments to the Social Security Act permitted the AFDC and TADC families to keep the first $30 and one third of monthly earnings above $30 without having the sum deducted from the welfare allowance. Part time earnings of teenagers are completely exempted in New York City from the calculation of the welfare allowance. Nevertheless, according to Elizabeth Durbin's analysis, less than five percent of the AFDC cases in 1967 were receiving supplementation for low earnings and the proportion had changed little in the preceding 10 years. Only a slight improvement had occurred by 1969; data for May indicate 6.4 percent of the AFDC cases were obtaining supplementation to earnings.

It would appear that the incentive is not sufficient but here is the rub. There is already some degree of inequity among those who have never been on welfare and, therefore do not receive the incentive payment and those who are on welfare. The latter may be obtaining as much as an additional $125 a month for the same work.

The question remains, therefore, whether in view of the present relationship between welfare benefits and wage rates for unskilled and semi-skilled jobs, an incentive can be offered sufficient to entice welfare recipients into employment without disturbing the non-welfare population working at the same low paid jobs, and without encouraging them to get on welfare at least for a while so that they can benefit from the incentive to leave the welfare rolls.

It would appear from our analysis that one cannot explain the tripling of the caseload since 1961 in either the unavailability of jobs or the unemployability of all but a few of the adults on welfare. This is not, of course, to say that jobs are available for all the adults on welfare or that all the women on AFDC could make appropriate arrangements for the care of their children. But the evidence appears to indicate that a significant fraction of the AFDC women could find work but are disinclined to take the jobs available to them because the monetary gain does not outweigh the inconvenience of working.

Note on Domestic Work for Welfare Recipients

One of the major job opportunities available to welfare recipients is domestic work. The District Court's recital of the facts in Woolfolk v. Brown, 325 F.Supp. 1162 (E.D.Va.1971), aff'd 456 F.2d 652 (4th Cir. 1972), paints a typical picture of the assignment of recipients to such work.

The eligibility technician in charge of Vivian Woolfolk's case testified that she presented the case to the local welfare board for termination after Miss Woolfolk had failed on the appointed day to appear for employment for reasons which "didn't seem too valid." (Carson depos., 77). On Sunday, September 14, 1970, Miss Woolfolk's work was to commence. On Thursday, the 18th, she appeared at the welfare office and explained that she had had a sore throat on Sunday. No inquiry was made to determine whether the job offer was still open on Thursday.

Nor was Miss Woolfolk informed that a cutoff of her benefits was being considered at that visit or at a subsequent one later on Thursday, when she reported with a doctor's certificate stating that she could work the next day. (Id., 77–79). On Friday, September 19th, her case was closed by the welfare board, thereby terminating benefits to her and her child.

The Superintendent of the Bedford County Welfare Department was chiefly responsible for offering Miss Woolfolk an employment opportunity (Goode depos., 7). The job involved babysitting for one small child all day, responsibility for four others, aged eight through seventeen, from about 3:30 until 5:00 p. m., serving dinner, and washing dishes. The pay was $20.00 per week, plus five days' room and board. Miss Woolfolk would live in a house trailer on the property, and if she did not desire to bring her daughter, Helen, with her, the child would be left with her grandmother. To the superintendent's knowledge, Miss Woolfolk's prior work experience was restricted to babysitting (Id., 13). The employment offer was made for that reason and on account of its proximity to Miss Woolfolk's home, in view of her lack of transportation (Id., 41). It was made prior to any visit to the job site (Id., 31) or examination of the living arrangements (Id., 33).

It was the general practice of the Bedford welfare office to keep a list of available jobs on hand and to offer positions deemed suitable to welfare recipients (Id., 27). No definable standards of suitability exist (Id., 28). No job training is available to persons offered work rule jobs (Id., 29). The ineligibility which flows from refusal to accept a job is considered "rather permanent." However, if one reapplies for benefits, the question of need is reexamined, and in practice aid will be granted if the job is not still available (Id., 46–47).

The three Calloway plaintiffs, sisters, were offered the same job in the course of a single telephone call (Carson depos., 82). This was also a babysitting job, an opening for one person, involving caring for two small children at a home some fifteen to twenty miles distant from the Calloway plaintiffs' residence (Carson depos., 82). When they each in turn declined the offer, on April 8, 1970, their cases were submitted to the welfare board; aid was terminated at the April 17th welfare board meeting. On May 12th, when the Calloways came to get food assistance from the welfare office, their AFDC cases were reopened after a telephone inquiry disclosed that the job was no longer open.

The local welfare office was aware from earlier unrelated contacts with the prospective employer of his general home situation. The procedure to determine the suitability of the employment was extremely informal in other respects as well:

Q. Is an accepted procedure in your office to offer jobs over the telephone?

A. No, we do not generally do it this way. The man had to have someone that day or was trying to find someone that day. We knew something about his home situation, and we knew the Calloway girls, and we felt that this was a job that one of them could do because one of them had said when she worked the other two would take care of her children. And this was the plan for each one; if one wouldn't go then we tried the others.

Q. To your knowledge was any counseling given to any of the Calloways after the Board made the determination to cut them off?

A. What type of counseling do you refer to?

Q. Counseling of the type referred to in the WIN manual, as to when someone refuses referral into the WIN program?

A. No, there was no counseling of this type given.

Assignments of this nature would not qualify under the WIN program. What are the policy arguments for and against forcing welfare mothers to work as domestics? It is well known that some legislators whose wives have trouble finding good maids prefer requiring such work. Would this be a fruitful way of reducing welfare rolls?

WORK IN AMERICA

Report of a Special Task Force to the Secretary of H.E.W. (1972).

* * *

WORK AND WELFARE

In original conception and intent, welfare is an income maintenance program for those who cannot take care of themselves. The main programs provide categorical aid to the blind, the aged, the disabled, and to families with dependent children (a program originally designed to make it possible for widows and mothers without employable husbands to stay at home and raise their children.)

Increasingly, however, the original purposes and definitions of welfare have lost their force, especially with respect to the Aid to Families with Dependent Children. What was originally defined as a population dependent on the larger community for maintenance and support tends now to be defined in the public's mind as a population of malingerers who ought to be forced to accept work. The result is that persons who cannot take jobs or, by social agreement, should not take jobs, are now the target of programs designed to make them take jobs.

This change in public perception and policy has two main roots. One is the frustration born of the now-certain knowledge that the need for a federal public assistance program will always be with us and will not, as was originally hoped, wither away as a result of the growth of a comprehensive contributory social insurance system. The other is the change from widows and orphans to unmarried mothers and illegitimate children as models or prototypes of the ADC family. ("The ADC example we always thought about," remembers the first Executive Secretary of the Social Security Board, "was the poor lady in West Virginia whose husband was killed in a mining accident, and the problem of how she could feed those kids.") Where the original model of the miner's widow evoked compassion, the new model of the unwed mother evokes deep and widespread resentment.

Underneath the resentment and the frustration, and giving rise to them, are a host of unverified assumptions about the character and composition of the welfare population: most poor people don't want to work; most people on welfare are black; welfare mothers have babies to increase their welfare benefits; people on welfare live well and easy; most people on welfare want to be on welfare; etc.

Every one of these assumptions is demonstrably false as a generalization, and is true only in the occasional particular. The facts are that most poor people are not on welfare and the majority of poor people not only want to work but do work, year round and full time; black families, though over-represented, make up less than half of the AFDC caseload; the average monthly payment per recipient on AFDC is $49.-60; most mothers on AFDC do want to work—it is not difficult to add to the factual side of this misunderstood issue.

What is so terribly damaging to the prospect of developing constructive programs for dealing with the problems of welfare is that these false stereotypes of poor people, black people, and AFDC families are widely held by the general public. The negative attitudes of most Americans about welfare thus constrain national leaders in their development of policy. Indeed, the existence of these feelings leads to a situation in which the public's "price" for welfare reform is the inclusion of mandatory work requirements for those on welfare, including mothers.

The variety of recent attempts to reform the welfare system are characterized by the inclusion of mandatory work provisions. These reflect the public's belief that there are many people on welfare who don't belong there, who could and should be working, and that we can deal with "the welfare mess" by forcing these people off the rolls. Realistically, then, we cannot expect a welfare reform program that does not have a work requirement for mothers until there is general public agreement that the great majority of people on welfare belong there (in the sense that they have no other place to go). The only able-bodied adults on welfare are those on the AFDC rolls, but since less than 5 percent of the families receiving AFDC include an able-bodied man, the only category of recipients with any potential for joining the work force are women with dependent children, the very persons AFDC was designed to assist in staying home.

From the analysis we present in this section, the present public attitudes may very well lead to a worse welfare problem in the future. A welfare program with a compulsory work requirement for mothers will not help the mothers, the children, or the society at large, and, as we will discuss later, it will not enhance the all-important role of the central provider in establishing family stability. We believe that the alternative presented here, that of viewing mothers as working and of making jobs available for central providers, would better achieve the major objectives of the general public—a decreasing welfare caseload in the long run.

Should Welfare Mothers be Required to Take a Job?

The question of whether the mother in a fatherless family (76 percent of AFDC families) should take a job or not is a complex one. It is not even clear that anyone other than the mother has the legal or moral right to make that decision, or that anyone other than the mother can make the decision that is best for her and her children. Some mothers prefer outside jobs to keeping house and raising children; others prefer to stay home. To force all AFDC mothers to do one or the other is to do violence to what we know about human development and family relationships: mothers who work because they prefer to work, and mothers who stay home because they prefer to stay home, probably make better and happier mothers (and children) than those who do one or the other because of circumstances or coercion. It follows that the public interest and the interests of the mother and her children will be best served if the mother herself makes the choice. This choice, of course, must be essentially a free one: a decision either way must not carry with it any special penalties, rewards or forfeitures.

The easiest part of the problem has to do with those women now on AFDC—perhaps a majority—who, other things being equal, would prefer to work and support their families. But other things are not equal. They do not take jobs because there aren't suitable child care fa-

cilities, or because the costs associated with having a job and paying for child care often leave them with less than they would be receiving on welfare. These women do not need to be coerced into the labor force; they need the freedom to join it: adequate child care facilities and a decent job at a living wage.

The more difficult part of the problem lies with those AFDC mothers who choose to remain home and raise their children themselves. More accurately, the problem lies not with them but rather with our system of public values regarding women and women's roles and our definition of work. When we say to the AFDC mother, for example, "You must go to work or take work-training in order to be eligible for public assistance," we are, in effect, telling her that, from society's point of view, she is not now working, that keeping house and raising children are not socially useful, at least not as useful as "a job." But we are able to make this judgment of the AFDC mother who stays home and raises her children only because we make this same judgment of all housewives.

Thus, the public devaluation of keeping house and raising children is, for the AFDC mother, only a special case of the more general problem faced by women throughout our society. Indeed, it is one of the principal sources of the deep discontent experienced by women in all social classes. The failure of society to acknowledge housekeeping and childrearing as socially useful work on a par with paid employment makes it increasingly difficult for the married woman who is "just a housewife" to see herself as a valued contributor in the eyes of her family, her neighbors, and the larger society. The pressures generated by such social values tend to push women into the labor force in their search for recognition as full and valued participants in society. The result is that some women who would perhaps prefer to remain at home are, in effect, pushed into the labor force against their will.

It is with the AFDC mother who would prefer to stay home that the social undervaluing of housekeeping and childrearing appears in its clearest, most perfect form. In this case, it is precisely the social undervaluing of housekeeping and childrearing that provides the rationale for telling her that she must take a job to be eligible for welfare, and also for the notion that she is "getting something for doing nothing."

The clear fact is that keeping house and raising children is work—work that is, on the average, as difficult to do well and as useful to the larger society as almost any paid job involving the production of goods or services. The difficulty is not that most people don't believe this or accept it (we pay lip service to it all the time) but that, whatever our private and informal belief systems, we have not, as a society, acknowledged this fact in our public system of values and rewards. Such an acknowledgment might begin with simply counting housewives in the labor force, assigning a money value to their work and including it in the calculation of the gross national product, and including housewives in social security or other pension systems. The question arises, "if the housewife is to be considered 'employed,' who is her employer?" One answer might be, her husband's employer, for it is the wife's labor and her support that enables her husband to do whatever he does for the man or the firm he works for. In this case, the husband and the wife would be viewed as a production unit and money for the housewife's pension plan might take the form of a payroll tax paid by the employer or shared by him and his employees. In the case of widows or other husbandless women with dependent children who do not work outside the home, they, too,

would be "covered" workers, self-employed, and pay their own retirement premiums out of their own resources or, if on welfare, out of their welfare checks. Alternatively, one might consider them simply public service workers and pay the premiums out of the general fund.

In either event, the choice confronting the AFDC mother would no longer be between taking a job or receiving no assistance (which is really no choice at all) but rather the choice between working at home, in her own house with her own children, or working outside the home. In the long run, such a change in the choice offered to welfare mothers would not only cost less, but it would also permit the welfare family to keep its self-respect and at the same time enlarge an important area of choice in our society.

DUBLINO v. NEW YORK STATE DEPT. OF SOCIAL SERVICES

Excerpt from Amicus Curiae Brief of National Welfare Rights Organization, et al.

Introduction

The operation of the [New York] Work Rules [described in the opinion at pp. 194–201, supra] has had practically no real impact on the alleviation of need for public assistance, and the known facts as to the characteristics of recipients of Aid to Families with Dependent Children (AFDC) and Home Relief (HR) would have indicated to any knowledgeable person that this would be the predictable result.

It is well known that there are very few recipients who are employable in the sense of being ready for direct entry into jobs. A 1971 state report found less than 3% of the total number of individuals on assistance, or under 54,000 people, to be employable but not employed, even using a definition of employability which considered anyone to be employable whose age, physical and mental capacity, and household circumstances would permit employment including "many * * who have never been employed as well as those who lack education, training or skill necessary to obtain employment currently." 104th Annual Report of the New York State Board of Social Welfare and the New York State Department of Social Services, published March 1971 at p. 1. Clearly, therefore, the work program is not even relevant to the overwhelming majority of recipients and, yet, the rights of all applicants are being severely burdened under the purported justification of offering employment to relieve dependence. Even for the "employables" there is clearly no real possibility of meaningful employment without a program of training and upgrading of skills. There is also obviously no real possibility that any substantial number of real jobs could be found even if the individual were provided with the skills.* This is in fact demonstrated by the results of the program to date.

With upwards of 100,000 people referred to SES, [State Employment Service]** reporting twice a month, only 15,755 welfare recipients found jobs during the period July 1971–December 1971 and, it is admitted "that not all are placed

in permanent positions", i. e., positions which offer employment for as little as 3 months or longer. Letter of Commissioner Wyman to Governor Rockefeller, Sixth Monthly Report on Work Program dated February 1, 1972. Clearly, many of these individuals would have secured employment on their own in any case and in fact, it is not clear to what extent the 15,000 figures may include individuals who did secure jobs themselves.*** Also, many of them are unemployed again already and more will be so shortly.

And what of the jobs. Few recipients have been placed at anything approaching a decent wage. The state even admits placing people in jobs paying less than $1.85 an hour. ($1.85 an hour = $74.00 a week). It is questionable whether either the individual or his society becomes more "healthy" by using his dependence to subsidize the continuation of industries and employers who pay substandard wages. In fact, the very presence of such a captive source of labor guarantees that those employers will be able to resist the normal free market pressures which might otherwise compel them to raise wages to a level of adequacy. Thus the state tells thousands of its citizens whose poverty has already deprived them of a decent education and

---

* Only 2,947 persons were placed in jobs after WIN training in 1970, although New York has 14,800 work and training slots. This was attributed to the fact that:

"The program has been adversely affected by a lack of employment opportunities caused by the general business slowdown during the past year and by a shortage of day care facilities." Annual Report of the State Board, supra, at 7.

Since that time the unemployment rate among the poor has greatly increased and is now 9.7%. Washington Post, Feb. 25, 1972 at A3.

** It is interesting to note that with the maze of press releases and statistics released each month by the defendants, it is impossible to ascertain the precise number of individuals subjected to the Work Rules to date.

*** A 1971 study of the AFDC program based on data as of January 1971 found that in N.Y.S., 12.4% of AFDC mothers were employed or in training, 2.3% were awaiting WIN enrollment and 3% were actively seeking work (total 17.7%) as opposed to 4.4% who might be available for employment but were not actively seeking work. Findings of the 1971 AFDC Study, NCSS Report AFDC–1(71), Table 21. That report also noted that there were more first-time recipients, and a decrease in average time on assistance and in long-term assistance cases, pointing to a rise in short-term use of AFDC as a means of support during a period of financial need, page 9. Similar findings as to the employment status of mothers were reached in 1969. Characteristics of AFDC families in N.Y.S., May 1969, prepared by N.Y.S.D.S.S., Program Analyses Reports No. 44, at 36.

otherwise hindered their ability to attain an adequate standard of living, that because of their dependence they must submit to being the instruments to support continuation of this system of institutionalized inhumanity and lack of respect for one's fellow human beings. Amicii's members find neither dignity or self-respect in knowing that their financial need compels them to subject themselves to further exploitation.

Then too, there are the numbers of people who have been required to take jobs which they find personally repugnant or even frightening or hazardous. Amicii certainly do not espouse any theory that a person's worth is measured by the status or wages of his or her job, but it is axiomatic that not all people can perform all jobs. Some work requires particular characteristics of personality, ego, intestinal fortitude, or whatever. For example, not all women would be comfortable employed as a go-go dancer or barmaid just as not all men would feel secure as a housing guard.† Examples could be endless; however, the New York program makes no provision for considering suitability of a job or assessing the need and capabilities of the particular individual.

This then, is what the program has achieved in relation to its stated goal. Placement of less than 1% of recipients in jobs, many only temporary and/or at substandard wages and/or offensive to the individual. This also is all it can achieve because of the facts of the situation.

Admittedly, the picture we have painted here so far seems slightly incredible. Certainly it seems that the Governor and the legislature cannot have been so misinformed, mistaken, or naive as to expend time and effort on a "major restructuring" of the program which would

have no real impact on dependency and could not have been expected to have any. Amicii agree wholeheartedly. While no real impact could be expected through placement of recipients in employment, a very real impact could have been foreseen and is resulting. This is a process of reducing assistance costs through attrition.

The more requirements, the more processes, the more applicants or recipients can be expected to fall into the void and disappear. Make it hard enough to do what is required to qualify for assistance and it can be certain that a substantial number of people just won't be able to get over all the hurdles.*

Historically, there have always been more people who could qualify for assistance than chose to do so. In 1960 it was concluded that there were 716,000 people in New York City alone living at or below the welfare level and not receiving assistance. The Enemies of the Poor, James Graham, Random House, 1970, at 203. Other studies have found as many as 13% of people not on the rolls to be eligible. *A Strategy to End Poverty,* Cloward & Piven, The Nation, May 2, 1966. As late as 1967, New York City Welfare Commissioner reported that "there were nearly as many eligible families off the relief rolls as there are on." N. Y. Times, May 18, 1967, editorial. This fact was attributed in New York as elsewhere to a deliberate suppression of information by welfare officials as to eligibility, to the fact of a "grueling bureaucratic obstacle course" to qualification,

---

† One of the assignments in the N.Y.C. program, N.Y. Times, July 28, 1971.

* This appears to be a general principle of administration in the N.Y. welfare program. After being advised of a series of incorrect and lawless actions taken by New York City Department in denying aid to a particular applicant, an official commented "She is not hip to welfare. * * * She doesn't know the game. It happens all the time. But if she's strong and holds out in the hotel, they'll have to find her a decent place." N.Y. Times, January 22, 1972, pp. 31, 60.

and the establishment of arbitrary and restrictive practices and conditions that included examination of such things as the individual's sexual behavior. *We've Got Rights—The No-Longer Silent Welfare Poor*, Cloward & Piven, The New Republic, August 5, 1967, at 25.

However, the late 60's brought a new phenomenon; the poor finally began to realize that the "welfare stigma" was a hoax which had been foisted on them, and a growing body of law began to limit the state's right to impose restrictive eligibility conditions which invaded the privacy and rights of the recipients. HEW also finally began to address the existence of these problems and to take at least limited initiatives to restrain such state action. Handbook of P.A.A. part IV, §§ 2000–2400 re Application, Determination of Eligibility and Assistance, promulgated 2/8/68, §§ 6000–6500 re Fair Hearings promulgated 2/8/68.

The state appears to have gone to great lengths to obscure the facts as to some of the burdens which the program imposes. Thus it is not possible to ascertain the full facts as to the percentage of those who have reported to SES regularly and repeatedly and have never even been referred to a job interview or the percentage of those who have pursued one or many such referrals without securing any job.** One only knows that in each

** For example, the report dated September 22, 1971 states

" * * * 13,320 recipients * * * have failed to comply with the requirements that they report, accept work, job referrals, or training

" * * * 7,530 recipients, *56.5% of those who failed to comply with reporting requirements*, have had their cases reviewed * * * and a final determination * * * made

" * * * Of those cases which have been disposed of, 4,217, 56% have been dropped from the welfare rolls."

Thus the state nowhere gives the simple figure as to how many people failed to report to SES. These reports are also noteworthy for the consistent misuse and mis-

case it is the majority. Each instance of a reporting without a referral or a referral without a placement is of course money spent which was desperately needed for food, clothing or other essentials of life.

The facts are similarly hidden as to the most direct form of arbitrary action, the total numbers of people who have been misclassified or who have missed a reporting date because of illness. It is known, however, that out of only 44,946 cases (those cases which were reviewed during August through December because of a question as to cooperation with the work rules), it was determined that 16,239 people should never have been required to report to SES in the first place and that another 6,313 were ill on the reporting date or otherwise validly unable to report. Clearly this is only the tip of the iceberg. There are many thousands more in the same situation among the remaining undetermined cases of questioned eligibility as well as the thousands misclassified who are continuing to report to SES over and over, simply because they can't find their way out of the program and they dare not risk the summary suspension of benefits which would ensue should they fail to report.

Finally there are those countless numbers who have done everything required, whether or not they ever should have been included in the process to begin with, but who have been completely lost in the administrative morass which has resulted from the shuffling of forms and

characterization of the figures. Thus it is clear that the only figure as to non-compliance which could have even a surface appearance of accuracy is the final one, 4,217, i. e., an individual has not failed to comply merely because an event has occurred which may be totally permissible under the work rules. Even more interestingly the state mischaracterizes all the reviewed cases as failures to report to SES although they clearly represent a percentage of the total number of people whose actions raised an eligibility question during the month.

checks between SES and DSS. However, no one seems to think it worthwhile to count the number of people who reported to SES as directed only to find their checks not there or who were cut off after they were referred back to DSS for verification of medical problems; the recipient can find his or her way from one office to the other but the systems used by DSS and SES are not quite so sophisticated. One can only wonder as to whether the gross inadequacy of the mechanisms in use results from overwhelming incompetence or from deliberate intent. Either is a sad commentary on the caliber of the public servants of this state.

For all these people there has been serious financial and personal hardship without purpose or logic. The financial hardship extends from the severe reduction in money available to meet basic needs because of the cost of reporting and referrals, to the drastic injury of complete and immediate loss of the grant.

NOTE

The foregoing brief argues that the failure of work requirements demonstrates that they have little to do with work as such, but rather are part of "a process to reduce assistance costs through attrition." Does this help explain why requirements are preferred over incentives? If so, is there any way to effectively shape this argument to provide a basis for judicial relief, or is it a point on which only legislative relief can be sought?

DO THE POOR WANT TO WORK? *

Leonard Goodwin.
(1972).

To be effective, welfare and manpower policies for the poor must be based on knowledge of how poor people

* © 1972 The Brookings Institution, Washington, D.C.

view life and work. Evidence from this study unambiguously supports the following conclusion: poor people—males and females, blacks and whites, youths and adults—identify their self-esteem with work as strongly as do the nonpoor. They express as much willingness to take job training if unable to earn a living and to work even if they were to have an adequate income. They have, moreover, as high life aspirations as do the nonpoor and want the same things, among them a good education and a nice place to live. This study reveals no differences between poor and nonpoor when it comes to life goals and wanting to work.

This conclusion may seem somewhat paradoxical. If poor persons, especially welfare recipients, really regard work as important for their self-esteem, why are they not working and moving out of poverty? Why are welfare rolls increasing rather than decreasing?

The paradox would be easily explained if one could show that the poor covered in this study were merely giving responses they thought middle-class persons wished to hear, but the data as adjusted for respondent bias give little evidence of gross distortion. Instead, the implicit behavioral theory on which the paradox is based must be considered. It assumes a direct connection between the goal of self-respect through work and actual work activity. Such a theory may fail to explain events because it is too simple— goals and actions are not necessarily linked directly. Actions tend to be guided most strongly by orientations that emphasize beliefs and intentions.

Thus, for black women on welfare the orientation that is directly linked to work activity combines belief and intention elements and measures acceptability of welfare. Women who find welfare most acceptable tend to show the lowest work activity. By itself, this finding might suggest that poor women prefer welfare to work. The data also indicate, however, that ratings on this orientation are sensitive to encounters in the work world. Women in the Work Incentive Program (WIN) who were terminated from it without jobs—who experienced another failure in the work world—showed a marked increase in the acceptance of welfare score over their score when they entered WIN, demonstrating that the concrete experience of failure directly and negatively influenced this work orientation. The picture that emerges is one of black welfare women who want to work but who, because of continuing failure in the work world, tend to become more accepting of welfare and less inclined to try again. Given this insight, what should policy be on requiring welfare mothers to work?

* * *

It is in this context that the latest federal efforts to provide public service employment for welfare recipients should be judged. If these jobs provide dignity, training, and sufficient income, they can be of help to the poor. If the jobs are ill-paid and regarded by employers and employees as "make-work," they may prove even more discouraging to the poor than no jobs at all. Welfare recipients who want training and jobs should not be denied the opportunity, but the training and support should be of the quality that makes occupational success a reasonable probability.

The consequences of failure in the work world should be considered not only from the point of view of the mothers, but from that of their children as well. The data suggest that poor black mothers have a substantial influence on the work orientations of their sons, including those measuring acceptability of welfare and lack of confidence, and that the sons' adherence to these two orientations may lead to both early school dropout and low work activity. Hence, stringent work requirements for welfare mothers, which are likely to lead to additional experiences of failure, can psychologically damage not only the mothers but also their children.

Mothers who are unable to support themselves and their families can be supported at a decent level by public funds without fear of damage to their work ethic or that of their sons. If the support is given, as Gilbert Steiner has suggested, "in a framework of honorable dependency," it will carry with it no social stigma, and the recipient mothers and children may be less likely to suffer from the feeling of inadequacy that inhibits subsequent work activity. But welfare payments, honorable or otherwise, are unlikely to be large enough to enable families to move up to middle-class circumstances— they serve only as a holding measure. The opportunity to move up would be enhanced if there were two breadwinners in the family rather than one, so an intact family has a potential economic advantage.

Moving Up

A striking feature of the outer-city black families in this study, who have made it out of the ghetto, is that their economic viability often depends on the joint income of husband and wife. The husbands, with only a tenth grade education on the average, are working at jobs that are not much different from those of men in the WIN program or men still in the ghetto. The outer-city blacks, however, despite having the high level of insecurity common to poor blacks, have stayed on their jobs. And most important, they have stayed married to women who on the average have an eleventh grade education and bring in almost 30 percent of the family income. The implication for policy here is that efforts to eliminate poverty should include incentives for a husband and wife to stay together as a family unit.

Job training for the poor might be thought of in family terms. Special benefits could be given to a husband and wife who participated in programs to gain new skills that would qualify them for jobs providing substantial joint income. At the same time, special efforts could be made to help the children of these adults succeed academically. Day care with a strong educational component for preschool children might serve the dual purpose of freeing a mother to work if she wished and providing special benefits to the child. In view of the negative results of past governmental efforts to aid the poor, such as WIN, however, one cannot help questioning whether such programs would really help.

A more equitable distribution of the tax burden would probably have greater economic effect than governmental "training" programs. If the poor were to pay a much lower proportion of their income in taxes than do the affluent, they would have more money to pay for training or day care themselves. Additional subsidies could be paid directly to heads of families who worked full time yet did not earn enough to move out of poverty.

Income is not the only issue involved in a family's moving out of poverty. There is a psychological component as well, to judge from the responses of the outer-city black family members. Both the outer-city parents and their children show lack of confidence and extreme consciousness of their marginal social status. The psychological stress of moving from lower to middle class may be great, and not every poor person may want or be able to accommodate to it. The situation may be especially difficult for the father who has less education than his wife and knows that he, unlike his white counterpart, can by himself barely support his family in middle-class status. This man is known to have a great lack of confidence in his abilities, and those with high scores on the lack of confidence

orientation earn the least income. Why these outer-city black men remain with their families and work hard to support them, while others with similar educational background do not, is a question of fundamental significance to which insufficient research has been directed.

In any case, attempts to help people overcome poverty and achieve social mobility should recognize the interplay between psychological and economic factors. An increase in family income of a few hundred dollars a year may in theory be enough to raise a family above some economically defined "poverty line." But such an amount is unlikely to generate a burst of confidence that would enable them to transform the ghetto into a better place to live or leave it for a better neighborhood. While a substantial rise in income might encourage some families to decide to move to a middle-class neighborhood, such a decision would not be a purely economic one: it would also be based on perceptions of ability to succeed. This study has clearly pointed to the tendency of poor blacks to be very uncertain about their ability. The limitation of using economic measurements alone is that they may show many rising above poverty because of government transfer payments, when socially and psychologically the urban ghettos remain unchanged.

The foregoing is not a criticism either of economic analysis or of proposals for guaranteeing income to the poor, but should provide a basis for moving beyond the often-expressed concern that transfer payments to the poor may take away their incentive to work. Excessive concern that a relatively low level of guaranteed income—around the poverty level—would cause people to drop out of the work force reflects a misunderstanding of the life and work orientations of the poor. They are no more likely to settle for this meager income and cease working than are middle-class people. Preliminary results from a work incentive experiment with low-income (intact) families, conducted by the University of Wisconsin, support this view.

The plight of the poor cannot be blamed on their having deviant goals or a deviant psychology. The ways in which the poor do differ from the affluent can reasonably be attributed to their different experiences of success and failure in the world. There is ample evidence to suggest that children who are born poor face discriminatory barriers to advancement in the educational and occupational worlds, which thrust them into failure much more consistently than their middle-class counterparts. Appropriate policies would enable more poor people to experience success. While success cannot be guaranteed, the probability of its attainment for larger numbers of the poor might be increased in two ways. The first is to lessen the risk of failure by removing discriminatory barriers so that, for example, more poor people become eligible for better jobs; the second, to reduce the cost of failure, when it does occur, by providing a guaranteed income at least a small margin above the poverty level. Poor families should be given enough economic security and low-risk opportunity to rise in status, according to their desire and ability, without being overwhelmed by failure induced by inequities in the social system.

THE POOR SHOULD BE PAID BONUSES

F. Helmut Weymar.
Social Policies for America in the Seventies:
Nine Divergent Views 55 (R.
Theobald ed. 1969).

The more is given the less the people will work for themselves, and the less they work the more their poverty will increase. TOLSTOI, 1892

Tolstoi's warning expresses well the American public's deep-seated suspicion of welfare programs. To increase aid to the poor, so the argument goes, is to encourage laziness. In light of this concern, it is ironic that today's welfare programs are structured so as to subvert, rather than harness, the beneficial forces generated by personal financial incentives.

* * *

An Incentive Bonus Program

Since no effective effort has been made to date utilizing special employment incentives to encourage the poor, what should be done? I submit that the poor should be offered unambiguously attractive incentives to upgrade their skills, and to find and hold employment using these upgraded skills. What would the key requirements of such a program be?

First, the incentives offered should be money in a considerable amount, sufficient to clearly offset the high effective tax rates incorporated in existing and proposed welfare programs.

Second, the incentives must be structured so as to foster relatively long-term career aspirations. This requirement reflects the fact that "the notion of a career, which plays such a significant part in the lives of middle class individuals, is hardly developed in the lower class." [17] If any substantial number of the poor are to attain incomes well above the poverty level, they must develop at least rudimentary career aspirations.

Third, the offer of special employment incentives must be coupled with a coordinated effort assuring the poor of the opportunity to earn these incentives. That is, prospective incentive recipients must be guaranteed ready access to such training, relocation, and employment-counseling programs as are necessary if they are to increase their earnings substantially.

[17] Suzanne Keller, The American Lower Class Family (Albany, New York State Division for Youth, 1966), p. 18.

Fourth, and finally, the expected returns from an incentive program must be attractive enough relative to other programs aiding the poor to warrant the expenditure of funds in this area.

Given these requirements, I propose the adoption of an incentive bonus program having the following characteristics:

Payments—An eligible person would be paid a $1.00 bonus for each $1.00 gain in his annual earned income. Half of this would be paid at the end of the year during which the income increase was achieved, and half would be paid five years later, providing that the increased income level had been maintained. Bonuses would be paid on all income gains up to the point where the recipient was earning 150 percent of his defined poverty income level. Thus, if an individual had a defined poverty income level of $3,000, he would be eligible for bonus payments until such time as his earnings had reached $4,500.

Eligibility—Any person who has been earning less than 150 percent of his family's defined poverty level for at least three years would be eligible for incentive bonuses.

Administration—Payments would be made by designated offices attached to local community action programs, welfare departments, or training programs. The primary function of the incentive bonus administrator would be to ensure that the increased motivation afforded bonus recipients would be matched by the opportunity to earn the bonuses offered. Given the family situations and the limited educational and employment backgrounds of most of the poor, it seems clear that increased incentives alone would be unlikely to draw a majority of these persons into effective labor market participation. At least three additional supporting steps would have to be taken.

First, day-care programs would have to be made available to mothers with preschool and primary-school children.

Second, adult education and vocational training programs would have to be utilized to upgrade reading, writing, and basic mathematical abilities, and to provide useful skills.

Third, and most important, a program would have to exist for the design and implementation of employment ladders for incentive recipients. Even after an initial practical period of adult education and vocational training, many recipients would still be unable to obtain the remunerative and secure kinds of jobs which might be expected to stave off future poverty. For such persons a training-employment sequence or ladder would likely be needed: adult education and training, first job (work experience), more training, better job, high skill training, final job. In order to provide useful employment ladders for individual incentive recipients, the activities of several local agencies would have to be coordinated: the welfare department, various training programs, the board of education, and various employment agencies, to name the key offices involved.

In effect acting as a career counselor, the incentive bonus administrator would be responsible for ensuring the availability of these supporting efforts to bonus recipients.

Fiscal Costs and Benefits—Crude estimates of the fiscal costs and benefits of such an incentive bonus program can be derived based on reasonable assumptions regarding administrative costs and the increased rates of employment and earnings induced by the bonuses. The results of this exercise indicate that in the case of AFDC recipients bonus program investments might yield a fiscal rate of return of between 3 and 17 percent per annum, while in the case of previously underemployed persons not on welfare the return might fall between 1 and 8 percent per annum. The assumptions are as follows.

Each incentive bonus administrative officer might cost about $15,000 per year including salary and overhead, and at any one point in time might counsel an average of seventy-five successful bonus recipients. Thus the administrative costs per successful recipient would run about $200 per year, and if the average length of bonus eligibility were five years, the total administrative cost per successful recipient would be $1,000. A typical AFDC success might increase her earnings from zero to $4,500 per year, thus earning bonuses totaling $4,500. Similarly, a typical success who was previously underemployed but not on welfare might earn bonuses of $2,000 by increasing his annual income from $2,500 to some point above 150 percent of his defined poverty level, here assumed to be $3,000. Thus, the total administrative plus bonus investment in an AFDC success would be $5,500, while in the case of a previously underemployed bonus recipient the investment would be $3,000.

The fiscal returns to providing an AFDC recipient with remunerative employment would be substantial. In 1964 the national average annual AFDC payment per recipient was about $375, or about $1,500 for a family of four. The successful employment of the AFDC head of a household of four would not only considerably improve the economic well-being of that household, but from a fiscal

point of view it would also bring an immediate annual saving of $1,500. In addition, the newly employed wage earner would generate total federal, state, and local taxes on the order of $300 per year. Thus the total annual fiscal return in the case of an AFDC success would be roughly $1,800. In the case of a previously underemployed father with four dependents, a new income level of, say, $6,000 per year would bring an increase in total annual tax revenues of roughly $450.

To convert these estimated fiscal costs and returns into a simple rate of return measure, the fact that some of the successful bonus recipients would have succeeded anyway, without the added bonus incentives, needs to be taken into account. The fiscal returns derived from these cases cannot be attributed to the bonus program. The table below indicates the simple rates of return to bonus program investments in AFDC and underemployed cases, where the portion of all successes which can be directly attributed to the bonus incentive effect is alternatively assumed to be 10 percent, 30 percent, and 50 percent. If, for example, 30 percent of the AFDC successful transitions into the labor force were attributable to bonuses (i. e. would not have happened without bonuses), then the annual fiscal return due to these cases, averaged over all successes, would be 30 percent of $1,800, or $540. This would yield a 9.8 percent simple rate of return on the average $550 bonus program investment per AFDC success.

Percent of Successes Attributable to Bonuses	AFDC Cases			Underemployed Cases		
	Average Investment	Average Return	Simple Rate of Return	Average Investment	Average Return	Simple Rate of Return
10	$5,500	$180	3.3%	$3,000	$ 45	1.5%
30	5,500	540	9.8	3,000	135	4.5
50	5,500	900	16.4	3,000	225	7.5

Other Benefits—Of course, the primary objective of an incentive bonus program for the poor would not be to maximize fiscal returns. These returns are

of interest only because they would reduce the net cost of the program, and
broaden the program's popular appeal.

The main benefits of increasing the
economic well-being of the poor need be
reviewed here only briefly. First, the individual who achieves self-sufficiency attains increased economic freedom and,
concurrently, a heightened sense of personal dignity. Further, he is likely to
provide a more effective economic upbringing for his children, in the sense
that they will more likely be able to fend
for themselves as they mature. The shift
of many individuals from unemployment
or underemployment to modern, productive jobs would strengthen the general
economy. In money terms, if two million individuals raised their average annual earned income by an average of
$4,000, the Gross National Product
would increase by $8 billion. Successful
steps toward solving the economic problems of poor families, via employment,
would go a long way toward eliminating
or at least reducing the need to deal with
the problems of poor communities.
Families with raised incomes would be
better able to pay economic rents, or to
own their own homes. They would be
better able to assume a share of their
communities' tax burden, thereby paying
for needed services.

Motivation: The Gap in the War on Poverty

In concluding, let me point out two
positions which I am *not* advocating in
proposing an incentive bonus program.

I am not arguing against giving money
to the poor, whether through existing
welfare programs or through a negative
income tax. The need for such programs
is clear; the level of support provided
by today's programs is manifestly too
low, especially for those disabled persons
for whom self-support is impossible.
But one should ask why the American

people—usually so generous—are reluctant to give more money to the poor.
The answer, I believe, is that the public
is convinced that the poor would become
lazy if guaranteed a decent living. If aid
is to be increased for those who cannot
support themselves, the electorate must
be assured that those who can support
themselves will make every effort to do
so. The adoption of an incentive bonus
program would be a step toward providing that assurance.

I am not downgrading the central importance of remedial education and vocational training, either. Without well-co-
ordinated programs in these areas, increased employment incentives could lead
only to increased frustration. What I am
advocating is the use of incentive bonuses
to provide unusually strong motivation
for the poor to enter and make full use
of training programs. The prevailing incentive approach used in our welfare system today is one of deprivation and
harassment. The aim often seems to be
to support life at a level just unbearable
enough so that anyone who can possibly
get off welfare will do so. But as with
ropes, people are more readily pulled
than pushed. New York City Welfare
Commissioner Mitchell Ginsberg has observed: "Under current regulations and
practices, the welfare system is basically
designed to save money rather than save
people, and the tragedy is that it ends up
doing neither." [18] The objective of the
incentive bonus program proposed here is
to replace the push of deprivation with
the pull of motivation.

It should be clear from the above that
an incentive bonus program would
complement, rather than compete with,
existing or proposed welfare and manpower programs. It would complement
welfare programs insofar as it would off-

[18] Institute of Public Administration, Developing New York City's Human Resources
(New York, 1966), Vol. I, p. 32.

set the employment disincentives these programs inevitably incorporate. It would complement training and relocation efforts insofar as it would heighten the appeal of these programs to prospective bonus recipients.

The concern for motivation that underlies this proposal is not original. In deliberating on the subject of poverty, a group within the President's Council of Economic Advisers identified the poverty cycle as follows:

"Poverty"

leads to

"Cultural and Environmental

obstacles to *motivation*"

which leads to

"Poor health, and inadequate

education, and low mobility

limiting *Earning Potential*"

which leads to

"Limited income opportunities"

which lead to

"Poverty" [19]

As it has evolved, the war on poverty has included a many-pronged attack aimed at increasing the earning potential of the poor, without adequately considering their motivation. The proposed incentive bonus program is designed to fill this gap.

THE WORK INCENTIVE TRAP

Edward V. Sparer.
(From The Rights of Americans: What They
Are—What They Should Be,
N. Dorsen ed. 1971).*

The "work incentive" proposal seems widely attractive. Economists Milton Friedman and James Tobin endorse it. Congress accepted a limited version in

[19] Daniel P. Moynihan, "What Is Community Action," The Public Interest (Fall 1966), pp. 3–8.

* © 1971 Pantheon Books/A Division of Random House, Inc.

1967 for AFDC recipients (allowing 30 percent of income to be retained), and President Nixon has proposed that the "work incentive" be broadened to 50 percent and be applied to all families with children whose income falls below his proposed federal floor. Welfare recipients, by and large, like the idea; some are even enthusiastic. (Why should their job income be "taxed 100 percent"?) The nonwelfare working poor like it; their total income would be raised. All America seems united on a good idea; who ever said that the different classes have different interests?

It is, I suspect, a trap. There are at least four closely related problems: (1) it is extremely expensive to finance a good "work incentive" and an adequate base grant for those who cannot work; (2) as illustrated by President Nixon's proposal, it is the base grant which will be sacrificed in favor of the incentive, thus leaving those who cannot work with an inadequate grant; (3) it pumps most new money to be put into a welfare system into federal subsidy for every sweatshop, every menial job, every poorly paid job in the country; and (4) it thereby conditions survival of the needy poor on their willingness to accept menial jobs, just as effectively as the most harshly administered work test—or perhaps even more effectively.

Thus, when the 1969 White House Conference on Hunger and Malnutrition was considering the NWRO proposal that it support the $5,500 welfare line for all persons in need, Robert Harris was quick to advise the participants what was wrong with the proposal. On the assumption that $5,500 was necessary for decent survival, Harris calculated that to guarantee such income would require $20 billion more in income maintenance programs, a manageable figure (once we abandon war-making). But, he argued, without either a work test or work incentive, it would cost far more because many persons would not work at lower-paid jobs when they could get $5,500 without such jobs. A 50 percent work incentive on a $5,500 base would cost some $70 billion more, an unmanageable figure, and subsidize persons making up to $11,000 a year. This is purely ridiculous. Harris argued, naturally, that the solution would be to lower the base grant —even though $5,500 is not high enough to support a family decently.

We must identify our primary concern. Is it to guarantee that people who cannot or should not work will have enough aid so as to live with minimum decency, or to assure that people who can work will do so regardless of what work they are forced to accept? Suppose a welfare system offered an adequate grant to all those in need (with income below it) and a right to refuse work which paid less than the welfare grant. If private business and government were forced to reorganize the economy to ensure that it provided purposeful and well-paying work, would not this be desirable? Are we not producing the opposite result when we subsidize (through the "work incentive") the most pointless and exploitive jobs in the economy while denying decent welfare grants to those who cannot work?

Note on Incentives in Supplemental Security Income Program

The new SSI program incorporates work incentives which are substantially more generous than the $30 per month plus one-third exclusion available to AFDC recipients. There is, first of all, a basic exclusion of the first $240 per year of all income, earned or unearned. § 1612(b)(2), 42 U.S.C.A. § 1382a(b)(2). On top of this, the next $780 of earned income plus one-half of all additional earned income is also excluded from welfare budget computations. § 1612(b)(4), 42 U.S.C.A. § 1382a(b)(4)(A). Put in aggregate monthly terms, this is the exclusion of the first $85 per month plus one-half the remain-

der of earned income. Moreover, as to blind and disabled (but not aged) recipients, the SSI program goes even further. Both blind and disabled are permitted to exclude

"Such additional amounts of other income, where such individual has a plan for achieving self-support approved by the Secretary, as may be necessary for the fulfillment of such plan" § 1612(b)(4)(A)–(B), 42 U.S.C.A. § 1382a(b)(4)(A)–(B).

Finally, blind recipients only are permitted an additional exclusion for "expenses reasonably attributable to the earning" of income.

Several questions may be raised about these work incentive provisions (or "income disregards" as they are sometimes called). Are these provisions adequate to encourage work? What justification is there for the hierarchy among blind, disabled and aged in the degree of generosity of the disregard? Why is even the least generous of the three so much greater than the disregard permitted to AFDC recipients? (Surely the explanation is not that Congress wishes AFDC recipients to have less incentive to work.)

And, finally, what are we to make of the special "self-support/fulfillment" benefit extended to blind and disabled recipients? The House Committee Report gives only one example of a situation where this might be invoked.

"A blind person, for example, might be getting $80 per month from a brother, in addition to, say, $100 a month he is earning himself. If the money from his brother were being saved for the establishment of a business—possibly a magazine stand or small store—which could help make him self-supporting, the money could be excluded if the Secretary approved his plan for self-support." H.R.Rep. No. 92–231, 92nd Cong., 1st Sess. 152 (1971).

If this is all that the provision is intended to cover, it is unnecessary, since the brother could easily establish a special purpose trust to accumulate the money for the recipient and insulate it from the welfare budget. But it is clear that the language of the provision is broad enough to exclude more than merely brotherly contributions, and therein lies the problem.

Is it wise to give this kind of open-ended discretion to an administrator? What rights does a recipient have to check arbitrary use of this broad discretionary power? Beyond these administrative law issues, there is also the public policy question: why should special protection be given to those who can afford to save some money when those who cannot afford to save any of their outside income are presumably more needy?

There is no doubt that the problem raised by the hypothetical case in the Committee Report is a sympathetic one. But we should not lose sight of the fact that it injects a note of social paternalism into a program which seems to be moving away from that and toward a more fixed, nondiscretionary minimum income support. Is there any way to accommodate the problem of the recipient who wants to become a capitalist without raising these problems?

SECTION 4. DETERMINATION OF THE BENEFIT LEVEL AND RELATED PROBLEMS

A. INTRODUCTION

Introductory Note on Benefit Determinations

The basic element in the fixing of benefits is the "standard of need," the amount which is calculated to be necessary to sustain an appropriate standard of living. Federal law nowhere prescribes what this amount is to be for the catagorical programs, or even what the targeted level for a standard of living is to be. Rather, the Federal categorical programs simply provide that coverage is available to "needy" persons who otherwise qualify, and leave it up to the states to determine who is "needy." Each state has of course set standards of need, using various approaches. The general approach is to prescribe a basic amount varying according to family size, and then to provide for certain adjustments to take account of special needs of recipients. In some states, the basic amount covers only a narrow group of items and the special needs provisions are a major part of the computation; in other states the basic amount covers virtually all normal needs and special needs provisions are taken into account only in limited situations. There are also varying approaches to determining what items are to be included in the standard of need (e. g., is any amount to be included for recreational costs?), and what dollar costs are to be assigned to each item. The Department of Health, Education and Welfare suggests use of Bureau of Labor Statistics data, but that is by no means a mandatory requirement. Standards of need are generally set below the traditional poverty line. The standard of need is sometimes known as the recipients' "budget."

Once the standard of need is determined, the next step is, normally, to offset the recipients' income and resources against need to determine the amount of the recipients' "budget deficit." Here again, the states have a large measure of discretion, although Federal law does impose some constraints. States are to take account of "expenses reasonably attributable to the earning of any such income" in computing the amount of available income. See, 42 U.S.C.A. § 602(a)(8).

[handwritten marginalia: Problem: state budget restraints do not allow full payment to all recipients]

Certain items of income are to be mandatorily disregarded—e. g., part-time earnings of a child who is still in school; "the first $30 plus one-third of the remainder" of monthly earnings of each individual recipient. 42 U.S.C. § 602(a)(8)(A). Within these limitations, states are free to take account of any income and resources, including such "resources" as a recipient's recovery on a tort claim and a recipient's rights of support from other responsible relatives. See pp. 281–295, infra.

The final step in the process is to determine the "level of benefits" or the actual "level of payment" to the recipient. There is no requirement that this be equal to the budget deficit, i. e. the amount necessary to bring the recipient up to the standard of need. Only a minority of states pay the full need. Some states limit payment through maximum grant provisions. Sometimes stated as an individual maximum and sometimes as a family maximum, these provisions place an absolute ceiling on the amount which may be paid. Dandridge v. Williams, supra, involved the Maryland family maximum. Ward v. Winstead, 314 F.Supp. 1225 (N.D.Miss.1970), app. dismissed 400 U.S. 1019 (1971), which involved the Mississippi individual maxima, illustrates just how low these maxima can be. Mississippi AFDC grants were limited to $12.00 per month for the third and subsequent children in a family. The other general approach to limiting levels of payment is use of a percentage reduction—a provision which limits grants to a defined percentage of the standard of need.

The end result—with limited standards of need and frequent severe restrictions on payment even under those limited standards—has been a modest level of payment in the most generous states and grossly inadequate payment in the less generous. This has provoked much litigation aimed at increasing levels of benefits, based on both constitutional and statutory grounds.

This litigation all involved the AFDC program and remains directly applicable to it. It also has implications for the adult programs, but the recent enactment of the Supplemental Security Income (SSI) Program has substantially modified the benefit computation process for persons in the adult categories. As to them, there is now a Federally pegged standard of need ($1,560 for an individual; $2,340 for an individual with eligible spouse) and the Federal government pays the full budget deficit in all cases. State discretion nonetheless continues to be important because states have the option to supplement the Federal grant and thereby raise the level of benefits. See pp. 22–23, supra.

ROSADO v. WYMAN

Supreme Court of the United States, 1970.
397 U.S. 397, 90 S.Ct. 1207, 25 L.Ed.2d 442.

Mr. Justice HARLAN delivered the opinion of the Court.

The present controversy, * * * involves the compatibility of the New York Social Services Law, McKinney's Consol. Laws, c. 55 (c. 184, L.1969) with § 402 (a)(23), 42 U.S.C. § 602(a)(23) Supp. IV, 1968), of the Federal Social Security Act of 1935.

* * *

In 1967 the Administration introduced omnibus legislation to amend the social security laws. The relevant AFDC proposals provided for more adequate assistance to welfare recipients and set up several programs for education and training accompanied by child care provisions designed to permit AFDC parents to take advantage of the training programs. In the former respect the AFDC proposals paralleled other provisions that put forward amendments to adjust benefits to

[Handwritten marginalia at top: "Rule ✓ States' goal = administrative efficiency — and here, did not a flat grant, system did not provide for "need" at all"]

[Handwritten marginalia right: "The grant has to be related to "need" criteria"]

recipients of other categorical aid to reflect the rise in the cost of living. Thus, in its embryo stage § 402 was § 202(b) of the Administration bill, H.R. 5710, 90th Cong., 1st Sess. (1967), which would have added to § 402(a) of the Social Security Act the following clause:

> "(14) provide (A), effective July 1, 1969, for meeting (in conjunction with other income that is not disregarded under the plan and the other resources) *all the need* as determined in accordance with the standards applicable under the plan for determining need of individuals eligible to receive aid to families with dependent children (and such standards shall *be no lower than the standards for determining need in effect* on January 1, 1967) and (B) effective July 1, 1968, for an annual review of such standards and (to the extent prescribed by the Secretary) for up-dating such standards to take into account changes in living costs." (Emphasis added.)

Section 202(b), however, was stillborn and no such provision was contained in the ultimate bill reported out by the House Ways and Means Committee. See H.R. 12080, 90th Cong., 1st Sess.

The Administration's renewed efforts, on behalf of a mandatory increase in benefit payments under the categorical assistance programs,[15] met with only lim-

ited success, resulting in § 213(a) of the Senate version which provided for a mandatory $7.50 per month increase in the standards and benefits for the adult categories and § 213(b) which is, in substance, the present § 402(a)(23). The Committee's comment on § 213(b), to the effect that States would be required "to price their standards * * * to reflect changes in the cost of living," tracks the statutory language.[16]

[Handwritten marginalia right: "Rule I case: p 269"]

> their own state assistance standards, and to update these standards periodically to keep pace with changes in the cost of living." Hearings before the Senate Committee on Finance on H.R. 12080, Part I, at 216 (90th Cong., 1st Sess., August 1967). See also testimony of Wilbur Cohen. Id., at 255–259.

[16] The comment to § 213 in the Senate Report reads:

> "Social security benefits have been increased 15 percent across the board by the committee with a minimum of $70, for an average increase of 20 percent. However, there is no similar across-the-board increase in the amount of benefits payable to aged welfare recipients. * * * In view of this situation and the need to recognize that the increase in the cost of living since the last change made in the Federal matching formula in 1965 also is detrimental to the well-being of these recipients, the committee is recommending a further change in the law. It is proposed that the law be amended to provide that recipients of old-age assistance, aid to the blind, and aid to the permanently and totally disabled shall receive an average increase in assistance plus social security or assistance alone (for the recipients who do not receive social security benefits) of $7.50 a month. * * *

> "To accomplish these changes, the States would have to adjust their standards and any maximums imposed on payments by July 1, 1968, so as to produce an average increase of $7.50 from assistance alone or assistance and social security benefits (or other income). Any State which wishes to do so can claim credit for any increase it may have made since December 31, 1966. Thus, no State needs to make an increase to the extent that it has recently done so.

> "States would be required to price their standards used for determining the amount of assistance under the AFDC program by July 1, 1969 and to reprice them at least annually thereafter, adjusting the standards and any maximums imposed on pay-

[15] Secretary Garner testified:

> "The House bill does nothing to improve the level of state public assistance. As things stand today, the States are required to set assistance standards for needy persons in order to determine eligibility—but they need not make their assistance payments on the basis of these standards. The result is that welfare payments are much too low in a good many States. That is a widely accepted fact among all who are concerned with these programs; indeed, it is probably the most widely agreed-upon fact among welfare experts today.

> "We strongly urge you to adopt the Administration's proposal requiring States to meet need in full as they determine

The Conference Committee eliminated the Senate provision in § 213 which would have required an annual adjustment for cost of living, and § 402 was enacted. It now provides:

Fed Stat.

"[The States shall] provide that by July 1, 1969, the amounts used by the State to determine needs of individuals will have been adjusted to reflect fully changes in living costs since such amounts were established and any maximums that the State imposes on the amount of aid paid to families will have been proportionately adjusted."

C

The background of § 402 reveals little except that we have before us a child born of the silent union of legislative compromise. Thus, Congress, as it frequently does, has voiced its wishes in muted strains and left it to the courts to discern the theme in the cacophony of political understanding. Our chief resources in this undertaking are the words of the statute and those common-sense assumptions that must be made in determining direction without a compass.

Reverting to the language of § 402 we find two separate mandates: first, the States must re-evaluate the component factors that comprise their need equation; and, second, any "maximums" must be adjusted.

We think two broad purposes may be ascribed to § 402: First, to require States to face up realistically to the magnitude of the public assistance requirement and lay bare the extent to which their programs fall short of fulfilling actual need; second, to prod the States to apportion their payments on a more equitable basis. Consistent with this interpretation of § 402, a State may, after recomputing its standard of need, pare down payments to

ments to reflect changes in living costs." S.Rep.No.744, at 169–170 (90th Cong., 1st Sess., 1967); see also id., at 293, U.S.Code Cong. & Admin.News 1967, pp. 3006–3007.

accommodate budgetary realities by reducing the percent of benefits paid or switching to a percent reduction system, but it may not obscure the *actual* standard of need.

Cong. Intent

The Congressional purpose we discern does not render § 402 a meaningless exercise in "bookkeeping." Congress sometimes, legislates by innuendo, making declarations of policy and indicating a preference while requiring measures which, though falling short of legislating its goals, serve as a nudge in the preferred directions. In § 402 Congress has spoken in favor of increases in AFDC payments. While Congress rejected the mandatory adjustment provision in the administration bill, it embodied in legislation the cost-of-living exercise which has both practical and political consequences.

It has the effect of requiring the States to recognize and accept the responsibility for those additional individuals whose income falls short of the standard of need as computed in light of economic realities and placing them among those eligible for the care and training provisions. Secondly, while it leaves the States free to effect downward adjustments in the level of benefits paid, it accomplishes within that framework the goal, however modest, of forcing a State to accept the political consequence of such a cutback and bringing to light the true extent to which actual assistance falls short of the minimum acceptable. Lastly, by imposing on those States that desire to maintain "maximums" the requirement of an appropriate adjustment, Congress has introduced an incentive to abandon a flat "maximum" system, thereby encouraging those States desirous of containing their welfare budget to shift to a percentage system which will more equitably apportion those funds in fact allocated for welfare and also more accurately reflect the real measure of public assistance being given.

While we do not agree with the broad interpretation given § 402 by the District

Court,[17] we cannot accept the conclusion reached by the two-judge majority in the Court of Appeals—that § 402 does not affect New York.[18] It follows from what we fathom to be the congressional purpose that a State may not redefine its standard of need in such a way that it circumnavigates around the requirement of re-evaluating its existing standard. This would render the cost-of-living reappraisal a futile, hollow, and, indeed, a deceptive gesture, and would avoid the consequences of increasing the numbers of those eligible and facing up to the failure

to allocate sufficient funds to provide for them.

These conclusions, if not compelled by the words of the statute nor manifested by legislative history, represent the natural blend of the basic axiom—that courts should construe all legislative enactments to give them some meaning—with the compromise origins of § 402, set forth above. This background, we think, precludes the more adventuresome reading that petitioners and the District Court would give the statute. See n. 17, supra. This reading is also buttressed by the fact that this construction has been placed on the statute by the Department of Health, Education and Welfare.[19] While, in view of Congress' failure to track the Administration proposals and its substitution without comment, of the present compromise section. HEW's construction commands less than the usual deference that may be accorded an administrative interpretation based on its expertise, it is entitled to weight as the attempt of an experienced agency to harmonize an obscure enactment with the basic structure of a program it administers. Cf. Zuber v. Allen, 396 U.S. 168, 192, 90 S.Ct. 314, 327, 24 L.Ed.2d 345 (1969); Udall v. Tallman, 380 U.S. 1, 85 S.Ct. 792, 13 L.Ed.2d 616 (1965).

D

While the application of the statute to the New York program is by no means simple, we think the evidence adduced supports the ultimate finding of the District Court, unquestioned by the Court of Appeals, that New York has, in effect, impermissibly lowered its standard of need by eliminating items that were included prior to the enactment of § 402.

* * *

[The opinion goes on to describe how this reduction in the standard of need was

---

[17] The District Court, while disclaiming any construction of § 402(a)(23) that would preclude converting to a flat grant system by averaging, concluded: "section 402(a)(23) precludes a state from making changes resulting in either reduced standards of need or *levels of payments*." 304 F.Supp., at 1377. (Emphasis added.) An extensive alteration in the basic underlying structure of an established program is not to be inferred from ambiguous language which is not clarified by legislative history. Such legislative history as there is suggests the opposite. The Senate's failure to adopt the Administration's proposals and its failure to provide for AFDC recipients an increase like that provided for the adult program, notwithstanding a proposed amendment to that effect by Senator McGovern gives rise to an inference, not negatived by the noncommittal and unilluminating comments of the committee, see n. 16, supra, that Congress had no such purpose. These considerations, we think, foreclose the broad construction adopted by the District Court.

[18] While it might be technically said that there was no majority holding on the merits in the Court of Appeals, this overlooks Judge Hays' preface to his discussion of the merits: "Although we are persuaded that the district judge had no power to adjudicate this action, we turn to a brief discussion of the merits, since our decision does not rest solely on jurisdictional grounds." 414 F.2d, at 178. Chief Judge Lumbard disavowed reaching the merits but expressly disagreed with Judge Feinberg, 414 F.2d, at 181. In these circumstances, it would be hypertechnical to conclude that the merits had not been faced and decided below such as to make a remand desirable prior to review and decisions by this Court. Cf. Barlow v. Collins, 397 U.S. 159, 90 S.Ct. 832, 25 L.Ed.2d 192 (1970).

[19] The regulations and explanations are set forth in the Government's amicus memorandum.

the effect of a shift from an item by item computation of need to a flat grant basis.]

We do not, of course, hold that New York may not, consistently with the federal statutes, consolidate items on the basis of statistical averages. Obviously such averaging may affect some families adversely and benefit others. Moreover, it is conceivable that the net payout, assuming no change in the level of benefits, may be somewhat less under a streamlined program. Providing all factors in the old equation are accounted for and fairly priced and providing the consolidation on a statistical basis reflects a fair averaging, a State may, of course, consistently with § 402 redefine its method for determining need. A State may, moreover, as we have noted, accommodate any increases in its standard by reason of "cost-of-living" factors to its budget by reducing its level of benefits. What is at the heart of this dispute is the elimination of special grants in the New York program, not the system of maximum grants based on average age. Lest there be uncertainty we also reiterate that New York is not foreclosed from accounting for basic and recurring items of need formerly subsumed in the special grant category by an averaging system like that adopted in the 1968 New York City experiment with cyclical grants.

* * *

Note on Rosado v. Wyman

Rosado represents one of the numerous litigative battles fought by a contemporary welfare rights movement that first emerged on the national scene in the mid-1960's. Buttressed by Great Society programs, the movement challenged the welfare system with a legion of militant anti-poverty groups working in tandem with the organized poor.

Since its initial years, the movement's tactics have been unquestionably influenced by a strategy to achieve welfare reform first suggested by Richard A. Cloward and Frances Fox Piven in the spring of 1966:

> [A] vast discrepancy exists between the benefits to which people are entitled under public welfare programs and sums which they actually receive. * * * for every person on the [welfare] rolls at least one more probably meets existing criteria of eligibility but is not obtaining assistance.

> This discrepancy is not an accident stemming from bureaucratic inefficiency; rather it is an integral feature of the welfare system which, if challenged, would precipitate a profound financial and political crisis. The force for that challenge, and the strategy we propose, is a massive drive to recruit the poor *onto* the welfare rolls.

> * * *

> A series of welfare drives in large cities would, we believe, impel action on a new federal program to distribute income, eliminating the present public welfare system and alleviating the abject poverty which it perpetrates. Widespread campaigns to register the eligible poor for welfare aid, and to help existing recipients obtain their full benefits, would product bureaucratic disruption in welfare agencies and fiscal disruption in local and state governments. These disruptions would generate severe political strains and deepen existing divisions among elements in the big-city Democratic coalition. * * * To avoid a further weakening of that historic coalition, a national Democratic administration would be constrained to advance a federal solution to poverty that would override local welfare failures, local class and racial conflicts and local revenue dilemmas.[1]

[1] Cloward and Piven. A Strategy to End Poverty, The Nation, May 2, 1966, at 510.

Essential to implementing the type of reform strategy envisaged by Cloward and Piven were the "neighborhood service centers" that proliferated throughout the 1960's. By 1968, the Office of Economic Opportunity alone had funded one or more such centers in some 870 communities.[2] Staffed by social workers, lawyers, churchmen, students and poor people themselves, the centers offered a variety of services that rendered the poor less impotent in their dealings with public welfare agencies. Typical of these services were those provided by the highly effective storefront offices of New York City's Mobilization for Youth:

They totaled up scores of welfare [recipients'] budgets to detect underbudgeting; they placed telephone calls to a bewildering number of functionaries and sometimes accompanied families to see officials in person. They argued and cajoled; they bluffed and threatened. * * * 'When I go to welfare,' one Stanton Street [MFY] staff member declared, 'I don't wait around for the stall. If I don't get treated with respect, I start hollering for the supervisor, and then I threaten legal action.' * * * Staff members, in short, took sides with the poor. * * * And they did help them to get many things, which was what drew people to the centers. * * *

As time passed, however, storefront staff members began to feel frustrated by the need to deal with the same grievances over and over again. * * * Instead, the center administrators began to think about group action; rather than bargaining separately on behalf of each of fifty clients for fifty separate clothing grants, why not bargain once on behalf of a group of fifty? * * * And so, after three years of taking in-

dividual complaints, a community organizer was hired to work out of the [MFY] center on Stanton Street, and an MFY attorney was assigned to work with him.[3]

Undoubtedly, Mobilization for Youth and other similar organizations had a significant impact on the size of local welfare rolls. A study conducted in Baltimore, for example, showed that during the space of one year the AFDC caseload in the area serviced by the city's first OEO neighborhood anti-poverty agency increased by 36.6 per cent while the city's total AFDC caseload during the same period grew by only 8.6 per cent. "All the agency did * * * was to make people aware of the availability of AFDC [and] to stimulate the use of [it]." [4]

While restrictions on the availability of public assistance were being weakened by neighborhood workers and organizations they were also being challenged in the courts. Durational residency requirements, man-in-the-house and employable-mother rules, "midnight raids," and the lack of due process in welfare administration were all subjected to a frontal legal assault. The impact of these efforts on the size of the welfare rolls defies precise measurement. Nevertheless, it is clear that in combination with the other aspects of the burgeoning welfare rights movement they were largely responsible for the vast rise in public assistance payments that took place during the 1960's.

Between 1960 and 1968, applications for public assistance rose 85 per cent on a

---

[2] S. Levitan, The Great Society's Poor Law: A New Approach to Poverty 128 (1969).

[3] F. Piven and R. Cloward, Regulating the Poor: The Functions of Public Welfare 291–3 (1971).

[4] Maryland State Department of Public Welfare, A Report on Caseload Increase in Aid to Families With Dependent Children Program, 1960–66 (Research Report No. 2 1967). [Cited in Regulating the Poor at 289.]

nationwide basis. As the number of applications rose, so did the proportion of them approved. In 1960, only 55 per cent of the individuals requesting public assistance received it. By 1968, this figure had grown to 70 per cent in the nation as a whole and to 78 per cent in the Northeast. From December 1964 to February 1969, welfare rolls in the 78 Northern urban counties rose 80 per cent. Even more dramatic were the increases in several large metropolitan centers. The rolls in New York, for example, jumped 137 per cent, and those in Los Angeles 145 per cent.[5]

The results of this trend were assayed in a recent speech by Senator Russell Long (Chairman of the Senate Finance Committee, which has jurisdiction over welfare legislation). He attacked "welfare activists, including the Government-paid corps of attorneys for the Office of Economic Opportunity" for "loading down the welfare rolls with millions of people who were never intended to be there" through victories in residency and man-in-the-house rule cases.

Senator Long warned:

The most obvious threat of the so-called welfare reform is that it would start by doubling the welfare rolls and set an irresistible foundation to redouble and then to double again, the list of recipients.[6]

That indeed appeared to be the case with the AFDC program, where reformers had focused their attention. The total AFDC roll rose from 3,073,000 recipients in 1960 to 6,086,000 in 1968 (up 98 per cent) and continued upward to 9,660,000 in 1970.[7]

Measured in dollar costs rather than numbers of recipients, the results are even more striking. Expenditures for public assistance almost doubled from $4.04 billion in 1959–60 to $7.83 billion in 1966–67, and doubled again to $14.43 billion in 1969–70, an overall increase of 257 per cent in a decade.[8] By comparison, the prior decade, before the upswing in welfare awareness, showed an increase of only 62 per cent, from $2.49 billion in 1949–50 to the $4.04 billion of 1959–60.

The feature of this welfare reform movement which led to *Rosado* was mass campaigns to procure those "special grants" authorized by statute but denied in practice. The following account of one such campaign appeared in the New York *Daily News* during the fall of 1967:

'Okay, honey, here's your list,' the woman with the white hat said to the thinner woman. 'Now you sit right down here and check off everything you don't have. And when you get all done, you go in there and tell them you want it. If they give you any trouble about it, you just come out and let me know. I'll go in there with you and squeeze it out of them people.'

The woman with the white hat was an officer of one of the city's more than 100 welfare client organizations. And she was doing her part in a nationwide campaign designed to 'bring the welfare system to its knees, right now.'

Her group had mimeographed a list of more than 200 items of clothing, furniture and household equipment,

---

[5] Piven and Cloward, supra note 3, at 331–5.

[6] Senate Comm. on Finance, Address of Hon. Russell B. Long, Welfare Reform—Or Is It? 92d Cong. 1st Sess. (Comm.Print 1971).

[7] Id.

[8] Skolnick and Dales, Social Welfare Expenditures, 1970–71, Soc.Sec.Bull. Dec. 1971, at 3, 5. Preliminary estimates for 1970–71 show a further increase to $18.63 billion; the increase from 1969–70 to 1970–71 being as great as total expenditures in 1959–60. These figures take no account of medicaid, a major new program in the 1960's. It is estimated that this program cost $6.5 billion for 1970–71. Id.

items which must, according to state law, be given to every individual who is receiving public assistance.

* * *

Of course, there is nothing extravagant on the list. And the city's welfare laws state that each relief recipient should be given those items he lacks at the time he comes onto the relief rolls.

But as a matter of fact, only between 2% and 3% of all welfare clients in the city are completely up to standard, and if the 97% or 98% who lack certain items should demand those items en masse—which they are now doing—the system could be financially brought to its knees.

* * *

The organizations also have provided hundreds of reliefers with legal assistance in preparing for 'fair hearings,' appeals based on complaints of unfair treatment.

One lawyer representing welfare clients reported that he has been winning special grants of $300 to $1,000 for each client who appealed on the ground that the Welfare Department has failed to enforce its minimum standards of assistance.

* * *

The State Department of Social Services, which conducts all fair hearings, has had to hire additional hearing examiners to cope with the massive new demands for hearings, and the snarl of red tape has backed up all the way to Albany.[9]

The New York City special grants campaign went a long way toward creating the type of fiscal and administrative crisis that Cloward, Piven and other strategists

had deemed essential for major welfare reform. As a result of the campaign, the number of time consuming fair hearings conducted in New York jumped from 5 per month to 50 per day.[10] In 1965, New York City spent about 40 dollars per welfare recipient for special grants. By 1968, this figure had skyrocketed to 100 dollars.[11]

In order to counter the threat posed by special grant campaigns, New York state officials abolished special grants in New York City during August 1968 and substituted a flat grant system. Welfare rights advocates countered with the lawsuit that resulted in the Supreme Court's *Rosado* opinion. In response to the Supreme Court, New York again revised its schedule of welfare benefits and adopted a new program of flat grants for the entire state. Nevertheless, on remand in *Rosado,*[12] the district court ruled that the new level of New York's welfare payments for upstate residents still placed it in violation of the Social Security Act. The state was ordered to either reformulate its payments once more or face the prospect of losing all federal public assistance funds.

Much to the chagrin of welfare reformers, the victory gained in *Rosado* was shortlived. In 1971, the New York State Legislature did what had previously been considered unthinkable and cut the benefit levels paid to AFDC recipients from 100 per cent to 90 per cent of their need.

New York's public assistance cutback was not unique. Faced with an administrative and fiscal crisis in their welfare programs, several states have taken sim-

---

[9] Clendenin and Singleton, Relief on the Rocks? "If the Book Says I Should Have It, I Want It," Daily News (New York), October 26, 1967, at 48, col. 1–2.

[10] Clendenin and Singleton, Relief on the Rocks? New Hard Boiled Plan May Cook Golden Egg, Daily News (New York), October 27, 1967, at 46, col. 2.

[11] Piven and Cloward, supra note 3, at 325.

[12] Rosado v. Wyman, 322 F.Supp. 1173 (E. D.N.Y.1970).

ilar measures. Combined with the continued failure of the federal government to liberalize public assistance programs, at least AFDC, these developments have played a role in convincing some formerly optimistic welfare rights strategists that their crisis promoting tactics are capable of producing momentary financial benefits for the poor, but not the long term economic reallocation that they desire.[13] But one message for lawyers is clear. While litigation tactics are an important part of modern reform strategy, they are not a panacea.

Problem

Prior to 1969 Wisconsin had developed a standard of need consisting of various "allowances" (e. g., "combined allowance" for food, clothing, etc., "shelter allowance," and "special needs allowance"). In 1969 this standard was updated to reflect cost of living increases. In the case of a family of four, the combined allowance was increased from $149 per month to $167 per month. At the same time the state altered its system for determining the actual level of benefits. Formerly, recipients were paid 100% of the standard of need, less their income or resources. As of 1969, however, the legislature decreed that AFDC payments were not to exceed 120% of the national average payments, as compared to 130–140% which had been paid. Pursuant to this mandate, the level of benefits was computed in the following manner: Starting with the old (pre-1969) combined allowance ($149 for a family of four), a "rated reduction" of $8 per person was subtracted ($32 for a family of four), and a set dollar amount was added for "common items" to cover several items formerly within the "special needs allowance" ($9 for a family of four). This total ($126 for a family of four) constituted a new "basic allowance" which pur-

ported to cover all items formerly within the combined allowance plus several former special needs items. A housing allowance and other special needs allowances were added to this and any family income or resources were subtracted to arrive at the actual grant.

Is this new Wisconsin system challengeable? See Alvarado v. Schmidt, 317 F. Supp. 1027 (W.D.Wisc.1970).

JEFFERSON v. HACKNEY

Supreme Court of the United States, 1972.
406 U.S. 535, 92 S.Ct. 1724, 32 L.Ed.2d 285.

Mr. Justice REHNQUIST delivered the opinion of the Court.

Appellants in this case challenge certain computation procedures which the State of Texas uses in its federally assisted welfare program. Believing that neither the Constitution nor the federal welfare statute prohibits the State from adopting these policies, we affirm the judgment of the three-judge court below upholding the state procedures.

I

Appellants are Texas recipients of Aid to Families with Dependent Children (AFDC). They brought two class actions, which were consolidated in the United States District Court for the Northern District of Texas, seeking injunctive and declaratory relief against state welfare officials. A three-judge court was convened pursuant to 28 U.S. C.A. § 2281.

The Texas State Constitution provides a ceiling on the amount the State can spend on welfare assistance grants.[1] In

---

[13] See generally Piven and Cloward, supra note 3.

[1] Originally, the Texas Constitution prohibited all welfare programs. Section 51 of Art. III of the Constitution, Vernon's Ann.St., provided that the legislature "shall have no power to make any grant or authorize the making of any grant of public moneys to any individual, association of in-

order to allocate this fixed pool of welfare money among the numerous individuals with acknowledged need, the State has adopted a system of percentage grants. Under this system, the State first computes the monetary needs of individuals eligible for relief under each of the federally aided categorical assistance programs.[2] Then, since the constitutional ceiling on welfare is insufficient to bring each recipient up to this full standard of need, the State applies a percentage reduction factor[3] in order to arrive at a reduced standard of need in each category which the State can guarantee.

Appellants challenge the constitutionality of applying a lower percentage reduction factor to AFDC than to the other categorical assistance programs. They claim a violation of equal protection because the proportion of AFDC recipients who are Black or Mexican-American is higher than the proportion of the aged, blind or disabled welfare recipients who fall within these minority groups. Appellants claim that the distinction between the programs is not rationally related to the purposes of the Social Security Act, and violates the Fourteenth Amendment for that reason as well. In their original

dividuals, municipal or other corporations whatsoever. * * *" However, beginning in 1933, exceptions to this rule were added to the state constitution in § 51–a, which now allows participation in the federal welfare programs, but limits state financing to the sum of $80,000,000. The legislature cannot exceed this welfare budget without a state constitutional amendment.

[2] Old Age Assistance (OAA), 42 U.S.C.A. § 301 et seq.; Aid to Families with Dependent Children (AFDC), 42 U.S.C.A. § 601 et seq.; Aid to the Blind (AB), 42 U.S.C.A. § 1201 et seq.; Aid for the Permanently and Totally Disabled (APTD), 42 U.S.C.A. § 1351 et seq.

[3] At the present time these factors are: OAA—100%; AB—95%; APTD—95%; and AFDC—75%. At the time this suit was instituted the AFDC percentage was 50%, but it was raised to 75% following a recent amendment of § 51–a. See n. 1, supra.

complaint, appellants also argued that any percentage reduction system violated § 402(a)(23) of the Social Security Act of 1935, as amended, 81 Stat. 898, 42 U.S.C.A. § 602(a)(23), which required each State to make certain cost of living adjustments to its standard of need.

The three-judge court rejected appellants' constitutional arguments, finding that the Texas system is neither racially discriminatory nor unconstitutionally arbitrary. The court did, however, accept the statutory claim that Texas' percentage reductions in the AFDC program violate the congressional command of § 402(a)(23). 304 F.Supp. 1332 (N.D. Tex.1969).

Subsequent to that judgment, this Court decided Rosado v. Wyman, 397 U.S. 397, 90 S.Ct. 1207, 25 L.Ed.2d 442 (1970). *Rosado* held that although § 402(a)(23) required States to make cost of living adjustments in their standard of need calculations, it did not prohibit use of percentage reduction systems which limited the amount of welfare assistance actually paid. 397 U.S., at 413, 90 S.Ct. at 1218. This Court then vacated and remanded the first *Jefferson* judgment for further proceedings consistent with *Rosado*. Jefferson v. Hackney, 397 U. S. 821, 90 S.Ct. 1517, 25 L.Ed.2d 807 (1970).

On remand, the District Court entered a new judgment, denying all relief. Then, in a motion to amend the judgment, appellants raised a new statutory claim. They argued for the first time that although a percentage reduction system may be consistent with the statute, the specific procedures which Texas uses for computing that reduction violate the congressional enactment. The District Court rejected this argument and denied without opinion appellants' motion to amend the judgment. This appeal under 28 U.S.C.A. § 1253 then followed, and we noted probable jurisdiction. 404 U. S. 820, 92 S.Ct. 115, 30 L.Ed.2d 47 (1971).

II

[handwritten margin note: whether = States' method of determining % figure is valid.]

Appellants' statutory argument relates to the method which the State uses to compute the percentage reduction when the recipient also has some outside income. Texas, like many other States,[4] first applies the percentage reduction factor to the recipient's standard of need, thus arriving at a reduced standard of need that the State can guarantee for each recipient within the present budgetary restraints. After computing this reduced standard of need, the State then subtracts any nonexempt[5] income in order to arrive at the level of benefits that the recipient needs in order to reach his reduced standard of need. This is the amount of welfare the recipient is given.

Under an alternative system used by other States, the order of computation is reversed. First, the outside income is subtracted from the standard of need, in order to determine the recipient's "un-

met need." Then, the percentage reduction factor is applied to the unmet need, in order to determine the welfare benefits payable.

The two systems of accounting for outside income yield somewhat different results.[6] Under the Texas system all welfare recipients with the same needs have the same amount of money available each month, whether or not they have outside income. Since the outside income is applied dollar for dollar to the reduced standard of need, which the welfare department would otherwise pay in full, it does not result in a net improvement in the financial position of the recipient. Under the alternative system, on the other hand, any welfare recipient who also has outside income is in a better financial position because of it. The reason is that the percentage reduction factor there is applied to the "unmet need," after the income has been subtracted. Thus, in effect, the income-earning recipient is able to "keep" all his income, while he receives only a percentage of the remainder of his standard of need.[7]

---

[4] Nineteen of the 26 States that use a percentage reduction system follow the Texas procedure of accounting for outside income. See Memorandum for the United States as Amicus Curiae 8, 15–16.

[5] A certain portion of earned income must be exempted as a work incentive. See 42 U.S.C.A. § 602(a)(8).

---

[6] Assuming two identical families, each with a standard of need of $200, and outside, nonexempt income of $100, the two systems would produce these results:

Texas System	*Alternative System*
$ 200 (need)	$ 200 (need)
× .75 (% reduction factor)	—100 (outside income)
$ 150 (reduced need)	$ 100 (unmet need)
—100 (outside income)	× 75 (% reduction factor)
$ 50 (benefits payable)	$ 75 (benefits payable)

[7] Assuming two families with identical standards of need, but only one with outside income, the alternative system leaves more money in the hands of the family with outside income:

Outside Income	*No Outside Income*
$ 200 (need)	$ 200 (need)
—100 (outside income)	— 0 (outside income)
$ 100 (unmet need)	$ 200 (unmet need)
× .75 (% reduction factor)	× .75 (% reduction factor)
$ 75 (benefits payable)	$ 150 (benefits payable)
TOTAL INCOME (outside income plus benefits payable = $175	TOTAL INCOME (outside income plus benefits payable) = $150

Each of the two systems has certain advantages. Appellants note that under the alternative system there is a financial incentive for welfare recipients to obtain outside income. The Texas computation method eliminates any such financial incentive, so long as the outside income remains less than the recipient's reduced standard of need.[8] However, since Texas' pool of available welfare funds is fixed, any increase in benefits paid to the working poor would have to be offset by reductions elsewhere. Thus, if Texas were to switch to the alternative system of recognizing outside income, it would be forced to lower its percentage reduction factor, in order to keep down its welfare budget. Lowering the percentage would result in less money for those who need the welfare benefits the most—those with no outside income—and the State has been unwilling to do this.

Striking the proper balance between these competing policy considerations is of course not the function of this Court. "There is no question that States have considerable latitude in allocating their AFDC resources, since each State is free to set its own standard of need and to determine the level of benefits by the amount of funds it devotes to the program." King v. Smith, 392 U.S. 309, 318–319, 88 S.Ct. 2128, 2134, 20 L.Ed. 2d 1118 (1968) (footnotes omitted).[9] So long as the State's actions are not in violation of any specific provision of the Constitution or the Social Security Act, appellants' policy arguments must be addressed to a different forum.

*   *   *

In Rosado v. Wyman, supra, the Court reviewed the history of this section and rejected the argument that it had worked any radical shift in the AFDC program. Id., 397 U.S. at 414 and n. 17, 90 S.Ct. at 1218.

*   *   *

Instead, the statute was meant to require the States to make cost of living adjustments to their standards of need, thereby serving "two broad purposes":

> "First, to require States to face up realistically to the magnitude of the public assistance requirement and lay bare the extent to which their programs fall short of fulfilling actual need; second, to prod the States to apportion their payments on a more equitable basis." Id., at 412–413, 90 S.Ct., at 1218.

Texas has complied with these two requirements. Effective May 1, 1969, the standard of need for AFDC recipients was raised 11% to reflect the rise in the cost of living, and the State shifted from a maximum grant system to its present percentage reduction system. In this way, the State has fairly recognized and exposed the precise level of unmet need, and by using a percentage reduction system it has attempted to apportion the State's limited benefits more equitably.

Although Texas has thus responded to the "two broad purposes" of § 402(a) (23), appellants argue that Congress also intended that statute to increase the total number of recipients of AFDC, so that more people would qualify for the subsidiary benefits which are dependent on receipt of AFDC cash assistance.[10] The

---

[8] Under the Texas system, once the income rises above the reduced standard of need the individual no longer receives any cash assistance. He then would have a financial incentive, since his income would be rising above the maximum he could expect from the welfare system.

[9] For a general review of the statutory scheme, see Rosado v. Wyman, 397 U.S., at 407–412, 90 S.Ct., at 1215–1218.

[10] Certain care and training provisions of the Social Security Act are available only to those who receive money payments under the categorical assistance programs. See 42 U.S.C.A. § 602(a)(14), (15); 42 U.S.C.A. §§ 602 (a)(19), 632; 42 U.S.C.A. § 1396a(a)(10). Under the Texas computation procedures, those whose income exceeds their reduced standard of need receive no cash benefits and

Texas computation procedures are thought objectionable since they do not increase the welfare rolls to quite the same extent as would the alternative method of recognizing outside income.

We do not agree that Congress intended § 402(a)(23) to invalidate any state computation procedures that do not absolutely maximize individual eligibility for subsidiary benefits. The cost of living increase that Congress mandated would, of course, generally tend to increase eligibility,[11] but there is nothing in the legislative history indicating that this was part of the statutory purpose.

* * *

III

We turn, then, to appellants' claim that the Texas system of percentage reductions violates the Fourteenth Amendment. Appellants believe that once the State has computed a standard of need for each recipient, it is arbitrary and discriminatory to provide only 75% of that standard to AFDC recipients, while paying 100% of recognized need to the aged, and 95% to the disabled and the blind. They argue that if the State adopts a percentage reduction system, it must apply the same percentage to each of its welfare programs.

This claim was properly rejected by the court below. It is clear from the

statutory framework that although the four categories of public assistance found in the Social Security Act have certain common elements, the States were intended by Congress to keep their AFDC plans separate from plans under the other titles of the Act.[15] A State is free to participate in one, several, or all of the categorical assistance programs, as it chooses. It is true that each of the programs is intended to assist the needy, but it does not follow that there is only one constitutionally permissible way for the State to approach this important goal.

This Court emphasized only recently, in Dandridge v. Williams, 397 U.S. 471, 485, 90 S.Ct. 1153, 1161, 25 L.Ed.2d 491 (1970), that in "the area of economics and social welfare, a State does not violate the Equal Protection Clause merely because the classifications made by its laws are imperfect." A legislature may address a problem "one step at a time," or even "select one phase of one field and apply a remedy there, neglecting the others." Williamson v. Lee Optical Co., 348 U.S. 483, 489, 75 S.Ct. 461, 465, 99 L.Ed. 563 (1955). So long as its judgments are rational, and not invidious, the legislature's efforts to tackle the problems of the poor and the needy are not subject to a constitutional straitjacket. The very complexity of the problems suggests that there will be more than one constitutionally permissible method of solving them.

The standard of judicial review is not altered because of appellants' unproven allegations of racial discrimination. The

thus do not qualify for these subsidiary benefits, although they do have "unmet need" qualifying them for aid under the alternative computation procedure.

[11] The Court in *Rosado* recognized this as one of several effects attributable to § 402 (a)(23). 397 U.S., at 413, 90 S.Ct. at 1218. See also id., at 409 n. 13, 90 S.Ct., at 1216. The Court did not, however, hold that each one of these effects was intended by Congress. In fact, the *Rosado* holding as to the "two broad purposes" of Congress was stated above, and the Texas system is perfectly consistent with it. The Court mentioned widened eligibility simply as one of several possible effects that *might* follow from the statute as so construed.

[15] Each categorical assistance program is embodied in a separate title of the Social Security Act, see n. 2, supra, and requires a state plan independent of the plans under the other titles. In 1962, however, Congress enacted 42 U.S.C.A. §§ 1381–1385, which for the first time enabled States to combine their plans, *but only for the non-AFDC programs.* Thus, while Congress has now enabled States to adopt a common plan for the other programs, it considered AFDC sufficiently different so as to require an independent plan.

three-judge court found that the "payment by Texas of a lesser percentage of unmet needs to the recipients of the AFDC than to the recipients of other welfare programs is not the result of racial or ethnic prejudice and is not violative of the federal Civil Rights Act or the Equal Protection Clause of the 14th Amendment." The District Court obviously gave careful consideration to this issue, and we are cited by its opinion to a number of subsidiary facts to support its principal finding quoted above. There has never been a reduction in the amount of money appropriated by the legislature to the AFDC program, and between 1943 and the date of the opinion below there had been five increases in the amount of money appropriated by the legislature for the program, two of them having occurred since 1959.[16] The overall percentage increase in appropriation for the programs between 1943 and the time of the District Court's hearing in this case was 410% for AFDC, as opposed to 211% for OAA and 200% for AB. The court further concluded:

"The depositions of Welfare officials conclusively establish that the defendants did not know the racial make-up of the various welfare assistance cate-

gories prior to or at the time when the orders here under attack were issued."

Appellants in their brief in effect abandon any effort to show that these findings of fact were clearly erroneous, and we hold they were not.

Appellants are thus left with their naked statistical argument: that there is a larger percentage of Negroes and Mexican-Americans in AFDC than in the other programs,[17] and that the AFDC is funded at 75% whereas the other programs are funded at 95% and 100% of recognized need. As the statistics cited in the footnote demonstrate, the number of minority members in all categories is substantial. The basic outlines of eligibility for the various categorical grants are established by Congress, not by the States; given the heterogeneity of the Nation's population, it would be only an infrequent coincidence that the racial composition of each grant class was identical to that of the others. The acceptance of appellants' constitutional theory would render suspect each difference in treatment among the grant classes, however lacking in racial motivation and however otherwise rational the treatment might be. Few legislative efforts to deal with the

---

[16] Since the original opinion below, there has been an additional increase. Following a constitutional amendment, see n. 3, supra, the appropriation has risen from $6,150,000 to $23,100,000.

---

[17]

Program	Year	Percentage of Negroes and Mexican-Americans	Percentage of White-Anglos	Number of Recipients
OAA	1969	39.8	60.2	
	1968	38.7	61.3	230,000
	1967	37.0	63.0	
APTD	1969	46.9	53.1	
	1968	45.6	54.4	4,213
	1967	46.2	53.8	
AB	1969	55.7	44.3	
	1968	54.9	45.1	14,043
AFDC	1969	87.0	13.0	
	1968	84.9	15.1	136,000
	1967	86.0	14.0	

difficult problems posed by current welfare programs could survive such scrutiny, and we do not find it required by the Fourteenth Amendment.[18]

Applying the traditional standard of review under that amendment, we cannot say that Texas' decision to provide somewhat lower welfare benefits for AFDC recipients is invidious or irrational. Since budgetary constraints do not allow the payment of the full standard of need for all welfare recipients, the State may have concluded that the aged and infirm are the least able of the categorical grant recipients to bear the hardships of an inadequate standard of living. While different policy judgments are of course possible, it is not irrational for the State to believe that the young are more adaptable than the sick and elderly, especially because the latter have less hope of improving their situation in the years remaining to them. Whether or not one agrees with this state determination, there is nothing in the Constitution which forbids it.[19]

no strict scrutiny of state program

[18] In James v. Valtierra, 402 U.S. 137, 91 S.Ct. 1331, 28 L.Ed.2d 678 (1971), it was contended that a California referendum requirement violated the Fourteenth Amendment because it imposed a mandatory referendum in the case of an ordinance authorizing low income housing, while referenda with respect to other types of ordinances had to be initiated by the action of private individuals. The Court responded:

"But of course a lawmaking procedure that 'disadvantages' a particular group does not always deny equal protection. Under any such holding, presumably a State would not be able to require referendums on any subject unless referendums were required on all, because they would always disadvantage some group. And this Court would be required to analyze governmental structures to determine whether a gubernatorial veto provision or a filibuster rule is likely to 'disadvantage' any of the diverse and shifting groups that make up the American people." 402 U.S., at 142, 91 S.Ct., at 1334.

[19] Just as the State's actions here do not violate the Fourteenth Amendment, we conclude that they do not violate Title VI of the Civil Rights Act of 1964, 42 U.S.C.A. § 2000d. The Civil Rights Act prohibits dis-

Dissent

Similarly, we cannot accept the argument in Mr. Justice MARSHALL'S dissent that the Social Security Act itself requires equal percentages for each categorical assistance program. The dissent concedes that a State might simply refuse to participate in the AFDC program, while continuing to receive federal money for the other categorical programs. See *post*, at p. 1746. Nevertheless, it is argued that Congress intended to prohibit any middle ground—once the State does participate in a program it must do so on the same basis as it participates in every other program. Such an all-or-nothing policy judgment may well be defensible, and the dissenters may be correct that nothing in the statute expressly rejects it. But neither does anything in the statute approve or require it.[20]

crimination in federally financed programs. We have, however, upheld the findings of nondiscriminatory purpose in the percentage reductions used by Texas, and have concluded that the variation in percentages is rationally related to the purposes of the separate welfare programs. The Court's decision in Griggs v. Duke Power Co., 401 U.S. 424, 91 S.Ct. 849, 28 L.Ed.2d 158 (1971), is therefore inapposite. In *Griggs*, the employment tests having racially discriminatory effects were found not to be job-related, and for that reason were impermissible under the specific language of Title VII of the Civil Rights Act. Since the Texas procedure challenged here *is* related to the purposes of the welfare programs, it is not proscribed by Title VI simply because of variances in the racial composition of the different categorical programs.

[20] The dissent cites the 1950 amendments to the Social Security Act as support for its novel statutory theory that States must provide equal aid levels in each welfare category. The 1950 amendments included "a revised method of determining the Federal share of assistance costs," 95 Cong.Rec. 13932, so that the Federal Government would pay a substantially equal percentage of matching funds to state plans in each of the categorical assistance programs. See S.Doc. No.208, 80th Cong., 2d Sess., 101. But this revision of the grant-in-aid formula in § 403 of the Act was not accompanied by any corresponding amendment of § 402, the section of the Act dealing with congressional limitations on state AFDC programs. Indeed,

In conclusion, we re-emphasize what the Court said in Dandridge v. Williams, 397 U.S., at 487, 90 S.Ct., at 1162–1163:

"We do not decide today that the [state law] is wise, that it best fulfills the relevant social and economic objectives that [the State] might ideally espouse, or that a more just and humane system could not be devised. Conflicting claims of morality and intelligence are raised by opponents and proponents of almost every measure, certainly including the one before us. But the intractable economic, social, and even philosophical problems presented by public welfare assistance programs are not the business of this Court. * * * [T]he Constitution does not empower this Court to second-guess state officials charged with the difficult responsibility of allocating limited public welfare funds among the myriad of potential recipients."

Affirmed.

Mr. Justice MARSHALL, with whom Mr. Justice BRENNAN joins; and Mr. Justice STEWART joins as to Part I only, dissenting. *strict scrutiny*

Appellants, recipients of Aid to Families with Dependent Children (AFDC) in Texas, brought this action to challenge two distinct aspects of the Texas AFDC program. First, appellants challenge the manner in which Texas arrives at the amount it will pay to persons who are needy. Second, they urge that Texas acts illegally in providing more money

proponents of the 1950 amendments explicitly recognized and endorsed the long-standing policy that the Federal Government sets only minimum AFDC standards, while leaving the States "wide discretion both in determining policies and in setting standards of need." S.Doc.No.208, supra, at 101. The enactment of a modified grant-in-aid formula hardly suggests Congress' intent to engage in "extensive alteration of the basic underlying structure of an established program." Rosado v. Wyman, 397 U.S., at 414 n. 17, 90 S.Ct., at 1219.

for persons receiving aid under other social welfare legislation than for persons receiving AFDC aid. The Court rejects both claims. I dissent.

[Statutory discussion of sections 402 (a)(23), 402(a)(10) and 402(a)(8) omitted]

* * *

II

Appellants also challenge the percentage reduction figure itself. It is agreed that Texas has established an identical standard of need for the four social welfare programs that it administers—Old Age Assistance (OAA), Aid to the Blind (AB), Aid for the Permanently and Totally Disabled (APTD), and AFDC. But Texas provides 100% of recognized need to the aged and 95% to the disabled and the blind while it provides only 75% to AFDC recipients. It is this disparity to which appellants object.

A. Appellants base their primary attack on the Fourteenth Amendment; they argue that the percentage distinctions between the other welfare programs and AFDC reflect a racially discriminatory motive on the part of Texas officials. Thus, they argue that there is a violation of the Equal Protection Clause. I believe that it is unnecessary to reach the constitutional issue which appellants raise, and therefore, I offer no opinion on its ultimate merits. I do wish to make it clear, however, that I do not subscribe in any way to the manner in which the Court treats the issue.

If I were to face this question, I would certainly have more difficulty with it than either the District Court did or than this Court seems to. The record contains numerous statements by state officials to the effect that AFDC is funded at a lower level than the other programs because it is not a politically popular program. There is also evidence of a stigma that seemingly attaches to AFDC recipients and no others. This Court noted in King v. Smith, 392 U.S., at 322, 88 S.Ct. at 2136, that AFDC recipients were often frowned upon by the community. The evidence also shows that 87% of the AFDC recipients in Texas are either Negro or Mexican-American. Yet, both the District Court and this Court have little difficulty in concluding that the fact that AFDC is politically unpopular and the fact that AFDC recipients are disfavored by the State and its citizens have nothing whatsoever to do with the racial makeup of the program. This conclusion is neither so apparent, nor so correct in my view.

Moreover, because I find that each one of the State's reasons for treating AFDC differently from the other programs dissolves under close scrutiny, as is demonstrated, infra, I am not at all certain who should bear the burden of proof on the question of racial discrimination. Nor am I sure that the "traditional" standard of review would govern the case as the Court holds. In Dandridge v. Williams, supra, on which the Court relies for the proposition that strict scrutiny of the State's action is not required, the Court never faced a question of possible racial discrimination. Percentages themselves are certainly not conclusive, but at some point a showing that state action has a devastating impact on the lives of minority racial groups must be relevant.

The Court reasons backwards to conclude that because appellants have not proved racial discrimination, a less strict standard of review is necessarily tolerated. In my view, the first question that must be asked is what is the standard of review and the second question is whether racial discrimination has been proved under the standard. It seems almost too plain for argument that the standard of review determines in large measure whether or not something has been proved. Whitcomb v. Chavis, 403 U.S. 124, 149, 91 S.Ct. 1858, 1872, 29 L.Ed.

2d 363 (1971); Gomillion v. Lightfoot, 364 U.S. 339, 81 S.Ct. 125, 5 L.Ed.2d 110 (1960).

These are all complex problems, and I do not propose to resolve any of them here. It is sufficient for me to note that I believe that the constitutional issue raised by appellants need not be reached, and that in choosing to reach it, the Court has so greatly oversimplified the issue as to distort it.

B. Appellants also challenge the distinction between programs under Title VI of the 1964 Civil Rights Act, 42 U.S. C.A. § 2000d:

"No person in the United States shall, on the ground of race, color, or national origin, * * * be subjected to discrimination under any program or activity receiving Federal financial assistance."

Only last Term in Griggs v. Duke Power Co., 401 U.S. 424, 91 S.Ct. 849, 28 L. Ed.2d 158 (1971), we had occasion to strike down under Title VII of the 1964 Act, 42 U.S.C.A. § 2000e, employment practices that had a particularly harsh impact on one minority racial group and that could not be justified by business necessity. We indicated in that case that "good intent or absence of discriminating intent does not redeem employment procedures or testing mechanisms that operate as 'built-in headwinds' for minority groups." Id., at 432, 91 S.Ct., at 854. We said, in fact, that "Congress directed the thrust of the Act to the *consequences* of employment practices, not simply the motivation." Ibid. (emphasis in original). That decision even placed the burden on the employer "of showing that any given requirement must have a manifest relationship to the employment in question." Ibid.

There has been a paucity of litigation under Title VI, and I am not prepared at this point to say whether or not a similar analysis to that used in *Griggs* should be used in Title VI cases. This is a question of first impression in this Court, and I do not think we have to reach it in this case. I include this section only to make plain that I do not necessarily reject the argument made by appellants; I simply do not reach it.

C. This brings me to what I believe disposes of the question presented: the disparity between the various social welfare programs is not permissible under the federal statutory framework.

The four social welfare programs offered by Texas are funded in part by the Federal Government. Each program is governed by a separate statute: OAA, 42 U.S.C.A. § 301 et seq.; AFDC, 42 U.S.C.A. § 601 et seq.; AB, 42 U.S.C.A. § 1201 et seq.; APTD, 42 U.S.C.A. § 1351 et seq. No State is compelled to participate in any program, and any State that wants to participate can choose to do so in one, several, or all of the programs.

There is no doubt that States are free to choose whether or not to participate in these programs, and it is also clear that each State has considerable freedom to allocate what it wants to one or more programs by establishing different standards of need to compute eligibility for aid. King v. Smith, 392 U.S., at 318–319, 88 S.Ct., at 2133–2134. It is also true, however, that the basic aims of the four programs are identical. Indeed, when Congress first enacted the programs in 1935, it viewed them all as necessary to provide aid to families unable to obtain income from private employment. The beneficiaries of the various programs shared the basic characteristics of need and dependence. H.R.Rep. No. 615, 74th Cong., 1st Sess., 3. While the programs as they now exist go well beyond merely furnishing financial assistance as they did originally they still maintain similar goals.

Moreover, all four programs were simultaneously amended in 1956 to provide for social and rehabilitative services to enable all needy individuals to attain the maximum economic and personal independence of which they were capable. Each program now requires a State to describe in its plan for each social welfare program it administers the services it offers to accomplish this objective. See 42 U.S.C.A. §§ 302(a)(11); 602(a)(14); 1202(a)(12); 1352(a)(11).

Congress has given the States authority to set different standards of need for different programs. But where, as here, the State concludes that the standard of need is the same for recipients of aid under the four distinct statutes, it is my opinion that Congress required that the State treat all recipients equally with respect to actual aid. In other words, as I read the federal statutes, they are designed to accomplish the same objectives, albeit for persons disadvantaged by different circumstances.

States clearly have the freedom to make a bona fide determination that blind persons have a greater need than dependent children, that adults have a higher standard of need than children, that the aged have more need than the blind, and so forth.

But, in this case, Texas made an independent determination of need, and it determined that the need of all recipients was equal. In this circumstance, I find nothing in the federal statute to enable a State to favor one group of recipients by satisfying more of its need, while at the same time denying an equally great need of another group. The purposes and objectives of the statutes are the same, those eligible for aid are suffering equally, and Congress intended that once a State chose to participate in the programs similarly situated persons would be treated similarly.

Everything in this record indicates that the recipients of the various forms of aid are identically situated. Although the District Court accepted the State's contentions that there are differences between AFDC and other recipients which warranted different treatment under the federal statutes, I find each of the reasons offered totally unpersuasive.

First, Texas argues that AFDC children can be employed, whereas recipients of other benefits cannot be. Assuming *arguendo* that this is true, it is an argument that falls of its own weight. Whatever income the children earn is subtracted from need, or it is excluded from consideration under § 402(a)(8) to encourage self-help. Thus, income is already reflected in the computation of payments, or it is excluded in order that a specific legislative goal may be furthered. Thus, income is irrelevant in any explanation of the differences between the percentage reductions applied to the various programs. It should also be noted that a recipient's income is also taken into consideration in programs other than AFDC. See 42 U.S.C.A. §§ 302(a)(10)(A); 1202(a)(8); 1352(a)(8).

Second, the State maintains that AFDC families can secure help from legally responsible relatives more easily than recipients under other programs. Assuming again for purposes of discussion that this is true, it should be plain that any support from any relatives is subtracted from the State's grant. Moreover, appellants properly point out that recipients of aid in non-AFDC programs often have a source of aid unavailable to AFDC recipients—the federal old age insurance, 42 U.S.C.A. § 201 et seq. Thus, there is no substance to this argument.

Third, Texas points to the likelihood of future employment for AFDC recipients, a likelihood that it says is nonexistent for older persons and others who receive aid. Federal law provides that a State may only consider income that is currently available in allocating funds. 45 CFR § 233.20(a)(3)(ii). This contention is therefore irrelevant.

The State makes only two other arguments. One has already been rejected. Texas urges that the purposes of the federal programs differ, but the history belies this contention. The other is that the numbers of AFDC recipients is rising and this program should therefore bear the burden of monetary limitations. The obvious problem with this argument is that one fundamental purpose of AFDC aid is to enable people to escape the welfare rolls. But, under the Texas system, the aid is presently insufficient, people are unable to escape from dependency, and the rolls became larger. Had Texas not funded AFDC at a lower level than other programs, it is possible that the number of recipients would not have grown so large. The State's argument is a self-fulfilling prophecy on which it cannot rely to penalize AFDC recipients. Furthermore, there is nothing in the federal legislation to indicate that aid is to be reduced in a program merely because the number of beneficiaries of that program increases at a more rapid rate than in other programs. On the contrary Congress has indicated that increased eligibility for AFDC is desirable, see 42 U.S.C.A. § 602(a)(23); Rosado v. Wyman, supra. It would be extreme irony if AFDC recipients were penalized by a State because their numbers grew in accordance with congressional intent.

The conclusion that I draw from the statutes is that Congress intended equal treatment for all persons similarly situated. Congress left to the States the determination of who was similarly situated by permitting States to determine levels of need. Since Texas has decided that AFDC recipients have precisely the same need as recipients of other social welfare benefits, it is my opinion that the federal legislation requires equal treatment for all.

This conclusion finds support in the legislative history of the 1950 amendments to the social welfare legislation. In those amendments Congress made clear its intent to put AFDC recipients on a par with recipients of other welfare aid.

> "Today more than 1.1 million children under 18 years of age are receiving aid to dependent children through the State-Federal program because one or both of their parents are dead, absent from the home, or incapacitated. These children, regardless of the State in which they now live, will someday find their place in the productive activities of our Nation. Many of these children will be seriously handicapped as adults because in childhood they are not receiving proper and sufficient food, clothing, medical attention, and the other bare necessities of life. The national interest requires that the Federal Government provide for dependent children *at least on a par* with its contributions toward the support of the needy aged and blind." S.Doc.No. 208, 80th Cong., 2d Sess., 105 (emphasis added).

Congress recognized that "families with dependent children need as much in assistance payments as do aged and blind persons." Id., at 106. It concluded that sound national policy was "for the States to provide payments for aid to dependent children comparable to those for the needy aged and blind." Ibid. It is evident that Congress rejected the notion that where AFDC recipients had the same need as other welfare beneficiaries, they should get less money. As Senator Benton said on the floor of the Senate:

> "There seems no reasonable basis for such inequitable treatment of mothers and of children by the Federal Government.

> "All of us with children know that it costs as much if not more to rear children in health, decency, and self-respect than to maintain an adult. It is surely no less important to make

this investment in our future citizens than it is to provide decently for those who have retired. * * *" 96 Cong.Rec., 8813–8814.

In the 1950 amendments, Congress increased the federal funding of AFDC so that its beneficiaries would receive treatment equivalent to that received by beneficiaries of the other federal-state social welfare legislation. Where the needs of the people receiving aid under the various programs differed, Congress recognized that the amount of aid forthcoming should also differ. But, where need was determined by the State to be equal for all recipients, Congress intended that all should receive an equal amount of aid. S.Doc.No.208, 80th Cong., 2d Sess., 108. There is absolutely no indication in any subsequent congressional action that the intent of Congress has changed.

Accordingly, I would reverse the judgment of the District Court and remand the case for formulation of relief consistent with this opinion.

[Dissenting opinion of Mr. Justice DOUGLAS, concurred in by Mr. Justice BRENNAN, omitted.]

Note on Statewideness Requirements

Another group of provisions of the Social Security Act which acts as a constraint on state discretion in establishing categorical assistance programs are Sections 402(a)(1) and 402(a)(3), 42 U.S.C.A. §§ 602(a)(1), 602(a)(3), which fix certain requirements of statewideness under the AFDC program. Analogous provisions exist in the other Federal categorical programs.

In Boddie v. Wyman, 434 F.2d 1207 (2d Cir. 1970), aff'd mem., 402 U.S. 991 (1971), recipients in upstate counties in New York successfully challenged provisions in the state AFDC program which establish differential standards of need and levels of payment between them and residents of the New York City area. They prevailed on the following argument, quoted from Brief for Appellees in the Court of Appeals:

"Titles IV and XVI of the Social Security Act require, in identical language, that a state plan for Aid to Families with Dependent Children or for Aid to the Aged, Blind or Disabled must

'provide that it shall be in effect in all political subdivisions of the State, and, if administered by them, be mandatory upon them.' §§ 402(a) (1) and 1602(a)(1) of the Act, 42 U.S.C.A. §§ 602(a)(1) and 1382 (a)(1).

This requirement of statewide operation of public assistance plans is buttressed by the further requirements that there be state financial participation in such plans, §§ 402(a)(2) and 1602 (a)(2) of the Act, 42 U.S.C.A. §§ 602(a)(2) and 1382(a)(2), and that there be a single state agency either to administer such plans or to supervise their administration, §§ 402(a)(3) and 1602(a)(3) of the Act, 42 U.S. C.A. §§ 602(a)(3) and 1382(a)(3).

"The concrete meaning of statewideness in public assistance administration can best be demonstrated in light of a consideration of the historical backdrop to and the legislative history of the entry of the federal government into the public assistance field. This consideration ultimately leads to the conclusion that the statewideness requirements mean that intrastate differences in the public assistance standard of need and amount of benefits based on the place of residence of the recipients must represent only differences, objectively determined, in the cost of those items for which the standard of need is intended to provide. As we shall explain below,

appellants have not complied with these requirements.

"Prior to the assumption by the federal government in 1935 of primary responsibility in the field of public assistance, public aid to the poor was a matter entirely of state and local concern. The implications of this fact in terms of unequal treatment of equally needy individuals within a state formed an important part of the legislative context in which the Social Security Act of 1935 was enacted. One of the primary purposes of federal involvement in public assistance was the elimination of the discretionary power of local officials that had frequently resulted in irrational intrastate differences in amounts of assistance paid to equally needy individuals. Families within each state were often subjected to totally arbitrary variances in providing for their basic needs, from some amount to zero, depending on the local county's disposition to provide budgetary allocations for the poor. Serious inequities thus resulted whereby families in entirely similar situations were provided drastically different allowances.

* * *

"It was in light of this fact of gross intrastate inequalities in public assistance payment levels that the President proposed and Congress enacted the requirements of statewide operation, state financial participation, and a single state administrative agency as conditions for the receipt of federal funds for public assistance under the Social Security Act. Of all provisions of the Act, these three have been characterized as having had 'the greatest effect upon the organization and administration of public welfare agencies in the states.' Brown, Public Relief, 1929 to 1939, 350 (1940). When the program of Aid to the Permanently and Totally Disabled was added to the Act in 1950,

P.L. 734, 81st Cong., 64 Stat. 477 (1950), and when the combined program of Aid to the Aged, Blind, or Disabled was enacted in 1962, P.L. 87–534, 76 Stat. 172 (1962), the three statewideness requirements were inserted in those titles as well.

"It was established at the outset of administration of the Act that the statewideness requirements mandate statewide uniformity in standards of assistance. Rejecting the argument that the requirement of statewide operation did not imply uniform statewide standards,

'[t]he [Social Security] Board [predecessor of the Department of Health, Education and Welfare] point[ed] out that uniform standards did not mean uniform payments, if the cost of living varied throughout the state, but only that persons with the same resources and needs should be treated the same. Actually, it was demonstrated in the course of time that the wide variations in payment within a state bore little relationship to variations in the cost of living. In fact, it was discovered that with the exception of rent, the variation in the cost of living was surprisingly small throughout a state, even between rural and urban areas.' Altmeyer, *The Formative Years of Social Security* 81 (1968).

"Treating alike 'persons with the same resources and needs' implies that the same needs will be met as to such persons throughout the state; that the budgetary components that comprise a public assistance grant will be the same in each case; and that differences in grant levels * are permissible only to

reflect differences, objectively determined, in the cost of the component items that comprise the public assistance grant."

B. RECOVERY OF RECIPIENTS' OTHER RESOURCES

PHILPOTT v. ESSEX COUNTY WELFARE BOARD

Supreme Court of the United States, 1973. 409 U.S. 413, 93 S.Ct. 590, 34 L.Ed.2d 608.

Mr. Justice DOUGLAS delivered the opinion of the Court.

Wilkes,[1] one of the petitioners, applied to respondent, one of New Jersey's welfare agencies, for financial assistance based upon need by reason of permanent and total disability. As a condition of receiving assistance, a recipient is required by New Jersey law to execute an agreement to reimburse the county welfare board for all payments received thereunder.[2] The purpose apparently is to enable

the Court the fact that should appellants determine that they are unwilling or unable to meet need in full on the basis of a statewide standard, any adjustments made in payment level must be accomplished 'by methods applied uniformly statewide.' 45 C.F.R. § 233.20(a)(3)(viii). Cf. Rosado v. Wyman, supra.

[1] The payment in controversy is in a bank account under the name of petitioner Philpott in trust for Wilkes.

[2] N.J.S.A. 44:7–14(a) provides: "Every county welfare board shall require, as a condition to granting assistance in any case, that all or any part of the property, either real or personal, of a person applying for old age assistance, be pledged to said county welfare board as a guaranty for the reimbursement of the funds so granted as old age assistance pursuant to the provisions of this chapter. The county welfare board shall take from each applicant a properly acknowledged agreement to reimburse for all advances granted, and pursuant to such agreement, said applicant shall assign to the welfare board, as collateral security for such advances, all or

---

* Since New York currently purports to be meeting 100 per cent of need, the theoretical distinction between the standard of need and the actual grant level has no practical effect. However, we call to the attention of

the Board to obtain reimbursement out of subsequently discovered or acquired real and personal property of the recipient.

Wilkes applied to respondent for such assistance in 1966 and he executed the required agreement. Respondent determined Wilkes' monthly maintenance needs to be $108; and finding that he had no other income, respondent fixed the monthly benefits at that amount and began making assistance payments, no later than January 1, 1967. The payments would have been less, if Wilkes were receiving federal disability insurance benefits under the Social Security Act and respondent advised him to apply for those federal benefits.

In 1968 Wilkes was awarded retroactive disability insurance benefits under the Social Security Act, 42 U.S. 423, covering the period from May 1966 into the summer of 1968. Those benefits, calculated on the basis of $69.60 per month, for 20 months and $78.20 per month for six months, amounted to $1,864.20. A check in that amount was deposited in the account which Philpott holds as trustee for Wilkes. Under New Jersey law, we are told, the filing of a notice of such a reimbursement agreement has the same force and effect as a judgment. 59 N.J. 75, 80, 279 A.2d 806.

Respondent sued to reach the bank account under the agreement to reimburse. The trial court held that respondent was barred by the Social Security Act, 42 U. S.C.A. § 407, from recovering any amount from the account.[3] 104 N.J.

Super. 280, 249 A.2d 639. The Appellate Division affirmed. 109 N.J.Super. 48, 262 A.2d 227. The Supreme Court reversed.[4] 59 N.J. 75, 279 A.2d 806. The case is here on a petition for a writ of certiorari which we granted.

On its face the Social Security Act in § 407 bars the State of New Jersey from reaching the federal disability payments paid to Wilkes. The language is all inclusive [5]—"none of the moneys paid or payable under this subchapter shall be subject to execution, levy, attachment, garnishment, or other legal process." The moneys paid as retroactive benefits were "moneys paid * * * under this subchapter"; and the suit brought was an attempt to subject the money to "levy, attachment * * * or other legal process."

New Jersey argues that if the amount of social security benefits received from the Federal Government had been made monthly, the amount of state welfare benefits could have been reduced by the amount of the federal grant. We see no reason to base an implied exemption from § 407 on that ground. We see no reason why a State, performing its statutory duty to take care of the needy, should be in a preferred position as compared with any other creditor. Indeed, since the Federal Government provides one-half of the funds for assistance under the New Jersey program of disability relief, the State concededly, on recovery of any sums by way of reimbursement, would have to account to the Federal Government for the latter's share.

---

part of his personal property as the board shall specify."

[3] 42 U.S.C.A. § 407 provides:
"The right of any person to any future payment under this subchapter shall not be transferable or assignable, at law or in equity, and none of the moneys paid or payable or rights existing under this subchapter shall be subject to execution, levy, attachment, garnishment, or other legal process, or to the operation of any bankruptcy or insolvency law."

[4] Since respondent did not claim a right to the entire federal payment but only to the amount by which its own payments would have been reduced had the federal benefits been received currently rather than retroactively and because the stipulated facts were ambiguous as to when respondent actually began making assistance payments, the court remanded for a determination of the precise amount of respondent's claim.

[5] Supra, n. 3.

The protection afforded by § 407 is to "moneys paid" and we think the analogy to veterans' benefits exemptions which we reviewed in Porter v. Aetna Casualty Co., 370 U.S. 159 is relevant here. We held in that case that veterans' benefits deposited in a savings and loan association on behalf of a veteran retained the "quality of moneys" and had not become a permanent investment. Id., at 101.

In the present case, as in *Porter,* the funds on deposit were readily withdrawable and retained the quality of "moneys" within the purview of § 407. The Supreme Court of New Jersey referred to cases [6] where a State which has provided care and maintenance to an incompetent veteran at times is a "creditor" for purposes of 38 U.S.C.A. § 3101 and at other times is not. But § 407 does not refer to any "claim of creditors" but imposes a broad bar against the use of any legal process to reach all social security benefits. That is broad enough to include all claimants, including a State.

The New Jersey court also relied on 42 U.S.C.A. § 404, a provision of the Social Security Act which permits the Secretary to recover overpayments of old age, survivors, or disability insurance benefits. But there has been no overpayment of federal disability benefits here and the Secretary is not seeking any recovery here. And the Solicitor General, speaking for the Secretary, concedes that the pecuniary interest of the United States in the outcome of this case, which would be its aliquot share of any recovery, is not within the ambit of § 404.

By reason of the Supremacy Clause the judgment below is

Reversed.

[6] See Savoid v. District of Columbia, 110 U.S.App.D.C. 39, 288 F.2d 851; District of Columbia v. Reilly, 102 U.S.App.D.C. 9, 249 F.2d 524. See decision at 59 N.J. 75, 85, 279 A.2d 806.

Notes

1. Is there any more general theory on which to challenge or limit state recoveries from resources acquired by recipients? In Snell v. Wyman, 281 F. Supp. 853 (S.D.N.Y.1968), the plaintiffs brought a broad challenge to New York's recovery rules based on a variety of constitutional theories. Under these rules New York welfare officials had the right to attach the proceeds of a tort claim recovered on by a recipient and the right to attach the proceeds of insurance recoveries by a recipient, as well as the right to take all other kinds of personal or real property obtained by a recipient. This right was not, however, used to recover the proceeds of earnings of the recipient. The majority of a three-judge court, per Judge Frankel, dismissed all the due process, equal protection and supremacy clause claims out of hand. Judge Kaufman dissenting, however, thought that the manner in which harsh recovery rules limited an individual's ability to achieve personal independence caused the rules to conflict with constitutionally protected "liberty" under the Fourteenth Amendment. Do constitutional developments since 1968 make this dissenting argument more or less likely of success today?

2. One limitation on the power of a state to make recoveries in federally supported programs is suggested by Cooper v. Laupheimer, 316 F.Supp. 264 (E.D. Pa.1970). There a Pennsylvania regulation provided for reduction of current grant payments to recover prior overpayments or duplicate payments. The regulation was struck down as

> repugnant to the provisions of the [Social Security] Act in its total disregard of the concept of need. Congress established only two prerequisites for eligibility: need and dependency. The Pennsylvania regulation must be measured against these criteria, even though it deals with reduction of aid rather

than conditions of eligibility, because it was the intent of Congress that need and dependency be the only two conditions restricting receipt of AFDC grants. * * * The Pennsylvania regulation ignores the Department's own prior determination that the family is in need and that a specified amount of semi-monthly aid must be provided to meet those needs. 316 F. Supp. at 269.

Accord, Evans v. Department of Social Services, 22 Mich.App. 633, 178 N.W.2d 173 (Ct.App.1970) (similar attempted recovery of fraudulently obtained payments barred). This reasoning you will recognize as another version of the § 402 (a)(10)—§ 406 reasoning employed in King v. Smith, supra, and Townsend v. Swank, supra. How could a state ever recover overpayments or fraudulently obtained payments without running afoul of the *Cooper* and *Evans* reasoning?

Problems

1. The overpayment problem is addressed directly in the new SSI program. Section 1631(b), 42 U.S.C.A. § 1383 (b), provides that overpayments are to be recovered "by appropriate adjustments in future payments" to the recipient. It also calls for appropriate provision to be made to "avoid penalizing [a recipient] who was without fault." Assume you represent an SSI recipient who has received overpayments because he neglected to promptly advise of a supplemental source of income, but who now has nothing other than his SSI grant on which to subsist. Is there any basis for him to lawfully resist an attempt to obtain recoupment out of his current grants?

2. A provision in the new SSI programs imposes money penalties on recipients for failure or delays without good cause in reporting "changes in circum-

stances relevant to eligibility." The penalty is $25 for the first offense and increases to $100 for the third and subsequent offense. See § 1631(e)(2), 42 U.S.C.A. § 1383(e)(2), in appendix. What sense does it make to use money penalties as a remedy imposed on persons who are, by definition, on the brink of subsistence? Are such penalties vulnerable to constitutional attack?

C. RELATIVE RESPONSIBILITY

Introductory Note on Relative Responsibility

Among the "resources" which a welfare department may deem available to an applicant for public assistance are the obligations of support owed him by a more or less extended net of related persons. The existence of these obligations may affect the welfare department's operations and the applicant's benefits in a variety of ways. Very commonly the welfare department will seek to enforce these obligations itself either to recover payments which it has made or to compel direct support of the applicant by the obligated relative. When a department seeks to mobilize such resources for the support of the applicant, problems involving the applicant's participation often arise. How broad is the applicant's duty to "cooperate" with the department in securing these resources? Can the local welfare department terminate assistance simply because of the applicant's refusal to pursue related parties with the requisite aggressiveness? Another possible solution to the problem might be for the department simply to assume that these support obligations are being fulfilled, whatever the reality. Though few would advocate so sweeping a disregard of an applicant's actual situation, many smaller questions involving assumptions and burdens of proof may be resolved in favor of departmental economy.

Departmental reliance upon support obligations raises major issues of distributive justice and efficacy in public assistance administration. Though consanguinity has been traditionally recognized as an acceptable basis for the allocation of support costs, that criterion is markedly discordant with the ability-to-pay notions which determine so much of the modern allocation of public costs. Particularly where an extended net of liable relatives is recognized under state law, the wisdom of departing from the normal general-revenue tax base may be questioned. Indeed, even where one is dealing with the relation of father to son, one finds the reports replete with cases in which the biological nexus is paralleled by no ties of familiarity, affection or support,— cases which raise grave doubt as to the ultimate significance of simple blood relationship for the problems at hand.

Moreover, whatever the conclusions one may reach on such matters, one must contend with the fact that reluctance to precipitate enforcement of support obligations causes many applicants to refrain from seeking public assistance. The aversion to trenching upon the already stretched resources of another household has caused many, particularly among the elderly, to prefer private penury to public assistance. Whatever the gain derived from reliance upon support obligations, its cost is some degree of frustration of the central purpose of public assistance.

DEPARTMENT OF MENTAL HYGIENE v. KIRCHNER

Supreme Court of California, In Bank, 1964. 60 Cal.2d 716, 36 Cal.Rptr. 488, 388 P.2d 720.

SCHAUER, Justice. Defendant administratrix appeals from a judgment on the pleadings, in the sum of $7,554.22, entered against her in an action by the

Department of Mental Hygiene of the State of California to recover the alleged cost of care, support, maintenance and medical attention supplied to Auguste Schaeche, mother of defendant's intestate, as a committed inmate of a state institution for the mentally ill. As will appear we have concluded that the statute upon which the judgment is based violates the basic constitutional guaranty of equal protection of the law, and that the judgment should be reversed.

Plaintiff in its complaint alleges in substance that in January 1953 the mother, Mrs. Schaeche, was adjudged mentally ill and by the court committed to Agnews [2] State Hospital where she had remained under confinement to the date the complaint was filed in April 1961; that the decedent, Ellinor Vance, was Mrs. Schaeche's daughter "and as such was legally responsible" for her committed mother's care and maintenance at Agnews; that pursuant to section 6651 [3] of the Welfare and Institutions Code the Director of Mental Hygiene determined the rate for such care and maintenance, and "said charges were made continuously for every month" Mrs. Schaeche was a "patient" at Agnews; that for the period of August 25, 1956, through August 24, 1960, such charges totaled $7,554.22, none of which had been paid; that the daughter died on August 25, 1960, and in November 1960 plaintiff filed against the daughter's estate its creditor's claim

[2] Welfare and Institutions Code section 6500: "There are in the State the following state hospitals for the care and treatment of the insane, the mentally ill, and the mentally disordered: * * * 3. Agnews State Hospital near the City of San Jose. * * *"

[3] Welfare and Institutions Code section 6651: "The rate for the care, support, and maintenance of all mentally ill persons and inebriates at the state hospitals * * * where there is liability to pay * * * shall be reviewed each fiscal year and fixed at the statewide average per capita * * * as determined by the Director of Mental Hygiene. * * *"

for $7,554.22, which was rejected, and which sum plaintiff now seeks to recover.

Defendant in her answer denies that her intestate, the daughter, "was legally responsible" for the mother's care and maintenance furnished by the state at Agnews "or any other place whatsoever"; denies any indebtedness to plaintiff; and furthermore alleges that the incompetent mother herself owns (in her guardianship estate) some $11,000 in cash, to which resort should first be had before attempt is made by the state to charge her children with the costs of her care. More specifically, defendant directly challenges the right of a state to statutorily impose [4] liability upon, and collect from, one adult for the cost of supporting another adult whom the state has committed to one of its hospitals for the mentally ill or insane. Both parties moved for judgment on the pleadings, the court granted plaintiff's motion and denied that of defend-

ant, and from the ensuing judgment defendant appeals.

In support of the judgment plaintiff department relies upon the declaration in section 6650 of the Welfare and Institutions Code that "The husband, wife, father, mother, or *children* of a mentally ill person or inebriate * * * shall be liable for his care, support, and maintenance in a state institution of which he is an inmate. * * *" (Italics added.)

The department, citing Guardianship of Thrasher (1951) 105 Cal.App.2d 768, 234 P.2d 230, and Dept. of Mental Hygiene v. Black (1961) 198 Cal.App.2d 627, 18 Cal.Rptr. 78, asserts flatly that the liability purportedly imposed by section 6650 upon the persons therein designated is not only, in the language of the section, "a joint and several liability," but is absolute and unconditional, and that "the fact that the patient has assets of her own becomes completely immaterial." In Thrasher it was held (pp. 776–778 [3–8] of 105 Cal.App.2d, pp. 235–236 of 234 P.2d) that the husband of an incompetent committed to a state mental hospital was under the duty to support her therein even though she had estate of her own. That case is of small help to plaintiff here; manifestly, the basic obligation and relevant status of the *husband* arose from the marriage contract to which he was a consenting party and no consideration was given to the question as to whether imposing liability upon one spouse for support of the other in a state institution denies equal protection of the law to the servient spouse. (See also Estate of Risse (1957) 156 Cal.App. 2d 412, 421 [7], 319 P.2d 789). However, in Black the court held the mother of a mentally ill person to be liable for the cost of the latter's support in a state hospital, with the declaration (p. 632 [2] of 198 Cal.App.2d, p. 81 of 18 Cal. Rptr.) that by reason of the provisions of section 6650 there was no merit to the

---

[4] *Historical Background:*

At common law there was no liability on a child to support parents, or on parents to support an adult child. (See, e. g., County of Los Angeles v. Frisbie (1942) 19 Cal.2d 634, 645–646 [11], 122 P.2d 526; Duffy v. Yordi (1906) 149 Cal. 140, 141–142, 84 P. 838, 4 L.R.A.,N.S., 1159 ("at common law there was no legal obligation on the part of the child to [support a parent] * * * such obligation depends entirely upon statutory provisions"); Napa State Hospital v. Flaherty (1901) 134 Cal. 315, 316–317, 66 P. 322, 323 ("The right to maintain any action against the father for the support of an adult child, if any such right exists, is purely a creation of the statute. No such right existed at common law"); 44 C.J.S. Insane Persons §§ 73–75, pp. 175, fn. 79; 176, fn. 81; 183 fn. 79; 67 C.J.S. Parent and Child §§ 17, 24, pp. 704–705, 727–728; 39 Am.Jur., pp. 710–712; 41 Am.Jur., pp. 684–687.) We recognize that various states have undertaken from time to time to create an obligation upon children to support indigent parents and upon parents to support indigent adult children; some states have even purported to create and impose a support obligation on brothers and sisters and on grandparents and grandchildren. (See 41 Am.Jur., pp. 684–686, §§ 6–7; 67 C.J.S. Parent and Child §§ 17, 24, pp. 705, 728.)

contention "that the personal assets of the incompetent patient must first be exhausted before liability is imposed on responsible relatives." (See also County of Lake v. Forbes (1941) 42 Cal.App.2d 744, 747 [3, 5], 109 P.2d 972, and Janes v. Edwards (1935) 4 Cal.App.2d 611, 612, 41 P.2d 370, involving other and different statutes.) We proceed to the fundamental issue tendered by the case before us.

Recently in Department of Mental Hygiene v. Hawley (1963) 59 Cal.2d 247, 28 Cal.Rptr. 718, 379 P.2d 22, the department, relying upon this same section 6650, attempted to collect from a father for the cost of care, support and maintenance in a state hospital for the mentally ill or insane of his son who had been charged with crime, but before trial of the criminal issue (and obviously without adjudication of that issue) had been found by the court to be insane and committed to such state hospital. We there held (pp. 255–256 [6] of 59 Cal.2d, p. 723 of 28 Cal.Rptr., p. 27 of 379 P.2d) that "The enactment and administration of laws providing for sequestration and treatment of persons in appropriate state institutions—subject of course, to the constitutional guaranties—who would endanger themselves or others if at large is a proper state function; being so, it follows that the expense of providing, operating and maintaining such institutions should (subject to reasonable exceptions against the inmate or his estate) be borne by the state." (Italics added.) We further held that recovery could not constitutionally be had against the father of the committed patient. The holding is dispositive of the issue before us. Whether the commitment is incidental to an alleged violation of a penal statute, as in Hawley, or is essentially a civil commitment as in the instant case, the purposes of confinement and treatment or care in either case encompass the protection of society from the confined person, and his own protec-

tion and possible reclamation as a productive member of the body politic. Hence the cost of maintaining the state institution, including provision of adequate care for its inmates, cannot be arbitrarily charged to one class in the society; such assessment violates the equal protection clause.

Although numerous cases can be cited wherein so-called support statutes have been sustained against various attacks, research has disclosed no case which squarely faced, considered, discussed and sustained such statutes in the light of the basic question as to equal protection of the law in a case wherein it was sought to impose liability upon one person for the support of another in a state institution. No such constitutional issue appears to have received either consideration or documented resolution in Dept. of Mental Hygiene v. McGilvery (1958) supra, 50 Cal.2d 742, 329 P.2d 689 (see pp. 754–761, esp. p. 760 [22], 329 P.2d pp. 694–699, esp. p. 699 wherein in this respect it is commented merely that "the present claim of unlawful classification may not properly be sustained"); neither is there any mention of either the United States or the California Constitutions in Department of Mental Hygiene v. Shane (1956) 142 Cal.App.2d Supp. 881, 299 P.2d 747, relied on in McGilvery with the statement (p. 752 [6] of 50 Cal.2d, p. 693 of 329 P.2d), "The present case cannot be distinguished from that case." It is axiomatic that cases are not authority for propositions not considered (McDowell and Craig v. City of Santa Fe Springs (1960) 54 Cal.2d 33, 38 [5], 4 Cal.Rptr. 176, 351 P.2d 344; Maguire v. Hibernia S. & L. Soc. (1944) 23 Cal. 2d 719, 730 [4], 146 P.2d 673, 151 A.L.R. 1062), and the Shane case obviously does not give substance to McGilvery on the subject constitutional issue.

We note that in Hoeper v. Tax Commission (1931) 284 U.S. 206, p. 217,

52 S.Ct. 120, p. 122, 76 L.Ed. 248, family relationship was not found an adequate basis for sustaining a statute under which the state attempted to assess an income tax against the husband measured in part by his wife's separate property income; the court there observed, "The state is forbidden to deny due process of law or *the equal protection of the laws for any purpose whatsoever.*" (Italics added.) Further, in Estate of Tetsubumi Yano (1922) 188 Cal. 645, 656–657 [14], 206 P. 995, blood relationship was found insufficient to constitute a basis for discrimination against a citizen minor whose father because of his race was (under a then held valid statute) ineligible for citizenship. (See also Oyama v. California (1948) 332 U.S. 633, 68 S.Ct. 269, 92 L.Ed. 249.) It is established in this state that the mere presence of wealth or lack thereof in an individual citizen cannot be the basis for valid class discrimination (Dribin v. Superior Court (1951) 37 Cal.2d 345, 348–350 [1], 231 P.2d 809, 24 A.L.R. 2d 864 [holding that a statute purporting to authorize a divorce from an insane spouse but limiting it to only those who could prove financial responsibility, constituted "arbitrary and unreasonable class discrimination"]) and in the same case (37 Cal.2d at p. 352 [11], 231 P.2d at p. 813, 24 A.L.R.2d 864) we declared "It is elementary that 'The insane have always been regarded as subject to control on the part of the state, *both for their protection and for the protection of others.*'" (Italics added.)

Lastly, in resolving the issue now before us, we need not blind ourselves to the social evolution which has been developing during the past half century; it has brought expanded recognition of the *parens patriae* principle (see 44 C.J. S. Insane Persons § 3, p. 48; 67 C.J.S. p. 624; 31 Words & Phrases 99–101) and other social responsibilities, including The California Rehabilitation Center

Act (added Stats.1961, ch. 850, p. 2228) and divers other public welfare programs to which all citizens are contributing through presumptively duly apportioned taxes. From all of this it appears that former concepts which have been suggested to uphold the imposition of support liability upon a person selected by an administrative agent from classes of relatives designated by the Legislature may well be re-examined. Illustrative of California's acceptance of this principle is the provision of section 6655 of the Welfare and Institutions Code that payment for the care and support of a patient at a state hospital "shall not be exacted * * * if there is likelihood of the patient's recovery or release from the hospital and payment will reduce his estate to such an extent that he is likely to become a burden on the community in the event of his discharge from the hospital." Thus, the state evidences concern that its committed patient shall not "become a burden on the community in the event of his discharge from the hospital," but at the same time its advocacy of the case at bench would seem to indicate that it cares not at all that relatives of the patient, selected by a department head, be denuded of *their* assets in order to reimburse the state for its maintenance of the patient in a tax supported institution. Section 6650 by its terms imposes absolute liability upon, and does not even purport to vest in, the servient relatives any right of control over, or to recoup from, the assets of the patient. A statute obviously violates the equal protection clause if it selects one particular class of persons for a species of taxation and no rational basis supports such classification. (See Blumenthal v. Board of Medical Examiners (1962) 57 Cal.2d 228, 237 [13], 18 Cal.Rptr. 501, 368 P.2d 101; Bilyeu v. State Employees' Retirement System (1962) 58 Cal.2d 618, 623 [2], 25 Cal.Rptr. 562, 375 P.2d 442.) Such a concept for the state's taking of a free man's property manifestly denies him equal protection of the law.

Anything found in Dept. of Mental Hygiene v. McGilvery (1958) supra, 50 Cal.2d 742, 754–761 [11–25], 329 P.2d 689 or in cases relying thereon (see e. g., Dept. of Mental Hygiene v. Black (1961) supra, 198 Cal.App.2d 627, 632 [2], 18 Cal.Rptr. 78; Estate of Setzer (1961) 192 Cal.App.2d 634, 637–638 [1], 13 Cal.Rptr. 683) contrary to the views herein expressed must be deemed disapproved.

The judgment is reversed and the cause is remanded with directions to enter judgment for defendant.

GIBSON, C. J., and TRAYNOR, McCOMB, PETERS, TOBRINER, and PEEK, JJ., concur.

_____

DEPARTMENT OF MENTAL HEALTH v. COTY

Supreme Court of Illinois, 1967.
38 Ill.2d 602, 232 N.E.2d 686.

HOUSE, Justice. This suit is another attack on the constitutionality of the reimbursement sections of the Mental Health Code. (Ill.Rev.Stat.1961, chap. 91½, pars. 9–19 through 9–25.) Section 9–19 provides that certain patients in a State hospital are liable for maintenance charges, and if the patient is unable to pay or his estate is insufficient, the patient's parents together with other designated members of the family are liable.

The action was instituted by the Attorney General of Illinois against the defendant, Louis Coty, the father of a mentally retarded son in Lincoln State School to collect for the treatment, detention and training of defendant's minor son as provided by statute. The Department filed a motion for summary judgment and the defendant submitted a second motion to strike and dismiss on the basis of Federal

constitutional and other objections. The circuit court of Cook County overruled defendant's motion and entered a judgment on the Department's motion. Defendant appeals to this court on the ground that the claim was in violation of the equal-protection clause of the fourteenth amendment of the Federal constitution.

This court upheld the constitutionality of the reimbursement provisions of the Mental Health Code in Kough v. Hoehler, 413 Ill. 409, 109 N.E.2d 177. (See also Department of Public Welfare v. Haas, 15 Ill.2d 204, 154 N.E.2d 265.) Defendant concedes the issue has been resolved under the State constitution but he argues that the question of conformity with the Federal constitution has been raised but not urged and rests this review exclusively on Federal grounds. He argues that assertion of the Department's claim denies him equal protection under the fourteenth amendment for several reasons. First, he complains that this proceeding was instituted after enactment of the new Health Code in 1963, and before its effective January 1, 1964, date against him but not against all liable relatives of other patients. Apparently, his objection on this phase is twofold. The new Act contains a five-year limitation and since a portion of the claim against him goes back well beyond five years he contends that no proceeding should be instituted in the interim between enactment and the effective date. The short answer is that the defendant's liability had already accrued and it is generally recognized that suits may be commenced at any time prior to the expiration of a limitation. (See Vol. 34, Am. Jur., sec. 23, pp. 30–31.) There is no merit to the argument that because some, but not all, delinquent relatives were sued that defendant suffered discrimination. Neither an individual nor the State is under any obligation to sue upon every cause of action which may accrue and failure to do so does not render a claim upon which suit is filed discriminatory.

Defendant's next charge of unequal protection is bottomed on the argument that only one small segment of a class (the parents of a mentally retarded child confined in a hospital) are directed to pay monthly charges in addition to their State and local taxes. This view follows the reasoning of Department of Mental Hygiene v. Kirchner (1964), 60 Cal.2d 716, 36 Cal.Rptr. 488, 388 P.2d 720, where it was said: " 'The enactment and administration of laws providing for sequestration and treatment of persons in appropriate state institutions * * * who would endanger themselves or others if at large is a proper state function; being so, it follows that the expense of providing, operating and maintaining such institutions should * * * be borne by the state.' Whether the commitment is incidental to an alleged violation of penal statute * * * or is essentially a civil commitment * * * the purposes of confinement and treatment or care in either case encompass the protection of society from the confined person and his own protection and possible reclamation as a productive member of the body politic. Hence the cost of maintaining the state institution, including provision of adequate care for its inmates, cannot be arbitrarily charged to one class in the society; such assessment violates the equal protection clause." After granting *certiorari* the Supreme Court vacated the judgment of the California Supreme Court and remanded for a determination by that court as to whether its decision was based on the California constitution or solely on the Federal constitution. (380 U.S. 194, 85 S.Ct. 871, 13 L.Ed.2d 753.) The California court thereafter held its decision to be based solely on its State constitution, thereby precluding review.

There is a solid array of authority contrary to the California view. Practically all States have reimbursement provisions or family-based repayments in their statutory plans and those courts which have acted upon them have, without exception, given their approval. (See e. g., In re Mansley's Estate (1916), 253 Pa. 522, 98 A. 702; State v. Bateman (1922), 110 Kan. 546, 204 P. 682; State v. Webber (1955), 163 Ohio St. 598, 128 N.E. 2d 3; Thomas v. State (1960), 241 Iowa 1072, 44 N.W.2d 410.) We think these cases state the better view.

It is next contended that section 9–23 (Ill.Rev.Stat.1953, chap. 91½, par. 9–23), which provides that the State's Attorney, upon request of the Department, shall file suit against persons refusing to pay the charges, grants to the State's Attorney the exclusive authority to act. This argument is based on the fact that the Attorney General and State's Attorneys have concurrent powers, that the legislature presumably knew of such concurrent powers, and that by specifically delegating authority to the State's Attorneys the legislature thereby limited the power of the Attorney General. The Appellate Court, First District, relying upon such well known cases as Fergus v. Russel, 270 Ill. 304, 110 N.E. 130, and People ex rel. Barrett v. Finnegan, 378 Ill. 387, 38 N.E.2d 715, recently held: "We conclude from the foregoing that the Attorney General of the State of Illinois, as chief law officer of the state, possessed both the common-law power and the statutory authority to act on behalf of the Department of Health * * *." (Department of Mental Health v. Salmar, 82 Ill.App.2d 450, 453–454, 226 N.E.2d 511, 512.) We are in accord with that view. As pointed out in Fergus v. Russel, the common-law powers of the Attorney General were preserved to him by the constitution and while the General Assembly can impose additional power and duties upon him, it cannot strip him of his common-law powers. There was no error in the filing of this proceeding by the Attorney General.

The judgment of the circuit court of Cook County is therefore affirmed.

Judgment affirmed.

Note on Relative Responsibility

Despite the broad language of the *Kirchner* opinion, a number of subsequent California lower court decisions have imposed liability upon individuals for the cost of public services rendered to their relatives. See County of Alameda v. Kaiser, 238 Cal.App.2d 815, 48 Cal.Rptr. 343 (1965); In re Dudley, 239 Cal.App.2d 401, 48 Cal.Rptr. 790 (1966); County of Alameda v. Espinoza, 243 Cal.App.2d 534, 52 Cal.Rptr. 480 (1966); In re Shaieb, 250 Cal.App. 2d 553, 58 Cal.Rptr. 631 (1967); Department of Mental Hygiene v. O'Connor, 246 Cal.App.2d 24, 54 Cal.Rptr. 432 (1966); Department of Mental Hygiene v. Kolts, 247 Cal.App.2d 154, 55 Cal.Rptr. 437 (1966). In County of San Mateo v. Boss, 3 Cal.3d 962, 92 Cal. Rptr. 294, 479 P.2d 654 (1971), the California Supreme Court gave its approval to these decisions and indicated that *Kirchner* was intended to bar relative responsibility in only a rather narrow group of situations:

> [W]e did recognize in *Kirchner* that the costs of * * * [public] care could, consistently with equal protection, be charged to those persons who had a preexisting duty to support the recipient of the care. * * * In a line of decisions since *Kirchner* imposition of liability upon the estate of the recipient of welfare, upon the recipient's spouse, and, where the recipient was a minor, upon his parents, has been upheld as constitutional. In each of these cases, it was found that the person upon whom liability was imposed owed a preexisting duty of support to the recipient of the public assistance. Since the state discharges that duty of support to the extent it provides welfare assistance, it may reasonably seek reimbursement from those whose duty it discharges. Such a preexisting duty of support provides a rational ground for classification of those who must bear a disproportionate amount of the costs of the welfare program. [footnotes omitted] 3 Cal. 3d at 967–68, 92 Cal.Rptr. at 297, 479 P.2d at 657.

Courts in several other states have also upheld relative responsibility laws. See Groover v. Essex County Welfare Bd., 264 A.2d 143 (D.C.Ct.App.1970); Jesmer v. Dundon, 64 Misc.2d 594, 315 N. Y.S.2d 514 (Fam.Ct.1970); Kerr v. State Public Welfare Commission, 470 P. 2d 167 (Ct.App.Or.1970); State Revenue Div. of Dept. of Treasury v. Raseman's Estate, 18 Mich.App. 91, 170 N. W.2d 503 (Ct.App.1969). But cf. Rowe v. Dept. of Mental Hygiene, 247 Md. 542, 233 A.2d 769 (1967) (imposing liability on wife for husband's care in state mental hospital violates state constitutional provision protecting her from debts of husband).

Does this mean that relatives could be required to pay the cost of room and board in a prison for a convict? See County of Alameda v. Espinoza, supra; Jesmer v. Dundon, supra. What is the legal status of the following statutes?

SOUTH CAROLINA CODE LAWS
§§ 20–303, 15–1228—
15–1231 (1952).

DOMESTIC RELATIONS

§ 20–303. **Husband's and father's obligation to support wife and children.**

Any able-bodied man or man capable of earning or making a livelihood who shall, without just cause or excuse, abandon or fail to supply the actual necessaries of life to his wife or to his minor unmarried legitimate or illegitimate child or children dependent upon him shall be guilty of a misdemeanor and, upon conviction thereof, shall be imprisoned for a term of not exceeding one year or be liable to a fine of not less than three hundred dollars nor more than fifteen hundred dollars, or both, in the discretion of the court. If a fine be imposed the court may in its discretion order that a portion of the fine be paid to a proper and suitable person or agency for the maintenance and support of the defendant's wife or minor unmarried legitimate or illegitimate child or children.

JUVENILE AND DOMESTIC RELATIONS COURTS

§ 15–1228. Liability of husband to support wife and children.

A husband is hereby declared to be chargeable with the support of his wife and children and, if possessed of sufficient means or able to earn such means, may be required to pay for their support a fair and reasonable sum according to his means, as may be determined by the court.

§ 15–1229. Liability of mother to support child.

When the father of a child is dead, is incapable of supporting his child or cannot be found within the State, the mother of such child is hereby declared to be chargeable with its support and, if possessed of sufficient means or able to earn such means, may be required to pay for its support a fair and reasonable sum according to her means, as may be determined by the court.

§ 15–1230. Liability of grandparents to support child.

When the father of a child included in a petition for support is dead or when the court, in its judgment, is unable to secure adequate support for such child from its parents and the child's grandparents are of sufficient means to support it such grandparents are hereby declared to be chargeable with the support of such grandchild and may be required to pay a fair and reasonable sum according to their means, as may be determined by the court.

§ 15–1231. Liability of stepparent to support stepchild.

The stepparent of a child is declared legally chargeable with the support of a stepchild likely to become a public charge provided it is shown to the satisfaction of the court that such stepparent had knowledge of the child's existence at the time of such stepparent's marriage.

———

N.J.S.A. §§ 44:1–140, 141 (1930).

44:1–140. Relatives chargeable

a. The father, grandfather, mother, grandmother, children, and husband or wife, severally and respectively, of a poor, old, blind, lame or impotent person or other poor person or child not able to work, shall, if of sufficient ability, at his or their charge and expense, relieve and maintain the poor person or child in such manner as shall be ordered, after due notice and opportunity to be heard, by any county or municipal director of welfare, or by any court of competent jurisdiction upon its own initiative or the information of any person.

b. The provisions of this section shall apply to the minor children of a mother whose husband shall fail properly to support and maintain such children when by reason thereof they are likely to become a public charge.

c. The provisions of this section shall not apply to any person 55 years of age or over except with regard to his or her spouse, or his or her natural or adopted child under the age of 21 years.

Amended by L.1968, c. 446 § 1, eff. Feb. 19, 1969.

44:1–141. Compelling support by relatives

If any of the relatives mentioned in section 44:1–140 of this title shall fail to perform the order or directions of the overseer with regard to the support of the poor person, or if the poor person is supported at public expense, the court of common pleas of the county wherein the poor person has a legal settlement, or the family court of the municipality wherein the person has a legal settlement, upon the complaint of the overseer of the poor or two residents of the municipality or county may summon the persons chargeable before it as in other actions, summon witnesses, and order, adjudge and decree that the able relatives pay such sum for each poor person as the circumstances may require in the discretion of the court, and as will maintain him or them and relieve the public of that burden; but nothing contained in this section shall be construed to grant jurisdiction for the trial of any of such cases to a recorder's court or family court in a county having a criminal judicial district court. Violation of any such order shall constitute a contempt of court.

* * *

The county through its governing body may also bring appropriate action at law in any court of competent jurisdiction to recover any money due for the relief, support and maintenance of a poor person against a person chargeable by law therefor.

LEWIS v. MARTIN

Supreme Court of the United States, 1970.
397 U.S. 552, 90 S.Ct. 1282, 25 L.Ed.2d 561.

Mr. Justice DOUGLAS delivered the opinion of the Court.

Appellants are mothers and children who receive welfare assistance under California law. At the time these actions were commenced, California law provided that payments to a "needy child" who "lives with his mother and a stepfather or an adult male person assuming the role of spouse to the mother although not legally married to her"—known in the vernacular as a MARS—shall be computed after consideration is given to the income of the stepfather or MARS. The California law conclusively presumes that the needs of the children are reduced by the amount of income available from the man in the house whether or not they are in fact available or actually used to meet the needs of the dependent children.

Following our decision in King v. Smith, 392 U.S. 309, 88 S.Ct. 2128, 20 L.Ed.2d 1118, HEW promulgated a regulation reaffirming its earlier rulings that the income of a man not ceremonially married to the mother of the dependent children may not be treated as available to the children unless there is proof that he has made actual contributions.[4] Even where the man is ceremonially married to the mother but is not the real or adoptive father his income may not be treated as available to the children unless he is legally obligated to support the child by state law.[5]

These suits by appellants were brought in a three-judge District Court to declare the California law and regulations invalid. That court dismissed the complaints, holding the HEW regulations were invalid. 312 F.Supp. 197. The cases are here on appeal and we noted probable jurisdiction. 396 U.S. 900, 90 S.Ct. 237, 24 L.Ed.2d 176.

The Social Security Act defines a dependent child as a "needy child * * * who has been deprived of parental support or care by reason of the death, continued absence from the home, or physical or mental incapacity of a parent,

---

[4] 45 CFR § 203.1.

[5] Id., § 203.1(a).

and who is living with" a specified relative. 42 U.S.C.A. §§ 606(a). This is the Aid to Families with Dependent Children Program (AFDC) which we discussed in King v. Smith.

The federal statute provides that state agencies administering AFDC plans "shall in determining need (of an eligible child), take into consideration any other income and resources (of the child) * * * as well as any expenses reasonably attributable to the earning of such income." 42 U.S.C.A. § 602(a)(7).

This directive was implemented by a regulation of HEW, effective July 1, 1967, which, as then worded, provided in part:

"[O]nly income and resources that are, in fact, available to an applicant or recipient for current use on a regular basis will be taken into consideration in determining need and the amount of payment." [6]

We stated in King v. Smith, supra, at 319, 88 S.Ct. at 2134, n. 16, that those regulations "clearly comport with" the Act. And as we have noted, shortly after King v. Smith, HEW promulgated a new regulation [7] which provided in pertinent part:

"(a) A State plan for aid and services to needy families with children * * * must provide that the determination whether a child has been deprived of parental support or care by reason of the death, continued absence from the home or physical or mental

incapacity of a parent * * * will be made only in relation to the child's natural or adoptive parent, or in relation to a child's stepparent who is ceremonially married to the child's natural or adoptive parent and is legally obligated to suport the child under State law of general applicability which requires stepparents to support stepchildren to the same extent that natural or adoptive parents are required to support their children.

"(b) The inclusion in the family, or the presence in the home, of a 'substitute parent' or 'man-in-the-house' or any individual other than one described in paragraph (a) of this section is not an acceptable basis for a finding of ineligibility or for assuming the availability of income by the State. * * * [I]n the consideration of all income and resources in establishing financial eligibility and the amount of the assistance payment, *only such net income as is actually available for current use on a regular basis will be considered, and the income only of the parent described in paragraph (a) of this section will be considered available for children in the household in absence of proof of actual contributions.* (Emphasis added).

In other words, the regulations explicitly negate the idea that in determining a child's needs, a stepfather (*i. e.,* a man married to a child's mother who has not adopted the child and is not legally obligated to support the child under state law) or a MARS may be presumed to be providing support. [8]

---

[6] HEW Handbook of Public Assistance Administration, Pt. IV, § 3131.7. In its present form the regulation provides:

"(ii) * * * in establishing financial eligibility and the amount of the assistance payment: * * * (c) only such net income as is actually available for current use on a regular basis will be considered, and only currently available resources will be considered." 45 CFR § 233.20(a)(3)(11), 34 Fed.Reg. 1395.

[7] 45 CFR § 203.1.

[8] An exception is a person, where presence is deemed essential to the well-being of the recipient of assistance and who is included in the family budget unit for calculation of need. See 42 U.S.C.A. § 602(a)(7) which provides:

"A State plan * * * must * * * provide that the State agency shall, in determining need, take into consideration any

We said in King v. Smith that AFDC aid can be granted "only if 'a parent' of the needy child is continually absent from the home." 392 U.S., at 313, 88 S.Ct. at 2131. If the stepfather or MARS is a "parent" within the meaning of the federal Act, any federal matching assistance under the AFDC program for children living with a MARS or stepfather would not be available to appellants. The three-judge court said that "The HEW regulation, by requiring proof of actual contributions from a MARS, reduces the expectation of Congress to a mere hope." 312 F.Supp. 202. We disagree. We traversed the entire spectrum of that question in King v. Smith, and find it unnecessary to restate again the legislative history of the relevant statutes. We concluded that Congress "intended the term 'parent' in § 406(a) of the Act * * * to include only those persons with a legal duty of support." 392 U.S., at 327, 88 S.Ct. at 2138. And we went on to say:

"It is clear, as we have noted, that Congress expected 'breadwinners' who secured employment would support their children. This congressional expectation is most reasonably explained on the basis that the kind of breadwinner Congress had in mind was one who was legally obligated to support his children. We think it beyond reason to believe that Congress would have considered that providing employment for the paramour of a deserted mother would benefit the mother's

children whom he was not obligated to support.

"By a parity of reasoning, we think that Congress must have intended that the children in such a situation remain eligible for AFDC assistance notwithstanding their mother's impropriety." Id., at 329, 88 S.Ct. at 2139–2140.

That reasoning led us to invalidate Alabama's "substitute father" regulation. Like reasoning leads us to hold, contrary to the three-judge District Court, that the HEW regulation is valid. We only add that HEW might reasonably conclude that only he who is as near as a real adoptive father would be has that consensual relation to the family which makes it reliably certain that his income is actually available for support of the children in the household. HEW may, in other words, reasonably conclude that an obligation to support under state law must be of "general applicability" to make that obligation in reality a solid assumption on which estimates of funds actually available to children on a regular basis may be calculated.

Any lesser duty of support might merely be a device for lowering welfare benefits without guaranteeing that the child would regularly receive the income on which the reduction is based, that is to say, not approximate the obligation to support placed on and normally assumed by natural or adoptive parents. That reading of the Act and of King v. Smith certainly cannot be said to be impermissible.

Our decision in King v. Smith held only that a legal obligation to support was a necessary condition for qualification as a "parent"; it did not also suggest that it would always be a sufficient condition. We find nothing in this regulation to suggest inconsistency with the Act's basic purpose of providing aid to "needy" children, except where there is a "breadwinner" in the house who can

---

other income and resources of any child or relative claiming aid to families with dependent children, or of any other individual (living in the same home as such child and relative) whose needs the State determines should be considered in determining the need of the child or relative claiming such aid, as well as any expenses reasonably attributable to the earning of any such income; * * *."

The so-called AFDC "essential person" is also covered by regulation. See 45 CFR § 233.20(a)(2)(vi), 34 Fed.Reg. 1394.

be expected to provide such aid himself. HEW, the agency charged with administering the Act, has apparently concluded that as a matter of current, practical realities, the relationship of the MARS to the home is less stable than that of the stepfather who at least has the additional tie of the ceremonial marriage, and that the likelihood of the MAR's contributing his income to the children—even if legally obligated to do so—is sufficiently uncertain in the absence of the marriage tie, to prevent viewing him as a "breadwinner" unless the bread is actually set on the table. Nothing in this record shows that this administrative judgment does not correspond to the facts. We give HEW the deference due the agency charged with the administration of the Act, see, e. g., Red Lion Broadcasting Co., Inc. v. FCC, 395 U.S. 367, 381, 89 S.Ct. 1794, 1802, 23 L.Ed.2d 371; Zemel v. Rusk, 381 U. S. 1, 11–12, 85 S.Ct. 1271, 1278, 14 L. Ed.2d 179. In the absence of proof of actual contribution, California may not consider the child's "resources" to include either the income of a nonadopting stepfather who is not legally obligated to support the child as is a natural parent, or the income of a MARS—whatever the nature of his obligation to support.

California on remand is foreclosed from arguing that its assumption-of-income provisions are consistent with the Act as applied to MARS; the State is limited to demonstrating that those provisions may be retained under the Act as applied to nonadopting stepfathers by showing that the legal obligation placed on such stepparents is consistent with the obligation required by the federal regulation.

Whether in that posture of the case California's laws and regulations are inconsistent with the federal standard is a question that the District Court did not reach. The cases are therefore reversed

and remanded so that such an adjudication can be made.

It is so ordered.

Reversed and remanded.

[Dissenting opinions of Mr. Justice BLACK and Mr. Chief Justice BURGER, omitted.]

SECTION 5. THE WELFARE PROCESS

A. INTRODUCTION

The materials in this section are designed to focus attention on selected problems arising in the course of the administration of public assistance. Following an introductory discussion by Professor Handler of the potentialities and limitations of the lawyer's role in this process, there come materials devoted to the process of eligibility determination, the relation of the Fourth Amendment to certain departmental investigatory practices, the appropriate timing of hearings, and the various procedural problems arising out of the so-called "Fair Hearing."

CONTROLLING OFFICIAL BEHAVIOR IN WELFARE ADMINISTRATION

54 Calif.L.Rev. 479 (1966).
Joel F. Handler.

Lawyers have always been concerned with controlling the actions of government. *What is new today is that attention has shifted to welfare administration.* The shift, of course, reflects the larger national interest in civil rights and poverty. The legal profession's reaction to the national interest has been an increasing awareness and apparent (if somewhat halting) willingness to do something about providing legal services for the underprivileged, the Negro, and the dependent poor. Within these broader shifts in attitudes, it is natural that lawyers would begin to concern themselves with the problems raised by government activity in the welfare field. Public welfare has been around a long time; attention is now being directed at it as part of the broad national movement for civil justice.

To a very considerable extent, lawyers cast the problem in traditional terms: How can the socially approved interests of the individual be protected in the government welfare programs? * * *

It is to the danger or threats to the freedom and dignity of the individual that the recent literature of the lawyers has turned. A good way to discuss the issues is to examine the work of Professor Charles Reich. His three articles —Midnight Welfare Searches and the Social Security Act,[6] The New Property,[7] and Individual Rights and Social Welfare: The Emerging Legal Issues [8]— have received a great deal of attention. They purport to define some of the more important issues, and suggest how we should solve them. Much new legal research adopts Reich's analysis and approach.[9]

Reich catalogues certain "ills" of present-day welfare administration. Welfare officials have attempted to impose moral codes on welfare recipients. Privacy has been unnecessarily invaded under the guise of eligibility and need investigations. Welfare laws sometimes impose financial responsibility on relatives of welfare recipients that are much broader than duties imposed on relatives of nonwelfare persons. The residence of welfare recipients is usually restricted; in some states, there are "removal" laws. Several states require work or vocational retraining as a condition of receiving aid. Public housing authorities may deny admission or terminate leases of people who have police records or whom the authorities think keep undesirable company or engage in immoral conduct. Often welfare recipients are required to take loyalty oaths not required of the general public. Under the means test, welfare officials have great powers over the family budget; independence is restricted by official supervision. * * *

The remedies or solutions that Reich proposes have a ring familiar to lawyers. In welfare the government should not be allowed to impose any conditions that would be unconstitutional if imposed on persons not on welfare; government can't "buy up" constitutional rights. The substantive provisions of welfare statutes must be stripped of all that is not relevant to the purposes of the programs, such as loyalty requirements for tenants in government housing. In addition, "to the extent possible, delegated power to make rules ought to be confined within ascertainable limits, and regulating agencies should not be assigned the task of enforcing conflicting policies. Also agencies should be enjoined to use their powers only for the purposes for which they were designed." But because it is so difficult to define in statutes what is relevant and to confine administrative discretion, Reich puts heavy emphasis on "basic" procedural safeguards. "In the case of a decision removing a family from

---

[6] 72 Yale L.J. 1347 (1963).

[7] 73 Yale L.J. 733 (1964).

[8] 74 Yale L.J. 1245 (1965).

[9] See, e. g., the statement of purposes of the newly established Project on Social Welfare Law at the New York University School of Law, 1 Welfare Law Bull., Dec. 1965, p. 1 * * * and Columbia University School of Social Work: Center on Social Welfare Policy and Law, Memorandum on the "social welfare law testing" function of the Center 1. This memorandum has been reprinted in Practical Lawyer, April 1966.

public housing, or a decision denying aid to families with dependent children, generally the matter is finally determined at some level within the appropriate agency, after investigation by the agency, and with comparatively informal procedures, if any, available to the persons affected." He calls for "full adjudicatory procedures." Reich is not very specific about what he means by this ("procedures can develop gradually and pragmatically") but appears to favor quite strongly the following: advance notification and publication of regulations that will govern future agency decisions; notice of proposed action, including a "full statement of the basis for it"; a trial-type hearing with the right to be represented by counsel; a separation of functions of investigator and judge; a decision based on competent evidence in the record; reasons in support of the decision; and "some form of review" (perhaps "within the agency, and, ultimately, in the courts"). Finally, Reich develops his idea of "entitlement." His conclusion is that the poor are entitled to welfare as a matter of "right" and not of "privilege." "The idea of entitlement is simply that when individuals have insufficient resources to live under conditions of health and decency, society has obligations to provide support, and the individual is entitled to that support as of right." At the risk of oversimplification, the objective of this position is to promote individual security by rejecting the case law justifying government interference on the ground that what the individual is claiming is a "mere gratuity" rather than a "right."

Reich's strategy is quite clear. What he wants to do, in essence, is elevate the position of the welfare recipient to a position similar to that of a person whose business interests are regulated by government. In business regulation, government agencies are dealing with a "right" —property. Constitutional limits, more

or less, are applicable. Through the years statutory and judicially-imposed procedural safeguards have developed. Reich introduces his argument for procedural safeguards in the welfare field by talking about and listing specifically the types of procedural safeguards developed in business regulation. * * *

The fact of the matter is that even in the administration of business regulation, very little of the type of control of administrative behavior that Reich talks about exists. It is now commonplace to reiterate that the informal procedures are truly "the lifeblood of the administrative process." Davis estimates that "perhaps eighty or ninety per cent of the impact of the administrative process involves discretionary action in absence of safeguards of hearing procedures." These are cases which are disposed of without a trial-type hearing or a record upon which the decision is based. Sometimes the informal adjudication consists of "settlement cases"—the party is entitled to a formal hearing if he wants one, but the case is settled prior to the hearing. In others, sometimes called the "pure administrative process," no formal hearings are provided prior to the formal decision (for example, inspection or tests of physical properties). * * *

Reich, in drawing upon the analogy of the administration of business regulation to support his arguments for "judicializing" welfare administration, seems to give the impression that administrative decisions are generally carried out with all the procedural safeguards: advance publication of rules, notice, formal trial-type hearings, competent and relevant evidence, decisions based on the record. His description leaves out the most significant area: informal administration, where none of these procedural safeguards are used. He is quite wrong in asserting that lawyers have made a "practical reality" of the judicial-type procedures. The existing evidence points in the opposite direction. According to persons intimate with the administrative process, it seems rare indeed when judicial-type procedures are used to attempt to control administrative behavior. * * *

Whatever the injustice committed at the administrative level, the opportunity to go to court means that ultimately the rights of the individual will be secure against lawless administrative behavior. Of course, there have been instances where appellate courts have checked lawless administrative behavior; and it might be demonstrated that the availability of judicial review does have some impact on some administrative agencies. But, in the main, it seems doubtful to rely on reviewing courts to accomplish significant changes in administrative behavior. First, much of the informal administrative process is not susceptible to judicial review. Second, at least in federal administrative law, the impact of the reviewing courts has been characterized as sporadic, clumsy, and largely ineffective. The courts have been concerned almost exclusively with matters of procedure; what the agencies *do* to people and their property is largely beyond judicial scrutiny, as long as procedural steps are properly taken or adequate "findings" are made. * * *

The importance of the discussion in the preceding section does not lie solely in exposing some of the futility and difficulties in the attempt to judicialize the administration of business regulation. It sheds light on some of the basic aspects of administrative processes; the lessons learned in the administration of business regulation should help in avoiding the pitfalls of attempting to control official behavior in welfare administration by imposing similar techniques.

I will use as my example the AFDC program, which is a grant-in-aid program administered under the Social Security Act. The Act sets forth relatively few mandatory requirements on the states as conditions for participation (for example, a state can have a residence requirement but it cannot be for longer than one year); most of the federal statutory provisions are permissive (for example, a state may extend the program where need is caused by the unemployment of a parent). As stated earlier, the federal statute generally leaves to the states the determination of the criteria of need, the levels of income and other sources that will be included in the budget, and the levels of income to be paid to the families (subject to a federally imposed maximum). In Wisconsin, as well as many other states, the state agency (Wisconsin States Department of Public Welfare, Division of Public Assistance) supervises the program, but the actual administration is carried on by county welfare agencies. The Wisconsin Division of Public Assistance assists the counties in the development of their programs, supervises their activities, and advises the local agencies of federal and state requirements. At both the federal and state levels there has been a conscious attempt to provide flexibility and a large measure of autonomy and discretion at the county level.

One of the discretionary decisions that is made at the county level is whether the AFDC mother should work. When the program was first enacted, the policy was to provide financial assistance so that the mother would not have to leave the home in order to work. Attitudes have changed, and it is now recognized that in certain situations if the mother has a job it may be beneficial to both the mother and the children (assuming adequate day care). Whether the mother should work or not is a decision that must be made on the basis of each family's needs. One of the dangers, of course, is that mothers will be "encouraged" to work in order to save public money, since her earnings will be included in the family budget. The Wisconsin regulations go to great length in suggesting criteria to be used by the county caseworkers in making this decision. The caseworkers are specifically told that the mother should work only if her working will contribute to the strengthening of family life and promote other rehabilitative goals; the decision must not be made in order to save public money.

Assume that in a particular case, a caseworker decides that the mother should work. Assume further that this decision was made to save public money and that it was not in the "best interests" of the family. The mother, for example, is genuinely reluctant to leave her children in the hands of the available day-care help. To a very great extent, the mother already has the "rights" that Reich calls for. In distinguishing the Social Security Act from other welfare programs, he says that "the framers of the Act had a clear concept concerning the 'right' to public assistance, and provided devices to protect these rights. Thus, in the program for aid to families with needy children, the Act requires that states afford an opportunity for a fair hearing to any individual whose claim is denied or not acted upon with reasonable promptness * * *." Wisconsin faithfully implements the purpose of the Social Security Act to provide procedural regularity and fairness. There is advance publication of the rule governing the situation; indeed, the fullness and clarity of the Wisconsin regulation is probably unusual. The state statute provides for a prompt, fair hearing not only when a claim is denied but also when an individual is dissatisfied with the amount of the grant. The regulations set forth detailed procedures which display a careful balance between fairness and informality. The appeal is heard by a special representative of the state Division of Public Assistance, and not by the county welfare department. Yet, it is easy to see how Reich's program of rights will be of little use to the mother in this type of situation.

One of the critical facts to realize is that at the point where the caseworker tells the mother that she must take a job, the mother is still in the program. She and her family are currently receiving assistance and she will probably not be able to support her family with her earnings; besides, she does not want to leave her children. She knows that tomorrow and the next day the same caseworker will be making other decisions that affect vitally her level of living and style of life. * * *

In short, in calculating whether to fight the decision about working, the mother has to weigh the costs to her ongoing relationship with the local agency; what will happen to her tomorrow if she disagrees with the caseworker this time and "goes over his head"? She is now beginning to think that in the "long run" it would be "better" for her family if she agreed with the caseworker and went to work. Reich is absolutely right in stating that caseworkers in these situations have great power over their clients. What he fails to realize is that this power largely nullifies a program of rights.

Note

In their study of the Texas fair hearing system Alexander W. Bell and G. Todd Norvell report that for 1966 only .49% of grant terminations or reductions were appealed by recipients. Of these appeals, 55% were decided in favor of recipients. They contrast this with an 8.7% appeal rate from federal district court decisions and a 21.7% reversal rate. The authors go on to conclude that for a variety of reasons including illiteracy, unassertiveness, and lack of understanding of rights, the fair hearing procedure is a paper right more than a reality. Texas Welfare Appeals: The Hidden Rights, 46 Texas L. Rev. 223 (1967).

To what extent does the Supreme Court decision in Goldberg v. Kelly deal with such problems and those raised in Professor Handler's article?

B. ADMINISTRATIVE DETERMINATIONS

GOLDBERG v. KELLY

Supreme Court of the United States, 1970.
397 U.S. 254, 90 S.Ct. 1011, 25 L.Ed.2d 287.
[Opinion printed at p. 59, supra.]

REGULATIONS OF THE DEPARTMENT OF HEALTH, EDUCATION AND WELFARE

45 C.F.R. § 205.10 (1971).

[The following are revised regulations on fair hearings promulgated by HEW after the Goldberg v. Kelly decision.

In examining these regulations, note particularly the requirement in §§ 205.10 (a)(1) and 205.10(a)(3) of a *state* agency hearing; the partial exemption in § 205.10(a)(5)(iii)(*a*)(1) for decisions which are not ones of "fact or judgment relating to the individual case"; the inclusion in § 205.10(a)(5) of aid reductions as well as aid terminations; the 15 day notice requirement in § 205.10(a) (5)(i); the requirement of an informal pre-hearing conference imposed by § 205.10(a)(5)(ii); and the group hearing requirements in § 205.10(a)(3)(v). To what extent are these and other aspects of the regulations demanded by Goldberg v. Kelly; to what extent has HEW gone beyond the demands of that decision?]

§ 205.10 Fair hearings.

(a) *State plan requirements.* A State plan under title I, IV–A, X, XIV, XVI or XIX of the Social Security Act must provide for a system of fair hearings under which:

(1) The single State agency responsible for the program will be responsible for fulfillment of fair hearings provisions.

(2) Every claimant will be informed in writing at the time of application and at the time of any action affecting his claim:

(i) Of his right to fair hearing;

(ii) Of the method by which he may obtain a hearing;

(iii) That he may be represented by legal counsel, or by a relative, friend, or other spokesman, or he may represent himself; and

(iv) Of any provision for payment of legal fees by the agency.

(3) An opportunity for a fair hearing before the State agency will be granted to any individual requesting a hearing because his claim for financial or medical assistance is denied, or is not acted upon with reasonable promptness, or because he is aggrieved by any other agency action affecting receipt, suspension, reduction, or termination of such assistance or by agency policy as it affects his situation. Under this requirement:

(i) A request for a hearing is defined as any clear expression (oral or written) by the claimant (or person acting for him, such as his legal representative, relative, or friend) to the effect that he wants the opportunity to present his case to higher authority.

(ii) The freedom to make such a request must not be limited or interfered with in any way, and agency emphasis must be on helping the claimant to submit and process his request, and in preparing his case, if needed.

(iii) The claimant must be provided reasonable time in which to appeal an agency action.

(iv) The fair hearing shall include consideration of:

(*a*) Any agency action, or failure to act with reasonable promptness, on a claim for financial or medical assistance, which includes undue delay in reaching a decision on eligibility or in making a payment, refusal to consider a request for or undue delay in making an adjustment in payment, and suspension or discontinuance of such assistance in whole or in part;

(*b*) The agency's interpretation of the law, and the reasonableness and equitableness of the policies promulgated under the law, if the claimant is aggrieved by their application to his situation;

(*c*) Agency decision regarding:

(*1*) Eligibility for financial or medical assistance in both initial and subsequent determinations,

(*2*) Amount of financial or medical assistance or change in payments,

(*3*) The manner or form of payment, including restricted or protective payments, even though no Federal financial participation is claimed, and

(*4*) Conditions of payment, including work requirements.

(v) States may respond to a series of individual requests for fair hearings by conducting a single group hearing. States may only consolidate cases in which the sole issue involved is one of an agency policy. In such a situation, each individual must be given the right to withdraw from the group hearing in favor of an individual hearing. If recipients request a group hearing on such an issue the State must grant it. In all group hearings, whether initiated by the State or by the claimants, the policies governing fair hearings must be followed. Thus, each individual claimant must be permitted to present his own case and be represented by his own lawyer.

(vi) The agency shall not deny or dismiss a request for a hearing except where it has been withdrawn by claimant in writing, or abandoned.

(4) Hearing procedures will be issued and publicized by the State agency for the guidance of all concerned.

(5) In cases of any proposed action to terminate, suspend or reduce assistance:

(i) The State or local agency will give timely and adequate advance notice detailing the reasons for the proposed action. Under this requirement:

(*a*) "Timely" means that the notice is mailed at least 15 days before the action is to be taken.

(*b*) "Adequate advance notice" means a written notice that includes details of reasons for the proposed agency action, explanation of the individual's right to conference, his right to request a fair hearing and the circumstances under which assistance is continued if a fair hearing is requested.

(ii) If, within the advance notice period, the individual responds by indicating his wish for an agency conference, an opportunity is provided for the recipient (or his representative) to discuss his situation with agency staff, obtain an explanation of the reasons for the proposed action, and present information to show that the proposed action is incorrect. Under this requirement:

(*a*) During this conference, the recipient is given the opportunity to speak for himself or be represented by legal counsel or by a friend or other spokesman.

(*b*) The opportunity for a conference does not in any way diminish the recipient's right to a fair hearing.

(iii) (*a*) In cases in which there is a request for a fair hearing within the advance notice period:

(*1*) Assistance is continued until the fair hearing decision is rendered and through a period consistent with the State's established policies for issuance of payments unless a determination is made by the State agency, in accordance with criteria issued by the Social and Rehabilitation Service, that the issue is one of State agency policy and not one of fact or judgment relating to the individual case, including a question of whether the State agency rules or policies were correctly applied to the facts of the particular case.

(2) The agency promptly informs the claimant in writing if assistance will be discontinued, based on the State agency's determination.

(b) Alternatively, the State may provide for continuing assistance in all cases. In cases in which a fair hearing is requested after expiration of the advance notice period, the State may provide for an additional period during which time the request for a hearing will result in reinstatement of assistance to be continued until the fair hearing decision.

(6) Information and referral services are provided to help claimants make use of any legal services available in the community that can provide legal representation at the hearing.

(7) The hearing will be conducted at a time, date and place convenient to the claimant, and adequate preliminary written notice will be given.

(8) The hearings will be conducted by an impartial official (or officials) of the State agency. Under this requirement, the hearing official must not have been involved in any way with the action in question.

(9) When the hearing involves medical issues such as those concerning a diagnosis, or an examining physician's report, or the medical review team's decision, a medical assessment other than that of the person or persons involved in making the original decision will be obtained at agency expense from a source

satisfactory to the claimant and made part of the record if the hearing officer or the appellant considers it necessary.

(10) The claimant, or his representative, will have adequate opportunity:

(i) To examine all documents and records used at the hearing at a reasonable time before the date of the hearing as well as during the hearing;

(ii) At his option, to present his case himself or with the aid of others including legal counsel;

(iii) To bring witnesses;

(iv) To establish all pertinent facts and circumstances;

(v) To advance any arguments without undue interference;

(vi) To question or refute any testimony or evidence, including opportunity to confront and cross-examine adverse witnesses.

(11) Prompt, definitive, and final administrative action will be taken within 60 days from the date of the request for a fair hearing, except where the claimant requests a delay in the hearing.

(12) The claimant will be notified of the decision, in writing, in the name of the State agency and, to the extent it is available to him, of his right to judicial review.

(13) When the hearing decision is favorable to the claimant, or when the agency decides in favor of the claimant prior to the hearing, the agency will make corrective payments retroactively to the date the incorrect action was taken or such earlier date as is provided under State policy.

(14) Recommendations of the hearing officer or panel shall be based exclusively on evidence and other material introduced at the hearing. The verbatim transcript of testimony and exhibits, or an official report containing the substance of what transpired at the hearing,

together with all papers and requests filed in the proceeding, and the recommendations of the hearing officer or panel will constitute the exclusive record for decision by the hearing authority and will be available to the claimant at a place accessible to him or his representative at any reasonable time.

(15) Decisions by the hearing authority, rendered in the name of the State agency, shall specify the reasons for the decision and identify the supporting evidence. They shall be binding on the State and local agency. Under this requirement:

(i) No person who participated in the local decision being appealed will participate in a final administrative decision on such a case;

(ii) The State agency is responsible for seeing that the decision is carried out promptly.

(16) The State agency will establish and maintain a method for informing, at least in summary form, all local agencies of all fair hearing decisions by the hearing authority and the decisions will be accessible to the public (subject to provisions of safeguarding public assistance information).

(17) In respect to title XIX, when the appeal has been taken on the basis of eligibility determination, the agency responsible for the determination of eligibility for medical assistance, if different from the single State agency administering the medical assistance plan, shall participate in the conduct of the fair hearing.

(b) *Federal financial participation.* Federal financial participation is available for the following items:

(1) Payments of assistance continued pending a hearing decision;

(2) Payments of assistance made to carry out hearing decisions, or to take corrective action after an appeal but prior to hearing, or to extend the benefit of a hearing decision or court order to others in the same situation as those directly affected by the decision or order. Such payments may be retroactive in accordance with applicable Federal policies on corrective payments.

(3) Payments of assistance within the scope of Federally aided public assistance programs made in accordance with a court order.

(4) Service costs incurred by the agency, at the applicable matching rates, for:

(i) Providing legal counsel to represent clients at hearings or in judicial review;

(ii) Providing transportation for the claimant, his representative and witnesses to and from the place of the hearing;

(iii) Meeting other expenditures incurred by the client in connection with the hearing.

(5) Administrative costs incurred by the agency in carrying out the hearing procedures, including expenses of obtaining an additional medical asssessment.

Note on the Response to Goldberg v. Kelly and the New HEW Regulations

Events after the *Kelly* decision should be disturbing to those who perceive a major Supreme Court decision as the final resolution of an issue. First, of course, the *Kelly* decision had legal effect only in New York. The companion case of Wheeler v. Montgomery, 397 U.S. 280 (1970), decided the same day as *Kelly,* also extended the effective legal impact to California. Separate legal action was required in each other state where welfare officials did not voluntarily adjust their practices. See, e. g., Mothers' and Childrens' Rights Organization v. Sterrett, [1968–1971 Transfer Binder] CCH Pov.L.Rep. ¶ 11,582 (N.D.Ind.1970); Barnett v. Lindsay, 319 F.Supp. 610 (D.C.Utah 1970); Woods v. Miller,

[1968–1971 Transfer Binder] CCH Pov.L.Rep. ¶ 13,025 (D.Nev.1971); Smith v. Graham, [1968–1971 Transfer Binder] CCH Pov.L.Rep. ¶ 12,992 (D.C. Kan.1971). It is not clear that this state-by-state compliance effort has been completed even at the time of this writing— almost three years after the *Kelly* decision, and two years after the promulgation of the HEW regulations.

While the problems of state-by-state implementation should have been anticipated, the implementation problems in New York City, the focal point of *Kelly*, may come as some surprise. The New York welfare administrators were under specific court injunction, and moreover, they had a reputation for liberality. They might have been expected to comply fully, albeit reluctantly, with the decision and regulations. Such was not the case. Follow up litigation was filed in late 1971 complaining that the *Kelly* requirements were being systematically ignored and that the HEW Regulation was being openly defied. Almenares v. Wyman, 334 F.Supp. 512 (S.D.N.Y.1971), aff'd, 453 F.2d 1075 (2d Cir. 1971), cert. denied 405 U.S. 944 (1972). The factual pattern was described in the Second Circuit decision:

> The plaintiffs in this action are three women recipients of AFDC benefits. Maria Almenares received a letter from the City dated July 12, 1971, advising that on July 16, her semi-monthly grant of $120.50 would be reduced to $6.35 because of non-payment of rent, which she alleged she was withholding pursuant to N. Y. Real Property Action and Procedure Law § 755, and receipt of support money from her husband, the extent of which she denied; allegedly no opportunity for a hearing, State or local, was offered. Cresencia Garcia received notice dated April 14, 1971, that her grant would be reduced as of May 16—in fact, she alleges that, without further notice, the reduction became effective on May 1— from $117 semi-monthly to $93.60 because of alleged endorsement of checks which she claimed she had not received. Local agency review was not had until July 9, after assistance had already been reduced; the decision was adverse but Mrs. Garcia claimed the hearing did not afford due process because the hearing examiner was not impartial and because she was denied the right to confront the evidence against her. Janet Rodriguez received notice early in July, 1971, that her semi-monthly grant of $117.30 would be suspended (later modified to a reduction to $27.45) because she had been working, a fact which she denied. No pre-termination or pre-reduction hearing, State or local, was afforded since, as the City now asserts, discontinuance or reduction was "mandated by law," * * *. Before decision of the motion for a preliminary injunction, eight other recipients of AFDC benefits were allowed to intervene. Allegedly four had suffered or were threatened with termination and four with substantial reductions of their grants. Six had been advised of their right to a City hearing and four had received this; the others claimed they had not been so advised. All those who had received hearings alleged that these did not comply with due process. Five of the eight allegedly had assistance reduced or terminated prior to any hearing.

A variety of jurisdictional and procedural defenses were rejected and the courts found the defense on the merits to be "unimpressive." (What do you think that defense was?)

Nonetheless, immediate relief was not forthcoming. The district court entered an injunction ordering full compliance with HEW regulations on November 4, 1971. However, because of stays pending appeal and delays to permit adminis-

trative implementation of the relief ordered, this full relief was delayed at least
until late March, 1972, and possibly later,
depending upon Supreme Court action
in the case. However, on January 12,
1972, the plaintiffs were already back in
court to complain that interim relief ordered by the court had not been put into
effect and, by mid-February, contempt
proceedings were under way in the district court. These resulted in a threatened
series of penalties, including monetary
treble damages in some instances, which
began to produce some compliance but
the issue continued to remain in serious
doubt at the end of 1972.

What do you expect is the compliance
situation in states without an active group
of welfare reform lawyers to doggedly
pursue the matter? Assuming that the
New York plaintiffs fully succeed in their
litigation, how much practical effect will
that have on the caseworker-client dynam-
ic described by Handler, supra? What
other approach might be taken to control administrative arbitrariness?

As a final note to this saga, we insert
the following excerpt from an August 14,
1972 press release of the New York City
Department of Social Services as a reminder that the judicial forum is only
one locale where these battles are being
fought.

Mayor John V. Lindsay and Human
Resources Administrator/Social Services Commissioner Jule M. Sugarman
have called on the White House to
change a new "Fair Hearing" welfare
process required by federal regulations,
charging that the present regulations
as interpreted by the Federal Courts,
"could result in the loss of millions of
tax dollars."

In a letter to Elliot Richardson,
Secretary of Health, Education and
Welfare, the two officials cited the new
regulations as "administrative absurdi-
ties" which "strain the public toler-

ance" and "stand to defeat any effort
to reduce the number of ineligibles on
the assistance rolls."

* * *

According to Mr. Sugarman, the new
regulations required his Department
to grant nearly $5 million in assistance
to cases marked for closing or grant
reduction during the month of June,
as opposed to about $1 million for
April, the last month before the regulatory change. In addition, he estimates
that the new system has resulted in
grants of an additional half million
dollars to the mushrooming number of
recipients requesting Fair Hearings.

* * *

To illustrate a completely ludicrous
situation created by the new procedure,
he pointed out that the City is in the
process of placing about 400 welfare
recipients in full-time City jobs, paid
at standard rates. It was assumed that
the Department of Social Services
would be able to terminate these
clients' Public Assistance aid on the
day they received their first regular
City paychecks.

"But the State has informed us that
we must issue a Fair Hearing notice
before we terminate the welfare checks,
and inform the client that he has a
right to be continued on Public Assistance until he has exercised his State
review option. This even though he is
employed in the job that we arranged
for him. To say the least, such a procedure will only foster more contempt
for the entire public assistance system,"
Commissioner Sugarman commented.

The letter noted with alarm the
trend in Fair Hearing requests under
the new regulations. In April 1972,
the last full month of operations under
the old procedures, the Department
mailed out 12,500 Fair Hearing notices.
In June, the first full month under new
regulations, that figure rose to 36,000.

The April figure for requests for Fair Hearings was 1,000; that number rose to 2,000 requests in June.

Mr. Sugarman said:

"We are now getting persistent reports from the welfare community that at least some of the clients are already thinking of the procedures as a new hustle, which has grave implications for our current program to tighten eligibility requirements, especially among our addict caseload. This could lead to a widespread cynical resort to these new procedures and virtually smother the system in paperwork."

Mayor Lindsay and Commissioner Sugarman said "the procedures which were previously in effect achieved a balance between the rights of welfare clients and the responsibilities of government while the new procedures "harm both the taxpayer and the viability of a public assistance system which must serve those in need."

An internal study conducted by Donna Kirchheimer of the New York City Human Resources Administration following the above press release concluded that certain claims made in it were inaccurate. Specifically, the study reported that

(1) Monthly costs in increased benefits due to the new regulations were 1.27 million rather than $4 million as claimed;

(2) it was unfair to describe the regulations as a "new hustle" because there was no evidence that frivolous appeals were on the upswing. The percentage of hearings decided favorably to recipients increased from 17.3% to 19.8% after the regulations went into effect. Combined with "No Issue" decisions in which the Department withdrew its proposed adverse action, recipients actually prevailed in 49.4% of fair hearings. Moreover, there was no increase in recipient defaults at hearings.

What legal significance do these findings have?

USE OF THE DECLARATION IN PUBLIC ASSISTANCE

Public Welfare Reporting Center of National Study Service, Inc., Facts About Welfare Series, Report No. 2, May, 1969 at 1–11.

The use of the declaration represents a new and simplified approach to eligibility determination in public assistance to needy people. It is not surprising that questions have been raised about the new procedure, as it represents a decided departure from past practice and a major change from previous operating requirements which received great emphasis by Federal, state and local authorities over many years.

In the interests of the public, each aspect of eligibility of a person applying for financial assistance was verified through some objective source. The caseworker first gathered all the facts concerning eligibility from the person asking for help, along with whatever verifications the applicant could furnish. He then spent hours and often days of time verifying each fact necessary to establish eligibility such as income, debts, age, school attendance of older children, legal residence, etc.

The use of the declaration eliminates much of this routine verification. The declaration is an application form designed to be completed by the applicant. In this application, he sets forth all the facts required to establish his eligibility. In the absence of any reason to doubt the facts set forth, they are accepted as a valid basis for decision by the public welfare department. As a safeguard, a sample of accepted cases is selected for complete verification. According to Federal regulations, if more than three per cent of the cases in the sample are found to be ineligible, the agency must institute 100 per cent verification of the eligibility factors causing the errors until the problems have been corrected. Federal requirements also call for conspicuous notice on the application form of the penalties for fraud.

The idea behind this plan is not really new. It is similar to procedures used to check on the accuracy of statements made by individuals as they file their income tax returns. The concept was first applied in public assistance administration in 1962. In that year, the State of Alabama introduced the plan by establishing continuing eligibility in the adult categories of public assistance—Old Age Assistance, Aid to the Blind, and Aid to the Disabled. During the next four years, a number of states experimented successfully with this method, and by 1966, the Federal Bureau of Family Service was certain enough of its validity to encourage its use in its official Handbook. It was first required as a procedure for eligibility determination for certain applicants for the Work Experience and Training Program in January, 1967.

By November, 1968, about half the states had tested the new approach, and Secretary Wilbur H. Cohen proposed making the procedure mandatory for all public assistance categories by July 1, 1969. When this policy change was published as required in the *Federal Register,* (30 days are allowed for reactions) there were many comments submitted, both pro and con. The opposition was primarily focused on two issues: expecting the states to move so quickly without sufficient opportunity for planning, and the possibility, some thought, of a rapid increase in case load. Just before he left office, and after clearance with his successor Robert H. Finch, Secretary Cohen published new regulations which require only that the states experiment with the declaration in all public assistance programs in some part of the state by July 1, 1969, and if the test results warrant, that they install the simplified method in all categories by stated dates beginning on October 1, 1969 for Old Age Assistance and ending on April 1, 1970 with Aid to Families with Dependent Children.

[Ed. Note: This regulation was modified, as of February 26, 1970 to delay the statewide requirement of a declaration system to July 1, 1971 for OAA, AB, and APTD, and to postpone it indefinitely as to AFDC. See 45 C.F.R. § 205.20 (1970). Subsequently, with the enactment of the Supplemental Security Income Program to replace the adult categorical programs, Congress barred the declaration system even as to adult assistance.]

The great interest in simplifying eligibility determination in public assistance stems from a number of factors. Among these are: (a) concern over the voluminous paper work which is very costly and which takes a disproportionate amount of caseworker time, permitting little activity other than the procedures associated with eligibility; [1] (b) concern over the delay between the application for and the approval of a grant, due to the complexities and verifications involved in the traditional application process; (c) increasing questions as to whether the periodic individual redeterminations are essential to assure case load validity; (d) progress toward simplification of budgets, making it easier to determine the size of the grant on an objective basis; [2] (e) need to free

[1] For example, a "survey by the Cuyahoga County Welfare Department revealed that 77% of the worker's time was spent on procedures and paper work, leaving almost no time for other problems of the client." Stein, Herman D., Editor, The Crisis in Welfare in Cleveland, Report of the Mayor's Commission, Case Western Reserve University, Cleveland, 1969, p. 30.

[2] See Winston, Ellen and White, Gladys O., "Simplifying Need to Determination in Public Assistance," Welfare in Review, October, 1967, pp. 1–5.

caseworkers so that they have time to provide social services and to carry out the objectives of the 1962 services amendments to the Social Security Act and related 1967 legislation; (f) recognition of the importance of treating people with dignity and protecting their self-respect, objectives militated against by detailed investigations of their circumstances and behavior; (g) growing support for the principle of the applicant as the principal source of information about his circumstances; and (h) increased recognition of the honesty of applicants in reporting facts within their knowledge and competence.

* * *

The most important question to be considered in relation to the use of the declaration is whether eligibility can be determined as accurately by the new method as by the traditional method for case investigation. As was indicated above, the Federal agency has established a tolerance level of 3 per cent in the use of declarations. This means that audits should not result in a finding of more than 3 per cent of the cases ineligible at the time the determinations were made. A few states have carried out extensive testing so that objective results are becoming available and all report that they are within the established limit.

Alabama checked a sample in each of the adult categories of at least 5 per cent of cases approved during the 12 months ending August 31, 1964. The total number of cases reviewed was 9,677 so that the sample exceeded 480 cases. It was necessary to terminate only 9 cases, a proportion considerably lower than the three per cent tolerance level, recognized by the Federal agency.[3]

In Maine, where a number of improvements in the administration of public as-

sistance, including the introduction of self-declarations, were carried out over a period of several years, the per cent of ineligible cases in the adult categories decreased from 8 per cent in 1964, under the old methods for eligibility determination, to 1 per cent in 1968.

The State Commissioner in Iowa, one of the relatively few states already using the declaration method statewide for all public assistance programs, in a letter to the Public Welfare Reporting Center, reported as follows:

"As to the effectiveness of the declaration method for determining eligibility, Quality Control findings indicate that, for this year ending March 31, 1968, the estimated per cent of eligible Aid to Dependent Children cases in Iowa was 98.7 per cent. In the adult programs of Old Age Assistance, Aid to the Blind and Aid to the Disabled, the study revealed that 97.2 per cent were eligible."

While the validity of self-declarations has been rather widely accepted for the adult categories, far more questions have been raised with respect to Aid to Families with Dependent Children, the program generally subject to the most criticism and certainly the most difficult to administer equitably. Hence the report from Iowa quoted above and the following one from the Marin County, California Department of Public Social Services for the period April 1, 1968 through October 1, 1968 are particularly timely. During the six month period, applications and redeterminations of eligibility were completed for 664 Aid to Dependent Children Families. Validation studies were made on 177 cases or 27 per cent with comparisons between cases in which information was obtained by interview (99 cases) and by a self-administered declaration (78 cases). In each group, one case was found ineligible.

[3] "A Simplified Method of Establishing Continuing Eligibility in the Adult Categories," Alabama Social Welfare, January–February, 1965, p. 13.

" * * * the information obtained on a self-administered declaration in this sample was as reliable and accurate as the information obtained through an interview-administered declaration method." [4]

Although less information is available, there is some indication that the declaration method results in substantial saving of staff time and expense. The substantive costs of eligibility determination under the declaration and the conventional system have been compared by Maine:[5]

"For Fiscal year 1968, during which time the declaration method of determining eligibility was followed, the average unit cost of eligibility determination (for the adult programs) approximated . . . . . $6.30"

"For Fiscal year 1965, during which time the conventional method of determining eligibility determination was followed the average cost of eligibility determination approximated—$22.-50." [6]

According to a report from Wisconsin, "The time estimates required to review the declaration form and prepare a budget range from a low of 20 minutes to a high of 3 hours. The latter figure tends to occur because of various internal procedures rather than because of any state and Federal requirements. The average amount of time required to complete the process is approximately one hour." [7]

[4] "An Approach to Manpower Utilization by Means of Functional Specialization of Public Welfare Staff and the Use of an All-Program Declaration of Eligibility," Progress Report, April 1, 1968, through October 1, 1968, Marin County Department of Public Social Services, California Project No. 323A, p. 14.

[5] Related costs of case maintenance are also included in the unit cost.

[6] Material made available by Commissioner Dean Fisher, M.D., in attachment to letter dated February 6, 1969.

[7] Wisconsin Self-Declaration Project, Department of Health and Social Services, Sec-

While the experience with the state-wide programs is too short and involves too few states to give conclusive results concerning the effect on caseloads, it should be noted that from November, 1965 to November, 1968, the trends in Old Age Assistance in Iowa, Maine and Utah (statewide users of the declaration) were similar to the national trends. In aid to Families with Dependent Children, the percentage increase in the case load was below the increase for the country as a whole.

WELFARE IN NEW YORK CITY: THE ROLE OF ADMINISTRATION

Blanche Bernstein.
City Almanac,* February 1970, at 9–10.

As with all other aspects of welfare, one can find considerable differences of view regarding the extent to which the Department of Social Services is responsible for the increase in the welfare caseload, particularly since 1965.

Lawrence Podell, formerly Research Director in the Department of Social Services, in his study for the Joint Legislative Committee to Review the Social Service Law of New York State dealt at some length with "the liberalized acceptance thesis." He notes the charges made that departmental policy makers frequently stated, without evidence, that there were twice as many entitled to relief as were receiving it and that the welfare system encouraged desertion and abandonment. Podell does not believe there is sufficient evidence available to conclude that the expression of these views influenced the actual administration of the welfare system.

tion 1115, Project #275, Second Progress Report, January, 1969, p. 1.

* Published by Center for New York City Affairs, New School for Social Research.

It is, however, easy to underestimate the influence of what the French call the "ambiance" or what is inadequately translated as the atmosphere or general climate. The views of the administration can indeed have an impact on staff, as any well organized bureaucrat knows, and the margin for interpretation in individual situations can be substantial. As a group of Dr. Podell's critics pointed out, it is possible that in earlier years the general policy was to deny relief if there was any basis for the denial and now the policy is to give relief if there is any legitimate basis for doing so.

The impact of the ambiance is not only on the staff, but on the potential welfare recipient. If important public officials are constantly suggesting that the welfare system encourages family breakdown *because* the father must leave the home for the family to be eligible for welfare, that even more persons ought to be on relief, that jobs suitable to the unskilled are increasingly difficult to find, and that in any event the jobs do not pay a decent wage, this can only be regarded as encouragement to applying for and staying on relief. The statistics do show, in any event, that AFDC applications rose from 51,559 in 1961 to 94,552 in 1968, the percentage of applications accepted increased from 55.7 to 79.3 percent, and the ratio of case closings which rose from 1961 to 1965 declined in the subsequent years. One must bear in mind that at the same time, the welfare rights organizations were active in promoting claimants rights to welfare, as were some of the organizations supported by funds available from the poverty program, and these activities may have had some impact on the welfare caseload.

It needs to be stated clearly that no objection can be made to the activities of either public officials or welfare rights groups if the end result is that more poor people *who do not have other alternatives* apply for and receive the welfare grants to which they are entitled. The real question is to what extent these activities provided a disincentive for seeking other ways of obtaining income.

Another factor in the situation has been that as the welfare load increased, staff requirements were greatly enlarged. Between January 1966 and December 1968 the staff grew from 16,000 to 27,500 including 10,300 caseworkers and 3,200 case supervisors. This was combined with the high turnover rate of 61 percent which meant that the staff during the last few years included a high proportion of inexperienced personnel. At the same time, the centralized training and orientation period for workers was reduced from three weeks to two days, and training was in effect shifted to on-the-job-training.

The study on the Administration of AFDC in New York City found evidence which suggests that the higher the percentage of case worker turnover, the higher the percentage of poor using AFDC: the city had the second highest percentage of turnover in the 11 cities studied. It also found that New York had the largest percentage of new employees among the cities studied and that the average age of its caseworkers was the lowest. In other words New York City's caseworkers were not only new at their jobs, but many of them were also young. Further, in terms of the proportion of caseworkers with professional orientation, New York ranked low and in terms of the number of "recipient-oriented" caseworkers it ranked high. All these factors are related to a higher proportion of poor on AFDC.

In the light of these findings it is fair to suggest that the ambiance created by welfare officials in combination with the large infusion of new and inexperienced personnel may be responsible for some part of the increase in the caseload in recent years, but how large a part one cannot say.

On the other hand, HRA and the Department of Social Services have developed a number of new programs to promote employment of the AFDC mothers. The Family Day Care program, though limited in scope, was an innovative way of employing some AFDC mothers to care for the children of others, freeing them for employment. The regular day care program has not expanded as rapidly, however, as appropriated funds allowed. Employment programs instituted by the Manpower Career and Development Agency, the Work Incentive program (WIN) and the efforts of the Division of Employment and Rehabilitation have resulted in some women moving into jobs but the results so far have been relatively minor.

In this situation of a permissive atmosphere and inexperienced staff, the subject of administrative practices cannot be closed without some reference to the Self Declaration which has been tried experimentally in a number of districts. The Administrator of the Human Resources Administration, Mitchell Ginsberg, has been the foremost exponent of the Self Declaration on the grounds that the potential welfare recipient should be accorded the same degree of confidence as the taxpayer making a self declaration of his income. He and some other welfare officials are satisfied with the results of the experiments, which in their view, indicate that the level of cheating was as low in welfare centers which used the Self Declaration as in centers which carried on the usual investigation of the financial status of the applicant. Others, notably Lawrence Podell, have grave doubts that the Self Declaration will keep the lid on cheating. Podell points out that acceptance rates were substantially higher in the centers experimenting with the Self Declaration than in centers following the usual procedures; a higher rate of acceptance does not necessarily mean a higher rate of ineligibility but it is presumptive evidence.

At best one would have to admit that the studies which have been undertaken so far have been based on small samples and do not provide a firm base for a decision which can have far reaching consequences. Further, the studies which have been carried out cannot reflect the impact over time of the use of this looser procedure.

For neither defenders nor critics of the system have pointed out that the analogy of the welfare client to the taxpayer is faulty. The government does not rely exclusively on the taxpayers self-declaration. It long since has had, as a check, the W–2 form filled out by employers on all salaries and wages paid and, more recently, reports from banks and corporations on interest and dividend payments. Further, from time to time, and more or less energetically, it seeks to catch up with the various devices dreamed up by ingenious taxpayers to hide income from the revenue collector.

We are all aware of the widespread belief that the self employed, whether doctors, consultants, or sidewalk vendors are less likely to report earnings fully than those on a payroll. The proponents of the Self Declaration are relying rather heavily on a benign view of human nature. There is no reason to believe that the poor are less honest than the relatively well-to-do, but there is no reason to believe that they are more honest either. It would appear, therefore, that unless some substitute for the W–2 form for those receiving welfare benefits is developed, the wisdom of eliminating the present type of investigation, except for the aged, blind and disabled must be questioned.

Note

Ms. Bernstein's critique of welfare administration concludes that a declaration system is unwise "except for the aged, blind, and disabled." What justification is there for treating these adult categories differently from AFDC (that is, other than the differing racial composition of the adult categories and AFDC which was raised as an issue in Jefferson v. Hackney, p. 268, supra)? Apparently Congress does not perceive the reasons, for it has now barred the declaration system even as to adult programs in enacting SSI. Section 1631(e)(1)(13) of SSI, 42 U.S.C.A. § 1383(e)(1)(B), requires that eligibility "not be determined solely on the basis of declarations by the applicant." Why, in light of the data discussed above, was this rule imposed which is so administratively burdensome and contrary to the interests of individual privacy?

C. INVESTIGATIONS

PARRISH v. CIVIL SERVICE COMMISSION

Supreme Court of California, 1967.
66 Cal.2d 260, 57 Cal.Rptr. 623, 425 P.2d 223.

TOBRINER, Justice. In the present case an Alameda County social worker, discharged for "insubordination" for declining to participate in a mass morning raid upon the homes of the county's welfare recipients, seeks reinstatement with back pay on the ground that such participation would have involved him in multiple violations of rights secured by the federal and state Constitutions. He urges that his superiors could not properly direct him to participate in an illegal activity and that he could not, therefore, be dismissed for declining to follow such directions.

The county acknowledges that it has subsequently abandoned the method of mass morning raids to determine welfare eligibility and that such operations are now forbidden by the applicable state and federal regulations.[1] Since these regulations were not in force at the time of the plaintiff's dismissal, however, we must determine whether he could properly refuse to participate in the welfare raids on the ground that they infringed rights of constitutional dimension.

For the reasons set forth in this opinion we have decided that the county's failure to secure legally effective consent to search the homes of welfare recipients rendered the mass raids unconstitutional. We have determined further that, even if effective consent had been obtained, the county could not constitutionally condition the continued receipt of welfare benefits upon the giving of such consent. We have therefore held, for these two independently sufficient reasons, that the project in which the county directed the plaintiff to take part transgressed constitutional limitations. In light of plaintiff's knowledge as to the scope and methods of the projected operation, we have concluded that he possessed adequate grounds for declining to participate.

On November 21, 1962, the Board of Supervisors of Alameda County ordered the county welfare director to initiate a series of unannounced early-morning searches of the homes of the county's welfare recipients for the purpose of detecting the presence of "unauthorized males."[2] The searches were to be mod-

[1] The state and federal regulations which bar such searches are, respectively, section V(B) of "Special Methods of Investigation," Department of Social Welfare Bulletin No. 624 (revised), effective September 1, 1963, and section 2220, item 1, and section 2230, item 1, of the United States Department of Health, Education and Welfare, Handbook of Public Assistance Administration, issued March 18, 1966, requiring state conformance therewith by July 1, 1967.

[2] Welfare and Institutions Code section 11351 (formerly § 1508) provides that the amount of a grant on behalf of a needy child is to be computed after considering the income of any adult male "assuming the role

eled on a Kern County project popularly known as "Operation Weekend."

Neither in planning nor in executing the searches did the county authorities attempt to secure appropriate search warrants. The social workers who conducted the searches were not required or permitted to restrict them to the homes of persons whom they had probable cause to arrest, or even to the homes of those welfare recipients whose eligibility they had any reason to doubt. Indeed, as will later appear, the majority of persons whose homes were searched were under no suspicion whatever and were in fact subjected to the raid for that very reason.

The Alameda County searches, popularly and reportorially dubbed "Operation Bedcheck," commenced on Sunday, January 13, 1963, at 6:30 a. m.[3] Although the county welfare department contained a 10-man fraud unit whose members ordinarily investigated all cases of suspected fraud, that unit could not adequately staff an operation of the sweep contemplated by the supervisors. Accordingly, despite the fact that the county's social workers did not ordinarily conduct fraud investigations, their services were necessary for this undertaking.

Since the social workers lacked experience with the techniques employed by the fraud investigators they received special instruction in the procedures to be followed. Their superiors instructed them to work in pairs with one member covering the back door of each dwelling while the recipient's own social worker presented himself at the front door and sought admittance. Once inside, he would proceed to the rear door and admit his companion. Together the two would conduct a thorough search of the entire dwelling, giving particular attention to beds, closets, bathrooms and other possible places of concealment.

Plaintiff was one of the social workers chosen to participate in the first wave of raids. Upon learning the nature of the proposed operation, he submitted a letter to his superior declaring that he could not participate because of his conviction that such searches were illegal. After plaintiff had explained his position to the division chief and the welfare director, he was discharged for insubordination.

"Insubordination can be rightfully predicated only upon a refusal to obey some order which a superior officer is entitled to give and entitled to have obeyed." (Garvin v. Chambers (1924) 195 Cal. 212, 224, 232 P. 696, 701; Sheehan v. Board of Police Commrs. (1925) 197 Cal. 70, 78, 239 P. 844; Forstner v. City and County of San Francisco (1966) 243 Cal.App.2d 625, 52 Cal.Rptr. 621.) Plaintiff contends that his superiors were not entitled to compel his participation in illegal searches and urges that such participation might have exposed him to severe penalties under federal law.[4]

of spouse" to the child's mother, whether married to her or not.

[3] At the civil service commission proceeding the welfare department's division chief testified: "We indicated that the operation should start at 6:30 A.M. [I]f they were using County automobiles * * * they should leave the County lot at 6:30 A.M. If they were leaving directly from their home * * * the call should start at approximately 6:30 as the first call."

[4] One who, clothed with the authority of a state agency, invades and searches a home without a warrant and without probable cause to effect an arrest upon the premises may incur civil liability to the occupant under section 1983 of title 42 of the United States Code. (See Monroe v. Pape (1961) 365 U.S. 167, 81 S.Ct. 473, 5 L.Ed.2d 492; Cohen v. Norris (9th Cir. 1962) 300 F.2d 24, 31, 32; Beauregard v. Wingard (S.D.Cal.1964) 230 F.Supp. 167, 173–177.) Moreover, under section 242 of title 18 of the United States Code, wilful participation in a state-directed activity which infringes any right secured by the federal Constitution is a misdemeanor, punishable by a fine of not more than $1,000 or imprisonment for not more than one year, or both. (See United States v. Price (1966) 383 U.S. 787, 86 S.Ct. 1152, 16 L.Ed.2d 267; Screws v. United States (1945) 325 U.S. 91,

Accordingly we must determine, as the central issue in the present case, the constitutionality of the searches contemplated and undertaken in the course of the operation. By their timing and scope those searches pose constitutional questions relating both to the Fourth Amendment's stricture against unreasonable searches and to the penumbral right of privacy and repose recently vindicated by the United States Supreme Court in Griswold v. State of Connecticut (1965) 381 U.S. 479, 85 S.Ct. 1678, 14 L.Ed.2d 510.[5]

At the outset we must identify the standards which govern the constitutionality of such searches. Although misrepresentation of welfare eligibility constitutes a crime, by virtue both of special legislation directed to that evil (Welf. & Inst.Code, §§ 11265, 11482 [formerly §§ 1563, 1577]) and the general grand theft statutes (Pen.Code, §§ 484, 487; see People v. Bailey (1961) 55 Cal.2d 514, 516–518, 11 Cal.Rptr. 543, 360 P.2d 39; People v. Ryerson (1962) 199 Cal.App.2d 646, 649–650, 19 Cal.Rptr. 22), the county nevertheless contends that the searches undertaken in the course of the operation need not meet the standards ordinarily applied to searches for evidence of crime. It predicates this contention upon its claim that the searches were designed primarily to secure proof of welfare ineligibility so as to reduce the number of persons on welfare rather than to lay the basis for criminal prosecutions.[6]

* * *

On the basis of the foregoing analysis we conclude that the searches contemplated and undertaken in the course of the operation in the present case must be deemed unconstitutional unless the county can show compliance with the standards which govern searches for evidence of crime. The county concedes that it sought no warrants for these searches [8] and that it lacked probable cause to arrest any person in any of the homes searched, but contends that the searches took place pursuant to effective consent, freely and voluntarily given. (People v. McLean (1961) 56 Cal.2d 660, 664, 16 Cal.Rptr. 347, 365 P.2d 403; People v. Burke (1956) 47 Cal.2d 45, 49, 301 P.2d 241.)

The alleged consent to search.

Our first task is to analyze the county's argument that the raids entailed no unlawful searches because the authorities instructed the searchers to refrain from forcing their way into any home. They were, instead, to report any refusal of entry to their superiors for such further action as might be deemed appropriate. The record indicates that, under the county's established practice, a reported refusal of entry could serve as a basis for terminating welfare benefits. The record also establishes that welfare recipients must depend to a remarkably high degree upon the continued favor of their social workers, who are vested with wide discretion to authorize or prohibit specific expenditures.[9] Accordingly, we

65 S.Ct. 1031, 89 L.Ed. 1495; People v. Cahan (1955) 44 Cal.2d 434, 436, 282 P.2d 905, 50 A.L.R.2d 513.) (But see Note, Federal Judicial Review of State Welfare Practices (1967) 67 Colum.L.Rev. 84, 96 fn. 76.)

5 See, generally, Symposium on the Griswold Case and the Right of Privacy (1965) 64 Mich.L.Rev. 197.

6 The county cannot now effectively preclude the possibility that, in an appropriate case, it would have undertaken criminal proceedings on the basis of evidence secured in the operation. That possibility suggests the danger that "the administrative officer who

invades the privacy of the home may be only a front for the police who are thus saved the nuisance of getting a warrant." (Abel v. United States (1960) 362 U.S. 217, 242, 80 S.Ct. 683, 699, 4 L.Ed.2d 668 [Douglas, J., dissenting].)

8 Since the searches were made without warrants, the county of course bears the burden of justifying them. (See People v. Henry (1967) 65 Cal.2d 842, 56 Cal.Rptr. 485, 423 P.2d 557, and cases there cited.)

9 This discretion, limited by no standard and subject to no appeal, heightens the peril

must determine whether the threat of sanctions necessarily implicit in a request for entry under such circumstances vitiated the apparent consent which the searchers sought to secure from the occupants.

With increasing frequency the courts have denied the efficacy of any consent to a search obtained by covert threats of official sanction or by implied assertions of superior authority. The courts have been quick to note the disparity of position between a government agent and an ordinary citizen; they have taken cognizance of the threat of unspecified reprisals which inheres in the official request for admission. (See, e. g., Pekar v. United States (5th Cir. 1963) 315 F. 2d 319, 324–325; Canida v. United States (5th Cir. 1958) 250 F.2d 822, 825, and cases there cited.) As the court stated in Judd v. United States (D.C. Cir. 1951) 190 F.2d 649, 651, "The Government must show a consent that is 'unequivocal and specific' [citation], 'freely and intelligently given.' [Citation.] Thus 'invitations' to enter one's house, extended to armed officers of the law who demand entrance, are usually to be considered as invitations secured by force. [Citation.] A like view has been taken where an officer displays his badge and declares that he has come to make a search [citation], even where the householder replies 'All

faced by any recipient bold enough to deny entry. Not surprisingly, none of the recipients were so daring here. (See Respondent's Reply Brief, p. 10.) In Shelton v. Tucker (1960) 364 U.S. 479, 81 S.Ct. 247, 5 L.Ed. 2d 231, the court struck down a statute requiring teachers to report their membership in any organization, noting that "[s]uch interference with personal freedom is conspicuously accented when the teacher serves at the absolute will of those to whom the disclosure must be made—those who any year can terminate the teacher's employment without bringing charges, without notice, without a hearing, without affording an opportunity to explain." (364 U.S. at p. 486, 81 S.Ct. at p. 251.) Cf. Note, op. cit. supra, 67 Colum.L.Rev. 84, 93.)

right.' [Citation.] Intimidation and duress are almost necessarily implicit in such situations; if the Government alleges their absence, it has the burden of convincing the court that they are in fact absent." (Accord, Channel v. United States (9th Cir. 1960) 285 F.2d 217, 219–221.)

Thus in Johnson v. United States (1948) 333 U.S. 10, 68 S.Ct. 367, 92 L.Ed. 436, the United States Supreme Court voided a conviction based upon evidence secured after the defendant had admitted officers who told her that they wanted "to talk to [her] a little bit." (333 U.S. at p. 12, 68 S.Ct. at p. 368.) The court concluded that "[e]ntry to defendant's living quarters * * * was demanded under color of office. It was granted in submission to authority rather than as an understanding and intentional waiver of a constitutional right." (333 U.S. at p. 13, 68 S.Ct. at p. 368.) Similarly, in United States v. Slusser (S.D. Ohio 1921) 270 F. 818, 819, the court declared: "The search so permitted * * * after declaration by the prohibition officer, with a display of his badge, that they were there to search the premises, was not by such consent as will amount to a waiver of constitutional rights, but, on the contrary, is to be attributed to a peaceful submission to officers of the law." (See also Amos v. United States (1921) 255 U.S. 313, 317, 41 S.Ct. 266, 65 L.Ed. 654; People v. Henry, supra, 65 Cal.2d 842, 56 Cal. Rptr. 485, 423 P.2d 557; People v. Shelton (1964) 60 Cal.2d 740, 745–746, 36 Cal.Rptr. 433, 388 P.2d 665, and cases there cited.)

Our case proceeds far beyond a mere request for admission presented by authorities under color of office. Thus we need not determine here whether a request for entry, voiced by one in a position of authority under circumstances which suggest that some official reprisal might attend a refusal, is itself sufficient to vitiate an affirmative response by an individual who had not been apprised of his Fourth Amendment rights.[10] The persons subjected to the instant operation confronted far more than the amorphous threat of official displeasure which necessarily attends any such request. The request for entry by persons whom the beneficiaries knew to possess virtually unlimited power over their very livelihood posed a threat which was far more certain, immediate, and substantial.[11] These circumstances nullify the legal effectiveness of the apparent consent secured by the Alameda County searchers.[12] Both this court and the Supreme Court of the United States have recently emphasized the heavy burden which the government bears when it seeks to rely upon a supposed waiver of constitutional rights.[13] The county has not sustained that burden here.

[10] See United States v. Nikrasch (7th Cir. 1966) 367 F.2d 740, 744; United States v. Blalock (E.D.Pa.1966) 255 F.Supp. 268; People v. Henry, supra, 65 Cal.2d 842, 56 Cal. Rptr. 485, 423 P.2d 557: Note, Consent Searches: A Reappraisal After Miranda v. Arizona (1967) 67 Colum.L.Rev. 130.

[11] In Lynumn v. State of Illinois (1963) 372 U.S. 528, 534, 83 S.Ct. 917, 920, 9 L.Ed. 2d 922, the United States Supreme Court regarded a threat that "state financial aid for [the defendant's] children would be cut off" as an important element of coercion in determining the voluntariness of defendant's confession.

[12] In a recent article devoted entirely to the problem of nighttime welfare searches, Professor Charles Reich canvasses the available authorities and concludes that "there is no theory under which it can be said that public assistance recipients consent, expressly or impliedly, to searches of their homes. The official demand for entrance is sufficient to render any apparent consent involuntary and the threat of loss of public assistance underscores the coercive nature of the demand for entry." (Reich, Midnight Welfare Searches and the Social Security Act (1963) 72 Yale L.J. 1347, 1350.) (See also ten Broek, California's Dual System of Family Law: Its Origin, Development and Present Status (1965) 17 Stan.L.Rev. 614, 670.)

[13] See, e. g., Miranda v. State of Arizona (1966) 384 U.S. 436, 475–476, 86 S.Ct. 1602,

The consequences of failure to consent.

Even if we could conclude, however, that the consent secured by the Alameda County searchers constituted a knowing and fully voluntary waiver of Fourth Amendment rights, that conclusion would not establish the constitutionality of the operation involved in this case. That operation rested upon the assumption that a welfare agency may withhold aid from recipients who do not willingly submit to random, exploratory searches of their homes; from its inception, the operation contemplated the use of such searches to threaten the withdrawal of welfare benefits from anyone who insisted upon his rights of privacy and repose. In light of the resulting pressure upon welfare recipients to sacrifice constitutionally protected rights, the ultimate legality of the operation in which the plaintiff refused to participate must turn on whether the receipt of welfare benefits may be conditioned upon a waiver of rights embodied in the Fourth Amendment.

In Bagley v. Washington Township Hospital Dist. (1966) 65 Cal.2d 499, 55 Cal.Rptr. 401, 421 P.2d 409, and Rosenfield v. Malcolm (1967) 65 Cal.2d 559, 55 Cal.Rptr. 505, 421 P.2d 697, this court recently reviewed the so-called "doctrine of unconstitutional conditions," [14] concluding that the power of

16 L.Ed.2d 694; Brookhart v. Janis (1966) 384 U.S. 1, 4, 7, 86 S.Ct. 1245, 16 L.Ed.2d 314; People v. Stewart (1965) 62 Cal.2d 571, 581, 43 Cal.Rptr. 201, 400 P.2d 97, aff'd sub nom. Miranda v. State of Arizona, supra, 384 U.S. 436, 497–499, 86 S.Ct. 1602.

[14] A sampling of the more informative decisions and articles on this subject would include: Sherbert v. Verner (1963) 374 U.S. 398, 83 S.Ct. 1790, 10 L.Ed.2d 965; Speiser v. Randall (1958) 357 U.S. 513, 78 S.Ct. 1332, 2 L.Ed.2d 1460; Hannegan v. Esquire, Inc. (1946) 327 U.S. 146, 66 S.Ct. 456, 90 L.Ed. 586; Fort v. Civil Service Commission (1964) 61 Cal.2d 331, 38 Cal.Rptr. 625, 392 P.2d 385; Danskin v. San Diego Unified Sch. Dist. (1946) 28 Cal.2d 536, 171 P.2d 885; O'Neil, Unconstitutional Conditions: Welfare Benefits with Strings Attached (1966) 54 Cal.L. Rev. 443; Comment, Unconstitutional Con-

government to decline to extend to its citizens the enjoyment of a particular set of benefits does not embrace the supposedly "lesser" power to condition the receipt of those benefits upon any and all terms.

When, as in the present case, the conditions annexed to the enjoyment of a publicly-conferred benefit require a waiver of rights secured by the Constitution, however well-informed and voluntary that waiver, the governmental entity seeking to impose those conditions must establish: (1) that the conditions reasonably relate to the purposes sought by the legislation which confers the benefit; (2) that the value accruing to the public from imposition of those conditions manifestly outweighs any resulting impairment of constitutional rights; and (3) that there are available no alternative means less subversive of constitutional right, narrowly drawn so as to correlate more closely with the purposes contemplated by conferring the benefit. (Bagley v. Washington Township Hospital Dist., supra, 65 Cal.2d 499, 55 Cal.Rptr. 401, 421 P.2d 409; Rosenfield v. Malcolm, supra, 65 Cal.2d 559, 55 Cal.Rptr. 505, 421 P.2d 697; see Note, op. cit. supra, 67 Colum.L.Rev. 84, 101 & fn. 104; cf. Symposium on the Griswold Case and the Right of Privacy, op. cit. supra, 64 Mich.L.Rev. 197, 251.)

Although we can conceive of unusual situations in which the government might properly predicate continued welfare eligibility upon consent to unannounced early-morning searches, the record fails to develop any justification for such a condition here. Under some circumstances the county might be able to establish that a requirement of consent to such searches would facilitate the detection of frauds which deplete the welfare fund. As noted above, we would then be called

ditions: An Analysis (1961) 50 Geo.L.J. 234; Note, Unconstitutional Conditions (1960) 73 Harv.L.Rev. 1595.

upon to decide whether the benefits derived from the imposition of such a condition outweighed the corresponding impairment of constitutional rights. We could not resolve this issue upon the record now before us, because the evidence adduced in the present case fails to establish the incidence of welfare fraud or the efficacy of mass morning raids in reducing such fraud.[15]

In any event the instant operation does not meet the last of the three requirements which it must satisfy: so striking is the disparity between the operation's declared purpose and the means employed, so broad its gratuitous reach, and so convincing the evidence that improper considerations dictated its ultimate scope, that no valid link remains between that operation and its proffered justification.

* * *

[We fully recognize the importance of ferreting out fraud in the inexcusable garnering of welfare benefits not truly deserved. Such efforts, however, must be, and clearly can be, conducted with due regard for the constitutional rights of welfare recipients.] The county welfare department itself has now abandoned the technique of investigation which it pursued here; we may thus rest assured that it will develop other more carefully conceived procedures. It is surely not beyond the competence of the department to conduct appropriate investigations without violence to human dignity and within the confines of the Constitution.

The judgment is reversed and the cause is remanded to the trial court with directions to enter judgment in accordance with this opinion.

TRAYNOR, C. J., and PETERS, MOSK, BURKE and PEEK, JJ.

15 By a series of doubtful rulings, plaintiff was prevented from introducing evidence which he claimed would demonstrate that such searches were neither necessary nor effective.

DISSENTING OPINION

McCOMB, Justice.

I dissent. I would affirm the judgment for the reasons expressed by Mr. Justice Taylor in the opinion prepared by him for the Court of Appeal in Parrish v. Civil Service Commission (Cal. App.) 51 Cal.Rptr. 589.

WYMAN v. JAMES

Supreme Court of the United States, 1971.
400 U.S. 309, 91 S.Ct. 381, 27 L.Ed.2d 408.

Mr. Justice BLACKMUN delivered the opinion of the Court.

This appeal presents the issue whether a beneficiary of the program for Aid to Families with Dependent Children (AFDC) [1] may refuse a home visit by the caseworker without risking the termination of benefits.

The New York State and City social services commissioners appeal from a judgment and decree of a divided three-judge District Court holding invalid and unconstitutional in application § 134 of the New York Social Welfare Law, McKinney's Consol.Laws, c. 55,[2] § 175 of

[1] In Goldberg v. Kelly, 397 U.S. 254, 256 n. 1, 90 S.Ct. 1011, 1014, 25 L.Ed.2d 287 (1970), the Court observed that AFDC is a categorical assistance program supported by federal grants-in-aid but administered by the States according to regulations of the Secretary of Health, Education, and Welfare. See New York Social Welfare Law §§ 343-362. Aspects of AFDC have been considered in King v. Smith, 392 U.S. 309, 88 S.Ct. 2128, 20 L.Ed. 2d 1118 (1968); Shapiro v. Thompson, 394 U.S. 618, 89 S.Ct. 1322, 22 L.Ed.2d 600 (1969); Goldberg v. Kelly, supra; Rosado v. Wyman, 397 U.S. 397, 90 S.Ct. 1207, 25 L.Ed.2d 442 (1970); and Dandridge v. Williams, 397 U.S. 471, 90 S.Ct. 1153, 25 L.Ed.2d 491 (1970).

[2] "§ 134. Supervision

"The public welfare officials responsible * * * for investigating any application for public assistance and care, shall maintain close contact with persons granted public assistance and care. Such persons shall

the New York Policies Governing the Administration of Public Assistance,[3] and §§ 351.10 and 351.21 of Title 18 of the New York Code of Rules and Regulations,[4] and granting injunctive relief.

be visited as frequently as is provided by the rules of the board and/or regulations of the department or required by the circumstances of the case, in order that any treatment or service tending to restore such persons to a condition of self-support and to relieve their distress may be rendered and in order that assistance or care may be given only in such amount and as long as necessary. * * * The circumstances of a person receiving continued care shall be reinvestigated as frequently as the rules of the board or regulations of the department may require."

Section 134-a, as added by Laws 1967, c. 183, effective April 1, 1967, provides:

"In accordance with regulations of the department, any investigation or reinvestigation of eligibility * * * shall be limited to those factors reasonably necessary to insure that expenditures shall be in accord with applicable provisions of this chapter and the rules of the board and regulations of the department and shall be conducted in such manner so as not to violate any civil right of the applicant or recipient. In making such investigation or reinvestigation, sources of information, other than public records, shall be consulted only with the permission of the applicant or recipient. However, if such permission is not granted by the applicant or recipient, the appropriate public welfare official may deny, suspend or discontinue public assistance or care until such time as he may be satisfied that such applicant or recipient is eligible therefor."

[3] "Mandatory visits must be made in accordance with law that requires that persons be visited at least once every three months if they are receiving * * * Aid to Dependent Children * * *."

[4] "Section 351.10. *Required Home Visits and Contacts.* Social investigation as defined and described * * * shall be made of each application or reapplication for public assistance or care as the basis for determination of initial eligibility.

"a. Determination of initial eligibility shall include contact with the applicant and at least one home visit which shall be made promptly in accordance with agency policy * * *."

"Section 351.21. *Required Contacts.* Contacts with recipients and collateral sources shall be adequate as to content and frequency and shall include home visits, office in-

James v. Goldberg, 303 F.Supp. 935 (S.D.N.Y.1969). This Court noted probable jurisdiction but, by a divided vote, denied a requested stay. 397 U.S. 904, 90 S.Ct. 921, 25 L.Ed.2d 85.

The District Court majority held that a mother receiving AFDC relief may refuse, without forfeiting her right to that relief, the periodic home visit which the cited New York statutes and regulations prescribe as a condition for the continuance of assistance under the program. The beneficiary's thesis, and that of the District Court majority, is that home visitation is a search and, when not consented to or when not supported by a warrant based on probable cause violates the beneficiary's Fourth and Fourteenth Amendment rights.

Judge McLean, in dissent, thought it unrealistic to regard the home visit as a search; felt that the requirement of a search warrant to issue only upon a showing of probable cause would make the AFDC program "in effect another criminal statute" and would "introduce a hostile arm's length element into the relationship" between worker and mother, "a relationship which can be effective only when it is based upon mutual confidence and trust"; and concluded that

terviews, correspondence, reports on resources and other documentation."

Section 369.2 of Title 18 provides in part: "(c) *Welfare of child or minor.* A child or minor shall be considered to be eligible for ADC if his home situation is one in which his physical, mental and moral well-being will be safeguarded and his religious faith preserved and protected. (1) In determining the ability of a parent or relative to care for the child so that this purpose is achieved, the home shall be judged by the same standards as are applied to self-maintaining families in the community. When, at the time of application, a home does not meet the usual standards of health and decency but the welfare of the child is not endangered, ADC shall be granted and defined services provided in an effort to improve the situation. Where appropriate, consultation or direct service shall be requested from child welfare."

the majority's holding struck "a damaging blow" to an important social welfare program. 303 F.Supp., at 946.

I

The case comes to us on the pleadings and supporting affidavits and without the benefit of testimony which an extended hearing would have provided. The pertinent facts, however, are not in dispute.

Plaintiff Barbara James is the mother of a son, Maurice, who was born in May 1967. They reside in New York City. Mrs. James first applied for AFDC assistance shortly before Maurice's birth. A caseworker made a visit to her apartment at that time without objection. The assistance was authorized.

Two years later, on May 8, 1969, a caseworker wrote Mrs. James that she would visit her home on May 14. Upon receipt of this advice, Mrs. James telephoned the worker that, although she was willing to supply information "reasonable and relevant" to her need for public assistance, any discussion was not to take place at her home. The worker told Mrs. James that she was required by law to visit in her home and that refusal to permit the visit would result in the termination of assistance. Permission was still denied.

On May 13 the City Department of Social Services sent Mrs. James a notice of intent to discontinue assistance because of the visitation refusal. The notice advised the beneficiary of her right to a hearing before a review officer. The hearing was requested and was held on May 27. Mrs. James appeared with an attorney at that hearing.[5] They continued to refuse permission for a worker to visit the James home, but again, express-

[5] No issue of procedural due process is raised in this case. Compare Goldberg v. Kelly, supra, 397 U.S. 254, 90 S.Ct. 1011 (1970), and Wheeler v. Montgomery, 397 U.S. 280, 90 S.Ct. 1026, 25 L.Ed.2d 307 (1970).

ed willingness to cooperate and to permit visits elsewhere. The review officer ruled that the refusal was a proper ground for the termination of assistance. His written decision stated:

"The home visit which Mrs. James refuses to permit is for the purpose of determining if there are any changes in her situation that might affect her eligibility to continue to receive Public Assistance, or that might affect the amount of such assistance, and to see if there are any social services which the Department of Social Services can provide to the family."

A notice of termination issued on June 2.

Thereupon, without seeking a hearing at the state level, Mrs. James, individually and on behalf of Maurice, and purporting to act on behalf of all other persons similarly situated, instituted the present civil rights suit under 42 U.S.C.A. § 1983. She alleged the denial of rights guaranteed to her under the First, Third, Fourth, Fifth, Sixth, Ninth, Tenth, and Fourteenth Amendments, and under Subchapters IV and XVI of the Social Security Act and regulations issued thereunder. She further alleged that she and her son have no income, resources, or support other than the benefits received under the AFDC program. She asked for declaratory and injunctive relief. A temporary restraining order was issued on June 13, James v. Goldberg, 302 F. Supp. 478 (S.D.N.Y.1969), and the three-judge District Court was convened.

II

The federal aspects of the AFDC program deserve mention. They are provided for in Subchapter IV, Part A, of the Social Security Act of 1935, 49 Stat. 620, as amended, 42 U.S.C.A. §§ 601–610. Section 401 of the Act, 42 U.S.C.A. § 601, specifies its purpose, namely, "encouraging the care of dependent children in their own homes or in the homes

of relatives by enabling each State to furnish financial assistance and rehabilitation and other services * * * to needy dependent children and the parents or relatives with whom they are living to help maintain and strengthen family life * * *." The same section authorizes the federal appropriation for payments to States which qualify. Section 402, 42 U.S.C.A. § 602, provides that a state plan, among other things, must "provide for granting an opportunity for a fair hearing before the State agency to any individual whose claim for aid to families with dependent children is denied or is not acted upon with reasonable promptness"; must "provide that the State agency will make reports. * * * as the Secretary [of Health, Education, and Welfare] may from time to time require"; must "provide that the State agency shall, in determining need, take into consideration any other income and resources of any child or relative claiming aid"; and must "provide that where the State agency has reason to believe that the home in which a relative and child receiving aid reside is unsuitable for the child because of the neglect, abuse, or exploitation of such child, it shall bring such condition to the attention of the appropriate court or law enforcement agencies in the State, * * *" Section 405, 42 U.S.C.A. § 605, provides that

"Whenever the State agency has reason to believe that any payments of aid * * * made with respect to a child are not being or may not be used in the best interests of the child, the State agency may provide for such counseling and guidance services with respect to the use of such payments and the management of other funds by the relative * * * in order to assure use of such payments in the best interests of such child, and may provide for advising such relative that continued failure to so use such payments will result in substitution there- for of protective payments * * * or in seeking the appointment of a guardian * * * or in the imposi- tion of criminal or civil penalties * * *."

III

When a case involves a home and some type of official intrusion into that home, as this case appears to do, an im- mediate and natural reaction is one of concern about Fourth Amendment rights and the protection which that Amend- ment is intended to afford. Its empha- sis indeed is upon one of the most pre- cious aspects of personal security in the home. "The right of the people to be secure in their persons, houses, papers, and effects * * *." This Court has characterized that right as "basic to our free society." Wolf v. Colorado, 338 U. S. 25, 27, 69 S.Ct. 1359, 1361, 93 L.Ed. 1782 (1949); Camera v. Municipal Court, 387 U.S. 523, 528, 87 S.Ct. 1727, 1730, 18 L.Ed.2d 930 (1967). And over the years the Court consistently has been most protective of the privacy of the dwelling. See, for example, Boyd v. United States, 116 U.S. 616, 626–630, 6 S.Ct. 524, 530–532, 29 L.Ed. 746 (1886); Mapp v. Ohio, 367 U.S. 643, 81 S.Ct. 1684, 6 L.Ed.2d 1081 (1961); Chimel v. California, 395 U.S. 752, 89 S.Ct. 2034, 23 L.Ed.2d 685 (1969); Vale v. Louisiana, 399 U.S. 30, 90 S.Ct. 1969, 26 L.Ed.2d 409 (1970). In *Camera* Mr. Justice White, after noting that the "translation of the abstract pro- hibition against 'unreasonable searches and seizures' into workable guidelines for the decision of particular cases is a diffi- cult task," went on to observe,

"Nevertheless, one governing princi- ple, justified by history and by cur- rent experience, has consistently been followed: except in certain carefully defined classes of cases, a search of private property without proper con-

sent is 'unreasonable' unless it has been authorized by a valid search war- rant." 387 U.S., at 528–529, 87 S.Ct., at 1730–1731.

He pointed out, too, that one's Fourth Amendment protection subsists apart from his being suspected of criminal be- havior. 387 U.S., at 530, 87 S.Ct., at 1731.

IV

This natural and quite proper protec- tive attitude, however, is not a factor in this case, for the seemingly obvious and simple reason that we are not concerned here with any search by the New York social service agency in the Fourth Amendment meaning of that term. It is true that the governing statute and regu- lations appear to make mandatory the initial home visit and the subsequent pe- riodic "contacts" (which may include home visits) for the inception and con- tinuance of aid. It is also true that the caseworker's posture in the home visit is perhaps, in a sense, both rehabilitative and investigative. But this latter aspect, we think, is given too broad a character and far more emphasis than it deserves if it is equated with a search in the tra- ditional criminal law context. We note, too, that the visitation in itself is not forced or compelled, and that the bene- ficiary's denial of permission is not a criminal act. If consent to the visitation is withheld, no visitation takes place. The aid then never begins or merely ceas- es, as the case may be. There is no entry of the home and there is no search.

V

If however, we were to assume that a caseworker's home visit, before or sub- sequent to the beneficiary's initial quali- fication for benefits, somehow (perhaps because the average beneficiary might feel she is in no position to refuse consent to the visit), and despite its interview nature, does possess some of the characteristics of a search in the traditional sense, we nevertheless conclude that the visit does not fall within the Fourth Amendment's proscription. This is because it does not descend to the level of unreasonableness. It is unreasonableness which is the Fourth Amendment's standard. Terry v. Ohio, 392 U.S. 1, 9, 88 S.Ct. 1868, 1873, 20 L.Ed.2d 889 (1968); Elkins v. United States, 364 U.S. 206, 222, 80 S.Ct. 1437, 1446, 4 L.Ed.2d 1669 (1960). And Mr. Chief Justice Warren observed in *Terry* that "the specific content and incidents of this right must be shaped by the context in which it is asserted." 392 U.S., at 9, 88 S.Ct., at 1873.

There are a number of factors which compel us to conclude that the home visit proposed for Mrs. James is not unreasonable:

1. The public's interest in this particular segment of the area of assistance to the unfortunate is protection and aid for the dependent child whose family requires such aid for that child. The focus is on the *child* and, further, it is on the child who is *dependent*. There is no more worthy object of the public's concern. The dependent child's needs are paramount, and only with hesitancy would we relegate those needs, in the scale of comparative values, to a position secondary to what the mother claims as her rights.

2. The agency, with tax funds provided from federal as well as from state sources, is fulfilling a public trust. The State, working through its qualified welfare agency, has appropriate and paramount interest and concern in seeing and assuring that the intended and proper objects of that tax-produced assistance are the ones who benefit from the aid it dispenses. Surely it is not unreasonable, in the Fourth Amendment sense or in any other sense of that term, that the State have at its command a gentle means, of limited extent and of practical and

considerate application, of achieving that assurance.

3. One who dispenses purely private charity naturally has an interest in and expects to know how his charitable funds are utilized and put to work. The public, when it is the provider, rightly expects the same. It might well expect more, because of the trust aspect of public funds, and the recipient, as well as the caseworker, has not only an interest but an obligation.

4. The emphasis of the New York statutes and regulations is upon the home, upon "close contact" with the beneficiary, upon restoring the aid recipient "to a condition of self-support," and upon the relief of his distress. The federal emphasis is no different. It is upon "assistance and rehabilitation," upon maintaining and strengthening family life, and upon "maximum self-support and personal independence consistent with the maintenance of continuing parental care and protection, * * *" 42 U.S.C.A. § 601; Dandridge v. Williams, 397 U.S. 471, 479, 90 S.Ct. 1153, 1158, 25 L.Ed.2d 491 (1970), and Mr. Justice Marshall dissenting at 510, 90 S.Ct. at 1174. It requires cooperation from the state agency upon specified standards and in specified ways. And it is concerned about any possible exploitation of the child.

5. The home visit, it is true, is not required by federal statute or regulation.[6] But it has been noted that the visit is "the heart of welfare administration"; that it affords "a personal, rehabilitative orientation, unlike that of most federal programs"; and that the "more pronounced service orientation" effected by Congress

---

[6] The federal regulations require only periodic redeterminations of eligibility. HEW Handbook of Public Assistance Administration, pt. IV, § 2200(d). But they also require verification of eligibility by making field investigations "including home visits" in a selected sample of cases. Pt. II, § 6200(a)(3).

with the 1956 amendments to the Social Security Act "gave redoubled importance to the practice of home visiting. * * *" Rehabilitation, Investigation and the Welfare Home Visit, 79 Yale L.J. 746, 748 (1970). The home visit is an established routine in States other than New York.[7]

6. The means employed by the New York agency are significant. Mrs. James received written notice several days in advance of the intended home visit.[8] The date was specified. Section 134–a of the New York Social Welfare Law, effective April 1, 1967, and set forth in n. 2, supra, sets the tone. Privacy is emphasized. The applicant-recipient is

[7] See e. g., Ark.Stat. 83–131 (1968): Ala., Manual for Administration of Public Assistance, pt. I–8 (1968 rev.); Ariz., Regulations promulgated pursuant to Revised Statute § 46–203, Reg. 3–203.6 (1968); Cal. State Dept. of Social Welfare Handbook, C–012.50 (1964); Colo. c. 119, Art. 9, C.R.S.1963 (1967 Supp.), as amended c. 279 Session Laws, 1969; Fla. Public Assistance c. 100; Ga. Division of Social Administration—Public Assistance Manual pt. III, § V(D)(2), pt. VIII(A)(1)(b) (1969); Ill.Stat. Public Aid Code 23 § 4–7; Ind.Stat. 52–1247, Dept. Pub. Welfare, Rules & Regs., Reg. 2–403 (1965); Mich. Public Assistance Manual, Item 243(3)(F) (Rev.) (1967); Miss. Code 1942 § 7177 (Laws of 1940, c. 294); Mo. Public Assistance Manual, Dept. of Welfare, § III (1969); Nebraska, State Plan and Manual Regulations, pt. IX, §§ 5760, 5771; N. J., Manual of Administration, Division of Public Welfare, pt. II, §§ 2120, 2122 (1969); N. M. Public Welfare Act, 13–1–13, Health and Social Services Dept. Manual, §§ 211.5, 272.11; S. C. Dept. of Public Welfare Manual, Vol. IV(D)(2); S.Dak.L.1967, 28–7–7 (formerly SDC 1960 Supp. 55.3805); Tenn.Code Ann. 14–301 et seq. 37–309, Public Assistance Manual, Vol. II, p. 212 (1968 rev.); Wisc. Public Assistance Law § 49.19(2).

[8] It is true that the record contains 12 affidavits, all essentially identical, of aid recipients (other than Mrs. James) which recite that a caseworker "most often" comes without notice; that when he does, the plans the recipient had for that time cannot be carried out; that the visit is "very embarrassing to me if the caseworker comes when I have company"; and that the caseworker "sometimes asks very personal questions" in front of children.

made the primary source of information as to eligibility. Outside informational sources, other than public records, are to be consulted only with the beneficiary's consent. Forcible entry or entry under false pretenses or visitation outside working hours or snooping in the home are forbidden. HEW Handbook of Public Assistance Administration, Part IV, §§ 2200(a) and 2300; 18 N.Y.C.R.R. §§ 351.1, 351.6, and 351.7. All this minimizes any "burden" upon the homeowner's right against unreasonable intrusion.

7. Mrs. James, in fact, on this record presents no specific complaint of any unreasonable intrusion of her home and nothing which supports an inference that the desired home visit had as its purpose the obtaining of information as to criminal activity. She complains of no proposed visitation at an awkward or retirement hour. She suggests no forcible entry. She refers to no snooping. She describes no impolite or reprehensible conduct of any kind. She alleges only, in general and nonspecific terms, that on previous visits and, on information and belief, on visitation at the home of other aid recipients, "questions concerning personal relationships, beliefs and behavior are raised and pressed which are unnecessary for a determination of continuing eligibility." Paradoxically, this same complaint could be made of a conference held elsewhere than in the home, and yet this is what is sought by Mrs. James. The same complaint could be made of the census taker's questions. See Mr. Justice Marshall's opinion, as United States Circuit Judge, in United States v. Rickenbacker, 309 F.2d 462 (C.A.2 1962), cert. denied, 371 U.S. 962, 83 S.Ct. 542, 9 L.Ed.2d 509. What Mrs. James appears to want from the agency which provides her and her infant son with the necessities for life is the right to receive those necessities upon her own informational terms, to utilize the Fourth Amendment as a wedge for imposing

those terms, and to avoid questions of any kind.[9]

8. We are not persuaded, as Mrs. James would have us be, that all information pertinent to the issue of eligibility can be obtained by the agency through an interview at a place other than the home, or, as the District Court majority suggested, by examining a lease or a birth certificate, or by periodic medical examinations, or by interviews with school personnel. 303 F.Supp. at 943. Although these secondary sources might be helpful, they would not always assure verification of actual residence or of actual physical presence in the home, which are requisites for AFDC benefits,[10] or of impending medical needs. And, of course, little children, such as Maurice James, are not yet registered in school.

9. The visit is not one by police or uniformed authority. It is made by a caseworker of some training[11] whose

primary objective is, or should be, the welfare, not the prosecution, of the aid recipient for whom the worker has profound responsibility. As has already been stressed, the program concerns dependent children and the needy families of those children. It does not deal with crime or with the actual or suspected perpetrators of crime. The caseworker is not a sleuth but rather, we trust, is a friend in need.

10. The home visit is not a criminal investigation, does not equate with a criminal investigation, and despite the announced fears of Mrs. James and those who would join her, is not in aid of any criminal proceeding. If the visitation serves to discourage misrepresentation or fraud, such a byproduct of that visit does not impress upon the visit itself a dominant criminal investigative aspect. And if the visit should, by chance, lead to the discovery of fraud and a criminal prosecution should follow,[12] then, even assuming that the evidence discovered upon the home visitation is admissible, an issue upon which we express no opinion, that is a routine and expected fact of life and a consequence no greater than that which necessarily ensues upon any other discovery by a citizen of criminal conduct.

11. The warrant procedure, which the plaintiffs appear to claim to be so precious to them, even if civil in nature, is not without its seriously objectionable features in the welfare context. If a warrant could be obtained (the appellees afford us little help as to how it would be obtained), it presumably could be applied for *ex parte,* its execution would require no notice, it would justify entry by force, and its hours for execution[13]

work they are employed to do, we must assume that the caseworker possesses at least some qualifications and some dedication to duty.

[12] See, for example, New York Social Welfare Law § 145.

[13] New York Code Crim.Proc. § 801.

[9] We have examined Mrs. James' case record with the New York City Department of Social Services, which, as an exhibit, accompanied defendant Wyman's answer. It discloses numerous interviews from the time of the initial one on April 27, 1967, until the attempted closing in June 1969. The record is revealing as to Mrs. James' failure ever really to satisfy the requirements for eligibility; as to constant and repeated demands; as to attitude toward the caseworker; as to reluctance to cooperate; as to evasiveness; and as to occasional belligerency. There are indications that all was not always well with the infant Maurice (skull fracture, a dent in the head, a possible rat bite). The picture is a sad and unhappy one.

[10] Section 406(a) of the Social Security Act, as amended, 42 U.S.C.A. § 606(a); § 349, subd. B, par. 1 of the New York Social Welfare Law.

[11] The *amicus* brief submitted on behalf of the Social Services Employees Union Local 371, AFSCME, AFL–CIO, the bargaining representative for the social service staff employed in the New York City Department of Social Services, recites that "caseworkers are either badly trained or untrained" and that "[g]enerally, a caseworker is not only poorly trained, but also young and inexperienced * * *." Despite this astonishing description by the union of the lack of qualification of its own members for the

would not be so limited as those prescribed for home visitation. The warrant necessarily would imply conduct either criminal or out of compliance with an asserted governing standard. Of course, the force behind the warrant argument, welcome to the one asserting it, is the fact that it would have to rest upon probable cause, and probable cause in the welfare context, as Mrs. James concedes, requires more than the mere need of the caseworker to see the child in the home and to have assurance that the child is there and is receiving the benefit of the aid which has been authorized for it. In this setting the warrant argument is out of place.

It seems to us that the situation is akin to that where an Internal Revenue Service agent, in making a routine civil audit of a taxpayer's income tax return, asks that the taxpayer produce for the agent's review some proof of a deduction the taxpayer has asserted to his benefit in the computation of his tax. If the taxpayer refuses, there is, absent fraud, only a disallowance of the claimed deduction and a consequent additional tax. The taxpayer is fully within his "rights" in refusing to produce the proof, but in maintaining and asserting those rights a tax detriment results and it is a detriment of the taxpayer's own making. So here Mrs. James has the "right" to refuse the home visit, but a consequence in the form of cessation of aid, similar to the taxpayer's resultant additional tax, flows from that refusal. The choice is entirely hers, and nothing of constitutional magnitude is involved.

VI

Camara v. Municipal Court, supra, 387 U.S. 523, 87 S.Ct. 1727, 18 L.Ed.2d 930 (1967), and its companion case, See v. City of Seattle, 387 U.S. 541, 87 S.Ct. 1737, 18 L.Ed.2d 943 (1967), both by a divided Court, are not inconsistent with our result here. Those cases concerned,

respectively, a refusal of entry to city housing inspectors checking for a violation of a building's occupancy permit, and a refusal of entry to a fire department representative interested in compliance with a city's fire code. In each case a majority of this Court held that the Fourth Amendment barred prosecution for refusal to permit the desired warrantless inspection. Frank v. Maryland, 359 U.S. 360, 79 S.Ct. 804, 3 L.Ed.2d 877 (1959), a case which reached an opposing result and which concerned a request by a health officer for entry in order to check the source of a rat infestation, was pro tanto overruled. Both Frank and Camara involved dwelling quarters. See had to do with a commercial warehouse.

But the facts of the three cases are significantly different from those before us. Each concerned a true search for violations. Frank was a criminal prosecution for the owner's refusal to permit entry. So, too, was See. Camara had to do with a writ of prohibition sought to prevent an already pending criminal prosecution. The community welfare aspects, of course, were highly important, but each case arose in a criminal context where a genuine search was denied and prosecution followed.

In contrast, Mrs. James is not being prosecuted for her refusal to permit the home visit and is not about to be so prosecuted. Her wishes in that respect are fully honored. We have not been told, and have not found, that her refusal is made a criminal act by any applicable New York or federal statute. The only consequence of her refusal is that the payment of benefits ceases. Important and serious as this is, the situation is no different than if she had exercised a similar negative choice initially and refrained from applying for AFDC benefits. If a statute made her refusal a criminal offense, and if this case were one concerning her prosecution under that statute, *Camara* and *See* would have conceivable pertinency.

VII

Our holding today does not mean, of course, that a termination of benefits upon refusal of a home visit is to be upheld against constitutional challenge under all conceivable circumstances. The early morning mass raid upon homes of welfare recipients is not unknown. See Parrish v. Civil Service Comm., 66 Cal. 2d 260, 57 Cal.Rptr. 623, 425 P.2d 223 (1967); Reich, Midnight Welfare Searches and the Social Security Act, 72 Yale L.J. 1347 (1963). But that is not this case. Facts of that kind present another case for another day.

We therefore conclude that the home visitation as structured by the New York statutes and regulations is a reasonable administrative tool; that it serves a valid and proper administrative purpose for the dispensation of the AFDC program; that it is not an unwarranted invasion of personal privacy; and that it violates no right guaranteed by the Fourth Amendment.

Reversed and remanded with directions to enter a judgment of dismissal.

It is so ordered.

Reversed and remanded with directions.

Mr. Justice WHITE concurs in the judgment and joins the opinion of the Court with the exception of Part IV thereof.

Mr. Justice DOUGLAS, dissenting.

We are living in a society where one of the most important forms of property is government largesse which some call the "new property."[1] The payrolls of government are but one aspect of that "new property." Defense contracts, highway contracts, and the other multi-

[1] See Reich, The New Property, 73 Yale L.J. 733, 737–739.

farious forms of contracts are another part. So are subsidies to air, rail, and other carriers. So are disbursements by government for scientific research.[2] So are TV and radio licenses to use the air space which of course is part of the public domain. Our concern here is not with those subsidies but with grants that directly or indirectly implicate the *home life* of the recipients.

In 1969 roughly 126 billion dollars were spent by the federal, state, and local governments on "social welfare."[3] To farmers alone, whose numbers totalled 128,987, nearly four billion was paid, in part for not growing certain crops.[4] Those payments were in some instances very large, a few running a million or more a year. But the majority were payments under $5,000 each.

Yet almost every beneficiary whether rich or poor, rural or urban, has a "house"—one of the places protected by the Fourth Amendment against "unreasonable searches and seizures."[5] The question in this case is whether receipt of largesse from the government makes the *home* of the beneficiary subject to access by an inspector of the agency of oversight, even though the beneficiary objects to the intrusion and even though the Fourth Amendment's procedure for access to one's *house* or *home* is not followed. The penalty here is not, of course, invasion of the privacy of Barbara James, only her loss of federal or state largesse. That, however, is merely rephrasing the problem. Whatever the

[2] See Ginzberg, What Science Policy? Columbia Forum, Fall 1970, p. 12.

[3] See Appendix I to this opinion.

[4] See Appendix II to this opinion.

[5] "The right of the people to be secure in their persons, houses, papers, and effects, against unreasonable searches and seizures, shall not be violated, and no Warrants shall issue, but upon probable cause, supported by Oath or affirmation, and particularly describing the place to be searched, and the persons or things to be seized."

semantics, the central question is whether the government by force of its largesse has the power to "buy up" rights guaranteed by the Constitution.[6] But for the assertion of her constitutional right, Barbara James in this case would have received the welfare benefit.

We spoke in Speiser v. Randall, 357 U.S. 513, 78 S.Ct. 1332, 2 L.Ed.2d 1460, of the denial of tax exemptions by a State for exercise of First Amendment rights.

"It cannot be gainsaid that a discriminatory denial of a tax exemption for engaging in speech is a limitation on free speech. * * * To deny an exemption to claimants who engage in certain forms of speech is in effect to penalize them for such speech. Its deterrent effect is the same as if the State were to fine them for this speech." Id., at 518, 78 S.Ct., at 1338.

Likewise, while second-class mail rates may be granted or withheld by the government, we would not allow them to be granted "on condition that certain economic or political ideas not be disseminated." Hannegan v. Esquire, Inc., 327 U.S. 146, 156, 66 S.Ct. 456, 461, 90 L. Ed. 586.

In Sherbert v. Verner, 374 U.S. 398, 83 S.Ct. 1790, 10 L.Ed.2d 965, a State providing unemployment insurance required recipients to accept suitable employment when it became available or lose the benefits. An unemployed lady was offered a job requiring her to work Saturdays but she refused because she was a Seventh Day Adventist to whom Saturday was the Sabbath. The State cancelled her unemployment benefits and we reversed, saying:

"The ruling forces her to choose between following the precepts of her religion and forfeiting benefits, on the one hand, and abandoning one of the precepts of her religion in order to

6 See 73 Harv.L.Rev. 1595, 1599.

accept work, on the other hand. Governmental imposition of such a choice puts the same kind of burden upon the free exercise of religion as would a fine imposed against appellant for her Saturday worship.

"Nor may the South Carolina court's construction of the statute be saved from constitutional infirmity on the ground that unemployment compensation benefits are not appellant's 'right' but merely a 'privilege.' It is too late in the day to doubt that the liberties of religion and expression may be infringed by the denial of or placing of conditions upon a benefit or privilege. * * * to condition the availability of benefits upon this appellant's willingness to violate a cardinal principle of her religious faith effectively penalizes the free exercise of her constitutional liberties." Id., at 404, 406, 83 S.Ct., at 1794, 1795.

These cases are in the tradition of United States v. Chicago, M. St. P. & P. R. Co., 282 U.S. 311, 328–329, 51 S.Ct. 159, 163–164, 75 L.Ed. 359[7] where Mr. Justice Sutherland, writing for the Court said:

" * * * the rule is that the right to continue the exercise of a privilege granted by the state cannot be made to depend upon the grantee's submission to a condition prescribed by the state which is hostile to the provisions of the federal Constitution." Id., at 328–329, 51 S.Ct. at 164.[8]

7 And see Hale, Unconstitutional Conditions and Constitutional Rights, 35 Col.L. Rev. 321 (1935); Frost & Frost Trucking Co. v. Railroad Commission, 271 U.S. 583, 594, 46 S.Ct. 605, 607, 70 L.Ed. 1101.

8 Flemming v. Nestor, 363 U.S. 603, 80 S.Ct. 1367, 4 L.Ed.2d 1435, is not in accord with that tradition. There we upheld the right of Congress to strip away accrued social security benefits. Nestor, an alien, came to this country in 1913. From the enactment of the Social Security Act until 1955 Nestor and his employers contributed payments to the fund. In 1955 Nestor became eligible for

What we said in those cases is as applicable to Fourth Amendment rights as to those of the First. The Fourth, of course, speaks of "unreasonable" searches and seizures, while the First is written in absolute terms. But the right of privacy which the Fourth protects is perhaps as vivid in our lives as the right of expression sponsored by the First. Griswold v. Connecticut, 381 U.S. 479, 484, 85 S.Ct. 1678, 1681, 14 L.Ed.2d 510. If the regime under which Barbara James lives were enterprise capitalism as, for example, if she ran a small factory geared into the Pentagon's procurement program, she certainly would have a right to deny inspectors access to her *home* unless they came with a warrant.

old-age benefits. One year later he was deported for having been a member of the Communist Party between 1933 and 1939—a time when it was perfectly legal to be a member. In 1954 Congress passed a law which provided for the loss of social security benefits for anyone deported for having been a member of the Communist Party. Like the law providing for deportation for membership this law, too, was fully retroactive. Thus Nestor was deported after he had retired based on a law condemning membership in the Communist Party at the time when it was legal to be a member, and stripped of his retirement income based on a law which was triggered by that deportation. We upheld the constitutionality of the 1954 law by a 5–4 majority.

The majority stated Nestor's property had not been taken without due process because Nestor had no property rights; his interest was "non-contractual" and could "not be soundly analogized to that of the holder of an annuity." 363 U.S., at 609–610, 80 S.Ct., at 1372. The majority then went on to hold social security benefits were only protected from congressional action which is "utterly lacking in rational justification." Id., at 611, 80 S.Ct. 1367.

If it was unconstitutional in *Speiser* to condition a tax exemption on a limitation on freedom of speech, it was equally unconstitutional to withhold a social security benefit conditioned on a limitation of freedom of association. A right-privilege distinction was implicitly rejected in *Speiser* and explicitly rejected in *Sherbert*. Today's decision when dealing with a state statute joins *Flemming* as an anomaly in the cases dealing with unconstitutional conditions.

That is the teaching of Camara v. Municipal Court, 387 U.S. 523, 87 S.Ct. 1727, 18 L.Ed.2d 930, and See v. City of Seattle, 387 U.S. 541, 87 S.Ct. 1737, 18 L.Ed.2d 943. In those cases we overruled Frank v. Maryland, 359 U.S. 360, 79 S.Ct. 804, 3 L.Ed.2d 877, and held the Fourth Amendment applicable to administrative searches of both the *home* and a business. The applicable principle, as stated in *Camara* as "justified by history and by current experience" is that "except in certain carefully defined classes of cases, a search of private property without proper consent is 'unreasonable' unless it has been authorized by a valid search warrant." 387 U.S., at 528–529, 87 S.Ct., at 1731. In *See,* we added that the "businessman, like the occupant of a residence, has a constitutional right to go about his business free from unreasonable official entries upon his private commercial property." Id., 387 U.S., at 543, 87 S.Ct., at 1739. There is not the slightest hint in *See* that the Government could condition a business license on the "consent" of the licensee to the administrative searches we held violated the Fourth Amendment. It is a strange jurisprudence indeed which safeguards the businessman at his place of work from warrantless searches but will not do the same for a mother in her *home.*

Is a search of her home without a warrant made "reasonable" merely because she is dependent on government largesse?

Judge Skelly Wright has stated the problem succinctly:

"Welfare has long been considered the equivalent of charity and its recipients have been subjected to all kinds of dehumanizing experiences in the government's effort to police its welfare payments. In fact, over half a billion dollars are expended annually for administration and policing in connection with the Aid to Families with Dependent Children program. Why such large sums are necessary for administration and policing has never been adequately explained. No such sums are spent policing the government subsidies granted to farmers, airlines, steamship companies, and junk mail dealers, to name but a few. The truth is that in this subsidy area society has simply adopted a double standard, one for aid to business and the farmer and a different one for welfare." Poverty, Minorities, and Respect For Law, 1970 Duke L.J. 425, 437–438.

If the welfare recipient was not Barbara James but a prominent, affluent cotton or wheat farmer receiving benefit payments for not growing crops, would not the approach be different? Welfare in aid of dependent children, like social security and unemployment benefits, has an aura of suspicion.[9] There doubtless are frauds in every sector of public welfare whether the recipient be a Barbara James or someone who is prominent or influential. But constitutional rights— here the privacy of the *home*—are obviously not dependent on the poverty or on the affluence of the beneficiary. It is the precincts of the *home* that the Fourth Amendment protects; and their

[9] Juvenal wrote

"Poverty's greatest curse, much worse than the fact of it, is that it makes men objects of mirth, ridiculed, humbled, embarrassed." Satires (Indiana Univ. Press 1958), p. 39.

In the 1837 Term the Court held in City of New York v. Miln, 11 Pet. 102, 9 L.Ed. 648, that New York could require ships coming in from abroad to report the names, ages, etc. of every person brought to these shores. The Court said: "We think it is as competent and as necessary for a state to provide precautionary measures against the moral pestilence of paupers, vagabonds, and possibly convicts: as it is to guard against the physical pestilence, which may arise from unsound and infectious articles imported, or from a ship, the crew of which may be labouring under an infectious disease."

I regretfully conclude that today's decision is ideologically of the same vintage.

privacy is as important to the lowly as to the mighty.[10]

"* * * studies tell us that the typical middle income American reaches retirement age with a whole bundle

[10] An individual who refuses to allow the home visit could either be a welfare recipient at the time or an applicant for assistance. In neither case would the outcome of the refusal be different.

If the mother is already a recipient, Social Service Regulation 351.21 requires continuing contacts at home between the recipient and the social worker. Should a recipient refuse a visit then § 175 of the Policies Governing the Administration of Public Assistance ("Mandatory visits must be made in accordance with law that requires that persons be visited * * *.") would require termination. When the decision to "discontinue, suspend or reduce" benefits is made, the recipient would receive a hearing under § 351.-26 at which the recipient could present "written and oral relevant evidence and argument to demonstrate why his grant should not be discontinued, suspended or reduced." Since § 134 of the Social Services Law requires visits, the refusal to allow the visit would apparently be dispositive of the matter.

That seems to be conceded here by the commissioner. In light of that fact, the failure of appellee, who went to a hearing and was denied relief, to pursue any further state remedy seems irrelevant as the only question posed was the constitutionality under the Fourth Amendment of the termination of assistance for failure to agree to the warrantless entry into her home.

Except in very limited circumstances (Social Service Regulations 351.10 and 372 (Emergency Assistance)) an initial home visit and investigation is necessary before receiving benefits. Should a potential recipient refuse the initial visit, she would be notified under 351.14(b) of the reason for the denial. Then she could request a "fair hearing" under Board Rule 85 and Social Service Regulation 358. Again it appears that refusing the visit would be dispositive of the claim.

The extent to which a person could receive emergency assistance after refusal of a visit is unclear. Social Service Regulation 372.3 recognizes that emergency assistance could be available to a person while the "fair hearing" is pending. It would seem, however, that implicit in 372.3 is the notion that, if the claim is disposed of, then the emergency assistance would terminate. Also emergency assistance is limited to periods not in excess of 30 consecutive days in any 12-month period. Regulation 372.1.

of interests and expectations: as home-owner, as small investor, and as social security 'beneficiary.' Of these, his social security retirement benefits are probably his most important resource. Should this, the most significant of his rights, be entitled to a quality of protection inferior to that afforded his other interests? It becomes the task of the rule of law to surround this new 'right' to retirement benefits with protections against arbitrary government action, with substantive and procedural safeguards that are as effective in context as the safeguards enjoyed by traditional rights of property in the best tradition of the older law." [11]

It may be that in some tenements one baby will do service to several women and call each one "mom." It may be that other frauds, less obvious, will be perpetrated. But if inspectors want to enter the precincts of the home against the wishes of the lady of the house, they must get a warrant. The need for exigent action as in cases of "hot pursuit" is not present for the lady will not disappear; nor will the baby.

I would place the same restrictions on inspectors entering the *homes* of welfare beneficiaries as are on inspectors entering the *homes* of those on the payroll of government, or the *homes* of those who contract with the government, or the *homes* of those who work for those having government contracts. The values of the *home* protected by the Fourth Amendment are not peculiar to capitalism as we have known it; they are equally relevant to the new form of socialism which we are entering. Moreover, as the numbers of functionaries and inspectors multiply, the need for protection of the individual be-

comes indeed more essential if the values of a free society are to remain.

What Lord Acton wrote Bishop Creighton [12] about the corruption of power is increasingly pertinent today:

"* * * I cannot accept your canon that we are to judge Pope and King unlike other men, with a favorable presumption that they did no wrong. If there is any presumption it is the other way against holders of power, increasing as the power increases. Historic responsibility has to make up for the want of legal responsibility. Power tends to corrupt and absolute power corrupts absolutely. Great men are almost always bad men, even when they exercise influence and not authority: still more when you superadd the tendency or the certainty of corruption by authority."

The bureaucracy of modern government is not only slow, lumbering, and oppressive; it is omnipresent. It touches everyone's life at numerous points. It pries more and more into private affairs, breaking down the barriers that individuals erect to give them some insulation from the intrigues and harassments of modern life.[13] Isolation is not a constitutional guarantee; but the sanctity of the sanctuary of the *home* is such—as marked and defined by the Fourth Amendment, McDonald v. United States, 335 U.S. 451, 453, 69 S.Ct. 191, 192, 93 L.Ed. 153. What we do today is to depreciate it.

I would sustain the judgment of the three-judge court in the present case.

---

[11] Jones, The Rule of Law and the Welfare State, 58 Col.L.Rev. 143, 154–155 (1958).

[12] Acton, Essays on Freedom and Power edited by Herman Finer, 364 (1948).

[13] Mass raids upon the homes of welfare recipients are matters of record. See Parrish v. Civil Service Commission, 66 Cal.2d 260, 57 Cal.Rptr. 623, 425 P.2d 223, where an inspector was discharged because he refused to engage in such "illegal activity" and was granted relief by way of back pay.

APPENDIX I

STATISTICAL ABSTRACT OF THE UNITED STATES, 1970, p. 277.

Social Welfare Expenditures, by Source of Funds and Public Program:
1967 to 1969

(In millions of dollars)

Program	1967		1968		1969 (prel.)	
	Federal	State and local	Federal	State and local	Federal	State and local
Total	53,244	46,449	60,548	51,497	68,595	58,206
Social insurance	30,544	6,724	35,391	7,302	40,824	7,896
Old-age, survivors, disability, health ins. ..	24,581	(X)	28,748	(X)	33,389	(X)
Health insurance for the aged	3,395	(X)	5,347	(X)	6,598	(X)
Railroad retirement	1,278	(X)	1,417	(X)	1,547	(X)
Public employee retirement [1]	3,725	2,178	4,167	2,416	4,739	2,740
Unemployment ins. and employment serv.[2]..	790	1,963	373	2,055	932	2,021
Railroad unemployment insurance	38	(X)	46	(X)	45	(X)
Railroad temporary disability insurance ...	38	(X)	36	(X)	58	(X)
State temporary disability insurance [3].....	(X)	530	(X)	574	(X)	635
Hospital and medical benefits	(X)	54	(X)	55	(X)	58
Workmen's compensation [4]	94	2,054	103	2,257	114	2,500
Hospital and medical benefits	14	681	15	750	17	833
Public aid	5,244	3,567	6,455	4,637	7,851	5,592
Public assistance	4,266	3,567	5,250	4,637	6,389	5,592
Vendor medical payments	1,157	1,226	1,760	1,821	2,186	2,235
Other [5]	979	—	1,205	—	1,462	—
Health and medical programs [6]	3,681	4,128	4,233	4,038	4,497	4,321
Hospital and medical care	1,596	2,658	1,835	2,708	1,967	2,827
Civilian programs	164	2,658	187	2,708	200	2,827
Defense Department [7]	1,432	(X)	1,648	(X)	1,766	(X)
Maternal and child health programs [8]	139	171	161	176	192	190
Medical research	1,290	65	1,479	69	1,401	73
School health (educational agencies)	(X)	178	(X)	190	(X)	204
Other public health activities [9]	373	667	427	434	551	527
Medical facilities construction	284	389	332	461	386	500
Defense Department	50	(X)	29	(X)	59	(X)
Other	234	389	305	461	327	500
Veterans programs	6,857	23	7,329	33	7,996	40
Pensions and compensations [10]	4,487	(X)	4,716	(X)	5,041	(X)
Health and medical programs	1,346	(X)	1,465	(X)	1,585	(X)
Hospital and medical care	1,250	(X)	1,372	(X)	1,478	(X)
Hospital construction	49	(X)	46	(X)	54	(X)
Medical and prosthetic research	47	(X)	46	(X)	53	(X)
Education	297	(X)	466	(X)	671	(X)
Life insurance [11]	548	(X)	504	(X)	503	(X)
Welfare and other	179	23	179	33	197	40
Education [12]	5,279	30,389	5,108	33,648	5,079	37,954
Elementary and secondary	2,497	25,247	2,638	28,065	2,472	31,963
Construction [13]	33	3,937	35	4,184	34	4,620
Higher	2,089	4,400	1,807	4,800	1,943	5,100
Construction	710	900	474	1,000	431	1,100
Vocational and adult [13]	552	742	519	783	514	891
Housing	283	95	325	103	446	110
Other social welfare	1,356	1,524	1,706	1,736	1,903	2,293
Vocational rehabilitation, total	319	91	363	106	431	127
Medical services and research	78	17	98	26	116	31
Institutional care [14]	15	880	23	1,015	26	1,495
School meals	442	147	544	162	624	171
Child welfare [15]	47	406	50	453	50	500
Special OEO programs [16]	452	(X)	608	(X)	647	(X)
Social welfare, not elsewhere classified [17]..	81	(X)	118	(X)	124	(X)

— Represents zero.
X Not applicable.
[1] Excludes refunds to those leaving service. Federal data include military retirement.
[2] Includes compensation for Federal employees and ex-servicemen, and trade adjustment and cash training allowances.
[3] Programs operate in 4 States only: Calif., N. J., N. Y., and R. I.
[4] Benefits by private insurance carriers, State funds, and self-insurers.
[5] Work relief, other emergency aid, surplus food for the needy, food stamps, and Job Corps, Neighborhood Youth Corps, and Work-Experience programs under the Economic Opportunity Act.
[6] Excludes domiciliary care in institutions other than mental or tuberculosis, and services included with other programs in social welfare series.
[7] Includes cost of medical care for military dependent families.
[8] Includes services for crippled children.
[9] Excludes water supply and sanitation services.
[10] Includes burial awards.
[11] Excludes servicemen's group life insurance.
[12] Federal expenditures for administrative costs (Office of Education) and research not shown separately but included in total.
[13] Construction costs of vocational and adult education programs included under elementary-secondary expenditures.
[14] Represents primarily surplus food for nonprofit institutions.
[15] Represents primarily child welfare services under title V of the Social Security Act.
[16] Includes community action, migrant workers, and VISTA programs and all administrative expenses of the Office of Economic Opportunity.
[17] Includes administrative expenses of the Secretary of Health, Education, and Welfare; Indian welfare; aging activities; certain manpower activities; and other items.

Source: Dept. of Health, Education, and Welfare, Social Security Administration; Social Security Bulletin, December 1969.

APPENDIX II

Hearings, S. Committee on Appropriations, H. R. 17923, 91st Cong., 2d Sess., 1971, Pt. 3, p. 1979.

U. S. Department of Agriculture
Agricultural Stabilization and Conservation Service
ASCS Payments to Producers, All Programs,[1]
Calendar Year 1969

	Amount	Percent of total
Total payments	$3,794,996,353	100
Payments below $5,000	2,078,439,326	55
Payments $5,000 or above	1,457,635,442	38
Undistributed[2]	258,921,585	7

ASCS Payments by Size Groupings $5,000 and over
(Excludes sugar and wool payments)

Range	Number	Amount
$5,000 to $7,499	61,330	$ 370,839,000
$7,500 to $9,999	25,859	222,488,754
$10,000 to $14,999	21,147	254,979,861
$15,000 to $24,999	12,856	242,547,832
$25,000 to $49,999	6,029	200,524,421
$50,000 to $99,999	1,404	91,191,225
$100,000 to $499,999	346	55,113,824
$500,000 to $999,999	11	7,668,176
$1,000,000 and over	5	12,282,349
Total	128,987	$1,457,635,442

Mr. Justice MARSHALL, whom Mr. Justice BRENNAN joins, dissenting.

Although I substantially agree with its initial statement of the issue in this case, the Court's opinion goes on to imply that the appellee has refused to provide information germane to a determination of her eligibility for AFDC benefits. The record plainly shows, however, that Mrs. James offered to furnish any information that the appellants desired and to be interviewed at any place other than her home. Appellants rejected her offers and terminated her benefits solely on the ground that she refused to permit a home visit. In addition, appellants make no contention that any sort of probable cause

exists to suspect appellee of welfare fraud or child abuse.

Simply stated, the issue in this case is whether a state welfare agency can require all recipients of AFDC benefits to submit to warrantless "visitations" of their homes. In answering that question, the majority dodges between constitutional issues to reach a result clearly inconsistent with the decisions of this Court. We are told that there is no search involved in this case; that even if there were a search, it would not be unreasonable; and that even if this were an unreasonable search, a welfare recipient waives her right to object by accepting benefits. I emphatically disagree with all three conclusions. Furthermore, I believe that binding regulations of the Department of Health, Education, and Welfare prohibit appellants from requiring the home visit.

[Ed: Constitutional point omitted.]

II

The Court's examination of the constitutional issues presented by this case has constrained me to respond. It would not have been necessary to reach these questions for I believe that HEW regulations, binding on the States, prohibit the unconsented home visit.[5]

---

[1] Includes acreage diversion payments on cotton, feed grain, and wheat; price support payments on cotton and feed grain; wheat marketing certificates; cost-share payments under the Agricultural Conservation Program, emergency conservation and Appalachia programs; land retirement and conservation assistance payments under the cropland conversion, cropland adjustment, and conservation reserve programs; and the milk indemnity payment program. Does not include any price support loans or purchases, and payments under the Sugar Act and the National Wool Act.

[2] Includes payments to producers under the Sugar Act and the National Wool Act and payments to vendors for costs of conservation materials and services and funds transferred to other agencies for conservation technical services under the Agricultural Conservation Program; promotion fund deduction withheld under the National Wool Act which were transferred to the National Sheep Producers Council.

[5] It is a time-honored doctrine that statutes and regulations are first examined by a reviewing court to see if constitutional questions can be avoided, Ashwander v. T.V.A., 297 U.S. 288, 346–348, 56 S.Ct. 466, 482–484, 80 L.Ed. 688 (1936) (Brandeis, J., concurring): see, e. g., Dandridge v. Williams, 397 U.S. 471, 90 S.Ct. 1153, 25 L.Ed.2d 491 (1970); King v. Smith, 392 U.S. 309, 88 S.Ct. 2128, 20 L.Ed.2d 1118 (1968). The court below chose not to invoke this doctrine, and litigation in this Court has emphasized the constitutional issues. However, the nonconstitutional questions were briefed by an *amicus curiae* and appellants responded fully in their Reply Brief. The parties may prefer a decision on constitutional grounds; but we, of course, are not bound by their litigation strategies.

The federal Handbook of Public Assistance Administration provides:

> "The [state welfare] agency especially guards against violation of legal rights and common decencies in such areas as entering a home by force, *or without permission*, or under false pretenses; making home visits outside of working hours, and particularly making such visits during sleeping hours; * * *" Part IV, § 2300(a) (emphasis supplied).

Although the tone of this language is descriptive, HEW requirements are stated in terms of principles and objectives, Handbook, Part I, § 4210(3); and appellants do not contend that this regulation is merely advisory. Instead, appellants respond with the tired assertion that consent obtained by threatening termination of benefits constitutes valid permission under this regulation. There is no reason to suspect that HEW shares this crabbed view of consent. The Handbook, itself, insists on careful scrutiny of purported consent, Part IV, § 2400. Section 2200(a) is designed to protect the privacy of welfare recipients, and it would be somewhat ironic to adopt a construction of the regulation which provided that any person who invokes his privacy rights ceases to be a recipient.

Appellants next object that the home visit has long been a part of welfare administration and has never been disapproved by HEW. The short answer to this is that we deal with only the *unconsented* home visit. The general utility and acceptance of the home visit casts little light on whether HEW might prefer not to impose the visit on unwilling recipients. Appellants also remind us that the Federal Government itself requires a limited number of home visits for sampling purposes. However, while there may well be a special need to employ mandatory visits as a part of quali-

ty control samples, Mrs. James' home was not a part of such a sample. Furthermore appellants admit that § 2200(a) governs the quality control program; so it is not clear that unconsented home visits are allowed even for sampling purposes. Although there appears to be no regulatory history, appellants tell us § 2200(a) merely permits a recipient to refuse a particular home visit and does not allow him to forbid home visits altogether. I suppose that one could read such a limitation into the section, but given the regulation's explicit language, given that HEW does not require home visits and views the visits as only one of several alternative sources of eligibility information, given HEW's concern for the privacy of its clients, and given the durable principle of this Court that doubtful questions of interpretation should be resolved in a manner which avoids constitutional questions, United States v. Delaware & Hudson Co., 213 U.S. 366, 407, 29 S.Ct. 527, 535, 53 L.Ed. 836 (1909), I would conclude that Mrs. James is protected by § 2200(a).

III

In deciding that the homes of AFDC recipients are not entitled to protection from warrantless searches by welfare caseworkers, the Court declines to follow prior caselaw and employs a rationale that, if applied to the claims of all citizens, would threaten the vitality of the Fourth Amendment. This Court has occasionally pushed beyond established constitutional contours to protect the vulnerable and to further basic human values. I find no little irony in the fact that the burden of today's departure from principled adjudication is placed upon the lowly poor. Perhaps the majority has explained why a commercial warehouse deserves more protection than does this poor woman's home. I am not convinced; and therefore, I must respectfully dissent.

Note

1. The Department of H.E.W. has recently addressed itself to the issue of home visits in setting out new guidelines for a program of "quality control" over public assistance caseloads. These guidelines are designed to tighten up policing procedures and impose very strict standards upon state welfare departments. As to home visits, the guidelines provide:

> "Most interviews will be held in the home. However, it may be held elsewhere and *the client may request that it be held elsewhere.*" (Emphasis added.) U. S. Dept. of H. E. W., Q.C. Manual: Quality Control in Public Assistance III–S (1972).

These guidelines were promulgated after the decision in Wyman v. James, and it is therefore clear that this tolerant attitude toward home visits was not legally compelled. What other reason might explain it?

2. You will recall that Townsend v. Swank and Carleson v. Remillard, pp. 159–178, supra, seems to prohibit the states from imposing eligibility conditions beyond those embodied in the Federal categorical definitions, absent clear Congressional authorization for the additional conditions. Why is New York's home visit requirement not an additional condition which is prohibited under the Townsend-Remillard doctrine?

D. JUDICIAL REVIEW

ROSADO v. WYMAN

Supreme Court of the United States, 1970.
397 U.S. 397, 90 S.Ct. 1207, 25 L.Ed.2d 442.

[Procedural issues only. Substantive portions of opinion printed at p. 260, supra.]

Mr. Justice HARLAN delivered the opinion of the Court.

The present controversy, which involves the compatibility of the New York Social Services Law, McKinney's Consol. Laws, c. 55 (c. 184, L.1969) with § 402 (a)(23), 42 U.S.C.A. § 602(a)(23) (Supp. IV, 1968), of the Federal Social Security Act of 1935, arises out of a pendent claim originally included in petitioner's complaint bringing a class action challenging § 131–a of the same New York statute as violative of equal protection by virtue of its provision for lesser payments to Aid For Dependent Children recipients in Nassau County than those allowed for New York City residents. Pursuant to the recommendation of Judge Weinstein, a three-judge court was convened on April 24, 1969, and a hearing was held. 304 F.Supp. 1350.

* * *

B

A further reason given to support the contention that the District Court should have declined to exercise jurisdiction is that the Department of Health, Education, and Welfare was the appropriate forum, at least in the first instance, for resolution on the merits of the questions before us, and that at the time this action came to Court HEW was "engaged in a study of the relationship between Section 602(a)(23) and Section 131–a." 414 F.2d, at 176 (opinion of Judge Hays).[8]

[8] In order to evaluate this argument, it is necessary to understand the mechanism by which HEW reviews state plans under the AFDC program. States desiring to obtain federal funds available for AFDC programs are required to submit a plan to the Secretary of HEW for his approval. 42 U.S.C.A. § 601. Once initially approved, federal funds are provided to the State until a change in its plan is formally disapproved. 42 U.S. C.A. § 604(a). The Secretary must afford the State notice of an alleged noncompliance with federal requirements and an opportunity for a hearing. Ibid. If after notice and hearing the Secretary finds that the State does not comply with the federal requirements, he is directed to make a total or partial cutoff of federal funds to the State. Ibid. 42 U.S.C.A. § 1316 describes the ad-

Petitioners answer, we think correctly, that neither the principle of "exhaustion of administrative remedies" nor the doctrine of "primary jurisdiction" has any application to the situation before us. Petitioners do not seek review of an administrative order, nor could they have obtained an administrative ruling since HEW has no procedures whereby welfare recipients may trigger and participate in the Department's review of state welfare programs. Cf. Abbott Laboratories v. Gardner, 387 U.S. 136, 87 S.Ct. 1507, 18 L.Ed.2d 681 (1967); K. Davis, Administrative Law § 19.01 (1965); L. Jaffe, Judicial Control of Administrative Action 425 (1965).

That these formal doctrines of administrative law do not preclude federal jurisdiction does not mean, however, that a federal court must deprive itself of the benefit of the expertise of the federal agency which is primarily concerned with these problems. Whenever possible the district courts should obtain the views of HEW in those cases where it has not set forth its views, either in a regulation, published opinion, or in cases where there is real doubt as to how the Department's standards apply to the particular state regulation or program.[9]

ministrative procedures which the Secretary must afford a State before cutting off funds, and also provides for review in the courts of appeals of the Secretary's action at the behest of the State. Whether HEW could provide a mechanism by which welfare recipients could theoretically get relief is immaterial. It has not done so, which means there is no basis for the refusal of federal courts to adjudicate the merits of these claims.

[9] As we observed in Southwestern Sugar & Molasses Co., Inc. v. River Terminals Corp., 360 U.S. 411, 420, 79 S.Ct. 1210, 1216, 3 L.Ed.2d 1334 (1959), that an issue is "one appropriate ultimately for judicial rather than administrative resolution, * * * does not mean that the courts must therefore deny themselves the enlightment which may be had from a consideration of the relevant * * * facts which the administrative agency charged with regulation of the transaction * * * is peculiarly well equipped

The District Court, in this instance, made considerable effort to learn the views of HEW. The possibility of HEW's participation, either as a party or an *amicus*, was explored in the District Court and the Department at that stage determined to remain aloof. We cannot in these circumstances fault the District Court for proceeding to try the case.

* * *

III.

New York is, of course in no way prohibited from using only state funds according to whatever plan it chooses, providing it violates no provision of the Constitution. It follows, however, from our conclusion that New York's program is incompatible with § 402, that petitioners are entitled to declaratory relief and an appropriate injunction by the District Court against the payment of *federal* monies according to the new schedules, should the State not develop a conforming plan within a reasonable period of time.

We have considered and rejected the argument that a federal court is without power to review state welfare provisions or prohibit the use of federal funds by the States in view of the fact that Congress has lodged in the Department of HEW the power to cut off federal funds for noncompliance with statutory requirements. We are most reluctant to assume Congress has closed the avenue of effective judicial review to those individuals most directly affected by the administration of its program. Cf. Abbott Laboratories v. Gardner, 387 U.S. 136, 87 S. Ct. 1507, 18 L.Ed.2d 681 (1967); Association of Data Processing v. Camp, 397 U.S. 150, 90 S.Ct. 827, 25 L.Ed.2d 827 (1970); Barlow v. Collins, 397 U. S. 159, 90 S.Ct. 832, 25 L.Ed.2d 192

to marshal and initially to evaluate." See also Far East Conference v. United States, 342 U.S. 570, 574–575, 72 S.Ct. 492, 494–495, 96 L.Ed. 576.

(1970). We adhere to King v. Smith, 392 U.S. 309, 88 S.Ct. 2128, 20 L.Ed.2d 1118 (1968), which implicitly rejected the argument that the statutory provisions for HEW review of plans should be read to curtail judicial relief and held Alabama's "substitute father" regulation to be inconsistent with the federal statute. While *King* did not advert specifically to the remedial problem, the unarticulated premise was that the State had alternative choices of assuming the additional cost of paying benefits to families with substitute fathers or not using federal funds to pay welfare benefits according to a plan that was inconsistent with federal requirements.

The prayer in the District Court in King v. Smith, as in the case before us, was for declaratory and injunctive relief against the enforcement of the invalid provision. 277 F.Supp. 31 (D.C.M.D. Ala.1967). We see no justification in principle for drawing a distinction between invalidating a single nonconforming provision or an entire program. In both circumstances federal funds are being allocated and paid in a manner contrary to that intended by Congress. In *King* the withholding of benefits based on the invalid state regulation resulted in overpayments to some recipients, assuming a constant state welfare budget, and a corresponding misallocation of matching federal resources. In the case before us, noncompliance with § 402 (a)(23) may result in limiting the welfare rolls unduly and thus channeling the matching federal grants in a way not intended by Congress. We may also assume that Congress would not countenance the circumnavigation of the political consequences of § 402, see Part C, supra, by permitting States to use federal funds while obscuring the actual extent to which their programs fall short of the ideal.

Unlike King v. Smith, however, any incremental cost to the State, assuming a desire to comply with § 402, is massive;

nor is there a discrete and severable provision whose enforcement can be prohibited. Accordingly, we remand the case to the District Court to fix a date which will afford New York an opportunity to revise its program in accordance with the requirements of § 402 if the State wishes to do so. The District Court shall retain jurisdiction to review, taking into account the views of HEW should it care to offer its recommendations, any revised program adopted by the State, or, should New York choose not to submit a revamped program by the determined date, issue its order restraining the further use of federal monies pursuant to the present statute.

In conclusion, we add simply this. While we view with concern the escalating involvement of federal courts in this highly complicated area of welfare benefits,[23] one that should be formally placed under the supervision of HEW, at least in the first instance, we find not the slightest indication that Congress

[23] The judiciary is being called upon with increasing frequency to review not only the viability of state welfare procedures, e. g., Goldberg v. Kelly, 397 U.S. 254, 90 S.Ct. 1011, 25 L.Ed.2d 287 and Wheeler v. Montgomery, 397 U.S. 280, 90 S.Ct. 1026, 25 L.Ed. 2d 307 (1970); Wyman v. James, 303 F. Supp. 935 (D.C.S.D.N.Y.1969), prob. juris. noted, 397 U.S. 904, 90 S.Ct. 921, 25 L.Ed.2d 85 (1970) (inspections of the house), but the substance and structure of state programs and the validity of innumerable individual provisions. See, e. g., Shapiro v. Thompson, 394 U.S. 618, 89 S.Ct. 1322, 22 L.Ed.2d 600 (1969) (residing requirements); King v. Smith, supra (substitute father); Solman v. Shapiro, 300 F.Supp. 409, aff'd 397 U.S. 5, 90 S.Ct. 25, 24 L.Ed.2d 5 (1969); Lewis v. Stark, 312 F.Supp. 197 (D.C.N.D.Cal.1968) (prob. juris. noted, 396 U.S. 900, 90 S.Ct. 237, 24 L.Ed.2d 176 (1969) ("man-in-the-house rule"). At least two other actions have been instituted to review various aspects of state programs in light of the statutory provisions involved in this case. See Lampton v. Bonin, 299 F.Supp. 336, 304 F.Supp. 1384 (D.C.E.D. La.1969); Jefferson v. Hackney, 304 F.Supp. 1332 (D.C.N.D.Tex.1969); cf. Wyman v. Rothstein, 303 F.Supp. 339; Williams v. Dandridge, decided today, 397 U.S. 471, 90 S.Ct. 1153, 25 L.Ed.2d 491 (1970).

meant to deprive federal courts of their traditional jurisdiction to hear and decide federal questions in this field. It is, of course, no part of the business of this Court to evaluate, apart from federal constitutional or statutory challenge, the merits or wisdom of any welfare programs, whether state or federal, in the large or in the particular. It is, on the other hand, peculiarly part of the duty of this tribunal, no less in the welfare field than in other areas of the law, to resolve disputes as to whether federal funds allocated to the States are being expended in consonance with the conditions that Congress has attached to their use. As Mr. Justice Cardozo stated, speaking for the Court in Helvering v. Davis, 301 U.S. 619, 645, 57 S.Ct. 904, 910, 81 L.Ed. 1307 (1937): "When [federal] money is spent to promote the general welfare, the concept of welfare or the opposite is shaped by Congress, not the states." Cf. Lassen v. Arizona ex rel. Arizona Highway Dept., 385 U.S. 458, 87 S.Ct. 584, 17 L.Ed.2d 515 (1967).

The judgment of the Court of Appeals is reversed and the case is remanded to that court for further proceedings consistent with this opinion.

It is so ordered.

Reversed and remanded.

Mr. Justice DOUGLAS, concurring.

While I join this opinion of the Court, I add a few words.

*   *   *

II

The fact that the Department of Health, Education, and Welfare is studying the relationship between the contested provision of the New York statute and the relevant section of the Social Security Act is irrelevant to the judicial problem. Once a State's AFDC plan is initially approved by the Secretary of Health, Education, and Welfare, federal

funds are provided the State until the Secretary finds, after notice and opportunity for hearing to the State, that changes to the plan or the administration of the plan are in conflict with the federal requirements. Social Security Act § 404(a), 49 Stat. 628, as amended, 42 U.S.C.A. § 604(a) (1964 ed., Supp. IV).

The statutory provisions for review by HEW of state AFDC plans [1] do not permit private individuals, namely present or potential welfare recipients, to initiate or participate in these compliance hearings. Thus, there is no sense in which these individuals can be held to have failed to exhaust their administrative remedies by the fact that there has been no HEW determination on the compliance of a state statute with the federal requirements. In the present case, that problem was discussed in terms of the District Court's discretion to refuse to exercise pendent jurisdiction. The argument for such a refusal has little to commend it. HEW has been extremely reluctant to apply the drastic sanction of cutting off federal funds to States which are not complying with federal law. Instead, HEW usually settles its differences with the offending States through informal negotiations. See Note, Federal Judicial Review of State Welfare Practices, 67 Col.L.Rev. 84, 91–92 (1967).[2]

Whether HEW could provide a mechanism by which welfare recipients could theoretically get relief is immaterial. It has not done so, which means there is no basis for the refusal of federal courts to adjudicate the merits of these claims. Their refusal to act merely forces plaintiffs into the state courts which certainly are no more competent to decide the federal question than are the federal courts. The terms of the New York statute are clear, and there is no way in which a

[1] The procedure by which HEW reviews state plans is set out in the opinion of the Court, p. 1214 n. 8.

[2] See Appendix.

state court could interpret the challenged law in a way which would avoid the statutory claim pressed here.

State participation in federal welfare programs is not required. States may choose not to apply for federal assistance or may join in some, but not all, of the various programs, of which AFDC is only one. That a State may choose to refuse to comply with the federal requirements at the cost of losing federal funds is, of course, a risk that any welfare plaintiff takes. Such a risk was involved in King v. Smith, 392 U.S. 309, 88 S.Ct. 2128, 20 L.Ed.2d 1118, which attacked Alabama's "substitute father" regulation as inconsistent with the Social Security Act. As long as a State is receiving federal funds, however, it is under a legal requirement to comply with the federal conditions placed on the receipt of those funds; and individuals who are adversely affected by the failure of the State to comply with the federal requirements in distributing those federal funds are entitled to a judicial determination of such a claim. King v. Smith, supra. The duty of a State, which receives this federal bounty to comply with the conditions imposed by Congress was adverted to by Mr. Justice Cardozo who wrote for the Court in Steward Machine Co. v. Davis, 301 U.S. 548, 597–598, 57 S.Ct. 883, 895–896, 81 L.Ed. 1279, sustaining the constitutionality of the Social Security Act:

"Alabama is seeking and obtaining a credit of many millions in favor of her citizens out of the Treasury of the nation. Nowhere in our scheme of government—in the limitations express or implied of our Federal Constitution —do we find that she is prohibited from assenting to conditions that will assure a fair and just requital for benefits received."

As he also said, speaking for the Court in Helvering v. Davis, 301 U.S. 619, 645, 57 S.Ct. 904, 910, 81 L.Ed. 1307,

a companion case to *Steward Machine Co.*:

"When money is spent to promote the general welfare, the concept of welfare or the opposite is shaped by Congress, not the states."

Where the suit involves an alleged conflict between the state regulation and the federal law, neither the United States nor the Department of Health, Education, and Welfare is a necessary party to such an action. The wrong alleged is the State's failure to comply with federal requirements in its use of federal funds, not HEW's failure to withhold funds from the State.

Whether HEW should withhold federal funds is entrusted to it, at least as a preliminary matter, by § 404(a) of the Social Security Act.[3] Whether the courts have any role to perform beyond ruling on an alleged conflict between the state regulation and the federal law is a question we need not reach.

[3] Section 404(a) of the Act provides: "In the case of any State plan for aid and services to needy families with children which has been approved by the Secretary, if the Secretary, after reasonable notice and opportunity for hearing to the State agency administering or supervising the administration of such plans, finds—

"(1) that the plan has been so changed as to impose any residence requirement prohibited by section 602(b) of this title, or that in the administration of the plan any such prohibited requirement is imposed, with the knowledge of such State agency, in a substantial number of cases; or

"(2) that in the administration of the plan there is a failure to comply substantially with any provision required by section 602(a) of this title to be included in the plan;

"[T]he Secretary shall notify such State agency that further payments will not be made to the State (or, in his discretion, that payments will be limited to categories under or parts of the State plan not affected by such failure) until the Secretary is satisfied that such prohibited requirement is no longer so imposed, and that there is no longer such failure to comply. Until he is so satisfied he shall make no further payments to such State (or shall limit payments to categories under or parts of the State plan not affected by such failure)."

APPENDIX

DEPARTMENT OF HEALTH, ED-UCATION, AND WELFARE

Office of the Secretary
Washington, D. C. 20201

December 29, 1969

Mr. George R. Houston

Associate Librarian

The Supreme Court of the United States

1st Street & East Capitol, N. W.

Washington, D. C. 20543

Dear Mr. Houston:

This relates to your conversation with me on December 29 concerning statements made in the last paragraph and footnote 55 on page 91 of volume 67, Columbia Law Review, January 1967, that this Department had not responded to a complaint and petition for hearing filed by Georgia and Arkansas claimants.

The author of the Law Review article is correct. There was, in fact, no response to the request for a conformity hearing. Had we replied to the letter, however, we would have stated, as we usually do in such cases, that conformity hearings are held only on the initiative of this Department when a determination has been made that the deficiencies in a state program are such that the state, under its applicable laws, cannot, or the responsible official, will not, voluntarily bring the state into compliance.

Letters such as the one you refer to may, however, trigger action by this Department when the contents bring to light conformity matters of which the Department has not been made aware of as a result of its own audits.

To date this Department has initiated conformity hearings in connection with the state plans of Nevada and Connecticut. In view of the fact that the imposition of sanctions against states which are found to be out of conformity are mandatory, we exert every effort at our command to bring a state into conformity without the necessity of a formal hearing.

If you have any further questions, please let us know.

Very truly yours,
Robert C. Mardian,
General Counsel

Mr. Justice BLACK, with whom THE CHIEF JUSTICE joins, dissenting.

Petitioners are New York welfare recipients who contend that recently enacted New York welfare legislation which reduces the welfare benefits to which they are entitled under the Aid to Families with Dependent Children (AFDC) program is inconsistent with the federal AFDC requirements found in § 402(a)(23), of the Social Security Act 42 U.S.C.A. § 602(a)(23). The New York statute which petitioners are challenging, § 131–a of the New York Social Services Law, was enacted on March 31, 1969, Little more than a week later on April 9, petitioners filed their complaint challenging this statute. The Court today holds that "the District Court correctly exercised its discretion by proceeding to the merits" of petitioners' claim that the federal and state statutes are inconsistent. At 1212. The Court reaches this conclusion despite the fact that the determination whether a State is following the federal AFDC requirements is clearly vested in the first instance not in the federal courts but in the Department of Health, Education, and Welfare (HEW); despite the fact that at the very moment the District Court was deciding the merits of petitioners' claim HEW was performing its statutory duty of reviewing the New York legislation to determine if it was at odds with § 402(a)(23); and despite the fact that if HEW had been given enough time to make a decision with regard to the New York legislation, its decision might have obviated the need for this and perhaps many other lawsuits. I regret that I cannot join an opinion which fails to give due consideration to the unmistakeable intent of the Social Security Act to give HEW primary jurisdiction over these highly technical and difficult welfare questions, which affirms what is to me a clear abuse of discretion by the District Court, and which plunges this Court and other federal courts into an ever-increasing and unnecessary involvement in the administration of the Nation's categorical assistance programs administered by the States.[1]

Under the AFDC program, 42 U.S. C.A. §§ 601–610, the Federal Government provides funds to a State on the condition that the State's plan for supplementing and distributing those funds to needy individuals satisfies the various federal requirements set out in the Social Security Act. By statute, the Secretary of HEW is charged with the duty of reviewing state plans to determine if they comply with the now considerable list of federal requirements, 42 U.S.C.A. § 602, and his approval of such a plan, and only his approval, qualifies the state program for federal financial assistance. 42 U.S.C.A. § 601. So that HEW may determine whether the state plan continues at all times to meet the federal requirements, each State is required by regulation to submit all relevant changes, such as new state statutes, regulations, and court decisions, to HEW for its review. 45 CFR § 201.3. If, after affording the State reasonable notice and an opportunity for a hearing, HEW determines that the state plan does not conform to the federal requirements, the federal agency then has a legal obligation to terminate federal aid to which the State would otherwise be entitled. 42 U.S.C.A. §§ 604, 1316. 45 CFR § 201.5. Waiver by the Secretary of any of the federal requirements is permitted only where the Secretary and state welfare officials have together undertaken a "demonstration" or experimental welfare project. 42 U.S.

C.A. § 1315. The administrative procedures which the Secretary must afford a State before denying or curtailing the use of federal funds are elaborated in 42 U.S.C.A. § 1316, and this section also provides that a State can obtain judicial review in a United States court of appeals of an adverse administrative determination.

This unified, coherent scheme for reviewing state welfare rules and practices was established by Congress to ensure that the federal purpose behind AFDC is fully carried out. The statutory provisions evidence a clear intent on the part of Congress to vest in HEW the primary responsibility for interpreting the federal Act and enforcing its requirements against the States. Although the agency's sanction, the power to terminate federal assistance, might seem at first glance to be a harsh and inflexible remedy, Congress wisely saw that in the vast majority of cases a credible threat of termination will be more than sufficient to bring about compliance. These procedures, if followed as Congress intended, would render unnecessary countless lawsuits by welfare recipients. In the case before the Court today it is undisputed that HEW had by the time of the proceedings in the District Court commenced its own administrative proceedings to determine whether § 131–a conforms to the Social Security Act's provisions. The agency had requested the New York welfare officials to provide detailed information regarding the statute and was preparing to make its statutorily required decision on the conformity or nonconformity of § 131–a. It was at this point, when HEW was in the midst of performing its statutory obligation, that the District Court assumed jurisdiction over petitioners' claim and decided the very state-federal issue then pending before HEW. Both Judge Hays and Judge Lumbard on the Court of Appeals were of the opinion that the District Court abused its discretion in finding that it had jurisdiction over this statu-

---

[1] This precise issue was not so clearly and sharply presented in King v. Smith, 392 U.S. 309, 88 S.Ct. 2128, 20 L.Ed.2d 1118 (1968), which I joined. See id., at 317 n. 11, 88 S.Ct. 2133, 326 n. 23, 88 S.Ct. 2138.

tory claim, and both judges relied in part on the pendency of the identical question before the federal agency. 414 F.2d 170, 176, 181 (1969). Judge Lumbard's reasoning is instructive:

"[H]ere, as Judge Hays points out, the federal claim seems more apt for initial resolution by the Department of Health, Education and Welfare, than by the courts. The two issues upon a resolution of which this claim turns—the practical effect of § 131–a and the proper construction of § 602(a)(23) of the Social Security Act—both are exceedingly complex. The briefs and arguments of the parties, and the varying judicial views they have elicited, have demonstrated the wisdom of allowing HEW, with its expertise in the operation of the AFDC program and its experience in reviewing the very technical provisions of state welfare laws, an initial opportunity to consider whether or not § 131–a is in compliance with § 602(a)(23). This is HEW's responsibility under the Social Security Act, see 42 U.S.C.A. § 1316 (Supp. 1969). I believe that the district court should have declined to exercise its jurisdiction, thus permitting HEW to determine the statutory claim asserted by plaintiffs, for the Department already had initiated review proceedings concerning § 131–a." 414 F.2d, at 181.

I agree with the Court of Appeals that the District Court abused its discretion in taking jurisdiction over this case, but I would go further than holding that the District Court's action was a mere abuse of discretion. Ensuring that the federal courts have the benefit of HEW's expertise in the welfare area is an important but by no means the only consideration supporting the limitation of judicial intervention at this stage. Congress has given to HEW the grave responsibility of guaranteeing that in each case where federal AFDC funds are used, federal policies

are followed, and it has established procedures through which HEW can enforce the federal interests against the States. I think these congressionally mandated compliance procedures should be the exclusive ones until they have run their course. The explicitness with which Congress set out the HEW compliance procedures without referring to other remedies suggests that such was the congressional intent. But more fundamentally, I think it will be impossible for HEW to fulfill its function under the Social Security Act if its proceedings can be disrupted and its authority undercut by courts which rush to make precisely the same determination that the agency is directed by the Act to make. And in instances when HEW is confronted with a particularly sensitive question, the agency might be delighted to be able to pass on to the courts its statutory responsibility to decide the question. In the long run, then, judicial pre-emption of the agency's rightful responsibility can only lead to the collapse of the enforcement scheme envisioned by Congress, and I fear that this case and others have carried such a process well along its way. Finally, there is the very important consideration of judicial economy and the prevention of premature and unnecessary lawsuits, particularly at this time when the courts are overrun with litigants on every subject. If courts are permitted to consider the identical questions pending before HEW for its determination, inevitably they will hand down a large number of decisions which could have been mooted if only they had postponed deciding the issues until the administrative proceedings were completed. For all these reasons I would go one step further than the Court of Appeals majority and hold that all judicial examinations of alleged conflicts between state and federal AFDC programs prior to a final HEW decision approving or disapproving the state plan is fundamentally inconsistent with the enforcement scheme created by Congress and hence such suits should be completely precluded. This preclusion of judicial action does not, of course, necessarily mean that the individual welfare recipient has no legal remedies. The precise questions of when and under what circumstances individual welfare recipients can properly seek federal judicial review are not before the Court, however, and I express no views about those issues.[2]

E. CONFORMITY HEARINGS

MEMORANDUM OF DEPARTMENT OF HEALTH, EDUCATION AND WELFARE
(1971)
BACKGROUND ON WELFARE COMPLIANCE ACTION

Recently, wide attention has been given to an incident in a Federal compliance action regarding California's welfare programs. However, this is only one aspect of a much broader series of developments involving many of the States. This memo is intended to portray the actions that we have taken and the results achieved thus far.

Necessity for Compliance Actions

The welfare provisions of the Social Security Act are among the most complex administrative laws that the Federal Government administers. The States and localities administer the Federally-aided public assistance programs for the aged, the blind, and disabled, for families with dependent children, and for medical assistance. If the State plan meets applicable conditions under the Social Security Act and HEW regulations, the Federal Government must under the law pay a substantial portion of the expenditures under the programs; in all, some $10 billion in Federal funds annually. HEW

has the administrative responsibility for seeing to it that the State plans for the expenditure of this vast amount of money and operations under the plans comply with the Federal requirements.

If a State does not comply, HEW's only remedy provided by the Social Security Act is to cut off Federal funds, after giving the State notice and opportunity for hearing. In the continuing Federal-State relationship, this unsatisfactory sanction is invoked only with great reluctance. Every effort is made to obtain compliance through discussion, technical assistance and negotiations. With over 200 State plans, and several thousand plan amendments a year, almost all questions are resolved in this manner. From 1936 through 1968, only 14 compliance hearings were called.

Federal enforcement has not, however, been consistent. When this administration took office, a "credibility gap" of major proportions existed. States were disregarding Federal law and regulations openly. The previous administration took no action to stop these violations of law and therefore the States felt no compulsion to comply.

In addition to pressure from the organized welfare rights group, who asked that *all* laws whether applying to individuals or to States be equally enforced, the Department was severely criticized by the Supreme Court for not acting administratively. In addition, the House Ways and Means Committee report on Family Assistance noted that States were not complying with the requirement of the Social Security Act and stated that " * * * It expects the Department of Health, Education, and Welfare to take whatever steps may be necessary to assure full and prompt compliance with the requirement of Federal law."

At approximately the same time, the Secretary was sued by welfare recipients because, it was alleged, he was not carrying out his responsibilities under the Act.

---

[2] The issues are canvassed in Note, Federal Judicial Review of State Welfare Practices, 67 Col.L.Rev. 84 (1967).

Attempting to apply the law fairly and consistently at a time when effectiveness of the Governmental process is being questioned, the Secretary determined that the President's commitment to restore respect for law demanded compliance by welfare recipients and State agencies alike.

Moreover, to avoid securing compliance not only was engendering contempt for Federal integrity by citizens and State officials, but raised the prospect of overburdening the Federal courts with what is essentially an administrative responsibility, further compounding the difficulty of law enforcement.

Action Taken

To attack this problem, HEW's Social and Rehabilitation Service first organized its regional staff to take regular inventory of compliance issues in all States and make this information open to the public. A more orderly procedure of time limited negotiating with agencies was instituted. We intensified our efforts to resolve all questions by negotiations but found that our credibility could not be established without proceeding to a hearing, looking to cutoff of Federal funds if the State did not comply. Hearing notices were issued to Nevada and Connecticut in November 1969; to California, Indiana, Nebraska, and Arizona in July 1970; and to Missouri in October 1970. Appendix A contains a complete chronology on each State. [Only Ariz., Ind., and Neb. included herewith.]

* * *

Prehearing Process

As soon as a new law is passed the States are notified. To the extent possible new requirements are made effective far enough in the future to allow for change in State law and administrative action. Regional staff work with the State agency and in most cases the State voluntarily complies.

If by the effective data, no action is taken, efforts are made at negotiating

compliance first with the Welfare Director and then with the Governor. Only after all attempts have failed is a hearing offered to the State.

The Hearing Process

* * * In contrast to the negotiations to obtain compliance, the hearing process itself is quasi-judicial, with orderly steps set forth in published regulations (45 CFR Part 213). The parties are the State, HEW, and representatives of welfare recipients and others with an interest who, pursuant to court decision, may intervene as a matter of right and participate fully in the proceedings. A hearing examiner presides at the hearing, and his recommended decision, together with the transcript and the briefs of the parties, is submitted to the Administrator, SRS, who issues the final decision of HEW, which may be appealed to the U.S. Court of Appeals.

The hearing is directed solely to the question of whether the State is in compliance with Federal requirements, and the decision both of the hearing examiner and the SRS Administrator must be made on the basis of the official record. This accords with the HEW regulations and the requirements of the Administrative Procedure Act.

Nevertheless, both before, during and after the hearing, HEW may negotiate with the State to obtain compliance. If the State submits plan amendments which appear to be approvable, the SRS Administrator must distribute it to any third parties to the hearing for comment, and after considering the comments he may approve the amendment and withdraw the issue from the hearing.

If a State is found out of compliance, Federal funds must be withdrawn, as prescribed by the Social Security Act, beginning no later than the beginning of the next calendar quarter and continuing until the State comes into compliance.

* * *

APPENDIX A
COMPLIANCE HEARING—ARIZONA
ISSUES AND CHRONOLOGY

State: Arizona

Major Issues:

1) The State plan includes a provision for terminating aid payments to recipients who are residents of the State after a temporary absence of 90 days.

2) Disregards are applied to the net amount of income rather than to the gross as required by Federal law.

3) Children of an AFDC family who are living with relatives rather than their natural parent will not continue to receive assistance unless the Welfare Department or the relatives have legal custody of them.

4) The State has not fulfilled the requirement of establishing, at the State and local levels, an advisory committee for AFDC and CWS.

Chronology:

1) Informal negotiations began in the Regional Office in 1968 for issue number 1 and in 1969 for the other three issues. These negotiations included field visits, numerous letters and telephone conversations.

2) State put on notice.	June 17, 1970
3) Response by Welfare Commissioner Graham to June 17th letter inviting Administrator or a representative to Arizona for discussions.	June 23, 1970
4) Negotiations in Arizona between State and Administrator's representative	July 1, 1970
5) Hearing called.	July 8, 1970
6) Letter from Governor Williams to The Secretary requesting information on the hearing procedures.	July 24, 1970
7) Response by the Administrator to the Governor's July 24th letter.	August 10, 1970
8) Letter from Governor inviting the Administrator or a representative to Arizona for a final attempt at negotiations before the hearing.	July 24, 1970
9) Hearing Examiner appointed.	July 27, 1970
10) Request by State for a 120 day continuance of the hearing (denied by the hearing examiner).	July 29, 1970

11) Negotiations in Arizona between State and Administrator's representative.	August 4, 1970
12) John C. Montgomery met with Governor Williams on behalf of the Secretary at the National Governors' Conference. The discussion centered on the scheduled conformity hearing and the State's repeated request for a 120 day continuance.	August 11, 1970
13) Hearing held.	August 18–19, 1970
14) Examiner's proposed decision.	November 27, 1970
15) Letters concerning hearing sent to the Administrator from Senator Goldwater.	December 9, 1970 December 15, 1970
16) Comments by parties on Examiner's proposed decision in which the State suggests that the Administrator hold a hearing to consider the validity of HEW regulations.	December 17, 1970
17) Notice sent to all parties by the Administrator calling a hearing on January 20, in Phoenix for consideration of the validity of HEW regulations.	January 13, 1971
18) Hearing presided over by the Administrator.	January 20, 1971
19) Administrator issued his decision finding the State out of compliance on all four issues.	January 26, 1971
20) State petitioned to the U. S. Court of Appeals for the Ninth Circuit to review Administrator's decision and penalty order, and to stay the order pending their decision.	February 5, 1971
21) Court granted State's petitions.	February 22, 1971

COMPLIANCE HEARING—INDIANA
ISSUES AND CHRONOLOGY

State: Indiana

Major Issues: 1) The State has not made proportionate adjustments in its individual and family maximums or its shelter maximums as required by Section 402(a)(23) of the Social Security Act.

2) The State plan does not provide for payments on behalf of AFDC children to vendors.

Chronology:

1)	Informal negotiations.	July 1, 1969– January 1970
2)	Administrator warned State of seriousness of problem.	January 28, 1970
3)	State put on notice	June 9, 1970
4)	Hearing called	July 8, 1970
5)	Hearing Examiner appointed	July 27, 1970
6)	Hearing held	September 1–2, 1970
7)	Examiner's proposed decision	November 19, 1970
8)	Letter sent from Administrator asking parties to comment on his intention to remove the part of issue No. 1 concerning shelter maximums.	December 7, 1970
9)	Letter from Administrator to State Welfare Administrator advising that he will remove the shelter maximums part of issue No. 1 when the State confirms that the new plan has been implemented.	January 8, 1971
10)	Administrator issued his decision finding the State out of compliance with fund cutoff effective April 1, 1971.	January 18, 1971

Next Steps:

1) It is expected that the Governor will sign corrective legislation to resolve the issue which was recently passed by the Legislature.

COMPLIANCE HEARING—NEBRASKA
ISSUES AND CHRONOLOGY

State: Nebraska

Major Issues:

1) The State has not submitted amended plan material updating its assistance standards or making proportionate adjustments in its maximums as required by Section 402(a)(23) of the Social Security Act.

2) The question is whether the Nebraska law on responsibility of a stepfather falls in the category which allows the State to consider his income available for support of his stepchildren.

Chronology:

1)	Informal negotiations	July 1, 1969– January 1970
2)	Administrator warned State of seriousness of problem.	January 28, 1970
3)	State put on notice	June 9, 1970
4)	Hearing called	July 8, 1970
5)	Hearing Examiner appointed	July 27, 1970

6)	Hearing held	September 10, 1970
7)	Examiner's proposed decision	November 19, 1970
8)	Administrator issued his decision finding the State out of compliance with fund cutoff effective April 1, 1971	January 18, 1971

Next Steps: 1) It is expected that the State Legislature will take action to resolve the issues.

APPENDIX E

COMPLIANCE HEARINGS IN PUBLIC ASSISTANCE PROGRAMS

The public assistance programs are authorized by various titles of the Social Security Act. They are:

> Old Age Assistance (Title I)
> Aid to Families with Dependent Children (Title IV)
> Aid to the Blind (Title X)
> Aid to the Permanently Disabled (Title XIV)
> Aid to the Aged, Blind & Disabled (Title XVI) (combined program which replaced programs operated under Title I, X and XIV)
> Medical Assistance (Title XIX)

Each State may, if it chooses, participate in these so-called categorical programs. If the State chooses to participate, the Federal Government share in the cost of the program (generally 50% or more). In return, the State must agree to meet Federal rules and requirements.

In addition to the categorical programs many States also have general assistance available to meet the needs of persons who do not fall into one of the Federally assisted programs.

In the case of a State which does not meet Federal requirements either because its plan does not conform or because in practice the requirement is not being met, Federal payments must be withheld for the entire program or for the part of the program which is being violated.

Prior to the withholding of funds the State must be offered an opportunity for a hearing. The hearing process is governed by the Administrative Procedure Act and by special regulations.

If after being provided an opportunity for a hearing the State is dissatisfied with the decision, it may appeal directly to the United States Court of Appeals. If the State is dissatisfied with that Court's decision, it may then appeal to the United States Supreme Court.

The following hearings have been called and/or held.

1.   1936, North Carolina
     Question of statewide operation of Aid to Blind program. Hearing held June 1936. State rules out of compliance. State made satisfactory changes. No funds withheld.

2. **1937, Missouri**

Questions of inefficient operation, inaccurate reporting of expenditures, inaccurate statistical reporting, and single State agency. Hearing scheduled in June 1937. *Hearing not held*; State submitted acceptable plan.

3. **1937, Illinois**

Questions of inefficient administration, denial of fair hearing, inaccurate reporting, inaccurate accounting methods and records in old age assistance program. Hearing held July 1937. State rules out of compliance, State made satisfactory changes; no funds withheld.

4. **1938, Oklahoma**

Questions of inefficient operation and denial of fair hearings. Hearings held in February 1938. State found out of compliance; funds stopped. State made satisfactory changes; funds resumed, retroactive.

5. **1938, Ohio**

Questions of inefficient administration, inaccurate reporting, denial of fair hearings in old age assistance program. Hearing held September 1938. State did not appear for hearing. State ruled out of compliance; funds stopped in October. In November, State made satisfactory changes; funds were resumed. The State lost $1,338,160 in Federal funds for October 1938. These funds have never been restored.

6. **1940, Kansas**

Question of whether certain boarding homes were public or private institutions—Federal matching is not available in public institutions. Hearing held August 1940. Institutions were ruled public. Federal matching for old age and aid to the blind recipients in these institutions was terminated.

7. **1941, Georgia**

Questions of protection of public assistance records and whether State had merit system. *No hearing held*; questions resolved by negotiation.

8. **1943, Texas**

Question of State law which allowed a $250 exemption of earned income in old age assistance program. *Hearing not held*; question resolved by negotiation.

9. **1943, Colorado**

Question of failure to take all income and resources into account in determining eligibility. Hearing held February 1944. State ruled out of compliance. No loss of funds; State made satisfactory changes.

10. **1944, Louisiana**

State requested hearing on the right of Federal Government to limit matching of payments in old age assistance program. *No hearing held*; matter settled at informal conference.

11. 1949, New Mexico

Question of denial of assistance to needy Indians. Hearing held February 1949. State ruled out of compliance. State made satisfactory changes; no loss of funds.

12. 1949, Arizona

Question of denial of assistance to needy Indians. Hearing held February 1949. State ruled out of compliance. State made satisfactory changes; no funds withheld.

13. 1951, Indiana

Question of State law that would allow public access to public assistance records. Hearing held May 1951. State found out of compliance; funds withheld. Court review upheld decision. State appeal dismissed as moot after the Social Security Act was modified, referred to as the "Jenner Amendment," in 1951 to allow access to records as long as the records are not used for commercial or political purposes. Withheld funds were restored to the State.

14. 1952, Arizona

Question of plan to exclude reservation Indians from new aid to the disabled program. Hearing held April 1952. Plan found not approvable; court later dismissed Arizona appeal. No loss of funds since program was not in operation. State submitted new plan in 1962, which was approved.

15. 1960, Louisiana

Questions of inefficient administration, denial of fair hearings, and the State's "suitable home" policy which in effect denied assistance to otherwise eligible children because they lived in a so-called "unsuitable home." Hearing held November 1960. State ruled out of compliance. State made satisfactory changes; no funds withheld.

16. 1965, Alabama

State refused to submit Civil Rights plan to HEW. Hearing started October 1965. State ruled out of compliance April 1966. Hearing examiner recommended funds be withheld. Secretary ordered funds withheld January 1967; State filed injunction in U. S. District Court in Alabama to prohibit HEW from withholding funds. Injunction granted. In August 1967, the U. S. Court of Appeals in New Orleans vacated the injunction and upheld HEW's order to terminate Federal funds. State petitioned to the Supreme Court, petition was denied. State submitted approvable plan material; no loss of funds.

17. 1968, Georgia

State requested a hearing on a proposed State regulation to establish waiting lists for AFDC applicants. Plan ruled not acceptable; State withdrew plan.

18. 1969, Nevada

Questions related to the absence of a Work Incentive (WIN) program, the ceiling on the amount of earned income disregarded in determining amount of assistance; and failure to provide day care. Hearing scheduled for January 1970; postponed pending appeal by National

Welfare Rights Organization to be full party to the hearings. Court ruled in favor of National Welfare Rights Organization. In the meantime, State submitted approvable State plan. *No hearing held.*

19. 1969, Connecticut

Questions related to disregard of income in determining amount of assistance, failure to test simplified eligibility, the eligibility of children in cases where an unrelated male is living with a woman, Medicaid payments, and failure to submit required plan for service programs in AFDC. Hearing scheduled January 1970, postponed pending appeal by National Welfare Rights Organization to be full party to hearing. U. S. Court of Appeals for the District of Columbia ruled, June 9, 1970, in favor of NWRO. Hearing resumed December 1970.

20. 1970, Arizona

Questions of termination of aid payments to recipients who have been temporarily absent from the State for 90 days, the method of disregarding earned income, the provision that a caretaker-relative must have legal custody of a child whose siblings are also receiving AFDC in the home of their natural parents in order for the child to be eligible for AFDC, and whether the State plan provided for an AFDC–CWS State advisory committee. Hearing was held August 18, 1970. State found out of compliance by Administrator. State petition for review and stay of decision and penalty accepted by Court of Appeals.

21. 1970, California

Questions of adjusting AFDC payment maximums according to 402 (a)(23), the consideration of stepparents and certain siblings as essential persons, and the State-wideness of the adult social services program. The hearing was held August 25, 1970. Hearing Examiner recommended State be found out of compliance. State has submitted plan material. Decision issued and rescinded by Administrator on January 8, 1970, pending outcome of litigation in State Courts.

22. 1970, Indiana

Questions of adjusting AFDC payment and shelter maximums according to 402(a)(23) and provisions for vendor payments. The hearing was held September 1, 1970. On January 18, 1971, Administrator found State out of compliance and ordered a fund cutoff effective April 1, 1971.

23. 1970, Nebraska

Questions of updating the assistance standard and the adjusting of AFDC payment maximums according to 402(a)(23), and the State law regarding the obligation of a stepfather for the support of his stepchildren. The hearing was held September 10, 1970. On January 18, 1971 the Administrator found the State out of compliance and ordered a fund cutoff effective April 1, 1971.

24. 1970, Missouri

Questions of updating assistance standards and adjusting AFDC maximums according to 402(a)(23), reduction in amount of medical care and services provided, failure to provide home health services, and promptness in acting on applications. Hearing held January 19, 1971.

Notes

1. The series of hearings during 1969–71 resulted in a combination of State compliance efforts, HEW compromises and much litigation. No funds were ever actually withheld, so Ohio's loss of funds in 1938 (see ¶ 5 above) remains the only such event in history.

2. The flurry of activity described in the above memorandum seems now to have been a temporary abberation, more than a fundamental change in policy. Since these events H.E.W. has called no conformity hearings in the past several years despite the fact that, by H.E.W.'s own admission, dozens of state programs are out of compliance with Federal law, some seriously so. There are cynical explanations for this weak enforcement policy—that key H.E.W. officials are not seriously concerned about state defections or are politically motivated not to challenge them. But there is also a more innocent explanation—that the conformity hearing process with its single remedy of a fund cutoff is poorly suited to any real enforcement role.

It was proposed, as part of the general welfare reform that has already resulted in SSI and which is still underway as to AFDC, that more flexible enforcement mechanisms be established. These are described in the following excerpt from the House Ways and Means Committee Report on H.R. 1:

Additional remedies for State noncompliance

The Administration has asked your committee for legislation providing additional methods for obtaining State compliance under the grant programs of the Social Security Act. The Secretary may now withhold or terminate Federal matching funds when he has determined that a State is not complying with Federal law or regulation. Your committee's bill would provide that he may prescribe other methods to correct administrative non-compliance, including establishing a timetable for corrections and a requirement that persons incorrectly denied benefits by the State be paid retroactively. Federal matching would continue as long as the Secretary is assured that the timetable is being followed. In addition, the Secretary would be authorized, as a means of securing compliance, to request the Attorney General to bring suit against the State. The provision would be effective on enactment. H. R.Rep. No. 92–231, 92d Cong., 1st Sess. 205–206 (1971).

These provisions were, however, not enacted. Is there any reason not to give H.E.W. this administrative flexibility?

SECTION 6. ALTERNATIVES FOR THE FUTURE

ON COMPARING INCOME MAINTENANCE ALTERNATIVES *

Theodore Marmor.
The American Political Science Review
(March 1971).

Major social policy decisions in America are not made by intellectuals, particularly academic intellectuals. Nonetheless, social critics, particularly academic intellectuals, extensively discuss the problems of income distribution and poverty. The gross national discussion has grown so large, in fact, that it appears we have a new service industry—one that does a lot of thinking about poverty. True, it has yet to *do* much about poverty, but "firms" within this industry write about poverty, argue about poverty, and generate papers for conferences at an accelerating rate and with escalating volume. The industry's growth has so expanded in the last ten years that some find it necessary to identify the division of this intellectual labor. Advocates of the negative income tax (NIT), for instance, are known by some producers of competing ideas as the "nit-wits."

The net effect of research efforts in the sixties was not to create a consensus concerning what ought to be done about poverty. There has been some agreement that the eventual answer would be an income maintenance program, but there has been less agreement about which plan is best. In the summer of 1968 at a joint congressional hearing on income maintenance, no less than two dozen intellectuals appeared before the committee to offer no less than two dozen different schemes on how the income of the poor might be maintained.[1]

Not only is there a proliferation of proposals, they have often been badly presented for intelligent policy choice. Discussion of family allowances, negative income taxes, and other cash transfer programs proceeds, as Lee Rainwater has said, " * * * either in the form of a catalogue of different proposals * * or shortsighted polemics about the superiority of some one method." [2]

Commonly, plans are grouped according to administrative method even when their social welfare goals are substantially different. For example, negative income tax plans of vastly different scope and benefit levels are grouped under the same rubric even though they are clearly not alternative means to solving the same problem. The proposal identified with Yale economist James Tobin—a major anti-poverty scheme featuring a $2600 guarantee level, universal eligibility, and a $5200 cut-off point—contrasts sharply with low-level negative income tax plans. One such plan, formulated by Robert Lampman to supplement the wages of the working poor, calls for a $750 guarantee and a $3000 cut-off point for a four-person family.[3] The Tobin plan, because of its universal and high benefits, would cost approximately $26 billion, some five times more than the estimated $5.0 billion cost of the Lampman plan. These two plans are alike in administrative mechanism but have little else in common, since they were designed as solutions to different problems.

[1] Income Maintenance Programs, Hearings Before the Subcommittee on Fiscal Policy of the Joint Economic Committee, Congress of the United States, Joint Economic Committee, 90th Congress, 2nd Session, Vol. I, June, 1968.

[2] Lee Rainwater to author, May, 1968. An example of cataloguing income maintenance alternatives can be found in Christopher Green, Negative Taxes and the Poverty Problem (Washington, D. C.: The Brookings Institution, 1967). James Vadakin, Family Allowances (Miami: University of Miami Press, 1968) illustrates special pleading for one mechanism of cash transfer in this case one defined by the age characteristics of the recipients. Variations in the nature of family allowances are substantial; European nations have programs so different that little is gained by grouping them as if they served common ends with comparable efficiency. Milton Friedman has disassociated his version of a welfare-replacing NIT from more generous negative tax plans such as James Tobin's. See Time, "Welfare and Illfare: The Alternatives to Poverty," December 13, 1968. For support of the idea that concepts like NIT do not sufficiently describe a class of programs, see "Comment: A Model Negative Income Tax Statute," Yale Law Journal, 78 (December 1968), p. 270, n. 6. The editors assert, " 'negative income tax' has no precise meaning," and add that, when they refer to "negative income tax," they mean their own proposal.

[3] Tobin, et al., "Is a Negative Income Tax Practical," Yale Law Journal, 77 (November 1967); and Robert Lampman, Wisconsin Law Review, 2 (1969), pp. 543–544. The plan mentioned—Negative Rates Plan for the Working Poor—is but one of many schemes Lampman has put forward. It is used here to illustrate a type of negative income tax, not Lampman's view of the most appropriate scheme.

There are proposals, on the other hand, which employ differing administrative mechanisms to deal with similar problems. Consider the Brazer child allowance scheme which proposes a universal yearly benefit of $600 per child, the elimination of tax exemptions for children, and a special recoupment tax which decreases the net value of child allowances as income increases. In effect, this plan provides a guarantee of $1200 for a family with two children, a cut-off point of more than $10,000, and a net cost of approximately $12 billion. Though more restricted in coverage than the Tobin negative income tax scheme, the Brazer plan would "remove an appreciable proportion of presently poor families" from poverty.[4] Both proposals are substantial anti-poverty measures, and, as such, have more in common than either does with the low-level negative income tax plan which Lampman proposed as a device to supplement wages and thus extend welfare transfers to the working poor.

The task of this paper is set by the confusions which have plagued the debate over cash transfer alternatives. It seeks to clarify choices in income maintenance, making explicit the trade-offs between competing objectives that are required of policymakers, but which are often obscured by polemics about the advantages or disadvantages of particular transfer mechanisms (e. g., negative income taxes, child allowances, demogrants).

The next section distinguishes among the goals of reforming the present system of public assistance, substantially reducing American poverty, and making both the tax system and the social distribution of income more equitable. Then follows a discussion of six criteria for evaluating and comparing alternative measures to one or another of these goals. The paper concludes with an application of the evaluative scheme to the welfare reform alternatives considered by the Nixon Administration in the spring of 1969.

I. Problems of Poverty and Income Distribution

The income maintenance schemes so widely discussed in the 1960s addressed at least three separable clusters of problems: the crisis of the welfare poor, the difficulties of all low-income Americans, and the inequities of the present distribution of income in the United States.

The first set of problems—identified with the crisis of the "welfare poor"—involves persons curently receiving benefits and those eligible for them under federal and state assistance programs. The most controversial programs include Aid to Families with Dependent Children (AFDC)[5] and general assistance. Both hostile critics and sympathetic analysts of public assistance seem to agree that there is a "crisis." What this crisis consists of differs from analyst to analyst, but the following issues emerge:[6]

[4] Harvey Brazer, "Tax Policy and Children's Allowances," Children's Allowances and the Economic Welfare of Children, Report of a Conference. (Citizen's Committee for Children of New York, Inc., 1968), p. 142.

[5] Eligibility for AFDC requires that the family be needy, fatherless (or include an incapacitated father), and include children under 18; that the unemployed parent and/or mother accept a job or training for a job if offered (or else lose the benefits); and that, under the "Man in the House" Rule which applied in many states, the mother be moral. "Poverty, Income Sources and Income Maintenance Programs," The President's Commission on Income Maintenance Programs, (Background Paper No. 2, May 18, 1968), p. 11. In 1961, the AFDC–UP program was instituted, permitting benefits to households headed by unemployed, able-bodied men. Only 25 states had adopted this program by 1969, and less than 100,000 families were receiving its benefits. Poverty Amid Plenty: The American Paradox (Washington, D. C.: U. S. Government Printing Office, 1969) p. 47.

[6] For a typical example of (a), see The Advisory Council on Public Welfare, Having the Power, We Have the Duty, Report to the Secretary of Health, Education, and Welfare (Washington, D. C.: Government

(a) inadequacy of payment levels;

(b) disparity of payments between one geographical area and another (beyond cost of living differentials), and among various categories of public assistance recipients;

(c) administrative injustices and arbitrariness, including the alleged stigma of being on welfare, which also serves to deter eligible and deserving persons from applying;

(d) the financial costs of increasing the benefits and the number of eligibles who might seek benefits;

(e) the unfortunate effects of public assistance upon family cohesiveness and work behavior;

(f) the social divisiveness and inequity of welfare programs aiding only certain groups of the poor and excluding others, most notably the working poor.

The dimensions of these problems are not agreed upon; "remedies" to these various difficulties are not obviously compatible or complementary. The numerous plans which have been offered as solutions to the welfare crisis have differed markedly in the priorities they set among these issues.

The second set of problems focuses on poverty in America, the number of persons with incomes below the poverty line, and the amount by which their incomes fall short of that standard (the poverty gap).[7] The non-welfare poor comprise the most obvious target from this perspective. Nearly two-thirds of the poor do not qualify for public assistance, which limits benefits to widows, orphans, abandoned families, the aged, sick, and disabled. Most of those whose income falls below the poverty line are those legally ineligible for assistance because of the restrictive categories now used. One substantial group of nonwelfare poor is the long-term unemployed who are bypassed because of limitations in unemployment insurance benefits, or the lack of universal coverage within public assistance.[8] However, most of the non-welfare poor are from families in which at least one adult member is working.

Printing Office, 1966), p. 2, which asserts that "public assistance payments are so low and so uneven that the Government is, by its own standards and definitions, a major source of the poverty on which it has declared unconditional war." For (b) see the discussion of welfare's "inequitable treatment of marginal nonrecipients" in Jacobus tenBroek, "California's Dual System of Family Laws: Its Origin, Development and Present Status," Stanford Law Review, 16 (March 1964), 257–317; (July 1964), 900–981; Vol. 16 (April 1965), 614–682; and William A. Johnson and Robert Rosenkranz, "Public Assistance" in Cities in Trouble: An Agenda for Urban Research, Anthony H. Pascal (ed.) (Memorandum RM–5603–RC, the Rand Corp., August, 1968), p. 87. For (c) see Charles A. Reich, "Individuals Rights and Social Welfare: The Emerging Issues," Yale Law Journal, 75 (June 1965). This theme is understandably stressed by welfare rights' groups, and raised in almost all discussion of public welfare. See also Having the Power, We Have the Duty, Advisory Council on Public Welfare, p. 74, for the warning that "there is great urgency for the emphatic assertion of public welfare's accountability for the protection of individual rights, and for the scrupulous observance of the individual rights of the people it serves." For (d) see the illustrative remarks by Congresswoman Griffiths in the 1968 Hearings of the Joint Economic Committee, supra, n. 1; and Daniel P. Moynihan, "The Crises in Welfare," The Public Interest, No. 10 (Winter, 1968), p. 4. For (e) see Herbert J. Gans, "The Negro Family: Reflections on the Moynihan Report," The Moynihan Report and the Politics of Controversy, Rainwater and Yancey (eds.) (Cambridge, Mass.: M.I.T. Press, 1967), p. 454. For (f) see Moynihan, and the work by Lampman, among others on how the American system of transfer payments affects the poor, Lampman, supra, n. 3.

[7] The official poverty line in 1969 was $3550 for an urban family of four. The poverty gap was $12 billion in 1966; see J. A. Kershaw, Government Against Poverty, (Chicago: Markham, 1970), p. 148.

[8] For data on the characteristics of the unemployed, see the discussion of employability in The President's Commission on Income Maintenance Programs, Background Papers, pp. 63–66.

Discussion of the nonwelfare poor has focused on how to expand or alter the existing categories in order to include those poor who are now ineligible for assistance; and, given the large number of working poor, how to build work incentives into cash transfers directed towards this group. Availability of work is central to discussion surrounding the long-term unemployed, but not the working poor, since that group already participates in the work force. Rather, aiding the working poor raises the issue of how to supplement income without reducing the incentive to work. Robert Lampman's low level negative income tax is one welfare reform plan that expands coverage while retaining work incentives.[9]

The third set of problems involves the unequal distribution of wealth and income in contemporary America. Here the problem of poverty is not only that many Americans are unable to command a subsistence income, or that the public welfare system has built-in indignities and difficulties. Rather, poverty is viewed as relative deprivation, and the critical difficulties are those of an income distribution in which the relative gap between the very poor and the median wage-earner is widening, not narrowing. The ratio of the poverty line to median income has fallen considerably over the past decade. In 1959 the poverty line was 47 percent of median income; in 1968 it was 36 percent.[10]

[9] See outline in Robert J. Lampman, "Steps to Remove Poverty from America," Paper prepared for delivery at the Wisconsin Symposium, January 13, 1968.

[10] For a definition of poverty in relative terms, see Victor Fuchs, "Redefining Poverty," The Public Interest, No. 8 (Summer 1967), 88–95. Martin Rein discusses the difficulties in absolutist, "bread-basket" conceptions of poverty in Louis Ferman, et al., (eds.), Poverty in America (2d ed., Ann Arbor: University of Michigan Press, 1968), pp. 116–133. English social critics have recognized the problem of fixed poverty lines for some time. For a cogent critical view (directed against the views of Rowntree),

Those interested in relative poverty are typically concerned with equity questions as well. Not only does the lower one-fifth in the national distribution of income control "to small" a proportion of the nation's wealth, but from this perspective the operation of the tax system also confers benefits which are socially unjustifiable. Two illustrations should make this point clearer. One equity issue is the way tax exemptions (such as child exemptions in the positive income tax) confer benefits in the form of tax savings whose value increases progressively with family income.[11] Another is the

see Peter Townsend, "The Definition of Poverty," Paper presented at the Colloquium on Handicapped Families, Bureau de Recherches Sociales, held under the auspices of UNESCO, (Paris, 10–12, February, 1964), pp. 6–10. For information on income distribution changes, see Poverty Amid Plenty: An American Paradox, pp. 38–39.

[11] It is extraordinary how difficult it is to convince the skeptics that tax exemptions are functional equivalents of direct government expenditures. See H. Aaron, "Tax Exemptions—The Artful Dodge," Trans-Action, 6 (March 1969), 4–6, for a statement of both the problem and the good reasons one has for treating tax exemptions and direct benefits as fiscal equivalents. It should be added that the *political process* affecting the two forms of transfers differs, and that there may be great differences in the legitimacy associated with particular forms. As Aaron says, suppose, "yesterday on the floor of Congress, Senator Blimp introduced legislation to provide cash allowances for most of the aged. Senator Blimp's plan is unique, however, in that it excludes the poor. The largest benefits, $70 per month, are payable to aged couples whose real income exceeds $200,000 per year. The smallest benefits, $14 per month, would be payable to couples with incomes between $1600 and $2600. Widows, widowers, and unmarried aged persons would receive half as much as couples. No benefits would be payable to those with very low incomes." Aaron remarks that "one can hardly imagine any public figure" introducing such legislation, for fear of being derided "in the press, by his constituency, and on the floor of the Congress. So one would think. But this system of 'old age allowances' has actually existed for many years, not as an expenditure program, but as a part of our tax system," through the double exemption granted aged couples.

privileged treatment (through exemptions and other tax devices) of particular forms of income (the capital gains tax) and of certain forms of economic risk (the oil depletion allowance).[12] These illustrations of privileged tax treatment raise questions of equity which differ sharply from the issues of the welfare and non-welfare poor. Accordingly, such a focus calls for a range of solutions quite different from those relevant to the problems of the welfare poor and low-income Americans.[13]

II. Alternative Income Maintenance Plans: Criteria for Comparison

I now want to turn to six criteria by which alternative means to a given poverty problem might be usefully compared. These criteria, while not exhaustive, represent the major considerations typically raised by American policy makers. Explicitly using them illuminates the choices among competing goals which a particular transfer scheme represents.

Adequacy. One of the most prominent standards of evaluation in any given income transfer program is the *adequacy of the benefit level.* Discussions of adequacy imply prior stipulation of the relevant standard against which benefits are measured. In other words, for any given conception of an appropriate poverty line,

the gap between that line and the present income of the poor constitutes the "adequacy problem." Any transfer plan's benefits constitute some more or less adequate means to fill that gap.[14]

At least two indicators of adequacy should be used. The first is the proportion of the national poverty gap filled by a given transfer program. This indicator provides an answer to the question, "how adequate an antipoverty program is a given plan?" This criterion may be referred to as *aggregate program adequacy.* Second, the adequacy of grants to particular beneficiaries—*individual adequacy*—can be measured by guarantee levels.

Commonly, the Social Security Administration's poverty line is adopted as a reference point.[15] Those persons below

---

[12] Tax reform was the subject of extended hearings before the House Committee on Ways and Means during the spring of 1969. For the range of reform proposals see Tax Reform Studies and Proposals, U. S. Treasury Department, Joint Publication, Committee on Ways and Means, and Committee on Finance, 91st Congress, 1st Session, February 5, 1969, (Washington, D. C.: U. S. Government Printing Office).

[13] The argument is not that programs related to one problem have no effect on other social ills; they do. But consider the difference between treating changes in chidren's tax exemptions as a tax reform issue and as an antipoverty remedy. A more equitable treatment of children's tax exemptions would not necessarily involve enough money to relieve poverty substantially.

[14] The differences between reforming welfare and eradicating poverty come out sharply in how analysts regard the adequacy criterion. Some, like the editors of the Yale Law Journal, take it as given that desirable programs will have a guarantee level set at the poverty line. Indeed, they question whether the "SSA poverty line—the 'minimum money income required to support an average family * * * at the lowest level consistent with the standard of living prevailing in this country'—" is adequate, "even if it has gained wide acceptance." Yale Law Journal, 78 (December 1968), p. 298, n. 91. On the other hand, welfare reforms costing approximately five billion dollars were in 1970 considered by the Congress. It is clearly possible to evaluate such low-adequacy alternatives by other criteria, and this may be very important if budgetary constraints rule out what the Yale editors seek.

[15] The poverty index set by the SSA is the minimum income per household of a given size, composition, and nonfarm status. In 1966 the Agriculture Department Economy Food Plan, which is the core of the poverty index, provided for total food expenditures of 75 cents a day per person (in an average four-person family). The index adds twice this amount to cover all family living items other than food. It has been adjusted for price changes since 1959; but has not kept pace with the increase in median income. Consequently, there was a larger absolute gap between median family income and the poverty line in 1969 than in 1959. Mollie Orshansky, "The Shape of Poverty in 1966," Social Security Bulletin, U. S. Department

the line are said to have less than minimally adequate income. The adequacy of a transfer program can then be evaluated from two perspectives: the degree to which benefits lift a recipient to the poverty line, and the extent to which total benefits fill the $12 billion gap between incomes of persons below and above the poverty line. Thus, the poverty line provides a basis for judging the adequacy of benefits directed to the welfare poor or, in a universal program, to all low-income Americans. The concern for adequacy may also be a criterion for tax reform if it focuses on the level of benefits for the poor in the form of more generous exemptions and deductions.

Although adequacy is not always the prime consideration in anti-poverty efforts, it is the principal preoccupation with militant welfare rights organizations and welfare reformers, particularly social workers and welfare critics, whose perspective is dominated by setting minimum floors of protection against various contingencies of living.[16]

of Health, Education, and Welfare, (Social Security Administration, March 1968), p. 5.

[16] I am indebted to Robert Lampman for a suggested typology of poverty reformers. He distinguishes three perspectives; that of welfare (minimum floors of protection); of social insurance (security against *variability* of income over time through insurance); and of tax and public finance (equity of treatment, work incentives). Lampman emphasizes that each mentality directs attention selectively and ignores issues of great importance to the others. Thus, public finance experts are horrified by the inequitable treatment of welfare beneficiaries in different categories and in different states, and by the high marginal tax rates public assistance formally requires. Such considerations are less salient to welfare reformers who focus on adequacy of benefits, the speed with which destitution is relieved, etc. Social insurance advocates are more likely to evaluate transfers by the sense of entitlement they involve, the predictability of future benefits, and security they offer large classes of Americans, not especially the poor. This suggestive typology has yet to be worked out, but offers a way of comparing trans-

Stigma. The degree of stigma associated with the source, form and administration of income maintenance programs is the second criterion—one that has been emphasized in some criticisms of the current welfare system. Generally speaking, social insurance programs, in which benefits are limited to contributors, have few stigmatizing associations. The recipients of welfare benefits, however, are often stigmatized as lazy, improvident, and content to live off the charity of others; and welfare benefits are conferred after a sometimes degrading investigation of the means and perhaps the morals of the potential recipient. Alvin Schorr has framed this concern in the telling phrase, "a means-tested program is a mean program."[17]

Those who, like Schorr, are preoccupied with reducing stigma typically turn to non-means-tested programs (like Social Security or child allowances) even when this involves less adequate benefits and much higher program costs. Means-tested programs, they argue, fail to reach all those whom the program is intended to serve, since many eligible to receive benefits are reluctant to apply. This underutilization, of course, has the added effect of keeping down the expense of welfare programs: stigma may be viewed as a means of rationing the use of government programs in which conferring benefits to all those eligible would sharply increase government expenditures.[18]

fers that could be added to the approach I am suggesting.

[17] Alvin L. Schorr, Explorations in Social Policy (New York: Basic Books, Inc., 1968), p. 62.

[18] The experience with the Kerr-Mills Medical Assistance law brings out this point. Generous in theory, only 32 states had workable programs by 1963, three years after enactment. Theodore Marmor, The Politics of Medicare (London: Routledge & Kegan Paul Ltd., 1970).

Finally, one must say that knowledge about the extent of stigma and its causes is impressionistic. How obnoxious the "obnoxious means test" really is remains a question needing an answer before this criterion can be intelligently employed.[19] But the lack of knowledge in public policy is seldom a barrier to either strong views or policy action. And so it is in income maintenance debates that allegations about the causes, effects, and ways of eliminating stigma are presented and received as though stigma were precisely understood.

Equitable Efficiency. Weisbrod defines equitable efficiency as the degree to which "actual redistribution of income coincides with the desired redistribution." To illustrate, Weisbrod describes:

> a manpower retraining program which may be intended to benefit the hard core unemployed—those who cannot find regular employment even under 'full employment' conditions. But, as the program is actually administered, it may (1) miss many in the hard core group, while at the same time, (2) aid a number of less needy persons.[20]

Those concerned with efficiency argue that these effects reduce the desirability of a program. Considerations of equita-

ble efficiency bring out how successfully (or unsuccessfully) a given program delivers benefits to a program's target population, and to no one else.

Weisbrod has introduced a useful distinction between two types of efficiency calculations. One efficiency consideration, he says, is the "degree to which programs intended to benefit group A also benefit group B." This might be termed *vertical efficiency*. The second issue is the degree to which "programs intended to benefit group A reach all of this group." Weisbrod refers to this as *horizontal efficiency*.

a. vertical efficiency. The vertical efficiency of a program may be defined as the ratio of benefits received by intended beneficiaries to total benefits distributed. If payments are made only to intended beneficiaries, the program's vertical efficiency ratio is 1.[21]

Vertical efficiency can be conceived as a measure of cost effectiveness: the greater the vertical efficiency ratio the smaller the per-unit cost of benefits to the target groups. Thus, between two programs that bring equal benefits to a given target group, the program having the higher vertical efficiency ratio, *ceteris paribus,* will be the least costly.

This conception of vertical efficiency implies that benefits to non-needy persons should be given a weight of zero. At least two objections can be made to this interpretation, as Weisbrod points out. First, there may be other than redistributional grounds for wanting to distribute benefits to the nonpoor (administrative simplicity, for example). Secondly, vertical efficiency may conflict with another criterion. For example, the extent to which a program limits benefits to those

---

[19] Some evidence has recently been gathered in Wisconsin indicating that the poor are not as hostile to the means test as commonly asserted. Handler and Hollingsworth found that "the clients reported very little evidence of hostility toward their case-worker or coercion in the administration of social services." Joel F. Handler and Ellen Jane Hollingsworth, "The Administration of Social Services in AFDC: The Views of Welfare Recipients," Institute for Research on Poverty, University of Wisconsin, Discussion Paper 37, p. 39.

[20] Burton A. Weisbrod, "Collective Action and the Distribution of Income: A Conceptual Approach," The Analysis and Evaluation of Public Expenditure: The PPB System, Vol. 1, A Compendium of Papers, Subcommittee on Economy in Government, Joint Economic Committee, U. S. Congress, 91st Congress 1st Session, (Government Printing Office: Washington, D. C., 1969), p. 184.

[21] As Weisbrod says, "a ratio of unity would thus indicate that all resources of the program are being devoted to the target group and do not benefit any others." Ibid., p. 185.

within the poverty class may contribute to the stigma associated with such a program. This conflict is implicit in Schorr's comment about the meanness of means-tested programs.[22]

The problem of weighting benefits to nonneedy persons is more complicated, however, than simply avoiding stigma. A critical objection to programs with less vertical efficiency is that there may be resentment against windfall gains to those outside the target group. One of the objections to negative income tax proposals is that plans for transferring income to the poor must involve sizeable payments to persons who are clearly not poor in order to provide a "meaningful floor of income and to avoid a very high tax on incremental income." [23] (Taxes here refer to the reductions in benefit payments per additional dollar of family income). The magnitude of this difficulty would be revealed by the vertical efficiency ratio, though the revelation of the difficulty in no way resolves it.

b. *horizontal efficiency.* Horizontal efficiency may be defined as the "ratio of the number of beneficiaries in the target group to the total number of persons in the target group." The smaller the proportion of the target group (all presumably deserving) being aided, the lower the horizontal efficiency ratio.

It ought to be noted, however, that the *horizontal efficiency* criterion differs from the adequacy standard. Clearly inadequate payments could go to all persons within a target group and thus lead one to rank a program high on horizontal efficiency and low on adequacy. The trade-off between these two criteria—at any given dollar cost of a program—is again a problem of weighting yet to be solved.

Incentive Effects: Work and Family. The work incentive effects of cash transfers is a fourth criterion of importance. Regardless of the administrative mechanism, any transfer program must answer three different questions: What shall be the level of the income guarantee (the maximum benefit)? How shall that benefit be reduced as earnings vary from zero (the tax rate)? And what shall be the cut-off point (the earnings level at which no benefits are paid)? [24]

The appropriate level of taxation on cash transfers depends in part on the effort of the tax rate on the work behavior of various groups in the population. That information is not known in any precise way.[25] The result is that analysts work from rules of thumb of the following sort: any income guarantee will reduce some work effort if the marginal tax on earnings is more than zero; or the desire to work is so great in American society that tax rates up to 50 percent will not greatly reduce work-force participation.

The absence of information about work incentives does not reduce the issue's political salience. Indeed, the existence of strong feelings about what the poor (and near poor) will or will not do under various incentive schemes is what prompted the Institute for Research on Poverty at the University of Wisconsin to undertake the Graduated Work Incentive Experiment which involves testing of several negative tax schemes on the

---

[22] See also D. P. Moynihan's remarks about stigma and community reactions to transfer programs in his "Crises in Welfare," The Public Interest, No. 10 (Winter 1968), 3–29.

[23] See Weisbrod., supra, n. 19, p. 187.

[24] Outlined in Christopher Green, op. cit., pp. 126–130.

[25] In most of the literature proposing various income maintenance plans, guarantee levels are so low that to consider many heads of four-person families would give up higher incomes to loaf on $1500 or so per year is ludicrous and in violation of our common sense. Yet, for political reasons, there is still concern over incentive effects of such plans.

work responses of some 800 New Jersey families. Figure 1, representing a moderately high negative income tax plan, illustrates the choices that must be made among (1) guarantee level, (2) tax rate, and (3) cut-off point.[26] A program guaranteeing $2500 when earnings are zero with a "tax" rate of 50 percent entails a cut-off point of $5000. If one specifies any two of the three variables, the value of the third variable is determined. The plan illustrated in the figure below sacrifices vertical efficiency for adequacy and substantial work incentives.

The concern about work incentives is part of the larger worry about the relation of transfer schemes to economic growth, productive efficiency, and allocative efficiency. Macroeconomic effects might be taken as another criterion of evaluation. In this paper, the work incentives issue is presented as a proxy for those broader concerns, as well as a salient political issue in its own right. All government redistribution involves what Musgrave calls the allocation and stabilization "functions" of the state.[27]

[26] David Wilkinson, "Foxtracks Across Ice," unpublished paper, University of Wisconsin, provides an illustration of this point. He visualizes the plan "as a line from a reel anchored to the top of an economic ladder. The line assures that the family won't drop below a certain rung. At the same time it assists a family moving up the ladder, though with decreasing payout as the family gets closer to the top. The reel and line represent an income assistance system working in conjunction with the family's own efforts to increase total income with earnings. The line won't lift the full weight of the family to the top, but it continues to be of assistance until the family gets there. The maximum vertical length of the line represents the level of support minimally guaranteed. The lift of the line represents the tax rate applied to earnings, with a smaller tax rate producing more lift than a larger rate. The break-even level corresponds to the top of the ladder, the point where all the line is reeled in."

[27] R. Musgrave, The Theory of Public Finance, (New York: McGraw-Hill, 1959), ch. 1.

The distribution of government goods and services between regions changes both the distribution of income and the allocation of productive resources. Giving money to the poor simply raises this issue more directly and dramatically. What effect will given transfer schemes have on work performance, the mobility of labor, the process of automation in low-wage industries, or the price of labor? All such questions are called for in evaluating transfer programs. And, it should be added here, transfer schemes may promote different family structures by the way the family unit is defined and the treatment of young adult dependents and

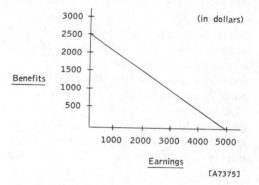

Figure 1.   A Negative Income Tax Plan

related adults other than mother and father. These important issues have received most attention from legal scholars.[28]

Program Costs. The costs of a transfer program may refer to total expenditures at all levels of government or the net increment to the federal budget, taking into account savings in other present federal, state, and local income transfer programs.

Program costs to any unit of government are very difficult to predict. Specifying the tax rate, cut-off point, and

[28] See, for example, W. Klein, "Some Basic Problems of Negative Income Taxation," Wisconsin Law Review, (Summer 1966)

guarantee level does not tell how workers will behave. Consequently, the number of persons who will be in a specified income range cannot be unambiguously determined from present data on the poor. Nor can the amount of the poverty "gap" be precisely measured, except retrospectively. The best that can be done is to make reasonable assumptions (perhaps alternative assumptions) about the work response to various plans and estimate program costs on that basis.

The allocation of program costs involves both the governmental unit whose expenditures are affected and the taxpayers who finance the program. Minimum federal payment levels for public assistance, for example, are advocated by some as if the purpose is to increase the total payments to public assistance beneficiaries. But, in fact, the demand for such changes comes prominently from beleaguered state and local governments eager to shift the burden of welfare payments to the federal government. Hence, one of the cost issues is which level of the political system will finance what proportion of any given transfer scheme. Program costs can be treated as either a criterion or a constraint. That is, one can ask, what is the cost of plan X compared to plan Y? Or one can ask how plans compare on other dimensions, subject to the constraint that their program costs fall within a specifed range.

Political Support. The relationship between political and economic costs and benefits is widely discussed but not well understood. As with program costs, political costs can be treated as a constraint or a variable. That is, given the political acceptability of two programs, they can be compared on the basis of the other criteria. Or, they can be compared according to the political support (and opposition) they will probably generate. The conceptual and measurement prob-

lems involved, however, are extraordinary.

Political support means the nature and extent of approval for a given program. One may speak of mass support and use polling data as an indicator of it. Public opinion polls recently have shown that more than a majority of those with opinions about income maintenance favored guaranteed employment plans, while less than a majority favored income guarantees.[29] Equally important for present purposes is support by governmental elites, particularly congressional elites. There are few ways one can accurately measure such support before decisive tests (like a vote) are taken. Votes on other redistributive issues are one indicator, but not a fully reliable one. Party positions on the questions offer another clue when combined with knowledge of the pattern of party cohesion on redistributive matters.

A good example of noting political costs and benefits, but not taking them into account in comparing the desirability of transfer programs, can be found in the *Yale Law Journal's* comment on

the relation between the [*Yale Law Journal's* model] NIT proposal and the increasingly urgent demands for a wholesale reform of public assistance. Any modification of public assistance programs that took into account all the serious criticisms of present welfare efforts—as, for example, do the

[29] In response to a question about guaranteeing every family an income of at least $3200 a year (for a family of four), with the government making up the differences the following results were obtained: favor —36%; oppose—58%; no opinion—6%. Results of a question about providing enough work so that each family that has an employable wage earner would be guaranteed a wage of about $60 a week or $3200 a year were: favor—78%; oppose—18%; no opinion—4%. American Institute of Public Opinion, Gallup Opinion Index, Report No. 37, July, 1968, pp. 23–24.

recommendations of the U.S. Advisory Council on Public Welfare—would result in a system of distributing benefits strikingly similar to that outlined in the model statute. The NIT and public assistance reforms are not so much alternative ways of dealing with poverty as they are alternative ways of dealing with Congress, and the choice between them is chiefly one of political strategy. Since the NIT completely escapes the faulty concepts and spotted history of public assistance, it still ranks as the preferable approach.[30]

III. Evaluating Income Maintenance Alternatives: The Nixon Administration's Choice in Welfare Reform, 1969

This concluding section illustrates how one might use the criteria just outlined to compare income maintenance schemes. The two welfare reform proposals chosen for this purpose—the Nathan task force plan and the Finch/Moynihan proposal to extend welfare benefits to poor families with children—had a timely relevance in 1969. They constituted the major options considered by the Republican Administration in the spring of that year. The subsequent developments in welfare reform—the presidential sponsorship of a family assistance plan that differs somewhat from either of the initial options discussed here, the passage of the welfare reform bill in the House of Representatives and the defeat of the bill within the Senate Finance Committee in the summer of 1970—reduce the timeliness, not the analytical significance, of the following illustrative comparison. It should be noted as well that the evaluative criteria could as easily be applied to other classes of cash transfer plans, whether they are addressed to welfare, poverty or income redistribution issues.

Different welfare reform proposals proceed from different views of the present system of public assistance. Before comparing our two illustrative welfare reforms, some preliminary remarks should be made about the demographic, administrative, and financial attributes of contemporary public assistance. Federal assistance goes to five state-federal programs: old age assistance (OAA), aid to families with dependent children (AFDC), aid to blind (AB), aid to the permanently and totally disabled (ATPD), and aid to the medically indigent (Medicaid). There are residual relief programs in each state which are financed wholly by state and/or local funds. The latter programs are collectively referred to as general relief or general assistance and do not receive federal supervision or funding.[31]

TABLE 1. NUMBER OF PUBLIC ASSISTANCE RECIPIENTS (IN THOUSANDS)

December of Year	Total	OAA	AFDC	AB	APTD	GA
1945	3,623.5	2,056	943	71.5	—	553
1951	5,657.2	2,701	1,041	97.2	124	694
1957	6,016.0	2,487	2,398	108.0	281	742
1963	7,379.9	2,052	3,930	96.9	464	737
1966	8,073.7	2,073	4,666	83.7	588	663
1967	8,893.0	2,073	5,309	82.6	646	782
1968	9,725.0	2,028	6,086	80.7	702	827

SOURCE: The President's Commission on Income Maintenance Programs, **Background Papers**, (GPO, 1970), p. 235.

[30] Yale Law Journal, 78 (December 1968), p. 282.

[31] The following discussion draws on work of the staff of the President's Commission on Income Maintenance Programs which presented its final report Poverty Amid Plenty: The American Paradox, in November, 1969.

Federal participation in public assistance was originally designed to help states support persons who were unable to work because of age, blindness, or absence of a wage-earner. Since 1950, new groups and purposes have been included. Aid to the partially and totally disabled was enacted in 1950; in 1960, medical assistance for the aged was enacted as the Kerr-Mills program. In the early 1960s, an unemployed parent amendment permitted AFDC benefits to families where the father was in the home and unemployed (AFDC–UP, now operative in 25 states). Two other legislative developments in the 1960s were of importance: in 1962, rehabilitative services were provided under public assistance and, in 1967, new amendments were passed which sought to get AFDC recipients to work through incentives (job training, day care, financial inducements) and sanctions (denying aid to those considered able but unwilling to work). Categorical public assistance, in summary, was designed for the nonworking poor, and only recently has focused upon problems of rehabilitation and employment.

The number of persons receiving public assistance has grown sharply since 1945. Part of the growth is attributable to the inclusion of new categories of assistance, but the AFDC program is clearly the source of most of the growth. The distribution of recipients for one month, by year and type of program, is presented in Table 1.

The growth in AFDC has dominated much of the discussion of public welfare, or "illfare," as *Time* magazine once put it. The distribution of poor persons *within* public assistance, however, does not point up the proportion of the poor excluded. Less than two-fifths of the twenty-five million who were poor in 1968 received aid from any public assistance programs.[32] Public assistance comprises programs for a minority of the poor. The crisis of welfare is thus only a part of the problem of American poverty.

Public assistance provides federal grants-in-aid to all states for cash payments to individuals and families in need. AFDC receives less federal assistance than the other programs, and the federal share under all the programs varies with the income level of the state. Of the $6 billion spent in 1966 on all public assistance programs, including administrative costs, about 60 percent, or $3.5 billion, came from the federal government. The extent of federal participation over time is presented in Table 2.

The administration of public assistance is discretionary, local, and uneven. Eligible persons are "needy" by virtue of destitution. The definition of destitution varies among the states. Moreover, state grants do not typically pay the difference between their definition of "need" and current income. In some states the "need" for a family of four is $280 per month and a family with no income gets that amount. In other states the "need" is $194, but the family with no income receives only $40. States vary in the requirements for granting assistance as well. In some states there were no residence tests; in others, a would-be recipient had to have lived in the state five of the past nine years and the year immediately preceding assistance. However, the 1969 Supreme Court decision in *Shapiro v. Thompson* ruled such residency tests unconstitutional for federally assisted programs.

The above characterization of public assistance entails no obvious reformist perspective. One may applaud or denounce the extent to which states with

[32] The President's Commission on Income Maintenance Programs. Poverty Amid Plenty: The American Paradox, p. 115.

TABLE 2. FEDERAL FINANCIAL PARTICIPATION
IN PUBLIC ASSISTANCE

Year	Total	Percent of Total		
	(millions of dollars)	Federal	State	Local
1945	987.9	40.7	47.8	12.5
1951	2,382.8	47.6	41.6	10.8
1957	3,090.3	51.3	37.0	11.7
1963	4,712.6	55.5	32.7	11.5
1966	6,652.0	58.6	30.7	10.8
1968	9,346.0	56.1	32.1	11.8

Source: President's Commission on Income Maintenance Programs, **Background Papers,** p. 235.

unequal resources differently define and support their categorically poor. The extraordinary growth of AFDC might, in one view, be evidence that the states are discovering the needs that exist; in another view, it is a sign of moral decay in want of immediate attention. There are those who think the problem with welfare is that we have too much of it; some are worried about too much administration and others are upset about too many recipients. Then, there are those who see the problem as too little public welfare, either in the sense that too few of the poor are eligible or, within the current system, too little is provided the recipients both in cash and incentives to improve their income position.

Critics of welfare often proceed as if everyone agreed on the nature and ranking of these problems. That is simply not true. Despite the fact that most advocates of welfare reform begin with the same opening salvo of objections to public assistance (indeed the criticisms have become clichés through endless listing), the classification of issues does not bring with it a decision rule. This failure occurs because a decision rule requires *both* a classificatory and a weighting scheme, and only the former is available. My thesis is that a weighting scheme also requires clear, explicit presentation of criteria to be weighted. I have tried to do that and now want to apply those criteria to two illustrative welfare reform proposals and make a first step toward a systematic comparative evaluation.

The two proposals were the chief options under discussion by President Nixon's Urban Council during the spring of 1969. Both plans were directed towards reducing inequities within the present welfare system. One, popularly known as the Nathan plan after presidential appointee Richard Nathan, proposed decreasing state variation in benefit levels through a national minimum standard for the present categories of public welfare, to be administered by the present federal-state welfare apparatus. This plan will be referred to as Uniform State Benefits (USB). The second proposal extended income assistance to poor families with children, which would be administered by the Social Security Administration, and will be referred to as Federal Family Benefits (FFB), though it was known more widely as the Finch-Moynihan proposal.

Both plans seek to reduce inequities presently affecting individuals and states. The inequities for individuals arise from the fact that federal matching formulas are insufficient tools to reduce the variation in state treatment of similar welfare recipients. At the lower level, poor states are encouraged, but not required to provide minimum payments that satisfy the barest conception of subsistence income. The wealthier the state (in per capita income) the lower the proportion of federal support for more generous grants. Hence, welfare generosity is a heavy fiscal burden, one which some states (and state legislators) find politically intolerable.

The similarities between proposals USB and FFB are striking. Both would cost the federal government approximately two billion dollars per year. Both would entail savings to financially hard-pressed states. Both provide for a national welfare minimum. The general income support program (FFB), while not universal, provides payments to all families with children and, thus, is much broader in scope than current AFDC and AFDC–UP programs. It is broader in that the income status of the family is the sole criterion of eligibility; this contrasts sharply with the fatherless-family criterion in AFDC and the unemployed father standard of eligibility in AFDC–UP. While both programs establish minimum welfare standards nationwide, their distribution of the federal financial increment (less than two billion dollars) to the poor and to state treasuries differ. Both the similarities and the differences are revealed clearly by evaluating the programs by the six criteria introduced in the second part of this paper, as shown in Table 3.

TABLE 3.   COMPARISON OF TWO WELFARE REFORM PROPOSALS: UNIFORM STATE
BENEFITS (USB) AND FEDERAL FAMILY BENEFITS (FFB)

Criteria for Comparison	Indicators	USB	FFB
Adequacy	• 4-person family guarantee • Poverty gap filled	$1500 or 42% of $3500 poverty line * 1.5/12, .7/12	$1500 or 42% of $3500 poverty line 2/12, 1.3/12
Stigma		no improvement	some improvement
Efficiency Horizontal Vertical	• Ratio of transfer benefits, poor to nonpoor • Amount of poverty gap filled to total benefits	.4 1 7/15	.8 1 13/20
Work Incentive		$30/month income disregard + 67% tax rate thereafter	$50/month income disregard + 50% tax rate thereafter
Program Cost †	• Federal Cost • State saving	$1.5 billion $800 million	$2 billion $710 million
Political Support	• Mass support for some reform • Bureaucratic support • Congressional support	+ — uncertain	+ + uncertain
Problem Focus		disparity of payments by State and category (b) ‡	inequitable exclusion of the poor (the working poor especially) from public assistance (f) ‡

* The first ratio compares total federal program costs to the poverty gap: the second is a ratio of only the transfer amount to the $12 billion poverty gap.
† Excluding food and training programs.
‡ See enumeration of welfare issues in Part I.

Adequacy. The first indicator in Table 3 measures the *individual adequacy* of benefit guarantees. By this standard there is no substantial difference between FFB and USB: both guarantee $1500 to a family of four (or about $31 per month for each family member.) If one takes tax rate provisions into account, FFB appears more adequate than USB; since FFB "taxes" earnings less heavily than USB, it would provide higher average payments to recipients earning the same wages.

The second indicator provides two measures of *aggregate program adequacy*: (1) the ratio of total program costs to the $12 billion poverty gap, the ratio being approximately 1.5/12 under USB and 2/12 under FFB; and (2) the ratio of benefits for the poor to the poverty gap, by which standard FFB is somewhat more adequate.

It should be clear that although FFB ranks higher on adequacy than USB, both programs are inadequate when judged by the current poverty standard. The Social Security definition of minimum income for a family of four ($3500) is not approximated in either program. The $1500 guarantee represents 42% of the poverty line, while the higher FFB program costs ($2 billion) represent one-sixth of the poverty income gap. These points alone serve to demonstrate how welfare reform can proceed quite apart from serious efforts to eradicate financial poverty, either individual or aggregate.

Stigma. Neither program represents a major effort to reduce the stigma allegedly associated with public assistance. USB is an effort to make public assistance less inequitable among states and among different categories of beneficiaries. FFB is directed towards the inequitable exclusion of poor, male-headed families with an employed father. But neither program makes public welfare less selective in the sense of transferring income to the nonpoor. On the other hand, FFB proposes that the family benefit be administered by the Social Security Administration, an administrative system considered less stigmatized than welfare agencies. Some reduction of stigma is associated with FFB on this basis. USB, in comparison, promises no substantial change.

a. Vertical Efficiency. Both programs satisfy this criterion because the ratio of benefits received by the poor to total transfer benefits is 1. This is the case only for the transfer portion of the program. That is, nonpoor persons receive no benefits; no "leakage" of that kind takes place. But, taking into account the state "savings" changes the vertical efficiency ratio for each program. For USB, it is $7/15$'s; for FFB, $13/20$'s. Another way of expressing the relative poverty intensity is to compare poverty relief to state financial relief: the ratio of poverty relief to state relief in USB is $7/8$'s; in FFB, $13/4$'s.

On the first measure, both programs are vertically efficient. On the second, FFB is far more vertically efficient; 65 percent of its costs represent direct expenditures for the poor, compared with 47 percent of USB going directly to the poor. Since the two programs involve similar levels of federal expenditures, the efficiency ratio makes a useful distinction. Knowing that FFB is more vertically efficient than USB does not, however, tell us how important that criterion is—that is, what weight to give it. However, the comparison avoids difficulties that arise in describing two programs of vastly different cost. A $28 billion program with a vertical efficiency ratio of .5 may appear to be far more "efficient," from this perspective, than the $2 billion FFB program with a vertical efficiency ratio of .65. But this is the case only by mixing the adequacy and vertical efficiency criteria.

b. Horizontal efficiency. Program USB is substantially less efficient, horizontally, than FFB. Indeed, increased horizontal efficiency in public welfare is the chief goal of the family benefit program. Since public assistance aids only about 40 percent of the poor, its horizontal efficiency ratio is .4. Since families headed by a man who works account for the major portion of those excluded from assistance, FFB has a much higher horizontal efficiency ratio, approximately .8. Conversely, USB is relatively inefficient on this dimension, since it retains the current categories of public assistance.

USB subordinates horizontal efficiency to financial relief of states. FFB seeks greater horizontal efficiency at the price of somewhat less financial relief to states. However, this is true only when one looks at the cash transfer portion of the programs. Any additional work and food programs would change these comparisons slightly, but, for present purposes, we will ignore that complication.

Work Incentives. USB provides for a continuation of the present Work Incentive Program (WIN) scheme under AFDC. Under WIN there is an earning exemption of $30, a 67 percent tax rate on additional earnings, and a training-employment program exclusively for AFDC recipients. FFB provides more financial incentives to work than USB, but does not compel recipients to seek training or work. The FFB tax rate is 50 percent, which means that the $1500 guarantee is combined with a cut-off point of $3000. In addition, individuals receive $50 per month as a special incentive for taking job training.

FFB also provides incentives to the state to *move* welfare clients into training. It does so because the trainee would continue to receive his family benefit, any amount he might be receiving from the state to supplement that payment, plus the bonus incentive of $50 per month. States giving families additional benefits under FFB (as would surely be the case in the larger industrial states) could gain substantially from widespread use of this training-payment provision. The training program would cost an additional $600 million if 150,000 training positions were created. Currently, there are 88,000 training positions budgeted under the WIN program, of which 35,000 are filled. At an average cost of $4000/position WIN would cost $325 million when fully utilized.

Program Costs. The additional federal cost of FFB, including the adult categories but exclusive of food and training programs, is approximately $2 billion. Of this, approximately $710 million results in savings to the states. The estimated cost of USB is $1.5 billion, of which roughly $800 million represents dollar-for-dollar savings for the states.[33]

---

[33] All of the financial cost estimates are for Fiscal Year 1972. This postponement of program initiation reflects a number of considerations: the administration's budget-cutting in 1969, the political gains of future as against present expenditures, and the assumption that passage of welfare reform would take perhaps two years. It perhaps should be added that USB cost estimates were understated by some $400 million because no allowance was made for increased

Neither estimate, of course, takes into account what the states might do with their "savings"; hence, there can be no precise estimate of total governmental costs of the programs plus state supplementary schemes.

The program costs criterion is more difficult to apply than it appears. If we take only direct transfers into account, the programs involve incomparable federal program costs: $1.5 billion for USB, $2 billion for FFB. Two complications arise, however. The first is the addition of training and food stamp programs which raise federal expenditures to approximately $4 billion. The comparison in Table 3 involves only the cash transfers, and this may confuse more than illuminate. But even for cash transfers, the program costs are very hard to gauge. It is impossible to know what the work response will be and, hence, the federal costs over time. The above estimates are made as if the poor tomorrow would act precisely as they do today. Nonetheless, there is reason to believe the costs are not markedly understated. Few heads of four-person families would voluntarily quit work to receive FFB's $1500 guarantee. And USB does not assist the working poor.

Political Support. Both programs share whatever diffuse political support exists for "doing something about welfare." FFB directs itself toward the AFDC problem and, through a sleight-of-hand name change, would, in the words of one promoter, "eliminate the much criticized AFDC program." USB directs itself to another aspect of the AFDC problem, the migration of welfare clients to large urban centers. FFB hopes to encourage families to leave welfare and also diminishes incentives for divorce and desertion presently found in AFDC programs. USB retains these unfortunate incentives

numbers of beneficiaries, according to OEO economists I interviewed in 1970.

but provides inducements for families in the less wealthy states to stay there. The support for stemming migration and discouraging desertion of fathers is, however, extremely hard to measure. Congressional committees with welfare jurisdiction are well represented with members declaring "widespread" support for doing something about the welfare mess. It is precisely the unspecified extent and nature of support for action that gives discretion to the congressional elites who judge options like USB and FFB.

The mass public's opinions are equally distant from the legislative system. Whatever diffuse hostility exists towards AFDC in the larger public could be used to justify either USB or FFB. Where the two programs differ most sharply— as, for example, on the question of whether geographical inequity is less pressing than the exclusion of the working poor from public assistance—public opinion is unformed and unlikely to be crucial in the decision-making process. Both programs tap other widespread anxieties: the desire for making work more attractive for welfare clients; the financial problems of the states and localities in meeting welfare costs; and the current preoccupation with food programs. Referring back to our six criteria, it is clear that USB and FFB differ most sharply on the weight given to horizontal equity in a welfare reform that does not address itself to eradicating poverty.

The political costs and benefits from improving the horizontal efficiency of public assistance are easiest to estimate at the federal administrative level. The gains of substance are evidence from either a welfare or public finance perspective. Professional reformers within the bureaucracy have for some years been seeking universal public assistance based on income criteria rather than the present categorical scheme which defines eligibility in terms of the *cause* of low income (blindness, disability, old age, etc.). If

bureaucratic support is the only measure, then FFB without doubt ranks higher. Neither proposal proposes to do away with state administration of other adult programs; hence, one cannot contrast them in terms of the jurisdictional squabbles raised.

A measure of political support, as central as bureaucratic preferences, is the anticipated reactions of Congress. The political costs of USB arise from its failure to deal with the problems of the working poor and its relatively lower horizontal efficiency. Its advocates, however, would argue that the congressional system directly represents the financial interests of states and localities, and that only a minority of the Congress stands for interests of the working poor and welfare efficiency. This argument rests, however, on the assumption that widespread congressional support for each feature of welfare reform is the precondition for enactment (the consensus view of political support). If, in contrast, one assumed sufficient general support for a large class of welfare reforms, the greater equity and efficiency of FFB would be decisive. Bureaucratic support for equity and efficiency would greatly assist in creating the minimum favorable coalition in the finance committees of the Congress. Only if it appeared that a determined majority could develop *against* FFB would one say that the political support criterion dictated selection of USB.[34]

[34] Predictions of support for a particular welfare reform proposal cannot be simply inferred from opinions about a program's principles. Politicians choose between proposals in constrained circumstances; the failure to distinguish approval of a program from willingness to support it has confounded predictions about the fate of welfare reform. A recent article, for example, claimed that no "income by right" proposals are "politically feasible in the near future because few people want them." On the basis of interviews with fifty congressmen and an unspecified number of federal officials, Cavala and Wildavsky concluded

The politics of welfare reform provide a striking illustration of the characteristic political processing of redistributive policies.[35] The role of the bureaucracy in that arena is one of balancing the interests known to be involved in income redistribution. The Congress ratifies or refuses the bargains that are expressed in the legislative initiatives brought to it. The evaluative effort we have been making represents the comparative analysis that was in fact made of USB and FFB within the Nixon Administration in the spring of 1969.[36]

that few political actors approved of income-by-right plans. Hence, they argued, "the President will not support [such a plan] and the Congress would not pass it if he did." In October, 1969, President Nixon sent to the Congress a $5 billion welfare reform bill, including a negative income tax for families with children similar to FFB. In early 1970 the House Committee on Ways and Means overwhelmingly supported the President's bill (by a vote of 21–3), an action which virtually assured House passage of the Family Assistance Act. No one could have predicted this sequence of events from presidential, congressional, or mass opinions about the desirability of income guarantee plans. The President faced a choice of whether to take action on the crises in public welfare and, subsequently, what type of welfare reform to propose. The Ways and Means Committee was not asked to express views on income guarantees, but to choose whether to support the Nixon welfare reform or some alternative course of action (including inaction). This episode suggests the difficulties of measuring political support for particular, constrained policy options by inquiring of politicians whether they approve of a broad class of policy principles. Bill Cavala and Aaron Wildavsky, "The Political Feasibility of Income By Right," Public Policy, (Winter 1970), pp. 321, 349.

[35] For a characterization of the redistributive "political arena," see Theodore Lowi, "American Business, Case Studies and Political Theory," World Politics, 16 (1963–64).

[36] On October 2, 1969, President Nixon sent to the Congress the Family Assistance Act of 1969, a plan modeled after FFB with the addition of a work requirement, child care

Constrained by a $2 billion budgetary allowance for additional cash transfers, committed to welfare reform, concerned about the pressures to relieve the states of part of their welfare burden, uncertain about what will reduce welfare rolls, federal officials had to compare programs by criteria whose weights are uncertain. If we have been unable to provide those weights and, hence, the basis for a simple decision rule, at least we have isolated some important criteria and discussed some of the issues involved in giving them weights.

IV. Conclusion

This paper has sought to clarify the choices among income maintenance alternatives, not to advocate a particular policy option. It began by distinguishing among the goals of reforming the present welfare system, substantially reducing American poverty, and making both the tax system and the social distribution of income more equitable. The second part set forth six criteria by which the desirability of competing income transfer schemes could be judged. The third section illustrated the use of these evaluative criteria by comparing two welfare reform plans that were before the Nixon Administration in 1969. Overall, the paper has sought to clarify the problems that exist in choosing among income maintenance alternatives and the necessity of giving relative weight to conflicting criteria.

provisions, somewhat different work incentives, and more than twice the estimated program costs. These changes from the FFB alternative would require a separate discussion of policy developments outside the scope of this paper, but of continuing interest. For a discussion of various aspects of the Nixon Administration's proposed Family Assistance Bill, see New Generation, 52 (Winter 1970).

TOWARDS A MORE ADEQUATE PROVISION FOR THE RELIEF OF NEED: PATTERNS FOR THE FUTURE

Paul M. Dodyk.

Many of the judicial opinions reproduced above have worked important changes bringing prompt betterment to hundreds of thousands of people. These are achievements not to be demeaned, but current thought seeks grander alternatives offering possibilities of total resolution. Two principal alternatives have emerged from the numerous schemes of reform which have been spun in public discussion of the poverty problem. These alternatives have frequently been referred to as the Demogrant (or social dividend) and the Guaranteed Annual Income (or negative income tax).

The Demogrant

The central idea around which various demogrant proposals have clustered is extremely simple. Based on the notion that a wealthy democratic society owes each of its members an equal duty of minimal support, the plan envisages the weekly or semimonthly payment of a social dividend to every man, woman and child. Instructed by the sorry history of our present system of local need assessment, the plan contemplates centralized federal determination of the amount paid. Various suggestions have been made as to the proper amount of the dividend. One thing is clear, however, to abolish poverty, the social dividend must be sufficient *in itself* to sustain the recipient at minimally acceptable levels of health and decency. For present purposes, this means that the dividend must at least equal the HEW poverty threshold for the family group in question. Anything less would fail of the purpose underlying most schemes of wholesale reform, which is the abolition of poverty. Needless to say, the amount payable would be shorn of family maxima, percentage reduction, and like practices currently in vogue.

The demogrant shares with its rival, the guaranteed annual income, insistence upon the view that the dividend is something to which a person is entitled *as of right,* with no strings attached. The social dividend is a legal entitlement untainted by charity or the welfare lady's discretion. It is the fundamental public obligation owed to every person by virtue of his membership in society. For its receipt, nothing is demanded: no residence time need be served, no complaints filed against absent spouses or other relations, no relationships severed with promising suitors, no admission granted to nocturnal surprise visitors from the department. By establishing the social dividend as a right unencumbered by behavioral conditions, its proponents hope to do away with what ten Broek has called America's "dual system of laws," and free those dependent upon the government for sustenance from any distinctive behavioral constraints.

The most important distinguishing characteristic of the demogrant—its *sine qua non*—is that it abjures any connection with the concept of need. Unlike other devices for the abolition of poverty, the demogrant would be made available to everyone, irrespective of his other sources of income. Moreover, although the amount of the dividend would be such that it alone would be sufficient for purposes of subsistence, the amount paid would not vary with the individual's other income. From the narrow, tight-fisted confines of today's categories—OAA, AB, APTD, AFDC—the demogrant goes to the extreme of total universality, including in its sweep every man, woman and child. It is in this universality and the concomitant divorce from considerations of need that the demogrant's proponents, such as Evelyn Burns, see its great advantage:

"The negative income tax, is, however, not truly revolutionary because in the last analysis it still relates the right to receive socially provided income to some concept of need . . . [I]t would still have the population divided into two obvious groups, those who are 'poor' enough to qualify for the negative tax, and the remainder. Some people would still have to be differentiated from others on the basis of economic status.

"The universal payment or guaranty, on the other hand, would have the advantage of treating all people equally. The question of the level of the guaranty would be of interest to all. It would not merely be a question of what was suitable for 'the poor'.

"It is for these reasons that if we should ever contemplate a shift away from the present complicated structure of social security programs, with their different and often offensive or arbitrary eligibility conditions and their varying benefit levels, I hope we shall move toward the demogrant rather than some version of the negative income tax."

The advantages anticipated by the demogrant's supporters are manifold and central. First, the demogrant would simplify administrative burdens and reduce related costs by doing away with the need for eligibility determinations; gone would be today's inquiry into needs, income and property. Second, it would enhance the system's acceptability by removing from it the stigma associated with a program designed for the poor. Many feel that any means test is demeaning and that it will reproduce, to some degree, that reluctance to apply which cripples the reach of current welfare programs. Finally and most importantly, there is a less tangible advantage—one more difficult to express. There is the sense that the demogrant, eschewing all means tests, is preferable for the simple reason that it does not assume the existence of two classes in American Society, the poor and the well-to-do. It is preferable because of its unifying assumption that all Americans are to be treated alike.

That, in brief, is the demogrant. No doubt, it could, if implemented, abolish poverty, defined in terms of monetary insufficiency and measured in accordance with the HEW standards. All one need do is to make sure that the social dividend is high enough to bring every recipient above the HEW threshold. Moreover, if the dividend is truly unconditional, if we take care to avoid building the old constraints into our new utopia, great strides will be made toward reestablishing the full measure of personal liberty, family integrity, and simple dignity for the poor.

The difficulty is that the gross cost of such a plan would, very roughly, be somewhat in excess of $200 billion. An expense of this magnitude, which would approximately double the Federal budget, is obviously not practicable. The demogrant is feasible only if coupled with substantial reform of the Federal tax structure—notably the Federal income tax—to make it more truly progressive. Such tax reform would assure that the demogrant would be largely recaptured from upper income families; and it could generate sufficient additional revenues to make the funding of the demogrant for poor and middle income families within the realm of possibility. Make no mistake about it. This would entail a substantial redistribution of income from the top half of the income strata to the bottom half. Whether the American public is prepared to make this effort is doubtful.

Yielding to the political economy of the situation may therefore entail some retreat from the total universality of the demogrant. If it is too costly to pay the social dividend to all, we must restrict it to some. To whom? Recognizing this problem, many proponents of the demogrant have fallen back to the Family Allowance (or Children's Allowance as it is sometimes known). Writing in *The Public Interest,* Mr. Moynihan proposes an American family allowance system of $8.00 per month for every child under six, and $12.00 per month for every child over six and under seventeen.[1]

Such a system would have considerable advantages as a contribution to the assault on poverty. For demogrant devotees, the family allowance's cardinal virtue is that it does not temporize with the means test, as it is payable to all children, irrespective of need. It is, moreover, a proposal with ample precedent in Western Europe and elsewhere, which can be invoked to counter the parade of horribles which opponents of income redistribution would muster. It is aimed at the group which is the largest single constituent of our poor. The cost is not prohibitive; Mr. Moynihan estimates it at some $9 billion. Politically it has the virtue of being aimed at a group which is innocent of any responsibility for its plight. In the same vein, the fact that it reaches all families can be expected to win support for it outside our poorest classes.

The problem is, of course, that the proposal offers no prospect of abolishing poverty. That it would do nothing for the 1,700,000 families without children (approximately one-third of the total number of poor families) is of course obvious. But even among children, the family allowance is at best a partial solution. Mollie Orshansky, one of the most distinguished of the poor's statisticians, estimates that a payment of $25.00 per month per child, more than double the Moynihan proposal, will remove from poverty only 36.2% of poor families with children, and somewhat less than half (45.4%) of the children (for 1965).

[1] Moynihan, "The Crises in Welfare". The Public Interest, Winter, 1968, No. 10, at 3, 26.

Moreover, the cost of even such piecemeal relief, $20.9 billion, is substantial. Inclusion of the allowance in taxable income will reduce the cost to $17.8 billion. Of this amount, only $4.2 billion will reach the poor, a consequence serious indeed when it is purchased at a cost which may well exhaust this country's redistributive capacity for the foreseeable future.

Increasing the payment to $50 per month, produces more impressive results, bringing 77% of our children out of poverty. But here the costs become very high indeed, involving an expenditure of $41.2 billion ($35 billion after tax) to put $8.4 billion in the hands of the poor.

This disproportion between cost and benefit to the poor is endemic in the entire demogrant family of proposals. The simple truth is that any transfer proposal which defines eligible recipients without reference to need is bound to involve a total expenditure greatly in excess of the benefit to the poor. There is doubtless great appeal to a thorough-going repudiation of the means test, but is the benefit so gained worth the cost; that is, will the pursuit of a public assistance program which is free of the means test stigma result in affording the poor diminished benefits because of the expense of making benefits available to those who are not needy. If so, can we sensibly trade the abolition of poverty away for a children's allowance which lifts but half our children out of poverty? Given the limitations upon our redistributive capacities which any realist must recognize, this may very well be the shape of the choice before us.

Reluctance to trade abolition for the values to be gained from eliminating the means test is reinforced by the thought that much of the opposition to the means test springs from the particularly humiliating and demanding form which it takes under our current welfare laws. Much of today's patina of disabling associations can perhaps be done away with even though the new system retains some means test. Doubtless this would require abandonment, not amendment of the existing welfare system, for the stigma of years past will doubtless continue to afflict any program identified with it. Perhaps integration with another body of laws, such as the Social Security Old Age, Survivors and Disability Insurance complex or the Internal Revenue System would aid in altering the image. Current eligibility-determination procedures could be replaced by some simplified system of declaring needs and income. Property rules could be liberalized, and the doctrine of relative responsibility eliminated.

Most important, however, any system which holds promise of disbursing assistance to the poor without the disabling associations of categorical assistance must be based on public acceptance of the notion that our productive processes, though privately owned, are held in trust to be managed for the common benefit, and that such management entails the right of every person to a standard of living compatible with prevailing notions of health and decency.

In the context of such a world, the existence of a means test need not carry with it all of today's burdensome and humiliating connotations. Perhaps some measure of indignity would remain ineradicable, but it may be possible to reduce the dignitary offense to so slight a dimension that its elimination could not sensibly be traded for the far more immediate and meaningful boon of universal material sufficiency.

The Guaranteed Annual Income

Equally prominent in recent discussion of the poverty problem is the Guaranteed Annual Income (GAI), a scheme which is also sometimes inelegantly labelled "The Negative Income Tax.[2] Though

the idea is not a new one, its prominence in current discussion seems to date from 1962 when Milton Friedman espoused it in his work, *Capitalism and Freedom.* Since the concept's reintroduction, the idea has atracted widespread support, including popularization by James Tobin, Robert Lampman, Earl Rolph, and George Break, all distinguished economists.

The essential difference between the demogrant and the guaranteed annual income lies in the fact that the latter is directed expressly at the needy. Where the demogrant seeks to ensure that no one lives in need by reaching everyone, the guaranteed annual income reaches only the poor. The basic concept is again very simple: [3] all you have to do is find all the poor people and give them enough money so that they are not poor anymore.

Under this system, anyone whose income falls below HEW's poverty index figure for a family group of his composition and location would be entitled to receive GAI payments. In its simplest form, the guaranteed annual income would supply the family with enough money to bring its annual income up to the appropriate index level. Thus, for 1970 an urban family of four with outside income of $1,000 would receive $2,841 to bring their total income up to $3,841; the "poverty gap" would be eliminated.

In contrast to today's categorical assistance system, the guaranteed annual income would not be limited to preferred classes of the worthy poor; it will seek to reach every person in need. Eligibility and the amount of payment would be centrally determined, although the amount may vary with regional differences in the cost of living.

---

[2] Whatever shape the relief of need takes after the inevitable disintegration of categorical assistance, let us hope that the new utopia comes attired in nomenclature more appealing than that of the negative income tax.

[3] Though its implementation may involve numerous and nettlesome practical problems.

Like the demogrant, the guaranteed annual income must be regarded as a fundamental legal right. Indeed, some would have us elevate the GAI to constitutional status, a sentiment which has also found expression in the talk among poverty lawyers of a "right to life" suit. Whether one is to seek constitutional sanctity for the right or to rest content with humbler statutory assurances, the GAI must be based on recognition of the principle that every person has a right to a standard of living compatible with prevailing notions of health and decency. The right is conferred upon all members of society without conditions requiring any distinctive standards of behavior. No intrusion upon domestic privacy, no constraints upon personal conduct, no disruption of family, no humiliating inquiry is to be countenanced.

Mechanically, the system would operate by having each family head submit a declaration of his anticipated income for the coming year. If this declaration shows a deficiency, the family will receive weekly or semimonthly GAI payments. Significant change in circumstances would require an amended declaration. No eligibility investigation comparable to today's humiliating probing would be required as a matter of regular routine; the fraud hunt would be conducted by occasional audit as it is under our tax system.

The numerous similarities between this procedure and current administration of the federal income tax have given rise to widespread suggestion that the new GAI system be integrated with the tax process. This notion seemed even more attractive when the Council of Economic Advisers' original poverty line, $3,000, exactly matched the sum of personal exemptions ($600 per person) and minimum standard deductions ($200 plus $100 per person) available to a family of four.[4] In-

tegrating the two would also have the advantage of separating the new system from the stigma-ridden categorical assistance program, though at the cost of association with a system which most people find at least mildly unpleasant, though for radically different reasons.

The dovetailing is, however, not nearly as neat as some have assumed. From an administrative point of view, the payment of funds with the speed and frequency required to relieve need contemplates a wholly different operation than today's tax collection requires. More seriously, the notion that we would use the Internal Revenue Code's current concept of "taxable income" to measure eligibility and need verges on the ludicrous. Use of that concept would classify as poor many whose income runs to millions of dollars annually (albeit nontaxable income). Provisions such as the exclusion of municipal bond interest from income and the special deduction from capital gains would serve no useful purpose in a GAI system. Moreover, a fully developed GAI system would doubtless entail a considerable body of distinctive rules. Thus, some provison would likely be made respecting the ownership of property, as regards both eligibility and amount of payment. Similarly, some restrictions would likely be placed on the individual's freedom to choose what family group is used as a basis for application.

---

[4] This approach has now been adopted to some extent as part of the tax reforms of 1969 and 1971. The minimum standard deduction has been replaced with a "low income allowance" of $1,100 per family which was designed to assure that, when added to the personal exemption of $750 per person (as of 1973), no family with income below the poverty line will have to pay a federal income tax. However, since this system does not pay out any subsidy to low income persons—it merely removes them from the income tax rolls—it is not yet a GAI or negative income in the sense discussed. Moreover, the failure to provide for adjustments to the low income allowance which would take account of adjustments in the cost of living has resulted in the continued imposition of federal income tax upon the poor even as defined by the spartan standards of the HEW poverty index.

As compared with the demogrant, the guaranteed annual income has the great advantage of being economically manageable without other major reforms. By focussing on the needy, the GAI is capable of eliminating poverty efficiently, without disbursing large amounts of money to the nonpoor. Where the Family Allowance puts only $1.00 into the hands of the poor for $5.00 spent, the guaranteed annual income is channelled directly to the poor. Moreover, the GAI is capable of eliminating poverty at a cost which is well within our material and political capacities; and most importantly, it is capable of doing so now. The cost of such an enterprise has been estimated at $10.1 to $12.3 billion,[5] assuming that the rest of the world holds still as we change over from categorical assistance to the guaranteed annual income.

These estimates indulge in the unrealistic assumption that there will be no offsetting adjustments in the other income received by the poor. Adjusting for the possibly induced fall in earnings by the poor could raise these estimates by $2.1 to $8.4 billion, depending on the magnitude of the reduction.

Plan Cost (in billions of dollars) [6]

$12.3	Earnings not reduced
14.4	Earnings drop 25%
16.5	Earnings drop 50%
18.6	Earnings drop 75%
20.7	Earnings drop 100%

While these cost estimates undoubtedly must be increased to take account of inflation since 1964–65, to say that the United States cannot "afford" this range of expenditure would be difficult. With our gross national product having exceeded $1,150 billion, the most expensive of the plans comes to less than 2% of current GNP. Nor can it be persuasively argued that the plan's adoption would result in a disproportionate allocation of resources to social welfare, when the sorry fact is that the United States ranks near the bottom in comparison with its Western European peers in that regard. Not only does our gross national product dwarf the expenditures required, it is also now increasing annually by nearly $100 billion a year.

If additional revenues were needed for a GAI, it could be raised without increasing tax rates by repealing the many preferential provisions which now pock our income tax structure. The total cost of these preferences, such as percentage depletion, the capital gains deduction, the nontaxability of municipal bond interest amounts to well over seventy billion dollars annually. Moreover, much of the revenue lost through such preferences is made up by the levying of taxes on the poor at demanding rates, who pay an estimated 20 to 30% of their meagre fare over to the government (most significantly, through local property taxes, state

[5] The Statistical Abstract for 1971 (Wash., D.C.1971) estimates the total gap between actual incomes and the S.S.A. Poverty Index at $17.2 billion for 1959, $14.7 billion for 1964 and $10.1 billion for 1969. Mollie Orshansky estimates the total gap between actual incomes and the S.S.A. Poverty Index at $11 billion for 1965. See Orshansky, "Who Was Poor in 1966", Children's Allowances and the Economic Welfare of Children (Citizens Committee for Children of New York, 1968) 48. Christopher Green estimates the cost of a guaranteed annual income of the sort described at $12.3 billion for 1964. Green, Negative Taxes and The Poverty Problem 141 (Brookings, 1967). His estimate differs from Orshansky's not only in time, but also in the fact that he does not use the S.S.A. Index, but rather a base of $1,500 for an individual plus $500 per additional family member. The $3,000 figure thus yielded for a family of four would approximate the S.S.A.'s typical urban family figure for 1964. Though it is true that the S.S.A. figure stood at $3,841 for 1970, the concomitant decrease from 34.1 million to 24.3 million poor from 1964 to 1969 would offset this increase, so that Green's cost estimates should still indicate the proper general order of magnitude. It should also be noted that these estimates exclude administrative costs.

[6] These computations are based on Green's study. Green, op. cit. supra, at 141.

sales taxes, and federal social security taxes). The notion of paying for the GAI by eliminating tax preferences, of redirecting funds from those who have avoided their public burden to those who are unfairly forced to bear it, has a certain appeal to it, though taking a realistic view of the matter, one would have to concede that the linkage would likely prove politically suicidal to both efforts.

Objections to a guaranteed annual income arise from sources apart from the problem of expense. On the crudest level, one does hear it said that the poor's poverty is a matter of their own making. It is a condition for which they are responsible, a just consequence of their chosen course of conduct. In particular, the image which most impedes progress toward some more rational system for the relief of need is the shiftless, lazy pauper partying it up on a tax-supported dole. Closely related to such objections is the notion that the guaranteed annual income will exert an even more stifling influence upon work and self-improvement than our present system of categorical assistance, which at least is limited to presumed unemployables.[7]

Of these charges, there is much to be said. First, the notion that voluntary, unjustified refusal to work plays a significant role in causing today's poverty seems wholly mistaken. The contrary is made clear by even the most cursory glance at who it is we are talking about. Of the 24.3 million poor, 9.8 million are children. One can hardly chastize them for refusal to work, or hold them responsible, for of all people, these children are surely innocent. Another 4.8 million are aged—persons over 65, who if not innocent of their fate, have reached the time of rest and forgiveness. Surely, we are at a point in time and affluence such that our economic well-being need not rest on the economically coerced labor of the

aged. Another three million are mothers of children under 18; of these 1.8 million also serve as the heads of their households. Given the deplorable state of child care facilities in this country, it seems impossible to frame our social welfare policies on the assumption that these women should leave their children and seek employment. More fundamentally, one may question the wisdom of depriving these women of the freedom to rear their own children. Given the state of our economic power, there seems scant reason to deprive the mothers of poverty of that freedom to associate with their children which is enjoyed by the well-to-do. Finally, one has 1.1 million heads of household who find themselves in poverty though they were employed at least 40 weeks during the year, and another three-quarters of a million who were ill, disabled or involuntarily unemployed.[8] None of these groups is fairly characterized by the shiftless image which seems to dominate so much of our public discussion of poverty, yet collectively they amount to a sizeable majority of the poor. Whatever else may be the cause of the poor's plight, it is not stubborn refusal to take employment; whatever else may be the cure, it is not stubborn insistence that they get a job.

Even if this is true, there remains the worry that, whatever the case today, any change to a more generous, less restrictive system will induce widespread withdrawal from the labor force. There is doubtless cause for such concern, but one must be careful to isolate the ways in which the guaranteed annual income may exert disincentive pressures. First, the GAI, like the current welfare system, makes it possible for a person to survive without seeking employment; the consequences of unemployment are made less dire. The differences between the two systems are (1) that the GAI will reach all the

---

[7] And more recently, those who are involuntarily unemployed.

[8] For August 1969. See Statistical Abstract of the United States, 1971, p. 322.

needy (not just the aged, blind, disabled, and families with dependent children), and (2) that the GAI will afford a level of support which is more nearly adequate.

Second, the GAI, in the form described above, also exerts disincentive pressure by removing all economic benefit from earnings below the poverty index level. Thus, if the father of a four-person family, earning $2,000 a year has the opportunity to earn another $500, why should he, since his GAI will decline by exactly that amount? Indeed, why should he continue to hold the $2,-000 job, particularly if that job is menial, dirty, and boring?

Such disincentive pressure is unfortunate both because of its adverse economic impact on production, and because of its sapping effect on the individual. The latter form of this pressure is not, however, a necessary feature of the guaranteed annual income. The GAI can as easily be designed so that the recipient derives substantial economic benefit from his employment. This could be accomplished by the simple expedient of reducing a person's GAI payment by only 50% (not 100%) of his outside earnings. Thus, a four-person family earning $2,000 would receive $2,841; that is $2,841 − 50% × $2,000 for a total income of $4,831. The family would benefit by 50% of its earnings.[9]

Such an alteration would doubtless greatly ease the system's disincentive pressures, but it would be costly. In addition to the $10 to $12.3 billion required to bridge the poverty gap, one must add the cost of allowing the poor to retain 50% of their earnings, which would result in substantial expenditure.[10]

Moreover, any such change entails accepting extension of the system above the poverty line and the costs thereof. Thus, a family just under the poverty line, with $3,800 in earned income, would be entitled to receive $1,941 (i. e., $3,841 − 50% ($3,800)),[11] a total income of $5,-741. Not only would the system extend beyond the poor by paying them more than is needed to lift them out of poverty; it would also necessarily reach persons who were not previously poor. One could hardly raise the $3,800-a-year family to $5,741 and do nothing for the $4,-000-a-year family. The most straightforward way of dealing equitably with this problem would be to open the GAI to all persons, reducing their payments by 50% of their earnings and 100% of their unearned income.[12] Such an extension would transform the GAI from a system aimed exclusively at the poor to one which reaches well into the lower reaches of the middle class. More precisely, the system would extend benefits to families of four with earned income of $7,682 or less,[13] though distributing

---

[9] There arises here a problem of integration with the Federal income tax. Generally speaking the GAI payments should be included in a taxpayer's gross income. The low income allowance should, however, be increased so that no tax is due until a family's income crosses the poverty threshold. It is also probably unwise, from an incentive standpoint, to design the system so that the individual retains less than 50% of the first $1,000 earned. For earnings in excess of $1,000, it may be possible to reduce GAI payments by 50% and impose the income tax as well, which in the lowest brackets would make for an effective rate of tax on earnings of about 65%.

[10] Green's efforts resulted in an estimate of $8,835,000 of earnings inuring to the poor in 1964, op. cit. supra at 23.

[11] That family would also have to pay an income tax on all but the first $1,000 of earned income. See note 9 supra.

[12] The increased income would also bear an income tax of about 15%–20% at current rates. See note 9 supra.

[13] That is, assuming a poverty floor of $3,841 and reducing the GAI payment by 50% of earnings. Since the purpose of the incentive version of the GAI is to encourage employment, unearned income is offset by a 100% reduction in the GAI. Thus, a family of four with $3,841 or more in un-

rather little to those at the upper end of that range.

The additional cost of extending the GAI to the near-poor would be substantial. Although no current estimate of such costs is available, earlier estimates of the cost of such a work incentive scheme predicted additional costs of 75% of the basic poverty gap.[14] Assuming a poverty gap of $10 to $12 billion, the added cost would be $7.5 to $9 billion.[15] Whether the gain is worth the cost is a matter about which reasonable men may differ. Some of the added cost would be sustained in any event through the doubtless greater reduction in earnings induced by the "pure" GAI system. Moreover, the effect which the system has in placing funds in the hands of families which find themselves just above the poverty line cannot be lamented as a wholly unmitigated evil. The S.S.A. index with which we are working is drawn along rather stringent lines, so that some measure of assistance to such families is easily defensible as a matter of humanitarian redistributive policy. Moreover, the extension of the system to the near-poor may serve some of the purposes sought in the demogrant's avoidance of the means test by reaching a somewhat broader segment of our people. In contrast

to such universal payment schemes as the Family Allowance, the plan remains a very efficient mechanism for channelling funds to the poor, placing a majority of the funds disbursed into such hands.

It of course remains true that this suggestion deals with only one of the disincentive features of the GAI. Though a family now stands to gain from its efforts, it is still guaranteed a certain minimal level of material sufficiency whether or not its members seek work. It is insulated against the most dire deprivation. Such insulation will erode some of today's incentive pressures.[16] Some GAI proponents, such as Milton Friedman have responded to this problem by making the GAI payments fall short of that minimal level necessary for health and decency and so preserving deprivation's incentive pressures. One wonders, however, whether such a course of action is necessary or wise. The S.S.A. poverty index is an extremely stringent standard of living. It is a far cry from the abundant life, and it seems unlikely that a very large number of Americans will willingly settle for such a life if opportunities of betterment are available. More important, does the United States today require the props of destitution and deprivation to bolster its economic position? Need an economy whose gross national product has crossed the thousand billion dollar mark resort to such cruel and undiscriminating methods of coercing labor? Continuing resort to deprivation as a work incentive would, under our fortunate circumstances, be objectionable even if it were visited only upon those whom one wishes to encourage; it is rendered the more objectionable when, as is inevitably the case, it is incidentally visited upon

earned income would be ineligible for the GAI.

[14] See Dodyk et al., Cases and Materials on Law and Poverty, 315 (1st ed. 1969).

[15] And perhaps somewhat more if one allows for loss of work effort under this scheme. Whether any adjustment should be made is debatable. Until very recently, our welfare system has contained an implicit 100% tax rate as welfare payments were reduced dollar for dollar to take account of earnings, and recent improvements have contributed rather feeble incentive provisions. Moreover, some would support repeal of minimum wage laws as a concomitant of the GAI and so remove this barrier to employment, though such a move would arouse vehement and well-grounded opposition despite the possible employment gains.

[16] We should not forget that the transition from today's system to the GAI is a change of degree. The programs which are now in use afford some measure of protection against destitution. The change will merely enhance, to some largely unpredictable degree, pressures which already are felt.

others innocent of their condition, most notably the children. The choice to be made is between the abolition of poverty and the preservation of *its* incentives; no compromise is possible.

Under the GAI it is said that not only will the poor get lazy; they will get children—by the millions. And as anyone knows, too many children is a bad thing. Much the same worry underlies some of the more objectionable features of categorical assistance, such as family maximums, suitable homes, and substitute fathers. Most persons would be prone to agree that there are getting to be too many people around here. But it seems highly doubtful that the GAI would induce an uncontrollable baby-boom. The spartan allowance contemplated would hardly make procreation a profitable enterprise, and despite the many virtues of sex, comfort still has its attractions.

Moreover, there is little if any empirical evidence that the GAI would result in an increase in population growth. The Scandinavian countries, which have had far more liberal social welfare provisions since the Second World War have experienced birth rates lower than those of the United States. Similarly, the population expansion programs of the totalitarian governments in Italy and Germany produced no great upsurge in population growth, despite a variety of financial inducements. Even more germane is the fact that American and Canadian birth rates have shown remarkable parallelism in recent years, despite the introduction and liberalization of a children's allowance program in Canada.

With no stronger empirical or *a priori* basis for assuming that the GAI will result in a population upsurge, any argument against the abolition of poverty based on such fears is difficult to indulge. The social gain from abolition is immediate, demonstrable, and important. Much suffering will be avoided. This cannot be doubted. Given these gains, one is entitled to a much more persuasive showing than has been made before one can take the baby-boom argument seriously. Particularly is this the case now that scientific advances have given us so much more control over our numbers. With these advances making population control possible through means which are so much less onerous and so much less offensive to egalitarian principle, there seems no reason to choose that method of population control which would perpetuate poverty.

To a connoisseur of panaceas, the guaranteed annual income may seem a rather thin gruel. To the accusation that the true utopia is not described in these pages, one can only plead guilty. The GAI speaks to only one aspiration: the abolition of poverty. Even here one's goals are extremely modest. The system described is one which will guarantee everyone only a minimal level of material sufficiency. If material progress continues as in the years past, there should be a growing margin of available resources for increasingly generous provision for income maintenance as well as for other needed social investment and services.

SUMMARY OF FAMILY ASSISTANCE PROVISIONS OF H.R. I

THE PROPOSED "SOCIAL SECURITY AMENDMENTS OF 1971"

As Reported to the House of Representatives on May 26, 1971. (House Report No. 92–231).

*   *   *

IV. PROVISIONS RELATING TO FAMILY PROGRAMS

The present program of aid to families with dependent children (AFDC) would be repealed effective July 1, 1972, and two new totally Federal programs would take effect on that day. The new programs would be adopted for a period of five years (through fiscal year 1977) in order to give Congress an opportunity to review their operation before continuing them in subsequent years. The new programs would be established by a new Title XXI in the Social Security Act. A description of the two new programs follows:

Families in which at least one person is employable would be enrolled in the Opportunities for Families Program, administered by the Department of Labor. Families with no employable person would be enrolled in the Family Assistance Plan administered by the Department of Health, Education, and Welfare.

A—OPPORTUNITIES FOR FAMILIES PROGRAM

Registration for employment and training

Every member of a family who is found to be available for work by the Secretary of Health, Education, and Welfare would be required to register for manpower services, training and employment.

An individual would be considered available for work unless such person—

(1) Is unable to work or be trained because of illness, incapacity, or age;

(2) Is a mother or other relative caring for a child under age 6 (age 3 beginning July 1974);

(3) Is the mother or other female caretaker of a child, if the father or another adult male relative is in the home and is registered.

(4) Is a child under the age of 16 (or a student up to age 22);

(5) Is needed in the home on a continuous basis because of illness or incapacity of another family member.

Nevertheless, any person (except one who is ill, incapacitated, or aged) who would be exempted from registering by the above provisions could voluntarily register.

Every person who registered (other than a volunteer) would be required to participate in manpower services or training and to accept available employment. An individual could not be required to accept employment however—

(1) If the position offered is vacant due to a strike, lockout, or other labor dispute;

(2) If the wages and other employment conditions are contrary to those prescribed by applicable Federal, State, or local law, or less favorable than those prevailing for similar work in the locality, or the wages are less than an hourly rate of $3/4$ of the highest Federal minimum wage ($1.20 per hour under present law);

(3) If membership in a company union or non-membership in a bona fide union is required;

(4) If he has demonstrated the capacity to obtain work that would better enable him to achieve self-sufficiency, and such work is available.

Child care and other supportive services

The Secretary of Labor directly or by using child care projects under the jurisdiction of the Department of Health, Education, and Welfare, would provide for child care services for registrants who require them in order to accept or continue to participate in manpower services, training, employment, or vocational rehabilitation.

The Secretary of Labor would be authorized funds to provide child care by grant or contract. Families receiving such services might also be required to pay all or part of the costs involved.

Health, vocational rehabilitation, family planning, counseling, social, and other supportive services (including physical examinations and minor medical services) would also be made available by the Secretary of Labor to registrants as needed.

Operation of manpower services, training and employment programs

The Secretary of Labor would develop an employability plan designed to prepare recipients to be self-supporting. The Secretary would then provide the necessary services, training, counseling, testing, coaching, program orientation, job training, and followup services to assist the registrant in securing employment, retaining employment, and obtaining opportunities for advancement.

Provision would also be made for voluntary relocation assistance to enable a registrant and his family to be self-supporting.

Public service employment programs would also be used to provide needed jobs. Public service projects would be related to the fields of health, social service, environmental protection, education, urban and rural development and redevelopment, welfare, recreation, public facility and similar activities. The Secretary of Labor would establish these programs through grants or by contract with public or nonprofit agencies or organizations. The law would provide safeguards for workers on such jobs and wages could not be less than the higher of the prevailing or applicable minimum wage or the Federal minimum wage.

Federal participation in the costs of an individual's participation in a public service employment program would be 100 percent for the first year of his employment, 75 percent for the second year, and 50 percent for the third year.

States and their subdivisions that receive Federal grants would be required to provide the Secretary of Labor with up-to-date listings of job vacancies. The Secretary would also agree with certain Federal agencies to establish annual or other goals for employment of members of families receiving assistance.

Allowances of individuals participating in training

An incentive allowance of $30 per month would be paid to each registrant who participates in manpower training (States would have the option of providing an additional allowance of up to $30). Necessary costs for transportation and similar expenses would also be paid.

Utilization of other programs

The Secretary of Labor would be required to integrate this program as needed with all other manpower training programs involving all sectors of the economy and all levels of government.

Rehabilitation services for incapacitated family members

Family members who are incapacitated would be referred to the state vocational rehabilitation service. A quarterly review of their incapacities would usually be made.

Each such incapacitated individual would be required to accept rehabilitation services that are made available to him, and an allowance of $30 would be paid him while he receives such services. (States would have the option of providing an additional allowance of up to $30.) Necessary costs for transportation and similar expenses would also be paid.

Evaluation and research; reports

The Secretary of Labor would be authorized to conduct research and demonstrations of the program and directed to make annual evaluation reports to the President and the Congress. An appropriation of $10,000,000 would be authorized for these purposes.

B—FAMILY ASSISTANCE PLAN

Payment of benefits

All eligible families with no member available for employment would be enrolled and paid benefits by the Secretary of Health, Education, and Welfare.

Rehabilitation services and child care for incapacitated family members

Family members who are unemployable because of incapacity would be referred to State vocational rehabilitation agencies for services. A quarterly review of their incapacities would usually be made. Such persons would be required to accept services made available, and would be paid a $30 per month incentive allowance plus transportation and other related costs. (States would have the option of providing an additional allowance of up to $30.)

Child care services would also be provided if needed to enable individuals to take vocational rehabilitation services.

Evaluation and research; reports

The Secretary of Health, Education, and Welfare would be authorized to conduct research and demonstrations of the family assistance plan and directed to make annual evaluation reports to the President and the Congress. An appropriation of $10,000,000 would be authorized for this purpose.

C—DETERMINATION OF BENEFITS

Uniform determinations

Both Secretaries would be required to apply the same interpretations and applications of fact to arrive at uniform determinations of eligibility and assistance payment amounts under the two family programs.

Eligibility for and amount of benefits

Family benefits would be computed at the rate of $800 per year for the first two members, $400 for the next three members, $300 for the next two members and $200 for the next member. This would provide $2,400 for a family of four, and the maximum amount which any family could receive would be $3,600. A family would not be eligible if it had countable resources in excess of $1,500.

If any member of the family fails to register, take required employment or training, or accept vocational rehabilitation services, the family benefits would be reduced by $800 per year.

Benefits would be determined on the basis of the family's income for the current quarter and the three preceding quarters.

After a family has been paid benefits for 24 consecutive months, a new application would be required which would be processed as if it were a new application.

The Secretary could determine that a family is not eligible if it has very large gross income from a trade or business.

Families would have to apply for all other benefits available to them in order to be eligible.

Definition of income

Earned income would follow generally the definition of earnings used in applying the earnings limitation of the social security program. Unearned income means all other forms of income among which are benefits from other public and private programs, prizes and awards, proceeds of life insurance not needed for last illness and burial (with a maximum of $1,500), gifts, support, inheritances, grants, dividends, interests and so forth.

The following items would be excluded from the income of a family:

1. Earnings of a student regularly attending school, with limits set by the Secretary.

2. Irregular earned income of an individual of $30 or less in a quarter and

irregular unearned income of $60 or less in a quarter.

3. Earned income used to pay the cost of child care under a schedule prescribed by the Secretary.

4. The first $720 per year of other earned income plus one-third of the remainder.

5. Assistance based on need received from public or private agencies, except veterans' pensions.

6. Training allowances.

7. The tuition part of scholarships and fellowships.

8. Home produce.

9. One-third of child support and alimony.

10. Foster care payments for a child placed in the family by a child placement agency.

The total of the exclusions under (1), (2), and (3) above could not exceed $2,000 for a family of four rising by $200 for each additional member to an overall maximum of $3,000.

Exclusions from resources

A family cannot be eligible for payments if it has resources in excess of $1,500. In determining what is included in the $1,500 amount, the following items are excluded:

1. The home to the extent that its value does not exceed a reasonable amount.

2. Household goods and personal effects not in excess of a reasonable amount.

3. Other property which is essential to the family's self-support.

An insurance policy would be counted only to the extent of its cash surrender value except that if the total face value of all such policies with respect to an individual is $1,500 or less, no cash surrender value will be counted.

The Secretary would prescribe periods of time, and manners in which, property must be disposed of in order that it would not be included as resources.

Meaning of family and child

A family would be defined as two or more related people living together in the United States where at least one of the members is a citizen or a lawfully admitted alien and where at least one of them is a child dependent on someone else in the family.

No family will be eligible if the head of the household is an undergraduate or graduate student regularly attending a college or university. Benefits would not be payable to an individual for any month in which he is outside the United States.

The term "child" means an unmarried person who is not the head of the household, and who is either under the age of 18 or under the age of 22 if attending school regularly.

Appropriate State law would be used in determining relationships.

The income and resources of an adult (other than a parent or the spouse of a parent) living with the family but not contributing to the family would be disregarded.

If an individual takes benefits under adult assistance, he could not be eligible for family benefits.

Optional State supplementation

If a State decides to supplement the basic Federal payment, it would be required to provide benefit amounts that do not undermine the earnings disregard provision. A State could agree to have the Federal Government make the supplementary payments on behalf of the

State. If a State agrees to have the Federal Government make its supplemental payments, the Federal Government would pay the full administrative costs of making such payments, but if it makes its own payments the State would pay all of such costs.

States could but would not be required to cover under medicaid persons who are made newly eligible for cash benefits under the bill.

The Federal Government, in administering supplemental benefits on behalf of a State, would be required to recognize a residency requirement if the State decided to impose such a requirement.

D—PROCEDURAL AND GENERAL PROVISIONS

Payments and procedures

The Secretary would be permitted to pay the benefits at such times as best carry out the purposes of the title and could make payments to a person other than a member of the family or to an agency where he finds inability to manage funds. The Secretary's decision would be subject to hearing and review.

The family benefits could not be paid to an individual who failed to register, or take work, training or vocational rehabilitation.

Cash advances of $100 or less could be paid if an applicant appears to meet all the eligibility requirements and is faced with a financial emergency.

The Secretary may arrange for adjustment and recovery in the event of overpayments or underpayments, with a view toward equity and avoiding penalizing people who were without fault.

People who are, or claim to be, eligible for assistance payments, and who disagree with determinations of the Secretary, could obtain hearings if they request

them within 30 days. Final determinations would be subject to judicial review in Federal district courts, but the Secretary's decisions as to any fact would be conclusive and not subject to review by the courts. The Secretary would also be given authority to appoint qualified people to serve as hearing examiners without their having to meet the specific standards prescribed under the Administrative Procedure Act for hearing examiners.

The right of any person to any future benefit would not be transferable or assignable, and no money payable under this title would be subject to execution, levy, attachment, garnishment, or other legal process.

In addition, the Secretary would establish necessary rules and regulations dealing with proofs and evidence, and the method of taking and furnishing the same, in order to establish the right to benefits.

Each family would be required to submit a report of income within 30 days after the end of a quarter and benefits would be cut off if the report was not filed. If a family failed, without good cause, to report income or changes in circumstances as required by the Secretary, it would be subject to a penalty of $25 the first time, $50 the second time and $100 for later times.

The head of any Federal agency would be required to provide such information as the Secretary of HEW needs to determine eligibility for benefits under this title.

Penalties for fraud

A penalty of $1,000 or 1 year imprisonment, or both, would be provided in the case of fraud under the program.

Administration

Both the Secretary of Health, Education, and Welfare and the Secretary of

Labor could perform their functions directly, through other Federal agencies, or by contract. An additional Assistant Secretary is authorized in the Department of Labor to head up the new program in that Department.

Child care

The Secretaries of Labor and Health, Education, and Welfare are each given the authority and responsibility for arranging day care for their respective recipients under the Opportunities for Families Program and the Family Assistance Plan who need such day care in order to participate in training, employment, or vocational rehabilitation. Where such care can be obtained in facilities developed by the Secretary of Health, Education, and Welfare, these would be utilized.

Insofar as possible, arrangements would be made for after school care with local educational agencies. All day care would be subject to standards developed by the Secretary of Health, Education, and Welfare, with the concurrence of the Secretary of Labor. Both Secretaries would have authority to make grants and contracts for payment of up to 100 percent of the cost of care. The Secretary of Health, Education, and Welfare would have total responsibility for construction of facilities. $700 million would be authorized for the provision of child care services in the first fiscal year, and such sums as Congress may appropriate in subsequent years. In addition, $50 million would be authorized for construction and renovation of child care facilities for each fiscal year.

Obligations of parents

A deserting parent would be obligated to the United States for the amount of any Federal payments made to his family less any amount that he actually contributes by court order or otherwise to the family.

Any parent of a child receiving benefits who travels in interstate commerce to avoid supporting his child would be guilty of a misdemeanor and subject to a fine of $1,000, imprisonment for 1 year, or both.

The Secretary would report to appropriate officials cases of child neglect or abuse which came to his attention while administering the program.

Local committees to evaluate program

Local advisory committees would be set up throughout the country, with a minimum of one in each State, which would evaluate and report on the effectiveness of the elements of the program designed to help people become self-supporting. Each committee would be composed of representatives from labor, business, and the public, as well as public officials not directly involved in the administration of the programs.

V. OTHER RELATED ASSISTANCE PROVISIONS

ADOPTION AND FOSTER CARE SERVICES UNDER CHILD WELFARE

Authorizations of $150 million for fiscal year 1972 and higher amounts for subsequent years would be provided for payments to the States to support foster care and related services.

PROVISIONS RELATED TO NEW ASSISTANCE PROGRAMS

Effective date for adult assistance and family programs

Major changes made in the assistance programs would be effective July 1, 1972. The child care provisions would become effective upon enactment of the bill. The amendments which provide benefits to families where the father and mother are both present, neither is incapacitated, and the father is not unemployed (the "working poor") would become effective January 1, 1973.

Prohibition against participation in food stamp program by recipients of payments under family and adult assistance programs

The bill would amend the Food Stamp Act of 1964 by providing that families and adults eligible for benefits under the assistance programs in this bill would be excluded from participation in the food stamp program.

Special provisions for Puerto Rico, the Virgin Islands, and Guam

There would be special provisions for Puerto Rico, the Virgin Islands, and Guam. The amounts used in the family assistance plan and the aid to the aged, blind, and disabled (other than the $720 amount of annual earnings to be disregarded and the $30 per month incentive allowances) would be adjusted by the ratio of the per capita income of each of these jurisdictions to the per capita income of the lowest of the 50 States.

Determination of medicaid eligibility

The Secretary would be able to enter into agreements with States under which the Secretary would determine eligibility for medicaid both for those eligible for Federal payments and the medically needy in cases where the State covered the medically needy. The State would pay half of the Secretary's additional administrative costs arising from carrying out the agreement.

Effective date.—July 1, 1972.

Transitional administration of public assistance

The Secretary of Health, Education, and Welfare could enter into agreements with States under which a State would administer the Federal assistance program for a period of up to one year from the beginning of the program.

Limitations on increases in State welfare expenditures

States would be guaranteed that, if they make payments supplementary to the Federal adult or family programs, it would cost them no more to do so than the amount of their total expenditures for cash public assistance payments during calendar year 1971, to the extent that the Federal payments and the State supplementary payments to recipients do not exceed the payment levels in effect under the public assistance programs in the State for January 1971. The value of food stamps would be taken into account in computing whether the guarantee would go into effect if the State pays in cash the value of food stamps. Most States would save money under the provisions of the bill; this provision would guarantee that no State would lose money.

Limitation on Federal expenditures for social services

The Federal Government would continue to provide 75 percent matching funds to the States for child care and family planning services on an open-end appropriation basis. Federal matching for other specified social services would be limited to the amounts appropriated by the Congress.

PUBLIC ASSISTANCE AMENDMENTS EFFECTIVE IMMEDIATELY

Additional remedies for State noncompliance with provisions of assistance titles

The Secretary would be able to require States to make payments to people who did not receive all money due them because the State failed to comply with a Federal requirement.

The Secretary could require a State which is in noncompliance with a Federal requirement to set up a timetable and method for assuring compliance, or could request the Attorney General to bring suit to enforce the Federal requirements.

Effective date.—Enactment.

Statewideness not required for services

A State would be permitted to furnish social services in one area of a State without being required to furnish such services in all geographic areas of the State.

Effective date.—Enactment.

Optional modification in disregarding income under AFDC

States would be permitted, between enactment and July 1, 1972, to modify their present AFDC programs so as to substitute the earnings disregard provisions in the family assistance provisions (cost of child care, plus $720, plus one-third of the remainder) for provisions of present law (the first $30 and one-third of the remainder after which actual work expenses are deducted).

A State could also apply the maximum dollar limits in the family programs on child care and student earnings ($2,000 for a family of four rising to $3,000 for a family of nine or more) to its present AFDC program.

Effective date.—Enactment.

Individual programs for family services not required

States would no longer be required to prepare a separate plan of services for each individual who is eligible for AFDC.

Effective date.—July 1, 1972, or earlier if the State so chooses.

Enforcement of support orders

States would be required to secure support for a spouse of a parent from the other parent (of children receiving assistance payments) where he has deserted or abandoned his spouse, utilizing reciprocal arrangements with other States to obtain or enforce court orders for support.

Effective date.—July 1, 1972, or earlier, if the State plan so provides.

Separation of social services and cash assistance payments

Each State would be required to submit a proposal to the Secretary by January 1, 1972 providing for the administrative separation of handling eligibility for cash payments and the provision of social services by July 1, 1972.

Increase in Federal matching to States for costs of establishing paternity and collecting child support payments

Federal matching would be increased from 50 percent to 75 percent for State costs incurred in establishing the paternity of AFDC children and locating and collecting support from their absent parents.

Effective date.—Enactment.

Vendor payments for special needs

States would be permitted to provide for non-recurring items of special need by means of vendor payments.

Increase in Federal matching—WIN program

Effective immediately, the Federal matching under the WIN program would be increased from 80 to 90 percent. This provision expires June 30, 1972.

* * *

Potential fiscal year 1973 costs of Assistance provisions under H.R. 1

[In billions of dollars; negative amounts indicate decreases]

	Federal			State and local[1]			Net cost to all governments
	Current law	H.R. 1	Net cost	Current law	H.R. 1	Net cost	
Payments to families	$3.9	[2]$5.8	$1.9	$3.3	$3.1	-$0.2	$1.7
Less savings from public service jobs		-.3	-.3				-.3
Subtotal	3.9	5.5	1.6	3.3	3.1	-.2	1.4
Payments to adult categories	2.2	4.1	1.9	1.4	1.5	.1	2.0
Cost of cash assistance	6.1	9.6	3.5	4.7	4.6	-.1	3.4
Federal cost of "hold harmless" provision		1.1	1.1		-1.1	-1.1	
Food programs	2.4	1.0	-1.4				-1.4
Cost of maintenance payments	8.5	11.7	3.2	4.7	3.5	-1.2	[3]2.0
Child care	.3	.8	.5				.5
Training	.2	.5	.3				.3
Public service jobs		.8	.8				.8
Supportive services		.1	.1				.1
Administration	.4	1.1	.7	.4		-.4	.3
Cost of related and support activities	.9	3.3	2.4	.4		-.4	2.0
Total cost of program	9.4	15.0	5.6	5.1	3.5	-1.6	4.0
Impact of other programs		-.1	-.1				-.1
Grand total	9.4	14.9	5.5	5.1	3.5	-1.6	3.9

[1] Assumes that the States, through supplemental programs, maintain benefit levels including the value of food stamp bonuses.
[2] Includes only 6 months of payments to families in which both parents are present, neither is incapacitated, and the father is employed. The effective date for this provision is Jan. 1, 1973.
[3] Net benefit increases to recipients.

Projected recipients under current law and persons eligible for assistance under H.R. 1, fiscal years 1973–1977

(In millions)

	1973	1974	1975	1976	1977
Persons eligible for benefits under H.R. 1:					
Persons in families:					
Not now covered under present programs	9.1	8.1	7.2	6.4	5.7
Covered under present programs	10.3	10.6	10.9	11.2	11.5
Aged, blind and disabled	6.2	6.6	7.1	7.2	7.2
Total eligibles under H.R. 1	25.6	25.3	25.2	24.8	24.4
Recipients under current law:					
Persons in families with dependent children	11.6	12.6	13.6	14.7	15.8
Aged, blind and disabled	3.4	3.4	3.5	3.5	3.6
Total recipients under current law	15.0	15.0	17.1	18.2	19.4

Potential State savings under assistance provisions of H.R. 1 [1]

[In millions of dollars]

	1973	1974	1975	1976	1977
Alabama	$ 32.4	$ 38.4	$ 45.4	$ 47.2	$ 49.1
Alaska	2.5	3.1	3.7	4.4	5.1
Arizona	21.5	22.6	23.8	25.2	26.5
Arkansas	19.7	20.4	21.3	22.1	22.9
California	234.9	294.9	356.5	402.5	447.7
Colorado	13.3	16.6	19.8	21.5	23.1
Connecticut	21.3	25.7	30.2	34.8	39.1
Delaware	1.8	2.1	2.5	3.0	3.6
District of Columbia	12.6	17.0	21.5	23.4	25.1
Florida	170.3	177.8	185.3	192.9	200.2
Georgia	57.8	53.4	55.0	56.7	58.3
Hawaii	7.0	7.8	8.6	9.6	10.7
Idaho	1.5	1.9	2.2	2.8	3.4
Illinois	62.1	78.9	95.6	112.4	129.2
Indiana	8.6	10.5	12.6	14.7	16.9
Iowa	26.7	28.6	30.5	32.6	34.6
Kansas	14.2	15.6	17.0	18.7	20.3
Kentucky	12.6	13.6	14.5	15.5	16.3
Louisiana	65.4	68.5	71.7	74.9	78.1
Maine	3.6	4.4	5.4	6.4	7.5
Maryland	41.9	44.7	47.5	50.4	53.2
Massachusetts	44.3	57.3	70.4	83.7	96.9
Michigan	45.4	58.2	71.2	84.2	97.2
Minnesota	15.2	19.4	23.8	28.1	32.6
Mississippi	23.3	24.2	25.2	26.4	27.5
Missouri	12.1	14.9	20.5	22.6	24.7
Montana	2.5	2.7	2.9	3.2	3.5
Nebraska	3.1	3.9	4.7	5.6	6.6
Nevada	1.1	1.2	1.2	1.8	2.1
New Hampshire	2.3	2.9	3.6	4.4	5.2
New Jersey	50.1	64.4	78.6	93.1	107.6
New Mexico	7.3	7.8	8.2	8.7	9.1
New York	188.4	238.7	289.2	339.6	390.1
North Carolina	31.9	33.0	34.1	35.2	36.4
North Dakota	1.2	1.2	1.4	1.8	2.2
Ohio	64.0	69.3	74.6	79.9	85.3
Oklahoma	38.3	40.2	42.0	43.9	45.6
Oregon	15.9	17.4	18.9	20.5	22.0
Pennsylvania	51.3	69.9	88.5	107.2	125.9
Rhode Island	6.3	7.7	9.3	11.0	12.7
South Carolina	13.8	14.5	15.2	16.0	16.7
South Dakota	2.5	2.8	3.3	3.7	4.3
Tennessee	34.2	35.1	36.1	37.0	38.0
Texas	57.1	59.7	61.4	65.1	67.7
Utah	3.4	3.6	3.9	4.3	4.7
Vermont	1.1	1.3	1.7	2.1	2.5
Virginia	10.4	12.9	15.5	18.2	20.9
Washington	11.4	15.9	20.6	25.2	30.0
West Virginia	18.3	18.7	19.2	19.7	20.3
Wisconsin	33.3	35.5	37.6	39.9	42.1
Wyoming	1.2	1.3	1.5	1.9	2.2
Guam	.22	.22	.32	.33	.33
Puerto Rico	26.1	27.6	29.1	30.7	32.2
Virgin Islands	1.1	1.2	1.2	1.4	1.4
Total	1,643.8	1,911.1	2,185.5	2,438.1	2,687.4

[1] Assumes that the States, through supplemental payments, maintain January 1971 payment levels including the value of food stamps and agree to Federal administration of supplemental payments.

CONGRESSIONAL ACTION ON H.R. 1

Center on Social Welfare Policy and Law,
2 Welfare L. News No. 3 (Nov. 1972).

The years of congressional skirmishing over welfare reform were temporarily halted late last month with the passage of a bill which provides for changes in Social Security, Medicare, Medicaid and the adult welfare programs, but leaves AFDC largely intact. We review here the developments which led to that result and the prospects for future congressional action on welfare * * *.

H.R. 1 as drafted by the House Committee on Ways and Means and its Chairman, Wilbur Mills of Arkansas, federalized both the family and the adult welfare programs and contained numerous changes in OASDI, Medicaid, and Medicare. [For a summary critique of H.R. 1 as originally drafted, see Vol. 1, No. 1 of the *Welfare Law News* (June 1971).]

Although the Ways and Means' version of H.R. 1 was less generous than President Nixon's original welfare reform proposal of 1969, the Administration supported the Committee bill.

A group of organizations headed by the AFL–CIO, the UAW, the League of Women Voters, and Common Cause, urged the House to support H.R. 1, in view of the fact that the vote would be up-or-down (Social Security bills in the House are traditionally not subject to amendment). These groups believed that the changes they supported would have to await Senate action.

The National Welfare Rights Organization and the Coalition for Adequate Welfare Reform Now, a group headed by the National Council of Churches, opposed H.R. 1, arguing that it was unwise to rely on the Senate for the many changes they believed essential.

Debate on H.R. 1 in the House began on June 21, 1971, under a "limited open rule," permitting it to be subject to only one amendment. This amendment, a motion to strike Title IV of the bill (the title containing the Family Assistance Plan and the Opportunities for Families Program, "FAP-OFF") sponsored by the Congressional Black Caucus, lost 234–187. The bill then passed the House and was sent to the Senate.

The Committee on Finance, chaired by Senator Long, took testimony from Administration witnesses in July 1971 and conducted further hearings in early September on the child care provisions of the bill. The Committee then turned to other legislative matters.

Liberalizing amendments to H.R. 1 were introduced in the Senate by Senator Ribicoff in October 1971 (Amendment No. 559). Senator Harris thereafter also introduced a welfare reform bill somewhat more liberal than the Ribicoff amendments (S. 2747), and Senator McGovern introduced the NWRO bill, the most generous of the three major alternative welfare packages (S. 2372). A comparison of these proposals with the House-passed version of H.R. 1 is found at V Clearinghouse Review 508 (January 1972).

The Finance Committee resumed hearings on H.R. 1 in January, 1972, and completed its public hearings on February 15. The Committee's version of H.R. 1 was not reported out, however, until September 27, 1972, the day on which debate on the bill began.

The Committee bill, which was 989 pages long (said to be one of the longest pieces of legislation in the history of Congress), differed substantially from the House version of H.R. 1. In place of the FAP-OFF provisions of the House bill, the Finance Committee's version would have established, effective January 1, 1974, a "guaranteed employment opportunity" program for able-bodied heads of families with children, (except mothers with children under six years of age), administered by a federal Work Administration composed of three board members appointed by the President.

The agency was to give first priority to placing persons in regular employment. If such employment paid between $1.50 and $2.00 an hour the Work Administration would have given the employee a "wage supplement" equal to ¾ of the difference between the salary and $2.00. A person dissatisfied with a placement in regular employment could not leave without temporary loss of eligibility for "guaranteed employment", unless he or she was granted permission by the Work Administration pursuant to a petition which could be filed after 30 days of service on the job.

The "guaranteed employment" for those not given regular employment would have been, in essence, work-for-relief in private non-profit or public agencies by which an individual would work up to 32 hours per week at $1.50 per hour to enable him or her to earn up to (but no more than) $48 per week (the guaranteed compensation under the program). It was also contemplated that the Work Administration would contract out recipients for temporary work with public or private employers (such as farmers or housewives) for a fee equal to the prevailing wage. The individuals in the program would not be deemed employees and would not be protected by any state or federal law (other than the Act) regulating the hours of work, rates of pay or other conditions of employment, except that persons contracted out to private employers would be covered by Social Security if a private employee in that position would be. For the children of individuals placed in guaranteed employment, after-school child care, if needed, would have been satisfied by any member of the family, whether a minor or an adult, who would be found capable of providing supervision. Guaranteed job

placements for mothers with young children "would include cleaning up and beautifying their apartments or homes [and] training in providing a pleasing home atmosphere with child-centered activities * * *". (Finance Committee Report, p. 422.) Only persons placed in public service jobs would have been eligible for the "wage supplement".

Persons engaged in regular or guaranteed employment would also have become eligible for an annual "work bonus" up to $400.

Those unable to work would have remained within the existing AFDC program, which was to be amended so as to deny eligibility to, among others, two-parent families headed by an able-bodied male, families headed by a woman with no children under six, individuals who were neither United States citizens nor aliens admitted for permanent residence, persons who had not resided in the state for varying amounts of time, unborn children, mothers who failed to cooperate in establishing paternity or securing child support, drug addicts, alcoholics, families with stepfathers or "men-in-the-house", and families headed by an unemployed parent who was participating in a strike.

Other changes in the current AFDC program would have included a prohibition on use of the declaration method for determining eligibility, the elimination of food stamp eligibility a restriction of fair hearing rights, a change in the income disregard so as to decrease the work incentive, a restriction of the confidentiality protections of recipients, and broad authorization for states to make protective payments to recipients rather than cash assistance grants. A federal parent-locater service was to be established to track down and obtain support from absent parents, utilizing the services of the United States Attorney General, legal services attorneys, and regional blood-typing laboratories to determine paternity. The use of federal funds to finance welfare litigation * * * was to be prohibited. A federal Child Care Bureau was established to provide day care for working parents.

Pending the inauguration of the "guaranteed employment" program in 1974, states were to be permitted to institute their own interim AFDC "work relief" programs whereby recipients would be forced to work for no pay other than the welfare grant. The provision authorizing such work relief was, in essence, a reenactment of the Community Work and Training Program ("CWTP"), 42 U.S.C. § 609, a program that had been repealed as of July 1, 1968. See 45 C.F.R. § 233.140. The new CWTP, unlike its predecessor, would not have required state workmen's compensation coverage.

These changes in Title IV of the bill were explicitly designed to reverse almost every major court decision of the past five years.

In addition, a more restrictive version of the federalized adult welfare programs than that which passed the House was included in the Finance Committee version of H.R. 1, and substantial changes in the OASDI and Medicaid-Medicare programs were made. The Committee Report explaining the amendments to H. R. 1 was 1,285 pages long.

The debate on H.R. 1 on the Senate floor began September 27 and continued with daily interruptions to consider other matters, until approximately 1 a. m. on the morning of October 6, when the Senate voted final passage of its version of H.R. 1. The events of these two weeks are difficult to chronicle because of the confusion on the Senate floor which provoked complaints from the Senators themselves from time to time.

Generally speaking, amendments to the OASDI and Medicare programs were the subject of much of the debate and action for the first few days but were fairly noncontroversial. On Saturday, September 30, Title III (the federalization of the adult welfare programs) passed substantially without opposition, as did the work bonus provisions of the Finance Committee bill.

During the next week, Senator Kennedy was unsuccessful in his attempts to amend the new Medicaid provisions which would have restricted eligibility and otherwise reduced services.

It was soon apparent that the focus of controversy, as expected, would be Title IV, as neither the Committee's version nor the House-passed bill were thought to be able to command a majority. The coalition headed by the AFL–CIO (described above) had supported throughout the Senate consideration the Ribicoff Amendment to H.R. 1 as a substitute for Title IV. In the year since those amendments had been introduced, however, Senator Ribicoff had been meeting with high officials in HEW to work out a compromise between his amendments and the Administration-backed H.R. 1. The Administration refused to endorse the compromise, opposed the Finance Committee version of H.R. 1, and announced that the only acceptable version of H.R. 1 was that which had passed the House.

The NWRO-Coalition for Adequate Welfare Reform group opposed both Titles IV and V (which contained restrictive amendments to both the family and the adult welfare programs) of the Committee bill and focused its efforts on proposals to delete these provisions, as well as to amend the restrictions on Medicaid eligibility contained in Title II. They remained opposed to the Ribicoff-Administration compromise as well, because they thought it did not represent a high enough opening bid to take into a Senate-House Conference Committee on H.R. 1 and therefore would result in a final bill which was no more beneficial to recipients than the House-passed version of H.R. 1.

On Tuesday, October 3, the Ribicoff compromise was called up for debate. At the conclusion of the debate, a motion to table the amendment made by Senator Long passed, 52–34, thus defeating the Ribicoff proposal.

On the following day an alternative to the Committee's version of Title IV was introduced by Senator Roth (an earlier Roth proposal had been withdrawn). His original proposal would generally have replaced all of Title IV (except the child support-parent locater provisions, the Child Care Bureau, and the wage supplement) with an authorization for the Secretary of HEW to "test", for a two to four year period, in an unlimited number of states, the House-passed and Finance Committee versions of H.R. 1 and the Ribicoff-Administration compromise, but would not have amended any other provisions of the Committee bill. The Administration opposed the Roth testing proposal.

When the Roth proposal was reintroduced, it was not available in printed form but the Senate was informed that it contained substantially the same provisions as his earlier amendment. Because of the way the Roth proposal came up, under Senate parliamentary rules the only course open to the Senators opposed to the Roth amendment, led by Senator Ribicoff, was a motion to recommit H.R. 1 with instructions to delete Titles IV and V. Senator Long immediately offered a motion to table the Ribicoff motion to recommit. It was clear that this was to be the key vote on Title IV, since the Ribicoff compromise had been defeated the day before and the Senate was thought to be anxious to vote for some substitute to the Committee's Title IV which seemed "non-controversial", e. g., a "test". The offering of the unprinted Roth amendment, the motion to recommit, and the motion to table that motion, had come up very quickly, and some Senators later complained that they were not familiar with all aspects of the amendment. In

any event, the vote on the motion to table carried by a vote of 44–41.

* * *

The Roth amendment then passed, 46–40. Amendments proposed by Senators Stevenson and Percy, some of which included alternative "testing" schemes, which would have been substituted for the Roth amendment, were then defeated by greater majorities.

At the end of the day, there was considerable debate as to whether or not the Senate was acting in a confused and non-deliberative manner. It was clear that a number of Senators felt that they had not understood what they were voting on that day.

Indeed, the next day, when the Roth amendment became available in printed form in the Congressional Record, many followers of the debate learned that the Roth proposal which was adopted, unlike the earlier Roth proposal, included within its text (and therefore its passage reflected an affirmative vote on) the cash-out of food stamps for recipients of the new Title III program for adult welfare recipients, the prohibition against the use of federal funds to finance welfare litigation, the repeal of the Brooke amendment, and authorization for the states to reinstitute CWTP "work relief" programs whereby recipients could be required to work for no pay other than their welfare grant, all of which were also contained in the original Senate Finance Committee bill.

Late on Thursday an amendment by Senator Case was successful in striking the food stamp cash-out, Senator Brooke was able to get agreement to repeal the Brooke amendment repealer, and Senator Mondale prevailed in his attempt to strike the Child Care Bureau and funnel the money authorized for it to existing day care options. But an amendment by Senator Cranston to strike the restrictive legal services provision was defeated, 38–35. In addition, amendments by Senators Buckley and Young, which were not available in printed form at the time they were voted on and were not explained to the Senate, were adopted by voice vote, thereby reinstating a number of the restrictive AFDC provisions which were contained in the original Committee bill.

Just before the final vote was taken, at shortly before 1:00 on the morning of October 6, concern was again expressed that the Senators had not known what they were doing when they voted on the various amendments.

The vote on final passage was 68 yeas and 5 nays, with Senators Allen, Chiles, Fannin, Mansfield, and Stevenson voting nay.

The Senate version of H.R. 1 now included amendments to the OASDI program and the Medicaid and Medicare programs, as well as a federalized welfare program for adult recipients. With respect to AFDC recipients, a pilot program to test various welfare reform measures was authorized, a work bonus and wage supplement provided, the states were permitted to run "work relief" programs, a complex federal-state system for pursuing absent parents and subjecting them to civil and criminal penalties for their non-support was established, restrictions were imposed on legal services attorneys in bringing welfare suits, and restrictions on the rights of current AFDC and AABD recipients were imposed. In AFDC, these included the imposition of 90-day durational residency requirements before one could receive aid, a decrease in the earned income disregard, a requirement that all welfare recipients obtain Social Security numbers as a condition of welfare eligibility, a prohibition against use of the declaration system, a prohibition against aid to unborn children, restrictions on current confidentiality protections, a prohibition against aid to non-citizens or aliens not admitted for permanent residence, a restriction on fair hearing requirements,

and a prohibition against the granting of AFDC to alcoholics and drug addicts.

In AABD, the Senate action eliminated the requirement that social services be available statewide, permitted states to charge for the furnishing of welfare manuals to recipients and others, authorized states to make rent payments for welfare recipients directly to landlords, repealed recent HEW regulations requiring the separation of social services from daily casework functions, restricted current fair hearing requirements, and authorized states to impose residency requirements on persons absent from a state for more than 90 days.

The House-Senate Conference Committee hastily convened on Wednesday, October 11, amidst pressures from NWRO, the Coalition for Adequate Welfare Reform Now, the AFL–CIO, the UAW, the League of Women Voters, Common Cause, the ACLU, and many other organizations, to delete from the bill Titles IV and V, which contained the pilot program, the work relief provision, the restrictions on legal services, and the child locator provisions, as well as the amendments to the current AFDC and AABD program. Because the conferees were unable to agree on whether to accept the House version of Title IV or the Senate's conglomeration of changes affecting the current family program in the limited time remaining before adjournment of Congress, and perhaps because of the aforesaid pressures from organizations, all of these provisions except those applicable to the adult welfare recipients were dropped in Conference. [These adult provisions established the new SSI program discussed elsewhere in these materials.] (However the provision requiring recipients to obtain Social Security numbers had been contained in Title I as well, and thus became law despite its elimination from Title IV.) The Conference Committee's version of H.R. 1 was signed into law by the President on October 30, 1972.

Appendix A

STATUTORY APPENDIX TO CHAPTER I

SOCIAL SECURITY ACT—PROVISIONS GOVERNING AFDC AND SSI

42 U.S.C.A. §§ 601–610, 630–644, 1381–1383c.

[Words stricken through are part of pre-1972 law. Words underscored were added, effective July 1, 1972, by the Talmadge Amendments. See pp. 210–212, infra. Sections 1381–1383c containing the SSI program were newly enacted on October 30, 1972 to take effect on January 1, 1974.]

SUBCHAPTER IV.—GRANTS TO STATES FOR AID AND SERVICES TO NEEDY FAMILIES WITH CHILDREN AND FOR CHILD-WELFARE SERVICES

Part A.—Aid to Families with Dependent Children

§ 601. Appropriations

For the purpose of encouraging the care of dependent children in their own homes or in the homes of relatives by enabling each State to furnish financial assistance and rehabilitation and other services, as far as practicable under the conditions in such State, to needy dependent children and the parents or relatives with whom they are living to help maintain and strengthen family life and to help such parents or relatives to attain or retain capability for the maximum self-support and personal independence consistent with the maintenance of continuing parental care and protection, there is authorized to be appropriated for each fiscal year a sum sufficient to carry out the purposes of this part. The sums made available under this section shall be used for making payments to States which have submitted, and had approved by the Secretary, State plans for aid and services to needy families with children.

As amended Jan. 2, 1968, Pub.L. 90–248, Title II, § 241(b)(1), 81 Stat. 916.

§ 602. State plans for aid and services to needy families with children; contents; approval by Secretary

(a) A State plan for aid and services to needy families with children must (1) provide that it shall be in effect in all political subdivisions of the State, and, if administered by them, be mandatory upon them; (2) provide for financial participation by the State; (3) either provide for the establishment or designation of a single State agency to administer the plan, or provide for the establishment or designation of a single State agency to supervise the administration of the plan; (4) provide for granting an opportunity for a fair hearing before the State agency to any individual whose claim for aid to families with dependent children is denied or is not acted upon with reasonable promptness; (5) provide (A) such methods of administration (including after January 1, 1940, methods relating to the establishment and maintenance of personnel standards on a merit basis, except that the Secretary shall exercise no authority with respect to the selection, tenure of office, and compensation of any individual employed in accordance with such methods) as are found by the Secretary to be necessary for the proper and efficient operation of the plan, and (B) for the training and effective use of paid subprofessional staff, with particular emphasis on the full-time or part-time employment of recipients and other persons of low income, as community services aides, in the administration of the plan and for the use of non-paid or partially paid volunteers in a social service volunteer program in providing services to applicants and recipients and in assisting any advisory committees established by the State agency; and (6) provide that the State agency will make such reports, in such form and containing such information, as the Secretary may from time to time require, and comply with such provisions as the Secretary may from time to time find necessary to assure the correctness and verification of such reports; (7) except as may be otherwise provided in clause (8), provide that the State agency shall, in determining need, take into consideration any other income and resources of any child or relative claiming aid to families with dependent children, or of any other individual (living in the same home as such child and relative) whose needs the State determines should be considered in determining the need of the child or relative claiming such aid, as well as any expenses reasonably attributable to the earning of any such income; (8) provide that, in making the determination under clause (7), the State agency—

(A) shall with respect to any month disregard—

(i) all of the earned income of each dependent child receiving aid to families with dependent children who is (as determined by the State in accordance with standards prescribed by the Secretary) a full-time student or part-time student who is not a full-time employee attending a school, college, or university, or a course of vocational or technical training designed to fit him for gainful employment, and

(ii) in the case of earned income of a dependent child not included under clause (i), a relative receiving such aid, and any other individual (living in the same home as such relative and child) whose needs are taken into account in making such determination, the first $30 of the total of such earned income for such month plus one-third of the remainder of such income for such month; (except that the provisions of this clause (ii) shall not apply to earned income derived from participation on a project maintained under the programs established by section 632(b)(2) and (3) of this title); and

(B)(i) may, subject to the limitations prescribed by the Secretary, permit all or any portion of the earned or other income to be set aside for future identifiable needs of a dependent child, and (ii) may, before disregarding the amounts referred to in subparagraph (A) and clause (i) of this subparagraph, disregard not more than $5 per month of any income;

except that, with respect to any month, the State agency shall not disregard any earned income (other than income referred to in subparagraph (B)) of—

(C) any one of the persons specified in clause (ii) of subparagraph (A) if such person—

(i) terminated his employment or reduced his earned income without good cause within such period (of not less than 30 days) preceding such month as may be prescribed by the Secretary; or

(ii) refused without good cause, within such period preceding such month as may be prescribed by the Secretary, to accept employment in which he is able to engage which is offered through the public employment offices of the State, or is otherwise offered by an employer if the offer of such employer is determined by the State or local agency administering the State plan, after notification by him, to be a bona fide offer of employment; or

(D) any of such persons specified in clause (ii) of subparagraph (A) if with respect to such month the income of the persons so specified (within the meaning of clause (7)) was in excess of their need as determined by the State agency pursuant to clause (7) (without regard to clause (8)), unless, for any one of the four months preceding such month, the needs of such persons were met by the furnishing of aid under the plan; (9) provide safeguards which restrict the use or disclosure of information concerning applicants and recipients to purposes directly connected with the administration of aid to families with dependent children; (10) provide, effective July 1, 1951, that all individuals wishing to make application for aid to families with dependent children shall have opportunity to do so, and that aid to families with dependent children shall be furnished with reasonable promptness to all eligible individuals; (11) effective July 1, 1952, provide for prompt notice to appropriate law-enforcement officials of the furnishing of aid to families with dependent children in respect of a child who has been deserted or abandoned by a parent; (12) provide, effective October 1, 1950, that no aid will be furnished any individual under the plan with respect to any period with respect to which he is receiving old-age assistance under the State plan approved under section 302 of this title; (13) provide a description of the services which the State agency makes available to maintain and strengthen family life for children, including a description of the steps taken to assure, in the provision of such services, maximum utilization of other agencies providing similar or related services; (14) provide for the development and application of a program for such family services, as defined in section 606(d) of this title, and child-welfare services, as defined in section 625 of this title, for each child and relative who receives aid to families with dependent children, and each appropriate individual (living in the same home as a relative and child receiving such aid whose needs are taken into account in making the determination under clause (7)), as may be necessary in the light of the particular home conditions and other needs of such child, relative, and individual, in order to assist such child, relative, and individual to attain or retain capability for self-support and care and in order to maintain and strengthen family life and to foster child development; (15) provide—

(A) for the development of a program for each appropriate relative and dependent child receiving aid under the plan, and each appropriate individual (living in the same home as a relative and child receiving such aid) whose needs are taken into account in making the determination under clause (7), with the objective of—

(i) assuring, to the maximum extent possible, that such relative, child, and individual will enter the labor force and accept employment so that they will become self-sufficient, and

(ii) preventing or reducing the incidence of births out of wedlock and otherwise strengthening family life,

(B) for the implementation of such programs by

(i) assuring that such relative, child, or individual who is referred to the Secretary of Labor pursuant to clause (19) is furnished child care services and that in all appropriate cases family planning services are offered them, and

(ii) in appropriate cases, providing aid to families with dependent children in the form of payments of the types described in section 606(b)(2), and

(A) for the development of a program, for each appropriate relative and dependent child receiving aid under the plan and for each appropriate individual (living in the same home as a relative and child receiving such aid) whose needs are taken into account in making the determination under clause (7), for preventing or reducing the incidence of births out of wedlock and otherwise strengthening family life, and for implementing such program by assuring that in all appropriate cases family planning services are offered to them, but acceptance of family planning services provided under the plan shall be voluntary on the part of such members and individuals and shall not be a prerequisite to eligibility for or the receipt of any other service under the plan; and

(B) to the extent that services provided under this clause or clause (14) are furnished by the staff of the State agency or the local agency administering the State plan in each of the political subdivisions of the State, for the establishment of a single organizational unit in such State or local agency, as the case may be, responsible for the furnishing of such services;".

(C) that the acceptance by such child, relative, or individual of family planning services provided under the plan shall be voluntary on the part of such child, relative, or individual and shall not be a prerequisite to eligibility for or the receipt of any other service or aid under the plan,

(D) for such review of each such program as may be necessary (as frequently as may be necessary, but at least once a year) to insure that it is being effectively implemented,

(E) for furnishing the Secretary with such reports as he may specify showing the results of such programs, and

(F) to the extent that such programs under this clause or clause (14) are developed and implemented by services furnished by the staff of the State agency or the local agency administering the State plan in each of the political subdivisions of the State, for the establishment of a single organizational unit in such State or local agency, as the case may be, responsible for the furnishing of such services;

(16) provide that where the State agency has reason to believe that the home in which a relative and child receiving aid reside is unsuitable for the child because of the neglect, abuse, or exploitation of such child it shall bring such condition to the attention of the appropriate court or law enforcement agencies in the State, providing such data with respect to the situation it may have; (17) provide—

(A) for the development and implementation of a program under which the State agency will undertake—

(i) in the case of a child born out of wedlock who is receiving aid to families with dependent children, to establish the paternity of such child and secure support for him, and

(ii) in the case of any child receiving such aid who has been deserted or abandoned by his parent, to secure support for such child from such parent (or from any other person legally liable for such support), utilizing any reciprocal arrangements adopted with other States to obtain or enforce court orders for support, and

(B) for the establishment of a single organizational unit in the State agency or local agency administering the State plan in each political subdivision which will be responsible for the administration of the program referred to in clause (A);

(18) provide for entering into cooperative arrangements with appropriate courts and law enforcement officials (A) to assist the State agency in administering the program referred to in clause (17)(A), including the entering into of financial arrangements with such courts and officials in order to assure optimum results under such program, and (B) with respect to any other matters of common concern to such courts or officials and the State agency or local agency administering the State plan; (19) provide—

(A) for the prompt referral to the Secretary of Labor or his representative for participation under a work incentive program established by part C of—

(i) each appropriate child and relative who has attained age sixteen and is receiving aid to families with dependent children,

(ii) each appropriate individual (living in the same home as a relative and child receiving such aid) who has attained such age and whose needs are taken into account in making the determination under section 602(a)(7), and

(iii) any other person claiming aid under the plan (not included in clauses (i) and (ii), who after being informed of the work incentive programs established by part C, requests such referral unless the State agency determines that participation in any of such programs would be inimical to the welfare of such person or the family;

except that the State agency shall not so refer a child, relative, or individual under clauses (i) and (ii) if such child, relative, or individual is—

(iv) a person with illness, incapacity, or advanced age,

(v) ~~so remote from any of the projects under the work in-~~
~~centive programs established by part C that he cannot effectively~~
~~participate under any of such programs;~~

~~(vi) a child attending school full time, or~~

~~(vii) a person whose presence in the home on a substantially~~
~~continuous basis is required because of the illness or incapacity of~~
~~another member of the household;~~

(A) that every individual, as a condition of eligibility for aid under
this part, shall register for manpower services, training, and employment as provided by regulations of the Secretary of Labor, unless such
individual is—

(i) a child who is under age 16 or attending school full time;

(ii) a person who is ill, incapacitated, or of advanced age;

(iii) a person so remote from a work incentive project that
his effective participation is precluded;

(iv) a person whose presence in the home is required because
of illness or incapacity of another member of the household;

(v) a mother or other relative of a child under the age of six
who is caring for the child; or

(vi) the mother or other female caretaker of a child, if the
father or another adult male relative is in the home and not excluded by clause (i), (ii), (iii), or (iv) of this subparagraph (unless he has failed to register as required by this subparagraph or
has been found by the Secretary of Labor under section 633(g)
to have refused without good cause to participate under a work incentive program or accept employment as described in subparagraph (F) of this paragraph);

and that any individual referred to in clause (v) shall be advised of her
option to register, if she so desires, pursuant to this paragraph, and
shall be informed of the child care services (if any) which will be
available to her in the event she should decide so to register;

(B) that aid under the plan will not be denied ~~by reason of such~~
~~referral~~ by reason of such registration or the individual's certification
to the Secretary of Labor under subparagraph (G) of this paragraph,
or by reason of an individual's participation on a project under the
program established by section 632(b)(2) or (3);

(C) for arrangements to assure that there will be made a non-
Federal contribution to the work incentive programs established by
part C by appropriate agencies of the State or private organizations of
~~20~~ 10 per centum of the cost of such programs, as specified in section
635(b);

(D) that (i) training incentives authorized under section 634,
and income derived from a special work project under the program established by section 632(b)(3) shall be disregarded in determining the
needs of an individual under section 602(a)(7), and (ii) in determining
such individual's needs the additional expenses attributable to his participation in a program established by section 632(b)(2) or (3) shall
be taken into account;

~~(E) that, with respect to any individual referred pursuant to sub-~~
~~paragraph (A) who is participating in a special work project under~~

the program established by section 632(b)(3), (i) the State agency, after proper notification by the Secretary of Labor, will pay to such Secretary (at such times and in such manner as the Secretary of Health, Education, and Welfare prescribes) the money payments such State would otherwise make to or on behalf of such individual (including such money payments with respect to such individual's family), or 80 per centum of such individual's earnings under such program, whichever is lesser and (ii) the State agency will supplement any earnings received by such individual by payments to such individual (which payments shall be considered aid under the plan) to the extent that such payments when added to the individual's earnings from his participation in such special work project will be equal to the amount of the aid that would have been payable by the State agency with respect to such individual's family had he not participated in such special work project, plus 20 per centum of such individual's earnings from such special work project; and

(F) that if and for so long as any child, relative, or individual (certified to the Secretary of Labor pursuant to subparagraph (G) referred to the Secretary of Labor pursuant to subparagraph (A)(i) and (ii) and section 407(b)(2) has been found by the Secretary of Labor under section 633(g) to have refused without good cause to participate under a work incentive program established by part C with respect to which the Secretary of Labor has determined his participation is consistent with the purposes of such part C, or to have refused without good cause to accept employment in which he is able to engage which is offered through the public employment offices of the State, or is otherwise offered by an employer if the offer of such employer is determined, after notification by him, to be a bona fide offer of employment—

(i) if the relative makes such refusal, such relative's needs shall not be taken into account in making the determination under clause (7), and aid for any dependent child in the family in the form of payments of the type described in section 606(b)(2) (which in such a case shall be without regard to clauses (A) through (E) thereof) or section 608 will be made;

(ii) aid with respect to a dependent child will be denied if a child who is the only child receiving aid in the family makes such refusal;

(iii) if there is more than one child receiving aid in the family, aid for any such child will be denied (and his needs will not be taken into account in making the determination under clause (7)) if that child makes such refusal; and

(iv) if such individual makes such refusal, such individual's needs shall not be taken into account in making the determination under clause (7);

except that the State agency shall for a period of sixty days, make payments of the type described in section 606(b)(2) (without regard to clauses (A) through (E) thereof) on behalf of the relative specified in clause (i), or continue aid in the case of a child specified in clause (ii) or (iii), or take the individual's needs into account in the case of an individual specified in clause (iv), but only if during such period such child, relative, or individual accepts counseling or other services (which the State agency shall make available to such child, relative, or individual) aimed at persuading such relative, child, or individual, as the case may be, to participate in such program in accordance with the determination of the Secretary of Labor; and

(G) that the State agency will have in effect a special program which (i) will be administered by a separate administrative unit and the employees of which will, to the maximum extent feasible, perform services only in connection with the administration of such program, (ii) will provide (through arrangements with others or otherwise) for individuals who have been registered pursuant to subparagraph (A), in accordance with the order of priority listed in section 633(a), such health, vocational rehabilitation, counseling, child care, and other social and supportive services as are necessary to enable such individuals to accept employment or receive manpower training provided under part C, and will, when arrangements have been made to provide necessary supportive services, including child care, certify to the Secretary of Labor those individuals who are ready for employment or training under part C, (iii) will participate in the development of operational and employability plans under section 633(b); and (iv) provides for purposes of clause (ii), that when more than one kind of child care is available, the mother may choose the type, but she may not refuse to accept child care services if they are available.

* * *

(20) effective July 1, 1969, provide for aid to families with dependent children in the form of foster care in accordance with section 608 of this title; (21) provide that the State agency will report to the Secretary, at such times (not less often than once each calendar quarter) and in such manner as the Secretary may prescribe—

(A) the name, and social security account number, if known, if each parent of a dependent child or children with respect to whom aid is being provided under the State plan—

(i) against whom an order for the support and maintenance of such child or children has been issued by a court of competent jurisdiction but who is not making payments in compliance or partial compliance with such order, or against whom a petition for such an order has been filed in a court having jurisdiction to receive such petition, and

(ii) whom it has been unable to locate after requesting and utilizing information included in the files of the Department of Health, Education, and Welfare maintained pursuant to section 405 of this title,

(B) the last known address of such parent and any information it has with respect to the date on which such parent could last be located at such address, and

(C) such other information as the Secretary may specify to assist in carrying out the provisions of section 610 of this title;

(22) provide that the State agency will, in accordance with standards prescribed by the Secretary, cooperate with the State agency administering or

supervising the administration of the plan of another State under this part—

(A) in locating a parent residing in such State (whether or not permanently) against whom a petition has been filed in a court of competent jurisdiction of such other State for the support and maintenance of a child or children of such parent with respect to whom aid is being provided under the plan of such other State, and

(B) in securing compliance or good faith partial compliance by a parent residing in such State (whether or not permanently) with an order issued by a court of competent jurisdiction against such parent for the support and maintenance of a child or children of such parent with respect to whom aid is being provided under the plan of such other State; and

(23) provide that by July 1, 1969, the amounts used by the State to determine the needs of individuals will have been adjusted to reflect fully changes in living costs since such amounts were established, and any maximums that the State imposes on the amount of aid paid to families will have been proportionately adjusted.

(b) The Secretary shall approve any plan which fulfills the conditions specified in subsection (a) of this section, except that he shall not approve any plan which imposes as a condition of eligibility for aid to families with dependent children, a residence requirement which denies aid with respect to any child residing in the State (1) who has resided in the State for one year immediately preceding the application for such aid, or (2) who was born within one year immediately preceding the application, if the parent or other relative with whom the child is living has resided in the State for one year immediately preceding the birth.

(c) The Secretary shall, on the basis of his review of the reports received from the States under clause (15) of subsection (a) of this section, compile such data as he believes necessary and from time to time publish his findings as to the effectiveness of the programs developed and administered by the States under such clause. The Secretary shall annually report to the Congress (with the first such report being made on or before July 1, 1970) on the programs developed and administered by each State under such clause (15).

§ 603. Payment to States; computation of amounts

(a) From the sums appropriated therefor, the Secretary of the Treasury shall (subject to subsection (d)) pay to each State which has an approved plan for aid and services to needy families with children, for each quarter, beginning with the quarter commencing October 1, 1958—

(1) in the case of any State other than Puerto Rico, the Virgin Islands, and Guam, an amount equal to the sum of the following proportions of the total amounts expended during such quarter as aid to families with dependent children under the State plan (including expenditures for premiums under part B of subchapter XVIII of this chapter for individuals who are recipients of money payments under such plan and other insurance premiums for medical or any other type of remedial care or the cost thereof)—

(A) five-sixths of such expenditures, not counting so much of any expenditure with respect to any month as exceeds the product of $18 multiplied by the total number of recipients of aid to families with dependent children for such month (which total number, for purposes of this subsection, means (i) the number of individuals with respect to whom such aid in the form of money payments is paid for such month, plus (ii) the number of other individuals with respect to whom expenditures were made in such month as aid to families with dependent children in the form of medical or any other type of remedial care, plus (iii) the number of individuals, not counted under clause (i) or (ii), with respect to whom payments described in section 606(b)(2) of this title are made in such month and included as expenditures for purposes of this paragraph or paragraph (2)); plus

(B) the Federal percentage of the amount by which such expenditures exceed the maximum which may be counted under clause (A), not counting so much of any expenditure with respect to any month as exceeds (i) the product of $32 multiplied by the total number of recipients of aid to families with dependent children (other than such aid in the form of foster care) for such month, plus (ii) the product of $100 multiplied by the total number of recipients of aid to families with dependent children in the form of foster care for such month; and

(2) in the case of Puerto Rico, the Virgin Islands, and Guam, an amount equal to one-half of the total of the sums expended during such quarter as aid to families with dependent children under the State plan (including expenditures for premiums under part B of subchapter XVIII of this chapter for individuals who are recipients of money payments under such plan and other insurance premiums for medical or any other type of remedial care or the cost thereof), not counting so much of any expenditure with respect to any month as exceeds $18 multiplied by the total number of recipients of such aid for such month; and

(3) in the case of any State, an amount equal to the sum of the following proportions of the total amounts expended during such quarter as found necessary by the Secretary of Health, Education, and Welfare for the proper and efficient administration of the State plan—

(A) 75 per centum of so much of such expenditures as are for—

(i) any of the services described in clauses (14) and (15) of section 602(a) of this title which are provided to any child or relative who is receiving aid under the plan, or to any other individual (living in the same home as such relative and child) whose needs are taken into account in making the determination under clause (7) of such section,

(ii) any of the services described in clauses (14) and (15) of section 602(a) of this title which are provided to any child or relative who is applying for aid to families with dependent children or who, within such period or periods as the Secretary may prescribe, has been or is likely to become an applicant for or recipient of such aid, or

(iii) the training of personnel employed or preparing for employment by the State agency or by the local agency administering the plan in the political subdivision; plus

(B) one-half of the remainder of such expenditures.

The services referred to in subparagraph (A) shall include only—

(C) services provided by the staff of the State agency, or of the local agency administering the State plan in the political subdivision: *Provided*, That no funds authorized under this part shall be available for services defined as vocational rehabilitation services under the Vocational Rehabilitation Act (i) which are available to individuals in need of them under programs for their rehabilitation carried on under a State plan approved under such Act, or (ii) which the State agency or agencies administering or supervising the administration of the State plan approved under such Act are able and willing to provide if reimbursed for the cost thereof pursuant to agreement under subparagraph (D), if provided by such staff, and

(D) subject to limitations prescribed by the Secretary, services which in the judgment of the State agency cannot be as economically or as effectively provided by the staff of such State or local agency and are not otherwise reasonably available to individuals in need of them, and which are provided, pursuant to agreement with the State agency, by the State health authority or the State agency or agencies administering or supervising the administration of the State plan for vocational rehabilitation services approved under the Vocational Rehabilitation Act or by any other State agency which the Secretary may determine to be appropriate (whether provided by its staff or by contract with public (local) or nonprofit private agencies);

except that services described in clause (ii) of subparagraph (C) hereof may be provided only pursuant to agreement with such State agency or agencies administering or supervising the administration of the State plan for vocational rehabilitation services so approved; and except that, to the extent specified by the Secretary, child-welfare services, family planning services, and family services may be provided from sources other than those referred to in subparagraphs (C) and (D). The portion of the amount expended for administration of the State plan to which subparagraph (A) applies and the portion thereof to which subparagraph (B) applies shall be determined in accordance with such methods and procedures as may be permitted by the Secretary.

(4) Repealed. Pub.L. 90–248, Title II, § 201(e)(3), 81 Stat. 880.

(5) in the case of any State, an amount equal to the sum of—

(A) 50 per centum of the total amount expended under the State plan during such quarter as emergency assistance to needy families with children in the form of payments or care specified in paragraph (1) of section 606(e) of this title, and

(B) 75 per centum of the total amount expended under the State plan during such quarter as emergency assistance to needy families with children in the form of services specified in paragraph (1) of section 606(e) of this title.

The number of individuals with respect to whom payments described in section 606(b)(2) of this title are made for any month, who may be included as recipients of aid to families with dependent children for purposes of paragraph (1) or (2), may not exceed 10 per centum of the number of other recipients of aid to families with dependent children for such month. In computing such 10 percent, there shall not be taken into account individuals with respect to whom such payments are made for any month in accordance with section 602(a)(19)(F) of this title.

(b) The method of computing and paying such amounts shall be as follows:

(1) The Secretary shall, prior to the beginning of each quarter, estimate the amount to be paid to the State for such quarter under the provisions of subsection (a) of this section, such estimate to be based on (A) a report filed by the State containing its estimate of the total sum to be expended in such quarter in accordance with the provisions of such subsection and stating the amount appropriated or made available by the State and its political subdivisions for such expenditures in such quarter, and if such amount is less than the State's proportionate share of the total sum of such estimated expenditures, the source or sources from which the difference is expected to be derived, (B) records showing the number of dependent children in the State, and (C) such other investigation as the Secretary may find necessary.

(2) The Secretary of Health, Education, and Welfare shall then certify to the Secretary of the Treasury the amount so estimated by the Secretary of Health, Education, and Welfare, (A) reduced or increased, as the case may be, by any sum by which he finds that his estimate for any prior quarter was greater or less than the amount which should have been paid to the State for such quarter, and (B) reduced by a sum equivalent to the pro rata share to which the United States is equitably entitled, as determined by the Secretary of Health, Education, and Welfare, of the net amount recovering during any prior quarter by the State or any political subdivision thereof with respect to aid to families with dependent children furnished under the State plan; except that such increases or reductions shall not be made to the extent that such sums have been applied to make the amount certified for any prior quarter greater or less than the amount estimated by the Secretary of Health, Education, and Welfare for such prior quarter.

(3) The Secretary of the Treasury shall thereupon, through the Fiscal Service of the Treasury Department and prior to audit or settlement by the General Accounting Office, pay to the State, at the time or times fixed by the Secretary of Health, Education, and Welfare, the amount so certified.

(c) Notwithstanding any other provision of this Act, the Federal share of assistance payments under this part shall be reduced with respect to any State for any fiscal year after June 30, 1973, by one percentage point for each percentage point by which the number of individuals certified, under the program of such State established pursuant to section 602(a) (19) (G), to the local employment office of the State as being ready for employment or training under part C, is less than 15 per centum of the average number of individuals in such State who, during such year, are required to be registered pursuant to section 602(a)(19)(A).

(d) (1) Notwithstanding subparagraph (A) of subsection (a)(3) the rate specified in such subparagraph shall be 90 per centum (rather than 75 per centum) with respect to social and supportive services provided pursuant to section 602(a)(19)(G).

(2) Of the sums authorized by section 401 to be appropriated for the fiscal year ending June 30, 1973, not more than $750,000,000 shall be appropriated to the Secretary for payments with respect to services to which paragraph (1) applies.

§ 604. Stopping payments on deviation from required provisions of plan or failure to comply therewith

(a) In the case of any State plan for aid and services to needy families with children which has been approved by the Secretary, if the Secretary, after reasonable notice and opportunity for hearing to the State agency administering or supervising the administration of such plan, finds—

(1) that the plan has been so changed as to impose any residence requirement prohibited by section 602(b) of this title, or that in the administration of the plan any such prohibited requirement is imposed, with the knowledge of such State agency, in a substantial number of cases; or

(2) that in the administration of the plan there is a failure to comply substantially with any provision required by section 602(a) of this title to be included in the plan;

the Secretary shall notify such State agency that further payments will not be made to the State (or, in his discretion, that payments will be limited to categories under or parts of the State plan not affected by such failure) until the Secretary is satisfied that such prohibited requirement is no longer so imposed, and that there is no longer any such failure to comply. Until he is so satisfied he shall make no further payments to the State (or shall limit payments to categories under or parts of the State plan not affected by such failure).

(b) No payment to which a State is otherwise entitled under this part for any period before September 1, 1962, shall be withheld by reason of any action taken pursuant to a State statute which requires that aid be denied under the State plan approved under this part with respect to a child because of the conditions in the home in which the child resides; nor shall any such payment be withheld for any period beginning on or after such date by reason of any action taken pursuant to such a statute if provision is otherwise made pursuant to a State statute for adequate care and assistance with respect to such child.

§ 605. Use of payments for benefit of children

Whenever the State agency has reason to believe that any payments of aid to families with dependent children made with respect to a child are not being or may not be used in the best interests of the child, the State agency may provide for such counseling and guidance services with respect to the use of such payments and the management of other funds by the relative receiving such payments as it deems advisable in order to assure use of such payments in the best interests of such child, and may provide for advising such relative that continued failure to so use such payments will result in substitution therefor of protective payments as provided under section 606 (b)(2) of this title, or in seeking appointment of a guardian or legal representative as provided in section 1311 of this title, or in the imposition of criminal or civil penalties authorized under State law if it is determined by a court of competent jurisdiction that such relative is not using or has not used for the benefit of the child any such payments made for that purpose; and the provision of such services or advice by the State agency (or the taking of the action specified in such advice) shall not serve as a basis for withholding funds from such State under section 604 of this title and shall not prevent such payments with respect to such child from being considered aid to families with dependent children.

§ 606. Definitions

When used in this part—

(a) The term "dependent child" means a needy child (1) who has been deprived of parental support or care by reason of the death, continued absence from the home, or physical or mental incapacity of a parent, and who is living with his father, mother, grandfather, grandmother, brother, sister, stepfather, stepmother, stepbrother, stepsister, uncle, aunt, first cousin, nephew, or niece, in a place of residence maintained by one or more of such relatives as his or their own home, and (2) who is (A) under the age of eighteen, or (B) under the age of twenty-one and (as determined by the State in accordance with standards prescribed by the Secretary) a student regularly attending a school, college, or university, its equivalent, or regularly attending a course of vocational or technical training designed to fit him for gainful employment;

(b) The term "aid to families with dependent children" means money payments with respect to, or (if provided in or after the third month before the month in which the recipient makes application for aid) medical care in behalf of or any type of remedial care recognized under State law in behalf of, a dependent child or dependent children, and includes (1) money payments or medical care or any type of remedial care recognized under State law to meet the needs of the relative with whom any dependent child is living (and the spouse of such relative if living with him and if such relative is the child's parent and the child is a dependent child by reason of the physical or mental incapacity of a parent or is a dependent child under section 607 of this title), and (2) payments with respect to any dependent child (including payments to meet the needs of the relative, and the relative's spouse, with whom such child is living, and the needs of any other individual living in the same home if such needs are taken into account in making the determination under section 602(a)(7) of this title) which do not meet the preceding requirements of this subsection, but which would meet such requirements except that such payments are made to another individual who (as determined in accordance with standards prescribed by the Secretary) is interested in or concerned with the welfare of such child or relative, or are made on behalf of such child or relative directly to a person furnishing food, living accommodations, or other goods, services, or items to or for such child, relative, or other individual, but only with respect to a State whose State plan approved under section 602 of this title includes provision for—

(A) determination by the State agency that the relative of the child with respect to whom such payments are made has such inability to manage funds that making payments to him would be contrary to the welfare of the child and, therefore, it is necessary to provide such aid with respect to such child and relative through payments described in this clause (2);

(B) undertaking and continuing special efforts to develop greater ability on the part of the relative to manage funds in such manner as to protect the welfare of the family;

(C) periodic review by such State agency of the determination under clause (A) to ascertain whether conditions justifying such determination still exist, with provision for termination of such payments if they do not and for seeking judicial appointment of a guardian or other legal representative, as described in section 1311 of this title, if and when it appears that the need for such payments is continuing, or is likely to continue, beyond a period specified by the Secretary;

(D) aid in the form of foster home care in behalf of children described in section 608(a) of this title; and

(E) opportunity for a fair hearing before the State agency on the determination referred to in clause (A) for any individual with respect to whom it is made;

(c) The term "relative with whom any dependent child is living" means the individual who is one of the relatives specified in subsection (a) of this section and with whom such child is living (within the meaning of such subsection) in a place of residence maintained by such individual (himself or together with any one or more of the other relatives so specified) as his (or their) own home.

(d) The term "family services" means services to a family or any member thereof for the purpose of preserving, rehabilitating, reuniting, or strengthening the family, and such other services as will assist members of a family to attain or retain capability for the maximum self-support and personal independence.

(e)(1) The term "emergency assistance to needy families with children" means any of the following, furnished for a period not in excess of 30 days in any 12-month period, in the case of a needy child under the age of 21 who is (or, within such period as may be specified by the Secretary, has been) living with any of the relatives specified in subsection (a)(1) of this section in a place of residence maintained by one or more of such relatives as his or their own home, but only where such child is without available resources, the payments, care, or services involved are necessary to avoid destitution of such child or to provide living arrangements in a home for such child, and such destitution or need for living arrangements did not arise because such child or relative refused without good cause to accept employment or training for employment—

(A) money payments, payments in kind, or such other payments as the State agency may specify with respect to, or medical care or any other type of remedial care recognized under State law on behalf of, such child or any other member of the household in which he is living, and

(B) such services as may be specified by the Secretary;

but only with respect to a State whose State plan approved under section 602 of this title includes provision for such assistance.

(2) Emergency assistance as authorized under paragraph (1) may be provided under the conditions specified in such paragraph to migrant workers with families in the State or in such part or parts thereof as the State shall designate.

§ 607. Dependent children of unemployed parents; termination date; definition

(a) The term "dependent child" shall, notwithstanding section 606(a) of this title, include a needy child who meets the requirements of section 606(a)(2) of this title, who has been deprived of parental support or care by reason of the unemployment (as determined in accordance with standards prescribed by the Secretary) of his father, and who is living with any of the relatives specified in section 606(a)(1) of this title in a place of residence maintained by one or more of such relatives as his (or their) own home.

(b) The provisions of subsection (a) of this section shall be applicable to a State if the State's plan approved under section 602 of this title—

(1) requires the payment of aid to families with dependent children with respect to a dependent child as defined in subsection (a) of this section when—

(A) such child's father has not been employed (as determined in accordance with standards prescribed by the Secretary) for at least 30 days prior to the receipt of such aid,

(B) such father has not without good cause, within such period (of not less than 30 days) as may be prescribed by the Secretary, refused a bona fide offer of employment or training for employment, and

(C)(i) such father has 6 or more quarters of work (as defined in subsection (d)(1) of this section) in any 13-calendar-quarter period ending within one year prior to the application for such aid or (ii) he received unemployment compensation under an unemployment compensation law of a State or of the United States, or he was qualified (within the meaning of subsection (d)(3) of this section) for unemployment compensation under the unemployment compensation law of the State, within one year prior to the application for such aid; and

(2) provides—

(A) for such assurances as will satisfy the Secretary that fathers of dependent children as defined in subsection (a) will be certified ~~referred~~ to the Secretary of Labor as provided in section 602(a)(19) within thirty days after receipt of aid with respect to such children;

(B) for entering into cooperative arrangements with the State agency responsible for administering or supervising the administration of vocational education in the State, designed to assure maximum utilization of available public vocational education services and facilities in the State in order to encourage the retraining of individuals capable of being retrained; and

(C) for the denial of aid to families with dependent children to any child or relative specified in subsection (a) of this section—

(i) if, and for so long as, such child's father is not currently registered with the public employment offices in the State, and

(ii) with respect to any week for which such child's father receives unemployment compensation under an unemployment compensation law of a State or of the United States.

(c) Notwithstanding any other provisions of this section, expenditures pursuant to this section shall be excluded from aid to families with dependent children (A) where such expenditures are made under the plan with respect to any dependent child as defined in subsection (a), (i) for any part of the 30-day period referred to in subparagraph (A) of subsection (b)(1), or (ii) for any period prior to the time when the father satisfies subparagraph (B) of such subsection, and (B) if, and for as long as, no action is taken (after the 30-day period referred to in subparagraph (A) of subsection (b)(2)), under the program therein specified, to ~~refer~~ certify such father to the Secretary of Labor pursuant to section 602(a)(19).

(d) For purposes of this section—

(1) the term "quarter of work" with respect to any individual means a calendar quarter in which such individual received earned income of not less than $50 (or which is a "quarter of coverage" as defined in section 413(a)(2) of this title), or in which such individual participated in a community work and training program under section 609 of this title or any other work and training program subject to the limitations in section 609 of this title, or the work incentive program established under part C;

(2) the term "calendar quarter" means a period of 3 consecutive calendar months ending on March 31, June 30, September 30, or December 31; and

(3) an individual shall be deemed qualified for unemployment compensation under the State's unemployment compensation law if—

(A) he would have been eligible to receive such unemployment compensation upon filing application, or

(B) he performed work not covered under such law and such work, if it had been covered, would (together with any covered work he performed) have made him eligible to receive such unemployment compensation upon filing application.

§ 608. Payment to States for foster home care of dependent children; definitions

Effective for the period beginning May 1, 1961—

(a) the term "dependent child" shall, notwithstanding section 606(a) of this title, also include a child (1) who would meet the requirements of such section 606(a) or of section 607 of this title except for his removal after April 30, 1961, from the home of a relative (specified in such section 606(a)) as a result of a judicial determination to the effect that continuation therein would be contrary to the welfare of such child, (2) whose placement and care are the responsibility of (A) the State or local agency administering the State plan approved under section 602 of this title, or (B) any other public agency with whom the State agency administering or supervising the administration of such State plan has made an agreement which is still in effect and which includes provision for assuring development of a plan, satisfactory to such State agency, for such child as provided in paragraph (f)(1) and such other provisions as may be necessary to assure accomplishment of the objectives of the State plan approved under section 602 of this title, (3) who has been placed in a foster family home or child-care institution as a result of such determination, and (4) who (A) received aid under such State plan in or for the month in which court proceedings leading to such determination were initiated, or (B)(i) would have received such aid in or for such month if application had been made therefor, or (ii) in the case of a child who had been living with a relative specified in section 606(a) of this title within 6 months prior to the month in which such proceedings were initiated, would have received such aid in or for such month if in such month he had been living with (and removed from the home of) such a relative and application had been made therefor;

(b) the term "aid to families with dependent children" shall, notwithstanding section 606(b) of this title, include also foster care in behalf of a child described in paragraph (a) of this section—

(1) in the foster family home of any individual, whether the payment therefor is made to such individual or to a public or nonprofit private child-placement or child-care agency, or

(2) in a child-care institution, whether the payment therefor is made to such institution or to a public or nonprofit private child-placement or child-care agency, but subject to limitations prescribed by the Secretary with a view to including as "aid to families with dependent children" in the case of such foster care in such institutions only those items which are included in such term in the case of foster care in the foster family home of an individual.

(c) the number of individuals counted under clause (A) of section 603(a)(1) of this title for any month shall include individuals (not otherwise included under such clause) with respect to whom expenditures were made in such month as aid to families with dependent children in the form of foster care; and

(d) services described in paragraph (f)(2) of this section shall be considered as part of the administration of the State plan for purposes of section 603(a)(3) of this title;

but only with respect to a State whose State plan approved under section 602 of this title—

(e) includes aid for any child described in paragraph (a) of this section, and

(f) includes provision for (1) development of a plan for each such child (including periodic review of the necessity for the child's being in a foster family home or child-care institution) to assure that he receives proper care and that services are provided which are designed to improve the conditions in the home from which he was removed or to otherwise make possible his being placed in the home of a relative specified in section 606(a) of this title, and (2) use by the State or local agency administering the State plan, to the maximum extent practicable, in placing such a child in a foster family home or child-care institution, of the services of employees, of the State public-welfare agency referred to in section 722(a) of this title (relating to allotments to States for child welfare services under sections 721–728 of this title) or of any local agency participating in the administration of the plan referred to in such section, who perform functions in the administration of such plan.

For purposes of this section, the term "foster family home" means a foster family home for children which is licensed by the State in which it is situated or has been approved, by the agency of such State responsible for licensing homes of this type, as meeting the standards established for such licensing; and the term "child-care institution" means a nonprofit private child-care institution which is licensed by the State in which it is situated or has been approved, by the agency of such State responsible for licensing or approval of institutions of this type, as meeting the standards established for such licensing.

§ 609. Community work and training programs

Provisions Inapplicable to Any State with respect to Any Quarter Beginning After June 30, 1968. Section 204(c)(2) of Pub.L. 90–248. Title II, Jan. 2, 1968, 81 Stat. 892, provided that: "The provisions of section 409 of the Social Security Act [this section] shall not apply to any State with respect to any quarter beginning after June 30, 1968."

§ 610. Assistance by Internal Revenue Service in locating parents; appropriations; transfer of moneys

(a) Upon receiving a report from a State agency made pursuant to section 602(a)(21) of this title, the Secretary shall furnish to the Secretary of the Treasury or his delegate the names and social security account numbers of the parents contained in such report, and the name of the State agency which submitted such report. The Secretary of the Treasury or his delegate shall endeavor to ascertain the address of each such parent from the master files of the Internal Revenue Service, and shall furnish any address so ascertained to the State agency which submitted such report.

(b) There are hereby authorized to be appropriated such sums as may be necessary to carry out the provisions of subsection (a) of this section. The Secretary shall transfer to the Secretary of the Treasury from time to time sufficient amounts out of the monies appropriated pursuant to this subsection to enable him to perform his functions under subsection (a) of this section.

* * *

Part C.—Work Incentive Program for Recipients of Aid under State Plan Approved under Part A

§ 630. Statement of Purpose

The purpose of this part is to require the establishment of a program utilizing all available manpower services, including those authorized under other provisions of law, under which individuals receiving aid to families with dependent children will be furnished incentives, opportunities, and necessary services in order for (1) the employment of such individuals in the regular economy, (2) the training of such individuals for work in the regular economy, and (3) the participation of such individuals in ~~special work projects~~ public service employment, thus restoring the families of such individuals to independence and useful roles in their communities. It is expected that the individuals participating in the program established under this part will acquire a sense of dignity, self-worth, and confidence which will flow from being recognized as a wage-earning member of society and that the example of a working adult in these families will have beneficial effects on the children in such families.

§ 631. Authorization of appropriations—Transfers of moneys

(a) There is hereby authorized to be appropriated to the Secretary of Health, Education, and Welfare for each fiscal year a sum sufficient to carry out the purposes of this part. The Secretary of Health,

Education, and Welfare shall transfer to the Secretary of Labor from time to time sufficient amounts, out of the moneys appropriated pursuant to this section, to enable him to carry out such purposes.

(b) Of the amounts expended from funds appropriated pursuant to subsection (a) for any fiscal year (commencing with the fiscal year ending June 30, 1973), not less than 33⅓ per centum thereof shall be expended for carrying out the program of on-the-job training referred to in section 632 (b)(1)(B) and for carrying out the program of public service employment referred to in section 632(b)(3).

(c) Of the sums appropriated pursuant to subsection (a) to carry out the provisions of this part for any fiscal year (commencing with the fiscal year ending June 30, 1973), not less than 50 percent shall be allotted among the States in accordance with a formula under which each State receives (from the total available for such allotment) an amount which bears the same ratio to such total as—

(1) in the case of the fiscal year ending June 30, 1973, and the fiscal year ending June 30, 1974, the average number of recipients of aid to families with dependent children in such State during the month of January last preceding the commencement of such fiscal year bears to the average number of such recipients during such month in all the States; and

(2) in the case of the fiscal year ending June 30, 1975, or in the case of any fiscal year thereafter, the average number of individuals in such State who, during the month of January last preceding the commencement of such fiscal year, are registered pursuant to section 602 (a)(19)(A) bears to the average number of individuals in all States who, during such month, are so registered.

§ 632. Establishment of programs

(a) The Secretary of Labor (hereinafter in this part referred to as the Secretary) shall, in accordance with the provisions of this part, establish work incentive programs (as provided for in subsection (b) of this section) in each State and in each political subdivision of a State in which he determines there is a significant number of individuals who have attained age 16 and are receiving aid to families with dependent children. In other political subdivisions, he shall use his best efforts to provide such programs either within such subdivisions or through the provision of transportation for such persons to political subdivisions of the State in which such programs are established.

(b) Such programs shall include, but shall not be limited to, (1)(A) a program placing as many individuals as is possible in employment, and (B) a program utilizing on-the-job training positions for others, (2) a program of institutional and work experience training for those individuals for whom such training is likely to lead to regular employment, and (3) a program of special work projects public service employment for individuals for whom a job in the regular economy cannot be found.

(c) In carrying out the purposes of this part the Secretary may make grants to, or enter into agreements with, public or private agencies or organizations (including Indian tribes with respect to Indians on a reservation), except that no such grant or agreement shall be made to or with a private employer for profit or with a private nonprofit employer not organized for a public purpose for purposes of the work experience program established by clause (2) of subsection (b) of this section.

~~(d) Using funds appropriated under this part, the Secretary, in order to carry out the purposes of this part, shall utilize his authority under the Manpower Development and Training Act of 1962, the Act of June 6, 1933, as amended (48 Stat. 113), and other Acts, to the extent such authority is not inconsistent with this Act.~~

(d) In providing the manpower training and employment services and opportunities required by this part, the Secretary of Labor shall, to the maximum extent feasible, assure that such services and opportunities are provided by using all authority available to him under this or any other Act. In order to assure that the services and opportunities so required are provided, the Secretary of Labor shall use the funds appropriated to him under this part to provide programs required by this part through such other Act, to the same extent and under the same conditions (except as regards the Federal matching percentage) as if appropriated under such other Act and, in making use of the programs of other Federal, State, or local agencies (public or private), the Secretary of Labor may reimburse such agencies for services rendered to persons under this part to the extent such services and opportunities are not otherwise available on a non-reimbursable basis.

(e) The Secretary shall take appropriate steps to assure that the present level of manpower services available under the authority of other statutes to recipients of aid to families with dependent children is not reduced as a result of programs under this part.

(f)(1) The Secretary of Labor shall establish in each State, municipality, or other appropriate geographic area with a significant number of persons registered pursuant to section 602(a)(19)(A) a Labor Market Advisor Council the function of which will be to identify and advise the Secretary of the types of jobs available or likely to become available in the area served by the Council; except that if there is already located in any area an appropriate body to perform such function, the Secretary may designate such body as the Labor Market Advisory Council for such area.

(2) Any such Council shall include representatives of industry, labor, and public service employers from the area to be served by the Council.

(3) The Secretary shall not conduct, in any area, institutional training under any program established pursuant to subsection (b) of any type which is not related to jobs of the types which are or are likely to become available in such area as determined by the Secretary after taking into account information provided by the Labor Market Advisory Council for such area.

§ 633. Operation of program

(a) The Secretary shall provide a program of testing and counseling for all persons ~~referred~~ certified to him by a State, pursuant to section ~~602~~ 602(a)(19)(G), and shall select those persons whom he finds suitable for the programs established by clauses (1) and (2) of section 632 (b). Those not so selected shall be deemed suitable for the program established by clause (3) of such section 632(b) unless the Secretary finds that there is good cause for an individual not to participate in such program. The Secretary, in carrying out such program for individuals certified to him under section 602(a)(19)(G), shall accord priority to such individuals in the following order, taking into account employability potential: first, unemployed fathers; second, mothers, whether or not required to register pursuant to section 602(a)(19)(A), who volunteer for participation under a work incentive program; third, other mothers, and pregnant women, registered pursuant to section 602(a)(19)(A), who are under 19 years of age; fourth, dependent children and relatives who have attained age 16 and who are not in school or engaged in work or manpower training; and fifth, all other individuals so certified to him.

~~(b) The Secretary shall develop an employability plan for each suitable person referred to him under section 602 which shall describe the education, training, work experience, and orientation which it is determined that each such person needs to complete in order to enable him to become self-supporting.~~

(b)(1) For each State the Secretary shall develop jointly with the administrative unit of such State administering the special program referred to in section 602(a)(19)(G) a statewide operational plan.

(2) The statewide operation plan shall prescribe how the work incentive program established by this part will be operated at the local level, and shall indicate (i) for each area within the State the number and type of positions which will be provided for training, for on-the-job training, and for public service employment, (ii) the manner in which information provided by the Labor Market Advisory Council (established pursuant to section 632(f) for any such area will be utilized in the operation of such program, and (iii) the particular State agency or administrative unit thereof which will be responsible for each of the various activities and functions to be performed under such program. Any such operational plan for any State must be approved by the Secretary, the administrative unit of such State administering the special program referred to in section 602(a)(19)(G), and the regional joint committee (established pursuant to section 639) for the area in which such State is located.

(3) The Secretary shall develop an employability plan for each suitable person certified to him pursuant to section 602(a)(19)(G) which shall describe the education, training, work experience, and orientation which it is determined that such person needs to complete in order to enable him to become self-supporting.

(c) The Secretary shall make maximum use of services available from other Federal and State agencies and, to the extent not otherwise available on a nonreimbursable basis, he may reimburse such agencies for services rendered to persons under this part.

(d) To the extent practicable and where necessary, work incentive programs established by this part shall include, in addition to the regular counseling, testing, and referral available through the Federal-State Employment Service System, program orientation, basic education, training in communications and employability skills, work experience, institutional training, on-the-job training, job development, and special job placement and followup services, required to assist participants in securing and retaining employment and securing possibilities for advancement.

(e)(1) In order to develop ~~special work projects~~ public service employment under the program established by section 632(b)(3), the Secretary shall enter into agreements with (A) public agencies, (B) private nonprofit organizations established to serve a public purpose, and (C) Indian tribes with respect to Indians on a reservation, under which individuals deemed suitable for participation in such a program will be provided work which serves a useful public purpose and which would not otherwise be performed by regular employees.

(2) Such agreements shall provide—

~~(A) for the payment by the Secretary to each employer a portion of the wages to be paid by the employer to the individuals for the work performed.~~

(A) for the payment by the Secretary to each employer, with respect to public service employment performed by any individual for such employer, of an amount not exceeding 100 percent of the cost of providing such employment to such individual during the first year of such employment, an amount not exceeding 75 percent of the cost of providing such employment to such individual during the second year of such employment and an amount not exceeding 50 percent of the cost of providing such employment to such individual during the third year of such employment;

(B) the hourly wage rate and the number of hours per week individuals will be scheduled to work ~~on special work projects~~ in public service employment for such employer;

(C) that the Secretary will have such access to the premises of the employer as he finds necessary to determine whether such employer is carrying out his obligations under the agreement and this part; and

(D) that the Secretary may terminate any agreement under this subsection at any time.

~~(3) The Secretary shall establish one or more accounts in each State with respect to the special work projects established and maintained pursuant to this subsection and place into such accounts the amounts paid to him by the State agency pursuant to section 602(a)(19)(E). The amounts in such accounts shall be available for the payments specified in subparagraph (A) of paragraph (2). At the end of each fiscal year and for such period of time as he may establish, the Secretary shall determine how much of the amounts paid to him by the State agency pursuant to section 602 (a)(19)(E) where not expended as provided by the preceding sentence of this paragraph and shall return such unexpended amounts to the State, which amounts shall be regarded as overpayments for purpose of section 603(b)(2).~~

(4) No wage rates provided under any agreement entered into under this subsection shall be lower than the applicable minimum wage for the particular work concerned.

(f) Before entering into a project under section 632(b)(3), ~~any of the programs established by this part~~, the Secretary shall have reasonable assurances that—

(1) appropriate standards for the health, safety, and other conditions applicable to the performance of work and training on such project are established and will be maintained,

(2) such project will not result in the displacement of employed workers,

(3) with respect to such project the conditions of work, training, education, and employment are reasonable in the light of such factors as the type of work, geographical region, and proficiency of the participant,

(4) appropriate workmen's compensation protection is provided to all participants.

(g) Where an individual ~~referred~~ certified to the Secretary of Labor pursuant to section 602(a)(19)~~(A)~~(G)(i) and (ii) refuses without good cause to accept employment or participate in a project under a program established by this part, the Secretary of Labor shall (after providing opportunity for fair hearing) notify the State agency which ~~referred~~ certified such individual and submit such other information as he may have with respect to such refusal.

(h) With respect to individuals who are participants in ~~special work projects~~ public service employment under the program established by section 632(b)(3), the Secretary shall periodically (but at least once every six months) review the employment record of each such individual while on such special work project and on the basis of such record and such other information as he may acquire determine whether it would be feasible to place such individual in regular employment or on any of the projects under the programs established by section 632(b)(1) and (2).

§ 634. Incentive payments and allowances for transportation and other costs

(a) The Secretary is authorized to pay to any participant under a program established by section 632(b)(2) an incentive payment of not more than $30 per month, payable in such amounts and at such times as the Secretary prescribes.

"(b) The Secretary of Labor is also authorized to pay, to any member of a family participating in manpower training under this part, allowances for transportation and other costs incurred by such member, to the extent such costs are necessary to and directly related to the participation by such member in such training."

§ 635. Federal assistance

(a) Federal assistance under this part shall not exceed 90 per centum of the costs of carrying out this part. Non-Federal contributions may be cash or in kind, fairly evaluated, including but not limited to plant, equipment, and services.

(b) Costs of carrying out this part include costs of training, supervision, materials, administration, incentive payments, transportation, and other items as are authorized by the Secretary, but may not include any reimbursement for time spent by participants in work, training, or other participation in the program; ~~except that with respect to special work projects under the program established by section 632(b)(3), the costs of carrying out this part shall include only the costs of administration.~~

§ 636. Period of enrollment

(a) The program established by section 632(b)(2) shall be designed by the Secretary so that the average period of enrollment under all projects under such program throughout any area of the United States will not exceed one year.

(b) Services provided under this part may continue to be provided to an individual for such period as the Secretary determines (in accordance with regulations prescribed ~~by the Secretary after consultation~~ jointly by him and ~~with~~ the Secretary of Health, Education, and Welfare) is neces-

sary to qualify him fully for employment even though his earnings disqualify
him from aid under a State plan approved under section 602.

§ 637. Relocation of participants

The Secretary may assist participants to relocate their place of residence when he determines such relocation is necessary in order to enable them
to become permanently employable and self-supporting. Such assistance shall
be given only to participants who concur in their relocation and who will be
employed at their place of relocation at wage rates which will meet at least
their full need as determined by the State to which they will be relocated.
Assistance under this section shall not exceed the reasonable costs of transportation for participants, their dependents, and their household belongings
plus such relocation allowance as the Secretary determines to be reasonable.

§ 638. Participants not Federal employees

Participants in ~~projects under~~ programs established by this part
shall be deemed not to be Federal employees and shall not be subject to
the provisions of laws relating to Federal employment, including those
relating to hours of work, rates of compensation, leave, unemployment compensation, and Federal employee benefits.

§ 639. Rules and regulations

~~The Secretary may issue such rules and regulations as he finds necessary to carry out the purposes of this part. Provided, That in developing
policies for programs established by this part the Secretary shall consult
with the Secretary of Health, Education, and Welfare~~.

The Secretary and the Secretary of Health, Education, and Welfare
shall, not later than July 1, 1972, issue regulations to carry out the purposes
of this part. Such regulations shall provide for the establishment, jointly
by the Secretary and the Secretary of Health, Education, and Welfare, of
(1) a national coordination committee the duty of which shall be to establish
uniform reporting and similar requirements for the administration of this
part, and (2) a regional coordination committee for each region which shall
be responsible for review and approval of statewide operational plans developed pursuant to section 633(b)."

* * *

§ 641. Evaluation and research

The Secretary shall (jointly with the Secretary of Health, Education, and Welfare) provide for the continuing evaluation of the work incentive programs established by this part, including their effectiveness in
achieving stated goals and their impact on other related programs. He
also may conduct research regarding ways to increase the effectiveness of
such programs. He may, for this purpose, contract for independent evaluations of and research regarding such programs or individual projects under
such programs. For purposes of sections 635 and 643, the costs of carrying
out this section shall not be regarded as costs of carrying out work incentive programs established by this part.

"Nothing in this section shall be construed as authorizing the Secretary
to enter into any contract with any organization after June 1, 1970, for
the dissemination by such organization of information about programs authorized to be carried on under this part."

§ 642. Technical assistance for providers of employment or training

~~(a) The Secretary shall make an agreement with any State which is able and willing to do so under which the Governor of the State will create one or more panels to review applications tentatively approved by the Secretary for the special work projects in such State to be established by the Secretary under the program established by section 632(b)(3).~~

~~(b) Each such panel shall consist of not more than five and not less than three members, appointed by the Governor. The members shall include one representative of employers and one representative of employees; the remainder shall be representatives of the general public. No special work project under such program developed by the Secretary pursuant to an agreement under section 633(e)(1) shall, in any State which has an agreement under this section, be established or maintained under such program unless such project has first been approved by a panel created pursuant to this section.~~

<u>The Secretary is authorized to provide technical assistance to providers of employment or training to enable them to participate in the establishment and operation of programs</u> authorized to be established by section 632(b)."

§ 643. Collection of state share

If a non-Federal contribution of ~~20~~ <u>10</u> per centum of the costs of the work incentive programs established by this part is not made in any State (as specified in section 602(a)) the Secretary of Health, Education, and Welfare may withhold any action under section 604 because of the State's failure to comply substantially with a provision required by section 602. If the Secretary of Health, Education, and Welfare does withhold such action, he shall, after reasonable notice and opportunity for hearing to the appropriate State agency or agencies, withhold any payments to be made to the State under sections 3(a), 603(a), 1003(a), 1403(a), 1603(a), and 1903(a) until the amount so withheld (including any amounts contributed by the State pursuant to the requirement in section 602(a)(19)(C)) equals ~~20~~ <u>10</u> per centum of the costs of such work incentive programs. Such withholding shall remain in effect until such time as the Secretary has assurances from the State that such ~~20~~ <u>10</u> per centum will be contributed as required by section 602. Amounts so withheld shall be deemed to have been paid to the State under such sections and shall be paid by the Secretary of Health, Education, and Welfare to the Secretary. Such payment shall be considered a non-Federal contribution for purposes of section 635.

§ 644. Agreements with other agencies providing assistance to families of unemployed parents

(a) The Secretary is authorized to enter into an agreement (in accordance with the succeeding provisions of this section) with any qualified State agency (as described in subsection (b)) under which the program established by the preceding sections of this part C will (except as otherwise provided in this section) be applicable to individuals ~~referred~~ <u>certified</u> by such State agency in the same manner, to the same extent, and under the same conditions as such program is applicable with respect to individuals ~~referred~~ <u>certified</u> to the Secretary by a State agency administering or supervising the administration of a State plan approved by the Secretary of Health, Education, and Welfare under part A of this title.

(b) A qualified State agency referred to in subsection (a) is a State agency which is charged with the administration of a program—

(1) the purpose of which is to provide aid or assistance to the families of unemployed parents,

(2) which is not established pursuant to part A of title IV of the Social Security Act,

(3) which is financed entirely from funds appropriated by the Congress, and

(4) none of the financing of which is made available under any program established pursuant to title V of the Economic Opportunity Act.

(c)(1) Any agreement under this section with a qualified State agency shall provide that such agency will, with respect to all individuals receiving aid or assistance under the program of aid or assistance to families of unemployed parents administered by such agency, comply with the requirements imposed by ~~section 602(a)(15) and~~ section 602(a)(19)~~(F)~~ in the same manner and to the same extent as if (A) such qualified agency were the agency in such State administering or supervising the administration of a State plan approved under part A of this title, and (B) individuals receiving aid or assistance under the program administered by such qualified agency were recipients of aid under a State plan which is so approved.

(2) Any agreement entered into under this section shall remain in effect for such period as may be specified in the agreement by the Secretary and the qualified State agency, except that, whenever the Secretary determines, after reasonable notice and opportunity for hearing to the qualified State agency, that such agency has failed substantially to comply with its obligations under such agreement, the Secretary may suspend operation of the agreement until such time as he is satisfied that the State agency will no longer fail substantially to comply with its obligations under such agreement.

(3) Any such agreement shall further provide that the agreement will be inoperative for any calendar quarter if, for the preceding calendar quarter, the maximum amount of benefits payable under the program of aid or assistance to families of unemployed parents administered by the qualified State agency which is a party to such agreement is lower than the maximum amount of benefits payable under such program for the quarter which ended September 30, 1967.

(d) The Secretary shall at the request of any qualified State agency referred to in subsection (a) of this section and upon receipt from it of a list of the names of individuals rereferred to the Secretary, furnish to such agency the names of each individual on such list participating in a <u>public service employment</u> ~~special work project~~ under section 633(a)(3) whom the Secretary determines should continue to participate in such ~~project~~ employment. The Secretary shall not comply with any such request with respect to an individual on such list unless such individual has been ~~referred~~ <u>certified</u> to the Secretary by such agency under such section ~~602(a)(15)~~ <u>602(a)(19)(G)</u> for a period of at least six months.

SUBCHAPTER XVI—SUPPLEMENTAL SECURITY INCOME FOR THE AGED, BLIND, AND DISABLED

§ 1381.   Statement of Purpose; authorization of appropriations

For the purpose of establishing a national program to provide supplemental security income to individuals who have attained age 65 or are blind or disabled, there are authorized to be appropriated sums sufficient to carry out this subchapter.

§ 1381a.   Basic entitlement to benefits

Every aged, blind, or disabled individual who is determined under part A to be eligible on the basis of his income and resources shall, in accordance with and subject to the provisions of this subchapter, be paid benefits by the Secretary of Health, Education, and Welfare.

PART A—DETERMINATION OF BENEFITS

§ 1382.   Eligibility for benefits—Definition of eligible individual

(a)(1) Each aged, blind, or disabled individual who does not have an eligible spouse and—

(A) whose income, other than income excluded pursuant to section 1382a(b) of this title, is at a rate of not more than $1,560 for the calendar year 1974 or any calendar year thereafter, and

(B) whose resources, other than resources excluded pursuant to section 1382b(a) of this title, are not more than (i) in case such individual has a spouse with whom he is living, $2,250, or (ii) in case such individual has no spouse with whom he is living, $1,500,

shall be an eligible individual for purposes of this title.

(2) Each aged, blind, or disabled individual who has an eligible spouse and—

(A) whose income (together with the income of such spouse), other than income excluded pursuant to section 1382a(b) of this title, is at a rate of not more than $2,340 for the calendar year 1974, or any calendar year thereafter, and

(B) whose resources (together with the resources of such spouse), other than resources excluded pursuant to section 1382b(a), are not more than $2,250,

shall be an eligible individual for purposes of this subchapter.

Amounts of benefits

(b)(1) The benefit under this subchapter for an individual who does not have an eligible spouse shall be payable at the rate of $1,560 for the calendar year 1974 and any calendar year thereafter, reduced by the amount of income, not excluded pursuant to section 1382a(b) of this title, of such individual.

(2) The benefit under this title for an individual who has an eligible spouse shall be payable at the rate of $2,340 for the calendar year 1974 and any calendar year thereafter, reduced by the amount of income, not excluded pursuant to section 1382a(b) of this title, of such individual and spouse.

Period for determination of benefits; redetermination of eligibility and amount of benefits; effective date of application

(c)(1) An individual's eligibility for benefits under this subchapter and the amount of such benefits shall be determined for each quarter of a calendar year except that, if the initial application for benefits is filed in the second or third month of a calendar quarter, such determinations shall be made for each month in such quarter. Eligibility for and the amount of such benefits for any quarter shall be redetermined at such time or times as may be provided by the Secretary.

(2) For purposes of this subsection an application shall be considered to be effective as of the first day of the month in which it was actually filed.

Limitations on amount of gross income earned; definition of gross income

(d) The Secretary may prescribe the circumstances under which, consistently with the purposes of this subchapter, the gross income from a trade or business (including farming) will be considered sufficiently large to make an individual ineligible for benefits under this subchapter. For purposes of this subsection, the term 'gross income' has the same meaning as when used in chapter 1 of the Internal Revenue Code of 1954.

Limitation on eligibility of certain individuals

(e)(1)(A) Except as provided in subparagraph (B), no person shall be an eligible individual or eligible spouse for purposes of this subchapter with respect to any month if throughout such month he is an inmate of a public institution.

(B) In any case where an eligible individual or his eligible spouse (if any) is, throughout any month, in a hospital, extended care facility, nursing home, or intermediate care facility receiving payments (with respect to such individual or spouse) under a State plan approved under subchapter XIX of this chapter, the benefit under this subchapter for such individual for such month shall be payable—

(i) at a rate not in excess of $300 per year (reduced by the amount of any income not excluded pursuant to section 1382a(b) of this title) in the case of an individual who does not have an eligible spouse;

(ii) at a rate not in excess of the sum of the applicable rate specified in subsection (b)(1) of this section and the rate of $300 per year (reduced by the amount of any income not excluded pursuant to section 1382a(b)) in the case of an individual who has an eligible spouse, if only one of them is in such a hospital, home, or facility throughout such month; and

(iii) at a rate not in excess of $600 per year (reduced by the amount of any income not excluded pursuant to section 1382a(b) of this title) in the case of an individual who has an eligible spouse, if both of them are in such a hospital, home, or facility throughout such month.

(2) No person shall be an eligible individual or eligible spouse for purposes of this subchapter if, after notice to such person by the Secretary that it is likely that such person is eligible for any payments of the type enu-

merated in section 1382a(a)(2)(B) of this title, such person fails within 30 days to take all appropriate steps to apply for and (if eligible) obtain any such payments.

(3)(A) No person who is an aged, blind, or disabled individual solely by reason of disability (as determined under section 1382c(a)(3) of this title) shall be an eligible individual or eligible spouse for purposes of this subchapter with respect to any month if such individual is medically determined to be a drug addict or an alcoholic unless such individual is undergoing any treatment that may be appropriate for his condition as a drug addict or alcoholic (as the case may be) at an institution or facility approved for purposes of this paragraph by the Secretary (so long as such treatment is available) and demonstrates that he is complying with the terms, conditions, and requirements of such treatment and with requirements imposed by the Secretary under subparagraph (B).

(B) The Secretary shall provide for the monitoring and testing of all individuals who are receiving benefits under this subchapter and who as a condition of such benefits are required to be undergoing treatment and complying with the terms, conditions, and requirements thereof as described in subparagraph (A), in order to assure such compliance and to determine the extent to which the imposition of such requirement is contributing to the achievement of the purposes of this subchapter. The Secretary shall annually submit to the Congress a full and complete report on his activities under this paragraph.

Individuals outside the United States; determination of status

(f) Notwithstanding any other provision of this subchapter, no individual shall be considered an eligible individual for purposes of this subchapter for any month during all of which such individual is outside the United States (and no person shall be considered the eligible spouse of an individual for purposes of this title with respect to any month during all of which such person is outside the United States). For purposes of the preceding sentence, after an individual has been outside the United States for any period of 30 consecutive days, he shall be treated as remaining outside the United States until he has been in the United States for a period of 30 consecutive days.

Individuals deemed to meet resources test

(g) In the case of any individual or any individual and his spouse (as the case may be) who for the month of December 1973 was a recipient of aid or assistance under a State plan approved under subchapter I, X, XIV, or XVI, the resources of such individual or such individual and his spouse shall be deemed not to exceed the amount specified in sections 1382(a)(1)(B) and 1382(a)(2)(B) of this title during any period that the resources of such individual or individual and his spouse (as the case may be) does not exceed the maximum amount of resources, as specified in the State plan (above referred to, and as in effect in October 1972) under which he or they were entitled to aid or assistance for the month of December 1972.

Individuals deemed to meet income test

(h) In determining eligibility for, and the amount of, benefits payable under this section in the case of any individual or any individual and his spouse (as the case may be) who is blind (as that term is defined under a State plan approved under subchapter X or XVI as in effect in October 1972) and who for the month of December 1973 was a recipient of aid or assistance under a State plan approved under subchapter X or XVI, there shall be disregarded an amount equal to the greater of the amounts determined as follows—

(1) the maximum amount of any earned or unearned income which could have been disregarded under the State plan (above referred to, and as in effect in October 1972), or

(2) the amount which would be required to be disregarded under section 1382a of this title without application of this subsection.

§ 1382a. Income; definition of earned and unearned income; exclusions from income

(a) For purposes of this subchapter, income means both earned income and unearned income; and—

(1) earned income means only—

(A) wages as determined under section 203(f)(5)(C); and

(B) net earnings from self-employment, as defined in section 411 (without the application of the second and third sentences following subsection (a)(10), and the last paragraph of subsection (a)), including earnings for services described in paragraphs (4), (5), and (6) of subsection (c); and

(2) unearned income means all other income, including—

"(A) support and maintenance furnished in cash or kind; except that in the case of any individual (and his eligible spouse, if any) living in another person's household and receiving support and maintenance in kind from such person, the dollar amounts otherwise applicable to such individual (and spouse) as specified in subsections (a) and (b) of section 1382 shall be reduced by 33⅓ percent in lieu of including such support and maintenance in the unearned income of such individual (and spouse) as otherwise required by this subparagraph;

(B) any payments received as an annuity, pension, retirement, or disability benefit, including veterans' compensation and pensions, workmen's compensation payments, old-age, survivors, and disability insurance benefits, railroad retirement annuities and pensions, and unemployment insurance benefits;

(C) prizes and awards;

(D) the proceeds of any life insurance policy to the extent that they exceed the amount expended by the beneficiary for purposes of the insured individual's last illness and burial or $1,500, whichever is less;

(E) gifts (cash or otherwise), support and alimony payments, and inheritances; and

(F) rents, dividends, interest, and royalties.

(b) In determining the income of an individual (and his eligible spouse) there shall be excluded—

(1) subject to limitations (as to amount or otherwise) prescribed by the Secretary, if such individual is a child who is, as determined by the Secretary, a student regularly attending a school, college, or uni-

versity, or a course of vocational or technical training designed to prepare him for gainful employment, the earned income of such individual;

(2) the first $240 per year (or proportionately smaller amounts for shorter periods) of income (whether earned or unearned) other than income which is paid on the basis of the need of the eligible individual;

(3)(A) the total unearned income of such individual (and such spouse, if any) in a calendar quarter which, as determined in accordance with criteria prescribed by the Secretary, is received too infrequently or irregularly to be included, if such income so received does not exceed $60 in such quarter, and (B) the total earned income of such individual (and such spouse, if any) in a calendar quarter which, as determined in accordance with such criteria, is received too infrequently or irregularly to be included, if such income so received does not exceed $30 in such quarter;

(4)(A) if such individual (or such spouse) is blind (and has not attained age 65, or received benefits under this subchapter (or aid under a State plan approved under section 1202 or 1382 of this title) for the month before the month in which he attained age 65, (i) the first $780 per year (or proportionately smaller amounts for shorter periods) of earned income not excluded by the preceding paragraphs of this subsection, plus one-half of the remainder thereof, (ii) an amount equal to any expenses reasonably attributable to the earning of any income, and (iii) such additional amounts of other income, where such individual has a plan for achieving self-support approved by the Secretary, as may be necessary for the fulfillment of such plan,

(B) if such individual (or such spouse) is disabled but not blind (and has not attained age 65, or received benefits under this subchapter (or aid under a State plan approved under section 1352 or 1382 of this title) for the month before the month in which he attained age 65), (i) the first $780 per year (or proportionately smaller amounts for shorter periods) of earned income not excluded by the preceding paragraphs of this subsection, plus one-half of the remainder thereof, and (ii) such additional amounts of other income, where such individual has a plan for achieving self-support approved by the Secretary, as may be necessary for the fulfillment of such plan, or

(C) if such individual (or such spouse) has attained age 65 and is not included under subparagraph (A) or (B), the first $780 per year (or proportionately smaller amounts for shorter periods) of earned income not excluded by the preceding paragraphs of this subsection, plus one-half of the remainder thereof;

(5) any amount received from any public agency as a return or refund of taxes paid on real property or on food purchased by such individual (or such spouse);

(6) assistance described in section 1382(e)(a) of this title which is based on need and furnished by any State or political subdivision of a State;

(7) any portion of any grant, scholarship, or fellowship received for use in paying the cost of tuition and fees at any educational (including technical or vocational education) institution;

(8) home produce of such individual (or spouse) utilized by the household for its own consumption;

(9) if such individual is a child one-third of any payment for his support received from an absent parent; and

(10) any amounts received for the foster care of a child who is not an eligible individual but who is living in the same home as such individual and was placed in such home by a public or nonprofit private child-placement or child-care agency.

§ 1382b.   Resources; exclusions from resources; disposition of resources

(a) In determining the resources of an individual (and his eligible spouse, if any) there shall be excluded—

(1) the home (including the land that appertains thereto), to the extent that its value does not exceed such amount as the Secretary determines to be reasonable;

(2) household goods, personal effects, and an automobile, to the extent that their total value does not exceed such amount as the Secretary determines to be reasonable;

(3) other property which, as determined in accordance with and subject to limitations prescribed by the Secretary, is so essential to the means of self-support of such individual (and such spouse) as to warrant its exclusion;

(4) such resources of an individual who is blind or disabled and who has a plan for achieving self-support approved by the Secretary, as may be necessary for the fulfillment of such plan; and

(5) in the case of Natives of Alaska, shares of stock held in a Regional or a Village Corporation, during the period of twenty years in which such stock is inalienable, as provided in section 7(h) and section 8(c) of the Alaska Native Claims Settlement Act.

In determining the resources of an individual (or eligible spouse) an insurance policy shall be taken into account only to the extent of its cash surrender value; except that if the total face value of all life insurance policies on any person is $1,500 or less, no part of the value of any such policy shall be taken into account.

(b) The Secretary shall prescribe the period or periods of time within which, and the manner in which, various kinds of property must be disposed of in order not to be included in determining an individual's eligibility for benefits. Any portion of the individual's benefits paid for any such period shall be conditioned upon such disposal; and any benefits so paid shall (at the time of the disposal) be considered overpayments to the extent they would not have been paid had the disposal occurred at the beginning of the period for which such benefits were paid.

§ 1382c.   Definitions

(a)(1) For purposes of this subchapter, the term "aged, blind, or disabled individual" means an individual who—

(A) is 65 years of age or older, is blind (as determined under paragraph (2)), or is disabled (as determined under paragraph (3)), and

(B) is a resident of the United States, and is either (i) a citizen or (ii) an alien lawfully admitted for permanent residence or otherwise permanently residing in the United States under color of law (including any alien who is lawfully present in the United States as a result of the application of the provisions of section 203(a)(7) or section 212(d)(5) of the Immigration and Nationality Act).

(2) An individual shall be considered to be blind for purposes of this subchapter if he has central visual acuity of 20/200 or less in the better eye with the use of a correcting lens. An eye which is accompanied by a limitation in the fields of vision such that the widest diameter of the visual field subtends an angle no greater than 20 degrees shall be considered for purposes of the first sentence of this subsection as having a central visual acuity of 20/200 or less. An individual shall also be considered to be blind for purposes of this subchapter if he is blind as defined under a State plan approved under subchapter X or XVI of this chapter as in effect for October 1972 and received aid under such plan (on the basis of blindness) for December 1973, so long as he is continuously blind as so defined.

(3)(A) An individual shall be considered to be disabled for purposes of this subchapter if he is unable to engage in any substantial gainful activity by reason of any medically determinable physical or mental impairment which can be expected to result in death or which has lasted or can be expected to last for a continuous period of not less than twelve months (or, in the case of a child under the age of 18, if he suffers from any medically determinable physical or mental impairment of comparable severity). An individual shall also be considered to be disabled for purposes of this subchapter if he is permanently and totally disabled as defined under a State plan approved under subchapter XIV or XVI of this chapter as in effect for October 1972 and received aid under such plan (on the basis of disability) for December 1973, so long as he is continuously disabled as so defined.

(B) For purposes of subparagraph (A), an individual shall be determined to be under a disability only if his physical or mental impairment or impairments are of such severity that he is not only unable to do his previous work but cannot, considering his age, education, and work experience, engage in any other kind of substantial gainful work which exists in the national economy, regardless of whether such work exists in the immediate area in which he lives, or whether a specific job vacancy exists for him, or whether he would be hired if he applied for work. For purposes of the preceding sentence (with respect to any individual), 'work which exists in the national economy' means work which exists in significant numbers either in the region where such individual lives or in several regions of the country.

(C) For purposes of this paragraph, a physical or mental impairment is an impairment that results from anatomical, physiological, or psychological abnormalities which are demonstrable by medically acceptable clinical and laboratory diagnostic techniques.

(D) The Secretary shall by regulations prescribe the criteria for determining when services performed or earnings derived from services demonstrate an individual's ability to engage in substantial gainful activity. Notwithstanding the provisions of subparagraph (B), an individual whose services or earnings meet such criteria, except for purposes of paragraph (4), shall be found not to be disabled.

(4)(A) For purposes of this subchapter, any services rendered during a period of trial work (as defined in subparagraph (B)) by an individual who is an aged, blind, or disabled individual solely by reason of disability (as determined under paragraph (3) of this subsection) shall be deemed not to have been rendered by such individual in determining whether his disability has ceased in a month during such period. As used in this paragraph, the term 'services' means activity which is performed for remuneration or gain or is determined by the Secretary to be of a type normally performed for remuneration or gain.

(B) The term 'period of trial work', with respect to an individual who is an aged, blind, or disabled individual solely by reason of disability (as determined under paragraph (3) of this subsection), means a period of months beginning and ending as provided in subparagraphs (C) and (D).

(C) A period of trial work for any individual shall begin with the month in which he becomes eligible for benefits under this subchapter on the basis of his disability; but no such period may begin for an individual who is eligible for benefits under this subchapter on the basis of a disability if he has had a previous period of trial work while eligible for benefits on the basis of the same disability.

(D) A period of trial work for any individual shall end with the close of whichever of the following months is the earlier:

(i) the ninth month, beginning on or after the first day of such period, in which the individual renders services (whether or not such nine months are consecutive); or

(ii) the month in which his disability (as determined under paragraph (3) of this subsection) ceases (as determined after the application of subparagraph (A) of this paragraph).

(b) For purposes of this subchapter, the term 'eligible spouse' means an aged, blind, or disabled individual who is the husband or wife of another aged, blind, or disabled individual and who has not been living apart from such other aged, blind, or disabled individual for more than six months. If two aged, blind, or disabled individuals are husband and wife as described in the preceding sentence, only one of them may be an 'eligible individual' within the meaning of section 1382a of this title.

(c) For purposes of this subchapter, the term 'child' means an individual who is neither married nor (as determined by the Secretary) the head of a household, and who is (1) under the age of eighteen, or (2) under the age of twenty-two and (as determined by the Secretary) a student regularly attending a school, college, or university, or a course of vocational or technical training designed to prepare him for gainful employment.

(d) In determining whether two individuals are husband and wife for purposes of this subchapter, appropriate State law shall be applied; except that—

(1) if a man and woman have been determined to be husband and wife under section 416(h)(1) of this title for purposes of subchapter II of this chapter they shall be considered (from and after the date of such determination or the date of their application for benefits under this subchapter, whichever is later) to be husband and wife for purposes of this subchapter, or

(2) if a man and woman are found to be holding themselves out to the community in which they reside as husband and wife, they shall

be so considered for purposes of this subchapter notwithstanding any other provision of this section.

(e) For purposes of this subchapter, the term "United States", when used in a geographical sense, means the 50 States and the District of Columbia.

(f)(1) For purposes of determining eligibility for and the amount of benefits for any individual who is married and whose spouse is living with him in the same household but is not an eligible spouse, such individual's income and resources shall be deemed to include any income and resources of such spouse, whether or not available to such individual, except to the extent determined by the Secretary to be inequitable under the circumstances.

(2) For purposes of determining eligibility for and the amount of benefits for any individual who is a child under age 21, such individual's income and resources shall be deemed to include any income and resources of a parent of such individual (or the spouse of such a parent) who is living in the same household as such individual, whether or not available to such individual, except to the extent determined by the Secretary to be inequitable under the circumstances.

§ 1382d. Rehabilitation services for blind and disabled individuals—Referral by Secretary of eligible individuals to appropriate State agency; review by Secretary of individual's blindness or disability and need for services

(a) In the case of any blind or disabled individual who—

(1) has not attained age 65, and

(2) is receiving benefits (or with respect to whom benefits are paid) under this subchapter,

the Secretary shall make provision for referral of such individual to the appropriate State agency administering the State plan for vocational rehabilitation services approved under the Vocational Rehabilitation Act, and (except in such cases as he may determine) for a review not less often than quarterly of such individual's blindness or disability and his need for and utilization of the rehabilitation services made available to him under such plan.

Acceptance by referred individuals of services; payment by Secretary to State agency by costs of providing services to referred individuals

(b) Every individual with respect to whom the Secretary is required to make provision for referral under subsection (a) shall accept such rehabilitation services as are made available to him under the State plan for vocational rehabilitation services approved under the Vocational Rehabilitation Act; and the Secretary is authorized to pay to the State agency administering or supervising the administration of such State plan the costs incurred in the provision of such services to individuals so referred.

Refusal by referred individuals to accept services

(c) No individual shall be an eligible individual or eligible spouse for purposes of this subchapter if he refuses without good cause to accept vocational rehabilitation services for which he is referred under subsection (a) of this section.

§ 1382e. Supplementary assistance by State or subdivision to needy individuals—Exclusion of cash payments in determination of income of individuals for purposes of eligibility for benefits; agreement by Secretary and State for Secretary to make supplementary payments on behalf of State or subdivision

(a) Any cash payments which are made by a State (or political subdivision thereof) on a regular basis to individuals who are receiving benefits under this subchapter or who would but for their income be eligible to receive benefits under this subchapter, as assistance based on need in supplementation of such benefits (as determined by the Secretary), shall be excluded under section 1382a(b)(6) of this title in determining the income of such individuals for purposes of this subchapter and the Secretary and such State may enter into an agreement which satisfies subsection (b) under which the Secretary will, on behalf of such State (or subdivision) make such supplementary payments to all such individuals.

Agreement between Secretary and State; contents

(b) Any agreement between the Secretary and a State entered into under subsection (a) shall provide—

(1) that such payments will be made (subject to subsection (c) of this section) to all individuals residing in such State (or subdivision) who are receiving benefits under this subchapter, and

(2) such other rules with respect to eligibility for or amount of the supplementary payments, and such procedural or other general administrative provisions, as the Secretary finds necessary (subject to subsection (c) of this section) to achieve efficient and effective administration of both the program which he conducts under this subchapter and the optional State supplementation.

Residence requirement by State or subdivision for supplementary payments; disregarding of amounts of certain income by State or subdivision in determining eligibility for supplementary payments

(c)(1) Any State (or political subdivision) making supplementary payments described in subsection (a) of this section may at its option impose as a condition of eligibility for such payments, and include in the State's agreement with the Secretary under such subsection, a residence requirement which excludes individuals who have resided in the State (or political subdivision) for less than a minimum period prior to application for such payments.

(2) Any State (or political subdivision), in determining the eligibility of any individual for supplementary payments described in subsection (a) of this section, may disregard amounts of earned and unearned income in addition to other amounts which it is required or permitted to disregard under this section in determining such eligibility, and shall include a provision specifying the amount of any such income that will be disregarded, if any.

Payment to Secretary by State of amount equal to expenditures by Secretary as supplementary payments; time and manner of payment by State

(d) Any State which has entered into an agreement with the Secretary under this section which provides that the Secretary will, on behalf of the

State (or political subdivision), make the supplementary payments to individuals who are receiving benefits under this subchapter (or who would but for their income be eligible to receive such benefits), shall, at such times and in such installments as may be agreed upon between the Secretary and such State, pay to the Secretary an amount equal to the expenditures made by the Secretary as such supplementary payments.

PART B—PROCEDURAL AND GENERAL PROVISIONS

§ 1383. Procedure for payment of benefits—time, manner, form and duration of payment; promulgation of regulations

(a)(1) Benefits under this subchapter shall be paid at such time or times and in such installments as will best effectuate the purposes of this subchapter, as determined under regulations (and may in any case be paid less frequently than monthly where the amount of the monthly benefit would not exceed $10).

(2) Payments of the benefit of any individual may be made to any such individual or to his eligible spouse (if any) or partly to each, or, if the Secretary deems it appropriate to any other person (including an appropriate public or private agency) who is interested in or concerned with the welfare of such individual (or spouse). Notwithstanding the provisions of the preceding sentence, in the case of any individual or eligible spouse referred to in section 1382(e)(3)(A) of this title, the Secretary shall provide for making payments of the benefit to any other person (including an appropriate public or private agency) who is interested in or concerned with the welfare of such individual (or spouse).

(3) The Secretary may by regulation establish ranges of incomes within which a single amount of benefits under this subchapter shall apply.

(4) The Secretary—

(A) may make to any individual initially applying for benefits under this subchapter who is presumptively eligible for such benefits and who is faced with financial emergency a cash advance against such benefits in an amount not exceeding $100; and

(B) may pay benefits under this subchapter to an individual applying for such benefits on the basis of disability for a period not exceeding 3 months prior to the determination of such individual's disability, if such individual is presumptively disabled and is determined to be otherwise eligible for such benefits, and any benefits so paid prior to such determination shall in no event be considered overpayments for purposes of subsection (b) of this section.

(5) Payment of the benefit of any individual who is an aged, blind, or disabled individual solely by reason of blindness (as determined under section 1382c(a)(2)) or disability (as determined under section 1382c(a)(3)), and who ceases to be blind or to be under such disability, shall continue (so long as such individual is otherwise eligible) through the second month following the month in which such blindness or disability ceases.

Overpayments and underpayments; adjustment, recovery, or payment of amounts by Secretary

(b) Whenever the Secretary finds that more or less than the correct amount of benefits has been paid with respect to any individual, proper adjustment or recovery shall, subject to the succeeding provisions of this subsection, be made by appropriate adjustments in future payments to such individual or by recovery from or payment to such individual or his eligible spouse (or by recovery from the estate of either). The Secretary shall make such provision as he finds appropriate in the case of payment of more than the correct amount of benefits with respect to an individual with a view to avoiding penalizing such individual or his eligible spouse who was without fault in connection with the overpayment, if adjustment or recovery on account of such overpayment in such case would defeat the purposes of this subchapter, or be against equity or good conscience, or (because of the small amount involved) impede efficient or effective administration of this subchapter.

Hearing for eligible individual or eligible spouse where eligibility or amount of benefit is in question; time for request for hearing; time for determinations pursuant to hearing; finality and conclusiveness of determinations of Secretary

(c)(1) The Secretary shall provide reasonable notice and opportunity for a hearing to any individual who is or claims to be an eligible individual or eligible spouse and is in disagreement with any determination under this subchapter with respect to eligibility of such individual for benefits, or the amount of such individual's benefits, if such individual requests a hearing on the matter in disagreement within thirty days after notice of such determination is received.

(2) Determination on the basis of such hearing, except to the extent that the matter in disagreement involves the existence of a disability (within the meaning of section 1382c(a)(3)), shall be made within ninety days after the individual requests the hearing as provided in paragraph (1).

(3) The final determination of the Secretary after a hearing under paragraph (1) shall be subject to judicial review as provided in section 405(g) of this title to the same extent as the Secretary's final determinations under section 405; except that the determination of the Secretary after such hearing as to any fact shall be final and conclusive and not subject to review by any court.

Applicability of procedural requirements; prohibition or assignment of payments; appointment of hearing examiners; representation of claimants; maximum fees; violations; penalties

(d)(1) The provisions of section 407 of this title and subsections (a), (d), (e), and (f) of section 405 of this title shall apply with respect to this part to the same extent as they apply in the case of subchapter II of this chapter.

(2) To the extent the Secretary finds it will promote the achievement of the objectives of this subchapter, qualified persons may be appointed to serve as hearing examiners in hearings under subsection (c) without meeting the specific standards prescribed for hearing examiners by or under subchapter II of chapter 5 of Title 5.

(3) The Secretary may prescribe rules and regulations governing the recognition of agents or other persons, other than attorneys, as hereinafter provided, representing claimants before the Secretary under this subchapter, and may require of such agents or other persons, before being recognized as representatives of claimants, that they shall show that they are of good character and in good repute, possessed of the necessary qualifications to en-

able them to render such claimants valuable service, and otherwise competent to advise and assist such claimants in the presentation of their cases. An attorney in good standing who is admitted to practice before the highest court of the State, Territory, District, or insular possession of his residence or before the Supreme Court of the United States or the inferior Federal courts, shall be entitled to represent claimants before the Secretary. The Secretary may, after due notice and opportunity for hearing, suspend or prohibit from further practice before him any such person, agent, or attorney who refuses to comply with the Secretary's rules and regulations or who violates any provision of this paragraph for which a penalty is prescribed. The Secretary may, by rule and regulation, prescribe the maximum fees which may be charged for services performed in connection with any claim before the Secretary under this subchapter, and any agreement in violation of such rules and regulations shall be void. Any person who shall, with intent to defraud, in any manner willfully and knowingly deceive, mislead, or threaten any claimant or prospective claimant or beneficiary under this subchapter by word, circular, letter, or advertisement, or who shall knowingly charge or collect directly or indirectly any fee in excess of the maximum fee, or make any agreement directly or indirectly to charge or collect any fee in excess of the maximum fee, prescribed by the Secretary, shall be deemed guilty of a misdemeanor and, upon conviction thereof, shall for each offense be punished by a fine not exceeding $500 or by imprisonment not exceeding one year, or both.

Administrative requirements prescribed by Secretary; criteria; reduction of benefits to individual for noncompliance with requirements

(e)(1)(A) The Secretary shall, subject to subparagraph (B), prescribe such requirements with respect to the filing of applications, the suspension or termination of assistance, the furnishing of other data and material, and the reporting of events and changes in circumstances, as may be necessary for the effective and efficient administration of this subchapter.

(B) The requirements prescribed by the Secretary pursuant to subparagraph (A) shall require that eligibility for benefits under this title will not be determined solely on the basis of declarations by the applicant concerning eligibility factors or other relevant facts, and that relevant information will be verified from independent or collateral sources and additional information obtained as necessary in order to assure that such benefits are only provided to eligible individuals (or eligible spouses) and that the amounts of such benefits are correct.

(2) In case of the failure by any individual to submit a report of events and changes in circumstances relevant to eligibility for or amount of benefits under this subchapter as required by the Secretary under paragraph (1), or delay by any individual in submitting a report as so required, the Secretary (in addition to taking any other action he may consider appropriate under paragraph (1)) shall reduce any benefits which may subsequently become payable to such individual under this title by—

(A) $25 in the case of the first such failure or delay,

(B) $50 in the case of the second such failure or delay, and

(C) $100 in the case of the third or a subsequent such failure or delay,

except where the individual was without fault or good cause for such failure or delay existed.

Furnishing of information by Federal agencies

(f) The head of any Federal agency shall provide such information as the Secretary needs for purposes of determining eligibility for or amount of benefits, or verifying other information with respect thereto.

§ 1383a.   Fraudulent acts; penalties

Whoever—

(1) knowingly and willfully makes or causes to be made any false statement or representation of a material fact in any application for any benefit under this subchapter,

(2) at any time knowingly and willfully makes or causes to be made any false statement or representation of a material fact for use in determining rights to any such benefit,

(3) having knowledge of the occurrence of any event affecting (A) his initial or continued right to any such benefit, or (B) the initial or continued right to any such benefit of any other individual in whose behalf he has applied for or is receiving such benefit, conceals or fails to disclose such event with an intent fraudulently to secure such benefit either in a greater amount or quantity than is due or when no such benefit is authorized, or

(4) having made application to receive any such benefit for the use and benefit of another and having received it, knowingly and willfully converts such benefit or any part thereof to a use other than for the use and benefit of such other person,

shall be guilty of a misdemeanor and upon conviction thereof shall be fined not more than $1,000 or imprisoned for not more than one year, or both.

§ 1383b.   Administration

The Secretary may make such administrative and other arrangements (including arrangements for the determination of blindness and disability under section 1382c(a)(2) and (3) in the same manner and subject to the same conditions as provided with respect to disability determinations under section 421 of this title) as may be necessary or appropriate to carry out his functions under this subchapter.

§ 1383c.   Eligibility for medical assistance of aged, blind, or disabled individuals under States medical assistance plan; determination by Secretary pursuant to agreement between Secretary and State; costs

The Secretary may enter into an agreement with any State which wishes to do so under which he will determine eligibility for medical assistance in the case of aged, blind, or disabled individuals under such State's plan approved under subchapter XIX of this chapter. Any such agreement shall provide for payments by the State, for use by the Secretary in carrying out the agreement, of an amount equal to one-half of the cost of carrying out the agreement, but in computing such cost with respect to individuals eligible for benefits under this subchapter, the Secretary shall include only those costs which are additional to the costs incurred in carrying out this subchapter.

Chapter 2

SELECTED PROBLEMS IN FAMILY
LAW AND POVERTY

SECTION 1. INTRODUCTION

A. A GENERAL VIEW

UNEQUAL PROTECTION: POV-
ERTY AND FAMILY LAW
FOSTER AND FREED

42 Ind.L.J. 192 (1967).*

MARRIAGE, DIVORCE, AND POVERTY

To an appreciable extent the law of marriage and divorce has priced itself out of the market. The financial obligations incurred as an incident to marriage may make it a luxury that the poor cannot afford and desertion may become the practical way to escape from either a putative or legal marital relationship. In England, before the Matrimonial Causes Act of 1857, desertion was the common mode of terminating an unsatisfactory relationship; dissenting sects and various groups had their own extra-legal customs, and parliamentary divorce was available only to the extremely wealthy. Even annulment or *a mensa et thoro* divorce, the alternatives available in the ecclesiastical courts, were too costly for the average Englishman. Thus of necessity, all but the wealthy were forced to resort to some form of self-help when a marital situation became intolerable.

In this country, too, among some subcultures, custom rather than law tradi-

tionally has governed the creation and termination of informal marital relationships.[11] Informal terminations of marriages are not uncommon for those informally entered into, and in the fifteen states retaining the institution of common law marriage there may be difficult factual questions due to the uncertainty of the distinction between legal and putative common law marriage. To the parties involved, "common law marriage" may mean either an at will liaison of uncertain duration, or a private contract of marriage, and especially among the poor, "common law divorce" may be resorted to in either event. There is the superstition in some parts of the country that if a spouse has been absent for five or seven years, the deserted party automatically is entitled to remarry, and there are instances of "law office divorce" where the parties assume that once a divorce complaint has been filed they are free to remarry and that the decree is a mere technicality.

There is a grave danger that something comparable to concubinage may develop in this country due to the financial obligations incurred by marriage and the expense of divorce. In many Latin American countries the children of concubines constitute over 50 percent of all live births.[13] Although the Roman Catho-

[11] See Foster, Common Law Divorce, 46 Minn.L.Rev. 43 (1961).

[13] See Arraros, Concubinage in Latin America, 3 J.Family Law 330 (1964), who reports the illegitimacy rate of all live births in 1958 in Panama was 73.9% and in Guatemala 71.6%. The Antilles, Honduras, Do-

lic hierarchy has disapproved of concubinage, unrealistic dogma and poverty have combined to make concubinage a socially acceptable institution for the impoverished masses. Unrealistic divorce laws and poverty in the United States likewise may combine to produce extralegal relationships and a high rate of illegitimacy.

When one considers that one-fourth to one third of the American population is afflicted with a combination of low income, low educational attainment, and substandard housing, the inevitability of irregular relationships and illegitimacy becomes apparent. Almost one-third of American families in 1959 had an annual income of less than $4,000; almost 40 million persons twenty-five years old and over in 1960 had no more than an eighth grade education; and in the same year over a quarter of all housing units in the United States were classified as deteriorated, dilapidated, or lacking in plumbing facilities. Income, education, and housing together with other factors such as age and religious affiliation, are all related to customs regarding marriage and divorce. Actually, socio-economic factors have much more to do with family stability and instability than do the usual symptoms set forth as grounds for divorce.

Sociologists have found that there is a rough inverse correlation between class position and rate of divorce. Those classified as professional, semi-professional, and proprietors are the least divorce prone, while laborers, service workers, and the unskilled or semi-skilled have the highest incidence of divorce. Moreover, the greatest degree of divorce proneness is among the lower income groups. The factors of location and mo-

minican Republic, El Salvador, Nicaragua, and Venezuela, all reported over 50 per cent. Most of the illegitimate children resulted from concubinage, although some were produced by casual meretricious relationships.

bility are, however, connected to low income and menial work. Moreover, among the very poor, the expense puts divorce out of the question. It also has been noted that conclusions from such studies may not be applicable to the Negro population which shows no comparable decrease in the incidence of divorce with increased income and educational achievement.

General economic conditions also affect the overall rate of divorce, and it has been said that the incidence of marriage and the incidence of divorce follow the business cycle. The marriage and divorce rates are relatively low in depression years and correspondingly high during years of prosperity. It should not be assumed, however, that economic adversity necessarily draws families closer together, for after the worst of the depression period is passed, there usually is a rapid rise in the divorce rate. It is likely that embittered and estranged couples merely bide their time until they can afford divorce.

With reference to educational achievement and family breakdown, in general there appears to be a correlation between degree of education and marriage stability. However, it is difficult to isolate the educational factor from other ones such as occupation, income, housing, social background, and age. One study reports that "not only are grammar-school educated persons more likely to *divorce* (at twice the *rate* of those of college education) but that they divorce on the average nine years earlier than do college people who divorce." Another study, however, showed that by educational level "divorcees" divided into 10 percent for the grade school group, 71 percent for the high school class, and 19 percent for the college grade. From these studies, and others, it has been concluded that "to some extent as regards divorce, family stability may be associated with higher educational accomplishment at the college level, but not at the high school level." In the case of Negroes, the divorce rate appears to remain approximately the same without reference to the amount of formal education.

Housing conditions obviously have a great impact upon both marriage and divorce. The availability of and means to pay for suitable living accommodations often are major factors in determining when couples will marry. Substandard housing or lack of separate living accommodations are important elements in family breakdown. The current programs for slum clearance, public housing, and relocation have as one objective the provision of better housing to increase family stability.

The inter-relation between poverty and family instability may be approached from another angle. Professor tenBroek cites a 1962 California study of some 86,-000 AFDC families (aid to families with dependent children program) which disclosed that of that number 77,000 were cases where the father was absent from the home. In 9,000 of those cases the fathers were absent because they were deceased, imprisoned, or had been deported or excluded, and in the remaining 68,355 cases they were "voluntarily absent." In the latter category of "voluntarily absent" fathers there were some 18,429 who were separated by divorce, annulment, or judicial separation; 10,473 who had separated without court decree; 5,647 cases of illegal desertion; 25,721 cases where the couples were never married and never lived together; and 8,085 cases where they had never married but lived together. The same study also reported that of the 249,000 children in California who in 1962 received AFDC, 37.2 percent were born to parents who never were married to each other. Insofar as compliance with marriage and divorce law is concerned, 49,000 of the 77,000 absent father cases were ones where there never had been a legal marriage, or there

was desertion or separation without a court decree.

The California study also made a breakdown by ethnic background for the percentage of "voluntarily absent" fathers, i. e., those not deceased, imprisoned, or deported, as compared with the total receiving AFDC. It was found that 68 percent of the white fathers were voluntarily absent from the home, 71 percent of the Mexican fathers, and 89 percent of the Negro fathers. In addition, half of the white fathers who were estranged were divorced or legally separated, as compared with 19.1 percent of the Mexican fathers, and 14.3 percent of the Negro fathers. While only 25.1 percent of the white fathers had never been married to the mother, 57.4 percent of the Mexican fathers and 62.3 percent of the Negro fathers had never been married to the mothers.

Although the California report, and other studies such as the Moynihan Report, are significant in disclosing the extent to which ethnic background is related to family patterns, poverty is much more widespread among Mexicans and Negroes, and their opportunity for economic advancement has been rare.[29] It appears that a combination of economic, historical, and cultural reasons account for the relative frequency of resort to custom instead of law on the part of some ethnic groups. When free legal aid services are made available to the poor, experience shows that they will resort to the legal processes, and in the case of divorce, the recent report from the "judicare" program in twenty-six rural counties in Wis-

[29] See Miller, Race, Poverty, and the Law, 54 Calif.L.Rev. 386 (1966). Negro unemployment hovers around two to three times that of white workmen and that which is described as "employment" for Negroes is all too often marginal work that requires supplemental aid or assistance. Address by President Lyndon B. Johnson, Howard University, June 4, 1965. See also Young, To Be Equal; ch. 3 (1964).

consin shows that the greatest demand for legal services on the part of indigents is in regard to family problems. In its first six weeks of operation, 84 percent of the cases were requests for divorce. Of eighty-six cases, sixty-three were for divorce, and nine were custody and support actions. This startling experience had its counterpart in England where in 1950, when legal services were provided for the poor, 80 percent of the cases first reported were for divorce, although the percentage subsequently leveled off at about 40 percent.

In New York City, the experience of the Mobilization for Youth project has been that the poor, if they ever consult lawyers, tend to delay until they are confronted with a crisis. Domestic relations cases and claims for support predominate "because the lower the average income the higher the rate of broken families." Before the advent of the poverty program, however, legal aid services in the vast majority of cities having legal aid were not provided for divorce or annulment cases, although in some instances non-support cases were handled by legal aid. Regardless of the motivations or rationale behind the policy decision not to provide legal aid for divorce cases, the practical consequence inevitably was to force the poor to by-pass law and to perpetuate "common law" marriage and "common law" divorce. * * *

It may be argued that economic compulsion to remain married and the expense of divorce serve the socially desirable purpose of promoting family stability. In our society, however, such rarely is the case. In real life, the parties become estranged, and when able to do so form new informal family relationships. Poverty usually promotes extra-legal action rather than a resignation to and endurance of an intolerable situation. The poor resort to desertion and propagate illegitimate children in large measure because law has priced itself out of the market. The law itself is not discriminatory, but in operation it produces discrimination because historically the indigent cannot afford the luxury of formal justice.

ALIMONY, SUPPORT, AND POVERTY

Professor tenBroek in his discussion and analysis of the origin, development, and present status of a "dual system" of family law, summarizes the differences between the two systems as follows:

> One is public, the other private. One deals with expenditure and conservation of public funds and is heavily political and measurably penal. The other deals with the distribution of family funds, focuses on the rights and responsibilities of family members, and is civil, nonpolitical, and less penal. One is for underprivileged and deprived families; the other for the more comfortable and fortunate.[41]

The historical origins of public assistance and the husband's duty to support his family are traced to the Elizabethan Poor Laws, whereas matrimonial property law and alimony are derived from the common law and statute. Professor tenBroek's conclusion that these separate systems are "inherently unequal" and that poverty is always an arbitrary criterion for governmental classification that poses an issue under the equal protection clause, has been challenged.[42] In fact it has been said in rebuttal that "indigence is not yet the source of a right to demand benefits, supported by a correlative governmental duty to provide them. But no one can doubt that government may choose to create certain benefits and make them available only to the indigent; too much

41 tenBroek, California's Dual System of Family Law: Its Origin, Development and Present Status, 16 Stan.L.Rev. 257, 257–258 (1965) pt. 1.

42 Lewis & Levy, Family Law and Welfare Policies—The Case for "Dual Systems," 54 Calif.L.Rev. 751 (1966). . . .

governmental action is based on the essentially unchallenged assumption that it may."

* * *

* * * How does the dual system perceived by tenBroek work out in practice? He points out that the family law of the poor reflects a different conception of marital rights and duties relating to property and support. Husband and wife are not seen as semi-independent partners, standing in a contractual relationship to each other, but as having a single, undivided, and unseparated interest in a common pool of family resources derived from the income of both spouses. The family law of the poor places greater emphasis upon the community, less upon the individuals; greater emphasis upon meeting the needs of both spouses for support, less upon individual rights to separate property and income. Only after family resources are depleted may public assistance be obtained. All of this, according to tenBroek, flows from the traditional policy of minimizing the public cost of supporting the poor and first tapping whatever family resources are available.

It is true that initially, under the Poor Laws, the husband's obligation to support his family was imposed by the temporal courts in order to reimburse the parish for its expenditures in maintaining his family. The common law action by creditors for necessaries was the only other sanction recognized.[48] The ecclesiastical courts, however, also recognized a hus-

band's moral obligation to support his family and applied their own sanctions to compel him to do so. It also should be remembered that the duty to support and the sanctions for its enforcement were developed at a time when the husband was lord and master and upon marriage acquired the wife's personalty, except her paraphernalia, and took over the management of her realty, pocketing the rents and profits therefrom. This vestige of feudalism, although mitigated for the wealthy by trustee devices recognized in chancery, had profound consequences under the common law, and despite Married Women's Property Acts, traces of it persist to this day. For purposes of the present discussion, however, the important thing is that although reimbursement of the parish may have been the original basis for the husband's duty to support his family, in time his duty to support came to be regarded as reciprocal to his control, management, and ownership of matrimonial property. Such was true, with qualifications, with reference to both his duty to support and his duty to pay alimony in the event of a divorce *a mensa et thoro*. Perhaps there was no early common law sanction closely resembling those imposed under modern support and welfare laws because the ecclesiastical courts claimed jurisdiction over such marital offenses as desertion and nonsupport, and there was no temporal interest perceived until parish expenditures under the Poor Laws led naturally to a demand for reimbursement instead of the ecclesiastical sanction of penance.

Insofar as the Poor Laws and welfare legislation treat husband and wife as partners and as having a single, undivided, and unseparated interest in a common pool of family resources, it may be argued that this system better reflects contemporary social and individual values. The community property regime may be more in accord with the expectations and roles

---

[48] Paulsen, Support Rights and Duties, 9 Vand.L.Rev. 709 (1956). It has been suggested that the duty of support flows from the wife's common law position as a near-chattel. Crozier, Marital Support, 15 B.U. L.Rev. 28 (1935). It also has been claimed that the duty is founded on feudal principles. A Support and Wife's Duty to Render Services, 29 Va.L.Rev. 857 (1943). Actually, however, the true basis for the duty is that it is a fair return for the ownership and control over her property which he obtains by marriage.

of modern middle class Americans who tend to view marriage as a partnership enterprise with a division of labor and as entailing mutual obligations and privileges. In practice, the matrimonial property law of a majority of states tends to favor the husband at the expense of the wife, although such undue preference may be compensated for in the rules pertaining to alimony. It might be socially desirable to place alimony on a more realistic basis by which actual need and ability to pay are the paramount considerations (and the award may be to either spouse), but also to adopt the community property concept for the distribution of property upon divorce and annulment. The current utilization of alimony to compensate for the inequity occasioned by obsolete matrimonial property laws causes a great deal of difficulty and confusion, whereas if the termination of a marriage were viewed as the dissolution of a partnership, contemporary notions of the economic nature of the marriage relationship would be better served.

It may be persuasively argued that the economics of family law in most states illustrate two wrongs trying to make it right. The wife ordinarily is at a disadvantage insofar as distribution or partitioning of property is concerned; the husband frequently is victimized by the law of support and alimony. Because of Married Women's Property Acts, there no longer is a reciprocal basis for the husband's support and alimony obligation. The notion that such duties persist without regard to the means or earning potential of the wife is difficult to justify in an era when employment opportunities for women may be equal to or exceed those for men.

Another difference between support obligations under welfare laws and those imposed by other laws is the effect given to marital fault. Fault may be relatively insignificant under welfare laws, and a wronged spouse may be required to pay minimal support to a wrongdoer. Although such a policy may have been motivated by the desire to decrease assistance costs, it makes good sense to stress actual need and ability to pay, since such issues are easier to resolve than the elusive problem of marital fault. In the case of alimony, and to some extent in non-support cases, fault becomes a crucial issue and a red herring that impairs economic justice. Moreover, fault need not be given such effect, for even under parliamentary divorce the guilty wife got a "compassionate allowance."

In addition to the greater emphasis on fault in divorce law, there also are differences as to the criteria employed for determining what the extent of the obligation is, who the obligors are, and which courts process the case. The so-called "means test," that is, whether a person has sufficient means and falls within a designated family relationship, controls the support obligation under welfare legislation. In the case of alimony, the commonly accepted standard is that the wife, where possible, is to be awarded a sum that will enable her to live in the style and manner she enjoyed during coverture. In most states alimony is awarded only to a wife or former wife, whereas under welfare legislation a wife of sufficient means may be ordered to contribute minimal support for a destitute husband. Some welfare laws also compel either or both parents to contribute to the support or maintenance of adult children who otherwise may become public charges, or compel children to contribute to the support of destitute parents.[57] The legal

---

[57] tenBroek (pt. 3), supra note 41, at 645–46, criticizes saddling relatives with responsibility and cites welfare authorities to the same effect. He says that "liability of relatives creates and increases family dissension and controversy, weakens and de-

obligation also may be extended to step-parents and may run between grandparents and grandchildren. In states such as New York, a different court processes support cases; divorce cases are handled by a higher court in the judicial hierarchy. The clientele, procedure, and courtroom atmosphere is substantially different in the two courts, the support court ordinarily serving a lower socio-economic strata than the divorce court. Typically, in metropolitan support courts, irate wives queue up for the "instant justice" that is forced down the throats of embittered husbands.

In the case of the very poor, contact with family law, when it does occur, usuailly is made in support court, where the "means test" is employed and the question of marital fault may not be relevant, and where the primary purpose is to tap a possible source of funds before the destitute relative is entitled to public assistance. Although this primary purpose for invoking the jurisdiction of the support court is properly challenged by tenBroek and defended by others, both the "means test" and the subordination of the fault issue are concepts which could improve the rules pertaining to alimony.

* * *

The assumption in both our welfare law and alimony law that upon marriage a husband is saddled with a lifelong duty to support a wife or ex-wife who does not remarry is most questionable in an age when women have clamored for and achieved equality. Such an assumption makes women more equal than equal. Even if the husband's obligation is conditioned upon actual need and ability to

stroys family ties at the very time and in the very circumstances when they are most needed, imposes an undue burden on the poor * * * and is therefore socially undesirable, financially unproductive, and administratively unfeasible."

pay, the assumed obligation is questionable. It is an incident of status rather than of contract. Even the economic basis of the assumption is suspect, due to the notorious difficulties in collecting support and alimony awards. * * *

In the case of the more prosperous, the husband's duty to support or pay alimony may be an unpleasant but tolerable burden, but where a poor or low income husband is involved, even a minimal order may constitute a great hardship or impossible burden. Of necessity, he may become a fugitive. Moreover, if he remarries or establishes a new family, further complications inevitably arise, making his primary obligation to the first family unrealistic. In short, both support and alimony law occasion hardship to poor and lower income husbands and in application often force the man into defiance of the law or prevent him from living in dignity. Either a "means test" should be employed in a realistic fashion, or a new approach should be made to the problem of separated or divorced families. It might be possible to follow the example of unemployment compensation and to devise some form of social security insurance against family breakdown. Husbands might welcome such a plan; it might be actuarily sound, and it would be more certain than compliance with support orders. The objection that such an insurance plan would precipitate divorce or family breakdown is unrealistic.

* * *

CHILD CUSTODY AND POVERTY

Custody disputes are rarely litigated among the poor and when they do arise they usually occur otherwise than as an incident to divorce. Of course, with increased free legal services to the poor, it may be anticipated that there will be an increase in such litigation. At the present time, however, a non-judicial issue over custody is more apt to arise as an incident in the administration of the AFDC program.

For example, welfare regulations may require that before AFDC may be awarded, the case worker must decide whether a bona fide offer of a free home made by a parent, relative, or other person should be considered a "resource." [70] A mother who has become destitute may be denied AFDC because of the availability of other resources. Such denials may be a lever to force the mother to give custody to the father or some other relative. Obviously, the child's best interests should be the controlling principle, and the grant or withdrawal of AFDC funds should not be utilized to control custody or to force a mother to give up her children. Nor should withdrawal of assistance funds be used as leverage to force marital reconciliations.

The actual custody of children also is affected in some states by a one-year residency requirement for granting public assistance. This requirement is an inhospitable survivor of the Elizabethan Poor Laws' "settlement" principle. The migration of the mother may be inhibited and she may be deterred from moving to a better labor market, or she may have to place her children with someone else if she moves, because AFDC will be unavailable at the new location. Both the "free home" and residency limitations reflect the economizing or "minimizing the cost" orientation of our welfare laws and in operation lend themselves to prejudiced application.

It should be noted, however, that the AFDC program, designed to permit children to be cared for in the home, is a tremendous improvement over the situation which prevailed when poor children were placed in orphanages. Under AFDC the mother may be able to maintain

the household, although to some extent her parental control is subject to the guidance of social workers who may intervene and give advice or pass judgment upon household management, child rearing, and budget matters. Such intervention may be a welcome service or busybody snooping, depending upon the circumstances.

In a few custody cases poverty may be a factor in determining placement. To some extent it is tied in with such proper criteria as the wholesomeness of the home environment and other factors pertaining to the child's welfare. For example, in a recent North Carolina case the custody of a child was transferred from the mother to the father where it was shown that the mother lived in a trailer, worked long hours as a waitress, and earned only $17.96 a week.[73] The father lived with his parents in a large house where the child would have her own room. In another recent case,[74] the court refused to change custody from the father where he maintained a good home and the mother, who had remarried, worked from late afternoon until midnight. The California court in Harris v. Harris,[75] changed custody from the mother to the father, who was a doctor with a good income, where it was shown that the children were neglected, dressed poorly, and lived in a house without toilet facilities, and that the mother when drunk lay around the house nude, and sometimes stayed out all night with men. A Pennsylvania mother, who lived in a trailer camp, also lost the custody of her six-year-old daughter to the father where it was shown that

[70] Kay & Philips, Poverty and the Law of Custody, 54 Calif.L.Rev. 717, 727 (1966).

[73] Matter of Teresa Ann Bowman, 264 N. C. 590, 142 S.E.2d 349 (1965).

[74] Grace v. Cummings, 253 Miss. 794, 179 So.2d 836 (1965).

[75] 186 Cal.App.2d 788, 9 Cal.Rptr. 300 (Dist.Ct.App.1960).

she neglected the child and frequently took her to bars.[76]

* * *

SOCIAL CLASS AND ADOPTION

Class and race distinctions have a profound effect upon placement and adoption. There is a constant demand for, and a relatively short supply of, white children born to middle class mothers. There also may be a lesser market for the children of poor white mothers. In the case of non-white poverty groups, however, there is virtually no demand.[78] Mothers from the latter class often are not permitted to relinquish their children to agencies for adoption because of the practical impossibility of locating adoptive homes. About 90 percent of adopted children are white although 60 percent of all illegitimate children are non-white. Probably no more than 500 to 1,000 families in the United States have taken multiracial children for adoption.[79]

In addition to the discriminatory effect of current demand, the rules for matching the adopted child to the adopting parents may have the same effect, whether intended or not. The attempt to match ethnic background, religion, physical characteristics, intelligence, and the like restricts the opportunity for placement and the opportunity to adopt. Probably, in most states welfare agencies would not place a Negro child in a white home, or a white child in a Negro home, regardless of the wishes of the parties or the suitability of the home.[80] * * *

* * * There is a need for critical judicial and legislative re-evaluation of the criteria applied in adoption and custody placements to discern which rules are reasonable or unreasonable in a democratic society. It is not surprising that the press and the public became angry over Commissioner Fitzsimmons' initial refusal to permit the adoption of four-year-old, blonde Beth Liuni by forty-eight-year-old, dark complexioned parents.[82] The irrelevancy of coloration in that case was obvious when compared with their shared mutual love and affection. * * * Due process and equal protection concepts should be applied to child placement. * * * It *is* a denial of equal protection to discriminate by arbitrary classification so that Negro children cannot be placed in white homes that welcome them.

So far we have been looking at the function of the agency and the courts' function in adoption cases and the discrimination that may be built into the law or rules and regulations. It also is of interest that the institution of adoption may mean different things in different social classes. Professor Jeffery, a distinguished sociologist, has pointed out that the adoptive parents from the upper class usually are childless and unrelated

---

[76] Commonwealth v. Sabo, 198 Pa.Super. 161, 181 A.2d 921 (1962).

[78] See Kay & Philips, supra note 70, at 738.

[79] Time, January 27, 1967, p. 76.

[80] See Katz, Judicial and Statutory Trends in the Law of Adoption, 51 Geo.L.J. 64, 75–77 (1962), and for an enlightened decision, see In re Adoption of a Minor, 228 F.2d 446 (D.C.Cir.1955). The Standards for Adoption promulgated by the Childhood Welfare League of America state that racial background in itself should not be a major criterion in the selection of a home for a child.

[82] See Fitzsimmons' v. Liuni, 51 Misc.2d 96 (Family Ct., Ulster County 1966), rev'd, 274 N.Y.S.2d 798 (App.Div.1966). The January 17, 1967, issue of The New York Times reported that Commissioner Fitzsimmons' reluctantly signed the necessary papers so that Beth might be adopted by the Liuni family with whom she has lived for four and a half years, having been placed in that home when she was five days old. Commissioner Fitzsimmons had opposed the adoption as an "improper placement" because of the difference in color of Beth and the Liunis, the age (48) of the adopting parents, and Mrs. Liuni's prior hospitalization for emotional or mental illness.

to the out-of-wedlock children they adopt, and that the adoption is for the purpose of acquiring a child for the family, i. e., to create a new social and familial relationship where one did not previously exist.[83] The middle class, however, usually adopts from the "divorce" and "parent" rather than the "out-of-wedlock" category, and typically the natural mother after divorce remarries and the second husband adopts the child. The social function is to legalize an existing social relationship. Lower class adoptions usually are from the "other" and "family" categories; the typical case is one where the children are in the care of relatives. The purpose may be to qualify for relief benefits, and the social function may be to provide a type of social service for dependent and neglected children.

According to this study, in their operation adoption laws tend to accord a service to middle and upper class families. Unwed middle and upper class mothers have a seller's market for their illegitimate offspring. The children of the poor and minority groups do not enjoy similar advantages. The consequences of illegitimacy are alleviated for some, but not for others. The unwanted child of a college co-ed may readily find a good home, but the chances are that the child of a domestic must be absorbed into a family which already has too many mouths to feed. Of course, in human terms, the latter home may be better because of warmth and affection, but it also may be an environment which spawns desperation and delinquency. We do not begrudge any children their opportunity to acquire adoptive parents; we merely lament the fact that the opportunity is not open to all and that arbitrary or discriminatory barriers all too often have been raised to prevent the placement of children in good homes. * * *

---

[83] See Jeffery, Social Class and Adoption Petitioners, 9 Social Problems 354 (1962).

PAULSEN, JUVENILE COURTS, FAMILY COURTS, AND THE POOR MAN †

54 Calif.L.Rev. 694 (1966).*

I

THE SETTING IN THE COURT

"IT IS A POOR MAN'S COURT." Martin Tolchin, a reporter for the New York Times, referred to the New York Family Court.[1] The judgment was correct when it was written in 1964 and it is correct today. For evidence we need look no further than the waiting rooms of that court and their population. Each morning a hundred stories of poverty are suggested by the faces and the personal effects of those who wait to appear before the judges. The cold atmosphere of the room only intensifies the feelings of helplessness, fear, and frustration which accompany poverty. "[C]ourtrooms are bare, toilet walls are defaced. The court's waiting rooms resemble those at hospital clinics. Negro and Puerto Rican families predominate, and many regard the trappings of justice with bitterness and suspicion."[2]

Impersonal attendants perform their duties with clipped routine, underscoring alienation. In the waiting rooms of the larger New York boroughs it is not unusual for fifty or sixty persons to be gathered. As each case is called the name

---

† The material for this article was largely taken from the New York Family Court and from the author's personal observation in that court. It is submitted that most juvenile courts in large cities would leave similar impressions. The Family Court has jurisdiction over delinquency, neglect, support, adoption, paternity, and family offense matters, but not annulment, separation, or divorce.

* Copyright 1966 by the California Law Review; reprinted by permission.

[1] Tolchin, Experts Wonder if Family Court is Doing its Job, N. Y. Times, Jan. 18, 1964, p. 24, col. 3.

[2] Ibid.

II

THE RESPONDENTS IN THE COURT

A. The Juvenile Court

of the respondent is shouted out in full voice by a court employee dressed like a police officer. The name of the youngster is likely to be sounded a second time if he does not leap forward immediately, lest a moment be wasted. Observers find it ironic to recall the words of the Illinois Family Court Act, which expressed the intended spirit of the New York law as well: "The children * * * as far as practicable * * * shall be treated not as criminals but as children in need of aid, encouragement and guidance." [3]

The courtrooms themselves are scarcely less disconcerting than the waiting rooms. In a busy court all sorts of court attendants and probation officers come and go during a hearing. Respondents, I am certain, would be surprised to learn that the proceeding is a "private" hearing.

The Honorable Florence Kelley, Administrative Judge of the New York Family Court, put it: "No one is at home in this court." A poor family brought before a juvenile court judge journeys into a foriegn land. In New York City, the judge, a relatively well-paid member of the upper middle class, is a college graduate and the possessor of a law degree. He is, thus, separated by education and way of life from most of those who are paraded before him every day. The probation officer to whom a youngster may be assigned is also a college graduate. Though he may have been recruited from the same economic and social class as the youngster in his charge, he has by effort and energy risen from it. Even the court officers and clerks are better paid and, to some extent, better educated than most of those who come with their children. The poor are certainly not "at home" in this atmosphere with these people.

* * *

Delinquent conduct is, of course, found among children of the upper and middle classes, but official rates of delinquency are higher among the poor. "Sociologists know that delinquency rates rise in disorganized neighborhoods, those without a stable culture, inhabited by socially and economically disadvantaged groups. There are many such areas in New York City; their rates of delinquency and adolescent crime are high." [6] A map showing the distribution of delinquency in New York City (based on police records and Children's Court cases in 1958) reveals that the worst areas were three neighborhoods of great poverty: Harlem, the South Bronx, and the Bedford-Stuyvesant area of Brooklyn.[7]

Certainly in the great cities of the nation the overwhelming number of children processed through the juvenile court are the children of the poor. The upper and middle classes show surprising agility in keeping their delinquent children out of the court. In some cases we can be sure that a petition has not been filed against an offending middle-class youngster because restitution has been supplied to the victim of the child's misconduct. In other cases, the upper and middle-class youths have been shielded against juvenile court adjudications by their parents' ability to provide privately arranged corrective treatment. After an adjudication, a person of means can often arrange for the use of private facilities not available to the poor.

One imaginative researcher has called our attention to the fact that the very

[3] Ill.Laws 1953, § 1, at 1089.

[6] Juvenile Delinquency Evaluation Project of the City of New York, Final Report No. II, Delinquency in the Great City 1 (1961).

[7] Id. at 13.

philosophy of the juvenile court with its emphasis on "saving" the child, on treatment rather than punishment, may itself be puzzling or, indeed, seem foolish to the young respondents.[8] Most youngsters raised on the street know that aggressive acts are followed by swift retribution. They not only know it, but they accept it as right. When a boy from the slums is ushered into the court because of unlawful conduct, he may think it strange to be confronted by officials moved by a philosophy of help rather than punishment. The skepticism of the youngster, it is fair to guess, colors his perception of the court's task. Measures designed to help or to provide treatment can very easily be perceived as punishment, simply because it is incredible to the juvenile that anything but punishment would follow the acts in which he was engaged. Perhaps, in the final analysis, this difficulty of communication is not so common because many courts are a good bit more punitive than the official theory admits.

Dr. Elliott Studt has a further point. She argues that today teenagers are bored, contemptuous, and impatient with the juvenile court because it is degrading for a teenager to be dealt with as a "child." Teenagers are likely to see the court and its staff "as inept and essentially unable to deal with realities." For example, she reports a comment about a probation officer: "I guess he tried to help. Mostly he lectured, I guess." The juvenile court is also likely to be unpopular with parents because:

[T]hese parents feel that the judge and his representative, the probation officer, have taken over in the name of the community the functions and responsibilities of parenthood * * *. Increased inadequacy, unnecessary dependency, a flagrant refusal to perform normal parental duties, and a hostile use of the court against the child are possible behavioral results.

These views suggest that the aims of the court have misfired in relation to the respondents and their families. What the court attempts is sometimes frustrated by the very tools it uses.

The poor may be the principal customers of juvenile court services, but the operation of the court generally is not arranged for their convenience. In most cases the chief concern of those who administer the court is to meet the convenience of the judges and the staff. An enormous amount of time is wasted by the parents of children pulled into court. Little or no attempt is made to space appointments for court hearings. Everyone is told to come at 9:30 in the morning, and the reception rooms fill with employed mothers and fathers who lose more wages with each passing hour.

Waiting to appear in court is not only expensive for those the court must serve, but the waiting often proves to be futile. A case scheduled to be heard may not be ready and an adjournment will have to be ordered, with the consequent loss of another day's pay for parents. Children's courts in this country generally do not function with the equivalent of the prosecutor, someone who clearly carries the task of preparing the "state's case"— making certain that necessary witnesses are present on a given day and that those witnesses can establish the basis for juvenile court action. Postponement can be a disaster for a family of limited means, supported by an income of wages paid by the hour.

The fact that those who go to a juvenile court are generally the poor (in the big cities at least) transforms the court into a class institution, a fact which may inhibit its development and, indeed, may have an impact on all sorts of legislative

---

8 See Younghusband, The Dilemma of the Juvenile Court, 33 Social Service Rev. 10, 14–17 (1959).

choices. The following quotation is found in a confidential mimeographed report of an important study group in one state considering the question whether child abuse cases should be reported to a department of social services or to the police. "According to statistics, many child abuse cases come from within families well-placed financially and of repute. In considering help to such families, reporting to the police, and taking court actions right away may not be appropriate."

B. The Family Court

If we speak not simply of children's cases in court, but of the adult cases in a family court which does not process divorce or annulment cases, the clear impression remains that the cases heard are those of the poor man. Certainly in New York City the entire Family Court possesses a proletarian flavor. In general, it is the daughters of the poor who bring filiation proceedings. Middle-class people, not deigning to spice their marital arguments with minor assaults, do not generally appear in the Family Offenses Term. Support orders not entered in connection with "matrimonial actions" (annulment, divorce, separation, or dissolution actions, which in New York are heard not in the Family Court but in the Supreme Court) are infrequently sought by persons of means.

In New York, the Family Court and the Surrogate's Court have concurrent jurisdiction over adoptions.[12] According to the original plan, this scheme was to end after two years, on September 1, 1964. From that date forward exclusive jurisdiction was to be lodged in the Family Court. The effective date for ending concurrent jurisdiction has been moved ahead from year to year. Several factors have been responsible for failure to place adoptions exclusively in the Family Court. The surrogates and their

friends at the bar have resisted the move for selfish reasons; some persons have argued that the Family Court in New York City lacked facilities to handle the case load. Yet, in the background was another matter: a feeling that adoptive parents should not find it necessary to "rub elbows" with those who normally occupy the waiting room benches. Indeed, partly in order to meet this point, the newly organized "Adoption Term" in the New York Family Court is presently housed in a building quite apart from any other part of the court.

It is a common belief among New York social workers that the Family Court does not possess annulment, separation, or divorce jurisdiction because of notions related to class divisions. How would it be possible for the judges who preside over the delinquent, the neglected, and husbands who refuse to pay small support orders, to handle intelligently the complex separation agreements of the well-to-do?

III

THE JURISDICTION OF THE JUVENILE COURT

Jurisdictional provisions of a juvenile court act are likely to reach disproportionate numbers of the children of the poor. Juvenile courts throughout the United States may assert authority over "neglected" children. Poor children fall into the "neglect" category more frequently than the offspring of the well-to-do. Parents adjudged guilty of neglect are often self-centered persons, not truly interested in their children, who do not have the means to provide substitutes for ordinary care and affection. An alcoholic mother in a low income family failing to get her children off to school creates a problem of neglect. The alcoholic, suburbanite wife of a successful executive, on the other hand, may be able to avoid the issue by hiring a competent

---

[12] N.Y.Family Ct.Act § 641.

nurse. One suspects that many cases of the physical abuse of children are rooted in the despair occasioned by a lack of means to provide comfort and variety in living.

A statute which defines a neglected child as one who is without proper care because his parent or guardian "neglects or refuses to provide," may sometimes be applied to a youngster with parents who are paupers, not parents who refuse to share what they have. What one regards as proper care may, indeed, be a matter of dispute reflecting class and cultural differences.[13] Standards of child rearing adequate in one cultural setting may seem appalling in another. Neglect defined as raising a child in an environment which is "injurious or dangerous" may create a hazard for parents without means. Unhappily, the environment of the poor is often injurious and dangerous.

It is not suggested that juvenile courts do, in fact, take the children of the poor and give them to the rich. The sheer difficulty of finding new homes for neglected children is a powerful deterrent against pushing the definition of neglect to the limit. Yet the fact remains that a child of parents who are very poor stands in danger of a court-ordered separation from his parents to an extent which children of the middle and upper classes do not.

In defining juvenile delinquency, older juvenile court acts in the United States provide a description of life in the lower economic classes appropriate to a novel by Charles Dickens. The Illinois Juvenile Court Act of 1905 defined a delinquent child as any male over the age of 17 who breaks the law and who:

> knowingly associates with thieves, vicious or immoral persons; or who, without just cause and without consent of its parents or custodian, absents it-

self from its home or place of abode, or who is growing up in idleness or crime; or who knowingly frequents a house of ill-repute; or who knowingly frequents any policy shop or place where any gaming device is operated; or who frequents any saloon or dram shop where intoxicating liquors are sold; or who patronizes or visits any public poolroom or bucket shop; or who wanders about the streets in the night time without being on any lawful business or occupation; or who habitually wanders about any railroad yards or tracks or jumps or attempts to jump onto any moving train; or who enters any car or engine without lawful authority; or who habitually uses vile, obscene, vulgar, profane, or indecent language; or who is guilty of immoral conduct in any public place or about any schoolhouse.

Children so described are hardly drawn from the choir of a fashionable Anglican congregation.

It is true that modern juvenile court acts generally do not contain such old-fashioned phrases and, further, it is true that these provisions have not often been invoked. Nevertheless, the phrases give us insight into the thinking of the founders of the juvenile court movement in respect to the kinds of children for which the court was created.

Jurisdictional formulations of delinquency often include vague phrases such as "engaging in conduct harmful to himself or others," "incorrigible," or "a child who is beyond the control of his parents or other custodian." Certainly such imprecise language has formed the basis for adjudications of delinquency in the case of Negro children engaged in civil rights demonstrations. One suspects that it can often be used generally against the children of the poor. Once more, such language may permit adjudications of delinquency for conduct related to cultural differences between economic classes.

13 See Chilman, Child Rearing and Family Relationship Patterns of the Very Poor, Welfare in Review, Jan. 1965, p. 9.

Legislation does not choose the children who are actually brought into juvenile court. The decision whether to file a delinquency petition against a certain boy, a decision of considerable consequence to the youngster, is ordinarily within the province of the man on the beat. Therefore, an officer's opinion about the behavior of children in his neighborhood becomes an important matter. Indeed, where officers are generally stationed in the community is a factor affecting delinquency rates in so far as those rates are measured by arrests and court appearances. It is disturbing to read the finding of a study of police practices in Allegheny County, Pennsylvania, which asserts that defiance on the part of a youngster will lead to a juvenile court appearance more quickly than any other response.[15] "Such damage to the dignity of the police will lead to court referral even in a minor case." Another study finds that boys who were:

> contrite, respectful and fearful had a greater chance of being released without citation or arrest than another who has committed the same offense, but was rude, obstinate, or even cool, i. e. interacted with the police as if the encounter were a routine event. Further, the youth's demeanor was often mentioned by police officers as the justification for arrest; appearance and stance as indicators of disrespect for conventional values became, for juveniles, a criteria for construing law violation.[16]

It is reasonable to believe that deprived youngsters, reared in an atmosphere mistrustful of law and lawmen, are likely to be seriously disadvantaged by such police attitudes.

IV

THE PROBLEMS OF COURTS FOR CHILDREN AND FAMILIES

Because juvenile courts and family courts serve large numbers of the poor, the poor experience, in full force, the troubles raised by the problems of those courts. Most of the charges made against these courts have spoken of untrained judges whose talents are not wisely used, of careless, slipshod procedure, and of ill-informed dispositional judgments together with inadequate facilities for care and treatment.

A. The Judges

Arguments for the creation of a specialized juvenile court or family court always bring out the point that the cases which come to these courts require a judge with special training and understanding. At the very least, the judge should be able to use expertly the social and psychological information which his staff gathers for him. Making the point real is still a dream in almost every court. By and large, special experience is lacking, politics still plays a major role in judicial selection, understanding and mutual confidence between the judges and the court staff are often absent. In many courts the judges are not specialists at all. In smaller communities juvenile court work will only be a small part of the judge's total caseload. In some city courts, district or circuit court judges rotate in and out of juvenile or family court assignments.

In New York City the family court judges change location from time to time, sitting, for example, two months in Manhattan after two months in the Bronx. One of the most distinguished of the New York justices, the Honorable Justine Wise Polier, reported the results of some research which justified a harsh

---

[15] Goldman, The Differential Selection of Juvenile Offenders for Court Appearances, 1950 (unpublished thesis in Sociology Dep't, University of Chicago), cited in Handler, The Juvenile Court and the Adversary System: Problems of Function and Form, 1965 Wis. L.Rev. 7, 18 n. 52.

[16] Center for the Study of Law and Society, Annual Rep. 1962–63, at 10 (University of California, Berkeley), cited in Handler, supra note 15, at 19 n. 52.

judgment of the practice. "Not infrequently a case was heard by as many as eight or ten judges before final disposition." [17] Judge Polier's research established that "a majority of the children have their cases disposed of by a judge who had not held the initial hearing and had not heard the case on the return of the social investigation during the second month." This rotation system "minimizes the continuity and consistency needed in the handling of cases invoving family relationships." Each new judge confronted with any aspect of a pending juvenile case can only orient himself, as quickly as possible, from written papers without insight gained from personal contact. Furthermore, the probation staff, in attempting to deal with the problems of a single family, are confused and frustrated by the varying attitudes among the judges.

Judge Polier's research, directed to the Juvenile Term of the New York Family Court in Manhattan during 1961, established another striking fact. The twelve judges who sat in Juvenile Term during the year varied greatly in their rate of dismissing petitions alleging juvenile delinquency:

> Twelve judges rotated; each served four or five weeks. The rate of dismissal of children charged with delinquency varied from 2.2 per cent by one judge to 24.9 per cent by another judge; the average was 13.8 per cent. Where neglect was alleged, the rate of dismissal varied from 0.5 per cent to 23.1 per cent; the average was 3.3 per cent.

The Children's Courts Project at the Columbia Law School will soon publish findings which establish the fact of disparity in adjudication rates even more dramatically. These findings suggest, like those of Judge Polier, that in a court founded on the notions that justice

should regard the individual and that results should fit the particular respondent, an exceedingly important factor determining whether or not a youngster is adjudicated a juvenile delinquent is the person of the judge before whom he is called to appear. The "good news" of individualized justice becomes, in the phrase of my associate, Professor Louis Swartz, the "luck of the draw." * * *.

D. Disposition

The catalogue of complaints regarding dispositions in juvenile courts runs from charges of abuse of discretion to an absence of the institutions which might carry out wise judgments.

The flexible powers of the juvenile court have been misused in the south in connection with civil rights demonstrations.[31] The 1965 report of the U. S. Commission on Civil Rights reports that in Jackson, Mississippi, Americus, Georgia, and St. Augustine, Florida, juveniles who had been arrested in demonstrations "were threatened with imprisonment and, as a condition of exoneration or release, were forced to promise that they would not participate in future civil rights activities."

In Jackson, Mississippi, over one-half of the demonstrators arrested were juveniles. Release of the children to their parents was conditioned on the parents doing everything possible to prevent further participation in demonstrations. In Americus, approximately 125 juveniles were arrested and about fifty were placed on probation on condition that they would not associate with certain civil rights leaders.

Many juveniles in Americus were arrested for a long period of time and detained without bail or hearing. The report tells the story of a fourteen-year-old Negro girl who was charged with assault

---

[17] Polier, A view from the Bench 12 (1964).

[31] U. S. Comm'n on Civil Rights, Law Enforcement, A Report on Equal Protection in the South 80–83 (1965).

with intent to kill, unlawful assembly, rioting, and aiding an attempt to escape. Bail was set at 12,000 dollars. She spent eighty-seven days in jail without a hearing.

In St. Augustine the juvenile court judge sent a letter to Negro leaders stating that parents ought not to permit children to take part in demonstrations, after which juveniles in picket lines were removed by the police. Four youngsters who refused to promise that they would refrain from demonstration activity spent six months in the county jail and reform schools until they were released in January 1964.

In Maryland, juveniles who participated in a sit-in were committed to a state training school pending the hearing of an appeal from an adjudication of delinquency. An appeal on this issue was unsuccessful because the Maryland High Court took the view that the trial court had not abused its discretion. It is pleasant to record that after another appeal the adjudications of delinquency were reversed. The adjudications, grounded on a "sit-in," and therefore an alleged criminal trespass, were held to be improper. Entering a theatre without tickets, lying on the theatre floor, and using profane language were, indeed, criminal activities; nevertheless, they were not a basis for a finding of delinquency under the Maryland law. A determination of delinquency in Maryland requires an additional finding by the juvenile court judge that by reason of the offensive act the youngster is "in need of care or treatment * * *." The Maryland court said, "In the main the demonstrations in which they participated were conducted by adults who, although disorderly in many instances, were not engaged in acts involving moral turpitude." The adult demonstrators had either been required to pay minimum fines or the cases had been dismissed. "Incarceration of these children beyond the immed-iate need for their protection could hardly be supported."

* * *

Not only is there a lack of placement facilities in New York for PINS, but placement facilities for certain neglected children are almost nonexistent. It is especially difficult to place neglected children of Puerto Rican and Negro backgrounds, with the result that these children are kept in temporary shelters for very long periods of time. Judge Polier's study of the New York Family Court as of April 30, 1963, found that 14.5 per cent of the Negroes in temporary shelter care had been kept there for over one year. No white child had been in temporary care for such a long time. Only fourteen per cent of white children had been in temporary care for over five months. In contrast, Judge Polier reported, "39.5 per cent of the neglected Negro children and twenty-two per cent of the Puerto Rican children remained in the shelters for six months or more on repeated court remands pending court disposition." She affirmed that in New York there is only one significant shelter boarding home program for non-white neglected children involving long term placement.

"Caseloads in the juvenile term now defy any possibility of probation work." The Polier study discovered that forty-nine New York City juvenile probation officers were carrying caseloads ranging from 117 to 256 children. With such caseloads probation officers can only consult the Social Service Exchange, get a formal report from school, and hold an office interview with the child and one parent. There can be no attempt to study the causes of family problems or to work out a sophisticated plan of treatment.

The probation staff in New York City is not very well-trained. Typically the New York probation officer assigned to work with juveniles has a college degree, but it may represent work in a field quite foreign to social work. The officer may or may not have taken a few professional courses. Usually he has become a probation officer after serving for a number of years as a social investigator in the Welfare Department, thus meeting the experience qualifications of the New York City civil service. Typically, a person on the probation staff with a Master's Degree in social work is a case supervisor and thus one step removed from first-hand contact with the youngsters supposedly to be benefitted by being in the charge of a trained expert.

We perhaps need to be reminded about the shocking state of some of our institutions. A recent magazine article described the main characteristics of Junior Village, an institution for "dependent" or "neglected" children in Washington, D. C. The author asserts that the City of "Washington is running a great factory of retardation and mental illness" because the Village is "too big, too crowded, and desperately understaffed, involuntarily inflicts severe—often permanent damage on small children."

The crowded conditions of Junior Village reflect the fact that foster care is underdeveloped in the nation's capitol. The number of homeless children has been rising, and the number of places to take care of them has not. The problem is particularly acute for Negroes; ninety-seven per cent of the children at Junior Village are Negroes.

In the Village, mental retrogression occurs, it is charged, because the children are isolated "to a degree that would be impossible even in the most disorganized family." The child is parted not only from his parents, but from his brothers and sisters, because the institution segregates children by age and sex. The children are further separated from the adult world by the eight-hour shift. The author argues, "One counselor gets him up in the morning, another puts him to bed

at night, a third appears if he wakes in the night, and the following morning he sees a fourth face because the first counselor has a day off." The birthdays of children are celebrated collectively, one a month, with a communal birthday cake.

The damage to the children is often irreversible. Treatment in Junior Village leaves them impaired "in their ability to receive and return affection, to control their impulses, and to use their minds." Ironically, it is expensive in terms of public money as well as in terms of the waste of human resources to keep a child in an institution. A child costs 300 dollars a month at Junior Village, a handsome sum which few middle-class people are able to mount for their own children's needs.

Clearly, more resources more intelligently used can minimize some of the inconveniences and harms of the present system. Long-term, meaningless detentions in detention facilities can be avoided. Disposition of cases can be speeded up, educational opportunities can be extended. But what of the fundamental point of the reformers? *Do* we or *could* we have the tools for restructuring character by any program, however well-financed?

In 1920, a commentator observed that the juvenile court idea was designed to carry out "the duty of the state to give to the child who has made a slip another chance; to reclaim him, if possible, as a normal, useful member of society, and to shield him from the handicap and baneful atmosphere of criminal courts and jails." [69] How much of the goal is attainable? To some extent, surely, we can "shield him" from the harms and horrors of the criminal jail and the accusing atmosphere of a criminal courtroom. The juvenile court can give the child "who has made a slip" a second chance. We

---

[69] Towne, Shall the Age Jurisdiction of Juvenile Courts be Changed?, 10 J. American Institute Crim.L. and Crim. 493, 497 (1920).

can rely on the warning which a child might take from an appearance in court to educate him a bit. The court mechanism gives us the means whereby the community can respond to a child's harmful conduct, can inform the youngster and other children that such conduct is not condoned, without at the same time taking harmful measures which might themselves create more trouble. The third task, the task to "reclaim him," is the troublesome one. We of course "reclaim" by giving a second chance and by preventing the harms the criminal law system can do, but can we in any other sense "reclaim" great numbers of children, and if so, by what techniques? The question and the challenge which we put to the reformers is precisely here. What are the means of change? Do they work? How expensive are they? How much is hope and how much is fact? The questions are put in no spirit of hostility. Those of us in the law who have been concerned with juveniles and their court would like nothing better than to hear reassuring, affirmative answers.

Any answer which requires thousands of dollars of treatment for each offender of any serious degree is in practical effect a useless response. A recommendation of one hundred sessions of therapy does not give an item for mass production. We in 1966 seek with somewhat less assurance than in 1900 a hopeful answer to the question: What can the clinic do to change character? A useful answer will have to produce a correctional flivver—a useful, inexpensive, sturdy model (or line of models) which, because of its low cost, can be made available to all.

If we lack the means to perform miracles of human reclamation, should the juvenile court experiment be abandoned rather than merely modified by the introduction of more formal procedure derived from the criminal courts and by becoming somewhat less ready to under-take drastic intervention? In my view, such an abandonment would be quite wrong. An important reason why the juvenile court has survived is the grim prospect of the alternative. For example, in October 1965, a fourteen-year-old Colorado boy began serving a four to five year sentence in the state penitentiary on a rape charge growing out of an assault on a nine-year-old girl. The maximum penalty for the offense was five years. The judge could have sent the boy to a reformatory where better facilities for rehabilitation were available. Nevertheless, the Colorado law permits the imposition of such severe punitive treatment.

The young people who are brought to court, so many of them the children of the poor, would hardly benefit from being taken to a tribunal dealing with adult criminals. Juvenile courts, imperfect as they are, surely prevent some harm simply by doing less damage than the criminal courts would do to children in their middle teens. Acts done by teenagers may cause great damage, thus evoking cries of rage from the community. Often the juvenile courts, by an adjudication of delinquency, avoid harsh regimens of treatment. A great many youthful offenses are not significant indices of bad character. As to these, the juvenile court can reassure the community without destroying the life of the youngster by making an adjudication and thereafter leaving the youngster to treat himself.[72]

---

[72] Cf. Note, Juvenile Delinquents: The Police, State Courts, and Individualized Justice, 79 Harv.L.Rev. 775, 810 (1966): "If the system is maintained in the face of extremely limited treatment facilities and incompetent prediction methods, it might be well to establish a 'presumption' that a juvenile involved is more likely than not to reform himself as he matures. Considering the present number of police and intake 'settlements' and court 'continuances,' it may be said that such a 'presumption' is already in effect informally; but express recognition of the desirability of keeping the child out of treatment may have a good deal of value."

B. ACCESS TO THE COURTS IN RELATION TO FAMILY PROBLEMS

BODDIE v. CONNECTICUT

The Supreme Court of the United States, 1971.
401 U.S. 371, 91 Sup.Ct. 780, 28 L.Ed.2d 113.

Mr. Justice HARLAN delivered the opinion of the Court.

Appellants, welfare recipients residing in the State of Connecticut, brought this action in the Federal District Court for the District of Connecticut on behalf of themselves and others similarly situated, challenging, as applied to them, certain state procedures for the commencement of litigation, including requirements for payment of court fees and costs for service of process, that restrict their access to the courts in their effort to bring an action for divorce.

It appears from the briefs and oral argument that the average cost to a litigant for bringing an action for divorce is $60.

There is no dispute as to the inability of the named appellants in the present case to pay either the court fees required by statute or the cost incurred for the service of process. The affidavits in the record establish that appellants' welfare income in each instance barely suffices to meet the costs of the daily essentials of life. * * *

Appellants * * * commenced this action in the Federal District Court seeking a judgment declaring that Connecticut's statute and service of process provisions, "requiring payment of court fees and expenses as a condition precedent to obtaining court relief [are] unconstitutional [as] applied to these indigent [appellants] and all other members of the class which they represent."
* * *

Our conclusion is that, given the basic position of the marriage relationship in this society's hierarchy of values and the concomitant state monopolization of the means for legally dissolving this relationship, due process does prohibit a State from denying, solely because of inability to pay, access to its courts to individuals who seek judicial dissolution of their marriages.

I

At its core, the right to due process reflects a fundamental value in our American constitutional system. Our understanding of that value is the basis upon which we have resolved this case.

Perhaps no characteristic of an organized and cohesive society is more fundamental than its erection and enforcement of a system of rules defining the various rights and duties of its members, enabling them to govern their affairs and definitively settle their differences in an orderly, predictable manner. Without such a "legal system," social organization and cohesion are virtually impossible; with the ability to seek regularized resolution of conflicts individuals are capable of interdependent action that enables them to strive for achievements without the anxieties that would beset them in a disorganized society. Put more succinctly, it is this injection of the rule of law that allows society to reap the benefits of rejecting what political theorists call the "state of nature."

American society, of course, bottoms its systematic definition of individual rights and duties, as well as its machinery for dispute settlement, not on custom or the will of strategically placed individuals, but on the common-law model. It is to courts, or other quasi-judicial official bodies, that we ultimately look for the implementation of a regularized, orderly process of dispute settlement. Within this framework, those who wrote our original Constitution, in the Fifth Amendment, and later those who drafted the Fourteenth Amendment, recognized the centrality of the concept of due process in the operation of this system. Without this guarantee that one may not be deprived of his rights, neither liberty nor property, without due process of law, the State's monopoly over techniques for binding conflict resolution could hardly be said to be acceptable under our scheme of things. Only by providing that the social enforcement mechanism must function strictly within these bounds can we hope to maintain an ordered society that is also just. It is upon this premise that this Court has through years of adjudication put flesh upon the due process principle.

Such litigation has, however, typically involved rights of defendants—not, as here, persons seeking access to the judicial process in the first instance. This is because our society has been so structured that resort to the courts is not usually the only available, legitimate means of resolving private disputes. Indeed, private structuring of individual relationships and repair of their breach is largely encouraged in American life, subject only to the caveat that the formal judicial process, if resorted to, is paramount. Thus this Court has seldom been asked to view access to the courts as an element of due process. The legitimacy of the State's monopoly over techniques of final dispute settlement, even where some are denied access to its use, stands unimpaired where recognized, effective alternatives for the adjustment of differences remain. But the successful invocation of this governmental power by plaintiffs has often created serious problems for defendants' rights. For at that point, the judicial proceeding becomes the only effective means of resolving the dispute at hand and denial of a defendant's full access to that process raises grave problems for its legitimacy.

Recognition of this theoretical framework illuminates the precise issue presented in this case. As this Court on more than one occasion has recognized, marriage involves interests of basic importance in our society. See, e. g., Loving v. Virginia, 388 U.S. 1 (1967); Skinner v. Oklahoma, 316 U.S. 535 (1942); Meyer v. Nebraska, 262 U.S. 390 (1923). It is not surprising, then, that the States have seen fit to oversee many aspects of that institution. Without a prior judicial imprimatur, individuals may freely enter into and rescind commercial contracts, for example, but we are unaware of any jurisdiction where private citizens may covenant for or dissolve marriages without state approval. Even where all substantive requirements are concededly met, we know of no instance where two consenting adults may divorce and mutually liberate themselves from the constraints of legal obligations that go with marriage, and more fundamentally the prohibition against remarriage, without invoking the State's judicial machinery.

Thus, although they assert here due process rights as would-be plaintiffs, we think appellants' plight, because resort to the state courts is the only avenue to dissolution of their marriages, is akin to that of defendants faced with exclusion from the only forum effectively empowered to settle their disputes. Resort to the judicial process by these plaintiffs is no more voluntary in a realistic sense than that of the defendant called upon to defend his interests in court. For both groups this process is not only the paramount dispute-settlement technique, but, in fact, the only available one. In this posture we think that this appeal is properly to be resolved in light of the principles enunciated in our due process decisions that delimit rights of defendants compelled to litigate their differences in the judicial forum.

II

* * *

A

Prior cases establish, first, that due process requires, at a minimum, that absent a countervailing state interest of overriding significance, persons forced to settle their claims of right and duty through the judicial process must be given a meaningful opportunity to be heard. * * *

B

Our cases further establish that a statute or a rule may be held constitutionally invalid as applied when it operates to deprive an individual of a protected right although its general validity as a measure enacted in the legitimate exercise of state power is beyond question. Thus, in cases involving religious freedom, free speech or assembly, this Court has often held that a valid statute was unconstitutionally applied in particular circumstances because it interfered with an individual's exercise of those rights.

III

Drawing upon the principles established * * * we conclude that the State's refusal to admit these appellants to its courts, the sole means in Connecticut for obtaining a divorce, must be regarded as the equivalent of denying them an opportunity to be heard upon their claimed right to a dissolution of their marriages, and, in the absence of a sufficient countervailing justification for the State's action, a denial of due process.[8]

[8] At least one court has already recognized the special nature of the divorce action. Justice Sobel in a case like that before us took note of the State's involvement in the marital relationship:

"Marriage is clearly marked with the public interest. In this State, a marriage cannot be dissolved except by 'due judicial proceedings. * * *' We have erected by

The arguments for this kind of fee and cost requirement are that the State's interest in the prevention of frivolous litigation is substantial, its use of court fees and process costs to allocate scarce resources is rational, and its balance between the defendant's right to notice and the plaintiff's right to access is reasonable.

In our opinion, none of these considerations is sufficient to override the interest of these plaintiff-appellants in having access to the only avenue open for dissolving their allegedly untenable marriages. Not only is there no necessary connection between a litigant's assets and the seriousness of his motives in bringing suit, but it is here beyond present dispute that appellants bring these actions in good faith. Moreover, other alternatives exist to fees and cost requirements as a means for conserving the time of courts and protecting parties from frivolous litigation, such as penalties for false pleadings or affidavits, and actions for malicious prosecution or abuse of process, to mention only a few. In the same vein we think that reliable alternatives exist to service of process by a state-paid sheriff if the State is unwilling to assume the cost of official service. This is perforce true of service by publication which is the method of notice least calculated to bring to a potential defendant's attention the pendency of judicial proceedings. * * * We think in this case service at defendant's last known address by mail and posted notice is equally effective as publication in a newspaper.

statute a money hurdle to such dissolution by requiring in many circumstances the service of a summons by publication * *. This hurdle is an effective barrier to [plaintiff's] access to the courts. The loss of access to the courts in an action for divorce is a right of substantial magnitude when only through the courts may redress or relief be obtained." Jeffreys v. Jeffreys, 58 Misc.2d 1045, 1056, 296 N.Y.S.2d 74, 87 (1968). * * *

We are thus left to evaluate the State's asserted interest in its fee and cost requirements as a mechanism of resource allocation or cost recoupment. Such a justification was offered and rejected in Griffin v. Illinois, 351 U.S. 12 (1956). In *Griffin* it was the requirement of a transcript beyond the means of the indigent that blocked access to the judicial process. While in *Griffin* the transcript could be waived as a convenient but not necessary predicate to court access, here the State invariably imposes the costs as a measure of allocating its judicial resources. Surely, then, the rationale of *Griffin* covers this case.

IV

In concluding that the Due Process Clause of the Fourteenth Amendment requires that these appellants be afforded an opportunity to go into court to obtain a divorce, we wish to re-emphasize that we go no further than necessary to dispose of the case before us, a case where the *bona fides* of both appellants' indigency and desire for divorce are here beyond dispute. We do not decide that access for all individuals to the courts is a right that is, in all circumstances, guaranteed by the Due Process Clause of the Fourteenth Amendment so that its exercise may not be placed beyond the reach of any individual, for, as we have already noted, in the case before us this right is the exclusive precondition to the adjustment of a fundamental human relationship. The requirement that these appellants resort to the judicial process is entirely a state-created matter. Thus we hold only that a State may not, consistent with the obligations imposed on it by the Due Process Clause of the Fourteenth Amendment, pre-empt the right to dissolve this legal relationship without affording all citizens access to the means it has prescribed for doing so.

Reversed. * * *

[The concurring opinion of Mr. Justice DOUGLAS is omitted].

Mr. Justice BRENNAN, concurring.

I join the Court's opinion to the extent that it holds that Connecticut denies procedural due process in denying the indigent appellants access to its courts for the sole reason that they cannot pay a required fee. "[C]onsideration of what procedures due process may require under any given set of circumstances must begin with a determination of the precise nature of the government function involved as well as of the private interest that has been affected by governmental action." Cafeteria & Restaurant Workers Union v. McElroy, 367 U.S. 886, 895 (1961); Goldberg v. Kelly, 397 U.S. 254, 263 (1970). When a State's interest in imposing a fee requirement on an indigent is compared to the indigent's interest in being heard, it is clear that the latter is the weightier. It is an unjustifiable denial of a hearing, and therefore a denial of due process, to close the courts to an indigent on the ground of nonpayment of a fee.

But I cannot join the Court's opinion insofar as today's holding is made to depend upon the factor that only the State can grant a divorce and that an indigent would be locked into a marriage if unable to pay the fees required to obtain a divorce. A State has an ultimate monopoly of all judical process and attendant enforcement machinery. As a practical matter, if disputes cannot be successfully settled between the parties, the court system is usually "the only forum effectively empowered to settle their disputes. Resort to the judicial process by these plaintiffs is no more voluntary in a realistic sense than that of the defendant called upon to defend his interests in court." Ante, at 376–377. In this case, the Court holds that Connecticut's unyielding fee requirement violates the Due Process Clause by denying appellants "an opportunity to be heard upon their claimed right to a dissolution of their marriages" without a sufficient countervailing justification. Ante, at 380. I see no constitutional distinction between appellants' attempt to enforce this state statutory right and an attempt to vindicate any other right arising under federal or state law. If fee requirements close the courts to an indigent he can no more invoke the aid of the courts for other forms of relief than he can escape the legal incidents of a marriage. The right to be heard in some way at some time extends to all proceedings entertained by courts. The possible distinctions suggested by the Court today will not withstand analysis.

In addition, this case presents a classic problem of equal protection of the laws. The question that the Court treats exclusively as one of due process inevitably implicates considerations of both due process and equal protection. Certainly, there is at issue the denial of a hearing, a matter for analysis under the Due Process Clause. But Connecticut does not deny a hearing to everyone in these circumstances; it denies it only to people who fail to pay certain fees. The validity of this partial denial, or differentiation in treatment, can be tested as well under the Equal Protection Clause.   *   *   *

Mr. Justice BLACK, dissenting. This is a strange case and a strange holding. Absent some specific federal constitutional or statutory provision, marriage in this country is completely under state control, and so is divorce.   *   *   *

The institution of marriage is of peculiar importance to the people of the States. It is within the States that they live and vote and rear their children under laws passed by their elected representatives. The States provide for the stability of their social order, for the good morals of all their citizens, and for the needs of children from broken homes. The States, therefore, have particular interests in the kinds of laws regulating their citizens when they enter into, maintain, and dissolve marriages. The power of the States over marriage and divorce is complete except as limited by specific constitutional provisions. Loving v. Virginia, 388 U.S. 1, 7–12 (1967).

The Court here holds, however, that the State of Connecticut has so little control over marriages and divorces of its own citizens that it is without power to charge them practically nominal initial court costs when they are without ready money to put up those costs. The Court holds that the state law requiring payment of costs is barred by the Due Process Clause of the Fourteenth Amendment of the Federal Constitution. Two members of the majority believe that the Equal Protection Clause also applies. I think the Connecticut court costs law is barred by neither of those clauses.

It is true, as the majority points out, that the Court did hold in Griffin v. Illinois, 351 U.S. 12 (1956), that indigent defendants in criminal cases must be afforded the same right to appeal their convictions as is afforded to a defendant who has ample funds to pay his own costs. *   *   *

Civil lawsuits, however, are not like government prosecutions for crime. Civil courts are set up by government to give people who have quarrels with their neighbors the chance to use a neutral governmental agency to adjust their differences. In such cases the government is not usually involved as a party, and there is no deprivation of life, liberty, or property as punishment for crime. Our Federal Constitution, therefore, does not place such private disputes on the same high level as it places criminal trials and punishment. There is consequently no necessity, no reason, why government should in civil trials be hampered or handicapped by the strict and rigid due process rules the Constitution has provided to protect people charged with crime. *   *   *

SECTION 2. ILLEGITIMACY AND THE CONSTITUTION

In the common law system an illegitimate child had no relatives. Gradually the law recognized a parent-child relationship between mother and illegitimate child. The law generally still disadvantages illegitimate children by excluding them from various statutory benefits which legitimate children possess. In the past few years, few cases have been decided by the Supreme Court of the United States striking down some of the discriminations against illegitimate children and recognizing certain rights in respect to the fathers of such children. The fact that a mother has given birth to an illegitimate child is frequently a factor in an adjudication of neglect.

See Section on Neglect, supra p. 531.

People v. Allen, supra p. 472, is presented as still another aspect of the problems which arise respecting the importance of status.

WEBER v. AETNA CASUALTY & SURETY COMPANY

Supreme Court of the United States, 1972.
406 U.S. 164, 92 S.Ct. 1400, 31 L.Ed.2d 768.

Mr. Justice POWELL delivered the opinion of the Court.

The question before us, on writ of certiorari to the Supreme Court of Louisiana, concerns the right of dependent unacknowledged, illegitimate children to recover under Louisiana workmen's compensation laws benefits for the death of their natural father on an equal footing with his dependent legitimate children. We hold that Louisiana's denial of equal recovery rights to dependent unacknowledged illegitimates violates the Equal Protection Clause of the Fourteenth Amendment. Levy v. Louisiana, 391 U.S. 68 (1968). Glona v. American Guarantee and Liability Insurance Company, 391 U.S. 73 (1968).

On June 22, 1967, Henry Clyde Stokes died in Louisiana of injuries received during the course of his employment the previous day. At the time of his death Stokes resided and maintained a household with one Willie Mae Weber, to whom he was not married. Living in the household were four legitimate minor children, born of the marriage between Stokes and Adlay Jones Stokes who was at the time committed to a mental hospital. Also living in the home was one unacknowledged illegitimate child born of the relationship between Stokes and Willie Mae Weber. A second illegitimate child of Stokes and Weber was born posthumously.

On June 29, 1967, Stokes' four legitimate children, through their maternal grandmother as guardian, filed a claim for their father's death under Louisiana's workmen's compensation law. The defendant employer and its insurer impleaded Willie Mae Weber who appeared and claimed compensation benefits for the two illegitimate children.

Meanwhile, the four legitimate children had brought another suit for their father's death against a third-party tortfeasor which was settled for an amount in excess of the maximum benefits allowable under workmen's compensation. The illegitimate children did not share in this settlement. Subsequently the employer in the initial action requested the extinguishment of all parties' workmen's compensation claims by reason of the tort settlement.

The trial judge awarded the four legitimate children the maximum allowable amount of compensation and declared their entitlement had been satisfied from the tort suit settlement. Consequently, the four legitimate children dismissed their workmen's compensation claim.

Judgment was also awarded to Stokes' two illegitimate offspring to the extent that maximum compensation benefits were not exhausted by the four legitimate children. Since such benefits had been entirely exhausted by the amount of the tort settlement, in which only the four dependent legitimate offspring participated, the two dependent illegitimate children received nothing.

I

For purposes of recovery under workmen's compensation, Louisiana law defines children to include "only legitimate children, stepchildren, posthumous children, and illegitimate children acknowledged under the provisions of Civil Code Articles 203, 204 and 205." Thus legitimate children and acknowledged illegitimates may recover on an equal basis. Unacknowledged illegitimate children, however, are relegated to the lesser status of "other dependents" under § 1232(8) of the workmen's compensation statute and may recover *only* if there are not enough surviving dependents in the preceding classifications to exhaust the maximum allowable benefits. Both the Louisiana Court of Appeal and a divided Louisiana Supreme Court sustained these statutes over appellants' constitutional objections, holding that our decision in *Levy*, supra, was not controlling.

We disagree. In *Levy*, the Court held invalid as denying equal protection of law, a Louisiana statute which barred an illegitimate child from recovering for the wrongful death of its mother when such recoveries by legitimate children were authorized. The Court there decided that the fact of a child's birth out of wedlock bore no reasonable relation to the purpose of wrongful death statutes which compensate children for the death of a mother. As the Court said in *Levy*:

"Legitimacy or illegitimacy of birth has no relation to the nature of the wrong allegedly inflicted on the moth-

er. These children, though illegitimate, were dependent on her; she cared for them and nurtured them; they were indeed hers in the biological and in the spiritual sense; in her death they suffered wrong in the sense that any dependent would." Levy v. Louisiana, supra, 391 U.S., p. 72. * *

Here, as in *Levy,* there is impermissible discrimination. An unacknowledged illegitimate child may suffer as much from the loss of a parent as a child born within wedlock or an illegitimate later acknowledged. So far as this record shows, the dependency and natural affinity of the unacknowledged illegitimate child for her father were as great as those of the four legitimate children whom Louisiana law has allowed to recover.[7] The legitimate children and the illegitimate child all lived in the home of the deceased and were equally dependent upon him for maintenance and support. It is inappropriate, therefore, for the court below to talk of relegating the unacknowledged illegitimate "to a less favorable position as are other dependent relatives such as parents." The unacknowledged illegitimate is *not* a parent or some "other dependent relative"; in this case she is a *dependent child,* and as such is entitled to rights granted other *dependent children.*

Respondent contends that our recent ruling in Labine v. Vincent, 401 U.S. 532 (1971), controls this case. In *Labine,* the Court upheld, against constitutional objections, Louisiana intestacy laws which had barred an acknowledged illegitimate child from sharing equally with legitimate children in her father's estate. That deci-

---

[7] The affinity and dependency on the father of the posthumously born illegitimate child is, of course, not comparable to that of offspring living at the time of their father's death. This fact, however, does not alter our view of the case. We think a posthumously born illegitimate child should be treated the same as a posthumously born legitimate child, which the Louisiana statutes fail to do.

sion reflected, in major part, the traditional deference to a State's prerogative to regulate the disposition at death of property within its borders. *Labine, supra,* p. 538. The Court has long afforded broad scope to state discretion in this area. Yet the substantial state interest in providing for "the stability of * * * land titles and in the prompt and definitive determination of the valid ownership of property left by decedents," In re Vincent, La.App., 229 So.2d 449 (1969), is absent in the case at hand.

Moreover, in *Labine* the intestate, unlike deceased in the present action, might easily have modified his daughter's disfavored position. As the Court there remarked:

> "Ezra Vincent could have left one-third of his property to his illegitimate daughter had he bothered to follow the simple formalities of executing a will. He could, of course, have legitimatized the child by marrying her mother in which case the child could have inherited his property either by intestate succession or by will as any other legitimate child." *Labine,* supra, 401 U.S., p. 539.

Such options, however, were not realistically open to Henry Stokes. Under Louisiana law he could not have acknowledged his illegitimate children even had he desired to do so.[9] The burdens

---

[9] La.Civ.Code Art. 204, * * * prohibits acknowledgment of children whose parents were incapable of contracting marriage at the time of conception. Acknowledgment may only be made if the parents could contract a legal marriage with each other. Decedent in the instant case remained married to his first wife—the mother of his four legitimate children—until his death. Thus, at all times he was legally barred from marrying Willie Mae Weber, the mother of the two illegitimate children. It therefore was impossible for him to acknowledge legally his illegitimate children and thereby qualify them for protection under the Louisiana Workmen's Compensation Act. See also Williams v. American Emp. Ins. Co., 237 La. 101, 110 So.2d 541 (1959), where the Louisiana Supreme Court held that a posthumous-

of illegitimacy, already weighty, become doubly so when neither parent nor child can legally lighten them.

* * *

II

Having determined that *Levy* is the applicable precedent we briefly reaffirm here the reasoning which produced that result. The tests to determine the validity of state statutes under the Equal Protection Clause have been variously expressed, but this Court requires, at a minimum, that a statutory classification bear some rational relationship to a legitimate state purpose. * * * Though the latitude given state economic and social regulation is necessarily broad, when state statutory classifications approach sensitive and fundamental personal rights, this Court exercises a stricter scrutiny, * * *.

The Louisiana Supreme Court emphasized strongly the State's interest in protecting "legitimate family relationships," 242 So.2d, at 570, and the regulation and protection of the family unit has indeed been a venerable state concern. We do not question the importance of that interest; what we do question is how the challenged statute will promote it. As was said in *Glona:*

> "* * * we see no possible rational basis * * * for assuming that if the natural mother is allowed recovery for the wrongful death of her illegitimate child, the cause of illegitimacy will be served. It would, indeed, be farfetched to assume that women have illegitimate children so that they can be compensated in damages for their death." Glona v. American Guarantee and Liability Insurance Co., 391 U.S. supra, p. 75, * * *

Nor can it be thought here that persons will shun illicit relations because the off-

---

ly born illegitimate child cannot be classified as a child entitled to workmen's compensation benefits, as defined under La.Rev.Stat. § 23:1021(3).

spring may not one day reap the benefits of workmen's compensation.

It may perhaps be said that statutory distinctions between the legitimate and illegitimate reflect closer family relationships in that the illegitimate is more often not under care in the home of the father nor even supported by him. The illegitimate, so this argument runs, may thus be made less eligible for the statutory recoveries and inheritances reserved for those more likely to be within the ambit of familial care and affection. Whatever the merits elsewhere of this contention, it is not compelling in a statutory compensation scheme where dependency on the deceased is a prerequisite to anyone's recovery, and where to the acknowledgment so necessary to equal recovery rights may be unlikely to occur or legally impossible to effectuate even where the illegitimate child may be nourished and loved. * * *

The status of illegitimacy has expressed through the ages society's condemnation of irresponsible liaisons beyond the bonds of marriage. But visiting this condemnation on the head of an infant is illogical and unjust.[13] Moreover, imposing disabilities on the illegitimate child is contrary to the basic concept of our system that legal burdens should bear some relationship to individual responsibility or wrongdoing. Obviously, no child is responsible for his birth and penalizing the illegitimate child is an ineffectual—as well as an unjust—way of deterring the parent. Courts are powerless to prevent the social opprobrium suffered by these hapless children, but the Equal Protection Clause does enable us to strike down discriminatory laws relating to status of birth where—as in this case—the classification is justified by no legitimate state interest, compelling or otherwise.

Reversed and remanded.

The concurring opinion of Mr. Justice BLACKMUN is omitted.

Mr. Justice Rehnquist, dissenting.

* * *

While the Court's opinion today is by no means a sharp departure from the precedents on which it relies, it is an extraordinary departure from what I conceive to be the intent of the framers of the Fourteenth Amendment and the import of the traditional presumption of constitutionality accorded to legislative enactments. Nowhere in the text of the Constitution, or in its plain implications, is there any guide for determining what is a "legitimate" state interest, or what is a "fundamental personal right." The traditional police power of the States has been thought to embrace any measure thought to further the well-being of the State in question, subject only to the specific prohibitions contained in the Federal Constitution. That Constitution of course contains numerous guarantees of individual liberty, which I would have no trouble describing as "fundamental personal liberties," but the right of illegitimate children to sue in state court to recover workmen's compensation benefits is not among them.

The relationship of the "legitimate" state interest and "fundamental personal right" analysis to the constitutional guarantee of equal protection of the law is approximately the same as that of "freedom of contract" to the constitutional guarantee that no person shall be deprived of life, liberty, or property without due process of law. It is an invitation for judicial exegesis over and above the commands of the Constitution, in which values that cannot possibly have their source

---

[13] See, e. g., Gray and Rudovsky, The Court Acknowledges the Illegitimate: Levy v. Louisiana and Glona v. American Guarantee and Liability Insurance Co., 118 U.Pa. L.Rev. 1 (1969). A comprehensive study of the legal status of illegitimacy and the effects thereof is H. Krause, Illegitimacy: Law and Social Policy (1971); reviewed by Wadlington, 58 Va.L.Rev. 188 (1972).

in that instrument are invoked to either validate or condemn the countless laws enacted by the various States.   *   *   *

In the instant case I cannot condemn as irrational Louisiana's distinction between legitimate and illegitimate children. In a statutory compensation scheme such as this, the State must inevitably draw rather fine and arbitrary lines. For example, Louisiana declares that parents will have priority in this scheme over first-cousins, regardless of the degree of dependency or affection in any given case. Surely, no one would condemn this classification as violative of the Fourteenth Amendment, since it is likely to reflect fairly the unarticulated intent of the decedent. Similarly, the State might rationally presume that the decedent would have preferred the compensation to go to his legitimate children, rather than those illegitimates whom he has not acknowledged.

Although the majority argues that "the state interest in minimizing problems of proof is not *significantly* disturbed by our decision," at 1406 (emphasis added), it clearly recognizes, as it must, that under its decision additional and sometimes more difficult problems of proof of paternity and dependency may be raised. This is particularly true with respect to petitioner's posthumous child, who was not born until after the death of his father. I believe that a State's desire to lessen these problems under its statutory scheme is a rational basis for difference in treatment of the two classes.

Finally, the majority apparently draws some comfort from the fact that the illegitimate children here could not have been acknowledged, since the decedent remained married to another woman while he raised these children. However, I do not believe that it follows from this fact that the statutory classification is irrational. On the contrary, this element of the statutory scheme points up another

possible legislative purpose which I do not believe this Court should so freely dismiss. Louisiana, like many other States, has a wide variety of laws designed to encourage legally recognized and responsible family relationships. I believe this particular statutory provision, forbidding acknowledgment of illegitimate children when the parents were not free to marry (in this case because the father was already married to another woman), might be considered part of that statutory pattern designed to discourage formation of illicit family relationships. Whether this is a wise state policy, or whether this particular statute will be particularly effective in advancing it, are not matters for this Court's determination.

All legislation involves classification and line drawing of one kind or another. When this Court expands the traditional "reasonable basis" standard for judgment under the Equal Protection Clause into a search for "legitimate" state interests which the legislation may "promote," and "for fundamental personal rights" which it might "endanger," it is doing nothing less than passing policy judgments upon the acts of every state legislature in the country.

———

STANLEY v. ILLINOIS

Supreme Court of the United States, 1972.
405 U.S. 645, 92 S.Ct. 1208, 31 L.Ed.2d 551.

[The Supreme Court held unconstitutional a proposition of Illinois Law according to which the children of unwed fathers became wards of the State upon the death of the mother. The Illinois law presumed that unwed fathers were unfit to raise their children. Mothers of either illegitimate or legitimate children and fathers of legitimate children could be deprived of them only after a hearing respecting the fitness of the father or mother. The Stanleys had lived together for eighteen years and produced three children].

WHITE, J. The Court has frequently emphasized the importance of the family. The rights to conceive and to raise one's children have been deemed "essential," Meyer v. Nebraska, 262 U.S. 390, 399 (1923), "basic civil rights of man," Skinner v. Oklahoma, 316 U.S. 535, 541 (1942), and "[r]ights far more precious * * * than property rights," May v. Anderson, 345 U.S. 528, 533 (1953). "It is cardinal with us that the custody, care and nurture of the child reside first in the parents, whose primary function and freedom include preparation for obligations the state can neither supply nor hinder." Prince v. Massachusetts, 321 U.S. 158, 166 (1944). The integrity of the family unit has found protection in the Due Process Clause of the Fourteenth Amendment, Meyer v. Nebraska, supra, at 399, the Equal Protection Clause of the Fourteenth Amendment, Skinner v. Oklahoma, supra, at 541, and the Ninth Amendment, Griswold v. Connecticut, 381 U.S. 479, 496 (1965) (Goldberg, J., concurring).

Nor has the law refused to recognize those family relationships unlegitimized by a marriage ceremony. The Court has declared unconstitutional a state statute denying natural, but illegitimate, children a wrongful death action for the death of their mother, emphasizing that such children cannot be denied the right of other children because familial bonds in such cases were often as warm, enduring, and important as those arising within a more formally organized family unit. Levy v. Louisiana, 391 U.S. 68, 71–72 (1968). "To say that the test of equal protection should be the 'legal' rather than the 'biological' relationship is to avoid the issue. For the Equal Protection Clause necessarily limits the authority of a State to draw such 'legal' lines as it chooses." Glona v. American Guarantee Co., 391 U.S. 73, 75–76 (1968).

These authorities make it clear that, at the least, Stanley's interest in retaining custody of his children is cognizable and substantial.

It may be, as the State insists, that most unmarried fathers are unsuitable and neglectful parents. It may also be that Stanley is such a parent and that his children should be placed in other hands. But all unmarried fathers are not in this category: some are wholly suited to have custody of their children. This much the State readily concedes, and nothing in this record indicates that Stanley is or has been a neglectful father who has not cared for his children. Given the opportunity to make his case, Stanley may have been seen to be deserving of custody of his offspring. Had this been so, the State's statutory policy would have been furthered by leaving custody in him.

* * * [T]he Constitution recognizes higher values than speed and efficiency. Indeed, one might fairly say of the Bill of Rights in general, and the Due Process Clause in particular, that they were designed to protect the fragile values of a vulnerable citizenry from the overbearing concern for efficiency and efficacy which may characterize praiseworthy government officials no less, and perhaps more, than mediocre ones.

Procedure by presumption is always cheaper and easier than individualized determination. But when, as here, the procedure forecloses the determinative issues of competence and care, when it explicitly disdains present realities in deference to past formalities, it needlessly risks running roughshod over the important interests of both parent and child. It therefore cannot stand.

Bell v. Burson, 402 U.S. 535 (1971) held that the State could not, while purporting to be concerned with fault in suspending a driver's license, deprive a citizen of his license without a hearing which would assess fault. Absent fault, the State's declared interest was so attenuated that administrative convenience was insufficient to excuse a hearing where evidence of fault could be considered. That drivers involved in accidents as a statistical matter, might be very likely to have been wholly or partially at fault did not foreclose hearing and proof in specific cases before licenses were suspended.

We think the Due Process Clause mandates a similar result here. The State's interest in caring for Stanley's children is *de minimis* if Stanley is shown to be a fit father. It insists on presuming rather than proving Stanley's unfitness solely because it is more convenient to presume than to prove. Under the Due Process Clause that advantage is insufficient to justify refusing a father a hearing when the issue at stake is the dismemberment of his family. * * *

The State of Illinois assumes custody of the children of married parents, divorced parents, and unmarried mothers only after a hearing and proof of neglect. The children of unmarried fathers, however, are declared dependent children without a hearing on parental fitness and without proof of neglect. Stanley's claim in the state courts and here is that failure to afford him a hearing on his parental qualifications while extending it to other parents denied him equal protection of the laws. We have concluded that all Illinois parents are constitutionally entitled to a hearing on their fitness before their children are removed from their custody. It follows that denying such a hearing to Stanley and those like him while granting it to other Illinois parents is inescapably contrary to the Equal Protection Clause.

Mr. Chief Justice BURGER, with whom Mr. Justice BLACKMUN concurs, dissenting. * * *

In * * *, I agree with the State's argument that the Equal Protection Clause is not violated when Illinois gives full recognition only to those father-child relationships that arise in the context of family units bound together by legal obligations arising from marriage or from adoption proceedings. Quite apart from the religious or quasi-religious connotations which marriage has—and has historically enjoyed—for a large proportion of this Nation's citizens, it is in law an essentially contractual relationship, the parties to which have legally enforceable rights and duties, with respect both to each other and to any children born to them. Stanley and the mother of these children never entered such a relationship. The record is silent as to whether they ever privately exchanged such promises as would have bound them in marriage under the common law. See Cartwright v. McGown, 121 Ill. 388, 398 (1887). In any event, Illinois has not recognized common law marriages since 1905. Ill.Rev.Stat., c. 89, § 4. Stanley did not seek the burdens when he could have freely assumed them.

Where there is a valid contract of marriage, the law of Illinois presumes that the husband is the father of any child born to the wife during the marriage; as the father, he has legally enforceable rights and duties with respect to that child. When a child is born to an unmarried woman, Illinois recognizes the readily identifiable mother, but makes no presumption as to the identity of the biological father. It does, however, provide two ways, one voluntary and one involuntary, in which that father may be identified. First, he may marry the mother and acknowledge the child as his own; this has the legal effect of legitimatizing the child and gaining for the father full recognition as a parent. Ill.Rev.Stat., c. 3, § 12–8. Second, a man may be found to be the biological father of the child pursuant to a paternity suit initiated by the mother; in this case, the child remains illegitimate, but the adjudicated father is made liable for the support of the child until the latter attains age 18 or is legally adopted by another. Ill. Rev.Stat., c. 1063¾, § 152.

Stanley argued before the Supreme Court of Illinois that the definition of "parents," set out in Ill.Rev.Stat., c. 37, § 701–14, as including "the father and mother of a legitimate child, or the survivor of them, or the natural mother of an illegitimate child, [or] * * * any adoptive parent," violates the Equal Protection Clause in that it treats unwed mothers and unwed fathers differently. Stanley then enlarged upon his equal protection argument when he brought the case here; he argued before this Court that Illinois is not permitted by the Equal Protection Clause to distinguish between unwed fathers and any of the other biological parents included in the statutory definition of legal "parents."

The Illinois Supreme Court correctly held that the State may constitutionally distinguish between unwed fathers and unwed mothers. Here, Illinois' different treatment of the two is part of that State's statutory scheme for protecting the welfare of illegitimate children. In almost all cases, the unwed mother is readily identifiable, generally from hospital records and alternatively by physicians or others attending the child's birth. Unwed fathers, as a class, are not traditionally quite so ease to identify and locate. Many of them either deny all responsibility or exhibit no interest in the child or its welfare; and, of course, many unwed fathers are simply not aware of their parenthood.

Furthermore, I believe that a State is fully justified in concluding, on the basis of common human experience, that the biological role of the mother in carrying and nursing an infant creates stronger bonds between her and the child than the bonds resulting from the male's often casual encounter. This view is reinforced by the observable fact that most unwed mothers exhibit a concern for their offspring either permanently or at least until they are safely placed for adoption, while unwed fathers rarely burden either the mother or the child with their attentions or loyalties. Centuries of human experience buttress this view of the realities of human conditions and suggest that unwed mothers of illegitimate children are generally more dependable protectors of their children than are unwed fathers. While these, like most generalizations, are not without exceptions, they nevertheless provide a sufficient basis to sustain a statutory classification whose objective is not to penalize unwed parents but to further the welfare of illegitimate children in fulfillment of the State's obligations as *parens patriae*.[4]

Stanley depicts himself as a somewhat unusual unwed father, namely, as one who has always acknowledged and never doubted his fatherhood of these children. He alleges that he loved, cared for, and supported these children from the time of their birth until the death of their mother. He contends that he consequently must be treated the same as a married father of legitimate children. Even assuming the truth of Stanley's allegations, I am unable to construe the Equal Protection Clause as requiring Illinois to tailor its statutory definition of "parents" so meticulously as to include such unusual unwed fathers, while at the same time excluding those unwed, and

---

4 When the marriage between the parents of a legitimate child is dissolved by divorce or separation, the State, of course, normally awards custody of the child to one parent or the other. This is considered necessary for the child's welfare, since the parents are no longer legally bound together. The unmarried parents of an illegitimate child are likewise not legally bound together. Thus, even if Illinois did recognize the parenthood of both the mother and father of an illegitimate child, it would, for consistency with its practice in divorce proceedings, be called upon to award custody to one or the other of them, at least once it had by some means ascertained the identity of the father.

generally unidentified, biological fathers who in no way share Stanley's professed desires.

* * *

Note

In Storm v. None, 57 Misc.2d 342, 291 N.Y.S.2d 515 (N.Y.Fam.Ct. Kings County 1968), Judge Polier wrote:

"The history of the legislation in New York State, concerning the right to support from the fathers of children born out-of-wedlock, provides an example of the diminishing but continuing discriminatory treatment of such children. The imposition of some obligation on the natural father was first imposed in New York under a criminal statute and subsequently under the Domestic Relations Court Act. Enforced for long years under a quasi-criminal proceeding, orders for support were niggardly and geared to relieving the taxpayer rather than to providing adequately for the support of a child.

"In 1962, when the unified Family Court Act for the State of New York took effect it transferred jurisdiction of filiation proceedings from the Court of Special Sessions to the Family Court. While generally regarded as a progressive statute, the new law largely maintained the discriminatory features of the preceding statutes in regard to the rights of children born out-of-wedlock:

1. Under the Family Court Act, the law continues to impose a statute of limitations in favor of the father of children born out-of-wedlock.

2. The *prima facie* presumption that the father of a child born in wedlock shall have sufficient means to support his minor children, is omitted from those sections of the Act dealing with support of children born out-of-wedlock.

3. The father of a minor child, born in wedlock, is held chargeable with the support of his minor child and if possessed of sufficient means or able to earn such means, may be required to pay for his support a fair and reasonable sum according to his means, as the court may determine. In contrast for a child born out-of-wedlock the law provides that each parent * * * is liable for the necessary support and education of the child and for the child's funeral expenses.

4. For the child born in wedlock, the statute provides that the court has continuing jurisdiction * * until its judgment is completely satisfied and may modify, set aside or vacate any order issued in the course of the proceeding. No comparable provision for continuing jurisdiction is set forth in Article V concerning children born out-of-wedlock.

5. The statute defining the right to support of children born out-of-wedlock authorizes agreements or compromises made by the mother or authorized persons, and sets forth that they become binding both on the mother and child when approved by the court, and that they bar other remedies for the support and education of the child.

6. Such agreements or compromises have been held to bar subsequent actions to determine paternity and so may deprive the child of his right to inheritance.

In sharp contrast the rights of a child born in wedlock have been protected against agreements and even judgments that prove improvident so far as a child's rights are concerned.

" * * * [S]tate statutes which discriminate against children on the basis of a classification as to whether they were born in or out-of-wedlock must be held to violate the Equal Protection Clause of the Constitution. Certainly there is no area in which such statutes should be more carefully scrutinized than where the support, the care, and the education of a child depend on their interpretation."

IN THE MATTER OF GUARDIANSHIP OF HARP

Court of Appeals of Washington, 1972.
6 Wash.App. 701, 495 P.2d 1059.

ARMSTRONG, Judge. The petitioner, Carl Hansen, sought a guardianship of his 2 illegitimate children. The trial court refused to take testimony and held that the petition, even if true, would not justify appointment of the father as guardian. Petitioner appeals from a denial of his petition.

The primary question raised in this appeal is whether the putative father is entitled to be appointed guardian of the persons of his illegitimate children while they remain living in the care, custody and control of their mother. We agree with the trial court that the putative father does not have this right.

The petition alleged facts, which if true, would raise a serious question of the fitness of the mother to have custody of the children. The paternity of the father had been established in a filiation proceeding.

In the trial court, petitioner contended that the mother of the children was incapable of fulfilling her responsibilities as the children's natural guardian due to an excessive drinking problem and overall unhealthy home environment. He sought guardianship not for the purpose of gaining the children's custody or control of their estate, but rather for the purpose of gaining the authority to oversee and direct the mother's allocation of support money and overall care and welfare of the children. He also sought guardianship in hopes of accomplishing the following: (a) to change the surnames of the children to his own, (b) to gain rights of reasonable visitation, (c) to make the children beneficiaries of his social security and provide for them by way of inheritance, and (d) to adopt the children in the event of the abandonment by their mother.

The trial court concluded that the mother of an illegitimate child is the natural guardian and any rights of the father are secondary to those of the mother. In essence, the trial court reasoned that to grant a petition in guardianship while the children remain in the mother's custody, in her home, would result in an unjustified encumbering of the mother's natural rights and accordingly dismissed the petition for failure to state a claim upon which relief could be granted. We agree that the putative father would not be entitled to be appointed guardian of his children under the circumstances of this case.

At the time of the trial of this case (as well as the time of argument of this appeal) the putative father of illegitimate children had very limited rights. The mother of the illegitimate child was deemed to be the natural guardian and legally entitled to its care and custody. The rights of the father to custody and control of the child, although superior to any other person, were inferior to the rights of the mother. Wade v. State, 39 Wash.2d 744, 238 P.2d 914 (1951). Our state filiation statute provides that if the mother is a suitable person she shall be awarded the custody and control of her illegitimate child. If she is not a suitable person, then the court may deliver the care and custody of the child to any reputable person including the father.   RCW 26.24.190.[1]

Upon the death of the mother of an illegitimate child, who has not been adopted, the putative father is entitled to custody and control of the child (1) if he is a fit person and (2) if the welfare of the child would be served.   In re Moore's Estate, 68 Wash.2d 792, 415 P.2d 653 (1966).   This right has been diluted by the express provisions of the adoption statutes, which provide that the putative father's consent to adoption of the children is not necessary.   RCW 26.32.030; RCW 26.32.040.   No notice of the adoption hearing need be given the father of an illegitimate child.   RCW 26.32.080 (5).

On April 3, 1972 the United States Supreme Court substantially increased the rights of the putative father of illegitimate children.   *   *   *

The court held that the putative father's rights as a parent were protected by the due process clause of the Fourteenth Amendment.   He was, therefore, entitled to a hearing to determine his fitness as a parent before his children were taken from him.   The state cannot merely presume that unmarried fathers are unsuitable and neglectful parents.   Parental fitness must be established on the basis of individual proof, whether or not the parenthood was sanctified by marriage.   Stanley v. Illinois, 405 U.S. 645, 92 S.Ct. 1208, 31 L.Ed.2d 551 (1972).

Obviously, the filiation and adoption statutes are now unconstitutional insofar as they fail to recognize the newly deter-

mined constitutional rights of the putative father.   We shall not endeavor to unravel the complexities involved in giving notice to a putative father to permit him due process in a determination of fitness to retain the custody of his children, or the change in his rights in adoption proceedings.   We commend that process to the legislature.   In any event, those questions are beyond the issues of this case.

With the current state of the law in mind, we address ourselves to the propriety of appointing the putative father of the illegitimate children their guardian notwithstanding the fact that they would remain living with the mother under her care, custody and control.   In determining the feasibility of granting the father's petition we take note of the requirement of RCW 11.88.030(8) that in a petition for appointment of a guardian, the petition is required to set forth the reason why the appointment of a guardian is sought, the interest of the petitioner in the appointment and whether the appointment is sought as guardian of the person, the estate or both.   Implicit within this provision is the requirement that before a court will appoint a guardian it must be shown that such appointment is necessary and reasonable.   39 Am.Jur. 2d § 19 (1968).

In the instant case petitioner does not seek the children's custody nor could he be appointed guardian of their estate since no estate exists.   Petitioner thus seeks guardianship of the person, not in the usual sense, but rather for the primary purpose of gaining the authority to oversee and control the mother's allocation of support money and overall care and welfare of the children.   Such a purpose is clearly not consistent with the purposes for which guardianship is intended.   To appoint petitioner guardian for the purpose of overseeing the mother's activities regarding her care and provision for the children would clearly stand

[1] RCW 26.24.190 provides: "If the mother be a suitable person she shall be awarded the custody and control of said child; if she be not a suitable person, the court may deliver the care and custody of said child to any reputable person, including the accused, charitable or state institution.   Such order and judgment may further provide, in the discretion of the court, that the surname of the accused shall henceforth be the lawful surname of such child."

in derogation of her custodial control of the children. Further, to create a dual control in these circumstances would not only constitute an unnecessary appointment of a guardian, but more significantly, subject the mother to continual interference by the putative father, thereby increasing the likelihood of friction within the home and adding to her burdens as a mother. The father of children born in wedlock would not be accorded these rights if the mother had been awarded custody of the children.

We conclude that the father of illegitimate children has no right to appointment as guardian of the persons of the children while they remain in the care, custody and control of their mother. Although the mother of illegitimate children is ordinarily the proper person to be appointed as guardian of the person and estate of the children, we can conceive of situations when the putative father would be the proper person to be appointed guardian. If the father had obtained custody and control of the children, either through juvenile court or an equitable proceeding, he would be the proper person to be appointed guardian of the persons and estate of the children. If the mother of the children had custody and control of the children and the putative father had set up funds for the welfare of the children, beyond his duty of support, the father might very well be the proper person to be appointed guardian of the estate of the children. The recent decision of the United States Supreme Court in Stanley v. Illinois, supra, has created an uncharted sea in the determination of the rights of putative fathers to their illegitimate children.

The trial court pointed out that the father is not without a remedy if his real concern is the welfare of the children. His petition clearly establishes the need of an investigation by the juvenile court. Pursuant to RCW 13.04.060 he is entitled to petition the juvenile court to obtain that court's protective services if the children are determined to be dependent children. In the exercise of its discretion, if the juvenile court finds that the mother is not a suitable person to have the custody and control of the child, then the custody and control may be awarded to the father as sanctioned by RCW 26.-24.190.

If the juvenile court finds the children to be dependent and awards custody of the children to the mother, in the discretion of the court, the father may acquire visitation rights. In determining whether the putative father should have visitation rights to his illegitimate children the best interests and welfare of the children are of paramount importance. See Annot., Right of Putative Father to Visit Illegitimate Child, 15 A.L.R.3d 887 (1967). * * *

Judgment affirmed.

PEOPLE v. ALLEN

Court of Appeals of New York, 1970.
27 N.Y.2d 108, 313 N.Y.S.2d 719.

JASEN, Judge. In 1962, the Legislature enacted section 812 of the Family Court Act, vesting the Family Court with "exclusive original jurisdiction over any proceeding concerning acts which would constitute disorderly conduct or an assault between spouses or between parent and child or between members of the same family or household." Subsequently, the act was amended to substitute "harassment, menacing, reckless endangerment, an assault or an attempt[ed] assault" for "or an assault".

In each of the cases before us, we are called upon to consider, for the first time, whether an unceremonialized informal or illicit relationship, not recognized elsewhere as a common-law marriage, qualifies for treatment as a spousal or family relationship, within the meaning of the statute.

Defendant Allen was convicted, upon his plea of guilty, of assault in the third degree, in the Supreme Court, Kings County, and sentenced to a term of one year's imprisonment. The plea was accepted in satisfaction of an indictment charging him with sodomy upon a female. According to the defendant, he had known the victim for 15 years and had lived with her for approximately three years—first in Chicago, and then in New York. Allen concedes that Illinois does not recognize common-law marriages and that he was not married to the victim of the sodomy.

Defendant Echols was convicted, upon his plea of guilty, of attempted assault in the second degree, in the Supreme Court, Bronx County, and sentenced to an indeterminate period of imprisonment not to exceed four years. The plea was accepted in satisfaction of an indictment for burglary in the first degree, assault in the first and second degrees, and possession of a dangerous weapon—all resulting when he broke into an apartment and stabbed his former girl friend with an ice pick. Echols apparently had lived with the complainant with some degree of regularity for 11 years and their relationship resulted in two children. During this period, and up to the present time, Echols was married to another woman from whom he had been separated for 12 years.

Defendant Christmas was convicted in Nassau County Court, after a jury trial, of assault in the second degree and possession of a dangerous weapon, and sentenced to a term of 1½ years' imprisonment. The facts, as to his relationship with the female victim involved in the assault, are in dispute. Christmas testified that he had known her for six or seven years; that he had slept with her on many occasions; and that for one and one-half years he had shared the same living quarters with her. The complainant, however, denied ever living with Christmas.

Each of these appellants raises the same argument on this appeal—that the assault charges on which they were convicted should have been transferred to the Family Court, as provided for in section 812 of the Family Court Act, because the complainant was a member of the same family or household as the defendant; and that the assault in question grew out of the intimate "family" relationship between the parties occupying the same "household".

The courts passing on this issue are divided—one view is to disregard the absence of a solemnized marriage and consider only whether the parties are living as a single domestic unit; and the other approach has required a legal marriage between the parties to qualify for Family Court treatment.

We agree with the second view and conclude that the Family Court lacks jurisdiction in these cases. We read the "family" and "household" categories of section 812 to confer jurisdiction on the Family Court over disputes arising in relationships only where there is legal interdependence, either through a solemnized marriage or a recognized common-law union.

The Legislature, in enacting article 8 of the Family Court Act, had as its aim the preservation of the family unit. Realizing that the intervention of the criminal law did not always serve that end, the Legislature sought to avoid the use of penal sanctions in certain well-defined situations where intra-family or intra-household assault had occurred and to provide, instead, conciliation and other practical assistance to the parties involved, through the Family Court.

Implicit in the legislation is the proposition that the family or household unit which is sought to be preserved must be one whose continued existence is consistent with both public policy and the laws of this State. Certainly, making available conciliation procedures, as contemplated by the Family Court Act, to such informal and illicit relationships as those before us, would clearly be contrary to public policy by conferring the privileges of Family Court services to a relationship which the Legislature has chosen not to recognize.

It matters not that, in reality, many such informal relationships exist in our State. Regardless of the frequency of its occurrence, such informal or illicit relationships remain unrecognized and should not be afforded the protective jurisdiction of the Family Court.

Although not controlling in our decision, we need only mention the tremendous burden that would be imposed on the Family Court, if we were to sustain the Family Court's jurisdiction over these relationships. For example, in each instance, it would be necessary to conduct a pretrial hearing to determine if there is a "unity of living arrangement, and of social [and] economic * * * interdependence" in order to qualify for Family Court treatment. (People v. Williams, 24 N.Y.2d 274, 281, 300 N.Y.S. 2d 89, 94, 248 N.E.2d 8, 13.) It should also be abundantly clear that these informal and transitory living arrangements often preclude effective conciliation.

In addition, there are procedures available to combat other problems created by such relationships. Support proceedings for the benefit of the children may be instituted regardless of the marital status of the parties. (Domestic Relations Law, § 33.) Restraining orders or jail, if necessary, can fulfill the parties' need for physical protection. Thus, there appears that little can be gained by transferring such cases to the Family Court.

In sum, then, we hold that the "family" and "household" categories of section 812 of the Family Court Act confer jurisdiction on the Family Court over disputes arising in relationships only where there is legal interdependence, either through a solemnized marriage or a recognized common-law union.

In each case, the judgment of conviction should be affirmed.

BERGAN, Judge (dissenting in part).

In the cases of Allen and Echols the records indicate long sustained relationships with the women who were victims of the assaults as "members of the same * * * household" (N.Y.Const., art. VI, § 13, subd. b; Family Ct. Act, § 812).

These situations established no marital or other legal family status for these men and women, but the continued stable relationships together made them "members" of the "same" household within the meaning of the Constitution and the statute. The language obviously embraces others than lawfully married people. (People v. James, 55 Misc.2d 953, 287 N.Y.S.2d 188; People v. Johnson, 48 Misc.2d 536, 265 N.Y.S.2d 260.)

The joint household status continued for long periods. Echols had lived with the complainant for about 11 years and they had two children together; Allen had lived with the complainant for three years. In the case of Christmas the record does not indicate any relationship in the same household with the complainant.

The statute (Family Ct. Act, § 812) grants exclusive first instance jurisdiction to the Family Court over assaults between members of the same household (People v. Johnson, 20 N.Y.2d 220, 282 N.Y.S. 2d 481, 229 N.E.2d 180). * * *

The court in People v. Haynes, 26 N.Y.2d 665, 666, 308 N.Y.S.2d 391, 392, 256 N.E.2d 545, 546, expressly reserved the question whether "an un-ceremonialized illicit relationship, how-ever persistent, qualifie[d] for treat-ment" under the Family Court Act.

That question is now here and a plain reading of the Constitution and the stat-ute would bring the Allen and Echols cases within the jurisdiction of the Family Court if the indications in the record of the nature of the relationships are estab-lished. For this purpose there should be a hearing.

The judgment in Christmas should be affirmed; the judgments in Allen and Echols should be modified by remitting the cases to the Supreme Court for a hear-ing (People v. Haynes, supra).

In People v. Allen: SCILEPPI and BREITEL, JJ., concur with JASEN, J.; GIBSON, J., concurs in result only; BERGAN, J., dissents and votes to modi-fy in a separate opinion in which FULD, C. J., and BURKE, J., concur.

Judgment affirmed.

In People v. Echols: SCILEPPI and BREITEL, JJ., concur with JASEN, J.; GIBSON, J., concurs in result only; BERGAN, J., dissents and votes to modi-fy in a separate opinion in which FULD, C. J., and BURKE, J., concur.

Judgment affirmed.

In People v. Christmas: FULD, C. J., and BURKE, SCILEPPI, BERGAN, BREITEL and GIBSON, JJ., concur.

Judgment affirmed.

SECTION 3. DELINQUENCY AND "BAD" CHILDREN

A. CHILDREN WHO COMMIT CRIMES

A short excursion into the theory be-hind the juvenile court and the basic question of how delinquency might be reduced may at first seem unrelated to family law. Yet the relationship is strong. Almost everyone agrees that one cause of delinquency is the failure of families to function adequately. Many delinquents are, in fact, neglected chil-dren as well. Furthermore, most treat-ment plans build on the family where its structure presents some ground for hope. The very heart of the juvenile court scheme emphasized the fact that the state was to exercise a parental func-tion.

As the materials indicate the relation-ship between poverty and delinquency is clear enough.

For lack of space these materials do not deal with problems of intake (screen-ing out those cases which need not go to court for formal adjudication) nor with the problems of informal disposition. Of course, by far the greatest number of de-linquents are dealt with in the early stages before the fact finding hearing. See Note, Juvenile Delinquency: The Police, State Courts, and Individualized Justice, 79 Harv.L.Rev. 775 (1966); Handler and Rosenheim, Privacy in Welfare: Public Assistance and Juvenile Justice, 31 Law and Contemp.Prob. 377, 395–401, 408–409 (1966); Sheridan, Juve-nile Court Intake, 2 J.Fam.Law 139 (1962); U. S. Children's Bureau, Stand-ards for Juvenile and Family Courts (Pub. No. 437) pp. 57–60 (1962); Note, Rights and Rehabilitation in the Juvenile Courts, 7 Col.L.Rev. 281 (1967).

IN THE MATTER OF GAULT

Supreme Court of the United States, 1967.
387 U.S. 1, 87 S.Ct. 1428, 18 L.Ed.2d 527.

Mr. Justice FORTAS delivered the opinion of the Court.

This is an appeal under 28 U.S.C.A. § 1257(2) from a judgment of the Su-preme Court of Arizona affirming the dismissal of a petition for a writ of habeas corpus. 99 Ariz. 181, 407 P.2d 760 (1965). The petition sought the release of Gerald Francis Gault, petitioners' 15-year-old son, who had been committed as a juvenile delinquent to the State Industrial School by the Juvenile Court of Gila County, Arizona. The Supreme Court of Arizona affirmed dismissal of the writ against various arguments which included an attack upon the constitutionality of the Arizona Juvenile Code because of its alleged denial of procedural due process rights to juveniles charged with being "delinquents." The court agreed that the constitutional guarantee of due process of law is applicable in such proceedings. It held that Arizona's Juvenile Code is to be read as "impliedly" implementing the "due process concept." It then proceeded to identify and describe "the particular elements which constitute due process in a juvenile hearing." It concluded that the proceedings ending in commitment of Gerald Gault did not offend those requirements. We do not agree, and we reverse. * * *

I.

* * *

[Gerald Francis Gault was taken into custody by the sheriff of Gila County on June 8, 1964, as a result of a verbal complaint by a neighbor about a lewd telephone call which she received. Gerald was at that time still subject to a six month juvenile court probation order. Both of the boy's parents were at work when he was picked up, and no notice was left at his home. More than 8 hours after he had been taken into custody, Gerald's brother was able to ascertain that he was at the Children's Detention Home. Mrs. Gault went to the home and was informed that a hearing would be held the next day at the Juvenile Court.

On the day of the hearing, a petition was filed with the Court by the deputy probation officer which "made no reference to any factual basis for the judicial action * * * it initiated." This petition was never served on the Gaults. At this hearing, only members of Gerald's immediate family and two probation officers were present. The complainant did not appear to testify, no one was sworn, no transcript or record was made, and no memorandum or record of the substance of the proceedings was prepared.

On June 11 or 12, Gerald was released and Mrs. Gault received a note from the probation officer. It was on plain paper, rather than on a letterhead, and stated that a further hearing would be held on June 15. At this hearing, Gerald was again accompanied only by members of his family and the complainant was not present.

At the habeas corpus hearing on August 17, the witnesses differed in their recollections as to Gerald's testimony at both prior hearings.]

At [the] June 15 hearing a "referral report" made by the probation officers was filed with the court, although not disclosed to Gerald or his parents. This listed the charge as "Lewd Phone Calls." At the conclusion of the hearing, the judge committed Gerald as a juvenile delinquent to the State Industrial School "for the period of his minority [that is, until 21], unless sooner discharged by due process of law." An order to that effect was entered. It recites that "after a full hearing and due deliberation the Court finds that said minor is a delinquent child, and that said minor is of the age of 15 years."

No appeal is permitted by Arizona law in juvenile cases. On August 3, 1964, a petition for a writ of habeas corpus was filed with the Supreme Court of Arizona and referred by it to the Superior Court for hearing.

At the habeas corpus hearing on August 17, Judge McGhee was vigorously cross-examined as to the basis for his actions.

He testified that he had taken into account the fact that Gerald was on probation. He was asked "under what section of * * * the code you found the boy delinquent?"

* * *

In substance, he concluded that Gerald came within ARS § 8–201–6(a), which specifies that a "delinquent child" includes one "who has violated a law of the state or an ordinance or regulation of a political subdivision thereof." The law which Gerald was found to have violated is ARS § 13–377. This section of the Arizona Criminal Code provides that a person who "in the presence of or hearing of any woman or child * * * uses vulgar, abusive or obscene language, is guilty of a misdemeanor. * * *" The penalty specified in the Criminal Code, which would apply to an adult, is $5 to $50, or imprisonment for not more than two months. The judge also testified that he acted under ARS § 8–201–6 (d) which includes in the definition of a "delinquent child" one who, as the judge phrased it, is "habitually involved in immoral matters." [6]

Asked about the basis for his conclusion that Gerald was "habitually involved in immoral matters," the judge testified, somewhat vaguely, that two years earlier, on July 2, 1962, a "referral" was made concerning Gerald, "where the boy had stolen a baseball glove from another boy

[6] ARS § 8–201–6, the section of the Arizona Juvenile Code which defines a delinquent child, reads:

"'Delinquent child' includes:

"(a) A child who has violated a law of the state or an ordinance or regulation of a political subdivision thereof.

"(b) A child who, by reason of being incorrigible, wayward or habitually disobedient, is uncontrolled by his parent, guardian or custodian.

"(c) A child who is habitually truant from school or home.

"(d) A child who habitually so deports himself as to injure or endanger the morals or health of himself or others."

and lied to the Police Department about it." The judge said there was "no hearing," and "no accusation" relating to this incident, "because of lack of material foundation." But it seems to have remained in his mind as a relevant factor. The judge also testified that Gerald had admitted making other nuisance phone calls in the past which, as the judge recalled the boy's testimony, were "silly calls, or funny calls, or something like that."

The Superior Court dismissed the writ, and appellants sought review in the Arizona Supreme Court. That court stated that it considered appellants' assignments of error as urging (1) that the Juvenile Code, ARS § 8–201 to § 8–239, is unconstitutional because it does not require that parents and children be apprised of the specific charges, does not require proper notice of a hearing, and does not provide for an appeal; and (2) that the proceedings and order relating to Gerald constituted a denial of due process of law because of the absence of adequate notice of the charge and the hearing; failure to notify appellants of certain constitutional rights including the rights to counsel and to confrontation, and the privilege against self-incrimination; the use of unsworn hearsay testimony; and the failure to make a record of the proceedings. Appellants further asserted that it was error for the Juvenile Court to remove Gerald from the custody of his parents without a showing and finding of their unsuitability, and alleged a miscellany of other errors under state law.

The Supreme Court handed down an elaborate and wide-ranging opinion affirming dismissal of the writ and stating the court's conclusions as to the issues raised by appellants and other aspects of the juvenile process. In their jurisdictional statement and brief in this Court, appellants do not urge upon us all of the points passed upon by the Supreme Court of Arizona. They urge that we hold the Juvenile Code of Arizona invalid on its face or as applied in this case because contrary to the Due Process Clause of the Fourteenth Amendment, the juvenile is taken from the custody of his parents and committed to a state institution pursuant to proceedings in which the Juvenile Court has virtually unlimited discretion, and in which the following basic rights are denied:

1. Notice of the charges;

2. Right to counsel;

3. Right to confrontation and cross-examination;

4. Privilege against self-incrimination;

5. Right to a transcript of the proceedings; and

6. Right to appellate review.

* * *

II.

The Supreme Court of Arizona held that due process of law is requisite to the constitutional validity of proceedings in which a court reaches the conclusion that a juvenile has been at fault, has engaged in conduct prohibited by law, or has otherwise misbehaved with the consequence that he is committed to an institution in which his freedom is curtailed. This conclusion is in accord with the decisions of a number of courts under both federal and state constitutions.

This Court has not heretofore decided the precise question. * * * and we direct our attention

We do not in this opinion consider the impact of these constitutional provisions upon the totality of the relationship of the juvenile and the state. We do not even consider the entire process relating to juvenile "delinquents." For example, we are not here concerned with the procedures or constitutional rights applicable to the pre-judicial stages of the juvenile process, nor do we direct our attention

to the post-adjudicative or dispositional process. See note 48, infra. We consider only the problems presented to us by this case. These relate to the proceedings by which a determination is made as to whether a juvenile is a "delinquent" as a result of alleged misconduct on his part, with the consequence that he may be committed to a state institution. As to these proceedings, there appears to be little current dissent from the proposition that the Due Process Clause has a role to play. The problem is to ascertain the precise impact of the due process requirement upon such proceedings.

From the inception of the juvenile court system, wide differences have been tolerated—indeed insisted upon—between the procedural rights accorded to adults and those of juveniles. In practically all jurisdictions, there are rights granted to adults which are withheld from juveniles. In addition to the specific problems involved in the present case, for example, it has been held that the juvenile is not entitled to bail, to indictment by grand jury, to a public trial or to trial by jury. It is frequent practice that rules governing the arrest and interrogation of adults by the police are not observed in the case of juveniles.

* * *

The history and theory underlying this development are well-known, but a recapitulation is necessary for purposes of this opinion. The juvenile court movement began in this country at the end of the last century. From the juvenile court statute adopted in Illinois in 1899, the system has spread to every State in the Union, the District of Columbia, and Puerto Rico. The constitutionality of juvenile court laws has been sustained in over 40 jurisdictions against a variety of attacks.[15]

15 See Paulsen, Kent v. United States: The Constitutional Context of Juvenile Cases, 1966 Sup.Ct.Review 167, 174.

The early reformers were appalled by adult procedures and penalties, and by the fact that children could be given long prison sentences and mixed in jails with hardened criminals. They were profoundly convinced that society's duty to the child could not be confined by the concept of justice alone. They believed that society's role was not to ascertain whether the child was "guilty" or "innocent," but "What is he, how has he become what he is, and what had best be done in his interest and in the interest of the state to save him from a downward career." [16] The child—essentially good, as they saw it—was to be made "to feel that he is the object of [the State's] care and solicitude" not that he was under arrest or on trial. The rules of criminal procedure were therefore altogether inapplicable. The apparent rigidities, technicalities, and harshness which they observed in both substantive and procedural criminal law were therefore to be discarded. The idea of crime and punishment was to be abandoned. The child was to be "treated" and "rehabilitated" and the procedures, from apprehension through institutionalization, were to be "clinical" rather than punitive.

These results were to be achieved, without coming to conceptual and constitutional grief, by insisting that the proceedings were not adversary, but that the State was proceeding as *parens patriae*. [18] The Latin phrase proved to be a great help to those who sought to rationalize the exclusion of juveniles from the constitutional scheme; but its meaning is murky and its historic credentials are of dubious relevance. The phrase was taken from chancery practice, where, however, it was used to describe the power of the State to act *in loco parentis* for the purpose of protecting the property interests and the person of the child. But there is no trace of the doctrine in the history of criminal jurisprudence. At common law, children under seven were considered incapable of possessing criminal intent. Beyond that age, they were subjected to arrest, trial, and in theory to punishment like adult offenders. In these old days, the State was not deemed to have authority to accord them fewer procedural rights than adults.

The right of the State, as *parens patriae*, to deny to the child procedural rights available to his elders was elaborated by the assertion that a child, unlike an adult, has a right "not to liberty but to custody." He can be made to attorn to his parents, to go to school, etc. If his parents default in effectively performing their custodial functions—that is, if the child is "delinquent"—the state may intervene. In doing so, it does not deprive the child of any rights, because he has none. It merely provides the "custody" to which the child is entitled. [21] On this basis, proceedings involving juveniles were described as "civil" not "criminal" and therefore not subject to the requirements

---

[16] Julian Mack, The Juvenile Court, 23 Harv.L.Rev. 104, 119–120 (1909).

[18] Id., at 109; Paulsen, op. cit. supra, note 15, at 173–174. There seems to have been little early constitutional objection to the special procedures of juvenile courts. But see Waite, How Far Can Court Procedure Be Socialized Without Impairing Individual Rights, 13 J.Am.Inst. of Crim.L. & Crim. 339, 340 (1922): "The Court which must direct its procedure even apparently to do something *to* a child because of what he *has done*, is parted from the court which is avowedly concerned only with doing something *for* a child because of what he *is* and *needs*, by a gulf too wide to be bridged by any humanity which the judge may introduce into his hear-

ings, or by the habitual use of corrective rather than punitive methods after conviction."

[21] See, e. g., Shears, Legal Problems Peculiar to Children's Courts, 48 A.B.A.J. 719, 720 (1962) ("The basic right of a juvenile is not to liberty but to custody. He has the right to have someone take care of him, and if his parents do not afford him this custodial privilege, the law must do so."); Ex parte Crouse, 4 Whart. 9, 11 (Sup.Ct.Pa.1839); Petition of Ferrier, 103 Ill. 367, 371–373 (1882).

which restrict the state when it seeks to deprive a person of his liberty.

Accordingly, the highest motives and most enlightened impulses led to a peculiar system for juveniles, unknown to our law in any comparable context. The constitutional and theoretical basis for this peculiar system is—to say the least—debatable. And in practice, as we remarked in the Kent case, supra, the results have not been entirely satisfactory.[23] Juvenile court history has again demonstrated that unbridled discretion, however benevolently motivated, is frequently a poor substitute for principle and procedure. In 1937, Dean Pound wrote: "The powers of the Star Chamber were a trifle in comparison with those of our juvenile courts. * * *" The absence of substantive standards has not necessarily meant that children receive careful, compassionate, individualized treatment. The absence of procedural rules based upon constitutional principle has not always produced fair, efficient, and effective procedures. Departures from established principles of due process have frequently resulted not in enlightened procedure, but in arbitrariness. The Chairman of the Pennsylvania Council of Juvenile Court Judges has recently observed: "Unfortunately, loose procedures, high-handed methods and crowded court calendars, either single or in combination, all too often, have resulted in depriving some juveniles of fundamental rights that have resulted in a denial of due process."

Failure to observe the fundamental requirements of due process has resulted in instances, which might have been avoided, of unfairness to individuals and inadequate or inaccurate findings of fact and unfortunate prescriptions of remedy. Due process of law is the primary and indispensable foundation of individual freedom. It is the basic and essential term in the social compact which defines the rights of the individual and delimits the powers which the State may exercise.[26]

---

[23] "There is evidence * * * that there may be grounds for concern that the child receives the worst of both worlds: that he gets neither the protections accorded to adults nor the solicitous care and regenerative treatment postulated for children." 383 U.S., at 556, 86 S.Ct., at 1054, citing Handler, The Juvenile Court and the Adversary System: Problems of Function and Form, 1965 Wis.L. Rev. 7; Harvard Law Review Note; and various congressional materials set forth at 383 U.S., at 546, n. 5, 86 S.Ct., at 1049.

On the other hand, while this opinion and much recent writing concentrate upon the failures of the juvenile court system to live up to the expectations of its founders, the observation of the Nat'l Crime Comm'n Report should be kept in mind:

"Although its shortcomings are many and its results too often disappointing, the juvenile justice system in many cities is operated by people who are better educated and more highly skilled, can call on more and better facilities and services, and has more ancillary agencies to which to refer its clientele than its adult counterpart." Id., at 78.

[26] The impact of denying fundamental procedural due process to juveniles involved in "delinquency" charges is dramatized by the following considerations: (1) In 1965, persons under 18 accounted for about one-fifth of all arrests for serious crimes (Nat'l Crime Comm'n Report p. 55) and over half of all arrests for serious property offenses (id., at 56), and in the same year some 601,000 children under 18, or 2% of the total population of that age, came before juvenile courts (Juvenile Court Statistics—1965, Children's Bureau Statistical Series, No. 85, p. 2 (1966)). About one out of nine youths will be referred to juvenile court in connection with a delinquent act (excluding traffic offenses) before he is 18 (Nat'l Crime Comm'n Report, p. 55), Cf. also Wheeler & Cottrell, Juvenile Delinquency—Its Prevention and Control (Russell Sage Foundation, 1965), p. 2; Report of the President's Commission on Crime in the District of Columbia (1966) (hereinafter cited as D.C.Crime Comm'n Report), p. 773. Furthermore, most juvenile crime apparently goes undetected or not formally punished. Wheeler and Cottrell, supra, observe that "Almost all youngsters have committed at least one of the petty forms of theft and vandalism in the course of their adolescence." Id., at 28–29. See also Nat'l Crime Comm'n Report, at p. 55, where it is stated that "self-report studies reveal that perhaps 90 percent of all young people have committed at least one act for which they could have been brought to juvenile court." It

As Mr. Justice Frankfurter has said: "The history of American freedom is, in no small measure, the history of procedure." But in addition, the procedural rules which have been fashioned from the generality of due process are our best instruments for the distillation and evaluation of essential facts from the conflicting welter of data that life and our adversary methods present. It is these instruments of due process which enhance the possibility that truth will emerge from the confrontation of opposing versions and conflicting data. "Procedure is to law what 'scientific method' is to science."

It is claimed that juveniles obtain benefits from the special procedures applicable to them which more than offset the disadvantages of denial of the substance of normal due process. As we shall discuss, the observance of due process standards, intelligently and not ruthlessly administered, will not compel the State to abandon or displace any of the substantive benefits of the juvenile process. But it is important, we think, that the claimed

benefits of the juvenile process should be candidly appraised. Neither sentiment nor folklore should cause us to shut our eyes, for example, to such startling findings as that reported in an exceptionally reliable study of repeaters or recidivism conducted by the Stanford Research Institute for the President's Commission on Crime in the District of Columbia. This Commission's Report states:

"In fiscal 1966 approximately 66 percent of the 16- and 17-year-old juveniles referred to the court by the Youth Aid Division had been before the court previously. In 1965, 56 percent of those in the Receiving Home were repeaters. The SRI study revealed that 61 percent of the sample Juvenile Court referrals in 1965 had been previously referred at least once and that 42 percent had been referred at least twice before." Id., at 773.

Certainly, these figures and the high crime rates among juveniles to which we have referred (supra, note 26), could not lead us to conclude that the absence of constitutional protections reduces crime, or that the juvenile system, functioning free of constitutional inhibitions as it has largely done, is effective to reduce crime or rehabilitate offenders. We do not mean by this to denigrate the juvenile court process or to suggest that there are not aspects of the juvenile system relating to offenders which are valuable. But the features of the juvenile system which its proponents have asserted are of unique benefit will not be impaired by constitutional domestication. For example, the commendable principles relating to the processing and treatment of juveniles separately from adults are in no way involved or affected by the procedural issues under discussion. Further, we are told that one of the important benefits of the special juvenile court procedures is that they avoid classifying the juvenile as a "criminal." The juvenile offender is now classed as a "delinquent." There

---

seems that the rate of juvenile delinquency is also steadily rising. See Nat'l Crime Comm'n Report, p. 56; Juvenile Court Statistics, supra, pp. 2–3. (2) In New York, where most juveniles are represented by counsel (see note 69, infra) and substantial procedural rights are afforded (see, e. g., notes 80, 81, 99, infra), out of a fiscal year 1965–1966 total of 10,755 juvenile proceedings involving boys, 2,242 were dismissed for failure of proof at the fact-finding hearing; for girls, the figures were 306 out of total of 1,051. New York Judicial Conference, Twelfth Annual Report, pp. 314, 316 (1967). (3) In about one-half of the States, a juvenile may be transferred to an adult penal institution after a juvenile court has found him "delinquent" (Delinquent Children in Penal Institutions, Children's Bureau Pub. No. 415 (1964), p. 1). (4) In some jurisdictions a juvenile may be subjected to criminal prosecution for the same offense for which he has served under a juvenile court commitment. However, the Texas procedure to this effect has recently been held unconstitutional by a federal district court judge, in a habeas corpus action. Sawyer v. Huack, 245 F.Supp. 55 (D.C.W.D.Tex. 1965). (5) In most of the States the juvenile may end in criminal court through waiver (Harvard Law Review Note, p. 793).

is, of course, no reason why this should not continue. It is disconcerting, however, that this term has come to involve only slightly less stigma than the term "criminal" applied to adults. It is also emphasized that in practically all jurisdictions, statutes provide that an adjudication of the child as a delinquent shall not operate as a civil disability or disqualify him for civil service appointment. There is no reason why the application of due process requirements should interfere with such provisions.

Beyond this, it is frequently said that juveniles are protected by the process from disclosure of their deviational behavior. * * * This claim of secrecy, however, is more rhetoric than reality. Disclosure of court records is discretionary with the judge in most jurisdictions. Statutory restrictions almost invariably apply only to the court records, and even as to those the evidence is that many courts routinely furnish information to the FBI and the military, and on request to government agencies and even to private employers. Of more importance are police records. In most States the police keep a complete file of juvenile "police contacts" and have complete discretion as to disclosure of juvenile records. Police departments receive requests for information from the FBI and other law-enforcement agencies, the Armed Forces, and social services agencies, and most of them generally comply. Private employers word their application forms to produce information concerning juvenile arrests and court proceedings, and in some jurisdictions information concerning juvenile police contacts is furnished private employers as well as government agencies.

In any event, there is no reason why, consistently with due process, a State cannot continue, if it deems it appropriate, to provide and to improve provision for the confidentiality of records of police contacts and court action relating to juveniles. * * *

Further, it is urged that the juvenile benefits from informal proceedings in the court. The early conception of the juvenile court proceeding was one in which a fatherly judge touched the heart and conscience of the erring youth by talking over his problems, by paternal advice and admonition, and in which, in extreme situations, benevolent and wise institutions of the State provided guidance and help "to save him from a downward career." Then, as now, goodwill and compassion were admirably prevalent. But recent studies have, with surprising unanimity, entered sharp dissent as to the validity of this gentle conception. They suggest that the appearance as well as the actuality of fairness, impartiality and orderliness—in short, the essentials of due process may be a more impressive and more therapeutic attitude so far as the juvenile is concerned. For example, in a recent study, the sociologists Wheeler and Cottrell observe that when the procedural laxness of the "parens patriae" attitude is followed by stern disciplining, the contrast may have an adverse effect upon the child, who feels that he has been deceived or enticed. They conclude as follows: "Unless appropriate due process of law is followed, even the juvenile who has violated the law may not feel that he is being fairly treated and may therefore resist the rehabilitative efforts of court personnel." [37] Of course, it is not sug-

[37] Juvenile Delinquency—Its Prevention and Control (Russell Sage Foundation, 1966), p. 33. The conclusion of the Nat'l Crime Comm'n Report is similar: "[T]here is increasing evidence that the informal procedures, contrary to the original expectation, may themselves constitute a further obstacle to effective treatment of the delinquent to the extent that they engender in the child a sense of injustice provoked by seemingly all-powerful and challengeless exercise of authority by judges and probation officers." Id., at 85. See also Allen, The Borderland of Criminal Justice (1964), p. 19.

gested that juvenile court judges should fail appropriately to take account, in their demeanor and conduct, of the emotional and psychological attitude of the juveniles with whom they are confronted. While due process requirements will, in some instances, introduce a degree of order and regularity to juvenile court proceedings to determine delinquency, and in contested cases will introduce some elements of the adversary system, nothing will require that the conception of the kindly juvenile judge be replaced by its opposite, nor do we here rule upon the question whether ordinary due process requirements must be observed with respect to hearings to determine the disposition of the delinquent child.

Ultimately, however, we confront the reality of that portion of the juvenile court process with which we deal in this case. A boy is charged with misconduct. The boy is committed to an institution where he may be restrained of liberty for years. It is of no constitutional consequence—and of limited practical meaning—that the institution to which he is committed is called an Industrial School. The fact of the matter is that, however euphemistic the title, a "receiving home" or an "industrial school" for juveniles is an institution of confinement in which the child is incarcerated for a greater or lesser time. * * *

In view of this, it would be extraordinary if our Constitution did not require the procedural regularity and the exercise of care implied in the phrase "due process." Under our Constitution, the condition of being a boy does not justify a kangaroo court. The traditional ideas of juvenile court procedure, indeed, contemplated that time would be available and care would be used to establish precisely what the juvenile did and why he did it—was it a prank of adolescence or a brutal act threatening serious consequences to himself or society unless cor-

rected? Under traditional notions, one would assume that in a case like that of Gerald Gault, where the juvenile appears to have a home, a working mother and father, and an older brother, the Juvenile Judge would have made a careful inquiry and judgment as to the possibility that the boy could be disciplined and dealt with at home, despite his previous transgressions.[41] Indeed, so far as appears in the record before us, except for some conversation with Gerald about his school work and his "wanting to go to * * * Grand Canyon with his father," the points to which the judge directed his attention were little different from those that would be involved in determining any charge of violation of a penal statute. The essential difference between Gerald's case and a normal criminal case is that safeguards available to adults were discarded in Gerald's case. The summary procedure as well as the long commitment were possible because Gerald was 15 years of age instead of over 18.

If Gerald had been over 18, he would not have been subject to Juvenile Court proceedings. For the particular offense immediately involved, the maximum punishment would have been a fine of $5 to $50, or imprisonment in jail for not more than two months. Instead, he was committed to custody for a maximum of six years. If he had been over 18 and had committed an offense to which such a sentence might apply, he would have been entitled to substantial rights under

[41] The Juvenile Judge's testimony at the habeas corpus proceeding is devoid of any meaningful discussion of this. He appears to have centered his attention upon whether Gerald made the phone call and used lewd words. He was impressed by the fact that Gerald was on six months' probation because he was with another boy who allegedly stole a purse—a different sort of offense, sharing the feature that Gerald was "along." And he even referred to a report which he said was not investigated because "there was no accusation" "because of lack of material foundation." * * *

the Constitution of the United States as well as under Arizona's laws and constitution. The United States Constitution would guarantee him rights and protections with respect to arrest, search and seizure, and pretrial interrogation. It would assure him of specific notice of the charges and adequate time to decide his course of action and to prepare his defense. He would be entitled to clear advice that he could be represented by counsel, and, at least if a felony were involved, the State would be required to provide counsel if his parents were unable to afford it. If the court acted on the basis of his confession, careful procedures would be required to assure its voluntariness. If the case went to trial, confrontation and opportunity for cross-examination would be guaranteed. So wide a gulf between the State's treatment of the adult and of the child requires a bridge sturdier than mere verbiage, and reasons more persuasive than cliché can provide. * * *

In Kent v. United States [383 U.S. 541] we stated that the Juvenile Court Judge's exercise of the power of the State as *parens patriae* was not unlimited. We said that "the admonition to function in a 'parental' relationship is not an invitation to procedural arbitrariness." With respect to the waiver by the juvenile court to the adult of jurisdiction over an offense committed by a youth, we said that "there is no place in our system of law for reaching a result of such tremendous consequences without ceremony—without hearing, without effective assistance of counsel, without a statement of reasons." We announced with respect to such waiver proceedings that while "We do not mean * * * to indicate that the hearing to be held must conform with all of the requirements of a criminal trial or even of the usual administrative hearing; but we do hold that the hearing must measure up to the essentials of due process and fair treatment." We reiterate

this view, here in connection with a juvenile court adjudication of "delinquency," as a requirement which is a part of the Due Process Clause of the Fourteenth Amendment of our Constitution.[48]

We now turn to the specific issues which are presented to us in the present case.

III.

NOTICE OF CHARGES

Appellants allege that the Arizona Juvenile Code is unconstitutional or alternatively that the proceedings before the Juvenile Court were constitutionally defective because of failure to provide adequate notice of the hearings. No notice was given to Gerald's parents when he was taken into custody on Monday, June 8. On that night, when Mrs. Gault went to the Detention Home, she was orally informed that there would be a hearing the next afternoon and was told the reason why Gerald was in custody. The only written notice Gerald's parents received at any time was a note on plain paper from Officer Flagg delivered on Thursday or Friday, June 11 or 12, to the effect that the judge had set Monday, June 15, "for further hearings on Gerald's delinquency."

A "petition" was filed with the court on June 9 by Officer Flagg, reciting only that he was informed and believed that

[48] The Nat'l Crime Comm'n Report recommends that "Juvenile courts should make fullest feasible use of preliminary conferences to dispose of cases short of adjudication." Id., at 84. See also D.C.Crime Comm'n Report, pp. 662–665. Since this "consent decree" procedure would involve neither adjudication of delinquency nor institutionalization, nothing we say in this opinion should be construed as expressing any views with respect to such procedure. The problems of pre-adjudication treatment of juveniles, and of post-adjudication disposition, are unique to the juvenile process; hence what we hold in this opinion with regard to the procedural requirements at the adjudicatory stage has no necessary applicability to other steps of the juvenile process.

"said minor is a delinquent minor and that it is necessary that some order be made by the Honorable Court for said minor's welfare." The applicable Arizona statute provides for a petition to be filed in Juvenile Court, alleging in general terms that the child is "neglected, dependent, or delinquent." The statute explicitly states that such a general allegation is sufficient, "without alleging the facts." There is no requirement that the petition be served and it was not served upon, given, or shown to Gerald or his parents.[50]

* * *

We cannot agree with the [Arizona] court's conclusion that adequate notice was given in this case. Notice, to comply with due process requirements, must be given sufficiently in advance of scheduled court proceedings so that reasonable opportunity to prepare will be afforded, and it must "set forth the alleged misconduct with particularity." It is obvious, as we have discussed above, that no purpose of shielding the child from the public stigma of knowledge of his having been taken into custody and scheduled for hearing is served by the procedure approved by the court below. The "initial hearing" in the present case was a hearing on the merits. Notice at that time is not timely; and even if there were a conceivable purpose served by the deferral proposed by the court below, it

would have to yield to the requirements that the child and his parents or guardian be notified, in writing, of the specific charge or factual allegations to be considered at the hearing, and that such written notice be given at the earliest practicable time, and in any event sufficiently in advance of the hearing to permit preparation. Due process of law requires notice of the sort we have described— that is, notice which would be deemed constitutionally adequate in a civil or criminal proceeding. It does not allow a hearing to be held in which a youth's freedom and his parents' right to his custody are at stake without giving them timely notice, in advance of the hearing, of the specific issues that they must meet. Nor, in the circumstances of this case, can it reasonably be said that the requirement of notice was waived.

IV.

RIGHT TO COUNSEL

Appellants charge that the Juvenile Court proceedings were fatally defective because the court did not advise Gerald or his parents of their right to counsel, and proceeded with the hearing, the adjudication of delinquency and the order of commitment in the absence of counsel for the child and his parents or an express waiver of the right thereto. * * * The [Arizona] court argued that "The parent and the probation officer may be relied upon to protect the infant's interests."

* * *

We do not agree. Probation officers, in the Arizona scheme, are also arresting officers. They initiate proceedings and file petitions which they verify, as here, alleging the delinquency of the child; and they testify, as here, against the child. And here the probation officer was also superintendent of the Detention Home. The probation officer cannot act as counsel for the child. His

---

[50] Arizona's Juvenile Code does not provide for notice of any sort to be given at the commencement of the proceedings to the child or his parents. Its only notice provision is to the effect that if a person other than the parent or guardian is cited to appear, the parent or guardian shall be notified "by personal service" of the time and place of hearing. ARS § 8–224. The procedure for initiating a proceeding, as specified by the statute, seems to require that after a preliminary inquiry by the court, a determination may be made "that formal jurisdiction should be acquired." Thereupon the court may authorize a petition to be filed. ARS § 8–222. It does not appear that this procedure was followed in the present case.

role in the adjudicatory hearing, by statute and in fact, is as arresting officer and witness against the child. Nor can the judge represent the child. There is no material difference in this respect between adult and juvenile proceedings of the sort here involved. In adult proceedings, this contention has been foreclosed by decisions of this Court. A proceeding where the issue is whether the child will be found to be "delinquent" and subjected to the loss of his liberty for years is comparable in seriousness to a felony prosecution. The juvenile needs the assistance of counsel to cope with problems of law, to make skilled inquiry into the facts, to insist upon regularity of the proceedings, and to ascertain whether he has a defense and to prepare and submit it. * * * Just as in Kent v. United States, [supra * * *] we indicated our agreement with the United States Court of Appeals for the District of Columbia Circuit that the assistance of counsel is essential for purposes of waiver proceedings, so we hold now that it is equally essential for the determination of delinquency, carrying with it the awesome prospect of incarceration in a state institution until the juvenile reaches the age of 21.

During the last decade, court decisions, experts, and legislatures have demonstrated increasing recognition of this view. * * *

The President's Crime Commission has recently recommended that in order to assure "procedural justice for the child," it is necessary that "Counsel * * * be appointed as a matter of course wherever coercive action is a possibility, without requiring any affirmative choice by child or parent." [65] * * *

---

[65] Nat'l Crime Comm'n Report, pp. 86–87. The Commission's statement of its position is very forceful:

"The Commission believes that no single action holds more potential for achieving procedural justice for the child in the juve-

We conclude that the Due Process Clause of the Fourteenth Amendment requires that in respect of proceedings to

nile court than provision of counsel. The presence of an independent legal representative of the child, or of his parent, is the keystone of the whole structure of guarantees that a minimum system of procedural justice requires. The rights to confront one's accusers, to cross-examine witnesses, to present evidence and testimony of one's own, to be unaffected by prejudicial and unreliable evidence, to participate meaningfully in the dispositional decision, to take an appeal have substantial meaning for the overwhelming majority of persons brought before the juvenile court only if they are provided with competent lawyers who can invoke those rights effectively. The most informal and well-intentioned of judicial proceedings are technical; few adults without legal training can influence or even understand them; certainly children cannot. Papers are drawn and charges expressed in legal language. Events follow one another in a manner that appears arbitrary and confusing to the uninitiated. Decisions, unexplained, appear too official to challenge. But with lawyers come records of proceedings; records make possible appeals which even if they do not occur impart by their possibility a healthy atmosphere of accountability.

"Fears have been expressed that lawyers would make juvenile court proceedings adversary. No doubt this is partly true, but it is partly desirable. Informality is often abused. The juvenile courts deal with cases in which facts are disputed and in which, therefore, rules of evidence, confrontation of witnesses, and other adversary procedures are called for. They deal with many cases involving conduct that can lead to incarceration or close supervision for long periods, and therefore juveniles often need the same safeguards that are granted to adults. And in all cases children need advocates to speak for them and guard their interests, particularly when disposition decisions are made. It is the disposition stage at which the opportunity arises to offer individualized treatment plans and in which the danger inheres that the court's coercive power will be applied without adequate knowledge of the circumstances.

"Fears also have been expressed that the formality lawyers would bring into juvenile court would defeat the therapeutic aims of the court. But informality has no necessary connection with therapy; it is a device that has been used to approach therapy, and it is not the only possible device. It is quite possible that in many instances lawyers, for all their commitment to formality, could do

determine delinquency which may result in commitment to an institution in which the juvenile's freedom is curtailed, the child and his parent must be notified of the child's right to be represented by counsel retained by them, or if they are unable to afford counsel, that counsel will be appointed to represent the child.

* * *

V.

CONFRONTATION, SELF-INCRIMINATION, CROSS-EXAMINATION

Appellants urge that the writ of habeas corpus should have been granted because of the denial of the rights of confrontation and cross-examination in the Juvenile Court hearings, and because the privilege against self-incrimination was not observed. The Juvenile Court Judge testified at the habeas corpus hearing that he had proceeded on the basis of Gerald's admissions at the two hearings. Appellants attack this on the ground that the admissions were obtained in disregard of the privilege against self-incrimination. If the confession is disregarded, appellants argue that the delinquency conclusion, since it was fundamentally based on a finding that Gerald had made lewd re-

more to further therapy for their clients than can the small, overworked social staffs of the courts.

*   *   *   *   *   *

"The Commission believes it is essential that counsel be appointed by the juvenile court for those who are unable to provide their own. Experience under the prevailing systems in which children are free to seek counsel of their choice reveals how empty of meaning the right is for those typically the subjects of juvenile court proceedings. Moreover, providing counsel only when the child is sophisticated enough to be aware of his need and to ask for one or when he fails to waive his announced right are not enough, as experience in numerous jurisdictions reveals.

"The Commission recommends:

"Counsel should be appointed as a matter of course wherever coercive action is a possibility, without requiring any affirmative choice by child or parent."

marks during the phone call to Mrs. Cook, is fatally defective for failure to accord the rights of confrontation and cross-examination which the Due Process Clause of the Fourteenth Amendment of the Federal Constitution guarantees in state proceedings generally.

Our first question, then, is whether Gerald's admission was improperly obtained and relied on as the basis of decision, in conflict with the Federal Constitution. * * *

We shall assume that Gerald made admissions of the sort described by the Juvenile Court Judge, as quoted above. Neither Gerald nor his parents was advised that he did not have to testify or make a statement, or that an incriminating statement might result in his commitment as a "delinquent."

The Arizona Supreme Court rejected appellant's contention that Gerald had a right to be advised that he need not incriminate himself. It said: "We think the necessary flexibility for individualized treatment will be enhanced by a rule which does not require the judge to advise the infant of a privilege against self-incrimination."

In reviewing this conclusion of Arizona's Supreme Court, we emphasize again that we are here concerned only with proceedings to determine whether a minor is a "delinquent" and which may result in commitment to a state institution. Specifically, the question is whether, in such a proceeding, an admission by the juvenile may be used against him in the absence of clear and unequivocal evidence that the admission was made with knowledge that he was not obliged to speak and would not be penalized for remaining silent. In light of Miranda v. Arizona, 384 U.S. 436, 86 S.Ct. 1602, 16 L.Ed.2d 694, 10 A.L.R.3d 974 (1966), we must also consider whether, if the privilege against self-incrimination is available, it can effectively be waived unless counsel is present or the right to counsel has been waived.

*   *   *

The privilege against self-incrimination is, of course, related to the question of the safeguards necessary to assure that admissions or confessions are reasonably trustworthy, that they are not the mere fruits of fear or coercion, but are reliable expressions of the truth. The roots of the privilege are, however, far deeper. They tap the basic stream of religious and political principle because the privilege reflects the limits of the individual's attornment to the state and—in a philosophical sense—insists upon the equality of the individual and the State. In other words, the privilege has a broader and deeper thrust than the rule which prevents the use of confessions which are the product of coercion because coercion is thought to carry with it the danger of unreliability. One of its purposes is to prevent the State, whether by force or by psychological domination, from overcoming the mind and will of the person under investigation and depriving him of the freedom to decide whether to assist the State in securing his conviction.

It would indeed be surprising if the privilege against self-incrimination were available to hardened criminals but not to children. The language of the Fifth Amendment, applicable to the States by operation of the Fourteenth Amendment, is unequivocal and without exception. And the scope of the privilege is comprehensive. As Mr. Justice White, concurring, stated in Murphy v. Waterfront Commission, 378 U.S. 52 (1964), at 94, 84 S.Ct. 1594, 12 L.Ed.2d 678, at 704:

"The privilege can be claimed in *any proceeding*, be it criminal or civil, administrative or judicial, investigatory or adjudicatory * * * it protects *any disclosures* which the witness may reasonably apprehend *could be used in a criminal prosecution or which could lead*

to other evidence that might be so used." (Emphasis supplied.)

*   *   *

Against the application to juveniles of the right to silence, it is argued that juvenile proceedings are "civil" and not "criminal," and therefore the privilege should not apply. It is true that the statement of the privilege in the Fifth Amendment, which is applicable to the States by reason of the Fourteenth Amendment, is that no person "shall be compelled in any *criminal case* to be a witness against himself." However, it is also clear that the availability of the privilege does not turn upon the type of proceeding in which its protection is invoked, but upon the nature of the statement or admission and the exposure which it invites. The privilege may, for example, be claimed in a civil or administrative proceeding, if the statement is or may be inculpatory.

It would be entirely unrealistic to carve out of the Fifth Amendment all statements by juveniles on the ground that these cannot lead to "criminal" involvement. In the first place, juvenile proceedings to determine "delinquency," which may lead to commitment to a state institution, must be regarded as "criminal" for purposes of the privilege against self-incrimination.

*   *   *

It is also urged, as the Supreme Court of Arizona here asserted, that the juvenile and presumably his parents should not be advised of the juvenile's right to silence because confession is good for the child as the commencement of the assumed therapy of the juvenile court process, and he should be encouraged to assume an attitude of trust and confidence toward the officials of the juvenile process. This proposition has been subjected to widespread challenge on the basis of current reappraisals of the rhetoric and realities of the handling of juvenile offenders.

* * *

We conclude that the constitutional privilege against self-incrimination is applicable in the case of juveniles as it is with respect to adults.

* * *

The "confession" of Gerald Gault was first obtained by Officer Flagg, out of the presence of Gerald's parents, without counsel and without advising him of his right to silence, as far as appears. The judgment of the Juvenile Court was stated by the judge to be based on Gerald's admission in court. Neither "admission" was reduced to writing, and, to say the least, the process by which the "admissions" were obtained and received must be characterized as lacking the certainty and order which are required of proceedings of such formidable consequences. Apart from the "admission," there was nothing upon which a judgment or finding might be based. There was no sworn testimony. Mrs. Cook, the complainant, was not present. The Arizona Supreme Court held that "sworn testimony must be required of all witnesses including police officers, probation officers and others who are part of or officially related to the juvenile court structure." We hold that this is not enough. No reason is suggested or appears for a different rule in respect of sworn testimony in juvenile courts than in adult tribunals. Absent a valid confession adequate to support the determination of the Juvenile Court, confrontation and sworn testimony by witnesses available for cross-examination were essential for a finding of "delinquency" and an order committing Gerald to a state institution for a maximum of six years.

The recommendations in the Children's Bureau's "Standards for Juvenile and Family Courts" are in general accord with our conclusions. They state that testimony should be under oath and that only competent material and relevant evidence under rules applicable to civil cases should be admitted in evidence.[98] * * *

As we said in Kent v. United States, 383 U.S. 541, 554, 86 S.Ct. 1045, 1053, 16 L.Ed.2d 84 (1966), with respect to waiver proceedings, "there is no place in our system of law for reaching a result of such tremendous consequences without ceremony * * *." We now hold that, absent a valid confession, a determination of delinquency and an order of commitment to a state institution cannot be sustained in the absence of sworn testimony subjected to the opportunity for cross-examination in accordance with our law and constitutional requirements.

VI.

APPELLATE REVIEW AND TRANSCRIPT OF PROCEEDINGS

* * *

This Court has not held that a State is required by the Federal Constitution "to provide appellate courts or a right to appellate review at all." In view of the fact that we must reverse the Supreme Court of Arizona's affirmance of the dismissal of the writ of habeas corpus for other reasons, we need not rule on this

[98] Standards, pp. 72–73. The Nat'l Crime Comm'n Report concludes that "the evidence admissible at the adjudicatory hearing should be so limited that findings are not dependent upon or influenced by hearsay, gossip, rumor, and other unreliable types of information. To minimize the danger that adjudication will be affected by inappropriate considerations, social investigation reports should not be made known to the judge in advance of adjudication." Id., at 87 (bold face eliminated). See also Note, Rights and Rehabilitation in Juvenile Courts, 67 Col.L. Rev. 281, 336 (1967): "At the adjudication stage, the use of clearly incompetent evidence in order to prove the youth's involvement in the alleged misconduct * * * is not justifiable. Particularly in delinquency cases, where the issue of fact is the commission of a crime, the introduction of hearsay—such as the report of a policeman who did not witness the events—contravenes the purposes underlying the Sixth Amendment right of confrontation." (Footnote omitted.)

question in the present case or upon the failure to provide a transcript or recording of the hearings—or, indeed, the failure of the juvenile court judge to state the grounds for his conclusion.

*   *   *

For the reasons stated, the judgment of the Supreme Court of Arizona is reversed and the cause remanded for further proceedings not inconsistent with this opinion.

It is so ordered.

Mr. Justice BLACK, concurring.

*   *   *

The juvenile court planners envisaged a system that would practically immunize juveniles from "punishment" for "crimes" in an effort to save them from youthful indiscretions and stigmas due to criminal charges or convictions. I agree with the Court, however, that this exalted ideal has failed of achievement since the beginning of the system. *   *   *

I consequently agree with the Court that the Arizona law as applied here denied to the parents and their son the right of notice, right to counsel, right against self-incrimination, and right to confront the witnesses against young Gault. Appellants are entitled to these rights, not because "fairness, impartiality and orderliness—in short, the essentials of due process" require them and not because they are "the procedural rules which have been fashioned from the generality of due process," but because they are specifically and unequivocally granted by provisions of the Fifth and Sixth Amendments which the Fourteenth Amendment makes applicable to the States. *   *   *

[The concurring opinion of Mr. Justice WHITE, and the opinion of Mr. Justice HARLAN, concurring in part and dissenting in part, are omitted.]

Mr. Justice STEWART, dissenting.

The Court today uses an obscure Arizona case as a vehicle to impose upon thousands of juvenile courts throughout the Nation restrictions that the Constitution made applicable to adversary criminal trials. I believe the Court's decision is wholly unsound as a matter of constitutional law, and sadly unwise as a matter of judicial policy.

Juvenile proceedings are not criminal trials. They are not civil trials. They are simply not adversary proceedings. Whether treating with a delinquent child, a neglected child, a defective child, or a dependent child, a juvenile proceeding's whole purpose and mission is the very opposite of the mission and purpose of a prosecution in a criminal court. The object of the one is correction of a condition. The object of the other is conviction and punishment for a criminal act.

*   *   *

The inflexible restrictions that the Constitution so wisely made applicable to adversary criminal trials have no inevitable place in the proceedings of those public social agencies known as juvenile or family courts. And to impose the Court's long catalog of requirements upon juvenile proceedings in every area of the country is to invite a long step backwards into the Nineteenth Century. In that era there were no juvenile proceedings, and a child was tried in a conventional criminal court with all the trappings of a conventional criminal trial. So it was that a 12-year-old boy named James Guild was tried in New Jersey for killing Catharine Beakes. A jury found him guilty of murder, and he was sentenced to death by hanging. The sentence was executed. It was all very constitutional.

A state in all its dealings must, of course, accord every person due process of law. And due process may require that some of the same restrictions which the Constitution has placed upon criminal trials must be imposed upon juvenile proceedings. For example, I suppose that all would agree that a brutally coerced confession could not constitutionally be considered in a juvenile court hearing. But it surely does not follow that the testimonial privilege against self-incrimination is applicable in all juvenile proceedings. Similarly, due process clearly requires timely notice of the purpose and scope of any proceedings affecting the relationship of parent and child. Armstrong v. Manzo, 380 U.S. 545, 85 S.Ct. 1187, 14 L.Ed.2d 62. But it certainly does not follow that notice of a juvenile hearing must be framed with all the technical niceties of a criminal indictment. * * *

In any event, there is no reason to deal with issues such as these in the present case. The Supreme Court of Arizona found that the parents of Gerald Gault "knew of their right to counsel, to subpoena and cross examine witnesses, of the right to confront the witnesses against Gerald and the possible consequences of a finding of delinquency." 99 Ariz. 181, 185, 407 P.2d 760, 763. It further found that "Mrs. Gault knew the exact nature of the charge against Gerald from the day he was taken to the detention home." 99 Ariz. at 193, 407 P.2d at 768. And, as Mr. Justice White correctly points out, * * * ante, no issue of compulsory self-incrimination is presented by this case.

I would dismiss the appeal.

———

J. W. POLIER, A VIEW FROM THE BENCH: THE JUVENILE COURT 55–57

(National Council on Crime and Delinquency, 1964).*

The Law Guardian

* * *

Although the law guardian's role is still in the process of development,

* Copyright 1964 by the National Council of Crime Delinquency; reprinted by permission.

several problems have already emerged which require careful study. To what extent should the law guardian serve in the same role as private counsel? Since the child and parents cannot secure counsel, is he—unlike private counsel—denied the privilege of refusing to serve or withdrawing from a case? To what extent is it his duty to advise the child to remain silent and to do everything in his power to secure a dismissal even when he knows that the child has committed the act and is a danger to himself or to the community? The last question is illustrated by a case in which it was alleged that a fifteen-year-old girl had attempted to poison her stepfather, according to the petition filed by her mother, a deaf-mute. After advising the child to remain silent, the law guardian moved for dismissal on the ground that the evidence was hearsay. Subsequently, the stepfather appeared and testified that he had seen the girl place roach powder in his wine. The girl admitted that she had done so and that she knew it might kill him. After an adjudicatory finding, she was remanded to a psychiatric hospital for observation and committed as mentally ill.

The question of the responsibility of the law guardian requires clarification. Some law guardians advise children to take the stand and speak the truth. They regard the responsibility to do everything possible to avoid "conviction and sentence" (or "adjudication and disposition") as inappropriate in a juvenile court, holding that the ultimate interest of the child requires full disclosure of the evidence so that appropriate services or treatment will be provided. Others take the position that their loyalty and responsibility belong exclusively to the respondent to whom they have been assigned. They make maximum use of the "right to remain silent," even when the parents would prefer to have the child speak and the child himself wants to.

They see their role as counsel for the defense whose task is to secure a dismissal by every legal means, including the right to remain silent. Sometimes this position is defended on the ground that the facilities for treatment and rehabilitation available to the court are so inadequate that a finding of delinquency may lead to inappropriate detention or placement more likely to injure the child than help him.

Many intermediate positions are taken which seem to shift not only with the individual law guardian's philosophy, background, training, skill, and personality, but with the individual case and, indeed, with the judge before whom the case is to be heard.

Aside from the question of responsibility to his client, the law guardian finds it almost impossible to play a constructive role at the dispositional hearing at this time because the sheer volume of cases and his lack of knowledge of community and placement services reduce his function to one of urging probation or accepting whatever placement is recommended by the probation officer or ordered by the court. Even in the significant number of neglect cases where remands in temporary care are continued for many months, intervention to seek re-investigation or work with the families is generally beyond his capacity.

Another matter requiring further study is the extent to which the record of probation efforts to work with the family or secure appropriate placement, the psychiatric reports, and the probation recommendation should be shared with the law guardian prior to the dispositional hearing. If the law guardian's role is to be more than nominal at the dispositional hearing, additional staff must be engaged, new procedures must be developed, and appropriate rules of court must be adopted. * * *

PAULSEN, JUVENILE COURTS AND THE LEGACY OF '67

43 Indiana L.J. 527, 536–540 (1968).*

The Lawyer's Role

It has so far been argued that if lawyers come into juvenile courts in large numbers the operation of these courts will be greatly changed. Is this true because lawyers operate badly, even heartlessly in juvenile court? Judge Whitlach of Cleveland has said, "[a] few members of the Bar proceed with the attitude that they are the savior of the child if they can prevent an adjudication of delinquency, despite the validity of the complaint and the obvious need of the child for the care and protection that the court can give him." [47] His complaint has been echoed by Judge Toner: "[a]n increasing number of lawyers proceed with the attitude that they must prevent an adjudication of delinquency regardless of its validity and the obvious needs of the child and the assistance that can be provided by the court." [48]

Do these comments mean that lawyers should not move to suppress illegally obtained evidence if suppression would release a guilty youth who "needed" treatment? Should a child's lawyer not challenge the use of a confession taken in violation of law if the statement seems quite trustworthy? If parents and child decide to invoke the right of silence should not the attorney assist them to vindicate the right? The assigned lawyer is assigned as the child's lawyer, the child's advocate. Is there not something of a fraud in-

* Copyright 1968 by the Indiana Law Journal; reprinted by permission.

[47] Whitlach, The Gault Decision—Its Effect on the Office of Prosecuting Attorney, 41 Ohio B.J. 41 (January 8, 1968).

[48] Address by Judge John J. Toner, Ohio Association of Juvenile Court Judges, Jan. 23, 1968.

volved in suggesting an undisclosed but a more unclelike role for counsel? Will not the respondent and his parents count on the lawyer to be an advocate—one who will carry out their instructions? Indeed, is a lawyer trained to be wise regarding the question: does this child need treatment from the state?

The New York Family Court Act,[49] establishing the "law guardian" system —the most comprehensive design for organizing legal services in children's courts—contains little to indicate that the New York legislature thought that juvenile court lawyers were to function in a special way. True, the name "law guardian" suggests the role of wise friend as well as legal counselor, but the statute nowhere expresses the view that the term is actually anything but an attractive name designed, perhaps, to muffle criticism of the Act's sponsors. On the contrary, words suggesting a lawyer's traditional role are employed at significant points. The Act affirms, "minors have a right to the assistance of counsel of their own choosing or of law guardians in neglect proceedings * * * and in proceedings to determine juvenile delinquency * * *." [50] The law guardian for the poor is thus equated with retained counsel. Further, the "law guardians" are defined as "attorneys * * * designated * * * to represent minors." [51] The statute goes on to express "a finding that counsel is often indispensible to a practical realization of due process and may be helpful in making reasoned determinations of fact and proper orders of disposition. This part establishes a system of law guardians to realize these purposes." [52] The purposes, then, are: "realization of due process," "reasoned

determination of fact," and "proper orders of disposition." No mention is made of seeing to it that a child who "needs" help receives it.

In short the legislature of New York, except for the use of the term to describe the lawyers to be assigned to the indigent, gives no hint that a lawyer acts improperly if he asserts all defenses and puts the state to its proof.

There is need for a lawyer in juvenile court and, so it seems to the author, a lawyer who acts as an advocate. He is to test the strength of the petitioner's case, to challenge that which can be challenged, and to question that which is open to question. There is no hint in Mr. Justice Fortas' *Gault* opinion that an advocate's action, which could block an adjudication by proper invocation of law or by appropriate challenge to the adequacy of proof, ought not to be taken because adjudication and commitment would benefit the child. Quite the contrary:

> [t]he probation officer cannot act as counsel for the child. His role in the adjudicatory hearing, by statute and in fact, is as arresting officer and witness against the child. Nor can the judge represent the child. There is no material difference in this respect between adult and juvenile proceedings of the sort here involved. In adult proceedings, this contention has been foreclosed by decisions of this Court. A proceeding where the issue is whether the child will be found to be delinquent and subjected to the loss of his liberty for years is comparable in seriousness to a felony prosecution. The juvenile needs the assistance of counsel to cope with problems of law, to make skilled inquiry into the facts, to insist upon regularity of the proceedings, and to ascertain whether he has a defense and to prepare and submit it. The child "requires the guiding hand

---

[49] N.Y.Family Ct.Act (McKinney 1963).

[50] N.Y.Family Ct.Act § 241 (McKinney 1963).

[51] Id. § 242.

[52] Id. § 241.

of counsel at every step in the proceedings against him." [53]

Indeed, Mr. Justice Fortas has rejected the propriety of a lawyer's role at the dispositional stage which is limited merely to being "helpful" to the child and instead emphasized the need to put forth the best affirmative case for him. In the Court of Appeals opinion in *Kent* [54]—a case involving the procedural requirements appropriate to a proceeding to determine whether the case of a sixteen year old should be transferred to criminal court—that court stated that the lawyer's role was to present "anything on behalf of the child which might help a court in arriving at a decision; it is not to denigrate the staff's submissions and recommendations." [55] Mr. Justice Fortas sharply disagreed with the court of appeals: "[o]n the contrary, if the staff's submissions include materials which are susceptible to challenge or impeachment, it is *precisely* the role of counsel to 'denigrate' such matter." [56] Mr. Justice Fortas went on to say that in respect to "critically important" decisions, the material which the judge uses to reach his decision ought to "be subjected, within reasonable limits having regard to the theory of the Juvenile Court Act, to examination, criticism and refutation." [57] The language does not suggest that there is a great difference between the task of a lawyer in a juvenile court and the task of a lawyer in an ordinary criminal case.

A full exploitation of all of the rights of a child in juvenile court will carry the consequence that some guilty youths will escape adjudication. For some young persons this escape may not be, in ultimate terms, a happy occurrence; if juvenile court treatment is beneficial, the beneficial opportunity for the child will be lost. If it is destructive to the child's character for him to go free if he is guilty, that corrupting lesson will be learned in some cases. One cannot have it both ways if the juvenile court is to function as part of the general legal system.

Granted that counsel is properly an advocate, ought not a lawyer seek to achieve what is "best for the child" through persuasion? Should not a lawyer urge a youngster to speak out and admit his guilt? Should not counsel influence his client in proper cases to take advantage of a regimen of character-building through probation or placement in an institution devoted to child care? [58] An affirmative answer puts the lawyer-advocate in the role of a guardian of the person. In the author's view, these roles are not happily united. This position has been articulated by the Supreme Court of Vermont in *In re Dobson*:

> [a]n attorney can effectively argue the alternative courses open to a client only to one assumed to be capable of making a discriminating choice. The minor is presumed incapable and under disability, hence the need of a guardian ad litem to weigh alternatives for him. Yet a lawyer attempting to function as both guardian ad litem and legal counsel is cast in the quandry of acting as both attorney and client, to the detriment of both capacities and the

---

53 387 U.S. 1, 36, 87 S.Ct. 1428, 18 L.Ed.2d 527 (1967) (footnotes omitted).

54 Kent v. United States, 119 U.S.App.D.C. 378, 343 F.2d 247 (1965), reversed 383 U.S. 541, 84 S.Ct. 1045, 16 L.Ed.2d 84 (1966).

55 Id. at 258.

56 Kent v. United States, 383 U.S. 541, 563, 86 S.Ct. 1045, 16 L.Ed.2d 84 (emphasis added).

57 Id.

58 Mr. Charles Schinitsky, Attorney in Charge, Family Court Branch of the Legal Aid Society, New York City, has discussed the duty of a law guardian in New York in relation to his client. See Paulsen, The Constitutional Domestication of the Juvenile Court 1967 Sup.Ct.Rev. 233, 262–264. Mr. Schinitsky concludes, "We do not believe that it is the duty of a law guardian, or of any other attorney, to urge a child to assist the state in securing his conviction."

possible jeopardizing of the infant's interests. The counseling of minors called for by 33 V.S.A. § 678 is best provided by a separation of the roles of guardian ad litem and attorney.[59]

There is one final point about the effects of a child's right to counsel. If many lawyers examine, criticize, and refute information submitted to the court by the probation staff at the dispositional stage of the proceeding, we can predict a certain kind of difficulty for the court. The members of the court staff may well see a useful role for lawyers at the factfinding or adjudicatory stage. If nothing else, television has instructed everyone that counsel has a place at a hearing designed to answer the question, "did he do it?" In contrast, few in the probation staff will take kindly to the challenges put by lawyers to a probation officer's recommendations regarding the disposition of an adjudicated delinquent. The questions asked by advocates seem like an attack on the officer's professional qualifications and his integrity. The staff is likely to view lawyers as interlopers, as persons who will destroy a possible relationship between the probation officer and the respondent, or as misguided amateurs interfering with the benefits which can be derived from a court acting upon expert information.

The staff, it is submitted, is quite mistaken in writing off the contribution which a lawyer can make to a dispositional hearing. A lawyer can articulate the point of view of a family which may be frightened, vulnerable, and without an articulate spokesman. He can bring new suggestions to the mind of the judge. He can call attention to the inadequate basis of some recommendations. At the dispositional stage wise decision-making

can also benefit from "constant, searching, and creative questioning." [60]

* * *

Notes

(1) New Jersey Rules of Court, Rule 6:9–1 (excerpts):

"(c) Offenses to be Listed on the Formal and Informal Calendars. All juvenile complaints which in the opinion of the judge may result in the institutional commitment of the juvenile shall be listed for hearing on the formal calendar, to be heard in accordance with paragraph (d) of this rule. All other complaints shall either be listed on the informal calendar or, in the discretion of the judge, may be referred to a juvenile conference committee or a referee for hearing in accordance with Rules 6:2–2 and 6:2–3.

"(d) Conduct of Formal Calendar. Where the complaint charges the juvenile with causing death, the county prosecutor shall appear at all hearings and prosecute the complaint on behalf of the State. In any other case on the formal calendar, the court may request a prosecuting attorney in accordance with Rule 6:3–5. The court shall provide for the representation of the juvenile, his parents, guardian, or custodian by counsel in accordance with Rule 6:3–4(c). At any such hearing, the court may, in its discretion, conduct the examination of witnesses, but the prosecuting attorney, if any, and counsel for the juvenile, his parents, guardian, or custodian, shall be permitted to participate in such examination and to present evidence, call witnesses and examine or cross-examine all witnesses with respect to any issue to be decided by the court.

"(e) Conduct of Informal Calendar. Complaints listed on the informal calen-

---

[59] 125 Vt. 165, 168, 212 A.2d 620, 622 (1965).

[60] Report of the Attorney General's Committee on Poverty and the Administration of Criminal Justice 10 (1963).

dar shall be conducted in summary manner and may result in any disposition provided in Rule 6:9–11 except commitment. The judge may conduct the examination of witnesses, but if the juvenile, his parents, guardian, or custodian are represented by counsel, such counsel shall be permitted to participate in the hearing and to present evidence, call and examine or cross-examine witnesses. At any stage of the hearing of a complaint listed on the informal calendar, the court may, in its discretion, suspend the hearing and transfer the complaint to the formal calendar to be heard in accordance with the provisions of paragraph (c) of this rule. The hearing on the formal calendar shall be conducted de novo and any statements made by the juvenile at the hearing on the informal calendar shall not be admissible in evidence.

"(f) Hearing after Finding Proof of Delinquency. After hearing of a juvenile complaint, if the court finds beyond a reasonable doubt that the evidence is sufficient to support an adjudication of delinquency, it may either adjudicate delinquency or postpone adjudication and, in either event, order an inquiry into the habits, mode of life, physical or mental condition of the juvenile and such other matters as may be of assistance to the court in determining the disposition of the complaint that will best serve the welfare of the juvenile."

(2) *Gault* left open a number of constitutional issues. The right to a transcript of the proceedings, to have the judge state the grounds for his conclusion and to appellate review were raised but not ruled upon in the opinion itself. However, "Mr. Justice Fortas' opinion * * * [in *Gault*] did call attention to the unfortunate consequences that can attend the failure to provide for appeals, for recording proceedings, and for a statement of reasons by the judge. The language reads like a warning shot, fired

to gain the attention of state court judges and lawmakers. It will not go unheeded by the prudent." Paulsen, The Constitutional Domestication of the Juvenile Court, 1967 Sup.Ct.Rev. 233, 237–238 (P. Kurland ed.)

Although *Gault* provides the juvenile with the right to counsel, the scope of this right is not made clear. Will the right extend to the intake and dispositional stages, or will it be limited to actual juvenile court proceedings? See Paulsen, The Constitutional Domestication of the Juvenile Court, 1967 Sup.Ct. Rev. 233, 256–57 (P. Kurland ed.)

"While it is a fair guess that the Supreme Court will not soon require counsel at the intake stage either because other needs for legal service have first call on the available supply of talent and money or because pre-judicial juvenile proceedings are something special, a constitutional right to counsel at the stage of disposition will surely emerge. The Crime Commission was quite correct in calling attention to the importance of counsel at a dispositional hearing. '[I]n all cases children need advocates to speak for them and guard their interests, particularly when disposition decisions are made.' [Report of the President's Commission on Law Enforcement and Administration of Justice: The Challenge of Crime in a Free Society 86 (1967)]

"The high importance of having a lawyer present at a dispositional hearing is not recognized by everyone. To some the dispositional decision ought to be left to those experts in achieving beneficial changes in human behavior. For these, the choices to be made are clinical or educational. 'How can we best serve the needs of this child?' is the classic way of putting the issue. The answer, however, will often turn on facts that ought to be tested by the 'constant, searching, creative questioning' of the adversary process. Experts, particularly experts who must deal with large numbers of cases, grow weary, make mistakes, take short cuts, bend to frustration, and, in some cases, respond to dislike and prejudice.

"Judge Lindsay G. Arthur of Minneapolis has this to say about a lawyer's task of 'validating' the work of experts:

A psychological report is an imposing document, exuding science, overawing the laity. But it can be based on mistakes. A social investigation is magnificent in its detail and completeness. But it is based heavily on hearsay. Hearsay can be unreliable as centuries of experience have demonstrated, and mistakes are unacceptable. A lawyer, familiar with the family, trained to analyze, experienced in cross-examination, can ensure that the disposition will be based on reliable facts and valid conclusions. As a corollary, the lawyer must know the contents of the reports and most lawyers can be relied on to be discreet in their disclosure of these contents to the family. [National Council of Juvenile Court Judges, Counsel for the Child 29 (1964).]

"Besides, the dispositional decision will be made by a judge, not the expert, in any event. A poor expert's advice needs testing; a skilled expert's recommendations deserve support. A family has a point of view at the time of disposition that they may be unable to articulate. In the great cities of America, the children of the dispossessed come to juvenile court in large numbers. These children and their parents need a voice—literally a 'mouthpiece.' In addition, a good lawyer's brain is another resource that can be put to the question 'What are the various dispositional choices?'

"Finally, a lawyer has an important role in preserving communication be-

tween the court and the respondent (and his family):

Experience demonstrates another function of lawyers, possibly their most valuable at the dispositional stage: to interpret the family to the Court and to interpret the Court to the family. Parents feel easier, they feel protected, they are far more apt to accept and cooperate in the disposition which may of itself make the disposition possible. And the Court can revert to objectivity in weighing plans and facts and conclusions." [Id. at 32]

McKEIVER v. PENNSYLVANIA

Supreme Court of the United States, 1971.
403 U.S. 528, 91 S.Ct. 1976, 29 L.Ed.2d 647.

Mr. Justice BLACKMUN announced the judgments of the Court and an opinion in which THE CHIEF JUSTICE, Mr. Justice STEWART, and Mr. Justice WHITE join.

These cases present the narrow but precise issue whether the Due Process Clause of the Fourteenth Amendment assures the right to trial by jury in the adjudicative phase of a state juvenile court delinquency proceeding.

The issue arises understandably, for the Court in a series of cases already has emphasized due process factors protective of the juvenile:

[Mr. Justice BLACKMUN'S discussion of the prior cases is omitted save for In re Winship].

6. In re Winship, 397 U.S. 358 (1970), concerned a 12-year-old charged with delinquency for having taken money from a woman's purse. The Court held that "the Due Process Clause protects the accused against conviction except upon proof beyond a reasonable doubt of every fact necessary to constitute the crime with which he is charged," 397 U.S., at 364,

90 S.Ct., at 1073, and then went on to hold, at 368, 90 S.Ct., at 1075, that this standard was applicable, too, "during the adjudicatory stage of a delinquency proceeding."

From these cases—it is apparent that:

1.   Some of the constitutional requirements attendant upon the state criminal trial have equal application to that part of the state juvenile proceeding that is adjudicative in nature.   Among these are the rights to appropriate notice, to counsel, to confrontation and to cross-examination, and the privilege against self-incrimination.   Included, also, is the standard of proof beyond a reasonable doubt.

2.   The Court, however, has not yet said that *all* rights, constitutionally assured to an adult accused of crime also are to be enforced or made available to the juvenile in his delinquency proceeding.   Indeed, the Court specifically has refrained from going that far:

> "We do not mean by this to indicate that the hearing to be held must conform with all of the requirements of a criminal trial or even of the usual administrative hearing; but we do hold that the hearing must measure up to the essentials of due process and fair treatment." *Gault*, 387 U.S., at 30, 87 S.Ct., at 1445.

3.   The Court, although recognizing the high hopes and aspirations of Judge Julian Mack, the leaders of the Jane Addams School and the other supporters of the juvenile court concept, has also noted the disappointments of the system's performance and experience and the resulting widespread disaffection. *Kent*, 383 U.S., at 555–556; *Gault*, 387 U.S., at 17–19.   There have been, at one and the same time, both an appreciation for the juvenile court judge who is devoted, sympathetic, and conscientious, and a disturbed concern about the judge who is untrained and less than fully imbued with an understanding approach to the complex problems of childhood and adolescence.   There has been praise for the system and its purposes, and there has been alarm over its defects.

4.   The Court has insisted that these successive decisions do not spell the doom of the juvenile court system or even deprive it of its "informality, flexibility, or speed." *Winship*, 397 U.S., at 366.   On the other hand, a concern precisely to the opposite effect was expressed by two dissenters in *Winship*. Id., at 375–376.

II

With this substantial background already developed, we turn to the facts of the present cases:

No. 322.   Joseph McKeiver, then age 16, in May 1968 was charged with robbery, larceny, and receiving stolen goods (felonies under Pennsylvania law, Pa. Stat.Ann., Tit. 18, §§ 4704, 4807, and 4817 (1963)) as acts of juvenile delinquency.   At the time of the adjudication hearing he was represented by counsel.[2]   His request for a jury trial was denied and his case was heard by Judge Theodore S. Gutowicz of the Court of Common Pleas, Family Division, Juvenile Branch, of Philadelphia County, Pennsylvania.   McKeiver was adjudged a delinquent upon findings that he had violated a law of the Commonwealth.   Pa.Stat. Ann., Tit. 11, § 243(4) (a) (1965).
* * *

Edward Terry, then age 15, in January 1969 was charged with assault and battery on a police officer and conspiracy (misdemeanors under Pennsylvania law, Pa.Stat.Ann., Tit. 18, §§ 4708 and 4302 (1963)) as acts of juvenile delinquency.

---

[2] At McKeiver's hearing his counsel advised the court that he had never seen McKeiver before and "was just in the middle of interviewing" him.   The court allowed him five minutes for the interview.   Counsel's office, Community Legal Services, however, had been appointed to represent McKeiver five months earlier.   App. 2.

His counsel's request for a jury trial was denied. * * *

The Supreme Court of Pennsylvania granted leave to appeal in both cases and consolidated them. The single question considered, as phrased by the court, was "whether there is a constitutional right to a jury trial in juvenile court." The answer, one justice dissenting, was in the negative. In re Terry, 438 Pa. 339, 265 A.2d 350 (1970). We noted probable jurisdiction. 399 U.S. 925 (1970).

The details of the McKeiver and Terry offenses are set forth in Justice Roberts' opinion for the Pennsylvania court, 438 Pa., at 341–342, nn. 1 and 2, 265 A.2d, at 351 nn. 1 and 2, and need not be repeated at any length here. It suffices to say that McKeiver's offense was his participating with 20 or 30 youths who pursued three young teenagers and took 25 cents from them; that McKeiver never before had been arrested and had a record of gainful employment; that the testimony of two of the victims was described by the court as somewhat inconsistent and as "weak"; and that Terry's offense consisted of hitting a police officer with his fists and with a stick when the officer broke up a boys' fight Terry and others were watching.

No. 128. Barbara Burrus and approximately 45 other black children, ranging in age from 11 to 15 years, were the subjects of juvenile court summonses issued in Hyde County, North Carolina, in January 1969.

The charges arose out of a series of demonstrations in the county in late 1968 by black adults and children protesting school assignments and a school consolidation plan. Petitions were filed by North Carolina state highway patrolmen. Except for one relating to James Lambert Howard, the petitions charged the respective juveniles with wilfully impeding traffic. The charge against Howard was that he wilfully made riotous noise and was disorderly in the O. A. Peay School in Swan Quarter; interrupted and disturbed the school during its regular sessions; and defaced school furniture. The acts so charged are misdemeanors under North Carolina law. N.C.Gen. Stat. §§ 20–174.1 (1965 and Supp. 1969), 14–132(a), 14–273 (1969). * * *

In each case the court found that the juvenile had committed "an act for which an adult may be punished by law." A custody order was entered declaring the juvenile a delinquent "in need of more suitable guardianship" and committing him to the custody of the County Department of Public Welfare for placement in a suitable institution "until such time as the Board of Juvenile Correction or the Superintendent of said institution may determine, not inconsistent with the laws of this State." * * * In its turn the Supreme Court of North Carolina deleted that portion of the order in each case relating to commitment, but otherwise affirmed. In re Burrus, 275 N.C. 517, 169 S.E.2d 879 (1969). Two justices dissented without opinion. We granted certiorari. 397 U.S. 1036 (1970).

The right to an impartial jury "[i]n all criminal prosecutions" under federal law is guaranteed by the Sixth Amendment. Through the Fourteenth Amendment that requirement has now been imposed upon the States "in all criminal cases which—were they to be tried in a federal court—would come within the Sixth Amendment's guarantee." This is because the Court has said it believes "that trial by jury in criminal cases is fundamental to the American scheme of justice." Duncan v. Louisiana, 391 U.S. 145, 149, 88 S.Ct. 1444, 1447, 20 L.Ed.2d 491 (1968).

This, of course, does not automatically provide the answer to the present jury trial issue, if for no other reason than that the juvenile court proceeding has not yet been held to be a "criminal prosecution," within the meaning and reach of the Sixth Amendment, and also has not yet been regarded as devoid of criminal aspects merely because it usually has been given the civil label. * * *

Little, indeed, is to be gained by any attempt simplistically to call the juvenile court proceeding either "civil" or "criminal." The Court carefully has avoided this wooden approach. Before *Gault* was decided in 1967, the Fifth Amendment's guarantee against self-incrimination had been imposed upon the state criminal trial. Malloy v. Hogan, 378 U.S. 1 (1964). So, too, had the Sixth Amendment's rights of confrontation and cross-examination, Pointer v. Texas, 380 U.S. 400 (1965), and Douglas v. Alabama, 380 U.S. 415 (1965). Yet the Court did not automatically and peremptorily apply those rights to the juvenile proceeding. A reading of *Gault* reveals the opposite. And the same separate approach to the standard-of-proof issue is evident from the carefully separated application of the standard, first to the criminal trial, and then to the juvenile proceeding, displayed in *Winship*. 397 U.S., at 361 and 365.

Thus, accepting "the proposition that the Due Process Clause has a role to play," *Gault*, 387 U.S., at 13, 87 S.Ct., at 1436, our task here with respect to trial by jury, as it was in *Gault* with respect to other claimed rights, "is to ascertain the precise impact of the due process requirement." Id., at 13–14.

V

The Pennsylvania juveniles' basic argument is that they were tried in proceedings "substantially similar to a criminal trial." They say that a delinquency proceeding in their State is initiated by a petition charging a penal code violation in the conclusory language of an indictment; that a juvenile detained prior to trial is held in a building substantially similar to an adult prison; that in Philadelphia juveniles over 16 are, in fact, held in the cells of a prison; that counsel and the prosecution engage in plea bargaining; that motions to suppress are routinely heard and decided; that the usual rules of evidence are applied; that the customary common-law defenses are available; that the press is generally admitted in the Philadelphia juvenile courtrooms; that members of the public enter the room; that arrest and prior record may be reported by the press (from police sources, however, rather than from the juvenile court records); that, once adjudged delinquent, a juvenile may be confined until his majority in what amounts to a prison (see In re Bethea, 215 Pa.Super. 75, 76, 257 A.2d 368, 369 (1969), describing the state correctional institution at Camp Hill as a "maximum security prison for adjudged delinquents and youthful criminal offenders"); and that the stigma attached upon delinquency adjudication approximates that resulting from conviction in an adult criminal proceeding.

The North Carolina juveniles particularly urge that the requirement of a jury trial would not operate to deny the supposed benefits of the juvenile court system; that the system's primary benefits are its discretionary intake procedure permitting disposition short of adjudication, and its flexible sentencing permitting emphasis on rehabilitation; that realization of these benefits does not depend upon dispensing with the jury; that adjudication of factual issues on the one hand and disposition of the case on the other are very different matters with very different purposes; that the purpose of the former is indistinguishable from that of the criminal trial; that the jury trial provides an independent protective factor; that experience has shown that jury trials in juvenile courts are manageable; that no reason exists why protection traditionally accorded in criminal proceedings should be denied young people subject to involuntary incarceration for lengthy periods; and that the juvenile courts deserve healthy public scrutiny.

VI

All the litigants here agree that the applicable due process standard in juvenile proceedings, as developed by *Gault* and *Winship*, is fundamental fairness. As that standard was applied in those two cases, we have an emphasis on fact-finding procedures. The requirements of notice, counsel, confrontation, cross-examination, and standard of proof naturally flowed from this emphasis. But one cannot say that in our legal system the jury is a necessary component of accurate factfinding. There is much to be said for it, to be sure, but we have been content to pursue other ways for determining facts. Juries are not required, and have not been, for example, in equity cases, in workmen's compensation, in probate, or in deportation cases. Neither have they been generally used in military trials. In *Duncan* the Court stated, "We would not assert, however, that every criminal trial—or any particular trial—held before a judge alone is unfair or that a defendant may never be as fairly treated by a judge as he would be by a jury." 391 U.S., at 158. * * * And in Williams v. Florida, 399 U.S. 78, (1970), the Court saw no particular magic in a 12-man jury for a criminal case, thus revealing that even jury concepts themselves are not inflexible.

We must recognize, as the Court has recognized before, that the fond and idealistic hopes of the juvenile court proponents and early reformers of three generations ago have not been realized. The devastating commentary upon the system's failures as a whole, contained in the President's Commission on Law Enforcement and Administration of Justice, Task Force Report: Juvenile Delinquency and Youth Crime 7–9 (1967), reveals the depth of disappointment in what has been accomplished. Too often the juvenile court judge falls far short of that stalwart, protective, and communicating figure the system envisaged. The community's unwillingness to provide people and facilities and to be concerned, the insufficiency of time devoted, the scarcity of professional help, the inadequacy of dispositional alternatives, and our general lack of knowledge all contribute to dissatisfaction with the experiment.[5]

The Task Force Report, however, also said, id., at 7, "To say that juvenile courts have failed to achieve their goals is to say no more than what is true of criminal

---

[5] "What emerges, then, is this: In theory the juvenile court was to be helpful and rehabilitative rather than punitive. In fact the distinction often disappears, not only because of the absence of facilities and personnel but also because of the limits of knowledge and technique. In theory the court's action was to affix no stigmatizing label. In fact a delinquent is generally viewed by employers, schools, the armed services—by society generally—as a criminal. In theory the court was to treat children guilty of criminal acts in noncriminal ways. In fact it labels truants and runaways as junior criminals.

"In theory the court's operations could justifiably be informal, its findings and decisions made without observing ordinary procedural safeguards, because it would act only in the best interest of the child. In fact it frequently does nothing more nor less than deprive a child of liberty without due process of law—knowing not what else to do and needing, whether admittedly or not, to act in the community's interest even more imperatively than the child's. In theory it was to exercise its protective powers to bring an errant child back into the fold. In fact there is increasing reason to believe that its intervention reinforces the juvenile's unlawful impulses. In theory it was to concentrate on each case the best of current social science learning. In fact it has often become a vested interest in its turn, loathe to cooperate with innovative programs or avail itself of forward-looking methods." Task Force Report 9.

courts in the United States. But failure is most striking when hopes are highest."

Despite all these disappointments, all these failures, and all these shortcomings, we conclude that trial by jury in the juvenile court's adjudicative stage is not a constitutional requirement. We so conclude for a number of reasons:

1. The Court has refrained, in the cases heretofore decided, from taking the easy way with a flat holding that all rights constitutionally assured for the adult accused are to be imposed upon the state juvenile proceeding. What was done in *Gault* and in *Winship* is aptly described in Commonwealth v. Johnson, 211 Pa.Super. 62, 74, 234 A.2d 9, 15 (1967):

"It is clear to us that the Supreme Court has properly attempted to strike a judicious balance by injecting procedural orderliness into the juvenile court system. It is seeking to reverse the trend [pointed out in *Kent*, 383 U.S., at 556, 86 S.Ct. 1045] whereby 'the child receives the worst of both worlds: * * *.' "

2. There is a possibility, at least, that the jury trial, if required as a matter of constitutional precept, will remake the juvenile proceeding into a fully adversary process and will put an effective end to what has been the idealistic prospect of an intimate, informal protective proceeding.

3. The Task Force Report, although concededly pre-*Gault,* is notable for its not making any recommendation that the jury trial be imposed upon the juvenile court system. This is so despite its vivid description of the system's deficiencies and disappointments. Had the Commission deemed this vital to the integrity of the juvenile process, or to the handling of juveniles, surely a recommendation or suggestion to this effect would have appeared. The intimations, instead, are

quite the other way. Task Force Report 38. Further, it expressly recommends against abandonment of the system and against the return of the juvenile to the criminal courts.[6]

4. The Court specifically has recognized by dictum that a jury is not a necessary part even of every criminal process that is fair and equitable. Duncan v. Louisiana, 391 U.S., at 149–150, n. 14, and 158.

5. The imposition of the jury trial on the juvenile court system would not strengthen greatly, if at all, the fact-finding function, and would, contrarily,

---

[6] "Nevertheless, study of the juvenile courts does not necessarily lead to the conclusion that the time has come to jettison the experiment and remand the disposition of children charged with crime to the criminal courts of the country. As trying as are the problems of the juvenile courts, the problems of the criminal courts, particularly those of the lower courts, which would fall heir to much of the juvenile court jurisdiction, are even graver; and the ideal of separate treatment of children is still worth pursuing. What is required is rather a revised philosophy of the juvenile court based on the recognition that in the past our reach exceeded our grasp. The spirit that animated the juvenile court movement was fed in part by a humanitarian compassion for offenders who were children. That willingness to understand and treat people who threaten public safety and security should be nurtured, not turned aside as hopeless sentimentality, both because it is civilized and because social protection itself demands constant search for alternatives to the crude and limited expedient of condemnation and punishment. But neither should it be allowed to outrun reality. The juvenile court is a court of law, charged like other agencies of criminal justice with protecting the community against threatening conduct. Rehabilitating offenders through individualized handling is one way of providing protection, and appropriately the primary way in dealing with children. But the guiding consideration for a court of law that deals with threatening conduct is nonetheless protection of the community. The juvenile court, like other courts, is therefore obliged to employ all the means at hand, not excluding incapacitation for achieving that protection. What should distinguish the juvenile from the criminal courts is greater emphasis on rehabilitation, not exclusive preoccupation with it." Task Force Report 9.

provide an attrition of the juvenile court's assumed ability to function in a unique manner. It would not remedy the defects of the system. Meager as has been the hoped-for advance in the juvenile field, the alternative would be regressive, would lose what has been gained, and would tend once again to place the juvenile squarely in the routine of the criminal process.

6. The juvenile concept held high promise. We are reluctant to say that, despite disappointments of grave dimensions, it still does not hold promise, and we are particularly reluctant to say, as do the Pennsylvania appellants here, that the system cannot accomplish its rehabilitative goals. So much depends on the availability of resources, on the interest and commitment of the public, on willingness to learn, and on understanding as to cause and effect and cure. In this field, as in so many others, one perhaps learns best by doing. We are reluctant to disallow the States to experiment further and to seek in new and different ways the elusive answers to the problems of the young, and we feel that we would be impeding that experimentation by imposing the jury trial. The States, indeed, must go forward. If, in its wisdom, any State feels the jury trial is desirable in all cases, or in certain kinds, there appears to be no impediment to its installing a system embracing that feature. That, however, is the State's privilege and not its obligation.

7. Of course there have been abuses. The Task Force Report has noted them. We refrain from saying at this point that those abuses are of constitutional dimension. They relate to the lack of resources and of dedication rather than to inherent unfairness.

8. There is, of course, nothing to prevent a juvenile court judge, in a particular case where he feels the need, or when the need is demonstrated, from using an advisory jury.

* * * [It] is of more than passing interest that at least 28 States and the District of Columbia by statute deny the juvenile a right to a jury trial in cases such as these. The same result is achieved in other States by judicial decision. In 10 States statutes provide for a jury trial under certain circumstances.

10. Since *Gault* and since *Duncan* the great majority of States, in addition to Pennsylvania and North Carolina, that have faced the issue have concluded that the considerations that led to the result in those two cases do not compel trial by jury in the juvenile court. * * *

* * *

12. If the jury trial were to be injected into the juvenile court system as a matter of right, it would bring with it into that system the traditional delay, the formality, and the clamor of the adversary system and, possibly, the public trial. It is of interest that these very factors were stressed by the District Committee of the Senate when, through Senator Tydings, it recommended, and Congress then approved, as a provision in the District of Columbia Crime Bill, the abolition of the jury trial in the juvenile court. S.Rep.No.91–620, pp. 13–14 (1969).

13. Finally, the arguments advanced by the juveniles here are, of course, the identical arguments that underlie the demand for the jury trial for criminal proceedings. The arguments necessarily equate the juvenile proceeding—or at least the adjudicative phase of it—with the criminal trial. Whether they should be so equated is our issue. Concern about the inapplicability of exclusionary and other rules of evidence, about the juvenile court judge's possible awareness of the juvenile's prior record and of the contents of the social file; about repeated appearances of the same familiar wit-

nesses in the persons of juvenile and probation officers and social workers— all to the effect that this will create the likelihood of pre-judgment—chooses to ignore it seems to us, every aspect of fairness, of concern, of sympathy, and of paternal attention that the juvenile court system contemplates.

If the formalities of the criminal adjudicative process are to be superimposed upon the juvenile court system, there is little need for its separate existence. Perhaps that ultimate disillusionment will come one day, but for the moment we are disinclined to give impetus to it.

Affirmed.

Mr. Justice WHITE, concurring.

* * *

For the most part, the juvenile justice system rests on more deterministic assumptions. Reprehensible acts by juveniles are not deemed the consequence of mature and malevolent choice but of environmental pressures (or lack of them) or of other forces beyond their control. Hence the state legislative judgment not to stigmatize the juvenile delinquent by branding him a criminal; his conduct is not deemed so blameworthy that punishment is required to deter him or others. Coercive measures, where employed, are considered neither retribution nor punishment. Supervision or confinement is aimed at rehabilitation, not at convincing the juvenile of his error simply by imposing pains and penalties. Nor is the purpose to make the juvenile delinquent an object lesson for others, whatever his own merits or demerits may be. A typical disposition in the juvenile court where delinquency is established may authorize confinement until age 21, but it will last no longer and within that period will last only so long as his behavior demonstrates that he remains an unacceptable risk if returned to his family. Nor is the authorization for custody until 21 any measure of the seriousness of the particular act that the juvenile has performed.

Against this background and in light of the distinctive purpose of requiring juries in criminal cases, I am satisfied with the Court's holding. To the extent that the jury is a buffer to the corrupt or overzealous prosecutor in the criminal law system, the distinctive intake policies and procedures of the juvenile court system to a great extent obviate this important function of the jury. As for the necessity to guard against judicial bias, a system eschewing blameworthiness and punishment for evil choice is itself an operative force against prejudice and short-tempered justice. Nor where juveniles are involved is there the same opportunity for corruption to the juvenile's detriment or the same temptation to use the courts for political ends. * * *

For me there remain differences of substance between criminal and juvenile courts. They are quite enough for me to hold that a jury is not required in the latter. Of course, there are strong arguments that juries are desirable when dealing with the young, and States are free to use juries if they choose. They are also free if they extend criminal court safeguards to juvenile court adjudications, frankly to embrace condemnation, punishment, and deterrence as permissible and desirable attributes of the juvenile justice system. But the Due Process Clause neither compels nor invites them to do so.

Mr. Justice BRENNAN, concurring in the judgment in No. 322 and dissenting in No. 128.

I agree with the plurality opinion's conclusion that the proceedings below in these cases were not "criminal prosecutions" within the meaning of the Sixth Amendment. For me, therefore, the question in these cases is whether jury trial is among the "essentials of due process and fair treatment," * * *

In my view, therefore, the due process question cannot be decided upon the basis of general characteristics of juvenile proceedings, but only in terms of the adequacy of a particular state procedure to "protect the [juvenile] from oppression by the Government," Singer v. United States, 380 U.S. 24, 31 (1965), and to protect him against "the complaint, biased, or eccentric judge." Duncan v. Louisiana, 391 U.S. 145, 156 (1968).

Examined in this light, I find no defect in the Pennsylvania cases before us. The availability of trial by jury allows an accused to protect himself against possible oppression by what is in essence an appeal to the community conscience, as embodied in the jury that hears his case. To some extent, however, a similar protection may be obtained when an accused may in essence appeal to the community at large, by focusing public attention upon the facts of his trial, exposing improper judicial behavior to public view, and obtaining, if necessary, executive redress through the medium of public indignation. Of course, the Constitution, in the context of adult criminal trials, has rejected the notion that public trial is an adequate substitution for trial by jury in serious cases. But in the context of juvenile delinquency proceedings, I cannot say that it is beyond the competence of a State to conclude that juveniles who fear that delinquency proceedings will mask judicial oppression may obtain adequate protection by focusing community attention upon the trial of their cases. For, however much the juvenile system may have failed in practice, its very existence as an ostensibly beneficent and noncriminal process for the care and guidance of young persons demonstrates the existence of the community's sympathy and concern for the young. Juveniles able to bring the community's attention to bear upon their trials may therefore draw upon a reservior of public concern unavailable to the adult criminal defendant. In the Pennsylvania cases before us, there appears to be no statutory ban upon admission of the public to juvenile trials. * * * I agree that the judgment in No. 322 must be affirmed.

The North Carolina cases, however, present a different situation. North Carolina law either permits or requires exclusion of the general public from juvenile trials. * * * The cases themselves, which arise out of a series of demonstrations by black adults and juveniles who believed that the Hyde County, North Carolina, school system unlawfully discriminated against black schoolchildren, present a paradigm of the circumstances in which there may be a substantial "temptation to use the courts for political ends." And finally, neither the opinions supporting the judgment nor the respondent in No. 128 has pointed to any feature of North Carolina's juvenile proceedings that could substitute for public or jury trial in protecting the petitioners against misuse of the judicial process. * * * Accordingly, I would reverse the judgment in No. 128. * * *

Mr. Justice DOUGLAS, with whom Mr. Justice BLACK and Mr. Justice MARSHALL concur, dissenting.

The concurring opinion of Mr. Justice HARLAN is omitted.

We held in In re Gault, 387 U.S. 1, 13, that "neither the Fourteenth Amendment nor the Bill of Rights is for adults alone." As we noted in that case, the Juvenile Court movement was designed to avoid procedures to ascertain whether the child was "guilty" or "innocent" but to bring to bear on these problems a "clinical" approach. Id., at 15, 16, 87 S.Ct., at 1437, 1438. It is, of course, not our task to determine as a matter of policy whether a "clinical" or "punitive" approach to these problems should be taken by the States. But where a State uses its juvenile court proceedings to prosecute a juvenile for a criminal act and to order "confinement" until the child reaches 21 years of age or where the child at the threshold of the proceedings faces that prospect, then he is entitled to the same procedural protection as an adult.

_____

PAULSEN, CHILDREN'S COURT: GATEWAY OR LAST RESORT?

Columbia University Forum, Summer 1967, Volume X, Number 2, p. 4.*

The *Gault* decision works a revolutionary change in the law applicable to erring children by establishing that all "fact-finding" hearings in juvenile courts (i. e., hearings in which it is determined what the respondent has done) "must measure up to the essentials of due process and fair treatment." The decision is built upon the premise that the juvenile court system has failed to provide the care and treatment that the theory underlying it had posited. The language of uplift has masked an ugly reality. "Training" schools are often nothing more than prisons for the young, and children may be incarcerated there by proceedings containing few of the safeguards provided for adult offenders. "So wide a gulf between the State's treatment of the adult and of the child," the opinion of Mr. Justice Fortas states, "requires a bridge sturdier than mere verbiage and reasons more persuasive that clichés can provide."

"**The** essentials of due process and fair treatment" include, in the Court's eyes, the giving of adequate and timely notice of the petition so the youngster and his parents have the opportunity to respond. Further, in fact-finding hearings "which may result in commitment" the child is entitled to be represented by counsel and, if the parents are unable to afford a lawyer, the state must provide one. Due

process will require that the "constitutional privilege against self-incrimination is applicable in the case of juveniles as it is with respect to adults." Without a valid confession, a determination of delinquency cannot be sustained "in the absence of sworn testimony subjected to the opportunity for cross-examination." * *

The reformers of the turn of the century and those who were persuaded by them held the highest hopes. Until a "better and finer agency may be evolved * * * the juvenile court will remain to serve as a fountain of mercy, truth and justice to our handicapped children." This sentiment appears in the final words of the final chapter of Herbert Lou's Juvenile Courts in the United States. Published in 1927, the book was until recently the most widely consulted work in its field. Every page of it reflects the sure conviction that these specialized courts for children are among man's most noble creations.

The juvenile court was created near the turn of the century by men and women possessed of a passion for social justice. The concerned citizens who secured the passage of juvenile court acts in almost every state within a few years after the landmark Illinois Act of 1899 were aroused by women's rights, prison reform, the plight of the immigrant poor, as well as by the need to protect children. The reformers were optimists. They saw the social order as basically good but believed that it ought to be brought up to date and some of the cruelty taken out of it. Women should have the vote, prisoners should be taught a trade, immigrants should be afforded equal opportunity, and wayward youth should be saved.

A child in trouble was not likely to be saved in 1899. If he were over seven, he could be convicted of crime. After conviction he would find himself branded for life with the criminal's stigma; he might be placed in an institution designed for hardened criminals and mixed with the general prison population. In part, the juvenile court movement was a reaction to this harsh and cruel system of cutting off a life's potential before the life had truly begun.

And in part, the reformers were skeptical about the entire process of criminal justice. Obviously, the system of conviction, punishment, and release had not contained crime. If anything, it made men worse. It embraced in its operation nothing designed to lift men up or to help them with their difficulties. Certainly this arrangement, based on uncertain theories of deterrence, in turn founded on a medieval conception of free will, would not in the reformers' eyes be appropriate to the twentieth century.

The new court was to emphasize correctional change in the individual child. The source of each young offender's forbidden deeds was to be discovered and eliminated by treatment. Medical attention was to be given those whose misbehavior resulted from physical ills. Psychological techniques were to be applied to the mentally disturbed. Special teaching would overcome behavior problems rooted in miseducation. A probation officer's guidance and counsel would strengthen the youth's own resources. Indeed, the juvenile court was often compared to a clinic or a school. The reformers had a firm and naïve belief that a body of science—medical, social, and psychological—did exist that could work beneficial changes in troubled children if only the law would open the door to its application. "The problem for determination by the judge is not," wrote Judge Julian Mack in 1908, "has this boy or girl committed a specific wrong, but what is he, how has he become what he is, and what had best be done in his interest and in the interest of the state to save him from a downward career." The child should be changed and restored, not branded and lost.

The juvenile court was to be staffed by expert, specialized judges knowledgeable in the behavioral sciences, filled with love for children; by probation officers with extensive training and light caseloads; by medical and psychological personnel who were to provide the needed auxiliary services.

The specialized court was to employ a flexible procedure geared to the individual case. Nothing should remind a respondent youngster of a criminal court—no jury, no robes, no formal courtroom trappings. The rules of evidence which exclude much relevant information only made more difficult the task of getting to the bottom of things. Lawyers were not needed because the court did not employ an adversary procedure. The aim of the process was to help the youngster. Lawyers would only introduce a useless element of conflict. Even the trial hearing itself was perceived as part of the treatment process. "Seated at a desk, with the child at his side, where he can on occasion but his arm around his shoulder and draw the lad to him, the judge, while losing some of his judicial dignity, will gain immensely in the effectiveness of his work." The words are again those of Judge Mack.

How could such a court meet the standards of American constitutions? After all, a youngster could lose his liberty by procedures far too streamlined to pass muster in the criminal courts. The juvenile court, asserted the reformers, was a civil not a criminal court. It employed chancery doctrines, in particular, the concept of *parens patriae*—the idea that the state is the ultimate parent of all. Constitutional guarantees, in short, were traded for rehabilitation, education, and salvation. * * *

The 1967 Report of the President's Commission on Law Enforcement and the Administration of Justice also makes a sharp break with the traditional theory regarding the juvenile court. Herbert

Lou said that youngsters were brought to court so that "the handicapped children of the community who come before it may be adjusted, protected, corrected, and developed into useful members of society." In contrast, the report of the President's Commission affirms that "delinquency is not so much an act of individual deviancy as a pattern of behavior produced by a multitude of pervasive societal influences well beyond the reach of action by any judge, probation officer, correctional counsellor or psychiatrist." The chief weapons in the fight against delinquency are to be social and economic means rather than attempts to effect change in individual offenders. The report urges improvement in schools, housing, employment opportunities, occupational training programs, and the strengthening of the family.

The formal juvenile court system and its pronouncements of delinquency, the report said, "should be used only as a last resort." The report does not present the juvenile court as an instrument for saving youth; instead it cites numerous studies that indicate that the court is a corrupter of youth. The draftsmen of the report recommend that children be kept away from the juvenile court's formal adjudication in as many cases as possible. They recommend the establishment of youth service bureaus, to be located in neighborhood community centers and required to receive both delinquent and non-delinquent children referred by police, parents, schools and other agencies. Each bureau would embrace a broad range of services designed to assist young people in their problems. The report further recommends that juvenile courts should make the fullest feasible use of "preliminary conferences" to allow for out-of-court adjustments and settlements at the level of court intake. A further device to avoid adjudication is contained in the suggestion that juvenile courts should employ consent decrees wherever

possible in the hope that the agreements to undertake rehabilitative treatment might free the respondent from the stigma of adjudication and at the same time make certain that an erring youth who needs it will undertake a treatment plan. For the cases that must come to court the report urges the introduction of procedures that will guarantee a fair hearing for finding the facts regarding the child's acts as well as a just process for determining questions of disposition. In particular, the Commission urges that lawyers be provided for juveniles. "It is essential," the report states, "that counsel be appointed by the juvenile court for those who are unable to provide their own."

Whatever hope there was (and I think there was little) for the juvenile court to be a gateway to a supermarket of services for regeneration has been drained away by the passing of time and the emergence of a new order of social values.

"Delinquency," invented as a soft substitute for the word "crime," is now a cruel term itself. Why?

The dreams were inflated dreams—cut off from the hard realities of the world. The cities, counties, and states were never willing or able to provide the juvenile court with the resources its theory required. Few judges have reached the level of performance that the reformers expected. Probation staffs have been inadequately trained and given such large numbers to supervise that nothing but the most perfunctory attention can be given most cases. Most courts do not have access either to adequate auxiliary services or to a wide range of institutions for the help of the adjudicated delinquent.

Would the problem of today's juvenile court disappear suddenly if immense new resources would be made available? No, I think not.

The dream believed too much in man's capacity—here and now—to effect correctional change. Within the population of teen-agers there are a number of dangerously anti-social persons who present a great threat to the community and about whose rehabilitation no one has a firm idea. A youth can inflict a grievous injury which cannot go unremarked and yet the tools are not at hand "to save him from a downward career." Thus we have in fact employed juvenile court adjudications to repress rather than to re-educate. The desire to save outruns the possibility of doing so.

The aspirations of the reformers have, in fact, been turned upside down. A contact with the juvenile court not only is unlikely to assist a youngster to become a better citizen but, according to respectable theory today, it is likely to lead him into further delinquency. The "saving" institution may be a corrupter of youth. A recent publication of the Russell Sage Foundation puts the matter this way: "If the labeling hypothesis is correct, official intervention may further define the youth as delinquent in the eyes of neighbors, family members, and peers, thus making it more difficult for him to resume conventional activities."

The reformers thought of most criminal procedure as a product of a dark age —technical, impeding the discovery of truth, useful only to pettifogging lawyers. Today, the aspects of the Bill of Rights that set standards in criminal procedure are perceived as milestones marking the progress of man's march to freedom.

Little by little we have learned again that informality can become the curtain behind which error, weariness, indifference, unseemly hate and prejudice can operate. The misuse of power by juvenile court judges in the South, little inhibited by statutory or constitutional norms, has been documented by the Civil Rights Commission. A trickle of appellate cases further suggests that injustice flowing from an abundance of discretionary power is not regional in this country.
* * *

The stance of the reformers no longer fits the 1960s. Listen to Judge Mack again. "Most of the children who come before the court are, naturally, the children of the poor. In many cases the parents are foreigners, frequently unable to speak English, and without an understanding of American methods and views. What they need, more than anything else, is kindly assistance. * * *" Is this the way we see delinquency, the delinquent, and the remedy for the problem? The respondent in the juvenile court, especially in the city, is apt to be of the poor; he is often a Negro. His parents are unlikely to be foreigners and may speak English reasonably well. The problems of the slum-bred delinquent will not yield to an offer of "kindly assistance."

The demand for more legal norms has also been fed by an old American practice: the unconscionable manipulation of law and legal process. *Gault* provides a moving example. The juvenile court judge who committed him was unclear about the exact statute under which young Gault was adjudicated. He took into account an unproved prior instance of alleged misconduct. He did not require the complaining witness to testify. Gault's parents were not given notice according to the proper legal form. The events fit the suspicion: the judge believed young Gault should be disciplined. It did not matter much how it was to be accomplished.

The Court, legislatures, and the President's Commission all point to a new juvenile court that will be quite different from the one proposed by the reformers. The new court is to be a court of last resort, not a gateway to rehabilitation and re-education. It will be a court very much like other courts, differing principally in its great emphasis upon (but not exclusive concern with) the rehabilitation of children *before* the formal trial. The new court will be challenged by the old problem: What can the state, in fact, do to help the youthful offender and reduce crime among the young? Orderliness can correct some abuses but surely it cannot create new opportunities.

Like the reformers, the Supreme Court, the legislatures, and the President's Commission are moved by a concern to serve children. They would do it differently, of course: where the intention was once to get the troubled child into the courts as fast as possible, the aim will now be to keep him out of court altogether, if that is possible. There is a deeper difference in respect a matter other than the method of proceeding. Fundamentally, the conviction is no longer shared that crime can be reduced or children, in large numbers, "saved" by the tactic of treating the individual deviant. Institutional rehabilitation, if not a myth, is at least unreachable in practice. More than law is required. Cure is not the characteristic of "last resort" expedients. Patient attack on basic social evils, together with sorrowful, helpful but firm response to those who cause serious harm, are the actions that commend themselves to the 1960s. Like the recommended programs of 1900, they will take money, determination, and love. Whether the outcome will be happier is in the balance.

IN THE MATTER OF CROMWELL

Court of Appeals of Maryland, 1963.
232 Md. 409, 194 A.2d 88.

HENDERSON, Judge. These cases came before us at an earlier stage, on petitions to release the appellants from the custody of the training schools to which they had been committed as juvenile delinquents, pending the hearing of these appeals. We declined to do so, holding that the temporary commitments violated no constitutional principle, and that the trial court was not clearly wrong in declining to release these children to the custody of their mothers under the circumstances of the case. We took judicial notice of the fact that the Governor had sent the State Militia to Cambridge to prevent threatened outbreaks of violence. We pointed out that the trial court may well have felt that it was in the best interests of the children that they be removed from the scene of danger, where they would be safe from the physical injuries they might suffer if they remained at home and persisted in their past course of participating in protests against racial segregation that were not always peaceful or law-abiding. Ex parte Cromwell, 232 Md. 305, 192 A.2d 775.

We advanced these appeals for hearing, and the case was heard on a stipulated statement of facts in lieu of a transcript of proceedings. We take judicial notice of the facts that the militia is still in Cambridge and that a Charter Amendment designed to clear the air, by forbidding discrimination in restaurants and certain other places of public accommodation, was defeated by popular vote on October 1, 1963.

The appellants, Dwight Cromwell and Dinez White, contend that they were denied their constitutional rights under the Fourteenth Amendment to the Federal Constitution, in that the court found them to be juvenile delinquents simply because of their participation in civil rights demonstrations. They argue that in picketing the Board of Education and in walking down the streets of Cambridge, they were merely exercising a right of free speech and assembly. The other three demonstrations in which they participated were "sit-ins" of privately operated places of public accommodation. They argue that these actions did not constitute unlawful trespass or disturbances of the peace, to justify a conviction either under the State Trespass Law (Code (1957), Art. 27, sec. 577), or the State Disorderly Conduct Law (Code (1957), Art. 27, sec. 123), or the local law of Dorchester County, P.L.L. (1961 Ed.) Art. 10, sec. 91 (Disorderly Conduct).

The Juvenile Court Act (Code (1957), Art. 26, sec. 52(e)) provides:

" 'Delinquent child' means a child (1) who violates any law or ordinance, or who commits any act which, if committed by an adult, would be a crime not punishable by death or life imprisonment; (2) who is incorrigible or ungovernable or habitually disobedient or who is beyond the control of his parents, guardian, custodian or other lawful authority; (3) who is habitually a truant; (4) who without just cause and without the consent of his parents, guardian or other custodian, repeatedly deserts his home or place of abode; (5) who is engaged in any occupation which is in violation of law, or who associates with immoral or vicious persons; or (6) who so deports himself as to injure or endanger the morals of himself or others."

The appellants were each 15 years of age when arrested on charges of disorderly conduct in connection with the "sit-in" demonstrations. Being of an age where the Juvenile Court has exclusive jurisdiction under Code (1957), Art. 26, sec. 53, in the absence of waiver under sec. 54, they were charged with delinquency in the juvenile court, on petitions assigning as the only reasons therefor, disorderly conduct on three occasions identified by dates in one case, and on four occasions in the other. At the hearing they were represented by counsel.

In the previous appeal we expressed no opinion as to the validity of the finding of delinquency, stating that the only matter then before us was the propriety of the ruling that the infant petitioners

be lodged in the training schools pending the determination of these appeals. The question reserved is now before us. We have no difficulty in holding that there was evidence before the trial court to support a finding that each child had committed acts, which if committed by an adult, would have constituted the crimes of trespass and disorderly conduct. We refer particularly to an incident mentioned in our prior opinion, where they entered the Dorset Theatre without tickets while a show was in progress, lay on the floor, used profane language and refused to leave until arrested. If we assume, without deciding, that children have the same rights of protest enjoyed by adults, such conduct, we think would justify a conviction in the case of adults. See Bell v. State, 227 Md. 302, 305, 176 A.2d 771, and cases there cited. (The Supreme Court granted certiorari in this case and in the earlier case of Griffin v. State, 225 Md. 422, 171 A.2d 717, and these cases will be argued, or reargued in the current term.) Under the existing law, unless and until it be declared unconstitutional by the Supreme Court of the United States, we find no violation of the Fourteenth Amendment in the assertion of a private proprietor's right to choose his customers, or to eject those who are disorderly or enter without paying a charge imposed upon all patrons.

But the difficulty in the case at bar is that a mere finding of a basis for delinquency is not enough. Code (1957) Art. 26, sec. 54, provides that when the jurisdiction of the Juvenile Court is invoked the "judge shall then determine whether or not such child comes within any of the aforesaid terms *and is, by reason thereof, in need of care or treatment* within the provisions and intent of this subtitle." Sec. 61 provides that the case shall be dismissed if the "judge determines that the child is not within the jurisdiction of the court *or that the child is not in need of care or treatment*

* * *." (Italics supplied.) Such need in the case at bar arises out of the threatened physical harm to the appellants, if they should persist in participating in public demonstrations which might lead to violence. If public demonstrations were discontinued for any reason, or if some guaranty were offered that the appellants would be effectively prevented by their parents or guardians from participating, we think it is clear that there would be no need for other or further care or treatment on that score.

While we hold that the disorderly conduct shown was sufficient to support the finding of delinquency, the conduct of these appellants, standing alone, was not so fundamentally wrong as to require permanent treatment, as distinguished from temporary custodial care. In the main, the demonstrations in which they participated were conducted by adults who, although disorderly in some instances, were not engaged in acts involving moral turpitude. It appears that the adult demonstrators were either dismissed, when charged with disorderly conduct, or that minimum fines were imposed. Incarceration of these children beyond the immediate need for their protection could hardly be supported. * * *

Decree reversed and case remanded, with costs.

Note

Wheeler & Cottrell, Juvenile Delinquency: Its Prevention and Control 39–40 (Russell Sage Foundation 1966): "Standard forms of probation, based upon individually oriented social casework, have been supplemented in recent years by two other forms of treatment, either of which may be employed in an institutional setting or while offenders are free in the community. One set of programs is founded upon what has been called guided group interaction, in which the attitudes and norms maintained by a group of delinquents is the focus of change, rather than the behavior and attitudes of any one of its members. The basis for this approach is the normative support for delinquency that comes from the peer group; hence it is thought that, by working with the values of the peer group as a unit, rather than with the individual, the system can be changed. In such programs the group itself has a stake in the fate of its members for they participate with the staff in solving problems.

"A second and related kind of program is one which uses the delinquent himself as an agent of change or therapy for others. The rationale behind this program is that the youth will learn conventional modes of behavior by being placed in conventional roles, with all the responsibilities such roles entail. In his efforts to help others, it is assumed, he will lose some of his antisocial tendencies and gain direct experience in performing in conventional ways. These programs are not unlike those of Alcoholics Anonymous and Synanon in their using the deviant himself as an agent of change.

"Among the most promising alternatives to full incarceration are various kinds of treatment programs operating in the community, but with the offender spending part of the day in a treatment center. One such program was introduced at the adult level as early as 1913 through the Huber Law in the State of Wisconsin. Current examples are the Provo and Essex Fields experiments designed for about twenty boys at a time, with the subjects living at home while working a full day and then participating in group sessions based upon the model of guided group interaction. The most important feature of these programs is that the youths remain in the community where their problems arose. Whatever efforts at change they make are therefore not restricted by the artificialities of institutional settings. The results from such projects appear promising, although evaluation is not easy and has been plagued by technical difficulties.

"A different type of treatment program has been sponsored by the California Youth Authority. The Community Treatment Project, as it is called, is similar to the Provo and Essex Fields experiments in that it operates within the community and is designed to serve youths who might otherwise be incarcerated. But the assumptions underlying the program and the nature of the program are somewhat different. It begins with a classification of offenders into interpersonal maturity levels. Each type defines a different problem and requires different treatment. The result is a rich matrix of treatment programs designed for different types of delinquents. The Community Treatment Project is still in the process of evaluation; but it, along with the Provo and Essex Fields experiments, provides a good example of the possibilities of developing forms of treatment short of incarceration which appear to be at least as successful in outcome as more severe methods.

"Another way of increasing the range of alternatives available to sentencing authorities and therapeutic agents is the development of different types of institutional settings with great variations in the length of time persons spend in them. It may well be that whatever impact is obtained by staying in an institution is accomplished during the first two weeks or months of that stay and conceivably within the first few days. Extremely short terms, of course, do not allow for intensive treatment over a long period of time in a controlled environment. But the obvious advantages of very short terms would seem to require that the burden of proof should be on those who argue that a long term is really necessary. In a short-term stay, the offender

may not lose his standing in his school, nor will he necessarily suffer the presumed stigma of commitment to a traditional penal institution. It seems most reasonable to attempt the development of short-term programs, particularly if educational or vocational programs, which often require several months to complete, can be carried out within the community instead of within an institutional setting."

B.   NON-CRIMINAL CONDUCT

Juvenile Court statutes throughout the country owing various formulations empower the juvenile courts to exercise the state's authority over children who are engaged in various forms of conduct thought to be immoral or harmful to the child (including failure to attend school). In some statutes such persons are called persons-in-need-of-supervision, in other statutes "incorrigibles" or "wayward minors". Most frequently, children are brought before the juvenile court for noncriminal conduct because they have disobeyed their parents.

BRAUN v. STATE

Supreme Court of North Dakota, 1966.
145 N.W.2d 482.

KNUDSEN, Justice. The appellant Jeanette Braun was committed by the Juvenile Court of Richland County to the State Industrial School by order dated April 18, 1966, having been * * *

There is no doubt that the defendant Jeanette was a delinquent child within the meaning of the statutes, and the court was correct in so finding and in assuming jurisdiction over her.* However,

* 5 N.D.Cent.Code § 27–16–08 (1960)
27–16–08.   Jurisdiction.—Except as otherwise provided by law, the [juvenile]

the question arises: Was the order committing her to the State Industrial School for the best interests of Jeanette Braun and of the State of North Dakota?

Jeanette had been living at the home of her parents at Wahpeton, North Dakota, and had been attending high school. On or about February 4, 1966, Jeanette, with four other girls, in her bedroom, drank two six-packs of beer, of which

court shall have original jurisdiction in all proceedings:

1. Concerning any child [defined as "a person less than eighteen years of age," 5 N.D.Cent.Code § 27–16–07 (1960)] residing in or who is temporarily within the county:

   a. Who has violated any city or village ordinance or law of this state or of the United States;

   b. Who has deserted his home without sufficient cause or who is habitually disobedient to the reasonable and lawful commands of his parents, guardians, or other custodians;

   c. Who habitually associates with dissolute, vicious, or immoral persons, or who is leading an immoral or vicious life;

   d. Who, being required by law to attend school, willfully and habitually absents himself therefrom, or who habitually violates the rules and regulations thereof;

   e. Whose parent or other person legally responsible for the care and maintenance of such child, neglects or refuses, when able so to do, to provide proper or necessary support, education as required by law, medical, surgical, or other care necessary for his health, morals, or well-being, or who is abandoned by his parents, guardian, or other custodian, or who is otherwise without proper custody or guardianship;

   f. Whose home, by reason of neglect, cruelty, drunkenness, or depravity on the part of the parent or person having the custody or control of such child, is an unfit place for such child to live;

   g. Who engages in an occupation or who is in a situation dangerous or injurious to the health, safety, or morals of himself or others.

* * *

Jeanette and her friend drank all but two cans. The next morning Jeanette and her friend, who stayed overnight, were late for school. Jeanette attended her first class, skipped her second class, and during the third class had some difficulty with her teacher because of giggling and laughing, and otherwise cutting up. The incident was reported by the school authorities to the Juvenile Commissioner who filed a petition with the district court praying the court to make provision for such child as the court may deem proper. A hearing was held on the petition on February 23, 1966, and on March 7 the court issued its order determining Jeanette to be a delinquent child within the meaning of the statutes, further ordering that the child should remain in the custody of her parents and placed on probation for a period of six months with the Juvenile Commissioner. It was further ordered that as a condition of probation that she be placed in a school to finish her high school. Jeanette at this time was sixteen years of age and a Junior in the Wahpeton high school. Jeanette had dropped out of school in her sophomore year to have an illegitimate child out of wedlock. She finished her sophomore year by correspondence.

The parents were unable to place Jeanette in any high school because the Wahpeton high school and the Hankinson Academy refused to accept Jeanette. Jeanette and her parents were brought before the court again on April 5, 1966, because of their failure to place Jeanette in school. It was brought out at this hearing that Jeanette was pregnant and planned on being married. The court ordered a clinical examination to determine whether or not she was pregnant. Thereafter, on the 18th day of April, 1966, the court ordered Jeanette committed to the State Industrial School at Mandan.

The Industrial School sent Jeanette to the Florence Crittenton Home at Fargo as the Industrial School had no facilities for the care of pregnant girls. While she was at the Florence Crittenton Home she and her father and Ronald Kelly, the father of her unborn child went to Sisseton, South Dakota, where she and Mr. Kelly were married. After her marriage she returned to her home as the Florence Crittenton Home would not keep a married woman. Shortly thereafter the marriage was annulled as Jeanette had not obtained the order of the juvenile court or of the superintendent of the State Industrial School granting Jeanette permission to marry, as required by § 14–10–07, N.D.C.C.* Thereafter, on July 25, 1966, Jeanette filed the motion for a new trial or for a rehearing before the juvenile commissioner and the district court, which motion was denied. The affidavit of Ronald Kelly attached to the motion states that he is the father of the unborn child; that he is 22 years of age; that on May 27, 1966, he graduated from the Wahpeton School of Science; that he and Jeanette are very much in love and are desirous of becoming married; that his father has purchased a home situated on two acres of land in Renville County next to the farming operations of affiant and his father for the purpose of providing a good and suitable home for him and Jeanette and their children; that affiant is engaged in farming with his father and his brother, the farm consist-

* 3 N.D.Cent.Code § 14–10–27 (1960)

14–10–07. Marriage of minors under supervision of juvenile court may be annulled. —A minor, while under the supervision or custody of the juvenile court or the superintendent of the state training school, shall not marry without the order of the juvenile court or of the superintendent of the state training school, as the case may be. Any such marriage made without such order is subject to annulment in a proceeding brought in district court by the state's attorney or by any person authorized by law to bring such annulment action. A person knowingly aiding, abetting, or encouraging such marriage is guilty of a misdemeanor.

ing of seventeen and a half quarters of land; that at the hearing on April 5 he appeared at the courthouse to tell the court that he and Jeanette wanted to get married but was informed that he could not attend the hearing and he was not able to testify; that he has been charged with statutory rape and the fact that the said statutory rape charge is still pending has nothing to do with this affiant's desire to enter into said marriage, and that the desire to marry is because of the love of the parties for each other and the desire to give a name to their unborn child and to live together as man and wife.

The affidavit of Jeanette Braun states that she is very much in love with Ronald Kelly and that she desires to be legally married to him and to give her unborn child a name and a permanent family home.

The affidavit of Mathew Braun and Ramona Braun, parents of Jeanette Braun, states that they are desirous that their daughter Jeanette be married to Ronald Kelly and they are confident that he will prove to be a good husband and father, and that the unborn child of their daughter be born in wedlock.

With the foregoing statement of facts in mind we will consider the question: Was the order of commitment to the State Industrial School for the best interests of Jeanette Braun and the State of North Dakota? * * *

In the case under consideration we have a girl, now 17 years of age at the time of the hearing, who has given birth to one illegitimate child and is about to give birth to another within the next month or so, unless she is permitted to marry the father of her unborn child. There are instances of other indiscretions on the part of Jeanette over the past few years of drinking beer on a few occasions. Her school work has been haphazard and her grades vary from incompletes to A. The record does not disclose any other indiscretions than her sexual indiscretions and the beer drinking. It appears to us that, though this situation is serious, there was another alternative than that of committing her to the State Industrial School, and that is to have permitted these young people to marry. Certainly the State Industrial School is not an institution for pregnant girls as they have no facilities to care for them. It appears that Ronald Kelly comes from a substantial farm family, well able to provide a good home for himself and his wife and child.

We therefore determine it is not for the best interests of the minor to continue in effect the commitment to the State Industrial School. We think that it is for the best interests of the minor and the State of North Dakota that these two young people be permitted to marry, and we therefore hold that the court abused its discretion in failing to relieve the minor of her commitment to the State Industrial School. The court had another alternative in permitting her to be married to the father of her unborn child. It appears that the juvenile court did not seriously consider this alternative. Mr. Kelly apparently is well able to care for a wife and children and these young people should be given the opportunity to show that they can accommodate themselves to a normal life.

The order entitled Order Denying Motion for New Trial or Rehearing is reversed and remanded to the district court sitting as a juvenile court with direction to enter an order pursuant to Rule 60(b), supra, relieving Jeanette Braun from the order committing Jeanette Braun to the State Industrial School dated April 18, 1966, and with further direction to enter an order pursuant to § 14–10–07, N.D. C.C., granting permission to Jeanette Braun to marry Ronald C. Kelly.

We wish to point out, however, that our holding in this case is based only on the special facts of this case and is not to be considered as a proper or recommended solution in all cases involving premarital indiscretions.

TEIGEN, C. J., and ERICKSTAD, STRUTZ and MURRAY, JJ., concur.

COMMONWEALTH v. BRASHER

Supreme Judicial Court of Massachusetts,
1971.

270 N.E.2d 389.

QUIRICO, Justice. On May 3, 1969, a complaint issued from a District Court alleging that the defendant "being between seven and seventeen years of age, is a delinquent child in that during the one month last past before the making of this complaint, at Fall River * * * [she] was a stubborn child and did refuse to submit to the lawful and reasonable commands of * * * Michael T. Walsh whose commands said Dianne Brasher was bound to obey.* (Violation of Chapter 272, sec. 53, General Laws)." [1] The defendant was tried in the District Court and was adjudged a delinquent child. She appealed to the Superior Court where she was again tried and adjudged a delinquent child. On July 2, 1969, the court ordered the defendant committed to the custody of the Youth Service Board (now the Depart-

---

* Dianne was near her fifteenth birthday at the time of the occurrences giving rise to the case. [Ed.]

[1] General Laws c. 272, § 53, as amended through St.1959, c. 304, § 1, provides: "Stubborn children, runaways, common night walkers, both male and female, common railers and brawlers, persons who with offensive and disorderly act or language accost or annoy persons of the opposite sex, lewd, wanton and lascivious persons in speech or behavior, idle and disorderly persons, prostitutes, disturbers of the peace, keepers of noisy and disorderly houses and persons guilty of indecent exposure may be punished by imprisonment in a jail or house of correction for not more than six months, or by a fine of not more than two hundred dollars, or by both such fine and imprisonment."

ment of Youth Services), suspended execution of the order for three years, and placed her on probation on condition that she be placed in the home of a named individual at Lowell.**

The case is before us on two principal issues raised by the defendant's bill of exceptions. The first issue is whether the statutes under which the defendant is being prosecuted are constitutional. The defendant contends that they are not for the reasons that (a) they deal with a subject matter which is beyond the State's police power, and (b) they are unconstitutionally vague and indefinite. The second issue is whether the evidence presented at the trial is sufficient to warrant a conviction, assuming the constitutionality of the statutes.

The constitutional issue raised by the defendant is directed at the part of G.L. c. 272, § 53, which provides punishment for stubborn children, and for this reason it will be helpful to review the history and development of this part of the statute. This provision appears to have originated in an act passed by the House of Deputies of the Colony of the Massachusetts Bay in New England on August 22, 1654, stating that "it appeares by too much experience that divers children & servants doe behave themselves too disrespectively, disobediently, & disorderly towards their parents, masters, & gouvernors, to the disturbance of families, & discouragement of such parents & gouvernors", and providing "corporall punishment by whiping, or otherwise," for such offenders. Mass.Bay Records, Vol. III (1644–1657) 355. Mass.Col.Laws (1887 ed.) 27. * * *

[The Court then briefly discussed the history of the Colonial provision in the State's law.]

[T]he provision relating to stubborn children * * * has remained basically the same.

Before discussing this particular case, it is appropriate to note that it is but the latest in a recent series of cases involving attacks, on constitutional grounds, on various provisions of G.L. c. 272, § 53. In Alegata v. Commonwealth, 353 Mass. 287, 302–304, 231 N.E.2d 201, we upheld the provision for punishment of disorderly persons. In Thomes v. Commonwealth, 355 Mass. 203, 243 N.E.2d 821, we upheld the provision for punishment of common night walkers. In Commonwealth v. Jarrett, Mass., 269 N.E.2d 657, we upheld the provision for punishment of disturbers of the peace. In Joyner v. Commonwealth, Mass., 260 N.E.2d 664, 666, we held that the words "stubborn children" as used in § 53 did not include "those who have attained their eighteenth birthday," and we therefore were not required to pass on the constitutional attack on the statute. In the case now before us, the person raising the constitutional question is a child born on July 7, 1954. We must therefore now consider and decide the constitutional question which we did not reach in the *Joyner* case. In doing so we shall deal separately with the several grounds on which the defendant's claim of unconstitutionality is based.

1. The principal ground upon which the defendant relies is that G.L. c. 272, § 53, in so far as it deals with stubborn children, is so vague and indefinite that it "leaves judges and jurors free to decide, without any legally fixed standards, what is prohibited and what is not in each particular case," and therefore violates the due process clause of the Fourteenth Amendment to the Constitution of the United States. The basic constitutional requirements in this regard were considered and discussed, with full citation of authorities, in our recent *Alegata, Thomes* and *Jarrett* cases cited above, and it is unnecessary to repeat the discus-

** According to defendant's counsel (in August, 1972) an application for certiorari in the Supreme Court of the United States in the *Brasher Case* was never filed because Dianne Brasher fled the home in which she was placed and disappeared. [Ed.]

sion here. Applying those constitutional requirements to the part of § 53 which is before us, we think that it is constitutionally adequate. * * *

We note, as we did in the *Jarrett* case, that § 53 does not purport to create or to define new crimes, but rather it prescribes the penalties for persons committing acts theretofore long recognized by our law as amounting to criminal offences. Therefore, the elements of the crime which is identified by the use of the descriptive words "stubborn children" are not to be determined solely on the basis of the inclusion of those words in § 53. We must start by considering the language of the 1654 Colonial law which said that it was "for the ready prevention" of the evil of children who behave themselves "to disrespectively, disobediently, & disorderly towards their parents, masters & gouvernors." Mass.Bay Records, Vol. III (1644–1657) 355. Mass.Col.Laws (1887 ed.) 27. * * *

We also note, as we did in the *Thomes* case, the permitted forms of complaints and indictments which are set forth in G.L. c. 277, § 79. * * * As to stubborn children the statutory form is: "That A. B., a minor, during the three months next before the making of this complaint, was a stubborn child, and stubbornly refused to submit to the lawful and reasonable commands of C. D., whose commands said A. B. was bound to obey." * * *

The elements which the Commonwealth is required to prove beyond a reasonable doubt in order to constitute the crime commonly identified by use of the words "stubborn children" are the following: (a) that a person having authority to give a child under the age of eighteen lawful and reasonable commands which such child is bound to obey gave such a command to a child; (b) that the child refused to submit to the command, and the refusal was stubborn in the sense that it was wilful, obstinate and persistent

for a period of time. The person giving the command is usually one of the child's parents, but it may be another person, as it was in this case. The defendant does not question that such other person, on the particular facts of this case, occupied such a position toward the defendant that he was authorized to give her lawful and reasonable commands which she was bound to obey. Single, infrequent or isolated refusals to obey such commands do not constitute a crime. Neither do manifestations of stubbornness which do not amount to refusals to obey commands. The law clearly does not make mere expressions of disagreement or differences of views or opinions between parent and child a crime on the part of the child. But it does not permit or excuse stubborn refusals by children to obey reasonable and lawful commands of their parents or persons similarly situated on a claim that it is merely the exercise of a right of dissent.

2. The defendant argues further that it is beyond the limits of the police power of the Commonwealth to make laws for the punishment of stubborn children for the reasons (a) that they punish children for disobeying commands having only moral, but not legal sanctions, and (b) that they constitute an impermissible intrusion into the privacy of family life.

The fact that a child is under a moral obligation to obey his parents does not preclude the Legislature, in the exercise of its police power, from making that same obligation a legal one, with criminal penalties for its breach. It has never been contended, nor can it be properly contended, that because it is morally wrong to steal or to do harm to the person of another, or to kill him, the Legislature is without power to make such conduct a crime and to prescribe penalties for the crime.

The argument that a law for the punishment of children who stubbornly disobey their parents is unconstitutional because it is an impermissible intrusion into the privacy of family life is without merit. * * *

The rights and obligations of members of families in relation to each other have been regulated by laws for centuries. 1 Blackstone, Commentaries (9th ed.) 446–454. In that time the law has always imposed a duty upon parents to support, provide for and protect the children they bring forth. This is an obligation which they owe to their children, but its breach is also a crime against society. In more recent times the law in this regard has been expanded to include the obligation to provide educational guidance. G.L. c. 273, § 1. To enable the parents to discharge that responsibility, the law gives them the custody of and right of control over their children. That carries with it the power to exercise whatever authority is reasonably necessary for the purpose, and to make all reasonable decisions for the control and proper functioning of the family as a harmonious social unit. Roe v. Doe, 36 App.Div.2d 162, 318 N.Y.S.2d 973. It permits the parents to give reasonable commands to their children and to require the children to obey those commands. The children in turn owe the parents an obligation to acknowledge and submit to their authority and to obey their reasonable and lawful requests and commands. In short, the governing authority for the proper operation, control and discipline of the family unit is vested in the parents.

While the State defers to the parents with respect to most decisions on family matters, it has an interest in insuring the existence of harmonious relations between family members, and between the family unit and the rest of the public society. To protect this interest, the State may properly require that unemancipated children obey the reasonable and lawful commands of their parents, and it may impose criminal penalties on the children if they persistently disobey such commands. The State is not powerless to prevent or control situations which threaten the proper functioning of a family unit as an important segment of the total society. It may properly extend the protection of its laws in aid of the head of a family unit whose reasonable and lawful commands are being disobeyed by children who are bound to obey them. The making of such laws is within the power of the Legislature "to make, ordain, and establish, all manner of wholesome and reasonable Orders, laws, statutes, and ordinances, directions and instructions, either with penalties or without; * * * as * * * [it] shall judge to be for the good and welfare of this Commonwealth, and for the government and ordering thereof, and of the subjects of the same." Part II, c. 1, § 1, art. 4, of the Constitution of Massachusetts.

A substantial portion of the defendant's brief is devoted to the statement of facts and arguments of a sociological nature criticizing our present statutes governing proceedings against juvenile offenders, criticizing the physical facilities available for the detention of such offenders, and suggesting that many of the children confined in such facilities do not belong there. It also suggests that stubbornness in a child "may be symptomatic of a psychological defect in the child or inadequacy in the parent or both." Arguments of this type are not relevant to the legal issues presented for our decision. They would be more appropriate if addressed to the Legislature which has the power to change the statutes if it is persuaded that such changes are needed. We do not have that power.

3. The only remaining issue raised [2] is whether the evidence was sufficient, if

[2] The defendant's brief contains an argument that because the proceedings against her were brought under G.L. c. 119, §§ 52–59, rather than under §§ 24–29 of the same chap-

believed, to constitute proof of the elements of the offence charged in the complaint. We hold that it was. In its light most favorable to the prosecution, the evidence permitted the trial judge, sitting without jury, to find the following facts. The defendant lived at the Deaconess Home where the complainant, Michael T. Walsh, was employed. On May 2, 1969, the defendant was to see a doctor for a complete physical examination and she refused to do so. On that same occasion she became a little angry, slammed a few doors, and refused to obey the request of the house mother not to slam doors and not to swear. At a staff meeting of the home the defendant was placed in group 4 which is a nonprivilege group. On several occasions she was away from the home with knowledge that she should have been at the home. At some time she was outside the home, probably talking with the boys, and she knew she was not to be outside the home. She had several temper outbursts during which she would not respond to commands of the house parents. On May 2, 1969, and on other occasions she used vile and vulgar language of a kind formerly used only by common railers engaged in gutter brawls. It need not be spread on

ter, she was denied the equal protection of law. It is not shown by the record before us that this question was raised before the trial judge but, if it was, it is without merit. Sections 24–29 relate to children who because of the death, absence, unavailability, incompetence or neglect of parents or guardians are in need of care, and they authorize the placing of such children in the custody of the Department of Public Welfare. By contrast, proceedings under §§ 52–59 are brought against children who are alleged to be delinquent by reason of their own misconduct in violating one of the criminal laws. This different treatment of children under the different sections of the statute is based on a reasonable distinction between those in need of care by reason of parental default or neglect, and those in need of discipline by reason of their own violation of a criminal law. This does not violate the defendant's constitutional right to the equal protection of law.

our permanent records. That language was used at times contemporaneously with the defendant's disobedience of the orders of those in charge of the home and it forms a part of the setting in which the disobedience occurred. The evidence was sufficient to support the finding of the judge that the defendant was delinquent by reason of her stubborn refusal to submit to the lawful and reasonable commands of a person whose commands she was bound to obey.

Exceptions overruled.

Notes

1. In In re Walker, 188 S.E.2d 731 (N.C.App.1972) Valerie Walker was found delinquent for the behavior set forth below, for violating the conditions set forth in a prior court order requiring her to alter the course of that behavior and for "not responding" to disciplinary actions taken by the school authorities. The report of the case states: Katherine Walker, mother of Valerie, testified that she lives with her husband and seven small children, including Valerie; that she works, and when she returns from work most of the time Valerie is not home and has not done the chores which have been assigned to her to do, such as cleaning her room, the bathroom and washing dishes; that Valerie tells her she has been with Vanessa Cunningham at Mrs. Cunningham's home and that she has told Valerie not to leave without telling her where she is going; that Valerie had been to Paradise Inn and bought a sandwich and she had told her not to go to Paradise Inn; that Paradise Inn has a bad reputation and is no place for a fourteen-year-old girl; that Valerie has stayed out at night till 1:00 o'clock and her mother did not know where she was.

The mother further testified that she had seven children at home but ten children in all; the oldest child at home is twenty-one, another twenty and one nineteen and then Valerie and then three children younger than Valerie. She testified, Valerie is lazy. She's a lazy child. No, I don't have no complaints. All I want her to do is do like a child should and act like one and not an adult. That's right; I have no complaints other than she acts like an adult and not like a child.

Howard King, the Assistant Principal of Mendenhall Junior High School, testified that Valerie had been enrolled in Mendenhall Junior High School from September 8, 1971; that she was in special education with a group of students who had a great deal of difficulty in adjusting.

Mr. King further testified that he had had numerous conferences with Valerie and that one problem was that in her physical education class she refused to dress out in there or obey the teacher; that he had had difficulty in communicating with Valerie and that she would not give him any reason for her conduct; that she would suck her thumb and would not talk and would then begin to talk and it was impossible to keep her quiet and "it doesn't have any meaning to what we're talking about". He further testified that Valerie was large for her age and as compared to the other children in the class. He further testified that Valerie was sent by her teachers to the office practically every day in school; that she does not fit into the classroom and disrupts whatever the teachers try to do; that if he had any way to get her home, he would have suspended her each day; that as it is, all they can do with her at school is to have her sit in the office and let her sit there and that she occasionally gets up and leaves; that Valerie does not respond to any methods of discipline available at the school.

The probation officer testified that Valerie had had problems at her previous school and was having the same problems at the school she was now attending; that Valerie's attitude was bad and she would not cooperate.

2. The Revised Code of the State of Washington, 13.04.010 defines a dependent child as a person under eighteen * * * "(7) Who is incorrigible; that is, who is beyond the power of his parents, guardian or custodian by reason of conduct or nature of said child * * *."

In In re Jackson, 6 Wash.App. 962, 497 P.2d 259 (Wash.App.Div. 1, Panel One, 1972) the Appellate Court stated: The constitution, however, does not require impossible standards of specificity in penal statutes. It requires only that a questioned statute convey a sufficiently definite warning as to proscribed conduct when measured by common practice and understanding. And, the test will be met if there are well-settled and ordinarily understood meanings for the words employed when viewed in the context of the entire statutory provision.

Children of ordinary understanding know that they must obey their parents or those persons lawfully standing in a parent's place. Therefore, the phrase "beyond the control and power of his parents" gives fundamentally fair notice to the child of a pattern of behavior that might cause him or her to be considered incorrigible.

3. See S. Katz v. W. Schroeder, Disobeying a Father's Voice, 57 Mass.L.Q. 43 (1972) and Gesicki v. Oswald, 336 F.Supp. 371 (D.C., S.D.N.Y.1971).

IN RE MARIO

Family Court, City of New York, New York County, 1971.
65 Misc.2d 708, 317 N.Y.S.2d 659.

NANETTE DEMBITZ, Judge. The major issue in this proceeding under the Family Court Act is the appropriate and constitutional treatment for a 13 year old boy who is a long-time school truant and beyond parental control in regard to his school attendance; he was on this ground adjudicated a "Person in Need of Supervision" under sections 712, 732 and 752 of the Family Court Act.[1]

On the basis of the facts detailed below, the Court finds that this respondent's placement in the Warwick State Training School for Boys, as recommended by his probation officer, will promote his welfare and his psychological and social development. Respondent's attorney argues that the Warwick placement is nevertheless interdicted by Matter of Lloyd, 33 A.D.2d 385, 308 N.Y.S.2d 419 (1st Dept., 1970) and Matter of Jeanette P., 34 A.D.2d 661, 310 N.Y. S.2d 125 (2nd Dept., 1970), each reversing a training school placement of a "Person in Need of Supervision" (generally and hereinafter abbreviated as "PINS"). Respondent further urges the constitutional point, strenuously debated during and ever since the enactment of the Family Court Act in 1962 but not heretofore adjudicated, that the restraint imposed by training school placement of a PINS—a child who has committed no crime under the Penal Law— violates the guarantees of the Fourteenth Amendment of the United States Constitution of due process and equal protection of law.

This Court holds that restraint of a parentally uncontrollable school truant by a training school is constitutional if this Court reasonably finds that this restraint will benefit the child, even though the child is only self-harming rather than harmful to others and even though analogous conduct on the part of an adult would not constitute a crime nor subject the adult to any restraint.

I. *Benefits of Warwick State Training School Placement for Respondent*

The issue highlighted by *Lloyd* and *Jeannette P.* (cited above) is that training school placement is inappropriate for some PINS children, who need merely removal from their own homes to substitute-residences of the type used for children neglected by their parents—generally termed "open" facilities. However, considering the conduct and patterns of this respondent, not only is no open facility available for him but also placement in the Warwick State Training School appears more desirable.

1. *Facts about Respondent*

The uncontroverted facts, briefly summarized, are that efforts by this Court and its probation officers over the past 8 months to induce the thirteen year old respondent, a long-time school truant, to resume school, have completely failed. Because of his refusal to attend the public school to which he was assigned, he was accepted in the special individualized day-school maintained by the Office of Probation for truants, and an expert probation officer unsuccessfully attempted to persuade him to try it. While respondent's hours improved for a few weeks following his first court appearances 7 and 8 months ago, since then he remains out of the house most nights until 2 or 3 a. m. despite admonitions from his mother, apparently "with older boys" but without revealing his whereabouts or activities; he habitually sleeps until 3 or 4 p. m. As to his home circumstances, respondent lives with his mother and siblings in a slum neighborhood on a public assistance budget; he shares a room with an 18-year-old brother who has been out of school and out of work for over a year and is actively homosexual.[2]

---

[1] During the major portion of this proceeding, a Person in Need of Supervision was defined as a male under 16 or female under 18 who is "an habitual truant or is incorrigible, ungovernable or habitually disobedient and beyond the lawful control of his parents, guardian or lawful custodian." (Fam.Ct. Act, sec. 712, prior to an amendment effective Sept. 1, 1970).

[2] A report from the "Children and Youth Comprehensive Medical Care Program of

An open facility to which respondent's probation officer referred him for placement, rejected him on the basis that he required "a more structured setting," and the Office of Probation reported that "in view of his non-cooperation with the several school plans" and other factors, applications to other open facilities would likewise prove futile. In the Court's opinion also, mere removal of respondent from his own home to the improved environment of an open facility would not at this juncture of his life motivate him to attend a school in the community regularly (that being a condition of residence in most open facilities) nor to return therefrom to the facility at the required hour.[3]

2. Program of Warwick State Training School [4]

Warwick State Training School, established "for the training and care of chil-

Roosevelt Hospital," stating it had been treating respondent's family for several years, strongly recommended his placement because "he is running the streets." The court psychiatrist also recommended respondent's placement, "in a treatment oriented facility," without specifying the type of treatment; there is no indication in the body of the report that psychiatric treatment or individual psychotherapy would be appropriate or beneficial.

All reports considered by the court are disclosed to respondent's attorney, pursuant to section 746 of the Family Court Act.

[3] When the probability of a child's success in an open facility is low, his placement there may be positively detrimental. Thus, PINS cases are frequently terminated without the child's improvement nor a training school placement, because by the time the child's placement on probation and in an open facility have both been tried and failed, he is no longer at an age or stage of development when a training school might benefit him.

[4] Since it is unfeasible to take prolonged testimony from training school representatives in every case in which a training school placement is contemplated, the statements in the text are based on such testimony in another proceeding, published reports of the Department of Social Services, information

dren" (Social Services Law, sec. 425) and situated on 740 acres of rural land, is a cottage-type institution for boys from $12\frac{1}{2}$ to 15, each cottage housing houseparents and a maximum of 25 boys. The program consists of attendance at a school on the grounds in the morning, with special remedial reading techniques for boys like respondent who read below the third grade level; and vocational training, shop-work, sports, recreation, and counseling for the remainder of the day. The school emphasizes incentives to good performance, and periodic excursions to the local theater, the Catskill Game Farm, dances with a nearby girls' institution, etc. are co-ordinated with the incentive program.

The school superintendent holds a degree as a Master of Social Work as also do the School's Director and Assistant Director of Social Services; a psychologist and six social workers are employed full-time; five additional psychologists a half-day a week; and a psychiatrist part-time daily. Each boy's cottage assignment and program is determined on the basis of periodic staff conferences as to his educational, social and psychological progress. Visits by parents, during which the parents can confer with the child's counsellor or social worker, are encouraged; paroles for weekends and for longer periods, such as a two week Christmas home-visit, are customary.

3. Alleged Undesirable Effects of Training-School

While respondent does not criticize the Warwick program, as such, its concomitant effects are attacked. A training-school placement of a PINS, it is argued, means that a child who has not committed any violation of law harmful to others, is placed together with dangerous juvenile

directly from Warwick, and on progress reports received from Warwick as to other placed children, which reveal its program and approach.

delinquents,[5] and thereby learns aggression and criminality. However, in regard to this street-wise respondent this possibility must be compared to his nightly learning on the streets. Further, it obviously is possible for the training school authorities to segregate PINS in a separate school from delinquents (See Social Services Law, sec. 427(2)), or certainly in separate cottages, classes, and groups in a school, if in their educated and expert judgment such separation is beneficial.

Again, the significance in respondent's life of the stigma which attaches to a training-school returnee, must be evaluated in the light of his present poor prognosis as an unschooled, undisciplined street-running teen-ager. Finally, any sense of injustice that a PINS might suffer from placement with delinquents (against whom criminal acts have been proved) would have less basis for a youth like respondent who has repeatedly violated specific mandates as to school attendance and curfew, in a pattern condemned by community standards. As to the recent statement of the White House Conference on Children, as quoted in the press and by respondent's attorney, that no child under 14 should be placed in a training school, it seems to this Court that the chance of the 13½ year old respondent's benefiting educationally, psychologically and socially from Warwick would be less if he passed yet more months in his present way of life.

II. *Restraints Imposed by Warwick Placement*

Warwick's premises are not walled or fenced, nor are the rooms or buildings locked except for the outer doors at night and except for the Administration Building. The location of the buildings in the midst of farm country some distance from the highway, serves as a deterrent to boys' eloping; in 1970 out of hundreds of boys at Warwick there were seven elopements. If a boy leaves Warwick without permission or fails to return after a home-visit, an arrest warrant can be issued to return him and in one instance in 1970 handcuffs were used for this purpose. It is in these respects that Warwick differs from the open facilities; it is physically easier for a child to elope from the latter, and if he does so he is not forced to return.

As to management of the boys within the school, there is no "strip" or "isolation" room at Warwick like that recently described in connection with a girls' training school,[6] nor is the procedure there followed of depriving the child of his clothing and of all occupation or recreation ever used at Warwick. For boys who require removal from their regular program, a dormitory is maintained in the Administration Building (that building being locked) in which there is TV, a pool table, and other equipment.

While courts are reluctant to interfere with the internal management of institutions, they cannot refrain from considering whether practices of a State institution unconstitutionally infringe on an inmate's liberties or invalidate his commitment there. This Court must consider the propriety of the use of physical force by training-school authorities against respondent, its only alternative being to refrain from a beneficial placement until specific and adequate regulations are adopted by the Department of Social Services.

Since the sole purpose of respondent's placement at Warwick is rehabilitation rather than deterrence—no acts presently

---

[5] A delinquent is a person under the age of 16 who commits "any act which, if done by an adult, would constitute a crime." (Fam. Ct.Act, sec. 731.)

[6] See Lollis v. New York State Department of Social Services, 322 F.Supp. 473 (S.D.N.Y.), decided December 18, 1970, describing such a room but noting that the record established "that isolation is never invoked at five of the twelve training schools and rarely at two others."

dangerous to the community having been proved against him,—the Court views any use of physical force to reinstitutionalize him in the event of his elopement as inappropriate and unreasonable, in part because the need for such force would be indicative of the failure of the rehabilitative program. (The placement order will therefore prohibit the use of such force.) Similarly, forcing respondent to remain in the special unit in the Administration Building for a prolonged period would likewise demonstrate such a failure and the unreasonableness of retaining him at Warwick for the purpose of rehabilitation. Compare People ex rel. Ceschini v. Warden; People ex rel. Smith v. La-Vallee, cited above; Clatterbuck v. Harris, 295 F.Supp. 84, 86 (D.D.C., 1968). While the Court is reluctant to assume the function of prescribing the maximum period for which School authorities can treat respondent in such unit, in the absence of any regulation establishing a maximum the Court will do so in its placement order.

III. Consistency of Placement Order with Appellate Division Decisions

While training-school placements for particular PINS children were reversed in Matter of Lloyd, 33 A.D.2d 385, 308 N.Y.S.2d 419 (1st Dept., 1970) and in Matter of Jeanette P., 34 A.D.2d 661, 310 N.Y.S.2d 125 (2d Dept., 1970), neither indicate that training school placement is invalid for all PINS. Nor can these decisions be interpreted, as it has been argued, to interdict training-school placements whenever parental neglect in a broad sense exists. For, delinquent as well as PINS conduct appears in the great majority of Family Court cases to stem primarily from parental inadequacies in relation to the child, with his economic and social milieu as a secondary factor. And treatment possibilities must be measured in large part by the modes of conduct the child has developed by the time the case comes to court.

The inadequacies of respondent's mother were passive—an inability to motivate or control him or to maintain a well-kept home [8]—as distinguished from the active rejection or harsh discipline which is manifested by some PINS' parents and which makes additional coercion of the child by the State seem peculiarly unfair. Nor was respondent's mother neglectful with respect to the particular issue of trying to secure his school attendance. Indeed, if respondent's mother had failed in this respect, she, rather than respondent, would be guilty of a violation of the Education Law, and respondent would not be deemed a truant (see Education Law, sec. 3212(3)). Training school placement, appropriate because of respondent's truancy, and the other factors described above, is not rendered either unjust or inappropriate by his mother's parenting inadequacies.

IV. Constitutionality of Family Court Act, as Here Applied

1. Definition of "Person in Need of Supervision"

While the statutory definition of a PINS as an *"habitual* truant" may lack mathematical precision,[9] there is no vio-

[8] A neglect petition filed at the Court's direction against respondent's mother by her public assistance worker, was withdrawn because she was already willingly—without coercion—participating in counseling and supportive services (at Roosevelt Hospital), cooperating in all proposals to aid her children, and showing improvement.

[9] The Court of Appeals has indicated that habitual truancy can refer to anything more than "a single act of truancy" (People v. Pikunas, 260 N.Y. 72, 74, 182 N.E. 675, 676). And under the amendment of section 712 of the Family Court Act, effective Sept. 1, 1970, substituting the phrase "who does not attend school, in accord with the provisions of part one of article sixty-five of the education law" for the phrase "who is an habitual truant," any unexcused absence apparently would be sufficient to constitute the child a PINS (see Education Law, secs. 3205, 3210). However, in practice this Court applies a much more lenient standard.

lation of due process in its application herein nor in the customary manner of its application by this Court. As in the instant case, the established procedure of the Family Court in truancy cases is first to place the child on parole or probation in the community, imposing specific requirements as to regular school attendance (as well as requirements in aid thereof such as a night-time curfew); placement is effected only if such specific conditions are disobeyed. Thus, respondent had adequate notice and warning of specific directions to be obeyed to avoid placement.

Indeed, under this Court's procedure in truancy cases imposition of placement is analogous to imprisonment for contempt for violation of an injunction; and here as there, the requirement of specificity adheres to the court order rather than the underlying statute.

As to the discretion to order placement after fact-findings of habitual truancy and of violation of specific orders of parole or probation, the requirements of due process are more than met, so long as respondent's counsel has—as he had here—an opportunity to know and controvert the facts considered by the Court, and so long as the placement order is a reasonable rehabilitative measure. Compare Williams v. New York, 337 U.S. 241; People ex rel. Smith v. LaVallee, * * * 29 A.D.2d at p. 250, 287 N. Y.S.2d at p. 604.

2. *Constitutionality of Restraint by Training School Placement of Respondent's Liberty*

Undoubtedly respondent's placement in Warwick State Training School imposes a restraint on his liberty, for he submits to transportation and residence there due to the threat of State authority. But the argument that respondent has committed no crime or act harmful to others, does not establish that the restraint is unconstitutional. Restraints are

constitutionally imposed in many circumstances for rehabilitative and remedial purposes, rather than for punishment. Robinson v. California, 370 U.S. 660, 665, 82 S.Ct. 1417, 8 L.Ed.2d 758: Matter of James, 22 N.Y.2d 545, 551, 553, 293 N.Y.S.2d 531, 535, 537, 240 N.E. 2d 29, 32, 33; People ex rel. Ceschini v. Warden, cited above. The restraint imposed on respondent is in this Court's opinion constitutional because reasonable rehabilitative measures are justified by respondent's truancy.

Compulsory education laws, in effect in New York since 1894, are intended for the welfare of the future adult as well as for the welfare of the state. People v. Eckerold, 211 N.Y. 386, 391, 393, 105 N.E. 670, 671, 672; People v. Turner, 277 App.Div. 317, 319, 98 N. Y.S.2d 886, 888 (4th Dept., 1950). It has never been questioned that the State can "require that all children of proper age attend some school." Pierce v. Society of Sisters, 268 U.S. 510, 534; see also Meyer v. Nebraska, 262 U.S. 390, 400–402; Oregon v. Mitchell, 400 U.S. 112, dec. Dec. 21, 1970. It necessarily follows, and is equally unquestioned, that the State acts constitutionally when it enforces the requirement of school attendance against both parents and children.

Thus, a child who is absent unlawfully is subject to arrest without a warrant for return to his assigned school (Education Law, sec. 3213), and, if he truants habitually without the acquiescence of his parents, to "confinement, maintenance and instruction" in an institution as a school delinquent (sec. 3214).

The purpose of that provision "is to compel the 'habitual and incorrigible truants' to learn—to become educated, not for the good of the individual alone, but for that of the collectivity also." Ackley v. Bd. of Education, 174 App.Div. 44, 47, 159 N.Y.S. 249, 251 (2d Dept., 1916).

It is true that the State does not exercise control over adults in comparable respects. Thus, doubt has been voiced as to the State's power to compel able-bodied persons to work in order " 'to remove the temptation to lead a life of crime or become public charges.' " (Fenster v. Leary, 20 N.Y.2d 309, 315, 282 N.Y.S.2d 739, 744, 229 N.E.2d 426, 431). However, despite the new equation of children with adults with respect to some rights, the eternal verity of the child's biological and psychological differences—his immaturity and plasticity—continues to evoke many different legal restrictions as well as privileges for the child.[13] And, while "the condition of being a boy does not justify a kangeroo court" (Matter of Gault, 387 U.S. 1, 28), the condition of being a boy *does* entail dependence on the part of the child and a reciprocal responsibility on the part of adults.

Adult responsibility, falling initially upon the parent, is recognized in a complex of legal duties, rights, and powers. Thus, the parent has a duty of financial support (Fam.Ct.Act, art. 4) as well as the right and power to discipline, the Penal Law providing: "A parent * * * entrusted with the care and supervision of a minor * * * may use physical force * * * upon such minor * * * when and to the extent that he reasonably believes it necessary to maintain discipline or to promote the welfare of such minor * * *" (Penal Law, sec. 35.10.)

While the doctrine of *parens patriae* does not permit any unfairness in judicial

procedure towards juveniles (Matter of Gault * * *), in this Court's opinion the vitality of that doctrine continues in that the State has the power to perform the parental role of insuring the child's education and training, when the parent is unable to control him sufficiently to perform it. If children were permitted the same freedom of choice as adults, they might well be unequipped when they attain adulthood to exercise *any* freedom of choice—specifically, without any education or training, they would be unable to choose to work in a job for which they in fact have the potential. Enforcement against the child of the compulsory school law appears still to be constitutional.

The Court concludes, on the basis of the facts stated above as to the respondent and as to the Warwick State Training School for Boys, that his placement there is a reasonable rehabilitative measure directed towards the education required by the compulsory education law, and that his placement at Warwick is therefore constitutional.

Respondent is placed in the Warwick State Training School for nine months (the period to be extended if the need be shown), subject to the special conditions as to the use of physical force against him and as to confinement within such school specified in the order of placement. Submission on March 10, 1971, by Warwick State Training School of report on respondent's progress, is requested.

Note

In In re Peters, 188 S.E.2d 619 (Ct. App.N.C., 1972). Eddie Peters was adjudicated a delinquent for failure to attend 12 out of the first 26 days of school. The case report states: "The evidence on behalf of Eddie is to the effect that he missed school as he was under a doctor's care; that he is fifteen years old and in the ninth grade; that he does better in some subjects than in others; and that he

---

13 E. g., a child under a certain age is not subject to criminal jurisdiction (Penal Law, sec. 30.00), can avoid certain of his contracts (Gen.Obligations Law, sec. 3–101), is especially protected in regard to sexual activity and danger from adults (Penal Law, art. 260), cannot work in certain occupations (Labor Law, sec. 133), cannot marry (Dom.Rels.Law, sec. 15–a), and can be restricted in his reading-matter (see Butler v. Michigan, 352 U.S. 380, 77 S.Ct. 524, 1 L.Ed.2d 412).

is pretty sure he was failing some subjects but that he was doing good in shop and science and part of physical education; that he is physically larger than most of the children in school; that he likes to work with his hands and would rather be out working than going to school. He testified,

' * * *   I work afternoons from 4:00 until 9:00 at night during the week, and on Saturdays and Sundays at Jarrell and Sons Kenco Station. I use the money that I earn to buy my clothes and what other needs arise. If I do not have anything that I need that week I give the money to my mother for whatever she needs to do with it. At present I am living at home with my mother and my two (2) sisters who are 20 years old and 16 years old. * * * My mother works, and leaves home at 6:30 in the morning. She usually gets me up for school and then comes home around 5:00. I see my father every day or so.

'I feel a responsibility about being the man of the household now. I have felt this way for a long time.

'I have worked at different places before. Sometimes I have worked for nothing just because I like to work, and it keeps me out of trouble. I have not been in any other trouble other than that which has occurred at school.'

"Leona Epperson Peters, the mother of Eddie, testified that she and her husband had been separated since March of 1970, and that Eddie's school problems had gotten worse since the separation; that Eddie resented his father having left home; that what he testified to about working and helping is true; that she had had no trouble with Eddie other than school-related problems; that Eddie had had a lot of trouble with his health and had had pneumonia every year and that last year he had been in the hospital three weeks with a chest problem. * * *

"CAMPBELL, Judge. * * * In the present hearing the only evidence before the Court and the facts found by the Court were that the juvenile had missed twelve out of the first twenty-six days of the school term. All of the evidence was to the effect that Eddie was a good worker, liked to work, and used his earnings for worthwhile purposes. He missed considerable school because of poor health, and it can be assumed this was due to the fact that he did not like to go to school. Is this sufficient evidence to justify putting this fifteen-year-old boy in an institution for delinquents?

"We note that the North Carolina Penal System Study Committee organized by the North Carolina Bar Association at the request of Governor Robert W. Scott has filed a preliminary report dated May 1, 1972, entitled 'As the Twig Is Bent, A Report on the North Carolina Juvenile Correction System.' In this Report the following appears:

'The Committee is of the opinion that approximately fifty percent of the children in our training schools should never have been sent there. This opinion is shared by staff personnel of the training schools, child psychiatrists and psychologists who are professionally involved with these students. * * * The only offense that many of the students have committed is that they do not like or cannot adjust to school.'

"The instant case is a good example of this situation. Eddie obviously is a child who should be afforded some technical training where he can use his hands and develop his aptitudes along that line and have some motivation. He obviously does not take to book learning. Forcing him into a classical schoolroom introduces a disruptive element which is not good for the school, the teachers, the other students and likewise is not good for Eddie.

"Suffice it to say that in the instant case the findings entered by the judge do not support the judgment ordering Eddie into the custody of the Board of Youth Development to be placed in a school or institution."

WISCONSIN v. YODER

Supreme Court of the United States, 1972.
406 U.S. 205, 92 S.Ct. 1526, 32 L.Ed.2d 15.

[The Supreme Court of the United States held that Wisconsin could not compel parents, members of the Old Order Amish religion, to send their children, aged 15 and 14, to high school. Such an action, the Court said, would violate the free exercise of religion provision of the First Amendment (made applicable to the States by the Fourteenth) on the ground that the Amish believe that the values taught in high school are destructice of the faith.]

BURGER, C. J. " * * * [I]n order for Wisconsin to compel school attendance beyond the eighth grade against a claim that such attendance interferes with the practice of a legitimate religious belief, it must appear either that the State does not deny the free exercise of religious belief by its requirement, or that there is a state interest of sufficient magnitude to override the interest claiming protection under the Free Exercise Clause."

" * * * In evaluating * * * [claims of encroachment on free exercise of religion] we must be careful to determine whether the Amish religious faith and their mode of life are, as they claim, inseparable and interdependent. A way of life, however virtuous and admirable, may not be interposed as a barrier to reasonable state regulation of education if it is based on purely secular considerations; to have the protection of

the Religion Clauses, the claims must be rooted in religious belief.

" * * * [T]he unchallenged testimony of acknowledged experts in education and religious history, almost 300 years of consistent practice, and strong evidence of a sustained faith pervading and regulating respondents' entire mode of life support the claim that enforcement of the State's requirement of compulsory formal education after the eighth grade would gravely endanger if not destroy the free exercise of respondents' religious beliefs."

"Aided by a history of three centuries as an identifiable religious sect and a long history as a successful and self-sufficient segment of American society, the Amish in this case have convincingly demonstrated the sincerity of their religious beliefs, the interrelationship of belief with their mode of life, the vital role which belief and daily conduct play in the continued survival of Old Order Amish communities and their religious organization, and the hazards presented by the State's enforcement of a statute generally valid as to others. Beyond this, they have carried the even more difficult burden of demonstrating the adequacy of their alternative mode of continuing informal vocational education in terms of precisely those overall interests that the State advances in support of its program of compulsory high school education. In light of this convincing showing, one which probably few other religious groups or sects could make, and weighing the minimal difference between what the State would require and what the Amish already accept, it was incumbent on the State to show with more particularity how its admittedly strong interest in compulsory education would be adversely affected by granting an exemption to the Amish."

[Justices Powell and Rehnquist did not participate.]

DOUGLAS, J., dissenting * * *

On this important and vital matter of education, I think the children should be enitled to be heard. While the parents, absent dissent, normally speak for the entire family, the education of the child is a matter on which the child will often have decided views. He may want to be a pianist or an astronaut or an ocean geographer. To do so he will have to break from the Amish tradition.

It is the future of the student, not the future of the parents, that is imperilled in today's decision. If a parent keeps his child out of school beyond the grade school, then the child will be forever barred from entry into the new and amazing world of diversity that we have today. The child may decide that that is the preferred course, or he may rebel. It is the student's judgment, not his parent's, that is essential if we are to give full meaning to what we have said about the Bill of Rights and of the right of students to be masters of their own destiny.[3] If he is harnessed to the Amish

way of life by those in authority over him and if his education is truncated, his entire life may be stunted and deformed. The child, therefore, should be given an opportunity to be heard before the State gives the exemption which we honor today.

The views of the * * * children in question were not canvassed by the Wisconsin courts. The matter should be explicitly reserved so that new hearings can be held on remand of the case.

In the majority opinion, Chief Justice BURGER made response to Mr. Justice DOUGLAS' point:

"Contrary to the suggestion of the dissenting opinion of Mr. Justice DOUGLAS, our holding today in no degree depends on the assertion of the religious interest of the child as contrasted with that of the parents. It is the parents who are subject to prosecution here for failing to cause their children to attend school, and it is their right of free exercise, not that of their children, that must determine Wisconsin's power to impose criminal penalties on the parent. The dissent argues that a child who expresses a desire to attend public high school in conflict with the wishes of his parents should not be prevented from doing so. There is no reason for the Court to consider that point since it is not an issue in the case. The children are not parties to this litigation. The State has at no point tried this case on the theory that respondents were preventing their children from attending school against their expressed desires, and indeed the record is to the contrary. The State's position from the outset has been that it is empowered to apply its compul-

---

[3] The court below brushed aside the students' interests with the off-hand comment that "when a child reaches the age of judgment, he can choose for himself his religion." 49 Wis.2d 430, 182 N.W.2d 549. But there is nothing in this record to indicate that the moral and intellectual judgment demanded of the student by the question in this case is beyond his capacity. Children far younger than the 14- and 15-year-olds involved here are regularly permitted to testify in custody and other proceedings. Indeed, the failure to call the affected child in a custody hearing is often reversible error. See, e. g., Callicott v. Callicott, 364 S.W.2d 455 (Tex.Civ.App.) (reversible error for trial judge to refuse to hear testimony of eight-year-old in custody battle). Moreover, there is substantial agreement among child psychologists and sociologists that the moral and intellectual maturity of the fourteen-year-old approaches that of the adult. See, e. g., J. Piaget, The Moral Judgment of the Child (1948); Elkind, Children and Adolescents 75–80 (1970); L. Kohlberg, Moral Education in the Schools: A Development View, in R. Muuss, Adolescent Behavior and Society 199–200 (1971); W. Kay; Moral Development 172–183 (1968); A. Gesell & F. Ilg, Youth: The Years From Ten

to Sixteen 175–182 (1956). The maturity of Amish youth, who identify with and assume adult roles from early childhood, see M. Goodman, The Culture of Childhood 92–94 (1970), is certainly not less than that of children in the general population.

sory attendance law to Amish parents in the same manner as to other parents —that is, without regard to the wishes of the child. That is the claim we reject today.

"Our holding in no way determines the proper resolution of possible competing interests of parents, children, and the State in an appropriate state court proceeding in which the power of the State is asserted on the theory that Amish parents are preventing their minor children from attending high school despite their expressed desires to the contrary. Recognition of the claim of the State in such a proceeding would, of course, call into question traditional concepts of parental control over the religious upbringing and education of their minor children recognized in this Court's past decisions. It is clear that such an intrusion by a State into family decisions in the area of religious training would give rise to grave questions of religious freedom comparable to those raised here and those presented in Pierce v. Society of Sisters. On this record we neither reach nor decide those issues."

SECTION 4. NEGLECT

A. PHYSICAL ABUSE, DISCOVERY, PROOF AND "TREATMENT"

NEW JERSEY STATUTES ANNOTATED, TITLE 30:4c–11 to 30:4c–15.

30:4C–11. Application for care or custody, verification and investigation; acceptance of care or custody

Whenever it shall appear that any child within this State is of such circumstances that his welfare will be endangered unless proper care or custody is provided, an application setting forth the facts in the case may be filed with the Bureau of Childrens Services by a parent or other relative of such child, by a person standing in loco parentis to such child, by a person or association or agency or public official having a special interest in such child or by the child himself, seeking that the Bureau of Childrens Services accept and provide such care or custody of such child as the circumstances may require. Such application shall be in writing, and shall contain a statement of the relationship to or special interest in such child which justifies the filing of such application. The provisions of this section shall be deemed to include an application on behalf of an unborn child when the prospective mother is within this State at the time of application for such services.

Upon receipt of an application as provided in this section, the Bureau of Childrens Services shall verify the statements set forth in such application and shall investigate all the matters pertaining to the circumstances of the child. If upon such verification and investigation it shall appear (a) that the welfare of such child will be endangered unless proper care or custody is provided; (b) that the needs of such child cannot properly be provided for by financial assistance as made available by the laws of this State; (c) that there is no person legally responsible for the support of such child whose identity and whereabouts are known and who is willing and able to provide for the care and support required by such child; and (d) that such child, if suffering from a mental or physical disability requiring institutional care, is not immediately admissible to any public institution providing such care; then the Bureau of Childrens Services may accept and provide such care or custody as the circumstances of such child may require.

30:4C–12. Complaint; investigation; hearing; order making child ward of court; duration of order; extension

Whenever it shall appear that the parent or parents, guardian, or person having custody and control of any child within this State is grossly immoral or unfit to be entrusted with the care and education of such child, or shall fail to provide such child with proper protection, maintenance and education, or is of such vicious, careless or dissolute habits as to endanger the welfare of such child, a written or oral complaint may be filed with the Bureau of Childrens Services by any person or by any public or private agency or institution interested in such child. When such a complaint is filed by a public or private agency or institution, it shall be accompanied by a summary setting forth the reason for such complaint and other social history of the child and his situation which justifies such complaint; or, if this is not feasible, such summary shall be made available to the Bureau of Childrens Services as soon thereafter as possible.

Upon receipt of a complaint as provided in this section, the Bureau of Childrens Services shall investigate, or shall cause to be investigated, the statements set forth in such complaint. If the circumstances so warrant, the parent, parents, guardian, or person having custody and control of the child shall be afforded an opportunity to file an application for care, as provided in section 11 of this act. If the parent, parents, guardian, or person having custody and control of the child shall refuse to permit or shall in any way impede investigation, and the bureau determines that further investigation is necessary in the best interests of the child, the bureau may thereupon apply to the Juvenile and Domestic Relations Court of the county where the child resides, for an order directing the parent, parents, guard-

ian, or person having custody and control of the child to permit immediate investigation. The court, upon such application, may proceed to hear the matter in a summary manner and if satisfied that the best interests of the child so require may issue an order as requested.

If, after such investigation has been completed, it appears that the child requires care and supervision by the Bureau of Childrens Services but the parent, parents, guardian, or person having custody and control of the child continue to refuse to apply for care in the manner provided in section 11, the bureau may apply to the Juvenile and Domestic Relations Court of the county where the child resides for an order making the child a ward of the court and placing such child under the care and supervision of the Bureau of Childrens Services.

The court, at a summary hearing held upon notice to the Bureau of Childrens Services, and to the parent, parents, guardian, or person having custody and control of the child, if satisfied that the best interests of the child so require, may issue an order as requested, which order shall have the same force and effect as the acceptance of a child for care by the bureau as provided in section 11 of this act; provided, however, that such order shall not be effective beyond a period of 6 months from the date of entry unless the court, upon application by the Bureau of Childrens Services, at a summary hearing held upon notice to the parent, parents, guardian, or person having custody of the child, extends the time of the order.

Note

Governor's Committee on Juvenile Justice, "A Study of the Administration of Juvenile Justice in California," Part II, 68–69 (1960):

"An effective well-rounded program for dependent and neglected children must include preventive services in addition to case work, foster care and institutional placement. This preventive casework program is commonly known as 'protective services.' In more specific terms, protective services refer to those social services provided to protect children when there is evidence that they are being neglected, abused, cruelly treated, or in moral danger. Protective services are ordinarily provided to the parents although the service is on behalf of the children, when the parents fail to provide the minimum care, guidance, and protection which the child needs for healthy growth.

"While protective services constitute casework, they differ from routine social work in at least two respects. First, the social agency normally has to exercise initiative and reach out to aid families by helping them realize that child neglect exists. By demonstrating the resources for help which are available in the community and in existing agencies they can aid the parents. Secondly, if the parents cannot profit from the help offered, the agency has the right and the responsibility to seek legal authority, if necessary, to protect the welfare of the children.

"Based on the experience of social agencies, most parents who neglect their children are not as a rule willfully neglectful, but disturbed people who are so engrossed with their own problems that they are unmindful of their children's needs. In addition, most child welfare experts contend that the child's best opportunity for healthy personality development requires that he grow up in his own home with his own parents. Small demonstration projects have shown that if protective services are provided on any scale, substantial public savings can be achieved in terms of averting public assistance and in terms of the cost of foster care. Of equal importance, failure to protect children from neglect is costly in terms of impeding the healthy develop-

ment of the child and in reducing his potential contribution to society as an adult. Neglected children may become serious behavior problems, deserting parents, or may suffer from mental illness in their adulthood. Indeed, society pays a high cost for the neglectful treatment of children during their formative years."

IN RE MARION FRANCES

Family Court of New York, Juvenile Term, 1966.

49 Misc.2d 372, 267 N.Y.S.2d 566.

JUSTINE WISE POLIER, Judge. This case raises serious question as to the adequacy of New York legislation to protect the "battered" or abused child, the procedures under the legislation, and its implementation in New York City.

The first neglect petition on her behalf was filed by the Society for the Prevention of Cruelty to Children on November 5, 1965, when she was nearly three years old.

Earlier in 1965, Sydenham Hospital had reported to the Protective Unit of the Department of Welfare suspicion that injuries they found on August 18, 1965, could not have resulted from a fall in a bathtub as reported by the stepfather, and that this was a "battered child". The medical testimony before the court presented hospital findings including marked redness of both legs, softening of soles of both feet, bluish areas on the buttocks and legs, and red areas on back and chest. There were also discolored areas on the back, chest, abdomen, legs, face, forehead and neck. The lesions were suggestive of belt or strap marks. The abrasions were suggestive of finger nail marks. The child was extremely docile, apprehensive, petrified, but became less fearful during the hospital stay. On August 24, 1965, on the decision of the Protective Unit, the child was discharged to the parents with a referral for clinic care. There was no record of subsequent clinic attendance. There was no referral for court action.

Two months later this small child was taken to a different hospital (Harlem) on October 16, 1965 by the mother. At that time the physician could not obtain a history of the injury from the mother. Physical finding, however, included a lesion on the buttocks that appeared to be a healing second degree burn and a second lesion on the right leg. Treatment was given in the hospital and the mother was directed to take the infant to the clinic for further care. Although the examining physician testified that in his opinion the injuries were at least six to twelve hours old, he testified that it was not his business to investigate.

The suspicion of the first hospital was promptly reported to the Protective Unit. The second injury was not reported. On the undertaking of the Protective Unit in August to supervise the child, the child was discharged to the parents. The supervision was delegated to a professionally untrained worker, who made one visit on September 21, 1965 and one on October 22, 1965. He did not secure the written report from Sydenham Hospital until October 8, 1965. When it was then decided to "double-check", the investigator went out on a visit two weeks later. The child had already received the second injuries. The child was not present, and he did not investigate although the parents mentioned that the child had received a minor bruise from being pushed against a radiator by a dog.

It was only through the fortunate incident of a family wedding later in October, 1965 that the grandmother called to take the child and discovered burns, raw open sores all over the baby's rectum, and bruises on her forehead and arms. It was she who took the baby home and called the Society for the Prevention of Cruelty to Children. When their representative

called and observed the infant's condition, he insisted on hospital examination, notified the Department of Welfare and filed a neglect petition in this court.

At the hearing on December 21, 1965, both the mother and stepfather gave a history of the child having fallen while being bathed by the stepfather to explain the first injuries in August. They sought to explain the second injuries as resulting from the baby being pushed against a radiator by a dog. The mother, aged 19, testified that the child was born out of wedlock and that she had married the stepfather, who was also 19, some five months earlier. Both the mother and father were defensive and evasive throughout their testimony as to how this infant had been injured. A finding of neglect was made and the child was paroled in the custody of the maternal grandmother.[1] Psychiatric studies of the mother and stepfather were ordered.

Spurred by reports of an increase in the number and violence of attacks on infants and young children by parents and caretakers, at a symposium in 1961 on "The Battered Child" at the American Academy of Pediatrics, the Children's Bureau undertook to assemble the information and start action. It had earlier developed a legislative guide to assure identification, protection and treatment for such children.[2]

In a 1963 pamphlet, the Children's Bureau took the position that cases of injury inflicted by parents "must be promptly called to the attention of appro-

---

[1] See, in the Matter of S., 46 Misc.2d 161, 259 N.Y.S.2d 164 (1965). The court there held that the condition of the infant spoke for itself and permitted a finding of neglect when an infant suffers serious injuries in a home for which there is no satisfactory explanation.

[2] U. S. Department of H. E. and W. Proposals for Drafting Principles and Suggested Language for Legislation on Public Welfare and Youth Services, Children's Bureau 1957, Note 1, p. 5.

priate agencies of government for investigation and such action as reasonably may be indicated, whether these cases are referred to social welfare agencies or the courts".[3] To secure prompt reporting the proposed legislation required that when a physician had reasonable cause to suspect that physical injury had been inflicted by a parent or person responsible for the care of a child, neither he nor the institution should have any discretion in the matter of notifying the appropriate police authority. The elements for such reasonable judgment were seen as:

The absence of the reasonably explainable results through accident

The infliction of the injuries in the family setting

The judgment based on his professional experience

The proposed legislation presupposed existence of adequate applicable and social machinery for the protection of children and the handling of persons responsible. It required immediate investigation by the police or the public welfare agency and further assumed the matter would be brought before the juvenile court, and possibly subject adults to criminal court jurisdiction.

Since 1963 the U. S. Children's Bureau has actively promoted legislation to require physicians to report cases where there was evidence that injuries might have been inflicted by parents or persons having custody of a child.

In 1960 only one state, California, had legislation to protect children from physical abuse. In August, 1965, Mrs. Oettinger, Chief of the Children's Bureau, announced that 46 states had adopted such laws of which 25 states had acted in 1965.[4] In making this announcement,

Mrs. Oettinger stated she saw the legislation as a necessary but only first step in getting at the problem. While acknowledging that there was no exact knowledge as to how many "battered babies" there were in the U. S. she stated that "we do know the number is growing." Mrs. Oettinger noted that the cases were "not limited to any one segment of our population—either by level of income or occupation." The importance

Bureau Release, August 26, 1965. Only Alabama, Hawaii, Mississippi, Virginia and the District of Columbia had failed to enact abuse statutes.

The State of Illinois, Department of Children and Family Services, issued regulations requiring all physicians who had reason to believe an injury of a child under 16 years was due to physical abuse or neglect to make immediate report to the Department. Such reports may also be made to the local law enforcement agency with notice to the Department. The Department on such notice is required to make immediate investigation and provide directly or through a voluntary agency the protective services required to prevent further abuse. It is also required to file a petition in the appropriate court to seek removal of the child when it is deemed necessary. Children and Family Service Regulation, No. 2, 42, June 1, 1965.

In Colorado reporting by physician, where there is cause to believe injuries of a child are not due to accident is made mandatory to the proper law enforcement agency. "Law Enforcement Agency" is defined to mean the police department in incorporated municipalities and the office of the sheriff in unincorporated areas. In turn, the law enforcement agency is required to submit such reports to the Colorado State Department of Public Welfare which is charged with investigation, the provision of protective services, and the institution of court action where indicated. Colorado Revised Statutes, 1963 Ch. 22 Article 13.

In 1963 Pennsylvania enacted a law making it mandatory on physicians, interns, residents, hospitals and pharmacies to report on "injuries by deadly weapon or criminal act". Under the Pennsylvania Act Adults are to be reported to the Chief of Police; children under 18 to the presiding judge of the juvenile court or to the community child protective agency where such court or service exists. In their absence reporting is to be rendered to the police. Act 492 of August 24, 1963, Amending Act of June 24, 1939, Commonwealth of Pennsylvania.

[3] U. S. Department of H. E. and W. The Abused Child, Principles and Suggested Language for Legislation on Reporting of the Physically Abused Child. (1963).

[4] U. S. Department of Health, Education and Welfare Administration, Children's

of providing protective services and substitute homes where needed to protect a child from further and serious injury was emphasized.

In 1963 the Journal of the American Medical Association wrote:

"It is likely that it (physical abuse of children) will be found to be a more frequent cause of death than such well recognized and thoroughly studied diseases as leukemia, cystic fibrosis and muscular distrophy, and may well rank with automobile accidents and the toxic and infectious encephalitis as causes of acquired disturbances of the central nervous system." [5]

A subsequent study by a group of workers in the Massachusetts SPCC reported the growing evidence of physical abuse by parents, repeated injuries, and instances of deaths from various areas of the country. This specific report sought to gather and analyze data on 134 cases involving about 200 children who were reported to have been abused during one year.[6] In 86 percent of these cases the abuse was committed by either the mother or the father. These parents were found to have many problems and to be relatively young. Three distinct clusters of personality characteristics were identified: 1. hostility and aggressiveness traceable to early childhood experience;[7] 2. rigidity, compulsiveness and lack of warmth; 3. strong feelings of passivity and dependence where parents competed

with their children for love and attention of their spouses. In this group general depression was frequently interwoven as part of the personality pattern; 4. significant degree of physical disability among fathers who were dependent on mothers for support.

It was found that generally one child in the family was selected for abuse, and once begun there was a tendency for the abuse to be repeated against the selected child.

In making treatment decisions three factors appear of primary importance: (1) the degree and extent of pathology in the family; (2) the apparent need of immediate protection for the child; and (3) the prognosis for success in helping the parent to effect change.

In reviewing the literature the investigators found an unfortunate separation of the medical aspects, the psychiatric aspects and the legal aspects of these problems. They recognized the importance of continuing social work for these families, but found that once identified, community responsibility for dealing with the problems was inadequate. They saw the need for a more comprehensive approach which would include protection of the child and social treatment of the family.

Legislation without thoughtful implementation that includes adequate diagnostic and casework treatment services was viewed as unsound.

"Even gross criteria must be developed to differentiate the parents who can utilize professional help from those whose personality development has been so arrested, twisted, warped and fixed that the most highly skilled professional staff cannot now help them develop into adequate parents * * * Someone must bear the responsibility for identifying and acting on behalf of the child whose right to health conflicts seriously with the rights of parents who cannot be helped to meet

---

[5] The Battered Child Syndrome, Editorial, CLXXXI (1962) P. 42.

[6] Physical Abuse of Children, An Agency Study by Bryant and others, Child Welfare March 1963. PP. 125–130.

[7] In the instant case, it was found that the stepfather had been known to this court before he was seven on a series of neglect petitions. Both parents were narcotic addicts who had repeatedly abandoned their children. A psychiatric study done in 1961 when he was fifteen noted the boy's anger with his parents because they had children but were not ready to act as parents.

their responsibilities before the child sustains physical or emotional injury." [8]

While accurate histories are seldom obtainable, the development of the use of X-ray has given additional confidence to the experienced clinician who suspects deliberate injury to an infant or young child.[9] Dr. Finberg, Chief of the Division of Pediatrics at Montefiore Hospital, reports that while the history given is usually that the baby either fell from a bed or chair or that an arm or leg became caught in the slat of a crib, "when something was found on X-ray, such as fracture, the odds have been four out of five (80%) that the trauma was deliberate and not accidental."

With such objective tools and such clinical experience, one must question whether it is sound to leave the determination of whether the infant or young child is to be released to the adults who had care of the child to non-medical personnel in the Department of Welfare without full investigation by a court.

Present legislation in New York seems peculiarly inadequate to protect the "bat-

tered child" in a big city like New York.[10] It would seem that several amendments should be considered to make the law more effective.

1. The law should require that not only a physician, but that any teacher, registered nurse, visiting nurse, or social worker, acting in an official capacity and believing that a child has been abused or neglected shall report the case to the police.[11]

2. A written report to the responsible protective service should be required from any physician or hospital without delay where there is suspicion that a child has been abused or battered.

3. Immediate reporting should be required to the police by physicians or hospitals as well as to the Protective Service of the Department of Welfare.

4. The Department of Welfare Protective Services Unit should be required to employ licensed social workers to investigate all cases of reported battered or abused children.

5. Where there is evidence of willful neglect or abuse the Department of Welfare Protective Services Unit should be required to file a petition in the Family Court to secure a prompt hearing and adjudication.

The serious nature of the charge of "battering" or physical abuse of a child

[8] Helen E. Boardman, Who Insures the Child's Right to Health? Child Welfare League of America, The Neglected Battered Child Syndrome, July 1963, P. 7. Mrs. Boardman had previously presented "a series of 12 parents believed to have inflicted trauma: six of the children were under 12 months and all were under 3½ years of age. All but one had a history of repeated injuries. Three were dead. Two of them had died of injuries that occurred after the parent had been convicted and placed on probation. * * * This indicates the high degree of wishful thinking by courts and protective services and of the damage of assuming such parents have learned their lesson or should automatically be given 'another chance'". See Marion C. Morris and Robert W. Gould, Role Reversal: A Concept in Dealing with the Neglected, Battered Child Syndrome, Child Welfare League of America, The Neglected Battered Child Syndrome, July 1963, P. 33.

[9] See Dr. Lawrence Finberg, A Pediatrician's View of the Abused Child, Child Welfare, January 1965.

[10] During the period of August 1, 1964 through July 31, 1965, 73% of the reports of suspected injuries inflicted on children under Sec. 483–d of the Penal Code came from New York City. See Administrative Letter, N. Y. Department of Social Welfare, November 30, 1965.

[11] Such a provision is reported to have been recently added by the Ohio Legislature under its House Bill 218. See, New York University School of Law, Welfare Law Bulletin, No. 2, February 1966, P. 5.

by a parent or guardian requires a judicial determination, where a court can subpoena witnesses and provide a forum in which all evidence can be submitted. The continuation of supervision by a social agency, without such an adjudication, fails to provide adequate protection for the child or a determination to which the parents or guardian are entitled.

Finally, in New York City where anonymity is so easily achieved, it would seem that some procedure should be developed so that where there has been suspicion of abuse, a central clearing house would register such cases, and such information would immediately be available to any hospital which subsequently examined a child. There is no doubt that in the instant case the infant would, with such information, not have been released by Harlem Hospital after emergency care only to be subjected to further abuse. A method of identification for follow-up purposes is now being used in one area in Pennsylvania on a voluntary basis.[12]

The case of Marion is but one example of the inadequate protection now afforded under existing legislation. No report of

---

[12] Freda G. Reinitz, Special Registration Project on the Abused Child, Child Welfare, Feb. 1965, P. 103. Beginning in February, 1964 the Philadelphia-Camden Social Service Exchange initiated a project which has since grown to include, in its Planning Committee, representatives of the Juvenile Aid Division of the Police Department (to whom cases are reported under the law), the protective agencies, the juvenile court, various units of the Public Health Department and selected social agencies. Through the project any case in which there is evidence of neglect or abuse of such order as to require referral for protective care is to receive a special designation "a Red X". This supplements but does not supersede the mandatory reporting. The purpose of the "Red X" is to alert agencies that the reporting agency had information that it was prepared to discuss if a child or his siblings come to attention for medical and protective care. This is an experimental plan which is being followed to find how cracks between services may be closed, to improve case finding and achieve more effective service in the hope that more children can be saved from irreparable damage.

the serious first injuries discovered by Sydenham Hospital was made to either the police or the court. The worker assigned by the Protective Services Unit was untrained and could not through monthly visits protect this infant from further abuse. No real service was rendered to the parents. The second hospital to which the infant was taken in October had no knowledge of the previous history at Sydenham. The reports of both hospitals were not submitted in writing until long after the incidents. In short, neither "protection" for the infant nor services to the parents were provided in timely or meaningful fashion. The law, as written, and its implementation in New York City fail to assure either.

It is directed that this child shall be discharged to the maternal grandmother under the supervision of the court. Visitation by the mother shall be arranged in the home of the grandmother on the mother's request, but the mother is directed not to remove the child, or take the child out except in the presence of the grandmother. The mother and stepfather are referred for casework services to a family case work agency. Order of protection to maternal grandmother to include terms of visitation. Progress report to be submitted to this court on September 15, 1966.

IN RE VULON CHILDREN

Family Court of Bronx County, Juv. Ct., 1968.
56 Misc.2d 19, 288 N.Y.S.2d 203.

NANETTE DEMBITZ, Judge. This neglect proceeding was initiated by a caseworker of the Bureau of Child Welfare of New York City, by a petition praying for a determination that the three Vulon children are neglected by both their father and mother within the meaning of article 3 of the Family Court Act. At the close of a lengthy hearing, the petition was dismissed.

Once a determination of neglect is made, the Court acquires not only broad authority to control the life of the family but even to deprive the parents of their cardinal right to the custody of their children (New York Family Court Act, secs. 353 to 355, Family Court Rules, rules 3.6, 3.7). Accordingly, a finding of neglect cannot be made lightly; the Court should exercise "its jurisdiction to interfere with parental guardianship reluctantly, and only upon strong and convincing proof of unfitness on the part of the parent or material benefit to the child." See Matter of Cole, 212 App.Div. 427, 429, 208 N. Y.S. 753, 755 (4th Dept., 1925). Compare People ex rel. Kropp v. Shepsky, 305 N.Y. 465, 469, 113 N.E.2d 801, 804 (1953).

This standard of judicial caution must be observed in applying this Court's mandate to dismiss a neglect petition if its allegations "are not established, or if the court concludes that its aid is not required on the record before it * * *" (Family Court Act, sec. 351). The Court dismissed the petition herein on both of these grounds.

The hearing showed without contradiction—and indeed from the mouths of petitioner's own witnesses—that Mr. and Mrs. Vulon are hard-working and devoted parents with an intact family, who maintain a well-kept apartment. The children—Maurice, aged 13, Marie, 10, and Michelle, 8, all attending a Catholic school, have good school records with respect to both studies and behavior, and are not known to have ever been the subject of any type of complaint at school or in the community. The Court's interview with the children (in the presence of the attorneys for all parties) revealed them to be well-spoken, well-dressed, well-groomed, and apparently well cared for. How then did this family become involved with the City's Bureau of Child Welfare?

The Bureau's petition alleges that the three children are left alone and unattended from 3:30 to 5:30 P.M. on week-days; that after Michelle was admitted to Lincoln Hospital "with severe injury to the vaginal area * * * the hospital reported Michelle as an abused child whose injuries were most likely the result of rape, and the circumstances surrounding this incident were unexplained by the parents." [2] The undisputed evidence shows that these allegations are misleading in significant respects.

Both Mr. and Mrs. Vulon work to support the family, Mrs. Vulon as an IBM key punch operator. She arrives home from work at 5:30 or a few minutes before. The three children generally return from school between 3:30 and 4:30 and then stay in the apartment doing homework. It is questionable whether it would constitute "neglect" to leave habitually well-behaved children of ages 13, 10 and 8, unattended in an apparently secure apartment in the afternoon for the two hours alleged in the petition; possibly self-responsibility to this limited extent, in a family where parents show an overall affection and concern, may not only be harmless but beneficial. In any event, Mrs. Vulon testified without contradiction that since the troubling incident here involved she had secured some one to stay in the apartment in the afternoons until she returns from work. Thus there

2 Under section 383–b of the New York Social Services Law, the hospital has the duty of reporting to an appropriate public welfare official any case where there is "reasonable cause to suspect that a child under the age of sixteen * * * has had serious physical injury inflicted upon him by other than accidental means, or whose condition gives indication of other serious abuse of maltreatment * * *". This section was added by the Laws of 1967, c. 631, sec. 2, effective Sept. 1, 1967, and was derived from a law of 1964. See Paulsen, Child Abuse Reporting Laws, 67 Columbia Law Review (1967) 1, as to social desirability of such reporting laws and their recent enactment throughout the United States.

is no evidence that the children are likely to be unattended; this Court's statutory mandate is—as in legal principle it must be—to determine whether, despite any past deficiency, children are at the time of the hearing suffering or likely to suffer from neglect (Family Court Act, sec. 312).

The evidence showed that on the afternoon of the incident in issue—which was a partial school holiday—Maurice was in and out of the home doing errands, Marie was washing dishes, and Michelle was first using the vacuum cleaner and then taking a bath, Marie heard Michelle exclaim from the bathroom and saw she was bleeding. Mrs. Vulon came home shortly thereafter, and although the bleeding was not extreme took Michelle to Prospect Hospital. There, because no physician was available, she was referred to Lincoln Hospital. By the time of her arrival at Lincoln the bleeding was more profuse and a physician recommended a surgical procedure under anesthesia for remedial and exploratory purposes. One source of suspicion against the family appears to have been that Mrs. Vulon did not immediately consent to surgery for her daughter; she testified that she had wanted to wait for her husband to arrive from Prospect Hospital, where he had expected to meet them. (Mrs. Vulon, who emigrated from Haiti in 1958, speaks poor English). The father arrived shortly; consent was given forthwith; and the child's condition was soon remedied.

The Lincoln Hospital physician called by petitioner testified that the bleeding was attributable to a laceration of the vagina of about an inch; that he could not estimate the source of the laceration with any certainty except that rape probably was *not* the cause; that the condition was probably due to "trauma" of some other type and could have been self-inflicted.

The erroneous suspicion of rape—which persisted apparently because of a failure to consult this knowledgeable physician—underlay petitioner's allegation as to the parents' failure to explain the circumstances of Michelle's bleeding. Mrs. Vulon did explain the circumstances to petitioner and other interrogators to the extent she could ascertain them from the children. There is no indication that she knew or could have known anything more than she recounted. What she failed to do was to accept the mistaken allegation of rape and to aid the Bureau in its exploration of this suspicion. According to petitioner, the parents "refused to believe that their child had been raped. They stated that they would not go into any conversation about rape with their children. They explained that in their country, a child did not learn about sex until the child was about 15 years of age; nor did the mother want me to discuss this with the child."

No doubt Mrs. Vulon's perturbation (described by petitioner) about the erroneous rape theory was due in part to the great damage that this charge would have inflicted on Maurice, the only suspect, who was an exemplary student in a Catholic school, aspiring to the priesthood. Though Mrs. Vulon apparently was herself concerned and frustrated that she was unable to ascertain the exact source of Michelle's bleeding, it was to the benefit rather than the detriment of her children that she refused to succumb to the mistaken suspicion of rape or to give it further currency.

Petitioner's attorney argued that neglect should be inferred from the parental failure to explain the basis for Michelle's bleeding. When there is insufficient evidence as to whether or not parents are responsible for a child's injury, an inference of parental abuse or lack of attention may, under special circumstances, be drawn from the injury itself coupled with the lack of explanation (for example, when a young baby has recurrent fractures, explicable only by either blows or serious falls). In the case at bar, however, it cannot be inferred—nor has it even been suggested—that the parents contributed directly to Michelle's condition (which the father believed, perhaps correctly, was due to some esoteric disease process). Further, considering the now-established improbability of rape and the possibility of a self-inflicted wound, it appears unlikely that Michelle's situation would have been any different if an adult had been in the apartment. In any event, any possible fault in supervisory care has been remedied, as noted above.

Prosecution of this petition was largely attributable, it is clear, to the parents' refusal of the Bureau's request that they consent to their children's examination by the Court psychiatrist. Such examination apparently was viewed in part by the Bureau as a possible method of determining whether Max committed the non-existent rape. So intent was the Bureau on its proposal that its attorney approached the Court ex parte before the hearing to ask it to order such examinations.

The failure to seek psychiatric aid was not alleged in the petition and therefore cannot, under the Family Court Act, the CPLR, or the due process guarantee of the Constitution be passed upon in this proceeding as an element of neglect. Even if properly alleged, however, the parents' rejection of psychiatric aid would not under the circumstances of this case and with the suspicion of rape eliminated, constitute neglect. The Vulons believe that their children's welfare will not be served by probing into the frightening episode of Michelle's bleeding by social workers or psychiatrists, and indeed indicate that the repetitive references to the incident to which the children have already been subjected were detrimental.

This judge personally has confidence in the psychiatric method and in free discussion with children of sex-related experiences. However, one cannot say that this approach has been so successful with our youth that the State can force parents—particularly in a family with a distinctive cultural pattern—to accept it, unless the need and the likelihood of benefit is clear.

It is the function of the trial court "which has seen and heard the witnesses" to determine whether neglect exists (see Cole, above, 212 App.Div. 427, at p. 428, 208 N.Y.S. 753, at p. 755). This Court believes from observation of these parents and children that they have an affectionate, mutually-respecting and beneficial relationship. A good faith appraisal by responsible and concerned parents, such as the Vulons, of the best way to handle a problem of child development on which reasonable men can differ in their value judgments, is not neglect. See Matter of Richards, 166 Misc. 359, 2 N.Y.S.2d 608 (Ch.Ct.Chenango, 1938); dismissal of petition affirmed, 255 App.Div. 922, 7 N.Y.S.2d 722 (3rd Dept., 1938). Compare Matter of Urdianyk, 27 A.D.2d 122, 123, 276 N.Y.S. 2d 386, 387 (4th Dept., 1967). While it was necessary and proper to conduct some investigation of whether Michelle's unusual condition indicated abuse or lack of care, the State cannot, without more justification than here appears, override the liberty of the parents, protected by the Constitution, to bring up their children as they think best. See Meyer v. State of Nebraska, 262 U.S. 390, 399, 43 S.Ct. 625, 67 L.Ed. 1042 (1923).

Petition dismissed.

Note

For a discussion of the social and legal problems involved in child abuse cases and the "battered child syndrome," see Paulsen, Parker and Adelman, "Child Abuse Reporting Laws—Some Legislative History," 34 George Wash.L.Rev. 482

(1966); Paulsen, "The Legal Framework for Child Protection," 66 Col.L. Rev. 679 (1966); and Paulsen, "Child Abuse Reporting Laws—The Shape of the Legislation," 67 Col.L.Rev. 1 (1967).

NEW YORK SOCIAL SERVICES LAW (1969)

§ 383–a. Register of child abuse cases

The department shall maintain and keep up-to-date a statewide register of all cases of child abuse reported in the state. Any individual or organization authorized by law to receive reports of such cases shall report all cases received by it to the department. The board may promulgate rules and the department may adopt regulations to implement this section.

§ 383–b. Reports of injury, abuse or maltreatment of children under sixteen years of age

1. Any physician, surgeon, dentist, osteopath, optometrist, chiropractor, podiatrist, resident, intern registered nurse, hospital personnel engaged in the admission, examination, care or treatment of persons or Christian Science practitioner having reasonable cause to suspect that a child under the age of sixteen years, brought to him or coming before him for admission, examination, care or treatment, has had serious physical injury inflicted upon him by other than accidental means, or whose condition gives indication of other serious abuse or maltreatment, shall report or cause reports to be made in accordance with the provisions of this section; provided, that where said physician, surgeon, dentist, osteopath, optometrist, chiropractor, podiatrist, registered nurse, resident, intern or such hospital personnel attends such child in his capacity as a member of the staff of a hospital or similar institution, he shall notify the person in charge of the institution, or his designee, who shall report or cause reports to be made in accordance with this section.

1–a. Any social services worker or school official having reasonable cause to suspect that a child under the age of sixteen years has had serious physical injury inflicted upon him by other than accidental means, or whose condition gives indication of other serious abuse or maltreatment, shall report or cause reports to be made in accordance with the provisions of this section.

1–b. Any report filed pursuant to this section shall be admissible in evidence in any proceedings relating to child abuse.

2. An oral report shall be made as soon as practicable by telephone, to be followed within forty-eight hours by a report in writing, to the public welfare official of the city or county in which the person reporting maintains his place of business. Such reports shall contain the names and addresses of the child and his parents or other person responsible for his care, if known; the child's age; the nature and extent of the child's injuries, abuse or maltreatment, including any evidence of prior injuries, abuse or maltreatment; and any other information which the person reporting believes might be helpful in establishing the cause of the injuries and the identity of the person or persons responsible therefor. The public welfare official shall maintain and keep up-to-date a central register of all cases reported under this section together with the final disposition thereof. Each public welfare official receiving reports under this section shall transmit a copy of each such report to the department which shall maintain and keep up-to-date a statewide central register of all reports made in the state.

An additional copy of each such report shall be forwarded by the public welfare commissioner to the society for the prevention of cruelty to children or other duly authorized child protective agency in his respective city or county if a prior request for such copies has been made to such official in writing by the society or agency.

3. The public welfare official shall investigate or cause to have investigated the cases of injury, abuse or maltreatment reported under this section and shall offer protective social services to prevent injury to the child, to safeguard his welfare, and to preserve and stabilize family life wherever possible.

4. Any person or institution participating in good faith in the making of a report pursuant to this section shall have immunity from any liability, civil or criminal, that might otherwise be incurred or imposed as the result of the making of such report.

5. Neither the physician-patient privilege, as set forth in section forty-five hundred four of the civil practice law and rules, nor the privilege attaching to confidential communications between husband and wife, as set forth in section forty-five hundred two of the civil practice law and rules, shall be a ground for excluding evidence regarding a child's injuries, abuse or maltreatment, or the cause thereof, in any judicial proceeding resulting from a report pursuant to this section.

§ 383–c. Temporary detention of an abused child

Any physician treating an abused child under sixteen years shall have the right to keep such child in his custody until such time as the custody of the child has been transferred to the appropriate police authorities.

IN RE S.

Family Court, New York City, Richmond County, 1971.
66 Misc.2d 683, 322 N.Y.S.2d 170.

RALPH E. CORY, Judge.* The instant cases arose by the filing of a child abuse petition in Kings County Family Court. * * *

After a fact-finding hearing the court found that child abuse was not established and the charges were reduced to neglect as to the child Terry. In the dispositional hearing,** Terry was remanded to the Angel Guardian Home. The remand was subsequently vacated and Terry was ordered returned to the respondents, the child's parents. Both parents are recent immigrants, the mother a Yugoslavian native and the father an Albanian native. The parents were to receive instruction in the care of children, proper health and safety and the prevention of injuries. They were also to obtain cribs, rather than permitting their children to sleep on the floor and mats. Finally, after many adjournments in which the respondents failed to appear, a warrant was executed and the parents appeared in court with Fred. The child abuse petition was amended to add Fred and he was remanded to the Commissioner of Social Services. Terry was hospitalized for the second time for dehydration, bruises and

* The children are represented by the Legal Aid Society.

** The New York Family Court Law makes provisions for an adjudication and an "abused" child, as well as a provision for an adjudication of "neglected" child. The Abused Child Act established special proceeding and is Article 10 of the Family Court Act. Article 3 of that act deals with the case of the "neglected" children.

In the rest of the nation children who are "abused" are included in general concepts of neglect. The New York statute provides for special, expeditious handling of "abused" child cases.

bites and other serious injuries. Both respondents were then remanded to Bellevue Hospital for observation and complete medical and psychiatric examinations because of long hysterical outbursts in court where they were physically removed with great difficulty. Family Court Act, Section 251. The children were on continued remand away from their home and Fred was deleted from the original petition on consent of the corporation counsel, law guardian and the attorney for the respondents. Before the conclusion of the fact-finding hearing on the instant petition, a new infant baby girl, Mary, was born to the respondent mother on March 20, 1971.

A new petition was drawn to have Mary declared neglected in that she was in danger of being found neglected since there is presently before this Court a petition to have Terry declared abused and Fred to be neglected.

After listening to oral argument by the corporation counsel who demanded that the new infant child be removed from the parental home on the grounds there would be substantial probability that the child will be found to be abused or neglected under Article 10, Family Court Act Section 1028(b) and *that she was in grave imminent danger to her life and limb*, and arguments in opposition by the attorney for the respondents that such drastic action without one scintilla of evidence that a baby four days old had been neglected would be a serious violation of due process, this Court temporarily remanded the infant to the Commissioner of Social Services Angel Guardian Home and ordered a hearing on this issue.

There is thus before this Court for decision two petitions in which a fact-finding hearing has been held. Even though the original neglect petition is not before this Court for decision, it is nevertheless before the court for an adjourned dispositional hearing in view of the subsequent injuries to Terry, as well as the original neglect petition of Terry, since the two petitions are inseparable and cannot be severed by virtue of the fact that both petitions involve the *same* child. * * *

Prior to the fact-finding hearing on the instant petitions alleging abuse of Terry and neglect of Fred, the attorney for the respondent parents has brought on . . . several motions as follows:

The preponderance of evidence rule for a proceeding under Article 10, Family Court Act, is neither logical nor constitutional. Due process requires that a finding under Article 10 be made only on proof *beyond a reasonable doubt*.

This motion is *denied*. Article 10, Family Court Act, sets forth no crime or criminal penalties involved—its objective is "to help protect children from injury or mistreatment and to help safeguard their physical, mental, and emotional well-being." Section 1011, Family Court Act.

The Family Court has jurisdiction over proceedings under Article 10, for the protection of children, notwithstanding the fact that a criminal court also has or may be exercising jurisdiction over the facts alleged in the petition or complaint. Section 1013(b), Family Court Act.

The respondents hereunder are not therefore criminal defendants as would require the reasonable doubt standard of proof applicable in criminal cases or in juvenile delinquency cases in the Family Court. * * *

Respondent's attorney brings on a motion that the privilege against self-incrimination contained in the Fifth Amendment of the U. S. Constitution and made applicable to the States through the Fourteenth Amendment applies to a fact-finding hearing under Article 10 in the Family Court. Respondents contend that the presumption created by Section 1046(a)(ii) that " * * * proof of injuries sustained by a child or of the condition of a child of such a nature as would ordinarily not be sustained or exist except by reason of the acts or omissions of the parent or other person responsible for the care of such child shall be *prima facie evidence of child abuse or neglect,* as the case may be, of the parent or other person legally responsible". (emphasis supplied)

This motion is *denied.* There is no violation of respondents' rights of privilege against self-incrimination. He is not required to take the stand and testify in child abuse or neglect proceedings. However, once the petitioner who has instituted child neglect proceedings under this Article 10 has established existence of child's injuries which are substantial in character while the child was in the lawful custody of his parents, then petitioner is deemed to have established a prima facie case and the burden of going forward with the proof, shifts from the petitioner to the respondents who are then required to offer satisfactory explanation concerning injuries. Matter of Young, supra, 50 Misc.2d 271, 270 N.Y.S.2d 250. * * *

Proof of abuse by a parent or parents is difficult because such actions occur ordinarily in the privacy of the home without outside witnesses. Without satisfactory explanation by the parents—a finding of neglect against the parent will be made—this is the Court's responsibility to the child. Matter of S. (1965) 46 Misc.2d 161, 259 N.Y.S.2d 164; Matter of Young, 50 Misc.2d 271, 270 N.Y.S. 2d 250.

Both of these cases uphold the present statutory presumption of Section 1046(a) (ii) permitting an inference of neglect or child abuse to be drawn from the child's age or condition unless the respondent

parents take the stand and offer satisfactory proof to negate the prima facie case established by statute if the injuries to the child are not satisfactorily explained. It may be a difficult decision for the respondents and their attorneys. It is a question of procedure and legal options for the defense, not one of the constitutionality of incrimination. The witness is not exonerated from answering merely because he declares that in doing so he would incriminate himself. It is for the court to say whether his silence is justified. * * *

The attorney for the respondent brings on a third motion, that since the charges against the respondent can form the basis of a subsequent felony prosecution by direct operation of the Family Court hearing, respondents are entitled to a *trial by jury* as a matter of constitutional due process.

This motion is *denied.* * * *

A proceeding under Article 10 of the Family Court Act is a civil proceeding and there are no penal provisions such as imprisonment for more than six months involved. In fact, no crime is involved at all. * * *

With respect to the Sixth Amendment, the within proceeding is not criminal in nature. The Statute (Article 10, Family Court Act) is not punitive. It is designated to *rescue the child.* Its object is not to *punish parents* but to safeguard children. This purpose is inconsistent with the granting of jury trials. To require a jury trial would bring a good deal more formality to the court without demonstrating that it would be better fact finding process than trial before a judge. * * *

As for the instant petitions involving child abuse and neglect, a long fact finding hearing was conducted over several days, including expert testimony by doctors and psychiatrists who were active in the case from its inception. The respondent parents took the stand themselves, after the various motions described above, brought by their attorney, had been denied.

The respondent parents steadfastly claimed under oath that they did not know how their child Terry had sustained such serious injuries. A catalogue of these injuries from the expert medical and psychiatric testimony, color photographs and hospital records revealed that the child Terry was acutely ill with pressure on the brain. There was bleeding in the head, compatible with trauma and malformation or defects of birth ruled out. The child has a cyst on the brain; brain damage is evident with structural lesions demonstrable. Trauma is the sustaining of injury by external force, not of internal or natural causes. Expert medical testimony stated that the injuries sustained by the child Terry are not consistent with a simple fall. The extent of the injuries would rule this out. In answer to a question by defense counsel, the chief medical expert testified that the injuries to the brain would be compatible with the child being hit on the head with a baseball bat.

It was also testified to that there were human bites distributed over the child's body which were black and then turned red. Rash and skin disorders were ruled out because of the peculiar distribution over the entire body.

The child Terry is still in critical condition in Maimonides Hospital where she was just brought by her parents in an ambulance with the police on November 6, 1970. The prognosis is extremely guarded. None of this expert medical testimony or the hospital records of the serious condition of the child was effectively rebutted.

The hospital records, the medical history including reports filed pursuant to Social Services Laws Sec. 383–a and under the Family Court Act Sec. 1046

(a)(iv) and Section 1038 and testimony by psychiatric experts who interviewed and treated respondents reveal that the mother is a Yugoslavian illiterate while her husband is an Albanian illiterate. Both were recent immigrants to this country and did not speak English. All court hearings except one were conducted with official Albanian interpreters present except in one instance where, however, the attorney for the respondents was present, a permissible procedure under Section 1042 of the Family Court Act. Testimony of the psychiatrists from their reports and memory revealed that the respondent mother, a Moslem, went with her husband to a Moslem shrine in Michigan to "get the curse on the baby Terry removed". The respondent mother when confronted with the nature of the child's injuries and the documented medical, neurological and radiological evidence insisted that the child was fine until the day of hospital admission when she woke up sick; that the bites were inflicted by her two and one-half year old brother and that the prior injuries to the child about fifteen months ago were due to being pushed off a table by the two and one-half year old. She contended Yugoslavian children bite, as an explanation for the bite marks distributed over the child Terry's body. The respondent mother also contended she was out of the room when the baby Terry fell off the table. When told that the child Terry was blind and comatose, the respondent mother claimed that Terry was fine and ready to go home which led the examining psychiatrists to conclude that she suffered from severe depression with possibility of delusions, although she denied hallucinations, suicidal and homicidal ideation.

Her husband, the respondent father, was employed as a porter. He testified he left home to go to work as a porter at 6:00 a. m. on November 6, 1970 and when he called his wife later, as was his custom, she informed him the child Terry was very sick and to come home right away. When he arrived home, the baby was rushed to the hospital. The respondent mother never left the home without her husband and when he was away, she stayed indoors at all times, presumably in deference to the Moslem custom in her native land. She did not even know how to contact him by telephone causing a delay of some six hours from when she first discovered the child was seriously ill at 8:00 a. m. until her husband arrived home at 2:00 p. m. Nor did she have the presence of mind to call a neighbor to summon emergency aid or assistance.

Both parents testified that three days before November 6, 1970 when the child became seriously ill, the baby Terry was playing in the kitchen and a tricycle fell on her face, causing slight injuries. Both also testified that they remonstrated with their son Fred, telling him not to hit his baby sister. No other explanation was ever offered as to what happened to Terry during the intervening three days when she woke up seriously ill and was rushed to the hospital later in the day. No plausible explanation of accidental means was ever offered to explain the injuries. There was no testimony that the child was ever out of the custody of the parents and thus no third party could have inflicted the injuries unless it was caused by Fred. The mother had previously explained to the psychiatrists and hospital staff that the previous injury to Terry had been caused by her brother's pushing her off the table. There was no testimony that the child fell from a very high place such as out of a window or down a long stairway that could conceivably cause such serious injuries. Even if the child Fred beat his sister constantly as to cause such injuries, there was no testimony offered by the parents to prevent such beatings.

After a careful analysis of the above facts and circumstances and the credible evidence adduced from all the testimony, there is ample proof of child abuse by the respondent parents as to Terry and neglect as to Fred * * *.

The quality of the evidence here, based on the strong statutory presumption, not rebutted or overcome by the respondents, is not strained or colored and well within the credible evidence based on all the facts and circumstances of the case. In child protective proceedings, the law must be practical and realistic—standards well met in the ascertainment of truth or serious attempts threat by the long fact-finding hearing in this case. The law of neglect and child abuse under the new Article 10, Family Court Act, does not require a legal straight jacket where all the evidence must fit into predetermined slots of minute exactitude. No branch of the law is a perfect science. * * *

As to the neglect petition concerning the infant baby Mary, born to the respondent mother on March 20, 1971, there is a finding of neglect under Section 1028 of the Family Court Act after a hearing. This is based on the exercise of discretion of the Family Court as parens patriae to avoid an imminent risk to the child's life or health in view of the findings on the other petition of child abuse and neglect against the other children. Section 1028(b), Family Court Act.

Attorney for the respondents argues that not one scintilla of evidence has been shown to indicate abuse or neglect on the new-born baby and to remove the child is a violation of due process, and a violation of their constitutional rights.

Section 1012(f)(i)(B) foresaw the dangers in the instant neglect petition, that the new-born child would be in imminent danger because of assaultive parents, by providing the words—"or a *substantial risk* thereof" in describing parents who fail to exercise a minimum degree of care. The legislative intent here is clear to guard against a child not only whose physical, mental or emotional condition has been impaired but " * * * *is in imminent danger of becoming impaired* * * * " Section 1012(f)(i), Family Court Act. (Emphasis supplied)

There has already been a finding of neglect against respondent parents on child Terry on an original child abuse petition. After a long fact-finding hearing just concluded, the respondents have been held to have abused the same child Terry (a finding of child abuse). The record is therefore sufficient to make the conclusion inescapable that the new-born female baby (Mary) is likely to suffer serious harm from improper guardianship. The record is also clear that in both findings of neglect and child abuse, a female child Terry has been involved. The new-born child is also female. The psychiatrists from Bellevue who testified indicated the Moslem belief of the respondent mother (part of the hospital record revealed to them) favored the male born. There is no direct proof in the record however that this fact alone had anything to do with the serious injuries suffered by the female child Terry. The record is also clear that the male child Fred has been unharmed and never assaulted by the parents at any time. The mother was acquainted with this Moslem custom in her native Yugoslavia and there had been some evidence in her own family history as relayed by her to the hospital authorities. There is ample proof in the record that both parents are ignorant of proper child care and supervision, and serious injuries have occurred to the child Terry as a direct result of the respondents' acts of omission and commission. At the same time there is some direct uncontradicted testimony that the parents were either unable or unwilling to control the male child Fred in the household,

allowing him to bite his sister severely, to push her off the table causing the fracturing of Terry's ribs and on mother's own testimony that she was out of the room when this happened. These are warning signs that this Court or any court faced with a similar problem could not safely ignore. * * *

The child Fred is declared to be a neglected child on the same legal reasoning as above set forth as to the child Mary. In addition, there is some uncontradicted evidence that the child Fred was allowed to beat and severely bite his baby sister Terry. According to the mother's statements the child Fred pushed the child Terry off a table causing her severe injuries. The mother testified she was out of the room at the time. There is no direct evidence, however, that the child Fred was ever abused by his parents. There is ample evidence, however, of improper supervision and guardianship under the statute by respondent parents in their inability to control Fred resulting in serious injuries to Terry. * * *

Because of the fact-finding hearings establishing *neglect* and *abuse* upon the child Terry and the serious injuries suffered by this child, this case is referred to the District Attorney of Richmond County in accordance with Section 1014 as to whether or not any violation of the Penal Law of New York State is involved (assault, etc.). The Clerk of Court is directed to make all files in this matter available for examination to the District Attorney of Richmond County and/or his authorized representatives. * * *

All of the children are continued on remand as heretofore to the Commissioner of Social Services until May 4, 1971, the date of the Dispositional Hearing. The child Terry is in Maimonides Hospital and the children Fred and Mary at the Angel Guardian Home.

TERR & WATSON, THE BATTERED CHILD REBRUTALIZED: TEN CASES OF MEDICAL—LEGAL CONFUSION

124 Amer.J.Psychiat. 10, pp. 1432–1439 (1968).*

* * * Over a two-year period we studied ten cases of suspected child abuse at the University of Michigan. These cases were referred to us by our department of pediatrics or the local juvenile court. In each case we interviewed both parents and the child in question. Siblings were interviewed whenever indicated. In cases which came to court hearings we provided reports and/or verbal testimony. In addition we offered psychiatric treatment at our institution for those cases in which this was recommended. We continued to consult with the courts until our services were no longer required. Finally, all cases were reviewed at later dates for further developments or difficulties. * * * In each of the ten cases studied we found confusion and lack of direction in both the legal and medical-social handling of the children and their families. Lawyers, prosecuting attorneys, juvenile court workers and judges, criminal court judges, divorce court workers, and legislators shared in this confusion and lack of direction.

1. *Effects of the Adversary Process*

In the heat of legal contest, lawyers representing the parents may ignore the interests of the child. For example, let us consider Denise, a recently adopted nine-year-old girl who had been subjected to 226 lashes with a belt for failure to bring home her homework papers. Denise's mother, in addition to doing most of the beating, had attempted to breast feed the nine-year-old, check her genitals daily for signs of masturbation, and engage her in games of *Sorry* whenever Denise confessed the impulse to masturbate.

The parents' lawyer chose to overlook all evidences of severe sexual and hostile provocations to this child. Instead he threatened numerous appeals and delay tactics in the determination of custody in order to protect his clients' rights to Denise. In this case countless delays would guarantee insecurity for this girl throughout most of her childhood despite her desperate need for permanent roots.

It appears that a lawyer representing battering parents may find himself in a dilemma. If the lawyer *knows* of the child's injury but helps the parents avoid incrimination (or being found at fault), he may help perpetrate a truly dangerous situation for the child. On the other hand, if he decides to tell the juvenile court judge what he knows, he may be breaching, or at least feel he is breaching, his duty to the parents. (We must ask in this regard: If we wish to protect children fully, should not lawyers report child abuse too?) The lawer's decision will probably depend upon his view of the community's treatment programs versus the community's punitive intentions.

2. *Effects of Prosecution*

A second important problem arises in the office of the prosecutor. The prosecutor feels he is "obliged" to prosecute the battering parent, but he has no similar sense of obligation to keep a family intact and functioning. Many factors enter into his decision to prosecute. First he needs sufficient evidence to "win" the case, preferably an admission by the parent or observation by eyewitnesses. For instance, prosecutors dropped two cases of severe brain injuries in babies because of "lack of evidence." In these cases, the offending parents vigorously denied purposeful abuse. In one, a mother, recently released from a mental institution, insisted that her eight-month-old son Ricky's bilateral subdural hematomas were caused when he hit his own head with his bottle. This story was readily accepted by a prosecutor. * * * Of the ten cases studied three were prosecuted. All of these three were self-admitted, purposeful, visible, and publicly notorious. Four cases were reported but not prosecuted. In each of these the abuse was denied or said to be "accidental." The wounds were well healed or hidden, and the stories had been kept out of the newspapers. The other three cases were not reported to the prosecutor.

Now let us consider the effect of legal punishment upon these cases. One mother, after serving a jail sentence for child abuse, committed three more similar offenses. A second mother who had served her jail sentence stood a good chance of getting her child back despite numerous medical and social work opinions against return of the child. In general, then, prosecution and punishment when used alone served only to increase the child's time in psychological limbo and did nothing to help clarify the child's future status in regard to adequate parental care.

Prosecutors, by delaying their decision to prosecute, may cause the waste of considerable time and effort which had gone into treatment. One mother and father received homemaker services, three months of intensive casework, and several psychiatric interviews by the time the prosecutor decided to initiate criminal action. Another couple two years after an alleged child abuse episode still await its legal resolution, even though they have undergone successful psychotherapy in the meantime.

As long as the issue of prosecution remains undecided, it is very difficult for parents to enter wholeheartedly into a treatment program. While a therapist should always inform parents that reports of their progress will be made available to the juvenile court, it is legally and medically self-defeating when such reports are to be sent to the prosecutor who is seeking incriminating evidence. * * * The juvenile court contributes to the confusion in battered child cases.

It appears to us that the crux of the difficulty in juvenile courts is the court's failure at the outset of a case to formulate a definite plan which sets forth all of the long- and short-range alternatives. * * * When one child has been battered it is very important that the juvenile court include all of the children in the family in the initial investigation and planning. In our study of eight couples with more than one child, three had been suspected of battering more than one youngster in the family. * * * Not only court workers but also juvenile court judges delay and fail to exert authority in battered child cases. Of seven cases handled in juvenile court hearings, final rulings of custody had not been obtained in four cases at the conclusion of the study. The shortest elapsed time had then been one year. * * * Finally, in considering the law's confusion in regard to battered child cases, we note the effects of the legislation itself. Originally most states passed child-abuse reporting statutes for the purpose of remedying the problem by treatment of the families (9). Statutes which require that reports be made to police departments or prosecutor's offices interfere with these widely accepted treatment aims. When, as in Michigan, a state requires reporting to both a treatment agency and an agency concerned with punishment, a conflict is set up which impedes the effective management of cases. * * * Doctors, social agencies, and nurses share responsibility with the law for the lack of communication and planning in battered child cases. Doctors frequently fail to report these cases. Of our ten cases, two were never reported to any authority. To the best of our knowledge this did not occur because the doctors wished to avoid court appearances. Rather, the failures to report were examples of either failure to diagnose child abuse or overconfidence in the voluntary nature of relationships with patients. * * * Having examined the many medical and legal stumbling blocks encountered by the battered child, we wish to offer some general proposals to relieve the confusion. Of course we are aware that every county and every state has its own statutes, courts, and treatment facilities. However, there are some principles which we believe transcend these differences.

First we wish to emphasize the importance of a treatment plan in the initial stages of working with the abused child and his family. The plan must allow for full and efficient use of the community's medical, social, and legal resources. One central agency is needed to set up the treatment plan, to facilitate interagency communication, and to bear ultimate responsibility for carrying out the plan. We feel that the juvenile court or the child protective service agency working closely with the juvenile court is the most appropriate unit to direct and coordinate this planning. Therefore we would hope that every battered child case comes to the immediate attention of the juvenile court. (The term juvenile court will henceforth be used to include child protective agency also.)

The sequence of planning is very important. The issue of prosecution must be settled before any treatment plan can go into effect. Prosecutors, when urged to do so, are able to decide within a few weeks whether or not to criminally prosecute a case. After the decision to prosecute is made, the juvenile court proceeds to weigh permanent termination of parental rights versus temporary placement of the child. Early planning is undertaken also for future juvenile court supervision and treatment of the parents if their child is to be returned to them at the time of acquittal or release from prison.

Let us assume that the prosecutor has decided not to initiate criminal action. What is the next step in planning? The juvenile court worker considers whether there is sufficient evidence of repeated abuse, a particularly severe injury, or parental disinterest in the child to press immediately for permanent termination of parental rights. If termination appears to be necessary, the parents may be helped through casework to understand their inability to cope with the child so that they voluntarily seek termination of their parental rights or at least desist from fighting such action in court.

On the other hand, there are a great many cases in which there is some doubt about eventual return of the child or in which there is insufficient evidence to terminate parental rights. In these cases there are two possible avenues of planning. One of these is removal of the battered child to a foster home or institution while the parents are treated to determine whether the child will eventually be returned to them (4). We take issue with this commonly used approach because we have found that after the disruptive child is removed, parents are no longer under stress and come to feel that they have changed, only to resume their former behavior when the child is returned to them.

We would propose a second approach in dealing with cases in which family restoration remains in doubt. After a reported battering, the child becomes a temporary ward of the juvenile court and returns to the parents, while certain safeguards are employed. The parents are required to undergo a few months' diagnostic trial of penetrating conjoint interviews (15) to determine their capability for insight and change. Safeguards include almost daily checks of the child by community health, social work, and/or educational personnel, as well as provision of homemaker services (6, 13), if available, for the mother. Another desirable safeguard is the appointment by the court of an attorney to represent the child's interests.

The backbone of this plan, however, is the diagnostic trial of conjoint parental interviews previously mentioned. These sessions will offer the parents a chance to observe their interactions with each other and with the child and to come to grips with some of their unrealistic ideas about the child. Such interviews may be conducted by a psychiatrist, psychologist, or social worker. After several sessions the therapist will have a firm, well-documented opinion about the family's future chances with the abused child. Termination of rights may come about if abuse continues even under supervision or if the family is unable to begin to improve with treatment.

On the other hand, if some improvement comes about in the trial period, a strong basis has been laid for continuing parental conjoint or individual therapy with court worker, social agency, or physician. We feel it would be wise for the court to invoke temporary custody for at least a year in cases in which the child will continue to live at home.

Finally, in order to provide the best therapeutic chance for the battered child it is necessary to draft statutes aimed at rehabilitation so that mandatory physicians' reports will result in treatment programs rather than punishment procedures.

In summary, we wish to emphasize that the process of handling battered children must continue to be a complex multi-agency process. One agency or one person cannot deal with the problems of the battered child alone. We have found that the handling will fail without the backup of juvenile court jurisdiction. Parents who ordinarily are inaccessible to more traditional voluntary treatment approaches may respond to treatment if a court insists upon it.

Note

Client Choice and the Offering of Protective Services

Freedom of the welfare client to make his own choices has long been a basic tenet of professional social work philosophy. This concept is not always followed by agencies offering protective services. Witness for example, the restrictions placed upon a Minneapolis mother by a juvenile court as reported in 3 Law in Action No. 5 (Sept. 1968):

"The case in Minneapolis stemmed from a Welfare Department allegation that one poor mother of six children was an unfit parent.

"She was accused, in essence, of her children's truancy, of mismanagement of her AFDC money, and of having an adult male companion. A petition by the county, to the Juvenile Court, asked that her parental rights be terminated forever and that her children be handed over to the Commissioner of Public Welfare. But, after a hearing was held, the court did not see fit to take the children from their mother. Instead, the court made an order relating to the woman's future conduct.

"She was ordered not to write any checks, lest she be found in contempt of court. The order also provided that it would be sufficient ground to terminate her parental rights if the woman should write a check and it bounced. Moreover, the order stated that it would be sufficient evidence to terminate her parental rights, in addition to being contemptuous of the court, if she should write five or more checks—whether or not they bounced.

"Nine months later, the county attorney petitioned for a contempt order, alleging that the mother had failed to pay her bills within 15 days of due date, and further alleging that she had failed to write medical excuses from school for some of her children. The woman was found guilty of contempt, and was sentenced to 90 days in jail. Simultaneously with her incarceration, the Welfare Department picked up her children and dispersed them among six different foster homes."

The family was reunited and the mother given control of her affairs after two years of litigation by O.E.O. attorneys.

The following analysis of the British system by Professor Handler attempts to explain why protective agencies and their personnel are willing to take over management of a client's day-to-day affairs:

"Interest in providing more effective preventive personal social services for families at risk is growing apace in Great Britain. Since 1963, children's departments have been given responsibility for providing preventive casework services; and they are to be given additional responsibilities under the new white paper, Children in Trouble. But what do preventive services mean to families at risk? What consequences do current policies in personal social services have for the freedom of welfare clients?

"The dominant model or image that most social workers have of their relationship with their clients is patterned after the private psychiatrist-client relationship. In that relationship, the client voluntarily comes to the professional for help and the task of the professional is to examine the so-called 'presenting problem,' establish a therapeutic relationship, and work out a 'constructive' plan of rehabilitation or at least devices for controlling the more destructive or obnoxious forms of behaviour. The client, in this private arrangement, is dependent in the sense that he feels the need for professional help, but the core of the relationship is voluntary. There are no legal, economic, or overt social compulsions. The professional, therefore, feels free to give his advice and the client, to a considerable extent, is free to take it or leave it.

"Child care officers have adopted the therapeutic rhetoric of the psychiatrist— their role is to get behind the presenting problem and restructure the family to abate major problems and to prevent them from recurring. (This, of course, is what preventive work means in the law and what the officers are charged with doing.) But people who come to children's departments have specific, tangible requests—a child to be received into care, a threatened eviction, an electricity cut-off, a truancy notice. Nevertheless, according to the social work rhetoric, disposing of the immediate problem, without more, is unprofessional, potentially destructive, and can create even further dependency. All casework services have to be—in their terms—'constructive'— part of a 'plan.'

"However, the crucial difference between the psychiatric model and the child care officer relationship lies in the differences in the social characteristics. [The children's department stands in a very powerful position vis-a-vis the client. The agency is a dispenser of rewards and benefits (which includes the staving off of more serious sanctions) that the families sorely need. These rewards and benefits are levers that the officers use in the casework plan. The casework plan means changing behaviour to conform to what the child care officer thinks is proper.] * * *

"[Punitive legal sanctions constitute only one part of the reward and punishment system administered by the departments. The total system of rewards and punishments is developed out of the relationship between the agency and its clients —why the clients and the children's departments are dealing with each other and how they are dealing with each other. The reasons for the relationship affect significantly the character of the relationship.] * * *

"[One is struck by the virulence of the hangover of the concept of pauperism. In the 19th century, poverty and pauperism were synonymous with moral decay and linked causally with criminality. Failure to earn a living was a form of deviant behaviour. The persistence of this moralistic attitude toward the welfare client and the pathological theory of poverty are present in the Children's and Young Persons Act. Both the Ingleby report, which led to the 1963 act, and the act itself justify preventive work, in large part, on crime prevention grounds. The attitudes of the child care officers as well as the policies of the departments are dressed up versions of 19th century programme criteria: we must be careful lest we increase dependency.]

"Not infrequently, 'success' with families at risk is judged in terms of the regular payment of bills. The operative social work principles in the children's departments today are remarkably similar to those of the Charity Organisation Society, founded about 100 years ago. The close supervision of the spending of money is little different from the old system of relief in kind; poor people cannot be trusted to spend money that isn't 'theirs.'

"In fairness, it should be recognised that children's departments are, for the most part, reactive agencies. To a large extent they are trapped by circumstances beyond their control. They are not responsible for delinquency, slum schools, low levels of assistance, the shortage of housing, the wage stop, the Ministry of Social Security's administration of special grants, poverty and ill-health. They have limited resources (particularly financial and material), heavy caseloads, and seem to move from crisis to crisis. There is no intensive casework in fact. Success in their terms does mean imposing their standards of behaviour on their clients. But it should be made clear that these standards are no more than what is minimally required to survive in a market-dominated society and to preserve the barest semblance of family stability and decency in disorganised and disturbed situations. In many instances child care officers have had to do practically everything for families during extended crises. Child care officers are forced to select.

They tend to select families who respond to services. Given the present position of the children's departments, this approach is probably rational. Even so, there are cases where extensive financial and material assistance is given without any real hope of change.

"The coercive aspects of the casework relationship, in my judgment, are not primarily due to lack of professional training or the personalities of the officers. Indeed, most of the officers who generated the data for this study were as highly trained as could reasonably be expected and appeared to me to be very hard-working, humane people operating under trying conditions. The coercion stems from the structural position of the agencies which gives them enormous power over clients. Child care officers are authority figures. They are extensions of other authoritative agencies—the police, the schools, the health agencies—or the key to desperately needed benefits. The brokering activities of the children's departments give them the power to do things that clients want.

"Ironically, this power of the officers will be increased by the current policy efforts to coordinate the work of the various statutory departments. To the extent that the police cooperate with the children's department, the latter becomes part of the administration of justice. Housing authorities use the children's departments to allocate priority rehousing. At least one Ministry of Social Security area office sends applicants for special grants first over to the children's department for its approval. Coordination is the wave of the future, but one of its consequences is to increase the discretionary levers in the hands of children's departments.

"It is therefore time for children's officers—and other social workers—to reconsider their psychiatrist-client relationship with those they seek to help. They are administrative officials exercising governmental powers." Handler, "The Coercive Children's Officer" New Society, 3 Oct. 1968, No. 314.

CHENEY, SAFEGUARDING LEGAL RIGHTS IN PROVIDING PROTECTIVE SERVICES

13 Children 87 (1966).

In protective services, the social worker is part of an administrative agency, separate from the juvenile court and empowered to provide the type of supervision to the home that a court may order, but solely on the basis of a social study in which legal considerations may be absent. The standards of care expected of the family under this supervision are set by the agency at its own discretion and may vary as the needs of therapy require. Moreover, the agency's criteria for intervention can be based on a lesser degree of neglect than is necessary to sustain an adjudication of neglect in the juvenile court; for the purpose of protective services is to treat incipient neglect and to resort to the court only when effective treatment has proved to be impossible.

"Neglect," however, is a concept which permits no degree of certainty, either in legal definition or social application. Most neglect statutes are broadly drawn. Such phrases as "proper care" and "conditions prejudicial to a child's well-being" define the conditions on which the State may act. These standards do no more than import vague subjective tests into a legal criterion. Commentators on the juvenile court generally agree that protection from this vagueness must be found in the wisdom of judges rather than in the detail of statute. But they also recognize that the vagueness "enables judges to conceal any kind of result behind * * * pious intonation(s) * * * " and "encourages slipshod decisions which stop short of workmanlike analysis and the decision of important legal issues."

Even when judges try to articulate a legal or social criterion of neglect, which could be a guideline for a protective worker, the results are not uniform. Judicial standards for parental care range from a "reasonably prudent man" test carried over from the law of negligence to a "demonstrated incapacity or something akin to criminal neglect." Perhaps the standard most generally followed is, as Monrad Paulsen suggests, the minimum quality of care which the community will tolerate. One judge, in a well-justified dissent, said that a decision should be based on "all of the many-colored hues going to make up the spectrum of life." Thus there is no agreement on the fundamental question of what standard of care the law requires of parents.

To make matters worse, there are almost no written juvenile court opinions dealing with neglect, and few appellate decisions. * * *

Social work as a profession does not provide any clearer criteria. Its emphasis on the emotional and psychological well-being of the child makes social workers less likely than many judges to interfere with family life on the basis of such forms of value preference such as religion or political beliefs. But their goal of emotional well-being is also based on value preferences.

A social worker may assume for himself a hierarchy of social values and conclude that families are providing children with what they need if they are, for example, adventuresome and generous, motivated by a desire to foster social responsibility, and endowed with spiritual qualities. But such values make precision in goal definition impossible. * * *

Any number of factors may be relevant in determining what a child's well-being requires. For example, when a child comes to the attention of the protective agency, should the agency intervene because the child's religious training is neglected, as has sometimes been done, or because his parents strongly advocate communism, as has also been done, or because a racial intermarriage disturbs the family's relationship to the community, as was alleged in a case in Connecticut?

Once the agency decides to intervene, what goals should be set? Should the child be removed to a family of greater wealth or social status or with more acceptable political beliefs? Or, if the child is not removed from his home, should the family be reorganized to strengthen religion or education, or to promote the child's physical well-being, or to make him respect his parents, or to promote family love, or all of these?

What is needed are clear standards and an administrative procedure designed to expose the criteria actually applied in any case to close legal and social scrutiny. * * *

[A] protective statute should exclude the right to intervene in family life because of the parent's behavior unless there is some direct evidence that it is adversely affecting the child. * * *

Where a person's liberty is involved, the general proposition is that procedural due process requires a hearing in which some tribunal passes on the State's right to intervene. Most protective statutes do not provide for hearings. They either ignore the requirement or they rely on the fiction that families given protective services always accept them voluntarily.

True, a parent confronted by a protective worker can obtain a hearing simply by vigorously refusing to accept the services and awaiting the agency's determination to file a neglect petition in the juvenile court. But most parents who are confronted with an offer of protective services may be uncertain of their legal position and may acquiesce only because advice from a social worker seems less threatening than court action. Moreover, many such parents may be recipients of public assistance and may believe that refusing the worker's offer of service may

jeopardize their means of sustenance. * * *

The best way to meet this obligation is to require a hearing within 60 to 90 days *after* services are offered the family on a voluntary basis under statutory authorization. If the hearing were required *before* any offer of services, the program would be indistinguishable from the present protective supervision used by the juvenile court, and would introduce the element of coercion so apt to produce hostility in parents. Allowing for the *voluntary* acceptance of the offer of services could promote the social worker's chances of developing the kind of helping relationship which can displace hostility with genuine cooperation. And, if the services prove officious, the court could readily terminate them.

The issue at this hearing—unless either protective worker or parent determined that a formal adjudication of neglect should be made—should be limited to the question of whether or not protective services were being administered within the definitions of neglect contained in the protective act and thus may continue. This procedure would not require the judge to become an administrator of the child protective agency. It would give the courts a function especially suited to them: judging whether the State is legitimately intervening in family life to advance the social welfare. * * *

The final question raised by due process requirements is whether a family should have a right to counsel at the hearing. Since juvenile court hearings need not provide a defendant with the safeguards required in criminal proceedings, counsel is, perhaps, not mandatory. But the absence of procedural safeguards in juvenile courts is not universally applauded. A benevolent deprivation is just as real as a malevolent one. * * *

The best way to assure both that due process of law is observed and that the values on which decisions are made are clearly stated is by providing parents with counsel if they cannot do so themselves, * * * Lawyers could help force those persons concerned with child neglect to grapple with the basic social and legal questions involved.

WYMAN v. JAMES

Supreme Court of the United States, 1971.
400 U.S. 309, 91 S.Ct. 381, 27 L.Ed.2d 408.
[Reprinted at p. 319, supra.]

Notes

1. R. A. Burt, Forcing Protection on Children and Their Parents: The Impact of Wyman v. James, 69 Michigan Law Review 1259 (1971): "The state's protective purposes in insisting that Mrs. James accept its assistance or suffer serious loss of benefits played an important role in the Wyman decision. Only a few years ago, in In re Gault, the Court refused to defer to a state's similarly beneficent motives when it was asked to withhold the imposition of procedural safeguards in juvenile delinquency proceedings. *Wyman* does not overrule *Gault*. But the suppositions underlying the two cases are vastly different."

2. For an excellent discussion of the *James* case, see Dembitz, "The Good of the Child Versus the Rights of the Parent: The Supreme Court Upholds the Welfare Home—Visit," 86 Political Science Quarterly, p. 389 (1971).

B. LIFE STYLES AND NEGLECT

IN RE YARDLEY

Supreme Court of Iowa, 1967.
260 Iowa 259, 149 N.W.2d 162.

GARFIELD, Chief Justice. This is a juvenile proceeding under chapter 232,

Code, 1966 (chapter 215 Laws 61st G.A. 1965), asking that six children of Wanda Yardley be declared "neglected", within the meaning of Code section 232.2 subd. 15 (section 3 of the Act) and the parent-child relationship between the children and their parents terminated. Following a hearing the relief was granted as to all the children except the youngest and their mother, age 34, has appealed.

The action was instituted by filing a petition on January 4, 1966 by a child welfare worker for the Wapello County Department of Social Welfare in Ottumwa. Counsel for the mother appeared in resistance to the petition. Counsel for the father of the five oldest children, Wanda's divorced husband, also appeared and took part in the hearing (on January 31 and February 4) but consented that the relief sought be granted.

Wanda obtained the divorce from Donald Yardley, Sr., September 10, 1963 because he was living with another woman, his present wife. Wanda was granted custody of Donald, Jr., born June 21, 1951, Pamela, born May 31, 1954 and Sandra, born July 26, 1961. Donald, Sr., was awarded custody of Theresa, born January 6, 1956 and Joseph, born January 30, 1959. Wanda's youngest was not born until June 20, 1965.

Wanda never married again. Father of her youngest is a man from Milwaukee whom she met in a tavern in Ottumwa and knew only three weeks. He has furnished no support for the child and apparently does not know it exists. The home in which Wanda and four of her children lived is owned by her father who has a separate room of his own there.

Theresa and Joseph were unhappy at their father's, returned to their mother's in September, 1964 and lived there much of the subsequent time. Donald, Sr., and his present wife have a young child of their own and his wife has three older children who live with them. Donald drives a moving van and is gone from home most of the time. Wanda's principal income consists of payments from Aid to Dependent Children (A.D.C.).

The case was referred to the child welfare branch of the Department of Social Welfare in April, 1964 following complaints the children were being neglected. Petitioner told Wanda it was claimed she was leaving the children alone while she went to taverns and that she was having a man in her home. This Wanda denied. The house was found to be cluttered and untidy, the kitchen had unwashed dishes piled up, beds were unmade and without sheets or proper bedding. In 18 to 25 visits to the home by the time of the hearing petitioner found it in much the same condition as at first. Other social welfare workers confirmed this.

In March, 1965 petitioner received a complaint that Wanda had thrown a shoe at the child Theresa and ruptured a blood vessel in her eye. Wanda admitted this but insisted she intended no injury. In April (1965) Wanda was found to be 7½ months pregnant with the child born out of wedlock. She insisted on keeping the child who was born in Ottumwa, rather than consent to its adoption.

When about to be confined in childbirth Wanda obtained a 17-year-old girl, Helen Guard, to come to the home and care for the children. Helen had dropped out of school when halfway through the tenth grade. She stayed in the home about a month, cared for the children, prepared their meals and kept house. Helen became 18 on October 25 and Wanda's father consented that she come there then to make her home. She was still living there at the time of the hearing. Some of Wanda's troubles stem from Helen's presence in the home.

Helen admitted as a witness a divorced man named Buck stayed with her in the back bedroom all of about three or four nights. The children who usually slept in that bed were required to give it up on these occasions. Wanda was at home and, according to Helen, did not object to such conduct. Another man who was "stewed up" came to see Helen and spent the night in the home although she said they were not "together" on this occasion. There is evidence Helen also entertained him in the bedroom at least once. Both men were friends of Wanda with whom she frequently danced at taverns or so-called clubs.

Wanda testified she did not approve Helen's entertaining men in the home or consent to it and did not know Buck spent the night there until she got up the next day. We infer from her testimony that her claimed lack of prior knowledge of his presence there is mainly based on the fact she did not see him and Helen together on the bed. Wanda also testified the man who was "stewed up" should have been ordered out of the house.

Helen testified she was not pregnant "for sure" but had not had a medical check-up.

Wanda's need of a baby-sitter was largely due to her frequenting taverns and clubs where liquor was sold and dancing permitted. She usually went to a tavern Friday or Saturday nights and sometimes one other evening during the week. She would leave home at 8:30 or 9:00 and return between 11:30 and one. Donald, Jr., testified his mother was usually in by one or 1:30. Her father would take her to a tavern or club many evenings and she would return home with someone she saw there or in a taxi. Wanda testified she formerly went to taverns more frequently and stayed later—until 2 a. m. When she bought her own drinks they were usually pop but if someone bought hard liquor for her she would drink it.

About every other Monday evening Wanda "baby-sat" with six children while their mother went bowling. Sometimes Wanda stayed all night with this friend. On the Friday and Saturday nights following birth of her baby on Sunday Wanda went to a tavern and stayed, according to her, until 12 and one. There is evidence she was away from home all of Friday night. It was shown without objection that Helen Guard told the paternal grandparents of the five children on Saturday afternoon she was worried about Wanda—she was just off somewhere drinking.

Donald, Jr., 14 at trial time, smoked cigarettes regularly but testified he was trying to stop; his mother bought cigarettes for him and the man Wanda said should have been ordered out of the home gave Donald cigarettes once. Donald was in the seventh grade in school at the time of the hearing. He and two of the other children were in "special education" part of the time. The last of June, 1965 Wanda told a social worker Donald had been a great deal of trouble lately and, so far as she was concerned, he could stay with his father.

Wanda's father provided little, if any, guidance for the children. He approved her frequenting taverns if she enjoyed it and someone stayed with the children. He did not know Wanda was pregnant with the last baby until six weeks before birth.

There is a good deal of evidence the children had enough food to eat, adequate clothes to wear and were kept fairly clean. What the children lacked was proper parental direction, moral guidance and good example. There was evidently a complete lack of religious training either in or out of the home.

Petitioner testified the local welfare office received constant complaints concerning the home and Wanda was highly emotional and immature. The office asked permanent removal of the children from the home and termination of parental rights.

There is other evidence of course but enough has been summarized to indicate what the record contains.

The trial court found the children were "neglected" within the meaning of chapter 215, section 3, subd. 15 Laws, Sixty-first General Assembly (section 232.2, subd. 15, Code, 1966), in that the father had abandoned the two children placed in his custody, all the children were "without proper parental care because of the faults or habits of (their) parents * * or other custodian" and were "living under conditions injurious to (their) mental * * * health or welfare."

When the petition was filed on January 4, 1966, the court found it appeared the welfare of the children required their temporary custody be immediately assumed by the juvenile court and ordered them delivered to the county board of social welfare pending further order (see chapter 215, section 8, Code, 1966, section 232.7). The record indicates this was done.

In the final decree, dated April 20, 1966, the order for temporary custody was terminated as to the baby (then ten months old) and he was ordered returned to Wanda subject to strict supervision by the county department of social welfare. The cause was continued as to the baby to be reviewed in one year. As to the other five children the parent-child relationship was terminated and their custody transferred to the county social welfare department. (See chapter 215, section 34, subd. 3, par. b, Code section 232.33, subd. 3, par. b.) * * *

II. Appellant has assigned errors relied upon for reversal as in appeals in law cases. The first of these is in admitting hearsay evidence. The others are errors (2) in the court's findings of fact, (3) in finding the children were "neglected", and (4) in ordering termination of the parental relationship of appellant. The second and third of these really challenge the sufficiency of the evidence to support the findings and the fourth is a similar challenge to the order referred to.

Ordinarily we do not review such errors as 2, 3, and 4 where our review is de novo. In such matters we review the facts as well as the law and draw what we think are proper conclusions therefrom. Gilbrech v. Kloberdanz, 252 Iowa 509, 515, 107 N.W.2d 574, 578; Arnold v. Arnold, 257 Iowa 429, 433, 133 N.W.2d 53, 56. * * *

[The discussion of the first assigned error is omitted.]

IV. This mainly leaves the question whether the evidence, as we have reviewed it, is sufficient to support depriving this mother of five of her six children. With the modification referred to infra we think it does.

Section 42 of chapter 215 (Code section 232.41) provides: "The court may upon petition terminate the relationship between parent and child: * * *

"2. If the court finds that one or more of the following conditions exist: * *

"b. That the parents have substantially and continuously or repeatedly refused to give the child necessary care and protection. * * *

"d. That the parents are unfit by reason of debauchery * * * or other conduct found by the court likely to be detrimental to the physical or mental health or morals of the child.

"e. That following an adjudication of neglect or dependency, reasonable efforts under the direction of the court have failed to correct the conditions leading to the termination."

It will be noticed that "d" above grants broad power to the court that we think authorized termination of the parent-child relation here.

In re Morrison, supra, 259 Iowa 301, 144 N.W.2d 97, 103, seems to be our only decision under the Juvenile Court Law enacted in 1965 by the Sixty-first General Assembly. Although the grounds for terminating the parent-child relation there were somewhat stronger than here, the opinion contains much that is applicable:

"It is well established in matters of this kind that the primary consideration is the welfare and best interest of the child. (citation) While there is a presumption that the best interest of the child will be served by leaving it with its parents, this is not conclusive. (citation) Obviously, there was substantial evidence presented here to overcome that presumption. We do not overlook the right of a child to the care, support and affection of his parents, and of the parents' right to custody unless by their conduct they forfeit that right. Nevertheless, we must recognize that the State, as parens patriae, has the duty to see that every child within its borders receives proper care and treatment.

"We do not overlook the fact that these children were kept clean and well-fed, that their physical home life was about average for persons of their parents' means, and that they attended church frequently. We credit the parents for that and, were it not for the obvious atmosphere of unwholesomeness generated by the words and deeds of these parties, we would perhaps be more hesitant to dissolve this parent-child relationship. * * * They need and must have proper guidance and must be furnished a healthy mental and moral atmosphere by those who have their custody and control."

What is said in Stubbs v. Hammond and State ex rel. Wiley v. Richards, cited in the quoted excerpt, is also to be commended. (Unlike In re Morrison, there was evidently no church attendance here.)

Incidentally, the Morrison opinion upholds the validity of the statute as against the charge parts of it are too vague and unconstitutional.

V. As before stated, the trial court's final decree dated April 20, 1966, ordered the baby returned to Wanda subject to strict supervision by the county department of social welfare and continued the cause as to him to be reviewed in one year. After referring to this provision appellant's brief and argument suggests opportunity should have been given Wanda to correct whatever faults and deficiencies were found relative to her conduct with respect to all the children.

We think there is merit in this suggestion as applied to any of the five older children who have not been adopted by others under the provisions of Code chapter 600 at the time this opinion is filed.

Section 59 of chapter 215 (Code section 232.58) provides: "The pendency of an appeal * * * shall not suspend the order of the juvenile court regarding a minor and shall not discharge the minor from the custody of the * * * agency to whose care the minor has been committed or placed unless otherwise ordered by the Supreme Court on application of an appellant."

No application for an order under this provision was made to us pending the appeal. See in this connection Savery v. Eddy, 242 Iowa 822, 840–844, 45 N.W. 2d 872, 47 N.W.2d 230, 48 N.W.2d 230.

While we feel sufficient grounds existed for the order of termination when made, it is possible conditions in the home or Wanda's conduct have improved to the point where some or all of the children may properly be returned to her. We are reluctant to approve taking the children from their mother permanently without giving her another opportunity to show she is now capable of caring for them in a manner not detrimental to their mental

health or morals. Such a showing would accord with the declaration of section 2 of chapter 215 (Code section 232.1) that a child "shall receive, preferably in his home, the care, guidance and control that will conduce to his welfare and the best interests of the state, * * *."

We modify the decree to provide for the taking of additional evidence in the trial court as to whether conditions in the home and Wanda's conduct at the time of hearing it are such that custody of the children should be returned to her and for such further orders with reference thereto as may be proper.

Modified, affirmed and remanded.

All Justices concur.

IN RE RAYA

Court of Appeals, Third District of California, 1967.

255 Cal.App.2d 260, 63 Cal.Rptr. 252.

PER CURIAM. The Superior Court of Sacramento County, sitting as a Juvenile Court, has adjudged the two minors, Timateo (Timothy) and Frances Raya, 9 and 7 years of age, respectively, to be dependent children within the meaning of Welfare and Institutions Code section 600, subdivision (a).[1] Five court orders are involved. Their net effect was to remove said children from the custody of both their parents; Henrietta Raya, the mother (who prior to the first of such

[1] Said section provides in part:

"Any person under the age of 21 years who comes within any of the following descriptions is within the jurisdiction of the juvenile court which may adjudge such person to be a dependent child of the court:

"(a) Who is in need of proper and effective parental care or control and has no parent or guardian, or has no parent or guardian willing to exercise or capable of exercising such care or control, or has no parent or guardian actually exercising such care or control."

(Section 600, subdivision (b), also includes a child "whose home is an unfit place for him by reason of neglect, cruelty, or depravity of either of his parents * * *.")

orders had had the children in her custody) and Isidro Raya, the father. Under the latest of said orders the children were placed in the Sacramento Receiving Home "pending suitable placement by the Sacramento County Welfare Department." The orders are appealable and have priority on appeal. (Welf. & Inst.Code, § 800.) They were appealed both by the father and the mother. Appearing on behalf of the children, the Public Defender has filed a brief supporting the parents' appeals. On September 20, 1967, we issued a temporary stay of execution and placed the children in the custody of their mother. The appeals have been argued.

Basic facts are that in the course of the hearing of a divorce action it developed that the couple, separated, were each presently cohabiting with partners of the opposite sex under a consensual extramarital, but long lasting, arrangement; that Mrs. Raya and her consort, William Mendoza, have had four children out of wedlock while Mr. Raya and his mistress, a Miss Fernandez, have had three children. Miss Fernandez, unmarried, also had had a child before the Raya-Fernandez liaison.

Mr. and Mrs. Raya separated in 1960. They have not lived together since. At the time of the separation Mrs. Raya took the two children with her and they have been with her until the court orders described.

As soon as Raya and Miss Fernandez commenced living together a divorce was contemplated but at the time Raya lacked funds to pay the legal expense. (Both families have been on relief sporadically. The Department of Social Welfare has known of the extramarital status of the two couples.) On February 7, 1967, Raya filed a divorce action; this through the Sacramento Legal Aid Society, whose policy to give financial assistance in proper domestic relations matters for the benefit of parties with substandard financial means is recent. The purpose here was to effect a change in the relationship of both couples, who have expressed an intent to marry as soon as this may legally be accomplished. (The report of the probation officer hereinafter mentioned credits the sincerity of this intent.) The Raya divorce will be final in February 1968. Mr. Raya's divorce complaint alleges Mrs. Raya to be a fit and proper person to have custody of the children.

During the pendency of the divorce a probation report was ordered. The report, dated April 18, 1967, includes these facts: The Mendoza-Raya family resides in a three-bedroom home in a low rent district. The home is being purchased by the couple. It is described as "neat, clean and quite comfortable * * * and furnished with all necessary facilities." The children lived in the Raya-Mendoza household and accepted Mr. Mendoza as their father and he was a father to them. The Rayas separated when the children were very young and since that time they had had little or no contact with their natural father. When they subsequently learned that their natural father was Raya, they became quite disturbed. The report states the children appear well cared for and Raya concedes that Mrs. Raya has been a good mother who gives the children good parental care. The Mendoza-Raya home is one block from the school which the children attend. Their school attendance record is good and they are doing exceptionally well in school. The report's appraisal in this regard is: "These children appear to be happy, healthy, normal youngsters and well cared for * * * bright friendly." The entire family, of the Catholic faith, attend church each Sunday.

Raya has contributed something to the support of the children but has also been before the Domestic Relations Division of the Sacramento County District Attorney's office for some remissness in this regard. The report's evaluation and recommendation includes: "Your officer is of the opinion that the mother of Timothy and Francis Ray [sic] is a person of good moral character and that she is properly caring for said minors and, too, is seeing that they receive an education as well as spiritual training, and your officer feels that inasmuch as we do have children here of tender age who are in need of maternal love, care, guidance, training, discipline and education, it is to their best interests and welfare that they continue in the custody of their mother. * * * [with] an opportunity to visit with their natural father and to become better acquainted with him."

The *facts* in this report apparently have been accepted by the trial court; but its *conclusions* were not. In fact, a minute order of March 21, 1967 (before the date of the report) reads: "Court finds both parents unfit. Refer to Juvenile Court under 600 A W & I Code. To be heard in Dept. 6 sitting as Juvenile Court." The matter was again referred to the County Probation Office, which thereafter filed petitions alleging the two Raya children were minors described in section 600, subdivision (a), of the Welfare and Institutions Code (see fn. 1). A hearing was held on the petition on June 23, 1967. Attorneys representing both parents were present, also Public Defender Kenneth Wells, who had been assigned by the court to represent the minors. A new probation report was then heard. Its factual determinations were substantially as stated above. Its recommendation, however, was that which later became the court's order. Testimony was also given by Raya, Mrs. Raya, and their respective intended spouses. Their testimony did not substantially differ from the facts in the reports.

Separate orders covering each minor have been made. Two orders were made on June 23, 1967. They declared the children to be dependent children under section 600, subdivision (a). The first (in each case) committed them to the joint supervision of the probation officer and county welfare department. Modified orders the same day changed the custody of the children to their maternal grandmother. Those orders were in turn modified three months later, on September 20, 1967. (The court at that time had learned the maternal grandmother was living with her "husband" out of wedlock.) The last order removed the children from the grandmother's custody and placed them, as stated above, in the receiving home.

The trial court found, utilizing the language of section 600, subdivision (a), that the children had "no parent or guardian actually exercising proper and effective care and control and continue[s] to be in need of such care and control," in that each of the natural parents had lived in unmarried cohabitation for more than the five preceding years. This finding cannot be disturbed on appeal if there is substantial evidence to support it. (In re Macidon, 240 Cal.App.2d 600, 607, 49 Cal.Rptr. 861; In re Corrigan, 134 Cal.App.2d 751, 754–755, 286 P.2d 32.) The evidence before the court supplied no substantial support for the finding.

In wardship proceedings the welfare of the child is the paramount concern. (In re Farley, 162 Cal.App.2d 474, 478, 328 P.2d 230; In re Corrigan, supra, 134 Cal.App.2d at p. 754, 286 P.2d 32.) Section 600, subdivision (a), of the Welfare and Institutions Code permits an adjudication of wardship when proper and effective parental care or control is lacking. The phrase "proper and effective" offers at best a dim light to discern the point at which a juvenile court is authorized to invade and supplant a parent-child relationship. In one sense the phrase expresses an objective identical with the judicially expressed goal of the child's welfare. In another sense it connotes parental fitness or unfitness. (See Marr v. Superior Court, 114 Cal.App.2d 527, 530, 250 P.2d 739.) Additional coloration may be gained from the notion of the "neglected child," whose home environment exposes him to physical or moral detriment.[2]

However this may be, the statutory criterion of improper and ineffective parental care denotes a fairly extreme case. A dominant parental right to custody of the child pervades our law. (See Prob. Code, § 1407; Civ.Code, § 197; Roche v. Roche, 25 Cal.2d 141, 143–144, 152 P.2d 999; Stever v. Stever, 6 Cal.2d 166, 168–170, 56 P.2d 1229; In re Campbell's Estate, 130 Cal. 380, 382, 62 P. 613; 2 Armstrong, California Family Law, pp. 993–1018.) Although expressed more often in divorce and guardianship cases, the dominating right of a parent to custody of his child plays a role in the interpretation of section 600, subdivision (a). Many homes, however blessed by marital vows, fall short of an ideal environment for children. It may be safely assumed that the Juvenile Court Law was not intended to expose such homes to wholesale intervention by public authorities. "It is cardinal with us that the custody, care and nurture of the child reside first in the parents, whose primary function and freedom include preparation for obligations the state can neither supply nor hinder." (Prince v. Commonwealth of Massachusetts, 321 U.S. 158, 166, 64 S.Ct. 438, 442, 88 L.Ed. 645, quoted in Roche v. Roche, supra, 25 Cal.2d at p. 144, 152 P.2d 999.) Thus before section 600, subdivision (a), authorizes the drastic step of judicial intervention, some threshold level of deficiency is demanded. Although a home environment may appear deficient when measured by dominant socioeconomic standards, interposition by the powerful arm of the public authori-

ties may lead to worse alternatives.[3] A juvenile court may possess no magic wand to create a replacement for a home which falls short of ideal.[4] California appellate decisions in wardship cases of the "dependent child" variety demonstrate rather extreme cases of neglect, cruelty or continuing exposure to immorality. (See In re Farley, supra, 162 Cal.App.2d 474, 328 P.2d 230; In re Schubert, 153 Cal. App.2d 138, 313 P.2d 968; In re Corrigan, supra, 134 Cal.App.2d 751, 286 P.2d 32; Marr v. Superior Court, supra, 114 Cal.App.2d 527, 250 P.2d 739; In re Halamuda, 85 Cal.App.2d 219, 192 P.2d 781; In re Schultz, 99 Cal.App. 134, 277 P. 1049; Ex parte Hunter, 45 Cal. App. 505, 188 P. 63.)

When section 600, subdivision (a), is so viewed, the present facts fall far short of that level of improper and ineffective control which might justify an adjudication of public wardship. Nonconflicting evidence demonstrated that the children were happy, healthy and well adjusted in the home provided by their mother and Mr. Mendoza; that the mother and Mr. Mendoza were satisfying the children's need for familial love, security and physical well-being. The fact that the mother had established a home and was living with a man to whom she was not married supplied the sole evidence which might conceivably support the finding. This piece of evidence was inextricably coupled with a group of accompanying circumstances: (1) the relationship was stable, not casual or promiscuous; (2) poverty alone had prevented the Rayas' divorce and the mother's marriage to Mr. Men-

---

[2] See Kay & Philips, Poverty and the Law of Child Custody, 54 Cal.L.Rev. 717, 733 et seq.

[3] See, e. g., Kay & Philips, op. cit. supra (fn. 2) pp. 736–738.

[4] See Paulsen, Juvenile Courts, Family Courts, and the Poor Man, 54 Cal.L.Rev. 694, 699. In another context, it has been observed that juvenile courts sometimes lack facilities and techniques for adequate performance in a parens patriae capacity. (Kent v. United States, 383 U.S. 541, 555–556, 86 S.Ct. 1045, 16 L.Ed.2d 84, per Fortas, J.)

doza; (3) as soon as poverty ceased to be a barrier—that is, shortly after the Sacramento Legal Aid Society broadened its program to provide legal counsel in such cases—a divorce was instituted, which would legitimize the Rayas' relationships and permit them to establish homes according to prevailing norms. The juvenile court did not face a situation in which the natural parent had surrendered to unmarried cohabitation as her permanent condition, nor need we consider such a case. Given time and freedom from outside interference, the Mendoza-Raya household was in process of transformation into an established family unit. If the wardship order did not block that process, it at least disrupted it and inflicted upon the children the pain and disarray of removal from home and family pending completion of the process. The potential legitimation of relationships cannot be ignored or discounted. (Guardianship of Smith, 42 Cal.2d 91, 94, 265 P.2d 888, 37 A.L.R.2d 867; see also, concurring opinion, 42 Cal.2d at p. 98, 265 P.2d at p. 892.) In Corrigan, supra, the mother's failure to take curative action was a negative factor in determining her ability to exercise parental control. (134 Cal.App.2d at p. 755, 286 P.2d 32.) Progress toward a cure is a positive factor. The juvenile court's findings took account only of the mother's past and present relationship and ignored the impending legitimation of that relationship. " * * * past indiscretions do not necessarily demonstrate present unfitness * * *." (Guardianship of Smith, supra, concurring opinion, 42 Cal. 2d at p. 98, 265 P.2d at p. 892.)

There was no debate but that poverty had played a major role in producing the home situation which evoked the wardship order. Adequately financed couples can afford divorce. Many take the step nonchalantly, quickly severing their marriages in jurisdictions which invite such business and changing mates with great readiness. The children of quickie marriages and quickie divorces need never find themselves in homes characterized by a permanent liaison such as Mrs. Raya's. For centuries the law has termed such liaisons meretricious or adulterous. Perhaps, in this day of casually created and broken marriages, the label should be applied with less readiness when poverty is a prime factor in producing the relationship. There is a danger here of imposing standards adapted to the well-to-do, who can usually pay for the forms of legitimacy, and ill-adapted for the poor, who frequently cannot.[5] Attempts to apply "across the boards" standards to rich and poor alike may avoid a theoretical discrimination and create a practical one.[6]

Able and vigorous counsel have urged upon us competing moral considerations. On the one hand we are told that there are subcultures in American society whose economic poverty bars them from access to divorce and impels the formation of non-marital households; that the Aid to Dependent Children provisions of the Welfare and Institutions Code contemplate support of children in their own homes even though, by a 1961 amendment, a "male person assuming the role of spouse" lives in the household; that the 1961 amendment evidences legislative sanction for such non-marital households among needy citizens; that this sanction should be observed in the application of those sections of the Welfare and Institutions Code forming the Juve-

[5] See Foster and Freed, Unequal Protection: Poverty and Family Law, 42 Ind.L.J. 192, 198–199; tenBroek, California's Dual System of Family Law: Its Origin, Development, and Present Status, 17 Stan.L.Rev. 614, 617–621. The court does not overlook Penal Code section 269a, declaring guilty of a misdemeanor every person "who lives in a state of cohabitation and adultery * * *."

[6] See Lewis and Levy, Family Law and Welfare Policies: The Case for "Dual Systems," 54 Cal.L.Rev. 748–780; Weyrauch, Dual Systems of Family Law: A Comment, 54 Cal.L.Rev. 781–791.

nile Court Law. On the other hand, we are told that reversal of the wardship order will evince judicial disrespect for the marriage institution and set the seal of judicial approval on adulterous relationships.

If abstract legal propositions fail to decide concrete cases, abstract moral dogmas accomplish even less. The safest moral guides for the courts are those crystallized in the statutes and case law. In determining whether the evidence supported an adjudication of Mrs. Raya's parental incapacity, the court neither excuses nor condemns. It simply decides that in these particular circumstances the finding of parental incapacity was unjustified by the facts.

Counsel for the appealing parents argue that "depravity" of the parent is a ground of wardship under subdivision (b) of section 600; that depravity alone controls in wardship cases resting upon parental immorality; that the statutory requisite of depravity cannot be evaded by utilizing some lesser degree of immorality as the sole basis for a finding of improper parental care or control under subdivision (a) of section 600. Since the present adjudication does not meet the less stringent terms of section 600, subdivision (a), there is no point in deciding whether the more stringent terms of section 600, subdivision (b), control.

Finally, we deal with an assertion that In re Corrigan, supra, 134 Cal.App.2d 751, 286 P.2d 32, and In re Schultz, supra, 99 Cal.App. 134, 277 P. 1049, are binding precedents, requiring the juvenile court to adjudicate wardship by force of *stare decisis*. The cited decisions sustained wardship adjudications where the mother (in Schultz, a woman *in loco parentis*) was exposing the children to her extramarital sexual activity. It would be simple to point to factual distinctions between those cases and this; or to counterbalance them with another child cus-

tody decision where the reviewing court reversed an order taking children from the mother under circumstances comparable to the present. (Ashwell v. Ashwell, 135 Cal.App.2d 211, 286 P.2d 983.) We know of no principle, however—and none has been cited to us—substituting *stare decisis* for individualized determinations in these cases.

The judgments are reversed with directions to dismiss the wardship petitions.

IN RE H CHILDREN

Family Court, City of New York, Queens County, 1970.
65 Misc.2d 187, 317 N.Y.S.2d 535.

M. MICHAEL POTOKER, Judge.[*] Petitioner's charge of child neglect under Article 10 of the Family Court Act is predicated on his wife's living in the same household with their five minor children and a paramour.

The facts are conceded. On September 13, 1970 respondent left the marital home with her five minor children, whose ages range from five to thirteen, and took up residence with her paramour in his one-family home. The children occupy two rooms on the upper floors while respondent and her paramour, with whom she has been intimate, share a bedroom on a lower floor. Respondent stated that she has instituted an action for divorce and, upon its being granted, intends to inter-marry with her paramour.

Respondent further testified that her paramour is supporting the household and that he is very good to the children, so much so, that they are doing much better in school and no longer truant.

Not at issue in this proceeding is the fact that respondent may very well have been justified in removing herself and their children from petitioner's home be-

---

[*] The children were represented by the Legal Aid Society.

cause of alleged misconduct on part of petitioner.

The question facing the court is whether respondent's conduct absent proof of present and discernible harm suffered by the children constitutes neglect under Article 10 of the Family Court Act.

Article 10—Child Protective Proceedings, formerly Article 3, is designed to establish procedures to help protect children from injury or mistreatment and to help safeguard their physical, mental and emotional well-being (Section 1011, Family Court Act).

No more objective or workable concept of neglect has been set by the courts than that contained in People ex rel. Wallace v. Labrenz, 411 Ill. 618, 104 N.E.2d 769 (1952): "Neglect, however, is the failure to exercise the care that the circumstances justly demand. It embraces wilful as well as unintentional disregard of duty. It is not a term of fixed and measured meaning. It takes its content always from specific circumstances, and its meaning varies as the context of surrounding circumstances changes."

In the Matter of Anonymous, 37 Misc. 2d 411, 238 N.Y.S.2d 422, a neglect proceeding was initiated by the father of three children who alleged that the children were neglected due to the immoral and improper conduct of their mother in that said mother entertained male companions in her home and in the presence of her children. In sustaining the allegations made by petitioner the Court held as follows:

"Our courts will continue to insist upon a high level of moral conduct on the part of custodians of children, and will never succumb to the Hollywood type of morality so popular today, which seems to condone and encourage the dropping of our moral guard. We have not yet reached the point where, when parents who have tired of each other's company, may be free to seek other companionship with complete disregard of the moral examples they are setting for their children. This is the crux of the case at bar." 37 Misc.2d at 412, 238 N.Y.S.2d at 423.

* * *

Isolated instances of infidelity can be overlooked (Kruczek v. Kruczek, Sup., 29 N.Y.S.2d 385), but for a married woman to live with a man with five minor children of her undissolved marriage transcends the area of an isolated occurrence.

In Johnson v. Johnson, 47 Misc.2d 805, 263 N.Y.S.2d 404, aff'd. 25 A.D. 2d 672, 268 N.Y.S.2d 403, a divorce action involving a mother's adultery, the Court said: "Such an example is a potent force in the formulation of a child's own standards of proper conduct." 47 Misc. 2d 308, 809, 263 N.Y.S.2d 408.

Neglect statutes are concerned with parental behavior only and solely as it adversely affects the child presently or in future. Spouses willing to betray each other need have no fear for the court's intervention providing however such actions do not in any manner whatsoever impair or tend to impair the physical, mental or emotional condition of a child.

In a neglect proceeding, the court's duty is to determine whether, despite any past deficiency, children are at time of hearing suffering or likely to suffer from neglect (Matter of Vulon, 56 Misc.2d 19, 288 N.Y.S.2d 203) unlike custody cases where the welfare and best interests of a child dictate its immediate removal from the custody of the guilty parent.

The gods visit the sins of the fathers upon the children (*Phrixus,* Fragment 970). Here the sins of the mother are being visited upon the children and as *parens patriae* (Finlay v. Finlay, 240 N.Y. 429, 148 N.E. 624, 40 A.L.R. 937) we are duty bound to intervene.

Who can deny that the children herein, more particularly the older ones who have reached the impressionable ages of thirteen and twelve, do not now or might not in the immediate future suffer detrimental damage attributable to the adulterous act of their mother. I submit that neglect as defined by the Act includes not only present harm being inflicted upon a child by the conduct of a parent but anticipates any harm that might be suffered by a child in the future as a result thereof (Section 1012, Family Court Act).

A finding of neglect is justified when there is a direct relationship between the mother's adultery and her children's welfare so that her immoral behavior would be directly detrimental to their best interest if the condition persists unabated.

I find that petitioner has sustained the allegations of his petition by a fair preponderance of credible evidence. Accordingly the children named therein are adjudicated neglected children pursuant to Article 10 of the Family Court Act.

The matter is referred to the Probation Department for investigation and report returnable on February 10, 1971.

IN RE KARR

Family Court, City of New York, Richmond County, May 20, 1971.
66 Misc.2d 912, 323 N.Y.S.2d 122.

RALPH E. CORY, Judge. The instant neglect petition alleges that the "Respondent neglected his child Margery Karr, under Section 1012 of the Family Court Act, in that he *abandoned* the child on December 26, 1966 and the child has resided with the Petitioner since that date. On October 17, 1970, the Respondent contacted the Petitioner and demanded that the child be surrendered to him so that he could bring it to some religious cult in Brooklyn permanently.

The Respondent has a history of mental and emotional illness and has been confined to a state hospital * * *."

A full fact finding hearing was held in which the petitioner had several witnesses testify on his behalf and *one* witness testified for the respondent who did not take the stand. This Court concludes that the child was placed with the *petitioner* voluntarily by the respondent father and with the *consent* of the petitioner on December 26, 1966. The petitioner and respondent are not related. The credible testimony, unrebutted, revealed that the respondent father contacted the petitioner and inquired about his daughter several times in the intervening years from the alleged act of abandonment (December 26, 1966) to the date of the petition (October 21, 1970). He also had some visitation privileges with his daughter during that period. The respondent also offered to pay some of the expenses incurred by the petitioner in caring for the child, to the limited extent of his income, an offer which was *refused* by the petitioner. This testimony was not rebutted. Accordingly, there was no proof adduced in any way, manner or form that this child had been abandoned by her parent. Under the facts and circumstances of this case, there never was any *abandonment with no intention of returning. There was no renouncing and forsaking of the child by the father.* The leaving of the child by the respondent with the petitioner was a *voluntary arrangement acceptable to both sides* and such an act never ripened into *abandonment* since the necessary element of *intent to abandon* is entirely *lacking* as revealed by the credible evidence above set forth. There is no abandonment therefore as defined in the statute. Family Court Act, Section 1012(f)(i)(B), (f)(ii). The attorney for the child (Legal Aid Society) conceded in his summation that there was no abandonment of the child in this case.

It is axiomatic in the law of neglect that the parent sought to be charged with neglect must have *custody, care and control* of the child during the period when neglect charges are alleged against the parent. Section 1012 of the Family Court Act is very specific in defining a "neglected child". Since the respondent did not have custody of the child during the period of the alleged neglect in the petition, he cannot be held responsible for the physical, mental or emotional condition of the child being impaired or in imminent danger of being impaired as the result of the failure of the parent to exercise a minimum degree of care. There is no such allegation in the petition, nor does the petition allege the person legally responsible for the child's care (the petitioner) exercised improper care or failed to exercise a minimum degree of care.

There was also no credible proof adduced that the respondent failed to supply the child with adequate food, clothing, shelter, education, medical or surgical care, though financially able to do so. Because of the petitioner's voluntary acceptance of custody of the child and his expressed willingness to do so as if she were his own child, the parent or respondent father was not required to supply the child with adequate food, clothing, shelter, education, medical or surgical care. Again he had no *custody* of the child and no neglect charge could be brought against him on this basis. Despite this however, the respondent father as parent made such an offer to the extent of his limited financial capacity, which offer was refused by the petitioner. This is the *antithesis of neglect* as it involves some demonstration of positive parental concern. Again, since the father never had custody of the child during the period of neglect in the petition, he could never be held responsible for improper supervision or guardianship by allowing to be inflicted harm or a substantial risk thereof, including the risk of excessive corporal punishment; or by using drugs or alcoholic beverages to the extent he loses self control of his actions or by any other acts of a similarly serious nature requiring the aid of this Court. There was no proof or testimony adduced as to these important elements of neglect against the respondent because he never had care, custody and control of the infant child during the time specified in the petition. Therefore none of the elements of neglect, including abandonment, required by the statute defining a neglected child have been proven or sustained. Family Court Act, Section 1012(f).

The petition alleges that the respondent had a history of mental and emotional illness and that he was confined at one time in a State Hospital. The fact that the respondent had a previous history of mental and emotional illness and had been confined at one time in a State Hospital is not conclusive as to whether the respondent father is *now suffering from mental or emotional illness at the time of the hearing.* No medical or psychiatric proof was submitted by the petitioner that the respondent had not been properly discharged from the State Hospital where he had been confined. The fact that a person may at one time have been a mental patient or confined to a State Hospital is not *neglect per se.* It is not *unfitness per se.* Even if it is conceded it is some form of imperfection, is not *unfitness.* People ex rel. Geismar v. Geismar, 184 Misc. 897, 908, 54 N. Y.S.2d 747. The imperfection must ripen into unfitness by connecting the actual elements or indicia of neglect stemming from such unfitness under the statute. None of these elements has been proven by the credible testimony in the instant case.

Furthermore, in neglect proceedings, the court's duty is to determine *whether despite any past deficiency,* children at the time of the hearing are suffering or likely to suffer from neglect. Matter of Vulon Children, 56 Misc.2d 19, 288 N.Y.S.2d 203. Such terms as physical, mental or emotional condition of the child is in *imminent danger of becoming impaired* or in providing the child with improper supervision or guardianship by unreasonably inflicting or allowing to be inflicted harm or a *substantial risk thereof* as set forth in the statute do not apply to *future* acts of neglect unconnected or not based on *present findings of neglect.* The term *"imminent danger of becoming impaired"* and *"substantial risk of harm"* apply to a substantial probability that the child will be found to be abused or neglected under Article 10 of the Family Court Act, and that the child is in grave imminent danger to her life and limb. Such facts do not exist under the proof presented in the instant petition. Such terms and their effective application presuppose a previous finding of neglect or child abuse. No such finding can take place in the instant petition for the reasons above set forth.

The instant petition then boils down and is predicated almost entirely on the allegation that the respondent father intended to bring his child up in some religious cult in Brooklyn to which he belonged. This cult was identified at the hearing as the International Society for Krishna Consciousness, Inc., a religious corporation chartered under the laws of the State of New York. According to the witness for the respondent, the head of the Brooklyn chapter of the organization, the movement is 5,000 years old. Their membership live in a communal relationship in a compound in Brooklyn while sleeping accommodations are provided in separate areas for married persons and single persons. Many children are in the movement and the organization runs a grade school with the necessary curriculum. It is not a religious school but the cult is a branch of the Krishna religion. Dietary laws are followed and the members eat their meals on the floor. The adult members of the organization do not work. The movement is supported by endorsements, the publication of books and pamphlets, the sale of incense and from the solicitation of funds on street corners where its members in colorful bizarre attire with shaven heads and prayer beads and long robes chant in the name of God to propagate a consciousness of the Krishna movement and to systematically propagate spiritual knowledge to society at large and to educate all peoples in the technique of spiritual life in order to check the imbalance of values in life and to achieve real unity and peace in the world and generally for similar other purposes set forth in the Certificate of Incorporation.

Testimony was in conflict as to whether or not children in the movement solicit funds and whether or not such solicitation is "begging".

Accordingly, the issue solely before this Court as to this portion of the petition is whether membership and life in this cult by the child, the subject of the petition, will be an act of neglect if the respondent father takes her into this movement as a way of life as he concededly has stated he will do?

It is impossible for this Court to decide this important and broad question on the basis of the neglect petition before it. Such questions are too conjectural, too far in the future, too remote and too uncertain for this Court to act now. The evidence presented in the instant case is far from sufficient to decide *permanent custody.* Article 10 of the Family Court Act is for the effective protection of children, their health, safety and welfare. Under this neglect petition, none of the indicia of neglect has been shown or proven to comply with the statute. Family Court Act, Section 1012(f).

Article 10 of the Family Court Act is designed to establish procedures to help protect children from injury or mistreatment and to help safeguard their physical, mental and emotional well being. It is designed to provide a due process of law for determining when the State, through its Family Court, may intervene against the wishes of the parent on behalf of the child so that his needs are properly met. Family Court Act, Section 1011. This statute is not a vehicle for recrimination against parents or their constitutional rights—including upbringing of children in the future. The law does not require, nor can it require, conformity in religious beliefs. The bizarre, the "off beat", the strange as well as the normal sects or denominations of worship are equally protected under the Constitution, without fear or favor. United States Constitution, Amendment I. What is rank heresy to some, is orthodoxy to others and vice versa.

The law properly provides for intervention by society when parental care is deemed dangerously faulty or insufficient. But the question is one of degree and the law must be flexible enough so that the State may intrude upon the sanctity of the family only in the most justifiable circumstances. Paulsen, "The Legal Framework for Child Protection in New York", 66 Columbia Law Review as reported in Columbia Journal of Law and Social Problems, Volume 7, Number 1, Winter 1971, p. 59.

The court should exercise its jurisdiction to interfere with paternal guardianship reluctantly and only upon strong and convincing proof of unfitness on the part of the parent or material benefit to the child. *Finding of neglect of child cannot be made lightly.* Matter of Vulon Children, *supra.* Accordingly, this

Court has no authority on the basis of the present petition before it, to grant what would be in effect *injunctive relief* of the type sought to be enforced here —that it will be neglect per se, neglect in futuro, for the respondent father to take his child, the subject of this petition, into this movement to which he now belongs.

This question should be decided by a full *habeas corpus proceeding* where custody of the child only would be the sole determination, to hear and determine at length with sufficient witnesses and expert testimony, for the best *interests and welfare* of the child, unencumbered by any questions of neglect or collateral inquiries as in the instant petition.

On the basis of all of the foregoing, this Neglect Petition is dismissed in its entirety.

C. NEGLECT AND THE INADEQUATE PARENT

IN RE TURNER

Court of Common Pleas of Stark County, Ohio, 1967.
12 Ohio Misc. 171, 231 N.E.2d 502.

MILLIGAN, Judge. This matter came on for hearing, upon an affidavit or complaint filed April 24, 1967, charging that a three-day-old child appears to be a dependent child; that Carl Swoveland is the legal father and Paulette Turner, a.k.a. Paulette Swoveland, is the legal mother. The affidavit was signed by Susan Albu, supervisor, Stark County Welfare Department.

The hearing was held May 8, 1967. The mother was represented by counsel.

The court makes the following findings of fact:

(1) On May 8, 1967, the court ordered placement with Stark County Wel-

fare, pending final determination upon receipt of a psychological report, to be made by agreement of all parties. The report having been completed and delivered to counsel for the family and to the court, and neither party having anything further to add, this matter is here for final determination.

(2) The mother of this infant is 15 and will be 16 on October 28, 1967. She has had an eighth grade education. Her employment to date consists of brief employment as an aide at a nursing home where her mother was employed.

(3) The mother's parents have had a stormy life with frequent moving and a rather constant pattern of financial deprivation since 1951.

(4) Paulette began a pattern of delinquent behavior in the community by disobeying her mother, truancy at home by staying away from home overnight, and associating meretriciously with other boys, in 1966. Her mother complained of this conduct to the Stark County Juvenile Court probation department.

(5) Paulette claims she was raped at age 13, and has had intercourse many times since.

(6) On September 21, 1966, following the filing of a delinquency complaint on September 2, 1966, by Relda Valentine, probation officer; Stark County Juvenile Court found Paulette to be a delinquent girl. The charge was that Paulette was delinquent by (a) incorrigibility at home (failure to subject herself to the reasonable control of her mother by reason of being wayward or habitually disobedient); (b) having sexual intercourse and being pregnant (so deporting herself as to injure or endanger the morals or health of herself or others); (c) breaking and entering an uninhabited building in Florida; and (d) attempting to enter the marriage relationship in Florida, without legal authority, with one Carl Swoveland, cur-

rently an inmate of the Florida State Prison. (Case No. 24927) She was "remanded to the Stark County Detention Home, pending placement." Thereafter, on October 13, 1966, the court committed Paulette to the custody of the Stark County Welfare Department, and this department provided maternity care.

(7) On April 1, 1966, the Juvenile & Domestic Relations Court of Hillsborough County, Florida, found Paulette delinquent, and released her to the custody of her father, Wilbur Turner, on probation. (Exhibits "A" and "B".)

(8) On December 17, 1965, Paulette participated in a pretended ceremonial marriage at Sarasota Florida. Paulette's mother and father were witnesses. (Exhibit "C".)

(9) In 1966, while the "pretended husband" was in jail in Florida, Paulette became pregnant in Stark County with the child who is the subject of this action. Her "pretended husband" is not the father of this child. Paulette claims that a married man is the father.

(10) Since her release from maternity care, Paulette has lived with her mother. She is not employed or enrolled in school. Paulette's father is currently in the south, running a truck stop. Her mother works at a nursing home and earns $60 every two weeks.

(11) Paulette's "pretended husband" expects parole in October, 1967. He has provided no support for Paulette since his incarceration, except an income tax refund. Paulette claims he has money in a Florida bank.

(12) There was no derogatory testimony concerning the physical surrounding of Paulette's residence. Paulette has adequate food, clothing, and shelter.

(13) At no time since birth has this child been in the custody of, or under control of, Paulette.

Is Baby Girl Turner, a.k.a. Baby Girl Swoveland, a dependent child?

Conclusions of Law

The issue is determined by reference to Section 2151.04, Revised Code, which defines a "dependent child" as any child:

"(A) Who is homeless or destitute or without proper care or support, through no fault of his parents, guardian, or custodian;

"(B) Who lacks proper care or support by reason of the mental or physical condition of his parents, guardian, or custodian;

"(C) Whose condition or environment is such as to warrant the state, in the interests of the child, in assuming his guardianship * * *"

It has been held that children whose parents are adulterous, childish, and selfish; speak vilely of each other to the children; and allow a close association between the children and immoral persons; are "dependent children." In re Douglas, Ohio Juv., 164 N.E.2d 475, 82 Ohio Law Abst. 170. See, also, In re Dake, Ohio Juv., 180 N.E.2d 646, 87 Ohio Law Abst. 483.

It is the finding and holding of this court that a child born to a 15-year-old girl who has a substantial record of delinquency, including numerous acts of sexual intercourse with different men; failure to respond to the reasonable control and discipline of her mother; has an eighth-grade education; and attempts to enter into a ceremonial marriage in Florida—prior to her pregnancy by a man other than her "husband"; and is also a delinquent child by the commission of a felony, where the father of the child is a married man and the "husband" of the mother is currently serving a sentence in the Florida State Penitentiary, and where the mother's family situation is financially and emotionally unstable—such child is a "dependent child," even though the child has never been in the custody of the natural mother.

Counsel for the family raise the question: "How can a child be found 'dependent' where there has never been an opportunity for the natural mother to provide a home and failure on her part?"

Although it is true that the state of dependency must exist on the date of the hearing, and it is further true that the court may not speculate upon a set of facts that do not exist; it is equally clear that the court, in an examination of the then existing facts, has not only the right, but the duty, to interpret the status of the parties with a view to determining whether or not the parent or parents is or are able, physically and emotionally, to provide proper care and support. The responsibility of the court to examine the conditions and environment within which the child would live, in the event the court were to find the child "not dependent," is material by the specific language of the statute. Also, the interests of the child are to be considered.

It is, therefore, the finding of this court that Baby Girl Turner, a.k.a. Baby Girl Swoveland, is a "dependent child."

Coming to the matter of the disposition, this court, in addition to the facts presented on the issue of dependency, has carefully examined the psychological examination and evaluation of the mother of this child. This examination was extensive, and numerous revealing tests were administered by the psychologist. He notes:

"Although she has engaged in a considerable variety of delinquent and socially-objectionable experiences, she remains a rather naive, unsophisticated person who lives on a very simple level and whose basic needs appear to be those of warmth, love, acceptance, and affection; the kinds of basic gratification which Paulette has apparently found in her heterosexual relationships.

" * * * There is considerable evidence of depression and of pronounced feeling of personal inadequacy in the face of a threatening, unfavorable, depriving environment.

" * * * Intellectual inadequacy does not appear to be primary in the total pattern of ineptness presented by the girl."

The psychologist notes that Paulette has compelling needs for physical affection, which would be promoted by the return of the child to her; that, in addition, she needs adolescent-level activities and the opportunity for developing additional skills. In conclusion, he states:

"Although she expresses a certain level of mother-interest, she simultaneously demonstrates ongoing adjustment problems involving compelling needs for love and affection, adolescent reaction to authority figures, and a social acting-out tendencies, conditions which suggest poor prognosis for successful self-management and poorer prognosis for success in the role of wife and mother."

This court believes that the best interests of this child, together with those of her infant mother, will be served by granting permanent custody, pursuant to the provisions of Section 2151.35, Revised Code, to the Stark County Welfare Department. Hopefully, Paulette will develop the kinds of skills and value-systems that she will need to effectively live within our culture; and, hopefully also, this child will be given the opportunity of being raised in a normal, healthy family relationship.

Exceptions to Paulette Swoveland. Costs waived.

Permanent custody granted.

IN RE P.

Family Court, City of New York, New York County, 1972.
71 Misc.2d 965, 337 N.Y.S.2d 203.

JUSTINE WISE POLIER, Judge. An increasing number of guardianship petitions and actions to terminate parental rights so as to free children in foster care for adoption are being brought to the Family Court. When contested, they present a clash between the assertion of parental rights as traditionally maintained and the assertion of the rights of children in terms of what is set forth as in their best interest. In the contested actions the parents have failed or are alleged to have failed to function as parents, but have not renounced what they regard as their parental right to have their child returned to their custody in the future when, or if, they request such return.

Frequently parents have shown little or no active interest in a child for long periods of time, or, indeed, until they receive notice of the action to terminate parental rights and free the child for adoptive placement. The parent may never have provided a home, may have maintained no real contact with the child, and may have no plans for making a home for the child. Still, the possible termination of parental rights comes as a jolt and is seen as punishment, forfeiture of what is theirs, and as a threat to self-esteem which must be fought.

A set of English decisions were recently cited to illustrate the current tensions in law in England as well as in the United States concerning the rights of children in relation to the rights of competing adult claimants.[1] In an adoption proceeding initiated by foster parents who

[1] Professor Joseph Goldstein, Address on the Occasion of the Twentieth Anniversary of the Hampstead Child Therapy Clinic, London, July 1972.

had had a child since birth and for whom the mother had requested adoption, the mother sought to withdraw consent when the child was one year old. The English Act allows dispensing with consent only if the court is satisfied that the parent (a) abandoned, neglected or ill-treated the infant, or (b) is withholding consent unreasonably.

The judge in the court of first instance dispensed with consent to adoption holding that it was unreasonable for the biological mother to fail to take into account the child's welfare, since removal from the only home the child had known would disturb the child emotionally and might cause a psychological disturbance. This decision was described by Professor Goldstein as changing the spirit of the statute and reversing the paramount consideration that had traditionally been accorded to the biological parent and had failed to take into account the child's welfare.

The decision and order of adoption was unanimously reversed by the Lords of Justice of the Court of Appeals in 1970, but was subsequently reinstated by the House of Lords in April 1971. [Re W. (an infant) [1970] 3 ALL E.R. 990 6 [1971] 2 ALL E.R. 49]

In recent years the legislature in New York as in other states has begun to look more closely at the consequence for children of public policies and laws which fail to safeguard the welfare of children. Laws to protect children against neglect and abuse have been strengthened. The Social Services Law was amended in 1969 so as to authorize the institution of adoptive proceedings on the basis of abandonment for six months instead of a year.[2]

The first permanent neglect statute (Family Court Act, Article 6) in New York was enacted in 1959 in order to make possible the termination of parental rights and the adoption of children, when parents, though physically and financially able, did not maintain meaningful contacts with children in foster care and plan for their return home. (Secs. 614(d), 622) It was only in 1971 that the statute was amended to relieve an authorized agency from pleading and proving efforts to strengthen the parental relationship when it pleaded and proved that such efforts "would be detrimental to the moral and temporal welfare of the child."[3]

Growing concern for the hurts suffered by children who are placed and who are left in foster care year after year with diminishing hope of ever returning to their natural parents or being adopted has

[2] L.1969, c. 640 eff. July 1, 1969. In referring to the 1969 amendment Surrogate Midonick wrote:

"At long last we see the Legislature coming to grips with the basic conflict between parental rights and infants' rights. Too often a preoccupation with parental rights tends to blur the essential right of an infant to end the limbo of foster care (or shelter boarding care) and secure permanent parental home either with his natural or adoptive parents. Parental 'rights' must not be emphasized to the point of denying the child a parental 'home.'" In the Matter of Jennifer "S"., 69 Misc.2d 942, 946, 330 N.Y.S.2d 872, 876.

In the final decision of this case 69 Misc. 2d 951, 955, 333 N.Y.S.2d 79, 84, Judge Midonick made a finding of abandonment and gave guardianship to the agency having the child's custody with authorization to consent to adoption. It is noteworthy that in doing so the Surrogate stated: " * * * now hold, that children too have a right to the protection of due process of law, and that a combination of parental abandonment and agency failure to promote the parent-child relationship cannot override the substantial best interest of an innocent child, under both Social Services Law § 384 and of the Family Court Act §§ 611, 614 and 622."

[3] L.1971, c. 901, Sec. 2 eff. June 25, 1971. The State Department of Social Services, in a memorandum, favoring the proposed amendment, supported the requirement that an authorized agency should make diligent efforts to strengthen the relationship between the child and its parents "but only when it is alleged and proven that such efforts will not be detrimental to the moral and temporal welfare of the child." Memorandum dated March 16, 1971.

been expressed in the literature and studies throughout the field of child care.

A recent study by the Bureau of Child Welfare of all New York City children in foster care who had had no contact with either parent during the preceding six months revealed the extent to which children are still left in a state of uncertainty by being legally chained to parents who give little hope of ever acting as parents. Unfreed from such chains they remain in foster home care without any claim to permanent status year after year. Although parental contact was defined liberally to include telephone calls, letters, cards and gifts as well as visits to a child, nearly one third or 6,487 children had had no contact in over 6 months. Of this group nearly 60 per cent had been in placement for more than four years. The study noted that few were legally freed for adoption even though many probably had no realistic possibilities for returning home and a large number had been in placement for a long period of time, some for their entire lives. Concern was expressed that most of the children in the study would grow up in foster homes, and would neither be returned to their parents nor adopted.[4]

In the hope of preventing such children from becoming "lost" children, legislation authorizing periodic review by the Family Court of all children in foster care for a continuous period of twenty-four months was enacted in 1971.[5] In 1972 the filing of petitions for such review was made mandatory in regard to the authorized agency charged with the care, custody or guardianship of a child. In addition, the legislation authorized filing of petitions for review by another authorized agency having supervision of such foster care or by the foster parents or parents in whose home the child resides or has resided during the twenty-four months. The Family Court is required on the proof adduced to enter an order of disposition in accordance with "the best interest of the child". Such order may direct continuance of foster care, the return of the child, the initiation of a proceeding to legally free such child for adoption, or that the child be placed for adoption in the foster family where he resides or with other person or persons. Such cases must now be reviewed at least every 24 months where children continue in foster care.[6]

The legislature has thus expressed its intent to assure to children judicial review so that they will not be left without homes and will, where possible, be given the opportunity to grow up in homes where they will receive good care together with the sense of belonging and being loved that is essential to healthy development.

Each step taken toward this end by the legislature and the courts creates rights of children which in turn deprive parents of traditional immunities from custodial consequences for failure to fulfill their duties as parents. Increasingly the correlative rights of children and the duties of parents are thus becoming articulated. The task of implementation still lies ahead.

While the legislation can provide guidelines for adjudicating the question of permanent neglect and can provide safeguards to assure due process, there can be no single or final definition that will encompass the myriad variations in the social histories, parental attitudes or actions, the conditions of the parents and the life prospects for the child. Adjudication on a case by case basis is essential if the conflicting claims of parents and children are to be justly evaluated and

---

4 New York City Department of Social Services, Census of Children in Care, Who May Need Adoption Planning, Prepared by Bellisfield, Pettiford, Allen and Hyde, July 1971. (See pp. 1, 2, 19, 24, 32, 52).

5 L.1971 c. 97.

6 Laws of 1972, c. 940 eff. July 8, 1972.

determined. The instant case is representative of many in which such conflicting claims are presented to the court. It requires a re-examination of the rights of the parents and of their three children in the light of recent legislation and judicial decisions in this state.

The Edwin Gould Services, an authorized child caring agency, seeks to have three children declared permanently neglected and the rights of their parents permanently terminated so that the children may be freed for legal adoption by the foster parents, who have been caring for them. The respondents, the biological parents, of the three children, oppose the petition and contend that their parental rights should not be permanently terminated.

It is agreed that the three children are under eighteen years of age and that they are in placement with the petitioner, an authorized agency in conformity with the statutory requirements for initiating a proceeding to permanently terminate parental rights. There is no contention that the respondent-parents are not physically or financially able to care for their children. Two contested issues are before this court in this action:

1. Did the authorized agency make the "diligent efforts to encourage and strengthen the parental relationship" as required by the Family Court Act prior to the amendment of June 25, 1971, and, if not, can it avail itself of the relief as authorized by that amendment?

2. Did the parents notwithstanding the diligent efforts of the agency fail "for a period of more than one year following placement * * * substantially and continuously or repeatedly to maintain contact with and plan for the future of the child [three children]?

Cooper et al., Cs. Law & Poverty 2d Ed. ACB—37

On the question of "diligent efforts to encourage and strengthen the parental relationship" the petitioner moved in July 1971, after the filing of the petition but before the trial, to amend the petition to claim the relief from diligent efforts allowed by the June 1971 amendment where the agency pleads and proves that "such efforts would be detrimental to the moral and temporal welfare of the child." * * * Although this court ruled in an interim decision that the statute as amended could be applied in this case, the evidence submitted to this court at the trial makes it unnecessary to reach that issue in this case.

On the basis of 115 facts to which the parties stipulated and the testimony of the agency caseworker, the evidence establishes by more than a fair preponderance of the evidence that the petitioner exerted diligent and continuing efforts to encourage and strengthen the parental relationship from 1965 when they received Dominic in care until February 1970 when they for the first time refused further visits to the parents.

The record establishes that within two months after Dominic's birth on October 2, 1963, the mother secured public assistance and an apartment in which she lived with him for only one month. The mother then left him with an unrelated neighbor from whose home he was removed by the police to the New York Foundling Hospital. After care in the hospital and several temporary boarding homes from December 26, 1963 to June 1, 1965, Dominic was placed by the petitioner in the foster home where he has continued to live for over seven years.

Attempts by the petitioner to contact the parents in June and July 1965 and in September and October 1967 were left unanswered. In November 1967, mail addressed to the mother was returned by the Post Office marked "unclaimed". In the absence of any responses or initiation of contacts by either parent after June 1965, the petitioner requested the Department of Social Services for permission to plan for adoption on January 19, 1968. Nevertheless when the father called the agency in February 1968, and the worker learned that the parents had been in a drug program she tried to help the parents to get appropriate housing and public assistance. Despite failures to keep appointments following this call the worker did arrange to have the parents see Dominic on May 15, 1968.

Within a month of this visit with Dominic, his younger siblings Barbara (born April 2, 1966) and Abby (born September 1, 1967) were placed by the Commissioner of Social Services with the petitioner on June 14, 1968 for foster home care. These two children had been adjudged neglected by the Family Court on December 28, 1967, and had been removed for temporary care by the court, and subsequently placed with the Commissioner of Social Services.

Although the parents were informed that the two younger children would also be in the care of the petitioner, no word was heard from either parent until the mother called in December 1968. Again there was no follow through until the father called in February 1969 when an appointment was made for February 14, 1969. This appointment was not kept and there was no further word from either parent until the father called on November 12, 1969. Despite all past failures, the petitioner arranged for a family reunion for the parents with the three children on December 9, 1969, but the parents did not appear. One more such family reunion was planned for January 14, 1970 and this time the parents did appear.

On reviewing the record, the Edwin Gould Services came to the judgment in February 1970 that to arrange for further visitation by the parents would not

be in the best interest of the children. At that time Dominic had spent at most three months of his life with his mother, and had been visited since 1965 only twice in 1968 and once in 1970, or a total of three times in over four and one half years. Barbara and Abby had been in placement with the petitioner since June 14, 1968 and had been visited by the parents at only one family reunion on January 14, 1970, one year and eight months after placement with the petitioner.

This record provides clear and convincing evidence that the petitioner made repeated and diligent efforts despite the non-cooperation of the parents to encourage and strengthen the parental relationship for a period of over four and one-half years. The agency was certainly under no statutory duty to continue its efforts when it came to the conclusion that to do so would be injurious to the children or contrary to the best interests of the children. By promptly advising the father of the agency's decision to terminate visits and of his right to counsel so that the court could determine the issue of permanent neglect, the agency acted in forthright fashion and exercised its responsibility both to the children and to the parents.

That the agency came to be convinced that adoption would be in the best interests of the children is no bar to a finding of permanent neglect. Nor can the diligent efforts required by the statute prior to 1971 be interpreted to require efforts without end to the detriment of a child. In re Klug, 32 A.D.2d 915, 302 N.Y.S. 2d 418.

This record, likewise, provides clear and convincing evidence that the parents, notwithstanding the agency's efforts have failed for periods of far more than one year following placement of their three children substantially and continuously or repeatedly to maintain contact with their children, and plan for their future. No meaningful contacts have been maintained by the parents since the placement of the children with the petitioner. The occasional and sporadic requests to visit with no follow-through followed by repeated absences of long duration do not fulfill even minimal parental obligations and cannot be regarded as beneficial to the children. In the Matter of Clear, 65 Misc.2d 323, 318 N.Y.S.2d 876; Soames v. Spence-Chapin Adoption Service, N.Y.L.J., Feb. 1, 1972, P. 16, Col. 6.

The duty to plan for the future of children in placement is not an alternative obligation but an additional responsibility of parents. (Family Court Act Secs. 614, 622). However, even if this were not so, the record negates respondents' conclusion that their search for a drug rehabilitation program suited to their needs constitutes planning for the future of their children. Serious and continuing drug involvement with intermittent efforts toward freeing themselves of their habits in a succession of detoxification and treatment programs followed by return to the use of heroin cannot be viewed as supporting the contention of serious planning or the ability to plan for the future of the children. Planning by a parent for the future has been interpreted to mean to formulate and to act to accomplish a feasible and realistic plan for a child. Matter of Stephen B., 60 Misc. 2d 662, 303 N.Y.S.2d 438.

Finally, respondents urge that the court should take into consideration that their failure to maintain contact with their children must be weighed in the light of the "class mores of poor, black, and unschooled persons", and the "impossible barriers" created by requirements that they comply "with the customs of bourgeois urban existence". Counsel for the respondents states that respondents concede with hindsight that they "should have acted the way our society demands all its members act, with civility, urbanity and deference". No such demands were made by the petitioner in this case, and respondents' rationalizations seem rather to be a belated attempt to justify their continuous failure to function as parents throughout the lives of their children. The plea of counsel seems to urge that to understand all concerning the problems of the parents must result in excusing all that parents do to or fail to do for their children.

This plea must be rejected. To accept it would constitute regression to the period when the rights of parents were treated as absolute, and would negate the rights of children as developed by the legislature and courts of the State of New York. It would require courts to sanction less protection for the children of poor, black and uneducated than for children of more privileged parents thus violating their constitutional right to equal protection under the law.

The three children, Barbara, Dominic and Abby P. are adjudicated to be permanently neglected children as defined by Article 6 of the Family Court Act. In view of the record in this case this court finds that the moral and temporal interests of these children require that the custody of the parents be permanently terminated. Custody of the three children is awarded to the petitioner so that the children may be freed for adoptive placement, and petitioner is directed to proceed to secure such adoptive placement as speedily as possible.

IN RE BONEZ

New York Family Court, New York County, 1966.
48 Misc.2d 900, 266 N.Y.S.2d 756.

JUSTINE WISE POLIER, Judge. In 1962 the Legislature, in enacting the new Family Court Act, imposed the requirement that when children were placed away from their homes by this Court, placement could be extended only on regular judicial review. The comments of the Joint Legislative Committee on Court Reorganization note that:

"This section is designed to assure an annual review of a placement and establishes a technique for holding the agency accountable for its treatment of the child and its program."

The care of the three children in these proceedings for whom extended placement was requested by the agencies with whom they were placed evidence the wisdom of the Joint Legislative Committee and the Legislature in providing for such review. It also evidences the need for facilities and personnel through which the Legislative intent can be implemented. Finally, it presents the classic and tragic story of what is happening to abandoned, neglected non-white children whose only hope for growing up in a permanent home is through adoption.

Ellen, the four year old little girl who was born out of wedlock, had been abandoned by her mother at the age of eight months in May 1962. Since then, although she has no family to which she can be returned, she has been placed in a congregate shelter and in three foster homes. Describing her as of superior intelligence and beauty the agency saw the problem of adoptive placement as due to "her dark skin coloring despite the fact that she is an appealing, attractive, alert child."

Since 1965, when the case appeared for judicial review on an application for extension of placement, the court has requested that the voluntary agency having custody should actively seek an adoptive home. It was not until October that the agency, in the absence of a suitable adoptive home, agreed to make referrals to seven other adoption agencies for an adoptive placement. Two of these agencies have responded positively and agreed to seek an adoptive home.

Martin who is nearly two years of age was abandoned when he was in a hospital as a new-born infant. Found neglected by this court, he was placed in congregate care and remained in such care until he was 16 months old. Then he was placed in a foster home where he still remains. He was described as an adorable and responsive infant with white complexion and keen features at eight months of age. The agency having custody, however, stated that chances of adoption were slim for Negro and Puerto Rican children, and requested extension of placement for 18 months just before his first birthday in January 1965.

The court requested the voluntary agency to seek adoptive placement and requested the Department of Welfare to report on what resources they could provide. The Department notified the court that it did not accept Catholic or Jewish families, and that its direct adoption services were "set up to implement private voluntary agencies to assist with Protestant Negro children."

When the court insisted on studies of this child and adoptive planning, many months passed before the voluntary agency reported, in September 1965, that the child had been "cleared for adoption" by its psychologist. The mother was located and agreed to surrender the child for adoption. The voluntary agency reported in October that Martin had been referred to their adoption unit, and that a surrender had been sought through the Department of Welfare in November. One month later, the voluntary agency reported that the Department of Welfare would not take a surrender from the mother since "no home was available for the child at this time." The requirement that a specific home be available before a mother is permitted to surrender a child is generally imposed when a child is non-white. In this case its imposition endangered adoption since the mother had disappeared on two occasions. The Department now imposed another condition to accepting a surrender, that the court commit to the Department of Welfare, thus surrendering jurisdiction and with it, all responsibility for the welfare of this child.

Such restrictive requirements, conditioning the acceptance of surrenders of children born out of wedlock, seem inconsistent with the powers and duties of the Commissioner of Public Welfare as set forth in the Social Welfare Law [See 398, 6(f)]:

"When in his judgment it is advisable for the welfare of the child, (he shall) accept the surrender of a child by an instrument in writing in accordance with the provisions of this chapter. Any inconsistent provision of law notwithstanding, the acceptance by the public welfare official of an absolute surrender of a child born out of wedlock from the mother of such child shall relieve her and her parents from any and all liability for the support of such child."

Bess Parsons, four years of age, is the youngest of eight children, all of whom have either been abandoned by their parents or removed from their parents because of neglect during the past thirteen years. Six children now in placement, the first having been placed in 1952, have never been visited by either parent. Despite such abandonment, no action has ever been taken, by either the voluntary agencies for these children, who will continue as agency boarders and whose support will total well over a quarter of a million dollars by the time the public subsidies are ended and these children have to go out into a world in which they belong to no one.

The history of the parents is replete with mutual abuse, alcoholism, indifference to the children, and emotional disturbance. Three of the children were never taken home by the parents when they were born, and were placed by the Department of Welfare in 1954, 1956 and 1959. The only child over whom this court now has jurisdiction was born in 1961, and removed by this court as neglected in 1962. The father died in 1963 and the mother is entitled to and is receiving social security. Although entitled to social security for this child and the five others still in placement, she has made no plans to care for her or for the other children and has not even visited them. In fact, despite urging by the agencies having custody, she has refused to do so.

This court was requested to extend placement in January 1965 for further agency care. On reviewing the record of this child and that of her siblings, this court felt that such extension was not in the best interest of this abandoned child. Instead, it continued a remand for a report from the Department of Welfare on what efforts had been made to work with the parents toward the return of the children or to terminate parental rights and free them for adoption. No satisfactory answer was ever received. Although the clinical study of the child reported Bess to be an "attractive, small but well-proportioned four year old Negro child" and "reflected the child's ability to function at or above her own age level in social situations," the Department of Welfare expressed the conclusion that adoption was neither a realistic nor feasible plan. This position can only be explained on the assumption that a non-white child is not entitled to or cannot be considered for adoptive placement by the Department unless Protestant and Negro.

Counsel for the agency which has resisted referral of this healthy, attractive non-white child for adoptive care, has stated in court that his agency believes in only limited application of the statutory authorization to free a child for adoption where there is permanent neglect. It regards foster home care as meeting all the child's needs.

This court cannot agree that it can approve extended placement for this abandoned four year old little girl, whose father is dead and whose mother has refused to visit her or plan for her, although able to do so. To approve extended placement and so authorize public subsidy for year after year would mean that this child, like her older siblings, will be destined for a series of foster home placements and become just one more agency child without a family.

This child has no legal status in the foster family, and the foster parents have no legal responsibility to provide continuing care beyond their convenience or desire to do so. Two of her siblings have been in three different foster homes since placement in the same agency. Studies of foster homes throughout the country show the high percentage of cases in which children in foster homes are moved through a succession of placements until they become rootless and incapable of any sense of belonging.

In view of the record and this court's obligation to act in the best interest of each child, it must now seek a permanent home by all adoption agencies in this area through the probation department.

On review of the applications for extended placement in these three cases, this court finds that the granting of such application would not be in the best interest of these three children. They are healthy, intelligent, attractive toddlers in need of permanent homes in which they can find the security that only adoptive parents can provide. The extensions requested do not offer promise of permanent homes, and each extension makes adoptive placement less likely.

In the case of Ellen the abandonment by the mother, her subsequent death and the unfitness of the putative father clearly demonstrate the need for adoptive placement. In the case of Martin the abandonment by the mother and her decision to surrender for adoption leave no question that he is entitled to adoption. Bess has been in placement since she was one, unvisited by either parent, and her mother, the surviving parent, has failed and refused to visit her in three years or to plan for her return home though able to do so. There could be no clearer case of permanent neglect.

This court has through repeated requests and adjournments for twelve months sought the cooperation of the voluntary agencies having custody of these children placed by this court, in order to secure adoptive placements. It is unfortunate that the planning for adoptive placement was not initiated by the agencies. However, at the present time the agency having custody of Ellen and Martin is now seeking adoptive placement. In the case of Bess, the agency has opposed such placement. While the views of social agencies are entitled to respectful consideration, this court cannot abdicate the responsibility under the law for determining what is in the best interest of a child.

In seeking to secure implementation of the Court's finding that these three children required adoptive placement, it received no cooperation from the Department of Welfare. Rather it was confronted with non-responsiveness, non-cooperation and obstructive tactics. Requests by the Court for information on available services were left unanswered. The Bureau of Child Welfare rejected referrals on the ground these were not Protestant Negro children. The surrender of Martin by his mother, who had twice disappeared, was not accepted.

The conclusion seems inescapable that the Department of Welfare, which has largely delegated its responsibility for the care of dependent and neglected children to voluntary agencies, is providing only infinitesimal adoptive services for Protestant Negro children. Without determining the constitutionality of public services that are restricted by race and religion, this Court is satisfied that procedure under such discriminatory policies cannot govern the Court's determination of what is in the best interest of these children.

Provisions in the Family Court Act requiring annual judicial review of placements and the provisions for the permanent termination of parental custody by reason of permanent neglect both establish the clear legislative intent to prevent the indefinite placement of children away from home, their loss of visibility, and the failure to plan adequately for them. It is the duty of this Court to see that these provisions shall be implemented on behalf of all children without regard to race, color, or religion. It cannot condone discriminatory implementation either by a public or private agency so long as this Court has jurisdiction and, therefore, responsibility for the welfare of a child.

In the cases of Ellen Bonez and Martin Ruiz where the voluntary agency is now seeking adoptive placement in cooperation with other adoption services, the remands are continued to January 17, 1966 for report on such placement.

In the case of Bess Parsons, where the agency has refused to refer for adoption, extension of placement is denied. Probation is directed to make referrals for adoptive placement directly to all adoption agencies in this area and report. The remand is continued to January 17, 1966 for such report.

Note

One of the children in In re Bonez came before Judge Polier again in In re Bess P., 52 Misc.2d 528, 276 N.Y.S. 2d 257 (Fam.Ct.N.Y.County, Juvenile Term, 1966):

"* * * [C]haritable institutions have not taken the position that they alone are the arbiters of whether children may be returned to responsible parents. They and the public departments have, however, failed to take positive steps to rehabilitate families, to terminate parental rights or to seek adoptive placements. As a result hundreds of infants and small children continue to drag out their lives in institutions and successive foster homes without ever becoming a part of any family or achieving a sense of belonging. And all this is done through the continuing public subsidy of care without exercise of what should be regarded as a requirement of accountability by the public department for the expenditure of public funds and for continuing review of what care is in the best interest of each child. * * *

"To correct this situation insofar as children within the jurisdiction of the new Family Court were concerned the legislature imposed a specific requirement on this court that when children were placed away from their home by this court, placement could be extended only on regular judicial review. The comments of the Joint Legislative Committee on Court Reorganization, reflecting the legislative purpose of this requirement, note that:

'This section is designed to assure an annual review of a placement and establishes a technique for holding the agency accountable for its treatment of the child and its program.' * * *

"On January 10, 1966 this court * * refused the application for extension of placement for Bess and two other children * * * [and] has continued to seek cooperation from both the Department of Welfare and the voluntary agencies. It has met with no practical response. The voluntary agencies have apparently closed ranks lest this court should be able to question their right to determine what kind of care is in the best interest of Bess. Despite the clear responsibility placed on the Department of Welfare 'for the assistance and care of any person who resides or is found in its territory and who is in need of public assistance and care which he is unable to provide for himself,' the Department has repeatedly defaulted in its obligation to non-white children. It has limited its adoptive services to Protestant Negro children and has despite full awareness of the inadequate adoptive services for other non-white children refused to accept referrals as in the instant case.

"This court in the face of such resistance and in the absence of power to command the necessary facilities must acknowledge its inability to act in accordance with the needs and best interest of Bess. It cannot extend placement to an agency which regards foster home care as all that this child needs. The only alternative is to discharge this child to the Commissioner of Welfare. In doing so this court urges that the Commissioner shall review the policies and procedures of the Bureau of Child Welfare so that children abandoned by their parents and in need of adoptive homes shall not in the future be referred to child care agencies without hope of adoptive placement because of race, color or religion. It also urges that the policy and practices of the Bureau of Child Welfare shall be modified so as to provide equal and direct services for all children without regard to race, color or religion. Without such changes the racist and religious barriers to equal services to such children as Bess will continue to deny them the equal protection to which they are entitled.

"Bess is discharged to the Commissioner of Welfare effective December 27, 1966."

IN THE INTEREST OF S. K. L. v. SMITH

Missouri Court of Appeals, St. Louis District, 1972.
480 S.W.2d 119.

SIMEONE, Judge. This is a proceeding under §§ 211.441 to 211.511, RSMo

1969, V.A.M.S.,[1] in which the Juvenile Officer of St. Louis County filed proceedings seeking to terminate the parental rights of the mother with reference to her three minor children. In each of these cases, which were consolidated on trial below and now on appeal, the Circuit Court, Juvenile Division, of St. Louis County entered its order terminating the parental rights of the mother and she has appealed.

On December 14, 1970, the Juvenile Officer of St. Louis County Juvenile Court filed petitions in the Juvenile Court to terminate the rights of the parents to the three children, S.K.L., G.W.L. and C.L.L., on the grounds that the parents have "abandoned" said children and have "wilfully, substantially and continuously or repeatedly neglected said child[ren] and refused to give said child[ren] necessary care and protection." Summons was duly served on the mother and publication of notice was given to the father.

The three children were respectively 7, 9 and 11 years of age at the time of the hearing. S.K.L. was born on December 26, 1960; G.W.L. was born on October 14, 1962; and C.L.L. was born on October 24, 1964.[2]

In December, 1968, the three children were placed in foster care and have been in the custody of Family Services, St. Louis County Welfare Office and have

[1] All references to statutes and rules are to RSMo 1969, V.A.M.S. and V.A.M.R., unless otherwise indicated. For a history of our statutes on termination of parental rights, see In re M_____, Mo.App., 393 S.W.2d 109, 116 fn. 5–8; In re M_____, Mo.App., 446 S.W.2d 508, 510, fn. 2. Our termination statutes were adopted for the first time in 1959 by the General Assembly.

[2] The mother admitted that another man was the father. No issue was raised as to this fact in the briefs. "[N]either past neglect of parental duty nor isolated transgressions against the moral law necessarily render an individual person unfit to have custody of his or her child * * *" In re C_____, Mo.App., 468 S.W.2d 689, 691.

been supported by ADC–FC funds of the State of Missouri.

Trial was held on June 8, 1971. The evidence of the Juvenile Officer consisted of the testimony of two social workers. Miss Ann Middleton, a social worker with Family Services since August of 1969, having graduated with a degree in social behavorial science the previous June, was the worker for C.L.L. and G.W.L. Miss Terry Fillmore was the worker assigned to S.K.L. The evidence of Miss Middleton showed that there were some thirteen contacts with the mother over the period of the year in question, December 14, 1969–December 14, 1970. These contacts of Miss Middleton with the mother show, in substance, that on various occasions the mother did not request to see or visit her children; that she did not send clothes, gifts or birthday cards to her children; that in December, 1969, she did not respond to a get-well card and Christmas card which her son sent to her while in the hospital after being encouraged to do so by Miss Middleton. Miss Middleton testified that "I feel that the children have very good potential and they are doing well in foster care. I don't feel that Mrs. L * * * is able to provide them the stability and the stimulation and incentive they need to perform to capacity. I think they would be better off in an adoptive home." The evidence shows that the mother was often in a hospital for leg ulcers and varicose veins.

Miss Fillmore, the social worker for S. K.L., testified that there were no telephone calls or gifts or messages or presents of any kind for the children and that the mother never requested to visit the daughter, S.K.L.

The appellant (mother) who had a sixth grade education with an eighth grade equivalency and her oldest daughter, Charlotte, also testified. The mother attempted to explain some of the reasons

why she did not see her children more often. She stated, "I didn't know I could make arrangements for it." She admitted that Miss Middleton asked her "sometimes" why she didn't "get together with your kids" but the mother "didn't think they'd bring them out to the home or anything." She testified that "Sometimes I asked her how they [the children] are." When asked why she didn't ask more frequently about them, she replied she didn't know. During the period between December 14, 1969 and December 14, 1970, she worked as a maid and earned $40.00–$50.00 per week but did not buy presents for the children because "I didn't even know I was supposed to—could—I didn't know if I could send them any." She said that she wanted to have her children back when her legs were better and that she did not ask to see her children because "I thought they were maybe supposed to make the arrangements." The mother stated that she used her crocheting ability to make items both for gifts and for sale and gave them to people she knew "real good." But she never crocheted anything for her children.

On November 16, 1970, when Miss Middleton visited the mother at her home, she discussed the "possibility" of terminating her parental rights to the children. Present at that time was the oldest daughter, Charlotte, age seventeen. Miss Middleton explained that the children had been in foster care for almost two full years and "explained termination to her." She also reviewed the needs of the children, the mother's plans for herself, and her expectations for her children. Charlotte at this time was expecting a child and expressed interest in helping provide a home for the children if this could be arranged. But Miss Middleton felt that this plan was "quite unrealistic."

At the time of the hearing the mother lived in a second story three-room apartment. It had a small kitchen, a small living room and a large bedroom, and "the homemaking standards appear[ed] to be very good."

When asked if she knew the reason for the hearing, the mother replied, "Well, something about the kids is all I know."

On June 14, 1971, the court entered its order terminating the parental rights of the mother on the ground "that it appears by clear, cogent and convincing evidence that for one year or more immediately prior to the filing of the Petition herein that said adult natural mother has abandoned said child and has wilfully, substantially and continuously neglected said child and has refused to give the child necessary care and protection." The court also ordered a hearing after proper service on the termination of the father's parental rights. After motion for rehearing the case was duly appealed to this court.

The mother urges in her brief that the court erred in finding by "clear, cogent and convincing evidence" that for one year or more immediately prior to the filing of the petition that the mother has abandoned the children and wilfully, substantially and continuously neglected and refused to give the children necessary care and protection. The respondent, Juvenile Officer, on the other hand urges that there was "clear, cogent and convincing evidence of abandonment and neglect" and that it was in the best interest and welfare of the children to terminate the parental rights.

The case is before us for review de novo and it is the duty of this court to make our own independent findings of fact and conclusions of law. Rule 73.01 (d); Renfro v. Jackson County Juvenile Court, Mo.App., 369 S.W.2d 616, 621; In re M——, Mo.App., 393 S.W.2d 109, 110[1].

Proceedings for termination of parental rights under statutory authority are of the

"utmost gravity." In the Interest of D—J— A— v. Smith, Mo.App., St. Louis District, 477 S.W.2d 718, 1972.[3]

This court stated in In re Taylor, Mo. App., 419 S.W.2d 473, 475, that "The action for termination of parental rights is designed to extinguish forever the pre-existing legal rights of the parents with respect to their child and is the subject of specialized legislation. The power of the juvenile court to effectuate such a result is in its entirety the creation of the statute; it does not otherwise exist * * *." The General Assembly and the courts have recognized that both by law and by nature parents have the primary right as against the world to their children. It is an inherent natural right. It is axiomatic therefore, that parents are not to have their rights to their children terminated except upon "clear, cogent and convincing" evidence of one or more of the grave reasons specified by law. In re Taylor, supra, at 476. The legislature did not intend by statute to provide that the "* * * relationship of parent and child might be lightly cast aside for any paternalistic sociological theory. Rather, the statute sets out only grave and compelling grounds for the action, essential to the welfare and protection of the child, and it should be so viewed and carefully applied." Renfro v. Jackson County Juvenile Court, supra, 369 S.W.2d at 621. Whoever seeks to invoke powers of termination carries the full burden of proof.

In 1959, for the first time, our legislature enacted laws specifically authorizing the courts to terminate the rights of a parent. It seems scarcely necessary to re-emphasize that this is an awesome power

---

[3] See Note, Termination of Parental Rights, 14 U.Kan.L.Rev. 117; See also Legislative Guides for the termination of parental rights and responsibilities and the adoption of children, U. S. Department of Health, Education and Welfare, Publication No. 394–1961.

conferred upon the courts and before it is exercised there must be strict and literal compliance with the statutory scheme. In re C——, Mo.App., 468 S.W.2d 689, 691.

The pertinent statute is § 211.441. It provides: "1. The juvenile court may, upon petition filed as provided in other cases of children coming under the jurisdiction of the court, terminate all rights of parents to a child when it finds that such termination is in the best interest of the child and one or more of the following conditions are found to exist:

     *   *   *   *   *

(2) When it apears by clear, cogent and convincing evidence that for one year or more immediately prior to the filing of the petition

(a) The parents have abandoned the child;

(b) The parents have willfully, substantially and continuously or repeatedly neglected the child and refused to give the child necessary care and protection;

(c) The parents, being financially able, have willfully neglected to provide the child with the necessary subsistence, education or other care necessary for his health, morals or welfare or have neglected to pay for such subsistence, education or other care when legal custody of the child is lodged with others;

(d) The parents are unfit by reason of debauchery, habitual use of intoxicating liquor or narcotic drugs or repeated lewd and lascivious behavior, which conduct is found by the court to be seriously detrimental to the health, morals, or well-being of the child;

     *   *   *   *   *"

Under the statutory provisions the power of the court is dependent upon the existence of one or more of the special conditions.

The cases that have been decided by the courts of this state show that, before termination of parental rights is ordered, there must be grave and compelling reasons. Renfro v. Jackson County Juvenile Court, supra (chronic alcoholism); In re M——, supra, (physical violence); In re C——, supra, (promiscuity and neglect);[4] In re Burgess, Mo.App., 359 S.W.2d 484, (physical abuse and neglect); In re C., C., and C., Mo.App., 380 S.W.2d 510, (adoption case—common drunk and neglect); White v. DeSpain, Mo.App., 453 S.W.2d 697, (horrible living conditions, a neglect case); Drake v. King, Mo.App., 446 S.W.2d 455, (refusal to care for children); In re J.L.L., Mo. App., 402 S.W.2d 629, (physical abuse and neglect); In the Interest of D—— J—— A—— v. Smith, supra, (no abandonment found).

The basis for the court's order on June 8, 1971, was that the mother had abandoned the children and wilfully, substantially and continuously neglected the children and refused to give the children necessary care and protection. "Abandonment" implies a wilful, positive act such as deserting the child. The wilfulness of neglect on the other hand is more of a negative proposition, or simply the failure to perform the duty with which the parent is charged by law according to acceptable community standards. The neglect,[6] in order to be wilful must be

---

[4] The mother made no effort to provide a home or even an acceptable substitute. "[A] parent has a duty to attempt to provide his child with a home in which the child will be housed, fed, clothed and educated, at least according to acceptable community standards. The appellant has not provided such a home in this case." "In candor, the appellant has simply drifted from one man to another. * * *" In re C——, Mo.App., 468 S.W.2d 689, 693, 692.

[6] Under § 211.031(1) the Juvenile Court has jurisdiction over children in proceedings because "(a) The parents or other persons legally responsible for the care and support of the child neglect or refuse to provide proper support, education which is required

intentional, deliberate and without just cause or excuse. As pointed out elsewhere, the term "neglect" is a general and a negative proposition meaning simply the failure to perform the duty with which a parent is charged by the law and by conscience. Wilful neglect must exclude acts which occur because of events which are beyond the control of the parent and which are not his fault. In re C——, supra, 468 S.W.2d at 693, citing In re C., C., and C., supra, and In re Taylor, supra.

We hold that there was insufficient "clear, cogent and convincing" evidence that the mother in this case abandoned or "willfully, substantially and continuously or repeatedly neglected the child[ren] and refused to give the child[ren] necessary care and protection." § 211.441, subd. 1(b). The mother from her testimony in the record appears to be a confused, handicapped, sickly and uneducated woman, although she did read books and had a sixth grade education. She was constantly in and out of hospitals and clinics for varicose veins and ulcerated legs. She relied on Miss Middleton for all sorts of aid and help.[7] She testified that she did not understand that she could see her children, or communicate with

by law. * * *" § 211.441, subd. 1 requires a much stronger test for termination: "(b) The parents have *willfully*, substantially and continuously or repeatedly neglected the child *and refused* to give the child necessary care and protection; * * *" (emphasis added). See also Note, The Custody Question and Child Neglect Rehearings, 35 U.Chi.L. Rev. 478.

[7] Kadushin, Child Welfare Services, at 234 reports: "The most successful approach [of social workers] seems to be one that directs itself to situational changes rather than psychological changes. Neglectful parents appear to be childlike in their dependency * * * Like children, they simultaneously welcome and resent being told, in clear, unequivocal terms, what to do. * * * According to Kaufman: 'The worker assumes the role of autonomous ego for these parents. He adopts a kindly but firm supportive parental role. [50, p. 196].' "

them or send them gifts. On one occasion when she expressed a desire to visit one of her children in the hospital she was discouraged from doing so by the social worker. On another occasion when her oldest daughter, Charlotte, suggested they try to make a home for the children, the social worker told her that the plan was "quite unrealistic." The mother expressed interest in her children by asking for pictures of the children in foster care; she also requested the hospital visit. The evidence that she merely failed to request to see her children during the critical year, that she did not send gifts and did not respond to a suggestion by the social worker to a gift sent by one of the children does not rise to the status of "clear, cogent and convincing" evidence to terminate *forever* the mother's rights in her children. No challenge was made as to the conduct of the mother. No question was raised as to her morality. She was not charged with abuse of the children. Hence we do not find under the circumstances an abandonment or a wilful, substantial, continuous or repeated neglect and refusal to give the children necessary care and protection.

The respondent relies on In re Slaughter, Mo.App., supra. There the appeal was from a decree of adoption rendered by the Juvenile Court under § 453.010, et seq. The natural mother appealed. The petition alleged that a child was declared neglected and dependent and made a ward of the court under the supervision of the state agency for the reason that the natural parents had wilfully abandoned and neglected the child.

The *Slaughter* decision is distinguishable. There was no evidence of any kind that the mother in *Slaughter* ever attempted to care for the child nor expressed an interest in the child. Here, at least the mother expressed interest in the children on more than one occasion.

We do not believe that the doctrine in *Slaughter* controls under the circumstances of this case. Rather, under the facts in the present case, we find the decision in In re Taylor, supra, more persuasive. In that case the court held that where the parents were ignorant of the actual locations in which their children were placed by the Division of Welfare, their failure to maintain active contacts with the children could not be considered wilful neglect. In re Taylor, supra, 419 S.W.2d at 476.

What really is the core issue here is whether or not parental rights may be terminated on the ground that the children would be "better off" in another home.[8] The General Assembly has not authorized such action nor adopted such a statute; it has authorized termination only when there is clear evidence that one or more of the statutory conditions is satisfied. We do not believe that either we or the Juvenile Court which has done and is doing so much good for neglected children, has authority to terminate parental rights because the court thinks children would be "better off" with someone else. In the extreme this could lead to a redistribution of a great mass of the minor population.[9] The General Assembly of this State, in its wisdom, has not given courts such authority.

The best interests of the child are of course, to be considered, and are of great importance, but one or more of the conditions specified in § 211.441 must be fulfilled. We hold that the required conditions were not satisfied under the facts in this case.

We believe that the overwhelming majority of our Missouri citizens hold the relationship between parent and child to be of the utmost importance, and it is only when grave and compelling reasons exist that that relationship may be severed. We hold that these reasons have not been shown under the facts in this case.

The judgment is reversed.

BRADY, C. J., and DOWD, SMITH and WEIER, JJ., concur.

IN RE SEGO

Court of Appeals of Washington, Division 1,
Panel One, 1972.
7 Wash.App. 457, 499 P.2d 881.

HOROWITZ, Chief Judge. This is an appeal from a juvenile court order permanently depriving Ronnie L. Sego of the custody of his daughter, about 5, and his son, about 3½ years of age. The controlling issue, among others involved, is whether the findings on which the deprivation order is based are supported by clear and convincing evidence. We hold that they are not and remand the case for additional testimony.

Sego, apparently a young man, returned in 1960 with an honorable discharge after 3 years of army service. While in the service, he acquired a habit of excessive drinking which he continued upon his return. He testified, "I would get emotionally upset and couldn't control myself." Following a history of marital discord, he shot and killed his wife, the mother of his two children. At that time the daughter was a little over 2 and the son about 9 months of age. The court found that "during these drinking periods the father * * * evidenced a vicious, mean disposition, which culminated in the killing of the mother of said children." Finding 3. Following the killing, Sego pleaded guilty to second degree murder and also pleaded guilty to armed robbery and escape. In March 1969 the court sentenced him to concurrent prison terms, 25 years on the first

8 Miss Middleton stated that "I think they would be better off in an adoptive home."

9 See the discussion in Simpson, The Unfit Parent, 39 Univ. of Detroit Law Journal, 347, 355.

two convictions, and 10 years on the third. Sego has been serving his terms in Walla Walla ever since.

On January 9, 1969, at an emergency hearing after Sego's arrest, the Clallam County Juvenile Court, upon the assumption that the children were "dependent" within the meaning of the Juvenile Court Act, made the children wards of the court and authorized their placement in a foster home. On January 24, 1969, the Juvenile Court, after a hearing in which Sego was represented by counsel, reaffirmed the dependent status of the children and continued their foster home care under the supervision of the (then) State Department of Public Assistance. On April 25, 1969, a further hearing was held. Sego was again represented by counsel. The Clallam County Juvenile Court reaffirmed the dependency and wardship status of the children, awarded the children's temporary custody to their maternal aunt and her husband, Mr. and Mrs. William Lee Johnson of Skagit County, Washington, and transferred jurisdiction over the children to the Skagit County court below, Juvenile Department.

Meanwhile, Sego made an especially good record of rehabilitation at the Walla Walla penitentiary. He took active steps to stop his drinking habit and, in connection therewith, became active in Alcoholics Anonymous. He took advantage of counseling and therapy services, attended Bible classes, and enrolled in an 18-month course at Walla Walla Community College to help qualify himself as a machinist. As a result, he secured a 5-year reduction in his sentences. This reduction meant that with good behavior, he was scheduled for release November 11, 1980. In addition, Sego was scheduled for a progress hearing in April 1972 which could result in early release. The evidence showed that his prospects for release by October 1972, when he completes his machinist's course, are good. The

evidence also showed that he could probably qualify for minimum security furlough status. Such status would enable Sego to go on furlough outside of prison from time to time to visit his children. The court found:

> That while evidence was introduced, tending to indicate that Mr. Sego has a remarkable record in rehabilitation at the Department of Institutions, such apparent rehabilitation is against a background of the structured life at the penitentiary, where he has endured none of the responsibilities attendant his duties as a father and head of the household.

Finding 5.

Following the award of temporary custody of the Sego children, the Johnsons established a fine home for them. According to a December 3, 1970 report prepared by Mr. Paradis of the Department of Social and Health Services, Division of Public Assistance, the Johnsons gave the children excellent care and wanted to adopt them. The report states "the Sego children have * * * acquired a much needed sense of being loved, security, and belonging on a permanent basis." The report then

> strongly recommend[ed] that Ronnie Lee Sego be permanently and totally deprived of all rights to care for said minors * * * and that [the children] be placed in adoptive status with responsibility for placement * * * to be with the Department of Social and Health Services.

The report stated that Sego's expected release date from Walla Walla would be November 11, 1985. Prior to the Paradis report, the Department had opposed visits by the children to their father, although no Juvenile Court order forbade them. The children visited the father on only one occasion when taken to Walla Walla by Sego's parents. The Paradis report does not show that Mr. Paradis ever met Sego.

On February 24, 1971, the court's probation officer and Mr. Paradis, the latter acting on behalf of the department, filed the petition below. The petition referred to "the murder of his wife." It stated that Sego would not, in the "foreseeable future [be] capable of providing for the care, control and custody of the said minor children." It alleged that the children were "entitled to a home situation that approximates as nearly as possible a natural home." The petition prayed that the court "consider permanent deprivation of these minor children from their father * * * " and that consideration be given to alternative relief.

At the hearing below, petitioners were represented by the Skagit County prosecuting attorney. Sego appeared in person and by his attorney. The children appeared by a Skagit County attorney appointed by the court as guardian ad litem for the children, and who filed a report with his recommendations. The Johnsons, although not parties to the proceedings, appeared by their attorney who participated through the guardian ad litem. At the conclusion of the hearing, the court filed a memorandum decision favoring permanent deprivation, and stated:

This Court does not reach this decision easily nor with peace of mind. Mr. Sego has the strongest of all rights known to the law in his claim for his blood children. He presents a very sympathetic and appealing picture as one who has attempted with all his strength to rehabilitate himself, cure his unfortunate habits, and overcome his past rash behavior. He indicates a deep love and concern for his children, and a real desire to reunite with them.

* * * [Nevertheless] [h]aving undertaken their care and protection, the Court must do all it can, consistent with the facts of the case, to permit of [sic] a happy, normal, well-adjusted life for these small, innocent children.

He then entered findings, conclusions and order permanently depriving Sego of the custody of his children and placing them in adoptive status. On December 27, 1971, he entered a further order denying Sego any further visitation rights of his children. This appeal followed.

Sego * * * contends that the court below had no jurisdiction to enter the order appealed from because the children were not "dependent" within the meaning of RCW 13.04.010. It is clear that unless the children are in dependent status, the juvenile court is without jurisdiction to terminate Sego's rights of permanent custody. In re Hudson, 13 Wash.2d 673, 126 P.2d 765 (1942).

Sego claims the children are not dependent because, from the beginning, both the paternal and maternal relatives of the children have been willing to provide support, care and maintenance for the children. We disagree with Sego's contention. The willingness and ability of other relatives to furnish the children's support and maintenance does not destroy the otherwise existing dependency status of such minor children.

RCW 13.04.010 defines a dependent child as one under 18:

(1) Who has no home * * *; or

(2) * * * who has no parent or guardian * * * capable of exercising, proper parental control.

In the instant case the children were dependent because they had "no home" (see In re Day, 189 Wash. 368, 65 P.2d 1049 (1937)), and have had no parent "capable of exercising proper parental control." The mother is dead and the father is serving his sentences.

Sego's remaining assignments of error deal with claimed improper admission of evidence and the insufficiency of the evidence to support the findings and conclusions. * * *

Sego * * * [objected] to the qualifications of the juvenile probation officer to testify that a denial of the petition would be harmful to the children. The testimony was not given in response to a hypothetical question. It is, therefore, difficult to determine just what facts she relied on in expressing her opinions. There was no showing that she had ever seen or interviewed Sego. Notwithstanding her general educational background, her qualifications to express the opinions she expressed, without interviewing Sego and the children, were at best debatable. Had the court sustained Sego's objection to her qualifications, we would have upheld his ruling as a proper exercise of discretion. * * * During her cross-examination it appeared she had talked to the children on only one occasion, when she took them to be interviewed by Dr. Kaufman, a psychiatrist. However, there was no showing of the nature or extent of the information she then received, except there was no conversation concerning the children's father. * * * [U]nder the circumstances, we cannot say that the error, if any, in admitting the testimony was prejudicial. The weight of the testimony is another matter.

We recognize that we may not substitute our findings for those of the trial court if the findings are supported by substantial evidence. Thorndike v. Hesperian Orchards, Inc., 54 Wash.2d 570, 343 P.2d 183 (1959). If, however, the findings are not so supported, *Thorndike* does not apply. Thus, scintilla evidence is insufficient to support a finding. Hewitt v. Spokane, Portland & Seattle Ry., 66 Wash.2d 285, 402 P.2d 334 (1965). See State v. Zamora, 6 Wash.App. 130, 491 P.2d 1342 (1971). Similarly, a mere preponderance of the evidence does not meet the higher standard of "clear, cogent and convincing" evidence. In re Estate of Reilly, 78 Wash.2d 623, 479 P.2d 1 (1970); Holmes v. Raffo, 60 Wash.2d 421, 374 P.2d 536 (1962). As *Reilly* points out, 78 Wash.2d at 640, 479 P.2d at 11, in overturning the trial court's findings on testamentary capacity and undue influence, "Evidence which is 'substantial' to support a preponderance may not be sufficient to support the clear, cogent, and convincing requirements with which we are faced."

An appellate court called to determine whether substantial evidence supports a finding may properly review the evidence to determine if it is clear, cogent and convincing. Should the appellate court find the requisite standard of proof has not been met, then it may be said the exercise of the court's discretion, based upon such unsupported finding "has been exercised upon a ground, or to an extent, clearly untenable or manifestly unreasonable." Friedlander v. Friedlander, 80 Wash.2d 293, 298, 494 P.2d 208, 211 (1972).

* * *

The natural parent's right to the custody and control of his minor child is a "sacred right." In re Hudson, supra. It is a right protected by the state and federal due process clauses. Stanley v. Illinois, 405 U.S. 645, 92 S.Ct. 1208, 31 L. Ed.2d 551 (1972); Sheldon v. Sheldon, 47 Wash.2d 699, 289 P.2d 335 (1955); In re Petrie, 40 Wash.2d 809, 246 P.2d 465 (1952). It is a right to be abridged only "for the most powerful reasons." In re Day, supra. The remedy should be one "imperatively demanded." See In re Neff, 20 Wash. 652, 655, 56 P. 383 (1899), quoted with approval in In re Ward, 39 Wash.2d 894, 896, 239 P.2d 560 (1952). A "clear" case must be proved. State ex rel. Cummings v. Kinne, 8 Wash.2d 1, 11, 111 P.2d 222 (1941). See Barstad v. Barstad, 74

Wash.2d 295, 298, 444 P.2d 691 (1968). A "plain showing" should be made out. In re Ward, supra, 39 Wash. 2d at 897, 239 P.2d 560, * * *.

The phrases "powerful reasons", "imperatively demanded", "clear case" and "plain showing" support the conclusion that a clear, cogent and convincing showing must be made to justify the entry of an order of permanent deprivation.[1]

The occasions for an order of permanent deprivation include those described in RCW 26.32.040 dealing with the grounds when, in adoption cases, the consent of the natural parent is excused. On the issue of parental fitness, in the absence of other grounds, it is difficult to improve upon the phrase "wilful substantial lack of regard for parental obligations" used in RCW 26.32.040(4). See In re Adoption of Lybbert, supra. Cf. RCW 13.04.140. A father's inability to perform his parental obligations because of imprisonment is bound up with the issue of parental fitness and child welfare. Imprisonment, per se, however, is insufficient to justify an order of permanent deprivation. In re Staat, 287 Minn. 501, 178 N.W.2d 709 (1970). On the other hand, the fact and cause of

imprisonment are properly considered in resolving the issue of permanent deprivation. In re Staat, supra, 178 N.W.2d at 713. See RCW 26.32.040(1). The court seeks to protect both the rights of the parent and the rights of the child. Sheldon v. Sheldon, 47 Wash.2d at 703, 289 P.2d 335. Furthermore, findings in permanent deprivation cases should be prepared with a "high degree of particularity". Wallin v. Wallin, Minn., 187 N.W.2d 627 (1971).

The integrity of the parental relationship is at least as important as the integrity of a legal instrument such as a contract or a deed when reformation is sought for mutual mistake. In the latter case, reformation will not be granted merely on a showing of possible, or even probable, error. Preponderance of the evidence is not enough. The evidence must be "clear, cogent and convincing" sufficient to establish "certainty of error." Neal v. Green, 71 Wash.2d 40, 426 P.2d 485 (1967). Such certainty exists in "a clear case." A case cannot be said to be made out by clear and convincing evidence if there is a serious or substantial doubt concerning the correctness of the conclusion sought. Paulsen v. Coombs, 123 Utah 49, 253 P.2d 621 (1953).

In reviewing an order of permanent deprivation, it is to be remembered that such an order utilizes a remedy of utmost severity and harshness. A temporary change of custody is capable of later change. A final order of deprivation, especially when followed by adoption is virtually irreversible. The difference in the severity of the remedies imposed requires a more substantial showing to support a case of deprivation than to support relief less drastic. Thus, an order providing for temporary, divided or partial custody will be upheld even without having to go so far as to show that the father has abandoned or disowned his child, or that he has willfully or consciously re-

---

[1] In cases involving separating a child from his parents, including cases of permanent deprivation, there is substantial outside case support for the "clear", "cogent and convincing", "clear and convincing" and "clear, cogent and convincing" evidence rules. In re Simmons Children, W.Va., 177 S.E.2d 19 (1970); State ex rel. Kiger v. Hancock, 153 W.Va. 404, 168 S.E.2d 798 (1969); In re Spence-Chapin Adoption Service v. Polk, 29 N.Y.2d 196, 324 N.Y.S.2d 937, 274 N.E.2d 431 (1971); In re Adoption of Sarver, 444 Pa. 507, 281 A.2d 890 (1971); In re Rogers, 492 P.2d 324 (Okl.1971); Green v. Sherman, Iowa, 173 N.W.2d 843 (1970); In re Roe v. Doe, 29 N.Y.2d 188, 324 N.Y.S.2d 71, 272 N.E.2d 567 (1971); Potter County Child Welfare Unit v. Charlow, 454 S.W.2d 214 (Tex.Civ.App.1970).

In some cases, the clear, cogent and convincing evidence rule is required by statute. In re Taylor (Smallen v. Taylor), 419 S.W.2d 473 (Mo.App.1967); In re M———, 446 S.W. 2d 508 (Mo.App.1969).

fused to perform his parental obligations, or that he has followed a consistent pattern of child abuse or cruelty. Yet, in the absence of other grounds, a showing of "willful substantial lack of regard for parental obligations" should be required if an order of permanent deprivation is to be entered. See In re Adoption of Lybbert, supra, 75 Wash.2d at 675, 453 P.2d at 652.

It is recognized that parental custodial rights, although not to be ignored, must yield to the welfare requirements of the child. Sheldon v. Sheldon, supra, 47 Wash.2d at 703, 289 P.2d 335. The child's welfare includes regard for the child's physical, mental, moral and emotional development. Under Washington law, in the words of Myers v. Myers, 21 Wash.2d 19, 21, 149 P.2d 926, 927 (1944), dealing with custody, "We have said many times that each case must be considered upon its own facts and the situation then before the court." This means that a parent's misconduct, whether or not criminal in character, does not necessarily and automatically give rise to permanent child deprivation. It is still a matter for factual determination whether the conduct is of such character as to demonstrate parental unfitness and substantial interference with the child's welfare. If parental traits of character are shown to be capable of correction, such traits may not require deprivation. See In re Sickles, 42 Wash.2d 17, 252 P.2d 1063 (1953). It would be inappropriate, however, to use deprivation of custody as a method of punishment. Thompson v. Thompson, 56 Wash.2d 244, 352 P.2d 179 (1960). No doubt permanent deprivation is justified to avoid permanent damage to the children. Before resorting to the drastic irreversible remedy of deprivation, however, alternatives must be considered. Thus, a loving aunt and uncle may be willing to continue as temporary custodians to give their niece and nephew a feeling of security and a "needed sense of being loved" even if the court declines to enter an order of permanent deprivation. The availability of such an alternative might reasonably militate against the entry of an order of permanent deprivation in the absence of further clear and convincing evidence that permanent deprivation is nevertheless required. See generally, on considerations pertinent to custody matters, H. Clark, Domestic Relations §§ 17.2, 17.4(c), 17.5, 17.7 (1968).

The record here raises a serious doubt whether the findings in support of the permanent deprivation order are supported by clear and convincing evidence. The court's deprivation order is predicated in substantial part on the finding that permanent deprivation is required "if permanent damage [to the children] is to be avoided." Finding 8. The findings, including Finding 8, and the conclusions based thereon, rest in substantial measure on expert testimony introduced on behalf of petitioners.

Petitioner Paradis, author of the December 3, 1970 report recommending permanent deprivation, had worked with the children and the Johnsons, but did not report having ever met or interviewed Sego. He did not testify. The only expert witnesses testifying in support of the deprivation order were the petitioner juvenile probation officer and the casework supervisor of petitioner Paradis. Sego is strongly critical both of the qualifications of either witness to testify and of the weight apparently attached to their testimony. It would unduly prolong this opinion to summarize the entire testimony of each of these witnesses. It is to be noted, however, that notwithstanding each witness had general educational qualifications, neither testified on the basis of any personal interview had with Sego, and the casework supervisor had never even seen, much less interviewed, the children. We have already pointed out the juvenile probation officer had seen the children on only one occasion in July 1971, and the very limited nature of the information she then received as disclosed by the record. Prior to the hearing, she had assumed that Sego's prison term would end in 1985. This assumption appears to have been an important factor in the opinion she expressed. She conceded "If I knew for a fact it was going to be much sooner then my recommendation might be changed."

The casework supervisor testified concerning her familiarity with the children based on her familiarity with "their record" and "their general living conditions." She was present during the court proceedings and heard the testimony. She "familiarized herself with some of the exhibits, including the report of Dr. Kaufman," she being a former student of Dr. Kaufman. To what extent she considered Sego's rehabilitation status does not specifically appear. She testified that based on her educational background, experience and knowledge of the case, she believed "very strongly that the deprivation should be completed and the children should be legally free." She believed deprivation should be promptly had. The reasons she relied on were "the age of the children and the trauma the children have already gone through." She testified that "whether Mr. Sego is in prison or not is really beside the point" because "there is no way we can erase what happened and the children are going to require * * * a great deal of stability in a normal-type family as we must raise children." Neither she nor the juvenile probation officer gave any testimony concerning whether, if the court denied permanent deprivation, nevertheless, because of the love that the Johnsons had for the Sego children, the Johnsons, in the children's interest, would seek to have them "gradually accept the tragedy of the whole thing."

Dr. Kaufman, the psychiatrist, apparently found it necessary to interview the children before he expressed an opinion on the matter of permanent deprivation. He, too, had never interviewed Sego. He prepared a report dated August 20, 1971, which was admitted into evidence by agreement of the parties. In that report he stated he had received two letters, one from the director of the Mental Health Unit at the penitentiary, and the other from the Division of Public Assistance, Mount Vernon, office, "concerning the record of the Sego family * * *." The record does not disclose the information contained in either letter. He further reported that he interviewed the children in July 1971, and at the same time saw Mrs. Johnson. Dr. Kaufman's report states:

> [I]t was apparent that the children have had good care recently. They both appeared healthy both physically and emotionally. They related to each other and to their aunt very well. * *

> Rhonda talked about her father, stated that she hadn't seen him for some time. She also talked about her grandparents, all in a very positive way. All in all, I would say that the Sego children * * * are functioning quite well within their age limits and show good bright intelligence. The little boy has no knowledge of the situation with his father or his late mother. The little girl is aware of the situation to the extent of her ability to make reasonable judgment at the age of four years, nine months, which is certainly limited.

The report continues:

> I can only say that there is certainly no indication that Rhonda and John Sego should not be returned to their father upon his release from the penitentiary and can show that he can provide a stable home and has consistent employment. Certainly, because of his incarceration, even on the crime of homicidal action in relation to their

mother, he should not have to suffer being deprived of his children. * *

Therefore, it would be my professional opinion that the children should not be arbitrarily removed from Mr. Sego's eventual custody just because of his incarceration but, on the other hand, he should have an opportunity of proving his stability and capability of setting up a suitable home for the children within a prescribed period of time after his release from the penitentiary before the children would or should be placed with him.

The guardian ad litem, appointed by the court to represent the minor children, filed his report and recommendations September 1, 1971. At that time Dr. Kaufman's report had not been received. The guardian ad litem's report reviewed Sego's history and the results of the guardian ad litem's visit to the Johnson home where he first met the two children. He stated that the children appeared "to be happy and appear to have adjusted very well to this home environment," and that "Mrs. Johnson * * * and her husband are desirous of adopting the two Sego children." Concerning the father, he reported:

Ronnie Lee Sego is a quiet, well-mannered and sensitive individual. He has apparently been able to adjust to this situation with his wife, and has evidently adjusted quite well at the State Penitentiary * * *. [F]rom the very beginning Mr. Sego has been concerned about the welfare of the children. * * *

The guardian ad litem assumed that Mr. Sego's probable date of release from the penitentiary would be "within some three to four years." He nevertheless stated:

It is my opinion that the welfare of the two minor children would not be served by granting the petition of the Juvenile Department to deprive Mr.

Sego of these rights. I believe Mr. Sego would be able to provide a suitable home and environment for these two children upon his release from the State Penitentiary. If the deprivation petition were granted, it would put the children in the situation of having in effect lost both their parents, instead of just one. I recognize that the trauma associated with the murder of one parent by the other is particularly powerful. However, I believe both children will be able to adjust to the situation in the custody and control of their natural father, Ronnie Lee Sego.

At the time of the hearing, no one knew for certain the outcome of Sego's progress hearing then scheduled for April 1972 on the matter of early release. Sego's prison counselor and the Protestant chaplain at the penitentiary were each hopeful for a favorable outcome of the progress hearing. Furthermore, with the consent of the interested parties, the court took judicial notice of the juvenile court hearings held in Clallam County in January and April 1969. However, only the statement of facts and orders from the April hearing have been incorporated into the record on appeal. We are handicapped in our review of the findings without the records of the January 1969 hearings.

The court's memorandum decision, which preceded the entry of findings, expressly states that the court did not "reach this decision easily nor with peace of mind." The court's difficulties may have been caused, at least in part, by the nature of the evidence on which he was compelled to rely. Had a clear case been made out, the court might not have felt it necessary to express the doubts to which he refers in his memorandum decision.

On this state of the record, additional evidence should be taken to remove any serious doubt concerning the propriety of the orders appealed from. The genuine concern of everyone connected with this case for the children's welfare is apparent. The children are still wards of the trial court, entitled to its continuing protection. The issue of permanent deprivation—the real controversy—needs further exploration. That need can best be met by remand for taking additional evidence rather than dismissal for want of convincing evidence. * * *

Expert witnesses can each testify, preferably in person concerning matters relevant to Sego's fitness and possible prospective permanent damage to the children, after each will have interviewed both the father, the children, and the Johnsons, and ascertained the Johnsons' continued willingness to keep the children and do what their love of the children requires of them. We do not intend, by what we say here, to limit evidence otherwise admissible. Upon review of the totality of all pertinent facts at the conclusion of the remanded hearing, conclusions may be reached on the issue of permanent deprivation free of the difficulties we have discussed. In remanding this case for additional evidence, we do not mean to express any opinion on the final disposition of this case. Daugherty v. Daugherty, supra. See RCW 26.32.040(1).

We make no change in the order of the trial court denying visitation rights to Mr. Sego. Pending the remanded hearing, the trial court is free to exercise its discretion on the matter of visitation. Upon the conclusion of the remanded hearing, the trial court will determine visitation rights based on its disposition of the matter of permanent deprivation.

The judgment is reversed with directions to hold further proceedings consistent with this opinion.

D. DAY CARE

MEYER, THE IMPACT OF URBANIZATION ON CHILD WELFARE

Child Welfare, October 1967, p. 433.*

In considering the impact of urbanization on child welfare, I am dismayed to discover myself in agreement with Marshall MacLuhan's notion that we go through our lives looking through a rear-view mirror. I think what he means by this is that it is not really possible to comprehend our present existence because we are going through it, so we tend to live out what has already passed. One of MacLuhan's illustrations of this idea is that the present television medium thrives largely on the movies of yesterday, and those movies derive largely from the books that preceded them. Similarly, it has seemed to me that, although we are talking about the impact of urbanization on child welfare today, the impact has actually been felt for many decades and, like television movies, our child welfare programs may well be based upon long-past rural cultures. I suppose it would follow that, since we are now ready to think about urbanization, we may be very well on our way into a different kind of social organization, although we are not aware of it: we might be talking about our present a few decades from now.

* * *

Urban Characteristics

First, some thoughts about urbanization. Although cities existed over 5000 years ago, the metropolis that we refer to when we talk about urban life goes back only about 100 years. The suburb is a fusion of city and country, and the

* Reprinted by special permission of Child Welfare League of America from *Child Welfare*.

futuristic megalopolis is conceived of as an extensive array of metropolises and suburbs. Beyond these loose definitions we can only use descriptive characteristics when we talk about urban life; the rest is rather soft data. * * *

Interdependence

The metropolis exists on a scale that transcends individual control, with a population that is highly interdependent. We require public transportation, police, fire, sanitation, and health and welfare departments, courts, community hospitals, and public schools. We rely on department stores and supermarkets on organized entertainment, tenants' organizations, labor unions, professional associations, and so forth. The complex structures that are necessary to meet the basic needs of people living in urban conditions are obviously far beyond the control, if not the comprehension, of the individual and his family. This characteristic of urban life is vital to our discussion of the impact of urbanization on child welfare, and we will come back to it.

For the moment we might take notice of a rural myth that seems to conflict with these urban realities, namely that the average American family is self-reliant and that those families who rely upon social and other services are dependent, immature, or sick. (The term used a century ago was "immoral.") This notion is indeed a rural myth—modern urban life rests upon an intricate network of organized systems, and no one any longer is self-reliant in the way that our pioneering ancestors were.

Population Density

A second characteristic of the metropolis is the density of population. Statistics indicate that 96 million people, or 53 percent of the population of this country, are concentrated in 213 urban areas occupying only .7 percent of the na-

tion's land. A more impressive fact is that 52 million Americans lived in only 16 urbanized areas in 1960. Of the 196.6 million people in America 70 percent live in urban centers and one half of this number are under 30. With this high degree of population density there are inevitable strains due to crowdedness, multiple ethnic living, and excessive demands upon social institutions. Without question housing limitations have had a particular impact upon family structure. We will return to this idea again when we discuss the impact of this characteristic of urbanization on child welfare.

But first let me comment upon our second rural myth, which suffers mightily in the face of the urban realities we have just mentioned. This myth is that the basis of American life is the extended family: if child care is threatened by the loss, disability, or breakdown of parents, there is always a relative or neighbor living in the home or nearby who will be willing to provide care. This simply is not true and could not be true in urban life, where space is at a premium and housing units are constructed for the minimum number of people in the nuclear family, if not for people who are unattached to any family structure. Thus, the urban condition has become the human condition for most of our population, and the family that has few relatives with the resources to care for children is not for our purposes different, alien, or dependent. Rather, it is the average urban family.

Employment

A third important urban characteristic is the reliance upon a money income derived from wage employment. This means that families thrive better when they have more money, and thus employment takes on high value for mothers as well as for fathers. Currently, 8 million mothers who work have children under 18. Another way of saying this is that

15 million children, 23 percent of all children under 18, have mothers who work. Once against we notice a fact of urban life that, as we shall discover, has important implications for child welfare.

Another effect of the reliance on a money income is related to the values placed upon children in a family and to the implications this has for family planning. For example, child labor laws restrict the employment of children in the city; there are few jobs they can do with safety, and therefore they are more of a financial burden to families than they were when more families lived on the farms and children did chores that were necessary to the sustenance of the family.

Here against we confront a rural myth in opposition to an urban reality. As long as there is no guaranteed minimum income and no children's allowance, and as long as money is a requisite of city life, women will work to supplement the family income. This is no longer a rural country in which we can anticipate that the mother will be at home to care for the children, to greet them on their return from school, to cook with loving care, and to provide a relaxed and unpressured home life—if, indeed, this ever was an accurate picture of American family life.

*   *   *

Social Work and Child Welfare

Let us turn to the field of social work. As we look at the nature of child welfare services in the framework of the rural myths and urban realities we have been discussing, perhaps we can project the kind of organization and delivery of service that would be most appropriate to the present urban environment of families and children. Since "child welfare" is still a vague concept, it is important for us to agree upon a definition of what we are to discuss here. In the broadest sense, we might view child welfare "as a way of stating a social goal—the general welfare of children with special attention to those economically and socially deprived." In this sense we would include social insurances and developmental services under the heading of child welfare. Or, in a narrower sense, we might view child welfare as the preventive and therapeutic services ordinarily provided by child welfare agencies—casework, foster care, adoption, group care, homemaker services, day care, and protective services. Here we would not include financial assistance (we assume for the sake of argument that AFDC has not been a good example of service through child welfare programs). For the sake of clarity, I will begin with the latter, functional definition of child welfare and then proceed to the former, developmental definition.

The Function of Child Welfare

An important problem is that child welfare programs may not be relevantly connected with existing needs. The reason for this, once again, is that the major service programs in organized child welfare reflect rural myths even as they ignore urban realities.

Historically, child welfare in this country has developed its identity as a field of practice through varied and imaginative child care programs designed to substitute for the child's own family.

*   *   *

A look at some statistics as of March 31, 1965, tells us the scope of these programs: A total of 697,300 children were receiving service from public and voluntary child welfare agencies and institutions in the United States. Thirty percent of these children were receiving foster family care, 16 percent were in institutions, 10 percent were in adoptive homes, and 42 percent lived with parents and relatives. Two percent had other kinds of living arrangements. Almost

700,000 is a large number of children, indeed. But there are in this country over 70 million children, most of whom live in urban centers facing the strains to which we referred earlier in this paper. Moreover, 14.8 million of the nation's children are considered by any current definition to be living in poverty, a condition that we have observed places an additional burden upon family life in the city. Although one might argue that it is not the responsibility of child welfare agencies to care for all of the children in the country, it would be safe to say that the .01 percent of the children in the country who are served by the bulk of the child welfare programs do not suggest that these programs are meeting the problems of population density in the cities in any mass way: we seem to be using an abacus rather than a computer in counting the numbers of children we are serving.

*   *   *

The Development of Child Welfare

What has gone wrong? How is it that this expensive, highly invested, carefully nurtured program seems not to have lived up to its own high standards? It is beyond dispute that foster care has succeeded and will always succeed when it is utilized for some special children who have no other special needs and are placed with some highly selected and very special foster parents—parents who might indeed need to be well subsidized in order to carry out their demanding role. The statistics I mentioned earlier, however, while representing only a tiny portion of American children, also represent 30 percent of all children served by child welfare programs. These figures suggest that foster family care is not presently being used as a very specialized service, but rather as a modality that strives to meet urban problems of family breakdown on a broad, undifferentiated scale. This approach is somewhat like trying to put out a tenement fire with a glass of water.

I think we have here another example of foster care reflecting the rural myth rather than the urban reality. When I was a social work student 20 years ago, Dorothy Hutchinson used to talk forcefully about the precise conditions under which placement should occur. I think she was absolutely correct when she said at that time that if children were to be separated from their parents, and placed in foster care, it should only be done when parents were dead, disabled as far as child care was concerned, or gone from the scene, or if the parent-child relationship was so destructive that the child could not thrive unless he were removed from his home. This description of justifiable reasons for placement made us feel sanguine, for 20 years ago these conditions may have actually existed as causes for which reasonable cures in placement could be achieved.

In the past two decades, however, much has happened to change those conditions as well as the reasonable cures for them. First, improvements in public health, physical rehabilitation, and medicine has cut down considerably on death and disability as major reasons for placement. Second, if parents are truly gone from the scene, there has been a broadening of adoption practice in the last 20 years that has provided for permanent placement of older children and children with moderate handicaps, and there has been less reliance upon physical matching and economic adequacy in adoptive parents. Thus, the concrete reasons for foster placement have decreased markedly.

Current Problems and Services

Foster Care

The major reason for placement today was a selective reason for placement 20 years ago, and thus the supply and demand factor was more in balance. That reason is, of course, emotional disturbance—characterological or behavioral problems of parents, with the resultant effect upon their children, and the disturbance of the children themselves. But we have said that urbanization contributes to the visibility of family tensions, that there is a state of normalness that pervades urban life, that family structures are changing and there are less personal resources available to rely on, that the sheer density of population has resulted in a comparable increase of psychosocial disorder, and that poor families (who are represented in the major portion of foster care statistics) have all of these urban problems compounded by poverty. If this is the social state of urban families in general, are we then to seek foster placement for all urban children? And were we to pursue such a Kafka-like plan, where would we find foster parents who were untouched by the very same problems and urban tensions? As far as this question of foster parents is concerned, have we not been trying to find them in suburbs, without confronting the basic realities of urban life?

It is, I think, a rural myth to believe that we can always substitute a better family life for children than the one in which they presently live. Where is the better family? And what have we gained for children when we have not guaranteed them the good future that we had intended? Is it not an aspect of the urban reality that all families have urban-conditioned problems, and that the rural model of family life belongs in the past?

Adoption

Let us turn our attention now to some other child welfare services that have been confronted by the reality of urbanization, even though they have often been organized around the myth of a rural America. We have alluded to adoption practices, which have a more recent origin in this country than foster care, and which have seemed to be somewhat more responsive to changing times. The absolute standards of parent selection, parent-child matching, financial comfort, and physical standards of the home have given way to more relative considerations as the balance of supply and demand has shifted. Yet adoption too, serving only 10 percent of the small number of children being served by child welfare agencies, is no more real than foster care as a mass solution for a mass problem, and for the same reasons. We have noted that there are decreasing numbers of children available for adoption because of absence of parents; and due to medical progress in treating sterility, there are decreasing numbers of people who are unable to have their own children. Adoption, then, may well become the highly selective process for highly selected children that adoptive programs were structured to become.

At this point, we must comment upon the rise in illegitimacy, for one might suppose that as the number of out-of-wedlock babies increases, substitute care through adoption and foster care would develop as the solution to their parenting.

Are we then to develop a social policy that will provide for 276,000 illegitimate babies, or 6 percent of the live births in 1964? In 1965, 142,000 children were adopted in the United States. Although there is a 6 percent increase in adoptions each year, it seems that we are being beaten by the numbers game. If there is one certain characteristic of urbanization, it is that population density differentiates urban life from rural life, and social solutions for child welfare problems need to be related to numbers of children; it is one of those urban realities that has been with us for years and that we should now be able to talk about.

Three aspects of urbanization that we have considered—changes in norms of behavior and modes of family life, the necessity to rely on institutional structures rather than on the family to meet our needs, and the increase in population density—make it clearer to us why the field of child welfare has begun to promote more socially viable programs to meet the needs created by urbanization.

Group Care

The use of group care, for example, is an interesting illustration. Everyone would agree that mass institutions are no solution for any child care needs; we are referring to the many other varieties of group care programs. Treatment residences for selected disturbed children, cottage-type small group care programs for children who merely need placement away from home, apartment residences for older children, way-stations or shelters for temporarily homeless children, and the host of special group homes for unmarried mothers, delinquents, narcotic addicts, and so forth, are group programs of this kind. Group care, it seems to me, could, by and large, be a modern kind of program, meeting a need that has been specifically created by urbanization.

First, it is a more realistic service as far as the large number of children cared for is concerned, and thus deals appropriately with the fact of urban population density. Second, it makes it more possible for a child to share in his own natural family's identity even though he may be living away from the family. The child is not asked to assume two identities that must inevitably conflict for him. Third, there is no problem of role confusion of foster parents. Fourth, the feeling of exclusion from the child's life does not contribute to the distance of the natural parents. Finally, group care reflects the urban reality that family breakdown in this decade is not a sickness but a general urban phenomenon and, there-

fore, that pursuance of a substitute family for a child is not a fruitful child welfare solution.

In the light of these factors the 16 percent figure for group care services seems paltry, particularly since there is a steady annual decline noted in institution care as compared with provision of foster family care services. The prevailing trend suggests that by 1975 there will be a 45 percent increase over 1965 in foster care, accompanied by a 22 percent drop in institution care.

Protective Services

A word about protective services is important here, for we are observing the gradual flourishing of what had once been a miniscule program in comparison with other child welfare services. In 1961, protective service agencies ranked third in the number of children served by public child welfare agencies and seventh in the number served by voluntary child welfare agencies. Child abuse and neglect may well be diseases of urban civilization—much as heart disease, accidents, and cancer are considered to be medical disease of civilization. The increase in recorded cases of child neglect and abuse has had a salutary effect upon child welfare programs, for today child protection seems to have an increased professional status.

I am not certain about the term "protective services" because, aside from the obvious cases of gross abuse in the group of so-called battered children, I am not sure that protective services have not already become a catchall of neglect cases, made visible in large numbers due to urbanization. My guess is that many cases handled by protective services should not be regarded as protective in the narrow sense at all. Such cases may well be representative of most families living in conditions of poverty in the inner cities, and it may be that it is not at all accurate to call them a syndrome. Nevertheless, although we do not have a nosology of "abused children," the increase of professionalism in protective services has been well worth the effort expended in this area. Caseworkers, functioning under what may well be the wrong title for that service, have stumbled upon the vital urbanized service that may meet the individual needs of families straining to adapt to the exacting, frustrating demands of urban life. Once the abused child syndrome is isolated from all other cases of urban-caused neglect, perhaps the bulk of casework services now being administered in protective service programs will move into another kind of service structure to form the basis of a thoroughly modern, urban, neighborhood preventive child welfare service. We shall see.

Homemaker Services

Homemaker services, as well, seem to me to be a response to the urban condition. These may be temporary or long-term; on call for emergency duty and on a 24-hour basis; and with or without a total casework plan being part of the eligibility for the service. Homemaker services are so economical, financially and socially, compared to the costs of services required if preventive services are not available, that we should all wonder why it has taken so long for us to develop them, even to the extent they now exist. Statistical accounting is negligible, but we know the number of homemakers is only a token in comparison with the need. Such programs confront the reality of family life today, which is ridden with pressures and emergencies and relies upon public and private structures for its continuation. With the vastly increasing numbers of one-parent families, homemaker services are indicated when that parent is unable to care for his or her children; one-parent families are extremely vulnerable. Moreover, since extended family life has gone the way of

the family farm, the intimate functions of child care that were once carried out by relatives must be translated to a socially provided structure that will reflect the urban reality rather than the rural myth.

Day Care

Day care services have also been a long time in coming, considering that we have known for years that increasing numbers of women work in this country. At last our urban communities and child welfare programs have begun to respond to the reality that demands that day care be a flexible social instrument providing care for children in families or groups, for the working day or only for a few hours so that mothers can shop or rest and care for their own needs. Obviously, mothers will then be better able to care for the needs of their children, too. According to the Children's Bureau, however, which has instituted a statistical reporting system as of September 1965, 37 states cared for only 4582 children in licensed day care centers and family day care programs. (This figure would not be accurate if we included nonlicensed and nursery programs.)

It seems to me that protective services, group care, homemaker services, and day care services will soon be going in a different direction from foster care and adoption services. The latter began as specialized services, and before we knew it they were being utilized to meet need on a grand scale—something they could not possibly do in an urban environment. On the other hand, the group care, homemaker, and day care services also began as specialized programs, and waited almost too long before the field became aware of their significance as modern urban-conditioned programs. Perhaps now we will be observing a slow reversal of the trend, with foster care and adoption returning to their specialities and the other services approaching the problem of providing mass devices to meet mass need.

Casework

And what of casework as the core of all these services? Casework, too, has been affected by the present urban situation. Our method is one that can be utilized in a variety of situations and in the face of new knowledge; it is fortunately not bound to the rural myth, even though we seem to be having quite a problem in adjusting it to the urban reality. Child welfare practitioners know all too well that the casework process fails when the social service alternatives are limited. For example, when we determine that an acting-out child must be separated from a mother who has a borderline psychiatric diagnosis and cannot cope with her home responsibilities, the most perceptive diagnostically-oriented caseworker cannot overcome the obstacles inherent in having so narrow a choice of foster parents who will be more capable than the natural mother of dealing with the child. The caseworker, moreover, cannot overcome the reality of urban life when he must place a poor child from an ethnic minority group living in an inner city. Where can the child be placed? With whom? How long will the placement last? What tools can he use to help the natural parent prepare to take the child back? Casework methodology must also adapt to the urban realities: there is no "better" home, there is no model family life just beyond the edge of the slum. The child in placement will not be made over into a new identity, and he will at last return to his slum in dreams, if not in reality. There is, in sum, no individualized casework cure for the urban condition, but there are other, more realizable goals that might better be pursued. We can consider these now in the context of child welfare as a goal for all children; as a developmental service in the urban world of today. Our present dated conception of services meets neither the requirement of keeping up with the quantitative need, nor that of providing appropriate services in the light of the kind of need.

Positive Response to Urbanization

Turning from MacLuhan's rear-view mirror, let us for once look forward through the windshield and view the real urban world that we have been discussing. Ironically, we must fantasize a bit in order to do this, and must comment on the future when we really ought to be talking about the present child welfare scene.

What would we foresee as child welfare practice that reflects the impact of urbanization? First, I would expect that the field of child welfare would, as someone has said, break down its own walls and see itself as responsible for the welfare of children—even, with the help of other fields of practice in social work, for 70 million children. But that subject must be pursued elsewhere.

In an adequate urban child welfare program, we would take cognizance of the value of the city neighborhood as the smallest feasible social unit that will mitigate the depersonalization of urban life. In this neighborhood structure there would be a complex of family and child welfare services, for without such a network the service alternatives would be too separate to meet the reality of urban living. In this family- and child-welfare-service complex the social necessities of urban life would be available for every family. With a few additions, the array of services is familiar to us.

First, income security through some social insurance system would make the most economic and social sense, but even without it and with a continuation of public assistance as the core mode of income maintenance, our array of services would have validity. Second, the neighborhood family and child welfare service would provide a day care program that would be so flexible that working mothers or hard-pressed mothers would be able to use it realistically to meet their requirements. The day care center would not, of course, concern itself with obstacles to eligibility.

Third, the neighborhood service program would have homemakers available for emergencies, and for short-term and long-term service to families who needed it. The homemakers might come from the neighborhood itself, and this would contribute to the income needs of the people we would be trying to help.

Fourth, there would be a vast program of casework services to families who are experiencing strain in interpersonal relationships and social functioning. Caseworkers would be inventive and would utilize methods of crisis intervention and would strive to develop increasing social competence rather than personality change as they worked with the families and children. They would use group methods and family treatment freely and would supervise nonprofessional staff in many of the necessary tasks.

Fifth, a protective service in this neighborhood center would deal primarily with child abuse, because the presence of caseworkers, homemaker services, and day care services would undoubtedly cut down considerably on the incidence of child neglect in that community.

Sixth, there would be an arrangement of group care facilities, perhaps overlapping other neighborhood areas, for with the preventive services we have described there would not be the pressing placement need in any one neighborhood.

Seventh, there would be adoptive services available for the decreasing number of children and adoptive parents who would need them, and there would be therapeutic group and foster family place-

ments to be used for specific, diagnostically supported reasons. Finally, in keeping with the census data, there would be a host of newly devised services for youth.

Were such a scheme provided for urban children, it might not be as necessary to fit them into the services at hand in the absence of real treatment-planning alternatives. It seems to me that the impact of urbanization has been felt already: in child welfare we have the expertise, the tools, and the clear vision necessary to face the urban reality.

WHAT DAY CARE OUGHT TO BE

Patricia G. Bourne.
The New Republic, February, 1972, p. 18–23.

When we talk about day care we are usually talking about three things. One is full-day care and protection of children whose parents are at work * * * The second is nursery schools, an enriching experience supplementing family life for the child. These programs have traditionally been half-day or three mornings a week, which means that they are not an option for the children of working mothers. The third, so new and so fragile that it is not yet clear that we can call it a tradition, is that of compensatory education.

Because "day care" has historically served children whose parents worked, it has been considered as something for people who are either too poor to too crass to stay home with their children. As the combination of work and motherhood has spread from the relatively small ranks of the very poor, who had no choice, to the professionals, who chose to work for reasons of self-fulfillment, the stigma associated with being a working mother has diminished. But the stigma associated with allowing someone else to *raise* your children for you has not diminished at all.

For the same reasons that day care is acceptable to the American family ethos, it is also gaining in some quarters a new kind of stigma. Because day care is hands-off regarding child-rearing, it also lacks the qualities of nurturing, developing or educating young children. * *

Private day nurseries, run for profit, and licensed (or not), are also a long-standing day care tradition. As with day care homes, licensing standards have related primarily to the adequacy of physical facilities and some minimum staff-child ratio of 1 to 10 or 12. The service provided is basically babysitting, whether you are poor and receiving care courtesy of the welfare department, or whether you are paying yourself.

Federal involvement in day care began during the Depression as part of WPA. But the first significant full-day group care program was created by the Lanham Act in 1941 to provide care for the children of mothers who were desperately needed in the war economy. This program was implemented with astonishing speed (and mixed results) and dismantled just as quickly when the war ended. Continuation of these programs was contingent upon state willingness to assume responsibility—California was the one state to do so. * * *

The primary source of federal support for day care has been Title 4A of the Social Security Act, as amended, in 1967. Under the AFDC Section, state welfare departments are enabled to provide day care benefits to every AFDC family and to those judged as past and potential recipients. These funds are disbursed on a three-to-one local matching-share basis; thus their use is contingent upon the willingness of state, county, city or some private source to provide one-quarter of the costs.

The second piece of Title 4A is the Work Incentive Program (WIN); it allows payment, again on a three-to-one matching basis, for day care services when the mother is enrolled in a WIN training program.

Title 4B of the Social Security Act, as amended, 1967, provides something called child welfare services. Grants are made to state welfare departments to provide services to children regardless of financial status. This program expended only $1.5 million in 1970 (as contrasted to $94 million under Title 4A, AFDC), and even some knowledgeable welfare department day care specialists have not heard of it.

In looking back over this brief review of federal participation in the support of day care services, three points stand out: 1) the federal government has gone to some pains to stay out of the business of *providing* day care services; they will *pay for services* that are provided by a local public agency or a nonprofit group. 2) Funding is, with the one exception of an almost invisible program, explicitly for and limited to the welfare or near-welfare population. 3) Funds for day care for the poor are almost always contingent upon participation in the labor force or some training program in preparation for participation in the labor force. Federal participation in day care has been explicitly and almost solely linked to programs designed to limit the welfare rolls.

There is one irony in this chronicle of federal participation: in order for any provider of services to receive federal funds, he must meet what are called the Federal Interagency Guidelines. The irony is that the bureaucrats assigned the task of setting these standards came up with a requirement of a staff/child ratio of one-to-five (as opposed to the 1 to 10 or 12 usual in state-licensed custodial programs), and they require an educational, nutritional and parent-participation component among others.

The nursery school movement has stressed the importance of the early years, not so much as a time for learning but as a time for critical emotional development. Children needed to learn to play with their peers, to cooperate, to tolerate those restrictions on their freedom arising from their membership in a community.

In 1964, as part of the War on Poverty, a bright-eyed hope-filled new program was begun called Head Start. Putting down Head Start as misguided boondoggle is now chic with both the right and the left. Its payoffs in terms of its stated goals have certainly not been proven—nor disproven. But the influence of Head Start is undeniable. A program of compensatory education for "culturally disadvantaged" children, it was part and parcel of an attempt at basic social reform.

We have seen that day care really means: 1) *care and protection of children while their parents work.* This tradition of day care has steadfastly avoided anything which will *appear* to be a usurpation of the family's child-rearing role. 2) *Nursery school in full-day form.* Here child-rearing functions are also carefully not usurped. It is a complement to and extension of the family environment. Nursery schools are often of the cooperative genre with the mother participating at least one morning a week and perhaps even taking classes in child development. 3) *Compensatory education.* Here we are not raising the child *for* the parents, but *making up* for what is seen as inadequate parental child-rearing. Some effort as in Head Start and especially in Parent Child Centers is made to educate the parents in the ways of child-rearing.

When one reads over what has been written about day care since it became a popular topic, one begins to get some feel that we are coming to a rough consensus about what day care ought to be. It should of course care for and protect our children; it should connect the child's worlds of home and day care; it should provide an environment that fosters his development of a sense of self, self-worth and security, and his ability to get what he wants and needs from the environment around him; and one which stimulates and develops his cognitive and sensory abilities. But when we take a closer look, we are not at all close to an agreement on what day care ought to be. The disagreement is wide on what *kind* of child care we want and on how much we are willing to spend for it.

The diversity of views could be spun out almost indefinitely. There is only one common denominator: care for the children of working mothers. Beyond that there is no possibility of agreeing on a definition. The common denominator is the lowest common denominator. The coalition that has formed around day care is really a coalition based on the needs of women in the labor force, *not* a coalition based on the needs of young children.

The second point on which there is a seeming consensus but, in fact, a wide disagreement, is on the amount of money we are willing to invest in care for children. Let us take a very rough look at day care costs, with school systems as a reference point.

An extravagant school district like Berkeley, California, spends about $1400 per year per child. The national average is more like $800. The *cheapest* custodial day care in California costs $1200 per year per child. As with schools, the costs are in the teachers. The $1200 day nursery figure pays for a program which employs an adult (usually an untrained one) for every 10 or 12 children. Federal Interagency Guidelines, mentioned earlier, require one adult for every five children; all instructors must have academic degrees. An OEO funded study of "exemplary" day care programs and systems around the country shows that those which maintain a one-to-five adult/child *contact-hour ratio* and which have first-rate educational developmental, health and parent involvement components are costing between $2500 and $3500 per year per child.

Will those in favor of getting welfare women out to work be willing to pay $5000 for care for a woman's two children in order to save $2400 on her AFDC grant? Will a woman whose earning power is $6000–8000 be willing to spend $5000 of it for child care in the private market? If she isn't, can the franchisers now entering the business with enthusiasm make a profit? Will industry and labor unions be willing to provide that magnitude of fringe benefit?

* * *

It would seem that if we are to have quality day care services in the public *or* private sector—quality even in the most limited sense of a reasonably adequate adult/child ratio—we will have to be willing to assume at least a portion of its costs for all who use it, as yet another public responsibility.

* * *

In the short run, * * * I am pessimistic. I feel that neither the public sector *nor* the private individual is, at this point, willing to spend sums on the order of $2500 to $3500 per year per child during the working day—willing, that is, if the issue is drawn solely around the needs of children. I would argue that day care must be placed in the larger context of national priorities in pragmatic American style. We have seen that lawmakers have been willing to pay for child care if it is a means to a valued end, such as getting women off the welfare rolls and into the labor force. Perhaps we must, for the time being, accept

these kinds of national priorities and play on them.

This strategy of piecemeal picking and poking at the present system may strike those who have hoped for a bold and straightforward initiative as incredibly depressing. I would argue simply that a politically acceptable bold initiative at this point in history would have to take such a form that it would be a genuine disservice to the nation's children.

———

THE CHILD DEVELOPMENT PROGRAMS PROPOSED BY AMENDMENTS TO THE ECONOMIC OPPORTUNITY ACT IN 1971.

[The child development provisions of the proposed 1971 amendments to the Economic Opportunity Act of 1964 are found in Senate Document 92–48 (92d Congress, First Session) pp. 11–43. The legislation authorized the appropriation of $2 billion for the fiscal year ending June 30, 1973. Section 501 of Title V sets forth the Congressional findings and the purpose of the program.]

———

"TITLE V—CHILD DEVELOPMENT PROGRAMS

STATEMENT OF FINDINGS AND PURPOSE

Sec. 501. (a) The Congress finds that—

(1) millions of children in the Nation are suffering unnecessary harm from the lack of adequate child development services, particularly during early childhood years;

(2) comprehensive child development programs, including a full range of health, education, and social services, are essential to the achievement of the full potential of the Nation's children and should be available to chil-

dren whose parents or legal guardians shall request them regardless of economic, social, and family backgrounds;

(3) children with special needs must receive full and special consideration in planning any child development programs and, pending the availability of such programs for all children, priority must be given to preschool children with the greatest economic and social need;

(4) while no mother may be forced to work outside the home as a condition for using child development programs, such programs are essential to allow many parents to undertake or continue full- or part-time employment, training, or education;

(5) comprehensive child development programs not only provide a means of delivering a full range of essential services to children, but can also furnish meaningful employment opportunities for many individuals, including older persons, parents, young persons, and volunteers from the community; and

(6) it is essential that the planning and operation of such programs be undertaken as a partnership of parents, community, and State and local government with appropriate assistance from the Federal Government.

(b) It is the purpose of this title to provide every child with a fair and full opportunity to reach his full potential by establishing and expanding comprehensive child development programs, and services designed to assure the sound and coordinated development of these programs, to recognize and build upon the experience and success gained through the Headstart program and similar efforts, to furnish child development services for these children who need them most, with special emphasis on preschool programs for economically disadvantaged children, and for children of working

mothers and single parent families, to provide that decisions on the nature and funding of such programs be made at the community level with the full involvement of parents and other individuals and organizations in the community interested in child development, and to establish the legislative framework for child development services.

Section 512 of the legislation set forth how the funds could be used.

USES OF FUNDS

Sec. 512. Funds available for this part may be used (in accordance with approved applications) for the following services and activities:

(1) planning and developing child development programs, including the operation of pilot programs to test the effectiveness of new concepts, programs, and delivery systems;

(2) establishing, maintaining, and operating child development programs, which may include—

(A) comprehensive physical and mental health, social, and cognitive development services necessary for children participating in the program to profit fully from their educational opportunities and to attain their maximum potential;

(B) food and nutritional services (including family consultation);

(C) rental, remodeling, renovation, alteration, construction, or acquisition of facilities, including mobile facilities, and the acquisition of necessary equipment and supplies;

(D) programs designed (i) to meet the special needs of minority group, Indian, and migrant children with particular emphasis on the needs of children from bilingual families for the development of skills in English and the other language spoken in the home, and (ii) to meet the needs of all children to understand the history and cultural backgrounds of minority groups which belong to their communities and the role of members of such minority groups in the history and cultural development of the Nation and of the region in which they reside;

(E) a program of daily activities designed to develop fully each child's potential;

(F) other specially designed health, social, and educational programs (including after school, summer, weekend, vacation, and overnight programs);

(G) medical, dental, psychological, educational, and other appropriate diagnosis, identification, and treatment of visual, hearing, speech, nutritional, and other physical, mental, and emotional barriers to full participation in child development programs, including programs for preschool and other children who are emotionally disturbed;

(H) prenatal and other medical services to expectant mothers who cannot afford such services, designed to help reduce malnutrition, infant and maternal mortality, and the incidence of mental retardation and other handicapping conditions, and postpartum and other medical services (including family planning information) to such recent mothers;

(I) incorporation within child development programs of special activities designed to identify and ameliorate identified physical, mental, and emotional handicaps and special learning disabilities and, where necessary because of the severity of such handicaps, establishing, maintaining, and operating separate child development programs designed primarily to meet the needs of handicapped children, including emotionally disturbed children;

(J) preservice and inservice education and other training for professional and paraprofessional personnel;

(K) dissemination of information in the functional language of those to be served to assure that parents are well informed of child development programs available to them and may become directly involved in such programs;

(L) services including in-home services, and training in the fundamentals of child development, for parents, older family members functioning in the capacity of parents, youth, and prospective parents;

(M) use of child advocates, consistent with the provisions of this title, to assist children and parents in securing full access to other services, programs, or activities intended for the benefit of children;

(N) programs designed to extend comprehensive prekindergarten early childhood education techniques and gains (particularly parent participation) into kindergarten and early primary grades (one through three), in cooperation with local educational agencies, including the use of former assistant Headstart teachers or similar early childhood education teachers as instructional aides (in addition to those employed by the schools involved) working closely with classroom teachers in the kindergarten and such early primary grades in which are enrolled children they taught in Headstart or other early childhood education programs, providing for full participation of parents of the children involved in program planning, implementation, and decision-making and for career development opportunities and advancement through continuing education and training for the instructional aides involved (including teacher salaries, educational stipends for tuition, books, and tutoring, career counseling, arrangements for academic credit for independent study, fieldwork based on their teaching assignments, and preservice and inservice training) and for the classroom teachers and principals involved; and

(O) such other services and activities as the Secretary deems appropriate in furtherance of the purposes of this part; and

(3) staff and other administrative expenses of Child Development Councils established and operated in accordance with this part.

The money was to be spent through "prime sponsors", i. e., "State, locality, combination of localities, Indian tribe or organization, public or non-profit organizations or agencies." The prime sponsors were to be designated by the Secretary of Health, Education and Welfare. He could approve a prime sponsorship plan, for example, submitted by any locality which has the population of 5,000 persons or over.

Each prime sponsor was to establish a child development council.

CHILD DEVELOPMENT COUNCILS

Sec. 514. (a) Each prime sponsor designated under section 513 shall establish and maintain a Child Development Council composed of not less than 10 members as follows—

(1) not less than half of the members of such Council shall be parents of children served in child development programs under this part; and

(2) the remaining members shall be appointed by the chief executive officer or the governing body, whichever is appropriate, of the prime sponsor to represent the public, but (A) not less than half of such members shall be persons who are broadly representative of the general public, including government agencies, public and pri-

vate agencies and organizations in such fields as economic opportunity, health, education, welfare, employment and training, business or financial organizations or institutions, labor unions, and employers, and (B) the remaining members, the number of which shall be either equal to or one less than the number of members appointed under clause (A), shall be persons who are particularly skilled by virtue of training or experience in child development, child health, child welfare, or other child services, except that the Secretary may waive the requirement of this clause (B) to the extent that he determines, in accordance with regulations which he shall prescribe, that such persons are not available to the area to be served.

At least one-third of the total membership of the Child Development Council shall be parents who are economically disadvantaged. Each Council shall select its own chairman.

(b) In accordance with procedures which the Secretary shall establish pursuant to regulations, each prime sponsor designated under section 513 shall provide, with respect to the Child Development Council established and maintained by such prime sponsor, that—

(1) the parent members described in paragraph (1) of subsection (a) of this section shall be chosen by the membership of Headstart policy committees where they exist, and, at the earliest practicable time, by project policy committees established pursuant to section 516(a)(2) of this part;

(2) the terms of office and any other policies and procedures of an organizational nature, including nomination and election procedures, are appropriate in accordance with the purposes of this part;

(3) such Council shall have responsibility for approving basic goals, poli-

cies, actions, and procedures for the prime sponsor, including policies with respect to planning, general supervision and oversight, overall coordination, personnel, budgeting, funding of projects, and monitoring and evaluation of projects; and

(4) such Council shall, upon its own initiative or upon request of a project applicant or any other party in interest, conduct public hearings before acting upon applications for financial assistance submitted by project applicants under this part.

Section 571 of the legislation defined "children" as "individuals who have not attained the age of 15."

The same section defined Child Development Programs as "programs provided on a full-day or part-day basis which provide the educational, nutritional, social, medical, psychological, and physical services needed for children to attain their full potential."

RICHARD NIXON, VETO MESSAGE—ECONOMIC OPPORTUNITY AMENDMENTS OF 1971

Senate Document No. 92–48, 92d Cong., First Session (December 9, 1971).

* * *

But the most deeply flawed provision of this legislation is Title V, "Child Development Programs."

Adopted as an amendment to the OEO legislation, this program points far beyond what this administration envisioned when it made a "national commitment to providing all American children an opportunity for a healthful and stimulating development during the first five years of life."

Though Title V's stated purpose, "to provide every child with a full and fair opportunity to reach his full potential" is certainly laudable, the intent of Title V is overshadowed by the fiscal irresponsibility, administrative unworkability, and family-weakening implications of the system it envisions. We owe our children something more than good intentions.

We cannot and will not ignore the challenge to do more for America's children in their all-important early years. But our response to this challenge must be a measured, evolutionary, painstakingly considered one, consciously designed to cement the family in its rightful position as the keystone of our civilization.

Further, in returning this legislation to the Congress, I do not for a moment overlook the fact that there are some needs to be served, and served now.

One of these needs is for day care, to enable mothers, particularly those at the lowest income levels, to take full-time jobs. Federal support for State and local day care services under Head Start and the Social Security Act already totals more than half a billion dollars a year—but this is not enough. That is why our H.R. 1 welfare reform proposals, which have been before the Congress for the past 26 months, include a request for $750 million annually in day care funds for welfare recipients and the working poor, including $50 million for construction of facilities. And that is why we support the increased tax deductions written into the Revenue Act of 1971, which will provide a significant Federal subsidy for day care in families where both parents are employed, potentially benefitting 97 percent of all such families in the country and offering parents free choice of the child care arrangements they deem best for their own families. This approach reflects my conviction that the Federal Government's role wherever possible should be one of assisting parents to purchase needed day care services in the private open market, with Federal involvement in direct provision of such services kept to an absolute minimum. * * *

* * * [T]he child development envisioned in this legislation would be truly a long leap into the dark for the United States Government and the American people, I must share the view of those of its supporters who proclaim this to be the most radical piece of legislation to emerge from the Ninety-second Congress. * * *

Specifically, these are my present objections to the proposed child development program:

First, neither the immediate *need* nor the desirability of a national child development program of this character has been demonstrated.

Secondly, day care centers to provide for the children of the poor so that their parents can leave the welfare rolls to go on the payrolls of the nation, are already provided for in H.R. 1, my workfare legislation. To some degree, child development centers are a duplication of these efforts. Further, these child development programs would be redundant in that they duplicate many existing and growing Federal, State and local efforts to provide social, medical, nutritional and education services to the very young.

Third, given the limited resources of the Federal budget, and the growing demands upon the Federal taxpayer, the expenditure of two billions of dollars in a program whose effectiveness has yet to be demonstrated cannot be justified. And the prospect of costs which could eventually reach $20 billion annually is even more unreasonable.

Fourth, for more than two years this administration has been working for the enactment of welfare reform, one of the objectives of which is to bring the family together. This child development program appears to move in precisely the opposite direction. There is a respectable

school of opinion that this legislation would lead toward altering the family relationship. Before even a tentative step is made in this direction by their government, the American people should be fully consulted.

Fifth, all other factors, being equal, good public policy requires that we enhance rather than diminish both parental authority and parental involvement with children—particularly in those decisive early years when social attitudes and a conscience are formed, and religious and moral principles are first inculcated.

Sixth, there has yet to be an adequate answer provided to the crucial question of who the qualified people are, and where they would come from, to staff the child development centers.

Seventh, as currently written, the legislation would create, ex nihilo, a new army of bureaucrats. By making any community over 5,000 population eligible as a direct grantee for HEW child development funds, the proposal actively invites the participation of as many as 7,000 prime sponsors—each with its own plan, its own council, its own version of all the other machinery that has made Head Start, with fewer than 1,200 grantees, so difficult a management problem.

Eight, the States would be relegated to an insignificant role. This new program would not only arrogate the initiative for preschool education to the Federal Government from the States—only 8 of which even require kindergarten at present. It would also retain an excessive measure of operational control for such education at the Federal level, in the form of the standards and program guidelines to be set down by the Secretary of HEW.

Ninth, for the Federal Government to plunge headlong financially into supporting child development would commit the vast moral authority of the National Government to the side of communal approaches to child rearing over against the family-centered approach.

This President, this Government, is unwilling to take that step.

PRESS RELEASE FROM THE OFFICES OF SENATORS WALTER F. MONDALE AND JACOB K. JAVITS, May 3, 1972

Senate Committee Approves Child Development Bill

WASHINGTON, D. C., May 3—The Senate Labor and Public Welfare Committee approved today a bipartisan, modified version of the child development bill which was vetoed last year. * * *

The Committee bill is designed to take into account the Administration's concerns about this legislation as expressed in the President's veto message last December. The Committee members emphasized that the compromise bill reflects their desire to resolve reasonable differences between the Administration and Congress.

Senators Mondale, Nelson, Javits and Taft are the principal supporters of the legislation this year.

Senators Mondale, Nelson, Javits and Taft pointed out the following changes which have been made in response to the concerns expressed by the President:

—This is a separate three-year bill, unlike last year's provisions which were attached to the OEO legislation.

—In order to meet objections regarding the delivery system and workability of the program, and to increase State involvement, localities seeking to run their own program must have populations of at least 25,000. This compares with a 5,000 population requirement from the vetoed bill. It reduces the number of eligible applicants from 7,000 to 2,000.

—Authorizations for the first operational year have been reduced by 40 per

cent * * * from $2 billion in the vetoed bill to $1.2 billion in this bill.

—The administration of the program has been simplified by increasing the administrative and policy powers of Governors and Mayors serving as prime sponsors, and eliminating the administrative responsibilities of the child development councils.

—Effective dates of the program have been postponed a year with FY 73 for planning and FY 74 and 75 for implementation.

—The first $500 million are reserved for Head Start.

—10% of the funds are reserved for State plans designed to coordinate programs within each State and prevent unnecessary duplication and inconsistencies.

—In order to experiment with the possibility for even greater State involvement, the bill permits the Secretary to select up to five States, on a demonstration basis, which will administer and serve as prime sponsors for all of the areas and localities in that State.

—The needs for staffing and training have been anticipated by increasing the authorization for planning and training from $100 million to $150 million and reserving up to 10% of the funds for staff training during the next two years.

—Local flexibility and local initiative have been protected within those areas under state prime sponsorship by assuring that councils composed of local officials and parents approve the State child development plan for that area and approve the project the State decides to fund in that area.

—Parent participation is emphasized by requiring at least 50% parent representation on councils that approve curriculum, policy and funding for child development programs.

—The bill retains the fee schedule from the vetoed bill * * * which provides free services to poor children, modest fees for children of families with incomes between $4300 and $7000, and a sliding scale fee schedule for families with higher incomes, but includes a new provision prepared by Senator Javits to permit local prime sponsors to obtain permission to charge less, in areas with high costs of living.

—Clarifies the previous bill's safeguards and protections for very young children.

—In order to draw on the experience of public schools and encourage continuity between preschool and school-age programs, the bill reserves five per cent of the funds for special innovative programs run by educational agencies.

—Funds for model programs, at the Secretary's discretion have been increased from five to 10 per cent.

—Authorizes the Secretary of HEW to coordinate other existing child care programs with programs funded under this Act as a result of an amendment offered by Senator Javits.

A RADICAL, DIRECT, SIMPLE, UTOPIAN ALTERNATIVE TO DAY-CARE CENTERS

William Shannon.
New York Times Magazine, April 30, 1972,
p. 71.

Last Dec. 9, President Nixon vetoed an antipoverty bill which had as its major component the Comprehensive Child Development Act of 1971, sponsored by Senators Walter Mondale, Minnesota Democrat, and Jacob Javits, New York Republican. The child-development bill, one of the most far-reaching measures ever passed by Congress, ranking in financial cost and social implications with Medicare or Federal aid to education, deserves much more thorough discussion than it has received. * * *

The Mondale bill which President Nixon vetoed is based on the theory that a big investment of money and effort in children, especially in the years from birth to 6, would save some of them from disasters later on and might actually reduce the amount of money that society now has to spend on juvenile-delinquent centers, prisons, mental hospitals, and other kinds of human repair and rehabilitation. In asserting the Government's comprehensive interest in these formative early years, the bill has many precedents, such as the long campaign against child labor, the public health effort to cut down infant mortality, the White House conferences on children and youth held once a decade since 1909, and the widely popular Head Start program enacted as a part of the poverty program.

Building on the Head Start model, the bill would go far beyond merely providing a convenient place near home or work where an employed mother could leave a child. It would establish child-development centers in every community. A child could get one, two or more meals, depending upon how many hours he stayed each day. A center would contract with outside doctors or clinics to provide medical, dental and psychiatric diagnosis and care. It would begin the education of preschool children and make available to them, as well as to older children, "summer, weekend, vacation and overnight programs." Parents would serve on the board of the center, and, if unemployed, they might be enlisted as volunteer workers or paid employes. In some circumstances, a mother might be paid to care for four or five children—her own as well as others—in her own home. This is called "family day care." Where needed, a professional or a trained volunteer would be sent out from the center to instruct and assist uneducated, inexperienced or under-confident mothers in baby and child care. * * *

The Mondale bill covers all children from birth through 14. There is comparatively little controversy, however, about the older children in the 6-to-14 age group who attend school. For them, the problem is primarily to find a place where they can play or otherwise usefully occupy themselves for two or three hours after school until their parents pick them up.

* * *

Although children from every kind of family could conceivably participate, the real emotional force behind the drive for comprehensive child development is the desire of liberal, compassionate people to improve the chances in life of children from the nation's worst-off families— migrant laborers and sharecroppers, unemployed miners in Appalachia, impoverished Mexicans, Puerto Ricans, Indians and blacks. Two-thirds of the places in the child-development centers would be reserved for the children of these low-income families. * * *

If a desire to improve the lot of impoverished children is one force behind proposals for comprehensive child development, the program's political appeal is enhanced by the benefits it offers three other groups of families. There are the families in modest economic circumstances with husbands who work but barely earn a subsistence income and wives who work part-time or full-time to pay for a few comforts beyond the family's necessities; these are the "working poor." A second group consists of middle-class women who ordinarily would not have to work when their children are small but who are driven back into the job market prematurely because of divorce, or the death or illness of their husbands. Third, there are the families in which husbands earn a satisfactory income but the women work by choice. These middle-class wives often argue for day care in terms of women's "liberation."

A fourth category might be families in which the husbands earn adequate incomes and wives do not pursue careers, but might do so if high-quality day care were available. In other words, comprehensive day care is not only a response to the increasing number of working mothers but its existence would probably serve to accelerate that trend. * * *

The opposition in and out of Congress has formed on both economic and cultural grounds. In the original version of his bill, Mondale proposed spending $2-billion in the first year of operation.

* * *

Politics aside, however, President Nixon's argument against actively encouraging the shift from the family to the day-care center as the prime agent in child-rearing goes to the heart of the issue. Are child-development centers desirable for any children other than the most damaged and deprived? The unpopular truth is that any community facility—call it a day-care center or a child-development center—is at best an inadequate, unsatisfactory substitute, and at worst a dangerous, destructive substitute for a child's own mother.

In the months of infancy, a child's whole universe consists of himself and the person who feeds him, dresses him and responds to his cries and other signals for attention. Although the development of a human being is imperfectly understood since babies cannot talk, intensive research by Dr. Margaret Mahler and other experts on what psychiatrists call the "separation-individuation process" shows that in the period from approximately 6 months of age to 2 years, critically important events are taking place in the formation of a child's personality. During those months, he learns that his mother is not just an extension of himself, that he is a person in his own right, that his mother can leave him and that there are other persons in the world besides himself and her.

Superficially, it is true that anybody can feed a baby or change his diapers. But in the most profound emotional sense, a baby's whole sense of himself depends upon the warmth and consistency of the relationship that he has with the person who takes care of him. If he is indifferently or inconsistently treated by a succession of various adults—as he would tend to be if left in a day-care center for 8 or 10 hours a day—he is truly a deprived child. Psychological research indicates that anxieties, depression, passivity and other serious handicaps may develop. From 2 to 3 years of age, a toddler learning to talk and to run about can begin to stutter or suffer other impairments, from slight to serious, if he is subjected to severe emotional upheaval —such as a shift from family care to day care. In the years from 3 to 6, other important though less dramatic stages of development unfold in the child's life. For these reasons, most well-run nursery schools which serve middle-class and upper-class families rarely take children before they are 2½ or 3 years old, and do not keep them more than three or four hours a day until they are at least 5 years old.

Day-care centers have become important institutions in this country in recent years as the number of working mothers has increased, but other nations have had much longer and more extensive experience with them. Dr. Dale Meers, a Washington psychiatrist, has reported on a study of programs in the Soviet Union, Hungary, East Germany, Czechoslovakia, Greece, Israel and France. The report, published by the U. S. Office of Economic Opportunity and entitled "International Day Care: A Selective Review and Psychoanalytic Critique," is hardly an encouraging document. In the Soviet Union, Dr. Meers reports, senior officials who run the day-care centers do not make use of them for their own children. "Their preference [is] to use their incomes to employ someone to care for their children at home." Dr. Meers found that Hungarian officials hoped eventually to eliminate day care for children under 3 because of the "manifest unhappiness" of the child. In Czechoslovakia, the best day care "appeared hygienic, sterile and depressing." In every country, Communist and non-Communist alike, officials encountered serious problems of staffing and rapid turnover.

"Nursing staff covertly resist continuity of care of one or more babies. Indeed, it was a common experience, internationally, that care-givers often could not readily identify their children by name and, with babies, did not know with certitude whether each one had been fed. * * * The younger and less active the child in the day nursery, the smaller the amount of attention be received.

"Multiple mothering all too frequently provides an uncoordinated octopus. The multiplicity of care-givers, their overlapping of shifts, their replaceability for illness or holidays, their departures for other employment, all leave the very young child accommodating first to one and then to another."

The enthusiasts of day care more often point to Israel where many children are communally reared in the kibbutz. * * *

Israeli practices in communal child rearing are the subject of intense controversy both within Israel and among outside experts. The evidence is not all in because really thorough scientific studies are only now being conducted, but there is some indication, as Dr. Bruno Bettelheim reported in his book, "The Children of the Dream," that kibbutz-raised children show significant personality differences from children raised in the conventional family. For example, the kibbutz children get along well with their peers and are very loyal to their group, but often seem incapable of deep emotional attachments and creative intensity.

There is a radical alternative to child-care centers which I believe would avoid the staffing difficulties, the psychic risks and the other drawbacks of communal care: Pay mothers to take care of their own children in their own homes.

Many years ago, Dr. Benjamin Spock put forward the ideal solution in his characteristically simple, straight-forward language. In "Baby and Child Care," he wrote: "Some mothers have to work to make a living. Usually their children turn out all right because some reasonably good arrangement is made for their care. But others grow up neglected and maladjusted. It would save money in the end if the Government paid a comfortable allowance to all mothers of young children who would otherwise be compelled to work. * * * It doesn't make sense to let mothers go to work making dresses in a factory or tapping typewriters in an office, and have them pay other people to do a poorer job of bringing up their children."

A comparison of costs suggests that the Federal Government, if it chooses to do so, can as easily pay a mother to take care of her own children as to finance them in a day-care facility. Most working mothers, unless they have high professional qualifications, would consider themselves fortunate if they found work paying $150 a week ($7,800 a year). After deductions for Federal and state income taxes, Social Security, union dues, lunches and carfare, their take-home pay would be about $100 a week, or $5,200 a year. To provide the kind of comprehensive child care which the Mondale bill envisages could easily cost $2,600 a year a child. If that sum were paid directly to the mother of two children, she would have as much income as if she went out to work. * * *

True equality between the sexes is wholly desirable, but the liberation of women must not become a potential defeat for young preschool children. Women should not try to combine a full-time job with raising small children. It is a rare and exceptionally gifted woman who does something more important in the outside world than she does during those critical first six years when she is helping to form the personality and character of a child.

Essentially, it is a matter of making a rational choice. If a young woman decided to join the Peace Corps, she would know that she was signing up for two years of her life. If she decided to go to medical school, she would know that she was committing herself to four years of hard work. I suggest that if a woman decides to have a baby, she should know that she is signing up for six years before she can return to work full time.

The direct, simple method of paying parents to stay at home with their children is perhaps utopian, basically because Americans do not believe in the family as much as they think they do. No one can say when or if Americans will reinvigorate those values which make parenthood the most serious human vocation, which are essential to sustain happy, effective families and which, if practiced, would truly make this country what it now mistakenly thinks it is—a child-centered society.

Chapter 3

HOUSING

SECTION 1. A STATISTICAL BACKDROP

A. HOUSING NEEDS

In Title XVI of the Housing and Urban Development Act of 1968, the Congress initiated the preparation of a plan to meet all of the nation's housing needs and eliminate all of its substandard housing in ten years, or by the end of fiscal year 1978. Reports on progress in meeting the plan's targets and revisions in the plan are to be made annually. Further, estimates of the need for housing over the period are to be updated regularly.

The first table below contains an estimate of the nation's housing needs, prepared by the Department of Housing and Urban Development in connection with the Second Annual Report on National Housing Goals (1970). The succeeding table states the production goals which have been set in accordance with the estimated needs. The third table indicates the early role of housing subsidies in meeting the production goals.

TABLE 1

HOUSING NEEDS: ESTIMATES FOR FISCAL YEARS 1969–1978
(MILLIONS OF UNITS)

Item	Number
For net additional household formation	13.5
To permit an increase in vacant units	3.5
To compensate for demolitions, casualty, and other losses of nondilapidated units other than mobile homes	2.0
To permit removal of all existing dilapidated units	1.8
To permit the removal of all units becoming dilapidated over the decade	3.5
To permit the replacement of mobile homes scrapped over the decade	1.2
Rehabilitations of nondilapidated, substandard units:	
(a) Without subsidy	1.7
(b) With subsidy	1.0
Subtotals:	
(a) New units and nonsubsidized rehabilitations	27.2
(b) New units and subsidized rehabilitations	26.5
Total need, including publicly assisted rehabilitations	28.2

Source: Message from the President of the United States, Second Annual Report on National Housing Goals, 1970.

TABLE 2

HOUSING GOALS, FISCAL YEARS 1969–1978, AND ACTUAL OR ESTIMATED PRODUCTION, FISCAL YEARS, 1969–1972
(PROJECTIONS ARE IN THOUSANDS AND ACTUAL UNITS ARE ROUNDED TO THOUSANDS)

Fiscal year	Total production	Subsidized units			Unsubsidized units		
		Total	New Starts	Rehabil- itations	Total	New Starts	Mobile home shipments
Total ten-year goal	26,000	6,000	5,000	1,000	20,000	16,000	4,000
1969 Goal	2,001	198	155	43	1,803	1,440	363
Actual	1,997	192	163	29	1,806	1,437	369
1970 Goal	1,850	310	260	50	1,540	1,090	450
Actual [a]	1,792	335	302	33	1,457	1,056	401
1971 Previous goal [b]	2,040	505	445	60	1,535	1,060	475
Low estimate	2,070	530	480	50	1,540	1,120	420
High estimate	2,120	—	—	—	1,590	1,170	—
1972 Previous goal [b]	2,330	650	575	75	1,680	1,230	450
Low estimate	2,295	695	620	75	1,600	1,180	420
High estimate	2,765	—	—	—	2,070	1,650	—
1973	2,650	695	595	100	1,955	1,505	450
1974	2,930	730	600	130	2,200	1,800	400
1975	3,085	730	595	135	2,355	1,955	400
1976	3,060	730	595	135	2,330	1,980	350
1977	3,060	730	595	135	2,330	1,980	350
1978	2,994	722	585	137	2,272	1,960	312

[a] Preliminary.

[b] From Second Annual Report on National Housing Goals, 1970.

Source: Third Annual Report on National Housing Goals, 1971.

TABLE 3

SUBSIDIZED HOUSING PRODUCTION BY TYPE OF STRUCTURE AND BY PROGRAM, FISCAL YEARS 1969–1972
(NUMBERS IN THOUSANDS)

Fiscal Year			1–4 Family units			Multifamily units			
		Total	Total	HUD	USDA programs	Total	Low-rent public housing	HUD privately owned	USDA programs
1969	Total	192	48	15	33	144	70	71	3
	New starts	163	32	8	24	131	64	65	2
	Rehabilitations	29	17	7	10	12	6	6	[a]
1970	Total	335	127	79	48	208	97	108	3
	New starts	302	107	69	38	195	90	102	3
	Rehabilitations	33	19	9	10	13	7	6	[a]
1971 (EST.)	Total	532	264	174	90	268	100	163	5
	New starts	481	234	160	74	247	94	148	5
	Rehabilitations	52	30	14	16	21	6	15	[a]
1972 (EST.)	Total	696	327	231	96	369	95	269	5
	New starts	622	288	207	82	334	90	239	5
	Rehabilitations	73	38	24	14	35	5	29	[a]

[a] Less than 500.

Note: These data are also available by calendar year in the Third Annual Report on National Housing Goals.

Source: Third Annual Report on National Housing Goals, 1971.

B. HOUSING CHARACTERISTICS

TABLE 4
GENERAL HOUSING CHARACTERISTICS: 1970 AND 1960

Item	1970	1960
All housing units	68,627,366	58,326,357
All year-round housing units	67,607,842	56,583,892
Vacant-seasonal and migratory	1,019,524	1,742,465
Population in housing units	197,353,275	175,263,469
Per occupied unit	3.1	3.3
Owner	NA	3.4
Rental	NA	3.1
Tenure, race, vacancy status		
Owner occupied	39,862,346	32,796,720
White	36,945,977	30,823,194
Negro	2,578,083	} 1,973,526
Other	338,286	
Renter occupied	23,554,976	20,227,155
White	19,526,946	17,056,622
Negro	3,626,826	} 3,170,533
Other	401,204	
Vacant Year-round	4,190,520	3,560,017
For sale only	475,842	521,780
For rent only	1,650,055	1,453,046
Other vacant	2,064,623	1,585,191
Median number of rooms	5.0	4.9
Units in structures		
1 unit	46,900,548	43,758,556
2 units or more	18,859,968	13,789,663
Mobile homes or trailers	1,847,326	766,565
Plumbing facilities		
With all plumbing facilities		48,537,001
All year-round units	62,930,316	NA
All occupied units	59,634,023	NA
1.01 or more persons per room	4,467,107	NA
Negro occupied units	5,154,598	NA
1.01 or more persons per room	916,315	NA
Lacking some or all plumbing facilities		9,777,783
All year-round units	4,677,526	NA
All occupied units	3,783,299	NA
Negro occupied units	1,050,311	NA
All occupied units	63,417,322	53,023,875
Median number of persons per unit	2.7	3.0
Persons per room		
1.00 or less	58,200,445	46,910,402
1.01 to 1.50	3,806,272	4,210,550
1.51 or more	1,410,605	1,902,923
Value		
Specified owner occupied	31,867,883	26,171,774
Less than $5,000	1,935,558	3,181,622
$5,000 to $9,999	4,964,570	6,746,549
$10,000 to $14,999	6,398,130	7,632,176
$15,000 to $19,999	6,430,245	4,723,113
$20,000 to $24,999	4,670,003	1,899,591
$25,000 to $34,999	4,431,780	1,227,219
$35,000 to $49,999	2,042,545	} 761,504
$50,000 or more	995,052	
Median	$17,000	$11,900
Contract rent		
Specified renter occupied	22,325,029	19,293,718
Less than $40	1,873,975	4,401,144
$40 to $59	2,923,367	5,052,206
$60 to $79	4,094,842	4,441,170
$80 to $99	3,298,439	2,133,938
$100 to $119	2,518,813	} 1,509,414
$120 to $149	3,022,343	
$150 to $199	2,271,021	} 370,052
$200 or more	995,491	
No cash rent	1,326,738	1,385,794
Median	$90	$58

Source: Dept. of Commerce, Bureau of the Census, **1960 Census of Housing** and **1970 Census of Housing**, Advance Report.

TABLE 5

MONTHLY COST OF SHELTER IN THREE LIVING STANDARDS FOR A FOUR
PERSON URBAN FAMILY: SPRING 1969

Living Standard	Homeowner shelter expense		Renter shelter expense	
	Amount	As percent of total budget	Amount	As percent of total budget
Total				
Lower [a]	—	—	$ 89	16.3%
Intermediate	$171	19.9%	115	14.6
Higher	214	17.5	180	15.3
Metropolitan areas				
Lower [a]	—	—	91	16.4
Intermediate	177	20.3	118	14.8
Higher	223	17.7	192	15.8
Nonmetropolitan areas				
Lower [a]	—	—	81	15.7
Intermediate	141	18.3	98	13.7
Higher	176	16.4	125	12.5

[a] The living arrangement in the lower standard is limited to rental housing only.

Notes:

Family consists of employed husband, age 38; a wife not employed outside the home; and two children, a girl age 8 and boy of 13.

3 living standards—In 1967, the Bureau of Labor Statistics began to estimate budgetary costs on the basis of three standards of living instead of just one. The original moderate living standard represented the estimated cost required to maintain the family at a level of adequate living to satisfy prevailing standards of what was necessary for health efficiency, nurture of children, and participation in community activities. Now two more cost estimates represent the costs of maintaining the family at living standards higher and lower than the moderate.

Homeowner shelter expenses includes average annual mortgage interest and principal payments, taxes, insurance, fuel, utilities, and repair and maintenance costs.

Renter shelter expense includes contract rent plus estimated costs of fuel and utilities where these are not part of the rent, and insurance on household contents.

Source: Dept. of Labor, Bureau of Labor Statistics, Three Budgets for an Urban Family of Four Persons, Spring 1969, News Release, December 1970.

C. THE ECONOMICS OF SLUMLORDISM

THE TENEMENT LANDLORD

George Sternlieb.
pp. 76–82, 88–89, 93–96 (1966).

SLUM OPERATIONS AND PROFITABILITY

How profitable is the operation of slum tenements? What kinds of rates of return can be expected in this type of property? What are the risk factors, such as vacancies and housing code enforcement, which shape the landlord's attitude? Are rents collected personally, or by intermediaries?

Operating Ratios of Slum Properties

There is considerable difficulty in securing reasonably reliable expense data for slum tenements. Previous efforts have been made using income tax returns as a source of information on repairs, maintenance, and profitability. These returns, when analyzed over a period of years, frequently indicate arithmetic errors and substantial misstatements. Data gathered by the New York State Temporary State Housing Commission in the course of the Upper West Side Renewal Project would seem to indicate total operating expenses before depreciation and debt service of somewhere between 50 percent and 60 percent. (See Exhibit 4–1.)

EXHIBIT 4–1

EXPENSE ITEMS AS A PERCENT OF GROSS INCOME *
(MEDIANS)

	Apartment Buildings Owned by		Single-Room-Occupancy Buildings
	Institutions	Others	
Real estate taxes	17.5	18.0	16.3
Utilities	3.2	3.3	3.9
Fuel	7.8	6.3	5.3
Insurance	3.1	2.4	2.1
Repairs and painting	11.2	7.6	7.4
Wages	11.2	8.4	11.6
Other	6.8	6.0	5.5
Total operating expense	60.9	52.1	52.0

* Data for estimates are based on 126 usable accounts from records of the City Tax Department between 1954 and 1956.
Source: N. Y. S. Temporary State Housing Rent Commission, Prospects for Rehabilitation, p. 89.

In a somewhat similar study of the West Side urban renewal area of New York City by Chester Rapkin, the estimate of the ratio of net operation income to gross is cited as "somewhere in the vicinity of 40 percent to 50 percent on the average—a proportion that compares favorably with return on other rental property in New York City." [2]

EXHIBIT 4–2

CONSOLIDATED OPERATING STATEMENT FOR OLD-LAW TENEMENTS (WALK-UPS)
BY QUALITY OF STRUCTURE AND MAINTENANCE AND INCOME

	Good-Condition and Well-Maintained Percent of Gross	Poor-Condition and Poorly-Maintained Percent of Gross
Real estate taxes	20.8	15.0
Utilities	3.5	5.1
Fuel	11.0	11.4
Insurance	4.0	7.3
Repairs and painting	10.6	12.6
Wages	5.3	6.4
Other	6.6	6.0
Total oper. expense	61.8	63.8
Net oper. income	38.2	36.2
Gross income	100.0	100.0

Source: Rapkin, The Real Estate Market in an Urban Renewal Area, p. 72.

As Exhibit 4–2 indicates, real estate taxes are the number one expense of good-condition and poor-condition buildings. Net operating income is actually lower for poor-condition and poorly-maintained parcels than for those which are in good condition and are well maintained. (The validity of data presented in this table is dependent upon the honesty of the landlords in compiling it, and the adjustments made by the researcher.)

For the purposes of this study, the researchers were fortunate enough to have available to them the complete records of a major tenement management company. Using the service of a firm of certified public accountants, the one hundred fifty parcels for which data of varying completeness was available were reduced to thirty-two parcels, all within the study areas and possessing complete documentation. Expense analyses were then developed for these parcels as shown in

[2] Chester Rapkin, The Real Estate Market in an Urban Renewal Area (N.Y.C. Planning Commission, 1959), p. 65.

Exhibit 4–3. The results agree closely with the experience reported in New York. The sum of the medians of expenditure, for example, is 61 percent of gross income. Taxes are 21 percent of gross, closely followed by repairs and maintenance at 18.15 percent. The management figure shown here includes 7 percent for management fees.

There is a considerable range of variation in total expense percentages. As will be noted later in more detail, this range of variation is indicative of the risk factors which surround the operating of slum properties. In turn, they obviously limit the number of people interested in going into high risk areas and, as a complement of this, increase the rate of return required.[3]

Trends

Have these expense ratios increased over the last several years? There seems to be substantial evidence that this has been the case.

Leo Grebler, in his study, Real Estate Investment Experience, (Columbia University Press, 1955) has developed data for walk-up apartments from the 1920–24 period through 1945–49. These data would indicate that net income as a percentage of gross income has dropped by one-half from 59 percent to 28 percent. The Journal of Property Management in a 1964 study of walk-ups of twelve to twenty-five units which were built before 1920, indicated that the average ratio of expenses to gross rent collections was around 60 percent, and that this per-

centage has increased sharply because of static gross income in the face of increasing costs.

EXHIBIT 4–3

OPERATING RATIOS OF 32 SLUM PROPERTIES

	Percent Expense to Income	
Category	Median	Interquartile Range
Management	13.33	9.82–16.13
Utilities	5.73	3.79–11.30
Services and fees	2.81	1.72– 4.77
Repairs and maintenance ..	18.15	12.62–28.27
Taxes	21.02	16.31–33.12
Sum of the medians	61.04	

Expense Breakdown

Management	Utilities
1. Superintendent	5. Electricity
2. Insurance	6. Water
3. Management (7% usually)	7. Fuel
4. Plans for bath	

Service and Fees

8. Advertising
9. Accounting
10. Legal
11. Constable

12. { Patent security / Accident / Miscellaneous }

13. Services
14. Rental fee
15. Returned security
16. Returned deposit
17. Fire permit
18. Inspection fees

Repairs and Maintenance

19. Exterminator
20. Central maintenance
21. Hardware supplies
22. Painting
23. Plumbing—allowance boiler
24. Cleaning
25. Other repairs
26. Glass
27. Electric fixtures
28. Hall lights
29. Stove—gas heater
30. Garbage cans
31. Ceiling plastering

Return on Investment

The profitability of investment in slum properties is as much a function of financial leverage as the percentage of return on gross income. In the next chapter tenement trading and financing are discussed in more detail, but it is worthwhile noticing here, for example, that if a tenement was purchased for four times its gross rent roll, a fairly generous multiplier, the yield before depreciation and financing charges based on the data presented would be 10 percent, i. e. 40 percent of 25 percent. If, instead of paying cash, the investor were able to secure a mortgage for 50 percent of the purchase price at a 6 percent interest figure, the yield would go up to 14 percent on his cash investment. Rapkin estimates

---

[3] The expenses indicated by this analysis are roughly corroborated by a study by Louis Winnick, Rental Housing * * *, p. 279, which presents the distribution of gross rent income for 201 FHA 608 projects for areas as of 1955. For New York walk-ups, for example, operating costs, plus real estate taxes, were 51.1%. This did not include any officers' salaries or management costs. If the 7% figure which has been indicated in this operating ratio data was included, it would increase the total to 58.1%.

that old-law tenements return 9.3 percent on the total consideration in the West Side Urban Renewal Project. Brownstones return an estimated 10.7 percent and all types of elevator apartments combined return 9.3 percent.

Sporn, conducting a study of one hundred twenty-three parcels in Milwaukee, showed an average rate of return on *equity* of 19.8 percent. (This does not take into account the owners' activity and/or wages in regard to personal labor and collections, etc.)

The actual return on investment figures obviously varies enormously, depending in substantial measure on the financing available. An example is the history of Parcel 553 in our study area, a six-family, three-story apartment in Area 3B. This was sold in October, 1962 for $16,500, with a savings and loan association taking back a $13,500 mortgage. In August, 1964 the mortgage was refinanced with another savings and loan association with the understanding that central heating equipment would be installed. This new mortgage was for $20,000. The owner made the improvements but the cost of central heat was less than the increment in the new financing and, therefore, his initial cash investment of $3,000 was essentially returned to him. The apartments are six-room flats, and rents now are between $90 and $100 per month for a gross rent roll of $6,000 per year, with interest charges of $1,200 and taxes of $1,100. Assuming all other costs including heat probably run no more than $1,000, the return is about $2,700 per year before depreciation and amortization on essentially no cash investment. (In justice to the owner, it should be pointed out that this is a very well-maintained and well-run parcel. The low expense figures which have been imputed are a function of the modernization and basic care with which the parcel has been handled.)

Cash-Flow Accounting

In appraising return on real estate investments, the basic consideration used by nearly all the landlords in this study were those of *cash flow*. Amortization, therefore, is considered an expense while depreciation charges are not. Given the relatively short-term nature of financing available for tenement purchase and improvements, the effects of this type of accounting on the rates of return demanded is all too clear.

Typical Returns on Value

To determine the return on the total value of tenement parcels required some method of assessing the value. In Exhibit 4–4, based on the thirty-two parcels examined in Exhibit 4–3, two approaches to this problem are presented. The first uses the assessment value which is nominally 100 percent; the second uses a multiplier of four times gross income, which in terms of the current market is undoubtedly high.

On the former base the thirty-two parcels, which were examined earlier, yield an average return of 12.04 percent and a median of 8.65 percent; on the latter basis the equivalent figures are 8.53 percent and 7.25 percent. Again it should be noted that there is a wide range within the interquartile figure.

* * *

Rent Collection Procedure

To give some feeling for the flavor of the rent collection procedure, it is worthwhile to describe the one used by the largest single tenement landlord in this study— an owner of more than two hundred tenement parcels in Newark.

All rents are due monthly at the landlord's office. If they are not paid by the tenth of the month, a note goes to the tenant. A dispossession notice is sent out on the twenty-seventh of the month. According to this owner, at least 75 percent of their rents are paid by check or

EXHIBIT 4–4

RETURN ON TOTAL PRICE OF THIRTY-TWO SLUM TENEMENTS

| | VALUE FIGURE | | CONTRIBUTION TO FINANCING AS A PERCENT OF VALUE | |
| | | | Contrib. Fin. | Contrib. Fin. |
Parcel No.	Tax Figure × 100/6.6	4 × Gross Income	Tax Figure × 100/6.6	4 × Gross Income
A1	$18,500.00	$20,872.00	11.4%	10.1%
2	20,606.00	12,952.00	3.0	4.8
3	20,394.00	15,172.00	10.6	14.3
4	2,606.00	11,220.00	54.5	12.7
5	19,606.00	24,156.00	8.6	7.0
6	16,394.00	16,176.00	8.7	8.8
7	11,697.00	18,324.00	47.2	30.1
8	14,697.00	15,628.00	8.0	7.5
9	14,803.00	19,460.00	—	—
10	10,697.00	17,680.00	—	—
11	13,803.00	24,552.00	12.1	6.8
12	14,000.00	19,760.00	7.7	5.4
13	33,606.00	62,324.00	10.8	5.8
14	28,000.00	16,612.00	5.4	9.1
15	28,000.00	9,188.00	—	—
16	17,394.00	12,632.00	10.2	14.1
17	10,394.00	18,780.00	17.6	9.7
18	10,803.00	19,212.00	4.0	2.3
19	5,500.00	8,900.00	4.6	2.8
20	14,803.00	23,544.00	6.6	4.1
21	17,303.00	18,572.00	10.3	9.6
22	17,394.00	19,760.00	4.7	4.1
23	6,500.00	9,556.00	22.8	15.5
24	18,000.00	12,820.00	5.5	7.7
25	12,106.00	16,204.00	14.0	10.4
26	14,394.00	17,960.00	12.5	10.0
27	18,894.00	15,060.00	—	—
28	14,500.00	20,120.00	8.1	5.8
29	14,303.00	17,948.00	7.0	5.6
30	20,394.00	24,668.00	6.1	5.1
31	15,000.00	18,840.00	6.1	4.8
32	13,606.00	24,732.00	9.0	4.9
Average	15,897.00	18,856.00	12.04	8.53
Interquartile Range			6.10–11.75	5.00–10.05
Median			8.65	7.25

money order and are received in the office. The other 25 percent are paid in person. In the course of an hour while the interviewer was in the office, at least eight people came in to pay the rent. Many of the tenants pay weekly even though the rents are ostensibly on a monthly basis. By this means they essentially budget their rent payments. Despite the brisk pace of warning and eviction notices, the landlord still finds that he gets stuck with a two-month-run bill on evictions, because of the time it takes for court proceedings to result in an official eviction notice.

In sum then, tenement parcels are returning, before debt service and depreciation, approximately 40 percent of the gross rentals received by the landlord. The actual return on investment in terms of the overall parcel value is clearly in the neighborhood of 10 to 12 percent. The range of variation both in expenses and in net return is considerable. A major factor affecting this is the variation of gross income as a function of the vacancy rates. It is the vacancy rate which determines a substantial part of the upward flexibility of the rent structure as well as the extent of gross rental. Let us examine this very significant function in detail.

Vacancy Rates

The basic fact of tenement ownership in hard-core Newark is that vacancy rates are very high. In 1950 only 0.7 percent of Newark's nonseasonal, sound-condition dwelling units were vacant. By 1960 this had increased to 4.1 percent; and in the author's opinion has substantially increased since then. The vacancy factor is concentrated in the hard-core slums.

The dynamics of this change are clear-cut. In the MPC attitude study cited earlier, Central Ward residents (roughly co-terminous with Area I) indicated the most substantial pattern of forecasted intent to move out. At the time the area was cited in the study as having a vacancy rate of 4 percent, i. e. four out of every one hundred contacts of the survey interviewers proved to be empty dwelling units. Even at this time the vacancy rate in the Central Ward was double the overall figure for the entire city.

* * *

The Effect of High Vacancy Rates

The effect of high vacancy rates is much more complex than might be thought at first glance. As yet, for example, they have rarely resulted in rent *reductions.* As Grebler [9] pointed out, a substantial exposure to high vacancy rates over time is required before the market adjusts price to meet the decreased demand. On the other hand, the high vacancy rate certainly inhibits rent increases. The fear of raising rents in a weak market is compounded of two elements; the possibility of ending up with substantial vacancies, and, perhaps even more significantly, the fear that in order to secure tenants at the

increased rates the landlord must take in lower categories of tenantry.

One Negro owner stated: "The only man who can afford the increased rates around here would be the man without roots, a drifter, and they're no good." *The availability of housing for Negroes in better areas of Newark, as well as in the surrounding suburbs, limits the number of people with capacity and willingness to pay high rents in the slum areas. The willingness of tenement owners to make improvements, threfore, is substantially inhibited by the feeling that there would be limited demand for better, i. e. higher rent, apartments.* The controller of a small hospital who owns two parcels in our sample area typified the attitude when he claimed:

Any increase in rents immediately results in vacancies even with the improvements; that's why the tenants are willing to stay in cold-water flats. This type of tenant cannot afford the increase in rents to offset taxes for improvements. The financial economy of the people don't permit it. They're big families with little or no employment.

The fear of losing the tenants one knows for the tenants one doesn't know, upon raising rents, also serves as an inhibitor. The attitude of a fifty-nine-year-old Portugese resident-owner and construction worker was representative of a substantial number of landlords. He said, "I couldn't raise the rents because I would get bad tenants, and that's the worst thing you can have." Faced with reassessment on this particular parcel and a lid on rents, this owner maintains the place but is very loath to put money into it.

Vandalism

In the face of a weak market, the fear of vacancies is a compound not only of the fear of loss of rent, but also, and perhaps equally, the fear of vandalism that goes

[9] Leo Grebler, Experience in Urban Real Estate Investment (N.Y.: Columbia University, 1955), pp. 182–183.

with vacancy. A major real estate holder said:

> Some tenants might appreciate certain improvements and, therefore, might pay some additional rents, whereas other tenants wouldn't care or couldn't pay more, and as a result some might move out. I wouldn't want to take the chance of vacancy. Vacancies lead to vandalism and looting. It's better business to be fully rented at the expense of getting top dollar.

Subsequent chapters will examine the effect of the poor rental market as an inhibitor of improvements despite tax and/or mortgage easements. It should be noted here, however, that the landlord's fear of substantial vacancies is a very real one. A fairly typical process is for the landlord of a six-family house to lose two or three tenants at once. Either he rents to undesirable tenants and thus drives out the balance of his tenantry, or he runs the risk of a group of delinquents moving into one of the vacant apartments by breaking through a window or by kicking down a door and proceeding to vandalize the premises. It is not uncommon to find that bathroom fixtures and piping are removed to be sold to junk dealers. Lighting fixtures and other elements of value are often removed also. The end result frequently is a vacant parcel with little residual value.

An example in point is a parcel currently assessed at $1,600 for land and $7,000 for building in the hard-core area. The classic pattern of several tenants moving out at once developed. Vandals got into one of the empty apartments and the remaining tenants then moved out. The building was boarded up and shortly thereafter was gutted by the neighborhood teenagers. It was sold in 1963 for $4,500, half its prior cost. This sale was accomplished only by means of a purchase money mortgage of $4,000.

The prevalence of vacant parcels, which was noted in an earlier chapter, has an enormously deleterious effect on surrounding land values as well as upon the overall neighborhood as a place in which to live, and these abandonments do not disappear from the scene. The reasons for this longevity of vacant parcels are indicated in Grebler's study of housing market behavior.

> In the removal of slums the action of market forces alone appears to be related not so much to physical or economic depreciation, as to alternative uses for the land, particularly the rate of which nonresidential can replace residential land use. This rate is dependent upon the speed and locational pattern of urban growth.

These observations of Grebler, based upon his study of a fifty-year period in the life of slums in New York's Lower East Side, indicate that unless the basic areas of slums in Newark regain some of their lost vitality, these blotches will die slowly at best. The land, with no improvement upon it, has literally no use and no value. Certainly, high tax rates levy a penalty against the owners of such unproductive shells, but this is relatively minor compared with the realization of loss which would accompany the shell's removal. As noted in Chapter 2, municipal policy enforcement of those sections of the housing code which call for demolition of vacant parcels is far from rigorous.

Risk and Return

It is the risk factor, typified by the vacant parcel, which raises the required threshold of return on investment in slum properties. In a sense, the very weakness of the market has increased the rewards which potential buyers of slum tenements require in return for their investment. The risks also, as shall be seen again and again in the following chapters, limit the *kind* of investor who is attracted to slum tenements. Both of these limitations are increased by the fear of housing inspection. One observer put it very aptly:

Landlords may suddenly be confronted with enthusiastic, if often short-lived, campaigns to enforce long dormant occupancy in building codes. Such campaigns are not inherently undesirable, nor is the rental market unable to adjust to consistent standards of code enforcement. But sporadic drives, together with the wide gulf that exists between the standard recited in statutory codes and actual enforcement, create many uncertainties; uncertainty is a notoriously uncongenial climate for investors.

The high rate of current return demanded by investors in slum tenements can be summarized as a compound of the fear of costly code crackdowns; the basic weakness of the market, both in terms of rental increases and securing full tenancy; the risk of outright loss through the complete abandonment of a parcel; and in substantial part, the pejoratives which society heaps upon the "slum lord." All of these combine to shape the nature of the trading market in slum tenements— the buying and selling, the maintenance and will to rehabilitate, the very charac-

teristics of the landlords who become involved in tenements—all are closely shaped and defined by the realities of the market.

In sum, high vacancy rates have been looked forward to by urban planners who have felt strongly that the major inhibitor to appropriate code enforcement and rehabilitation efforts was the lack of housing for those displaced. While this potential is now being made available through the actions of the market, the landlord's will and desire to upgrade his parcels, with some exceptions discussed, are being eroded by the relative lack of profitability of those parcels. Faced with a weak market, the entrepreneur can do one of three things:

1. Sell out, or

2. Do as little as possible in terms of new investment and wait for "better times," or

3. Upgrade his holdings so as to attract either higher paying or a more stable tenantry.

Which shall the landlord choose?

D. LOW–RENT PUBLIC HOUSING

TABLE 6

LOW-RENT PUBLIC HOUSING: SUMMARY OF CHARACTERISTICS OF FAMILIES WHO MOVED IN DURING THE SIX MONTHS ENDED MARCH 31, 1970, BY RACE

Characteristics	All families [a]	White	Negro and other
Number moving in	89,899	44,432	44,977
Percent	100	100	100
Receiving assistance or benefits, total	69	72	66
Assistance with or without benefits	43	32	55
Benefits only	25	40	11
Not receiving assistance or benefits	31	28	34
Veterans and servicemen	17	22	12
No service connection	76	69	83
Not known	7	10	5
Age of head of family			
Under 25	23	17	29
25–34	23	17	29
35–44	12	9	15
45–54	7	6	8
55–64	9	10	7
65 and over	26	41	11
Elderly families as percent of total	36	52	19
Number of minors			
None	38	56	20
One or two	32	25	39
Three or four	19	14	24
Five or six	8	5	11
Seven or more	3	1	5
Mean number of minors	1.78	1.15	2.42
Number of persons			
One	26	39	12
Two	21	23	20
Three or four	30	24	36
Five or six	15	10	20
Seven or eight	6	3	8
Nine or more	2	1	4
Mean number of persons	3.16	2.54	3.78
Gross rent			
Under $20.00	1	*	1
$20.00–29.99	8	8	8
30.00–39.99	19	23	14
40.00–49.99	20	24	15
50.00–59.99	20	19	20
60.00–69.99	14	12	16
70.00 and over	19	14	25
Median gross rent			
All families	$50.00	$46.00	$55.00
Elderly families	$41.00	$40.00	$45.00
Mean gross rent			
All families	$52.43	$49.38	$55.57
Elderly families	$43.85	$42.53	$47.60
Median income			
All families	$2,501	$2,265	$2,792
Elderly families	$1,755	$1,741	$1,798

[a] Includes families for whom data on race are not available.

* Less than 0.5 percent.

SECTION 2. THE CLIENT SEEKS YOUR ADVICE

A. LANDLORD FAILS TO MAINTAIN "FIT" SHELTER

THE LANDLORD AND THE TENANT AT COMMON LAW: A LAW FOR LANDLORDS

In the absence of statute or agreement, landlords owe their tenants very few duties. The common law does, of course, imply a covenant for quiet enjoyment in every rental agreement, except when such covenant contradicts some express term of the lease. To prove a breach of the covenant for quiet enjoyment, the tenant must establish (a) a *substantial* interference with his use of the demised premises; and (b) the fact that this interference has been caused by the lessor, or by someone having title paramount to that of the lessor, or by someone who derived authority for his acts from the lessor.

If the tenant proves a breach, he recovers his damages and, if sued for the rent may plead "constructive eviction," provided he has vacated the premises; this exonerates him from further leasehold duties. If the landlord has *himself* interfered with the tenant's use by evicting the tenant physically from part of the premises (partial actual eviction), courts have let the tenant occupy the remaining portion rent free until the interference ends. Smith v. McEnany, 170 Mass. 26, 48 N.E. 781 (1897). The rationale: a wrong doer may not apportion his own wrong.

Partial actual eviction occurs rarely, and constructive eviction (rescission) is not usually a very potent weapon. To begin with, the tenant often faces a Hobson's choice: either endure the interference or move into other quarters not as desirable as those left behind—a situation that cannot change while decent housing for the poor remains desperately short. Moreover, before the tenant can establish that his quiet enjoyment has been disrupted, he must first show that the landlord is legally required to halt the interference. To illustrate: tenant complains of a drunken, noisy upstairs neighbor. Courts have said that landlord has no duty to stop the disturbance; therefore, landlord has not himself interfered with tenant's enjoyment. (One might argue that any occupant who is regularly allowed to behave disruptively derives authority for his acts from the landlord.) To give a second—and more common—illustration: tenant complains that his apartment is rat infested. At common law, courts have held that the landlord need not warrant that the premises are habitable. In the absence of *this* antecedent duty, tenant can not prove that landlord's inaction has caused a substantial interference with his enjoyment. Similarly, the common law has exacted no duty from the landlord that he repair and maintain the premises; therefore unheated quarters resulting from a landlord's refusal to fix a broken boiler do not *legally* deny the tenant quiet enjoyment. Finally, even where landlord has expressly agreed to maintain the premises, many courts have advanced the principle of independent covenants, that is, the landlord's duty to repair is independent from the tenant's duty to pay rent. This has meant that the tenant may not treat the breach of a repair covenant as equivalent to a breach of the covenant of quiet enjoyment permitting tenant to vacate the premises and rescind the lease if his use has been substantially impaired. Instead the tenant has had to look to his rights in damages.

With the advent of housing codes, landlord's duties for the maintenance of safe, fit, and healthful premises have enlarged greatly. The pages that follow describe housing codes and discuss the methods and difficulties of enforcement. Following this discussion, we will consider how the "common law" of landlord and tenant has recently begun to respond to the many duties that housing codes now impose upon landlords.

HOUSING CODE ENFORCEMENT: SANCTIONS AND REMEDIES *

Judah Gribetz and Frank P. Grad.

66 Colum.L.Rev. 1254 (1966).

* * *

The beginning of modern code enforcement in America may be placed at the turn of the century, with the enactment in 1901 of the Tenement House Act for New York City. Thus, housing codes and code enforcement for the benefit of the inhabitants are of very recent origin, when compared, for instance, with the common law antiquities of the law of landlord and tenant. Prior to our century, to be sure, there had been building codes and other laws relating to dwellings, but their major concern had been the protection of the city from conflagration and building collapse. Regulations to protect the tenants themselves were scant, and were generally limited to provisions aimed at preventing nuisances and limiting the spread of communicable disease. The need for housing codes to protect the inhabitants themselves is a fairly recent phenomenon of the growth of cities.

A few large eastern cities passed housing codes near the turn of the century. Prior to 1954 there had been some 56 housing codes enacted in the entire country. In 1954, in an effort to safeguard federal funds spent on local redevelopment programs which could not succeed

---

* Excerpts from this article are interspersed throughout this section. It will be hereinafter designated as "Housing Code Enforcement—Grad and Gribetz."

---

in providing adequate housing without a related community-wide effort, Congress enacted the "workable program requirement" requiring the community to develop a "workable program * * * to eliminate and prevent the development or spread of slums and urban blight." Certification of a workable program by the HHFA Administrator was made a statutory condition to urban renewal loan and capital grant assistance, public housing aid, and FHA mortgage insurance. Housing Act of 1954, § 303, 68 Stat. 623, as amended, 42 U.S.C.A. § 1451 (c) (Supp. I, 1965). The Administrator prescribed several requirements for a workable program, including the adoption of local housing codes and preparation of plans for their enforcement. The 1964 Housing Act amendments directed the Administrator to make the workable program as effective as possible and also directed that, beginning in 1967, he could not certify or recertify a workable program unless the locality has had in effect a housing code for at least 6 months and the Administrator was satisfied that it is carrying out an effective program of enforcement. As a result of the workable program requirement, more than 1,000 communities have enacted housing codes since 1954.

* * *

HOUSING CODES AND THEIR ENFORCEMENT

Legislative Drafting Research Fund of Columbia University (Oct. 1966).

The essential contents (though not the standards) of housing codes * * * have remained unchanged since the Model Tenement House Act developed by Veiller, which formed the basis for the New York Tenement House Law enacted in 1901. Although housing codes may regulate other, additional matters, their core content consists of 1) requirements for proper maintenance, including cleanliness and repair; 2) requirements for lighting and ventilation; 3) requirements for fire safety; 4) requirements for equipment and facilities, including sanitary facilities, water supply, sewerage and drainage, heating and electrical equipment; and 5) requirements respecting minimum space and maximum occupancy. Finally, housing codes contain provisions for administration and enforcement, including a delineation of responsibilities for compliance by the owner and by the occupant.

A review of standards in existing housing codes indicates broad similarities in the codes of different municipalities, with most, if not all, of the newer codes (adopted after the 1954 workable program requirement came into being) following one of four or five model housing ordinances to a considerable extent. The Model Codes, in turn, show considerable similarity among themselves. The relatively few housing codes that preceded the 1954 workable program requirement were generally adopted in the early years of this century, and generally appear to be adaptations—with updating amendments—of Veiller's Model Tenement House Act or of its New York counterpart.

LEGAL REMEDIES FOR HOUSING CODE VIOLATIONS *

Frank P. Grad.
(Prepared for the National Commission on Urban Problems. Research Report No. 14, 1968) pp. 7–8.

Housing Codes as Function of State and Local Lawmaking

Before undertaking a general examination of the code enforcement process, it may be well to consider what body of

* Excerpts from this article are interspersed throughout this section. It will be hereinafter designated as "Legal Remedies for Housing Code Violations—Grad."

of law is included under the term "housing code." The most common usage of the term covers the large mass of municipal ordinances, entitled "housing code," "housing maintenance code," "residential property maintenance code," or some other, similarly descriptive term. Municipal housing codes are ordinances adopted by a municipality, either by special authorization or enabling legislation enacted by the state legislature, or pursuant to the municipality's general powers under its charter or under appropriate local home-rule provisions. The municipal housing codes, however, are only one source of relevant legislation, for in many instances the state enabling legislation itself will contain important provisions. Most commonly, the enabling legislation provides for the manner in which municipal housing codes may be enforced—and hence, these state law provisions assume particular significance for the enforcement process. A number of states— Connecticut, Iowa, Massachusetts, Michigan, Minnesota, New Jersey and Pennsylvania—have enacted state housing codes, one of them truly applicable to the entire state, others applicable only to certain cities, or to municipalities falling into a particular classification. A number of other states, such as California and New York, have extensive state housing legislation, but permit municipalities to adopt codes that are not inconsistent with the state law and that may be more stringent than the state code. There are, moreover, in all states general provisions, usually procedural, but sometimes substantive in nature, relating to the criminal process and to other enforcement sanctions, that are relevant to, and may affect housing code enforcement efforts. But apart from such general provisions, it is noteworthy that most of the newer code enforcement sanctions and remedies must be looked for in state legislation, rather than in the local housing codes themselves.

Most municipalities are authorized to prosecute violations of ordinances—including housing codes—as misdemeanors; frequently, too, municipalities may collect civil penalties for such breaches of their local laws. But that is where the authorization usually ends—and under the well-known "Dillon's Rule" municipal powers must be narrowly construed.[19] Hence, the power to use equitable remedies—including injunctions and receiverships—must be specially granted by state law, as was only recently emphasized by the invalidation of a municipally enacted receivership law.[20] So too, the power to make repairs and to impose the cost as a lien on the property would seem to require state legislation, particularly when a prior lien is involved that would affect rights under existing state law relating to mortgages and other liens on land. So, too, ownership, leasing, and conveyance of real property are matters of primary state jurisdiction, and the newly emerging field of private code enforcement through the so-called tenant rent strike remedies consequently rests on state law enactments, rather than on provisions in municipal housing codes or other municipal ordinances. When we discuss "housing code enforcement," therefore, and especially in the context of legal aspects of enforcement, the term "housing code" means considerably more than a particular municipal code. Realistically, it includes the entire body of state and local law that prescribes housing standards and that may be relied upon to provide the source of power or authority for enforcement sanctions and remedies. When we look toward the improvement of sanctions and remedies in code enforcement, moreover, it follows that we must generally look to state law, either to provide the remedy, or to enable the municipality to provide it, because the municipalities themselves generally lack the power to legislate effectively in the remedial field.

ADMINISTRATIVE CODE OF CITY OF NEW YORK

CHAPTER 26

TITLE D

HOUSING MAINTENANCE CODE

§ D26–1.01 *Short title.*—This title shall be known and may be cited as the "housing maintenance code."

ARTICLE 10

OBLIGATIONS OF OWNER AND TENANT; DUTY TO REPAIR

§ D26–10.01 *Duties of owner.*—a. The owner of a multiple dwelling shall keep the premises in good repair.

b. The owner of a multiple dwelling, in addition to the duty imposed upon him by subsection (a) of this section, shall be responsible for compliance with the requirements of this code, except insofar as responsibility for compliance is imposed upon the tenant alone. * * *

§ D26–10.03 *Duties of tenant.*—a. A tenant shall, in addition to complying with all provisions of this code and the multiple dwelling law applicable to him, be responsible for violations of this code to the extent that he has the power to prevent the occurrence of a violation. A tenant has the power to prevent the occurrence of a violation if:

(1) it is caused by his own wilful act or that of a member of his family or household, or a guest; or

(2) it is the result of his gross negligence, neglect or abuse, or the gross

---

19 The rule was first formulated by Justice Dillon in his opinion in City of Clinton v. Cedar Rapids & M. R. R. R., 24 Iowa 455 (1868).

20 City of St. Louis v. Golden Gate Corp., 421 S.W.2d 4 (Mo.1967).

negligence, neglect or abuse of a member of his family, or household or a guest. * * *

§ D26–10.07 *Owner's right of access.*—No tenant shall refuse to permit the owner, or his agent or employee, to enter his dwelling unit or other space under his control to make repairs or improvements required by this code or other law or to inspect such apartment or other space to determine compliance with this code or any other provision of law, if the right of entry is exercised at a reasonable time and in a reasonable manner. The department may by regulation restrict the time and manner of such inspections. * * *

ARTICLE 12
PAINTING

§ D26–12.01 *Painting of public parts and within dwellings.*—

b. In occupied dwelling units in a multiple dwelling, the owner shall:

(1) paint or cover the walls and ceilings with wallpaper or other acceptable wall covering; and

(2) repaint or re-cover the walls and ceilings with wallpaper or other acceptable wall covering every three years, and more often when required by contract or other provisions of law.

ARTICLE 13
EXTERMINATION AND RAT ERADICATION

§ D26–13.03 *Rodent and insect eradication; mandatory extermination.*—
a. The owner or occupant in control of a dwelling shall keep the premises free from rodents, and from infestations of insects and other pests, and from any condition conducive to rodent or insect and other pests life.

b. When any premises is subject to infestation by rodents or insects and other pests, the owner or occupant in control shall apply continuous eradication measures.

c. When the department makes the determination that any premises are infested by rodents, insects or other pests, it may order such eradication measures as the department deems necessary.

ARTICLE 15
WATER SUPPLY

§ D26–15.01 *Water supply to buildings.*—The owner of a dwelling shall provide and maintain a supply of pure and wholesome water sufficient in quantity and at sufficient pressure to keep all plumbing fixtures adequately supplied for their sanitary maintenance. Where water mains are available in the street, every dwelling shall be supplied with water from such mains. The owner shall keep the water free from connection to any unsafe water supply or from cross-connections to any drainage system.

ARTICLE 16
SEWERS AND DRAINAGE

§ D26–16.01 *Maintenance of sewer connections and plumbing fixtures.*—The owner of a dwelling shall properly maintain and keep in good repair the plumbing and drainage system, including water closets, toilets, sinks and other fixtures.

ARTICLE 17
HEAT AND HOT WATER

§ D26–17.01 *Central heat or electric or gas heating system; when required.*—Except as otherwise provided in this article, every multiple dwelling and every tenant-occupied one- or two-family dwelling shall be provided with heat from a central heating system constructed in accordance with the provisions of the building code and the regulations of the department. A system of gas or electric heating provided for each dwelling unit may, if approved by the department, be utilized in lieu of a central heating system if

(1) the system is lawfully in use on the effective date of this code; or

(2) the system is approved by the appropriate city agencies having jurisdiction and is installed in a structure or building erected, converted, substantially rehabilitated, or completely vacated, after the effective date of this code.

§ D26–17.03 *Minimum temperature to be maintained.*—During the period from October 1 through May 31, centrally-supplied heat, in any dwelling in which such heat is required to be provided, shall be furnished so as to maintain, in every portion of such dwelling used or occupied for living purposes:

(1) between the hours of six a. m. and ten p. m., a temperature of at least 68 degrees Fahrenheit whenever the outside temperature falls below 55 degrees; and

(2) between the hours of ten p. m. and six a. m., a temperature of at least 55 degrees Fahrenheit whenever the outside temperature falls below 40 degrees.

§ D26–17.07 *Supply of hot water; when required.*—Except as otherwise provided in this article, every bath, shower, washbasin and sink in any dwelling unit in a multiple dwelling or tenant-occupied one-family or two-family dwelling shall be supplied at all times between the hours of six a. m. and midnight with hot water at a constant minimum temperature of 120 degrees Fahrenheit from a central source of supply constructed in accordance with the provisions of the building code and the regulations of the department. Gas or electric water heaters may, if approved by the department, be utilized in lieu of a central source of supply of hot water if such heaters

(1) are lawfully in use on the effective date of this code; or

(2) are approved by the appropriate city agencies having jurisdiction and are installed in a structure or building erected, converted, substantially rehabilitated, or completely vacated after the effective date of this code.

SUBTITLE IV
ADMINISTRATION
ARTICLE 40
POWERS AND FUNCTIONS OF THE DEPARTMENT

§ D26–40.01 *Power to make regulations.*—The department shall have power to promulgate such regulations as it may consider necessary or convenient to interpret or carry out any of the provisions of this code.

§ D26–40.03 *Power to issue orders.*—a. The department shall have power to issue notices and orders to secure compliance with the requirements of this code, of the multiple dwelling law, and of other state and local laws that impose requirements on dwellings. * * *

ARTICLE 41
REGISTRATION

§ D26–41.01 *Registration; time to file.*—a. The owner of a dwelling required to register under this article shall register with the department in accordance with the provisions of this article.

b. A registration statement shall be filed:

(1) for every existing multiple dwelling. * * *

(2) prior to the issuance of a certificate of occupancy, for any multiple dwelling hereafter erected, or any dwelling or building hereafter altered or converted to a multiple dwelling.

(3) on or before July 1, 1970, for all one- and two-family dwellings whose owner does not reside within the city and thereafter not later than ten days after the owner of a one- or two-

family dwelling removes his residence from the city.

(4) within such time as provided in section D26–41.05, in the case of a change of ownership where registration is required under this article.

§ D26–41.03 *Registration statement; contents.*—a. The registration statement shall include the following information:

(1) An identification of the premises by block and lot number, and by the street numbers and names of all streets contiguous to the dwelling, or by such other description as will enable the department to locate the dwelling.

(2) An identification of the owner by name, residence and business address. If the owner is a corporation, the identification shall include the name and address of such corporation together with the names, residences and business addresses of the officers. * * *

(3) If the dwelling is a multiple dwelling, the name and address of a managing agent designated by the owner to be in control of and responsible for the maintenance and operation of such dwelling and to authorize, on behalf of the owner, the correction of any emergency conditions or the making of any emergency repairs for which the owner is responsible under the provisions of the multiple dwelling law or this code. * * *

(4) If the dwelling is a multiple dwelling, the number of a telephone within a radius of 50 miles of the city limits where an owner or officer, if the owner is a corporation, or the managing agent may reasonably be expected to be reached at all times.

(5) If the dwelling is a one- or two-family dwelling and the owner does not reside within the city, the name and address of a natural person who is over the age of twenty-one years and a resident of the city, designated by the owner to receive service of notices, orders or summonses issued by the department. * * *

§ D26–41.21 *Failure to register; penalties.*—a. A person who is required to file a statement of registration or an amendment of a statement of registration or any other statement required under this article and who fails to file as required may, whenever appropriate, be punished under the provisions of article 52 of this code, and he shall be subject to a civil penalty of not less than two hundred and fifty and not more than five hundred dollars, recoverable by the department by civil action in a court of appropriate jurisdiction.

b. An owner who is required to file a statement of registration under this article and who fails to file as required shall be denied the right to recover possession of the premises for non-payment of rent during the period of non-compliance, and shall, in the discretion of the court, suffer a stay of proceedings to recover rents, during such period. In any action to recover possession under section 711 of the real property actions and proceedings law, the owner shall set forth his registration number issued by the department, and shall allege that he has filed a statement of registration and shall annex a copy of the receipt of such registration to his petition.

SUBTITLE V
LEGAL REMEDIES AND ENFORCEMENT
ARTICLE 50
ENFORCEMENT ACTIONS AND PROCEEDINGS IN GENERAL

§ D26–50.11 *Responsibility of stockholders of corporations owning multiple dwellings declared nuisances.*—a. The term "nuisance" shall be held to embrace public nuisance as known at common law or in equity jurisprudence. Whatever is dangerous to human life or detrimental to health, and whatever dwelling is overcrowded with occupants or is not provided with adequate ingress or egress or is not sufficiently supported, ventilated, sewered, drained, cleaned or lighted in reference to its intended or actual use, and whatever renders the air or human food or drink unwholesome, are also severally, in contemplation of this section, nuisances. All such nuisances are unlawful.

b. Whenever the department shall certify that any multiple dwelling, or any part of its premises, or the plumbing, sewerage, drainage, lighting or ventilation thereof, is in a condition or in effect dangerous to life or detrimental to health, the department may, after giving notice to the owner and an opportunity to be heard at a hearing held for such purpose, declare the same, to the extent it may specify, a public nuisance. Such declaration shall be filed in the central violation file as provided by section 328 of the multiple dwelling law, if applicable, or as a public record in the department. The officers of a corporation upon which notice of such hearing has been served * * * shall serve similar notice on all stockholders of record of the corporation and other persons known to be stockholders or beneficial owners of the stock of the corporation. A stockholder upon whom such notice has been served shall serve similar notice upon any persons holding a beneficial interest in his stock.

"e." Whenever a multiple dwelling shall have been declared a public nuisance to any extent pursuant to subsection (b) of this section, and such declaration shall have been filed as therein provided, all officers, directors and persons having an interest, as holder or beneficial owner thereof, in more than ten per cent of the issued and outstanding stock of any corporation * * * shall, in addition to all other liabilities and penalties provided in this code and elsewhere, be jointly and severally liable for all injury to person or property thereafter sustained by any tenant of such multiple dwelling or any other person by reason of the condition constituting such public nuisance and for all costs and disbursements including attorney's fees of any suit brought by such tenant or other person.

ARTICLE 52
CRIMINAL PENALTY

§ D26–52.01 *Penalties; false statements.*—Any person who

(1) violates any provision of this title; or

(2) violates, or fails to comply with, any requirement of an order of the department; or

(3) makes, or causes any other person to make, any false or misleading statement on any registration statement, notice, or other document required to be filed pursuant to this title, or on any application, or any accompanying document, for the granting of any determination or to cause any other action by the department pursuant to this code; shall be guilty of an offense punishable, for a first offense, by a fine of not more than five hundred dollars or by imprisonment for not more than thirty days, or by both such fine and imprisonment; and for a second or subsequent offense consisting of the continuance or recurrence of the same violation in the same dwelling, by a fine of not more than one thousand dollars or by imprisonment for not more than one year, or by both such fine and imprisonment.

ARTICLE 53
INJUNCTIVE RELIEF

§ D26–53.01 *Injunctions; mandatory and prohibitory.*—The department may institute an action in a court of competent jurisdiction for an order requiring the owner of property or other responsible person to abate or correct any violation of this code, or to comply with an order or notice of the department, or for such other relief as may be appropriate to secure continuing compliance with this code. An action for injunctive relief hereunder may be brought in addition to other sanctions and remedies for violations of the code, or may be joined with any action for such other sanctions and remedies except criminal prosecution.

ARTICLE 54
REPAIRS BY DEPARTMENT

§ D26–54.01 *Power to cause or order correction of violations.*—a. Whenever the department determines that, because of any violations of this title or other applicable law, any dwelling or part of its premises is dangerous to human life and safety or detrimental to health, it may

(1) cause the dwelling to be repaired, altered, cleansed, or otherwise improved so as to correct such conditions, or

(2) order the owner of the dwelling or other responsible party to repair, alter, cleanse or otherwise improve the dwelling so as to correct such conditions.

b. An order issued pursuant to the preceding subsection shall state the violations involved and the corrective action to be taken, and shall fix a time for compliance, which shall be not less than 21 days from the date of service of the order, except that where immediate danger to health or safety exists or is threatened, a shorter period for compliance may be fixed.

c. Any order not complied with within the stated time for compliance may be executed by the department.

§ D26–54.05 *Recovery of expenses of repair.*—All expenses incurred by the department in causing the correction of unlawful conditions pursuant to section

D26–54.01(a) (1) or in executing an order pursuant to section D26–54.01(c) * * * shall constitute a debt recoverable from the owner and a lien upon the building and lot, and upon the rents and other income thereof. The provisions of article 57 shall govern the effect and enforcement of such debt and lien.

ARTICLE 55
RECEIVERSHIP

§ D26–55.01 *Grounds for appointment of receiver.*—Whenever the department certifies that any condition in violation of this title or other applicable law in any multiple dwelling or any part of its premises constitutes a serious fire hazard or is a serious threat to life, health or safety, it may, upon failure of the owner to comply with an order to correct such conditions issued pursuant to section D26–54.01 of this code, apply for the appointment of a receiver to repair and correct the violations.

§ D26–55.03 *Notice to owner, mortgagees and lienors.*—a. If the department intends to seek the appointment of a receiver to remove or remedy a condition described in the preceding section, it shall serve upon the owner, along with the order pursuant to section D26–54.01 of this code, a notice stating that in the event the violations covered by the order are not removed or remedied in the manner and within the time specified therein, the department may apply for the appointment of a receiver of the rents, issues and profits of the property with rights superior to those of the owner and any mortgagee or lienor. * * *

§ D26–55.05 *Order to show cause.*—a. The department, upon failure of the owner to comply with an order under section D26–55.03 within the time provided therein, may thereafter apply to a court of competent jurisdiction in the county where the property is situated for an order directing the owner and any mortgagees or lienors of record to show cause why the commissioner of real estate should not be appointed receiver of the rents, issues and profits of the property and why the receiver should not remove or remedy such condition and obtain a lien in favor of the department of real estate against the property having the priority provided in article 57 of this code to secure repayment of the costs incurred by the receiver in removing or remedying such conditions. Such application shall contain (a) proof by affidavit that an order of the department has been issued, served on the owner, mortgagees and lienors, and filed, in accordance with section D26–55.03; (b) a statement that a serious fire hazard or a serious threat to life, health, or safety continued to exist in said dwelling after the time fixed in the department order for correction of the condition, and a description of the dwelling and conditions involved; (c) a brief description of the nature of the work required to remove or remedy the condition and an estimate as to the cost thereof. * * *

§ D26–55.11 *Powers and duties of receiver.*—a. A receiver appointed pursuant to this article shall have all of the powers and duties of a receiver appointed in an action to foreclose a mortgage on real property, together with such additional powers and duties as herein granted and imposed. He shall not be required to file any bond.

b. The receiver shall with all reasonable speed remove violations in the dwelling and its premises, including those constituting a fire hazard or a threat to life, health or safety. He may also, in addition to ordinary repairs, maintenance and replacement, make other improvements to effect a rehabilitation of the property, in such fashion as is consistent with maintaining safe and habitable conditions over the remaining useful life of the dwelling. He shall have the power to let contracts or incur expenses therefor in accordance

with the provisions of law applicable to contracts for public works except that advertisement shall not be required for each such contract. Notwithstanding any provision of law, the receiver may let contracts or incur expenses for individual items of repairs, improvements or supplies without the procurement of competitive bids where the total amount of any such individual item does not exceed twenty-five hundred dollars.

c. The receiver shall collect the accrued and accruing rents, issues and profits of the dwelling and apply the same to the cost of the repairs and improvements authorized in subsection (b), to the payment of expenses reasonably necessary to the proper operation and management of the property, including insurance and the fees of the managing agent, and the necessary expenses of his office as receiver, the repayment of all monies advanced to the receiver by the department of real estate to cover the costs incurred by the receiver and interest thereon; and then, if there be a surplus, to unpaid taxes, assessments, water rents, sewer rents, and penalties and interest thereon, and then to sums due to mortgagees or lienors. If the income of the property shall be insufficient to cover the cost of the repairs and improvements, or of the expenses reasonably necessary to the proper operation and management of the property and other necessary expenses of the receiver, the department of real estate shall advance to the receiver any sums required to cover such cost and expenses and thereupon shall have a lien against the property having the priority provided in article 57 for any such sums so advanced with interest thereon.

§ D26–55.15 *Recovery of expenses of receivership; lien of receiver.*—a. The expenditures made by the receiver pursuant to section D26–55.11 shall, to the extent that they are not recovered from the rents and income of the property collected by the receiver, constitute a debt of the owner and a lien upon the building and lot, and upon the rents and income thereof. Except as otherwise provided in this section, the provisions of section 57 shall govern the effect and enforcement of such debt and lien; references therein to the department shall, for purposes of this article be deemed to refer to the receiver and, after his discharge, the department of real estate.

ARTICLE 56
VACATE ORDERS

§ D26–56.01 *Power to order dwelling vacated.*—a. Any dwelling or part thereof, which, because of a structural or fire safety hazard, defects in plumbing, sewage, drainage, or cleanliness, or any other violation of this code or any other applicable law, constitutes a danger to the life, health, or safety of its occupants, shall be deemed to be unfit for human habitation.

b. The department may order or cause any dwelling or part thereof which is unfit for human habitation to be vacated.

ARTICLE 57
RECOVERY OF EXPENSES

§ D26–57.01 *Action against the owner for recovery of expenses.*—The department may bring an action against the owner of a dwelling for the recovery of any costs, expenses and disbursements incurred by it under any provision of this code making such expenses a debt recoverable from the owner. The institution of any such action shall not suspend or bar the right to pursue any other remedy provided by law for the recovery of such expenses, and such action may, subject to jurisdictional limitations, be joined with the enforcement of any such other remedy or any other claim against the owner relating to the same premises.

§ D26–57.03 *Lien on premises.*—A lien created pursuant to the provisions

of article 54 or 55 of this code shall, except to the extent otherwise provided in this article, have priority over all other liens and encumbrances on the premises, except taxes and assessments. The effect of, and proceedings involving, such lien shall, except as otherwise provided in this article, be governed by the provisions of law regulating mechanics' liens.

§ D26–57.11 *Levy on rents.*—a. The department may serve upon any person liable for rent or other compensation for the occupancy of premises subject to this article a notice containing:

(1) a statement of the contents of a certificate under section D26–57.05 (a), or of a judgment in an action under section D26–57.01 or in an action to enforce a lien under this article;

(2) a statement of the amount remaining due under such certificate or judgment; and

(3) a demand that rent thereafter be paid to the department as it comes due. Service of the notice shall be made by personal delivery of a copy thereof, or by registered mail.

b. Upon receipt of such notice, the person to whom it is directed shall pay any rent due, and future rent as it comes due, to the department in the manner set forth in the demand. The department may, upon failure to pay, sue for rent due. In such suit, the validity of proceedings prior to the issuance of the notice under subsection (a) of this section shall not be subject to question.

c. The department shall issue a receipt for each sum paid under this section. Such payment and receipt shall for all purposes have the same legal effect as payment to or a receipt from the owner or other person authorized to collect rent. No person shall be subject to any proceedings for the recovery of possession or other relief, or any penalty or forfeiture, arising out of his failure to pay to any person any sum paid to the department under this section.

d. The department shall, at the time of service of any notice under subsection (a), give the owner and agent notice by registered mail at their last registered addresses or other address, if known, of such action. Unless within 12 days of such notice suit has been instituted by or on behalf of the owner to restrain such action or recover from the department any sums collected, the action of the department shall not be subject to challenge.

e. Upon collection of the total sum owing to the department, it shall forthwith serve upon each person served with a demand under subsection (a) a notice cancelling such demand.

LEGAL REMEDIES FOR HOUSING CODE VIOLATIONS—GRAD

Constitutionality of Housing Codes

While questions will occasionally arise as to whether particular procedural or remedial aspects of housing legislation will meet the constitutional requirements of due process of law, the power of the state or of a municipality to impose housing standards by way of a housing code is no longer open to question.[23] The power to impose reasonable standards for housing conditions and housing maintenance is part of the state's police power to protect public order, health, safety, and welfare of the people.[24] The police power, an attribute of every sovereign government, is limited primarily by the constitutional protection of the people against deprivation of life, liberty, and

property without due process of law.[25] Thus, housing regulations will be valid as long as they bear a demonstrable relationship to public health, safety and welfare, and do not deprive the owner of the housing of his property interests without due process of law.[26] Courts today have developed a very broad concept of the police power over private property, and prevailing social, as well as legal attitudes toward the rehabilitation of property and its maintenance have progressed considerably since the time 80 years ago when the New York Court of Appeals, reversing the lower courts and over a sharp dissent, upheld the "radical" requirement that New York City tenements be furnished with running water on each floor, but reassured owners that if any legislature would go to such absurd lengths as to require a private bathroom for each apartment (which it doubted) surely no court in the land would let such a law stand.[27]

Although there were some recent cases in which similar issues were raised,[28]

[23] See, e. g., Health Dept. v. Rector of Trinity Church, 145 N.Y. 32, 39 N.E. 833 (1895); Tenement House Dept. v. Moeschen, 179 N. Y. 325, 72 N.E. 231 (1904), aff'd per curiam 203 U.S. 583, 27 S.Ct. 781, 51 L.Ed. 328 (1906); Queenside Hills Realty Co. v. Wilson, 294 N.Y. 917, 63 N.E.2d 116 (1945) aff'd sub. nom. Queenside Hills Realty Co. v. Saxl, 328 U.S. 80, 66 S.Ct. 850, 90 L.Ed. 1096 (1946).

[24] See cases cited supra, note 23.

[25] U.S.Const., 5th Amend.; See, e. g., Nebbia v. New York, 291 U.S. 502, 54 S.Ct. 505, 78 L.Ed. 940 (1934).

[26] For a brief discussion of the limits of the police power imposed by due process, with particular reference to regulations of public health, see, Grad, Public Health Law Manual, pp. 5, 37–40 (1965).

[27] Health Dept. v. Rector of Trinity Church, supra, note 23.

[28] Early Estates, Inc. v. Housing Board of Review, 93 R.I. 227, 174 A.2d 117 (1961) upheld Providence, R. I., housing code requirements of hallway lights, as a proper exercise of the police power, but invalidated provisions of the same code, requiring installation of hot water in a third-floor tenement. With two judges dissenting, the court held that the latter requirement was not expressly authorized by state law, because it was "not necessarily related to sanitation or public health and welfare, nor is such requirement reasonably necessary to make dwellings and dwelling premises fit for human habitation." To the same effect, Gates Co. v. Housing Appeals Board of Columbus, 10 Ohio St.2d 48, 225 N.E.2d 222 (1967). See also Philbrick v. White, 106 N.H. 340, 211

housing codes have been upheld almost uniformly against such due process attacks.[29]

Another common basis for constitutional challenge to housing codes has been the common state constitutional provision that the legislative power is vested in the legislature. Essentially, the argument is reduced to an assertion that the delegation of the power to pass a housing code to the municipality is an improper delegation of legislative power. There is no substantial force left to this argument, however, because such a delegation to a municipality is now well-recognized and uniformly approved.[30] The argument that the municipality had no power (short of express delegation) to adopt remedial provisions that go beyond state law is, however, regularly made and may be difficult to reckon with when the municipality has adopted repair or receivership remedies, or has otherwise attempted to modify state law relating to the ownership, sale or leasing of property.[31]

A third kind of constitutional challenge to housing codes that is frequently encountered focuses on the allegedly retroactive effect of such legislation. In one sense, it is true that higher maintenance and occupancy standards affect existing buildings, and by that token impose the new and higher requirements retroactively. When a housing code requires that there be separate toilet facilities for the occupants of every apartment where prior construction requirements merely provided for one toilet on each floor, the owner will be required to meet the cost of the additional facilities, though it may strike him that the new requirement compels him to alter a condition that was previously legal—he is caught "retroactively." When a city requires in its housing code that henceforth all dwellings shall be supplied with central heat and hot water, the owner of the cold water tenement will be required to put in the necessary boiler, pipes and radiators, even though his building was constructed in full compliance with the requirements of the building code some forty or fifty years ago.[32] But although the owner may feel that he has been dealt with unfairly if he is convicted or otherwise penalized for failing to provide the newly required facilities, his grievance is really with progress, not with the law.

The new standard is *not* a retroactive law in the sense in which a constitutionally objectionable *ex post facto* law is retroactive,[33] because the owner is not being punished for the past lack of facilities, but only for failing to provide the facilities *after* the effective date of the new legal requirement. Thus, the new stand-

A.2d 852 (1965) invalidating Concord housing code because its provisions did not comply procedurally with the state enabling act.

[29] City of Bakersfield v. Miller, 64 Cal.2d 93, 48 Cal.Rptr. 889, 410 P.2d 393 (1966); Apple v. Denver, 154 Colo. 166, 390 P.2d 91 (1964); Lester v. City of St. Petersburg, 183 So.2d 589 (Fla.App.1966); City of Chicago v. Miller, 27 Ill.2d 211, 188 N.E.2d 694 (1963); Kaukas v. City of Chicago, 27 Ill.2d 197, 188 N.E.2d 700 (1963); City of Louisville v. Thompson, 339 S.W.2d 869 (Ky.App.1960); Givner v. Commissioner of Health of Baltimore City, 207 Md. 184, 113 A.2d 899 (1955); Paquette v. City of Fall River, 338 Mass. 368, 155 N.E.2d 775 (1959); Adamec v. Post, 273 N.Y. 250, 7 N.E.2d 120 (1937); Ajootian v. Housing Bd. of Review of Providence, 98 R.I. 370, 201 A.2d 905 (1964); Richards v. City of Columbia, 227 S.C. 538, 88 S.E.2d 683 (1955); Boden v. City of Milwaukee, 8 Wis. 2d 318, 99 N.W.2d 156 (1959).

[30] See, e.g. State of Connecticut v. Schaffel, 4 Conn.Cir. 234, 229 A.2d 552 (1966); McBriety v. Baltimore, 219 Md. 223, 148 A.2d 408 (1959); Apple v. City of Denver, supra, note 29.

[31] See, e.g. City of St. Louis v. Golden Gate Corp., 421 S.W.2d 4 (Mo.1967).

[32] E.g. Health Dept. v. Rector of Trinity Church, supra, note 23; Tenement House Dept. v. Moeschen, 179 N.Y. 325, 72 N.E. 231 (1904), aff'd. per curiam, 203 U.S. 583, 27 S.Ct. 781, 51 L.Ed. 328 (1906); City of Louisville v. Thompson, supra, note 29. Contra: Early Estates, Inc. v. Housing Bd. of Review, supra, note 28.

[33] E. g. U.S.Const. Art. I, § 9.

ards are prospective in operation, and not retroactive in the legal sense, because the owner cannot claim any vested interest in having the law remain unchanged. If an owner were able to assert such an interest in the immutability of the law, then it becomes impossible ever to raise standards in existing dwellings. With isolated exceptions,[34] therefore, the courts have rejected such constitutional objections based on *ex post facto* or retroactivity grounds.[35] * * *

Questions

What if the owner proves he is unable financially to comply with the higher standards: Should the ordinance still be enforced against him? Is there a constitutional basis for the owner's defense? Might he also have a defense akin to the contract doctrine of impossibility? Is he legally any better off than an owner who has let his premises run down and *then* is not able to pay whatever it costs to remove code violations? Cf. People v. Rowen, 9 N.Y.2d 732, 174 N.E.2d 331 (1961) (Court of Appeals, without opinion, unanimously reversed conviction of owner unable to finance $42,500 expenditure to install 22 water closets and central heating in two Old Law Tenements; buildings assessed at $30,000). If the courts refuse to convict an owner who cannot afford to comply with a higher standard, may the municipality then vacate the buildings as unfit for human habitation? Alternatively, may the city finance the rehabilitation itself and charge back the cost to the building owner?

Do standards of fitness yield to economic realities?

34 Early Estates, Inc. v. Housing Bd. of Review, supra, note 28.

35 Queenside Hills Realty Co. v. Saxl, 328 U.S. 80, 66 S.Ct. 850, 90 L.Ed. 1096 (1946). See also cases cited supra, note 32, and Apple, City of Bakersfield, Chicago v. Miller, Kaukas, Louisville v. Thompson, Adamec, and Paquette cases cited supra, note 29.

LEGAL REMEDIES FOR HOUSING CODE VIOLATIONS—GRAD

Basic Issues of Code Enforcement

The problems of housing codes are very largely problems of enforcement: the key issues today tend to relate not so much to the development and enactment of an adequate set of housing standards, but to the means of securing compliance with such standards as have become law. Despite the fact that codes vary considerably in comprehensiveness and in level of standards required, the most striking housing deficiencies represent cases of unenforced codes. Thus, general compliance with the most elementary code requirement—the general maintenance provision requiring a dwelling to be kept "in good repair" or "in clean and sanitary condition"—or even with the public health laws against "nuisances" and "conditions dangerous to life and health" that predate the codes—would work a dramatic improvement in the living conditions of millions of the Nation's poorest households.

To say this is simply to observe that even more than most laws, housing codes are of little value without effective enforcement devices, vigorously pursued; it is by no means to imply that raising housing standards is simply a matter of finding and employing the proper code enforcement methods. Even with respect to those aspects of the housing problem which are amenable to a code enforcement approach rather than demanding more radical action, the particular legal techniques seem often to be less important than the manner in which they are administered and the environment in which they must function. For example, in most cases the number and nature of the legal tools available to an enforcement department are of much less practical importance than the adequacy of the number of inspectors it has at its disposal. Again, if a code standard is raised so as to require an expensive improvement in existing dwellings, experience in large cities has shown that no combination of enforcement laws will produce compliance on the part of the marginal property owner if financing that he can afford does not exist or is not made available. * * * [Moreover] if owners of rental housing, faced with a legal requirement to make expensive improvements, decide that it would be cheaper to close down or demolish the buildings, the result—especially if the tenants are of low income and housing is in short supply—may well be worse than if the higher standard had not been imposed. In the absence of rent control and subject to any outstanding leases, there is ordinarily nothing to prevent an owner from taking his building off the housing market; and major limitations on this right would represent a more radical intrusion on private property than would be constitutionally permissible. Thus the municipality, in the process of enforcing the code, almost inevitably must look to tax incentives or other means of encouraging the improvements; and it may well find itself having to engage in an active repair program. * * Finally, the types of activities that seek to achieve code compliance are far wider than the ordinary concept of law enforcement would suggest. In addition to the various methods of ordering or coercing compliance by departmental or court action, enforcement agencies are typically empowered to move directly to eliminate unlawful conditions: traditionally by negative means such as vacating or demolishing an unfit building, and increasingly through the rendition of services, by various repair programs (usually with provisions, which may or may not be effective, for recovering the cost from the owner). In the most heralded new development, tenants themselves are encouraged to seek legal remedies against noncomplying landlords. In addition to all these coercive remedies, the code enforcement agency or other departments of government may be prepared to offer encouragements to community improvement ranging from education and consultation through the furnishing of better neighborhood services to the offer of substantial financing and tax advantages to owners who wish to rehabilitate.

Code Enforcement in Large and Small Settings

The nature of the code enforcement task may vary widely, depending on its setting. Significant differences exist both between types of community and different types of housing within a community. * * *

The inherent differences between the large city and the other communities in which housing codes have been enacted only recently suggest a need for critical examination of generalizations based on experience in certain special contexts. Most analyses of code enforcement have dealt with the large metropolitan center; in fact, most general discussions of various aspects of enforcement look largely at a single city. To speak of rent strikes and of the experience of a long period of enforcement in an almost exclusively apartment-house setting is to speak of New York City; an evaluation of widespread use of injunctions will be based largely on Chicago experience; to discuss special education programs for tenant violators is chiefly to speak of Baltimore's Housing Clinic, and so on. More comparative analysis will become possible as experience with housing codes is accumulated in greater variety of settings.

In addition to the nature of the community, the type of housing to which a code is being applied—in terms both of the individual buildings and the neighborhood—makes a great difference. The basic distinction, which runs through the entire subject of enforcement, is of course that between the private home and the tenant-occupied building, especially where the latter is a multi-family dwelling with non-resident owners. It does not seem to be much of an exaggeration to say that the term "code enforcement" really means two different things in these two different settings. There are further differences, depending on the quality of the housing supply. A very different approach may be called for, depending on whether the task to be done is meeting the minor day-to-day problems of a neighborhood of good housing, making an intensive effort to uphold standards in an area threatened with decline or to reverse deterioration that has actually set in, or doing what code enforcement can do to alleviate the problems of a hard-core slum that must ultimately yield to redevelopment.

HOUSING CODE ENFORCE-MENT—GRAD AND GRIBETZ

The Inadequacy of the Criminal Sanction

Departmental repairs, injunctions, and civil penalties, as well as other sanctions, have long been authorized. But prior to the institution of the receivership program, the vacate order and criminal prosecution were the only sanctions consistently employed. The vacate order, though inherently the most effective remedy, is tied to the existence of an adequate vacancy ratio, particularly in low-rent housing. Thus, the vacate order is likely to remain an extraordinary sanction for quite some time. This leaves criminal prosecution as the only sanction routinely relied on in New York during the past fifty years. The trouble with criminal prosecution for housing violations—as well as for the scores of other state and local regulations of health and safety—is that in hard-core cases it does not work. The remedy is inadequate as a cure or a deterrent; it does not result in repairs of buildings or in deterrence of recalcitrant owners. Fur-

thermore, the sanction is fraught with procedural and conceptual difficulties that make it unsuitable as a contemporary code enforcement device.

A. *The Imposition of the Sanction*

In New York City there are some 20,-000 prosecutions for housing violations every year, most of them heard in a special part of the criminal courts. Each of the prosecutions involves several separate counts of violation, and may involve as many as a hundred separate violations. And yet, in 1965 the average fine per case (not per violation) was under fourteen dollars. Calculated per violation, the average fine was said to be about fifty cents. Many violations so penalized have been outstanding for months, if not years, and many of them are of a hazardous nature. These inconsequential penalties are not the result of inadequate provisions of the law; on the contrary, the New York statutes allow the imposition of very heavy fines, ranging up to $1,000 per violation for repeated offenders, and provide for jail sentences of up to six months.[101] Yet fines have remained min-

---

[101] There is a rather bewildering array of criminal penalties available for housing violations. Most violations of the Multiple Dwelling Law, which is the basic state law governing housing, are punishable as misdemeanors, for a first offense by fine up to $500 and by imprisonment not exceeding 30 days, or both. Second and subsequent violations are punishable by a fine up to $1,000 or by imprisonment up to 6 months, or both. It should be noted, however, that in the context of housing violations, the concept of repeat violations has an unusually restrictive meaning, for a second or subsequent offense is defined as one "arising from the failure to remove the violation upon which the first offense was based. * * *" McKinney's N.Y.Mult.Dwell.Law § 403(1) (Supp.1965).

Violations of the Multiple Dwelling Code, which is a local law, constituting Title D of Chapter 26 of the New York City Administrative Code, are treated as "offenses," a lesser category of infractions than misdemeanors, with the first conviction punishable by fine up to $500, or, upon failure or refusal to pay the fine, by imprisonment not

imal and landlords find it cheaper to pay the fine than to make the repair. Jail sentences for "slumlords" are practically never imposed, and hence remain an empty threat.[102]

Criminal prosecution involves a number of procedural difficulties that make it an inappropriate remedy for coping with contemporary enforcement problems. Speed is one of the purported advantages of the criminal process; the prompt imposition of sanctions, regardless of severity, is said to serve a deterrent purpose in and of itself. Yet, housing cases remain pending in the criminal court for many months, and even years. The basic reason for delays in disposition is the requirement of personal appearance by the defendant. In a criminal prosecution the court is concerned with the culpability of the *defendant*, rather than the condition of the *building*.

exceeding 30 days. Second or subsequent offenses, as previously defined, are punishable by fine of not less than $10 nor more than $1,000, or by imprisonment up to 1 year, or by both fine and imprisonment. New York City, N.Y., Admin.Code § D26–8.0 (1964).

Housing violations involving infractions of the New York City Health Code (which has the force of law, though enacted by a five-member appointive Board of Health, N.Y. City, N.Y., Charter § 558) are punishable as misdemeanors. N.Y.City, N.Y., Charter § 558(d). If a willful violation is charged, McKinney's N.Y.Pub.Health Law § 12–b (effective Sept. 1967) authorizes a fine up to $2,000, imprisonment up to 1 year, or both.

Other penalty provisions are applicable to electrical code, fire prevention code, and other violations. The diversity of penalties arises from the broad variety of laws and ordinances that are involved in "code enforcement." The situation is further aggravated by the fact that a single condition may violate different provisions of laws, so that the range of penalties may well depend on the law selected as a basis for prosecution, or, as a practical matter, on the municipal department which first notes and then prosecutes for the violation.

[102] In 14,786 convictions, only 36 defendants were sentenced to jail for housing violations. 1963 New York City Criminal Court Ann.Rep. 12–15.

Moreover, a criminal court cannot proceed until it has personal jurisdiction of the accused, and personal jurisdiction is not complete until the defendant is in the court's presence. Thus, even though a defendant may have been properly served with a criminal summons, and even though his failure to appear in response to the summons may make him liable to further penalties, the court cannot proceed with the case until the defendant shows up. It might be added that in fact most housing summonses are not properly served because they are served by mail rather than by personal delivery. Hence, to a considerable extent, code enforcement—even in the criminal courts—must rely on the voluntary cooperation of the great majority of landlord defendants.

When owners do eventually appear in court, adjournments and delays are frequent, and cases may be adjourned several times. Furthermore, procrastination works in favor of the offending owner, since delay is unlikely to increase his fine and allows him to play a waiting game with respect to repairs. He can wait until the very last moment and then plead for an opportunity to meet code requirements. Usually the court will adjourn the case and order a reinspection report from the Department. Then, making his repairs just before reinspection, the owner will claim that he has fully cooperated with the Department. If the reinspection report is favorable, the court will probably accept the defendant's plea in mitigation and will impose a light fine—even where violations have been outstanding for many months. Thus, neither the severity of the criminal penalty nor the certainty and speed of its imposition are likely to bring about compliance.

B. *The Conceptual Hurdle* * * *

The reluctance of the criminal courts to treat housing offenders with the severity reserved for "real" criminals has long been a problem. It has bedevilled code enforcement from its early days and is reflected in the unsanctioned practice in the New York courts of allowing the substitution of a corporate defendant for the real defendant to avoid tainting housing defendants with a criminal record. The growing reliance on the criminal law and on strict criminal liability to deal with economic and administrative offenses has long been criticized by leading jurisprudential thinkers. It has been said that the result of imposing strict criminal liability in such cases was "merely to impose a nominal tax on illegal enterprise" because strict liability does not distinguish between categories of offenders. Since penalties under any system of strict liability are likely to be light, "there can hardly be any doubt that strict liability is a futile gesture so far as unscrupulous persons are concerned. * * *"

Thus, the nature of the criminal remedy and its lack of effectiveness in code enforcement are interrelated. It is obvious that the volume and nature of housing violations make it practically impossible to look for intent and wrongful knowledge on the part of the owner in every case. It follows that if we continue to rely on criminal prosecutions, the doctrine of strict liability will be essential. But strict liability, the definition of "absolute" crimes regardless of intent, invariably leads to a trivializing of the offense, to judicial nullification by a refusal to impose penalties that are capable of deterrence. The criminal sanction in housing code enforcement thus becomes incapable of drawing clear distinctions between the hard-core recalcitrant and the less serious occasional offender who needs to be prodded into compliance.

The emphasis in code enforcement today is on achieving compliance by bringing about the repair and rehabilitation of dwellings. But neither the tenants nor the municipality can have a sense of ac-

complishment when owners are convicted and sentenced to pay a fine if the condition of the dwellings themselves remains unchanged. Routine criminal prosecutions for housing violations have never worked very well to correct hard-core slum conditions. Now they have become totally irrelevant since the demand is increasingly for remedies that will more assuredly lead to the improvement of conditions in substandard housing.

Injunctions

The injunction, an order of the court addressed to a defendant, commanding or prohibiting specified conduct, with failure to comply punishable as a contempt of court, is a most useful sanction, because of its great flexibility. Instead of punishing for past conduct, it compels compliance with the requirements of law in the future. Unlike other less discriminating remedies, it allows the court to fit the contents of its order to the specific circumstances of the case, and to the specific defendant. This very flexibility makes the remedy one of useful application in housing code enforcement.

The injunctive remedy has been on the books in many states for many years. In fact, it was indirectly provided for in the first modern housing law, the New York Tenement House Act of 1901, and its first recorded use occurred in the famous case of Tenement House Dept. v. Moeschen,[1] in 1904, in which the Tenement House Act was upheld both by the state's highest court, as well as, subsequently, by the United States Supreme Court, as was that law's provision requiring the removal of "school sinks"—sewer-connected privies—from tenement yards. Although the authority for injunctions, both mandatory and prohibitory, was even more clearly stated in sub-

---

[1] 179 N.Y. 325, 72 N.E. 231, aff'd 203 U.S. 583, 27 S.Ct. 781, 51 L.Ed. 328 (1906).

sequent New York legislation,[2] the remedy fell into disuse soon after the *Moeschen* case, and no recourse has been had to it in New York in recent years. Its employment in selected cases has been urged, however, in a recent New York study of housing code enforcement sanctions.[3]

A similar disuse of injunctions long authorized by law [4] is encountered in other states. Some use of the remedy has been made in recent years in California, where, largely under the provisions of the California Health and Safety Code,[5] which are quite similar to the New York authorization, rather sweeping mandatory injunctions have been granted, ordering extensive repairs and reconstruction or the reconversions of dwellings to conditions prior to their illegal alteration.[6]

Some use of housing injunctions has been made also in Philadelphia.[7]

The only city in which injunctions have been used with any regularity is Chicago, where the law authorizing mandatory injunctions became one of the standard techniques of code enforcement. In 1963, the Chicago Department of Buildings obtained 178 mandatory injunctions against housing violations;[8] in 1964, it obtained 223.[9] The total number of injunctions secured is especially striking, since the Chicago courts have not merely issued perfunctory orders in the words of the statute, but have sought to shape effective decrees suited to end special problems. The Chicago effort is noteworthy, too, because the courts have insisted in housing injunctions cases not only on the joinder of all interested parties,[10] but also on the retention of jurisdiction for as long as necessary for a "complete determination of the controversy." [11] Injunctions have apparently become so well established an enforcement device in Chicago that few challenges to their use have been attempted—and where attempted, they were quickly disposed of.[12]

The use of injunctions in code enforcement thus stands on sound ground. Even

---

[2] N. Y. Multiple Dwelling Law § 306 as enacted by N.Y.L.1929, c. 713. The section allows the code enforcement agency to "institute any appropriate action or proceeding to prevent such unlawful construction, alteration, conversion or maintenance, to restrain, correct or abate such violation or nuisance, to prevent the occupation of said dwelling or structure or any part thereof, or to prevent any illegal act, conduct or business in or about such dwelling, structure or lot."

[3] Grad, Weiss & Hack, Legal Remedies in Housing Code Enforcement in New York City, 87, 95–98 (Legislative Drafting Research Fund of Columbia University, 1965). For a history of the New York experience in using injunctive remedies, see ibid., 90–93.

[4] For statutes authorizing injunctive relief in housing cases, see e. g. Smith-Hurd Ill.Ann.Stat. ch. 24 § 11–31–2; Iowa Code Ann. §§ 413.113–413.114; Mass.Gen.Laws Ann. c. 143 § 57; Mich.Comp.Laws Ann. § 125.502; Minn.Stat.Ann. § 460.75; N.J.Stat. Ann. § 55:11–17 (1964); McKinney N.Y.Mult. Dwell.Law § 306; Purdon Pa.Stat.Ann. tit. 53, § 4102; Chicago Munic.Code § 39–6; Memphis Code § 3007.13; N.Y.C. Housing Maintenance Code, §§ D26–53.01—D26–53.07.

[5] § 17981.

[6] See e. g., People v. Morehouse, 74 Cal.App. 2d 870, 169 P.2d 983 (1946) (mandatory preliminary injunction granting ordered extensive improvements and repairs); City and County of San Francisco v. Meyer, 208 Cal. App.2d 125, 25 Cal.Rptr. 99 (1962) (owner of

illegally converted building ordered to reconvert, alter building so as to lawfully accommodate increased occupancy, or demolish it); Knapp v. City of Newport Beach, 186 Cal.App.2d 669, 9 Cal.Rptr. 90 (1960) (owner ordered to virtually reconstruct building, at cost equal to twice its present value).

[7] Note. Enforcement of Municipal Housing Codes, 78 Harv.L.Rev. 801, 827 (1965).

[8] 1963 Chicago Dep't of Buildings Ann.Rep. 6.

[9] 1964 Chicago Dep't of Law Ann.Rep. 95.

[10] Chicago v. Miller, 27 Ill.2d 211, 188 N.E. 2d 694, appeal dismissed, 375 U.S. 11, 84 S. Ct. 68, 11 L.Ed.2d 40 (1963).

[11] See 78 Harv.L.Rev. supra, note 7, at 827. See also Chicago v. 934 Willow Bldg. Corp., 36 Ill.App.2d 72, 183 N.E.2d 572 (1962).

[12] See cases cited, supra, notes 10 and 11, and Chicago v. Larson, 31 Ill.App.2d 450, 176 N.E.2d 675 (1961).

aside from specific authorizations, municipal authorities have long had the power to enjoin public nuisances.[13] To the extent that a housing violation constitutes a nuisance—either because it may be regarded as a common law nuisance, or because it has been so designated by statute—an injunction clearly will issue. Injunctive relief has also been available for a long time to deal with illegal acts or conditions that constitute a threat to the public health, safety and welfare, where legal remedies would be inadequate.

Injunctions have long been authorized in the field in which housing standards originated—public health—and health boards and health officers have frequently sought and been granted the assistance of equity to enforce public health requirements, particularly in the abatement of nuisances.[14] Health and housing laws overlap in many jurisdictions, and in many municipalities housing standards are still enforced by health officers. There is no reason, therefore, why a useful sanction in public health enforcement generally should not be relied on with greater frequency in housing enforcement.

One objection that may be raised to the use of injunction in code enforcement is the traditional doctrine that "equity will not enjoin a crime," and since housing violations are generally treated as crimes, injunctions should not be sought. The doctrine, though still given lip-service, is no longer good law. Not only has it been discredited in private proceedings,[15] where it had its origin, but it has been clearly rejected in cases where the aid of equity is sought by public agencies, particularly where injunctive relief for the correction of violations has been authorized by statute.[16]

Thus it appears that injunctive relief can be an effective sanction in housing enforcement, though it may require more extensive preparation and more careful presentation of a case, in order that full advantage may be taken of the court's power to frame a decree to deal with the special problems of each case. Preliminary injunctions are among the swiftest remedies, with special applicability in emergency situations; however, a court proceeding leading to a permanent injunction may be fairly lengthy—possibly not a significant objection, in the light of the usual delays in criminal prosecutions.

Because proceedings for injunctions require greater care in preparation and are likely to be more extended, as well as because a proper defendant must be found and served so as to be personally responsible for the execution of the decree, such equitable proceedings cannot be recommended as an appropriate remedy in all cases. The remedy would be appropriate, however, in cases of dwellings that require major repairs; in instances where higher standards have been made applicable to existing dwellings so that major improvements are necessary, or in instances where there has been prolonged and persistent failure to furnish required services.[17]

---

13 4 Pomeroy, Equity Jurisprudence § 1349 (5th ed. Symons): Rhyne, Municipal Law, §§ 26–21, 26–25 (1957).

14 Grad, Public Health Law Manual, 129–131, 133–136 (1965).

15 See, e.g., Graceland Corp. v. Consolidated Laundries Corp., 7 A.D.2d 89, 180 N.Y.S. 2d 644 (1958).

16 See Developments in the Law: Injunctions, 78 Harv.L.Rev. 994, 1019. But see City of Harahan v. Olson, 250 La. 999, 200 So. 874 (1967) (no housing injunction can be granted in the absence of statutory authorization).

17 Cf. 78 Harv.L.Rev. supra note 7, at 827: "Many chancery judges would undoubtedly consider injunction and civil contempt too drastic a sanction for the ordinary nonhazardous violation. When the violation is hazardous, however, injunctive relief may be an appropriate and effective device."

In all of these instances the great flexibility of the injunctive remedy is of great value. A defendant who pleads hardship need neither be excused nor ordered to do the impossible. Under an appropriate drawn decree, the court may direct compliance—unless there is an emergency situation—as funds become available, or it may even order the defendant to collect rents, and apply them, after expenses, to no other purpose than the designated repairs. A defendant could be ordered, too, to account periodically to the court until he has fully complied.

*   *   *

Governmental Repair Programs
Housing Code Enforcement

State and Municipal Governments have long had the power to repair dwellings, to remove major health hazards, fire, or safety hazards endangering the occupants, when the owner refuses or fails to repair them.[1] Frequently the municipality's power to make repairs on private property under these circumstances was, and, under some laws, still is part of the right to order premises to be vacated for repair or demolition. As has been pointed out, the power of the government to make repairs to remove hazards to life and health is an ancient one, derived from the governmental power to abate nuisances and public health hazards. However, it has been used relatively infrequently until recent times. And even now—just as in the past—the use of the power has been largely restricted to a few jurisdictions.[3] Among major cities, its substantial employment has been restricted almost exclusively to the City of New York. The limited use of the remedy is explainable, as will presently appear, by cost factors and by practical aspects of the operation of code enforcement agencies.

The New York Experience

The repair remedy has its origin in a provision of the original New York Tenement House Law of 1901.[4] The pertinent provision of the Tenement House Law, later carried over into the Multiple Dwelling Law,[5] established that the housing department is empowered to declare a multiple dwelling or any part thereof to be a public nuisance whenever it is able to certify that such dwelling or any of its parts, or the plumbing, sewerage, drainage, lighting, or ventilation thereof is in a condition or in effect dangerous to life or health. Upon such a finding the department is authorized to issue a written order, effective no less than 21 days after service, requiring that the defect be corrected. The period of compliance may be shortened in cases of immediate hazard to occupants of adjoining property or to the general public.

The law further provides that in the event of failure of compliance with the order, its terms may be executed by the department, its agents or contractors. The department is also granted authority to let out contracts for repairs in accordance with provisions for the letting of contracts for public works. If the department undertakes the repair work in this fashion, it may recover its expenses in one of a number of ways. It may sue

---

[1] E. g., West's Ann.Cal.Health & Safety Code § 17982; Conn.Gen.Stat.Rev. § 19–344; Iowa Code § 413.115; Mass.Gen.Laws Ann. c. 143 §§ 4, 53, 80, 88; Baltimore Housing Code § 1303. * * * Also, demolition statutes ordinarily provide for repair as the first alternative.

[3] Note, Enforcement of Municipal Housing Codes, 78 Harv.L.Rev. 801, 835 (1965).

[4] The Tenement House Law of 1901 was the first modern housing code. There had, of course, been general provision in earlier public health legislation, authorizing orders to cleanse, purify and repair dwellings, and, in default of compliance, to permit the department to do so on the owner's behalf, charging him for the cost. See Grad, Public Health Law Manual, 104–113 (1965).

[5] N.Y.Mult.Dwell.Law § 309.

the owner personally and recover a judgment against him, and if the judgment remains unpaid, the department then has an ordinary judgment lien on the property. But the department does not have to proceed against the owner personally. It may instead simply file a lien for the expenses necessarily incurred, in the same manner and with the same effect as a mechanic's lien. Such a lien becomes conclusive unless the party against whose property the lien is claimed brings a proceeding to discharge the lien within six months after actual notice of its filing.

The department furthermore is granted a lien on the rents of the property, and may collect the cost of repairs directly out of rents after serving upon the tenant an appropriate order, or a transcript of the judgment, where obtained, together with an affidavit of its expenses.[5a] A separate procedure is also provided for in the law whereunder the department could immediately proceed to "cause" the repairs to be made. In that event no prior order to the owner is necessary, and summary repair with an immediate filing of a lien for expenses may be undertaken.

*   *   *

In the early 1960's New York undertook a substantial rat eradication program. This program, undertaken by the Department of Health, was also based on municipal repair provisions (continued in local law), whereunder the Health Department (rather than the Building Department) was authorized to correct building conditions and to impose a lien on the premises for the cost. The Health Department's rat eradication program proceeded under the Department's repair powers.

In attempting to recover its costs, the Department went so far as to file liens against properties affected for the expenses of rat eradication measures. However, the City's recoveries in the rat eradication program were very minimal, because the amount involved in extermination in each building rarely exceeded $50. Any further efforts at recovery after the lien was placed were unwarranted because the cost of collection would have exceeded the amount of the eventual recovery.[10]

Following its experience with the rat eradication program, New York City undertook an emergency repair program of considerably more substantial scope.[11] In this particular program the provisions of the New York Multiple Dwelling Law were not used because the City attempted to surmount the potential difficulties of having to serve owners and mortgagees before obtaining a prior lien for repair costs. The program was based, instead, on a longstanding provision of the Administrative Code of the City of New York which had never previously been used.[12] It gives the Department of Health a prior lien and a rent lien for expenses incurred in the correction of conditions dangerous to health.

The program officially began with a resolution of the Board of Health of the City of New York on January 29, 1965, which declared any building in the City containing conditions dangerous to life and health to be a public nuisance, and it directed all persons having an interest in such a building to abate the nuisance

---

5a [Ed. What are the practical and legal differences between a lien on the rents and a lien on the property?]

10 Gribetz & Grad, Housing Code Enforcement: Sanctions and Remedies, 66 Colum.L. Rev. 1254, 1274 (1966).

11 The account of New York City's repair program that follows is largely based on The Department of Buildings of the City of New York, A Program for Housing Maintenance and Emergency Repair, 42 St. John's L.Rev. 165 (October 1967), hereinafter cited as "Emergency Repair" with page number. The article is a collaborative effort of Charles G. Moerdler Esq., then Commissioner of Buildings, and his legal staff.

12 N.Y.C.Admin.Code §§ 564–21.0, 564–24.0.

immediately. This resolution was intended to fulfill the legal requirement of notice to the owner before repair actions by the Department could be taken. In effect, the City chose to give notice to *all* owners having buildings with serious violations simultaneously by way of a general proclamation, rather than giving notice individually by legal service.

The City appropriated $1 million as a revolving fund for the repair of dwellings in urgent and immediate need of such repair. * * * Procedures for designating specific buildings for repair and for the recovery of moneys expended were established in October of 1965. The Building Department was to notify the Committee which buildings were designated, the Health Department was to make the requisite certification under the Board of Health resolution, and then the Health Department was to direct the Department of Real Estate to undertake the actual repairs. * * * Where repairs exceeded $50, the Corporation Counsel would secure and furnish a title search. The Secretary would send a letter to all persons responsible as owners or as managers, making a demand for the amount of expenses. If no payment for expenses was forthcoming from the owner or mortgagees, the Secretary then sought reimbursement out of rents payable by the tenants. * * *

The results of the program for its first year and a half of operation, from January 1965 through July 1966, can only be described as mixed and inconclusive. The Department of Real Estate incurred liabilities in excess of $1 million under the emergency repair program. Recoupment, however, amounted to only about $21,500. In other words, only about 2 percent of expenditures were recovered. On the other hand, some 3,561 buildings received some form of emergency repairs. The receipts of $21,500 consisted of slightly more than one-half of collections from landlords and slightly less than one-half from rents paid by tenants to the City under rent liens.

The program was at least partially successful in terms of its repair objectives. It undoubtedly served to prevent considerable misery among tenants living in a substantial number of tenements. The repair action though not nearly as prompt as would seem to be desirable, was considerably more speedy than if the normal route of criminal prosecution of landlords had been followed, particularly because many of the owners of buildings subjected to emergency repairs were either absentee landlords whose whereabouts were unknown, or hard-core recalcitrants, who would not have repaired even had they been convicted of violations.[17]

The criticisms of the program fall into a number of categories. First, it is clearly an expensive program in that recovery of costs is slow and is likely to remain slow. Second, the emergency repair program pointed up the need for more immediate availability of inspection and other personnel with authority to order the making of emergency repairs. * * The criticism of the time it took to make repairs arose from the experience that even minor repairs—including leaking pipes, broken windows, lack of lights in the halls or minor boiler defects—were delayed because an outside contractor had to be hired when the need for the repair had been verified and the repair ordered. It has been suggested that the City should maintain its own repair crews for such minor repairs. On the other hand, however, it has been said that the loss of efficiency was made up for, at least to some extent, by the advantage gained in using indigenous personnel in making the repairs, thereby providing useful training

[17] Emergency Repair, at 181–182.

and experience in areas where they are most necessary.[18]

The problem with recoupment of costs arose out of a number of circumstances. Only a few liens, and no priority liens, appear to have been secured under the program. There were instances when a great deal of money was poured into the repair or maintenance of structures abandoned by the owner, where the City failed to secure its interests by obtaining title to the structures and lot by foreclosure. Priority liens diminish the costs of the City when the properties previously repaired under the emergency repair program are ultimately acquired by the City in the course of urban renewal. Other methods of securing recovery of expenses have also been suggested, including the use of rent payments withheld by the Department of Welfare [19] under the so-called "Spiegel Law" where rent withholding was based on the failure of the owner to comply with housing standards.[19A]

The City's Emergency Repair Program is being continued and its administrative operations have been simplified.[21] It is being funded by additional appropriations from time to time. Although recent figures on amounts spent on emergency repairs are not available,[22] it is clear that the repair program will never be self-liquidating, and that whatever funds are invested in emergency repairs will never be fully recovered. It seems to be the fate of so-called revolving funds in this area that they will revolve very little if at all. * * *

In a number of instances municipal repairs may be treated as assessable improvements, and the cost of the repair may then simply be added to other special assessments on the property and they may be collected in the same manner as real estate taxes. This is a useful device. No instances have been found, however, where this device was either challenged or upheld. This is of some significance, because emergency repairs do not normally fall into the same category of improvements for which special assessments have been authorized and recognized in the past. * * *

An example of this method of recovery of repair costs is furnished by the City of Rochester, N.Y., where a repair program has been going on since about 1962. Starting with a budget of only a few thousand dollars in the early years, the program is budgeted for more than $600,000 for the fiscal year 1967–68. The city hires contractors to make the repairs, and charges the owner for the full cost plus a handling charge of 5 percent, plus an additional 10 percent penalty. The amount of costs and the handling charges and penalties are added to the owner's tax bill as assessments. It is reported that this method for collection is very effective, and that the city has recovered its full repair costs—perhaps even more—as a result of penalty and handling charges! When an owner does not pay his assessments, he is subject to tax foreclosure in the usual course. The Rochester procedure has not, apparently, been tested in court.[26] * * *

---

18 Ibid., at 182–183.

19 Ibid., at 183–184.

19A [Editors: Cf. Farrell v. Drew, p. 690, infra. In the cases or urban renewal and rent withholding however, the moneys that the city would recoup are taxpayer moneys. Is it any easier to "disguise" repair lien moneys as welfare payments or as land acquisition costs than it would be to get a direct appropriation for housing rehabilitation? Should benefits flowing from tax expenditures ever be disguised?]

21 1966 N.Y.C.Dep't Bldgs.Ann.Rep., pp. 265–268.

22 The departmental report, supra, note 21, cites activities but provides no cost figures.

26 Report of Rochester, N. Y. repair experience was made available to the author by Mr. Robert Hale. See Report of Study on "Present State of Housing Code Enforcement," undertaken by NAHRO for the National Commission on Urban Problems (1968).

Because of the natural reluctance of municipalities to undertake programs that are open-ended and that may ultimately involve the municipality in repair expenses that it cannot recoup, it is essential that recovery provisions be strengthened by providing expressly for priority liens and rent liens, rather than, as do most repair laws at present, providing merely for the imposition of a non-priority lien by the municipality. Municipalities should as far as possible recover their expenses, especially because they are more likely to use their repair powers fully when their chances of recovering expenses are improved.

In working out arrangements for (possibly Federal) financial assistance to emergency repair programs, distinction will have to be drawn between governmental repair as part of a program of rehabilitation, and the kind of "first aid" operation here discussed. Since higher housing standards are required to obtain Federal funds for rehabilitation projects, such a distinction is essential, because such higher standards obviously should not apply with respect to repair programs in areas that are not considered ultimately salvageable. Whether "economically feasible" or not, the need is enormous and must be met on humanitarian, rather than economic grounds. * * *

Receivership

One of the most effective and massive remedies for dwellings with major violations is the court appointment of a receiver to manage a building, collect the rents and use them for required repairs and rehabilitation, and restore the building to its owner once it has been repaired and the expenses incurred by the receiver have been repaid.

Receivership is now authorized in six states;[18] in four of them the authorizing

legislation was enacted or became effective so recently that there has been no significant experience with the remedy.[19] Receivership is generally considered an "extraordinary remedy," and hence it has been authorized by *state* legislation. In the one instance where an attempt was made to provide for it by city ordinance without special state authorization—St. Louis—the ordinance was promptly invalidated.[20] * * * The only jurisdiction that has utilized the remedy consistently over the past three or four years is Chicago—New York City abandoned the remedy at the end of 1965 when a change of administration took place—and there have hardly been any new receivership proceedings instituted in New York City for about two years! [25]

The New York City Experience * * *

Passed in 1962, the New York receivership law [31] authorizes the code enforcement agency of New York City to petition for the appointment of a receiver whenever an owner fails or refuses to remedy conditions that have been certified by the agency as "a nuisance * * which constitutes a serious fire hazard or is a serious threat to life, health or safety. * * *"

If the court would find, following a hearing, that proof of a hazardous nuisance was sufficient, and that the facts

18 Conn.Gen.Stat. § 19–347b (Supp.1965); Smith-Hurd Ill.Ann.Stat. ch. 24, § 11–31–2 (Supp.1966); Burns' Ind.Ann.Stat. § 48–6144

(1963); Mass.Gen.Laws Ann. c. 111, § 127h (Supp.1966); N.J.Stat.Ann. § 40:48–2.12h (Supp.1965); McKinney's New York Mult. Dwell.Law § 309.

19 Connecticut, initially passed in 1965, amended to allow commencement of receiverships by tenants in 1967; Massachusetts, effective April 1966; New Jersey, effective 1962, but not applied.

20 City of St. Louis v. Golden Gate Corp., 421 S.W.2d 4 (Mo.1967).

25 During 1966, the first year of the new administration, 4 new receivers were appointed. These appointments had apparently been the results of proceedings begun in 1965. 1966 N.Y.C.Bldgs. Dep't Ann.Rep. 260.

31 N.Y.Mult.Dwell.Law § 309, as amended by L.1962, c. 492.

warranted granting the application, it appointed the Commissioner of Real Estate as receiver. * * *

In the event that the income was insufficient to pay for the costs of repair, the Department of Real Estate could advance money from a special repair and receivership revolving fund, and obtain a lien for such advances on all future rents, issues, and profits. This lien survived both the discharge of the receiver after his accounting to the court, and foreclosure by any mortgagee or lienor who had received notice, until all advances were fully paid.[31A] In 1965, when it became apparent that repayment out of rents through the prior rent lien would generally take a long time, the receivership law was amended to provide for a prior lien on the fee, or the property itself.[33]

The constitutionality of the receivership law, with special reference to its prior rent lien features, was upheld in 1964[34] (before the amendment that provided for a prior lien on the fee) against the same claims of denial of due process that had been raised 26 years earlier in the *Central Savings Bank* case.[35] * *

[The decision did not however, give any indication as to whether the priority lien on the fee—authorized in the 1965 amendment[36]—would pass muster, because that question was not before the court. But the entire tenor of the opinion would lead one to conclude that if the court were today presented with the determination whether the creation of a senior lien on the fee would be considered an unconstitutional impairment of the mortgagee's contract, or—procedural aspects aside—a violation of due process, the decision would be different from that in *Central Savings.*] . . .

Effectiveness of Receivership in New York

In the opinion of responsible public officials and qualified observers, the receivership law proved a most effective remedy during the three or four years of its application. Up to the end of 1965, when new receivership proceedings were no longer instituted, 679 cases were investigated for receivership, and proceedings were actually begun in about 450 of these. By April 1966, some 120 buildings had had receivers appointed.[38] But this does not provide the full picture of the success of the receivership remedy, for at least 20 percent of the 450 receivership proceedings begun were closed because the owner had shown substantial compliance even before the show-cause hearing, the first formal step in the appointment of a receiver. The Department, moreover, gave every encouragement to the owner who demonstrated a clear intent to start repairs immediately and entered into numerous compliance agreements. The point has also been made that the mere availability of the remedy has operated as a potential threat to noncomplying owners, resulting in substantial improvements in buildings not directly affected.[39]

31A [Editors: New York State had an earlier receivership law, passed in 1937, and invalidated one year later, Central Savings Bank v. City of New York, 279 N.Y. 266, 18 N.E.2d 151 (1938). Procedural due process objection to the notice provisions, as well as substantive due process criticism of the prior lien arrangement, grounded the Court's opinion. The 1962 act successfully avoided the defects in the earlier law, note 34 infra. Before the Court struck down the 1937 Act, repairs had been made on some 1300 buildings.]

33 N.Y.Sess.Laws L.1965, c. 144, and c. 919, eff. May 11, 1965.

34 Matter of Dep't of Buildings of the City of New York, 14 N.Y.2d 291, 200 N.E.2d 432 (1964). See also, Matter of Dep't of Buildings v. Soltzer, 16 N.Y.2d 915, 264 N.Y.S.2d 701, 212 N.E.2d 154 (1965).

35 Supra, note 31A.

36 Supra, note 33.

38 Gribetz & Grad, Housing Code Enforcement: Sanctions and Remedies, 66 Colum.L. Rev. 1254, 1273 (1966).

39 Gribetz & Grad, supra, note 38.

Receivership proved to be a most effective and direct remedy for seriously deteriorated and substandard buildings. Of all the available sanctions, receivership alone provided for *certain* removal of all serious hazards, and the restoration of at least minimal legal habitability. The remedy was effective, because it afforded an opportunity to make a careful selection of buildings appropriate for massive repair. The receivership procedure, too, assured that all of the parties concerned or involved with the deteriorated condition of the building could be notified and brought together with comparative ease. In addition to the owner—who no longer would stand to gain from his unavailability for service, as in a criminal proceeding—and the municipality, the proceeding also involved the mortgagee, who stood to lose some of the benefits of his silent partnership in slum ownership unless he acted to protect his investment.

The limitations on the receivership remedy in New York, which were effectively to suspend the use of the remedy, were primarily financial. It might be argued that a municipality should restore dwellings to safe and sanitary conditions meeting minimum legal requirements for decent shelter without regard to the ultimate recoupment of its investment. Nevertheless, almost three years' operation under the receivership program made it plain that rent liens were insufficient to allow for the amortization of repair costs within a reasonable time. Because of long neglect, the average repair cost for each building taken into receivership turned out to be over $25,000. Because rentals in receivership buildings were generally low—and were kept low by rent control—and maintenance costs high, the rent return available to satisfy the receiver's lien on the average building was no greater than $1,000 per month.[40]

The failure to recoup expenses over a reasonable period meant that the modest revolving fund was seriously depleted, and the program became self-limiting.

Initially, it had been anticipated that the city, by taking over some receivership buildings on tax foreclosure, would recoup its costs upon subsequent resale. This was a reasonable possibility since payment of taxes remained a continuing obligation of the owner, and the receiver would pay taxes only after the costs of repair, operation, and management had been met. But it turned out that neither rent liens nor tax foreclosures provided a reliable method of repayment. During the first 2½ years of operation, only 10 percent of the 1½ million dollars spent had been recovered. This experience then led to the 1965 amendment of the law, which provided for a prior receivership lien on the fee that would survive the discharge of the receiver. The idea was that once a building had been made livable, the city would be able to foreclose on its lien and, possibly, resell the building, for the chance of resale after full repair of the building was considered favorable.

The theory of the amendment has not been tested, for only a very few receivership proceedings were initiated after the amendments became effective, and the amendment was not applicable retroactively to receiverships begun prior to its effective date.

Ever since the beginning of the receivership program there had been a lively debate on whether the condition of the building and its need for rehabilitation ought to be the decisive factor in selecting it for receivership treatment; or whether the economic feasibility of rehabilitation and recoupment of costs out of rents within a reasonable time ought to be determinative.[42] * * * In

---

[40] Frank Lazarus, then Commissioner of the Department of Real Estate, quoted in the New York Times, April 8, 1965, p. 21, col. 1.

[42] Frank Lazarus, then Commissioner of the Department of Real Estate, the agency charged by law with statutory receivership

the long run economic considerations won the day in convincing the city administration of the necessity of discontinuing the program. This decision, while warranted to some extent by the City of New York's serious fiscal plight, was opposed by many knowledgeable persons, including the City Commissioner of Buildings.[43]

It has been pointed out that the effectiveness of the receivership remedy, even in financial terms, should not be measured in the amount of money recovered by way of prior liens on the rents or prior lien foreclosures. * * * Depriving the owner of the right to manage his property is a stronger deterrent than small criminal fines. Thus neighboring owners are stimulated by receivership to bring their own buildings into legal compliance. It was stated by the Commissioner of Buildings of the City of New York, who was largely responsible for the program,

In calculating the cost of continuing an effective receivership program, results

of slum buildings, had earlier estimated that the cost of removing violations from receivership buildings averaged almost $20,000 per building without hope of recovery and that the continuance of the program would put the City deeply in the red. N. Y. Times, Feb. 12, 1964, p. 1. In response, James Farmer, then National Director of CORE, stated:

> If 1,000 buildings were so repaired by the City—and this would be a major breakthrough—it would cost only $20 million, or just about two-thirds of 1 per cent of the city budget.

> It's a question of priorities. The World's Fair loan was more than $40 million. That was a risk loan without lasting benefit. The city lost money on such a loan in 1939–1940. So what are the priorities: Finance or human health?

N. Y. Times, Feb. 13, 1964, p. 20.

43 See note 38, supra. The Department of Buildings, under Commissioner Charles Moerdler, kept referring cases for receivership, but they were stopped at the level of the Department of Real Estate, whose cooperation, under established procedures, was necessary.

to date establish that receivership is a means of inducing several dollars of private improvement for every dollar of city expenditure. We have obtained desired code compliance in more than twice the number of buildings than those that resulted in the appointment of receivership.[44]

The Chicago Experience

Chicago's receivership program, the first in the country, began without any express statutory authorization, with an imaginative use of statutory construction, and of inherent and statutory equity powers by the courts. * * * Under a 1953 amendment of what was then the Illinois Cities and Villages Act, a municipality was authorized to "make application to any court of competent jurisdiction for an injunction requiring compliance" with city ordinances "or for such other order as the court may deem necessary or appropriate to secure such compliance."[45] The courts adopted the theory, and a number of receiverships were allowed without special statutory authorization upon application of the City of Chicago and, relying on its general equity powers, the Illinois courts went so far as to appoint receivers of buildings in violation of housing standards at the application of tenants in the buildings.

In 1965, receivership was placed on even more secure ground in Illinois, when the statute which had expressly provided only for injunctions was amended to authorize specifically the granting of receiverships. By its terms the statute provided that the municipality has the power to make application for the appointment of a receiver when, upon due investigation, any building located within an urban conservation area, as designated pursuant to the Illinois Urban Community Conservation Act, fails to conform to

44 Gribetz, New York City's Receivership Law, 21 J.Housing 297, 300 (1964).

45 Ill.Rev.Stat. ch. 24 § 11–31–2.

the standards and provisions of such a conservation plan, and if the owner of the building fails, after due notice, to make appropriate repairs so that the building will conform to the plan.

The Illinois receivership law further provides that an action for receivership be given precedence on the calendar. If a receiver is appointed by the court the receiver is given a prior lien on the rents to cover the cost of repairs, and he is also given the right to issue notes or receivership certificates paying "such interest as the court may fix." These receivership notes or certificates are to be negotiable, and when sold or transferred by the receiver, they become a first lien upon the property and its rents and other income. As soon as the purchaser files his notice of lien in the appropriate recorder's office, the lien of the receiver's note or certificate may be enforced by foreclosure in the same manner as a mortgage. Suit to foreclose must be commenced within two years after default. The law further provides that the court may authorize the receiver "to enter into such agreements and to do such acts as may be required to obtain first mortgage insurance on the receiver's notes or certificates from an agency of the federal government."

It should be noted that under the Illinois receivership statute receivership may be applied for if the building "fails to conform to the standards and provisions of" the applicable conservation plan. Unlike the New York statute, the Illinois provision does not require that especially hazardous defects be shown. Moreover, the compliance required is compliance with the standards of the conservation plan, not with the standards of the generally applicable housing ordinance. Thus the standards of repair that must be met by the owner—or by the receiver, if a receiver is appointed—are higher than ordinary housing code standards. Unlike the New York stat-

ute, the Illinois law does not require that a government agency be appointed receiver nor does it have elaborate requirements for notice on mortgagees or lienors. In actual practice just as great care is taken in Chicago to give notice and to join in the proceeding all of the interested parties as is the case in New York. In Chicago this is done under the general provisions of the rules of civil practice, which require such joinder if a party is to be bound by the judgment.

It is reported that the Chicago receivership program has been most effective. Since the beginning of the program in the early sixties, from eight to nine hundred receivership proceedings have been undertaken and some six hundred buildings are currently in receivership. The program was speeded up considerably after receivership was expressly authorized by the 1965 amendment of the law.

One of the organizations that has been most frequently designated as receiver is the Chicago Dwellings Association. The Chicago Dwellings Association is a limited dividend corporation, a subsidiary of the Chicago Housing Authority, which was originally organized pursuant to state law to build middle-income housing. The latest reports of the Chicago Dwellings Association show that by June 3, 1967, the Association had been appointed receiver for 374 buildings with 4,112 dwelling units. Receivership was completed and the receiver discharged in 286 buildings with 3,353 units. Currently, some 88 buildings with 759 units are being held in receivership by the Association.

It appears that the Chicago Dwellings Association has worked closely with the Chicago Housing Authority and the Chicago Department of Buildings in the selection of buildings for receivership. Somewhat less attention is paid in Chicago than in New York to the problem of economic feasibility of rehabilitation at the time receivership proceedings are instituted. It appears that receivership is increasingly being used, in fact, as a device to ferret out the truth with respect to the economic feasibility of rehabilitation.

Once the receiver is appointed, he investigates the situation, and if the building cannot be rehabilitated in an economic fashion, he reports back to the court with that information. Following such an adverse report, the owner will frequently agree to the entry of a demolition order. Thus receivership has actually served not only the end of rehabilitation but also the purpose of demolition of deteriorated buildings where rehabilitation is no longer practicable.[45a] * * *

It is noteworthy of receiverships in Chicago, according to reports from the Chicago Dwellings Association, that half the receivership buildings have three units or fewer. It is said that though financing the rehabilitation is easier in larger buildings, it is the smaller ones that are most likely to be badly deteriorated and in need of repair.[49]

A test case is presently pending, Gerick v. Chicago Title & Trust Company.[50] The circuit court of Cook County has already granted specific performance to a receiver in his suit to compel performance of a contract to purchase receivers' certificates as a valid first mortgage upon the real estate. It appears that the Chicago Title & Trust Company has been unwilling to insure receivers' certificates as a prior lien in the absence of a clear

holding by the highest court of Illinois. As a result, receivers' certificates have not been commercially marketable thus far, and receiverships have heretofore had to be financed out of public funds. If the test case is eventually affirmed by the Illinois Supreme Court,[50a] the marketability of receivership certificates would be assured and the road would be open to an enormous increase in receivership activities.[51]

HOUSING CODE ENFORCE-MENT—GRAD AND GRIBETZ

TOWARD A NEW CIVIL REMEDY

A. *Tailoring the Remedy*

The primary need in code enforcement is for an adequate range of legal sanctions to deal with the spectrum of housing problems of differing severity. The great majority of owners are law-abiding and usually need little more than notice of a code violation from the Department before they will make repairs. A smaller number of owners may need a determined push from the Department before they will comply. The number of hard-core, persistent violators, who require a major legal effort to compel them into compliance, is actually quite small, although an inordinate amount of the Department's time and means may go into bringing them to book. Thus, remedies of varying severity must be devised to deal differently with different groups. But all of the remedies must aim at inducing—

45a [Editors: Almost one-half of the receivership cases involving the Chicago Dwellings Association have resulted in demolition orders.]

49 The preceding account of the Chicago receivership experience is based on information received in April 1968 from Professor Julian H. Levi, Professor of Urban Studies, Division of Social Sciences, University of Chicago, who is counsel of the Chicago Dwellings Association.

50 66 CH 6882.

50a [We were unable to find an appellate citation. Eds.]

51 Cf. Dep't of Housing and Urban Development, Dep't of Justice and Office of Economic Opportunity, Tenants' Rights: Legal Tools for Better Housing 2 (Report on a National Conference on Legal Rights of Tenants, 1967).

both directly and indirectly—the future repair and rehabilitation of structures by their owners. The emphasis must be on solving the difficulties created by the problem *building*—not on the useless enterprise of punishing the troublesome *owner*.

The purposes of diversification of treatment in housing code enforcement are best served by emphasizing civil rather than criminal sanctions. Civil and economic remedies, such as receivership, the vacate order, and other remedies that affect the owner's rent roll have always been more effective than criminal prosecution. Since housing violations are basically economic offenses, the way to deal with them is through the imposition of economic sanctions.

To devise a promising program of civil, rather than criminal enforcement of housing standards, several steps would seem to be necessary. First, routine reliance on criminal prosecutions ought to be abandoned by repealing most of the provisions for criminal penalties. Criminal prosecution for housing violations ought to be retained only for the few, exceptional, cases where criminal intent or reckless defiance of legal requirements can be proven. Second, for the routine criminal prosecutions so abandoned there ought to be substituted a new economic sanction, namely, a mandatory civil penalty. This fine could be fixed by law at so much per violation per day, possibly graduated depending on the seriousness of the violation—the full cumulative amount to be recoverable by civil action, and, if not promptly paid by the owner, then collectible directly out of the building's rents. Third, all legal aspects of code enforcement ought to be consolidated in a single court of civil jurisdiction, with power to exercise its jurisdiction both *in personam* against the responsible party and *in rem* against the building. The court should operate somewhat like a "social" court (like fam-

ily court, for instance), and should have continuing jurisdiction to deal with the building and the responsible parties until full compliance with code requirements is assured. In order to afford the court full opportunity to exercise its consolidated jurisdiction, it should have jurisdiction of routine actions for the collection of civil penalties, actions for the collection of expenses incurred by the municipality in the repair or demolition of dwellings, proceedings for injunctive relief, receivership actions, actions by tenants to compel code compliance, including proceedings for summary dispossess for non-payment of rent in which the existence of housing violations has been raised as a defense, as well as of any other action or proceeding in which the existence of code violations is an issue.

B. *The Operation of the Cumulative Civil Penalty*

Perhaps the best method of explaining the operation of the proposed civil penalty is by way of an example. Assume that in the course of a housing inspection four housing violations are noted. A violation notice is then sent to the owner or agent, informing him of the existence of the violations and giving him notice that unless the violations are removed by a certain date—two or three weeks from the date of the notice in the case of non-hazardous violations—he shall become liable to a civil penalty fixed by law at three dollars per violation for each day, after the date of notice, prior to the removal of the violations. In the case of hazardous violations, the date for compliance might be advanced, or the Department might specify the need for "forthwith" or immediate compliance. On the date set for compliance, or as soon thereafter as possible, the Department would reinspect, and if there has been compliance, the matter would be closed and the owner would receive a notice to that effect. If he has failed to comply, the Department would face essentially the same problem it has now in cases of noncompliance—whether to take the case to court immediately or to seek compliance through further administrative action.

Assuming that the owner repairs three weeks after the date set for compliance, the Department could sue for a civil penalty of $252, a figure arrived at by multiplying the amount of the fine, three dollars, by the number of violations, four, by twenty-one, the number of days the violation had remained uncorrected. The Department could proceed to legal action at any time after the period for compliance has elapsed; under those circumstances, the action would not be for a fixed amount but for such amount of statutory penalties as might be shown to be due. If a persistent offender failed to make repairs during the pendency of the action, the court would have to calculate the penalty from the date of reinspection to the date of judgment. The defendant could limit the amount of the penalty by making repairs during the pendency of the action, notifying the Department that he had done so, and requesting that the violation be dismissed as of record. Because the penalty imposed would depend in each case on the length of time a violation had remained uncorrected, the Department would have to be prepared to make reinspections quite promptly. Although the length of time a violation has existed could well be a triable issue, provision could be made by law—possibly in the form of certain presumptions—for the possibility that prompt reinspection is not feasible in every case.

To avoid any misconception, we emphasize that it is the *principle* of a mandatory, cumulative per diem penalty that is proposed, not a three dollar per day per violation penalty as such. Perhaps the per diem penalty ought to be much less for certain run-of-the-mill violations, and higher for very serious ones. The precise formula can be worked out so long as the principle of a fixed penalty, small in itself but cumulative and varying in its impact according to the length of time violations remain unrepaired, is established.

C. *The Enforcement of the Remedy*

1. *Constitutionality.* From the constitutional point of view, there is no great difficulty in drafting legislation that will meet the objective. The imposition of civil penalties for the violation of police power regulations has been upheld, as has the validity of cumulative penalties. As long as a defendant may challenge and have judicially reviewed the Department's finding of a violation, without running the risk of paying a huge cumulative penalty for the full period of noncompliance if the issue is eventually decided against him, due process requirements are satisfied. Whether or not a jury trial would be necessary would depend on the particular state's constitution; in New York, in any event, a civil penalty action would not require trial by jury.

2. *Fairness.* A scheme of mandatory and cumulative civil penalties as here proposed is somewhat novel, but it is likely to operate more effectively than the present system of criminal prosecutions—mainly because the proposal seems inherently fair. The example of a proposed three dollar penalty per violation per day is less than the usual parking ticket, and the penalty would not begin to run until the offender has had an adequate time for compliance. Moreover, the offender has it within his power to reduce the amount of the penalty by making repairs promptly. Furthermore, the amount of the penalty is determinable in advance. The remedy is an economic penalty, and the offender has the opportunity to calculate how much his noncompliance will cost him; no calendar jockeying to get before an easy judge, or tem-

porary, time-wasting pleas of "not guilty" can affect the amount of the penalty. The fixed fine, too, removes the gambling element from housing cases; there is no chance that an owner with long-continued, serious violations will get away with an insignificant fine, nor is there a risk that the owner with few or minor violations who intended to repair promptly will unexpectedly suffer severe penalties. Finally, the remedy is less likely to encounter judicial nullification, because, unlike criminal prosecution, it does not subject the decent owner who is caught with violations on his property to the risk of a lifetime criminal record.

3. *Procedural Advantages*. Although the remedy is fair, it nonetheless has major potential for economic deterrence. Even though a penalty of some three dollars per day per violation is very low, an owner who permits several violations to persist for more than a few weeks will be liable to a civil penalty many times the average criminal fine of fifteen dollars presently imposed. Thus, the offender will have a very real incentive to make repairs promptly, particularly because the civil remedy presents fewer procedural obstacles to enforcement than criminal prosecution.

Unlike a criminal court, a civil court does not require the personal presence of the defendant in order to proceed. Not even personal service of process on the owner would be necessary; the Department could proceed *in rem* against the building itself merely by posting the summons on the building and mailing a copy to the owner listed in the Department registry (whether he is the actual owner or not). The penalty would be recoverable in any event by a rent lien, collectible out of the current rents. Thus, the "phantom landlord" whose whereabouts are never known when he is to be served with a summons would be deprived of his advantages—in fact, he might find it more advantageous to regis-

ter voluntarily so that he may at least get notice of any action taken against the building.

4. *A Side Effect: Revenue Production*. Aside from providing a real economic incentive to prompt repair and code compliance by the owners directly involved, the civil penalty is likely to benefit the aims of prompt rehabilitation of dwellings in another way. Unlike the criminal process, which has yielded mere pittances in fines, the civil penalty may be expected to yield substantial revenues, at least in its early years. Penalties collected could be specially earmarked by the city, to be used as a revolving fund for the making of repairs under a receivership or other direct repair program.

---

1. Repair and Offset

MARINI v. IRELAND

Supreme Court of New Jersey, 1970.
56 N.J. 130, 265 A.2d 526.

HANEMAN, J. This matter concerns the appealability of County District Court landlord and tenant dispossess judgments; the scope of a landlord's duty to make repairs; and the right to offset the cost of such repairs against accruing rent on the failure of the landlord to make same, if found to be required.

On or about April 2, 1969, plaintiff, landlord, and defendant, tenant, entered into a one-year lease for an apartment located in a two-family duplex building at 503–B Rand Street, Camden, New Jersey. The annual rent of $1,140 was agreed to be paid in monthly installments of $95. The lease incorporated a covenant of quiet enjoyment but did not include a specific covenant for repairs.

On or about June 25, 1969, defendant alleges that she discovered that the toilet in the leased apartment was cracked and water was leaking on to the bathroom floor. She further alleges that repeated attempts to inform plaintiff of this condition were unsuccessful. On or about June 27, 1969, defendant hired one Karl T. Bittner, a registered plumber, to repair the toilet. Bittner repaired the toilet at a cost of $85.72, which the tenant paid.

On July 15, 1969, defendant mailed plaintiff a check for $9.28 together with the receipt for $85.72 in payment of the July rent. Plaintiff challenged the offsetting of the cost of the repair and demanded the outstanding $85.72.

When his demands were refused, plaintiff instituted a summary dispossess action for nonpayment of rent in the Camden County District Court pursuant to N.J.S.A. 2A:18-53(b) alleging the nonpayment of the July rent in the amount of $85.72 and August rent of $95. A hearing was had on August 15, 1969. Plaintiff argued that he was entitled to the $85.72 because he had no duty to make repairs and consequently, defendant's payment of the cost of repair could not be offset against rent.

The judge conceived the issue as entirely a legal one and determined that the facts which defendant alleged did not create a duty upon the landlord to make repairs. Thus, without trying out the issues tendered by defendant, he found a default in payment of rent of $85.72 (July) and $95 (August) plus costs and rendered a judgment for possession. Defendant appealed to the Appellate Division.

On August 29, 1969, a judge of the Appellate Division granted a temporary stay of the judgment for possession and the warrant of eviction. The Appellate Division granted a stay pending appeal on September 23, 1969 and ordered de-

fendant to pay all the rents then due except the contested July rent. The Appellate Division also then denied plaintiff's cross-motion to dismiss the appeal. Before the Appellate Division heard argument, this Court certified the case on its own motion. R. 2:12-1.

The issues which evolve on this appeal are: Did defendant's claimed right to offset her cost of repairs against rent raise a "jurisdictional" issue. If the answer to that query is in the affirmative, did the landlord have a duty to repair and may the issue of failure to comply with such duty be raised in a dispossess action. Also involved in the latter question is the right of the tenant to make repairs upon the landlord's failure to so do and the right to offset the cost thereof against rent.

N.J.S.A. 2A:18-53 provides in part:

"Any lessee or tenant * * * of any houses, buildings, lands or tenements, * * * may be removed from such premises by the county district court of the county within which such premises are situated, in an action in the following cases:

*   *   *   *   *

"b. Where such person shall hold over after a default in the payment of rent, pursuant to the agreement under which the premises are held."

N.J.S.A. 2A:18-59 reads:

"Proceedings had by virtue of this article shall not be appealable except on the ground of lack of jurisdiction. The landlord, however, shall remain liable in a civil action for unlawful proceedings under this article."

* * * We hold, therefore, that equitable as well as legal defenses asserting payment or absolution from payment in whole or part are available to a tenant in a dispossess action and must be considered by the court. Denial of a motion by defendant directed at the complaint

for failure to make adequate factual allegations, or of a motion at the conclusion of the trial for failure to supply proof that the amount of rent alleged in the complaint is in default, both going to the question of jurisdiction, are each appealable.

Insofar as Peters v. Kelly, 98 N.J. Super. 441, 237 A.2d 635 (App.Div. 1968), conflicts with the foregoing it is overruled.

It becomes necessary to consider the merits of defendant's equitable defense that the failure of the landlord to repair the toilet constituted a breach of the covenant of habitability or quiet enjoyment and gave rise to defendant's entitlement to self-help, permitting her to repair the toilet and offset the cost thereof against her rent. We need not concern ourselves with the covenant of quiet enjoyment as will hereafter become apparent.

We are here concerned with the lease of premises for residential purposes. The lease provides:

"WITNESSETH, that the said party of the first part hath let, and by these presents doth grant, demise and to farm let unto the said party of the second part, all that contains 4 rooms and bath, apartment situated in the city and county of camden [sic.], state [sic.] of New Jersey, known and designated as 503—B Rand Street.

* * * * *

"nor use or permit any part thereof to be used for any other purpose than dwelling * * *."

As the lease contains no express covenant to repair, we are obliged to determine whether there arises an implied covenant, however categorized, which would require the landlord to make repairs.

A lease was originally considered a conveyance of an interest in real estate. Thus, the duties and obligations of the parties, implied as well as express, were dealt with according to the law of property and not of the law of contracts. In Michaels v. Brookchester, Inc., 26 N.J. 379 (1958) this Court said at p. 382, 140 A.2d 199, at p. 201:

"Historically a lease was viewed as a sale of an interest in land. The concept of *caveat emptor,* applicable to such sales, seemed logically pertinent to leases of land. There was neither an implied covenant of fitness for the intended use nor responsibility in the landlord to maintain the leased premises. Bauer v. 141–149 Cedar Lane Holding Co., 24 N.J. 139, 145, 130 A.2d 833 (1957); Bolitho v. Mintz, 106 N.J.L. 449, 148 A. 737 (E. & A. 1930). This principle, suitable for the agrarian setting in which it was conceived, lagged behind changes in dwelling habits and economic realities. 1 American Law of Property (1952), § 3.78, p. 347. Exceptions to the broad immunity inevitably developed."

The guidelines employed to construe contracts have been modernly applied to the construction of leases. 3 Thompson on Real Property 377 (1959). See also 6 Williston on Contracts, 3d ed. Jaeger, § 890A, p. 592 (1962):

"There is a clearly discernible tendency on the part of the courts to cast aside technicalities in the interpretation of leases and to concentrate their attention, as in the case of other contracts, on the intention of the parties, * * *."

In Pines v. Perssion, 14 Wis.2d 590, 111 N.W.2d 409 (Sup.Ct.Wis.1961), the court stated at p. 412:

"Legislation and administrative rules, such as the safeplace statute, building codes and health regulations, all impose certain duties on a property owner with respect to the condition of his premises. Thus, the legislature has made a policy judgment—that it is socially (and politically) desirable to impose these duties on a property owner—which has rendered the old common law rule obsolete. To follow the old rule of no implied warranty of habitability in leases would, in our opinion, be inconsistent with the current legislative policy concerning housing standards. The need and social desirability of adequate housing for people in this era of rapid population increases is too important to be rebuffed by that obnoxious legal cliché, *caveat emptor*. Permitting landlords to rent 'tumbledown' houses is at least a contributing cause of such problems as urban blight, juvenile delinquency and high property taxes for conscientious landowners."

In Reste Realty Corporation v. Cooper, 53 N.J. 444 (1969), this Court said at p. 452, 251 A.2d 268, at p. 272:

"Moreover, an awareness by legislatures of the inequality of bargaining power between landlord and tenant in many cases, and the need for tenant protection, has produced remedial tenement house and multiple dwelling statutes. See e. g., N.J.S.A. 55:13A–1 et seq. and the regulations thereunder; see generally Fuerstein and Shustack, 'Landlord and Tenant—The Statutory Duty to Repair,' 45 Ill.L.Rev. 205 (1950); Annotation, 17 A.L.R.2d 704 (1951). It has come to be recognized that ordinarily the lessee does not have as much knowledge of the condition of the premises as the lessor. Building code requirements and violations are known or made known to the lessor, not the lessee. He is in a better position to know of latent defects, structural and otherwise, in a building which might go unnoticed by a lessee who rarely has sufficient knowledge or expertise to see or to discover them. A prospective lessee, such as a small businessman, cannot be expected to know if the plumbing or wiring sys-

tems are adequate or conform to local codes. Nor should he be expected to hire experts to advise him. Ordinarily all this information should be considered readily available to the lessor who in turn can inform the prospective lessee. These factors have produced persuasive arguments for re-evaluation of the *caveat emptor* doctrine and, for imposition of an implied warranty that the premises are suitable for the leased purposes and conform to local codes and zoning laws."

See also Lemle v. Breeden, 462 P.2d 470 (Sup.Ct.Hawaii 1969).

A covenant in a lease can arise only by necessary implication from specific language of the lease or because it is indispensable to carry into effect the purpose of the lease. In determining, under contract law, what covenants are implied, the object which the parties had in view and intended to be accomplished, is of primary importance. The subject matter and circumstances of the letting give at least as clear a clue to the natural intentions of the parties as do the written words. It is of course not the province of the court to make a new contract or to supply any material stipulations or conditions which contravene the agreements of the parties. Kampf v. Franklin Life Ins. Co., 33 N.J. 36, 161 A.2d 717 (1960); Washington Construction Co., Inc. v. Spinella, 8 N.J. 212, 84 A.2d 617 (1951); City of Camden v. South Jersey Port Commission, 4 N.J. 357, 73 A.2d 55 (1950); McBride v. Maryland Casualty Co., 128 N.J.L. 64, 23 A.2d 596 (E. & A.1942). Terms are to be implied not because

"they are just or reasonable, but rather for the reason that the parties must have intended them and have only failed to express them * * * or because they are necessary to give business efficacy to the contract as written, or to give the contract the effect which the parties, as fair and reasonable men, presumably would have agreed on if, having in mind the possibility of the situation which has arisen, they contracted expressly in reference thereto. See 12 Am.Jur., Contracts, sec. 239; 14 Am.Jur., Covenants, Conditions and Restrictions, sec. 14." William Berland Realty Co. v. Hahne & Co., 26 N.J.Super. 477, 487, 98 A.2d 124, 129 (ch. 1953), modified 29 N.J. Super. 316, 102 A.2d 686 (App.Div. 1954).

See also Silverstein v. Keane, 19 N.J. 1, 115 A.2d 1 (1955). Cragmere Holding Corp. v. Socony Mobil Oil Co., 65 N.J. Super. 322, 167 A.2d 825 (App.Div. 1961).

So here, the lease expressly described the leased premises as "4 rooms and bath, apartment" and restricted the use thereof for one purpose,—"dwelling." Patently, "the effect which the parties, as fair and reasonable men, presumably would have agreed on," was that the premises were habitable and fit for living. The very object of the letting was to furnish the defendant with quarters suitable for living purposes. This is what the landlord at least impliedly (if not expressly) represented he had available and what the tenant was seeking. In a modern setting, the landlord should, in residential letting, be held to an implied covenant against latent defects, which is another manner of saying, habitability and livability fitness. See Hyland v. Parkside Investment Co., Inc., 10 N.J.Misc. 1148, 162 A. 521 (Sup.Ct. 1932). It is a mere matter of semantics whether we designate this covenant one "to repair" or "of habitability and livability fitness." Actually it is a covenant that at the inception of the lease, there are no latent defects in facilities vital to the use of the premises for residential purposes because of faulty original construction or deterioration from age or normal usage. And further it is a cove-

nant that these facilities will remain in usable condition during the entire term of the lease. In performance of this covenant the landlord is required to maintain those facilities in a condition which renders the property livable.

It is eminently fair and just to charge a landlord with the duty of warranting that a building or part thereof rented for residential purposes is fit for that purpose at the inception of the term and will remain so during the entire term. Of course, ancillary to such understanding it must be implied that he has further agreed to repair damage to vital facilities caused by ordinary wear and tear during said term. Where damage has been caused maliciously or by abnormal or unusual use, the tenant is conversely liable for repair. The nature of vital facilities and the extent and type of maintenance and repair required is limited and governed by the type of property rented and the amount of rent reserved. Failure to so maintain the property would constitute a constructive eviction.

It becomes necessary to consider the respective rights and duties which accompany such an implied covenant. We must recognize that historically, the landlord's covenant to alter or repair premises and the tenant's covenant to pay rent were generally regarded as independent covenants. The landlord's failure to perform did not entitle the tenant to make the repair and offset the cost thereof against future rent. It only gave rise to a separate cause of action for breach of covenant. Duncan Development Co. v. Duncan Hardware, Inc., 34 N.J.Super. 293 at 298, 112 A.2d 274 (App.Div. 1955), cert. denied 19 N.J. 328, 116 A. 2d 829 (1955); Stewart v. Childs Co., 86 N.J.L. 648, 92 A. 392 (E. & A. 1914). This result also eventuated from the application of the law of real estate rather than of contract. The concept of mutually dependent promises was not originally applied to the ascertainment of whether covenants in leases were dependent or independent. However, presently we recognize that covenants are dependent or independent according to the intention of the parties and the good sense of the case. Higgins v. Whiting, 102 N.J.L. 279, 131 A. 879 (Sup.Ct.1925); 3 Thompson on Real Property, § 1115 (1959 Replacement).

In Higgins v. Whiting, supra, the court said at pp. 280 and 281, 131 A. at p. 880 concerning the test of dependency of express covenants:

"In 24 Cyc. 918, it is said that covenants are to be construed as dependent or independent according to the intention and meaning of the parties and the good sense of the case. Technical words should give way to such intention. 7 R.C.L. 1090, § 7. So, the rule is thus stated; where the acts or covenants of the parties are concurrent, and to be done or performed at the same time, the covenants are dependent, and neither party can maintain an action against the other, without averring and proving performance on his part. 13 Corpus Juris 567.

*   *   *   *   *

"In the present case, the covenant to pay rent and the covenant to heat the apartment are mutual and dependent. In the modern apartment house equipped for heating from a central plant, entirely under the control of the landlord or his agent, heat is one of the things for which the tenant pays under the name 'rent.' "

Our courts have on a case by case basis held various lease covenants and covenants to pay rent as dependent and under the guise of a constructive eviction have considered breach of the former as giving the right to the tenant to remove from the premises and terminate his obligation to pay rent. See McCurdy v. Wyckoff, 73 N.J.L. 368, 63 A. 992 (Sup.Ct.1906); Weiler v. Pancoast, 71 N.J.L. 414, 58 A. 1084 (Sup.Ct.1904); Higgins v. Whiting, 102 N.J.L. 279, 131 A. 879 (Sup.Ct.1925); Stevenson Stanoyevich Fund v. Steinacher, 125 N.J.L. 326, 15 A.2d 772 (Sup.Ct.1940).

It is of little comfort to a tenant in these days of housing shortage to accord him the right, upon a constructive eviction, to vacate the premises and end his obligation to pay rent. Rather he should be accorded the alternative remedy of terminating the cause of the constructive eviction where as here the cause is the failure to make reasonable repairs. See Reste Realty Corporation v. Cooper, supra, footnote 1, 53 N.J. pp. 462, 463, 251 A.2d 268. This latter course of action is accompanied by the right to offset the cost of such repairs as are reasonable in the light of the value of the leasehold against the rent. His pursuit of the latter form of relief should of course be circumscribed by the aforementioned conditions.

If, therefore, a landlord fails to make repairs and replacements of vital facilities necessary to maintain the premises in a livable condition for a period of time adequate to accomplish such repair and replacements, the tenant may cause the same to be done and deduct the cost thereof from future rents. The tenant's recourse to such self-help must be preceded by timely and adequate notice to the landlord of the faulty condition in order to accord him the opportunity to make the necessary replacement or repair. If the tenant is unable to give such notice after a reasonable attempt, he may nonetheless proceed to repair or replace. This does not mean that the tenant is relieved from the payment of rent so long as the landlord fails to repair. The tenant has only the alternative remedies of making the repairs or removing from the premises upon such a constructive eviction.

We realize that the foregoing may increase the trials and appeals in landlord and tenant dispossess cases and thus increase the burden of the judiciary. By way of warning, however, it should be noted that the foregoing does not constitute an invitation to obstruct the recovery of possession by a landlord legitimately entitled thereto. It is therefore suggested that if the trial of the matter is delayed the defendant may be required to deposit the full amount of unpaid rent in order to protect the landlord if he prevails. Also, an application for a stay of an order of removal on appeal should be critically analyzed and not automatically granted.

In the light of the foregoing we find it unnecessary to pass on defendant's other grounds of appeal.

Reversed and remanded for trial in accordance with the above.

For reversal and remandment: Chief Justice WEINTRAUB and Justices JACOBS, FRANCIS, PROCTOR, HALL, SCHETTINO and HANEMAN—7.

For affirmance: None.

Notes on Repair and Offset

1. In Garcia v. Freeland Realty, Inc., 63 Misc.2d 937, 314 N.Y.S.2d 215 (Civ. Ct.1970), tenant sued to recover (1) the cost of plaster and paint needed to repair his apartment's walls, and (2) the reasonable value of his labor, computed at $7.00 an hour for 10 hours. The record established that the tenant's two very young children had been eating plaster and paint flakes from walls that the landlord had refused to repair.

Although the court gave judgment to the tenant and cited the Marini decision, the court narrowed the Marini rationale. Judicial notice was taken that New York City slum children often suffered serious lead poisoning (and sometimes mental retardation) from eating plaster and paint flakes. [The New York Times had reported 25,000 to 35,000 cases yearly.] Calling the condition of the tenant's walls one of emergency, the court held that the tenant could remove this menace to his children's health and charge the cost to the landlord, since the landlord (under New York law) might well be liable in tort if any child was poisoned. In other words, the tenant was free to head off an actionable tort resulting from the landlord's inaction.

Why might the landlord have been liable in tort? In Altz v. Leiberson, 233 N.Y. 16, 134 N.E. 703 (1922), a tenant, injured by a falling ceiling in his apartment, sued and recovered judgment from a landlord who had breached the statutory duty to repair. Judge Cardozo concluded his opinion with the following observation:

> "We may be sure that the framers of this statute, when regulating tenement life, had uppermost in thought the care of those who are unable to care for themselves. The legislature must have known that unless repairs in the rooms of the poor were made by the landlord, they would not be made by anyone. The duty imposed became commensurate with the need. The right to seek redress is not limited to the city or its officers. The right extends to all whom there was a purpose to protect."

Yet the New York courts did not extend this logic beyond the tort area, holding (in two Appellate Division decisions) that a tenant could not charge back repair costs where landlord failed (as required by statute) to paint or repair. Davar Holdings, Inc. v. Cohen, 255 App.Div. 445, 7 N.Y.S.2d 911 (1938) aff'd without opinion, 280 N.Y. 828, 21 N.E.2d 882 (1939); Emigrant Industrial Savings Bank v. 108 W. 49th St. Corp., 255 App.Div. 570, 8 N.Y.S. 2d 354 (1938), aff'd without opinion,

280 N.Y. 791, 21 N.E.2d 620 (1939). In both cases, the courts said that housing code duties were enforceable by the municipality only.

In the *Garcia* case, Judge Goodell might have limited the earlier cases to their (quite unusual) facts; instead, he modified the "no repair and offset" rule whenever a tenant's health was jeopardized. And, thus, the common law inched forward. A few months later, a different trial judge (Sandler of East Haven Associates "fame," infra) took the next inch. See Jackson v. Rivera, 318 N.Y.S. 2d 7 (Civ.Ct.1970) (tenant able to make and offset a $22 "emergency" repair of a toilet that did not work).

2. Some states, by statute, have long given the tenant either a limited or an open-ended privilege to repair and offset. Below are two examples:

WEST'S ANN.CAL.CIV.CODE § 1942

"If within a reasonable time after notice to the lessor, of dilapidations which he ought to repair, he neglects to do so, the lessee may repair the same himself, where the cost of such repairs do not require an expenditure greater than one month's rent of the premises, and deduct the expenses of such repairs from the rent, or the lessee may vacate the premises, in which case he shall be discharged from further payment of rent, or performance of other conditions."

OKL.STAT.ANN. TIT. 41, § 32

§ 32. When lessee may repair

"If within a reasonable time after notice to the lessor of dilapidations which he ought to repair, he neglects to do so, the lessee may repair the same himself and deduct the expense of such repairs from the rent, or otherwise recover it from the lessor; or the lessor may vacate the premises, in

which case he shall be discharged from further payment of rent, or performance of other conditions."

Is there any practical justification for denying tenants the privilege of repair-and-offset? Or, as in the California statute, limiting the expenditure for which offset is available?

3. Assume that the state recognizes a repair-and-offset rule:

a. May the tenant, who performs the work himself, charge for his time? If so, at what rate? Cf. Garcia v. Freeland Realty, Inc., supra.

b. Before embarking on the repairs, must tenant first give landlord a reasonable chance to do the work? If so, what is reasonable? Might reasonable depend upon the degree of tenant's inconvenience if the work remains undone, or on the peril to the tenant's health, or on the landlord's previous record of making repairs? Should tenant be reimbursed if he goes ahead without first giving landlord notice and a fair chance to do the work? In that connection, suppose that the tenant does the work perfectly and at a cost no greater than the landlord would have incurred?

c. Suppose that the tenant does the work perfectly—after landlord refuses to act—but at a cost greater than "the fair and reasonable value" of the labor and materials (alternatively, at a cost greater than the landlord would have incurred): May the tenant recoup his entire outlay? Suppose that the tenant imperfectly does the work: What then are his risks?

d. In the name of "repairs," what work may the tenant order? Suppose, for example, there is an electrical short which requires urgent attention, and also a long-standing incapacity in the electrical wiring system preventing tenant from using major appliances:

May tenant, while the electrician is repairing the short, also order the rewiring even though the installation of heavier wiring is a form of capital improvement?

e. Realistically, how valuable is the repair-and-offset remedy for low-income tenants who are not able to do much of the repair work themselves? What if tenant orders the work, but does not pay for it: May the unpaid artisan file a mechanic's lien against the property? Cf. 79 A.L.R. 962 (1932); 163 A.L.R. 992 (1946); 4 A.L.R. 685, 687 (1919).

What new financing and administrative procedures seem called for to insure a steady level of repairs as part of a code enforcement program?

f. The *Marini* and (to a lesser extent) *Garcia* decisions privilege the tenant to make the repairs when landlord refuses to act. Might it be argued that the privilege is coupled with a duty—i. e., the tenant *must* act (if he can reasonably do so) to eliminate conditions perilous to his health and safety, and that tenant assumes the risk of his failure to act?

g. The common-law imposed no duty upon landlords to repair, but if landlord undertook to make repairs voluntarily (or by covenant), he was liable to his tenants for injuries caused by his negligence or unskillfulness in making repairs, or in leaving the premises in an unsafe condition. Marks v. Nambil Realty Co., Inc., 245 N.Y. 256, 157 N.E. 129 (1927), 150 A.L.R. 1373 (1944). Compare May v. 11½ East 49th St. Co., 269 App.Div. 180, 54 N.Y.S. 2d 860 (1945), aff'd 296 N.Y. 599, 68 N.E.2d 881 (1946) (Marks rule does not apply where work done by independent contractor). Should tenant who voluntarily makes repairs also be subject to liability if he completes the repairs negligently? To take a specific case: Suppose that tenant, while repairing hallway stairs, fails properly to tack down the carpeting and a second tenant trips and injures himself. Does the injured tenant have a claim against the tenant who repaired? Since a fellow-tenant may very well be uninsured and totally unable to pay any judgment rendered against him, what value has the suit? Can it be argued successfully that the "repairing" tenant—for the purpose of these repairs—acted as landlord's agent?

h. The cases that we have seen deal with repairs within the tenant's own apartment. Are there any reasons why the doctrine should not extend to repairs in the common areas or in an apartment of a neighboring tenant (a) where the condition threatens the acting tenant's health or safety, (b) where the condition threatens the acting tenant's property, (c) where the condition interferes with the acting tenant's comfort? In short, can we have a tenant (or a tenant's association) acting as a building "ombudsman," curing code violations as they occur and applying all expenditures against future rent? Would we need a statute to achieve this? How would you draft the statute?

2. Suspension of Rent

BROWN v. SOUTHALL REALTY COMPANY

Court of Appeals of District of Columbia, 1968.

237 A.2d 834.

QUINN, Judge. This appeal arises out of an action for possession brought by appellee-landlord, against appellant-tenant, Mrs. Brown, for nonpayment of rent. The parties stipulated, at the time of trial, that the rent was in the arrears in the amount of $230.00. Mrs. Brown contended, however, that no rent was due under the lease because it was an illegal contract. The court held to the contrary and awarded appellee possession for non-payment of rent.

Although counsel for appellant stated at oral argument before this court that Mrs. Brown had moved from the premises and did not wish to be returned to possession, she asserts that this court should hear this appeal because the judgment of the court below would render certain facts res judicata in any subsequent suit for rent. * * *

Thus, because the validity of the lease and the determination that rent is owing will be irrevocably established in this case if the judgment of the trial court is allowed to stand, we feel that this appeal is timely made.

Although appellant notes a number of errors, we consider the allegation that the trial court erred in failing to declare the lease agreement void as an illegal contract both meritorious and completely dispositive, and for this reason we reverse.

The evidence developed, at the trial, revealed that prior to the signing of the lease agreement, appellee was on notice that certain Housing Code violations existed on the premises in question. An inspector for the District of Columbia Housing Division of the Department of Licenses and Inspections testified that the violations, an obstructed commode, a broken railing and insufficient ceiling height in the basement, existed at least some months prior to the lease agreement and had not been abated at the time of trial. He also stated that the basement violations prohibited the use of the entire basement as a dwelling place. Counsel for appellant at the trial below elicited an admission from the appellee that "he told the defendant after the lease had been signed that the back room of

the basement was habitable despite the Housing Code Violations." In addition, a Mr. Sinkler Penn, the owner of the premises in question, was called as an adverse witness by the defense. He testified that "he had submitted a sworn statement to the Housing Division on December 8, 1964 to the effect that the basement was unoccupied at that time and would continue to be kept vacant until the violations were corrected."

This evidence having been established and uncontroverted, appellant contends that the lease should have been declared unenforceable because it was entered into in contravention to the District of Columbia Housing Regulations, and knowingly so.

Section 2304 of the District of Columbia Housing Regulations reads as follows:

No persons shall rent or offer to rent any habitation, or the furnishings thereof, unless such habitation and its furnishings are in a clean, safe and sanitary condition, in repair, and free from rodents or vermin.

Section 2501 of these same Regulations, states:

Every premises accommodating one or more habitations shall be maintained and kept in repair so as to provide decent living accommodations for the occupants. This part of the Code contemplates more than mere basic repairs and maintenance to keep out the elements; its purpose is to include repairs and maintenance designed to make a premises or neighborhood healthy and safe.

It appears that the violations known by appellee to be existing on the leasehold at the time of the signing of the lease agreement were of a nature to make the "habitation" unsafe and unsanitary. Neither had the premises been maintained or repaired to the degree contemplated by the regulations, i. e., "designed to make a premises * * * healthy and safe." The lease contract was, therefore, entered into in violation of the Housing Regulations requiring that they be safe and sanitary and that they be properly maintained.

In the case of Hartman v. Lubar, 77 U.S.App.D.C. 95, 96, 133 F.2d 44, 45 (1942), cert. denied, 319 U.S. 767, 63 S.Ct. 1329, 87 L.Ed. 1716 (1943), the court stated that, "[t]he general rule is that an illegal contract, made in violation of the statutory prohibition designed for police or regulatory purposes, is void and confers no right upon the wrongdoer." The court in Lloyd v. Johnson, 45 App. D.C. 322, 327 (1916), indicated:

> To this general rule, however, the courts have found exceptions. For the exception, resort must be had to the intent of the legislature, as well as the subject matter of the legislation. The test for the application of the exception is pointed out in Pangborn v. Westlake, 36 Iowa 546, 549, and approved in Miller v. Ammon, 145 U.S. 421, 426, 36 L.Ed. 759, 762, 12 Sup. Ct.Rep. 884, as follows: "We are, therefore, brought to the true test, which is, that while, as a general rule, a penalty implies a prohibition, yet the courts will always look to the subject matter of it, the wrong or evil which it seeks to remedy or prevent, and the purpose sought to be accomplished in its enactment; and if, from all these, it is manifest that it was not intended to imply a prohibition or to render the prohibited act void, the court will so hold and construe the statute accordingly."

Applying this general rule to the Housing Regulations, it may be stated initially that they do provide for penalties for violations. A reading of Sections 2304 and 2501 infers that the Commissioners of the District of Columbia, in promulgating these Housing Regulations, were endeavoring to regulate the rental of housing in the District and to insure

for the prospective tenants that these rental units would be "habitable" and maintained as such. The public policy considerations are adequately stated in Section 2101 of the District of Columbia Housing Regulations, entitled "Purpose of Regulations." To uphold the validity of this lease agreement, in light of the defects known to be existing on the leasehold prior to the agreement (i. e., obstructed commode, broken railing, and insufficient ceiling height in the basement), would be to flout the evident purposes for which Sections 2304 and 2501 were enacted. The more reasonable view is, therefore, that where such conditions exist on a leasehold prior to an agreement to lease the letting of such premises constitutes a violation of Sections 2304 and 2501 of the Housing Regulations, and that these Sections do indeed "imply a prohibition" so as "to render the prohibited act void." Neither does there exist any reason to treat a lease agreement differently from any other contract in this regard.

Thus, for this reason and those stated above, we reverse.

Reversed.

Notes on Brown v. Southall Realty Co.

The holding of the *Southall* case has been followed in Diamond Housing Corporation v. Robinson, 257 A.2d 492 (D.C.App.1969) in circumstances where the owner knew of the violations, though they had not been officially noted. The theory of illegal contract was not followed in Saunders v. First National Realty Corporation, 245 A.2d 836 (D.C.App. 1968) where the violations appeared only after the lease was signed; thus, the lease was not illegal from its inception. The theory of illegality of contract has also been upheld in the case of Jensen v. Salisbury, CV12–6808–1934 (Conn.Civ. Ct., 12th Cir., Sept. 9, 1968). Various writers, in discussing the theory of illegality of contract as applied to leases in violations of housing codes, have indicated their belief that the theory allows the tenant to escape the obligations of the lease but does not provide him with a right to remain in the premises indefinitely. Note, Leases and the Illegal Contract Theory, 56 Geo.L.J. 920 (1968); Note, Tenants' Rights in the District of Columbia: New Hope for Reform, 18 Cath.L.Rev. 80 (1968); Note, Brown v. Southall Realty Co., 30 U.Pitt.L.Rev. 134 (1968). The matter has been explained in Diamond Housing Corp. v. Robinson, supra, in which the court expressly clarified its opinion in Brown v. Southall. When a lease is void and unenforceable, the court held, the tenant becomes a tenant at sufferance, and his tenancy may be terminated (under the D. C. code) on thirty days' notice. The court added that a landlord is not under an obligation to rent his property, and if he is unwilling to put the property into habitable, safe and sanitary condition, "he may and should properly terminate the tenancy and withdraw the property from the rental market. * * *" (257 A.2d at 495).

The following contains a good summary of recent developments in warranty and illegality of contract theories, M. Moskowvitz, Rent Withholding and The Implied Warranty of Habitability—Some New Breakthroughs, 4 Clearinghouse Review 49 (1970).

JAVINS v. FIRST NATIONAL REALTY CORP.

United States Court of Appeals, District of Columbia Circuit, 1970.
138 U.S.App.D.C. 369, 428 F.2d 1071.

J. SKELLY WRIGHT, Circuit Judge. These cases present the question whether housing code [1] violations which arise dur-

[1] Housing Regulations of the District of Columbia (1956). [Some footnotes have been omitted].

ing the term of a lease have any effect upon the tenant's obligation to pay rent. The Landlord and Tenant Branch of the District of Columbia Court of General Sessions ruled proof of such violations inadmissible when proffered as a defense to an eviction action for nonpayment of rent. The District of Columbia Court of Appeals upheld this ruling. Saunders v. First National Realty Corp., 245 A.2d 836 (1968).

Because of the importance of the question presented, we granted appellants' petitions for leave to appeal. We now reverse and hold that a warranty of habitability, measured by the standards set out in the Housing Regulations for the District of Columbia, is implied by operation of law into leases of urban dwelling units covered by those Regulations and that breach of this warranty gives rise to the usual remedies for breach of contract.

I

The facts revealed by the record are simple. By separate written leases, each of the appellants rented an apartment in a three-building apartment complex in Northwest Washington known as Clifton Terrace. The landlord, First National Realty Corporation, filed separate actions in the Landlord and Tenant Branch of the Court of General Sessions on April 8, 1966, seeking possession on the ground that each of the appellants had defaulted in the payment of rent due for the month of April. The tenants, appellants here, admitted that they had not paid the landlord any rent for April. However, they alleged numerous violations of the Housing Regulations as "an equitable defense or [a] claim by way of recoupment or set-off in an amount equal to the rent claim," as provided in the rules of the Court of General Sessions. They offered to prove

"[t]hat there are approximately 1500 violations of the Housing Regulations of the District of Columbia in the building at Clifton Terrace, where Defendant resides, some affecting the premises of this Defendant directly, others indirectly, and all tending to establish a course of conduct of violation of the Housing Regulations to the damage of Defendants * * *."

Settled Statement of Proceedings and Evidence, p. 2 (1966). Appellants conceded at trial, however, that this offer of proof reached only violations which had arisen since the term of the lease had commenced. The Court of General Sessions refused appellants' offer of proof and entered judgment for the landlord. The District of Columbia Court of Appeals affirmed, rejecting the argument made by appellants that the landlord was under a contractual duty to maintain the premises in compliance with the Housing Regulations. Saunders v. First National Realty Corp., supra, 245 A.2d at 838.

II

Since, in traditional analysis, a lease was the conveyance of an interest in land, courts have usually utilized the special rules governing real property transactions to resolve controversies involving leases. However, as the Supreme Court has noted in another context, "the body of private property law * * *, more than almost any other branch of law, has been shaped by distinctions whose validity is largely historical." [6] Courts have a duty to reappraise old doctrines in the light of the facts and values of contemporary life—particularly old common law doctrines which the courts themselves created and developed. As we have said before, "[T]he continued vitality of the common law * * * depends upon its ability to reflect contemporary community values and ethics."

The assumption of landlord-tenant law, derived from feudal property law, that a lease primarily conveyed to the ten-

ant an interest in land may have been reasonable in a rural, agrarian society; it may continue to be reasonable in some leases involving farming or commercial land. In these cases, the value of the lease to the tenant is the land itself. But in the case of the modern apartment dweller, the value of the lease is that it gives him a place to live. The city dweller who seeks to lease an apartment on the third floor of a tenement has little interest in the land 30 or 40 feet below, or even in the bare right to possession within the four walls of his apartment. When American city dwellers, both rich and poor, seek "shelter" today, they seek a well known package of goods and services [9]—a package which includes not merely walls and ceilings, but also adequate heat, light and ventilation, serviceable plumbing facilities, secure windows and doors, proper sanitation, and proper maintenance.

Professor Powell summarizes the present state of the law:

"* * * The complexities of city life, and the proliferated problems of modern society in general, have created new problems for lessors and lessees and these have been commonly handled by specific clauses inserted in leases. This growth in the number and detail of specific lease covenants has reintroduced into the law of estates for years a predominantly contractual ingredient. In practice, the law today concerning estates for years consists chiefly of rules determining the construction and effect of lease covenants. * * *" [10]

Ironically, however, the rules governing the construction and interpretation of

[6] Jones v. United States, 362 U.S. 257, 266, 80 S.Ct. 725, 733, 4 L.Ed.2d 697 (1960).

[9] See, e. g., National Commission on Urban Problems, Building the American City 9 (1968). The extensive standards set out in the Housing Regulations provide a good guide to community expectations.

[10] 2 R. Powell, Real Property ¶ 221 [1] at 179 (1967).

"predominantly contractual" obligations in leases have too often remained rooted in old property law.

Some courts have realized that certain of the old rules of property law governing leases are inappropriate for today's transactions. In order to reach results more in accord with the legitimate expectations of the parties and the standards of the community, courts have been gradually introducing more modern precepts of contract law in interpreting leases.[11] Proceeding piecemeal has, however, led to confusion where "decisions are frequently conflicting, not because of a healthy disagreement on social policy, but because of the lingering impact of rules whose policies are long since dead."[12]

In our judgment the trend toward treating leases as contracts is wise and well considered. Our holding in this case reflects a belief that leases of urban dwelling units should be interpreted and construed like any other contract.[13]

III

Modern contract law has recognized that the buyer of goods and services in an industrialized society must rely upon the skill and honesty of the supplier to assure that goods and services purchased are of adequate quality. In interpreting most contracts, courts have sought to protect the legitimate expectations of the buyer and have steadily widened the seller's responsibility for the quality of goods and services through implied warranties of fitness and merchantability. Thus without any special agreement a merchant will be held to warrant that his goods are fit for the ordinary purposes for which such goods are used and that they are at least of reasonably average quality. Moreover, if the supplier has been notified that goods are required for a specific purpose, he will be held to warrant that any goods sold are fit for that purpose. These implied warranties have become widely accepted and well established features of the common law, supported by the overwhelming body of case law. Today most states as well as the District of Columbia have codified and enacted these warranties into statute, as to the sale of goods, in the Uniform Commercial Code.

Implied warranties of quality have not been limited to cases involving sales. The consumer renting a chattel, paying for services, or buying a combination of goods and services must rely upon the skill and honesty of the supplier to at least the same extent as a purchaser of goods. Courts have not hesitated to find implied warranties of fitness and merchantability in such situations. In most areas product liability law has moved far beyond "mere" implied warranties running between two parties in privity with each other.

The rigid doctrines of real property law have tended to inhibit the application of implied warranties to transactions involving real estate. Now, however, courts have begun to hold sellers and developers of real property responsible for the quality of their product. For ex-

---

[11] E. g., Medico-Dental Building Co. v. Horton & Converse, 21 Cal.2d 411, 418, 132 P.2d 457, 462 (1942). See also 1 American Law of Property § 3.11 at 202–205 (A. Casner ed. 1952); Note, The California Lease—Contract or Conveyance?, 4 Stan.L.Rev. 244 (1952); Friedman, The Nature of a Lease in New York, 33 Cornell L.Q. 165 (1947).

[12] Kessler, The Protection of the Consumer Under Modern Sales Law, 74 Yale L.J. 262, 263 (1964).

[13] * * * We also intend no alteration of statutory or case law definitions of the term "real property" for purposes of statutes or decisions on recordation, descent, conveyancing, creditors' rights, etc. We contemplate only that contract law is to determine the rights and obligations of the parties to the lease agreement, as between themselves. The civil law has always viewed the lease as a contract, and in our judgment that perspective has proved superior to that of the common law. See 2 M. Planiol, Treatise on the Civil Law § 1663 et seq. (1959); 11 La.Stat. Ann., Civil Code, Art. 2669 (1952).

ample, builders of new homes have recently been held liable to purchasers for improper construction on the ground that the builders had breached an implied warranty of fitness. In other cases courts have held builders of new homes liable for breach of an implied warranty that all local building regulations had been complied with. And following the developments in other areas, very recent decisions and commentary [25] suggest the possible extension of liability to parties other than the immediate seller for improper construction of residential real estate.

Despite this trend in the sale of real estate, many courts have been unwilling to imply warranties of quality, specifically a warranty of habitability, into leases of apartments. Recent decisions have offered no convincing explanation for their refusal [26]; rather they have relied without discussion upon the old common law rule that the lessor is not obligated to repair unless he covenants to do so in the written lease contract.[27] However, the Supreme Courts of at least two states, in recent and well reasoned opinions, have held landlords to implied warranties of quality in housing leases. Lemle v. Breeden, S.Ct.Hawaii, 462 P.2d 470 (1969); Reste Realty Corp. v. Cooper, 53 N.J. 444, 251 A.2d 268 (1969). See also Pines v. Perssion, 14 Wis.2d 590, 111 N.W.2d 409 (1961). In our judgment, the old no-repair rule cannot co-exist with the obligations imposed on the landlord by a typical modern housing

code, and must be abandoned [28] in favor of an implied warranty of habitability.[29] In the District of Columbia, the standards of this warranty are set out in the Housing Regulations.

IV

A. In our judgment the common law itself must recognize the landlord's obligation to keep his premises in a habitable condition. This conclusion is compelled by three separate considerations. First, we believe that the old rule was based on certain factual assumptions which are no longer true; on its own terms, it can no longer be justified. Second, we believe that the consumer protection cases discussed above require that the old rule be abandoned in order to bring residential landlord-tenant law into harmony with the principles on which those cases rest. Third, we think that the nature of today's urban housing market also dictates abandonment of the old rule.

The common law rule absolving the lessor of all obligation to repair originated in the early Middle Ages.[30] Such a rule was perhaps well suited to an agrarian economy; the land was more impor-

[25] Comment, Liability of the Institutional Lender for Structural Defects in New Housing, 35 U.Chi.L.Rev. 739 (1968).

[26] E. g., Kearse v. Spaulding, 406 Pa. 140, 176 A.2d 450 (1962); Susskind v. 1136 Tenants Corp., 43 Misc.2d 588, 251 N.Y.S.2d 321 (1964); Rubinger v. Del Monte, N.Y.S.Ct., App.T., 217 N.Y.S.2d 792 (1961).

[27] The cases which recite this old rule are legion. A representative sampling is cited in 32 Am.Jur. Landlord and Tenant § 655 n. 14 (1941).

[28] As far as tort liability is concerned, we have previously held that the old common law rule has been changed by passage of the housing code and that the landlord has a duty to maintain reasonably safe premises. See Note 52 infra.

[29] Although the present cases involve written leases, we think there is no particular significance in this fact. The landlord's warranty is implied in oral and written leases for all types of tenancies.

[30] The rule was "settled" by 1485, 3 W. Holdsworth, A History of English Law 122–123 (6th ed. 1934). The common law rule discussed in text originated in the even older rule prohibiting the tenant from committing waste. The writ of waste expanded as the tenant's right to possession grew stronger. Eventually, in order to protect the landowner's reversionary interest, the tenant became obligated to make repairs and liable to eviction and damages if he failed to do so. Ibid.

tant [31] than whatever small living structure was included in the leasehold, and the tenant farmer was fully capable of making repairs himself.[32] These historical facts were the basis on which the common law constructed its rule; they also provided the necessary prerequisites for its application.[33]

Court decisions in the late 1800's began to recognize that the factual assumptions of the common law were no longer accurate in some cases. For example, the common law, since it assumed that the land was the most important part of the leasehold, required a tenant to pay rent even if any building on the land was destroyed.[34] Faced with such a rule and the ludicrous results it produced, in 1863

the New York Court of Appeals declined to hold that an upper story tenant was obliged to continue paying rent after his apartment building burned down.[35] The court simply pointed out that the urban tenant had no interest in the land, only in the attached building.

Another line of cases created an exception to the no-repair rule for short term leases of furnished dwellings.[36]

These as well as other similar cases [38] demonstrate that some courts began some time ago to question the common law's assumptions that the land was the most important feature of a leasehold and that the tenant could feasibly make any necessary repairs himself. Where those assumptions no longer reflect contemporary housing patterns, the courts have created exceptions to the general rule that landlords have no duty to keep their premises in repair.

It is overdue for courts to admit that these assumptions are no longer true with regard to all urban housing. Today's urban [39] tenants, the vast majority of whom live in multiple dwelling houses, are interested, not in the land, but solely in "a house suitable for occupation." Fur-

---

[31] The land was so central to the original common law conception of a leasehold that rent was viewed as "issuing" from the land: "[T]he governing idea is that the land is bound to pay the rent * * *. We may almost go to the length of saying that the land pays it through [the tenant's] hand." 2 F. Pollock & F. Maitland, The History of English Law 131 (2d ed. 1923).

[32] Many later judicial opinions have added another justification of the old common law rule. They have invoked the time-worn cry of *caveat emptor* and argued that a lessee has the opportunity to inspect the premises. On the basis of his inspection, the tenant must then take the premises "as is," according to this reasoning. As an historical matter, the opportunity to inspect was not thought important when the rule was first devised. See Note 30 supra.

[33] Even the old common law courts responded with a different rule for a landlord-tenant relationship which did not conform to the model of the usual agrarian lease. Much more substantial obligations were placed upon the keepers of inns (the only multiple dwelling houses known to the common law). Their guests were interested solely in shelter and could not be expected to make their own repairs. "The modern apartment dweller more closely resembles the guest in an inn than he resembles an agrarian tenant, but the law has not generally recognized the similarity." J. Levi, P. Hablutzel, L. Rosenberg & J. White, Model Residential Landlord-Tenant Code 6–7 (Tent.Draft 1969).

[34] Paradine v. Jane, Aleyn 26, 82 Eng.Rep. 897 (K.B.1947); 1 American Law of Property, supra Note 11, § 3.103.

[35] Graves v. Berdan, 26 N.Y. 498 (1863).

[36] 1 American Law of Property, supra Note 11, § 3.45 at 267–268, and cases cited therein.

[38] The cases developing the doctrines of "quiet enjoyment" and "constructive eviction" are the most important. See 2 R. Powell, supra Note 10, ¶ 225 [3]. See also Gladden v. Walker & Dunlop, 83 U.S.App.D.C. 224, 168 F.2d 321 (1948) (landlord has duty to maintain portions of apartment "under his control" including plumbing, heating and electrical systems); J. D. Young Corp. v. McClintic, Tex.Civ.App., 26 S.W.2d 460 (1930) (implied covenant of fitness in lease of building under construction); Steefel v. Rothschild, 179 N.Y. 273, 72 N.E. 112 (1904) (duty to disclose latent defects).

[39] In 1968 more than two thirds of America's people lived in the 228 largest metropolitan areas. Only 5.2% lived on farms. The World Almanac 1970 at 251 (L. Long ed.). More than 98% of all housing starts in 1968 were non-farm. Id. at 313.

thermore, today's city dwelling usually has a single, specialized skill unrelated to maintenance work; he is unable to make repairs like the "jack-of-all-trades" farmer who was the common law's model of the lessee. Further, unlike his agrarian predecessor who often remained on one piece of land for his entire life, urban tenants today are more mobile than ever before. A tenant's tenure in a specific apartment will often not be sufficient to justify efforts at repairs. In addition, the increasing complexity of today's dwellings renders them much more difficult to repair than the structures of earlier times. In a multiple dwelling repair may require access to equipment and areas in the control of the landlord. Low and middle income tenants, even if they were interested in making repairs, would be unable to obtain any financing for major repairs since they have no long-term interest in the property.

Our approach to the common law of landlord and tenant ought to be aided by principles derived from the consumer protection cases referred to above. In a lease contract, a tenant seeks to purchase from his landlord shelter for a specified period of time. The landlord sells housing as a commercial businessman and has much greater opportunity, incentive and capacity to inspect and maintain the condition of his building. Moreover, the tenant must rely upon the skill and *bona fides* of his landlord at least as much as a car buyer must rely upon the car manufacturer. In dealing with major problems, such as heating, plumbing, electrical or structural defects, the tenant's position corresponds precisely with "the ordinary consumer who cannot be expected to have the knowledge or capacity or even the opportunity to make adequate inspection of mechanical instrumentalities, like automobiles, and to decide for himself whether they are reasonably fit for the designed purpose." Henningsen v. Bloomfield

Motors, Inc., 32 N.J. 358, 375, 161 A.2d 69, 78 (1960).[42]

Since a lease contract specifies a particular period of time during which the tenant has a right to use his apartment for shelter, he may legitimately expect that the apartment will be fit for habitation for the time period for which it is rented. We point out that in the present cases there is no allegation that appellants' apartments were in poor condition or in violation of the housing code at the commencement of the leases.[43] Since the lessees continue to pay the same rent, they were entitled to expect that the landlord would continue to keep the premises in their beginning condition during the lease term. It is precisely such expectations that the law now recognizes as deserving of formal, legal protection.

Even beyond the rationale of traditional products liability law, the relationship of landlord and tenant suggests further compelling reasons for the law's protection of the tenants' legitimate expectations of quality. The inequality in bargaining power between landlord and tenant has been well documented.[44] Tenants have very little leverage to enforce demands for better housing. Various impediments

[42] Nor should the average tenant be thought capable of "inspecting" plaster, floorboards, roofing, kitchen appliances, etc. To the extent, however, that some defects are obvious, the law must take note of the present housing shortage. Tenants may have no real alternative but to accept such housing with the expectation that the landlord will make necessary repairs. Where this is so, caveat emptor must of necessity be rejected.

[43] In Brown v. Southall Realty Co., 237 A.2d 834 (1968), the District of Columbia Court of Appeals held that unsafe and unsanitary conditions existing at the beginning of the tenancy and known to the landlord rendered any lease of those premises illegal and void.

[44] See Edwards v. Habib, 130 U.S.App.D.C. 126, 140, 397 F.2d 687, 701 (1968); 2 R. Powell, supra Note 10, ¶ 221 [1] at 183; President's Committee on Urban Housing, A Decent Home 96 (1968).

to competition in the rental housing market, such as racial and class discrimination [45] and standardized form leases,[46] mean that landlords place tenants in a take it or leave it situation. The increasingly severe shortage [47] of adequate housing further increases the landlord's bargaining power and escalates the need for maintaining and improving the existing stock. Finally, the findings by various studies of the social impact of bad housing has led to the realization that poor housing is detrimental to the whole society, not merely to the unlucky ones who must suffer the daily indignity of living in a slum.

Thus we are led by our inspection of the relevant legal principles and precedents to the conclusion that the old common law rule imposing an obligation upon the lessee to repair during the lease term was really never intended to apply to residential urban leaseholds. Contract principles established in other areas of the law provide a more rational framework for the apportionment of landlord-tenant responsibilities; they strongly suggest that a warranty of habitability be implied into all contracts [49] for urban dwellings.

B. We believe, in any event, that the District's housing code requires that a warranty of habitability be implied in the leases of all housing that it covers. * * *

[45] President's Committee, supra Note 44, at 96; National Commission, supra Note 9, at 18–19; G. Sternlieb, The Tenement Landlord 71 (1966).

[46] R. Powell, supra Note 10, ¶ 221 [1] at 183 n. 13.

[47] See generally President's Committee, supra Note 44.

[49] We need not consider the provisions of the written lease governing repairs since this implied warranty of the landlord could not be excluded. See Henningsen v. Bloomfield Motors, Inc., supra Note 19; Kay v. Cain, 81 U.S.App.D.C. 24, 25, 154 F.2d 305, 306 (1946). See also Note 58, infra.

The 75 pages of the Regulations provide a comprehensive regulatory scheme setting forth in some detail: (a) the standards which housing in the District of Columbia must meet; (b) which party, the lessor or the lessee, must meet each standard; and (c) a system of inspections, notifications and criminal penalties. The Regulations themselves are silent on the question of private remedies.

Two previous decisions of this court, however, have held that the Housing Regulations create legal rights and duties enforceable in tort by private parties. In Whetzel v. Jess Fisher Management Co., 108 U.S.App.D.C. 385, 282 F.2d 943 (1960), we followed the leading case of Altz v. Lieberson, 233 N.Y. 16, 134 N.E. 703 (1922), in holding (1) that the housing code altered the common law rule and imposed a duty to repair upon the landlord, and (2) that a right of action accrued to a tenant injured by the landlord's breach of this duty. As Judge Cardozo wrote in *Lieberson:*

"* * * We may be sure that the framers of this statute, when regulating tenement life, had uppermost in thought the care of those who are unable to care for themselves. The Legislature must have known that unless repairs in the rooms of the poor were made by the landlord, they would not be made by any one. The duty imposed became commensurate with the need. The right to seek redress is not limited to the city or its officers. The right extends to all whom there was a purpose to protect. * * * *"

134 N.E. at 704. Recently, in Kanelos v. Kettler, 132 U.S.App.D.C. 133, 135, 406 F.2d 951, 953 (1968), we reaffirmed our position in *Whetzel,* holding that "the Housing Regulations did impose maintenance obligations upon appellee [landlord] which he was not free to ignore."

The District of Columbia Court of Appeals gave further effect to the Housing

Regulations in Brown v. Southall Realty Co., 237 A.2d 834 (1968). There the landlord knew at the time the lease was signed that housing code violations existed which rendered the apartment "unsafe and unsanitary." Viewing the lease as a contract, the District of Columbia Court of Appeals held that the premises were let in violation of Sections 2304 [53] and 2501 [54] of the Regulations and that the lease, therefore, was void as an illegal contract. In the light of *Brown,* it is clear not only that the housing code creates privately enforceable duties as held in *Whetzel,* but that the basic validity of every housing contract depends upon substantial compliance with the housing code at the beginning of the lease term. The *Brown* court relied particularly upon Section 2501 of the Regulations which provides:

"Every premises accommodating one or more habitations shall be maintained and kept in repair so as to provide decent living accommodations for the occupants. This part of this Code contemplates more than mere basic repairs and maintenance to keep out the elements; its purpose is to include repairs and maintenance designed to make a premises or neighborhood healthy and safe."

By its terms, this section applies to maintenance and repair during the lease term. Under the *Brown* holding, serious failure to comply with this section before the lease term begins renders the contract void. We think it untenable to find that this section has no effect on the contract after it has been signed. To the contrary, by signing the lease the landlord has undertaken a continuing obligation to the tenant to maintain the premises in accordance with all applicable law. * * *

We therefore hold that the Housing Regulations imply a warranty of habitability, measured by the standards which they set out, into leases of all housing that they cover.

V

In the present cases, the landlord sued for possession for nonpayment of rent. Under contract principles,[61] however, the tenant's obligation to pay rent is dependent upon the landlord's performance of his obligations, including his warranty to maintain the premises in habitable condition. In order to determine whether any rent is owed to the landlord, the tenants must be given an opportunity to prove the housing code violations alleged as breach of the landlord's warranty.[62]

At trial, the finder of fact must make two findings: (1) whether the alleged violations [63] existed during the period for which past due rent is claimed, and (2) what portion, if any or all, of the tenant's obligation to pay rent was suspended

[53] "No person shall rent or offer to rent any habitation, or the furnishings thereof, unless such habitation and its furnishings are in a clean, safe and sanitary condition, in repair, and free from rodents or vermin."

[54] See infra.

[61] In extending all contract remedies for breach to the parties to a lease, we include an action for specific performance of the landlord's implied warranty of habitability.

[62] To be relevant, of course, the violations must affect the tenant's apartment or common areas which the tenant uses. Moreover, the contract principle that no one may benefit from his own wrong will allow the landlord to defend by proving the damage was caused by the tenant's wrongful action. However, violations resulting from inadequate repairs or materials which disintegrate under normal use would not be assignable to the tenant. Also we agree with the District of Columbia Court of Appeals that the tenant's private rights do not depend on official inspection or official finding of violation by the city government. Diamond Housing Corp. v. Robinson, 257 A.2d 492, 494 (1969).

[63] The jury should be instructed that one or two minor violations standing alone which do not affect habitability are *de minimis* and would not entitle the tenant to a reduction in rent.

by the landlord's breach. If no part of the tenant's rental obligation is found to have been suspended, then a judgment for possession may issue forthwith. On the other hand, if the jury determines that the entire rental obligation has been extinguished by the landlord's total breach, then the action for possession on the ground of nonpayment must fail.[64]

The jury may find that part of the tenant's rental obligation has been suspended but that part of the unpaid back rent is indeed owed to the landlord. In these circumstances, no judgment for possession should issue if the tenant agrees to pay the partial rent found to be due. If the tenant refuses to pay the partial amount, a judgment for possession may then be entered.

The judgment of the District of Columbia Court of Appeals is reversed and the cases are remanded for further proceedings consistent with this opinion.[67]

So ordered.

Circuit Judge ROBB concurs in the result and in Parts IV–B and V of the opinion.

---

[64] As soon as the landlord made the necessary repairs rent would again become due. Our holding, of course, affects only eviction for nonpayment of rent. The landlord is free to seek eviction at the termination of the lease or on any other legal ground.

[67] Appellants in the present cases offered to pay rent into the registry of the court during the present action. We think this is an excellent protective procedure. If the tenant defends against an action for possession on the basis of breach of the landlord's warranty of habitability, the trial court may require the tenant to make future rent payments into the registry of the court as they become due; such a procedure would be appropriate only while the tenant remains in possession. The escrowed money will, however, represent rent for the period between the time the landlord files suit and the time the case comes to trial. In the normal course of litigation, the only factual question at trial would be the condition of the apartment

Notes to Javins v. First National Realty Co.

1. The court draws heavily upon the sale of goods analogy, asserting that only historical differences explain why the "seller" of land *did* not (as did the seller of goods) warrant fitness. History aside, what present day factors argue for or against treating the lease of an apartment and the sale of an auto in the same way?

2. According to the opinion (see note 63), one or two *minor* violations standing alone might not affect habitability. In that event, tenant's defense fails and the landlord gets judgment for possession. Should tenants (or their lawyers) have to risk guessing wrong as to what violations are minor and what violations are not? If you were the tenant's lawyer and wanted to protect him (and your own inner peace) against a bad guess, what procedural steps might you recommend to accompany your *Javins* type defense? Is the standard for a successful defense different where the tenant (as here) stays and refuses to pay rent than it would be if the tenant vacated and refused to pay rent on the claim of constructive eviction? When a state court adopts the *Javins* rule, should code enforcement officials then promulgate a list of violations affecting habitability? (see, e. g., note 1, page 696, infra)?

---

during the time the landlord alleged rent was due and not paid.

As a general rule, the escrowed money should be apportioned between the landlord and the tenant after trial on the basis of the finding of rent actually due for the period at issue in the suit. To insure fair apportionment, however, we think either party should be permitted to amend its complaint or answer at any time before trial, to allege a change in the condition of the apartment. In this event, the finder of fact should make a separate finding as to the condition of the apartment at the time at which the amendment was filed. This new finding will have no effect upon the original action; it will only affect the distribution of the escrowed rent paid after the filing of the amendment.

If this were done, however, might someone then argue against the validity of any code provision whose violation did not affect habitability, the argument being that the regulatory power rests on dangers to health, safety etc.? Looking at this issue differently, what constitutes habitability (or unhabitability)?

3. The court remanded this case for trial, principally to allow proof as to what portion ("whether *any or all*") of the tenant's obligation to pay rent was suspended by the landlord's breach. The court explicitly recognized that the landlord might be entitled to some of the rent. At the trial, which party has the burden of coming forward to establish the (reduced) rental value of the premises? What form of proof is required? Is it realistic to expect that poor tenants can present the (expert?) testimony that will establish (or contradict the owner's evidence of) rental value? Do you see any solution to this procedural difficulty?

4. Suppose that the trial jury finds that the tenant's entire rental obligation has been extinguished by the landlord's breach: If the landlord refuses to repair, may the tenant remain indefinitely and pay no rent? Earlier the D.C.Ct. of Appeals had held—in the case of a void and unenforceable lease—that the tenant becomes an occupant at sufferance, subject to summary dispossess, Diamond Housing Corp. v. Robinson, 257 A.2d 492 (D.C.App.1969). Is there any reason to treat the tenant's status differently (and less protectively) where the lease is void ab initio than where the lease becomes unenforceable after the term begins? In logic? In practice? If the *Diamond Housing* rule were to apply to a *Javins*-type situation, wouldn't this invite landlords to concede that their premises were uninhabitable whenever a difficult tenant pleaded a *Javins*-type defense, and one month later then sue to recover possession from an occupant at sufferance—a 2-step form of retaliatory eviction? And doesn't the logic of *Diamond Housing* also apply to an instance where the tenant's rent is partly suspended and the landlord fails to repair?

5. Suppose that the trial jury finds that a tenant's entire rental is extinguished by the landlord's breach: thereafter, landlord undertakes a repair program requiring six months to complete. Is the landlord entitled to collect any rent before the end of six months? Do you see any feasible scheme for gradual restoration of the tenant's rent as repairs proceed?

6. *Javins* was a landlord-initiated suit to recover possession. The court found an implied covenant of habitability. Is this promise one that the tenant can sue specifically to enforce? In short: is there any way that tenants can compel their landlords to provide habitable quarters (other than through municipal code enforcement proceedings)?

7. Consider very carefully what you think the impact will be on housing conditions and shelter costs generally if all rental agreements are deemed to include an implied covenant of habitability (fitness).

8. Should there be serious concern that the remedy of summary dispossess may become even less summary if tenants can routinely assert a *Javins*-type defense? Presently, most eviction actions based on non-payment of rent are uncontested, but even a "defenseless" tenant can often obtain a short stay of eviction simply by asking for it. Will the caseload in landlord-tenant courts become unmanageable if the issue of habitability is raised in every suit? And is there (should there be) any way to screen the tenant genuinely trying to improve his environment from the tenant who has neither intention to stay or to pay?

9. The Oregon Forcible Entry and Wrongful Detainer Statute provides for

summary dispossess for non-payment of rent. The Statute bars a defense based on the landlord's breach of a duty to maintain the premises, unless the landlord is seeking a judgment for unpaid rent as well as for immediate possession. The United States Supreme Court has held that this limitation on triable issues does not deprive tenants of Due Process or Equal Protection. Lindsey v. Normet, 405 U.S. 56, 92 S.Ct. 862, 31 L.Ed.2d 36 (1972).

In a state having an Oregon-type statute, how would you as the tenant's lawyer raise the issue of uninhabitability?

10. What are the arguments for or against a court-made rule that no landlord may sue to recover rent or possession without alleging and proving that the premises are free of all code violations (except those caused by the occupant)?

11. The *Javins* decision has been widely discussed: Comment appears at 39 Geo.Wash.L.Rev. 152–65 (1970); 6 Harv.Civ.Rights L.Rev. 193–204 (1970); 84 Harv.L.Rev. 729–38 (1971); 16 Howard L.J. 366–79 (1971); 55 Minn. L.Rev. 354–61 (1970).

12. The *Javins* opinion cites the earlier Hawaii decision, Lemle v. Breeden, 51 Haw. 426, 462 P.2d 470 (1969). There tenant sued to recover a $1,190 deposit when he discovered that he was sharing his luxurious ocean-front house with a colony of rats. Tenant stayed around only for three days and three nights, sleeping(?) huddled together with his family in the downstairs living room. In deciding for the tenant, the Court might have rested its holding on one of the common-law exceptions to the "no warranty of fitness" rule—a short term rental of *furnished* quarters. Ingalls v. Hobbs, 156 Mass. 348, 31 N.E. 286 (1892). Instead, the court seized the opportunity to incorporate an implied warranty of habitability in *all* rental transactions. It does not appear that

the landlord had violated a local housing code.

In its opinion the court seems to assume that it could have decided the case more traditionally on a constructive eviction theory (tenant had vacated); but this assumed that landlord had an antecedent duty to exterminate; otherwise, how could he have breached his covenant for quiet enjoyment? The court then explains that constructive eviction (i. e., quiet enjoyment) offers less flexibility than habitability:

> "It is a decided advantage of the implied warranty doctrine that there are a number of remedies available. The doctrine of constructive eviction, on the other hand, requires that the tenant abandon the premises within a reasonable time after giving notice that the premises are uninhabitable or unfit for his purposes." 51 Hawaii 426, 434–35, 462 P.2d 470, 475.

Is this distinction necessary? Why not subsume the covenant of habitability under the covenant for quiet enjoyment, and give tenants the option of suspending rent where landlord's neglect has made the premises uninhabitable?

13. Suppose that the tenant in Lemle v. Breeden had seen evidence of rat infestation before he signed the lease: could landlord have urged successfully that tenant took the premises in an "as is" condition—i. e., that tenants may sometimes waive their right to a covenant of habitability?

14. Once again, the British have been able to unshackle their common-law heritage more easily than we have. The English Housing Act, 1957, 5 & 6 Eliz. 2, c. 56 provides:

> [There is an implied condition] notwithstanding any stipulation to the contrary, * * * that the house is fit for human habitation at the commencement of the tenancy and an undertaking * * * that the house

will be kept so fit by the landlord during the tenancy.

However, the Act applies only to low-rent housing, bearing a maximum monthly rental of £80 in London and £52 elsewhere.

15. Other recent implied warranty of habitability decisions include: Academy Spires, Inc. v. Jones, 108 N.J.Super. Ct. 395, 261 A.2d 413 (1970); Amanuensis, Ltd. v. Brown, 65 Misc.2d 15, 318 N.Y.S.2d 11 (Civ.Ct.1971); Jack Spring, Inc. v. Little, 50 Ill.2d 351, 280 N.E.2d 208 (1972); Kline v. Burns, 276 A.2d 248 (N.H.1971); Hinson v. Delis, 26 Cal.App.3d 62, 102 Cal.Rptr. 661 (1972). But see Graham v. Wisenburn, 39 A.D.2d 334 (1972) (court refuses to extend implied warranty to tenant-occupied one-family house).

EAST HAVEN ASSOCIATES v. GURIAN

Civil Court, New York City, 1970.
64 Misc.2d 276, 313 N.Y.S.2d 927.

LEONARD H. SANDLER, J. The most important of the several interesting issues presented by the proof in this case is whether or not the doctrine of constructive eviction is available to a residential tenant when a landlord is responsible for conditions that render part of the premises uninhabitable, and the tenant abandons that part but continues to reside in the rest of the premises. Put in another way, the question is whether New York law should recognize the doctrine of partial constructive eviction as a counterpart to partial actual eviction precisely as it has recognized for over a century constructive eviction as a counterpart to actual eviction. (See Dyett v. Pendleton, 8 Cow. 727.)

After a careful review of the authorities, I have concluded that the concept of partial constructive eviction is sound in

principle, is supported by compelling considerations of social policy and fairness, and is in no way precluded by controlling precedent.

On May 26, 1963, the defendant entered into a lease with the then owner of 301 East 69 Street, with respect to apartment 18E under which the defendant agreed to pay rent for the apartment from December 1, 1963 to November 30, 1966 in the amount of $425 per month. The apartment in question had a terrace.

In April, 1966, the plaintiff acquired the building. At the end of July, 1966, the defendant and his family vacated the apartment and refused to pay rent for the months of August, September, October and November, 1966, the remaining period of the lease. Accordingly, plaintiff sued for the total of the four months rent, for the reasonable value of legal services, and for specific items of damages allegedly caused by the defendants. As to the last, I find the proof wholly deficient and these claims are accordingly dismissed.

The defense to the suit for rent rests upon the claim that the defendant was constructively evicted from the apartment as a result of the misconduct and neglect of the landlord, which allegedly rendered the terrace uninhabitable.

In addition, the defendant sues for damages to his furniture caused by the landlord's neglect, but this claim clearly must fail since the proof established that the damage complained of occurred before the plaintiff acquired the building. Finally, the defendant seeks return of his security in the amount of $425.

The central factual issue turns on the condition of the terrace and the factors causing that condition.

I find that from early 1965 the central air conditioner emitted quite steadily a green fluid and a stream of water overflow that fell in significant quantities on the terrace. I further find that the incinerator spewed forth particles of ash that were deposited in substantial part upon the terrace. The result was to render the terrace effectively unusable for its intended purposes, and the defendant and his family promptly abandoned the terrace, although it had been a prime factor in inducing them to enter the lease.

Nevertheless, I am unable to conclude that the departure of the defendant and his family from the apartment at the end of July, 1966 constituted their constructice eviction from the entire premises. The evidence clearly discloses that the terrace had become unusable no later than the early spring of 1965, and quite possibly earlier. The law is clear that the abandonment must occur with reasonable promptness after the conditions justifying it have developed. (See 1 Rasch, Landlord and Tenant, § 877, and cases cited.)

Unquestionably, this rule should be given a flexible interpretation in light of the practical difficulties these days in finding satisfactory apartments. Moreover, tenants have a right to rely on assurances that the landlord will correct the objectionable conditions.

Although the question is troublesome, I have concluded that a delay of at least 17 months in moving, without any significant proof of an early sustained effort to find other apartments, cannot be reconciled with the current requirements of law.

Turning to the issue of partial eviction, the proof quite plainly established that the terrace had been promptly abandoned once the condition complained of had developed. I am satisfied that conforming the pleadings to the proof to permit consideration of the issue of partial eviction would serve the interests of justice. (CPLR 3025, subd. [c].)

Although the matter is not clear, I am inclined to believe that the proof before

me spelled out an actual partial eviction. It seems to me that the tangible and concrete physical character of the substances falling on the terrace provides a substantial basis for such a finding.

However, I do not rest my decision on that ground in view of the decision of the New York Court of Appeals in Barash v. Pennsylvania Term. Real Estate Corp. (26 N.Y.2d 77). Although the facts of the *Barash* case do not preclude such a finding, the wording of the opinion plainly suggests a disposition to define actual eviction rather narrowly. I therefore turn to consider the status of partial constructive eviction under New York law.

In his authoritative treatise, Rasch flatly asserted that constructive eviction requires "surrender of the entire possession by the tenant." (See 1 Rasch, Landlord and Tenant, § 876.)

None of the cases he cites, however, supports that sweeping assertion. These cases, with many others, repeat the general formula that constructive eviction requires abandonment of the premises. None of the cases I have examined squarely address the question here presented of the legal effect of abandonment of only that part of the premises rendered uninhabitable.

The doctrine of constructive eviction was developed by analogy to actual eviction on the basis of a very simple and obvious proposition. If a tenant is effectively forced out of leased premises as a result of misconduct by a landlord that substantially impairs enjoyment of the leased premises, the same legal consequences should follow as though the evicted were physically evicted.

In the eloquent landmark decision that firmly established constructive eviction in New York law, Dyett v. Pendleton (8 Cow. 727, supra) the following was said at page 734: "Suppose the landlord had established a hospital for the small pox, the plague, or the yellow fever, in the remaining part of this house; suppose he had made a deposit of gunpowder, under the tenant, or had introduced some offensive and pestilential materials of the most dangerous nature; can there be any hesitation in saying that if, by such means, he had driven the tenant from his habitation, he should not recover for the use of that house, of which, by his own wrong, he had deprived his tenant? It would need nothing but common sense and common justice to decide it."

Why should a different test be applied where the tenant, through comparable means, is effectively deprived of the use of part of his residence, and abandons that part? Ought not the same consequences to follow as would follow an "actual partial eviction"?

I am unable to see any basis in "common sense and common justice" for treating the two situations differently.

Support for this view appears in the careful phrasing of the first decision to establish the requirement of abandonment in constructive eviction cases (Edgerton v. Page 20 N.Y. 281, 284, 285). The Court of Appeals squarely rested the requirement on the unfairness of suspending rent while the tenant continued to occupy the "entire premises." "I cannot see upon what principle the landlord should be absolutely barred from a recovery of rent, when his wrongful acts stop short of depriving the tenant of the possession of *any portion* of the premises. * * * The true rule, from all the authorities is, that while the tenant remains in possession of the *entire premises* demised, his obligation to pay rent continues."

While some later opinions have been less carefully worded, I know of none that requires a different result.

While the view here expressed seems to me inherent in "common sense and

common justice" that gave rise originally to the doctrine of constructive eviction, the result is independently compelled by considerations of fairness and justice in the light of present realities.

It cannot be seriously disputed that a major shortage in residential housing has prevailed in our metropolitan area for several decades. The clear effect has been to undermine so drastically the bargaining power of tenants in relation to landlords that grave questions as to the fairness and relevance of some traditional concepts of landlord-tenant law are presented.

The very idea of requiring families to abandon their homes before they can defend against actions for rent is a baffling one in an era in which decent housing is so hard to get, particularly for those who are poor and without resources. It makes no sense at all to say that if part of an apartment has been rendered uninhabitable, a family must move from the entire dwelling before it can seek justice and fair dealing.

Accordingly, I hold that when the defendant and his family ceased to use the terrace, a partial constructive eviction occurred with the same legal consequences as attends a partial "actual" eviction.

These consequences were comprehensively defined in Peerless Candy Co. v. Halbreich (125 Misc. 889). It is clear that from the time of the partial eviction, the defendant had the right to stop paying rent. Accordingly, I find against the plaintiff on its action for rent and legal expenses, and for the defendant on his action to recover the security deposit of $425.

Judgment should be entered for the defendant for $425 with interest from August 1, 1966.

Notes to East Haven Associates v. Gurian

1. The facts in Barash v. Pennsylvania Terminal Real Estate Corp., 26 N.Y.

2d 77, 308 N.Y.S.2d 649, 256 N.E.2d 707 (1970), were these: Tenant charged landlord with wrongful failure to air-condition his offices evenings and weekends, causing the offices to become "hot, stuffy, and unusable and uninhabitable" at those times. Claiming a partial actual eviction, tenant sought an order relieving him from payment of rent. Two lower courts refused to dismiss the tenant's complaint, but the Court of Appeals reversed.

"The tenant, who has not abandoned the premises, asserts that there has been an actual eviction, though partial only, thus permitting him to retain possession of the premises without liability for rent. To support this contention it is claimed that failure to supply fresh air constitutes actual eviction, if only, albeit, during the hours after 6:00 P.M. and on weekends. * * *

"All that tenant suffered was a substantial diminution in the extent to which he could benefically enjoy the the premises. Although possibly more pronounced, tenant's situation is analogous to cases where there is a persistent offensive odor, harmful to health, arising from a noxious gas, an open sewer * * *, or defective plumbing * * *. In all such cases there has been held to be only a constructive eviction. * * * Given these well-established rules, proper characterization of the instant failure to ventilate follows easily. * * * The tenant has neither been expelled nor excluded from the premises, nor has the landlord seized a portion of the premises for his own use or that of another. He has, by his alleged wrongful failure to provide proper ventilation, substantially reduced the beneficial use of the premises. * * * Since the eviction, if any, is constructive and not actual, the tenant's failure to abandon the premises makes the first cause of action insufficient in law. * * *"

2. "The fallacy * * * is quite evident and manifest. Applying 'common sense and common justice,' a tenant deprived of the beneficial use and enjoyment of a portion of the demised premises cannot be placed in a better bargaining advantage than a tenant who is deprived of the beneficial use and enjoyment of the entire demised premises. For, if a tenant must abandon the demised premises to claim the benefit of a total constructive eviction, then, certainly, a tenant deprived of the beneficial use and enjoyment of a portion of the premises must either vacate the said premises or pay rent if he elects to remain in possession." [Leonforte, J., in dismissing defense of partial constructive eviction where tenant unable to use the terrace of his fourth-floor apartment, but remained in possession] Zweighaft v. Remington, 66 Misc. 2d 261, 263, 320 N.Y.S.2d 151, 153 (Civ.Ct.1971).

Who has the better of the argument, Judge Sandler or his brother, Leonforte?

NEW YORK MULTIPLE DWELLING LAW (SUPP.1965)

§ 302–a. *Abatement of rent in the case of serious violations*

1. The provisions of this section shall apply to all cities with a population of two million or more.

2. a. A "rent impairing" violation within the meaning of this section shall designate a condition in a multiple dwelling which, in the opinion of the department, constitutes, or if not promptly corrected, will constitute, a fire hazard or a serious threat to the life, health or safety of occupants thereof.

b. The determination as to which violations are "rent impairing" shall be made in the following manner. Within six months after the enactment of this section, the department shall promulgate a list of conditions constituting violations of the provisions of this chapter and of any regulations promulgated pursuant to the provisions of subdivision four of section three of this chapter. Such list shall contain a brief description of the condition constituting the violation, the section of this chapter or regulation violated, and the order number assigned thereto. The department may from time to time change the number or description of violations on such list, as may seem appropriate to the department. Such list shall be available at all times to the public.

c. At the time of the promulgation of the list of violations, the department shall also designate, by reference to the order number, those violations which it proposes to classify as rent impairing as above defined. Within thirty days thereafter, the department shall hold a public hearing at which all persons interested may be heard as to the propriety of the classification of such violations as rent impairing. At least twenty days' notice of such hearing shall be given by publication in the city record or other publication in which official notices of the city are regularly published. Within a reasonable time after the hearing, the department shall make and publish a list of those violations which are classified as rent impairing. Any person interested may, within four months thereafter, seek a review by the supreme court of the propriety of the classification of any of such violations as "Rent Impairing" by a special proceeding pursuant to article seventy-eight of the civil practice law and rules. No other body or officer shall have the power to review said classification.

d. The department may at any time change the number or description of rent impairing violations but no such change

shall be made except in the manner above set forth after notice and public hearing.

3. a. If (i) the official records of the department shall note that a rent impairing violation exists in respect to a multiple dwelling and that notice of such violation has been given by the department, by mail, to the owner last registered with the department and (ii) such note of the violation is not cancelled or removed of record within six months after the date of such notice of such violation; then for the period that such violation remains uncorrected after the expiration of said six months, no rent shall be recovered by any owner for any premises in such multiple dwelling used by a resident thereof for human habitation in which the condition constituting such rent impairing violation exists, provided, however, that if the violation is one that requires approval of plans by the department for the corrective work and if plans for such corrective work shall have been duly filed within three months from the date of notice of such violation by the department to the owner last registered with the department, the six-months period aforementioned shall not begin to run until the date that plans for the corrective work are approved by the department; if plans are not filed within said three-months period or if so filed, they are disapproved and amendments are not duly filed within thirty days after the date of notification of the disapproval by the department to the person having filed the plans, the six-months period shall be computed as if no plans whatever had been filed under this proviso. If a condition constituting a rent impairing violation exists in the part of a multiple dwelling used in common by the residents or in the part under the control of the owner thereof, the violation shall be deemed to exist in the respective premises of each resident of the multiple dwelling.

b. The provisions of subparagraph a shall not apply if (i) the condition referred to in the department's notice to the owner last registered with the department did not in fact exist, notwithstanding the notation thereof in the records of the department; (ii) the condition which is the subject of the violation has in fact been corrected, though the note thereof in the department has not been removed or cancelled; (iii) the violation has been caused by the resident from whom rent is sought to be collected or by members of his family or by his guests or by another resident of the multiple dwelling or the members of the family of such other resident or by his guests, or (iv) the resident proceeded against for rent has refused entry to the owner for the purpose of correcting the condition giving rise to the violation.

c. To raise a defense under subparagraph a in any action to recover rent or in any special proceeding for the recovery of possession because of non-payment of rent, the resident must affirmatively plead and prove the material facts under subparagraph a, and must also deposit with the clerk of the court in which the action or proceeding is pending at the time of filing of the resident's answer the amount of rent sought to be recovered in the action or upon which the proceeding to recover possession is based, to be held by the clerk of the court until final disposition of the action or proceeding at which time the rent deposited shall be paid to the owner, if the owner prevails, or be returned to the resident if the resident prevails. Such deposit of rent shall vitiate any right on the part of the owner to terminate the lease or rental agreement of the resident because of non-payment of rent.

d. If a resident voluntarily pays rent or an installment of rent when he would be privileged to withhold the same under subparagraph a, he shall not thereafter have any claim or cause of action to recover back the rent or installment of rent so paid. A voluntary payment within the meaning hereof shall mean payment other than one made pursuant to a judgment in an action or special proceeding.

e. If upon the trial of any action to recover rent or any special proceeding for the recovery of possession because of non-payment of rent it shall appear that the resident has raised a defense under this section in bad faith, or has caused the violation or has refused entry to the owner for the purpose of correcting the condition giving rise to the violation, the court, in its discretion, may impose upon the resident the reasonable costs of the owner, including counsel fees, in maintaining the action or proceeding not to exceed one hundred dollars.

* * *

In the case below, the New York Court of Appeals considers the validity of the Spiegel Law, which grants to welfare tenants a remedy similar to that which section 302–a of the Multiple Dwelling Law gives all New York City tenants.

FARRELL v. DREW

Court of Appeals of New York, 1967.
19 N.Y.2d 486, 281 N.Y.S.2d 1, 227 N.E.2d 824.

Chief Judge FULD. The sole issue, on this direct appeal from orders of the Civil Court of the City of New York, is the constitutionality of section 143–b of the Social Welfare Law, known as the Spiegel Law, providing rent abatement for welfare tenants who live in buildings that contain a "violation of law * * * which is dangerous, hazardous or detrimental to life or health."

Petitioner landlord brought these summary eviction proceedings for nonpayment of rent, which were consolidated for trial, against three welfare recipients who were tenants in the same building. The Welfare Department, which had been making the rent payments for these tenants directly to the landlord (Social Welfare Law, § 143–b, subd. 1), appeared on their behalf as *amicus curiae*, asserting as a defense that in the apartment of a fourth tenant who was not a welfare recipient there existed a dangerous and hazardous condition which rendered the building unsafe for *all* occupants. The trial court held that the Spiegel Law was constitutional and, after finding that a hazardous condition existed in the building, dismissed the eviction proceedings.

The Legislature made clear, by its "Declaration of purpose and necessity" (L.1962, ch. 997, § 1), that it was prompted to pass section 143–b of the Social Welfare Law in order to alleviate

"certain [existing] evils and abuses * * * which have caused many tenants, who are welfare recipients, to suffer untold hardships, deprivation of services and deterioration of housing facilities because certain landlords have been exploiting such tenants by failing to make necessary repairs and by neglecting to afford necessary services".

The legislation, designed to operate as an effective weapon in the fight against slum housing in general (see 1963 Opns. Atty.Gen. 181, 182; Gribetz and Grad, Housing Code Enforcement, 66 Col.L. Rev. 1254, 1282), was adopted only after it became apparent that existing sanctions, including criminal sanctions, were inadequate to cope with the problems of building law enforcement. (See Gribetz and Grad, Housing Code Enforcement, 66 Col.L.Rev. 1254, 1275–1281.) Confronted with this situation, the Legislature responded by enacting not only the rent abatement statute now before us (Social Welfare Law, § 143–b) but also the 1962 Receivership Law (Multiple Dwelling Law, § 309) which we held constitutional several years ago. (See Matter of Department of Bldgs. of City of N. Y. [Philco Realty Corp.], 14 N.Y.2d 291, 251 N.Y.S.2d 441, 200

N.E.2d 432; Matter of Department of Bldgs. of City of N. Y. [Soltzer], 16 N.Y.2d 915, 264 N.Y.S.2d 701, 212 N.E.2d 154.)

In the cases before us, the landlord does not challenge the Legislature's power to require that building law violations be corrected. Her attack is directed solely against the sanction chosen by the Legislature to attain its objective of safe housing. Specifically, her contention is that the rent abatement provided by section 143–b works a denial of equal protection of the laws, a deprivation of property without due process and an unconstitutional impairment of contractual rights.

Although the landlord lacks standing to complain that the statute discriminates in favor of tenants who are welfare recipients (see, e. g., Matter of Guardian Life Ins. Co. v. Chapman, 302 N.Y. 226, 238, 97 N.E.2d 877, 883; Thompson v. Wallin, 276 App.Div. 463, 466, 95 N. Y.S.2d 784, 788, affirmed 301 N.Y. 476, 95 N.E.2d 806; United States v. Raines, 362 U.S. 17, 21 80 S.Ct. 519, 4 L.Ed.2d 524), she is entitled to urge that it denies equal protection of the laws on the ground that it is aimed only at *landlords* of welfare recipients. However, it is settled that such legislation is not unconstitutional as long as a "reasonable basis" exists for differentiating among the members of the same class. (Citations omitted) As we wrote in the Durham Realty Corp. case, which involved a statute barring eviction of tenants who paid a "reasonable" rent (230 N.Y., at p. 447), "One class of landlords is selected for regulation because one class conspicuously offends; one class of tenants has protection because all who seek homes cannot be provided with places to sleep and eat. Those who are out of possession, willing to pay exorbitant rentals, or unable to pay any rentals whatever, have been left to shift for themselves. But such classifications deny to no one the equal protection of the laws. The distinction between the groups is real and rests on a substantial basis."

In the situation presented by the cases before us, it is the landlords of welfare recipients who, the Legislature found, "conspicuously offend". To be sure, they are not the only landlords who fail to make repairs in slum dwellings. But welfare recipients have even less freedom than other tenants of deteriorated buildings in selecting a place to live (see, e. g., Matter of Schaeffer v. Montes, 37 Misc. 2d 722, 729, 233 N.Y.S.2d 444, 451), and the landlords of welfare recipients, secure in their receipt of rents directly from public funds have even less incentive than other landlords to make repairs. Under circumstances such as these, if the Legislature chooses to select one class of landlords and impose a special sanction against them, the equal protection clause does not forbid it. (See Ferguson v. Skrupa, 372 U.S. 726, 732–733, 83 S.Ct. 1028).

It is likewise clear that the State may, in the exercise of its police power, provide for the curtailment of rent payments to landlords as a means of inducing them to eliminate dangerous housing conditions. (Citations omitted) We have, in the past, upheld and applied statutes or regulations, not too unlike the one before us, which provide for (1) rent reduction (citations omitted.)

Nor is the statute subject to criticism on constitutional grounds because it does not, in so many words, call for notice and hearing to the landlord. The simple fact is that both are implicit in the statutory scheme. By providing that a violation of the building laws is "a valid defense"—to be pleaded as such—in a summary eviction proceeding (subd. 5, par. [a]), the section affords the landlord ample notice of the violation and full opportunity to refute the claim and litigate the issue. In short, the statute "import[s] a hearing" (Matter of De-

partment of Bldgs. of City of N. Y. [Philco Realty Corp.], 14 N.Y.2d 291, 302, 251 N.Y.S.2d 441, 450, 200 N.E. 2d 432, 439) and, as already indicated, the landlord before us actually received a full hearing with respect to both the existence and hazardous character of the violation in question.

It is clear, too, that section 143–b does not effect any unconstitutional impairment of the landlord's contractual rights. "If the legislation before us 'is addressed to a legitimate end and the measures taken are reasonable and appropriate to that end' ", this court declared in the *Philco Realty* case (14 N.Y.2d at pp. 297–298), "it may not be stricken as unconstitutional, even though it may interfere with rights established by existing contracts. (Home Bldg. & Loan Assn. v. Blaisdell, 290 U.S. 398, 438, 54 S.Ct. 231, 240, 78 L.Ed. 413.) It is 'fundamental' * * * that 'the state may establish regulations reasonably necessary to secure the general welfare of the community by the exercise of its police power although the rights of private property are [thereby] * * * curtailed and freedom of contract is abridged.' " And, after noting that contracts are made subject to the exercise of the State's power when justified, we went on to say that, whether this protective power of the State be treated as "an implied condition of every contract and, as such, as much part of the contract as though it were written into it" or as " 'an exercise of the sovereign right of the Government to protect the * * * general welfare of the people * * * paramount to any rights under contracts between individuals' " (East New York Bank v. Hahn, 326 U.S. 230, 232–233, 66 S.Ct. 69, 70, 90 L.Ed. 34), it is " 'settled law' " that " 'the interdiction of statutes impairing the obligation of contracts does not prevent the State from exercising such powers as * * * are necessary for the general good of the public, though contracts previously entered into between individuals may thereby be affected.' " (Home Bldg. & Loan Assn. v. Blaisdell, 290 U.S. 398, 437, 54 S.Ct. 231, 239.) The remedial legislation challenged in the case before us is reasonably aimed at correcting the evil of substandard housing and may not be stricken as unconstitutional even though the means devised to accomplish that result may, to some extent, impair the obligation of the landlord's contract.

The appellant's remaining points bear on the wisdom rather than the constitutionality of this legislation and require no discussion. As we have sought to demonstrate, section 143–b of the Social Welfare Law is free from any constitutional impediment.

The orders appealed from should be affirmed, with costs.

VAN VOORHIS, J. (dissenting). A mere statement of the provisions of section 143–b (subds. 2, 5) of the Social Welfare Law in their application to this case, should be enough to demonstrate its unconstitutionality, both as denying the equal protection of the law and depriving appellant of property without due process of law (U.S.Const., 5th and 14th Amdts.; N.Y.Const., art. I, § 6). Tenants on welfare (as distinct from tenants not receiving public relief) are exempted from payment of rent, as well as dispossession, for any period during which there is outstanding anywhere in the building any violation of law relating to dangerous or hazardous conditions or conditions detrimental to life or health. There are no building violations in any of the three apartments in this building from which tenants—who have not paid their rent—are sought to be evicted. There is no violation anywhere in the building which is dangerous or hazardous to these welfare tenants or detrimental to their health. It happens that in the apartment of a fourth tenant—not a wel-

fare recipient—a door did not fit properly. The inspector testified that, when he called it to the landlord's attention, it had been repaired "but still the door would bind slightly. In other words, it would not close fully." The inspector added: "The tenant seemed happy, but I wouldn't accept it." Of course, that tenant, in whose apartment this "violation" existed, is obliged to continue to pay his rent out of his own pocket because he is not receiving public relief. The statute discriminates with, as it seems to me, no constitutional basis for classification, in favor of those who do not support themselves. Because of the fact that this door will not completely close, the tenants of three other apartments in the building, because they are on relief, whose apartments contain no violations, are permitted to continue to live there at the expense of the landlord without paying rent. The Welfare Department has appeared *amicus* in behalf of the tenants to save money for the city at the expense of the owner of the apartment house. As the Civil Court Judge who dismissed these petitions in summary proceedings said correctly in another case (Matter of Schaeffer v. Montes, 37 Misc. 2d 722, 723, 233 N.Y.S.2d 444, 446) this *"is said to be the first law of its kind in the United States."* This is not remarkable if constitutional safeguards are to continue to have any further relation to real property of this character. Its constitutionality is in no manner sustained by the rent control cases such as People ex rel. Durham Realty Corp. v. La Fetra (230 N.Y. 429, 130 N.E. 601, 16 A.L.R. 152); Teeval Co. v. Stern (301 N.Y. 346, 93 N.E.2d 884); Twentieth Century Assoc. v. Waldman (294 N.Y. 571, 63 N.E.2d 177), or Block v. Hirsch (256 U.S. 135, 41 S.Ct. 458, 65 L.Ed. 865). The only suggestion of relationship to the public safety in an effort to relate it to the police power is that, unless this door (which is not a fire door) were completely closed, if a fire started in this nonwelfare tenanted apartment, it might spread slightly more rapidly into other portions of the building. If the door fitted perfectly, there would be no obligation on the tenant to keep it closed. Any fire hazard, the building inspector admitted, was a very remote possibility. It would be a safe assumption that there are many doors somewhere in apartments in multiple dwellings in New York City which do not completely close, and many more that are not always kept closed. But even if the spreading of fire were a probability, what possible relationship could there be to the public safety in denying dispossess warrants in these cases? It could only mean that these welfare tenants would continue to be subjected to this fictitious hazard.

This statute recites that it was adopted to aid in eliminating slums. It would be related to that objective if payment for the use and occupation of the apartments were channeled to the landlord in such manner that the landlord would be required to spend it for the improvement of the property, but these provisions of this statute are unrelated to that end. They prevent the rent from being paid in any manner so that it could be used for repairs or improvements. Such provisions have no relation to slum clearance except to prevent it.

Not only does this constitute deprivation of property without due process of law, but it denies the equal protection of the law to owners of dwellings occupied by tenants who are on public relief. This is illustrated by the circumstance that this landlord can continue to collect rent from the tenant not on relief in whose premises this trivial violation exists.

The orders appealed from should be reversed and dispossess warrants issued.

Judges BURKE, BERGAN, KEATING and BREITEL concur with Chief Judge FULD; Judge VAN VOORHIS

dissents and votes to reverse in an opinion in which Judge SCILEPPI concurs.

Orders affirmed.

———

NOTE: RENT WITHHOLDING AND THE IMPROVEMENT OF SUBSTANDARD HOUSING *

53 Calif.L.Rev. 304, 331–332, 334–336 (1965).

* * *

III

RENT WITHHOLDING OUTSIDE OF NEW YORK

A. Tenant Organized Rent Strikes

Tenant led rent strikes have been organized in several areas outside of New York City. They are likely to continue to appear throughout the country as tactics of protest within the civil rights movement. However, it is probable that they will not meet with such success as has been witnessed in New York since elsewhere there are generally no adequate legal theories upon which tenants may safely withhold their rent. Moreover, since rent control has been extinguished nearly everywhere but in New York City, even if a court should rule that rent need not be paid as long as a dwelling remains in a dangerous condition, the effect of such a holding could be undercut by a landlord exercising his right to recover possession of the premises upon the expiration of the tenant's lease. In the common event that the slum tenant simply has a month-to-month tenancy, this can be done in most jurisdictions by giving a thirty-day notice to quit. The only alternative would be to hold that when dangerous code violations exist in a unit, they will be a defense not only to an action for rent, but also to the landlord's right to recover possession upon termination of the lease. This would in effect give the tenant a judicially created lease for as long as the condition remains.

In most jurisdictions the success of a rent strike will depend primarily upon its "nuisance value," and its ability to create public interest in the needs of the slum areas. The latter effect of a rent strike can be of considerable importance. A good deal of publicity depicting the squalor and deterioration of the slums usually accompanies a rent strike, and may result in increased pressure on the landlords from the code enforcement agencies and the legislature.

It would be possible, of course, for a state to enact a law similar to the one presently proposed in New York enabling a tenant to withhold his rent upon the failure of his landlord to eliminate dangerous violations and permit the existence of such violations to be a defense to the landlord's action for nonpayment. Even in the absence of rent and eviction control, such an act would embody some of the coercive effects of the New York legislation. The statute might further provide that the existence of hazardous violations suspends the landlord's ability to recover possession upon the termination of the tenant's lease. This would protect the slum tenant from a landlord's evasion of the purposes of the statute in the situations where he may evict by serving a notice to quit. It is probable that where the existence of substandard housing is widespread and the official means of enforcement have proven grossly inadequate such a law would be advisable. The value of rent withholding as an enforcement technique in this situation lies in its directness, and in its bypassing the ineffectual and probably understaffed enforcement agency. The justification for the extreme measure lies in the seriousness of the problem and the continued failure of other means of enforcement.

*   *   *

CONCLUSION

The tenant led rent strike is more a symptom than a cure. It is primarily a weapon of protest rather than an effective device for bringing a lasting solution to the problems of slum housing. When the rent strike arises it indicates the accepted methods of creating an adequate supply of standard low cost housing have broken down. Where the technique has been given a statutory basis it serves both as a reasonably satisfactory channel for protesting an intolerable situation and as a substitute for the normal methods of code enforcement. As the latter, however, it suffers from several defects. First, there is no guarantee that the sanction will be consistently applied. Since the use of the method depends upon the tenants' own initiative, it may be invoked sporadically with some owners being subjected to what is admittedly a heavy sanction while others get by with an occasional fine, or perhaps no penalty at all. This disparity of application neither creates a respect for the law and a willingness to comply voluntarily with the minimum standards, nor ensures a uniformly adequate supply of housing. Secondly, this type of enforcement technique is apt to be too harsh and inflexible. The best housing law enforcement program is the one where compliance can be obtained through persuasion, and where actual resort to the penal sanctions is rarely necessary. Where the tenants themselves administer and apply these heavy penalties, landlord-tenant relationships will become strained, and the opportunity to persuade compliance will be diminished. Furthermore, the potential uses of these heavy sanctions would tend to make investment in low rent property unattractive, possibly resulting in even less new construction in low cost housing and in transfers of the existing accommodations to speculators interested only in a quick depreciation and resale. It is only when the problem has reached the point where the traditional means of enforcement have completely failed that these considerations must yield to the immediate safety and welfare of the tenants. In such a case rent withholding legislation is justified.

Welfare rent withholding is not subject to some of these criticisms since it is administered by an official agency, and presumably will be consistently and rationally applied. The more serious criticisms of this technique relate to the effect of forced withholding and relocation upon the welfare recipients. Even so, the use of the device is a recognition that the normal enforcement methods have proven unsatisfactory.

Overriding all criticisms of the wisdom and effectiveness of rent withholding are the inadequacies inherent in any attempt merely to coerce compliance with housing laws. Substandard buildings are usually old, and they can be repaired and maintained according to ever rising standards for only so long. Eventually they must be torn down and replaced with new housing adapted to the needs of low income families. Neither rent strikes nor any other means of housing law enforcement can bring this about directly. What the rent strikes can and do accomplish is to indicate dramatically the need that exists. This need has not been fully met by the present sources of residential construction. The signs seem to point to the necessity for greater participation by the federal government, either through subsidies to private contractors, or, more directly, through the public housing program. Whatever the source of the cure, until there is a more effective commitment to this area of housing construction, rent strikes are likely to continue to appear, and, irrespective of their usefulness as an enforcement device, repeatedly indicate the need for more standard low cost homes.

* * *

Notes on statutory suspension of rent

1. The New York City Department of Buildings has designated 57 code violations as "rent impairing." Cf. New York Mult. Dwelling Law, section 302–a at § 2a. They range from defective faucets and inadequate lighting in the laundry room to structural defects, vermin, and the lack of a legal second means of egress. A challenge to this list of violations failed. Matter of 10 W. 28th St. Corp. v. Moerdler, 52 Misc.2d 109, 275 N.Y.S.2d 144 (Sup.Ct.1966).

2. A tenant wishing to raise a section 302–a defense must first deposit whatever rent landlord claims is owed, id. at § 3c. Does this requirement unconstitutionally deprive tenant of the use of his money for an indefinite period of time without any prior opportunity to be heard as to the accuracy of the amount? Faced with this claim, a trial judge invalidated the deposit requirement. Amanuensis, Ltd. v. Brown, 65 Misc.2d 15, 318 N.Y.S.2d 11 (Civ.Ct.1971). The opinion relied heavily on Sniadach v. Family Finance Corp., 395 U.S. 337, 89 S.Ct. 1820, 23 L.Ed.2d 349 (1969), where the Supreme Court struck down on procedural due process grounds a Wisconsin statute forcing an employer, upon service of a summons in a garnishment action, to withhold up to 50 percent of the employee's wages, without any opportunity for the employee to be heard. Does the analogy convince you? [The Sniadach opinion is reprinted in full and discussed—Chapter 5, infra.]

3. Section 302–a and Art. 7–A of the Real Prop. Act. & Proc. Law, infra, both were enacted in 1965 in response to a massive wave of rent strikes which arose in New York's slums two years earlier. A salient difference between the two statutes is that section 302–a is strictly defensive—a tenant unhappy about code violations can validate his refusal to pay rent only after the landlord sues him.

In this respect, section 302–a resembles the long-standing but seldom utilized section 755 of the Real Prop. Act. & Proc. Law, which permits New York State tenants to deposit the rent due if the landlord sues for possession or for non-payment of rent. Upon tenant's showing of outstanding violations amounting in seriousness to a constructive eviction, the court may then stay proceedings and also direct the release of all deposited rentals to a contractor or materialman who makes the necessary repairs. As a condition to the continuing stay of proceedings, tenant must deposit all rentals as they become due. There is not, however, any positive mechanism for launching the repairs, and unlike the remedy of section 302–a, where tenant's rent obligation is suspended, a tenant relying on section 755 continues to pay out moneys for a slummy apartment. Shouldn't section 302–a and section 755 both be amended to give courts discretionary power to name a receiver who will remove the violations? If such discretionary power becomes available, what factors should a judge consider before exercising the power?

ARTICLE 7–A, N. Y. REAL PROPERTY ACTIONS AND PROCEEDINGS LAW (SUPP.1965)

SPECIAL PROCEEDINGS BY TENANTS OF MULTIPLE DWELLINGS IN THE CITY OF NEW YORK FOR JUDGMENT DIRECTING DEPOSIT OF RENTS AND THE USE THEREOF FOR THE PURPOSE OF REMEDYING CONDITIONS DANGEROUS TO LIFE, HEALTH OR SAFETY

§ 769. *Jurisdiction; court; venue.* 1. A special proceeding by tenants of a multiple dwelling in the city of New York for a judgment directing the deposit of rents into court and their use for the purpose of remedying conditions dangerous to life, health or safety may be maintained in the civil court of the city of New York. * * *

§ 770. *Grounds for the proceeding.* One-third or more of the tenants occupying a multiple dwelling located in the city of New York may maintain a special proceeding as provided in this article, upon the ground that there exists in such multiple dwellings or in any part thereof a lack of heat or of running water or of light or of electricity or of adequate sewage disposal facilities, or any other condition dangerous to life, health or safety, which has existed for five days, or an infestation by rodents, or any combination of such conditions.

§ 771. *Commencement; notice of petition; time and manner of service.* 1. A special proceeding prescribed by this article shall be commenced by the service of a petition and notice of petition. A notice of petition may be issued only by a judge or the clerk of the court.

2. The notice of petition shall specify the time and place of the hearing on the petition and state that if at such time, a defense to such petition is not interposed and established by the owner or any mortgagee or lienor of record, a final judgment may be rendered directing that the rents due on the date of entry of such judgment from the petitioning tenants and the rents due on the dates of service of such judgment on all other tenants occupying such multiple dwelling, from such other tenants, shall be deposited with the clerk of the court, and any rents to become due in the future from such petitioners and from all other tenants occupying such multiple dwelling shall be deposited with such clerk as they fall due; and that such deposited rents shall be used, subject to the court's direction, to the extent necessary to remedy the condition or conditions alleged in the petition. * * *

§ 772. *Contents of petition.* The petition shall:

1. Allege material facts showing that there exists in such multiple dwelling or any part thereof one or more of the following: a lack of heat or of running water or of light or electricity or of adequate sewage disposal facilities, or any other condition dangerous to life, health or safety, which has existed for five days, or an infestation of rodents.

2. Allege the number of petitioners making the petition and that they constitute one-third or more of the tenants of said multiple dwelling in occupancy thereof.

3. Allege a brief description of the nature of the work required to remove or remedy the condition and an estimate as to the cost thereof.

4. Allege the amount of rent due from each such petitioner, monthly.

5. State the relief sought. * * *

§ 775. *Defenses.* It shall be a sufficient defense to the proceeding, if the owner or any mortgagee or lienor of record establish that:

a. The condition or conditions alleged in the petition did not in fact exist or that such condition or conditions have been removed or remedied; or

b. Such condition or conditions has been caused by a petitioning tenant or tenants or members of the family or families of such petitioner or petitioners or of their guests or by other residents of the multiple dwelling or their families or guests; or

c. Any tenant or resident of the multiple dwelling has refused entry to the owner or his agent to a portion of the premises for the purpose of correcting such condition or conditions.

§ 776. *Judgment.* The court shall render a final judgment either

a. Dismissing the petition for failure to affirmatively establish the allegations thereof or because of the affirmative establishment by the owner or a mortgagee or lienor of record of a defense or defenses specified in section seven hundred seventy-five of this article; or

b. Directing that (1) the rents due on the date of the entry of such judgment from the petitioning tenants and the rents due on the dates of service of the judgment on all other tenants occupying such multiple dwelling, from such other tenants, shall be deposited with the clerk of the court; (2) any rents to become due in the future from such petitioners and from all other tenants occupying such multiple dwelling shall be deposited with such clerk as they fall due; (3) such deposited rents shall be used subject to the court's direction, to the extent necessary to remedy the condition or conditions alleged in the petition and (4) upon the completion of such work in accordance with such judgment, any remaining surplus shall be turned over to the owner, together with a complete accounting of the rents deposited and the costs incurred; and granting such other and further relief as to the court may seem just and proper. A certified copy of such judgment shall be served personally upon each non-petitioning tenant occupying such multiple dwelling. * * * Any right of the owner of such multiple dwelling to collect such rent moneys from any petitioning tenant of such multiple dwelling on or after the date of entry of such judgment, and from any non-petitioning tenant of such multiple dwelling on or after the date of service of such judgment of such non-petitioning tenant as herein provided, shall be void and unenforceable to the extent that such petitioning or non-petitioning tenant, as the case may be, has deposited such moneys with the clerk of the court in accordance with the terms of such judgment, regardless of whether such right of the owner arises from a lease, contract, agreement or understanding heretofore or hereafter made or entered into or arises as a matter of law from the relationship of the parties or otherwise. It shall be a valid defense in any action or proceeding against any such tenant to recover possession of real property for the non-payment of rent or for use or occupation to prove that the rent alleged to be unpaid was deposited with the clerk of the court in accordance with the terms of a judgment entered under this section. * * *

§ 778. *Appointment of administrator*

1. The court is authorized and empowered, in implementation of a judgment rendered pursuant to section seven hundred seventy-six or seven hundred seventy-seven of this article, to appoint a person other than the owner, a mortgagee or lienor, to administer the rent moneys or security deposited with the clerk subject to the court's direction. Such person shall be an attorney and counsellor at law duly qualified to practice law in this state or a certified public accountant or a real estate broker licensed in this state. Such administrator is authorized and empowered in accordance with the direction of the court, to order the necessary materials, labor and services to remove or remedy the conditions specified in the judgment, and to make disbursements in payment thereof. Such administrator, shall, upon completion of the work prescribed in such judgment, file with the court a full accounting of all receipts and expenditures for such work.

2. The court may allow from the rent moneys or security on deposit a reasonable amount for the services of such administrator.

3. The administrator so appointed shall furnish a bond, the amount and form of which shall be approved by the court. The cost of such bond shall be paid from the moneys so deposited.

Notes on Article 7–A

1. Article 7–A was enacted in 1965 and has survived constitutional attack. Matter of Himmel v. Chase Manhattan Bank, 47 Misc.2d 93, 262 N.Y.S.2d 515 (Civ.Ct.1965). The building was hardly a slum, being described in the opinion as a "fine and elegant 14 story apartment residence," whose tenants had complained of inadequacies in the central air conditioning, rodent infestation, frequent elevator breakdown, and poor security against crimes.

An early evaluation of Article 7–A, made after it had been in operation for two years, concluded:

"Article 7–A proceedings can be efficacious in providing needed relief for tenement dwellers. Too often, however, too much is expected of the remedy. In the cases surveyed where rehabilitation was considered relatively successful, there was at most a seven-to-one ratio between the cost of repairs and the monthly rent roll. However, contingencies such as tenants' vacating the premises or not paying rent may make this seven-to-one ratio too optimistic to serve as a rule of thumb. Even when the repairs are of a sufficiently limited scope, the remedy may fail because of its complete dependence on volunteers who lack the time—and often the competence—to complete a rent strike successfully.

"The statute itself should be amended to clarify the administrator's powers and duties. Now generally ignored, the requirement that the administrator withdraw funds from the court should be replaced by statutory provision for payment of rents directly to the administrator. To prevent the innumerable delays now occurring, the emergency nature of the statute should be emphasized by more explicit prohibition of adjournments. The shortage of competent administrators could be alleviated by allowing the court to appoint persons other than attorneys, certified public accountants, or real estate brokers.

"Requiring the expertise of individual volunteers and the resources of privately or governmentally sponsored community organizations, the Article 7–A proceeding is not truly a tenants' remedy. Bypassing the City Agencies, the rent strike "tacitly assumes that there may be situations where the municipality may be unable to act with sufficient speed or decisiveness." When competently and not overambitiously employed, the rent strike provides an effective emergency measure for checking slight deterioration of tenements. But a piecemeal approach with a private remedy is no panacea for the slums." Note, Tenant Rent Strikes, 3 Colum.J.Law & Soc.Prob. 1, 16 (1967).

A more recent survey of Article 7–A voices much the same guarded optimism. Note, Article 7–A Revisited: New York City's Statutory Rent Strike Law, 8 Colum. J.Law & Soc.Prob. 523 (1972). The writer estimates that eighty 7–A petitions were filed throughout New York City in 1970 and again in 1971.

2. A 1966 Pennsylvania statute, the Pennsylvania Rent Withholding Act, Act of January 24, 1966, P.L. (1965) 1534, § 1, as amended, 35 P.S. § 1700–1 (Supp. 1970), combines features of the New York laws above. The statute provides for the local certification of dwellings as "unfit for human habitation" (term not defined); in that event, any tenant may automatically put his rent into escrow, and, thereupon, is immune from eviction. Six months later, if the dwelling has not yet been certified as "fit for human habitation," the tenant gets back all monies paid into escrow. During the escrow period the tenant may not be evicted. In DePaul v. Kauffman, 441 Pa. 386, 272 A.2d 500 (1971), building owners attacked the statute as unconstitutionally vague, a taking of property without due process, and an impairment of the obligation of contract. They lost despite a claim that the delays in getting an improvement loan prevented the completion of repairs within the requisite six months so as to avoid forfeiture of the rentals. Contrast the Pennsylvania statute with the New York statutes. If the goal is *improved* housing conditions, which statutory approach is the better?

In Klein v. Allegheny County Health Department, 441 Pa. 1, 269 A.2d 647 (1970), the Supreme Court held that the statute permitted successive six-months periods of rent escrow.

3. Michigan has enacted broad new legislation which gives the tenant some new defenses against the landlord as well as a new cause of action. In every residential lease the landlord is deemed to covenant an implied warranty of habitability and fitness. In addition, tenants have been given a cause of action against landlords for the violation of statutory health and safety standards. Mich.Comp. L. Sec. 554.139 (Supp.1969). The tenant may defend against a summary eviction proceeding on the grounds that the landlord has himself breached the lease. Mich.Comp.L. Sec. 600.5637(5) (Supp. 1969). Michigan has also enacted a statutory protection against retaliatory eviction. Mich.Comp.L. Sec. 600.5646 (4) (Supp.1969). Michigan has also made provision for the payment of rent into escrow for the continued existence of violations; escrow funds may be used for defraying the cost of repairs. The law was applied in Goodloe v. Goodman Bros., C.A. No. 109864 (Mich.Cir.Ct., Wayne County, June 1968) 15 Welf. Law Bull. 18 (Dec.1968) where the court enjoined a landlord from continuing summary eviction proceedings against

rent-striking tenants and ordered the rent paid into court. Tenants had claimed breach of warranty, illegal contract, and partial eviction as defenses. The Michigan retaliatory eviction law was applied in Oliver v. Sweeney, No. DA 114 (Mich. Civ.Ct. June 8, 1970).

4. New York City is seeking legislation to require landlords to post a security deposit of one month's rent on each apartment to guarantee that repairs would be made when necessary. The Town of Ridgefield, New Jersey has passed a similar law. N.Y.Times, Oct. 10, 1972, p. 35, col. 7.

3. Criminal Process

NEW YORK REAL PROPERTY LAW (McKINNEY'S 1968)

§ 235. Wilful violation of the terms of a lease

Any lessor, agent, manager, superintendent or janitor of any building, or part thereof, the lease or rental agreement whereof by its terms, expressed or implied, requires the furnishing of hot or cold water, heat, light, power, elevator service, telephone service or any other service or facility to any occupant of said building, who wilfully or intentionally fails to furnish such water, heat, light, power, elevator service, telephone service or other service or facility at any time when the same are necessary to the proper or customary use of such building, or part thereof, or any lessor, agent, manager, superintendent or janitor who wilfully and intentionally interferes with the quiet enjoyment of the leased premises by such occupant, is guilty of a violation.

NOTE: The New York Penal Law § 10.00 (McKinney's 1967) defines "violation" as an offense for which a sentence to a term of imprisonment in excess of fifteen days cannot be imposed. Prior to 1967, a guilty landlord could have been punished by imprisonment in a county jail or workhouse for a term not exceeding six months.

B. LANDLORD FAILS TO MAINTAIN PHYSICALLY SAFE PREMISES AND TENANT IS INJURED OR CRIMINALLY ASSAULTED

WHETZEL v. JESS FISHER MANAGEMENT CO.

United States Court of Appeals, District of Columbia Circuit, 1960.
108 U.S.App.D.C. 385, 282 F.2d 943.

BAZELON, Circuit Judge. In Bowles v. Mahoney, this court adhered to the common-law rule that "absent any statutory or contract duty, the lessor is not responsible for an injury resulting from a defect which developed during the term."[1] Since that case was decided, the Commissioners of the District of Columbia have promulgated regulations concerning maintenance and repair of residential property. The primary question here presented is whether these regulations impose a "statutory * * * duty" on the lessor not presented in Bowles v. Mahoney. We conclude that they do.

The issue arises upon an appeal from a summary judgment entered against the plaintiffs below. Their amended complaint alleged that on March 1, 1956, Audrey Whetzel rented an apartment from the appellee for $75.00 per month upon a one-year lease which did not affirmatively place the burden of repairs, other than those caused by the tenant's negligence, on either party.[2] On June

[1] 1952, 91 U.S.App.D.C. 155, 159, 202 F.2d 320, 323, certiorari denied 1953, 344 U.S. 935, 73 S.Ct. 505, 97 L.Ed. 719.

[2] The lease provided that the lessee would "keep the premises in good order and condition and surrender the same at the expira-

30, 1956, four months after she entered into possession, the entire bedroom ceiling fell, causing the injuries of which she complains.[3] The principal theory of her action is that the appellee, with knowledge of the defect, negligently permitted the ceiling to remain in an unsafe condition.[4]

I. The Applicable Law

Appellant contends that the Housing Regulations establish a standard of con-

tion of the term herein in the same order in which they are received, *usual wear and tear and damage resulting from acts not caused by the Tenant's negligence excepted.*" (Emphasis supplied.) The landlord reserved the right of access to the premises "at any time for the purpose of inspection * * * or for the purpose of making any repairs the landlord considers necessary or desirable." The tenant agreed to give the landlord "prompt notice of any defects or breakage in the structure, equipment or fixtures of said premises," and promised not to make structural alterations or additions without permission.

For a discussion of the effect of statutes requiring the landlord to repair in cases where a lease places the duty of repair squarely upon the tenant, see Feuerstein & Shestack, Landlord and Tenant—The Statutory Duty to Repair. 45 Ill.L.Rev. 205, 220 (1950). Cf. Michaels v. Brookchester, Inc., 1958, 26 N.J. 379, 140 A.2d 199, 204.

[3] Mrs. Whetzel's husband, a co-plaintiff, sued for medical expenses and loss of consortium. Her son, also a co-plaintiff, claimed injury through loss of his mother's support, maintenance and attention. They have also appealed from summary judgment. Since their right to recover is contingent upon hers, we will, for the sake of simplicity, treat the case as if Mrs. Whetzel were the sole appellant.

[4] The amended complaint also alleged that the appellee (1) negligently failed to warn appellant of the latent defect, of which it had knowledge; (2) fraudulently misrepresented the premises as fit for occupancy; (3) negligently performed an agreement to redecorate, and to undertake the necessary plastering; and (4) breached the agreement to redecorate and plaster. On this appeal appellants urge only that the complaint was improperly dismissed because of the duty imposed by the Housing Regulations. For that reason we do not consider the other counts of the amended complaint.

duct for the landlord, which, if negligently breached, allows an injured tenant to recover. They rely heavily on the landmark case of Altz v. Lieberson, 1922, 233 N.Y. 16, 134 N.E. 703, 704.

That case also involved a tenant injured by a falling ceiling. Judge Cardozo, writing for the New York Court of Appeals, held that the New York Tenement House Law, which provided that "every tenement house and all the parts thereof shall be kept in good repair," thus "changed the ancient rule" and imposed upon landlords a duty that "extends to all whom there was a purpose to protect." That statute did not specify who had the duty of repair; nor did it speak of tort liability. It only authorized penalties in criminal enforcement proceedings.[5] Nevertheless, the court held that:

> The Legislative must have known that unless repairs in the rooms of the poor were made by the landlord, they would not be made by anyone. The duty imposed became commensurate with the need. The right to seek redress is not limited to the city or its officers.

Other jurisdictions have accepted the view that regulations which explicitly or implicitly require a landlord to repair may render him liable for injuries resulting from a failure to comply.[6] Indeed, in

[5] New York Tenement House Act, New York Sess.Laws 1909, ch. 99, § 124.

[6] Rimco Realty & Investment Corp. v. La Vigne, 1943, 114 Ind.App. 211, 50 N.E.2d 953 (Landlord liable for loss caused by fire originating in a garbage chute, such chutes being illegal in tenement houses); Morningstar v. Strich, 1950, 326 Mich. 541, 40 N.W.2d 719, 721, (Owner liable for injuries resulting from defective radiator under statute providing that "every dwelling * * * shall be kept in good repair by the owner"); Evers v. Davis, 86 N.J.L. 196, 90 A. 677 (1914) (Complaint alleging that death resulted from absence of a fire escape and that failure to provide fire escapes violates the Tenement Housing Act states a cause of action against

our own case of Hill v. Raymond, 1935, 65 App.D.C. 144, 81 F.2d 278, we held that building regulations establishing certain standards for interior stairways were admissible as evidence of a landlord's negligence in failing to illuminate and to maintain a common stairway. See also Nielsen v. Barclay Corp., 1958, 103 U.S. App.D.C. 136, 138 note 8, 255 F.2d 545, 547 note 8.[7]

The view expressed in these cases is fully consistent with "the almost universal American and English attitude * * * that where legislation pre-

owner); Daniels v. Brunton, 1951, 7 N.J. 102, 80 A.2d 547, 549 (Owner liable for injury in demised premises under statute providing that "Every tenement house * * * shall be * * * maintained in good repair" and rendering owner criminally responsible for breach thereof); Michaels v. Brookchester, Inc., 1958, 26 N.J. 379, 140 A.2d 199 (Same); Doster v. Murr, 1937, 57 Ohio App. 157, 12 N.E.2d 781 (Owner of building leased to a single tenant liable for injury caused by absence of a stairway hand-rail under statute providing that "owner * * * lessees * * * or proprietors" shall provide and maintain such fixtures); cf. Tvedt v. Wheeler, 1897, 70 Minn. 161, 72 N.W. 1062; Beard v. General Real Estate Corp., 10 Cir., 1956, 229 F.2d 260.

Contra: Chambers v. Lowe, 1933, 117 Conn. 624, 169 A. 912, 913 (Legislature did not intend that statute providing that tenements "shall be kept in good repair" should render owner liable for injuries occurring in parts of building not used in common); Johnson v. Carter, 1934, 218 Iowa 587, 255 N.W. 864, 93 A.L.R. 774 (Same); Garland v. Stetson, 1935, 292 Mass. 95, 197 N.E. 679 (Same); Corey v. Losse, Mo.1937, 297 S.W. 32 (Ordinance providing that owner or lessee shall keep tenement in good repair could not constitutionally impose tort liability upon owner).

See generally, Feuerstein & Shestack, Landlord and Tenant—The Statutory Duty to Repair, 45 Ill.L.Rev. 205 (1950); Annotation, 17 A.L.R.2d 704 (1951).

[7] In a case imposing tort liability upon landlords for injuries resulting from repairs which they or their contractors negligently perform, we said, "There is a practical as well as a logical reason [for this result] * * *. Today insurance * * * is available. Liability for an unsafe condition of the premises no longer is a substantial hardship." Bailey v. Zlotnick, 1957, 80 U.S.App. D.C. 117, 149 F.2d 505, 507, 162 A.L.R. 1108.

scribes a standard of conduct for the purpose of protecting life, limb, or property from a certain type of risk, and harm to the interest sought to be protected comes about through breach of the standard from the risk sought to be obviated, then the statutory prescription of the standard will at least be considered in determining civil rights and liabilities." 2 Harper & James, Torts 997 (1956). See also Restatement, Torts § 286 (1934); Prosser, Torts 152–64 (2d ed. 1955); Thayer, Public Wrong and Private Action, 27 Harv.L.Rev. 317 (1914).

This axiom of tort law tacitly recognizes that the continued vitality of the common law, including the law of torts, depends upon its ability to reflect contemporary community values and ethics: Holmes, The Common Law 1, 120–21, 149, 162–63 (1881); Cardozo, The Nature of the Judicial Process 24–25, 108 (1921); O'Meara, Natural Law and Everyday Law, 5 Natural Law Forum 85 (1960). An essential element of tort liability is the breach of a duty of care owed. Palsgraf v. Long Island R. R., 1928, 248 N.Y. 339, 162 N.E. 99, 59 A.L.R. 1253. Whether or not a duty of care exists is, basically, a question of law. Harper & James, Torts § 18.8 (1958). A penal statute which is imposed for the protection of particular individuals establishes a duty of care based on contemporary community values and ethics. The law of torts can only be out of joint with community standards if it ignores the existence of such duties. See Evers v. Davis, 1914, 86 N.J.L. 196, 90 A. 677; Morris, The Role of Criminal Statutes in Negligence Actions, 49 Colum. L.Rev. 21 (1949).

The courts have not agreed, however, on the precise effect to be given a breach of a statute. A majority of American courts hold that the unexcused violation of a statute which is intended to protect a class of persons, of which the plaintiff is a member, against the type of harm which has in fact occurred is negligence *per se*. That is to say, such violation is negligence as a matter of law and the jury must be so instructed. Prosser, Torts 161 (1955). But a substantial and growing number of jurisdictions hold that violation of a penal statute is "only evidence of negligence which the jury may accept or reject as it sees fit." Ibid.

Commentators have pointed out that the *per se* rule may create serious rigidities and inequities. See, e. g., 2 Harper & James, Torts § 17.6 (1958); Morris, The Relation of Criminal Statutes to Tort Liability, 46 Harv.L.Rev. 453 (1933). Strictly applied, the *per se* rule can, for instance, render negligent as a matter of law a defendant who has taken all due precautions,[8] and bar recovery of a plaintiff who is likewise free from fault in all but a technical sense. Prosser, Torts 162–63 (1955); Morris, The Role of Criminal Statutes in Negligence Actions, 49 Colum.L.Rev. 21, 29 (1949); Prosser, Contributory Negligence as a Defense to a Violation of Statute, 32 Minn.L.Rev. 105 (1948). Courts adhering to the *per se* rule have generally recognized its inadequacies and developed such doctrines as "statutory purpose" and "justifiable violation" in an effort to return to the jury responsibility for determining whether reasonable care was exercised in the circumstances.

This jurisdiction has adopted these exceptions. In a leading case, we held that "violation of an ordinance intended to promote safety is negligence. If by creating the hazard which the ordinance was intended to avoid, it brings about the harm which the ordinance was intended to prevent, it is a legal cause of the harm." Ross v. Hartman, 1943, 78 U.S.App.D.C. 217, 218, 139 F.2d 14, 15,

158 A.L.R. 1370.[9] Accord, Danzansky v. Zimbolist, 1939, 70 App.D.C. 234, 105 F.2d 457; Richardson v. Gregory, No. 15576, 108 U.S.App.D.C. 263, 281 F. 2d 626. * * *

II. The Instant Case

Turning to the instant case, we must determine the authority of the District of Columbia Housing Regulations and their effect upon the landlord's duty of care toward his tenants. * * *

* * * Section 2301 provides that "No owner, licensee, or tenant shall occupy or permit the occupancy of any habitation in violation of these regulations." Section 2501 directs, *inter alia,* that:

> "Every premises accommodating one or more inhabitations shall be maintained and kept in repair so as to provide decent living accommodations for the occupants. This part of the Code contemplates more than mere basic repairs and maintenance to keep out the elements; its purpose is to include repairs and maintenance designed to make a premises or neighborhood healthy and safe."

And more specifically § 2504 requires:

> "Each interior wall or ceiling shall be structurally sound and free of loose plaster or other loose structural or surfacing material. Each interior wall or ceiling shall be free of holes and wide cracks."

Thus it appears that § 2301 imposes upon the appellee a duty of care toward its tenants. This duty can be satisfied either by making the necessary repairs or by terminating use of the premises as a place of human habitation. Breach of that duty is, according to the principles

---

[8] Harper & James give the example of a defendant whose automobile tail lights go out, despite all due precaution, shortly before an accident. Harper & James, Torts 999 (1958).

[9] There we found that a defendant, who had left his automobile unlocked in violation of traffic regulations, was negligent as a matter of law and liable for injuries sustained by third persons at the hands of one who stole the car.

which we have discussed, at least evidence of negligence.

But § 2301 also creates a duty of care which the appellant owes to herself. Breach of this duty is likewise at least evidence of contributory negligence. The question then is, does her contributory negligence so clearly appear from the face of the complaint that she is not entitled to go to trial? We think not.

In the first place, even if she were contributorily negligent *per se,* there would remain for the jury the question of proximate cause. Richardson v. Gregory, No. 15576, 108 U.S.App.D.C. 263, 281 F.2d 626. Second, the pleadings and affidavits which constitute the present record do not provide an adequate basis for determining whether the plaintiff-appellant was contributorily negligent as a matter of law by occupying non-conforming premises.

It is possible that facts may be developed at trial which would warrant a charge of negligence or contributory negligence as a matter of law. But we think that these are questions generally for the jury to resolve upon consideration of all the circumstances bearing on negligence and contributory negligence—including but by no means limited to the regulatory violation, reasonable efforts if any to comply with the regulations, and circumstances excusing their violation. Hecht Co. v. McLaughlin, 1954, 93 U.S.App. D.C. 382, 214 F.2d 212.

For example, recovery would be barred if the jury finds that in the total circumstance of the case the tenant unreasonably exposed herself to danger by failing to vacate the premises or to keep them in repair. Some of the more obviously relevant circumstances would include the lease provisions, if any, concerning the duty to repair and the landlord's right of entry for that purpose; the latent or patent character of the defect and tenant's knowledge, or opportunity for knowledge thereof; who repaired previous defects,

if any; the amount of rental and term of lease, on the one hand, against the extent and nature of the defect and cost of repair on the other; and the bargaining position of the parties in entering into the lease.[15] In the present case, the jury would also consider, for example, the fact that the defective ceiling is a common wall with the floor of the apartment above, over which a tenant has virtually no control.

Appellee contends, however, that even if the jury must weigh the duty imposed by the Housing Regulations upon the lessee, summary judgment was nonetheless appropriate because there are uncontradicted affidavits in the record showing that appellee had no notice of the defect in the ceiling. We think actual knowledge is not required for liability; it is enough if, in the exercise of reasonable care, appellee should have known that the condition of the ceiling violated the standards of the Housing Code. Prosser, Torts 6 (1955).

We cannot say that upon a trial a jury could not reasonably find that appellee should have known of the condition of the ceiling. The bathroom ceiling, located just off the bedroom in appellant's apartment, had fallen and been repaired not long before appellant took possession. On New Year's Eve of 1956, just two months before appellant moved in, the livingroom ceiling of the adjoining apartment also fell. On April 1, 1956, appellant noticed a leak in her bedroom ceiling, and reported it to the janitor who was able to stop the leak by adjusting the radiator in the apartment above. But there is no evidence that he then inspected appellant's ceiling to determine if it had been weakened. Just before appellant moved in, appellee hired a contractor to inspect and repair the plaster in appellant's apartment. The contractor's affidavit, executed three years after

---

[15] See Kay v. Cain, 1946, 81 U.S.App.D.C. 24, 154 F.2d 305.

the event, stated that he "carefully inspected and examined the entire apartment" and found "the plaster in the ceiling of the bedroom * * * in good sound condition." Appellant filed no counter affidavits. But in the circumstances of this case, such failure does not "compel acceptance as true of fact alleged in the movant's affidavits" for the purpose of summary judgment. Cellini v. Moss, 1956, 98 U.S.App.D.C. 114, 116, 232 F.2d 371, 373, quoting Subin v. Goldsmith, 2 Cir., 1955, 224 F.2d 753, 759. In view of the fact that the ceiling fell only four months after the alleged inspection, the jury might reasonably find that the inspection was negligently performed. Cf. Washington Loan & Trust Co. v. Hickey, 1943, 78 U.S.App. D.C. 59, 137 F.2d 677.

It follows from all that we have said that the District Court erred in granting summary judgment on the first count of appellants' amended complaint. We therefore reverse the judgment as to that count and remand with directions to proceed to trial. As to the other counts, we affirm since appellants make no point on appeal with respect to them.[16]

So ordered.

WILBUR K. MILLER, Circuit Judge, dissents.

KLINE v. 1500 MASSACHUSETTS AVENUE APARTMENT CORP.

United States Court of Appeals, District of Columbia Circuit, 1970.
141 U.S.App.D.C. 370, 439 F.2d 477.

WILKEY, Circuit Judge. The appellee apartment corporation states that there is "only one issue presented for review * * * whether a duty should be placed on a landlord to take steps to protect tenants from foreseeable criminal acts committed by third parties". The District

[16] See note 4, supra.

Court as a matter of law held that there is no such duty. We find that there is, and that in the circumstances here the applicable standard of care was breached. We therefore reverse and remand to the District Court for the determination of damages for the appellant.

I

The appellant, Sarah B. Kline, sustained serious injuries when she was criminally assaulted and robbed at approximately 10:15 in the evening by an intruder in the common hallway of an apartment house at 1500 Massachusetts Avenue. This facility, into which the appellant Kline moved in October 1959, is a large apartment building with approximately 585 individual apartment units. It has a main entrance on Massachusetts Avenue, with side entrances on both 15th and 16th Streets. At the time the appellant first signed a lease a doorman was on duty at the main entrance twenty-four hours a day, and at least one employee at all times manned a desk in the lobby from which all persons using the elevators could be observed.[1] The 15th Street door adjoined the entrance to a parking garage used by both the tenants and the public. Two garage attendants were stationed at this dual entranceway; the duties of each being arranged so that one of them always was in position to observe those entering either the apartment building or the garage. The 16th Street entrance was unattended during the day but was locked after 9:00 P.M.

By mid-1966, however, the main entrance had no doorman, the desk in the lobby was left unattended much of the time, the 15th Street entrance was generally unguarded due to a decrease in garage personnel, and the 16th Street en-

[1] Miss Kline testified that she had initially moved into the building not because of its central location, but also because she was interested in security, and had been impressed by the precautions taken at the main entrance.

trance was often left unlocked all night. The entrances were allowed to be thus unguarded in the face of an increasing number of assaults, larcenies, and robberies being perpetrated against the tenants in and from the common hallways of the apartment building. These facts were undisputed, and were supported by a detailed chronological listing of offenses admitted into evidence. The landlord had notice of these crimes and had in fact been urged by appellant Kline herself prior to the events leading to the instant appeal to take steps to secure the building.[3]

Shortly after 10:00 PM on November 17, 1966, Miss Kline was assaulted and robbed just outside her apartment on the first floor above the street level of this 585 unit apartment building. This occurred only two months after Leona Sullivan, another female tenant, had been similarly attacked in the same commonway.

II

At the outset we note that of the crimes of violence, robbery, and assault which had been occurring with mounting frequency on the premises at 1500 Massachusetts Avenue, the assaults on Miss Kline and Miss Sullivan took place in the hallways of the building, which were under the exclusive control of the appellee landlord. Even in those crimes of robbery or assault committed in individual apartments, the intruders of necessity had

to gain entrance through the common entry and passageways.[4] These premises fronted on three heavily traveled streets, and had multiple entrances. The risk to be guarded against therefore was the risk of unauthorized entrance into the apartment house by intruders bent upon some crime of violence or theft.

While the apartment lessees themselves could take some steps to guard against this risk by installing extra heavy locks and other security devices on the doors and windows of their respective apartments, yet this risk in the greater part could only be guarded against by the landlord. No individual tenant had it within his power to take measures to guard the garage entranceways, to provide scrutiny at the main entrance of the building, to patrol the common hallways and elevators, to set up any kind of a security alarm system in the building, to provide additional locking devices on the main doors, to provide a system of announcement for authorized visitors only, to close the garage doors at appropriate hours, and to see that the entrance was manned at all times.

The risk of criminal assault and robbery on a tenant in the common hallways of the building was thus entirely predictable; that same risk had been occurring with increasing frequency over a period of several months immediately prior to the incident giving rise to this case; it was a risk whose prevention or minimization was almost entirely within the power of the landlord; and the risk materialized in the assault and robbery of appellant on November 17, 1966.

III

In this jurisdiction, certain duties have been assigned to the landlord because of his *control* of common hallways, lobbies,

[3] Appellant Kline testified that one could hardly fail to notice the police cars about the building after each reported crime. She further testified that in 1966, before her assault, she herself had discussed the crime situation with Miss Bloom, the landlord's agent at the premises, and had asked her "why they didn't do something about securing the building". Moreover, the record contains twenty police reports of crimes occurring in the building in the year 1966, showing that in several instances these crimes were an almost daily occurrence. Such reports in themselves constitute constructive notice to the landlord.

[4] The plaintiff testified that she had returned to her apartment after leaving work at 10:00 PM. We are in agreement with the trial court that her assailant was an intruder. * * *

stairwells, etc., used by all tenants in multiple dwelling units. This Court in Levine v. Katz, 132 U.S.App.D.C. 173, 174, 407 F.2d 303, 304 (1968), pointed out that:

> It has long been well settled in this jurisdiction that, where a landlord leases separate portions of property and reserves under his own control the halls, stairs, or other parts of the property for use in common by all tenants, he has a duty to all those on the premises of legal right to use ordinary care and diligence to maintain the retained parts in a reasonably safe condition.

While Levine v. Katz dealt with a physical defect in the building leading to plaintiff's injury, the rationale as applied to predictable criminal acts by third parties is the same. The duty is the landlord's because by his control of the areas of common use and common danger he is the only party who has the *power* to make the necessary repairs or to provide the necessary protection.

As a general rule, a private person does not have a duty to protect another from a criminal attack by a third person. We recognize that this rule has sometimes in the past been applied in landlord-tenant law, even by this court.[6] Among the reasons for the application of this rule to landlords are: judicial reluctance to tamper with the traditional common law concept of the landlord-tenant relationship; the notion that the act of a third person in committing an intentional tort or crime is a superseding cause of the harm to another resulting therefrom; the oftentimes difficult problem of determining foreseeability of criminal acts; the vagueness of the standard which the landlord must meet; the economic consequences of the

imposition of the duty; and conflict with the public policy allocating the duty of protecting citizens from criminal acts to the government rather than the private sector.

But the rationale of this very broad general rule falters when it is applied to the conditions of modern day urban apartment living, particularly in the circumstances of this case. The rationale of the general rule exonerating a third party from any duty to protect another from a criminal attack has no applicability to the landlord-tenant relationship in multiple dwelling houses. The landlord is no insurer of his tenants' safety, but he certainly is no bystander. And where, as here, the landlord has notice of repeated criminal assaults and robberies, has notice that these crimes occurred in the portion of the premises exclusively within his control, has every reason to expect like crimes to happen again, and has the exclusive power to take preventive action, it does not seem unfair to place upon the landlord a duty to take those steps which are within his power to minimize the predictable risk to his tenants. * * *

Upon consideration of all pertinent factors, we find that there is a duty of protection owed by the landlord to the tenant in an urban multiple unit apartment dwelling.

Summarizing our analysis, we find that this duty of protection arises, first of all, from the logic of the situation itself. If we were answering without the benefit of any prior precedent the issue as posed by the appellee landlord here, "whether a duty should be placed on a landlord to take steps to protect tenants from foreseeable criminal acts committed by third parties," we should have no hesitancy in answering it affirmatively, at least on the basis of the facts of this case.

As between tenant and landlord, the landlord is the only one in the position to take the necessary acts of protection re-

---

6 Applebaum v. Kidwell, 56 App.D.C. 311, 12 F.2d 846 (1926); Goldberg v. Housing Authority of Newark, 38 N.J. 578, 186 A.2d 291, 10 A.L.R.3d 595 (1962); but see Ramsay v. Morrissette, 252 A.2d 509 (D.C.App.1969) and Kendall v. Gore Properties, 236 F.2d 673 (D. C.Cir. 1956).

quired. He is not an insurer, but he is obligated to minimize the risk to his tenants. Not only as between landlord and tenant is the landlord best equipped to guard against the predictable risk of intruders, but even as between landlord and the police power of government, the landlord is in the best position to take the necessary protective measures. Municipal police cannot patrol the entryways and the hallways, the garages and the basements of private multiple unit apartment dwellings. They are neither equipped, manned, nor empowered to do so. In the area of the predictable risk which materialized in this case, only the landlord could have taken measures which might have prevented the injuries suffered by appellant. * * *

Secondly, * * * there is implied in the contract between landlord and tenant an obligation on the landlord to provide those protective measures which are within his reasonable capacity. Here the protective measures which were in effect in October 1959 when appellant first signed a lease were drastically reduced. She continued after the expiration of the first term of the lease on a month to month tenancy. As this court pointed out in Javins v. First National Realty Corp., 138 U.S.App.D.C. 369, 428 F.2d 1071 (1970), "Since the lessees continued to pay the same rent, they were entitled to expect that the landlord would continue to keep the premises in their beginning condition during the lease term. It is precisely such expectations that the law now recognizes as deserving of formal, legal protection. * * *

IV

We now turn to the standard of care which should be applied in judging if the landlord has fulfilled his duty of protection to the tenant. Although in many cases the language speaks as if the standard of care itself varies, in the last analysis the standard of care is the same—reasonable care in all the circumstances. The specific measures to achieve this standard vary with the individual circumstances. It may be impossible to describe in detail for all situations of landlord-tenant relationships, and evidence of custom amongst landlords of the same class of building may play a significant role in determining if the standard has been met.

* * *

We therefore hold in this case that the applicable standard of care in providing protection for the tenant is that standard which this landlord himself was employing in October 1959 when the appellant became a resident on the premises at 1500 Massachusetts Avenue. The tenant was led to expect that she could rely upon this degree of protection. While we do not say that the precise measures for security which were then in vogue should have been kept up, (e. g., the number of people at the main entrances might have been reduced if a tenant-controlled intercom-automatic latch system had been installed in the common entryways), we do hold that the same relative degree of security should have been maintained.

The appellant tenant was entitled to performance by the landlord measured by this standard of protection whether the landlord's obligation be viewed as grounded in contract or in tort. As we have pointed out, this standard of protection was implied as an obligation of the lease contract from the beginning. Likewise, on a tort basis, this standard of protection may be taken as that commonly provided in apartments of this character and class in this community, and this is a reasonable standard of care on which to judge the conduct of the landlord here.

V

Given this duty of protection, and the standard of care as defined, it is clear that the appellee landlord breached its duty toward the appellant tenant here. The risk of criminal assault and robbery on any tenant was clearly predictable, a risk of which the appellee landlord had specific notice, a risk which became reality with increasing frequency, and this risk materialized on the very premises peculiarly under the control, and therefore the protection, of the landlord to the injury of the appellant tenant. The question then for the District Court becomes one of damages only. To us the liability is clear.

Having said this, it would be well to state what is *not* said by this decision. We do not hold that the landlord is by any means an insurer of the safety of his tenants. His duty is to take those measures of protection which are within his power and capacity to take, and which can reasonably be expected to mitigate the risk of intruders assaulting and robbing tenants. The landlord is not expected to provide protection commonly owed by a municipal police department; but as illustrated in this case, he is obligated to protect those parts of his premises which are not usually subject to periodic patrol and inspection by the municipal police. We do not say that every multiple unit apartment house in the District of Columbia should have those same measures of protection which 1500 Massachusetts Avenue enjoyed in 1959, nor do we say that 1500 Massachusetts Avenue should have precisely those same measures in effect at the present time. Alternative and more up-to-date methods may be equally or even more effective.

Granted, the discharge of this duty of protection by landlords will cause, in many instances, the expenditure of large sums for additional equipment and services, and granted, the cost will be ultimately passed on to the tenant in the form of increased rents. This prospect, in itself, however, is no deterrent to our acknowledging and giving force to the

duty, since without protection the tenant already pays in losses from theft, physical assault and increased insurance premiums.

The landlord is entirely justified in passing on the cost of increased protective measures to his tenants, but the rationale of compelling the landlord to do it in the first place is that he is the only one who is in a position to take the necessary protective measures for overall protection of the premises, which he owns in whole and rents in part to individual tenants.

Reversed and remanded to the District Court for the determination of damages.

MacKINNON, Circuit Judge, dissenting: I respectfully dissent from the panel decision that the plaintiff has proved liability as a matter of law. My inability to join in that disposition of the case is based primarily in my disagreement as to what facts were proved at the trial of that issue by the court without a jury. In my view the panel opinion errs by overstating the facts which might be construed as being favorable to appellant and by failing to recognize gross deficiencies in appellant's proof, thereby applying a more strict standard of responsibility to the landlord than the opinion actually states to be the law.

One difficulty here is that the trial court sitting without a jury held as a matter of law that there was no rule requiring the operator of the apartment building to use due care to exclude intruders by locking doors or posting doormen at entrances so as to protect tenants against crimes committed by intruders and others. It never considered whether the facts proved liability if the duty did exist. Against such a procedural background the panel opinion here comes to a different conclusion on the duty owed by the landlord to its tenants and then proceeds to find defendant liable on the facts as a matter of law. This necessarily involves a *de novo* consideration of the facts on a cold record and subjects the result to all the imperfections inherent in any decision arrived at under such handicaps. Here, those handicaps are magnified by the fact that the case was tried to the court without a jury and this necessarily had some tendency to steer the facts toward the issues that became uppermost in the court's mind as the case progressed and away from the issues upon which the court now reverses the trial court. The result in my view is a record that cannot support the panel decision.

*   *   *

As for the claim that appellant was led to believe she would get the same standard of protection in 1966 that was furnished in 1959, there is obviously nothing to this point. She was not led to expect that. She personally observed the changes which occurred in this respect. They were obvious to her each day of her life. And since her original lease had terminated and her tenancy in 1966 was on a month to month basis, whatever contract existed was created at the beginning of the month and since there was no evidence of any alteration in the security precautions during the current month, there is no basis for any damage claim based on contract.

The panel opinion is an excellent argument for a high degree of security in apartments and many of its contentions have considerable weight to them but in my opinion they overstate the security that can reasonably be afforded. The hysteria of apartment dwellers in an inner city plagued with crime [8] is understand-

able but they are not any more exposed there than they are on the streets or in office buildings and they cannot expect the landlord to furnish the equivalent of police protection that is not available from the duly constituted government in the locality.[9] In my opinion the decision in Goldberg v. Housing Authority of Newark, 38 N.J. 578, 186 A.2d 291, 10 A.L.R.2d 595 (1962) answers all appellant's arguments. It is just too much, absent a contractual agreement, to require or expect a combination office-apartment building such as is involved here to provide police patrol protection or its equivalent in the block-long, well-lighted passageways. Yet nothing short of that will meet the second guessing standard of protection the panel opinion practically directs. If tenants expect such protection, they can move to apartments where it is available and presumably pay a higher rental, but it is a mistake in my

---

[8] This court is well aware of the high level of crime in various areas of Washington. About two-thirds of our cases on appeal presently involve criminal offenses. Also the daily newspapers are full of the details of various crimes. The Washington Post of June 19, 1970, p. B 5, stated: "Asleep in rooms, 5 guests robbed in downtown hotel." The story referred to three rooms on the ninth floor of the Statler Hilton Hotel, one of the most prestigious in the city. This is five times as many robberies as had occurred at 1500 Massachusetts Avenue prior to this case. Under the panel opinion, now the Statler Hilton Hotel would practically be required to patrol the upper hotel rooms. The *Post* news story also reported 21 daylight robberies, 4 assaults and 8 thefts, all of which occurred before 6 P.M. This is a fairly typical day in Washington.

[9] Plaintiff's complaint here is partly based on the claim that the landlord was required to maintain a reasonable number of guards. The allegation of the complaint alleged that appellee was negligent in not "taking reasonable precautions in the evening hours of maintaining a *reasonable* number of guards upon the premises so as to protect your plaintiff in her person and in her property." (Emphasis added). To require apartment landlords to employ guards to protect tenants against criminal depredations would be very costly and raise many troublesome questions. How much training should they have? Should such guards be armed? What would be their liability and that of the landlord if they killed an alleged offender in the commission of a criminal act? When duly appointed and trained city policemen are subjected to grand jury indictment for killing criminals caught in the act, the liability and exposure of an apartment house guard and his landlord to criminal and civil process under similar circumstances could be very substantial.

judgment to hold an office-apartment building to such a requirement when the tenant knew for years that such protection was not being afforded.

* * *

It is my conclusion that appellant did not sustain her burden of proof that the owner of the apartment building failed to exercise reasonable care and I would affirm the decision of the very distinguished and learned trial judge. Accordingly, I dissent.

Notes on Unsafe Premises

1. Tenant was raped at knife point while asleep in her top floor apartment in New York City's East Village (a high crime area). Her assailant entered from a fire escape into a bedroom window. A portion of the window glass had been broken two weeks earlier, but the landlord had ignored the tenant's repeated plea that the glass be fixed. Tenant recovered a $10,000 judgment against landlord based on the landlord's *negligent* failure to obey the Housing Code. The court refused, however, to decide whether landlord also had a *contractual* duty to protect tenants from foreseeable violence. Smith v. ABC Realty Co., 66 Misc.2d 276, 322 N.Y.S.2d 207 (Civ.Ct. 1971).

The Appellate Court overturned the judgment, holding that defendant's negligence was not the proximate cause of the plaintiff's injuries. 71 Misc.2d 384, 336 N.Y.S.2d 104 (App.T.1972). See also Hall v. Fraknoi, 69 Misc.2d 470, 330 N.Y.S.2d 637 (Civ.Ct.1972) (landlord's failure to install front door locks and a hall buzzer system not the proximate cause of the knifepoint robbery of the tenant in the building's lobby).

2. The court in the *Kline* opinion articulates both a tort and implied contract theory to support plaintiff's recovery. In tort, landlord must protect tenants from reasonably foreseeable and pre-

ventable harm. In implied contract, according to the opinion, landlord must maintain the level of protection that existed when the tenancy began. Note that this duty may be sometimes broader, sometimes narrower than the duty "to provide those protective measures which are within [landlord's] reasonable capacity." (Opinion at page 709).

Under contract theory, might Mrs. Kline have sued the landlord even before the slugging? Might she have rescinded her lease? Might she have remained in possession and refused to pay rent? What of the landlord's argument that the implied duty to furnish protection must be recast against the level of protection currently existing each time tenant renews her lease?

Suppose that A becomes a tenant in 1969 and B becomes a tenant in 1970. During 1969, the level of protection declines. In 1971, B is assaulted. Can B hold landlord to the level of protection that landlord impliedly agreed to furnish A? What if A's tenancy had already expired when B's injury occurred?

Might the level of protection remain steady while the degree of security drops (or rises)? Should the implied covenant be stated in terms of protection or security?

3. More on the alternative contract and tort theories of landlord liability:

a. Effect upon insurance coverage—

The typical landlord's general liability insurance policy excludes "liability assumed by the *insured* under any contract agreement except an incidental contract." Incidental contract is defined to include "any written lease of premises * * *" If the *Kline* decision rested only on contract, would this exclusionary language exculpate the insurer?

b. Measure of damages—

Contract law limits recovery to general damages (here, the diminution in rental value resulting from the breach) and to special damages flowing naturally from the breach or specifically contemplated by the parties. Hadley v. Baxendale, 156 Eng.Rep. 145 (Ex.1854). Does Mrs. Kline's personal injury meet the Hadley v. Baxendale test? How would the courts treat a lease clause exculpating the landlord (or limiting a recovery to general damages) should landlord breach his contract duty to maintain protective services? Note that courts or statutes generally void clauses exculpating landlords from negligence. See, e. g., McKinney's N.Y.Gen. Obligation Law § 5–321 (1964).

c. Remedies other than Money Damages—

What are the tenant's remedies under a contract theory? Under a tort theory? Cf. Comment, 71 Colum.L.Rev. 275, 291–94 (1971).

4. Liability Insurance Rates

The most significant factor in the setting of premium rates is geographical location. Rates for the same category of structure (no elevators, some commercial tenants) on Manhattan's "decaying" lower East Side are 4.27 times greater than on the borough's "fashionable" East Side. These differences do not reflect the existence of a *Kline* duty. Comment, 71 Colum.L.Rev 275, 300 (1971). What is the likely effect of a *Kline* rule on liability insurance rates? Will insurers even be willing to insure in high crime areas? If not, what then?

5. The Economic Impact of the Kline Rule:

"It would seem that the most effective direct measure for protecting tenants is to provide guard or doorman service. This would also be the most costly measure, as may be readily illustrated. In New York City, for example, the average salary for service employees and doormen is rapidly approaching $140 per week, the minimum annual cost of providing round-the-clock doorman or guard service in that city would, then, be approximately $22,-000. It seems reasonable to assume that costs in other metropolitan areas would not be significantly less. Consequently, in a middle income apartment house with 100 apartment units and an average monthly rental of $200 per unit, the cost of providing twenty-four hour guard or doorman service would consume almost 10 percent of the annual rent roll of $240,000. If the landlord passed on the entire cost to the tenants, the increase in the monthly rental rate would be about $18.50 per apartment unit. A far greater per-apartment burden would be imposed on those smaller structures in which lower income tenants normally live. For example, if the owner of a twenty-five unit structure with an average monthly rental of $125 per unit were to provide a comparable level of protection, the $22,-000 cost figure would consume nearly 60 percent of the annual rental income. To cover this cost completely, the landlord would have to increase the monthly unit rental rate by approximately $73." Comment, 71 Colum.L.Rev. 275, 298 (1971)

6. In crime-ridden areas, where foreseeable risks are greatest, how can protection be given that is not much too expensive? Will the real impact of the *Kline* rule be felt only in higher income buildings?

7. Suppose that tenant is assaulted while residing in a municipally owned public housing project. To what degree do doctrines of sovereign immunity disable tenant from bringing suit on either a tort or implied contract theory? Cf. Knox Hill Tenant Council v. Washington, 39 U.S.L.W. 2474, 145 U.S.App.D. C. 122, 448 F.2d 1045 (1971).

C. LANDLORD SEEKS TO EVICT A TENANT FOR REASONS OTHER THAN FOR NON–PAYMENT OF RENT

---

1. Retaliatory Eviction

McQUEEN v. DRUKER

United States Court of Appeals,
First Circuit, 1971.
438 F.2d 781.

COFFIN, Circuit Judge. Appellees are tenants in a 500 unit apartment complex, Castle Square, in the South End of Boston—the same subsidized housing facility constructed and operated under section 221(d)(3) of the National Housing Act, 12 U.S.C.A. § 1715*l*(d)(3), which was involved in Hahn v. Gottlieb, 430 F.2d 1243 (1st Cir. 1970). This suit originated when appellant landlord, in accordance with the terms of the lease, notified these tenants in May, 1970, that it was not to be renewed after the July 31, 1970 termination date. Appellees brought this action under 42 U.S.C.A. § 1983, asserting jurisdiction under 28 U.S.C.A. §§ 1331, 1343, and seeking an injunction against their threatened eviction; a declaration that eviction must be predicated on cause, with notice, hearing and assurance of alternative housing; and compensatory and punitive damages.

The district court found sufficient federal and state involvement to make applicable the due process clauses of the Fifth and Fourteenth Amendments and the First Amendment. It enjoined the eviction, and made two declarations of rights and responsibilities. First, it declared that the statutory scheme for § 221(d)(3) housing impliedly requires a good-cause notice to evict and that state court proceedings, observing this substantive federal ruling, would provide procedural due process. Second, it declared that, since "the chief reason" for the landlord's notice to quit was "association-al activities" on behalf of fellow tenants, petitions to the Federal Housing Authority, and litigation, the First and Fourteenth Amendments barred any eviction so grounded. 317 F.Supp. 1122 (D. Mass.1970).

The large problem for us is whether the landlord's action in exercising his contractual right under the lease not to renew and in seeking to evict appellees, can rationally be said to be such "state action" as to call into play the Fourteenth Amendment. More precisely, the question is whether the landlord, though not an ostensible agent of the state, has such a relationship with the state that his activities take on the color of state law. United States v. Price, 383 U.S. 787, 794 n. 7, 86 S.Ct. 1152, 16 L.Ed.2d 267 (1966). The district court, relying on Colon v. Tompkins Square Neighbors, 294 F.Supp. 134 (S.D.N.Y.),[4] as well as on Burton v. Wilmington Parking Authority, 365 U.S. 715, 81 S.Ct. 856, 6 L.Ed.2d 45 (1961), and Marsh v. Alabama, 326 U.S. 501, 66 S.Ct. 276, 90 L.Ed. 265 (1946), reasoned that "With respect to Castle Square, the federal and state governments have elected to place their power, property, and privilege behind the landlords' authority over the tenants, and have insinuated themselves into a position of interdependence with the landlords."

The landlord claims that this case involves only "a regulation of the operations of a private business, not a vesting in it of the functions of government" and argues, citing Grossner v. Trustees of Columbia University in the City of New York, 287 F.Supp. 535, 548 (S.D.N.Y.

---

[4] This case dealt with very similar facts. We do not feel that *Colon* is inconsistent with the subsequent Second Circuit case, McGuane v. Chenango Court, Inc., 431 F.2d 1189 (1970), which seems to hold only that mere receipt of mortgage insurance under the National Housing Act does not make a private apartment house owner an agency of a state. With this proposition we of course agree as our discussion indicates.

1968), that "the receipt of money from the State is not, without a good deal more, enough to make the recipient an agency or instrumentality of the Government". He attacks the court's finding in the words of Mr. Justice Harlan's dissent in *Wilmington Parking Authority,* supra, 365 U.S. at 727, 81 S.Ct. at 862, as the result of "undiscriminatingly throwing together various bits and pieces". We do not agree. Our scrutiny of the landlord-state relationship indicates far less privateness in the landlord's enterprise, far more of a governmental function, and "a good deal more" than receipt of governmental financial help. They are inescapably the "bits and pieces" on which an ultimate judgment must rest after "sifting facts and weighing circumstances", *Wilmington Parking Authority,* supra, 365 U.S. at 722, 81 S.Ct. 856. We concede that little guidance in making a principled decision is found in such serpentine words as "insinuated", *Wilmington Parking Authority,* supra, 365 U.S. at 725, 81 S.Ct. 856, "involved", Reitman v. Mulkey, 387 U.S. 369, 380, 87 S.Ct. 1627, 18 L.Ed.2d 830 (1967), "entwined", Evans v. Newton, 382 U.S. 296, 301, 86 S.Ct. 486, 15 L.Ed.2d 373 (1966), or "intertwining", *Grossner,* supra, 287 F.Supp. at 548. Commentators have varied in approving or disapproving this lack of precision, but all have recognized it. Recognizing that the state coloration required by § 1983 is inevitably opaque, we nevertheless hazard our analysis.

Defendant purchased the Castle Square property from the Boston Redevelopment Authority (BRA), which had condemned it in connection with its urban renewal program. The federal incentive to private entrepreneurs, inducing them to take part in helping achieve the national objective of providing housing for needy and displaced families, is insurance of mortgage loans up to 90 per cent of a project's cost, supplementation of mortgagors' interest payments above 3 per cent, and assurance of a 6 per cent return on investment through rent adjustments. In addition to limiting the exposure of private enterprise, the federal law imposes requirements which must be adopted by participating states. For example, federal law requires that, in disposing of urban renewal property, the BRA must place restrictions on the use of property in order to ensure that it is used in accordance with approved urban renewal plans or for low or moderate income housing. 42 U.S.C.A. §§ 1460 (c)(4), 1455, and 1457. State law requires similar restrictions. Mass.Gen. Laws ch. 121, §§ 26YY and 26LL.

Consequently, the BRA has required the landlord through a lengthy Land Disposition Agreement to adhere to many standards governing the physical plant (e. g., prior approval for construction, improvements and demolition, a minimum investment in works of art, facilities for the handicapped, equal employment opportunity); limitations on rental agreements as to amount, duration, and increases; admissions policies (e. g., income levels of applicants, priority to four classes of displaced persons and four classes of commercial occupants, and allowing the Boston Housing Authority to select tenants for 10 per cent of the residential units); [6] management (e. g.,

---

[6] By subsequent agreement between the landlord and the BHA this commitment was raised to a maximum option of 25% as part of the BHA's leased housing program, under which the BHA guarantees rental payments. In addition, the City of Boston has granted the landlord a concessionary tax rate of 15% of income. Both these arrangements decrease the landlord's risk of non-payment of rents, the former by assuring the landlord of at least 25% of his rents each month without recourse to collection efforts, and the latter by pegging his tax obligations to rents actually received. Although the regulatory agreement with the FHA assures the landlord a 6% return, altering the rent schedules to produce such a return necessarily involves some delay. The arrangements with the

use solely in accordance with the South End Urban Renewal Plan, consultation with BRA "with respect to its rental program, including preparation of advertising matter, brochures, leases, establishment of rental offices, and all aspects of said program which relate to or have an effect upon the selection of tenants", inspection at all reasonable hours); transfer of title (e. g., compliance with any "conditions * * * the Authority may find desirable in order to achieve and safeguard the purposes of the Massachusetts Housing Authority Law, and the Plan.").

The state supervision of the "private" operations here seems to us to be more than the placing of state "power, property and prestige" behind the discriminatory action of a private restaurateur-lessee in a public building. Burton v. Wilmington Parking Authority, supra, 365 U.S. at 725, 81 S.Ct. 856. Here the landlords are, in return for an assured consideration, and subject to specific and continuing oversight, helping the state realize its specific priority objective of providing for urban renewal displacees and its more general goal of providing good quality housing at rents which can be afforded by those of low and moderate income. The stronger posture of government supervision present in this case is not unrelated to the fact that the government has chosen to attract the participation of private persons in carrying out a specific governmental purpose. In Evans v. Newton, 382 U.S. 296, 86 S.Ct. 486, 15 L.Ed.2d 373 (1966), the Court held that a park, serving the community and having a municipal purpose, could not be insulated from the effect of the Fourteenth Amendment by transfer of title to private trustees. It also observed that "If the municipality remains entwined in the management and control of the park, it remains subject to the restraints of the

BHA and the City therefore act to ease the financial shock sustained during this required lead time.

Fourteenth Amendment just as the private utility in Public Utilities Comm'n v. Pollak, 343 U.S. 451, 462, [72 S.Ct. 813, 96 L.Ed. 1068], remained subject to the Fifth Amendment because of the surveillance which federal agencies had over its affairs." 382 U.S. at 301, 86 S. Ct. at 489. Here the function, while perhaps not so traditionally governmental as parks, fire or police services, or libraries, is today one of the major concerns of most cities of substantial size. And to the performance of that function by the landlord, governmental authority contributes significant operational surveillance.

We view our task of "sifting facts and weighing circumstances" as one to be done to the end of determining when it is fair and reasonable to hold an individual subject to the same duties of observance of constitutional rights as are imposed on a governmental unit. Mere receipt or financial subsidy and subjection to some regulation are the conditions of much of our societal life. Neither factor—or both together—is dispositive of "state action". But, while we disavow any effort to be definitive, we conclude that at least when a specific governmental function is carried out by heavily subsidized private firms or individuals whose freedom of decision-making has, by contract and the reserved governmental power of continuing oversight, been circumscribed substantially more than that generally accorded an independent contractor, the coloration of state action fairly attaches.

This brings us to the implications of the applicability of the Fourteenth Amendment to the landlord's pending action to evict appellees. Appellant's burden is to establish that the district court's finding was clearly erroneous. We have examined the record and find abundant evidence supporting the district court's determination. The appellant distributed a flyer to all tenants announcing his intention to evict the appellees including as a reason "the many confrontations * * * with the McQueens" as compelling his actions. The manager of Castle Square in his testimony admitted telling the appellees' counsel that the conflict with the McQueens had become a "cause celebre" and that the landlord could not tolerate being confronted. The appellant did not deny that his motive was retaliatory at least in part. He presented in addition a panoply of alternate reasons for the eviction, all of which had been unsuccessfully tendered previously in state eviction proceedings against the McQueens. The court was well within its bounds to discount these grounds and find the dominant and primary motive one of retaliation against the appellees for their exercise of First Amendment rights. Cf. NLRB v. Billen Shoe Co., 397 F.2d 801 (1st Cir. 1968). This established, it must follow that, whatever other rights or privileges may be available, appellees are at least protected from this eviction.[9]

The appellees in addition request a further declaration that the Castle Square landlord may not evict a tenant without giving notice of good cause for the eviction accompanied by a hearing thereupon in order to satisfy due process. Because of our disposition of this appeal on the grounds stated above, we do not have to reach this latter question. As far as this tenant is concerned, the landlord may not

evict him for holding over after termination of his lease because, as found by the district court, the eviction was brought because of the exercise by the tenants of their First Amendment Rights. The procedural rights of a tenant whose eviction is not motivated by constitutionally impermissible reasons is not presented by this appeal. Furthermore, we doubt whether any "case or controversy" is involved when a tenant requests a declaration of procedural rights as to an imagined future eviction which has never been threatened. The Declaratory Judgment Act requires more concreteness than this. Aetna Life Ins. Co. v. Haworth, 300 U.S. 227, 57 S.Ct. 461, 81 L.Ed. 617 (1937); 6A Moore ¶ 57.12. Finally, while Thorpe v. Housing Authority of the City of Durham, 393 U.S. 268, 89 S.Ct. 518, 21 L.Ed.2d 474 (1968), laid down the procedural rights of tenants in wholly public housing projects as a result of nonconstitutional analysis, we are disinclined to attempt to define any additional constitutional rights of tenants in a § 1983 case in the absence of a more real crucible of controversy.

The judgment of the district court is affirmed insofar as it enjoins appellant from proceeding further with respect to his May 20, 1970 notice of termination of the McQueen tenancy and with respect to the proceedings for eviction of the McQueens which appellant began in the Boston Municipal Court on August 31, 1970.

* * *

Note: The court in McQueen v. Druker refused to deal with the procedural rights of a tenant facing eviction from a subsidized, but privately owned section 221(d)(3) project. The procedural rights of *public* housing tenants are discussed fully in Escalera v. New York City Housing Authority, infra.

[9] Indeed, the particular activity engaged in by appellees is within the spirit if not the letter of the Massachusetts law giving a tenant a right of action against a landlord "who threatens or takes reprisals * * * for reporting * * * a suspected violation of any health or building code or of any other municipal by-law or ordinance, or state law or regulation which has as its objective the regulation of residential premises * * *." Mass.Gen.Laws Ch. 186, § 18. Cf. also Edwards v. Habib, 130 U.S.App.D.C. 126, 397 F.2d 687 (1968).

EDWARDS v. HABIB

United States Court of Appeals, District of
Columbia Circuit, 1968.
130 U.S.App.D.C. 126, 397 F.2d 687.
Certiorari denied 393 U.S. 1016, 89 S.Ct. 618,
21 L.Ed.2d 560, 1969.

Before DANAHER, WRIGHT and
McGOWAN, Circuit Judges.

WRIGHT, Circuit Judge. In March
1965 the appellant, Mrs. Yvonne Edwards, rented housing property from the
appellee, Nathan Habib, on a month-to-
month basis. Shortly thereafter she complained to the Department of Licenses
and Inspections of sanitary code violations which her landlord had failed to
remedy. In the course of the ensuing
inspection, more than 40 such violations
were discovered which the Department
ordered the landlord to correct. Habib
then gave Mrs. Edwards a 30-day statutory notice [1] to vacate and obtained a default judgment for possession of the
premises. Mrs. Edwards promptly
moved to reopen this judgment, alleging
excusable neglect for the default and also
alleging as a defense that the notice to
quit was given in retaliation for her complaints to the housing authorities. Judge
Greene, sitting on motions in the Court
of General Sessions, set aside the default
judgment and, in a very thoughtful opinion, concluded that a retaliatory motive,
if proved, would constitute a defense to
the action for possession. At the trial
itself, however, a different judge apparently deemed evidence of retaliatory motive irrelevant and directed a verdict for
the landlord.

[1] 45 D.C.Code § 902 (1967), Notices to
quit—Month to month:

"A tenancy from month to month, or from
quarter to quarter, may be terminated by a
thirty days' notice in writing from the landlord to the tenant to quit, or by such a notice
from the tenant to the landlord of his intention to quit, said notice to expire, in
either case, on the day of the month from
which such tenancy commenced to run."

Mrs. Edwards then appealed to this
court for a stay pending her appeal to
the District of Columbia Court of Appeals, and on December 3, 1965, we
granted the stay, provided only that Mrs.
Edwards continue to pay her rent. Edwards v. Habib, 125 U.S.App.D.C. 49,
366 F.2d 628 (1965). She then appealed to the DCCA, which affirmed the
judgment of the trial court. 227 A.2d
388 (1967). In reaching its decision the
DCCA relied on a series of its earlier
decisions holding that a private landlord
was not required, under the District of
Columbia Code, to give a reason for evicting a month-to-month tenant and was free
to do so for any reason or for no reason
at all. The court acknowledged that the
landlord's right to terminate a tenancy
is not absolute, but felt that any limitation on his prerogative had to be based
on specific statutes or very special circumstances. Here, the court concluded,
the tenant's right to report violations of
law and to petition for redress of grievances was not protected by specific legislation and that any change in the relative
rights of tenants and landlords should be
undertaken by the legislature, not the
courts. We granted appellant leave to
appeal that decision to this court. We
hold that the promulgation of the housing code by the District of Columbia
Commissioners at the direction of Congress impliedly effected just such a
change in the relative rights of landlords
and tenants and that proof of a retaliatory motive does constitute a defense to
an action of eviction. Accordingly, we
reverse the decision of the DCCA with
directions that it remand to the Court of
General Sessions for a new trial where
Mrs. Edwards will be permitted to try
to prove to a jury that her landlord who
seeks to evict her harbors a retaliatory
intent.

*   *   *

But we need not decide whether judicial recognition of this constitutional

defense is constitutionally compelled. We need not, in other words, decide whether 45 D.C.Code § 910 could validly compel the court to assist the plaintiff in penalizing the defendant for exercising her constitutional right to inform the government of violations of the law for we are confident that Congress did not intend it to entail such a result.

45 D.C.Code § 910, in pertinent part provides:

"Whenever * * * any tenancy shall be terminated by notice as aforesaid [45 D.C.Code § 902, see Note 1 supra], and the tenant shall fail or refuse to surrender possession of the leased premises, * * * the landlord may bring an action to recover possession before the District of Columbia Court of General Sessions, as provided in sections 11–701 to 11–749."

And 16 D.C.Code § 1501, in pertinent part, provides:

"When a person detains possession of real property * * * after his right to possession has ceased, the District of Columbia Court of General Sessions * * * may issue a summons to the party complained of to appear and show cause why judgment should not be given against him for restitution of possession."

These provisions are simply procedural. They neither say nor imply anything about whether evidence of retaliation or other improper motive should be unavailable as a defense to a possessory action brought under them. It is true that in making his affirmative case for possession the landlord need only show that his tenant has been given the 30-day statutory notice and he need not assign any reason for evicting a tenant who does not occupy the premises under a lease. But while the landlord may evict for any legal reason or for no reason at all, he is not, we hold, free to evict in retaliation for his tenant's report of housing code violations to the authorities. As a matter of statutory construction and for reasons of public policy, such an eviction cannot be permitted.

The housing and sanitary codes, especially in light of Congress' explicit direction for their enactment, indicate a strong and pervasive congressional concern to secure for the city's slum dwellers decent, or at least safe and sanitary, places to live. Effective implementation and enforcement of the codes obviously depend in part on private initiative in the reporting of violations. Though there is no official procedure for the filing of such complaints, the bureaucratic structure of the Department of Licenses and Inspections establishes such a procedure, and for fiscal year 1966 nearly a third of the cases handled by the Department arose from private complaints. To permit retaliatory evictions, then, would clearly frustrate the effectiveness of the housing code as a means of upgrading the quality of housing in Washington.

As judges, "we cannot shut our eyes to matters of public notoriety and general cognizance. When we take our seats on the bench we are not struck with blindness, and forbidden to know as judges what we see as men." Ho Ah Kow v. Nunan, C.C.D.Cal., 12 Fed.Cas. 252, 255 (No. 6546) (1879). In trying to effect the will of Congress and as a court of equity we have the responsibility to consider the social context in which our decisions will have operational effect. In light of the appalling condition and shortage of housing in Washington, the expense of moving, the inequality of bargaining power between tenant and landlord, and the social and economic importance of assuring at least minimum standards in housing conditions, we do not hesitate to declare that retaliatory eviction cannot be tolerated. There can be no doubt that the slum dweller, even though his home be marred by housing code violations, will pause long before he complains of them if he fears eviction as a consequence. Hence an eviction under the circumstances of this case would not only punish appellant for making a complaint which she had a constitutional right to make, a result which we would not impute to the will of Congress simply on the basis of an essentially procedural enactment, but also would stand as a warning to others that they dare not be so bold, a result which, from the authorization of the housing code, we think Congress affirmatively sought to avoid.

The notion that the effectiveness of remedial legislation will be inhibited if those reporting violations of it can legally be intimidated is so fundamental that a presumption against the legality of such intimidation can be inferred as inherent in the legislation even if it is not expressed in the statute itself. Such an inference was recently drawn by the Supreme Court from the federal labor statutes to strike down under the supremacy clause a Florida statute denying unemployment insurance to workers discharged in retaliation for filing complaints of federally defined unfair labor practices. While we are not confronted with a possible conflict between federal policy and state law, we do have the task of reconciling and harmonizing two federal statutes so as to best effectuate the purposes of each. The proper balance can only be struck by interpreting 45 D.C.Code §§ 902 and 910 as inapplicable where the court's aid is invoked to effect an eviction in retaliation for reporting housing code violations.

This is not, of course, to say that even if the tenant can prove a retaliatory purpose she is entitled to remain in possession in perpetuity. If this illegal purpose is dissipated, the landlord can, in the absence of legislation or a binding contract, evict his tenants or raise their rents for

economic or or other legitimate reasons, or even for no reason at all. The question of permissible or impermissible purpose is one of fact for the court or jury, and while such a determination is not easy, it is not significantly different from problems with which the courts must deal in a host of other contexts, such as when they must decide whether the employer who discharges a worker has committed an unfair labor practice because he has done so on account of the employee's union activities. As Judge Greene said, "There is no reason why similar factual judgments cannot be made by courts and juries in the context of economic retaliation [against tenants by landlords] for providing information to the government."

Reversed and remanded.

Notes on Retaliatory Eviction

1. The leases in McQueen v. Druker were for a term of years which expired on July 31, 1970. Although the leases required landlord to notify the tenants formally that the term would end and that they would have to leave by July 31, the landlord's "election" is technically very different from the election in a month-to-month tenancy, as in Edwards v. Habib. A term of years ends automatically unless both parties elect to renew the term; a periodic tenancy continues automatically unless one party or both elects to end the tenancy. Is this a technical difference that the court in McQueen v. Druker should have considered?

---

2. At least 14 states have adopted legislation recognizing retaliatory eviction in some form as a defense: They are California, Connecticut, Delaware, Hawaii, Illinois, Maine, Maryland, Massachusetts, Michigan, Minnesota, New Jersey, New York, Pennsylvania, and Rhode Island.

3. After validating the tenant's defense of retaliatory eviction in Markese v. Cooper, 70 Misc.2d 478, 333 N.Y.S.2d 63 (County Ct.1972), the judge continued:

Unfortunately, the matter does not rest here. I recognize the myriad problems which now confront a trial court. For example, what remedy shall it permit the tenant here if she is successful? It is precisely here that legislation, if it existed, would set forth definite remedial standards that would apply uniformly throughout the State. Unfortunately, any remedy must now be applied on a case-by-case basis that guarantees considerable diversity until, ultimately, there has emerged a pattern which all courts can follow.

Another problem which the trial court must face is the standard of proof that will be required to prove the tenant's defense and the criteria to be employed. For example, how does one go about proving a retaliatory motive, and must it be the dominant or paramount motive, or need it be only a substantial one?

* * *

As to the remedy to be afforded, it is clear that a tenant may not remain upon the premises indefinitely solely by reason of a successful defense of retaliatory eviction. In Edwards v. Habib (397 F.2d 687, *supra*), the court cautioned that even if a tenant can prove a retaliatory purpose he would not be entitled to remain in possession in perpetuity. "If this illegal purpose is dissipated, the landlord can, in the absence of legislation or a binding contract, evict his tenants or raise their rents for economic or other legitimate reasons, or even for no reason at all." (p. 702).

Unfortunately, Judge Wright did not set forth how or when such illegal

purpose is "dissipated" nor did he define the outer limits of its baneful influence. Here again the trial court has been left with a principle, but without a palpable, tangible procedure.

* * *

And since the eviction proceedings would be tainted by an unlawful motive, damages should be made available to the tenant. These would be compensatory and special damages * * *, and, in a proper case, could be exemplary or punitive as well * * *.

* * *

Unfortunately, unless the Legislature acts, these admittedly incomplete standards will have to suffice until the slow hand of experience shapes new and better ones.

* * *

70 Misc.2d at 489, 333 N.Y.S.2d at 74.

4. The Uniform Residential Landlord and Tenant Act, drafted and approved by the National Conference of Commissioners on Uniform State Laws (1972), contains the following Article:

Article V

RETALIATORY CONDUCT

SECTION 5.101 *Retaliatory Conduct Prohibited.*

(a) Except as provided in this section, a landlord may not retaliate by increasing rent or decreasing services or by bringing or threatening to bring an action for possession after:

(1) the tenant has complained to a governmental agency charged with responsibility for enforcement of a building or housing code of a violation applicable to the premises ma-

terially affecting health and safety; or

(2) the tenant has complained to the landlord of a violation under Section 2.104 [landlord to maintain premises]; or

(3) the tenant has organized or become a member of a tenant's union or similar organization.

(b) If the landlord acts in violation of subsection (a), the tenant is entitled to the remedies provided in Section 4.107 [the greater of treble damages or 3 months' rent] and has a defense in any retaliatory action against him for possession. In an action by or against the tenant, evidence of a complaint within [1] year before the alleged act of retaliation creates a presumption that the landlord's conduct was in retaliation. The presumption does not arise if the tenant made the complaint after notice of a proposed rent increase or diminution of services. "Presumption" means that the trier of fact must find the existence of the fact presumed unless and until evidence is introduced which would support a finding of its non-existence.

(c) Notwithstanding subsections (a) and (b), a landlord may bring an action for possession if:

(1) the violation of the applicable building or housing code was caused primarily by lack of reasonable care by the tenant, a member of his family, or other person on the premises with his consent; or

(2) the tenant is in default in rent; or

(3) compliance with the applicable building or housing code requires alteration, remodeling, or demolition which would effectively deprive the tenant of use of the dwelling unit.

* * *

Discuss this proposal in the light of the foregoing questions, note 3 supra.

2. Claim of Undesirability

_____

NOTE: PUBLIC LANDLORDS AND PRIVATE TENANTS: THE EVICTION OF "UNDESIRABLES" FROM PUBLIC HOUSING PROJECTS *

77 Yale L.J. 988 (1968).

The congressionally announced policy underlying the public housing program is to provide "decent, safe and sanitary dwellings for families of low income." Beyond this goal of physically adequate shelter, it is suggested that public housing should contribute to a sense of community and stability often missing in urban low-income neighborhoods. Reality, however, has wandered far from these ideals. While housing projects represent, for those families who get in, a physical improvement over the tenements replaced, the cost of walls with fewer rats and stairways that do not collapse has frequently been unwelcome, unnecessary intrusions into the personal lives of tenants. Public housing authorities tend to treat residents not as the reason for their existence, but as a threat to the peace and quiet of their highrise towers.[3]

* * *

Inside the project, the manager has a difficult time with many of his tenants.

* Reprinted by permission of the Yale Law Journal Company, and Fred B. Rothman & Company from The Yale Law Journal, Vol. 77, p. 988.

[3] The poor record of some public housing authorities in dealing with their tenants has finally attracted the official attention of HUD. In a circular dated February 7, 1967, on the subject of "Termination of Tenancy in Low-Rent Projects," [hereinafter cited as Circular 2-7-67], the Assistant Secretary for Renewal and Housing Assistance informed local authorities that "within the past year increasing dissatisfaction has been expressed with eviction practices in public low-rent housing projects." The Circular went on to require that the authorities adopt somewhat fairer procedures.

As public housing has been increasingly opened to the lowest income groups within society—the permanently poor—its population of so-called problem families has grown. These families—large, without regular income, often fatherless, ignorant of the fundamentals of sanitation and housekeeping—are costly to the project and tarnish its image in the community. They drive or frighten away more prosperous tenants, depriving public housing of stabler occupants. Unable to pay much rent in the first place, problem families are the most frequent rent defaulters.

Caught between this crossfire, public housing authorities sometimes lay too hasty and heavy a hand on project residents.[9] Unreasonable or unnecessary restrictions are imposed; sensible regulations are applied in wooden, senseless fashion. A Chicago project evicted tenants for organizing "quarter parties" where food and drinks were sold on the premises at nominal prices. In New Orleans a housing authority permitted a blind tenant to keep his seeing-eye dog only after a protracted wrangle. Many authorities do not allow tenants to conduct any type of business in their units, though encouragement of entrepreneurial activities among the poor is supposedly part of the anti-poverty plan. Residents often cannot host overnight guests, a galling reminder to them not to make themselves too much at home in public housing.

Many tenants whose leases are terminated have not violated a particular rule, but by their conduct have made themselves "undesirable" occupants.

This all-purpose rubric lends itself easily to abuse. A project manager in New York City evicted the families of teenage gang members as a matter of course. With similar Draconian logic, a housing authority terminated the lease of a woman because her adult son was an addict, though he did not live with his mother and apparently made no trouble when he visited her. Having an illegitimate child commonly marks the tenant as an undesirable. Housing authorities have also drawn the bounds of desirability to exclude political activists. A resident of a North Carolina project received a notice to vacate within twenty-four hours after she was elected president of a tenant union organization.[18]

Over-eager efforts to reform tenants, head off trouble, and keep the project quiet and peaceful injure not only the tenants who are expelled for no good reason, but also the tenants who remain and, consequently, the entire public housing program. The injury to the evicted tenant and his family is plain enough. Suddenly ejected from one home with little or no time to find another, they suffer materially and emotionally. Loss of sanctuary and familiar surroundings, coupled with a feeling of helplessness against the dispossessor, make an eviction—especially an unjust one—a painful, sometimes traumatic experience.[19] In

---

[9] Dunham & Grundstein, Impact of a Confusion of Social Objectives on Public Housing: A Preliminary Analysis, 12 Marriage & Family Living, 103, 109 (1955). Usually, public housing tenant leases impose two to five times the number of restrictions found in ordinary leases; they are also enforced more strictly. See also A. Schorr, Slums and Social Insecurity, 112 (1963).

[18] Housing Authority of City of Durham v. Thorpe, 267 N.C. 431, 148 S.E.2d 290 (1966), vacated and remanded, 386 U.S. 670, 87 S. Ct. 1244, 18 L.Ed.2d 394 (1967) (per curiam). The authority contended that the election was not the reason for the termination, though it gave no other. See also Cummings v. Weinfeld, 177 Misc. 129, 30 N.Y.S.2d 36 (Sup.Ct.1940), where a tenant of a quasi-public limited-dividend housing development was evicted when he attempted to organize a tenants' union.

[19] Studies of low-income families displaced by urban renewal suggest that the emotional injury can be grave. One sociologist found that a forced change of residence caused long periods of depression in at least forty per cent of the families forced out of Boston's

relocating, the ousted tenant usually finds that he must pay more rent for less housing—frequently for substandard housing.[20] The role of public housing and other urban renewal projects in reducing the supply of low-income shelter and thus forcing rents up adds a rueful touch of irony to the family's plight. Finally, terminating a lease on grounds of undesirability marks the tenant a troublemaker and may effectively bar his admission to other public housing.

* * *

ESCALERA v. NEW YORK CITY HOUSING AUTHORITY

United States Court of Appeals, Second Circuit, 1970.

425 F.2d 853, certiorari denied 400 U.S. 853, 91 S.Ct. 54, 27 L.Ed.2d 91.

J. JOSEPH SMITH, Circuit Judge. Appellants are tenants in New York City public housing projects. They brought four suits in the United States District Court for the Southern District of New York against the New York City Housing Authority [hereinafter cited as "HA"] and certain individuals as officers of the HA, in the form of class actions on behalf of themselves and all tenants similarly situated. The complaints invoked jurisdiction under the Civil Rights Act, 28 U.S.C.A. § 1343(3) (1962), and alleged the deprivation of appellants' right to due process secured by the Fourteenth Amendment to the Constitution and of their rights under the United States Housing Act of 1937, 42 U.S.C.A. § 1401 et seq. (1962). They sought injunctive and declaratory relief against certain alleged practices of the HA, 28 U.S.C.A. §§ 2201, 2202 (1962), 42 U.S.C.A. § 1983 (1970), and in two instances (Haywood and Lockman) a money judgment for additional rents which had been paid.

Appellants sought a preliminary injunction by filing an order to show cause. Defendant then moved pursuant to Rule 12(b) of the Federal Rules of Civil Procedure to dismiss the actions for, *inter alia,* failure to state a claim upon which relief could be granted, lack of jurisdiction, lack of substantial federal question, and failure to exhaust administrative remedies, and because the federal courts should abstain from considering these actions pending a determination by New York state courts in the first instance.

After the parties submitted affidavits, argument on the motions was heard before District Judge Sylvester J. Ryan. Thereafter by an opinion of October 31, 1968 (67 Civ. 4236, 4306, 4307, 4414 S.D.N.Y.), and judgment of the next day, Judge Ryan granted defendants' mo-

---

West End. Fried, Grieving for a Lost Home: Psychological Costs of Relocation, in Urban Renewal: The Record & The Controversy 359 (J. Wilson ed. 1966). Since the lower economic classes seem to have a greater need for external stability and geographic identity in their lives, the shock of displacement is more severe to most of them than it would be to middle class families. Id. 365–66.

20 A survey of urban renewal relocation in forty-one cities revealed that eighty per cent of displacees paid higher rents in their new homes, though one- to two-thirds of them ended up in sub-standard dwellings. A. Schorr, supra note 9, at 63. In 26 cities which provided little or no assistance in relocation, seventy per cent of the displaced families moved into substandard housing, while in the 15 cities where such assistance was offered, only half that proportion did not find adequate new shelter. Id. 66. The U. S. Housing & Home Finance Agency, now assimilated into HUD, responded to critical studies with one of its own, showing that almost all displacees relocated in respectable housing and at only a small increase in rent. U. S. Housing & Home Finance Agency, The Housing of Relocated Families: Summary of a Census Bureau Survey, in Urban Renewal: The Record and the Controversy 341–45 (J. Wilson ed. 1966). One student of the path-

ology of urban renewal, however, saw obvious statistical juggling in the HHFA report. Hartman, A Comment on the HHFA Study of Relocation, in Urban Renewal: The Record and the Controversy 353–58 (J. Wilson ed. 1966).

tion, and dismissed the actions on the merits. We find error in the dismissal of these actions and remand to the district court to consider appellants' application for preliminary relief and to hold a trial on the merits.

The instant class actions challenge the constitutionality of the procedures used by the HA in three different types of actions: (1) termination of tenancy on the ground of non-desirability; (2) termination of tenancy for violation of HA rules and regulations; and (3) assessment of "additional rent" charges under the HA lease for undesirable acts by tenants. The HA, a corporate governmental agency financed by federal, state and city funds, administers the largest public housing program in the country, housing more than 144,000 families.

I.

* * *

A. Termination for Non-desirability.

Tenants in HA projects are required to sign month-to-month automatically renewable leases which can be terminated at the end of any month by either party upon the giving of one month's notice. Leases are terminated by the giving of one month's notice if the tenant is found to be non-desirable.[1]

If a tenant's undesirable acts persist to the point where the project manager decides he should recommend the termination of the tenancy on the ground of non-desirability, the manager has a meeting with the tenant at which he informs the tenant of his proposed recommendation, reviews with the tenant the informa-

tion in the tenant's folder (which contains the entire history of the tenancy), and discusses the undesirable activity in question. The tenant is given a chance to explain his activity.

If after the meeting the project manager still wishes to recommend termination for non-desirability, the tenant is notified that he may submit a written statement to be sent with the project manager's recommendation and the tenant's folder to the HA Tenant Review Board [hereinafter cited "TRB"].

The TRB consists of eight officers of the HA. They consider the tenant's folder and the project manager's recommendation, and if they make a preliminary determination of the tenant's non-desirability, they inform the tenant in writing that they are "considering a recommendation" of termination, that he may appear before the TRB to tell his side of the case if he requests an appearance in 10 days, and that if he so requests an appearance he will be informed of the nature of the conduct under consideration. If the tenant fails to request an appearance within 10 days, the preliminary determination of non-desirability is made final by the TRB Chairman.

If the tenant makes a timely request for an appearance, he is sent a form letter telling him the time and place of the scheduled hearing, the general definition of a non-desirable tenant (as set out in footnote 1, supra), a short, often one-sentence, statement of the nature of the particular non-desirable conduct under consideration,[2] and the fact that he may

---

[1] A family is non-desirable if it constitutes "* * * a detriment to health, safety or morals of its neighbors or the community; an adverse influence upon sound family and community life; a source of danger or a cause of damage to the property of the Authority; a source of danger to the peaceful occupation of other tenants, or a nuisance." Tenant Review Handbook, Ch. VII, ¶ I, Appendix B at 4.

[2] The plaintiffs in the instant cases received the following notification of their non-desirable conduct.

Mr. and Mrs. Rolle: "Record of anti-social activities and arrests of your son, Fred, Jr., constituting a threat to the peace and safety of the community."

Mr. and Mrs. Humphrey: "Illegal acts of Mr. Humphrey, having an adverse effect on the project and its tenants."

bring any person to help represent him at the hearing.

A panel of two or more, usually three, of the TRB members is present at the hearing. The HA ordinarily presents no witnesses, but rather has a panel member read a summary of the entries in the tenant's folder. The tenant or his representative is permitted to comment about the entries or question witnesses in that regard. The tenant is generally not permitted to see the contents of the folder, the names of those who complained of his non-desirable activity, or the summary of the entries.[3] The rules and regulations governing the TRB and its panels in non-desirability cases, set out in the TRB "Handbook" are not made available to the tenant, even upon request. No transcript of the hearing is maintained.

Despite the summary notification to the tenant prior to hearing of the conduct under consideration, the panel decides whether the tenant is non-desirable on the basis of the tenant's entire folder;[4] thus the decision may be based in whole or in part on entries in the folder although the tenant received no notification prior to the hearing that the TRB was considering these entries, or indeed the decision may rest in some part on items in the folder about which the tenant is not notified even at the hearing.

If the panel decides that the tenant is non-desirable, the Chairman of the TRB

[3] In the case of plaintiff Rolle, upon demand of counsel, the TRB panel permitted counsel to inspect the folder at the premises of the hearing, and offered to grant an adjournment of the hearing if one were requested. In the case of plaintiff Humphrey, however, the folder and the summary of its contents were not made available to the tenant despite repeated requests. Affidavits submitted on behalf of plaintiffs indicate that other tenants, not named in this suit, have been unable to gain access to their folders.

[4] Affidavit of Nancy E. LeBlanc in *Rolle*, January 15, 1967.

notifies the tenant that the panel has determined that the tenant is ineligible. No findings or reasons grounding the panel's determination are released. Thereafter the HA gives the tenant the required one month's notice under lease to terminate the tenancy, and notifies the tenant that he should vacate. If the tenant does not vacate, a holdover proceeding is commenced in the New York City Civil Court. The only issue in such a proceeding is the validity of the notice to terminate under the lease, and the determination of non-desirability cannot be put in question. * * *

The facts as to the instant plaintiffs may be quickly summarized. Proceedings were begun against the Rolles because of the alleged anti-social acts (such as statutory rape) of their son Fred, and against the Humphreys because Mr. Humphrey had been arrested on a narcotics charge several miles from the project. Both requested hearings. Counsel for Rolle demanded a variety of procedural safeguards sought in the present action, such as advance notice of the complete charge, a transcript of the hearing, confrontation and cross-examination of witnesses, an impartial hearing examiner, etc. Although the panel permitted Rolle's counsel to inspect the folder, it did not grant the other requests and Rolle refused to go forward with the hearing. Any further action by the HA with respect to Rolle was voluntarily postponed pending the outcome of this litigation. The Humphreys went through with the hearing although they were not permitted to inspect the folder, and were found to be non-desirable, and were given notice of termination and to vacate. No holdover action was brought due to the intervention of this action.

As to the procedures for termination on the ground of non-desirability, the appellants seek the following relief: (1) an injunction against evictions on this ground unless the following safeguards are afforded in connection with the hearing: (a) written notice prior to the hearing of all the grounds to be relied on in the decision; (b) notice of the rules and regulations governing the TRB panel at the hearing; (c) inspection of the tenant folder; (d) exclusion of items about which advance notice was not given; (e) confrontation and cross-examination of witnesses; (f) exclusion of hearsay items; (g) right to compel attendance of witnesses; (h) the keeping of a written record of the hearing; (i) impartial hearing examiner; (j) written decision with findings of facts and reasons; and (k) access to prior decisions as precedent; (2) an injunction against using a lease which permits the HA to evict simply by giving one month's notice and thus which permits the HA to evict without the above safeguards; (3) an injunction against the failure of the HA to negotiate new leases which provide safeguards which are constitutionally required; (4) a declaratory judgment that the present procedures are constitutionally deficient; and (5) an injunction against the termination of tenancies on grounds not set out in the lease or otherwise made known and which are too vague.

B. *Termination for Breach of Rules and Regulations.*

Tenants are required to sign the "Tenant Rules and Regulations" upon the execution of their lease agreements. This document is specifically referred to by the lease.

Violation of the rules and regulations is considered to be ground for termination of tenancy. The procedure for termination on this ground is quite simple. If the project manager feels that a tenant is ineligible for continued tenancy by virtue of a violation of the rules and regulations, he holds a meeting with the tenant at which the manager informs the tenant of the alleged violation and the possibility of termination. The tenant may tell his side of the story.

After the meeting, the project manager may decide the tenant is ineligible because of the violation, in which event he forwards the tenant's folder and a recommendation to terminate to the HA Central Office. The folder contains the manager's report on his meeting with the tenant and the tenant's responses. If the Central Office approves of the manager's determination, a notice to vacate after one month is sent to the tenant. If the tenant refuses to vacate, a holdover proceeding may be instituted as in the non-desirability cases.

The facts in regard to the instant plaintiffs, Mr. and Mrs. Escalera, are simple. For several years the Escaleras had a dog in violation of HA rules. They had been assessed "additional rent" (infra) for having the dog. In July, 1967, the project manager asked them about the dog, warning them that keeping the dog violated HA rules. Mr. Escalera informed the manager that the dog had been sold; the manager demanded written proof which was never provided. On September 29, 1967 the Escaleras received notice from the HA to vacate by October 31, 1967. Holdover proceedings were postponed due to the institution of the present suit.

As to the procedures for termination on the ground of violation of the HA rules and regulations, the appellants seek the following relief: (1) a preliminary injunction against the eviction of the Escaleras; (2) an injunction against evictions for rules violations if the tenant has not been afforded an opportunity to contest the reasons for termination; (3) an injunction against lease provisions which permit termination upon the giving of notice without giving reasons or a fair hearing to contest the reasons; (4) an injunction against failure by the HA to negotiate new leases providing at least minimum safeguards; and (5) a declaratory judgment that the present procedures are constitutionally deficient.

C. *"Additional Rent" Charges or Fines.*

The HA lease agreements by reference to the Tenant Rules and Regulations (which must be signed by tenants along with their leases) permit the HA to charge "additional rent" which must be paid, subject to landlord remedies for nonpayment of rent, in three types of circumstances: (1) for repair of damage to the premises; (2) for additional services provided for a tenant; and (3) for "liquidated damages" caused by a tenant or his family in violating the rules and requirements established by the HA for protection of its property and other tenants.

The amount of the "additional rent" is within the project manager's discretion. The project manager, if he feels an "additional rent" charge is warranted, may impose it after giving notice to the tenant.[5] If the tenant fails to pay the extra charge as part of his rent, the landlord may bring suit in the New York Civil Court to collect unpaid rent.

The "additional rent" charges assessed to instant appellants are as follows. The Humphreys paid a $3 charge for an allegedly clogged toilet. Mrs. Haywood paid a $5 charge for the alleged behavior of her brother, one Mullins, who was not a tenant and was not living in the project, and over whom Mrs. Haywood could exercise little control.[6] Another charge of $10 was assessed for

similar acts of her brother, and upon nonpayment and intervention of counsel, the charge was rescinded. The Lockmans were fined three times for alleged conduct of their son: (1) $2 for playing ball on HA property (the Lockmans contend he was on neighboring property); (2) $5 for riding a bicycle on HA walks (the Lockmans contend that he was only repairing the bicycle); and (3) $2 for another ball-playing incident which was reduced to $1 when the Lockmans argued that the grass would not be harmed due to the snow cover. The Lockmans paid these charges.

As to the procedures for assessing "additional rent" charges, appellants seek the following relief: (1) an injunction against the assessment of these charges without a prior fair hearing with the essential safeguards sought in the termination cases; (2) an injunction against requiring tenants to sign leases purporting to permit the assessment of these charges; (3) an injunction against failure to renegotiate leases; (4) an injunction against any further "additional rent" charges based on standards and conduct which are vague and not specifically made known to tenants; (5) a declaratory judgment that the present procedures are constitutionally deficient; and (6) a money judgment for the amount of the charges paid by Haywood and Lockman.

II.

Appellants challenge the constitutionality of the HA procedures for terminating tenancies on the grounds of non-desirability and breach of the rules and regulations and for assessing "additional rent" charges, contending that these procedures deny members of their classes their rights to due process of law. Although the termination of tenancy procedures afforded by the HA in this case admittedly satisfy the requirements of the Department of Housing and Urban Development circular of February 7,

---

5 The HA Management Manual requires the project manager to give the tenant an opportunity to tell his side of the story. The manager is also required to summarize the tenant's position and enter the summary in the tenant's folder.

6 Indeed, Mrs. Haywood attempted to dissuade her brother from visiting the project. She had him committed to a psychiatric ward for observation and she requested HA police to arrest him if he appeared at the project.

1967, considered by the Supreme Court in Thorpe v. Housing Authority of City of Durham, 393 U.S. 268, 89 S.Ct. 518, 21 L.Ed.2d 474 (1969), this is not dispositive of the question of whether the procedures satisfy the due process requirements of the Fourteenth Amendment. See Thorpe, supra, 393 U.S. at 283–284, 89 S.Ct. 518; In re Williams, 309 N.Y. S.2d 454 (Sup.Ct. Westchester County, April 10, 1970). But see Chicago Housing Authority v. Stewart, 43 Ill.2d 96, 251 N.E.2d 185 (1969), cert. denied, 397 U.S. 1000, 90 S.Ct. 1147, 25 L.Ed. 2d 410 (March 23, 1970).

Nor is it conclusive in the consideration of appellants' constitutional claims to argue that there is no constitutional right to continue living in public housing projects. See Chicago Housing Authority v. Blackman, 4 Ill.2d 319, 122 N.E. 2d 522, 524 (1954); Municipal Housing Authority v. Walck, 277 App.Div. 791, 97 N.Y.S.2d 488 (1950); cf. Lynch v. United States, 292 U.S. 571, 577, 54 S.Ct. 840, 78 L.Ed. 1434 (1934) (Brandeis, J.). The government cannot deprive a private citizen of his continued tenancy, without affording him adequate procedural safeguards even if public housing could be deemed to be a privilege. See Goldberg v. Kelly, 397 U.S. 254, 262–63, 90 S.Ct. 1011, 1017, 25 L.Ed.2d 285 (March 23, 1970); Willner v. Committee on Character & Fitness, 373 U.S. 96, 83 S.Ct. 1175, 10 L. Ed.2d 224 (1963); Greene v. McElroy, 360 U.S. 474, 79 S.Ct. 1400, 3 L.Ed.2d 1377 (1959); Hornsby v. Allen, 326 F.2d 605, 609 (5 Cir. 1964); Van Alstyne, The Demise of the Right-Privilege Distinction in Constitutional Law, 81 Harv.L.Rev. 1439, 1451–54 (1968); Note, Another Look at Unconstitutional Conditions, 117 U.Pa.L.Rev. 144 (1968).

Since these actions were dismissed at the pleadings stage, we must view the allegations in the complaints and support-

ing affidavits in the light most favorable to the appellants, see p. 857 supra; in this light we find that appellants have a claim for relief. Certain aspects of the alleged present HA procedures cannot stand without a convincing showing at trial that the HA has a compelling need for procedural expedition.

"The very nature of due process negates any concept of inflexible procedures universally applicable to every imaginable situation." Cafeteria & Restaurant Workers Union, Local 473 v. McElroy, 367 U.S. 886, 895, 81 S.Ct. 1743, 1748, 6 L.Ed.2d 1230 (1961); Dixon v. Alabama State Bd. of Education, 294 F.2d 150, 155 (5 Cir. 1961.) The minimum procedural safeguards required by due process in each situation, depend on the nature of the governmental function involved and the substance of the private interest which is affected by the governmental action. Goldberg v. Kelly, supra, 397 U.S. at 263, 90 S.Ct. at 1017; see Joint Anti-Fascist Refugee Committee v. McGrath, 341 U.S. 123, 162–163, 71 S. Ct. 624, 95 L.Ed. 817 (1951) (Frankfurter, J., concurring). Since these competing interests have not been fully developed at the trial level, it is not now appropriate for this court to prescribe the minimum necessary procedural requirements. However, if appellants can show at trial the existence of certain of the pleaded HA procedures, we hold that they will have made out a prima facie case for relief; the exact nature and extent of that relief can only be determined after trial.

A.

We consider first the procedures for terminating tenancies on the ground of non-desirability. We find this procedure may be deficient in four respects. First, summary notice such as that sent to the tenants here of the non-desirable conduct under consideration by the TRB is inadequate. See In re Williams, supra, 309

N.Y.S.2d at 460. The one-sentence notices sent to the present appellants were insufficient to notify them even of the particular conduct thought by the TRB to be most serious. But since the TRB bases its decision on the tenant's entire folder, detailed notice as to the particular conduct thought to be most serious would be inadequate to give the tenant advance notice of all the items which might be considered against him so that he might challenge these items.

The purpose of requiring that notice be given to the tenant before the hearing is to insure that the tenant is adequately informed of the nature of the evidence against him so that he can effectively rebut that evidence. The instant one-sentence summary notices are inadequate for this purpose. Willner v. Committee on Character & Fitness, 373 U.S. 96, 105, 107, 83 S.Ct. 1175, 10 L. Ed.2d 224 (1963); *Dixon*, supra, 294 F. 2d at 158–159. Nor does the conference between the project manager and the tenant cure the deficiency in the notice, see Goldberg v. Kelly, supra, 397 U.S. at 270, 90 S.Ct. at 1020, since the manager does not divulge all entries in the folder some of which may influence the TRB's decision.

Second, denying tenants access to the material in their folders, when the entire folder is considered by the TRB in its determination of eligibility, deprives the tenants of due process. Goldberg v. Kelly, supra, 397 U.S. at 270, 90 S.Ct. at 1021. A hearing at which the tenant can rebut evidence against him would be of little value if the TRB's ultimate decision can rest on items in the tenant's folder of which he has no knowledge and hence has had no opportunity to challenge. *Willner*, supra, 373 U.S. at 107, 83 S. Ct. 1175 (Goldberg, J., concurring).

If secrecy must be preserved as to some items in the tenant's folder, then these items may not be relied on in the decision of the HA. The decision must be based solely on the evidence adduced at the hearing. Goldberg v. Kelly, supra, 397 U.S. at 271, 90 S.Ct. at 1022. Although it is unnecessary to write a full judicial opinion, the HA should "demonstrate compliance with this elementary requirement" and "state the reasons for [its] determination and indicate the evidence [it] relied on." Id. at 271, 90 S.Ct. at 1022; see In re Williams, supra, 309 N. Y.S.2d at 460.

Third, denying the tenant the opportunity to confront and cross-examine persons who supplied information in the tenant's folder upon which HA action is grounded is improper. Goldberg v. Kelly, supra, 397 U.S. at 270, 90 S.Ct. at 1021; *Willner*, supra, 373 U.S. at 107, 83 S.Ct. 1175 (Goldberg, J., concurring); In re Williams, supra, 309 N.Y.S.2d at 460; see *Dixon*, supra, 294 F.2d at 159. "In almost every setting where important decisions turn on questions of fact, due process requires an opportunity to confront and cross-examine adverse witnesses." Goldberg v. Kelly, supra, 397 U.S. at 269, 90 S.Ct. at 1021.

Under the present procedures, it appears that often the tenant is not even advised as to the source of many of the entries in his folder; preliminary disclosure of this information is, of course, necessary before the tenant can decide whether to confront the person supplying the damaging entry in his folder. If disclosure of the names of persons supplying information in the folder, or the subsequent confrontation at a hearing between the tenant and such persons is deemed to be undesirable because of possible hostility amongst housing project neighbors, the HA may not base its determination on such information. Goldberg v. Kelly, supra, at 270, 90 S.Ct. at 1022; see Alderman v. United States, 394 U.S. 165, 89 S.Ct. 961, 22 L.Ed.2d 176 (1969); Silverthorne Lumber Co. v. United States, 251 U.S. 385, 40 S.Ct. 182, 64 L.Ed. 319 (1920).

Finally, we find that the HA's failure to disclose the rules and regulations in the TRB Handbook governing the TRB panel at the hearing concerning termination for non-desirability may be found to be improper. See Goldberg v. Kelly, supra, 397 U.S. at 271, 90 S.Ct. at 1022 ("The decision maker's conclusion as * * * must rely solely on the *legal rules* and evidence adduced at the hearing" [emphasis added]). Appellants allege that this information is necessary to adequate preparation of the tenant's substantive case before the TRB. If this is established at trial, these regulations must be made generally available prior to the hearing. The HA's argument, that the regulations contained in the Handbook are merely internal procedural guidelines, may be considered by the trial court in determining whether, in fact, the Handbook is necessary in preparing a tenant's case before the TRB.

B.

Next, we consider the procedures for terminating tenancies on the ground of violation of rules and regulations and for assessing "additional rent" charges. Each procedure would seem to suffer the first three deficiencies of the TRB procedure. The tenant should be notified in advance of the complete grounds for the proposed action; should have access to all the information upon which any decision will be based; and should be afforded the right to confront and cross-examine witnesses in appropriate circumstances. In addition, it would seem that the tenant should be afforded the opportunity to present his side of the case in the presence of an impartial official, not merely to the project manager who instituted the proposed action against the tenant.[7] Goldberg v. Kelly, supra, at

271, 90 S.Ct. at 1021; cf. In re Murchison, 349 U.S. 133, 136, 75 S.Ct. 623, 99 L.Ed. 942 (1955); Wasson v. Trowbridge, 382 F.2d 807, 813 (2d Cir. 1967); compare Administrative Procedure Act § 5, 5 U.S.C.A. § 554 (1966); Note, Public Landlords and Private Tenants: The Eviction of "Undesirables" From Public Housing Projects, 77 Yale L.J. 988, 994, 1004–05 (1968).

Although a full-fledged adversary hearing need not be afforded in all cases, the tenant must be adequately informed of the nature of the evidence against him and accorded an adequate opportunity to rebut the evidence. *Willner,* supra, 373 U.S. at 107, 83 S.Ct. 1175 (Goldberg, J., concurring). Indeed in the cases of violations of rules and regulations and of "additional rent" charges, the evidence against the tenant is quite likely to come from third parties. In such cases, the tenant should be permitted to challenge the person supplying that evidence. The language of Mr. Justice Frankfurter concurring in *Joint Anti-Fascist Refugee Committee,* supra, is apt:

"The validity and moral authority of a conclusion largely depend on the mode by which it was reached. Secrecy is not congenial to truth-seeking and

---

[7] In the case of termination on the ground of non-desirability, the TRB as a whole must approve the project manager's recommendation to terminate before there can be an appearance by the tenant before a panel of the TRB. Although this initial TRB approval of the manager's recommendation becomes final if the tenant does not request a hearing we are not convinced that the panel members' involvement in the initial approval precludes their unbiased participation on the panel at the hearing reviewing the recommendation of the project manager. See Goldberg v. Kelly, supra, at 271, 90 S.Ct. at 1022 ("[P]rior involvement in some aspects of a case will not necessarily bar [an] official from acting as a decision maker. He should not, however, have participated in making the determination under review."); In re Williams, 309 N.Y.S.2d 454 (Sup.Ct. Westchester County April 10, 1970); cf. Gonzales v. United States, 364 U.S. 59, 63, 80 S.Ct. 1554, 4 L.Ed.2d 1569 (1960); Marcello v. Bonds, 349 U.S. 302, 311, 75 S.Ct. 757, 99 L. Ed. 1107 (1955).

self-righteousness gives too slender an assurance of rightness. No better instrument has been devised for arriving at truth than to give a person in jeopardy of serious loss notice of the case against him and opportunity to meet it. Nor has a better way been found for generating the feeling, so important to a popular government, that justice has been done." 341 U.S. at 171–172, 71 S.Ct. at 649.

The HA's argument that the "additional rent" charges are provided for in the HA lease is not dispositive of the question of the fairness of the procedures under which said charges are imposed. Holloway v. Department of Housing and Urban Development, 418 F.2d 242 (5 Cir. 1969); see Vinson v. Greenburgh Housing Authority, 29 A.D.2d 338, 288 N.Y.S.2d 159 (1968), leave to appeal granted, (1969). Nor is it persuasive in the posture of this case to argue that a tenant may challenge the additional rent charges by refusing to pay them and by defending in court against the HA's suit for nonpayment of rent. The cost of defending in court and the hazards envisioned by a public housing tenant in refusing to pay rent, would probably dissuade all but the boldest tenant from contesting an "additional rent" charge in this manner. Nor can the small size of the "additional rent" charges be relied on to deny tenants automatically fair procedures. To be sure, the size of the charges is relevant to the question of the burdensomeness of the required procedures, but even small charges can have great impact on the budgets of public housing tenants, who are by hypothesis below a certain economic level. See Goldberg v. Kelly, supra, 397 U.S. at 264, 90 S.Ct. at 1017.

[The parts of the opinion that deal with jurisdiction, substantiality, case or controversy, abstention, state review and exhaustion of administrative remedies have been omitted.]

IV.

The minimum procedural requirements of due process under the Fourteenth Amendment must reflect the balance between the government's interest in efficient administration and the nature of the individual's interest being affected by governmental action. We hold only that granting every favorable inference to plaintiffs' complaints and affidavits, it appears that the HA's procedures are deficient in several specific aspects. Upon trial, the HA may be able to show great need for expedited procedures, or the plaintiffs may fail to substantiate all of their allegations. Therefore the fashioning of a remedy or a declaratory judgment must await the full trial of these actions.

Reversed and remanded for consideration of plaintiffs' motion for preliminary relief and for trial on the merits.

Notes and Questions on Eviction as a "Non-Desirable"

1. The opinion speaks of the HUD circular of February 7, 1967, discussed by the Supreme Court in Thorpe v. Housing Authority of City of Durham, 393 U.S. 268 (1969). This circular directed Local Authorities to inform any tenant facing eviction of "the specific reason(s) for [the] notice to vacate; thereupon, the tenant was to be given an opportunity to make such reply or explanation as he wished."

Previously, even this simple procedural safeguard was denied public housing tenants, who could be summarily evicted, without explanation, when their month-to-month (the standard) tenancy ended. See e. g., Walton v. City of Phoenix, 69 Ariz. 26, 208 P.2d 309 (1949). Some local authorities, on their own initiative, would inform the tenant, but once again, the month-to-month tenant had no common-law right to test the merits of the Authority's claim. Does a common-law tenant for a term of years enjoy greater procedural rights?

2. Prior to Escalera, a state court had directed a local authority to give reasons for terminating a month-to-month tenancy; otherwise the summary proceeding would fail. Affirming the lower court order, a divided (3–2) Appellate Division in Vinson v. Greenburgh Housing Authority, 29 A.D.2d 338, 288 N.Y.S.2d 159 (2d Sept. 1968) wrote as follows:

The Authority's return alleges no reason for the termination of the lease; it admits that the petitioners' attorney spoke to its attorney, who informed the former that the Authority was not required to give a reason for the eviction. The Authority claims as a defense that the notice validly terminated the lease and that its determination was neither a judicial nor a quasi-judicial act and hence not reviewable by the court.

Special Term in effect granted the relief sought by the petitioners, unless the Authority submit an appropriate return stating the grounds for its determination. Special Term reasoned that the petitioners had asserted grave charges of irresponsibility by the Authority and that the latter's contention that its exercise of discretion to terminate the lease was absolute could not be sustained. By permission of Special Term, the Authority appeals (CPLR 5701, subd. [c]).

The Authority argues that the provisions in the lease for its termination are plain and binding on both parties and cannot be modified by the court. To interfere with its determination by requiring an explanation, the Authority urges, imposes a burden not demanded from other landlords and thus discriminates unfairly and invalidly against it. On the other hand, the petitioners press on us the contention that the Authority may not act arbitrarily toward its ten-

ants, for otherwise a tenant might be evicted without cause or justification.

We meet, then, the question of the nature of the relationship between a housing authority and its tenants. Ordinarily, provisions in a lease permitting its termination upon the service of a notice of a stated period are enforcible by the landlord at will (Zule v. Zule, 24 Wend. 76; cf. Metropolitan Life Ins. Co. v. Carroll, 43 Misc. 2d 639, 251 N.Y.S.2d 693). The relationship between landlord and tenant is considered contractual simply; and the terms of the lease for termination, unless calling for a reasonable basis for action, may be exercised without explanation. But a housing authority is not an ordinary landlord, nor its lessees ordinary tenants.

Our Constitution recognizes low rent housing as a proper governmental function (N.Y.Const., art. XVIII). The Legislature, in response to its direction, has enacted the Public Housing Law.

* * *

Thus, our State has distinguished low rent housing as a human need to be satisfied through governmental action and has created by specific statutory provisions the structure of the relationship between the housing authority and the tenant. The statute consequently enters into and becomes a part of the lease; and its spirit and intent must be the guiding beacon in the interpretation of the terms of the lease.

" 'Due process of law,' is not confined to judicial proceedings, but extends to every case which may deprive a citizen of life, liberty, or property, whether the proceeding be judicial, administrative, or executive in its nature" (Stuart v. Palmer, 74 N.Y. 183, 190–191). Once the State embarks into the area of housing as a function of government, necessarily that function, like other governmental functions, is subject to the constitutional commands. Low rent housing is not the leasing of government-owned property originally acquired for a different purpose, but now surplus or not required for that purpose, on a sporadic or temporary basis (cf. United States v. Blumenthal, 3 Cir., 315 F.2d 351), where the traditional notions of private property might well be applied; rather, it imports a status of a continuous character, based on the need of the tenants for decent housing at a cost proportionate to their income, subject to the compliance by the tenants with reasonable regulations and the payment of rent when due. "The Government as landlord is still the government. It must not act arbitrarily, for, unlike private landlords, it is subject to the requirements of due process of law" (Rudder v. United States, 96 U.S.App. D.C. 329, 226 F.2d 51, 53). * * * We think that a housing authority cannot arbitrarily deprive a tenant of his right to continue occupancy through the exercise of a contractual provision to terminate the lease. In other words, the action of the housing authority must not rest on mere whim or caprice or an arbitrary reason.

Several considerations combine to justify the difference in treatment between governmental agencies and private individuals. Realistically, it must be acknowledged that the housing authority prescribes the terms of the lease and that the tenant does not negotiate with the authority in the usual sense (see, Reich, The New Property, 73 Yale L.J. 733, 749–752; Friedman, Public Housing and the Poor: An overview, 54 Cal.L.Rev. 642, 660; note, Government Housing Assistance to the Poor, 76 Yale L.J. 508, 512). In this condition of affairs, to impose a requirement of good faith and reasonableness on the party in the stronger

bargaining position when he exerts a contractual option is but a reflection of simple justice (cf. New York Cent. Iron Works Co. v. United States Radiator Co., 174 N.Y. 331, 66 N.E. 967; Wood v. Duff-Gordon, 222 N.Y. 88, 118 N.E. 214).

* * *

Moreover, in balancing the interests of the State against the interests of the individual, the advantages to the State are outweighed by the detriment to the individual, if we were to deny the tenant protection from an arbitrary termination of the lease. The eviction of a family in the income bracket eligible under the standards of public housing from its household is a serious blow. If, in fact, a mistake has been made in the accusation against the tenant of improper conduct or a violation of regulations, or if the reason for the ouster has no better basis than dislike or unjustified discipline, the requirement of the disclosure of the ground for the termination of the lease affords the tenant the opportunity to protest its exercise. On the other hand, the authority will suffer no more than delay in the ultimate eviction in the event the termination of the lease is made on reasonable grounds; and in the meantime the authority may control excessive misbehavior of the tenant through police action.

The declared purpose of the statute makes clear that low rent housing was considered to be permanent and not transitory and that, so long as the tenants remain qualified and do not violate the reasonable regulations of the State agency, they would not be evicted for grounds extrinsic to these requirements. So, the State policy was established in contemplation of "insanitary and substandard housing conditions owing to overcrowding and concentration of the population," as a result of which "the construction of new housing facilities, under public supervision in accord with proper standards of sanitation and safety and at a cost which will permit monthly rentals which persons of low income can afford to pay" is necessary; and it was acknowledged that "these conditions require the creation of the agencies, instrumentalities and corporations hereinafter prescribed, which are declared to be agencies and instrumentalities of the state for the purpose of attaining the ends herein recited" (Public Housing Law, § 2).

*   *   *

Once the field of housing as a utility has been encompassed by the State, we think that the traditional protection against the caprice of State agencies must be preserved. "Discretionary administrative power over individual rights * * * is undesirable *per se*, and should be avoided as far as may be, for discretion is unstandardized power and to lodge in an official such power over person or property is hardly conformable to the 'Rule of Law' " (Freund, Historical Survey in Growth of American Administrative Law, pp. 22–23).

The dissenting justices in *Vinson* agreed that public housing tenants do have a property right, which governmental agencies could not arbitrarily take from them. But the dissenters insisted that it was a property right circumscribed by the terms and conditions of the lease upon which it was founded.

The Illinois Supreme Court distinguished between governmental activities (arbitrariness not allowed) and proprietary activities (arbitrariness tolerated), and held that the Chicago Housing Authority was a "proprietary" landlord. Chicago Housing Authority v. Stewart, 40 Ill.2d 23, 237 N.E.2d 463 (1968). But can one find the governmental-pro-

prietary distinction in the Constitution? And is housing management less "governmental" then, let us say, insuring mortgages or paying urban renewal writedowns?

3. Shortly after the *Thorpe* decision, tenants' groups asked to negotiate with HUD on the rights of public housing tenants. With the National Associations of Housing and Redevelopment Officials (NAHRO) joining the discussions as an active third party, the negotiations resulted in two tentative drafts, one on leases and the other on grievance procedures. HUD has since issued circulars that generally embody these agreements. The circular on grievance procedures compels a hearing—if a tenant wishes—before an impartial official or a hearing panel. If representatives of managements are on the panel, tenants must be represented in equal numbers. A tenant is entitled to see the evidence against him, cross-examine witnesses, have the proceedings open or closed, and be represented by counsel. The final decision, which must be in writing, must contain the reasons and evidence relied on. Renewal & Housing Management, §§ 7465.8, 7465.9 (Feb. 22, 1971).

The fair hearing safeguards of *Escalera* and the HUD circulars resemble those constitutionally required in Goldberg v. Kelly, 397 U.S. 254 (1970), for the termination of welfare benefits which are more fully discussed in Chapter 1, supra. Is it a serious argument that equally rigorous administrative procedures are not needed to terminate welfare payments and public housing tenancies, since the tenant will always have his day in court before he is evicted? Cf. Caulder v. Housing Authority, 433 F.2d 998 (4th Cir. 1970) [dissenting opinion]. Can it be argued, contrarily, that a public housing tenancy—in view of the urgent shortage of standard, low-rent facilities—should be protected even more jealously than a welfare benefit? The loss of welfare frequently implies alternative income; but the loss of public housing (as a non-desirable) usually implies a return to squalor or unbearably higher rentals.

The HUD Circular states that the tenant may invoke the formal hearing procedures for "any LHA [Local Housing Authority] action or failure to act in accordance with the lease requirements, or * * * involving interpretation or application of LHA's regulations, policies or procedures which adversely affect the tenant's rights, duties, welfare or status." Renewal & Housing Management, § 7465.9 (Feb. 22, 1971). Presumably, this would include an eviction for any cause, including non-payment of rent; or the levying of a fine for rule violation. Could the tenant also invoke a hearing when the LHA sought to raise his rent? Would the hearing procedure be suitable for a tenant's complaint of poor maintenance or lack of services? If the tenant initiates a grievance and is dissatisfied with the outcome, what recourse does he have: judicial review? a de novo action? If the tenant by-passes the grievance machinery and relies initially upon the courts, can it be successfully asserted that he has failed to exhaust his administrative remedies?

For an elaborate inquiry into the statutory and constitutional basis for HUD's rule-making process in this area, see Lefcoe, HUD's Authority to Mandate Tenants' Rights in Public Housing, 80 Yale L.J. 463–514 (1971).

4. The *Thorpe* case directs attention to modes of tenant activity which, even when proved, would not let an LHA abruptly end a tenancy. The Durham (N.C.) Housing Authority served an eviction notice upon Joyce Thorpe (a month-to-month tenant) one day after her election as president of a project tenants' organization, but refused to explain its action. The North Carolina courts granted the eviction and cited common-law prece-

dent to justify the Authority's refusal to give any reason. The U.S. Supreme Court granted certiorari on December 5, 1966, but while the case was pending, HUD, on February 7, 1967, issued the aforesaid circular (note 1 supra), the court vacated the judgment below and remanded the case "for such further proceedings as may be appropriate in the light of the [Circular]." 386 U.S. 670 (1967).

On remand, the North Carolina Supreme Court refused to apply the HUD Circular on the ground that the HUD procedures did not apply to prior events (the eviction attempt had occurred 17 months earlier.) The United States Supreme Court again granted certiorari and, rejecting the "prospective-only" argument, once again reversed the state court judgment. The court refused, however, to rule on Mrs. Thorpe's contention that an eviction would violate her First Amendment rights of free speech and association; to do so would be premature. But the opinion noted the Housing Authority's concession that it would not evict any tenant for engaging in constitutionally protected activity. See also, Justice Douglas' concurring opinion in the earlier *Thorpe* decision, 386 U.S. 670, 674–681 (1967); Edwards v. Habib, 130 U.S. App.D.C. 126, 397 F.2d 687 (1968), cert. denied 393 U.S. 1016 (1969). See also Chicago Housing Authority v. Blackman, 4 Ill.2d 319, 122 N.E.2d 522 (1954) (Authority could not evict tenants for refusing to sign a loyalty oath which failed to distinguish between knowing and innocent membership in subversive organizations).

It is a safe bet that an Authority may not attempt to suppress speech or organization, or retaliatorily evict, or practice racial or religious discrimination; the Constitution deals emphatically with all such conduct by a governmental agency. Suppose, however, that on the facts of *Escalera*, the Authority proves after giving the tenants all necessary procedural safeguards that the Escaleras kept a dog in violation of LHA rules, or that Mrs. Haywood's brother (a non-tenant) behaved badly when he visited her, or that the Lockman sons insisted on playing ball on the grass. Having made its proof of these leasehold violations, would the Authority be entitled to an eviction? Putting the question differently: Does a public housing tenant have any substantive protection against removal whenever he is found to violate his tenancy (for reasons other than non-payment of rent)? At the very least, should offenses be classified as substantial (material) and insubstantial (non-material)? What criteria should we apply in defining whether a violation is substantial? Is a system of fines the best way for dealing with insubstantial breaches given the low-income (and often welfare) status of public housing tenants? Should the standards for eviction as an undesirable be roughly similar to the standards for non-selection of an applicant as a potentially undesirable tenant?

Can it be argued that the *Constitution* protects the public housing tenant against removal except for substantial cause? Make the argument. Does the argument reach moderate- or middle-income tenants who are living in projects subsidized through governmental low interest loans and interest reduction payments. (e. g., the FHA sec. 236 program)? Does the argument also reach low-income tenants living in privately owned units that have been leased to the Local Housing Authority under the section 23 program? Does the argument also reach the recipients of housing allowances (funded under the current HUD demonstration programs) who are living in privately owned units? Might it reach *all* tenancies, as long as housing remains in short supply: In short, should there be a "statutory" tenancy for *all* tenants? Or to put the question somewhat differently: Should all private landlords be deemed

public utilities, regulated both as to their rates and their manner of dealing with customers (tenants)?

5. Do (public housing) tenants enjoy any Constitutional protection against a landlord's (LHA's) unilateral decision to change the house rules and regulations, where the lease openly reserves this privilege (as leases invariably do)? Might public housing tenants now insist that the HUD hearing procedures, note 3 supra, cover an LHA's rule changes?

----

3. Landlord Seeks to Charge a Higher Rent

Introduction to Rent Control

Amout 70 percent of *all* residential rentals are periodic tenancies, usually from month-to-month. Either party to such a tenancy could, at common law, end the tenancy by giving notice to the other, one month in advance if the tenancy were from month-to-month, one week in advance if the tenancy were for shorter periods. The decision to terminate required neither explanation nor justification—only sufficient notice. And except for slight change in the length or manner of notice, statutory law, until the 1940s, generally reaffirmed the common-law.

With the advent of World War II, rent control fundamentally changed the landlord-and-tenant relationship. Quite evidently, it was not enough to fix ceiling rentals if the landlord could unilaterally end the tenancy. Tenants who could not stay to pay might be forced into a black market for scarce apartments. Thus all existing tenancies, at the end of one month if the tenancy were from month-to-month or at the end of the term if the tenancy were for a term of years, automatically became *statutory* tenancies. This meant that the power to terminate rested solely with the tenant unless landlord could meet one of the few specified exceptions (e. g., landlord wanted the unit for his own use). Tenant could exercise the power to terminate by giving one month's notice.

Federal rent controls ended in 1947, and thereafter most states allowed free market forces to determine rent levels. New York State asserted control until 1962, but after 1962 only New York City and Boston among major cities continued to fix rents. Convinced by 1971 that rent controls had aggravated both the shortage and condition of housing, the New York State legislature stripped the New York City of its power to retain ceilings upon vacated units, but city rent controls continued for tenants still in possession.

President Nixon's New Economic Policy, announced in August 1971, returned virtually *all* rentals to federal control, except where local regulation persisted.* Guidelines promulgated in December 1971 called for the fixing of a basic rental for every controlled unit, and for automatic annual increments (2.5 percent) to cover hikes in operating costs. Landlords could, in addition, recoup outlays for capital expenditures and higher real estate taxes.

But as suddenly as they had begun, Federal controls over rentals (and other prices) ended in January, 1973, when the nation moved into the so-called "Phase 3" era. Whether country-wide rent controls will reappear may depend upon the government's ability to curb inflation.

HAHN v. GOTTLIEB

United States Court of Appeals,
First Circuit, 1970.
430 F.2d 1243.

COFFIN, Circuit Judge. In this appeal, we are asked to decide whether

* But the Federal Rent Board was empowered to supersede local controls.

tenants in housing subsidized under § 221(d)(3) of the National Housing Act have the right to an administrative hearing and judicial review when their landlord proposes to increase rents.

Plaintiffs are members of a tenants' association at the Castle Square project in Boston (the project), a development of low-and middle-income housing financed under § 221(d)(3), as amended, 12 U.S.C.A. § 1715*l*(d)(3). Defendants Gottlieb and Druker (the landlord) are the current owners of the project. Prior to the expiration of the plaintiffs' leases in July 1969, the landlord filed a proposed monthly rent increase of $28 per apartment with defendant Flynn, Regional Director of the Federal Housing Administration. Plaintiffs sought an opportunity to be heard on the proposed increase; and, when the FHA failed to satisfy their request, they brought suit in the federal district court.

The district court initially granted plaintiffs' prayer for a preliminary injunction, then vacated its order when the FHA agreed to provide a hearing. The hearing was held before a member of the FHA's Boston staff. Several tenants gave graphic evidence concerning construction defects, which plaintiffs maintain were the cause of higher maintenance and operating costs. Plaintiffs also introduced expert evidence designed to show that the landlord could maintain a satisfactory rate of return on his investment with a smaller rent increase. Shortly after the hearing, defendant Flynn notified plaintiffs that he had granted a monthly increase of $22.00 per apartment, $11.00 effective immediately and $11.00 a year hence.

Plaintiffs immediately renewed their prayer for a preliminary injunction, complaining that the FHA had failed to afford them a "full and fair" hearing. However, the district court, reversing its original position, held that plaintiffs had no right to an FHA hearing and no standing to protest agency procedure in court. The court reasoned that under the National Housing Act, the Secretary of Housing and Urban Development (HUD), under whose jurisdiction the FHA falls, has the widest latitude in determining proper procedures; that, absent statutory authority, tenants had no right to be heard; and that plaintiffs had no legally protected interest since the government was acting under a contract to which plaintiffs were not parties.

On appeal, plaintiffs raise two main issues: first, they assert a constitutional right to a hearing, including opportunity to cross-examine adverse witnesses and an agency decision based on a formal record; and second, they claim a right to judicial review of adverse agency action.

I. *Statutory Scheme*

We begin our consideration of plaintiffs' claims by examining the statute, § 221(d)(3), as amended by the Housing Act of 1961, Public L. 87–70, 75 Stat. 149. The general goal of national housing policy is to provide "a decent home and a suitable living environment for every American family". 42 U.S.C.A. §§ 1441, 1441a. Section 221(d)(3) seeks to implement this goal by assisting "private industry in providing housing for low and moderate income families and displaced families." 12 U.S.C.A. § 1715l(a). This assistance to the private sector takes two forms. First, the FHA provides insurance on long-term mortgage loans covering up to 90 per cent of the project's cost, thus encouraging private investment in projects which would otherwise be too risky. Second, eligible borrowers can obtain below-market interest rates on FHA-insured loans, thus reducing the rentals necessary

to service the landlord's debt obligation.[2] 12 U.S.C.A. § 1715l(d)(5).

To administer this two-pronged program, the statute confers broad discretion on the Secretary of HUD. The Secretary is authorized to approve mortgagors and to supervise their operations "under a regulatory agreement or otherwise, as to rents, charges, and methods of operation, in such form and in such manner as in the opinion of the Secretary will effectuate the purposes of this section." 12 U.S.C.A. § 1715l(d)(3). Similar discretion is vested in the Secretary concerning eligibility for occupancy, 12 U.S.C.A. § 1715l(d)(3)(iii), construction standards, 12 U.S.C.A. § 1715l (f), terms of amortization, 12 U.S.C.A. § 1715l(d)(6), and consent to the release of the mortgagor, 12 U.S.C.A. § 1715l(e)(2).

Implementing these broad grants of authority, the Secretary has promulgated regulations concerning priorities and income limits for occupancy in § 221(d) (3) projects. 24 C.F.R. § 221.537. The Secretary also regulates the landlord's return on his investment by strictly supervising accounting practices, 24 C.F.R. § 221.531(b), and, in the case of limited distribution mortgagors like defendants Gottlieb and Druker, by setting a six per cent ceiling on return. 24 C.F.R. § 221.532(a). Applications for rent increases must be submitted to the FHA, which takes into account the rental income necessary to maintain a project's economic soundness and "to provide a reasonable return on the investment con-

[2] This is usually accomplished with the cooperation of the Federal National Mortgage Association, which agrees to purchase the mortgage note when construction is completed. Thus the private lender receives normal interest rates until the loan closing, at which point the FNMA purchases the loan and reduces interest rates to three per cent. See Fitzpatrick, FHA and FNMA Assistance for Multifamily Housing, 32 Law and Cont. Prob. 439, 448–453 (1967).

sistent with providing reasonable rentals to the tenants." 24 C.F.R. § 221.531 (c). FHA's agreement with the landlord in this case further provides that rental increases will be approved if necessary to compensate for increases in expense "over which the owners have no effective control".

These regulations illustrate that the success of a § 221(d)(3) project requires a flexible exercise of administrative discretion. The ultimate goal of the program is housing for low and middle income families, but this goal is to be achieved by expanding the range of housing needs which can be met by private enterprise. S.Rep.No.281, 87th Cong., 1st Sess. 3 (1961). To provide low-income housing while maintaining a sound investment requires considerable adaptability. We think Congress recognized this need for adaptability when it authorized the Secretary to regulate mortgagors by individual agreement as well as by general rule. Of course, the need for administrative flexibility does not of itself preclude an agency hearing or judicial review, but we must take care lest we kill the goose in our solicitude for the eggs.[3]

[3] This discussion should dispose of any objection to plaintiffs' standing to seek judicial review. Not only do the tenants allege injury in fact in the form of higher rents, but their interest in low-rent housing is "within the zone of interests" protected by the statute. Association of Data Processing Service Organizations, Inc. v. Camp, 397 U.S. 150, 90 S.Ct. 827, 25 L.Ed.2d 184 (1970); Barlow v. Collins, 397 U.S. 159, 164, 90 S.Ct. 832, 25 L.Ed.2d 192 (1970). The private defendants' argument that tenants were not the primary concern of Congress misses the mark; plaintiffs come within the circumference of those who "arguably" can show a protected interest. A.D.P.S.O. v. Camp, supra, 397 U.S. at 156, 90 S.Ct. 827. In this respect, they differ from the plaintiffs in Arnold Tours, Inc. v. Camp, 428 F.2d 359 (1st Cir. June 1, 1970), who could produce no evidence whatsoever to indicate that Congress was concerned with protecting their interests.

II. *Right to a Hearing*

Plaintiffs' initial claim is that they are entitled to a formal hearing before the FHA prior to the approval of any rent increase. This contention finds no support in the text of the National Housing Act. Plaintiffs claim, however, that both the right to a hearing and its procedural characteristics can be derived from the Due Process Clause of the Fifth Amendment.[4] Broadly speaking, resolution of this claim requires us to balance the interests of the government in the procedure adopted against the citizen's interest in greater safeguards. Goldberg v. Kelly, 397 U.S. 254, 263, 90 S.Ct. 1011, 25 L.Ed.2d 287 (1970). As an initial step in the weighing process, we must determine "the precise nature of the government function involved as well as of the private interest that has been affected by government action." Cafeteria & Restaurant Workers Union v. McElroy, 367 U.S. 886, 895, 81 S.Ct. 1743, 1748, 6 L.Ed.2d 1230 (1961); accord, Goldberg v. Kelly, supra, 397 U.S. at 263, 90 S.Ct. 1011. Then, since different standards of fairness have traditionally been associated with different types of proceedings, we must examine the nature of the FHA proceedings and the possible burdens and benefits which might flow from the rights asserted by plaintiffs. Hannah v. Larche, 363 U.S. 420, 442, 80 S.Ct. 1502, 4 L.Ed.2d 1307 (1960).

In this case, as we have seen, the primary role of the government is that

[4] We are satisfied that the Administrative Procedure Act does not apply to this case. Section 4 of the A.P.A., 5 U.S.C.A. § 553(a), exempts matters relating to public loans, benefits, and contracts from the statutory requirements for rule-making. Section 5 of the A.P.A., 5 U.S.C.A. § 554, applies only when there is an "adjudication", a term which implies a greater direct impact on individual interests than is true in our case. See Gart v. Cole, 263 F.2d 244, 251 (2d Cir.), cert. denied, 359 U.S. 978, 79 S.Ct. 898, 3 L.Ed.2d 929 (1959); see text infra.

of insurer for private investors. The government attempts to regulate its contractual relations with mortgagors in order to advance public welfare, but its freedom to pursue social goals is limited by the need to avoid excessive losses.[5] While the government may have less freedom as an insurer than it does as an employer, compare Cafeteria & Restaurant Workers Union v. McElroy, supra, 367 U.S. at 896–898, 81 S.Ct. 1743, the government needs considerable procedural flexibility in either case.

The private interest affected, on the other hand, is the interest of low and middle income families in housing they can afford. The government has not, however, undertaken to provide this assistance directly under the § 221(d)(3) program. Instead, the government provides a limited subsidy to private landlords, who then enter an ordinary lease arrangement with eligible tenants. Plaintiffs are not legally "entitled" to low rents in the same sense that the welfare recipient in Goldberg v. Kelly, supra, was entitled to basic sustenance under a system of categorical assistance. Compare 42 U.S.C.A. § 602(a)(10); King v. Smith, 392 U.S. 309, 316, 327, 88 S.Ct. 2128, 20 L.Ed.2d 1118 (1968). Moreover, the tenant's interest is not directly jeopardized each time the FHA approves a rent increase. The increase may be small, and rent supplement programs are available to those in greatest need. Thus the government action in this case poses a less serious threat to the private interest involved than the termination of welfare benefits in Goldberg v. Kelly, supra, which deprived the recipient of the means of existence, or the denial of a security clearance in Greene v. McElroy, 360 U.S. 474, 79 S.Ct. 1400, 3 L.Ed.2d 1377 (1959), which meant loss of employment, or the eviction in Escalera v. New York City Housing Authority, 425 F.2d 853 (2d Cir. April 29, 1970), which as a practical matter meant total loss of decent low-rent housing.

The proceeding in which plaintiffs seek to assert their interests is basically an informal rate-making process. The landlord who seeks a rent increase submits documentation to the FHA showing his expenses, return on investment, and the like. The FHA staff then examines his proposal in the light of the terms of the regulatory agreement, the broad criteria of the regulations, and current economic conditions. Plaintiffs seek to encumber these negotiations with a formal hearing, the right to cross-examine adverse witnesses, and an impartial decision-maker, who must state the reasons for his decision and the evidence on which he relies. These procedural safeguards are characteristic of adjudicatory proceedings, where the outcome turns on accurate resolution of specific factual disputes. See, e. g., Escalera v. New York City Housing Authority, supra; Randell v. Newark Housing Authority, 384 F.2d 151 (3d Cir. 1967), cert. denied, Avent v. Newark Housing Authority, 393 U.S. 870, 89 S.Ct. 158, 21 L.Ed.2d 139 (1968). Such safeguards are not, however, essential in "legislative" proceedings, such as rate-making, where decision depends on broad familiarity with economic conditions. Cf. Norwegian Nitrogen Products Co. v. United States, 288 U.S. 294, 303–305, 53 S.Ct. 350, 77 L.Ed. 796 (1933). As Professor Davis has pointed out, when decision turns on "legislative" rather than "adjudicative" facts, a formal adversary hearing may contribute little or nothing to the agency's

[5] The FHA is financed entirely by premiums on mortgage insurance. When a mortgagor fails, the FHA reimburses the mortgagee and takes over the project by assignment or foreclosure until a new purchaser can be found. Klaman, Public/Private Approaches to Urban Mortgage and Housing Problems, 32 Law and Cont.Prob. 250, 263 (1967); Fitzpatrick, supra n. 2 at 459–461. Obviously, under such a program, the FHA has a pressing interest in promoting the solvency of its mortgagors.

understanding of the issues. 1 K. Davis, Administrative Law § 7.02 at 413 (1958).

The distinction between "legislative" and "adjudicative" facts is particularly apt in this case, where it is the tenants rather than the landlord who seek a hearing. The tenants are unlikely to have special familiarity with their landlord's financial condition, the intricacies of project management, or the state of the economy in the surrounding area. Hopefully, the FHA can check the accuracy of the landlord's documentation without their assistance. They may be aware of construction defects in their own living areas, but if, contrary to § 1715*l*(d)(2), a building has been approved which does not conform to applicable standards, there would seem to be limited utility in rehearsing old mistakes each time a rental increase is sought. Of course, tenants' complaints about maintenance and living conditions ought to be heard, but such grievances can be dealt with without requiring a trial-type hearing with each rent increase. Indeed, an effective grievance system should be operable at all times, not merely when the landlord seeks to raise his rents. Thus the elaborate procedural safeguards which plaintiffs demand are unlikely to elicit essential information in the general run of cases.

These procedures would, however, place a significant burden on the relationship between the landlord and the FHA. At present, applications for rent increases are merely one aspect of an on-going relationship between insured and insurer. Plaintiffs would turn these applications into occasions for full-scale review of the relationship, as their conduct in the hearing they have already received illustrates. Such reconsideration may delay economically necessary rent increases and discourage private investors from entering the § 221(d)(3) program at all. Equally important, the project in question con-

tains some 500 tenants, each of whom has the same interest in low-rent housing. As Justice Holmes pointed out in Bi-Metallic Investment Co. v. State Bd. of Equalization, 239 U.S. 441, 445, 36 S.Ct. 141, 142, 60 L.Ed. 372 (1915):

"Where a rule of conduct applies to more than a few people it is impracticable that every one should have a direct voice in its adoption. The Constitution does not require all public acts to be done in a town meeting or an assembly of the whole." Accord, Bowles v. Willingham, 321 U.S. 503, 519, 64 S.Ct. 641, 649, 88 L.Ed. 892 (1944).

Applying the constitutionally relevant test, therefore, it seems to us that the government interest in a summary procedure for approving rent increases outweighs the tenants' interest in greater procedural safeguards. The procedures demanded by plaintiffs would place substantial additional burdens on the insurer-insured relationship without necessarily improving the fundamental fairness of the proceedings. We therefore hold that tenants in housing financed under § 221 (d)(3) of the National Housing Act are not constitutionally entitled to an administrative hearing on their landlord's proposals for increased rents.

III. *Judicial Review*

This brings us to plaintiffs' second major claim, that they are entitled to judicial review of FHA decisions to grant a rent increase. Since the National Housing Act does not explicitly bar resort to the courts, we address ourselves to the alternate exception to judicial review, recognized in section 10 of the Administrative Procedure Act: whether "agency action is committed to agency discretion by law". 5 U.S.C.A. § 701(a)(2). In approaching this question, we recognize a strong presumption in favor of review, which is overcome only by "clear and convincing evidence" that Congress intended to cut off review above the agency level. * * * In the absence of a clear declaration of Congressional intent, three factors seem to us determinative: first, the appropriateness of the issues raised for review by the courts; second, the need for judicial supervision to safeguard the interests of the plaintiffs; and third, the impact of review on the effectiveness of the agency in carrying out its assigned role. See Saferstein, Nonreviewability: A Functional Analysis of "Committed to Agency Discretion", 82 Harv.L.Rev. 367, 371 (1968).

Looking first to the appropriateness of judicial review, we note that courts are ill-equipped to superintend economic and managerial decisions of the kind involved here. This is not a case which can be resolved by "judicial application of canons of statutory construction." Compare Barlow v. Collins, supra at 166, 90 S.Ct. at 837. A partial list of the issues raised by plaintiffs either in the FHA hearing or in the court below includes: whether the landlord's increased operating costs were attributable to poor design and construction defects; whether and to what extent costs attributable to such defects should be absorbed by the landlord or passed on to the tenants; whether estimates of the vacancy rate, of commercial occupancy, and of managerial expenses were reasonable; and whether the FHA had properly determined the investment base for computing a reasonable return. Our only guides in answering such questions are the sometimes conflicting statutory goals of increased low-rent housing through private investment and the extremely broad regulatory criteria of maintaining "the economic soundness of the project" while insuring "a reasonable return on the investment consistent with providing reasonable rentals to tenants." 24 C.F.R. § 221.531(c). Under these circumstances, we willingly confess our incapacity to contribute intelligently to the general course of decisions on rents and charges.

The second consideration, the need for judicial intervention to protect plaintiffs' interest in low-rent housing, is by no means insubstantial. Plaintiffs' choices are limited; their bargaining power generally not strong. But, as we have already noted, plaintiffs' interests are not threatened by every rent increase, and other forms of relief, such as rent supplements, are available. We must, in addition, take into account the kind of program which Congress has erected to meet plaintiffs' needs. The National Housing Act does not provide categorical assistance to those in need of housing, nor does it erect detailed statutory safeguards to protect their interests, such as those provided for persons displaced by urban renewal. Compare 42 U.S.C.A. § 1455(c); Western Addition Community Organization v. Weaver, 294 F.Supp. 433, 441–443 (N.D.Cal.1969); see also Merge v. Sharott, 341 F.2d 989 (3d Cir. 1965). Instead Congress has attempted to meet plaintiffs' needs indirectly, by stimulating private investors to supply low-rent housing. Rents in such housing are to be regulated, but only "in such manner as in the opinion of the Secretary will effectuate the purposes of this section." 12 U.S.C.A. § 1715l(d)(3). Given this mechanism, we think plaintiffs' long-run interest may not be well served by a judicially-imposed system of review of all rent increases. Delay, the frictions engendered by the process of litigation, and the possibility—seldom discussed—of landlord appeals from FHA decisions in favor of tenants may lead to higher rentals and ultimately to less participation by private investors.

Turning finally to the impact of review on agency effectiveness, we think that resort to the courts might have a serious adverse impact on the performance of the FHA. Close judicial scrutiny inevitably leads to more formalized decision-making. This result may be tolerable and even desirable in some cases. However, FHA consideration of rent increases can recur as often as leases expire over the life of a forty-year mortgage. To impose the formalities which attend review on all these essentially managerial decisions seems to us inconsistent with the constant Congressional urgings to simplify procedures and expedite work. E. g., H.R.Rep.No.1585, 90th Cong., 2d Sess., 1968 U.S.Code Cong. and Ad.News, p. 2876.

Equally important, such review would discourage the increased involvement of the private sector which is the goal of § 221(d)(3). Landlords such as defendants are already subject to many restraints. Under § 221(d)(3), their plans must be approved and cost ceilings fixed; their rentals must pass agency scrutiny, and the return on their investment is fixed. Moreover, since government is so heavily involved, they may not discriminate in their admissions policy. Colon v. Tompkins Square Neighbors, Inc., 294 F.Supp. 134 (S.D.N.Y.1968). They are by definition attempting to serve displaced families and families of low and moderate income whose background of poverty and dislocation poses unique problems of accommodation. Were judicial review added to the already onerous burdens which the landlord assumes when he contracts with the FHA, the net effect would be to discourage private investment.

Notes on Rent Regulation

1. Beginning in 1968, the federal government began to phase out the section 221(d)(3) program [involved in *Hahn*], replacing it—as to new projects—with the section 236 "interest reduction" program, but this program, too, actively relies on limited-profit investors. The limitation on profits (to a six percent

annual return on investment), plus various cost-reduction subsidies, are designed to bring rentals within the means of moderate-income tenants. Rent regulation serves a dual purpose: to assure the economic viability of the project; to limit the investor's return. Thus the controlled rental should be both the minimum and the maximum charge for the unit. Just so with public utility rate-making!

Trouble arises when the income of subsidized tenants does not climb fast enough to meet increases in property taxes and other operating costs. Unlike public housing, where a tenant's rent is a fixed percentage of his income (although even there, rising costs have forced the percentage somewhat higher), the tenants in a section 221(d)(3) or section 236 project may have widely varying capacities to absorb rental increases; therefore, an across-the-board absolute increase in rent will result in much higher percentage-of-income increases for some tenants than for others. This causes tension between the goals of economic soundness and assured investor return on the one hand and relatively inexpensive housing for lower income families on the other hand.

One tack might be to adopt, whenever feasible, the public housing formula requiring that *all* subsidized tenants pay a designated part of their income for shelter. Thus, tenant A might pay more than tenant B pays for an identical unit; the aggregated rentals would provide the investor with his margin of profit. Since tenant A still pays below the market rental for his unit, can he complain legally that his rental dollar brings less shelter than does tenant B's?

An alternative tack is to charge equivalent rentals for equivalent units, but furnish rent supplements to tenants not able to pay comfortably the full rental charge. The court's opinion cites the federal rent supplement program (on the books since

1965) as mitigating the hardship on individual tenants ["Plaintiffs' interests are not threatened by every rent increase, and other forms of relief, such as rent supplements, are available"]. Available, but not readily! Never a favored program, rent supplement has benefited only 70,000 families from its adoption through fiscal 1972. Moreover, quite stringent guidelines limit the percentage of rent supplemented units within each 221(d)(3) or 236 project. Other limitations on the availability of rent supplements are the federal requirements that a local government must ask for rent supplements (and many have refused to do so), the income ceiling on families eligible for rent supplement (well below the income needed for 221(d)(3) housing), and the unwillingness of project sponsors to keep poorer families. For fuller discussion, see Lefcoe, HUD's Authority to Mandate Tenants' Rights in Public Housing, 80 Yale L.J. 463, 499–500 (1971).

2. The court's opinion makes much of a so-called distinction between "legislative [rate-making]" proceedings and adjudicatory, and after classifying the rent increase application as legislative, accepts Professor Davis' wisdom that a formal adversary hearing may contribute little or nothing to the agency's understanding of the issues. The court also depreciates the tenant's ability to handle such matters as the landlord's financial condition, the intricacies of project management, or the state of the economy in the surrounding area. Note, however, that at the court-ordered hearing to which they were no longer entitled, tenants had already succeeded in convincing FHA that landlord should get only $22.00 of the $28.00 monthly increase he was seeking, and even that increase was to be staged over two years. What forms of expert testimony must tenants present to challenge a landlord's application for increase? At the rate-making stage, can

the FHA be expected to act as the consumers' watchdog? ("Hopefully, the FHA can check the accuracy of the landlord's documentation without their assistance.") A pious hope?

Having rejected the tenants' claim for an agency hearing, the court uses similar argument to turn down judicial review. "Courts are ill-equipped to superintend economic and managerial decisions of the kind involved here." Since courts regularly review rate-making decisions of federal and state regulatory commissions, do the rents of a subsidized housing project present unique and potentially insoluble issues for appellate review? Suppose that the FHA grants rental increases which give the investor better than a six percent annual review: If Hahn v. Gottlieb remains the law, are the project's occupants without recourse? Suppose that tenants refuse to pay the increase and are sued for eviction for non-payment of rent: In the eviction proceeding, may tenants question whether landlord may validly charge the higher rent?

Are the constitutional issues bearing on the tenant's right to a hearing and judicial review any different in public housing than in subsidized, privately owned housing? Note the First Circuit's earlier readiness to find "government" in this very 221(d)(3) project. McQueen v. Druker, supra. Under the theory of Escalera, may public housing tenants obtain a formal hearing whenever an LHA applies to HUD for a rental increase? Whenever an LHA seeks to evict a tenant for refusing to pay the increase? Does the HUD Circular on grievance procedures, supra, require a hearing on proposed public housing rent increases?

3. Is it realistic that private investment *would* be discouraged if agency hearings and judicial review were added to the constraints facing 221(d)(3) or 236 sponsors? Even if this were provable, is it relevant in deciding the merits

of a constitutional claim that tenants have been denied procedural due process? Should the supplies of subsidized housing be subject to any less regulation than, let us say, the supplies of electrical power?

4. If the ultimate problem is that of poverty—the inability of tenants to pay rental increases, why bother to fashion elaborate procedural safeguards which may delay but not necessarily avert the duty to pay more rent?

5. Governmentally subsidized housing projects were not covered by the Stage II rent guidelines which limited regulated landlords to an annual 2.5 percent rent increase (plus the right to pass on higher real estate taxes). Why should subsidized landlords have been regulated less stringently than were non-subsidized landlords? Might a non-subsidized landlord, able to prove an annual investment yield below six percent, have validly challenged his regulation as a denial of equal protection?

SECTION 3. HOUSING SUB-SIDIES

A. WHY DO WE NEED HOUSING SUBSIDIES?

---

1. The Components of Housing Costs

REPORT OF THE NATIONAL COMMISSION ON URBAN PROBLEMS

Building The American City (1968) pp. 417–27.

THE COMPONENTS OF HOUSING COSTS

A few basic principles should be stated at the outset. *First*, whether housing is public or private, subsidized or unsub-

sidized, the basic components of costs are the same. The fact that the rent of a public housing tenant, for example, does not include amortization of development costs does not mean that there have been no such costs. It means simply that the burden of such costs is borne by society. Similarly, where the Government subsidizes various costs of private housing—such as interest rates or property tax deductions—the costs do not disappear, but rather are shifted from the tenants (or homeowners) to the government.[1]

Second, homeownership and rental housing involve, for the most part, the same basic cost elements; apparent differences reflect the manner in which payments are made rather than differences in cost components. The tenant pays the cost of insurance, mortgage amortization, maintenance, and the rest through his monthly rental payments, while the homeowner pays them directly. The one major item of cost which the tenant bears but the homeowner does not is the charge for management services, including salaries of management personnel and return on the owner's investment. The homeowner, in effect, performs his own management functions and realizes as a return on his investment only imputed rent and perhaps appreciation in the value of the property.

The costs of housing—whether rental or ownership—can be broken down in a

---

[1] There may, of course, be differences in the actual "level" of a particular cost component which vary with the public, private or subsidized nature of a particular project. Costs of management, for example, may differ because of differences between public and private pay scales. The cost of money (i. e., financing cost) will differ depending on whether the government borrows against its own credit, as in public housing and 221 (d)(3) housing, or subsidizes borrowing from private sources charging market interest rates, as in the new 235 and 236 programs. Building specifications, sources of supply, procedures and the like may also differ in ways which affect costs.

number of ways. They can be thought of in terms of the kind of economic resource involved (land, materials, investment capital, and labor) or the service for which the charge is made (construction, financing, insurance, etc.). One widely accepted method for considering costs is to distinguish operating and development costs. The former consist of charges for heat and utilities, maintenance and repairs, management services, taxes and other assessments, and insurance. Development costs are those involved in building and marketing the housing and include the costs of land, site improvement, construction, overhead, profit, marketing, interim and permanent financing. * * *

The single-family house

(1) *Development Costs.*—In 1966, new FHA 203 single-family housing was developed at a median value per house of $18,099, and an average sales price of $17,731. Only 25 percent of all such houses were valued at less than $15,000; 0.2 percent at less than $9,000. On the average, slightly less than 20 percent of FHA value was attributable to land and site improvement costs, with the remaining 80 percent accounting for all other development costs. This 80 percent amounted to $12.16 per square foot of living space. * * *

TABLE 2.—SELECTED COMPONENTS OF COST AS A PERCENTAGE OF TOTAL DEVELOPMENT COST FOR SINGLE-FAMILY HOUSES, 1966

Items	Representative	Range
Site	15	10–19
Construction:		
Direct	66	61–74
Indirect	3	2–5
Subtotal	84	80–87
Financing	3	1–4
Marketing	4	2–5
Administrative and general	6	5–8
Net profit before taxes	3	2–6

Source: Based on an NAHB survey, using model accounting system, of approximately 40 builders in all parts of the Nation in 1966, each producing an average of 30 to 100 homes per year. Selling prices of homes ranged from $10,000 to $100,000

* * * The remaining development costs—marketing, financing, profit, and overhead—vary within a range of 16 to 28 percent.

The home buyer normally pays for the development costs over time by means of a mortgage. Monthly payments are made to amortize the mortgage principal (development cost less down payment) and to cover interest on the unpaid balance.

(2) *Operating Costs.*—The homeowner directly pays the costs of maintaining his property and meeting current operating charges. Table 3 shows average operating expenses and their relationship to debt service and total monthly housing expense:

TABLE 3.—MONTHLY OWNERSHIP EXPENSE OF NEW FHA (203) HOUSES: 1966

Items	Average expense per month	Percent
Monthly expense for housing	$159.74	100.0
Debt service, principal and interest on mortgage and FHA insurance premium	93.80	58.7
Hazard insurance	4.05	2.3
Taxes and assessments	21.25	13.3
Maintenance and repair	9.66	6.1
Heating and utilities	23.67	14.8
Miscellaneous	7.36	4.6

Source: FHA 203 Homes, Series Data Handbook, a Supplement to FHA Trends (203b), 1966, RR 251. . . .

The sum of monthly debt service and operating expenses is the total housing expense to the homeowners. As table 3 shows, the average total expense on new FHA 203 houses in 1966 was $159.74. The range in the continental United States was from a low of $129.17 in Kentucky to $195.49 in California. The average FHA homeowner spent 27.7 percent of his net effective income [5] on his monthly housing expense.

[5] The FHA-estimated amount of the mortgagor's earning capacity, after deductions for Federal income taxes, that is likely to prevail during the first third of the mortgage term.

Assuming a 90-percent, 25-year mortgage on an $18,000 home (mortgage value equals $16,200) at a rate of 7 percent, for example, monthly payments will be $114.51. In 1966, the average debt service on FHA 203 houses was $93.80 a month.

Multifamily housing

Multifamily housing includes a variety of housing types. Under some definitions it contains every type of structure from two-family or semidetached units to high-rise apartments. In this discussion multifamily housing includes only structures containing three or more dwelling units. These consist of low-rise and high-rise buildings. Low-rise structures include row houses, garden apartments and other walkup buildings in which upper stories are accessible by stairs only. High-rise structures are buildings with elevators.

Because of this variety of housing types and the range of unit and room sizes in multifamily dwellings, average figures are even more suspect than those for single-family houses. Again, however, they are presented to provide a general idea of levels and relationships.

(1) *Development Costs.*—Table 5 presents figures for all HUD multifamily programs.

TABLE 5.—SELECTED COMPONENT COSTS OF HUD MULTIUNIT HOUSING: PROJECTS BEGUN IN 1966

	High	Median	Low
Development cost/unit ..	$36,001	$15,650	$ 7,702
Site cost/unit	6,361	2,252	265
Size, square feet/unit ..	1,954	963	433
Structure cost/square feet	[1] 29.69	12.49	6.82
Turner Apartment Index, costs/square feet	21.37	16.67	12.80

[1] This figure is abnormally high. The figure for the next highest is $21.16.

Sources: Department of Housing and Urban Development and Turner Construction Co. The Turner Index is based on unit prices for apartments built for private owners to rent on a commercial basis, which include luxury buildings.

The average of $15,650 per unit for total development costs, with an average structure cost of $12.49 per square foot, corresponds generally to figures of $18,099 and $12.16 for FHA 203 single-family housing.

* * * As with homeownership, the development costs of rental property are normally financed by a mortgage. With rental property, the debt service is included in the monthly rental charge.

(2) *Operating costs.*[6]—In addition to paying a pro rata share of interest and amortization of mortgage principal, the tenant pays for operating expenses in his monthly rent. These expenses are basically the same as those incurred by the homeowner, except that they include the cost of management services, which the homeowner provides for himself. * *

* * * The FHA value of new single-family FHA 203 housing in the postwar period has increased 100 percent since 1948. In the 1958–66 period, average sales price increased by 23.5 percent. A new price index from the Census Bureau, issued in July 1968, indicates an increase of approximately 10 percent in the sales prices of single family houses sold during the period 1963–67. * * *

Though comparable, detailed data on cost trends for rental housing are not available, it appears that similar increases —reflecting the same underlying trends in component costs—occurred in multifamily housing. * * *

* * * *Site costs*

The single most dramatic increase in the cost of a major component has occurred in site costs. The average site cost for FHA 203 houses in 1966, $3,-

[6] Most of the data on operating costs and monthly rentals was obtained from the Institute of Real Estate Management of the National Association of Real Estate Boards.

544, was more than 3⅓ times higher than the price of $1,049 in 1948. * *

* * * Site costs consist of the costs of land acquisition and site improvement, and both have increased at astounding rates. Land acquisition costs are a function of many factors, including population increases, distance from the central city or from major regional facilities, access to transportation, zoning, etc. Geographic differences are significant, though substantial increases in lot prices have occurred in virtually every part of the Nation. * * * In multifamily structures, the story is very much the same. Land acquisition costs for public housing in New York, for example, increased by 48 percent from 1957–59 to 1964–66, and for limited profit, moderate-income housing in New York these costs increased by 59 percent from 1957 to 1967.

Site improvement costs are incurred in preparing a site for building and providing required facilities for servicing the building once erected. Where redevelopment occurs or initial development takes place on an isolated lot in a builtup area, such costs involve preparing the site itself for the structure—clearing it, excavating, grading, landscaping, and the like—and connecting plumbing facilities to existing sewer and water systems. Where land is newly subdivided, site development costs may, in addition, include the provision of streets, curbs, sidewalks, gutters, street lighting, sewers, and a variety of other facilities required by a subdivision ordinance. * * *

* * * Site development cost increases have, in some places, outstripped even the very rapid rise in land acquisition costs. Thus, for example, the 59-percent increase in land acquisition costs for limited profit, moderate-income housing in New York between 1957 and 1967 was accompanied by a 150 percent increase in site improvement costs, mak-

ing for a total site cost increase of 79 percent.

Site improvement costs vary with the geographical nature of the area and characteristics of the terrain on which a particular project is located. More important, in most places, than peculiar geological conditions, however, are the requirements of local subdivision regulations, which prescribe standards for streets, curbs, lighting, and other utilities. * * *

* * * The different standards which cause the major variations in cost concerned street paving, sidewalks, and trees. [One township,] for example, requires subdividers only to construct gravel and oil topped roads and it has no requirements for sidewalks or trees.

Site improvement costs also depend on the size of lots and, more particularly, on the width of lots. Lot width determines the number of linear feet of improvements required to service one house, and each additional foot results in added costs.[10]

Structure costs

The costs of constructing the building itself represent the largest single element of development costs. Structure costs may be divided into four categories: (1) foundations, frame and shell; (2) interior finish; (3) mechanicals; and (4) major appliances. * * *

* * * The major ingredients in structure costs are labor and materials. * * * Direct labor costs represented slightly more than 40 percent of structure cost in 1966, with materials and job overhead making up the remainder.

Labor input, of course, varies with the particular operation to be performed. Thus, onsite labor for steel or concrete

---

[10] See a more complete discussion of the effects of zoning ordinances and subdivision regulations on site costs contained in Part III.

generally accounts for 20–25 percent of the total costs of these particular items. On the other hand, labor accounts for 75 percent of the cost of painting and decorating and 60 percent of the cost for masonry.

The materials and labor components appear to have increased at quite different rates. As of May 1968, the price of all construction materials had increased by 10.2 percent from the 1957–59 figures, according to the Wholesale Price Index. Variations among particular materials were substantial.

Wage rates for construction workers have increased steadily in recent years. Average hourly earnings and average weekly earnings for construction workers increased 53 and 57 percent during the period 1957–59 to May 1968, exclusive of fringe benefits. Union hourly wages in the building trades increased 44.6 percent from 1957–59 to 1967. Fringe benefits have also shown substantial increases. The special mechanical trades, including electricians, plumbers and other workers employed in heating, ventilation, air conditioning, generally experienced the highest wage increases.

Financing and closing costs.

Another major factor in the increasing costs of housing is the substantial increase in financing costs in recent years. Two basic types of financing costs must be considered. *First*, there is the so-called interim financing cost, which consists of financing costs incurred by the developer and builder during the time of land assembly, site preparation, construction and marketing but prior to the actual sale or rental of the structure. Money is needed during this period to finance the purchase of materials, labor and various other types of inputs. These costs may amount to as much as 6 percent or more of the selling price. * * * They are determined by the amount the developer or builder must borrow, the term of the

loan, and the interest rate. Thus, the cost of interim financing will generally increase as structure costs and the time required for construction increase. Normally the interest rate on interim financing is about the same as that on permanent financing, though the shorter term of interim financing loans may result in some minor variations. In tight money situations, the rate on interim financing will normally be somewhat higher than that on permanent financing, especially for multifamily construction.

The *second* type of financing cost is permanent financing—the cost required to amortize the selling price. Mortgage interest rates for permanent home mortgages are determined by a variety of complex economic factors of which construction activity and demand for home mortgages are only a part. National monetary policy and fiscal policy and the demand for funds by governments and individuals all play a part. Fluctuations in mortgage interest rates can be substantial, depending upon how these numerous factors converge at any one time. Moreover, differing local conditions and sluggish responses to demand and supply pressures in local areas make for differences in prevailing rates in various localities and regions at any one time.

Permanent financing charges are levied by the lender in two ways. First, they are imposed as the stated interest charges on the unpaid balance of the mortgage loan. In this form they are borne directly by the home owner and, in the case of rental property, by the tenant as one element of his monthly payments. Second, they take the form of points charged against the mortgage amount (one point equalling 1 percent of the principal) at the time the loan is made.

Charges for points arise primarily in connection with FHA-insured mortgages. They are a device by which the lender can achieve a market yield on his loan despite the imposition by FHA of a ceiling on stated interest rates. In recent years they have also been used in connection with conventional mortgages to increase yields where State usury laws impose ceilings below going market rates. Under FHA regulations the buyer of a house cannot be required to pay more than 1 point; the seller must pay the rest. In fact, the seller of new housing considers his payment for points as a cost and thus passes it along to the buyer in the selling price. * * *

The combination of the stated interest rate and points is the effective yield to the lender and, in one form or another, it is the buyer who bears these costs. Despite occasional short-term declines in home mortgage interest rates, the postwar trend in yields has been almost steadily upward. In the early 1950's, yields on conventional mortgages commonly were about 5¼ to 5½ percent. For the last few years, they have more normally been about 6½ percent, and still more recently they have gone above 7 percent. In response to these trends and in an effort to limit the number of points, several States have found it necessary to increase statutory interest ceilings. * * *

* * * Closely related to financing costs are closing costs, which include a package of charges related to obtaining permanent financing and transferring title to the property. Since such costs are normally paid for in the first instance by the buyer and not included in the selling price, they are often left out of cost computations. Such costs vary substantially depending on local "closing" and title insurance practices. * * * Average closing costs on FHA 203 houses in 1966 amounted to $394, or 2.2 percent of sales price. From 1957–59 to 1966, such costs increased by 33 percent.

Other Development Costs

In addition to site, structure, and financing costs, development costs include profit, overhead, marketing, and fees of various types (e. g., charges for the services of architects and lawyers). Considered together, these costs, as reported, range from 16 to 28 percent of total development costs. * * *

* * * Discussions with knowledgeable builders and real estate investors suggest that the average builder of single-family homes usually aims for a profit of 15 to 20 percent of gross sales, where profit includes gains on all cost components. Thus, for example, a builder may add an 8-percent fee on a house in which all cost factors add up to $20,000, making the selling price $21,600. One cost item may be $5,000 for land which in fact the builder acquired for only $1,000, 10 years earlier. If, after deducting property taxes and interest during the holding period, the profit on land amounts to $2,720, then total profit to the builder is $4,320 ($2,720 plus $1,600), or 20 percent.

Builders' overhead and profit and architects' fees are included as "fees"

TABLE 14.—MONTHLY PAYMENTS ON A $15,000 MORTGAGE AT VARIOUS TERMS AND INTEREST RATES

Term (years)	Interest rates (percent)							
	3½	4	4½	5	5½	6	6½	7
10.........	$148.33	$151.87	$155.46	$159.10	$162.79	$166.53	$170.32	$174.16
15.........	107.23	110.95	114.75	118.62	122.56	126.58	130.67	134.82
20.........	86.99	90.90	94.90	98.99	103.18	107.46	111.84	116.30
25.........	75.00	79.18	83.37	87.69	92.11	96.65	101.28	106.02
30.........	67.36	71.61	76.00	80.52	85.17	89.93	94.81	99.80
35.........	61.99	66.42	70.99	75.70	80.55	85.53	90.62	95.83
40.........	58.11	62.69	67.43	72.33	77.37	82.53	87.82	93.21
50.........	52.98	57.86	62.91	68.12	73.48	78.96	84.56	90.25

Source: Commercial and industrial mortgage tables, Mortgage Publications Co., Boston, Mass.

for HUD multifamily projects. Median
figures are generally about 11 percent.
Again, additional "profit" may be present in cost items not designated as
such. In a number of HUD programs—
including 220, 221(d)(3) (limited
dividend), 221(d)(4) and 231 (for
profit)—a 10-percent builder and sponsor's fee for profit and risk are allowed
by law. In others, a sliding scale guide is
generally used to determine an appropriate builder's fee, beginning at 10 percent for projects of up to $100,000 and
going down at higher amounts to a low
of 4.25 percent for projects over $12
million.

Operating Costs

Operating costs, as noted above, today
account for about one-half the rental
charge on multifamily homes. Of this
amount, heat, utilities, and property taxes
represent the largest items. * * *

Increases in operating expenses have
been among the most substantial percentage increases in costs. Heat and utilities
for FHA 203 housing increased by 30
percent from 1959 to 1966; maintenance
and repair rose by 33 percent; and taxes
and assessments by 40 percent during the
same period. * * *

2. The Existing Housing Subsidies

A DECENT HOME: THE REPORT OF THE PRESIDENT'S COMMIT-TEE ON URBAN HOUSING

(1968), pp. 59–79.

II. Principal Federal Housing Subsidy Programs

There are a great many Federal housing programs. Most are administered by
HUD, but the Veterans Administration,
the Farmers Home Administration, and
the Department of Defense all have significant housing programs of their own.
Many of the HUD programs, like the

traditional mortgage insurance programs
of FHA, do not involve the subsidization
of housing costs. The major HUD housing subsidy programs are outlined below.
* * *

Public Housing

Although the layman may refer to all
Government-assisted housing as "public
housing," the term is used by housing
professionals only to denote the specific
program begun in 1937. The Public
Housing program, as it has traditionally
operated, places responsibility for development, ownership, and management of
subsidized rental projects in the hands of
independent local government agencies
called housing authorities. A local housing authority cannot receive Federal assistance without the approval of both its
local government and the Housing Assistance Administration, a subdivision of
the Department of Housing and Urban
Development. Some state laws go further and require local government approval of specific sites. Some jurisdictions, like the entire states of California
and Texas, require that the Federal contract to support Public Housing projects
be approved by local voters in referenda.
Although practically all large cities have
established housing authorities, many
small jurisdictions, particularly suburban
ones, do not participate in the program.
For example, in 1967 less than half of
the localities with populations between
25,000 and 50,000 had housing authorities.

A housing authority generally can only
build within the boundaries of the local
jurisdiction which established it. In addition, since 1954 Public Housing projects cannot be built in areas which do not
have HUD-certified Workable Programs
for community improvement. Thus, local governments which do not wish to
have more subsidized projects located
within their boundaries can "veto" them
by simply letting their Workable Programs lapse. The result of all these

forces is that most urban Public Housing projects have been located in decaying areas of central cities.

Rents in Public Housing are lowered through a number of subsidies, both Federal and local. The cost of project development is financed with long-term tax-exempt local bonds. This tax exemption lowers direct debt retirement costs. The Federal Government makes annual contributions to the local housing authority which cover all costs of retiring the bonds. The Federal Government is also authorized to pay a local authority an additional $120 per year for the benefit of each family which is elderly, displaced, extremely poor, or contains four or more children. Lastly, public housing projects do not pay normal local real estate taxes but instead pay lower amounts in-lieu-of-taxes.

Because of these substantial subsidies, admission to public housing projects is restricted to families whose incomes are below limits established by the local housing authority under statutory Federal guidelines. At the end of 1964 the median income limit for admission for a family of two adults and two children, in localities within urbanized areas, was $4,-000. The highest limit ($5,760) was in New York City. The median income of all families admitted to Public Housing in recent years has been roughly $2,500. The median rent for all public housing units is approximately $45. Roughly one-half of all public housing units are occupied by Negro tenants and one-third by elderly persons. Given the inadequate coverage and size of welfare payments, there are still millions of families who are too poor to live in public housing projects. Even those who live there may have to commit a disproportionate share of their incomes to pay the low rents.

Local housing authorities also set income limits for continued occupancy of public housing, normally at 125 percent of the limits for admission. Until a few years ago, tenants who earned more than

the limits for continued occupancy were evicted—a practice widely believed to be damaging to incentives and to add to the instability within public housing. Recently, this practice has been softened somewhat.

The Public Housing program has been exclusively a rental program. Some recent efforts have been made to encourage ownership by tenants. For most of its history, Congressional pressure has required that projects have few amenities. This has proved to be short-sighted since many projects have been so distinctive in appearance that they have tended to stigmatize the neighborhoods in which they are located and the tenants themselves. Fortunately, in recent years there has been some change in attitude, and HUD has attempted, with some notable results, to encourage good design.

In 1967, the Public Housing program included some 650,000 units which housed almost 2.4 million persons. This figure dwarfs production totals under the other programs described below, principally because Public Housing was the only housing subsidy program in the United States until the last decade. Table 2–1 presents production figures for all Public Housing programs between 1939 and 1967. Production has been rather erratic, at least until recent years; the highest production peaks were reached in 1941 and 1952–53.

TABLE 2–1. LOW-RENT PUBLIC HOUSING UNITS COMPLETED, ACQUIRED, OR LEASED FOR CALENDAR YEARS 1939–67

1939	4,960	1954	44,293
1940	34,308	1955	20,899
1941	61,065	1956	11,993
1942	36,172	1957	10,513
1943	24,296	1958	15,472
1944	3,269	1959	21,939
1945	2,080	1960	16,401
1946	1,925	1961	20,965
1947	466	1962	28,682
1948	1,348	1963	27,327
1949	547	1964	24,488
1950	1,255	1965	30,769
1951	10,246	1966	31,483
1952	58,258	1967	38,756
1953	58,214		

Source: Housing Assistance Administration.

Some housing experts believe that the conventional Public Housing program as presently structured has proved to be an awkward method of producing housing. The requirement of local government approval of sites (not to mention problems raised by local referenda and the Workable Program requirement) has restricted the expansion of the program since Public Housing has rarely proved to be a popular neighbor. In addition, housing authorities have been criticized for using authoritarian management policies typified by complex tenant regulations. Surveys indicate that many poor families believe that public housing will not offer them an attractive living environment. Many even prefer to live in unsubsidized, substandard private buildings. HUD has recently begun to place careful controls on project size, on use of high rise structures, on design, and has encouraged more flexible management, all in an effort to make future public housing projects more attractive. * * *

At its inception Public Housing offered the private sector few opportunities to participate. The "conventional" system of developing public housing followed the usual public works format, limiting the role of the private entrepreneur to that of contractor. The private sector was afforded no opportunity to be a developer of housing (purchasing land, supervising the design, constructing the building, selling or leasing all or a portion of the completed project) or to be a builder (supervising the design and constructing the building) or even to be a manager of a completed project. However, in recent years opportunities for private participation in the development and management of public housing have been greatly expanded.

1. Turnkey 1 (Development)

The Turnkey process, started by the Department of Housing and Urban Development on an experimental basis in January of 1966, permits a local Public Housing authority to enter into a commitment to eventually purchase a housing project (land and building) from a private developer who has built the project in accordance with plans approved by the authority. The purchase price is established under a procedure set forth in the contract between the parties and contains ample protection for both. * * *

This Turnkey I program is very much like the turnkey process often employed by the private sector for the development of new plants. In this system the purchaser contracts with a builder to design and build a plant to certain specifications; a predetermined price is paid when the keys to the completed building are delivered.

The details of the Turnkey process in public housing are as follows:

a. *Selection of developer.* The local housing authority can accept solicited or unsolicited proposals for development of a project. The proposal should contain a preliminary price for land and building; a description of the site, including a city-wide map showing the relationship of the site to schools, shopping centers and transportation; a rough sketch of a feasible site plan with a rough sketch of the building and typical units, and description of the type of construction and heating system to be used.

b. *Letter designating turnkey developer.* The local authority selects a developer on the basis of the suitablility and feasibility of the proposal. No further selection or bidding process is required. Once selected, the authority will send a letter to the developer notifying him that his proposal has been approved and requesting him to prepare and submit preliminary plans, specifications, and a proposed sales price subdivided into land cost, construction cost, and architectural and engineering cost services.

c. Negotiation and execution of letter of intent. Upon receiving the "Letter Designating Turnkey Developer," the developer submits preliminary plans, outline specifications, evidence of ownership of the site (or that the developer will own the site prior to the start of construction), and a sales price. This submission must be complete enough to permit the local authority to obtain two independent land appraisals and construction cost estimates. On the basis of these independent estimates, the local authority negotiates a purchase price which is inserted in a Letter of Intent and executed by the developer and the authority and then approved by HUD.

The "Letter of Intent to Enter into Contract of Sale of Low-Rent Housing Project to Local Authority" obligates the parties to enter into a contract to sell the finished project when completed in accordance with plans prepared by the developer and approved by the local authority. The parties agree that the sale price shall be the lesser of (1) the price stated in the Letter of Intent or (2) the sum of (a) the negotiated land price, (b) architectural and engineering fees, and (c) the midpoint between two independent cost estimates based upon the final working drawings and detailed construction specifications. To protect the developer, the Letter provides that if the final cost estimate is less than 95 percent of the price stated in the Letter of Intent, and if the parties cannot negotiate an acceptable purchase price, then the developer may sell the site together with the plans, and the local authority must purchase the land and plans for a price equal to the stated value of the site and the stated cost of preparing plans and performing architectural and engineering services. If the parties agree not to sell the site, the developer must absorb the cost of the plans.

The Letter of Intent also contains a timetable for submission and approval of plans and execution of the Contract of Sale. In the event that there is a delay in the submission or approval of plans, the construction cost estimate is adjusted in accordance with the percentage change in the Department of Commerce composite cost index.

d. Execution of contract of sale. After execution of the Letter of Intent the developer prepares and submits working drawings and detailed specifications. The local authority obtains a cost estimate based upon these final plans. Once the final cost estimates are available, the parties execute the Contract of Sale. The price is determined in accordance with the pricing procedure set out in the Letter of Intent.

e. Construction and purchase. After execution of the Contract of Sale, work on the site proceeds. If required, Federal guarantees of interim financing can be arranged. Upon completion of the project, title is transferred to the local authority.

The program is based on the belief that involving the private sector in acquisition of sites and preparation of plans will produce public housing more quickly and at less cost. While precise results must await completion of a study now underway within the HAA, preliminary indications suggest that these objectives are being attained. * * *

2. Turnkey II Management

The Department of Housing and Urban Development has recently tried on an experimental basis the private *management* of housing projects owned by public authorities. This new practice, called Turnkey II, is a logical extension of the Turnkey I program. * * *

* * * At the present time management contracts are negotiated on the basis of an agreed budget plus a fixed fee. The local authority pays the direct expenses or reimburses the management firm for them. The management firm receives a fee based on that customarily paid for

comparable services in the locality. The firm is required to manage the project within the annual budget. The budget may be revised for good cause with approval by the local authority and HUD.

While almost any type of fee arrangement is legally possible, HUD's budget plus fixed fee contract protects both the public interest and the owner from excessive risks. The parties can negotiate a budget containing a maximum figure which affords the manager a reasonable operating margin. Since the public agency pays only actual costs, in the event the manager is able to operate economically, the savings are passed along to the public.

Turnkey II can also add variety to the type and character of the housing to be provided. The proposed Lavanburg Foundation development in New York City, one of the pilot projects announced by HUD, is an illustration. The Lavanburg Foundation, a nonprofit organization, proposes to develop and sell to the New York City Housing Authority on a Turnkey basis an undivided interest in the residential portion of a project which includes moderate-income housing and accompanying commercial, recreational, medical, and community facilities. In addition, the Foundation will retain complete management responsibility by negotiating a Turnkey II management contract for the Housing Authority's project activities. In this manner, public housing tenants will be provided with a conventional housing setting. Any Public Housing tenant whose income exceeds Public Housing levels will be permitted to remain in the development and will receive the benefits of the moderate-income assistance. The transfer of a tenant from one program to another would appear only as a book entry.

[Editors: There is also a Turnkey III program, which HUD announced September 18, 1967. This program offers ownership to public housing occupants. Typ-

ically, tenants are given lease-purchase contracts when they have earned, out of the self-maintenance of their units, a "sweat equity" of at least $350. A low-income family may, as its income increases, accelerate its acquisition of ownership by making extra contributions of money, which are added to its sweat equity. The program remains experimental.]

3. Leasing Program

The new Section 23 leasing program authorizes local Public Housing authorities to lease privately owned real estate for occupancy by families eligible for Public Housing. The difference between the rental received by the landlord and that part paid by the tenant—the subsidy —is contributed, subject to limitations as to amount, by the Federal Government.

HUD anticipates that in fiscal year 1969 the leasing techniques will account for approximately 16 percent of the total number of subsidized units to be provided under all Federal subsidy programs. Although only three years old, this program has proved the feasibility of subsidizing existing standard housing.

The leasing technique allows the private housing market to make existing standard housing units available to Public Housing authorities at market rentals. The private property owner executes a lease with the local housing authority. Selection of tenants is usually the function of the local authority. Rentals to be charged are decided by negotiation. The power to give notice to vacate is reserved to the local authority. The lease provisions fixing responsibility for maintenance and replacement (including redecoration) are required to conform to standard practice for the rental of other units in the building.

Section 23 of the U. S. Housing Act restricts the lease term to one to five years. However, with the approval of

HUD, the lease may contain renewal options to be exercised at the discretion of the parties or automatically, which could extend the term to 10 years, or longer in rare instances. The Section 10(c) leasing program permits leasing up to 40 years. This program, however, requires:

1. The existence of an approved "Workable Program," and

2. Partial tax exemption or tax remission by the local community.

* * *

Both the Section 10(c) and Section 23 programs limit the use of Federal subsidies to existing structures. While this will not prohibit local authorities from executing leases with developers prior to the construction of a property, it does expose the local authority and the developer of a new project to unnecessary risks since there is no absolute assurance that the Federal subsidies will be available. It increases the difficulties of financing low-income housing development. The restriction of the leasing program to existing structures and the limitations placed on the Section 23 lease term unnecessarily complicate a program which offers substantial opportunity for the private sector to develop public housing. * * *

202 and 221(d)(3) Below Market Interest Rate Programs

These two low-interest loan programs, although differing in details, use the same subsidy technique and are best analyzed together. The 202 program begun in 1959 is administered by the Housing Assistance Administration which is also responsible for Public Housing. The subsidy used is a direct loan from HUD to sponsoring nonprofit corporations, originally at an interest rate based on the oustanding Federal debt and since 1965 at a flat 3 percent interest rate. Profit-motivated sponsors are not permitted to own these projects; only elderly or handicapped persons may live in 202 projects. Current income limits for tenant eligibility are the lesser of: (1) $4,500 per year for single persons, and $5,400 per year for two person families; or (2) 80 percent of the appropriate 221(d)(3) BMIR limits. Under this program, HUD also provides the interim financing needed for construction, again at a 3 percent rate of interest. The permanent loans may have a term of up to 50 years and can cover up to 100 percent of the costs of a project. Projects built under 202 are *not* restricted to jurisdictions which have HUD-approved Workable Programs.

The 221(d)(3) Below Market Interest Rate program (221(d)(3) BMIR), a considerably broader program than 202 in terms of eligible sponsors and eligible tenants, was begun in 1961. FNMA is now authorized to purchase 221(d)(3) mortgages bearing interest rates of 3 percent. Unlike 202, profit-seeking corporations as well as nonprofit ones can own 221(d)(3) projects. FHA, which administers 221(d)(3), prevents undue profits by requiring cost certification and by controlling rent levels and the distribution of profits. Interim financing must be arranged with conventional private lenders at market interest rates. The maximum term for the low-interest permanent mortgages has been established by HUD regulation at 40 years. The mortgage can cover up to 100 percent of replacement costs for nonprofit and cooperative sponsors and 90 percent for profit-oriented sponsors.

The majority of 221(d)(3) projects consist of newly constructed row houses and walkup apartments. They are either rental projects or cooperatives. They must be located in communities which have Workable Programs, a requirement which has restricted use of 221(d)(3).

The availability of a 3 percent loan permits a reduction of monthly rents in 221(d)(3) and 202 units of roughly $30 to $40 below the rents which would be charged if they were financed with market-rate mortgages. The income limits for admission to 221(d)(3) BMIR projects are usually several thousand dollars higher than the limit for admission to public housing in the same area. Income limits are established by HUD and depend upon family size and geographic area. * * *

Both the 202 and 221(d)(3) programs have certain disadvantages inherent in any below-market interest rate programs. Federal accounting techniques require that a Government purchase of a mortgage be treated as an expenditure in the year of purchase, but no credit is given to the fact that a mortgage is an asset. The result is a substantial increase in the apparent Government deficit for the year in question. In addition, it is difficult to adjust the amount of subsidy provided to a project through a low-interest loan to the varying needs of individual families living in that project. As a result of these budgetary and flexibility problems, the more recent housing subsidy programs—Rent Supplements and the new Homeownership and Rental programs—rely not on low-interest loans but on annual Federal payments to reduce housing costs. This approach spreads out the budgetary impact over several decades and permits better correlation of the amount of subsidy with the needs of the recipient.

As of June 1967, 62,000 units of 221 (d)(3) BMIR housing had been completed or were under construction. Roughly one-half of these units had been built by profit-motivated developers and about one-half by nonprofit and cooperative sponsors. * * *

Rent Supplement

The Rent Supplement program was offered by the Administration in 1965 as a substitute for 221(d)(3) BMIR. Under the rent supplement technique, the tenant family pays 25 percent of its income toward rent, while the Federal Government pays directly to the landlord the difference between economic rent levels and the tenant's contribution. This approach has the advantages of keying the amount of subsidy to the tenant's need and of spreading the cost to the Federal Government over a long period. In its deliberations on the Housing Act of 1965, Congress did not accept the Administration's recommendation that the Rent Supplement program be aimed at moderate-income families as well as low-income families. Instead, it adopted the Rent Supplement program only after restricting eligibility for supplements to families whose incomes on admission are below the eligibility limits for Public Housing in the same locality. In addition, Congress continued the 221(d)(3) program instead of substituting the Rent Supplement program for it as the Administration had recommended.

In essence, the Rent Supplement program attempts to shift the responsibility for building and operating low-rent housing projects from the local housing authorities (relied on in the Public Housing program) to private groups, both profit-motivated and nonprofit. After receiving approval of a proposed project from FHA (which administers the program), the private housing owner finances his project with a private mortgage at the market interest rate. On completion of construction, the housing owner rents units in the project to any family he chooses. However, not all tenants in a project are eligible for supplements. To be eligible, a family must have a low income (one below limits established by the Secretary of HUD which themselves must be below the limit for admission to Public Housing in that area), have few assets, and be a member of one of the following deserving groups: elderly, handicapped, displaced by Government action or natural disaster, or now living in substandard housing. As mentioned, these eligible tenants pay 25 percent of their income toward rent, and the Federal Government pays any remainder directly to the landlord. Tenants who are not eligible for supplements pay the entire rent themselves. As a tenant's income rises, his supplement is reduced. For this reason, a family whose income rises substantially after admission to a Rent Supplement project is not required to leave it.

Congress passed the Rent Supplement program by the smallest of margins in 1965 and has since limited its implementation in a number of ways. The program has received few appropriations; in fact it has barely survived attacks during the appropriations stage. To mollify Congressional pressures, HUD has been forced to impose regulations on the program which have made it increasingly unworkable. One regulation requires that in no instance may a tenant receive a supplement which exceeds 70 percent of the fair market rental of the unit. Other regulations which have proved to be very damaging to the program establish specific dollar limits on construction costs and on maximum fair market rentals. These low maximums inhibit production and force those who do build to produce rather austere projects. Still other regulations flatly prohibit even some of the limited amenities allowed in 221(d) (3) BMIR projects.

The limits on maximum rents and construction cost have made the Rent Supplement program generally unworkable for new construction in major central cities outside the South and Southwest. In addition, the limitations on amenities have made the program much less attractive to builders since they now fear they will be unable to produce a project which will appeal to those ineligible for supplements. At present, both builders and FHA generally assume that at least 90 percent of the tenants in Rent Supple-

ment projects will in fact receive supplements. Thus, these regulations, which have been forced on HUD by Congressional pressure, defeat the Administration's goal of economically integrated tenancies within projects and scare away builders who are reluctant to own projects housing mostly low-income families.

The Appropriations Committees have also restricted the program through riders on appropriations bills. The Rent Supplement program as enacted is largely free of the Workable Program requirement. One rider has restricted location of Rent Supplement projects to localities which either have Workable Programs or whose governments approve the projects. Another rider has increased the equity requirements for nonprofit sponsors who receive special assistance from GNMA. Congress's hostility to the Rent Supplement program has severely restricted production under it. Twelve hundred units were started under the program in fiscal year 1967 and about 12,000 in fiscal year 1968. * * *

Section 236 Rental Housing Program

The new 236 program, part of the Housing Act of 1968, is designed to replace eventually both the 202 and 221(d) (3) programs. Like the Rent Supplement program, it relies on private developers—both nonprofit and profit-oriented—of rental or cooperative housing. The subsidy technique is similar to that used in the Rent Supplement program: tenants pay 25 percent of their income toward rent, and the Federal Government pays a supplement which makes up the difference between a tenant's payment and market rents. There is, however, a crucial difference. The maximum Federal payment on a unit lowers the rent to the level which would be achieved had the project been financed with a 1 percent mortgage. Thus, the primary difference between 236 and the Rent Supplement program is that the subsidy under 236 is not as deep.

The maximum Federal subsidy to a tenant per month will be about $50 to $60. This is not enough to reach the poorest families. To be eligible, a family's income (less $300 per child) must not exceed 135 percent of the limits for admission to Public Housing projects. Thus, 236 will serve primarily families whose incomes range between $4,000 and $6,500 per year. In high cost areas, such as Detroit, tenant incomes must be higher unless families chose to allocate more than 25 percent of gross income to housing. To alleviate this problem partially, 20 percent of the units of a 236 project can be occupied by tenants receiving Rent Supplement payments and who thus might have lower incomes.

In some communities the basic income limits for the 236 program may be too low to make the program economically feasible. Not only would the very poor not be able to afford these projects, but moderate-income families may be excluded because they exceed the rather low income limits. In many communities, particularly higher-cost urban centers, the income spectrum the 236 program can serve may have been narrowed so much that some builders will be reluctant to participate in the program for fear they will be unable to find enough eligible tenants willing to occupy the units. However, some relief is provided by a provision permitting 20 percent of the appropriations to be used for families whose incomes exceed the limits for admission, but whose incomes are still below 90 percent of the 221(d)(3) BMIR limits in that area (with $300 deductions for each minor child).

Despite this feasibility issue and the inability of the 236 program to reach very poor families, it has several advantages over the earlier moderate-income programs. It offers deeper subsidies

than those available under 202 and 221 (d)(3) BMIR by providing the equivalent of 1 percent loans instead of 3 percent loans. In addition, it avoids the budgetary impact problems raised by direct loan programs and provides a technique for adjusting the amount of subsidy to a tenant's income. Lastly, the program is not subject to the Workable Program requirement, which does apply to 221(d) (3). * * *

Homeownership Program—Section 235

The Homeownership program contained in the Housing Act of 1968 is a major landmark in the history of Federal housing legislation. Prior to its enactment, all major housing subsidy programs were limited to rental units, with cooperative housing units permitted in a few instances.

Assistance under the new Homeownership program generally will be restricted to new or substantially rehabilitated units. Private homebuilders will plan the housing and have it approved by FHA for inclusion in the program prior to the beginning of construction. When built, the houses will be sold to eligible buyers who will finance their purchases with FHA-insured market rate mortgages from private lenders. The subsidy technique used is similar to that in the Section 236 rental program. The Federal Government contracts to pay part of the homebuyer's mortgage payments. The maximum Government subsidy reduces the homebuyer's payment to that which he would owe if his purchase had been financed with a mortgage bearing an interest rate of 1 percent. Translated into dollars, the maximum subsidy will be about $40 to $70 a month, depending on the value of the house and the market interest rate. The actual amount of the subsidy may be somewhat less, depending on the income of the family buying the house. All families must devote at least

20 percent of their income to paying off the mortgage. (This figure of 20 percent is lower than the 25 percent used under the rental programs because the homebuyer must bear all utility charges, maintenance, and repair expenses himself.) As family income rises, the Federal payments due to the lender consequently will be gradually reduced and eventually eliminated. Because the maximum Federal subsidy is limited, the program will not be of much help to families with very low incomes. However, it will provide assistance to those in the broad range of incomes between $3,000 and $7,000 a year. Some examples might help explain how the program works. Assuming a $15,000, 35-year mortgage at 6¾ percent, the required monthly payment due the lender (counting principal and interest due on the mortgage, mortgage insurance premium, hazard insurance, and taxes) would be $125. A family with an annual income of $6,000 would pay $100 of this, while the Government would pay the remaining $25. A family with an annual income of $4,000 or less would pay $68 a month, and the Government would pay the remaining $57.

Houses built under the program will be of modest but adequate quality. In general, the mortgage on a house cannot exceed $15,000. A mortgage of up to $17,500 is allowed in high-cost areas and of up to $20,000 for large families in high-cost areas. Down payments would be low, as little as $200 for some families, and in no case greater than 3 percent of the value of the house.

During the debate in Congress, the hottest issue was whether the eligibility for assistance under the Homeownership program should be restricted to persons below certain income levels. Such limits, of course, were not strictly necessary since the amount of subsidy is automatically keyed to the homebuyer's income and thus the well-to-do could not have received any benefits even if there were no income limits. Congress eventually adopted income limits like those used in the Section 236 program. Assistance payments are restricted to homebuyers who, when they buy the houses, have incomes (less $300 per child) which do not exceed 135 percent of the income limits for admission to Public Housing projects in that locality. These limits are roughly $5,000–$6,000 per year for four-person families in major metropolitan areas.

Although the program is restricted primarily to new construction and substantial rehabilitation, a limited number of families, such as those displaced by Government action, can qualify for assistance in the purchase of an existing house. Public or private agencies will be hired to counsel families who need help in assuming the responsibilities of homeownership. Families which have imperfect but acceptable credit histories or irregular income patterns which would normally disqualify them from mortgage insurance under FHA programs, but who still make reasonably satisfactory risks, may participate in the program. * * *

[Editors: Despite, or perhaps because of the stepped-up volume of units subsidized under public housing and sections 235 and 236 from 1970–1972, see page 765 infra, the Nixon administration early in 1973 called for an 18-months moratorium in the issuance of new subsidy commitments. Whether these programs will be ultimately continued, modified, or replaced (possibly by a housing allowance scheme) is yet to be seen.]

Subsidies for Rehabilitation

All programs discussed above can be used to subsidize housing costs in rehabilitated dwellings. In addition to these programs, there are a number of relatively minor ones which can be used only for rehabilitation. Two of these, the Section 312 loan program and Section 115 rehabilitation grant program, can only be used within limited Urban Renewal or Concentrated Code Enforcement areas. In fact, they are administered by the Renewal Assistance Administration in HUD which is generally responsible for the Urban Renewal programs. The Section 312 program, enacted in 1964, provides direct 3 percent loans to homeowners, the proceeds of which can be used for rehabilitation and, if necessary, also for refinancing existing mortgages. The 312 program was the first to authorize Federal housing loans at less than the average cost of Federal borrowing.

The Section 115 rehabilitation grant program, also designed to support the Urban Renewal process, was begun in 1965. Only families who own and oc-cupy their own homes and who have very low incomes are eligible for these grants. The maximum grant now available is $3,000.

A third rehabilitation subsidy program, Section 221(h), was enacted in 1966. This program is extremely limited in scope. Its main significance is that it provided a historical precedent for the Homeownership program of 1968 into which it has been merged. Sponsors of 221(h) projects must be nonprofit organizations. These nonprofit sponsors acquire and rehabilitate single-family units and then sell them to families whose incomes are below Public Housing income limits. The subsidy provided is a 3 percent 25-year mortgage purchased by FNMA. This subsidy is often inadequate to enable these families to participate in the program. * * *

TABLE 2–2. AVERAGE OR MINIMUM REQUIRED RENTALS ON NEWLY CONSTRUCTED ONE- AND TWO-BEDROOM APARTMENTS UNDER DIFFERENT FEDERAL HOUSING PROGRAMS AND THE REQUIRED FAMILY INCOME IMPLIED AT SPECIFIED RENT-INCOME RATIOS *

Program	Required annual (monthly) rentals on units with—		Required income at rent-income ratios of 20 or 25 percent for families occupying—			
			One bedroom		Two bedrooms	
	One bedroom	Two bedrooms	20 percent	25 percent	20 percent	25 percent
207 average (no subsidy)	$2,270 ($189)	$2,719 ($227)	$11,350	$9,080	$13,595	$10,876
Public Housing average	905 (75)	1,161 (97)	4,525	3,620	5,805	4,644
Rent Supplement minimum	472 (39)	540 (45)	2,360	1,888	2,700	2,160
236 minimum	1,472 (123)	1,763 (147)	7,360	5,888	8,815	7,052
221(d) (3) BMIR average	1,664 (139)	1,993 (166)	8,320	6,656	9,965	7,972

* The calculations apply to Detroit in 1967 and cities with similar cost levels. Within the group of cities with more than 2 million inhabitants, Detroit had the lowest dwelling construction cost limits for Public Housing in 1966. They were at the same level as those in Dallas (population 1.1 million in 1960). Development cost limits in all other cases except the Rent Supplement program (RS) were assumed to be equal to those specified for 221(d)(3) BMIR. These were $14,150 for one-bedroom and $16,950 for a two-bedroom dwelling unit. No rent supplement projects have been completed in Detroit by 1967.
  Source: Von Furstenberg and Moskof: Federally Assisted Rental Housing Programs: Which Income Groups Have They Served or Whom Can They Be Expected To Serve?

HOUSE COMM. ON BANKING AND CURRENCY, SUBCOMM. ON HOUSING

92d Cong., 1st Sess., Pamels 467–470 (June 1971).

TABLE I.—BASIC CHARACTERISTICS OF MAJOR ACTIVE HOUSING SUBSIDY PROGRAMS

Characteristic	Public housing	Rent supplements	Sec. 236 rental	Sec. 235 homeownership	Rural housing (ownership)
1. Type of sponsor/owner.	Local housing authority	Nonprofit, cooperative, limited-distribution mortgagor.	Nonprofit, cooperative, limited-distribution mortgagor.	Eligible owners (see below).	Eligible owners (see below).
2. Type of housing.	New construction, acquisition and rehabilitation, leased existing housing, single or multifamily.	New or substantially rehabilitated, 5 or more units.	New or substantially rehabilitated projects, 5 or more units.	New, rehabilitated, existing. Single- or 2-family dwellings. Condominium units.	New, rehabilitated, existing. Single-family dwellings.
3. Eligible tenants/owners.	Low-income households; limits set by local authorities, typically $4,000 to $5,000 for 4-person family. Limits for continued occupancy higher than for admission.	Low-income households in same income range as public housing. Must be displaced by governmental action, elderly, handicapped or occupants of substandard housing. Supplements may also be paid to occupants of 221(d)(3), 202, 231 and 236 projects under limited circumstances.	Low-to-moderate income households with incomes up to 135 percent of public housing levels; 20 percent of payments may go to families above this level but not more than 90 percent of 221(d)(3) limits. Typical limits are $6,000 to $8,000 for 4-person family.	Low-to-moderate income households (Same as Sec. 236.)	Low- and moderate-income families residing in rural communities not more than 5,500 population. 1970 act increased limit to 10,000. Income limit is $8,000.
4. Mortgage or cost limits.	Determined by HUD on basis of prototype cost for type of structure and area. Current average cost of new units is about $20,000.	FHA unit limits for 221(d)(3) which vary by size and type of unit. Unit limit of $22,000 administratively applied.	Same as for 221(d)(3) and rent supplements (see previous column).	$18,000 ($21,000 in high-cost area); $21,000 for 5 or more person families ($24,000 in high-cost area).	No fixed limits. Units average $12,500.
5. Subsidy mechanism.	Federal payment of annual debt service on tax-exempt local authority bonds covering capital cost. In addition there are special subsidies for elderly, displaced, large families and those too poor to cover operating costs with 25 percent of their income.	Federal payments to cover difference between 25 percent of tenant income and fair market rent. Payment may not exceed 70 percent of fair market rent. Mortgages are FHA market rate, except for limited use of supplements to piggyback other subsidized programs.	Federal interest reduction payments on FHA insured market rate mortgages. Payments equal difference between amount required for principal, interest, and mortgage insurance premium and the same amount required if interest rate were 1 percent. Tenants must pay 25 percent of income for rent. If this exceeds operating cost plus principal and interest at 1 percent the excess payment is refunded to the Government.	Federal interest reduction payments to mortgagees on behalf of low-income homeowners with FHA insured market rate mortgages. Payments may not exceed difference between principal, interest, and mortgage insurance premium and principal and interest at 1 percent rate. Tenants must pay at least 20 percent of income toward principal, interest, insurance, and taxes.	Federally insured loans to rural homeowners. Interest rate is normally about 1 percent below market rate with Farmers Home Administration absorbing the difference in subsidy payments to loan purchasers. Loan rates may be reduced to as low as 1 percent in same manner as in sec. 235 program. About 20 percent of families so subsidized.
6. Administrative agency.	Department of Housing and Urban Development.	Department of Housing and Urban Development.	Department of Housing and Urban Development.	Department of Housing and Urban Development.	Department of Agriculture, Farmers Home Administration.

[A7407]

TABLE II.—FEDERAL COSTS OF MAJOR ACTIVE HOUSING SUBSIDY PROGRAMS

	Public housing	Rent supplements	Sec. 236 rental	Sec. 235 home-ownership	Rural housing
1. Annual budget obligations:					
Subsidy payments:					
Fiscal year 1971	$655,000,000	$47,000,000	$35,000,000	$117,000,000	[1] $40,000,000
Fiscal year 1972	$825,000,000	$91,000,000	$151,000,000[2]	$299,000,000[2]	[1] $57,000,000[3]
2. Administrative cost	[2]				
3. Average subsidy cost per unit (estimated payments, fiscal year 1971).	$700	$981	$871	$857	$163
4. Average subsidy cost per unit (estimated contract reservation, fiscal year 1971).	$1,480 (new conventional); $78 (special subsidies); $50 (estimated loss on tax exemption).	$1,500 (market-rate projects); $900 (236 piggy-back).	$1,113	$1,107	$163

[1] Due to asset sales transactions, actual outlays are negative. Amounts shown above are for premium interest payments to purchasers of housing loans—roughly the interest subsidy involved.

[2] HUD administrative expenses not separately identified by program. 1972 estimate for all subsidy programs is $33,000,000.

[3] Not separately identified but probably over $50,000,000 due largely to servicing costs.

TABLE III.—PRINCIPAL BENEFITS OF MAJOR ACTIVE HOUSING SUBSIDY PROGRAMS

	Public housing	Rent supplements [1]	Sec. 236, rental	Sec. 235, home-ownership	Rural housing (ownership)
1. Units assisted:					
(a) Total June 30, 1970	864,769	25,409	5,439	65,654	358,000
(b) Units added, fiscal year 1971	106,000	15,000	88,263	155,746	78,600
(c) Units added, fiscal year 1972	92,000	30,000	129,700	188,600	121,800
(d) Total June 30, 1972	1,062,769	70,409	223,402	409,990	558,400
2. Family income (median)	[2] $2,548	$2,185	$5,303	$5,760	$6,425
3. Monthly rents (median)	$50	$51	$115	[3] $85	[3] $105
4. Estimated monthly subsidy [4]	$60	$86	$73	$71	$14
5. Implied rent as percent of income ..	24	28	26	18	19
6. Nonwhite occupants (percent)	51	37	[5] 40	30	20
7. Elderly occupants (percent)	36	34	[5] 7	4	NA
8. Family size (median persons per unit)	3.6	3.2	[5] 3.3	4.0	NA

[1] Includes market rate projects only.
[2] Elderly, $1,753.
[3] Homeowners payment toward principal and interest. Excludes utilities and other homeowner operating expenses.
[4] Federal cash costs only.
[5] Data based on 221(d)(3) experience. Assumes sec. 236 experience will be similar.

TABLE V.—DISTRIBUTION OF SUBSIDIZED RENTAL HOUSING UNITS BY PROGRAM [1]

[In percent]

	Public housing	Rent supplements	Sec. 236 rental	Sec. 221(d)(3)	All four programs
1. Regional concentration by census region:					
(a) Northeast	31.8	10.2	3.2	27.6	30.0
(b) North central	20.5	17.5	33.7	33.4	22.9
(c) South	37.7	52.8	38.6	26.0	36.0
(d) West	10.0	19.5	24.5	13.0	11.1
2. Regional concentration relative to low-income population: [2] by census region:					
(a) Northeast	164	53	16	142	155
(b) North central	93	79	152	151	104
(c) South	83	117	85	57	79
(d) West	76	148	186	98	84
3. Intra-metropolitan distribution: [3]					
(a) Blighted area	([4])	27	22	35	10
(b) Other inner city area	([4])	25	5	14	16
(c) Other areas within city limits	([4])	39	61	37	47
(d) Suburban	([4])	9	12	14	27
4. Relation to other programs: [3]					
(a) Minority concentration	([5])	37	21	42	30
(b) Model cities areas	([5])	10	7	3	3
(c) Urban renewal areas	([5])	7	13	21	13

[1] Data drawn from unpublished paper by George M. Von Furstenberg "A Synopsis of Federally Assisted Rental Housing with Special Reference to the Distribution of Services by Size of Family and by Regions and States," 1970.
[2] 1968 census data, poverty level plus 25 percent.
[3] Based on FHA survey data, 1970.
[4] Data not available. About one-third to one-half estimated to be in blighted areas.
[5] Not available.

3. The Freedom of Choice Alternative: The Housing Allowance Approach

THE HOUSING ALLOWANCE APPROACH

Frank de Leeuw.

(This paper was prepared at the request of the Subcommittee on Housing of the Committee on Banking and Currency, U. S. House of Representatives, 92d. Cong., 1st Sess., and appears in Panels 541–547, 552–553 (June 1971).

I. INTRODUCTION

Discussion of housing allowances in this country has picked up notably in recent years, although proposals for a system of allowances or rent certificates date back at least to the 1930's. The President's Committee on Urban Housing was attracted to the idea of a housing allowance and recommended experimentation. The Housing Act of 1970 authorizes a housing allowance experiment; and two model cities programs include small allowance plans. Furthermore, some of the present housing programs—notably the Section 23 Leasing Program—resemble a housing allowance in some respects.

This paper summarizes work which has gone on for the past year at the Urban Institute on the housing allowance approach. The paper is organized around three issues: design, costs, and market effects. The section on design indicates the similarities and differences between housing allowances and other housing and income assistance programs, and describes three alternative housing allowance plans. The section on costs presents estimates of how many individuals and families there are which cannot afford "adequate housing" at a "reasonable percentage of income," and discusses the cost of meeting this "housing gap" through a housing allowance plan. The section on market effects discusses the extent to which housing allowances on a large scale would drive up rents without providing more housing services. It is very difficult to be at all certain about market effects, and our conclusions here are subject to revision as we learn more about housing market behavior.

The paper concludes with my own tentative evaluation of the housing allowance approach. At this stage in our work, it appears to me that housing allowances are feasible and are probably simpler and less costly than some of the more traditional housing programs, at least if allowances are not introduced suddenly on a large scale. It appears to me much more difficult, however, to make a case for more emphasis on housing allowances as compared to a reformed system of general income maintenance. If a housing allowance approach is adopted, furthermore, it will be very important to integrate it carefully into the entire system of income assistance and housing programs in operation.

II. DESIGN: THREE HOUSING ALLOWANCE PLANS

To place the housing allowance approach in perspective it is helpful to begin with a definition. Housing allowances are defined as "a general system of grants to low-income households intended to be spent largely on housing." The first part of the definition, "a general system of grants," means that housing allowances are not tied to particular newly-constructed or rehabilitated units. That is the obvious difference between the housing allowance approach and many existing housing programs. A vast portion of the existing housing stock would qualify for occupancy under a housing allowance, whereas it does not qualify under many current programs. The second part of the definition, "intended to be spent largely on housing," differentiates a housing allowance from a program of general income assistance. There would be an attempt to insure that a substantial proportion of any assistance under a housing allowance program was actually spent on housing. Under existing welfare programs the trend is away from any such earmarking of funds.

The housing allowance approach thus falls in between general income maintenance plans and many traditional housing programs. Income transfer programs such as social security or proposed family assistance plans tend to have a minimum of public participation in the actual provision of services. Housing programs such as Public Housing or Section 236 and its predecessors involve public participation at many stages in providing services. Housing allowances fall in between the two. There is some attempt to channel the assistance into a particular kind of service, but beyond that there is no detailed public participation in the provision of the service.

Requiring or encouraging an allowance to be spent on housing rather than on other goods and services is by no means a simple or costless process. Table 1 describes three plans under which an allowance might be channeled into housing, and lists some of the characteristics of each method. The first plan, called the rent certificate plan, is similar to a food stamp plan. An eligible household pays some percentage of its income, and in return receives a certificate worth more than its payment. The value of the certificate varies by size of household. The certificate can be redeemed only by a certified landlord; this requirement is what tends to channel the money into housing. In the form just described, a certificate plan could only apply easily to renter households. Low-income homeowners would have to be assisted through some other means.

The second plan, called the minimum-condition plan, pays a cash grant to a low-income household provided that the dwelling unit it occupies meets certain standards of plumbing, kitchen facilities, space per person, and other conditions. Again, the amount of the grant depends on a household's income and its size. The second plan resembles a program of general income assistance (the proposed family assistance plan, for example) with the additional requirement that in order to get assistance, a family must reside in a unit meeting certain minimum standards.

The third plan, labeled the percentage-of-rent plan pays each eligible household a subsidy equal to some fraction of its actual rental expenditures. The fraction would be largest for poorest households

TABLE 1.—3 HOUSING ALLOWANCE PLANS

Plan	Size of allowance	Form of payment	Conditions attached to allowance	Separate program for owner-occupants
1. Rent certificate	Difference between a "cost of adequate housing" and some percentage of household income.	Certificate redeemable by landlord.	Income below some cut-off level.	Yes.
2. Minimum housing condition.	do	Cash	Income below some cut-off level. Inspection and certification of unit.	No.
3. Percentage of rent	Percentage of actual rent paid; percentage declines as income rises.	do	Income below some cut-off level. Certification of rental cost.	Yes.

and would decline to zero as income rises to some breakeven point. Like the rent certificate plan, this plan applies in its simplest form only to renter households and there would have to be some other way of dealing with low-income home-owners.

Each of these plans is a feasible way to implement a system of housing allow-ances. Each has its administrative and economic advantages and drawbacks, de-tailed in a working paper;[2] but space permits only three general observations here. First, while the plans are listed as three alternative comprehensive pro-grams, there is no reason why they could not be combined with one another in various ways or combined with other types of income and housing programs. For example, the percentage-of-rent and minimum-condition plans could be com-bined by paying a percentage of rent to low-income households provided their units meet certain minimum conditions. Second, each of the plans requires a sub-stantial amount of administrative machin-ery—to determine eligibility, certify land-lords, inspect units, or verify rents, de-pending on the plan. Much of this work overlaps administrative functions of other federal or local programs and may offer opportunities for consolidation of admin-istration. Third, the outcome of any of the plans is highly sensitive to how allow-ance payments are treated under other in-come payment programs, and how these other programs—the main ones are social security and public assistance—affect elig-ibility and size of payment under a hous-ing allowance.

This third point requires some elabora-tion. Both the number of households eligible for a housing allowance and ac-tual payments to them will be much larger if the allowance is based on a concept of earned income—not including public as-

sistance, social security, or other transfer programs—than if it is based on income including these other benefits. Con-versely, public assistance and certain oth-er payments will be larger if they do not take account of housing allowance bene-fits than if they do. Thus, arrangements in which each assistance program "ig-nores" benefits under other programs tend to maximize the amount of assist-ance low-income families receive.

Arrangements in which one program "ignores" another, however, raise severe problems. One of them is that there may be no incentive, or very little incentive, for households in certain income ranges to increase their earned income; reduc-tions in benefits of all kinds approach or even exceed increases in earnings. Another problem is that such arrange-ments make it extremely difficult to move toward a simpler, more equitable system by allowing one comprehensive program gradually to replace some of the others. My feeling therefore is that a housing allowance program should be based on a comprehensive income concept including other transfer payments, and that these other transfer payments should be calcu-lated before determining eligibility and payments under an allowance.

Experimental housing allowance pro-grams planned or underway might well focus on a comparison of the benefits to participants, costs, and administrative problems of various housing allowance plans. A large-scale experimental proj-ect could try out several plans and per-haps more than one schedule of benefits under each plan, and compare what hap-pens to eligible households and what problems arise in administering the plans.

III. Costs: The Size of the Housing Problem

We turn now from issues of program design to issues of costs: specifically to the questions of (a) how many households in the United States can't afford adequate

2 See "The Design of a Housing Allow-ance," The Urban Institute, Washington, D. C.; Working Paper No. 112-25, 1970.

housing at a reasonable percentage of income and the size of the "housing gap" between what these households can afford and the cost of adequate housing, and (b) what the relationship is of these estimates to the likely cost of a housing allowance program. Answering these questions is one way to begin to develop an estimate of what it would cost to enable everyone to live in adequate housing.

A. THE SIZE OF THE "HOUSING GAP"

The concepts of "the cost of adequate housing" and "a reasonable percentage of income" are necessarily subjective. That does not mean that the concepts are meaningless, however; it is meaningful and useful to attempt to define them in a way which accords with general feelings in this country about desirable standards of housing and appropriate budget proportions devoted to housing. The definitions we have used are shown in Table 2.

The "cost of adequate housing" figures in the table refer to an area of average housing cost and to the year 1969. They would of course be lower for a low-cost area like the rural South, and higher for a high-cost area like Chicago; and they would be higher today than they were in 1969. They are based partly on experience under the Section 23 Leasing Program in various localities scattered throughout the country and partly on Bureau of Labor Statistics surveys of rental costs in 39 metropolitan areas.[3] They therefore embody the housing standards used in bringing units under lease in the Section 23 program and in selecting the sample of units in the BLS study. Generally speaking, these standards include structural soundness, complete plumbing and kitchen facilities, and absence of crowding, but very few "luxury" services such as air conditioning or extra bathrooms. The percentages in column (3) are approximately the average percentage which renter families spend on housing.

Equipped with these definitions, we can now ask the question of how many households there are which can't afford the costs listed in column (2) at the percentages of income listed in column (3). There are still problems in translating the definition into a set of estimates. It is necessary to take account of geographic differences in housing cost, equity in owner-occupied houses, and other complications. Even in an area of average costs, some households are able to buy adequate housing for less than the amounts in column (2), while others live in inadequate housing in spite of spending as much as the column (2) amounts or more. Let me refer at this point to the working paper by John Heinberg, which describes

TABLE 2.—DEFINITIONS OF HOUSING STANDARDS AND PERCENTAGES OF
INCOME, BY SIZE OF HOUSEHOLD (1969)

(1)	(2)		(3)
	Cost of adequate housing		"Reasonable percentage of income"
Size of household	Per year	Per month	
1 person	$ 840	$ 70	30–35
2 persons	1,032	86	25–30
3 persons	1,224	102	20–25
4 persons	1,320	110	20–25
5 persons	1,464	122	20–25
6 persons	1,608	134	20–25
7 plus persons	1,704	142	20–25

Note: The "per month" cost figures have been rounded.

[3] The BLS survey results for 1969 are reported in the U. S. Department of Labor, "Three Budgets for an Urban Family of Four Persons: Final Spring 1969 Cost Estimates," December 1970.

the problems and procedures in some detail.[4] For purposes of this paper it is sufficient simply to give the results.

The results are 12.8 to 16.8 million households which can't afford adequate housing at a reasonable percentage of income, and a "housing gap," as of 1969, of $5.1 to $7.0 billion between what these households can afford at a reasonable fraction of income and the cost of adequate housing for them. The range between the upper and lower figures is due to the range of percentages listed in column (3). HUD programs—principally public housing—were providing assistance for about 700 thousand of the 12.8 to 16.8 million households in 1969, and were filling about $0.4 billion of the "housing gap."

These estimates immediately provoke a number of questions. One of them is why the estimated number of households is so much larger than the number of substandard dwelling units as estimated from Census or other sources. The estimates of households are larger than the estimates of number of substandard units principally for three reasons. The first is that a count of substandard units does not take in those households which occupy adequate housing but do so only at a percentage of their income higher than what we have defined as "reasonable." The second is that a count of substandard units does not take account of those persons who dwell in standard units, but at a high density—households, that is, which reduce costs below the estimates in Table 2 at the expense of crowding. The third is that the standards embodied in the estimates of "the cost of adequate housing" probably average somewhat above the minimum requirements for a "standard" unit in Census tabulations.

[4] See "The Transfer Cost of a Housing Allowance: Conceptual Issues and Benefit Patterns," Working Paper No. 112-18. The Urban Institute, 1971.

The estimates also provoke questions about who these 12.8 to 16.8 million households are. The detailed calculations underlying the estimates indicate that 35 to 40 percent of them are single-person households, and 15 percent of them are households with six or more members (these large households, however, include 35 percent of the *individuals* in the full group). About 60 percent of them live in metropolitan areas. Low-income homeowners constitute 40 percent of them, an estimate which depends on the assumption that owner-occupancy of an adequate unit costs as much as rental housing but that owner-occupant incomes should be increased by five percent of their equity in the homes they occupy.

B.   THE COST OF AN ALLOWANCE PROGRAM

The "housing gap" estimate of $5.1 to $7.0 billion is not the same thing as an estimate of what a national housing allowance would cost. In the first place, the "housing gap" estimate fails to take account of the cost of administering a housing allowance program, with its earmarking requirements and its likely duplication of at least some functions of other income transfer programs. In the second place, the "housing gap" estimates fail to take account of the fact that a large-scale allowance program would itself drive up housing prices and rents, and would therefore increase the necessary cost of adequate shelter above the amounts which were used in defining the cost of adequate housing above. In the third place, and working in the opposite direction, HUD subsidy programs are currently filling some portion of the "housing gap" (the estimates, while they make no deductions for HUD subsidies, do allow for the contribution made by cash-grant programs such as social security and public assistance).

Our estimate is that the cost of administering a comprehensive allowance program would amount to $0.7 to $0.9 billion per year. We believe that the effect of a comprehensive allowance program on the housing market would raise the "cost of adequate housing" by something like 12 percent.[5] Basing an allowance on this higher cost would in turn increase the number of eligible households by about 2 million and the size of the "housing gap" by about $2 billion. HUD programs contributed about $0.4 billion toward closing the "housing gap" in 1969. Thus a crude estimate of the annual cost of enabling *every* household to occupy adequate housing at a reasonable percentage of income would be the $5.1–$7.0 billion gap plus $0.7–$0.9 billion plus $2.0 billion, minus $0.4 billion, or $7.4–$9.5 billion per year.[6]

Now under an actual allowance program it seems almost certain that only some fraction of all the households with a "housing gap" would elect to participate in the program. We probably know enough to design programs that would attract the vast majority of potentially eligible households, programs that would attract only a modest proportion of these households, programs that would appeal much more to large households than to small households, and programs that would affect decisions to participate in a number of other ways. The participation fraction, as well as the estimate of the "gap" itself, is highly sensitive to how generously low-income homeowners are treated under an allowance program and to what the cost of adequate housing is assumed to be for a homeowner.

[5] The 12 percent is the result of assuming that the increased housing demand due to the allowance amounts to about 40 percent of total housing expenditures by participants and that about 30 percent of the increased demand goes into higher rents (a fraction discussed in the next section of this paper).

[6] This estimate assumes no significant "work incentive" effects from a housing allowance program.

The estimate of program costs of $7.4 to $9.5 billion, for these reasons, is a *maximum* of what an allowance program would cost. An actual program would probably cost less than the maximum, and could cost only a small fraction of the maximum if it were designed initially to fill only a part of the "housing gap" or to appeal to only certain types of eligible households.

Even using the maximum cost (and the additional 2 million participating households), it is noteworthy that costs amount to only about $500 per year per household. This is much lower than the average subsidy per unit under many current federal housing programs. A small-scale allowance program, furthermore—for example, one which covered no more households than current HUD programs—would have still lower costs per household, since it would presumably affect prices and rents much less than a comprehensive program. A new unit of public housing, in contrast, involves an explicit annual subsidy of more than $1000 and involves further hidden subsidies in the cost of foregone state and local property tax revenues and foregone income tax revenues from holders of tax-exempt public housing bonds.

Why should there be such a large difference between this cost per household under the housing allowance approach and the cost under some of the conventional approaches? In the case of public housing, an important part of the explanation is that many of the households have extremely low incomes and hence large differences between the "cost of adequate housing" and a "reasonable" percentage of income. But that is not true of most of the other conventional programs, and does not explain all of the difference even for new public housing. I believe that one part of the explanation is that utilizing the existing stock is a much more cost-effective way of obtaining housing than bidding for resources in the new construction market. It is significant in this connection that the cost of a unit of existing housing under the Section 23 Leasing Program appear to be appreciably lower than costs per unit converted to an annual basis for new public housing.[7] * * *

C. EVALUATION

An evaluation of the housing allowance approach must be labeled "tentative" at this point. An experimental allowance program and additional statistical analysis may modify some judgments. Furthermore, the work we have done deals with the economics of housing allowances, not with their social or political effects.

With those caveats, my personal evaluation of the housing allowance approach can be summarized in four propositions.

First, a housing allowance program would succeed in improving the housing conditions of many low-income households. Although an allowance program would raise administrative problems and cause some increase in rents and housing prices, it would also bring about substantial change in the housing services received by participating households.

Second, there is a strong case in favor of more emphasis on housing allowances versus emphasis on some of the important existing housing programs. Housing allowances would act on a vast portion of the existing housing stock that many of our current programs don't directly affect at all, and the housing allowance approach may well result in more housing services per dollar spent than new construction-type subsidies.

---

[7] The cost comparison, part of current Institute work on the section 23 program, takes account of the greater durability of new public housing by amortizing the capital costs over 40 years. It does not put a money value on other differences between new public housing and leased existing housing, some of which favor one form of subsidy and some the other.

Third, it is difficult to make a case for emphasis on housing allowances versus emphasis on a reformed system of public assistance or general income maintenance. Housing allowances would probably involve a substantial expansion or duplication of the administrative functions of existing programs, and would probably have effects on rents that would be more severe than the corresponding price effects of general income maintenance. These seem to me substantial disadvantages. Any advantages of emphasizing housing assistance rather than general income assistance—advantages such as political support or contribution to slum neighborhood confidence—need to be weighed against these disadvantages.

Finally, the way in which a housing allowance relates to social security, public assistance, and other forms of income assistance has a critical effect on the outcome and political acceptability of an allowance program. A sensible way to relate a housing allowance to other programs would be to determine eligibility for the allowance and size of payment *after* calculation of other assistance payments, treating other payments as additions to income.

B. ELIGIBILITY PROCEDURES AND STANDARDS

PUBLIC HOUSING AND THE POOR: AN OVERVIEW
LAWRENCE M. FRIEDMAN

54 Calif.L.Rev. 642 (1966).

A. *Tenant Selection*

Tenant eligibility is determined by statute and local rule. Federal law makes relatively few demands on administration, insisting only that only poor persons be allowed in public housing. The Wagner-Steagall Act limited tenancy to "families of low income" who could not "afford to pay enough to cause private enterprise in their locality * * * to build an adequate supply of decent, safe, and sanitary dwellings for their use." Income limits were part of the federal law—the Act was restricted to families "whose net income at the time of admission does not exceed five times the rental." [68] Between 1949 and 1961, the federal statute specifically stated that public housing agencies were not to "discriminate against families, otherwise eligible for admission to [public] housing, because their incomes are derived in whole or in part from public assistance." Federal law also asks local agencies to adopt admission policies which "give full consideration" to their "responsibility for the rehousing of displaced families,—to the applicant's status as a serviceman or veteran," his age, disability, housing conditions, and urgency of housing need. Other than this, federal law is silent on eligibility for public housing; and indeed, the statute offers little guidance as to the administration of projects or the termination of tenancy. In the 1950's, during the palmy days of McCarthyism, the so-called "Gwinn amendment" briefly made non-membership in subversive organizations a condition of tenancy. The Gwinn amendment reminds us of the *possibility* that onerous conditions for eligibility can be written into federal law. On the other hand, the life of the Gwinn amendment was short and the reaction of courts quite hostile. The experiment has not been repeated.

State laws are not much more explicit than federal law. The states have followed the federal lead in prescribing income limits. More than thirty states have the five-to-one ratio or some variant; a few have a different ratio, or a flexible maximum coupled with a general requirement of poverty; a few simply delegate authority to local projects to fix rent scales.[75] Some states specifically provide for the problem of the over-income tenant; in New Jersey, for example, he may continue to occupy his quarters until his income is more than twenty-five per cent over the maximum for entry. A few states add a detail here or there—by spelling out their preference for veterans, for example. But in the main, tenant selection is controlled by the housing authorities themselves. Some of them have their own preference lists—giving special place or exemption from some prerequisite to veterans, to persons in desperate need of housing, or even to students.[78]

The selection process has not been carefully studied. If there were abuses, no one in government seemed to have heard of them. Within categories of preference, selection is made on a first-come-first-served basis, although screening out of "undesirables" is often practiced with the aid of social workers. If responsible officials discriminated among applicants there would be no machinery for correcting these abuses. We may be fairly confident that "discrimination" in the usual sense does not occur. One cannot think of any reasons offhand why officials should play favorites. Applicants are too poor to offer much of a bribe.

---

[68] 50 Stat. 888 (1937), as amended, 42 U.S. C.A. § 1402 (1964), as amended, 42 U.S.C.A. § 1402 (Supp. I, 1965). For families with three or more minor dependents, the ratio was six to one. In 1958 specific income-rent ratios were dropped from the statute, leaving the matter to the discretion of local authorities and state statutes; the federal statute still required that families be "of low income," however. 73 Stat. 680 (1959), as amended, 42 U.S.C.A. § 1402 (1964), as amended, 42 U.S. C.A. § 1402 (Supp. I, 1965).

[75] N.Y.Pub.Housing § 156 (six-to-one ratio); La.Rev.Stats, § 40:478 (1960) (no specific ratio, but a general requirement of "low income" and a list of factors to be considered); Mont.Rev.Codes Ann. § 35–103(18) (1961) ("low income" to be determined by local authority).

[78] San Francisco waives a one-year residency requirement for students. San Francisco Housing Authority, Low Rent Housing —Policy, Part I, sec. I, p. 3 (rev. Feb. 1964).

A class difference separates officials from applicants; a project manager is highly unlikely to have a cousin or sister-in-law anxious to be moved from the bottom to the top of the waiting list. This, indeed, is a general characteristic of welfare administration, as opposed to, for example, the enforcement of housing codes or the administration of regulatory programs that affect businessmen. The selection process is therefore likely to be fair, in the sense of conforming to general rules, and will remain fair in this sense even though applicants have no "rights" and no meaningful review. But though fair, selection may be blind, rule-bound, and unwilling to temper principle to the dictates of common sense. Recently complaints that filtered through legal aid services and agencies of the War on Poverty have brought some examples to light. One housing authority, for example, tried to evict two Puerto Rican brothers, seventeen and eighteen years old, after their mother died and left them orphaned, on the grounds that the authority could not enter into a lease with minors. The Housing Authority of New Bern, North Carolina, adopted a rule which called for the eviction of any tenant to whom "additional illegitimate children" were born during tenancy. Perhaps many additional injustices are hidden in the criteria of selection or in the manner in which screeners work and perceive their work. These injustices, however, are not easily cured. What reform calls for here is not enforcement of rules, but changes in rules. And that in turn requires political pressures upon management—a theme to which we shall return.

Race discrimination was not unknown in the early days of public housing; indeed, the Public Housing Authority deliberately encouraged segregation in some cities.[81] Race discrimination has been abandoned as policy by the PHA; race is no longer officially a criterion for eligibility or assignment to a project. Many Southern projects are still totally segregated. For example, there are seven projects in Anniston, Alabama—three all-white and four all-Negro. And there is a great deal of *de facto* segregation in public housing in the North. It is as distasteful to Negroes as *de facto* school segregation. The remedies are if anything more elusive. In many cities, a majority of public tenants are Negroes. This is true in Chicago, for example. Chicago has virtually no all-white housing projects; but it has many all-Negro projects; and in some projects the percentage of white tenants is far greater than the percentage of whites in public housing in general. Spreading the few white tenants equally throughout the city would simply drive many of them out of public housing, without benefiting the Negro particularly. Yet the present pattern *is* one of *de facto* segregation. Public housing is, by and large, located in Negro areas and is inhabited by Negroes. Projects are so large in the major urban areas that a project would be impossible for a white, middle-class community to digest, if some giant hand picked it up and transported it to the urban fringe. We have seen how political and social forces have transformed public housing into Negro ghetto housing. De facto segregation illustrates quite the opposite point from tenant selection. Here, the granting of formal rights to Negroes to demand desegregated projects would be meaningless in many cities, not because no real abuses exist, but because the problem is so basic that only a radical solution can remedy the matter; rights are not enough.
* * *

---

81 E. g., in San Diego, see Davis & McEntire, Residence and Race 320 (1960). In fairness to PHA, it ought to be pointed out that public housing accommodations were generally available to Negroes "in accordance with need * * * in striking contrast to the discriminatory distribution of local, state and Federal funds," and that it was white prejudice that defeated many attempts by housing officials to break out of the ghetto. Weaver, The Negro Ghetto 179 (1948).

HOLMES v. NEW YORK CITY HOUSING AUTHORITY

United States Court of Appeals,
Second Circuit, 1968.
398 F.2d 262.

Before: HAYS, ANDERSON, and FEINBERG, Circuit Judges.

ANDERSON, Circuit Judge. This class action was brought on September 9, 1966 by 31 named plaintiffs on behalf of themselves and all others similarly situated under the Civil Rights Act, 42 U. S.C.A. § 1983, and the Federal Constitution, challenging the procedures employed by the defendant New York City Housing Authority in the admission of tenants to low-rent public housing projects administered by it in New York City. The jurisdiction of the district court is predicated upon 28 U.S.C.A. § 1343(3).

The New York City Housing Authority is a public corporation created pursuant to the Public Housing Law of the State of New York for the purpose of implementing the State Constitution by providing "low-rent housing for persons of low income as defined by law * *" New York State Constitution, Art. XVIII, § 1. At the time of the complaint in this action, the Authority was providing housing facilities for more than 500,000 persons, in 152 public projects which it owned and administered in New York City. Approximately half of these were federal-aided projects, the remainder being supported by either State or local funds.

The eligibility requirements for prospective public housing tenants are set out in the Public Housing Law, and in resolutions adopted by the Authority pursuant to its rule-making power. Public Housing Law, § 37(1)(w). While these vary somewhat for federal, state, and local-aided projects, two requirements common to all are that the applicant's annual income and total assets not exceed specified limits, and that, at the time of admission, the applicant have been a resident of New York City for not less than two years. In addition each candidate must be situated in an "unsafe, insanitary, or overcrowded" dwelling, Resolution No. 62–7–473, § 3 (federal-aided projects), or living "under other substandard housing conditions," Resolution No. 56–8–433, § 4 (state-aided projects). Each of the plaintiffs in the present action is alleged to meet these requirements.

Each year the Authority receives approximately 90,000 applications out of which it is able to select an average of only 10,000 families for admission to its public housing projects. In doing so the Authority gives preference to certain specified classes of candidates, e. g., "site residents," families in "emergency need of housing," "split families," "doubled up and overcrowded families." Resolution No. 56–8–433, § 4.

In federal-aided projects the Authority is required to allocate the remaining apartments among non-preference candidates in accordance with "an objective scoring system" which is designed to facilitate comparison of the housing conditions of these applicants. Resolution No. 62–7–473, § 4(b). For state-aided projects, however, there is no similar regulation and we assume that this is also the case with local-aided projects. The plaintiffs in this action are all non-preference candidates seeking admission to any of the public housing projects run by the defendant.

In the complaint the named plaintiffs allege that although they have filed with the Authority a total of 51 applications for admission to its housing facilities, 36 in 1965 or earlier, and some as long ago as 1961, none has been advised in writing at any time of his eligibility, or ineligibility, for public housing.

The complaint cites numerous claimed deficiencies in the admissions policies and practices of the Authority. Regulations on admissions (other than those pertaining to income level and residence) are not made available to prospective tenants either by publication or by posting in a conspicuous public place. Applications received by the Authority are not processed chronologically, or in accordance with ascertainable standards, or in any other reasonable and systematic manner. All applications, whether or not considered and acted upon by the Authority, expire automatically at the end of two years. A renewed application is given no credit for time passed, or precedence over a first application of the same date. There is no waiting list or other device by which an applicant can gauge the progress of his case and the Authority refuses to divulge a candidate's status on request. Many applications are never considered by the Authority. If and when a determination of ineligibility is made (on any ground other than excessive income level), however, the candidate is not informed of the Authority's decision, or of the reasons therefor.

The complaint charges that these procedural defects increase the likelihood of favoritism, partiality, and arbitrariness on the part of the Authority, and deprive the plaintiffs of a fair opportunity to petition for admission to public housing, and to obtain review of any action taken by the Authority. The deficiencies are alleged to deprive applicants of due process of law in violation of the Fourteenth Amendment to the Federal Constitution.[2]

[2] The constitutional claims in the complaint are directed at local Resolutions or regulations (or the lack thereof) issued by the Authority, which have effect only within the City of New York. Public Housing Law § 31. No specific provision of the Public Housing Law or any other statute of general statewide application is called into question. Accordingly, a three-judge court is not required by 28 U.S.C.A. § 2281. See e. g., Moody v.

In the district court the defendant moved to dismiss the complaint for failure to state a claim within the court's civil rights jurisdiction. Alternatively it requested that the court refrain from the exercise of its jurisdiction under the doctrine of abstention.

On October 20, 1967, the motion was denied by the trial court which also refused abstention. Thereafter permission was granted to the defendant to take this interlocutory appeal under 28 U.S.C.A. § 1292(b). The issues here are whether the plaintiffs have stated a federal claim,[3] and, if so, whether the district court should proceed to the merits. We have concluded that the district judge was correct in answering each of these points in the affirmative and we, therefore, affirm his order.

Clearly there is sufficient in the complaint to state a claim for relief under § 1983 and the due process clause. One charge made against the defendant, which has merit at least in connection with state-aided projects where the Authority has adopted no standards for selection among non-preference candidates, is that it thereby failed to establish the fair and orderly procedure for allocating its scarce supply of housing which due process requires. It hardly need be said that the existence of an absolute and uncontrolled discretion in an agency of government vested with the administration of a vast program, such as public housing, would be an intolerable invitation to abuse. See Hornsby v. Allen, 326 F.2d 605, 609–610 (5 Cir. 1964). For this reason alone due process requires that selections among applicants be made in accordance with

Flowers, 387 U.S. 97, 101–102, 87 S.Ct. 1544, 18 L.Ed.2d 643 (1967).

[3] While this issue was not specifically mentioned in the defendant's § 1292(b) papers, we have decided to consider it in view of its close relationship to the other question, both of which have been fully briefed by the parties.

"ascertainable standards," id. at 612, and, in cases where many candidates are equally qualified under these standards, that further selections be made in some reasonable manner such as "by lot or on the basis of the chronological order of application." Hornsby v. Allen, 330 F. 2d 55, 56 (5 Cir. 1964) (on petition for rehearing). Due process is a flexible concept which would certainly also leave room for the employment of a scheme such as the "objective scoring system" suggested in the resolution adopted by the Authority for federal-aided projects.[4]

There is no merit in the Authority's contention that the plaintiffs are without standing to raise the due process objection. As applicants for public housing, all are immediately affected by the alleged irregularities in the practices of the Authority. Compare Thomas v. Housing Authority of City of Little Rock, 282 F. Supp. 575 (E.D.Ark.1967); Banks v. Housing Authority of City of San Francisco, 120 Cal.App.2d 1, 260 P.2d 668 (Dist.Ct.App.1953), certiorari denied 347 U.S. 974, 74 S.Ct. 784, 98 L.Ed. 1114 (1954); cf., Norwalk Core v. Norwalk Redevelopment Agency, Slip Opinion p. 2599 (2 Cir. June 7, 1968).

* * *

The principal argument which the Authority has pressed on this appeal is that the district court should have refused to exercise its jurisdiction under the judicially created "abstention" doctrine, which recognizes circumstances under which a federal court may decline to proceed with an action although it has jurisdiction over the case under the Constitution and the statutes. See generally Wright on Federal Courts § 52, at 169–177 (1963). We agree with the district judge that this is not an appropriate case for abstention.

At least in actions under the Civil Rights Act the power of a federal court to abstain from hearing and deciding the merits of claims properly brought before it is a closely restricted one which may be invoked only in a narrowly limited set of "special circumstances." Zwickler v. Koota, 389 U.S. 241, 248, 88 S.Ct. 391, 19 L.Ed.2d 444 (1967); cf. Allegheny County v. Mashuda Co., 360 U.S. 185, 188–189, 79 S.Ct. 1060, 3 L.Ed.2d 1163 (1959). In enacting the predecessor to § 1983, Congress early established the federal courts as the primary forum for the vindication of federal rights, and imposed a duty upon them to give "due respect" to a suitor's choice of that forum. Zwickler v. Koota, supra at 247–248; Harrison v. N. A. A. C. P., 360 U.S. 167, 180–181, 79 S.Ct. 1025, 3 L.Ed.2d 1152 (1959) (dissenting opinion). As a consequence it is now widely recognized that "cases involving vital questions of civil rights are the least likely candidates for abstention."

* * *

The ground for federal abstention upon which the Authority relies derives from the Supreme Court's decisions in Burford v. Sun Oil Co., 319 U.S. 315, 63 S.Ct. 1098, 87 L.Ed. 1424 (1943), and Alabama Public Service Commission v. Southern Railway Co., 341 U.S. 341, 71 S.Ct. 762, 95 L.Ed. 1002 (1951), discussed in Note, 59 Col.L.Rev., supra at 757–762. But in those cases the federal courts were asked to resolve problems calling for the comprehension and analysis of basic matters of state policy, see 319 U.S. at 332; 341 U.S. at 347, which were complicated by non-legal considera-

---

[4] The possibility of arbitrary action is not excluded here, however, by the existence of this reasonable regulation. The "scoring system" scheme will hardly assure the fairness it was devised to promote if, as the plaintiffs allege, some applicants, but not others, are secretly rejected by the Authority, are not thereafter informed of their ineligibility, and are thereby deprived of the opportunity to seek review of the Authority's decision, as provided by New York law under CPLR § 7803(3). Cf. Griffin v. Illinois, 351 U.S. 12, 76 S.Ct. 585, 100 L.Ed. 891, 55 A.L.R.2d 1055 (1955).

tions of a predominantly local nature, and which made abstention particularly appropriate. In contrast to the present case which presents only issues of federal constitutional law, *Burford* and *Alabama* involved situations to which concededly the "federal courts can make small contribution." 319 U.S. at 327. Equally important as a distinguishing factor is the fact that the state legislatures in those cases had specially concentrated all judicial review of administrative orders in one state court, see 319 U.S. at 325–327; 341 U.S. at 348; Note, 59 Col.L.Rev., supra at 759–760, in effect designating the state courts and agencies as "working partners" in the local regulatory scheme. 319 U.S. at 326. While this might be said to hold true in future cases in New York where the Authority makes a specific determination of ineligibility affecting a particular applicant for public housing,[6] it is certainly not so here where the very concern of the plaintiffs is that no such determinations have been made, and where New York law provides a remedy for the plaintiffs' ills which is dubious at the very best.[7] What we have

just said also serves to distinguish the recent case of Randell v. Newark Housing Authority, 384 F.2d 151 (3 Cir. 1967), cited by both parties, where the federal court action was "closely tied" to various landlord and tenant actions already pending before the courts of New Jersey. 384 F.2d at 157, n. 15.

Equitable considerations also favor the result reached by the district judge. The 31 named plaintiffs speak not only for themselves, but also for thousands of New York's neediest who may have been unfairly entrenched in squalor due to the alleged inadequacies of the Authority's procedures. The need for relief is thus immediate, and should not be aggravated further by delay in the courts. See Baggett v. Bullitt, 377 U.S. 360, 378–379, 84 S.Ct. 1316, 12 L.Ed.2d 377 (1964); Allegheny County v. Mashuda Co., supra at 196–197; England v. Louisiana State Bd. of Medical Examiners, 375 U.S. 411, 425–427, 84 S.Ct. 461, 11 L.Ed.2d 440

---

[6] Judicial review in the New York courts is available to any rejected public housing applicant under CPLR § 7803(3), where he may question "whether a determination was made in violation of lawful procedure, was affected by an error of law or was arbitrary and capricious or an abuse of discretion * * *." Once an administrative procedure has been instituted by the Authority which in all respects complies with Federal constitutional standards, then the great majority of claims arising out of the acceptance or rejection of applicants by the Authority will be matters entirely within the purview of the State courts, which sit in a "much better position * * * to ascertain the myriad factors that may be involved in a particular situation and to determine their proper weight." S.Rep.No.281, 87th Cong., 1st Sess. (1961) in 2 U.S.Code Cong. & Ad.News, at 1944; cf., Austin v. NYCHA, 49 Misc.2d 206, 267 N.Y. S.2d 309 (1966); Sanders v. Cruise, 10 Misc. 2d 533, 173 N.Y.S.2d 871 (1958).

[7] The only possibility for relief in the state courts in the present case where no deter-

mination as to the eligibility of any of the plaintiffs has been made, is by way of mandamus under § 7803(1), brought to compel the Chairman or Executive Director of the Authority "to perform a duty enjoined upon [him] by law," i. e., to issue regulations to remedy the procedural defects alleged in the complaint, as he is empowered to do under Resolutions applicable to both federal and state-aided projects. See Res.No. 56–8–433, § 9(i), (iii), and (iv); Res.No. 62–7–473, § 10 (i), (ii), and (iv). We do not think, however, that this section would provide the plaintiffs a "plain, adequate and complete" remedy in the state courts, Potwora v. Dillon, 386 F.2d 74, 77 (2 Cir. 1967), a necessary precondition to abstention. Compare Wright v. McMann, 387 F.2d 519, 523–524 (2 Cir. 1967). The restrictive New York case law supports this conclusion. See, e. g., Gimprich v. Board of Ed. of City of New York, 306 N.Y. 401, 118 N.E.2d 578 (1954) (mandamus does not lie to compel an act of administrative discretion); Grand Jury Ass'n of New York County, Inc. v. Schweitzer, 11 A.D.2d 761, 202 N.Y.S.2d 375 (1960) (petitioner must show "clear legal right" to mandamus); C. S. D. No. 2 of Towns of Coeymans, et al. v. New York State Teachers Retirement System, 46 Misc.2d 225, 259 N.Y.S.2d 585 (1965) (even then, relief may be denied in court's discretion).

(1964) (Justice Douglas concurring); Note, 80 Harv.L.Rev., supra at 606–607.

The order of the district court is affirmed.

HAYS, Circuit Judge (dissenting). I dissent.

The plaintiffs allege that applicants for public housing are not notified as to whether they are eligible, that they must refile their applications every two years and do not get priority because of earlier filing, and that the Housing Authority has not published and posted its regulations regarding selection of tenants. These complaints hardly seem to raise federal constitutional questions. See Chaney v. State Bar, 386 F.2d 962 (9th Cir. 1967), certiorari denied 36 U.S.L.W. 3390 (April 8, 1968); Powell v. Workmen's Comp. Board, 327 F.2d 131 (2d Cir. 1964); Sarelas v. Sheehan, 326 F.2d 490 (7th Cir. 1963), certiorari denied 377 U.S. 932, 84 S.Ct. 1334, 12 L.Ed.2d 296 (1964).

But even if we assume that some constitutional issues are raised, there are no allegations which tend to show that the individual plaintiffs have been denied rights. We should not entertain such a vague, uncertain, abstract and hypothetical complaint. See Birnbaum v. Trussell, 347 F.2d 86 (2d Cir. 1965).

Notes and Questions on Eligibility Procedures

1. Willie Sumpter sought admission to a White Plains (N.Y.) housing project. The Housing Authority's Executive Director told applicant at a personal interview that he was being rejected because of his criminal record (several traffic violations and disorderly conduct charges) and some trouble he once had with the police. Applicant argued that he was denied procedural due process because no evidentiary hearing had been afforded him.

Special Term agreed that applicant should have an evidentiary hearing. There, with the aid of counsel, if the applicant desired, he might confront and cross-examine any adverse witnesses and present his own arguments and evidence. Also, applicant was entitled to findings of fact upon which any adverse decision was based. Sumpter v. White Plains Housing Authority, 63 Misc.2d 654, 313 N.Y.S.2d 133 (Sup.Ct.1970).

The decision did not survive appeal. Applicant could only demand the personal interview required by section 156–a of the New York Public Housing Law at which the authority would tell him why he was not to get housing. The opinion spoke of the "administrative complication and burdens attendant upon the various housing authorities in the state [that] preclude the rigid requirement * * * for a full evidentiary hearing in each case of rejection." In New York City alone, 9,411 applicants were rejected in 1970. 36 A.D.2d 728, 320 N.Y.S.2d 472 (2d Dept. 1971).

Compare with Spady v. Mt. Vernon Housing Authority, 70 Misc.2d 270, 333 N.Y.S.2d 557 (Sup.Ct.1972). (Having been accepted as a proposed tenant, an individual could demand a hearing on the claim of ineligibility even though he had not yet taken possession of his apartment).

2. 42 U.S.C.A. § 1410(g)(4) (Supp.1971), which Congress added [after the Holmes decision] in the Housing and Urban Development Act of 1969, Pub.L.No.91–152, provides: (4) the public housing agency shall promptly notify (i) any applicant determined to be ineligible for admission to the project of the basis for such determination and provide the applicant upon request, within a reasonable time after the determination is made, with an opportunity for an *informal hearing* [italics added] on such determination, and (ii) any applicant de-

termined to be eligible for admission to the project of the approximate date of occupancy insofar as such date can be reasonably determined.

Does New York's requirement of a private interview, supra, satisfy the federal statutory requirement of an informal hearing? What makes a hearing informal: disregard of formal evidentiary rules and a relaxed atmosphere, or the absence of such procedural safeguards as right to counsel, confrontation of adverse witnesses, right to call friendly witnesses, published findings of fact? Should the procedures that are constitutionally required for the loss of benefits, cf. Escalera v. New York City Housing Authority, 425 F.2d 853 (2d Cir. 1970), p. 724 supra; Goldberg v. Kelly, 397 U.S. 254, 90 S.Ct. 1011, 25 L.Ed.2d 287 (1970), chapter 1, supra, apply equally for an initial refusal to grant benefits? If you do not advocate an Escalera type hearing for each of New York City's 9,411 applicants who were rejected in 1970, would you take any steps (beyond a private interview) to insure that applicants not be rejected arbitrarily? If courts are to review claims of arbitrary rejection, what minimum standards (as to probativeness) should the record satisfy: putting this question differently, might one argue that the right to review carries with it the right to a controverted hearing before an impartial fact-finder? Might the form of original "hearing" depend upon the reasons given for the proposed denial of eligibility: Compare, for example, a denial based on "undesirability" with a denial based on excess income. What, if any, discretion should be given local housing authorities in shaping their hearing procedures? Might review be lodged elsewhere than in the courts?

3. In New York City, where only one *qualified* applicant out of nine actually gets admitted in any year, the applicant's priority status becomes critically important. Should an applicant who is unhappy about his priority have an opportunity to challenge that status?

4. Where public housing is in desperately short supply, should all priorities be scrapped and qualifying applicants be admitted solely by lot or on a first come-first served basis? If you believe that some priorities are needed (more urgently, perhaps, because of the shortage), try to define a priority system.

THOMAS v. HOUSING AUTHORITY OF CITY OF LITTLE ROCK

United States District Court, E.D. Arkansas, W.D. 1967.
282 F.Supp. 575.

MEMORANDUM OPINION

HENLEY, Chief Judge. This is a class suit for declaratory and injunctive relief brought by plaintiffs, Alma Jean Thomas and Estella Watson, against The Housing Authority of The City of Little Rock, Arkansas, and George Millar, the Authority's Executive Director. Plaintiffs are both Negro women. They complain that they were denied admission to low rent housing facilities operated by the Housing Authority in Little Rock on the basis of the fact that both are the mothers of illegitimate children. They assert that the Housing Authority's "unwed mother" policy, presently to be described, is violative of the due process and equal protection clauses of the 14th Amendment to the Constitution of the United States. They also allege that the Housing Authority is practicing unlawful racial discrimination in the operation of its facilities, which alleged discrimination is forbidden by the 14th Amendment and by section 601 of the Civil Rights Act of 1964, 42 U.S.C.A. § 2000d. Subject matter jurisdiction is not questioned and is established.

The defendants deny that plaintiffs are entitled to the relief sought, and the cause is now before the Court on the cross-motions of the parties for summary judgment. Controlling facts are not in dispute.

The Housing Authority operates in Little Rock five public housing projects or facilities for the purpose of providing low rent housing accommodations for families of low income. The operation is conducted under a contract between the Housing Authority and the federal Public Housing Administration as provided by the Federal Housing Act of 1937, as amended, 42 U.S.C.A. § 1401 et seq. The Housing Authority is a body corporate and politic organized under the terms of the "Public Housing Act," adopted by the Arkansas Legislature in 1937, Ark.Stats.Ann., § 19–3001 et seq. There is no question that the Housing Authority is a public body, and that in administering the low rent housing program it is performing a public function in undertaking to provide safe, adequate, and decent housing for low income families in line with the declared findings and purposes of the federal and State statutes which have been mentioned.

The Little Rock Housing Authority has been in existence and operation for many years. The policy of the Housing Authority eschews racial discrimination in stated terms as follows:

"The Housing Authority of the City of Little Rock will accept applications for Low-Rent Public Housing in all projects, select tenants for all projects and assign applicants to dwelling units in all projects without regard to race, creed, color or national origin. The Housing Authority * * * will not discriminate because of race, creed, color or national origin in the sale, leasing, rental or other disposition of housing or related facilities (including land) included in the projects or in the use or occupancy thereof. The Housing Authority * * * will not, on account of race, color, creed or national origin deny to any family the opportunity to apply for such housing, nor deny to any eligible applicant the opportunity to lease or rent any dwelling in any project suitable to their (sic) needs."

While that stated policy facially satisfies the requirements of both the 14th Amendment and section 601 of the Civil Rights Act of 1964, the record reflects that three of the five projects have always been, and presumably still are, occupied solely by Negroes, and that the other two have always been, and presumably still are, occupied exclusively by white tenants. Further, materials of record indicate that the projects occupied by Negroes are identified as "Negro" facilities, and that the other projects are identified as "Caucasian" facilities. As of a comparatively recent date 384 white families were occupying the "Caucasian" facilities, and 705 Negro families were occupying the "Negro" facilities.

The record reflects that the unwed mother policy of which plaintiffs complain was adopted, perhaps informally, by the Commissioners of the Housing Authority in 1959 for the purpose of correcting a serious morals problem which had arisen in certain of the facilities. According to the discovery deposition of Director Millar, certain female tenants of the projects had been engaging in on-premises prostitution and sexual promiscuity to such an extent that older and more settled families of low income were unwilling to apply for admission to the facilities or to continue to reside therein.

The policy was formalized in 1962 and is now included in the Authority's manual of Revised Policy and Procedure. The relevant provision is as follows:

"SUBJECT: Selection of Tenants and Processing Applications.

* * * * * *

"V. *Definitions and Standards.*

"D. A Family—Consists of a 'head' and one or more other persons related to the 'head' by blood, marriage or adoption. Other persons, including foster children and members temporarily absent, may be considered a part of the family group if they are living or will live regularly with the family. To qualify as a family, there must have been a legal marriage. A single, separated or divorced family 'head' having children born out of wedlock shall not be eligible for admission or continued occupancy.

"A family shall not be eligible for admission or continued occupancy if any family member residing regularly with the family has a child or children born out of wedlock."

As stated, the policy was adopted to meet the 1959 situation which has been described. However, the record is silent as to the extent to which unwed mothers participated in the misbehavior against which the Housing Authority moved, and is likewise silent as to the extent to which that misbehavior resulted in illegitimate births.

Coming now to the facts of the instant case, both plaintiffs applied for admission to low rent housing on September 20, 1966. Copies of their applications are of record. The application of plaintiff Thomas reflects that she has three illegitimate children born between November 11, 1962, and October 6, 1965. She expressed a preference for assignment to Ives Homes, a Negro facility, or to Sunset Terrace, a Caucasian facility, in that order. The application of Watson shows that she has three illegitimate children born between June 12, 1964, and June 6, 1966. She expressed a preference for assignment to Hollingsworth Homes, a Negro facility.

It appears to be conceded that both applicants qualified, aside from the un-

wed mother policy, as heads of families of low income eligible for low rent public housing, and that space for both of them was available in the facilities for which preferences had been expressed. Both applications were denied solely by reference to the unwed mother policy of the Housing Authority.

On this phase of the case the question for decision is whether a local Housing Authority, administering a low rent public housing program, can validly exclude or evict from occupancy of such housing a family of low income on the sole ground that the head of the family or some member thereof has an illegitimate child or illegitimate children. To put the question slightly differently and in somewhat clearer focus, can the Little Rock Housing Authority validly deny admission to or evict from one of its projects an otherwise eligible low income family by an automatic application of the Authority's unwed mother policy? The question seems to be one of first impression.

In taking up that question, the Court will say preliminarily that on the unwed mother phase of the case the action meets the requirements for a class action set forth in Rule 23 of the Federal Rules of Civil Procedure, as amended in 1966, and the Court now holds that the two individual plaintiffs validly represent a "class" consisting of family groups adversely affected by the unwed mother policy and have standing to seek relief against that policy for the benefit of themselves and other members of the class.

As stated, the Housing Authority is a public body, not a private landlord; hence, it cannot act arbitrarily or capriciously in selecting and evicting its tenants. Rudder v. United States, 96 U.S. App.D.C. 329, 226 F.2d 51. Ark.Stats. Ann. § 19–3011(a) permits the Housing Authority to make needful bylaws, rules and regulations, not contrary to the statute, and necessary to carry into effect the powers and purposes of the agency.

While the statute vests a rule making power in the local Housing Authorities, the regulations and policies which they promulgate must be in harmony with the statute and must bear a reasonable relationship to the low rent housing program and the proper operation thereof. 2 Am.Jur.2d, Administrative Law, §§ 303–304; Asbury Hospital v. Cass County, N.D., 326 U.S. 207, 214, 66 S.Ct. 61, 90 L.Ed. 6; Panama Refining Co. v. Ryan, 293 U.S. 388, 426–430, 55 S.Ct. 241, 79 L.Ed. 446; Gulf, Colorado & Santa Fe R. Co. v. Ellis, 165 U.S. 150, 155–159, 17 S.Ct. 255, 41 L.Ed. 666.

It is at this point that controversy arises. The plaintiffs say that the classification expressed in the Housing Authority's unwed mother policy is unreasonable, arbitrary and capricious, that it has no reasonable relationship to the public housing program and is, in fact, contrary to the aims and objects of that program, and is designed purely as a punitive measure directed against poor people who have become the parents of illegitimate children.

The Housing Authority argues, on the other hand, that the regulation was within the power of the Authority to adopt; that it does not conflict with the low rent housing program; that it is legitimately and reasonably related to that program; that it is in fact necessary to the proper operation of the facilities, and that it is constitutional and valid.

That evils result from slum living is generally accepted; the wide range of alleged evils need not be detailed here. The theory of the low rent housing program is that if families of low income can be removed from the slums and placed in safe, sanitary and decent housing they will be motivated and enabled to lead better, healthier and more productive lives.

In passing upon the question at issue, due regard must be had to the humanitarian nature of the public housing. It is the function of the Housing Authority to carry out that program in the City of Little Rock, that is to say to provide housing for low income families. The Authority is not concerned with punishing people for past misconduct, sexual or otherwise.

The requirements of the federal and State statutes and of the contract between the Housing Authority and the Public Housing Administration relating to the eligibility of families of low income to be admitted to and to remain in the Authority's facilities do not deal specifically with the character, reputation or morals of tenants or prospective tenants.

However, it seems clear to this Court that the statutory and contractual eligibility requirements are minimal, and that the Authority must of necessity have the authority to prescribe reasonable criteria for the screening of applicants for admission and for the exclusion of those applicants with respect to whom illegal or disorderly conduct or conduct amounting to a nuisance may reasonably be anticipated. Further, the Authority must have the right to evict from the facilities tenants who are guilty of such conduct after admission.[3]

Unless the agency has that authority in those areas administration of the fa-

[3] This is not to suggest that the criteria for admission necessarily should be the same as for eviction. While the Housing Authority is operating its facilities in the implementation of a humanitarian program designed to help as many poor people as possible, the Housing Authority is also acting as a landlord collecting rents and managing dwelling units. In its capacity as a public landlord the Authority is, of course, concerned with the orderly and efficient administration of the facilities, and that particular concern may be directed more at families which have been admitted to the facilities than at families who are applying for initial admission.

cilities in an orderly and efficient manner will be disrupted, and, as counsel for the Housing Authority warns, the transplanted tenants may recreate within the facilities the slum environment from which they came. It should be remembered in this connection that many low income families will be helped by a change of their environment; other families and individual members thereof may be helped little if at all. Some people who were bad citizens in the slums will be bad citizens anywhere they may reside.

While the unwed mother policy of the Housing Authority doubtless had for its object the elimination of serious sexual misconduct within the facilities which might or might not involve violations of the criminal laws, the Court has come to the conclusion that the policy, as written, cannot be sustained.

In the Court's estimation the fatal vices of the policy are its inflexibility, and its general disharmony with the spirit and aim of the low rent housing program.

The prohibition of the present policy is absolute. It makes no distinction between the unwed mother with one illegitimate child and the unwed mother with ten of such children; it does not take into account the circumstances of the illegitimate birth or births, the age, knowledge, training or experience of the mother, or the possibility or likelihood of future illegitimate births. It completely overlooks the possibility that the mother has reformed, or that if placed in better surroundings she may lead a more conventional life.

Under the regulation, as written, if the head of a family or any member thereof has an illegitimate child, that family is automatically excluded from admission to the facilities, and if an illegitimate child is born into a family group which has been admitted to the facilities, the fact of the birth is an automatic basis for evic-

tion. In the Court's eyes the present regulation is drastic beyond any reasonable necessity in the context in which it was promulgated.

The policy would stand on better ground if it was capable of insuring that all of the tenants of the facilities would be persons of good conduct. That it is not so capable is too manifest to require discussion. The absence of illegitimate children from a family group does not establish the morality of the members of the group or insure lawful conduct of tenants of the Housing Authority.

More basically, an indiscriminate denial of access to public housing to families unfortunate enough to have or acquire one or more illegitimate children would be to deprive of the real or supposed benefits of the program many of the very people who need it most—the poorest and most ignorant of the poor. An administrative policy which involves such a denial does not square with the humane purpose of the low rent housing program.

It is not necessary for this Court to say in this case how far in the screening of its applicants a local Housing Authority may go in requiring as a condition of admission that the applicant show past conformity with the moral code generally accepted by the community, or how far such an Authority may go in requiring its tenants to conform to that code as a condition of continued occupancy of the facilities. It is sufficient for present purposes for the Court to hold, as it does hold, that a Housing Authority may not exclude from the benefits of public housing a low income family merely because of the incidence of illegitimacy within the family group. Such a policy simply has no place in the low rent housing program, and in that sense is arbitrary and capricious.

Before leaving the unwed mother policy, the Court wishes to emphasize that there are certain things which it is *not* holding.

The Court is not holding that the federal Constitution, the Public Housing Act, or the Arkansas statute, or the contract between the Housing Authority and the Public Housing Administration, require the Commissioners of the Authority or their subordinates to permit the facilities to be operated as brothels or places of assignation. The Housing Authority is not required to tolerate criminal activities within the facilities, or disorderly conduct, or conduct amounting to a nuisance or which seriously violates ordinary standards of decency.

Further, in passing upon an application for initial admission to the facilities the Housing Authority is not required to close its eyes to the fact that the head or a member of the family group has one or more illegitimate children. And the Court thinks that the Authority might permissibly formulate a policy giving some evidentiary or presumptive effect to the presence of illegitimate children in a family group, particularly where there are more than one of such children, where they are of recent birth, and where the births have followed each other in quick succession. If, as is the case of these plaintiffs, a woman has had three illegitimate children in a space of three years, the Court thinks that a Housing Authority as a condition for admitting the woman's family to tenancy in one of its facilities certainly may require some assurance that the family will be satisfactory low rent housing tenants notwithstanding the past conduct of the mother.

From what has just been said it follows that these two particular plaintiffs will not automatically be entitled to admission to the facilities. The Authority is perfectly free to consider under appropriate criteria whether a given unwed mother and her family should be admitted to the facilities. All that the Court

holds is that such a mother and family may not automatically be excluded or evicted from the facilities merely because of her status as an unwed mother.

* * *

Question

What is the practical significance of the *Thomas* case? Suppose that the Little Rock authority now takes the plaintiffs' applications, grants a private interview, and then notifies the applicants that because of the circumstances of their illegitimate motherhood, they are ineligible for public housing: Do the plaintiffs have any recourse?

MANIGO v. NEW YORK CITY HOUSING AUTHORITY

Supreme Court, Special Term, New York
County, Part I, 1966.
51 Misc.2d 829, 273 N.Y.S.2d 1003.

FRANCIS T. MURPHY, J. Petitioner, pursuant to article 78 of the CPLR, seeks a review and annulment of the determination of the New York City Housing Authority denying her and her family admission to tenancy in public housing operated by respondent.

Petitioner contends that she is qualified for tenancy and has complied with all of the required application procedures, and that the standards used by respondent to determine qualifications of tenancy deny her and her family the equal protection guaranteed by the 14th Amendment of the Constitution of the United States in that the said standards are arbitrary, capricious, unreasonable and unrelated to the declared purpose and public policy of the respondent.

Respondent is a public corporation organized and existing by virtue of the Public Housing Law of the State of New York. Pursuant to its legal authority respondent owns and operates low-rent public housing within the City of New York to provide housing accommodations in such properties for families of low income who qualify pursuant to law and to regulations made by the said respondent. Respondent, in the operation of its properties, has established eligibility requirements for applicants. These regulations and requirements are contained in Authority Resolution No. 12–9–683 entitled "Resolution Relating to Desirability as a Ground for Eligibility" and have been made a part of the record herein. Section 1 of the said resolution sets forth that nondesirability standards and procedures have been established to insure the health, safety, morals and comfort of public housing tenants, to protect the property of the Authority and to facilitate the proper administration by the Authority of its projects. The standards for judging nondesirability are set forth in section 2 of the said resolution as follows: "Section 2. *Ground for Eligibility*. It shall be a ground for eligibility for admission or continued occupancy in any Authority project, that the tenant or applicant is or will be a desirable tenant. The standard to be used in approving eligibility for admission or continued occupancy of a family shall be that the family will not or does not constitute (1) a detriment to the health, safety or morals of its neighbors or the community, (2) an adverse influence upon sound family and community life, (3) a source of danger to the peaceful occupation of the other tenants, (4) a source of danger or cause of damage to the premises or property of the Authority, or (5) a nuisance. In making such determination consideration shall be given to the family composition, parental control over children, family stability, medical and other past history, reputation, conduct and behavior, criminal record, if any, occupation of wage earners, and any other data or information with respect to the family that has a bearing upon its desirability, in-

cluding its conduct or behavior while residing in a project. Any applicant or tenant determined to be ineligible by virtue of the standard herein set forth shall be declared to be ineligible on the ground on Non-Desirability."

There can be no doubt that the respondent, to protect the large concentration of children and elderly persons who reside within its properties, must take steps to prevent the development of unsafe conditions therein. Without a proper screening of prospective tenants the dangers to those persons residing therein would be multiplied many times over.

In the case of Matter of Sanders v. Cruise (10 Misc.2d 533, 536, 173 N.Y. S.2d 871, 874) the court, in ruling upon a desirability resolution substantially similar to the instant one, said: "There can be no doubt that the Authority's [desirability] standard for continued occupancy is reasonable and necessary".

In the course of its routine investigation relating to the desirability of the petitioner as a tenant the respondent discovered, among other things, that petitioner's husband, during the past eight years, has been arrested seven times. On four of these occasions he has been adjudicated a youthful offender or a juvenile delinquent. On at least two occasions he has been incarcerated. In addition to the four juvenile and youthful offender offenses, he was, in 1964, arrested for disorderly conduct, found guilty and sentenced to 10 days in the Workhouse. In July of 1965 he was arrested for possession of drugs, which charge was ultimately dismissed. The record further reveals that the first juvenile delinquency adjudication was as a result of an altercation with one of the respondent's public housing guards.

Respondent, in applying the facts in the instant case to the eligibility resolution above set forth, has concluded that the background of petitioner's husband makes a clear case of nondesirability within the standards and regulations provided by respondent. This court agrees with the fundamental proposition advanced by petitioner that adjudication of a person as a youthful offender or juvenile delinquent, standing by itself, cannot be utilized to operate as a forfeiture of any right or privilege nor to disqualify that person from certain rights specified in the applicable statutes. However, this does not mean that an applicant's entire behavior pattern over a period of years may not be the proper subject of scrutiny by an administrative agency before granting a right or privilege such as eligibility to public housing. As was stated in the case of Matter of Strong v. Kennedy (29 Misc.2d 54, 55, 56, 210 N.Y.S.2d 588, 590): "It is not held here that adjudication of juvenile delinquency may never be taken into account in weighing the suitability for appointment of an individual. * * * Discrimination must be made between misbehavior which is isolated and arises out of the highspirited nature of youth and its inherent instability and misconduct which is continuous and basic."

There is ample in the record for the respondent to have concluded that petitioner's husband has been engaged in a course of conduct which is within the intendment of the nondesirability resolution. The transgressions of petitioner's husband have not been isolated, but have followed a continuous basic pattern over the course of the last several years. As recently as two years ago, he has been found guilty of disorderly conduct and sentenced to the Workhouse.

Accordingly, the court finds that in the circumstances presented the actions of the respondent were reasonable and the standards applied by said respondent with respect to petitioner's application were applied reasonably and justified the action taken by the said respondent. The petition is dismissed.

Notes on Eligibility Standards

1. The New York City Housing Authority, during much of the 1960s, placed all applicants into three categories: "clear and present danger" (ineligible); "potential problems" (possibly ineligible); eligible. "Clear and present danger" meant one of the following:

a. Contagious diseases which create a hazard for other tenants (tuberculosis, leprosy, etc.);

b. Past or present engagement in illegal occupations (prostitution, professional gambling, etc.);

c. Evidence that an individual is prone to violence;

d. Confirmed drug addiction;

e. Rape or sexual deviation (indecent exposure, mutual masturbation, etc.);

f. Grossly unacceptable housekeeping (causing fire hazard, foul odors, etc.);

g. Record of unreasonable disturbance of neighbors or destruction of property;

h. Other evidence of behaviour which endangers life, safety or morals.

The "potential problems" list was even longer, containing 22 categories. These included: lack of parental control, alcoholism, highly irregular work history, frequent separations of husband and wife ("our concern here is with the stability of the family unit"), family with minor children which does not include both parents, apparent mental retardation (of any member of the family), obnoxious conduct during processing of application.

Comment on the standards above. In doing so, consider the following attitudes:

a. The right to decent housing is everyone's right. There are neither deserving nor undeserving poor;

b. Families who are denied public housing as problem-ridden may benefit most from a fresh start in a decent housing environment;

c. A public landlord should be as discriminating as a private landlord. The Housing Authority must respect the well-being of *all* tenants in a project and attempt to screen out those applicants likeliest to disrupt or discomfort other occupants;

d. Public housing projects maintain a delicate financial balance. Therefore, housing authorities should be able to reject any applicant if they doubt he will pay his rent or if they believe he may cause excessive physical damage to his apartment;

e. Public and Congressional approval of public housing is essential to the program's financial support. Therefore, housing projects should be run as model communities; this means model tenants and highly selective admission practices.

f. Problem families are least able to compete for suitable housing in the private market. Therefore, they should be given special consideration as applicants for public housing.

g. No one should be denied eligibility on the *prediction* that he will be an undesirable tenant. There is time enough to terminate his benefits if he is undesirable in fact.

2. Because of the heavy demand for low-rent units, a local housing authority fixes a residency requirement of one year before an otherwise eligible family may file its application. Or: the authority permits immediate filing but will take no family before it has lived in the community for one year. Or: the authority permits immediate filing but assigns a lower priority to shorter-term residents than it assigns to longer-term residents. Are any of the procedures constitutionally valid? Cf. Cole v. Housing Authority, 312 F.Supp. 692 (D.C.R.I.1970); Shapiro v. Thompson, 394 U.S. 618, 89 S.Ct. 1322, 22 L.Ed.2d 600 (1969). (The full opinion in *Shapiro* is set out in Chapter 1, supra and discussed.)

SECTION 4. WHERE SHALL THE POOR LIVE?

ALTERNATIVES TO THE GILDED GHETTO

Kain & Persky
Public Interest, Winter 1969, pp. 74–87.

We are faced today with a spate of proposals and programs for improving the ghetto through economic development, renewal, and reconstruction. The intellectual basis of many of these proposals stems from a false analogy of the ghetto to an underdeveloped country in need of economic development. This oversimplified and misleading view ignores the strong linkages that tie the ghetto to the remainder of the metropolis and to the nation. When the nature of these linkages and the complex relationship between the ghetto and metropolitan development is understood, the potential destructiveness of these proposals becomes apparent. In this article we attempt to describe these interrelationships and the ghetto's consequent culpability for an expanded list of urban problems.

The Ghetto and the Metropolis

If we begin with the usual list of "ghetto problems" unemployment, low income, poor schools, and poor housing —it is easy to see the appeal of proposals aimed at making the ghetto livable. Moreover, casual observation of the slow pace of school desegregation, residential integration, and fair employment practices would indicate that the promise of integration and the gains achievable from the process are to be made only at an obscure point in the future. Thus, in the short run, the argument for ghetto improvement would have us view the ghetto as something of a community unto itself, a community that could substantially benefit from economic development and especially heavy investments of physical capital.

The weakness of this argument, however, is attested to by a growing body of evidence that indicates that (1) the above list of ghetto problems is much too short, because it ignores the serious implications of the growing ghetto for the metropolis as a whole and that (2) the ghetto itself is responsible for or seriously aggravates, many of the most visible problems of urban Negroes.

The central Negro ghetto has produced a significant distortion of metropolitan development, which has added substantially to problems in central city finance, metropolitan transportation, housing, and urban renewal. The decline of central cities has been hastened by a conviction in the white community, both individual and corporate, that the ghetto would continue its rapid expansion, carrying along its associated problems of concentrated poverty and social disorganization.

Although historically lower income groups have tended to live in central cities, this residential pattern was the result of a highly centralized employment structure. Low income households, constrained by limited housing and transportation budgets, clustered tightly around the work places in the densest accommodations available. High income households, by contrast, with more disposable income and preferences for less congested living conditions, found it expedient to commute to suburban areas where land costs were lower. These low-

er housing costs in suburban locations more than compensated them for the time, inconvenience, and out-of-pocket costs of commuting. Today, it still remains true that low income households cluster more closely around their work places than do high income households. However, with the accelerating pace of suburbanization of industry and jobs—itself no doubt due partly to the ghetto's expansion—these jobs are found less frequently in cities. Thus the poor are found less frequently in the central city; it is mainly the Negro poor who are found there. The inference is inescapable; *central cities are poor largely because they are black, and not the converse.*

The residential locations of whites in similar income groups support this contention. This is clearly shown in Table 1, which gives the proportion of low income whites and Negroes living in the suburban rings of the ten largest metropolitan areas (Table 1 also includes data for all whites and Negroes). For example, 45 per cent of Detroit's poor white families live in suburbs, but only 11 per cent of its poor Negro families do so. These figures belie the argument that Negroes are concentrated in central cities because they are poor. This finding is consistent with the work of numerous researchers who have concluded that little of the existing pattern of Negro residential segregation can be explained by income or other socioeconomic characteristics. One of the authors of this article has elsewhere estimated that, on the basis of Negro employment locations and of low income white residential choice patterns, as many as 40,000 Detroit Negro workers and 112,000 Chicago Negro workers would move out of central ghettos in the absence of racial segregation.[1]

[1] John R. Theyer, John F. Kain, and Martin Wohl, The Urban Transportation Problem (Cambridge, Mass.: Harvard University Press, 1965), pp. 164–165.

TABLE 1. PER CENT OF WHITE AND NEGRO FAMILIES (TOTAL AND POOR) LIVING
IN THE SUBURBAN RING OF THE TEN LARGEST URBANIZATION AREAS *

		WHITE		NEGRO	
		ALL FAMILIES	FAMILIES WITH INCOMES $3,000	ALL FAMILIES	FAMILIES WITH INCOMES $3,000
1	New York	27.8%	16.3%	9.4%	8.2%
2	Los Angeles	65.2	61.6	27.3	23.3
3	Chicago	47.6	37.2	7.7	5.9
4	Philadelphia	50.8	37.4	15.7	14.2
5	Detroit	58.9	44.9	12.1	11.3
6	San Francisco-Oakland	57.8	48.8	29.2	25.8
7	Boston	74.3	64.0	19.2	13.9
8	Washington	75.7	59.6	9.8	10.4
9	Pittsburgh	70.5	63.3	29.4	27.1
10	Cleveland	59.2	39.3	3.1	2.4

* For New York and Chicago the suburban ring is the difference between the SMSA and central city. For all other cities it is the difference between the urbanized area and central city. Both San Francisco and Oakland are counted as central cities.

This residential pattern imposed on the Negro has led to an unduly large proportion of poverty-linked services being demanded of central cities. At the same time, the expansion of the ghetto has encouraged the exodus of middle income whites. The result has been rapid increases in local government expenditures and a severe constraint on the ability of central cities to raise revenues. Hence, the current crisis in city finances. Although the problem can be handled in the short run by various schemes of redistributing governmental revenues, a preferable long-run solution would involve a major dispersal of the low income population, in particular the Negro. Central cities will continue to have a high proportion of the poor as long as they contain a large proportion of metropolitan jobs. However, there is no rationale for exaggerating this tendency with artificial restraints.

Housing, Transportation, Schools

Housing segregation has also frustrated efforts to renew the city. At first sight the logic of renewal is strong. By offering federal subsidies to higher income whites locating within their boundaries, central cities have hoped to improve their tax base. The same logic underlies community efforts to woo industry. However, to the extent that these groups consider the city an inferior location, because of the existence of the ghetto, such subsidies will continue to fail. As long as the ghetto exists, most of white America will write off the central city. Spot renewal, even on the scale envisioned in the Model Cities program, cannot alter this basic fact.

In this context, even the small victories of central cities are often of a pyrrhic nature. So long as the central business district (CBD) manages to remain a major employment location, the city is faced with serious transportation problems, problems that would be substantially reduced if more of the centrally employed whites were willing to reside in the city. To a great extent, the CBD stakes its existence on an ability to transport people rapidly over long distances. Pressures for more expressways and high-speed rail transit are understandable—and yet both encourage the migration to the suburbs. The city must lose either way, so long as the ghetto is a growing mass that dominates the environment of its core and the development of its metropolitan area.

From the above argument, it is clear that the impact of the ghetto on the processes of metropolitan development has created or aggravated many of our most critical urban problems. These costs are borne by Negroes and whites alike. However, the same interaction between the ghetto and metropolis has produced other important distortions whose costs fall almost exclusively on the Negro community. The ghetto has isolated the Negro economically as well as socially. In the first place, the Negro has inadequate access to the job market. For him, informal methods of job search, common to low skilled employment, are largely limited to the ghetto. Jobs may be plentiful outside of the ghetto, yet he will know little or nothing of these opportunities. Moreover, the time and cost necessary to reach many suburban jobs, frequently compounded by the radial character of public transit services, often will discourage Negroes from taking or even seeking such jobs. Granted that the ghetto generates a limited number of service jobs, this effect is more than offset by the discriminatory practices of nonghetto employers. Research on the distribution of Negro employment in Northern metropolitan areas indicates the importance of these factors, by demonstrating that the proportion of Negroes in an area's work force is dependent on that area's distance from the ghetto and the racial composition of the surrounding residential neighborhoods. These distributional characteristics also affect the level of Negro employment. Estimates indicate that as many as 24,000 jobs in Chicago and 9,-000 in Detroit may be lost to the Negro community because of housing segregation.[2] These figures are based on 1956 and 1952 data and may well underestimate the current situation. The continu-

ing trend of job decentralization also may have aggravated the situation.

De facto school segregation is another widely recognized limitation of Negro opportunities resulting from housing market segregation. A large body of evidence indicates that students in ghetto schools receive an education much inferior to that offered elsewhere. Low levels of student achievement are the result of a complex of factors including poorly trained, overworked, and undermotivated teachers, low levels of per student expenditures, inadequate capital plants, and the generally low level of students' motivation and aspiration. This last factor is, of course, related to the ghetto's poverty and social disorganization.

The continued rapid growth of central city ghettos has seriously expanded the realm of *de facto* segregation and limited the range of possible corrective actions. For example, in 1952, 57 per cent of Cleveland's Negro students went to schools with more than 90 per cent Negro enrollment. In 1962, 82 per cent went to such schools. By 1965, Chicago, Detroit, and Philadelphia all had more than 70 per cent of their Negro students in these completely segregated schools.[3]

* * *

Nothing less than a complete change in the structure of the metropolis will solve the problem of the ghetto. It is therefore ironic that current programs which ostensibly are concerned with the welfare of urban Negroes are willing to accept, and are even based on, the permanence of central ghettos. Thus, under every heading of social welfare legislation—education, income transfer, employment, and housing—we find programs that can only serve to strengthen the ghetto and the serious problems that it generates. In particular, these programs

[2] John F. Kain, "Housing Segregation, Negro Employment, and Metropolitan Decentralization." Quarterly Journal of Economics, LXXXII, No. 2 (May 1968), 175–197.

[3] U. S. Commission on Civil Rights, Racial Isolation in the Public Schools (Washington, D. C.: U. S. Government Printing Office, 1967), Vol. 1, p. 13.

concentrate on beautifying the fundamentally ugly structure of the current metropolis and not on providing individuals with the tools necessary to break out of that structure. The shame of the situation is that viable alternatives *do* exist. * * *

* * * An alternative approach would aim at drastically expanding the supply of low income housing *outside* the ghetto. Given the high costs of reclaiming land in central areas, subsidies equivalent to existing urban renewal expenditures for use anywhere in the metropolitan area would lead to the construction of many more units. The new mix by type and location would be likely to favor small, single-family homes and garden apartments on the urban periphery. Some over-building would be desirable, the object being the creation of a glut in the low income suburban housing market. It is hard to imagine a situation that would make developers and renters less sensitive to skin color.

These measures would be greatly reinforced by programs that increase the effective demand of Negroes for housing. Rent subsidies to individuals are highly desirable, because they represent the transfer of purchasing power that can be used anywhere in the metropolitan area. Other income transfer programs not specifically tied to housing would have similar advantages in improving the prospects of ghetto dispersal. Vigorous enforcement of open housing statutes would aid the performance of the "impersonal" market, perhaps most importantly by providing developers, lenders, and realtors with an excuse to act in their own self interest. * * *

* * * The conclusion is straightforward. Where alternatives exist, and it has been a major effort of this article to show that they do exist, considerable weight must be placed on their differential impact on the ghetto. Programs that

tend to strengthen this segregated pattern should generally be rejected in favor of programs that achieve the same objectives while weakening the ghetto. Such a strategy is not only consistent with the nation's long-run goals, but will often be substantially cheaper in the short run.

Note

The authors recommend—as a transitional phase—the suburbanization of the Negro which does not necessarily imply integration into white residential neighborhoods. Instead, clusters of predominantly non-white communities might disperse into the suburbs. Although separation would continue for years at least, job opportunities would improve for blacks, programs to reduce de facto school segregation through busing would become more feasible, and the pressures on white, middle-class city neighborhoods and on long-distance transport facilities would ease.

Do you agree with the authors? Can you devise a systematic program for dispersed non-white neighborhoods? What are the political, legal, fiscal, governmental, social, psychological difficulties that your program must try to surmount?

THE IDEA IS TO SAVE THE HOUSING THAT IS THERE

Frank S. Kristof.
N.Y. Times, Jan. 15, 1972, p. 31, col. 2.

The bitter conflict stirred by the Forest Hills public housing project raises grave questions of public housing policy. The problem is epitomized by Percy Sutton's question: "Where do black people and Puerto Rican people turn if they want to change their lives and not forever be restricted to the ghetto?"

The answers—which few persons seem willing to face—are that:

(1) within the foreseeable future there is no ready means of escape from the ghettos for the poor—be they whites, blacks, or Puerto Ricans, and

(2) new public housing has become the most costly, inefficient and ineffective method of dealing with this problem. It is costly because the $35,000-per-unit Forest Hills project requires a subsidy of some $4,000 per family per year in direct public outlays or in Federal or local taxes foregone ($5,000 annually in the Ruppert Breweries site).

It is inefficient because in the last five years the New York City Housing Authority, one of the most able and best-managed agencies in the business, has not been able to expend the limited funds made available for low-rent public housing. The combination of rapidly rising construction costs, high land costs, inflexible Federal regulations, growing local, and now Federal, opposition to the location of projects in the ghetto areas and wild opposition to the location of these projects in better areas have combined to nearly halt the construction of new low-rent projects.

It is ineffective because low-rent projects that reasonably could obtain acceptance in better neighborhoods are small-scale projects (i. e. 150–350 apartments), precisely the kind that the housing authority has not been able to build within Federal cost limits.

Forced to large-scale projects in order to overcome the cost problems, the authority is producing the 840-unit Forest Hills project which makes a mockery of the concept of "vest-pocket" housing. This project will create a new ghetto of some 2,500 poor persons—be they black or white.

But none of this discussion meets Mr. Sutton's basic question, "How do the blacks and Puerto Ricans escape the ghet-

tos?" Given the available resources and existing ground rules, poor blacks and Puerto Ricans cannot escape until employment income improves. The answer to the problem must be found in the 99 per cent of the city's housing termed "existing housing inventory."

About a third of the residential land area of the city has housing classed as old, deteriorating or needing repair or rehabilitation. This represents some 800,-000 housing units. The great proportion of the city's poor live in these areas. At least three-quarters of this housing basically is sound.

This housing today is deteriorating into slums and ultimate abandonment because of poor neighborhood conditions, low incomes of families, low rents and inadequate maintenance. The inadequate maintenance is caused by the city's conflicting and contradictory housing policies, cumbersome administrative structure, frequent shifts in key administrative personnel, and a total failure to harness the private sector into a cooperative working arrangement with the public sector.

Compared with the capital costs of new public—and publicly aided—housing of $35,000 to $40,000 per unit, some 600,-000 units of basically sound housing can be brought back to standard at an average of $8,000 per unit; only a small proportion—perhaps 100,000 units—require or warrant gutting and reconstruction. It is a fair estimate that no more than 100,000 to 150,000 units are in such poor shape that they require demolition. Thus the capital costs of programs required to save the existing housing stock would be less than one-quarter of that required to replace it. And it could be done more quickly and with much less wholesale relocation of families.

Most of the necessary programs are basically in existence. A large part of the Federal Section 236 one-per cent interest rate program would be shifted to rehabilitation activities. A reorganized municipal loan program would require a major infusion of new funds. Finally, it would require expansion of the Federal rent supplement program to all families eligible for this assistance (in terms of their income levels) and would permit use of these programs in all existing housing that has been rehabilitated or is being maintained in good condition.

Finally, steps would have to be taken to improve municipal services to the neighborhoods in sanitation, health, and protection. Only by conserving precious existing housing and upgrading existing neighborhoods can there be any hope for alleviating ghetto life within a reasonable period of time.

Frank S. Kristof is director of the division of economics and housing finance of the Urban Development Corporation of New York.

A. OFFICIAL SITE SELECTION PRACTICES

GAUTREAUX v. CHICAGO HOUSING AUTHORITY

United States District Court, E.D.N.D.Illinois, 1969.
296 F.Supp. 907.

MEMORANDUM OPINION

AUSTIN, DISTRICT JUDGE. Plaintiffs, Negro tenants in or applicants for public housing, sue on behalf of themselves and all others similarly situated alleging that defendants, the Chicago Housing Authority (CHA), a municipal corporation, and C. E. Humphrey, Exec-

utive Director of CHA, have violated their rights under the Fourteenth Amendment of the Constitution of the United States. Count I charges that defendants intentionally chose sites for family public housing and adopted tenant assignment procedures in violation of 42 U.S. C.A. Secs. 1981 and 1983 for the purpose of maintaining existing patterns of residential separation of races in Chicago. Count III alleges that regardless of their intentions defendants violated 42 U.S. C.A. Secs. 1981 and 1983 by failing to select family public housing sites in such locations as would alleviate existing patterns of residential separation. Counts II and IV repeat the allegations in Counts I and III respectively and demand relief under 42 U.S.C.A. Sec. 2000d (Section 601 of Title VI of the Civil Rights Act of 1964).

On March 2, 1967, this court denied defendants' motion to dismiss for failure to state a claim upon which relief can be granted as to Counts I and II and granted the motion as to Counts III and IV, 265 F.Supp. 582. Plaintiffs' remaining requests for relief include (1) a declaratory judgment pursuant to 28 U.S.C.A. Secs. 2201 and 2202 that defendants have selected sites in violation of plaintiffs' constitutional rights, (2) a permanent injunction against the racially discriminatory aspects of the public housing system, (3) an order directing defendants to submit and carry out a plan for selection of future sites to eliminate these discriminatory aspects, and (4) a declaratory judgment that plaintiffs have the right under 42 U.S.C.A. Sec. 2000d to end the use of federal funds to perpetuate the racially discriminatory aspects of the public housing system and an injunction against such use. Since March 2, 1967 the parties have amassed thousands of pages of depositions, affidavits and exhibits. Both parties now move for summary judgment on Counts I and II. * * *

II.   Discriminatory Site Selection Procedures

In choosing sites for public housing, the CHA is directed by statute to follow these criteria:

[E]limination of unsafe and unsanitary dwellings, the clearing and redevelopment of blighted and slum areas, the assembly of improved and unimproved land for development or redevelopment purposes, the conservation and rehabilitation of existing housing, and the provision of decent, safe, and sanitary housing accommodations.

Ill.Rev.Stats., Ch. 67½, Sec. 8.2.

The City Council must approve all sites before they are acquired. Ill.Rev.Stats., Ch. 67½, Sec. 9. However, CHA is not compelled to acquire or build upon all sites thus approved. Humphrey Dep., p. 107.

Plaintiffs charge that the procedure mainly used by defendants to maintain existing patterns of racial residential separation involved a pre-clearance arrangement under which CHA informally submitted sites for family housing to the City Council Alderman in whose ward the site was located. CHA admits the existence of this procedure. E. g., Humphrey Aff't., p. 7. The Alderman to whom White sites were submitted allegedly vetoed these sites because of the 90% Negro waiting list and occupancy rate would create a Negro population in the White area. Plaintiffs allege that the few White sites which escaped an Alderman's informal veto were rejected on racial grounds by the City Council when they were formally submitted by CHA for approval.

A.   Statistics on Sites Considered and Selected.

As of July, 1968, CHA had in operation or development 54 family projects at 64 sites in Chicago consisting of 30,-848 units. CHA Sept. 20 Brief, p. 7, (adopting figures in Baron Aff't. submitted by plaintiffs). Exclusive of the four segregated White projects, CHA's family housing tenants are 99% Negroes. Stipulation, July 29, 1968. Exclusive of the four projects, housing units now located in neighborhoods between 50% and 100% Negro represent 99½% of the total units operated by CHA; units in neighborhoods between 75% and 100% Negro are 92% of the total; and units in areas over 95% Negro are two-thirds of the total. Baron Aff't., Ex. A. A glance at a map depicting Negro areas of residence in Chicago confirms that the 50% to 90% Negro areas are almost without exception contiguous with 90% to 100% Negro areas and that the relatively small numbers of Chicago Negroes not concentrated in the over 90% areas are almost entirely concentrated in the over 50% areas. Baron Aff't., Ex. F. Therefore, given the trend of Negro population movement, 99½% of CHA family units are located in areas which are or soon will be substantially all Negro. Baron Aff't., Ex. G. It is incredible that this dismal prospect of an all Negro public housing system in all Negro areas came about without the persistent application of a deliberate policy to confine public housing to all Negro or immediately adjacent changing areas.

To sustain their burden of proving that defendants' past and present policies have deprived them of their constitutional rights, plaintiffs contend that, during the consideration of each of the five major family housing programs since 1954, White sites meeting all appropriate criteria were rejected for racial reasons. Mr. Humphrey's affidavit sets forth (a) the total number of sites initially selected by CHA which met criteria of slum clearance, cost limitations, accessibility to public facilities, and overall metropolitan planning, (b) White sites initially selected which met these same criteria, (c) the number of apartment units planned for the White sites initially selected as a percentage of the total apartment units planned for all sites selected, (d) White sites finally approved by the City Council, and (e) Negro sites approved.

	(a) Sites Initially Selected	(b) White Sites Initially Selected	(c) Per Cent of Units in White Sites Initially Selected	(d) White Sites Approved	(e) Negro * Sites Approved
1955 Program	25	4	45%	0	19
1956 Program	11	4	30%	0	5
1958 Program	11	2	31%	0	7
1965 Program	18	9	50%	0	9
1966 Program	38	22	50%	2	9

* The sites classified by Mr. Humphrey as in Negro neighborhoods were primarily in over 95% Negro neighborhoods, but a few sites so classified were in neighborhoods which were ⅓ White.

Mr. Humphrey estimates that the sites selected initially by CHA for the five programs totalled 7,883 White housing units and 10,901 Negro units for a total of 18,784 units. One of the two White sites finally approved in 1966 included 400 units and was located on vacant land bounded on one side by a predominantly Negro area and partially occupied by dilapidated Negro shacks. Humphrey Dep. II, p. 190. The mere fortuity that this site was included in a 72.8% White census tract does not make it relevant to negate the inference of a policy against choosing sites in White neighborhoods. The other White site approved in 1966 was planned for 36 units. CHA did not proceed formally to submit for City Council approval seven White sites in 1965 because "the Aldermen in whose Wards those sites were located advised of community opposition and indicated they were opposed to such sites in their Wards." Humphrey Aff't., p. 6. One White site in the 1965 program was not submitted to the City Council because the City Department of Development and Planning advised against its acquisition, presumably because it conflicted with other urban planning projects. The only White site formally submitted was dropped from consideration by the City Council Committee on Planning and Housing. In 1966 the Department of Development and Planning advised against all 20 of the White sites not formally submitted because it "either (a) disapproved the site, (b) recommended deferment or (c) advised of Aldermanic opposition." Humphrey Aff't., p. 9. Since the Department merely assumed CHA's admitted former role in the preclearance procedure, it must be inferred in the absence of a suggestion to the contrary by defendants that only a minimal number of White sites in 1966 were disapproved because they conflicted with other urban development projects.

Additional family sites not included in the five programs were developed in 1963 in a Negro neighborhood (346 units) and in 1965 in two White neighborhoods (12 units). CHA also operates 5,050 units of public housing for elderly persons of which 54½% are in substantially White neighborhoods. Fifty-seven per cent of 2,047 elderly housing units presently in development are in White neighborhoods. The Illinois statutory procedures applying to family housing projects, including the requirement of City Council approval, apply also to elderly housing projects. (Plaintiffs' Complaint is not directed to elderly housing.) But the relatively equal distribution between White and Negro elderly housing sites actually developed arises from circumstances which are not applicable to family housing sites. In selecting tenants for elderly housing Mr. Rose conceived a "proximity rule" under which the applications of persons living within a two block radius of the site of an elderly housing project were granted priority and successive priorities were given to persons living within concentric half mile circles. Rose Dep., p. 196. The "proximity rule" helped "very obviously" to obtain an Alderman's approval because it was a "fair assumption" that a White site would be occupied by Whites. Rose Dep., p. 197. CHA abandoned the "proximity rule" after the Commissioner of Public Housing Administration informed CHA that enforcement of the "proximity rule" would result in loss of federal funds. Letter of December 11, 1963, Rose Dep., Ex. 4. Before abandonment of the "proximity rule" the selection of elderly housing sites in White areas was consistent with a policy against placing Negroes in White neighborhoods, and after its abandonment a change to a policy of selecting all Negro sites would almost certainly have resulted in a loss of federal funds. Therefore, the circumstances surrounding the choice of sites for elderly housing tend to prove a purpose to perpetuate racial separation rather than to refute it. The mix of White and Negro elderly housing sites is not relevant except to show (as does the nearly identical mix between White and Negro family sites initially selected by CHA) what would probably have happened in the absence of a policy of eliminating White sites on racial grounds.

No criterion, other than race, can plausibly explain the veto of over 99½% of the housing units located on the White sites which were initially selected on the basis of CHA's expert judgment and at the same time the rejection of only 10% or so of the units on Negro sites.

* * *

C. Legal Consequences of the Site Selection Policies.

On March 2, 1967 this court ruled that "plaintiffs, as present and future users of the system, have the right under the Fourteenth Amendment to have sites selected for public housing projects without regard to the racial composition of either the surrounding neighborhood or of the projects themselves." 265 F. Supp. 582, 583. The statistics on the family housing sites considered during the five major programs show a very high probability, a near certainty, that many sites were vetoed on the basis of the racial composition of the site's neighborhood. In the face of these figures, CHA's failure to present a substantial or even a speculative indication that racial criteria were not used entitles plaintiffs to judgment as a matter of law. Jones v. Georgia, 389 U.S. 24, 88 S.Ct. 4, 19 L.Ed.2d 25 (1967) (finding of discrimination based entirely on jury selection statistics and absence of explanation); Hernandez v. Texas, 347 U.S. 475, 74 S.Ct. 667, 98 L.Ed. 866 (1954) (same). The additional evidence of intent, composed mostly of uncontradicted admissions by CHA officials, also establishes plaintiffs' right to judgment as a matter of law either considered alone or in combination with the statistics. Cypress v. Newport News General and Nonsectarian Hospital Assn., 375 F.2d 648 (4th Cir. 1967).

Defendants urge that CHA officials never entertained racist attitudes and that "the racial character of the neighborhood has never been a factor in CHA's selection of a suitable site." Humphrey Aff't., p. 2. In view of CHA's persistent selection of White sites at the initial stage before the pre-clearance procedure and the candor of its officials on deposition, these statements are undoubtedly true. It is also undenied that sites for the projects which have been constructed were chosen primarily to further the praiseworthy and urgent goals of low cost housing and urban renewal. Nevertheless, a deliberate policy to separate the races cannot be justified by the good intentions with which other laudable goals are pursued. Brown v. Board of Education of Topeka, Shawnee County, Kansas, 347 U.S. 483, 74 S.Ct. 686, 98 L.Ed. 873 (1954). It is also true that there is no evidence that the Aldermen who vetoed White sites were necessarily motivated by racial animus when they followed a policy of keeping Negroes out of White neighborhoods. Most Aldermen apparently talked to their constituents and received unfavorable reactions before exercising their informal vetoes. Humphrey Dep. I, pp. 116–117; Rose Dep., p. 59. But even if the Aldermen's informal surveys were correct in their uniform assessment of public opinion, they cannot acquiesce in the sentiment of their constituents to keep their neighborhoods White and to deny admission to Negroes via the placement of public housing. U. S. v. School District 151, 404 F.2d 1125, (7th Cir. Dec. 17, 1968), at p. 11 of the slip sheet opinion; cf. Reitman v. Mulkey, 387 U.S. 369, 87 S.Ct. 1627, 18 L.Ed.2d 830 (1967).

CHA finally contends that the impulse originating and sustaining the policy against choosing White sites came from the City Council. But by incorporating as an automatic step in its site selection procedure a practice which resulted in a racial veto before it performed its statutory function of formally presenting the sites to the City Council, CHA made those policies its own and deprived opponents of those policies of the oppor-

tunity for public debate. It is no defense that the City Council's power to approve sites may as a matter of practical politics have compelled CHA to adopt the pre-clearance procedure which was known by CHA to incorporate a racial veto. In fact, even if CHA had not participated in the elimination of White sites, its officials were bound by the Constitution not to exercise CHA's discretion to decide to build upon sites which were chosen by some other agency on the basis of race. Cooper v. Aaron, 358 U.S. 1, 78 S.Ct. 1401, 3 L.Ed.2d 5 (1958); Orleans Parish School Board v. Bush, 268 F.2d 78 (5th Cir. 1959). See also U. S. v. School District 151, supra, in which the court observed at footnote 7, "There is no doubt that Board members were under severe pressure from District residents and that performance of duty was made difficult. But this cannot excuse the unconstitutional conduct justifiably found on this record." Although neither the City Council nor its members individually are parties to this suit, they will be bound by any order entered in this case against CHA of which they have actual notice. FRCP 65(d).

III. Relief

Plaintiffs' motion for summary judgment is granted on Count I; defendants' motion is denied.

A final judgment embracing all claims for relief shall not be entered for 30 days. During that time the parties should attempt to formulate a comprehensive plan to prohibit the future use and to remedy the past effects of CHA's unconstitutional site selection and tenant assignment procedures. If the parties cannot agree, each party shall submit a proposed judgment order.

Summary judgment is denied as to both parties on Count II. Although this court held on March 2, 1967 that Count II states a claim upon which relief can be granted under 42 U.S.C.A. Sec. 2000d (Section 601 of Title VI of the Civil Rights Act of 1964), judgment on Count II would, in the context of this case, determine the propriety of granting a narrow, drastic kind of relief—that of enjoining the use of federal funds. The Public Housing Administration has already taken a position against denying federal funds in reply to a rather scanty presentation protesting the selection of a few sites on the basis of racial composition of their neighborhoods. Letter of October 14, 1965 from Marie C. McGuire, Commissioner of PHA, to Rev. Jerome Hall of the West Side Federation, Swibel Dep., Ex. 3. In addition to the uncertainty of whether PHA would hold it appropriate to deny funds under the facts as they are now known, it is not clear whether even a temporary denial of federal funds would not impede the development of public housing and thus damage the very persons this suit was brought to protect. The use of a threatened denial of funds to coerce compliance with the Constitution, if coercion is necessary, would seem to be a less efficient remedy than an injunction available under Count I. Therefore, summary judgment is denied without precluding plaintiffs from showing on the basis of more facts that denial of federal funds is an appropriate form of relief.

Two further results of CHA's participation in a policy of maintaining existing patterns of residential separation of the races must be mentioned. First, as Dr. Baron's Affidavit discloses, the 188,000 White families eligible for public housing have understandably chosen in the main to forego their opportunity to obtain low cost housing rather than to move into all Negro projects in all Negro neighborhoods. This is an ironic but predictable result of a segregationist policy of protecting Whites from less than half as many (76,000) eligible Negro families. Second, existing patterns of racial separation must be reversed if there is to be a chance of averting the desperately intensifying division of Whites and Negroes in Chicago. On the basis of present trends of Negro residential concentration and of Negro migration into and White migration out of the central city, the President's Commission on Civil Disorders estimates that Chicago will become 50% Negro by 1984. By 1984 it may be too late to heal racial divisions.

Notes on Official Site Selection Practices

1. The judgment order appears at Gautreaux v. Chicago Housing Authority, 304 F.Supp. 736 (N.D.Ill.1969). It divides Cook County and Chicago into a limited Public Housing Area (defined as census tracts having a 30 percent or more non-white population, and all sites within one mile therefrom) and a General Public Housing Area. It directs the Housing Authority to begin building at least 700 Dwelling Units in the General Public Area of the City of Chicago before initiating any new units elsewhere. Thereafter, the Authority would have to place at least 75 percent of both newly constructed and leased dwelling units within the General Public Area of the City of Chicago, although the Authority could meet one-third of that quota by finding sites within the General Public Area in the rest of Cook County if Chicago residents could occupy those units.

The order also limited the size of projects (the Authority would have to justify any project to be occupied by more than 120 *persons*), the concentration of the non-elderly poor within census tracts, and even the placement of families within buildings (no children above the third story).

Section VIII of the order read in part:

"CHA shall affirmatively administer its public housing system in every respect * * * to the end of disestablishing the segregated public housing system which has resulted from CHA's unconstitutional site selection and tenant assignment procedures. Without limiting the foregoing, (a) CHA shall use its best efforts to increase the supply of Dwelling Units as rapidly as possible in conformity with the provisions of this judgment order and shall take all steps necessary to that end, including making applications for allocations of federal funds and carrying out all necessary planning and development; * * *"

Judge Austin made his order binding both upon the officers and employees of the CHA and the members of the City Council.

After entry of the judgment order, supra, the Court issued five subsequent orders between September and November, 1969. Cf. Gautreaux v. Chicago Housing Authority, 436 F.2d 306, 308 (7th Cir. 1970). No appeal was taken from these orders. However, when the Chicago Housing Authority failed to submit any sites for City Council approval well into 1970, a series of conferences was held in the Judge's Chambers. At one of these meetings, in June, 1970, a CHA Commissioner stated that submission of sites to the City Council before the upcoming Mayoral election, scheduled for April, 1971, "would have adverse political consequences." The Court then modified its earlier order and directed that sites be submitted to the Plan Commission and City Council in accordance with a specific timetable. Appeal was unavailing, 436 F.2d 306 (7th Cir. 1970).

2. It is one thing for a court to find the Housing Authority's active discrimination in site selection and tenant assignment; quite something else for a court to see that the Housing Authority increase the supply of Dwelling Units "as rapidly as possible" and locate three-fourths of those Units in previously white areas. Consider whether (and, if so, why) it is harder for courts to monitor housing dispersal than to monitor school desegregation or legislative reapportionment. How might the court enforce its Order if (a) the City Housing Authority does not apply for HUD funds, (b) the City Council lets its Workable Program (precondition for public housing funds) lapse, (c) the City Council, after angry neighborhood protests, refuses to approve enough sites in white areas, (d) HUD, after angry congressional protest, refuses to commit funds for projects scheduled for white, middle-class neighborhoods?

3. The New York City Housing Authority has sought actively to place low-income projects into higher income neighborhoods. It has usually been a grim business. Typical is the fury that erupted in Forest Hills, Queens—a middle-class, Jewish community:

THE BATTLE OF FOREST HILLS —WHO'S AHEAD?

Walter Goodman.
N.Y. Times, Feb. 20, 1972, VI (Mag.), p. 8.

The pile drivers are driving at 108th Street and 62d Drive; the picketers are picketing, the epithets are flying. A monument to many of our urban aches and pains is rising on that soggy land in Queens, commemorating the ideals and the limitations of those who are trying to manage this poor city and the dangerously conflicting needs and emotions of those who are trying to live in it.

The Forest Hills-Rego Park project, unfortunately and unfairly, has become in these angry months a symbol for New York's entire scatter-site housing program and for much else about the city. Initiated in 1966, when it was welcomed in principle by everybody, the program called for construction of low-income apartment houses in middle-income neighborhoods, at the same time that efforts continued, under the Model Cities program, to rebuild the worst sections of Harlem, Bedford-Stuyvesant and the Southeast Bronx. To most people the term "scatter site" suggested fairly small, widely distributed developments, in contrast to the huge buildings that had come to stand for public housing since the nineteen-thirties. The new program was designed to take families out of the slums, sources of infection for so many social ailments, and to move the city toward the objective of racial and, incidentally, economic integration. * * *

The Forest Hills site, 8.46 unused acres, [has for its immediate surroundings] several seven-story apartment houses, one fancier 15-story building, with rentals starting at $200 a month and going much higher, modest garden developments that were showing signs of running down, a new elementary school and the usual tangle of Queens highways. As the Planning Commission stated in approving the site, it was in "a strong and thriving community," a place where lots of building was going on, where people wanted to live. According to the 1960 census, only 2 per cent of the 55,332 people in the 17 census tracts immediately surrounding the site were nonwhite, and 1 per cent were Puerto Rican, so it did not seem likely that a low-income project would "tip" the neighborhood into ghettoism. * * *

One uninviting feature (not counting the people who live there) was the nature of the land. Beneath the property runs a stream, known as Horse Brook, which makes for a mucky subsoil; the planners understood that pilings would have to be sunk, at unusual expense, for the buildings' foundations. * * * The original design calling for a total of

828 apartments in seven structures—one 22-story building, three 12-story buildings and three 10-story buildings—was later judged too expensive to put up because of the marshy soil. The cost per apartment would have run over what the Federal Government was prepared to pay.

The design was altered several times; architects were changed, and in 1969 the plans were finally revised to build three 24-story buildings with 840 apartments—the highest and largest of the city's scatter-site efforts by a substantial margin, with about twice as many apartments as the runner-up. Even its supporters in Forest Hills concede that living space for 2,500 or more people was not what the term "scatter housing" brought to most minds. But there seemed to be no choice: Fewer and higher buildings meant lower foundation costs per apartment.

* * *

As the plans were finally developed, they contained a number of changes and additions designed for community appeal: 340 of the 840 apartments would be set aside for elderly persons—that is, 40.5 per cent instead of the 30 per cent originally scheduled—and the number of apartments for large families would be cut sharply; a two-story community center would contain facilities for the elderly as well as for others, and there would be a one-story early-childhood center, with seven classrooms for 200 children. (Both would be open to the surrounding community.) * * *

The foregoing plans were all made without consulting the people of Forest Hills. That may have been mere self-defense on the planners' part, for residents had made it clear that they were in no humor for collaboration. The local planning board voted against the project unanimously. * * * Early in 1971, as final plans were approved, protests broke out again at open meetings in

Queens of the City Planning Commission. The protestors dominated the proceedings, and now some people who had been against the original idea of putting a high school on the site were calling for the school rather than low-income apartments. By May, when the Housing Authority issued a history of the project which noted that it "does have support in the community (while there is some opposition as well)," it was evident that the parenthesis was misplaced. Whatever support existed was being drowned in the cries of the opponents.

Emotions are running high in Forest Hills, in forms to which America's cities are by now accustomed: meetings, manifestoes and lawsuits, marching and picketing, a bit of stone-throwing, a lot of sloganeering—loud, rude slogans about John Lindsay ("Adolf Lindsay—the middle class will bury you!") and quieter, ruder ones about the prospective newcomers * * *

The objections to the new project are not very different from those raised against virtually every scatter-site project conceived since 1966, from Riverdale to Howard Beach. * * *

Will the new inhabitants "overwhelm" the neighborhood, as opponents warn, turning it into another Grand Concourse? Supporters make light of the impact of a couple of thousand newcomers on a "community of a half million people." But the "community" which will feel the project's impact most is much smaller than that—closer to 15,000 than to 500,-000. It is not as stable as some advocates contend, and further changes can be anticipated, such as more middle-class black families moving into the garden apartments near the project.

Forest Hills is by no means a crime-free garden—but it is not the South Bronx either. Many residents once lived in places where fear today keeps people behind locked and bolted doors after dark. And their experience tells them that the deterioration of neighborhoods is connected with the arrival of blacks. "They're scared to death," says Haskell Lazere, the American Jewish Committee's New York director. "I have never in my life felt a community to be so in terror." * * *

The Forest Hills fight has seen much waving of that tattered word "racism," but the fact of race does not explain the resistance to low-income housing throughout the country, unless it is tied in with the fact of class. In 1966, 700 residents disrupted a City Planning Commission meeting to protest the first set of Queens scatter sites, with statements like, "We improved our lot by struggle. The Negroes want everything for free. How much can we take? How much can we pay? We'd be better off on relief." Elinor C. Guggenheimer, then on the Planning Commission, commented: "What has been significant and alarming in the hearings has been the outspoken dislike and fear of the poor, expressed not only by the average residents of the middle-income areas, but by their elected officials. Vituperative references to the poor and to the importance of preserving class distinctions were applauded."

Today Jerry Birbach and many others speak of themselves as people who have worked hard to get where they are, only to see nonworking people moving into apartments ("with air conditioning?") which cost more than some existing homes. "I think that when they go back to their old neighborhoods and they see that they were destroyed by low-income families and lack of planning by the city, they have a right to be afraid." Afraid of the poor? Afraid of the blacks? It is not easy to sort out such fears.

The situation is aggravated by the fact that the most prominent protestors against the project are Jewish. To be sure, a number are not—Joseph Devoy, chairman of the local planning board, is a churchgoing man, and there are a couple of Negroes in the Forest Hills Residents Association—but the area is, after all, three-quarters Jewish, and some of the opposition is based on that reality. For the past decade, the large Conservative temples of Queens have been suffering a decline in membership, with younger families moving to the suburbs and older couples retiring to Florida. Some rabbis view the project as an additional spur to dispersal, a concern that Herbert Kahn, friend of scatter housing, dismisses somewhat lightly as "the whole bag of Jewish paranoia." The project represents a special threat to the Orthodox, many of whom have come to Queens from deteriorating and dangerous neighborhoods in other boroughs. Dr. Alvin Lashinsky, outgoing president of the Queens Jewish Community Council, which claims to speak for 53 religious groups, fears that the project will disrupt Jewish life, in particular for those who require a congenial, close-knit setting to carry on their observances, their schools, their traditions. Once settled, the Orthodox find it difficult to move. They grant that they themselves encountered opposition when they first arrived in Queens, but point out that they came family by family; the Government did not plunk them down en masse. They are incensed at what they see as the latest in a series of assaults on New York's Jewish middle class; they speak of teachers intimidated by "community control" and students discriminated against by "open admissions."

The Forest Hills fight has become a field day for haters of blacks, haters of Jews, haters of Lindsay, haters of the poor and haters of the middle class. It has encouraged posturing on all sides. * * * Even if the city had performed

better from the beginning, when it made its bad bargain, this project, like nearly every project, would have met resistance. It was beyond the powers of reasoned discourse to convert the Forest Hills Residents Association.

At present, no one believes that the project can simply be stopped. Opponents are pressing now for an accommodation of some sort, such as reducing the size of the buildings and the number of tenants especially welfare tenants. (Dr. Lashinsky's group would prefer a breakdown of 70 per cent middle-income, 20 per cent low-income, 10 per cent elderly.) The administration position, its public position at any rate, is that a substantial change at this time would mean the end of low-income housing in Forest Hills. As Mr. Elliott told a State Senate committee in December: "The plain fact is that scaling down the project means killing it. Costs would exceed Federal guidelines. It would need new, all but impossible to achieve, approvals. This would mean further delay and even higher costs. Those who say make it smaller are saying make it vanish."

As I write, closed talks aimed at some sort of understanding are being held. "The project will not be built," maintains Seymour C. Samuels, president-elect of the Queens Jewish Community Council. "It will be settled around the table or in the streets." * * *

There are practical, as well as political and psychological, difficulties in the way of making any major change new. A cutback to 12-story buildings, I am assured, would require city funds to meet the large additional costs. Given the condition of the municipal budget, that is no minor obstacle. To turn the project into something other than a low-income development would also involve changes in funding methods, and no one seems able to say whether such an arrangement could sensibly be worked out for Forest Hills. And even if new approvals would be forthcoming, if the delays would not be excessive, if the additional costs could be met, any change would be strenuously resisted on principle, by the city's black leadership and by liberal groups. Scatter housing in New York has a dim future. * * *

Note

What advice have you for the Housing Authority as it seeks to defuse the Forest Hills situation? What advice have you for the Housing Authority as it plans shelter for the poor in Staten Island or elsewhere in middle-class Queens? Is Forest Hills a classic case of an irrepressible conflict? Are we dealing with issues of white against black? Of "rich" against poor? Of aesthetics and property values? Of the quality of education? Of stark naked fear?

Should courts play a more active role in site selection, to the point, perhaps, of actually designating sites for low-income projects—on the argument that the judiciary can survive outraged protest, while local politicians and bureaucrats cannot? Alternatively, should HUD or some other federal agency play a heavier role—on the related argument that bureaucrats in Washington, D. C., can safely ignore outraged protest, while Mayor Lindsay and his aides cannot? In this connection, consider whether Congress should form a federal public housing agency to build low-income projects and then turn their management over to local authorities; this was how public housing began before a lower court held that the Constitution did not permit it. United States v. Certain Lands in City of Louisville, 78 F.2d 684 (6th Cir. 1935). The decision has been much criticized, and many believe it is no longer correct law (if ever it was).

SHANNON v. UNITED STATES DEPARTMENT OF HOUSING AND URBAN DEVELOPMENT

United States Court of Appeals,
Third Circuit, 1970.
436 F.2d 809.

OPINION OF THE COURT

GIBBONS, Circuit Judge. Plaintiffs-Appellants in this action are white and black residents (some homeowners and some tenants), businessmen in, and representatives of private civic organizations in the East Poplar Urban Renewal Area of Philadelphia. They sue in their own right, and as class representatives of others similarly situated pursuant to Rules 23 and 17(b) of the Federal Rules of Civil Procedure. The individual defendants are those federal officials of the Department of Housing and Urban Development responsible for implementing the several federal statutes on fair housing and urban development. The Department of Housing and Urban Development (HUD) is also named as a defendant. Their complaint seeks a preliminary and a final injunction against the issuance of a contract of insurance or guaranty, and against the execution or performance of a contract for rent supplement payments, for Fairmount Manor, an apartment project which, when the complaint was filed, was about to be constructed in the East Poplar Urban Renewal Area. Jurisdiction is claimed under 28 U.S.C.A. § 1331 (federal questions), under 28 U.S.C.A. § 1361 (mandamus against federal officials), under 28 U.S.C.A. § 1343 (civil rights), and 28 U.S.C.A. § 2201 (declaratory judgments). A number of substantive and procedural irregularities are alleged in the steps leading to federal approval of the contract of insurance and the approval of the project for a rent supplement contract. The essential substantive complaint is that the location of this type of project on the site chosen will have the effect of increasing the already high concentration of low income black residents in the East Poplar Urban Renewal Area. The essential procedural complaint preserved on appeal is that in reviewing and approving this type of project for the site chosen, HUD had no procedures for consideration of and in fact did not consider its effect on racial concentration in that neighborhood or in the City of Philadelphia as a whole.

The district court denied plaintiffs' application for a preliminary injunction. It also denied defendants' Rule 12 motion to dismiss for failure to state a claim or for lack of jurisdiction. The defendants then filed an answer alleging lack of standing on the part of the plaintiffs, sovereign immunity, administrative discretion, and due compliance with all substantive and procedural requirements of the applicable law. An accelerated final hearing followed. On October 7, 1969 the district court filed an opinion containing findings of fact and conclusions of law and entered a final judgment dismissing the complaint.

We have been advised by the parties, although the facts do not fully appear in the record, that while the suit was pending construction of Fairmount Manor proceeded to completion and that the project is now occupied. We have also been advised that no mortgage insurance contract has been issued by HUD insuring a permanent mortgage on the project.

Fairmount Manor is designated a "221(d)(3)" project. This type housing project is authorized by Section 221(d) (3) of the Housing Act of 1954, 68 Stat. 590, 599, 12 U.S.C.A. § 1715l(d) (3). This mode of assistance, designed to assist private industry in providing for low and moderate income families, 12 U.S.C.A. § 1715l(a), provides that HUD may insure mortgages on housing

owned by eligible sponsors for the entire replacement cost of the project. 12 U.S. C.A. § 1715l(d)(3)(iii). Sponsors eligible for such one hundred per cent mortgage insurance include private nonprofit corporations. Philadelphia Housing Development Corporation (PHDC) is an eligible nonprofit corporation which was formed for the express purpose of becoming a sponsor for Fairmount Manor. It made application to HUD for mortgage insurance under § 221(d)(3), 12 U.S.C.A. § 1715l(d)(3), which was approved on November 20, 1968. As is often the case with such nonprofit sponsors, there is a connection between the nonprofit sponsor and a commercial real estate developer, in this case Abram Singer & Sons (Singer).

Rent supplement contracts are authorized by § 101 of the Housing and Urban Development Act of 1965. 12 U.S. C.A. § 1701s. That statute authorizes HUD to contract with "housing owners" to make annual payments on behalf of "qualified tenants." "Qualified tenants" are individuals or families having incomes below the maximum permitted in the area for occupation of public housing dwellings, 12 U.S.C.A. § 1701s(c) (1), and who are occupying substandard housing, or have been displaced by condemnation or disaster, or are physically handicapped or aged. 12 U.S.C.A. § 1701s(c)(2). "Qualified tenants" are, in short, tenants who, but for the rent supplement contract pursuant to which the government pays part of their rent, would be living either in low rent public housing or in slum housing. "Housing owners," for purposes relevant to this case, are 221(d)(3) nonprofit sponsors.[1]

---

[1] 12 U.S.C.A. § 1701s(b). As further provided in this section such term also includes a private nonprofit corporation or other private nonprofit legal entity, a limited dividend corporation or other limited dividend legal entity, or a cooperative housing corporation, which is the owner of a rental or cooperative housing project financed under a State or lo-

Prior to its approval of Fairmount Manor for 221(d)(3) mortgage insurance, HUD approved PHDC as a "housing owner" and Fairmount Manor as a project eligible for 100 percent occupancy by "qualified tenants" receiving rent supplement assistance. Such approval did not require that PHDC rent only to "qualified tenants," but only that if it did so the government would pay a rent supplement for all such tenants. The record does not disclose what percentage of the tenants now occupying the project are "qualified tenants."

Fairmount Manor is located between 6th and 7th Streets and Fairmount Avenue and Green Street in North Philadelphia. It is within the East Poplar Urban Renewal Area, which is bounded, in turn, by 5th and 9th Streets and Spring Garden Street and Girard Avenue. East Poplar is the subject of an urban renewal plan. That plan was formulated by the Philadelphia Redevelopment Authority, which is a local public agency (LPA) within the meaning of the Housing Act of 1949. 42 U.S.C.A. § 1450 et seq. That statute authorizes HUD to advance loans and grants to local public agencies for urban renewal projects. The LPA first formulated an urban renewal plan for East Poplar on October 24, 1958. This plan was formally revised on five occasions, and the presently effective plan is the Fifth Amended Plan for East Poplar, dated June, 1964. Federal funds were made available for site acquisition and other purposes in connection with the East Poplar urban renewal plan pursuant to a Loan and Grant Contract between HUD and the LPA. * *

cal program providing assistance through loans, loan insurance, or tax abatement and which prior to completion or construction or rehabilitation is approved for receiving the benefits of this section. Subject to the limitations provided in subsection (h) of this section, the term "housing owner" also has the meaning prescribed in such subsection.

The original urban renewal plan, adopted in 1959, called for a combination of rehabilitation of structures by property owners in part of the area, and of site acquisition in another part. Within the tract to be acquired existing structures deemed non-salvageable were to be cleared, and salvageable structures were to be conveyed to a redeveloper for rehabilitation as single family and multi-family owner-occupied dwellings. In addition the redeveloper [Singer] was to erect 244 single family owner-occupied units. The changes approved in Amendments One through Five left these features of the Plan essentially unchanged.

Plaintiffs claim that in reliance on the original Plan and subsequent amendments, which contemplated redevelopment of the Fairmount Manor area primarily for single family owner-occupied homes, they made substantial investments, commitments, and in some cases home purchases. Rehabilitation of some 70 structures originally deemed salvageable did not proceed on schedule and these were eventually vandalized. * *

Of the 244 new single family dwellings only 70 have been erected to date. * * *

In 1966 * * *, Singer proposed a 221(d)(3) project with federal rent supplements, to be built by him for a non-profit sponsor. The LPA entered into a revised contract with Singer for such a project on September 26, 1967. This contract referred to a 221(d)(3) project for families of moderate income, but it is undisputed that at all times after the project was first discussed a 221(d)(3) project with rent supplements was contemplated. * * *

On November 3, 1967 the HUD Regional Administrator approved the proposed revision in the Plan (Exhibit P–61). There was no final approval for rent supplements, however, until September of 1968. * * *

Plaintiffs rely on two other statutes. These are Title VI of the Civil Rights Act of 1964, Pub.L. 88–352, Title VI, July 2, 1964, 78 Stat. 252, 42 U.S.C.A. § 2000d et seq., and Title VIII of the Civil Rights Act of 1968, Pub.L. 90–284, Title VIII, Apr. 11, 1968, 82 Stat. 81, 42 U.S.C.A. § 3601 et seq. The 1964 Act provides in part:

> No person in the United States shall, on the ground of race, color, or national origin, be excluded from participation in, be denied the benefits of, or be subjected to discrimination under any program or activity receiving Federal financial assistance. (42 U.S.C.A. § 2000d).

> Each Federal department which is empowered to extend Federal financial assistance to any program or activity, by way of grant, loan, or contract other than a contract of insurance or guaranty, is authorized and directed to effectuate the provisions of section 2000d of this title with respect to such program or activity by issuing rules, regulations, or orders of general applicability which shall be consistent with the achievement of the objectives of the statute authorizing the financial assistance in connection with which the action is taken. * * * (42 U.S.C.A. § 2000d–1).

The 1968 Act provides in part:

> It is the policy of the United States to provide, within constitutional limitations, for fair housing throughout the United States. (42 U.S.C.A. § 3601).

> (d) The Secretary of Housing and Urban development shall

> * * * * *

> (5) Administer the programs and activities relating to housing and urban development in a manner affirmatively to further the policies of this subchapter. (42 U.S.C.A. § 3608(d)(5)).

The 1968 Civil Rights Act in other sections prohibits a number of discriminatory practices in the sale, rental, financing or brokerage of housing, and provides, with respect to such practices, an enforcement machinery. 42 U.S.C.A. § 3610. The section quoted above, however, refers to the Secretary's duties with respect to HUD's own programs and activities.

Read together, the Housing Act of 1949 and the Civil Rights Acts of 1964 and 1968 show a progression in the thinking of Congress as to what factors significantly contributed to urban blight and what steps must be taken to reverse the trend or to prevent the recurrence of such blight. In 1949 the Secretary, in examining whether a plan presented by a LPA included a workable program for community improvement, could not act unconstitutionally, but possibly could act neutrally on the issue of racial segregation. By 1964 he was directed, when considering whether a program of community development was workable, to look at the effects of local planning action and to prevent discrimination in housing resulting from such action. In 1968 he was directed to act affirmatively to achieve fair housing. Whatever were the most significant features of a workable program for community improvement in 1949, by 1964 such a program had to be nondiscriminatory in its effects, and by 1968 the Secretary had to affirmatively promote fair housing.

The interrelationship of the Housing Act of 1949 and the 1964 Civil Rights Act is recognized in the regulations issued by HUD. 24 C.F.R. §§ 1.1–1.7. Those regulations do not apply to insurance or guaranty contracts, 24 C.F.R. § 1.3, but they do apply to urban renewal programs under the Housing Act of 1949, and to "any assistance to any person who is the ultimate beneficiary under such program or activity." 24 C.F.R. § 1.3(3). Such persons include rent supplement benefici-aries. The regulations provide:

> A recipient, in determining the *loca-tion or types of housing,* * * * *financial aid or other benefits* which will be provided under any such pro-gram or activity, or the class of per-sons to whom, or the situations in which, such housing, * * * finan-cial aid, or other benefits will be pro-vided * * * or the class of persons to be afforded an opportunity to par-ticipate in any such program or activi-ty, may not, directly or through con-tractual or other arrangements, utilize criteria or methods of administration *which have the effect of subjecting persons to discrimination because of their race* * * * *or have the effect of defeating or substantially impairing the objectives of the program or activ-ity as respect persons of a particular race, color or national origin.* (24 C. F.R. § 1.4(b)(2)(i)) (emphasis add-ed). * * *

The regulation marks a recognition by the agency charged with enforcement that the 1964 Act must be read *in pari mater-ia* with the other statutes dealing with housing and urban development. In particular in adopting an "effects" test rather than an "intention" test for review-ing local actions respecting location of types of housing, the regulation recog-nizes that the 1964 Act gave refined meaning to the requirement in the Hous-ing Act of 1949 of a "workable program for community improvement." 42 U.S. C.A. § 1451(c). While no regulations have been issued under that part of the Civil Rights Act of 1968 applicable to the administration of HUD's own programs, 42 U.S.C.A. § 3608(d)(5), that statute, too, must be read as a refinement of the "workable program for community im-provement" requirement.

The issue then, is whether, when HUD approved a change from an urban renew-al plan which contemplated substantial owner-occupied dwellings to a plan which contemplated 221(d)(3) dwellings with rent supplement assistance, the procedures which it followed were in adequate com-pliance with the 1949 Housing Act and the 1964 and 1968 Civil Rights Acts.

The defendants challenge the standing of these plaintiffs to raise that issue. The district court held that they had the req-uisite standing. We agree. * * *

But, say the defendants, even assuming standing in the Article III sense and in the sense of 5 U.S.C.A. § 702, this is a case of agency action committed to agency discretion by law. Neither in the Hous-ing Act of 1949, 42 U.S.C.A. § 1450 et seq., nor in the relevant provisions of the Housing Act of 1954, 12 U.S.C.A. § 1715*l*, and the Housing and Urban De-velopment Act of 1965, 12 U.S.C.A. § 1701s, do we find language which ex-pressly or by necessary implication would make unreviewable HUD's decision to permit modification of the East Poplar Urban Renewal Plan by substituting a different type of housing than was con-templated in earlier versions of the Plan. Congressional intent to commit agency action to unreviewable discretion must appear from "clear and convincing evi-dence." Abbott Laboratories v. Gardner, 387 U.S. 136, 141, 87 S.Ct. 1507, 18 L. Ed.2d 681 (1967). There is no such ev-idence in the statutes under which HUD acted in this case. * * *

[Plaintiffs] contend that an essential part of the East Poplar plan was that res-ident home ownership would tend to cre-ate a more stable and racially balanced environment. They contend that the change to 221(d)(3) rent supplement housing introduced into a neighborhood in which there were already a large num-ber of public low rent housing projects another project for the same socio-eco-nomic group. * * * A 221(d)(3) project with 100 percent rent supplement occupancy is the functional equivalent of a low rent public housing project.

The defendants assert that HUD has broad discretion to choose between alternative methods of achieving the national housing objectives set forth in the several applicable statutes. They argue that this broad discretion permitted HUD in this case to make an unreviewable choice between alternative types of housing. We agree that broad discretion may be exercised. But that discretion must be exercised within the framework of the national policy against discrimination in federally assisted housing, 42 U.S.C.A. § 2000d, and in favor of fair housing. 42 U.S.C.A. § 3601. When an administrative decision is made without consideration of relevant factors it must be set aside. Scenic Hudson Preservation Conf. v. FPC, supra, 354 F.2d at 612. Here the agency concentrated on land use factors and made no investigation or determination of the social factors involved in the choice of type of housing which it approved. Whether such exclusive concentration on land use factors was originally permitted under the Housing Act of 1949, since 1964 such limited consideration has been prohibited.

Oddly enough, HUD in its Low Rent Housing Manual recognizes that concentration of low rent public housing can have adverse social, and hence planning, consequences. Paragraph 4(g) of that manual provides:

> [a]ny proposal to locate housing only in areas of racial concentration will be *prima facie* unacceptable and will be returned to the Local Authority for further consideration.

If there is a distinction between the effects of site selection of low rent public housing and of 221(d)(3) rent supplement housing, such distinction has not been developed in the record before us. No similar regulations applicable to 221 (d)(3) projects or to the rent supple-

ment program have been issued, though these programs, operating in conjunction, would seem to have the same potential for perpetuating racial segregation as the low rent public housing program has had. See Gautreaux v. Chicago Housing Authority, 296 F.Supp. 907 (N.D.Ill.1969); Hicks v. Weaver, supra.

Defendants contend that the interests which plaintiffs seek to vindicate are adequately protected by the complaint and enforcement procedures of Title VIII of the Civil Rights Act of 1968, 42 U.S. C.A. §§ 3610–3613, and Title VI of the Civil Rights Act of 1964, 42 U.S.C.A. § 2000d–1. They contend plaintiffs could have and did not exhaust enforcement remedies therein provided. We do not agree. Those sections of the 1968 Act establish a complaint and enforcement procedure for the redress of discriminatory housing practices prohibited by §§ 804, 805 and 806 of the Act, 42 U.S.C.A. §§ 3604, 3605, 3606. The complaint and enforcement procedures do not pertain to the Secretary's affirmative duties under § 808(d)(5) of the 1968 Act, 42 U.S. C.A. § 3608(d)(5), or under the 1964 Civil Rights Act, or under the Housing Act of 1949. As to these affirmative duties judicial review of his actions is available as outlined hereinabove. Similarly, the procedures afforded under the Civil Rights Act of 1964 are designed to provide redress against specific discriminatory acts, and do not pertain to the adequacy of HUD procedures.

Finally, defendants contend that there was no evidence in the record below of discriminatory site selection in the location of rent supplement projects. The district court found:

> What proof there is on this question shows without dispute that rent subsidy housing is evenly and well disbursed within the city as well as without, in both ghetto and non-ghetto areas. (305 F.Supp. at 225).

Leaving to one side the plaintiffs' contention that this finding goes beyond the proof and is in any event the result of the district court's circumscription of evidence on that point, we think the finding is irrelevant. Congress has since 1949 refined its view of the factors relevant to achieving national housing objectives. At least under the 1968 Civil Rights Act, and probably under the 1964 Civil Rights Act as well, more is required of HUD than a determination that some rent supplement housing is located outside ghetto areas. Even though previously located rent supplement projects were located in non-ghetto areas the choice of location of a given project could have the "effect of subjecting persons to discrimination because of their race * * * or have the effect of defeating or substantially impairing accomplishment of the objectives of the program or activity as respect persons of a particular race. * * *" 24 C.F.R. § 1.4(b)(2)(i). That effect could arise by virtue of the undue concentration of persons of a given race, or socio-economic group, in a given neighborhood. That effect could be felt not only by occupants of rent supplement housing and low cost housing, but by occupants of owner-occupied dwellings, merchants, and institutions in the neighborhood. Possibly before 1964 the administrators of the federal housing programs could, by concentrating on land use controls, building code enforcement, and physical conditions of buildings, remain blind to the very real effect that racial concentration has had in the development of urban blight. Today such color blindness is impermissible. Increase or maintenance of racial concentration is prima facie likely to lead to urban blight and is thus prima facie at variance with the national housing policy. Approval of Fairmount Manor * * * produced a decision which failed to consider that policy. * * * Without in any way attempting to limit the agency in the exercise of its own ad-

ministrative expertise, we suggest that some considerations relevant to a proper determination by HUD include the following:

1. What procedures were used by the LPA in considering the effects on racial concentration when it made a choice of site or of type of housing? [7]

2. What tenant selection methods will be employed with respect to the proposed project?

3. How has the LPA or the local governing body historically reacted to proposals for low income housing outside areas of racial concentration?

4. Where is low income housing, both public and publicly assisted, now located in the geographic area of the LPA?

5. Where is middle income and luxury housing, in particular middle income and luxury housing with federal mortgage insurance guarantees, located in the geographic area of the LPA?

6. Are some low income housing projects in the geographic area of the LPA occupied primarily by tenants of one race, and if so, where are they located?

7. What is the projected racial composition of tenants of the proposed project?

8. Will the project house school age children and if so what schools will they attend and what is the racial balance in those schools?

9. Have the zoning and other land use regulations of the local governing body in the geographic area of the LPA had the effect of confining low income housing to

7. Cf., El Cortez Heights Residents and Property Owners Ass'n v. Tucson Housing Auth., 10 Ariz.App. 132, 457 P.2d 294 (1969).

certain areas, and if so how has this affected racial concentration?

10. Are there alternative available sites?

11. At the site selected by the LPA how severe is the need for restoration, and are other alternative means of restoration available which would have preferable effects on racial concentration in that area?

The foregoing considerations are confined to the geographic area served by the LPA. We do not suggest that by so confining our listing we would restrict HUD to a review of factors operating only within such geographic area. The time may come when, in order to achieve the goals of the national housing policy, HUD will have to take steps to overcome the effects of contrasts in urban and suburban land use regulations. What those steps should be we do not here suggest.

Nor are we suggesting that desegregation of housing is the only goal of the national housing policy. There will be instances where a pressing case may be made for the rebuilding of a racial ghetto. We hold only that the agency's judgment must be an informed one; one which weighs the alternatives and finds that the need for physical rehabilitation or additional minority housing at the site in question clearly outweighs the disadvantage of increasing or perpetuating racial concentration.

Thus the district court judgment dismissing the complaint must be reversed. This brings us to a consideration of possible remedies. The defendants suggest that because the project has been completed and occupied by rent supplement tenants there is no longer any relief which may feasibly be given. The completion of the project and the creation of intervening rights of third parties does indeed present a serious problem of equitable remedies. It does not, however, make the case moot in the Article III sense. Relief can be given in some form. For example, the court could order that the project mortgage not be guaranteed under § 221(d)(3) and that it be sold to a private profit-making owner. It could order that the project continue in nonprofit ownership as a 221(d)(3) project, but that the rent supplement tenants be gradually phased out and replaced with market rental tenants. Since the disposition which we propose to make will require a remand to the district court and then to the administrative agency, it may well be that no equitable relief at all will in the end be required. This suit for an injunction and for declaratory relief will have been no less appropriate a means for obtaining judicial review even if that should prove to be the case.

The final order of the district court will be vacated and the cause remanded to the district court for the entry of an injunctive order prohibiting further steps in the finalization of mortgage insurance or other federal financial assistance to the project until such time as HUD makes a determination in substantive and procedural conformance with this opinion as to whether the location of a 221(d)(3) project with 100 percent rent supplement occupancy will enhance or impede a workable program for community improvement in conformity with the Civil Rights Acts of 1964 and 1968. That order should impose an appropriate time limit for such determination. Because of the intervening rights of tenants and others not before the court the order need not in the interim require termination of rent supplement payments. The HUD determination shall be reviewable by the district court which at that time may make an appropriate final order.

Notes to Shannon v. HUD

HUD, on October 2, 1971, published its proposed criteria for the approval of project sites under the § 235(i), § 236, rent supplement and public housing programs. 36 Fed.Reg.No. 192. HUD would require its officials to evaluate each site (or sponsor) as "superior", "adequate", or "poor" in eight essentials:

(1) Satisfies a need for low(er) income housing;

(2) Offers minority housing opportunities;

(3) Offers improved location for low(er) income families;

(4) Bears relationship to orderly growth and development;

(5) Relationship of proposed project to physical environment;

(6) Sponsor's ability to perform;

(7) Offers potential for creating minority employment and business opportunities;

(8) Makes provision for sound housing management.

A "poor" rating on any criterion disqualifies the project. Projects having the most "superior" ratings will get the highest priority on funds.

Criterion 2 is explained:

2. Minority housing opportunities.

Objective: To provide minority families with opportunities for housing in a wide range of locations.

To open up nonsegregated housing opportunities that will contribute to decreasing the effects of past housing discrimination.

A *superior* rating shall be given if the proposed project (1) is located so that, within the housing market area, it will provide opportunities for minorities for housing outside existing areas of minority concentration; or, (2) will be located in an area which is substantially racially mixed and on the basis of factors such as existing demographic trends it appears that the project will have no significant effect on the proportion of minority to non-minority families; or (3) will be located in or near an area of minority concentration,

but the location is part of an Urban Renewal, or Model Cities Area, or other official local development plan which part will include housing which is expected to serve a wide range of income levels and a racially varied population. (The plan should not currently be experiencing unusual delays in execution, nor should there be any indication that such delays will be encountered.)

An *adequate* rating shall be given if the proposed housing will be located in or near an area of minority concentration, but is necessary to meet overriding housing needs which cannot otherwise feasibly be met in that housing market area. Such a need could be demonstrated, for example, by evidence that land costs for appropriately zoned land in all other acceptable locations in the housing market area are too high to accommodate such housing; the only other acceptable locations are in parts of the housing market area which are or are becoming areas of minority concentration; or the residents of the project area or prospective residents of the proposed housing have expressed a desire for the project to be built in or near that area because they have strong cultural, social or economic ties to it. A need based on strong cultural, social, or economic ties should be supported by citizens' participation in Model Cities planning, or resolutions or other communications from citizens' associations or other broadly based neighborhood groups; opposing views should be accorded full consideration.

All "adequate" ratings shall be accompanied by documented findings based upon relevant racial, socioeconomic and other data and information supporting both the overriding need and the unavailability of alternate housing. An overriding need may not serve as the basis for an "adequate" rating if the only reason the need cannot otherwise feasibly be met is that discrimination on the basis of race, color, or national origin renders sites outside areas of minority concentration unavailable.

A *poor* rating shall be given to any proposed project which does not satisfy any of the above conditions and to any proposed project which is likely to cause a substantially racially mixed area to become one of minority concentration.

Criterion 3 is explained:

3. Improved location for low(er) income families.

Objective: To avoid concentrating subsidized housing in any one section of a city or metropolitan area.

To provide low(er) income families with opportunities for housing in a wide range of locations.

To locate subsidized housing in neighborhoods containing facilities and services that are typical of those found in neighborhoods consisting largely of unsubsidized housing of a similar price range.

To locate subsidized housing in areas reasonably accessible to job opportunities.

A *superior* rating shall be given if the proposed project is to be located in a section (consisting of the project neighborhood and the surrounding neighborhoods) that contains little or no subsidized housing and (a) the project is, or will be in the near future, accessible to social, recreational, educational, commercial, health facilities and services, and other municipal services that are equivalent to or better than those typically found in neighborhoods consisting largely of unsubsidized housing of a similar price range; and (b) travel time and cost via public transportation or private auto from the neighborhood to employment providing a range of jobs for low(er) income workers (exclud-

ing elderly) is considered excellent for such families in the metropolitan area or town. A superior rating may also be given if the housing is to be located in an Urban Renewal, Model Cities Area or a New Community and such housing is required to fulfill, respectively, the Urban Renewal Plan, Comprehensive City Demonstration Programs, or New Community Development Plan approved under title VII of the Housing and Urban Development Act of 1970.

An *adequate* rating shall be given to a proposal (1) in a section already containing a significant amount of subsidized housing if the addition of the proposed housing will not establish the character of the section as one of subsidized housing and the housing will provide an expanded range of housing opportunity for low(er) income families; or, (2) in an undeveloped area, if the scale of the project will not be such that it establishes the character of the section as one of subsidized housing; and, in the event of either (1) or (2), (a) the project is, or will be in the near future, accessible to social, recreational, educational, commercial, health facilities and services, and other municipal services that are equivalent to those typically found in neighborhoods consisting largely of unsubsidized housing of a similar price range, and (b) travel time and cost via public transportation or private auto from the neighborhood to employment providing a range of jobs for low(er) income workers (excluding elderly) is reasonable for such families in the metropolitan area or town.

A *poor* rating shall be given if the proposed project is to be located in a section characterized as one of subsidized housing, or if the proposed project would establish the character of the section as one of subsidized housing; or facilities and services accessible to the project are inferior to those generally found in neighborhoods consisting largely of unsubsidized housing of a similar price range, and there is little likelihood for improvement in the near future; or travel time and cost to employment providing a range of jobs for low(er) income workers (excluding elderly) will be appreciably greater than that usually required in the metropolitan area or town.

The site selection criteria do not cover rehabilitation projects, § 235 existing housing, § 23 leases of existing housing having fewer than 25 units, and new projects of fewer than 5 units.

Discuss the soundness of these criteria.

2. The Douglas Commission wrote in 1968:

"Nevertheless, we must conclude that the principal reason for the failure of [urban renewal], over its first 18 years, * * * is that too many local and federal officials in it and too many of their allies and supporters did not understand its major purposes or did not take them seriously. Instead of a grand assault on slums and blight as an integral part of a campaign for 'a decent home and a suitable living environment for every American family,' renewal was and is too often looked upon as a federally financed gimmick to provide relatively cheap land for a miscellany of profitable or prestigious enterprises * * * [to provide] sites for uses other than low and moderate income housing—e. g., for public, civic, and educational purposes as well as commercial, industrial, and higher income housing * * *."

The National Commission on Urban Problems, Building the American City (1968), pp. 153, 154.

Documenting this conclusion, the Report noted that approximately 400,000 dwelling units had been demolished in urban renewal areas, inhabited mostly by low- and moderate-income persons. Fewer than 200,000 dwelling units had been planned to replace the units lost; of this number, only 74,000 would qualify for housing subsidy. The public housing count was 18,766! Id. at 163.

Congress has attempted to remedy this situation in a series of moves beginning in 1966: In a residential redevelopment, the locality must "provide a substantial number of units of standard housing of low and moderate cost." Pub.L. 89–754, § 703–a. Two years later, Congress was even more specific and required that of all housing units built in urban renewal projects, at least one-half must be for low- and moderate-income families and at least 20 percent for low-income families and individuals. Housing and Urban Development Act of 1968, § 512, 42 U.S.C.A. § 1455(f) (1969). Finally, in 1970, Congress imposed the most rigorous standards ever:

"If any urban renewal project * * * includes the demolition or removal of any residential structure * * *, there shall be provided in the area within which the local public agency has jurisdiction (by construction or rehabilitation) standard housing units for occupancy by low and moderate income families * * * at least equal in number to the number of units occupied by such families prior to the demolition or removal of such structure or structures * * *."

The requirement applies to projects "recognized" after Dec. 24, 1969, and may sometimes be waived by the secretary of HUD.

Pub.L. 91–152, Tit. II, §§ 205, 210, 42 U.S.C.A. § 1455(h) (Supp.1972).

Discuss the basic tension between the goals of dispersing low-income housing from within areas of racial and poverty concentration and of replacing—on a one-to-one basis—all units of lower income housing that are lost to urban renewal (or to any other governmental program—viz. highway construction).

3. The poor (mostly non-white) are everywhere in Newark, Washington, Cleveland and other major cities. Is it foolish to seek a purely Newark solution for the dispersal of its poor? Must we begin far more emphatically to think of county-wide or even metropolitan-wide alternatives? Consider, for example, the recent decision in the Richmond, Virginia, public school case, where a federal judge ordered two neighboring suburban school districts to work closely with the Richmond school board in preparing a plan for the racial integration of all three school districts. Bradley v. School Bd. of City of Richmond, 338 F.Supp. 67 (D.C. E.D.Va.1972), reversed 462 F.2d 1058 (4th Cir. 1972), cert. granted sub nom. School Bd. of City of Richmond v. State Bd. of Educ., 93 S.Ct. 936 (1973). And consider also HUD Secretary Romney's TACLE proposal for a metropolitan area planning competition. Wall St. J., Dec. 30, 1971, p. 20, col. 1.

B. EXCLUSIONARY ZONING AND OTHER PRACTICES

NATIONAL COMM'N ON URBAN PROBLEMS BUILDING THE AMERICAN CITY

411-17 (1968).

Many of the most serious problems facing the Nation's cities are metropolitan in scope. Problems of air and water pollution, transportation, open space, solid waste disposal, housing, and employment do not end at municipal borders. At the same time, land-use controls, which are important factors in the creation and solution of such problems, are lodged in local governments with virtually no supervision by metropolitan or State agencies.

The constituency served by local officials making land-use decisions is quite different from that of the metropolitan area as a whole, whose concerns are affected by those decisions. It is hardly surprising that the interests and desires of one small jurisdiction do not always conform to the needs of the larger area of which it is a part. It is understandable, for example, that local officials—and their constituents—may not want a regional waste disposal plant within their own borders. Indeed, many officials would prefer to have as little development as possible of any kind—to keep the community just as it is. The inevitability of regional development may be obvious; but, to local officials and their constituents, it may be equally obvious that much of it should be located somewhere else. Similarly, there may well be a recognition that low- and moderate-income families within the metropolitan area need to be housed somewhere; that they need to be housed within any given jurisdiction in the area is far less readily accepted.

The problem takes on momentous proportions when compounded by the reliance of local governments on the property tax as their major source of revenue. How land within their borders is used becomes not merely a question of esthetic and social sensitivity, it is a matter of governmental solvency. Land-use controls have become a major weapon in the battle for ratables.

The game of "fiscal zoning" requires the players—i. e., zoning jurisdictions—to attract uses which add more in property taxes or local sales taxes than they require in expensive public services and to exclude uses which do not pay their own way. In essence, this means that jurisdictions are influenced to seek industrial and commercial uses and luxury housing and discourage or prohibit such uses as housing for low- and moderate-income persons. A further refinement is the desire to exclude housing which attracts families with many children in favor of housing with no children or as few as possible—all this because children require schools, the most significant expenditure item of local governments. Low-income housing is bad from a purely fiscal perspective because it does not add to the tax rolls the same amount of assessed value as luxury housing and because it often brings large families into a community. In addition, the families occupying such housing may require welfare and, it is widely believed, more of other services from the local government than higher income families require.

Of course, there are sometimes important nonfiscal policies behind certain types of exclusionary land-use decisions. "Undesirable" uses such as junkyards are not very attractive. "Undesirable" people—minority groups and the poor—would not "fit in." Indeed, for many suburban dwellers it was just such "undesirable" aspects of the city that drove them out; and for central city dwellers who have managed to find neighborhoods which satisfy them, it may well be the absence of such "undesirables" that keeps them in. * * *

Large-lot zoning

The most widely discussed form of exclusion is large-lot zoning, by which a jurisdiction attempts to limit development in substantial portions of its territory to single-family residences on very large lots. The actual effects of this practice are not easy to isolate. Many factors determine the price which a particular lot will command in the market. In a weak market, large-lot zoning may make little difference, with a 4-acre tract selling for little more than a 2-acre tract, and both sizes providing sites for shacks. In a strong market, a change from a 4-acre minimum to a 2-acre minimum may not lower the price per lot since potential developers are concerned primarily with the number of units that can be built on a given tract and will bid up the price of the rezoned tract. Comparisons of different properties are difficult. A 2-

acre lot may be more valuable than a 4-acre lot because of factors unrelated to size—location, topography, etc. Broad comparisons thus become extremely suspect. Nevertheless, it does appear that land prices per lot do diminish as minimum lot size is reduced, though usually not commensurately with the change in size. That is to say, a half-acre lot will cost less than a 1-acre lot, but will cost more than half the price. Table 6 gives figures for three suburban jurisdictions which serve to illustrate the point.

Even where prices per lot do not differ markedly from zone to zone, it does appear that large-lot zoning can have significant effects on the cost of housing.

TABLE 6.—PRICE OF VACANT LOTS BY RESIDENTIAL ZONING CATEGORY IN GREENWICH, CONN., ST. LOUIS COUNTY, MO., AND MONTGOMERY COUNTY, MD.

Zone	Minimum area per dwelling unit	Median sales price per lot
Greenwich, Conn.: [1]		
R–A–4	4 acres	$18,000
R–A–2	2 acres	19,700
R–A–1	1 acre	18,000
R–20	20,000 sq. ft	12,500
R–12	12,000 sq. ft	8,500
R–7	7,500 sq. ft	8,000
R–6	7,500 sq. ft	9,000
St. Louis County, Mo.: [2]		
R–1	1 acre	5,000
R–2	15,000 sq. ft	2,000
R–3	10,000 sq. ft	1,500
R–4	7,500 sq. ft	1,111
R–5	6,000 sq. ft	800
Montgomery County, Md.: [3]		
R–A	2 acres	18,000
R–E	40,000 sq. ft	11,800
R–R	20,000 sq. ft	7,650
R–15C	15,000 sq. ft	5,400
R–90	9,000 sq. ft	4,000
R–60	6,000 sq. ft	3,600

[1] Based on actual sales in 1966.
[2] Based on interviews with local officials and developers.
[3] Based on actual sales in 1967, available selling prices in Lusk's Real Estate Directory for Montgomery County, 1967 edition, and interviews with real estate developers and appraisers.
Source: Study prepared for the Commission by Department of Urban Affairs, Urban Research Center, Hunter College of the City University of New York.

First, extensive large-lot zoning in a given area has the effect of substantially reducing the total amount of housing that can be accommodated. If demand for new housing is strong, this restriction of the supply of housing sites will increase residential land costs generally. Moreover, by limiting the amount of land for housing on smaller lots and multi-family units below that which the market demands, the prices for these sites may be increased.

Second, the increase in the total house-and-lot price may be greater than the increase in land price caused by large-lot zoning. Some builders will simply not build the same house on a large lot that they will on a smaller lot, believing that a larger house is necessary. Furthermore, many builders observe a rule of thumb that the price of a lot should be some specified percentage of the total price of house and lot, e. g., 20 percent. If such a rule is strictly observed, a $1,000 increase in lot cost will result in a $5,000 increase in the price of the finished house and lot.

Third, large-lot zoning generally results in added costs for land improvements. Depending on specific requirements in the zoning ordinance regarding lot width, the effect can be to increase significantly the required linear feet of streets, sidewalks, gutters, sewers and water lines. Table 7 suggests the magnitude of such added costs.

In some instances the fiscal objectives behind large-lot zoning are quite clear. In St. Louis County, for example, the Parkway School District has calculated that any home costing less than $26,274 does not pay its own way in educational costs. On this basis, district officials oppose any change in zoning to permit lots of less than a quarter-acre, below which they believe housing costing less than this amount can be built.

But the motives for large-lot zoning are generally not clear-cut. Rather they are a mixture of fiscal and non-fiscal factors. Where a community does not wish to bear the cost of extending water and sewer lines beyond present develop-

ment, it may limit new development to large lots so that it can be served by septic tanks and wells. Some communities think of large-lot zoning as a means of retarding development or preserving rural character or open space. And, in some instances, it is clearly viewed as a technique for keeping out "incompatible" people—lower-income groups and minorities.

Large-lot zoning is a common and widespread practice in many major metropolitan areas. Data are scarce, however, since few metropolitan planning agencies or other regional groups have attempted to make consolidated area zoning maps or compile data on the total zoning pattern in the area. A Commission survey shows that 25 percent of metropolitan area municipalities of 5,000-plus permit *no* single-family houses on lots of less than one-half acre. Of these same governments, 11 percent have some two-acre zoning; 20 percent have some one-to-two-acre zoning; 33 percent have some one-half-to-one-acre zoning; and more than 50 percent have some one-fourth-to-one-half-acre zoning.

* * *

TABLE 7.—LAND IMPROVEMENT COSTS PER LOT BY RESIDENTIAL ZONING CATEGORY IN ST. LOUIS COUNTY, MO., AND MONTGOMERY COUNTY, MD.

Zone	Minimum area per dwelling unit	Average frontage per lot (feet)	Improvement cost per lot [1]
St. Louis County, Mo.:			
R–1 ____	1 acre _____	125	$4,375
R–2 ____	15,000 sq. ft _.	100	3,500
R–3 ____	10,000 sq. ft _.	80	2,800
R–4 ____	7,500 sq. ft _.	65	2,275
R–5 ____	6,000 sq. ft _.	55	1,925
Montgomery County, Md.:			
R–A ____	2 acres _____	150	5,250
R–E ____	40,000 sq. ft _.	125	4,375
R–R ____	20,000 sq. ft _.	100	3,500
R–150 __	15,000 sq. ft _.	80	2,800
R–90 ___	9,000 sq. ft _.	75	2,625
R–60 ___	6,000 sq. ft _.	60	2,100

[1] Estimated locally at $35 a foot of frontage.

Source: Study prepared for the Commission by Department of Urban Affairs Urban Research Center, Hunter College of the City University of New York.

In Connecticut, more than half of the vacant land zoned for residential use in the entire State is for lots of 1 to 2 acres. In Greenwich, Conn., a community of about 65,000 within mass-transit commuting distance of New York City, more than four-fifths of the total undeveloped area is zoned for minimum lots of 1 acre or more—39 percent for 4 acres, 25 percent for 2 acres, and 17½ percent for 1 acre.

In Cuyahoga County, which contains the city of Cleveland, 85,200 acres of vacant land are zoned for single-family residential use. Of this amount, only 28,425 acres, or 33 percent, are zoned for one-half acre or less; 42,225 acres, or 50 percent, are zoned for one-half to 1.9 acres minimum lot sizes; and 14,550 acres, or 17 percent, are zoned for 2 acres or more. Thus, 67 percent of the vacant land zoned for single-family development in the core county of the Cleveland SMSA is zoned for minimum lots of one-half acre or more. In outlying Geauga County, for example, 85 percent of the residentially zoned area requires lots of 1 acre or more.

Exclusion of multiple dwellings

Perhaps an even more important form of exclusionary zoning is the limitation of residential development to single-family houses. Again, motives are undoubtedly mixed. Apartments are viewed by many suburban dwellers as central city structures, having no place in the "pastoral" setting of suburbia. Apartment dwellers are sometimes stereotyped as transients who, not having the permanent ties to the community which homeownership provides, will not be sufficiently concerned about the community or their own residences. But fiscal motives are also present. There is a concern that apartments—especially those which have large units and thereby can accommodate large families—will not pay their way. Where low- or moderate-income units are involved, both fiscal and social concerns increase.

Multifamily housing units generally provide the best opportunities for housing persons of low and moderate incomes. The rental nature of such housing, and the savings produced by spreading land costs over a greater number of units, place such housing within the means of many who could not afford new single-family houses. Furthermore, many of the publicly assisted housing programs are multifamily programs and depend on the existence of zoning for multifamily structures.

Most jurisdictions have some zoning for multifamily structures, and it appears that more suburban zoning jurisdictions are permitting them than in the past. A Commission survey shows that 87 percent of municipalities and New England-type townships of 5,000-plus have at least one district in which multifamily housing can be built. But the figure fails to reveal the way in which such zoning comes about. In many suburban jurisdictions zoning for multifamily housing occurs only through a piecemeal rezoning process. There is at any one time little undeveloped land available for multifamily construction. The price of land zoned for such purposes is thus inflated because of the uncertainty about the total amount of land that may become available. Of the undeveloped land zoned for residential purposes in the New York metropolitan area, for example, 99.2 percent is restricted to single-family dwellings.

Minimum house size requirements

The most blatant, though not most extensive, exclusionary practice takes the form of excluding housing which fails to contain a minimum floor area as set out in the zoning ordinance. Such requirements raise the lower limit of construction costs, and thus can be the most direct and effective exclusionary tool.

An extreme application of the technique is found in Bloomington, Minn., an affluent suburb of the Twin Cities. Bloomington imposes a 1,700-square-foot minimum floor area. At a square foot construction cost of $15.82, the average for FHA Section 203 housing in the Minneapolis area in 1966, the smallest house permitted would require $26,894.00 in construction costs alone. * * *

Exclusion of mobile homes

Exact figures are not available on the extent to which mobile homes are excluded from zoning jurisdictions, but it appears that a large number of governments exclude them entirely or limit them to industrial and commercial areas. A study in 1964 showed that in New York State, of 237 zoning ordinances reviewed, over half excluded mobile homes either explicitly or by imposing minimums relating to floor area, height, or other factors which mobile homes could not meet. Only 82 communities permitted mobile homes on individual lots, as distinguished from mobile home parks; and in all but 12 of these communities such lots had to be in areas zoned for industrial or commercial uses. Only 11 communities permitted mobile home parks to locate in residentially zoned areas.

The exclusion of mobile homes in large part reflects a stereotyping of their appearance and of their occupants. Many see mobile homes as unattractive and occupied by people who do not take care of their homes or neighborhood. Such images are often derived from viewing mobile homes in the midst of industrial districts, to which they are so often relegated. Moreover, there are sometimes fiscal reasons for exclusion in addition to those generally applicable to housing which might accommodate low- and moderate-income families. In many areas mobile homes are not taxable as real property. And in some States they are not subject to local personal property taxes because of special State levies, the imposition of which may exempt them from local taxes. In New York State, mobile homes are taxable as real property, and the fiscal motive for exclusion is accordingly reduced. The high exclusion rate in New York may thus indicate an even greater amount of exclusion in other States.

Unnecessary high subdivision requirements

Land improvement costs are becoming an increasingly important part of housing costs. Zoning, as discussed above, affects such costs by determining the number of linear feet of various improvements which are required to serve a given house. Subdivision regulations determine the precise specifications of such improvements, as well as the amount of land within a subdivision which can actually be devoted to housing. The more expensive these requirements are the greater the cost of housing.

Subdivision regulations differ widely from locality to locality. By demanding higher quality improvements, a jurisdiction can effectively increase the cost of housing and thereby exclude a greater number of potential home buyers from the market.

Administrative practices

Some of the most effective devices for exclusion are not discoverable from a reading of zoning and subdivision ordinances. Where rezoning is, in effect, necessary for many projects or where apartment development requires a special exception (as it does in some suburban communities), officials have an opportunity to determine the intentions of each developer with some precision. How many bedrooms will the units in his apartment house contain? What will be the rent levels? To whom does he plan to rent or sell? "Unfavorable" answers in terms of the fiscal and social objectives of such officials do not necessarily mean that permission will be denied outright. They may, however, mean long delays, attempts to impose requirements concerning dedications of land and provision of facilities over and above those which are properly required under the subdivision ordinance, and the like.

One witness heard by the Commission in Philadelphia stated the problem this way:

> Regulations are frequently written so that each apartment developer has to negotiate with the community in order to get in at all. He negotiates either to get a zoning amendment because there is no permitted area zoned for apartments in the community, or he negotiates in order to get a special exception because the zoning ordinance does not permit apartments outright. In both cases the negotiation process is one of trying to bid up the price or cost of the apartment structure in order to limit the number of people who can come in at lower cost. * * *

> A subdivision ordinance was used as a club in Abington against a veterans' cooperative which had intended to build about 250 free-standing houses which conformed with the zoning ordinance. This was in the late 1950's. I was a member * * *. It was an outright question of refusing to give the approval, and keeping the matter in the courts until the veterans' group broke up because they couldn't wait for housing. * * *

APPEAL OF GIRSH

Supreme Court of Pennsylvania, 1970.
437 Pa. 237, 263 A.2d 395.

ROBERTS, Justice. By agreement dated July 13, 1964, appellant contracted to purchase a 17½ acre tract of land,

presently zoned R–1 Residential,[1] in Nether Providence Township, Delaware County. Appellant agreed to pay a minimum of $110,000 (later changed by agreement to $120,000) for the property. He further agreed to request the Township Board of Commissioners to change the R–1 Residential zoning classification so that a high-rise apartment could be built on the property and to pay $140,000 if this request were granted.

Nether Providence is a first-class township with a population of almost 13,000 persons and an area of 4.64 square miles. Approximately 75% of the Township is zoned either R–1 or R–2 Residential, which permit the construction of single-family dwelling units on areas not less than 20,000 and 14,000 square feet, respectively. Multi-unit apartment buildings, although not *explicitly* prohibited, are not provided for in the ordinance. The Township contains the customary commercial and industrial districts, as well as two areas where apartments have been permitted and constructed only after variances were secured.

After the Board refused to amend the zoning ordinance, appellant sought a building permit to construct two nine-story luxury apartments, each containing 280 units.[2] The permit was refused since the R–1 Residential classification does not permit multiple dwellings. Appellant appealed to the Zoning Board of Adjustment and announced that he would attack the constitutionality of the zoning ordinance in lieu of seeking a variance. The Zoning Board sustained the ordinance and denied relief. The Court of Common Pleas of Delaware County af-

---

[1] R–1 Residential zones require minimum lot sizes of 20,000 square feet. The most common of the permissible land uses under the R–1 Residential classification is a single-family detached dwelling.

[2] Appellant stated in court that he would reduce the number of units per building to 216.

firmed, and appellant took this appeal. We hold that the failure of appellee-township's zoning scheme to provide for apartments is unconstitutional and reverse the decree of the court below.

Initially, it is plain that appellee's zoning ordinance indeed makes no provision for apartment uses. Appellee argues that nonetheless apartments are not explicitly *prohibited* by the zoning ordinance. Appellee reasons that although only single-family residential uses are provided for, nowhere does the ordinance say that there shall be no apartments. In theory, an apartment use by variance is available, and appellee urges that this case thus is different from prior cases in which we severely questioned zoning schemes that did not allow given uses in an *entire* municipality. See Exton Quarries, Inc. v. Zoning Board of Adjustment, 425 Pa. 43, 228 A.2d 169 (1967); Ammon R. Smith Auto Co. Appeal, 423 Pa. 493, 223 A.2d 683 (1966); Norate Corp. v. Zoning Board of Adjustment, 417 Pa. 397, 207 A.2d 890 (1965).

Appellee's argument, although perhaps initially appealing, cannot withstand analysis. It is settled law that a variance is available *only* on narrow grounds, i. e., "where the property is subjected to an unnecessary hardship, unique or peculiar to itself, and where the grant thereof will not be contrary to the public interest. The reasons to justify the granting of a variance must be 'substantial, serious and compelling.' " Poster Advertising Company, Inc. v. Zoning Board of Adjustment, 408 Pa. 248, 251, 182 A.2d 521, 523 (1962). In light of this standard, appellee's land-use restriction in the case before us cannot be upheld against constitutional attack because of the *possibility* that an *occasional* property owner may carry the heavy burden of proving sufficient hardship to receive a variance. To be constitutionally sustained, appellee's land-use restriction must be reasonable. If the failure to make allowance in the

Township's zoning plan for apartment uses is unreasonable, that restriction does not become any the more reasonable because once in a while, a developer may be able to show the hardship necessary to sustain a petition for a variance.[3] At least for the purposes of this case, the failure to provide for apartments anywhere within the Township must be viewed as the legal equivalent of an explicit total prohibition of apartment houses in the zoning ordinance.

Were we to accept appellee's argument, we would encourage the Township in effect to spot-zone a given use on variance-hardship grounds. This approach distorts the question before us, which is whether appellee must provide for apartment living as part of its *plan* of development. Cf. Eves v. Zoning Board of Adjustment, 401 Pa. 211, 164 A.2d 7 (1960).

By emphasizing the possibility that a given land owner *could* obtain a variance, the Township overlooks the broader question that is presented by this case. In refusing to allow apartment development as part of its zoning scheme, appellee has in effect decided to zone *out* the people who would be able to live in the Township if apartments were available.

---

[3] We must start with the basic proposition that absent more, an individual should be able to utilize his own land as he see fit. U.S.Const. Amends. V, XIV. Although zoning is, in general, a proper exercise of police power which can permissibly limit an individual's property rights, Village of Euclid, Ohio v. Ambler Realty Co., 272 U.S. 365, 47 S.Ct. 114, 71 L.Ed. 303 (1926), it goes without saying that the use of the police power cannot be unreasonable. E. g., Eller v. Board of Adjustment, 414 Pa. 1, 198 A.2d 863 (1964). If the zoning ordinance is unreasonable, it is no saving that some people may show the requisite degree of hardship to obtain a variance. The hardship necessary to sustain an application for a variance borders on economic disaster, but this provides no protection for the individual who is disadvantaged to a substantial, but lesser, extent. This infringement on this latter individual's right to use his own property cannot be allowed unless it is reasonable.

Cf. National Land and Investment Co. v. Easttown Twp. Board of Adjustment, 419 Pa. 504, 532, 215 A.2d 597, 612 (1965): "The question posed is whether the township can stand in the way of the natural forces which send our growing population into hitherto undeveloped areas in search of a comfortable place to live. We have concluded not. A zoning ordinance whose primary purpose is to prevent the entrance of newcomers in order to avoid future burdens, economic and otherwise, upon the administration of public services and facilities can not be held valid."

We emphasize that we are not here faced with the question whether we can compel appellee to zone *all* of its land to permit apartment development, since this is a case where *nowhere* in the Township are apartments permitted. Instead, we are guided by the reasoning that controlled in *Exton Quarries*, supra. We there stated that "The constitutionality of zoning ordinances which totally prohibit legitimate businesses * * * from an entire community should be regarded with particular circumspection; for unlike the constitutionality of most restrictions on property rights imposed by other ordinances, the constitutionality of total prohibitions of legitimate businesses cannot be premised on the fundamental reasonableness of allocating to each type of activity a particular location in the community." 425 Pa. at 58, 228 A.2d at 179. In *Exton Quarries* we struck down an ordinance which did not allow quarrying anywhere in the municipality, just as in Ammon R. Smith Auto Co. Appeal, supra, we did not tolerate a total ban on flashing signs and in *Norate Corp.,* supra, we struck down a prohibition on billboards everywhere in the municipality. Here we are faced with a similar case, but its implications are even more critical, for we are here dealing with the crucial problem of population, not with billboards or quarries. Just as

we held in *Exton Quarries, Ammon R. Smith,* and *Norate* that the governing bodies must make some provision for the use in question, we today follow those cases and hold that appellee cannot have a zoning scheme that makes no reasonable provision for apartment uses.

Appellee argues that apartment uses would cause a significant population increase with a resulting strain on available municipal services and roads, and would clash with the existing residential neighborhood. But we *explicitly* rejected both these claims in *National Land,* supra: "Zoning is a tool in the hands of governmental bodies which enables them to more effectively meet the demands of evolving and growing communities. It must not and can not be used by those officials as an instrument by which they may shirk their responsibilities. Zoning is a means by which a governmental body can plan for the future—it may not be used as a means to deny the future. * * * Zoning provisions may not be used * * * to avoid the increased responsibilities and economic burdens which time and natural growth invariably bring." 419 Pa. at 527–528, 215 A. 2d at 610. Cf. Delaware County Community College Appeal, 435 Pa. 264, 254 A.2d 641 (1969); O'Hara's Appeal, 389 Pa. 35, 131 A.2d 587 (1957). That reasoning applies equally here. Likewise we reaffirm our holding in *National Land* that protecting the character—really the aesthetic nature—of the municipality is not sufficient justification for an exclusionary zoning technique. 419 Pa. at 528–529, 215 A.2d at 610–611.

This case presents a situation where, no less than in *National Land,* the Township is trying to "stand in the way of the natural forces which send our growing population into hitherto undeveloped areas in search of a comfortable place to live." Appellee here has simply made a decision that it is content with things as they are, and that the expense or change in character that would result from people moving in to find "a comfortable place to live" are for someone else to worry about. That decision is unacceptable. Statistics indicate that people are attempting to move away from the urban core areas, relieving the grossly over-crowded conditions that exist in most of our major cities. Figures show that most jobs that are being created in urban areas, including the one here in question, are in the suburbs. New York Times, June 29, 1969, p. 39 (City Edition). Thus the suburbs, which at one time were merely "bedrooms" for those who worked in the urban core, are now becoming active business areas in their own right. It follows then that formerly "outlying", somewhat rural communities, are becoming logical areas for development and population growth—in a sense, suburbs to the suburbs. With improvements in regional transportation systems, these areas also are now more accessible to the central city.

In light of this, Nether Providence Township may not permissibly choose to only take as many people as can live in single-family housing, in effect freezing the population at near present levels. Obviously if every municipality took that view, population spread would be completely frustrated. Municipal services must be provided *somewhere,* and if Nether Providence is a logical place for development to take place, it should not be heard to say that it will not bear its rightful part of the burden.[4] Certainly it can protect its attractive character by requiring apartments to be built in accordance with (reasonable) set-back, open

space, height, and other light-and-air requirements,[5] but it cannot refuse to make any provision for apartment living. The simple fact that someone is anxious to build apartments is strong indication that the location of this township is such that people are desirous of moving in, and we do not believe Nether Providence can close its doors to those people.

It is not true that the logical result of our holding today is that a municipality must provide for all types of land use. This case deals with the right of people to *live on land*, a very different problem than whether appellee must allow certain industrial uses within its borders.[6] Apartment living is a fact of life that communities like Nether Providence must learn to accept. If Nether Providence is located so that it is a place

---

[4] Perhaps in an ideal world, planning and zoning would be done on a *regional* basis, so that a given community would have apartments, while an adjoining community would not. But as long as we allow zoning to be done community by community, it is intolerable to allow one municipality (or many municipalities) to close its doors at the expense of surrounding communities and the central city.

[5] As appellants indicate, the apartments here in question would cover only 2.7 acres of a 17.7 acre tract, would be located far back from the road and adjacent properties, and would be screened by existing high trees. Over half of the trees now on the tract would be saved.

It should be pointed out that much of the opposition to apartment uses in suburban communities is based on fictitious emotional appeals which insist on categorizing all apartments as being equivalent to the worst big-city tenements. See Babcock and Bosselman, Suburban Zoning and the Apartment Boom, 111 U.Pa.L.Rev. 1040, 1051–1072 (1963), wherein the authors also convincingly refute the arguments that apartments necessarily will: not "pay their own way"; cut off light and air; become slums; reduce property values; be destructive to the "character of the community"; and bring in "low-class" people.

[6] Even in the latter case, if the Township instituted a total ban on a given use, that decision would be open to at least considerable question under our decision in *Exton Quarries*, supra.

In addition, at least hypothetically, appellee could show that apartments are not appropriate on the site where appellant wishes to build, but that question is not before us as long as the zoning ordinance in question is fatally defective on its face. Appellee could properly decide that apartments are more appropriate in one part of the Township than in another, but it cannot decide that apartments can fit in *no* part of the Township.

where apartment living is in demand, it must provide for apartments in its plan for future growth; it cannot be allowed to close its doors to others seeking a "comfortable place to live."

The order of the Court of Common Pleas of Delaware County is reversed.

BELL, C. J., files a concurring opinion.

JONES, J., files a dissenting opinion in which COHEN and POMEROY, JJ., join.

BELL, Chief Justice (concurring).

This case poses for me a very difficult problem. One of the most important rights, privileges and powers which (at least until recently) has differentiated our Country from Communist and Socialist Countries, is the right of ownership and the concomitant use of property. The only limitation or restriction thereof was "sic utere tuo ut alienum non laedas" —a right to use one's property in any way and manner and for any purpose the owner desires, except and unless it injures the property of another, or endangers or seriously affects the health or morals or safety of others.

Then along came zoning with its desirable objectives. However, desirable or worthwhile objectives have too often been carried to an unfair or unwise or unjustifiable extreme, or an extreme which makes the Act or Ordinance illegal or unconstitutional.

This Ordinance cannot be sustained under the theory or unwitting pretense that it is necessary for, or has a substantial relationship to the protection of the health or morals or safety of the people of that Township, and, as Justice Roberts points out, it cannot and should not be legalized or Constitutionalized under the theory of "general welfare" *

or "public interest or worthy objectives." Furthermore, Courts, Legislators, zoning bodies and most of the public have forgotten or rendered meaningless Article I, Section 1, of the Constitution of Pennsylvania, which provides: "All men are born equally free and independent, and have certain inherent and indefeasible rights, among which are those of * * acquiring, possessing and protecting property * * *."

I believe that a County or Township can "reasonably" regulate the location, size, height, setbacks, light and air requirements, etc. of apartment houses or buildings, but that neither a County nor a Township can *totally prohibit* all apartment houses or buildings. Cf. Exton Quarries Inc. v. Zoning Board of Adjustment, 425 Pa. 43, 228 A.2d 169. Whether an ordinance which makes no provision for, or authorization of, apartment houses is equivalent to a total prohibition thereof raises (at least, for me) a difficult question. However, I have come to the conclusion that the present zoning ordinance (1) *in practical effect* amounts to a prohibition of apartment houses, and (2) cannot be saved or legalized by a right to a variance which is grantable only upon proof of (a) unnecessary hardship upon and which is unique or peculiar to the property involved, as distinguished from the hardship arising from the impact of the zoning ordinance upon the entire district, and (b) where the proposed variance will not be contrary to the public safety, health, morals or general welfare: DiSanto v. Zoning Board of Adjustment, 410 Pa. 331, 189 A.2d 135; Sheedy v. Zoning Board of Adjustment, 409 Pa. 655, 187 A.2d 907; Brennen v. Zoning Board of Adjustment, 409 Pa. 376, 187 A.2d 180; Joseph B.

---

* Aesthetics have no place or part in zoning either as support or justification for, or

rejection of any plan. Moreover, it is sometimes forgotten that very few can ever agree on what is or is not "aesthetic."

Simon .& Co. v. Zoning Board of Adjustment, 403 Pa. 176, 168 A.2d 317.

For these reasons, I concur in the Opinion of the Court.

JONES, Justice (dissenting).

Appellant attacks the constitutionality of the zoning ordinance in question on two levels. First, he maintains that it is unconstitutional for the Township to prohibit the construction of apartment buildings throughout the entire township. Second, he argues that the ordinance as applied to the Duer Tract in particular is unconstitutional because the property cannot reasonably be graded and developed for single-family residences.

The principles governing the disposition of cases involving a constitutional attack on a zoning ordinance have been oft-repeated in our case law. "The test of constitutionality of a zoning ordinance is whether it bears a substantial relation to the health, safety, morals or general welfare of the public: [Citing authority]. One who challenges the constitutionality of a zoning ordinance has no light burden and it is settled that before a zoning ordinance can be declared unconstitutional it must be shown that its provisions are clearly arbitrary and unreasonable, having no substantial relation to the public health, safety, morals or general welfare. If the validity of the legislative judgment is fairly debatable, the legislative judgment must be allowed to control: [Citing authorities]." Glorioso Appeal, 413 Pa. 194, 198, 196 A.2d 668, 671 (1964).[1]

Appellant's first argument is that the zoning ordinance is unconstitutional in that it makes no provision for apartment

buildings anywhere in the township. Appellant maintains that this Court looks askance at zoning ordinances which totally prohibit a legitimate use anywhere within the municipality, citing Exton Quarries, Inc. v. Zoning Board of Adjustment, 425 Pa. 43, 228 A.2d 169 (1967); Ammon R. Smith Auto Co. Appeal, 423 Pa. 493, 223 A.2d 683 (1966); Norate Corp. v. Zoning Board of Adjustment, 417 Pa. 397, 207 A.2d 890 (1965); Eller v. Board of Adjustment, 414 Pa. 1, 198 A.2d 863 (1964). Of these four cases, the authority most in point is Exton.[2] In Exton we struck down a zoning ordinance as unconstitutional which prohibited any and all quarrying within the township. We noted that the township was sparsely settled and that the proposed quarry would be located some distance from the nearest residential neighborhood. We held that "a zoning ordinance which totally excludes a particular business from an entire municipality must bear a more substantial relationship to the public health, safety, morals and general welfare than an ordinance which merely confines that business to a certain area in the municipality." (425 Pa. at 60, 228 A.2d at 179.)

The Township, in support of its position that the zoning ordinance in question is constitutional, cites two decisions of our Court. In Dunlap Appeal, 370 Pa. 31, 87 A.2d 299 (1952), we upheld an ordinance which forbid the construction of row houses, and in Mutual Supply Co. Appeal, 366 Pa. 424, 77 A.

[1] See also: National Land and Investment Co. v. Easttown Twp. Bd. of Adjustment, 419 Pa. 504, 511, 512, 215 A.2d 597 (1965); Colligan Zoning Case, 401 Pa. 125, 131, 162 A.2d 652 (1960); Bilbar Constr. Co. v. Easttown Twp. Bd. of Adjustment, 398 Pa. 62, 72, 141 A.2d 851 (1958).

[2] In Norate we struck down an ordinance which prohibited all "off-site" advertising signs anywhere within the township. In Ammon Smith we struck down a similar ordinance banning all flashing signs. In Eller we voided an ordinance requiring minimum set-offs for mushroom houses on the grounds that the set-offs would require a person to own approximately 69 acres before he could grow mushrooms. I conclude that none of these three cases is cogent authority for the position advanced by the appellant.

2d 612 (1951), we upheld an ordinance which permitted only single-family dwellings in the face of a challenge from a coal mining company which wanted to build coal mining structures on the surface of the land which were necessary for the mining operations below the surface.[3]

My research indicates that the exact question presented on this appeal has never been decided at the appellate level in this Commonwealth. The one decision I have found most directly on point is Lofmer, Inc. v. Board of Adjustment of Easttown Twp., 11 Chester Cty. R. 66 (1963), in which the Court of Common Pleas of Chester County upheld the constitutionality of a zoning ordinance which changed the applicable zoning classification to prohibit apartment buildings. The court held that the fact that a zoning ordinance makes no provision for a particular use of property in the township does not, ipso facto, make the ordinance unconstitutional. I am in agreement with this conclusion.

Exton, upon which the majority opinion places the most reliance, can be distinguished on two grounds. First, *Exton* involved the total prohibition of a valid use. The ordinance now before us does not involve a total prohibition; the ordinance simply does not make provision for apartment buildings. While at first blush this might appear to be a distinc-

tion without a difference, there is, in reality, an important difference. Apartment buildings are permissible—and, in fact, have been constructed—if a variance is granted. Therefore, it is not correct to say that the Township totally prohibits the construction of apartment buildings.[4]

Second, the natural expansion of the majority's conclusion is that Nether Providence must provide for all types of high-density, residential land use. This is an unsound result. It makes no more sense to require a rural township to provide for high-rise apartments than to provide for industrial zones; likewise, it would not make sense to require an industrial municipality to provide for agricultural uses. By concluding that the township must provide for high-rise apartments, the majority also impliedly holds that every possible use, having no greater detrimental effect, must also be allowed. In my opinion, this decision places us in the position of a "super board of adjustment" or "planning commission of last resort," a position which we have heretofore specifically rejected. National Land and Investment Co. v. Easttown Twp. Bd. of Adjustment, 419 Pa. 504, 521–22, 215 A.2d 597, 606–607 (1965).

Even if I were to accept appellant's logic, it must still be affirmatively demonstrated that high-rise apartment buildings are a *suitable* land use within the township. The court below held that appellant had failed to carry his burden of proof, and I find no fault in this decision. The evidence indicates that 90% of the township is presently already developed. A land planner and municipal consultant testified that he had studied the remaining undeveloped properties within the township and concluded that none of them was suitable for high-rise apartments. Furthermore, the township is residential in nature with a relatively

---

3 In *Mutual Supply*, we stated in pertinent part: "The exclusion of industrial use involves an exercise of legislative discretion under the existing facts and circumstances. In the present instance, there was evidence that 'the highest and best use of the area is residential.' Within a half-mile radius of Mutual's surface plot there are not less than forty residences of an average value of $30,000 each. Of course, if the ordinance's exclusion of industrial use would conclusively prevent the appellants from mining and removing their coal for which they have full mining rights without liability for surface support, then a different question would be presented." (366 Pa. at 430, 431, 77 A.2d at 615.)

4 Cf. Honey Brook Twp. v. Alenovitz, 430 Pa. 614, 243 A.2d 330 (1968).

sparse population. A high-rise apartment project would produce a significant increase in population which would tax the limited municipal services available in the township.[5] Accordingly, I find it impossible to say on the face of this record that a township such as Nether Providence is constitutionally required to make provision for high-rise apartments in its zoning ordinances.[6]

I turn now to appellant's second contention, viz., that the zoning ordinance permitting only single-family dwellings is unconstitutional as applied to the Duer Tract in particular. Appellant's first argument under this heading is that the ordinance has no relation to the public health, safety and welfare. I cannot agree. The proposed apartment complex would be the largest of its kind in Delaware County, housing an estimated 1,600 persons, and would increase the population of the township by 13%. We cannot refute the conclusion that such a large and rapid increase in population would place a strain on the township's limited municipal services and rural roads. Furthermore, except for the railroad tracks, the area surrounding the Duer Tract is composed exclusively of single-family dwellings. The proposed apartment towers would be incompatible with the existing residential neighborhood and would introduce a structure completely out of proportion to any other building in the township. Furthermore, the complex would present a density problem in this area of the township. The First Class Township Code specifically empowers local municipalities to zone for density;[7] I conclude that the ordinance in question is a proper application of that power.

Appellant's second argument is that the ordinance is unreasonable, arbitrary and discriminatory as applied to the Duer Tract because of the prohibitive expense involved in grading and preparing the land for single-family residences. There is no question that the property contains some topographical features which are less than desirable for the construction of single-family homes. The record is replete with conflicting testimony, however, as to how much expense would be required to grade the tract and divert the creek which runs through the property. There is evidence in the record to support the court's conclusion that these preparatory expenses would not make the cost of the homes prohibitively expensive. The court pointed out that a development of single-family houses is now being constructed on a neighboring tract which is very similar topographically to the Duer Tract. Furthermore, appellant made a firm commitment to buy the property regardless of whether he was successful in having the zoning classification changed. Apparently when he purchased the property, therefore, appellant concluded that he could successfully build and sell single-family homes on the tract.

Therefore, I would hold that the Township is *not* constitutionally required to

[5] Since I would hold that appellant failed to prove that high-rise apartments would be a suitable land use in the township, *Exton* is inapposite, for there was no question in *Exton* that quarrying was a suitable land use.

[6] Decisions in other jurisdictions support this conclusion. See, e. g., Valley View Village, Inc. v. Proffett, 221 F.2d 412, 418 (6th Cir. 1955), (per Potter Stewart, J.); Fanale v. Borough of Hasbrouck Heights, 26 N.J. 320, 139 A.2d 749, 752 (1958) (per Weintraub, C. J.); Connor v. Township of Chanhassen, 249 Minn. 205, 81 N.W.2d 789, 794–795 (1957); Fox Meadow Estates, Inc. v. Culley, 233 App. Div. 250, 252 N.Y.S. 178 (1931), aff'd per curiam, 261 N.Y. 506, 185 N.E. 714 (1933); Guaclides v. Borough of Englewood Cliffs, 11 N.J.Super. 405, 78 A.2d 435 (1951) (per William Brennan, J.).

[7] Act of June 24, 1931, P.L. 1206, art. XXXI, § 3101, as amended, 53 P.S. § 58101. This section has been repealed by the recently enacted Pennsylvania Municipalities Planning Code. The new Code also empowers municipalities to zone for density. Act of July 31, 1968, P.L. ——, No. 247, § 603(4), 53 P.S. § 10603(4) (pp).

provide for multiple-unit apartment buildings in its zoning ordinance and that the ordinance in question is not unconstitutional as applied to the Duer Tract.

I dissent.

COHEN and POMEROY, JJ., join in this dissenting opinion.

Notes on Exclusionary Zoning

1. The Town of New Castle, a rural community in northern Westchester County, New York, has a population of 14,700. It is one of nine towns and villages in the County that prohibit multifamily housing. On January 10, 1972, two trade associations of builders, architects, and apartment house owners sued to invalidate the Town's zoning ordinance for depriving them of the right to carry on their trade. Analyze this theory.

George Frank, director of the Builders Institute, one of the two plaintiffs, admitted that his suit might appear to be throwing the builders into a "strange alliance" with social reformers. N.Y. Times, Jan. 11, 1972, p. 32, col. 5.

If this suit succeeds, what is to keep plaintiffs from building only luxury apartments? Note, in this vein, that builder Girsh had wanted to construct 280 luxury units. Are there any individuals or groups having standing to intervene to argue for the interests of potential low income tenants. (Cf. the Madison Township Case, note 4, infra). If the New Castle ordinance is struck down, what should the decree provide: for an unrestricted right to build apartments anywhere in the Town? for a revised zoning ordinance that allows some apartment development? If the decree takes the latter form, and the Town sets aside five percent of the vacant, residentially zoned land for multiple dwellings, is a court likely to interfere any further with the legislative will? Note, in this connection,

the dissenting language of Justice Jones in Appeal of Girsh.

> "One who challenges the constitutionality of a zoning ordinance has no light burden * * * If the validity of the legislative judgment is fairly debatable, the legislative judgment must be allowed to control."

This may be boiler plate judicial prose, but it also fairly states the attitude of most courts.

2. While allowing apartments, the Prince George's County (Maryland) zoning ordinance fixes the number of bedrooms within a project. Not more than 40 percent of the apartments may contain two bedrooms; another 10 percent may contain three bedrooms [100 units = 160 bedrooms]. One builder sought to increase his bedroom mix from the permitted 367 up to 442. He argued, unsuccessfully, that the ordinance both unreasonably deprived him of property and denied equal protection to those large-sized families unable to afford the purchase of a single-family dwelling or unwilling to purchase one. Malmar Associates v. Board of County Commissioners for Prince George's County, 260 Md. 292, 272 A.2d 6 (Ct. App.1971).

Against the builder's argument that his plan would add only nine students to the elementary school system, the Court wrote:

> "Even nine additional students in an overcrowded school situation may well be sufficient to support the District Council's conclusion inasmuch as the line must be drawn at some point; and if the cup is already completely full, even one additional drop will make it overflow * * *"

The court cited the County's doubled population (357,000 to 700,000) during the 1960s and spoke of the pressing need to control density. Suppose, however, that the Prince George's ordinance had restricted even more stringently the percentage of two and three bedroom apartments: What criteria should a court consider against the claim that the regulation is unreasonable? Note, in this connection, that the Prince George's ordinance does not regulate the maximum number of bedrooms in one-family houses (zoning ordinances rarely—maybe never—do), and that many zoning ordinances require a minimum floor area for one family houses.

The court quickly rejected the builder's equal protection argument but on grounds other than that the plaintiff was asserting the equal protection rights of others. In the absence of a class action or an organizational plaintiff having a common interest with members of a deprived group (viz, the NAACP seeking to enforce the voting rights of poor, disenfranchised blacks), may plaintiff A become the spokesman for the constitutional rights of B?

3. In Oakwood at Madison, Inc. v. The Township of Madison, Docket No. L–7502–70PW (New Jersey Super.Ct., Middlesex County 1970) six low-income individuals joined two developers in attacking the Madison Township zoning ordinance. The individuals represented a class of non-residents who had failed to find housing they could afford within the Township.

Virtually all of Madison's vacant residential acreage was zoned for one or two acre lots, yet the town had had no new two acre development since the 1930's and only one acre subdivisions had been proposed after 1964. Testimony indicated that houses built on such large lots could not be sold for less than $45,000–50,000. The zoning ordinance also restricted multi-family development so that only 500 to 700 units could still be built within the town. Three bedroom apartments were banned, and no more than 20 percent of a project's units could contain two bedrooms.

The Court invalidated the entire Township Ordinance for failing to consider the housing needs of the region, and for failing to "promote a reasonably balanced and well-ordered plan for the entire municipality."

"In Madison Township's approach to the objective of balance, its attempted cure is a worse malady than whatever inbalance [re: fiscal · needs] existed. About 8000 acres of land, apparently prime for low or moderate income housing development, have been taken out of the reach of 90% of the population, prohibitive in land and construction costs. The acreage available for multi-family apartment units is miniscule. Families with more than one child are barred from multi-family apartments because of the one and two bedroom restrictions, restrictions without any guise of a health or safety purpose.

"The exclusionary approach in the ordinance under attack coincides in time with desperate housing needs in the county and region and expanding programs, Federal and state, for subsidized housing for low income families.

"Regional needs are a proper (Editors' query: necessary) consideration in local zoning * * * In pursuing the valid zoning purpose of a balanced community, a municipality must not ignore housing needs, that is, its fair proportion of the obligation to meet the housing needs of its own population and of the region. Housing needs are encompassed within the general welfare. The general welfare does not stop at each municipal boundary * * *."

Compare the court's argument in the Madison Township case with the rationale of Appeal of Girsh and the theory of the builders' complaint in the Town of New Castle suit, supra. Is the Madison Township ordinance fatally defective because it exceeds the power delegated to the Township by New Jersey's zoning enabling law, or because it deprives the builder plaintiffs of property without due process, or because it deprives the individual plaintiffs of some constitutionally protected right? Or is there some other reason?

4. The *Girsh* opinion relies heavily on the Court's earlier decision in National Land and Investment Co. v. Easttown Twp. Board of Adjustment, 419 Pa. 504, 215 A.2d 597 (1965). There the Court declared invalid a two acre minimum lot size requirement. The case is a landmark of sorts, for the Court refused to be easy hostage to the usual vague arguments (viz, congestion, rustic simplicity) that local bodies usually intone to justify low-density zoning. Later, in Appeal of Kit-Mar Builders, Inc., 439 Pa. 466, 268 A.2d 765 (1970), the Court indicated, in striking down a one-acre requirement, that sewerage problems could never excuse exclusionary zoning.

Minimum lot size requirements, if so excessively large as to discourage nearly all development, operate directly against poor and middle-class homebuyers alike. Indirectly, the requirements may cause special hardship for the poor by reducing the supply and thereby increasing the cost of smaller, buildable lots—if there are any. Paradoxically, therefore, a township that permits some new development on smaller lots may discriminate more against the poor than does a township that permits no new development on smaller lots.

5. Fiscal zoning has become a phrase of contempt, yet towns seem to have a legitimate interest both in achieving fiscal balance and in planning for orderly development. Fiscal balance must remain an elusive goal in any fast growing area as long as the funding for public education—the major item of local expenditure—remains so closely tied to the property tax base. In time, the property tax may be on its way out as the chief support vehicle for public education. Compare Serano v. Priest with San Antonio Independent School Dist. v. Rodriguez, set out in Chapter 1, supra. Until then, towns will continue to worry about balanced budgets, credit ratings, and debt ceilings, and who can say that is wrong.

Town planners also worry about the aesthetics and inefficiency of uncontrolled development. The homebuilder cares little about the cosmos; he will plant his houses wherever there is a buildable site without concern for the integration of housing with jobs, transportation, supporting government facilities, and certainly without concern for the indiscriminate waste of virgin land. By zoning large areas at so low a density that builders are curbed, a town gains the breathing pause necessary to plan for the next decade, and who can say that is wrong. Cf. Golden v. Town of Ramapo, 30 N.Y.2d 359, 285 N.E.2d 291 (1972).

What *is* wrong is the system of government that lets (*and* requires) each township to go it alone without any meaningful check or guidance from a central source and without any centralized system for the collection and redistribution of revenue.

JAMES v. VALTIERRA

Supreme Court of the United States, 1971.
402 U.S. 137, 91 Sup.Ct. 1331, 28 L.Ed.2d 678.

Mr. Justice BLACK delivered the opinion of the Court.

These cases raise but a single issue. It grows out of the United States Housing Act of 1937, 42 U.S.C.A. § 1401 et seq., which established a federal housing agency authorized to make loans and grants to state agencies for slum clearance and low-rent housing projects. In response, the California Legislature created in each county and city a public housing authority to take advantage of the financing made available by the Federal Housing Act. See California Health and Safety Code § 34240. At the time the federal legislation was passed the California Constitution had for many years reserved to the State's people the power to initiate legislation and to reject or approve by referendum any Act passed by the state legislature. California Const. Art. IV, § 1. The same section reserved to the electors of counties and cities the power of initiative and referendum over acts of local government bodies. In 1950, however, the State Supreme Court held that local authorities' decisions on seeking federal aid for public housing projects were "executive" and "administrative," not "legislative," and therefore the state constitution's referendum provisions did not apply to these actions.[1] Within six months of that decision the California voters adopted Article XXXIV of the state constitution to bring public housing decisions under the State's referendum policy. The Article provided that no low-rent housing project should be developed, constructed or acquired in any manner by a state public body until the project was approved by a majority of those voting at a community election.[2]

The present suits were brought by citizens of San Jose, California, and San Mateo County, localities where housing authorities could not apply for federal funds because low-cost housing proposals had been defeated in referendums. The plaintiffs, who are eligible for low-cost public housing, sought a declaration that Article XXXIV was unconstitutional because its referendum requirement violated: (1) the Supremacy Clause of the United States Constitution; (2) the Privileges and Immunities Clause; and (3) the Equal Protection Clause. A three-judge court held that Article XXXIV denied the plaintiffs equal protection of the laws and it enjoined its enforcement. 313 F.Supp. 1 (N.D.Cal. 1970). Two appeals were taken from the judgment, one by the San Jose City Council, and the other by a single member of the council. We noted probable jurisdiction of both appeals. 398 U.S. 949 (1970); 399 U.S. 925 (1970). For the reasons that follow, we reverse.

The three-judge court found the Supremacy Clause argument unpersuasive, and we agree. By the Housing Act of 1937 the Federal Government has offered aid to States and local governments for the creation of low-rent public housing. However, the federal legislation does not purport to require that local governments accept this or to outlaw local referendums on whether the aid should be accepted. We also find the privileges and immunities argument without merit.

---

[1] Housing Authority v. Superior Court, 35 Cal.2d 550, 557–558 (1950).

[2] "Section 1. No low rent housing project shall hereafter be developed, constructed, or acquired in any manner by any state public body until, a majority of the qualified electors of the city, town or county, as the case may be, in which it is proposed to develop, construct, or acquire the same, voting upon such issue, approve such project by voting in favor thereof at an election to be held for that purpose, or at any general or special election.

"For the purpose of this article the term 'low rent housing project' shall mean any development composed of urban or rural dwellings, apartments or other living accommodations for persons of low income, financed in whole or in part by the Federal Government or a state public body or to which the

Federal Government or a state public body extends assistance by supplying all or part of the labor, by guaranteeing the payment of liens, or otherwise. * * *

"For the purposes of this article only 'persons of low income' shall mean persons or families who lack the amount of income which is necessary (as determined by the state public body developing, constructing, or acquiring the housing project) to enable them without financial assistance, to live in decent, safe and sanitary dwellings, without overcrowding. * * *"

While the District Court cited several cases of this Court, its chief reliance plainly rested on Hunter v. Erickson, 393 U.S. 385 (1969). The first paragraph in the District Court's decision stated simply: "We hold Article XXXIV to be unconstitutional. Hunter v. Erickson. * * *" The court below erred in relying on *Hunter* to invalidate Article XXXIV. Unlike the case before us, *Hunter* rested on the conclusion that Akron's referendum law denied equal protection by placing "special burdens on racial minorities within the governmental process." Id., at 391. In *Hunter* the citizens of Akron had amended the city charter to require that any ordinance regulating real estate on the basis of race, color, religion, or national origin could not take effect without approval by a majority of those voting in a city election. The Court held that the amendment created a classification based upon race because it required that laws dealing with racial housing matters could take effect only if they survived a mandatory referendum while other housing ordinances took effect without any such special election. The opinion noted:

> "Because the core of the Fourteenth Amendment is the prevention of meaningful and unjustifiable official distinctions based on race, [citing a group of racial discrimination cases] racial classifications are 'constitutionally suspect' * * * and subject to the 'most rigid scrutiny. * * *' They 'bear a far heavier burden of justification than other classifications. * * *'" Id., at 391–392.

The Court concluded that Akron had advanced no sufficient reasons to justify this racial classification and hence that it was unconstitutional under the Fourteenth Amendment.

Unlike the Akron referendum provision, it cannot be said that California's Article XXXIV rests on "distinctions based on race." Id., at 391. The Article requires referendum approval for any low-rent public housing project, not only for projects which will be occupied by a racial minority. And the record here would not support any claim that a law seemingly neutral on its face is in fact aimed at a racial minority. Cf. Gomillion v. Lightfoot, 364 U.S. 339 (1960). The present case could be affirmed only by extending *Hunter,* and this we decline to do.

California's entire history demonstrates the repeated use of referendums to give citizens a voice on questions of public policy. A referendum provision was included in the first state constitution, Calif.Const. of 1849, Art. VIII, and referendums have been a commonplace occurrence in the State's active political life.[3] Provisions for referendums demonstrate devotion to democracy, not to bias, discrimination, or prejudice. Nonetheless, appellees contend that Article XXXIV denies them equal protection because it demands a mandatory referendum while many other referendums only take place upon citizen initiative. They suggest that the mandatory nature of the Article XXXIV referendum constitutes unconstitutional discrimination because it hampers persons desiring public housing from achieving their objective when no such roadblock faces other groups seeking to influence other public decisions to their advantage. But of course a lawmaking procedure that "disadvantages" a particular group does not always deny equal protection. Under any such holding, presumably a State would not be able to require referendums on any subject unless referendums were required on all, because they would always disadvantage some group. And this Court would be required to analyze governmental structures to determine

3 See, e. g., Crouch, Winston W. "The Initiative and Referendum in California," The Haynes Foundation, Los Angeles, 1950.

whether a gubernatorial veto provision or a filibuster rule is likely to "disadvantage" any of the diverse and shifting groups that make up the American people.

Furthermore, an examination of California law reveals that persons advocating low-income housing have not been singled out for mandatory referendums while no other group must face that obstacle. Mandatory referendums are required for approval of state constitutional amendments, for the issuance of general obligation long-term bonds by local governments, and for certain municipal territorial annexations. See Calif.Const. Art. XVIII, Art. XIII, § 40; Art. XI, § 2(b). California statute books contain much legislation first enacted by voter initiative, and no such law can be repealed or amended except by referendum. Calif.Const. Art. IV, § 24(c). Some California cities have wisely provided that their public parks may not be alienated without mandatory referendums, see, e. g., San Jose Charter, § 1700.

The people of California have also decided by their own vote to require referendum approval of low-rent public housing projects. This procedure ensures that all the people of a community will have a voice in a decision which may lead to large expenditures of local governmental funds for increased public services and to lower tax revenues.[4] It gives them a voice in decisions that will affect the future development of their own community. This procedure for democratic decision-making does not violate the constitutional command that no State shall deny to any person "the equal protection of the laws."

The judgment of the three-judge court is reversed and the case is remanded for dismissal of the complaint.

Reversed.

Mr. Justice DOUGLAS took no part in the consideration or decision of this case.

———

Mr. Justice MARSHALL, whom Mr. Justice BRENNAN and Mr. Justice BLACKMUN join, dissenting.

By its very terms, the mandatory prior referendum provision of Article 34 applies solely to

"any development composed of urban or rural dwellings, apartments or other living accommodations for persons of low income, financed in whole or in part by the Federal Government or a state public body or to which the Federal Government or a state public body extends assistance by supplying all or part of the labor, by guaranteeing the payment of liens, or otherwise."

Persons of low income are defined as

"persons or families who lack the amount of income which is necessary * * * to enable them, without financial assistance, to live in decent, safe and sanitary dwellings, without overcrowding."

The article explicitly singles out low-income persons to bear its burden. Publicly assisted housing developments designed to accommodate the aged, veterans, state employees, persons of mod-

---

[4] Public low-rent housing projects are financed through bonds issued by the local housing authority. To be sure, the Federal Government contracts to make contributions sufficient to cover interest and principal, but the local government body must agree to provide all municipal services for the units and to waive all taxes on the property. The local services to be provided include schools, police, and fire protection, sewers, streets, drains, and lighting. Some of the cost is defrayed by the local governing body's receipt of 10% of the housing project rentals, but of course the rentals are set artificially low. Both appellants and appellees agree that the building of federally-financed low-cost housing entails costs to the local com-

munity. Appellant Shaffer's Brief, at 34–35. Appellee's Brief, at 47. See also 42 U.S.C. §§ 1401–1430.

erate income, or any class of citizens other than the poor, need not be approved by prior referenda.*

In my view, Article 34 on its face constitutes invidious discrimination which the Equal Protection Clause of the Fourteenth Amendment plainly prohibits. "The States, of course, are prohibited by the Equal Protection Clause from discriminating between 'rich' and 'poor' *as such* in the formulation and application of their laws." Douglas v. California, 372 U.S. 353, 361 (1963). (Mr. Justice HARLAN, dissenting). Article 34 is neither "a law of general applicability that may affect the poor more harshly than it does the rich," ibid, nor an "effort to redress economic imbalances," ibid. It is rather an explicit classification on the basis of poverty—a suspect classification which demands exacting judicial scrutiny, see McDonald v. Board of Education, 394 U.S. 802, 807 (1969); Harper v. Virginia Board of Elections, 383 U.S. 663 (1966); Douglas v. California, 372 U.S. 353 (1963).

The Court, however, chooses to subject the article to no scrutiny whatsoever and treats the provision as if it contained a totally benign, technical economic classification. Both the appellees and the Solicitor General of the United States as *amicus curiae* have strenuously argued, and the court below found, that Article 34, by imposing a substantial burden solely on the poor, violates the Fourteenth Amendment. Yet after observing that the article does not discriminate on the basis of race, the Court's only re-

sponse to the real question in this case is the unresponsive assertion that "referendums demonstrate devotion to democracy, not to bias, discrimination, or prejudice." It is far too late in the day to contend that the Fourteenth Amendment prohibits only racial discrimination; and to me, singling out the poor to bear a burden not placed on any other class of citizens tramples the values that the Fourteenth Amendment was designed to protect.

I respectfully dissent.

Notes on Exclusionary Land Practices and the Denial of Equal Protection

1. The United States Supreme Court has further limited the suspect classification treatment of wealth. San Antonio Independent School District v. Rodriguez, —— U.S. ——, 93 S.Ct. 1278, —— L.Ed. 2d —— (1973) (school financing case). Reread the Rodriguez case, page 97 supra, and consider how the opinion might bear on local zoning laws that effectively preclude or sharpiy curtail housing for the poor.

2. The California referendum procedure applies only to conventional public housing projects. It does not cover either turnkey projects or leased units. Nor is there a referendum requirement for rent-supplemented units. Suppose now that California were to extend the referendum procedure to include *all* low-income subsidy programs: as the attorney for legal services, how would you deal with the Valtierra decision? What Valtierra-based arguments would you expect from the California State Attorney?

3. The Township of Mount Laurel, New Jersey, lies approximately 10 miles from Camden and 20 miles from Trenton. Four major planned-unit developments, containing 11,600 dwelling units to house almost 50,000 persons, are in the works. All comply generally with existing zoning which restricts housing to

---

* California law authorizes the formation of Renewal Area Agencies whose purposes include the construction of "low income, middle income and normal market housing," California Health and Safety Code §§ 33701 et seq. Only low income housing programs are subject to the mandatory referendum provision of Article 34 even though all of the agencies' programs may receive substantial governmental assistance.

single-family units; the homes are expected to sell for upwards of $30,000.

Three groups of individual plaintiffs joined the NAACP and CORE in attacking the zoning ordinance. One group of plaintiffs, resident in Mount Laurel, occupied substandard housing because they could find nothing better. A second group had once lived in Mount Laurel but the housing shortage had forced them out. The third group wanted to move to Mount Laurel; they could find jobs there, but no housing. The plaintiffs were all black and relatively poor. Significantly, the court's opinion does *not* mention the plaintiff's race.

In their complaint, plaintiffs sought a declaration that the defendants violated the Constitution and laws of the United States and the State of New Jersey inasmuch as they

"a. unlawfully discriminated against all plaintiffs solely on the basis of their economic status, and in effect, their race in the provision of standard housing;

. . .

"f. unlawfully failed to take affirmative action to provide standard housing for low and moderate income persons employed or expected to be employed in the business and industry which have located and are projected to locate in said Township; . . ."

After reviewing the minutes of various township committee meetings at which officials spoke of the need to be "selective" in approving subdivision plans, and after hearing that every development proposal "leaned into the direction of homes only for those of high income," the court held that Mount Laurel—through zoning —had practised economic discrimination by depriving the poor of the chance to secure subsidized housing. Accordingly, the town's zoning ordinance was declared invalid.

Judged by its craftsmanship, the opinion is simply awful. Grammarians would flinch at its diction and style, and one reads in vain for its constitutional parameters. But the court hews out a remedy that is breathlessly impressive.

The court accepts the plaintiffs' view that simply to invalidate the zoning ordinance would add little to the low- or moderate-income housing supply. Plaintiffs were not, after all, seeking to develop housing themselves. Moreover, the township might immediately enact a slightly revised ordinance that allowed some apartments, while less blatant forms of economic discrimination might still continue. Therefore, the court ordered the township immediately to make a study that would identify the housing need for low- and moderate-income persons (1) residing in the township; (2) presently employed by the municipality or in commercial and industrial uses in the township; (3) expected or projected to be employed by the municipality or in commercial and industrial uses, the development of which can reasonably be anticipated in the township.

Nor would a study be enough. For the court directed the township to prepare an *affirmative program* that would satisfy the projected need for low- and moderate-income units which "shall encompass the most effective and thorough means by which municipal action can be utilized to accomplish the goals as previously set forth." And, underscoring the urgency with which it viewed the issues, the court gave the township only 90 days to complete both the study and the drafting of an affirmative plan. Southern Burlington County NAACP v. Township of Mount Laurel, Docket No. L–25741–70–PW (N.J.Super.Ct., Burlington County, 1970).

4. California law authorizes a referendum procedure with respect to all proposed local legislation. Cal. Elections Code §§ 4051, 4052 (West 1961). A nonprofit sponsor, the Southern Alameda

Spanish Speaking Organization (SASSO), sought to build a 280-unit, federally funded, low- and moderate-income housing project. The Union City Council agreed to rezone the site for apartments, but opponents of the project perfected referendum proceedings before the rezoning ordinance could become effective. At the referendum election, the project lost 1149 to 845.

SASSO then sued. It argued that the referendum procedure could not validly be invoked to send a zoning decision to the electorate, since this would cause arbitrary and capricious land use controls, would violate Title VI of the Civil Rights Act of 1964 and Title VIII of the Civil Rights Act of 1968, and would also violate the Supremacy Clause of the United States Constitution (Article VI, § 2). A three-judge federal court sat unconvinced; the court's opinion presages the Supreme Court's decision in James v. Valtierra. Southern Alameda Spanish Speaking Organization v. City of Union City, 314 F. Supp. 967 (N.D.Cal.1970).

SASSO also argued that even if the referendum procedure did not on its face affront the laws cited above, the referendum was deliberately used to deprive plaintiffs of equal protection and due process, since the project opponents intended to prevent low-income, Spanish-speaking members of a minority group from occupying the proposed site. Conceding that plaintiffs had raised a factual issue, the court then held that they had not made a sufficient prima facie showing to warrant preliminary injunctive relief. "Although the referendum process admittedly resulted in rejection of rezoning the Baker Road property from agricultural-single family to multi-family classification, there is no more reason to find that this was done on the ground of invidious racial discrimination any more than on perfectly legitimate environmental grounds which are always and neces-

sarily involved in zoning issues." 314 F.Supp. at 973.

When neighbors fight a proposed low-income project, can't one assume (nine times out of ten) that the issues are not environmental? And if the neighbors are worried about the environment, isn't the legislature (or planning board) the place to explore that issue? Are plaintiffs correct in asserting that land-planning decisions cannot (and should not) be delegated to the electorate on a piecemeal basis?

Suppose that the following pattern emerges; whenever a parcel is rezoned for low-rent apartments, a referendum is held and the project is defeated; whenever a parcel is rezoned for luxury apartments, no referendum is held, or a referendum is held and the project is approved. What arguments would you make, in the light of Valtierra and SASSO, to challenge the referendum procedure? To support the procedure? How would you handle the intermediate case where the electorate occasionally approves a low-rent project? How vulnerable is a zoning ordinance that requires apartment developers but no one else to obtain prior city council approval, if the city council can show that it generously gives its approval?

Some states also have the initiative procedure allowing voters to introduce and pass legislation on their own accord. If a site is already zoned for apartments, might the electorate initiate a rezoning law in order to block a low-rent project? Cf. City of Scottsdale v. Superior Court, 103 Ariz. 204, 439 P.2d 290 (1968).

5. Is decent housing a "fundamental right," subjecting to strict judicial scrutiny any state law that interferes with efforts to achieve the right?

Not according to the Supreme Court:

["We do not denigrate the importance of decent, safe and sanitary housing. But the Constitution does not provide judicial remedies for every social and economic ill. We are unable to perceive in that document any constitutional guarantee of access to dwellings of a particular quality or any recognition of the right of a tenant to occupy the real property of his landlord beyond the term of his lease, without the payment of rent * * *. *Absent constitutional mandate,* the assurance of adequate housing and the definition of landlord-tenant relationships are legislative, not judicial, functions." (Emphasis supplied.)]

Lindsey v. Normet, 405 U.S. 56, 74, 92 S.Ct. 862, 874, 31 L.Ed.2d 36 (1972). Cf. also San Antonio Independent School District v. Rodriguez, —— U.S. ——, 93 S.Ct. 1278, 1296, —— L.Ed.2d —— (1973).

6. The right to travel argument: "[S]ubsidized housing is as essential to a poor person's ability to migrate to a state or among localities within it as are welfare benefits. . . . Because housing for the poor is in extremely short supply, and because it can only be effectively provided through the federal public housing program, it follows inexorably that by placing restrictions on public housing that are not placed on housing for groups other than the poor, a state can as effectively prevent the in-migration of the poor, as through the use of the blatant prohibitions in Edwards [v. California] or the prior residence requirements in Shapiro [v. Thompson]. * * * In its essence the right to travel is one of the most important of all the rights of United States citizens." Amicus Brief of The National Urban Coalition and Various Other Civil Rights groups at 47, 50, 51, James v. Valtierra, 402 U.S. 137 (1971).

*

Chapter 4

RACIAL DISCRIMINATION IN EMPLOYMENT

THE PROBLEM [a]

Present discrimination, the effects of past deprivation, and an economy that increasingly saves its rewards for the highly trained—these add up to poverty for millions of American blacks. Since every statistical measure reveals their plight, only a few are needed to illustrate it.

In 1970, the unemployment rate for nonwhites averaged 8.2 per cent, as contrasted with 4.5 per cent for whites.[b] To appreciate the size of an 8.2 per cent unemployment rate, consider the sense of crisis that pervades public discussion of the unemployment rate when it approaches 6 per cent for the nation as a whole. The unemployment rate for blacks has been above 6 per cent ever since the end of the Korean War and, except for 1970, has regularly been at least twice that for whites.[c]

When blacks do find jobs, they are likely to be poor ones. Half of all employed whites hold white-collar jobs, but only one in four black workers does. In the blue-collar category, more than one-third of the whites are craftsmen and foremen, but only one-fifth of the blacks are. The bottom classifications in the Labor Department's scale—service and farm workers—contain 15 per cent of the whites, 31 per cent of the blacks.[d]

The net effect of these statistics is to be seen in a comparison of family incomes. Thirty-nine per cent of all nonwhite families earn less than $5,000 a year; only 18 per cent of white families earn so little.[e]

To be sure, the economic status of blacks has been improving in a number of respects. Thus, blacks are not so heavily under-represented in some desirable employment categories as they once were. For example, whereas only 13 per cent of employed blacks were white-collar workers in 1957, 26 per cent found employment in this sector in 1969.[f] And by 1970, the median family income of

[a] Here and in other textual passages in this chapter the editors have borrowed freely from M. Sovern, Legal Restraints on Racial Discrimination in Employment (Twentieth Century Fund 1966). Some footnotes in cases and other borrowed material in this chapter have been omitted; others have been renumbered.

[b] Bureau of the Census, United States Department of Commerce and Bureau of Labor Statistics, United States Department of Labor, The Social and Economic Status of Negroes in the United States, 1970, at 48, Table 36.

[c] Ibid.

[d] Bureau of the Census, United States Department of Commerce, Statistical Abstract of the United States (1970), at 226, Table 335. The data used are for 1969.

[e] The Social and Economic Status of Negroes in the United States, 1970, supra note b, at 26, Table 17. The data used are for 1969.

[f] Statistical Abstract, supra note d.

blacks had climbed to $6,279 a year, a gain of about 50 per cent over 1960.[g]

Nonetheless, the 1970 median income for white families was $10,236, more than half again the black figure; [h] black men "who have completed four years of high school have a lower median income than white men who have completed only eight years of elementary school"; [i] and there were still 7.7 million blacks below the "poverty line" in 1970.[j]

Bringing blacks to full economic citizenship will be a long and complicated undertaking. All of the forms of racial discrimination practiced in our society will have to be contended with and much else will have to be done besides.

While all forms of discrimination contribute to the economic plight of blacks and while a host of public measures not specifically directed at discrimination can help alleviate it, this chapter will concentrate on one form of discrimination—discrimination in employment—and how the law responds to it. Other programs

[g] The Social and Economic Status of Negroes in the United States, 1970, supra note b, at 1, 27, Table 18.

[h] Ibid.

[i] Id. at 34.

[j] Id. at 35. "Families and unrelated individuals are classified as being above or below the low income level, sometimes called the poverty level, using cutoffs adjusted to take account of such factors as family size, sex and age of the family head, the number of children, and farm-nonfarm residence. At the core of this index was a nutritionally adequate food plan ('economy' plan) designed by the Department of Agriculture for 'emergency or temporary use when funds are low.' The low income cutoffs for farm families have been set at 85 percent of the nonfarm levels. These cutoff levels are updated every year to reflect the changes in the Consumer Price Index. The low income threshold for a nonfarm family of four was $3,968 in 1970, $3,743 in 1969, and $2,973 in 1959. In 1970, the low income threshold ranged from about $2,500 for a family of two persons to $6,400 for families of 7 or more persons. For a more detailed explanation, see Current Population Reports, Series P–23, No. 28." Id. at 2 n. 1.

to improve the condition of blacks have little chance of success unless the fight against job discrimination succeeds at the same time. Better education would be bitterly frustrating and training for skills would be an outrageous irony if employers and unions were left free to turn workers away because of their color.

S. HOLLAND, THE EMPLOYMENT SITUATION FOR NEGROES

Bureau of Labor Statistics, United States Department of Labor, 20 Employment and Earnings and the Monthly Report on the Labor Force, Sept. 1967, 11–26.

* * * The unemployment rate for Negro teenagers rose sharply in 1958, and, from 1958 through 1966, it remained between 24 and 30 percent. In other words, 1 out of 4 Negro youngsters seeking work is unsuccessful. * * *[k]

Employment problems in city slums. About 1 out of every 10 workers in the slums of 13 major cities was unemployed in November 1966—an unemployment rate nearly three times the national average.

* * *

The national figures on unemployment include all persons who were not employed and who actively sought work during the survey period. This is an objective standard which is reasonable and significant for most of the U. S. population, but it provides only a partial indication of the work problems which contribute to poverty in the slums. Many more slum residents have only part-time jobs, are earning too little to meet their own and their families' minimum subsistence needs, or are outside the labor force (though able to work) than are unemployed, in the sense that they are jobless and looking for work.

[k] The teenage unemployment rate for nonwhites was 29.1 percent in 1970. The Social and Economic Status of Negroes in the United States, 1970, at 49.

The following points summarize the [Labor] Department's findings regarding the 800,000 persons of working age in areas covered in its November surveys:

1. About 7 percent of the slum residents with jobs were employed only part-time, although they would have preferred full-time work. The comparable figure for the Nation as a whole was 2.3 percent.

2. Nearly two-fifths of the slum area families (and unrelated individuals) reported annual incomes under $3,000, compared with one-fourth in the United States as a whole.

3. A disproportionately large number of slum residents of working age were neither working nor looking for work, and so were not counted in the labor force. This labor force "nonparticipation rate" was 11 percent among men 20 to 64, compared with only 7 percent in the country generally.

4. A fifth or more of the adult men expected to be part of the population of these slum areas were not located by the November surveys. This finding parallels the Census "undercount" experience for nonwhite men.

As a first approach to measuring the entire area of joblessness and employment hardship, a "sub-employment" index has been constructed, based on these survey findings and other data and on a number of carefully considered estimates and assumptions.[1]

The average rate of sub-employment for the 10 slums surveyed was 34 percent. In other words, one out of every three slum residents who was already a worker, or should and could become one with suitable help, was either jobless or not earning enough to live above the poverty level.

Note

Though this chapter focuses on the problems of blacks, they are obviously not alone either in the ranks of the economically deprived or on the casualty lists of discrimination victims. See, for example, Committee for Economic Development, Training and Jobs for the Urban Poor 9 (1970): "Although poverty, as officially defined, has been decreasing during recent years in the country at large, in 1968 there were still 25.4 million persons 'in poverty' of whom about half lived in metropolitan areas. Of the total, approximately two-thirds

TABLE I.   UNEMPLOYMENT AND SUB-EMPLOYMENT RATES FOR SELECTED SLUM AREAS, NOVEMBER 1966

Slum Area	Unemployment rate	Sub-employment rate
Boston-Roxbury area	6.9	24
Cleveland-Hough and surrounding neighborhood	15.6	na
Detroit-Central Woodward area	10.1	na
Los Angeles-South Los Angeles	12.0	na
New Orleans—Several contiguous areas	10.0	45
New York:		
Harlem	8.1	29
East Harlem	9.0	33
Bedford-Stuyvesant	6.2	28
Philadelphia-North Philadelphia	11.0	34
Phoenix-Salt River Bed area	13.2	42
St. Louis-North Side	12.9	39
San Antonio-East and West sides	8.1	47
San Francisco-Oakland:		
San Francisco-Mission-Fillmore	11.1	25
Oakland-Bayside	13.0	na

[1] For an explanation of the subemployment index and a more detailed report on the November 1966 Urban Employment Survey, see Department of Labor, Manpower Report of the President, H.R.Doc.No.116, 90th Cong., 1st Sess., 73–88 (1967).

were whites and one-third nonwhites but the percentage of blacks in poverty (about 32 per cent) was over three times that of whites (10 per cent), and the percentage for Spanish-Americans, who are mainly counted as whites, was even higher than for blacks." And see The Social and Economic Status of Negroes in the United States, 1970 supra note b, at 33, Table 24, supporting in detail the assertion that, "Men earn more money than women for both Negro and white persons."

SECTION 1. THE CIVIL RIGHTS ACT OF 1964

A. TITLE VII—EQUAL EMPLOYMENT OPPORTUNITY [m]

DEFINITIONS

SEC. 701. For the purposes of this title—

(a) The term "person" includes one or more individuals, governments, governmental agencies, political subdivisions, labor unions, partnerships, associations, corporations, legal representatives, mutual companies, joint-stock companies, trusts, unincorporated organizations, trustees, trustees in bankruptcy, or receivers.

(b) The term "employer" means a person engaged in an industry affecting commerce who has fifteen or more employees for each working day in each of twenty or more calendar weeks in the current or preceding calendar year, and any agent of such a person, but such term does not include (1) the United States, a corporation wholly owned by the Govern-

ment of the United States, an Indian tribe or any department or agency of the District of Columbia subject by statute to procedures of the competitive service (as defined in section 2102 of title 5 of the United States Code), or (2) a bona fide private membership club (other than a labor organization) which is exempt from taxation under section 501(c) of the Internal Revenue Code of 1954, except that during the first year after the date of enactment of the Equal Employment Opportunity Act of 1972, persons having fewer than twenty-five employees (and their agents) shall not be considered employers.

(c) The term "employment agency" means any person regularly undertaking with or without compensation to procure employees for an employer or to procure for employees opportunities to work for an employer and includes an agent of such a person.

(d) The term "labor organization" means a labor organization engaged in an industry affecting commerce, and any agent of such an organization, and includes any organization of any kind, any agency, or employee representation committee, group, association, or plan so engaged in which employees participate and which exists for the purpose, in whole or in part, of dealing with employers concerning grievances, labor disputes, wages, rates of pay, hours, or other terms or conditions of employment, and any conference, general committee, joint or system board, or joint council so engaged which is subordinate to a national or international labor organization.

(e) A labor organization shall be deemed to be engaged in an industry affecting commerce if (1) it maintains or operates a hiring hall or hiring office which procures employees for an employer or procures for employees opportunities to work for an employer, or (2) the number of its members (or, where it is a labor organization composed of other

---

[m] 78 Stat. 253, 42 U.S.C.A. § 2000e et seq. (1964), as amended by 86 Stat. 103 (1972).

labor organizations or their representatives, if the aggregate number of the members of such other labor organization) is (A) twenty-five or more during the first year after the date of enactment of the Equal Employment Opportunity Act of 1972, or (B) fifteen or more thereafter, and such labor organization

(1) is the certified representative of employees under the provisions of the National Labor Relations Act, as amended, or the Railway Labor Act, as amended;

(2) although not certified, is a national or international labor organization or a local labor organization recognized or acting as the representative of employees of an employer or employers engaged in an industry affecting commerce; or

(3) has chartered a local labor organization or subsidiary body which is representing or actively seeking to represent employees of employers within the meaning of paragraph (1) or (2); or

(4) has been chartered by a labor organization representing or actively seeking to represent employees within the meaning of paragraph (1) or (2) as the local or subordinate body through which such employees may enjoy membership or become affiliated with such labor organization; or

(5) is a conference, general committee, joint or system board, or joint council subordinate to a national or international labor organization, which includes a labor organization engaged in an industry affecting commerce within the meaning of any of the preceding paragraphs of this subsection.

(f) The term "employee" means an individual employed by an employer except that the term "employee" shall not include any person elected to public office in any State or political subdivision of any State by the qualified voters thereof, or any person chosen by such officer to be on such officer's personal staff, or an appointee on the policy making level or an immediate adviser with respect to the exercise of the constitutional or legal powers of the office. The exemption set forth in the preceding sentence shall not include employees subject to the civil service laws of a State government, governmental agency or political subdivision.

(g) The term "commerce" means trade, traffic, commerce, transportation, transmission, or communication among the several States; or between a State and any place outside thereof; or within the District of Columbia, or a possession of the United States; or between points in the same State but through a point outside thereof.

(h) The term "industry affecting commerce" means any activity, business, or industry in commerce or in which a labor dispute would hinder or obstruct commerce or the free flow of commerce and includes any activity or industry "affecting commerce" within the meaning of the Labor-Management Reporting and Disclosure Act of 1959, and further includes any governmental industry, business or activity.

(i) The term "State" includes a State of the United States, the District of Columbia, Puerto Rico, the Virgin Islands, American Samoa, Guam, Wake Island, the Canal Zone, and Outer Continental Shelf lands defined in the Outer Continental Shelf Lands Act.

(j) The term "religion" includes all aspects of religious observance and practice, as well as belief, unless an employer demonstrates that he is unable to reasonably accommodate to an employee's or prospective employee's religious observance or practice without undue hardship on the conduct of the employer's business.

EXEMPTION

SEC. 702. This title shall not apply to an employer with respect to the employment of aliens outside any State, or to a religious corporation, association, educational institution, or society with respect to the employment of individuals of a particular religion to perform work connected with the carrying on by such corporation, association, educational institution, or society of its activities.

DISCRIMINATION BECAUSE OF RACE, COLOR, RELIGION, SEX, OR NATIONAL ORIGIN

SEC. 703. (a) It shall be an unlawful employment practice for an employer—

(1) to fail or refuse to hire or to discharge any individual, or otherwise to discriminate against any individual with respect to his compensation, terms, conditions, or privileges of employment, because of such individual's race, color, religion, sex, or national origin; or

(2) to limit, segregate, or classify his employees or applicants for employment in any way which would deprive or tend to deprive any individual of employment opportunities or otherwise adversely affect his status as an employee, because of such individual's race, color, religion, sex, or national origin.

(b) It shall be an unlawful employment practice for an employment agency to fail or refuse to refer for employment, or otherwise to discriminate against any individual because of his race, color, religion, sex, or national origin, or to classify or refer for employment any individual on the basis of his race, color, religion, sex, or national origin.

(c) It shall be an unlawful employment practice for a labor organization—

(1) to exclude or to expel from its membership, or otherwise to discriminate against any individual because of his race, color, religion, sex, or national origin;

(2) to limit, segregate, or classify its membership or applicants for membership, or to classify or fail or refuse to refer for employment any individual, in any way which would deprive or tend to deprive any individual of employment opportunities, or would limit such employment opportunities or otherwise adversely affect his status as an employee or as an applicant for employment, because of such individual's race, color, religion, sex, or national origin; or

(3) to cause or attempt to cause an employer to discriminate against an individual in violation of this section.

(d) It shall be an unlawful employment practice for any employer, labor organization, or joint labor-management committee controlling apprenticeship or other training or retraining, including on-the-job training programs to discriminate against any individual because of his race, color, religion, sex, or national origin in admission to, or employment in, any program established to provide apprenticeship or other training.

(e) Notwithstanding any other provision of this title, (1) it shall not be an unlawful employment practice for an employer to hire and employ employees, for an employment agency to classify, or refer for employment any individual, for a labor organization to classify its membership or to classify or refer for employment any individual, or for an employer, labor organization, or joint labor-management committee controlling apprenticeship or other training or retraining programs to admit or employ any individual in any such program, on the basis of his religion, sex, or national origin in those certain instances where religion, sex, or national origin is a bona fide occupational qualification reasonably necessary to the normal operation of that particular business or enterprise, and (2) it shall not be an unlawful employment practice for a school, college, university, or other educational institution or institution of learning to hire and employ employees of a particular religion if such school, college, university, or other educational institution or institution of learning is, in whole or in substantial part, owned, supported, controlled, or managed by a particular religion or by a particular religious corporation, association, or society, or if the curriculum of such school, college, university, or other educational institution or institution of learning is directed toward the propagation of a particular religion.

(f) As used in this title, the phrase "unlawful employment practice" shall not be deemed to include any action or measure taken by an employer, labor organization, joint labor-management committee, or employment agency with respect to an individual who is a member of the Communist Party of the United States or of any other organization required to register as a Communist-action or Communist-front organization by final order of the Subversive Activities Control Board pursuant to the Subversive Activities Control Act of 1950.

(g) Notwithstanding any other provision of this title, it shall not be an unlawful employment practice for an employer to fail or refuse to hire and employ any individual for any position, for an employer to discharge any individual from any position, or for an employment agency to fail or refuse to refer any individual for employment in any position, or for a labor organization to fail or refuse to refer any individual for employment in any position, if—

(1) the occupancy of such position, or access to the premises in or upon which any part of the duties of such position is performed or is to be performed, is subject to any requirement

imposed in the interest of the national security of the United States under any security program in effect pursuant to or administered under any statute of the United States or any Executive order of the President; and

(2) such individual has not fulfilled or has ceased to fulfill that requirement.

(h) Notwithstanding any other provision of this title, it shall not be an unlawful employment practice for an employer to apply different standards of compensation, or different terms, conditions, or privileges of employment pursuant to a bona fide seniority or merit system, or a system which measures earnings by quantity or quality of production or to employees who work in different locations, provided that such differences are not the result of an intention to discriminate because of race, color, religion, sex, or national origin, nor shall it be an unlawful employment practice for an employer to give and to act upon the results of any professionally developed ability test provided that such test, its administration or action upon the results is not designed, intended or used to discriminate because of race, color, religion, sex or national origin. It shall not be an unlawful employment practice under this title for any employer to differentiate upon the basis of sex in determining the amount of the wages or compensation paid or to be paid to employees of such employer if such differentiation is authorized by the provisions of section 6(d) of the Fair Labor Standards Act of 1938, as amended (29 U.S.C.A. § 206(d)).

(i) Nothing contained in this title shall apply to any business or enterprise on or near an Indian reservation with respect to any publicly announced employment practice of such business or enterprise under which a preferential treatment is given to any individual because he is an Indian living on or near a reservation.

(j) Nothing contained in this title shall be interpreted to require any employer, employment agency, labor organization, or joint labor-management committee subject to this title to grant preferential treatment to any individual or to any group because of the race, color, religion, sex, or national origin of such individual or group on account of an imbalance which may exist with respect to the total number or percentage of persons of any race, color, religion, sex, or national origin employed by any employer, referred or classified for employment by any employment agency or labor organization, admitted to membership or classified by any labor organization, or admitted to, or employed in, any apprenticeship or other training program, in comparison with the total number or percentage of persons of such race, color, religion, sex, or national origin in any community, State, section, or other area, or in the available work force in any community, State, section, or other area.

OTHER UNLAWFUL EMPLOYMENT PRACTICES

SEC. 704. (a) It shall be an unlawful employment practice for an employer to discriminate against any of his employees or applicants for employment, for an employment agency or joint labor-management committee controlling apprenticeship or other training or retraining, including on-the-job training programs to discriminate against any individual, or for a labor organization to discriminate against any member thereof or applicant for membership, because he has opposed any practice made an unlawful employment practice by this title, or because he has made a charge, testified, assisted, or participated in any manner in an investigation, proceeding, or hearing under this title.

(b) It shall be an unlawful employment practice for an employer, labor organization, employment agency, or joint labor-management committee controlling apprenticeship or other training or retraining, including on-the-job training programs, to print or publish or cause to be printed or published any notice or advertisement relating to employment by such an employer or membership in or any classification or referral for employment by such a labor organization, or relating to any classification or referral for employment by such an employment agency, or relating to admission to, or employment in, any program established to provide apprenticeship or other training by such a joint labor-management committee indicating any preference, limitation, specification, or discrimination, based on race, color, religion, sex, or national origin, except that such a notice or advertisement may indicate a preference, limitation, specification, or discrimination based on religion, sex, or national origin when religion, sex, or national origin is a bona fide occupational qualification for employment.

EQUAL EMPLOYMENT OPPORTUNITY COMMISSION

SEC. 705. (a) There is hereby created a Commission to be known as the Equal Employment Opportunity Commission, which shall be composed of five members, not more than three of whom shall be members of the same political party. Members of the Commission shall be appointed by the President by and with the advice and consent of the Senate for a term of five years. Any individual chosen to fill a vacancy shall be appointed only for the unexpired term of the member whom he shall succeed, and all members of the Commission shall continue to serve until their successors are appointed and qualified, except that no such member of the Commission shall continue to serve (1) for more than sixty days when the Congress is in session unless a nomination to fill such vacancy shall have been submitted to the Senate, or (2) after the adjournment sine die of the session of the Senate in which such nomination was submitted. The President shall designate one member to serve as Chairman of the Commission, and one member to serve as Vice Chairman. The Chairman shall be responsible on behalf of the Commission for the administrative operations of the Commission, and, except as provided in subsection (b), shall appoint, in accordance with the provisions of title 5, United States Code, governing appointments in the competitive service, such officers, agents, attorneys, hearing examiners, and employees as he deems necessary to assist it in the performance of its functions and to fix their compensation in accordance with the provisions of chapter 51 and subchapter III of chapter 53 of title 5, United States Code, relating to classification and General Schedule pay rates: Provided, that assignment, removal, and compensation of hearing examiners shall be in accordance with sections 3105, 3344, 5362, and 7521 of title 5, United States Code.

(b)(1) There shall be a General Counsel of the Commission appointed by the President, by and with the advice and consent of the Senate, for a term of four years. The General Counsel shall have responsibility for the conduct of litigation as provided in sections 706 and 707 of this title. The General Counsel shall have such other duties as the Commission may prescribe or as may be provided by law and shall concur with the Chairman of the Commission on the appointment and supervision of regional attorneys. The General Counsel of the Commission on the effective date of this Act shall continue in such position and perform the functions specified in this subsection until a successor is appointed and qualified.

(2) Attorneys appointed under this section may, at the direction of the Commission, appear for and represent the Commission in any case in court, provided that the Attorney General shall conduct all litigation to which the Commission is a party in the Supreme Court pursuant to this title.

(c) A vacancy in the Commission shall not impair the right of the remaining members to exercise all the powers of the Commission and three members thereof shall constitute a quorum.

(d) The Commission shall have an official seal which shall be judicially noticed.

(e) The Commission shall at the middle and at the close of each fiscal year report to the Congress and to the President concerning the action it has taken; the names, salaries and duties of all individuals in its employ and the moneys it has disbursed; and shall make such further reports on the cause of and means of eliminating discrimination and such recommendations for further legislation as may appear desirable.

(f) The principal office of the Commission shall be in or near the District of Columbia, but it may meet or exercise any or all its powers at any other place. The Commission may establish such regional or State offices as it deems necessary to accomplish the purpose of this title.

(g) The Commission shall have power—

(1) to cooperate with and, with their consent, utilize regional, State, local, and other agencies, both public and private, and individuals;

(2) to pay to witnesses whose depositions are taken or who are summoned before the Commission or any of its agents the same witness and mileage fees as are paid to witnesses in the courts of the United States;

(3) to furnish to persons subject to this title such technical assistance as they may request to further their com-

pliance with this title or an order issued thereunder;

(4) upon the request of (i) any employer, whose employees or some of them, or (ii) any labor organization, whose members or some of them, refuse or threaten to refuse to cooperate in effectuating the provisions of this title, to assist in such effectuation by conciliation or such other remedial action as is provided by this title;

(5) to make such technical studies as are appropriate to effectuate the purposes and policies of this title and to make the results of such studies available to the public;

(6) to intervene in a civil action brought under section 706 by an aggrieved party against a respondent other than a government, governmental agency or political subdivision.

(h) The Commission shall, in any of its educational or promotional activities, cooperate with other departments and agencies in the performance of such educational and promotional activities.

(i) All officers, agents, attorneys, and employees of the Commission, including the members of the Commission, shall be subject to the provisions of section 9 of the Act of August 2, 1939, as amended (the Hatch Act), notwithstanding any exemption contained in such section.

PREVENTION OF UNLAWLFUL EMPLOYMENT PRACTICES

SEC. 706. (a) The Commission is empowered, as hereinafter provided, to prevent any person from engaging in any unlawful employment practice as set forth in section 703 or 704 of this title.

(b) Whenever a charge is filed by or on behalf of a person claiming to be aggrieved, or by a member of the Commission, alleging that an employer, employment agency, labor organization, or joint labor-management committee controlling apprenticeship or other training or re-

training including on-the-job training programs, has engaged in an unlawful employment practice, the Commission shall serve a notice of the charge (including the date, place and circumstances of the alleged unlawful employment practice) on such employer, employment agency, labor organization or joint labor-management committee (hereinafter referred to as the 'respondent') within ten days and shall make an investigation thereof. Charges shall be in writing under oath or affirmation and shall contain such information and be in such form as the Commission requires. Charges shall not be made public by the Commission. If the Commission determines after such investigation that there is not reasonable cause to believe that the charge is true, it shall dismiss the charge and promptly notify the person claiming to be aggrieved and the respondent of its action. In determining whether reasonable cause exists, the Commission shall accord substantial weight to final findings and orders made by State or local authorities in proceedings commenced under State or local law pursuant to the requirements of subsections (c) and (d). If the Commission determines after such investigation that there is reasonable cause to believe that the charge is true, the Commission shall endeavor to eliminate any such alleged unlawful employment practice by informal methods of conference, conciliation, and persuasion. Nothing said or done during and as a part of such informal endeavors may be made public by the Commission, its officers or employees, or used as evidence in a subsequent proceeding without the written consent of the persons concerned. Any person who makes public information in violation of this subsection shall be fined not more than $1,000 or imprisoned for not more than one year, or both. The Commission shall make its determination on reasonable cause as promptly as possible and, so far as practicable, not later than one hundred and twenty days from the filing of the charge or, where applicable under subsection (c) or (d), from the date upon which the Commission is authorized to take action with respect to the charge.

(c) In the case of an alleged unlawful employment practice occurring in a State, or political subdivision of a State, which has a State or local law prohibiting the unlawful employment practice alleged and establishing or authorizing a State or local authority to grant or seek relief from such practice or to institute criminal proceedings with respect thereto upon receiving notice thereof, no charge may be filed under subsection (a) by the person aggrieved before the expiration of sixty days after proceedings have been commenced under the State or local law, unless such proceedings have been earlier terminated, provided that such sixty-day period shall be extended to one hundred and twenty days during the first year after the effective date of such State or local law. If any requirement for the commencement of such proceedings is imposed by a State or local authority other than a requirement of the filing of a written and signed statement of the facts upon which the proceeding is based, the proceeding shall be deemed to have been commenced for the purposes of this subsection at the time such statement is sent by registered mail to the appropriate State or local authority.

(d) In the case of any charge filed by a member of the Commission alleging an unlawful employment practice occurring in a State or political subdivision of a State, which has a State or local law prohibiting the practice alleged and establishing or authorizing a State or local authority to grant or seek relief from such practice or to institute criminal proceedings with respect thereto upon receiving notice thereof, the Commission shall, before taking any action with respect to such charge, notify the appropriate State or local officials and, upon request, afford

them a reasonable time, but not less than sixty days (provided that such sixty-day period shall be extended to one hundred and twenty days during the first year after the effective day of such State or local law), unless a shorter period is requested, to act under such State or local law to remedy the practice alleged.

(e) A charge under this section shall be filed within one hundred and eighty days after the alleged unlawful employment practice occurred and notice of the charge (including the date, place and circumstances of the alleged unlawful employment practice) shall be served upon the person against whom such charge is made within ten days thereafter, except that in a case of an unlawful employment practice with respect to which the person aggrieved has initially instituted proceedings with a State or local agency with authority to grant or seek relief from such practice or to institute criminal proceedings with respect thereto upon receiving notice thereof, such charge shall be filed by or on behalf of the person aggrieved within three hundred days after the alleged unlawful employment practice occurred, or within thirty days after receiving notice that the State or local agency has terminated the proceedings under the State or local law, whichever is earlier, and a copy of such charge shall be filed by the Commission with the State or local agency.

(f) (1) If within thirty days after a charge is filed with the Commission or within thirty days after expiration of any period of reference under subsection (c) or (d), the Commission has been unable to secure from the respondent a conciliation agreement acceptable to the Commission, the Commission may bring a civil action against any respondent not a government, governmental agency, or political subdivision named in the charge. In the case of a respondent which is a government, governmental agency, or political subdivision, if the Commission has been unable to secure from the respondent a conciliation agreement acceptable to the Commission, the Commission shall take no further action and shall refer the case to the Attorney General who may bring a civil action against such respondent in the appropriate United States district court. The person or persons aggrieved shall have the right to intervene in a civil action brought by the Commission or the Attorney General in a case involving a government, governmental agency, or political subdivision. If a charge filed with the Commission pursuant to subsection (b) is dismissed by the Commission, or if within one hundred and eighty days from the filing of such charge or the expiration of any period of reference under subsection (c) or (d), whichever is later, the Commission has not filed a civil action under this section or the Attorney General has not filed a civil action in a case involving a government, governmental agency, or political subdivision, or the Commission has not entered into a conciliation agreement to which the person aggrieved is a party, the Commission, or the Attorney General in a case involving a government, governmental agency, or political subdivision, shall so notify the person aggrieved and within ninety days after the giving of such notice a civil action may be brought against the respondent named in the charge (A) by the person claiming to be aggrieved or (B) if such charge was filed by a member of the Commission, by any person whom the charge alleges was aggrieved by the alleged unlawful employment practice. Upon application by the complainant and in such circumstances as the court may deem just, the court may appoint an attorney for such complainant and may authorize the commencement of the action without the payment of fees, costs,

or security. Upon timely application, the court may, in its discretion, permit the Commission, or the Attorney General in a case involving a govenment, governmental agency, or political subdivision, to intervene in such civil action upon certification that the case is of general public importance. Upon request, the court may, in its discretion, stay further proceedings for not more than sixty days pending the termination of State or local proceedings described in subsections (c) or (d) of this section or further efforts of the Commission to obtain voluntary compliance.

(2) Whenever a charge is filed with the Commission and the Commission concludes on the basis of a preliminary investigation that prompt judicial action is necessary to carry out the purpose of this Act, the Commission, or the Attorney General in a case involving a government, governmental agency, or political subdivision, may bring an action for appropriate temporary or preliminary relief pending final disposition of such charge. Any temporary restraining order or other order granting preliminary or temporary relief shall be issued in accordance with rule 65 of the Federal Rules of Civil Procedure. It shall be the duty of a court having jurisdiction over proceedings under this section to assign cases for hearing at the earliest practicable date and to cause such cases to be in every way expedited.

(3) Each United States district court and each United States court of a place subject to the jurisdiction of the United States shall have jurisdiction of actions brought under this title. Such an action may be brought in any judicial district in the State in which the unlawful employment practice is alleged to have been committed, in the judicial district in which the employment records relevant to such practice

are maintained and administered, or in the judicial district in which the aggrieved person would have worked but for the alleged unlawful employment practice, but if the respondent is not found within any such district, such an action may be brought within the judicial district in which the respondent has his principal office. For purposes of sections 1404 and 1406 of title 28 of the United States Code, the judicial district in which the respondent has his principal office shall in all cases be considered a district in which the action might have been brought.

(4) It shall be the duty of the chief judge of the district (or in his absence, the acting chief judge) in which the case is pending immediately to designate a judge in such district to hear and determine the case. In the event that no judge in the district is available to hear and determine the case, the chief judge of the district, or the acting chief judge, as the case may be, shall certify this fact to the chief judge of the circuit (or in his absence, the acting chief judge) who shall then designate a district or circuit judge of the circuit to hear and determine the case.

(5) It shall be the duty of the judge designated pursuant to this subsection to assign the case for hearing at the earliest practicable date and to cause the case to be in every way expedited. If such judge has not scheduled the case for trial within one hundred and twenty days after issue has been joined that judge may appoint a master pursuant to rule 53 of the Federal Rules of Civil Procedure.

(g) If the court finds that the respondent has intentionally engaged in or is intentionally engaging in an unlawful employment practice charged in the complaint, the court may enjoin the respondent from engaging in such unlawful employment practice, and order such affirmative action as may be appropriate, which may include, but is not limited to, reinstatement or hiring of employees, with or without back pay (payable by the employer, employment agency, or labor organization, as the case may be, responsible for the unlawful employment practice), or any other equitable relief as the court deems appropriate. Back pay liability shall not accrue from a date more than two years prior to the filing of a charge with the Commission. Interim earnings or amounts earnable with reasonable diligence by the person or persons discriminated against shall operate to reduce the back pay otherwise allowable. No order of the court shall require the admission or reinstatement of an individual as a member of a union, or the hiring, reinstatement, or promotion of an individual as an employee, or the payment to him of any back pay, if such individual was refused admission, suspended, or expelled, or was refused employment or advancement or was suspended or discharged for any reason other than discrimination on account of race, color, religion, sex, or national origin or in violation of section 704(a).

(h) The provisions of the Act entitled "An Act to amend the Judicial Code and to define and limit the jurisdiction of courts sitting in equity, and for other purposes," approved March 23, 1932 (29 U.S.C. 101–115), shall not apply with respect to civil actions brought under this section.

(i) In any case in which an employer, employment agency, or labor organization fails to comply with an order of a court issued in a civil action brought under this section, the Commission may commence proceedings to compel compliance with such order.

(j) Any civil action brought under this section and any proceedings brought under subsection (i) shall be subject to appeal as provided in sections 1291 and 1292, title 28, United States Code.

(k) In any action or proceeding under this title the court, in its discretion, may allow the prevailing party, other than the Commission or the United States, a reasonable attorney's fee as part of the costs, and the Commission and the United States shall be liable for costs the same as a private person.

SEC. 707. (a) Whenever the Attorney General has reasonable cause to believe that any person or group of persons is engaged in a pattern or practice of resistance to the full enjoyment of any of the rights secured by this title, and that the pattern or practice is of such a nature and is intended to deny the full exercise of the rights herein described, the Attorney General may bring a civil action in the appropriate district court of the United States by filing with it a complaint (1) signed by him (or in his absence the Acting Attorney General), (2) setting forth facts pertaining to such pattern or practice, and (3) requesting such relief, including an application for a permanent or temporary injunction, restraining order or other order against the person or persons responsible for such pattern or practice, as he deems necessary to insure the full enjoyment of the rights herein described.

(b) The district courts of the United States shall have and shall exercise jurisdiction of proceedings instituted pursuant to this section, and in any such proceeding the Attorney General may file with the clerk of such court a request that a court of three judges be convened to hear and determine the case. Such request by the Attorney General shall be accompanied by a certificate that, in his opinion, the case is of general public importance. A copy of the certificate and request for a three-judge court shall be immediately furnished by such clerk to the chief judge of the circuit (or in his absence, the presiding circuit judge of the circuit) in which the case is pending. Upon receipt of such request it shall be

the duty of the chief judge of the circuit or the presiding circuit judge, as the case may be, to designate immediately three judges in such circuit, of whom at least one shall be a circuit judge and another of whom shall be a district judge of the court in which the proceeding was instituted, to hear and determine such case, and it shall be the duty of the judges so designated to assign the case for hearing at the earliest practicable date, to participate in the hearing and determination thereof, and to cause the case to be in every way expedited. An appeal from the final judgment of such court will lie to the Supreme Court.

In the event the Attorney General fails to file such a request in any such proceeding, it shall be the duty of the chief judge of the district (or in his absence, the acting chief judge) in which the case is pending immediately to designate a judge in such district to hear and determine the case. In the event that no judge in the district is available to hear and determine the case, the chief judge of the district, or the acting chief judge, as the case may be, shall certify this fact to the chief judge of the circuit (or in his absence, the acting chief judge) who shall then designate a district or circuit judge of the circuit to hear and determine the case.

It shall be the duty of the judge designated pursuant to this section to assign the case for hearing at the earliest practicable date and to cause the case to be in every way expedited.

(c) Effective two years after the date of enactment of the Equal Employment Opportunity Act of 1972, the functions of the Attorney General under this section shall be transferred to the Commission, together with such personnel, property, records, and unexpended balances of appropriations, allocations, and other funds employed, used, held, available, or to be made available in connection with such functions unless the President submits, and neither House of Congress vetoes, a reorganization plan pursuant to chapter 9 of title 5, United States Code, inconsistent with the provisions of this subsection. The Commission shall carry out such functions, in accordance with subsections (d) and (e) of this section.

(d) Upon the transfer of functions provided for in subsection (c) of this section, in all suits commenced pursuant to this section prior to the date of such transfer, proceedings shall continue without abatement, all court orders and decrees shall remain in effect, and the Commission shal be substituted as a party for the United States of America, the Attorney General, or the Acting Attorney General, as appropriate.

(e) Subsequent to the date of enactment of the Equal Employment Opportunity Act of 1972, the Commission shall have authority to investigate and act on a charge of a pattern or practice of discrimination, whether filed by or on behalf of a person claiming to be aggrieved or by a member of the Commission. All such actions shall be conducted in accordance with the procedures set forth in section 706 of this Act.

EFFECT ON STATE LAWS

SEC. 708. Nothing in this title shall be deemed to exempt or relieve any person from any liability, duty, penalty, or punishment provided by any present or future law of any State or political subdivision of a State, other than any such law which purports to require or permit the doing of any act which would be an unlawful employment practice under this title.

INVESTIGATIONS, INSPECTIONS, RECORDS, STATE AGENCIES

SEC. 709. (a) In connection with any investigation of a charge filed under section 706, the Commission or its designated representative shall at all reasonable times have access to, for the purposes of examination, and the right to copy any evidence of any person being investigated or proceeded against that relates to unlawful employment practices covered by this title and is relevant to the charge under investigation.

(b) The Commission may cooperate with State and local agencies charged with the administration of State fair employment practices laws and, with the consent of such agencies, may for the purpose of carrying out its functions and duties under this title and within the limitation of funds appropriated specifically for such purpose, engage in and contribute to the cost of research and other projects of mutual interest undertaken by such agencies, and utilize the services of such agencies and their employees and, notwithstanding any other provision of law, pay by advance or reimbursement such agencies and their employees for services rendered to assist the Commission in carrying out this title. In furtherance of such cooperative efforts, the Commission may enter into written agreements with such State or local agencies and such agreements may include provisions under which the Commission shall refrain from processing a charge in any cases or class of cases specified in such agreements or under which the Commission shall relieve any person or class of persons in such State or locality from requirements imposed under this section. The Commission shall rescind any such agreement whenever it determines that the agreement no longer serves the interest of effective enforcement of this title.

(c) Every employer, employment agency, and labor organization subject to this title shall (1) make and keep such records relevant to the determinations of whether unlawful employment practices have been or are being committed, (2) preserve such records for such periods, and (3) make such reports therefrom, as the Commission shall prescribe by regulation or order, after public hearing, as reasonable, necessary, or appropriate for the enforcement of this title or the regulations or orders thereunder. The Commission shall, by regulation, require each employer, labor organization, and joint labor-management committee subject to this title which controls an apprenticeship or other training program to maintain such records as are reasonably necessary to carry out the purposes of this title, including, but not limited to, a list of applicants who wish to participate in such program, including the chronological order in which applications were received, and to furnish to the Commission, upon request, a detailed description of the manner in which persons are selected to participate in the apprenticeship or other training program. Any employer, employment agency, labor organization, or joint labor-management committee which believes that the application to it of any regulation or order issued under this section would result in undue hardship may apply to the Commission for an exemption from the application of such regulation or order and, if such application for an exemption is denied, bring a civil action in the United States district court for the district where such records are kept. If the Commission or the court, as the case may be, finds that the application of the regulation or order to the employer, employment agency, or labor organization in question would impose an undue hardship, the Commission or the court, as the case may be, may grant appropriate relief. If any person required to comply with the provisions of this subsection fails or refuses to do so, the United States district court for the district in which such person is found, resides, or transacts business, shall, upon application of the Commission, or the Attorney General in a case involving a governmental agency or political subdivision, have jurisdiction to issue to such person an order requiring him to comply.

(d) In prescribing requirements pursuant to subsection (c) of this section, the Commission shall consult with other interested State and Federal agencies and shall endeavor to coordinate its requirements with those adopted by such agencies. The Commission shall furnish upon request and without cost to any State or local agency charged with the administration of a fair employment practice law information obtained pursuant to subsection (c) of this section from any employer, employment agency, labor organization, or joint labor-management committee subject to the jurisdiction of such agency. Such information shall be furnished on condition that it not be made public by the recipient agency prior to the institution of a proceeding under State or local law involving such information. If this condition is violated by a recipient agency, the Commission may decline to honor subsequent requests pursuant to this subsection.

(e) It shall be unlawful for any officer or employee of the Commission to make public in any manner whatever any information obtained by the Commission pursuant to its authority under this section prior to the institution of any proceeding under this title involving such information. Any officer or employee of the Commission who shall make public in any manner whatever any information in violation of this subsection shall be guilty of a misdemeanor and upon conviction thereof, shall be fined not more than $1,000, or imprisoned not more than one year.

SEC. 710. For the purpose of all hearings and investigations conducted by the Commission or its duly authorized agents or agencies, section 11 of the National Labor Relations Act (49 Stat. 455; 29 U.S.C. 161) shall apply.

NOTICES TO BE POSTED

SEC. 711. (a) Every employer, employment agency, and labor organization, as the case may be, shall post and keep posted in conspicuous places upon its premises where notices to employees, applicants for employment, and members are customarily posted a notice to be prepared or approved by the Commission setting forth excerpts from or, summaries of, the pertinent provisions of this title and information pertinent to the filing of a complaint.

(b) A willful violation of this section shall be punishable by a fine of not more than $100 for each separate offense.

VETERANS' PREFERENCE

SEC. 712. Nothing contained in this title shall be construed to repeal or modify any Federal, State, territorial, or local law creating special rights or preference for veterans.

RULES AND REGULATIONS

SEC. 713. (a) The Commission shall have authority from time to time to issue, amend, or rescind suitable procedural regulations to carry out the provisions of this title. Regulations issued under this section shall be in conformity with the standards and limitations of the Administrative Procedure Act.

(b) In any action or proceeding based on any alleged unlawful employment practice, no person shall be subject to any liability or punishment for or on account of (1) the commission by such person of an unlawful employment practice if he pleads and proves that the act or omission complained of was in good faith, in conformity with, and in reliance on any written interpretation or opinion of the Commission, or (2) the failure of such person to publish and file any information required by any provision of this title if he pleads and proves that he failed to publish and file such information in good

faith, in conformity with the instructions of the Commission issued under this title regarding the filing of such information. Such a defense, if established, shall be a bar to the action or proceeding notwithstanding that (A) after such act or omission, such interpretation or opinion is modified or rescinded or is determined by judicial authority to be invalid or of no legal effect, or (B) after publishing or filing the description and annual reports, such publication or filing is determined by judicial authority not to be in conformity with the requirements of this title.

FORCIBLY RESISTING THE COMMISSION OR ITS REPRESENTATIVES

SEC. 714. The provisions of section 111 and 1114, title 18, United States Code, shall apply to officers, agents, and employees of the Commission in the performance of their official duties. Notwithstanding the provisions of sections 111 and 1114 of title 18, United States Code, whoever in violation of the provisions of section 1114 of such title kills a person while engaged in or on account of the performance of his official functions under this Act shall be punished by imprisonment for any term of years or for life.

SPECIAL STUDY BY SECRETARY OF LABOR

SEC. 715. There shall be established an Equal Employment Opportunity Coordinating Council (hereinafter referred to in this section as the Council) composed of the Secretary of Labor, the Chairman of the Equal Employment Opportunity Commission, the Attorney General, the Chairman of the United States Civil Service Commission, and the Chairman of the United States Civil Rights Commission, or their respective delegates. The Council shall have the responsibility for developing and implementing agreements, policies and practices designed to maximize effort, promote efficiency, and eliminate conflict, competition, duplication and inconsistency among the operations, functions and jurisdictions of the various departments, agencies and branches of the Federal Government responsible for the implementation and enforcement of equal employment opportunity legislation orders, and policies. On or before July 1 of each year, the Council shall transmit to the President and to the Congress a report of its activities, together with such recommendations for legislative or administrative changes as it concludes are desirable to further promote the purposes of this section.

EFFECTIVE DATE

SEC. 716. (a) This title shall become effective one year after the date of its enactment.

(b) Notwithstanding subsection (a), sections of this title other than sections 703, 704, 706, and 707 shall become effective immediately.

(c) The President shall, as soon as feasible after the enactment of this title, convene one or more conferences for the purpose of enabling the leaders of groups whose members will be affected by this title to become familiar with the rights afforded and obligations imposed by its provisions, and for the purpose of making plans which will result in the fair and effective administration of this title when all of its provisions become effective. The President shall invite the participation in such conference or conferences of (1) the members of the President's Committee on Equal Employment Opportunity, (2) the members of the Commission on Civil Rights, (3) representatives of State and local agencies engaged in furthering equal employment opportunity, (4) representatives of private agencies engaged in furthering equal employment opportunity,

and (5) representatives of employers, labor organizations, and employment agencies who will be subject to this title.

NONDISCRIMINATION IN FEDERAL GOVERNMENT EMPLOYMENT

SEC. 717. (a) All personnel actions affecting employees or applicants for employment (except with regard to aliens employed outside the limits of the United States) in military departments as defined in section 102 of title 5, United States Code, in executive agencies (other than the General Accounting Office) as defined in section 105 of title 5, United States Code (including employees and applicants for employment who are paid from nonappropriated funds), in the United States Postal Service and the Postal Rate Commission, in those units of the Government of the District of Columbia having positions in the competitive service, and in those units of the legislative and judicial branches of the Federal Government having positions in the competitive service, and in the Library of Congress shall be made free from any discrimination based on race, color, religion, sex, or national origin.

(b) Except as otherwise provided in this subsection, the Civil Service Commission shall have authority to enforce the provisions of subsection (a) through appropriate remedies, including reinstatement or hiring of employees with or without back pay, as will effectuate the policies of this section, and shall issue such rules, regulations, orders and instructions as it deems necessary and appropriate to carry out its responsibilities under this section.

The Civil Service Commission shall—

(1) be responsible for the annual review and approval of a national and regional equal employment opportunity plan which each department and agency and each appropriate unit referred

to in subsection (a) of this section shall submit in order to maintain an affirmative program of equal employment opportunity for all such employees and applicants for employment;

(2) be responsible for the review and evaluation of the operation of all agency equal employment opportunity programs, periodically obtaining and publishing (on at least a semi-annual basis) progress reports from each such department, agency, or unit; and

(3) consult with and solicit the recommendations of interested individuals, groups, and organizations relating to equal employment opportunity.

The head of each such department, agency, or unit shall comply with such rules, regulations, orders, and instructions which shall include a provision that an employee or applicant for employment shall be notified of any final action taken on any complaint of discrimination filed by him thereunder. The plan submitted by each department, agency, and unit shall include, but not be limited to—

(1) provision for the establishment of training and education programs designed to provide a maximum opportunity for employees to advance so as to perform at their highest potential; and

(2) a description of the qualifications in terms of training and experience relating to equal employment opportunity for the principal and operating officials of each such department, agency, or unit responsible for carrying out the equal employment opportunity program and of the allocation of personnel and resources proposed by such department, agency, or unit to carry out its equal employment opportunity program.

With respect to employment in the Library of Congress, authorities grant-ed in this subsection to the Civil Service Commission shall be exercised by the Librarian of Congress.

(c) Within thirty days of receipt of notice of final action taken by a department, agency, or unit referred to in subsection 717(a), or by the Civil Service Commission upon an appeal from a decision or order of such department, agency, or unit on a complaint of discrimination based on race, color, religion, sex or national origin, brought pursuant to subsection (a) of this section, Executive Order 11478 or any succeeding executive orders, or after one hundred and eighty days from the filing of the initial charge with the department, agency, or unit or with the Civil Service Commission on appeal from a decision or order of such department, agency, or unit until such time as final action may be taken by a department, agency, or unit, an employee or applicant for employment, if aggrieved by the final disposition of his complaint, or by the failure to take final action on his complaint, may file a civil action as provided in section 706, in which civil action the head of the department, agency, or unit, as appropriate, shall be the defendant.

(d) The provisions of section 706(f) through (k), as applicable, shall govern civil actions brought hereunder.

(e) Nothing contained in this Act shall relieve any Government agency or official of its or his primary responsibility to assure nondiscrimination in employment as required by the Constitution and statutes or of its or his responsibilities under Executive Order 11478 relating to equal employment opportunity in the Federal Government.

SPECIAL PROVISION WITH RESPECT TO DENIAL, TERMINATION AND SUSPENSION OF GOVERNMENT CONTRACTS

SEC. 718. No Government contract, or portion thereof, with any employer, shall be denied, withheld, terminated, or suspended, by any agency or officer of the United States under any equal employment opportunity law or order, where such employer has an affirmative action plan which has previously been accepted by the Government for the same facility within the past twelve months without first according such employer full hearing and adjudication under the provisions of title 5, United States Code, section 554, and the following pertinent sections: Provided, That if such employer has deviated substantially from such previously agreed to affirmative action plan, this section shall not apply: Provided further, That for the purposes of this section an affirmative action plan shall be deemed to have been accepted by the Government at the time the appropriate compliance agency has accepted such plan unless within forty-five days thereafter the Office of Federal Contract Compliance has disapproved such plan.

Notes

1. Title VII was originally enacted in 1964, to become effective the following year. Amendments to the law began to be offered even before it took effect and, eight years later, Congress passed and the President signed the Equal Employment Opportunity Act of 1972. The single most important change was the grant to the Equal Employment Opportunity Commission of the power to sue to enforce the statute. Before 1972, the EEOC could only conciliate complaints it found meritorious, while enforcement of Title VII in the courts was left to individual actions, with occasional help from the Attorney General of the United States. The 1972 change preserved the individual right of suit subject to conditions spelled out in the statute.

All of the 1972 amendments have been incorporated into the preceding text without the distraction of italics and brackets to indicate which provisions originated when. Students interested in a section-by-section analysis of the 1972 legislation and its impact on the 1964 law should consult Cong.Rec. §§ 3460–3463, March 6, 1972.

2. Title VII is considered at length in Berg, Equal Employment Under the Civil Rights Act of 1964, 31 Brooklyn L.Rev. 62 (1964); Symposium on Title VII, 7 B.C.Ind. & Com.L.Rev. 413 (1966); Bureau of National Affairs, The Civil Rights Act of 1964, Washington 1964; Sovern, Legal Restraints on Racial Discrimination in Employment, Twentieth Century Fund, New York, 1966; Note, Title VII, Civil Rights Act of 1964: Present Operation and Proposals for Improvement, 5 Colum.J. of L. and Soc.Probs. 1 (1969). Additional references can be found in the extensive Developments Note, Employment Discrimination and Title VII of the Civil Rights Act of 1964, 84 Harv.L.Rev. 1109 (1971). The legislative history of the original Title VII is collected in Equal Employment Opportunity Commission, Legislative History of Titles VII and XI of Civil Rights Act of 1964, Washington 1968. Current Developments are reported regularly in Bureau of National Affairs, Labor Policy and Practice, Vol. 6 (Fair Employment Practices) Washington and Commerce Clearing House, Employment Practices Guide, Chicago.

B. STATEMENT OF SELECTED ISSUES

The materials that follow, subdivided into the broad categories of substance and procedure, are intended to aid the student in his consideration of the key issues arising under Title VII. As will appear, many of those issues are also inherent in other anti-discrimination measures.

The critical substantive questions cluster around the concept of "discrimination." When do employers and unions "discriminate" by relying on standards which, though formulated in nonracial terms, place blacks at a disadvantage? Consider two brief extracts:

BONFIELD, THE SUBSTANCE OF AMERICAN FAIR EMPLOYMENT PRACTICES LEGISLATION

61 Northwestern Law Review 907,
956–57 (1967).

This means that the conduct which ultimately forms the basis of a finding of discrimination under the fair employment laws is prohibited only when it is coupled with a certain state of mind. "Thus, discrimination is essentially an equivocal act accompanied and inspired by the mental element of prejudice. It is the motive that distinguishes the [prohibited] act, not the act itself." However, a man is deemed to intend the natural consequences of his acts and therefore the act, the setting from whence it came, as well as its consequences may be probative of the employer's intent. That is, circumstantial evidence may also establish the requisite general intent. As a result, the motive behind an employer's conduct will make a nice question of fact in each case —a question which must be resolved before an evaluation of the unlawfulness of the conduct can be ascertained.

BLUMROSEN, BLACK EMPLOYMENT AND THE LAW 173–74

(Rutgers University Press 1971).

Title VII makes unlawful those actions which "adversely affect" employment opportunities of persons because of their race. Thus Title VII establishes a standard of conduct to effectuate the public interest represented by the statute. The body of law regulating in civil cases the relations of one person to another is called the law of tort. Thus Title VII establishes a body of "statutory tort law" regulating the relations of employers, unions and employment agencies toward minority group persons. In traditional legal terms, the tort we are concerned with would be classified as an intentional tort. This "intention" has nothing to do with the evil motive (mens rea) of the criminal law. Rather, it involves awareness that the acts of the defendant would inflict harm on the plaintiff. This awareness provides the element of "blameworthiness" which distinguishes the intentional from the negligent infliction of harm in modern tort law. The narrow concept of intent espoused by those who would restrict the application of Title VII and, strangely enough, by two commentators who otherwise seem friendly toward the objectives of Title VII, has no place in the modern law of tort. Rather, if the defendant is aware that his action is reasonably certain to adversely affect persons because of their race, he has the intention required by the law of tort.

————

What difference does it make whether the courts agree with Bonfield or Blumrosen? What are the implications for companies that hire only high school graduates? for employers relying on aptitude and achievement tests? for enterprises that refuse to hire applicants with a criminal record? for apprenticeship programs that give preference to the relatives of union members? for union contracts that preserve promotional opportunities for senior workers? Relevant materials are to be found below.

————

As with any regulatory system, so with Title VII—virtually all of the questions considered in administrative law and civil procedure courses are relevant. But enough cases have now been litigated under Title VII to give some procedural issues special prominence. Under what conditions may a complaint bring a class action? How are the limitations periods of Section 706 to be calculated? Materials relevant to these and related questions are to be found below.

Problems of proof permeate the whole subject. Watch for them in the section on Selected Substantive Issues. Additional materials on proving discrimination appear at pp. 916–920.

The subject of remedies is also a recurrent one, but it receives special attention at pp. 920–939.

Yet another set of procedural problems arises out of the varying anti-discrimination measures—state and federal—that may be brought to bear on a single claim of discrimination. Must some remedies be utilized before others? To what extent does the outcome in one forum bind the parties in another? And so on. Consideration of these issues is postponed to Section 3, after the materials on other anti-discrimination measures.

C. SELECTED SUBSTANTIVE ISSUES

---

1. Preferring Family and Friends

SOVERN, LEGAL RESTRAINTS ON RACIAL DISCRIMINATION IN EMPLOYMENT 177–82

(Twentieth Century Fund 1966).

Lefkowitz v. Farrell

On January 2, 1963, the Attorney General of New York filed a verified complaint with that state's Commission for Human Rights, charging various named respondents with discriminatory

administration of an apprenticeship training program. Heading the list of the accused was Mell Farrell, president of Local 28, Sheet Metal Workers International. Joined with him were the union itself; the Joint Apprenticeship Committee, composed equally of representatives of the union and representatives of two employer associations in the sheet metal industry; and individual members of the Joint Apprenticeship Committee. The union and the Committee were accused of discriminating against Negroes generally and against one James Ballard specifically in approving applicants for apprenticeship training; the individual respondents were charged with aiding and abetting the union and the Committee in their discriminatory practices.

The structure within which the discrimination was alleged to have occurred is typical of the skilled construction crafts generally. The Joint Apprenticeship Committee exists by virtue of a collective agreement between the union and two employer associations representing contractors engaged in sheet metal work on construction throughout New York City. That agreement provides for equal union and employer representation on the Committee and requires it "to formulate and make operative rules and regulations to govern eligibility, registration, education, transfer, service, hours and working conditions of duly qualified apprentices and the operation of an adequate apprentice system to meet the needs and requirements of the sheet metal trade in New York City." [8] That agreement also pro-

---

[8] The decisions of the Commission for Human Rights are not regularly reported. Its opinion and order in Lefkowitz v. Farrell have, however, been published in the Race Rel.Law Rep., Spring 1964, pp. 393–406. We will, therefore, cite this source when referring to those documents. The quotation in the text, however, comes not from the opinion or order, but from the commission's findings, which were published only in mimeograph and are not generally available. Since page references to this source would be of little

vided, the Commission for Human Rights found, "that apprentice candidates should be designated by the union subject to the approval of the JAC."

The program administered by the Joint Apprenticeship Committee is registered with the New York State Apprenticeship Council and subject to the Bureau of Apprenticeship and Training of the United States Department of Labor, about both of which more later. For four years the apprentice receives on-the-job and classroom instruction: at the beginning of the program he is paid 40 per cent of the journeyman rate; by his final semester he has moved up to 80 per cent. (Under the contract in force when the Commission for Human Rights rendered its decision, the journeyman rate was $6.15 per hour plus fringe benefits.)

Apprentices who complete the program "are regularly and invariably accepted for membership in Local 28," and this was virtually the only road to membership. It was, moreover, virtually the only road to employment as a sheet metal worker in the city of New York.

To be admitted to the program an applicant had to be not less than 18 nor more than 23 years old at the time of appointment, except that a veteran of the armed services could be taken up to the age of 25 if he applied before going into the service. This was the only express requirement. In practice, Local 28 "favored those who had a high school diploma or its equivalent and required that an applicant be sponsored by at least one member of Local 28, except that veterans were not required to be so sponsored."

This was the program into which James Ballard, a 22-year-old Negro Air Force veteran, sought admission in March 1962. Although he possessed the qualifications usually demanded by the Joint

Apprenticeship Committee, he was not among the 56 applicants accepted in June 1962, nor was he included in the groups designated in January and July 1963.

In the interim the attorney general had filed his complaint with the Commission for Human Rights and a member of the commission had been designated to look into the matter. After a preliminary investigation, he tried without success to conciliate the case. Finally, on August 2, 1963, a full seven months after the attorney general's complaint had been filed, the investigating commissioner issued a written determination that probable cause existed to credit the allegations of the complaint. After another month of fruitless conciliation attempts, the investigating commissioner set the case for public hearing before a panel of three other commissioners. The hearing began on September 23 and the last of 13 sessions was held on December 18; the submission of briefs was completed on February 2, 1964; the panel rendered its decision on February 26.

The commissioners were unanimous in finding the respondents guilty as charged. Their decision can usefully be viewed as resting on two separate but related sets of findings—one having to do with actual, present animus against Negroes, the other with the racially discriminatory consequences of nepotism. Present animus could fairly be inferred from the following combination of facts. (1) Local 28, with a complement of approximately 3,300 members, had never had a Negro member, nor had any Negro ever been accepted as a sheet metal apprentice. (2) Although the union claimed that James Ballard was not accepted for apprenticeship training "because it was its usual practice to consider and select apprentices in the order of their having filed their apprenticeship applications and that many applicants had filed before Ballard," the commission found ten completely undated applications among those picked for the

July 1962, January 1963, and July 1963 semesters, and all of the applicants designated for those semesters filed their papers after many other applicants who were passed over. (3) One Shelton, a Negro sheet metal worker, testified that while he was employed in a non-union shop, Local 28 unionized it and forced his reassignment to a truck driver's job; he tried repeatedly to gain entry into the union, but on one occasion a union official told him, as he put it, that Local 28 "did not have any Negroes in there and as soon as they did start taking them in, I would be one of the first," and on another the same official "still said they wasn't taking Negroes in." [9] (4) Two other Negroes seeking appointments as apprentices were also turned away for questionable reasons.

The respondents attempted to rebut the inference of animus against Negroes in several ways, but only one merits serious consideration. Their contention, in essence, was that the apprenticeship program kept out everybody but the friends and relatives of Local 28's members. While it was unfortunate that no Negroes had found their way into that select circle, many whites were similarly luckless, and so race could not be held the basis of Ballard's or any other Negro's exclusion. The commission could hardly ignore this argument, for its own findings included the following:

At least 80% of all apprentices in the entire JAC training program are related to members of Local 28.

In the designation of apprentices for the JAC training program, Local 28, as a general practice, gave preference to relatives of its members.

Even these findings, however, did not preclude the commission from finding a specific animus against Negroes, for they imply that at least a few places in the program were not assigned to relatives

and they leave unrebutted Shelton's testimony that he was twice told by a union business agent that the union would not accept Negroes. Consequently, had the commission wished to issue a narrowly based decision, it probably could have done so by finding simply that race prejudice did in fact infect the selection of sheet metal apprentices. The trouble with this approach, from the commission's point of view, is that it might conceivably have called for a more limited remedy than the one actually ordered; it would probably have created few new opportunities for Negroes; and it would certainly have lessened the case's importance as a precedent for other suits.

While the commission did specifically find that qualified Negroes were discriminated against because of their color, it did not stop there. Mindful of its broad mandate "to eliminate and prevent discrimination in employment," [10] the commission made a frontal attack on the union's nepotic selection of apprentices. At some points in its opinion the commission seems to say that an all-white group discriminates on the basis of race whenever it makes admission depend on relation to or sponsorship by a member. Thus, "Mostly the union members sponsor their relatives. The fact that there are no Negro union members to sponsor the Negro applicant makes the discrimination against him a racial one." [11] And "If this Commission were to permit unions having no Negro members to select applicants solely on the basis of their relationship to persons already admitted to membership, the Law's mandate would be violated." [12]

Notes

1. Is Title VII violated when a union excludes all but the relatives of members

[9] Race Rel.Law Rep., Spring 1964, p. 400.

[10] N.Y. Executive Law § 200.

[11] Race Rel.Law Rep., Spring 1964, p. 401.

[12] Ibid.

from desirable employment? Does the answer depend on the union's racial composition? If the union has only white members, does it matter how there came to be no blacks among them?

a. In Lefkowitz v. Farrell, the New York Commission for Human Rights found that until the end of 1946, Local 28 had been barred from accepting Negro members by the constitution of the Sheet Metal Workers' International Association. That finding was ample to support the inference that Local 28's all-white status was attributable in part to past discrimination against Negroes. Does a union discriminate because of race by preferring the relatives of members when its own past racial discrimination makes it impossible for any black to qualify for such a preference? Does it matter how far in the past that racial discrimination occurred?

b. In Local 53, Asbestos Workers v. Vogler, 407 F.2d 1055 (5th Cir. 1969), the Court of Appeals said:

"The District Court did no more than prevent future discrimination when it prohibited a continuing exclusion of Negroes through the application of an apparently neutral membership provision which was *originally* instituted at least in part because of racial discrimination and which served no significant trade-related purpose. While the nepotism requirement is applicable to black and white alike and is not on its face discriminatory, in a completely white union the present effect of its continued application is to forever deny to Negroes and Mexican-Americans any real opportunity for membership. See Ross v. Dyer, 5 Cir. 1963, 312 F.2d 191, 196; State Commissioner for Human Rights v. Farrell, 43 Misc.2d 958, 252 N.Y.S.2d 649 (1964). See also Quarles v. Phillip Morris, Inc., E. D.Va.1968, 279 F.Supp. 505, 516, 518–19; United States v. Local 189,

United Papermakers and Paperworkers, E.D.La.1968, 282 F.Supp. 39, 44–45. See M. I. Sovern, Legal Restraints on Racial Discrimination in Employment 181–82 (1966). In view of the general policies of racial discrimination in Louisiana, United States v. State of Louisiana, E.D.La.1963, 225 F.Supp. 353, 363–81 affirmed 1965, 380 U.S. 145, 85 S.Ct. 817, 13 L.Ed.2d 709 and Local 53's admitted policy of racial discrimination both prior to and following the effective date of the Act, the union cannot salvage the invalidity of this requirement by convincing us that it did not arise at least in part from racial bases."

2. Compare with Title VII section 296 (1–a) of New York's Executive Law:

"It shall be an unlawful discriminatory practice for an employer, labor organization, employment agency or any joint labor-management committee controlling apprentice training programs:

"(a) To select persons for an apprentice training program registered with the state of New York on any basis other than their qualifications, as determined by objective criteria which permit review. * * * "

3. In Kotch v. Board of Pilot Commissioners for the Port of New Orleans, 330 U.S. 552, 67 S.Ct. 910, 91 L.Ed. 1093 (1946), plaintiffs were challenging a Louisiana law that limited appointments as pilots to those who had served an apprenticeship under a certified state pilot. Plaintiffs claimed that incumbent pilots generally selected only their friends and relatives as apprentices. By a vote of five to four, the Supreme Court held that the pilotage law as administered did not violate the equal protection clause of the Fourteenth Amendment. Mr. Justice Rutledge dissented, saying:

"Conceivably the familial system wold be the most effective possible scheme for training many kinds of artisans or public servants, sheerly from the viewpoint of securing the highest degree of skill and competence. Indeed, something very worth while largely disappeared from our national life when the once prevalent familial system of conducting manufacturing and mercantile enterprises went out and was replaced by the highly impersonal corporate system for doing business.

"But that loss is not one to be repaired under our scheme by legislation framed or administered to perpetuate family monopolies of either private occupations or branches of the public service. It is precisely because the [Fourteenth] Amendment forbids enclosing those areas by legislative lines drawn on the basis of race, color, creed and the like, that, in cases like this, the possibly most efficient method of securing the highest development of skills cannot be established by law. Absent any such bar, the presence of such a tendency or direct relationship would be effective for sustaining the legislation. It cannot be effective to overcome the bar itself. The discrimination here is not shown to be consciously racial in character. But I am unable to differentiate in effects one founded on blood relationship." 330 U.S. at 566. Would plaintiffs have a claim under Title VII? Against whom?

4. "Local 28's view of apprenticeship openings as valuable patronage, to be dispensed in accordance with the wishes of the faithful, and the power to implement that view are held by many building trades locals. Construction craft unions have historically sought to limit entry into their labor markets in order to maximize work opportunities for their members. By controlling the number of apprentices, they can hold down present low-wage competition (since apprentices, who spend most of their training time on the job, can do some of a journeyman's work, their unlimited availability might cause contractors to hire fewer journeymen and more apprentices) while avoiding a future "surplus" of fully trained journeymen. Many employers are not disposed to resist: they perceive apprentices as a burden rather than a cheap manpower supply and would rather leave their training to others. In allocating the few apprenticeship openings available, union leaders have quite naturally responded to the wishes of their members by designating their relatives and friends. This is not only the natural response; it is also the one best calculated to build loyalty to the union and, not to be overlooked, to the leaders themselves.

"Control over apprenticeship openings is thus a highly sensitive matter for the building trades unions. They have a stake in the status quo of a sort that has no real parallel on the employer side. Consider Lefkowitz v. Farrell again: The sheet metal employers lost nothing of importance to them, but Local 28 lost much that was important to it.

"The implications for Negroes are baleful. Since many craft locals are almost all or entirely white, nepotic apprentice selection effectively bars Negroes from ever working in the crafts those locals control." Sovern, Legal Restraints on Racial Discrimination in Employment 187–88 (Twentieth Century Fund 1966).

———

The New York Commission for Human Rights' proceeding against Local 28, Sheet Metal Workers International, eventuated in a set of standards to govern the selection and training of sheet metal apprentices in New York City. See State Commission for Human Rights v. Farrell, 43 Misc.2d 958, 252 N.Y.S.2d 649 (Sup.Ct., Spec.Term, N.Y.County 1964). Selected portions of the standards follow. Lawyers have been known to snatch defeat from the jaws of victory by paying insufficient attention to the details of the final decrees entered in cases they have won. How would you rate the Commission's attorneys? Do the standards adequately protect minority youths seeking admission to apprenticeship programs? Do any provisions strike you as especially astute? Do you see any loopholes?

PART I

PURPOSES, INTENT AND PROCEDURE

A. NON-DISCRIMINATORY PROGRAM—Selection of apprentices will be made subject to the objective standards herein provided. Apprentices will be selected on the basis of qualifications alone, and all applicants will be afforded equal opportunity under these standards without regard to race, creed, color, national origin or physical or psychological handicaps, *provided however,* that if the physical or psychological handicaps affect the applicant's ability to perform the manual labors required by the trade, the applicant will not be accepted.

* * *

B. APPLICATIONS—All applicants who heretofore have applied, and all applicants who may hereafter apply for apprenticeship training shall be accorded equality of treatment in determining their eligibility to be appointed to the apprentice training program and shall be judged by the same set of objective standards. No preference in treatment shall be given between those who apply for admission de novo and those who have applied heretofore.

PART II

QUALIFICATIONS

A. NOTIFICATION OF REQUIREMENTS—A written statement of the qualifications for admission will be given to each applicant prior to the time when each applicant is first required to demonstrate his qualifications.

B. AGE PREREQUISITE—Applicants for Apprenticeship Training shall:

(a) be not less than 18 years of age, nor more than 23. * * * Service in the Armed Forces may extend the age limit to 25 years of age. * * *

(b) HIGH SCHOOL PREREQUISITE—. * * *
Applicants who file applications for admission to the Apprenticeship Training Program during 1969 and thereafter, shall have graduated from high school or have an equivalency certificate showing completion of high school studies.

(c) PHYSICAL EMOTIONAL PREREQUISITE—Be physically fit and emotionally stable for work in the trade. Each applicant who meets the age, educational and physical requirements shall be given an aptitude test and based upon the aptitude scores, personal interviews will be granted to the number determined in accordance with the formula hereinafter set forth.

C. ESTABLISHMENT OF QUALIFICATIONS—Qualifications shall be established by:

1. Certificate of age from Local Board of Education or certified photostat of birth certificate (attach to application).

* * *

4. Applicants for admission to apprenticeship training during 1969 or thereafter, a diploma or other proof of graduation from an accredited high school, or an equivalency certificate establishing equivalent education.

5. PROOF OF PHYSICAL FITNESS—A medical examination pursuant to the form herein set forth, shall be given at a time, place and by a physician designated by the Committee. Physical standards, based upon requirements of the trade, shall be established and revised, from time to time, by a Medical Advisory Panel appointed by the Committee.

D. APTITUDE TESTING. Applicants who satisfy the age, educational and physical requirements will be eligible for Aptitude tests to be given at a time and place designated by the Committee by the New York University Testing and Advisement Center, Washington Square East, New York City or by equivalent University testing center.

Test 1. Mental alertness.

2. Mechanical reasoning.

3. Space relations.

4. Mathematical Computations and Concepts.

5. Mathematical Analysis and problem solving.

Aptitude tests will be graded on a maximum score for all five tests to be 750 points.

E. INTERVIEWS—200% of the number of apprentices to be appointed who achieved the highest aptitude test scores shall be given a personal interview at a time and place and before a person or persons designated by the Committee. The interview procedures as established by the Committee, shall uniformly be applied to each applicant eligible for interview.

F. SELECTION SOLELY BY SCORES ATTAINED—Apprentices shall be appointed in order of rank, without regard to race, creed, color or national origin, after they have displayed qualifications in sufficient measure to meet minimum standards established by the committee.

G. INTERVIEW BOARD—Examining personnel for interview will be 50% representation from each of labor and management. Each interviewer will grade applicant individually in accordance with specific maximum point allocations for various categories.

H.　(1) MAXIMUM TOTAL SCORES—Total maximum score for any applicant shall be:

Tests .... 750 points
Interviews .150 points
900 points

(2) FINAL SELECTION— The final selection of applicants shall be based on the determination of the total number of apprentices to be appointed.

I. NOTIFICATION TO APPLICANTS.—Each applicant, at least 10 days prior to the commencement of the apprenticeship term for which he has applied, shall be:

1. Given written notification as to whether or not he has qualified for placement on the applicant list and, if he has so qualified, his ranking among the applicants. Further, such notification shall inform each qualified applicant whether or not he has been appointed and if not, the basis of nonappointment. The notification shall be sent by prepaid first class mail and the committee shall obtain from the postmaster, or his representative, a certificate of mailing showing the name and address of the addressee of the letter of notification.

2. Such notification shall set forth the terms of any appellate procedure afforded by the committee. Such appellate procedure shall provide for fi-

nal determination and written notification thereof within 30 days of the appeal.

*   *   *

4. Complete records of the selection process shall be maintained by the committee for two years, or the life of the applicant list, whichever is greater, and shall be made available to the Industrial Commissioner upon request. Such records shall include copies of any written examinations taken by or documents submitted by or in connection with each applicant and a brief summary of each interview, if any, including the judgment of the interviewer for each applicant.

J. APPLICATION FEES—Costs of examining procedures—Applicants shall be required uniformly to pay to the Committee, at the time of filing applications, a reasonable fee not to exceed $10.00 to cover the expenses of the examinations and examining procedures.

K. NOTIFICATION OF REJECTION—Applicants who are not accepted because of failure at any stage of qualification to meet the requirements and standards herein provided shall be notified as provided by Paragraph "I" above, but within ten (10) days after the decision is made by the Committee and the reasons for rejection shall be set forth in the notice and each applicant shall have the right of appeal hereafter set forth.

[The appeal provisions have been omitted.—Ed.]

*   *   *

PART VII

MISCELLANEOUS

(a) The Rules and Regulations of the Industrial Commissioner of the State of New York heretofore adopted or which may hereafter be adopted by him, in so far as they are not inconsistent with the

within Objective Standards governing the Admission of Apprentices and of the Order of the Court approving same, shall be deemed adopted into, and made part of, the within Objective Standards without specific inclusion.

(b) Any requirement for the advanced publication of notice of the intention of the Committee to accept applicants for new classes to be formed by the Committee, required to be given to any person or persons, or to any public body or bodies, by virtue of the provisions of any Federal or State law, or by virtue of the regulations of any governmental committee or officer having jurisdiction, shall be deemed incorporated into the within Objective Standards, and made a part hereof, without specific inclusion. * * *

Supplemental Opinion

In implementation of the order of this court dated November 6, 1964, the parties have reported that they have agreed upon the institution of an apprenticeship class of 65 to commence not later than March 15, 1965. A stipulation to that effect has been submitted, approved by the court, and marked "So Ordered". The foregoing is reasonably fair and will generally effectuate the purposes of the order herein. It is also expected that henceforth new classes will be instituted on a periodic basis. * * *

2. Seniority

LOCAL 189, UNITED PAPER-MAKERS v. UNITED STATES

United States Court of Appeals,
Fifth Circuit,
416 F.2d 980 (1969), certiorari denied
397 U.S. 919, 90 S.Ct. 926 (1970).

WISDOM, Circuit Judge. Title VII of the Civil Rights Act of 1964 prohibits discrimination in all aspects of employment. In this case we deal with one of the most perplexing issues troubling the courts under Title VII: how to reconcile equal employment opportunity *today* with seniority expectations based on *yesterday's* built-in racial discrimination. May an employer continue to award formerly "white jobs" on the basis of seniority attained in other formerly white jobs, or must the employer consider the employee's experience in formerly "Negro jobs" as an equivalent measure of seniority? We affirm the decision of the district court. We hold that Crown Zellerbach's job seniority system in effect at its Bogalusa Paper Mill prior to February 1, 1968, was unlawful because by carrying forward the effects of former discriminatory practices the system results in present and future discrimination. When a Negro applicant has the qualifications to handle a particular job, the Act requires that Negro seniority be equated with white seniority.

I.

A. The parties stipulated most of the basic facts. Crown Zellerbach (Crown) runs a paper mill at Bogalusa, Louisiana. The Company employs about 950 white workers and 250 Negro workers. Jobs there have always been organized hierarchically within "lines of progression". The jobs within each line for the most part are related functionally so that experience in one job serves as training for the next.

Until May 1964, the Company segregated the lines of progression by race, reserving some lines to white employees and others to Negroes. Local 189 of the United Papermakers and Paperworkers, the white local, had jurisdiction over the more desirable lines; Local 189–A, the Negro local, had jurisdiction over the left-overs. With very few exceptions, the lowliest white jobs paid more and carried greater responsibility than the most exalted Negro jobs. Promotion within each line was determined by "job seniority"; when a vacancy occurred, the workers in the slot below it could bid for the job, and the one who had worked the longest *in the job slot below* had priority.

The Company put new employees on "extra boards". These boards were labor pools used to fill temporary vacancies within the lines of progression. The senior men had first call on vacancies in the entry jobs at the bottom of the various lines. When lay-offs occurred, those at the bottom of the line were bumped back to the extra board. They had first claim, however, on any vacancies in their old jobs under "rights of recall". Crown segregated its extra boards, like its lines of progression, by race, one for Negroes and one for whites.

The Company merged the extra boards in May 1964. Whoever, regardless of race, had the longest term on the board now gained priority to bid on entry jobs in the white lines. Merger opened up the lines to Negro entrants, and helped the relatively recent Negro employees on the board. It did not help more senior Negroes already in the lines of progression. Moreover, the rights of recall gave any white who had served in a white line preference over others on the board in bidding on his old job. That fact slowed the advance of even newer Negro employees. A "transfer provision" added in 1965 enabled Negroes already in black lines of progression to bid on the bottom jobs in white lines on the basis of their "mill seniority", or time worked at the mill. This change meant that they did not have to become junior men on the extra board in order to bid on the starting job in previously white lines. It also meant that they did not have to surrender certain benefits accruing to mill seniority when they made the transfer.

Title VII went into effect with regard to Crown on July 2, 1965. Section 703 (a)(2) makes it unlawful for an employer

"to limit, segregate, or classify his employees in any way which would deprive or tend to deprive any individual of employment opportunities or otherwise adversely affect his status as an employee, because of such individual's race, color, religion, sex, or national origin." 42 U.S.C.A. § 2000e–2(a) (2).

Later in 1965 the Equal Employment Opportunity Commission discussed with the Company and the Papermakers the effect of Title VII on seniority arrangements. A letter from Herman Edelsberg, the Executive Director of the EEOC, stated that the Commission would be satisfied by the "non-discriminatory application of the seniority agreement established by collective bargaining," i. e. job seniority, provided that Crown discontinue segregation of the progression lines. The Chairman of the Commission, Franklin D. Roosevelt, Jr., met with representatives of the Company and the unions in December 1965 and declared that "application of the seniority system established by collective bargaining" would comply with the statute.

In January 1966 the unions and the Company amended the collective bargaining agreement so as to merge the progression lines within each department on the basis of existing pay rates. Except for one job in the plant, merger by pay rates merely meant tacking the Negro lines to the bottom of white lines. Whites on the extra boards who had rights of recall to jobs formerly entry jobs retained those rights to the same jobs, even though the positions were now in the middle of the merged lines. More importantly, Crown continued to award promotions according to job seniority: the man with the most years in the job slot below the vacancy had first call. Time worked in the mill counted for

nothing as such. As a necessary result, Negroes had no seniority in bidding for formerly white jobs except as against each other and new white employees. They could not have such seniority, since the Company had not allowed them into the white progression lines. Crown gave no recognition to years spent in the Negro lines, and continued to make years spent in formerly white jobs the determinative factor in awarding all former white jobs except those previously at the entry level. The system conditioned job advancement upon a qualification that the Company itself had limited racially, *regardless of whether the qualification—* seniority in previously white jobs—*was necessary to do the work.* The legality of that arrangement is the main issue here.

In February 1967, more than a year after the merger of the lines, the Office of Federal Contract Compliance entered the picture. That agency has responsibility for overseeing compliance with Executive Order 11246 requiring non-discrimination assurances from all employers who contract with the federal government. The OFCC attacked what the EEOC had previously seemed to approve, Crown Zellerbach's system of job seniority. In place of job seniority the OFCC proposed an "A + B" system which would combine an employee's time in the job below the vacancy and his total time at the mill in computing seniority. The Company accepted this compromise and tried to get the Papermakers to go along with it. The two locals, 189 and 189–A, both refused, although for different reasons. Crown thus faced a strike if it went ahead with the "A + B" system and the loss of future federal contracts if it did not. In January it notified the unions that it would install the "A + B" system unilaterally on February 1, 1968. Local 189, the white union, responded by voting to strike on that date. Local 189–A, the Negro union, refused to join in the strike warning, calling the "A + B" system "a step in the right direction".

The Government filed this suit on January 30, 1968, to enjoin the strike as an effort "to perpetuate a seniority and recall system which discriminates against Negro employees". The district court granted the injunction the next day. The United States then asked the courts to strike down the "A + B" system as illegal, and to require that mill experience alone become the standard of seniority. The Government now was asking the court to set aside job seniority in any form, a stronger measure than the one requested earlier by the OFCC, which in turn had gone beyond the original position of the EEOC. Local 189–A and two Negro employees intervened as plaintiffs on behalf of all Negro employees at the mill.

After a three-day hearing on job seniority, the district court issued an order on March 26, 1968, dealing with two issues that had been stipulated by the parties as severable from the eleven others in the case. The court continued in effect the injunction of January 31. It also held that job seniority "presently discriminate[s] against Negro employees at the mill whenever Negroes hired prior to January 1965 [when progression lines were merged] compete against white employees for promotion, demotion or selection for training". The court also found that job seniority, as a matter of fact, "is not necessitated by safety or efficiency factors * * *." It ordered the abolition of job seniority in favor of mill seniority "in all circumstances in which one or more competing employees is a Negro employee hired prior to January 16, 1966." The decree did not, by its terms, upset the use of job seniority in bidding that involved only whites or Negroes hired after the merger of the lines of progression.

In explaining its order, the court pointed out that the abolition of job seniority did not mean that affected Negro employees would be able to bid on any job in the mill solely on the basis of their years with the Company. They would still have to move up the lines of progression job-by-job. Among the competitors within the slot below a vacancy, however, time in the mill rather than time in the job would define seniority. As a further qualification of its order, the court disavowed any intention "to deny Crown the right to require that competing employees have the fundamental qualifications necessary to fill the vacant position."

* * *

B.   The stipulated issues are: "whether, under the facts and circumstances of this case, the job seniority system which was in effect at the Bogalusa paper mill prior to February 1, 1968, was unlawful" and, if so, "what is the necessary or appropriate standard or guideline for identifying the seniority of employees for purposes of promotion or demotion?"

The plaintiffs maintain that Crown's practice of awarding jobs on the basis of *job* seniority rather than *mill* seniority discriminates against Negroes, since they had no way of attaining job seniority in "white" slots until the recent desegregation of the plant. When Negroes bid for jobs above the former entry level of white lines of progression, Crown in effect penalized them for not having what it denied them on account of their race until a short time ago—"white" job seniority. Crown's system gives renewed effect to the old racial distinctions without the plaintiffs say, *the justification of business necessity.* The practice of awarding jobs by job seniority would, the plaintiffs assert, amount to present and prospective racial discrimination.

Crown and Local 189, the white union, maintain that Crown ceased to discriminate in 1966 when it merged the white and Negro lines of progression. That change, coupled with the merger of the extra boards in 1964 and the transfer provisions of 1965 removed all explicit racial classification at the Bogalusa mill. What remains, the defendants say, is a racially neutral system of job seniority. The fact that the system continues to prefer whites over previously hired Negroes in filling certain vacancies does not in itself show racial discrimination. That effect, the defendants argue, is merely an ineradicable consequence of extinct racial discrimination. They point to evidence that Congress meant Title VII to apply prospectively only. Competitive seniority has an honorable place in the history of labor,[7] and portions of the legislative history of the Act seem to immunize accrued rights of seniority against remedial measures. Thus Title VII § 703(h) specifically protects "bona fide seniority systems" from the operation of the Act. The defendants also maintain that insistence upon mill seniority would effective-

ly bestow preferential treatment upon one race, which the Act by its terms positively forbids.

I.

No one can quarrel with the broad proposition that Title VII operates only prospectively. By specific provision, the Act did not become effective at all until one year after the date of enactment. The central operative provision, § 703 (a), declares that "it *shall* be an unlawful employment practice" for an employer to discriminate. (Emphasis added.) Section 701(b) and (e) provide that for staggered effective dates: The Act applied on July 2, 1965, only to employers of 100 employees or more, extending to employers of 75, 50, and 25 at successive yearly intervals. The dispute is whether a seniority system based on pre-Act work credit constitutes present discrimination.

Although the effect of Title VII provoked considerable debate in Congress, the legislative history of the title is singularly uninstructive on seniority rights. Opponents of the Act warned that Title VII would destroy hard-earned seniority rights; proponents responded that it would not affect accrued seniority.[8]   In

---

[7] Cooper and Sobol, 82 Harv.L.Rev. 1601, fn. 2: "The use of competitive status seniority to govern promotions, demotions, and layoffs is a fundamental aspect of industrial relations in this country. In nearly all businesses of significant size whose employees are organized, a seniority system plays some role in determining the allocation of the work. Such systems are commonly accompanied by lines of progression or promotional ladders which establish an order of jobs through which employees normally are promoted.

"Seniority may be measured by total length of employment with the employer ('employment,' 'mill,' or 'plant' seniority), length of service in a department, ('departmental seniority'), length of service in a line of progression ('progression line' seniority), or length of service in a job ('job' seniority). Different measures of seniority sometimes are used in the same plant for different purposes. The variations and combinations of seniority principles are very great, but in all cases the basic measure is length of service, with preference accorded to the senior worker. Similarly, construction craft unions, which control the allocation of local work in their craft, have adopted referral rules based on length of service."

[8] "Title VII would have no effect on seniority rights existing at the time it takes effect." Justice Department statement. Cong. Record, April 8, 1964, p. 6986. "If a rule were to state that all Negroes must be laid off before any white man, such a rule could not serve as a basis for a discharge subsequent to the effective date of the title * * * but, in the ordinary case, assuming that seniority rights were built up over a period of time during which Negroes were not hired, these rights would not be set aside by taking effect of Title VII. Employer and labor organizations would simply be under a duty not to discriminate against Negroes because of their race. Any differences in treatment based on established seniority rights would not be based on race and would not be forbidden by the title." Ibid. "Title VII would have no effect on established seniority rights. Its effect is prospective and not retrospective. Thus, for example, if a business has been discriminating in the past and as a result has an all-white working

Quarles v. Philip Morris, Inc., E.D.Va. 1968, 279 F.Supp. 505, after a careful review of the legislative history, Judge John D. Butzner, Jr. concluded:

> Several facts are evident from the legislative history. First, it contains no express statement about departmental seniority. Nearly all of the references are clearly to employment seniority. None of the excerpts upon which the company and the union rely suggests that as a result of past discrimination a Negro is to have employment opportunities inferior to those of a white person who has less employment seniority. Second, the legislative history indicates that a discriminatory seniority system established before the act cannot be held lawful under the act. The history leads the court to conclude that Congress did not intend to require "reverse discrimination"; that is, the act does not require that Negroes be preferred over white employees who possess employment seniority. It is also apparent that Congress did not intend to freeze an entire generation of Negro employees into discriminatory patterns that existed before the act.

Perhaps the strongest argument for the *Quarles* construction of the Act is § 703(h):

> Section 703(h) expressly states the seniority system must be *bona fide*. The purpose of the act is to eliminate racial discrimination in covered employment. Obviously one character-

istic of a *bona fide* seniority system must be lack of discrimination. Nothing in § 703(h), or in its legislative history suggests that a racially discriminatory seniority system established before the act is a *bona fide* seniority system under the act. Quarles v. Philip Morris, Incorporated, E.D.Va.1968, 279 F.Supp. 505, 517.

We agree with this view.

II.

The defendants assert, paradoxically, that even though the system conditions future employment opportunities upon a previously determined racial status the system is itself racially neutral and not in violation of Title VII. The translation of racial status to job-seniority status cannot obscure the hard, cold fact that Negroes at Crown's mill will lose promotions which, *but for* their race, they would surely have won. Every time a Negro worker hired under the old segregated system bids against a white worker in his job slot, the old racial classification reasserts itself, and the Negro suffers anew for his employer's previous bias. It is not decisive therefore that a seniority system may appear to be neutral on its face if the inevitable effect of tying the system to the *past* is to cut into the employees *present* right not to be discriminated against on the ground of race. The crux of the problem is how far the employer must go to undo the effects of past discrimination. A complete purge of the "but-for" effects of previous bias would require that Negroes displace white incumbents who hold jobs that, but for discrimination, the Negroes' greater mill seniority would entitle them to hold. Under this *"freedom now"* theory, allowing junior whites to continue in their jobs constitutes an act of discrimination.

Crown and Local 189 advance a *"status quo"* theory: the employer may satisfy the requirements of the Act mere-

---

force, when the Title comes into effect, the employer's obligation would be simply to fill future vacancies on a non-discriminatory basis. He would not be obliged—or indeed, permitted—to fire whites in order to hire Negroes, or to prefer Negroes for future vacancies, or, once Negroes are hired, to give them special seniority rights at the expense of the white workers hired earlier." Memorandum by Senators Clark and Case. Bureau of National Affairs Operations Manual, The Civil Rights Act of 1964, p. 320. See Cooper and Sobol, fn. 2, 82 Harv.L.Rev. 1607–1609.

ly by ending explicit racial discrimination. Under that theory, whatever unfortunate effects there might be in future bidding by Negroes luckless enough to have been hired before desegregation would be considered merely as an incident of now extinguished discrimination.

A *"rightful place"* theory stands between a complete purge of "but-for" effects maintenance of the status quo. [sic] The Act should be construed to prohibit the *future awarding* of vacant jobs on the basis of a seniority system that "locks in" prior racial classification. White incumbent workers should not be bumped out of their *present* positions by Negroes with greater plant seniority; plant seniority should be asserted only with respect to new job openings. This solution accords with the purpose and history of the legislation.

Not all "but-for" consequences of pre-Act racial classification warrant relief under Title VII. For example, unquestionably Negroes, as a class, educated at all-Negro schools in certain communities have been denied skills available to their white contemporaries. That fact would not, however, prevent employers from requiring that applicants for secretarial positions know how to type, even though this requirement might prevent Negroes from becoming secretaries.

This Court recently struck down a nepotism membership requirement of a "white" union which shortly before had ceased overt discrimination. Local 53 of the International Association of Heat and Frost Insulators and Asbestos Workers v. Vogler, 5 Cir. 1969, 407 F.2d 1047. Under the nepotism rule, only the sons of members or close relatives living with members could become "improvers", and only "improvers" could be accepted into the union. Relationship to a member as a prerequisite to admission had the necessary effect of locking non-whites out of the union. The union

argued that the desire to provide family security was a rational non-racial basis for the rule and that since the nepotism requirement excluded all persons unrelated to members, regardless of their race, it could not, therefore, be called a racial classification. This court held that the rule served no purpose related to ability to perform the work in the asbestos trade and that it violated Title VII:

> The District Court did no more than prevent *future* discrimination when it prohibited a continuing exclusion of Negroes through the application of an apparently neutral membership provision which was *originally* instituted at least in part because of racial discrimination and which served no significant trade-related purpose. While the nepotism requirement is applicable to black and white alike and is not on its face discriminatory, in a completely white union the present effect of its continued application is to forever deny to Negroes and Mexican-Americans any real opportunity for membership.

In *Vogler* this Court made the point, citing *Quarles*, that "where necessary to insure compliance with the Act, the District Court was fully empowered to eliminate the present effects of past discrimination". *Vogler*, however, does not mesh completely with the facts in this case. The nepotism rule there, as the court pointed out, had scant relation to the operation of the business. It also had the inevitable effect of assuring the lily-white status of the union for all time. Nevertheless, the decision does support the position that reliance on a standard, neutral on its face, is no defense under the Act when the effect of the standard is to lock the victims of racial prejudice into an inferior position.

The controlling difference between the hypothetical typing requirement and the nepotism rule rejected in *Vogler* is *business necessity*. When an employer or union has discriminated in the past and when its present policies renew or exaggerate discriminatory effects, those policies must yield, unless there is an overriding legitimate, non-racial business purpose. Secretaries must be able to type. There is no way around that necessity. A nepotism rule, on the other hand, while not unrelated to the training of craftsmen, is not essential to that end. To be sure, skilled workers may gain substantial benefits from having grown up in the home of a member of the trade. It is clear, nonetheless, that the benefits secured by nepotism must give way because of its effective continuation and renewal of racial exclusion. That much was decided in *Vogler*.

The decisive question then is whether the job seniority standard, as it is now functioning at the Bogalusa plant, is so necessary to Crown Zellerbach's operations as to justify locking Negroes, hired before 1966, into permanent inferiority in their terms and conditions of employment. The record supports the district court's holding that job seniority is not essential to the safe and efficient operation of Crown's mill. The defendants' chief expert witness, Dr. Northrup, made it clear that he considered mill seniority "disastrous" only to the extent that it allowed *all* men in a slot to bid on the basis of their time at the mill. He stated that mill seniority in that sense would create labor unrest because its main effect would be to allow whites to "jump" other whites and Negroes to "jump" other Negroes. He also expressed fears about allowing anyone to bid on any vacancy in a line of progression, without requiring that he first advance job-by-job through the various levels below it. That problem might be solved, he stated, by imposing a residency requirement for training purposes. Dr. Northrup explicitly stated that job seniority does *not* provide the only safe or efficient system for governing promotions. He suggested, in

fact, an alternative "job credit" system that would give certain fractional seniority credit to victims of discrimination for the years in which they had been excluded from the white progression lines.

The court took account of Dr. Northrup's apprehensions in fashioning its decree. In place of job security [seniority?] the court ordered the institution of a mill seniority system carefully tailored to assure that no employee would have a right to a job that he could not perform properly. The court's decision put the emphasis where it belongs: absent a showing that the worker has the ability to handle a particular job, the entry job is the proper beginning for any worker. Under the court's decree, employees still must move up through the various lines of progression job-by-job. As a further restraint, if a certain minimum time is needed in one job to train an employee for the next a residency requirement may be imposed that will slow the rise of Negro employees. Under the system that is in effect at the mill now, and that is unaffected by the decree, that residency period is six months. To meet the problem of labor unrest that might result from "jumping" unrelated to racial issues, the court specifically limited its decree to instances in which Negroes hired before 1966 were among the bidders. Finally, and most importantly, both the court's decree and the existing collective bargaining agreement give Crown Zellerbach the right to deny promotions to employees who lack the ability or qualification to do the job properly.

All these precautions, we think, bear out the plaintiffs' assertion that there are satisfactory alternatives to job seniority at the Bogalusa mill. They lead us to conclude that the imposition of a system that perpetuates and renews the effects of racial discrimination in the guise of job seniority is not necessary or justified at Bogalusa. Job seniority, embodying as it does, the racially determined effects of a biased past, constitutes a form of present racial discrimination.

This case is not the first case to present to courts in this circuit the problem of dealing with a change in system that is apparently fair on its face but in fact freezes into the system advantages to whites and disadvantages to Negroes. In United States v. State of Louisiana, E.D. La.1963, 225 F.Supp. 353, a three-judge court had before it a new citizenship test adopted by the State Board of [Voters] Registration. The test was fair on its face and, perhaps, capable of fair administration. But it was a test that white voters, almost all of whom were registered, had not had to take. It was a difficult test for eligible Negroes, most of whom were not registered. The court enjoined the State from administering the test. "The promise of evenhanded justice in the future does not bind our hands in undoing past injustices". 225 F.Supp. at 396. The court said:

> The cessation of prior discriminatory practices cannot justify the imposition of new and onerous requirements, theoretically applicable to all, but practically affecting primarily those who bore the brunt of previous discrimination. * * *

The Supreme Court affirmed, adding: "the court has not merely the power but the duty to render a decree which will so far as possible eliminate the discriminatory effects of the past as well as bar like discrimination in the future." Louisiana v. United States, 1965, 380 U.S. 145, 85 S.Ct. 817, 13 L.Ed.2d 709. [Additional citations omitted.]

It might be said that in these cases the courts focussed on the unlawfulness of the prior discrimination. In Gaston County v. United States, 1969, 395 U.S. 285, 89 S.Ct. 1720, 23 L.Ed.2d 309, however, the Court's refusal to approve a voter literacy test was based on the inferior education inherent in segregated schooling. The automatic "triggering" provisions of the 1965 Voting Rights Act of 1965 [sic] had suspended Gaston County's literacy test because certain indicia chosen by Congress raised the presumption that the tests were being used to discriminate against Negroes seeking to register. In order to reinstate its test under the Act, Gaston County had to show that it had not used the test in the preceding five years "for the purpose or with the effect of denying or abridging the right to vote on account of race or color." The district court found, as a fact, that Gaston County's Negro schools had not provided educational opportunities equal to those available to whites. That alone, said the Supreme Court, would make the imposition of a literacy test an act of continuing discrimination. Neither the fair administration of the test, nor its legitimate public purpose could save it from condemnation under the Act.

III.

With specific regard to employment opportunities under Title VII, decisions by at least two district courts support our conclusion that facially neutral but needlessly restrictive tests may not be imposed where they perpetuate the effects of previous racial discrimination.

In Quarles v. Philip Morris, Inc., E.D. Va.1968, 279 F.Supp. 505, the first case to challenge the legality of a promotion system under Title VII, the employer had segregated the races by departments at its plant. The employer desegregated the plant but prohibited transfers from one department to another. It also required that the transferor bid on vacancies according to his departmental seniority, rather than his seniority at the plant. The effect was to deny to Negroes promotion into the better paying jobs, because they could not accumulate seniority in the fabrication and warehouse departments, where the better jobs lay. Quarles, a Negro employed in the prefabrication department, could not become a truck driver, a higher-rung position in an all-white department. The court held that the new arrangement violates the statute (279 F.Supp. at 513, 519):

"The present discrimination resulting from historically segregated departments is apparent from consideration of the situation of a Negro who has worked for ten years in the prefabrication department. * * * [He is required] to sacrifice his employment seniority and take new departmental seniority based on his transfer date. Thus a Negro with ten years employment seniority transferring * * * from the prefabrication department to the fabrication department takes an entry level position with departmental seniority lower than a white employee with years less employment seniority. These restrictions upon the present opportunity for Negroes result from the racial pattern of the company's employment practices prior to January 1, 1966. The restrictions do not result from lack of merit or qualification. A transferee under any plan must satisfy ability and merit requirements regardless of his seniority.

* * * * *

The court finds that the defendants have intentionally engaged in unlawful employment practices by discriminating on the ground of race against Quarles, and other Negroes similarly situated. This discrimination, embedded in seniority and transfer provisions of collective bargaining agreements, adversely affects the conditions of employment and opportunities for advancement of the class."

In Dobbins v. Local 212, IBEW, S.D. Ohio 1968, 292 F.Supp. 413, the union had formerly excluded nonwhites from membership. The effects of this practice had been doubly serious, since the union controlled hiring referrals within a certain geographic area. After opening its apprenticeship programs and membership to Negroes the union continued to prefer applicants who had previously worked under union contracts. This preferential referral system contained no explicit racial classification or discriminatory purpose. The court looked, nonetheless, to its inevitable discriminatory effect:

"A policy of giving priority in work referral to persons who have experience under the Local's Collective Bargaining Agreement is discriminatory when competent N[egroe]s have previously been denied the opportunity to work under the referral agreement by reason of their race." 292 F.Supp. at 445.

When the defendant's conduct evidences an "economic purpose" there is no discrimination under Title VII: "The limitation of either union or apprentice membership to a number far below the number necessary for the particular trade would be a discriminatory practice and pattern in a context involving an all W[hite] union membership with a previous history of discrimination. Louisiana v. United States, 380 U.S. 145, 85 S.Ct. 817, 13 L.Ed.2d 709 (1965). However, on a showing by a defendant that the limitation has nothing to do with any discriminatory intention but is related to reasonable economic purpose, the limitation in number is not unlawful." The court went on to hold the referral system illegal:

"Preference to union members in work referral is a violation of Title VII if that preference operates, after July, 1965, to continue to restrict the employment opportunities of N's who have been excluded from membership and work under union auspices because of their race. United States by Clark v. Local 189, United Papermakers and Paperworkers, 282 F.Supp. 39 (D.C.

La., 1968); Quarles v. Philip Morris, Inc., 279 F.Supp. 505 (D.C.Va., 1968)." 292 F.Supp. at 446.

Nothing that we said in Whitfield v. United Steelworkers, Local 2708, 5 Cir. 1958, 263 F.2d 546, cert. denied 360 U. S. 902, 79 S.Ct. 1285, 3 L.Ed.2d 1254, compels a different result. In that case Negro workers challenged a plan, negotiated through collective bargaining, purporting to do away with segregated lines of progression in a steel mill. There was no issue in *Whitfield* as to the measure of promotion from one job to another. *Quarles* distinguishes *Whitfield* (279 F. Supp. at 518):

> *Whitfield* does not stand for the proposition that present discrimination can be justified simply because it was caused by conditions in the past. Present discrimination was allowed in *Whitfield* only because it was rooted in the Negro employees' lack of ability and training to take skilled jobs on the same basis as white employees. The fact that white employees received their skill and training in a discriminatory progression line denied to the Negroes did not outweigh the fact that the Negroes were unskilled and untrained. Business necessity, not racial discrimination, dictated the limited transfer privileges under the contract.

In *Whitfield* the company had organized functionally-related jobs into two separate lines of progression, Line 1 (the skilled jobs) for whites and Line 2 (the unskilled jobs) for Negroes. Advancement in a line was based on knowledge and experience acquired in the next lower job. The company opened both lines on a non-racial basis, and added that Negroes in Line 2 would in the future have preference over new whites in applying for vacancies in Line 1. Except for variations in pay, the change had the effect of merging the lines into one, with the

formerly white line on top. In *Whitfield*, unlike the present case, the two lines were not so functionally related that experience at the top of the formerly black line could provide adequate training for the bottom jobs in the white line. The company therefore required that men moving into the formerly all-white Line 1 take a qualification test, one that the white incumbents had not been required to take. (The company had previously required 260 hours "probationary" experience instead.) Negroes objected to the test requirement on the ground that whites already working in Line 1 did not have to take the test to advance or remain in the line. The company also required, as we have said, that employees bidding into Line 1 from Line 2 start at the bottom job. Negroes in Line 2 protested that this requirement also discriminated against them because it meant that Negroes would have to take a wage cut in moving from the top job in Line 2 to the bottom job in Line 1. The plaintiffs brought the complaint under the *Steele* doctrine,[14] which requires certified unions to represent members of the bargaining unit on a non-discriminatory basis.

This Court rejected both of the plaintiffs' objections. We held that the qualification test was the " 'minimum assurance' the Company could have of efficient operations", and that the company and union had gone "about as far as they could go in giving negroes a preference in filling Number 1 line vacancies, consistent with being *fair to incumbents and consistent with efficient management.*" 263 F.2d at 550 (emphasis added.) The requirement that entrants into Line 1

[14] See Steele v. Louisville & Nashville R. Co., 323 U.S. 192, 65 S.Ct. 226, 89 L.Ed. 173, and Syres v. Oil Workers International Union, Local 23, 1955, 350 U.S. 892, 76 S.Ct. 152, 100 L.Ed. 785.

start at the bottom job was justified as a business necessity:

> *Such a system was conceived out of business necessity,* not out of racial discrimination. An employee without proper training and with no proof of potential ability to rise higher, cannot expect to start in the middle of the ladder, regardless of plant seniority. It would be unfair to the skilled, experienced, and deserving employee to give a top or middle job to an unqualified employee. It would also destroy the whole system of lines of progression, *to the detriment of efficient management* and to the disadvantage of negro as well as white employees having a stake in orderly promotion." 263 F. 2d at 550.

In United States by Clark v. H. K. Porter Co., N.D.Ala.1968, 296 F.Supp. 40, 90, the court rejected an attack by the Government upon "the procedure that the first man to [get] a job is the first to advance", i. e. job seniority, super-imposed, as here, upon a history of racial discrimination. The court found, as a matter of fact, that it was not "permissible" to assume "on the record in this case" that

> "with less than the amount of on-the-job training now acquired by reason of the progression procedure, employees could move into the jobs in the progression lines and perform those jobs satisfactorily and—more importantly—without danger of physical injury to themselves and their fellow employees." 296 F.Supp. at 91.

In other words, the record in that case, as the district court viewed it, showed that safety and efficiency, the component factors of business necessity, would not allow relaxation of the job seniority system. We see no necessary conflict between *Porter's* holding on this point and our holding in the present case.

* * *

When an employer adopts a system that necessarily carries forward the incidents of discrimination into the present, his practice constitutes on-going discrimination, unless the incidents are limited to those that safety and efficiency require. * * *

IV.

The defendants maintain that Congress specifically exempts seniority systems such as Crown's from the operation of Title VII. In support of their assertion the defendants cite that portion of § 703(h) which allows an employer to "apply different standards of compensation, or different terms, conditions, or privileges of employment *pursuant to a bona fide seniority* or merit system * * * provided that such differences are not the result of an intention to discriminate because of race, color, religion, sex, or national origin".

No doubt, Congress, to prevent "reverse discrimination" meant to protect certain seniority rights that could not have existed but for previous racial discrimination. For example a Negro who had been rejected by an employer on racial grounds before passage of the Act could not, after being hired, claim to outrank whites who had been hired before him but after his original rejection, even though the Negro might have had senior status but for the past discrimination. As the court pointed out in *Quarles,* the treatment of "job" or "department seniority" raises problems different from those discussed in the Senate debates: "a department seniority system that has its genesis in racial discrimination is not a bona fide seniority system." 279 F.Supp. at 517.

It is one thing for legislation to require the creation of *fictional* seniority for newly hired Negroes, and quite another thing for it to require that time *actually worked* in Negro jobs be given equal status with time worked in white jobs. To begin with, requiring employers to correct their pre-Act discrimination by creating fictional seniority for new Negro employees would not necessarily aid the actual victims of the previous discrimination. There would be no guaranty that the new employees had actually suffered exclusion at the hands of the employer in the past, or, if they had, there would be no way of knowing whether, after being hired, they would have continued to work for the same employer. In other words, creating fictional employment time for newly-hired Negroes would comprise preferential rather than remedial treatment. The clear thrust of the Senate debate is directed against such preferential treatment on the basis of race. That sentiment was codified in an important portion of Title VII, § 703(j):

"(j) Nothing contained in this subchapter shall be interpreted to require any employer, employment agency, labor organization, or joint labor-management committee subject to this subchapter to grant preferential treatment to any individual or to any group because of the race, color, religion, sex, or national origin of such individual or group on account of an imbalance which may exist with respect to the total number or percentage of persons of any race, color, religion, sex, or national origin employed by any employer, referred or classified for employment by any employment agency or labor organization, admitted to membership or classified by any labor organization, or admitted to, or employed in, any apprenticeship or other training program, in comparison with the total number or percentage of persons of such race, color, religion, sex, or national origin in any community, State, section, or other area, or in the available work force in any community, State, section, or other area." 42 U.S.C.A. § 2000e–2(j).

No stigma of preference attaches to recognition of time actually worked in Negro jobs as the equal of white time. The individual victims of prior discrimination in this case would necessarily be the ones—the only ones—to benefit by the institution of mill seniority, as modified in the decree. We conclude, in agreement with *Quarles,* that Congress exempted from the anti-discrimination requirements only those seniority rights that gave white workers preference over junior Negroes. This is not to say that *Whitfield* and *Quarles* and Title VII prohibit an employer from giving compensatory training and help to the Negro workers who have been discriminated against. Title VII's imposition of an affirmative duty on employers to undo past discrimination permits compensatory action for those who have suffered from prior discrimination.

V.

We find unpersuasive the argument that, whatever its operational effects, job seniority is immune under the statute because not imposed with the *intent* to discriminate. Section 703(h), quoted earlier, excludes from the strictures of Title VII different working terms dictated by "bona fide" seniority systems "provided that such differences are *not the result of an intention to discriminate because of race * * *."* [15] Here, however, if

[15] "In determining the meaning of 'intentional,' resort must be had almost entirely to legislative history. In its original form, 706(g) contained no such requirement; it was amended by Senator Dirksen's proposal, probably in response to opposition pressure. The first draft of the amendment contained the word 'willfully' instead of 'intentionally'; interpretative material was introduced into the record by Senator Dirksen:

The words 'willful and willfully' as ordinarily employed, mean nothing more than that the person, of whose actions or default the expressions are used, knows what he is doing, intends what he is doing, and is a free agent. * * *

Crown did not intend to punish Negroes as such by reinstituting job seniority, the differences between the job status of Negroes hired before 1966 and whites hired at the same time would have to be called the "result" of Crown's earlier, intentional discrimination. *Quarles* put it this way:

"The differences between the terms and conditions of employment for white [sic] and Negroes about which plaintiffs complain are the result of an intention to discriminate in hiring policies on the basis of race before January 1, 1966. The differences that originated before the act are maintained now. The act does not condone present differences that are the result of intention to discriminate before the effective date of the act, although such a provision could have been included in the act had Congress so intended. The court holds that the present differences in departmental seniority of Negroes and white [sic] that result from the company's intentional, racially discriminatory hiring policy before January 1, 1966 are not validated by the *proviso* of § 703(h)" 279 F.Supp. 517–518.

> The terms are also employed to denote an intentional act * * * as distinguished from an accidental act * * *
>
> This is precisely the situation which might exist if the words are not added. * * * Accidental, inadvertent, heedless, unintended acts could subject an employer to charges under the present language.

For reasons that are not apparent, this version was not enacted, and not until some time later was the amendment with the present language passed. The only significant difference between the two versions is the substitution of 'intentionally' for 'willfully' and there is no indication that any strengthening of the requirement was meant. It may be concluded that the Dirksen Amendment does not greatly narrow the coverage of section 706(g)." Note, Legal Implications of the Use of Standardized Ability Tests in Employment and Education, 68 Col.L.Rev. 691, 713 (1968).

Section 706(g) limits injunctive (as opposed to declaratory) relief to cases in which the employer or union has *"intentionally engaged in"* an unlawful employment practice. Again, the statute, read literally, requires only that the defendant meant to do what he did, that is, his employment practice was not accidental. The relevant legislative history, quoted in the margin, bears out the language of the statute on that point.

Section 707(a) allows the Attorney General to enforce the Act only where there is a "pattern or practice of resistance to the full enjoyment of any of the rights secured by this subchapter" and where the pattern or practice "is *intended* to deny the full exercise of the rights herein described". Defendants contend that no such condition existed here. The same point arose in *Dobbins*. The court rejected it (292 F.Supp. at 448):

"In reviewing statutes, rules or conduct which result in the effective denial of equal rights to Negroes or other minority groups, intention can be inferred from the operation and effect of the statute or rule or from the conduct itself. The conduct of defendant in the present case 'by its very nature' contains the implications of the required intent. Local 357, Intern. Broth. of Teamsters, etc. v. National Labor Relations Board, 365 U.S. 667 at 675, 81 S.Ct. 835, 6 L.Ed.2d 11 (1961) citing Radio Officers' Union, etc. v. National Labor Relations Board, 347 U.S. 17, 45, 74 S.Ct. 323, 98 L. Ed. 455 (1954). See also the remarks of then Senator Humphrey, 110 Cong. Rec. 14270 in reference to Title VII, 'Intention could be proved by or inferred from words, conduct or both.' Thus the Attorney General has a cause of action when the conduct of a labor organization in relation to N's or other minority groups has the effect of creating and preserving employment opportunities for W's only. Section 707 (a) of the Civil Rights Act of 1964."

Here, as in *Dobbins,* the conduct engaged in had racially-determined effects. The requisite intent may be inferred from the fact that the defendants persisted in the conduct after its racial implications had become known to them. Section 707 (a) demands no more.

VI.

The defendants contend that the letters and statements made by EEOC officials approving the merger of Crown's progression lines acted as a bar under § 713(b) of the Act to suit by either the Government or by the private plaintiffs Johnson, Hill, and Local 189-A. The relevant portion of § 713(b) reads as follows: "In any action or proceeding based on any alleged unlawful employment practice, no person shall be subject to any liability or punishment for or on account of (1) the commission by such person of an unlawful employment practice if he pleads and proves that the act or omission complained of was in good faith, in conformity with, and in reliance on any written interpretation or opinion of the Commission".

The key phrase in this provision is "written opinion or interpretation of the Commission". The EEOC published its own interpretation of the phrase in the Federal Register in June 1965, *before Title VII took effect and some six months before the public statements at issue here:* "Only (a) a letter entitled 'opinion letter' and signed by the General Counsel on behalf of the Commission or (b) matter published and so designated in the Federal Register may be considered a 'written interpretation or opinion of the Commission' within the meaning of section 713 of Title VII." 29 C.F.R. § 1601.30.

The statements that Crown relied upon to its supposed detriment in this case do not fall within either of the defined categories. They appeared neither as portions of the Federal Register or as designated "opinion letters" over the signature of the General Counsel. We have merely a letter from Mr. Edelsberg, Executive Director, and a statement of Mr. Roosevelt, the Chairman of the Commission. Mr. Edelsberg was not General Counsel, nor did his letter bear the "opinion letter" label. Mr. Roosevelt issued his statement orally. The regulation clearly requires more.

Courts give great weight to an agency's interpretation of the statute that it administers. The regulation here gives reasonable scope to the statutory provision. A broader reading might bind the Commission to informal or unapproved opinions volunteered by members of its staff.

We cannot help sharing Crown Zellerbach's bewilderment at the twists and turns indulged in by government agencies in this case. We feel compelled to hold, however, that neither the statement by Chairman Roosevelt nor the letter by Executor Director Edelsberg provides a legal defense to the present suit.

VII.

Our main conclusions may be summarized as follows: (1) Crown's job seniority system carries forward the discriminatory effects integral to the company's former employment practices. (2) The safe and efficient operation of the Bogalusa mill does not depend upon maintenance of the job seniority system. (3) To the extent that Crown and the white union insisted upon carrying forward exclusion of a racially-determined class, *without business necessity,* they committed, with the requisite intent, in the statutory sense, an unfair employment practice as defined by Title VII.

The district court thoughtfully worked a decree studded with provisos to protect the employer from the imposition of unsafe or inefficient practices and at the same time prevent racial discrimination. The decree also specifically provides that job seniority may still apply to bidding between one white employee and other. [sic] By making the decree applicable only to bidding that involves Negroes hired before 1966, the district court limited the remedy to the scope of the illegal conduct. The judgment of the district court is affirmed.

ON PETITION FOR REHEARING AND PETITION FOR RE-HEARING EN BANC

PER CURIAM:

The Petition for Rehearing is denied and no member of this panel nor Judge in regular active service on the Court having requested that the Court be polled on rehearing en banc, (Rule 35 Federal Rules of Appellate Procedure; Local Fifth Circuit Rule 12) the Petition for Rehearing En Banc is denied.

Notes

1. What do you think of the court's distinction of its decision in Whitfield v. United Steelworkers, Local 2708? Do you regard United States v. Hayes International Corp., 415 F.2d 1038, 1042 n. 6 (5th Cir. 1969) as an improvement? There the court of appeals noted that the lower court had relied on Whitfield, "wherein it was held that a union which in the past had negotiated discriminatory contracts was presently only required to cease such practices and had no obligation to remove the continuing effects of past discrimination. Whitfield was not a Title VII case and therefore is not controlling. Furthermore, to the extent that it can be read as limiting the power of courts to order 'such affirmative action as may be appropriate,' 42 U.S.C.A. § 2000e–5(g), to simply barring any further application of discriminatory practices, Whitfield is inconsistent with the words of the statute, its purposes and the

thrust of recent cases in this circuit. [Citations omitted.]" Is the Fifth Circuit's statement of Whitfield in Hayes consistent with its statement of Whitfield in the main case?

In Taylor v. Armco Steel Co., 429 F.2d 498 (5th Cir. 1970), the very seniority system that the court had approved in Whitfield came before it again. Judge Wisdom, who wrote the court's opinions in both Whitfield and the main case, wrote again. He said: "Within the context of the NLRA and *Steele, Whitfield* is defensible. Today, however, the Court must reverse and remand this case to the district court for proceedings consistent with Title VII * * * and the decisional development of the law in other circuits." 429 F.2d at 499.

If Whitfield is defensible under the NLRA, why is it indefensible under Title VII? Is Whitfield defensible under the NLRA? See pp. 989–985 infra.

2. A problem analogous to that considered in the main case is posed by union referral systems that give preference to job applicants with previous experience in a locality, under a particular union's collective agreements, or in an industry. Where past union discrimination has prevented blacks from obtaining the requisite experience, the apparent "colorblindness" of such experience requirements has not prevented courts from striking them down. United States v. Sheet Metal Workers International, Local 36, 416 F.2d 123 (8th Cir. 1969); Dobbins v. Local 212, IBEW, 292 F.Supp. 413 (S.D. Ohio 1968). Do you attach any significance to the distinction that in the seniority cases at least some of the workers who have suffered from the defendant's past discrimination are readily identifiable, while the immediate beneficiaries of the referral decisions may well be workers quite different from those who suffered from the defendants' past discrimination?

3. Suppose that you are counsel to the black employees in a plant with a his-

tory like that of the employer in the main case. Suppose further that you are offered a settlement that would entitle your clients to transfer from their present departments to vacancies in previously all-white departments in accordance with their plant seniority. Two conditions are explicitly attached to the offer of settlement. First, the transfer option may only be invoked when the employee is capable of performing the job with a brief break-in period. And, second, if he survives the break-in period, the employee's job rights will thereafter be governed by his departmental seniority in the new department. Will you recommend acceptance of the offer? If not, what modifications will you seek?

In answering the foregoing questions, consider, in addition to the main case, United States v. Bethlehem Steel Corp., 446 F.2d 652 (2d Cir. 1971), and Robinson v. Lorillard Corp., 444 F.2d 791 (4th Cir. 1971), both of which grant "seniority carryover" and "rate retention." Both opinions also cite a number of other decisions relevant to the issues posed in these notes. And see Hicks v. Crown Zellerbach, 321 F.Supp. 1241 (E.D.La.1971). Robinson v. Lorillard also upholds the right of members of the affected class to back pay. Accord, e. g., Bowe v. Colgate-Palmolive Co., 416 F.2d 711 (7th Cir. 1969).

4. Suppose that in 1967, a large manufacturing company completely integrated its lines of progression, offered special training to its black workers and promoted them in accordance with their plant seniority (when they were able to do the job after training). In addition, to make up for previously discriminatory hiring practices, the company instituted a vigorous program to recruit blacks. During the years 1967 through 1970, 40 per cent of all new employees were black—bringing the total of black employees in the plant to 25 per cent. Economic setbacks have now forced the company to

lay off several thousand employees. In accordance with the collective bargaining agreement in effect at the plant, the company is laying off the workers with the lowest plant seniority. Forty-three per cent of the workers laid off are black. Are any of the black workers who have been laid off entitled to relief under Title VII? Should they be entitled to relief? What theories would you argue on behalf of the laid-off black workers? on behalf of the company? on behalf of the union? Would it make any difference whether the company had discriminated after July 2, 1965?

5. Can difficulties posed for plaintiffs by Title VII's effective date be avoided by reliance on other theories of action? Consider Sections 2 and 3 infra.

6. See Blumrosen, Seniority and Equal Employment Opportunity: A Glimmer of Hope, 23 Rutgers L.Rev. 268 (1969); Doeringer, Promotions Systems and Equal Employment Opportunity, 19 Ind.Rel.Res.Ass'n 278 (1966); Gould, Seniority and the Black Worker: Reflections on Quarles and its Implications, 47 Tex.L.Rev. 1039 (1969); Note, Title VII, Seniority Discrimination and the Incumbent Negro, 80 Harv.L.Rev. 1260 (1967).

3. Testing and Other Requirements

GRIGGS v. DUKE POWER COMPANY

Supreme Court of the United States, 1971.
401 U.S. 424, 91 S.Ct. 849, 28 L.Ed.2d 158.

Mr. Chief Justice BURGER delivered the opinion of the Court.

We granted the writ in this case to resolve the question whether an employer is prohibited by the Civil Rights Act of 1964, Title VII, from requiring a high school education or passing of a standardized general intelligence test as a condition of employment in or transfer to jobs when (a) neither standard is shown to be significantly related to successful job performance, (b) both requirements operate to disqualify Negroes at a substantially higher rate than white applicants, and (c) the jobs in question formerly had been filled only by white employees as part of a longstanding practice of giving preference to whites.

Congress provided, in Title VII of the Civil Rights Act of 1964, for class actions for enforcement of provisions of the Act and this proceeding was brought by a group of incumbent Negro employees against Duke Power Company. All the petitioners are employed at the Company's Dan River Steam Station, a power generating facility located at Draper, North Carolina. At the time this action was instituted, the Company had 95 employees at the Dan River Station, 14 of whom were Negroes; 13 of these are petitioners here.

The District Court found that prior to July 2, 1965, the effective date of the Civil Rights Act of 1964, the Company openly discriminated on the basis of race in the hiring and assigning of employees at its Dan River plant. The plant was organized into five operating departments: (1) Labor, (2) Coal Handling, (3) Operations, (4) Maintenance and (5) Laboratory and Test. Negroes were employed only in the Labor Department where the highest paying jobs paid less than the lowest paying jobs in the other four "operating" departments in which only whites were employed. Promotions were normally made within each department on the basis of job seniority. Transferees into a department usually began in the lowest position.

In 1955 the Company instituted a policy of requiring a high school education for initial assignment to any department except Labor, and for transfer from the

Coal Handling to any "inside" department (Operations, Maintenance, or Laboratory). When the Company abandoned its policy of restricting Negroes to the Labor Department in 1965, completion of high school also was made a prerequisite to transfer from Labor to any other department. From the time the high school requirement was instituted to the time of trial, however, white employees hired before the time of the high school education requirement continued to perform satisfactorily and achieve promotions in the "operating" departments. Findings on this score are not challenged.

The Company added a further requirement for new employees on July 2, 1965, the date on which Title VII became effective. To qualify for placement in any but the Labor Department it became necessary to register satisfactory scores on two professionally prepared aptitude tests, as well as to have a high school education. Completion of high school alone continued to render employees eligible for transfer to the four desirable departments from which Negroes had been excluded if the incumbent had been employed prior to the time of the new requirement. In September 1965 the Company began to permit incumbent employees who lacked a high school education to qualify for transfer from Labor or Coal Handling to an "inside" job by passing two tests—the Wonderlic Personnel Test, which purports to measure general intelligence, and the Bennett Mechanical Aptitude Test. Neither was directed or intended to measure the ability to learn to perform a particular job or category of jobs. The requisite scores used for both initial hiring and transfer approximated the national median for high school graduates.[3]

The District Court had found that while the Company previously followed a

---

[3] The test standards are thus more stringent than the high school requirement, since they would screen out approximately half of all high school graduates.

policy of overt racial discrimination in a period prior to the Act, such conduct had ceased. The District Court also concluded that Title VII was intended to be prospective only and, consequently, the impact of prior inequities was beyond the reach of corrective action authorized by the Act.

The Court of Appeals was confronted with a question of first impression, as are we, concerning the meaning of Title VII. After careful analysis a majority of that court concluded that a subjective test of the employer's intent should govern, particularly in a close case, and that in this case there was no showing of a discriminatory purpose in the adoption of the diploma and test requirements. On this basis, the Court of Appeals concluded there was no violation of the Act.

The Court of Appeals reversed the District Court in part, rejecting the holding that residual discrimination arising from prior employment practices was insulated from remedial action.[4] The Court of Appeals noted, however, that the District Court was correct in its conclusion that there was no finding of a racial purpose of invidious intent in the adoption of the high school diploma requirement or general intelligence test and that these standards had been applied fairly to whites and Negroes alike. It held that, in the absence of a discriminatory purpose, use of such requirements was permitted by the Act. In so doing, the Court

of Appeals rejected the claim that because these two requirements operated to render ineligible a markedly disproportionate number of Negroes, they were unlawful under Title VII unless shown to be job-related.[5] We granted the writ on these claims. 399 U.S. 926, 90 S.Ct. 2238, 26 L.Ed.2d 791.

The objective of Congress in the enactment of Title VII is plain from the language of the statute. It was to achieve equality of employment opportunities and remove barriers that have operated in the past to favor an identifiable group of white employees over other employees. Under the Act, practices, procedures, or tests neutral on their face, and even neutral in terms of intent, cannot be maintained if they operate to "freeze" the status quo of prior discriminatory employment practices.

The Court of Appeals' opinion, and the partial dissent, agreed that, on the record in the present case, "whites fare far better on the Company's alternative requirements" than Negroes.[6] This consequence would appear to be directly traceable to race. Basic intelligence must have the means of articulation to mani-

---

[4] The Court of Appeals ruled that Negroes employed in the Labor Department at a time when there was no high school or test requirement for entrance into the higher paying departments could not now be made subject to those requirements, since whites hired contemporaneously into those departments were never subject to them. The Court of Appeals also required that the seniority rights of those Negroes be measured on a plantwide, rather than a departmental, basis. However, the Court of Appeals denied relief to the Negro employees without a high school education or its equivalent who were hired into the Labor Department after institution of the educational requirement.

[5] One member of that court disagreed with this aspect of the decision, maintaining, as do the petitioners in this Court, that Title VII prohibits the use of employment criteria which operate in a racially exclusionary fashion and do not measure skills or abilities necessary to performance of the jobs for which those criteria are used.

[6] In North Carolina, 1960 census statistics show that, while 34% of white males had completed high school, only 12% of Negro males had done so. U. S. Bureau of the Census, U. S. Census of Population: 1960, Vol. 1, Part 35, Table 47.

Similarly, with respect to standardized tests, the EEOC in one case found that the use of a battery of tests, including the Wonderlic and Bennett tests used by the Company in the instant case, resulted in 58% of whites passing the tests, as compared with only 6% of the blacks. Decision of EEOC, CCH Empl.Prac.Guide, Paragraph 17,304.53 (Dec. 2, 1966). See also Decision of EEOC 70–552, CCH Empl.Prac.Guide, Paragraph 6139 (Feb. 19, 1970).

fest itself fairly in a testing process. Because they are Negroes, petitioners have long received inferior education in segregated schools and this Court expressly recognized these differences in Gaston County v. United States, 395 U.S. 285, 89 S.Ct. 1720, 23 L.Ed.2d 309 (1969). There, because of the inferior education received by Negroes in North Carolina, this Court barred the institution of a literacy test for voter registration on the ground that the test would abridge the right to vote indirectly on account of race. Congress did not intend by Title VII, however, to guarantee a job to every person regardless of qualifications. In short, the Act does not command that any person be hired simply because he was formerly the subject of discrimination, or because he is a member of a minority group. Discriminatory preference for any group, minority or majority, is precisely and only what Congress has proscribed. What is required by Congress is the removal of artificial, arbitrary, and unnecessary barriers to employment when the barriers operate invidiously to discriminate on the basis of racial or other impermissible classification.

Congress has now provided that tests or criteria for employment or promotion may not provide equality of opportunity only in the sense of the fabled offer of milk to the stork and the fox. On the contrary, Congress has now required that the posture and condition of the job seeker be taken into account. It has—to resort again to the fable—provided that the vessel in which the milk is proffered be one all seekers can use. The Act proscribes not only overt discrimination but also practices that are fair in form, but discriminatory in operation. The touchstone is business necessity. If an employment practice which operates to exclude Negroes cannot be shown to be related to job performance, the practice is prohibited.

On the record before us, neither the high school completion requirement nor the general intelligence test is shown to bear a demonstrable relationship to successful performance of the jobs for which it was used. Both were adopted, as the Court of Appeals noted, without meaningful study of their relationship to job-performance ability. Rather, a vice president of the Company testified, the requirements were instituted on the Company's judgment that they generally would improve the overall quality of the work force.

The evidence, however, shows that employees who have not completed high school or taken the tests have continued to perform satisfactorily and make progress in departments for which the high school and test criteria are now used.[7] The promotion record of present employees who would not be able to meet the new criteria thus suggests the possibility that the requirements may not be needed even for the limited purpose of preserving the avowed policy of advancement within the Company. In the context of this case, it is unnecessary to reach the question whether testing requirements that take into account capability for the next succeeding position or related future promotion might be utilized upon a showing that such long range requirements fulfill a genuine business need. In the present case the Company has made no such showing.

The Court of Appeals held that the Company had adopted the diploma and test requirements without any "intention to discriminate against Negro employees." We do not suggest that either the District Court or the Court of Appeals erred in examining the employer's intent; but

[7] For example, between July 2, 1965, and November 14, 1966, the percentage of white employees who were promoted but who were not high school graduates was nearly identical to the percentage of non-graduates in the entire white work force.

good intent or absence of discriminatory intent does not redeem employment procedures or testing mechanisms that operate as "built-in headwinds" for minority groups and are unrelated to measuring job capability.

The Company's lack of discriminatory intent is suggested by special efforts to help the undereducated employees through Company financing of two-thirds the cost of tuition for high school training. But Congress directed the thrust of the Act to the *consequences* of employment practices, not simply the motivation. More than that, Congress has placed on the employer the burden of showing that any given requirement must have a manifest relationship to the employment in question.

The facts of this case demonstrate the inadequacy of broad and general testing devices as well as the infirmity of using diplomas or degrees as fixed measures of capability. History is filled with examples of men and women who rendered highly effective performance without the conventional badges of accomplishment in terms of certificates, diplomas, or degrees. Diplomas and tests are useful servants, but Congress had mandated the common-sense proposition that they are not to become masters of reality.

The Company contends that its general intelligence tests are specifically permitted by § 703(h) of the Act.[8] That section authorizes the use of "any professionally developed ability test" that is not "designed, intended, *or used* to discriminate because of race * * *." (Emphasis added.)

The Equal Employment Opportunity Commission, having enforcement responsibility, has issued guidelines interpreting § 703(h) to permit only the use of job-

---

[8] Section 703(h) applies only to tests. It has no applicability to the high school diploma requirement.

related tests.[9] The administrative interpretation of the Act by the enforcing agency is entitled to great deference. See e. g., United States v. City of Chicago, 400 U.S. 8, 91 S.Ct. 18, 27 L.Ed. 2d 9 (1970); Udall v. Tallman, 380 U. S. 1, 85 S.Ct. 792, 13 L.Ed.2d 616 (1965); Power Reactor Development Co. v. Electricians, 367 U.S. 396, 81 S. Ct. 1529, 6 L.Ed.2d 924 (1961). Since the Act and its legislative history support the Commission's construction, this affords good reason to treat the Guidelines as expressing the will of Congress.

Section 703(h) was not contained in the House version of the Civil Rights Act but was added in the Senate during extended debate. For a period, debate revolved around claims that the bill as proposed would prohibit all testing and force employers to hire unqualified persons simply because they were part of a group formerly subject to job discrimination.[10] Proponents of Title VII

---

[9] EEOC Guidelines on Employment Testing Procedures, issued August 24, 1966, provide: "The Commission accordingly interprets 'professionally developed ability test' to mean a test which fairly measures the knowledge or skills required by the particular job or class of jobs which the applicant seeks, or which fairly affords the employer a chance to measure the applicant's ability to perform a particular job or class of jobs. The fact that a test was prepared by an individual or organization claiming expertise in test preparation does not, without more, justify its use within the meaning of Title VII."

The EEOC position has been elaborated in the new Guidelines on Employee Selection Procedures, 35 Fed.Reg. 12333 (August 1, 1970). These Guidelines demand that employers using tests have available "data demonstrating that the test is predictive of or significantly correlated with important elements of work behavior comprising or relevant to the job or jobs for which Guidelines are being evaluated." Id., at § 1607.4(c).

[10] The congressional discussion was prompted by the decision of a hearing examiner for the Illinois Fair Employment Commission in Myart v. Motorola Co. (The decision is reprinted at 110 Cong.Rec. 5662 (1964).) That case suggested that standardized tests on which whites performed better

sought throughout the debate to assure the critics that the Act would have no effect on job-related tests. Senators Case of New Jersey and Clark of Pennsylvania, comanagers of the bill on the Senate floor, issued a memorandum explaining that the proposed Title VII "expressly protects the employer's right to insist that any prospective applicant, Negro or white, *must meet the applicable job qualifications.* Indeed, the very purpose of Title VII is to promote hiring on the basis of job qualifications, rather than on the basis of race or color." (Emphasis added.) 110 Cong.Rec. 7247.[11] De-

spite these assurances, Senator Tower of Texas introduced an amendment authorizing "professionally developed ability tests." Proponents of Title VII opposed the amendment because as written, it would permit an employer to give any test, "whether it was a good test or not, so long as it was professionally designed. Discrimination could actually exist under the guise of compliance with the statute." Remarks of Senator Case, 110 Cong.Rec. 13504.

The amendment was defeated and two days later Senator Tower offered a substitute amendment which was adopted verbatim and is now the testing provision of § 703(h). Speaking for the supporters of Title VII, Senator Humphrey, who had vigorously opposed the first amendment, endorsed the substitute amendment, stating: "Senators on both sides of the aisle who were deeply interested in Title VII have examined the text of this amendment and have found it to be in accord with the intent and purpose of that title." 110 Cong.Rec. 13724. The amendment was then adopted.[12] From the sum of the legislative history relevant in this case, the conclusion is inescapable that the EEOC's construction of § 703(h) to require that employment tests be job-related comports with congressional intent.

---

than Negroes could never be used. The decision was taken to mean that such tests could never be justified even if the needs of the business required them. A number of Senators feared that Title VII might produce a similar result. See remarks of Senators Ervin, 110 Cong.Rec. 5614–5616; Smathers, id., at 5999–6000; Holland, id., at 7012–7013; Hill, id., at 8447; Tower, id., at 9024; Talmadge, id., at 9025–9026; Fulbright, id., at 9599–9600; and Ellender, ibid.

[11] The Court of Appeals majority, in finding no requirement in Title VII that employment tests be job-related, relied in part on a quotation from an earlier Clark-Case interpretative memorandum addressed to the question of the constitutionality of Title VII. The Senators said in that memorandum: "There is no requirement in Title VII that employers abandon bona fide qualification tests where, because of differences in background and education, members of some groups are able to perform better on these tests than members of other groups. An employer may set his qualifications as high as he likes, he may test to determine which applicants have these qualifications, and he may hire, assign, and promote on the basis of test performance." 110 Cong.Rec. 7213.

However, nothing there stated conflicts with the later memorandum dealing specifically with the debate over employer testing, 110 Cong.Rec. 7247 (quoted from in the text above), in which Senators Clark and Case explained that tests which measure "applicable job qualifications" are permissible under Title VII. In the earlier memorandum Clark and Case assured the Senate that employers were not to be prohibited from using tests that determine *qualifications.* Certainly a reasonable interpretation of what the Senators meant, in light of the subsequent memorandum directed specifically at employer

testing, was that nothing in the Act prevents employers from requiring that applicants be fit for the job.

[12] Senator Tower's original amendment provided in part that a test would be permissible "if * * * in the case of any individual who is an employee of such employer, such test is designed to determine or predict whether such individual is suitable or trainable with respect to his employment in the particular business or enterprise involved * * *." 110 Cong.Rec. 13492. This language indicates that Senator Tower's aim was simply to make certain that job-related tests would be permitted. The opposition to the amendment was based on its loose wording which the proponents of Title VII feared would be susceptible to misinterpretation. The final amendment, which was acceptable to all sides, could hardly have required less of a job relation than the first.

Nothing in the Act precludes the use of testing or measuring procedures; obviously they are useful. What Congress has forbidden is giving these devices and mechanisms controlling force unless they are demonstrably a reasonable measure of job performance. Congress has not commanded that the less qualified be preferred over the better qualified simply because of minority origins. Far from disparaging job qualifications as such, Congress has made such qualifications the controlling factor, so that race, religion, nationality, and sex become irrelevant. What Congress has commanded is that any tests used must measure the person for the job and not the person in the abstract.

The judgment of the Court of Appeals is, as to that portion of the judgment appealed from, reversed.

Mr. Justice BRENNAN took no part in the consideration or decision of this case.

Notes

1. The Chief Justice's reference to the stork and the fox, for those whose recollections of Aesop have faded, is to the following fable:

A Fox one day invited a Stork to dinner, and being disposed to divert himself at the expense of his guest, provided nothing for the entertainment but some thin soup in a shallow dish. This the Fox lapped up very readily, while the Stork, unable to gain a mouthful with her long narrow bill, was as hungry at the end of dinner as at the beginning. The Fox meanwhile professed his regret at seeing his guest eat so sparingly. The Stork said little but begged that the Fox would do her the honor of returning her visit. Accordingly, he agreed to dine with her on the following day. He arrived true to his appointment and the dinner was ordered forthwith. But

when it was served up he found to his dismay that it was contained in a narrow necked vessel, down which the Stork readily thrust her long neck and bill, while the Fox was obliged to content himself with licking the neck of the jar.

The moral: apparently neutral devices may be discriminatory when applied to different groups in society.

2. Would the Court have reached the same conclusion if Duke Power had no history of racial discrimination?

3. At page 886 supra, the Court observes that, "The evidence, however, shows that employees who have not completed high school or taken the tests have continued to perform satisfactorily and make progress in departments for which the high school and test criteria are now used." Suppose the record had been silent on this point. Would that have affected the outcome?

4. In future cases, which party will have the burden of persuasion on the various issues relevant to a test's validity?

5. What if a new, job-related test were now administered to Duke Power employees wishing to transfer from one department to another? Could such a test be used to determine future promotions at Duke Power?

6. What purpose was served by the addition of Section 703(h) to Title VII?

7. At page 886 supra, the Court declares that, "The Act proscribes not only overt discrimination but also practices that are fair in form, but discriminatory in operation. The touchstone is business necessity. * * *" What constitutes a "business necessity"? Consider Robinson v. Lorillard Corp., 444 F.2d 791, 797–800 (4th Cir. 1971):

It is in determining whether a practice is unlawfully discriminatory that the business necessity test does come into play. The courts have recognized that respondents are sometimes justified in continuing an employment practice regardless of its differential racial impact. The classic example of an acceptable practice is an employer's policy, in filling secretarial positions, of hiring only applicants who can type even though, especially in a limited geographical area, it may be much more difficult for Negroes than for whites to obtain the necessary training and experience.

The business necessity test has evolved as the appropriate reagent for detecting which employment practices are acceptable and which are invalid because based on factors that are the functional equivalent of race. For example, Local 189, United Papermakers & Paperworkers, AFL–CIO, CLC v. United States, supra, was concerned with the validity of a seniority system which, as in our case, was itself neutral but perpetuated the effects of previous racial discrimination in hiring. The Fifth Circuit formulated this expression of the governing test:

> The controllng [sic] difference between the hypothetical typing requirement and the nepotism rule rejected in *Vogler* is *business necessity.* When an employer or union has discriminated in the past and when its present policies renew or exaggerate discriminatory effects, those policies must yield, unless there is an overriding legitimate, non-racial business purpose.

416 F.2d at 989 (Emphasis in original). The Tenth Circuit has framed the test a little differently in Jones v. Lee Way Motor Freight, 431 F.2d 245 (1970), which also involved a neutral transfer policy which perpetuated the effects of prior racial hiring practices: "When a policy is demonstrated to have discriminatory effects, it can be justified only by a showing that it is necessary to the safe and efficient operation of the business." 431 F.2d at 249.

Griggs v. Duke Power Co., supra, presented a slightly more complicated factual situation. * * *

Collectively these cases conclusively establish that the applicable test is not merely whether there exists a business purpose for adhering to a challenged practice. The test is whether there exists an overriding legitimate business purpose such that the practice is necessary to the safe and efficient operation of the business. Thus, the business purpose must be sufficiently compelling to override any racial impact; [5] the challenged practice must effectively carry out the business purpose it is alleged to serve; [6] and there must be available no acceptable alternative policies or practices which would better accomplish the business purpose advanced, or accomplish it equally well with a lesser differential racial impact.

Lorillard advances three "cogent business interests" for maintaining its

---

[5] The desire of a union to insure family security by restricting new membership to the sons and close relatives of present members may constitute a legitimate "business purpose." But it cannot override the racial impact where present union membership is all-white. See Local 53, International Association of Heat & Frost Insulators and Asbestos Workers v. Vogler, 407 F.2d 1047 (5th Cir.1969).

[6] In the *Griggs* case the Supreme Court held that "Congress has placed on the employer the burden of showing that any given requirement must have a manifest relationship to the employment in question." 401 U.S. 424, 91 S.Ct. at 854. The Court concluded that Duke Power failed to carry that burden in arguing that its educational standards were necessary to upgrade the quality of the work force:

On the record before us, neither the high school completion requirement nor the general intelligence test is shown to bear a demonstrable relationship to successful performance of the jobs for which it was used.

401 U.S. 424, 91 S.Ct. at 853.

departmental seniority system. The first is captioned "Industry Practice and Previous Experience." The substance of this point is that the Greensboro plant was the successor to an earlier Jersey City plant, and the practices at the old site were simply transplanted into the new operation. Lorillard further asserts that its seniority system is similar to those in other collective bargaining agreements in the tobacco industry. These submissions might have some force were it neecssary to establish a bad motive or discriminatory intent as one element in a Title VII suit. But neither maintenance of the status quo nor conformance to precedent is a legimate business purpose that will vindicate an otherwise unlawful practice.

Lorillard's second argument is that the seniority system was only adopted under union pressure, and that, "A company would probably never establish a seniority system of its own accord * * *." At first blush this appears to be a rather forceful statement that the seniority system serves no business purpose. But Lorillard's apparent point is that it was forced either to accept the system or endure a strike.

Avoidance of union pressure also fails to constitute a legitimate business purpose which can override the adverse racial impact of an otherwise unlawful employment practice. The rights assured by Title VII are not rights which can be bargained away—either by a union, by an employer, or by both acting in concert. Title VII requires that both union and employer represent and protect the best interests of minority employees. Despite the fact that a strike over a contract provision may impose economic costs,[8] if a discrimina-

tory contract provision is acceded to the bargainee as well as the bargainor will be held liable.

Lorillard's third argument, entitled "Efficiency, Economy and Morale," comes closest to stating a legitimate business purpose. The most forceful point under this heading is the assertion that employees will perform a job more efficiently if they have prior experience at other jobs within the same department. However, this "efficiency" business purpose fails to withstand scrutiny for a number of reasons. First, the record is barren of any real evidence that the jobs in the formerly all-white departments are so complex and interrelated that progression through a series of jobs is necessary to efficient performance of the more difficult tasks.

Second, there is direct evidence to the contrary in the fact that the seniority system ordered into effect by the District Court had been originally proposed *by Lorillard* in the course of negotiating the 1968 collective bargaining agreement. The District Court added only the red-circling requirement to remove the wage rate barrier to transfers. Third, Lorillard's efficiency argument is clearly inconsistent with its earlier argument that the seniority system would never have been adopted if the union had not forced it upon the company. Fourth, the order of the District Court specifically provides for a preliminary trial period on

---

[8] While considerations of economy and efficiency will often be relevant to determining the existence of business necessity, dollar cost alone is not determinative. For ex-

ample, although there undoubtedly are significant costs involved in validating tests, Griggs requires that employment tests be abandoned if not specifically validated as job-related. Analogous is Diaz v. Pan American World Airways, 442 F.2d 385 (5th Cir. 1971), where the court explicitly held that mere customer preference would not justify continuation of a discriminatory hiring policy, even in the context of a sex discrimination case which, unlike race cases, is subject to a "bona fide occupational qualification" exception. At 386.

the job. If the transferee is unable to perform satisfactorily, the transfer does not become final and the employee returns to his old job.

Finally, it is difficult to imagine how even the necessity for job progression could constitute the business necessity which would justify a departmental seniority system that perpetuated the effects of prior discriminatory practices. For, after all, seniority is necessarily an inefficient means of assuring sufficient prior job experience. It may take only six months to learn a job well and become qualified for advancement. Yet the vagaries of chance may present an opportunity for advancement in only six weeks or not for six years. When some employees have been discriminatorily denied entry to the department, an alternative promotion system could advance the employee who has been discriminated against if he has the greatest employment seniority and has served a necessary minimum time in his present job or has satisfactorily established his capacity to handle the job. Such an alternative plan would accomplish the business purpose "equally well with a lesser differential racial impact."

We recognize Lorillard's point that changing the seniority system may frustrate the expectations of employees who have established departmental seniority but not employment seniority in the preferable departments. However, Title VII guarantees that all employees are entitled to the *same* expectations regardless of "race, color, religion, sex, or national origin." Where some employees now have lower expectations than their co-workers because of the influence of one of these forbidden factors, they are entitled to have their expectations raised even if the expectations of others must be lowered in order to achieve the statutorily mandated equality of opportunity.

We also recognize that some additional administrative costs may be imposed by the order of the District Court. But we have already noted that avoidance of the expense of changing employment practices is not a business purpose that will validate the racially differential effects of an otherwise unlawful employment practice.

* * *

Consider too Bowe v. Colgate-Palmolive Co., 416 F.2d 711, 715–718 (7th Cir. 1969):

Colgate uses an unusual system of plant-wide seniority due to the uncertainty from week to week as to which jobs in the plant will operate. Each week, every employee completes a job preference sheet for the following week with job assignments being made on the basis of seniority. The seniority system is bifurcated into separate eligibility lists for men and women. While men may bid for jobs plant wide, women are restricted to jobs which do not require lifting more than 35 pounds. The history and mechanics of this unusual system are fully set out at 272 F.Supp. 340–347. The Union also bears responsibility for this system since it continued to abide by it as enshrined in the contract in force on the effective date of Title VII and since it preserved some parts of the system in its 1966 contract with Colgate. However, as shown below, there is no liability on the part of the Union due to the failure of any of the plaintiffs to comply with the jurisdictional requisites for filing a suit against the Union.

The trial court carefully analyzed the various facts relating to the weight-lifting restriction and concluded that Colgate had acted reasonably and in the interest of the safety of its female employees in imposing the 35-pound restriction. 272 F.Supp. at 353–357, and 363–366. While this was a carefully reasoned and conscientious approach, we hold it error as it is based on a misconception of the requirements of Title VII's anti-discrimination provisions.

The trial court relied on 42 U.S.C.A. § 2000e–2(e) which permits discrimination in hiring by sex where sex "is a bona fide occupational qualification reasonably necessary to the normal operation of that particular business or enterprise" and § 2000e–3(b) which similarly permits discrimination in job advertisements where sex "is a bona fide occupational qualification for employment." The court also relied on § 2000e–7 which states that the Act shall not be deemed to relieve those covered under it from any liability imposed by state law, except where such law would require the doing of "any act which would be an unlawful employment practice under this subchapter." Thus, the court succumbed to the erroneous argument that state laws setting weight-lifting restrictions on women were not affected by Title VII.

* * *

If anything is certain in this controversial area, it is that there is no general agreement as to what is a maximum permissible weight which can be safely lifted by women in the course of their employment. The states which have limits vary considerably. Most of the state limits were enacted many years ago and most, if not all, would be considered clearly unreasonable in light of the average physical development, strength and stamina of most modern American women who participate in the industrial work force. Almost all state limits are below the 33 to 44.1 pounds recommended by an investigatory committee of the International Labor Organization (I.L.O.) in March, 1964. Even those limits were rejected by the I.L.O. and the provision finally adopted in I.L.O. Convention No. 127 (June 28, 1967) simply states

that no worker should transport loads "which, by reason of its weight is likely to jeopardize his health or safety" and that the maximum weight of loads for women "shall be substantially less than that permitted for adult male workers." At the same time, Recommendation 127 was adopted stating that the maximum load for an adult male should be 55 kg. or 121 pounds. While there was no agreement as to a maximum load for women, the I.L.O. experts individually suggested limits ranging from 60.5 to 76.9 pounds, virtually twice the limit agreed to by the court below.

We agree with the Secretary of Labor insofar as he stated that it is best to consider individual qualifications and conditions, such as the physical capability and physiological makeup of an individual, climatic conditions, and the manner in which the weight is to be lifted. See also, Cheatwood v. South Central Bell Telephone & Telegraph Co., 303 F.Supp. 754 (D.C.Ala. 1969). There is a significant difference in job requirements which must be considered just as carefully as the physiological capabilities of individual employees. Thus, there are probably very few plant workers (male or female) who could not lift a 38-pound case with a handle and move it 10 feet once during a shift. If, however, the case had to be moved further, or more frequently, or lifted to a shoulder-height shelf, the degree of exertion is increased and the number of those capable of performing it is diminished.

Accordingly, we hold that Colgate may, if it so desires, retain its 35-pound weight-lifting limit as a general guideline for all of its employees, male and female. However, it must notify all of its workers that each of them who desires to do so will be afforded a reasonable opportunity to demonstrate his or her ability to perform more strenuous jobs on a regular basis. Each employee who is able to so demonstrate must be permitted to bid on and fill any position to which his or her seniority may entitle him or her. On remand, the court shall study the problem together with the parties and devise and adopt a system which will afford this opportunity to each employee desiring it.

* * *

Compare the EEOC's Sex Discrimination Guidelines, 29 C.F.R. §§ 1604.1 to 1604.10, as last amended on March 30, 1972. Selected portions follow:

Sec. 1604.2 Sex as a Bona Fide Occupational Qualification.—(a) The Commission believes that the bona fide occupational qualification exception as to sex should be interpreted narrowly. Labels —"men's jobs" and "women's jobs"— tend to deny employment opportunities unnecessarily to one sex or the other.

(1) The Commission will find that the following situations do not warrant the application of the bona fide occupational qualification exception:

(i) The refusal to hire a woman because of her sex based on assumptions of the comparative employment characteristics of women in general. For example, the assumption that the turnover rate among women is higher than among men.

(ii) The refusal to hire an individual based on stereotyped characterizations of the sexes. Such stereotypes include, for example, that men are less capable of assembling intricate equipment; that women are less capable of aggressive salesmanship. The principle of non-discrimination requires that individuals be considered on the basis of individual capacities and not on the basis of any characteristics generally attributed to the group.

(iii) The refusal to hire an individual because of the preferences of co-workers, the employer, clients or customers except as covered specifically in subparagraph (2) of this paragraph.

(2) Where it is necessary for the purpose of authenticity or genuineness, the Commission will consider sex to be a bona fide occupational qualification, e. g., an actor or actress.

(b) Effect of sex-oriented State employment legislation. (1) Many States have enacted laws or promulgated administrative regulations with respect to the employment of females. Among these laws are those which prohibit or limit the employment of females, e. g., the employment of females in certain occupations, in jobs requiring the lifting or carrying of weights exceeding certain prescribed limits, during certain hours of the night, for more than a specified number of hours per day or per week, and for certain periods of time before and after childbirth. The Commission has found that such laws and regulations do not take into account the capacities, preferences, and abilities of individual females and therefore discriminate on the basis of sex. The Commission has concluded that such laws and regulations conflict with and are superseded by Title VII of the Civil Rights Act of 1964. Accordingly, such laws will not be considered a defense to an otherwise established unlawful employment practice or as a basis for the application of the bona fide occupational qualification exception.

(2) The Commission has concluded that State laws and regulations which discriminate on the basis of sex with regard to the employment of minors are in conflict with and are superseded by Title VII to the extent that such laws are more restrictive for one sex. Accordingly, restrictions on the employment of minors

of one sex over and above those imposed on minors of the other sex will not be considered a defense to an otherwise established unlawful employment practice or as a basis for the application of exception.

(3) A number of States require that minimum wage and premium pay for overtime be provided for female employees. An employer will be deemed to have engaged in an unlawful employment practice if:

(i) It refuses to hire or otherwise adversely affects the employment opportunities of female applicants or employees in order to avoid the payment of minimum wages or overtime pay required by State law; or

(ii) It does not provide the same benefits for male employees.

(4) As to other kinds of sex-oriented State employment laws, such as those requiring special rest and meal periods or physical facilities for women, provision of these benefits to one sex only will be a violation of Title VII. An employer will be deemed to have engaged in an unlawful employment practice if:

(i) It refuses to hire or otherwise adversely affects the employment opportunities of female applicants or employees in order to avoid the provision of such benefits; or

(ii) It does not provide the same benefits for male employees. If the employer can prove that business necessity precludes providing these benefits to both men and women, then the State law is in conflict with and superseded by Title VII as to this employer. In this situation, the employer shall not provide such benefits to members of either sex.

(5) Some States require that separate restrooms be provided for employees of each sex. An employer will be deemed to have engaged in an unlawful employ-

ment practice if it refuses to hire or otherwise adversely affects the employment opportunities of applicants or employees in order to avoid the provision of such restrooms for persons of that sex.

* * *

Sec. 1604.9 Fringe Benefits.—(a) "Fringe benefits" as used herein, includes medical, hospital, accident, life insurance and retirement benefits; profit-sharing and bonus plans; leave; and other terms, conditions, and privileges of employment.

(b) It shall be an unlawful employment practice for an employer to discriminate between men and women with regard to fringe benefits.

(c) Where an employer conditions benefits available to employees and their spouses and families on whether the employee is the "head of the household" or "principal wage earner" in the family unit, the benefits tend to be available only to male employees and their families. Due to the fact that such conditioning discriminatorily affects the rights of women employees, and that "head of household" or "principal wage earner" status bears no relationship to job performance, benefits which are so conditioned will be found a prima facie violation of the prohibitions against sex discrimination contained in the Act.

(d) It shall be an unlawful employment practice for an employer to make available benefits for the wives and families of male employees where the same benefits are not made available for the husbands and families of female employees; or to make available benefits for the wives of male employees which are not made available for female employees; or to make available benefits to the husbands of female employees which are not made available for male employees. An example of such an unlawful employment practice is a situation in which wives of male employees receive maternity benefits while female employees receive no such benefits.

(e) It shall not be a defense under Title VII to a charge of sex discrimination in benefits that the cost of such benefits is greater with respect to one sex than the other.

(f) It shall be an unlawful employment practice for an employer to have a pension or retirement plan which establishes different optional or compulsory retirement ages based on sex, or which differentiates in benefits on the basis of sex. A statement of the General Counsel of September 13, 1968, providing for a phasing out of differentials with regard to optional retirement age for certain incumbent employees is hereby withdrawn.

Sec. 1604.10 Employment Policies Relating to Pregnancy and Childbirth. —(a) A written or unwritten employment policy or practice which excludes from employment applicants or employees because of pregnancy is in prima facie violation of Title VII.

(b) Disabilities caused or contributed to by pregnancy, miscarriage, abortion, childbirth, and recovery therefrom are, for all job-related purposes, temporary disabilities and should be treated as such under any health or temporary disability insurance or sick leave plan available in connection with employment. Written and unwritten employment policies and practices involving matters such as the commencement and duration of leave, the availability of extensions, the accrual of seniority and other benefits and privileges, reinstatement, and payment under any health or temporary disability insurance or sick leave plan, formal or informal, shall be applied to disability due to pregnancy or childbirth on the same terms and conditions as they are applied to other temporary disabilities.

(c) Where the termination of an employee who is temporarily disabled is caused by an employment policy under which insufficient or no leave is available, such a termination violates the Act if it has a disparate impact on employees of one sex and is not justified by business necessity.

8. United States v. Sheet Metal Workers International, Local 36, 416 F. 2d 123, 135 (8th Cir. 1969), describes the following examination procedure for admission to Local 36: "The applicant is then scheduled to take a test which is administered by the apprentice instructor, Edward Schultz—a Local 36 member. The examination consists of three sets of written questions—the Purdue Sheet Metal Test, a layout problem and a welding test. The testing time varies from one to four hours. Schultz notes the scores on the test sheets and adds personal comments as to why a person is or is not qualified. No passing score is established. Neither the test sheets nor the scores on them are forwarded to anyone. Schultz simply notifies the Business Agent that the applicant is qualified or that he is not qualified." Is this procedure lawful? Do you desire any additional information?

9. The widespread use of tests in employment screening makes the subject of testing critically important to any attorney interested in equal employment opportunity. Many of the issues are highly technical. How should a test be validated? Of what significance is the racial composition of the groups used to conduct a validity study? How important is the choice of a passing score?

Other questions pose difficult policy choices. Should a company be allowed to test applicants for low-level jobs with examinations validated for jobs well up the line of progression? In answering this question, does it matter whether most beginners actually reach the higher-level jobs? Whether training for the higher-level jobs is provided on the way up? May a "valid" test nonetheless be unlawful? Consider the following passage from Cooper and Sobol, Seniority and Testing Under Fair Employment Laws: A General Approach to Objective Criteria of Hiring and Promotion, 82 Harv. L.Rev. 1598, 1661–62 (1969):

"On the other hand, there are several situations in which even a complete empirical validity study showing a test to be valid is not enough to satisfy fair employment requirements. One such situation is that in which the predictive value of a 'valid' test is slight in comparison with the discriminatory impact of the test. Test validity is not an all or nothing proposition. It does not mean that every person who scores low on the test will perform less well on the job than every person who scores high, but only that, based on the group involved in the study, there is a greater probability that a high scorer on the test will perform well than that a low scorer will. The degree of this probability is the degree of validity of the test. The well established pattern even for 'valid' tests is one of relatively low validity. Yet some test consultants recommend use of a test if it has any statistically significant validity. This means in many cases that a test which statistically accounts for only four or five per cent of all the variance in successful job performance is considered valid. Even the most valid tests rarely account, in statistical terms, for more than twenty-five per cent of job performance. In a case where a test with low validity has a highly adverse impact on blacks, use of test scores as a major factor in employment decisions is likely to be unnecessarily prejudicial to blacks. Assume, for purposes of illustration, that a 'general intelligence' test is given to potential football players. Football is to some extent a game of wits and the kind of academic background needed to score well on a test may be a factor in a player's success. It would be absurd, however, to select football players largely on the basis of test

scores because there are so many other factors that go into playing success. Any coach who did so would be unnecessarily discriminating against groups with weaker educational backgrounds—including of course, blacks. The problem raised by this situation where a test has low validity but is highly prejudicial to blacks has been recognized by a panel of experts appointed to review the OFCC order on testing, but the order as now written does not deal with it."

10. If testing is discouraged, what is to take its place? Under what circumstances does a company violate Title VII by allowing the evaluations of supervisors to govern promotions? See Rowe v. General Motors Corp., 457 F.2d 348 (5th Cir. 1972):

"With this background—which is either uncontradicted or based upon credible evidence which the Judge did not under controlling legal principles * * discredit—we think it clear that the promotion/transfer procedures as applied violate Title VII in several particulars which can be briefly capsulated:

(i) The foreman's recommendation is the indispensable single most important factor in the promotion process.

(ii) Foremen are given no written instructions pertaining to the qualifications necessary for promotion. (They are given nothing in writing telling them what to look for in making their recommendations.)

(iii) Those standards which were determined to be controlling are vague and subjective.

(iv) Hourly employees are not notified of promotion opportunities nor are they notified of the qualifications necessary to get jobs.

(v) There are no safeguards in the procedure designed to avert discriminatory practices."

What additional facts would you expect to find in the "background" referred to by the court?

In August, 1970, the Equal Employment Opportunity Commission promulgated the following guidelines. Are you satisfied by its answers to the foregoing questions:

EQUAL EMPLOYMENT OPPORTUNITY COMMISSION GUIDELINES ON EMPLOYEE SELECTION PROCEDURES

35 Fed.Reg. 12333 (1970).

§ 1607.1   Statement of purpose

(a) The guidelines in this part are based on the belief that properly validated and standardized employee selection procedures can significantly contribute to the implementation of nondiscriminatory personnel policies, as required by Title VII. It is also recognized that professionally developed tests, when used in conjunction with other tools of personnel assessment and complemented by sound programs of job design, may significantly aid in the development and maintenance of an efficient work force and, indeed, aid in the utilization and conservation of human resources generally.

(b) An examination of charges of discrimination filed with the Commission and an evaluation of the results of the Commission's compliance activities has revealed a decided increase in total test usage and a marked increase in doubtful testing practices which, based on our experience, tend to have discriminatory effects. In many cases, persons have come to rely almost exclusively on tests as the basis for making the decision to hire, transfer, promote, grant membership, train, refer or retain, with the result that candidates are selected or rejected on the basis of a single test score. Where tests are so used, minority candidates frequently experience disproportionately high rates of rejection by failing to attain score levels that have been established as minimum standards for qualification.

It has also become clear that in many instances persons are using tests as the basis for employment decisions without evidence that they are valid predictors of employee job performance. Where evidence in support of presumed relationships between test performance and job behavior is lacking, the possibility of discrimination in the application of test results must be recognized. A test lacking demonstrated validity (i. e., having no known significant relationship to job behavior) and yielding lower scores for classes protected by Title VII may result in the rejection of many who have necessary qualifications for successful work performance.

(c) The guidelines in this part are designed to serve as a workable set of standards for employers, unions and employment agencies in determining whether their selection procedures conform with the obligations contained in Title VII of the Civil Rights Act of 1964. * * *

§ 1607.2   "Test" defined

For the purpose of the guidelines in this part, the term "test" is defined as any paper-and-pencil or performance measure used as a basis for any employment decision. * * * The term "test" includes all formal, scored, quantified or standardized techniques of assessing job suitability including, in addition to the above, specific qualifying or disqualifying personal history or background requirements, specific educational or work history requirements, scored interviews, biographical information blanks, interviewers' rating scales, scored application forms, etc.

§ 1607.3 Discrimination defined

The use of any test which adversely affects hiring, promotion, transfer or any other employment or membership opportunity of classes protected by Title VII constitutes discrimination unless: (a) the test has been validated and evidences a high degree of utility as hereinafter described, and (b) the person giving or acting upon the results of the particular test can demonstrate that alternative suitable hiring, transfer or promotion procedures are unavailable for his use.

§ 1607.4 Evidence of validity

(a) Each person using tests to select from among candidates for a position or for membership shall have available for inspection evidence that the tests are being used in a manner which does not violate § 1607.3. Such evidence shall be examined for indications of possible discrimination, such as instances of higher rejection rates for minority candidates than nonminority candidates. Furthermore, where technically feasible, a test should be validated for each minority group with which it is used; that is, any differential rejection rates that may exist, based on a test, must be relevant to performance on the jobs in question.

(b) The term "technically feasible" as used in these guidelines means having or obtaining a sufficient number of minority individuals to achieve findings of statistical and practical significance, the opportunity to obtain unbiased job performance criteria, etc. It is the responsibility of the person claiming absence of technical feasibility to positively demonstrate evidence of this absence.

(c) Evidence of a test's validity should consist of empirical data demonstrating that the test is predictive of or significantly correlated with important elements of work behavior which comprise or are relevant to the job or jobs for which candidates are being evaluated.

(1) If job progression structures and seniority provisions are so established that new employees will probably, within a reasonable period of time and in a great majority of cases, progress to a higher level, it may be considered that candidates are being evaluated for jobs at that higher level. However, where job progression is not so nearly automatic, or the time span is such that higher level jobs or employees' potential may be expected to change in significant ways, it shall be considered that candidates are being evaluated for a job at or near the entry level. This point is made to underscore the principle that attainment of or performance at a higher level job is a relevant criterion in validating employment tests only when there is a high probability that persons employed will in fact attain that higher level job within a reasonable period of time.

* * *

§ 1607.5 Minimum standards for validation

(a) For the purpose of satisfying the requirements of this part, empirical evidence in support of a test's validity must be based on studies employing generally accepted procedures for determining criterion-related validity, such as those described in "Standards for Educational and Psychological Tests and Manuals" published by American Psychological Association, 1200 17th Street N.W., Washington, D.C. 20036. Evidence of content or construct validity, as defined in that publication, may also be appropriate where criterion-related validity is not feasible.

* * *

(b) Although any appropriate validation strategy may be used to develop such empirical evidence, the following minimum standards, as applicable, must be met in the research approach and in the presentation of results which constitute evidence of validity:

(1) Where a validity study is conducted in which tests are administered to applicants, with criterion data collected later, the sample of subjects must be representative of the normal or typical candidate group for the job or jobs in question. This further assumes that the applicant sample is representative of the minority population available for the job or jobs in question in the local labor market. Where a validity study is conducted in which tests are administered to present employees, the sample must be representative of the minority groups currently included in the applicant population. If it is not technically feasible to include minority employees in validation studies conducted on the present work force, the conduct of a validation study without minority candidates does not relieve any person of his subsequent obligation for validation when inclusion of minority candidates becomes technically feasible.

(2) Tests must be administered and scored under controlled and standardized conditions, with proper safeguards to protect the security of test scores and to insure that scores do not enter into any judgments of employee adequacy that are to be used as criterion measures. * * *

(3) The work behaviors or other criteria of employee adequacy which the test is intended to predict or identify must be fully described. * * *

(4) In view of the possibility of bias inherent in subjective evaluations, supervisory rating techniques should be carefully developed, and the ratings should be closely examined for evidence of bias. In addition, minorities might obtain unfairly low performance criterion scores for reasons other than supervisors' prejudice, as when, as new employees, they have had less opportunity to learn job skills. The general point is that all criteria need to be examined to insure freedom from factors which would unfairly depress the scores of minority groups.

(5) Differential validity. Data must be generated and results separately reported for minority and nonminority groups wherever technically feasible. Where a minority group is sufficiently large to constitute an identifiable factor in the local labor market, but validation data have not been developed and presented separately for that group, evidence of satisfactory validity based on other groups will be regarded as only provisional compliance with these guidelines pending separate validation of the test for the minority group in question. (See § 1607.9.) A test which is differentially valid may be used in groups for which it is valid but not for those in which it is not valid. In this regard, where a test is valid for two groups but one group characteristically obtains higher test scores than the other without a corresponding difference in job performance, cutoff scores must be set so as to predict the same probability of job success in both groups.

(c) In assessing the utility of a test the following considerations will be applicable:

(1) The relationship between the test and at least one relevant criterion must be statistically significant. This ordinarily means that the relationship should be sufficiently high as to have a probability of no more than 1 to 20 to have occurred by chance. However, the use of a single test as the sole selection device will be scrutinized closely when that test is valid against only one component of job performance.

(2) In addition to statistical significance, the relationship between the test and criterion should have practical significance. The magnitude of the relationship needed for practical significance

or usefulness is affected by several factors, including:

(i) The larger the proportion of applicants who are hired for or placed on the job, the higher the relationship needs to be in order to be practically useful. Conversely, a relatively low relationship may prove useful when proportionately few job vacancies are available;

(ii) The larger the proportion of applicants who become satisfactory employees when not selected on the basis of the test, the higher the relationship needs to be between the test and a criterion of job success for the test to be practically useful. Conversely, a relatively low relationship may prove useful when proportionately few applicants turn out to be satisfactory;

(iii) The smaller the economic and human risks involved in hiring an unqualified applicant relative to the risks entailed in rejecting a qualified applicant, the greater the relationship needs to be in order to be practically useful. Conversely, a relatively low relationship may prove useful when the former risks are relatively high.

§ 1607.6   Presentation of validity evidence

The presentation of the results of a validation study must include graphical and statistical representations of the relationships between the test and the criteria, permitting judgments of the test's utility in making predictions of future work behavior. (See § 1607.5(c) concerning assessing utility of a test.) Average scores for all tests and criteria must be reported for all relevant subgroups, including minority and nonminority groups where differential validation is required. Whenever statistical adjustments are made in validity results for less than perfect reliability or for restriction of score range in the test or the criterion, or both, the supporting evidence from the validation study must be presented in detail. Furthermore, for each test that is to be established or continued as an operational employee selection instrument, as a result of the validation study, the minimum acceptable cutoff (passing) score on the test must be reported. * *

§ 1607.7   Use of other validity studies

In cases where the validity of a test cannot be determined pursuant to § 1607.4 and § 1607.5 (e. g., the number of subjects is less than that required for a technically adequate validation study, or an appropriate criterion measure cannot be developed), evidence from validity studies conducted in other organizations, such as that reported in test manuals and professional literature, may be considered acceptable when: (a) The studies pertain to jobs which are comparable (i. e., have basically the same task elements), and (b) there are no major differences in contextual variables or sample composition which are likely to significantly affect validity. Any person citing evidence from other validity studies as evidence of test validity for his own jobs must substantiate in detail job comparability and must demonstrate the absence of contextual or sample differences cited in paragraphs (a) and (b) of this section.

§ 1607.8   Assumption of validity

(a) Under no circumstances will the general reputation of a test, its author or its publisher, or casual reports of test utility be accepted in lieu of evidence of validity. Specifically ruled out are: assumptions of validity based on test names or descriptive labels; all forms of promotional literature; data bearing on the frequency of a test's usage; testimonial statements of sellers, users, or consultants; and other nonempirical or anecdotal accounts of testing practices or testing outcomes.

(b) Although professional supervision of testing activities may help greatly to insure technically sound and nondiscriminatory test usage, such involvement alone shall not be regarded as constituting satisfactory evidence of test validity.

§ 1607.9   Continued use of tests

Under certain conditions, a person may be permitted to continue the use of a test which is not at the moment fully supported by the required evidence of validity. If, for example, determination of criterion-related validity in a specific setting is practicable and required but not yet obtained, the use of the test may continue: *Provided:* (a) The person can cite substantial evidence of validity as described in § 1607.7(a) and (b); and (b) he has in progress validation procedures which are designed to produce, within a reasonable time, the additional data required. It is expected also that the person may have to alter or suspend test cutoff scores so that score ranges broad enough to permit the identification of criterion-related validity will be obtained.

§ 1607.10   Employment agencies and employment services

(a) An employment service, including private employment agencies, State employment agencies, and the U. S. Training and Employment Service, as defined in section 701(c), shall not make applicant or employee appraisals or referrals based on the results obtained from any psychological test or other selection standard not validated in accordance with these guidelines.

(b) An employment agency or service which is requested by an employer or union to devise a testing program is required to follow the standards for test validation as set forth in these guidelines. * * *

§ 1607.11   Disparate treatment

The principle of disparate or unequal treatment must be distinguished from the concepts of test validation. A test or other employee selection standard—even though validated against job performance in accordance with the guidelines in this part—cannot be imposed upon any individual or class protected by Title VII where other employees, applicants or members have not been subjected to that standard. Disparate treatment, for example, occurs where members of a minority or sex group have been denied the same employment, promotion, transfer or membership opportunities as have been made available to other employees or applicants. Those employees or applicants who have been denied equal treatment, because of prior discriminatory practices or policies, must at least be afforded the same opportunities as had existed for other employees or applicants during the period of discrimination. Thus, no new test or other employee selection standard can be imposed upon a class of individuals protected by Title VII who, but for prior discrimination, would have been granted the opportunity to qualify under less stringent selection standards previously in force.

§ 1607.12   Retesting

Employers, unions and employment agencies should provide an opportunity for retesting and reconsideration to earlier "failure" candidates who have availed themselves of more training or experience. In particular, if any applicant or employee during the course of an interview or other employment procedure claims more education or experience, that individual should be retested.

§ 1607.13   Other selection techniques

Selection techniques other than tests, as defined in § 1607.2, may be improperly used so as to have the effect of discriminating against minority groups. Such techniques include, but are not restricted to, unscored or casual interviews and unscored application forms. Where there are data suggesting employment discrimination, the person may be called upon to present evidence concerning the validity of his unscored procedures as well as of any tests which may be used, the evidence of validity being of the same types referred to in §§ 1607.4 and 1607.5. Data suggesting the possibility of discrimination exist, for example, when there are differential rates of applicant rejection from various minority and nonminority or sex groups for the same job or group of jobs or when there are disproportionate representations of minority and nonminority or sex groups among present employees in different types of jobs. If the person is unable or unwilling to perform such validation studies, he has the option of adjusting employment procedures so as to eliminate the conditions suggestive of employment discrimination.

Notes

1. Is a job interview a test? In hiring new associates, may a law firm prefer graduates of the schools the partners attended?

2. The Department of Labor's Office of Federal Contract Compliance, which is responsible for overseeing compliance with the equal employment opportunity assurances given by employers who contract with the federal government, has testing guidelines of its own which are the substantial equivalent of the EEOC Guidelines. See 36 Fed.Reg. 19307 (1971).

3. How do the following three excerpts affect your appraisal of the EEOC Guidelines? of Griggs v. Duke Power?

FLEISCHMAN, LET'S BE HUMAN

(National Labor Service January 1968).

The Federal Equal Employment Opportunity Commission last year investigated a complaint by a Negro who charged that a company was discriminating against him by requiring the passing of an I.Q. test for promotion to the job of forklift operator. The test involved is used very widely throughout the country. Here are three questions from the test.

1. *Clutter, clatter.* Do these words have a similar meaning? Contradictory? Mean neither the same nor opposite?

2. *Piteous, pitiable.* Do these words have a similar meaning? Contradictory? Mean neither the same nor opposite?

3. *Parasite, parasol.* Do these words have a similar meaning? Contradictory? Mean neither the same nor opposite?

If the applicant gets these questions right, can he drive a forklift? Some may answer that, even if it does not indicate performance on the forklift, it indicates I.Q. Stephen N. Schulman, then Chairman of EEOC, asks what difference I.Q. makes if the individual cannot drive a forklift. Moreover, he insists, it does not even indicate I.Q. but rather familiarity with the verbal facility required in white society. Indicating how the test may be applying culturally biased values—biased against the Negro—Schulman offers another test which is deliberately designed to be culturally biased in favor of the Negro and against the white.

1. If a man is called a "blood," then he is—a) a fighter, b) a Mexican-American, c) a Negro, d) a hungry hemophile, e) a red man or Indian.

2. Cheap chittlings will taste rubbery unless they are cooked long enough. How soon should you quit cooking them to eat and enjoy them? 45 minutes, 2 hours, 24 hours?

3. A "gas head" is a person who has —a) a fast moving car, b) stable of "lace," c) "process," d) habit of stealing cars, e) long jail record for arson.

How would you feel if your job depended on the extent to which you could answer this test? You'd probably reply that it has nothing to do with your job. But was the other test more relevant to the forklift operator?

The Negro who failed the first test had driven a forklift for five years with the Federal government, and had passed a test there, with a score of 90, about its actual operation.

COOPER AND SOBOL, SENIORITY AND TESTING UNDER FAIR EMPLOYMENT LAWS: A GENERAL APPROACH TO OBJECTIVE CRITERIA OF HIRING AND PROMOTION

82 Harvard Law Review 1598, 1642–45 (1969).

Some tests have an obvious relevance to business needs and can clearly be justified for reasonable use as a criterion for employment decisions. A typist must know how to type and a welder to weld. A proofreader must be reasonably proficient at proofreading. The use of narrow skill tests to measure these abilities directly has not raised difficult questions under equal employment laws. But the so-called "aptitude" tests, which are not so obviously related to the demands of the job, are of more questionable legality. The test most frequently challenged is the Wonderlic Personnel Test, a very general test with questions on arithmetic, vocabulary and verbal reasoning which appear to be highly related to formal education. Another test commonly challenged is the Test of Mechanical Comprehension, which questions understanding of basic physical principles such as leverage and centrifugal force by using illustrated questions.

It is sometimes argued that standardized intelligence tests are inherently related to business needs on the ground that every employer is entitled to prefer more intelligent employees. Similarly, mechanical comprehension tests are some-

times thought of as related to business needs in any industrial situation where machinery is used. This notion misconceives the function of tests. Industrial employers need people who can do industrial jobs better; to the extent that requires a certain mental capacity, the employer can be said to need a more "intelligent" employee or one with certain kinds of comprehension. But a paper and pencil test asking general questions does not necessarily measure the relevant mental capacity. It measures the capacity to answer the questions on the test. This may or may not be related to the capacity to perform well on particular jobs.

Contrary to popular belief, the likelihood that scores on any particular aptitude test will correlate significantly with performance on any particular job is very slim indeed. Standardized employment testing is not a space-age science. The tests most widely used in industry were developed during or before World War II, and many date back to World War I. Hundreds of careful studies by industrial psychologists investigating the "validity" of these standardized tests have shown that test scores commonly bear little or no relationship to job performance. An eminent industrial psychologist in the field of aptitude testing, Dr. Edwin Ghiselli of the University of California, recently reviewed all the available data on the predictive power of standardized aptitude tests and was forced to conclude that in trades and crafts aptitude tests "do not well predict success on the actual jobs," [24] and that in industrial occupations "the general picture is one of quite limited predictive power." [25] In many situations there is actually a negative relationship between test scores and job success.[26] The lay reputation of tests is

[24] E. Ghiselli, The Validity of Occupational Aptitude Tests 51 (1966).

[25] Id. at 57.

[26] See, e. g., id. at 46.

plainly running ahead of their accomplishments.

Predictive accuracy is particularly uncertain when tests are administered to a mixed racial group. A basic assumption underlying prediction from test scores is what might be called the "equal exposure" assumption. A test measures how well a person has learned various skills and retained certain information. To the extent an entire group tested has had equal opportunity to learn these skills and information, test scores might be expected to bear some relationship to how well persons in the group can learn something else, such as doing a job, at least where the level of learning ability needed for the job approximates that measured by the test. But when this equal exposure assumption is false—as it surely is in the case of comparisons between blacks and whites—the already shaky basis for test predictions is drastically undercut. * * *

NOTE, EMPLOYMENT DISCRIMINATION AND TITLE VII OF THE CIVIL RIGHTS ACT OF 1964

84 Harvard Law Review 1109, 1128–1130 (1971).

The Guidelines' language is too stringent in several ways. First, the requirement that the employer not test for skills higher than those needed to fill entry positions unless promotion is "nearly automatic" is too narrow. It is true, of course, that an IQ test for unskilled jobs which are "blind alleys," in that there are no formalized promotion procedures, is likely to be of little usefulness except for discrimination; verbal aptitude seldom qualifies a man for essentially mechanical tasks. But "blind alley" jobs are relatively rare in industry. Even if there is no high probability that employees will advance to higher positions, there is often a significant possibility. If a test helps the employer to predict whether a worker will be promotable, it will be in his interest to hire as many predicted "promotables" as he can at the going wage rate, so that the quality of the group from which he makes his final selections will be maximized. Proscribing tests in this situation discriminates against applicants who are more productive, and thus may offend the color blindness constraint of Title VII. An entry level employee who is trainable for a number of tasks is simply more valuable than one who is not. Moreover, the legislative history suggests that some senators saw "trainability" as an appropriate qualification for which to test.

A second instance of the Guidelines' excessive stringency is the requirement that to escape mere "provisional compliance" tests must be "differentially validated." "Differential validity" is the notion that tests can be valid for one race but not for another, or that a lower score for one race may be equally as predictive of job success as a higher score is for another. But differential validity is a "hypothesis for which, at the present time, there is insufficient factual evidence to affirm or deny with confidence." Even if the concept has merit, applying it raises almost insurmountable difficulties. In requiring generation of data separately for each minority group, the Commission significantly increases the expense and difficulty of validation, despite the lack of evidence that differential validity is a phenomenon that occurs with any significant frequency. One prominent psychologist has suggested that only one of twenty corporations could adequately validate a test for different races. Moreover, if there are situations in which tests are differentially valid, the phenomenon may be more a product of cultural deprivation than of race. Whites who are culturally deprived may be as much the victims of differential validity as are blacks. Where this is true, requiring tests to be validated by racial groups rather than by socio-economic groups and making adjustments in the passing score according to race, could be very damaging to culturally deprived white workers. They would be judged by the high standards applied to their more advantaged racial fellows, while suffering from the same deprivations as minority workers.

A third respect in which the Guidelines are too strict is the requirement that an employer affirmatively show that alternative suitable hiring, transfer, or promotion policies are not available to him. This requirement applies although the employer has a valid test that predicts job performance for both blacks and whites. If this test leaves blacks underrepresented in his company, the employer must show that there are no other criteria as high in predictive validity by which a larger number of blacks could be hired. This is no easy showing. For example, assume the hiring officer has a validated test which results in an eight percent black work force in a twenty percent black region. How does he go about showing that an extended interview, with elaborate rating scales, would not give equally productive workers and increase the black percentage? And if he has two valid tests, one of which has a more significant differential impact on minorities than the other, must he use only the test which leads to greater employment of blacks even if the two tests, used together, significantly enhance his predictive powers? The alternative showing requirement is, on its face, impossible to follow.

The Guidelines, if applied as strictly as their language allows, would encourage many employers to use a quota system of hiring.

Notes

1. Students who wish to pursue the subject further would do well to read pages 1120–1140 of the Harvard Law Review Note; Cooper and Sobol; Kirk-

patrick et al., Testing and Fair Employment (N.Y.U.Press 1968); Note, Legal Implications of the Use of Standardized Ability Tests in Employment and Education, 68 Colum.L.Rev. 691 (1968); Ruch and Ash, Comments on Psychological Testing, 69 Colum.L.Rev. 608 (1969); and Wallace et al., Testing of Minority Group Applicants for Employment, EEOC Research Rep. 1966–7 (1966).

2. Legal attacks need not, of course, be the only strategy for minority groups stymied by testing requirements. In a number of instances, special tutoring has proved extraordinarily successful. State Commission for Human Rights v. Farrell, 52 Misc.2d 936, 277 N.Y.S.2d 287, aff'd 27 A.D.2d 327, 278 N.Y.S.2d 982 (N.Y.Sup.Ct., Spec. Term, N.Y. County 1967), a byproduct of Lefkowitz v. Farrell, supra at 860, rejected the claim of Sheet Metal Workers, Local 28, that the tutoring afforded minority applicants for apprenticeship training gave them an unfair advantage and rendered the tests inaccurate measuring devices. (Twenty-four of the thirty-two blacks who took the test passed; one obtained a perfect score; and 12 of the top 15 applicants were black.)

What should the result be where valid, job-related tests are given, but because of financial inability to take preparation courses being offered, economically disadvantaged applicants score lower than applicants with greater financial means?

GREGORY v. LITTON SYSTEMS

United States District Court, C.D. California, 1970.

316 F.Supp. 401, affirmed as modified, 472 F.2d 631, Ninth Circuit, 1972.

IRVING HILL, District Judge. This action arises under Title VII of the Civil Rights Act of 1964. * * *

Plaintiff, a negro, seeks back pay, attorney's fees, and injunctive relief on behalf of himself and others similarly situated, as a result of alleged discrimination in withdrawing an offer of employment previously made. He does not seek reinstatement or an order requiring him now to be employed by Defendant. Pre-Trial was waived.

Many of the facts were stipulated, including those related in the paragraph which follows:

On or about February 7, 1968, Plaintiff applied for employment with Defendant (sometimes also referred to herein as "Litton") as a sheet metal mechanic in its Data Systems Division. After verifying his references, Litton, on March 14, 1968, offered Plaintiff employment to start March 18, 1968. Plaintiff accepted the offer. Litton had no knowledge at the time of this offer and acceptance that Plaintiff had previously been arrested. In fact, Plaintiff had previously been arrested on fourteen different occasions in situations other than minor traffic incidents. But he had never been convicted of any criminal offense. Thirteen of these arrests had occurred before 1959. Litton has a "standard policy" of not hiring applicants who have been arrested "on a number of occasions" for things other than minor traffic offenses. In effectuating that policy, Litton requires new employees, before entering their duties, to fill out a form called "Preliminary Security Information," which requires a listing of all arrests other than those involving minor traffic offenses. When Plaintiff's said arrest record was disclosed on the form on March 14, 1968, Litton, under its said policy, withdrew its offer of employment. The offer was withdrawn solely because of the arrest information furnished. Litton's policy required that it withdraw its offer of employment without consideration of Plaintiff's race. The decision to withdraw the offer of employment was in no way predicated on any national security clearance regulations.

Based on the evidence introduced at the trial, I find the further facts set forth in the following-numbered paragraphs.

1. Litton's said policy of disqualifying frequently-arrested persons from employment was objectively applied and was enforced without reference to race, color, religion, sex, or national origin. Litton does employ persons who have previously been arrested and has several hundred such persons now employed on the rolls of its Data Systems Division. But these are cases in which the employees have not suffered arrest on "a number of occasions." Incidentally, Litton has never precisely defined what constitutes "a number of occasions."

2. There is no evidence to support a claim that persons who have suffered no criminal convictions but have been arrested on a number of occasions can be expected, when employed, to perform less efficiently or less honestly than other employees. In fact, the evidence in the case was overwhelmingly to the contrary. Thus, information concerning a prospective employee's record of arrests without convictions, is irrelevant to his suitability or qualification for employment. In recognition of this irrelevance, the County of Los Angeles, a large-scale employer, has ceased to ask for arrest information in applications for employment.

3. Negroes are arrested substantially more frequently than whites in proportion to their numbers. The evidence on this question was overwhelming and utterly convincing. For example, negroes nationally comprise some 11% of the population and account for 27% of reported arrests and 45% of arrests reported as "suspicion arrests." Thus, any policy that disqualifies prospective employees because of having been arrested once, or more than once, discriminates in fact against negro applicants. This discrimination exists even though such a policy is objectively and fairly applied as between applicants of various races. A sub-

stantial and disproportionately large number of negroes are excluded from employment opportunities by Defendant's policy.

4. The discrimination which is inherent in the use of Litton's said policy is not excused or justified by any business necessity.

5. If Litton is permitted to continue obtaining information concerning the prior arrests of applicants for employment which did not result in convictions, the possible use of such information as an illegally discriminatory basis for rejection is so great and so likely, that, in order to effectuate the policies of the Civil Rights Act, Litton should be restrained from obtaining such information. However, Litton should be permitted to obtain and inspect information which is on the public record concerning the prosecution and trial of any prospective employee, even if the proceeding eventually resulted in an acquittal. Records of arrests which do not result in formal prosecution or trial, are not matters of public record.

Certain legal propositions govern this case.

The policy of Defendant under which Plaintiff was denied employment, i. e., the policy of excluding from employment persons who have suffered a number of arrests without any convictions, is unlawful under Title VII. It is unlawful because it has the foreseeable effect of denying black applicants an equal opportunity for employment. It is unlawful even if it appears, on its face, to be racially neutral and, in its implementation, has not been applied discriminatorily or unfairly as between applicants of different races. See United States v. Sheet Metal Workers International Ass'n Local Union No. 36, 416 F.2d 123 (8th Cir. 1969); Local 189, United Papermakers and Paperworkers v. United States, 416 F.2d 980 (5th Cir. 1969). See also Gaston County v. United States, 395 U.S. 285, 89 S.Ct. 1720, 23 L.Ed.2d 309 (1969). In a situation of this kind, good faith in the origination or application of the policy is not a defense. An intent to discriminate is not required to be shown so long as the discrimination shown is not accidental or inadvertent. The intentional use of a policy which in fact discriminates between applicants of different races and can reasonably be seen so to discriminate, is interdicted by the statute, unless the employer can show a business necessity for it. In this context "business necessity" means that the practice or policy is essential to the safe and efficient operation of the business. Local 189, United Papermakers and Paperworkers v. United States, supra. As previously stated, the Court finds that the policy in question is not justified or excused by business necessity in this case.

It is apparent from what has been said above that Plaintiff is entitled to a judgment. In this area of the law, even where the action is not a Civil Rule 23 class action, equitable relief may be granted both for the protection of Plaintiff and for the protection of other applicants similarly situated. Jenkins v. United Gas Corp., 400 F.2d 28 (5th Cir. 1968); cf. Culpepper v. Reynolds Metals Co., 421 F.2d 888 (5th Cir. 1970). See generally Newman v. Piggie Park Enterprises, 390 U.S. 400, 88 S.Ct. 964, 19 L.Ed.2d 1263 (1968) (dictum). Such injunctive relief will be given in this case, even though Plaintiff seeks no present employment by Defendant. Cf. Jenkins v. United Gas Corp., supra.

Relief will be granted as follows:

1. Plaintiff shall have a money judgment by way of compensatory damages for the difference between what he has earned since Defendant's offer of employment was withdrawn and what he would have earned had he been employed by Defendant. The parties have stipu-

lated that that sum is $4,400. Punitive damages are denied.

2. As provided in the statute, attorney's fees are awardable against Defendant and in favor of Plaintiff's attorney. The amount awarded is $5,000.00, plus normally allowable costs. In addition, Defendant shall pay to Plaintiff's counsel the cost of the deposition of Wolfgang, statutory witness fees paid, travel expenses for the witnesses Wolfgang and Christensen, cost of the transcript of the Court's oral decision, cost of copying exhibits and briefs, all as claimed in the Equal Employment Opportunity Commission's brief filed July 16, 1970. Other items claimed are denied.

3. Defendant is enjoined as follows:
A. From continued discrimination against plaintiff and other persons similarly situated because of their race, arising out of prior arrests involving no conviction.

B. From seeking from applicants for employment, by questionnaires, forms, or verbally, information concerning their prior arrests which did not result in conviction.

C. From utilizing as a factor in determining any condition of employment including hiring, promotion, and termination, any record of arrest which did not result in conviction.

D. In view of the fact that arrest information, which is not a matter of public record, can apparently be obtained cheaply and easily from sources other than the applicant, Defendant will be restrained from seeking, obtaining, or considering, in connection with employment of applicants, information concerning arrests of such applicants which did not result in conviction, provided, however, that this shall not prohibit Defendant from seeking and obtaining information on the public record, but provided further that public record information concerning arrests

alone may not be utilized, as provided in C above as a factor in determining any condition of employment.

Nothing contained in the injunction shall prohibit or preclude the Defendant from complying with any requirement of national security clearance regulations. Nothing contained in the injunction shall prohibit the Defendant from seeking, ascertaining, considering, or using information concerning criminal convictions of applicants or existing employees. The matter of how, and to what extent, information concerning criminal convictions may be considered and used, is not before me in this case and I mean to express no opinion on any aspect of that question.

Notes

1. Can Litton refuse to hire applicants who have actually been tried on criminal charges? If they were acquitted? Convicted?

2. May an employer enforce a company policy against wage garnishments by dismissing workers whose wages have been garnished more than once? Would such a policy "discriminate" in violation of Title VII? Would it be justified by "business necessity"? See Johnson v. Pike Corp., 332 F.Supp. 490 (D.C.C.D. Cal.1971).

3. Company markets its products through door-to-door salesmen. Each new man is hired on a probationary basis for two weeks and assigned to any available route. In order to be hired for a permanent position, he must attain a sales volume during this two-week period equal to one-half the average volume on the route over the past three years. A black salesman was hired and assigned a route in a predominantly white area of Long Island. Although previously successful in other sales jobs, he failed to meet the minimum sales volume and was denied a permanent position. Does he have a Title VII claim?

4. Other questionable employment barriers are considered in Yeager, Litigation Under Title VII of the Civil Rights Act of 1964, the Construction Industry and the Problem of the "Unqualified" Minority Worker, 59 Geo.L.J. 1265 (1971).

D. SELECTED PROCEDURAL PROBLEMS

Title VII, like any complex system for the enforcement of rights, gives rise to an infinite number of procedural issues. These can only be sampled here. For helpful consideration of a great many more, see Note, Employment Discrimination and Title VII of the Civil Rights Act of 1964, 84 Harv.L.Rev. 1109, 1195–1275 (1971); see also Coleman, Title VII of the Civil Rights Act: Four Years of Procedural Elucidation, 8 Duquesne L. Rev. 1 (1970).

1. Class Actions and Limitations Periods

In assessing the importance of the following case, keep in mind that it was decided before passage of the Equal Employment Opportunity Act of 1972. At the time it was decided, a complainant could, as now, move the Equal Employment Opportunity Commission by filing with it a charge claiming that he had been aggrieved by an unlawful employment practice. He had to do this "within ninety days after the alleged unlawful employment practice occurred. * * *" The Commission was then to investigate the charge, and if it found reasonable cause, to attempt to conciliate the case. The main difference between the old procedures and the new was that if the Commission was "unable to obtain voluntary compliance" within thirty days (plus thirty more if the Commission believed it could use them fruitfully), the Commission itself could not sue. It was merely to notify the complainant that it had failed and he was then free to bring a lawsuit on his own "within thirty days thereafter."

MILLER v. INTERNATIONAL PAPER CO.

United States Court of Appeals,
Fifth Circuit, 1969.
408 F.2d 283.

Before GEWIN and BELL, Circuit Judges, and BOOTLE, District Judge.

GEWIN, C. J.: The appellants in this case are five Negroes who are employed by the appellee International Paper Company. They brought suit in the District Court for the Northern District of Mississippi on behalf of themselves and others similarly situated against the company, four local unions and three international unions, alleging racial discrimination in violation of Title VII of the Civil Rights Act of 1964. The district court entered summary judgment for the defendants-appellees on the grounds (1) that a class action could not be maintained on behalf of persons who have not filed charges with the Equal Employment Opportunity Commission and (2) that the suit had not been filed within the time permitted by the statute. * * *

I

After having made vociferous and vigorous contentions in their briefs supporting the district court's class-action holding, the appellees conceded during oral argument that their position is now untenable under the holding in Oatis v. Crown Zellerbach Corp.,[78] decided by this court subsequent to the decision below. We held in Oatis that membership

[78] 398 F.2d 496 (5th Cir. 1968).

in the class cannot be restricted to individuals who have filed charges with the EEOC prior to the institution of suit.[79] The district court here was apparently of the view that, since the filing of a charge with the EEOC is a jurisdictional prerequisite to filing suit, those individuals who had not filed charges with the EEOC could not be included in a class of persons who could properly file suit. Substantively, the district court's syllogism is inviolable. This court was quite clear in the *Oatis* case [80] and in Jenkins v. United Gas Corp.[81] that a complainant under Title VII cannot bypass the EEOC. The effect of a contrary holding would be virtually to eliminate the commission established by Congress to encourage fair employment practices. The fallacy of the district court's reasoning is that the matter is primarily procedural rather than substantive and thus the question is one of simple expediency. In this posture, it is perfectly clear that no procedural purpose could be served by requiring scores of substantially identical grievances to be processed through the EEOC when a single charge would be sufficient to effectuate both the letter and the spirit of Title VII.

II

The district court held that, under section 706(e) of the Act, a charging party has sixty days after filing his charge with the EEOC to bring suit and, if he fails, "the action and the right of action no longer exist, and the defendant is exempt from liability."

The pertinent part of section 706(e) provides:

If within thirty days after a charge is filed with the Commission * * * (except that * * * such period may be extended to not more than sixty days upon a determination by the Commission that further efforts to secure voluntary compliance are warranted), the Commission has been unable to obtain voluntary compliance with this subchapter, the Commission shall so notify the person aggrieved and a civil action may, within thirty days thereafter, be brought against the respondent named in the charge * * *.

The appellants brought this suit in the district court some five and a half months after filing their charges with the EEOC. However, the suit was filed within thirty days after the EEOC notified the appellants that voluntary compliance had not been achieved.

Since by the explicit terms of section 706(e) the EEOC has up to sixty days to attempt conciliation, the limitation period applicable to the complainant could in no event be sixty days after the filing of charges with the EEOC. By stacking the thirty-day post-notice period on top of the sixty-day conciliation period, it would not be completely unreasonable to argue that the applicable limitation period is ninety days from the filing of the charges. But even that construction is untenable. Suppose, for example, a party files a charge with the EEOC and the latter, after holding the charge for exactly sixty days, mails notice of failure to effect voluntary compliance; the charging party receives the notice two days after mailing and then on the thirtieth day thereafter files suit in the district court. Here, every

---

[79] The court in Oatis indicated that a Title VII class action is subject to two basic limitations:

First, the class action must * * * meet the requirements of Rule 23(a) and (b)(2). Next, the issues that may be raised by plaintiff in such a class action are those issues that he has standing to raise (i. e., the issues as to which he is aggrieved, see § 706(a) * * *), and that he has raised in the charge filed with the EEOC pursuant to § 706(a).

398 F.2d at 499. See Jenkins v. United Gas Corp., 400 F.2d 28, 33–35 (5th Cir. 1968).

[80] 398 F.2d at 497–98.

[81] 400 F.2d 28, 30 (5th Cir. 1968).

term of the statutory provision has been complied with and yet, if the aggregated periods fixed the time within which suit must be filed, the charging party would be two days too late. This logical discrepancy is a clear portent that the two time periods provided in section 706(e) were not intended to apply as an aggregation.

* * *

The confusion concerning the time limitations seems to stem from the inclusion in section 706(e) of both a time limitation on the conciliation efforts of the EEOC and a time limitation on the charging party's right to file suit. The provision states that the EEOC has thirty days, or sixty days if needed, to attempt conciliation by informal means. It also provides that the charging party has thirty days within which to file suit after receiving notice from the EEOC that voluntary compliance has not been achieved.[82]

Section 706(e) of the Act provides that notice of failure to conciliate shall be sent by the EEOC and "within thirty days thereafter" the aggrieved person may file suit. It is clear from this provision that the limitation period applicable to the charging party does not begin to run until notice of the failure to obtain voluntary compliance has been sent and received. Thus the question is whether the EEOC, by its failure to observe the limitation period applicable to it—if, indeed, it did fail[85]—can abrogate an aggrieved person's right to a judicial determination of this charge. Considering the incongruity inherent in aggregating the two periods set forth in section 706(e) and the harsh effect an affirmative answer would have on aggrieved persons, it is hardly surprising that all but one of the decisions on point have answered the question in the negative.[86] We hold that the thirty-day limitation period applicable to charging parties under section 706(e) does not begin to run until notice of the failure to achieve voluntary compliance

---

[82] As the Seventh Circuit has observed, one missing link in the temporal chain is how long the EEOC has to serve notice after the lapse of the conciliation period. Choate v. Caterpillar Tractor Co., 402 F.2d 357, 361 (7th Cir. 1968). The EEOC originally took the position that the notice must be sent "within a reasonable time after the expiration of the statutory period, or after an earlier disposition of the charge." EEOC General Counsel's Opinion, October 25, 1965, CCH Employ.Prac.Guide Para. 17,252.32. However, the EEOC's regulations now indicate that notice will not be served prior to the processing of the charge unless the charging party demands notice. 29 C.F.R. § 1601.25a(b) (1966). In this same vein, a number of district court decisions have held that the limitation period on conciliation is directory rather than mandatory. See, e. g., Kendrick v. American Bakery Co., 58 LC Para. 9146 (N.D.Ga.1968); Pullen v. Otis Elevator Co., 292 F.Supp. 715 (N.D.Ga.1968); Harris v. Orkin Extermination Co., 293 F.Supp. 104, 58 LC Para. 9134 (N.D.Ga.1968); Dent v. St. Louis-San Francisco Ry., 265 F.Supp. 56, 58 (N.D.Ala.1967), rev'd on other grounds, 406 F.2d 399 (5th Cir. 1968) [No. 24810, January 8, 1969]. Since this limitation period does not affect the rights and duties of the charging party, we find no occasion in this case to express an opinion on this matter.

[85] Again, we express no opinion on the question whether the EEOC did in fact exceed the limitation period applicable to it. See note 82 supra. The decision of that issue must await the presentation of a factual setting which places it in a brighter focus and a clearer perspective than the present case.

[86] Choate v. Caterpillar Tractor Co., 402 F.2d 357, 361 (7th Cir. 1968); Mondy v. Crown Zellerbach Corp., 271 F.Supp. 258, 261 (E.D. La.1967), rev'd on other grounds sub nom. Oatis v. Crown Zellerbach Corp., 398 F.2d 496 (5th Cir. 1968); Dent v. St. Louis-San Francisco Ry., 265 F.Supp. 56, 58 (N.D.Ala. 1967), rev'd on other grounds, 406 F.2d 399 (5th Cir. 1968) [No. 24810, January 8, 1969]; Ward v. Firestone Tire & Rubber Co., 260 F. Supp. 579, 580 (W.D.Tenn.1966); Kendrick v. American Bakery Co., 58 LC Para. 9146 (N. D.Ga.1968); Pullen v. Otis Elevator Co., 292 F.Supp. 715 (N.D.Ga.1968); Harris v. Orkin Exterminating Co., 293 F.Supp. 104, 58 LC Para. 9134 (N.D.Ga.1968); Contra Cunningham v. Litton Indus., 56 LC Para. 9078 (C.D.Cal.1967).

has been sent by the EEOC and received by the aggrieved person.[87]

The unions advance two additional grounds for upholding the district court's grant of summary judgment as to them. First, they contend that the court lacked jurisdiction of the case because they were not named in the charges which the appellants filed with the EEOC. This circuit has already made clear—and we have reiterated in this opinion—that charging parties cannot bypass the EEOC. Therefore, if charges of employment discrimination have not been filed against the unions, the appellants' right to file suit against the unions has not ripened. Assuming the presence of these facts, the district court's grant of summary judgment would be correct as to the unions. However, we are unable to determine on the record now before us whether or not the unions were named in the EEOC charges. * * * Therefore, this matter must be decided by the district court upon remand.

* * *

VI

In conclusion, it may be observed that on the surface the present case concerns only the meaning of certain statutory provisions. But beneath the legal facade a faint hope is discernible rising like a distant star over a swamp of uncertainty and perhaps of despair. Those who love their work may sometimes forget that a successful human community requires the performance of many vapid and colorless tasks. Even the most tedious physical labor is endurable and in a sense enjoyable, however, when the laborer knows that his work will be appreciated and his progress rewarded. "Work without hope," said Coleridge, "draws nectar in a sieve, And hope without an object cannot live." The ethic which permeates the American dream is that a person may advance as far as his talents and his merit will carry him.[92] And it is unthinkable that a citizen of this great country should be relegated to unremitting toil with never a glimmer of light in the midnight of it all.

The judgment of the district court is reversed and the case is remanded for further proceedings not inconsistent with this opinion.

Reversed and remanded.

Notes

1. To what extent, if at all, do the 1972 amendments to Title VII affect the court's conclusions?

2. Part I of the court's opinion contains a summary of its decision in Oatis v. Crown Zellerbach Corp. concerning class actions under Title VII. Of what significance are the principles laid down by the court?

---

[87] The EEOC has adopted this view of section 706(e). EEOC General Counsel's Opinion, October 25, 1965, CCH Employ.Prac. Guide Para. 17,252.32 (1966). As the administrative body charged with investigation and negotiation of rights under Title VII, its construction of the statute must be given considerable weight. See Udall v. Tallman, 380 U.S. 1, 15 (1965); Skidmore v. Swift & Co., 323 U.S. 134, 139–140 (1944); Cox v. United States Gypsum Co., 284 F.Supp. 74, 78 (N.D. Ind.1968); 1 Davis Administrative Law Treatise § 5.06 (1958). § 5.06 (1958).

We should point out that there is no intimation in our holding that EEOC could defeat an aggrieved person's right to sue by refusing to issue the required notice. In the event of an outright refusal, the grievant could file suit within a reasonable time after the lapse of the conciliation period. The EEOC's regulations are not inconsistent with this view. See 29 C.F.R. § 1601.25a(b) (1966).

[92] See Sovern, Legal Restraints on Racial Discrimination in Employment 212 (1966). One Reviewer of Professor Sovern's excellent and scholarly book suggests that the principle of individual merit excludes consideration of non-merit factors. Rosen, Book Review, 81 Harv.L.Rev. 276, 278 (1967). This criticism is obviously unfounded; recognition of merit is simply the first level of basic social justice.

In Oatis itself, the court added:

"Additionally, it is not necessary that members of the class bring a charge with the EEOC as a prerequisite to joining as co-plaintiffs in the litigation. It is sufficient that they are in a class and assert the same or some of the issues. This emphasizes the reason for Oatis, Johnson and Young to appear as co-plaintiffs. They were each employed in a separate department of the plant. They were representative of their respective departments, as Hill was of his, in the class action. They, as co-plaintiffs, must proceed, however, within the periphery of the issues which Hill could assert. Under Rule 23(a) they would be representatives of the class consisting of the Negro employees in their departments so as to fairly and adequately protect their interests. This follows from the fact that due to the inapplicability of some of the issues to all members of the class, the proceeding might be facilitated by the use of subclasses. In such event one or more of the co-plaintiffs might represent a subclass. It was error, therefore, to dismiss appellants. They should have been permitted to remain in the case as plaintiffs but with their participation limited to the issues asserted by Hill."

What does the presence of Oatis, Johnson and Young as co-plaintiffs add to Hill's class action?

"A closely related question is whether the plaintiff is able to protect the interests of the class fairly and adequately. For example, in Johnson v. Georgia Highway Express, Inc. [417 F.2d 1122 (5th Cir. 1969)], the issue was whether a black employee claiming to have been discharged because of his race had standing to sue for black employees victimized by discriminatory 'hiring, firing, promotion, and maintenance of facilities.' If

the thrust of the Title VII class action is seen as directed against the underlying policy of discrimination, the plaintiff should be able to raise any aspects of the discriminatory policy which might potentially affect him. Using this rationale, the *Johnson* court found that the plaintiff had standing to sue on behalf of all present and future employees as well as discharged employees of the same class.

"The Fifth Circuit's 'across the board' class action concept goes a long way toward effectuating the public interest. But it nonetheless should not be applied before a careful examination is made to be certain that the plaintiff really does fairly and adequately represent the interests of the class for which he purports to act. If a complainant alleges a policy of discrimination, he has in one sense alleged an issue common to all claimed instances of discrimination in the plant. Relief as against all the discriminatory practices, however, must be contingent upon proof that each is in fact prohibited conduct. When the complainant has proven that his discharge, for instance, was racially motivated, he has not thereby proven the claims of all those he purports to represent—i. e., members of his race who allege discriminatory hiring, firing, promotions, testing, seniority, etc. The complainant may not have enough interest in or knowledge about these other instances of allegedly unfair conduct to present the best case which could be made against them. If one is prepared to accept the Fifth Circuit's view as to commonality of interest, then at least full and adequate representation should not be quickly presumed, since the consequences in terms of res judicata are serious." Note, Employment Discrimination and Title VII of the Civil Rights Act of 1964, 84 Harv.L.Rev. 1109, 1220–1221 (1971). Compare Huff v. N. D. Cass Co., 468 F.2d 172 (5th Cir. 1972), petition for rehearing granted.

3. What is the effect on a pending class action claiming discriminatory promotion practices of plaintiff's acceptance of a promotion? In Jenkins v. United Gas Corp., 400 F.2d 28 (1968), the Fifth Circuit held that the promotion did not render the suit moot either as to the employee individually or as to the class he represented. Plaintiff was still claiming lost wages and attorneys' fees and seeking protection against discrimination in the future. "[W]hile we do not here hold that such a 'private Attorney General' is powerless absent court approval to dismiss his suit, see F.R.Civ.P. 41(a)(2); the court, over the suitor's protest, may not do it for him without ever judicially resolving by appropriate means (summary judgment, trial, etc.) the controverted issue of employer unlawful discrimination." 400 F.2d at 33.

Suppose the charging party had accepted the promotion before starting suit? Would he have standing to maintain it? Suppose he were tendered the promotion and declined it?

4. In footnote 79 supra, the court says that, "[T]he issues that may be raised by plaintiff in such a class action are those . . . that he has raised in the charge filed with the EEOC. * * *" What does that mean? Compare King v. Georgia Power Co., 295 F.Supp. 943, 947 (N.D.Ga.1968), holding that a civil action may raise "that range of issues that would have been the subject matter of conciliation efforts between EEOC and the employer." The King standard was quoted approvingly by the Court of Appeals for the Fifth Circuit in Sanchez v. Standard Brands, Inc., 431 F.2d 455, 467 (5th Cir. 1970). In Edwards v. North American Rockwell Corp., 291 F.Supp. 199, 203 (D.C.Cal.1968), the court declared that "Any allegations in the Complaint referring to matters occurring after the filing of a charge must necessarily be considered as allegations concerning which no charge has been filed for pur-

poses of this Court's subject matter jurisdiction." Additional authorities are collected in A.B.A. Section of Labor Relations Law, 1971 Rep. of the Committee on Equal Employment Opportunity Law 60.

The Sanchez case, supra, describes the charge form at p. 458:

"The Commission's charge form is a relatively simple one-page form, obviously designed to be utilized by even the most unsophisticated and unlettered layman. Three specific portions of the form are relevant for purposes of this case. One portion calls for an explanation of the factual basis of the charge of discrimination; the complainant is asked to 'explain what unfair thing was done to you.' Another part of the form calls for the complainant to specify whether the discrimination alleged was 'because of' (a) 'race or color,' (b) 'religious creed,' (c) 'national origin,' or (d) 'sex'; a row of boxes is provided—one for each category of discrimination—and the complainant is asked to 'please check one.' Still another portion of the form asks the complainant to state 'the most recent date on which this discrimination took place.'"

5. When the time allowed for the bringing of a private suit was 30 days instead of the present 90, Goodman v. City Products Corp., 425 F.2d 702 (6th Cir. 1970), affirmed the dismissal of an action filed 31 days after the plaintiff received notice of EEOC's inability to conciliate. Do any of the materials in Section 2 infra suggest a possible remedy?

6. "The failure to allege that the complaint was filed with the EEOC within 90 days of the alleged unfair employment practices is of no importance, for the violations of Title VII alleged in the complaint may be construed as 'continuing' acts." King v. Georgia Power Co., 295 F.Supp. 943, 946 (N.D.Ga.1968). Though a discriminatory lay-off is not

a "continuing act," a discriminatory failure to recall from lay-off may be. Cox v. U.S. Gypsum Co., 409 F.2d 289 (7th Cir. 1969); and see Tippett v. Liggett & Myers Tobacco Co., 316 F.Supp. 292 (M.D.N.C.1970).

2. Proving Discrimination

JONES v. LEE WAY MOTOR FREIGHT, INC.

United States Court of Appeals, Tenth Circuit, 1970.
431 F.2d 245, certiorari denied 401 U.S. 954, 91 S.Ct. 972, 28 L.Ed.2d 237.

BREITENSTEIN, Circuit Judge. The plaintiffs-appellants, four Negro truck drivers employed by defendant-appellee Lee Way Motor Freight, Inc., allege in their complaint that the company's refusal to grant requested transfers was an unlawful employment practice in violation of Title VII of the 1964 Civil Rights Act, 42 U.S.C.A. § 2000e et seq. The case was heard on answers to interrogatories and stipulated testimony. The district court found that the company's no-transfer policy was established for "rational and bona fide considerations" and was indiscriminately applied. Relief was denied, Jones v. Lee Way Motor Freight, Inc., W.D.Okl., 300 F.Supp. 653, and this appeal followed. Jurisdiction is found under 42 U.S.C.A. § 2000e–5(f).

The company has two categories of drivers, line (over the road) and city. Line drivers receive higher wages, and line jobs are generally considered superior to city jobs. Each group is covered by a separate union contract. Company policy prohibits transfers between the two groups. In 1964, 1966, and 1968, there were 353, 516, and 542 line drivers respectively. At all pertinent times all of the line drivers were white. For the same years the company employed 52,

169, and 196 city drivers of which 12, 33, and 38 (or about 20%) were Negro.

The no-transfer policy was initiated in 1957. The company says that it adopted the policy for valid reasons which include inability of transferees to adjust to new working conditions, difficulties such as seniority because each category is covered by a different union contract, and the retraining required for both the transferee and his replacement. There is no claim that the policy has been unfairly or discriminately applied.

Plaintiffs, employed as city drivers at the company's Houston terminal before July 2, 1965, the effective date of the Act, sought transfers to the line category in 1966. The requests were denied on the basis of the no-transfer policy. The plaintiffs went to the Equal Employment Opportunity Commission, which found reasonable cause to believe that the company was engaging in unlawful employment practices. Voluntary compliance was not achieved, and the plaintiffs brought this suit.

The essence of plaintiffs' claim is that application of the superficially neutral no-transfer policy to them is discriminatory because it locks them in inferior jobs which were the only ones available in the days of the company's discriminatory hiring practices. They say that although the policy may be rational, it cannot be justified as necessary to the business, and therefore is an unlawful employment practice which violates § 2000e–2(a). To sustain their position, the plaintiffs rely heavily on cases holding that Title VII affords relief from present effects of past discrimination.

Plaintiffs do not rest their claim on discriminatory hiring and cannot, because they were hired before the Act became effective. However, discriminatory hiring is essential to their case because it is the premise of the argument that the no-transfer policy is discriminatory. The plaintiffs emphasize the employment statistics and urge that the district court misapprehended the value of this evidence in disclosing the company's pre-Act employment practices. In racial discrimination cases, statistics often demonstrate more than the testimony of many witnesses, and they should be given proper effect by the courts. [Citations omitted.]

In the case at bar, the statistics show that at no time between July 1, 1964, and March 1, 1968, did the company employ a single Negro line driver in spite of the fact that there were between 353 and 542 men in that category. Although all city drivers during this period were not Negroes, all Negro drivers were city drivers. The line driver group is sufficiently larger than the city driver group that approximately 80% of the white drivers are in the line category. In short, there were no Negro line drivers; most whites were line drivers; and all Negroes were city drivers.

In the light of the large number of line drivers, the statistics establish a prima facie case that during the 1964–1968 period race was a factor in staffing the two driver categories. See Turner v. Fouche, 396 U.S. 346, 360, 90 S.Ct. 532, 24 L.Ed. 2d 567. Nothing in the record leads us to believe that the situation was any different in preceding years. The company's conclusory claims that it has never discriminated against Negroes in hiring line drivers do not overcome this prima facie case. Turner v. Fouche, supra, and Dailey v. City of Lawton, 10 Cir., 425 F.2d 1037. True, no specific instances of discrimination have been shown. However, because of the historically all-white make-up of the company's line driver category, it may well be that Negroes simply did not bother to apply. See United States v. Sheet Metal Workers, supra, 416 F.2d 123, at 132, and Lea v. Cone Mills Corp., M.D.N.C., 301 F. Supp. 97, 102.

In any event, lack of specific instances does not rebut the fact that at no time before the institution of this action had the company employed a Negro line driver. The company's claimed recent efforts to recruit Negro line drivers and its hiring of two in August, 1968, do not change the situation, because our concern is with the employment practices at the time when the plaintiffs were hired. We conclude that when the plaintiffs were hired, the driver categories were staffed along racial lines to the extent that no Negroes would be hired as line drivers.

The next question is whether the pre-Act discriminatory hiring practices make application to the plaintiffs of the uniform and neutral no-transfer policy an unfair employment practice in violation of § 2000e–2(a). * * *

* * *

Since Quarles, numerous cases have held that superficially neutral policies violate Title VII if their effect is to perpetuate past racial discrimination. See Local 189, United Papermakers and Paperworkers v. United States. * * *

* * *

A neutral policy which is inherently discriminatory may nevertheless be valid if it has business justification. The district court found that the no-transfer policy was "established as a result of other rational and bona fide considerations." Plaintiffs do not challenge this finding as such. Rather they contend that the court should have applied the more stringent, and correct, test of business necessity and that, measured against this standard, the no-transfer policy is not justifiable.

* * *

The remedial nature of Title VII requires the adoption of the business necessity test. If employers or unions could pursue, upon a showing of mere rationality, neutral policies which have the effect of perpetuating past discrimination, the value of the principles developed in Quarles and subsequent cases would be eroded. When a policy is demonstrated to have discriminatory effects, it can be justified only by a showing that it is necessary to the safe and efficient operation of the business. See Local 189, United Papermakers and Paperworkers v. United States, supra, 5th Cir., 416 F.2d at 989.

The three reasons advanced to justify the no-transfer policy are (1) bad experience with transfers in the past, (2) cost of training both the transferee and his replacement, and (3) grievances and other problems which might arise from the fact that the job categories are covered by different union contracts. There is no contention that the policy, adopted in 1957, seven years before the passage of the Act, was other than a bona fide effort by the company to resolve what it considered to be real problems. Although the reasons advanced in justification are concededly not insubstantial, we believe that they fall short of demonstrating business necessity.

The difficulties resulting from previous transfers, basically that the transferee had difficulty in adjustment and often requested retransfer, might be largely alleviated by screening plaintiffs in the same way that prospective line drivers are interviewed. The plaintiffs' willingness to pursue this case indicates that they genuinely want to be line drivers and militates against any conclusion that the company's experience with them will be the same as it was with previous transferees.

The training costs are somewhat illusory. To fill a line driver vacancy with a new hire rather than a transferee will entail as much training if not more because a transferee has some knowledge of company policy and procedure. The

training of a new city driver to replace the transferee will entail some costs, but we believe that these would not be substantial enough to outweigh the detriment to the plaintiffs of permanently locking them in city drivers' jobs.

Much the same might be said of the potential personnel problems occasioned by transfers and resulting from two union contracts. These may never develop. The record shows that in the case of the one city driver who was inadvertently allowed to transfer, the union sided with him when the company tried to return him to his previous job. We will not accord this contention greater weight than the plaintiffs' rights under Title VII. In short, we are not persuaded that the no-transfer policy is essential to the safe, efficient operation of the company's business.

To summarize, we hold that the no-transfer policy, as applied to plaintiffs, is an unlawful employment practice within the meaning of § 2000e–2(a) because it perpetuates past discrimination, by preventing them from now having jobs which were formerly denied to them because of their race, and because it does not satisfy the business necessity test. Although the company did not adopt the policy with the intention of discriminating, the practice was followed deliberately, not accidently. We conclude that the company "is intentionally engaging in an unlawful employment practice" within the meaning of § 2000e–5(g).
* * *

Section 2000e–5(g) authorizes the district court to "order such affirmative action as may be appropriate." In our opinion the no-transfer policy cannot be used to bar these plaintiffs from application for line jobs without surrendering their positions as city drivers. The company must consider such applications and judge them by the same standards as all other applicants. This form of relief will alleviate to some extent the present consequences of the company's past hiring policies. On the basis of the record presented and the statements of counsel at the time of argument, we express no opinion on the seniority problems which may arise in the event that one of the plaintiffs qualifies and is accepted for a line job.

*   *   *

Notes

1. Is evidence that there are no blacks in an employer's work force admissible to prove discrimination? Is it dispositive? What can be inferred from such evidence? What else would you like to know? about the community in which the employer is located? about the nature of the work? about turnover rates? In addition to the main case, see, e. g., Parham v. Southwestern Bell Tel. Co., 433 F.2d 421 (8th Cir. 1970); United States v. Jacksonville Terminal Co., 451 F.2d 418 (5th Cir. 1971), certiorari denied, 4 EPD ¶ 7774 (1972).

2. See Note, An American Legal Dilemma—Proof of Discrimination, 17 U. of Chi.L.Rev. 107, 120 (1949):

"Generally the evidence tending to establish that an employer has discriminated against an individual can be divided into three categories (1) evidence of general discriminatory employment patterns and practices in the plant; (2) evidence that the complainant is qualified for the job in question; (3) evidence showing that the reasons given by the employer for his actions are unsubstantiated or are mere pretext.

"The evidence described in the first category is again evidence of discrimination against a group used to establish the probability of discrimination against the individual complainant. It is clear that this evidence alone without further evidence of the kind described

in the second category would not be enough to justify an order requiring the employer to take affirmative action toward the complainant."

3. What if an employer has an integrated work force? Does that bar a finding of discrimination?

4. Under what circumstances is evidence that a respondent discriminated before the effective date of Title VII admissible to prove that it discriminated after the statute's effective date? See United States v. Jacksonville Terminal Co., supra note 1. In Dobbins v. Local 212, I.B.E.W., 292 F.Supp. 413, 444 (S.D. Ohio 1968), the court said:

"11. In considering whether defendants are discriminating in violation of Title VII, evidence of the defendants' conduct prior to July 2, 1965, is relevant. Such past conduct may illuminate the purpose and effect of present policies and activities and show that policies which appear neutral are in fact designed to presently discriminate. Discrimination by labor unions, based on race or color, was illegal long before July 2, 1965. Steele v. Louisville & N. R. Co., 323 U.S. 192, 65 S.Ct. 226, 89 L.Ed. 173 (1944). Pre-Act discrimination does not furnish the basis for any relief under Title VII. United States v. Sheet Metal Workers, 280 F.Supp. 719 (1968, Mo.), particularly at page 728. The pattern or practice based on which a successful Title VII action may be maintained must be shown to have been one which existed or took place after, and not before, July 2, 1965. Its effect is prospective and not retrospective. (Interpretive Memorandum of Title VII, Senators Clark and Case, 110 Cong. Rec. 7213.) From the same Memorandum: 'The principle purpose * * is to obtain future compliance.'

"While only a post-Act practice or pattern may furnish the basis for a

Title VII claim, evidence of conduct pre-Act is competent and relevant for a number of purposes. One of them, for example, would be to aid in the determination of whether or not a particular practice or pattern, or system had been originally instigated by reason of anything discriminatory based on race or color. Obviously, if it was, the continuance for a day after July 2, 1965, would be discriminatory. If it was not—or stated otherwise, if it was adopted originally for a purpose having nothing to do with discrimination and for a legitimate economic purpose—the continuance could not be 'per se' discriminatory. As another example of relevance, the Act requires an inquiry into the 'intention' of the defendant, and that is true whether the case is a private one or one brought by the Attorney General. See 2000e–5 and 2000e–6. In each situation the plaintiff has the burden of proving 'intentional' engagement (in 5) and 'intended to deny' (in 6). It is hornbook that even in the criminal field, in which evidence of prior conduct should be held more tightly in line than in a civil case, evidence of prior criminal activity is frequently competent and relevant to the question of 'intent' of the defendant. It must necessarily follow that the same is true to a greater extent in the civil field. To take another and practical example from this case—the question whether a given examination administered after the Act was or was not a discriminatory 'chilling' is much more approachable if it can be compared with pre-Act examinations than if it is approached in a vacuum. It is, therefore, concluded that pre-Act activity for a reasonable time before July 2, 1965—a reasonable time in this case being approximately six years—is competent and relevant, not for any substantive purpose; not for supplying proof of an essential ele-

ment of the plaintiff's case; not for any purpose of visiting the sins of the forefathers on a present-day defendant; but for the purpose of interpreting post-Act activity and for the purpose of determining the intention—post-Act—of the defendant. While it should be limited to a reasonable length of time, latitude should be accorded a defendant for the purpose of counter-explanation. For example—taken from this case—if the evidence had been cut off at the five or six year stage, it would have indicated that some W's who did not have applications filed were examined at a time when N's were not; actually they did have applications filed prior to the six-year period."

5. The Dobbins case, supra note 4, offers other examples of evidence that may be helpful in an employment discrimination case.

6. How does an attorney obtain evidence of the kind discussed in the preceding notes?

3. Remedies

If the following case were to arise under Title VII, would any modifications of the district court's decree be necessary? desirable?

CARTER v. GALLAGHER

United States Court of Appeals,
Eighth Circuit, 1972.
452 F.2d 315, modified on rehearing en banc,
452 F.2d 315.
Certiorari denied, 4 EPD ¶7818 (1972).

Before MATTHES, Chief Judge, VAN OOSTERHOUT, Circuit Judge and EISELE, District Judge.

VAN OOSTERHOUT, Circuit Judge. This is an appeal by defendants from decree enjoining them from holding examinations and setting standards for the purpose of determining qualifications of applicants for positions on the Minneapolis Fire Department until various racially discriminatory practices are corrected as directed in the trial court's decree and providing for absolute minority preference in employment of twenty minority persons.

This action for injunctive and declaratory relief was brought by five Blacks on behalf of themselves and all persons similarly situated. The classes represented by plaintiffs are:

(a) All those Black, Indian and other minority persons presently applying for employment with the Minneapolis Fire Department.

(b) All those Black, Indian and other minority persons in the City of Minneapolis who are not applicants for employment with the Minneapolis Fire Department either because their applications were not approved or because they believed that equal employment opportunity is denied to Black, Indian and other minority applicants for such employment.

For convenience the plaintiffs and the classes they represent will usually be referred to as minority persons.

The defendants, who are sued in their official capacity and individually, are Gallagher, Glover and Canfield, the members of the Civil Service Commission of the City of Minneapolis; Proctor, the Personnel Director of the Commission; and Fire Chief Hall.

The court permitted the case to proceed as a class action. No challenge is made to class representation.

The Minneapolis Commission on Human Relations has intervened on behalf of plaintiffs. Fire Fighters Association of Minneapolis, Associated Fire Fighters of Minnesota and International Association of Fire Fighters have jointly filed amici curiae brief in support of defendants' position.

*   *   *

Plaintiffs assert that the recruitment, examination and hiring practices of defendants with respect to the fire department deny Blacks, Indians and other members of minority groups the right to due process of law and equal protection of the law guaranteed by the Fourteenth Amendment and the right not to be discriminated against in employment by reason of race as guaranteed by 42 U.S.C.A. § 1981.

This case was tried to the court. Much of the evidence was stipulated. An evidentiary hearing was held, a number of witnesses were produced and examined. The evidence to the extent necessary will be discussed in the course of the opinion.

Judge Larson made 146 findings of fact, which generally upheld plaintiffs' contentions, and appropriate conclusions of law. Based thereon, he entered a decree, not reported, on March 9, 1971, which reads as follows:

*   *   *

"On the basis of the record and the proceedings herein, the evidence presented to the Court, the arguments of counsel, and the findings of fact and conclusions of law filed in this case this date, it is the ORDER, JUDGMENT and DECREE of this Court:

"1. That the defendants herein, their successors in office, agents, servants, and employees, and all persons in active concert or participation with them, give absolute preference in certification as fire fighters with the Minneapolis Fire Department to twenty (20) Black, American-Indian, or Spanish-surnamed-American applicants for fire fighter who qualify for such positions on the basis of the examinations given pursuant to the Minneapolis Civil Service Commission fire fighter examination plan number 8326, or subsequent examination plans, and who meet the requirements of said examination plans as amended pursuant to paragraph seven (7) of this Decree.

"2. That the defendants herein, their successors in office, agents, servants, and employees, and all persons in active concert or participation with them

(a) establish an eligibility list of all Black, American-Indian, or Spanish-surnamed-American applicants for the position of fire fighter with the Minneapolis Fire Department who qualify for such positions on the basis of the examinations given pursuant to the Minneapolis Civil Service Commission fire fighter examination plan number 8326 and who meet the requirements of said examination plan as amended pursuant to paragraph seven (7) of this Decree, and

(b) rank said minority applicants in order of their relative standing on said examinations with those persons eligible for a veterans preference or for a residence preference given such preference on said eligibility list, and

(c) proceed with the certification of fire fighter applicants from the full eligibility list established on the basis of said examinations only after twenty positions have been filled from the eligibility list established pursuant to paragraph 2(a) of this Decree or after all persons on the eligibility list established pursuant to paragraph 2(a) of this Decree have been offered certification for the position of fire fighter with the Minneapolis Fire Department and have had a period of five (5) business days within which to accept or reject such certification.

(d) in the event that all preferred minority positions are not filled from the register established by examination plan number 8326, the same procedure will be followed on succeeding examination plans until all such twenty (20) preferred positions are filled by minority applicants.

"3. That the defendants herein, their successors in office, agents, servants and employees, and all persons in active concert or participation with them, are enjoined from enforcing the provisions of Minnesota Statutes § 197.45 and the provisions of the Minneapolis City Charter, chapter 19, sections 7 and 15, insofar as such enforcement is in conflict with the Order of the Court contained in paragraph one (1) of this Decree.

"4. That the defendants Gallagher, Canfield, Glover, Proctor, and White, their successors in office, agents, servants, and employees, and all persons in active concert or participation with them, shall reopen the application period for the next examination for the position of fire fighter for the primary purpose of receiving applications from Blacks, American-Indians, or Spanish-surnamed-American persons for a period of two weeks to commence forthwith upon the completion and implementation of the affirmative recruitment program required pursuant to paragraph five (5) of this Decree.

"5. That the defendants herein, their successors in office, agents, servants, and employees, and all persons in active concert or participation with them, shall prepare and submit to the Court and counsel for the plaintiffs and the plaintiff-intervenor, no later than two weeks from the date of this Decree a plan for affirmative action for the recruitment of Black, American-Indian, and Spanish-surnamed-American persons for the position of fire fighter with the Minneapolis Fire Department, which plan shall include:

(a) Provision for the active participation in such affirmative action program of all the defendants in this action,

(b) Provision for consultation by the defendants herein and members of the staff of the Minneapolis Civil Service Commission with representatives of the City and community agencies and groups which have direct contact with the minority community in Minneapolis, and

(c) Provision for pretest tutoring sessions involving personnel from the Civil Service Commission staff and from the Minneapolis Fire Department, and

(d) Provision for the maximum feasible use of all communication media most likely to reach the minority community in Minneapolis, and

(e) Incorporation in the promotional material used, including all advertising used, of a statement referring to the Court's Order granting a minority preference as set forth in paragraph one (1) of this Decree, a statement regarding all changes made in examination plan number 8326 as set forth in paragraph seven (7) of this Decree, and a statement regarding the availability of pretesting tutoring sessions established pursuant to paragraph 5(c) of this Decree.

"6. That the defendants Gallagher, Canfield, Glover, Proctor and White, their successors in office, agents, servants, and employees, and all persons in active concert or participation with them, shall not give examinations pursuant to the Minneapolis Civil Service Commission examination plan number 8326 until the following action has been taken:

(a) The written examination for fire fighter with the Minneapolis Fire Department given pursuant to said examination plan has been validated by procedures commensurate with those set forth in the Equal Employment Opportunity Commission Guidelines on Employment Testing Procedures set forth in 35 F.R. 12333, et seq. (Aug. 1, 1970), 29 C.F.R. §§ 1607.1 to 1607.14, and

(b) The Court and counsel for the plaintiffs and the plaintiff-intervenor have been given copies of said written examination for fire fighter with the Minneapolis Fire Department and copies of all reports, including a resumé of any oral reports, which are made by the defendants, their employees, or any consultant working with them, regarding validation studies of said written examination provided that such copies of said written examination and such copies of said reports may be given to the court and coun-

sel for the plaintiff and the plaintiff-intervenor subject to a protective order in a form approved by the Court, and

(c) Counsel for the plaintiffs and the plaintiff-intervenor have been given notice at least two weeks prior to the date scheduled for administration of said written examination, and

(d) All action required by paragraphs four (4), five (5), seven (7) and eight (8) of this Decree has been completed.

"7. The defendants Gallagher, Canfield, Glover, Proctor, and White, their successors in office, agents, servants, and employees, and all persons in active concert or participation with them, shall make the following permanent changes in the Minneapolis Civil Service Commission fire fighter examination plan number 8326 and all subsequent examination plans:

(a) Delete therefrom any reference to the applicant's arrest record, and

(b) Incorporate in said fire fighter examination plan provisions to the effect that:

(i) no person will be rejected as an applicant for the position of fire fighter with the Minneapolis Fire Department by reason of the conviction of any felony or felonies at any time prior to five years from the date of application or by reason of the conviction of any misdemeanor or misdemeanors at any time prior to two years from the date of application, provided that the applicant was not incarcerated upon the conviction of any felony or misdemeanor during said five or two year periods, and

(ii) no person will be rejected as an applicant for the position of fire fighter with the Minneapolis Fire Department by reason of the conviction of any felony, misdemeanor, or other criminal act, or the conviction of felonies, misdemeanors, or other criminal acts, except upon a written finding by the Civil Service Commission after notice to the applicant and an opportunity to respond in person or in writing that

a. the act or acts upon which such convictions were based, considering the circumstances in which it occurred, involve behavior from which it can reasonably be inferred that such applicant cannot adequately fulfill the duties of a fire fighter with the Minneapolis Fire Department.

(c) Delete from said fire fighter examination plan the requirement that an applicant must have a high school diploma or a G.E.D. certificate by the time he is hired, provided that an entering fireman may be required within two years of entering upon duty to obtain a high school diploma or a G.E.D. equivalency certificate, and

(d) Change the minimum age requirement as stated in said fire fighter examination plan from twenty years to eighteen years, and change the maximum age limit from thirty years to thirty-five years, provided that the maximum age may be reduced to thirty at such time as there are twenty Blacks, American-Indians and Spanish-surnamed-Americans employed by the Minneapolis Fire Department.

"8. That the defendants, their successors in office, agents, servants, and employees, and all persons in active concert or participation with them, shall

(a) refrain from requesting or considering any information regarding an applicant's arrest record when determining the eligibility of an applicant for a position with the Minneapolis Fire Department, and

(b) incorporate all the changes ordered in Minneapolis Civil Service Commission fire fighter examination plan number 8326 pursuant to paragraph seven

(7) of this Decree in all information, pamphlets, announcements or other material utilized as part of the affirmative recruitment program undertaken pursuant to paragraph five (5) of this Decree.

"9. That the defendants herein, their successors in office, agents, servants, and employees, and all persons in active concert or participation with them, shall

(a) within six months of the date of the Order, submit to the Court and counsel for the plaintiffs and the plaintiff-intervenor, a plan for affirmative action to assure that all recruitment, examination, and hiring practices followed in obtaining employees for the Minneapolis Fire Department are designed to assure equal employment opportunities for Blacks, American-Indians and Spanish-surnamed-Americans, which affirmative plan shall include procedures commensurate with the Equal Employment Opportunity Commission Guidelines on Employment Testing Procedures set forth in 35 F.R. 12333, et seq. (Aug. 1, 1970), 29 C.F.R. §§ 1607.1–1607.14 to insure that all examinations given to applicants for employment with the Minneapolis Fire Department are validated to insure that they do not discriminate against Blacks, American-Indians, and Spanish-surnamed-Americans, and that the results obtained will provide a reasonable prediction of job performance with the Minneapolis Fire Department, and

(b) to report forthwith to the Court and counsel for the plaintiffs and the plaintiff-intervenor the number and names of all Blacks, American-Indians, and Spanish-surnamed-Americans who are certified as fire fighters pursuant to fire fighter examination number 8326, and

(c) to report forthwith to the Court and counsel for the plaintiffs and plaintiff-intervenor the names of all Black, American-Indian, and Spanish-surnamed-American applicants who are not found eligible for certification as fire fighters with the Minneapolis Fire Department or who, after being found eligible for such certification, are not in fact certified at any time when eligible candidates are being certified, together with a statement as to the reasons for the failure to find such applicants eligible or the failure to certify them, and

(d) to report forthwith to the Court and counsel for the plaintiffs and the plaintiff-intervenor the name of any Black, American-Indian, or Spanish-surnamed-American applicant for fire fighter with the Minneapolis Fire Department who, having been certified for such employment, subsequently is dismissed or who subsequently terminates his employment, together with a statement as to the reason for such dismissal or termination.

"10. That the Court shall maintain continuing jurisdiction of this action."

*   *   *

Defendants urge that the court's judgment and decree should be reversed and vacated for the following reasons:

I. The District Court lacks jurisdiction to determine plaintiffs' claims.

II. Substantial evidence is lacking to support certain specified findings of fact, the resulting conclusions of law, and the decree and judgment.

III. The court wrongly deprived the Civil Service Commission of discretionary powers vested in it under the provisions of the Minneapolis Home Rule Charter and the rules of the Minneapolis Civil Service Commission.

IV. The court abused its discretion in granting injunctive relief since the record shows the Commission has taken steps to insure that the examination and other employment standards will not be discriminatory.

V. The court erred in ordering absolute minority preference in employment of twenty minority persons.

VI. The court erred in granting other injunctive relief.

Such contentions will be considered in the order just stated.

*   *   *

II.

Defendants urge that some 27 specified findings of fact out of the 146 findings made by the trial court are not supported by substantial evidence. Such argument is summarily made. We have carefully examined the record and are convinced that the procedures existing prior to the commencement of this suit for testing applicants' eligibility for a fireman's position were racially discriminatory. The evidence shows that of the 535 men in the fire department none are Black, Indian or Mexican-Americans. Only two Blacks had served on the fire department in the recent past. Blacks constituted 6.44% of the Minneapolis population in 1970. The court found the all-White fire department was the result of past discriminatory hiring practices and procedures. Statistical evidence can make a prima facie case of discrimination. Parham v. Southwestern Bell Telephone Co., 8 Cir., 433 F.2d 421, 426. The court found that there was no substantial evidence to rebut the inference of racial discrimination based upon the statistics.

Subsequent to the commencement of this action, the record reflects that the Commission recognized that its written examination was racially discriminatory. Substantial changes were made in its content. Consideration of the arrest record of applicants was eliminated and other changes were made. The record shows that Fire Chief Hall took a strong position against recruitment and employment of Blacks.

The court made no express finding of bad faith or evil motives on the part of the defendants. Neither 42 U.S.C.A. §§ 1981 nor 1983 incorporates any requirement that discrimination be wilfull or intentional. In an analogous situation arising under Title 7 of the Civil Rights Act, the Supreme Court states: "good intent or absence of discriminatory intent does not redeem employment procedures or testing mechanisms that operate as 'built-in headwinds' for minority groups and are unrelated to measuring job capability." Griggs v. Duke Power Co., 401 U.S. 424, 91 S.Ct. 849, 28 L. Ed.2d 158 (March 8, 1971).

Defendants' own testimony affirmatively shows the testing procedure in issue prior to the commencement of the action was racially discriminatory.

* * *

V.

Defendants most vigorous attack upon the injunction decree is directed toward paragraph 1 creating absolute preference in fire department employment to twenty minority persons who meet the qualifications for the position under the revised qualification standards established by the decree. Paragraphs 2 and 3 of the decree implement the provisions of paragraph 1.

Defendants contend that such minority preference order violates the Fourteenth Amendment in that it discriminates against White applicants whose qualifications are found to be superior to those of the minority applicants upon the basis of approved and acceptable job related tests and standards, and who, but for the minority preference requirement, would be entitled to priority in employment.

Plaintiffs, citing Louisiana v. United States, 380 U.S. 145, 85 S.Ct. 817, 13 L.Ed.2d 709, and Swann v. Charlotte-Mecklenburg Board of Education, 402 U.S. 1, 91 S.Ct. 1267, 28 L.Ed.2d 554 (1971), urge that the District Court has the power and duty to exercise its equitable powers to fashion a remedy which will so far as possible eliminate the present effects of past discrimination as well as bar like discrimination in the future.

Courts of equity have a broad power to fashion an effective remedy. However, the power to provide an effective remedy affords no basis for depriving others of a constitutionally protected right. Plaintiffs in effect concede this in their brief when they state: "Initially, we assume the obvious—that the District Court could not order the city official to take any action which would itself be unconstitutional."

Thus we reach the crucial question which is whether giving absolute preference to twenty minority applicants who meet the qualification tests infringes upon the constitutional rights of white applicants whose qualifications are established to be superior. The trial court based the minority preference on violation of 42 U.S.C.A. § 1981 which reads:

"All persons within the jurisdiction of the United States shall have the same right in every State and Territory to make and enforce contracts, to sue, be parties, give evidence, and to the full and equal benefit of all laws and proceedings for the security of persons and property as is enjoyed by white citizens, and shall be subject to like punishment, pains, penalties, taxes, licenses, and exactions of every kind, and to no other."

Plaintiffs in their brief properly state the law as follows:

"For the past 90 years the Supreme Court has recognized that the Congress intended section 1981 to have as broad a scope as the Fourteenth Amendment where state action is involved. In Strauder v. West Virginia, 100 U. S. 303, 25 L.Ed. 664 (1880), the Court stated with respect to Rev.Stat.

1977 (now section 1981) that 'this Act puts in the form of a statute what had been substantially ordained by the Constitutional Amendment.' 100 U. S. at 312. In context the Court is referring to the Fourteenth Amendment. On the same day, in Virginia v. Rives, 100 U.S. 313, 317–318, 25 L.Ed. 667 (1880), the Court treated the Civil Rights Act and the Fourteenth Amendment as coextensive in substance. The close relationship between the Civil Rights Act of 1866 and the Fourteenth Amendment has been consistently emphasized by the Court. * * * "

Section 1981 and the Fourteenth Amendment by their plain and unambiguous language accord equal rights to all persons regardless of race. We believe that § 1981 and the Fourteenth Amendment proscribe any discrimination in employment based on race, whether the discrimination be against Whites or Blacks, * * *

Under the charter and the civil service provisions properly administered preference is to be accorded to the fire fighter applicant having the highest rating. Under the court's minority preference provision, a White person who, in a subsequently conducted examination fairly conducted and free of racial discrimination, obtains a higher rating than a minority person is denied employment solely because he is a White man. The fact that some unnamed and unknown White person in the distant past may, by reason of past racial discrimination in which the present applicant in no way participated, have received preference over some unidentified minority person with higher qualifications is no justification for discriminating against the present better qualified applicant upon the basis of race.

In our view, no authority has been cited which would support such racial discrimination. We are convinced that the minority preference provision of the

decree discriminates in favor of minority persons and against Whites whose qualifications are fairly established to be superior to minority persons given preference by the decree.

School integration cases such as *Swann,* supra, are clearly distinguishable. Whites have no constitutional right to insist upon segregated schools. No constitutional rights of Whites are involved in decrees ordering school integration.

Cases such as Local 53 of Int. Ass'n of Heat & Frost I. & A. Workers v. Vogler, 5 Cir., 407 F.2d 1047, are distinguishable. In *Vogler,* the court upheld the trial court's finding that three Blacks and one Mexican had applied for union membership and had been discriminatorily denied membership solely upon the basis of their race. The court ordered the union to give such identified persons union membership. The relief was granted to specific persons who were wrongly denied membership. Moreover, the issue of reverse discrimination was not raised or considered by the court.

In our present case, there is no claim or showing made that plaintiffs were identified members of the class who made prior applications for employment and were denied employment solely because of race. Thus we do not have a situation where a specified minority person having superior qualifications to a White fire fighter applicant has shown that he, himself, has been damaged or injured by a discriminatory refusal of employment.

VI.

Defendants claim the injunctive relief granted is too broad in other respects. In *Griggs,* supra, the standard laid down for determining the validity of tests and job standards is thus stated:

"The Act proscribes not only overt discrimination but also practices that are fair in form, but discriminatory in operation. The touchstone is business necessity. If an employment practice which operates to exclude Negroes cannot be shown to be related to job performance, the practice is prohibited." 401 U.S. 424, 431, 91 S.Ct. 849, 853.

Such standard is appropriate to test the relief granted upon the basis of the record made in this case. We shall proceed to examine and determine the validity of the relief granted in paragraphs 4 to 10, inclusive, of the decree, supra.

We affirm and approve the provisions of paragraphs 4 and 5 requiring the reopening of applications for the next examination and the requirement that an affirmative plan for recruitment of minority persons be promptly submitted to the court for approval. We disapprove, however, of that part of paragraph 5(e) which requires publicity for the minority preference provision which we have heretofore disapproved.

The provisions of paragraph 6 are approved and affirmed except for the modification of paragraph 6(d) to the extent that it is consistent with the views expressed in this opinion.

The provisions of paragraph 7(a) relating to the elimination of applicants' arrest records is approved.

The provisions of paragraph 7(b), particularly subdivision (i) thereof, are too broad. The parties agree that a conviction of a felony or misdemeanor should not per se constitute an absolute bar to employment. We are persuaded by defendants' argument that applicants' conviction records, at least in cases of aggravated offenses and multiple convictions, may have a bearing on the suitability of an applicant for a fire department position both from the standpoint of protecting fellow firemen and the public. The trial court in its discretion may require the defendants to submit to it for approval a rule with respect to the consideration to be given to an applicant's con-

viction record, which at a minimum should not treat conviction as an absolute bar to employment. We would not consider any rule giving fair consideration to the bearing of the conviction upon applicant's fitness for the fire fighter job to be inappropriate.

The provisions of paragraph 7(c) relating to educational requirements are approved and affirmed. We note that no complaint is made that the court did not go far enough in this respect.

The provision of paragraph 7(d) reducing the minimum age requirement is disapproved. Absent racial discrimination, it is appropriate for employers to fix age requirements. There is no adequate evidentiary basis to support a finding that the minimum age requirement is racially discriminatory.

By reason of past racial discrimination, we approve the 7(d) temporary enlargement of the maximum age requirement from thirty to thirty-five years.

The provisions of paragraph 8 are adequately covered by other provisions of the decree.

By reason of the lapse of time from the entry of the decree and the likelihood that changes have subsequently been made, the provisions of paragraph 9 of the decree can to the extent necessary be best realized under the continuing jurisdiction provisions of paragraph 10.

We agree that the court should maintain continuing jurisdiction of this action for a sufficient period of time to reasonably assure it that racial discrimination has been eliminated in filling positions on the fire department. The court may require such reports and information as it deems necessary and issue such orders as may be required to accomplish the objective of eliminating racial discrimination in the employment of fire fighters.

The trial court's determination that past racial discrimination against minority persons applying for fire fighters' positions has been established is affirmed. The court's decree to the extent that it gives absolute preference to twenty applicants is reversed and vacated. In other respects, the court's decree and judgment is affirmed to the extent indicated in this opinion.

The case is remanded for further proceedings consistent with the views herein expressed.

Costs are taxed two-thirds to defendants-appellants and one-third to plaintiffs-appellees.

Before MATTHES, Chief Judge, VAN OOSTERHOUT, Senior Circuit Judge, and MEHAFFY, GIBSON, LAY, HEANEY, BRIGHT, ROSS and STEPHENSON, En Banc.

On Petition For Hearing En Banc.

GIBSON, Circuit Judge.

A panel of this court composed of Matthes, Chief Judge, Van Oosterhout, Senior Judge, and Eisele, District Judge from the Eastern District of Arkansas sitting by designation, in an opinion, authored by Judge Van Oosterhout, sustained the order and opinion of the Honorable Earl R. Larson, District Court of Minnesota, finding that the employment practices and procedures for determining qualifications of applicants for positions on the Minneapolis Fire Department were racially discriminatory in violation of the Equal Protection Clause of the Fourteenth Amendment and the Civil Rights Act of 1870, 42 U.S.C.A. § 1981, and approved a number of corrective practices ordered so as to eliminate all racially discriminatory practices; but disapproved that part of Judge Larson's order providing for absolute minority preference in the employment of the next 20 persons to be hired by the department. The case was brought as a class action and relief was extended to minority groups as a class.

The panel opinion, while sustaining most of Judge Larson's findings and or-

ders granting affirmative relief, did not approve of the absolute preference in Fire Department employment to 20 minority persons who met the qualifications for the positions under the revised qualification standards established by the decree and held that the absolute preference order infringed upon the constitutional rights of white applicants whose qualifications are established to be equal or superior to the minority applicants.

* * *

A petition for rehearing en banc by the appellees was granted but limited solely to the issue of the appropriate remedy. The cause was resubmitted to the court en banc on briefs of the various parties and intervenors and without oral argument. The United States filed a brief as amicus curiae on behalf of the plaintiffs on the rehearing.

The facts are contained in the panel opinion and need not be repeated here. The fact of past racially discriminatory practices and procedures in employment by the Fire Department is accepted and clearly evidenced by the fact that of the 535 men in the Fire Department none are from minority groups. We are thus here concerned only with the appropriateness of the remedy ordered by the District Court. The absolute preference of 20 minority persons who qualify has gone further than any of the reported appellate court cases in granting preference to overcome the effects of past discriminatory practices and does appear to violate the constitutional right of Equal Protection of the Law to white persons who are superiorly qualified.

The panel opinion has recognized the illegality of the past practices, has ordered those practices abandoned, and the affirmative establishment of nondiscriminatory practices and procedures. There is, as the panel pointed out, no claim or showing made that the plaintiffs were identifiable members of the class who had made prior applications for employment and were denied employment solely because of race. This latter situation could be remedied immediately by ordering the employment of such persons. However, in dealing with the abstraction of employment as a class, we are confronted with the proposition that in giving an absolute preference to a minority as a class over those of the white race who are either superiorly or equally qualified would constitute a violation of the Equal Protection Clause of the Fourteenth Amendment to the Constitution.

* * *

Admittedly the District Court has wide power sitting as a court of equity to fashion relief enforcing the congressional mandate of the Civil Rights Acts and the constitutional guarantees of the Equal Protection of the Law; and clearly, courts of equity have the power to eradicate the effects of past discriminations. Parham v. Southwestern Bell Telephone Co., 433 F. 2d 421 (8th Cir. 1971). We are not here concerned with the anti-preference treatment section 703(j) of Title VII of the Civil Rights Act of 1964, 42 U.S.C.A. § 2000e–2(j), as this class action is predicated under § 1981 of the old Civil Rights Act and the provisions of the Fourteenth Amendment. However, even the anti-preference treatment section of the new Civil Rights Act of 1964 does not limit the power of a court to order affirmative relief to correct the effects of past unlawful practices. United States v. IBEW, Local No. 38, 428 F.2d 144 (6th Cir.), cert. denied, 400 U.S. 943, 91 S.Ct. 245, 27 L.Ed.2d 248 (1970).

Although this case is not predicated upon Title VII of the Civil Rights Act of 1964 and most of the cases that have dealt with the issue of remedying past discriminatory practices along with prohibiting present discriminatory practices are under that Act, the remedies invoked in those cases offer some practical guidelines in dealing with this issue.

As the panel opinion points out most of these cases deal with discriminations to a specified individual who has been presently discriminated against on account of race, and the remedy is there easily applied as the individual who has been discriminated against can be presently ordered employed without running into the constitutional questions involved in granting preference to any one class over another. However, in United States v. Ironworkers Local 86, 43 F.2d 544 (9th Cir. 1971), cert. denied 404 U.S. 984, 92 S.Ct. 447, 30 L.Ed.2d 367 (1971) the Ninth Circuit approved the district court decree ordering building construction unions to offer immediate job referrals to previous racial discriminatees and also approved a prospective order requiring the unions to recruit sufficient blacks to comprise a 30 per cent membership in their apprenticeship programs. This was ordered in Seattle which had a black population of approximately 7 per cent. See, United States v. Local No. 86, Int. Ass'n of Bridge S., D. and R. Ironworkers et al., 315 F.Supp. 1202 (W.D.Wash.1970).

In Local 53 of Int. Ass'n of Asbestos Workers v. Vogler, 407 F.2d 1047 (5th Cir. 1969), the trial court ordered the immediate admission into the union of three Negroes who were racially discriminated against in their application for membership and voided a local membership rule that in effect made the union a self-perpetuating nepotistic group, specifically ordering the union to develop objective criteria for membership and prospectively ordering the alternating of white and Negro referrals.

In United States v. Central Motor Lines, Inc., 325 F.Supp. 478 (W.D.N.C. 1970), the trial court issued a preliminary injunction requiring the motor carrier to hire six Negro drivers "promptly," (apparently within two weeks from the date of the order), and that any future drivers hired were to be in an alternating ratio of one black to one white.

Cases arising from Executive Order #11246, prohibiting all contractors and subcontractors on federally financed projects from discriminating in their employment practices, have also upheld plans which establish percentage goals for the employment of minority workers. See Contractors Association of Eastern Pa. v. Secretary of Labor, 442 F.2d 159 (3d Cir. 1971) (upholding the "Philadelphia Plan" requiring minority employment goals in the construction trades ranging from 19 per cent-26 per cent); Joyce v. McCrane, 320 F.Supp. 1284 (D. N.J.1970) (requiring contractors to employ 30 per cent-37 per cent minority journeymen).

It is also appropriate to note that precedent from our own Circuit establishes that the presence of identified persons who have been discriminated against is not a necessary prerequisite to ordering affirmative relief in order to eliminate the present effects of past discrimination. In United States v. Sheet Metal Workers Local 36, 416 F.2d 123 (8th Cir. 1969), we required substantial changes in union referral systems. In connection with this holding, Judge Heaney noted:

"We recognize that each of the cases cited in n. 15 to support our position can be distinguished on the ground that in each case, a number of known members of a minority group had been discriminated against after the passage of the Civil Rights Act. Here, we do not have such evidence, but we do not believe that it is necessary. The record does show that qualified Negro tradesmen have been and continue to be residents of the area. It further shows that they were acutely aware of the Locals' policies toward minority groups. It is also clear that they knew that even if they were permitted to use the referral system and become members of the union, they

would have to work for at least a year before they could move into a priority group which would assure them reasonably full employment. In the light of this knowledge, it is unreasonable to expect that any Negro tradesman working for a Negro contractor or a nonconstruction white employer would seek to use the referral systems or to join either Local." Id. at 132.

It may also be pointed out that in actions under Title VII of the Civil Rights Act, 42 U.S.C.A. § 2000e et seq., Congress has specifically granted authority to the trial courts to "order such affirmative action as may be appropriate, which may include * * * *hiring of employees* * * *." 42 U.S.C.A. § 2000e—5(g) (emphasis added).

None of the remedies ordered or approved in the above cases involved an absolute preference for qualified minority persons for the first vacancies appearing in an employer's business, in contrast to the remedy ordered in the instant case. The absolute preference ordered by the trial court would operate as a present infringement on those nonminority group persons who are equally or superiorly qualified for the fire fighter's positions; and we hesitate to advocate implementation of one constitutional guarantee by the outright denial of another. Yet we acknowledge the legitimacy of erasing the effects of past racially discriminatory practices. Louisiana v. United States, supra. To accommodate these conflicting considerations, we think some reasonable ratio for hiring minority persons who can qualify under the revised qualification standards is in order for a limited period of time, or until there is a fair approximation of minority representation consistent with the population mix in the area. Such a procedure does not constitute a "quota" system because as soon as the trial court's order is fully implemented, all hirings will be on a racially nondiscriminatory basis, and it could well be that many more minority persons or less, as compared to the population at large, over a long period of time would apply and qualify for the positions. However, as a method of presently eliminating the effects of past racial discriminatory practices and in making meaningful in the immediate future the constitutional guarantees against racial discrimination, more than a token representation should be afforded. For these reasons we believe the trial court is possessed of the authority to order the hiring of 20 qualified minority persons, but this should be done without denying the constitutional rights of others by granting an absolute preference.

Ideas and views on ratios and procedures may vary widely but this issue should be resolved as soon as possible. In considering the equities of the decree and the difficulties that may be encountered in procuring qualified applicants from any of the racial groups, we feel that it would be in order for the district court to mandate that one out of every three persons hired by the Fire Department would be a minority individual who qualifies until at least 20 minority persons have been so hired.

Fashioning a remedy in these cases is of course a practical question which may differ substantially from case to case, depending on the circumstances. In reaching our conclusion in the instant case, we have been guided to some extent by the following considerations:

(1) It has now been established by the Supreme Court that the use of mathematical ratios as "a starting point in the process of shaping a remedy" is not unconstitutional and is "within the equitable remedial discretion of the District Court." Swann v. Charlotte-Mecklenburg Board of Education, 402 U.S. 1, 25, 91 S.Ct. 1267, 1280, 28 L.Ed.2d 554 (1971).

(2) Given the past discriminatory hiring policies of the Minneapolis Fire De-

partment, which were well known in the minority community, it is not unreasonable to assume that minority persons will still be reluctant to apply for employment, absent some positive assurance that if qualified they will in fact be hired on a more than token basis.

(3) As the panel opinion noted, testing procedures required to qualify applicants are undergoing revision and validation at the present time. As the tests are currently utilized, applicants must attain a qualifying score in order to be certified at all. They are then ranked in order of eligibility according to their test scores (disregarding for present purposes the veteran's preference). Because of the absence of validation studies on the record before us, it is speculative to assume that the qualifying test, in addition to separating those applicants who are qualified from those who are not, also ranks qualified applicants with precision, statistical validity, and predictive significance. See generally, Cooper & Sobel, Seniority and Testing under Fair Employment Laws: A General Approach to Objective Criteria of Hiring and Promotion, 82 Harv.L.Rev. 1598, 1637–1669 (1969). Thus, a hiring remedy based on an alternating ratio such as we here suggest will by no means necessarily result in hiring less qualified minority persons in preference to more qualified white persons.

(4) While some of the remedial orders relied on by the plaintiffs and the Government ordered one to one ratios, they appear to be in areas and occupations with a more substantial minority population than the Minneapolis area. Thus we conclude that a one to two ratio would be appropriate here, until 20 qualified minority persons have been hired.

The panel opinion is adopted as the opinion of the court en banc with the exception of that part relating to the absolute preference.

The District Court properly retained jurisdiction pending full implementation of its decree and the remedy. Cause is remanded for further proceedings consistent with this opinion.

All costs of the appeal are to be assessed three-fourths against the defendant-appellants and one-fourth against the plaintiffs-appellees.

MATTHES, Chief Judge (concurring).

As the panel opinion shows, I was opposed to the absolute preference requirement as enunciated in the district court's opinion. Upon consideration of the petition for rehearing en banc, and briefs filed in support and opposition to the rehearing, I have concluded that the remedy fashioned by the opinion authored by Judge Gibson is appropriate and should be granted. Accordingly, I concur in the majority opinion on the petition for rehearing en banc.

VAN OOSTERHOUT, Senior Circuit Judge (dissenting).

For reasons stated in Division V of the panel opinion in this case, reported at 452 F.2d 324, I dissent from the en banc mandatory determination that one out of three persons hired by the Fire Department shall be a minority person until at least twenty minority persons are hired. Such provision in my opinion is vulnerable to the same constitutional infirmity as Judge Larson's absolute preference provision. This court's minority preference provision will not discriminate against as many white applicants as Judge Larson's decree but it will still give some minority persons preference in employment over white applicants whose qualifications are determined to be superior under fairly imposed standards and tests.

Employment preferences based on race are prohibited by the Fourteenth Amendment. This case is distinguishable from Swann v. Charlotte-Mecklenburg Board of Education relied upon by the majority in that whites have no right to insist upon segregated schools, while white as well as Black applicants cannot be denied employment on the basis of race.

I agree that a court of equity has broad power to frame an appropriate decree but such power does not extend to establishing provisions which deprive persons of constitutionally guaranteed rights.

Present and future applicants for firemen positions are in no way responsible for past discrimination. Plaintiffs have not shown that any plaintiff now seeking employment has personally suffered as a result of past discrimination by being denied employment over a less qualified white person. Past general racial discrimination against Blacks under the circumstances of this case does not justify unconstitutional present racial discrimination against white applicants. The court should of course go as far as is constitutionally permissible to eliminate racial discrimination in employment of firemen. Substantial steps in that direction have been taken by other provisions of Judge Larson's decree and the panel opinion.

MEHAFFY, Circuit Judge, joins in this dissent.

In the conciliation agreement provisions which follow, respondent company undertook to remedy a long history of discriminatory practices. Had the case not been settled, how many of the company's undertakings could have been ordered in a Title VII decree?

EQUAL EMPLOYMENT OPPORTUNITY COMMISSION WASHINGTON, D. C. 20506

Case Nos. 5–7–235, 5–7–237, 5–7–520 and 5–7–521.

In the Matter of the Conciliation Between

EQUAL EMPLOYMENT OPPORTUNITY COMMISSION, THOMAS MANN, JAMES LASSITER, ARTHUR FORD, REVEREND J. C. FAUNTLEROY, ET AL.

CONCILIATION AGREEMENT

II. GENERAL REMEDIAL ACTION

1. *Evaluation of Jobs*

a. The Company and the Commission shall forthwith undertake a general review to determine if Negro employees are improperly classified with respect to the jobs they are performing and the rates they are paid relative to white employees doing the same or substantially equivalent work. With respect to several job categories in which, predominantly, Negroes are employed and there is no direct basis for comparison with rates of pay of white employees, a review will be made of such categories to determine whether the rate of pay is discriminatorily depressed on the basis of race.

b. To conduct this review, the Company shall as soon as possible but no later than 45 days from the date of this Agreement, retain at its expense an expert in job evaluation and statements of work content, knowledgeable in race relations, who is acceptable to the Commission, to make this determination. In the event an expert acceptable to the Commission is not designated within 45 days, the parties shall forthwith reconvene for the sole purpose of designating the expert. The expert shall report his findings to the Company and the Commission. The Company shall implement the decision of the expert by re-classifying such employ-ees and/or adjusting the rate of pay accordingly within a period of 30 days from the date of determination. The Company shall supply said expert with adequate staff and facilities and shall make available all records and other information necessary to perform this function. Such review shall be concluded within 120 days of the appointment of the expert, unless the expert requests and the Commission agrees to a reasonable extension of time for this purpose.

c. The scope of the review is to be general, and shall not be limited by or to the complaint of individual employees. However, this review will encompass the rate and classification of any Negro employee who requests such a review. If, as a result of this review, the Commission believes that an employee's job is improperly classified relative to jobs held by white employees or that a rate is lower than that paid white employees performing the same or substantially equivalent work, the Commission shall so notify the Company which will take appropriate action to correct the situation. As a part of this review procedure, there shall be developed written statements of the work content for all jobs involved, which reflect the work actually performed.

d. The expert described above may be an individual, management consultant or operations research organization. Both the Commission and the Company may nominate persons or organizations to be retained as the expert. It shall be the expert's responsibility to conduct the review set forth in the first paragraph of this section.

2. *Promotion to Supervisor and Other Positions, Upgrading and Vacancies*

a. As the Company's last report to the Government showed that only 32 of 1997 persons employed by the Company as "Officials and Managers" were Negroes, the Company agrees that, to comply affirmatively with Title VII of the Civil Rights Act of 1964, the Executive Order of the President and the Regulations of Departments and Agencies of the Federal Government, it will afford affirmative opportunities for promotion to and within supervisory levels, including staff supervisors, junior and senior quartermen, foremen and assistant foremen, assistant superintendent and superintendent, to qualified Negroes employed by the Company. Accordingly, the Company agrees to revise its promotion policies and practices with a view to improving opportunities for qualified Negro personnel for promotion to and within supervisory levels, as follows:

b. An inventory of the skilled Negro employees, indicating their seniority (defined as continuous service with the shipyard) and qualifications, and an inventory of the seniority and qualifications of the last 100 persons promoted to quarterman positions prior to July 2, 1965, will be conducted jointly by the Company and by Industrial Employment Policy Specialists of the Department of Defense as an interested party, and in the interests of contract compliance, commencing within 30 days of the date of this Agreement. Within 60 days of the conclusion of the inventory, a list of those Negro employees whose seniority and qualifications exceed those of white employees among the 100 persons described above will be developed jointly by the Company and by the Industrial Employment Policy Specialist and will constitute the order of placement, as supervisory positions open, for which the employee's qualifications are relevant, until the list is exhausted. Refusals of Negro employees to accept offers of promotions to supervision must be documented in each case.

c. Provided however, that where the Company desires to fill a vacancy with an employee with greater seniority or qualifications than Negro employees on the list, the Company may present his qualifications in writing to the Commission, along with a demonstration of special circumstances and unusual need for which it wishes to promote said employee. If the Commission is satisfied that the request is free of discrimination on the basis of race, color, religion or national origin, it shall grant the request. All appointments to supervisory posts shall be made without regard to the race of the employees who will be subject to such supervision.

d. Prior to the completion of the list described above and its use as a basis for selection of supervisors, supervisory vacancies may develop. Said vacancies will be filled by qualified Negro employees. Where the Company has special reasons for desiring to fill any such vacancy with a white employee, it shall first notify the Commission in writing, stating its reasons. If the Commission is satisfied that the request is free of discrimination, it shall grant the request.

e. Any disagreement between the Company and the Industrial Employment Policy Specialists, with respect to matters described in the first paragraph of this section, shall be resolved by the expert mentioned above, if appointed and available, and otherwise by the Commission.

3. *Promotion and Transfer to Non-Supervisory Positions*

a. The Company agrees to post at the Employment Office, Yard Personnel Office, and at all normal access gates into the yard, notices of the existence of all job vacancies. Applications to fill such vacancies will be considered and qualified applicants for such jobs shall be selected on the basis of their length of service where their skill, ability, and efficiency are fairly equal.

b. The Company shall permit employees from predominantly Negro job classifications to transfer to vacancies in other departments for which they are qualified. If, within two weeks, the employee is unable to perform in the new job, he may return to his old job. If the vacancy to which he transfers is a lower rate step in his classification, he will be transferred at his rate before the transfer.

c. Employees in predominantly Negro departments shall be given the first opportunity for training in programs in which they are qualified to enter.

d. The Company will apply a liberal policy in the application of this section to advance the basic purpose of this Agreement.

e. To comply affirmatively with Title VII and Executive Orders in the matter of promotion and training, the Company agrees to undertake an intensive re-evaluation of the skills of its Negro employees, to institute training programs to develop and improve the skill levels of such employees, and to promote and adjust compensation on the basis of such re-evaluation and/or training. Opportunities to acquire skills necessary for upgrading shall be afforded Negro employees on a nondiscriminatory basis so that they acquire a rounded work experience.

f. The qualifications of all Negro applicants for employment will be reviewed and measured against minimum qualifications for all job classifications. Such applicants will be given full consideration for filling vacancies in all such job classifications for which they may qualify. Review of applicant qualifications shall be concluded within 60 days after the date of this Agreement.

4. *Adjustment of Rate: Promotional Opportunities*

In order to adjust the pay rate and classification of Negro employees who may have been discriminatorily denied or delayed in their advancement through the wage and job structure of the Company, the following is agreed to:

a. To determine Company practices with respect to the rate and conditions of promotions of white employees both within steps of job classifications and from one job classification to another, control groups will be picked by a random sample method from the Fitters Department (X–11), the Painters Department (X–33), and Storekeepers (0–53).

b. The sample selected from each department shall be sufficient to trace the pattern of employment history of white employees in the department from the time of their original hiring.

c. From this sample there will be derived a profile of the rate and conditions for promotion of white employees.

d. This profile shall be developed jointly by the expert described in section 1 and the Industrial Employment Policy Specialists, Department of Defense.

e. Thereafter, the expert would compare the history of progression and promotion of individual Negro employees in said departments with the profile.

f. Upon establishment that a Negro employee has not moved up through the grades within the classification in which he is presently employed as rapidly as the norm or standard derived from the sample for white employees, he shall forthwith be assigned the first grade in his job classification, or such other grade as he would have achieved had his history followed the normal progression indicated in the study unless the Company demonstrates from such records as it keeps which are themselves not the product or result of discrimination, that the employee was not promoted for reason of physical handicap, improper attendance or other conduct on the premises. Considerations of the employee's skill and ability are not germane to this section. The burden of demonstrating that from Company records that the employee should not be upgraded is on the Company.

g. Where the expert finds that the Negro employee would have been promoted beyond his classification had the white rate of progress been followed, the Company may assert that the employee is not and cannot become qualified for promotion to the higher classification, using the same standard for promotion between classes heretofore used for white employees as derived from the sample.

h. If the evaluator finds that the Negro employee has such qualifications for promotion, or can achieve them through reasonable training, he shall be placed on a preferential promotion list and given at an appropriate time such training as may be reasonably necessary to equip him for promotion. Such promotion shall be given when need arises for additional members of the next higher class.

i. The sample and its results will apply to other departments to which reasonably applicable. Thereupon the expert shall apply the same standards of comparison of Negro employment records against the promotion and upgrading profile of white employees and the same actions will be taken as a result of that comparison as described in paragraphs 6 and 7.

j. If a further sample is needed, the department or departments from which it is to be drawn shall be discussed with the Commission. The expert will apply the results of any such further sample alone or in conjunction with the previous sample in such departments as are agreed upon in the manner described in paragraphs 6 and 7.

k. The entire Negro labor force will be reviewed in the manner set out above.

l. The Company may as a part of this process, and in its discretion, seek to determine if white employees have been unfairly treated in respect to ingrade progressions or promotions, and to attempt, in the event such unfairness is found, to correct it.

5. *Apprenticeship Programs*

As the Company's last report to the Government (Form 40) showed that only 6 of the 506 apprentices enrolled in the apprenticeship program were Negroes, the Company agrees that, to provide affirmatively for equal employment opportunity, apprenticeship classes shall henceforth be filled as follows:

a. The Company shall, within 30 days of this Agreement, estimate the number of vacancies in the program for the coming year. Similar estimate shall be made each succeeding 12 months.

b. The Company agrees that qualified employees now on the payroll shall have first opportunity to fill apprenticeship classes during the next two years. For these employees, the Company agrees to accept a high school diploma or academic equivalent for admission, to accept employees up to the age of 25 years as entering apprentices, to accept married students as apprentices, to keep such as apprentices should they marry during the course of apprenticeship, and not to debar any employee from the apprenticeship program because of previous attendance at college or other institution of higher education.

c. A list of Negro employees eligible for the apprenticeship program under these provisions shall be compiled and shall be available to the Commission. Rejections of this opportunity by employees on the list shall be obtained in writing, with a copy to the Commission.

d. In filling vacancies in the apprenticeship classes, the Company agrees to exercise its utmost efforts to see that substantial numbers of Negroes are included in such classes. To this end the Company agrees, (1) to include in its recruitment efforts the predominantly Negro schools in the labor market area; and (2) to notify civil rights organizations in said area of this Agreement and to solicit such organizations to send qualified applicants for such programs. The Commission shall, upon request, supply a list of such organizations. Copies of such notices and solicitations shall be furnished by the Company to the Commission. The parties to this Agreement recognize as a natural result of this recruitment effort that the ratio of Negro to white apprentices in any given year should approach the ratio of Negro to white employees and the ratio of Negro to whites in the labor market area but this provision shall not be construed to require or permit the rejection of any qualified applicant on the basis of his race or color.

e. When the Company has filled one-third of the estimated vacancies in any apprenticeship class for each year through the foregoing procedures, it shall notify the Commission of the proportion of Negro employees enrolled in the class, and the Company shall not fill more than half the remaining vacancies until the Commission has responded. The Commission's response can be expected within two weeks. If it appears to the Commission that adequate numbers of Negro employees will not be enrolled in the class, the Commission may propose additional reasonable recruiting steps which the Company shall undertake to assure the fulfillment of its obligations under this section.

f. The Company shall integrate the apprenticeship faculty by October 1, 1966, and the apprenticeship Selection Committee forthwith.

g. Apprenticeship requirements shall be reviewed by the Company and the Commission within the next 60 days to determine whether increased numbers of Negroes can be appointed consistent with the maintenance of the requirements for qualified apprentices. After this review, the Commission may propose other reasonable steps to increase the number of Negro apprentices, and the Company shall take such steps.

h. All other training programs, formal and informal, including crash training, patternmaking and tack welding programs, shall be open to employees without regard to race or color. The Company shall post in conspicuous places and otherwise publicize information to all its employees concerning the availability of these programs, and shall actively encourage Negro participation in these programs.

Notes

1. See Blumrosen, The Newport News Agreement, One Brief Shining Moment in the Enforcement of Equal Employment, in Blumrosen, Black Employment and the Law 328–407 (Rutgers University Press 1971).

2. The public accommodations title of the Civil Rights Act of 1964 contains language virtually identical to Section 706(k)'s grant of judicial discretion to award "a reasonable attorney's fee" to the prevailing party. In Newman v. Piggie Park Enterprises, 390 U.S. 400, 88 S.Ct. 964, 19 L.Ed.2d 1263 (1968), the Supreme Court construed that language to mean that attorneys' fees should "ordinarily" be awarded to prevailing plaintiffs. In Robinson v. Lorillard Corp., 444 F.2d 791, 804 (4th Cir. 1971), the court held the Piggie Park standard applicable in Title VII cases.

3. Section 707(g) authorizes courts, among other things, to "order such affirmative action as may be appropriate. * * *" What does that mean? "Affirmative action" is also called for by

Executive Order 11246. See pp. 946–964 infra for an indication of how the executive order's requirement is implemented. Does "affirmative action" in Title VII mean the same thing as "affirmative action" in Executive Order 11246?

SECTION 2. OTHER SOURCES OF THE RIGHT NOT TO BE DISCRIMINATED AGAINST

A. STATE FAIR EMPLOYMENT PRACTICES LAWS

Most states and many municipalities have fair employment practices laws and the literature commenting on them is voluminous. For comprehensive treatments see, e. g., Bonfield, State Civil Rights Statutes: Some Proposals, 49 Iowa L.Rev. 1067 (1964), Institutional Analysis of the Agencies Administering Fair Employment Practice Laws, 42 N.Y.U.L. Rev. 823 (1967), Substance of American Fair Employment Legislation, 61 Northwestern L.Rev. 907, 62 Northwestern L.Rev. 19 (1967); Bureau of National Affairs, State Fair Employment Practice Laws and Their Administration, Washington, 1964; Norgren and Hill, Toward Fair Employment, Columbia University Press, New York, 1964; Sovern, Legal Restraints on Racial Discrimination in Employment, Twentieth Century Fund, New York, 1966; Sutin, The Experience of State Fair Employment Commissions: A Comparative Study, 18 Vand.L.Rev. 965 (1965); Note, The Right to Equal Treatment: Administrative Enforcement of Anti-Discrimination Legislation, 74 Harv.L.Rev. 526 (1961). For detailed consideration of particular state statutes, see e. g., Auerbach, The 1967 Amendments to the Minnesota State Act Against Discrimination and the Uniform Law Commissioners' Model Anti-Discrimination Act: A Comparative Analysis and Evaluation, 52 Minn.L.Rev. 231 (1967); Blumrosen, Antidiscrimination Laws in Action in New Jersey: A Law-Sociology Study, 19 Rutgers L.Rev. 189 (1965); Higbee, Development and Administration of the N.Y. State Law Against Discrimination, University of Alabama, 1966; Note, The California FEPC: Stepchild of State Agencies, 18 Stan.L. Rev. 187 (1965). The National Conference of Commissioners on Uniform State Laws has adopted a Model Anti-Discrimination Act. The Act and an accompanying article by its draftsman, Professor Dorsen, appear in 4 Harv.J. Legis. 212 (1967).

The state laws are generally similar to Title VII in their substantive reach, different in their modes of enforcement. Where Title VII relies on the courts to decide cases that cannot be conciliated, the typical state statute depends on the administrative process. An administrative agency will serve as the primary forum to hear discrimination cases, entering cease and desist orders against those found to have violated the law. Courts will usually be involved only in reviewing administrative determinations. The New York law is unusual in giving discrimination victims a choice of a court action or an administrative remedy. N.Y. Exec.Law § 297(9).

B. THE CONSTITUTION OF THE UNITED STATES

Excerpts from the Constitution of the United States

Fifth Amendment

No person shall * * * be deprived of life, liberty, or property, without due process of law * * *.

Thirteenth Amendment

Section 1. Neither slavery nor involuntary servitude, except as a punishment for crime whereof the party shall have been duly convicted, shall exist within the United States, or any place subject to their jurisdiction.

Section 2. Congress shall have power to enforce this article by appropriate legislation.

Fourteenth Amendment

Section 1. [N]o State shall make or enforce any law which shall abridge the privileges or immunities of citizens of the United States; nor shall any State deprive any person of life, liberty, or property, without due process of law; nor deny to any person within its jurisdiction the equal protection of the laws.

* * *

Section 5. The Congress shall have power to enforce, by appropriate legislation, the provisions of this article.

ETHRIDGE v. RHODES

United States District Court, Southern
District of Ohio, 1967.
268 F.Supp. 83.

OPINION AND ORDER

KINNEARY, District Judge. This is a class action for declaratory and injunctive relief brought by plaintiffs, William Ethridge and Jerome Welch, on their behalf, and on behalf of all others similarly situated, against defendants, James A. Rhodes, Governor of the State of Ohio, Alfred Gienow, Director of the Ohio Department of Public Works, and John D. Herbert, Treasurer of the State of Ohio. The jurisdiction of this action is asserted under the Fourteenth Amendment to the Constitution of the United States, Title 28, United States Code, Sections 1331, 1343(3) and 2201, and

Title 42, United States Code, Sections 1981 and 1983.

The Amended Complaint alleges that defendants, as duly elected and appointed officials of the State of Ohio, are about to enter into contracts for the construction of the Medical Basic Sciences Building on the campus of The Ohio State University, at Columbus. Plaintiffs seek to enjoin the State of Ohio from entering into such contracts on the ground that such action will be a deprivation, under color of state law, of their privileges and immunities as citizens of the United States as secured to them by the equal protection and due process clauses of the Fourteenth Amendment to the Constitution of the United States and Title 42, United States Code, Sections 1981 and 1983. It is charged that this activity violates these provisions inasmuch as it represents a continuation of state participation in a pattern of discrimination against plaintiffs, and the class they represent, in access to job opportunities on construction projects financed by federal and state funds, solely on the basis of their race.

* * *

Plaintiff, William Ethridge, has been employed for the past fourteen and one-half years as an aircraft electrician by North American Aviation, Inc., Columbus, Ohio. He has received instruction in electronics in both civilian and military schools, and his present employment involves the installation of electrical equipment and the reading of blueprints dealing with all phases of electrical work. Ethridge has also done some part-time work in the areas of commercial and residential wiring.

This plaintiff has made repeated attempts to gain admission to Local 683, International Brotherhood of Electrical Workers. He has been unable to gain admission because the two union officials, whom he has been told he must contact, have been "out" each time he sought to contact them. He has been unable to acquire an application form for admission to this union because he has been told that the application form must be notarized by one of the union officials who were consistently unavailable. His attempts to secure employment directly with construction contractors have been met with the answer that they do all of their hiring through the union.

Plaintiff, Jerome Welch, a college graduate, is presently employed as a high lift and bulldozer operator by Craig and Sons, Columbus, Ohio. He received instruction in heavy equipment operation and obtained a diploma in that field from the Interstate School, Muncie, Indiana.

This plaintiff's attempts to gain admission to Local 18, International Union of Operating Engineers, has met with doubtful results. While he has been able to obtain a "work permit," contractors have told him that before he can be employed he must present a "book" to signify that he is a fully pledged member of the union. The union officials whom Welch has to see in order to gain full membership in the union have also been "out" on every occasion that he has attempted to contact them.

Bids from contractors were received by the State of Ohio for the construction of the Medical Basic Sciences Building, and after review, contracts were sent to at least four contractors for their signatures. While these contracts have been signed and returned by the contractors and have not been signed by state officials, a declaration of intention to sign them has been made by state officials.

At least one of the contractors who has signed such a contract refused to submit a "responsive bid," that is, one containing the following assurance in compliance with the antidiscrimination provisions of the defendant Governor's executive order dealing with construction contracts:

ASSURANCE

The undersigned hiring source, in response to the Executive Order issued by Governor James A. Rhodes on June 15, 1966, as amended December 30, 1966, hereby gives its assurance to _____ as follows:

(1) Admission to the full referral facilities of this hiring source, both as to apprentices and journeymen, is open on equal terms to all qualified persons without discrimination based on race, color, religion, national origin or ancestry.

* * *

Upon discovering that no responsive bids were submitted in the category of heating, ventilating and air conditioning, defendant Gienow requested and received from defendant Rhodes a waiver of application of the assurances requirement to this contract.

In order for plaintiffs to prevail in their contention that this Court has jurisdiction of this action under the Fourteenth Amendment, it is incumbent on plaintiffs to prove that there is "state action" resulting in a denial of equal protection of the laws—that is, action which results in racial discrimination. The Fourteenth Amendment was aimed at state, rather than individual, abridgment of individual rights. Burton v. Wilmington Parking Authority, 365 U.S. 715, 81 S.Ct. 856, 6 L.Ed.2d 45 (1961); Simkins v. Moses H. Cone Memorial Hosp., 323 F.2d 959 (4th Cir. 1963). Similarly, in order to prevail on the question of this Court's jurisdiction under Title 42, United States Code, Section 1983, plaintiffs must prove that defendants acted "under color of state law" to deprive a citizen of the United States of rights, privileges, or immunities secured by the Constitution and laws of the United States. Monroe v. Pape, 365 U.S. 167, 81 S.Ct. 473, 5 L.Ed.2d 492 (1961).

Defendants are aware that a number of unions have not referred Negroes for employment on the construction of other buildings erected by the State of Ohio on the campus of The Ohio State University. Defendants know to a certainty that many of the unions which will be used as labor sources by the proposed contractors on the Medical Basic Sciences Building project do not now have any Negro members. And the defendants also know that union officials responsible for admission to these unions have been persistently "out" or unavailable to Negroes who seek membership in such unions. Thus, the evidence presented establishes defendants' knowledge of a pattern of discrimination against Negroes, solely on the basis of their race, as to admission and referral by certain of the craft unions which will be used as labor sources for this project. There is, in addition, uncontroverted proof that no steps have been taken by the responsible union officials to correct such inequities.

The testimony of J. Parker Garwick, president of Garwick and Ross, the low bidder on the general contract, indicates that his company plans to secure its labor force only through union referrals. Although certain unions which Garwick and Ross plans to use as hiring sources on this project have never before referred Negroes, the Garwick and Ross bid was unqualified—giving the assurance required by the executive order. Garwick and Ross plans to implement its assurance by making requests for Negro workers. If no Negroes are referred, this company intends to take no further steps to assure that its hiring source does not discriminate.

Stephen E. Lance, Ohio State University Constructor and the person designated by the University as the person in charge of the equal employment program, aptly summed up the situation which will inevitably and automatically exist on this project under present plans, —that is, qualified Negroes in certain crafts will not be able to get jobs. Since the contractors will hire only through unions, and a majority of the craft unions do not have Negro members and will not refer non-member Negroes, the contractors will hire only non-Negroes in a majority of the crafts needed to work on this project.

The Fourteenth Amendment proscription of racial discrimination does not extend to the acts of non-governmental persons such as union officials. Civil Rights Cases, 109 U.S. 3, 3 S.Ct. 18, 27 L.Ed. 835 (1883). However, when a state has become a joint participant in a pattern of racially discriminatory conduct by placing itself in a position of interdependence with private individuals acting in such a manner—that is, the proposed contractors acting under contract with unions that bar Negroes—this constitutes a type of "state action" proscribed by the Fourteenth Amendment. Burton v. Wilmington Parking Authority, supra. Thus, as in the instant suit, where a state through its elected and appointed officials, undertakes to perform essential governmental functions—herein, the construction of facilities for public education—with the aid of private persons, it cannot avoid the responsibilities imposed on it by the Fourteenth Amendment by merely ignoring or failing to perform them. Ibid.

Plaintiffs have correctly asserted jurisdiction under § 1983. This statute is intended to allow redress against official representatives of the state who abuse their positions. It was enacted as a means for enforcing the provisions of the Fourteenth Amendment against those who act as officials of the State, whether they act in accordance with their authority or misuse it. Monroe v. Pape, supra.

The officials of the State of Ohio, through the testimony of the defendant, Director of Public Works, have displayed a shocking lack of concern over the realities of this whole situation and the inevitable discrimination that will result from entering into and performing under the proposed contracts with the proposed contractors. This Director testified that non-discrimination is just another provision of the contract, and his best solution for correcting discrimination, if and when it occurs, is to invoke the sanctions of the performance bond. This solution is totally inadequate for the elimination of the pattern of discrimination that has been allowed to exist. Defendants' failure to assure qualified minority workers equal access to job opportunities on public construction projects by acquiescing in the discriminatory practices of contractors and craft unions clearly falls within the proscription of the Fourteenth Amendment, and a cause of action is stated under § 1983. In a venture, such as this one, where the state as a governmental entity becomes a joint participant with private persons, the restrictions of the Fourteenth Amendment apply not only to the actions of the state but also to the acts of its private partners —the contractors—and the state is bound to affirmatively insure compliance with the constitutional provisions. Burton v. Wilmington Parking Authority, supra. Since this section imposes civil liability, proof of a "specific intent to deprive a person of a federal right" is not required as under the criminal civil rights statutes. Monroe v. Pape, supra.

We come next to the question of the procedural availability of the injunction remedy in this case. The plaintiffs are here seeking an extraordinary remedy. It must be established that the threatened injury is irreparable and that no other adequate remedy exists. Stated otherwise, it must be proved that plain, complete, practical and efficient means of effecting justice may be obtained only through the prompt administration of an injunction in equity. Local 499, IBEW v. Iowa Power & Light Co., 224 F.Supp. 731 (S.D.Iowa 1964).

Defendants assert that the threatened injury is not irreparable and that an injunction is not the only adequate remedy because Title 42, United States Code, Section 2000e–1–15, and Ohio Rev. Code, ch. 4112, provide a remedy for the specific injury set out in the Complaint. It is alleged that through the commissions set up by these statutes and judicial enforcement of their orders, any person found to have been discriminated against could gain access to labor organizations and awarded a back pay differential for the pecuniary damages suffered through the discriminatory exclusions from work on the project. However, it is quite apparent from the evidence presented that the threatened injury is not fully reparable through the utilization of the procedures set out in both the federal and state statutes.

Moreover, while the statutory provisions may serve to redress the pecuniary damage resulting from discrimination, they do not take a single step toward mending the psychological damage to both the party discriminated against and others in the class he represents. It is evident from the testimony of the several sociologists who appeared as witnesses in this case that discrimination in the area of employment stunts the educational and technical potential development of the class subject to such inequities. This Court is also mindful of the evidence submitted by experts in cases dealing with discrimination in other areas of life. Such evidence pointed out that segregation and discrimination not only denote inferiority of the class discriminated against, but also retard the development of that class, and that in cases in which this type of activity receives the sanction of the government, the impact is even greater. See, e. g., Brown v. Board of Education, 349 U.S. 294, 75 S.Ct. 753, 99 L.Ed. 1083 (1955); 347 U.S. 483, 74 S.Ct. 686, 98 L.Ed. 873, 38 A.L.R.2d 1180 (1954). Injuries of this kind are not subject to any sort of monetary valuation. Thus, the pecuniary awards allowed under the federal and state statutes provide no adequate remedy.

Apart from the question of the reparability of discrimination by money damages, the Director of the Ohio State Civil Rights Commission testified that the Commission has been ineffectual in remedying discrimination in the craft unions. The Director further testified that even with the powers available to the Commission, the case by case approach which must be followed by that body results in too long a delay before any meaningful steps will be made toward eliminating discrimination. In view of the requirement that the state administrative remedy be sought before use of the federal administrative remedy, Title 42, United States Code, Section 2000e 5(b) (See Senate Discussion, June 4, 1964), the delay in administration is compounded. Thus, the federal administrative remedy also lacks any sort of speedy effectiveness.

ORDER

In accordance with and for the reasons stated in the foregoing Opinion, the Court determines that the named plaintiffs and all other persons similarly situated are threatened with and will suffer irreparable injury if the defendants are not restrained, enjoined and mandated in the particulars contained in the injunctive order made herein, and that they have no other adequate remedy.

It is, therefore, ordered, adjudged and decreed that James A. Rhodes, as Governor of the State of Ohio, John D. Herbert, as Treasurer of the State of Ohio, and Alfred Gienow, as Director of Public Works of the State of Ohio, their successors in office, agents, representatives, and employees be and each of them, is hereby restrained and enjoined from:

(1) Entering into the contracts already submitted by defendants to, and on their parts executed by, the construction firms of Garwick and Ross, Huffman-Wolf, States Electric, Gesling Company, and others, for the construction of a building, designated as the Medical Basic Sciences Building, on the campus of The Ohio State University at Columbus, under the proposal and agreements which bind such contracting firms in their intended performance of the said contracts;

(2) Entering into contracts for the construction of said Medical Basic Sciences Building with any persons who are bound by any agreement, or otherwise, to secure their labor force exclusively or primarily from any organization or source that does not supply or refer laborers and craftsmen without regard to race, color, or membership in a labor union;

(3) Entering into contracts for the construction of the said Medical Basic Sciences Building with any persons who are bound by any agreement, or otherwise, with a labor organization, which requires, as a condition of employment, that employees hired by such persons become members of labor organization within a certain number of days after employment, and membership in such labor organizations is not equally available to all persons without regard to race or color.

It is further ordered, adjudged and decreed that:

(1) With respect to the construction of the said Medical Basic Sciences

Building, James A. Rhodes, as Governor of the State of Ohio, John D. Herbert, as Treasurer of the State of Ohio, and Alfred Gienow, as Director of Public Works of the State of Ohio, their successors in office, agents, representatives, and employees may enter into contracts only with persons who will obligate themselves and be legally eligible and prepared actually to secure a labor force only from sources that will reasonably insure equal job opportunities to all qualified persons, including journeymen and apprentice craftsmen and laborers, without regard to race, color, or membership or non-membership in a labor union.

(2) Jurisdiction of all matters related to, connected with, and which may arise out of this Opinion and Order be, and they are hereby, specifically retained by this Court.

Notes

1. Why hasn't the State satisfied its obligations under the Constitution by enacting legislation outlawing discrimination?

2. If you were counsel to plaintiffs in a situation like the one that gave rise to Ethridge v. Rhodes, would you pursue the course followed by Ethridge's lawyer or invoke Title VII? Why?

3. *Accord* with Ethridge v. Rhodes, Todd v. Joint Apprenticeship Committee, 223 F.Supp. 12 (N.D.Ill.1963), remanded with instructions to dismiss as moot, 332 F.2d 243 (7th Cir. 1964), certiorari denied 380 U.S. 914, 85 S.Ct. 880, 13 L.Ed.2d 800 (1964). But see Gaynor v. Rockefeller, 15 N.Y.2d 120, 256 N.Y.S.2d 584, 204 N.E.2d 627 (1965); cf. Waters v. Paschen Contractors, Inc., 227 F.Supp. 659 (N.D.Ill. 1964). In Todd, the district court or-

dered the offending union and related defendants to cease discriminating against Negro applicants. The court of appeals directed dismissal because the construction contract on which the suit had been founded was completed the day after the district court entered its order.

Hadnott v. Laird, 317 F.Supp. 379 (D. C.D.C.1970), affirmed 463 F.2d 304 (D.C.Cir.1972), a suit against the Secretary of Defense of the United States, accepted the defense of sovereign immunity and distinguished Ethridge v. Rhodes on the ground that it was an action against state officials not involving the sovereign immunity of the federal government. The district court went on to say:

"But even if the sovereign immunity doctrine did not dispose of this action, it would be dismissed because of plaintiffs' failure to pursue the administrative remedies afforded them." 317 F.Supp. at 383.

The remedies contemplated by the court were those created by Executive Order 11246, infra, and Title VII. The Court of Appeals affirmed on the exhaustion of administrative remedies ground without reaching the sovereign immunity theory.

James v. Ogilvie, 310 F.Supp. 661 (N.D.Ill.1970), also distinguishes Ethridge, saying:

"In the *Ethridge* case, testimony of the Director of the Ohio State Civil Rights Commission indicated that Ohio's administrative remedies were too slow to be meaningful. No such evidence is before us. On the present record, issuance of temporary injunctive relief would be unwarranted. * *

"In conclusion we do not dismiss this action, neither do we afford any temporary relief. [We will entertain a motion] that this action be held in abeyance until such time as the plaintiffs attempt to pursue available state remedies or show cause why such remedies are ineffective to protect their rights. * * *" 310 F.Supp. at 665.

4. Ethridge v. Rhodes is commented on in Marcus, Union Discrimination Checked: Ethridge v. Rhodes Rouses a Slumbering Giant, 14 How.L.J. 76 (1968); Note, 17 Amer.L.Rev. 92 (1967); Casenote, 81 Harv.L.Rev. 690 (1968); Comment, 46 No.Car.L.Rev. 149 (1967).

C. NONDISCRIMINATION PROVISION IN FEDERAL CONTRACTS, WITH EMPHASIS ON AFFIRMATIVE ACTION, PREFERENTIAL TREATMENT AND RELATED MATTERS

EXCERPTS FROM EXECUTIVE ORDER 11246

30 Fed.Reg. 12319 (1965), as amended by E.O. 11375, 32 Fed.Reg. 14303 (1967); E.O. 11478, 34 Fed.Reg. 12985 (1969), 42 U.S.C.A. § 2000e note (1970).

PART II. NONDISCRIMINATION IN EMPLOYMENT BY GOVERNMENT CONTRACTORS AND SUBCONTRACTORS

Subpart A. Duties of the Secretary of Labor

Sec. 201. The Secretary of Labor shall be responsible for the administration of Parts II and III of this Order and shall adopt such rules and regulations and issue such orders as he deems necessary and appropriate to achieve the purposes thereof.

Subpart B. Contractors' Agreements

Sec. 202. Except in contracts exempted in accordance with Section 204 of this Order, all Government contracting agencies shall include in every Government contract hereafter entered into the following provisions:

"During the performance of this contract, the contractor agrees as follows:

"(1) The contractor will not discriminate against any employee or applicant for employment because of race, color, religion, sex, or national origin. The contractor will take affirmative action to ensure that applicants are employed, and that employees are treated during employment, without regard to their race, color, religion, sex, or national origin. Such action shall include but not be limited to the following: employment, upgrading demotion or transfer; recruitment or recruitment advertising; layoff or termination; rates of pay or other forms of compensation; and selection for training, including apprenticeship. The contractor agrees to post in conspicuous places, available to employees and applicants for employment, notices to be provided by the contracting officer setting forth the provisions of this nondiscrimination clause.

"(2) The contractor will, in all solicitations or advertisements for employees placed by or on behalf of the contractor, state that all qualified applicants will receive consideration for employment without regard to race, color, religion, sex, or national origin.

"(3) The contractor will send to each labor union or representative of workers with which he has a collective bargaining agreement or other contract or understanding, a notice, to be provided by the agency contracting officer, advising the labor union or workers' representative of the contractor's commitments under Section 202 of Executive Order No. 11246 of September 24, 1965, and shall post copies of the notice in conspicuous places available to employees and applicants for employment.

"(4) The contractor will comply with all provisions of Executive Order No. 11246 of Sept. 24, 1965, and of the rules, regulations, and relevant orders of the Secretary of Labor.

"(5) The contractor will furnish all information and reports required by Executive Order No. 11246 of September 24, 1965, and by the rules, regulations, and orders of the Secretary of Labor, or pursuant thereto, and will permit access to his books, records, and accounts by the contracting agency and the Secretary of Labor for purposes of investigation to ascertain compliance with such rules, regulations, and orders.

"(6) In the event of the contractor's noncompliance with the nondiscrimination clauses of this contract or with any of such rules, regulations, or orders, this contract may be cancelled, terminated or suspended in whole or in part and the contractor may be declared ineligible for further Government contracts in accordance with procedures authorized in Executive Order No. 11246 of Sept. 24, 1965, and such other sanctions may be imposed and remedies invoked as provided in Executive Order No. 11246 of September 24, 1965, or by rule, regulation, or order of the Secretary of Labor, or as otherwise provided by law.

"(7) The contractor will include the provisions of Paragraphs (1) through (7) in every subcontract or purchase order unless exempted by rules, regulations, or orders of the Secretary of Labor issued pursuant to Section 204 of Executive Order No. 11246 of Sept. 24, 1965, so that such provisions will be binding upon each subcontractor or vendor. The contractor will take such action with respect to any subcontract or purchase order as the contracting agency may direct as a means of enforcing such provisions including sanctions for noncompliance: *Provided, however,* That in the event the contractor becomes involved in, or is

threatened with, litigation with a subcontractor or vendor as a result of such direction by the contracting agency, the contractor may request the United States to enter into such litigation to protect the interests of the United States."

Sec. 203. (a) Each contractor having a contract containing the provisions prescribed in Section 202 shall file, and shall cause each of his subcontractors to file, Compliance Reports with the contracting agency or the Secretary of Labor as may be directed. Compliance Reports shall be filed within such times and shall contain such information as to the practices, policies, programs, and employment policies, programs, and employment statistics of the contractor and each subcontractor, and shall be in such form, as the Secretary of Labor may prescribe.

(b) Bidders or prospective contractors or subcontractors may be required to state whether they have participated in any previous contract subject to the provisions of this Order, or any preceding similar Executive order, and in that event to submit, on behalf of themselves and their proposed subcontractors, Compliance Reports prior to or as an initial part of their bid or negotiation of a contract.

(c) Whenever the contractor or subcontractor has a collective bargaining agreement or other contract or understanding with a labor union or an agency referring workers or providing or supervising apprenticeship or training for such workers, the Compliance Report shall include such information as to such labor union's or agency's practices and policies affecting compliance as the Secretary of Labor may prescribe: *Provided,* That to the extent such information is within the exclusive possession of a labor union or an agency referring workers or providing or supervising apprenticeship or training and such labor union or agency shall refuse to furnish such information to the contractor, the contractor shall so certify to the contracting agency as part of its Compliance Report and shall set forth what efforts he has made to obtain such information.

(d) The contracting agency or the Secretary of Labor may direct that any bidder or prospective contractor or subcontractor shall submit, as part of his Compliance Report, a statement in writing, signed by an authorized officer or agent on behalf of any labor union or any agency referring workers or providing or supervising apprenticeship or other training, with which the bidder or prospective contractor deals, with supporting information, to the effect that the signer's practices and policies do not discriminate on the grounds of race, color, religion, sex, or national origin, and that the signer either will affirmatively cooperate in the implementation of the policy and provisions of this Order or that it consents and agrees that recruitment, employment, and the terms and conditions of employment under the proposed contract shall be in accordance with the purposes and provisions of the Order. In the event that the union or the agency shall refuse to execute such a statement, the Compliance Report shall so certify and set forth what efforts have been made to secure such a statement and such additional factual material as the contracting agency or the Secretary of Labor may require.

Sec. 204. The Secretary of Labor may, when he deems that special circumstances in the national interest so require, exempt a contracting agency from the requirement of including any or all of the provisions of Section 202 of this Order in any specific contract, subcontract, or purchase order. The Secretary of Labor may, by rule or regulation, also exempt certain classes of contracts, subcontracts, or purchase orders (1) whenever work is to be or has been performed outside the United States and no recruitment of workers within the limits of the United States is

involved; (2) for standard commercial supplies or raw materials; (3) involving less than specified amounts of money or specified numbers of workers; or (4) to the extent that they involve subcontracts below a specified tier. The Secretary of Labor may also provide, by rule, regulation, or order, for the exemption of facilities of a contractor which are in all respects separate and distinct from activities of the contractor related to the performance of the contract: *Provided,* That such an exemption will not interfere with or impede the effectuation of the purposes of this Order: *And provided further,* That in the absence of such an exemption all facilities shall be covered by the provisions of this Order.

Subpart C—Powers and Duties of The Secretary of Labor and The Contracting Agencies

Sec. 205. Each contracting agency, shall be primarily responsible for obtaining compliance with the rules, regulations, and orders of the Secretary of Labor with respect to contracts entered into by such agency or its contractors. All contracting agencies shall comply with the rules of the Secretary of Labor in discharging their primary responsibility for securing compliance with the provisions of contracts and otherwise with the terms of this Order and of the rules, regulations, and orders of the Secretary of Labor issued pursuant to this Order. They are directed to cooperate with the Secretary of Labor and to furnish the Secretary of Labor such information and assistance as he may require in the performance of his functions under this Order. They are further directed to appoint or designate, from among the agency's personnel, compliance officers. It shall be the duty of such officers to seek compliance with the objectives of this Order by conference, conciliation, mediation, or persuasion.

Sec. 206. (a) The Secretary of Labor may investigate the employment practices of any Government contractor or subcontractor, or initiate such investigation by the appropriate contracting agency, to determine whether or not the contractual provisions specified in Section 202 of this Order have been violated. Such investigation shall be conducted in accordance with the procedures established by the Secretary of Labor and the investigating agency shall report to the Secretary of Labor any action taken or recommended.

(b) The Secretary of Labor may receive and investigate or cause to be investigated complaints by employees or prospective employees of a Government contractor or subcontractor which allege discrimination contrary to the contractual provisions specified in Section 202 of this Order. If this investigation is conducted for the Secretary of Labor by a contracting agency, that agency shall report to the Secretary what action has been taken or is recommended with regard to such complaints.

Sec. 207. The Secretary of Labor shall use his best efforts, directly and through contracting agencies, other interested Federal, State, and local agencies, contractors, and all other available instrumentalities to cause any labor union engaged in work under Government contracts or any agency referring workers or providing or supervising apprenticeship or training for or in the course of such work to cooperate in the implementation of the purposes of this Order. The Secretary of Labor shall, in appropriate cases, notify the Equal Employment Opportunity Commission, the Department of Justice, or other appropriate Federal agencies whenever it has reason to believe that the practices of any such labor organization or agency violate Title VI or Title VII of the Civil Rights Act of 1964 or other provision of Federal law.

Sec. 208. (a) The Secretary of Labor, or any agency, officer, or employee in the executive branch of the Government designated by rule, regulation, or order of the Secretary, may hold such hearings, public or private, as the Secretary may deem advisable for compliance, enforcement, or educational purposes.

(b) The Secretary of Labor may hold, or cause to be held, hearings in accordance with Subsection (a) of this Section prior to imposing, ordering, or recommending the imposition of penalties and sanctions under this Order. No order for debarment of any contractor from further Government contracts under Section 209 (a)(6) shall be made without affording the contractor an opportunity for a hearing.

Subpart D. Sanctions and Penalties

Sec. 209. (a) In accordance with such rules, regulations, or orders as the Secretary of Labor may issue or adopt, the Secretary or the appropriate contracting agency may:

(1) Publish, or cause to be published, the names of contractors or unions which it has concluded have complied or have failed to comply with the provisions of this Order or of the rules, regulations, and orders of the Secretary of Labor.

(2) Recommend to the Department of Justice that, in cases in which there is substantial or material violation or the threat of substantial or material violation of the contractual provisions set forth in Section 202 of this Order, appropriate proceedings be brought to enforce those provisions, including the enjoining, within the limitations of applicable law, of organizations, individuals, or groups who prevent directly or indirectly, or seek to prevent directly or indirectly, compliance with the provisions of this Order.

(3) Recommend to the Equal Employment Opportunity Commission or the De-

partment of Justice that appropriate proceedings be instituted under Title VII of the Civil Rights Act of 1964.

(4) Recommend to the Department of Justice that criminal proceedings be brought for the furnishing of false information to any contracting agency or to the Secretary of Labor as the case may be.

(5) Cancel, terminate, suspend, or cause to be cancelled, terminated, or suspended, any contract, or any portion or portions thereof, for failure of the contractor or subcontractor to comply with the nondiscrimination provisions of the contract. Contracts may be cancelled, terminated, or suspended absolutely or continuance of contracts may be conditioned upon a program for future compliance approved by the contracting agency.

(6) Provide that any contracting agency shall refrain from entering into further contracts, or extensions or other modifications of existing contracts, with any noncomplying contractor, until such contractor has satisfied the Secretary of Labor that such contractor has established and will carry out personnel and employment policies in compliance with the provisions of this Order.

(b) Under rules and regulations prescribed by the Secretary of Labor, each contracting agency shall make reasonable efforts within a reasonable time limitation to secure compliance with the contract provisions of this Order by methods of conference, conciliation, mediation, and persuasion before proceedings shall be instituted under Subsection (a) (2) of this Section, or before a contract shall be cancelled or terminated in whole or in part under Subsection (a)(5) of this Section for failure of a contractor or subcontractor to comply with the contract provisions of this Order.

* * *

Sec. 211. If the Secretary shall so direct, contracting agencies shall not en-

ter into contracts with any bidder or prospective contractor unless the bidder or prospective contractor has satisfactorily complied with the provisions of this Order or submits a program for compliance acceptable to the Secretary of Labor or, if the Secretary so authorizes, to the contracting agency.

PART III. NONDISCRIMINATION PROVISIONS IN FEDERALLY ASSISTED CONSTRUCTION CONTRACTS

Sec. 301. Each executive department and agency which administers a program involving Federal financial assistance shall require as a condition for the approval of any grant, contract, loan, insurance, or guarantee thereunder, which may involve a construction contract, that the applicant for Federal Assistance undertake and agree to incorporate, or cause to be incorporated, into all construction contracts paid for in whole or in part with funds obtained from the Federal Government or borrowed on the credit of the Federal Government pursuant to such grant, contract, loan, insurance, or guarantee, or undertaken pursuant to any Federal program involving such grant, contract, loan, insurance, or guarantee, the provisions prescribed for Government contracts by Section 202 of this Order or such modification thereof, preserving in substance the contractor's obligations thereunder, as may be approved by the Secretary of Labor, together with such additional provisions as the Secretary deems appropriate to establish and protect the interest of the United States in the enforcement of those obligations. Each such applicant shall also undertake and agree (1) to assist and cooperate actively with the administering department or agency and the Secretary of Labor in obtaining the compliance of contractors and subcontractors with those contract provisions and with the rules, regulations, and relevant orders of the Secretary, (2) to obtain and to furnish to the administering department or agency and to the Secretary of Labor such information as they may require for the supervision of such compliance, (3) to carry out sanctions and penalties for violation of such obligations imposed upon contractors and subcontractors by the Secretary of Labor or the administering department or agency pursuant to Part II, Subpart D, of this Order, and (4) to refrain from entering into any contract subject to this Order, or extension or other modification of such a contract with a contractor debarred from Government contracts under Part II, Subpart D, of this Order.

Notes

1. The Secretary of Labor's responsibilities under Executive Order 11246 have been delegated to the Director of the Office of Federal Contract Compliance. The OFCC has issued rules and regulations further defining the duties of contractors. Obligations of Contractors and Subcontractors, 41 C.F.R. § 60–1 (1970) as amended, 35 Fed.Reg. 10,660 (1970). For references to "Order No. 4" and the OFCC's testing guidelines, see p. 963 infra and p. 903 supra, respectively.

2. What result if an individual brings suit claiming that a contractor has violated his contractual pledge not to discriminate? See Farkas v. Texas Instruments, 375 F.2d 629 (5th Cir. 1967), certiorari denied 389 U.S. 977, 88 S.Ct. 480, 19 L.Ed.2d 471 (1968); Farmer v. Philadelphia Electric Co., 329 F.2d 3 (3rd Cir. 1964); Todd v. Joint Apprenticeship Committee, 223 F.Supp. 12 (N.D.Ill.1963), remanded with instructions to dismiss as moot, 332 F.2d 243 (7th Cir. 1964), certiorari denied 380 U.S. 914, 85 S.Ct. 880, 13 L.Ed.2d 800 (1964). Cf. Trustees of Tufts College v. Volpe Construction Co., 264 N.E.2d 676 (Sup.Jud.Ct. of Mass.1970), hold-

ing that a university, required by Section 301 of Executive Order 11246 to insert the equal opportunity clause in agreements with contractors in order to obtain federal assistance for the construction of a dormitory, can sue to enforce the contractor's promise to take affirmative action; Hadnott v. Laird, 317 F.Supp. 379 (D.C.D.C.1970), summarized at p. 945 supra.

3. After protracted proceedings and conciliation efforts, Secretary of Labor Shultz decided to accept a company offer to improve its recruitment practices despite his reservations about the settlement. In the Matter of Allen-Bradley Co., OFCC Docket No. 101–68. The Secretary said in part:

> I would prefer that the commitment specify additional procedures to correct the Company's violations with regard to its recruiting practices, its recruiting sources, and its image as an employer which discriminates.

> Notwithstanding my less than complete satisfaction with the program offered by the Company, my decision to accept it has been further influenced by other important factors. The first is my respect for the efforts of the blue-ribbon panel, chaired by Professor Meltzer, which assisted in mediating issues in this case coupled with my belief that the recommended "fruits of mediation," which I commissioned, should not be dismissed lightly.

> Secondly, it has been brought to my attention that substantial progress is being made by the Allen-Bradley Company in rectifying the violations found by the Panel. In this regard, it is my understanding that not only have recruiting violations been cured, but there have been substantial increases in the hiring of minorities by the Company. We should be mindful that it

is substance and results which concern us in the Equal Opportunity Program.

In light of my reservations, however, it is my further decision to direct a review of the entire equal opportunity posture of the Allen-Bradley Company by the OFCC, and such other compliance agencies as may be appropriate, six months after the date of this decision. That review shall examine the Company's compliance with the program it has proposed and I have herein accepted, to determine whether the results desired have been achieved. The review shall cover testing and other such standards for employment, upgrading and promotion which may be in use; the affirmative action plan which is required to be developed and kept on file by the Company; and other such practices as may be related to the Company's total compliance posture.

Compare the Newport News agreement, at pp. 934–938 supra, with the Allen-Bradley settlement.

4. Presidential anti-discrimination orders are discussed in, among others, Manning and Domesick, Title VII's Relationship and Effect on Executive Order 11246, 7 B.C.Ind. & Com.L.Rev. 561 (1966); Powers, Federal Procurement and Equal Employment Opportunity, 29 Law & Contemp.Prob. 468 (1964); Sovern, Legal Restraints on Racial Discrimination in Employment, Twentieth Century Fund, New York, 1966; Speck, Enforcement of Nondiscrimination Requirements for Government Contract Work, 63 Colum.L.Rev. 243 (1963); Note, Executive Order 11246: Anti-Discrimination Obligations in Government Contracts, 44 N.Y.U.L.Rev. 590 (1969); Note, Employment Discrimination and Title VII of the Civil Rights Act of 1964, 84 Harv.L.Rev. 1109, 1275–1304 (1971).

CONTRACTORS ASSOCIATION OF EASTERN PENNSYLVANIA v. SECRETARY OF LABOR

United States Court of Appeals,
Third Circuit.
442 F.2d 159 (1971).
Certiorari denied 404 U.S. 854, 92 S.Ct. 98,
30 L.Ed.2d 95.

Before HASTIE, Chief Judge, and McLAUGHLIN and GIBBONS, Circuit Judges.

OPINION OF THE COURT

GIBBONS, Circuit Judge. The original plaintiff, the Contractors Association of Eastern Pennsylvania (the Association) and the intervening plaintiffs, construction contractors doing business in the Philadelphia area (the Contractors), appeal from an order of the district court which denied their motion for summary judgment, granted the motion of the federal defendants to dismiss the Association complaint for lack of standing, and granted the cross-motion of the federal defendants for summary judgment.
*   *   *

The complaint challenges the validity of the Philadelphia Plan, promulgated by the federal defendants under the authority of Executive Order No. 11246. That Plan is embodied in two orders issued by officials of the United States Department of Labor, dated June 27, 1969 and September 23, 1969, respectively.

*   *   * In summary, they require that bidders on any federal or federally assisted construction contracts for projects in a five-county area around Philadelphia, the estimated total cost of which exceeds $500,000, shall submit an acceptable affirmative action program which includes specific goals for the utilization of minority manpower in six skilled crafts: ironworkers, plumbers and pipefitters,

steamfitters, sheetmetal workers, electrical workers, and elevator construction workers.

Executive Order No. 11246 requires all applicants for federal assistance to include in their construction contracts specific provisions respecting fair employment practices, including the provision:

> "The contractor will take affirmative action to ensure that applicants are employed, and that employees are treated during employment, without regard to their race, color, religion, sex or national origin."

The Executive Order empowers the Secretary of Labor to issue rules and regulations necessary and appropriate to achieve its purpose. On June 27, 1969 Assistant Secretary of Labor Fletcher issued an order implementing the Executive Order in the five-county Philadelphia area. The order required bidders, prior to the award of contracts, to submit "acceptable affirmative action" programs "which shall include specific goals of minority manpower utilization." The order contained a finding that enforcement of the "affirmative action" requirement of Executive Order No. 11246 had posed special problems in the construction trades. Contractors and subcontractors must hire a new employee complement for each job, and they rely on craft unions as their prime or sole source for labor. The craft unions operate hiring halls. "Because of the exclusionary practices of labor organizations," the order finds "there traditionally has been only a small number of Negroes employed in these seven trades."[8]

The June 27, 1969 order provided that the Area Coordinator of the Office of Federal Contract Compliance, in conjunction with the federal contracting and administering agencies in the Philadelphia area, would determine definite standards for specific goals in a contractor's affirmative action program. After such standards were determined, each bidder would be required to commit itself to specific goals for minority manpower utilization. The order set forth factors to be considered in determining definite standards, including:

> "1) The current extent of minority group participation in the trade.
>
> 2) The availability of minority group persons for employment in such trade.
>
> 3) The need for training programs in the area and/or the need to assure demand for those in or from existing training programs.
>
> 4) The impact of the program upon the existing labor force."

Acting pursuant to the June 29, 1969 order, representatives of the Department of Labor held public hearings in Philadelphia on August 26, 27 and 28, 1969. On September 23, 1969, Assistant Secretary Fletcher made findings with respect to each of the listed factors and ordered that the following ranges be established as the standards for minority manpower utilization for each of the designated trades in the Philadelphia area for the following four years:

Identification of Trade	Until 12/31/70	Range of Minority Group Employment for 1971	for 1972	for 1973
Ironworkers	5%–9%	11%–15%	16%–20%	22%–26%
Plumbers & Pipefitters	5%–8%	10%–14%	15%–19%	20%–24%
Steamfitters	5%–8%	11%–15%	15%–19%	20%–24%
Sheetmetal workers	4%–8%	9%–13%	14%–18%	19%–23%
Electrical workers	4%–8%	9%–13%	14%–18%	19%–23%
Elevator construction workers	4%–8%	9%–13%	14%–18%	19%–23%

[8] The order of June 27, 1969 listed "roofers and water proofers" among the trades underrepresented by minority craftsmen.

The order of September 23, 1969 dropped this category from the list, leaving the six trades previously named.

The order of September 23, 1969 specified that on each invitation to bid each bidder would be required to submit an affirmative action program. The order further provided:

"4. No bidder will be awarded a contract unless his affirmative action program contains goals falling within the range set forth * * * above. * * *

* * * * * *

6. The purpose of the contractor's commitment to specific goals as to minority manpower utilization is to meet his affirmative action obligations under the equal opportunity clause of the contract. This commitment is not intended and shall not be used to discriminate against any qualified applicant or employee. Whenever it comes to the bidder's attention that the goals are being used in a discriminatory manner, he must report it to the Area Coordinator of the Office of Federal Contract Compliance of the U. S. Department of Labor in order that appropriate sanction proceedings may be instituted.

* * * * * *

8. The bidder agrees to keep such records and file such reports relating to the provisions of this order as shall be required by the contracting or administering agency."

In November, 1969, the General State Authority of the Commonwealth of Pennsylvania issued invitations to bid for the construction of an earth dam on Marsh Creek in Chester County, Pennsylvania. Although this dam is a Commonwealth project, part of the construction cost, estimated at over $3,000,000 is to be funded by federal monies under a program administered by the Department of Agriculture. The Secretary of Agriculture, one of the federal defendants, as a condition for payment of federal financial assistance for the project, required the inclusion in each bid of a Philadelphia Plan Commitment in compliance with the order of September 23, 1969. On November 14, 1969, the General State Authority issued an addendum to the original invitation for bids requiring all bidders to include such a commitment in their bids. It is alleged and not denied that except for the requirement by the Secretary of Agriculture that the Philadelphia Plan Commitment be included, the General State Authority would not have imposed such a requirement on bidders.

The Association consists of more than eighty contractors in the five-county Philadelphia area who regularly employ workers in the six specified crafts, and who collectively perform more than $150,000,000 of federal and federally assisted construction in that area annually. Each of the contractor plaintiffs is a regular bidder on federal and federally assisted construction projects. The complaint was filed prior to the opening of bids on the Marsh Creek dam. It sought injunctive relief against the inclusion of a Philadelphia Plan Commitment requirement in the invitation for bids. * * *

The complaints of the Association and the Contractors refer to the fact that the Comptroller General of the United States has opined that the Philadelphia Plan Commitment is illegal and that disbursement of federal funds for the performance of a contract containing such a promise will be treated as unlawful.[10] The

10 Comp.Gen.Op., Letter to Sec. of Labor George P. Shultz, August 5, 1969, 115 Cong. Rec. 17,201–04 (daily ed. Dec. 18, 1969). The Comptroller General had objected to earlier efforts at implementing the "affirmative action" aspect of Exec.Order No. 11246 on the ground that these plans failed to inform prospective bidders of definite minimum standards for acceptable programs. In his negative opinion letter in response to the original Philadelphia Pre-Award Plan, he had also adverted to the possibility of conflict with Title VII of the Civil Rights Act of 1964. * * * The Title VII objections

plaintiffs point out that the withholding of funds after a contractor has commenced performance would have catastrophic consequences, since contractors depend upon progress payments, and are in no position to complete their contracts without such payments. They allege that the Philadelphia Plan is illegal and void for the following reasons:

1. It is action by the Executive branch not authorized by the constitution or any statute and beyond Executive power.

2. It is inconsistent with Title VII of the Civil Rights Act of 1964.

3. It is inconsistent with Title VI of the Civil Rights Act of 1964.

4. It is inconsistent with the National Labor Relations Act.

5. It is substantively inconsistent with and was not adopted in procedural accordance with Executive Order No. 11246.

6. It violates due process because
   a) it requires contradictory conduct impossible of consistent attainment;

   b) it unreasonably requires contractors to undertake to remedy an evil for which the craft unions, not they, are responsible;

   c) it arbitrarily and without basis in fact singles out the five-county Philadelphia area for discriminatory treatment without adequate basis in fact or law; and

   d) it requires quota hiring in violation of the Fifth Amendment.

The federal defendants moved both to dismiss the complaint under Rule 12(b)(1), Fed.R.Civ.P. and for summary judgment under Rule 56(b), Fed.R.Civ.P. They asserted that the plaintiffs lacked

became the heart of the opinion of August 5, 1969 which challenged the validity of the Revised Philadelphia Plan.

standing and that they were entitled to judgment as a matter of law. The plaintiffs moved for summary judgment. The district court held that the Association lacked standing to maintain the suit, that the Contractors had such standing, and that the Plan was valid, 311 F.Supp. 1002. It granted summary judgment for the federal defendants, and the plaintiffs appeal.

Standing

[W]e need not reach this issue, * * since the Contractor plaintiffs who as bidders are directly impacted by the requirement that they agree in their bid to comply with the Plan, clearly have standing. * * *

All plaintiffs have been represented by the same attorney, and the presence or absence of the Association as a plaintiff has no practical significance.

Executive Power

The plaintiffs contend that the Philadelphia Plan is social legislation of local application enacted by the Executive without the benefit of statutory or constitutional authority. They point out, probably correctly, that the Plan imposes on the successful bidder on a project of the Commonwealth of Pennsylvania record keeping and hiring practices which violate Pennsylvania law.[14] If the Plan was adopted pursuant to a valid exercise

[14] The Pennsylvania Human Relations Act, 43 P.S. § 951 et seq. (Supp.1970), specifically prohibits an employer from keeping any record of or using any form of application with respect to the race, color, religion, ancestry, sex or national origin of an applicant for employment. 43 P.S. § 955(b)(1). The Act also prohibits the use of a quota system for employment based on the same criteria. 43 P.S. § 955(b)(3). The record keeping prohibition may be of limited force due to certain requirements of Title VII of the Civil Rights Act of 1964. 42 U.S.C.A. § 2000e–8(c). Moreover, we do not know how the Pennsylvania courts or the Pennsylvania Human Relations Commission would react to a scheme of "benign" quota hiring.

of presidential power its provisions would, of course, control over local law. [Citations omitted.] But, say the plaintiffs, where there is neither statutory authorization nor constitutional authority for the Executive action, no substantive federal requirements may be imposed upon a contract between the Commonwealth and its contractor.

The district court's answer is that the federal government "has the unrestricted power to fix the terms, conditions and those with whom it will deal." For this proposition it cites Perkins v. Lukens Steel Co., 310 U.S. 113, 60 S.Ct. 869, 84 L. Ed. 1108 (1940) and King v. Smith, 392 U.S. 309, 333, 88 S.Ct. 2128, 20 L. Ed.2d 1118 (1968). Neither case is in point, however on the issue of Executive as distinguished from federal power. King v. Smith held that the Alabama substitute father regulation was inconsistent with the Social Security Act, 42 U.S.C.A. § 606(a), and points out that the federal government may impose the terms and conditions upon which its money allotments may be disbursed. The conditions referred to were imposed by Congress, not by the Executive branch. Perkins v. Lukens Steel Co. interprets the Public Contracts Act of June 30, 1936, which requires that sellers to the federal government pay prevailing minimum wages. It holds that an administrative determination of prevailing wages in a given industry made by the Secretary of Labor is not subject to judicial review on behalf of a potential seller.[17] The opinion contains the language:

"Like private individuals and businesses, the Government enjoys the unrestricted power to produce its own supplies, to determine those with whom it will deal, and to fix the terms and conditions upon which it will make needed purchases."

The quoted language refers to federal power exercised pursuant to a statutory mandate. The case is not in point on the issue of Executive power absent such a mandate.

The federal defendants and several amici contend that Executive power to impose fair employment conditions incident to the power to contract has been upheld in this circuit and in the Fifth Circuit. They cite Farmer v. Philadelphia Electric Company, 329 F.2d 3 (3d Cir. 1964) and Farkas v. Texas Instrument, Inc., 375 F.2d 629 (5th Cir.), cert. denied, 389 U.S. 977, 88 S.Ct. 480, 19 L.Ed.2d 471 (1967). Both cases discussed the Executive Order program for achieving fair employment in the context of Government contracts rather than federally assisted state contracts, and both assumed the validity of the Executive Order then applicable. Both cases held that even assuming the validity of the Executive Order, it did not give rise to a private cause of action for damages by a party subjected to discrimination. Discussion of the validity of the Executive Order was in each case dictum. Moreover, both *Farmer* and *Farkas* refer to 40 U.S.C.A. § 486 (a) as the source of the Executive power to issue the order. That subsection authorizes the President to prescribe such policies and directives as he deems necessary to effectuate the provisions of Chapter 10 of Title 40 [21] and Chapter 4 of Title 41.[22] These chapters deal with procurement of Government property and services, not with federal assistance programs. Thus even if *Farmer* and *Farkas* were holdings rather than dicta as to Executive power, the holdings would not reach the instant case. The validity of the Executive Order program as applied

---

[17] The actual holding of Perkins was subsequently nullified by Congress. 66 Stat. 308 (1952), 41 U.S.C.A. § 43a. See 4 K. Davis, Administrative Law § 28.06 (1958).

[21] Management and Disposal of Government Property.

[22] Procurement Procedures.

to the construction industry in state government contracts by virtue of federal assistance has not been litigated, so far as we have been able to determine, in any case reaching the courts of appeals.[23] Certainly no case has arisen which considers Executive power to impose, by virtue of federal assistance, contract terms in a state construction contract which are at variance with state law.

The limitations of Executive power have rarely been considered by the courts. One of those rare instances is Youngstown Sheet & Tube Co. v. Sawyer, 343 U.S. 579, 72 S.Ct. 863, 96 L.Ed. 1153 (1952). From the six concurring opinions and one dissenting opinion in that case, the most significant guidance for present purposes may be found in that of Justice Jackson:

"We may well begin by a somewhat oversimplified grouping of practical situations in which a President may doubt, or others may challenge, his powers, and by distinguishing roughly the legal consequences of this factor of relativity.

1. When the President acts pursuant to an express or implied authorization of Congress, his authority is at its maximum, for it includes all that he possesses in his own right plus all that Congress can delegate. In these circumstances, and in these only, may he be said (for what it may be worth) to personify the federal sovereignty. If his act is held unconstitutional under these circumstances, it usually means that the Federal Government as an undivided whole lacks power. A seizure executed by the President pursuant to an Act of Congress would be supported by the strongest of presumptions and the widest latitude of judicial interpretation, and the burden of persuasion would rest heavily on any who might attack it.

2. When the President acts in absence of either a congressional grant or denial of authority, he can only rely upon his own independent powers, but there is a zone of twilight in which he and Congress may have concurrent authority, or in which its distribution is uncertain. Therefore, congressional inertia, indifference or quiescence may sometimes, at least as a practical matter, enable, if not invite, measures on independent presidential responsibility. In this area, any actual test of power is likely to depend on the imperatives of events and contemporary imponderables rather than on abstract theories of law.

3. When the President takes measures incompatible with the expressed or implied will of Congress, his power is at its lowest ebb, for then he can rely only upon his own constitutional powers minus any constitutional powers of Congress over the matter. Courts can sustain exclusive presidential control in such a case only by disabling the Congress from acting upon the subject. Presidential claim to a power at once so conclusive and preclusive must be scrutinized with caution, for what is at stake is the equilibrium established by our constitutional system." [24]

Plaintiffs contend that the Philadelphia Plan is inconsistent with the will of Congress expressed in several statutes. We deal with these statutory contentions hereinafter. Thus for the moment we may set to one side consideration of Justice Jackson's third category, and turn to category (1), action expressly or impliedly authorized, and category (2), action in which the President has implied power to

[23] But cf. Weiner v. Cuyahoga Community College, 19 Ohio St.2d 35, 249 N.E.2d 907 (1969), cert. denied, 396 U.S. 1004, 90 S.Ct. 554, 24 L.Ed.2d 495 (1970); Ethridge v. Rhodes, 268 F.Supp. 83 (S.D.Ohio 1967).

[24] 343 U.S. at 635–638, 72 S.Ct. at 870–871 (footnotes omitted).

act in the absence of congressional pre-emption. To determine into which category the Philadelphia Plan falls a review of Executive Orders in the field of fair employment practices is helpful. [That review is omitted.]

While all federal procurement contracts must include an affirmative action covenant, the coverage on federally assisted contracts has been extended to construction contracts only. This choice is significant, for it demonstrates that the Presidents were not attempting by the Executive Order program merely to impose their notions of desirable social legislation on the states wholesale. Rather, they acted in the one area in which discrimination in employment was most likely to affect the cost and the progress of projects in which the federal government had both financial and completion interests. In direct procurement the federal government has a vital interest in assuring that the largest possible pool of qualified manpower be available for the accomplishment of its projects. It has the identical interest with respect to federally assisted construction projects. When the Congress authorizes an appropriation for a program of federal assistance, and authorizes the Executive branch to implement the program by arranging for assistance to specific projects, in the absence of specific statutory regulations it must be deemed to have granted to the President a general authority to act for the protection of federal interests. In the case of Executive Order Nos. 11246 and 11114 three Presidents have acted by analogizing federally assisted construction to direct federal procurement. If such action has not been authorized by Congress (Justice Jackson's first category), at the least it falls within the second category. If no congressional enactments prohibit what has been done, the Executive action is valid. Particularly is this so when Congress, aware of Presidential action with respect to fed-

erally assisted construction projects since June of 1963, has continued to make appropriations for such projects. We conclude, therefore, that unless the Philadelphia Plan is prohibited by some other congressional enactment, its inclusion as a pre-condition for federal assistance was within the implied authority of the President and his designees. We turn, then to a consideration of the statutes on which plaintiffs rely.

The Civil Rights Act of 1964

Plaintiffs suggest that by enacting Title VII of the Civil Rights Act of 1964, 42 U.S.C.A. § 2000e et seq., which deals comprehensively with discrimination in employment, Congress occupied the field. The express reference in that statute to Executive Order No. 10925 or any other Executive Order prescribing fair employment practices for Government contractors, 42 U.S.C.A. § 2000e–8(d), indicates, however, that Congress contemplated continuance of the Executive Order program. Moreover we have held that the remedies established by Title VII are not exclusive. Young v. International Telephone & Telegraph Co., 438 F.2d 757 (3d Cir. 1971).

But while Congress has not prohibited Presidential action in the area of fair employment on federal or federally assisted contracts, the Executive is bound by the express prohibitions of Title VII. The argument most strenuously advanced against the Philadelphia Plan is that it requires action by employers which violates the Act. Plaintiffs point to § 703 (j), 42 U.S.C.A. § 2000e–2(j):

"Nothing contained in this subchapter shall be interpreted to require any employer * * * [or] labor organization * * * to grant preferential treatment to any individual or to any group because of the race * * * of such individual or groups on account of an imbalance which may exist with respect to the total number or percentage of persons of any race * * * employed * * * in comparison with the total number or percentage of persons of such race * * * in the available work force in any community * * * or other area."

The Plan requires that the contractor establish specific goals for utilization of available minority manpower in six trades in the five-county area. Possibly an employer could not be compelled, under the authority of Title VII, to embrace such a program, although § 703(j) refers to percentages of minorities in an area work force rather than percentages of minority tradesmen in an available trade work force. We do not meet that issue here, however, for the source of the required contract provision is Executive Order No. 11246. Section 703(j) is a limitation only upon Title VII not upon any other remedies, state or federal.

* * *

Plaintiffs contend that the Plan, by imposing remedial quotas, requires them to violate the basic prohibitions of Section 703(a). * * *

Because the Plan requires that the contractor agree to specific goals for minority employment in each of the six trades and requires a good faith effort to achieve those goals, they argue, it requires (1) that they refuse to hire some white tradesmen, and (2) that they classify their employees by race, in violation of § 703(a). This argument rests on an overly simple reading both of the Plan and of the findings which led to its adoption.

The order of September 23, 1969 contained findings that although overall minority group representation in the construction industry in the five-county Philadelphia area was thirty per cent, in the six trades representation was approximately one per cent. It found, moreover, that this obvious underrepresentation was due to the exclusionary practices of the

unions representing the six trades. It is the practice of building contractors to rely on union hiring halls as the prime source for employees. The order made further findings as to the availability of qualified minority tradesmen for employment in each trade, and as to the impact of an affirmative action program with specific goals upon the existing labor force. The Department of Labor found that contractors could commit to the specific employment goals "without adverse impact on the existing labor force." Some minority tradesmen could be recruited, in other words, without eliminating job opportunities for white tradesmen.

To read § 703(a) in the manner suggested by the plaintiffs we would have to attribute to Congress the intention to freeze the status quo and to foreclose remedial action under other authority designed to overcome existing evils. We discern no such intention either from the language of the statute or from its legislative history. Clearly the Philadelphia Plan is color-conscious. Indeed the only meaning which can be attributed to the "affirmative action" language which since March of 1961 has been included in successive Executive Orders is that Government contractors must be color-conscious. Since 1941 the Executive Order program has recognized that discriminatory practices exclude available minority manpower from the labor pool. In other contexts color-consciousness has been deemed to be an appropriate remedial posture. Porcelli v. Titus, 302 F.Supp. 726 (D.N.J. 1969), aff'd, 431 F.2d 1254 (3d Cir. 1970); Norwalk CORE v. Norwalk Redevelopment Agency, 395 F.2d 920, 931 (2d Cir. 1968); Offermann v. Nitkowski, 378 F.2d 22, 24 (2d Cir. 1967). It has been said respecting Title VII that "Congress did not intend to freeze an entire generation of Negro employees into discriminatory patterns that existed before the Act." Quarles v. Philip Morris, Inc., supra, 279 F.Supp. at 514. The

Quarles case rejected the contention that existing, nondiscriminatory seniority arrangements were so sanctified by Title VII that the effects of past discrimination in job assignments could not be overcome.[47] We reject the contention that Title VII prevents the President acting through the Executive Order program from attempting to remedy the absence from the Philadelphia construction labor of minority tradesmen in key trades.

What we have said about Title VII applies with equal force to Title VI of the Civil Rights Act of 1964, 42 U.S.C.A. § 2000d et seq. That Title prohibits racial and other discrimination in any program or activity receiving federal financial assistance. This general prohibition against discrimination cannot be construed as limiting Executive authority in defining appropriate affirmative action on the part of a contractor.

We hold that the Philadelphia Plan does not violate the Civil Rights Act of 1964.

The National Labor Relations Act

The June 27, 1969 order, par. 8(b) provides:

> "It is no excuse that the union with which the contractor has a collective bargaining agreement failed to refer minority employees. Discrimination in referral for employment, even if pursuant to provisions of a collective bargaining agreement, is prohibited by the National Labor Relations Act and the Civil Rights Act of 1964. It is the longstanding uniform policy of OFCC that contractors and subcontractors have a responsibility to provide equal em-

ployment opportunity if they want to participate in federally involved contracts. To the extent they have delegated the responsibility for some of their employment practices to some other organization or agency which prevents them from meeting their obligations pursuant to Executive Order 11246, as amended, such contractors cannot be considered to be in compliance with Executive Order 11246, as amended, or the implementing rules, regulations and orders."

The union amici vigorously contend that the Plan violates the National Labor Relations Act by interfering with the exclusive union referral systems to which the contractors have in collective bargaining agreements bound themselves. Exclusive hiring hall contracts in the building and construction industry are validated by Section 8(f) of the National Labor Relations Act, 29 U.S.C.A. § 158(f).

* * *

It is clear that while hiring hall arrangements are permitted by federal law they are not required. Nothing in the National Labor Relations Act purports to place any limitation upon the contracting power of the federal government. We have said hereinabove that in imposing the affirmative action requirement on federally assisted construction contracts the President acted within his implied contracting authority. The assisted agency may either agree to do business with contractors who will comply with the affirmative action covenant, or forego assistance. The prospective contractors may either agree to undertake the affirmative action covenant, or forego bidding on federally assisted work. If the Plan violates neither the Constitution nor federal law, the fact that its contractual provisions may be at variance with other contractual undertakings of the contractor is legally irrelevant. Factually, of course, that variance is quite relevant. Factually it is en-

---

[47] The federal courts in overcoming the effects of past discrimination are expressly authorized in Title VII to take affirmative action. 42 U.S.C.A. § 2000e–5(g). See Vogler v. McCarty, 204 F.Supp. 368 (E.D.La.1968), aff'd. sub nom., International Ass'n Heat & Frost Insulation & Asbestos Workers v. Vogler, 407 F.2d 1047 (5th Cir. 1969).

tirely likely that the economics of the marketplace will produce an accommodation between the contract provisions desired by the unions and those desired by the source of the funds. Such an accommodation will be no violation of the National Labor Relations Act.

The absence of a judicial finding of past discrimination is also legally irrelevant. The Assistant Secretary acted not pursuant to Title VII but pursuant to the Executive Order. Regardless of the cause, exclusion from the available labor pool of minority tradesmen is likely to have an adverse effect upon the cost and completion of construction projects in which the federal government is interested. Even absent a finding that the situation found to exist in the five-county area was the result of deliberate past discrimination, the federal interest in improving the availability of key tradesmen in the labor pool would be the same. While a court must find intentional past discrimination before it can require affirmative action under 42 U.S.C.A. § 2000e–5(g), that section imposes no restraint upon the measures which the President may require of the beneficiaries of federal assistance. The decision of his designees as to the specific affirmative action which would satisfy the local situation did not violate the National Labor Relations Act and was not prohibited by 42 U.S.C.A. § 2000e–5(g).

Consistency with Executive Order No. 11246

* * *

Administrative action pursuant to an Executive Order is invalid and subject to judicial review if beyond the scope of the Executive Order. Peters v. Hobby, 349 U.S. 331, 75 S.Ct. 790, 99 L.Ed. 1129 (1955). But the courts should give more than ordinary deference to an administrative agency's interpretation of an Executive Order or regulation which it is charged to administer.

[Citations omitted.]

The Attorney General has issued an opinion that the Philadelphia Plan is valid,[50] and the President has continued to acquiesce in the interpretation of the Executive Order made by his designee. The Labor Department interpretation of the affirmative action clause must, therefore, be deferred to by the courts.

Plaintiffs also contend that the signing of the June 27, 1969 and September 23, 1969 orders by an assistant secretary rather than by the Secretary of Labor makes those orders procedurally invalid. Here they rely on § 401 which provides:

> "The Secretary of Labor may delegate to any officer, agency, or employee in the Executive branch of the Government, any function or duty of the Secretary under Parts II and III of this Order, except authority to promulgate rules and regulations of a general nature."

The Plan, they say, is a rule or regulation of a general nature, and could have been issued only by the Secretary. In the first place the Plan is not general. It is based upon findings as to the available construction manpower in a specific labor market. Moreover, the interpretation of § 401 made by the administrator requires the same deference from the courts as is required toward his other interpretations of the order. We will not second guess his delegation to the Assistant Secretary of the duty of enforcing the affirmative action covenant.

The Due Process Contentions

Plaintiffs urge that the Plan violates the Due Process Clause of the Fifth Amendment in several ways.

[50] Att'y Gen. Op., Letter to Sec. of Labor Shultz, Sept. 23, 1969, 115 Cong.Rec. 17,204–06 (daily ed. Dec. 18, 1969).

First, they allege that it imposes on the contractors contradictory duties impossible of attainment. This impossibility arises, they say, because the Plan requires both an undertaking to seek achievement of specific goals of minority employment and an undertaking not to discriminate against any qualified applicant or employee, and because a decision to hire any black employee necessarily involves a decision not to hire a qualified white employee. This is pure sophistry. The findings in the September 23, 1969 order disclose that the specific goals may be met, considering normal employee attrition and anticipated growth in the industry, without adverse effects on the existing labor force. According to the order the construction industry has an essentially transitory labor force and is often in short supply in key trades. The complaint does not allege that these findings misstate the underlying facts.

Next the plaintiffs urge that the Plan is arbitrary and capricious administrative action, in that it singles out the contractors and makes them take action to remedy the situation created by acts of past discrimination by the craft unions. They point to the absence of any proceedings under Title VII against the offending unions, and urge that they are being discriminated against. This argument misconceives the source of the authority for the affirmative action program. Plaintiffs are not being discriminated against. They are merely being invited to bid on a contract with terms imposed by the source of the funds. The affirmative action covenant is no different in kind than other covenants specified in the invitation to bid. The Plan does not impose a punishment for past misconduct. It exacts a covenant for present performance.

Some amici urge that selection of the five-county Philadelphia area was arbitrary and capricious and without basis in fact. The complaint contains a conclusive allegation to this effect. No supporting facts are alleged. It is not alleged, for example, that the specific goals for minority manpower utilization would be different if more or fewer counties were to be included in the September 23, 1969 order. The union amici do question the findings made by the Assistant Secretary of Labor, but the complaint, fairly read, does not put these findings in issue. We read the allegation with respect to the five-county area as putting in issue the legal authority of the Secretary to impose a specific affirmative action requirement in any separate geographic area. The simple answer to this contention is that federally assisted construction contracts are performed at specific times and in specific places. What is appropriate affirmative action will vary according to the local manpower conditions prevailing at the time.

Finally, the plaintiffs urge that the specific goals specified by the Plan are racial quotas prohibited by the equal protection aspect of the Fifth Amendment.

[Citations omitted.]

The Philadelphia Plan is valid Executive action designed to remedy the perceived evil that minority tradesmen have not been included in the labor pool available for the performance of construction projects in which the federal government has a cost and performance interest. The Fifth Amendment does not prohibit such action.

One final point. The plaintiffs contend that although there were cross-motions for summary judgment the district court, while it should have entered summary judgment in their favor, could not properly enter summary judgment against them. Several amici press this point on appeal even more strenuously than do plaintiffs. They contend that neither the finding of past discrimination by the craft unions made in the June 27, 1969 order nor the statistical findings as to availability of minority tradesmen, employee attrition, and industry growth made in the September 23, 1969 order should be accepted as true.

[T]he complaint to which the motions by the federal defendants was addressed nowhere challenges the factual underpinnings of the specific goals set forth in the September 23, 1969 order. Rather the complaint makes a legal attack upon the power of the Department of Labor to impose these goals as contractual commitments. Read generously the complaint can be construed to challenge the administrative procedures followed by the Assistant Secretary in determining these goals. We have dealt hereinabove with that challenge insofar as it questions compliance with the procedures specified in Executive Order No. 11246. Insofar as the complaint challenges on broader administrative law grounds the methods by which the Assistant Secretary assembled the data for the September 23, 1969 order, we hold that public hearings after notice were an appropriate means for the administrative agency to obtain the information needed for informed judgment. Cf. Shannon v. Department of Housing & Urban Development, 436 F. 2d 809 (3d Cir. 1971). No public hearing was held prior to the issuance of the June 27, 1969 order, which contains the Assistant Secretary's finding of past exclusionary union practices. He relied upon published data, however, which itself may have been sufficient to justify administrative action leading to the specification of contract provisions. We need not decide that issue, however, for in our view the data in the September 23, 1969 order revealing the percentages of utilization of minority group tradesmen in the six trades compared with the availability of such tradesmen in the five-county area, justified issuance of the order without regard to a finding as to the cause of the situation. The federal interest is in maximum availability of construction tradesmen for the projects in which the federal

government has a cost and completion interest. A finding as to the historical reason for the exclusion of available tradesmen from the labor pool is not essential for federal contractual remedial action.

The judgment of the district court will be affirmed.

Notes

1. Informative treatments of the Philadelphia Plan can be found in Leiken, Preferential Treatment in the Skilled Building Trades: An Analysis of the Philadelphia Plan, 56 Cornell L.Rev. 84 (1970); Nash, Affirmative Action Under Executive Order 11,246, 46 N.Y.U.L. Rev. 225 (1971); The Philadelphia Plan: Equal Employment Opportunity in the Construction Trades, 6 Colum.J. of Law and Social Problems 187 (1970). All three articles discuss analogous plans in other localities. For the text of the "Washington Plan", see 41 C.F.R. Part 60–5 (1971).

2. The Columbia piece offers the following summary of Order No. 4, 41 C.F. R. Part 60–2 (1971), the nearest thing to the Philadelphia Plan for federal contractors outside the construction industry:

By the terms of this Order, the contractors must consider nine factors: (1) minority population in the surrounding labor pool; (2) extent of minority unemployment; (3) percentage of minority work force relative to the total work force in the area; (4) availability of skilled minority workers in an area in which the contractor can reasonably recruit; (5) availability of skilled minority workers; (6) availability of promotable minority workers already employed by the contractor; (7) anticipated expansion, contraction and turnover of the work force; (8) existence of training facilities for minority workers; and (9) the degree of training which the contractor can reasonably undertake. In essence, both the Philadelphia Plan and Order 4 require the percentage of minority employees of a government contractor to equal the percentage of minority members in the qualified surrounding work force. 6 Colum.J. of Law and Social Problems at 196.

Is the final sentence of the passage just quoted consistent with the main case?

3. Accord with the main case, Southern Illinois Builders Ass'n v. Ogilvie, 5 EPD ¶ 8085 (7th Cir. 1972), upholding the "Ogilvie Plan"; Joyce v. McCrane, 320 F.Supp. 1284 (D.C.N.J.1970), upholding a New Jersey plan that set goals of 30 to 37% utilization of minority journeymen and emphasizing that, "Sanctions cannot be imposed under the Plan if the contractors strive to meet these goals and fall short." Cf. Weiner v. Cuyahoga Community College District, 19 Ohio St.2d 35, 249 N.E.2d 907 (1969), certiorari denied 396 U.S. 1004 (1970), holding that a bidder for a public construction contract can legally be required to submit an affirmative action plan as a condition of his bid, but asserting in a dictum that, "The establishment of a quota of employment of any particular minority would also be discriminatory in violation of the Civil Rights Act of 1964."

4. Rev.Code Wash.Anno. § 49.04.-100 provides that "Joint apprenticeship programs entered into under authority of chapter 49.04 RCW and which receive any state assistance in instructional or other costs, shall as a part thereof include entrance of minority races in such program, when available, in a ratio not less than the ratio which the minority race represents in population to the actual population in the city or trade area concerned. * * *" Compare the approach of New York Human Rights Law sec. 296(1–a), supra.

5. To what extent, if at all, do the Philadelphia Plan and comparable re-

quirements rest on the assumption that those governed by them have discriminated in the past? May more rigorous requirements be imposed on those actually found to have discriminated? Consider, for example, Local 53, Asbestos Workers v. Vogler, 407 F.2d 1047 (5th Cir. 1969), approving a district court order requiring a union that had violated Title VII to alternate job referrals, on a one-to-one basis, between blacks and whites until objective criteria for union membership were developed; United States v. Local 86, Ironworkers, 315 F.Supp. 1202 (W.D.Wash.1970), affirmed 443 F.2d 544 (9th Cir. 1971), requiring apprenticeship committees that had discriminated "to insure a minimum participation by blacks in the building trades' apprenticeship programs of 30 percent of each class" and contractors who had violated Title VII to "establish and maintain a preapprentice program [with stipulated numbers of jobs] for blacks, notwithstanding any provisions in the collective bargaining agreements to the contrary." 315 F.Supp. at 1247, 1248. And review Carter v. Gallagher, supra at p. 920. Cf. United States v. Montgomery County Bd. of Ed., 395 U.S. 225 (1969).

THE MODEL ANTI-DISCRIMINATION ACT APPROVED BY THE NATIONAL CONFERENCE OF COMMISSIONERS ON UNIFORM STATE LAWS, 1966

Section 310. [Imbalance Plans]

It is not a discriminatory practice for a person subject to this chapter to adopt and carry out a plan to fill vacancies or hire new employees so as to eliminate or reduce imbalance with respect to race, color, religion, sex, or national origin if the plan has been filed with the Commission under regulations of the Commission and the Commission has not disapproved the plan.

COMMENT: This section is designed to permit the adoption of voluntary plans to reduce or eliminate imbalance, subject to the power of the Commission to disapprove plans pursuant to its regulations. Several states have enacted similar provisions with respect to racial imbalance in schools.

———

KAPLAN, EQUAL JUSTICE IN AN UNEQUAL WORLD: EQUALITY FOR THE NEGRO—THE PROBLEM OF SPECIAL TREATMENT

61 Northwestern Law Review 363 (1966).

*   *   *

The problems involved in special and preferential treatment for the Negro are difficult and subtle ones. True, one can parody the whole idea by paraphrasing the pigs in George Orwell's Animal Farm and asserting that all men are equal, but Negroes are more equal than others. And admittedly, there is a certain irony in climaxing a long struggle in the name of equality by demanding inequality. The fact is, however, that even within our usual ideals of equality, a series of arguments can be made for special treatment for Negroes.

The first argument begins with the assertion that although we still have a long way to go in achieving a society where race is as irrelevant to the economic, political, or social rights of any individual as is his eye color, the great strides we have taken toward that goal in the last decade indicate that some time in the not-too-distant future we will approach that type of society in large areas of the United States. At that time, at the latest, we will have to attend to the problem of the many Negroes who have been casualties of our history of race relations. Though they will then be judged on their indi-

vidual worth alone, their history will have left them so educationally, economically, and psychologically disadvantaged that unless they receive special preference, they and the vast majority of their children will be condemned by our now color-blind society to perpetual deprivation in the midst of surrounding affluence.[16] If, the argument continues, preferential treatment for the Negro will be necessary when our society becomes color blind, how much more important is it today when our society imposes so many obstacles to achievement of equality by the Negro.

A somewhat different argument is based on the premise that we achieve true equality only by treating persons according to their need. Certainly we see no conflict between our ideals of equality and the granting of special treatment to the handicapped.[17] And we not only tax the poor at a lower rate than the rich but we have a whole variety of social programs which, while they do not actually produce equality, nonetheless treat the needy in a sense more favorably than the wealthy.

The treatment-according-to-need argument often uses the analogy of a foot-race in which one of the runners has been shackled for the entire time. We could not simply remove his chains and let the race continue. Not only would he then be far behind in the race, but also, from want of exercise and various other disabilities, he would be much less able to continue. The thrust of this argument is that the only treatment consistent with equality is one which does not merely allow the foot-race to proceed but which

[16] Kenyon, in Equality 76–93 (1965).

[17] See Miller, in Equality 29 (1965) "Large-scale hire-the-handicapped programs are undertaken without objection; yet loss of a leg is often less of a handicap than being born with a dark skin, and physical handicaps have not been deliberately inflicted as have racial handicaps."

somehow propels the last place runner back into contention.

Nor will it do to assert that this argument is fallacious in making a blanket assumption about Negroes, which applies to some, but not all. The ready reply is that our society often predicates special treatment upon judgments as to the needs of some but not all the members of a class, plus an unwillingness to draw distinctions exempting the relatively few who are not in need. Thus laws requiring shorter hours for women than for men are not based on the supposition that all women are frailer and less healthy than all men. The convenience of simple lines is important also, and it has been therefore argued that unless "looking at color" is used, "elaborate machinery" will have to be set up in many cases to determine "need * * * and social workism will be tremendously increased." [18]

Another argument for preferential treatment for Negroes invokes Aristotle's commutative rather than his distributive justice. This asserts that since our white society has enslaved and exploited the Negro, leaving him in far worse condition to compete in and enjoy the benefits of our society, it is only fair that each victim of this wrong be compensated for his injuries—whether or not he is presently in need. This is especially so, the argument goes, since the white society which damaged the Negro has been unjustly enriched by benefiting from slavery and cheap Negro labor. In addition, over and above the measurable financial loss inflicted, compensation may be claimed for pain, suffering and humiliation. There has, indeed, been some precedent for the recognition of this type of obligation. We have sought to compensate American Indians for lands taken away from their ancestors and, though to some the comparison may be odious, the West German government has paid millions of

dollars to Israel in reparation for Nazi crimes against Jews. This repayment of a debt theory avoids the thorny issue of the correspondence between color and need. Under this view, "the professional Negro, the Negro businessman, and those able to climb the ladder despite their handicaps would each be much further along than they are if it were not for the immoral practices of the white society," [19] and hence are legitimate objects of compensation.

The final category of arguments for granting special treatment to Negroes appeals to our self-interest rather than our morality. Some versions would have us treat the Negro in the United States as we would an underdeveloped country—a country with enormous possibilities both for productive power and for consuming the products of American industry. Advocates of this position point out that the bringing up of the Negro to full economic equality with the white man in the United States would at the present time increase the gross national product by $13 billion per year [20] and would in addition ease the drain on our economy caused by welfare expenditures and crime.[21] Others cite an even more in-

[18] Marcuse, in Equality 147 (1965).

[19] Id. at 149.

[20] Joint Economic Committee, 1964 Joint Economic Report, S.Rep.No.931, 88th Cong., 2d Sess. 61 (1965).

[21] Though one may argue that it is only insofar as it attempts to raise the level of the poor in the United States that special treatment for the Negro makes economic sense, two answers—inconsistent with each other but neither obviously false—can be given. The first proceeds from the fact that the Negro has been the object of intense discrimination to the conclusion that the depressed groups in our society contain an unusually high percentage of talented Negroes who with only a relatively slight push and at comparatively low cost can be raised from poverty. The second argument takes into account the psychological damage done the Negro by slavery and segregation and concludes that therefore additional effort will be required to overcome this specifically racial handicap. Compare, U. S. Bureau of the

tensely practical reason. Regardless of the needs of any other groups, Negroes, and more specifically, lower-class Negroes, are social dynamite. Now and for some time to come it will be these Negroes who most hate our white society, if not all whites personally. As their expectations rise they will find their present condition more and more intolerable and our only hope to avoid the most explosive and dangerous type of conflict is to grease the axle where it is squeaking and grant them special treatment.[22]

PREFERENCE IN EMPLOYMENT

For many reasons, by far the greatest pressure for preferential treatment for Negroes involves the employment area. The Negro unemployment rate is approximately twice that of the rest of the population and is concentrated most heavily among the young. Moreover, even among the employed, the Negro worker receives only 50% of the income of the white worker and this gap, at least in dollar terms, is widening—from 1951 to 1962 the average annual income of Negro male workers increased $963; that of white workers increased by $2,117.[23] Before the Negro can achieve anything else in our society he needs both the income from and the dignity of a job.[24]

Of course, one can argue that questions of preference for Negroes need never be faced, since a variety of completely color-blind programs—from training programs for the poor to massive public works

projects in the urban, and largely Negro, slums—will do more good. Moreover, it can be asserted that like all such controversies which involve distribution of the pieces of a static pie, the problem can be obviated merely by using a bigger pie. Admittedly, large allocations of resources toward training and finding employment for the unemployed, and all measures which produce a more prosperous economy, will not only benefit the Negro but probably do so much more than any practicable preference plan.[25] This does not make the problems of preference for Negroes irrelevant, however. For the foreseeable future we will still be faced with the facts that poverty will afflict a disturbingly large percentage of our population, and that, of those most afflicted, a disproportionately high percentage will be Negro. Moreover, no practicable amounts of public spending can cure either of these problems in the next generation or so. Indeed the other demands on government resources being what they are, it is very possible that any governmental effort will be accounted a success if it merely offsets the impact of automation—which seems to be abolishing just the jobs which we would expect large numbers of Negroes to begin moving into—leaving the situation no worse than it is today. In short, resources are limited, and even after we have allocated a "proper" amount to these problems, we will still be faced with the question of whether to stretch them further by somehow concentrating their benefits on the Negro. Of the methods of doing this, probably the most discussed has been that of employment preference.

Though any discussion of securing the Negro a larger share of our economic well-being through some type of employment preference raises dozens of issues,

Census Current Population Reports, Series P–20, No. 142, Negro Population: March 1964 at 7 (1965) with Young, To Be Equal 22 (1964).

[22] See, e. g., Report by the Governor's Commission on the Los Angeles Riots (1965).

[23] Moynihan Political Perspectives, in The Negro Challenge to the Business Community 76 (Ginzberg ed. 1964).

[24] Certainly one of the major reasons for the urgency of the employment problem is the effect of the problem of male unemployment upon the Negro family structure.

[25] It is estimated that a massive public works program in urban depressed areas would reach 72% of the nation's Negroes. Miller, in Equality 33 (1965).

we will concentrate our attention here on three main questions: first, can the government require private employers to prefer Negroes in hiring; second, to what extent may an employer be permitted to grant preferential treatment to Negroes if it so desires—especially in a jurisdiction covered by a fair employment law which prohibits discrimination against a job applicant because of his race; and third, under what conditions may Negroes be granted preference in public employment.

*   *   *

Let us then turn to the question of whether the government can require private employers to grant employment preference to Negroes. Although this question has, of course, a constitutional dimension, it is easier to consider, first, certain institutional and political constraints that will establish the relatively narrow limits in which any preference plan would have to operate. While these limitations are not directly related to any constitutional provision, they would of course exert a great influence on a court's determination of the permissible extent of governmental action in this area.

The operation of these constraints can be observed by examining the ways the government might compel the hiring of Negroes for jobs which others, by hypothesis, are better able to perform. Presumably, the establishment of one huge government hiring office to make all employment decisions would, for a host of reasons, be out of the question. At the other end of the spectrum would appear to be a quota system simply requiring an employer to maintain a given percentage of Negroes in his working force, but leaving the great bulk of the employment decisions in his hands. The individual employer than would be left to determine how to hire the necessary number of Negroes and how best to adapt his enterprise to their training and talents.

Though for this reason, a quota system would seem the easiest type of preference to enforce, it is not nearly so simple as might appear. Too low a quota might serve as a ceiling on Negro employment, while one too high might place an unrealistic and expensive burden upon the employer to find Negroes where none existed. Moreover, quotas would have to vary from industry to industry. It is one thing to expect a steel plant to employ 12% Negroes; it may be quite a different burden to expect an accounting firm to do this. A sensible quota system might then require consideration, for each different employer, of the different types of work done and the degree of skill and education which they required. The many industries which require the aid of their unions in determining job classifications bear witness to how difficult this is to do from above. Moreover, any large-scale setting of quotas is an extremely complex business. Since a major variable affecting this decision would be the availability of Negroes of a given level of competence, not only would the filling of quotas for one industry change the labor pool available for all the others, but the quotas would have to vary from city to city and area to area. Negro residential patterns, not only within cities but within the nation as a whole, are relatively inflexible; not only do some areas—especially near the centers of largest cities—have large concentrations of Negroes, but far larger areas have only a minute proportion.[26] In these areas, despite great inducement to Negroes, employers would be unable to fill any but a vanishingly small quota. It is, to be sure, possible that the very inflexibility of the quota system would force employers to train Negroes for occupancy of a much

[26] Although Negroes comprise 10.5% of the nation's population, there are eleven Northern states in which less than 1% of the population is Negro. U. S. Bureau of Census Statistical Abstract of the United States: 1965, at 26 (86th ed.)

larger range of jobs, and perhaps even to combat residential segregation by offering Negroes incentives to move into areas where their labor is in short supply. On the other hand, all that might result is bidding between different employers for the capable Negroes who already have jobs or are self-employed, while those who really need the preference would remain unaffected.

In theory, less rigid than the quota would be the simple requirement that the fact that a job applicant is a Negro should be weighed somehow in his favor. This view can mean merely that where two applicants, white and Negro, are equal in terms of ability to perform the job, the Negro should be selected.[27] Unfortunately, however, such a formulation has many disadvantages. Especially if the suitability for later promotion may be considered, the number of relevant qualities in which men may differ is so large that, in real life employment situations, equality of job applicants is relatively rare. Moreover, preference for the Negro, if it is to be more than marginally effective, must be considerably greater than this. On the other hand, if we are willing to throw aside exact equality and to demand only that preference be given to the Negro where approximate equality exists, the difficulty of setting standards by which employers can tell what is required of them becomes more serious, and the greater the differences of ability we consider as within the rubric of approximate equality, the greater this problem becomes.

Another method of giving preference to the Negro would be to follow the analogy of the veterans' preference on civil service examinations and require the hiring of the Negro if his ability was within a specific, measurable distance of

that of his white competitor. In principle, a Negro credit seems no less practicable than a veteran's credit. We must realize, however, that the decision as to the amount of the credit is not an easy one. If the credit is too small, it will not move enough of its beneficiaries into contention for jobs and if it is too large it may result in the hiring of incompetent employees at too great a social cost.

Moreover, the situation becomes much more complicated when we attempt to give preference to two different categories of applicants. Thus, if a veteran's credit of 10 points were already in effect and a Negro credit of, say, 10 points were superimposed upon it, a Negro veteran might receive too great a preference. One can conceive of a job market able to absorb, without a serious loss of efficiency, a 10 but not a 20 point credit. Of course, this might be remedied by allowing the use of one or the other but not both credits. One could argue however, that this discriminates against the Negro veteran as contrasted with other Negroes or, alternatively, as contrasted with other veterans. And though it is possible that one could take less than the sum of the two preferences, say 15 points for the Negro veteran, and still remain at the necessary competence level, there would be constant pressure to maintain each of the preferences at the maximum level consistent with obtaining employees of the necessary level of competence.

The main institutional problem with the analogy to the veterans' preference, of course, is that the great majority of jobs, especially those for which large numbers of Negroes are closest to being qualified, are not filled through the type of white collar tests where it is easy to specify a credit. Though in theory not impossible, it is a most difficult matter in most industries to devise any general quantifiable methods of giving specific degrees of preference to Negro applicants. For instance, if a generally ade-

---

[27] This is the position taken by Whitney Young of the National Urban League. Young, supra note 21 at 61.

quate worker received job preference through ignoring his lack of one particular skill, it might prove difficult to prevent his assignment to a job where that skill was essential.

Of course, governmental coercion is not the only method of inducing employers to give preference to Negroes. Subsidies could be paid, tax credits allowed, surplus property sold, or government contracts awarded to complaisant employers. The problem, however, is that this in no way lessens the problems of quotas and preferences which we have previously discussed. As soon as we attempt to determine which employers are now entitled to the government benefits, we must face these issues again.

In addition to the institutional difficulties in enforcing any system of job preference for Negroes, there are, of course, several other weighty arguments against such a scheme. First of all, an effective system of preference may be extremely expensive. Productive inefficiency can only result when better workers are rejected in favor of those less qualified. Presumably this explains why many of the advocates of employment preference for Negroes envision assembly lines or other routine work, where it is assumed that the output of two workers will be about the same even though there may be a considerable difference in their abilities. And even where the output of the two workers might be measurably different, one can be more comfortable advocating preference if he considers the type of work unimportant. Thus, though the advocates of preference in the retail selling trade seem to be willing to put up with the inconvenience this might entail, no one would recommend that preference be given to Negro brain surgeons. We feel that not only is this occupation very important, but that, in it, every little bit of skill is crucial.

The brain surgeon example also points up another difficulty with employment preference for Negroes. The consequences of any deficiency in the brain surgeon will not be spread thinly over society; rather they will be concentrated in the form of serious damage to a small number of almost randomly selected individuals. However, all preference schemes to a greater or lesser extent involve the unequal distribution of higher costs over society. One can even think of situations in which job preference for the Negro, by raising the cost of products which are consumed primarily by other Negroes will, in the long as well as the short run, be a net drain on the Negro's resources. For years, certain school systems have been giving preference to Negro teachers, either out of a desire to have Negroes better represented on their staffs, or else simply to man their Negro schools. It has only recently become apparent that in many cases the immediate advantages of employing less adequate Negro teachers have been more than counterbalanced by the disadvantages forced upon their usually Negro students.[28]

Preference for Negroes may backfire in other ways, too. For a host of reasons, the percentage of Negro women able to compete in the job market has been higher than that of Negro men. Even while we recognize that this is one of the basic causes of the damaged Negro family structure—one of the most serious and fundamental obstacles to equality for the Negro—we may be exacerbating the situation unless we use care to make certain that any quota or other preference plan does not result in the increased disproportion of employed Negro women over men.

Moreover, insofar as the Negro candidates for job preference are less quali-

[28] See Kaplan, Segregation Litigation and the Schools—Part III: The Gary Litigation, 59 Nw.U.L.Rev. 121, 152–55 (1965).

fied than their white competitors, firms in areas with a low concentration of Negroes will be aided at the competitive expense of those where a large Negro labor pool exists, thus influencing plant locations and expansions in a way so as to diminish the total job opportunities available to Negroes.

On the other hand, this economic argument can be overdone. Many desirable forms of social legislation exercise a distorting effect on our economy. Unemployment insurance often exerts a pressure on employers to avoid laying off workers where economically this would be the most efficient course. And even if this is regarded as forcing a business to bear the social cost of its off again, on again hiring policy, it is harder to make the same argument with respect to minimum wage laws. Moreover, in many areas, such as the building trades, the operation of the usual laws of supply and demand have been so frustrated by cartelization that it is hard to argue that the superimposition of some type of preference for Negroes would distort the economic production of goods in any significant way.

Probably more serious even than the "economic" difficulties with any preference scheme is the unfairness to those workers in competition with the preferred Negroes. Nor is it persuasive that such preference would more equitably spread unemployment over society—either on the simple theory that the unemployment rate among white workers is one-half that among Negroes, or on the somewhat more sophisticated theory that employment patterns in those areas where it is impractical to enforce any preferential treatment may for the foreseeable future favor whites.

The major problem with this type of argument is that it conceals a built-in assumption that a preference for Negroes will secure employment for them at the expense of the middle-class whites. The fact is, however, that preference for the Negro is, in today's world, discrimination against the members of those groups which are most similar to the Negro. It is the Puerto Rican, the Mexican, the Appalachian white and the American Indian who would feel the brunt of preferential treatment for the Negro, and it is just they who are least able to bear the burdens of preference for others. Put another way, the fallacy of talking about equalizing the burdens of unemployment is that it confuses the group with its members. Preference for the Negro simply means preference for individual Negroes on the grounds that they are Negroes. When we talk of raising the Negro to equality all we mean is that we wish to have more of those whom we consider Negroes participate more fully in the benefits of our society. Our society, however, contains large numbers of people of all races who, by any standard, do not have an adequate share of its benefits. They form what Gunnar Myrdal calls the underclass—the self-perpetuating group at the bottom level of our society who have lost the ability and the hope of moving up.[29] And though certainly the underclass contains a higher percentage of the nation's Negroes than of any other racial group (with the possible exception of the American Indian) at least two-thirds of its members are not Negroes and well over half of the Negro population of the U. S. does not belong to this underclass. In other words, the underclass forms just as distinctive a group in our society as does the Negro—and indeed membership in this group is a considerably better guide to the need for societal assistance or preference than is membership in the Negro "race." And though, with respect to the Negro members of this underclass, it is relatively easy to isolate specific types of deprivation at

[29] Myrdal, Challenge to Affluence 34–49 (1963).

the hands of society and thereby explain their present status, the chances are that if we examine all the other members, we will find that each of them, in one way or another, has somehow been injured by our society. At the very least, we can say that the great majority of the underclass have been without personal fault in their condition. Is it so very important,[30] then, that one very specific type of deprivation was visited upon the Negro members of the underclass? One can, of course, argue that the Negro member has special psychological problems which are not shared by the rest of the underclass. Assuming this is true, its relevance on the issue of job preference is hardly clear. Moreover, we know very little about the other members of the underclass and it is well within the realm of possibility that many of them have psychological problems equal to those of the Negro. Certainly, they have had to confront their own obvious failure without the ready excuse available to the Negro.

The Negro can, of course, be distinguished from the rest of the underclass on the ground that only he is the object of hostile discrimination in employment. Hence, it can be argued that the Negro who would be barred by his race from competing for many positions should be given preference, at least in some jobs, to make up for this and to put him on an equal footing with the rest of the underclass. Discriminating in the Negro's favor on this ground is rational, however, only if we assume the same individuals who suffer because of our preferring the Negro will be the beneficiaries of private anti-Negro discrimination. In fact, of course, this is not the case. Though perhaps discrimination against Mexicans or Puerto Ricans may not be as extensive as against Negroes, these groups are themselves often the targets of dis-

crimination and we are by no means redressing any balance by further discriminating against them in order to prefer Negroes.[31] This is even more clear where preference is given one group of Negroes to make up for discrimination against an entirely different group. It is hard to justify preference for New York Negroes on the ground that Alabama Negroes are the victims of discrimination.

More important even than the abstract justice of such preference is the effect it would have on American society. Regardless of whether a sophisticated analysis can show that the Negro is entitled to job preference at the expense of the rest of the underclass, it is most unlikely that the Negroes' competitors will agree. Quite the contrary; it is clear that any attempt to secure preferential treatment for Negroes in the employment area will be extremely divisive. In addition to the previously-mentioned groups, whose economic well-being is not perceptibly better than the Negro's, those most affected by job preference for the Negro would be the second generation Americans and the poor whites who have most bitterly resented his march toward equality. A major factor which has tended to weaken this opposition is our ethic that men are entitled to be treated on their individual worth alone. It is one thing to tell those in job competition with the Negro that because of tihs principle they can no longer enjoy an advantage which they (or, more likely, others) had previously enjoyed; it is very different to tell them that this principle must now be modified to put them at a disadvantage. Those who will feel the pinch most strongly have not only not benefited

---

[30] Except in the important sense politically that it is the Negroes who most show signs of rioting.

[31] An economist recently told the California Fair Employment Practices Commission that Mexican-Americans have a more severe employment handicap than Negroes. He cited language difficulties and occupations that are seasonal or short-term as major factors. San Francisco Chronicle, March 18, 1966, p. 9, col. 1.

from the exploitation of Negroes, but may in fact have been harmed by it—if only because this caused a depression in their own wage rates. In terms of education and training, as well as any other measurable standard, the members of the rest of the underclass are no better off than most Negroes; to attempt to give Negroes formal legal preference over them will only exacerbate what is already a serious source of tension. It has been argued that the poor Negro can move forward only by creating new alliances with poor whites. It is hard to think of a better way than preference to prevent this.

The divisive effect of preferential treatment exists, moreover, not only when it is instituted, but also when it ceases. The question of how one decides when to cease what all agree is to be only a temporary preferential treatment is a thorny one. Though it would seem easy to say that preferential treatment should cease when the average Negro reaches the same economic, social and educational level as the average white person, there is not even agreement on this. It has been argued, by analogy to the argument presented earlier of compensation for previous pain and suffering, that the preferential treatment should continue until the Negro has not only made up the distance he is behind in the foot-race,[32] but also until he is far enough ahead to repay him for the humiliations he has suffered.[33] And even if the attainment of simple equality is determined to be enough, one can think of literally a dozen different indices of equality which might be used by one side or the other in the battles over when to do away with preference. Some have recognized this problem, but dismissed it. They have argued that the basic idea, though necessary, is an affront to the

Negro's dignity, and hence that the Negro will not wish preferential treatment any longer than absolutely essential.[34] It is hard, however, to see why the Negro would be any more willing to give up a concrete economic advantage than have been the farmer and those benefited by protective tariffs. Experience indicates that whenever a temporary benefit is extended to any group there will always be members of it who will come to rely on it or claim that it has become, for some reason, a matter of right.

The divisiveness of preferential treatment extends beyond its institution and cessation. So long as preferential treatment for Negroes is institutionalized, a principle will have been established which will encourage constant effort by other ethnic groups to achieve the same kind of treatment. Although today the Negro is the only member of the underclass who is reasonably well organized, one can already see signs that this is changing, and that the value of organization is coming to be appreciated by several other minorities.[35] And though many arguments can be made that the Negro is entitled to spe-

[32] See * * * N. Y. Times, April 10, 1966, p. 1, "Shipyard in South Induced to Make Up For Past Bias":

[33] Marcuse, in Equality 151 (1965).

[34] Marcuse, in Equality 170 (1965). "No man, woman, or child likes to be singled out as needing special assistance; every individual wants to stand on his own two feet, and compensatory treatment beyond a certain point is an affront to pride and an insult to dignity. Particularly is this so when race is involved, and each minor example of preference is a continual reminder of racial differentiation. The Negro community itself will therefore demand no more compensation than is required to permit it to overcome those handicaps that past discrimination has caused; past that point, the Negro community will be as vehemently opposed to preferential treatment as some members of the white community are now."

[35] For example, the American Indian Association recently asked a doll manufacturing firm to stop production of a toy named "Nutty Mad Indian." The Association claims that the "grotesque, gyrating figure in war paint crazily banging a war drum" is "highly derogatory" to the 550,000 American Indian citizens and "especially humiliating to Indian children." San Francisco Chronicle, March 7, 1966.

cial treatment in a way that no other group is, we can expect to hear several other minorities present their cases.[36] It is after all hard to say that the moral claim of the Negro is so much greater than that of the American Indian, who once ruled the continent and was slaughtered wholesale, deprived of his land, and penned up upon reservations. In the tax field we have thus a paradigm of the departure from principle to bestow a benefit on one group, carrying with it the divisiveness caused by others who regard their claim as equally good. The legislative treatment of percentage depletion has become a constant headache, with one group after another demanding in, on the ground that it *has* as much right as the present beneficiaries.[37] And in the preference area an equal claim to that of the Negro may not be necessary. The Mexican-American may perhaps argue for preference not so much on the ground that his claim is as good as that of the Negro, but rather on the ground that his situation is closer to the Negro's than to those who must bear the burdens imposed by the preference system. Many authorities have argued for the separation principle of the First Amendment not because it protects religion from government, but rather because it minimizes the likelihood that the government will be drawn into religious controversies.[38] Any effort which would draw the government more than absolutely necessary into blatantly ethnic controversies may be suspect on that ground alone.[39]

The previously-mentioned argument that the Negro himself will wish to do away with the affront of preferential treatment highlights another important facet of the problem. Insofar as preferential treatment means more than merely picking a Negro who perhaps after a little training can do the job as well as the person to whom he was preferred, it means that the Negro worker in a given job will, on the average, be less competent than his white counterpart. It is hard to predict the psychological consequences of this, either for the Negro or for the white population. It is possible, of course, that they might not be serious at all—the capacity for self-delusion among Negroes may be no less than among automobile drivers, 87% of whom, we are told, regard themselves as better than average. On the other hand, it may be that enforced preferential treatment might actually dampen the motivation of Negroes who could never really know to what extent their achievements were based upon merit, and to what degree upon an artificial preference. One of the great problems of the Negro today results from the natural tendency of those who have been persecuted to think that they have deserved their ill-treatment.[40] Regardless of all other problems, so long as the Negro self-image is that of unworthiness, he can never achieve equality in our society. The institutionalization of preference for Negroes in employment may exacerbate rather than solve this problem.

36 When the first Puerto Rican civil rights organization was formed in New York in early 1964 the leader of the group commented, "If the only way people are going to listen is for us to start demonstrating then we'll have to do it." N. Y. Times, Jan. 3, 1964, p. 26, col. 5.

37 Stern, The Great Treasury Raid 267–77 (1964).

38 Katz, Religion and American Constitutions 13 (1964).

39 To be sure, local government is often drawn into blatantly ethnic controversies, e.

g., freeways running through the Negro neighborhood, urban renewal programs, and police review boards. State and federal governments have fewer of such problems where the ethnic elements arise from the specific applications of rules which appear on their face to be color-blind. Once one concedes that these ethnic confrontations (even where unavoidable) are undesirable, it becomes hard to argue that government should court them except for the most compelling reasons.

40 Clark, Prejudice and Your Child 37–65 (2d ed. 1963).

Finally, in addition to all these economic and political problems in compelling preference for Negroes, we come to what some may regard as a moral ground for rejecting such a step—that this would involve the government in the administration of racial classifications. Certainly, there is reason to avoid involving the government in what Boris Bittker calls the "dirty business" of litigating the race of an individual.[41] Our definitions of race are so vague as not to be susceptible of simple application. One can well imagine a case in which testimony would be necessary from "expert" witnesses as to the degree of kinkiness of hair, of skin color, of pinkness of palms and many other factors which go into our definitions of a Negro. Nor would these experts be the anthropologists who might be able to devise scientific measurements of the individual variables; the only real experts on determining who is a Negro are the racists, who have made a life study of the question—which they regard as the most important in the world. Nor, granting that race is merely a cultural construct, can one simply say that one is a Negro if the culture treats him as Negro. Not only is even this concept fuzzy at the edges, but some people are treated as Negroes in one environment, while in another they are regarded as white, Mexican or Puerto Rican. Perhaps we might be willing to swallow hard and accept the possibility of litigating an individual's race if we could be assured that we would actually have to do so only rarely, if at all. It is impossible to guarantee this, however. Although the previous litigation has involved attempts to prove that someone was a Negro over his denials, it is not at all obvious that all disputes will cease once the Negro is granted preference. True, in the current state of our society it is unlikely that a Nordic would insist

that he was Negro and voluntarily undertake all the attendant social problems, especially since his chances of success would be minimal. One could well imagine, however, that a Latin American might find the advantages of preference such as to induce him to claim to be a Negro. This may sound fanciful, but the fact is that in India, where preferential treatment in employment is given to ex-untouchables, impostership by members of other castes has caused a serious problem.[42]

The most important objection to racial classification, however, is unrelated to the morality of litigating the race of an individual. Far more serious is the fact that any legal classification by race weakens the government as an educative force. For the foreseeable future we will have a complex of laws requiring citizens in various of their activities to be color-blind. It is, of course, hoped that such laws will influence not only behavior but public opinion as to the morality of discrimination. Indeed, in all probability this latter effect is more important than the actual enforcement mechanisms of the law. The principle all these laws are attempting to establish can be phrased in various ways with different types of emphasis. One is that a man is entitled to be judged on his individual merit alone; another is that race is irrelevant to the worth of the individual. Whatever the formulation, however, a statute specifically granting Negroes a benefit tends to undermine the principle we are working so hard to establish. Preference for Negroes can thus be expected to be a major factor in preventing the education we are trying to bring about through a host of other laws. Evidence from the behavioral sciences demonstrates that people can be convinced by consistent logical or moral arguments, but that when spoken to by

[41] Bittker, The Case of the Checker-Board Ordinance: An Experiment in Race Relations, 71 Yale L.J. 1387, 1422 (1962).

[42] Isaacs, India's Ex-Untouchables 115 (1965).

two voices, they tend to listen only to the one they wish to hear.[43] When both voices are the government's, the citizenry may hear only the voice which says race is important and the worth of the individual less so. Perhaps one could stomach the use of racial classifications to provide preference for the Negro if one were confident that the result would be a massive crash-program which, by allocating enormous resources to the problem, would do the job in a minimum of time. The political realities of life are such, however, that this would probably not happen. The resources allocated to the Negro would most likely—or at least no court could assume the contrary—be woefully insufficient, and we would have then incurred all the disadvantages of racial classification for a meager benefit indeed. It is possible that in the completely color-blind world of the future, the educative force of principled action by the government in the racial area may no longer be important. In today's world, however, constant education in color blindness is essential.

One may, of course, question whether the society which we hope to build in the future should actually be completely color-blind. The presence of disparate groups in our culture contributes to its interest and its productivity, and one may well feel that we lose something when our Chinese restaurants are staffed by Negroes, Puerto Ricans, and Italians. Nevertheless, the history of the Negro in America is such that for many generations to come, classification of the Negro as a distinct group can only evoke bitter memories. At least with respect to the Negro, the type of society we probably should envision is one where color is completely irrelevant, not only to all governmental, but to all societal purposes. It may be that the only possible way that

this can be achieved is through inter-marriage so complete that the Negro no longer exists as a Negro.[44] Whether or not this is true, however, the government by making different rules for the white and the Negro can only increase the importance of race in our already race-ridden society.

This is not to say that data should be gathered by the census bureau completely without reference to race. It may be that such data, on balance, is more valuable than the mild erosion of the principle that it causes. However, where race is used as a criterion of governmental action impinging on the lives of individuals, and most important, where the government accords differential treatment to individuals solely because of their race, the erosion of the color-blindness principle by the government may become much more serious.

The damage that such governmental action can do is sometimes quite difficult to predict in advance. An argument can be made that the assimilation of the Puerto Ricans in New York was proceeding better before they were officially classified as Negroes for the purpose of perfectly, well-intentioned programs. The effect of the law has been to stamp them more clearly as a group apart, a designation to which both they and the rest of society could not help but react.

Although we have thus far discussed the question of government-imposed employment preference for Negroes strictly in terms of policy, the issue, of course, has strong constitutional overtones. In this area, however, it might not be an overstatement to say that there is very little difference between the constitutional and the policy approaches. One can say, though, that in the constitutional area we regard as a relevant consideration the problem of standards for decision as well

---

[43] Berelson & Steiner, Human Behavior 113 (1964).

[44] Podhoretz, as quoted in Time, May 20, 1966, p. 56.

as the political, economic and psychological effects of a challenged statute.

In considering standards—which is another way of stating the requirement of principled decision—we ask the type of question which often creates difficulty where the competency of the state to make choices is in issue. If a community can allow preferential treatment for Negroes, can it not do so also for American Indians or for Latin Americans? In a particular state it will be almost impossible for a court to determine that one is proper and the other unconstitutional —unless the court is willing to adopt the proposition that anything which helps the Negro goes, but that aid to other groups must meet stricter standards. And even if it does this, would the court then be able to strike down a statute which based the preference for the Negro on his percentage of Negro blood? Such an enactment could be defended on the theory that the more Negro ancestors an individual has had, the more he has suffered from the wrongs of society and the more deserving of preference he is. It might then be that such a preference which helped some Negroes would hurt others. More important, the standards problem does not merely end with asking whether the state could grant other groups the same preference as it grants the Negro. It raises the question of whether the state can prefer other groups without preferring the Negro. If the community can do this, might it prefer American Indians, to the disadvantage of the Negro? This in itself may not be so disturbing, but if one takes the view that the only reason we would permit such departures from color blindness is to aid the Negro, then the problem of standards becomes crucial.

We may note, as have others,[45] the irony that if a state law permitting job preference for Negroes were held unconstitutional, the Fourteenth Amendment, which was passed in an attempt to benefit the Negro, (and certainly never to harm him) would be used to prevent the state from helping him. The answer is that, unless aid for the Negro is the only value which the amendment enshrines, even this laudable objective must be reached with proper weight given the other values in our society.

Furthermore, in determining whether the state should be permitted to compel employment preference for Negroes, we should ask whether there is anything special about employment which should distinguish it from other areas of life. After all, the achievement of political power is one of the fastest ways to equality for an ethnic group. More specifically, it has been argued that in the North, as well as in the South, it will only be when the Negro holds political power that he will be able to use the government to secure equitable treatment for himself, and that in a sense, all other ways of advance are dependent upon this most basic achievement. When one considers also the psychological truth which has only lately begun to be realized, that for the dispossessed benefits granted are not nearly so sweet as benefits won, and that help, even from a benign overlord, is often seen as humiliating and patronizing, it would seem that a degree of political control over his own affairs is the essential condition for equality for the Negro. What then would be wrong with a state's giving Negroes preferential treatment at the ballot box—say, one man, two votes? If the neutral principle that the Constitution is color-blind is unduly simplistic and inappropriate for the complexities of today's world, why is the equally simple principle of one man, one vote entitled to gentler treatment?

Finally, in considering the issues of standards for the determination of whether racial classification is constitutionally permissible, we may be influenced by the

45 Bittker, supra note 41 at 1393.

fact that regardless of the area of life involved, it may be difficult in many practical situations to distinguish between preferential and hostile treatment. As a result, in deciding whether to depart from the easily applied principle of color-blindness, a court may be influenced by the fact that the upholding of well-intentioned preference today may serve as precedent for the allowance of most unpleasant treatment of minorities in the future.[46]

True, it is not obvious that all racial classifications are constitutionally improper. Though the principle that the Constitution is color-blind is an easily stated and applied one,[47] it may be that the broader terms of the equal protection clause allow a color line to be drawn by the state under certain circumstances.[48] For instance, a state might well be permitted to provide that anyone whose skin is darker than a certain shade (either attached as an exhibit or defined in terms of albedo or reflecting power) is negligent for walking on a road at night without wearing some light-colored item of clothing. This, however, is a very different type of classification from that contemplated in preference (or segregation) laws. Not only will some whom we define as non-Negro be included in the dark-skinned category and some Negroes excluded, but even more important, the classification appears to be made for a reasonable purpose to which color—as distinguished from race—is directly relevant.

So, too, it is conceivable that some future scientific discovery may show that in certain genes attached to what we consider Negroid characteristics are associated with specific diseases. Perhaps then a vaccination could be required of all those who appeared to have the relevant characteristics. Whether the state could then require a vaccination of all Negroes—on the theory that this social fact is an easily administerable and roughly accurate guide to the need for the medical treatment is another question indeed.

What may be characteristic of a majority of the members of a race is not necessarily a characteristic of the race. Thus, if there were a culture-free intelligence test and if, on it, Negroes averaged below whites, a segregation on the basis of a race would remain far more objectionable than one based on intelligence. Nor would it be possible to distinguish preferential treatment from racial segregation on the ground that the former is an attempt to improve a situation while the latter, at least as practiced, could only have the effect of increasing the problem which brought it into being. So far as the issue of racial classification is concerned, both policies involve the same problems. Moreover, while one can argue that the legislature must be permitted to use rough classifications if it is to legislate effectively, for a host of reasons one might not wish to allow the same freedom in the racial area. Be that as it may, the classifications based on the possession by Negroes of one specific characteristic are not apposite here. In both segregation and preferential treatment, racial classification has a social rather than a physical basis, and while the "physical" cases present many interesting issues, we need not trouble ourselves with them here.

As a result, though our discussion of the problems of preferential treatment in employment might tempt one to lay down

[46] The experience of the Jews with quota systems causes many to reject any "preferential" scheme. See, e. g., 2 Law Commentary 8 (1964).

[47] Present Supreme Court decisions leave some doubt as to the validity of the color-blindness principle. Compare the opinion of Mr. Justice Goldberg in Bell v. Maryland, 378 U.S. 226, 287–288, 84 S.Ct. 1814, 12 L.Ed. 2d 822 (1964), with that of Mr. Justice Black at pages 342–43.

[48] See Virginia Bd. of Elections v. Hamm, 379 U.S. 19, 379 S.Ct. 157, 13 L.Ed.2d 91, affirming 230 F.Supp. 156 (E.D.Va.1964).

the principle that the state may never use the social definition of an individual's race to determine whether he is to receive a benefit or bear a burden, the employment area does not provide a proper context for such a decision. In this area, preference for the Negro is objectionable on so many other grounds that it would be improper to rely on such a broad principle.

The principle may be tested further, however, if we ask a somewhat different question. To what extent may a government which prevents discrimination against Negroes, permit a private employer, who so wishes, to discriminate in their favor? We will assume that in the absence of a statute, a private employer may discriminate either in favor of or against members of any group. This has been going on for so long that it no longer raises any real questions. Presumably then, if a state wishes to aid the Negro and sees him as the victim of discrimination, it can pass anti-discrimination laws. And, if it feels that the majority of its employers are more likely to prefer Negroes, it can refuse to interfere with the employer's traditional freedom. The question, of course, comes up where the government wishes to have the best of both worlds—to restrain those who would discriminate against Negroes, while ignoring those who wish to prefer them.

First of all, it should be clear that many of the problems which are most serious when the government is attempting to compel preference disappear when the employer himself is permitted to decide whether and in what ways to give preference to Negroes. The lack of due process restraints upon high management of corporations, their larger arsenal of coercive and persuasive methods and the psychological identification of lower with upper management all make a corporate resolve to prefer Negroes considerably more effective than a governmental order.

Moreover, a preference for Negroes, determined and enforced by top management, causes many fewer difficulties than does such a governmental policy. The company which determines that it should employ more Negroes can make its own choice of how to go about this. It can impose quotas on departments formally or informally, or it can grant various types of preference to Negro applicants with far greater flexibility than could be done through governmental directives.

Moreover, such private discrimination is not so divisive as is the state-imposed variety. Given the traditionally broad scope allowed private industry to pick and choose whom it will hire, private preference violates fewer expectations of those in competition with the Negro—and since it raises fewer expectations among Negroes it would be easier to terminate. Moreover, to the white victim private discrimination would probably be less galling than the governmental variety. After all, it adds insult to injury when one receives the injury at the hands of the government which not only lives on his tax revenues, but also in theory, at least, is dedicated to his protection. Moreover, the fact that such discrimination is private means that it is, in general, less visible. Hence, on the simple theory that those who do not know cannot resent, such private job preference for the Negro is likely to be far less divisive than that imposed by the government.

Whatever the advantages of private preference over the governmentally-imposed variety, the problem becomes more complex where a "fair employment" statute in general terms forbids discrimination against any person on the grounds of his race. It can be argued, of course, that such a statute need not affect the preferential treatment at all, and that whatever administrative authority enforces the statute could merely ignore complaints against those accused of preferring Negroes. Though perhaps for a short while such a policy might be administered covertly, it would be very difficult to do this for any length of time. Complaints from non-Negroes who alleged that less-qualified Negroes were hired in their stead would sooner or later have to be adjudicated, and presumably the laying down of standards in this area would eventually force an overt acknowledgment that preference for Negroes is not to be treated the same way as preference for non-Negroes.

This, of course, would by no means return us to our original problem of enforced preferential treatment. Although the government would no longer be neutral on the issue, all the administrative decisions as to whether and to what extent to prefer Negroes would rest in private hands. However, though this might avoid the institutional problems of preference, the political problems would remain.

True, there would be a difference in the position of the government with respect to the non-Negro worker—but it is the difference between hitting someone and holding him while someone else does the hitting. It is more than likely that the divisiveness of this type of preference, in its institutional maintenance and cessation, would not be a great deal less than that of the government-imposed variety—though of course the fewer the employers who actually chose to prefer Negroes, the less the actual impact, and hence the less the divisiveness of such an arrangement.

On balance, though an exception in a fair employment law raises fewer practical problems than does governmentally-imposed preference, it would still probably be unconstitutional. Not only does such a plan make use of racial classifications, but a court could not help but be influenced by the fact that the employer who wishes to hire more Negroes does not really need an exception from a fair employment statute. A company which wishes to increase the number of Negroes it hires can do so in many informal ways which do not violate anti-discrimination statutes. Probably the most important method available to the employer is his control of information as to job opportunities. Though this is under no interpretation a preference, employers have been able to increase their hiring of Negroes simply by making it clear that they were willing to hire on the basis of merit alone and by broadcasting their employment wanted ads to the Negro community as well as the white one.[49] We enter an area akin to preference when the employer structures his employment information policy so as to reach Negroes more than whites. By recruiting in Negro neighborhoods, advertising in Negro newspapers and making use of Negro radio stations, the employer can gain access to a large pool of Negro labor. Moreover, insofar as no similar efforts are directed toward the non-Negro, the result will be that Negroes will be hired for positions over others who might, if they applied, be deemed more qualified.

In some ways this type of preference may be even more helpful to Negroes than simply choosing them over better qualified white applicants. One of the words most often used to describe the condition to which our history has reduced many Negroes is "apathy." There are differing degrees of apathy, however, and at least some Negroes who had ceased applying for employment have answered advertisements specifically aimed at them. Moreover, even those who presently are too immobilized to respond to such recruitment may not be so after more and more efforts have been extended to make them enter the job market.[50] This type

[49] Northrup & Rowan, The Negro and Employment Opportunity 126–29, 156–62 (1965).

[50] Id. at 147–54 relates the experience of the Lockheed-Georgia Company.

of preference is not only permitted by the usual fair employment law, but is far less divisive than the more blatant quotas and credits. Most people would probably regard the restrictions on whom an employer may select for a job as much stricter than those directing how he should advertise his requirements. And since the advertising policy will attract less attention than the selection policy, we may bring into play again the principle that one who does not know of the existence of a job opening cannot be aggrieved that someone else has filled it.

The employer's control of job information is only the most obvious means by which he might prefer Negroes while remaining within fair employment laws. In his complete discretion, and restrained only by economic considerations, he can locate plants in Negro areas or close the gap between the white and the Negro worker by giving various types of on-the-job training and by redefining the work assigned to different classes of employees.

Indeed, the relative case with which private business can implement a preference for Negroes has tempted organs of government to apply covert pressure on private employers to do so. Governmental benefits such as the awarding of contracts, which are often subject to the almost complete discretion of the contracting officer, provide a convenient and all too powerful handle.[51] At least in those areas where no real enforcement of non-

discriminatory hiring practices exists, a hint by a contracting officer or even a few questions on the issue may convince an employer that on his own initiative he wishes to prefer Negroes. It is true that this method, being covert, avoids certain of the serious disadvantages which flow from formally imposed preference. On the other hand, it is not only devotion to a rule of law which may make one leery of the effectuation of governmental policy by these means. Such a means of enforcing preference may not only be arbitrary and inefficient, but experience with the industrial loyalty security set-up[52] may strongly suggest the inadvisability of allowing such irrelevant considerations to influence use of the contracting power.

The distinction between the problems encountered by the government in compelling preference, and the flexibility with which an employer can implement his own desire to prefer Negroes becomes quite dramatic when one considers the case of public employment. Though it has been argued that the relevant constitutional restraints upon the state in its capacity as employer are no different from those which govern the rules it may impose on private employers,[53] there is a dearth of authority on the issue. Even if such a stringent rule were not adopted, however, it is clear that the Constitution exerts some restraints upon the state in its capacity as employer. In determining the exact extent of these restraints we would have to weigh the many disadvantages of allowing the state, albeit covertly, to draw color lines and, on the other, the fact that many of the institutional difficulties which prevent the state from overtly requiring private employers to

[51] The preferential resolve may also originate with the representatives of the office charged with enforcing the fair employment act. Whether through the threat of a publicized investigation which can be harmful even where it is not fruitful, or simply through persuasion, he sometimes can induce employers to give preference. One investigator of a fair employment commission, after describing his technique, commented "And if they say 'Are you suggesting that I prefer a man just because he's a Negro,' I say 'I'm talking about fair employment, not preference' and I get up and leave."

[52] See Greene v. McElroy, 360 U.S. 474, 79 S.Ct. 1400, 3 L.Ed.2d 1377 (1959).

[53] Linde, Justice Douglas on Freedom in the Welfare State: Constitutional Rights in the Public Sector, 39 Wash.L.Rev. 4, 31 (1964).

grant preferential treatment do not apply where the state itself is the employer. If only because the state can grant preference to Negroes more quietly than it can require other employers to do so, the public employment situation is different. Moreover, in public employment we have a much greater tradition that the state may consider factors which it could not impose upon private employers. Not only is the spoils system very much with us, but we are quite accustomed to hearing about different ethnic groups monopolizing certain state jobs. Moreover, in government employment there may be special reasons for giving a preference to Negroes. The symbolic effect on both foreign and domestic affairs created by having Negroes in the higher levels of government may make preference rational there, while at much lower levels, such as in urban police work, it may well be that a Negro can do his job better simply because he is a Negro.

It is probable, however, that in this area we are better off doing what is usually done with respect to the public employment area—insisting that pure ability to perform the job, unrelated to any considerations of ethnicity or politics—is the only proper determinant of government employment, while at the same time allowing the government to further, as discreetly as possible, whatever values preference may provide. We trust that the judiciary will use every means at its disposal to avoid entering this area—because of the difficulties of proof involved, because of its unwillingness to interfere with the internal administration of co-ordinate branches of government, and because the question on the merits is a difficult one. In a sense then, the limits of judicial cognizability and discretion to avoid questions become the limits on preference in governmental employment.

* * *

D. THE CIVIL RIGHTS ACT OF 1866

YOUNG v. INTERNATIONAL TEL. & TEL.

United States Court of Appeals, Third Circuit.
438 F.2d 757 (1971).

Before HASTIE, Chief Judge, and FREEDMAN and GIBBONS, Circuit Judges.

OPINION OF THE COURT

GIBBONS, Circuit Judge.

Plaintiff appeals from the order of the district court which dismissed his complaint for want of subject matter jurisdiction. The complaint seeks damages and injunctive relief with respect to alleged racial discrimination in employment. In reviewing a dismissal pursuant to Rule 12(b)(1) we must accept these allegations as true.

Plaintiff is a black citizen of the United States, a resident of Philadelphia, and a sheet metal journeyman. Defendant International Telephone & Telegraph Co., Nesbitt Division (Nesbitt) operates a plant in Philadelphia where it employs sheet metal workers. Defendant Local #19, Sheet Metal Workers International Association (Local #19) is an unincorporated trade union of sheet metal workers, having union contracts with employers of sheet metal workers in the Philadelphia area. Defendant Kern is the Vice-President of Local #19. Prior to 1965 there were no minority group members of Local #19 due to a policy of racial exclusion implemented by conspiracy between Local #19 and certain employers including Nesbitt, whereby employers kept minority workers in unskilled job classifications. In 1965 plaintiff was admitted to membership in Local #19 as a result of an order by the Philadelphia

Human Relations Commission requiring Nesbitt to reinstate plaintiff in a job category which required his admission to Local #19. Since his admission to Local #19 both it and Nesbitt have harassed plaintiff maliciously and wantonly, in retaliation for his enforcing his right of admission to the union, and pursuant to its general practice of discriminating against black employees. Plaintiff filed three complaints with the Philadelphia Human Relations Commission in an unsuccessful effort to end harassment by Nesbitt, but was eventually forced to seek other employment.

In 1969 Local #19 was composed of 1,688 journeymen, of whom only 17 were from minority groups. At the same time, at least 375 minority group workers were qualified to perform the same work as present members of Local #19 but were denied admission to the Union.

Defendant Hershman Sheet Metal Works, Inc. (Hershman) is an employer of Sheet Metal Workers at its plant in Philadelphia. On July 17, 1970 Hershman offered plaintiff employment and on July 20 he resigned from Nesbitt. When plaintiff went to Local #19 to notify it of his new job Kern informed him that Local #19's rules required that he be placed on the Out-of-Work List, in spite of the fact that Local #19's usual procedure with respect to white members is to grant immediate transfer when a new job has been secured by an individual member. On July 20 Local #19 notified Hershman that plaintiff could not work there, and as a result Hershman cancelled plaintiff's job.

Plaintiff on his own behalf seeks damages from Nesbitt, Hershman and Local #19 for lost wages since July 20, 1970, and temporary and permanent injunctions restraining Hershman from breaching his employment contract, and Local #19 from interfering with that contract. Claiming to act on behalf of all black sheet metal journeymen who are present and potential members of Local #19, pursuant to Rule 23(a) and (b)(2), Fed. R.Civ.P., he seeks temporary and permanent injunctions against Nesbitt, Hershman, and Local #19, restraining each from discriminating against blacks with respect to job opportunities and working conditions.

The complaint does not allege that plaintiff has pursued any remedies under Title VII of the Civil Rights Act of 1964. 42 U.S.C.A. § 2000e–5. Jurisdiction is asserted under 42 U.S.C.A. § 1981 and § 1985, and under 28 U.S.C.A. § 1343(1) and (4). The district court dismissed (1) because § 1981 is not applicable to discrimination in private employment, and (2) because plaintiff's failure to have invoked the administrative processes of Title VII of the 1964 Civil Rights Act is fatal to his cause. We reverse.

I. The Effect of 42 U.S.C.A. § 1981

Defendants contend that § 1981 does not give plaintiff a right of action for their acts of discrimination relating to his employment. That statute provides:

All persons within the jurisdiction of the United States shall have the same right * * * to make and enforce contracts * * * as is enjoyed by white citizens * * *.

Respondents contend that this section is not applicable to private acts of discrimination in employment because, having been enacted pursuant to congressional powers under the Fourteenth Amendment, it must be read as applicable only to state action. Courts of Appeals in two circuits have considered and rejected this contention, and we agree. Waters v. Wisconsin Steel Workers of Internat'l Harvester Co., 427 F.2d 476 (7th Cir.), cert. denied International Harvester Co. v. Waters, 400 U.S. 911, 91 S.Ct. 137, 27 L.Ed.2d 151 (1970); Sanders v. Dobbs Houses, Inc., 431 F.2d 1097 (5th

Cir. 1970).[1] These courts concluded that § 1981 was derived from the Civil Rights Act of 1866, 14 Stat. 27 (1866), that the 1866 Act was enacted pursuant to congressional powers under the Thirteenth Amendment, and that it was intended to prohibit acts of private discrimination.

In Jones v. Alfred H. Mayer Co., 392 U.S. 409, 88 S.Ct. 2186, 20 L.Ed.2d 1189 (1968), the Supreme Court held that 42 U.S.C.A. § 1982, which was derived from § 1 of the Civil Rights Act of 1866, prohibited all racial discrimination, public and private in the sale or rental of property. The constitutionality of this enactment was upheld on the basis of congressional power to enforce the Thirteenth Amendment. If, as plaintiff contends, § 1981 was derived from the same 1866 statute, Jones v. Alfred H. Mayer Co., supra, and the subsequent case of Sullivan v. Little Hunting Park, 396 U.S. 229, 90 S.Ct. 400, 24 L.Ed.2d 386 (1969) control. Defendants argue, however, that § 1981 is derived not from the 1866 Act, but from the Act of 31 May, 1870, 16 Stat. 140, 144. In one sense this is true, for after the adoption of the Fourteenth Amendment, Congress in the 1870 Civil Rights Act, in order to insure that the prohibitions of the 1866 Act were supported by that Amendment as well as the Thirteenth, restated verbatim parts of the 1866 Act including the part which in the 1866 Act was the nearest counterpart of § 1981. The part of the 1866 Act dealing with property (now § 1982) was not restated in 1870. When in 1874 prior acts were codified the two sections became sections 1977 and 1978 of the Revised Statutes of 1874. The codification acknowledges the 1866 Act for the derivation of § 1978 (now § 1982) but acknowledges the 1870 Act for the derivation of § 1977 (now § 1981). Where there is any difference in language between the 1866 and 1870 Acts the 1870 Act is for present purposes broader since it applied to all persons within the jurisdiction of the United States, not just to citizens. Nothing in this history shows any congressional intent in 1870 or in 1874 not to rely upon the Thirteenth Amendment or to restrict what is now § 1981 to cases involving state action.[2]

The Supreme Court evidently concludes that both § 1981 and § 1982 were enacted under Thirteenth Amendment powers for in Jones v. Alfred H. Mayer Co., supra, it discussed Hodges v. United States, 203 U.S. 1, 27 S.Ct. 6, 51 L.Ed. 65 (1906), a case involving § 1977 of the Revised Statutes (now § 1981) and an employment situation in which the Court had taken a restricted view of congressional power under the Thirteenth Amendment. The court said, "Insofar as *Hodges* is inconsistent with our holding today, it is hereby overruled." 392 U.S. at 441 n. 78, 88 S.Ct. at 2205. Sullivan v. Little Hunting Park, supra, considered a complaint based on both § 1981 and § 1982. While the holding in that case refers to § 1982 neither the majority nor the dissent draws any distinction between the two sections. Thus the indication in Jones v. Alfred H. Mayer Co., supra, of common lineage of the two sections may still be relied upon. We

---

[1] Accord, State of Washington v. Bough Constr. Co., 313 F.Supp. 598 (W.D.Wash., N.D.1968); Clark v. American Marine Corp., 304 F.Supp. 603 (E.D.La.1969) (dictum); United States v. Medical Society of South Carolina, 298 F.Supp. 145 (D.S.C.1969) (dictum); Dobbins v. Local 212, IBEW, 292 F.Supp. 413 (S.D.Ohio 1968) (dictum). The district court relied on two cases rejecting the cause of action. Harrison v. American Can Co., 2 F.E.P. 1 (S.D.Ala.1969); Smith v. North American Rockwell Corp., 50 F.R.D. 515 (N.D.Okla.1970). Since the decision in Sanders v. Dobbs Houses, Inc., supra, the *Harrison* case is no longer authoritative even in the Southern District of Alabama.

[2] See Note, Racial Discrimination in Employment under the Civil Rights Act of 1866, 36 U.Chi.L.Rev. 615 (1969); Larsen, New Law of Race Relations, 1969 Wis.L.Rev. 470.

conclude, therefore, that this case falls within the holdings of Jones v. Alfred H. Mayer Co., supra, and Sullivan v. Little Hunting Park, supra, and § 1981 is applicable to private acts of discrimination.

Defendants also contend that assuming the applicability of § 1981 to certain private acts of discrimination, a fair reading of the statute precludes the construction that it was intended to apply to the employment situation. We cannot agree. In the context of the Reconstruction it would be hard to imagine to what contract right the Congress was more likely to have been referring. Certainly the recently emancipated slaves had little or nothing other than their personal services about which to contract. If such contracts were not included, what was? Certainly the situation of former slaves with respect to their labor was a matter of grave concern in the Congress when the 1866 Act was passed.[4] We therefore reject the strained reading of § 1981 suggested by defendants.

Since this appeal arises on the pleadings, it presents no precise issue as to the relief which would be available assuming that § 1981 prohibits private discrimination in employment. Sullivan v. Little Hunting Park, supra, indicates that 28 U.S.C.A. § 1343(4) creates federal jurisdiction to award damages or equitable relief, and that on the authority of 42 U.S.C.A. § 1988 a district court may draw from federal or state sources an appropriate federal rule of damages. 396 U.S. at 238–240, 90 S.Ct. 400. Thus, unless another statute has repealed § 1981 by necessary implication, the dis-

trict court had jurisdiction to grant all the relief which plaintiff requested.

II. The Effect of 42 U.S.C.A. § 2000e et seq. on § 1981

Defendants contend that Title VII of the Civil Rights Act of 1964 did by necessary implication deprive the district court of jurisdiction. There could have been no intentional repealer, since in 1964 the Congress had no knowledge that private discrimination was prohibited by either § 1981 or § 1982. Jones v. Alfred H. Mayer Co., supra, was not decided until 1968. In that case the Supreme Court referred to the rules of statutory construction of Posadas v. National City Bank, 296 U.S. 497, 503, 56 S.Ct. 349, 352, 80 L.Ed. 351 (1936):

> There are two well-settled categories of repeals by implication—(1) Where provisions in the two acts are in irreconcilable conflict, the latter act to the extent of the conflict constitutes an implied repeal of the earlier one; and (2) if the latter act covers the whole subject of the earlier one and is clearly intended as a substitute, it will operate similarly as a repeal of the earlier act. But, in either case, the intention of the legislature to repeal must be clear and manifest; otherwise, at least as a general thing, the latter act is to be construed as a continuation of, and not a substitute for, the first act and will continue to speak, so far as the two acts are the same, from the time of the first enactment.

Applying these rules of statutory construction, we hold that Title VII of the 1964 Act does not deprive the district courts of jurisdiction over actions brought under § 1981 to remedy private discrimination in employment.

Title VII prohibits discrimination in employment on the basis of race, color, religion, sex, or national origin, by specified groups of employers, labor unions

---

[4] See, e. g., Report of Maj. Gen. C. Schurz at 16–25, S.Exec.Doc.No.2, 39th Cong., 1st Sess. (Dec. 19, 1865); Cong.Globe, 39th Cong., 1st Sess., at 1160 (H.P.) (March 2, 1866) (remarks of Rep. Windom), at 156 (S.P.App.) (March 8, 1966) (remarks of Sen. Morril), at 1833 (H.P.) (April 7, 1866) (remarks of Rep. Lawrence).

and employment agencies. 42 U.S.C.A. § 2000e–2. Discrimination on the basis of religion, sex, or national origin, but not on the basis of race or color—is permitted where the qualification is "reasonably necessary in the normal operation of that particular business or enterprise * * *." 42 U.S.C.A. § 2000e–2(c). Only employers in interstate commerce, employing 25 or more employees are covered. 42 U.S.C.A. § 2000e(b). The Act does not cover the United States or State Governments or Indian Tribes. 42 U.S.C.A. § 2000e(b)(1). It does not cover private clubs, 42 U.S.C.A. § 2000e (b)(2), or the employment of individuals performing educational functions for educational institutions. 42 U.S.C.A. § 2000e–1. Thus with respect to employers covered, Title VII coverage is narrower than § 1981. It is broader in coverage of classes of victims of discriminatory acts. And since § 1981 covers other contract rights besides that of employment as well as rights other than the right to contract, Title VII clearly does not cover the whole subject of the earlier act. We are not dealing with a statute intended as a substitute. The remaining question is whether in any respects the two statutes are in irreconcilable conflict.

* * *

Defendants contend that the provisions for deferral to state agencies for sixty days and for EEOC conciliation efforts for thirty days are in irreconcilable conflict with § 1981 and that exhaustion of these steps in the administrative process should be considered as jurisdictional prerequisites to a district court suit charging discrimination in private employment. They argue for a pre-emption of the field by the Title VII administrative remedies, to the exclusion of the federal courts, at least until after the administrative remedies have run their course.

Imposing the duty on the EEOC to defer to state or local agencies for sixty days certainly is no evidence of a congressional intention to deprive other appropriate forums of their jurisdiction. At most it indicates an intention to take advantage of existing state agencies having expertise and experience, and thereby to shield the new federal agency from an overburdening caseload. That this must have been the intention is evidenced by the fact that deferral to state or local agencies is only temporary. If results have not been accomplished in sixty days the EEOC must begin its investigation. We cannot read into the statute an intention on the part of Congress to vest exclusive jurisdiction in state or local agencies even during the sixty days during which the EEOC must defer to such agencies when in many instances deferral by the EEOC will end before the state or local agency acts on the case.

The statutory duty of the EEOC to attempt conciliation presents a more complex issue. Here an intention to substitute conciliation and persuasion for friction and contention in the delicate field of labor-management relations is evident. At the same time no reference is made in the statute or in such legislative history as is available to any limitation on the jurisdiction of other agencies.[8] Yet the Congress was aware that the courts and the National Labor Relations Board deal with racial discrimination by unions and employers. [Citations omitted.]

Several courts have already recognized that there is concurrent jurisdiction between the EEOC and the NLRB. Local Union No. 12, United Rubber, Cork, Linoleum and Plastic Workers of America, A.F.L.–C.I.O. v. N. L. R. B., 368 F.2d 12 (5th Cir. 1966), cert. denied, 389 U.S. 837, 88 S.Ct. 53, 19 L.Ed.2d

---

[8] In fact, Senator Tower introduced an amendment which would have excluded any federal agency but the EEOC from dealing with practices covered by Title VII. That amendment was defeated by more than a 2–1 margin. 110 Cong.Rec. 13650–52 (1964).

99 (1967); United Packinghouse, Food and Allied Workers Int'l Union, A.F.L.–C.I.O. v. N L R B, [infra at 994]. There is nothing in the language of the statute which casts doubt on the validity of these holdings. Nor is there anything in the language of the statute indicating an intention to deprive the district courts of any pre-existing jurisdiction, known or unknown.

In Waters v. Wisconsin Steel Works of Internat'l Harvester Co., supra, the Seventh Circuit considered the same argument made by the defendants with respect to the necessary effect of the EEOC duty to conciliate and said:

> Because of the strong emphasis which Congress placed upon conciliation, we do not think that aggrieved persons should be allowed to by-pass the Commission without good reason. We hold, therefore, that an aggrieved person may sue directly under section 1981 if he pleads a reasonable excuse for his failure to exhaust EEOC remedies. 427 F.2d at 487.

In that case the plaintiff alleged facts which the court found to be a sufficient justification for failure to proceed before the Commission. Defendants would have us accept the *Waters* case as holding that either exhaustion of EEOC administrative procedures or some justification for nonexhaustion is a jurisdictional prerequisite for an employment discrimination suit. It is not at all clear that the Seventh Circuit intended its *Waters* opinion to go that far. But in any event such a holding would not be warranted by any language in Title VII and we decline to so hold. As will be developed hereinafter, due regard to the conciliation jurisdiction of the EEOC can be afforded by the district courts short of the erection of a jurisdictional bar.

Defendants contend that there is an irreconcilable conflict between § 1981 and Title VII because of the difference in applicable statutes of limitations. There is no federal statute of limitations applicable to § 1981, and the federal courts would look to the most nearly analogous state statute of limitations. See Henig v. Odorioso, 385 F.2d 491 (3d Cir. 1967), cert. denied 390 U.S. 1016, 88 S.Ct. 1269, 20 L.Ed.2d 166 (1968). A charge generally must be filed with the Commission, within ninety days after the alleged unlawful practice occurred. This protective limitation on the business of a new federal agency gives no indication of any congressional intention to limit access to the courts. When the Commission notifies the charging party of its inability to achieve conciliation that party may, within thirty days of such notice, commence a civil action in the district court. 42 U.S.C.A. § 2000e–5(c). There is a distinctly separate Title VII purpose for this thirty day statute of limitations, not applicable to § 1981. Title VII provides:

> Upon application by the complainant and in such circumstances as the court may deem just, the court may appoint an attorney for the complainant and may authorize the commencement of the action without the payment of fees, costs, or security. Upon timely application, the court may, in its discretion, permit the Attorney General to intervene in such civil action if he certifies that the case is of general public importance. 42 U.S.C.A. § 2000e–5(c).

In a Title VII action there is also a provision for the award of reasonable attorney's fees to the prevailing party. 42 U.S.C.A. § 2000e–5(k). Moreover, as we pointed out hereinabove, many acts of discrimination other than those coming under § 1981 are prohibited by Title VII. Limiting access to the court under Title VII, therefore, involves governmental and judicial interests distinctly different and greater than are involved under § 1981. The different governmental interests include the broader coverage of Title VII and the possibility of participation in the lawsuit by the Attorney General. The different judicial interests include the possibility of waiver of fees and costs, imposition of counsel fees, and appointment of counsel. The difference in applicable statutes of limitations is in these circumstances no argument for implied repeal or even for the application of the Title VII statute of limitations to § 1981 actions. In Sanders v. Dobbs Houses, Inc., supra, the Fifth Circuit had before it a § 1981 suit commenced forty-six days after the EEOC had notified plaintiff of its inability to achieve conciliation. It held that the action could proceed. It rejected the contention that there was irreconcilable conflict and hence pre-emption by the later statute. We agree.

We conclude that nothing in Title VII of the Civil Rights Act of 1964 imposes any jurisdictional barrier to a suit brought under § 1981 charging discrimination in pivate employment.

III. Implementing the Conciliation Policy of Title VII

We do not suggest by this holding that in the course of a suit under § 1981 the conciliation features of Title VII should be entirely disregarded. Even in a suit arising under Title VII the district courts are told:

> Upon request, the court may, in its discretion, stay further proceedings for not more than sixty days pending the termination of State or local proceedings described in subsection (b) of this section or the efforts of the commission to obtain voluntary compliance. 42 U.S.C.A. § 2000e–5(e).

Most § 1981 cases, and in particular most class actions under § 1981, will seek equitable relief. Obviously the availability of conciliation by the EEOC is a factor to be considered in the exercise of discretion in granting such re-

lief. This is particularly the case with preliminary injunctions. There is ample scope, within the traditional bounds of discretion in the application of equitable remedies, for the district courts to develop on a case by case basis an accommodation between their jurisdiction under § 1981 and the conciliation efforts of the Commission. There may be cases, indeed, where conciliation will be more successful because carried out while a preliminary injunction has preserved, for an aggrieved employee, the status quo.

In this connection we call to the district court's attention the Commission's power, under 42 U.S.C.A. § 2000e–4(f):

> (4) upon request of (i) any employer, whose employees or some of them, or (ii) any labor organization, whose members or some of them, refuse or threaten to refuse to cooperate in effectuating the provisions of this subchapter, to assist in such effectuation by conciliation or such other remedial action as is provided by this subchapter.

This power apparently may be exercised by the EEOC at any time, even during the pendency of a lawsuit brought pursuant to § 1981. The district courts may well find it appropriate to suggest to defendants in certain cases such resort to the healing remedies of conference, conciliation, and persuasion.

Title VII is in our view "a continuation of, and not a substitute for" § 1981. Cf. Posadas v. National City Bank, supra, 296 U.S. at 503, 56 S.Ct. at 352. By fashioning equitable relief with due regard to the availability of conciliation and by encouraging in appropriate cases a resort to the EEOC during the pendency of § 1981 cases the courts will carry out the policies of both statutes. The order dismissing the complaint for lack of subject matter jurisdiction will be reversed, and the case remanded to the district court for further proceedings consistent with this opinion.

Notes

1. As the court in the main case makes clear, it regards Jones v. Alfred H. Mayer Co., 392 U.S. 409, 88 S.Ct. 2186, 20 L.Ed.2d 1189 (1968), as controlling. The following extracts suggest the main lines of the Supreme Court's analysis in Jones v. Mayer:

That broad language [referring to § 1 of the Civil Rights Act of 1866] we are asked to believe, was a mere slip of the legislative pen. We disagree. For the same Congress that wanted to do away with the Black Codes *also* had before it an imposing body of evidence pointing to the mistreatment of Negroes by private individuals and unofficial groups, mistreatment unrelated to any hostile state legislation. * * * The congressional debates are replete with references to private injustices against Negroes—references to white employers who refused to pay their Negro workers, white planters who agreed among themselves not to hire freed slaves without the permission of their former masters, white citizens who assaulted Negroes, or who combined to drive them out of their communities.

* * *

In light of the concerns that led Congress to adopt it and the contents of the debates that preceded its passage, it is clear that the Act was designed to do just what its terms suggest: to prohibit all racial discrimination, whether or not under color of law, with respect to the rights enumerated therein. * * *

As its text reveals, the Thirteenth Amendment "is not a mere prohibition of state laws establishing or upholding slavery, but an absolute declaration that slavery or involuntary servitude shall not exist in any part of the United States." Civil Rights Cases, 109 U.S. 3, 20; 3 S.Ct. 18, 28, 27

L.Ed. 835. It has never been doubted, therefore, "that the power vested in Congress to enforce the article by appropriate legislation," ibid., includes the power to enact laws "direct and primary, operating upon the acts of individuals, whether sanctioned by state legislation or not." Id., at 23, 3 S.Ct., at 30.

* * *

* * * Surely Congress has the power under the Thirteenth Amendment rationally to determine what are the badges and the incidents of slavery, and the authority to translate that determination into effective legislation. Nor can we say that the determination Congress has made is an irrational one. For this Court recognized long ago that, whatever else they may have encompassed, the badges and incidents of slavery—its "burdens and disabilities"—included restraints upon "those fundamental rights which are the essence of civil freedom, namely, the same right * * * to inherit, purchase, lease, sell and convey property, as is enjoyed by white citizens." Civil Rights Cases, 109 U.S. 3, 22, 3 S.Ct. 18, 29, 27 L.Ed. 835. * * *

392 U.S. at 427–428, 436, 438, 440–441.

2. In his dissenting opinion in Jones v. Mayer, Mr. Justice Harlan noted that Title VIII of the Civil Rights Act of 1968 contained comprehensive fair housing provisions and went on to observe: "I think it particularly unfortunate for the Court to persist in deciding this case on the basis of a highly questionable interpretation of a sweeping, century-old statute which, as the Court acknowledges, contains none of the exemptions which the Congress of our own time found it necessary to include in a statute regulating relationships personal in nature. In effect, this Court, by its construction of § 1982, has extended the coverage of fed-

eral 'fair housing' laws far beyond that which Congress in its wisdom chose to provide in the Civil Rights Act of 1968." 392 U.S. at 478.

The argument was continued in Sullivan v. Little Hunting Park, also relied on by the main case. The Supreme Court majority disposed of the point this way:

> It is suggested, not by any party but by the dissent, that any relief should await proceedings under the Fair Housing Act of 1968. 82 Stat. 810, 42 U.S.C.A. (Supp. IV) § 3601 et seq. But these suits were commenced on March 16, 1966, two years before that Act was passed. It would be irresponsible judicial administration to dismiss a suit because of an intervening Act which has no possible application to events long preceding its enactment. 396 U.S. at 240.

How solid a foundation for the main case is Jones v. Alfred H. Mayer Co.?

3. If you were counsel to a victim of employment discrimination, what factors would lead you to sue under the Civil Rights Act of 1866 rather than proceed under Title VII? to proceed under Title VII in preference to a suit under the 1866 statute?

4. In Dobbins v. Local 212, I.B.E. W., 292 F.Supp. 413, 444 (S.D.Ohio 1968), the court said: "There being no Federal statute of limitations with respect to a Civil Rights Act of 1866 case, the most adaptable State statute governs. See Mulligan v. Schlachter, 389 F.2d 231 (6th Cir. 1968). The most applicable Ohio statute is R.C. of Ohio 2305.09(d) —four years." In Waters v. Wisconsin Steel Works of International Harvester Co., cited in the main case, the Court of Appeals for the Seventh Circuit held that the cognate statute of limitations was Illinois' catchall of five years rather than the 120 days allowed for the filing of a claim with the Illinois anti-discrimination commission. The court was moved by the differences between the administrative and judicial remedies.

5. The issue of whether a plaintiff may bypass the EEOC and seek an independent remedy under § 1981 has now been considered by three courts of appeals. Each has acknowledged the availability of § 1981, with the Seventh Circuit suggesting the qualification quoted in the main case. The Fifth Circuit did not have to confront the exhaustion issue in Sanders v. Dobbs Houses, Inc., cited in the main case, because the plaintiff had already been to the EEOC; however, in Caldwell v. National Brewing Co., 443 F. 2d 1044 (5th Cir. 1971), certiorari denied, 92 S.Ct. 931 (1972) the court lined up with the Third Circuit and held that prior recourse to Title VII's administrative procedures is not a jurisdictional prerequisite to a § 1981 action.

6. Lee v. Southern Home Sites Corp., 444 F.2d 143 (5th Cir. 1971), raised the question "whether attorney's fees should be awarded to successful plaintiffs who charged that the defendant violated 42 U.S.C.A. § 1982 by refusing to sell lots to Negroes on the same terms the defendant sold lots to whites." 444 F.2d at 143. The court answered: "We hold that attorney's fees are part of the effective remedy a court should fashion to carry out the congressional policy embodied in Section 1982." 444 F.2d at 144. The court left little doubt that it would give the same answer in a suit under § 1981.

E. THE NATIONAL LABOR RELATIONS AND RAILWAY LABOR ACTS

The impact of federal labor legislation on employment discrimination is best explored in the context of the traditional Labor Law course. Nevertheless, students of racial discrimination in employment should have some awareness of labor law's relevance to their concerns. Accordingly, the following extracts offer a general introduction to: (1) the scope of the duty of fair representation; and (2) possible modes of enforcing that duty.

SOVERN, LEGAL RESTRAINTS ON RACIAL DISCRIMINATION IN EMPLOYMENT 144–45, 154–56, 160–61

(Twentieth Century Fund 1966).

THE DUTY OF FAIR REPRESENTATION: RATIONALE AND SCOPE

The Steele Case

Under both the N.L.R.A. and the R. L.A., a union selected by a majority of the employees in a unit appropriate for collective bargaining becomes the exclusive representative of all the employees in the unit, and not only of those who wish to be represented by that union. Once the choice is made, all are bound by collective agreements negotiated by the representative selected and none may elect to have another union bargain for him or even to bargain for himself. Because the majority's choice is imposed upon everyone in this way, the Supreme Court has consistently held that these statutes require the union chosen to represent everyone in the unit fairly. The leading case is Steele v. Louisville & N. R. R.,[4] a suit under the Railway Labor Act by a Negro locomotive fireman against the railroad that employed him and the all-white union that represented

him. Steele alleged that the union, which he was compelled to accept as his collective bargaining representative because it was the choice of a majority of the firemen in the railroad's employ, had sought and obtained from the railroad a collective agreement that discriminated against Negroes. Holding that if the allegations were proved, Steele and his fellow Negro firemen would be entitled to judicial relief, the Supreme Court said:

> So long as a labor union assumes to act as the statutory representative of a craft, it cannot rightly refuse to perform the duty, which is inseparable from the power of representation conferred upon it, to represent the entire membership of the craft. While the statute does not deny to such a bargaining labor organization the right to determine eligibility to its membership, it does require the union, in collective bargaining and in making contracts with the carrier, to represent non-union or minority union members of the craft without hostile discrimination, fairly, impartially, and in good faith.[5]

If the statute were not so interpreted, the Court indicated, it might well be unconstitutional.

* * *

Employers' Derivative Liability

An employer cannot knowingly participate in a union's violation of its duty of fair representation without exposing himself to joint liability with it. If, for example, an employer accedes to a union request that he dismiss a worker because of his race, the employer can plainly be ordered to restore the worker to his job and almost certainly can be compelled to pay him his lost wages.[6]

---

[4] 323 U.S. 192, 65 S.Ct. 226, 89 L.Ed. 173 (1944); accord, e. g., Conley v. Gibson, 355 U.S. 41, 78 S.Ct. 99, 2 L.Ed.2d 80 (1957) (Railway Labor Act); Syres v. Oil Workers, 350 U.S. 892, 76 S.Ct. 152, 100 L.Ed. 785 (1956) (National Labor Relations Act); Graham v. Brotherhood of Locomotive Firemen, 338 U.S. 232, 70 S.Ct. 14, 94 L.Ed. 22 (1949) (Railway Labor Act); Tunstall v. Brotherhood of Locomotive Firemen, 323 U.S. 210, 65 S.Ct. 235, 89 L.Ed. 187 (1944) (Railway Labor Act).

[5] 323 U.S. at 204.

[6] Richardson v. Texas & N. O. R. R., 242 F.2d 230 (5th Cir. 1957); Central of Ga. Ry. v. Jones, 229 F.2d 648 (5th Cir. 1956), certiorari denied, 352 U.S. 848, 77 S.Ct. 32, 1 L.Ed. 2d 59 (1956).

Perhaps too an employer is jointly responsible for a union's breach of duty even when that breach takes the form of failing to resist his discrimination. When an employer makes a discriminatory demand and the union offers no resistance, he knows or should know that it is defaulting on its duty. If the employer shares responsibility with the union in this circumstance, a ban on *employer* discrimination has found its way into both the R.L.A. and the N.L.R.A. The practical effect could be far-reaching: if a union violates its duty by failing to resist employer discrimination, and if the employer is jointly responsible for the union's violation merely by virtue of his taking advantage of its nonresistance, an employer whose employees are unionized risks a violation of the applicable labor relations law whenever he practices employment discrimination. The National Labor Relations Board has already taken a large step toward this proposition by flatly declaring that "[C]ollective bargaining agreements which discriminate invidiously are not lawful under the Act * * * and both unions and employers are enjoined by the Act from entering into" them.[7] Whether this view will prevail remains to be seen.

THE HISTORICAL ROLE OF THE COURTS

The duty of fair representation was first articulated in the courts, and for most of the twenty-two years since the *Steele* case enforcement has rested mainly with them. State as well as federal courts have been held competent to enforce the duty, and both have been free to award damages, injunctions, or both in appropriate cases.

[In Vaca v. Sipes, 386 U.S. 171, 87 S.Ct. 903, 17 L.Ed.2d 842 (1967), the Supreme Court rejected the argument that the National Labor Relations Board has exclusive jurisdiction to enforce the duty in cases arising under the National Labor Relations Act.]

THE ROLE OF THE NLRB

The ample powers of the judiciary notwithstanding, Negro resistance to union discrimination has only rarely included reliance on the unequivocal holdings in *Steele* and the decisions following it. Any of the busy state FEPC's receives far more employment complaints from Negroes in one year than all of the courts have received under *Steele* in over 20 years. In part, this may be attributable to the expense of obtaining counsel familiar with the intricacies of our federal labor legislation and of pursuing the matter through the courts. In other words, the high cost of suing has probably sapped the right to be represented fairly of much of its efficacy.

While we generally leave litigants in the courts to find and pay their own way, one who complains to the National Labor Relations Board can have these burdens borne for him. Once he complains, investigation and if the results of the investigation warrant it, prosecution of his claim will be undertaken by subordinates of the General Counsel of the NLRB, without cost to the complainant. Consequently, it becomes important to know whether violations of the duty of fair representation lie within the Board's powers of correction. If they do, relief from union discrimination can be sought without straining the limited financial resources of Negro workers and civil rights organizations.

Since the duty of fair representation is implicit, not expressed, in the National Labor Relations Act, the statute is silent on how that duty is to be enforced. Nevertheless, the possibilities for the NLRB are fairly obvious. They fall into two basic categories: refusal by the Board to

---

[7] Local 1367, International Longshoremen's Association, 148 N.L.R.B. No. 44 (1964). And see Local No. 12, United Rubber Workers (Business League of Gadsden), 150 N.L.R.B. No. 18 (1964) * * *.

aid unions to become or remain exclusive representatives when they can be expected to abuse the power that this position entails; and unfair labor practice proceedings. The discussion begins, then, with a consideration of the Board's responses to the argument that it should refuse to assist to the status of exclusive representative a union that cannot be expected to discharge its duty. It continues by considering whether a union commits an unfair labor practice if it fails in its duty of fair representation.

*   *   *

We have considered four ways in which the Board can refuse to help a union become or remain an exclusive representative: (1) rescind certification; (2) refuse to certify; (3) withhold an order to bargain; and (4) remove the contract bar. The Board has actually invoked sanctions 1 and 4 against unions that have abused their powers as exclusive representative and has indicated a willingness to use sanction 2 against a union that persists in representing unfairly. We have suggested that sanction 3 would also be appropriate.

The effectiveness of these measures should not be exaggerated. Rescission of certification obviously holds no fears for uncertified unions, a category into which the great majority of unions still fall. In addition, many certified unions, if obliged to, could get along quite well without their certifications. It follows that the refusal to certify is also a remedy of limited utility. The withholding of orders to bargain would reach some unions not vulnerable to rescission and denial of certification, but this remedy too is useless against unions that do not have to call for help from the Board because they already have well-established bargaining relationships that are not likely to be broken off, nor will this sanction reach unions strong enough to cow recalcitrant employers. Removing the contract bar is no more potent: it obviously cannot hurt

until a petition for a representation election is filed, and such petitions are not filed against well-entrenched unions.

While the remedies we have been discussing are not likely to make strong unions tremble, the weak, in the labor movement as elsewhere, are numerous enough to matter. Given the choice between abandoning racist policies and doing without the Board's imprimatur, some of these will surely choose to cease discriminating.

Unfair Labor Practice Proceedings

Unfair labor practice proceedings constitute a far more powerful sanction than the Board remedies discussed so far because they eventuate, when the charge is well founded, in a cease and desist order directing the respondent to fulfill his obligations under the law. Such an order, when enforced by a federal court of appeals, is backed up by the court's contempt powers. If, therefore, violation of the duty of fair representation is an unfair labor practice, a violator can be ordered to represent fairly and can be fined or imprisoned for disobedience of that order.

Until 1962, the NLRB had never held unfair representation to be an unfair labor practice. Since then, it has repeatedly done so. Some of the approaches employed in the Board's recent decisions pose serious theoretical difficulties. * *

[In spite of those difficulties, the Board's view that unfair representation is an unfair labor practice has fared well in the courts. See Truck Drivers, Local 568 v. NLRB, 126 U.S.App.D.C. 360, 379 F.2d 137 (D.C.Cir. 1967); NLRB v. Local 1367, I.L.A., 368 F.2d 1010 (5th Cir. 1966), certiorari denied, 389 U. S. 837, 88 S.Ct. 58 (1967); Local 12, United Rubber Workers v. NLRB, 368 F. 2d 12 (5th Cir. 1966), certiorari denied 389 U.S. 837, 88 S.Ct. 53 (1967). But see NLRB v. Miranda Fuel Co., 326 F.2d 172 (2d Cir. 1963).]

Notes

1. United Packinghouse Workers v. NLRB, 135 U.S.App.D.C. 111, 416 F.2d 1126, certiorari denied 396 U.S. 903, 90 S.Ct. 216, 24 L.Ed.2d 179 (1969), constitutes a major addition to the law governing employer liability under the N.L.R.A. Sovern, The Right to Equal Employment Opportunity, in Dorsen, The Rights of Americans 23, 36–38 (1971) contains the following commentary:

"The duty of an employer under the NLRA and RLA to refrain from racial discrimination against his employees has always been seen as a derivative of the union's duty. It was generally assumed that an employer who wanted to indulge his taste for bigotry was free to do so as far as federal labor legislation was concerned unless a union was implicated. * * * The simplest example of employer freedom of action under the labor laws was the employer who, without a union in the plant or otherwise on the scene, chose to hire Negroes only in the lowest labor grades and to keep them there. The assumption was that as far as the national labor laws were concerned, such an employer was free to discriminate on the basis of race. The Court of Appeals for the District of Columbia may well have thrown out that assumption in Packinghouse Workers v. NLRB.

" * * * Judge J. Skelly Wright, writing for the Court of Appeals, admitted that he could find 'no cases in which an employer's policy of discrimination as such was alleged to be a violation of the Act. * * * ' He also acknowledged: 'In order to hold that employer racial discrimination violates Section 8(a)(1) it must be found that such discrimination is not merely unjustified, but that it interferes with or restrains discriminated employees from exercising their statutory right to act concertedly for their aid or protection, as guaranteed by Section 7 of the Act.'

"Then, in an ingenious reformulation of the issue, he says: '[I]n the context of employer racial discrimination, the question reduces to whether that discrimination inhibits its victims from asserting themselves against their employer to improve their lot.' He goes on to answer the question by concluding that racial discrimination does have such an inhibiting effect. He says:

This effect is twofold: 1) racial discrimination sets up an unjustified clash of interests between groups of workers which tends to reduce the likelihood and the effectiveness of their working in concert to achieve their legitimate goals under the Act: and 2) racial discrimination creates in its victims an apathy or docility which inhibits them from asserting their rights against the perpetrator of the discrimination. *We find that the confluence of these two factors sufficiently deters the exercise of Section 7 rights as to violate Section 8(a)(1).* (Emphasis in original)

" The crucial point is that there is nothing, either in the words of the court's opinion or in the logic of its rationale, that would limit the decision to unionized enterprises. The court itself notes that Section 7 'protects concerted activity by workers to alleviate oppressive working conditions, regardless of whether their activity is channeled through a union, through collective bargaining, or through some other means.' It follows from this decision that any employer covered by the NLRA who engages in racial discrimination is vulnerable to a proceeding under that statute. Since the National Labor Relations Board has the cease and desist powers that the EEOC lacks, and since, according to *Packinghouse Workers,* the NLRA outlaws racial discrimination by employers as well as unions, the decision effectively converts the NLRA into a comprehensive fair employment practices law.

"If the National Labor Relations Act were a brand new law, Judge Wright's opinion might have some claim to plausibility, although there would be difficulties with it in any event. But the statute is 34 years old. In all that time no one had ever supposed that Congress enacted a fair employment practices law back in 1935, least of all Congress. The decision does not seem likely to survive."

2. Sovern, Legal Restraints on Racial Discrimination in Employment 263 (Twentieth Century Fund 1966) contains an extensive bibliography on the National Labor Relations and Railway Labor Acts. For additional references, see Boyce, Racial Discrimination and the National Labor Relations Act, 65 Nw.U.L. 232 (1970).

SECTION 3. WHICH REMEDY?

PECK, REMEDIES FOR RACIAL DISCRIMINATION IN EMPLOYMENT: A COMPARATIVE EVALUATION OF FORUMS

46 Washington Law Review 455, 456–457
(1970).

Among the factors to be considered in a comparative evaluation of forums and bases for obtaining relief from racial discrimination in employment are the following: (1) the parties proceeded against—employers, employer associations, employment agencies, or unions; (2) the status of the complainant— whether employed or a union member; (3) the possibility that a collective bargaining agreement may affect the employment involved; (4) the limitation periods within which proceedings must be initiated; (5) the effect of proceeding in one forum upon remedies which might be available in other forums; (6) the type of relief available in the forum; (7) the provisions for payment of attorneys' fees or for obtaining attorneys' services; (8) the investigatory and discovery procedures which are available; and (9) special defenses applicable to particular proceedings.

RIOS v. REYNOLDS METALS CO.

United States Court of Appeals,
Fifth Circuit, 1972.
467 F.2d 54.

Before BELL, DYER and CLARK, Circuit Judges.

BELL, C. J.: Title VII of the Civil Rights Act of 1964 makes it unlawful for an employer to discriminate against an employee on the basis of race, color, religion, sex, or national origin. 42 U.S.C.A. § 2000e. The Act provides a procedure whereby an aggrieved employee may obtain relief from injuries caused by discriminatory employment practices. This procedure culminates in a civil action by the employee where other measures fail. The question presented on this appeal is whether this judicial remedy is available to an employee who first submits his claim to arbitration under an anti-discrimination clause in a collective bargaining agreement between his employer and his union and receives an adverse arbitral determination of the issues he ultimately presents to the court under Title VII.

We touched on this question in a peripheral manner in a prior decision of this court. Hutchings v. United States Industries, Inc., 5 Cir., 1970, 428 F.2d 303. There we held that the doctrines of election of remedies and res judicata did not bar a subsequent suit under Title VII where the rights and remedies at issue in an arbitration proceeding differed from the rights and remedies at issue under Title VII. We left for the future

"* * * the question whether a procedure similar to that adopted by the Labor Board in deferring to arbitration awards when certain standards are met might properly be adopted in Title VII cases." Id. at 314, n. 10. The more important fact in *Hutchings* was that the collective bargaining agreement and arbitral process did not expressly include the employer obligation under Title VII. There we said:

> "In view of the dissimilarities between the contract grievance-arbitration process and the judicial process under Title VII, it would be fallacious to assume that an employee utilizing the grievance-arbitration machinery under the contract and also seeking a Title VII remedy in court is attempting to enforce a single right in two forums. We do not mean to imply that employer obligations having their origin in Title VII are not to be incorporated into the arbitral process. When possible they should be. See generally Gould, Labor Arbitration of Grievances Involving Racial Discrimination, 118 U.Pa.L.Rev. 40 (1969). But the arbitrator's determination under the contract has no effect upon the court's *power* to adjudicate a violation of Title VII rights."

Here the employer obligation in issue under Title VII is expressly included in the arbitral process under the collective bargaining agreement.[1] We also have

---

[1]   GRIEVANCE PROCEDURE
ARTICLE VI

Section 1. It is agreed that any employee may present a grievance to the Company in matters pertaining to the application and interpretation of this agreement and it is agreed that such grievance will be processed in accordance with the procedure outlined herein.

An employee who wishes to present a grievance shall first discuss this grievance with his immediate supervisor. The employee will, if he wishes, be accompanied by his Union representative. Failing to resolve such griev-

a prejudgment determination by an arbitrator of an issue which is the same issue as that which the employee subsequently presented to the district court.

In the case at bar the district court held that the arbitrator's determination of this issue barred the civil action under Title VII. For reasons to be stated, we reverse and remand for further proceedings.

I. Appellant Rios was employed at a plant operated by Reynolds Metals Company, appellee. Rios applied for a position as mechanic pipefitter, a position then vacant. After passing a written examination, he assumed the new post on a trial basis. About one month later he was demoted to his former position.

Pursuant to the provisions of the collective bargaining agreement between Reyn-

---

ance, it may be reduced to writing and presented to the supervisor and answered by him.

* * *

Failing satisfactory adjustment, the Union shall take up the grievance with the Director of Labor Relations for further handling. The Director of Labor Relations shall give his answer within thirty (30) days from the time the matter is referred to him.

Failing satisfactory adjustment by the Director of Labor Relations, the grievance may be submitted to arbitration by either party.

In the event a single arbitrator cannot be selected by the parties, the Federal Mediation and Conciliation Service Director, by mutual request, shall be asked to submit a list from which the parties to the dispute shall select an arbitrator.

If they fail to make a selection from the list, then the Director of said Service shall be asked to appoint an arbitrator outside the original list.

The decision of the arbitrator shall be final and binding on all affected parties. Expenses of the arbitrator, including his fee, shall be paid equally by the Company and the Union.

* * *

NONDISCRIMINATION
ARTICLE XXXVII

Section 1. The Company and the Union agree not to discriminate against any employee because of race, color, creed, national origin, sex, or Union activity in all matters pertaining to hiring, wages, hours, and working conditions.

olds and the Aluminum Workers International Union, Rios filed a grievance in which he claimed that he had not been given a reasonable trial period at his new assignment. Arbitration ensued. At the arbitration hearing, in response to questions raised by his union representative, Rios maintained that one reason for his demotion was that Reynolds had discriminated against him because he was a Mexican-American. The arbitrator rejected this contention and determined that Rios had been given fair treatment during the trial period. The arbitrator concluded that Rios was demoted because he was unable to perform the new job satisfactorily.

Rios initiated this action in the district court before the arbitration hearing was held. The arbitrator's decision followed and thereafter, in light of the decision of the arbitrator, Reynolds moved for summary judgment. Reynolds contended that Rios, having submitted to arbitration, was bound by the arbitrator's determination. The district court accepted this contention.

II. The settlement of labor disputes by arbitration is a favored national labor policy.

[Citations omitted.] For this reason, in developing principles that will govern the availability of judicial relief under Title VII, we must carefully assess the impact of judicial action upon the favored arbitral remedy.

The viability of arbitration depends on the willingness of courts to enforce the arbitrator's award without reopening issues resolved by him. Thus, in such cases, courts customarily defer to the arbitrator's determination. They restrict their inquiry to the single question whether, under the terms of the collective bargaining agreement, the arbitrator had power to decide the issues he decided. If he had such power, his decision is binding. See, e. g., United Steelworkers v. Enterprise Wheel & Car Corp., supra, 363 U.S. at 596.

The question here is whether a similar approach should be followed when, in the first instance, the issues decided by the arbitrator are cognizable in the federal court by virtue of Title VII, which manifests a strong national policy against discriminatory employment practices. We conclude that the traditional approach to the arbitration process is not warranted in this context.

The remedy afforded by Title VII is supplemental. It exists apart from analogous remedies provided by contract or by federal or state law. Indeed, aggrieved employees may seek relief under Title VII without first involving or exhausting available alternative legal or contractual remedies. See Caldwell v. National Brewing Company, 5 Cir. 1971, 443 F.2d 1044; King v. Georgia Power, 295 F.Supp. 943 (N.D.Ga.1968).[2] In addition, we have said that even where an employee does pursue an alternative remedy in cases involving Title VII rights, the federal court is to be "the final arbiter." *Hutchings,* supra, 428 F.2d at 313.

It does not follow, however, that the policies of Title VII require that an employee who has submitted his claim to binding arbitration must always be given an opportunity to relitigate his claim in court. In some instances such a requirement would not comport with elementary notions of equity, for it would give the employee, but not the employer, a second chance to have the same issue resolved. More importantly, such a requirement would tend to frustrate the national policy favoring arbitration. An employer would have little incentive to agree to arbitrate under a system where only the

---

2 This treatment of the supplemental remedy of Title VII is not unlike that given the supplemental remedy of 42 U.S.C.A., § 1983. See Monroe v. Pape, 1961, 365 U.S. 167, 183, 81 S.Ct. 473, 5 L.Ed.2d 492; McNeese v. Board of Education, 1963, 373 U.S. 668, 674, 83 S. Ct. 1433, 10 L.Ed.2d 622; Damico v. California, 1967, 389 U.S. 416, 88 S.Ct. 526, 19 L.Ed.2d 647; Wilwording v. Swenson, 1971, 404 U.S. 249, 92 S.Ct. 407, 30 L.Ed.2d 418.

employee, in the event of an adverse arbitral determination, would have an opportunity to relitigate the matter in court.

This, of course, assumes that the national policy favoring arbitration of labor disputes should include grievances concerning rights which are guaranteed by Title VII. As we have noted, the teaching of *Hutchings* is that they may be included in the grievance-arbitration process. But as *Hutchings* holds, the determination in the arbitration process has no effect upon the power of the federal court to adjudicate a violation of rights under Title VII. The question thus becomes whether the courts may accommodate the national arbitration process policy to Title VII proceedings without thwarting the congressional intent in Title VII to eliminate discriminatory practices in employment. We conclude that the policy which favors arbitration and the remedial policy of Title VII may be accommodated by a procedure which was alluded to in *Hutchings* but saved for decision on another day. It is that a district court may, under limited circumstances, defer to a prior arbitration award.

The apparent analogy is to the deferral procedure followed by the National Labor Relations Board in the exercise of its discretionary powers under the National Labor Relations Act. See Lodge No. 12, etc. v. Cameron Iron Works, 5 Cir., 1958, 257 F.2d 467, 473; Spielberg Manufacturing Co., 112 NLRB 1080 (1955).

As we recognized in Lodge No. 12, etc. v. Cameron Iron Works, supra, a prior arbitration award does not divest the NLRB of its statutory jurisdiction to effectuate the policies of the National Labor Relations Act. But we recognized as well that a given controversy may be cognizable both as an arbitrable grievance under a collective bargaining agreement, and as a labor dispute under the National Labor Relations Act. Where such a coincidence of issues exists, it is within the discretionary power of the NLRB to defer to findings made by the arbitrator.

In exercising this power, the NLRB has recognized the limits of its discretion and has developed minimum standards on which to structure the decision to defer *vel non*. In *Spielberg Manufacturing Co.*, 112 NLRB at 1082, the Board stated that where "the proceedings appear to have been fair and regular, all parties have agreed to be bound, and the decision of the arbitration panel is not clearly repugnant to the purposes and policies of the Act," it is proper for the Board to defer to a prior arbitration award involving the same issues. This practice has been approved by the courts and reaffirmed by the NLRB as being consistent with national labor policy. See, e. g., Carey v. Westinghouse Corp., 1964, 375 U.S. 261, 270, n. 7. Lodge No. 12, etc. v Cameron Iron Works, supra.

We hold that the federal district court in the exercise of its power as the final arbiter under Title VII may follow a like procedure of deferral under the following limitations. First, there may be no deference to the decision of the arbitrator unless the contractual right coincides with rights under Title VII. Second, it must be plain that the arbitrator's decision is in no way violative of the private rights guaranteed by Title VII, nor of the public policy which inheres in Title VII. In addition, before deferring, the district court must be satisfied that (1) the factual issues before it are identical to those decided by the arbitrator; (2) the arbitrator had power under the collective agreement to decide the ultimate issue of discrimination; (3) the evidence presented at the arbitral hearing dealt adequately with all factual issues; (4) the arbitrator actually decided the factual issues presented to the court; (5) the arbitration proceeding was fair and regular and free of procedural infirmities. The burden of proof in establishing these conditions of limitation will be upon the respondent as distinguished from the claimant.

In essence, this procedure will amount to a review of the arbitration proceeding in cases involving Title VII rights. It is not as broad as the procedure followed in general grievance-arbitration cases where the court looks only to the question whether under the terms of the collective bargaining agreement the arbitrator had power to decide the issues he decided. *United Steelworkers,* supra, 363 U.S. at 596. Neither is it as broad as the policy of deferral under res judicata principles which we have applied in cases where facts previously determined by the Labor Board are presented in collateral proceedings in the federal courts. [Citations omitted.] [3]

Reversed and Remanded for further proceedings not inconsistent herewith.

Notes

1. As the main case makes plain, a particular discriminatory act or practice may be subject to a variety of remedial systems. The notes that follow deal with conflict, overlap and accommodation between those systems.

[3] It is to be observed that our holding may be somewhat in line with the result which has evolved in the Sixth Circuit in a series of cases beginning with Dewey v. Reynolds Metals Co., 6 Cir. 1970, 429 F.2d 324, aff'd without opinion by an equally divided court, 402 U.S. 689, 91 S.Ct. 2186, 29 L.Ed.2d 267 (1971), and ending with Newman v. Avco Corp., 6 Cir. 1971, 451 F.2d 743. Under the Sixth Circuit's approach it now appears that a claimant who has received an adverse arbitration award must be permitted to relitigate his claim in court unless certain conditions are met. Thus, the arbitration proceeding must have been fair and impartial. The issue presented to the court under Title VII must be the same as the issue decided by the arbitrator under the collective bargaining agreement. The arbitrator must have had power, under the collective bargaining agreement, to decide the issues he decided. Newman v. Avco, supra. These conditions reproduce in part the minimum criteria for deferral, which we have set out.

2. Suppose that one party to a contract dispute before an arbitrator wishes him to consider Title VII but the other does not. What is the arbitrator's responsibility? The question is discussed and references cited in Sovern, When Should Arbitrators Follow Federal Law? in Proceedings of the Twenty-Third Annual Meeting of the National Academy of Arbitrators 29 (Bureau of National Affairs 1970).

3. What bearing do the main case and the Sixth Circuit's decisions summarized by the court in footnote 3 have on these related questions: Must a complainant exhaust a grievance procedure created by a collective bargaining agreement before bringing a Title VII suit? When, if ever, must a complainant elect between the Title VII and grievance procedure remedies? When, if ever, is a Title VII suit barred by prior recourse to contractual grievance machinery?

In Dewey v. Reynolds Metals Co., the Sixth Circuit said:

> "The question in our case is not whether arbitration and resort to the courts could be maintained at the same time; rather our case involves the question whether suit may be brought in court *after* the grievance has been finally adjudicated by arbitration." 429 F.2d at 332.

And consider Bowe v. Colgate-Palmolive Co., 416 F.2d 711, 715 (7th Cir. 1969):

> "Accordingly, we hold that it was error not to permit the plaintiffs to utilize dual or parallel prosecution both in court and through arbitration so long as election of remedy was made after adjudication so as to preclude duplicate relief which would result in an unjust enrichment or windfall to the plaintiffs."

Edwards and Kaplan, Religious Discrimination and the Role of Arbitration Under Title VII, 69 Mich.L.Rev. 599, 641–

653 (1971); Meltzer, Labor Arbitration and Overlapping and Conflicting Remedies for Employment Discrimination, 39 U. of Chi.L.Rev. 30 (1971); and Gould, Labor Arbitration of Grievances Involving Racial Discrimination, cited in the main case, contain analyses and references pertinent to the questions raised in this note as well as to those raised in note 2. See also Platt, The Relationship Between Arbitration and Title VII of the Civil Rights Act of 1964, 3 Ga.L.Rev. 398 (1968).

Materials relevant to the overlap between Title VII and the Civil Rights Act of 1866 are to be found at pp. 982–990 supra.

4. Tipler v. E. I. duPont deNemours and Co., 443 F.2d 125 (6th Cir. 1971), holds that the National Labor Relations Board's adverse determination on a claim of discriminatory discharge does not bar a Title VII action. For other discussions of the relationship of Title VII to the National Labor Relations Act, see, e. g., Fuchs and Ellis, Title VII: Relationship and Effect on the National Labor Relations Board, 7 B.C. Ind. & Com.L.Rev. 575 (1966); Rosen, Division of Authority Under Title VII of the Civil Rights Act of 1964: A Preliminary Study in Federal-State Interagency Relations, 34 Geo.Wash.L.Rev. 846 (1966); Comment, Racial Discrimination on the Jobsite: Competing Theories and Competing Forums, 12 U.C.L.A.L.Rev. 1186 (1965); Comment, Jurisdictional Conflicts in Minority Employment Relations: NLRB and EEOC, 2 U.San Fran.L.Rev. 149 (1967).

5. Sections 706(c) and (d) and 708, supra, contain the essentials of Title VII's attempt to accommodate to state law. They leave many questions unanswered. See, e. g., Blumrosen, Black Employment and the Law 64–73, 79–83 (Rutgers University Press 1971); Peck, Remedies for Racial Discrimination in Employment: A Comparative Evaluation of Forums, 46 Wash.L.Rev. 455, 460–461 (1970); Rosen, Division of Authority Under Title VII of the Civil Rights Act of 1964: A Preliminary Study in Federal-State Interagency Relations, 34 Geo.Wash.L.Rev. 846 (1966); Severn, Legal Restraints on Racial Discrimination in Employment 93–96 (Twentieth Century Fund 1966).

VOUTSIS v. UNION CARBIDE CORP.

United States Court of Appeals,
Second Circuit, 1971.
452 F.2d 889, certiorari denied 4 EPD
¶ 7813, 1972.

Before LUMBARD, FEINBERG, and OAKES, Circuit Judges.

OAKES, C. J.: Appellant, Marina Voutsis, a former employee of appellee, Union Carbide, appeals from the dismissal of her complaint charging appellee with sex discrimination. The summary judgment dismissal was for failure to state a claim because appellant had filed her complaint with intervenor United States Equal Employment Opportunity Commission (hereinafter EEOC) too *soon*, that is, before the expiration of the 60-day period prescribed for deferral to state administrative and judicial proceedings in 42 U.S.C.A. § 2000e–5(b), and on the further ground that she had foreclosed federal action by electing to pursue her state remedies by entering into, and was bound by, "a settlement" with Union Carbide in the state proceedings. The opinion below, reaffirmed in a rehearing and reported at 321 F.Supp. 830, 834 (S.D.N.Y.1970), relied on Washington v. Aerojet-General Corp., 282 F. Supp. 517 (C.D.Cal.1968), and on Love v. Pullman Co., 430 F.2d 49, aff'd on rehearing, 430 F.2d at 56–58 (10th Cir.

1970), cert. granted 401 U.S. 907 (1971).

* * *

The rather stormy Senate debate leading up to the passage of the Act made it plain that, as a compromise, Congress was seeking "to give States * * * a reasonable opportunity to act under State law before the commencement of any Federal proceedings by individuals who alleged discrimination." A search of the debates, however, has failed to shed any light on the question whether the words "no charge may be filed" were intended to be construed literally as the trial court felt bound to do, or whether a more reasonable construction was intended, requiring only that federal authorities defer to state proceedings for a limited period of time in order to give the state or local agency "an opportunity to handle the problem under State or local law."

We agree with Judge Fahy, dissenting in Love v. Pullman Co., supra at 54, and with District Judge MacBride, in Antonopulos v. Aerojet-General Corp., 295 F. Supp. 1390, 1395 (E.D.Cal.1968), that the intent of Title VII is remedial and that plaintiffs under it should not be held accountable for a procedural prescience that would have made a Baron Parke happy or a Joseph Chitty proud. See also Local 5, IBEW v. EEOC, 398 F.2d 248, 249 (3rd Cir. 1968), cert. denied 393 U.S. 1021 (1969).

Our conclusion that the complaint was properly filed pursuant to the statute is made easier by the EEOC regulation. Under the regulation, a copy of a complaint filed prematurely with the Commission is promptly transmitted to the appropriate local or state agency, while the complaint itself is held by the EEOC until termination of the local or state proceedings or the lapse of the 60-day statutory waiting period, whichever occurs first, and then it is considered to be filed.

An interpretation of this nature, made by the agency charged with Title VII enforcement, is to be accorded considerable deference by the courts. * * * To place an unnecessary stumbling block in the private litigant's path, particularly when the national enforcement agency has carried out the federal mandate of accommodation to state action, would be hypertechnical and overly legalistic, and would improperly shield a discriminatory organization from the reach of civil litigation. * * *

Nor do we find that appellant elected to pursue state remedies exclusively by entering into a "settlement" with the employer in the state action. In the "settlement" of August 12, 1969, appellee agreed to "offer to the complainant within 30 days after the date of this stipulation the opportunity to accept employment in a non-exempt, non-routine administrative position with higher pay points and a higher salary level conforming to similar assignments within Union Carbide. * * *" This vague "settlement" left open a number of questions— e. g., what is a "non-routine administrative position"—which have yet to be finally answered in the New York State proceedings, despite two appeals and an elapsed time of more than two years. State Division of Human Rights v. Union Carbide Corp., 35 App.Div.2d 664, 315 N.Y.S.2d 401 (1st Dep't 1970); State Division of Human Rights v. Union Carbide Corp., 34 App.Div.2d 636, 310 N.Y.S.2d 396 (1st Dep't 1970). We understand that the case is again before the Division of Human Rights, on remand from the Appellate Division, for the purpose of making a record appropriate for judicial scrutiny.

The Congressional policy here sought to be enforced is one of eliminating employment discrimination, and the statutory enforcement scheme contemplates a resort to the federal remedy if the state machinery has proved inadequate. The federal remedy is independent and cumulative, cf. Vaca v. Sipes, 386 U.S. 171, 177–80 (1967), and it facilitates comprehensive relief. Oatis v. Crown Zellerbach Corp., 398 F.2d 496, 498 (5th Cir. 1968) (class action permissible). While plaintiff may ultimately achieve some individual relief in the state proceedings which might bar her from duplicate relief here, Bowe v. Colgate-Palmolive Co., 416 F.2d 711, 715 (7th Cir. 1969), the federal claim allows the district court to conduct a "full scale inquiry into the charged unlawful motivation in employment practices," Jenkins v. United Gas Corp., 400 F.2d 28, 33 (5th Cir. 1968), and to award broad relief, perhaps for the entire class of employees of which appellant is a member. * * * The "harsh" and "technical" procedural rule of election of remedies, Great American Ins. Co. v. Merchants & Manufacturers Mutual Ins. Co., 423 F.2d 1143, 1146 (6th Cir. 1970), is not applicable to a Title VII civil rights plaintiff, because the purposes underlying enactment of that Title were clearly based on the congressional recognition that "* * * state and local FEPC laws vary widely in effectiveness. In many areas effective enforcement is hampered by inadequate legislation, inadequate procedures, or an inadequate budget. Big interstate industry cannot effectively be handled by the States." The system of remedies is a complementary one, with the federal remedy designed to be available after the state remedy has been tried without producing speedy results.

We also agree with the conclusion of the Fifth, Sixth and Eighth Circuits that the doctrines of *res judicata* and *collateral estoppel* do not bar appellant as a matter of law. Tipler v. E. I. DuPont deNemours & Co., 443 F.2d 125 (6th Cir. 1971) (prior determination by NLRB); Taylor v. Armco Steel Co., 429 F.2d 498 (5th Cir. 1970) (judicial determination prior

to Civil Rights Act); Hutchings v. United States, 428 F.2d 303 (5th Cir. 1970) (arbitration award); Norman v. Missouri Pacific R. R., 414 F.2d 73 (8th Cir. 1969) (judicial determination under Railway Labor Act). But see Dewey v. Reynolds Metals Co., 429 F.2d 324 (6th Cir. 1970), aff'd per curiam without opinion, 402 U.S. 689 (1971) (4–4 decision) (arbitration award interpreting collective bargaining contract).

We express no opinion, however, on the question whether appellant could, without the federal commission's consent, bind herself to a settlement after filing her federal complaint. Cf. D. A. Schulte, Inc. v. Gangi, 328 U.S. 108 (1946); see 29 C.F.R. § 1601.9 (EEOC consent required to withdraw suit). Suffice it to say here that no settlement has been effectuated with or without EEOC consent.

We reverse and remand, with instructions to the district court to proceed in an expeditious manner in accordance with this opinion.

Notes

1. In Love v. Pullman Co., 404 U.S. 522, 92 S.Ct. 616, 30 L.Ed.2d 679 (1972), a unanimous Supreme Court agreed with the Court of Appeals for the Second Circuit in approving the EEOC's method of dealing with complaints that should have gone to a state agency first. The court said:

"Nothing in the Act suggests that the state proceedings may not be initiated by the EEOC acting on behalf of the complainant rather than by the complainant himself, nor is there any requirement that the complaint to the state agency be made in writing rather than by oral referral. Further, we cannot agree with the respondent's claim that the EEOC may not properly hold a claim in 'suspended animation,' automatically filing it upon termination of the state proceedings."

2. See Crosslin v. Mountain States Tel. and Tel. Co., 422 F.2d 1028 (9th Cir. 1970), holding that section 706's requirement of prior recourse to a state agency applies even though the state agency does not have the power to grant "a suitable remedy for the aggrieved person." Plaintiff did not complain to the Arizona Civil Rights Commission before filing with the EEOC. Though "the only sanction or remedy specified by Arizona civil rights laws appears to be a criminal penalty—a fine of not to exceed $300," the court of appeals directed dismissal of plaintiff's Title VII action. The Supreme Court vacated and remanded for reconsideration, 400 U.S. 1004, 91 S.Ct. 562, 27 L.Ed.2d 618 (1971). On remand, the district court denied defendant's motion to dismiss, 4 EPD ¶ 7577 (D.Ariz.1971).

*

Chapter 5

CONSUMER PROTECTION

INTRODUCTORY NOTE

The condition of poverty is usually thought of as one of too few assets and too little income, but it has two other defining characteristics as well: too many debts and too high a level of current expenditure. Aside from mortgage payments or rent, most debt and expenditure is attributable to purchases of consumer goods. Since the poor, by definition, have little income, it is essential that they get their money's worth. Yet they have reason to believe that they are exploited almost every time they buy.

Consider food, for example. It is often alleged that supermarkets charge more for the same items in low-income neighborhoods than they do in middle-class areas, or that food is shipped to poor neighborhoods for sale after it has gone unsold for several days in a chain's middle-class branches. Although studies have not supported this conclusion, they have found that the large chain stores, which can take advantage of economies of scale, are more often located in wealthier neighborhoods; thus, the poor must more often shop at "mom and pop" grocery stores offering lower quality food at higher prices.[1] Nor are the supermarket chains building new branches in the inner city; land is cheaper and operating costs are lower in suburban shopping centers.

Higher prices for daily small purchases can be bad enough, but the most acute consumer problems of the poor stem from purchases of durables (such as furniture, automobiles, and appliances) and services (such as correspondence lessons, self-defense instruction, reducing classes). Although poor persons may have little cash at any one time, they may commit themselves to paying hundreds or thousands of dollars for goods or services by signing instalment contracts or borrowing from various types of financial institutions. Exploitation in such transactions can have drastic consequences. The affected consumers may have to pay for many years for merchandise of little value, and if they fail to do so, they may not only lose the goods but may have their salaries garnisheed, their bank accounts attached, much of their household furniture seized and even their homes levied upon. It is not uncommon for them to lose their jobs, because despite legislation forbidding it,[2] many employers resist the bookkeeping expenses associated with wage garnishment by discharging garnisheed employees.[3] Consumer debt problems also severely affect the marriages and health of the debtors.[4]

"Much of the violence in recent civil disorders has been directed at stores and other commercial establishments in disadvantaged Negro areas. In some cases,

[1] See Federal Trade Commission Economic Report on Food Chain Selling Practices in the District of Columbia and San Francisco (1969).

[2] 15 U.S.C.A. § 1674 (1968).

[3] See authorities collected in Comment, Consumer Legislation and the Poor, 76 Yale L.J. 745, 746 n. 6 (1967).

[4] Caplovitz, Debtors in Default, Report to U. S. Office of Economic Opportunity No. NY–CAP–66–9702 at 14–13 to 14–20 (1971) (Soon to be published as a book under the name Consumers in Trouble).

rioters focused on stores operated by white merchants who, they apparently believed, had been charging exorbitant prices or selling inferior goods. Not all the violence against these stores can be attributed to "revenge" for such practices. Yet it is clear that many residents of disadvantaged Negro neighborhoods believe they suffer constant abuses by local merchants.

"Significant grievances concerning unfair commercial practices affecting Negro consumers were found in 11 of the 20 cities studied by the Commission. The fact that most of the merchants who operate stores in almost every Negro area are white undoubtedly contributes to the conclusion among Negroes that they are exploited by white society.

"It is difficult to assess the precise degree and extent of exploitation. No systematic and reliable survey comparing consumer pricing and credit practices in all-Negro and other neighborhoods has ever been conducted on a nationwide basis. Differences in prices and credit practices between white middle-income areas and Negro low-income areas to some extent reflect differences in the real costs of serving these two markets (such as differential losses from pilferage in supermarkets), but the exact extent of these differential real costs has never been estimated accurately. Finally, an examination of exploitative consumer practices must consider the particular structure and functions of the low-income consumer durables market.

Installment Buying

"This complex situation can best be understood by first considering certain basic facts:

'Various cultural factors generate constant pressure on low-income families to buy many relatively expensive durable goods and display them in their homes. This pressure comes in part from continuous exposure to commercial advertising, especially on television. In January 1967, over 88 percent of all Negro households had TV sets. A 1961 study of 464 low-income families in New York City showed that 95 percent of these relatively poor families had TV sets.

'Many poor families have extremely low incomes, bad previous credit records, unstable sources of income, or other attributes which make it virtually impossible for them to buy merchandise from established large national or local retail firms. These families lack enough savings to pay cash, and they cannot meet the standard credit requirements of established general merchants because they are too likely to fall behind in their payments.

'Poor families in urban areas are far less mobile than others. A 1967 Chicago study of low-income Negro households indicated their low automobile ownership compelled them to patronize primarily local neighborhood merchants. These merchants typically provided smaller selection, poorer services, and higher prices than big national outlets. The 1961 New York study also indicated that families who shopped outside their own neighborhoods were far less likely to pay exorbitant prices.

'Most low-income families are uneducated concerning the nature of credit purchase contracts, the legal rights and obligations of both buyers and sellers, sources of advice for consumers who are having difficulties with merchants, and the operation of the courts concerned with these matters. In contrast, merchants engaged in selling goods to them are very well informed.

'In most states, the laws governing relations between consumers and merchants in effect offer protection only to informed, sophisticated parties with understanding of each other's rights and obligations. Consequently, these laws are little suited to protect the rights of most low-income consumers.

"In this situation, exploitative practices flourish. Ghetto residents who want to buy relatively expensive goods cannot do so from standard retail outlets and are thus restricted to local stores. Forced to use credit, they have little understanding of the pitfalls of credit buying. But because they have unstable incomes and frequently fail to make payments, the cost to the merchants of serving them is significantly above that of serving middle-income consumers. Consequently, a special kind of merchant appears to sell them goods on terms designed to cover the high cost of doing business in ghetto neighborhoods." Report of the National Advisory Commission on Civil Disorders 274–75 (Bantam ed. 1968).

The plan of this section of the book is first to examine common selling practices and the primarily pertinent legal doctrines —fraud, misrepresentation and unconscionability. Second, the materials discuss problems arising from the institution of credit *per se,* as opposed to the underlying sales—these topics include rate regulation and disclosure and the rules governing debt collection. Finally, the text offers readings on existing and proposed consumer remedies, both private and public.

SECTION 1. SELLING

Note on Sales Tactics

No sterile summary can accurately describe the varied techniques used to bilk the poor; the very names of some of the tactics—such as the bait and switch,[1]

[1] The store advertises merchandise at a low price. But salesmen tell customers who

the T.O.,[2] and the chain referral [3]—suggest the world of the con men. Many of

respond that the advertised merchandise is unavailable or confide that it is of poor quality. They "switch" the customers to higher-priced models. This tactic, of course, is not confined to low-income retailers.

[2] Or "turnover".

The salesman starts by showing the customer a pile of junk for $198. One store keeps its bait furniture piled in a dark corner, lit by a naked lightbulb. It is painted battleship gray, every stick of it, down to what used to be the chrome legs on the dinette table. If you wanted to give a salesman a heart attack, all you'd have to do is say, "Okay, I'll take it." "You don't want this stuff," he says. "It'll fall apart in a couple of months. Besides, a person like you can afford something better. Let me show you something a little bit better." The salesman then takes the stiff upstairs in an elevator, but not before shaking him down for a $50 deposit for the privilege of "seeing the warehouse." The elevator gets "stuck" after the first trip up and doesn't get unstuck until the stiff has been signed up for a bill of goods. The idea of the T.O. is to show the stiff successively more expensive suites of furniture without letting him get discouraged about the price.

When he begins to look green around the gills the first time around, the salesman turns him over to another salesman who is introduced as the "assistant manager." The A.M. immediately "sandbags"—knocks 50 per cent off—whatever the first salesman quoted. The stiff is so taken aback that he lets the A.M. build him up again. Just before he begins to feel weak again, the A.M. turns him over to the "manager," who slashes the A.M.'s prices "as a special favor to you." The manager will try to build him up to, say, $800 or $1,000. If the stiff says he "wants to think about it" and tries to leave, he finds that the elevator is on the fritz. The "owner" now appears, knocks off a hundred bucks or two, and this usually convinces the stiff to sign. At which point the elevator suddenly clicks into action. C. Karpel, Ghetto Fraud on the Installment Plan, New York Magazine, May 26, 1969, pp. 24–25. Reprinted by permission of William Morris Agency, Inc. Copyright © 1969 by Craig Karpel.

[3] The customer is told that he is not really making a purchase, but is joining a money-making plan. He will get a commission on every new customer he successfully refers to the seller, enabling him to recoup the cost of the merchandise and then some. The cus-

the worst frauds are perpetrated by door-to-door sellers, although consumer fraud is by no means limited to this type of selling.

A few attempts have been made to describe the flavor of deceptive selling schemes.[4] None of them fully capture the psychological devices by which salesmen take consumers into their confidence by using their idiom, insisting on first names, and, importantly, by remaining with the potential buyers for hours until they are worn down to the point of signing the contracts. The following ma-

tomers he refers can get commissions, too, and he will get commissions on their sales as well, and so on down the pyramid. As with a chain letter, the bubble soon bursts.

[4] Caplovitz, The Poor Pay More, 12–31 (1967); Karpel, supra note 2; Schrag, Counsel for the Deceived (1972); Schrag, "Bleak House 1968, A Report on Consumer Test Litigation" 44 N.Y.U.L.Rev. 115, 118–20 (1969) Carper, Not with a Gun (1973).

terials, from a case brought by a government agency, constitute one of the best available records of door-to-door sales techniques. The first portion—the "authorized presentation"—is collected from materials supplied to the New York City Department of Consumer Affairs by the company in question, which used a large fleet of salesmen to make about 1500 sales a year in customers' homes—always by referral from other customers. The second portion—the affidavits—describes what actually happened during the sales, as reported by the customers, two of whom were actually agency employees who were tape-recording the salesmen's statements. In the litigation, the company and the salesmen denied that the salesmen made the alleged statements; the Department then revealed, in reply affidavits, that it had made concealed recordings.

AUTHORIZED DOOR-TO-DOOR SALES PRESENTATION OF COMPACT ELECTRA CORP.

INTRODUCTION

1. GOOD EVENING, _____ IS MY NAME. BILL AND MARY JONES ASKED ME TO STOP BY AND YOUR (wife or husband) SAID IT WOULD BE CONVENIENT AT (time). I'D LIKE TO STEP IN A MINUTE IF I'M WELCOME.
   (Visit at least 5 minutes)

2. HAVE YOU TALKED TO BILL OR MARY SINCE WE CALLED YOU? NO.

3. WELL, EVIDENTLY THEY LEFT IT UP TO ME TO EXPLAIN.
   * * *

4. ONE OF THE THINGS I WANT TO TALK ABOUT THIS EVENING IS SAVING MONEY. THIS IS SOMETHING WE ALL TALK ABOUT BUT FEW OF US EVER DO ANYTHING ABOUT. AND I THINK YOU'LL AGREE THAT SAVING MONEY IS JUST AS IMPORTANT AS MAKING MONEY. NOW, THE WAY I'M TALKING ABOUT SAVING MONEY IS THROUGH A SHOPPERS SERVICE AND THERE'S ONE THING I'D LIKE TO MAKE CLEAR AT THIS POINT. THIS SERVICE IS NOT FOR SALE. YOU COULDN'T BUY IT AT ANY PRICE.

5. THERE ARE TWO PRIMARY REASONS WHY A SHOPPERS'S SERVICE SAVES ITS MEMBERS BOTH TIME AND MONEY. FIRST OF ALL, MASS BUYING POWER. THOUSANDS OF FAMILIES BUYING AS A SINGLE UNIT TO GET THE LOWEST POSSIBLE QUANTITY PRICE. YOU'RE FAMILIAR WITH HEPTZ RENT-A-CAR. THEY BUY ALL FIRST LINE CARS FULLY EQUIPPED AND I'M SURE YOU REALIZE THEY BUY THAT PARTICULAR CAR FOR LESS THAN WE COULD. THE REASON IS THAT THEY BUY THOUSANDS OF CARS. THIS IS WHAT WE MEAN BY MASS BUYING POWER.

6. THE SECOND REASON IS FULL TIME PROFESSIONAL SHOPPERS, TO GET THE HIGHEST QUALITY PRODUCTS AT THE LOWEST POSSIBLE PRICES. LARGE COMPANIES SUCH AS THE HOLIDAY INNS HIRE HIGH PRICED PROFESSIONAL PEOPLE WHOSE ONLY JOB IS TO FIND THE BEST PRODUCT AT THE BEST PRICE. A SHOPPERS SERVICE GIVES ADVANTAGES TO ITS MEMBERS MUCH THE SAME AS HERTZ OR HOLIDAY INN RECEIVE.

7. IF, IN THE NEXT YEAR, YOU WERE ABLE TO BUY ALMOST EVERY PRODUCT YOU USE, ANYTHING FROM ASPIRIN TO AUTOMOBILES, THROUGH A SHOPPERS SERVICE I'M SURE YOU FOLKS REALIZE THAT YOU WOULD HAVE TO SAVE A GREAT DEAL OF MONEY. THE U. S. DEPARTMENT OF COMMERCE TELLS US THAT THE AVERAGE AMERICAN FAMILY SPENDS OVER $5,000.00 EACH YEAR MAINTAINING A HOME AND SUPPORTING A FAMILY. IF YOU SAVE JUST 10% YOU WOULD

HAVE TO SAVE $500.00 A YEAR. NOW I KNOW THAT I HAVEN'T GIVEN YOU ANY DETAILS, BUT ON THE STRENGTH OF WHAT I'VE TOLD YOU, IF YOU HAD A SERVICE LIKE THIS WOULD YOU USE IT? (Get answer)

(It is very important at this point to get a positive answer before continuing. If the customer seems unsure it means that they don't understand the shopping service. Simply re-explain it and ask again for a positive answer).

8. NOW, AS I TOLD YOU BEFORE, THIS SERVICE IS NOT FOR SALE, BUT MY COMPANY DOES ALLOW ME TO GIVE IT TO PEOPLE UNDER TWO CONDITIONS. FIRST, THAT THEY WOULD USE IT IF THEY HAD IT. AND THIS YOU'VE ALREADY ANSWERED. THE SECOND, IS THAT YOU WOULD RECOMMEND OUR PRODUCT JUST LIKE _____ AND _____ ARE DOING, AND THIS YOU CAN'T ANSWER BECAUSE YOU HAVEN'T SEEN IT. IF YOU FEEL THAT YOU CAN RECOMMEND IT, I WANT YOU TO TELL ME. IF NOT, THERE IS NO OBLIGATION. IS THAT FAIR ENOUGH.

9. FINE, I'LL STEP OUT TO THE CAR AND I'LL BE RIGHT BACK.

HISTORY

1. NOW FOLKS, I'D LIKE TO TELL YOU A LITTLE ABOUT THE COMPANY THAT MAKES THIS PRODUCT, BUT BEFORE I DO, I'D JUST LIKE TO SAY ONE THING. BILL AND MARY DIDN'T SEND ME OVER HERE TO WRESTLE YOU FOR YOUR POCKETBOOK OR INSULT YOU. ALL I WANT TO DO ON A VERY FRIENDLY BASIS, IS SHOW YOU THIS EQUIPMENT AND EXPLAIN THE SHOPPING SERVICE. IF YOU FEEL THAT YOU CAN PROFIT FROM IT THE SAME AS BILL AND MARY, WONDERFUL, AND IF NOT, I'LL THANK YOU FOR YOUR TIME AND BE ON ABOUT MY BUSINESS. FAIR ENOUGH?

2. I WORK FOR A LOCAL COMPANY WHO IS THE FRANCHISED DISTRIBUTOR FOR INTERSTATE ENGINEERING CORPORATION, WHO HAS FACTORIES THROUGHOUT THE WORLD. WHEN INTERSTATE WAS FIRST ORGANIZED IN 1937 THEY BUILT A LIGHT AIRCRAFT CALLED THE INTERSTATE CADET. WHEN THE SECOND WORLD WAR STARTED, THE GOVERNMENT USED HUNDREDS OF THESE CADETS AS TRAINERS FOR OUR PILOTS. THEY CALLED IT THE L-6.

3. ALSO, YOU HAVE HEARD OF LOCKHEED, NORTH AMERICAN, NORTHRUP, DOUGLAS AND BOEING. DURING THE WAR YEARS, INTERSTATE MADE PRECISION PARTS AND ASSEMBLIES THAT CONTRIBUTED TO THE PERFORMANCE OF AIRCRAFT MANUFACTURED BY THESE COMPANIES.

4. INTERSTATE BUILT THE ACTUATING CYLINDERS THAT OPEN AND CLOSE THE BOMB BAY DOORS ON THE B-29. THEY ALSO BUILT THE ENTIRE FUSELAGE FOR THE NAVY'S AD-6. THIS WAS A CARRIER BASED BOMBER AND THEY CALLED IT THE WORK HORSE OF THE NAVY. THEY ALSO BUILT THE FUSELAGE FOR THE HILLER HELICOPTER.

5. AFTER THE WAR INTERSTATE USED ITS TREMENDOUS TECH-
NICAL KNOWLEDGE IN SUPPLYING VITAL COMPONENTS FOR
THIS NATION'S MISSILE DEFENSE SYSTEM ON THE ATLAS,
NIKE, JUPITER AS WELL AS MANY OTHER MISSILES. INTER-
STATE IS A PRIME CONTRACTOR ON THE NAVY'S POLARIS
PROGRAM. THIS IS WHERE THEY FIRE THE POLARIS MIS-
SILE FROM NUCLEAR SUBS UNDER WATER. THEY DESIGNED
AND BUILT THE MISSILE FIRING TEST INSTRUMENTATION
THAT WAS USED.

6. I THINK YOU WILL AGREE THAT INTERSTATE HAS A BACK-
GROUND AS AIR SPECIALISTS. (As an afterthought) I'VE BEEN
CALLED AN AIR SPECIALIST, TOO—A HOT AIR SPECIALIST.

7. WHAT DO YOU THINK I HAVE IN THE BOX?

* * *

[The salesman returns with a vacuum cleaner, which he demonstrates. The
price is $425 cash, or approximately $525 on a 3-year contract.]

CLOSE

THAT IS THE COMPACT. * * * WHAT DO YOU THINK OF IT?
CAN YOU SEE WHERE THE COMPACT IS A BENEFIT OVER AND
ABOVE WHAT YOU ARE PRESENTLY USING?

IS THE COMPACT SOMETHING YOU COULD RECOMMEND TO YOUR
FRIENDS JUST AS BILL AND MARY HAVE RECOMMENDED IT TO
YOU?

YOU BUY THE COMPACT LIKE ANYTHING ELSE. THE COMPACT,
POLISHAIRE, EVERYTHING YOU SEE IS JUST $_____ -CASH- OR
AS MANY DO. THE BUDGET PLAN—$_____ DOWN AND $_____
A MONTH. THAT'S REALLY GREAT, ISN'T IT?

NOW WHEN BILL AND MARY PURCHASED THEIR COMPACT WE
GAVE THEM A WONDERFUL OPPORTUNITY TO POSSIBLY OFF-
SET THE COST OF IT AND WE DID IT ALL THROUGH THE USE OF
OUR OWN ADVERTISING BUDGET.

I WOULD LIKE TO ASK YOU A QUESTION * * * IN YOUR OPIN-
ION WHAT IS THE REAL PURPOSE OF ADVERTISING? (Get answer.)

IN OTHER WORDS, THE MAIN PURPOSE OF ADVERTISING IS TO
ACQUAINT PEOPLE WITH THE PRODUCT, ISN'T THAT TRUE?
IN FACT, MANY MAJOR COMPANIES SPEND MILLIONS OF DOL-
LARS EVERY MONTH ADVERTISING THEIR PRODUCTS. FOR EX-
AMPLE . . . I AM SURE YOU ARE FAMILIAR WITH THE JOHN-
NY CARSON SHOW. IT COSTS $16,000 TO BUY ONE MINUTE ON
THIS SHOW. DO YOU THINK THAT WE COULD SHOW YOU EVERY-
THING WE HAVE SHOWN YOU THIS EVENING IN ONE MINUTE ON
THE JOHNNY CARSON SHOW? (Get answer.)

NO MATTER WHAT WE SHOWED YOU IN ONE MINUTE ON THE
JOHNNY CARSON SHOW, DO YOU THINK THAT IT WOULD CON-
VINCE YOU TO GO DOWN AND BUY THE COMPACT? (No.) THAT'S
RIGHT! WE KNOW THAT THAT KIND OF ADVERTISING IS REAL-
LY EXPENSIVE AND DOESN'T GET THE KIND OF RESULTS WE
WANT. JUST BECAUSE SOME GUY ON T. V., IN A MAGAZINE, OR
ON A BILLBOARD TELLS YOU TO BUY HIS PRODUCT, YOU DON'T
ALWAYS DO IT, DO YOU, JOE?

NOW WE ARE NO DIFFERENT FROM ANYONE ELSE—WE MUST ADVERTISE THE COMPACT. HOWEVER, WE MUST ADVERTISE IN SUCH A WAY AS TO ASSURE OUR COMPANY OF RESULTS. WHEN BILL AND MARY BOUGHT THEIR COMPACT THEY DECIDED TO HELP US ADVERTISE. FOR EXAMPLE, WITHOUT THEIR HELP I WOULDN'T BE HERE THIS EVENING, WOULD I? TO SHOW OUR APPRECIATION TO THEM WE HAVE MADE IT POSSIBLE FOR THEM TO ACTUALLY SAVE HUNDREDS OF DOLLARS. HELEN, YOU PROBABLY RUN THE HOUSEHOLD. SAVING MONEY IS THE SAME AS MAKING MONEY, ISN'T IT? DO YOU AGREE WITH THAT, JOE? IN OTHER WORDS, A PENNY SAVED IS A PENNY EARNED, RIGHT? IF I WERE TO SHOW YOU A WAY WHERE YOU AND HELEN WOULD BE ABLE TO SAVE ON THE AVERAGE OF FROM $10 TO $20 A MONTH, YOU WOULDN'T BE MAD, WOULD YOU?

JOE AND HELEN, THE UNITED STATES BUREAU OF CENSUS STATES THAT THE AVERAGE AMERICAN FAMILY SPENDS $5,-047.00 EACH YEAR. OVER A 20 YEAR PERIOD THIS ADDS UP TO OVER $100,000.00. MUCH OF THIS MONEY IS SPENT YEAR AFTER YEAR FOR SUCH THINGS AS AUTOMOBILES, CLOTHING, FURNITURE, FOOD, DRUGS, AND OTHER FAMILY NEEDS. THE AVERAGE FAMILY SPENDS THESE HARD EARNED DOLLARS WITHOUT EVER HAVING THE TIME OR EXPERIENCE TO GET THE BEST BUYS POSSIBLE. NOW JOE AND HELEN, YOU AND I BOTH KNOW THAT ANY COMPANY THAT HAD $100,000.00 TO SPEND WOULD HAVE A PURCHASING AGENT, A MAN WHO WOULD GO OUT AND GET THE BEST BUYS POSSIBLE FOR THE LEAST AMOUNT OF MONEY. HELEN, LET ME ASK YOU A QUESTION—WHO IS THE PURCHASING AGENT IN YOUR HOME? THEN ABOUT THE BEST YOU CAN DO, HELEN, IS TO GO OUT. LOOK IN THE NEWSPAPER, AND WATCH THE SALES TO TAKE ADVANTAGE OF THOSE OFFERS. RIGHT? (Right.) IF YOU ARE ANYTHING LIKE MY WIFE YOU PROBABLY BURN UP MORE GAS LOOKING FOR BARGAINS THAN YOU SAVE ON THE BARGAIN ITSELF. RIGHT?

IN ORDER TO LET YOU TAKE ADVANTAGE OF THE TREMENDOUS BUYING POWER THE TYPICAL AMERICAN FAMILY HAS, WE WILL GIVE YOU, ABSOLUTELY FREE, A MEMBERSHIP IN FAMILY BUYING SHOPPING SERVICE THAT CAN BE WORTH HUNDREDS OF DOLLARS TO YOU! IT MEANS SIMPLY THIS: BY PURCHASING THE COMPACT SYSTEM TONIGHT AND HELPING US ADVERTISE, YOU HAVE THE RIGHT TO BUY AT TREMENDOUS SAVINGS ALMOST EVERY STANDARD PRODUCT ON THE AMERICAN MARKET TODAY FROM AUTOMOBILES TO ASPIRIN. IN OTHER WORDS, NATIONWIDE SERVES AS YOUR PERSONAL PURCHASING AGENT WHOSE JOB IT IS TO GET THE BEST BUYS POSSIBLE FOR YOUR FAMILY. NOW, HERE IS EXACTLY WHAT I MEAN.

WHAT IS A RECENT MAJOR PURCHASE YOU HAVE MADE. (Get answer.) WHERE DID YOU GET IT?

WHEN YOU BOUGHT THAT (item) YOU PAID FOR LOTS OF THINGS YOU DIDN'T GET. FOR EXAMPLE: RETAIL ADS, SALES COMMISSIONS, AND STORE PROFIT. THROUGH FAMILY BUYING YOU WOULD HAVE SAVED THIS EXPENSE. WHEN YOU DEAL DIRECTLY THROUGH MAXIMUM DISCOUNT BUYING SOURCES IT'S EASY

TO SAVE $10 TO $20 EVERY MONTH. CAN YOU SEE HOW THIS WOULD BE A BENEFIT TO YOUR FAMILY?

THE BEAUTIFUL THING ABOUT THIS PROGRAM IS THAT YOU SAVE ON THE ITEMS YOU ARE NOW BUYING. IN OTHER WORDS, YOU DON'T HAVE TO BUY ANYTHING DIFFERENT OR UNUSUAL TO SAVE MORE THAN THE COST OF THE COMPACT SYSTEM. NOW, HERE IS A PARTIAL LIST OF THE MERCHANDISE THAT IS AVAILABLE TO YOU AT TREMENDOUS SAVINGS. (Show list.) ISN'T THIS FANTASTIC!!

HERE ARE SOME TYPICAL EXAMPLES OF SAVINGS OFFERED TO MEMBERS THROUGH NATIONWIDE. (Give 3 Examples.) ALL WE ASK IS THAT YOU RECOMMEND THE COMPACT TO 15 OF YOUR CLOSE FRIENDS AND RELATIVES JUST AS BILL AND MARY HAVE DONE. NOW REMEMBER, YOU DON'T HAVE TO BE AFRAID THAT WE ARE GOING TO HIGH PRESSURE OR INSULT YOUR FRIENDS. WE DO TWO THINGS: SHOW THE COMPACT AND EXPLAIN THE SHOPPING PROGRAM TO THEM, AND THE REST IS UP TO THEM.

HELEN, I AM SURE IF YOU KNEW A WAY YOU COULD SHOW YOUR NEIGHBORS HOW THEY COULD SAVE FROM $10 TO $20 EVERY MONTH YOU WOULD TELL THEM, WOULDN'T YOU? SO YOU ARE REALLY DOING THEM A FAVOR BY GIVING THEM THE OPPORTUNITY TO SEE THE COMPACT AND THE SHOPPING PROGRAM, AREN'T YOU? ANOTHER THING * * * WHEN YOU GIVE US THE NAMES WE ASK THAT BOTH THE HUSBAND AND WIFE BE TOGETHER FOR THREE REASONS: ONE, WE ONLY PRESENT THIS PROGRAM ONE TIME—THAT DOESN'T MEAN YOU CANNOT BUY THE COMPACT LATER—YOU CAN BUY IT ANYTIME. BUT IT DOES MEAN THAT THIS IS THE ONLY OPPORTUNITY THEY WILL HAVE TO GET THE SHOPPING PROGRAM. SECOND, AND MOST IMPORTANT WE DON'T WANT THE MAN TO THINK SOME HIGH PRESSURE SALESMAN TRIED TO SELL HIS WIFE A BILL OF GOODS. ANOTHER THING WE HAVE FOUND IS, THE HUSBAND GETS JUST AS EXCITED ABOUT FAMILY BUYING AS THE WIFE DOES.

I WANT YOU TO UNDERSTAND THAT THIS SHOPPING PROGRAM CAN BE WORTH HUNDREDS AND MAYBE EVEN THOUSANDS OF DOLLARS IN SAVINGS. THAT'S IF YOU USE IT. IF YOU DON'T USE THIS PROGRAM YOU WOULDN'T SAVE A NICKEL, WOULD YOU? THE REASON WE ARE ABLE TO GIVE IT TO YOU AT NO COST IS JUST AS I EXPLAINED EARLIER. THIS IS THE WAY WE SPEND OUR ADVERTISING DOLLARS. WE PAY YOUR INITIATION FEE AND GIVE YOU THIS CERTIFICATE WHICH IS GOOD FOR ONE FULL YEAR. IF, AT THE END OF THAT TIME, YOU WANT TO RENEW YOUR MEMBERSHIP, IT COSTS YOU ONLY $12.00 A YEAR. IT WOULD CERTAINLY BE WORTH THAT, WOULDN'T IT? JOE AND HELEN, YOU'VE ALREADY SAID YOU REALLY LOVE THE COMPACT AND THAT YOU WOULD BE WILLING TO RECOMMEND IT TO YOUR FRIENDS. AFTER SEEING THE SHOPPING PROGRAM I KNOW YOU ARE ANXIOUS TO START SAVING MONEY RIGHT NOW, SO I'LL JUST FIX THIS UP.

(Head down—Close on telephone number) JUST GIVE ME YOUR PHONE NUMBER AND I'LL FIX IT UP.

OBJECTIONS

1. "I can't afford it!"
   (Smile)

The objection that practically every salesman in the U. S. gets the most is "I can't afford it"; some people say it who don't mean it at all. There are two reasons why a person would tell me "I can't afford it,"—one is he doesn't have $ (full amt.) to give me right now—that's no problem because we have this set up on a payment basis and before your 1st payment would be due in 30 days you will have received your membership kit from Family Buying and, I'm sure, will have picked out some things you were to buy anyway that will save you more than what the payments will be.

The other reason a person would say I can't afford it is because he doesn't have $ (monthly payment) to make a payment with. If this is true I will be the first guy in town to tell you don't fool with it, but as I said earlier, Bill and Mary bought the Compact and they have received their free Family Buying Membership. They wanted you to have the same opportunity.

One other thing I want to say is if I have said anything that you don't understand or anything you don't believe please ask me about it because if you don't take advantage of this, and it's my fault, I have unintentionally cheated you out of several thousand dollars.

Now I'm going to pack it up and the decision is yours.

(Back off chair.)

IF PEOPLE UNDERSTAND YOU AND BELIEVE YOU THEY WILL BUY

2. If after the above answer people still say "I can't afford it."

If I ask you an honsest question will you give me an honest answer in return? (Answer) If your refrigerator or freezer went bad in the morning would you buy another one. (Yes.) Everyone I have ever asked that question said yes because too many things would go to waste without a refrigerator and I couldn't afford not to have one. The amount of money you would waste without a refrigerator would not be more than the amount you will waste by buying at retail the rest of your life.

If people question you too much on how it all works and you don't know —don't fib to them. Give them the T. V. set story. Don't be smart or cute —people don't like that, but this little story gets the job done in practically all cases.

If after a couple of closes you feel you are getting the run around— nickel and dime excuses, real politely tell them: "You know it's silly for me to sit here and try to convince you to save your money through smart buying—I apologize because that decision is strictly yours." (Back off chair.)

IF PEOPLE UNDERSTAND YOU AND BELIEVE YOU THEY WILL BUY.

AFFIDAVITS OF BESS MYERSON, ROY MORRISON, ERNESTINE NUGENT, BETTY WHITE, ISABEL LITTLE, AND MARIA HERNANDEZ, AND REPLY AFFIDAVITS OF MARIA HERNANDEZ AND ISABEL LITTLE, IN GRANT V. COMPACT ELECTRA CORP., INDEX NO. 49060/70 (S.CT. NEW YORK CO., N. Y.)

SUPREME COURT OF THE STATE OF NEW YORK
COUNTY OF NEW YORK

BESS MYERSON GRANT, as Commissioner of the Department of Consumer Affairs of the City of New York,

Plaintiff,

vs

COMPACT ELECTRA CORP., NORTHEAST DISCOUNT CORP. and HYMAN SINDELMAN,

Defendants,

AFFIDAVIT

STATE OF NEW YORK
COUNTY OF NEW YORK } SS.:

BESS MYERSON GRANT, being duly sworn, deposes and says:

1. I am the Commissioner of the Department of Consumer Affairs of the City of New York and the plaintiff herein. I make this affidavit in support of plaintiff's application for a temporary restraining order and a preliminary injunction enjoining the defendants from false and deceptive representations and practices in connection with the sale of vacuum cleaners. The nature of the temporary and preliminary relief sought in this application is set forth in more specific detail in the final paragraph of this affidavit.

2. Plaintiff, acting pursuant to the provisions of Chapter 64, Title A of the Administrative Code of the City of New York, is about to commence an action to enjoin the defendants from making use of unfair, deceptive and unconscionable trade practices in the selling of vacuum cleaners.

3. By § 2203d–4.0(d) of the Administrative Code of the City of New York plaintiff is expressly empowered to make application to the Supreme Court for an order enjoining deceptive or unconscionable trade practices in the sale of consumer goods or in the collection of consumer debts.

4. In the discharge of my official duties, I caused an investigation to be made by my staff of the business practices of the defendants. Information gathered by our investigation with respect to the trade practices, sales methods and representations to induce sales and collect on installment sales contracts of the defendants is presented herein in the affidavits of Maria Hernandez, Isabel Little, Roy Morrison, Ernestine Nugent and Betty White attached hereto as plaintiff's Exhibit "I" and referred to hereinafter as the "Hernandez and others' affidavits".

5. In the course of our departmental investigation I learned that Compact Electra Corp. sells vacuum cleaners by gaining access to consumers' homes by offering consumers, by mail or telephone, a free gift. The consumer is never told that the sender of the postcard or the telephone caller

offers the gift in connection with the sale of a vacuum cleaner. This fact is evidenced by the postcard itself, annexed hereto as plaintiff's exhibit "2" and by paragraph 2 of the affidavit of Betty White submitted herein. (plaintiff's Exhibit "1").

6. I and my staff learned in the course of our investigation that salesmen for the defendant Compact Electra Corp. regularly made the following representations and engaged in the following practices with respect to an organization known as Family Buying Power: (See plaintiff's Exhibit "1" —Hernandez affidavit.)

a) The purchaser of a vacuum cleaner will receive a lifetime membership in Family Buying Power, a so-called consumer's "wholesale" buying club.

b) Certain items are available through Family Buying Power at prices specified by the Compact Electra salesman.

c) Every type of merchandise except food is available through Family Buying Power.

d) Family Buying Power is owned and operated by Compact Electra Corp.

e) The cost of the vacuum cleaner, $423.95 plus finance charges, can be recouped by savings available to the consumer through Family Buying Power.

7. Upon information and belief, the false and deceptive nature of these representations by Compact Electra salesmen was confirmed by statements made to Mr. Stephen Newman of my staff by Mr. Robert Dortch, president of that organization [Family Buying Power]. He interviewed Mr. Dortch on June 25, 1970 at the office of Family Buying Power in Cranbury, New Jersey.

8. Upon information and belief, in the course of the interview, Mr. Dortch stated that, contrary to defendant Compact Electra's representations:

a) The memberships in Family Buying Power offered free by defendant Compact Electra to induce sales of its vacuum cleaners are for one year only and are not lifetime memberships.

b) Only a limited range of products are available to members of Family Buying Power. Excluded are products that are fair-traded; products of local rather than national distribution; products that are house brands.

c) Prices at which members are able to buy are by no means wholesale prices; Mr. Dortch does not approve of the term "wholesale" to describe his organization.

d) Family Buying Power does not guarantee specific prices or a specific price reduction for items members may wish to buy.

e) Even with the discounts available to members of Family Buying Power, it would be virtually impossible for purchasers to recoup the cost of the vacuum cleaner in one year.

f) Family Buying Power is not owned, controlled or operated by the defendant Compact Electra Corp.

9. As attested by the affidavit of Betty White, submitted herein, (plaintiff's Exhibit "1") the representations by defendant Compact Electra's

salesmen that the prospective purchaser or buyer is entitled to a free gift are false and deceptive. The gift offered, of trifling value, is not in fact free. It is given only if the prospective purchaser actually buys the vacuum cleaner and gives the salesman the names of ten additional prospective customers.

10. It is the custom for Compact Electra salesmen to make, as part of their sales methods, the following additional statements and representations and indulge in the following practices as attested in the affidavits of Hernandez et al, (plaintiff's Exhibit "1") in order to induce prospective buyers to sign additional sales contracts for the purchase of vacuum cleaners:

a) The salesman is prepared to leave the vacuum cleaner with the consumer with absolutely no obligation on the part of the consumer and that the consumer can later decide not to accept the vacuum cleaner although he has signed a contract.

b) The document tendered to the consumer for signature is not a contract but merely a "receipt" for the vacuum cleaner, or an application for membership in Family Buying Power.

c) The salesman would write on the consumer's copy of the contract, but not on Compact's copy, that the sale was conditional upon approval by the signing consumer's spouse, thereby relieving the consumer from any obligation if the spouse did not approve the purchase.

d) The salesman would leave his telephone number, in case the consumer later decided not to purchase the vacuum cleaner so that the consumer could contact the salesman and have him pick up the vacuum cleaner.

e) The salesman states that finance charges assessed by Compact are at rates as low as those charged by a bank for a loan.

11. As attested by the affidavits of Hernandez, et al submitted herein all of those representations and practices are false and deceptive in that:

a) Compact *does hold* the consumer fully liable on a signed contract, contrary to its salesmen's representation that the consumer has a trial period after signature, during which he may choose not to buy the vacuum cleaner.

b) The document offered for signature is in fact not a receipt for the vacuum cleaner left on a trial basis, or a membership in Family Buying Power; the document is actually a contract to purchase the Compact vacuum cleaner.

c) Salesmen represent that the signed contract is not binding until approved by the purchaser's spouse, whereas Compact holds the purchaser liable under the contract whether approved by the spouse or not.

d) Although salesmen represent that consumers can call them at home, at a telephone number given, to cancel an order before they submit it to the company, the phone number given is that of the offices of Compact Electra Corp. Upon calling the consumers are told that no one would come to take the machine away, and that they would have to pay.

e) Salesmen represent that the annual percentage rate of interest of 18% charged by Compact as evidenced by the contract of Ernestine Nugent annexed hereto as plaintiff's exhibit "3" is the same as that charged by banks for loans. However, banks do not, and under New

York Banking Law Section 108(4)(b), cannot charge more than six dollars per annum discount per one hundred dollars of the face amount, or 13.8% interest for personal loans.

12.   In the course of our investigation I learned that the defendant Compact Electra Corp. assigns its retail installment sales contracts to the defendant Northeast Discount Corp. Thereafter Compact Electra represents to its customers, that, once a contract is so assigned, the customer has no recourse against Compact Electra. Northeast Discount threatens to sue customers who refuse to pay for vacuum cleaners on the ground the salesman made deceptive representations. That such representations are made by Compact salesmen is attested by the affidavits attached hereto of Roy Morrison and Betty White.

13.   The representations made by Compact Electra Corp. and Northeast Discount Corp. as set forth in paragraph 12 above are false and deceptive in that

a) Compact Electra and Northeast Discount are wholly owned and operated by defendant Hyman Sindelman. They share the same office at 246–14 Jamaica Avenue, Bellerose, New York. These statements were told to Mr. Newman by Mr. Sindelman himself at a hearing at the office of the Department of Consumer Affairs on July 7, 1970.

b) The only business of Northeast Discount is to send out collection notices to customers of Compact Electra. (Sindelman testimony)

c) The officers and employees of Compact Electra have full knowledge and control over accounts transferred to Northeast Discount for collection. (Sindelman testimony)

14.   According to the records of the County Clerk, New York County, State of New York, Hyman Sindelman and certain corporations owned by him were the subjects of an injunction action in 1964 by the Attorney General. The action, Index No. 42129/63 was brought on the grounds that the defendants engaged in persistent fraudulent selling practices in connection with retail sales of vacuum cleaners. The core of Sindelman's fraudulent sales methods was a so-called "Bond of Friendship" offered prospective customers. The injunction issued against Sindelman and his corporations by this court was affirmed after modification by the Appellate Division, First Dept. and by the Court of Appeals. The case is reported as Matter of People v. Compact Associates, 22 A.D.2d 129 (1964) aff'd 17 N.Y.2d 758 (1966). In its opinion the Appellate Division at page 133 made the following findings in part:

"3.   That * * * corporate respondents' salesmen made representations beyond what was authorized by said respondents to the effect that no sale was being made, that the prospective purchaser was only giving a receipt for the machine left by him, that the purchase price was less than that stated, and other false and fraudulent representations to induce conditional sales contracts to be made."

"4.   That the method of selling authorized by corporate respondents provides a ready cover for its salesmen to exceed their authority and use fraudulent means to obtain sales contracts by concealing the basic nature of the transaction in the initial stage . . ."

* * *

"6.   That the sales practices of respondent corporations amounted to persistent fraud."

15.   Nevertheless, as the affidavits of Hernandez, et al (plaintiff's Exhibit "1") submitted herein demonstrate, defendant Sindelman, now operating through a new corporation, Compact Electra, is still engaged in persistent fraudulent selling practices making use of a new deceptive scheme based on the so-called consumer's buying club "Family Buying Power" to replace the discredited "Bond of Friendship" stratagem.

16.   As described in detail herein the defendants Compact Electra Corp. and its president Hyman Sindelman are currently engaged in false, deceptive and unconscionable practices in selling vacuum cleaners. On information and belief, these defendants currently have 30 or more salesmen operating daily in New York City as their agents in making these false and deceptive representations. These salesmen operate in all sections of the city including areas where most of the residents are low income people, many with poor understanding of English. According to a statement made to the Department of Consumer Affairs by defendant Sindelman, Compact Electra is currently selling about 1,500 vacuum cleaners a year in New York City. Our departmental investigation has revealed that, since January 1970, Compact Electra has begun lawsuits against 156 persons in Kings County Civil Court alone.

17.   For these reasons a temporary restraining order, as requested in the final paragraph herein, is necessary. It is or should be noted that the temporary restraining order requested seeks to restrain defendants from false, misleading and unconscionable practices. It will not interfere with their sales activities if such activities are carried on without false and misleading representations and practices. The harm that may be inflicted upon many residents of this city subject to the false and deceptive sales activities of the defendants far outweighs any possible inconvenience or harm to the defendants in requiring them to confine their efforts to truthful selling pending the argument of the plaintiff's motion for a preliminary injunction.

18.   No prior application has been made for the relief here sought or for any other provisional remedy. * * *

/S/————————————
Bess Myerson Grant

————

AFFIDAVIT

[Omissions are references to exhibits filed in court]

STATE OF NEW YORK ⎫
                              ⎬ SS.:
COUNTY OF KINGS   ⎭

ROY MORRISON, being duly sworn, deposes and says:

1.   I reside with my wife and 2 children at 2 East 53d Street, Brooklyn, New York. I am employed by Humble Oil & Refining Co. located at 293 Green Street, Brooklyn, New York.

2.   On February 18, 1970, Mr. Bernie Brenner came to my home. He said that he had been referred to me through a friend of my wife.

3.   Mr. Brenner told me that he was a salesman of Compact Electra cleaning systems, consisting of a vacuum cleaner, hair dryer, massaging vibrator, and several other attachments. He had such an appliance with him when he called at my house.

4.   Before talking about the vacuum cleaner, Mr. Brenner told me that if I were to purchase a Compact Electra vacuum cleaner, he would enroll me in a wholesale buyers club for life at no additional cost to me beyond the cost of the vacuum cleaner.

5.   He said that the only way to become a member of this club was to buy his entire vacuum cleaning system.

6.   He said that membership in this club would allow me to buy such things as a car, a sewing machine, a bedroom or a living room set, or whatever other things we needed at wholesale prices. All we would have to do is to go to the warehouse which Mr. Brenner's company maintained and pick out what we wanted. If they did not have what we wanted, all we would have to do would be to go into any store, take down the model number of the item we wanted, send the number to the wholesale buyers club, and we would be able to get it from the club at wholesale.

7.   After explaining the wholesale buyers club to me, Mr. Brenner told me about the construction of the vacuum cleaner, and said that it was "fully guaranteed."

8.   He also said that the cost was $400 plus tax which I could pay over a three year period. Mr. Brenner also asked me to give him the names of 10 friends of mine whom he could call on.

9.   I told Mr. Brenner that he would have to give me a day or two so that I could decide whether or not I wanted to purchase the vacuum cleaner.

10.   Mr. Brenner was very persistent and kept on trying to talk me into buying the vacuum cleaner immediately, rather than waiting a day or two. He told me that he would leave it with me, and that if I decided that I did not want to buy the vacuum cleaner, I could call him the next day and inform him of my decision. Then he would come back to my home and pick up the machine.

11.   Mr. Brenner told me that he would leave the vacuum cleaner with me, and that if I didn't want to keep it, I could call him the next day so that he could come and pick it up.

12.   By this time it was between 8:00 and 9:00 in the evening. My wife was ill, and to get him to leave, and in view of what he had said, I signed the document which he had brought with him.

13.   Before leaving, Mr. Brenner gave me a gift of some items for my wife. They included a can of paint, a very small can of furniture polish, a very small container of pine oil, and some detergent for washing dishes. I still have these "gifts" and have never used any of them.

14.   I called Mr. Brenner early the next morning, February 19, 1970, at the telephone number (445–2750) which he gave me the previous evening, but I was told that Mr. Brenner was not there. I intended to tell him that I did not want to buy the vacuum cleaner.

15.   I called several more times that day—with the same purpose in mind—and have continued to try to get Mr. Brenner at that number, but I have never been able to reach him.

16.   During my first call on the morning of February 19, 1970, I explained to the person at the number which Mr. Brenner gave me that Mr. Brenner said that I could return the machine to him with no obligation. The person told me that I was mistaken, that I had signed a contract for the purchase of the vacuum cleaner, and that they would not be able to take it back.

17. I went to see an attorney, Mr. John L. Phillips, 523 Nostrand Avenue, Brooklyn, New York, who told me that he would mail my copy of the contract back to the Compact Electra Company with a letter telling them to come and collect the machine from my home. No one ever came to pick up the machine.

18. About three or four days after February 18, 1970, I called the number which Mr. Brenner had give me and again they told me there was nothing they could do for me because the contract had been turned over to Northeast Discount Corp., P. O. Box 299, Floral Park, N. Y.

19. I called Northeast Discount Corp. and explained to them that Mr. Brenner had told me that I could cancel the contract. But they told me that I had signed a contract for the purchase of the vacuum cleaner and that I would have to pay for it. I was told if I did not pay, I would be sued and my salary would be garnisheed.

20. About two or three weeks after February 18, 1970, I received a payment book from Northeast Discount Corp., which I took to Attorney John L. Phillips. Mr. Phillips told me that he would write a letter to Northeast and send the payment book back to them.

21. Several weeks later, I began receiving threatening letters and notices from Northeast Discount Corp. * * * I also received many telephone calls from Northeast telling me to pay. On May 16, 1970, Northeast sent me a letter, a copy of which is annexed hereto as Exhibit "A–3" telling me that they would take drastic measures if I did not pay within 5 days.

22. I returned to see Attorney Phillips and let him know what was happening, but he never kept any file or copies of the letters he had sent to Compact Electra and to Northeast Discount Corp.

23. To this day, I have only paid four dollars ($4.00) which was my deposit with Mr. Brenner when he left the vacuum cleaner overnight at my house on February 18, 1970, for me to decide whether or not I wanted to buy it.

24. I have never used the vacuum cleaner which Mr. Brenner left. When he first came to my house, it was packed in a sealed box. Mr. Brenner unpacked the vacuum cleaner in order to demonstrate its operation, proceeded to spill some sand on my floor, and then cleaned it up with his vacuum cleaner. Since Mr. Brenner's demonstration, I have kept the vacuum cleaner in the original box in which he brought it.

25. In response to notices for payment which I received from the attorney for Northeast Discount Corp., Theodore Decker, 246–16 Jericho Turnpike, Bellerose, New York, I wrote a letter to Mr. Decker explaining all of the circumstances of my alleged "purchase" of a vacuum cleaner.

26. During the second week of July, 1970, and after I had made a complaint to the Department of Consumer Affairs of the City of New York, Mr. Decker telephoned me and told me that the president of Compact Electra was willing to let me out of the contract. I told Mr. Decker that I would have to contact the Department of Consumer Affairs first. Mr. Decker replied that the Department of Consumer Affairs couldn't get me out of the contract and that only Compact Electra could do this. He said that not only would the company let me out of the contract, but the president of Compact Electra would be happy to meet me personally.

27. I returned the entire vacuum cleaning system to the offices of Compact Electra at 246–14 Jamaica Avenue, Bellerose, New York on approximately July 17, 1970. The president of Compact Electra, Mr. Sindelman, was not present when I returned the machine. ．．．

Roy Morrison

EXHIBIT "A–3" TO AFFIDAVIT OF ROY MORRISON

IF YOU ARE SUED　＊　＊　＊

on a debt and the Court gives Judgment against you, you are in serious trouble.

AN EXECUTION CAN BE ISSUED AGAINST YOU

Then an Officer of the Court may seize your goods, attach your wages, bank account or other property.

He may also be instructed to bring you and your family into Court and force you and them to tell under oath what property you own. This will be expensive and embarrassing to you.

In addition, a Judgment hanging over your head will cost you many times the amount of the debt, in loss of credit and respect in your community.

IT'S IMPOSSIBLE TO ESCAPE A JUDGMENT

For a Judgment may be renewed and thus remain in effect until paid—and it may be recorded everywhere.

Your debt will have to be paid some day, so to save expense, loss of credit and embarrassment to you and your family, you MUST take care of it immediately.

AFFIDAVIT

STATE OF NEW YORK ⎱
COUNTY OF KINGS ⎰ SS.:

ERNESTINE NUGENT, being duly sworn, deposes and says:

1. I reside with my husband at 1334 Eastern Parkway, Brooklyn, New York.

2. On April 15, 1970, Mr. John Robateau came to my home and introduced himself as a salesman for Compact Electra Corp. He said he had been referred to me by a friend of mine.

3. Mr. Robateau told me that he was selling vacuum cleaners and that my purchase would also entitle me to membership in a wholesale buyers club for life at no extra cost. He said this club would allow me to purchase at the wholesale price such items as furniture, electrical appliances, rugs, and televisions.

4. He then demonstrated the vacuum cleaner to me, stating that it was fully guaranteed. He also showed me several attachments which he said

came with the machine—hair dryer, venetian blind cleaner, and a massaging vibrator. He stated that the cost was $400, plus tax and easy credit terms.

5.   Mr. Robateau then handed me a paper which he said was a referral form on which I was to list the names of several friends of mine that might be interested in buying this vacuum cleaner. I have retained this form, a copy of which is annexed hereto as Exhibit "C–1". He then gave me a second form, stating that it was merely a membership agreement in the buyers club which I was to sign. I told him that I was not interested in buying the vacuum cleaner because I already had one, but that I would like to join the buyers club if it was not also necessary to purchase the machine. He assured me that this would not obligate me in any way towards the purchase of the vacuum cleaner. He stated, though, that this was the only time that I could sign up to become a member of this buying club and therefore I had better sign right now.

6.   I then signed the paper. * * * and Mr. Robateau stated that he would leave the vacuum cleaner at my apartment on a three week trial basis. At the end of that time, if I did not want the machine I could call him and he would come and pick it up, again obligating me in no way.

7.   Before leaving, Mr. Robateau gave me what he said were gifts for becoming a member of the buyers club. These gifts consisted mainly of household items such as furniture polish and dishwashing soap. I still have those items, but they have never been used. He also left some brochures describing the operations of the buyers club.

8.   Mr. Robateau then stated that he was in a hurry and when I asked him for the membership agreement form that I had signed, rather than giving it to me, he stuffed it into the box containing the vacuum cleaner and left.

9.   I then became suspicious and upon reading the form, I realized that I had been misled into signing a contract. That same day, April 15, 1970, I called the Compact Electra Company to advise them that I wanted the vacuum cleaner removed from my apartment. I told them that their salesman, Mr. Robateau had said that I was under no obligation and could return the machine any time within three weeks, but they said that I had signed the contract and was therefore bound. I have also written to them several times by registered mail. * * *, but they have neither replied to these requests nor taken back the machine.

10.   During the week of April 20, 1970, I received a payment book from Northeast Discount Corp. demanding payment for purchase of this vacuum cleaner. Since that time I have received two threatening letters from this company, one during the first week of July, 1970 and the other on the 1st of August, 1970. Both of these letters demanded immediate payment of what was owing, stating that garnishment proceedings against my salary would be commenced if I did not comply.

11.   To this date, the only money that I have payed is the $3.95 charge which Mr. Robateau stated was the membership fee to join the buyers club. I have paid no other money and have not used this machine in any way.

Ernestine Nugent

AFFIDAVIT

STATE OF NEW YORK ⎫
COUNTY OF KINGS ⎬ SS.:
⎭

BETTY WHITE, being duly sworn, deposes and says:

1. I live at 327 Sterling Street, Brooklyn, New York, with my husband and child.

2. In October, 1968, I received a telephone call from a man telling me that he had a free gift for me. He did not tell me what the gift was. I was curious about what the gift was, so I invited the man to stop by my house. He also did not mention during this telephone call that he was a salesman of Compact Electra vacuum cleaners.

3. On October 28, 1968, at about 7:00 p. m. the man who had called me about the free gift came to my home. He introduced himself to me as Bernie Brenner.

4. Mr. Brenner had with him my "gift," which turned out to be a small cardboard representation of a house. * * *

5. Pictured on this house are the "gifts" which Mr. Brenner would give me. However, the gift which Mr. Brenner had spoken about on the phone as being "free" had some conditions attached to it. He now said that he would be glad to give me the gift only if I recommended to him the names of 10 persons upon whom he could call. Furthermore, the gift would be mine for "free" only if I purchased a Compact Electra vacuum cleaner.

6. Mr. Brenner also explained to me something called Family Buying Power. He said that if I bought a vacuum cleaner from him, I would be given a free, lifetime membership in a wholesale buying club that would allow me to buy a great many things at a considerable saving.

7. Mr. Brenner demonstrated the operation of the vacuum cleaner for me, as well as the operation of some of the attachments, including a hair dryer, room sprayer, and massager.

8. Mr. Brenner told us that the cost of the vacuum cleaner was $329.95 plus tax of $16.50, and that our monthly payment would be $13.95 for 30 months.

9. It was about 10:00 in the evening and Mr. Brenner had been at our house for about three hours. We were getting tired and wanted him to leave. So, my husband and I decided to purchase the vacuum cleaner. We both signed the contract. * * * I was under 21 years of age at that time.

10. When I signed the contract, Mr. Brenner gave me the allegedly "free" gift. It consisted of sample sizes of toothpaste, mouthwash, aspirin, spray starch, and fabric softener.

11. I began making instalment payments on the vacuum cleaner within about one month of the date of purchase. My payments were sometimes for $13.95 as called for in the contract, but on occasion I made larger payments in order to pay for the vacuum cleaner more rapidly than 30 months.

12. In the course of Mr. Brenner's visit to us on October 28, 1968, he mentioned that he played basketball. Since my husband also liked to play, Mr. Brenner gave him his telephone number, which he said was his home telephone number, to call him if my husband ever wanted to play basketball.

13. My husband became ill several months after purchasing the vacuum cleaner. He had his first attack of asthma which permitted him to work only sporadically. Until this time, we were unaware that he suffered from asthma. Therefore, when my husband became ill and had to stop work, I attempted to telephone Mr. Brenner at the phone number he had given my husband. I wanted to explain that my husband was ill, and that we would not be able to continue to make payments on the vacuum cleaner because of our sudden loss in income.

14. However, when I called the number that Mr. Brenner had given us, it turned out not to be Mr. Brenner's home telephone number as he had said. Instead, I found myself speaking with someone in the office of Compact Electra.

15. I explained our financial situation to the person who answered the telephone at Compact Electra, and asked them to come and pick up the vacuum cleaner because I would not be able to continue my payments on it.

16. Compact Electra refused to pick up the vacuum cleaner. They told me that I had signed a contract and that there was no way they could let me out of it. Furthermore, they said that the contract had been turned over to Northeast Discount Corp., and that Compact Electra no longer could do anything about it.

17. I began receiving collection notices shortly thereafter from Northeast Discount Corp. * * * The notices demanded that I resume making my payments and threatened suit if I did not. These notices were signed by a Mr. Greene.

18. I called back Compact Electra and asked to speak with Mr. Greene so that I could explain my financial circumstances to him. However, they told me that Mr. Greene could not be reached until 10:00 p. m. and that there was no one else who could help me in this matter.

19. I also began receiving collection notices and demands for payment. * * * from an attorney for Northeast Discount Corp., Mr. Theodore Decker. I also called Mr. Decker and explained my financial situation to him, but he said that he was unable to help me.

20. In the meantime, I also received a notice from Family Buying Power on March 11, 1969, that one year had elapsed since I had become a member, and that I owed them $12.00 if I wanted to renew my membership. This was difficult for me to understand for two reasons. First, I had become a member of Family Buying Power in October, 1968, when I purchased the vacuum cleaner. Therefore, one year had not yet elapsed by March, 1969. Second, Mr. Brenner had told me that my membership in Family Buying Power which he was giving me as a gift for purchasing a Compact Electra vacuum cleaner was a lifetime membership, and that it was absolutely free. Thus, I could not see why I had to pay $12.00 to renew a membership that was supposed to be free for life.

21. On February 10, 1970, my husband received a summons in the mail from Norman S. Langer, the attorney for Compact Electra. This summons indicated that my husband was being sued by Compact Electra.

22. Then, in May 1970, my husband received another document from Norman S. Langer. * * * In this document, which is a notice of default judgment, it is stated that service of the summons and complaint was personally made upon my husband, Dorsey White. However, my husband,

Dorsey White, never had a summons or complaint served personally upon him in this suit. The only "service" upon the defendant was by mail on February 10, 1970. Neither myself nor my husband was ever served personally.

Betty White

AFFIDAVIT

STATE OF NEW YORK⎱
             ⎰ SS.:
COUNTY OF NEW YORK⎱

ISABEL LITTLE, being duly sworn, deposes and says:

1. I am a student at the College for Human Services, 201 Varick Street, New York, N. Y. As part of a work-study program I work for the Department of Consumer Affairs of the City of New York, 80 Lafayette Street, New York, N. Y.

2. On June 15, 1970, a salesman of Compact Electra vacuum cleaning systems, called at my home at 170 Madison Street, New York, N. Y. I had previously called him by telephone and requested that he demonstrate his product for me. This salesman identified himself to me only as "Shelly."

3. Shelly told me that if I bought a Compact Electra vacuum cleaner from him, I would receive a free membership in a club called Family Buying Power.

4. He said that membership in this club would allow me to purchase items that I might want at wholesale prices. This large amount of savings would provide me with enough money to pay for the Compact Electra vacuum cleaner.

5. According to Shelly, not only was this membership absolutely free to me, if I bought a vacuum cleaner from him, but it was also a life-time membership. He told me that this means that I would not have to pay any fee to remain a member of Family Buying Power.

6. Shelly showed me a membership certificate for Family Buying Power. The certificate indicated that membership was for one year. This confused me because Shelly had already said that membership in Family Buying Power was life-time.

7. I asked Shelly about this contradiction. He explained that Compact Electra used to give a one-year membership in Family Buying Power to its customers. But now, according to Shelly, Compact Electra gives a life-time membership to its customers. He said that even though the certificate says that membership is for one year, it is really a life-time membership, and there is no additional cost to the member for the life-time membership.

8. Shelly said that the only way in which I could become a member of Family Buying Power was to purchase a Compact Electra vacuum cleaner. He said that there was no other way for a person living in New York City to become a member of Family Buying Power other than through buying a vacuum cleaner from Compact Electra. The reason for this, according to Shelly, is that Compact Electra has the franchise and control of Family Buying Power for all of New York, New Jersey, and Connecticut.

9. I asked Shelly if Compact Electra is the same program as Family Buying Power. His reply was that the two programs "tie in" with each other, and that Compact Electra "controls this wholesale service."

10. Shelly also told me that if I waited to make my purchase of the Compact Electra at some later date, I would not be able to receive a membership, free or otherwise, in Family Buying Power. He said that it would be a shame to lose this opportunity because people in other parts of the country paid as much as $360.00 just to join Family Buying Power.

11. I didn't understand how I would be able to save so much money by buying through Family Buying Power. Shelly said that the reason I would be able to enjoy such large savings was because Family Buying Power provides a way for its members to buy directly from manufacturers, jobbers, distributors, and importers.

12. I asked Shelly what kinds of things I would be able to buy from Family Buying Power. He said that I would be able to buy anything I wanted through my membership so "long as it's sold in a store," except for food.

13. Shelly said that buying through Family Buying Power would help me, among other things, to:

a. save $300 to $1000 on an automobile;

b. save 50% on some furniture;

c. save one-third to one-half on any brand of television that can be bought in a retail store;

d. purchase a 16-volume set of encyclopedias selling for $159.00 in Macy's for $34.50;

e. purchase a $179.00 Singer automatic zig-zag sewing machine in a walnut console cabinent for $58.00;

f. purchase a bedroom set selling for $229, $300, $350, or $400 in various stores for $125;

g. purchase a watch selling for $49 in Busch Jewelers for $19.00;

h. purchase a stereo selling for $369.00 in Sachs Quality Stores for $186.00;

i. purchase a $129.00 hand-tailored man's wool or silk suit for $43.00, or a $130.00 ladies' suit for $32.00.

14. Shelly said that these were just some examples of the things I would be able to buy through the wholesale buying service. He also said that I would be able to purchase many small items such as aspirin, razor blades, shaving cream, and toothpaste from Family Buying Power at wholesale prices.

15. After explaining Family Buying Power, Shelly gave me some information about the Compact Electra vacuum cleaner that he was selling. Shelly told me that the vacuum cleaner has a 25-year guarantee on metal parts and life-time free service, and that the vacuum cleaner "would never lose pressure." He said, for example, if a customer were to hit the vacuum cleaner with a sledge hammer and smash it to bits, Compact Electra would replace the vacuum cleaner free if the damage occurred within 25 years of the initial purchase.

16. Shelly told me that the vacuum cleaner has several attachments. These attachments permit it to operate as an air filter, vaporizor, deodori-

zor, hair dryer, spray gun for DDT and for other sprays, vibrating massager, and a waxer, buffer, and polisher.

17. The total price for the vacuum cleaner and all of these attachments was $399.00 plus tax of $24.00.

18. I did not have to pay the entire price immediately in cash. According to Shelly, I could pay whatever I could afford each week, and "get the money back through Family Buying Power."

19. He said that I would become a member of the wholesale club from the date of the demonstration, even before I began making payments on the vacuum cleaner. Shelly kept talking as if I had told him that I was going to buy the vacuum cleaner, although I had said that it was too expensive for me.

20. He said what Compact Electra does, in effect, is to send the customers' payments back to them. He said, for example, each month I might make a payment of $5.00 on the vacuum cleaner, and with the wholesale service it would be just like having my $5.00 payment sent back to me.

21. Shelly told me that when I wanted to buy something, I would just send the money to the wholesale service. I asked him the name of the service. He told me that it was called the Executive Buying Corporation, and it was also called Family Buying Power.

22. Shelly said that for tax purposes they had split up their company into different corporations. He said their names are Compact Electra, Compact Island, Compact Associates, Compact Bellerose, and Compact Discount. According to Shelly, the reason for having all those corporations is that they can split up the money and put a little in each corporation and save money on taxes this way.

23. Shelly told me that I could purchase the vacuum cleaner on time for $400.00. I would have to pay a finance charge of $40.00 for each year that I took to pay.

24. He said that if I were to borrow $500.00 from a bank to pay for the vacuum cleaner, I would have to pay finance charges of $50.00 per year for two years.

25. He said that he had no control over finance charges because they are regulated by New York State.

26. Shelly said that if I wanted to, I could pay him only $3.95 in cash. This would leave an unpaid balance of $420.00.

27. He said that he would leave the vacuum cleaner with me regardless of the amount of the deposit so long as I signed the contract right then and there. I could pay the balance of $420.00 in 18 monthly payments of $26.83; or I could pay in 24 monthly payments of $20.00 each. If I chose the latter method of payment, finance charges would be $42.00 per year, or $84.00 for two years.

28. His rapid explanation of the finance charges, of how much I would have to put down and borrow and of how long I would have to pay left me confused.

29. I explained to Shelly that my financial situation was not good enough right now to buy the vacuum cleaner. I asked him if he could come back in about a month and a half. He said that he could.

30. However, Shelly kept trying very hard to sell me the vacuum cleaner right then and there. He said he would leave the vacuum cleaner with

me with a deposit of only $1.00 if I would sign the contract. But I told him that I didn't want to sign any papers.

31. He said that when he came back in a month and a half, I would still have to sign the contract. However, if I didn't sign the contract on his present visit, I would forever relinquish the opportunity to join the wholesale buying club. He also said that it was a shame that I would lose out on a deal that would save me between $300.00 and $500.00.

Isabel Little

AFFIDAVIT

STATE OF NEW YORK   } SS.:
COUNTY OF BRONX

MARIA HERNANDEZ, being duly sworn, deposes and says:

1. I am a student at the College for Human Services, 201 Varick Street, New York, N. Y. As part of a work-study program I work for the Department of Consumer Affairs of the City of New York, 80 Lafayette Street, New York, N. Y.

2. On June 1, 1970, at about 11:00 a. m., Mr. John Robateau, a salesman of Compact Electra vacuum cleaning systems, called at my home at 304 East 156th Street, Bronx, New York, in response to my previous telephone request that he demonstrate his product for me.

3. Mr. Robateau told me that his company would take care of service and repairs for the vacuum cleaner free for life. Then he said that the guarantee was for 25 years, after which service was free, but that I would have to pay for replacement parts. Finally, he told me that the guarantee was in effect for my own lifetime, not the lifetime of the vacuum cleaner. The result of these conflicting statements was that I was confused as to what kind of guarantee the vacuum cleaner actually had.

4. Mr. Robateau told me that because the Compact Electra vacuum cleaner never loses its suction, it will work forever.

5. Mr. Robateau also explained that he had a program, called Family Buying Power, that would help me to pay for the entire vacuum cleaner. Family Buying Power would allow me to buy many things at a price below the normal retail price, and that after a couple of months or a couple of years of buying things through this program I would have saved enough to pay for the vacuum cleaner completely.

6. Mr. Robateau said that Compact Electra has a contract with Family Buying Power, and that Family Buying Power is like a branch of Compact Electra. Then he told me that Compact Electra is the owner of Family Buying Power.

7. When I asked Mr. Robateau what kinds of things I would be able to buy through my membership in Family Buying Power, he informed me that I could get everything I needed except food, including custom-tailored clothes, medicines, dishwashers, radios, automobiles, stereo sets, washing machines, air conditioner, and other appliances.

8.   He said that some examples of savings that I would receive would be:

a. $329 stereo set for $179;

b. $771 dining room set for $495;

c. $29 blender for $19;

d. $4900 Pontiac Bonneville for $3900.

9.   Mr. Robateau told me that the reason that I could save so much money by buying directly through Family Buying Power was that it would allow me to buy directly from the distributor.   He said Family Buying Power has about one million members.

10.   Mr. Robateau said that he would give me a free lifetime membership in Family Buying Power if I purchased a Compact Electra vacuum cleaner from him.   Compact Electra would rather give its customers a free lifetime membership in Family Buying Power so that they would recommend more customers to Compact Electra instead of spending money on advertising.   This way the money that would have been spent on advertising is used to buy memberships in Family Buying Power as a reward to its customers for recommending more customers.

11.   Mr. Robateau gave me a form, annexed hereto as Exhibit "E–1", for me to recommend other customers to him.

12.   According to Mr. Robateau, if I did not buy the vacuum cleaner at that time, I would not be able to be enrolled as a member of Family Buying Power, even if I later decided to buy the vacuum cleaner.

13.   Mr. Robateau told me that if I signed the contract, he could take a deposit from me and leave the vacuum cleaner, and that I could subsequently "get out of the contract" if my husband didn't like the vacuum cleaner.   Mr. Robateau promised me that he would not send in the contract that night.

14.   When I still hesitated to sign, Mr. Robateau told me he would do something for me which he had never done before.   He would write "on approval by husband" or "not valid until approved by your husband" on my copy of the contract.   Then if my husband did not approve, Mr. Robateau said he would come back and destroy the contract and take back the vacuum cleaner.

15.   Mr. Robateau said that when I discussed the matter of purchasing the vacuum cleaner with my husband, I could tell him that the contract had not yet been approved even though I had signed it, and that the document which I signed was merely a receipt to indicate that Mr. Robateau had left the vacuum cleaner at my house, pending my husband's approval.

16.   Mr. Robateau gave me a telephone number at which I could call him if I wanted to cancel the contract.   He said that it was his home telephone number and that his wife would be home all day to take a message.

17.   When I later called Mr. Robateau at the number which he gave me, I was told that I was speaking with the office of Compact Electra, and not Mr. Robateau's home.

18.   A Miss Johnson then told me that I could become a member of Family Buying Power if I changed my mind and decided to buy the vacuum cleaner at a later date.   This was directly contrary to what Mr. Robateau had told me.

————————————

Maria Hernandez

SUPREME COURT OF THE STATE OF NEW YORK
COUNTY OF NEW YORK

BESS MYERSON GRANT, as Commissioner of
the Department of Consumer Affairs of the City
of New York,

Plaintiff,

vs.

COMPACT ELECTRA CORP., NORTHEAST
DISCOUNT CORP. and HYMAN SINDEL-
MAN,

Defendants.

AFFIDAVIT

STATE OF NEW YORK
COUNTY OF KINGS   SS.:

BETTY WHITE, being duly sworn, deposes and says:

1. I reside at 327 Sterling Street, Brooklyn, New York.

2. This is my second affidavit in support of the motion by the Commissioner of Consumer Affairs for a preliminary injunction. My first affidavit, sworn to August 7, 1970, described the many falsehoods and misrepresentations used by the defendants' salesman to induce me to purchase a Compact Electra vacuum cleaner.

3. I make this affidavit to describe the deceit used by the Compact salesman to induce me to fill out the document entitled "Questionnaire" (defendants' Exhibit "B") [introduced to discredit Ms. White's affidavit].

4. I filled out this questionnaire at the time of the sale, at the insistence of the Compact salesman, Bernard Brenner. Mr. Brenner pleaded with me to compliment him, saying that my favorable report would help him gain a promotion in salary which he badly needed. He claimed that he had a young wife at home who was very sickly, and that he had five very young children. He told me he needed any extra money he could get to pay for his wife's medical care and to support his family.

5. His story was so pitiful that I felt sorry for him. Although I knew nothing about the vacuum cleaner or about Family Buying Power except what he had just told me, I complimented Mr. Brenner and expressed my satisfaction with the machine and with his sales presentation in the Questionnaire he provided.

6. I later discovered the many fraudulent statements Mr. Brenner had made to me in his sales pitch. I now regard Mr. Brenner's conduct and sales presentation as completely fraudulent and deceitful.

Betty White

SUPREME COURT OF THE STATE OF NEW YORK
COUNTY OF NEW YORK

BESS MYERSON GRANT, as Commissioner of the Department of Consumer Affairs of the City of New York,
 	
                   Plaintiff,
 	
        vs.
 	
 COMPACT ELECTRA CORP., NORTHEAST DISCOUNT CORP. and HYMAN SINDELMAN,
                        Defendants.
	REPLY AFFIDAVIT

STATE OF NEW YORK ⎫
COUNTY OF BRONX ⎬ ss.
⎭

MARIA HERNANDEZ, being duly sworn, deposes and says:

1. I make this affidavit in reply to the affidavit of JOHN ROBATEAU, defendants' vacuum cleaner salesman. In his affidavit, Mr. Robateau denies having made certain fraudulent statements to me when he delivered his sales presentation in my home. His denials, however, are demonstrably false. His sales presentation was recorded by me, with my consent, on a tape recorder which was out of Mr. Robateau's view. Consequently, I can quote the exact words Mr. Robateau used in making all the misrepresentations he specifically denies having made.

2. In particular, Mr. Robateau denies making the following false statements:

(a) that membership in Family Buying Power enables the consumer to purchase merchandise directly from the distributor; and that such purchasing is possible because Family Buying Power has about one million members;

(b) that Family Buying Power can supply any item of merchandise except food;

(c) that Compact Electra owns Family Buying Power;

(d) that he gave me his telephone number (so that I could call him if I wanted to cancel the contract).

3. Mr. Robateau's exact words in making the above misrepresentations were:

(a) "With the membership that we give you, this membership will allow you to buy directly from the distributor, just as if you were buying in quantity. What makes that possible is because Family Buying Power has about a million members."

(b) "Every single thing that you walk into the store to buy with the exception of food you can get through the club."

(c) "It's [Family Buying Power] like a branch. . . . They [Compact Electra] are the owner but it's a different branch."

(d) "The copy [of the contract] that I leave with you, I'll put 'on approval by husband.' [If he doesn't approve] I'll come back and destroy it and take back the machine. * * * I'll give you my home phone."

4. The tape recording also reveals the additional distortions and false-hoods described in my original affidavit, and not specifically denied by Mr. Robateau.

MARIA HERNANDEZ

SUPREME COURT OF THE STATE OF NEW YORK
COUNTY OF NEW YORK

BESS MYERSON GRANT, as Commissioner of the Department of Consumer Affairs of the City of New York, <div align="center">Plaintiff,</div> <div align="center">vs.</div> COMPACT ELECTRA CORP., NORTHEAST DISCOUNT CORP. and HYMAN SINDELMAN, <div align="right">Defendants.</div>	REPLY AFFIDAVIT

STATE OF NEW YORK } ss.
COUNTY OF NEW YORK }

ISABEL LITTLE, being duly sworn, deposes and says:

1. I make this affidavit in reply to the affidavit of SHELLY LIEBER-MAN, defendants' vacuum cleaner salesman. In his affidavit, Mr. Lieber-man denies having made certain fraudulent statements to me when he delivered his sales presentation in my home. His denials, however, are demonstrably false. His sales presentation was recorded by me, with my consent, on a tape recorder which was out of Mr. Lieberman's view. Consequently, I can quote the exact words used by Mr. Lieberman in making all the misrepresentations he specifically denies having made.

2. In particular, Mr. Lieberman denies making the following false statements:

    a. that Family Buying Power is a "wholesale" buyers club;

    b. that Compact Electra gives free lifetime memberships in Family Buying Power to its customers;

    c. that every article of merchandise except food, and every brand of every article, is available through the buying club;

    d. that what Compact Electra does, in effect, is to send that customer's payments back to them through the wholesale service.

3. Mr. Lieberman's exact words in making the above misrepresentations were:

    a. "We have to save you money through the wholesale service, because if we don't you could sue my company—we misrepresented to you * * *. We set this up with the Better Business Bureau when this was brought into the New York area * * * they know about this wholesale service."

Mr. Lieberman used the word "wholesale" to describe Family Buying Power more than a dozen times.

b. "Anything that the people want for the rest of their life they can get from manufacturers, jobbers, distributors and importers * * all wholesale."

c. "Whether its anything from aspirin to automobiles, we can get it wholesale."

"Doesn't matter what the brand is."

d. "Suppose I tell you that this product really doesn't cost the people any money. In fact by a person getting this product, they can make roughly $300—$500 a year profit."

"Some people want to pay $20 a month [for the Compact] and let's say they pay the $20—and they get it back from the company. That's what's happening. This wholesale service is designed to save a person money."

4. The tape recording also reveals the additional distortions and falsehoods described in my original affidavit, and not specifically denied by Mr. Lieberman.

_____

Isabel Little

Note on Grant v. Compact Electra Corp.

1. Is the authorized portion of this sales presentation deceptive? Which specific phrases are misleading, if any? Can a court find an offer deceptive even if it cannot point to specific false statements? Of what relevance is the fact that the introductory section, which can last up to forty-five minutes, discusses "saving money" but does not disclose what product is for sale, nor even that the caller is selling something? Does the seller have any obligation affirmatively to disclose his purpose?

2. Assuming that door-to-door selling serves some purpose, how can a company in this business ensure that its salesmen observe company policy and do not engage in unauthorized exaggeration? Should it give them lectures? Withhold commissions until it confirms with customers that they were told only the truth? Fire salesmen caught misleading customers? Is it possible to police a large sales force composed of people who have a strong incentive (a commission ranging from 15% to 40%) for making a sale on every presentation?

3. Some states have enacted statutes giving "home solicitation" buyers one, two or three days to cancel the sale by mailing the seller notice of their intention to cancel. See, e. g., Uniform Consumer Credit Code (UCCC) § 5.204. This type of reform has been criticized as insufficient for these reasons: (A) It is not economical for the seller to deliver goods he may have to take back until after he is sure that the sale will go through; he therefore withholds delivery for three days. But the consumer does not realize that he wishes to cancel until he sees the goods, and by that time it is too late. In the case of services, such as "Family Buying Power," the consumer may not realize until months later that what he has agreed to purchase is of little value to him. (B) Many families, particularly those of low income, cannot make cancellation decisions in three days in any event, but could do so in a longer period of time. The longer the period, the greater the difficulty for businesses to keep their books. (C) If notice of cancellation is to be made by ordinary mail, companies can claim that they did not receive the notice; if registered mail, return-receipt requested is required, low-income consumers may have difficulty exercising their rights because of the complexity and expense of the procedure. (D) Unscrupulous sellers can circumvent the law by back-dating contracts so that the cancellation notice appears to have been sent too late. See Comment, "A Case Study of Consumer Legislation: the Elimination of Negotiability and the Cooling-Off Period," 78 Yale L.J. 618 (1969) ("One firm conclusion of this study is that a cooling-off period of such short length benefits customers very little" Id. at 628.) and Schrag, "On Her Majesty's Secret Service: Protecting the Consumer in New York," 80 Yale L.J. 1529, 1563–64 (1971). The National Consumer Act, a model statute prepared by the OEO National Consumer Law Center at Boston College Law School, would automatically cancel a door-to-door sale unless the customer specifically affirms the transaction in a subsequent writing. NCA §§ 2.501–2.504 (First Final Draft 1970). Is this a disguised attempt to prohibit door-to-door sales? What arguments can be made against prohibition?

4. In the *Compact* case, plaintiff claimed not only that the defendant made deceptive statements concerning savings that could be achieved through "Family Buying Power," but that it used Northeast Discount Corporation to make claims as purported assignee of Compact, though Northeast was owned by the man who owned Compact. What harm was there in this?

5. Does door-to-door selling serve a valuable purpose? To what extent are

the poor unable to shop in stores, or get credit from stores? See Caplovitz, The Poor Pay More 49–57 (1967).

6. The court's opinion: "Although the defendants deny that they have committed any fraudulent or deceptive trade practices, they nonetheless have agreed to refrain from all but three of the practices which the plaintiff seeks to enjoin through a preliminary injunction. Since there is complete agreement as to these practices except for the three mentioned, the imposition of an injunction seems unduly harsh and unnecessary. Such relief is readily available if defendants are found to be violating the agreement and representations they make to the court herein. * * *" Grant v. Compact Electra Corp., N.Y.L.J. March 20, 1971 (S.Ct.N.Y.Co.1971).

THOR FOOD SERVICE CORP. v. MAKOFSKE

Supreme Court of New York, 1961.
28 Misc.2d 872, 218 N.Y.S.2d 93.

BIRDIE AMSTERDAM, Justice. This non-jury action is predicated upon an alleged breach of a written retail installment contract entered into between plaintiff and the defendants. Defendants seek to resist payment upon the claim of fraud in the inducement.

The contract concerns plaintiff's sale to defendants on the installment payment plan of a refrigerator-freezer combination at the agreed price of $1,342.80. Executed on March 15, 1960, the contract provides for 36 monthly installments of $37.30 each, commencing April 28, 1960, with acceleration of all payments, at plaintiff's option, on ten days' continued default of any installment.

The freezer was delivered to the defendants on March 17, 1960. They concede they never made a complaint, nor do they now in respect of its condition or functioning. They further concede they

have made no payments whatever on the appliance although they have made use thereof and still retain it. They contend, by way of affirmative defense, that plaintiff's salesman represented to them that plaintiff "would satisfy all of the food needs of the defendants and the members of their family for not more than $100.00 per month"; that they believed the representation to be true, relied thereon, and were thereby induced to execute the contract; that their reasonable food requirements could not and were not thereafter provided for the sum so represented; that they wrote plaintiff on May 4, 1960, that they elected to rescind the contract. At this point it is to be noted that the contract itself makes no mention whatever of food supply to or purchase by the defendants. This will be discussed further hereinafter.

Defendants are husband and wife. He is a police officer—she takes care of the household. They have three infant children aged one, five and seven years, respectively. The husband testified that, pursuant to an advertisement issued by plaintiff concerning a food freezer plan, he wrote the plaintiff for information. Thereupon a sales representative of the plaintiff called upon the defendants. They discussed and told him of their eating habits and that they expended $25 a week for their food requirements. Therewith the salesman prepared an itemized list of specified foods, consisting of groups of varied packaged meats, groceries, dairy products, vegetables, etc., for use over a four-month period (Defts' Exh. E). Defendants claim he told them that the cost of the freezer and their food needs would be $95 to $100 per month. They admit that prior to signing the contract they carefully went over said prepared list and they suggested extra items, which were added thereto, all for the total sum of $260; that they were also given a food plan certificate (Defts' Exh. B), by which they were entitled through the North Shore Packing Co., Inc. (which is designated as the exclusive food purveyor for plaintiff), to certain benefits therein specified, to wit: free home delivery of food, freedom of selection with no minimum requirement, free home-economist service to assist with food orders, custom cutting of meats to personal specifications, the privilege of purchasing food at volume savings prices, unconditional guarantee of all meats as to quality, guaranteed to be U.S. Government inspected prime and choice grades only, and nationally advertised brands of groceries. Admittedly defendant husband signed a statement (Defts' Exh. C) that he understood the service was not on a trial basis and that on or about March 24, 1960 the defendants received each and every one of the specified itemized foods as per the afore-stated list (Defts' Exh. E).

Defendants testified that about a week thereafter they realized that the food would not last for a four-month period; that they tried to contact the salesman by telephone but were unsuccessful; that on May 4, 1960 they caused a letter to be sent by their attorney to plaintiff demanding it take back the freezer and rescinding the contract. They admitted that their food needs fluctuated from time to time; that they consumed all the food (which they paid for after being advised to do so by their attorney); and that they utilized the freezer in the interim period.

The issue therefore presented is whether defendants established their defense of actionable fraud in the inducement of the contract for the sale of the freezer.

The law is well established and needs no citation of authority for the holding that the essential elements of "fraud" are representation, falsity, scienter, deception and injury. The representation must be definite and specific, materially false, made with the speaker's knowledge of its falsity, with fraudulent intent, and must be relied upon by the other party who must be ignorant of its falsity and caused to suffer loss. Averments of mere opinions and promises of indefinite matters are not sufficient. The false representation relied upon must relate to a past or existing fact, or something equivalent thereto; as distinguished from a mere estimate or expression of opinion (Benz v. Kaderbeck, 241 App.Div. 583, 585, 272 N.Y.S. 558, 561). Fraud must be established by clear and convincing factual proof (Lowendahl v. Baltimore & Ohio Railroad Company, 247 App.Div. 144, 158, 287 N.Y.S. 62, 76, affirmed 272 N.Y. 360, 6 N.E.2d 56; Fein v. Starrett Television Corporation, 280 App.Div. 670, 673, 116 N.Y.S.2d 571, 573; Lynch v. Gibson, 254 App.Div. 47, 3 N.Y.S.2d 672, affirmed 279 N.Y. 634, 18 N.E.2d 36). Fraud may not rest alone on conjecture or supposition. Woolson v. Waite, 158 Misc. 764, 767, 286 N.Y.S. 619, 623, affirmed 247 App. Div. 855, 286 N.Y.S. 624.

Mindful of these legal authorities and principles enunciated, we test the facts adduced and the defense in the light of the foregoing pronouncements. The basic problem presented is whether defendants can establish upon all the evidence misrepresentation by plaintiff or its agent, and reliance upon the misrepresentation. Viewing the contract itself, it speaks only of a "freezer" giving its make, model and serial number. Nothing else but the conditional sale of a freezer is provided for in this contract. Nowhere are the sale and payments therefor conditioned upon the additional sale to defendants, and purchase by them of foods, etc., nor is any mention made of same. The written contract sued on herein contains and constitutes the entire agreement between the parties and makes no reference to or incorporation therein of any supplemental agreement relating to foodstuffs, groceries and the like. It contains the further proviso that "This is our entire agreement and cannot be changed orally.

"Notice to the Buyer.

"1. Do not sign this agreement before you read it or if it contains any blank space."

Were we dealing here with a generally vague contract or illiterate defendants, our task would be simple. Here, however, we have defendants who are sophisticated, intelligent individuals. Their own testimony established that they were well aware of the food requirements for their entire family; that they were well aware of the fluctuations of their food needs. I am satisfied, and the only inference I can draw upon the sum total of the evidence before me, is that they well knew what they were signing as far as the contract for the freezer was concerned and that they knew what they were buying and that the purchase of the freezer was not on a trial basis. In so far as the alleged representation by plaintiff's salesman is concerned, I conclude his statements to the defendants cannot be considered to constitute other than his opinion—a mere estimate of the food supply necessary to satisfy the possible food consumption of defendants' family, consisting of two adults and three infants. In my opinion it was nothing more than an estimated opinion to which the law of fraud does not extend. Moreover, the proof is not clear and convincing that defendants placed reliance upon the representation they alleged. Obviously they knew better than the salesman the extent of their food requirements. As hereinbefore stated, they carefully examined and went over the itemized list prepared for them by the salesman and they made quite a number of additions and changes thereto.

In light of the evidentiary facts adduced and the circumstances presented, a finding of fraud in the inducement is not warranted.

Accordingly, it is my considered view and I am persuaded to the ultimate conclusion that no actionable fraud has been demonstrated and that plaintiff is entitled to recover for the sale price of its freezer. Judgment is directed in its favor against the defendants in the sum of $1,342.80, together with the costs and disbursements of this action. The Clerk is directed to enter judgment accordingly.

All motions on which decision was reserved are resolved in accordance with this determination. This constitutes the decision of the Court, pursuant to section 440 of the Civil Practice Act.

Note on Puffing, Standards of Truthfulness and Mass Media Advertising

1. Food freezer swindles were the most notorious consumer fraud perpetrated on urban low-income and working-class buyers in the 1960's. "The deep freezer that purportedly pays for itself out of savings from the accompanying food plan is currently a very popular racket. Many poor families sign contracts for these freezers, only to learn, when they later receive their copy of the contract and the payment book, that the quoted price was far below the price which they have to pay. Moreover, instead of obtaining bargain buys on food, these families soon discover that the prices charged are actually higher than supermarket prices and that the quality of the food delivered each month deteriorates." Caplovitz, The Poor Pay More xviii (1967). Typically, the seller visited the prospect's home and spent one or two hours drawing up massive lists of types of food "just so that you can see how much this plan would save you." Like Compact representatives, who dwelled upon "Family Buying Power" rather than the sale of a vacuum cleaner, freezer salesmen emphasized the food, and the money

that a family could save. As a seeming afterthought at the end of a visit, they would add "You do have a freezer to put this in, don't you?" When the customer responded negatively, the salesman would indicate that the monthly price he had quoted included payments on a freezer. Then he would extend a sheaf of papers and say, "Just sign here and here." The customer thereby signed two separate contracts—one for a supply of food, and one for the purchase of a freezer. As in the *Thor* case, the latter contract typically contained a "parol evidence" clause. In addition to *Thor*, see Toker v. Perl, 103 N.J.Super. 500, 247 A.2d 701 (1968), aff'd other grounds 108 N.J.Super. 129, 260 A.2d 244 (A.D.1970), Milford Finance Corp. v. Lucas, 8 UCC Reporting Service 801 (A.D.Mass.1970).

Does the *Thor* court correctly recite the applicable legal standards? If so, are they appropriate to transactions involving dealers and consumers, as opposed to purely commercial transactions? Why does the court differentiate between promises about "past or existing fact" and promises about the adequacy of the seller's future services?

2. Is a trial an effective means of reproducing for the court the true nature of the salesman's pitch? Does the court appear concerned with the relative emphasis which the salesman placed on the food transaction, as opposed to the freezer purchase? Why were the buyers not entitled to rely on the opinion of a professional, who counseled customers every day about their food requirements?

3. Section 5 of the Federal Trade Commission Act, 15 U.S.C.A. § 45(a)(1) (as amended) (1938), enforceable only in administrative proceedings initiated by the Commission, prohibits "unfair methods of competition in commerce, and unfair or deceptive acts or practices in commerce." Is this a more appropriate standard for consumer protection than state decisional law concerning fraud and misrepresentation, or is it too vague to be practicable? See Matter of Tashof, F.T. C. Complaints and Orders 1967–70, para. 18,606, p. 20,941 (1968), Tashof v. F. T.C., 141 U.S.App.D.C. 274, 437 F.2d 707. The Uniform Deceptive Trade Practices Act, which by 1971 had been adopted in approximately eight states, prohibits engaging in any one of eleven specified practices, or "any other conduct which similarly creates a likelihood of confusion or misunderstanding."

4. A man with a high school education saw an advertisement for an automobile in the newspaper, and visited the dealer's lot in Milwaukee, in the month of March, to look at the car. In response to the buyer's question, the dealer said that the car "was full power and air conditioning and everything." The dealer then let him drive the car for an hour and a half. The dealer meanwhile, was advertising the car as "factory air conditioned." After he purchased the car, he discovered that it was not in fact equipped with air conditioning. Although the trial court granted damages to the buyer, the Supreme Court of Wisconsin reversed, holding his reliance on the salesman's statement unjustifiable as a matter of law. Williams v. Rank and Sons Buick, 44 Wis.2d 239, 170 N.W.2d 807 (1969).

5. "Action on a negotiable promissory note dated January 30, 1953, in the original principal sum of $275.58 payable in eighteen monthly installments of $15.31 each, the first of which was due March 15, 1953, executed by defendants, Carl D. and Jewell D. Charlton, who are husband and wife, payable to the order of Compact Sales Co. * * *

"In their answer, defendants pleaded *fraud in the factum*, i. e., that their signatures were obtained 'by trick, artifice and fraud' on the part of one C. A. Stubblefield (hereinafter referred to as Stubblefield), an agent of Howard Stubblefield, who did business under the trade name of Compact Sales Co. (hereinafter referred to as Compact), in that Stubblefield 'asked them to sign what he falsely stated and represented to them to be (and what they believed to be) a receipt' for a vacuum cleaner but which was, in fact, the note (and chattel mortgage) in suit. Defendants further pleaded *fraud in the inducement,* i. e., that Stubblefield falsely stated that Compact 'was seeking a person' in the area of defendants' home on R.F.D. 1, Neosho, Missouri, to make appointments for representatives of Compact to demonstrate vacuum cleaners in other homes under an arrangement known (and hereinafter referred to) as a 'club plan,' whereby Compact would pay to the person making such appointment $25 for each vacuum cleaner sold as a result thereof; that 'only one person would be selected to make appointments' within an area extending 'from * * * Granby in Newton County to Southwest City in McDonald County'; and that, relying upon such false representations, defendant, Jewell D. Charlton, was induced to accept 'said position' and to sign a 'club plan.' Defendants denied that plaintiff was a holder in due course and asserted that it took the note with full knowledge of 'the scheme and methods' used to defraud defendants.

"The evidence upon trial tended to support the averments of defendants' answer. Stubblefield, coming to defendants' home at night, 'wanted us to act as agent for him and make appointments for him to sell vacuum sweepers to other people and we were to get paid ($25) for each sweeper he sold someone'—'he said we could have the territory from Granby to Southwest City, be the only ones through there to make appointments.' After admittedly having read it in full, Mrs. Charlton signed a 'club plan,' a single-spaced typewritten sheet which stated the 'conditions for acceptance as club member' and the 'acceptance' by Compact but included no reference to

territory. Then Stubblefield said that 'he would like to leave a vacuum sweeper in our home since we were going to be an agent for him and he would like for us to sign a receipt showing he had left it in good hands.' Stubblefield 'had a clip board with the papers on it and the club plan was on top and we signed that and under it was the two lines of the receipt and we signed that.' When asked why she read the 'club plan' but not the 'receipt,' her reply was 'well, he was getting ready to leave and said he was in a hurry and would we sign those papers and the receipt and club plan'; but, when plaintiff's counsel immediately put the direct inquiry as to whether Stubblefield 'gave you plenty of time to read them if you wanted to read them,' Mrs. Charlton conceded 'I guess I could have.' Mrs. Charlton subsequently learned that she was not 'sole agent' for Compact; and, although she made some appointments for demonstrations, she 'didn't turn them in—I told them what was up.'

"Plaintiff purchased the Charlton note for $225 on February 5, 1953, and 'soon after' defendants 'got a card from (plaintiff) saying that they had purchased a note against us for a vacuum sweeper,' to which Mrs. Charlton responded by letter dated February 20, 1953, *'when we bought our Compact cleaner we understood from the salesman that the Co. took care of the mortgage—we did not intend to get mixed up with any Finance Co. when we bought it.'* At the trial, Mrs. Charlton insisted that Stubblefield had said nothing about sale of a vacuum cleaner to defendants and that they had not purchased one. Strangely and perhaps significantly, Mr. Charlton, who also signed the 'receipt' (actually the note), did not testify. * * *

"Although their exact ages are not shown, it is apparent that defendants are neither elderly nor infirm. There is no suggestion that Mr. Charlton, employed at the Neosho plant of *Pet Milk Com-*

pany, is illiterate; and, the record affirmatively shows that his wife, employed at a drive-in restaurant, can read and write, for she admittedly read in full the single-spaced typewritten sheet referred to as the 'club plan' and her well-composed letter of February 20, 1953, to plaintiff was written in ink in a flowing hand so neat and legible that it might well be the envy of every member of this court. Although Stubblefield's suave and extravagant assurances of the quick and easy financial rewards to accrue from Mrs. Charlton's appointment under the 'club plan' may have temporarily disarmed defendants of all suspicion and engendered an unwarranted confidence in this utter stranger, the fact remains that defendants intended to sign the paper upon which their signatures appear. Thus, our case is *not* one where parties, having read the instrument presented to them, have signed another and different instrument fraudulently substituted by deft manipulation, nor where persons, unable to protect their own interests by reason of illiteracy, infirmity or impairment of sight, have been deceived by fraudulent representations as to the character of the paper presented or by misreading of the paper, nor where one's request to read an instrument just signed has been denied; but, defendants' plaint in the instant suit is simply that the paper, which stranger Stubblefield blandly denominated a receipt, actually was a note.

"That '(t)he * * * law affords to every one reasonable protection against fraud in dealing; but it does not go to the romantic length of giving indemnity against the consequences of indolence and folly or a careless indifference to the ordinary and accessible means of information' [2 Kent's Comm. 485] is a timeless truth as compelling today [Dickinson v. Bankers Life & Casualty Co., Mo.App., 283 S.W.2d 658, 663(7)] as when so graphically expressed by Chancellor Kent more than one hundred twenty-five years

ago. See also Dyrssen v. Union Electric Light & Power Co., 317 Mo. 221, 295 S.W. 116, 118. Our courts frequently have proclaimed that '(i)t is trite law that a person is expected to learn what an instrument contains before he signs it, either by reading or having it read, or by having its contents stated by some one on whom he has a right to rely, the circumstances considered, and provided either method of obtaining the information is available without too great inconvenience.' Passing the obvious import of Mrs. Charlton's letter of February 20, 1953, to plaintiff, we have searched the record in vain for any material fact or circumstance which would distinguish this case from those in which our courts repeatedly have imposed liability on makers who carelessly and negligently have signed notes in professed reliance on the false representations of others that the papers were receipts or contracts (or duplicate copies thereof). There was no relationship of trust or confidence between defendants and Stubblefield who came to them in the night as a complete stranger. That he was in a hurry to leave was not a unique factor; and, *even if* Stubblefield had kept his hand on the clipboard while defendants signed (and there is not a word of testimony that he did), this would not have differentiated the instant case from others in which a showing of similar tactics had not served to relieve from liability. On defendants' own evidence, we think it clear that there is no basis in the instant case for submission of the defense of *fraud in the factum*."

Local Finance Co. v. Charlton, 289 S. W.2d 157 (Mo.App.1956).

6. The judges in these cases expect consumers to be cynical about sales talk. To what extent do these judges unrealistically project their own cynicism and "sophistication" onto the buyers in question? Is such projection warranted? A 1971 survey of 130 Columbia Law School students in a course on consumer protec-

tion revealed that only 25% of them thought that when a department store advertised a "storewide" sale, it reduced the prices of more than eight percent of the types of merchandise it carried, but 72% of the students thought that most consumers would expect more than eight percent of such types to be discounted. Should judges similarly take pains to distinguish between their own "sophisticated" reactions to advertising and the possibly different reactions of the public at large? Between their reactions and the reactions of the buyers in the individual cases they are adjudicating?

Does frequent misrepresentation and exaggeration in mass media advertising lead judges to expect falsity in selling offers and to expect others, also, to assume that salesmen lie? How can a judge hold the Thor Food Service Corp. to high standards of honesty when Proctor and Gamble claims on television that "Crisco splatters 35% less when you're frying chicken" without telling viewers less than *what?* Consider other common examples of lack of candor: Shell gasoline is claimed to improve gasoline mileage because it is platformated; the advertiser does not mention that all major American gasolines are plaformated. Anacin is said to have "the ingredients your doctor recommends"; the ingredient referred to is aspirin. USDA standards specify that packaged chicken chow mein need contain only 6% chicken. This dialogue was used by Sterling Drug Co. until a government agency intervened:

BAYER ADVERTISEMENT

Man: Excuse me.

Man: Sorry, but do you have anything for a headache?

Man: Nothing stronger than aspirin? (Picture shows someone giving him a tin of Bayer aspirin)

Woman: You look intelligent. You should know—all the major

pain relievers work mainly with aspirin.

Man: C'mon.

Woman: Look at their labels. They all rely on aspirin.

Man: Aspirin?

Woman: Aspirin is what doctors recommend, and Bayer is the only one that's 100% aspirin.

Man: I'll take two.

Merck and Co. advertised that Sucrets "relieve sore throat pain fast and kill even Staph and Strep germs with a special pain relieving antiseptic. Hexylresorcinol. So, when minor sore throat strikes and brings fiery pain, Sucrets relieve sore throat pain and kill even Staph and Strep germs." Actually, Sucrets could not kill such bacteria in a manner that was medically significant, could not effectively attack viruses which caused viral sore throats, and were not helpful in curing existing throat infections. Doherty, Clifford, Steers and Shenfield, Inc. v. FTC, 392 F.2d 921 (1968). Campbell Soup Co. advertised its vegetable soup by photographing a bowl of it into which had been placed clear glass marbles; the marbles sank, forcing the vegetables to the surface so that the soup appeared to contain more vegetables than it actually did. Matter of Campbell Soup Co., FTC Complaints and Orders, 1967–70 Transfer Binder, 18897, pp. 21231–32. False mass media advertising is so prevalent that among businessmen themselves—or at least among subscribers to the Harvard Business Review—only 30% believe that advertisements "present a true picture of the product advertised." Greyser and Reece, Businessmen Look Hard at Advertising, Harvard Business Review, Vol. 49, No. 3 (May-June 1971) p. 18.

Should lawyers attempt to change this situation through new legislation? Through litigation? Through increased public enforcement of existing laws? Or is it better to accept current standards and urge laymen to accept them also? Should all false advertising statutes be repealed so that the public would not be misled into expecting protection?

"There are some kinds of talk which no sensible man takes seriously, and if he does he suffers from his credulity. If we were all scrupulously honest, it would not be so; but, as it is, neither party usually believes what the seller says about his own opinions, and each knows it. Such statements, like the claims of campaign managers before election, are rather designed to allay the suspicion which would attend their absence than to be understood as having any relation to objective truth." Judge Learned Hand, in Vulcan Metals Co. v. Simmons Manufacturing Co., 248 F. 853, 856 (2d Cir. 1918). (Judge Hand was careful to distinguish between contracts between merchants and contracts in which the parties were not "on an equality." Ibid. This distinction has not always been observed. Even as between merchants, should the doctrine of "puffing" be restricted to discourage exaggeration in the commercial climate?)

SECTION 2. UNCONSCION-ABILITY

UNIFORM COMMERCIAL CODE
SECTION 2–302 AND
OFFICIAL COMMENT

§ 2—302. **Unconscionable Contract or Clause**

(1) If the court as a matter of law finds the contract or any clause of the contract to have been unconscionable at the time it was made the court may refuse to enforce the contract, or it may enforce the remainder of the contract without the unconscionable clause, or it may so limit the application of any unconscionable clause as to avoid any unconscionable result.

(2) When it is claimed or appears to the court that the contract or any clause thereof may be unconscionable the parties shall be afforded a reasonable opportunity to present evidence as to its commercial setting, purpose and effect to aid the court in making the determination.

Official Comment

Prior Uniform Statutory Provision: None.

Purposes

1. This section is intended to make it possible for the courts to police explicitly against the contracts or clauses which they find to be unconscionable. In the past such policing has been accomplished by adverse construction of language, by manipulation of the rules of offer and acceptance or by determinations that the clause is contrary to public policy or to the dominant purpose of the contract. This section is intended to allow the court to pass directly on the unconscionability of the contract or particular clause therein and to make a conclusion of law as to its unconscionability. The basic test is whether, in the light of the general commercial background and the commercial needs of the particular trade or case, the clauses involved are so one-sided as to be unconscionable under the circumstances existing at the time of the making of the contract. Subsection (2) makes it clear that it is proper for the court to hear evidence upon these questions. The principle is one of the prevention of oppression and unfair surprise (Cf. Campbell Soup Co. v. Wentz, 172 F.2d 80, 3d Cir. 1948) and not of disturbance of allocation of risks because of superior bargaining power. The underlying basis of this section is illustrated by the results in cases such as the following:

Kansas City Wholesale Grocery Co. v. Weber Packing Corporation, 93 Utah 414, 73 P.2d 1272 (1937), where a clause limiting time for complaints was held inapplicable to latent defects in a shipment of catsup which could be discovered only by miscroscopic analysis; Hardy v. General Motors Acceptance Corporation, 38 Ga.App. 463, 144 S.E. 327 (1928), holding that a disclaimer of warranty clause applied only to express warranties, thus letting in a fair implied warranty; Andrews Bros. v. Singer & Co. (1934 CA) 1 K.B. 17, holding that where a car with substantial mileage was delivered instead of a "new" car, a disclaimer of warranties, including those "implied," left unaffected an "express obligation" on the description, even though the Sale of Goods Act called such an implied warranty; New Prague Flouring Mill Co. v. G. A. Spears, 194 Iowa 417, 189 N.W. 815 (1922), holding that a clause permitting the seller, upon the buyer's failure to supply shipping instructions, to cancel, ship, or allow delivery date to be indefinitely postponed 30 days at a time by the inaction, does not indefinitely postpone the date of measuring damages for the buyer's breach, to the seller's advantage; and Kansas Flour Mills Co. v. Dirks, 100 Kan. 376, 164 P. 273 (1917), where under a similar clause in a rising market the court permitted the buyer to measure his damages for non-delivery at the end of only one 30 day postponement; Green v. Arcos, Ltd. (1931 CA) 47 T.L.R. 336, where a blanket clause prohibiting rejection of shipments by the buyer was restricted to apply to shipments where discrepancies represented merely mercantile variations; Meyer v. Packard Cleveland Motor Co., 106 Ohio St. 328, 140 N.E. 118 (1922), in which the court held that a "waiver" of all agreements not specified did not preclude implied warranty of fitness of a rebuilt dump truck for ordinary use as a dump truck; Austin Co. v. J. H. Tillman

Co., 104 Or. 541, 209 P. 131 (1922), where a clause limiting the buyer's remedy to return was held to be applicable only if the seller had delivered a machine needed for a construction job which reasonably met the contract description; Bekkevold v. Potts, 173 Minn. 87, 216 N.W. 790, 59 A.L.R. 1164 (1927), refusing to allow warranty of fitness for purpose imposed by law to be negated by clause excluding all warranties "made" by the seller; Robert A. Munroe & Co. v. Meyer (1930) 2 K.B. 312, holding that the warranty of description overrides a clause reading "with all faults and defects" where adulterated meat not up to the contract description was delivered.

2. Under this section the court, in its discretion, may refuse to enforce the contract as a whole if it is permeated by the unconscionability, or it may strike any single clause or group of clauses which are so tainted or which are contrary to the essential purpose of the agreement, or it may simply limit unconscionable clauses so as to avoid unconscionable results.

3. The present section is addressed to the court, and the decision is to be made by it. The commercial evidence referred to in subsection (2) is for the court's consideration, not the jury's. Only the agreement which results from the court's action on these matters is to be submitted to the general triers of the facts.

WILLIAMS v. WALKER-THOMAS FURNITURE CO.

United States Court of Appeals, District of Columbia Circuit, 1965.
350 F.2d 445.

J. SKELLY WRIGHT, Circuit Judge. Appellee, Walker-Thomas Furniture Company, operates a retail furniture store in the District of Columbia. During the period from 1957 to 1962 each appellant in these cases purchased a number of household items from Walker-Thomas, for which payment was to be made in installments. The terms of each purchase were contained in a printed form contract which set forth the value of the purchased item and purported to lease the item to appellant for a stipulated monthly rent payment. The contract then provided, in substance, that title would remain in Walker-Thomas until the total of all the monthly payments made equaled the stated value of the item, at which time appellants could take title. In the event of a default in the payment of any monthly installment, Walker-Thomas could repossess the item.

The contract further provided that "the amount of each periodical installment payment to be made by [purchaser] to the Company under this present lease shall be inclusive of and not in addition to the amount of each installment payment to be made by [purchaser] under such prior leases, bills or accounts; *and all payments now and hereafter made by [purchaser] shall be credited pro rata on all outstanding leases, bills and accounts* due the Company by [purchaser] at the time each such payment is made." (Emphasis added.) The effect of this rather obscure provision was to keep a balance due on every item purchased until the balance due on all items, whenever purchased, was liquidated. As a result, the debt incurred at the time of purchase of each item was secured by the right to repossess all the items previously purchased by the same purchaser, and each new item purchased automatically became subject to a security interest arising out of the previous dealings.

On May 12, 1962, appellant Thorne purchased an item described as a Daveno, three tables, and two lamps, having total stated value of $391.10. Shortly thereafter, he defaulted on his monthly payments and appellee sought to replevy all the items purchased since the first trans-

action in 1958. Similarly, on April 17, 1962, appellant Williams bought a stereo set of stated value of $514.95.[1] She too defaulted shortly thereafter, and appellee sought to replevy all the items purchased since December, 1957. The Court of General Sessions granted judgment for appellee. The District of Columbia Court of Appeals affirmed, and we granted appellants' motion for leave to appeal to this court.

Appellants' principal contention, rejected by both the trial and the appellate courts below, is that these contracts, or at least some of them, are unconscionable and, hence, not enforceable. In its opinion in Williams v. Walker-Thomas Furniture Company, 198 A.2d 914, 916 (1964), the District of Columbia Court of Appeals explained its rejection of this contention as follows:

"Appellant's second argument presents a more serious question. The record reveals that prior to the last purchase appellant had reduced the balance in her account to $164. The last purchase, a stereo set, raised the balance due to $678. Significantly, at the time of this and the preceding purchases, appellee was aware of appellant's financial position. The reverse side of the stereo contract listed the name of appellant's social worker and her $218 monthly stipend from the government. Nevertheless, with full knowledge that appellant had to feed, clothe and support both herself and seven children on this amount, appellee sold her a $514 stereo set.

"We cannot condemn too strongly appellee's conduct. It raises serious questions of sharp practice and irresponsible business dealings. A re-

[1] At the time of this purchase her account showed a balance of $164 still owing from her prior purchases. The total of all the purchases made over the years in question came to $1,800. The total payments amounted to $1,400.

view of the legislation in the District of Columbia affecting retail sales and the pertinent decisions of the highest court in this jurisdiction disclose, however, no ground upon which this court can declare the contracts in question contrary to public policy. We note that were the Maryland Retail Installment Sales Act, Art. 83 §§ 128–153, or its equivalent, in force in the District of Columbia, we could grant appellant appropriate relief. We think Congress should consider corrective legislation to protect the public from such exploitive contracts as were utilized in the case at bar."

We do not agree that the court lacked the power to refuse enforcement to contracts found to be unconscionable. In other jurisdictions, it has been held as a matter of common law that unconscionable contracts are not enforceable.[2] While no decision of this court so holding has been found, the notion that an unconscionable bargain should not be given full enforcement is by no means novel. In Scott v. United States, 79 U.S. (12 Wall.) 443, 445, 20 L.Ed. 438 (1870), the Supreme Court stated:

> " * * * If a contract be unreasonable and unconscionable, but not void for fraud, a court of law will give to the party who sues for its breach damages, not according to its letter, but only such as he is equitably entitled to. * * * "[3]

[2] Campbell Soup Co. v. Wentz, 3 Cir., 172 F.2d 80 (1948); Indianapolis Morris Plan Corporation v. Sparks, 132 Ind.App. 145, 172 N.E.2d 899 (1961); Henningsen v. Bloomfield Motors, Inc., 32 N.J. 358, 161 A.2d 69, 84–96, 75 A.L.R.2d 1 (1960). Cf. 1 Corbin, Contracts § 128 (1963).

[3] See Luing v. Peterson, 143 Minn. 6, 172 N.W. 692 (1919); Greer v. Tweed, N.Y.C.P., 13 Abb.Pr., N.S., 427 (1872); Schnell v. Nell, 17 Ind. 29 (1861); and see generally the discussion of the English authorities in Hume v. United States, 132 U.S. 406, 10 S.Ct. 134, 33 L.Ed. 393 (1889).

Since we have never adopted or rejected such a rule,[4] the question here presented is actually one of first impression.

Congress has recently enacted the Uniform Commercial Code, which specifically provides that the court may refuse to enforce a contract which it finds to be unconscionable at the time it was made. 28 D.C.Code § 2–302 (Supp. IV 1965). The enactment of this section, which occurred subsequent to the contracts here in suit, does not mean that the common law of the District of Columbia was otherwise at the time of enactment, nor does it preclude the court from adopting a similar rule in the exercise of its powers to develop the common law for the District of Columbia. In fact, in view of the absence of prior authority on the point, we consider the congressional adoption of § 2–302 persuasive authority for following the rationale of the cases from which the section is explicitly derived.[5] Accordingly, we hold that where the element of unconscionability is present at the time a contract is made, the contract should not be enforced.

Unconscionability has generally been recognized to include an absence of meaningful choice on the part of one

[4] While some of the statements in the court's opinion in District of Columbia v. Harlan & Hollingsworth Co., 30 App.D.C. 270 (1908), may appear to reject the rule, in reaching its decision upholding the liquidated damages clause in that case the court considered the circumstances existing at the time the contract was made, see 30 App.D.C. at 279, and applied the usual rule on liquidated damages. See 5 Corbin, Contracts §§ 1054–1075 (1964); Note, 72 Yale L.J. 723, 746–755 (1963). Compare Jaeger v. O'Donoghue, 57 App.D.C. 191, 18 F.2d 1013 (1927).

[5] See Comment, § 2–302, Uniform Commercial Code (1962). Compare Note, 45 Va. L.Rev. 583, 590 (1959), where it is predicted that the rule of § 2–302 will be followed by analogy in cases which involve contracts not specifically covered by the section. Cf. State of New York Law Revision Commission, Report and Record of Hearings on the Uniform Commercial Code 108–110 (1954) (remarks of Proofessor Llewellyn).

of the parties together with contract terms which are unreasonably favorable to the other party.[6] Whether a meaningful choice is present in a particular case can only be determined by consideration of all the circumstances surrounding the transaction. In many cases the meaningfulness of the choice is negated by a gross inequality of bargaining power.[7] The manner in which the contract was entered is also relevant to this consideration. Did each party to the contract, considering his obvious education or lack of it, have a reasonable opportunity to understand the terms of the contract, or were the important terms hidden in a maze of fine print and minimized by deceptive sales practices? Ordinarily, one who signs an agreement without full knowledge of its terms might be held to assume the risk that he has entered a one-sided bargain.[8] But when a party of little bargaining power, and hence little real choice, signs a commercially unreasonable contract with little or no knowledge of its terms, it is hardly likely that his consent, or even an objective manifestation of his consent, was ever given to all the terms. In such a case the usual rule that the terms of the agreement are not to be questioned [9] should be abandoned and the court should consider whether the terms of the contract are so unfair that enforcement should be withheld.[10]

In determining reasonableness or fairness, the primary concern must be with the terms of the contract considered in light of the circumstances existing when the contract was made. The test is not simple, nor can it be mechanically applied. The terms are to be considered "in the light of the general commercial background and the commercial needs of the particular trade or case." [11] Corbin suggests the test as being whether the terms are "so extreme as to appear unconscionable according to the mores and business practices of the time and place."

---

[6] See Henningsen v. Bloomfield Motors, Inc., supra Note 2; Campbell Soup Co. v. Wentz, supra Note 2.

[7] See Henningsen v. Bloomfield Motors, Inc., supra Note 2, 161 A.2d at 86, and authorities there cited. Inquiry into the relative bargaining power of the two parties is not an inquiry wholly divorced from the general question of unconscionability, since a one-sided bargain is itself evidence of the inequality of the bargaining parties. This fact was vaguely recognized in the common law doctrine of intrinsic fraud, that is, fraud which can be presumed from the grossly unfair nature of the terms of the contract. See the oft-quoted statement of Lord Hardwicke in Earl of Chesterfield v. Janssen, 28 Eng.Rep. 82, 100 (1751):

"* * * [Fraud] may be apparent from the intrinsic nature and subject of the bargain itself; such as no man in his senses and not under delusion would make * * *."

and cf. Hume v. United States, supra Note 3, 132 U.S. at 413, 10 S.Ct. at 137, where the Court characterized the English cases as "cases in which one party took advantage of the other's ignorance of arithmetic to impose upon him, and the fraud was apparent from the face of the contracts." See also Greer v. Tweed, supra Note 3.

[8] See Restatement, Contracts § 70 (1932); Note, 63 Harv.L.Rev. 494 (1950). See also Daley v. People's Building, Loan & Savings

Ass'n, 178 Mass. 13, 59 N.E. 452, 453 (1901), in which Mr. Justice Holmes, while sitting on the Supreme Judicial Court of Massachusetts, made this observation:

"* * * Courts are less and less disposed to interfere with parties making such contracts as they choose, so long as they interfere with no one's welfare but their own. * * * It will be understood that we are speaking of parties standing in an equal position where neither has any oppressive advantage or power * * *."

[9] This rule has never been without exception. In cases involving merely the transfer of unequal amounts of the same commodity, the courts have held the bargain unenforceable for the reason that "in such a case, it is clear, that the law cannot indulge in the presumption of equivalence between the consideration and the promise." 1 Williston, Contracts § 115 (3d ed. 1957).

[10] See the general discussion of "Boiler-Plate Agreements" in Llewellyn, The Common Law Tradition 362–371 (1960).

[11] Comment, Uniform Commercial Code § 2–307.

1 Corbin, op. cit. supra Note 2.[12] We think this formulation correctly states the test to be applied in those cases where no meaningful choice was exercised upon entering the contract.

Because the trial court and the appellate court did not feel that enforcement could be refused, no findings were made on the possible unconscionability of the contracts in these cases. Since the record is not sufficient for our deciding the issue as a matter of law, the cases must be remanded to the trial court for further proceedings.

So ordered.

DANAHER, Circuit Judge (dissenting):

The District of Columbia Court of Appeals obviously was as unhappy about the situation here presented as any of us can possibly be. Its opinion in the *Williams* case, quoted in the majority text, concludes: "We think Congress should consider corrective legislation to protect the public from such exploitive contracts as were utilized in the case at bar."

My view is thus summed up by an able court which made no finding that there had actually been sharp practice. Rather the appellant seems to have known precisely where she stood.

There are many aspects of public policy here involved. What is a luxury to some may seem an outright necessity to others. Is public oversight to be required of the expenditures of relief funds? A washing machine, e. g., in the hands of a relief client might become a fruitful source of income. Many relief clients may well need credit, and certain business establishments will take long chances on the sale of items, expecting their pricing policies will afford a degree of protection commensurate with the risk. Perhaps a remedy when necessary will be found within the provisions of the "Loan Shark" law, D.C.Code §§ 26–601 et seq. (1961).

I mention such matters only to emphasize the desirability of a cautious approach to any such problem, particularly since the law for so long has allowed parties such great latitude in making their own contracts. I dare say there must annually be thousands upon thousands of installment credit transactions in this jurisdiction, and one can only speculate as to the effect the decision in these cases will have.[1]

I join the District of Columbia Court of Appeals in its disposition of the issues.

Note on Unconscionable Clauses

It should be noted that the Court in *Williams* did not hold the contract unconscionable; it merely remanded to the lower court for findings on the issue. What type of findings was the lower court directed to make? Which factors would be of primary relevance: those peculiar to the individual transaction or those pertinent to the commercial context?

For example, the Court noted that Mrs. Williams was on welfare. How strongly should this weigh? If this factor is held pertinent, would the doctrine of unconscionability tend to decrease the granting of credit to welfare recipients, as the dissenting judge seemed to fear? To what extent is it important that the seller *knew* she was on welfare? Should sellers be discouraged from selling expensive appliances to poor people who want to buy them?

---

[12] See Henningsen v. Bloomfield Motors, Inc., supra Note 2; Mandel v. Liebman, 303 N.Y. 88, 100 N.E.2d 149 (1951). The traditional test as stated in Greer v. Tweed, supra Note 3, 13 Abb.Pr., N.S., at 429, is "such as no man in his senses and not under delusion would make on the one hand, and as no honest or fair man would accept, on the other."

[1] However the provision ultimately may be applied or in what circumstances, D.C.Code § 28–2–301 (Supp. IV, 1965) did not become effective until January 1, 1965.

Suppose this unlikely dialogue had occurred:

Seller: You're on welfare. I'd like to sell you the stereo, but my company says I can't, because we wouldn't be sufficiently sure that you could pay us back.

Mrs. Williams: That's too bad. I'd really like the stereo.

Seller: I could sell it to you if you'd get your brother, who earns a good salary, to guarantee the contract.

Mrs. Williams: No, I hate to make other people responsible for my debts.

Seller: Well, then, although I was going to give you our Form A, in which our only security for the credit would have been the stereo itself and the right to sue you personally in the event you stopped paying, I'll give you Form B, which you've used before, which says that if you don't pay we can take back everything you've bought from us which isn't fully paid for, and which prevents you from completing payments on the stereo until everything is paid for.

In other words, if Mrs. Williams had clearly understood what she was doing, and had bargained over the cross-collateral clause, would a finding of unconscionability have been precluded? Or is that clause itself so grossly unfair that it should not be enforced even if the buyer understood it? "One cannot tell from the statute whether the key concept is something to be predicated on the bargaining process or on the bargain or on some combination of the two, that is, * * * whether it is procedural or substantive." Leff, "Unconscionability and the Code—The Emperor's New Clause," 115 U.Pa.L.Rev. 485, 488 (1966). The Leff article is the leading work on the theory and history of Section 2–302.

What evidence would you expect "the parties" to present to the lower court on the "commercial setting, purpose and effect" of the clause or the contract? Could the plaintiff have avoided the defense of unconscionability by showing that other stores in the neighborhood used the clause? By showing that "of the thirty-seven jurisdictions which have statutes regulating retail installment sales, only one has a provision making add-on clauses impermissible"? Leff, supra, at 554. Would evidence that the "effect" of such a clause enabled the store to make a little more money cut for or against the store? See Leff, supra, at 544–46.

Curiously, the most extensive judicial development of the unconscionability section of the Code has come not in review of particular "small-print" clauses such as the one involved in *Williams,* but in cases in which it is claimed that the contract term most important to the buyer— and most likely, perhaps, to be understood by him—is unconscionable: the price.

AMERICAN HOME IMPROVEMENT, INC. v. MacIVER

Supreme Court of New Hampshire, 1964.
105 N.H. 435, 201 A.2d 886.

This is an agreed case submitted on exhibits and certain stipulated facts. The plaintiff seeks to recover damages for breach by the defendants of an alleged agreement for home improvements. The agreement (Exhibit No. 1) was signed by the defendants April 4, 1963 and it provided that the plaintiff would "furnish and install 14 combination windows and 1 door" and "flintcoat" the side walls of the defendants' property at a cost of $1,759. At the same time the defendants signed an application for financing to a finance corporation (Exhibit No. 2). This application also contained a blank note and a blank power of attorney to the finance corporation which were undated and were signed by the defendants. The application stated the total amount due, the number of months that payments were to be made (60) and the monthly payment but did not state the rate of interest. The defendants received a copy of exhibit 2 on April 4, 1963.

"At some time after April 7, 1963, the defendants received notice of approval of the application for financing * * * Exhibit A." This exhibit stated that the application for credit in the net amount of $1,759 had been approved and that the monthly payments would be $42.81 for 60 months "including principal, interest and life and disability insurance."

"It is further agreed that on or about April 9, 1963 the defendants notified the plaintiff to cease work on the defendants' premises, and plaintiff complied. By April 9, 1963, the plaintiff had done a negligible amount of work on the premises but had already paid a sales commission of Eight Hundred Dollars ($800.00) in reliance upon the contract. It is agreed that the plaintiff did not willfully violate any provision of RSA 399–B."

The defendants moved to dismiss on the ground that the action could not be maintained because the plaintiff failed to comply with the provisions of RSA 399–B (supp); Laws 1961, 245:7 which requires disclosure of finance charges to the borrower by the lender. The Court (Grimes, J.) reserved and transferred without ruling questions of law arising out of the defendants' motion to dismiss.

KENISON, Chief Justice. RSA 399–B:2 (supp) as enacted by laws 1961, 245:7 provides as follows: "*Statement Required.* Any person engaged in the business of extending credit shall furnish to each person to whom such credit is extended, concurrently with the consummation of the transaction or agreement to extend credit, a clear statement in writing setting forth the finance charges, expressed in dollars, rate of interest, or monthly rate of charge, or a combination thereof, to be borne by such person in connection with such extension of credit as originally scheduled." Credit is de-

fined broadly in the act and includes any " * * * contract of sale of property or services, either for present or future delivery, under which part or all of the price is payable subsequent to the making of such sale or contract * * *." RSA 399–B:1 I (supp). The definition of finance charges " * * * includes charges such as interest, fees, service charges, discounts, and other charges associated with the extension of credit." RSA 399–B:1 II.

The first question is whether credit was extended to the defendants in compliance with the statute. The application for financing (Exhibit No. 2) and the approval of the financing (Exhibit A) informed the defendants of the monthly payments, the time credit was extended (60 months) and the total amount of the credit extended but neither of them informed the defendants the rate of interest, or the amount of interest or other charges or fees they were paying. This is not even a token compliance with the statute which requires " * * * a clear statement in writing setting forth the finance charges, expressed in dollars, rate of interest, or monthly rate of charge or a combination thereof * * *." RSA 399–B:2 (supp). The obvious purpose of the statute was to place the burden on the lender to inform the borrower in writing of the finance charges he was to pay. This burden was not met in this case. Annot. 116 A.L.R. 1363. Disclosure statutes are designed to inform the uninformed and this includes many average individuals who have neither the capability nor the strength to calculate the cost of the credit that has been extended to them. Economic Institutions and Value Survey: The Consumer in the Market Place—A Survey of the Law of Informed Buying, 38 Notre Dame Lawyer 555, 582–588 (1963); Ford Motor Co. v. F. T. C., 6 Cir., 120 F.2d 175, 182 (6th Cir. 1941). RSA 399–B:3 (supp) provides that "[n]o person shall extend credit in contravention of this chapter." We conclude that the extension of credit to the defendants was in violation of the disclosure statute.

The parties have agreed that the plaintiff did not willfully violate the disclosure statute and this eliminates any consideration of RSA 399–B:4 (supp) which provides a criminal penalty of a fine of not more than five hundred dollars or imprisonment not more than sixty days, or both. This brings us to the second question whether the agreement is "void so as to prevent the plaintiff from recovering for its breach."

"At first thought it is sometimes supposed that an illegal bargain is necessarily void of legal effect, and that an 'illegal contract' is self-contradictory. How can the illegal be also legal? The matter is not so simple." 6 A. Corbin, Contracts, s. 1373 (1962). The law is not always black or white and it is in the flexibility of the gray areas that justice can be done by a consideration of the type of illegality, the statutory purpose and the circumstances of the particular case. "It is commonly said that illegal bargains are void. This statement, however, is clearly not strictly accurate." 5 Williston, Contracts (Rev. ed. 1937) s. 1630. The same thought is well summarized in 6 A. Corbin, Contracts, s. 1512 (1962): "It has often been said that an agreement for the doing of that which is forbidden by statute is itself illegal and necessarily unenforceable. This is an unsafe generalization, although most such agreements are unenforceable." This section was cited in the recent case of William Coltin & Co. v. Manchester Savings Bank, 105 N.H. 254, 197 A.2d 208, holding unenforceable a contract for a broker's commission for the sale of real estate without a license in violation of a statute.

In examining the exhibits and agreed facts in this case we find that to settle the principal debt of $1,759 the defendants signed instruments obligating them to pay $42.81 for 60 months, making a total payment of $2,568.60, or an increase of $809.60 over the contract price. In reliance upon the total payment the defendants were to make, the plaintiff paid a sales commission of $800. Counsel suggests that the goods and services to be furnished the defendants thus had a value of only $959, for which they would pay an additional $1,609.60 computed as follows:

"Value of goods and services		$ 959.00
Commission	800.00 ⎫	
Interest and carrying charges	809.60 ⎬	1,609.60
Total payment		$2,568.60"

In the circumstances of the present case we conclude that the purpose of the disclosure statute will be implemented by denying recovery to the plaintiff on its contract and granting the defendants' motion to dismiss. Burque v. Brodeur, 85 N.H. 310, 158 A. 127; Park v. Board of Aviation Trustees for City of Manchester, 96 N.H. 331, 76 A.2d 514; Albertson & Co. v. Shenton, 78 N.H. 216, 98 A. 516.

There is another and independent reason why the recovery should be barred in the present case because the transaction was unconscionable. "The courts have often avoided the enforcement of unconscionable provisions in long printed standardized contracts, in part by the process of 'interpretation' against the parties using them, and in part by the method used by Lord Nelson at Copenhagen." 1 Corbin, Contracts, s. 128 (1963). Without using either of these methods reliance can be placed upon the Uniform Commercial Code (U.C.C. 2–302(1)). See RSA 382–A:2–302(1) which reads as follows: "If the court as a matter of law finds the contract or any clause of the contract to have been unconscionable at the time it was made the court may refuse to enforce the contract, or it may enforce the remainder of the contract without the unconscionable clause, or it may so limit the application of any unconscionable clause as to avoid any unconscionable result."

Inasmuch as the defendants have received little or nothing of value and under the transaction they entered into they were paying $1,609 for goods and services valued at far less, the contract should not be enforced because of its unconscionable features. This is not a new thought or a new rule in this jurisdiction. See Morrill v. Bank, 90 N.H. 358, 365, 9 A. 2d 519, 525; "It has long been the law in this state that contracts may be declared void because unconscionable and oppressive * * *."

The defendants' motion to dismiss should be granted. In view of the result reached it is unnecessary to consider any other questions and the order is

Remanded.

All concurred.

FROSTIFRESH CORP. v. REYNOSO

District Court of New York, Nassau County, Second District, 1966.
52 Misc.2d 26, 274 N.Y.S.2d 757.

FRANCIS J. DONOVAN, Judge.

DECISION AFTER TRIAL

Plaintiff brings this action for $1364.-10, alleging that the latter amount is owed by the defendants to the plaintiff on account of the purchase of a combination-refrigerator-freezer for which they agreed to pay the sum of $1145.88. The balance of the amount consists of a claim for attorney fees in the amount of $227.-35 and a late charge of $22.87. The only payment made on account of the original indebtedness is the sum of $32.00.

The contract for the refrigerator-freezer was negotiated orally in Spanish between the defendants and a Spanish speaking salesman representing the plaintiff. In that conversation the defendant husband told the salesman that he had but one week left on his job and he could not afford to buy the appliance. The salesman distracted and deluded the defendants by advising them that the appliance would cost them nothing because they would be paid bonuses or commissions of $25.00 each on the numerous sales that would be made to their neighbors and friends. Thereafter there was submitted to and signed by the defendants a retail installment contract entirely in English. The retail contract was neither translated nor explained to the defendants. In that contract there was a cash sales price set forth of $900.00. To this was added a credit charge of $245.88, making a total of $1145.88 to be paid for the appliance.

The plaintiff admitted that cost to the plaintiff corporation for the appliance was $348.00.

No defense of fraud was set forth in the pleadings and accordingly such defense is not available.

However, in the course of the trial, it did appear to the court that the contract might be unconscionable. The court therefore continued the trial at an adjourned date to afford a reasonable opportunity to the parties to present evidence as to the commercial setting, purpose and effect of the contract.

The court finds that the sale of the appliance at the price and terms indicated in this contract is shocking to the conscience. The service charge, which almost equals the price of the appliance is in and of itself indicative of the oppression which was practiced on these defendants. Defendants were handicapped by a lack of knowledge, both as to the commercial situation and the nature and terms of the contract which was submitted in a language foreign to them.

The question presented in this case is simply this: Does the court have the power under section 2–302 of the Uniform Commercial Code to refuse to enforce the price and credit provisions of the contract in order to prevent an unconscionable result.

It is normally stated that the parties are free to make whatever contracts they please so long as there is no fraud or illegality (Allegheny College v. National Chautauqua County Bank, 246 N.Y. 369, 159 N.E. 173, 57 L.R.A. 980).

However, it is the apparent intent of the Uniform Commercial Code to modify this general rule by giving the courts power "to police explicitly against the contracts or clauses which they find to be unconscionable. * * * The principle is one of the prevention of oppression and unfair surprise." (See the official comment appended to the statute in the note on page 193, McKinney's Uniform Commercial Code, volume 62½ Part I.)

The comment cites Campbell Soup Company v. Wentz, 3 Cir., 172 F.2d 80, to illustrate the principle. It is interesting to note that the Wentz case involved oppression with respect to the price Campbell Company agreed to pay for carrots, the price specified in the contract being $23.00 to $33.00 a ton. In the particular case Wentz, the farmer, refused to deliver carrots at the contract price, since the market price at such time had increased to $90.00 a ton. The Court of Appeals said "We think it too hard a bargain and too one-sided an agreement to entitle the plaintiff to relief in a court of conscience" (p. 83).

In the instant case the court finds that here, too, it was "too hard a bargain" and the conscience of the court will not permit the enforcement of the contract as written. Therefore the plaintiff will not be permitted to recover on the basis of the price set forth in the retail installment contract, namely $900.00 plus $245.85 as a service charge.

However, since the defendants have not returned the refrigerator-freezer, they will be required to reimburse the plaintiff for the cost to the plaintiff, namely $348.00. No allowance is made on account of any commissions the plaintiff may have paid to salesmen or for legal fees, service charges or any other matters of overhead.

Accordingly the plaintiff may have judgment against both defendants in the amount of $348.00 with interest, less the $32.00 paid on account, leaving a net balance of $316.00 with interest from December 26, 1964.

FROSTIFRESH CORP. v. REYNOSO

Supreme Court of New York, Appellate Term, Second Department, 1967.
54 Misc.2d 119, 281 N.Y.S.2d 964.

Seller's action to recover amount allegedly due under installment contract for refrigerator-freezer. The District Court, Nassau County, Second District, Francis J. Donovan, J., 52 Misc.2d 26, 274 N.Y.S.2d 757, determined that contract was unconscionable and limited seller to recovery of cost of refrigerator-freezer, and seller appealed. The Supreme Court, Appellate Term, held that evidence warranted finding that contract was unconscionable, but that seller could recover net cost for refrigerator-freezer, plus reasonable profit, in addition to trucking and service charges necessarily incurred and reasonable finance charges.

Reversed for new trial with respect to damages.

PER CURIAM.

Judgment unanimously reversed, without costs, and a new trial ordered limited to an assessment of plaintiff's damages and entry of judgment thereon.

While the evidence clearly warrants a finding that the contract was unconscionable (Uniform Commercial Code, § 2–302), we are of the opinion that plaintiff should recover its net cost for the refrigerator-freezer, plus a reasonable profit, in addition to trucking and service charges necessarily incurred and reasonable finance charges.

JONES v. STAR CREDIT CORP.

Supreme Court of New York, Special Term,
Nassau County, Part III, 1969.
59 Misc.2d 189, 298 N.Y.S.2d 264.

SOL M. WACHTLER, Justice. On August 31, 1965 the plaintiffs, who are welfare recipients, agreed to purchase a home freezer unit for $900 as the result of a visit from a salesman representing Your Shop At Home Service, Inc. With the addition of the time credit charges, credit life insurance, credit property insurance, and sales tax, the purchase price totalled $1,234.80. Thus far the plaintiffs have paid $619.88 toward their purchase. The defendant claims that with various added credit charges paid for an extension of time there is a balance of $819.81 still due from the plaintiffs. The uncontroverted proof at the trial established that the freezer unit, when purchased, had a maximum retail value of approximately $300. The question is whether this transaction and the resulting contract could be considered unconscionable within the meaning of Section 2–302 of the Uniform Commercial Code which provides in part:

> (1) If the court as a matter of law finds the contract or any clause of the contract to have been unconscionable at the time it was made the court may refuse to enforce the contract, or it may enforce the remainder of the contract without the unconscionable clause, or it may so limit the application of any

unconscionable clause as to avoid any unconscionable result.

> (2) When it is claimed or appears to the court that the contract or any clause thereof may be unconscionable the parties shall be afforded a reasonable opportunity to present evidence as to its commercial setting, purpose and effect to aid the court in making the determination. L.1962, c. 553, eff. Sept. 27, 1964.

There was a time when the shield of "caveat emptor" would protect the most unscrupulous in the marketplace—a time when the law, in granting parties unbridled latitude to make their own contracts, allowed exploitive and callous practices which shocked the conscience of both legislative bodies and the courts.

The effort to eliminate these practices has continued to pose a difficult problem. On the one hand it is necessary to recognize the importance of preserving the integrity of agreements and the fundamental right of parties to deal, trade, bargain, and contract. On the other hand there is the concern for the uneducated and often illiterate individual who is the victim of gross inequality of bargaining power, usually the poorest members of the community.

Concern for the protection of these consumers against overreaching by the small but hardy breed of merchants who would prey on them is not novel. The dangers of inequality of bargaining power were vaguely recognized in the early English common law when Lord Hardwicke wrote of a fraud, which "may be apparent from the intrinsic nature and subject of the bargain itself; such as no man in his senses and not under delusion would make." The English authorities on this subject were discussed in Hume v. United States, 132 U.S. 406, 411, 10 S.Ct. 134, 136, 33 L.Ed. 393 (1889) where the United States Supreme Court characterized (p. 413, 10 S.Ct. p. 137) these as "cases in which one party took advantage of the other's ignorance of arithmetic to impose upon him, and the fraud was apparent from the face of the contracts."

The law is beginning to fight back against those who once took advantage of the poor and illiterate without risk of either exposure or interference. From the common law doctrine of intrinsic fraud we have, over the years, developed common and statutory law which tells not only the buyer but also the seller to beware. This body of laws recognizes the importance of a free enterprise system but at the same time will provide the legal armor to protect and safeguard the prospective victim from the harshness of an unconscionable contract.

Section 2–302 of the Uniform Commercial Code enacts the moral sense of the community into the law of commercial transactions. It authorizes the court to find, as a matter of law, that a contract or a clause of a contract was "unconscionable at the time it was made", and upon so finding the court may refuse to enforce the contract, excise the objectionable clause or limit the application of the clause to avoid an unconscionable result. "The principle", states the Official Comment to this section, "is one of the prevention of oppression and unfair surprise". It permits a court to accomplish directly what heretofore was often accomplished by construction of language, manipulations of fluid rules of contract law and determinations based upon a presumed public policy.

There is no reason to doubt, moreover, that this section is intended to encompass the price term of an agreement. In addition to the fact that it has already been so applied (State by Lefkowitz v. ITM, Inc., 52 Misc.2d 39, 275 N.Y.S.2d 303; Frostifresh Corp. v. Reynoso, 52 Misc.2d 26, 274 N.Y.S.2d 757, revd. 54 Misc.2d 119, 281 N.Y.S.2d 964; Ameri-can Home Improvement, Inc. v. MacIver, 105 N.H. 435, 201 A.2d 886, 14 A.L. R.3d 324), the statutory language itself makes it clear that not only a clause of the contract, but the contract in toto, may be found unconscionable as a matter of law. Indeed, no other provision of an agreement more intimately touches upon the question of unconscionability than does the term regarding price.

Fraud, in the instant case, is not present; nor is it necessary under the statute. The question which presents itself is whether or not, under the circumstances of this case, the sale of a freezer unit having a retail value of $300 for $900 ($1,-439.69 including credit charges and $18 sales tax) is unconscionable as a matter of law. The court believes it is.

Concededly, deciding the issue is substantially easier than explaining it. No doubt, the mathematical disparity between $300, which presumably includes a reasonable profit margin, and $900, which is exorbitant on its face, carries the greatest weight. Credit charges alone exceed by more than $100 the retail value of the freezer. These alone, may be sufficient to sustain the decision. Yet, a caveat is warranted lest we reduce the import of Section 2–302 solely to a mathematical ratio formula. It may, at times, be that; yet it may also be much more. The very limited financial resources of the purchaser, known to the sellers at the time of the sale, is entitled to weight in the balance. Indeed, the value disparity itself leads inevitably to the felt conclusion that knowing advantage was taken of the plaintiffs. In addition, the meaningfulness of choice essential to the making of a contract, can be negated by a gross inequality of bargaining power. (Williams v. Walker-Thomas Furniture Co., 121 U. S.App.D.C. 315, 350 F.2d 445.)

There is no question about the necessity and even the desirability of instalment sales and the extension of credit. Indeed, there are many, including welfare recipients, who would be deprived of even the most basic conveniences without the use of these devices. Similarly, the retail merchant selling on instalment or extending credit is expected to establish a pricing factor which will afford a degree of protection commensurate with the risk of selling to those who might be default prone. However, neither of these accepted premises can clothe the sale of this freezer with respectability.

Support for the court's conclusion will be found in a number of other cases already decided. In American Home Improvement, Inc. v. MacIver, supra, the Supreme Court of New Hampshire held that a contract to install windows, a door and paint, for the price of $2,568.60, of which $809.60 constituted interest and carrying charges and $800. was a salesman's commission was unconscionable as a matter of law. In State by Lefkowitz v. ITM, Inc., supra, a deceptive and fraudulent scheme was involved, but standing alone, the court held that the sale of a vacuum cleaner, among other things, costing the defendant $140 and sold by it for $749 cash or $920.52 on time purchase was unconscionable as a matter of law. Finally, in Frostifresh Corp. v. Reynoso, supra, the sale of a refrigerator costing the seller $348 for $900 plus credit charges of $245.88 was unconscionable as a matter of law.

One final point remains. The defendant argues that the contract of June 15, 1966, upon which this suit is based, constitutes a financing agreement and not a sales contract. To support its position, it points to the typed words "Refinance of Freezer A/C #6766 and Food A/C #56788" on the agreement and to a letter signed by the plaintiffs requesting refinance of the same items. The request for "refinancing" is typed on the defendant's letterhead. The quoted refinance statement is typed on a form agreement

entitled "Star Credit Corporation—Retail Instalment Contract". It is signed by the defendant as "seller" and by the purchasers as "buyer". Above the signature of the buyers, they acknowledge "receipt of an executed copy of this RETAIL INSTALMENT CONTRACT" (capitalization in original). The June 15, 1966 contract by defendant is on exactly the same form as the original contract of August 31, 1965. The original, too, is entitled "Star Credit Corporation—Retail Instalment Contract". It is signed, however, by "Your Shop At Home Service, Inc." Printed beneath the signatures is the legend "Duplicate for Star". In substance and effect, the agreement of June 25, 1966 constitutes a novation and replacement of the earlier agreement. It is, in all respects, as it reads, a Retail Instalment Contract.

Having already paid more than $600 toward the purchase of this $300 freezer unit, it is apparent that the defendant has already been amply compensated. In accordance with the statute, the application of the payment provision should be limited to amounts already paid by the plaintiffs and the contract be reformed and amended by changing the payments called for therein to equal the amount of payment actually so paid by the plaintiffs.

Note on Unconscionable Pricing

1. In each of these cases, why was the transaction unconscionable? Consider them one at a time, and then attempt to state the principle for which they stand.

In *MacIver*, note that the Court characterizes the sale as one in which the defendants "were paying $1609 for goods and services valued at far less." The court thus excludes two components of the price—the commission and the finance charges—from what it considers to be the "goods and services" purchased.

Why is commission to be excluded? Would the court exclude from the "value" other elements of selling overhead such as advertising expenses or the gasoline used by the salesman on his way to survey the customer's home? The court did not claim that the commission was out of line with accepted business practice in the trade. Was this because the court knew that it was out of line or because such a commission was unreasonably high even if it conformed to trade practice?

Calculate the interest rate which defendants were charged by using the monthly repayment formula $Rate = \dfrac{24C}{L(N+1)}$ where C is the cost of the loan, L is the amount of the loan, and N is the number of payments to be made. Was this percentage out of line with prevailing rates? See Leff, "Unconscionability and the Code—The Emperor's New Clause," 115 U.Pa.L.Rev. 485 (1966) at 550, nn. 264–65 and accompanying text.

2. The principles underlying the *Frostifresh* opinions are even cloudier than those in *MacIver*, because the Court recites several factors peculiar to that case without specifying their significance: (1) the contract was negotiated orally in Spanish, (2) the buyer could not afford the appliance, (3) the seller knew the buyer was about to become unemployed, (4) the seller "deluded" the buyer, but the defense of fraud "was not set forth in the pleadings and accordingly such defense is not available."

Most of the opinion dwells not upon these facts, but upon the price which the Court found "shocking to the conscience." The Court specifically mentions two indicia of "oppression":

(1) The service charge of $246 imposed on $900, over a three year period ($32 × 36 monthly payments = approximately $1146.). What was the annual percentage rate? Was it within the limits permitted by New York State Personal Property Law § 404 (1957)?

(2) The cash price of $900 compared to the store's cost of $348. This latter figure is apparently the cost of the item alone, exclusive of overhead. How does the mark-up compare to markups in the appliance industry generally? To retail mark-ups in the economy as a whole? Should the Court have inquired about the seller's rate of profit? If so, which calculation is pertinent: profit as a percentage of gross sales or as a return on invested capital?

The trial court awarded the plaintiff only its wholesale cost of the freezer. Was it equitable to deny the company legal fees for collecting on an unconscionable contract, where the company was allowed to collect a partial judgment? Was it equitable to deny service charges even on the $348 to which the court held the seller entitled? Why was the company denied the right to recover the commissions that it actually paid to its salesman? On the other hand, why did the court award the seller two years' back interest, dating from the default in payment?

The appellate court permitted the seller to recover not only its net cost for the appliance, but also (1) trucking, (2) finance charges, (3) "service charges" and (4) "a reasonable profit." If the contract was unconscionable, why should recovery of these charges be permitted? What are the "service charges" referred to? How was the lower court to determine, on remand, what profit was reasonable? What if the seller had been operating at a loss? Under the appellate court's formula, what components, if any, that went into the $1146 price would be denied to the seller?

3. In *Jones*, unlike *MacIver* or *Frostifresh*, the Court compared the price of the goods to their "retail value" rather than to the company's own cost. Was this a preferable manner of proceeding? The court went to the brink of holding

that outrageous pricing could alone sustain a finding of unconscionability, then drew back. What would be the effects of such a holding?

One effect would be that both merchants and consumers' representatives would be better able to forecast, without having to litigate each case, that a court would hold a particular contract unconscionable. At present, the doctrine does not deter even extreme cases of overpricing, because courts routinely recite the presence of such factors as poverty and language, facts peculiar to each case upon which the result may depend. A "price alone" decision might at least set some outer limits on permissible mark-up. Would this be desirable? Reducing the section "to a mathematical ratio formula," at least in price cases, might also enable consumers' attorneys to try cases expeditiously, without having to prove, in each case, at great expense, all the circumstances of the sale and the buyer's educational level, income and habits.

The buyer might also be relieved of the burden of proving that the high cost/price ratio was not justified by reasonable overhead expenses or by prevailing competitive conditions; these are facts normally in the seller's knowledge and are difficult and costly for the buyer to obtain, even using discovery. See Schrag, "Bleak House 1968: A Report on Consumer Test Litigation," 44 N.Y.U.L.Rev. 115, 133–51 (1969). And a clearer statement of the objective facts constituting unconscionable pricing would facilitate settlement, since not every case would have to be tried to determine whether the buyer was pitiful enough to qualify for special treatment. For these reasons, some consumers' representatives would prefer more objective statements of the doctrine, such as an objective price formula. Are courts in sympathy with that desire? What does the court in *Jones* mean when it says that "It may, at times, be [a ratio formula]"?

Why did the Court in *Jones* leave the parties where they stood, with the seller entitled to keep the payments the buyer had already made? Why did it not compute the amount to which the seller was entitled based upon those charges it found "legitimate," and require a rebate of the balance to the buyer? Does the court's disposition support the principle that "Possession is nine tenths of the law"? See also Toker v. Westerman, 8 UCC Reporting Service 798, 113 N.J. Super. 452, 274 A.2d 78 (1971).

4. These three cases constitute almost the entire body of law on price unconscionability. See also Central Budget v. Sanchez, 53 Misc.2d 620, 279 N.Y.S. 391 (Civ.Ct.N.Y.1967); Toker v. Perl, 103 N.J.Super. 500, 504, 247 A.2d 701 (1968) aff'd other grounds 108 N.J. Super. 129, 260 A.2d 244 (A.D.1970); Patterson v. Walker-Thomas Furniture Co., 277 A.2d 111 (D.C.App. May 10, 1971); Morris v. Capitol Furniture & Appliance Co., 280 A.2d 775 (D.C.App. August 16, 1971). Do they provide real guidance toward deciding new cases? Consider the following problem.

A poor, English-speaking consumer, who earns $4500 in a canning factory, is visited by a door-to-door salesman. The consumer has a 10th grade education. His wife, who has an eighth-grade education and works in a cafeteria for $4000 a year, sits in on the transaction. Without making any fraudulent statements, the salesman persuades the couple to sign a three-year instalment contract for the purchase of a freezer, at a total price of $1145. The freezer is an off-brand model, and the buyers are told that the price includes a three year service warranty. The seller will pay them $25 for referrals of new customers, up to a maximum of two referrals.

Three weeks later, when neighbors see the freezer, they tell the buyers that they have been "had," because brand name freezers of similar capacity can be purchased in department stores for $350 and even in ghetto neighborhood stores for $600. The buyers consult you, an attorney for the Legal Aid Society. Do you have enough information to judge whether or not you can in good faith claim that the contract was unconscionable?

Suppose you consult an expert, who examines the appliance and says that the parts of the unit are worth $75. Now do you have enough information to be confident that, under the precedents, your claim of unconscionability will stand up? Do you have enough if he says that even calculating the labor of assembly and manufacturer's profit, the finished $1145 machine is worth $180?

Assume that you commence discovery proceedings (but see Patterson v. Walker-Thomas Furn. Co., 277 A.2d 111 (D.C. App. May 10, 1971) and Schrag, "Bleak House 1968: A Report on Consumer Test Litigation, 44 N.Y.U.L.Rev. 115 at 133–52 (1969)), and discover that the price of $1145 has the following explanation:

The salesman is an independent contractor who operates a "leased department" in the store from which he operates; the store lets him use its space, name, good will and some supporting services, functions as seller when he makes sales, and provides financing. The costs are as follows:

Raw materials used in making freezer		$ 75
Manufacturer's labor, profit, other overhead		105
Subtotal		180
Transportation from midwestern assembly plant to east coast warehouse		35
Subtotal		215
East coast regional distributor's warehouse costs, administrative expenses, other overhead and reasonable profit		115
Subtotal		330
Transportation of freezer to buyer's residence		12
Subtotal		342
Store's overhead: value of space used by salesman for his office; advertising of store's name to promote good will, taxes, interest on bank loans, and pro-rata valuation of ancillary personnel such as store guards and elevator operator		145
Subtotal		487
Store's profit		33
Subtotal		520
Salesman's net commission (he sells one freezer a week, so his income is approximately $10,000 a year)		200
Subtotal		720
Payment to former customer who referred purchaser		25
Subtotal		745
Three year service contract with independent repair service		20
Subtotal		765
Salesman's personal overhead: depreciation on car used for house calls, answering service, accountant, his own advertising and printing, insurance, legal fees, etc.		58
Subtotal		823
Sales tax on above at 7%		57
Subtotal		880
Finance charge on above at 18% per annum (on declining balance) for three years		265
TOTAL		1145

If mark-up is pertinent to the issue of unconscionability, how should it be computed? Which figure should be the "original" price and which the "marked-up" price to which it is compared? Should the price be held not unconscionable because the seller's profit was less than 3% of the total selling price? Or should elements of the price other than profit be considered? If so, which of the above charges should be deemed impermissible and therefore (1) excluded from the base on which mark-up is computed, or (2) included in the calculation of how great a mark-up was effectuated? Which, if any, should be excluded from the base *and* included in the mark-up?

5. Note that if the buyer had purchased an empty carton instead of a freezer, less than $200 might be saved from the final price. Would the sale of an empty carton for $945 to an educated consumer be per se unconscionable, or could such a transaction be redeemed by a showing of justifiable overhead? How significant a difference is made by placing in that carton a freezer which cost $180 to manufacture, and raising the total by $180?

6. Is the ratio of manufacturing costs to distribution costs in the above problem unrepresentative of the pricing pattern in ghetto sales? In sales generally? How much does it cost to manufacture the soda in a 10 cent bottle of soda? In that same bottle sold for 25 cents in a restaurant? How much does it cost to make a record which sells for $5.98, compared to the cost of designing and producing the record jacket, advertising the record, distributing it to record stores, paying interest on loans to the manufacturer and distributors, etc.?

7. Do you think that the cases reported above have had any effect on the prices of consumer durables or services in the low-income or any other market? If not, are the courts whistling in the wind?

8. Special problems arise when the doctrine of the unconscionability of the price is considered in conjunction with state statutes setting ceilings on the rate of finance charges which may be imposed. These ceilings generally range between 12% and 18%, on the declining balance, of the amount financed (the "cash price" of the goods). However, low-income retailers (and perhaps all retailers) cannot break even on extensions of credit at these rates—their losses as a result of default, and their costs of credit investigation, credit processing, money and collection greatly exceed the amount the law allows them to recover by way of finance charges imposed on buyers. They cope by raising the "cash prices" of the goods to cover that portion of credit costs not reimbursed by finance charges. In many cases of low-income sellers, this is merely a matter of the style employed in filling out contracts; no customers can afford to purchase the items for cash in any event, so the "cash price" is fictitious to begin with, and inflating it is a minor variation in the type of fiction employed.

With this in mind, consider the following variation on the above problem:

The store buys a freezer for $300. Its overhead and profit are $200, so it would like to sell the freezer to cash customers for $500. But no one in the community has $500, so it must sell on credit. Its costs in extending credit are very high, so that even if it made no profit on the credit component of the sale, it would have to charge $500 in finance charges on a three-year contract. Other things being equal, its contracts would show

CASH PRICE	$ 500
FINANCE CHARGE	500
TOTAL	$1000

However, since state law limits the finance charge to, say, 18% per annum, the company which makes no cash sales, pegs its prices this way:

CASH PRICE	$ 782
FINANCE CHARGE	218
TOTAL	$1000

Does this violate the state law limiting finance charges? If so, is the law also violated by the hundreds of major American retailers who routinely raise their cash prices to cover credit costs uncompensated by finance charges under existing ceiling legislation? See National Retail Merchants Ass'n, Economic Characteristics of Department Store Credit (1969). If the seller routinely discounted such contracts to a finance company for $500 would a court be more likely to say that the ceiling had been violated? If so, would a distinction between an independently financed and a self-financed credit sale be logically valid?

On the other hand, if the above transaction does not violate state law, must the concept of price unconscionability be imported to scrutinize the $782 cash price, in order to give any meaning to the state ceiling legislation? In other words, can state control over credit charges in the sale of merchandise be enforced without some legal control over cash prices as well, and is unconscionability the only legal tool which courts presently have to exercise that control?

To what extent do the reported decisions on price unconscionability regard mark-ups attributable to the expenses associated with credit as particularly suspicious, a position which could be justified by reference to the enforcement of ceiling legislation? To what extent, on the other hand, do these courts consider such components of mark-up to be particularly justifiable? Note that in *Jones,* the court remarks, "Similarly, the retail merchant selling on instalment or extending credit is expected to establish a pricing factor which will afford a degree of protection commensurate with the risk of selling to those who might be default prone."

The following study underscores the urgency of these inquiries, for it suggests that

1) low-income retailers do not make greater profits than do general retailers; if their prices are unconscionable, the illegality must have something to do with the sellers' high costs, rather than their profits; and

2) a substantial proportion of low-income retailers' higher costs are attributable to the costs of extending credit: investigation, processing, money, risk, collection and legal expenses.

EXCERPT FROM FTC, ECONOMIC REPORT ON INSTALLMENT CREDIT AND RETAIL SALES PRACTICES OF DISTRICT OF COLUMBIA RETAILERS, pp. ix-xi, 17–20 (1968)

SUMMARY AND CONCLUSIONS

This report presents the results of a survey of installment credit and sales practices involving household furnishings and appliances in the District of Columbia. The purpose of the survey was to obtain a factual picture of the finance charges, prices, gross margins and profits, legal actions taken in collecting delinquent accounts, and the assignment relationships between retailers and finance companies. The survey covered those D. C. retailers of furniture and appliances having estimated sales of at least $100,000 for the year 1966. The 96 retailers providing data had combined sales of $226 million, which represented about 85 percent of the sales of furniture, appliance, and department store retailers in the District of Columbia.

Use of Installment Credit by D.C. Retailers

Sixty-five retailers with combined sales of $151 million indicated regular use of consumer installment sales contracts. The remainder sold only for cash or on a regular or revolving charge account basis. This report focuses primarily on retailers using installment contracts. These retailers were classified into two groups: those appealing primarily to low-income customers and those appealing to a more general market.

D.C. stores varied widely in their use of installment credit. Some general market discount appliance stores made very few sales on credit. At the other extreme, a number of low-income market retailers sold entirely on installment credit.

Installment credit was used much more extensively by retailers selling to low-income consumers than by retailers selling to other consumers. Low-income market retailers used installment credit in 93 percent of their sales. The comparable figure for general market retailers was 27 percent.

Customer Characteristics of Low-Income Market Retailers

A sample of installment sales contracts and credit applications was analyzed to identify the customer characteristics of low-income market retailers. The analysis revealed substantial differences between customers of the low-income market retailers and all residents of the District of Columbia. The average family size was larger—4.3 persons compared to an average of 3.5 persons for the District of Columbia. Almost half of the families of customers in the sample had five or more members. The median family income during 1966 of the sample customers was $348 per month. This is very low considering the larger than average size of the families. The Bureau of Labor Statistics recently estimated that the

maintenance of a moderate standard of living for four in Washington, D.C., requires a monthly income of $730.

Most customers were engaged in low-paying jobs. The largest proportion, 28 percent, were Service Workers, such as waitresses and janitors. Second in importance were Operatives (including such occupations as taxi drivers and laundry workers). Laborers and Domestic Workers also represented a significant share of the sample. Together, these 4 major occupational groups accounted for 75 percent of the customer sample. In comparison, only 36 percent of the general population in the District was classified in these low-paying occupational groups. There were 31 welfare recipients in the sample, accounting for 6 percent of all customers in the sample. There were also a number of customers in the sample dependent on social security, alimony, support payments, and income received from relatives.

A review of credit references noted in the 486 contracts subjected to detailed analysis revealed that 70 percent indicated no credit references or references with low-income market retailers only. Only 30 percent of the customers of this retailer, therefore, had established credit with general market retailers.

Gross Margins and Prices of Low-Income Market Retailers

The survey disclosed that without exception low-income market retailers had high average markups and prices. On the average, goods purchased for $100 at wholesale sold for $255 in the low-income market stores, compared with $159 in general market stores.

Contrasts between the markup policies of low-income and general market retailers are most apparent when specific products are compared. Retailers surveyed were asked to give the wholesale and retail prices for their two best-selling models in each product line. These price data are typical of the large volume of products sold by each class of retailer.

For every product specified, low-income market retailers had the highest average gross margins reported. When similar makes and models are compared, the differences are striking. For example, the wholesale cost of a portable TV set was about $109 to both a low-income market and a general market retailer. The general market retailer sold the set for $129.95, whereas the low-income market retailer charged $219.95 for the same set. Another example is a dryer, wholesaling at about $115, which was sold for $150 by a general market retailer and for $300 by a low-income market retailer.

Operating Expenses and Net Profits of Retailers Surveyed

Despite their substantially higher prices, net profit on sales for low-income market retailers was only slightly higher and net profit return on net worth was considerably lower when compared to general market retailers. It appears that salaries and commissions, bad-debt losses, and other expenses are substantially higher for low-income market retailers. Profit and expense comparisons are, of course, affected by differences in type of operation and accounting procedures. However, a detailed analysis was made for retailers of comparable size and merchandise mix to minimize such differences.

Low-income market retailers reported the highest return after taxes on net sales, 4.7 percent. Among the general market retailers, department stores had the highest return on net sales, 4.6 percent. Furniture and home furnishings stores earned a net profit after taxes of 3.9 percent; and appliance, radio, and television retailers were the least profitable with a net profit of only 2.1 percent on sales.

Low-income market retailers reported an average rate of return on *net worth* after taxes of 10.1 percent. Rates of return on net worth varied considerably among various kinds of general market retailers. Appliance, radio, and television retailers reported the highest rate of return after taxes, 20.3 percent of net worth. Next in order were furniture and home furnishings retailers with 17.6 percent and department stores with 13 percent on net worth.

* * *

Operating Expenses and Net Profits

Not all of the low-income market retailers covered in this survey maintained and submitted financial statements adequate for detailed analysis of expenses and net profit. Likewise, most of the small-volume general market retailers did not submit detailed financial statements. Of the 18 low-income market retailers, however, 10 submitted statements permitting some analysis of specific expense items. These 10 low-income market retailers were matched with 10 general market retailers of comparable size and mix of merchandise who submitted statements permitting a comparative analysis of expenses and profits.

A comparison of expenses and profits as a percent of sales for the matched samples of 10 low-income market retailers and 10 general market retailers of furniture and appliances is shown in table II–5. The 10 low-income market retailers paid only 37.8 percent of their sales revenue for the merchandise they sold, while the cost of goods sold by the general market retailers was 64.5 percent of their sales revenue. As previously noted, low-income market retailers sell comparable merchandise at much higher retail prices, which accounts for this wide difference in cost of merchandise as a percentage of sales. The remaining gross margin for the 10 low-income market retailers was 62.2 percent and for the 10 general market retailers, 35.5 percent of sales. The gross margin to cover expenses and net profit was 26.7 percentage points higher for the low-income market retailers.

TABLE II–5.—COMPARISON OF EXPENSES AND PROFITS AS PERCENT OF SALES FOR
10 LOW-INCOME MARKET RETAILERS AND 10 GENERAL MARKET RETAILERS
OF FURNITURE AND APPLIANCES IN THE DISTRICT OF COLUMBIA, 1966

Revenue component	10 low-income market retailers	10 general market retailers	Difference in margins and ratios	
			Percentage points	Percent of total
1966 net sales	$5,146,395	$5,405,221		
	Percent	Percent		
Operating ratios as percent of sales	100.0	100.0		
Cost of goods sold	37.8	64.5		
Gross profit margin	62.2	35.5	+ 26.7	100.0
Salary and commission expense [1]	28.2	17.8	+ 10.4	38.9
Advertising expense	2.1	3.9	− 1.8	− 6.7
Bad-debt losses [2]	6.7	.3	+ 6.4	24.0
Other expenses [3]	21.3	11.2	+ 10.1	37.8
Total expenses	58.3	33.2	+ 25.1	94.0
Net profit return on sales	3.9	2.3	+1.6	6.0

[1] Includes officer's salaries.
[2] Includes amounts held back by finance companies to cover bad-debt losses.
[3] Other expenses, including taxes, after deduction of other income.

Source: FTC Survey.

Practically all of the substantially higher gross margin of the 10 low-income market retailers was offset by higher expenses and did not result in markedly higher net profit as a percentage of sales. As shown in the right-hand columns of table II–5, of the total difference in gross margin of 26.7 percentage points, 94 percent of the difference (25.1 percentage points) was accounted for by higher expenses and 6 percent of the difference (1.6 percentage points) was accounted for by higher net profits on sales of low-income market retailers.

More than one-third (38.9 percent) of the higher gross margin of the 10 low-income market retailers was spent on salary and commission expense. This expense item included all employees' compensation and officers' salaries and was 28.2 percent of sales for low-income market retailers, compared to 17.8 percent of sales for general market retailers. A major reason for low-income market retailers' higher personnel expense is believed to be their use of outside salesmen who canvass house-to-house or followup requests for home demonstrations and often make collections of installment payments at the home of the customer. Several of the 10 low-income market retailers pay their outside salesmen-collectors commissions on both sales and collections. Other reasons for higher personnel costs of low-income market retailers could be that they have more sales personnel and pay higher rates of compensation compared to small-volume general market retailers; and since they finance all or a larger proportion of their own installment contracts, they require more employees to keep records of small payments on installment credit accounts.

The proportion of sales revenue spent on advertising was higher for the 10 general market retailers than for the 10 low-income market retailers. This is consistent with the lack of extensive citywide advertising among the low-income market retailers in the total sample. The difference in advertising ratios was 1.8 percentage points. The 10 general market retailers spent 3.9 percent of their sales revenue on advertising, while the advertising by the 10 low-income market retailers amounted to 2.1 percent of their sales revenue.

Higher bad-debt losses of low-income market retailers accounted for about one-fourth (24 percent) of the total difference in gross margins. It was evident from analysis of financial statements, finance charges, and retail prices of low-income market retailers that they often charge higher prices anticipating that part of the increased revenue will cover higher collection expenses of their method of doing business. For the group of 10 low-income market retailers, bad-debt loss was 6.7 percent of sales, while comparable size general market retailers had bad-debt losses of less than 1 percent of sales.

Other expenses accounted for more than one-third (37.8 percent) of the higher gross margin of low-income market retailers. The remaining items of expense amounted to 21.3 percent of sales for the 10 low-income market retailers and to 11.2 percent of sales for the 10 general market retailers. Items of occupancy, delivery, and administrative expense were included among the other expenses, but a comparative analysis of these items could not be made because of inconsistency in expense account classifications and accounting methods. Nevertheless, there were certain items of expense that appeared more often and in larger proportionate amounts on the low-income market retailers' statements, which account for part of their higher ratio of other expenses to sales. Since most of the low-income market retailers financed their own installment sales, the expense of processing this credit and interest on borrowed funds appeared as substantial items on their statements. Legal and professional fees were larger items of expense among low-income market retailers, reflecting cost of suits filed for the collection of delinquent accounts. Insurance costs were generally higher as a percentage of sales for these retailers.

Net profit as a percentage of sales for the 10 low-income market retailers was 3.9 percent, as compared to 2.3 percent for the 10 general market retailers. This difference of 1.6 percentage points in higher net profit for the low-income market retailers amounted to less than one-tenth (6 percent) of the total difference in gross margins. The business methods employed by low-income market retailers involved substantially higher costs which offset the higher prices charged, leaving no markedly higher net profit as a percentage of sales.[9]

Net profit after taxes as a percent of owner equity was also determined for these two groups of retailers. This average net profit was 12.7 percent for the 10 low-income market retailers and 8.1 percent for 9 out of the 10 general market retailers.[10] The variation in rates of return on owner's equity within each group

[9] Statistical tests were applied to analyze differences in profit and cost elements for the 10 low-income and 10 general market retailers compared in this section. These tests have limited validity because of the small number of observations and the non-random method by which the retailers were selected. They suggest, however, that the differences in profit rates indicated do not justify rejecting the hypothesis that profits are actually similar for both groups of retailers. Similar tests applied to gross margins and other elements of expense, notably salaries, bad debts, and other expenses, appear to justify accepting the hypothesis that expense experience for the two groups of retailers is different.

[10] One of the 10 small-volume general market retailers had to be omitted from the net return on owners' equity analysis because of incomplete financial statement information.

of retailers was so great as not to warrant a conclusion that rates for one group were different from those of the other.

Note

1. In view of the difficulty of judicial application of the doctrine of unconscionable pricing, it may be desirable to supply administrative guidance. As of 1971, one statute, the New York City Consumer Protection Law of 1969, had been enacted to accomplish this result. The statute permits the Commissioner of Consumer Affairs to write regulations defining practices as unconscionable, taking into account certain factors:

NEW YORK CITY ADMINISTRATIVE CODE

§§ 2203d-10, 2.0(b), and 3.0.

§ 2203d–1.0 **Unfair trade practices prohibited.**—No person shall engage in any deceptive or unconscionable trade practice in the sale, lease, rental or loan or in the offering for sale, lease, rental, or loan of any consumer goods or services, or in the collection of consumer debts.

§ 2203d–2.0(b). **Definition * *. Unconscionable trade practice.** Any act or practice in connection with the sale, lease, rental or loan or in connection with the offering for sale, lease, rental or loan of any consumer goods or services, or in the extension of consumer credit, or in the collection of consumer debts which unfairly takes advantage of the lack of knowledge, ability, experience or capacity of a consumer; or results in a gross disparity between the value received by a consumer and the price paid, to the consumer's detriment; provided that no act or practice shall be deemed unconscionable under this title unless declared unconscionable and described with reasonable particularity in a local law, or in a rule or regulation promulgated by the commissioner. In promulgating such rules and

regulations the commissioner shall consider among other factors: (1) knowledge by merchants engaging in the act or practice of the inability of consumers to receive properly anticipated benefits from the goods or services involved; (2) gross disparity between the price of goods or services and their value measured by the price at which similar goods or services are readily obtained by other consumers; (3) the fact that the acts or practices may enable merchants to take advantage of the inability of consumers reasonably to protect their interests by reason of physical or mental infirmities, illiteracy or inability to understand the language of the agreement, ignorance or lack of education, or similar factors; (4) the degree to which terms of the transaction require consumers to waive legal rights; (5) the degree to which terms of the transaction require consumers to jeopardize money or property beyond the money or property immediately at issue in the transaction; and (6) definitions of unconscionability in statutes, regulations, rulings and decisions of legislative, or judicial bodies in this state or elsewhere.

§ 2203d–3.0 **Regulations.**—The commissioner may adopt such rules and regulations as may be necessary to effectuate the purposes of this title, including regulations defining specific deceptive or unconscionable trade practices.

Such rules and regulations may supplement but shall not be inconsistent with the rules, regulations and decisions of the Federal Trades Commission and the Federal courts in interpreting the provisions of Section 5(a)(1), or the Federal Trade Commission Act, 15 U.S.C.A. 45(a)(1), or the decisions of the courts interpreting General Business Law § 350 and Uniform Commercial Code § 2–302.

Problem

With the above statute as your authority, draft regulations governing unconscionable practices in the sale of (a) appliances and (b) furniture, pursuant to this statute. The major difference between the two commodities is that the models and styles of furniture sold in low-income areas are likely to be entirely different from those sold in middle-class areas; comparisons of prices from store to store will therefore be more difficult. Consider the impact of your regulation on low-income retailers and their customers, and the practicability of enforcement. For example, if the regulation is sufficiently objective in its standards to be enforceable, will it prevent high-cost low-income retailers from doing business? If so, will the poor be unable to purchase durables, by virtue of being unable to obtain credit from general market retailers? Is this desirable?

SECTION 3. REGULATION OF THE CONSUMER CREDIT INDUSTRY

A. LIMITATIONS ON CREDIT CHARGES

M. BENFIELD, MONEY, MORTGAGES AND MIGRAINE— THE USURY HEADACHE

19 Case West.Res.L.Rev. 819, 838 ff. (1968).

* * * All 48 States with general usury laws except Arkansas have a series of statutory or judicial exceptions which substantially diminish the impact of the general rate limitation. The most common of these exceptions are discussed in the following sections.

(1) The Small Consumer Borrower Exemption from Usury Statutes.—Many consumer borrowers undoubtedly need

legislative protection from sellers and lenders who overreach on credit transactions. A substantial portion of small loans to consumers are emergency loans to tide the borrower over a financial rough spot caused either by an unexpected expense, temporary unemployment, or by the borrower's inability to handle his financial affairs. Such a borrower needs money quickly to protect himself from inconvenience, discomfort, or loss of property to existing creditors. This necessitous borrower usually is willing to pay almost any rate to get a loan and often would in the absence of legislative controls.

Also, it is an unfortunate fact that many consumers are unintelligent or naive in money matters and, in the absence of some legislative limits on rates, would pay very high rates without fully understanding either the rate or its effect. However, if one accepts the fact that consumers are of differing credit worthiness, he must also accept the fact that legislative ratemaking in the consumer area cannot take the form of price fixing for every class of customer without resulting in serious inequality among borrowers. Therefore, rates set by statute in the consumer area probably should be set at some outside conscionable limit with the expectation that most transactions will take place at lower rates. It is clear, however, that the present general usury rates are too low to allow any substantial amount of consumer financing to be done under them.[100]

One of the most fantastic episodes of 19th century laissez faire business profit taking occurred in the small loan business between 1870 and around 1910. The general usury statute maximums then (6 to 12 percent), as now, were not high enough to permit profitable lending of

---

[100] On the costs of the consumer credit industry, see J. Chapman & R. Shay, The Consumer Finance Industry (1967).

small amounts at legal rates. In the large industrial cities, however, there were many wage earners who could not control their financial situation and who were often in desperate need of small amounts of cash to pay medical bills or to tide them over periods of unemployment. The need could not be satisfied within the usury structure, so it was satisfied outside it. Small loan lenders operated openly and advertised in nearly every city of any size in the United States in spite of the fact that in every State except Massachusetts they were lending at illegal rates.[101] The interest rates charged ranged from a reasonable 3 percent per month to 33 percent per month and even higher.

*   *   *

In the early years of this century, the Russell Sage Foundation became interested in small loan problems and sponsored the development of the Uniform Small Loan Law which attacked the problem of high rate consumer loans by (1) fixing realistic legal rates (originally $3\frac{1}{2}$ percent per month on small loans); (2) requiring small loan lenders to be licensed and subject to regulation by State authorities; and (3) subjecting lenders to criminal penalties for violation of the small loan law.[105] Laws patterned more or less closely after the Uniform Small Loan Law were soon adopted in a number of States and there is presently legislation in all States except Arkansas which permits small loans to be made at rates higher than the general usury rates.[106] The

original maximum loan amount under the Uniform Small Loan Law was $300 and a number of States still have this limitation, though other States have much higher small loan law ceilings.[107]

The enactment of the small loan laws substantially improved the position of the consumer-borrower of small sums by supplanting low usury rates with higher rates which provided a reasonable profit for credit suppliers. Social science researchers have made it clear that such laws do lower interest rates to consumers and that, in their absence, in more recent times, rates have been five or six times higher than the small loan rates.[108]

(2) Industrial and Installment Loan Laws.—In addition to the small loan laws just discussed, most States have installment or industrial loan laws or both under which rates in excess of those allowed by the usury statutes may be charged. Industrial loan acts are statutory approvals of the Morris Bank Plan which was developed around 1910 by Arthur Morris to secure a yield greater than that permitted under the usury laws. *   *   *

Installment loan laws which authorize lenders to charge higher than usury rates on installment loans exist in about four-fifths of the States. In all States with such laws banks may lend at the installment loan rates and in some States only banks may lend at such rates. In other States, various types of lenders, and, in a few States, all lenders, may lend at the installment loan rates.

---

101 L. Robinson & R. Nugent, Regulation of the Small Loan Business 38–73 (1935).

105 [D. Gallert, W. Hilborn & G. May, Small Loan Legislation 27–28 (1932)] at 89–94. The most recent (7th) draft of the Uniform Small Loan Law is set out in B. Curran [Trends in Consumer Credit Legislation (1965)] at 144–57.

106 1 CCH Installment Credit Guide ¶ 41 (Aug. 17, 1966); see B. Curran, supra note 105. Rates presently range from approximately 12 percent to 40 percent. Most rates range around 3 percent per month for the first $300 and generally scale down in a series

of steps on larger amounts if the law covers loans higher than $300.

107 1 CCH Installment Credit Guide ¶ 41 (Aug. 17, 1966); B. Curran, supra note 105, at 20–21.

108 D. Gallert, W. Hilborn & G. May, supra note 105; L. Robinson & R. Nugent, supra note 101; see Simpson, Cost of Loans to Borrowers Under Unregulated Lending, 8 Law & Contemp.Prob. 73 (1941) for a study of small loan rates in some Southern States in the late thirties.

The rate provisions usually provide that a dollar discount or add-on may be charged at the beginning of the loan. These provisions, like the industrial loan provisions, result in a simple annual interest yield on installment loans which is approximately double the stated add-on or discount rate. In 17 States there is no maximum on the amount which may be loaned under installment loan provisions —and in those States, the installment loan law becomes, in effect, a special general usury law applying to all loans repayable in installments.[113] In the other States there are limits on the amounts which may be loaned at installment loan rates ranging from as low as $1,000 in Wyoming to $15,000 in Illinois. The installment loan rates are usually around 12 percent simple annual interest and in only two States are they higher than 15 percent on amounts larger than $1,000.[114]

In addition to the small loan, industrial loan, and installment loan laws, most States have special provisions for credit unions and pawnbrokers which allow them to charge more than the general usury rates for loans. Also, many States have special statutory provisions authorizing higher rates for home improvement loans, check loans, second mortgage loans, and others.[115]

The small loan, industrial loan, and installment loan laws and other special consumer lending laws, together carve out a massive area of credit which is not subject to the general usury laws.[116] These statutes, not the general usury laws, are now, it should be observed, the statutes which apply to control practically all consumer borrowing except home mortgage loans. This is particularly significant since perhaps the single most influential reason given for retention of usury laws is protection of the necessitous consumer-borrower.

(3) The "Time-Price" Exception to General Usury Laws.—As just pointed out, all States except Arkansas have concluded that the best solution to the problems of consumer credit is the statutory creation of exceptions to the general usury laws permitting lenders to charge higher rates under controlled conditions. Likewise, all States except Arkansas give similar treatment to credit sales of goods either through the "time-price doctrine" or through various retail installment sales acts which have replaced the time-price rules.[117]

Under the time-price doctrine a seller of goods may fix one price for a sale for cash and another for a sale on credit and the difference in price is not considered to be an interest charge, but rather is considered to be merely a higher price for the goods which the merchant may

---

[113] The 17 States and the maximum simple annual interest yield on installment loans are as follows:

Alabama	10.90%
Kansas	10.90%
N. Carolina	11.58%
Delaware	11.58%
Kentucky	9.58%
Oregon	10.90%
Georgia	10.90%
Maryland	11.58%
S. Carolina	12.68%
Hawaii	26.14%
Nebraska	12%
Texas	14.45%
Indiana	15.68%
New Mexico	12.68%
Vermont	11.58%
Virginia	11.58%
W. Virginia	11.58%

These rates are interpolated from the information given in 1 CCH Installment Credit Guide ¶ 48 (Aug. 17, 1966).

[114] Hawaii (26.14 percent) and Indiana (15.68 percent). Id.

[115] See B. Curran, Trends in Consumer Credit Legislation 45–52, 75–76, 79–82 (1965). For a typical second mortgage statute, see Ohio Rev.Code Ann. §§ 1321.51–.60 (Page Supp.1967).

[116] B. Curran, Trends in Consumer Credit Legislation (1965), gives an excellent general survey of the many laws creating special rates for consumer transactions.

[117] Id. at 83–123.

charge to cover the risks of selling on credit.[118] The principle was first announced in an 1827 English case [119] and the first American case recognizing the doctrine appeared in Missouri in 1856.[120] From its mid-19th century beginnings, the time-price doctrine swept across the country and it was not until the 1950's that two States, Arkansas and Nebraska, overruled their prior cases, and held a credit sale of goods to be subject to usury or small loan statutes.[121]

The time-price doctrine and the rule that a purchase of a note or contract obligation at less than its face value is not subject to usury laws became the twin pillars supporting the great modern credit sale society.[122] The dealer sold on credit at a "time-price" and then sold the resulting conditional sales contract or account to a finance company. Since neither transaction was subject to usury laws, the rate charged to customers could be sufficiently high to provide a good return for the extension of credit and the finance company could purchase at a discount big enough to give it a good profit. Through this use of the two rules, banks and sales finance companies were able to avoid usury and small loan laws.[123] The time-price doctrine, therefore, came to be used to allow banks and finance companies to charge rates for financing which they could not have charged had they been dealing directly with the buyer.

* * * The purchaser of a new automobile may either borrow money from a bank or finance company and pay cash for the automobile or he may buy the automobile on credit from the dealer. In either case the economic result is the same, especially in view of the fact that in most cases the dealer who finances a sale immediately transfers the paper to a bank

---

[118] As stated in the leading American case, Hogg v. Ruffner, 66 U.S. (1 Black) 115, 118–119, 17 L.Ed. 38 (1861):

[I]t is manifest that if A propose to sell to B a tract of land for $10,000 in cash, or for $20,000 payable in ten annual instalments, and if B prefers to pay the larger sum to gain time, the contract may not be called usurious. A vendor may prefer $100 in hand to double the sum in expectancy, and a purchaser may prefer the greater price with the longer credit; and one who will not distinguish between things that differ, may say, with apparent truth, that B pays a hundred percent for forbearance, and may assert that such a contract is usurious; but whatever truth there may be in the premises, the conclusion is manifestly erroneous. Such a contract has none of the characteristics of usury; it is not for the loan of money, or forbearance of a debt.

[119] Beete v. Bidgood, 108 Eng.Rep. 792 (K.B. 1827). The concept, however, has a long history. Mention of the "time-price doctrine" appears as early as the 12th century when Pope Alexander III rejected it and ruled that credit sales at prices above the cash price were usurious. S. Homer, A History of Interest Rates 70 (1963). However, later scholastics managed to work in a higher price for credit sales as a part of the "just-price doctrine." Salin, Just Price, 8 Encyc.Soc.Sci. 504, 506 (1932).

[120] Mitchell v. Griffith, 22 Mo. 515 (1856). The court held that the doctrine did not apply where all of the $6,289 purchase price of land was paid except $379.72 for which 2½ months credit was given.

[121] B. Curran, supra note 116, contains a general discussion of the significance of the time-price doctrine. For a more detailed discussion, see Britton & Ulrich, The Illinois Retail Installment Sales Act—Historical Background and Comparative Legislation, 53 Nw.U.L.Rev. 137 (1958); Warren, Regulation of Finance Charges in Retail Installment

Sales, 68 Yale L.J. 839 (1959); Consumer Credit Symposium: Developments in the Law, 55 Nw.U.L.Rev. 303 (1960). Nebraska has now adopted a retail instalment sales act permitting higher than usury rate credit charges in installment sales. See B. Curran, supra note 116.

[122] The usury statutes apply only to extensions of credit, that is, to cases in which an obligor promises to pay money in the future in return for a present advance. However, the sale by a person to whom money is due of his right to receive the money for a sum less than the amount due is not a transaction subject to the usury laws since the seller himself does not promise to pay money in the future. Cases are collected in Annot., 143 A.L.R. 238 (1943).

[123] See Britton & Ulrich, supra note 121, at 140–44; Warren, supra note 121, at 857.

or sales finance company which, through a different office, would probably have loaned the purchase price directly to the buyer. In determining the "time-price" the seller usually uses a chart furnished him by his financing agency which shows the price which should be charged to produce the desired yield. In such circumstances, to say that the additional charge is not equivalent to an interest charge gets very farfetched indeed.

* * *

In this area, as in others, it can be assumed that the courts were "doing" better than they were "saying." So long as general usury laws were the alternative to the time-price doctrine, the time-price doctrine was the better choice. Holding that sales were subject to general usury statutes would have forced sellers into illegal transactions or into various subterfuges to avoid their impact. And the small loan and installment loan laws which ordinarily involved the concept of a licensed lender and substantial State regulartory authority did not adequately fit the thousands of retailers in the various States.

* * *

The need for regulation of installment sellers in a way similar to the regulation of consumer lenders was recognized a good many years ago; the first installment sales act took effect in Indiana in 1935.[129] Today 43 States and the District of Columbia have retail installment sales laws fixing the maximum finance charge which may be imposed in credit sales.[130] These acts vary in coverage,

some covering only motor vehicles, some only goods other than motor vehicles, and some which are so-called "all goods acts" covering sales of all kinds of goods. Some of the statutes are limited to sales for nonbusiness purposes while others apply generally to all credit sales.

The net effect of the evolution from the time-price doctrine to regulation through retail installment sales acts is to subject credit sales to regulation and rates very similar to those provided under small loan and installment loan acts and to leave another huge area of credit free from usury statute control.

(4) Exemptions for Loans to Corporations.—The time-price doctrine and small loan, installment loan, industrial loan, and similar laws take most nonreal estate consumer credit from under the general usury statutes. The exemptions for loans to corporations exclude from the usury laws loans at the other end of the lending spectrum.

Note

In today's consumer credit market, different kinds of institutions extend credit under various legal controls and various rates. For example, a consumer who needs but does not have $300 to buy a television might get a 7% per annum passbook loan from his savings bank, with his savings account as collateral, or an 11% loan from a commercial bank, or a 6% loan from a credit union operated by his employer or labor union, or a loan from a small loan company at between 20% and 40%, or he might use a store credit card and pay credit charges ranging from 0% to 18%, depending on state law and local custom. Or he might sign a contract with the store for the extension of store credit, which the store might hold itself while collecting from him, or might assign to a sales finance company, so that he paid that institution from month to month. Or he might use a bank credit

[129] See Britton & Ulrich, supra note 121, at 151 n. 59; 1 CCH Installment Credit Guide ¶ 35 (Aug. 17, 1966).

[130] The States which have no statutes regulating finance charge rates in credit sales are North Carolina, Rhode Island, South Carolina, Virginia, West Virginia, and Wyoming. 1 CCH Installment Credit Guide ¶ 35, at 1502–27, 1553–83 (Aug. 17, 1966). In Arkansas, credit sales are subject to the general 10 percent usury law.

card, or a reserve checking account to obtain bank credit at from 12% to 18%.

However, not all of these institutions lend to the same borrowers; each type tends to have its own clientele as well as its own rate structure. For example, only the employed can borrow from the job-related credit unions that generally offer the cheapest rates. Only relatively wealthy individuals will be able to obtain loans from most banks, and the banks discourage loans under $1000 because fixed processing costs for bank loans are high. Less wealthy people are thrown back on retailers and sales finance companies to finance purchases, and persons who are poorer still are forced to use the highest-cost legitimate credit institutions, the small loan companies. Finally, the poor (who, some argue, need credit most) are unable to get credit at all, except perhaps from loan sharks.

In other words, economic conditions have generated several separate types of lending institutions, each with its own set of rates, and each with a corresponding separate risk pool. One type of institution (banks) deals primarily with the rich, and offers the lowest rates; another (small loan companies) services the working class, and offers credit at much higher rates. At rates between those of banks and those of loan companies, retailers and others extend credit to the middle class. The evolution of legal rules governing interest rate ceilings has encouraged this trend by which the poor pay more; separate laws, which evolved independently to provide exceptions from state usury regulation, apply to separate institutions.

This set of affairs mirrors economic segregation and stratification found throughout society. For example, wealthy middle-class suburban communities, which have zoned out the poor and are relatively free of such costly burdens as crime, grime and welfare, are able to spend more on their schools than are less

wealthy cities, perpetuating inequality. Middle class persons are able to join group health and life insurance plans, providing them with financial advantages not available to the poor. Similar examples of lawful devices by which the rich stay rich and the poor stay poor are sprinkled throughout this book.

From one perspective, this state of affairs, at least with respect to credit, seems inevitable, perhaps even desirable; why *shouldn't* a group of people be permitted to persuade a lender that as a group they are more likely to repay on time than are average citizens, and that therefore they should get lower rates? The largest, wealthiest corporations, after all, get the prime rate of corporate lending, much lower than the interest rate charged to "mom and pop" companies.

However, reasoning which justifies economic discrimination against the poor may seem overly smug to some, and in others it may breed revolutionary sentiment. ("Marat, we're poor/And the poor stay poor," runs the people's refrain from Peter Weiss's Marat/Sade).

Should consumer credit legislation attempt to force institutions to distribute to wealthier borrowers, to taxpayers, or to some other group, some of the costs of lending to the poor? If so, how should this be accomplished?

For example, by threatening demonstrations or appealing to sentiments of benevolence or guilt, poverty organizations have from time to time convinced general market retailers to participate in experimental programs to extend credit to selected low-income families, so that they could obtain both merchandise and credit at fair prices, free from the markups and high-pressure salesmanship that characterize the ghetto market. See The Urban Coalition, Consumer Credit and the Low Income Consumer (1969). To the extent that stores suffer losses from such experiments and pass those losses on to all of their customers, most of whom are wealthier than the poor people participating in the program, they are reversing the trend and causing the rich to subsidize the poor. For example, in 1968 Kann's Department Store in Washington, D.C. gave a limited amount of credit—$50 each—to 500 poor people. Despite screening by a poverty organization to eliminate over-extended debtors, and despite the fact that each participant had to attend a credit education class before obtaining credit, the poor consumers' delinquency ratio was twice that of Kann's regular customers. Ibid at 39. Late payments increase a lender's interest and collection expenses, and force him to raise his prices for all his customers. Is this desirable?

The following models are among many that could be designed in connection with major revisions of the statutes governing the extension of consumer credit. Which of them would you support?

A) Continuation of the present system, which is itself less than a perfect "free market" model. For example, many states grant lenders' licenses only to loan companies which can show that the issuance of a license would be to the public "convenience and advantage"; this really means that installment lending is oligopolistic or cartelized in each market area, and legal enforcement of scarcity keeps rates high, in the name of prevention of alleged cut-throat competition. Furthermore, retail credit ceilings are unrealistically low, so part of the cost of credit is passed along to all buyers in the form of higher merchandise prices. To that extent, users of retail credit are subsidized by those who pay cash. Note that the high cost of administration of the nation's bank credit card systems is collected largely

through "discounts" (percentage commissions) which banks charge participating merchants, rather than through finance charges imposed on consumers who use the cards; here too, whatever increased net costs the merchants bear are passed on to all customers, who to that extent subsidize cardholders.

B) Elimination of rate ceilings and licensing restrictions, and reliance on competition to produce a fair market rate, coupled with a requirement that each individual institution give each of its customers the same rate. Thus, a particular finance company or store would have to make a determination as to who would be included in its risk pool, and could not discriminate within the pool. On one city street might co-exist a 12% loan company, a 20% loan company, a 50% loan company and a 250% loan company, and a consumer would go from one to another until he found one willing to accept him.

C) Elimination of ceilings and restrictions as above, while authorizing credit grantors to charge differential rates to different classes of borrowers—6% to the rich and 100% to the poor. Everyone might be able to obtain credit at *some* rate from such an institution. To insure that individual rates were being assigned on some rational basis such as a forecast of the likelihood of repayment, rather than, say, racially, a statute might require the creditor to test the borrower by some objective point system—e. g., two points for each year of continuous residence in the city, one point for each thousand dollars of salary, one point for being married, etc.—in order to determine his rate.

Do these last two models presuppose that until the country becomes genuinely committed, politically, to income redistribution, it is foolish, unjust and politically naive to attempt to give poor people consumer credit which the free market would deny them? Is that a correct premise?

D) Raise ceilings to approximately 40%, relying basically on competition to produce market rates below that figure, but providing that upper limit to keep the lid on charges in less competitive sub-areas of the economy. Such a limit might variously be viewed as either the prevention of "unconscionable" rates of interest, or the deliberate exclusion from the credit market of persons so poor that, in the judgment of those who lend and those who govern, they should not be borrowing for fear that they may over-extend themselves. See Uniform Consumer Credit Code §§ 2.201, 2.207, 3.201, 3.508, 3.602. Would such a proposal adequately take account of the fears that led the Russell Sage Foundation to recommend higher ceilings at the turn of the century? That is, if the poor were unable to obtain loans at 36%, and no higher rate were authorized, would they be content with the reasoning of the statute or seek out loan sharks? Do loan sharks hover in the modern ghetto or are contemporary loan sharks more interested in overextended commercial borrowers?

E) Reduction of present ceilings to rates lower than those at which credit can economically be extended. This might tend to restrict the direct lending industry, in favor of those who extend sale credit and can hide their credit costs in their cash prices, thus forcing increased subsidy of credit buyers by cash buyers.

Of course, this proposal would also have the tendency to reduce the total amount of consumer credit extended in the United States, currently more than 100 billion dollars. Can this proposal be justified on either of the following theories?

1) It is desirable to use every available device to reduce economic inequality in the United States. Giving the poor credit is like giving them money and should be promoted. Favoring sale credit over loan credit is democratic; it is harder for stores to turn customers away than for lending institutions to do so. Furthermore, the above proposal can be coupled with a law requiring stores to lend to certain categories of low-income persons; say, any person earning more than $4000 a year, or any person who has not defaulted on previous debts to a greater extent than $500. Then the poor would have the opportunity to shop at the same stores as the rich, and would not be barred by the unavailability of retail credit at those stores; furthermore, they would pay the same prices for both merchandise and credit as other buyers. Prices of goods would rise substantially, but would be effectively higher for the rich and lower for the poor than at present.

2) To the extent that such legislation reduced credit and perhaps, in turn, sales, it would have desirable side effects, because the United States is in any event overly concerned with consumption and with the production of goods instead of public services. A cut-back in credit would significantly reduce use of the private automobile with its attendant homicide and environmental damage; it would also com-

bat inflation, reduce the rate of accumulation of solid wastes, discourage advertising for the purpose of making people buy what they do not need, and cut back on consumption of unnecessary durables, such as automobiles with the latest styling changes.

F) In connection with proposals (A) through (E) above, provision of federal guarantees for extension of consumer credit to the poor. See the proposed Community Credit Expansion Act, S. 2146 (90th Cong), and discussion by its sponsor, Sen. William Proxmire, Congressional Record, May 13, 1969, S. 5090–5104. Can guarantees which reduce rates for the poor be justified if the working poor, or the lower-middle class is excluded? Who should be eligible to participate? How much would such a system cost the public in taxpayer subsidies to pay for (a) defaults and delinquencies by the debtors involved and (b) the cost of administration? What devices should a government agency adopt to insure (a) that the loans it guarantees are repaid, and (b) that persons who default on such loans do not receive them and default on them repeatedly? That is, would involvement of the government in lending, even as guarantor, lead to more forceful collection practices than private lenders now engage in? What is the record of the Internal Revenue Service and of state educational loan programs in this regard? Is the government as free as a private party to decide to forbear? And should persons who default on a government guaranteed loan be barred from credit forever? If not, is there any way to prevent this phenomenon from occurring?

B.　TRUTH IN LENDING

To date, the most extensive federal involvement in the regulation of consumer credit has been enactment and enforcement of the Consumer Credit Protection Act (Truth-in-Lending is Title I) in 1968. See 15 U.S.C.A. § 1601 ff. The law, and the Federal Reserve Board's interpretive regulations, 12 C.F.R. § 226, provide detailed requirements concerning the written disclosure of specified credit information in consumer credit agreements. The most important disclosures required are the amount of finance charges and the percentage rate of such charges as a proportion of the declining balance.

For eight years, the political battle over enactment of this legislation was bitterly contested; the fight was so fierce and so occupied concerned politicians that virtually no other consumer protection legislation was passed during the years of the Democratic administration. Was it worth it? Even before the bill became law, some observers predicted that it would have virtually no effect, particularly on the problems of the poor. One such skeptical account is printed below, followed by a press release purporting to document the utility of the law during its first year of operation. Do the results of the study confirm or rebut Prof. Kripke's forecast?

GESTURE AND REALITY IN CONSUMER CREDIT REFORM

Homer Kripke *
44 N.Y.U.L.Rev. (1969).

Two major efforts toward reform of consumer credit by statute culminated in the summer of 1968. First, Congress passed the "Truth-in-Lending Bill" [1] which had been pending before the Senate since 1961 [2] and which was finally passed by nearly unanimous action by the Senate and then, with substantial additions, by the House.[3] Second, the National Conference of Commissioners on Uniform State Laws (NCCUSL) promulgated, and the American Bar Association approved, the Uniform Consumer Credit Code (UCCC), for enactment by the states.

The federal bill, by voluntarily renouncing the operative effect of its provisions in a state which has comparable provisions,[4] has given a powerful impetus to the rapid enactment of state legislation in this field. Whether or not the states adopt the UCCC (and at this writing it is too early to tell), this code will remain the touchstone for consideration of all state legislation in the field for some years.

It is therefore appropriate and timely to consider what has been accomplished and what remains to be done. On this point the writer finds himself largely a dissenter from the received view that the federal legislation is a great step forward. It accomplishes a little something, but very little compared to what could have been done with the energy expended.

I

THE "PUT-ON"

It is not too much to say that the strong support of witnesses,[5] public officials, legal aid workers, and consumer representatives for the concept of full disclosure of the rate of finance charges and other aspects of a consumer credit transaction—as proposed to be required by the Senate bill during seven long years of

---

* Professor, New York University School of Law, J.D.1933, Michigan. The author served as Consultant on Consumer Leasing on the Staff of the Special Committee on Retail Sales, Consumer Credit, Small Loans and Usury which prepared the UCCC.

[1] The Truth-in-Lending Bill is Title I of the Consumer Credit Protection Act, Pub.L. No.90–321, 82 Stat. 146 (May 29, 1968) [hereinafter CCPA]. As originally passed by the Senate, S. 5, 90th Cong., 1st Sess. (1967), the bill contained only what is now the Truth-in-Lending title.

[2] Earlier versions of the bill were: S. 2755, 86th Cong., 2d Sess. (1960); S. 1740, 87th Cong., 1st Sess. (1961); S. 750, 88th Cong., 1st Sess. (1963); S. 2275, 89th Cong., 1st Sess. (1965).

[3] The House introduced its own bill, H.R. 11601, 90th Cong., 1st Sess. (1967). The Subcommittee on Consumer Affairs of the House Committee on Bankruptcy and Currency held hearings thereon, amended the bill in committee and again on the floor, then substituted its own text for that of the Senate bill, S. 5, and passed the Senate bill. The Conference Committee made further changes, but the bill is basically in the House form.

[4] CCPA §§ 123, 305.

[5] The more recent hearings in the field of consumer credit are cited as follows:

Hearings on S. 5 Before the Subcomm. on Financial Institutions of the Senate Comm. on Banking and Currency, 90th Cong., 1st Sess. (1967) [hereinafter Banking Hearings].

Hearings on H.R. 11601 Before the Subcomm. on Consumer Affairs of the House Comm. on Banking and Currency, 90th Cong., 1st Sess., pts. 1, 2 (1967) [hereinafter House Hearings].

Hearings on S. 316, S. 2589, S. 2590, S. 2592 Before the Subcomm. on Business and Commerce of the Senate Comm. on the District of Columbia, 90th Cong., 1st & 2d Sess. (1968) [hereinafter D.C. Hearings].

Hearing on the FTC Report on Credit Practices Before the Subcomm. on Financial Institutions of the Senate Comm. on Banking and Currency, 90th Cong., 2d Sess., ser. 90–93 (1968) [hereinafter Hearing on Door-to-Door Sales].

Hearings on S. 1599 Before the Consumer Subcomm. of the Senate Comm. on Commerce, 90th Cong., 2d Sess. (1968) [hereinafter Commerce Hearings].

hearings and legislative activity and by comparable "little Douglas bills" or truth-in-lending bills in the states—was a "put-on." [6] Many of them knew that disclosure would have only a slight effect on the evils about which they were testifying and agitating; yet everyone acted as if disclosure bills would solve the problem.[7]

It was not surprising that the vast discrepancy between the evils of deception and fraud, set forth in the testimony, and the disclosure remedy would escape the attention of popular writers who reasonably inferred that disclosure would remove the evils about which the witnesses were testifying. Such details as the fact that the widely-hailed Massachusetts Truth-in-Lending Bills had had very little impact [8] failed to diminish the enthusiasm of the popular writers for the same thing on a national scale.[9]

So far as the witnesses are concerned, the causes of the put-on are somewhat more difficult to understand. The writer does not, of course, mean to sug-

gest that anyone was wilfully deceiving the congressional committees or the public. To understand why they deceived themselves is somewhat more complex. The reasons are a compound of superficial knowledge, concealing basic misunderstanding of the status of the instalment credit business, and a great deal of wishful thinking based on the unconscious hope that the simple disclosure solution would avoid the necessity of facing up to the hard and expensive decisions that would be necessary if one really wanted to attack the evils.

First, the spokesmen on the consumer side did not really understand the instalment credit business. The statistics that some of them used as to the size of "finance companies" lumped together the figures on consumer credit with those of commercial instalment sales and the quite different businesses of factoring, commercial receivables financing, etc. Second, and more importantly, they failed to distinguish in their minds the tremendous difference between instalment credit, as available in the purchase of new cars, high grade used cars, and appliances from reputable dealers in middle-class contexts and the totally different problem of instalment credit in the poverty areas, marked by ignorance on the part of the buyer, enticement, the bait of easy terms, fraudulent practices, shoddy merchandise, unreliable dealers, garnishment, and oppressive collection methods.[10] While no sharp line between these areas could be drawn by a definition, there is in fact a significant distinction.

In the middle-class areas—where the consumer has mobility; some training in shopping; some experience in personal planning and, therefore, some restraint against impulse buying; some ability at price shopping; and occasionally some understanding of the amount of finance

---

[6] For the morphology of the put-on, see Brackman, The Put-On, New Yorker, June 24, 1967, at 34.

[7] For a summary of the expressions of the myth that a uniform method of disclosure would give the consumer the knowledge to shop effectively, see Note, Consumer Legislation and the Poor, 76 Yale L.J. 745, 747–49 (1967) [hereinafter Yale Note]. Much of this thinking was that of Senator Paul Douglas, first proponent of the Truth-in-Lending Bill. The student author of the Yale Note rejects this view: "Whatever its validity for the middle class, this model is almost always inapplicable to the purchases of the poor." Id. at 749. After Truth-in-Lending was enacted into law, the Senate's professional staff assistant expressed the same recognition of reality. McLean, The Federal Consumer Credit Protection Act, 24 Bus.Law. 199 (1968).

[8] Mass.Gen.Laws Ann. ch. 140A (Supp. 1969); id. ch. 255D (Supp.1969). For the effects of this statute, see notes 22, 23 infra.

[9] The Truth about Credit is Coming, Consumer Reports, Aug. 1968, at 428; Fritchey, Truth-in-Lending Gains, N. Y. Post, Aug. 21, 1967, at 26, col. 3; Porter, More Truth in Lending, N. Y. Post, June 3, 1968, at 47, col. 1.

[10] See D. Caplovitz, The Poor Pay More 137–55 (paperback ed. 1967).

charges—disclosure in a prescribed form will undoubtedly do some good by making comparison easier. In a nation of 200 million people, there will certainly be some who will profit from standardized disclosure. But the writer has elsewhere argued that the amount of good to be accomplished will be relatively small and will by no means fulfill the high expectations, because the middle class buyer has already learned where credit is cheapest.[11] The writer there pointed out that statistical efforts to determine whether the consumer understood the cost of financing were merely unimpressive confirmation of the compelling economic fact visible to anyone who wanted to see: that the comparatively high-priced sales finance companies catering to middle-class buyers had lost position to banks providing financing at lower rates. Within six months after those views were expressed, they were amazingly confirmed by the fact that the three largest independent sales finance companies, which had been significant financial intermediaries between basic sources of savings and users of consumer credit for two generations, had lost or were on their way to losing their independent existence. The characteristic of these companies was that they showed low earnings growth potential despite earnest efforts to diversify into other financial and non-financial enterprises. It was the judgment of the financial community that their long-established borrowing power and existing long-term debt at favorable interest rates could be more advantageously used than in consumer credit.[12]

---

[11] Kripke, Consumer Credit Regulation: A Creditor-Oriented Viewpoint, 68 Colum.L.Rev. 445, 455–69 (1968).

[12] Associates Investment Corporation disappeared into the maw of Gulf and Western Corporation. Commercial Credit Corporation became a subsidiary of Control Data Corporation.

Most impressive of all was the proposal that C.I.T. Financial Corporation become a

Thus, for the middle-class consumer, the battle for competitive pricing of credit had been essentially won before it was aided by the disclosure statutes. In the poverty context, however, the problem as to disclosure was and is different. How much good will disclosure do in this context?

In the first place, the congressional hearings are full of stories of consumers who never understood even that they had to pay a finance charge, although the papers which they had signed showed a finance charge and a total cost far in excess of the cash price quoted to them.[13]

---

subsidiary of Xerox Corporation. C.I.T., the largest independent company (and largest of all after General Motors Acceptance Corporation) was immune from an involuntary takeover, because of its financial strength and the large holdings of the founding families; but it had had a low growth rate and low earnings multiple, which made it difficult to use its stock for acquisitions. See C.I.T.'s Treadmill, Forbes Magazine, Oct. 15, 1967, at 27. An opportunity to bring its earnings under the shelter of the earnings multiple of Xerox Corporation must have seemed attractive to its officers. But there was wide discussion in the financial community as to whether the deal made any sense other than as a juggling of price-earnings ratios, since Xerox did not need C.I.T.'s credit strength. The deal was dropped after having been publicly announced, reputedly because of the opposition of large institutional holders of Xerox. Metz, Market Place, N. Y. Times, Nov. 15, 1968, at 66, cols. 7–8.

Note also the merger of G.A.C. Corp., formerly General Acceptance Corporation, with Gulf American Corporation, a land development company. See also the financial difficulties of Automobile Banking Corporation, a consumer finance organization. N. Y. Times, Aug. 5, 1968, at 57, cols. 3–7.

[13] Statement of Mr. Virgil Anderson, House Hearings, supra note 5, at 1189: "At the first point I want to stress to the Committee that when I purchased this freezer I was unaware of the additional charges that I was confronted with, also with the financing of this freezer." See also id. at 1189, 1190. Statement of Ida L. Bryant, D.C. Hearings, supra note 5, at 44: "I thought I had asked the proper questions of the salesman and I understood that the set would cost $195 plus $25 tax. It really makes me mad that I was never told about any finance charges or in-

For this kind of consumer, it is unlikely that disclosure in writing, in a different prescribed form, is going to make any difference. Recognizing this fact, the Federal Trade Commission, although its officials have repetitiously been strong advocates of the disclosure statute,[14] has gone so far as to require oral disclosure in an order in a fraud case in the light of its assertion that consumers do not understand written disclosure.[15]

In the second place, there is much evidence that some consumers in the poverty areas understand very well that they are being bilked by high cash prices and high finance charges, even before the new legislation takes effect; but they also know that merchants or credit agencies with lower charges are not going to extend credit to them.[16] A person who scarce-

ly knows where the money for his next meal is coming from is not going to worry much about the risk involved in obtaining some needed goods when he does not know where next month's and next year's instalments are coming from.

A third reason that disclosure is a wholly inadequate solution in poverty areas is that, even when accompanied with rate regulation, it is concerned only with the admitted credit charges in a transaction. But a very substantial portion of all consumer credit is sale credit —i. e., it consists of credit extended in the first instance by the seller or dealer, whether or not he subsequently transfers the credit obligation to a bank or finance company. The total profitability of a credit sale transaction depends on the

---

terest or any other charges." Statement of Christine Hardy, id. at 48: "The price of the set was listed at $229.00 with sixteen payments of $16.50 each. I was told nothing about any finance charges. * * *" See also D. Caplovitz, supra note 10, at 137–55.

[14] Letter of Chairman Paul Rand Dixon, Banking Hearings, supra note 5, at 24–25; statement of Chairman Dixon, House Hearings, supra note 5, at 272–77; testimony of Chairman Dixon, D.C. Hearings, supra note 5, at 150–62. See also his statement in Hearing on Door-to-Door Sales, supra note 5, at 2–17.

[15] Leon A. Tashof, No. 8714, at 50 (F.T.C. Dec. 2, 1968). Presumably, the FTC was speaking of a prior similar order when it said in June 1968: "In addition, for the first time the Commission required that a disclosure be made orally as well as in writing, on the theory that most consumers, and especially low-income consumers, will not be really aware of any such written disclosure in a conditional sale contract, regardless of its conspicuousness." Federal Trade Comm'n, Report on District of Columbia Consumer Protection Program 10 (1968) [hereinafter FTC Protection Report].

[16] Statement of Miss Shirley Kronberg, Hotel, Motel and Club Employees Union, House Hearings, supra note 5, at 1173–74:

It has been our experience that consumer education by itself * * * is not doing much good.

We have gone to great lengths to educate our membership about shopping for cash, about comparison shopping. * * *

We find that people know what is right, but they are not able to pursue a course which will give them the best purchase.

The largest single reason is that they cannot get credit in a creditable establishment.

* * *

I recognize the value of the Truth in Lending Bill and the good it will do for the literate, the educated. * * *

It is the people who walk into a store and whose entire transaction is oral * * * who believe the salesman when he tells them "This will cost you $2.00 a week". * * * He doesn't know how many months, how many years, how much the service charges, how much he is paying for financing. * * *

See also the statement of Miss Mary Tarcher, Director of the Legal Aid Society, id. at 1187. See D. Caplovitz, supra note 10, at 73:

A 31-year-old Negro mother of two children living on welfare expresses a fairly typical opinion: "[B]ut by buying from these fellows I get some of the things I have to have sooner."

"Many stores won't give credit to welfare families. * * *"

Well aware that she is a "poor credit risk," and of the higher charges she pays, she * * * finds the peddler the only available source of what she wants to buy. (Emphasis in original.)

combination of the merchandise profit and the financing profit. If a seller is restricted in the finance rate involved, either by maximum rate legislation or by a competitive desire to advertise "low finance rates" or "low bank rates," he can forego part of the possible finance profit, increase his cash selling price, and make the profit there.[17] The forces of competition, of course, in some contexts, restrict the amount of cash selling price that may be quoted; but in the poverty areas, where the potentialities of abuse are greatest, the salutary effects of competition are the least effective. The ghetto shopper is not a comparison shopper and does not have access to the lowest prices.[18] The Consumer Credit Protection Act (CCPA) totally failed to deal with this enormous loophole in the effect of disclosure and rate regulation. In contrast, the authors of the UCCC saw and expressed the problem clearly [19] and dealt with it as best they could by a provision making it evidence of unconscionability to charge more than going prices to persons in like positions.[20] This provision is all to the good, but it necessarily leaves open an enormous number of questions.

Even before the CCPA goes into effect on July 1, 1969, it is already possible to forecast its effect from the experience of the widely-heralded Massachusetts Truth-in-Lending statutes.[21] The latter have had very little effect, and this was already clear before the CCPA was finally enacted.[22] To the extent that they have had effect, the Massachusetts statutes seem to have been costly to the consumer by suppressing advertised rate competition and by causing finance charges to be buried in cash prices.[23]

That the truth in lending provisions of the CCPA will have very little impact in the poverty areas as to which the most concern is expressed has been largely conceded by strong proponents of the legislation. The Chairman of the Federal Trade Commission has admitted this:

> Mr. Dixon. [W]e found that in some instances retailers took all credit costs and put them in the asking price —just hid them, you see.
>
> Now if we pass a truth-in-lending bill and this should be the developing practice, truth in lending is not going to reach the problem in the ghetto.
>
> Senator Sparkman. * * * A great many people seem to think the disclosure of finance charges will solve the problem.
>
> * * *

---

[17] See colloquy, text accompanying note 24 infra; Jordan & Warren, The Uniform Consumer Credit Code, 68 Colum.L.Rev. 387, 393–94 (1968); Spanogle, Why Does the Proposed Uniform Consumer Credit Code Eschew Private Enforcement?, 23 Bus.Law. 1039, 1049 (1968). See also President's Committee on Consumer Interests, Position Statement on the UCCC, Dec. 3, 1968, in NCCUSL, Major Statements in Support of the Uniform Consumer Credit Code Filed with the Massachusetts Committee on the Judiciary, January 29, 1969, Boston, Massachusetts 20 [hereinafter Major Statements].

[18] D. Caplovitz, supra note 10, at 49–57; Yale Note, supra note 7, at 762–65 and authorities cited therein.

[19] Jordan and Warren, note 17, supra.

[20] Uniform Consumer Credit Code § 6.111 (3)(c) (Rev. Final Draft 1968) [hereinafter UCCC].

[21] Mass.Gen.Laws Ann. ch. 140A (Supp. 1969); id. ch. 255D (Supp.1969).

[22] N. Y. Times, May 25, 1968, at 45, col. 6: "If the experience of a Massachusetts statute on credit is any barometer, the public's reaction to being told precisely what its annual interest on credit buying amounts to will be practically nil." This conclusion is supported in detail in Note, A Survey of Experience Under the Massachusetts Retail Installment Sales Act, 9 B.C.Ind. & Com. L.Rev. 1020 (1968), and by Pullen, The Impact of Truth-in-Lending Legislation—The Massachusetts Experience, Research Report to the Federal Reserve Bank of Boston No. 43 (1968).

[23] Pullen, supra note 22, at 23–27, 49.

But my thinking is that there are a lot of things involved not covered by disclosure.[24]

Similar recognition has been shown by a professional staff member of the Senate committee which was the forum for the long drive to enact the Truth-in-Lending Bill [25] and by the draftsmen of the UCCC.[26] Yet neither the Federal Trade Commission nor the Senate committee ever took steps to have the bill amended to encompass credit abuses that could not be reached by disclosure, but which were before them not only in the drafts of the UCCC then in process but also in the Commission's own studies of the evils requiring remedy.[27]

[24] Hearing on Door-to-Door Sales, supra note 5, at 10.

[25] McLean, supra note 7, at 206:

[B]ut at least a very vocal reason and a very substantial part of the rhetoric which attempted to justify both the truth-in-lending and the Consumer Credit Code project was to provide relief to the poor, to help the people living in urban ghettos from being victimized by the high cost of credit. * * *

Reform in the area of disclosure is certainly needed, but I think it will be the middle income consumer that will obtain the greatest benefit. * * *

[N]ow that we have largely solved the problems of middle class America (assuming the States will enact the Consumer Credit Code) I think we still have peculiar problems with low income consumers. Here I think we need to adopt a rifle shot approach as opposed to a shotgun approach.

See also the commentaries of Messrs. Miskell and Mov, id. at 221–24 respectively.

[26] Jordan & Warren, Disclosure of Finance charges: A Rationale, 64 Mich.L.Rev. 1285, 1321 (1966) indicates that disclosure will be of minimal influence to the marginal consumer whose problem is not credit charges but rather credit itself.

[27] See FTC Protection Report, supra note 15, at 17–22, with a long list of recommendations for state action. The only recommendation for federal legislative action, id. at 21, was to pass the pending Bill on Door-to-Door Sales, S. 1599, 90th Cong., 1st Sess. (1967).

NATIONAL COMMISSION ON CONSUMER FINANCE, PRESS RELEASE

For Release for
Sunday, March 21, 1971

COMMISSION ANALYZES EFFECTIVENESS OF TRUTH IN LENDING LAW

About 30 percent of American consumers who did not know the annual percentage rates charged for consumer credit in June 1969 have become aware of those rates under the Federal Truth in Lending Act, the National Commission on Consumer Finance reported today.

Despite this marked improvement, however, the Commission staff analysis disclosed that more than half of the users of installment credit remained unaware of the annual percentage rate.

In measuring the effectiveness of Truth in Lending after 15 months of its operation, the Commission found that 2 out of 5 Americans surveyed (38.3 percent) were aware of the rate charged for various forms of installment credit in 1970 compared with only 1 out of 7 (14.5 percent) before the law took effect.

Users of retail revolving credit (department store accounts, gasoline credit cards, etc.) were found to be more knowledgeable about the rates charged than users of installment credit, both before and after the new Federal law went into operation. Approximately 35 percent knew the annual rate for open end credit prior to the start of the Truth in Lending Act on July 1, 1969; by September 1970, more than half of revolving credit users (55.7 percent) knew the rates charged for that type of credit.

Commission Chairman Ira M. Millstein made public today tabulations of "changes in awareness of annual percentage rates" compiled from a staff analysis of answers to nationwide surveys made by the Federal Reserve Board in June 1969 and in September 1970.

"The term 'annual percentage rate' of the finance charge is the key measuring device under Truth in Lending for comparing the true cost of different forms of credit," Chairman Millstein explained.

"Obviously this concept is not yet well understood by a majority of the people using five specific categories of installment credit—personal loans, home improvement loans, new car financing, used car financing, and furniture and appliance credit. But the significant increase in awareness of rates during the first year of operation of Truth in Lending indicates that the concept is now much better understood than it was. There remains much to be done, however, to make the annual percentage rate concept more comprehensible to those who use credit—and particularly to those with low income and less than a high school education," he said.

The Commission staff analysis was based on an evaluation of answers given to Federal Reserve Board interviewers by heads of households in two polls taken 15 months apart. Of the thousands interviewed in each of the two surveys, only those who said they had used some type of consumer credit were asked for the specific rates they had been charged. The 1969 survey covered transactions in a 1-, 3- or 5-year period before Truth in Lending; the 1970 survey covered transactions after the start of Truth in Lending. Some preliminary tabulations of the responses in both surveys were made public by the Federal Reserve Board in January 1970.

The data collected by the Federal Reserve Board were turned over to the National Commission on Consumer Finance which was created by the Consumer Credit Protection Act. Title IV of that Act directs the Commission to make a thorough study of the consumer credit industry, the Truth in Lending Act and other means to insure the informed use of credit by consumers.

Before analyzing replies to the Federal Reserve surveys, Commission staff studied the actual rates charged for the five categories of consumer installment credit in various regions of the country, then compared responses given by those interviewed by the Federal Reserve with the actual rates.

Respondents were classified as "aware" of the rates they had been charged for installment credit if their answers fell within the following ranges:

for new autos—8 percent and above;

for used autos—11 percent and above;

for furniture and appliances—12 percent and above;

for home improvements—8 percent and above;

for personal loans—12 percent and above (finance companies)

8 percent and above (all others).

Those whose answers fell outside the limits (61.7 percent) were considered by Commission staff to have been "unaware" of the actual rates charged.

A separate analysis of responses on retail revolving (open end) credit compared with rates actually charged showed a much higher level of awareness. For this type of credit respondents were classified as "aware" if they reported annual percentage rates from 12 through 18 percent or monthly rates not exceeding 2 percent per month.

Gains in awareness were not evenly distributed among consumers when classed by education, age, income, region, race, and source of credit. Increased awareness of finance charges was generally greater for consumers with higher income and educational levels. It was also greater if they were white rather than black, if they were not residents of a poverty area and if they lived in the western part of the United States.

Chairman Millstein said that because of wide variations in mortgage interest rates during the 6 years covered by the two surveys, the Commission staff had been unable to make the kind of analysis for mortgage credit that it had made for installment and retail revolving credit. Analysis of awareness for bank credit card annual percentage rates is still to be made, he added.

Besides Chairman Millstein, Commission members now include Senators John J. Sparkman (D.-Ala.); William Proxmire (D.-Wisc.); and John G. Tower (R.-Tex.); Representatives Leonor K. Sullivan (D.-Mo.); Henry B. Gonzalez (D.-Tex.); and Lawrence G. Williams (R.-Pa.); Dr. Robert W. Johnson of Purdue University and Douglas M. Head, former Attorney General of Minnesota. Representatives Gonzalez and Williams were recently named by House Speaker Carl Albert to replace Representatives Wright Patman and Seymour Halpern. Mr. Head was named by President Nixon to replace former Chairman Robert Braucher, who is now on the Supreme Judicial Court of Massachusetts.

Note

Is the *concept* of disclosure irrelevant to the poor, or is Truth-in-Lending simply an inadequate method of making disclosure accomplish its goal? See Comment, "Consumer Legislation and the Poor," 76 Yale L.J. 745 (1967). Though the Comment argues that low-income consumers lack all of the characteristics of those for whom disclosure would be valuable, its author, Eric Schnapper, later petitioned the Federal Reserve Board, on behalf of the NAACP Legal Defense Fund and other organizations, to add to the Truth-in-Lending regulations a requirement that creditors print certain rescission notices on their contract forms. The notices would say: "If you are unable to understand the contents of this agreement because you cannot read English, you may cancel any credit transaction made pursuant to this agreement within a reasonable time after you have obtained a translation of it or a complete explanation of its contents from any person of your choice other than the creditor. * * *" The Schnapper amendment would also provide: "If all the required disclosures and the required notice are made in a foreign language in addition to English, the words 'either English or [name of foreign language]' may be substituted for 'English' in that notice." *Matter of Canas,* Petition for Initiation of Rule Making Procedure (1971). The idea was to give creditors a strong incentive—fear that many contracts would otherwise be rescindable indefinitely—to insure that the consumer was given a copy of the contract in a language he could read, and to explain the contract to an illiterate consumer. Would such a device work?

Should the Truth-in-Lending law be amended to require oral disclosures to low-income consumers, on the theory that they do not read the fine print in written credit agreements? To require oral disclosure to all consumers? Would such a provision be enforceable? Would it have harmful effects on business which outweigh any beneficial effects for consumers?

In October, 1971, the Federal Reserve Board decided not to require foreign language disclosures under the Truth-in-Lending Law. 2 C.C.H.Pov.L.Rep. para. 13,956, p. 13,238 (1971).

C. THE HOLDER-IN-DUE-COURSE DOCTRINE

A Hopefully Historical Note

At least until 1972, a special problem plaguing users of instalment credit was the holder-in-due-course doctrine. Sellers of goods and services would require consumers to sign negotiable promissory notes, which they would then indorse to banks or finance companies with whom they did business on a regular basis. The third-party purchaser of the paper would then claim the rights of a holder in due course of commercial paper; specifically, freedom from any claims or defenses that the buyer might have asserted against the seller with whom he dealt.

For example, if a man purchased a food freezer or vacuum cleaner from door-to-door salesman, and signed such a note, he would soon learn that the note had been sold to a bank, and he would be told to make his monthly payments to that institution. However, the man might stop making his payments when he discovered that he'd been cheated by the salesman's fraudulent statements about the nature of the merchandise. In a suit by the bank on the note, the buyer would not be permitted to assert defenses (other than "real" defenses, see UCC 3–305), provided that the bank took the note in good faith, for value, and without notice of the buyer's defenses. If the seller deliberately lied to the buyer about the goods, if the merchandise was unmerchantable, or even if the goods were never delivered (failure of consideration), the buyer would have to pay. Of course, he would still have a right of action against the seller, but asserting it would require finding the seller solvent and initiating a new proceeding against him, rather than merely interposing a defense.

Similar results were achieved by printing in retail instalment contracts a clause whereby the buyer waived all of his claims and defenses as against innocent third-party purchasers. Such clauses were made valid by UCC 9–206 "subject to any statute or decision which establishes a different rule for buyers of consumer goods."

The abolition of this doctrine was for years one of the primary goals of consumer spokesmen. Even its one-time supporters recognized the hardship that it caused in consumer cases, and recommended its limitation to transactions among dealers, rather than those between dealers and consumers. Compare Kripke, "Chattel Paper as a Negotiable Specialty Under the Uniform Commercial Code," 59 Yale L.J. 1209 (1950) with Kripke, "Consumer Credit Regulation: A Creditor-Oriented Viewpoint," 68 Colum.L.Rev. 445, 469–73 (1968)

Successful judicial attacks on the doctrine, once a rarity, Commercial Credit Corp. v. Childs, 199 Ark. 1073, 137 S. W.2d 260 (1940), became, in the late 1960's, more common. Unico v. Owen, 50 N.J. 101, 232 A.2d 405 (1967); Morgan v. Reasor, 69 Cal.2d 881, 73 Cal.Rptr. 398, 447 P.2d 638 (1968). Legislation to limit its use in consumer cases was enacted in a few states. N.Y. Pers.Prop.L. § 403, (as amended 1970); Calif.Civil Code § 1804.2 (1967); Uniform Consumer Credit Code § 2.404, alt. A.

Nevertheless, in 1971, the doctrine was still applied to cut off the rights of consumers in approximately 40 states. Furthermore, its restriction (except in Massachusetts, see Mass.Gen.Laws ch. 255 § 12(f) (1970)) did not apply to third-party credit cards, such as bank credit cards, which were rapidly replacing instalment contracts as a method of financing instalment sales. Agreements drafted by banks pertaining to the use of these cards required buyers to waive defenses as against their banks.

To eliminate this problem on a nationwide basis, the Federal Trade Commission proposed and held hearings on, a trade regulation rule which would read as follows:

§ 433.1   Definitions

For purposes of this part, the following definitions shall apply:

(a) *Consumer goods or services.* Goods or services purchased or leased primarily for personal, family, or household purposes, including courses of instruction or training regardless of the purpose for which they are taken.

(b) *Seller.* Any person, partnership, corporation, or association, engaged in the retail sale or lease of consumer goods or services to a consumer.

(c) *Consumer.* Any buyer or lessee of consumer goods or services.

(d) *Consumer transaction.* Any sale or lease of consumer goods or services by a seller to a consumer.

(e) *Consumer note.* Any negotiable promissory note or other negotiable instrument of indebtedness, or any retail installment contract whether negotiable or nonnegotiable, executed by a consumer in connection with a consumer transaction. "Consumer note" shall not include a check given in current payment of a presently due consumer obligation, if the check is dated at or before the date of its issuance, or at the time of its issuance is postdated not more than 10 days, and collection thereof through banking channels is initiated by the payee within 7 days of the date of the check.

(f) *Credit card issuer.* Any person, partnership, corporation, or association, including a bank, which by agreement extends to a cardholder the right to use a credit card in connection with a consumer transaction.

(g) *Cardholder.* Any consumer who enters into an agreement with a credit card issuer extending to such consumer the right to use a credit card in connection with a consumer transaction.

(h) *Related creditor.* Any person, partnership, corporation, or association, which is engaged in making loans to consumers to enable payment to be made for consumer goods or services and which either participates in or is directly connected with the consumer transaction. Without limiting the scope of the immediately preceding language, there shall be a rebuttable presumption that a creditor is a related creditor under any one of the following circumstances:

(1) The creditor is a person related by blood or marriage to the seller or to the seller's spouse.

(2) The creditor prepared, supplied or furnished the seller with the forms or documents used to evidence or secure the consumer loan.

(3) The seller prepared, supplied or furnished the creditor with the forms or documents used to evidence or secure the consumer loan.

(4) The creditor is directly or indirectly controlled by, under common control of, or is otherwise affiliated with the seller.

(5) The creditor and the seller are engaged in a joint venture to produce consumer obligations payable either directly or by transfer to the creditor.

(6) The creditor directly or indirectly pays the seller any consideration for the referral of consumer borrowers.

(7) The seller guaranteed the consumer loan or otherwise assumed the risk of loss by the creditor upon the loan.

(8) The creditor made five or more loans within a 1-year period the proceeds of which are used in transactions with the same seller following referral of the consumer to the creditor by the seller.

(9) (i) The creditor knew or had reason to know that the loan proceeds would be used in whole or in substantial part to pay the seller for an obligation of the consumer, and (ii) the creditor had notice that the seller failed or refused to perform contracts with the consumers, or

failed to remedy complaints within a reasonable time.

§ 433.2 Prohibited acts and practices: Sellers

In any consumer transaction it constitutes an unfair and deceptive act or practice for a seller to:

(a) Obtain a consumer note and fail to have inscribed upon the face of such note, in 10 point bold face type the following statement:

NOTICE

CONSUMER NOTE

It is agreed that any holder of this instrument takes this instrument subject to all claims and defenses which would be available to the maker in an action arising out of the contract which gave rise to the execution of this instrument, notwithstanding any agreement to the contrary. Recovery by the maker under this provision shall not exceed the full amount of this intrument.

(b) Take or receive from a consumer any agreement, contract or other obligation which contains:

(1) Any waiver of rights or remedies with respect to any assignee of such agreement, contract, or other obligation, which would accord to such assignee rights and remedies superior to those possessed by the seller with whom the consumer dealt.

(2) Any provision by which the consumer agrees not to assert against any assignee of the seller a claim or defense arising out of the consumer transaction, which claim or defense could be asserted against the seller.

(c) Engage in such a transaction financed by a related creditor unless the financing arrangements between the consumer and the related creditor conform to § 433.2(e) and permit the consumer to maintain against the related creditor any claim or defense arising out of the consumer transaction up to the full amount financed.

(d) Enter into any agreement, contract, or other obligation, for participation in a credit card plan with any credit card issuer who:

(1) Takes or receives from a cardholder any agreement, contract, or other obligation, except one conforming to paragraph (b) of this section, which contains any provision whereby the cardholder agrees not to assert against the issuer claims or defenses arising out of consumer transactions arranged with the issuer's credit card, up to the full amount financed with the credit card in that transaction.

(2) Places any time limitation on the rights of a credit card holder to assert claims or defenses arising out of a consumer transaction which is shorter than the period in which payments are to be made for the sale or lease or the date of final delivery of the goods or the completion of the furnishing of the services, whichever is longest.

(e) Place any time limitation on the rights of a consumer to assert claims or defenses arising out of a consumer transaction which is shorter than the period in which payments are to be made for the sale or lease or the date of final delivery of the goods or the completion of the furnishing of the services, whichever is longest; or to engage in a consumer transaction financed by a related creditor where the financing arrangements specify a shorter period of time within which the consumer may raise a claim or defense.

§ 433.3 Consumer notice required: Consumer notes

If any consumer transaction requires or involves the execution of a consumer note it constitutes an unfair and deceptive act or practice for a seller to fail to attach to the consumer's receipt or copy of the contract a note in the same language (e. g., Spanish) as that principally used in the consumer transaction containing the following information and statements:

KEEP THIS NOTICE OF YOUR RIGHTS

You have just signed a Consumer Note. It may be sold to a bank or finance company. If so, you will make payments to that bank or finance company, not to the seller. Keep your copy of the Consumer Note with this Notice.

You have the right to expect:

To receive the goods or services promised.

That the seller will fix any defects he promised to fix.

Service on the product if promised by the seller.

That the seller will come through on his part of the bargain.

If you can prove your rights were violated, you have the right:

To refuse payment.

To sue for money already paid.

To tell your side of the story in court if you are sued for nonpayment.

It will be easier to prove your rights were violated if:

You complain to the seller as soon as possible after you find fault with the goods or services. Keep a copy of your letter, or take a friend if you complain in person.

You ask the seller to make good on his promise and he does not. Keep a copy of your letter, or take a friend if you complain in person.

You can show the seller has gone out of business or cannot be located.

You keep all receipts, repair bills, and other papers.

If you have any questions about your rights, get in touch with:

A lawyer.

Your local legal aid society.

Your local or State Consumer Protection Office.

Your neighborhood legal services office.

Your small claims court.

The law stands behind you. Nothing you sign will cause you to lose these rights.

The Federal Trade Commission requires that this notice be given to you. This notice applies only to the goods or services you bought when you got this notice.

§ 433.4 Consumer notice required: related creditors

If any consumer transaction is financed by a related creditor it constitutes an unfair and deceptive act or practice for a seller to fail to attach to the consumer's receipt or copy of the contract a notice in the same language (e. g., Spanish) as that principally used in the consumer transaction containing the following information and statements:

KEEP THIS NOTICE OF YOUR RIGHTS

You have just borrowed money to make this purchase from a bank or finance company. You will make payments to the bank or finance company, not to the seller.

You Have the Right to Expect:

To receive the goods or services promised.

That the seller will fix any defects he promised to fix.

Service on the product if promised by the seller.

That the seller will come through on his part of the bargain.

If You Can Prove Your Rights Were Violated, You Have the Right:

To refuse payment.

To sue for money already paid.

To tell your side of the story in court if you are sued for nonpayment.

It Will Be Easier To Prove Your Rights Were Violated If:

You complain to the seller as soon as possible after you find fault with the goods or services. Keep a copy of your letter, or take a friend if you complain in person.

You ask the seller to make good on his promise and he does not. Keep a copy of your letter, or take a friend if you complain in person.

You can show the seller has gone out of business or cannot be located.

You keep all receipts, repair bills, and other papers.

If You Have Any Questions About Your Rights, Get In Touch With:

A lawyer.

Your local legal aid society.

Your local or State Consumer Protection Office.

Your neighborhood legal services office.

Your small claims court.

The Law Stands Behind You. Nothing You Sign Will Cause You To Lose These Rights.

The Federal Trade Commission requires that this notice be given to you. This notice applies only to the goods or services you bought when you got this notice.

As this book goes to press, the Commission has not acted upon the new proposed rule. However, the editor expects that it will adopt the rule, or a similar rule, in the near future, and assumes, therefore, that extended discussion of the controversy is not necessary in this volume because it will soon be moot. If he is in error, the reader should consult the following materials:

1. Littlefield, "Good Faith Purchase of Consumer Paper: The Failure of the Subjective Test," 39 S.Calif.L.Rev. 48 (1966).

2. Littlefield, "Preserving Consumer Defenses: Plugging the Loophole in the New UCCC," 44 N.Y.U.L.Rev. 272 (1969).

3. Jordan and Warren, "The Uniform Consumer Credit Code," 68 Colum. L.Rev. 387, 433–38 (1968) and cases cited therein.

SECTION 4. DEBT COLLECTION

Although a majority of defaults among poor people who have obtained installment credit are probably occasioned by a sudden loss of income (e. g., a lay-off or discharge) or an unexpected drain on available cash (e. g., medical bills or funeral expenses), a substantial number —perhaps 30%—are "protest defaults" occasioned by some fault of the creditor. See Caplovitz, Debtors in Default, Table 4.1 at 4–8 (1970). Many of these protests are based upon facts which legally might constitute whole or partial defenses to creditors' claims for the balance due. For example, if the goods fell apart, the seller may have breached a warranty of merchantability. If the consumer did not receive the same merchandise he saw in the store, the seller may have breached an express warranty. See UCC 2–313. If the consumer stopped paying because he saw the same merchandise at a middle-income store at one-third the price, he may have a claim of unconscionability.

If the salesman misled him about the goods or about such ancillary services as a "lifetime discount," he may be entitled, theoretically, to rescind the contract on the ground of fraud.

In evaluating common collection devices, consider among other things, (1) the degree to which they encourage or inhibit the assertion and vindication of legitimate consumer claims and defenses, and (2) the degree to which it is appropriate to enforce collection against a consumer who stopped paying because of (a) a perceived grievance (b) loss of income (c) emergency expenses, and (d) unwillingness to repay. What percentage of cases fall into each category? In addition, to the extent that defaults are committed by irresponsible "deadbeats" and business losses are generally passed on to consumers, would a "reform" or "weakening" of collection methods require consumers generally to bear the costs occasioned by those who default? Would this be fair?

––––––––

A. INFORMAL DEVICES

––––––––

Normally, a creditor's first response to a delinquent account is to dun.

Often he sends from four to twenty-four increasingly strident letters to the debtor, urging him to pay the alleged debt and threatening various actions if he does not.

One type of dun threatens litigation, and warns of additional costs that will be imposed if the consumer is sued:

AUTOMATED CREDIT OF MANHATTAN
60 EAST 42ND STREET
NEW YORK, N. Y. 10017

JANUARY 8, 1971

MAIL PAYMENT TO:
AUTOMATED CREDIT OF MANHATTAN

MISS SARAH _____   60 EAST 42ND STREET
APT 1R   NEW YORK, N. Y. 10017

_____

NEW YORK N Y

CHECK PAYABLE TO:
YOUR MAID SERVICE

AMOUNT DUE:
$ 12.60

PLEASE RETURN UPPER PORTION WITH PAYMENT

DEAR MISS: 02–18

WE HAVE ADVISED OUR CLIENT THAT WE ARE CONTACTING OUR ATTORNEYS IN YOUR AREA. A SUMMONS TO APPEAR IN COURT WILL BE SERVED UPON YOU. WHEN A JUDGMENT IS OBTAINED AGAINST YOU, ALL COURT COSTS, DISBURSEMENTS AND INTEREST CHARGES WILL BE ADDED TO YOUR BILL.

THIS EXTREME ACTION CAN ONLY BE AVOIDED BY YOUR SETTLING THIS ACCOUNT IMMEDIATELY.

YOURS TRULY,
LEGAL PROCESSING DIVISION
MARVIN E. SCOTT

947–7225   524–6793   524–6798

R & R UNLIMITED CORP.

2 WEST 31st STREET
(CORNER 5th AVE. – SUITE 301)
NEW YORK, N. Y. 10001

Creditor   Great Leaders

Balance Due $158.00

April 2, 1971

Edith _____
_____
Woodside, NY 11377

THIS IS OUR LAST REQUEST FOR PAYMENT BEFORE ACTION

DEAR Madam:

WE HAVE BEEN RETAINED BY THE ABOVE-MENTIONED COMPANY TO COLLECT AN OUTSTANDING BALANCE WHICH IS LONG PAST DUE.

YOU ARE THEREFORE GIVEN NOTICE THAT UNLESS YOUR ACCOUNT IS PAID IN FULL WITHIN SEVEN (7) DAYS FROM RECEIPT OF THIS LETTER, WE WILL BE COMPELLED TO REFER SAME TO THE <u>CREDITOR'S ATTORNEY</u> TO COLLECT THROUGH <u>LEGAL PROCEDURE</u>.

THIS PROCEDURE WILL ENTAIL <u>ADDITIONAL COSTS</u>, WHICH WILL BE ADDED TO YOUR PRESENT BALANCE, UNLESS PAYMENT IS REMITTED AS REQUESTED WITHIN SEVEN (7) DAYS.

VERY TRULY YOURS,

C. S. FISKE
R & R UNLIMITED CORP.

P.S. IMPORTANT:—SEND ALL REMITTANCES AND COMMUNICATIONS TO THIS OFFICE.

REFERENCE: CIVIC READING CLUB $134.00

48 Hour Notice
JUN 7 = 1971

FINAL NOTICE OF COURT ACTION

32081

To: Mr. And Mrs. Ronald _____
35-20 _____ Street _____ 44c
Corona, New York

CREDIT ASSOCIATES INTERNATIONAL INC.
DATE.
594 GRAND CONCOURSE
CREDITOR.
AMT. Due BRONX, NEW YORK.

Final notice of court action 48 hours from hereof our lawyers will file
proceedings against you without further notice, because you have failed
or neglected to comply with request for payment.   Cost of legal action,
to you, court costs as much as $50.00.

THIS AMOUNT MAY BE ADDED TO YOUR ACCOUNT UNLESS YOU
COMPLY WITH THE ABOVE 48 HOUR NOTICE LEGAL DEPT.

If You Are Sued On a Debt. . . .
and the Court gives Judgment against you, you are in a SERIOUS
SITUATION.

An Execution can be Issued Against You!
Then an Officer of the Court may seize your goods, attach your wages,
bank account or other property.

He may also be instructed to bring you and your family into Court and
force you and them to tell under oath what property you own.
This will be expensive and embarrassing to you.

In addition, a Judgment hanging over your head will cost you many times
the amount of the debt, in loss of credit and respect in the community.

It's Impossible to Escape a Judgment.
For a Judgment may be renewed and thus remain in effect until paid—
and it may be recorded everywhere.

Your debt will have to be paid some day, so to save expense, loss of
credit and embarrassment to you and your family take care of it NOW.

CAUTION
CHECKS OR MONEY ORDERS
MUST BE MADE OUT TO:
CREDIT ASSOCIATES INTERNATIONAL, Inc.
FOR PROPER CREDIT

[A7337]

Questions

1.   Are these letters, or any of them,
overly intimidating? Misleading? Should
the creditor be required to inform the
consumer that the consumer may have a
just claim or defense, and that he has a
right to withhold payment and test the
creditor's claim in court?   Should these
letters note that no additional costs—
indeed, no costs at all—will be imposed
if the debtor prevails in the threatened
lawsuit?

2.   Is it improper for a creditor or collection agency to threaten a lawsuit if it
has a right to bring one but as a practical
matter, for economic reasons, never does

so? What if it does so in a random 5% of cases, for the purpose of making its threats true and credible?

3. Is it more or less desirable for the creditor to make his threats vague, as in the following letters?:

THIRD NOTICE — PAST DUE PAYMENT

WE'VE TRIED TO BE FAIR AND PATIENT * * *

BECAUSE WE WANT YOU AS A FRIEND AND CUSTOMER. BUT— MUCH AS WE REGRET IT—MORE DRASTIC ACTION MUST BE TAKEN TO COLLECT THIS ACCOUNT UNLESS A SUBSTANTIAL PAYMENT IS MADE WITHIN THE NEXT FIVE DAYS. AMOUNT DUE IS $_____

YOUR CREDIT IS A VALUABLE ASSET, PROTECT IT!

NORTHEAST DISCOUNT CORP.
     (212) 895–0885
     (516) 775–2910   **Consumer Credit Department**

If payment has already been made, please disregard this notice.

ENCYCLOPEDIA BRITANNICA—GREAT BOOKS— F. E. COMPTON

Jul. 15, 1971

Mr. _____   ACCOUNT NUMBER
_____   R 417–010558
Arverne N.Y. 11692

Dear Mr. _____

YOUR CONTRACT IS IN DEFAULT IN THE AMOUNT OF $38.30!

If you will refer to the contract which you signed, you will realize the significance of the above statement.

We hesitate to employ drastic collection measures whch might prove costly and embarrassing to you, yet we cannot continue to carry your account in its present condition.

Our next step depends entirely upon the consideration given this letter.

Sincerely,

Collection Manager

NR:af

Suits filed and judgments obtained against debtors are recorded by local credit bureaus, and the information made available to local creditors to whom the debtor may later apply for new credit. (The debtor's right to see and correct derogatory information in his file if it plays a role in denying him credit is reg-ulated by the Fair Credit Reporting Act, 15 U.S.C.A. § 1681 ff. (1971)). The information is also available to creditors elsewhere in the country, through a nationwide network of credit reporting agencies. Is it improper to threaten the debtor with the issuance of a derogatory report to the local credit bureau? With the fact that institution of an action will be reported to the bureau? With the fact that the bureau will be informed if the creditor prevails in an action? What, if anything, is objectionable in the following letter?

AUTOMATED CREDIT OF MANHATTAN
60 EAST 42ND STREET
NEW YORK, N. Y. 10017

DECEMBER 22, 1970

MISS SARAH _____
APT 1R

_____

NEW YORK N Y

MAIL PAYMENT TO:
AUTOMATED CREDIT OF MANHATTAN
60 EAST 42ND STREET
NEW YORK, N. Y. 10017

CHECK PAYABLE TO:
YOUR MAID SERVICE

AMOUNT DUE:
$ 12.60

PLEASE RETURN UPPER PORTION WITH PAYMENT

DEAR MISS: 02–04

SINCE OUR FIRST REMINDER HAS NOT PRODUCED A RESPONSE FROM YOU, WE MUST CONCLUDE THAT YOU ARE NOT CONCERNED WITH THE IMPORTANCE OF COMPUTERIZED CREDIT INFORMATION.

THE INFORMATION WE HAVE GATHERED WILL NOW BE AVAILABLE ON A NATIONWIDE BASIS TO ALL BANKS, RETAIL AND COMMERCIAL ESTABLISHMENTS AND CREDIT CARD ORGANIZATIONS. THESE DATA MAY ALSO INCLUDE OTHER DEBTS UNCOVERED BY OUR COMPUTERS.

WE STRONGLY URGE THAT YOU IMMEDIATELY REMIT THE AMOUNT DUE.

YOURS TRULY,

COMPUTER AUDITS DIVISION
WARREN R. ANDERSON

If duns to the debtor's home produce no response, it is not unusual for the creditor to write to his employer, hinting that if the creditor is forced to sue the debtor and garnishee his salary, the employer will suffer bookkeeping expenses in connection with the garnishment. Knowing this, 83% of employers accede to requests to counsel employees to settle with their alleged creditors, and 40% of that 83% warn debtors that they may be penalized by the employer if they do not settle.[1]

---

[1] Affidavit of David Caplovitz, based upon unpublished study, filed in National Assn. of Installment Companies, Inc. (Commercial Lawyers Conference) v. Grant, 65 Misc.2d 897, 318 N.Y.S.2d 966 (1971), aff'd 37 A.D.2d 955, 326 N.Y.S.2d 539 (1st Dept. 1971), Record filed in the Appellate Division at 108–09.

GREAT LEADERS, INC.

P.O. Box 107, Homecrest Station • Brooklyn, N. Y. 11229 • Tel. 769–6306

ATTENTION: PAYROLL DEPT.

RE:

```
┌ Vinnie _____        ┐                    Home _____
│ 44 _____ Ave.                            Office _____
└ Bklyn., N.Y. 11225 ┘
```

Gentlemen:

    The above named employee has an account with us, and according to our recent investigation is still in your employ. The account is seriously delinquent.

    Business courtesy dictates that we advise you of our intent to seek judgment and subsequent garnishee since all requests for payment have been ignored.

    Before we take further action, we ask your cooperation in discussing the mutual expense and inconvenience of litigation with this employee.

    We would appreciate your completing this form, after you have discussed the matter, and returning it in the enclosed prepaid envelope.

Very truly yours,

M. A. ARTHUR
Credit Manager

Employed from _____ to _____ Salary $_____ per _____
Position _____ Soc. Sec. No. _____
Amount of Present Salary Attachments $_____ No. _____

If no longer employed, please indicate:

Date and reason for termination _____
Present Employer _____
Present Address _____
Remarks:

Signature _____
Title _____
Company _____
Address _____
_____
Date _____

Are letters of this type libelous? Are they an invasion of the debtor's privacy, or otherwise tortious? See Block, "Creditor's Pre-judgment Communication to Debtor's Employer: An Evaluation," 36 Bklyn.L.Rev. 95 (1969). Legislation to prohibit such communications was upheld in Commercial Lawyers Conf. v. Grant, 65 Misc.2d 897, 318 N.Y.S.2d 966 (Sup. Ct.N.Y.1971), aff'd 37 A.D.2d 955, 326 N.Y.S.2d 539 (1st Dept., 1971).

Creditors also make frequent use of repeated telephone calls to low-income debtors, their family, friends, neighbors and employers, to persuade them to pay alleged debts. See record of Hearing on Abusive Collection Practices before the New York Regional Office of the Federal Trade Commission, Sept. 13–16, 1971. The following excerpt from a training manual published by the American Collectors' Assn. is illustrative of the tactics of the more "reputable" segment of the collection industry:

"Punch Lines" for collectors

There follows an assortment of "catch" phrases and word-pictures that have been gleaned from some of the more successful telephone collectors in the business. This is by no means a complete list; neither are these phrases necessarily suited for every collector's use, but they will serve to open the imagination of the collector so that he, in turn, may take parts of these and add some of his own. When you find a phrase that works, write it down and use it if suitable in every similar situation. If it works, that's what counts;

APPEAL	WORDING
Protect your credit:	"It took you years and years of hard work and sacrifice to build up the good record you own—are you going to jeopardize it all with this one bad bill?"
	"What is your credit rating worth to you? Surely it's worth more than this account, isn't it?"
	"You can't expect anyone else to extend you credit if you haven't even paid for this old bill yet, can you?"
Honesty:	"I don't know of a living soul who would ever accuse you of dishonesty. But really, when you buy something on time, and don't pay for it, it's the same thing;"
	"You'll sure feel better when you get this bill off your conscience."
Job Security:	"Your boss pays his bills on time, and I think I know how he feels about people who don't. He has some slow accounts on his books, too."
	"Nobody wants to hire a fellow with bills in a collection agency. For one thing he is usually thinking about his bills instead of his job."
Miscellaneous:	"You're not going to stake everything you worked so hard for on a little account like this, are you?"
	"Think of all the times you have helped your friends out of a jam . . . now's the time you need their help."
	"You have to have insurance to drive your car, and insurance companies are checking people's credit ratings pretty closely before renewing policies."

Handling Common Responses

Debtors offer dozens of excuses why they cannot or will not pay their bills. The reasons they give and the problems they present are many and varied. The following are a few of the most common responses, and a brief explanation of how they can be handled.

1. Some of the situations you will meet are:

     a. Some debtors will offer to make partial payments. We must realize that not every debtor is able to pay in full; however, this is our primary goal. The debtor should never be pressed to the point where he will be able to use a refusal to accept partial payments as an excuse for not paying at all. Strive in every case for payment in full, but have your program ready to switch when you recognize that it is not possible to accomplish this.

        All payment plans set up with the debtor should leave the impression that you are really doing him a special favor, and he dare not violate your confidence. In cases where you feel that a phone call will make little impression on the debtor, insist that no payment agreements can or will be made on the phone and that he must come into the office.

     b. The debtor may say he will pay the creditor direct, because he feels he can get a better deal from the creditor. He figures he can talk the creditor into:

        (1) Withdrawing the claim from your hands
        (2) Taking less than the full amount
        (3) Taking small payments

Your creditor certainly does not wish to be placed in such a compromising situation.

     c. When the debtor threatens bankruptcy, you may choose one of two courses:

        (1) Meet it boldly: "Bankruptcy, you say?" If you can't pay this bill, how can you pay the expenses of filing bankruptcy?" "It will cost you money either way—wouldn't it be easier just to pay this bill?"

        (2) Pass over the threat as if it were meaningless. Your exhibiting the slightest alarm at hearing this will only encourage him to use it on you and the rest of his creditors until the day when someone has the misfortune to "call" him on it and he will be forced to file to avoid being known as a "bluffer."

     d. The debtor may claim that his account is "outlawed." This means only that resort to legal prerogatives is no longer available and does not in any way mean that he may not or should not pay the bill. The debtor knows this; he is using another excuse for non-payment. The appeal to pride and honesty may work.

2. Many times you will not be able to get information on the debtor because you are not able to reach him or he refuses to give any.

     a. If you are unable to catch the debtor at home, take the information home with you and call him during the evening or over the weekend. The collection business knows no conventional business hours.

b. If the debtor himself doesn't want to give you any information about himself, be firm with him. For example, he may not wish to tell you where he is working. The reason is that he fears garnishment, so you may use the following approach: "Look, Mr. Jones, all I have to do is dial a couple of numbers when we are through talking, and I can find out where you are working. You may as well cooperate. I can get this information with or without your help."

c. Occasionally a debtor will hang up on you. Immediately dial again with a firm voice saying something to the effect, "If you hang up on me again, it will cost you plenty." To allow the debtor to get by with this too easily will only encourage him to use this means of ending unpleasant conversation in the future.

d. If you feel that you are getting nowhere with the debtor, you may want to "turn over" the call to another person, who will take over with an entirely different approach. In telephone collection, the telephone "turn over" is expressed "T. O." The new voice on the phone is often an important sounding one with the title of "Manager." This tactic could be used more often in collection agencies than it is.

3. More often than not, you will have to call back the debtor who failed to keep his promise to pay.

a. The best approach to take is to start from scratch on the second call adopting a little firmer attitude. Who failed, you or the debtor? Sure, the debtor failed to keep his word, but this could be predicted. Maybe you failed too, in not hitting the right appeal or in not having the debtor thoroughly convinced.

b. A broken promise should be followed up just as soon as you are positive that the promise has been broken. The debtor knows he made the promise and he knows he is breaking it. If his telephone rings, it will prove to him you are watching him closely and that he had better pay because you DO mean business.

c. It might be wise to remind the debtor of your telephone conversation. If you, as a collector haven't made an impression, the debtor feels only relief when the conversation ends and may "forget" to send you his payment. Some collectors, to add emphasis, will send out a short note confirming the promise and re-stating the exact time when payment is expected. This note reaches the debtor the following morning and serves to reinforce his promise.

4. Many debtors are physically handicapped, suffering from a prolonged illness or on pension. Many of these debtors will definitely be unable to earn enough to pay the bill. Or they may use this as an excuse for not paying. Know what the real story is, listen with sympathy, and then if you feel they can pay, try this: "There is an old saying that if you knew your neighbor's troubles, you would never trade." We all have troubles of some kind. Now about this bill * * *"

B. FORMAL DEVICES

If the various forms of dunning are not effective to obtain payment of the debt, creditors may choose one or more methods of collection provided for by statute. These include repossession, replevin, and personal suit against the debtor, followed by execution against salary (garnishment), home, bank accounts, and tangible personal property.

If the standard-form contract signed by the debtor has so provided, the creditor may repossess the merchandise which has not been fully paid for. The method of repossession is governed by the following sections of the Uniform Commercial Code:

UNIFORM COMMERCIAL CODE SECTIONS 9—501 TO 9—507

PART 5

Default

§ 9—501. Default; Procedure When Security Agreement Covers Both Real and Personal Property

(1) When a debtor is in default under a security agreement, a secured party has the rights and remedies provided in this Part and except as limited by subsection (3) those provided in the security agreement. He may (1) reduce his claim to judgment, (2) foreclose or (3) otherwise enforce the security interest by any available judicial procedure. If the collateral is documents the secured party may proceed either as to the documents or as to the goods covered thereby. A secured party in possession has the rights, remedies and duties provided in Section 9—207. The rights and remedies referred to in this subsection are cumulative.

(2) After default, the debtor has the rights and remedies provided in this Part, those provided in the security agreement and those provided in Section 9—207.

(3) To the extent that they give rights to the debtor and impose duties on the secured party, the rules stated in the subsections referred to below may not be waived or varied except as provided with respect to compulsory disposition of collateral (subsection (1) of Section 9—505) and with respect to redemption of collateral (Section 9—506) but the parties may by agreement determine the standards by which the fulfillment of these rights and duties is to be measured if such standards are not manifestly unreasonable:

(a) subsection (2) of Section 9—502 and subsection (2) of Section 9—504 insofar as they require accounting for surplus proceeds of collateral;

(b) subsection (3) of Section 9—504 and subsection (1) of Section 9—505 which deal with disposition of collateral;

(c) subsection (2) of Section 9—505 which deals with acceptance of collateral as discharge of obligation;

(d) Section 9—506 which deals with redemption of collateral; and

(e) subsection (1) of Section 9—507 which deals with the secured party's liability for failure to comply with this Part.

(4) If the security agreement covers both real and personal property, the secured party may proceed under this Part as to the personal property or he may proceed as to both the real and the personal property in accordance with his rights and remedies in respect to the real property in which case the provisions of this Part do not apply.

(5) When a secured party has reduced his claim to judgment the lien of any

levy which may be made upon his collateral by virtue of any execution based upon the judgment shall relate back to the date of the perfection of the security interest in such collateral. A judicial sale, pursuant to such execution, is a foreclosure of the security interest by judicial procedure within the meaning of this section, and the secured party may purchase at the sale and thereafter hold the collateral free of any other requirements of this Article.

§ 9—502. Collection Rights of Secured Party

(1) When so agreed and in any event on default the secured party is entitled to notify an account debtor or the obligor on an instrument to make payment to him whether or not the assignor was theretofore making collections on the collateral, and also to take control of any proceeds to which he is entitled under Section 9—306.

(2) A secured party who by agreement is entitled to charge back uncollected collateral or otherwise to full or limited recourse against the debtor and who undertakes to collect from the account debtors or obligors must proceed in a commercially reasonable manner and may deduct his reasonable expenses of realization from the collections. If the security agreement secures an indebtedness, the secured party must account to the debtor for any surplus, and unless otherwise agreed, the debtor is liable for any deficiency. But, if the underlying transaction was a sale of accounts, contract rights, or chattel paper, the debtor is entitled to any surplus or is liable for any deficiency only if the security agreement so provides.

§ 9—503. Secured Party's Right to Take Possession After Default

Unless otherwise agreed a secured party has on default the right to take possession of the collateral. In taking possession a secured party may proceed without judicial process if this can be done without breach of the peace or may proceed by action. If the security agreement so provides the secured party may require the debtor to assemble the collateral and make it available to the secured party at a place to be designated by the secured party which is reasonably convenient to both parties. Without removal a secured party may render equipment unusable, and may dispose of collateral on the debtor's premises under Section 9—504.

§ 9—504. Secured Party's Right to Dispose of Collateral After Default; Effect of Disposition

(1) A secured party after default may sell, lease or otherwise dispose of any or all of the collateral in its then condition or following any commercially reasonable preparation or processing. Any sale of goods is subject to the Article on Sales (Article 2). The proceeds of disposition shall be applied in the order following to

(a) the reasonable expenses of retaking, holding, preparing for sale, selling and the like and, to the extent provided for in the agreement and not prohibited by law, the reasonable attorneys' fees and legal expenses incurred by the secured party;

(b) the satisfaction of indebtedness secured by the security interest under which the disposition is made;

(c) the satisfaction of indebtedness secured by any subordinate security interest in the collateral if written notification of demand therefor is received before distribution of the proceeds is completed. If requested by the secured party, the holder of a subordinate security interest must seasonably furnish reasonable proof of his interest, and unless he does so, the secured party need not comply with his demand.

(2) If the security interest secures an indebtedness, the secured party must account to the debtor for any surplus, and, unless otherwise agreed, the debtor is liable for any deficiency. But if the underlying transaction was a sale of accounts, contract rights, or chattel paper, the debtor is entitled to any surplus or is liable for any deficiency only if the security agreement so provides.

(3) Disposition of the collateral may be by public or private proceedings and may be made by way of one or more contracts. Sale or other disposition may be as a unit or in parcels and at any time and place and on any terms but every aspect of the disposition including the method, manner, time, place and terms must be commercially reasonable. Unless collateral is perishable or threatens to decline speedily in value or is of a type customarily sold on a recognized market, reasonable notification of the time and place of any public sale or reasonable notification of the time after which any private sale or other intended disposition is to be made shall be sent by the secured party to the debtor, and except in the case of consumer goods to any other person who has a security interest in the collateral and who has duly filed a financing statement indexed in the name of the debtor in this state or who is known by the secured party to have a security interest in the collateral. The secured party may buy at any public sale and if the collateral is of a type customarily sold in a recognized market or is of a type which is the subject of widely distributed standard price quotations he may buy at private sale.

(4) When collateral is disposed of by a secured party after default, the disposition transfers to a purchaser for value all of the debtor's rights therein, discharges the security interest under which it is made and any security interest or lien subordinate thereto. The purchaser takes free of all such rights and interests even though the secured party fails to comply with the requirements of this Part or of any judicial proceedings

(a) in the case of a public sale, if the purchaser has no knowledge of any defects in the sale and if he does not buy in collusion with the secured party, other bidders or the person conducting the sale; or

(b) in any other case, if the purchaser acts in good faith.

(5) A person who is liable to a secured party under a guaranty, indorsement, repurchase agreement or the like and who receives a transfer of collateral from the secured party or is subrogated to his rights has thereafter the rights and duties of the secured party. Such a transfer of collateral is not a sale or disposition of the collateral under this Article.

§ 9—505. Compulsory Disposition of Collateral; Acceptance of the Collateral as Discharge of Obligation

(1) If the debtor has paid sixty per cent of the cash price in the case of a purchase money security interest in consumer goods or sixty per cent of the loan in the case of another security interest in consumer goods, and has not signed after default a statement renouncing or modifying his rights under this Part a secured party who has taken possession of collateral must dispose of it under Section 9—504 and if he fails to do so within ninety days after he takes possession the debtor at his option may recover in conversion or under Section 9—507(1) on secured party's liability.

(2) In any other case involving consumer goods or any other collateral a secured party in possession may, after default, propose to retain the collateral in

satisfaction of the obligation. Written notice of such proposal shall be sent to the debtor and except in the case of consumer goods to any other secured party who has a security interest in the collateral and who has duly filed a financing statement indexed in the name of the debtor in this state or is known by the secured party in possession to have a security interest in it. If the debtor or other person entitled to receive notification objects in writing within thirty days from the receipt of the notification or if any other secured party objects in writing within thirty days after the secured party obtains possession the secured party must dispose of the collateral under Section 9—504. In the absence of such written objection the secured party may retain the collateral in satisfaction of the debtor's obligation.

§ 9—506. Debtor's Right to Redeem Collateral

At any time before the secured party has disposed of collateral or entered into a contract for its disposition under Section 9—504 or before the obligation has been discharged under Section 9—505(2) the debtor or any other secured party may unless otherwise agreed in writing after default redeem the collateral by tendering fulfillment of all obligations secured by the collateral as well as the expenses reasonably incurred by the secured party in retaking, holding and preparing the collateral for disposition, in arranging for the sale, and to the extent provided in the agreement and not prohibited by law, his reasonable attorneys' fees and legal expenses.

§ 9—507. Secured Party's Liability for Failure to Comply With This Part

(1) If it is established that the secured party is not proceeding in accordance with the provisions of this Part disposition may be ordered or restrained on appropriate terms and conditions. If the dis-

position has occurred the debtor or any person entitled to notification or whose security interest has been made known to the secured party prior to the disposition has a right to recover from the secured party any loss caused by a failure to comply with the provisions of this Part. If the collateral is consumer goods, the debtor has a right to recover in any event an amount not less than the credit service charge plus ten per cent of the principal amount of the debt or the time price differential plus 10 per cent of the cash price.

(2) The fact that a better price could have been obtained by a sale at a different time or in a different method from that selected by the secured party is not of itself sufficient to establish that the sale was not made in a commercially reasonable manner. If the secured party either sells the collateral in the usual manner in any recognized market therefor or if he sells at the price current in such market at the time of his sale or if he has otherwise sold in conformity with reasonable commercial practices among dealers in the type of property sold he has sold in a commercially reasonable manner. The principles stated in the two preceding sentences with respect to sales also apply as may be appropriate to other types of disposition. A disposition which has been approved in any judicial proceeding or by any bona fide creditors' committee or representative of creditors shall conclusively be deemed to be commercially reasonable, but this sentence does not indicate that any such approval must be obtained in any case nor does it indicate that any disposition not so approved is not commercially reasonable.

––––––––

On paper, these rules appear to be fair and reasonable, and to ensure that the debtor's account is credited with the value of the item repossessed; only if the amount realized by sale of the item is less than the amount owed the creditor may the debtor be sued personally for the balance.

Questions

How far is the creditor allowed to go in retaking the merchandise without "breaching the peace"? May he jump start an automobile in the middle of the night in front of the debtor's home? In the debtor's garage? May he use a skeleton key to enter the debtor's house when the debtor is not home, to take back a partially paid-for washing machine? May he disguise himself as a repairman or a student taking a survey to get into the debtor's house?

When the creditor sells the merchandise, must he notify the debtor in advance? Must he hold an auction? May the creditor sell the merchandise to someone he knows? To himself? What is the difference between a public and a private sale?

PROFIT ON DEFAULT: AN ARCHIVAL STUDY OF AUTOMOBILE REPOSSESSION AND RESALE

Philip Shuchman *

22 Stanford L.Rev. 20 (1969).

* * *

I. INTRODUCTION TO THE LEGAL MODEL

A. *The Legal Model and Its Background*

Most personal property sold to the retail public by installment sale is regulated

---

* L.L.B.1953, M.A.1957, University of Pennsylvania Professor of Law, University of Connecticut. Thanks are due to the Hon. John J. Daly, Chief Judge of the Circuit

by the Uniform Commercial Code (now in effect in 49 of the states) [6] as supplemented or superseded by various kinds of consumer protection legislation in many states. Because automobiles were the first major items of personal property to be sold on credit, the rights and remedies of the parties to retail installment sales of automobiles are regulated by separate legislation in many states or have become part of "all-goods" acts, as in Connecticut and most other states.[7] Fifty-two percent of all cars are sold on credit.[8] The amounts involved are substantial both in the aggregate and in terms of installment payments as a percentage of disposable income.[9] Hence

Court of Connecticut, for permitting us to rummage through the court's files; also to the Hon. John J. Tynan, Commissioner of Motor Vehicles, for making the department records available to us and for providing the assistance of his staff.

Most of the data were gathered by law students at the University of Connecticut: Miss Marilyn A. Seichter and Messrs. Henry S. Cohn, Richard A. Gerken, Archie Hovanesian, Herbert F. Rosenberg, and Anthony W. Slusarz, Jr. The design of the study, the interpretations of the data, and other commentary are the writer's responsibility.

[6] The only state that has not adopted the Uniform Commercial Code is Louisiana.

[7] See B. Curran, supra note 2, at 254–55 (Chart II). One conspicuous exception to the pattern of separate treatment for automobile installment contracts is the recent Federal Consumer Credit Protection Act of 1968, 82 Stat. 146. Effective July 1, 1969, the Act requires creditors to divulge the simple annual interest rate, equivalent to the add-on or discounted interest. Additional provisions limiting creditors' garnishment remedies will become effective July 1, 1970.

[8] U. S. Bureau of the Census, Dep't of Commerce, Statistical Asbtract of the United States 565 (Table 820) (88th ed. 1967).

[9] As of March 1969, $34.3 billion was outstanding in automobile consumer paper, which amounts to 38% of the $89.7 billion total for all retail-installment credit. U. S. Bureau of the Census, Dep't of Commerce, Statistical Abstract of the United States 460 (Chart 664) (1969); cf. Wall Street Journal, July 2, 1968, at 2, col. 2. The 1954–55 National Survey of the Federal Reserve System

separate regulation seems appropriate. An additional and important consideration for our purposes is the existence of a widespread and relatively open market in used cars. No other common subject of the retail-installment sale has regionally accepted prices with so many sales outlets.

The repossession and subsequent resale of automobiles in Connecticut is regulated almost exclusively by the Retail Installment Sales Financing Act (RISFA) [10] —a fairly typical "all-goods" act. Briefly sketched, RISFA provides that upon default in the payment of any installment of the time purchase price, the lienholder or secured party (who may be the seller or a financial institution that purchased the obligation secured by the car, the so-called chattel paper) has the right to repossess the car. That can be done without any prior notice to the installment buyer.[11] If the consumer is not given notice of intention to repossess, however, he has 15 days within which to redeem the collateral.[12]

The repossessed automobile may then be sold at either public or private sale.[13]

Before 1961, the creditor was required to notify the defaulting buyer in writing of the time and place of a sale of either type. In what was termed a minor and merely formal change, however, the Connecticut Legislature in 1961 rescinded the requirement of notification if the repossessed car was to be resold at private sale,[14] so written notice must now be given to the buyer whose car has been repossessed only if the resale is to be public.[15] The secured party is not required in all instances to sell the repossessed collateral in settling the account of the defaulting purchaser. If the purchaser has paid less than 60 percent of the time-sale price, the repossessor is not obliged to resell the collateral unless the defaulting purchaser demands resale by written notice.[16] If the consumer has paid more than 60 percent of the time-sale price, the creditor is required to sell the collateral.[17]

The proceeds of the resale are to be applied, first, to the expense of the sale, second, to the payment of repossession and storage costs pending resale, and, third, to the satisfaction of the balance due under the retail installment contract.[18] A 15-percent attorney's collection fee may be added to the balance due on the sale

---

showed a median of 11% of disposable income allocated to installment payments for new cars for those with incomes under $5000; for all consumers a median of 22% of disposable income went to pay for new cars purchased on credit. 4 Nat'l Bureau of Econ. Research, Board of Governors of the Federal Reserve System, Consumer Instalment Credit 87–88 (1957) [hereinafter cited as Consumer Instalment Credit]. There is no reason to think the figures would be much different 15 years later, or as applied to a sample of used-car purchases.

[10] Conn.Gen.Stat.Ann. §§ 42–83 to –100 (Supp.1969), amending Conn.Gen.Stat.Ann. §§ 42–83 to –100 (1960).

[11] Id. § 42–98(b). Similar provisions exist in the laws of other states. See, e. g., Md. Ann.Code art. 83, § 141(b) (1965); Mass.Ann. Laws ch. 255, § 13I(a) (1968); Pa.Stat. tit. 69, § 623A (1965).

[12] Conn.Gen.Stat.Ann. § 42–98(c) (1960).

[13] Conn.Gen.Stat.Ann. §§ 42–98(d), (c) (Supp.1969), amending Conn.Gen.Stat.Ann. §§ 42–98(d), (e) (1960). For equivalent provisions see, e. g., Mass.Ann.Laws ch. 255, § 13I(c)

(1968); Pa.Stat. tit. 69, § 626B (1965). Ill. Ann.Stat. ch. 121½, § 580 (Smith-Hurd Supp. 1969), gives the parties to a retail installment sale of an automobile the rights and remedies contained in article 9 of the Uniform Commercial Code.

[14] 9 Conn. General Assembly, House Proceedings, pt. 2, at 889 (1961).

[15] Conn.Gen.Stat.Ann. § 42–98(d) (Supp. 1969), amending Conn.Gen.Stat.Ann. § 42–98 (d) (1960).

[16] Conn.Gen.Stat.Ann. §§ 42–98(d), (e) (Supp. 1969). Other states have established minimums for required public sale ranging from 50% of the cash-sale price to 80% of the time-sale price. See B. Curran, supra note 2, at 112.

[17] Conn.Gen.Stat.Ann. §§ 42–98(d), (e) (Supp. 1969).

[18] Conn.Gen.Stat.Ann. § 42–98(f) (1960).

contract;[19] delinquency and collection charges, and court costs may also be imposed.[20]

RISFA provides that "if the proceeds of resale are not sufficient to defray the * * * expenses * * * and the balance due under the contract, the holder of the contract may recover the deficiency from the retail buyer. * * * "[21] That is accomplished by a separate legal action termed a deficiency-judgment proceeding.[22] If a deficiency judgment is obtained, the next step may be attachment of the debtor's property or other execution process, usually an order for garnishment of the debtor's wages, which follows default in a weekly payment order of the court.[23]

But the formal legal picture is only a distant approximation of the actual practices. It is to that later reality that we now turn.

B. *Economic Aspects of the Legal Model*

The financers largely create both the legal and economic models that regulate the retail installment sale of cars. The financers provide the forms to be used for the dealer contract and for the retail installment sale. Moreover, it is the financers who decide the dollar terms of the retail installment sale. Contractual arrangements for the purchase of the dealer's chattel paper depend largely upon the respective economic leverage of the dealer and the financer. Sometimes the dealer obtains his inventory financing with the condition that he then discount his retail installment contracts to that financer.[24] Inventory financing is less profitable and sometimes difficult to get at all. But the purchase of retail chattel paper is generally profitable business for which there is more competition between financers. The nature of the dealer's business—the kind of chattel paper he generates as measured by the frequency of defaults—is said to be another factor in the bargaining process.

With occasional variants, there are five categories of dealer-financer agreements for disposition of the dealer's paper: (1) nonrecourse; (2) full recourse; (3) full repurchase; (4) limited repurchase; and (5) optional repurchase.[25] First, a deal-

19 Id. § 42–91. Similar provisions appear in Md.Ann.Code art. 83, § 145 (1965) (not exceeding 15%); 12 Minn.Stat.Ann. § 168.71(a) (3) (Supp.1969) (not exceeding 15%); Mo.Ann. Stat. tit. 24, § 365.100(2) (1968) (not exceeding 15%); N.J.Stat.Ann. § 17:16C–42(b) (1963) (allowing attorney's fees up to 20% on the first $500 and 10% on the balance); N.Y. Pers.Prop.Law § 302(7) (McKinney 1962) (not exceeding 15% of the amount due and payable plus court costs).

20 Conn.Gen.Stat.Ann. § 42–91 (1960). Equivalent provisions are to be found, e. g., in Cal.Civ.Code § 2983.4 (West Supp.1968); Md.Ann.Code art. 83, § 145 (1965); Mass.Ann. Laws ch. 255, §§ 13*I*(c)(1), (2) (1969); 12 Minn. Stat.Ann. § 168.71(3) (Supp.1969); Tex.Rev. Civ.Stat.Ann. art. 5069–7.03(6) (Supp.1968); Mo.Ann.Stat. tit. 24, § 365.100(2) (1968).

21 Conn.Gen.Stat.Ann. § 42–98(g) (1960). Similar statutes include Cal.Civ.Code § 2983.2 (West Supp.1968); Md.Ann.Code art. 83, § 143 (b)(4) (1957); Mass.Ann.Laws ch. 255, § 13*I*(d) (Supp.1969); Pa.Stat.Ann. tit. 69, § 627 (1965).

22 Conn.Gen.Stat.Ann. § 42–98(g) (1960).

23 Conn.Gen.Stat.Ann. § 52–361(b) (Supp. 1969), amending Conn.Gen.Stat.Ann. § 52–361 (b) (1960).

24 However, a few states prohibit manufacturers from using coercive practices to ensure that the dealer, the retail seller, "transfers installment sales contracts to the manufacturer's * * * designee." B. Curran, supra note 2, at 113, citing Ind.Ann.Stat. §§ 58–909, –910, –921, –924 (1961); N.C.Gen.Stat. § 1243– 20 (1953); Wis.Stat.Ann. § 218.7 (1958). In the writer's experience coercion is unnecessary. The scarcity and expense of inventory financing and the desire for the financier's goodwill are decisive. See Skilton, Cars for Sale: Some Comments on the Wholesale Financing of Automobiles, 1957 Wis.L.Rev. 352, 355–56.

25 See, e. g., Chrysler Credit Corporation Form 84–291–0515, Conn.1965.

er may sell, assign, or dispose of his paper without recourse; the dealer then has no legal obligation to the financer in the event of the consumer's default. Second, the dealer may dispose of his paper with full recourse: He agrees to repurchase the chattel paper for the balance due in the event of default. The burden is thus on the dealer to repossess the vehicle, resell it, and if need be, proceed against the consumer for a deficiency judgment. Or, the dealer may ignore the collateral and simply institute suit against the consumer for the balance due plus the vigorish allowed under state statutes. Third, the dealer may enter into a full-repurchase agreement. In this case the financer usually repossesses the car, delivers it to the dealer, and then assigns all his rights in the chattel paper to the dealer who pays the financer the balance due on the retail installment contract. Fourth, the dealer may negotiate a limited-repurchase agreement. The agreement is similar to the full-repurchase agreement, except that the dealer obligates himself for the balance due on the retail installment contract only up to a specified maximum. Fifth, under an optional-repurchase agreement, the financer may, and in some instances must, repossess the car. The dealer then buys the car from the financer either at a price fixed in advance, or for the balance due on the chattel paper, which will be the maximum fixed price. The financer or the dealer will then proceed against the consumer.

The particular economic arrangement chosen often reflects a compromise, with parties fitting projected profit to levels of anticipated risk. In all except the first of these arrangements (nonrecourse) between dealer and financer, the dealer is apt to have a reserve account made up of the accumulated rebates of finance charges [26] and commissions from

the sale of credit life insurance and collision insurance on the vehicle, although the latter two are often separately handled. But if the dealer's credit is good or the financer is satisfied that the dealer is solvent and reliable, the chattel paper may simply be purchased at some rate below that charged the retail customer. For example, if the consumer has paid 7 percent add-on or discount, the dealer may be charged 5 percent. That may be done on a monthly arrangement or settled upon the completion of each transaction. If there is no reserve account for defaults, the dealer's liability may be attended upon each default.

Thus the dealer's rebate—a portion of which is usually held in a reserve account—may be 2 percent per annum on the full amount financed. Hence, where a car is financed for $3000 over 3 years, the dealer's rebate from the total finance charge will be about $180. If the dealer wants a nonrecourse arrangement, the bargaining item for that consideration will be a reduction in the rebate rate. Typically, the dealer will have to lose about half of one percent per annum, or about $45 of the $180 rebate. That alone might be worth selling the chattel paper without any responsibility in the event of the retail customer's default. But losing one-quarter or more of the finance rebate is not the only economic consideration. For it is said that financers will not purchase from that dealer the chattel paper of any even slightly questionable retail accounts, and this leverage is usually of greater concern to the dealer. For without available financing, most dealers would be badly hurt, perhaps even put out of business.

(not including insurance commissions); the financer holds back 1% to 5% of the total finance charge to create a reserve against the dealer's defaulted accounts. These practices have not changed appreciably over the past several years. See Shuchman, Consumer Credit by Adhesion Contracts II, 35 Temp. L.Q. 281, 294 (1962).

---

[26] The full rebate of the finance charge to the dealer is said to range from 25% to 40%

But whatever its variant, the economics of the legal model involved provide no incentive for the financer and little incentive for the dealer to resell the repossessed car at the highest price obtainable in an open market at the time and place of repossession. For the financer is almost always paid by the dealer; and the dealer can often recover his loss by proceeding against his customer, or by the financer's execution process against the other assets of the final debtor, the retail buyer who has defaulted. What is implicit in the above description should be evident: Buyers have almost no influence on these legal arrangements.

II. THE LEGAL MODEL AT WORK

A. *A Few Illustrative Cases*

Ordinarily, little is known of the interstitial transactions by which the secured party disposes of the repossessed automobile. But the occasional defenses undertaken by various legal aid groups present some dramatic illustrations. In Chrysler Credit Corp. v. Thomas,[27] answers to the defendant's interrogatories revealed that the car had been purchased in March 1966, for a net cash price of $2605. Defendant defaulted after having paid a total of $1835. On May 1, 1967, the financer repossessed the car and then promptly resold it to the original dealer on May 18 for $400. On that date (of the first or wholesale resale) the repossessed car had a *Redbook* [28] re-

tail value of $850 to $900 and a *Redbook* wholesale value of about $700. Five weeks later the car was again resold (the second or retail resale) for $995 in cash, a sum two-and-a-half times the sale price of five weeks earlier. Of course, the $400 resale price was the basis for the deficiency-judgment claim.

Again in Russell Pontiac, Inc. v. Loveless [29] the defendants bought the car in April 1966 for a cash price of $1661 (a time-sale price of $2764). The car was repossessed by the financer on March 2, 1967, and sold to the original dealer for $450. The original dealer as plaintiff made a deficiency claim of $598, based on the first (or wholesale) resale. That dealer's "nominee" dealer then resold the car again four weeks later to a retail buyer for $1550 in cash, nearly three-and-a-half times its selling price a month earlier. The *Redbook* retail value of the car at repossession was about $1925 and the wholesale value about $1375, assuming the car had no power equipment or other "extras."

Finally, Chorches Motors, Inc. v. Sears [30] reveals a net purchase price of $2156, not including the finance package or the trade-in allowance; the chattel paper was sold to the financer on the same date as the execution of the retail installment sale (and, as usual, on the financer's forms). Five months later, upon default, there was an unpaid balance of $1157. The plaintiff-dealer claimed a sale (to himself) for the sum of $500 as disposition of the repossessed collateral. This sale (subsequently not proved to the court's satisfaction) was

---

27 Chrysler Credit Corp. v. Thomas, No. CV–7–685–11988 (7th Cir. Ct. Conn., April 1, 1968). Copies of the pleadings were kindly provided by William H. Clendenin, Jr., of the New Haven Legal Assistance Association.

28 The so-called *Redbook* is a publication of the National Automotive Publishers. It lists by model and year (and standard equipment packages) three prices for all automobiles: the retail, wholesale, and finance values. It is used by the Connecticut Department of Motor Vehicles and by most financing agencies and automobile dealers in Connecticut. The *Redbook* is published eight times a year

and broken down by geographic areas, one of which is New England.

29 Russell Pontiac, Inc. v. Loveless, No. CV–16–6712–6836 (16th Cir.Ct.Conn., Dec. 15, 1967). Copies of the pleadings were kindly provided by Professor Neil O. Littlefield of the University of Connecticut Law School.

30 Chorches Motors, Inc. v. Sears, No. CV–12–6605–7565 (12th Cir.Ct.Conn., May 9, 1966).

claimed to have taken place on December 6, 1965, less than three weeks after repossession. Then, on February 1, 1966, the plaintiff-dealer made good his obligation to the financer by payment of $965 (apparently almost the full balance due on the retail installment contract less credits for unearned interest and insurance premium rebates). On March 23, 1966, some three-and-a-half months after the abortive first resale of the collateral, the plaintiff-dealer again resold the repossessed car, this time to another retail buyer for $1075, more than twice its earlier "resale" price. Of course, the deficiency judgment of $465 claimed was calculated by subtraction of the $500, first-resale proceeds, from the $965 that the plaintiff-dealer paid the financer. The *Redbook* retail value of the car at the date of the first resale was about $1000 and the wholesale value about $700.

Each of the three cases is marked by a disparity between the first (wholesale) resale price, which forms the basis for determining any deficiency, and the dealer's subsequent (retail) resale price, and also by a disparity between the first-resale price and the *Redbook* values. The practices and the results in these hedgehog-like illustrations appear typical of our larger sample. These three cases reveal the system in microcosm.

B. *Introduction to the Realities as Shown by an Empirical Study of the Legal Model*

In our sample, most of the used cars sold on credit were repossessed within ten to eleven months from the date of the original installment-sale contract.[31] After default, most creditors mail out form letters notifying the purchaser of his delinquency. Then if the default is not promptly cured, repossession takes

place, usually late at night. A few daylight repossessions take place in parking lots if the consumer-debtor's place of employment is known. The police are immediately notified of the repossession [32] so that they can be responsive to complaints of thefts by owners of repossessed cars. The first (or wholesale) resale takes place shortly after repossession. RISFA gives the consumer, the retail buyer, fifteen days within which to redeem the car that is the collateral for the loan.[33] After the two-week period following repossession, the car is promptly sold. On the average, the first resale takes place about 32 days after repossession and usually within a week of the first time the car could be lawfully sold.[34] So far as the legal model regulates practices, its effects end at that point. The "sale" that disposes of the collateral is deemed to have taken place,[35] and the basis for the deficiency judgment is the price of that sale.

What transactions legally constitute a "resale," whether public or private, and what facts constitute a "public sale" are both questions too indefinite to answer given the disparate judicial constructions of the phrases. Typical of the problems that have arisen are the extent of the public notice required, the time for giving of notice, and the form and contents of the notice. The time and place of the

---

[31] The median for all 83 litigated cases is 299 days. The average is 365 days. See Appendix, Table A1, line 1, col. 1.

[32] Conn.Gen.Stat.Ann. § 42–98(a) (1960).

[33] Conn.Gen.Stat.Ann. § 42–98(c) (1960). The repossessors keep the vehicles for 15 days whether or not the debtor asserts his right to redemption as allowed by RISFA.

[34] See Appendix, Table A1, col. 2. Although the average reflects data from only 29 of the 83 litigated cases, the small number of extreme variations from the median (18 days) suggests that the general pattern is prompt first resale.

[35] Cf. Associates Discount Corp. v. Weldon, 4 Conn.Cir.Ct. 351, 231 A.2d 671 (App.Div.), petition for appeal denied, 154 Conn. 750, 228 A.2d 559 (1967); J. F. England's Sons, Inc. v. Liggett, 82 S.D. 656, 152 N.W.2d 583 (1967).

sale have also been disputed at length.[36] We assume a "public" sale to be an auction-type sale open to the public and with some minimum effective notice to the public and to the party affected.

But the problem what is or is not a public sale is of little moment, for RISFA nowhere requires a public sale. The repossessor shall resell "at public or private sale." [37] If there is any discernible difference between public and private resales, it is that the secured party may buy the car at the public sale.[38] RISFA is silent on the question whether the secured party may buy the car at private sale. But since there exists a possibility of judicial interpretation that the secured party cannot buy for a fishcake at private sale and still obtain his deficiency judgment, the written notices to the consumer state that a public sale will be held. About half the Circuit Court records that specified the type of sale declared that a public sale was held. The remaining files were not informative on the question what kind of sale took place.

The private sale that disposes of the repossessed car is by no means an arm's-length transaction. For the typical first "sale" following repossession is from the financer, the secured party in the Uniform Commercial Code terminology,[39] to the assignor of the chattel paper, the dealer who originally sold the vehicle on credit, or to another friendly dealer.

Upon default, the financer repossesses the automobile and "resells" it to a dealer in the first instance. Sometimes the dealer-buyer is the original dealer who sold the car; more often it appears to be his "nominee." If the original dealer had one of the usual recourse arrangements with the financer, he may insist upon a fair resale price, or may himself purchase the vehicle at a price sufficient to satisfy his contractual arrangements with the financer. Or, the price may be arbitrarily determined, possibly based on the likelihood of collection from the retail customer. For the financer is indifferent to the allocation of the dealer's payment of the balance due on the installment contract. For example, if the balance due upon default is $1500, the dealer may give the financer two checks: one for $500, which represents the wholesale purchase price of the car, and another check for $1000, which is the balance of his contractual responsibility to the financer. But the $500 "sale price" is the basis for the deficiency-judgment claim, for that part of the transaction represents the disposition of the collateral within the meaning of the retail-installment sales financing acts in most states. The full "price" of that sale—whatever the allocation—appears to be about equal to the net balance then due the financer, without any additional charges to the dealer and sometimes with a discount. The first resale—the legally cognizable disposition of the collateral—is thus at best a wholesale transaction from the financer to a dealer. The financer merely wants to be made whole. The dealer, however, has another aim: He is legally obliged to pay the financer, but it is then his burden to recover any deficiency from the retail buyer. This is normally accomplished by the deficiency-judgment proceeding that finally results in execution on the judgment by wage garnishment.

The typical practice when the financer has no contractual ties with respect to the disposition of that car is to make a few inquiries by telephone to dealers of his acquaintance in the area. The highest of the two or three bids is said to be the

36 Elm Buick Co. v. Moore, 150 Conn. 631, 192 A.2d 638 (1963); Annot., 49 A.L.R.2d 15 (1956), Annot., 4 A.L.R.2d 575 (1949).

37 Conn.Gen.Stat.Ann. §§ 42–98(d), (c) (Supp. 1969).

38 See Conn.Gen.Stat.Ann. § 42–98(d) (1960); cf. Uniform Commercial Code § 9–504.

39 Uniform Commercial Code § 9–105(i).

selling price,[40] and the financer or dealer then seeks a deficiency judgment against the consumer for the balance plus the repossession costs and other expenses. If the dealers are economically rational they will not bid more than the wholesale value of the car, except in the rare case where a dealer has a specific buyer anxious to have that particular model. In no event do such sales appear to be "open to the public" in the conventional meaning of that phrase or, indeed, open to anyone except those solicited by the financer. If the prices offered by the dealers are too low, the financer will "buy" the car for himself.

The dealers and financers appear to believe that a sale from the secured party (usually the financer) for a sum well below wholesale price to the original dealer or to another dealer is, in fact and at law, a proper public sale. Since it is the legal model that controls over well reasoned common sense and the empirical realities, they may be right. No advertising is necessary or utilized; nor need the sale be conducted by an auctioneer or even held at a used-car lot where such collateral is normally sold.[41] The public need not be invited to attend; not even the used-car dealers in the area are invited. But only a few dealers are solicited to offer bids, usually without having seen the car and only on the basis of a telephone call.

Thus the first (or wholesale) resale of the car is by "public" or by private sale, either to the repossessor himself or to another automobile dealer, but not to a retail customer.[42] In all our cases the sale was back to the original dealer or to another used-car dealer. As a result the defaulting purchaser can hope to reduce his debt by no more than the wholesale value of the car. Our data in 83 cases indicate that the consumer did not fare even this well on the first resale.

C. Empirical Data: The Low-Level Model

1. The first resale.

The price of the first resale averaged only 51 percent of the *Redbook* retail price of the car on the date of repossession.[43] Even if one assumes *Redbook* wholesale value as the proper standard for measuring the dealer's proceeds at first resale, average proceeds from the first resale amounted to only 71 percent of *Redbook* wholesale at repossession.[44] In only 17 of 83 cases did first-resale prices equal or exceed *Redbook* whole-

---

[40] The interrogatories and answers in Associates Discount Corp. v. Barham, No. CV–6–6712–33883 (6th Cir.Ct.Conn., Dec. 21, 1967), are laconic but wonderfully descriptive. Copies of the pleadings were kindly provided by Stephen Rose of the New Haven Legal Assistance Association: "Q1. What was the date, time, place and character, public or private, of the resale? A. October 19, 1967, 10:00 a. m., public sale, 53 Randolph Avenue, Waterbury, Conn. Q2. To whom was the automobile resold? A. To the plaintiff. * * * Q5. Was more than one bid received at the resale? A. Yes. Q6. If the answer to question five is yes, state the names of the other bidders, the amounts bid, and the conditions under which such bids were offered or solicited. A. Joe's Used Cars, Welton Street, Waterbury, Connecticut, $700; Imperial Auto Body, Industrial Lane, Waterbury, Connecticut, $675.00; John Storto, 47 Randolph Avenue, Waterbury, Connecticut, $675.00. *All bids were solicited and obtained by telephone.*" (Emphasis added.)

[41] See, e. g., Associates Discount Corp. v. Weldon, 4 Conn.Cir. 351, 355, 231 A.2d 671, 673 (App.Div.), petition for appeal denied, 154 Conn. 750, 228 A.2d 559 (1967).

[42] That resale price cannot necessarily be discovered from any public record because only taxable sales need be fully reported. Conn.Gen.Stat.Ann. §§ 12–430, 14–166, 14–169 (1960). See Appendix, section B.

[43] See Appendix, Table A1, col. 14. Since these are now all used cars and there is less than a month between repossession and first sale, the difference in the value of the car between the two dates is negligible, probably not more than 1%.

[44] See Appendix, Table A1, col. 13.

sale.[45]   Thus even if one accepts the re-possessor's legal right to sell the repos-sessed car in the wholesale market, he is not very efficient in that regard. This striking lack of efficiency is again ap-parent when first resale prices are com-pared with the prices at which dealers buy and sell at their weekly wholesale auc-tions, where the average price is 93 per-cent of *Redbook* wholesale.[46] Little more than a quarter of the first resales dis-played comparably high resale prices.[47]

These data reveal an alarming and most inequitable situation: The default-ing consumer would be better off were his repossessed car, which he purchased at retail, sold within the wholesale price structure, provided that the mechanics of the resale were reasonably conducive to realistic pricing or merely as efficient as the usual transaction between dealers in used cars.

The low prices at first resale cannot be attributed to the cars' condition. The re-possessed cars were not wrecked; more-over, if a car had been seriously dam-aged, the secured party was reimbursed for the loss as payee of a collision insur-ance policy required by the retail install-ment sale contract.[48] Examination of about 20 repossessed automobiles con-ducted during a prestudy revealed that all could be driven and that all appeared in normal condition. It is a reasonable in-ference that most of the repossessed cars

in the larger sample could be driven and were in normal condition. Only two of nearly 150 cars in the full survey were "junked" after repossession.

In nearly half the cases examined, the difference between the actual first resale

TABLE 1

AVERAGE RELATIVE EFFICIENCY AS A PERCENTAGE OF REDBOOK VALUE

	First Resale	Second Resale
Price of sale / Redbook retail at sale	51%	92%
Price of sale / Redbook wholesale at sale	71%	—

TABLE 2

AVERAGE RATIOS OF SALE PRICES TO NET TOTAL CLAIM

	First Resale	Second Resale
Price of sale / Net total claim	51%	86%
Redbook wholesale at sale / Net total claim	77%	—
Redbook retail at sale / Net total claim	108%	97%

in the wholesale market and an equally swift first resale in the retail market would have meant the difference between a deficiency judgment and full satisfac-tion of the debt.[49] In the 83 litigated cases the actual price of the first resale averaged only 51 percent of the repos-sessor's net claim.[50] If the first resale had been made at retail *Redbook*, the average price would have yielded 108 percent of the repossessor's net claim.[51] Similarly, if one demanded only *Redbook* wholesale of the first resale, the resulting

---

[45] See Appendix, Table A2, line 1.

[46] See Table 5 and text accompanying notes 96–99 infra.

[47] See Appendix, Table A2, line 1.

[48] Every contract examined in our study showed an item of cost for collision insurance, usually with a $50 or $100 deductible clause. The insurance premium is paid by the debtor, who also pays interest on the financing of the premium (from which the dealer gets a commission). Some financers also have a blanket policy providing them with collision coverage on all cars financed by them in the event that the original insurance lapses or is discontinued, or if the other coverage is dis-claimed.

[49] See Appendix, Table A1, col. 18. A sale at *Redbook* retail at the date of the whole-sale resale would have eliminated deficiency in 40 of our 83 cases.

[50] The median price of the first resale was 52% of the net claim. See Appendix, Table A1, col. 12.

[51] See Appendix, Table A1, col. 18.

price would have covered 77 percent of the total claim compared to 51 percent of the net claim produced by the actual proceeds from the wholesale resale.[52]

2. *The second resale.*

In sharp contrast to the first or wholesale resale is the subsequent retail resale. This sales takes place on a dealer's used-car lot in the normal business manner. Typically, the second resale takes place three to five months after repossession.[53] Unlike the timing of the first resale, an average of 32 days after repossession, the dealers await a better market in which to sell when they keep all the proceeds. Even more revealing are the prices at the second resale, which average 92 percent of *Redbook* retail value on the day of the sale.[54] By comparison, the price of the first resale—the sale determinative of the purchaser's credit against his debt—was only 51 percent of *Redbook* retail and 71 percent of *Redbook* wholesale.[55] The difference between the second resale figure of 92 percent of *Redbook* retail and the first resale figure of 71 percent of *Redbook* wholesale suggests a significant disparity in the dealer's economic incentive between the first (wholesale) resale and the second (retail) resale—still assuming that the wholesale market was the proper market for the first resale.[56]

A comparison between the price of the retail resale and the repossessor's net claim again emphasizes the frightful position of the defaulting purchaser. Because of the lapse of time, second resale even at full *Redbook* retail will not entirely satisfy the repossessor's claim. The *Redbook* resale value of the car has declined and now will equal, on the average, only 97 percent of the average claim,[57] rather than 108 percent on the day of repossession.[58] However, the actual price at the second or retail resale yielded 86 percent of the purchaser's debt.[59] In short, the difference between the first and second resales amounted to more than one-third of the claim against the purchaser: 35 percent, or the difference between 86 percent and 51 percent of the debt.

The data indicate that if the dealer or financer were to sell the repossessed car promptly at retail, the average price obtained would be about 108 percent of what is unilaterally calculated as the deficiency claim. Thus it is evident that if repossessors sold the repossessed automobiles at retail as quickly as they actually sell them at wholesale the number of deficiencies would decline sharply. And, if deficiency judgments were eliminated, the defaulting purchaser would be spared his own and the repossessor's court costs, and the 15 percent attorney's collection fee, reducing the amount of the total claim even further. But even if a deficiency-judgment action were necessary, the enhanced first resale price would significantly decrease the size of the deficiency owed by the defaulting purchaser.

D. *Collection Fees and Other Expenses*

1. *The consumer's burden.*

One prophetic 19th century jurist with a fundamentalist morality discussing a 5-percent attorney's fee for collection *and* costs of suit rhetorically asked what might

---

[52] See Appendix, Table A1, cols. 17, 12.

[53] See Appendix, Table A1, col. 3 (average of 147 days and median of 105 days between repossession and the date of the transfer-of-title form filed with the Connecticut Department of Motor Vehicles).

[54] See Appendix, Table A1, col. 16 (median is 100%).

[55] See Appendix, Table A1, cols. 12, 13.

[56] If the proper market for the first resale were the retail market, the apparent disparity in dealer incentive would of course be even more pronounced.

[57] See Appendix, Table A1, col. 19 (median is 94%).

[58] See Appendix, Table A1, col. 18.

[59] See Appendix, Table A1, col. 15 (median is 87%).

"be supposed as the natural result to the community from the execution of this agreement?"

It would be the condition of future loans, at banks, that the borrower should pay the expenses of collection. * * * The brokers in this state would hold a general jubilee; and as their sense of morality and law usually expands with their hopes of gain, in proportion to the borrower's necessity they would find, probably, additional items of *costs,* as the means of a legalized extortion upon their loans. In our opinion, such agreements are against the public policy of the country, and ought not to be enforced in courts of justice.[60]

Twentieth century legislators and uniform commissioners appear to be of a different opinion.

RISFA provisions,[61] allowing the suing creditor the costs of repossession and storage, court costs, and a 15-percent attorney's collection fee, exhibit the same permissive approach found in provisions of the Uniform Commercial Code and the Uniform Consumer Credit Code.[62] A neutral observer of the automobile financing system might find this anomalous. In litigated disagreements between transacting businessmen, each party ordinarily bears his own costs and legal fees. But when a businessman deals with an installment buyer the situation is quite different. For those standard form agreements have a provision unique to the adhesion contract: Instead of each party paying his own costs and legal fees, the consumer-debtor pays his own, and he also pays the costs and legal fees of the dealer or financer, his adversary. The costs seem arbitrary and high. The legal fees in our sample *always* amounted to 15 percent of the balance due on the contract. Every deficiency-judgment case examined (all those in the original group of about 150) had a 15-percent attorney's collection fee.[63] The maximum permissible statutory charge was, as always, the minimum actually imposed. I have never heard it satisfactorily explained why the creditor of a consumer installment buyer is entitled to exact costs and charges and a 15-percent attorney's collection fee, while no creditor of a businessman can impose such standardized costs, charges, and fees. Contractual provisions for payment of attorney's fees have been held void as against public policy in at least eight states.[64] The cases are decided on a variety of grounds: that such provisions are oppressive; that they are penalties, or usurious and apt to promote litigation. Moreover, the sentiment in some of these states is so strong that attorney's collection fees even in promissory notes that have been executed and were to be performed in other states cannot be enforced in the forum state.[65] Yet it does not appear that this prohibition has seriously impeded the business of installment sellers and their financers in such states.[66]

---

[60] State v. Taylor, 10 Ohio 378, 381 (1841) (emphasis in original).

[61] Conn.Gen.Stat.Ann. § 42-91 (1960) (attorney's fees, court costs, and delinquency charges); id. § 49-98(f) (repossession and storage expenses).

[62] Uniform Consumer Credit Code §§ 2.413-.414 (Revised Final Draft 1969); Uniform Commercial Code § 9-504(1)(a) ("reasonable attorneys' fees and legal expenses * * * to the extent provided for in the agreement and not prohibited by law"). The Uniform Consumer Credit Code can be found at 2 CCH Consumer Credit Guide 5002 et seq. (1969).

[63] Smaller dealers and financers are said to pay their lawyers one-third of what is collected, plus costs. Lawyers doing such work have generally confirmed this.

[64] See Annot., 54 A.L.R.2d 1053 (1957); Annot., 17 A.L.R.2d 288, 313 (1951).

[65] See Annot., 54 A.L.R.2d 1053 (1957).

[66] The Commissioners on Uniform State Laws allowed for that possibility in Alternative A of the Uniform Consumer Credit Code § 3.404, which prohibits the enforcement of contractual provisions "for the payment by the debtor of attorney's fees." Uniform Consumer Credit Code § 3.404.

If the security agreement must provide for payment of attorney's fees by the consumer, the amount should be set by the court after the completion of execution process—not upon default, and not based upon an arbitrary 15-percent standard. Since most deficiency judgments are entered by default (see Table 3), fees should be low. Certainly the fee in default cases bears no relation to the amount of the claim.[67]

2. The consumers' rights and remedies.

There should arise the question why the consumer-debtor is not given something of the same rights or their equivalent. If the dealer or financer defaults in his performance of the contract, which he has drawn for his own use and to which the consumer-debtor must assent if he wishes to do such business at all, what rights does the consumer-debtor have? RISFA answers that question in a manner peculiar to consumer-credit legislation. For a *willful* violation of the statutory provisions—the qualification is two-fold: The violations are limited to the statutory requirements and the violations must be willful—the creditor is prohibited from recovering his costs and charges.[68] An additional penalty of a fine (from $25 to $100) may be imposed for a willful violation by the creditor.[69] However,

the balance due on the installment contract can still be recovered. The creditor can get all his bread whether the consumer-debtor was guilty of an unintentional breach of the contract or a willful breach. His intent makes no difference. But the consumer-debtor cannot recover *his* costs, charges, and attorney's fees resulting from the creditor's breach of the contract, whether willful or not.[70]

E. The Consumer Defends and Other Myths

Given the assumption that the consumer-debtor and the seller or financer are both "parties" in the same sense that is meaningful within the framework of the adversary system, present repossession and resale practices may be acceptable. For then one also assumes the consumer-debtor will, if aggrieved, file responsive pleadings and initiate discovery proceedings. Only in that way has he any chance to obtain the details of the machinations that follow the repossession of his automobile. Yet it is evident that the assumptions and what is implicit in them are fictional: that the consumer has knowledge that there is or may be a legal problem [71] or that counsel could help (although to a very limited extent given the legal model) or that he has the financial wherewithal to retain counsel. There is no basis in the realities of the social and economic situation to pretend that these are both "parties" so that the same label

---

[67] See Project, Resort to the Legal Process in Collecting Debts from High Risk Credit Buyers in Los Angeles—Alternative Methods for Allocating Present Costs, 14 U.C.L.A.L. Rev. 879, 896 (1967).

[68] Conn.Gen.Stat.Ann. § 42–99 (1960). The statute requires that the creditor "approved of or had knowledge of [the] violation and after such approval or knowledge retained the benefits, proceeds, profits or advantages accruing from such violation or otherwise ratified such violation." Id.

[69] Although there is a minor problem of statutory construction, I assume the fine cannot be imposed on a burden of proof less than that required for forfeiture of charges and costs. Compare Conn.Gen.Stat.Ann. § 42–99 (1960) with id. § 42–100.

[70] Moreover, it is questionable whether the Uniform Consumer Credit Code provisions for penalties and attorney's fees in the case of a creditor's violations will make any significant or even perceptible difference. See Uniform Consumer Credit Code § 5.202. Apart from the high incidence of deficiency judgments by default, there is the serious question whether private counsel can afford to undertake such an action on a contingent-fee arrangement and whether the publicly funded legal aid groups can represent an indigent client in a claim for damages.

[71] G. Sykes, Legal Needs of the Poor in the City of Denver (1968).

properly describes both the financer and the consumer.

In only one of 150 cases examined before obtaining sufficient information for the eventual sample did the defaulting consumer retain counsel to protect his interests.[72] Of the 87 cases forming the basis of this part of the study, 74 cases resulted in default judgment for lack of appearance, two cases revealed a defense, and in two cases the consumer appeared himself to agree to a stipulated weekly payment. No information was available in nine cases. The plaintive pleading in a statistically typical repossession case appears below.[73]

Later examination of the 87 Circuit Court files is fairly revealing of the subsequent course of what is euphemistically termed litigation over the rights of the consumer. Seventy-four of these 87 cases resulted in default judgment for lack of an appearance.

The actions for deficiency judgments are almost always commenced by abode service.[74] Connecticut law does not require that any effort at personal service

be made; service at the last known abode of the defendant is considered equivalent to personal service.[75] Of the 87 cases, two failed to show the type of service of record; 15 more, or less than 1 in 5, were by personal service, and 70 of the 85 were abode service.

In only two cases of the 87 actions for deficiency judgments was a defense interposed; in two more cases a stipulation (an agreement between the parties for weekly payments) was arranged. Nine cases had nothing of record or no default had yet been entered. But as Table 3 shows, when it came to execution process, either by wage garnishment or against the defendant's property, 50 of the 87 defendants could be found, or at least their employers located for personal service.

After the entry of default judgment, the procedural steps in Connecticut require that plaintiff request an order for weekly payments to satisfy the debt now evidenced by the deficiency judgment obtained by default.[76] Of the 87 cases, 14 are incomplete or provide no information at that stage. Seventy-one of the remaining 73 show weekly payment orders. The two stipulations for weekly payments are included in the total of 71 weekly payment orders.

The next step, wage garnishment or property execution or both, can be ordered only after default in the weekly payment order.[77] In addition to the 14 incomplete or unknown cases in the weekly payment group, there are 21 more cases in which no action to garnish wages has been taken, although in those cases still

---

[72] See Appendix, Section A, infra. The appearance of a lawyer would be of record in the docket entries, or in the file of the case, or both.

[73] *"Motion to reopen default*

              CV–14–673–27712

"I paid $3,476.00 for the car, they took it back because I know longer could pay for it, they sold car for $1900.00 dollars, this is a 1966 Pontaic Tempest worth $3,400 dollars for $1900.00 dollars is not wright in my eyes.

"They want $496.00 for damgdes do you think this is right I don't. I gave them down payment $850.00 dollors made three payments of $95.47 which is $285.00 dollors that makes it $1,135.00 with down payment thank you"

[74] How often abode service gives actual notice is questionable. A local study still in progress has offered preliminary indications that personal service at least elicits more appearances and results in fewer defaults. See Committee on Legal Assistance, Does a Vendee Under an Installment Sales Contract Receive Adequate Notice of a Suit Instituted by a Vendor?, 23 Record of N.Y.C.B.A. 263 (1968); 3 Colum.J.L. & Soc.Prob. 17 (1967).

[75] Conn.Gen.Stat.Ann. § 52–57 (1960): "Except as otherwise provided, process in any civil action shall be served by leaving [a copy of the complaint] with the defendant, *or* at his usual place of abode, in this state." (Emphasis added.)

[76] Id. § 52–361(a) (1960).

[77] Conn.Gen.Stat.Ann. § 52–361(b) (Supp. 1969), amending Conn.Gen.Stat.Ann. § 52–361(b) (1960).

pending, that right remains available to the plaintiff.[78] There were six executions issued upon the property of the defendants, two of which also involved wage garnishment orders. Hence to summarize the 87 cases: 39 result in wage garnishments; 4 result in property execution; 2 more have both these collec-

tion devices, and 2 are disposed of in weekly payments arranged by stipulation of the parties. Five cases had no execution process. The dispositions of the remaining 35 cases are unknown of record or pending and incomplete. Table 3 summarizes the results of each stage of litigation.

TABLE 3

SUMMARY OF DISPOSITION OF CONSUMER LITIGATION

	No. Cases	Percent
1. Appearance at trial		
Default	74	85 [a]
Defense or stipulation	4	5
Unknown	9	10
Total	87	100
2. Weekly payment orders		
Payment order issued	71	82
No payment order	2	2
Unknown (5 + 9)	14	16
Total	87	100
3. Execution		
Wage garnishment only	39	45
Property execution only	4	5
Both wage garnishment and property execution	2	2
Neither wage garnishment nor property execution	5	6
Weekly payment by stipulation	2	2
Pending and unknown (21 + 14)	35	40
Total	87	100

[a] The 74 defaults constitute 95% of the 78 known cases.

———◆———

F. Does It Matter Who Finances, Resells, and Sues for Deficiency?

Given that in more than half the deficiency-judgment actions following repossession and resale of the collateral, the secured party or his assignee appears to recover his "paper" loss by wage garnishment or other execution process, there is little incentive for the secured party to resell the used car at the highest price obtainable.[79] And how especially true that

is when a resale in the most inefficient of wholesale markets will satisfy the legal requirements of disposition by resale for purposes of establishing a loss upon which the claim for deficiency judgment will be founded. Consider again the following: First, the dealer can buy the equivalent car at a wholesale auction for about 90 to 95 percent of the current wholesale value. Second, after default and repossession, the financer will often "resell" the car to the original dealer at a price well below wholesale value. Or, the financer may

[78] Those debtors may, of course, have been obedient to the weekly payment order.

[79] See Jordan & Warren, The Uniform Consumer Credit Code, 68 Colum.L.Rev. 387, 441 (1968). The authors state that "[s]o long as the creditor can sell [the collateral of the secured transaction] to himself, as he can under the Uniform Commercial Code section

9–504, it is in his interest to buy the [collateral] at a low price, thus increasing the amount of the deficiency left to be recovered from the debtor." Id. The same incentives exist when the financer, as secured party, resells to the original dealer, and the financer is the plaintiff in the deficiency action.

be paid the balance due on the retail installment contract and "resell" the car at the dealer's direction; or the financer may resell the car to one of the dealers whose sales he finances. Whatever way the transaction is sliced, the sale price is about 71 percent of wholesale value.[80] If the dealer's recourse agreement requires him to repurchase the car, he can proceed against the retail customer for the difference between the wholesale resale price and the full balance due on the retail installment contract (plus the allowable vigorish). Fourth, if the dealer as plaintiff-reseller cannot recover his deficiency following a resale to himself at less than the wholesale value, he can bestow a favor upon another dealer who presumably will "pat him on the back" when that other dealer repossesses a car. Fifth, more often than not, the repossessing dealer can have both: The deficiency is recoverable from the consumer and the other dealer may return the favor by selling him another repossessed car at far below the current wholesale price. Thus the present legal model in most states, and under the Uniform Commercial Code and the various RISFA's, creates no incentive to help the defaulting consumer. On the contrary, the existing legally accepted practices create an optimum means for lawfully fleecing him.

Table 4 summarizes the data by permutations of the respective parties in each possible status: Whether the dealer or another person financed the sale; whether the dealer or the financer was the plaintiff in the deficiency-judgment proceeding; and whether the first (or wholesale) buyer was the original dealer or another dealer. In our sample no separate financers were buyers at the first sale, although the reported cases[81] reveal that occurrence

and those engaged in the business advise that occasionally the transaction is in that form.

It seemed a plausible hypothesis that where the original dealer was the plaintiff in the deficiency-judgment action, the ratio of the *Redbook* retail price over the total claim (line 8 of Table 4) would be largest; that is, the repossessed car would have been sold at wholesale for proportionately less. Although that hypothesis is partially supported by columns 1 and 3 of line 8, the remaining data qualify such an inference. On the whole, however, the various aspects of the legal model in operation seem to show that the several permutations of the parties as wholesale buyers and plaintiffs make little difference (or at least none readily explicable) from the standpoint of the consumer-debtor.[82]

G. *Other Observations on Defaulting Consumers*

It is generally asserted by spokesmen for the financing institutions that no lender deliberately undertakes questionable accounts, those apt to default;[83] and that those consumer-debtors who do pay are penalized because the financers' losses are recouped by means of higher charges necessarily imposed upon them.[84] At least as regards automobiles sold by retail installment, those may be irrelevant rather than untrue comments. If our data

Corp. v. Beckwith, 23 Conn.Supp. 362, 183 A.2d 755 (Cir.Ct.App.Div.1962).

[82] The arrangements of record may fail to correspond to the underlying contractual arrangements. Some outside dealers may not be independent of the original dealer; and some dealers are said to own financers. Or, unknown unrelated variables, not included in our typology, may account for these results.

[83] See, e. g., Kripke, Consumer Credit Regulation: A Creditor-Oriented Viewpoint, 68 Colum.L.Rev. 445, 448–49 (1968).

[84] Felsenfeld, Some Ruminations About Remedies in Consumer-Credit Transactions, 8 B.C.Ind. & Cum.L.Rev. 535 (1967).

[80] See Appendix, Table A1, col. 13.

[81] See Associates Discount Corp. v. Weldon, 4 Conn.Cir.Ct. 351, 231 A.2d 671 (App.Div.), petition for appeal denied, 154 Conn. 750, 228 A.2d 559 (1967); cf. Universal C.I.T. Credit

TABLE 4
VARIATION IN EFFICIENCY AND PROCEEDS

	1	2	3	4	Total/Average
1. Financed by	F [a]	F	D [b]	F	
2. Plaintiff at deficiency proceeding	D	F	D	F	
3. Purchaser of collateral	D	D	B [c]	B	
4. Number of cases	20	9	19	35	83
5. $\dfrac{\text{First resale price}}{\textbf{Redbook} \text{ wholesale at first resale}}$ (%)	78	92	72	61	71
6. $\dfrac{\text{First resale price}}{\textbf{Redbook} \text{ retail at first resale}}$ (%)	58	69	44	47	51
7. $\dfrac{\text{First resale price}}{\text{Net total claim}}$ (%)	62	51	43	46	51
8. $\dfrac{\textbf{Redbook} \text{ retail at first resale}}{\text{Net total claim}}$ (%)	119	105	107	103	108
9. $\dfrac{\text{First resale price}}{\text{Second resale price}}$ (%)	60	73	71	61	65
10. $\dfrac{\text{Second resale price}}{\textbf{Redbook} \text{ retail at second resale}}$ (%)	110	105	76	86	92
11. $\dfrac{\text{Second resale price}}{\text{Net total claim}}$ (%)	116	94	68	76	86

[a] "F" denotes financer. [b] "D" denotes original dealer. [c] "B" denotes outside dealer.

———— ◆ ————

are at all reliable, the dealer or financer has little reason to be discouraged in his business affairs by the likelihood of default. In the event, he is apt to be fully compensated for the time and trouble occasioned by repossession and resale. For there certainly *appears* to be some substance to the claims of additional profits on resales following repossession. However, Professor Kripke earnestly believes that

the archetype of the creditor as rapaciously eager to repossess, to profit hugely by resale and otherwise to oppress the debtor, is´ in large part an arch-myth, at least as applied to creditors catering to middle-class buyers. In the first place, resale markets for consumer goods with the exception of automobiles are so poor that the alleged resale profits are a fantasy. More important, a company of institu-

tional size simply cannot afford the amount of individual handling by persons capable of making decisions that would be necessary to operate oppressively. Even if every dollar of principal and finance charge is ultimately realized by collection, an account that requires individual collection handling yields a loss.[85]

The middle-class, non-automobile situation described by Professor Kripke is so very different from the realities we found. But, apart from what seem his acts of faith, what propositions of fact has Professor Kripke put forward? What exceptions or limitations are involved in his assertions? First, automobiles as the subject of retail-installment sales are apparently excluded; thus some 40 percent of consumer installment credit is not considered. Second, the

[85] Kripke, supra note 83, at 448.

quoted paragraph does not seem to apply to low-income groups, just those who have the most need for and make the most use of retail installment credit.[86] Third, the individual handling that is required for oppressive measures in defaulted consumer installment accounts is claimed to be too expensive. In fact, it is said to be so costly that even if all the principal and finance charges (and the default charges, court costs and attorneys' collection fees?) were to be collected, such accounts would still be losers. This last item needs more response.

The accounts in default are handled in groups with printed forms leaving only a few blanks to be filled in. Moreover, the suit papers are picked up by the sheriff or other process server in fair piles from lawyers who usually do little else for their livelihood and have the entire process organized in routines that are both aesthetically pleasing and economically worthwhile.[87] There is rarely any litigation; almost all such claims result in default judgments.[88] There need be no venal creditor to produce the desired and frightful results. They can be accomplished by any benign, law-abiding financer or installment seller. The present legal model and the practices it permits are all that is needed for oppressive measures. And because of the sanguine views of the Uniform Commissioners and their financer-clients, the prospective legal

model, the Uniform Consumer Credit Code, will be little better.

Also, the institutional lender often looks to the retail installment seller (or his reserve account) for payment in the event of default. Hence Professor Kripke's limitation to lenders tends to distort. If "lenders" includes retail installment sellers as well as their financers, a recent Federal Trade Commission Report on retail-installment sellers of household furnishings indicates that default followed by legal action comes as no surprise. Rather, their data "suggest a marketing technique which includes actions against default as a normal matter of business rather than as a matter of last resort." [89] The F.T.C. survey found that among eleven low-income market retailers in the District of Columbia, "one court judgment was obtained for every $2200 of sales" (probably one in nine or ten accounts), and that "low-income market retailers make extensive use of the courts in collecting debts." [90] Our data tend to show motivations for quick defaults and repossessions on the part of automobile dealers and their financers, with special application to used cars presumably purchased on credit by similar low-middle-income groups.[91] The employment of full-time repossessors by financers and some of the larger volume dealers bespeaks anticipation of defaults that will occasion repossession, and in sufficient numbers.[92]

---

86 See U. S. Federal Trade Comm'n, Economic Report on Installment Credit and Retail Sales Practices of District of Columbia Retailers 5, 7 (1968): "[I]nstallment credit transactions accounted for 92.7 percent of the total sales of the 18 low-income–market retailers. In contrast, installment credit accounted for only 26.5 percent of the total sales of general-market retailers." Id. at 5. The "general-market retailer" is defined as one who sells to a broad consumer market or primarily to middle- and high-income groups.

87 See Project, supra note 67, at 890–92.

88 See Table 3 and text accompanying notes 71–78 supra.

89 U. S. Federal Trade Comm'n, supra note 86, at xv.

90 Id. at xiii.

91 Credit buyers of new cars have been found to have lower incomes, smaller liquid-asset holdings, and smaller net worth than cash buyers, 4 Consumer Instalment Credit, supra note 9, at 28.

92 U. S. Att'y for the Southern District of N. Y., Dep't of Justice, Report on the Work of the Consumer Fraud Unit 16 (1968). "Investigations have disclosed a pattern of sales of certain used cars at many times their original cost, followed by a cycle of repossession, repurchase of the car at a low price at auction and further resale at many times

There are enough defaults to make economically worthwhile the salary of the night-type who accomplishes the actual physical retaking of the car. One cannot, in this context, dismiss the matter as the derelictions of a few "deadbeats." Rather, our observations and inferences are consistent with the Federal Trade Commission report that default followed by repossession, deficiency-judgment proceedings, and wage garnishment is accepted as normal business routine.

III. ALTERNATIVES TO THE PRESENT LEGAL MODEL: THE LEAST DISPLACEMENT

A self-executing practice regulating repossession and resale of automobiles as collateral would be an improvement over the present legal model. Under one such rule, the court would refuse to entertain the action, notwithstanding the defendant's failure to appear, unless the specified minimum information was clearly set forth.[93] By a rule of practice or procedure the courts could also provide a more explicit definition of "public sale" as contrasted with the usual private sale.

Yet it seems evident from this study and from examination of the few reported cases that give the actual figures, that it will make very little difference whether this information is given of record and whether the resale is public or private. The considerable debate over proper notice to the affected parties [94] and the advantage of public over private resales (and what constitutes a proper public sale) is nearly irrelevant to empirical reality. Three important particulars intrude. First, unless the conduct of a public sale is something on the order of the wholesale model described below,[95] the public resale prices are not apt to approximate the retail market values of the vehicles at the time of sale, if retail is the accepted standard. Second, lacking effective public resale procedures, private resales may be better if regulated so that there are good incentives for prompt resale at the highest prices obtainable; perhaps as part of such a practice a floor could be put on the resale price of each repossessed car. But third, the paramount consideration is to abandon the patent fiction that if the consumer is given legal remedies for adequate protection, he will assert those rights with any significant frequency.

Accordingly, the remainder of this section is devoted to consideration of three alternative models—the dealers' wholesale auction market, the Uniform Consumer Credit Code, and the Uniform Commercial Code. None provides a complete solution, yet each displays key elements in an equitable system of repossession and resale. After examining each of these models, an historical model—

---

that price to a new customer." Id. No supporting data are given.

93 This could be accomplished by a court-enacted rule, since the only question involved would be the completeness required of the statement of the elements of the cause of action in the pleadings. Such minimum information regarding the history of the account might include the following: original cash sale price, wholesale value of trade-in, cash down payment; collision insurance, credit life insurance, any other charges (itemized); total debt based on original contract (time sale price); payments made on account (itemized); balance due at time of default; date of repossession; cost of repossession; storage costs (total per day) and storage location; photocopy of the original contract; notice of the sale given (how and to whom); when, where, and how the car was resold; the actual cash resale price; rebates of (1) unearned finance charges and (2) unearned insurance premiums (collision, credit life, etc.).

94 See, e. g., Norton v. National Bank of Commerce, 240 Ark. 143, 398 S.W.2d 538 (1966) (decided under and construing section 9–504(3) of the Uniform Commercial Code); Mallicoat v. Volunteer Finance & Loan Corp., 415 S.W.2d 347, 350 (Tenn.Ct.App.1966) (responsive to the question whether the sale was conducted in a "commercially reasonable" manner by reference to "lack of notice, known to the creditor"); Elm Buick Co. v. Moore, 150 Conn. 631, 192 A.2d 638 (1963).

95 See Section III–A infra.

strict foreclosure—is shown to provide an effective alternative to the present legal model.

A. *The Dealers' Wholesale Auction: An Alternate Model*

One gets some notion how economical and efficient an auction sale of used cars can be when both parties to the sale are dealers engaged in the business of buying and selling used cars. The model is a public auction sale of automobiles held weekly at Warehouse Point, Connecticut. This is a wholesale auction and only dealers are permitted to buy and sell. The enterprise appears to be commercially viable, probably quite successful. The auction offers nearly 300 cars at each weekly sale. There are separate lanes for recent cars and for cars more than two model years old. The proprietors advise that over the past ten years more than 70 percent of the cars put up for sale at the auction have been sold.

The cars are subdivided into three categories: model years from 1962 and before; 1963 and 1964 models; models from 1965 through 1968. These categories were as of July 1968 and are adjusted annually in October when the new model year begins. Cars in the oldest category are auctioned at a per-car cost of $12 to the seller and $7 to the buyer. The two groups of more recent cars are auctioned with charges of $14 to the seller and $9 to the buyer. These charges include an insured title to the vehicle and examination by the auctioneer's mechanic, described below. The auction company permits two tries at making the sale at a price acceptable to the seller. The auction is something of a legal hybrid but appears to be a conditional auction subject to acceptance by the seller when the bidding is completed.

The other terms of the auction sale are revealing of the efficiency and candor of transactions between dealers. Cars sold for $305 or less are taken "as is" except for major mechanical defects, such as cracked cylinder blocks, and in any case where the buyer claims that there has not been "fair play," which connotes a variety of deceptive practices. All cars sold for more than $305 are subject to inspection by the buyer and his test-driving the vehicle. In this category any major mechanical defects are considered cause for "rejection," which in this context may mean recision. Upon request the buyer may have the car examined by the mechanic employed for that purpose by the auction company. The mechanic, equipped with a device similar to a stethoscope, determines from the noise of the motor whether there is a defect that would warrant "rejection." The mechanic is skilled enough to satisfy the dealers who attend. In the event of continued disagreement, the management of the auction company appears empowered to make the final decision by a binding arbitration ruling. There are no reports of difficulties in this legal system and apparently there have never been any appeals to state-created courts.

In an effort to gauge the efficiency of the dealers' auction, we attended a typical session at Warehouse Point. The 92 sales that took place during the time we attended constitute our sample. This is a systematic sampling that appeared from an examination of the used cars yet to be sold fully representative of the larger group of more than 200 cars to be sold on that day.[96] Two of the student researchers had considerable experience with automobiles and were, in most cases, able to judge whether the condition of the car was normal for its age. Given the efficiency and economy of this transactional

---

[96] Table A1 and Table 5 (condensed for publication) include fairly equivalent spreads as regards the vehicle makes and years. We have no reason to think the samples not comparable by reason of preponderances of any make or year.

model, and that it is an almost classic open market, the average prices approximated the ideal of the model, the current wholesale price. The cumulative-averages column of Table 5 summarizes the dealers' wholesale auction: The 92 cars sold for an average of 93 percent of the wholesale price on that date in that area, as measured by the *Redbook* for that six-week period in New England. If we eliminate two cars thought to have been used by police and sold at far less than their wholesale values (37 and 42 percent), the model is even better. The remaining 90 used cars were sold at an average price of nearly 95 percent of the then wholesale value.

Given that the appropriate standard is the wholesale price (the price at which the dealer can buy or sell and the maximum that the car is worth to the dealer) the dealers' auction produces good results. The used cars are sold at an average of nearly 95 percent of the then *Redbook* wholesale values.[97]

TABLE 5

DEALERS' WHOLESALE AUCTION

Model Year	Number		Percent of Redbook Wholesale
1968	2		101
1967	6		80
1966	15		89
1965	12		102
1964	15		87
1963	15		89
1962	14		101
1961	13		94
	Total	92	Average 93
	Total [a]	90	Average [a] 95

[a] Without the two "police" cars.

Viewed as a possible alternative model, the wholesale auction has noteworthy advantages. The sale is held every Wednes-

day during every week of the year. The proprietors think the element of habit on the part of dealers who attend regularly and the 20-year continuity of the operation are major factors in the large attendance, which, during our day of observation, ran on the order of 200 to 300 buyers and sellers at all times during a rainy day. The auction company also publishes its own weekly list of the prices at which specific models of cars were sold at the last week's sale. The list is mailed to some 2300 active dealers in New England, New Jersey, and New York.[98] These are not only buyers and sellers of acumen and experience but their business is accomplished under pleasant circumstances without puffing and with some fair assurances of honest dealings. The considerable publicity and good attendance, combined with the good facilities for buyers and sellers, result in a fair approximation of the ceiling of the wholesale model.[99]

* * *

The Uniform Commercial Code * * provide[s] that if the disposition of collateral produces a surplus, the creditor must account for that to the consumer; if the proceeds of the collateral leave a balance still due on the contract, the consumer is liable on a deficiency judgment.[112] The preceding sentence is one

---

[97] Some of the dealers at the wholesale auction use the so-called *Blackbook*, which is published weekly and contains only wholesale prices. The *Blackbook* has four wholesale values for different conditions of the car, while the *Redbook* allows only for "normal" condition of the car. Most dealers appeared to be using the *Redbook* and the *N.A.D.A.* book, which are comparable.

[98] But based on examination of the license plates, only Connecticut dealers and a few from Massachusetts attended on the day we observed the auction sale.

[99] Moreover, the operation is more than economically feasible. Assuming that not less than 10,500 cars are sold annually, the auction company certainly appears to be a profitable enterprise, for, in addition to the gross commission of about $220,000 on sales, there are concessions of various kinds on the premises and a cafeteria which was very well attended during our day of observation. Also noteworthy is that, for the costs of $19 to $23 per vehicle, the plant and facilities are clean and adequate.

[112] Uniform Commercial Code § 9–504(2); Uniform Consumer Credit Code § 5.103;

of those wonderfully equitable sounding balances. Better than a one-sided freedom of contract theory, these provisions really look fair in the "what's-sauce-for-the-gander" style. Except that the whole proposition is a formal and empty statement about things that do not occur in fact. Such arrant nonsense is not to be received with good grace from the Uniform Commissioners to whom, one would suppose, reality has a greater appeal than a priori formalities. In our study we found no surpluses; the proceeds from the typical first resale amounted to about 51 percent of the balance due from the defaulting consumer.[113] I surmise that there are hardly ever any surpluses of which the consumer-debtor or any court takes cognizance. The realities of the legal model make the "surplus" situation a sport. They are such as to give one pause: What are these scholars talking about?[114]

———◆———

If repossession and resale results in a deficiency, or if the creditor chooses not to repossess (or to replevy under a court order, which enables him to call upon the sheriff to do the physical retaking and obviates the need to avoid a breach of the peace), a suit may be instituted against the debtor personally. The quality of justice doled out to consumer credit debtors in the low-level civil courts in urban areas is nothing short of scandalous.

Conn.Gen.Stat.Ann. §§ 42–98(f), (g) (1960). The UCCC provisions are phrased as a modification of the UCC, restricting deficiencies to purchases of more than $1000. See Jordan & Warren, supra note 79, at 440–41.

[113] See Appendix, Table A1, col. 12.

[114] Another respectable example is the recent (and formally accurate) statement that "[t]he debtor is given the right * * * to compel a resale to protect his equity in the repossessed collateral." Jordan & Warren, supra note 79, at 440–41.

CONSUMERS IN TROUBLE [*]

David Caplovitz.

Seeking a Judgment: The Role of the Courts in the Collection Process

When extrajudicial methods of collection fail, creditors are likely to enlist the courts in the collection process. Of course, they hope to collect the debt by invoking the power of the court, but even if they do not collect, a judgment against the debtor is still of value for income tax purposes. Bad debts are worth 50 cents in deductions on every tax dollar. Since we sampled [more than 900] default-debtors from court records, each, by definition, had been sued.[1] Thus, we now confront the debtors not merely as persons in default, but as defendants in legal actions. We consider in this chapter the stages of the legal process leading up to judgment.

Service of Process

Central to the American judicial system is the concept embodied in the four-

[*] This article is condensed from Chapter 11 of the forthcoming book Consumers in Trouble to be published by Appleton Century Crafts, Educational Division, Meredith Corporation. Copyright © 1973 Meredith Corporation. Reprinted by permission.

[1] It happens that in four of the 438 Detroit cases, the process server recorded that he was unable to find the debtor and thus the legal action was stopped. Our interviewers did find these four persons and learned about their debt problem. That such cases of admitted nonservice occurred only in Detroit, calls attention to city variations in both the stage at which the case is recorded and the information about the case appearing in the docket book. In Chicago and Detroit, where process serving is an activity of the court, the case is entered in a docket book at the time at which the creditor requests service. In New York, where process serving is a private industry, the case is entered in a docket book only when proof of service is filed. The confirmation of judgment book in Chicago records whether service was made. In Detroit, the comparable information appeared only in the file of the case. The two-stage process in Detroit resulted in the four cases of nonservice slipping into the sample.

teenth amendment that prohibits a citizen from being deprived of his rights or property without due process of the law. The doctrine of due process requires that a person be notified of any legal action taken against him in order that he may defend himself in court. In consumer actions, this means that the debtor has to be properly notified of the legal action instituted by the creditor.

The issue of service of process in these three jurisdictions provides an unusual opportunity to study the efficacy of procedural laws, for the rules governing service of process in New York are quite different from those in Chicago and Detroit. One major difference is that process serving in New York is a private industry, responding to the profit motive. Any person 21 years of age or older may serve a summons and a number of process serving firms exist in New York which handle the bulk of the business. In contrast, in Michigan and Illinois, as in most other states, process serving is carried out by an official of the court, the sheriff's office or a bailiff. The entrepreneurial character of process serving in New York results in a number of illegal shortcuts that we shall soon note.

In all three jurisdictions, the process server is required to attempt personal service, that is, must try to hand the summons and complaint (which are printed on the same form) to the debtor. But in Chicago and Detroit, the rules regarding substitute service are (or were) much more lenient than in New York. Should the process server in Chicago or Detroit not find the debtor at home, he is permitted to hand the summons to any person 21 years of age or older in the household and then mail a copy to the debtor. Until recently, the process server in New York was required to prove that he had made several attempts at personal service

on different days before substitute service was permitted.[2]

The method of service is related to yet another difference between New York law and that in the other jurisdictions— the length of time the debtor has to respond. If personal service is made in New York, the debtor is given only 10 days to answer the summons. If substitute service is employed, the debtor in New York is given up to 30 days to respond before the creditor can claim a default judgment. In Illinois and Michigan the debtor is given about 15 days to respond *regardless* of method of service.

The fees that can be charged for process serving are quite low in all these jurisdictions, ranging at the time of our study from $1.50 per summons in New York to $4.00 per summons in Detroit, with additional charges for mileage in Chicago. These fees are paid initially by the plaintiff but are passed on to the defendant, being added to the amount sought in the judgment.

One final difference exists between process serving in New York and the other two jurisdictions. The Soldiers and Sailors Relief Act, passed by the Federal government years ago, prohibits *default* judgments against members of the armed services on the theory that a member of the military may be unable to show up in court to defend himself because he is off fighting a war or is on assignment in some other jurisdiction. Thus, before a default judgment (or in Chicago, a confession of judgment confirmed) can be obtained, an affidavit of nonmilitary service must be filed with the court. In Chicago and Detroit, the burden of filing this affidavit rests with the plaintiff and his attorney, presumably because they know that at the time of the initial trans-

---

[2] The New York law was changed in September of 1970, permitting substitute service to be made in much the same way as in the other jurisdictions.

action the debtor was not in military service. But in New York the convention is that the process server makes the determination of whether the debtor is a civilian, and it is he who files the affidavit of nonmilitary service. Perhaps one reason for this custom is that the process server is entitled to charge an additional $2.00 for filing the affidvait of nonmilitary service. Because of this fee, they do not hesitate to file such affidavits even when the defendant is an elderly woman. This New York procedure creates an additional strain toward personal service or at least the allegation of personal service for unless he can see the debtor, the process server is in no position to judge his military or civilian status. Many of these variations in the rules have a significant bearing on the *method* of service, but there is a prior topic to be considered, whether service, regardless of method, is made at all.

City Variations in Rate of Service

The New York system has been widely criticized for stimulating "sewer service," a term that refers to summonses being thrown away (down the sewer) rather than served, and false affidavits of service being signed by unscrupulous process servers and their firms. Regardless of whether service is actually made, the New York system (which at one time or another has been investigated by the State Attorney General's office, the United States Attorney's office and the City of New York's Department of Consumer Affairs) involves other evasions of the law. Various investigations have disclosed that the employees of process serving firms sign large numbers of summonses in *blank*. These men come only once a week to collect summonses for their territory and phone in the results of their efforts each day. The central office then fills out the affidavits signed in blank and someone in the central office with the authority to do so notarizes them, thereby

committing perjury. This illegal short-cut both speeds up the process of filing suit (no small matter when several creditors may be competing to collect from the same debtor) and saves the process server the expense of making frequent trips to the central office.[3]

As this suggests, the violation of the debtor's right of notification is much more likely to occur in New York than in Chicago or Detroit.[4] The data show this to be so. Service of process was most effective in Detroit as 84 per cent of the sampled debtors in that city reported that they received the summons and complaint. In Chicago, 71 per cent said they had been served, but in New York, only a bare majority, 54 per cent reported re-

---

[3] The United States Attorney's office in the Southern District of New York successfully prosecuted several process servers for "sewer service" under the Civil Rights Act. See U. S. v. Barr, 295 F.Supp. 889 (S.D.N.Y., 1969). One of the men convicted in these cases admitted that he never served a summons outside of Brooklyn, his base of operations, but the U. S. Attorney's office found a number of affidavits of service filed against debtors in other boroughs bearing this man's signature. This provides some indication of the callous attitude of the process serving firms. They do not even bother to match the signed-in-advance affidavits with debtors who could have been served by the process server. Thus, every debtor outside of Brooklyn who was sued on the basis of a summons signed by this man was denied due process. The U. S. Attorney's office could find many of these cases by going through the files. Yet it would be powerless to take action against the creditors, for each of the innumerable creditors would have to be made the object of a separate legal action. This condition thus differs from a class action in which a large number of persons join forces to sue a single defendant.

[4] Some 42 Detroit cases are omitted from this analysis. Thirty-eight are replevin actions in which the plaintiff is seeking to repossess goods, a process that does not involve advance notification. A writ is left with the debtor at the time of repossession informing him that he has 14 days in which to challenge the plaintiff's right to the goods and have them returned to him. The other four are the cases in which the process server was unable to make service.

ceiving the summons. Even though some respondents may have wittingly or unwittingly reported incorrectly on this issue, such errors only affect the absolute percentages for each city and would in no way undermine the sharp intercity differences found.[5]

A Note on Debtor's Awareness of the Suit

In all three cities combined, 29 per cent of the debtors claimed that they were never served with a summons. How then, if at all, did these debtors find out about the legal action against them? In earlier research we found that some debtors learned about the law suit only when their employers told them about the garnishment order and then it was often too late to save their jobs, much less defend their legal rights in court. Table 11.1 shows the distribution of debtors in each city according to how they learned that they were being sued.

When debtors do not learn about the suit from the summons, they are most likely to learn about it from their employer in connection with a garnishment notice. This turns out to be true for 10 per cent of the debtors in the aggregate and

TABLE 11.1

How Debtor First Learned of Suit, by City

Source	Chicago	Detroit	New York	Three City Total
Summons	71%	84%	54%	72%
Employer	12	5	13	10
Creditor	5	3	11	6
Notice of Default Judgment	– –	– –	5	2
Other	2	1	6	2
Unaware of Suit	11	7	12	9
	101%	100%	101%	101%
N	(311)	(395)	(332)	(1038)

for a somewhat higher proportion in Chicago and New York. Perhaps the most striking finding in Table 11.1 is that almost one in every ten (nine per cent) had no idea that they were sued until told so by the interviewer although they were aware of some problem with the creditor designated by the interviewer. Such debtors were most common in New York, 12 per cent, but Chicago virtually matched this percentage (11 per cent). The Detroit debtors, no doubt because of the more effective system of notification in that city, were most likely to know that they had been sued. (These debtors unaware of the suit may be persons who had worked out settlements with their creditors, or they may be persons removed from the labor market and thus able to escape garnishment proceedings against them.)

Responding to the Summons

The debtor who has been served with notice is, of course, free not to respond, in which case he subjects himself to a default judgment (or a confirmation of judgment in Chicago). He may not respond because he feels that he has no valid defense or for a host of other reasons that we shall soon examine. But it

[5] To refresh the debtor's memory on this matter of service, the respondent was shown a standard summons and complaint form and asked whether he had ever received such a document.

is important to note that responding to a summons is by no means the same as having a day in court and, in fact, is no guarantee against a *default* judgment. Rather it represents but the first stage in a process which may eventuate in a trial before a judge.

The summons informs the debtor that he must appear in court within a specified period of time or on or before a specific date in order to file an answer to the plaintiff's complaint against him. The answer consists of a written document setting forth the debtor's reasons for not paying the debt. The process of filing an answer varied somewhat among the three cities at the time of our survey in 1967. It was perhaps most complicated in Chicago. If the debt was less than $200, the Chicago debtor who appeared on the due date was immediately assigned a trial date and was not required to file a written answer. But if the debt was greater than $200, the debtor who responded was given three copies of a standard answer form. He was told to return one copy to the court within ten days, to mail another copy to the creditor's attorney, and to keep one copy for himself. He was then assigned a date three weeks hence to appear in the "Answer Call Room" at which time he would learn the date that his case was set for trial. Thus, if adhered to strictly, the Chicago procedure in debts over $200 could involve three appearances *before* the trial, one on the date specified in the summons to receive the answer form, another within the next ten days, a third three weeks later to learn about the trial date. Apparently the practice in Chicago, at least in cases where the debtor was represented by a lawyer, was to ignore the ten day request for the answer and to file the answer on the twenty-first day, thus eliminating one of the three steps.[7]

In both Detroit and New York, the procedure for filing an answer was and is rather simple. When the debtor appears in court with his summons, he is given a standard form to fill out. The clerk will help him fill it out or may even fill it out for him. The answer is thus filed at the time the defendant appears. Moreover, the defendant does not have the responsibility of sending a copy of his answer to the plaintiff's attorney, the theory being that the latter can always come to court and read the answer once he receives the notice of the trial.

In each jurisdiction, filing an answer, whatever its merits, requires the court clerk to schedule a trial (which the plaintiff's attorney can avoid by moving for a summary judgment or by requesting postponements, discovery proceedings, etc.). But, in fact, the clerks in each jurisdiction are likely to exercise some discretion. We know this to be true in New York where we have interviewed some "answer" clerks. They told us that when the debtor does not have a *legitimate* answer, they advise him not to file and risk the burden of further court costs. The question arises as to how the clerks define a legitimate answer. They apparently have no difficulty with an answer involving violations of expressed or implied warranties, but it is not clear what advice they give when the debtor claims that he was misled about the price or other terms of the sale. Moreover, the New York clerks told us that they do not regard such reasons for default as "I lost my job" or "I was sick" or "I am too poor to pay" valid defenses, even though under the emerging doctrine of "unconscionability" some merit might be found in such answers. In short, moti-

---

[7] Since 1967, Illinois law has simplified its answer process in two respects. First, the $200 ceiling for a verbal answer and immediate trial date has been raised to $1000. For cases above this amount, the debtor is now permitted to file an answer within ten days of the summons and at that time is assigned a trial date. Thus the entire Answer Call Room procedure has been eliminated.

vated by the desire to save the debtor-defendant additional court costs (and perhaps to avoid crowding the court calendar with frivolous cases), the clerks exceed their authority and usurp some of that of a judge. Such "discretionary justice" has been well documented in the criminal area in studies of the police.[8] We now see that it also exists in civil law with court clerks as the agents of discretionary justice.

Whatever the procedure for filing an answer, we are not now concerned with the number of answers actually filed, but rather with the number of debtors who responded to the summons and presumably tried to file an answer.[9] All the debtors who were served were asked:

> "Did you or someone representing you go to court when you got the summons?"

The wording of the question allowed for a representative of the debtor, such as a lawyer, appearing in court for him. The direct question of whether the debtor did in fact respond to the summons suffers from the same possibilities of respondent error or bias as the question of whether a summons was received. But it is not immediately clear what direction such bias might take. Presumably, if the debtor was ready to admit being served, he might be under pressure to admit that he answered even when he did not. But to falsify a response to the summons would place additional strains on the debtor for he would then have to explain why the outcome was not more favorable (for, as we shall see, the outcome is almost invariably *un*favorable to

the debtor). Further room for error is introduced by the fact that the person being interviewed was sometimes the spouse of the debtor who may have been misled about the debtor's behavior. Moreover, some debtors may have thought that their representatives did appear in court when they did not. In short, there are numerous reasons for questioning the validity of the *absolute* percentages based on the reports of our respondents. In one of the three cities, Chicago, it is actually possible to determine the extent of reported error on this question. As noted, any Chicago defendant who answered the summons by the required date was automatically assigned either to a trial at some future date (if his debt was under $200) or to the "Answer Call Room" (if his debt was above $200) where at a later time he would be assigned a trial date. The clerks manning the confirmation of judgment book in Chicago presumably exercised no discretion whatsoever. If the summons was served and the debtor did not appear, his case was stamped "ex parte judgment confirmed," the Chicago variant of a default judgment. If he did appear, his case was set down for either the Answer Call Room or for trial. It turns out that 66 Chicago debtors responded to the summons according to the confirmation book, but some 79 Chicago debtors told us that either they themselves or some representative of theirs answered the summons. The "true" figure comes to 30 per cent of those who received the summons, the reported figure, to 36 per cent. This discrepancy of six percentage points presumably represents respondent error.[10] But, as in the previous analysis, we are less interested in the absolute percentages (although they have considerable importance as crude estimates of the reality) than we are in the *differences*

---

[8] See for example, Jerome H. Skolnick, Justice Without Trial: Law Enforcement in a Democratic Society (New York: John Wiley and Sons, 1966).

[9] The New York clerks that we spoke to claimed that about one out of every three or four persons who respond do not have legitimate answers and are discouraged from filing.

[10] It is possible that in a few of these cases the debtor successfully had his judgment reopened.

among the three cities under study. For this purpose we shall deal with the debtors' reports on whether or not they answered the summons.

We have seen that New York lags far behind Chicago and Detroit when it comes to service of process, but improper service turns out to be only the tip of the iceberg. Upon further examination, the breakdown of the New York judicial system in consumer actions is even more complete than the figures on service imply. Even those New York debtors who are served hardly ever show up in court (four per cent), in marked contrast with the substantial minorities in Chicago (36 per cent) and Detroit (34 per cent).

The four per cent in New York represents a mere eight persons out of the 178 who claimed they received a summons. In contrast, more than a third of the Chicago debtors and a similar number of the Detroit debtors who were served responded to the summons.[11] How is the incredibly poor record for appearances in New York to be explained? Those who said they did not go to court were asked to explain why. Surprisingly, this "reason" question sheds little light on the very low rate of appearances in New York. The kinds of reasons offered were quite varied but they did not differ substantially from city to city. Table 11.7 shows the categories with the largest frequencies as well as those of particular interest.

By far the most common reason for not appearing in court in each jurisdiction

TABLE 11.7

Reasons for Not Appearing in Court in Response to the Summons, by City

	Chicago	Detroit	New York
1. Tried to settle and thought court action was discontinued	33%	28%	21%
2. Advised not to go to court by plaintiff's attorney or own attorney or case being handled by some professional	13	13	9
3. Thought debt settled and did not owe more money	5	6	10
4. Unable to go; sick or could not afford loss of day's pay	16	8	12
5. No particular reason; forgot	10	14	11
6. Couldn't pay; no defense	7	14	8
7. Received summons too late to go to court	4	3	3
8. Did not know that he was supposed to go to court	3 } 4%	6 } 7%	15 } 19%
9. Afraid to go to court	1	1	4
Total per cent *	92%	93%	93%

* The percentages do not total 100 because we have omitted a miscellaneous category as well as the "no answer" cases.

(ranging from a third of the Chicago cases to a fifth of the New York cases) is that the debtor, presumably stimulated by the initiation of the law suit, has arranged for some kind of settlement with

11 On the basis of the entire sample, including those who claim they were not served, the response rate comes to 25 per cent in Chicago, 26 per cent in Detroit, and two per cent in New York.

the creditor's attorney. These debtors are of the impression, often mistaken, that the court action has been discontinued. The next two categories are closely related to the first in that the debtor was either under the impression that the debt had been settled and that therefore the court action was no longer appropriate or he did not appear on the advice of either his own attorney or the lawyer for the defendant (more typically the latter). These cases, too, imply that some process of negotiation or settlement was going on outside of court which would make a court appearance unnecessary. These three categories account for 40 to 50 per cent of the "no show" cases. The group of debtors who were unable to appear either because of illness or fear of losing a day's work is perhaps not as large as might have been expected, ranging from eight per cent in Detroit to 16 per cent in Chicago. Of considerable significance are the figures for the "no defense" category. A number of judges in these courts are well aware of the extraordinarily high proportion of default judgments in consumer actions (a topic discussed later in this chapter), but they are not alarmed for they reason that this indicates merely that the debtor knows he is at fault and sees no point of risking further court costs by making an appearance and asking for a trial.[12] As these data show, fewer than 10 per cent of the Chicago and New York debtors who did not appear gave such a reason and in Detroit the figure is only 14 per cent. Obviously, this popular theory is not supported by the reasons offered spontaneously by the debtors to explain their nonappearance. Just as we found that some consumers got into trouble because they forgot to pay their bills, so we find that this brand of irresponsibility explains why some failed to answer the summons. Approximately 10 per cent in each jurisdiction (a somewhat higher proportion in Detroit—14 per cent) answered the query about why they did not appear by saying that there was no particular reason or that they simply forgot.

[12] See, for example, the testimony of Judge Gittelson, the former administrator of the New York City Civil Court, before the New York State Senate Committee on Codes, which held hearings on garnishment laws, July 10, 1969.

Although the types of reasons reviewed so far show some intercity variation, they do not shed much light on New York's very poor record for appearances. But the last two categories of Table 11.7 provide one clue to that city's poor record. Fifteen per cent of the New York debtors, a substantially higher proportion than in the other two cities, told us that they did not know that they were supposed to appear in court, that, in short, they did not understand the meaning of the summons. Moreover, four per cent of the "no show" New York cases reported that they were *afraid* to appear in court. This figure takes on significance only when compared with the rate of such fear in the other cities—one per cent. These two categories of reasons conjure up the debtor who is confused by the intricacies of urban life, the new migrant from a more traditionalistic culture. In New York, such persons are apt to be Puerto Ricans who suffer a language barrier. That some New York debtors did not know that they were supposed to appear in court might be explained by their inability to read the summons which, until very recently, was printed only in English. The last two categories account for about a fifth of the reasons for nonappearance in New York, a rate much higher than in the other cities. But the ignorance-fear-confusion hypothesis explains only part of the "no show" phenomenon in New York. It is most appropriate for the Puerto Rican debtors but they constitute only a quarter of the sample and obviously not all of them were unassimilated newcomers.

More significant reasons for the failure of New York debtors to respond are not revealed by their volunteered explanations. Among these is the widespread abuse of the rules of venue. Unlike the other three cities in our sample, New York encompasses five counties, each of which has its own branch of the city's civil court in which these actions are brought. In Chicago and Detroit, the chances are quite high that both the debtor and the creditor reside within the jurisdiction of the court. This is not so in New York. Although we sampled cases only from the New York County Court, the county corresponding to Manhattan, only 25 per cent of the New York debtors lived in Manhattan. The rest lived in the other boroughs or outside the city. (Some 22 New York debtors, seven per cent of the sample, lived outside the city limits.) The venue rule permits actions to be brought either in the county of the defendant's residence or in that of the plaintiff. This rule is biased against the debtor, for in many instances the sale takes place at the debtor's home, although the creditor is located in a distant borough or outside the city. In such cases, it is permissible for the creditors to bring the suit in the counties where their businesses are located even though the debtors may never have been there.[13] Although all the suits were brought in Manhattan's court, only 55 per cent of the plaintiffs were located in Manhattan. Cases in which *either* the defendant or the plaintiff resided in Manhattan came to 66 per cent of the sample, leaving some 34 per cent in which the overly generous rule of venue was clearly violated. The callous nature of this system is captured in the reply of Brand Jeweler's attorney to a reporter who asked him why he files the cases of this Brooklyn firm, whose customers reside for the most part in Brooklyn, in the Manhattan court: "Because that's the court nearest to my office."[14]

Thus the victims of Brand Jeweler's confidence game are sued in the Manhattan court because Brand Jeweler happens to employ a Manhattan attorney. Perhaps another reason is that the attorney knows that this will make it more difficult for the defendant to respond to the summons.

That fully three-quarters of the New York debtors did not live in the same borough in which they were being sued would appear to be a factor in the failure of all but a handful to answer the summons, although virtually none of the debtors offered as a reason for their nonappearance their not knowing where the court was located, how to get to it, or the trip being too difficult.

A comparison of the summonses used in Chicago, Detroit and New York calls attention to yet another possible reason for the failure of New York debtors to respond. In both language and type face, the New York summons is much more difficult to understand than those used in Chicago and Detroit. In both of these cities, key parts of the summons appear in large bold face type, set off from other parts, whereas in New York, the essential points are lost in legal verbiage. Moreover, in both Chicago and Detroit, the time for responses is the same whether personal or substitute service was made and therefore there is no ambiguity as to when the debtor should respond. In contrast, the New York summons tries to explain the difference in response time according to method of service.

These differences become obvious when we consider the actual language that appears on the summonses. In all three cities, the summonses are headed by the name of the court in which they are issued, followed by the names and addresses of the plaintiff, defendant, and plaintiff's attorney, the date at which the summons was issued or served and in Chicago and Detroit, the signature of the court clerk. (This does not appear on

---

[13] For example, we once interviewed a Harlem woman who bought a deep freezer from a door-to-door salesman employed by a firm in New Rochelle. She received a summons informing her to appear at the Westchester County Court, a summons that did not even indicate the city in which this court was located.

[14] See Craig Karpel, "Ghetto Fraud on the Installment Plan," in New York Magazine, May 26th and June 2nd, 1969.

the New York summons because service of summons is not a court responsibility in New York.) For present purposes, the critical parts of these summonses are their communications addressed to the defendants. In Chicago, the language of the summons differed according to whether the suit was an open one or one based on a confession of judgment contract. Since the Chicago sample was based exclusively on the confirmation of judgment book, the appropriate summons is the one served on debtors who had signed confession of judgment contracts. This document contains the following message for the defendant:

To each defendant:

YOU ARE SUMMONED and required either:

1. To appear in person in the office of the Clerk of this Court in Room No. 602 in the Chicago Civic Center, Chicago, Illinois, at 2 o'clock P.M., on ———, 19—, and file your appearance in writing with the clerk of said Court, or

2. To cause your appearance in writing to be filed in said action by yourself or attorney.

IF YOU DO NOT APPEAR OR CAUSE YOUR APPEARANCE TO BE FILED, THE JUDGMENT BY CONFESSION FOR $——— AND COSTS ENTERED AGAINST YOU ON ———, 19—, MAY BE CONFIRMED.

It should be noted that in this summons for a confirmation of judgment the debtor is provided with a date (and even a particular hour) when he must appear in order to challenge the judgment. The penalty for not appearing is communicated to the debtor in large bold face type set off from the rest of the message. The message to the defendant on the Detroit summons also appears in large bold face type.

NOTICE TO THE DEFENDANT

IF YOU CARE TO CONTEST THIS CASE, YOU OR AN ATTORNEY OF YOUR CHOICE MUST APPEAR AND FILE A PLEA OR ANSWER IN THE CLERK'S OFFICE, ROOM 1101, CITY COUNTY BUILDING, WITHIN FIFTEEN (15) DAYS AFTER DATE OF SERVICE OF THIS SUMMONS UPON YOU. IF YOU DO NOT, THE PLAINTIFF CAN TAKE JUDGMENT AGAINST YOU FOR THE AMOUNT CLAIMED IN THE ATTACHED STATEMENT.

This message to the defendant is even clearer than that in the Chicago summons for the Detroit debtor is not confused by options. Like the Chicago summons, the critical information appears in large bold face type.

In contrast, the messages directed to the defendant in the New York summons read as follows:

YOU ARE HEREBY SUMMONED to appear in the Civil Court of the City of New York, County of New York, at the office of the Clerk of the said court at 111 Centre Street in the County of New York, City and State of New York, within the time period provided by law as noted below to make answer to the complaint which is annexed hereto; upon your failure to answer, judgment will be taken against you for the relief demanded in the complaint, together with the costs of this action.

Dated, New York, N.Y. ——— 19—
Plaintiff's Address

[Name and Address of
Plaintiff's Attorney]

NOTE: The law provides that:

(a) If this summons is served by its delivery to you personally within the City of New York, you must appear and answer within TEN days after such service; or

    (b) If this summons is served by delivery to any person other than you personally, or is served outside the City of New York, *or by publication, or by any means other than personal delivery to you within the City of New York,* you are allowed THIRTY days after the proof of service thereof is filed with the Clerk of this Court within which to appear and answer.

The communications to the debtor-defendant in this summons are contained in but three sentences or parts, the first of which contains 91 words, the second, about personal service, 29 words, and the third, about substitute service, 67 words. (Actually the second and third constitute a single sentence.) The long first sentence contains three messages: first, it tells the debtor that he is being summoned to court; second, it tells him the address of the court; and third it tells him that if he fails to appear, he will be subjected to a default judgment for the "relief demanded in the complaint." Unlike the summonses in Chicago and Detroit, these vital messages all appear in the same lower case type face of a single sentence. It talks about "the time period provided by law as noted below," about the complaint "which is annexed hereto" and about "relief demanded in the complaint together with the costs of this action." A summons so designed is hardly apt to communicate with the typical debtor who tends to be rather poorly educated; moreover, it falls far short of the clarity of the summonses in the other two cities.

    One further irony of the New York summons should be noted. Its cumbersome language notwithstanding, it does try to tell the debtor who received substitute service that he has up to 30 days in which to respond, whereas those served personally must respond within 10 days. But we know that New York process

servers almost always *claim* personal service, when in fact, only about a fifth of those served at all are served personally. Thus if the typical New York debtor *could* understand the abstruse language of the summons and made his appearance *after* the tenth day, he would more than likely find that he was the victim of a default judgment. Without the assistance of an attorney, there is little that the debtor can do to rectify such an injustice, for it is a matter of his word against that of the process server. Although New York law attempts to give greater protection to the debtor not served personally, it actually has the opposite effect. It encourages such a defendant to respond too late to protect his rights in the law suit.

    Apart from the reasons which the debtors themselves offered for their nonappearance, we have identified two "structural" factors that might account for the poor showing of the New York judicial system, the venue issue and the complicated, hard to understand summons form.[15] To these, we may add a third, the *location* of the court house. The Chicago summons directs the debtor to a particular room in a particular building, the Chicago Civic Center, in downtown Chicago. This building has become such a landmark and its location is so central to the city, that there is hardly a Chicago resident not familiar with it. The Court

[15] The contrast between what we have called "structural" reasons and the reasons that the debtors themselves offered for their nonappearance calls attention to a methodological dispute that still remains unresolved. The historians of methodology in the social sciences might well note this discussion for it concerns the relative merits of "reason analysis" in which the researcher allows the actors to explain their behavior in terms of an exhaustive scheme of *possible* reasons provided by the researcher and "correctional analysis" in which the researcher *infers* causes of social phenomena through his statistical manipulations of the data. For a discussion of this debate and a less than satisfactory resolution, see Harry Kalven and Hans Zeisel, The American Jury (Boston: Little and Brown, 1966), ch. 7.

of Common Pleas in Detroit is also located in the center of the downtown section of the city. But this is *not* true of the Civil Court of the City of New York, County of New York (Manhattan). The New York summons provides an address: 111 Centre Street. This address is some three miles from the center of New York's downtown section, Times Square. The numerical grid system in Manhattan makes it quite easy for a stranger to get around most sections. But the courthouses of Manhattan as well as City Hall are located in the old section of the city, the very tip of lower Manhattan where the streets have names rather than numbers. This part of New York is well known to the vast numbers of middle class persons who work on Wall Street, or in the city's large banks or for local government. But the average Harlem or Bedford-Stuyvesant or East Bronx resident rarely, if ever, has occasion to visit this area. In fact, he is likely to know it only if he has had brushes with the law, for this is where the criminal courts are located. For the typical resident of a low-income neighborhood in New York, 111 Centre Street is not only a mysterious address, but it is far removed from the debtor's residence. Although we have no way of proving it, for we did not ask the New York debtors if they knew where 111 Centre Street is, it would seem that the remote location of the New York courthouse is another important reason for the low answer rate in that city.

A Postscript on New York

In the opening chapter we noted that this study provides a photograph of the consumer credit system and its breakdowns as of 1967. The system has been changing at an ever increasing rate. Thus the procedural rules in effect in 1967 were modified in certain respects by the fall of 1970. Oddly enough, the findings of this research have played some role in the procedural changes that have

been instituted. Some of the findings of this chapter have been presented in public speeches, in testimony before legislative bodies and in informal gatherings of consumer advocates. The finding on the violation of venue reached the ears of the recently appointed Administrative Judge of the Civil Court, Edward Thompson. He is concerned about the rights of debtors and in the spring of 1970 he called a meeting of the leading collection lawyers and announced to them that henceforth they must file their suits in the county where either the plaintiff or the defendant resides, a ruling that went into effect in mid-June of 1970. During the first week, some 1200 summonses were rejected because of violation of venue.[16] In the second week, about 500 summonses were rejected on this ground, and each succeeding week has seen fewer and fewer violations, with the result that by mid-September, 1970, only about 50 summonses in all five counties were rejected because of improper venue.

It would be misleading, however, to imply that a system can be so easily changed, in this instance by the edict of an administrative judge. Those who have fought for social reform know that battles are not so readily won, and the sociological functionalists know that social systems tend to follow some law of inertia. And so may be the case with the venue reform instituted by Judge Thompson. At this writing, in the fall of 1970, Judge Thompson is being sued by the association of collection lawyers who claim that the judge has no right to interpret venue in so strict a fashion and in doing so, he is, in essence, making law, a function of the state legislature.

Another change in New York procedure takes cognizance of the large proportion of Spanish-speaking defendants in these actions. A new state law that

---

16 In New York, the action commences with the filing of the affidavit of service of process.

went into effect September 1, 1970, requires all summonses in consumer credit suits to be printed in both Spanish and English. Still another recent procedural change requires the plaintiff to send notification of a default judgment to the defendant at least seven days before the default judgment can be claimed.[17] In instances of personal service this has the effect of raising the time for claiming default judgments from ten to seventeen days and in instances of substitute service, the minimum period for the default judgment is raised from 30 to 37 days. The purpose of this notification process is to offset the widely publicized scandal of sewer service. The theory is that the debtor with a valid defense who was not served will now have an opportunity to appear in court and challenge the judgment.

Even when those opposed to reforms designed to protect the consumer fail to have them rescinded, it is not clear that the reforms have any real impact on the system. Thus the venue ruling has been in effect for three months but the clerks of the Manhattan court are not aware of any increase in the response rate. The Spanish language summons is only one month old, but again the clerks are not aware of a sudden increase in Puerto Rican defendants making appearances. Finally, the notice of default judgment, which has been law for several years, has not led to any rash of reopened judgments. In the concluding chapter we shall consider the issue of when reforms are meaningful and when they are not, but it may be noted now that modifications made to improve the system may have no impact.

* * *

[17] This can be done by regular mail. The plaintiff must file some proof that he mailed this notice, usually a certificate of mailing that can be purchased at the post office for five cents or so.

The Legal Outcome of the Case: The Rarity of Trials

We have seen that some five per cent of the Chicago, Detroit and New York debtors filed answers with the court (all but two of these debtors being located in Chicago or Detroit). One might assume that at least these people had their "day in court" in the sense that their case was heard by a judge. But those familiar with legal process know that filing an answer in itself is no guarantee of a trial. Answers filed by debtors, especially by those without legal counsel, tend to be easily challenged by the plaintiff's attorney. He is likely to apply for a summary judgment based on the debtor's faulty answer. (It will be recalled that the plaintiff's attorney is always notified of the defendant's answer and is given an opportunity to study it before the trial date.) Faulty answers are quite common, given the holder-in-due course doctrine. Debtors may file answers based on the breach of expressed or implied warranties on the part of the seller, but this defense has no bearing on a law suit brought by the holder-in-due course. In short, filing an answer is a much broader concept than "having a day in court" in which a judge makes a determination based on the merits of the case. As we shall see, this meaning of a "day in court" rarely occurs in consumer actions, even though a substantial minority of debtors had valid defenses and a number did file answers.

All debtors, regardless of whether they said they received a summons or responded to one, were asked whether their case "ever came to trial before a judge." The respondents clearly had difficulty with this seemingly straightforward factual question. If there is reason to suspect some exaggeration with respect to the question of answering the summons or filing an answer, there is even more reason to doubt the validity of the debtor's response to the question about a trial.

Some 14 per cent of *all* Chicago debtors *claimed* that their case was tried before a judge. In Detroit, six per cent of all the debtors made this claim and in New York, only one per cent (three debtors) did. But closer examination of these cases indicates that the debtors had little understanding of what is meant by a trial and in fact hardly any of them did have trials. For example, in Chicago, 44 debtors said that their case had gone to trial but 26 of these cases were stamped "ex parte judgment confirmed," meaning that the debtor had not shown up on the due date and that he was the victim of a default judgment. Of the remaining 18 cases in which the debtor had made an appearance by the due date, almost all did *not* come to trial according to the court records. An examination of the questionnaires in these Chicago cases in which the debtor *thought* his case came to trial uncovered a number of reasons for the debtor's confusion. Thirteen had filed for bankruptcy and they apparently had their bankruptcy proceeding in mind when asked about a trial. Another 20 of these Chicago debtors *assumed* that a trial must have occurred because they received notice of a judgment against them, incorrectly believing that a judgment can result only from the deliberations of a court. Since they learned of a judgment against them, they presumed that a trial must have occured in their absence. Of the remaining 11 cases in which Chicago debtors claimed a trial took place, no ready explanation could be found for this belief in nine of them, and in only two cases did the court record confirm that a trial had occurred. The check of the court records revealed that there actually were seven trials in the Chicago sample, although in five of the cases the debtor did not know that a trial had occurred. But all five of these debtors had retained lawyers and it is quite posisble that their lawyers represented them in court in their absence. The creditor won in four of these trials and the debtor won in three suggesting that if more debtors were to have had their cases heard by a judge the rate of outcomes favorable to them would increase.

The Detroit picture is similar. In that city, 28 of the 438 debtors claimed that a trial had occurred. In five of these cases the debtor confused a bankruptcy proceeding with a trial of the merits of the creditor's suit and in at least five cases, the debtor assumed that the judgment against him meant that a trial had occurred. A check of the court records indicated that in only a few of these cases did the defendant actually appear before a judge. Thus, 20 of these 28 cases were recorded as default judgments; in three cases the action against the defendant was dismissed because the plaintiff failed to appear at the trial and two cases were dismissed on other grounds.[18]

In New York, the picture is even more strange. Three debtors *claimed* that their case had either come to trial or was scheduled for trial. A check of the docket books some three years later showed that three New York cases had been scheduled for trial.[19] But in only one instance did these cases overlap and there is no evidence that the trial actually took place since no judgment has been entered in the docket book. Such evidence is also lacking for the other two cases which, according to the docket book, were set for trial. A check of the questionnaires in these two instances shows that these debtors worked out a settlement with the creditor and knew nothing about a trial.

[18] The files were missing in three of these cases and we were unable to determine the outcome.

[19] It will be recalled that only one of the New York debtors who responded to the summons filed an answer. That three New York cases were scheduled for trial suggests that a few debtors managed to file answers even though they did not initially respond to the summons.

Of the two New Yorkers who incorrectly claimed that their case had gone to trial, one was apparently referring to a bankruptcy proceeding and the other was the victim of a default judgment. Perhaps, he, like some of the debtors in the other cities, assumed that a judgment meant that a trial had occurred. In short, after consulting a court clerk who checked a book recording trials, we can report that *no* trials occurred in the sample of New York debtors.

As all this makes amply clear, hardly any debtor-defendants appeared before judges in our three sample cities. As far as we can tell from the court records, none of the 332 New York debtor-defendants had a trial; in Detroit, only a handful, as few as three and as many as 11 *may* have had an appearance before a judge, a group which includes cases in which either the plaintiff did not show up or the action was dismissed "with prejudice" meaning that the defendant could not again be sued on the same grounds. But even among this handful of Detroit debtors whose cases resulted in favorable outcomes, there is no evidence that a trial actually took place. It is quite possible that of the more than 1000 Chicago, Detroit and New York debtors interviewed, only seven, all in Chicago, actually had their cases tried before a judge. These figures underscore the vast discrepancy between the *appearance* of judicial outcomes and their reality. Courts render judgments in consumer actions even though a judge is rarely called upon to decide the relative merits of the plaintiff's and defendant's case. The concept of "judgment" is largely a facade for routinized bureaucratic procedures that have nothing to do with the actions of officials known as "judges." [20] The accusation that the courts operate merely as collection agencies for creditors irrespective of the debtor-defendants' defenses finds much merit in these findings.

Remaining to be considered is an examination of the outcomes of these law suits according to the court records. It is widely suspected that the overwhelming majority of these actions result in default judgments. The data on hand bear this out. In each of the three cities, at least nine out of every ten of these cases ended in a default judgment, as can be seen from Table 11.10.[21]

[20] A crude parallel might be found in the criminal law where the great majority of the cases result in negotiated pleas rather than trials. In the criminal area the presumption has been that virtually all of those who "cop a plea" are indeed guilty and are benefitting from the tradeoff. A careful study of the criminal process might well disclose that this presumption is as fallacious as the view that the debtors who never have their day in court are indeed at fault. Our data have shown that this assumption is not valid for a substantial minority of debtors. Were they to have had adequate legal representation and trials, they would have escaped the judgments against them. A comparable study in the criminal field might also disclose that the bargained plea covers up considerable injustices to defendants.

[21] Excluded from this table are the 38 replevin actions in Detroit and the four Detroit cases in which service was not made. It may be noted that in replevin cases the debtor is served with a writ at the time of the repossession informing him that he has up to 14 days in which to challenge the plaintiff's claim to the goods. If he does not exercise this right, then a default judgment is entered against him. In only one of the 38 replevin actions in Detroit did the debtor show up in court to challenge the repossession and his motion to quash the replevin was denied by the judge. Thus had we counted the replevin cases in Detroit, some 37 default judgments out of a possible 38 would have been added to the total, bringing default judgments in Detroit, slightly above those in other cities.

TABLE 11.10

Legal Outcome of Case According to Court Records in Each City

	Chicago	Detroit	New York
A. Default Judgments	91%	91%	92%
B. Other Outcomes, Favorable to the Plaintiff			
Case dismissed-discontinued because creditor satisfied	4	5	2
Trial: creditor won	1	---	---
No judgment (but questionnaire indicates settlement)	---	---	5
C. Outcome Probably Favorable to Defendant			
Trial: debtor won	1	---	---
Action dismissed because of debtor's bankruptcy	1	☆	☆
Action dismissed because: a) neither party appears b) plaintiff fails to appear or c) dismissed with prejudice	---	4	---
Answer filed by defendant, no further action	1	---	---
Judgment vacated against one of the spouses in initial suit	1	---	---
	100%	100%	99%
N ☆	(308)	(387)	(328)

☆ A few cases in each city are omitted from this tally because the forms containing their court identification numbers were lost in the course of data processing and we were thus unable to check their legal outcome some three years later when all the court records were re-examined.

———◆———

Table 11.10 is divided into three parts. The first, which accounts for at least 90 per cent of the outcomes in each city, refers to default judgments, judgments automatically awarded to the plaintiff regardless of the merits of the case because the defendant failed to appear. The second part of the table shows the outcomes that were favorable to the plaintiff even though they did not involve default judgments and the third part shows the frequency of outcomes favorable to defendants or at least outcomes in which the debtor did not have to pay.

In Chicago and New York almost all of the non-default judgment cases represented settlements favorable to the creditor, whereas in Detroit, the nine per cent that were not default judgments were more evenly split between outcomes favorable to the plaintiff and those favorable to the defendant (five per cent vs. four per cent). One sign of the inefficiency of the New York system is that in eighteen cases (five per cent) there was no indication in the court record of any outcome. A check of the questionnaires showed that these debtors had worked out settlements with their creditors and we include them in the second part of the table for this reason. (Apparently, the plaintiff's lawyer in these cases did not notify the court of the outcome nor did the court request this information from him.) When the results in all three cities are combined, the debtor-defendant turns out to be the winner in only three per cent of the cases. This figure must be judged against the 19 per cent who claimed fraud as a reason for not paying and an additional eight per cent who cited payment misunderstandings. As noted, the laws regarding warranty, misrepresentation, type face on contracts and other facets of the transaction are such that many more than the quarter of these debtors who insisted that they were not at fault would undoubtedly have been successfully defended had they the benefit of legal counsel and a trial. The fact that the legal actions against the debtors in our sample resulted in creditor victories in all but three per cent of the cases (91 per cent being default judgments and another six per cent cases in which the creditor was sufficiently successful in exacting payments from the debtor that he either moved to dismiss the case or did not claim a judgment) is strong support for the notion that the courts act as collection agencies rather than judicial bodies in the field of consumer credit.

Note on the Debtor in Court

Your editor's personal experience with low-income consumers suggests two additional reasons why few defendants—even those who actually receive a summons—appear. For one thing, many are utterly alienated from the legal system, and regard the court with as much hostility as they regard their creditor; both are perceived as components of an oppressive system. The debtor fights against that system by refusing to play by its rules, by not cooperating; he defaults. Also, the summons is often the fifteenth or twentieth dun that the debtor has received from the creditor; he has successfully ignored the previous nineteen, and may assume that nothing terrible will happen to him if he ignores this one, either.

As the Caplovitz study shows, between 92% and 97% of defendants lose by default. But what of the three or four percent who enter an appearance? They almost never have trials, for Caplovitz' study of more than a thousand cases revealed only eight trials, all of them in Chicago.

These debtors may be divided into two categories: the small minority who have counsel, and the great majority who do not. A small proportion of consumer credit defendants are aware of the existence of Legal Aid or Legal Services Programs, so that lawyers for the poor are occasionally asked to represent them. However, many such defendants are turned away by legal aid programs, because consumer credit debtors tend to be wage-earners (that is how they obtained credit), even if marginally so, who earn slightly more than the eligibility limits of the programs (which are usually approximately $3500 or $4000 plus $500 per dependant). Some programs turn away eligible debtors because they are too overwhelmed by urgent eviction, welfare and family law cases to accept consumer problems. Many legal services lawyers also shy away from consumer cases because they may require time-consuming analysis of unfamiliar commercial law. And private attorneys frequently charge a minimum of between $50 and $200 for an initial interview and the opening of a file.

However, if the debtor does obtain the services of an attorney, he will quickly be able to obtain a highly favorable settlement. The attorney will call the creditor's lawyer and threaten to defend the action and insist on a trial. The creditor cannot afford a trial; producing witnesses to testify to the sale, delivery and non-payment, even if no complex legal questions are involved, will cost more than the amount of the claim. Collection lawyers make money for themselves and their clients on one thing alone: *volume*. They can well afford to write off those few cases in which debtors appear by counsel, while obtaining default judgments in 92% of the cases and settling most of the balance on terms favorable to them.

If the debtor does not have counsel, he faces the various obstacles discussed by Caplovitz which stand between him and answering the summons, and he can be subjected to discovery and a wide variety of motions, such as motions challenging his answer and a motion for summary judgment. Most defendants appearing *pro se* will be perplexed by the arrival, in the mail, of these technically worded motions, but if they ignore them, they will lose their cases. To answer these motions they will have to compose written papers and file them in the right place, which is nearly impossible for a layman to do, or appear personally (losing a day's work) to argue their side on the day that the court is hearing motions.

Should the unrepresented debtor withstand all of the motions directed at him, and be present on the day his trial is scheduled, he has only to insist on a trial to stand an excellent chance of winning his case. He may have numerous defenses, but even if he has none, he is likely to win at trial because the creditor will withdraw at that point, finding it not worth his while, economically, to produce witnesses as to sale, delivery and non-payment in order to prove his case. But if the trial is scheduled in a high-volume urban court (the Civil Court of the City of New York entertains half a million actions a year, twenty-five hundred a day), the debtor may face severe pressure from the judge to settle with his creditor's attorney in the corridor, rather than insisting on a trial. In such courts, "dispositions" of cases is a crucial measure of a judge's effectiveness; the judge may be required to file monthly reports with administrative judges indicating how many cases he disposed of. Trials, which substantially reduce his rate of disposition, will reveal the judge to be less efficient than his colleagues who "knock heads together." Thus many debtors who do answer *pro se*—a majority of them, according to some observers of the process—are forced by the judges into rushed negotiations with the creditor's attorney in a courtroom corridor. They are never told that the attorney did not bring his witnesses with him to court, making a victory for the defendant likely if only he refuses to settle.

Consider the awesome system we have created: on relatively small claims (up to $1000), the creditor cannot afford to sue, and the debtor cannot afford to defend. For both of them, the dispute-resolution mechanism is too costly to invoke, relative to what they perceive is at stake in the creditor's claim. In such a situation, the creditor should always lose, because, theoretically, as the plaintiff, he bears the burden of going forward.

But in fact, the debtor almost always loses, for three reasons:

(1) The creditor can afford to *say*, formally, that he is going to litigate the case fully. He does this by serving and filing a summons and complaint, which costs him less than ten dollars. By contrast, for reasons both economic and psychological, at least 92% of debtors do not *say* (by filing an answer) that they are going to defend, and in our legal system, if you don't say what you are going to do, you lose by default.

(2) Those debtors who do answer encounter another version of the inequality of economic power. For five or ten dollars, the creditor's attorney can prepare and mail to the debtor motion papers or interrogatories, which few low-income consumers are prepared to cope with on their own. If they try, they usually have to spend one or more days in court, conferring with the clerk and appearing to resist or respond to the motion. Each time, they have to miss work.

(3) The *pro se* debtors who withstand the motions may still lose because the judges may have a stake in encouraging settlements rather than trials, and the unrepresented consumer is at an obvious disadvantage both of information and of bargaining power when he negotiates with an attorney.

Of course, it is just those retailers who sell to the poor who most frequently invoke the assistance of this system.

**FTC, ECONOMIC REPORT ON IN-
STALLMENT CREDIT AND RE-
TAIL SALES PRACTICES OF
DISTRICT OF COLUMBIA RE-
TAILERS 33–34 (1968)**

JUDGMENTS, GARNISHMENTS, AND REPOSSESSIONS BY RETAILERS

When an account under an installment sales contract becomes delinquent, the holder of that contract can proceed to collect by several legal means. A judgment can be obtained that will permit repossession of the merchandise or garnishment of the wages of the purchaser.[6] If the retailer has assigned the contract *without* recourse, the finance company or bank takes the risk of loss and proceeds to exercise its legal rights. Consequently, retailers are not involved in the collection process if they assign without recourse. If a delinquent account comes back to the retailer who has assigned *with* recourse or if an account originally financed by the retailer himself becomes delinquent, the retailer does not become involved in legal processes if he turns the account over to a collection agency. For these reasons, many retailers in this survey had no records on this volume of judgments, garnishments, or repossessions.

Eleven low-income market retailers obtained 2,690 judgments in 1966. Their legal actions resulted in 1,568 garnishments and 306 repossessions (table III–9). In contrast, general market retailers reported very few judgments. The 8 furniture and home-furnishings stores providing such data reported only 70 judgments for the year 1966. Low-income market retailers obtained almost that number of judgments in an average *week*. One large department store, whose 1966 sales far exceeded the total for the entire low-income market group, reported only 29 judgments.

TABLE III–9.—JUDGMENTS, GARNISHMENTS, AND REPOSSESSIONS ON DELINQUENT
INSTALLMENT CONTRACTS REPORTED BY DISTRICT OF
COLUMBIA RETAILERS, 1966

Type of retailers	Number of retailers reporting	Total judgments	Judgments resulting in:	
			Garnishments	Repossessions
Low-income market retailers	11	2,690	1,568	306
General market retailers:				
Appliance, radio, and television retailers	3			3
Furniture and home-furnishings retailers	8	70	26	13
Department stores	1	29	9	
Total	23	2,789	1,603	322

Source: FTC Survey.

To gain additional perspective on the extent to which the courts are being used as a collection agency, the number of suits

[6] Repossession can be accomplished without court action by the holder of the installment conditional sales contract. In such instances, if the proceeds of a public sale of the repossessed item does not cover the unpaid balance plus fees, the holder can still sue on the contract and get a judgment for the deficiency.

filed in 1966 by the surveyed retailers in their own names was determined from the records of the District of Columbia Court of General Sessions. These suits included actions for collection of 30-day, revolving credit, and installment contract accounts. They did *not* include suits filed by collection agencies as assignees of retailers' accounts. During 1966, the 18 low-income market retailers in this study filed 3,030 suits, the equivalent of one suit for every $2,599 of their net sales. Among the general market retailers in the sample, 22 appliance stores filed 53 suits; 22 furniture stores, 207; and 3 department stores, 356 (table III–10). All together, there were only 616 suits filed by the 47 general market retailers, which averaged one suit for every $232,299 of their net sales.

An additional unknown number of suits involving default on merchandise credit sales was filed by collection agencies. Various retailers may prefer to assign delinquent paper to a collection agency. This shifts the responsibility for obtaining legal assistance and minimizes whatever risk of bad publicity credit suits might incur.

TABLE III–10.—DEBT SUITS FILED IN THE DISTRICT OF COLUMBIA BY LOW-INCOME MARKET AND GENERAL MARKET RETAILERS, 1966

Type of retailers	Number of suits filed	Number of retailers	Net Sales 1966 ($000)	Net Sales per debt suit
Total sample of low-income market and general market retailers	3,646	65	$150,970	$41,406
Low-income market retailers	3,030	18	7,874	2,599
General market retailers:	616	47	143,096	232,299
Appliance, radio, and television	53	22	25,089	473,377
Furniture and home-furnishings	207	22	26,643	128,710
Department stores	356	3	91,364	256,840

Source: District of Columbia Court of General Sessions, Debt Suit Files; FTC Survey.

Nevertheless, it is clear that general market retailers resort to the courts, either directly or indirectly, much less frequently than do low-income market retailers. If the 47 general market retailers had obtained judgments at the same rate as did the low-income market retailers, a very large number of court cases would have occurred. Instead of the 616 judgments which they actually obtained, general market retailers would have had a total of 55,000 judgments if they had filed one suit for every $2,599 in sales, as did the low-income market retailers (table III–10). In fact, the total number of suits in 1966 involving claims of $10,000 or less was 49,000, only a part of which were claims for payment for merchandise purchases. The latter figure involved claims for a multitude of causes: auto accidents, small loan defaults, failure to pay utility bills and the like. Clearly, a number of low-income market retailers have come to view the courts as an inte-

gral part of their credit-collection system and in so doing have put a heavy burden on our legal system.

Questions

1. Would it be desirable to require that plaintiffs in consumer credit cases attach to their summonses a list of all legal aid and legal services offices in town, and advise the defendant to seek help from them? Such a proposal has been made by the Consumer Affairs Committee of the Association of the Bar of the City of New York, after two years of discussion, but at this writing it has received little enthusiasm from legal services groups and negative reaction from the court system. Would any substantial increase in the number of consumer defendants who seek legal services paralyze neighborhod law offices? Would any substantial increase in the number of consumer defendants filing answers and insisting on trials paralyze the courts? If

so, can it be defended on a theory analogous to the thesis that overloading the welfare system with eligible clients will cause a crisis leading, after a period of hardship, to an improved system? See Cloward and Piven, A Strategy to End Poverty, The Nation, May 2, 1966, at 510.

2. Should consumer credit litigants be required to discuss their dispute informally before any trial? See Leff, "Ignorance, Injury and Spite: The Dynamics of Coercive Collection", 80 Yale L.J. 1 (1970).

3. Much of the advantage which the litigation system gives to creditors results from the economies of scale that creditors' attorneys achieve. By virtue of their specialization in collection work and their high volume, they are able to process hundreds of cases a week in essentially the same way, at a relatively low unit cost. No parallel system keeps the costs down for debtor-litigants; even legal aid services are not specialized in the sense of having lawyers who do nothing but consumer cases on a mass basis. But suppose that a few young lawyers sought a foundation grant to establish a legal services organization to specialize in the representation of consumer debtors, using printed forms as often as possible to minimize costs. How many attorneys would it need per ten thousand cases filed by creditors? How would it make its presence known to its potential clients? Could it consult court records of summonses filed, and send form letters to the defendants offering free representation? See American Bar Assn., Code of Professional Responsibility, Disciplinary Rule No. DR 2–101. Could it put up posters in the slums, advertising its services? See unpublished opinion, Report of the Committee on Legal Ethics and Grievances of the Bar Associaton of the District of Columbia in the Matter of Advertising conducted by Monroe H. Freedman and the Stern Community Law Firm, March 10, 1972.

Would State Bar Associations resist the establishment of such a service? What would be the likely sources of support and opposition?

Execution of Judgment

After he has lost a suit, whether by default or otherwise, the consumer can be forced to pay in any of a variety of ways. His bank account may be attached, his real or personal property seized, and his salary garnished. (If sewer service has occurred, the consumer's first notice that he has been sued may be an attachment or garnishment.)

Except in Pennsylvania, which, with Texas, does not permit wage garnishment, attachment of the judgment debtors' homes to satisfy debts arising from the purchase of consumer goods is relatively rare, though the home-owning consumer who has no attachable salary may have to worry about this potential remedy because homestead exemptions are relatively low. See, e. g., Vernon's Mo. Stats.Ann., tit. 35, § 513, 475 (1952) ($1500 to $3000 home); Ga.Code Ann., § 51–1301 (1965) ($200 to $500 home). Attachment of personalty, and particularly of salaries, is the normal, and for most creditors, the least expensive means of enforcing a judgment.

GANNON, "SEIZING PAY," FROM THE WALL STREET JOURNAL, REPRINTED IN HOUSE OF REPRESENTATIVES, SUBCOMMITTEE ON CONSUMER AFFAIRS, HEARINGS ON CONSUMER CREDIT PROTECTION ACT 765–66 (1967)

SEIZING PAY—UNIONS, FIRMS, LAWYERS SEEK TO CURB GARNISHING AS ITS INCIDENCE RISES—IT LEADS TO BANKRUPTCY, FIRING

AND RELIEF ROLLS, THEY SAY;
AUTO WORKER KILLS HIMSELF—
DEDUCTING $500,000 AT INLAND

(By James P. Gannon, Staff Reporter of The Wall Street Journal)

CHICAGO.—One payday in January, auto worker Carl W. Clark discovered his entire week's take-home pay of $112.39 had been turned over to the state of Indiana for delinquent state income taxes. Beset by debts, he asked officials at Ford Motor Co.'s plant in suburban Chicago Heights, Ill., for his accrued vacation pay to tide him over.

Next payday, he learned Indiana—the state where he used to live—had received $208.84 out of his $363.93 in wages and vacation pay. The 24-year-old father of a young boy, not knowing how much he owed Indiana tax collectors, (the two deductions actually satisfied the claim) became despondent over the pay loss. Two days later, Carl Clark placed a .22 calibre rifle under his chin and shot a bullet into his brain.

This suicide has spurred anew wide-ranging inquiries into the consequences of consumer debt problems. Under special scrutiny is the rising number of wage garnishments and other forms of pay seizure by creditors, including state and Federal tax collectors. The spotlight on pay attachment also has illuminated a misery-multiplying debtor's course that runs from garnishment and loss of job to bankruptcy and going on relief.

The activity on pay-seizure problems is intensifying on several fronts. Labor unions are campaigning to restrict wage garnishment laws in many states. Legal experts are drafting a uniform consumer credit code that they hope will be enacted in each state. An Illinois Congressman is seeking legislation limiting the amount of wages than can be taken at one time to pay back taxes. And business and financial interests, anxious to avoid any image-blackening, are accelerating joint efforts to aid over-burdened debtors.

BUY NOW, PAY LATER

The cause of the wage-attachment problem is overuse of credit, easy to find in America's debt-fueled economy. Consumer debt outstanding rose to $86 billion in 1965, up 12% from 1964 and 50% from 1961. A convenience to most people, readily available credit is a curse to many others, who can't or won't use it wisely. They're the ones facing garnishment troubles.

Because wage garnishments are issued by thousands of local courts, there aren't any national statistics on their volume. But checks of big courts in some metropolitan areas indicate more and more workers are finding part of their wages confiscated to pay overdue debts.

In Chicago, the Cook County Circuit Court issued 84,513 garnishments last year, 15% more than in 1964 and 72% more than in 1961. The marshal of the municipal courts of Los Angeles County served 114,972 wage garnishments in the fiscal year ended last June 30, up 6% from the prior year, and garnishments there this year are running at an annual rate of 122,000. Court officials in New York, Cleveland and other big cities also cite rising garnishment totals.

The figures don't disclose the full extent of pay impounding. They don't include the huge volume of wage "assignments," which are legally distinct but similar in effect to garnishments. Under a wage assignment, a debtor pledges his future wages to repay the debt if he defaults; execution of the wage assignment doesn't normally require a court judgment, as a garnishment usually does. The garnishment figures also don't include tax levies, such as that in the Carl Clark case.

MR. REED'S PLIGHT

The records of Inland Steel Co. indicate how widespread wage attachment can be. Each payday the company makes such deductions from the paychecks of about 2,000 of its 22,000 production employes in the Chicago area, says Dorothy A. Lascoe, who handles this chore. Inland annually pays out more than $500,000 of withheld wages to creditors, she adds.

Who are the people behind the statistics? Most often, they are working men like Franchot Tone Reed, a 29-year-old tire mounter for a Chicago-area truck manufacturer, who learned of garnishment the hard way.

In 1964 Mr. Reed traded his 1956 Plymouth in on a 1950 Cadillac and signed an installment sales contract to pay $1,200 for the aging car in 48 weekly payments of $25. After he defaulted, the dealer repossessed the car and had Mr. Reed's wages attached to pay off the contract. The deduction took 15% of his pay, the legal limit on garnishments in Illinois.

To "get cut loose" from his debts and the garnishment, Mr. Reed filed bankruptcy late in 1964. Last year, Federal bankruptcy court in Chicago discharged Mr. Reed of $2,195 in debts, including bills for jewelry and clothing as well as the costly old Cadillac.

TRIGGERING BANKRUPTCY

As this case suggests, there is a connection between mounting garnishments and the steady rise in the number of personal bankruptcies in recent years. "Garnishment frequently triggers bankruptcy," says Linn K. Twinem, chairman of the American Bar Association's committee on consumer bankruptcy.

A record 180,323 bankruptcy cases were filed in Federal courts in the fiscal year ended last June 30, up from 171,719 in the prior year and 110,034 five years

earlier. Bankruptcy filings this year are expected to top 200,000. Personal bankruptcy filings accounts for 91% of the total.

Mr. Twinem says there is a "close relationship" between the severity of a state's garnishment law and its bankruptcies. California, which has a relatively tough garnishment law, led in bankruptcy filings in fiscal 1965 with 33,656. At the other extreme, three populous states that don't allow garnishments have dramatically lower bankruptcy-filing totals; Pennsylvania had 1,133, Florida 958 and Texas 661.

Garnishment often causes workers to lose their jobs. Many employers fire employes whose debt problems lead to excessive wage attachments, arguing that company handling of garnishment paperwork and court appearances by employes are costly and time-consuming. The Cook County Credit Bureau in Chicago surveyed 1,100 employers in 1964 and found that processing a single garnishment costs a company from $15 to $35; the estimated costs of garnishments to the surveyed employers totaled $12 million annually.

Few companies will discuss the firing of workers for garnishments. A personnel official at one General Motors Corp. plant near Chicago confirms union reports that 45 men were discharged at the plant for that reason last year. Another Chicago manufacturer admits firing "25 or 30" men for garnishments.

Union officials liken the practice of firing debt-burdened workers to the medieval custom of locking debtors in prison. "Under both practices, the debtor has a harder time paying his bills," says one. Most companies say they try to keep a man as long as he is making sincere efforts to straighten out his debts.

Employes fired for debt problems often wind up on relief rolls, social workers say. In a study of 827 persons applying for general asistance relief, the Cook County Department of Public Aid found that about 9% of the applicants had been fired from their jobs due to garnishments.

Questions

Although garnishment can cause severe family hardship, unemployment, and bankruptcy, it is defended as one of the least disruptive of creditor remedies. Proposals to abolish garnishment are met by the argument that more drastic remedies, such as seizure of the consumer's home, would then be resorted to, and if homestead exemptions were increased to protect the consumer's home, furniture and automobile, credit would dry up and consumers, particularly those of low income, would not be able to buy durables on credit at all. Of course, for the poor, this would mean that many desires for consumer goods would go unsatisfied, at the same time that those goods were being promoted extensively in the media— a potentially explosive situation. Furthermore, it is argued, the availability of garnishment is central to the consumer credit system because what credit is all about is enabling people to have goods and services now by agreeing to pay for them out of future income.

If garnishment were prohibited, why should anyone expect sellers to extend credit? Which remedies, and in what proportions, would you like to see available: repossession, replevin, garnishment, realty execution, personalty execution, damage to or destruction of credit rating, jail (see Carley, Debtors Behind Bars: A Stern Maine Law Stirs Legal Debate, Wall St. Journal, Dec. 26, 1968, p. 1.)? What exemptions would you create? What would be the effect of any changes you make in the status quo on (a) the availability of credit to the poor, (b) the price of credit (rate), and (c) where the prevailing rate is already at a legal limit, the price of goods?

Note on Creditor's Remedies and Constitutional Law

The excerpt from Caplovitz describes that aspect of the collection machinery which—imperfect as it is in practice— most closely conforms to a theoretical model of due process. Debtors are supposed to be notified of the initiation of a lawsuit against them, and they have the right, on paper, to appear and defend themselves. No due process right to the appointment of counsel in civil cases yet exists; the fact that defendants cannot *practically* be heard is not a concern of constitutional dimensions.

However, until very recently, many states also permitted creditors certain short cuts in obtaining their redress. For example, until 1969, seventeen states permitted creditors to attach wages at the outset of a lawsuit, instead of having to wait until judgment. Thus they could put intense pressure on the debtor-defendants to settle at once, instead of trying the case. (Of course, if the debtor did survive until trial and won the case, his back wages would be released).

This practice was challenged by the NAACP Legal Defense Fund and declared unconstitutional in Sniadach v. Family Finance Corp., 395 U.S. 337 (1969):

In this case the sole question is whether there has been a taking of property without that procedural due process that is required by the Fourteenth Amendment. We have dealt over and over again with the question of what constitutes "the right to be heard" (Schroeder v. New York, 371 U.S. 208, 212, 83 S.Ct. 279, 282, 9 L.Ed.2d 255) within the meaning of procedural due process. See Mullane v. Central Hanover Bank & Trust Co., 339 U.S. 306, 314, 70 S.Ct. 652, 657, 94 L.Ed. 865. In the latter case we said that the right to be heard "has little reality or worth unless one is informed that the matter is pending and can choose for himself whether to appear or default, acquiesce or contest." 339 U.S., at 314, 70 S.Ct., at 657. In the context of this case the question is whether the interim freezing of the wages without a chance to be heard violates procedural due process.

A procedural rule that may satisfy due process for attachments in general, see McKay v. McInnes, 279 U.S. 820, 49 S.Ct. 344, 73 L.Ed. 975, does not necessarily satisfy procedural due process in every case. The fact that a procedure would pass muster under a feudal regime does not mean it gives necessary protection to all property in its modern forms. We deal here with wages—a specialized type of property presenting distinct problems in our economic system. We turn then to the nature of that property and problems of procedural due process.

A prejudgment garnishment of the Wisconsin type is a taking which may impose tremendous hardship on wage earners with families to support. Until a recent Act of Congress, § 304 of which forbids discharge of employees on the ground that their wages have been garnished, garnishment often meant the loss of a job. Over and beyond that was the great drain on family income. As stated by Congressman Reuss:

"The idea of wage garnishment in advance of judgment, of trustee process, of wage attachment, or whatever it is called is a most inhuman doctrine. It compels the wage earner, trying to keep his family together, to be driven below the poverty level."

Recent investigations of the problem have disclosed the grave injustices made possible by prejudgment garnishment whereby the sole opportunity to be heard comes after the taking. Congressman Sullivan, Chairman of the

House Subcommittee on Consumer Affairs who held extensive hearings on this and related problems stated:

"What we know from our study of this problem is that in a vast number of cases the debt is a fraudulent one, saddled on a poor, ignorant person who is trapped in an easy credit nightmare, in which he is charged double for something he could not pay for even if the proper price was called for, and then hounded into giving up his pound of flesh, and being fired besides." 114 Cong.Rec. 1832.

The leverage of the creditor on the wage earner is enormous. The creditor tenders not only the original debt but the "collection fees" incurred by his attorneys in the garnishment proceedings:

"The debtor whose wages are tied up by a writ of garnishment, and who is usually in need of money, is in no position to resist demands for collection fees. If the debt is small, the debtor will be under considerable pressure to pay the debt and collection charges in order to get his wages back. If the debt is large, he will often sign a new contract of 'payment schedule' which incorporates these additional charges."

Apart from those collateral consequences, it appears that in Wisconsin the statutory exemption granted the wage earner is "generally insufficient to support the debtor for any one week."

The result is that a prejudgment garnishment of the Wisconsin type may as a practical matter drive a wage-earning family to the wall. Where the taking of one's property is so obvious, it needs no extended argument to conclude that absent notice and a prior hearing (cf. Coe v. Armour Fertilizer Works, 237 U.S. 413, 423, 35 S.Ct. 625, 628, 59 L.Ed. 1027) this prejudgment garnishment procedure violates the fundamental principles of due process.

The decision in *Sniadach* led poverty lawyers and others to challenge a variety of the "short-cut" creditors' remedies, with the following results:

1. *Prejudgment attachment of personal property*: In Randone v. Appellate Department, 5 Cal.3d 536, 96 Cal.Rptr. 709, 488 P.2d 13 (1971), the Supreme Court of California declared unconstitutional the prejudgment attachment of bank accounts. The defendant claimed that *Sniadach* could be distinguished because of its emphasis on wages as a special kind of property, uniquely necessary to the wage-earner, but the court ruled that *Sniadach* was a broad decision applying traditional notions of due process to prejudgment remedies; therefore, a taking without prior hearing could only be justified in an emergency. Though it was urged that restriction of creditors' remedies would reduce the amount of consumer credit extended by financial institutions, the court held that even if the claim were true, a state interest in promoting commerce could not justify the deprivation of individual constitutional rights.

2. *Confession of judgment.* At the end of the 1960's a few states still allowed confessions of judgment in consumer transactions; a contract clause would provide that the consumer authorized the creditor's attorney to represent him (the debtor), and to confess judgment against him in any court, without notice or hearing, in the event that he defaulted on the debt. This practice was challenged by an OEO Legal Services office in Swarb v. Lennox, 314 F.Supp. 1091 (1970), aff'd by default, 405 U.S. 191 (1972).

To meet the creditors' claim that the confession procedure effected no real harm because the debtor could reopen the judgment by motion, the consumers' lawyers proved the practice that belied the theory: (1) Such a motion could not be made by the debtor *pro se*, since it had to be accompanied by the transcripts of depositions, (2) the transcripts themselves cost a dollar per page, (3) according to the minimum fee schedule of the Philadelphia Bar Association, an attorney had to charge at least $150 for making a motion to reopen, and (4) while making his motion, the debtor had to post a bond to stay the sheriff's sale of his property.

The creditors nevertheless urged the court to distinguish *Sniadach* on the ground that the consumer who signed a confession of judgment *agreed* to the summary procedure; unlike Ms. Sniadach he voluntarily relinquished a waivable right (trial by jury). The legal services lawyers called Prof. Caplovitz to testify about his study of 236 Philadelphia judgment debtors; only 14% of them had understood that they were waiving their right to trial, while 22% believed that their contracts had contained no such clause, and 62% had no opinion one way or the other.

Impressed by this testimony, and applying the doctrine that the waiver of a constitutional right must be undertaken knowingly, Johnson v. Zerbst, 304 U.S. 458, 58 S.Ct. 1019, 82 L.Ed. 1461 (1938), the court held the procedure unconstitutional. It limited its judgment, however, to persons who earned less than $10,000 a year, on the theory that since only 4% of the debtors in the Caplovitz sample earned more than this amount, the court had no evidence that wealthier consumers did not understand what they were signing.

In Osmond v. Spence, 327 F.Supp. 1349 (1971), remanded 405 U.S. (1972), on remand again declaring confession of judgment unconstitutional, Civ. No. 3940 (D.Del. June 13, 1972), the Delaware confession statute was similarly challenged. No empirical data was presented to the court, but the procedure was held unconstitutionally applied to the named plaintiffs in the class action because "as the right of civil jury trial is fundamental, courts indulge every reasonable presumption against waiver." However, the court declined to extend the protection of its judgment to unnamed members of the class, although the dissenting judge would have declared it applicable to a class of persons who earned less than OEO poverty guidelines —$1900 for a single person, $3800 for a family of four, or $5600 for a family of seven.

In Douglas v. Beneficial Finance Co., 334 F.Supp. 1166, 4 CCH Consumer Credit Guide para. 99501, at p. 89, 466 (D.Alaska, 1971), the court declined to declare a confession statute unconstitutional, distinguishing Swarb on the ground that the empirical evidence there presented was not before the court—no one had flown Caplovitz to Alaska.

3. *Replevin.* Prejudgment replevin statutes generally permit a creditor to invoke the aid of a sheriff to obtain lawful possession of secured goods as to which the purchaser had defaulted. The court was authorized to issue ex parte orders permitting the retaking upon application by the creditor. Challenge to the procedure was successful in Laprease v. Raymours Furniture Co., 315 F.Supp. 761 (N.D.N.Y.1970) and Blair v. Pitchess, 5 Cal.3d 258, 96 Cal.Rptr. 42 (1971), though the courts reached the same results in somewhat different ways. Both courts held the procedure to violate the Fourth Amendment's guarantee against unreasonable and warrantless searches and seizures. In New York, the court also held that the Fifth Amendment was violated because "beds, stoves, mattresses, dishes, tables and other necessaries for ordinary day-to-day living are, like wages

in *Sniadach*, a 'specialized type of property presenting distinct problems in our economic system,' the taking of which on the unilateral command of an adverse party 'may impose tremendous hardships' on purchasers of these essentials." The California court saw no need to rely on this distinction, reading *Sniadach* as broadly as it did shortly afterward in *Randone*. And to the creditors' argument that replevin differed from prejudgment garnishment in that the goods in question were the creditor's (the debtor having defaulted), the court replied that such a contention constituted bootstrap reasoning, since the fact of ownership and default were to be determined in the subsequent proceeding on the merits.

In *Blair*, the record showed that most installment contracts contained clauses by which the debtor consented to the summary retaking procedure. Although Caplovitz did not testify, the court dismissed that theory, branding the agreements "contracts of adhesion" rather than genuine mutual understandings. See F. Kessler, "Contracts of Adhesion Some Thoughts About Freedom of Contract", 43 Colum.L.Rev. 629 (1943); Slawson, "Standard Form Contracts and Democratic Control of Lawmaking Power", 84 Harv.L.Rev. 529 (1971). This use of the concept of adhesion contract, to prevent the waiver of a *constitutional* right, seems more justifiable than applications of the theory to render inoperative other creditor rights secured in standard form contracts; at least it gives the concept some scope without requiring it to prove too much.

The Supreme Court settled the issue in Fuentes v. Shevin, 407 U.S. 67, 92 S.Ct. 1983, 32 L.Ed.2d 556 (1972), a challenge to the constitutionality, as applied to consumers, of the Pennsylvania and Florida replevin laws. The Court ruled (1) that the theory of *Sniadach*, supra, applied not only to necessities of life, but to all property interests, or at least to all "that cannot be characterized as de minimus", 407 U.S. at 90 n. 21; (2) possessory interests, as well as title, were deserving of protection against pre-hearing seizure; and (3) while the right to a hearing before summary deprivation of property can be waived, see D. H. Overmyer Co. v. Frick Co., 405 U.S. 174 (1972), at the very *least*, be clear". 407 U.S. at 95. The decision contains dicta ("appellees made no showing that the appellants were actually aware or made aware of the significance of the fine print now relied upon as a waiver") suggesting the burden-shifting theory of the district court in *Osmond* but did not explicitly go so far toward the protection of consumers' rights. The *Fuentes* majority (4–3, with Justices Powell and Rehnquist not participating) was so precarious as to guarantee that the consumer law reform movement would be holding its breath for several years as cases testing the validity of the other creditors' short cuts made their way to the Supreme Court.

Questions

Are the repossession provisions of the Uniform Commercial Code unconstitutional, at least as applied to consumer transactions? The creditor is entitled, by virtue of statute, to take possession of goods without notice or hearing. He says that the goods are his, because the debtor has defaulted, but *Fuentes* dismissed that claim in the replevin context. He says that the debtor agreed to the self-help retaking, but *Blair* and *Osmond* would at least presume the "agreement" to be invalid because not genuine, and a sociological study of consumer debtors who sign repossession clauses would probably indicate that few understand themselves to be authorizing self-help recoveries by their creditors. And all of the post-*Sniadach* cases cited above stand for the proposition that *Sniadach* is not limited to the protection of wages.

But repossession, unlike replevin, is accomplished by self-help; no court officer serves papers or is involved in the process in any other way. Does this feature of self-help repossession remove it from constitutional scrutiny on the ground that it does not involve state action? Or is state action sufficiently present when a state law permits an otherwise private company to retake possession without a prior hearing? At this writing, two federal district courts in California have answered this question with opposite results. Compare Adams v. Egley, 338 F.Supp. 614 (S.D.Calif.1972) with Oller v. Bank of America, 342 F.Supp. 21 (N. D.Calif.1972); the two cases are being appealed.

The same question arises with respect to the constitutionality of state wage assignment laws, which permit a creditor to require its debtors to execute separate contracts authorizing the creditor, without prior hearing, to seize a fixed percentage of the debtor's wages upon an alleged default. Unlike wage garnishment, wage assignment is contractual and while enforcement of wage assignments may involve state courts, no state official other than court personnel participate in the process. See Comment, "Wage Assignments: A Creditor Remedy in Need of Reform," 18 Wayne L.Rev. 1535, (1972).

SECTION 5.　CONSUMER REMEDIES

The excerpt from Caplovitz in the last section indicates that creditors, particularly those in the inner city, have neatly integrated litigation into their collection activities, that they use the courts efficiently and routinely to enforce contract claims. What about consumer-initiated cases?

Some cities have small claims courts in which individuals may sue companies more easily than in the regular courts, but such tribunals are rarely invoked by consumers in *credit* cases (because the debtors rely instead on withholding the money, leading to creditor-initiated action; also in many cities, such as New York, the small claims courts cannot entertain equitable claims such as demands for rescission or reformation), and they are underutilized by the poor. The number of consumer-initiated cases is but an insignificant fraction of the total number of consumer cases in the United States.

Yet it is tempting to imagine turning the tables by providing aggressive representation to low-income consumers. What would happen if a number of lawyers for the poor frequently brought massive damage actions, on a variety of theories, against the very creditors that were hounding their clients in other cases?

To a large extent, this question is unanswered, because most legal services programs have been too busy with their regular caseload to attempt to seize the initiative. While there have been some exceptions, such as California Rural Legal Assistance, Alaska Legal Services, and Neighborhood Legal Services in the District of Columbia, poverty lawyers have rarely attempted to take the offensive in consumer cases.

The editor believes that the assumption of such a role would enable lawyers for the poor to achieve a better balance of power between the creditors and the debtors in most low-income urban communities. But he does not think that it should be attempted without an appreciation of the frustrations that can be expected along the way—the delays, the procedural obstacles, the hostile attitude of many judges, and the burdens such a strategy places

on consumer clients. He has therefore described, at some length, his own experience initiating consumer test litigation as a staff attorney of the NAACP Legal Defense Fund. See Schrag, "Bleak House 1968: A Report on Consumer Test Litigation," 44 N.Y.U.L.Rev. 115 (1969).

An alternative to using the present formal system of consumer adjudication is *changing* it to facilitate participation by the more than 90% of debtors who now default, and by those who pay unjust claims because they fear the burden of threatened court action. The following proposal suggests one type of alternative to civil courts of inferior jurisdiction.

COMMITTEE REPORT

TOWARD THE INFORMAL RESOLUTION OF CONSUMER DISPUTES (1972)

BY THE SPECIAL COMMITTEE ON CONSUMER AFFAIRS

Association of the Bar of the City of New York.

This Association, through its Committees on Civil Rights, Legal Assistance and Consumer Affairs, has been concerned with both substantive and procedural legal problems faced by consumers in their dealings with vendors, finance companies, banks, administrative agencies, courts and lawyers. The Association's published reports on these subjects have called attention to the need for legislative and judicial reforms aimed at affording consumers both expanded rights and effective ways of asserting those rights.[1]

[1] E. g., Committee on Legal Assistance, "Does a Vendor under an Installment Sales Contract Receive Adequate Notice of a Suit Instituted by a Vendor," 23 Record of the Ass'n of the Bar 263 (1968); Committees on Grievances and Legal Assistance, "Improper Collection Practices," 23 Record of the Ass'n of the Bar 441 (1968); Committee on Civil Rights, "The Right to Counsel in Civil Cases," 24 Record of the Ass'n of the Bar 304 (1969); Committee on Legal Assistance, "Blueprint

It has become increasingly apparent, however, that existing judicial and administrative *procedures* often restrict the effective assertion of any *rights* in the consumer field. Finding these procedures to be a major obstacle to the enforcement of both new and old consumer rights, we describe in this report a proposed informal, decentralized judicial forum which may avoid many existing procedural injustices and obstacles. While we do not expect that such a model forum will readily be authorized, funded and established in all jurisdictions, we are hopeful that substantial progress can be made toward these ends in New York during the coming year.

Findings

In recent years the legal position of the consumer has been significantly improved, both in New York City [2] and elsewhere. [3] While equality between consumer and merchant has yet to be achieved or even approximated, the growth of consumer organizations and consumer awareness has resulted in statutes, regulations and judicial decisions which constitute a formidable corpus of "consumer rights." [4] These rights are primarily substantive. That is, they require vendors and creditors to comply with certain modes of business, conduct appropriate to a "fair marketplace" and to forego other modes of business conduct deemed deceptive or otherwise unfair. [5] At the same time, there has been a parallel recognition by consumers that their new rights are difficult to enforce in practice. [6] The consumer still lacks reliable and inexpensive procedures to enforce his rights and remedy even the most routine abuses.

(a) *The Consumer as Plaintiff.* Many such procedural shortcomings involve the failure of consumers to assert meritorious claims against vendors or creditors (or the failure of public agencies to assert such claims on the consumers' behalf). This is the problem of the missing plaintiff. Within this category, we identify the following procedural defects:

(i) The consumer may be unaware that he has a meritorious complaint.

(ii) Because of the relative informality of most consumer transactions, the consumer frequently may fail to retain (or to receive at all) factual documentation necessary to meet evidentiary requirements imposed by courts.

(iii) The consumer may be unfamiliar with the existence, location or operation of the forums or agencies which might serve him—and therefore

---

for Change," 25 Record of the Ass'n of the Bar 28 (1970); Committees on Consumer Affairs, Federal Legislation, Trade Regulation and Federal Courts, "Proposed Federal Legislation to Protect Consumers, Including Consumer Class Actions," 10 Reports of Committees of the Ass'n of the Bar 1 (1971).

[2] See, for example, the extraordinary variety of Consumer Protection Regulations promulgated by the NYC Department of Consumer Affairs pursuant to the Consumer Protection Law of 1969.

[3] For a more general summary, see State of New York Joint Legislative Committee on Consumer Protection, Fifth Annual Report, 1969–70.

[4] See, e. g., "Translating Sympathy for Deceived Consumers into Effective Programs for Protection," Note, 114 U. of Pa.L.Rev. 395 (1966) reprinted in Katz, ed., The Law and the Low Income Consumer, NYU Sch. of Law (1968); "Consumer Legislation and the Poor," Note, 76 Yale L.J. 745 (1967); Dole, Jr., "Merchant and Consumer Protection: The Uni-

form Deceptive Trade Practices Act," 76 Yale L.J. 485 (1967).

[5] See, e. g., 15 U.S.C.A. § 45(a)(1).

[6] See, e. g., "Translating Sympathy for Deceived Consumers into Effective Programs for Protection," supra; FTC, National Consumer Protection Hearings (1968); Caplovitz, Debtors in Default, Vol. II: The Events Following Upon the Default (Bureau of Applied Social Research, Columbia University, 1971) to be published. Law and Order Reconsidered, Report of the Task Force on Law and Law Enforcement to the National Commission on the Causes and Prevention of Violence at pp. 35–44.

may not know where or how to lodge a meritorious complaint.

(iv) The consumer may have had prior and unfavorable experiences with the forum or agency and have become disillusioned with its efficacy or fairness. This is especially true if the consumer was first introduced to the forum as defendant, but may also be true where earlier complaints were not redressed or acted upon.

(v) The consumer may find the forum or agency inconvenient because of its location, hours or procedures (which often require the expense of retaining a lawyer). In this situation, the cost to the consumer in lost working time, travel expense or attorney's fees may make it economically self-defeating for him to commence suit.

(vi) The consumer may find the forum or agency excruciatingly slow in hearing his complaint and reaching judgment or may find enforcement of a favorable judgment difficult and prolonged.

(vii) The consumer may feel that the forum or agency cannot fashion an adequate remedy, as when the forum cannot grant "consequential damages" for physical harm or is more concerned (as may be proper) with correction of generalized abuses than with individual redress.

(viii) Even if he is aware of his claim, able to substantiate it, and confident of the court's ability to vindicate his rights, the consumer may be unable to bear the expense and risk of responding to unrelated counterclaims which may be asserted against him.

(b) *The Consumer as Defendant.* The second category of procedural shortcoming affecting consumers involves their inability to assert, as defendants, meritorious defenses to claims of vendors and creditors. This is the problem of the missing defendant. The problem of the missing defendant is, if anything, more serious than that of the missing plaintiff. This is so because procedural defects often approach the outrageous and because their impact is greatest upon the poor.[7]

The procedural defects here include, in addition to those noted above with respect to the missing plaintiff:

(i) Improper or non-existent service of process, so that the defendant often lacks knowledge of the proceeding (so-called "sewer services").

(ii) Deliberate selection by suppliers of improper and inconvenient venue.

(iii) Antiquated forms of summons and complaint which, even when properly served, fail to alert the consumer to the fact and seriousness of the suit.

(iv) Calendar procedures which require multiple court appearances and concommitant absence from work.

(v) The extreme difficulty of obtaining a lawyer for individual consumer disputes in which the amount in controversy is often less than even a modest professional fee.

(vi) Suppliers' pre-judgment communications with employers, which chill the employee's willingness to defend for fear of jeopardizing their jobs.[8]

(c) *Alternative Remedial Responses.* The foregoing obstacles to consumer justice are relatively well-known. The responses have been diverse. They include:

[7] See "Consumer Legislation and the Poor," supra; Caplovitz, supra; "Abuse of Process: Sewer Service" 3 Colum.J. of Law & Social Problems, Inc. (June, 1967); "The Right to a Day in Court and the Consumer Defendant," 23 Record of the Ass'n of the Bar 586 (Nov., 1968).

[8] See "Improper Collection Practices," 23 The Record of The Association of the Bar of the City of N. Y. 441 (June, 1968).

(i) a marked increase in the number of governmental agencies charged with "consumer protection"; (ii) repeated calls for legislation authorizing "consumer class actions"; (iii) renewed interest in consumer problems by the OEO Legal Services Program; (iv) well-publicized experiments in "voluntary settlement" procedures by business associations; and (v) in New York City as least, considerable attention to the revitalization of the Small Claims Court.

The Committee has attempted to evaluate the potential of each of these responses to overcome the obstacles noted above. For the reasons stated below, we find that, even if adopted, none of these courses of action is likely materially to affect established patterns of consumer abuse.

(i) *Consumer Protection Agencies.* Considerable attention has been focused on recent federal and state efforts to establish specialized agencies in the consumer protection field.[9] Notwithstanding this attention, the Committee believes that statutory, budgetary and practical limitations on investigative and enforcement activities will preclude such agencies from protecting low and middle income consumers in all but the most flagrant cases of abuse or fraud. Most such agencies do not, in fact, have any significant enforcement powers of their own and must instead seek relief before other agencies or courts.

(ii) *Consumer Class Actions.* This Committee, in conjunction with three other Committees of the Association, recently issued a report urging Congressional enactment of a broad federal consumer class action bill.[10] In doing so, we cautioned that even as potentially powerful a remedy as federal class actions would have little, if any, impact on the routine abuses to which low income consumers are subjected on a daily basis. The vast majority of such abuses do not raise issues appropriate for class action resolution in either the federal or state courts. Indeed, those abuses deal with oral or written representations made to individual buyers, the condition or quality of particular goods or services, the extent to which payment has in fact been made, the adequacy of repairs and similar issues tied to individual consumer transactions. While we continue to believe in the necessity for federal class actions in the consumer field, it would be illusory to regard such a remedy as a cure for— or in fact genuinely responsive to— the pervasive procedural shortcomings discussed above.

(iii) *Legal Service Lawyers.* If individual, rather than class, representation is required to remedy most consumer grievances, one possible response to this need is to expand substantially the number of legal services attorneys available to furnish such representation

---

[9] See, e. g., H.R. 18067 and S. 4459. The following is a sampling of pending state legislation to establish or invigorate consumer agencies: Alabama—SB 199; Alaska—SB 13; Connecticut—SB 37, SB 104, SB 1015, SB 1037, SB 1415, HB 86, HB 5477, HB 6987, HB 7127, HB 8164, HB 8165, HB 8315, HB 8321, HB 8907, HB 9212; Georgia—HB 581; Hawaii—SB 856, SB 857, HB 7, HB 8; Illinois—SB 493, SB 1093, HB 1901, HB 2239, HB 2836; Iowa—SB 288; Kansas—SB 427; Kentucky—SB 53, HB 68; Maryland—SB 53; Michigan—SB 1061; New York—AB 6550, SR 120, AB 8496, AR 129; Ohio—HB 38, HB 249; Pennsylvania—HB 506; Puerto Rico— SB 1022, SB 1037, SJR 1487, HB 1389, HR 327, HR 394; South Carolina—HB 2119; Tennessee—SB 16; Vermont—SB 162; Wisconsin—SB 426, AB 1145, AB 1257.

[10] Committees on Federal Legislation, The Federal Courts, Consumer Affairs, and Trade Regulation of the Association of the Bar of the City of New York, Proposed Federal Legislation to Protect Consumers, Including Consumer Class Actions (1971); See also Senate Bill S. 3201 (91st Cong., 2d Sess.) Title II, and Committee on Federal Legislation, New York State Bar Association, Report on the Consumer Protection Class Action Jurisdiction Act, 42 NYSBJ (Jan. 1970).

and to encourage the private bar to assume broader *pro bono* responsibilities in the consumer field. However, given the budgetary constraints of the present Legal Services Program and the extremely limited public service efforts of the private Bar, it is inconceivable that any such expansion will be adequate, in the foreseeable future, to meet the demonstrated need for consumer assistance.[11] Furthermore, other legal needs of poor and middle-income families (welfare, landlord-tenant, matrimonial and criminal, for example) would have compelling claims on such expanded services even if they were available.

(iv) *Voluntary Arbitration Procedures.* The practical impossibility of securing a lawyer to represent every consumer plaintiff and defendant has led to a variety of proposals for voluntary dispute-settlement procedures.[12]

---

[11] In fact, OEO recently ordered the New York City Legal Services Program (CALS) to reduce average case loads from 200 cases per lawyer to 75. As a result, CALS could close its doors to all consumer cases for months or years. See NYLJ, Dec. 17, 1971, p. 1.

[12] See, however, "Friend or Foe? Better Business Bureau is Increasingly Assailed by Furious Consumers," Wall St. Journal, 9/18/70. The National Institute for Consumer Justice (see NYT, 1/27/71) is engaged in an evaluation of arbitral techniques in the consumer area. In an internal memorandum made available to the Committee, the Institute has described the following projects:

"A. Pennsylvania

Compulsory arbitration has been permitted in the courts of common pleas of Pennsylvania since 1952, and was extended to the Municipal Court of Philadelphia in 1958. The Philadelphia plan has been widely discussed (see Rosenberg and Shubin, "Trial by Lawyer: Compulsory Arbitration of Small Claims in Pennsylvania," 74 Harv.L.Rev. 448 (1961), and articles cited therein).

At present, apparently all claims of $500 to $10,000 filed in the County Court are submitted to arbitration by a panel of three lawyers (claims under $500 are apparently handled in the Municipal Court, acting as a small claims court). According to all reports, this has resulted in a tremendous re-

duction in the backlog of the courts. A report issued after the first decade of compulsory arbitration in Philadelphia noted that over 62,000 cases had been arbitrated and the average waiting period had been reduced to three months.

B. New York

In 1970, the New York State Legislature enacted legislation calling for the compulsory arbitration of money damage claims not exceeding $3,000. While the law has statewide application, it has been put into operation—on a pilot basis—in only one area, Monroe County (Rochester). Since September 1, 1970, cases for money damages up to $3,000 commenced in the City Court of Rochester have been assigned for trial by arbitration before a three-lawyer panel. These cases represent about 90% of the City Court's civil work load. As in Philadelphia, the parties are represented by counsel in nearly all cases. After one year of operation, 458 had been settled prior to hearing, and 655 tried. The civil court's backlog was cut from 1400 to 590.

The National Center for Dispute Settlement of the American Arbitration Association: Philadelphia Project

The American Arbitration Association founded the Center for Dispute Settlement in 1968 to develop mechanisms applying the concept of arbitration to the settlement of individual disputes arising in everyday life. A prototype neighborhood center opened in Philadelphia in 1969. Thirty per cent of its first nine months' cases involved consumer-merchant disputes. None of the 45 cases closed during that period, however, was successfully arbitrated, apparently for the primary reason that merchants were unwilling to submit to arbitration. Merchants claimed that customers delayed making complaints until "the last minute," a situation which purportedly led the merchants to a state of intransigence and refusal to submit to arbitration.

Other neighborhood centers are planned for other cities, but we do not as yet have any detailed information on them.

Better Business Bureaus: Arbitration Projects

Better Business Bureaus in a number of communities have been involved in arbitrating certain kinds of disputes for periods up to 15 years. One kind of dispute frequently handled by the Bureaus: complaints and problems arising out of laundry and dry cleaning. A Textile Arbitration Panel has been in operation in the Los Angeles area for six years. A similar panel operates in Atlanta, as well as several other cities.

The NICJ has contacted the Council of Better Business Bureaus, which is attempt-

These proposals, often advanced by business representatives, represent an important step forward in the consumer area. They do not, however, provide a sufficent basis for assuring the vindication of consumer rights on a continuing basis. The deed for such relief is, we believe, sufficiently urgent and compelling that society should not —and cannot—be satisfied with voluntary solutions on the part of a few suppliers who are sufficiently enlightened to appreciate the correlation between a fair marketplace and increased consumption of their goods or services. Nevertheless, we welcome those proposals which have been established on an experimental basis and believe that their results will prove helpful in achieving *compulsory* settlement procedures at the neighborhood level. In particular, the Committee is eager to evaluate the results of a pilot dispute settlement project currently under way in Washington, D. C. (under the guidance of the Consumer Arbitration Council of the American Arbitration Associations National Center for Dispute Settlement) and a consumer-business arbitration experiment being conducted by the Long Island Better Business Bureau.

(v) *Small Claims Courts.* Many large cities, including New York, have established Small Claims Courts which afford individual consumers an opportunity for relatively speedy, inexpensive and informal relief. Many such courts, however, as in New York City, prohibit actions by incorporated suppliers *against* consumers. The practical effect of this exclusion is to expose consumer defendants to suits in more formal, complex and expensive courts, in which (for the reasons cited above) the incidence of default judgments is intolerably high. Even for the consumer plaintiff, the Small Claims Court may be poorly located or confusing.[13] The jurisdictional limitations of many such courts ($500 in New York City) also bar many consumer complaints involving major appliances, instruction courses or automobile repairs. Notwithstanding their informal hearing procedures, such courts uniformly lack a full-time staff to assist the court in appraising the condition of merchandise or any mechanism to help consumers enforce judgments against recalcitrant suppliers.

Proposed Neighborhood Consumer Courts

We believe that the factors discussed above point toward the creation of decentralized, informal neighborhood tribunals for the special hearing of consumer complaints. We believe that such a forum, if properly implemented, would make a substantial contribution toward achieving prompt, just and inexpensive resolution of grievances by and against consumers.

The nature and general characteristics of the proposed tribunal (hereafter referred to as a "Consumer Court") are described below.

---

ing to act as a central clearinghouse for information on various BBB projects, and we expect to obtain more information from that source in the immediate future. The BBBs appear to be increasingly interested in promoting arbitration, and their progress in this area is worth watching."

In addition, the following committees have been set up by industry groups to handle consumer complaints: The Association of Home Appliance Manufacturers Committee; Major Appliance Consumer Action Panel; and Home Movers Independent Complaint Committee.

[13] See, however, "Small Claims Court Opens in Harlem," NYT 1/8/72 for a description of an on-going experiment in scheduling Small Claims Court sessions at 170 East 121st Street in addition to the regular sessions held downtown at 111 Centre Street. See also "Court with a Quiet Access to Justice," NYT 2/6/71. See also Schrag, "On Her Majesty's Secret Service: Protecting the Consumer in New York," 80 Yale L.J. 1529, 1543 (1971).

(a) *Number and Composition of Consumer Courts.* Ideally, each recognized geographical community within a large city should have its own Consumer Court. Budgetary limitations will determine the extent to which this goal is achieved in any jurisdiction. In general, we believe that one such Court for each State Assembly District would provide a minimum distribution formula. In New York City, a preferable standard would be one Consumer Court for each Community School District.

Once established, each such Court would include a Presiding Judge and a panel of from three to nine special Referees. Such Referees, who need not be lawyers, will be selected as follows: the appropriate body of judges will assemble an advisory council of 15 members which will consist of one-third consumer representatives, one-third vendor-credit representatives, and one-third independent parties. By majority vote the advisory council will recommend a city-wide list of Referees for assignment in each district where the Consumer Court will be located. The judges may, after appropriate inquiry concerning the character and competence of the recommended Referees, accept or reject any recommendations, and the advisory council will be expected to furnish additional recommendations in the event of rejections. Following their acceptance by the judges, Referees will be assigned within the relevant district in the discretion of the Presiding Judge of that district.

Each Court would have a clerk's office and other administrative staff, the function of which is described below.

(b) *Jurisdiction.* The proposed Consumer Court would have exclusive jurisdiction over all "consumer actions" in which the amount in controversy, exclusive of interest and costs (if any), does not exceed $3,000 (or, in the case of disputes involving automobiles or courses of instruction, $5,000). Both consumers and suppliers would be required to utilize this forum in lieu of all alternative forums presently available.

For jurisdictional purposes, "consumer actions" are suits:

(i) by suppliers and their assignees seeking payment and permitted interest and penalties in respect of goods sold or services rendered primarily for personal, household or family purposes;

(ii) by suppliers and their assignees seeking repossession or deficiency payments in respect of such goods;

(iii) by consumers seeking damages, rescission, reformation, refund, performance, repair, replacement or other legal or equitable relief arising out of the purchase of such goods or services;

(iv) by creditors for sums loaned (either directly or as "holders-in-due-course," assignees or credit card issuers), including permitted interest and penalties thereon, for the purchase of goods or services intended primarily for personal, household or family purposes;

(v) by debtors or vendees to have such loans and related obligations declared void or for other legal or equitable relief in respect thereto;

(vi) by small businesses (three or fewer full-time employees) with respect to goods purchased for resale to the public; and

(vii) by beneficiaries under personal property and medical or disability insurance policies.

Disputes described in item (vi) are included because of their similarity to the more orthodox consumer grievances insofar as they often require prompt, inexpensive, informal and convenient forums for their resolution. Neighborhood proprietors of extremely small businesses frequently face the same obstacles in this regard as individual consumers. Personal property and health insurance claims are included in item (vii) because the amounts involved in such claims, together with the other procedural obstacles stated above, often make full-scale litigation impracticable.

It is not essential that the proposed forum deal solely with consumer actions. Other categories of small claims may also be brought before this forum. Any broader jurisdiction should, however, carefully preserve a central concern with consumer actions for three reasons:

First, the assertion of existing legal rights by consumers will depend greatly on public realization that a forum exists which is especially concerned with the just treatment of consumers. A forum which makes the consumer the forgotten man, buried among other categories of suit, will quickly sink into deserved impotence.

Second, the effectiveness and legitimacy of the forum will depend in part upon the growing expertise of its Referees with consumer problems as a field of legal expertise, and with the particular factual issues that may recur in the neighborhood. Attention to too many legal areas may spell expertise in none.

Third, although there is much to be said in the abstract in favor of a broad jurisdiction which will include landlord-tenant, welfare, health care and related complaints, the proposed forum is admittedly an experiment, and as such requires modesty of ambition and careful consideration of its successes and failures. Too expansive a jurisdiction may assure operational and analytical confusion and failure.

(c) *Venue.* Venue will be a jurisdictional concept in the proposed Consumer Court. Improper complaints will therefore not be accepted for filing. Any judgment issued on an improperly filed complaint will be void, a determination to be made initially by the clerk. False statements as to venue will be regarded as prima facie evidence of perjury.

Venue will be proper either where the defendant resides or where the sale occurred, at the option of the plaintiff. A sale is deemed to occur at the sales office of the vendor; mail-order sales, however, and door-to-door or telephone sales are deemed to occur only at the residence of the vendee. Alternatively, venue may be set where the consumer (whether plaintiff or defendant) resides. This may be necessary to avoid the emergence of "collection-agency" forums in the vicinity of large department stores.

(d) *Initiating Suit.* To initiate suit, a plaintiff must furnish to the clerk, either in person or by mail, a completed summons and complaint form to be supplied by the Court. The clerk will be available to advise parties on how to complete the form.

The form of summons will be specially prepared to provide better warning to defendants of the fact and seriousness of suit. Where local conditions warrant, the summons will be in both English and other languages generally spoken in the district. The summons will specify the scheduled return date (to be set between 10 and 20 days after its issuance), as well as the addresses and telephone numbers of nearby legal aid offices and bar association referral services. The summons and complaint will also request the defendant to bring listed documentation to the hearing (e. g., contract forms, cancelled checks, etc.). At the same time, the plaintiff will be required to produce all pertinent documents (contract, proof of delivery and receipt, etc.) which are in his possession or otherwise available to him.

No formal answer will be required of the defendant. He must, however, either appear in Court at the scheduled time or complete and return to the clerk the form of Adjournment Request attached to the summons. If such request is received at least two days before the time of the scheduled hearing, the Court will grant a single three-day adjournment. Additional adjournments will be granted only in extraordinary circumstances and at the discretion of the Referee.

The Committee has considered and rejected an alternative approach which would permit the defendant to simply complete and return, prior to the scheduled hearing, a summary form of Tear-Off Answer. While the Tear-Off Answer holds considerable promise for reducing the incidence of default judgments in more conventional forums (for example, New York City's Civil Court), the absence of formal pleadings or calendar parts in the proposed Consumer Court makes such an innovation unnecessary. It would be both simpler and more efficient, we believe, for the defendant simply to appear and state his defense, if any, on the scheduled date.

Service will be effected through registered mail, return receipt requested. Mailing will be made by the clerk. In recommending this, the Committee does not condemn personal service. We believe, however, that personal service imposes an expense upon the consumer and vendor plaintiff which is not essential and which, in fact, often results in a less reliable form of service. Personal service may, of course, be appropriate in areas where mail delivery is unreliable.

(e) *Counterclaims.* As a general rule, no counterclaims will be permitted. In an informal forum it is easy enough for the defendant to initiate another action. However, counterclaims which arise out of the same transaction or occurrence may, in the discretion of the Referee, be asserted in order to settle related disputes between the parties.

(f) *Right to Counsel; Amicus Role.* Counsel would be encouraged in the Consumer Court. While the forum would not require a lawyer's procedural expertise, the Committee feels that substantive rights can be better identified and asserted with the assistance of counsel than by the parties alone. To this end, the summons will contain a statement indicating that counsel is available and showing the locations of nearby legal aid offices. However, because legal aid counsel may be unavailable, consumer parties may appear alone or through third-parties who are not attorneys. Such third-parties may include consumer groups or friends.

(g) *Technical Assistance; Expert Testimony.* Each Court will have available to it a full-time staff of experts to assist Referees in evaluating claims of defective merchandise or service. This staff will be available at the request of the plaintiff (made at the time of filing a complaint or, with the permission of the Court, at the time of the scheduled hearing) or the defendant (who may request such assistance at any time prior to the hearing, or with the Court's permission, at the hearing itself). The party requesting such assistance will incur a flat, one-time, modest charge payable at the time such assistance is requested. The expert will then inspect the goods (or services) in question and submit his report orally to the Referee on the hearing date (or, in the discretion of the Referee, any adjournment thereof). He will, of course, be subject to cross-examination by both parties.

In order to reduce the cost and increase the technical expertise of its staff, the Court may wish to schedule cases involving similar issues (for example, defective automobile repairs or broken furniture) for hearing on a single day.

(h) *Function of Referees.* In general, each case will be heard by a single Referee. However, upon motion of a party, approved by the Referee, or on the initiative of the Referee, a panel of three Referees may be convened to hear a case of special importance. The assignment of Referees to particular cases will generally be by lot.

The Referee will have the general powers of a court, including but not limited to:

(i) subpoenaing witness to appear;

(ii) subpoenaing books, papers, documents and other items of evidence;

(iii) physical inspection of evidence, either at the Court or at the consumer's or supplier's premises;

(iv) administering oaths;

(v) determining the admissibility of evidence and the form in which it is to be offered; and

(vi) deciding questions of law and fact in the cases submitted to them.

The Referee (or Referees) will, within five days after the hearing, file a report and award, signed by the Referee (or by at least two members of a three man panel); copies of the report will be mailed to the parties of their counsel.

(i) *Relief and Applicable Law.* Despite its informal procedure, the Court will apply substantive law and (except as stated below) will have the power to award any relief which may be proper in a court of law or equity.

In recommending the creation of a decentralized consumer forum, we recognize that the line between procedure and substance is not always clear, and that out of the proposed Consumer Court may come revised and expanded definitions of consumer rights. Thus, while we endorse the application of existing substantive law by Referees, we welcome the emergence of a "common law" which reflects the Court's growing expertise and familiarity with consumer problems. We particularly look for innovation in such areas as

voidness because of unconscionability [14] and equitable arrangements for payment of sums owed by the consumer.[15]

At the same time, we do not endorse the view that existing substantive law should be applied as little as possible or should be replaced by a general sense of what is fair on the facts. We regard existing substantive law as moving toward a just balancing of the legitimate rights of consumers and merchants and reject counsels of impatience and despair. Moreover, we do not believe that judges and Referees will tend to indulge an inherent anti-consumer bias by virtue of the Court's adherence to substantive law. On the contrary, we see the Consumer Court as an expression of the informed and impartial judgment of consumers and vendors alike that neither gains in the long run from the complex and frustrating procedures (and hence incompete rights) presently afforded consumers.

(j) *Defaults.* In the event that the defendant fails to appear at the scheduled hearing, the Referee may, in his discretion, conduct an inquest of the plaintiff to ascertain the principal facts bearing upon the complaint and determine whether such facts constitute a prima facie case against the defendant. In cases involving claims for liquidated damages, the Referee may, in lieu of an inquest, require of plaintiff and its counsel a verified affidavit affirming the plaintiff's allegations. However, the Court may (and, in our judgment, should) continue to conduct inquests where it suspects possible fraud, overreaching or other abuses by a plaintiff or where default judgments in such cases become routine. In general, the Referee will be expected to fashion an

[14] See Materials on Consumer Protection (1969) by Univ. of Pa. Law. Sch. Reg. H. Smith Community Lawyer Fellowship Program.

[15] See Hilliard & Hurt, "Wage Earners Plans under Chapter XIII of the Bankruptcy Act," 19 Bus.Lawyer 271 (1963).

appropriate remedy under the circumstances. Following the entry of such a judgment, the absent defendant may reopen the case only upon a showing before the Court that he was not properly served with the summons and complaint or has an excusable reason for default and a meritorious defense.

In the event of default by the plaintiff, the Referee will enter judgment for the defendant. The plaintiff will then be precluded from instituting an action in any court based upon the facts alleged in the complaint.

(k) *Appeals.* Any party may, within five days after an award is filed, file with the clerk a form requesting either (*i*) the vacating of such award on the ground that it was procured by fraud, corruption or other unlawful means; or (*ii*) the certification of such award for review on the ground that it involves a novel question of law (raised before the Referee) which is either important to the case or affects consumers and suppliers generally. Such request (to be briefly stated in a form supplied by the clerk, a copy of which will be forwarded to the opposing party), will be reviewed, without a hearing, by the Presiding Judge of the Court (or his designee). If, following such review, the Presiding Judge (or such designee) determines that such award should be vacated, he will reschedule the matter for a new hearing before a different Referee and advise the parties accordingly. If the Judge (or such designee) believes that the question of law involved in such award is novel and important to the case or of concern to consumers or suppliers generally, he may certify such award for review by a superior tribunal (which, in New York City, would presumably be the Appellate Term of the Supreme Court).

(l) *Enforcement of Judgment.* The judgment of the Referee should—absent appeal—result in automatic enforcement

action by marshals attached to the forum in the event of non-compliance within a period of 10 days.

(m) *Avoiding Vendor Domination.* To function properly, the Consumer Court must not become a collection agency for vendors.[16] At the same time, the consumer will be the chief victim of any attempt to limit the number of complaints which the forum will hear by any single plaintiff. Accordingly, this Committee opposes any limitations of access.[17]

(n) *Dealing With Patterns of Abuses.* The Consumer Court should not be empowered to entertain class action suits or to enjoin patterns of conduct until it has demonstrated its competency in handling individual grievances. It should, however, have the power to prevent abuses of judicial process and to bar use of default judgments and court proceedings as an instrument of fraud in the collection of invalid judgments. It should, additionally, maintain adequate records so that it can inform other agencies and forums of recurrent abuses. Submission to the Consumer Court should not shield a supplier against a class action suit.

Finality, the Shifting Dimensions of Due Process and Equal Protection for Consumers

It is evident that some features of the Consumer Court may raise questions of constitutional dimension. The proposed forum will, after all, be the compulsory place of hearing for the vast preponderance of consumer grievances. Yet it will seek to dispense with all but a few judges and completely eliminate jury trials,[18]

---

[16] "The poor do not collect in small claims courts; they are only collected from" Law and Order Reconsidered, supra, at p. 35.

[17] See N.Y.C.C.A. § 1809.

[18] See N.Y.S.Const. Art. 1 § 2; U.S.Const., Seventh Amendment; Minneapolis & St. L. R. Co. v. Bombois, 241 U.S. 211 (1916); Barton v. Barbour, 104 U.S. 126 (1881); Duignan v. U. S., 274 U.S. 231 (1927); Olesen v. Trust

minimize the formal rules of evidence;[19] utilize Referees who may not be lawyers; bar any appeal from its findings of fact; and provide only limited review of conclusions of law.[20]

The Committee believes that these features of the proposal can and should withstand attack under the due process requirements of the Fourteenth Amendment.[21] We believe this for two fundamental reasons: *first,* any contrary position risks offending the equal protection requirement that access to justice not depend upon the wealth of the litigant;[22] *second,* the inherently small amounts in dispute make it inefficient to embrace here the familiar technique of subsidizing the poor litigant so that he may have the same full-scale litigation opportunities as his wealthier opponent.[23]

Because we recognize that men of goodwill may differ on this point, we wish to identify some alternative approaches which the Committee has considered in the course of its deliberations. Some of these may be appropriate in the event of the invalidity of any particular feature of the proposals described above.

In order to defend the Consumer Court against a constitutional challenge based on

Co. of Chi., 245 F.2d 522 (7th Cir., 1957), cert. den. 355 U.S. 896 (1957).

[19] See N.Y.C.C.A. § 1804; 5 U.S.C.A. § 556 (d).

[20] Olesen v. Trust Co. of Chi., supra; U. S. v. Walker, 111 F.Supp. 455 (D.Conn.1952); Stunda v. U. S., 225 F.Supp. 973 (W.D.Missouri 1964); McGrath v. Kirstensen, 340 U.S. 162 (1950); Nat'l Union of Marine Cooks v. Arnold, 348 U.S. 37 (1954); Dist. of Col. v. Clowan's, 300 U.S. 617 (1937); Ohio ex rel. Bryant v. Apron Metropolitan Park District, 281 U.S. 74 (1930).

[21] See Hotel Martha Washington Management Co. v. Swinick, 322 N.Y.S.2d 139 (S.Ct., App.Term, 1st Dep't 1971).

[22] See Boddie et al. v. Connecticut et al., 401 U.S. 371 (1971); Griffin et al. v. Illinois, 351 U.S. 12 (1955); Lee v. Habid, 424 F.2d 891 (D.C.C.A.1970).

[23] See Hotel Martha Washington Management Co. v. Swinick, supra. See also B.N.A. Daily Executive Report 8–13–17 report on radio and direct interview with Robert Pitofsky, director of FTC's consumer protection bureau, which states:

"The Federal Trade Commission's top consumer protection official has labeled the nation's present judicial system as 'too expensive, too threatening, too cumbersome, and too time consuming to dispose of the typical complaint,' and proposed instead a national system of conciliation and arbitration for consumer complaints.

"Robert Pitofsky, director of FTC's consumer protection bureau, said in a UPI Wash-

ington Window radio program interview: 'What we're going to have to do is think our way into techniques of conciliation and arbitration that are cheap, quick, and understandable to consumers. Now, we've got a long way to go.'

"Mr. Pitofsky said in an interview with BNA that the present judicial system has failed 'in the one-on-one context: consumer against seller.' The present system, he declared, 'just wasn't designed to deal with this type of consumer problem.'

" 'There's tremendous exploitation and it's a cause of great frustration among people,' he added. Such exploitation, he said, takes the form of 'civil fraud' that people 'run into day in and day out where the judicial system seems to throw all its weight on the side of the seller and the collector of debts rather than the purchaser.'

" 'Any system of arbitration and conciliation, Mr. Pitofsky said, should be 'very informal' and in no way associated with the federal court system, since 'the expense and delay associated with the federal system are too ominous to the typical consumer.' Mr. Pitofsky explained that the type of consumer complaint system he envisions might be patterned after the European system of settling disagreements between consumers and businesses.

" 'There is now a President's Commission on Consumer Justice which is well staffed and well-financed which I hope will come out within the next year with a report on what can be done to supplement what I think are the deficiencies of our judicial system,' Mr. Pitofsky said. 'The FTC itself is looking into aspects of the judicial system like deficiency judgments and collection practices in an effort to try to eliminate the worst elements of abuse.'

" 'But there are no easy solutions to the problems associated with consumer justice, Mr. Pitofsky indicated. In fact, he admitted later that he had posed many more questions dealing with consumer problems than he prepared to answer. 'The problem is very complex,' he said. 'There is some progress being made there, but we've got a long way to go.' "

the plaintiff's or defendant's right to jury trial, we have considered permitting either party to request a 6-man jury upon the payment of the administrative costs associated with such a trial. It is clear, however, that even if few parties requested juries, the effectiveness of the Court would be seriously undermined. Although exercise of this privilege might be deterred through the imposition of costs approximating the actual expense of administering a jury system, such an approach would perpetuate what the Committee regards as the undesirable (and possibly unconstitutional) judicial practice of conditioning the exercise of procedural rights on a party's ability to pay. We therefore prefer to treat the question of jury trial on its merits and believe that, under the circumstances described in this report, such a privilege is not constitutionally required. If, however, the Committee is incorrect in this view, and the right to request a jury trial is required even in the proposed Consumer Court, we would suggest that the fees imposed in connection with such trials fully reflect the administrative costs occasioned thereby.

We have also considered relinquishing such other features of the proposal as may be necessary to preserve the finality of decisions by the forum. On the assumption that due process does not require any right of appeal,[24] we emphasize the crucial importance of having the litigation end with the decision of the Consumer Court. Any alternative is likely to relocate in the appellate tribunal all the procedural abuses which today afflict trial courts. While we can sympathize with endeavors to achieve a more flexible and liberal procedure for appeal, we fear that

the complex, expensive and time-consuming steps necessarily involved in appeals will chill the energies of consumers and significantly dilute the utility of the proposed Court.

An alternative approach, which we reject as a likely exercise in futility, is the creation of a subsequent right of a full-scale trial de novo at the request of the losing party. It is easy to describe how this would work, for the compulsory arbitration experiment of the Appellate Division, Fourth Department, has embraced this technique. Under that experiment the arbitration award is final, and judgment is entered thereon, unless (i) demand is made for a trial de novo or (ii) the award is vacated. In addition, demands for a trial de novo may be made by any party in any court which could have entertained the case in the absence of the required arbitration. The party so demanding must, within twenty days after the arbitration award is filed, file with the court clerk and serve upon all adverse parties a demand for trial de novo and an affidavit setting forth a substantial ground for this demand. The defendant must also, concurrently with the filing of the demand, reimburse the court clerk the fees paid to the arbitrators for their services. Such sums are not recoverable by defendant upon trial de novo or in any other proceeding. In any trial, the arbitrator may not be called as a witness nor may the report or award of the arbitrator be admitted in evidence.

While this approach strives to deter requests for a trial de novo, we question whether its deterrent impact will be felt by vendors or creditors. In substance, this approach seems merely to give the vendor or creditor an extra bite at the apple, with little real incentive to accept defeat before the informal forum. If, in practice, the Fourth Department approach *does* effectively deter appeals from adverse arbitration awards, we see

---

[24] See Olesen v. Trust Co. of Chi., supra; U. S. v. Walker, supra; Stunda v. U. S., supra; McGrath v. Kirstensen, supra; Nat'l Union of Marine Cooks v. Arnold, supra; Dist. of Col. v. Clowan's, supra; Ohio ex rel. Bryant v. Apron Metropolitan Park District, supra.

no reason why this result cannot be achieved directly in the manner suggested above for the proposed Consumer Court.

Conclusion

In recommending the creation of an informal Consumer Court for individual grievances, we do not intend to make exaggerated claims on its behalf. Not only is the challenge of providing remedies not the whole of the picture, but the informal forum is not the whole of providing remedies. An essential and significant role must also be played by formal forums in the reform of their own procedures; by consumers acting in formal legal proceedings both individually and in class actions; by business associations in creating workable grievance procedures; and by public agencies with the power to define and proscribe unfair trade practices and act (through the use of preliminary and permanent injunctions, restitution orders, civil damages and even criminal penalties) to enforce their rules. This proposal is not intended to diminish efforts in these areas. It *is* intended to indicate that state and local government, together with an imaginative judiciary, can make a significant contribution toward resolving consumer grievances by establishing, in each neighborhood, fast, inexpensive, informal and effective means for asserting established consumer rights. If, as intended, the new forum both draws from and sinks roots into the community in which it operates, the forum may, in time, serve to resolve other forms of private disputes as well and, by so doing, help expand the role of law in resolving broader conflicts within the community.

Respectfully submitted,

THE SPECIAL COMMITTEE ON
CONSUMER AFFAIRS

STEPHEN L. KASS, Chairman

JULIA C. ALGASE
EDWARD BRANSILVER

DAVID CAPLOVITZ
MARTIN COLE
ALBERT W. DRIVER, JR.
CARL FELSENFELD
EMILIO P. GAUTIER
RICHARD A. GIVENS
LEON S. HARRIS
LEON I. JACOBSON
RHODA KARPATKIN
HOMER KRIPKE
JAMES LACK
RICHARD S. LANE
MICHAEL B. MAW
DAVID PAGET
EDWARD A. PERELL
JAMES PRENDERGAST
BRUCE RATNER
DON ALLEN RESNIKOFF
IRVING SCHER
PHILIP G. SCHRAG

Separate Report of Albert W. Driver, Jr.

It is undoubtedly true, as the report states, that voluntary settlement procedures cannot be depended upon to vindicate all consumer rights. It is my opinion, however, that the ease and simplicity of the litigation procedures recommended in the majority's report can scarcely fail to discourage voluntary settlements unless strong impetus for such settlements is affirmatively provided.

Certainly sound public policy, to say nothing of respect for the taxpayers, requires that access to public tribunals be denied to all litigants who have not made meaningful efforts to compose their differences on a voluntary basis. This principle is recognized in the requirement, for example, of a demand and refusal as a prerequisite to many causes of action. In breach of warranty cases, the Uniform Commercial Code likewise requires that the seller be given notice of an alleged breach (§ 607(a)(3)) and in appropriate cases an opportunity to cure the defect in question (§ 2–508). More directly to the point, perhaps, is the "statement of readiness" rule adopted by the Appellate Division, which requires the plaintiff's attorney to solemnly represent, as a condition to placement on the trial calendar, that the subject of settlement has been unsuccessfully discussed.

Since the authors of the majority report have very wisely resolved not to seek changes in the substantive law, the defendant vendors are presumably assured of receiving advance notice and a prior demand for a redress of grievances before being sued in the neighborhood consumer court. What is lacking from the committee's proposal, however, is certain minimal assurance that a vendor anxious and willing to dispose of the problem without official prodding or intervention will be given adequate opportunity to do so and will not be made an object of court room scrutiny unless his voluntary settlement procedures have been invoked without success.

There are undoubtedly various ways to deal with the problem. The simplest, I suggest, would be to permit the vendor to establish as a complete affirmative defense that it had adopted a reasonable procedure for the voluntary settlement of disputes, that it had formally invited the plaintiff to utilize that procedure but that the plaintiff did not do so. To qualify as reasonable, the procedure in question should enable claims to be presented and disposed of within a specified time period, perhaps 20 days after notice unless extended at plaintiff's request. Requirements as to the place of inspection of merchandise would likewise have to meet the test of reasonableness.

Questions

1. Do you agree with the basic concept underlying this model: that simplification of the procedure for consumer dispute settlement is desirable? If so, do you agree with the particular suggestions contained in the report?

2. Specifically, what is the proper relation of courts to inhabitants in a city; should a court be truly a "neighborhood" forum, or should there be a court for each Congressional District or even larger area? Should it hear only consumer cases, on the theory that specialized judges will render more sensitive justice, or are specialized judges likely to become sympathetic to one side or the other after a while? If the latter, is either side more likely to win the bias of the court? How should notice be given to the parties, particularly the consumer? Personal service seems expensive, and requiring it leads to abuses, but on the other hand, much mail goes undelivered in low-income areas because of common mailbox theft and frequent changes of address.

Who should be the judges? Should they be appointed, elected by a wide constituency, elected by community groups, or selected by some other procedure? Should they have any legal training? For that matter, should they be directed to apply the "law" to a case, or should they only apply some sense of equity? If lay persons are to do the former task, what special training should they be given? Is the use of lay judges or arbitrators essential to community confidence in the tribunal and the process? Or, alternatively, should the decision-makers not be chosen by the community on the theory that they will become embroiled in bitter conflict and are likely to lack the confidence of many in faction-ridden poverty areas in any event?

How much formality is necessary to give the consumer a fair chance without making it difficult for him to participate? For example, should discovery be allowed? It permits harassment of debtors and multiple postponement of cases, yet may be necessary to the consumer's own preparation of a case where vital documents, such as the original contract, a statement of account, or correspondence is in the hands of the creditor. Similarly, the right to appeal gives creditors an opportunity to escalate the conflict to a more expensive and more formal forum; is it central to fair adjudication? Should counsel be permitted in the forum? If counsel is barred, poorly educated consumers will often face sophisticated representatives, while the tyranny of legal services caseloads denies a lawyer to most consumers. See Silver, "The Imminent Failure of Legal Services for the Poor: Why and How to Limit Caseload," 46 J. Urban L. 217 (1969).

Consumer Class Actions

Class actions, long used by shareholders in stock fraud cases and by minority and poverty groups in civil rights cases, have been proposed as a powerful tool of consumer protection. See Dole, Consumer Class Actions Under Recent Consumer Credit Legislation, 44 N.Y.U.L.Rev. 80 (1969); Starrs; The Consumer Class Action Part II—Considerations of Procedure, 49 B.U.L.Rev. 407 (1969); Eckhardt, Consumer Class Actions, 45 Notre Dame Law. 663 (1970); Schrag and Meltsner, "Class Action: A Way to Beat The Bureaucracies Without Increasing Them", The Washington Monthly, November, 1972, p. 55; and see generally the Congressional Hearings cited in Dole, The Settlement of Class Actions for Damages, 71 Colum.L.Rev. 971 at 972–73 n. 16.

In a class action, one consumer could sue on behalf of himself and all others similarly situated; that is, all others with respect to whom the company had violated the law in substantially the same way. A suit by one person for $100 in damages could become a suit by ten thousand injured consumers for a million dollar judgment. Of course, most consumer cases do not involve facts sufficiently similar to those other persons to justify class action treatment. But thousands of cases ripe for class treatment do arise every year: the store that uses the same false advertisement to sell to hundreds; the door-to-door company whose salesmen memorize the same untrue pitch; the manufacturer of expensive "health" gadgetry which is declared unsafe for human use after thousands have purchased it; the automobile manufacturer which releases thousands of cars with the same design defect; the creditor whose computational practices render his contracts usurious; the low-income retailer whose appliances are sold at unconscionable prices within that doctrine's contemporary meaning.

Class actions have the following advantages: (1) They are just, in that each victim gets compensation, and the violator is punished in proportion to the magnitude of his wrong; (2) they promote for consumers the efficiency that collection lawyers enjoy as a result of volume, because a single attorney can treat thousands of cases as one and avoid duplicative investigation, motion practice and proof; (3) they deter wrongdoing, because a violator is subject to huge claims or even bankruptcy; (4) they encourage the emergence of new legal manpower to represent consumers, because courts commonly award successful class action attorneys a substantial portion of the gross award or settlement, even a million dollar counsel fee for a very long and involved case for the recovery of enormous claims; (5) they attract publicity, and thus call attention to abuses of consumers; (6) they give consumers' legal representatives a weapon with which to extract concessions and reforms from companies that violate the law (in a sense, encouraging collective bargaining between equal forces instead of forcing individual consumers to try to deal with big stores); (7) they are one of the few ways to provide remedies to persons with modest claims.

The battle for the right to maintain consumer class actions has been waged primarily in the state courts, because with the exception of truth-in-lending consumer protection law is almost exclusively state law, over which the federal courts, applying their liberal class action Rule, F.R.C.P. 23, have no jurisdiction. Cf. Snyder v. Harris, 394 U.S. 332, 895 S.Ct. 1053 (1969) (to invoke diversity jurisdiction, each member of class must have claim exceeding $10,000; aggregation not permitted). Many state courts have treated the concept icily.

NEW YORK CPLR § 1005

§ 1005. Class actions

(a) When allowed. Where the question is one of a common or general interest of many persons or where the persons who might be made parties are very numerous and it may be impracticable to bring them all before the court, one or more may sue or defend for the benefit of all.

(b) Protective orders; notice. The court at any stage of the action may impose such terms as shall fairly and adequately protect the interests of the persons on whose behalf the action is brought or defended. It may order that notice be given in a prescribed manner:

1. of a proposed settlement; or

2. of entry of a judgment.

(c) Court approval for compromise, discontinuance and dismissal. A class action shall not be compromised, discontinued or dismissed by consent, by default or for neglect to prosecute except with the approval of the court.

HALL v. COBURN CORP.

Court of Appeals of New York, 1970.
26 N.Y.2d 396, 311 N.Y.S.2d 281.

BERGAN, Judge. These are two class actions brought by purchasers under retail sales contracts for recovery of the penalty prescribed by section 414 of the Personal Property Law, Consol.Laws, c. 41, for a willful violation of the Retail Installment Sales Act (Personal Property Law, art. 10). The violation claimed is that the type on certain printed parts of the installment contracts was less than 8 point in size (§ 402).

Plaintiff Hall and plaintiffs Russell allege they entered into different retail installment contracts for the purchase of carpeting with different sellers and that material parts of the written contracts "were printed in type smaller than eight-point". Each seeks the recovery of the "amount of the credit service charge" which measures the statutory penalty (Personal Property Law, § 414, subd. 2).

The pleadings are quite indefinite about the "class" for which the actions are maintained. The court is not told anything about the class or even, as a fact, that it exists. The Hall action is described as being brought by plaintiff for herself "and all other persons who bought merchandise by entering into retail installment contracts by signing Form 'N.Y. —COB 3—N.Y.', which contracts were subsequently purchased by the Coburn Corporation of America".

There follows the allegation in similar general terms that the "question which is the subject of this action" (i. e., the size of the type) "is one of common and general interest to all persons who bought merchandise by entering into retail installment contracts by signing Form 'N.Y. —COB 3—N.Y.', which contracts were subsequently purchased by the Coburn Corporation of America". The Russell pleading is identical.

To permit the maintenance of a class action by one contracting party on behalf of others who made different contracts solely because of a similarity in form of the instrument of contract would enlarge greatly the scope of the New York class action permitted by CPLR 1005 (subd. [a]) as it, and its identical predecessor, section 195 of the Civil Practice Act, have been construed by this court.

One thing seems clear from these decisions: that there must be more of a common interest than the fact that a number of persons made a number of quite different and unrelated contracts with a number of different and unrelated sellers using the same written form which is claimed to be illegal. This does not become a common question because the same finance company is the assignee of the contracts and prepared them for use by the contracting parties.

The principle was stated by Judge Lehman in Society Milion Athena v. National Bank of Greece, 281 N.Y. 282, 292, 22 N.E.2d 374, 377: "Separate wrongs to separate persons, though committed by similar means and even pursuant to a single plan, do not alone create a common or general interest in those who are wronged." This language was quoted with approval by Judge Fuld in 1965 in Gaynor v. Rockefeller, 15 N.Y.2d 120, 129, 256 N.Y.S.2d 584, 589, 204 N.E.2d 627, 631 and by Judge Stevens in his dissent in Onofrio v. Playboy Club of N. Y., 20 A.D.2d 3, 7, 244 N.Y.S.2d 485, 489, a dissent which was expressly made the basis of decision by this court (15 N.Y.2d 740, 741, 257 N.Y.S.2d 171, 172, 205 N.E.2d 308, 309).

There is some inconsistency in the cases in this court, but an overall appraisal of them would suggest that a basis for class action is not stated in these complaints. Mr. Uviller in his brief for the Bar Association as *amicus* observes that the cases in this court "seem to defy explanation in terms of a single principle" although he suggests that their most "consistent requirement" seems to be the allegation of identical facts as the basis for recovery.

But "identical facts" were pleaded in Onofrio v. Playboy Club of N. Y. where all the other club members were in the same legal position as the plaintiffs Onofrio et al. "Suing on Behalf of Themselves and All Other Members of Playboy Club of New York, Inc." (15 N.Y.

2d 740, 257 N.Y.S.2d 171, 205 N.E.2d 308, supra). This was true also of Gaynor v. Rockefeller where the discrimination alleged affected what Judge Fuld described as "all other members of the indeterminate class of * * * citizens who may have been the victims" of discrimination (15 N.Y.2d 120, 129, 256 N.Y.S.2d 584, 589, 204 N.E.2d 627, 631, supra).

The present cases are similar to Coolidge v. Kaskel, 16 N.Y.2d 559, 260 N.Y.S.2d 835, 208 N.E.2d 780. It was there alleged that a prospectus sent to purchasers of stock in a co-operative building violated a statute. The dissent of Judge Burke clearly points up the issue and suggests in that case a much stronger basis for a class suit than the present ones.

The principle laid down in Bouton v. Van Buren, 229 N.Y. 17, 127 N.E. 477, which involved the right of the owner of a brokerage account on margin to sue for accounting on behalf of herself and other owners of accounts based on improper practices of the broker, has been consistently followed (cf. Brenner v. Title Guar. & Trust Co., 276 N.Y. 230, 11 N.E.2d 890).

The broadest support for the right to bring a class action seems to be Kovarsky v. Brooklyn Union Gas Co., 279 N.Y. 304, 18 N.E.2d 287, decided in 1938. The gas company had been making a small, but illegal, charge for turning on gas after temporary discontinuance of service. Plaintiff sued on behalf of himself and other consumers similarly situated.

It was held he could maintain a representative action insofar as it sought injunction and declaratory judgment since this (especially the declaration) could affect all consumers of the gas company whose gas was turned off and on, but that plaintiff could not in any event maintain a representative action for an accounting of the charges that might have been paid (p. 314, 18 N.E.2d p. 290).

There is a rational nexus between consumers serviced by the same utility, but whatever might be said of that common interest the tendency of the cases which followed *Kovarsky* (supra) is to restrict rather than enlarge, the scope of class action.

The real sanction accorded by this court to class suits has been in the closely associated relationships growing out of trust, partnership or joint venture, and ownership of corporate stock (see, e. g., Lichtyger v. Franchard Corp., 18 N.Y.2d 528, 277 N.E.2d 377, 223 N.E.2d 869; Leibert v. Clapp, 13 N.Y.2d 313, 247 N.Y.S.2d 102, 196 N.E.2d 540; Case v. Indian Motorcycle Co., 300 N.Y. 513, 89 N.E.2d 246).

Since the weight of authority seems to interdict these actions, the question is whether the court should now revise the rule it has laid down to permit class suits in this situation. It is submitted that the poor are victimized by this type of credit practice; that public authority is impotent to help them; and only by permitting self-help class actions initiated by private individuals and their lawyers can the imbalance be redressed.

The real injustice of course, is the fact the poor have to pay more for carpets and for everything else they buy on credit than people who are able to pay outright. Mr. and Mrs. Russell, for example, paid $736.92 for a $549.02 carpet for their living room and bedroom. Mrs. Hall paid $826.56 for a $580 carpet. But this was not due to the small type of which plaintiffs complain. It was due to the addition of charges which are expressly permitted by statute law.

The lawful credit service charges are all spelled out in section 404 of the Personal Property Law and were complied with in these purchases. There was nothing small about the figures which were writ-

ten in. They were large enough for anyone to see and are boldly framed. Added to the $609 of Mrs. Hall's contract, which included sales tax on the basic $580, are $10.01 for credit life insurance, $23.82 for property insurance and $183.73 for "credit service charge". It is not suggested any of this is illegal, but it adds about 40% to the cost of her purchase. The Russell contract contains similar components.

If this is unfair, as it seems to be, the statute should be changed either to prohibit sales of this type or to reduce the legally permissible charges. On this essentially economic problem it is doubtful if any public good can be accomplished by making a finance company pay back legally permissible credit charges in an indefinite number of contracts because the type is too small on printed parts of the contract.

The small type of which plaintiffs complain was not concerned with the terms of the contract of sale itself. In large part it dealt with the remedies by repossession and recovery if the purchaser did not pay for the goods.

That a seller can get his goods back if they are not paid for is a common understanding and expectation of those who buy on credit. The terms of credit and protective insurance were also in small type, but the cost of the insurance items was boldly stated in writing next to printed references of sufficient size.

If the type were as large as the printer's font affords it would not make the slightest difference in the execution of these costly contracts by people who need goods but are unable to pay for them. The essential thing for a purchaser to be able to see in this contract is the exact amounts which make up the price and what has to be paid. These things are certainly stated in bold writing.

The public value of judicial sanction to this kind of class action which would harass a finance company underwriting credit sales without addressing itself to the real evil of retail credit buying is open to substantial doubt. The basic public problem is the heavy cost of credit to consumers.

The size of the contract type, although a technicality prescribed by statute, is still a technicality which does not reach the base of the problem.

Both congressional committees and the American Bar Association acting for the legal profession have been concerned with means of protecting consumers against fraudulent, deceptive or unfair trade practices.

Limitations on, or alternatives to, class actions have been considered as, for example, requiring a predetermination of unfair practice by a public agency or a court at suit of a public agency, before a class action might be instituted. Another alternative is a requirement that actions for recovery be maintained by the public agency itself.

These limitations would tend to answer the main objection to the privately maintained consumer class action; that without adequate public control they may become instruments of harassment benefiting largely persons who activate the litigation.

No significant public benefit is discernible from the acceptance of these present class actions which do not, on the merits asserted, justify present departure from the existing New York rule. The Legislature in the spring of 1970 created the State Consumer Protection Board, the public function of which will be to protect consumers from unfair practices. (L. 1970, ch. 294.)

Besides this there has previously been adequate public authority in New York to see to it that the requirement of law as to the size of type on contracts be followed and enforcement need not rest on privately instituted actions for the public benefit.

The Banking Department may control the form of defendant's contracts and make appropriate directions as to the size of type. Besides this, the violation of the statute is a misdemeanor (Personal Property Law, § 414) and the Attorney-General may institute a prosecution based on small type.

The orders should be affirmed, without costs.

FULD, C. J., and BURKE, SCILEPPI, BREITEL, JASEN and GIBSON, JJ., concur.

Orders affirmed.

Note

1. Plaintiffs' counsel, attorneys of the NAACP Legal Defense Fund, chose *Hall* as a test case because the similarity among members of the class was more obvious than with almost any other possible facts. Since only the contract forms were at issue, defendants would be unable to argue that individual differences in sales presentations or in reliance prevented the maintenance of a representative action. An earlier case had foundered on the theory, among others, that reliance on false advertising material may have varied from one consumer to another. Onofrio v. Playboy Club, 15 N.Y.2d 740, 257 N.Y. S.2d 171, 205 N.E.2d 308 (1965). Yet the court seems to have been offended that while the defendant had violated a statute, which provided for a penalty, the case did not portray a sufficiently evil company or practice. Did the Fund choose the wrong type of case?

2. The year after Hall was decided, a consumer class action was brought in New York against a company which had allegedly used an illegal method to compute amounts due on revolving accounts, resulting in unlawfully high finance charges. Here was a case in which, in the words of

Hall, the "basic public problem" of "the heavy cost of credit" was directly at issue. The court held that a class action for money damages was improper, citing *Hall*. "The actions herein represent an idea whose time may have come, but perhaps unfortunately, not in the courts of the State of New York." Zachary v. R. H. Macy & Co., 66 Misc.2d 974, 323 N.Y.S. 2d 757 (Sup.Ct.N.Y.Co.1971), rev'd other grounds, 39 A.D.2d 116, 332 N.Y.S. 2d 425 (1972), rev'd again on other grounds, 31 N.Y.2d 443, 340 N.Y.S.2d 908 (1972).

A class action statute identical to that of New York was at issue in the following case.

VASQUEZ v. SUPERIOR COURT

Supreme Court of California, 1971.
4 Cal.3d 800, 94 Cal.Rptr. 796, 484 P.2d 964.

MOSK, Justice. We consider whether a group of consumers who have bought merchandise under installment contracts may maintain a class action seeking rescission of the contracts for fraudulent misrepresentation on behalf of themselves and others similarly situated, against both the seller of a product and the finance company to which the installment contracts were assigned. We conclude that such an action will lie against the seller under the principles set forth in Daar v. Yellow Cab Co. (1967) 67 Cal.2d 695, 63 Cal.Rptr. 724, 433 P.2d 732, and that the assignee of the contract is a proper party to such an action under the circumstances presented here.

The action was brought by 37 named plaintiffs on behalf of themselves as well as others who are residents of San Joaquin and Stanislaus Counties and who purchased frozen food and freezers from Bay Area Meat Company. They each executed two retail installment sales contracts to finance the purchases, one in payment of the food, and the other for the freezer,

and a binder contract. These contracts were assigned by Bay Area to three finance companies, Avco Thrift, Sterling Finance Corporation, and Beneficial Finance Company of Turlock, which were also named as defendants.[1] Defendants demurred to the complaint on the ground that it did not state a cause of action, and the demurrers were sustained without leave to amend insofar as the complaint alleged a class action for fraud but were overruled on the fraud count as to the named plaintiffs. A second cause of action, also alleged as a class action, charged violation of the Unruh Act (Civ.Code, § 1801 et seq.) in that the installment contracts failed to meet the requirements of that act. The demurrers of all defendants were overruled as to the second cause of action.

In upholding the demurrers to the class action aspect of the fraud count, the trial court made it clear that it was not concerned with the sufficiency of the particular allegations to assert a class action but, rather, that in its view a class action for fraud may not be maintained by consumers.[2] * * *

We conclude, therefore, that since plaintiffs cannot appeal from the order which bars a substantial portion of their cause from being heard on the merits, their petition for a writ of mandate deserves consideration.

---

[1] For literary convenience, defendants in the trial court who are real parties in interest will be referred to hereinafter either as defendants or as Bay Area, Avco, Sterling, or Beneficial. The reference to "plaintiffs," who are petitioners in this proceeding, will, unless otherwise stated, refer collectively to both the named plaintiffs and the unnamed class members.

[2] After analyzing some California cases on the subject of class actions, the court stated in its ruling that many state decisions appear to have been unsympathetic to consumer class actions, that these cases may be outmoded and class actions may be permitted, but that appellate courts are better suited to decide this question than a trial court.

II

Thirty years ago commentators, in urging the utility of the class suit to vindicate the rights of stockholders, made this incisive observation: "Modern society seems increasingly to expose men to * * * group injuries for which individually they are in a poor position to seek legal redress, either because they do not know enough or because such redress is disproportionately expensive. If each is left to assert his rights alone if and when he can, there will at best be a random and fragmentary enforcement, if there is any at all. This result is not only unfortunate in the particular case, but it will operate seriously to impair the deterrent effect of the sanctions which underlie much contemporary law. The problem of fashioning an effective and inclusive group remedy is thus a major one." (Kalven and Rosenfield, Function of Class Suit (1941) 8 U.Chi.L.Rev. 684, 686.)

What was noteworthy in the milieu three decades ago for stockholders is of far greater significance today for consumers. Not only have the means of communication improved and the sophistication of promotional and selling techniques sharpened in the intervening years, but consumers as a category are generally in a less favorable position than stockholders to secure legal redress for wrongs committed against them. For these reasons, the desirability of consumers suing as a class for fraud or other improper conduct by predatory sellers has been the topic of much thoughtful analysis in recent years. Numerous commentators have urged adaptation of class proceedings to consumer frauds. (See, e. g., Starrs, The Consumer Class Action (1969) 49 B.U.L.Rev. 211–250, 407–513; Eckhardt Consumer Class Actions (1970) 45 Notre Dame Law 663; Goldhammer, The Consumer Class Action in California (1970) 45 L.A.Bar Bull. 235.)

Protection of unwary consumers from being duped by unscrupulous sellers is an exigency of the utmost priority in contemporary society. According to the report of the Kerner Commission, many persons who reside in low income neighborhoods experience grievous exploitation by vendors using such devices as high pressure salesmanship, bait advertising, misrepresentation of prices, exorbitant prices and credit charges, and sale of shoddy merchandise. State laws governing relations between consumers and merchants are generally utilized only by informed, sophisticated parties, affording little practical protection to low income families. (Report of National Advisory Commission on Civil Disorders (Bantam ed. 1968) pp. 275–276; Hester, Deceptive Sales Practices and Form Contracts—Does the Consumer Have a Private Remedy? 1968 Duke L.J. 831.) The alternatives of multiple litigation (joinder, intervention, consolidation, the test case) do not sufficiently protect the consumer's rights because these devices "presuppose 'a group of economically powerful parties who are obviously able and willing to take care of their own interests individually through individual suits or individual decisions about joinder or intervention.'" (Dolgow v. Anderson (E.D.N.Y.1968) 43 F.R.D. 472, 484.)

Frequently numerous consumers are exposed to the same dubious practice by the same seller so that proof of the prevalence of the practice as to one consumer would provide proof for all. Individual actions by each of the defrauded consumers is often impracticable because the amount of individual recovery would be insufficient to justify bringing a separate action; thus an unscrupulous seller retains the benefits of its wrongful conduct. A class action by consumers produces several salutary by-products, including a therapeutic effect upon those sellers who indulge in fraudulent practices, aid to legitimate business enterprises by curtailing illegitimate competition, and avoidance to the judicial process of the burden of multiple litigation involving identical claims. The benefit to the parties and the courts would, in many circumstances, be substantial.

In California, we do not lack authority on the subject of the amenability of consumer claims to class action litigation. Section 382 of the Code of Civil Procedure provides, "* * * when the question is one of a common or general interest, of many persons, or when the parties are numerous, and it is impracticable to bring them all before the Court, one or more may sue or defend for the benefit of all." In the leading case of Daar v. Yellow Cab Co., supra, 67 Cal. 2d 695, 63 Cal.Rptr. 724, 433 P.2d 732, we held that an individual plaintiff may under this section bring a class action on his own behalf and on behalf of other taxicab riders similarly situated to recover overcharges allegedly made by defendant company. *Daar* did not, like the present case, involve purported fraudulent misrepresentations, but the principles set forth there guide us in determining whether the class action mechanism is an appropriate vehicle to resolve a claim based upon such misrepresentations.

The class in *Daar* consisted of several thousand taxicab riders. Plaintiff sought to recover as damages the illegal overcharges received by defendant cab company from riders over the four years immediately preceding the commencement of the action. It was alleged that proof of a common or single state of facts and law would establish the right of each member of the class to recover, that the percentage of rate overcharge to each class member was identical, and that the amount of the overcharge could be calculated from defendant's books. In reversing the trial court's judgment based on sustaining a demurrer to the complaint, we concluded that two requirements must be met to sustain a class action. The first

is existence of an ascertainable class, and the second is a well-defined community of interest in the questions of law and fact involved.

As to the necessity for an ascertainable class, the right of each individual to recover may not be based on a separate set of facts applicable only to him.[5]

The requirement of a community of interest does not depend upon an identical recovery, and the fact that each member of the class must prove his separate claim to a portion of any recovery by the class is only one factor to be considered in determining whether a class action is proper. The mere fact that separate transactions are involved does not of itself preclude a finding of the requisite community of interest so long as every member of the alleged class would not be required to litigate numerous and substantial questions to determine his individual right to recover subsequent to the rendering of any class judgment which determined in plaintiffs' favor whatever questions were common to the class.

Substantial benefits both to the litigants and to the court should be found before the imposition of a judgment binding on absent parties can be justified, and the determination of the question whether a class action is appropriate will depend upon whether the common questions are

---

[5] *Daar* involved the question of identification of class members, an issue which, as we shall see, presents no serious obstacle to the maintenance of a class action here. In *Daar* it was held that the fact that individual taxicab riders could not be identified at the time the action was brought was not significant because a complete determination of the issues affecting the class (i. e., such as whether there was an overcharge and the total amount thereof) could be made without identification and without the appearance of the individual class members. An accounting could determine the total of the overcharges, we stated, and after the questions relating to the alleged impropriety of the charge and the total amount of the overcharge had been determined, each class member could come forward to prove his own separate damages.

sufficiently pervasive to permit adjudication in a class action rather than in a multiplicity of suits.

In applying these principles to the facts alleged in *Daar*, we concluded that the issues which were common among the class members would be the principal issues in any individual action, both in terms of time to be expended in their proof and of their importance, and that if a class suit were not permitted, a multiplicity of legal actions dealing with identical basic issues would be required in order to permit recovery by each of several thousand taxicab riders. The result would be manifold burdens on the parties and on the judicial process. Furthermore, efforts to seek recovery by an individual taxicab user would be unlikely as there was a relatively small loss to each class member and separate actions would not be economically feasible. Absent a class suit, a wrong-doing defendant would retain the benefits of its wrongs.

III

Sufficiency of the Allegations to State a Class Action

With these principles in mind, we turn to the allegations of the complaint which seeks to rescind the contracts on the ground that plaintiffs were induced to execute the instruments by the fraudulent representations of Bay Area. The complaint alleges that the same representations regarding the food and the freezers were made to each plaintiff, that Bay Area knew the representations were false, that they were made with intent to defraud, and that plaintiffs signed the agreements in reliance thereon. It is further alleged that plaintiffs are united in interest in that, inter alia, they have all signed contracts to purchase food and a freezer in reliance upon the misrepresentations, which in turn were based upon recitations by salesmen of a standard sales monologue contained in a training book

and sales manual. Proof of a common state of facts, it is alleged, will establish the right of each class member to rescind his contract.

1. *Ascertainability of the Class*

The first requisite for the maintenance of a class action, ascertainability of the class, presents no serious obstacle in this case. The complaint alleges that the members of the class are all those who have signed installment contracts with Bay Area for the purchase of meat and a freezer after January 1, 1966, who reside in Stanislaus or San Joaquin Counties, and who have paid or are obligated to pay money on the contracts to one of the defendants. It appears that there are approximately 200 persons in the class. Furthermore, it is alleged, the names and addresses of the class members may be ascertained from defendants' books.

2. *Community of Interest*

We next ascertain whether there are issues common to the class as a whole sufficient in importance so that their adjudication on a class basis will benefit both the litigants and the court. In this evaluation the mere fact that the transaction between Bay Area and each plaintiff was separately consummated is not determinative so long as each class member will not be required to litigate numerous and substantial issues to establish his individual right to recover.

In order to prevail plaintiffs must show that Bay Area made false representations with knowledge of their falsity, that these representations were made with intent to and did induce reasonable reliance by plaintiffs, and that plaintiffs suffered damages as a result. (Ach v. Finkelstein (1968) 264 Cal.App.2d 667, 674, 40 Cal.Rptr. 472.) Defendants assert that none of these elements may be proved by the device of a class action because each plaintiff entered into a separate transaction at a different time and proof of the fact of representation, its falsity, and reliance as to the named plaintiffs will not supply proof of these elements as to the absent members of the class. Thus, it is asserted, each member of the class must establish his right to recover on the basis of facts peculiar to his own circumstances, because of which the action may not be tried as a class suit.

a. *The Representations*

The representations conveniently fall into two categories: those concerning the contract for the purchase of the freezer and those relating to the frozen food contract. We examine them separately.

Plaintiffs allege that Bay Area's salesmen represented to each member of the class that the freezers were of high quality and guaranteed for a lifetime and that they were sold at a reasonable retail price.[6] It is asserted by plaintiffs that they can demonstrate these representations were in fact made to each class member without individual testimony because the salesmen employed by Bay Area memorized a standard statement containing the representations (which in turn were based on a printed narrative and sales manual) and that this statement was recited by rote to every member of the class. The demurrers must be deemed to admit these facts.[7] If plaintiffs can prove their allegations at the trial, an inference that the representations were made to each class member would arise, in which case it would be unnecessary to elicit the testimony of each plaintiff as to whether the representations were in fact made to him.

It is also alleged that the representations regarding the freezers were false, and that the prices charged for them were exorbitant, excessive and unconscionable, amounting to not less than twice the reasonable retail price. The falsity of these representations could be shown on a common basis since proof of the allegations regarding the quality and price of the freezers purchased by the named plaintiffs would provide proof as to all. Although it appears that not every member of the class purchased the same brand and model of freezer, it is likely that all the brands and models are represented among the 37 named plaintiffs and to the extent that this is not so evidence may be introduced to cure the omission.

We turn next to the alleged misrepresentations regarding the frozen food purchased by plaintiffs. It is averred that Bay Area salesmen represented to each class member that the food orders were sold at a wholesale rate, that each order would last a minimum of seven months, and that the total cost of a "seven-month" food order and a freezer would be less than the amount plaintiffs were spending each month for similar food at retail stores.

According to the allegations, a common sales recitation was also employed in the sale of the frozen food and, for the reasons discussed above regarding the freezer contracts, we assume for the present that these representations were in fact made to each plaintiff.

As to the falsity of the representations, we perceive no singular difficulty in proving on a common basis whether the food supplied by Bay Area was sold at wholesale rates. Defendants insist, however, that it would be impossible without the individual testimony of each plaintiff to demonstrate the falsity of the alleged representations that the supply of food would last for seven months. It is argued that each plaintiff must have given an estimate

---

[6] We do not discuss whether the allegations are sufficient to state a cause of action for fraud. The trial court has concluded that the complaint is sufficient in this regard in overruling defendants' demurrers insofar as the named plaintiffs are concerned.

[7] Defendants deny in their briefs that there was a standard sales manual and they assert that the recital did not contain the alleged misrepresentations. These are factual matters for determination by the trial court.

of his consumption to the salesman, that the accuracy of this estimate as well as the salesman's calculation of the amount of food required for a seven-month supply would vary in each case, and that individual proof of consumption of each plaintiff's family during the period would be required.

This contention is unpersuasive at the pleading stage of the proceedings because we cannot assume that plaintiffs will be unable to establish their allegations without the separate testimony of each class member; at least they must be afforded the opportunity to show that they can prove their allegations on a common basis. An examination of the contracts attached to the complaint indicates that Bay Area sold varying quantities of food to the several plaintiffs, but that each order was of a standard type. Thus, for example, customers who purchased Pack F received 119 pounds of beef and 123 pounds of assorted variety meats, vegetables, and fruit juices. Each type of food pack had a standard price.

The existence of these standard orders raises at least a rebuttable implication that the salesmen utilized a defined formula to determine the amount of food a particular family would need for a specified period of time. Whether this formula related to the size of the family, the amount the family spent for food each month [8] or a combination of factors, is not clear. If a formula was in fact utilized the alleged falsity of the representation regarding the length of time a food order would suffice can be demonstrated by proof of such factors as the average monthly consumption of food for a family of a particular size.

The final allegation of misrepresentation with regard to the frozen food is that Bay Area salesmen told plaintiffs the total cost of a "seven-month" food order and a freezer would be less than the amount each plaintiff was spending every month on food at retail stores. The thrust of this allegation is that it was represented the price differential between the cost of the food purchased from Bay Area and its retail value elsewhere would be adequate to pay for the freezers purchased by plaintiffs. It appears from what has been said above that this allegation, too, may be amenable to proof on a common basis.

There may be other methods by which plaintiffs can establish the alleged falsity of the representations regarding the food orders for the class as a whole. For the purpose of determining if the demurrers should have been overruled, it is sufficient that there is a reasonable possibility plaintiffs can establish a prima facie community of interest among the class members on the false representation issue. Plaintiffs' inability to do so, if that be the ultimate result, can be determined at a later stage of the proceeding.

b. *Reliance*

The next element which plaintiffs must prove in order to prevail is reliance upon the alleged misrepresentations. If they can establish without individual testimony that the representations were made to each plaintiff and that they were false, it should not be unduly complicated to sustain their burden of proving reliance thereon as a common element.

The rule in this state and elsewhere is that it is not necessary to show reliance upon false representations by direct evidence. "The fact of reliance upon alleged false representations may be inferred from the circumstances attending the transaction which oftentimes afford much stronger and more satisfactory evidence of the inducement which prompted the party defrauded to enter into the contract than his direct testimony to the same

---

[8] There is some indication in the record that salesmen asked prospective customers the amounts they spent on food each month and that this amount was written down in the course of the sale.

effect." (Hunter v. McKenzie (1925) 197 Cal. 176, 185, 239 P. 1090, 1094; Gormly v. Dickinson (1960) 178 Cal. App.2d 92, 105, 2 Cal.Rptr. 650; Thomas v. Hawkins (1950) 96 Cal.App.2d 377, 380, 215 P.2d 495; Mathewson v. Naylor (1937) 18 Cal.App.2d 741, 744, 64 P.2d 979; see Bank of St. Helena v. Lilienthal-Brayton Co. (1928) 89 Cal. App. 258, 262, 264 P. 546; 12 Williston on Contracts (3d ed. 1970) p. 480.)

Williston speaks in terms of a presumption: "Where representations have been made in regard to a material matter and action has been taken, in the absence of evidence showing the contrary, it will be presumed that the representations were relied on." (12 Williston on Contracts (3d ed. 1970) 480.) This rule is in accord with the Restatement. (Rest., Contracts, § 479, illus. 1.) Whether an inference (as held in Hunter v. McKenzie, supra, 197 Cal. 176, 185, 239 P. 1090) or a presumption (as described by Williston and the Restatement) of reliance arises upon proof of a material false representation we need not determine in this case. It is sufficient for our present purposes to hold that if the trial court finds material misrepresentations were made to the class members, at least an inference of reliance would arise as to the entire class.[9] Defendants may, of course, introduce evidence in rebuttal.

[9] The requirement that reliance must be justified in order to support recovery may also be shown on a class basis. If the court finds that a reasonable man would have relied upon the alleged misrepresentations, an inference of justifiable reliance by each class member would arise. It should be noted in this connection that a misrepresentation may be the basis of fraud if it was a substantial factor in inducing the plaintiff to act and that it need not be the sole cause of damage. (Wennerholm v. Stanford Univ. Sch. of Med. (1942) 20 Cal.2d 713, 717, 128 P.2d 522.) Plaintiffs suggest that individual proof of reliance may be dispensed with if, as they assert, fraud may be presumed from the alleged unconscionable price of the freezers. We need not discuss the merit of this theory since we conclude that if the trial court finds

Some federal class action cases in which stockholders have alleged fraud on the basis of printed misrepresentations in a corporation prospectus hold that individual proof may not be required to establish reliance by each stockholder. (See, e. g., Green v. Wolf Corporation (2d Cir. 1968) 406 F.2d 291, 301; Dolgow v. Anderson, supra, 43 F.R.D. 472, 491.) [10]

c. *Damages*

The final element of plaintiffs' cause of action is damages. *Daar* makes it clear that although ultimately each class member will be required in some manner to establish his individual damages this circumstance does not preclude the maintenance of the suit as a class action.[11]

3. *Summary*

The complaint alleges there is an ascertainable class and plaintiffs may be able to demonstrate a community of interest as to the elements of their claim of fraud, aside from the amount of damages suffered by each class member. They

that the alleged misrepresentations were material, it could find an inference or rebuttable presumption of reliance by each class member without his direct testimony.

[10] Beneficial cites Morris v. Burchard (S.D. N.Y.1971) 51 F.R.D. 530, in support of its position that individual proof of reliance is required. In *Morris* it was held that the fact of reliance could not be proved on a collective basis because the alleged misrepresentations to the class members were not similar. The present case is distinguishable, because here plaintiffs have alleged a community of interest as to the representations.

[11] Plaintiffs pray for return of the amounts they paid on the contracts, less the value of the food they consumed, a sum of $1,300 or less for most plaintiffs, and not more than $1,700 for any of them. In addition, they seek damages for injury to their credit standing in the community as a result of the outstanding obligation on the contracts and compensation for storing the unused freezers in their homes. These damages are alleged to amount to no more than $1,000 for any one plaintiff. Finally, they ask punitive damages of $5,000 each, alleging that defendants were guilty of oppression, fraud and malice.

should, in any event, be afforded the opportunity to demonstrate that proof of most of the important issues as to the named plaintiffs will supply the proof as to all. We conclude, therefore, that the trial court erred in sustaining the demurrers to the first cause of action on the ground that it did not allege a class action.

It may be, of course, that the trial court will determine in subsequent proceedings that some of the matters bearing on the right to recovery require separate proof by each class member. If this should occur, the applicable rule as stated in *Daar* is that the maintenance of the suit as a class action is not precluded so long as the issues which may be jointly tried, when compared to those requiring separate adjudication, justify the maintenance of the suit as a class action. If the questions which must be litigated separately are not numerous or substantial, it would be advantageous to the parties and the judicial system to allow the named plaintiffs to sue on behalf of the class.[12] * *

IV

Defendant's Contentions

Defendants insist that a class action is inappropriate under these circumstances. It is argued that the present case is distinguishable from *Daar* because there separate suits would have been impractical since the recovery of the individual class members would have been very small whereas in the present case each plaintiff's claim is sufficiently large to justify separate actions.

The complaint alleges that the total obligation of most class members on their contracts is less than $1,300. While the impracticability of bringing an individual action for comparatively small potential recovery is a consideration in favor of allowing a class action, it cannot be said that a potential recovery for each class member larger than a nominal sum necessarily militates against maintenance of such a suit. In a recent case we allowed an individual stockholder to sue on behalf of a class although the damages alleged for each member were substantially more than those prayed for in the present case. (See Jones v. H. F. Ahmanson & Co. (1969) 1 Cal.3d 93, 81 Cal.Rptr. 592, 460 P.2d 464.) We cannot conclude as a matter of law that consumers are entitled to less protection as a class than stockholders.[13] * * * [Reversed]

Question

How can you account for the radically different attitudes of the highest courts of New York and California, each of them unanimous, interpreting the same language?

PROPOSALS FOR CONSUMER CLASS ACTIONS IN FEDERAL COURTS

FEDERAL RULE OF CIVIL PROCEDURE NO. 23

Rule 23. Class Actions

(a) *Prerequisites to a Class Action.* One or more members of a class may sue

---

[12] The character of the issues which must be separately tried varies, of course, from case to case, but each must be tested by the rules set forth above. For example, in *Daar* each class member was required to prove that he rode in a taxicab during the period in issue and that he was overcharged a stated amount, but the total amount of damages to the class as a whole were not difficult to ascertain on a common basis since it was alleged that the exact amount of overcharges was known to the taxicab company and could be ascertained from its books and records.

[13] The United States Supreme Court has interpreted rule 23 of the Federal Rules of Civil Procedure (28 U.S.C.A.) as prohibiting the aggregation of separate and distinct claims to fulfill the $10,000 requirement for federal district court jurisdiction. (Snyder v. Harris (1969) 391 U.S. 332, 89 S.Ct. 1053, 22 L.Ed.2d 319.) Thus, a class action in the federal courts is not appropriate where the claim of each plaintiff is separate and distinct unless a class member has a claim of $10,000 or more.

or be sued as representative parties on behalf of all only if (1) the class is so numerous that joinder of all members is impracticable, (2) there are questions of law or fact common to the class, (3) the claims or defenses of the representative parties are typical of the claims or defenses of the class, and (4) the representative parties will fairly and adequately protect the interests of the class.

(b) Class Actions Maintainable. An action may be maintained as a class action if the prerequisites of subdivision (a) are satisfied, and in addition:

(1) the prosecution of separate actions by or against individual members of the class would create a risk of

(A) inconsistent or varying adjudications with respect to individual members of the class which would establish incompatible standards of conduct for the party opposing the class, or

(B) adjudications with respect to individual members of the class which would as a practical matter be dispositive of the interests of the other members not parties to the adjudications or substantially impair or impede their ability to protect their interests; or

(2) the party opposing the class has acted or refused to act on grounds generally applicable to the class, thereby making appropriate final injunctive relief or corresponding declaratory relief with respect to the class as a whole; or

(3) the court finds that the questions of law or fact common to the members of the class predominate over any questions affecting only individual members, and that a class action is superior to other available methods for the fair and efficient adjudication of the controversy. The matters pertinent to the findings include: (A) the interest of members of the class in individually controlling the prosecution or defense of separate ac-

tions; (B) the extent and nature of any litigation concerning the controversy already commenced by or against members of the class; (C) the desirability or undesirability of concentrating the litigation of the claims in the particular forum; (D) the difficulties likely to be encountered in the management of a class action.

(c) Determination by Order Whether Class Action to be Maintained; Notice; Judgment; Actions Conducted Partially as Class Actions.

(1) As soon as practicable after the commencement of an action brought as a class action, the court shall determine by order whether it is to be so maintained. An order under this subdivision may be conditional, and may be altered or amended before the decision on the merits.

(2) In any class action maintained under subdivision (b)(3), the court shall direct to the members of the class the best notice practicable under the circumstances, including individual notice to all members who can be identified through reasonable effort. The notice shall advise each member that

(A) the court will exclude him from the class if he so requests by a specified date; (B) the judgment, whether favorable or not, will include all members who do not request exclusion; and (C) any member who does not request exclusion may, if he desires, enter an appearance through his counsel.

(3) The judgment in an action maintained as a class action under subdivision (b)(1) or (b)(2), whether or not favorable to the class, shall include and describe those whom the court finds to be members of the class. The judgment in an action maintained as a class action under the subdivision (b)(3), whether or not favorable to the class, shall include and specify or describe those to whom the notice provided in subdivision (c)(2)

was directed, and who have not requested exclusion, and whom the court finds to be members of the class.

(4) When appropriate (A) an action may be brought or maintained as a class action with respect to particular issues, or (B) a class may be divided into subclasses and each subclass treated as a class, and the provisions of this rule shall then be construed and applied accordingly.

(d) Orders in Conduct of Actions. In the conduct of actions to which this rule applies, the court may make appropriate orders: (1) determining the course of proceedings or prescribing measures to prevent undue repetition or complication in the presentation of evidence or argument; (2) requiring, for the protection of the members of the class or otherwise for the fair conduct of the action, that notice be given in such manner as the court may direct to some or all of the members of any step in the action, or of the proposed extent of the judgment, or of the opportunity of members to signify whether they consider the representation fair and adequate, to intervene and present claims or defenses, or otherwise to come into the action; (3) imposing conditions on the representative parties or on intervenors; (4) requiring that the pleadings be amended to eliminate therefrom allegations as to representation of absent persons, and that the action proceed accordingly; (5) dealing with similar procedural matters. The orders may be combined with an order under Rule 16, and may be altered or amended as may be desirable from time to time.

(e) Dismissal or Compromise. A class action shall not be dismissed or compromised without the approval of the court, and notice of the proposed dismissal or compromise shall be given to all members of the class in such manner as the court directs. As amended Feb. 28, 1966, eff. July 1, 1966.

Note on Proposed Federal Class Action Legislation

Decisions such as Hall, coming at a time when the federal courts are facilitating increased use of class actions under Rule 23 in antitrust and stock fraud cases, see Eisen v. Carlisle and Jacquelin, 391 F.2d 555 (2d Cir. 1968) and —— F.2d —— (2d Cir., May 1, 1973); Dolgow v. Anderson, 43 F.R.D. 472 (E.D.N.Y. 1968), have led to pressure for Congressional reform of consumer class action law. Two different types of federal reforms have been suggested. One (see S. 1980, 91st Cong.) would permit classes of consumers to sue in the federal courts for violations affecting commerce of state statutory or decisional law for the benefit of consumers. Thus the federal courts would interpret and apply, in class action cases, the whole range of state consumer protection law, including the law of warranty, fraud, misrepresentation, credit limitations and unconscionability, as well as particular statutory protections such as prohibitions against undisclosed balloon payments. See N.Y.Pers.Prop.Law § 402 (3)(b)(2)(1969).

The other proposal, (see e. g., S. 3201 (91st Cong.)) urged by those who are uncomfortable at the prospect of federal courts applying state law so extensively, would prohibit, as a matter of federal law, many abhorrent consumer selling practices; violations of these federal laws could be redressed in class actions in federal courts because they would arise under federal law. In both instances, the Congress would waive the requirement that each individual plaintiff have a claim of $10,000, although to prevent actions in cases where the cost of distribution of the proceeds to the class would exceed the recovery itself, a minimum average claim of ten or fifteen dollars might be required.

In the 91st and 92nd Congress, opposition to class action proposals was more fierce than opposition to any other consumer protection legislation. A class action bill was reported favorably by the Senate Commerce Committee in the 91st Congress (S.Rep. 1124) (1970), but the bill never emerged from the House Commerce Committee, and so was allowed to die.

Opponents of class action legislation never declared themselves against the concept of consumer protection. Rather, they worried about encouragement of lawsuits which would "harass legitimate business" and "burden the federal courts".

HEARINGS ON CONSUMER PROTECTION, U. S. SENATE COMMITTEE ON COMMERCE SUBCOMMITTEE FOR CONSUMERS, WASHINGTON, D. C. (1970)

STATEMENT OF MILTON HANDLER, ATTORNEY, NEW YORK

* * *

The net effect of these provisions, I submit, would be to impose an intolerable burden on the Federal courts and subject accused wrongdoers to unjust harassment without resulting in any commensurate benefit to consumers.

Let me develop that.

The purpose of class suits has traditionally been to allow the courts to deal with a multiplicity of claims in an economical manner by permitting the actual parties to a litigation also to represent the interests of persons who are not before the court but who occupy substantially the same legal positions with respect to the controversy in question. The reasons for caution in the utilization of such a device are readily apparent. On the one hand, there is a danger to potential defendants, since a plaintiff with even a minuscule claim may increase the *in terrorem* effect of his action by invoking the claims of untold numbers of other persons; on the other hand, since absent

claimants are, in effect, made to stand or fall with their purported representatives, it is essential that there be every assurance that their interests are in fact being adequately represented.

Under this bill any Tom, Dick, or Harry can select himself to be the representative of all of the consumers of the United States without any check whatsoever by the courts.

In addition—as the courts have shown themselves to be acutely aware—the class action procedure can have the effect of instantly transforming an orderly lawsuit into a gigantic litigation burdening the court's resources beyond its capacity to manage or effectively control.

For these reasons, the draftsmen of rule 23 under the aegis of the Supreme Court took great pains to insure that class actions would be permitted only under carefully prescribed conditions.

In my prepared paper, I outline what those conditions are.

The necessity of applying the safeguards provided by rule 23 is particularly acute in the case of consumer claims. Here, the homogeneity which justifies such wholesale adjudication will often be lacking. Purchases are made by consumers at different times and places and from different sellers.

This is on the assumption that the suit will be allowed against the manufacturer, which is not always clear. The ultimate purchaser does not buy normally from the manufacturer. If the producer is being sued in a consumer class action, it will be on the basis of multiple purchases from multiple sellers under varying conditions and frequently varying prices.

Furthermore, there is every likelihood that a consumer-plaintiff's claim may be very small—under S. 3092 the defrauded purchaser of a $1 item could presumably bring suit on behalf of all other purchasers of that product in the United States.

Where there are thousands, millions, tens of millions, and even hundreds of millions of claimants, I ask: How are these claims to be processed by the courts? And what happens if the defendant insists upon its constitutional right to a jury trial on the issue of the amount of damages suffered by each individual claimant?

If this committee believes I am exaggerating, let me tell you there are pending in the Federal courts suits on behalf of every inhabitant of these United States. The bill you are presently considering would not only permit, but encourage and invite class actions on behalf of untold numbers of people.

The burden S. 3092 would impose on the Federal judiciary is further aggravated by the provision in the bill permitting class actions to be brought for claims based on any State statute or decisional law which may be found to be "for the benefit of consumers." Since the word "consumer" is defined to include anyone offered or supplied "interests in land" as well as goods, services, and intangibles, the effect of the bill is to extend Federal jurisdiction to all landlords and tenant disputes as well as to all contract and fraud cases affecting consumers.

I would like to ask this committee to consider how, as a practical matter, the limited resources of the Federal judiciary can be expected to cope with this flood of litigation.

The number of Federal judges as contrasted with the number of State court judges is infinitesimal. The Federal courts have very heavy responsibilities in the administraton of Federal criminal justice, in the trial of complex cases arising out of Federal statutes, such as antitrust, patents, trademarks, copyrights, and the like, in the interpretation of the host of new laws that go on the books each year, and in defending the constitutional rights of all of our citizens.

Just picture one of our district courts in which there is only a single judge, and let's suppose that one of these consumer class actions on behalf of millions of claimants were brought before him. He would be out of business for a year or 2 years or perhaps 10 years. What happens to all of his other judicial responsibilities?

It is no good for the Chief Justice of the United States to go around the country complaining about delays, it is no good for Members of Congress to complain about judicial delay, if, at the same time, we enact legislation which would destroy the judicial system because it would put burdens upon it which it is unable to discharge.

It is of no use to talk about crime waves if we don't give the judges time to try criminal cases.

The class action procedure proposed in S. 3092 may also result in great inequity for the potential defendants in such suits. In considering the interests of such persons—which would include virtually all of the businesses in America, both large and small—we should remember that we are talking about persons who, in the main, are not unscrupulous defrauders of the public. Many of the deceptive acts and practices which the Federal Trade Commission has dealt with in the past do not concern hard-core frauds. Whether or not the law has been violated is not always clear. To put a businessman to the expense of defending himself against a class suit may place him in a position where the costs of litigation by themselves can impose upon him a penalty completely disproportionate to the offense.

Moreover, these heavy expenses are incurred even if the defendant establishes his innocence. Ultimately these costs, like all costs of doing business, will be borne by the consumer.

It is for this reason, and others, that I think the idea of the consumer class suit will be self-defeating.

Let us consider for a moment the measure of damages which might be appropriate in the most common cases of consumer fraud. I suggest that the committee read the 11 enumerated practices in this bill and ask yourselves what will be the measure of damage applicable to each offense.

What, for example, would be the amount of damages which would be awarded to the victim of bait and switch advertising who was induced to purchase a product other than that advertised? How much should be awarded to the purchaser at a "going out of business sale" which in fact had been going on for 10 years?

Isn't it perfectly plain that in many of these situations a monetary recovery is unrealizable? Thus, for such cases, the effect of the proposed consumer class action would be nil. Zero multiplied by 100 million is still zero.

Lest I be charged with inconsistency, let me make clear that while in certain instances you are creating a remedy which would be meaningless because nobody can resort to it since there will be no recovery, I am also suggesting that you are creating a remedy for which, in other instances, there may be some recovery but at disproportionate cost to our society.

Let's examine the case where some definite amount of individual damage can be shown. It is reasonable to expect that such monetary claims will be relatively small—so small, in fact, that any recovery due to the consumer is likely to be largely eroded by the costs of litigation. In Gas Service Co. v. Coburn, a companion case with Snyder v. Harris, the plaintiff's claim amounted to $7.81.

Suppose you have a class action of thousands or millions of claims of that dimension and with the legislation overriding the decision of Snyder v. Harris, you permit the aggregation of all these small claims.

Now, the claims have to be processed. They don't process themselves. It is an easy matter under the bill to aggregate all the claims, but what happens after the aggregation? The cases have to be tried in court, liability has to be established, each claim has to be made out. This can be very costly.

There is first the cost of proving each claim. There is the cost of publishing or serving notice upon the class members. There is the cost of administration in the Federal courts. There are the fees of counsel. Is it not likely that the administrative costs may well exceed the amount of claim itself?

How much of this $7.81 overcharge for each consumer would remain after all these costs are paid?

I ask whether, in view of the dangers inherent in the class action device and the miniscule benefit individual consumers can expect, it would not be more in the public interest if the resources to be expended in conducting such litigation were allocated to some other consumer purpose?

Now, I come to what I would regard as constructive suggestions for the committee to consider in lieu of a remedy which I think is neither feasible nor desirable.

Mr. Chairman, it seems to me, on the basis of my experience in this area, that the important thing is to keep the stable locked before the horse is stolen.

What does that mean?

With proper enforcement most fraudulent schemes could be thwarted by the prompt issuance of preliminary injunctions. If fraud is promptly thwarted, people will not be victimized. Prevention will advance the public interest to a much greater extent than compensation.

Under the new legislation the Commission will have the power to seek such preliminary relief. So do some of the States under State law and those that have no such legislation should follow the lead of the Federal Government and the States that provide such relief.

The enforcement agencies, whether they be the Commission or the Attorney General, need adequate appropriations for the purposes of detection, investigation and litigation. Given the tools, the enforcement agencies should be able to stem the tide of misrepresentation by prompt and effective action.

An additional and especially effective means of preventing consumer frauds is one which the President stressed in his message on consumer protection. I am referring to consumer education and the distribution of information which can aid consumers in making intelligent purchasing decisions. The President indicated that the nationwide network of community action agencies might be one instrument for extending such education to the poor—who are the group most seriously victimized by consumer deception.

He further stated that he had requested that a new consumer bulletin be published on a regular basis.

I feel that this is one area in which every dollar spent can only mean saving untold dollars which would otherwise have to be expended in the infinitely more expensive task of attempting to remedy harm which has already occurred.

STATEMENT OF HERBERT H. SCHIFF, CHAIRMAN OF THE BOARD AND PRESIDENT OF SCOA INDUSTRIES, INC.; ACCOMPANIED BY EUGENE A. KEENEY, PRESIDENT OF THE AMERICAN RETAIL FEDERA- TION; AND JAMES M. GOLDBERG, VICE PRESIDENT, GOVERNMENT AFFAIRS DIVISION

Mr. SCHIFF. Mr. Chairman and members of the subcommittee, my name is Herbert H. Schiff. I am chairman of the board and president of SCOA Industries, Inc., of Columbus, Ohio, and I am appearing here today as chairman of the consumer relations committee of the American Retail Federation.

The American Retail Federation is a national organization which, through its 50 state and 29 national retail trade association affiliates, represents more than 800,000 retail establishments of all types.

A ball park figure would be that we represent about $150 billion worth of retail volume and we employ somewhere around 10 million people.

We appreciate the opportunity to appear here today to express retailing's views with regard to three bills which would broaden the authority of the Federal Trade Commission and which would provide access to the Federal court system for consumer class actions.

The retail industry, which acts as the purchasing agent for the consumer, believes that the interest of its customers is paramount. We believe that a customer who feels he has been defrauded, and who cannot obtain satisfaction through the normal complaint procedure, is entitled to a remedy.

In our own company, we have a policy to give the customer's money back immediately and then investigate the claim.

As Virginia Knauer, the President's Special Assistant for Consumer Affairs, has pointed out, the remedy should be "convenient, expeditious and effective." Underscoring these criteria is the fact that the vast majority of consumer complaints involve relatively small amounts, most often ranging from 10 cents to $100.

But what remedy is possible that would be fast, efficient, effective? No legislative proposal to date—and that includes the class action proposals pending before this subcommittee—meets these requirements. Class actions, as we will explain later, are a particularly unsuitable remedy in these instances. There are, however, existing approaches which are available to the consumer, and which, if pursued with vigor, could provide the remedy that is needed.

ALTERNATIVES TO CLASS ACTIONS

First, there is Federal Trade Commission enforcement of its section 5 authority. The FTC has, of course, been the target of many criticisms and suggestions in recent months—first through the report of the so-called "Nader's Raiders" and later through the investigation of the White House—requested special commission of the American Bar Association.

With these reports as guidelines, the new FTC Chairman, Caspar Weinberger, has taken steps to speed up the internal procedures within his agency. We are pleased that the Chairman has indicated he will reactivate the Commission's long-dormant Office of Program Review. We believe that if Chairman Weinberger is given a free hand to reorganize the agency as he sees fit, the FTC can play what he foresees as an "aggressive role" in protecting the consumer.

Second, the Commission should be given the authority to obtain preliminary injunctions in cases of consumer fraud. Even a revitalized FTC, with its programs and priorities firmly in mind, is limited in its effectiveness without this authority.

For this reason, the American Retail Federation supports S. 2246, the Deceptive Sales Act, introduced by the Distinguished chairman of this subcommittee. We recommend that amendments be added to S. 2246 to make it conform to the version of this bill which was passed by the Senate nearly 2 years ago. We would be pleased to submit legislative language.

In addition, we believe that S. 2246 should be amended to require the issuance of an FTC complaint prior to the time that a preliminary injunction is sought. This will assure that the Commission will not use the injunction technique as a substitute for actual investigation of an alleged violation of the laws which it administers.

A third alternative to class actions is more vigorous use of small claims courts throughout the country. We believe that such courts provide an effective means for fast, efficient, effective relief. If the procedures for using small claims courts are not widely known, then we suggest that more localities follow the lead of Mrs. Bess Myerson Grant in New York City. Her department of consumer affairs recently published a consumer-oriented brochure entitled, "How to Sue in Small Claims Court."

Fourth, the National Center for Dispute Settlement, an offshoot of the American Arbitration Association, has volunteered its efforts to help resolve consumer disputes.

In this same vein, it should be noted that Mrs. Knauer is using the authority of her Office of Consumer Affairs to help bring consumer and business together in settlement of the complaints which come across her desk. We support legislation which would make this Office a statutory one within the Executive Office of the President.

These are by no means the only alternatives to class actions. We believe, however, that they can work if used properly. We recommend efforts by both business and consumers to use these existing and suggested remedies more effectively.

The potential impact of indiscriminate consumer class actions on business is devastating. I might deviate to say this: We spend millions of dollars every year building up our names and our good will, and just one action calling it wrong can ruin everything you have done over the years.

Senator MOSS. Even if it isn't a successful action?

Mr. SCHIFF. Even if it isn't successful. This is the horror of it. It is unfortunate.

Senator MOSS. I am not sure I can accept that, but I am glad to have you respond.

Mr. SCHIFF. We have a difference of opinion, sir, but I respect yours.

This subcommittee is aware, I am sure, of the pending class action on the west coast involving a nationally known manufacturer of auto accessories. Being sued because of some allegedly defective truck tires, this defendant's potential liability is in excess of $400 million.

Other consumer class actions which are pending, while they may not involve such an enormous figure, still pose a staggering threat to business.

Because of the great recoveries possible, consumer class actions are a harsh, vindictive remedy which are used, not against those who perpetrate so-called "hardcore" fraud, but against reputable business.

I repeat, not against those who perpetrate so-called "hardcore" fraud, but against reputable business.

The consumer abuses against which class action legislation is being directed are those unconscionable practices which exploit the unsophisticated consumer on a widespread basis. But such consumer frauds are generally engaged in by fly-by-night operators or marginal businesses skirting the fringe of legality.

Such defendants would generally be judgment-proof against substantial awards, and for this reason would not fear the deterrent of a consumer class action. Further, class action lawyers will be uninterested in instituting suits against such businessmen. Accordingly, class action would be least effective where consumer abuses are most pronounced.

Class action defendants are generally not selected on the basis of their degree of guilt, but rather on their ability to pay substantial damages. I must say here we spend hundreds of thousands of dollars every year, and it goes into millions, just protecting ourselves by insurance against what may happen.

Experience demonstrates that the expectation of high legal fees at the expense of large businesses encourages "strike suits" which misuse the class action mechanism.

A decision to bring a class action is simply not based on a judgment that particular consumer problems require litigation in the public interest—the kind of judgment which would be made by a responsible public official. Instead, the determination to sue is placed in the hands of a private attorney who personally benefits from the litigation.

Plaintiffs' attorneys are simply not motivated to bring suit against those who are most likely to engage in widespread consumer frauds. They have no public interest to be concerned about. We do, sir. Thus, lawsuits will invariably be brought against financially sound enterprises who may be trapped with respect to insignificant, technical, or isolated violations—for which any responsible public official would seek from the businessman an assurance of greater care in the future or, at most, a minor penalty.

Private class action suits also involve a hardship on consumers.

First, they involve cumbersome and time-consuming procedures devoted to accumulating the interests of numerous individuals in a single proceeding, including questions involving the makeup of the class itself, intricate requirements for notice to all class members, protracted pretrial procedures, and extensive hearings.

Second, class action litigation will place heavy burden of management on the courts, already faced with heavy backlogs of pending cases. Because of the complex notice requirements, unwieldy pretrial procedures, protracted trials and difficult damage determinations which are inherent in class actions, there will be further delay. Is that a fast, efficient consumer remedy?

Third, the class action mechanism may actually prevent the settlement of consumer claims. Because the financial interest of the plaintiff's attorney is far more substantial than the interests of each member of the class, the lawyer, rather than the client, becomes the participating litigant and real party in interest, thereby abusing the judicial process.

The class action, with its promise of huge fees not commensurate with work expended, offers a bonanza to the lawyer who runs first to the courthouse to file suit rather than seek informal resolution of a claim. And I call that ambulance chasing.

Moreover, he has no interest in advising his clients to seek the assistance of a government agency or seek individual means of recovery. It is relatively simple for an enterprising law office to marshal an expansive list of clients through the class action notice provision. Thus, alternatives to class action litigation are not considered, and the remedial mechanisms otherwise available to the consumer are not utilized.

In addition, the rules governing procedure in a class action automatically operate to increase the number of plaintiffs by forcing all potential members into the litigation unless they affirmatively request exclusion. In this instance, the consumer who is a potential member of a class is easily persuaded to join the suit. The persuasion is even easier when the consumer does not feel he has been cheated or feels that his claim has been satisfied through self-help, is told that he can get "something for nothing" merely by declining to withdraw from the suit.

In conclusion, Mr. Chairman, the Federation believes that a private class action brought to remedy consumer abuses does not properly perform its intended task.

There are consumer protection vehicles presently in existence, and still others currently under consideration, which may do the job. Specifically, we recommend swift passage of legislation to give the Federal Trade Commission the authority to seek preliminary injunctions for consumer fraud. We have indicated our willingness to make suggestions on improving this proposal.

But before adopting inappropriate class action legislation, the other remedies should first be analyzed in order to determine if and how they fail to provide adequate consumer protection.

It has not yet been shown why these other remedies, particularly if vigorously enforced or strengthened, will be ineffective. Until such a demonstration is made, effort should not be misdirected to a "remedy" with nothing to offer other than large attorneys' fees and the opportunity to be vindictive with reputable business.

Thank you very much, Mr. Chairman.

Senator MOSS. Thank you, Mr. Schiff.

We certainly accept your offer to make suggestions about the proposal to give the Federal Trade Commission authority to seek preliminary injunctions, which is one of the matters before us, but to say

I am astonished to have you style a class action bill as one that provides the vehicle to be vindictive by the consumer is stating it mildly. Class action suits are not new to the law. We have them now in many things. In tort actions we can have class action suits. We have them all the time in antitrust. Why is it suddenly going to be a vehicle for vindictiveness if they are given to consumers who have suffered some kind of unfairness or misrepresentation or something of the sort in purchasing goods from a distributor or a manufacturer?

Mr. SCHIFF. Senator, you and I do not disagree on the fact that if something is wrong it should be righted. We do not disagree on it. We disagree on the means to get it.

We feel that the remedy is not through class action bills or class action.

A recent case in Pittsburgh on the new credit law is a suit against Gimbel Bros. for two and a half million dollars, not for violation of the law but a violation of a small technicality of print.

Now, Gimbel's credibility that they have spent years building up is being questioned in court.

Senator MOSS. Of course, I know nothing about the case, I have only your description of it, but I have enough faith in the courts to think if it is a small technicality in the print that there isn't going to be any recovery in a case like that.

Mr. SCHIFF. Sir, who do you seek the redress from on the good will that you have lost from your customers?

Senator MOSS. Of course, I don't agree with you on this, that merely filing a suit destroys the good will that has been built up by a distributor or a manufacturer of a product. As a matter of fact, I think it would require a recovery in the class action plus quite a bit of publicity

to be damaging to the good will that they have established over a period of time.

Mr. SCHIFF. The first publicity, sir, is all that is needed.

Senator MOSS. I accept that as your point of view, and there may be some damage in it, but I was interested in your suggestion here that they ought to make great use of the small claims court, and you commended Mrs. Grant because her department had put out a brochure telling people how to use this small claims court.

Why doesn't this same damage to reputation come if a whole flock of small claims court suits go on?

Mr. SCHIFF. A small case to recover anywhere from 10 cents to a hundred dollars or $500, sir, does not have the publicity of a hundred million dollar suit or a four hundred million dollar suit or a two and a half million dollar suit will have.

It will be the legitimate businessman who is trying his best to please the customer, because this is his livelihood, and he is going to be there for years, who will be affected. It will not be the merchant who daily fraudulently does things, because he will be out of business by the time that thing is settled. He will be elsewhere. He will not be in business.

This is the unfortunate thing of class actions, sir.

Senator MOSS. The kind of businessman you describe is the one I would expect would have a complaints department and an adjustment procedure so that he would arrive at an adjustment on his problem without being subjected to a class suit.

Mr. SCHIFF. Senator, we do $270 million of business, 80 percent at retail, in department stores and in shoe stores. We have a policy of our company which we rigidly enforce, and yet this does not mean that somebody of our 11,000 employees is not going to displease a customer.

When we receive a letter from a customer of complaint, that is the first time my office receives it, at the particular time we send a customer a check, we ask the regional manager who is in charge of the area as well as the district manager and the manager of the store to contact that customer and do everything in the world to please that customer because what that customer can say nice about us is much more important to us than he can say bad about us. We do that procedure.

But I cannot guarantee as we sit here right now that one of our people across this great Nation—we are in practically 44 of the 50 States—is not displeasing a customer. I don't care whether that customer is right or wrong, if that customer is dissatisfied, that is important to me, how to make that customer satisfied.

Senator MOSS. And I would agree with you very much, but I can't see that having one of your employees displease a customer could lay the basis for any kind of a class action.

Mr. SCHIFF. Sir, I wish you were right. It just takes one dissatisfied customer to tell one attorney, whom I will call an ambulance chaser, and the whole procedure starts.

All you have to do is check the records of insurance companies as to how many of these complaints are settled out of court and don't get into court, and settled for much, much more than the damage that allegedly happened to the customer, and I will take the customer's word for it that the damage did happen to him.

Senator MOSS. How could this dissatisfied customer and the lawyer get up a class all of a sudden to come in on an action because of something that one customer did not like?

Mr. SCHIFF. Are you familiar with the Playboy incident in California—I am not a lawyer, so I am not exactly sure of the case. I know I am quoting you approximate facts, but I may not be quoting you the complete facts—in which membership was charged at $25 a year and then a billing of $5 a year and then a surcharge of $8?

A class action bill was started and everybody was asked to have themselves included, and those who were excluded were even sued with the Playboy people. So, it was to your benefit to do it.

The individuals recovered their $8, but the lawyers got a nice fee.

Senator MOSS. I don't know whether you read the terms of this bill which first of all limits the attorney's fee to 10 percent unless the court makes a finding that this is not commensurate with the service that he is rendering.

Mr. SCHIFF. On $2 million that would be $200,000 and 10 percent of $400 million would be $40 million.

Senator MOSS. If that much damage has been committed, perhaps the attorney deserves a large attorney's fee—

Mr. SCHIFF. That is a lot of money and you may be out of business.

Senator MOSS (continuing). Having carried a case of that complexity to a successful conclusion.

I must say I don't share your appreciation about the failure of the Federal courts to be able to handle litigation or complaints that come before them, to winnow out suits that are frivolous—that are manufactured in any way—nor do I lack your faith in the disciplinary measures of the Bar Association and the courts for ambulance chasers, as you call this type of lawyer. Disciplinary actions are taken if this sort of thing goes on.

I could understand your apprehension. I am going to have to go down and make a quorum.

Mr. SCHIFF. Our testimony supports strengthening the FTC's ability to handle these matters, and our testimony also indicates that we believe Virginia Knauer's office should become a statutory one.

Our testimony does not support and we are against class action.

Senator MOSS. I am going to have to be excused for just a few moments.

I am sure Senator Pearson has some questions and will continue the hearing, and I will be back in just a moment.

Senator PEARSON (presiding). I understand your testimony. Let me ask you in relation to the class suit whether or not your position would remain the same and your opposition to it for the reasons you have stated if the class suit was authorized in the terms of the administration bill which provides for a triggering mechanism in the Attorney General's Office?

Mr. SCHIFF. As I understand the New York bill, and I am not as familiar with it as Mrs. Grant, I understand that there it comes from their office, and if there is recovery that their office makes sure—whether it is a corporation counsel who does it, but it is directed by law that when the relief is granted by the court, if there be relief, that it is given to the consumer where and when they can find them and the remainder goes back to the city.

We would be against that, but, on the other hand, we would be in favor of the Federal Trade Commission getting an injunction to stop the practice and making sure that the individual did get some relief.

Senator PEARSON. My question was directed toward one of the bills that is the subject of these hearings. The ad-

ministration bill indicates that before a class action may be brought that the Attorney General makes a judgment that a class action is legitimate.

Mr. SCHIFF. We oppose the President's proposals.

Senator PEARSON. Even with the triggering mechanism?

Mr. SCHIFF. Yes, sir.

Senator PEARSON. What would be your reason for that opposition?

Mr. SCHIFF. We do not believe in any class action of any type, sir. We believe it is damaging and irreparable to legitimate business. On the other hand, we do not take cognizance of those who do fraudulent practice. We know that if we do our business legitimately and we satisfy our customers daily to the point where even some of our members will take goods off sale if they do not fit the quality of their advertising requirements, we believe that that is sufficient. We do not believe in class action suits; therefore, we cannot support the President's bill.

Senator PEARSON. You do not believe that there will be any conceivable circumstances under which a class action would be justified?

Mr. SCHIFF. Sir, we do not believe there would be any circumstances, nor do we believe if it were enacted that for the relief it was trying to obtain that it would serve its purpose. We believe it would be definitely a weapon to punish legitimate business, because we believe that is the only place that anybody can get relief.

Senator PEARSON. I share with you —as a matter of fact, I believe I have got more confidence in the American businessman than you have in the American lawyer.

Mr. SCHIFF. Yes, sir.

Senator PEARSON. And I have got a great deal more confidence in the American judicial system to weed out frivolous complaints. I don't know whether you have ever been before a Federal judge in a pretrial hearing—

Mr. SCHIFF. Thank God, no.

Senator PEARSON. Well, maybe someday you will thank God there is one there, too, because the protection of rights works both ways, and I am sure many businessmen day in and day out rely upon the certainty and the equity of the law.

But in the Federal procedures when you go in there for pretrial procedures, you must show you have a legitimate case or the judge just says to you, "dismiss your case or we will go in and direct a verdict."

Mr. SCHIFF. Unfortunately, business spends millions of dollars on advertising its name.

Senator PEARSON. And they get it from consumers.

Mr. SCHIFF. They get it from the consumers. They spend this money advertising their name daily in the media. The same media other things, empowering the FTC to seek temporary restraining orders as well as rulemaking authority, assessment of civil penalties, and award of damages to injured consumers.

Do you support those recommendations of the FTC?

Mr. SCHIFF. Sir, we have not read his testimony as of yesterday, so I cannot comment at this particular point. I am sorry.

Senator MOSS. Does this seem to be inconsistent now to recommend availability of class action along with this power that the FTC would have?

Mr. SCHIFF. Sir, we are against class action in any manner or form.

Senator MOSS. You have mentioned this class action on the west coast which you said involved about $400 million. Is that the case of General Motors—the wheel case?

Mr. SCHIFF. Yes, sir.

Senator MOSS. In which General Motors subsequently acknowledged that the wheels supplied for their trucks were defective and they advised to replace them at the purchaser's own expense?

Mr. SCHIFF. I believe that is the case, sir. I am not familiar with all the detail. I am familiar with the implication if they are found to be doing wrong.

Senator MOSS. In this case I am certainly not shocked by the suit, but I am shocked by the practice that was brought to light and that gave rise to the suit; so, in this instance I certainly cannot agree with you that a class action should not lie in that case.

Mr. SCHIFF. Sir, I still feel there could have been other remedies. I am not familiar with all the details. I am sorry. I am not a lawyer.

Senator MOSS. Do you think, then, if we provided for severe criminal penalties against hard-core fraud, that that would be an alternative to this class action that you object to categorically?

Mr. SCHIFF. Yes, sir; and we also feel that a remedy has to be fast, efficient, and effective. The longer a thing draws out, the less the consumer can be protected, sir.

Senator MOSS. I think we can agree on that very much, which is one of the things that limits the effectiveness of the small claims court route I think; you cannot get resolved a situation that applies to a vast number of people in a quick, relatively short time, because they have all got to individually bring their suits.

Mr. SCHIFF. Nor will class action, sir.

Senator MOSS. That is your point of view.

Mr. SCHIFF. I respect yours; I think you respect mine, sir.

Senator MOSS. Yes, I do, and I appreciate your coming here.

———

The following bill incorporates both approaches to federalization of consumer class actions, and attempts to meet many of the arguments of the critics. See, e. g., section 6(b).

92d CONGRESS
  1st Session

H.R. 5630

* ———

IN THE HOUSE OF REPRE-
SENTATIVES

March 4, 1971

Mr. Eckhardt (for himself, Mr. Moss, Mr. Symington, Mr. Dingell, Mr. Van Deerlin, Mr. Murphy of New York, Mr. Adams, Mr. Rooney of Pennsylvania, Mr. Tiernan, Mr. Podell, Mr. Helstoski, Mr. Carney, Mr. Metcalfe, Mr. Roy, Mr. Rosenthal, Mrs. Sullivan, Mr. Kastenmeier, Mr. Edwards of California, Mr. Mikva, Mr. Scheuer, Mr. Conyers, Mr. Corman, Mr. Burton, Mrs. Griffiths, and Mr. Udall) introduced the following bill; which was referred to the Committee on Interstate and Foreign Commerce

———

A BILL

To provide implementation of the Federal Trade Commission Act to give in-

creased protection to consumers, and for other purposes.

Be it enacted by the Senate and House of Representatives of the United States of America in Congress assembled, That this Act may be cited as the "Consumer Class Action Act of 1971".

Sec. 2. Findings and Purpose.—The Congress finds that there is a Federal interest in curbing unfair and deceptive practices which affect commerce. Congress finds that it promotes the free flow of goods in commerce and promotes the public welfare to provide an adequate process for class actions on behalf of similarly situated consumers.

Sec. 3. Definitions.—As used in this title—

(a) "Unfair consumer practice" means any of the following:

(1) any material statement, whether oral, written, or by visual description or other representation of any kind, or by half-truth or intentional omission, in connection with the sale, lease, rental, or loan or the offering for sale, lease, rental, or loan of goods or services to consumers, or the extension of credit to consumers, or the collection of debts from consumers, which has the capacity, tendency, or effect of misleading or deceiving consumers. Such statements include, but are not limited to—

(A) offering goods or services intending not to sell them as offered;

(B) advertising goods or services intending not to supply reasonably expectable public demand, unless the advertisement accurately discloses the limitation;

(C) making misleading statements concerning the need for any goods, services, or repairs;

(D) making misleading statements concerning the rights, obligations, liabilities, privileges, or remedies of the consumer;

(E) representing that goods are new when they are not;

(F) representing that goods are of a particular standard, grade, quality, style, or model when they are not;

(G) making misleading statements concerning the reasons for, existence of, or amounts of price reductions or comparative price or value;

(H) representing that goods or services are those of another, when they are not;

(I) representing that goods or services have sponsorship, approval, origin, characteristics of safety, performance or nonpollution, ingredients, uses, benefits, or quantities that they do not have, or that a person has a sponsorship, approval, status, affiliation, or connection that he does not have;

(J) taking consideration for goods or services without delivering the goods, performing the services or refunding the consideration within a reasonable period of time;

(K) making misleading statements concerning the profitability, risk, or any other material respect of any business opportunity or venture, or preparation or course of study for same, intended to be embarked upon by a natural person;

(L) offering gifts, prizes, free items, or other gratuities without providing them as offered;

(M) making misleading statements concerning the existence, terms or probability of any rebate, additional goods or services, commission or discount offered as an inducement for the sale of goods or services to a consumer in return for

giving the supplier the names of prospective consumers or otherwise helping the offerer to enter into any other consumer transaction;

(N) threatening that a creditor will take action that he does not actually take in the regular course of business;

(2) the use or threat of physical force against consumers or the undue harassment or coercion of consumers;

(3) failure to return deposits or advance payments for goods not delivered or services not rendered, when no default or further obligation of persons making such deposits or advance payments exists;

(4) violations which give rise to civil liability under State statutory or decisional law for the benefit of consumers;

(5) any other action prohibited by rule of the Federal Trade Commission, in accordance with the provisions of section 6(g) of the Federal Trade Commission Act (15 U.S.C. 46(g)), as amended, provided that such rule:

(A) became effective prior to the time of the action complained of, and

(B) was expressly designated by the Federal Trade Commission as a rule intended to constitute the basis of civil liability under this Act.

(b) "Intentional", and "intending" refer to actual intent, intent presumed where objective circumstances indicate that the person acted with intent, or intent presumed where circumstances indicate that the supplier acted in disregard of reasonable safeguards or care;

(c) "Consumer" means any natural person who is offered or supplied goods or services for personal, family, or household purposes, or who is offered a personal business or moneymaking opportunity;

(d) "Goods" includes real property but does not include securities or interests in securities or aircraft to the extent regulated in design or construction;

(e) "Services" includes insurance services.

Sec. 4. It shall be unlawful for a person to commit any unfair consumer practice as defined in this Act if—

(a) his business affects commerce; or

(b) the violation or violations affect commerce.

Sec. 5. The district courts of the United States shall have original jurisdiction of civil class actions brought by a consumer or group of consumers under this Act on behalf of himself or themselves and all consumers similarly situated. The jurisdiction of district courts of the United States under this section shall be concurrent with that of the courts of the several States. If an action under this Act is brought in a court of a State, the provisions of rule 23 of the Federal Rules of Civil Procedure shall apply to such action to the same extent that such provisions apply in the case of an action brought in a United States district court.

Sec. 6. (a) In order for an action to be entertained under this Act, the court must find that the action is of such nature as to be entertainable under rule 23 of the Federal Rules of Civil Procedure.

(b) If the court finds that the case is entertainable under rule 23 of the Federal Rules of Civil Procedure, it may nevertheless decide, in its discretion, whether or not the controversy should be entertained or dismissed without prejudice to refiling the same in a court of competent jurisdiction of the State. In so determining the court shall consider—

(1) the nature and importance of the case;

(2) the condition of its docket and the likelihood that the matter would unduly delay other cases;

(3) the multidistrict or multistate nature of the matter; and

(4) the relative procedural advantages of trying the case in the Federal or in the State court.

(c) In order for an action to be entertained under this Act in a district court of the United States the court shall make a determination of whether or not the amount which can reasonably be expected to be the amount in controversy exceeds $25,000. If such amount cannot reasonably be expected to exceed $25,000, then the court shall not entertain the action. For the purposes of this paragraph, the aggregate claims for all members of the class shall be taken into account to make up such requisite amount, and, if injunctive relief is sought and may reasonably be expected to be appropriate, the court shall consider the probable damages to the class if injunctive relief were not granted as an item to making up such requisite amount.

Sec. 7. No person shall be a member of a class in an action under this Act unless the amount of his loss or claim exceeds $10.

Sec. 8. In any action under this Act, the court shall only award—

(a) injunctive and declaratory relief;

(b) restitution and actual damages;

(c) relief or penalties specifically provided for under any statute giving rise to a right within the jurisdiction of the court in a case arising under this Act; and

(d) costs of court as provided in section 14; and in no event shall award damages for personal injury or exemplary damages.

Sec. 9. In an action in a United States District Court under this Act based upon violations of State law, the law of the States shall be applied as if jurisdiction were based upon diversity of citizenship.

Sec. 10. Section 1441 of title 28, United States Code, shall not apply with respect to any action of which the district courts have jurisdiction solely by reason of the fact that the act complained of is alleged to be a violation of State statutory or decisional law for the benefit of consumers.

Sec. 11. At least thirty-five days prior to instituting an action under this Act, the prospective plaintiff or plaintiffs shall mail notice to the prospective defendant or defendants informing them, in general terms, of the nature of the alleged unfair consumer practice or practices. No action for monetary relief may be maintained if, within thirty days after the mailing of the notice, the prospective defendant or defendants—

(a) identify from business records all consumers similarly situated and notify them that appropriate refunds, credits, adjustments, replacements, or repairs will be made within thirty additional days; provided that where sales, leases, rentals, or loans were effected through misleading statements, the defendants must notify the affected consumers that their money will be refunded upon their tender of the merchandise or any unused portion of the services, and where consumer debts were collected through misleading statements, the defendants must notify the affected consumers that the money will be refunded upon request; and

(b) cease the alleged unfair consumer practice or practices. Evidence of compliance or attempted compliance with this section shall not be construed as an admission of engaging in an unlawful practice.

Sec. 12. Actions pursuant to this Act shall be administered, so far as feasible within the discretion of the court, to avoid a multiplicity of suits, to avoid duplicating or overlapping class actions, and to avoid expenses of litigation which unduly repress obtaining justice under the Act. Such administration shall include, but shall not be limited to, assessing the costs of any required notice of the action as justice requires and providing for the use of facilities of the court, including mailing privileges, in such manner as justice requires.

Sec. 13. Actions pursuant to this section for redress of consumer injury shall be administered, so far as practicable, to facilitate voluntary settlements. The court shall have authority, upon the tender of a reasonable settlement offer by the defendant or defendants to the entire class, to supervise the submission of such settlement offer to the class. The court may take reasonable steps to insure that the consumers in the class are afforded, so far as feasible as determined by the court, the opportunity to exercise an individual choice with respect to accepting or rejecting any settlement offer. The court shall insure that equal space for the presentation of views as to the merits of the offer shall be tendered to plaintiffs and defendants in the notice of the offer to the members of the class. The cost of communicating the offer, or subsequent offers, tendered under the provisions of this section to the members of the class, shall be borne by the defendants. Such settlement offers shall be completed as expeditiously as possible.

Sec. 14. Whenever a consumer shall prevail in an action brought pursuant to this section, he shall be allowed to recover, in addition to damages, the costs of suit, including attorneys' fees. Such costs may be awarded from money damages which the defendant owes to members of the class who cannot be located with due diligence. Upon termination of a class action under this Act, whether by judgment, settlement, or compromise, the court shall inquire into the reasonableness of attorneys' fees charged and revise such fees where necessary to assure that they are reasonable, taking into consideration, among other factors, the contingency of success, the actual time spent by attorneys in preparation and prosecution of the action, the difficulty of the case, the experience of plaintiffs' counsel, the amount recovered in the action, and the benefits to the public of the litigation.

Sec. 15.   An action to enforce any claim under this section shall be forever barred unless commenced within three years after the claim arose, except that in the case of an action dismissed without prejudice to be filed in a State court under section 9 this limitation shall be tolled between the time that the action is commenced in Federal court and one month after the Federal court dismisses the action without prejudice to refiling.

Sec. 16.   An action under this title may be brought in any district in which the claim arose or in which the defendant resides, is found, has an agent, is licensed to do business, or is doing business.

Sec. 17.   This Act shall not annul, alter, or affect in any manner the meaning, scope, or applicability of any Federal or State law except as specifically provided herein (as, for instance, in the case of application of Federal rule 23 in cases brought upon a claim under this Act in State court), including but not limited to laws concerning the provision of goods and services to consumers and Public Law 91–222 (84 Stat. 87), or limit in any way the availability of rights or remedies under such law.

Sec. 18.   If any provision of this Act is declared unconstitutional, or the applicability thereof to any person or circumstance is held invalid, the constitutionality of the remainder of the Act and the applicability thereof to other persons and circumstances shall not be affected thereby.

SECTION 6. CONSUMER PROTECTION AGENCIES

A.   THE FEDERAL TRADE COMMISSION

Prior to 1969, the nation's potentially most important consumer protection agency, the Federal Trade Commission, had compiled for itself an unrelieved record of mediocrity brought about by inadequate statutory authority, overly cautious interpretation of its mandate, fear of Congressional review, lack of sufficient budget, understaffing and use of the agency as a vehicle for political patronage.   The Nader Report on the Federal Trade Commission, printed in the Congressional Record for January 22, 1969 at p. 1539, and later published in much-abridged form as Cox, Fellmeth and Schulz, The Nader Report on the Federal Trade Commission (1970), simultaneously exposed the activities of the Commission and catalyzed dramatic change.   An American Bar Association Commission, created at the request of President Richard M. Nixon, reached essentially the same critical conclusions as the Nader study, ABA Commission to Study the Federal Trade Commission, Report (1969), and the President appointed, as the new FTC Chairman, Miles Kirkpatrick, who had been Chairman of the ABA Commission. Kirkpatrick, in turn, appointed Prof. Robert Pitofsky, who had been Counsel to the ABA Commission, as Director of the Bureau of Consumer Protection, which in recent years has been responsible for major changes in the pattern of FTC enforcement activity. For example, the Commission has proposed numerous new trade regulations for the protection of consumers, including abolition of the holder in due course doctrine for consumer transactions and has required companies to make public whatever data they have to substantiate objective advertising claims. Resolution of the Commission, 2 CCH Tr.Reg.Rep. Para. 7996 (1971). In addition, the Commission has sought new types of relief in connection with proceedings involving alleged deception of consumers:

(1) *Corrective advertising.* In Matter of Campbell Soup Co., FTC Complaints and Orders 1967–70 Transfer Binder, Para. 19261, pp. 21421–26 (1970), the Commission considered a demand by consumer protection organization, SOUP, that it not let a company off with merely a cease and desist order to stop a deceptive practice. Campbell Soup Co. had allegedly placed clear glass marbles in the bottom of a bowl of soup which it photographed for advertising purposes; the marbles caused the solid ingredients to rise to the surface, thus making the soup appear more dense than it really was. SOUP contended that deterrence of similar violations in the future, and correction of mistaken impressions created by years of false soup advertising, required a type of Commission order stronger than the order to cease and desist to which Campbell was prepared to consent. SOUP petitioned the Commission to require that future Campbell advertising disclose that prior advertisements had been challenged by the FTC as being deceptive, and that these corrective ads run for the same period of time that the challenged advertisements appeared, and in the same period. Although the Commission denied the petition "because we think that the Commission has other important matters to deal

with [and] the added amount of relief which might theoretically be obtained after years of protracted litigation is not worth the expenditure of resources which could be put to better use elsewhere," it declared that "we have no doubt as to the Commission's power to require such affirmative disclosures when such disclosures are reasonably related to the deception found and are required in order to dissipate the effects of that deception."

In its complaint in the "Hi-C" Case, Matter of Coca-Cola Co., 3 Tr.Reg.Rep. Para. 19603, p. 21648, modifying proposed complaint 3 Tr.Reg.Rep. Para. 19351, p. 21484, the FTC proposed to require a company to disclose in future advertisements that the Commission had found that Hi-C had been falsely advertised in the past to give consumers the erroneous impression that the drink was the nutritive equivalent of orange juice.

In Matter of I.T.T. Continental Baking Co., 3 Tr.Reg.Rep. Para. 19681 p. 21727 (1971), respondent consented to an order requiring it, for one year, to spend 25% of its advertising budget for Profile bread on FTC-approved advertisements containing statements that, contrary to possible interpretations of prior advertising, Profile is not effective for weight reduction.

(2) *Compensation.* With a few exceptions the Commission had not until recently taken upon itself the function of ensuring financial compensation to consumers already injured by an unlawful practice, even when thousands of persons may have been affected; it limited its intervention to halting the practice in question. But in Matter of Curtis Publishing Co., 3 Tr.Reg.Rep. Para. 19719, pp. 21754–62 (1971), the Commission affirmed that it had restitutionary power. The Curtis Publishing Company ceased to publish the Saturday Evening Post, for financial reasons. It did not offer refunds to most subscribers, but

instead switched them to Life Magazine, on an issue for issue basis. It also misled consumers into thinking that they could not demand a cash refund. The Commission overruled the decision of its hearing examiner that it was without legal power to order refunds to subscribers, but declined to order such refunds in this case. "[I]f adequate public interest grounds for granting restitution are present in a particular case, the benefit to private persons who may be restored to the status quo ante would be merely an incidental aspect of the Commission's order."

The Commissioners disagreed on the reason for declination to order restitution to the subscribers. One Commissioner did not participate; one concurred in the result without opinion. One reasoned that the Commission could not act because "[w]hether or not a Post subscriber was or is entitled to a refund for the remaining portion of his subscription depends upon the circumstances under which the subscription was written, the contract terms, the response of the subscriber to the opportunity to accept a substitute magazine and the law of the state where the subscription was made." Two Commissioners disagreed with this statement since "there can be no serious question but that under general principles of contract law, these subscribers had a right to a refund of money * * * if there were provisions in any of Curtis' contracts which allowed the publisher to substitute another magazine, or if perchance there were state laws giving a publisher such an option in the event of insolvency, respondent should be charged with the burden of bringing forth such facts." However, these Commissioners concurred in the result because Curtis was so near bankruptcy that it could not have made refunds; since, therefore, its obfuscation of the right to a cash refund could not have prejudiced anyone, its deception was not a material one, and the FTC Act was not violated.

The Commission's determination with respect to its power to order cash transfers to consumers bore fruit in the "Big Name Bingo" Case, Matter of Coca-Cola Co., Proposed Complaint, 3 Tr.Reg.Rep. Para. 19290, p. 21457 (1970). The Commission charged that the company had misled purchasers of Coca-Cola into thinking that they could win a $100 prize by solving a puzzle; an "undisclosed rule" not understood by persons "of average sophistication and skill in semantics"—namely, that some questions could have two answers—prevented thousands of people who submitted a correct answer to each question from getting their prizes. As a result, only a few people got the cash awards. The Commission proposed to order the company to "cease and desist from wrongfully withholding the earned prize of $100" from such people. The company initiated litigation to test the Commission's power in this regard.

Questions

1. What type of federal agency action is desirable for the prevention of consumer fraud and other abuses? Should the Federal Trade Commission establish neighborhood-level offices in poverty areas? See ABA Commission Report on the Federal Trade Commission at 55–62 (1969). What power should the FTC be able to exercise?

2. Can agencies be expected, under any circumstances, to protect consumers sufficiently, or, in view of political and budgetary considerations, will some kinds of private remedies, such as class actions, continue to be needed?

3. Legislation in the 92nd Congress would have provided a statutory basis for FTC assertion of the power to order restitution. "After an order of the Commission to cease and desist * * *

has become final * * * the Commission * * * may institute civil actions * * * to redress injury to consumers caused by the acts or practices which were the subject of the cease and desist order, including but not limited to, recision or reformation of contracts, the refund of money or return of property, public notification of the violation, and the payment of damages." S. 986 (91st Cong.) (Passed Senate, Nov. 8, 1971, Cong.Rec. p. S 17887, daily ed. Nov. 8, 1971, but died in committee in the House). Will enactment of this bill make any material difference in the quality of life or the degree of abuse in low-income areas?

State and local agencies

In general, state agency enforcement of consumer protection laws has been even worse, historically, than Federal Trade Commission enforcement. See, e. g., Center for the Analysis of Public Issues, "The New Jersey Office of Consumer Protection: A Promise Unfulfilled" (Princeton, N.J. 1970); Kripke, "Gesture and Reality in Consumer Credit Reform," 44 N.Y.U.L.Rev. 1, 44–46 (1969) ("If one talks to Legal Aid workers in New York, one gets an unflattering picture of the usefulness of the Attorney General's office in this field. He is told of persons waiting by the hour to be interviewed, with scant results. That office has no authority to bring civil suits on behalf of private litigants. Therefore, if it cannot effect an adjustment by telephone mediation, it drops the matter and refers the consumer to private counsel or legal service offices. It has brought few injunctions against fraudulent practices, and it is believed that it has not accomplished very much by voluntary stipulations to desist.").

The editor of this section has participated in an experiment to determine whether a local government, operating under optimal conditions of legislative authority, with adequate funding and virtually unlimited power to select attorneys to bring cases against violators, could make any significant dent in eliminating abuses against consumers. As Chairman of the New York City Consumer Advisory Counsel, he helped to draft a strong statute defining new powers, particularly restitutionary powers, for the New York City Department of Consumer Affairs. The law, passed in 1969, is reproduced at 80 Yale L.J. 1600 (1971).

After the statute had been enacted, the editor served for fifteen months directing the agency's Law Enforcement Division, which conducted investigations and brought cases under the law. His experience and conclusions cannot easily be summarized. For a description at moderate length see Schrag, "On Her Majesty's Secret Service: Protecting the Consumer in New York City," 80 Yale L.J. 1529 (1971). For the full story, including the editor's own view of the future role of government agencies in consumer protection, consult Schrag, Counsel for the Deceived (1972).

SECTION 7. CONCLUSION

Is consumer protection worth its cost? Almost all proposals for reform are met by the objection that they would impose on society—perhaps most heavily on precisely those who are sought to be protected—unacceptable burdens: higher prices, higher finance charges, higher taxes, reduced selling, reduced credit, overgrown bureaucracies, stifled competition, crowded courts. Undoubtedly, some proposed reforms bear too high a price tag. For example, creation of government apparatus to investigate and act upon every single consumer complaint would probably cost more than the value of eliminating marginal abuses (although at the present time we are probably far from the optimal level of government consumer fraud services, a condition which may be remedied in part by legislation pending the 93rd Congress to provide federal grants in aid to state and local consumer agencies. See S. 1177, Title III (92nd Cong), which passed the House but was killed by a Senate filibuster.). How can we tell whether any particular programs justify their projected costs? In the absence of hard data concerning the likely costs and benefits of such reforms as prohibiting garnishment or liberalizing class actions, should we act or postpone action?

It is particularly important to judge the cost of consumer reforms aimed at the poor, who, though they can least afford it, are victimized more than the middle class in almost every category of consumer problem. Having less money, they must make every purchase a good one, yet they are likely to be troubled by every kind of problem. Mass media advertising, much of it itself exaggerated, generates demand for costly goods they can buy only on credit. But those in lower income brackets can often obtain loan credit only from the sources charging the highest rates, and sale credit only from low-income retailers who are more likely to engage in sharp selling practices and resort quickly to such devices as repossession, litigation, and wage garnishment to obtain payment. In disputes with sellers or other creditors, low-income consumers are least able to use to advantage the dispute-settling machinery provided by the law.

It is often suggested that it would be improvident to tinker with the consumer credit system to solve the buying problems of the poor; that the system, while flawed, is basically harmonious, and that drastic restrictions on creditors' remedies, rate ceilings or selling methods, or greatly increased burdens pertaining to disclosure or government supervision, or the facilitation of contested litigation would drive ghetto suppliers from the market and leave the poor without the goods and services they need and desire. Commercial opponents of proposed consumer reforms sometimes claim that what the poor need is not consumer protection, but money. But few of them lobby for an adequate guaranteed annual income; they claim that lobbying for social welfare legislation is not a proper function of a department store, credit company, bank, or manufacturer.

"It may even be that under the present marketing arrangements in our society, unethical practices are an inevitable consequence of serving the wants of the poorest risks. Society now virtually presents the very poor risks with twin options: of foregoing major purchases or of being exploited. * * * In the final analysis, the consumer problems of low-income families cannot be divorced from the other problems facing them. Until society can find ways of raising their educational level, improving their occupational opportunities, increasing their income, and reducing the discrimination against them—in short, until poverty itself is eradicated—only limited solutions to their problems as consumers can be found." Caplovitz, The Poor Pay More 180, 192 (1967).

*

INDEX

References are to Pages

1208